1993	1992
Current liabilities		
Current maturities of long-term debt	$ 1.5	$ 1.9
Notes payable	386.7	210.0
Accounts payable	308.8	313.8
Accrued liabilities:		
Income taxes	65.9	104.1
Salaries and wages	76.5	78.0
Advertising and promotion	233.8	228.0
Other	141.4	135.2
Total current liabilities	1,214.6	1,071.0
Long-term debt	521.6	314.9
Nonpension postretirement benefits	450.9	407.6
Deferred income taxes	188.9	184.6
Other liabilities	147.7	91.7
Shareholders' equity		
Common stock, $.25 par value		
Authorized: 330,000,000 shares		
Issued: 310,292,753 shares in 1993 and 310,193,228 in 1992	77.6	77.5
Capital in excess of par value	72.0	69.2
Retained earnings	3,409.4	3,033.9
Treasury stock, at cost: 82,372,409 and 72,874,738 shares	(1,653.1)	(1,105.0)
Minimum pension liability adjustment	(25.3)	
Currency translation adjustment	(167.2)	(130.4)
Total shareholders' equity	1,713.4	1,945.2
Total liabilities and shareholders' equity	$ 4,237.1	$ 4,015.0

See notes to consolidated financial statements.

INTERMEDIATE ACCOUNTING

FIFTH EDITION

INTERMEDIATE ACCOUNTING

FIFTH EDITION

Jan R. Williams
University of Tennessee

Keith G. Stanga
University of Tennessee

William W. Holder
University of Southern California

The Dryden Press
Harcourt Brace College Publishers

Fort Worth   Philadelphia   San Diego   New York   Orlando   Austin   San Antonio
Toronto   Montreal   London   Sydney   Tokyo

Acquisitions Editor	Elizabeth Storey
Developmental Editor	Van Strength
Project Editor	Cheryl Hauser
Art Director	Jeanette Barber
Production Manager	Erin Gregg
Product Manager	Annie Todd
Marketing Assistant	Kipp Murray
Permissions Editor	Shirley Webster
Copy Editor	JaNoel Lowe
Indexer	Kristina Sanfilippo DeVico
Compositor	Beacon Graphics
Text Type	10/12 Times Roman

Material from Uniform CPA Examination Questions and Unofficial Answers, copyright © 1957 through 1987 by the American Institute of Certified Public Accountants, Inc., is adapted with permission.

Material from the Certificate in Management Accounting Examination, copyright © 1972 through 1984 by the National Association of Accountants, is adapted with permission. Permission has been received from the Institute of Certified Management Accountants of the Institute of Management Accountants to use questions and/or unofficial answers from past CMA examinations.

Cover and frontispiece photo illustration by Ben Britt Photography.

Address for orders:
The Dryden Press, 6277 Sea Harbor Drive, Orlando, FL 32887-6777
1-800-782-4479 or 1-800-433-0001 (in Florida)

Address for editorial correspondence:
The Dryden Press, 301 Commerce Street, Suite 3700, Fort Worth, TX 76102

ISBN: 0-03-006223-3

Library of Congress Catalog Card Number: 94-70732

Photo Credits appear on page 1277, which constitutes a continuation of the copyright page.

Printed in the United States of America

4 5 6 7 8 9 0 1 2 3   048   9 8 7 6 5 4 3 2 1

The Dryden Press
Harcourt Brace College Publishers

We dedicate this work to

Our wives:
Elaine Williams   Josie Stanga   Carolyn Holder

and our families
in appreciation of their support

The Dryden Press Series in Accounting

Introductory

Bischoff
Introduction to College Accounting
Third Edition

Principles

Hanson, Hamre, and Walgenbach
Principles of Accounting
Sixth Edition

Computerized

Bischoff and Wanlass
The Computer Connection: General Ledger and Practice Sets to accompany Introductory Accounting
Second Edition

Wanlass
Computer Resource Guide: Principles of Accounting
Fourth Edition

Financial

Backer, Elgers, and Asebrook
Financial Accounting: Concepts and Practices

Beirne and Dauderis
Financial Accounting: An Introduction to Decision Making

Porter and Norton
Financial Accounting: The Impact on Decision Makers

Stickney and Weil
Financial Accounting: An Introduction to Concepts, Methods, and Uses
Seventh Edition

Managerial

Ketz, Campbell, and Baxendale
Management Accounting

Maher, Stickney, and Weil
Managerial Accounting: An Introduction to Concepts, Methods, and Uses
Fifth Edition

Intermediate

Williams, Stanga, and Holder
Intermediate Accounting
Fifth Edition

Advanced

Huefner and Largay
Advanced Financial Accounting
Third Edition

Pahler and Mori
Advanced Accounting
Fifth Edition

Financial Statement Analysis

Stickney
Financial Statement Analysis: A Strategic Perspective
Second Edition

Auditing

Guy, Alderman, and Winters
Auditing
Third Edition

Rittenberg and Schwieger
Auditing: Concepts for a Changing Environment

Theory

Belkaoui
Accounting Theory
Third Edition

Bloom and Elgers
Foundations of Accounting Theory and Policy: A Reader

Bloom and Elgers
Issues in Accounting Theory and Policy: A Reader

Taxation

Duncan
Essentials of U.S. Taxation
Second Edition

Everett, Raabe, and Fortin
1995 Income Tax Fundamentals

Madeo, Anderson, and Jackson
Sommerfeld's Concepts of Taxation
1996 Edition

Reference

Bailey
Miller Comprehensive GAAS Guide
College Edition

Williams
Miller Comprehensive GAAP Guide
College Edition

Governmental and Not-for-Profit

Douglas
Governmental and Nonprofit Accounting: Theory and Practice
Second Edition

Ziebell and DeCoster
Management Control Systems in Nonprofit Organizations

The Harcourt Brace College Outline Series

Campbell, Grierson, and Taylor
Principles of Accounting I
Revised Edition

Emery
Principles of Accounting II

Emery
Intermediate Accounting I
Second Edition

Emery
Intermediate Accounting II

Frigo
Cost Accounting

Poteau
Advanced Accounting

Preface

The decade of the 1990s will be remembered as the decade of change in accounting education. Never before has the discipline placed so much emphasis on changing the education model for preparing students to enter the accounting profession.

The need for change in accounting education has resulted from several factors. The body of knowledge that students entering the profession must master is growing at an unprecedented rate. At the same time, the skills required for success in accounting practice—whether in public accounting, industry, government, or education—are expanding. No longer is it enough for students to only have a mastery of technical accounting material. Today they are expected to develop a broad background in areas such as computer science, economics, and finance, while at the same time developing high-level interpersonal skills, particularly the ability to communicate well and work in teams.

In addition to authoring *Intermediate Accounting,* we have been participants at the forefront of recent changes in accounting education. Jan Williams is currently Director of Education of the American Accounting Association and represents that organization as a member of the Accounting Education Change Commission (AECC). The AECC, an organization funded by the Big Six accounting firms, is intended to be a catalyst for change in accounting education. Jan has also been actively involved in the AICPA's program to change accounting education via the 150-hour education requirement. Keith Stanga has been involved in accounting education change through his role as an administrator of an accounting program. Keith currently serves as Head of the Department of Accounting and Business Law at The University of Tennessee. He and his faculty colleagues are working together in several specific areas to continuously improve the educational experience of accounting students at The University of Tennessee. William Holder has been deeply involved in the comprehensive curriculum revision project at the University of Southern California for the past five years. His efforts have been focused directly on the subject matter of this text as it relates to the redesigned curriculum. In addition, Bill's involvement with standard setting and his consulting experience with accounting litigation is reflected where appropriate to help put the student's mind on these aspects of financial accounting practice. We all teach intermediate accounting on a regular basis and are well aware of the importance of presenting high-level technical material in an interesting and challenging way.

From the first edition, the objective in writing this textbook was to provide the market with a book that maintains a unique balance between explanation of applied accounting practice and the conceptual framework on which practice is based. This objective, established in 1984, remains consistent with current trends in accounting education. With the help of users, reviewers, students, colleagues, and our publisher, we have sought to continuously improve our presentation with new material and proven pedagogical techniques.

The need for change in accounting education does not mean that traditional approaches to teaching and learning have no merit. We are sensitive to traditional needs of many faculty and students. Our goal has always been to blend the best of tradition in intermediate accounting with the innovations of the present and future. We believe the fifth edition of *Intermediate Accounting* accomplishes this goal.

FEATURES OF THE FIFTH EDITION

Retained Unique Approach in Early Chapters

We have retained the three early chapters that lay the foundation of balance between theory and practice for students.

- In Chapter 2, we present the broad accounting principles that underlie specific procedures currently used in the preparation of financial statements. We highlight these principles throughout the book in marginal heads as their application to specific reporting practices are illustrated.

- In Chapter 3, we introduce the student to the nature and measurement of the elements of financial statements, emphasizing alternatives to current practice at a level understandable to students at this point in their study of financial accounting.
- Chapter 4 reviews the four basic financial statements and emphasizes the important feature of articulation.

Learning Enhancements

We retained a unique feature we have had since the first edition—*noting accounting principles throughout the textbook in the margins.* Instructors have consistently said this feature helps students identify and understand the overall impact of the principles on accounting concepts and practice.

Boxed articles extend the subject of the chapter to show students actual business applications, often from perspectives outside the accounting profession such as those of investors and creditors. We have continued to *improve our flowcharts, diagrams, and other graphics* that summarize text material and enhance students' learning. As a part of this effort to provide greater visual appeal and permit more alternatives for emphasis, we have published this edition in a *new four-color format.*

Emphasis on Contemporary Issues

We stress contemporary financial reporting issues throughout the book in several ways. We provide students with *Kellogg's Financial Statements* as an appendix to the book and as the primary company referenced throughout the book, replacing Strawbridge & Clothier from the previous edition. In the fifth edition, we have *expanded references to international accounting,* pointing out varying reporting practices in different parts of the world. Where appropriate, we emphasize *how current financial reporting standards provide information that is useful in predicting future cash flows,* a primary objective of financial reporting as indicated in the FASB's conceptual framework. The emphasis on *current research,* which has characterized earlier editions, has been strengthened. Many items in the assignment materials include written requirements, and many of the *judgment cases have ethical considerations* similar to those students are likely to confront early in their professional careers. All of these features are intended to emphasize contemporary issues that are important for the preparation of future professionals.

Increased Emphasis on Real-World Applications

Each chapter opens with a carefully selected vignette and photo to interest students and to emphasize the importance of chapter concepts. Throughout the book, we use extensive examples, drawn from published financial statements of well-known companies. Realistic cases and material have been prepared that model the accounting practice.

New Financial Reporting Cases

Appearing at the end of Chapters 7 through 26, these cases are characterized by excerpts from published financial statements of actual companies. The questions following the cases require students to respond to the kinds of problems they are likely to face in practice, which require interpretation and have possible judgment implications.

Text Reorganized into Six Major Sections from Five

Intermediate accounting includes many procedures. We chose to organize the book into six major parts, or sections, to provide students with a framework to organize the material—a roadmap of sorts. The fifth edition is organized as follows:

Part I—Theoretical Foundation for Financial Reporting (Chapters 1–4)
Part II—Tools of Accounting (Chapters 5–6)
Part III—Asset Accounting (Chapters 7–13)
Part IV—Liability and Stockholders' Equity Accounting (Chapters 14–18)
Part V—Reporting Operations and Cash Flows (Chapters 19–22)
Part VI—Advanced Measurement and Disclosure Issues (Chapters 23–26)

A newly organized Part V includes discussion of issues related to reporting operations and cash flows. Of particular interest is Chapter 21, which covers the theoretical construct underlying revenue recognition and illustrates the application of that theory in the preparation of income statements in complex situations.

In response to users and reviewers, we added a sixth section, titled Advanced Measurement and Disclosure Issues. Chapters in this section, used in conjunction with the 1993 financial statements of Kellogg Company presented in an appendix to the book, are particularly useful to help students understand many of the most complex accounting and disclosure issues confronting the profession today.

Moved Forward Earnings per Share Coverage (Chapter 18)

Based on market feedback, we brought this coverage forward to strengthen the tie between EPS figures and debt and equity instruments that are discussed in Chapters 14–17, which directly precede it.

Extensively Updated

In the text, examples, illustrations, and assignment and test material, we have taken care to provide students and instructors with current material.

Of particular importance is the revision of Chapter 10 on the subject of investments. It reflects recent changes by the FASB to incorporate current value information in the financial statements. The broader implications of this development for financial reporting, as well as the specific application for investment accounting, are explored in Chapter 10.

In Chapter 21, we review many topics related to income presentation of a comprehensive income statement, which includes all of the irregular income items that the students will have studied.

Emphasis on Professional Judgment

In today's complex business environment, professional judgment by accountants is particularly important. Throughout the text, we refer to the importance of professional judgment. Each chapter ends with a brief discussion of the judgment implications of the subject of the chapter and is supported by judgment cases in the problem material. These features provide the instructor with an opportunity to remind students that professional accountants are constantly confronted with the need to apply carefully reasoned judgment as they carry out their responsibilities in the financial reporting process.

SUPPORTING PACKAGE MATERIAL

For the Student

- *Working Papers*
- *Checklist of Key Figures*
- Improved! *Spreadsheet Templates for Selected Assignment Problems*
- Improved! *Study Guide with Lotus 1-2-3 Applications Manual* In response to primary research with intermediate students, this edition of the study guide now includes several new features. The manual is prepared by James Rothwell, Ouachita Baptist University, and James Reeve, University of Tennessee.

- *Practice Set, Classic Toys and Trains*   This practice set allows the student to explore transactions of a small corporate merchandising company. It includes special journals and direct and indirect statements of cash flows. The practice set is available in manual or computerized versions and is prepared by Sandra Pelfrey and Gadis J. Dillon.

For the Instructor

- New! *Annotated Instructor's Edition*
- Improved! *Instructor's Manual and Instructor's Manual on disk*   For those instructors who wish to modify this material for their class notes, the instructor's manual is available on 3.5-inch disk. The instructor's manual is written by Jane Campbell of Kennesaw State College.
- *Solutions Manual*
- *Teaching Transparencies*
- Improved! *Solutions Transparencies*   In this edition, these transparencies have been enlarged and redesigned.
- Improved! *Test Bank*   Written by Larry A. Deppe, Westminster College, the test bank has hundreds of new questions. Many require critical thinking skills.
- *Computerized Test Bank*   Available in 3.5-inch, 5.25-inch Mac and Windows versions. This software offers four ways to select questions, a range of formatting options, and the option to easily add questions.

Special Packaging and Innovative Computerized Learning Materials

As with previous editions, we have a special packaging option for the textbook and *Miller GAAP Guide: College Edition,* by Jan Williams. A new computerized version of the *GAAP Guide* will allow students who like to study with a computer to research pronouncements by topic on this new version of the *GAAP Guide.*

ACKNOWLEDGMENTS

The fifth edition of *Intermediate Accounting* would not have been successfully completed without the help of many people. We would like to recognize those who have contributed to the writing, review, revision, and publication of *Intermediate Accounting.*

One of the most useful forms of input concerning a textbook is the expert evaluation of educators who invest time and effort in reviewing the manuscript at the request of the publisher. We received many thought-provoking reviews of our first four editions and gave careful consideration to all suggestions made. We gratefully acknowledge the contributions of the following individuals who were willing to assist us as we sought to improve the overall quality of this text in the fifth edition: Alex B. Ampadu, SUNY at Buffalo; Jack Armitage, University of Nebraska at Omaha; Ronald Campbell, North Carolina A&T State; Larry Deppe, Westminster College; Larry Falcetto, Emporia State University; Lucille Genduso, Nova University; Oscar J. Holzmann, University of Miami; Kenneth R. Lambert, University of Memphis; Martha Loudder, Texas A&M University; George Mead, Michigan State University; Lucille Montondon, Southwest Texas State University; Daniel J. O'Mara, Villanova University; and Larry Walther, University of Texas at Arlington. We also wish to thank the users of the fourth edition who responded to detailed questionnaires or otherwise offered suggestions.

We must thank our student and faculty colleagues at the University of Tennessee and the University of Southern California for their advice and counsel. Many useful suggestions from these individuals have been incorporated into this revision. The direct input from those studying the text and those teaching from it is invaluable to us.

We would like to express a special thanks to those individuals who assisted in the development of our improved supplements package this edition. First, we appreciate the efforts extended by Jane Campbell (Kennesaw State College) on the instructor's manual; James

Rothwell (Ouachita Baptist University) and James Reeve (University of Tennessee) for contributions to this and previous editions of the study guide, respectively. Also, we are grateful to Larry Deppe for the significant revision to the test bank.

We also appreciate the assistance and dedication of other supplement authors and contributors. They include Sandra Bitenc, Kent Finkle, Gadis Johnson, Sandra Pelfrey, Suzanne Pinac-Ward, Chandra Schrog, and Lyn Suberly.

Throughout the text, we cite authoritative accounting literature published by the American Institute of Certified Public Accountants (AICPA) and the Financial Accounting Standards Board (FASB). We are grateful for the work done by these organizations. We also acknowledge and thank the AICPA and The Institute of Management Accounting for allowing us to adapt material from past CPA and CMA examinations.

Our text includes many financial reporting examples taken from the published financial statements of U.S. corporations. We have also included several articles from business publications. We appreciate the willingness of these organizations to allow us to use this material, which greatly enhances the learning experiences of serious students of this book.

The people at The Dryden Press have provided guidance and motivation to this revision. Those on the editorial staff—Lyn Hastert, editor-in-chief; Elizabeth Storey, acquisitions editor; Van Strength, developmental editor—have shown great personal interest in the project, and their understanding of our lives outside of writing the book has made this edition possible. We are thankful for the skill of the production team: Cheryl Hauser has been meticulous in keeping us posted of the many deadlines and changes, and we appreciate the hard work of our designer, Jeanette Barber, our production manager, Erin Gregg, and our permissions editor Shirley Webster. Finally, the sales and marketing group of Dryden deserves our thanks for the success of the book to date, and we wholly support their effort in the fifth edition under the direction of Annie Todd, product manager for accounting.

A special acknowledgment goes to our families. Much of the credit for this book rightfully belongs to them.

Jan R. Williams
Keith G. Stanga
William W. Holder

Contents in Brief

Contents

Part VI Advanced Measurement and Disclosure Issues

The Financial Accounting Environment

OBJECTIVES

1. To introduce and discuss the topic of financial accounting.
2. To distinguish clearly between preparers, auditors, and users of financial statements.
3. To introduce the concept of generally accepted accounting principles.
4. To explain how generally accepted accounting principles have been developed.
5. To indicate the major sources of generally accepted accounting principles.
6. To discuss some major issues that are likely to affect the development of generally accepted accounting principles.
7. To introduce the subject of international accounting in a global economy.
8. To introduce the subject of ethics in accounting.

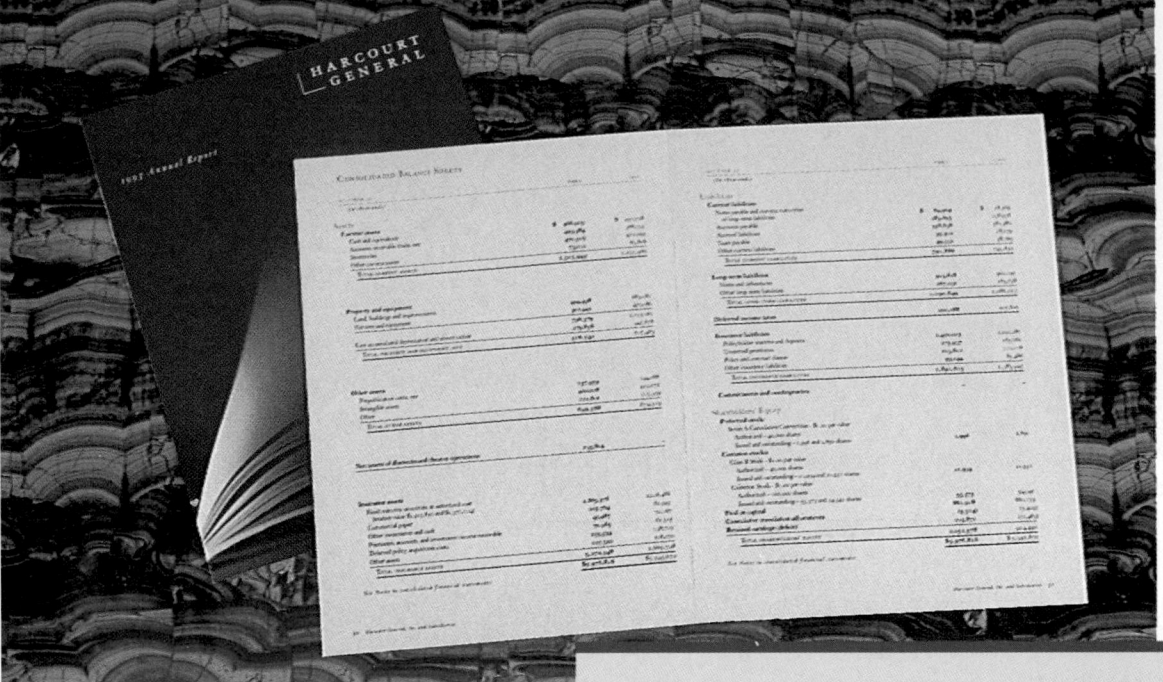

A recent commentary in *Business Week* complains that "if accounting is the language of business, too many companies speak in the balance-sheet equivalent of Aramaic."* The commentary criticizes the Financial Accounting Standards Board (i.e., the FASB, which is the private sector organization that sets accounting standards in the United States) for moving too slowly on controversial accounting issues and for being too heavily influenced by corporate interests. The article recommends some changes in the manner in which the FASB operates.

This chapter explains that the formulation of accounting principles is interesting and controversial. Accounting principles affect financial statements, which in turn affect investment and credit decisions. And these decisions help to determine how our society allocates its scarce resources, and ultimately, how well off all of us are.

---

*Dean Foust, "It's Time to Free the FASB Seven," *Business Week,* May 3, 1993, p. 144.

ACCOUNTING AS AN INFORMATION SYSTEM

Accounting *identifies, measures,* and *communicates* information about *economic entities for use* in making *economic decisions.* An accountant's primary task is therefore to supply information to help users, such as stockholders, bankers, and managers, make better decisions. These decisions determine how scarce resources are allocated within and among business enterprises. Accounting information helps society determine what goods and services to produce, as well as how and for whom to produce them. It should come as no surprise, then, that accounting is an exciting, often *controversial,* discipline.

Accounting is closely related to several fields of study, including economics, finance, psychology, sociology, communications theory, and political science. By applying psychological principles, for example, accountants learn how people process accounting information and how that information affects their decisions.

INTERNAL AND EXTERNAL USERS

The two types of accounting information users are internal and external. The primary *internal users* are managers, who need accounting information to assist them in basic planning and control. Because of their authority within their companies, managers can usually obtain the internal information they need. When providing information to managers, accountants are not constrained by generally accepted accounting principles, which are principles that have substantial authoritative support. Instead, they prepare whatever information management finds most useful. The branch of accounting concerned with providing information for internal users is called **managerial,** or **management, accounting.** Managerial accounting is the subject of other textbooks and courses.

External users are those outside the business enterprise who have or contemplate having a direct or an indirect interest in the enterprise. They include present and potential owners (stockholders), lenders, suppliers, employees, and customers, as well as financial analysts, stock exchanges, regulatory authorities, and the general public. Compared with management, external users generally have much less authority to request information. When preparing information for external users, accountants follow generally accepted accounting principles presently established by the Financial Accounting Standards Board. The use of such principles enhances the confidence and understanding of users and helps them to make more meaningful comparisons between companies.

Financial accounting is the branch of accounting that measures and reports the financial position of a business enterprise as well as changes in financial position. The main output of the financial accounting process is a set of basic, general-purpose financial statements. As illustrated in Chapter 4, the basic financial statements are the balance sheet, the income statement, the statement of cash flows, and the statement of retained earnings or statement of stockholders' equity. Financial accounting information is designed primarily to meet the needs of external users. This textbook deals with financial accounting. In this chapter we discuss the environment of financial accounting.

BASIC NEEDS OF EXTERNAL USERS

Although there are many types of external users, financial accounting has traditionally focused on meeting the needs of present and potential owners, such as preferred and common stock investors, and creditors, such as bankers and bondholders. Owners and creditors are the most obvious external groups that use financial statements. Moreover, information useful to investors and creditors is likely to be useful to other external users as well.

Fundamentally, investors and creditors invest or lend cash, and they want to know how much cash they will receive in return and when they will receive it. Stockholders, for example, typically make decisions *to buy, sell, or hold equity investments.* Before they exchange cash for shares of stock, they seek information that will help them to assess the amount, timing, and uncertainty of expected cash flows in the form of dividends and appreciated market prices. Similarly, commercial bank loan officers make decisions *to extend or not extend loans.* When making these decisions, bankers want information that will help them to assess their chances of receiving cash via interest and repayment of principal.[1]

Investment and credit decisions involve a comparison of expected cash outflows with expected cash inflows. In most cases, the outflows are known, based on, for example, the market price of the stock on the date of purchase or the amount of the loan requested. But the investor or creditor usually must *predict the amount of cash inflows* and *assess the risk that*

---

[1]*FASB Statement of Financial Accounting Concepts No. 1,* "Objectives of Financial Reporting by Business Enterprises," 1978, par. 25.

those inflows will be less than expected. What an investor or creditor would really like is a knowledge of the future. However, no one can supply such knowledge directly.

The expected cash flows to investors and creditors are related to the expected cash flows to the enterprise to which they have committed their funds. More precisely, "The prospects [of investors and creditors] for those cash receipts are affected by an enterprise's ability to generate enough cash to meet its obligations when due and its other cash operating needs, to reinvest in operations, and to pay cash dividends and may also be affected by perceptions of investors and creditors generally about that ability, which affect market prices of the enterprise's securities."[2]

For an enterprise to generate favorable cash flows over the long run, it must operate profitably and remain solvent. Thus, **profitability** and **solvency** are two basic factors that investors and creditors evaluate based on the information in financial statements. Profitability refers to the ability of an enterprise to generate earnings. Solvency refers to its ability to pay its debts when they come due. A company may be highly profitable yet be on the verge of bankruptcy due to a shortage of liquid assets such as cash and accounts receivable. Investors and creditors must therefore evaluate both aspects of a business enterprise.[3] Furthermore, if a business is to operate profitably and remain solvent, it must be *managed effectively*. Thus, financial statements can also be used to evaluate management's performance.

To summarize, investors and creditors provide cash, and they want to know how much cash they will receive in return and when they will receive it. To help resolve these questions, they use financial statements to

1. Make predictions.
2. Assess risk.
3. Evaluate profitability.
4. Evaluate solvency.
5. Evaluate management's performance.

These uses are interrelated.

GENERAL-PURPOSE FINANCIAL STATEMENTS

Even when we narrow the list of external users to owners and creditors, we find that these users make different kinds of decisions under a variety of circumstances. Bankers, for example, make short-term, intermediate-term, and long-term loans to many different types of customers, so their needs for certain items of accounting information may vary. Moreover, users differ in their abilities to read, analyze, and understand accounting information. An unsophisticated stockholder with virtually no understanding of accounting information contrasts with a chartered financial analyst who has met rigorous education, experience, and examination requirements and who renders professional advice on investment matters.

Clearly, the diversity of users poses a problem. Should accountants prepare "tailor-made" financial statements to meet the needs of a particular user? Or should accountants prepare a single, general-purpose set of financial statements to reasonably satisfy the needs of most users? Presently, financial accounting emphasizes general-purpose statements because (1) accountants believe that many users need similar information and (2) general-purpose statements are more favorable from a benefit/cost standpoint. As a general rule, *the benefits of information (including financial accounting information) should exceed the costs of providing and using it.* In general-purpose financial statements, accountants strive to

---

[2]*FASB Statement of Financial Accounting Concepts No. 1,* par. 37.

[3]Loyd C. Heath and Paul Rosenfield, "Solvency: The Forgotten Half of Financial Reporting," *Journal of Accountancy* (January 1979), pp. 48–54.

present information that is "comprehensible to those who have a reasonable understanding of business and economic activities and are willing to study the information with reasonable diligence."[4]

FINANCIAL STATEMENTS AND FINANCIAL REPORTING

The main output of the financial accounting process today is a set of basic, general-purpose **financial statements.** These statements are as follows:

1. A **balance sheet,** which summarizes an enterprise's financial position at a particular point in time.
2. An **income statement,** which summarizes an enterprise's income and the components of income over a period of time.
3. A **statement of cash flows,** which summarizes an enterprise's cash receipts and cash payments during a period of time.
4. A **statement of retained earnings,** which describes the changes in an enterprise's retained earnings during a period, or a **statement of stockholders' equity,** which describes the changes in retained earnings as well as in other accounts that compose stockholders' equity.

Actual examples of these financial statements appear in annual reports to shareholders. Companies also present them in other disclosure media such as registration statements and annual reports filed with the Securities and Exchange Commission. This textbook focuses on general-purpose financial statements including their related notes (footnotes), which are an integral part of the financial statements. To familiarize you with financial statements, we have reproduced a set of actual financial statements of Kellogg Company (a company that makes many well-known products, such as Corn Flakes and Frosted Flakes) on the endpapers (inside the front and back covers). Take a few minutes to review these statements now. We shall refer to them at various times throughout the book. Additionally, the Appendix contains most of the material presented in a recent annual report of Kellogg.

The output of the financial accounting process is not confined to financial statements. **Financial reporting** encompasses not only financial statements but also other means of communicating information that relates directly or indirectly to the financial accounting process. Corporate managers may communicate financial accounting information outside of the financial statements because they are required to do so by rule or custom or because they simply want to do so voluntarily.[5] Annual reports to shareholders, for example, include not only financial statements but also other information such as financial highlights and a multi-year summary of important financial figures. They also include **nonfinancial** information such as a description of major products and a listing of corporate officers and directors.[6]

Financial reporting provides a *major portion, but not all,* of the information needed by external users for making investment, credit, and similar decisions. Professional financial analysts, for example, usually gather and evaluate economic information (such as gross national product and interest rate figures) and industry information (such as weekly and monthly production figures provided for many industries) before they analyze information about individual companies. Also, many analysts obtain information by talking with representatives of corporate management.

---

[4]*FASB Statement of Financial Accounting Concepts No. 1,* par. 34.

[5]*FASB Statement of Financial Accounting Concepts No. 1,* par. 7.

[6]To summarize certain key terms, *financial accounting* is the branch of accounting concerned with measuring and reporting the financial position of a business enterprise and the changes that occur in financial position. *Financial statements* (i.e., balance sheet, income statement, statement of cash flows, and statement of retained earnings or statement of stockholders' equity) represent the main output of the financial accounting process. *Financial reporting* is a broad term that encompasses financial statements as well as other means of communicating information that relates directly or indirectly to the financial accounting process.

CHARACTERISTICS AND LIMITATIONS OF FINANCIAL STATEMENTS

Some of the more important characteristics and limitations that apply to present-day financial statements are briefly described below.[7]

1. **Financial nature.** The information in financial statements is primarily financial in nature. It is generally expressed in *units of money* regardless of changes in purchasing power.
2. **Business entities.** The information pertains to individual business entities (which may be a group of related companies) rather than to industries or to the entire economy.
3. **Estimates and judgment.** The information reflects estimates and judgment and is therefore inexact. Financial statements look more precise than they really are.
4. **Historical report.** The information reflects the financial effects of transactions and events that have already occurred. Financial statements do not contain future projections.
5. **General purpose.** The information is designed to reasonably meet the needs of many diverse users, particularly present and potential owners and creditors.
6. **Interrelatedness.** Financial statements are interrelated because measuring financial position is related to measuring changes in financial position. Thus, we say that financial statements **articulate** with one another.
7. **Summarization and classification.** The information is summarized and classified in a manner designed to help meet users' needs.
8. **Several measurement bases.** Financial statements reflect several measurement or valuation bases (e.g., accounts receivable are reported at net realizable value, plant assets are usually reported at their original cost less accumulated depreciation).
9. **A single source.** Financial statements are only one source of the information needed by investors and creditors.
10. **Cost.** Financial statements involve a cost to provide and use. They can be justified only if the benefits they provide exceed the costs.

OBJECTIVES OF FINANCIAL REPORTING

The objectives of financial reporting follow:[8]

1. To provide information useful in *investment, credit, and similar decisions.*
2. To provide information useful in *assessing cash flow prospects.*
3. To provide information about *enterprise resources, claims to those resources, and changes in them.*

Notice that the first objective is the most general; the next two are progressively more specific. Moreover, the third objective flows logically from the second, which in turn flows logically from the first. We explain these objectives more fully in the next chapter.

PREPARERS AND AUDITORS OF FINANCIAL STATEMENTS

Financial statements pertain to an entity such as a corporation. The **management** of that entity has the primary responsibility for preparing and disseminating its financial statements. Financial statements therefore contain **assertions** or **representations made by management,** such as sales, net income, and total assets.

Management's role in the financial reporting process has evolved over many years and is related to the fact that the corporation is the dominant medium for pooling productive resources in our economy. As corporations have grown in size, the separation between those who own the company (stockholders) and those who control it (managers) has widened. As a

---

[7]*APB Statement No. 4,* "Basic Concepts and Accounting Principles Underlying Financial Statements of Business Enterprises," 1970, par. 35, and *FASB Statement of Financial Accounting Concepts No. 1,* pars. 17–23.

[8]*FASB Statement of Financial Accounting Concepts No. 1,* pars. 34, 37, and 40. For an excellent critical review of these objectives, see Nicholas Dopuch and Shyam Sunder, "FASB's Statements on Objectives and Elements of Financial Accounting: A Review," *Accounting Review* (January 1980), pp. 1–21. Dopuch and Sunder (p. 8) believe that these objectives "are unlikely to help resolve major accounting issues or to set standards of financial reporting as the FASB had expected."

result, owners have demanded a periodic accounting from those to whom they have entrusted economic resources.

Many critics have charged that management has too much responsibility in the financial reporting process. They claim that since financial statements are reports *on* management's performance, management should have less responsibility for determining their contents. Despite the critics' views, the traditional position of the accounting profession has been that because managers are highly familiar with company objectives and operations, they are best suited to present pertinent information about the company to external parties.

To summarize, management has certain important **accountability** responsibilities to external parties. In discharging these responsibilities, management typically obtains the services of internal and external accountants.

INTERNAL ACCOUNTANTS

Management hires **internal accountants** (commonly called **industrial accountants** or **management accountants**) to work as employees within the company. Internal accountants perform many services, depending on the size and complexity of the enterprise. Perhaps their most distinguishing service is to produce and analyze many kinds of information designed to help management make better planning and control decisions. Should a company buy some new material-handling equipment? What is the optimal quantity of inventory for a company to order? When should a company order inventory? These are only a few of the questions that internal accountants can help to answer.

Internal accountants also design and implement accounting systems. In larger companies, they may serve on an **internal audit staff** that ensures that the company safeguards its assets, produces reliable accounting information, operates efficiently, and adheres to management's policies.

The internal accountant's most important services that relate to financial accounting are *collecting data* and *preparing the financial statements*. Internal accountants must therefore understand and apply the accounting principles we discuss throughout this text.

Some internal accountants have earned the **certificate in management accounting (CMA).** The CMA is the professional designation for management accountants. As you might expect, not all internal accountants have earned the CMA. Moreover, not all persons who have CMAs are internal accountants. Many people with CMAs work in public accounting, colleges and universities, government, and elsewhere. In addition to meeting certain other requirements, a person wishing to earn a CMA must pass a rigorous examination. Several assignment problems in this textbook have been adapted from recent CMA examinations.

EXTERNAL ACCOUNTANTS

Although most managers and internal accountants are both competent and honest, an independent outside party is needed to attest to the fairness of management's financial statements so that users will have more confidence in them. This is the major role of **external** or **public accountants.**

Certified public accountant (CPA) is the major professional designation of those who practice public accounting. Not all public accountants are CPAs; not all CPAs practice public accounting. To become a CPA, a person must satisfy certain education and experience requirements and pass a rigorous, uniform examination that the American Institute of Certified Public Accountants (AICPA) prepares and grades. The assignment material in this textbook contains many problems that we have adapted from CPA examinations.

Although CPA firms provide such services as tax advice and management advisory services, their primary service is **auditing** (often called the **attest function**). In an audit, CPAs serve management as independent contractors, but their primary responsibility is to external users of financial statements. Basically, an **audit** consists of an examination of a company's financial statements followed by the issuance of a report that expresses the auditor's opinion about whether the financial statements have been presented fairly in accordance with generally accepted accounting principles. The **audit report** lends credibility to management's financial statements so that users can be more confident that the statements accurately represent what they purport to represent. In other words, an audit adds reliability to financial statements.

The most common type of audit report is one in which the auditor issues an **unqualified opinion,** which means that the auditor believes that the financial statements have been presented fairly in accordance with generally accepted accounting principles. Exhibit 1–1 illustrates a standard audit report in which an unqualified opinion is given. The wording was adopted by the accounting profession in 1988. In the **opening paragraph,** the auditor identifies the financial statements that were audited. The second paragraph, called the **scope paragraph,** describes the nature of an audit. The third paragraph, called the **opinion paragraph,** presents the auditor's opinion on the financial statements.

Auditors may also render qualified opinions, adverse opinions, and disclaimers. A **qualified opinion** is given when the overall financial statements are fairly presented "except for" certain items (which the auditor discloses). An **adverse opinion** means that the financial statements have not been presented fairly in accordance with generally accepted accounting principles. Finally, a **disclaimer of opinion** means that the auditor could not evaluate the fairness of the financial statements and, as a result, expresses no opinion on them.

Publicly owned companies and thousands of nonpublicly owned companies usually issue audited financial statements once each year. The Securities and Exchange Commission and the stock exchanges require that the annual financial statements of companies subject to their jurisdiction be audited by independent CPAs. Bankers often require a company's audited statements before making loans. Even when no one requires audited statements, managers often obtain audits and issue the audited statements.

EXHIBIT 1–1

Unqualified Audit Report

Independent Auditor's Report

We have audited the accompanying balance sheet of X Company as of December 31, 19XX, and the related statements of income, retained earnings, and cash flows for the year then ended. These financial statements are the responsibility of the Company's management. Our responsibility is to express an opinion on these financial statements based on our audit.

We conducted our audit in accordance with generally accepted auditing standards. Those standards require that we plan and perform the audit to obtain reasonable assurance about whether the financial statements are free of material misstatement. An audit includes examining, on a test basis, evidence supporting the amounts and disclosures in the financial statements. An audit also includes assessing the accounting principles used and significant estimates made by management, as well as evaluating the overall financial statement presentation. We believe that our audit provides a reasonable basis for our opinion.

In our opinion, the financial statements referred to above present fairly, in all material respects, the financial position of X Company as of [at] December 31, 19XX, and the results of its operations and its cash flows for the year then ended in conformity with generally accepted accounting principles.

(Date)

SOURCE: *Statement on Auditing Standards No. 58,* "Reports on Audited Financial Statements," 1988, par. 8.

Auditors must be **competent** and **independent** of any company whose financial statements they audit. To be competent, auditors must have a working knowledge of the generally accepted auditing standards that govern how an audit should be conducted as well as generally accepted accounting principles, many of which we cover in this textbook. To be independent, auditors must be honest and must not have any financial or family interest in the company they are auditing. Auditors must be independent *in fact* and *in appearance.* Users of financial statements simply will not attribute much importance to the auditor's opinion unless they perceive that the auditor is independent of the company being audited.

Exhibit 1–2 provides an overview of the major parties directly involved in the financial reporting process. They include preparers, auditors, and users of financial statements.

GENERALLY ACCEPTED ACCOUNTING PRINCIPLES

Basically, accounting principles are guidelines for gathering and communicating accounting information.[9] Imagine what would happen if companies were free to choose whatever accounting principles they preferred. One company might report its inventory at historical cost (the actual cost to purchase or produce the inventory), while others might use replacement costs, current selling prices, or other measurements. Or one company might publish only an income statement while another might report only a balance sheet. Such a situation could seriously reduce the ability of users to make valid comparisons between companies.

To help overcome this problem, the accounting profession has given some accounting principles the special status of being **generally accepted accounting principles** (commonly called **GAAP**). Generally accepted accounting principles are those that have **substantial authoritative support.**[10] Specifically, they represent "the consensus at any time as to which economic resources and obligations should be recorded as assets and liabilities, which changes in them should be recorded, when these changes should be recorded, how the recorded assets and liabilities and changes in them should be measured, what information should be disclosed and how it should be disclosed, and which financial statements should be prepared." [11] Internal and external accountants must have a thorough knowledge of generally accepted accounting principles in order to prepare and attest to financial statements. Moreover, users should be familiar with these principles so that they can understand the nature and limitations of the information presented in financial statements.

EXHIBIT 1–2
Preparers, Auditors, and Users of Financial Statements

Preparers
(Management, using internal accountants)

→

Financial Statements
(Balance sheet, income statement, etc.)

→

Users
(Investors, creditors, etc.)

↑

Auditors
(External accountants)

---

[9]Accounting principles have also been called *standards, concepts, procedures, rules,* and *practices.*

[10]AICPA Special Bulletin, *Disclosure of Departures from Opinions of Accounting Principles Board* (October 1964), par. 3.

[11]*APB Statement No. 4,* par. 27.

In some ways, generally accepted accounting principles are similar to laws within our legal system in that generally accepted accounting principles are formulated *by people.* Thus, instead of having been discovered in nature, generally accepted accounting principles "have developed on the basis of experience, reason, custom, usage, and, to a significant extent, practical necessity." [12] These principles should and do *change* as conditions warrant. Furthermore, they are often *highly controversial,* as are laws that govern draft registration, drinking, gambling, and many other areas. Just as laws should be judged based on how much they contribute to the achievement of society's goals, generally accepted accounting principles should be evaluated on the basis of how much they contribute to the **objectives of financial accounting.** Unlike laws, however, generally accepted accounting principles in the United States have largely been determined within the *private sector* rather than the public sector (the government sector) of our economy.

Generally accepted accounting principles help to determine the information contained in financial statements. In turn, financial statements help to determine the outcome of investment and credit decisions that affect everyone's well-being. Preparers, auditors, and users of financial statements (including various organizations that represent preparers, auditors, and users) are very interested in GAAP because they are affected by them. It should come as no surprise, then, that GAAP have usually been formulated in an environment in which considerable *political pressures* exist. Each group interested in financial reporting attempts to argue persuasively for the kind of accounting it desires for a particular kind of economic event or item, and some individual or group must find an acceptable resolution. Although politics has generally not dominated accounting standard setting in the United States and should never be allowed to do so, *politics will likely always play an important role in the development of GAAP.* Recently, for example, Senator Joseph I. Lieberman (D-Conn.) considered proposing a bill that would direct "the Securities and Exchange Commission to neither permit nor require companies to show an expense for the cost of stock options." [13]

DEVELOPMENT OF GENERALLY ACCEPTED ACCOUNTING PRINCIPLES

Most of the progress made in the development of generally accepted accounting principles (standards) in the United States occurred during and after the 1930s. This progress was spurred by such factors as the growth of the corporate form of business organization in the early 1900s, with its separation of ownership from management; the introduction of income taxation in 1913, which made accounting records necessary for tax purposes; the intense criticism of corporate reporting practices in the financial press during the early part of this century; the stock market crash of 1929 and the depression that followed it; and the passage in 1933–1934 of federal legislation designed to help ensure that investors have adequate information on which to base their investment decisions.

Understanding generally accepted accounting principles requires a knowledge of the various organizations that have influenced their development. Primary among these are the American Institute of Certified Public Accountants, the Financial Accounting Standards Board, and the Securities and Exchange Commission. Publications by these and other organizations assist students of intermediate accounting and more advanced courses in financial accounting.

AMERICAN INSTITUTE OF CERTIFIED PUBLIC ACCOUNTANTS

The **American Institute of Certified Public Accountants (AICPA)** is the national professional organization of CPAs. In addition to many other useful publications, the AICPA publishes a monthly journal, *The Journal of Accountancy,* that deals primarily with issues that are of concern to practicing accountants.

---

[12]*APB Statement No. 4,* par. 139.

[13]Financial Accounting Standards Board, *Status Report No. 244* (Stamford, Conn.: FASB, August 31, 1993).

Committee on Accounting Procedure

The AICPA's first major involvement in developing accounting principles occurred in 1938 when it established the **Committee on Accounting Procedure (CAP).** The CAP was composed of 21 volunteer AICPA members, most of whom were practicing accountants. Its purpose was to further the development of accounting principles, primarily by reducing the number of alternatives available for a given type of transaction or item.

The CAP issued pronouncements called **Accounting Research Bulletins (ARBs),** which summarized the committee's views concerning the proper accounting treatment for various transactions and items. ARBs were designed to help practicing accountants resolve specific issues, such as depreciation and long-term construction-type contracts.

The assenting votes of two-thirds of the CAP's members were required to issue an ARB, and from 1939 to 1959, the CAP issued 51 ARBs. Although the CAP was dissolved in 1959, those ARBs that have not been superseded by professional pronouncements are still important sources of generally accepted accounting principles.

ARBs were primarily *advisory* in nature. Although accountants generally followed the principles recommended in the ARBs, they were not required to do so. The AICPA could only *encourage* its members to observe the ARBs since it lacked the authority to require compliance. Ultimately, the authority of the ARBs was based on their general acceptance within the financial community.

The CAP authorized the publication of **Accounting Terminology Bulletins.** As the name implies, their purpose was to explain and improve accounting terminology. The first eight bulletins were reissued in 1953 as *Accounting Terminology Bulletin No. 1.* Three more bulletins were later published.

Even though the ARBs helped to improve the quality of accounting practice, the CAP was criticized for several reasons. The primary criticism was the committee's failure to develop a coherent framework of objectives and broad principles within which to resolve specific accounting problems. Instead, the CAP followed a more expedient "piecemeal" approach, trying to resolve immediate problems on a case-by-case basis. A result was that the ARBs were sometimes inconsistent with one another. Other major criticisms were that the CAP permitted too many alternative accounting principles to exist, did not move quickly enough, and did not support conclusions with research.

Accounting Principles Board

In 1959 the AICPA replaced the CAP with the **Accounting Principles Board (APB),** which was responsible for developing accounting principles. This new committee consisted of 18 to 21 volunteer accountants who were drawn from public practice, industry, colleges and universities, and government. The primary pronouncements that the APB issued are called **Opinions.** These opinions presented the board's views concerning proper accounting in areas such as income taxes, earnings per share, and intangible assets. Issuance of an opinion required a two-thirds vote of the APB's members. From 1959 to 1973, the board issued 31 opinions. Although the APB was replaced in 1973 by the Financial Accounting Standards Board, opinions that have not been superseded are still important sources of generally accepted accounting principles.

APB Opinions often dealt with complex issues. Thus, the AICPA published a series of **Accounting Interpretations** (of APB Opinions) designed to guide practitioners in applying opinions. Interpretations were not, however, formal pronouncements of the APB.

During the early years of the APB's existence, the AICPA could not require practitioners to comply with APB Opinions. In October 1964, however, the AICPA's governing council adopted a recommendation that AICPA members "should see to it that departures from Opinions of the Accounting Principles Board (as well as effective Accounting Research Bulletins issued by the former Committee on Accounting Procedure) are disclosed, either in footnotes to financial statements or in the audit reports of members in their capacity as independent auditors." [14] In 1972 this recommendation was incorporated in **Rule 203** of the AICPA Code of Professional Conduct. It prohibits an AICPA member from expressing an opinion that financial statements conform with GAAP if the statements contain a material departure from an accounting principle established by the Financial Accounting Standards Board (as well as accounting principles established by effective ARBs and APB Opinions), unless the member can prove that, because of unusual circumstances, following such a principle would result in misleading financial statements. [15]

The AICPA has extended the original scope of *Rule 203* by requiring AICPA members to justify departures from Financial Accounting Standards Board standards that relate to the disclosure of information *outside* of the published financial statements, such as supplementary financial statements adjusted for the effects of inflation. [16] *Rule 203* is very important because it effectively requires that AICPA members either comply with authoritative accounting pronouncements or risk having to defend why they did not do so. Generally, few accountants want to assume such a risk.

When the AICPA established the APB, it also created a separate Accounting Research Division (within the AICPA). Unlike the CAP, the APB emphasis was placed on research. When it established the APB, the AICPA expected that the board's opinions would be influenced by the logical and thorough **Accounting Research Studies** conducted for the Research Division. These studies were designed as a basis to identify and discuss accounting problems, but the conclusions of the authors did not represent the official position of the AICPA. Fifteen Accounting Research Studies ultimately were published.

The Accounting Research Studies did not have as much impact on the APB's conclusions as was hoped when the Research Division was organized. For example, two of the earliest studies were expected to identify a set of basic postulates (assumptions) and broad principles that would serve as a logical foundation for the APB's Opinions. [17] After these studies were published in 1962, the APB merely acknowledged their contribution to accounting thought. But the board did not accept the studies because it believed that they were too radically different from the generally accepted accounting principles in existence at that time.

Although the APB made significant progress in the development of generally accepted accounting principles, it was criticized for most of the same reasons for which the CAP had been criticized earlier. Critics also charged that the views of large public accounting firms and the AICPA had, and were *seen* to have, too much influence on the APB's decisions. Some charged, for example, that public accountants on the board were hard pressed to criticize poor accounting principles that their own clients were using.

In response to these criticisms, the AICPA appointed a seven-person committee, chaired by Francis M. Wheat, to study the process of establishing accounting principles and to make recommendations for improvement. The Wheat Committee issued its report in March 1972, which led to the establishment of the Financial Accounting Standards Board.

FINANCIAL ACCOUNTING STANDARDS BOARD

Since July 1973, the **Financial Accounting Standards Board (FASB)** has been the official private sector body charged with establishing and improving generally accepted accounting

---

[14]AICPA Special Bulletin, *Disclosure of Departures from Opinions of Accounting Principles Board,* par. 1.

[15]*AICPA Professional Standards—Volume 2* (Chicago: Commerce Clearing House), ET Sec. 203.01.

[16]*AICPA Code of Professional Conduct* (New York: AICPA, 1988), p. 11.

[17]These studies are *Accounting Research Study No. 1*, "The Basic Postulates of Accounting" (New York: AICPA, 1961) by Maurice Moonitz, and *Accounting Research Study No. 3*, "A Tentative Set of Broad Accounting Principles for Business Enterprises" (New York: AICPA, 1962) by Robert T. Sprouse and Maurice Moonitz.

principles for business enterprises in the United States.[18] At its outset the board decided that ARBs and APB opinions should remain in force until superseded by an FASB pronouncement.

Like the CAP and the APB, the FASB formulates accounting principles in a committee context. However, the FASB now has several important characteristics that make it different from its predecessors:

1. The FASB consists of only *seven members.* It has considerably fewer members than its predecessors, which tends to reduce the time needed to respond to emerging problems.
2. All FASB members are *fully remunerated* and *serve full-time.* Whereas the members of the predecessor committees were part-time volunteers who continued to hold their positions elsewhere, FASB members must sever their ties with former employers before they serve on the board. This feature reduces the possibility of actual or apparent conflicts of interest.
3. FASB members are *not required to be CPAs.* In contrast, members of the predecessor committees were AICPA members and therefore were CPAs. This FASB characteristic reduces the likelihood that FASB pronouncements will reflect only the views of preparers and auditors of financial statements.
4. The FASB is an *independent body.* It is not part of the AICPA, as were its predecessors. This feature reduces the chances that FASB pronouncements will reflect, and be *seen* to reflect, only the views of the AICPA.

The FASB issues three major types of pronouncements:

1. **Statements of Financial Accounting Standards (SFASs).** These establish new or amend existing generally accepted accounting principles.
2. **Interpretations.** These clarify, explain, or elaborate on SFASs, APB Opinions, or ARBs. Interpretations are themselves a part of GAAP.
3. **Statements of Financial Accounting Concepts (SFACs).** These set forth objectives and concepts that the FASB uses as the basis for establishing and improving generally accepted accounting principles. SFACs do not establish generally accepted accounting principles within the scope of *Rule 203.*

In addition, the FASB's staff issues **Technical Bulletins** that are designed to provide guidance on certain financial accounting and reporting problems on a timely basis. Technical Bulletins generally deal with questions about how to implement existing standards in practice. Interested parties are invited to comment on proposed Technical Bulletins, and all Technical Bulletins are considered by the FASB at a public meeting. The FASB's staff also publishes *Qs and As* (Questions and Answers) to provide quick answers to certain narrow, technical questions that have been posed.

In 1984 the FASB established an **Emerging Issues Task Force (EITF)** composed of 17 persons who represent CPA firms, major companies, the FASB, and the SEC. This group meets every six weeks to resolve, on a timely basis, accounting problems associated with new types of transactions. The EITF publishes **consensus positions** that explain its views. By resolving short-term emerging issues fairly quickly, the EITF allows the FASB to focus on those longer-term, more pervasive issues that affect financial reporting.

At times, the FASB needs to change accounting principles because of such factors as changing business and economic circumstances, new informational needs of investors and creditors, advances in information technology, and abuses in the application of existing principles. In deciding whether to add a new project to its lengthy agenda, the FASB considers four criteria: pervasiveness of the accounting issue, availability of alternative solutions, technical feasibility of deriving a solution to the accounting problem, and practical

---

[18]The Wheat Committee recommended use of the term *standards* instead of *principles* because of confusion over the meaning of *accounting principles.* In this textbook we use the terms *principles* and *standards* interchangeably.

IT'S TIME TO FREE THE FASB SEVEN

If accounting is the language of business, too many companies speak in the balance-sheet equivalent of Aramaic. Accounting standards change so slowly, they often seem relics from another era. At times, that can have dire consequences. During the 1980s, for instance, hundreds of troubled thrifts engaged in wild—and disastrous—speculation, yet their balance sheets seemed to be in the black. That's because accounting rules let S&Ls book a debt security at its purchase price, masking how much it may have dropped in value. Only belatedly did taxpayers and shareholders learn about the multibillion-dollar losses.

Many experts place the blame for the creaky pace of rule changes squarely on the obscure organization empowered by the Securities & Exchange Commission to make accounting policy: the 20-year-old Financial Accounting Standards Board. Sure, the Norwalk (Conn.) organization sometimes seems to have a ferocious bark. In 1991, it forced companies to book charges for their huge retiree health-benefits liabilities, and on April 7, it voted to require them to deduct employee stock options from earnings. But FASB often takes a decade to go after the corporate ankle.

Wiggle Room

The reason: FASB's board is kept on a short leash by corporate interests, which have too much influence over its funding and membership. "It's doubtful you're going to have a standards board dedicated to substantial change," says John C. Burton, former SEC chief accountant.

FASB's seven board members—usually retired accountants—began studying the stock-options and health-benefits proposals back in 1984. And FASB decisions often contain loopholes. On April 13, FASB finally acted—under SEC pressure—to force banks and insurers to mark their debt instruments to current market value. Bowing to these institutions, however, FASB postponed making the requirement effective until 1997. It also gave banks and insurers wiggle room: If they claim they'll hold a bond until maturity, they can carry it at its purchase price.

Much of the heat comes from FASB trustees in the Financial Accounting Federation, which appoints FASB board members and approves its spending. Its 16 trustees are drawn from companies, accounting firms, government, and academe, but Corporate America is the most influential. In particular, the Business Roundtable, a group of CEOs from the biggest U.S. corporations, has pressed its party line on trustees. The Roundtable also urges accounting firms and consultants, who feed from the corporate trough, to provide self-serving expertise to FASB. In the mid-1980s, trustees voted to award Corporate America a second FASB seat. In 1990, they upped the number of board votes needed to approve a proposal, from four votes to five—making it tougher for reform initiatives.

Maverick Axed

Pro-Big Business trustees often lobby FASB members aggressively. FASB Chairman Dennis R. Beresford admits this is a problem: "Sometimes, we have to educate [the trustees] as to what the limits of their responsibilities are." Among the more blatant moves was their 1991 refusal to reappoint C. Arthur Northrop, a former IBM treasurer. Northrop frequently voted against executives on controversial issues. Says Paul B. Miller, accounting professor at the University of Colorado: "The trustees were created to protect the board from pressure, but instead they have become the implements of pressure."

It's time to free the FASB Seven from this outside influence—beginning with their financial support. Companies and their handmaiden accounting firms provide 35 percent of FASB's $15 million annual budget. Critics contend that some executives have threatened to withhold support if FASB doesn't vote their way.

A good solution is to require that corporations filing documents with the SEC pay a small sum each time to create a permanent endowment for FASB. Another remedy: Shift board appointment power to the SEC. Together, these measures would make it easier to update accounting rules. And corporate reports at last would reflect current conditions, not ancient history.

SOURCE: Dean Foust, "It's Time to Free the FASB Seven," *Business Week*, May 3, 1993, p. 144. Reprinted from November 22, 1993 issue of Business Week, copyright © 1993 by McGraw-Hill, Inc.

consequences.[19] When the FASB tentatively decides to change accounting principles in a particular area (for example, leases or pensions), people are vitally interested because of the considerable impact that financial statements have on the allocation of wealth in our society. The FASB therefore has an elaborate **due process system** that it follows diligently when developing new accounting principles.

The FASB tries to involve in its standard-setting process everyone who is interested in financial reporting and wants to participate. These people include preparers, auditors, users, and others. FASB members may therefore have backgrounds in financial analysis, industry, government, and academia, as well as in public accounting. FASB meetings are open to the

---

[19]Dennis R. Beresford, "The 'Balancing Act' in Setting Accounting Standards," *Accounting Horizons* (March 1988), p. 1.

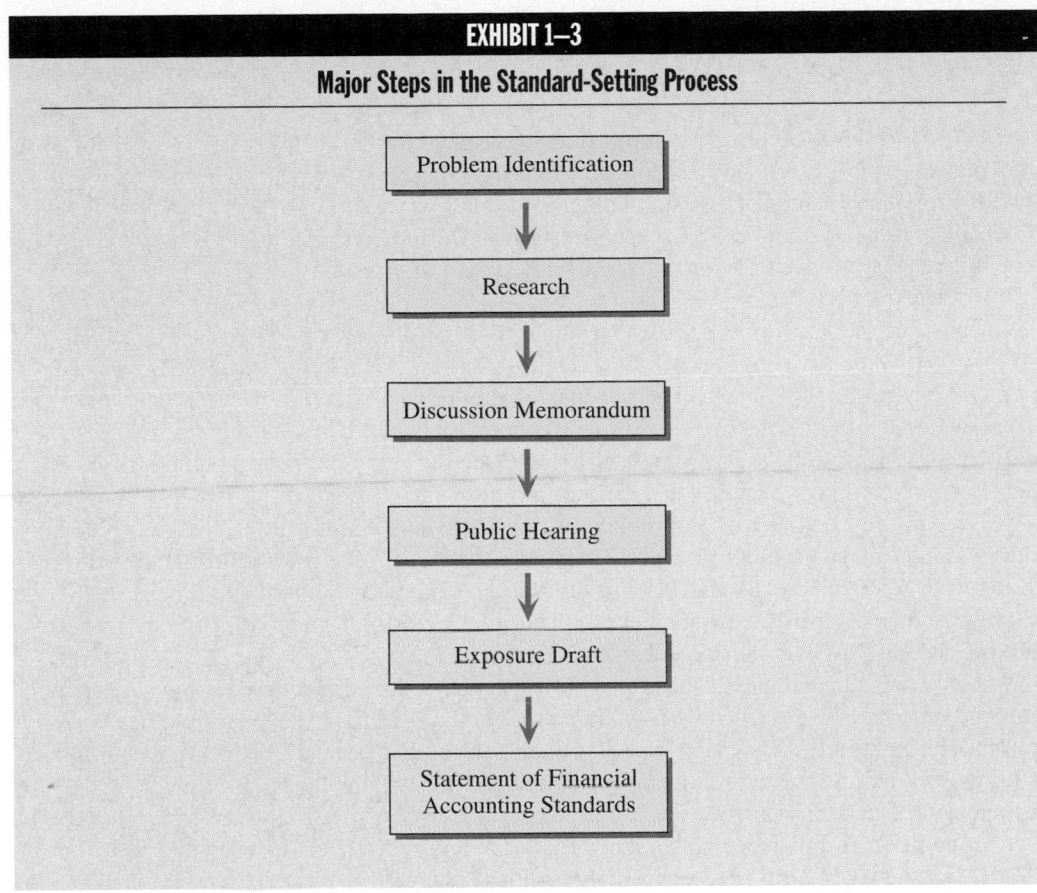

EXHIBIT 1–3

Major Steps in the Standard-Setting Process

Problem Identification

Research

Discussion Memorandum

Public Hearing

Exposure Draft

Statement of Financial Accounting Standards

public, and the board keeps a public record. The board's due process system of formulating an SFAS typically involves the following major steps, illustrated in Exhibit 1–3:[20]

1. The board *identifies an accounting problem* (such as accounting for leases or pension plans) and places the problem on its agenda.
2. The board appoints a task force of technical experts, which *conducts extensive research* on the problem.
3. The board issues a **Discussion Memorandum,** which summarizes the major issues and possible solutions and serves as the basis for public comment.
4. The board *conducts a public hearing* at which it invites interested parties to present their views.
5. The board issues an **Exposure Draft,** which is a *proposed* SFAS that is distributed for public comment.
6. The board *issues an SFAS* after it has analyzed public responses to the exposure draft. Issuing a pronouncement now requires an affirmative *vote of five of the seven FASB members.*[21]

The **Financial Accounting Foundation** is the independent entity whose board of trustees oversees the basic structure of the standard-setting process. In addition, the trustees

---

[20]The FASB follows similar steps when issuing Interpretations and SFACs.

[21]The Trustees of the Financial Accounting Foundation have changed the number of affirmative votes required from four (a simple majority) to five (a supermajority). The requirement for five assenting votes became effective on January 1, 1991. The Trustees made the change to ensure that the FASB would not likely issue a pronouncement when considerable dissent still exists among FASB members.

appoint members to the FASB and to the FASB's advisory council. They also secure private contributions to fund the FASB's operations. The trustees are appointed by a panel of representatives from several national organizations whose members have a knowledge of and an interest in corporate financial reporting.

The **Financial Accounting Standards Advisory Council** helps the FASB to set priorities and to establish ad hoc task forces. Moreover, the advisory council reacts to proposed FASB pronouncements and assists the board in other ways. Often the FASB appoints a task force to help the board resolve a specific problem. Members of the advisory council frequently serve on these task forces. The FASB is also assisted by full-time research and administrative staffs.

Thus far, the FASB has set accounting standards using a case-by-case approach similar to that of its predecessors. But one of the initial tasks undertaken by the FASB was a **Conceptual Framework Project.** The purpose of this project was to develop an authoritative, coherent structure of objectives and broad fundamentals of financial accounting. The FASB calls it a "constitution" that it hopes will lead to better, more consistent standards. This recently completed project will be discussed in more depth later in this chapter.

As you might expect, the existence of the FASB has changed the AICPA's role in the development of accounting principles. Currently, the AICPA has an **Accounting Standards Executive Committee (AcSEC).** This committee issues **Statements of Position (SOPs)** that are intended to influence the development of accounting principles in specialized areas not covered by FASB pronouncements.

AcSEC also distributes **Issues Papers,** which are designed to identify financial accounting and reporting issues (such as LIFO inventories) that AcSEC believes should be addressed or clarified by the FASB. Issues Papers present neutral discussions of various accounting issues as well as arguments on alternative solutions. Issues Papers normally include advisory conclusions that represent the views of at least a majority of AcSEC members.

In addition to publishing SOPs and Issues Papers, the AICPA also publishes **Industry Audit Guides** and **Industry Accounting Guides.** The guides are prepared by AICPA committees or task forces and usually deal with specialized financial reporting issues that pertain only to a particular industry (e.g., casinos). The guides are normally reviewed by AcSEC and the FASB before being issued. In November 1987, AcSEC began a series of **Practice Bulletins,** which focus on certain narrow accounting issues.

In addition to AcSEC, the AICPA has an **Auditing Standards Board (ASB).** The ASB develops auditing standards and enforces professional ethics.

Because accounting principles help to determine how resources are allocated in our economy, it is not surprising that the FASB, like its predecessor committees, often has had to deal with **political pressures** in addition to having to decide what is theoretically sound accounting. In 1979, for example, the Securities and Exchange Commission, acting under pressure from Congress and the Department of Energy, in effect forced the FASB to change the accounting principles it had developed for oil and gas producing companies. Why did the SEC take this action? One major reason was that many smaller producers claimed that the FASB's principles would force them to report lower earnings, thereby making it harder for them to raise capital. According to these smaller producers, this in turn would adversely affect the nation's ability to discover oil and gas. Clearly, the ability of the FASB to survive as a private sector, standard-setting body will depend to a large extent on how effectively it handles the many conflicting political pressures that are brought on it.

GOVERNMENTAL ACCOUNTING STANDARDS BOARD

In 1984 the Financial Accounting Foundation established the **Governmental Accounting Standards Board (GASB)** to formulate accounting standards for state and local governments. The GASB operates much like the FASB. It exists in the private sector, has five members, and follows a due process system when setting standards. The GASB and FASB have equal status as arms of the Financial Accounting Foundation. GASB standards apply to state and local governments; FASB standards apply to all other organizations.

In 1986 the AICPA designated the GASB's authoritative pronouncements as being within the scope of *Rule 203* of the AICPA's Code of Professional Conduct. Accountants and auditors must therefore apply GASB standards when presenting the financial statements of a state or local government. This textbook deals primarily with accounting for business enterprises and therefore does not cover GASB standards. These are usually covered in governmental accounting textbooks.

SECURITIES AND EXCHANGE COMMISSION

The level of stock prices in the United States declined dramatically between 1929 and 1933. This occurrence brought considerable public pressure for better disclosure of corporate information. In the midst of this pressure and of a severe depression, Congress enacted legislation that has had a tremendous influence on corporate financial reporting. Basically, Congress passed the **Securities Act of 1933** to improve the disclosures made by companies when they sell a *new* issue of securities to the public. Then it passed the **Securities Exchange Act of 1934** to improve the periodic disclosures made by companies whose shares are publicly traded. The 1934 Act created the **Securities and Exchange Commission (SEC)** as a public sector organization to enforce both of these disclosure statutes.

The SEC does not protect investors from sustaining losses. Instead, its basic purpose is to ensure that companies provide investors with adequate information on which to base their investment decisions. Accordingly, companies under SEC jurisdiction must report to the SEC a substantial quantity of information on a variety of different forms.[22] This information is available for public use. The most important corporate reports required by the SEC are the following:

1. **Registration statement.** This is a detailed report required under the 1933 Act when a company offers publicly its securities. It includes such information as the nature of the company's business, a description of the securities being registered, and audited financial statements.
2. **10-K report.** This is a detailed report that companies file annually under the 1934 Act. It discloses various corporate activities as well as audited financial statements. Companies usually disclose more in their 10-K reports than in their annual reports to shareholders.
3. **10-Q report.** This is a quarterly report filed under the 1934 Act. It is much less detailed than the 10-K. In addition to a description of various activities, the 10-Q report includes financial information that has been reviewed but not audited by an independent CPA.
4. **8-K report.** This report, required under the 1934 Act, explains a material event (such as a major acquisition or a lawsuit) that investors want to know about. An 8-K report usually must be filed within 15 days after a material event has occurred.

These reports reflect the SEC's concern that companies disclose relevant financial and non-financial information on a timely basis. The SEC also is concerned about the costs that companies must incur to comply with the various disclosure requirements. Accordingly, the SEC designed an **integrated disclosure system** that allows companies to avoid having to file duplicate copies of certain information that is already publicly available.

The SEC is also engaged in an ongoing project (known as the *Electronic Data Gathering, Analysis, and Retrieval System,* commonly called **EDGAR**) that will allow companies to file reports electronically, via computerized documents. At some time in the future, users

---

[22]In essence, the 1933 Act applies to a company when it makes a public offering of its securities. The 1934 Act applies mainly to companies whose securities are traded on a national securities exchange and to "over-the-counter" companies that have at least $5,000,000 in assets and at least 500 stockholders.

of financial statements may be able to obtain convenient access to the information contained in the SEC's electronic filings through their personal computers.

The primary sources of the SEC's financial information requirements are

1. **Regulation S-X.** This is the original source that prescribes the form and content of financial statements filed with the SEC. It is revised frequently.
2. **Accounting Series Releases (ASRs).** These are pronouncements that modify the SEC's financial information requirements.
3. **Staff Accounting Bulletins (SABs).** These are interpretations and practices followed by the SEC's staff in administrating the commission's disclosure requirements. SABs are not official rules or interpretations of the SEC itself.
4. **Financial Reporting Releases (FRRs).** These pronouncements were first issued in 1982 and are intended to replace ASRs. The first FRR is a codification of portions of ASRs that were relevant when it was issued.
5. **Accounting and Auditing Enforcement Releases (AAERs).** These pronouncements began in 1982 and deal with enforcement-related matters.

Since its inception, the SEC has had *broad legal authority to establish accounting and reporting standards.* To date, the Commission has largely delegated this authority to private sector organizations (the CAP, APB, and FASB). But the SEC can in effect veto the standards set by these organizations, and it has done so occasionally.[23] The SEC can effectively veto a standard set by the FASB by refusing to force companies to apply it in reports filed with the Commission. *Remember* that the SEC has statutory authority to prescribe accounting and reporting standards for companies under its jurisdiction.

Generally, the SEC and each of the private sector, standard-setting organizations have cooperated with each other. In *ASR No. 150,* the SEC indicated that it looked to the FASB to provide leadership in establishing and improving accounting principles. The SEC nevertheless has considerable influence on the development of accounting principles. The main ways that the SEC has exerted its influence are by responding to planned and existing pronouncements of the FASB and of its predecessors and by strongly encouraging these organizations to resolve emerging accounting problems.

During the 1970s the SEC played a more active role in developing accounting principles. Understanding the significance of the SEC's role is vital to the study of financial accounting.

OTHER INFLUENCES ON ACCOUNTING PRINCIPLES

The AICPA, FASB, and SEC are the organizations that have had the most influence in shaping generally accepted accounting principles for business enterprises. However, certain other organizations as well as the income tax law have had an important impact.[24]

Income Tax Law

The **income tax law,** as enacted by Congress, administered by the Internal Revenue Service, and interpreted by the courts, has influenced the development and the implementation of accounting principles. For example, many smaller businesses maintain accounting records primarily for income tax purposes. Moreover, to avoid having to maintain one set of books for financial accounting purposes and a different set for tax purposes, many companies use fi-

---

[23]In 1972 an APB member likened the SEC to top management and the APB to lower-level management. See Charles T. Horngren, "Accounting Principles: Public or Private Sector?" *Journal of Accountancy* (May 1972), pp. 37–41.

[24]Some students who have taken cost accounting may notice that we have not included the **Cost Accounting Standards Board (CASB)** in the following discussion. The CASB is a federal agency initially created by Congress in 1970. It is a public sector body charged with developing cost accounting standards for use by most businesses with large government contracts. The CASB was abolished in 1980 and reestablished in 1988. Overall, it has had a very limited impact on financial accounting.

nancial accounting principles that will reduce and postpone their income tax payments. Suppose that a company plans to use an accelerated depreciation method for tax purposes but has no strong theoretical reason to favor any particular depreciation method for financial reporting purposes. The company may choose the accelerated method for financial reporting purposes (as well as for tax purposes) to avoid the need for two sets of depreciation records.

Finally, the tax law states that if a company uses the last-in, first-out (LIFO) inventory method for tax purposes, it must also use LIFO for financial reporting purposes. We explain this conformity requirement in Chapter 8.

Although tax law has played a role in shaping generally accepted accounting principles, an important point to remember is that *the principles that a company should use for tax purposes are not necessarily the same as those it should use for financial accounting purposes.* Tax accounting focuses on the measurement of taxable income using principles established by tax laws. In contrast, a primary focus of financial accounting is the measurement of accounting income using generally accepted accounting principles. The objectives of the tax law are to *raise money* for the operation of the government and to achieve certain *social goals.* In contrast, the primary objective of generally accepted accounting principles is to *provide useful information* to investors, creditors, and other users. Because the objectives of tax accounting and financial accounting differ, we find that the principles of tax accounting frequently differ from those of financial accounting.

This textbook deals with financial accounting principles. In Chapter 18, we examine financial accounting issues that relate directly to corporate income taxes.

Interestingly, many accountants believe that income tax law often has played a major role in the "nondevelopment" of GAAP. For example, the use of current value accounting in a company's primary financial statements is not now a generally accepted accounting principle. One reason for the opposition is the fear that such accounting will "create new kinds of income" that the government will want to tax.

American Accounting Association

The **American Accounting Association (AAA)** is dominated by accounting educators, although many practicing accountants are active members. In addition to fostering improvements in accounting education and research, the AAA has helped to develop accounting principles, especially in the area of financial accounting theory.

AAA committees have traditionally followed a broader, more conceptual approach to the development of accounting principles than either the FASB or its predecessors. Publications of the AAA often concentrate on what accounting *should be* rather than on what it *is now.*

Unlike the FASB, the AAA is not an organization designed to promulgate accounting principles that practitioners must observe. The AAA has therefore not been highly concerned about whether the work of its committees receives immediate acceptance in practice. AAA publications often affect practice in indirect ways several years after they are published.

Included among many AAA publications are three journals: *The Accounting Review,* which publishes scholarly research in all areas of accounting; *Accounting Horizons,* which publishes applied accounting research; and *Issues in Accounting Education,* which publishes research that pertains to accounting education.

The AAA is actively involved in the work of the FASB. For example, an AAA representative serves on the panel that selects the trustees of the Financial Accounting Foundation, and an AAA committee reacts to FASB pronouncements.

Financial Executives Institute

The **Financial Executives Institute (FEI)** primarily comprises financial executives, such as controllers and treasurers, from large corporations. Members of this organization are an important subset of *preparers* of financial statements. Views expressed by FEI members have played a significant role in the development of generally accepted accounting principles.

The FEI publishes a journal called *Financial Executive,* and it has sponsored several important research studies in financial accounting. Like the AAA, the FEI has been actively involved in the work of the FASB.

Institute of Management Accountants

The **Institute of Management Accountants (IMA)** consists largely of industrial accountants. Traditionally, the IMA has focused on cost and managerial accounting. In recent years, however, it has increased its role in the development of financial accounting standards.

The IMA publishes a journal called *Management Accounting.* In addition, it has published several important research studies in financial accounting, and it administers the CMA program. Like the AAA and the FEI, the IMA has been actively involved in the FASB's work.

Financial Analysts Federation

The **Financial Analysts Federation (FAF),** a national organization of financial analysts, is one of the most knowledgeable and influential groups that *use* accounting information. A **financial analyst** is a person who analyzes information and renders professional advice on investment matters. Many analysts have earned the designation **Chartered Financial Analyst (CFA).** A CFA is an individual who has met certain education and experience requirements and who has passed a rigorous examination on such subjects as accounting, economics, financial analysis, portfolio management, and ethics.

The FAF publishes the *Financial Analysts Journal.* The organization maintains a strong interest in corporate financial reporting, and it plays an active role in the work of the FASB. Financial analysts frequently have served as participants in behavioral studies on the uses of accounting information.

Robert Morris Associates

Robert Morris Associates (RMA) is a national organization of bank loan and credit officers. As *users* of accounting information, commercial bank loan officers have influenced the development of generally accepted accounting principles. Much of this influence occurred around the beginning of this century, when bankers were the dominant external users of accounting information. Like financial analysts, bank loan officers often serve as participants in accounting research studies. RMA publishes *The Journal of Commercial Bank Lending.*

SOURCES OF GENERALLY ACCEPTED ACCOUNTING PRINCIPLES

As stated earlier, generally accepted accounting principles have substantial authoritative support. The accounting profession has never published a complete, official list of such principles. Furthermore, because the profession has not defined precisely what is meant by the phrase "substantial authoritative support," the boundary that separates generally accepted accounting principles from others is sometimes hazy. In practice, therefore, determining whether an accounting principle is generally accepted sometimes requires judgment. Accountants and auditors must be familiar with the sources of generally accepted accounting principles in order to answer difficult measurement and disclosure questions.

Statement on Auditing Standards No. 69 classifies generally accepted accounting principles for business enterprises in the five categories shown in Exhibit 1–4.[25] In general, these

---

[25]*Statement on Auditing Standards No. 69,* "The Meaning of Present Fairly in Conformity with Generally Accepted Accounting Principles in the Independent Auditor's Report" (New York: AICPA, 1992). This chapter provides an overview of the main ideas in *SAS 69* that apply to intermediate accounting. Readers who seek more details should examine *SAS 69.*

EXHIBIT 1–4

GAAP Hierarchy for Business Enterprises

Established Accounting Principles

Category A—FASB Statements of Financial Accounting Standards, FASB Interpretations, APB Opinions, and Accounting Research Bulletins. These sources represent the most authoritative sources of GAAP.

Category B—FASB Technical Bulletins, AICPA Industry Audit and Accounting Guides, and AICPA Statements of Position.

Category C—Consensus positions of the FASB Emerging Issues Task Force and AICPA Practice Bulletins.

Category D—AICPA Accounting Interpretations, Questions and Answers published by the FASB staff, as well as industry practices widely recognized and prevalent.

Other Accounting Literature

Category E—Includes such examples as FASB Concepts Statements, AICPA Issues Papers, International Accounting Standards Committee Statements, and accounting textbooks and journal articles.

SOURCE: Adapted from *Statement on Auditing Standards No. 69,* "The Meaning of Present Fairly in Conformity with Generally Accepted Accounting Principles in the Independent Auditor's Report" (New York: AICPA, 1992), p. 8.

---

categories are ranked from the most authoritative sources of GAAP (category A) to the least authoritative sources (category E). Categories A through D represent *established accounting principles;* category E encompasses *other accounting literature.* Accountants should always record transactions in accordance with the *substance* (true nature) of the transactions.

Category A contains pronouncements of an authoritative body designated by the AICPA council to establish accounting principles under *Rule 203* of the AICPA Code of Professional Conduct. An accountant should follow the accounting treatment indicated in a ***Rule 203* pronouncement** (i.e., a category A pronouncement) unless unusual circumstances exist that indicate that following the pronouncement would cause the financial statements to be *misleading.* If an accounting treatment is not specified in a category A pronouncement, the accountant should consult sources of established accounting principles in categories B, C, or D, in that order. Finally, if an accounting treatment is not covered in category A, B, C, or D, the accountant should consult other accounting literature (category E). When consulting sources in category E, the accountant should subjectively evaluate the authoritative status of the issuer or author. For example, FASB Concepts Statements would normally be more influential than textbooks or journal articles.

Although considerable progress has been made in the development of generally accepted accounting principles, much more work remains to be done. Some of the major issues that are likely to affect progress in this area are briefly discussed below.

CONCEPTUAL FRAMEWORK ISSUE

A project that may ultimately have the greatest overall impact on the accounting standard-setting process is the FASB's Conceptual Framework Project. As stated earlier, this project has sought to develop an authoritative, coherent structure of objectives and broad fundamentals of financial accounting. This structure will be the basis for developing new financial accounting standards and eliminating inconsistencies that exist in current standards. It should

FUTURE DEVELOPMENT OF GENERALLY ACCEPTED ACCOUNTING PRINCIPLES

provide a strong foundation to help the FASB resolve difficult accounting questions. The FASB also intends that the structure will help everyone who has an interest in financial accounting to better understand the nature and limitations of financial accounting information.

To give you a more concrete idea of what the FASB means by a conceptual framework, here are the major topics that the Conceptual Framework Project comprises:

1. Objectives of financial reporting by business enterprises.
2. Objectives of financial reporting by nonbusiness organizations.
3. Qualitative characteristics of accounting information.
4. Elements of financial statements.
5. Recognition and measurement in financial statements of business enterprises.

The development of an authoritative conceptual framework has taken a lot of time, and there have been no easy, clear-cut answers to the questions that have arisen. The conceptual framework will continue to evolve in the future, but changes in it will not likely occur as fast as changes in accounting standards. In the long run, the FASB's success as a policy-making organization will probably depend heavily on the success of the Conceptual Framework Project. Yet a conceptual framework is unlikely to be a panacea. Certain factors will limit its usefulness: (1) the accounting policy-making process entails complex social choices; (2) the conceptual framework may not be interpreted uniformly by all FASB members at a given time; and (3) the FASB membership will continue to change over time, thereby possibly altering the board's interpretation of the conceptual framework.[26]

ECONOMIC IMPACT ISSUE

Accounting principles affect the allocation of scarce resources in our society because they determine the content of financial statements that investors, creditors, and others use to make many important decisions. Perhaps less obvious but also very important is the fact that a *manager's behavior,* as reflected in various operating and financial decisions, often is influenced by the manager's knowledge of the information that accounting principles require. Indeed, some of a manager's compensation (i.e., bonus) often is determined by the amount of net income reported in the company's financial statements. For example, Disney's CEO was once awarded a contract that included "an annual cash bonus equal to 2% of Disney's net income in excess of a 9% return on equity. That clause alone resulted in a $6.8 million bonus [in 1988] when Disney's ROE hit 25%."[27]

A former chief accountant of the SEC has aptly stated that "the way you keep score determines at least in part the way you play the game."[28] Under current generally accepted accounting principles, for example, a company is not required to include all types of leases among its liabilities. Many people believe that if the FASB required companies to include all leases among their liabilities, companies would engage in fewer leasing transactions. Because of the actions of preparers and users of financial statements, accounting principles have an important *economic impact* on our society. Simply put, they help to determine who gets how much wealth.

In recent years, accounting principles have been directly linked to such issues as health care for retirees, bank lending policies, the merger movement, gross national product, national energy policy, and tax policy designed to encourage business investment. This fact has raised questions about whether and to what extent the FASB should be concerned with the

---

[26]See Charles T. Horngren, "Uses and Limitations of a Conceptual Framework," *Journal of Accountancy* (April 1981), pp. 86, 88, 90, 92, 94–95.

[27]John A. Byrne, Ronald Grover, and Todd Vogel, "Is the Boss Getting Paid Too Much?" *Business Week* (May 1, 1989), p. 52.

[28]"Why Everybody's Jumping on the Accountants These Days," *Forbes* (March 15, 1977), p. 39.

economic impact of the standards that it sets. When the FASB established standards for oil and gas producing companies, to use a recent example mentioned earlier, should the FASB have been concerned only with trying to do what it considered correct according to accounting theory, or should it also have been concerned with doing what some energy producers claimed was best for the nation's energy program?

During the 1970s and 1980s, the economic impact issue began to play an increasingly important role in the standard-setting process of both the APB and the FASB.[29] An awareness of this role helps to explain some of the generally accepted accounting principles that exist today.

In the future, the FASB is likely to be guided in its decisions primarily by the accounting theory that the board has adopted in its Conceptual Framework Project. However, the board will also consider the economic impact of its decisions by assessing the economic benefits and costs that its decisions are likely to produce. Doing this will not, of course, be easy.

PUBLIC VERSUS PRIVATE SECTOR ISSUE

As noted earlier, private sector organizations have played the dominant role in shaping the development of generally accepted accounting principles in the United States. Nevertheless, the SEC has the legal authority to prescribe accounting principles, and Congress can effectively tell the SEC what to do. Will Congress ever decide that accounting principles should be formulated in the public sector?

In the past, Congress has exerted relatively little direct influence on the standard-setting process. The most notable exceptions have been in the areas of LIFO inventory pricing, accounting for the investment tax credit, and accounting for oil and gas producing companies.

In 1976, however, a report issued by a House of Representatives subcommittee chaired by John E. Moss criticized the lack of uniformity in generally accepted accounting principles. Later that year, a Senate subcommittee chaired by Lee Metcalf issued a staff study that recommended that the federal government should establish financial accounting standards for publicly owned corporations. The same Senate subcommittee issued a report in 1977 that was much less critical of the accounting profession and the standard-setting process. In 1984 and 1985, a House of Representatives subcommittee chaired by John D. Dingell held hearings during which many criticisms of accounting standard-setting were expressed. This subcommittee seriously questioned whether existing accounting and auditing standards are sufficient to alert investors and creditors to potential business failures.

The accounting profession has responded to these Congressional criticisms in many ways, but presently it appears that Congress does not have a strong interest in creating a federal board to establish financial accounting standards. Nevertheless, the work of the Congressional subcommittees has shown that some elected officials are not pleased with the progress that private sector organizations have made in developing accounting standards.

Most accountants and other businesspeople believe strongly that standard setting should remain in the private sector. A survey of the preferences of 1,329 preparers, auditors, and users of financial reports "showed a clear preference for financial accounting reporting standards to be set within the private sector, by a body similar in composition to the current FASB."[30] The reasons for favoring the private sector determination of GAAP appear to be based on such important factors as objectivity, prestige and acceptability, expertise, competence, and image. Expertise is probably the most important of these factors.[31] A recent

---

[29]See Stephen A. Zeff, "The Rise of 'Economic Consequences,'" *Journal of Accountancy* (December 1978), pp. 56–63.

[30]Joshua Ronen and Michael Schiff, "The Setting of Financial Accounting Standards—Private or Public?" *Journal of Accountancy* (March 1978), p. 69.

[31]Ronen and Schiff, pp. 69–70.

Business Week article charged that the "FASB is kept on a short leash by corporate interests" who provide much of the FASB's financial support.[32] The article suggested that companies filing documents with the SEC be required to pay a small sum each time to create a permanent endowment for the FASB. Alternatively, the authority for appointing FASB members could be shifted from the Financial Accounting Foundation to the SEC.

In the final analysis, whether or not accounting standard setting remains in the private sector will likely depend on how successful the FASB is in satisfying the various groups who are interested in its decisions, including Congress.

UNIFORMITY VERSUS FLEXIBILITY ISSUE

People can usually think of several ways to account for a given type of transaction. Take depreciation, for example. Generally accepted accounting principles support the concept that depreciation is a cost allocation process. But even though most accountants may agree with this concept, several depreciation methods are currently used, such as straight line, double-declining balance, and sum-of-the-years'-digits. The depreciation method that a company uses will influence the amount of its net income and other financial statement variables. This fact and the fact that people use financial statements to make *comparisons* among companies are the basis for one of the accounting profession's oldest debates—uniformity versus flexibility of accounting principles.

Proponents of uniformity have argued that company managers have too many accounting options available to them. They believe that these options create confusion and reduce the ability of financial statement users to make meaningful comparisons. On the other side, proponents of flexibility believe that some alternatives should be allowed. These people believe that some flexibility is needed because each company is complex and unique.

Uniformity and flexibility are extremes disliked by most accountants. Strict uniformity would probably result in a "cookbook" prescribing everything from the detailed procedures for gathering data to the precise format to use for financial statements. At the opposite extreme, unlimited flexibility would make it difficult for users to make comparisons and would undermine the integrity of the financial reporting process. The critical issue, therefore, is where on the uniformity/flexibility continuum the accounting profession should be.

One of the major tasks of the FASB and its predecessors has been to eliminate undesirable accounting alternatives. In doing this today, accountants tend to emphasize the goal of **achieving comparability** rather than either uniformity or flexibility. A requirement for financial statements to be comparable is that any differences among the financial statements of different companies should reflect basic differences between the companies themselves, not merely differences between the accounting principles that they use. Achieving comparability requires "(1) identifying and describing the circumstances that justify or require the use of a particular accounting practice or method, [and] (2) eliminating the use of alternative practices under these circumstances."[33] Accomplishing this goal has not been and will not be easy. History reveals that when the accounting profession's critics believe that it has fallen short of achieving comparability, cries for more uniformity tend to become louder. An important determinant of the FASB's success will be the extent to which it contributes to comparability through an acceptable resolution of the uniformity/flexibility debate.

MARKET EFFICIENCY ISSUE

Market efficiency is an issue with important implications for the uniformity/flexibility debate and for other accounting matters. Basically, in an **efficient market,** stock prices behave

---

[32]Dean Foust, "It's Time to Free the FASB Seven," *Business Week* (May 3, 1993), p. 144.

[33]*APB Statement No. 4,* par. 102.

as if they fully reflect publicly available information, including that reported in general-purpose financial statements. Although the evidence is not yet conclusive, a large body of empirical literature in accounting and finance suggests that the stock market is highly efficient.

An efficient market reacts to financial statements in a sophisticated manner. It is not fooled when two companies use different accounting methods. Instead, it recognizes that the numbers were generated by different methods. A high degree of market efficiency implies that the market is strongly influenced by the decisions of people who have considerable knowledge of accounting and business. In other words, an efficient market tends to be dominated by *sophisticated* rather than naive users of financial statements.

An efficient market for accounting implies that many financial reporting issues can be resolved by a relatively simple strategy of **adequate disclosure.**[34] Consider the various depreciation methods discussed earlier. Those who believe that the market is highly efficient would argue that the reporting of several depreciation figures, each computed according to one of the widely used methods, involves only a small cost. Therefore, a company should use one method in its financial statements but disclose in the footnotes what depreciation would be under the other methods. Users who are presumed to be highly sophisticated can then adjust the statements to reflect the other methods if they want to do so.

Efficient-market research has not been fully accepted by all accounting authorities. The research pertains to the market as a whole, not to the behavior of individual investors. Moreover, it says nothing about the information needs of financial statement users, such as bankers, whose decisions do not directly involve publicly traded stocks. Nevertheless, the efficient-markets issue is one that may have an important effect on the course of standard setting in the United States.

BIG GAAP/LITTLE GAAP ISSUE

General-purpose financial statements must conform with generally accepted accounting principles. These principles apply to any business regardless of its size or ownership characteristics. But consider a small, closely held business such as a family-owned jewelry store or construction company. Do those who use the financial statements of these kinds of businesses (primarily owners and bankers) really need the same types of information as those who use the financial statements of such companies as Exxon, Chrysler, and Procter & Gamble? Many people say no. And as a result, some have argued that one set of generally accepted accounting principles (which they would call *big GAAP*) should apply to larger or publicly held companies, while a somewhat different set (*little GAAP*) should apply to smaller or closely held companies.

Proponents of the big GAAP/little GAAP view believe that general-purpose financial statements of smaller companies often are unnecessarily costly because they include information that users really do not want. Proponents also believe that the cost of presenting all this information effectively precludes smaller companies from presenting information that is not required by GAAP but that users would find more useful. As a result, they believe that present accounting standards tend to discriminate against smaller businesses.[35]

The accounting profession has never defined precisely what constitutes a large or a small company. Accountants conveniently use the catchy term "big GAAP/little GAAP" to refer to the broad question of whether differential accounting principles should exist for different types of companies, whether based on size or ownership characteristics, or both.

---

[34]See William H. Beaver, "What Should Be the FASB's Objectives?" *Journal of Accountancy* (August 1973), pp. 49–56.

[35]See "Report of the Committee on Generally Accepted Accounting Principles for Smaller and/or Closely Held Businesses," *Journal of Accountancy* (October 1976), pp. 116–120.

The number and complexity of pronouncements issued by the APB and the FASB have increased the importance of the big GAAP/little GAAP issue. The FASB is very concerned about this issue and has taken steps to reduce the financial reporting burden of smaller companies. In April 1978, for example, the FASB declared that nonpublic enterprises no longer are required to report earnings per share and segment information. In the following year, the board made its inflation accounting requirements applicable only to very large companies. The big GAAP/little GAAP controversy is likely to continue to influence the standard-setting process in the future. The issue is very important because the United States has about 7,000,000 private businesses compared to only about 10,000 public companies.

INTERNATIONAL ACCOUNTING IN A GLOBAL ECONOMY

Accounting is not the same in all countries. For example, U.S. and Canadian companies must report quarterly financial information; companies in Great Britain and Japan have no such requirement. U.S. and Australian accounting standards require companies to record accruals for deferred income taxes; companies in Switzerland and Germany do not have this requirement. Companies in France and Spain can use discretionary reserves to smooth income, while those in the United States and the Netherlands cannot.[36]

Accounting is strongly influenced by the **economic, political, and social environment** of the country in which it exists. For example, the annual inflation in Argentina has often exceeded 100%; not surprisingly, Argentine companies are required to make adjustments in their financial statements to reflect the effects of inflation. In contrast, recent annual inflation in the United States has been less than 5%, and U.S. companies are not required to make inflation-related adjustments.

The economic linkages between countries are becoming more pronounced. More and more companies are "thinking globally" when they seek access to debt and equity capital, raw materials, labor, and customers. In 1992 Exxon Corporation earned more than three-fourths of its revenues and net income in foreign countries and had more than half of its assets invested outside the United States. Although many large companies, such as Sony (Japan), Bayer (Germany), Nestlé (Switzerland), Coca-Cola (United States), Seagram (Canada), British Petroleum (United Kingdom), Michelin (France), and Volvo (Sweden) are well known internationally, many thousands of smaller companies also have international operations. **Multinational companies** (those companies that operate in more than one country) are becoming increasingly common throughout the world.

As companies become more international in scope, a need exists for accounting standards that allow users to make valid comparisons among the financial statements of companies located in different countries. In 1973, the **International Accounting Standards Committee (IASC)** was formed to develop **international accounting standards** and to promote harmonization between the accounting principles of different countries. The term **harmonization** refers to reducing or eliminating national differences in accounting principles.

The IASC represents more than 100 professional accounting bodies from about 80 countries. It is a private sector organization, headquartered in London, and comprises 14 voting members; it follows a due process approach to international standard setting. The IASC has no legal authority to force companies to use its standards. Support for IASC standards is voluntary except in countries (such as Malaysia and Pakistan) that have adopted IASC standards as GAAP. IASC standards tend to be less detailed than FASB standards. In recent years, the IASC has worked to enhance comparability by reducing the number of accounting alternatives available for the same type of economic event.

This textbook emphasizes U.S. accounting principles, most of which are consistent with international accounting standards. At several places in the remaining chapters, we point out

---

[36]Frederick D. S. Choi and Gerhard G. Mueller, *International Accounting,* 2nd ed. (Englewood Cliffs, N.J.: Prentice-Hall, 1992), p. 84.

certain differences between U.S. accounting principles and those in other countries. The intent is not to comprehensively cover international accounting standards but rather to help you acquire a global perspective on accounting. Coverage of certain international accounting topics is a traditional part of advanced accounting courses; some universities offer entire courses in international accounting.

ETHICS IN ACCOUNTING

Ethics has been a major news topic during the past several years. Television broadcasts and newspaper articles have bombarded us with stories about such practices as government officials making illegal sales of weapons to foreign countries, corporate officers making money in the stock market by using insider information, and companies profiting from products that are known to cause unreasonable health hazards.

Everyone should behave in a way that is both legally and morally defensible. To behave legally, of course, means to obey laws. Morality provides fundamental guidelines to help people resolve conflicts and live together in groups. Thus, to behave in an ethical (morally defensible) manner, a person must do what is right according to the current values of society.

When applying accounting principles and acting in other aspects of their professional lives, accountants have a *special* obligation to observe high standards of ethical behavior because of the trust confided in them by the users of financial statements. Investors and creditors must believe in the integrity of financial statements if the statements are to have any value. If accounting is to continue as a useful institution in our society, accountants must have credibility. An accountant who engages in an illegal or unethical act undermines the integrity of the entire financial reporting process.

According to an internationally known moral psychologist, a person must perform four processes in order to "behave morally":[37]

1. The person must interpret a situation in terms of what actions are possible, who would be affected by each action, and how the affected parties would regard the effects on their welfare.
2. The person must make a judgment about what action is morally right.
3. The person must emphasize moral values above other personal values and decide to do what is morally right.
4. The person must be strong enough to follow through with his or her decision to behave ethically.

Accountants experience many ethical dilemmas in their work. Some are fairly easy to recognize, such as management asking the accountant to deliberately misstate the company's revenues by recording sales that have not been made. Other dilemmas, though, are more subtle, and the accountant should always be "on guard" to recognize the ethical aspects of a situation. For example, management may ask the accountant to "use a little imagination" when making a routine estimate such as bad debts expense or warranty expense. The accountant should emphasize ethics when interpreting such a request.

If you are an accountant who encounters an ethical dilemma, you should try to resolve the problem in a calm, reasoned manner. Begin by evaluating all the facts and defining the ethical issues. Identify the parties who would be directly or indirectly affected by the ethical decision. Then determine the alternative courses of action and compare the consequences of each response. Next, make a decision that complies with high legal and moral standards of conduct. Finally, you must have the courage and willpower to follow through with your ethical decision.

---

[37]James R. Rest, *Moral Development: Advances in Research and Theory* (New York: Praeger, 1986), pp. 3–4. Moral judgment research has produced many interesting findings, including the following examples (pp. 176–177): 1. Moral judgment changes with time and formal education. 2. People develop moral judgment by becoming more aware of the social world and their place in it. 3. Moral education programs, especially those that emphasize peer discussions of controversial moral dilemmas, stimulate moral judgment development.

Fortunately, the accounting profession currently enjoys a high degree of moral credibility in the eyes of the general public. A 1989 news release indicated that in a nationwide survey of businesspeople, accountants were regarded as having the highest business ethics of 16 professions, ranking ahead of dentists and doctors.[38]

CONCLUDING REMARKS

Accounting seeks to identify, measure, and communicate information about economic entities that is useful in making economic decisions. Financial accounting is the branch of accounting that provides information about the financial position of a business enterprise and the changes that occur therein. Its primary focus is meeting the needs of external users such as stockholders and bankers. As you study the remaining chapters, *continually question* whether the accounting principles presented really aid the decision-making processes of external users. Do not assume that an accounting principle is desirable for society just because it is now generally accepted.

General-purpose financial statements constitute the main output of financial accounting. Accountants prepare these statements in accordance with generally accepted accounting principles, which are largely determined within the private sector of our economy. Because these principles constantly change, the study of accounting is a lifelong process.

For financial statements to be useful, they must help investors and creditors to assess "the amounts, timing, and uncertainty of prospective cash receipts from dividends or interest and the proceeds from the sale, redemption, or maturity of securities or loans."[39] To help investors and creditors assess their personal chances of receiving cash from a given enterprise, financial statements should provide information to help users "assess the amounts, timing, and uncertainty of prospective net cash inflows to the related enterprise."[40] Throughout this text, we shall refer many times to the "predicting future cash flows" objective of financial statements. Unfortunately, surprisingly little empirical research is available that relates directly to this important objective. The accounting profession still has much to learn about how well financial statements really help users to predict future cash flows.

In the following chapters, we examine the hows, whys, and so whats of intermediate accounting. The next chapter focuses on why and deals with the basic theory of general-purpose financial statements.

KEY POINTS

1. Accounting seeks to identify, measure, and communicate information about economic entities that is intended to be useful in making economic decisions. (Objective 1)
2. Financial accounting is the branch of accounting that is concerned with measuring and reporting the financial position of a business enterprise and the changes that occur in financial position. Financial accounting information is designed primarily to meet the needs of external users. (Objective 1)
3. External users of financial statements include present and potential owners, lenders, suppliers, employees, and customers, in addition to financial analysts, stock exchanges, regulatory agencies, and the general public. (Objective 2)
4. Investors and creditors use financial statements to make predictions, assess risk, and evaluate profitability, solvency, and management's performance. (Objective 2)
5. The basic financial statements are the balance sheet, income statement, statement of cash flows, and statement of retained earnings or statement of stockholders' equity. (Objective 2)
6. The management of an entity has the primary responsibility for preparing its financial statements. Managers in turn hire internal accountants to collect data and prepare the statements. (Objective 2)

---

[38]"Ethics Survey Ranks Accountants First," *Journal of Accountancy* (October 1989), p. 110.

[39]*FASB Statement of Financial Accounting Concepts No. 1,* par. 37.

[40]*FASB Statement of Financial Accounting Concepts No. 1,* par. 37.

7. Public (external) accountants examine financial statements and express an opinion about whether the statements have been prepared in accordance with generally accepted accounting principles. (Objective 2)

8. Auditors must be competent and independent from the companies they audit. (Objective 2)

9. Generally accepted accounting principles are those principles that have substantial authoritative support. (Objective 3)

10. The organizations that have had the most influence in developing generally accepted accounting principles are the Committee on Accounting Procedure, the Accounting Principles Board, the Financial Accounting Standards Board, and the Securities and Exchange Commission. (Objective 4)

11. Certain other organizations and the income tax law have also affected the development of generally accepted accounting principles. (Objective 4)

12. Experience, reason, custom, usage, and practical necessity are important factors in developing generally accepted accounting principles. (Objective 4)

13. FASB Statements of Financial Accounting Standards and Interpretations, APB Opinions, and Accounting Research Bulletins are the most authoritative sources of generally accepted accounting principles. (Objective 5)

14. Several important issues are likely to affect the development of generally accepted accounting principles. These include the FASB's Conceptual Framework Project, the economic impact issue, the public versus private sector issue, the uniformity versus flexibility issue, the market efficiency issue, and the big GAAP/little GAAP issue. (Objective 6)

15. Accounting is strongly affected by the economic, political, and social environment of the country in which it exists. The International Accounting Standards Committee develops international accounting standards and promotes harmonization between the accounting principles of different countries. (Objective 7)

16. Accountants have a special obligation to observe high standards of ethical conduct because of the considerable trust confided in them by the users of financial statements. (Objective 8)

QUESTIONS

1–1 What is the difference between internal and external users of accounting information?

1–2 What is financial accounting?

1–3 What is meant by the term general-purpose financial statements? Why does the accounting profession emphasize general-purpose statements instead of single-purpose statements?

1–4 What are three examples of accounting applications that illustrate the following point: "Financial statements are not usually as precise as they appear to be"?

1–5 What are five sources that investors and creditors commonly use to obtain information about specific companies?

1–6 What is the difference between financial statements and financial reporting?

1–7 What is the role of corporate management in the financial reporting process?

1–8 What do the professional designations of CMA and CPA mean?

1–9 What is an audit?

1–10 What do the following terms that relate to audit reports mean?

[a] Unqualified opinion
[b] Qualified opinion
[c] Adverse opinion
[d] Disclaimer of opinion

1–11 What is meant by the term *generally accepted accounting principles?*

1–12 How do the following types of pronouncements differ?

[a] Accounting Research Bulletins
[b] APB Opinions
[c] Statements of Financial Accounting Standards
[d] Statements of Financial Accounting Concepts
[e] FASB Interpretations

1–13 What is *Rule 203* of the AICPA Code of Professional Conduct? What is its significance?

1–14 What are the major differences between the FASB and its predecessor standard-setting bodies (the CAP and APB)?

1–15 What major steps does the FASB usually follow when formulating a Statement of Financial Accounting Standards?

1–16 What is the nature of the Securities Act of 1933 and the Securities Exchange Act of 1934?

1–17 What is the SEC's fundamental purpose?

1–18 What is the SEC's role in establishing accounting standards?

1–19 Why do the principles of income tax law often differ from the principles of financial accounting?

1–20 Of what significance are financial analysts and commercial bank loan officers to the accounting profession?

1–21 What are the various sources of generally accepted accounting principles, going from the most authoritative sources to the least authoritative sources?

1–22 What is the FASB's Conceptual Framework Project?

1–23 How do accounting principles affect the manner in which our society allocates its scarce resources?

1–24 What is the uniformity versus flexibility debate in financial accounting?

1–25 Do generally accepted accounting principles apply only to large companies? Explain.

1–26 What is the role of the International Accounting Standards Committee?

1–27 What does *morality* mean and why is it particularly important for accountants to observe high standards of moral behavior?

CASES

1–28 Sources of Information Assume that you have recently graduated from college and that your boss asks you to speak to a local civic organization of businesspeople. The topic of your speech is "Sources of Information That May Be Useful in Investment, Credit, and Similar Decisions."

INSTRUCTIONS

Identify the major sources that you should describe in your speech.

1–29 The Accounting Profession A friend of yours majoring in another business field has asked you what, if anything, besides the technical content of accounting courses distinguishes accounting from other business disciplines. He does not understand why accountants can become licensed by the state as certified public accountants and what role such individuals can play in the commercial process.

INSTRUCTIONS

Develop a response to your friend's question. In determining your response, consider the characteristics that distinguish a profession from other business or commercial endeavors. Also be sure to address the role of accounting in the functioning of our capital markets as well as its contribution to the management of business enterprises.

1–30 Accounting Principles At the completion of the Goody Department Store audit, the president asks about the meaning of the phrase "in conformity with generally accepted accounting principles" that appears in your audit report on the management's financial statements. He observes that the meaning of the phrase must include more than what he thinks of as "principles."

INSTRUCTIONS

[a] Explain the meaning of the term *accounting principles* as used in the audit report. (Do *not* discuss in this part the significance of "generally accepted.")

[b] The president wants to know how you determine whether or not an accounting principle is generally accepted. Discuss the sources of evidence for determining whether an accounting principle has substantial authoritative support.

[c] The president believes that diversity in accounting practice always will exist among independent entities despite continual improvements in comparability. Develop arguments that *support* his belief. (AICPA adapted)

1–31 Departures from GAAP You are preparing the financial statements for your company, a chain of retail clothing stores, when the president calls you in to discuss an accounting problem. The issue involves a transaction that the company has just completed and that has a substantial effect on reported earnings. There is an FASB Statement of Financial Accounting Standards that deals generally with the issue; however, the company's transaction does have a few characteristics that the FASB statement does not consider. The president wishes to account for the transaction in a way that would depart from the provisions of the FASB statement, and you can see some validity to her position. First, the transaction of the company is somewhat different from that contemplated by the FASB statement. While you do not consider the differences to be significant, you do believe that the accounting proposed by the president of your company would better portray the economic substance of the transaction. Nevertheless, you believe that accounting for the transaction in the fashion prescribed by the FASB is also reasonable. The president concludes the meeting with the following statement: "Study this issue for a while and write a position paper that lets me know your thinking. I know I can count on you to support my efforts to put our best foot forward in the marketplace."

INSTRUCTIONS

Respond to the president's charge. Use the information provided in the case and the material in Chapter 1 to prepare a response that you believe is consistent with the responsibilities of a professional accountant.

1–32 Standard-Setting Process An article about the FASB on the front page of *The Wall Street Journal* (April 30, 1984) stated that "critics all over the country are bombarding the seven-member board with a cacophony of complaints. Accountants increasingly accuse the FASB of moving too slowly — and of producing little of substance when it finally does act." The article also stated that "by one estimate, it [the FASB] mailed out more than three million documents last year and more than 100,000 letters. It receives up to 600 phone calls daily, many seeking advice on how to interpret its complex rules."

INSTRUCTIONS

[a] Explain why the formulation of accounting policy is considered highly controversial.
[b] Why does the FASB work at a pace that many critics regard as too slow when formulating accounting policy?

1–33 Politicization in Standard Setting Some accountants have said that the development and acceptance of generally accepted accounting principles (i.e., standard setting) is being politicized. Some use the term *politicization* in a narrow sense to mean influence by governmental agencies, particularly the SEC, on the development of generally accepted accounting principles. Others use the term more broadly to mean the compromising that takes place in bodies responsible for developing generally accepted accounting principles because of the influence and pressure of interested groups (e.g., SEC, AAA, IMA, businesses through their various organizations, financial analysts, bankers, and lawyers).

INSTRUCTIONS

[a] The CAP of the AICPA was established in 1938 and functioned until 1959, when it was replaced by the APB. In 1973 the FASB was formed and the APB dissolved. Explain how these groups were formed, their methods of operation, and the reasons for the demise of the CAP and the APB. Indicate whether these events show increasing politicization (in the broad sense) of accounting standard setting. Cite specific developments to support your answer.
[b] What arguments support the politicization of accounting standard setting?
[c] What arguments can be raised against the politicization of accounting standard setting?

(CMA adapted)

1–34 Income Tax Laws One of your friends is a law school student who recently decided to take an introductory course in financial accounting. After his first day of class, he tells you: "I'm having some trouble understanding what financial accounting is all about. In law school, I learned how to calculate income according to tax laws. Why aren't the tax laws used to calculate income in financial accounting?"

INSTRUCTIONS

[a] Answer your friend's question.
[b] Discuss the significance of income tax law in the development of generally accepted accounting principles.

1–35 Standard Setting for Leases For many years, the accounting profession has debated the merits of two primary methods of accounting for leases by lessees (i.e., companies that lease assets from other enterprises): (1) capitalization of leases, which means that lessees record the present value of expected future lease payments as an asset and liability, treat lease payments as reductions in the liability, and depreciate the recorded asset; and (2) expensing of lease payments as they are made with no initial recording of a lease asset or liability by the lessee.

When the FASB was discussing the issue of accounting for leases, it received a letter from a U.S. senator that read in part as follows:

A number of my associates in Congress and I are concerned with the possible effect of lease capitalization upon the financing costs of American industry—which costs enter into the eventual prices to the public of goods and services. In an inflationary period, such suggested accounting practice may have a marked effect upon the prices to the public of transportation, energy, food, and housing. It would be most unfortunate if a theoretical approach to financial disclosure assumed greater importance than the public good especially when effective and more acceptable accounting methods are available for the protection of the investor.

INSTRUCTIONS

[a] Identify the broad issue in accounting standard setting that underlies the senator's concern.
[b] What effect, if any, do *you* think the points raised in the senator's letter should have on the FASB's deliberations in the matter of accounting for leases?

1–36 Development Stage Companies   In 1975 the FASB issued *SFAS No. 7,* "Accounting and Reporting by Development State Enterprises." This pronouncement states that "an enterprise shall be considered to be in the development stage if it is devoting substantially all of its efforts to establishing a new business and either of the following conditions exists:

[a] Planned principal operations have not commenced.
[b] Planned principal operations have commenced but there has been no significant revenue therefrom" (par. 8).

In essence, *SFAS No. 7* concluded that development-stage companies must use the same accounting principles that established companies use. But when the Exposure Draft that preceded *SFAS No. 7* was issued, "some respondents to the Exposure Draft expressed concern that requiring development stage enterprises to present the same basic financial statements and to apply the same generally accepted accounting principles as established operating enterprises might make it difficult, if not impossible, for development stage enterprises to obtain capital" (par. 48).

INSTRUCTIONS

Identify and explain the broad issue that underlies the concern expressed by the respondents to the Exposure Draft that preceded *SFAS No. 7.*

1–37 General versus Detailed Standards   An article in *The Wall Street Journal* (Wednesday, August 3, 1988, p. 6) stated that "John Reed, chairman of Citicorp and chairman of the [Business] Roundtable's accounting principles task force, has been criticizing the FASB in meetings with SEC commissioners and managing partners of major accounting firms.... According to accountants and businessmen, Roundtable members are telling the SEC that some FASB rules use a 'cookbook' approach and are so narrow and detailed as to make implementation prohibitively costly. They have cited rules on pension costs and deferred taxes."

INSTRUCTIONS

When the FASB publishes an accounting standard, should the standard be written in a manner that is relatively general or relatively detailed in nature? Explain the rationale for your preference.

1–38 Effects of Accounting Principles   An article in *Forbes* (November 28, 1988, p. 170) stated that "foreign companies have a walloping advantage over U.S. companies in playing the takeover game in this country. The advantage is intangible, but it's a big advantage all the same." The article explains that when a U.S. company acquires another company, generally accepted accounting principles require the U.S. company to amortize any payment that is made for goodwill. The goodwill is amortized over a maximum period of 40 years and causes the acquiring company's net income to be lower by the amount of the amortization. In contrast, British accounting rules provide that when a British company acquires another enterprise, even one located in the United States, any amount paid for goodwill is immediately written off against stockholders' equity and is therefore never charged against the British company's net income.

INSTRUCTIONS

Do you believe that the British accounting rules for goodwill give British companies an advantage over U.S. companies when acquiring other firms? Present arguments to support your answer.

1–39 Market Efficiency Issue   At an open meeting in July 1981, it was stated that the SEC "intends to apply the efficient market theory ... to public offerings by widely followed companies to take advantage of periodic reports filed under the Securities Exchange Act prior to a new registration statement." (From "The Week in Review," Deloitte Haskins & Sells, July 31, 1981, p. 1.)

INSTRUCTIONS

[a] What is an efficient market?

[b] Briefly indicate how you think the SEC could apply the efficient market theory "to take advantage of periodic reports filed under the Securities Exchange Act prior to a new registration statement."

1–40 Big GAAP/Little GAAP Issue   In an open letter to the FASB, a large, international CPA firm stated that "we are genuinely concerned that you are not reacting to a serious problem. A recent exchange of correspondence between the AICPA and the FASB makes it clear to us that the present FASB does not intend to consider relief from onerous accounting and disclosure requirements for the thousands of smaller and/or closely held businesses across this country" (*The Wall Street Journal,* October 25, 1977, p. 24).

INSTRUCTIONS

[a] Take the position that the accounting profession should have one set of generally accepted accounting principles that apply to all companies, regardless of size or ownership characteristics. Develop arguments that support your position.

[b] Take the position that the accounting profession should have one set of generally accepted accounting principles for larger and/or publicly held companies and a somewhat different set for smaller and/or closely held companies. Develop arguments that support your position.

1–41 Expense Reimbursement   As an accountant for a medium-size company, you have recently returned from a five-day out-of-town assignment and are now completing your expense reimbursement form. Your employer has a written policy allowing you to claim reimbursement for your *actual daily cost of meals* up to a maximum of $30 per day. You are *not* required to provide receipts for the meals that you claim.

While you were on assignment, you ate meals for free at your aunt's home, but no one from your company knows because you worked on the assignment alone. You have learned through informal conversation that some of your fellow employees routinely request reimbursement for the maximum meal allowance of $30, even when the actual cost of their meals is much less.

INSTRUCTIONS

Would you claim reimbursement for the cost of your meals at the maximum daily rate allowed by your company ($30 × 5 days = $150)? Explain your answer.

Financial Accounting Theory

OBJECTIVE

1. To describe financial accounting theory as currently applied. The theory consists of the following components:
   a. Objectives
   b. Qualitative characteristics
   c. Assumptions
   d. Concepts and elements
   e. Broad principles
   f. Detailed principles
   g. Modifying conventions

Chambers Development, Inc., is a company that develops land-fills and whose stock had been very popular on Wall Street. Early in 1992, the company announced that it would start expensing the indirect costs of developing landfill sites. Previously, the company had capitalized these costs and had reported them as assets on the balance sheet.

The accounting change reduced 1991 net income by more than 50%, or $27 million. The change was also associated with a $1.4 billion reduction of Chambers' market valuation.

The issue of whether to capitalize or expense a cost can make a big difference in financial statements. To resolve this issue requires a knowledge of accounting theory and the ability to use professional judgment. Accounting theory is the subject of this chapter.

Roula Khalaf, "Fuzzy Accounting," *Forbes,* June 22, 1992, p. 96.

A ccounting theory has been defined "as a coherent set of hypothetical, conceptual, and pragmatic principles forming a general frame of reference for inquiring into the nature of accounting."[1] This chapter provides an overview of descriptive financial accounting theory as it pertains to general-purpose external reporting by business enterprises. Note carefully the following words in the preceding sentence:

1. **Overview.** In this chapter, we introduce the most important components of financial accounting theory. Entire textbooks have been devoted to explaining these and other components in more depth.

2. **Descriptive.** Descriptive theory refers to the ways in which accounting theory is currently applied. In contrast, normative theory attempts to prescribe how theory ought to be. This chapter is primarily descriptive.

[1]Eldon S. Hendriksen and Michael F. van Breda, *Accounting Theory,* 5th ed. (Homewood, Ill.: Irwin, 1992), p. 21.

3. **Financial accounting theory.** We present a logical framework that helps to explain why *financial* accounting is applied the way it is today.
4. **General-purpose external reporting.** The chapter focuses on a theoretical structure for general-purpose (rather than single- or limited-purpose), external (rather than internal) reporting.

A knowledge of accounting theory should help you to understand and apply generally accepted accounting principles (GAAP) as well as changes in them. Because accounting problems often appear routine, accountants sometimes bog down in the mechanics of problem solving and lose sight of the theory they seek to apply. For this reason, you should study this chapter carefully. Later, as you study other chapters, reread the appropriate sections of this chapter. Always strive for sound conceptual understanding that can help you to solve most accounting problems, whether you encounter them in a textbook, on an examination, or in the business world.

The accounting profession today does not have a single, comprehensive, generally accepted framework of accounting theory. As we pointed out in Chapter 1, however, the Financial Accounting Standards Board (FASB) has developed a conceptual framework that it hopes the financial community will accept. Recognize, therefore, that accounting is a relatively young and dynamic discipline for which a theoretical structure is still evolving. The theoretical framework presented in this chapter is based on several sources and represents descriptive financial accounting theory today.[2]

A MODEL

Exhibit 2–1 presents the theoretical components discussed in this chapter. These components are **objectives, qualitative characteristics, assumptions, concepts and elements, broad principles, detailed principles,** and **modifying conventions.**[3] A move from the top to the bottom of the exhibit represents a move from the general objectives to detailed principles, which are quite specific. Accountants traditionally have had less difficulty agreeing on the more general components of the model than on the more specific ones. Most accountants agree, for example, that an important accounting objective should be to provide useful information. On the other hand, less agreement exists about which principles the accounting profession should adopt to achieve the objective of providing useful information.

When studying the model of financial accounting theory, remember that the components are *not all independent of one another.* Many important *interrelationships* exist that are too complex to identify meaningfully in one model. Furthermore, accounting principles have not always developed on the basis of explicit objectives. As we pointed out in Chapter 1, many generally accepted accounting principles "have developed on the basis of experience, reason, custom, usage, and, to a significant extent, practical necessity."[4] For this reason, some accountants think that certain principles are inconsistent with certain objectives. These components may therefore change as a result of further development of accounting theory. Despite these limitations of the model, we believe that it provides a useful framework in which to study financial accounting.

OBJECTIVES OF FINANCIAL REPORTING

In 1978 the FASB issued *Statement of Financial Accounting Concepts No. 1,* "Objectives of Financial Reporting by Business Enterprises."[5] The objectives outlined in *SFAC No. 1* stem largely from the important needs of external users, who lack the authority to require the

[2]The framework that we present draws heavily from the works published by the FASB in its Conceptual Framework Project.

[3]The labels attached to certain components of the model vary somewhat in practice. *Principles,* for example, are sometimes called standards, concepts, procedures, rules, and practices.

[4]*APB Statement No. 4,* "Basic Concepts and Accounting Principles Underlying Financial Statements of Business Enterprises," 1970, par. 139.

[5]*FASB Statement of Financial Accounting Concepts No. 1,* "Objectives of Financial Reporting by Business Enterprises," 1978.

EXHIBIT 2–1

Financial Accounting Theory: A Model

Objectives

Financial reporting should provide information useful in investment, credit, and similar decisions.

Financial reporting should provide information useful in assessing cash flow prospects.

Financial reporting should provide information about enterprise resources, claims to those resources, and changes in them.

Qualitative Characteristics

Relevance	Reliability
Predictive value	Verifiability
Feedback value	Neutrality
Timeliness	Representational faithfulness

Assumptions

Economic entity
Periodicity
Going concern

Concepts and Elements

Financial Position	Changes in Financial Position
Assets	Revenues
Liabilities	Expenses
Owners' equity	Gains
	Losses
	Income
	Investments by owners
	Distributions to owners

Broad Principles

Monetary unit
Asset/Liability measurement
Revenue realization
Matching
Consistency
Disclosure

Modifying Conventions

Materiality
Industry practices
Conservatism
Substance over form

Detailed Principles

Covered throughout the text

information that they want about a given enterprise. Furthermore, the objectives are affected by the economic, legal, political, and social environment in the United States, and as a result, they may change over time. Finally, the objectives are affected by the characteristics and limitations of the information that financial reporting traditionally has provided.

SFAC No. 1 has identified three major objectives of financial reporting, which includes financial statements. These objectives are summarized in Exhibit 2–1. The first objective is the most general; the next two are progressively more specific.

USEFUL INFORMATION

The initial objective states that "financial reporting should provide information that is useful to present and potential investors and creditors and other users in making rational investment, credit, and similar decisions. The information should be comprehensible to those who have a reasonable understanding of business and economic activities and are willing to study the information with reasonable diligence."[6] This objective underscores the fact that financial reporting is not an end in itself. Instead, the *output* of the financial accounting process should serve as useful *input* for making rational investment, credit, and similar decisions in our society.

Traditionally, anyone proposing usefulness as an accounting objective has had to respond to these important questions: Useful to whom? And for what purpose? In stating its initial objective, the FASB's responses to these questions were quite broad. As a result, the scope of financial reporting is not confined to one, or even a few, user groups. Instead, financial reporting attempts to serve many diverse users. These users, however, are expected to understand business affairs and be willing to spend reasonable amounts of time and effort analyzing accounting information. Accountants should always try to produce reports that are understandable to these users. Naive users of accounting information should consider taking steps to improve their understanding of business matters, or they should rely on professional advisers. **Understandability** to *reasonably informed users* is therefore a desirable quality of useful accounting information.

Although providing useful information is the primary objective of financial reporting, accounting principles do not require companies to report all potentially useful information. Instead, a pervasive constraint stipulates that *accounting information should be provided only when the benefits of the information exceed the costs of providing and using it.* As you might imagine, trying to determine the benefits and costs of accounting information is highly subjective and can lead to honest differences of opinion between competent persons. Benefits of accounting information are enjoyed by preparers (such as improved access to capital markets and favorable impact on the company's public relations), users (better investment and credit decisions, for example), and consumers (steady supply of goods and services, more efficient functioning of the marketplace, and so forth). Preparers initially pay most of the costs, which are then passed on to users of financial statements and consumers of the company's goods and services.[7]

CASH FLOW PROSPECTS

Rational investment, credit, and similar decisions are made after careful consideration of such factors as expected cost, risk, and return. As noted in Chapter 1, investors and creditors invest and lend cash, and they want to know how much cash they will receive in return and when they will receive it. Information that helps to resolve these uncertainties is surely regarded as useful.

---

[6] *FASB Statement of Financial Accounting Concepts No. 1*, p. viii.

[7] *FASB Statement of Financial Accounting Concepts No. 2*, "Qualitative Characteristics of Accounting Information," 1980, par. 136.

Accordingly, the second objective is that "financial reporting should provide information to help present and potential investors, creditors, and other users in assessing the amounts, timing, and uncertainty of prospective cash receipts from dividends or interest and the proceeds from the sale, redemption, or maturity of securities or loans. Because investors' and creditors' cash flows are related to enterprise cash flows, financial reporting should provide information to help investors, creditors, and others assess the amounts, timing, and uncertainty of prospective net cash inflows to the related enterprise."[8] Note that this objective differentiates cash flows to investors and creditors from cash flows to a given enterprise to which they have committed funds. Chances of investors and creditors receiving cash via dividends, interest, and otherwise depend on the expected cash flows to the enterprise. If the enterprise succeeds in generating favorable cash flows, the probability of investors and creditors receiving favorable cash flows is increased.

The second objective recognizes that a business enterprise's primary goal is to increase its monetary wealth so that over time it can return the maximum amount of cash to its owners. A business enterprise attempts to increase its monetary wealth by using cash to generate more cash.[9] Enterprises that succeed in using cash to generate more cash are said to have **earning power.** The lifetime earnings of an enterprise are eventually measured by the excess of the cash generated and returned to owners over the amount they invested. For an enterprise to have earnings or earning power, it must have **cash-generating ability.**[10]

Financial reporting is useful only if it helps users to evaluate the enterprise's cash generating ability and to assess prospective net cash inflows. In subsequent chapters of this book, we stress the important point that alternative accounting principles should be evaluated in relation to their usefulness in predicting net cash inflows to the enterprise.

ENTERPRISE RESOURCES, CLAIMS, AND CHANGES

What information is helpful to investors, creditors, and other users in assessing prospective cash receipts from a business enterprise? *SFAC No. 1* responds to this question with the third major objective of financial reporting. This objective holds that "financial reporting should provide information about the economic resources of an enterprise, the claims to those resources (obligations of the enterprise to transfer resources to other entities and owners' equity), and the effects of transactions, events, and circumstances that change its resources and claims to those resources."[11]

Some of the most significant transactions and events that change a firm's resources and the claims to those resources are used to measure financial performance. The FASB stated that "the primary focus of financial reporting is information about an enterprise's performance provided by measures of earnings and its components."[12] Thus, investors and creditors may use past measures of earnings to help predict future earnings and, indirectly, to help predict their chances of receiving cash from a given enterprise.

The FASB believes that **accrual accounting** results in better performance measures than does cash basis accounting. The board has emphasized, however, that "accrual accounting provides measures of earnings rather than evaluations of management's performance, estimates of 'earning power,' predictions of earnings, assessments of risk, or confirmations or rejections of predictions or assessments. Investors, creditors, and other users of the

---

[8]*FASB Statement of Financial Accounting Concepts No. 1,* p. viii.

[9]*Report of the Study Group on the Objectives of Financial Statements,* "Objectives of Financial Statements" (New York: AICPA, 1973), p. 21.

[10]George H. Sorter, in collaboration with Martin S. Gans, Paul Rosenfield, R. M. Shannon, and Robert G. Streit, "Earning Power and Cash Generating Ability," *Objectives of Financial Statements* Vol. 2/Selected Papers (New York: AICPA, 1974), p. 110–116.

[11]*FASB Statement of Financial Accounting Concepts No. 1,* p. viii.

[12]*FASB Statement of Financial Accounting Concepts No. 1,* par. 43.

information do their own evaluating, estimating, predicting, assessing, confirming, or rejecting."[13] Thus, accountants provide useful historical measurements, but they cannot accurately predict the future and they surely do not make decisions for users. Interestingly, an empirical study has found that current earnings (based on accrual accounting) is a better predictor of a company's future cash flows than is information about current cash flows.[14]

While financial reporting focuses primarily on earnings, information about financial position as well as significant changes in financial position (besides earnings) is important when assessing an enterprise's cash flow prospects. Because management knows more about a firm than do outsiders, management's explanation of the financial impact of certain transactions, events, and circumstances often can enhance the usefulness of information.

QUALITATIVE CHARACTERISTICS OF ACCOUNTING INFORMATION

Given that the basic objective of external financial reporting is to provide information that is useful to people making rational economic decisions, a logical question is: What qualitative characteristics determine the usefulness of accounting information? Many studies have addressed this issue and have generally produced similar results.

The FASB believes that **relevance** and **reliability** are the two most fundamental qualitative characteristics of useful accounting information.[15] **Relevance** means "the capacity of information to make a difference in a decision by helping users to form predictions about the outcome of past, present, and future events or to confirm or correct prior expectations."[16] For example, when stockholders decide to buy, sell, or hold equity investments, earnings per share information is generally regarded as highly relevant. In contrast, the serial numbers of plant assets, although highly reliable, are irrelevant information.

The major characteristics of relevant information are the following.[17]

1. **Predictive value.** Information has predictive value when it can help users to increase the likelihood of correctly forecasting the outcome of events. For example, if "cash provided by operations" proves valuable in predicting loan default, it is said to have predictive value.
2. **Feedback value.** Information with feedback value enables users to confirm or correct expectations. A net income measure, for example, has feedback value if it can help stockholders to confirm or revise their expectations about a company's ability to generate earnings.
3. **Timeliness.** Information is timely when it is available to a decision maker before decisions are made. For example, one of the most important attributes of quarterly financial information is its timeliness.

To be relevant, information must have predictive value *or* feedback value or both, and it must be timely.

Reliability is "the quality of information that assures that information is reasonably free from error and bias and faithfully represents what it purports to represent."[18] In other words, users can trust that reliable measurements will accurately represent the reality that the measurements claim to represent. For example, most people consider the amount of cash that a company has in its bank account to be highly reliable information. However, information about a company's projected earnings per share 50 years from now is usually not very reliable.

Reliable information has three major characteristics.[19]

1. **Verifiability.** Information is considered verifiable when it is based on reasonable underlying evidence. Such evidence would permit all competent accountants to generate similar mea-

---

[13]*FASB Statement of Financial Accounting Concepts No. 1,* par. 48.

[14]Robert R. Greenberg, Glenn L. Johnson, and K. Ramesh, "Earnings versus Cash Flow as a Predictor of Future Cash Flow Measures," *Journal of Accounting, Auditing and Finance* (Fall 1986), pp. 266–277.

[15]*FASB Statement of Financial Accounting Concepts No. 2,* 1980, p. x.

[16]*FASB Statement of Financial Accounting Concepts No. 2,* p. xvi.

[17]*FASB Statement of Financial Accounting Concepts No. 2,* pp. xv–xvi.

[18]*FASB Statement of Financial Accounting Concepts No. 2,* p. xvi.

[19]*FASB Statement of Financial Accounting Concepts No. 2,* p. xvi.

surements under the same circumstances. The amount of a company's cash on hand, for example, usually is highly verifiable because accountants can simply count it.

Because of the need for verifiability, financial accounting is based primarily on the results of **arm's-length exchange transactions,** in which unrelated parties act in their own best economic interests. Some accountants refer to the verifiability characteristic as **objectivity.**

2. **Neutrality.** Information is neutral when it is free of bias toward a desired result or behavior. Accounting information would not be neutral if it systematically produced results that favored one group of users, such as bankers, over another, such as labor organizations.

3. **Representational faithfulness.** Information is representationally faithful when a measure or description agrees with the phenomenon that it claims to represent. A measure of a company's accounts receivable, for example, would have low representational faithfulness if it included a material amount of uncollectible accounts.

To be reliable, information must have all three characteristics described above.

Many accountants have argued that relevance and reliability may require important trade-offs. That is, to increase the relevance of accounting information, accountants may have to sacrifice some reliability, and vice versa. For example, generally accepted accounting principles call for reporting plant assets in the balance sheet at their historical cost. It is possible, however, that the current cost of plant assets is a more relevant, yet less reliable, measure than the historical cost of these assets. If so, the question then becomes: Which measure of plant assets, historical cost or current cost, results in information that is most useful? One of the great challenges of the accounting profession is to achieve an optimal balance between relevance and reliability to ensure that accounting information will be as useful as possible. Arriving at this balance requires considerable research and is likely to generate many interesting debates in the financial community.

ASSUMPTIONS

To provide information that is both relevant and reliable, and therefore useful, accountants begin by making certain **assumptions.** These assumptions, often called **postulates,** generally relate to things that are taken for granted. By starting with basic assumptions, other components in the theoretical framework may be logically derived.

ECONOMIC ENTITY ASSUMPTION

Applying the principles of accounting requires the identification of specific units of economic activity. Each unit serves as a focal point to guide the accountant's recording and reporting functions. Accordingly, accountants make the **economic entity assumption,** which says that *economic activities can be meaningfully associated with specific entities or units of accountability.* Typical examples of an economic entity are a person (such as a candidate for public office), a sole proprietorship, a partnership, and a corporation. The entity assumed may be somewhat narrow in scope, such as a division of a diversified company, or quite broad, as when consolidated financial statements are prepared for a group of corporations having common ownership. In any case, the name of the entity should appear at the top of the financial statements.

The economic entity assumption requires a careful separation of the financial affairs of a business (the entity) from the affairs of its owners and other businesses. For example, when a building contractor purchases lumber for an addition to his personal residence, this cost should not be included in the financial affairs of his building company.

Accountants sometimes ignore certain legal considerations when complying with the economic entity assumption. For example, the accounting records of a partnership must be kept separate and distinct from the records of the individual partners, even though the partners may be personally liable for partnership debts if liquidation occurs. Similarly, although a parent corporation and one or more subsidiaries constitute separate *legal* entities, accountants often prepare consolidated financial reports depicting the companies as a single *economic* entity.

PERIODICITY ASSUMPTION

The most reliable method of calculating a new firm's income is to wait until the firm is finally liquidated. At that time, lifetime income can be measured as the amount of resources paid by the firm to the owners over the amount paid in by the owners. Of course, measuring income only when a firm is terminated is not a practical way to satisfy the needs of financial statement users. Indeed, for information to be relevant and thereby have an impact on important decisions, it must be timely.

The need for timely dissemination of information has led accountants to make **the periodicity assumption:** *the economic activities of a firm can be meaningfully related to arbitrary time periods that are shorter than the firm's life.* In practice, annual, quarterly, and monthly time periods are commonly used. An annual period may be a calendar year, ending December 31, or a fiscal year, the end of which often coincides with the lowest point in a firm's business activities.

The economic activities of a typical business are complex and continuous. A new machine purchased by a manufacturing firm, for example, will likely last for several accounting periods. During these periods, the machine will be used—with raw materials, labor, and other machines—to produce a product that may be sold at some future date for a price that is now uncertain. Given this interaction and uncertainty, no one can precisely determine the benefits of the machine to the firm. Therefore, depreciation expense under accrual accounting cannot be precisely determined for a period shorter than the life of the machine. As this example shows, financial reporting for any brief period requires **estimates** and **professional judgment,** and the accountant's measurements are therefore often tentative. In general, as the time period becomes shorter, it becomes increasingly difficult to make meaningful estimates, and the reliability of accounting information is reduced.

GOING CONCERN (CONTINUITY) ASSUMPTION

The **going concern assumption** holds that *in the absence of evidence to the contrary, accountants assume that entity operations will continue for a reasonable period of time; that is, the entity will not be liquidated in the near future.* There is no assumption that the entity will exist permanently but simply that it will last at least long enough to fulfill its plans and commitments. This assumption is supported by the fact that most businesses expect to operate for extended periods of time. This expectation is fostered by our relatively stable economic, political, and social environment, in which laws and customs afford certain rights and protections.

The going concern assumption helps to provide a rationale for several important aspects of accounting. It permits assets to be defined as probable future economic benefits to a firm. Moreover, it lends support to the historical cost system of measurement, which is based on the premise that historical accounting information can be used to help predict interesting events. If, for example, the firm were expected to liquidate in the immediate future, assets would be better stated at their net realizable values. The going concern assumption also supports such interperiod allocation procedures as depreciation and amortization. It would not make sense, for example, to depreciate a new machine over 10 years if the company that owned it was expected to fold next year. Finally, the going concern assumption serves as a basis for conventional balance sheet classification. Why list certain liabilities as long term, for example, if the firm is expected to go out of business within six months?

The accountant should periodically reevaluate the logic of assuming a going concern for any given enterprise. Perhaps management would like to liquidate in the near future, or perhaps a long period of substantial losses will soon result in a forced liquidation. When evidence indicates that liquidation is imminent, the going concern assumption should be abandoned in favor of the quitting concern (i.e., liquidation) assumption, under which assets should be measured at their net realizable values and the priority rights of creditors should be reported. Accounting for companies under the quitting concern assumption is covered in advanced accounting courses.

The economic entity, periodicity, and going concern assumptions support certain basic **concepts** and **elements.** The concepts are financial position and changes in financial position. The elements that compose financial position are assets, liabilities, and owners' equity; these elements appear on an entity's balance sheet. The major elements that explain the changes in an entity's financial position are revenues, expenses, gains, losses, income, investments by owners, and distributions to owners. Revenues, expenses, gains, losses, and income appear on an entity's income statement, while investments by and distributions to owners are summarized on its statement of stockholders' equity. The relationship of concepts and elements is illustrated in Exhibit 2–2.

CONCEPTS AND ELEMENTS

FINANCIAL POSITION

The **financial position** of an entity is determined by its economic resources and the claims against those resources *at a particular point in time.*[20]
Financial position primarily consists of the following:

1. **Assets,** or the probable future economic benefits obtained or controlled by an entity as a result of past transactions or events. Examples are cash, merchandise inventory, and land.
2. **Liabilities,** or the probable future sacrifices of economic benefits arising from present obligations of an entity to transfer assets or provide services to other entities in the future as a result of past transactions or events. Examples are accounts payable, bonds payable, and unearned revenues.
3. **Owners' equity,** which is the residual interest in the assets of an entity that remains after deducting its liabilities. Examples of owners' equity are common stock, paid-in capital in excess of par value, and retained earnings.

CHANGES IN FINANCIAL POSITION

Changes in financial position are the result of certain events that occur *during a period of time.* The key elements that follow account for changes in financial position.[21]

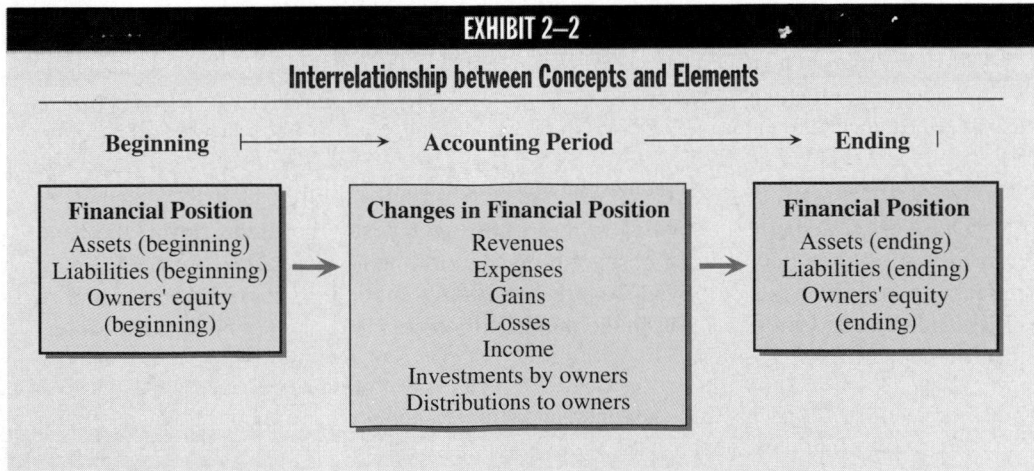

EXHIBIT 2–2

Interrelationship between Concepts and Elements

Beginning ⊢——————→ Accounting Period ——————→ Ending ⏐

Financial Position	Changes in Financial Position	Financial Position
Assets (beginning)	Revenues	Assets (ending)
Liabilities (beginning)	Expenses	Liabilities (ending)
Owners' equity (beginning)	Gains	Owners' equity (ending)
	Losses	
	Income	
	Investments by owners	
	Distributions to owners	

---

[20]The definitions of *assets, liabilities,* and *owners' equity* are based on *FASB Statement of Financial Accounting Concepts No. 6,* "Elements of Financial Statements," 1985.
[21]Definitions are based on *FASB Statement of Financial Accounting Standards No. 6,* 1985.

1. **Revenues,** that is, inflows or other enhancements of assets of an entity or settlements of its liabilities (or both) during a period, based on production and delivery of goods, provision of services, and other activities that constitute the entity's major operations. Examples are sales revenue, interest revenue, and rent revenue.

2. **Expenses,** which include outflows or other use of assets or incurrences of liabilities (or both) during a period as a result of delivering or producing goods, rendering services, or carrying out other activities that constitute the entity's major operations. Examples are cost of goods sold, salaries expense, and advertising expense.

3. **Gains,** or increases in owners' equity (net assets) from peripheral or incidental transactions of an entity and from all other transactions and events affecting the entity during a period, except those that result from revenues or investments by owners. Examples are a gain on the sale of plant assets and a gain on the early retirement of long-term debt.

4. **Losses,** or decreases in owners' equity (net assets) from peripheral or incidental transactions of an entity and from all other transactions and events affecting the entity during a period, except those that result from expenses or distributions to owners. Examples are losses on the sale of investments and on litigation.

5. **Income,** which results from adding all revenues and gains for a period and subtracting all expenses and losses for the period.

6. **Investments by owners** are increases in owners' equity resulting from transfers from other entities of something valuable in exchange for ownership interests. Although assets (typically cash) are usually received as investments by owners, the consideration may also include services or satisfaction of liabilities of the enterprise.

7. **Distributions to owners** are decreases in owners' equity resulting from transferring assets, rendering services, or incurring liabilities to owners. One example is dividends declared.

The elements described above are fairly broad. Although we have defined the term *assets,* for example, we have not yet stated what attribute of assets (e.g., historical cost or current value) should be reported on the balance sheet. To give the elements a more concrete and practical focus, we must consider broad and detailed principles as well as modifying conventions. Most of the broad and detailed principles enable the accountant to recognize various items in financial statements.

RECOGNITION IN FINANCIAL STATEMENTS

Recognition is the process of including an item in financial statements as an asset, liability, revenue, expense, or the like. A recognized item is represented by both words and numbers (e.g., Accounts Receivable $40,000), and the amount is included in the financial statement totals.

For an item to be recognized, the following criteria must be met:

1. **Definitions.** The item must meet the definition of an element of financial statements.
2. **Measurability.** The item must have a relevant attribute measurable with sufficient reliability.
3. **Relevance.** The information about the item must be capable of making a difference in user decisions.
4. **Reliability.** The information must be representationally faithful, verifiable, and neutral.

These criteria should be applied in the context of a cost-benefit constraint (the benefits of information should exceed the costs of producing it) and a materiality threshold. Note that the recognition criteria are derived from the qualitative characteristics of relevance and reliability and that the criteria help to make the definitions of the elements operational in resolving financial reporting issues.[22]

BROAD PRINCIPLES

To implement the concepts and elements, accountants apply certain generally accepted principles. Broad principles are those that have a pervasive impact on the form and content of financial statements. These principles relate to the basic accounting functions of **measurement** and **disclosure.**

---

[22]*FASB Statement of Financial Accounting Concepts No. 5,* "Recognition and Measurement in Financial Statements of Business Enterprises," 1984.

MONETARY UNIT PRINCIPLE

Quantification generally makes information more useful. Although it may be helpful to know that a firm generated net income during a particular period, it would be more helpful to know *how much*. Quantification decreases uncertainty about the firm's performance.

To quantify financial position and the changes in it, a measuring unit serves as a common denominator that permits variables (inventories, cost of goods sold, and so on) to be related to each other. It also permits the aggregation of diverse items using basic arithmetic operations (addition, subtraction, and so on). In a barter economy, any valuable resource (for example, cows) could be used as a measuring unit. In a more advanced economy, such as that of the United States, money is a widely accepted medium of exchange. It is a convenient, customary, and understandable way to express wealth as well as changes in wealth. The **monetary unit principle** maintains that *accountants should measure in units of money, that is, number of dollars, or nominal dollars.*

Monetary Unit

Money measures the command over goods and services, just as the mile measures distance and the pound measures weight. Unfortunately, as a measuring unit, money has a major drawback. Most measuring units remain stable over time, but the ability of money to command goods and services (its **general purchasing power,** or **GPP**) usually changes. During a period of inflation (a rise in the overall level of prices), the GPP of money declines. Conversely, during a period of deflation (a decline in the overall level of prices), the GPP of money rises. Clearly, the economic problem of inflation has persisted in the United States for many years. This phenomenon has resulted in financial statements that reflect dollars of *mixed,* rather than uniform, purchasing power. A dollar invested in plant assets 30 years ago, for example, may be combined in financial statements with a dollar that resulted from sales made yesterday. Many observers believe that this tends to distort interperiod and intercompany comparisons and thereby reduces the usefulness of financial statements.

To help make financial statements more useful, some people have proposed that accountants stop measuring in nominal dollars and begin measuring in **constant dollars,** that is, dollars that have *uniform,* rather than mixed, purchasing power. These proposals usually call for companies to issue **constant dollar financial statements,** a topic that we explain in Chapter 26. Current generally accepted accounting principles do not require companies to publish constant dollar financial statements. The prevailing thought in the financial community is that, given the imprecise nature as well as the costs of preparing and interpreting constant dollar financial statements, the distortive effects of inflation are not now sufficiently material to require a modification of the monetary unit principle. For this reason, we emphasize the monetary unit principle throughout the text.

ASSET/LIABILITY MEASUREMENT PRINCIPLE

The **asset/liability measurement principle** (which we shall sometimes refer to as the **measurement principle**) says that *assets and liabilities currently reported in financial statements are measured by different attributes, depending on the nature of the asset or liability and the relevance and reliability of the attribute measured.*[23] GAAP currently uses five different asset measurement attributes and specifies the circumstances when each is required:

Asset/Liability Measurement

1. **Historical cost** (often simply called *cost*) is the cash-equivalent payment actually made to acquire an asset and put it to its intended use. The historical cost of a new machine, for example, includes the net invoice price as well as transportation, setup, and break-in charges. Nonmonetary assets such as inventories; property, plant, and equipment; and intangible assets are ordinarily measured at historical cost.[24]

---

[23]*FASB Statement of Financial Accounting Concepts No. 5,* par. 66.

[24]Nonmonetary assets are those assets that cannot be expressed in terms of a fixed or predetermined number of dollars to be received by the reporting entity.

2. **Current cost** is the cash-equivalent payment that a company would have to make today to acquire the same asset. Accountants measure some inventories at current cost.

3. **Current exit value in orderly liquidation** is the amount of cash an asset could be sold for in an orderly liquidation. Some investments in marketable securities are measured using this attribute.

4. **Expected exit value in due course of business,** often called **net realizable value,** is the amount of cash or cash-equivalent value that a company expects to receive for an asset in the ordinary course of business, less the costs of completing and selling the asset. Accountants use expected exit values to measure accounts receivable and some inventories.

5. **Present value of expected cash flows** is the discounted amount of the net cash inflows that an asset is expected to produce. Accountants use this attribute to measure long-term receivables.

Five similar attributes are used in present practice to measure liabilities. In the next chapter, we further explain and illustrate the various asset and liability measurement attributes.

Each measurement attribute differs conceptually from the others, although different attributes often have the same dollar amounts. For example, the historical cost and current cost of a parcel of land are the same amount on the date that a company acquires the land. After the acquisition date, the two amounts usually differ.

Although current practice uses five different asset attributes, the historical cost attribute tends to dominate because of its wide use in measuring inventories, plant assets, and intangible assets. That is why current GAAP is commonly called **historical cost accounting.**

Historical cost is dominant for several reasons. First, people generally perceive it as the most reliable asset measurement attribute. Based on completed, arm's-length transactions, historical costs can be verified. Second, historical costs reliably measure an asset's current value on the date the asset was acquired. Third, if current values were more widely used, a company would need to revalue its assets and liabilities each time it prepared financial statements (annually, or perhaps even quarterly or monthly). Many people question whether the benefits of the resulting information would exceed the costs of providing it. Finally, government agencies, such as the Internal Revenue Service, require that historical cost measurements be used in reports, such as tax returns, filed with them. These legal requirements have caused the historical cost system of measurement to be widely understood and established in the business community.

Many accountants and financial analysts question the relevance of historical cost measurements. For example, land acquired 20 years ago for $50,000 would be reported on today's balance sheet at its historical cost even though it may now be worth $200,000. Historical cost critics would argue that the $50,000 amount is irrelevant to user decisions. Another limitation of historical cost is that its proper determination is sometimes difficult and often requires estimates, allocations, and judgment. For example, what is the historical cost of a new machine acquired in exchange for an old machine plus a two-year, noninterest-bearing promissory note? We answer this question, and many similar ones, in later chapters.

Recent FASB work in such areas as pension accounting, accounting for income taxes, and financial instruments indicates that the board is becoming increasingly concerned about the proper recognition and measurement of assets and liabilities in corporate balance sheets.

REVENUE REALIZATION PRINCIPLE

Companies engage in many different kinds of earning activities. Generally, these activities include planning, investing cash in productive assets, selling products or services to customers, collecting cash from customers, and providing warranty services. Collectively, a firm's earning activities constitute its earning process, and companies engage in this process with the goal of ultimately receiving more cash (hopefully much more) than they invested in productive assets. Because the goal of the earning process is to receive cash, it is logical for accountants to construct their measure of revenue based on past cash receipts or claims to future cash receipts that result from earning activities during an accounting period.

From a conceptual point of view, a firm generates revenue *continuously* during all phases of its earning process. In theory, therefore, accountants should initially measure revenue when a new product is planned and then measure additional revenue when the product is produced, when it is sold, and when cash is finally collected. As might be expected, measuring revenue during the early stages of an earning process is difficult because of the tremendous uncertainty about the amount of cash that the firm will ultimately receive.

Consequently, despite the theory that revenue is earned continuously, the accounting profession has had to resolve the following practical question: When can revenue be measured in a sufficiently reliable manner to enter it in the accounting records? The profession's answer to this question is found in the **revenue realization principle.** This principle states that *revenue should be recognized (recorded in the accounting records) when (1) the earning process is complete or virtually complete and (2) the amount and timing of revenue are reasonably determinable.* When these two conditions are met, most of the uncertainty about the existence and amount of revenue has been resolved and revenue can be measured with sufficient reliability.

Revenue Realization

The two conditions for revenue realization are normally satisfied when a product is sold (when title passes from the seller to the buyer). Thus, an asset such as inventory should generally be carried at historical cost until an increase in its value is verified by a sale transaction. At the time of sale, most of the significant earning activities have been completed, and objective evidence provided by an exchange transaction supports the existence and amount of revenue to be recorded. Furthermore, expenses incurred to produce the revenue are either known or can be estimated with reasonable accuracy. Therefore, the accountant can apply the matching principle to measure periodic income.

The revenue realization principle also governs the recognition of revenue from sources other than product sales. For instance, revenue generated by providing services is recorded when the services have been rendered and are billable. Furthermore, revenue, such as rent revenue and interest revenue, generated by allowing others to use enterprise resources is usually recorded as time passes or as the resources are used.

Because the revenue realization principle usually requires a sale, accountants measure revenue at the fair market value of the consideration received in the exchange transaction or the fair market value of the consideration given up, whichever is more clearly determinable. Moreover, the requirement that the earning process be complete or virtually complete implies that any amount received in advance of providing goods or services must be recorded as a liability, such as unearned subscriptions revenue, until it is earned.

Although the revenue realization principle *normally* requires accountants to record revenue only when a sale occurs, sale is not the only time when the two revenue realization conditions can be met. Contractors, for example, often engage in construction projects, such as office buildings and dams, that span several accounting periods. Rather than waiting until a contract is completed to measure revenue, contractors may choose to recognize revenue **during production** using the percentage-of-completion method. This method may be used when there is a definite contract price and when reasonable estimates of progress toward project completion can be made. As another example, revenue is sometimes recorded **at the completion of production,** before a sale has occurred. This procedure is appropriate for products, such as certain metals and agricultural commodities, for which a guaranteed market exists in which the firm can sell all that it has produced at a definite price. Finally, the recognition of revenue is sometimes delayed beyond the time of sale to the time **when cash is collected.** This occurs when significant uncertainty exists about the value of the assets received in the sale or the amount of additional expenses that will be incurred in connection with the sale. Under these circumstances, which occasionally pertain to certain kinds of installment sales, either the installment sales method or the cost recovery method may be appropriate for recognizing revenue. This discussion provides an introductory overview of the revenue realization principle; additional discussion appears in Chapter 21.

MATCHING PRINCIPLE

Matching

Today, the income statement is generally regarded as the most important financial statement, and net income is one of the most significant numbers that accountants compute. In measuring periodic income, accountants usually apply the revenue realization principle first to determine when revenue should be recognized. Then they turn to the matching principle to determine when expenses should be recognized. The **matching principle** says that *costs should be recognized as expenses when the goods or services represented by the costs contribute to revenue.* In other words, accountants should attempt to associate (match) the revenues of an accounting period with the expenses incurred to generate those revenues.

From a conceptual point of view, the matching principle implies that the accountant should determine the extent to which the goods and services represented by historical costs have contributed to revenues during the accounting period. Costs that have contributed to revenues should be expensed, and costs that are expected to contribute in the future should be **capitalized** (reported as assets). This approach is called **direct matching,** but from a practical standpoint, it can be applied only to certain kinds of costs. For instance, a manufacturing company's costs of direct materials and direct labor can be reasonably identified with its product (inventory). When the product is sold, sales revenue is recognized. Accordingly, because the direct materials and direct labor costs contributed directly to the sales revenue, those costs constitute expenses and should be reflected in the cost of goods sold. As another example, the costs of sales commissions can be directly related to the sales transactions. When sales revenue is recognized, the costs of related commissions should be expensed. Direct matching therefore involves associating expenses with revenues on the basis of a presumed **cause-and-effect relationship.**

Unfortunately, it is virtually impossible to accurately determine the extent to which the goods or services represented by most costs contribute to revenues. For example, when Sears, Roebuck & Company purchases a new computer for use in its accounting system, who can precisely determine the pattern of the computer's contribution to revenues? Or when Anheuser-Busch incurs advertising costs, who can accurately assess the pattern of future benefits to the company? The lack of answers to these and similar questions often makes direct matching impractical, and accountants must use **indirect matching.** This approach involves estimates, and the accountant may try to match revenues with expenses based on a **systematic and rational allocation** of historical costs, such as depreciation expense or amortization expense. At times, however, the accountant cannot make a systematic and rational allocation, either because of the uncertainty of future revenues or the difficulty of reliably associating certain costs with future revenues. Under these circumstances, costs are reported as expenses in the period in which they are incurred. This is called **immediate recognition** of costs as expenses. Examples of such costs are advertising and research and development. Note that accounting for these kinds of costs reflects the modifying convention of conservatism (discussed later in the chapter), the accountant's general guide for dealing with uncertain situations.

The revenue realization principle and the matching principle are the essence of the **accrual basis of accounting.** Under cash basis accounting, revenue is recorded only when received in cash, and expenses are recorded only when paid in cash. In contrast, accrual basis accounting requires recognition of revenue when earned (according to the revenue realization principle) and recognition of expenses when incurred (according to the matching principle). Differences between cash basis and accrual basis accounting are explained more fully in

FUZZY ACCOUNTING

A few months ago Chambers Development, Inc. (*Forbes*, Oct. 21, 1991) was the darling of Wall Street. Then, on March 17, the developer of landfills dropped a bombshell. Chambers said it would start expensing indirect costs related to developing landfill sites. The company had been capitalizing these costs, which include public relations and legal costs to obtain permits for landfills.

The change resulted in a $27 million charge to earnings, wiping out more than half the company's 1991 net income—and more than $1.4 billion of Chambers' market valuation.

The debate whether to expense or defer costs is one of the biggest in accounting. And it's heating up in the wake of the Chambers writeoff. The general rule is that companies can capitalize costs only when the costs provide benefits beyond the year in which they are incurred. But it's often difficult to determine if work done today will bring future revenue, and when.

Robert Willens, an accounting expert at Shearson Lehman Brothers, thinks Chambers' capitalization was perfectly valid. Why? Because, he argues, Chambers was simply matching the cost of obtaining permits against future landfill revenues. "There's a belief that conservative accounting is accurate accounting," says Willens, "but there's a larger principle you have to adhere to, and that's to match revenues with expenses."

But in a filing with the SEC, Chambers' accounting firm, Grant Thornton—it has since been fired—says it couldn't determine how much of the legal and public relations costs were attributable to the future development of the landfills. So the accountants wrote off everything. Chambers is undergoing a new audit, so the final chapter of the Chambers story won't be written until the summer.

Because the capitalization rules often aren't well defined, analysts and investors get nervous when companies seem to be aggressively capitalizing costs. For example: Short-sellers have been betting credit card issuer Advanta Corp. will eventually take a big writeoff. Why? Partly because Advanta capitalizes the costs of issuing the cards and amortizes them over five years. In 1991 Advanta deferred $24 million of such costs. Its net income last year was just $25 million. Yet its competitor MBNA Corp. expenses much of the costs within a year of when they're incurred.

Even when accountants have written specific rules on capitalization of costs, the rules are followed in a variety of ways. Take software development. The rules say a company can start capitalizing the cost of developing a product when it has reached the point of "technological feasibility." When is that? Microsoft doesn't capitalize any development costs. Most other software companies typically capitalize 10% to 20% of their total R & D budget.

But tiny ($18 million in revenues) Greensburg, Pa.–based Sulcus Computer capitalized over 60% of its $2.8 million R & D budget last year. "Maybe other companies' R & D departments haven't been as successful," says Robert Colleran, Sulcus chief financial officer. Maybe.

How can investors be protected against unexpected writeoffs that can send stocks plunging? Look for footnotes that describe a company's capitalization policy. Advanta, for instance, spells out its policies clearly. Chambers didn't. Also, look closely at what companies include in their "other assets" category on the balance sheet. That's where they tend to dump a lot of deferred costs that could come back to bite shareholders if they have to be written off.

Loren Kellogg, publisher of *Financial Statement Alert*, which scrutinizes accounting practices, cites Continental Medical Systems, an operator of rehabilitation hospitals, as one company where he has seen red flags. The company capitalizes costs it incurs to obtain government approval for its facilities as well as to develop the hospitals. For the fiscal year ended June 30, 1991, Continental reported $29 million in such deferred costs for some 30 facilities under development. Operating earnings: just $35 million.

Ultimately the answer lies in more detailed disclosure requirements. Had Chambers spelled out how much of its costs it was booking as assets, the writeoff wouldn't have been such a nasty surprise. Unfortunately, the market is full of Chambers Developments, waiting to happen.

SOURCE: Roula Khalaf, "Fuzzy Accounting," *Forbes* (June 22, 1992), p. 96. Reprinted by permission of Forbes Magazine, June 22, 1992, © Forbes, Inc., 1992

Chapter 3. To fully implement the accrual basis, the accountant must make certain adjusting entries at the end of every accounting period (as we explain in Chapter 5) so that the accountant can observe the principles of revenue realization and matching.

A final important point is that in conventional accounting, income measurement is closely related to asset and liability measurement. Thus, the balance sheet and the income statement are said to be "fundamentally related." Notice, for example, that measuring depreciation expense, in compliance with the matching principle, directly affects the reported measurement of the asset that is being depreciated. The term **articulation** refers to the fundamental relationship among all financial statements prepared according to GAAP. Because of articulation, an accounting principle designed primarily to match revenues with expenses on the income statement may sometimes have an undesirable effect on asset or liability measurements on the balance sheet. Likewise, an accounting principle designed to better measure assets and liabilities may sometimes have an undesirable effect on matching revenues with expenses. Many accounting principles developed long ago (e.g., inventory accounting, depreciation accounting) appear to have a matching orientation while many principles developed more recently (e.g., pension accounting, income tax accounting) appear to have an asset and liability measurement orientation.

CONSISTENCY PRINCIPLE

To formulate rational investment, credit, and similar decisions, users of accounting information typically make comparisons. Specifically, they compare circumstances of different companies (**intercompany comparisons**) and circumstances of a single company over time (**interperiod comparisons**). **Comparability** is therefore a desirable quality of useful accounting information that allows users to detect similarities in and differences between two underlying sets of objects or events.

Alternative generally accepted accounting principles exist in many areas of accounting. For example, in accounting for depreciation, a company may choose among the double-declining balance method, the sum-of-the-years'-digits method, the straight-line method, and others. Because a company may choose among these alternatives, intercompany comparisons based on financial statements may sometimes be distorted. Nevertheless, these alternatives exist because different companies face substantially different circumstances. The accounting profession recognizes that the validity of intercompany comparisons is enhanced when differences between the financial statements of different companies result from basic differences between the companies themselves or from the nature of their transactions, not merely from differences in accounting principles.[25] For this reason, the FASB and its predecessor committees have sought to eliminate alternative accounting principles that cannot reasonably be justified on the basis of differences in factual circumstances. In the past, for example, some companies capitalized research and development (R & D) costs, while others expensed R & D costs when incurred. The FASB stated that capitalizing most kinds of R & D costs could not be justified, and in 1974 the board issued *Statement of Financial Accounting Standards No. 2,* which basically requires companies to expense R & D costs when incurred. A major aim of this pronouncement was to enable financial statement users to make better comparisons between firms engaged in R & D activities.

The accounting profession is also highly concerned with interperiod comparisons, which help users of accounting information to discern important trends. Knowing past trends, users can presumably make more accurate predictions about their prospects of receiving cash from an enterprise. To improve the interperiod comparability of accounting infor-

Consistency mation, accountants observe the **consistency principle,** which holds that *accountants must measure and disclose information about an entity in the same manner from one accounting period to the next.* In other words, once a company adopts a certain set of accounting principles, it must observe them consistently over time. A company cannot use the first-in, first-out (FIFO) method of inventory cost determination in 1994; the last-in, first-out (LIFO) method in 1995; the average cost method in 1996; and so forth. It should be noted, however, that the consistency principle does not require a company to measure and disclose all information in the same manner in a single accounting period. For example, it does not prohibit a company from using the FIFO method for one part of its inventories and the average cost method for another part.

The consistency principle also does not prohibit a firm from changing from one accounting principle to another if it has a good reason for doing so. *Accounting Principles Board*

---

[25] *APB Statement No. 4,* par. 101.

Opinion No. 20 states that "the presumption that an entity should not change an accounting principle may be overcome only if the enterprise justifies the use of an alternative acceptable accounting principle on the basis that it is preferable."[26] The accounting profession has not yet defined precisely what it means by the term *preferable.* When a company changes from one accounting principle to another, it must clearly disclose the nature of, reason for, and dollar effects of the change. We cover accounting changes in Chapter 20.

The consistency principle is very important to independent auditors. The standard audit report that was adopted by the accounting profession in 1988 (see Exhibit 1–1 in Chapter 1) implies that the auditor is satisfied that the company has applied accounting principles on a consistent basis over time. On the other hand, if a company makes a change in an accounting principle that has a material effect on the financial statements, the auditor should refer to an explanatory paragraph of the audit report in the manner shown below:

> *As discussed in Note X to the financial statements, the Company changed its method of computing depreciation in 19X5.*[27]

If the auditor believes that the change in accounting principles has been appropriately accounted for and justified by management, the auditor may issue an unqualified opinion on the financial statements. If the auditor disagrees, however, the auditor renders a qualified or an adverse opinion.

An empirical study has shown that during a recent 10-year period, unsuccessful companies were more likely to make accounting changes than were successful companies. The study measured success as the total market return (including price appreciation and dividend yield) to shareholders during the 10-year period. Although accounting changes are often appropriate and desirable, the study suggests that some managers may try to modify their company's net income simply by making accounting changes.[28]

DISCLOSURE PRINCIPLE

The disclosure principle (often called *adequate, fair,* or *full disclosure*) is a significant and far-reaching component of accounting theory. In fact, the disclosure principle formed the basis for the securities legislation enacted in the United States in 1933 and 1934. In recognition of the prime importance of adequate disclosure, one of the generally accepted auditing standards of the AICPA holds that "informative disclosures in the financial statements are to be regarded as reasonably adequate unless otherwise stated in the [auditor's] report."[29]

Consistent with the accountant's aim to provide useful information, the **disclosure principle** calls for *revealing information that will be useful in the decision-making processes of reasonably informed users.* To determine an appropriate level of disclosure for a given company, an accountant must apply generally accepted accounting principles to the circumstances involved. This requires considerable **professional judgment.**

Disclosure

When disclosing information, the accountant must be an effective communicator. A delicate balance must be achieved between completeness and understandability. Although accountants want to issue complete financial reports, the understandability of the reports is impaired by excessive details. The disclosure principle requires that appropriate terminology be used in financial reports. Further, it implies that important information of an unfavorable nature should not be hidden by the use of crafty language, small type, and other means.

---

[26]*APB Opinion No. 20,* "Accounting Changes," 1971, par. 16.

[27]*Statement on Auditing Standards No. 58,* "Reports on Audited Financial Statements" (New York: AICPA, 1988), par. 35.

[28]Steven Lilien, Martin Mellman, and Victor Pastena, "Accounting Changes: Successful versus Unsuccessful Firms," *The Accounting Review* (October 1988), pp. 642–656.

[29]*AICPA Professional Standards—Volume 1,* AU Sec. 430.01.

Several methods of disclosure are commonly used. The most important information is presented in the **body of the financial statements.** For example, publicly held companies are required to disclose earnings per share information on the face of their income statements. **Notes** (footnotes) are an integral part of the financial statements and may effectively be used to disclose such facts as accounting policies, contractual restrictions, and certain details about leases. In addition, accountants use **schedules** to disclose such items as inventory (i.e., raw materials, work in process, and finished goods), operating expenses, and changes in the components of working capital. At times, **supplementary statements,** such as financial statements adjusted for inflation, constitute an effective method of disclosure.

Attempting to comply with the disclosure principle raises many interesting questions. For example, suppose that you are the independent auditor for a paper company. While examining the evidence for the financial statements, you discover that the company has violated an environmental protection statute. If the violation is discovered, the company could be sued for millions of dollars. How would you apply the disclosure principle under these circumstances? Clearly, adequate disclosure will continue to be a challenge in the years ahead.

DETAILED PRINCIPLES

Accountants use **detailed principles** to apply the broad principles. Detailed principles are highly specific, and more than one level of detailed principles may exist in a given area of accounting. Accountants often use the terms *procedures* and *methods* when referring to detailed principles. With plant assets, for example, accountants implement matching (a broad principle) by using depreciation (a detailed principle), which is computed by one of several methods (an even more detailed principle). Like broad principles, detailed principles relate to the basic accounting functions of measurement and disclosure.

Detailed principles are far too numerous to list and explain in this chapter. For this reason, they are covered in other chapters of this text and in other financial accounting courses. Accounting Research Bulletins (ARBs), APB Opinions, and FASB Statements of Financial Accounting Standards (SFASs) contain many detailed accounting principles.

MODIFYING CONVENTIONS

To be useful, accounting theory must be applied in the business world by individual accountants, who must use informed judgment to resolve many difficult questions. To help accountants resolve these questions practically and consistently, the accounting profession has adopted conventions (or customs) that modify basic accounting theory.

To a large extent, accountants apply these **modifying conventions** by using generally accepted rules of broad and detailed accounting principles; modifying conventions are therefore technically a part of generally accepted accounting principles. They are usually called *modifying conventions,* rather than *accounting principles,* because they cause the accountant to modify the "theoretically ideal" treatment of certain economic things and events. In other words, they enable the accountant in some cases to depart from a rigid interpretation of broad and detailed accounting principles. Modifying conventions may therefore be viewed as exceptions to accounting principles. These exceptions are justified on the grounds that accounting theory

1. Must yield information for which the benefits exceed the costs.
2. Must be applied in complex business enterprises among which facts and circumstances may differ substantially.
3. Must be applied under conditions of uncertainty.
4. Should focus on the economic substance of business transactions.

MATERIALITY

All FASB Statements of Financial Accounting Standards contain the following appendage: "The provisions of this Statement need not be applied to immaterial items." Although *all* transactions must be recorded and their effects ultimately reflected in the financial statements, the requirements of sound theory may be modified somewhat when dealing with immaterial items. For example, current generally accepted accounting principles require that extraordinary items (if material) be presented in a separate section of the income statement. This disclosure principle presumably results in useful information because a knowledge of extraordinary items should assist financial statement users to evaluate enterprise performance and to make important predictions. The question becomes: How large must an extraordinary item be to become material and thereby require separate disclosure? Clearly, a $100 tornado loss sustained by a multimillion-dollar company would not require separate disclosure, but would likely be combined with other items in the body of the income statement. Cluttering the financial statements with trivial details would be a disservice to statement users and may in some cases make the financial statements misleading. **Materiality,** therefore, refers to *"the magnitude of an omission or misstatement of accounting information that, in the light of surrounding circumstances, makes it probable that the judgment of a reasonable person relying on the information would have been changed or influenced by the omission or misstatement."* [30]

Materiality

When making materiality decisions, accountants must decide whether knowledge of a particular item of information would likely affect a decision made by an informed user of financial statements. The materiality evaluation is complicated by a lack of knowledge about the specific ways in which accounting information influences investment, credit, and similar decisions.

Materiality decisions may involve quantitative as well as qualitative considerations. Quantitative considerations refer to such factors as the effect of the item on the company's earnings trend or its relationship to key financial variables such as assets, liabilities, owners' equity, revenues, expenses, and net income. Qualitative considerations center around the basic nature of the item. Does the item result in a contractual violation? Does the item represent an illegal transaction such as a bribe paid to a foreign official? Does the item represent an insider transaction such as an interest-free loan made to the company president? Affirmative answers to these and similar questions may indicate that the item in question should be disclosed regardless of the dollar magnitudes immediately involved.

Materiality is one of the most complex, pervasive, and elusive components of accounting theory. Making materiality decisions requires considerable *judgment.* Because of differences in circumstances, an item that is judged material for one company may not necessarily be judged material for another one. To the dismay of some accountants, the accounting profession has not developed a comprehensive set of criteria to evaluate materiality dilemmas. A relatively small number of materiality guidelines are contained in authoritative accounting pronouncements about certain areas (e.g., earnings per share and segment reporting). The FASB's current position, however, is that "no general standards of materiality can be formulated to take into account all the considerations that enter into an experienced human judgment." [31]

An interesting study in this area used four case studies to compare auditors' materiality judgments with those of judges, corporate attorneys, bank lending officers, financial analysts, and credit managers. The findings indicate a lack of consensus within the auditor group and among the various other groups studied. [32]

---

[30]*FASB Statement of Financial Accounting Concepts No. 2,* p. xv.

[31]*FASB Statement of Financial Accounting Concepts No. 2,* p. xiii.

[32]Marianne Jennings, Dan C. Kneer, and Philip M. J. Reckers, "A Reexamination of the Concept of Materiality: Views of Auditors, Users, and Officers of the Court," *Auditing: A Journal of Theory and Practice* (Spring 1987), pp. 104–115.

INDUSTRY PRACTICES

Generally accepted accounting principles are intended for use in general-purpose external financial reporting by business enterprises. Accountants must therefore apply broad and detailed accounting principles to different kinds of companies. In applying these principles, accountants have found that certain industries (groups of similar companies) have peculiar characteristics that sometimes warrant a modification of accounting principles. The term **industry practices** pertains to *modifications of accounting principles necessitated by the unusual characteristics of some industries.* Because these modifications presumably enhance the usefulness of accounting information, they have become generally accepted within the accounting profession and are therefore a part of GAAP.

For example, the investment company industry consists of firms that sell their own shares of capital stock to the public and invest most of the proceeds in the securities of other entities. Thus, investment securities comprise most of the assets of a typical investment company. Given the importance of these securities and the fact that accountants can usually determine their market value in a sufficiently reliable manner, generally accepted accounting principles call for reporting the investment securities of investment companies at market value. Notice that this industry practice departs from historical cost measurement. Additionally, it constitutes an exception to the revenue realization principle because the statement of operations (income statement) for an investment company includes unrealized increases and decreases (i.e., not verified by actual sales) in the value of investment securities held. Interestingly, as we explain in Chapter 10, the FASB has recently changed the accounting principles for investments in debt and equity securities by all companies to require a greater use of current market values.

Industry practices cause many accounting principles to be modified. In fact, these practices have a significant impact on the published financial statements of such companies as banks, savings and loan associations, finance companies, life insurance companies, and public utilities. Knowledgeable preparers and users of external accounting information should be aware of industry practices and their role in the framework of GAAP. AICPA Industry Accounting and Audit Guides are excellent authoritative sources of information about industry practices.

CONSERVATISM

As stated earlier, accountants try to produce reliable measurements. Often these measurements must be made in the presence of significant uncertainties. For example, over what period will a company benefit from research and development costs or from advertising costs? Given the difficult nature of such questions, accountants cannot possibly prepare precise financial statements.

When accountants attempt to resolve measurement uncertainties, they recognize that corporate managers tend to be confident and optimistic (sometimes too optimistic) about their companies. Moreover, many managers desire to maximize their reported earnings each period. From the pragmatic standpoint of avoiding unfavorable legal exposure, it is less risky for the accountant to understate than to overstate net income and net assets. Therefore, most accountants adopt a cautious attitude toward the inherent risks and uncertainties of the measurement process. This attitude is reflected in the modifying convention of conservatism.

The **conservatism** convention holds that *when faced with significant uncertainties about the solution to an accounting problem, an accountant should favor the solution that least favorably affects net income and net assets of the current period.* Thus, conservatism is a practical and prudent, yet an imprecise, response to the problem of measurement risk. Implicit in the conservatism convention is the belief that, *when faced with significant uncertainties,* the accountant should observe the following moderating tendencies:

Industry Practices (margin note)

Conservatism (margin note)

1. Measure revenues and gains lower rather than higher and later rather than earlier.
2. Measure expenses and losses higher rather than lower and earlier rather than later.
3. Measure net income lower rather than higher.
4. Measure assets lower rather than higher.
5. Measure liabilities higher rather than lower.
6. Measure owners' equity lower rather than higher.

Ideally, the accountant's measurements should be neither overstated nor understated. Conservatism is not a license to deliberately understate net income and net assets. If a firm having cash of $100,000 reports only $25,000, this is not conservatism but inaccurate reporting.

Companies are *not required* to select the most conservative accounting treatment available in every situation. Thus, conservatism is not a basic accounting principle. Instead, it is more appropriately viewed as a modifying convention. For example, the common practice of immediately expensing the costs of major advertising programs is a modification of the matching principle, owing to the uncertainty associated with the existence and timing of future benefits.

Many examples of conservatism are found in accounting practice. These include the lower of cost or market rule for valuing inventories, accelerated depreciation and LIFO, recording goodwill only when purchased in an arm's-length transaction, amortizing organization costs over a relatively brief period even though the life of the firm is benefited, and immediately expensing most R & D and advertising costs even though they will likely benefit future periods.

Many users of financial statements support the conservatism convention. Bankers, for example, recognize that the cost of lending to an applicant who defaults is usually higher than the cost of not lending to a loan applicant who would not have defaulted. Accordingly, bankers tend to support conservatism, including the lower of cost or market rule for inventory valuation. Moreover, most financial analysts evaluate enterprise performance on the basis not only of the quantity but also the quality of reported earnings. An important factor when assessing quality of earnings is the extent to which a firm uses conservative accounting policies. All other things being equal, many analysts tend to look more favorably on a company that adopts conservative accounting policies. Such companies are sometimes said to have "conservative accounting personalities." In recent years, IBM Corporation has experienced a number of business difficulties, and critics have charged that the company's accounting policies have become considerably less conservative in such areas as recognition of revenue, accounting for investments in equipment, and accounting for the company's retirement plan. IBM has strongly defended all of its accounting policies.[33]

SUBSTANCE OVER FORM

Financial accounting is concerned with the legal as well as the economic effects of accountable events. But *when an apparent conflict exists between the economic substance and the legal form of a business transaction, accountants tend to emphasize economic substance.* To illustrate, computing earnings per share of common stock would appear to involve little more than dividing net income for a period by the average number of common shares outstanding. Certain securities, however, such as bonds that are convertible into common stock, may in substance be equivalent to common stock even though they are not common stock in legal form. *APB Opinion No. 15* therefore requires accountants to include these types of securities in earnings per share calculations under certain circumstances. By modifying the way

Substance over Form

---

[33]Michael W. Miller and Lee Berton, "As IBM's Woes Grew, Its Accounting Tactics Got Less Conservative," *The Wall Street Journal*, April 7, 1993, pp. A1, A8.

in which accountants had computed earnings per share numbers, the APB attempted to put economic substance over legal form.

As another example, accountants sometimes encounter long-term notes that have no stated interest rates. Such notes may result from transactions between related parties such as a parent corporation and one of its subsidiary companies. Legally, then, these notes do not bear interest. Nevertheless, the accounting profession recognizes that money has a time value, and as a result, the notes that companies typically issue contain interest even though the interest may not be explicitly stated. Accordingly, even though a long-term note may have no stated interest rate, *APB Opinion No. 21* requires accountants to impute (estimate and record) interest under certain circumstances.

As a final example of putting substance over form, current accounting principles require a lessee to report certain kinds of leases as assets and liabilities even though the lessee does not actually own the leased property. In substance, these leases convey to lessees certain rights that are almost identical to the rights held by companies that purchase rather than lease their property.

Putting substance over form requires judgment, and this aspect of accounting theory may appear somewhat vague to you at this point in your study. It should become clearer, though, after you have studied subsequent chapters.

PROFESSIONAL JUDGMENT

Throughout this textbook we emphasize that accountants must use professional judgment when applying accounting principles. For example, to apply the asset/liability measurement principle, an accountant would initially record an inventory purchase at historical cost. But what does historical cost mean in a specific instance? Should cost be determined before or after purchase discounts? Should cost include such elements as inbound transportation, insurance, inspection, handling, warehousing, and purchasing? Should cost be specifically identified, or should it reflect some assumption such as FIFO, LIFO, or weighted average?

As another example, when should an accountant stop making the going concern assumption for a particular company? How badly must a company perform financially for an accountant to assume a quitting concern? Would assuming a quitting concern tend to become a self-fulfilling prophesy for the company? If so, might this cause the company some problems?

As another example, how often should a company be allowed to change accounting principles? Is it acceptable for a company to change inventory costing methods, and thereby violate consistency, once every 50 years? Every 20 years? Every 5 years? Every year?

As a final example, when is R & D expense material? One might initially say that R & D is material when it exceeds a certain percentage of a company's net sales. But what if a large pharmaceutical company that depends heavily on R & D were to cut its R & D spending to only a tiny fraction of sales in a particular year? Might R & D expense become material because it has been reduced significantly? These are a few examples to illustrate that accounting is not a precise science and that applying accounting principles requires professional judgment.

CONCLUDING REMARKS

The authors cannot overemphasize the importance of developing a sound conceptual understanding of financial accounting. You should apply this understanding when solving the problems in this book. A procedural approach to solving problems, emphasizing mechanics and memorization, should be avoided. Accounting problems that appear in textbooks, on examinations, and in the business world often are complex and may vary in an endless number of ways. To solve these problems, accountants must have a solid base of theoretical knowledge, and they must use professional judgment. In the following chapters, we explain in more detail how theory applies to specific accounting issues, and *we highlight in the margin* the key elements of accounting theory explained in Chapter 2.

The model presented in this chapter explains most, but not all, of financial accounting as accountants apply it today. In Chapter 1, we explained that because accounting principles help to determine how scarce resources are allocated in our economy, the FASB and its predecessor committees often have had to deal with political pressures in addition to deciding what is theoretically sound accounting. We believe that some accounting principles exist primarily because of political pressures, not because they are consistent with the model. The existence of these principles, however, does not mean that the model is worthless. Instead, it simply reflects the reality that accounting is a pragmatic discipline concerned with producing information that ultimately affects the welfare of people. At appropriate places throughout the text, we point out accounting principles that do not appear to exist primarily because of the model.

In the next chapter, we explore certain aspects of descriptive accounting theory in greater depth. We also introduce some proposals that, if adopted, would change the basic information that accountants currently report.

KEY POINTS

1. Financial reporting should provide information (1) that is useful in investment, credit, and similar decisions; (2) that is useful in assessing cash flow prospects; and (3) about enterprise resources, claims to those resources, and changes in them. (Objective 1a)

2. Relevance and reliability are the two primary qualities of useful accounting information. (Objective 1b)

3. Financial accounting theory is based on three major assumptions or postulates: (1) economic entity, (2) periodicity, and (3) going concern. (Objective 1c)

4. The assumptions listed above support basic concepts and elements. The first basic concept is financial position, and its elements are assets, liabilities, and owners' equity. The second basic concept is changes in financial position, and its major elements are revenues, expenses, gains, losses, income, investments by owners and distributions to owners. (Objective 1d)

5. Accountants apply certain generally accepted principles to implement the concepts and elements. Broad principles have a pervasive impact on the form and content of financial statements. The broad principles of financial accounting are (1) monetary unit, (2) asset/liability measurement, (3) revenue realization, (4) matching, (5) consistency, and (6) disclosure. (Objective 1e)

6. Detailed principles are the highly specific ones that accountants use to apply the broad principles in practice. Detailed principles are numerous and are covered in subsequent chapters of this text and in other courses. (Objective 1f)

7. Modifying conventions may be viewed as exceptions to accounting principles. These conventions are (1) materiality, (2) industry practices, (3) conservatism, and (4) substance over form. (Objective 1g)

QUESTIONS

2-1 What is accounting theory?

2-2 What are the objectives of financial reporting? How are these objectives interrelated?

2-3 Why are explicitly stated objectives considered important in the development of a structure of accounting theory?

2-4 Why is it important for financial statements to help users predict the net cash inflows to a business enterprise?

2-5 In general, how much knowledge does the accounting profession expect the users of financial statements to have? Why is it important for the accounting profession to state, at least in general terms, how much knowledge it expects users to have?

2-6 What are the qualities of relevance and reliability? How do these qualities relate to the basic accounting objective of providing useful information?

2-7 What is the significance of the contention that relevance and reliability require important trade-offs?

2-8 Should the FASB require companies to report all information that users of financial statements regard as useful? Justify your answer.

2–9 What does each of the following accounting assumptions mean? (1) economic entity, (2) periodicity, and (3) going concern?

2–10 What is the concept of financial position? What are the elements that compose it?

2–11 What is the concept of changes in financial position? What are the elements that represent changes in financial position?

2–12 What is the monetary unit principle? Why is this principle criticized during periods of rapid inflation?

2–13 What does the asset/liability measurement principle mean? Why has the accounting profession traditionally preferred historical costs over current costs for measuring nonmonetary assets?

2–14 What does the revenue realization principle mean? When are the two conditions for revenue realization normally satisfied? At what times, other than at the time of sale, might it be appropriate under GAAP for a company to recognize revenue?

2–15 What does the matching principle mean? What are the differences between direct and indirect matching?

2–16 What are the differences between cash basis and accrual basis accounting?

2–17 What does the consistency principle mean? Why is this principle important to the users of financial statements?

2–18 Does the existence of the consistency principle mean that:

[a] A company must use the same depreciation method in a given year to account for all of its depreciable assets?

[b] All companies in the steel industry must use the same inventory cost determination method, such as FIFO or LIFO?

[c] A company can never change from one generally accepted accounting principle to another?

2–19 What is meant by the disclosure principle. In general, how does an accountant determine an appropriate amount of disclosure for a given company?

2–20 What is meant by the modifying convention of materiality? Why is materiality regarded as one of the most pervasive aspects of accounting theory?

2–21 What does the term *industry practices* mean? What are three industries in which industry practices affect the information reported in corporate financial statements?

2–22 What is meant by the modifying convention of conservatism? What do financial analysts mean when they say that certain companies have "conservative accounting personalities"?

2–23 What does the modifying convention of substance over form mean?

EXERCISES

2–24 Assumptions, Principles, and Conventions   Listed below are the assumptions, broad principles, and modifying conventions discussed in Chapter 2:

[a] Economic entity assumption
[b] Periodicity assumption
[c] Going concern assumption
[d] Monetary unit principle
[e] Asset/liability measurement principle
[f] Revenue realization principle
[g] Matching principle

[h] Consistency principle
[i] Disclosure principle
[j] Materiality
[k] Industry practices
[l] Conservatism
[m] Substance over form

INSTRUCTIONS

Select the letter corresponding to the assumption, broad principle, or modifying convention that best supports each of the following statements. *Do not use any letter more than once.*

[1] A bank's financial statements reflect some noticeable differences from those of most other types of companies.

[2] A company reports its financial statements in dollars that have mixed, rather than uniform, amounts of purchasing power.

[3] A company records a new machine at the cash-equivalent price paid to purchase it.

[4] A company estimates and records interest expense on a seven-year note payable that has no stated interest rate.

[5] A company reports major details about its leases in the notes to the financial statements.

[6] After adopting the first-in, first-out (FIFO) method of determining inventory costs, a company continues to use this method over time.

[7] A company that is uncertain about what depreciation method to use elects an accelerated method.

[8] A company allocates the cost of a patent to the accounting periods in which it helps to produce revenue.

[9] A small company separates its transactions from those of the owners.

[10] A company decides that whenever an asset costs less than $50, the cost will be charged to an expense account, even though the asset may benefit several accounting periods.

2–25 Assumptions, Principles, and Conventions Refer to the list presented in 2–24.

INSTRUCTIONS

Select the letter corresponding to the assumption, broad principle, or modifying convention that best supports each of the following statements. *Do not use any letter more than once.*

[1] Subscriptions received in advance by a magazine publisher are liabilities until the magazines are published.

[2] Large companies ordinarily publish a complete set of financial statements at least once a year, regardless of whether the financial results are good or bad.

[3] A company should always report the important details about its long-term liabilities.

[4] When a company prepares financial statements according to GAAP, it ignores changes in the purchasing power of the dollar.

[5] Accounts receivable are reported at their net realizable value.

[6] The cost of a building is charged to expense in the accounting periods in which the building helps to produce revenue.

[7] A company ordinarily does not separately list each account payable on its balance sheet.

[8] Leases on certain properties are reported as assets by companies that do not own the properties.

[9] The balance sheet of a small appraisal firm excludes the owner's personal automobile.

[10] The amounts reported in financial statements should not ordinarily reflect a liquidation of the business.

2–26 Assumptions, Principles, and Conventions Refer to the list presented in 2–24.

INSTRUCTIONS

Select the letter corresponding to the assumption, broad principle, or modifying convention that best supports each of the following statements. *Do not use any letter more than once.*

[1] Investors and creditors expect companies to issue financial reports at predetermined time intervals, not only when the financial results are favorable to the reporting company.

[2] Most users would not want a company to charge the cost of a new building to expense in the year of acquisition.

[3] Users expect to know certain details about a company's pension plan.

[4] Many users trust the reliability of historical cost valuations of plant assets.

[5] User decisions would not likely be affected if a company listed petty cash separately on the balance sheet.

[6] Many users of financial statements prefer accounting principles such as last-in, first-out (LIFO) and accelerated depreciation that tend to state a company's income on the "low side."

[7] Investors and creditors generally do not want financial statements to reflect a liquidation assumption unless it is likely that the firm will be liquidated in the near future.

[8] Users have trouble making interperiod comparisons when a company changes accounting principles from one year to the next.

[9] Many users believe that when convertible bonds are very similar to common stock, the bonds should be treated as common stock for the purpose of computing earnings per share.

[10] Most users of financial statements would not like for companies to record sales before title to the inventory passes from the seller to the buyer.

2–27 Assumptions, Principles, and Conventions Refer to the list presented in 2–24.

INSTRUCTIONS

Select the letter corresponding to the assumption, broad principle, or modifying convention that is most clearly *violated* by the accounting practice described in each statement below. *Do not use any letter more than once.*

[1] A company follows a policy of recording an item as an asset whenever the company is in doubt about whether the item is an asset or an expense of the current period.

[2] A company changes from LIFO to FIFO when accounting for inventories.

[3] A company that has been in business for 40 years prepares every financial statement in dollars that have the same amount of purchasing power.

[4] A company records sales after inventory has been produced but before it is sold.

[5] A company decides to publish financial statements only in years when it has good news to report.

[6] A company reports inventories, plant assets, and intangible assets at current cost amounts on the balance sheet date.

[7] An electronics company owned by Mike Hardy reports the cost of Hardy's swimming pool as an asset on the balance sheet.

[8] A company having 500 accounts receivable lists each account among the assets on the balance sheet.

[9] A company does not report the major details about its stockholders' equity.

[10] A company charges the cost of new office equipment to expense in the year of purchase although the equipment is expected to help produce revenue for many years.

2–28 Asset Measurement   Matt Company purchased a used delivery truck from Wall Company on July 1, 1996. Wall had acquired the truck new on July 1, 1995, for $25,000 and had taken $5,000 of depreciation for the fiscal year ending June 30, 1996. To acquire the truck, Matt issued to Wall 1,000 shares of Matt's $10 par value common stock. The stock was traded on a national stock exchange, and on July 1, 1996, it had a fair market value of $24 per share. A reputable local mechanic estimated that the truck was worth $21,500 cash on July 1, 1996. Matt had offered Wall this amount, but Wall refused. Immediately after Matt purchased the truck, Jones Company offered to buy it from Matt for $24,700 cash.

INSTRUCTIONS

[a] Record the appropriate journal entry on the books of Matt Company on July 1, 1996.

[b] Explain the rationale for your answer to [a].

2–29 Various Principles   Pauli Company recorded the following events as indicated during the current accounting period:

[1] The company gave its president a new swimming pool for her personal use at home.

Plant Assets	30,000	
Cash		30,000

[2] The company recorded depreciation on its office building. The dollar amount was correctly computed according to the straight-line method.

Retained Earnings	25,000	
Accumulated Depreciation		25,000

[3] An appraisal indicated that land acquired for $35,000 at the end of the previous accounting period was worth $40,000 at the end of the current period.

Land	5,000	
Gain from Holding Land		5,000

[4] Because the inflation rate during the current accounting period was 10%, the company reasoned that $40,000 of liabilities held throughout the period could now be paid using "cheaper" dollars.

Liabilities	4,000	
Purchasing Power Gain		4,000

[5] The company purchased a $12 pencil sharpener that was expected to last five years.

Miscellaneous Expense	12	
Cash		12

[6] The company purchased equipment on sale for $16,000 cash. The equipment would have cost Pauli $20,000 if it had not been on sale.

Equipment	20,000	
Cash		16,000
Revenue		4,000

[7] The company president accepted a three-month loan on the last day of the accounting period.

Accounts Receivable	10,000	
Cash		10,000

INSTRUCTIONS

[a] Using the theoretical model presented in the chapter, comment on the appropriateness of the manner in which Pauli Company has recorded each of the above events.

[b] Record the journal entries, if any, that Pauli should have made for each of these events.

CASES

2–30 Application of Accounting Theory   Rio Company has just acquired 100 shares of the outstanding common stock of Duke, Inc., a large company whose stock trades on a major stock exchange. Over the years, the accounting profession has discussed three major methods that Rio might use to account for its investment in Duke:

[1] *The cost method*   Here Rio would record the investment at historical cost on the date acquired and continue to report it at cost until sold.

[2] *The lower of cost or market method*   Here Rio would record the investment at historical cost on the date acquired. If, on the balance sheet date, the fair market value of the stock is *less than* historical cost, Rio would report the investment at the lower market value.

[3] *The market value method*   Here Rio would record the investment at historical cost on the date acquired. On the balance sheet date, Rio would report the investment at the market value, regardless of whether the market value was above or below Rio's historical cost.

INSTRUCTIONS

Discuss the major pros and cons of each of these methods within the context of accounting theory. Which method do you feel should be required as GAAP? Explain the reasoning that supports your answer.

2–31 Relationship between Objectives and a Detailed Principle   A company may occasionally change from one accounting principle to another. For example, it may change from the LIFO method of inventory pricing to the FIFO method and from the double declining balance method of depreciation to the straight-line method. *APB Opinion No. 20* (par. 17) states that "the nature of and justification for a change in accounting principle and its effect on income should be disclosed in the financial statements of the period in which the change is made." In the context of the theoretical model presented in Chapter 2, this requirement of *Opinion No. 20* is an example of a *detailed principle*.

INSTRUCTIONS

Explain how the detailed principle referred to above logically relates to the objectives of financial reporting.

2–32 Accrual versus Cash Basis   According to *SFAC No. 1,* a major objective of financial reporting is to provide information that helps stockholders, bankers, and others to assess their chances of receiving *cash* from a given enterprise. Nevertheless, the accounting profession believes that income statements prepared under the *accrual basis* of accounting are more useful than either *cash basis income statements* or *statements of cash receipts and disbursements*.

INSTRUCTIONS

[a] Distinguish clearly between the cash basis and the accrual basis of accounting.

[b] Distinguish clearly between (1) an accrual basis income statement, (2) a cash basis income statement, and (3) a statement of cash receipts and disbursements.

[c] Explain why an accrual basis income statement should be useful to stockholders, bankers, and other users when assessing their chances of receiving cash from a given enterprise.

2–33 Income and Value   The general manager of the Milburn Manufacturing Company received an income statement from his controller. The statement covered the calendar year 1994. "Joe," he said to the controller, "this statement indicates that a net income of $2 million was earned last year. You know the value of the company is not that much more than it was this time last year."

"You're probably right," replied the controller. "You see, there are factors in accounting that sometimes keep reported operating results from reflecting the change in the value of the company."

INSTRUCTIONS

Prepare a detailed explanation of the accounting conventions to which the controller referred. Include justification, to the extent possible, for the accounting methods generally used.

(AICPA adapted)

2–34 Fair Presentation of Income   Section 446 of the 1954 Internal Revenue Code states: "Taxable income shall be computed under the method of accounting on...which the taxpayer regularly computes his income in keeping his books"; the method employed shall "clearly reflect income." Among the permissible methods are "(1) the cash receipts and disbursements method" and "(2) an accrual method."

INSTRUCTIONS

Generally accepted accounting principles normally require the use of accrual accounting to "fairly present" income. If the cash receipts and disbursements method of accounting will "clearly reflect" taxable income, why does this method not usually also "fairly present" income?

(AICPA adapted)

2–35 Asset Measurement   In 1965, Meyer Company bought some land in Hawaii for $250,000. Today the land could be sold for $5,000,000.

INSTRUCTIONS

[a] In your opinion, would Meyer Company's financial statements be more useful to investors and creditors if the land were reported at $250,000 or at $5,000,000? Explain your answer.

[b] At what amount would generally accepted accounting principles require the land to be reported? Explain your answer.

2–36 Revenue Realization   After the presentation of your report on the examination of the financial statements to the board of directors of Finchum Publishing Company, one of the new directors says he is surprised the income statement assumes that an equal proportion of the revenue is earned with the publication of every issue of the company's magazine. He feels that the "crucial event" in the process of earning revenue in the magazine business is the cash sale of the subscription. He does not understand why—other than for the smoothing of income—most of the revenue cannot be "realized" in the period of the sale.

INSTRUCTIONS

Discuss the propriety of timing the recognition of revenue in Finchum Publishing Company's accounts with

[a] The cash sale of the magazine subscription.

[b] The publication of the magazine every month.

[c] Both events, by recognizing a portion of the revenue with the cash sale of the magazine subscription and a portion of the revenue with the publication of the magazine every month.

(AICPA adapted)

2–37 Economic versus Accounting Income   On May 5, 1995, Gibbs Corporation signed a contract with Shaw Associates under which Shaw agreed (1) to construct an office building on land owned by Gibbs, (2) to accept responsibility for obtaining financing for the project and finding tenants, and (3) to manage the property for 50 years. The annual profit from the project, after debt service, was to be divided equally between Gibbs Corporation and Shaw Associates. Shaw was to accept its share of future profits as full payment for its services in construction, obtaining finances and tenants, and management of the project.

By April 30, 1996, the project was nearly completed and tenants had signed leases to occupy 90% of the available space at annual rentals totaling $2,600,000. It is estimated that, after operating expenses and debt service, the annual profit will amount to $850,000. Shaw Associates believes that the economic benefit derived from the contract should be reflected on its financial statements for the fiscal year ended April 30, 1996. Management has directed that revenue be accrued in an amount equal to the commercial value of the services Shaw rendered during the year, that this amount be carried in contracts receivable, and that all related expenditures be charged against the revenue.

INSTRUCTIONS

[a] Explain the main difference between the economic concept of business income as reflected by Shaw's management and the measurement of income under GAAP.

[b] Discuss the factors to be considered in determining when revenue has been realized for the measurement of periodic income.

[c] Does the measurement of revenue and expense for the year by Shaw's management agree with generally accepted accounting principles? Support your opinion by citing the factors to be considered for asset measurement and revenue and expense recognition. (AICPA adapted)

2–38 Revenue Realization   Trotman Trading Stamps, Inc., was formed early this year to sell trading stamps throughout the Southwest to retailers who distribute the stamps gratuitously to their customers. Books for accumulating the stamps and catalogs illustrating the merchandise for which the stamps may be exchanged are given free to retailers for distribution to stamp recipients. Centers with inventories of merchandise premiums have been established to redeem stamps. Retailers may not return unused stamps to Trotman.

The following schedule expresses Trotman's expectations of a "normal month's activity," defined as the level of operations expected when expansion of activities ceases or tapers off to a stable rate. The company expects this level to be attained in the third year, when stamp sales will average $2,000,000 a month.

Month	Actual Stamp Sales	Merchandise Premium Purchases	Stamp Redemptions
6th	30%	40%	10%
12th	60	60	45
18th	80	80	70
24th	90	90	80
30th	100	100	95

Trotman plans to adopt an annual closing date at the end of each 12-month period.

INSTRUCTIONS

[a] Discuss the factors to be considered in determining when revenue should be recognized in measuring the income of a business enterprise.
[b] Discuss the accounting alternatives that should be considered by Trotman Trading for the recognition of its revenues and related expenses.
[c] For each accounting alternative discussed in [b], provide a balance sheet account and indicate how each should be classified. (AICPA adapted)

2–39 Cost, Expense, and Loss   You have been asked to deliver your auditor's report to the board of directors of Trombetta Manufacturing Corporation and to answer questions about the financial statements. After reading the statements, one director asks: "What are the precise meanings of the terms *cost, expense,* and *loss*? These terms sometimes seem to identify similar items and other times seem to identify dissimilar items."

INSTRUCTIONS

[a] Explain the meanings of these terms and their use in financial reporting under generally accepted accounting principles. Also discuss the distinguishing characteristics of the terms and their similarities and interrelationships.
[b] Classify each of the following items as a cost, expense, loss, or other category and explain how the classification of each item may change:

[1] Cost of goods sold.
[2] Bad debts expense.
[3] Depreciation expense for plant machinery.

[4] Organization costs.
[5] Spoiled goods.

[c] The terms *period cost* and *product cost* describe certain items in financial statements. Define these terms and distinguish between them. To what types of items does each apply?

2–40 Matching   You are an accountant employed by a large CPA firm. Redington Enterprises, one of your clients, is a manufacturer of paper and wood products. The company's president, Juanita Lopez, is having trouble understanding her company's most recent income statement, which you audited. "The matching principle of accounting doesn't seem to make sense," Lopez tells you. "I know the principle says that costs should be recognized as expenses when the goods or services they represent contribute to revenue. The question I have is how my company is supposed to *know when* the goods and services represented by our costs contribute to revenue. When we purchase a new machine for use in manufacturing, for example, it is used along with many other input factors to manufacture our products, which we then sell. Determining exactly how much the new machine contributes to revenues in a particular period is impossible. And I always thought that accountants tried to produce reliable information."

INSTRUCTIONS

[a] Answer the question that Lopez has raised.

[b] Explain how accountants try to make the matching principle operational.

[c] Describe how the matching principle is applied to account for each of the following types of costs and explain the rationale for each treatment.

    [1] Advertising costs.

    [2] Raw material costs.

    [3] Cost of equipment expected to last five years.

    [4] Cost of sales commissions.

    [5] Cost of a patent expected to benefit the company for seven years.

2–41 Matching   Hatchett Corporation builds and sells "shell houses." These are frame structures that are completely finished on the outside but are unfinished on the inside except for flooring, partition studding, and ceiling joists. Shell houses are sold chiefly to customers who are handy with tools and have time to do the interior wiring, plumbing, wall completion and finishing, and other work necessary to make the shell houses livable dwellings.

    Hatchett buys shell houses from a manufacturer in unassembled packages consisting of all lumber, roofing, doors, windows, and similar materials. Before building in a new area, Hatchett buys or leases land for its local warehouse, field office, and display houses. Display houses are erected at a total cost of from $6,000 to $10,000, including the cost of the unassembled packages. The chief cost is the unassembled packages; building is a short, low-cost operation. Old models are torn down or altered every three to seven years. Sample houses have little salvage value because dismantling and moving costs nearly equal the cost of an unassembled package.

INSTRUCTIONS

[a] A choice must be made between (1) expensing the costs of display houses in the period in which the expenditure is made and (2) spreading the costs over more than one period. Discuss the advantages of each method.

[b] Should Hatchett amortize the cost of display houses on the basis of (1) the passage of time or (2) the number of shell houses sold? Explain.   (AICPA adapted)

2–42 Matching   The general ledger of Good Times, Inc., a corporation engaged in the development and production of television programs for commercial sponsorship, contains the following accounts before amortization at the end of the current year:

Account	Balance (Debit)
Super Mario Sisters	$51,000
Groundhog Night	36,000
The Forgiven	17,500
Jessica Park	8,000
Studio Rearrangement	5,000

    An examination of contracts and records reveals the following:

[1] The first two accounts listed represent the total cost of completed programs that were televised during the accounting period just ended. Under the terms of an existing contract, *Super Mario Sisters* will be rerun during the next accounting period, at a fee equal to 50% of the cost of the first program televised. The contract for the first run produced $300,000 of revenue. The contract with the sponsor of *Groundhog Night* provides that he may, at his option, rerun the program during the next season at a fee of 75% of the cost of the first program televised.

[2] The balance in *The Forgiven* account is the cost of a new program, which has just been completed and is being considered by several companies for commercial sponsorship.

[3] The balance in the *Jessica Park* account represents the cost of a partially completed program for a projected series that has been abandoned.

[4] The balance of the Studio Rearrangement account consists of payments made to a firm of engineers, which prepared a report on using studio space and equipment more efficiently.

INSTRUCTIONS

[a] State the general principles of accounting that apply to the first four accounts.

[b] Describe how you would report each of the first four accounts in the financial statements of Good Times, Inc.

[c] In what way, if at all, does the Studio Rearrangement account differ from the first four?

(AICPA adapted)

2–43 Consistency Sidekick Tool Company is a large manufacturing concern that uses the FIFO method of inventory cost determination. The other major companies in Sidekick's industry use the LIFO method. At a recent stockholders' meeting, one of Sidekick's shareholders made the following statement:

"I'm having a lot of trouble comparing the performance of our company with that of others in the industry because we are the only company that uses FIFO. It seems to me that because of the *consistency principle* of accounting, we should be using LIFO so that our financial results will be consistent with those of our major competitors."

INSTRUCTIONS

Explain the consistency principle and evaluate the stockholder's statement.

2–44 Consistency and Matching Homer Company had used the first-in, first-out (FIFO) method of inventory cost determination from the year the company was organized (1986) until 1991. In 1991 the company changed to the last-in, first-out (LIFO) method. Management explained that the change was "to achieve a better matching of revenues and expenses." Assume that the current year is 1995 and that Homer's management wants to change back to FIFO. The reason management now gives for the change is "to achieve a better matching of revenues and expenses."

INSTRUCTIONS

In your opinion, should generally accepted accounting principles allow Homer to change back to FIFO in 1995? (For the purpose of answering this question, ignore income tax law.) Explain the rationale that supports your opinion.

2–45 Materiality As a recent college graduate, you have been hired as an accountant with the Hawthorne Company. Hawthorne recently sustained an extraordinary loss due to a flood. In accounting, an extraordinary gain or loss is one that is unusual in nature and not expected to recur in the foreseeable future. Generally accepted accounting principles require companies to disclose extraordinary gains and losses in a specially labelled section of the income statement *if* they are judged to be material. The reason for special disclosure is to highlight extraordinary items in an effort to permit investors and creditors to make more meaningful evaluations of management's performance and more accurate predictions of future cash flows. If an extraordinary gain or loss is not considered material, it may be combined with other items in the income statement and may not be reported in a special extraordinary items category.

Hawthorne's chief executive officer (CEO) has just entered your office and wants you to explain how the accounting profession would determine whether the extraordinary flood loss is material.

INSTRUCTIONS

Explain to Hawthorne's CEO the *general factors* that you believe should be considered in determining whether the flood loss is material. You need not attempt to develop precise, numerical materiality guidelines.

2–46 Materiality Assume that you are the independent auditor of a successful brewing company that spent approximately 5% of each sales dollar on advertising during each of the past 10 years. The company charges all advertising costs to expense in the period in which the costs are incurred, and in past years, it has separately disclosed the amount of advertising expense in its income statement.

This year management has decided to save money by curtailing its advertising; this expense for the year amounts to only 0.5% of sales. When examining the annual financial statements and the footnotes, you find no mention of advertising expense for the period. Upon asking management about the omission, you are told: "We have not disclosed advertising expense separately in our income statement because the amount clearly is immaterial. We don't want to clutter our financial statements, and thereby confuse our stockholders, by disclosing every minor detail concerning our operations. We have therefore included advertising in the 'other expenses' category of our income statement."

INSTRUCTIONS

[a] Evaluate management's contention that this year's advertising expense is immaterial.

[b] What disclosure relating to the company's advertising do you recommend for this year? Defend your answer from the standpoint of accounting theory.

2-47 Conservatism   Chris Graning has recently organized the HiCharge Company to produce and sell consumer electronic products. As company president, Graning is currently trying to determine the accounting principles that his company should use. He says that "we will need to use LIFO for our inventories and accelerated depreciation for our depreciable assets because these methods produce conservative results and are therefore required by GAAP."

INSTRUCTIONS

Explain to Graning what accountants mean by *conservatism*. In addition, explain whether conservatism will require HiCharge Company to use LIFO and accelerated depreciation or whether Graning should use some other criteria in deciding what methods to use.

Nature and Measurement of the Elements of Financial Statements

OBJECTIVES

1. To introduce the measuring units that may be used in financial statements.
2. To discuss the nature and measurement of assets, liabilities, and owners' equity.
3. To discuss the nature, measurement, and components of net income.
4. To discuss the usefulness of accounting net income.
5. To present the arguments favoring and opposing the publication of financial forecasts.

While virtually everyone agrees that cash on hand is an asset, the status of certain other assets has been more controversial. One highly controversial asset, goodwill, represents the capability of a company to produce earnings in excess of normal. As the following examples from 1992 financial statements suggest, goodwill is a significant asset on the balance sheets of many companies:

Company Name	Goodwill Amount	Goodwill as a Percentage of Total Stockholders' Equity
American Brands, Inc.	$3.1 billion	72%
Georgia Pacific	1.8 billion	72
Unisys	1.23 billion	55
H. J. Heinz	822 million	35
General Electric	7.4 billion	32

While U.S. companies are required by GAAP to record goodwill as an asset under certain circumstances, companies in Great Britain are not. This raises the following questions: What exactly are assets? And what is the nature of the other elements that belong in a company's financial statements? This chapter addresses these questions as well as others related to it.

In this chapter, we discuss assets, liabilities, owners' equity, revenues, expenses, gains, losses, and income. Financial forecasts also are discussed so that you may contrast their information with that traditionally reported in financial statements.

Most concepts discussed in this chapter are applied within generally accepted accounting principles (GAAP). Other concepts may be viewed as proposals for changing GAAP. If adopted by the accounting profession, these proposals would alter the present scope of accounting information.

This chapter provides a conceptual foundation that will help explain the strengths and limitations of conventional financial statements (i.e., statements prepared today in accordance with GAAP). The specific content of these statements is covered in Chapter 4. The conceptual foundation will also help you to understand some of the more serious proposals that have been made for changing conventional financial statements. We explain and illustrate these proposals more extensively in other chapters, particularly Chapter 26.

MEASUREMENT IN ACCOUNTING

Accounting is a measurement and disclosure discipline. That is, accountants measure the various elements of a company's financial statements, such as assets, liabilities, and revenues, and disclose their results to users in order to help them make better decisions. The information that accountants choose to measure and disclose should be useful, which means that it should be both relevant and reliable.

The term **measurement** refers to the assignment of numbers to objects, such as inventories and plant assets, and events, such as purchases and sales. Measurement allows us to use numbers to conveniently relate certain objects and events to others. If, for example, we are told that one box weighs 100 pounds and another weighs 200 pounds, we know how heavy the second box is relative to the first without ever having seen or lifted either box. In accounting, the term **valuation** conveys the same meaning as measurement. Accountants often say, for example, that a company's inventories are valued (measured) at a certain amount on the balance sheet.

The elements of financial statements are the subject matter of financial accounting and are the things accountants seek to measure. Users need measurements of assets, liabilities, and other elements to make rational investment, credit, and similar decisions. But in order to measure the elements, we must first select a measuring unit and a financial attribute to measure.

Monetary Unit

To illustrate, assume that a company owns some land that we want to measure for financial reporting purposes. The measuring unit could be constant dollars that measure purchasing power as of the balance sheet date, or it could be nominal dollars that reflect the dollar's purchasing power at the time the land was acquired. The monetary unit principle requires the use of nominal dollars in conventional financial statements. The land has several financial attributes, such as how much it actually cost, how much it would cost to replace, and how much it could be sold for. Which one of these financial attributes should we measure? Although historical cost is the financial attribute required in conventional financial statements, other attributes could result in more useful information. Determining which measuring unit and which financial attribute would provide the most useful information are two major challenges that the accounting profession has faced for many years. We explore these issues more fully in later sections of this chapter and in Chapter 26.

THE MEASURING UNIT

Financial statements are expressed in money, which measures command over goods and services in the economy. If the general level of prices of goods and services remained constant over time, money would not be a controversial measuring unit to use in financial statements. Under these circumstances, money received or paid 10 years ago could be compared meaningfully with money received or paid today, because both sums would represent the same amount of purchasing power or command over goods and services.

In reality, the general level of prices in the economy usually changes over time. An increase in the general price level means that money's command over goods and services has decreased; this is called **inflation.** Similarly, a decrease in the general price level—**deflation**—means that money's command over goods and services has increased. In the United States and in most other countries, inflation has existed for many years and is regarded by many people as simply a way of life. Between 1970 and 1980, for example, inflation in the United States was more than 100%. Persistent inflation has caused accountants to actively debate the pros and cons of the two measuring units that have been suggested for financial statements: **nominal dollars** and **constant dollars.**

A *nominal dollar* is one that has not been adjusted for inflation (or deflation); a *constant dollar* is one that has been adjusted. Dollars are adjusted for inflation or deflation by using a **general price-level index,** which is a measure that reveals how much the average price of a given group of goods and services has changed over time. General price-level indexes show the changes that have occurred over time in the overall level of prices in the economy. A general price-level index should be distinguished from a **specific price index,** which is a measure that reveals changes over time in the price of some relatively specific good or service, such as televisions or hospital care. The price of a specific good or service does not necessarily change at the same rate or even in the same direction as do prices in general. In a given year, for example, the inflation rate, which refers to prices in general, might be 10%, while the price of personal computers (a specific good) actually falls by 15%.

The most important general price-level indexes are the **Consumer Price Index for All Urban Consumers** and the **Gross National Product Implicit Price Deflator Index.** The federal government derives each index by monitoring the changes over time that occur in the prices of the "market basket." Each index has its own market basket, or predetermined group of goods and services. When constructing an index, a base period is selected and assigned an index number of 100. All other periods are then assigned index numbers that relate to the base. If prices in general rose by 10% in the period immediately following the base, for example, this period would be assigned an index number of 110.

To illustrate the nominal dollar and constant dollar measuring units, suppose that a company acquired land for $10,000 at the beginning of the current year, when the general price-level index was 100. At the end of the year, the general price-level index was 110, which means that the inflation rate during the year was 10%. In an ending balance sheet prepared according to GAAP, we would report the land at $10,000. This amount is simply the historical cost of the land measured in nominal dollars. However, if we wanted to measure the historical cost of the same land using year-end constant dollars, the land would be measured at $11,000 ($10,000 × 110/100). Observe that we measured the *historical cost* of the land in two ways; we did *not* measure its current market value. Using the nominal dollar measuring unit, we measured the historical cost at $10,000. Measured in constant dollars, the historical cost is $11,000. We derived different amounts simply because we used different measuring units. Because of inflation, we would need $11,000 at the end of the year to have the same purchasing power as $10,000 at the beginning.

As another example of nominal versus constant dollar measurement, suppose that a company buys a product costing $200 at the beginning of the year, when the general price-level index is 110, and sells it for $220 at the end of the year, when the general price-level index is 121. How much income did the company earn as a result of these events?

Measured in nominal dollars, as required under GAAP, the income is $20, as shown below:

Sales (measured when the general price-level index was 121)	$220
Less: Cost of product sold (measured when the general price-level index was 110)	200
Nominal dollar income	$ 20

Observe that the conventional nominal dollar income of $20 is the result of matching a revenue ($220) and an expense ($200) that are measured in dollars having *different amounts of purchasing power.* In contrast, the income measured in year-end constant dollars is zero, as shown below:

Sales (measured when the general price-level index was 121)	$ 220
Less: Cost of product sold (measured when the general price-level index was 121: $200 × 121/110 = $220)	220
Constant dollar income	$–0–

Under the nominal dollar approach, the company's income is $20 because the sale allowed the company to recover a larger *number of dollars* than were originally spent to buy the product. In contrast, under the constant dollar approach, income is zero because the sale merely allowed the company to recover the same *amount of purchasing power* that was originally invested in the product.

As a final example contrasting the nominal dollar and constant-dollar measuring units, suppose that at the beginning of the current year, you invested $1,000 in a savings account that will pay 6% interest on the last day of the year. Ignoring income taxes and assuming that the current annual inflation rate is 12%, how much income will you earn from your savings account during the year? The nominal dollar income, which ignores inflation, would simply equal the interest of $60 ($1,000 × 6%) to be paid at year-end. This amount suggests that you will be $60 richer at the end of the year. But because of inflation, you were actually better off with $1,000 at the beginning of the year than you will be with $1,060 at year-end. The constant dollar income for the period would reflect this reality by recognizing a loss of purchasing power as a result of holding cash during a period of inflation. On a constant dollar basis, you would actually have a *loss* of $60 for the year, computed as follows:

Interest revenue ($1,000 × .06)	$ 60
Less: Purchasing power loss from holding cash [($1,000 × 1.12) − $1,000]	120
Constant dollar loss	$ (60)

Purchasing power gains and losses exist when the measuring unit is constant dollars, but not when it is nominal dollars. These gains and losses occur as a result of holding *monetary assets* (cash or claims to a fixed number of dollars of cash) or *monetary liabilities* (obligations to pay a fixed number of dollars of cash) during periods of inflation or deflation. During a period of inflation, a company gains purchasing power by being in debt because the debt can be paid with dollars having less purchasing power. On the other hand, a company loses purchasing power by holding monetary assets, such as cash, accounts receivable, and notes receivable, during a period of inflation because the assets lose some of their potential for buying goods and services. The opposite results occur in periods of deflation. Purchasing power gains and losses are not presently reported in conventional financial statements because the measuring unit is the nominal dollar.

The desirability of using constant dollars as the measuring unit in financial statements has been one of the most widely discussed topics in financial accounting for several decades. Proponents claim that constant dollar measurements would be helpful to users of financial statements by revealing the impact of inflation on business enterprises. Opponents argue that constant dollar measurements are imprecise and costly and that inflation rates in the United States have not been high enough to warrant a departure from nominal dollar accounting. A. Gary Schilling, an economic consultant and investment adviser, is critical of the consumer price index (CPI) as a measure of inflation. He believes that over time, the CPI "doesn't record the effects of buying more of what's cheap and less of what's expensive. Nor does it properly adjust for quality improvements in goods and services.... It also slights new products.... Hot items like cellular phones, Rollerblades, mountain bikes, and Camcorders didn't really exist when the current market basket was set."[1]

Conventional financial statements are now prepared using nominal dollars, and we emphasize the use of nominal dollars in this textbook. As you read the remaining chapters, however, remember the distinction between nominal dollars and constant dollars and that the use of nominal dollars creates certain distortions in financial statements. You will understand financial statements much better if you are aware of their strengths and their limitations.

---

[1] A. Gary Shilling, "Inflation or Deflation?" *Forbes* (June 21, 1993), p. 252.

In Chapter 26 we explain constant dollar accounting in greater depth. We also discuss Financial Accounting Standards Board (FASB) *Statement of Financial Accounting Standards No. 33,* which from 1979 until 1984 required large corporations to report selected constant dollar measurements as supplementary information to their basic financial statements.[2]

Now that we have examined the measuring units available for financial statements, we shall discuss the nature and measurement of the major elements of financial statements.

ASSETS

NATURE OF ASSETS

In Chapter 2 we define **assets** as probable future economic benefits obtained or controlled by an entity as a result of past transactions or events.[3] Assets have three essential characteristics:

1. They embody probable future economic benefits.
2. Their economic benefits must accrue to a particular entity.
3. They are the result of transactions or events that have already occurred.

These characteristics pertain to *all* assets, such as cash, accounts receivable, merchandise inventory, land, and machinery. Historical cost is *not* an essential characteristic. Some assets, such as the land a city donates to attract a company to the area, may be acquired without cost.

The most important characteristic of an asset is the probable future economic benefits that usually result in net cash inflows to a company. A company may obtain the future economic benefits by exchanging the asset for something else of value or by using the asset. Two of a tire manufacturer's assets, for example, are the inventory of tires and the machinery used to make tires. The manufacturer usually derives benefits by exchanging the tire inventory for cash or claims to cash and by using the machinery to manufacture tires that can later be sold.

Because the economic benefits of an asset are received in the future, accountants sometimes are uncertain about whether a particular item constitutes an asset. Cash is obviously an asset because it can buy goods and services. Uncollectible accounts receivable are clearly not assets because of the absence of future benefits. But what about a new advertising program that a U.S. automobile manufacturer implements to convince consumers that they should buy American products? When the manufacturer spends money for the advertising, it hopes to derive future benefits. To an objective observer, however, the future benefits may be too uncertain to acknowledge as an asset.

To qualify as an asset, the economic benefits of an item must be controlled by a particular entity. Public highways and public parks are therefore not considered assets of a particular company. Although the company may regularly use the highways to transport goods and the parks to have employee picnics, it does not have the right to regulate the use of the highways and parks by others. However, private roads and parks that it has built on its own land are considered assets because it can regulate access by others.

In accounting, we define *assets* as probable future economic benefits rather than as physical objects. A subtle but important point is that the "bundle" of benefits, not the physical object itself, is the essence of an asset. A building, for example, is a physical structure that may provide many benefits such as office space and residual value after the building has been used. These *benefits* constitute the asset. At times, two or more entities may share the benefits that a building or other asset provides. In a building that is leased, for example, one party may have the right to use the property while another has the right to receive periodic rents and to realize the residual value of the property when the lease expires. In this case, the building provides economic benefits to both parties to the lease.

---

[2]*FASB Statement of Financial Accounting Standards No. 33,* "Financial Reporting and Changing Prices," 1979.
[3]*FASB Statement of Financial Accounting Concepts No. 6,* "Elements of Financial Statements," 1985, par. 25. The discussion of the nature of assets relies heavily on *SFAC No. 6.*

Assets may also result from past transactions or events of a particular entity. A 10-year-old machine becomes an asset to a particular company on the date the company acquires it, not when it was manufactured. Similarly, a machine that a company plans to acquire next year will not be an asset to the company until it is acquired.

MEASUREMENT OF ASSETS

Assets have several measurable financial attributes. As discussed in Chapter 2, conventional accounting emphasizes the historical cost attribute. That is the reason that financial statements today are frequently referred to as *historical cost financial statements.* But as we noted in the previous section, historical cost is not an essential characteristic of an asset. Furthermore, historical cost is not the only attribute that accountants measure. Indeed, the asset measurements reported in financial statements today reflect a *mixture of financial attributes.*

Asset/Liability Measurement

A company operates in both an input market and an output market, and exchange prices exist in both markets. The financial attributes that may be used for asset measurement fall into two general categories that correspond to these markets, as shown below:[4]

Market	Asset Measurement Category	Financial Attribute
Input	Input values	Historical cost
		Current cost
Output	Output values	Current exit value in orderly liquidation
		Expected exit value in due course of business
		Present value of expected cash flows

Fundamentally, an **input market** is one in which a company acquires goods and services from suppliers, employees, and others. An **input value** refers to a measure of the amount a company must give up to acquire the goods and services. In contrast, an **output market** is one in which a company sells its products to customers. An **output value** refers to a measure of the amount a company will receive in exchange for its product.

As we discuss these financial attributes, remember the following points:

1. Each attribute pertains to an existing asset.
2. Each attribute pertains to an actual transaction (one that has actually occurred), an expected transaction (one that is expected to occur), *or* a hypothetical transaction (one that would occur if certain circumstances existed).
3. Each attribute pertains to the past, the present, *or* the future.
4. Each attribute is used in practice for measuring certain kinds of assets under current GAAP.
5. Asset valuations (and income measurements) may differ significantly, depending on which financial attribute is used. Under certain circumstances, the measurement of two or more financial attributes of a given asset may result in the same dollar amounts. Nevertheless, each attribute differs conceptually from the others.

Historical Cost

As we discussed in Chapter 2, the **historical** or **acquisition cost** of an asset is the amount of the cash or cash-equivalent payment actually made to acquire the asset. Historical cost is therefore an input value based on an actual past transaction. In conventional financial statements, historical cost is generally used to measure inventories; property, plant, and equipment; and intangible assets.

---

[4]The discussion of financial attributes of assets relies heavily on *FASB Discussion Memorandum,* "Conceptual Framework for Financial Accounting and Reporting: Elements of Financial Statements and Their Measurement," 1976, pars. 402–437. The five financial attributes are also discussed in *FASB Statement of Financial Accounting Concepts No. 5,* 1984, pars. 66–70.

Historical costs are based on arm's-length exchange transactions that have actually occurred and can be verified by invoices, canceled checks, and other source documents. The historical cost of an asset equals its market value at the time the company acquired it. Changes in an asset's market value that occur after acquisition generally are ignored until the company sells it. Proponents emphasize that historical costs are objective and reliable while opponents argue that historical costs lack relevance because they fail to reflect current market values after a company acquires an asset.

Current Cost

The **current cost** of an asset is the amount of cash or cash-equivalent payment that a company would have to make today to acquire the same asset. Like historical cost, current cost is an input value, but unlike historical cost, it is based on a hypothetical present transaction. Suppose, for example, that a company owns land that it acquired a year ago for $20,000 (a historical cost). If the company would have to pay $25,000 for the land today, the land has a current cost of $25,000 to the company. Assuming that no inflation occurred during the year, the company has earned a $5,000 **holding gain** simply by holding the land during a time when its market value increased. In general, holding gains are not separately recognized under generally accepted accounting principles, which, as we have stated, are based primarily on historical costs. However, applying the lower of cost or market rule when measuring inventories sometimes results in current cost measurements and holding losses that appear in conventional financial statements. We explain this rule in Chapter 8.

Various methods can be used to determine the current costs of a company's assets. The current cost of a raw material may be determined by examining the prices listed in the supplier's current catalog. It is often possible to determine the current cost of certain equipment used in operations by applying specific price indexes that measure changes in the price of the equipment over time. Appraisals may be effectively used to determine the current cost of such assets as land and specialized machinery. As we discuss in Chapter 26, *SFAS No. 33* required certain large companies to report selected current cost measurements as supplementary information to their conventional financial statements. The major items required by *SFAS No. 33* were inventories, cost of goods sold, plant assets, and depreciation. In essence, *SFAS No. 33* was a large-scale experiment that focused on the preparation and use of current cost and constant dollar measurements. Now this kind of information is encouraged but not required.

Proponents argue that the use of current cost measurements in financial statements would help users to make more accurate predictions of future cash flows and more meaningful evaluations of a company's financial position and performance. Critics contend that current cost measurements are generally too subjective and unreliable to be useful in making investment and credit decisions.

Current Exit Value in Orderly Liquidation

The **current exit value** (also called *current market value*) of an asset is the amount of cash it could be sold for in an orderly liquidation. In other words, the current exit value of a machine tells us how much cash a company could receive if it were to sell the machine (not the entire business, only the machine) in an orderly manner as opposed to a forced sale. Current exit value is an output value based on a hypothetical present transaction. Accountants use current exit value in practice today to measure certain debt and equity securities that companies hold as investments as well as securities held by investment companies. In Chapter 10, we explain the relatively new accounting principles that exist in this area.

Recall that when an asset is measured at historical cost, changes in its market value are generally ignored until the time of sale. In contrast, when an asset is measured at current exit value, changes in its current exit value may be recognized in both the asset valuation and income. Assume, for example, that a company buys an inventory item on December 31, 1995, for $100. Assume further that the current exit value of the item on that date is $140, and the company actually sells it for $150 on March 3, 1996. Under the historical cost approach, the company would report the asset at $100 at the end of 1995 and would report income of $50 ($150 − $100) in 1996, when the asset is sold. The current exit value approach, in contrast, would require the company to report the asset at $140 at the end of 1995 and to report income of $40 ($140 − $100) during 1995 and $10 ($150 − $140) during 1996.

Proponents argue that current exit values are relevant because they reveal the cash receipts a company can command at the present time. On the other hand, critics maintain that companies acquire many assets for use rather than sale and that current exit value measurements of most assets are unreliable. Critics further argue that some intangible assets, work-in-process inventory, and specialized plant assets, such as an oil refinery in a foreign country that has an unstable government, have no current exit values.

Expected Exit Value in Due Course of Business

The **expected exit value** of an asset, often called **net realizable value,** is the amount of cash or cash-equivalent value that a company expects to receive for the asset in the ordinary course of business minus the costs of completing and selling the asset. Suppose, for example, that a company owns some partially completed inventory that could be sold as is for $6,000. Completing and selling the goods, which the company plans to do, will cost approximately $500, and it estimates that the completed goods can be sold for $8,000. Under these circumstances, the goods have a current exit value of $6,000. Their expected exit value in due course of business, however, is $7,500 ($8,000 − $500). Expected exit value is therefore an output value based on an expected future transaction. Changes that occur over time in an asset's expected exit value are recognized in both the asset valuation and income. In practice, expected exit values are used to measure accounts receivable and, under certain circumstances, to measure inventories.

An asset's expected exit value is relevant to users because it indicates the net amount of cash the company expects to receive for the asset in the future. Expected exit values, however, are generally subject to the same criticisms as current exit values.

Present Value of Expected Cash Flows

An economic fact universally accepted by rational businesspeople is that money has a time value, commonly called **interest.** Suppose that your neighbor (whom you trust) offers to give you in exchange for cash a written and signed IOU for $112 payable to you one year from now. How much cash would you be willing to pay for the IOU today, assuming you want to earn 12% interest on your investment? Clearly, you should not pay $112 because you would not earn any interest. The answer, of course, is $100 ($112 ÷ 1.12 = $100). We would say, then, that your neighbor's IOU has a **present value** (that is, a value at the present time) as an asset to you of $100. To determine the present value, we *discounted* the amount you would receive at the end of the year ($112) using a 12% discount rate.

Here's the point of the preceding exercise. Ultimately, the value of an asset to a company depends on the asset's ability to generate net cash inflows (cash inflows − cash outflows = net cash inflows) for the company in the future. Inventory, for example, has value because of the net cash inflows that generally result from the future sale. Equipment used in the manufacturing process has value because it is used to produce products that can later be sold to generate cash. The **present value** of an asset is the discounted amount of the net cash inflows that the asset is expected to generate. Present value, then, is an output value based on expected future transactions.

To determine the present value of an asset, we must discount all the expected net cash inflows. This process requires an estimate of (1) the *amount* of net cash inflows that an asset will generate, (2) the *timing* of those cash flows, and (3) the *discount rate*. Changes in an asset's present value are recognized in valuing it and in determining income. At this point, you should concentrate on *why* present value is an important financial attribute of assets. Computing present values is not difficult and is explained in Chapter 6.

Present value is widely regarded as the most relevant of the various asset valuation concepts. If measured reliably, present value is the most useful asset attribute in predicting cash flows to the business enterprise; it is therefore most compatible with the second objective of financial reporting, as discussed in Chapter 2. Assets are essentially expected future economic benefits, and present values tell us how much those benefits are currently worth to the company. The benefits are expressed as the net cash inflows that the company expects the asset to generate in the future. Little doubt exists that investors, creditors, and other users of financial statements would like to know the present values of a company's assets. The problem is that accountants cannot measure present values reliably for most types of assets. For example, a machine used in the manufacturing process is likely to be used with other machines, materials, and labor services to produce a product that the company hopes to sell in the future for some amount of cash. But who knows whether the product will actually sell, how much cash it will sell for, and when the company will receive the cash from the sale? Who knows how much cash is attributable to the machine we are trying to measure, exclusive of the other factors (e.g., materials, labor services, advertising) that are important in producing and selling the product? And what discount rate should we use to compute the present value? The difficulty of answering these kinds of questions is what makes the present value approach impractical for most types of assets. However, the present value approach is used in GAAP today for measuring certain long-term receivables under *Accounting Principles Board Opinion No. 21*.[5] The amount and timing of cash receipts for long-term receivables can usually be estimated with reasonable accuracy, and the discount rate used in practice is one that is reasonable at the time the receivable was created. The FASB is working on a major project that examines accounting measurements based on present value.

Summary

Asset/Liability Measurement

Exhibit 3–1 summarizes the financial attributes we have discussed. Although each attribute is used under GAAP to measure certain types of assets, the historical cost attribute is presently emphasized. Proponents of historical cost tend to emphasize the reliability of the measurement while proponents of each alternative to historical cost tend to emphasize the relevance of the measurement to users of a company's financial statements. Recall that relevance and reliability are the most important determinants of the usefulness of information. Assuming that relevance and reliability require important trade-offs, an important question facing the accounting profession is which financial attribute is in fact the most *useful* for decision making. Is it really the historical cost attribute, or is it another one?

LIABILITIES

NATURE OF LIABILITIES

In Chapter 2, we define **liabilities** as probable future sacrifices of economic benefits arising from present obligations of an entity to transfer assets or provide services to other entities in the future as a result of past transactions or events.[6] A liability has three essential characteristics:

1. It embodies a probable future sacrifice of economic benefits.
2. It obligates a particular entity to transfer assets or provide services in the future.
3. It is the result of a transaction or event that has already occurred.

---

[5]*APB Opinion No. 21*, "Interest on Receivables and Payables," 1971.
[6]*FASB Statement of Financial Accounting Concepts No. 6,* par. 35. The discussion of the nature of liabilities relies heavily on *SFAC No. 6.*

EXHIBIT 3–1

Financial Attributes of Assets

Financial Attribute	Description	Transaction	Time
Input Values			
Historical cost	Amount of cash or cash-equivalent payment actually made to acquire the asset	Actual	Past
Current cost	Amount of cash or cash-equivalent payment that a company would have to make today to acquire the same asset	Hypothetical	Present
Output Values			
Current exit value in orderly liquidation	Amount of cash the asset could be sold for in an orderly liquidation	Hypothetical	Present
Expected exit value in due course of business	Amount of cash or cash-equivalent value that a company expects to receive for the asset in the ordinary course of business, minus the costs of completing and selling the asset	Expected	Future
Present value of expected cash flows	Amount of discounted net cash inflows that the asset is expected to generate	Expected	Future

The essential characteristics of a liability are similar to those of an asset, except that an asset entitles an entity to *receive* economic benefits, whereas a liability obligates the entity to *pay* economic benefits. Most liabilities, such as accounts payable, are settled by paying cash, but some, such as the liability for magazine subscriptions paid in advance, require settlement in the form of services or assets other than cash. For a liability to exist, it is not necessary to know either its exact amount or the identity of the parties to whom the entity is obligated. For example, companies report liabilities under product warranties in their financial statements without knowing the identity of the customers whose products will become defective and require servicing. The dollar estimates are based on past experience.

The most significant characteristic of a liability is the duty or requirement to sacrifice economic benefits in the future, either by expending assets or providing services. Liabilities may be payable on demand, on certain maturity dates, or when certain specific events occur. Because a liability entails a probable future sacrifice, uncertainty often exists about whether a particular item qualifies as a liability. For example, accounts payable, interest payable, and wages payable are clearly liabilities because they represent probable future sacrifices. On the other hand, determining that an entity will probably lose a lawsuit and therefore have to pay damages is much more difficult and requires considerable judgment.

Most liabilities, such as bonds payable, are evidenced by contracts or other agreements and by the fact that the entity incurring the liability usually receives proceeds (cash, other assets, or services). However, contracts and the receipt of proceeds are not essential characteristics of a liability. Some liabilities, such as income taxes and lawsuit settlements, result from governmental or legal actions and do not involve proceeds to the entity. Other liabilities, such as donations to charity, result from discretionary actions by an entity's management and the entity does not receive proceeds.

A liability does not have to be legally enforceable, although most liabilities, such as notes payable, are. A liability may exist simply because an entity is bound by custom or tradition to provide money, goods, or services in the future. A liability for year-end bonuses, for example, may exist because a company has always paid such amounts even without a contractual requirement to do so. When an obligation is not legally enforceable, determining whether a liability really exists is often extremely difficult. Under such circumstances, an accountant must apply careful judgment.[7]

Probable future sacrifices alone do not constitute a liability. For a liability to exist, a particular entity must be obligated to transfer assets or provide services to other entities in the future as a result of past transactions or events. A company that has sold all of its inventory has no liability to pay for new inventory until acquired from another entity. Similarly, the amount shown in the next year's budget for labor services is not a liability until the company has received the services.

MEASUREMENT OF LIABILITIES

The five financial attributes discussed earlier for assets also pertain to liabilities.[8] But relative to asset measurement, liability measurement has received much less attention in the accounting literature. The measurement of a liability in practice is often the result of measuring the other side of the transaction that created the liability. When a company acquires an inventory item for $100 on credit, for example, the asset is measured at its historical cost of $100; the liability is also measured at $100, which is the amount the company expects to spend to liquidate the liability. In practice, a variety of financial attributes is used to measure liabilities.

Asset/Liability Measurement

Liabilities enable companies to delay payment. The cost of delaying payment is *interest,* or the time value of money. *Whether interest is explicitly stated or not, it is always inherent in liabilities.* Two issues in liability measurement therefore are (1) whether the interest should be separately recognized and (2) what rate should be used to recognize the interest.

Each of the following financial attributes pertains to a liability that presently exists. Although each attribute is conceptually unique, the measurement of two or more financial attributes of a given liability may result in the same dollar amount under certain circumstances. Measurements of liabilities and income may differ considerably, depending on the financial attribute used.

Present Value of Expected Cash Flows

Conceptually, a liability should be measured on a present-value basis, and many liabilities are currently measured this way. The **present value** of a liability is the discounted amount of the net cash outflows that are expected to be necessary to liquidate the liability. Suppose, for example, that a company has a debt of $1,000 that is payable one year from today. Assuming an interest rate of 12%, the present value of the liability today is $892.86 ($1,000 ÷ 1.12).[9] The $107.14 difference between $1,000 and $892.86 is the interest charge that the company will incur by being indebted during the coming year. Under the present-value approach, the interest would be separately recognized and accounted for.

Present-value measurements reflect the time value of money and are required in current practice when measuring certain long-term payables under *APB Opinion No. 21.* In practice, accountants apply the present value approach throughout the time a liability exists by using a discount rate equal to the market rate of interest at the time the liability was initially in-

---

[7]This issue is discussed in more detail in *FASB Statement of Financial Accounting Concepts No. 6,* pars. 40 and 203.

[8]The discussion of financial attributes of liabilities relies heavily on *FASB Discussion Memorandum,* "Conceptual Framework for Financial Accounting and Reporting: Elements of Financial Statements and Their Measurement," 1976, pars. 534–576. The five financial attributes are also discussed in *FASB Statement of Financial Accounting Concepts No. 5,* 1984, pars. 66–70.

[9]Computing present values is discussed more fully in Chapter 6.

curred. This discount rate is called the **historical market rate.** Very often the historical market rate is simply the interest rate stated in the loan agreement.

Expected Exit Value in Due Course of Business

The **expected exit value** of a liability is the amount of cash or cash-equivalent value that the company expects to pay to eliminate the liability in the ordinary course of business. The amount of the cash or cash-equivalent payment is not discounted to a present value. Assume that a company acquires some merchandise on credit. The goods cost $5,000, which it agrees to pay in 60 days. The expected exit value of the liability is $5,000.

Expected exit values show how much cash the company expects to spend to liquidate a liability, but they ignore the time value of money completely. In the example above, the interest on the $5,000 liability for 60 days is not separately considered. To illustrate this point more dramatically, assume that a company currently sells at par value $100,000, 12%, 20-year bonds that it expects to retire at maturity. The expected exit value of the bonds today would be $340,000 [$100,000 maturity value + $240,000 ($100,000 × 12% × 20) interest]. Recording the bond liability at $340,000 fails to reflect the economic reality that interest of $240,000 will be incurred during the 20-year life of the bonds. Under current GAAP, the company would measure the bond liability at $100,000, an amount equal to the present value of the interest and principal payments required to liquidate the bonds.

Expected exit values are used under GAAP for measuring many liabilities. For example, accounts payable to suppliers are usually measured at expected exit values. The interest is ignored because the credit period is usually relatively brief and therefore the interest is immaterial. As another example, liabilities for product warranties are usually measured at their expected exit value. In this case, the interest is ignored because the amount and timing of payment are too uncertain to permit a meaningful estimate of the interest.

Materiality

Historical Proceeds

The **historical proceeds** of a liability is the amount of the cash or cash-equivalent proceeds actually received when the liability was incurred. To illustrate, assume that a company receives $18,000 from magazine subscriptions paid in advance for three years. The company now is obligated to provide the magazines, and it would measure the liability for unearned subscriptions revenue at $18,000, the amount of the cash proceeds received.

Historical proceeds is generally used under GAAP to measure liabilities for products or services that a company has agreed to provide in the future. The time value of money is generally ignored for these types of liabilities because it is considered too impractical to measure.

Current Proceeds

The **current proceeds** of a liability is the amount of cash or cash-equivalent value that a company would receive today by incurring the same liability. The amount changes in response to changes in market interest rates and in the perceived risk of the company that has the liability. As market interest rates rise, the current proceeds of a given liability tend to decrease; similarly, as market interest rates fall, the current proceeds tend to increase.

To illustrate, suppose that on January 1, 1995, a company issues a $10,000, 10%, two-year note payable with interest of $1,000 ($10,000 × 10%) payable at the end of each year. On that date, the market rate of interest is 10%, and the company receives proceeds of $10,000, because the present value of the note (including the interest) at the market rate of interest is $10,000. On December 31, 1995, the company pays $1,000 of interest for the year 1995, the current market rate of interest is 12%, and the company's risk level is unchanged from the beginning of the year. Under these circumstances, the current proceeds of the note will be $9,821.43 on December 31, 1995. This amount equals the $10,000 face amount plus $1,000 of interest due at the end of 1996, divided by 1.12 ($11,000 ÷ 1.12 = $9,821.43). We are saying, then, that *if* the company were to issue on December 31, 1995, a $10,000, 10% note with one year remaining to maturity, it would obtain proceeds of $9,821.43. The current proceeds are less than $10,000 because the current market rate of interest (12%) exceeds the interest rate stated in the note (10%). A lender who invested $9,821.43 in the note at the end of 1995 would earn 12% interest (the current market rate) during 1996 [$9,821.43 + ($9,821.43 × 12%) = $11,000]. Notice that $9,821.43 is simply the present value of the note computed using the current market rate of interest (12%) at the end of 1995.

We emphasize that the note payable in the previous example would be reported at $10,000 (not $9,821.43) in conventional financial statements prepared at the end of 1995. This is so because $10,000 is the present value of the note at the end of 1995 computed using the market rate of interest that prevailed when the note was issued ($11,000 ÷ 1.10 = $10,000).

Under the current proceeds approach to liability measurement, the time value of money is measured using a current rather than a historical interest rate. Some people believe that the use of current proceeds would enhance the usefulness of financial statements for making predictions of cash flows and evaluations of management. But current proceeds departs from historical cost accounting and is not used for measuring liabilities under GAAP.

Current Exit Value in Orderly Liquidation

The **current exit value** of a liability is the amount a company would have to pay currently to eliminate the liability in an orderly manner. Assume, for example, that a company has $100,000 of bonds payable outstanding and that each of the 100 bonds was originally sold at par value of $1,000. Assume further that market interest rates have fallen since the bonds were issued and that each bond now has a market price of $1,050. In this example, the current exit value of the bonds is $105,000 ($1,050 × 100) because this is the amount the company would have to pay currently to retire the bonds by purchasing them in the market.

When a liability requires specified cash payments, such as the bond liability in the example above, the current exit value and current proceeds will usually be the same amount. Nevertheless, current exit value and current proceeds differ conceptually. *Current exit value* refers to how much a company would have to *pay* to eliminate the liability; *current proceeds* refers to how much a company would *receive* by incurring the liability. Some people argue that current exit values would be relevant to users when assessing an entity's ability to adapt to a changing environment. The counterargument is that most companies do not intend to eliminate all of their liabilities currently. Like current proceeds, current exit value measurements represent a departure from historical cost accounting and are not used when measuring liabilities in financial statements prepared in accordance with GAAP.

Summary

The various financial attributes of liabilities are summarized in Exhibit 3–2.

OWNERS' EQUITY

NATURE OF OWNERS' EQUITY

Owners' equity is "the residual interest in the assets of an entity that remains after deducting its liabilities."[10] In other words, owners' equity equals net assets, which are assets minus liabilities. Liabilities and owners' equity are similar in that they both represent **sources of assets.** That is, assets come from either creditors (liabilities) or owners (owners' equity). Therefore, liabilities and owners' equity represent **claims or interests in the assets of an entity.** Despite these similarities, liabilities and owners' equity *differ* in several important aspects:

---

[10]*FASB Statement of Financial Accounting Concepts No. 6,* par. 49. The discussion of the nature of owners' equity relies heavily on *SFAC No. 6.*

EXHIBIT 3–2

Financial Attributes of Liabilities

Financial Attribute	Description	Transaction	Time
Present value of expected cash flows	Amount of discounted net cash outflows that are expected to be necessary to liquidate the liability	Expected	Future
Expected exit value in due course of business	Amount of cash or cash-equivalent value that a company expects to pay to eliminate the liability in the ordinary course of business	Expected	Future
Historical proceeds	Amount of cash or cash-equivalent proceeds actually received when the liability was incurred	Actual	Past
Current proceeds	Amount of cash or cash-equivalent value that a company would receive today by incurring the same liability	Hypothetical	Present
Current exit value in orderly liquidation	Amount of cash that a company would have to pay currently to eliminate the liability in an orderly manner	Hypothetical	Present

1. Liabilities represent the interest of creditors in the assets of an entity; owners' equity represents the interest of owners.
2. Liabilities rank ahead of owners' equity when an entity's assets are distributed. A company may not pay dividends to owners until it has made the required interest and principal payments to creditors. Moreover, when a company is liquidated, liabilities must be paid before distributions can be made to owners.
3. The amount of liability payments is usually more certain than is the amount of payments to owners. Oral or written agreements, such as bond contracts, usually specify how much cash a company must pay to liquidate its liabilities. The amount of dividend payments to owners, however, is usually determined at the discretion of a company's board of directors.
4. The timing of liability payments is usually more certain than the timing of payments to owners. Many liabilities have specific maturity dates; owners' equity does not mature.

Owners' equity represents the interest of parties who stand to lose the largest amount if an entity is unsuccessful and to gain the largest amount if it is successful. Owners are the primary beneficiaries of an entity's net income, but they also must bear its losses. Owners' equity is originally created when owners invest cash or other assets in an entity. Subsequently, the interest of owners may be increased by additional investments and net income, and it may be decreased by distributions to owners (dividends) and net losses.

Owners' equity provides an important frame of reference when measuring a company's net income. In the absence of additional investments by owners or distributions to them during a period, net income for the period will equal the increase in owners' equity that occurred during the period.

MEASUREMENT OF OWNERS' EQUITY

As indicated earlier, owners' equity is a **residual figure** derived by deducting liabilities from assets. The measurement of owners' equity is therefore not an independent process. Instead, it depends on the valuations assigned to the individual assets and liabilities. Suppose that a company had only one asset, an account receivable with an expected exit value of $10,000,

Asset/Liability Measurement

and no liabilities. Under these circumstances, owners' equity would simply reflect the expected exit value measurement of $10,000 ($10,000 − $0). As we have seen, however, companies actually use a mixture of financial attributes (historical costs, expected exit values, present values, etc.) when measuring their individual assets and liabilities. Owners' equity therefore reflects a mixture of financial attributes. For this reason and because many assets and liabilities are simply too difficult to measure and report at all, owners' equity does not reveal the current market value of the company to its owners.

INCOME

In this section, we discuss the nature, measurement, components, and usefulness of net income. Many people believe that net income is the most important single number that appears in the financial statements. Unlike cash on hand, the net income for a typical business cannot be seen or counted. It is not surprising that income concepts have been a highly controversial topic in accounting and economics.

NATURE OF NET INCOME

The famous economist J. R. Hicks defined an individual's income as the maximum amount the person could consume in a period and still be as well off at the end of the period as he or she was at the beginning.[11] This definition can be adapted to a business enterprise: the **net income** of a business is the increase in the net assets (owners' equity) of the firm, assuming no new capital contributions by the owners or dividend distributions by the business.[12] More precisely, the net income for a period equals the ending owners' equity minus the beginning owners' equity plus dividends declared during the period minus additional capital contributions made during the period. To illustrate, assume that during a period, a company had ending owners' equity of $25,000, beginning owners' equity of $20,000, dividends declared of $10,000, and additional capital contributions of $3,000. Net income for the period would be $12,000 ($25,000 − $20,000 + $10,000 − $3,000).

The distinction between a **return of capital** and **return on capital** is important to the understanding of net income. Stockholders invest in companies to earn a return *on* capital, or an amount in excess of their original investment. A return *of* capital is simply an erosion of the capital invested in the firm. Net income occurs only after the capital used from the beginning of the period is maintained. This concept is known as **capital maintenance.** In the Hicksian sense, the same level of "well-offness" must be maintained before net income can be said to exist. Revenues must be applied to the recovery of the resources used in the business before any net income can result. The capital used in the business does not have to be physically replaced with the exact type of resources consumed. Capital maintenance is a measurement concept, not a statement of how managers should reinvest resources.

To illustrate the concept of capital maintenance, consider a retail store with all its capital invested in an inventory of 800 stereophonic tapes costing $5 each. If the retailer sells 600 tapes at $7 each, the total revenue is $4,200 (600 × $7). Therefore, at the end of the period, the retailer has 200 tapes and $4,200. To determine net income, we must deduct from $4,200 an amount that represents the capital invested in the 600 tapes that were sold. One way to do this is to deduct $3,000 (600 × $5) from the $4,200 as a return *of* capital and then consider the remaining $1,200 (600 × $2) as a return *on* capital (i.e., net income). The retailer need not actually replace the 600 tapes that were sold. Our objective in deducting $3,000 is merely to measure the capital consumed by the sale of 600 tapes so that we can

---

[11]R. Hicks, *Value and Capital* (Oxford: Clarendon Press, 1946), p. 172.

[12]Robert T. Sprouse and Maurice Moonitz, *Accounting Research Study No. 3,* "A Tentative Set of Broad Accounting Principles for Business Enterprises" (New York: AICPA, 1962), p. 54.

EXHIBIT 3–3
Reconciliation between Cash Flow and Revenue/Expense Recognition

	Cash Precedes Recognition	Cash Follows Recognition
Revenues	**Liability** Example: Unearned Rent Revenue	**Asset** Example: Accrued Interest Receivable
Expenses	**Asset** Example: Prepaid Insurance	**Liability** Example: Accrued Wages Payable

determine net income. In other words, $3,000 is a measure of the capital that the firm must maintain before net income can exist.[13]

Lifetime Net Income

The most definitive measure of net income can be made when a company is liquidated. At that time, the **lifetime net income** of the firm can be determined with certainty. Assuming no additional investments or withdrawals by owners, lifetime net income (or loss) would equal the cash initially invested by owners at the beginning of business, subtracted from the cash remaining for the owners at the end of business—after assets are liquidated and liabilities are satisfied. Over the life of the company, total revenues equal all cash receipts from earning activities (such as sales), and total expenses equal all cash disbursements for earning activities (such as payments to suppliers and employees). Lifetime net income therefore equals lifetime cash receipts from earning activities minus lifetime cash disbursements for earning activities, or net cash inflows from earning activities during the life of the company.

Periodic Net Income

Although the lifetime net income of an enterprise corresponds with its net cash flows from earning activities, it does not help the investor or creditor to make *timely* decisions. Investors and creditors are not interested in knowing the net income of a firm after final disposition of assets. Instead, they need periodic disclosures of operating performance in order to assess current investments and loans and to evaluate future capital commitments.

One function of an accountant is to provide statements of periodic net income. This presents a challenge because, in contrast to lifetime net income, periodic net income does not necessarily reflect cash flows for the period. At *some time* during the life of a company, a dollar should be received for every dollar of revenue reported by the company, but the cash receipts do not have to occur in the same period that the revenue is recognized. Likewise, at *some time* during the life of a company, a dollar should be spent for every dollar of expense reported by the company, but the cash payments do not have to occur in the same period that the expense is recognized. The accountant attempts to reconcile the recognition of revenues and expenses with the actual cash flows of past, present, and future periods. This reconciliation requires the recognition of certain assets and liabilities, as shown in Exhibit 3–3.

---

[13]Central to the concept of capital maintenance is the accountant's assessment of "well-offness." The accountant's definition of capital has a direct bearing on what is considered as net income. It is beyond the scope of this text to discuss the various concepts of capital. A lucid discussion can be found in Keith Shwayder, "The Capital Maintenance Rule and the Net Asset Valuation Rule," *Accounting Review* (April 1969), pp. 304–316.

The upper left cell of Exhibit 3–3 illustrates the situation in which cash inflow precedes the recognition of revenue. Consider a business that rents space in return for a fee received in advance. At the time the business collects the fee, there is no revenue, only the liability to provide rental space. The business recognizes revenue only as rental space is provided. Likewise, the lower left cell of Exhibit 3–3 represents the case of cash outflow preceding the recognition of an expense. This occurs when a business pays cash in exchange for future services, such as prepaid insurance. The prepaid insurance represents the right to future protection that is amortized as an expense only as the protection is received.

The upper right cell of the exhibit illustrates transactions in which cash inflow follows revenue recognition. An example is interest on an investment in the bonds of another company. If the interest has been earned as of the end of an accounting period, then the interest must be recognized as a receivable and as revenue, even though the business will not receive the cash associated with the interest until the next accounting period. The lower right cell concerns transactions in which cash outflow follows expense recognition. Frequently, at the end of a reporting period, an enterprise has received employee services for which it has not yet paid. The labor represents a liability that will later be compensated by actual cash payment.

In each case, revenue and expense recognition for the period do not exactly correspond to cash flows. Although cash flows are reconciled with revenues and expenses over the lifetime of a company, it is unreasonable to postpone income measurement until business is terminated. Instead, accountants have methods to measure periodic net income.

THE MEASUREMENT OF PERIODIC NET INCOME

The measurement of periodic net income depends on the valuation of assets and liabilities, since periodic net income is the change in the net assets for the period, assuming no new capital contributions or dividends. Periodic net income could be measured under a cash basis system or an accrual basis system.

Cash Basis Accounting versus Accrual Basis Accounting

Cash basis accounting defines revenues as cash inflows from earning activities, and expenses as cash outflows in earning activities. Frequently, cash inflows and outflows occur in different periods than the related accomplishments and efforts. For example, the purchase of machinery results in an immediate cash outflow but provides useful service over a period of years. **Accrual basis accounting** allows for such cases by recording the results of significant operating events when they occur rather than when cash is received or paid. Under accrual basis accounting, revenues are recognized when earned, regardless of when cash is received, and expenses are recognized when incurred, regardless of when cash is paid.

Because investors and creditors are interested in cash flows (see Chapter 2), a simple cash basis income statement may seem preferable to an accrual basis statement. Most accountants disagree. A cash basis system usually fails to provide valuable information about the earning capability of the firm. In addition, cash receipts and disbursements for successive periods are generally unrelated and can produce misleading trends.

Consider a college student who started a business, the Nimble Fingers Typing Service. The following events occurred during the first three months of the academic year.

September

Rented a microcomputer for $25 on account.

Purchased paper for $30 on account.

Placed an advertisement in the campus newspaper for $40 on account.

Typed several projects and charged customers a total fee of $200 on account.

October

Collected $200 in fees from customers.

November

Remitted payments to paper supplier, campus newspaper,
and office equipment lessor.

Exhibit 3–4 represents the income statement and balance sheet under cash accounting. Close examination of these financial statements reveals some difficulties of cash basis accounting. If we evaluated the performance of Nimble Fingers based on the monthly cash flow figures, our conclusions would change from month to month. For September we might conclude that the business accomplished nothing, because the financial statements contain all zeros. We know, however, that Nimble Fingers provided typing services throughout September.

October appears more promising with a large increase in net income, and we might conclude that the business is proving successful. This, however, is misleading, because we know, as early as the end of September, that of the $200 cash inflow reported in October, only $105 represents a return *on* invested capital, while the remaining $95 is a return *of* capital. This information is known, but the reporting is delayed under cash basis accounting.

The November income statement reports a net loss of $95. This turn of events leaves the outside observer unable to determine what might happen in December. The total net income for all three months is $105 ($0 + $200 − $95), which is accurate. What is not meaningful is the time period in which the $105 was disclosed. Under cash basis accounting, we must wait for the final cash payment in November before we have an accurate picture of the events for the first three months. The criticism is that this information was known with reasonable certainty as early as the end of September, but recognition was delayed until cash changed hands.

Accrual accounting alleviates these problems by recording net income when it was *earned* rather than when cash was collected or paid. Exhibit 3–5 presents the Nimble Fingers financial statements under accrual accounting. The information disclosed in September under accrual accounting differs markedly from that under cash accounting. Net income is disclosed in the period in which effort is applied to the typing business, and accomplishments accrue as the jobs are completed. All net income is disclosed in September, when the

---

EXHIBIT 3–4

Financial Statements for Nimble Fingers under Cash Basis Accounting

Income Statement
(month ending)

	September	October	November
Revenues	$–0–	$200	$–0–
Expenses	–0–	–0–	95
Net income (Loss)	$–0–	$200	$(95)

Balance Sheet
(last day of the month)

	September	October	November
Total assets (Cash)	$–0–	$200	$105
Owner's capital	$–0–	$200	$105

EXHIBIT 3–5

Financial Statements for Nimble Fingers under Accrual Basis Accounting

Income Statement
(month ending)

	September	October	November
Revenues	$200	$–0–	$–0–
Expenses	95	–0–	–0–
Net income	$105	$–0–	$–0–

Balance Sheet
(last day of the month)

	September	October	November
Cash	$–0–	$200	$ 105
Accounts receivable	200	–0–	–0–
Total assets	$ 200	$200	$ 105
Accounts payable	$ 95	$ 95	$–0–
Owner's capital	105	105	105
Total liabilities and owner's capital	$ 200	$200	$ 105

main activities of the business were completed. After September, only the incidental activities of collecting customer accounts and satisfying creditor obligations remain. The income statement reflects this by attributing zero earnings to October and November. The balance sheet includes Accounts Receivable and Accounts Payable among the assets and liabilities in order to reconcile cash flow with revenue and expense recognition (Exhibit 3–3).

In both cash basis and accrual basis accounting, the net income for a period equals the change in the net assets, and the lifetime net income is $105. The two methods differ in the assignment of income to periods. Under accrual accounting, revenues and expenses are recorded at the earliest appearance of objective evidence. This frequently precedes cash flow. As a result, accrual accounting assigns income to the period in which it is earned, which is often a more timely measurement than that of cash basis accounting.

Measuring Income under Accrual Accounting

Asset/Liability Measurement

The methods of measuring income under accrual accounting relate to the financial attributes used in measuring assets and liabilities, as discussed earlier in the chapter. Accrual basis income may be measured under historical cost, current cost, current exit value, expected exit value, and present value methods.

To illustrate the various methods of measuring income under accrual accounting, consider the wholesaler Horizon Sales, Inc. Horizon Sales has only one asset—an inventory of fur coats purchased on January 1, 1995. Information about the fur coats is as follows.

January 1, 1995
Fur coats are purchased at a cost of $100,000.

December 31, 1995
Current cost to replace the fur coats is $125,000.

Amount of cash that could be received in orderly liquidation (current exit value) of the fur coats is $133,000.

Amount of cash expected to be received for the fur
coats after selling costs (expected exit value)
is $135,000.

December 31, 1996

Fur coat inventory is sold for $144,000 on account.

January 1, 1997

$144,000 is collected from customers.

Historical Cost.   If the inventory of fur coats is measured under historical cost, recognition of income is delayed until the sale. This is consistent with the revenue realization principle, which requires that revenue be recorded only when the earning process is complete or virtually complete, and when the amount and timing of revenue are reasonably determinable. The objective evidence provided by the sale is usually necessary to satisfy the criteria for recognizing revenue. Therefore, net income of $44,000 ($144,000 − $100,000) would be recorded for Horizon Sales in 1996.

Revenue Realization

Current Cost.   Although historical cost is consistent with GAAP, it is helpful to understand the alternatives to conventional accounting methods. Under the current cost method, on December 31, 1995, Horizon Sales would write up the inventory to current cost ($125,000). The $25,000 difference between the beginning and ending balance of the inventory is called a **holding gain** (or holding loss if the ending balance was less than the beginning balance). The holding gain would be reported on the 1995 income statement. In 1996 the $19,000 difference between the selling price ($144,000) and the current cost valuation of the inventory on December 31, 1995 ($125,000) would be included in income.[14]

Current Exit Value.   If we assume that Horizon Sales reports the fur coats at their current exit value, the holding gain for 1995 would be $33,000. This is the increase in the current exit value of the inventory from the beginning to the end of the period ($133,000 − $100,000 = $33,000). Horizon's 1996 current exit value income on the sale of the fur coats would be $11,000 ($144,000 − $133,000).

Expected Exit Value.   As discussed previously, current exit value and expected exit value are likely to result in two different valuations of the same item because of the different assumptions used in each method. In the example of Horizon Sales, the holding gain for 1995 would be $35,000 ($135,000 − $100,000), while the expected exit value income recognized in 1996 would be $9,000 ($144,000 − $135,000).

Present Value of Expected Cash Flows.   To illustrate the measurement of earnings under present value, we must first assume that Horizon Sales knew when it purchased the fur coats on January 1, 1995, that $144,000 cash would be received for their sale two years later. This is, of course, an unrealistic assumption.[15] As a result, we illustrate present value income measurement for Horizon Sales, bearing in mind the limitations of this approach to assets and liabilities with uncertain future cash flows.

Horizon Sales invested $100,000 in an asset (fur coats) that will be worth $144,000 in two years. The *annual* rate of growth necessary to increase the inventory from its present

---

[14]If the current cost valuation of the inventory remained unchanged from December 31, 1995, to December 31, 1996, all of the $19,000 would be considered "current operating income." If, however, the current cost valuation of the inventory changed during 1996, the $19,000 would be separated into two parts, current operating income and holding gain. As an example, if the current cost valuation of the inventory was $134,000 on December 31, 1996, then $10,000 ($144,000 − $134,000) would be current operating income and $9,000 ($134,000 − $125,000) would be a holding gain. We discuss this more fully in Chapter 26.

[15]The assumption of perfect foreknowledge is not so unreasonable in the case of assets and liabilities resulting in fixed cash flows. Examples include notes receivable and payable, which are contracts for certain cash flows in the future. In these cases, a present value approach is generally accepted.

value of $100,000 to the future value of $144,000 is 20%.[16] For 1995 the investment is assumed to grow by 20%, or $20,000 ($100,000 × .20). Therefore, the inventory has a value of $120,000 on December 31, 1995. The $20,000, or the difference between the beginning and ending inventory valuation, is the income earned and reported in 1995. For 1996 the investment has a beginning value of $120,000. A 20% annual return on this amount yields $24,000 ($120,000 × .20) and increases the value of the inventory to $144,000. This is not a coincidence. The annual rate of return is determined so that the inventory balance increases to the selling amount of $144,000. The income earned in 1996 would be $24,000, and the increase in the inventory balance would reflect the 20% rate of return.

Summary.   The net income of Horizon Sales under all five methods is summarized in Exhibit 3–6. Clearly, the *total income* on the sale of the fur coats is $44,000. The question is *how to assign* the $44,000 return on investment to the two periods. Under GAAP (historical cost), the $44,000 is reported in 1996, the year of the sale. Under the four alternatives to historical cost, at least part of the $44,000 is reported in 1995. This points to a frequent criticism of historical cost, namely, the delay in recognizing income. Critics suggest that alternatives are generally more *timely* in the recognition of income and are therefore more relevant to users of financial statements in their attempts to predict future cash flows.

Historical cost proponents counter that the alternatives are too unreliable and also generate income numbers that are less likely to result in cash flows. For example, if the company sold the fur coats for only $100,000 on December 31, 1996, the current cost and exit value (current and expected) methods would recognize income in 1995 and a loss in 1996. Supporters of historical cost argue that the reporting of income in 1995 could have harmed users, because that income failed to materialize. The uncertainty of eventual cash realization was too great and resulted in the reversal in 1996 of income recognized in 1995.

COMPONENTS OF NET INCOME

Net income is composed of revenues, expenses, gains, and losses. Each component can be defined according to the asset/liability view or the revenue/expense view. According to the **asset/liability view,** the components of net income are defined by reference to definitions of assets and liabilities. Under the **revenue/expense view,** the components of net income are defined without reference to definitions of assets and liabilities. Both views are used in practice, but the FASB currently favors the asset/liability view implied in the following definitions, which we presented in Chapter 2:

1. **Revenues.**   Inflows or other enhancements of assets of an entity or settlements of its liabilities (or both) during a period, based on production and delivery of goods, provision of services, and other activities that constitute the entity's major operations. Examples are sales revenue, interest revenue, and rent revenue.
2. **Expenses.**   Outflows or other use of assets or incurrences of liabilities (or both) during a period as a result of delivering or producing goods, rendering services, or carrying out other activities that constitute the entity's ongoing major or central operations. Examples are cost of goods sold, salaries expense, and advertising expense.
3. **Gains.**   Increases in owners' equity (net assets) from peripheral or incidental transactions of an entity and from all other transactions and events affecting the entity during a period, except those that result from revenues or investments by owners. Examples are a gain on the sale of plant assets and a gain on the early retirement of long-term debt.
4. **Losses.**   Decreases in owners' equity (net assets) from peripheral or incidental transactions of an entity and from all other transactions and events affecting the entity during a period, except those that result from expenses or distributions to owners. Examples are losses on the sale of investments and on litigation.

---

[16]The annual rate of return can be determined with the aid of present value interest tables. Use of these tables is discussed in Chapter 6.

EXHIBIT 3-6

Net Income of Horizon Sales for 1995 and 1996 under Five Asset Valuation Methods

Method	1995	Net Income 1996	Total
Historical cost	$ –0–	$44,000	$44,000
Current cost	25,000	19,000	44,000
Current exit value	33,000	11,000	44,000
Expected exit value	35,000	9,000	44,000
Present value of expected cash flows	20,000	24,000	44,000

Notice the references to assets, liabilities, and owners' equity (net assets). The components of net income are *not* defined independently of definitions of assets and liabilities. In a sense, the definitions of assets and liabilities are the anchor, or reference point, for the definitions of revenues, expenses, gains, and losses. The FASB calls this the **asset/liability view.**

According to the alternative conceptual approach—the **revenue/expense view**—revenues, expenses, gains, and losses are defined without direct reference to definitions of assets and liabilities. Proponents of this view disagree about the correct definition of the components of income, but they generally view revenues as a measure of the operating accomplishments of the enterprise in a particular period and expenses as the efforts necessary to generate the revenues for the period. Fundamental to this position is the principle of matching expenses with revenues. Under the revenue/expense view, how we define assets and liabilities is secondary to how we define revenues and expenses. Assets and liabilities are essentially the debits and credits that remain after revenues and expenses are properly matched on the income statement.

Matching

Both the asset/liability view and the revenue/expense view are compatible with financial statements that *articulate* with one another. **Articulated financial statements,** which are the kind produced under GAAP, are fundamentally related or tied to one another.

The major issue in the asset/liability and revenue/expense controversy is which definition should take precedence. Critics of the revenue/expense view believe that the matching principle lacks objectivity. Furthermore, they believe that the income statement may be open to recognition of revenues and expenses that are not changes in enterprise assets or liabilities. Critics have suggested that such revenues and expenses are meaningless to understanding the change in wealth of a business. Under the revenue/expense view, the balance sheet can become a "dumping ground" for nonresources and nonobligations because of vague definitions of revenues and expenses. Supporters of the asset/liability view impose an objective limit on what will be considered as admissible revenues, expenses, gains, and losses. Only transactions that increase or decrease the assets or liabilities of an enterprise can be considered revenues or expenses.

As indicated earlier, current practice reflects a *combination of both views,* which makes the distinction between them difficult to observe. The FASB has decided to emphasize one view in order to guide future accounting policy decisions. Because the FASB has supported the asset/liability view, we have embraced this view throughout the conceptual discussion in this chapter.

USEFULNESS OF ACCOUNTING NET INCOME

In the mid-1960s, many critics of financial reporting argued that the net income number was meaningless. They based their opposition on continued adherence to historical cost, which they thought misrepresented reality. In addition, skeptics denounced the diversity of acceptable accounting methods (e.g., LIFO versus FIFO in inventory costing) for determining net

LIES, DAMNED LIES, AND THE BUDGET DEFICIT

Next time you hear a politician or newspaper reporter glibly throw around warnings of our looming $360 billion federal deficit, think of Bear, Stearns' respected economist, Lawrence Kudlow. "Why hyperventilate about the deficit?" asks Kudlow. "The reality is that the deficit isn't nearly as bad as people think." When it is calculated on a real economic basis, Kudlow thinks the deficit is probably around $45 billion.

Forty-five billion? That's a long way from the $269 billion that's commonly thought to be this year's deficit. Whether the deficit is $269 billion or $45 billion is something voters and political candidates might well want to know before ruling tax cuts out of the question.

What's at issue here is how Washington cooks its books. Government accounting ledgers show the deficit for this past fiscal year, ended Sept. 30, as a record $269 billion. For fiscal 1992, the figure is projected to top $360 billion. But the government's accounting system measures only cash transactions—the money that flows in and out of government coffers in a given year. It makes no attempt to relate those cash flows to the years in which the economic activity that generated them occurred.

Think of a simplified analogy to illustrate these timing differences. Suppose, for example, a bank teller were taking money from the till and losing it on the horses. The bank's owner, looking to sell out, covers up the fraud by replacing the stolen funds. Two years later the owner sells his stake and retrieves the funds he put in. That's when the bank discovers the fraud. When did the bank lose the money? Under cash accounting, the loss occurred when the bank discovered it. But in reality the bank's economic loss occurred every time the errant teller placed a losing bet.

Although it cannot uncover fraud, the accrual accounting method the Securities & Exchange Commission requires all publicly owned corporations to use in preparing their financials tries to capture the true timing of economic gains and losses. The accrual method matches revenues and associated expenses in each period.

What difference does it make whether the government uses cash accounting or accrual accounting? A huge difference.

Consider the S&L bailout. Simply put, the bailout involves an initial transfer of savings and loan assets from the private sector to the government—a cash outflow. In later years, the assets will be sold, creating another transfer payment, a cash inflow.

At this point, the Resolution Trust Corp. is seizing more assets than it's selling, causing the reported budget deficit to balloon. According to the Congressional Budget Office, net "spending" for deposit insurance (for S&L and bank bailouts) will reach $115 billion next year, nearly one-third of the total deficit. But starting in 1995, more assets will be sold than seized and the bailout will actually start lowering the deficit. These huge inflows and outflows are what one gets with cash-basis accounting.

Does that $115 billion spending for deposit insurance have much to do with what's currently going on in the goods-and-services economy? Most economists don't think so. They think the thrifts lost their money back in the 1980s; as with the bank teller, the money's long gone. But cash accounting doesn't recognize the fact, and treats the losses as if they were happening today. "The cash cost to the government is when it has to take the institutions over, but the economic cost happened back [in the 1980s]," notes a Congressional Budget Office analyst.

The problem with the S&L rescue is that the government did not adequately reserve for the threat of the bailout. The government kept the S&Ls afloat without increasing reserves, postponing the day of reckoning. Had the government provided enough of a cushion against which the failing thrifts' assets would have been written down as the assets turned sour, there would have been no $115 billion item in the fiscal 1992 budget.

Think of it this way: True accrual accounting would have measured the costs and revenues of economic activity as they took place. Without such accounting, expenses in this case were wildly understated in early years, and wildly overstated in later years. This back-ending of expenses may serve politicians well, but it doesn't provide much help to people trying to create reasonable economic policies.

For a rough measure of the deficit on which economic policy should be based—the "underlying deficit," as

income. They suggested that managers could disclose net income in various ways according to GAAP because of the lack of uniform measurement principles. Indeed, one author showed how identical firms could produce an earnings per share of either $.80 or $1.79, depending on the choice of accounting principles.[17] Critics asserted that such ambiguity reduced the credibility of accounting income numbers as a source of information to statement users. One financial analyst described the situation this way:

---

[17]The illustration was provided by Leonard Spacek, "Business Success Requires an Understanding of Unsolved Problems of Accounting and Financial Reporting," in J. Lories and R. Brealey (eds.), *Modern Developments in Investment Management* (New York: Praeger, 1972), pp. 630–644.

economists call the deficit associated with the real, ongoing economy—many turn to the national income and product accounts put out by the Commerce Department. According to these accounts, the deficit last year was only $166 billion, compared with the official figure of $220 billion put out by the government. How so? The Commerce Department's accounts exclude deposit insurance spending.

Doesn't the difference between what the thrifts lost and what the RTC will collect have to be funded—just as the bank must ultimately replace what the teller stole? Yes, but again that's just a transfer payment that can be raised in the capital markets. It is not something with which to saddle the productive economy.

Bear, Stearns' Kudlow goes a step further in his calculation of the country's underlying deficit. He notes that annual interest payments that are due on U.S. Treasury debt held by the public now total some $200 billion, accounting for about 75% of the official deficit.

But Kudlow argues that interest payments on the debt should be looked at separately from other budget outlays. They represent past budgetary decisions—payments for past spending—not purchases of goods or services today. Thus, says Kudlow, they properly relate to years past and have little impact on current economic activity.

So Kudlow subtracts from the $269 billion deficit figure about $200 billion of interest payments and another $67 billion of deposit insurance, and by accounting for some $44 billion of coalition contributions to the Gulf War, comes up with what he believes the real economic deficit for 1991 is: about $45 billion. Concludes Kudlow: "The issue is [the economy's] growth, not debt or the deficit. The reason the deficit [looks like] a problem right now is that the economy hasn't grown in three years." Kudlow believes cutting marginal tax rates and the capital gains tax is not only necessary to get the economy moving again, but also easily affordable, given the small size of the country's underlying deficit.

Perhaps the strangest aspect of federal accounting is that the government prepares neither an income statement nor a balance sheet. When the government invests in buildings, bridges, battleships and other capital equipment that serve the taxpayers for, say, 50 years, the accountants book the whole investment as an expense in the budget the first year. Using accrual accounting, a corporation would capitalize the investment and depreciate it over its useful life.

You could call the government's expense-it-all-immediately accounting practices highly conservative, but in reality they are foolish because they render the true economic deficit an even more elusive figure. Charges Northwestern University economist Robert Eisner, who has been arguing for years that the deficit is no problem: "Federal accounting has no resemblance to business accounting or anything sensible."

Economists like Eisner and Larry Kudlow are beginning to be heard. Last year's budget agreement with Congress authorized the Commerce Department to start devising a complete new set of financials for national income and product accounts—essentially a balance sheet and income statement for the country, prepared using accrual accounting techniques.

The figures will be adjusted for inflation, which many economists say will put the debt and deficit figures into a more realistic relationship with the underlying economy. Stanford University economist Michael Boskin, now head of the Bush Administration's Council of Economic Advisers, is actively pushing the project, which will probably be ready in 1995.

Note, however, that this won't put an end to politicians' cooking the books. More likely, a new set of recipes will be developed. Warns James Miller, U.S. Budget Director under Ronald Reagan: "Once you have a capital budget, it would be the propensity of politicians to load everything onto the books and borrow against it."

Having trouble paying teachers and health care workers? No sweat. Just capitalize them as investments in the country's future. Still, more realistic accounting rules for politicians are very much in order.

SOURCE: Roula Khalaf, "Lies, Damned Lies, and the Budget Deficit," *Forbes,* December 9, 1991, pp. 71, 74. Reprinted by permission of *Forbes Magazine,* December 9, 1991, © copyright Forbes, Inc.

The accountant defines it [earnings] as what he gets when he matches costs against revenues, making any necessary allocations of costs to prior periods; or as the change in the equity account over the period. These costs are not economic definitions of earnings but merely descriptions of the motions the accountant goes through to arrive at the earnings number.[18]

Matching

Fortunately, subsequent research on the usefulness of net income disclosures has lessened many of these concerns. One classic study investigated whether knowledge of the next year's net income would be sufficient to earn superior returns in the price of a company's

---

[18]Jack Treynor, "The Trouble with Earnings," *Financial Analysts Journal* (September 1972), p. 41.

stock.[19] Obviously, if such advance knowledge could not be used in profitable investment strategy, it would be of little value. Results of this study indicated that if just the direction of change in the next year's net income were known for a number of companies, investment decisions would consistently produce better-than-average returns. These results suggest that disclosure of net income has value for investors.

Although strong evidence indicates that the net income number is useful for investor decision making, it says nothing about the timeliness of net income disclosures. Such information could have already reached investors in other forms. Investors could use alternative sources of information, such as investment advisory services and government reports, to estimate the current earnings of a company.

A study was conducted to test the timeliness of net income disclosures.[20] It investigated whether present and potential investors reacted to the initial disclosure of the accounting net income number. Initial disclosure of a corporation's quarterly or annual earnings precedes the dissemination of quarterly or annual reports to shareholders. Major stock exchanges require listed companies to release earnings announcements to the press and wire services as soon as the information becomes available. Most U.S. corporations release earnings data via the Dow-Jones News Service (the Broad Tape), which is a financial news wire service. The earnings release is then printed in *The Wall Street Journal* the next business day. Exhibit 3–7 shows a typical annual and quarterly earnings announcement. If information in the preliminary earnings release had already reached investors, we would not expect investors to react to the net income disclosure. The study found that the volume of trading increases dramatically in the week the net income disclosure is released publicly, compared to the rest of the year. This finding supports the timeliness of net income disclosure.

Evidence strongly suggests that accounting net income is both useful and timely to investors in their buying and selling decisions. However, the question remains: Why do investors perceive the net income number as relevant information? The significance of net income can be viewed in two interrelated ways. In one sense, net income is a measure of *past* performance; in another sense, it is an indicator of *future* cash flows. These uses are discussed in the following sections.

Net Income as a Measure of Past Performance

A business begins operations by obtaining financing from its owners and possibly from creditors. It then uses the cash received to acquire labor, raw materials, plant, equipment, and other inputs of production. The goal of the organization is to convert these inputs into an output (product) whose value is greater than the sum of the inputs. This is accomplished by adding time, form, and place utility to the inputs. For example, grapes from the Rhine Valley can be pressed into wine; the bottled wine is then aged for several years, after which it may be shipped to The Plaza in New York. The inputs, including vineyard, winepress, storage area, and shipping, combine to produce a fine table wine that can be sold for an amount greater than the sum of the input costs. This is accomplished by adding time (the aging process), form (grapes to wine), and place (Germany to New York) to the product. This process can be characterized as the **earning process** of the firm.

The earning process and financing activities of a firm become interrelated through time. Firms must compete for investment dollars. The amount and cost of funds that a firm can obtain is a function of its earnings performance relative to other companies. Earnings tell owners and creditors how efficiently management converts inputs to outputs. Successful

[19]Ray Ball and Phillip Brown, "An Empirical Investigation of Accounting Income Numbers," *Journal of Accounting Research* (Autumn 1968), pp. 159–178.

[20]William Beaver, "The Information Content of Annual Earnings Announcements," *Journal of Accounting Research* (Supplement 1968), pp. 67–92.

EXHIBIT 3–7

Preliminary Earnings Announcement
Compaq Computer Corp. (N)

	Quarter Ending December 31	
	1993	**1992**
Sales	$2,202,000,000	$1,423,000,000
Net income	151,000,000	89,000,000
Avg shares	86,800,000	80,900,000
Shr earns (primary):		
Net income	1.74	1.11
Shr earns (fully diluted):		
Net income	1.73	1.10
	Year Ending December 31	
Sales	7,191,000,000	4,100,000,000
Net income	462,000,000	213,000,000
Avg shares	84,700,000	82,600,000
Shr earns (primary):		
Net income	5.45	2.58
Shr earns (fully diluted):		
Net income	5.35	2.52

SOURCE: *The Wall Street Journal,* January 27, 1994, p. C16.

---

firms, as demonstrated by past earnings activities, enjoy a competitive advantage in the financing markets. In contrast, less successful firms may find their sources of capital diminished or unavailable. The result can be the final liquidation of an inefficient firm.

The earnings of an enterprise can be viewed as a "report card" of management's performance. Did management responsibly utilize its resources? If not, the stockholders have two choices: they can replace existing management, or they can sell their interest in the firm. However, evaluating management performance can be difficult, especially if based solely on net income. Assume, for example, that the latest year-to-year net income results of a company show a 10% decrease. From this information alone, we might conclude that past performance is rather poor. However, if we know that during the same period, the net income of all firms in the economy decreased by an average of 30%, we might conclude that our company performed rather well. An informed user of financial statements should also recognize that some events affecting a company's performance, such as floods and earthquakes, are beyond management's control.

Net Income as a Predictor of Cash Flows

Net income helps investors and creditors not only to evaluate the past performance of a firm but also to predict the cash returns they will receive. For stockholders, the value of shares relates to future dividends. For example, the price of a share is generally higher when stockholders expect to receive larger dividends, all else equal. As a result, shareholders want information that helps them predict future dividends. Net income disclosures may be useful in this regard, because future dividends depend on future earnings.

As a first step in predicting cash flow, present earnings should be separated into a transitory component and a permanent component.[21] The **transitory component** of net income

---

[21]A more detailed discussion of these two components of earnings and reporting considerations can be found in *FASB Discussion Memorandum,* "Reporting Earnings" (Stamford, Conn.: FASB, 1979).

is that part which investors do not expect again in the near future. Transitory income can result from unusual or incidental activities of limited duration or in unconventional markets. For example, a publishing company purchases a downtown parking lot as the site of a future office building. Until construction begins, the company operates the parking lot and collects parking fees. The parking fees are income of limited duration (until construction begins), are incidental to the main function of the company (publishing), and are therefore not expected to continue. Transitory income (or loss) can also result from unusual events, such as a casualty loss from an earthquake or an expropriation of plant assets by a foreign country.

The **permanent component** of net income is the part that investors expect to continue. Permanent income results from the primary functions of the enterprise. In the publishing company, permanent income is generated from producing and marketing books. Permanent income is affected by changes in the demand for books, the price of the books, and the cost of making them.

Predictably, investors focus on permanent earnings, because only they are useful in predicting income. Transitory earnings are not expected to affect future income. Because accounting policy makers, such as the FASB, understand the importance of distinguishing between the two components of net income, various types of transitory earnings must presently be identified. In Chapter 4, we explore the reporting requirements for several of these nonrecurring events. Unfortunately, the financial reporting requirements for net income do not permit these two types of earnings to be clearly distinguished from each other.

Creditors and investors have similar needs. Whereas investors are concerned with the ability of the firm to pay dividends, creditors are interested in the ability of the firm to make interest and principal payments on loans. Both investors and creditors are forward looking in this regard. As a result, creditors also focus on the permanent component of net income in assessing the future earnings capability of the firm. Future earnings protect interest payments, because interest is paid to creditors before dividends are distributed to stockholders.

As the needs of investors and creditors are satisfied, so too are the needs of other users. Customers, for example, are interested in the longevity of the enterprise, especially if it provides warranty contracts or if the product line requires major support (as in the case of computer equipment). Employees are concerned with job security and compensation. In both cases, the permanent net income can help predict income.

In summary, a firm's earnings have proven useful in the investment decision. Net income reflects past performance and suggests future performance. Net income can tell financial statement users where the firm has been and, to a more limited degree, where it is going.

In present accounting practice, terms such as *net income* and *net earnings* are used interchangeably, and we make no distinction between them in this textbook. The FASB has indicated that in the future, however, it will attempt to enhance the usefulness of the income measurement by distinguishing between an enterprise's **earnings** and **comprehensive income.** Earnings will be considered a measure of an enterprise's performance during a period and will measure the extent to which revenues and gains associated with cash-to-cash cycles substantially completed during a period exceed the expenses and losses associated with the same cycles. Comprehensive income will be considered a broad measure comprising all recognized changes in owner's equity except those resulting from investments by owners and distributions to owners. Certain transactions and events (e.g., changes in the market values of investments in marketable equity securities classified as noncurrent assets) will be included in the determination of comprehensive income but will be excluded from earnings. The concepts of earnings and comprehensive income will likely evolve gradually over time. We explain the distinction between these concepts more fully in Chapter 21.

Thus far in this chapter, we have presented information about *past and current measurements.* However, financial statement users want information about the ability of a business to generate income *in the future.* Some observers have suggested that enterprises could provide this information directly to financial statement users in the form of published financial forecasts.

A **financial forecast** is a presentation that shows an enterprise's *expected* future financial position, results of operations, and cash flows based on conditions that management expects to exist and actions it expects to take. A financial forecast contrasts with a **financial projection,** which shows future financial position, results of operations, and cash flows that would exist if one or more *hypothetical* (but not expected) assumptions occurred. In other words, forecasts present what management expects to happen, whereas projections present what would happen if certain unexpected events (e.g., a labor strike) occurred. At the present time, neither of these two types of **prospective financial statements** is required by GAAP. However, some companies have in the past voluntarily disclosed financial forecasts, and considerable discussion has taken place about the desirability of requiring all companies to publish forecasts as a part of GAAP.

The construction of a financial forecast requires assumptions about the future state of the overall economy and the interaction of the firm with the economy. The accuracy of the forecasts relates directly to the accuracy of these assumptions. As a result, some people have advocated the publication of a range of forecasts during a given period. In this way, financial statement users would be aware of management's range of expectations, from pessimistic to optimistic, and could then select a scenario consistent with their own expectations.

In 1973 the Securities and Exchange Commission (SEC) reversed its long-standing opposition to public disclosure of financial forecasts by issuing guidelines for voluntary disclosures to be filed with the Commission. Since that time, there has been a great deal of interest in and controversy about the subject of mandated public disclosure of financial forecasts. In the rest of this section, we briefly discuss the arguments favoring and opposing public disclosure of financial forecasts.

BENEFITS OF PUBLIC DISCLOSURE

The major argument in favor of the required disclosure of financial forecasts is that it would provide useful information to users of financial statements. Proponents of required financial forecasts have argued that forecasts are essential for making more accurate predictions, which lead to informed investment and credit decisions. Investors and creditors could benefit from financial forecasts by learning about management's plans and expectations. Relative to the outside investor, management generally knows more about the firm and at least as much about the impact of the external environment. Empirical research shows that corporate managers can prepare more accurate financial forecasts for their companies than can ordinary investors who use simple statistical models to generate forecasts.[22] Evidence also suggests that corporate managers (who have the advantage of inside knowledge of the company) are somewhat more accurate than financial analysts (who have the advantage of objectivity) in forecasting performance.[23] Finally, research shows that management's forecasts have

---

[22]William Ruland, "The Accuracy of Forecasts by Management and by Financial Analysts," *The Accounting Review* (April 1978), pp. 439–447.

[23]Russell Barefield, Eugene E. Comiskey, and Charles L. McDonald, "Accuracy of Management and Security Analysts' Forecasts: Additional Evidence," *Journal of Business Research* (August 1979), pp. 109–115.

information content in that stock prices respond to the information contained in earnings forecasts.[24]

Managers could also benefit by the publication of financial forecasts. Financial forecasts put managers' reputations at stake and would give them strong incentive to achieve the forecasted figures. Moreover, preparing forecasts for publication forces managers to plan for the future. Such planning may enable them to take advantage of opportunities and avoid mistakes in judgment.

Some people have argued that reporting forecasts is in the public interest because it reduces the opportunities for privileged insiders to profit from information that is not publicly available. Further, certain forecasted information regularly appears in sources such as *The Wall Street Journal,* but the forecasts do not contain management's assumptions and are not subjected to the rigorous standards that would be applied if forecasts were a required part of GAAP.

COSTS OF PUBLIC DISCLOSURE

The publication of financial forecasts has some serious limitations. A major concern is the possible misinterpretation of the forecasts by financial statement users. Because many investors are untrained in the interpretation of financial forecasts, they are likely to be unaware of the uncertainty of forecasts. Statement users may also have difficulty interpreting the variety of assumptions underlying the forecast. Moreover, across various firms, different forecast assumptions would lead to difficulty in comparing forecasts.

Another possible source of misinterpretation is management's tendency to bias forecasts. Managers may present overly optimistic forecasts to place the firm in a favorable light. Such forecasts may help the firm obtain bank loans or may raise the stock price but may mislead unwary investors. Other managers may play it safe by issuing overly conservative forecasts that they are nearly certain to attain. The outside investor may be misled into selling the stock or avoiding its initial purchase, only to find that the company was more prosperous than anticipated. This limitation can be mitigated by having an independent auditor examine the reasonableness of the assumptions. The auditor's report would state that an examination of the underlying assumptions was made and that they were found reasonable. The report would also note that because assumptions can prove faulty, it is not a guarantee of future performance.

Management has long opposed the publication of financial forecasts because of the possible disclosure of sensitive information, such as major marketing, product, or investment strategies. Competitors could develop counterstrategies to block the firm from realizing its goals, which, of course, would not benefit the forecasting company or its shareholders.

Another serious limitation of financial forecasts is the potential legal liability. Do investors have legal recourse if actual results deviate sharply from the forecast? Blaming management for inaccurate forecasts is questionable when it has made an honest attempt to plan properly, make full disclosure, and manage as efficiently as possible. For example, the airlines could not have predicted the effect of the 1973 oil embargo on their operating costs. To hold the airlines responsible for inaccurate forecasts under these circumstances would be inequitable.

Some observers argue further that managers should not engage in the investment function by making financial forecasts. These critics suggest that financial forecasting is largely the domain of investors, who either reap the rewards of accurate forecasting or incur the penalty of inaccurate forecasting. A partner in the public accounting firm of Arthur Andersen &

---

[24]Stephen H. Penman, "An Empirical Investigation of the Voluntary Disclosure of Corporate Earnings Forecasts," *Journal of Accounting Research* (Spring 1980), pp. 132–160.

Co. has stated that "predictions of the future must be the responsibility of the investor. This is the essence of risk taking, and predicting and interpreting the future is the primary function in investment evaluation. No one can take to insure [through lawsuits] the results of future events." [25]

SUMMARY

The issue of mandated disclosure of financial forecasts will be controversial for some time. The SEC and the FASB have been emphasizing disclosures that have a future orientation. In contrast, most managers have opposed the concept for most of the reasons listed above. In terms of the qualitative characteristics we presented in Chapter 2, proponents of financial forecasts tend to argue that forecasts are relevant while opponents argue that the information lacks sufficient reliability. At this time, it is difficult to predict the outcome of this controversy.

CONCLUDING REMARKS

Financial accounting is constantly changing to achieve greater relevance and reliability. It is a discipline that has many interesting, conceptual controversies. An understanding of only the present system of GAAP will not likely be adequate for a person whose future career will be spent preparing or using financial statements. Indeed, the educational process of the professional accountant (and other professional persons) is continuous. You should think of a degree program in business as a foundation on which to build knowledge and skills that will adapt to changing circumstances in an exciting world.

In this chapter, we have presented a conceptual discussion of the nature and measurement of the elements of financial statements. Throughout this discussion, we have presented alternatives to the present accounting model to acquaint you with not only what is presently accepted but also what may be generally accepted in the future. An understanding of this chapter should broaden your understanding of accounting and should allow you to accommodate more contemporary accounting ideas. Moreover, this conceptual material should enhance your understanding of present generally accepted accounting principles. Current practice employs, to varying degrees, many of the ideas and valuation methods discussed in this chapter.

In Chapter 26, we use many of the concepts discussed in this chapter in more practical applications. In Chapter 4, we extend our presentation of GAAP for external reporting with an overview of the major financial statements.

KEY POINTS

1. Measurement refers to the assignment of numbers to objects and events. To measure the elements of financial statements, we must select a measuring unit and a financial attribute to measure. (Objective 1)
2. The measuring units that have been suggested for use in financial statements are nominal dollars and constant dollars. A nominal dollar has not been adjusted for inflation or deflation; a constant dollar has been adjusted. Conventional financial statements use nominal dollars. (Objective 1)
3. A general price-level index indicates changes over time in the overall level of prices in the economy. A specific price index indicates changes over time in the price of a specific good or service. (Objective 1)
4. Purchasing power gains and losses are reported when financial statements are presented in constant dollars. These gains and losses result from holding monetary assets or liabilities during periods of inflation or deflation. (Objective 1)
5. Assets are probable future economic benefits that accrue to an entity as a result of past transactions or events. (Objective 2)
6. Financial attributes of assets include historical cost, current cost, current exit value in orderly liquidation, expected exit value in due course of business, and present value of expected cash

[25]"Forecasting Earnings," *Forbes* (December 1, 1972), p. 37.

flows. Conventional financial statements reflect a mixture of these attributes, although historical cost is emphasized. (Objective 2)

7. Liabilities are probable future sacrifices of economic benefits that obligate an entity to transfer assets or perform services in the future as a result of past transactions or events. (Objective 2)

8. Important issues in liability measurement are (1) whether the interest inherent in a liability should be recognized separately, and (2) what interest rate should be used to recognize the interest. (Objective 2)

9. Financial attributes of liabilities include present value of expected cash flows, expected exit value in due course of business, historical proceeds, current proceeds, and current exit value in orderly liquidation. Conceptually, a liability should be measured on a present value basis; many liabilities are measured this way under GAAP. (Objective 2)

10. Owners' equity equals net assets, which are assets minus liabilities. Owners' equity is not measured as an independent element of financial statements. Instead, its valuation depends on the valuations assigned to the individual assets and liabilities. (Objective 2)

11. Net income measures the change in net assets for a period of time, assuming no new capital contributions by the owners or dividend distributions by the business. (Objective 3)

12. Net income should be recognized only after the capital used from the beginning of the period is maintained. (Objective 3)

13. Lifetime net income is the total income of an enterprise from inception to termination. Lifetime revenues of an enterprise equal the total cash received from earning activities, and lifetime expenses equal the total cash disbursed for earning activities. (Objective 3)

14. Periodic net income is the change in the wealth of a business over a short period of time, generally one year. (Objective 3)

15. Accrual basis accounting is generally preferred over cash basis accounting, because earnings disclosures are more timely and less subject to meaningless fluctuations. (Objective 3)

16. Net income measurement under accrual accounting depends on the valuation concepts used to measure assets and liabilities. Unlike lifetime net income, periodic net income is affected by the valuation concepts employed. (Objective 3)

17. Net income is composed of revenues, expenses, gains, and losses. Each component can be defined by the asset/liability or the revenue/expense view. According to the asset/liability view, the components of net income are defined by direct reference to definitions of assets and liabilities. Under the revenue/expense view, the components of net income are defined without reference to definitions of assets and liabilities. Both concepts are used in practice, but the FASB supports the asset/liability view. (Objective 3)

18. Strong evidence supports both the usefulness and timeliness of accounting net income. (Objective 4)

19. Accounting net income can be used to evaluate past performance and predict future earnings. (Objective 4)

20. Financial forecasts represent financial expectations of management. Considerable controversy presently exists about the possibility of requiring the publication of financial forecasts. Most people today believe that the costs of requiring companies to publish financial forecasts exceed the benefits. (Objective 5)

21. Major advantages of requiring companies to publish financial forecasts include providing useful information, providing certain managerial incentives, reducing opportunities for insider profits, and improving the forecast information that is currently published. Major disadvantages include possible misinterpretation by users, biased forecasts, competitive disadvantages, potential legal liability, and the philosophy that making future predictions is the responsibility of investors and creditors, not accountants. (Objective 5)

QUESTIONS

3-1   What does "measurement" mean? Why is measurement important in accounting?

3-2   What is the difference between nominal dollars and constant dollars? Which one of these measuring units does GAAP require? Why?

3-3   What is the difference between a general price-level index and a specific price index?

3-4   What are purchasing power gains and losses? Are they reported in conventional financial statements? Explain why or why not.

3–5 Identify three essential characteristics of assets and give ten examples of assets under GAAP.

3–6 Identify and define the financial attributes that may be used when measuring assets.

3–7 Identify three essential characteristics of liabilities and give 10 examples of liabilities under GAAP.

3–8 Identify and define the financial attributes that may be used to measure liabilities.

3–9 What does the term *owners' equity* mean? How does owners' equity differ from liabilities? Give five examples of items classified as owners' equity under GAAP.

3–10 In what manner is owners' equity similar to liabilities? How do owners' equity and liabilities differ?

3–11 How is owners' equity measured in conventional financial statements?

3–12 Provide a conceptual definition of *net income*.

3–13 Explain the term *capital maintenance*. Why is this concept important in determining income for a period?

3–14 What is lifetime net income? What are some distinguishing characteristics of lifetime net income? How does lifetime net income differ from periodic net income?

3–15 Define *cash basis accounting*. What are some disadvantages of this system?

3–16 Define *accrual basis accounting*. How can this system produce different periodic net income numbers for the same periods?

3–17 What are the advantages and disadvantages of using historical cost to determine income?

3–18 What are the components of net income? How are they similar?

3–19 How does the revenue/expense view differ from the asset/liability view?

3–20 Is accounting net income a useful number? What are the uses of the accounting net income disclosure?

3–21 What is a financial forecast? What are the major advantages and disadvantages of published forecasts?

PROBLEMS

3–22 Nominal Dollar versus Constant Dollar Measurement   Tim Rogers invested $600,000 in a parcel of land on January 1, 1996. He sold the land for $640,000 on December 31, 1996. The Consumer Price Index for All Urban Consumers was 100 on January 1, 1996, and 110 on December 31, 1996.

INSTRUCTIONS
[a] Compute the gain or loss on the sale in accordance with GAAP. Ignore income taxes.
[b] Compute the gain or loss on the sale in constant end-of-1996 dollars. Ignore income taxes.
[c] Based only on the information presented above, was Rogers better or worse off at the end of 1996 than at the beginning? Explain your answer.
[d] In your opinion, should financial statements continue to emphasize the nominal dollar measuring unit, or should they emphasize the constant dollar measuring unit? Present arguments that support your position.

3–23 Nominal Dollar versus Constant Dollar Measurement   At the beginning of 1996, Gwen Rich purchased 1,000 shares of Stanley Company's common stock for $50 per share. During 1996 the general price level *declined* by 10%. At the end of 1996, Rich sold the 1,000 shares for $48 per share.

INSTRUCTIONS
[a] Compute the gain or loss on the sale in accordance with GAAP. Ignore income taxes.
[b] Compute the gain or loss on the sale in constant end-of-1996 dollars. Ignore income taxes.
[c] Based only on the information presented above, was Rich better or worse off at the end of 1996 than at the beginning? Explain your answer.
[d] Did Rich have a purchasing power gain during 1996? Did she have a purchasing power loss during 1996? Explain your answers.

3–24 Purchasing Power Gains and Losses   On January 1, 1996, Paul, Inc., sold merchandise to Scalf, Inc., for $90,000 on account. Inflation was 10% during 1996, and as of December 31, 1996, Paul had not received the $90,000 payment due from Scalf.

INSTRUCTIONS

[a] Calculate the amount of purchasing power gain or loss for Paul and for Scalf.

[b] Explain why each company had a purchasing power gain or loss.

[c] Are purchasing power gains and losses reported in conventional financial statements? Why or why not?

3–25 Nature of Assets You have been asked to determine whether each of the following items is an asset of Purdy Company.

[1] One hundred shares of IBM's common stock that Purdy has purchased.

[2] A county-owned road constructed on land owned by Purdy.

[3] An order placed by Purdy for merchandise that the supplier has in a warehouse and will ship in 10 days.

[4] A patent, owned by Purdy, to produce a drug that has been linked to cancer and banned by the Food and Drug Administration. The drug will not be sold anywhere in the world.

[5] Ten $1,000, 12%, 20-year bonds of Chrysler Corporation that Purdy has purchased.

[6] The excellent credit reputation that Purdy has earned in the business community.

[7] A note receivable from a debtor who has been declared bankrupt and will not pay the amount owed to Purdy.

[8] A franchise that Purdy has acquired to market a successful product in three states.

[9] An order received from a customer for merchandise that Purdy will ship in five days.

[10] A machine that Purdy has purchased and received from a manufacturer.

[11] Merchandise owned by Jasper Company that Purdy is holding on consignment. (Purdy is the consignee or selling agent and will try to sell the goods for Jasper.)

[12] A noncancelable lease that gives Purdy the right to use a machine owned by Scott Company for five years, which is the estimated economic life of the machine.

[13] Cash received from a customer who has placed a prepaid order for merchandise to be shipped by Purdy in 30 days.

[14] A privately owned park that Purdy has built on its own land and that often is used by the city for sporting events.

[15] A parcel of land that has been given to Purdy by the county.

INSTRUCTIONS

Indicate whether each of the above items is an asset of Purdy Company, according to GAAP. Briefly explain the reason for each decision.

3–26 Nature of Liabilities You have been asked to determine whether each of the following items is a liability of Vinci Company on December 31, 1996.

[1] The cash outlay expected to be made on January 7, 1997, to purchase equipment on that date.

[2] The amount expected to be needed to provide warranty services to customers for products sold before the end of 1996.

[3] The expected cash outlay for employee wages that will be earned during 1997.

[4] The obligation to provide future issues of a monthly newsletter for which subscriptions were pre-paid during 1996.

[5] The obligation to provide merchandise to a customer who submitted a prepaid order on December 10, 1996.

[6] The obligation to fill orders expected to be made by regular customers during 1997.

[7] An obligation to distribute shares of Vinci's own common stock to Vinci's stockholders as a result of a 10% stock dividend declared on December 15, 1996, and distributable on January 10, 1997.

[8] The obligation that may be required to settle a lawsuit against Vinci Company that is pending on December 31, 1996. Vinci's attorneys expect to win the case.

[9] The obligation to retire at maturity $100,000, 12%, 10-year bonds issued at par value on December 31, 1996. (Interest on the bonds is to be paid annually, beginning on December 31, 1997.)

[10] The obligation to pay $120,000 interest ($100,000 × 12% × 10 years) on the bonds in [9].

[11] The burden associated with having earned a poor credit reputation during 1996.

[12] The obligation to provide office space to a tenant who paid six months of rent in advance on December 31, 1996.

INSTRUCTIONS

Indicate whether each of the above items is a liability, according to GAAP, of Vinci Company on December 31, 1996. Briefly explain the reason for each decision.

3–27 Cash versus Accrual Measurements   Saylor Company employs 10 people. Salaries are paid biweekly, and certain employees occasionally receive salary advances. The company also owns several warehouses that it leases to various tenants. Some tenants are required to pay rent before using the warehouses while others are allowed to use the warehouses before paying rent.

Saylor Company uses the conventional accrual basis of accounting, as required under GAAP. The amount of salaries expense for 1996 was $79,000, and the amount of cash received from warehouse tenants was $114,000. Selected information obtained from the company's comparative balance sheets is shown below:

	Dec. 31, 1995	Dec. 31, 1996
Prepaid salaries	$ 1,000	$ 3,000
Accrued salaries payable	5,000	2,500
Rent receivable	10,000	7,000
Unearned rent revenue	18,000	25,000

INSTRUCTIONS

[a] Compute the amount of cash paid for salaries during 1996.
[b] Compute the amount of rent revenue for 1996.

3–28 Cash versus Accrual Measurements   Ghori Company employs several consulting companies. Some of the companies require payments in advance of performing services while others bill Ghori Company after the services are rendered. Ghori Company also leases office space to several law firms. Some law firms are required to pay rent in advance of using their offices while others are allowed to use their offices before paying rent.

Ghori Company uses the conventional accrual basis of accounting, as required under GAAP. The amount of cash paid to consulting companies during 1996 was $64,000, and the amount of rent revenue earned from leasing office space was $78,000. Selected information obtained from the company's comparative balance sheets is shown below:

	Dec. 31, 1995	Dec. 31, 1996
Prepaid consulting fees	$ 2,000	$5,000
Accrued consulting fees payable	7,000	2,000
Rent receivable	6,000	8,000
Unearned rent revenue	10,000	4,000

INSTRUCTIONS

[a] Compute the amount of consulting expense for 1996.
[b] Compute the amount of cash received from leasing office space during 1996.

3–29 Cash versus Accrual Statements   During the last four months of the academic year, the yearbook committee of Bluebird State University produced and distributed the university's yearbook. It was published in April at a cost of $15 a copy. The selling price was $22 each. If ordered in advance, the yearbook sold for $18. The committee estimated that 9,000 yearbooks would be sold for the 1995–96 academic year.

In February the yearbook committee authorized the payment of $1,500, which was the amount left from last year's yearbook sales, to the local newspaper, the campus newspaper, and a local radio station for advertising to be provided in March. In March advance payments for 5,000 yearbooks were received. The printing of 9,000 yearbooks was completed in April and paid for on April 30. The difference between the cash on hand and the printing costs was made up by a short-term loan. In May all advance orders were filled and 3,500 more yearbooks were sold on a cash basis. The short-term loan of April was paid off in May, including an interest charge of $500. The unsold yearbooks were considered worthless and were therefore destroyed.

INSTRUCTIONS

[a] Prepare both cash basis and accrual basis income statements and balance sheets for February, March, April, and May. (The difference between assets and liabilities is termed "fund balance," because the yearbook operation has no owners.)
[b] What is the total income from the yearbook sales for the 1995–96 academic year under each method?
[c] From this problem, what is an obvious limitation of a cash basis system?

3–30 Measurement of Income   Fred Smiley Sales Company, an automobile dealership, started business on January 1, 1995, with $42,900 in cash. Smiley decided to "wait out" the current model year and start purchasing inventory when the 1996 models became available. As a result, the Smiley dealership purchased four new 1996 model automobiles on September 1, 1995. The costs of the new 1996 models were as follows:

Model	Cost
Astra	$ 8,800
Blaze	9,900
Cortez Deluxe	11,000
Dynasty Wagon	13,200

On November 1, the dealership sold the Astra for $10,340. On December 30, the manufacturer increased the wholesale price on the 1996 models by 10%. Smiley believed he could sell the Blaze, Cortez, and Dynasty for $12,210, $14,080, and $17,270, respectively, on December 31. The salespersons' commissions were equal to 5% of the sales price. During calendar year 1996, the Blaze was sold for $12,430 and the Cortez for $14,410. Smiley still held the 1996 Dynasty Wagon on the lot as of October 1, 1996. He discounted the vehicle and finally sold it for $14,630 on October 15. On December 31, 1996, Fred Smiley Sales Company ceased operations.

INSTRUCTIONS

[a] Determine the net income for Fred Smiley Sales Company for calendar years 1995 and 1996, assuming the automobile inventory is valued under (1) historical cost, (2) current cost, and (3) current exit value.

[b] What is the lifetime net income of the Smiley dealership under each valuation method?

[c] Which pattern of income flows do you believe is most fair and reasonable?

3–31 Measurement of Income   On January 1, 1995, Parti Beer Company began business with an $880,000 cash investment. The company did not intend to brew beer from raw materials but to use a newly developed aging process on beer purchased wholesale from other producers. After two years of aging by this special process, a top-quality premium beer was to result. One beer distributor was so impressed with the aging process that a contract was made for 20,000 barrels at a price of $60 a barrel, to be delivered and paid for on December 31, 1996.

On January 1, 1995, Parti purchased 20,000 barrels of freshly brewed beer at $20 a barrel in order to start the aging process, which cost $1 per barrel per month. On December 31, 1995, the wholesale price of beer aged one year was $38 a barrel. The company estimated it could sell the beer for $45 a barrel after only one year of aging. On December 31, 1996, the aging process was completed and the beer was delivered to the distributor.

INSTRUCTIONS

[a] Prepare balance sheets for December 31, 1995, for Parti Beer Company under the following four valuation methods: (1) historical cost, (2) current cost, (3) current exit value, and (4) expected exit value.

[b] What is the reported net income for 1995 and 1996 under each valuation method?

[c] Which pattern of income flows do you believe is most fair and reasonable?

3–32 Cash versus Accrual Statements   IVY State University's 1995–96 basketball season began on December 1, 1995, and will end on March 31, 1996. The ISU basketball arena (fully depreciated) holds 15,000 fans. The *number of home dates* per month is as follows: December, 7; January, 5; February, 5; and March, 5.

Five thousand seats per game are reserved for the ISU students at an admission price of $5 per student per game. The remaining seats are sold to alumni and other fans at a season ticket cost of $308. Season ticket orders are mailed on November 30. Season ticket holders have the choice of paying the $308 as a lump sum by December 6 (the first home date) or using a payment plan of $77 per month with the first payment due by December 7. Forty percent of the season ticket holders choose the payment plan.

The university also operates the concession stands, which cost $3,000 per game and generate $8,000 in cash revenues per game. All concession items are purchased COD seven days before a home date. There is no ending inventory of concession stand items on December 31.

The major cost to the university in managing the arena is the utility bill for heat and lighting. The university receives the utility bill on the fifth of each month for the previous month's usage. The arena uses no heat or lighting in the off season. Monthly usage during the basketball season is $240,000. Arena workers receive wages on a per game basis and are paid on the day following a home date. The payroll cost for a home date is $12,000. In addition, the university insures the arena at a cost of $24,000 per year. The insurance is paid in advance each December 1. The arena had $3,000 cash left from the preceding basketball season.

On December 31, 1995, after a particularly exciting game in which ISU upset its conference rival, the president of the university asks you to prepare financial statements for December. The president noticed that the arena was sold out for each of the home dates in December and, as a result, wants to know how much cash the arena operation is generating.

INSTRUCTIONS

[a] Prepare for the president an income statement for December and a balance sheet on December 31, 1995, under a cash basis assumption. Develop an alternative set of statements under an accrual approach. (Identify the difference between assets and liabilities as "fund balance" rather than owners' equity, because a university does not have shareholders.)

[b] Assuming the arena is used only for basketball, what will the arena operation earn for the period from December 1, 1995, to November 30, 1996?

[c] Show the president the shortcomings of cash basis financial statements in evaluating the arena's operating performance for December.

CASES

3–33 Income and Inflation The Brakebill Company was formed on January 1, 1995. On that date, stockholders contributed $50,000 to the company in exchange for 5,000 shares of Brakebill's common stock. The company placed the $50,000 in a noninterest-bearing checking account. For various unforeseen reasons, the company engaged in no further transactions during 1995. On December 31, 1995, the company still had $50,000 in its checking account. Assume the inflation rate during 1995 was 10%.

INSTRUCTIONS

[a] According to GAAP, what is the amount of Brakebill's net income (loss) for 1995? Explain your answer.

[b] In an economic sense, would Brakebill Company generally be considered better off or worse off at the end of 1995 than at the beginning? Explain your answer.

[c] If you were in charge of setting GAAP, how much net income (loss) would you require Brakebill to report for 1995? Explain your answer.

3–34 Nature of Liabilities Many companies promise to pay the cost of their employees' health care after they retire. In the past, generally accepted accounting principles have not required companies to include among their liabilities the obligations for postretirement health care benefits. Instead, companies have simply accounted for these costs as expenses when the costs were paid, which, of course, was after the employees retired. This is sometimes referred to as a *pay as you go* basis of accounting for these costs.

The FASB has recently studied this accounting issue and has argued that companies should be required to account for the cost of postretirement health care benefits during the periods in which the employees work for the company (i.e., before the employees retire). Such accounting would force many companies to report very large expenses and liabilities in their financial statements.

Many corporate managers have objected to the FASB's position, stating that such accounting is too imprecise and would cause many companies to drop or reduce postretirement health care benefits. The managers also claim that the FASB's approach would substantially reduce corporate net income and stockholders' equity and that some companies may even be forced to cut expenses in other vital areas, such as research and development.

In response to the managers' arguments, the FASB has argued that companies should be required to account for all of their obligations. Companies should not be excused from accounting for obligations just because they can only be estimated or because they adversely affect the company's financial statements.

INSTRUCTIONS

[a] Explain the theoretical rationale that supports the FASB's position on the accounting issue described above.

[b] Explain why you agree or disagree with the FASB's position.

[c] What is your opinion of the validity of the arguments that the corporate managers have raised?

3–35 Measurement of Liabilities On January 1, 1996, Amy Company borrowed $50,000 cash from Jeanne Company by signing a $50,000, 12%, two-year promissory note calling for interest of $6,000 ($50,000 × 12% = $6,000) to be paid at the end of 1996 and 1997. On that date, the market rate of interest for similar notes was 12%.

On December 31, 1996, Amy paid the $6,000 interest for 1996. At that time, the market rate of interest for notes similar to the one issued by Amy was 14%.

As the controller for Amy, you are trying to determine the amount the company should report for the note payable on December 31, 1996, in a balance sheet prepared in accordance with GAAP. You are considering the following alternatives:

[1] Report the note payable at $56,000. This amount equals the face amount of the note plus the interest that must be paid at the end of 1997 ($50,000 + $6,000 = $56,000).

[2] Report the note payable at $49,122.81. This amount equals the amount in [1], discounted for one year at the current market interest rate of 14% ($56,000 ÷ 1.14 = $49,122.81).

[3] Report the note payable at $50,000. This amount equals the amount in [1], discounted for one year at the market interest rate of 12% that was in effect when the note was issued ($56,000 ÷ 1.12 = $50,000).

INSTRUCTIONS

Which of the above alternatives should you select? Explain your answer.

3–36 Liabilities versus Owners' Equity Dawn Wright, an accountant employed by Wong Company, has asked for your help in deciding whether each of the items listed below should be reported in Wong Company's balance sheet as a liability or as stockholders' equity:

[1] An issue of subordinated income bonds that mature in 10 years. The bonds provide for interest at an annual rate of 12%, to be paid only in those years during which the company's income is sufficient to cover the interest.

[2] An issue of preferred stock that Wong is required to redeem on specified future dates. The stock confers no voting rights and has a stated cumulative dividend rate of 12%.

[3] An issue of preferred stock that Wong has an option to redeem at any time. The stock confers no voting rights and has a stated cumulative dividend rate of 13%.

INSTRUCTIONS

[a] Explain how the substance over form modifying convention relates to the reporting problem indicated above.

[b] Indicate whether each item listed above should be classified as a liability or as stockholders' equity. Explain your answers.

3–37 Measurement of Stockholders' Equity On December 31, 1996, Begley Corporation reported total assets of $10,000,000, total liabilities of $4,000,000, and total stockholders' equity of $6,000,000. The stockholders' equity consisted of common stock of $1,000,000 and retained earnings of $5,000,000. Begley had 100,000 shares of $10 par value common stock outstanding on December 31, 1996, and the market price per share on that date was $70.

INSTRUCTIONS

[a] Explain how stockholders' equity is measured in conventional accounting.

[b] Explain why the reported stockholders' equity of $6,000,000 does not equal the ending market price per share multiplied by the shares outstanding ($70 × 100,000 = $7,000,000).

3–38 Cash versus Accrual Discussion Firestone Foundation is a not-for-profit organization dedicated to the support of the arts in the surrounding communities. The large foundation has investments in real estate, stocks and bonds, and mortgages, as well as unpaid pledges from supporters. The real estate investments have outstanding mortgages. The foundation has been operating its accounting system on a cash basis since its inception in 1956. The trustees have embarked on a program to increase foundation activities, including an aggressive annual fund-raising campaign.

The trustees have decided that the foundation's accounting records should be audited annually and have engaged a CPA firm to conduct the first audit. One of the auditors recommends that the foundation convert its accounting system to an accrual basis from the cash basis. The auditor has stated that accrual accounting is used by profit-making companies but has not been used extensively by governmental or not-for-profit organizations. The auditor believes that accrual accounting has many advantages and would be very useful for Firestone Foundation.

INSTRUCTIONS

[a] Describe how the foundation's statement of financial position and statement of receipts and disbursements prepared on an accrual basis would differ from those prepared on a cash basis.

[b] Identify and briefly explain the advantages accrual accounting provides to profit-making companies that would also be applicable to Firestone Foundation.

[c] Explain how the trustees' ability to evaluate the performance of the foundation's executive director would be improved if the foundation used financial statements prepared on the accrual basis rather than the cash basis method of accounting.   (CMA adapted)

3–39 Measurement of Income Barry Ganno bought a four-bedroom home on January 1, 1995, for $285,000 cash. After this purchase, Ganno had only $45,000 cash left in his noninterest-bearing checking account. On December 31, 1995, Ganno could sell his house for $360,000 cash. At that time, he could engage in one of the following independent transactions:

[1] Sell the house and buy a similar four-bedroom home in the same town for $360,000.

[2] Sell the house and buy a similar four-bedroom home in another region of the country for $285,000.

[3] Sell the house and buy a similar four-bedroom home in another region of the country for $405,000.

[4] Sell the house and buy a six-bedroom home in the same town for $405,000.

[5] Not sell the house.

INSTRUCTIONS

[a] Determine the 1995 income (gain) Ganno would record for each of the independent situations above, according to GAAP. Assume no transaction costs or taxes. Also assume that Ganno is indifferent about regional location, and that all houses are of similar construction quality.

[b] How well does GAAP capture the economic substance of each transaction above?

3–40 Asset/Liability versus Revenue/Expense View The following definitions of assets and liabilities are given in *Accounting Terminology Bulletin No. 1* (New York: AICPA, 1953), pars. 26 and 27:

> **Asset**—*something represented by a debit balance that is or would be properly carried forward upon a closing of books of account according to the rules or principles of accounting.*
> **Liability**—*something represented by a credit balance that is or would be properly carried forward upon a closing of books of account according to the rules or principles of accounting.*

INSTRUCTIONS

Are the above definitions consistent with the asset/liability or the revenue/expense view? What deficiencies can you identify in the above definitions?

3–41 Usefulness of Forecasts You and a friend are discussing whether corporate managers should be required to report financial forecasts in their companies' published annual reports. Your friend argues, "Forecasts are useful information because investors and creditors want to know as much as possible about the future when they make their decisions. Usefulness is the primary objective of corporate financial reporting. Therefore, if information is useful, then GAAP should require companies to report it."

INSTRUCTIONS

[a] If a certain type of information really is useful, should GAAP require companies to report it?

[b] Summarize the arguments for and against the required disclosure of financial forecasts.

[c] In your opinion, should companies be required to disclose financial forecasts? Defend your answer.

3–42 Forecast Considerations and Assumptions Eland Electronics is a new company in the high-growth electronics field. It produces a unique electronic test package for the defense industry. Eland Electronics, which has been run very successfully as a private company for two years, will be making its first public offering of common stock within the next month. Naturally, the company wants to obtain the highest price possible for the new offering. The treasurer of the company, Tom Cason, has suggested that the publication of a three-year earnings forecast may enhance the offering price of the new shares.

INSTRUCTIONS

What factors must Cason consider in the construction of the earnings forecast? What shortcomings in the public disclosure of financial forecasts should Cason be aware of?

3–43 Forecast Considerations and Assumptions   Hotel management must make many assumptions in constructing financial forecasts. Listed below are some variables management may have to consider in making a financial forecast.

[1] Gasoline prices   [4] Characteristics of automobiles
[2] Aging population   [5] Land values
[3] Financing costs   [6] General economic conditions

The following background information comes from the annual report of Sleepy Inns of America, a fast-growing national motel chain.

The market which Sleepy Inns serves is broad and rapidly growing. Responding to today's more demanding traveler, we offer quality lodgings at better prices than our competitors. We cut out such expensive frills as elaborate lobbies, convention space, and meeting halls, and we pass the savings on to our guests. We offer all of the conveniences that travelers appreciate. Each of our strategically located properties provides a cluster of services in one convenient location — lodging, food, gasoline, gifts, and souvenirs.

INSTRUCTIONS

Explain how each of these variables may be interpreted by the managers of Sleepy Inns of America in constructing a financial forecast.

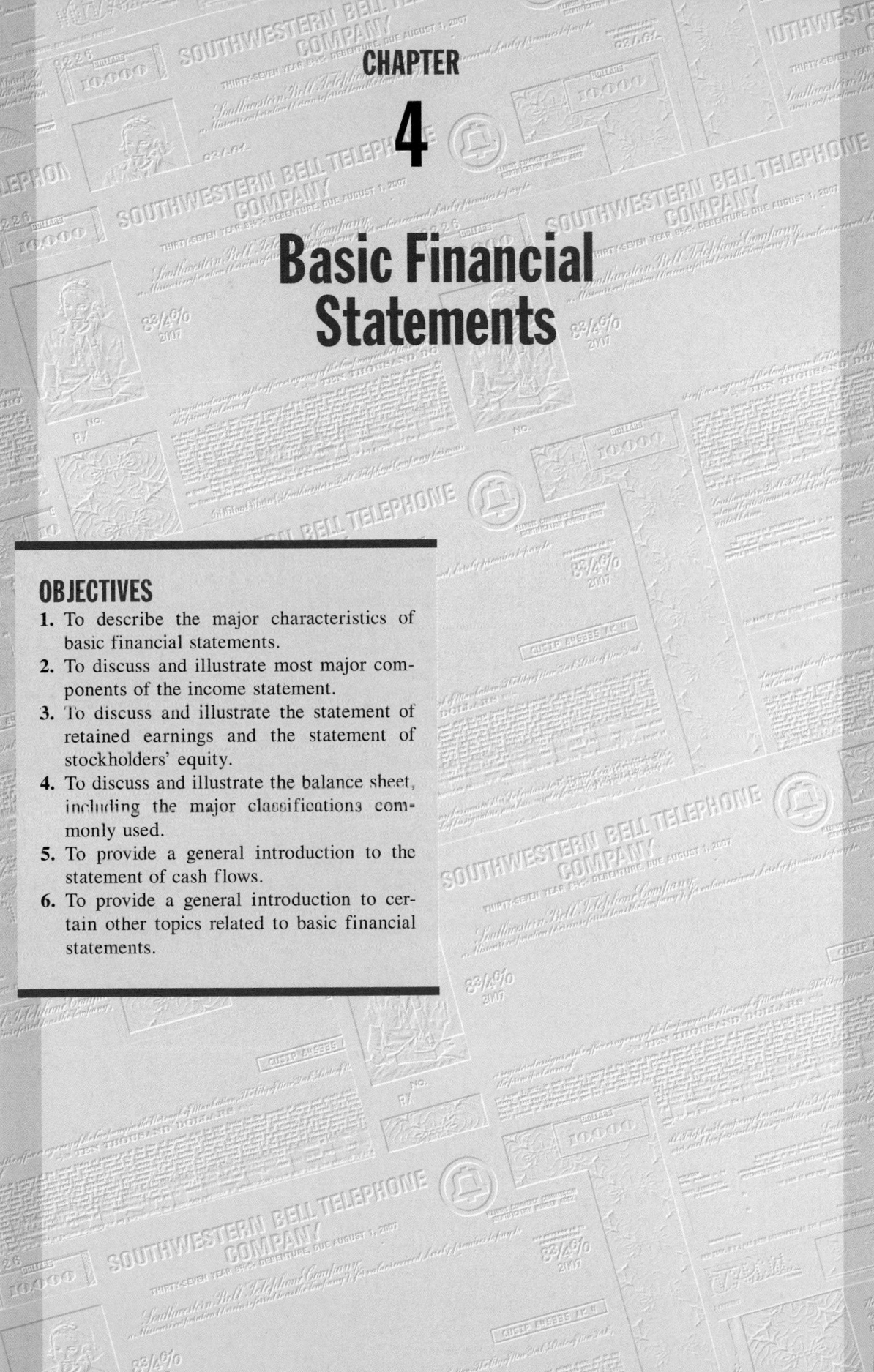

Basic Financial Statements

OBJECTIVES

1. To describe the major characteristics of basic financial statements.
2. To discuss and illustrate most major components of the income statement.
3. To discuss and illustrate the statement of retained earnings and the statement of stockholders' equity.
4. To discuss and illustrate the balance sheet, including the major classifications commonly used.
5. To provide a general introduction to the statement of cash flows.
6. To provide a general introduction to certain other topics related to basic financial statements.

Most companies prepare financial statements on a calendar-year basis, that is, at December 31. But many have adopted fiscal years that end at other times during the year. For example, Kmart ends its fiscal year in January, just after the Christmas season. Campbell Soup Company's fiscal year ends on July 31, just before tomatoes are harvested and when tomato inventories are at their lowest levels. Both companies initially chose their fiscal years to match their natural business cycles, although Campbell depends far less on tomatoes today than it once did. This allowed the companies to account for inventories when they are at the lowest levels. Many companies, especially smaller ones, have adopted noncalendar fiscal years to try to reduce the fees of and to get better service from their external accountants, who are usually booked up and charging full fees from January through April.

Whether a company uses a calendar-year accounting period or some other one, it must produce a complete set of basic financial statements at least once a year. These statements are the subject of this chapter.

Christopher Power, ed., Richard Greene, "Let's Get Fiscal," *Forbes,* April 30, 1984, pp. 102, 104.

CHARACTERISTICS OF BASIC FINANCIAL STATEMENTS

What was the net income of Exxon last year? Was this figure large or small in relation to the company's sales and to its stockholders' equity? What was the relationship last year between IBM's dividends and earnings? What proportion of General Motors' assets at the end of last year did the company finance through debt? How did General Electric use its cash last year? These are a few of the many questions that investors, creditors, and other users seek to answer based on information presented in the companies' financial statements.

The basic financial statements are the **balance sheet,** the **income statement,** the **statement of cash flows,** and the **statement of retained earnings** (or **statement of stockholders' equity**). Companies usually present basic financial statements in their annual reports to shareholders and in other disclosure media. The balance sheet summarizes the financial position of an enterprise *at a particular point in time.* The other basic statements summarize various changes in financial position that have occurred *during a period of time.*

As discussed in Chapter 2, the primary goal of a business enterprise is to increase its monetary wealth so that over time it can return the most cash to its owners. Business enterprises attempt to increase their monetary wealth by using cash to generate more cash. Financial statements help users to evaluate the enterprise's success in generating favorable cash flows. They help users to assess prospective net cash inflows to the enterprise and to assess their own chances of receiving cash from the enterprise.

Basic financial statements have several important characteristics:

1. They are only a **subset,** although an important subset, of the information needed by users for making rational investment, lending, and similar decisions.
2. They are primarily **historical** in nature.
3. They **summarize** information.
4. They reflect many **estimates.**
5. They are **general-purpose** reports designed to serve the needs of many different users.
6. They **articulate** with each other (i.e., they are **interrelated**).

Intermediate Accounting is a book about basic financial statements. The purpose of this chapter is to review the four basic financial statements in a manner that is compatible with the knowledge that you should have when entering intermediate accounting. By discussing all four financial statements in a single chapter, we can stress the important concept of articulation between financial statements. *Please take a moment to review your table of contents and observe that Part V (Chapters 19, 20, 21, and 22) of this book is titled "Reporting Operations and Cash Flows."* Chapter 4 (this chapter) presents the balance sheet and statement of stockholders' equity in detail; it also reviews most major aspects of the income statement and statement of cash flows. Chapter 21, which relies on the accounting change material presented in Chapter 20, explains additional income statement complexities at a time in your study when you will be better prepared to understand them. Likewise, Chapter 22 explains additional information about the statement of cash flows at a time in your study when you will be better able to understand it.

This chapter presents the statements in the order in which accountants typically prepare them (i.e., income statement, statement of retained earnings or statement of stockholders' equity, balance sheet, and statement of cash flows). To emphasize the interrelatedness of basic financial statements, the chapter illustrates a set of statements prepared for Sunrise Corporation.[1]

COVERAGE OF BASIC FINANCIAL STATEMENTS IN THIS TEXTBOOK

---

[1]A complete set of financial statements of Kellogg Company (a company that makes many well-known cereal products) is presented in the Appendix and inside the front and back covers of this book.

The authors recommend *Accounting Trends & Techniques* for additional examples of disclosures made in financial statements. This annual publication of the American Institute of Certified Public Accountants is based on a survey of the annual reports to shareholders of 600 companies.

INCOME STATEMENT

The **income statement,** generally regarded as the most important financial statement, is used in two major ways:

1. **To predict cash flows.**   Users of financial statements typically invest or lend cash, and they want to know *how much* cash they will receive in return and *when* they will receive it. Knowledge of a company's past income and its components helps users to predict more accurately the company's income and to better assess their own chances of receiving cash from the company.
2. **To evaluate management's performance.**   Users regard the income statement as an important indication of management's success. Stockholders typically want to reward good managers and replace poor ones.

From a societal standpoint, measurements reported on the income statement help to ensure that we put our scarce resources to their best uses and that the goods and services we want are available. If a company produces and distributes its products successfully, it should earn income. Moreover, a record of profitable operations should help the company to raise capital and other resources. Generally, resources should flow into companies that have unusually high incomes and out of those that sustain losses.

ELEMENTS OF THE INCOME STATEMENT

Accountants traditionally have measured a company's income by focusing on transactions that caused changes in the company's assets and liabilities during a period of time. These transactions include revenues, expenses, gains, and losses. As you might expect, accountants disagree about the best way to measure these components of a company's income. For example, we could measure expenses using current costs, current exit values, or historical costs. Traditionally, accountants have relied primarily on historical costs. Income measurement in conventional accounting involves primarily the *revenue realization, matching,* and *asset/liability measurement* principles, as discussed in Chapter 2.

Revenue Realization

Matching

Asset/Liability Measurement

The fundamental elements of the income statement and their relationships to net income are demonstrated in the following equation:

$$\text{Revenues} - \text{Expenses} + \text{Gains} - \text{Losses} = \text{Net Income}$$

A review of several definitions presented in Chapter 2 is appropriate at this point:[2]

1. **Revenues.**   Inflows or other enhancements of assets of an entity or settlements of its liabilities (or both) during a period, based on production and delivery of goods, provision of services, and other activities that constitute the entity's major operations.
2. **Expenses.**   Outflows or other use of assets or incurrences of liabilities (or both) during a period as a result of delivering or producing goods, rendering services, or carrying out other activities that constitute the entity's major operations.
3. **Costs.**   Sacrifices incurred in acquiring resources. We include the term *cost* here so that you can differentiate it from the term *expense*. Costs do not enter into the calculation of net income until they expire. An **expense** in conventional accounting is an **expired cost** (more precisely, an **expired historical cost**). In contrast, a *cost that has not yet expired* is reported as an *asset*.

---

[2]These definitions are based largely on *FASB Statement of Financial Accounting Concepts No. 6,* "Elements of Financial Statements," 1985, pars. 78, 80, 82, and 83.

4. Gains and losses. **Gains** are increases in owners' equity (net assets) from peripheral or incidental transactions of an entity and from all other transactions and events affecting the entity during a period, except those resulting from revenues or investments by owners. **Losses** are decreases in owners' equity (net assets) from peripheral or incidental transactions of an entity and from all other events affecting the entity during a period, except those that result from expenses or distributions to owners. Unlike revenues and expenses, which are measured and reported at *gross amounts,* gains and losses are measured and reported at *net amounts.* For example, if a company paid $70,000 for land and later sold it for $100,000, the company would report a $30,000 gain. This gain equals the gross selling price of $100,000, net of the land's cost of $70,000. In practice, gains are sometimes classified broadly as revenues; losses are sometimes classified broadly as expenses.

5. Net income. The net result of adding revenues and gains for a period and deducting expenses and losses for the period. Terms such as *earnings* and *profit* often are used as synonyms for *income.*

Several items that may appear on an income statement are somewhat peculiar and should be explained further at this time. These items include extraordinary gains and losses, unusual or infrequently occurring gains and losses, gains and losses resulting from the disposal of business segments, and the cumulative effect of a change in accounting principles.

Extraordinary Gains and Losses

Suppose that a company sustains a loss from an earthquake. Because this kind of loss is rare, users of financial statements could make more accurate predictions and more meaningful evaluations of management's performance if they knew about unusual and nonrecurring gains and losses. As a result, generally accepted accounting principles (GAAP) require companies to report material extraordinary gains and losses in a special section of their income statements.

Materiality

To be considered an extraordinary gain or loss, an event or transaction must meet *both* of the following criteria:[3]

1. **Unusual nature.** The underlying event or transaction should be highly unusual and clearly unrelated to, or only incidentally related to, the ordinary activities of the entity, considering the environment in which it operates.
2. **Infrequent occurrence.** The underlying event or transaction should not be expected to recur in the foreseeable future, considering the environment in which the entity operates.

Note that to be considered extraordinary, an item must be both unusual and nonrecurring.[4] The term **extraordinary item** therefore has a technical meaning in accounting that differs from the everyday connotation of items that are simply unusual or peculiar. Furthermore, the criteria require the accountant to consider the specific *characteristics of the company* as well as the *environment in which it operates.* For example, an accountant would be more likely to judge a loss from a hurricane as extraordinary if it were sustained by a company located in Iowa instead of one located on the Louisiana Gulf Coast.[5]

---

[3]*APB Opinion No. 30,* "Reporting the Results of Operations," 1973, par. 20.

[4]As is true of most rules, there are *exceptions* to the criteria for extraordinary items. The exceptions generally require that certain types of gains and losses be classified as extraordinary *regardless of the criteria in APB Opinion No. 30.* Those exceptions that pertain to intermediate accounting will be covered at appropriate places throughout the text. For example, the FASB in *Statement of Financial Accounting Standards No. 4* stated that gains and losses from extinguishment of debt should always be classified as extraordinary. We explain this exception in Chapter 15.

[5]We are referring to a loss in excess of insurance proceeds or a loss not covered at all by insurance.

Accountants must use *judgment* when applying the above criteria, which are inherently very restrictive and are rarely satisfied in practice.[6] In many cases, an event or transaction meets both criteria only as the direct result of a **major casualty** (such as an earthquake), an **expropriation** (takeover of property by a government), or a **prohibition** under a newly enacted law. To clarify these restrictions, the Accounting Principles Board (APB) indicated that the following items could be reported as extraordinary *only* if they resulted from a major casualty, expropriation, or prohibition:[7]

1. Write-downs or write-offs of receivables, inventories, equipment leased to others, or intangible assets.
2. Gains or losses from foreign currency transactions and translation of foreign currency financial statements.
3. Gains or losses on disposal of a segment of a business.
4. Other gains or losses from sale or abandonment of property, plant, or business equipment.
5. Effects of a strike, including those against competitors and major suppliers.
6. Adjustments of accruals on long-term contracts.

Below are some examples of events or transactions that meet both criteria and should therefore be judged as extraordinary:

1. A large portion of a tobacco manufacturer's crops are destroyed by a hailstorm. Severe damage from hailstorms in the locality where the manufacturer grows tobacco is rare.
2. A food canner destroys a large quantity of inventory because of a government ban on canned goods containing cyclamates. Government prohibitions of this kind rarely occur.
3. An earthquake destroys an oil refinery owned by a large multinational oil company. Earthquakes rarely occur in the area where the oil refinery is located.
4. A large company (Johnson & Johnson) incurred substantial costs when it withdrew all Tylenol capsule products from the market as a result of the criminal tampering with Tylenol Extra-Strength Capsules in the Chicago area during the third quarter of 1982. Clearly, the Tylenol case meets the criteria of unusual and nonrecurring.

In contrast, here are some examples of events or transactions that should *not* be judged extraordinary because they do not meet both criteria for extraordinary items:

1. A citrus grower's Florida crop is damaged by frost. Frost damage is normally experienced every three or four years. In this case, the criterion of infrequent occurrence is not met.
2. A company that operates a chain of warehouses sells the excess land surrounding one of its warehouses. When the company buys property to establish a new warehouse, it usually buys more land than it will use for the warehouse because it expects the land to appreciate in value. In the past five years, there have been two instances in which the company sold such excess land. Here the criterion of infrequent occurrence has not been met.
3. A large diversified company sells a block of shares from the portfolio of securities it has for investment purposes. This is the first sale from its portfolio. The criterion of unusual nature has not been met in this case because the company owns several securities.
4. A textile manufacturer with only one plant moves to another location. It has not relocated a plant in 20 years and has no plans to do so in the foreseeable future. Here the criterion of

---

[6]*Accounting Trends & Techniques,* 47th ed. (New York: AICPA, 1993), p. 377, reveals that only 84 extraordinary items were reported in the 600 annual reports examined. Of the 84 items, 77 were *exceptions* to the criteria for extraordinary items set forth in *APB Opinion No. 30* (see footnote 4).

[7]*APB Opinion No. 30,* par. 23.

unusual nature has not been met because, in general, moving from one location to another is a common business occurrence.[8]

Unusual or Infrequently Occurring Items

An accountant sometimes encounters a gain or loss that is unusual in nature *or* occurs infrequently, *but not both.* Such a gain or loss is therefore *not* extraordinary. Examples are gains or losses from the sale of plant assets, losses from inventory write-offs, and losses due to a strike. According to *APB Opinion No. 30,* these gains and losses should be reported as separate items in the income statement if they are material. They should *not* be reported in any way that implies that they are extraordinary in nature.

Materiality

In practice, the distinction between extraordinary items and unusual or infrequently occurring items is sometimes hazy. Accountants should be aware that, because the income statement reports management's performance, many managers want to report gains as nonextraordinary and losses as extraordinary. This tendency should not influence the accountant's judgment about whether a particular event or transaction is extraordinary.

Disposal of a Business Segment

The term **segment of a business** refers to "a component of an entity whose activities represent a separate major line of business or class of customer. A segment may be in the form of a subsidiary, a division, or a department, . . . provided that its assets, results of operations, and activities can be clearly distinguished, physically and operationally and for financial reporting purposes, from the other assets, results of operations, and activities of the entity."[9] A company may **dispose** of a segment of its business. For example, a company that has a furniture division and a clothing division may sell its clothing division.

Gains and losses from disposal of a business segment are *not* extraordinary items. Instead, they must be reported in a special income statement category called **discontinued operations.** *In Chapter 21, we discuss in detail the complex requirements for discontinued operations and illustrate how to report them in a comprehensive income statement.*

Changes in Accounting Principles

A company may occasionally change from one generally accepted accounting principle to another. For example, it may change from the first-in, first-out (FIFO) to the last-in, first-out (LIFO) method of inventory cost determination, or from the sum-of-the-years'-digits method to the straight-line method of computing depreciation. Such changes are called **changes in accounting principles,** and they are permitted under generally accepted accounting principles if the company can establish that the new principle is preferable to the old.

Changes in accounting principles are *not* extraordinary items. Instead, *most* changes in accounting principles are reported in a special income statement category called the **cumulative effect of a change in accounting principles.**[10] Financial reporting requirements for

---

[8]Most of the examples above were taken from *Accounting Interpretations of APB Opinion No. 30,* "Reporting the Results of Operations" (New York: AICPA, 1973).

[9]*APB Opinion No. 30,* par. 13.

[10]*APB Opinion No. 20,* "Accounting Changes," 1971, par. 20.

changes in accounting principles are complex. *In Chapter 20, we explain the subject of accounting changes. Then in Chapter 21, we illustrate how to report these changes in a comprehensive income statement.* Therefore, as explained near the beginning of the chapter, this chapter introduces you to the income statement; Chapter 21 explains additional income statement reporting details at a time when you will be better able to understand their meaning and significance.

INCOME STATEMENT FORMAT

The form and content of the income statement have been greatly affected by professional pronouncements relating to such issues as intraperiod income tax allocation, accounting changes, discontinued operations, extraordinary items, and earnings per share. These issues often are complex and require careful study before the implications of income statement reporting can be fully understood. For this reason, we review in this section the fundamental aspects of the income statement format. In Chapter 21, we consider some additional reporting complexities of the income statement.

The accounting profession has not adopted a uniform format for the entire income statement. Instead, it permits some flexibility, which enables the practicing accountant to structure an income statement that best fits the circumstances of the reporting entity. Nevertheless, many income statement disclosures (such as depreciation expense) are required by GAAP, and we discuss these required disclosures at appropriate places in this book. Accountants traditionally have presented the income statement in either a multiple-step or a single-step form.

Multiple-Step Form

A **multiple-step** income statement presents subtotals for gross margin and operating income before showing net income. Net income is therefore derived in intermediate steps. Exhibit 4–1 illustrates a multiple-step income statement for Sunrise Corporation. In practice, many details shown in this example may be condensed or may be reported in footnotes or parenthetically. For example, the income statement may begin with net sales if the accountant thinks that the revenue contra account balances are immaterial. Moreover, the accountant may report only the totals for cost of goods sold, selling expenses, and general and administrative expenses. The details may be presented separately in the footnotes.

Materiality

As Exhibit 4–1 suggests, a multiple-step format calls for deducting cost of goods sold from net sales to measure **gross margin on sales** (often called **gross profit on sales**). Gross margin is an intermediate measure of profitability that indicates the difference between the selling prices and costs of products sold during the accounting period. For example, the gross margin earned by companies that produce cereal products is currently about 50%.

To the extent possible, **operating expenses** usually are divided into two categories: **selling expenses** relate to the sale of the company's products; **general and administrative expenses** relate to the general operations of the business.

Income from operations (also called **operating income**) is a measurement of the company's profitability as a result of its primary business activities. **Other revenues** and **other expenses** are related to the secondary activities of the company; these two sections often are combined. Note that Sunrise Corporation correctly reported an unusual item (loss on sale of long-term investments) as "other expense." As stated earlier, items that are unusual or nonrecurring (but not both) must not be reported as extraordinary items.

Income before taxes and extraordinary item is an intermediate measure of income that would simply be called "income before taxes" if Sunrise Corporation did not have an extraordinary item. **Income tax** is the final expense deducted. The amount is determined by

EXHIBIT 4–1

Multiple-Step Income Statement

Sunrise Corporation
Income Statement
For the Year Ended December 31, 1996

Sales revenue			
Sales			$579,500
Less: Sales returns and allowances		$ 18,200	
Sales discounts		11,300	29,500
Net sales			550,000
Cost of goods sold			
Merchandise inventory, Jan. 1, 1996		$ 40,000	
Purchases	$340,000		
Less: Purchase returns and allowances	(20,000)		
Purchase discounts	(6,800)		
Add: Transportation-in	11,800		
Net purchases		325,000	
Cost of goods available for sale		$365,000	
Less: Merchandise inventory, Dec. 31, 1996		(35,000)	
Cost of goods sold			330,000
Gross margin on sales			220,000
Operating expenses			
Selling expenses			
Sales salaries	48,000		
Advertising	12,000		
Transportation-out	7,300		
Depreciation of delivery equipment	3,000		
Other selling expenses	2,700	$ 73,000	
General and administrative expenses			
Office salaries	27,100		
Utilities	9,900		
Supplies	7,700		
Insurance	5,800		
Depreciation of building	2,500		
Depreciation of office equipment	2,000		
Amortization	3,200		
Bad debts	4,500		
Other general and administrative expenses	1,800	64,500	
Total operating expenses			137,500
Income from operations			82,500
Other revenues			
Interest		$ 2,100	
Dividends		5,200	
Rent		7,200	
Gain on sale of equipment		6,500	21,000
			103,500
Other expenses			
Interest		$ 14,400	
Unusual item—loss on sale of long-term investments		5,100	19,500
Income before taxes and extraordinary item			84,000
Income tax expense			33,600
Income before extraordinary item			50,400
Extraordinary item—gain from expropriation of land, less applicable income tax expense of $16,000			24,000
Net income			$ 74,400
Per share of common stock			
Income before extraordinary item			$2.32
Extraordinary gain (net of tax)			1.20
Net income			$3.52

Above the line

multiplying the income before taxes and extraordinary item by the income tax rate, which we assume is 40%.[11] The amount therefore includes the income tax effect of all income statement items that appear before it. Income tax expense should always be shown separately, not combined with any other expenses.

Income before extraordinary item indicates how profitable the company was without considering the effects of the extraordinary item. Because extraordinary items are unusual *and* nonrecurring, many financial statement users rely heavily on the income before extraordinary item when they make predictions and evaluate management's performance.

The **extraordinary item** is presented next, as required by GAAP. In the exhibit, Sunrise Corporation reported an extraordinary *gain* because the proceeds received from a government expropriation of land exceeded the land's cost. An extraordinary gain or loss is always reported in a special income statement section. Further, the generally accepted accounting principle of **intraperiod tax allocation,** which is discussed in detail in Chapter 19, requires that the gross amount of an extraordinary gain be reduced by the amount of **income tax expense** associated with the gain. Similarly, it requires that the gross amount of an extraordinary loss be reduced by the amount of the **income tax reduction** associated with the loss. Extraordinary gains and losses are therefore always reported **net** of their income tax effects, or on a **net of tax basis.** Note in the exhibit that if the extraordinary gain had not been reported on a net of tax basis, the reported income tax expense (associated with income before taxes and extraordinary item) would have been $49,600 ($33,600 + $16,000). Income before extraordinary item would then have been reported as only $34,400 ($84,000 − $49,600). This error could cause some users to evaluate the company in a misleading (and in this case, less favorable) light. Special income statement categories for discontinued operations and the cumulative effect of a change in accounting principles are required by GAAP. In Chapter 21, we present a comprehensive income statement that includes these categories.

Net income includes the effects of all revenues, expenses, gains, and losses. The beneficiaries of net income are the stockholders, both preferred and common.

Earnings per share of common stock is a widely used financial measurement that appears below net income.[12] Its beneficiaries are *common* stockholders. In the simplest case, an accountant calculates earnings per share by dividing net income by the weighted average number of common shares outstanding during the period. Sunrise Corporation had preferred stock outstanding (see Exhibit 4–6). We therefore subtracted preferred dividends from net income when calculating earnings per share of common stock. Note that because Sunrise Corporation had an extraordinary item, it reported *three* per-share numbers: (1) income before extraordinary item, (2) extraordinary gain (net of tax), and (3) net income. Companies report these numbers separately to help users of financial statements make better predictions and more meaningful evaluations of management's performance. Calculating and reporting earnings per share can be extremely complex; we discuss and illustrate these complexities in Chapter 18.

Single-Step Form

In the **single-step** income statement, the accountant deducts total expenses from total revenues in a single step to measure net income. No separate disclosure is made of gross margin or operating income. Most companies that prepare single-step income statements deduct in-

---

[11]So that we can concentrate on the basic form and content of financial statements without being diverted by income tax calculations, we assume a tax rate of 40% for the financial statements presented in this chapter.

[12]Nonpublic enterprises are not required under generally accepted accounting principles to report earnings per share. Unless stated otherwise, you should assume in all end-of-chapter assignments that earnings per share is required.

EXHIBIT 4–2

Single-Step Income Statement

Sunrise Corporation
Income Statement
For the Year Ended December 31, 1996

Revenues		
Net sales		$550,000
Other revenues		21,000
Total revenues		571,000
Expenses		
Cost of goods sold	$330,000	
Selling expenses	73,000	
General and administrative expenses	64,500	
Interest	14,400	
Unusual item—loss on sale of long-term investments	5,100	
Total expenses		487,000
Income before taxes and extraordinary item		84,000
Income tax expense		33,600
Income before extraordinary item		50,400
Extraordinary item—gain from expropriation of land, less applicable income tax expense of $16,000		24,000
Net income		$ 74,400
Per share of common stock		
Income before extraordinary item		$2.32
Extraordinary gain (net of tax)		1.20
Net income		$3.52

NOTE TO STUDENTS: With either the multiple-step or the single-step form, generally accepted accounting principles require special income statement categories for discontinued operations and the cumulative effect of a change in accounting principles. In Chapter 21, we discuss and illustrate these categories. We also present a comprehensive income statement that includes these categories.

---

come tax as a separate, final item.[13] In Exhibit 4–2, we present a somewhat condensed, single-step income statement. Such condensation is not essential. Indeed, **condensed income statements** may be presented in either a multiple-step or a single-step format. A typical annual report contains a condensed income statement. As you can see by comparing Exhibits 4–1 and 4–2, extraordinary items are reported in a special income statement category, regardless of the format used. Moreover, the multiple-step and single-step formats always contain the same information after "income before taxes and extraordinary item."

Multiple-Step versus Single-Step Form

Many preparers and users of financial statements prefer the multiple-step form because it highlights gross margin and operating income. Others prefer the single-step form because it often is easier to understand and does not suggest a priority of expenses. In other words, the

---

[13]*Accounting Trends & Techniques,* 1993, p. 273.

format does not imply that a company must recover its cost of goods sold expense before it can recover any other expenses. In reality, of course, a company must cover all of its expenses if it is to have net income. Proponents of the single-step form also point out that the accounting profession has not clearly defined several terms often used in a multiple-step statement (especially *income from operations*). A survey of the annual reports of 600 companies indicated that in 1992, 211 of them used the single-step form and that 389 used the multiple-step form.[14]

STATEMENT OF RETAINED EARNINGS

The statement of retained earnings describes the changes in a company's retained earnings during a period and relates the income statement to the balance sheet. The retained earnings statement usually is fairly simple and may consist of three sections: (1) **prior period adjustments,** (2) **net income,** and (3) **dividends declared.** Users of financial statements can analyze the statement to determine whether any prior period adjustments exist and what relationship exists between a company's net income and its dividends.

A statement of retained earnings for Sunrise Corporation is shown in Exhibit 4–3.

PRIOR PERIOD ADJUSTMENTS

Prior period adjustments are charged or credited directly to retained earnings. These items do not appear on the income statement of the period in which they occur.

In 1977 the Financial Accounting Standards Board (FASB) issued *Statement of Financial Accounting Standards No. 16,* which greatly reduced the number of items that a company could report as prior period adjustments. In this pronouncement, the FASB stated:

> *Items of profit and loss related to the following shall be accounted for and reported as prior period adjustments and excluded from the determination of net income for the current period:*
>
> *1. Correction of an error in the financial statements of a prior period and*
> *2. Adjustments that result from realization of income tax benefits of preacquisition operating loss carryforwards of purchased subsidiaries.*[15]

The **correction of an error** that was made in the financial statements of a **prior period** is accounted for in the **current period** as a prior period adjustment.[16] The error may have resulted from mathematical mistakes, errors in selecting or applying accounting principles, or oversight or misuse of facts when the company prepared its erroneous financial statements.[17] Examples of errors are an overstatement of merchandise inventory at the end of the preceding period because of an inaccurate physical count and an understatement of previously reported depreciation because of an error in computation. A change from an accounting principle that is not generally accepted to one that is generally accepted is considered to be the correction of an error.

In practice, prior period adjustments due to errors are rare, yet they can sometimes have a significant effect on a company's financial statements. In its 1988 annual report, American Building Maintenance Industries, Inc., reported a prior period adjustment of $9,397,000. In

---

[14]*Accounting Trends and Techniques,* 1993, p. 273.

[15]*FASB Statement of Financial Accounting Standards No. 16,* "Prior Period Adjustments," 1977, par. 11. This pronouncement did not affect the manner of reporting accounting changes required or permitted by an FASB Statement or Interpretation, or an APB Opinion. We discuss the reporting of accounting changes in Chapter 20, where we see that adjustments to the opening balance of a company's retained earnings need not be confined to prior period adjustments.

[16]Moreover, when comparative statements are reported, erroneous amounts previously reported should be corrected.

[17]*APB Opinion No. 20,* par. 13.

EXHIBIT 4–3

Sunrise Corporation
Statement of Retained Earnings
For the Year Ended December 31, 1996

Retained earnings, Jan. 1, 1996, as previously reported		$ 45,600
Less: Prior period adjustment—correction of depreciation understatement in 1995 due to error, less applicable income tax effect of $2,000		3,000
Retained earnings, Jan. 1, 1996, as restated		42,600
Add: Net income		74,400
Subtotal		117,000
Less: Dividends declared on preferred stock ($.80 per share)	$ 4,000	
Dividends declared on common stock ($.60 per share)	12,000	16,000
Retained earnings, Dec. 31, 1996		$101,000

---

essence, this company does not carry insurance for property damage and personal liability and worker's compensation coverages. A 1988 analysis of insurance claims showed that in certain prior years, the company did not report the effect of claims that had been incurred.

A recent study has found that although corrections of prior years' income due to errors are rare, they are relatively more common when a firm has overstated, as opposed to understated, its income of prior periods. The study found that overstatements of income are more likely when firms have diffuse ownership, low growth in earnings, and few income-increasing GAAP alternatives. Overstatement errors appear to be less likely for those companies that have audit committees.[18]

An accountant must carefully distinguish a *correction of an error* from a **change in an accounting estimate.** A change in an accounting estimate results from the necessity for accountants to make many estimates. Changes in these estimates occur when new information or subsequent developments allow the accountant to make more accurate estimates. Examples include changes in estimates of uncollectible accounts receivable and changes in the estimated service lives or salvage values of plant assets. Changes in accounting estimates are *not* prior period adjustments. These changes should be accounted for in the period of change if the change affects that period only, or in the period of change and future periods if the change affects both.[19] We explain corrections of errors and changes in accounting estimates in Chapter 20.

Prior period adjustments that result from realization of income tax benefits of preacquisition operating loss carryforwards of purchased subsidiaries are not covered extensively in this text. Coverage of this topic is appropriate in advanced accounting courses.

As shown in Exhibit 4–3, a prior period adjustment is added to or deducted from the previously reported opening balance of retained earnings to derive a **restated (revised) opening balance.** Furthermore, a prior period adjustment is reported **net of its related income tax effect,** like that for extraordinary items. As we discuss in Chapter 19, the principle

---

[18]Mark L. DeFond and James Jiambalvo, "Incidence and Circumstances of Accounting Errors," *The Accounting Review* (July 1991), p. 643–655.
[19]*APB Opinion No. 20,* par. 31.

of intraperiod tax allocation requires that prior period adjustments be reported on a net of tax basis.

NET INCOME AND DIVIDENDS

The **net income** figure on the statement of retained earnings is taken directly from the income statement. When a company sustains a **net loss** during a period, the loss is deducted on the retained earnings statement.

Dividends declared during the period are deducted on the retained earnings statement and dividends per share ordinarily are disclosed. Dividends declared may be in the form of cash, other assets, or the company's own stock. Further, they may relate to both preferred and common stock. Note carefully that dividends declared are deducted on the statement because the declaration represents a reduction in retained earnings. Sometimes a company declares a dividend in one period but does not pay or distribute it until the next. As a result, dividends declared during a period may include an amount paid or distributed during the period and an amount that will be paid or distributed in the next period.

COMBINED STATEMENT OF INCOME AND RETAINED EARNINGS

Exhibit 4−4 illustrates a **combined statement of income and retained earnings.** Some accountants favor a combined statement of income and retained earnings because it integrates

---

EXHIBIT 4−4

Sunrise Corporation
Combined Statement of Income and Retained Earnings
For the Year Ended December 31, 1996

Net income*		$ 74,400
Add: Retained earnings, Jan. 1, 1996, as previously reported	$45,600	
Less: Prior period adjustment—correction of depreciation understatement in 1995 due to error, less applicable income tax effect of $2,000	3,000	
Retained earnings, Jan. 1, 1996, as restated		42,600
Subtotal		117,000
Less: Dividends declared on preferred stock ($.80 per share)	4,000	
Dividends declared on common stock ($.60 per share)	12,000	16,000
Retained earnings, Dec. 31, 1996		$101,000
Per share of common stock†		
Income before extraordinary item		$2.32
Extraordinary gain (net of tax)		1.20
Net income		$3.52

*The items shown in Exhibits 4−1 or 4−2 would appear above net income.

†Alternatively, earnings per share may be presented parenthetically in the body of the combined statement of income and retained earnings.

important and related information. Opponents claim that it may be too complicated for many users and deemphasizes net income by not placing this item at the bottom of the combined statement.

Sometimes a company also has changes in other accounts that comprise stockholders' equity. These changes occur as the company sells additional stock, buys and sells treasury stock, or engages in other kinds of capital stock transactions. Such changes must be disclosed in a separate statement, in the basic statements, or in the notes to the financial statements. Changes in the number of shares outstanding should also be disclosed.[20]

Many companies report all of these changes in a separate **statement of stockholders' equity.** This statement combines the retained earnings statement with one that shows changes in all the other components of stockholders' equity. As a result, a company that reports a statement of stockholders' equity need not report a separate retained earnings statement. A statement of stockholders' equity for Sunrise Corporation appears in Exhibit 4–5.

The **balance sheet** (sometimes called the **statement of financial position**) shows the financial position of an enterprise at a particular point in time. Investors, creditors, and other users of financial statements analyze an enterprise's balance sheet to evaluate such factors as **liquidity** (how close the assets are to cash realization), **capital structure** (what amount of assets has been financed by creditors and what amount by owners), and **financial flexibility** (the ability of a company to use its financial resources to adapt to change). Generally, companies that lack sufficient liquidity and financial flexibility, perhaps because virtually all of their assets are far removed from cash and a very large proportion of their capital structure consists of debt, are less able than other companies to take advantage of attractive investment opportunities or to absorb adverse changes in operating conditions. Companies

STATEMENT OF STOCKHOLDERS' EQUITY

Disclosure

BALANCE SHEET

EXHIBIT 4–5

Sunrise Corporation
Statement of Stockholders' Equity
For the Year Ended December 31, 1996

	Preferred Stock	Common Stock	Paid-In Capital in Excess of Par	Retained Earnings	Total
Balance, Jan. 1, 1996, as previously reported	$50,000	$ 60,000	$25,000	$ 45,600	$180,600
Less: Prior period adjustment—correction of depreciation understatement in 1995 due to error, less applicable income tax effect of $2,000				(3,000)	(3,000)
Balance, Jan. 1, 1996, as restated	50,000	60,000	25,000	42,600	177,600
Add: Net income				74,400	74,400
Less: Dividends declared on preferred stock ($.80 per share)				(4,000)	(4,000)
Dividends declared on common stock ($.60 per share)				(12,000)	(12,000)
Add: Common stock issued on Jan. 2, 1996 (8,000 shares)		40,000	15,000		55,000
Balance, Dec. 31, 1996	$50,000	$100,000	$40,000	$101,000	$291,000

[20]*APB Opinion No. 12,* "Omnibus Opinion—1967," 1967, par. 10.

without sufficient liquidity and financial flexibility are therefore more likely to fail than are other companies. The 1985 annual report of Texaco, Inc., contains an interesting disclosure that shows how a company's financial flexibility can sometimes be changed drastically. The disclosure includes the following:

> *There was a significant change in Texaco's financial flexibility at December 31, 1985 attributable to the December 10, 1985, judgment of the Texas State District Court against Texaco and for Pennzoil in the amount of $10.5 billion (excluding interest).*

The balance sheet was once regarded as the most important financial statement, but, as stated earlier, most users now regard the income statement as paramount. Nevertheless, the balance sheet may be regaining some attention. For example, a *Business Week* article stated that "investors, including the biggest bank trust departments, still look at earnings before they buy a security, but today the deal must also make sense in terms of a company's current ratio, debt/equity ratio, and return on investments. Corporations with balance sheets that cannot pass muster will find themselves closed out of the marketplace."[21] Moreover, the FASB is clearly giving renewed attention to the balance sheet, as indicated by its asset/liability view of earnings in the Conceptual Framework and its recent standards in such areas as pensions and income taxes.

ELEMENTS OF THE BALANCE SHEET

The following equation presents the three major elements of the balance sheet:

$$\text{Assets} = \text{Liabilities} + \text{Owners' Equity}$$

In Chapter 2, we defined these elements as follows:[22]

1. **Assets.**   Probable future economic benefits obtained or controlled by an entity as a result of past transactions or events.
2. **Liabilities.** Probable future sacrifices of economic benefits arising from present obligations of an entity to transfer assets or provide services to other entities in the future as a result of past transactions or events.
3. **Owners' equity.**   The residual interest in the assets of an entity that remains after deducting its liabilities.

BALANCE SHEET CLASSIFICATIONS

Generally accepted accounting principles require a company to report its assets, liabilities, and owners' equity in several classifications or categories. Although some flexibility is permitted in selecting and naming balance sheet categories and in grouping specific items into them, the following categories (in the order shown) are representative of those found in practice:

Assets
Current assets
Investments and funds ⎫
Property, plant, and equipment ⎬ Noncurrent assets
Intangible assets ⎭
Other assets

Liabilities
Current liabilities
Long-term liabilities

---

[21]"Focus on Balance Sheet," *Business Week* (June 7, 1976), p. 52.
[22]Based on *FASB Statement of Financial Accounting Concepts No. 6*, pars. 25, 35, and 49.

Owners' Equity
Paid-in capital
Capital stock
Preferred stock
Common stock
Paid-in capital in excess of par
Retained earnings

Exhibit 4–6 shows the **account form** of balance sheet for Sunrise Corporation. In this form, the liabilities and owners' equity are listed to the right of the assets. The **report form** and the **financial position form** are also acceptable. The report form shows the liabilities and owners' equity directly below the assets. The financial position form shows current liabilities deducted from current assets to determine working capital. Noncurrent assets are then added to working capital and noncurrent liabilities are deducted to arrive at owners' equity.[23]

The following discussion of each classification includes a brief indication of how some of the major items reported in it are valued on the balance sheet. You will see that although balance sheets are based largely on historical costs, they actually reflect several measurement attributes. Many of the remaining chapters in this book are organized within a balance sheet framework, and we explain in detail the nature and valuation of individual assets, liabilities, and owners' equity.

Asset/Liability Measurement

Assets

Current Assets. Current assets are cash and other assets that are reasonably expected to be realized in cash or sold or consumed during the normal operating cycle of the business or within one year from the balance sheet date, whichever is *longer*.[24] An **operating cycle** for a given enterprise is the *average time* that it takes to spend cash for inventory, sell the inventory in exchange for a receivable, and collect the receivable in cash. The cycle thus progresses from cash, through inventories and receivables, back to cash.

Most companies have operating cycles that are less than one year. Some companies, however, such as those involved in distilling, tobacco, and lumber operations, have longer operating cycles. A balance sheet of one of these companies may therefore contain current assets, such as inventory, for which cash realization is not expected within the next year.

Current assets are usually listed in the order of their liquidity. The most common current assets are cash, short-term investments, receivables, inventories, and prepaid expenses.

Cash (on hand and on deposit) is included among current assets only if it is available for current operations. Any cash that has been restricted for other purposes should be reported in the investments and funds section of the balance sheet. Cash is reported at its face amount.

Short-term investments are those that are readily marketable and that management *intends* to convert into cash within the next year or operating cycle, whichever is longer. Often they consist entirely of marketable securities such as stocks or bonds. Current accounting standards require these securities to be reported at fair value, as Chapter 10 explains.

Receivables represent claims to cash. Accounts receivable typically compose the largest dollar value of receivables. An estimated allowance for doubtful accounts should be deducted from the gross amount of accounts receivable so that the accounts are properly reported at their **net realizable value** (estimated amount collectible).

---

[23]*Accounting Trends & Techniques,* 1993, p. 127, indicates that in 1992, 178 of the 600 companies surveyed used the account form, 421 used the report form, and only 1 used the financial position form.

[24]*Accounting Research Bulletin No. 43,* "Restatement and Revision of Accounting Research Bulletins," 1953, Ch. 3, Sec. A, par. 4.

EXHIBIT 4–6

Sunrise Corporation
Balance Sheet
December 31, 1996

Assets

Current Assets

Cash		$ 22,500	
Marketable securities		40,000	
Accounts receivable	$ 55,000		
Less: Allowance for doubtful accounts	4,500	50,500	
Notes receivable		26,000	
Merchandise inventory (at lower of average cost or market)		35,000	
Prepaid expenses			
Supplies	5,350		
Insurance	4,650	10,000	
Total current assets			$184,000

Investments and Funds

Investment in Case Company common stock		41,800	
Land held for future plant site		55,000	
Plant expansion fund		48,700	
Total investments and funds			145,500

Property, Plant, and Equipment

Land		22,000	
Building	100,000		
Less: Accumulated depreciation	30,000	70,000	
Equipment	80,000		
Less: Accumulated depreciation	20,000	60,000	
Total property, plant, and equipment			152,000

Intangible Assets

Goodwill			38,500

Other Assets

Bond issue costs			8,000
Total assets			$528,000

Inventory in a merchandising company normally consists only of merchandise that is ready for sale to customers. On the other hand, the inventories of a manufacturing concern may consist of factory supplies, raw materials, work (goods) in process, and finished goods. Inventories are usually reported at the lower of cost or market value.

Prepaid expenses consist of such items as insurance, rent, advertising, taxes, and operating supplies. These items are not current assets in the sense that they will be converted into cash but rather in the sense that if they had not been paid for in advance, they would require the use of current assets during the next year or operating cycle. A prepaid expense is reported at the amount of its unexpired or unconsumed cost.

In practice, the distinction between current and noncurrent assets is sometimes hazy and is based in part on judgment, custom, and materiality. For example, a company that has a three-month operating cycle may report a two-year prepaid insurance policy as a current **Materiality** asset because the amount involved is immaterial. As another example, companies do not cus-

Liabilities and Stockholders' Equity

Current Liabilities

Accounts payable		$ 47,400	
Notes payable		12,000	
Interest payable		4,200	
Salaries payable		6,400	
Commissions payable		1,000	
Income tax payable		10,000	
Advances from customers		7,200	
Unearned rent revenue		4,800	
Total current liabilities			$ 93,000

Long-Term Liabilities

Bonds payable (10%, due Dec. 31, 2006)		150,000	
Less: Unamortized discount		6,000	144,000
Total liabilities			237,000

Stockholders' Equity

Paid-in capital			
Capital stock			
Preferred stock ($10 par, 8%, cumulative and nonparticipating, 10,000 shares authorized, 5,000 shares issued and outstanding)	$ 50,000		
Common stock ($5 par, 25,000 shares authorized, 20,000 shares issued and outstanding)	100,000	150,000	
Paid-in capital in excess of par		40,000	
Total paid-in capital			190,000
Retained earnings			101,000
Total stockholders' equity			291,000
Total liabilities and stockholders' equity			$528,000

tomarily report the following year's depreciation as a current asset, although a portion of plant assets will be consumed in the next year's operations.

Investments and Funds.   This category is used to report various types of investments and fund balances that management *intends* to hold for a period longer than the normal operating cycle or one year, whichever is longer, and that are *not* used in the business operations. Assets reported here need not be readily marketable. This category often is called **long-term investments,** or simply **investments.** Assets commonly included in this category are listed below:

1. Long-term investments in securities of other companies, such as stocks, bonds, and notes.
2. Investments in plant assets that are not currently used in operations, such as land held for a future plant site or for speculation.
3. Special fund balances accumulated for a particular purpose, such as future plant expansion.
4. Cash surrender value of life insurance policies.

The valuation basis used for assets in this category depends on the type of asset. For example, a special fund balance is normally reported at the amount accumulated in the fund; a long-term investment in bonds is usually reported at face value plus unamortized premium (or face value minus unamortized discount). Long-term stock investments may be reported at fair value or in accordance with the equity method of accounting, depending on the extent of ownership interest held. We discuss the valuation of investments and funds more fully in Chapter 10.

Property, Plant, and Equipment.   This section of the balance sheet reports assets that are tangible (have physical substance) and long lived and that are used in the business operations. **Plant assets** is a shorter title that refers to property, plant, and equipment. Examples of plant assets are business sites (the land on which the business is located), buildings, equipment, machinery, furniture, fixtures, tools, containers, and natural resources. Accountants ordinarily record depreciation or depletion on all plant assets except land.

Plant assets are reported on the balance sheet at their historical cost less any accumulated depreciation or depletion. The term **book value** (or **net book value**) refers to the difference between cost and accumulated depreciation or depletion.

Intangible Assets.   Intangible assets are long-lived resources that lack physical substance but convey valuable rights and privileges to the business. Examples include patents, copyrights, goodwill, trademarks, franchises, and organization costs. An accountant usually cannot measure the value of intangible assets with sufficient objectivity to report it in the balance sheet. Therefore, the accountant initially records an intangible asset at cost, based on a completed, arm's-length exchange transaction. The cost is then allocated in a systematic manner over the periods benefited through a process called **amortization.** The balance sheet valuation assigned to an intangible asset is therefore its cost less amortization taken to date. Companies rarely report accumulated amortization in a separate contra account.

Other Assets.   This category includes assets that do not fit conveniently into one of the other four categories. Ideally, accountants seldom use the other assets category because it is very general and because most assets can be classified in one of the other, more specific categories. Nevertheless, in practice, a wide variety of assets is reported as other assets.

Examples of other assets are machinery rearrangement costs, bond issue costs, long-term rental prepayments, and noncurrent deferred income tax assets. The valuation reported is usually the unallocated cost. Accountants sometimes use the term **deferred charges** (meaning simply **delayed debits**) to describe certain assets in this category. A deferred charge is essentially a long-term prepayment of an expense. Many accountants avoid this term because, technically speaking, buildings, patents, and similar assets classified elsewhere are also deferred charges.

Liabilities

Current Liabilities.   Current liabilities are "obligations whose liquidation is reasonably expected to require the use of existing resources properly classifiable as current assets or the creation of other current liabilities."[25] Notice that the definition of current liabilities is closely related to that of current assets. That is, if the satisfaction of a liability requires the use of existing current assets or the creation of other current liabilities, the liability is considered current for accounting purposes. Current liabilities include the following:[26]

1. Payables for items that have entered or relate directly to the operating cycle, such as accounts payable, wages payable, commissions payable, and income taxes payable.

[25]*Accounting Research Bulletin No. 43,* Ch. 3, Sec. A, par. 7.
[26]*Accounting Research Bulletin No. 43,* Ch 3, Sec. A, par. 7.

2. Collections received in advance of delivering goods or performing services, such as advances from customers for merchandise ordered or cash received for advance ticket sales.

3. Other obligations that will be liquidated through the use of current assets or the creation of other current liabilities within the next year or operating cycle, whichever is longer. Examples include short-term notes payable resulting from the purchase of equipment and the currently maturing portion of long-term debt.

Not all short-term obligations require the use of current assets or the creation of other current liabilities during the next year or operating cycle. For example, a bond issue that matures during the next year may be paid using cash accumulated in a sinking fund (classified in the Investments and Funds category), or a short-term note payable may be refinanced on a long-term basis. These obligations should be reported as long-term rather than as current liabilities. Current liabilities are normally listed in the order of their liquidation dates and are usually reported at the amount to be paid.

Working capital (sometimes called **net working capital**) is the difference between total current assets and total current liabilities. Working capital is an approximate measure of the net amount of a company's relatively liquid resources, and many creditors believe that it constitutes a margin of safety for paying short-term debts.[27] Companies without adequate working capital may be more likely than others to have liquidity problems.

Because many users of financial statements place emphasis on working capital and on the size of a company's **current ratio** (current assets *divided by* current liabilities), corporate managers have at times wanted to (incorrectly) report certain noncurrent assets as current and certain current liabilities as long term. Accountants and auditors must detect and request that management correct these errors before the financial statements are issued.

Long-Term Liabilities.   Long-term liabilities are obligations that will *not* require the use of current assets or the creation of other current liabilities within the next year or operating cycle, whichever is longer. In other words, this category comprises all liabilities other than those properly classified as current. Examples of long-term liabilities are bonds payable, long-term notes payable, deferred income taxes, long-term obligations under warranty contracts, obligations under capital leases, and pension obligations. Conceptually, a long-term liability should be measured on the date incurred at an amount equal to the present value of the expected future payments.

When bonds payable are reported, any premium associated with the bonds should be added to the face or maturity value; similarly, any discount should be subtracted. An obligation classified as long term sometimes requires the use of current assets or the creation of other current liabilities within the next year or operating cycle, whichever is longer. Such an obligation, along with any related premium or discount, should be reclassified as a current liability. An example is a five-year note payable that matures within the next year and will be paid using cash that is classified as a current asset.

Some companies use a **Deferred Credits** category to report certain long-term obligations, such as deferred income taxes and collections received in advance of performing services on a long-term basis. Deferred credits are simply delayed credits that will increase reported income in future periods.

Owners' Equity

Owners' equity is a measure of the owners' interests in the assets of a business. Traditionally, the accountant measures individual assets and liabilities directly. Owners' equity is simply a residual, indirect measurement whose value depends on the values assigned to assets and liabilities.

---

[27]For an interesting discussion of the limitations of the working capital concept, see Philip Fess, "The Working Capital Concept," *Accounting Review* (April 1966), pp. 266–270.

The three primary forms of business organization are sole proprietorships, partnerships, and corporations. In proprietorships and partnerships, owners' equity is usually summarized in a single capital account for each owner. The balance in a capital account summarizes the owner's investments and withdrawals as well as the owner's share of past net incomes and losses. The balance sheet of a proprietorship or partnership generally does not distinguish between amounts paid into the firm by owners and reinvested earnings, because state laws usually do not restrict the amount of withdrawals that a proprietor or partner can make. Creditors of proprietorships and partnerships are usually more interested in the personal financial conditions of the owners because, in the event of liquidation, owners may be held personally liable for business debts.

Corporations report owners' equity (usually called **stockholders'** or **shareholders' equity**) in two major categories: **Paid-In Capital** (often called **Contributed** or **Invested Capital**) and **Retained Earnings.** The use of these categories results in a stockholders' equity that is classified approximately according to *sources* of capital.

Historically, legal considerations have influenced the reporting of stockholders' equity. Because corporate stockholders cannot be held personally liable for company debts, state laws provide that corporations cannot distribute assets to stockholders if so doing would reduce owners' equity below a minimum amount known as **legal** or **stated capital.** The legal capital of a given company depends on the laws of the state in which it is organized.

Paid-In Capital.   This category is used to report amounts that stockholders have paid into the company in exchange for shares of stock. It may be divided further into capital stock and additional paid-in capital.

Capital stock includes both preferred and common stock. Here companies report the par or stated value per share multiplied by the number of shares issued. The total amount received is reported for stock that has no par or stated value. If a company has both preferred and common stock outstanding, it should report each type separately.

Paid-in capital in excess of par, or **additional paid-in capital,** represents amounts received in excess of the par or stated value of shares sold. Paid-in capital in excess of par may
Materiality   be presented as a single amount, but if several material sources of paid-in capital in excess of par exist, a breakdown by source may be helpful to financial statement users.

Retained Earnings.   Retained earnings, which represent a company's accumulated earnings less its dividends, are added to total paid-in capital when determining total stockholders' equity. A negative (debit) balance in retained earnings, called a **deficit,** occurs when a company's losses and dividends have exceeded its earnings. An accountant should simply deduct a deficit from total paid-in capital to arrive at total stockholders' equity.

The retained earnings category is sometimes divided into **appropriated** and **unappropriated** components. Companies may appropriate (or restrict) retained earnings for legal, contractual, or discretionary reasons. The amount appropriated is not available as a basis for declaring dividends during the time of appropriation. Companies usually disclose appropriations of retained earnings in the notes to their financial statements. Occasionally, however, a company may make a formal journal entry for the amount appropriated. This entry involves a debit to the Retained Earnings account and a credit to a Retained Earnings account appropriated for the designated purpose, such as future plant expansion. These kinds of entries ultimately produce balances in appropriated Retained Earnings accounts, such as Retained Earnings Appropriated for Future Plant Expansion or Retained Earnings Restricted by the Purchase of Treasury Stock. These accounts and their balances are reported as appropriated retained earnings.

When a company has created accounts for retained earnings appropriations, it reports the amount of its unappropriated retained earnings separate from the amounts appropriated. Unappropriated retained earnings are simply those available for declaring dividends.[28]

Companies sometimes purchase and hold shares of their own stock that they previously sold to investors. These shares constitute **treasury stock.** A company may acquire treasury stock for several reasons. For example, it may want to use the stock to satisfy employee stock option contracts or to effect a merger. Treasury stock is *not* an asset but a reduction in stockholders' equity. The vast majority of companies account for treasury stock at cost by debiting a treasury stock account for the cost of the shares purchased. The company later deducts the amount in the Treasury Stock account as the final account in the stockholders' equity section. Some companies account for treasury stock at par value; under this method, treasury stock is deducted in the capital stock subcategory of stockholders' equity. We explain the methods of treasury stock accounting in Chapter 16.

A complete set of financial statements includes a **statement of cash flows.**[29] The primary purpose of the statement of cash flows is to report information about a company's cash receipts and payments during a period. If used with the other basic financial statements, the statement of cash flows can help users to assess a company's ability to generate future net cash inflows, assess the company's ability to pay debts and dividends, evaluate the company's needs for external financing, assess the reasons for differences between income and related cash flows, and evaluate both the cash and noncash aspects of the company's investing and financing transactions during the period.

STATEMENT OF CASH FLOWS

Although the statement of cash flows provides considerable information about a company's current cash receipts and payments, the statement by itself does not provide a sound basis for making predictions about the company's future cash flows. Many current cash receipts result from decisions made in *past* periods (e.g., the decision made in an earlier period to invest in plant assets), and many current decisions involving cash payments are made to increase *future* cash receipts (e.g., the decision made in the current period to invest in plant assets). Thus, the statement of cash flows should be used with the other basic financial statements to help investors and creditors assess such important factors as an entity's liquidity, financial flexibility, profitability, and risk.

A statement of cash flows explains the change during the period in a company's cash. If a company invests in highly liquid short-term investments, such as U.S. Treasury bills, the statement should explain the change during the period in **cash and cash equivalents.**

The statement of cash flows is classified in *three major categories.*

1. **Investing activities** include lending money and collecting loans, acquiring and disposing of securities that are not cash equivalents, and acquiring and selling long-term productive assets.
   a. Investing activities that produce cash *inflows* include
      (1) Cash receipts from the collection (or sale) of loans made to other enterprises.
      (2) Cash receipts from the sale of assets such as investments in securities (other than cash equivalents) of other companies and property, plant, and equipment.
   b. Investing activities that produce cash *outflows* include
      (1) Cash outflows to make loans to other enterprises.
      (2) Cash payments to acquire assets such as investments in securities (other than cash equivalents) of other companies and property, plant, and equipment.

---

[28]A decision to declare dividends is, of course, influenced by many factors other than retained earnings.

[29]This section is based on *FASB Statement of Financial Accounting Standards No. 95,* "Statement of Cash Flows," 1987.

2. **Financing activities** include obtaining resources from owners and paying dividends, and obtaining resources from creditors and repaying the amounts borrowed.
   a. Financing activities that produce cash *inflows* include
      (1) Cash receipts from the issuance of debt securities (short-term or long-term).
      (2) Cash receipts from the issuance of equity securities.
   b. Financing activities that produce cash *outflows* include
      (1) Repayments of amounts borrowed.
      (2) Cash payments of dividends.
      (3) Cash payments to repurchase the company's own stock (treasury stock).
3. **Operating activities** include all transactions that are not properly classified as investing or financing activities. Operating activities include producing and selling goods and providing services. Generally, the cash flows from operating activities represent the cash effects of transactions that are reflected in income.
   a. Operating activities that produce cash *inflows* include
      (1) Cash receipts from the sale of goods or services to customers.
      (2) Cash receipts from interest, dividends, and other sources that do not represent investing or financing activities.
   b. Operating activities that produce cash *outflows* include
      (1) Cash payments for the acquisition of inventory.
      (2) Cash payments to employees and other suppliers of goods and services.
      (3) Cash payments for taxes.
      (4) Cash payments for interest.
      (5) Cash payments for other purposes that do not represent investing or financing activities.

Classification according to the three categories described above allows investors and creditors to assess significant relationships within and among a company's major activities: its operating, investing, and financing activities. The classification system provides useful information by linking cash flows that are often considered to be related, such as cash inflows from borrowing money and cash outflows to repay loans. An empirical study has confirmed that the three categories in the statement of cash flows have information content in that the stock market reacts to the information in a manner that economic theory predicts.[30]

Exhibit 4–7 shows the statement of cash flows for Sunrise Corporation. Preparation of such a statement requires comparative balance sheets as well as information that explains changes in the account balances during the period. We have *not included* all this information here, because at this point in your study, you should concentrate on the basic form of the statement and the general types of information it conveys. You cannot "verify" all the numbers in Exhibit 4–7, but that is not our purpose at this time. *After studying Chapter 4, you should have an introductory understanding of the nature and purpose of the statement of cash flows. In Chapter 22, we discuss the statement in detail and explain how to prepare it.*

As Exhibit 4–7 shows, the statement begins with cash flows from operating activities. Remember that operating activities encompass all transactions that are not properly classified as investing or financing activities. Net cash flow from operating activities does *not* include cash flows from certain transactions that are reflected in income but that are investing or financing activities. For example, Sunrise had an unusual loss on the sale of long-term investments during 1996 (as shown in Exhibit 4–1). The sale of long-term investments is really an investing activity, and, accordingly, the loss is reflected in the calculation of the proceeds from the sale of long-term investments ($10,900).

Net cash flow from operating activities should be prominently disclosed, because users of financial statements generally are interested in evaluating the ability of a company to generate cash through its operations. Some companies can generate net income but not much cash. Over the long run, a business ordinarily must generate cash through its own operations if it is to survive. A company cannot simply depend on raising cash through such means as

---

[30]J. Livnat and P. Zarowin, "The Incremental Information Content of Cash-Flow Components," *Journal of Accounting and Economics* (May 1990), pp. 25–46.

EXHIBIT 4–7

Sunrise Corporation
Statement of Cash Flows
For the Year Ended December 31, 1996

Cash Flows from Operating Activities		
Cash received from customers	$538,700	
Interest received	2,100	
Dividends received	5,200	
Rent received	8,400	
Cash provided by operating activities		$554,400
Cash paid to suppliers and employees	455,900	
Interest paid	14,200	
Taxes paid	47,300	
Cash disbursed for operating activities		517,400
Net cash flow from operating activities		37,000
Cash Flows from Investing Activities		
Short-term loans made	(18,000)	
Collections on short-term loans	8,000	
Purchases of long-term investments	(14,000)	
Proceeds from sale of long-term investments	10,900	
Purchases of property, plant, and equipment	(38,800)	
Proceeds from disposals of property, plant, and equipment	76,400	
Net cash provided by investing activities		24,500
Cash Flows from Financing Activities		
Proceeds of short-term debt	23,000	
Payments to settle short-term debt	(25,000)	
Proceeds of long-term debt	50,000	
Payments to settle long-term debt	(110,000)	
Proceeds from issuing common stock	55,000	
Dividends paid	(16,000)	
Net cash used by financing activities		(23,000)
Net increase in cash and cash equivalents		38,500
Cash and cash equivalents, Jan. 1, 1996		24,000
Cash and cash equivalents, Dec. 31, 1996		$ 62,500

borrowing or selling plant assets. In Exhibit 4–7 we see that Sunrise generated a positive net cash flow of $37,000 as a result of its operating activities during 1996.

Cash flows from investing activities are reported in the next category shown in Exhibit 4–7. Observe how the cash outflows associated with each of the investing activities are deducted from related cash inflows. The statement shows that Sunrise generated $24,500 from its investing activities during 1996, primarily from disposing of certain plant assets.

Cash flows from financing activities are also reported by subtracting cash outflows from related cash inflows, as shown in Exhibit 4–7. The statement shows that Sunrise's major financing activities during 1996 were the issuance of common stock and the settlement of a long-term note payable, thereby increasing the extent to which the firm relies on owner financing. Unlike the operating and investing activities, which *provided* cash during 1996, Sunrise's financing activities *used* cash of $23,000.

Taken together, Sunrise's operating, investing, and financing activities resulted in a net increase in cash and cash equivalents of $38,500. The term *cash and cash equivalents* (as opposed to *cash*) is used near the bottom of the statement because Sunrise has marketable securities. These short-term, highly liquid investments are considered to be part of the company's cash management program rather than a part of its operating, investing, or financing activities. Let us now *assume* that Sunrise had cash and cash equivalents of $24,000 at the beginning of 1996. If we add $24,000 to the $38,500 net increase in cash and cash equivalents, we find that Sunrise has cash and cash equivalents of $62,500 at the end of 1996.

Many other issues affect the form and content of the statement of cash flows. For example, when a company reports net cash flow from operating activities in the manner shown in Exhibit 4–7, a reconciliation of net income and net cash flow from operating activities must be provided in a separate schedule. This schedule is explained in Chapter 22.

RELATIONSHIP BETWEEN BASIC FINANCIAL STATEMENTS

As we have stated earlier, the basic financial statements **articulate** with each other. Their relationship is summarized in simplified terms in Exhibit 4–8.

A company's financial position at a particular moment in time is shown on the balance sheet. The other basic financial statements summarize various types of changes in financial position that have occurred during a period of time. The income statement explains the changes in financial position that are the result of earnings activities. The statement of retained earnings (or statement of stockholders' equity) explains certain changes in the equity component of financial position. Finally, the statement of cash flows summarizes all important cash receipts and payments during a period.

The income statement reports the revenues, expenses, gains, losses, and net income for a period. The net income explains a part of the change in retained earnings that is shown on the statement of retained earnings (or statement of stockholders' equity). The statement of cash flows summarizes the major cash-related activities that have occurred during the period. The income statement, statement of retained earnings (or statement of stockholders' equity), and statement of cash flows are tied together by the beginning and ending balance sheets. All of the basic financial statements articulate with each other because of the double entry system of accounting and because revenues, expenses, gains, losses, investments by owners, and distributions to owners represent flows associated with the economic resources and obligations presented on the balance sheet.

Articulation is an important financial statement concept to understand. A company's computation of depreciation on its plant assets, for example, affects not only the income statement (depreciation expense) but also the balance sheet (accumulated depreciation). Most people believe that articulation is desirable because it accurately reflects the nature of a company's economic activities. Benefits usually require sacrifices, and sacrifices usually produce benefits. Double entry accrual accounting, which we review in the next chapter, ensures that financial statements prepared according to GAAP will articulate.

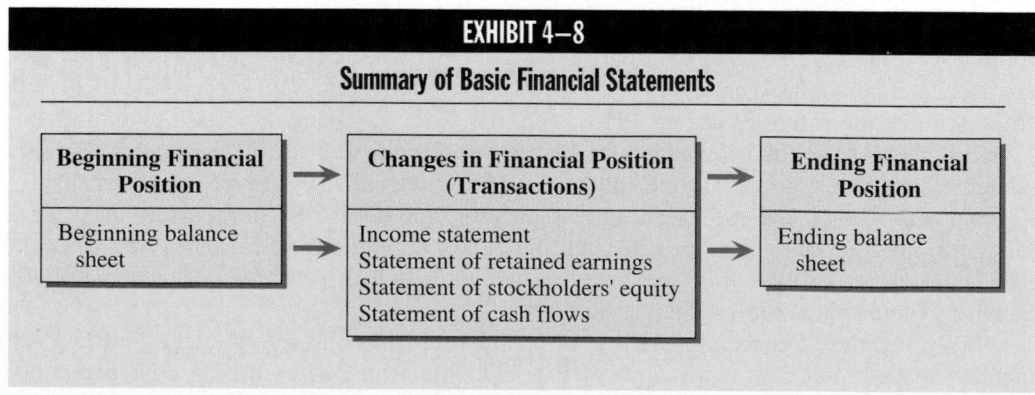

EXHIBIT 4–8

Summary of Basic Financial Statements

Beginning Financial Position	Changes in Financial Position (Transactions)	Ending Financial Position
Beginning balance sheet	Income statement Statement of retained earnings Statement of stockholders' equity Statement of cash flows	Ending balance sheet

A *minority* view holds that financial statements could be improved if articulation were not required. Proponents of this view believe that articulation is an unnecessary constraint that limits the usefulness of financial statements. To illustrate this view, most people believe that LIFO inventory costing is generally desirable for the income statement (because cost of goods sold is measured at recent cost prices) but undesirable for the balance sheet (because inventory is measured at outdated historical costs). In contrast, FIFO is generally viewed as desirable for the balance sheet but undesirable for the income statement. A proponent of non-articulated financial statements might argue that a company should be allowed to use LIFO on its income statement and FIFO on its balance sheet. Moreover, there is no need for the two statements to articulate. We emphasize that nonarticulated financial statements, although interesting, are *not* generally accepted today.

The **disclosure principle** requires an accountant to report information that might affect the decisions made by reasonably informed users of financial statements. To comply with this principle, an accountant usually must report in financial statements considerably more information than we have illustrated thus far in the chapter. Moreover, all of this information must be effectively communicated. In the remaining sections of this chapter, we shall discuss several other topics pertaining to basic financial statements.

To help you understand the kinds of information that companies actually report, we have included a set of financial statements of Kellogg Company in the endpapers of this book. Look over these statements now and refer to them frequently as you study the remaining chapters. Although the statements contain material that you have not yet encountered, you will understand them much better after you have studied this book.

OTHER FINANCIAL STATEMENT TOPICS

Disclosure

NOTES TO FINANCIAL STATEMENTS

As illustrated earlier, financial statements are summaries that consist of very few words and dollar amounts. **Notes to financial statements** (often called **footnotes**) report information that does not fit in the body of the statements without reducing the understandability of the statements. *Notes are an integral part of the financial statements and therefore must be prepared and read carefully.* The notes often require several pages.

Five major types of information are commonly disclosed in notes:

1. Information on **accounting policies.** As discussed below, a company must disclose the major accounting policies that it uses in preparing its financial statements.
2. Information on **subsequent events.** As discussed below, companies are required to disclose certain types of events that occur between the date shown on the balance sheet and the date on which the financial statements are issued.
3. Information on **contingencies.** Companies often disclose certain contingencies, which are events, such as pending lawsuits, involving uncertainty about possible gain or loss that will be resolved in the future. We discuss accounting for contingencies in Chapter 14.
4. Information on major **contracts, commitments,** and **restrictions.** Important details about leases and pension plans, for example, usually are reported in the notes.
5. Information that **amplifies data** presented in the body of the statements. For example, a company may provide a schedule that separates its inventories into raw materials, work in process, and finished goods.

Notes to financial statements should be concise, complete, and easily understood by a reader who has a reasonable understanding of business affairs and is willing to study the financial statements. The precise nature of disclosures required in notes is highly detailed. We discuss these disclosures more fully at appropriate places in most of the remaining chapters.

SUMMARY OF ACCOUNTING POLICIES

Knowledgeable users of financial statements recognize that the numbers reported in a company's financial statements depend on the accounting policies used to generate them. As a result, when analyzing a company's financial statements, users typically want answers to questions such as: What inventory cost determination method (such as FIFO, LIFO, or average cost) does the company use? What depreciation method (such as double declining balance, sum-of-the-years' digits, or straight line) does the company use?

To ensure that users have the information needed to answer these kinds of questions, *APB Opinion No. 22* requires a company to disclose the accounting policies that it uses. The term **accounting policies** refers to the specific principles and methods that a company has adopted for preparing its financial statements. The accounting policies that a company discloses should be those that (1) involve a selection from existing acceptable alternatives, (2) are peculiar to the reporting company's industry, or (3) are unusual or innovative applications of generally accepted accounting principles.[31]

A company should preferably disclose its accounting policies in a separate **summary of significant accounting policies.** This summary should precede the notes to the financial statements or appear as the first note.[32]

SUBSEQUENT EVENTS

Financial statements seldom are issued on the date shown on the balance sheet. Instead, a period of time usually elapses during which the accountants and auditors complete their work on the statements. During this period, called the **subsequent period,** many important
Materiality events can occur that have a material effect on the financial statements being prepared.

Subsequent events are events that occur during the subsequent period, that is, between the date shown on the balance sheet and the date on which the financial statements are issued. Exhibit 4–9 illustrates the subsequent period, during which subsequent events may occur, in relation to a set of 1996 financial statements. The subsequent period is January 1, 1997, to February 28, 1997.

There are two types of subsequent events. The first type consists of events that provide additional evidence about *conditions that existed on the balance sheet date* and that affect the estimates used in preparing the financial statements. The appropriate accounting for this type of subsequent event is to adjust the account balances reported in the financial statements

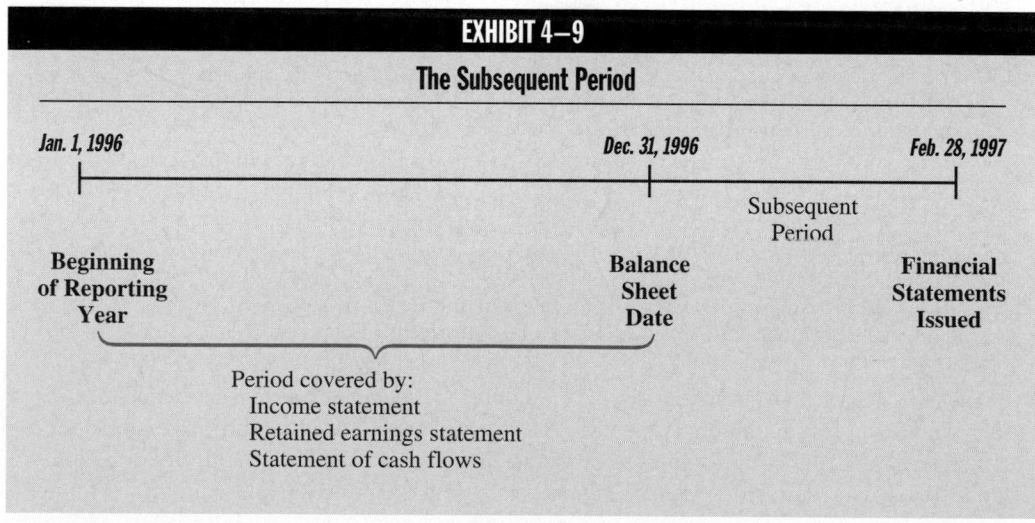

EXHIBIT 4–9

The Subsequent Period

Jan. 1, 1996   *Dec. 31, 1996*   *Feb. 28, 1997*

                                                                                Subsequent
                                                                                Period

Beginning   **Balance**   **Financial**
of Reporting   **Sheet**   **Statements**
Year   **Date**   **Issued**

Period covered by:
   Income statement
   Retained earnings statement
   Statement of cash flows

---

[31]*APB Opinion No. 22,* "Disclosure of Accounting Policies," 1972, par. 12.
[32]*APB Opinion No. 22, par. 15.*

AS IBM'S WOES GREW, ITS ACCOUNTING TACTICS GOT LESS CONSERVATIVE

To all outward appearances, International Business Machines Corp. ran into trouble with startling speed.

Even its harshest critics have been stunned by its nearly $5 billion of losses last year, its first layoffs in half a century and an unprecedented purge of top executives. Its stock has lost more than $70 billion in market value since it peaked in 1987. And the crisis has sparked a once-unthinkable move: IBM turned to an outsider, Louis V. Gerstner, to rescue it.

Now, considerable evidence suggests that IBM may have helped delay its day of reckoning with some surprisingly aggressive accounting moves. The moves didn't violate any laws or cause the company's fundamental business problems. Some, though not all, of the moves were fully disclosed to the public.

But some finance experts say that just as IBM's business started to sour, its accounting became markedly less conservative. "Since the mid-1980s, IBM has been borrowing from the future to bolster today's profits," says Thornton O'glove, a frequently critical San Francisco accounting expert and former publisher of the *Quality of Earnings* newsletter.

Booking Sales Quickly

Although IBM doesn't dispute any of the facts about the accounting changes, it takes strong issue with the conclusion by some experts that it was stretching to make its numbers look better, while pushing possible bad news into the future.

The evidence of the aggressive accounting comes on several fronts:

- IBM's former chief outside auditor, Price Waterhouse's Donald Chandler, wrote IBM a blistering 20-point memo in November 1988 suggesting that the company was reporting revenue that it might never get. For example, he criticized IBM for booking revenue when its products were shipped to dealers who could return them and sometimes even to its own warehouses—a far more aggressive approach than many companies take.
- For more than 10 years, IBM has quietly turned to Merrill Lynch & Co. and others to execute a rare financial maneuver that propped up the results of IBM's big leasing business. The maneuver allowed IBM to book immediately all the revenue from a long-term computer lease—even though the actual dollars would flow in only over the life of the lease. That didn't break any accounting rules, but some accountants term it an end-run that most blue-chip companies would avoid. Mr. Chandler called the revenue booster "troubling indeed" and urged IBM to take "immediate action" to use the maneuver less—advice that IBM ignored.
- Footnotes in IBM's annual reports disclose that, in 1984, it adopted more liberal accounting for its huge investments in equipment and for its retirement plan. The changes—a bit like removing a car's shock absorbers—enabled IBM to push the cost of its investments into the future. While

similar to moves at many other companies, they may have increased IBM's profits more than many investors realize. Although IBM disclosed details of the changes, it never said how much they lifted earnings—and still refuses to do so.

Policies Defended

IBM strongly defends all its accounting moves and says all the changes were made for prudent business reasons. In a 22-page response to questions, it writes: "When our accounting policies and practices are compared with others in our industry or other major corporations, they cannot be shown, even with perfect hindsight, to be other than thoughtful and prudent."

IBM calls the Chandler memo part of the normal give-and-take between a company and an auditor with a flair for peppery language. The company says it improved its procedures in response to some of his concerns but hasn't changed its general accounting philosophy and many of the practices at issue.

Mr. Chandler, who retired last year, at first declined to comment when reached at home. Later, in a statement released by IBM, he said his work with the company was "totally open and frank." Of his specific criticisms, he cautioned, "It's absolutely vital that they not be taken out of context." He said every "significant" matter he raised was "satisfactorily resolved" and noted that he consistently blessed IBM's financial statements with clean audit opinions.

Questions about IBM's accounting could be awkward for the wounded computer giant. IBM long enjoyed a reputation as the epitome of financial conservatism, with triple-A-rated debt and the bluest of blue-chip stocks. A pioneer in mandating rigorous workplace ethics, IBM requires all employees to swear that they have read a 28-page "Business Conduct Guidelines" manual that warns them against "not only reporting information inaccurately, but also organizing it in a way that is intended to mislead or misinform."

Over the past eight years, IBM has openly discussed its business troubles—but always with an upbeat tone and never foreshadowing the full dimensions of last year's staggering loss. Meanwhile, in the late 1980s, IBM's executives got enormous raises and bonuses, partly pegged to its earnings, and sanguine investors loaded up on its stock. The stock is languishing at $52 a share, down from a 52-week high of $100 and a 1987 peak of $175 a share.

SOURCE: Michael W. Miller and Lee Burton, "As IBM's Woes Grew, Its Accounting Tactics Got Less Conservative," *The Wall Street Journal* (April 7, 1993), pp. A1, A8. Reprinted by permission of The Wall Street Jounral, © 1993, Dow Jones & Company, Inc. All Rights Reserved Worldwide.

to reflect the new information. For example, the bankruptcy of a major customer 10 days after the balance sheet date usually reflects a condition (namely, the poor financial health of the customer) that existed on the balance sheet date, and the estimate of bad debts may therefore need to be revised upward to reflect the new information.

The second type of subsequent event provides evidence about *conditions that arose after the balance sheet date.* Events of this type do not result in adjustments of the account balances of the previous period. They may, however, require disclosure to prevent the financial statements from being misleading. Examples of subsequent events that require disclosure are the purchase of a business, the loss of inventories or plant assets due to a casualty, and the sale of a bond or capital stock issue.[33]

Obviously, a subsequent event also affects the financial statements of the period in which the event occurs. For example, in the context of Exhibit 4–9, a material sale of common stock that occurred on January 10, 1997, should be disclosed in the notes to the 1996 financial statements and recorded as a transaction of 1997. A more thorough treatment of subsequent events usually appears in auditing texts.

COMPARATIVE FINANCIAL STATEMENTS

The financial statements illustrated in this chapter were prepared for one period only. In practice, **comparative financial statements** are ordinarily presented for two or more periods, as shown in the financial statements in the endpapers of this book. Such statements are more useful than single-period statements because they reveal important trends. When comparative financial statements are presented, all elements reported in the current period's statements should be comparable to those reported for the prior period(s). Any exceptions must be clearly explained.

ROUNDING OF AMOUNTS

The dollar amounts in financial statements are usually rounded. A recent survey of the annual reports of 600 companies found that 45 rounded to the nearest dollar, 390 rounded to the nearest thousand dollars, and 165 rounded to the nearest million dollars.[34] Rounding is justified because of materiality and the many estimates in financial statements. Failure to round may imply a degree of precision that simply does not exist in financial statements.

Materiality

DISCLOSURE METHODS

Accountants use several methods of disclosure. Generally, the most important information is disclosed in the **body of the financial statements.** In addition to the account titles and amounts, **parenthetical disclosures** may be made in the body of the statements. For example, the interest rate and due date of bonds payable may be shown in parentheses on the balance sheet. Or a related asset and liability, such as inventory pledged as collateral on a note payable, may be cross-referenced by a parenthetical remark beside the respective title.

Notes to the financial statements are used to report details that simply do not fit conveniently in the body of the statements. In addition, accountants often use schedules (presented alone or as part of the notes) to report such information as major inventory categories and operating expense details. The use of such schedules is particularly appropriate when a company prepares condensed financial statements. At certain times, accountants may use **supplementary statements** effectively. Such statements may be used, for example, to present financial statements that have been adjusted for inflation.

---

[33]*Statement on Auditing Standards No. 1,* "Codification of Auditing Standards and Procedures" (New York: AICPA, 1972), Sec. 560, par. .06.

[34]*Accounting Trends & Techniques,* 1993, p. 32.

Future research in this area will likely study the effects of **graphic presentations** (e.g., line graphs, bar charts, pie charts) versus the more traditional tabular presentations of accounting information. The results of one such study suggest that no one form of presentation is best in all situations.[35]

AMOUNT OF DISCLOSURE

An elusive problem that the accountant faces when preparing financial statements is deciding on an appropriate **amount (extent) of disclosure.** Accountants want to prepare financial statements that are reasonably complete, yet understandable. Clearly, to achieve understandability, an accountant must summarize many details. The question is: To what extent can the accountant summarize and still present statements that are sufficiently complete and therefore in compliance with the disclosure principle?

Deciding on an appropriate amount of disclosure in a given case depends on such related factors as the objectives of the statements, GAAP, the circumstances involved, the modifying convention of materiality, and professional judgment. Statements prepared for bankers, for example, often are fairly detailed to satisfy the bankers' needs. Those prepared for publication in annual reports to shareholders often are highly condensed.

As a general principle, the **offsetting** of assets and liabilities in the balance sheet is improper except when a specific legal right of offset exists. For example, cash in a bond sinking fund should not be offset against the bond liability, even though the company intends to use the cash to pay the bonds.

As another general principle, material **related-party transactions** should be disclosed. Examples are loans made by the company to its management or to a subsidiary.

Disclosure

Materiality

TERMINOLOGY

The language of accounting is technical, consisting of some words whose meanings differ from their everyday connotations. To communicate effectively, accountants must select words and phrases that the average user of financial statements can understand.

There is no requirement that the financial statements contain the same account titles that appear in the general ledger. For example, *accounts receivable* in the general ledger is sometimes reported on the balance sheet as *amounts due from customers.*

The accounting profession has been very concerned with improving the terminology used in financial statements. *Accounting Terminology Bulletin No. 1,* for example, noted that accountants have used the term *reserve* to describe asset contra accounts, liability accounts, retained earnings appropriations, and loss accounts. To avoid confusion, the bulletin recommended that the use of *reserve* be limited to retained earnings appropriations. The bulletin further recommended that accountants stop using the term *surplus* because it may mislead users by connoting an amount in excess of that needed. Accountants should use *paid-in capital* or *contributed capital* instead of *paid-in surplus* or *capital surplus.* Likewise, the use of *retained earnings* is preferable to *earned surplus.*[36]

One reason that we mention these terminology recommendations is that the terms *not* recommended are still sometimes encountered in practice. We emphasize the use of modern, preferred terminology throughout the textbook. Remember that financial statements will not be useful if they do not communicate effectively.

AUDITOR'S REPORT

As explained in Chapter 1, financial statements often are accompanied by an independent auditor's report. Financial statements contain the representations of management. The

---

[35]Larry R. Davis, "Report Format and the Decision Maker's Task: An Experimental Investigation," *Accounting, Organizations and Society,* Vol. 14, No. 5/6, 1989, pp. 495–508.

[36]*Accounting Terminology Bulletin No. 1,* "Review and Résumé," 1953, pars. 57–70.

functions of an independent auditor are to *examine the statements* and *express an opinion* that lends credibility to management's representations. This enables users to have greater confidence in the statements. Exhibit 1–1 (Chapter 1) illustrates the wording of a standard audit report in which an unqualified opinion was given on the financial statements.

PROFESSIONAL JUDGMENT

Accountants must use professional judgment when preparing financial statements. They must help to provide answers to the following kinds of questions: Should raw materials, work-in-process, and finished goods inventories be reported separately on the balance sheet, or should they be combined into a single amount to report as inventories? If a company maintains 80 general ledger accounts for various expenses, how should it combine these accounts on an income statement to avoid reporting excessive details? If a company has accounts receivable, what should be the balance in the allowance for doubtful accounts? What is the likelihood that a company will lose a significant lawsuit that has been filed against it? What is a reasonable rate of return to assume that a company will earn on the assets in its pension fund? Generally accepted accounting principles do not answer all questions that arise during an accountant's work.

Used together, the four basic financial statements help users to predict cash flows to the enterprise and to assess their own chances of receiving cash. When presented with a challenging judgmental issue, an accountant should remember that a major objective of financial reporting is to provide information that helps users to predict cash flows (see Chapter 2). So if a company has 80 general ledger accounts for various expenses, the optimal level of detail to report is that which is most helpful to users for the purpose of predicting future cash flows. Although making this determination is quite challenging, the "predicting future cash flows" objective at least provides a framework that can be helpful when accountants make professional judgments.

The financial statements discussed in this chapter are directly related to the model of financial accounting theory that we explained in Chapter 2 (see Exhibit 2–1). You may wish to review Exhibit 2–1 now and consider the following important points:

1. Financial statements help to accomplish the *objectives* of financial reporting, which are to provide useful information, to provide information helpful in assessing cash flow prospects, and to provide information about enterprise resources, claims to those resources, and changes in them.

2. Financial statements seek to provide information that is both relevant and reliable. Recall that relevance and reliability are the primary *qualitative characteristics* of useful accounting information.

3. Financial statements reflect the *assumptions of* economic entity (the entity identified at the top of the financial statements), periodicity (annual periods, quarterly periods, etc.), and going concern.

4. The *concepts* of financial position and changes in financial position are reflected in financial statements. Assets, liabilities, and owners' equity are the *elements* that compose financial position, while revenues, expenses, gains, losses, income, investments by owners, and distributions to owners are the major *elements* that compose changes in financial position.

5. The *broad principles* of monetary unit, asset/liability measurement, revenue realization, matching, consistency, and disclosure are all reflected in financial statements.

6. Financial statements also reflect numerous *detailed principles* that we will cover throughout the textbook.

7. The *modifying conventions* of materiality, industry practices, conservatism, and substance over form also affect financial statements.

CONCLUDING REMARKS

Financial statements are the culmination of an accountant's work. They constitute the *output* of the accounting information system and serve as *input* for investment, credit, and similar decisions that help to determine how resources are allocated in our society.

Financial statements are summaries that are primarily historical. They are interrelated and general purpose, and they reflect many estimates. Underlying the information reported in financial statements are many important measurement and disclosure principles that we discuss throughout the textbook.

All financial statements bear the name of the reporting entity, the title of the statement, and the date or period of time covered. The balance sheet presents financial position at a particular point in time; the other basic statements present various changes in financial position during a period of time.

The financial statements discussed in this chapter are currently reported under generally accepted accounting principles. To help ensure that companies provide financial statements regularly, accountants follow certain steps during an accounting period. These steps, collectively called the *accounting cycle,* are presented in the next chapter.

KEY POINTS

1. The basic financial statements are the balance sheet, the income statement, the statement of cash flows, and the statement of retained earnings (or statement of stockholders' equity). (Objective 1)
2. Basic financial statements have several important characteristics:
   a. They are only a subset of the information needed by users for making rational investment, lending, and similar decisions.
   b. They are primarily historical in nature.
   c. They summarize information.
   d. They reflect many estimates.
   e. They are general-purpose reports designed to serve the needs of many different users.
   f. They articulate with one another. (Objective 1)
3. Extraordinary gains and losses result from events or transactions that are unusual in nature *and* not expected to recur in the foreseeable future. (Objective 2)
4. A multiple-step income statement presents subtotals for gross margin and operating income; a single-step income statement does not. (Objective 2)
5. Prior period adjustments, such as the correction of an error made in the financial statements of a prior period, should be charged or credited directly to retained earnings. (Objective 3)
6. The major balance sheet categories are
   a. Assets
      Current assets
      Investments and funds
      Property, plant, and equipment
      Intangible assets
      Other assets
   b. Liabilities
      Current liabilities
      Long-term liabilities
   c. Owners' equity
      Paid-in capital
         Capital stock
            Preferred stock
            Common stock
         Paid-in capital in excess of par
      Retained earnings (Objective 4)
7. The statement of cash flows provides information about the cash receipts and cash payments of an entity during a period. (Objective 5)
8. Notes (footnotes) are an integral part of the basic financial statements. (Objective 6)
9. The role of an independent auditor is to examine financial statements and express an opinion on them. (Objective 6)

QUESTIONS

4–1 What are the basic financial statements?

4–2 How do financial statements relate to the need of users to predict the amount and timing of net cash inflows they will receive as a result of their investment or credit decisions?

4–3 What are some important characteristics of the basic financial statements?

4–4 What are the criteria used to determine whether a gain or loss is extraordinary?

4–5 Why does the accounting profession require that extraordinary gains and losses be presented in a special section of the income statement?

4–6 What are three examples of an extraordinary item? (Do not use the examples presented in the chapter.)

4–7 May gains and losses from disposal of a business segment and from changes in accounting principles be included in the extraordinary items category? Explain your answer.

4–8 How does a multiple-step differ from a single-step income statement?

4–9 What are the advantages of using a multiple-step format for presenting the income statement? What are the advantages of using a single-step format?

4–10 What does the term *prior period adjustments* mean? How should prior period adjustments be reported in the financial statements?

4–11 Suppose that in 1996 a company changes its estimate of the *total* useful life of its 12-year-old building from 30 years to 40 years. For accounting purposes, what kind of event is this, and how should it be accounted for?

4–12 What does the term *current assets* mean? Cite five examples of current assets.

4–13 Why are special fund balances and the cash surrender value of life insurance not usually reported among the current assets?

4–14 What does the term *current liabilities* mean? Cite five examples of current liabilities.

4–15 What do the terms *working capital* and *current ratio* mean?

4–16 What are the various categories that may be used in the stockholders' equity section of the balance sheet?

4–17 What is treasury stock? Is it an asset? Explain your answer.

4–18 What are the major categories of a statement of cash flows? Briefly describe them.

4–19 How do a cash basis income statement, a statement of cash receipts and disbursements, and a statement of cash flows differ? Which one is required by GAAP?

4–20 Why are the notes to the financial statements important to users?

4–21 What does the term *subsequent events* mean? Indicate the two types (i.e., categories) of subsequent events and the appropriate accounting treatment for each type in the financial statements of the period preceding the subsequent event.

4–22 What factors should affect an accountant's decision about how detailed a given set of financial statements should be?

4–23 Why is terminology considered an important aspect of accounting?

4–24 What are the roles of management and the independent auditor in relation to a set of financial statements?

EXERCISES

4–25 Cost of Goods Sold   The following information pertains to Lin, Inc., for the 1996 accounting period:

Transportation out	$ 9,500	Transportation in	$ 7,100
Purchases	160,000	Sales discounts	5,200
Sales returns	11,200	Purchase returns	6,000
Inventory, Dec. 31	25,800	Purchase discounts	3,000
Purchase allowances	2,300	Advertising	28,000
Sales	290,000	Sales allowances	3,600
Inventory, Jan. 1	40,000		

INSTRUCTIONS

[a] Prepare the Cost of Goods Sold section of Lin, Inc.'s income statement for 1996.
[b] Compute the gross margin for 1996.
[c] Indicate how the accounts not used in [a] and [b] should be classified in the income statement for 1996.

4–26 Income Statement Formats   The following information pertains to the 1996 accounting period of Jones Company:

Cost of goods sold	$170,000
Dividend revenue	6,000
General and administrative expenses	21,000
Interest expense	5,000
Interest revenue	9,000
Net sales	290,000
Selling expenses	29,000
Income tax rate	40%
Number of common shares outstanding	10,000

INSTRUCTIONS

[a] Prepare a multiple-step income statement for 1996.
[b] Prepare a single-step income statement for 1996.

4–27 Income Statement Sections   Rio Company has been manufacturing and selling computers, household appliances, and medical supplies since 1984. The following events occurred during the company's 1996 accounting period:

[1] The company sold its computer division.
[2] The company lost one of its manufacturing plants because of an earthquake.
[3] The company lost its inventory held in a Middle Eastern country because of a government expropriation.
[4] The company sold its household appliance division.
[5] The company adopted the FIFO method of inventory cost determination. Prior to 1996, the company used the average cost method.
[6] The company adopted the straight-line method of accounting for all depreciable assets. Prior to 1996, the company used the double-declining balance method.

INSTRUCTIONS

Assume that each of the above events is material and qualifies for reporting in one of the following income statement sections: (1) discontinued operations, (2) extraordinary items, and (3) cumulative effect of a change in accounting principles. In what section should each event be reported?

4–28 Retained Earnings Statement   At the beginning of its 1996 calendar-year accounting period, Totten, Inc., had retained earnings of $83,000. During 1996 the company earned a net income of $51,000 and declared cash dividends of $25,000 on its common stock. None of these dividends had been paid as of year-end. In addition, the company discovered that because of a mathematical error, depreciation expense had been overstated by $10,000 in 1995.

The company's income tax rate was 40% in 1995 and 1996. The company had 5,000 shares of common stock outstanding throughout 1996.

INSTRUCTIONS

Prepare a statement of retained earnings for Totten for 1996.

4–29 Combined Statement of Income and Retained Earnings   The following information pertains to the 1996 calendar-year accounting period of Nellis Corporation:

Number of common shares outstanding throughout the year	10,000
Cost of goods sold	$161,200
Dividends declared	50,000
Loss from earthquake (extraordinary item)	20,000
General and administrative expenses	41,000
Loss due to write-off of worthless equipment (unusual item)	17,000
Net sales	468,000
Selling expenses	48,800

ADDITIONAL INFORMATION

Nellis Corporation reported retained earnings of $167,000 on December 31, 1995. During 1996 the company discovered that because of a material counting error, ending inventory for 1995 had been overstated by $16,000. The company's income tax rate was 40% in 1995 and 1996.

INSTRUCTIONS

Prepare a combined statement of income and retained earnings for Nellis Corporation for 1996. Use the single-step format.

4–30 Working Capital   The following information pertains to Maltais Company on December 31 of the current year:

Equipment	$240,000
Accumulated depreciation—equipment	40,000
Accounts receivable	27,000
Prepaid insurance	3,000
Short-term notes payable	12,000
Cash	30,000
Bonds payable maturing in 20 years	110,000
Total assets	358,000
Land	50,000
Accounts payable	30,000
Allowance for doubtful accounts	2,000
Merchandise inventory	34,000
Short-term investments	16,000
Wages payable	4,000
Total liabilities	171,000
Premium on bonds payable	15,000

INSTRUCTIONS

Compute Maltais Company's working capital on December 31. Show all of your work clearly.

4–31 Property, Plant, and Equipment and Long-Term Liabilities   Listed below are some of the account balances of Oakley Oil Company on December 31, 1996, the end of the company's annual accounting period:

Land held for future building site	$ 63,000
Oil deposit	800,000
Term bonds payable (10%, due June 30, 2007)	400,000
Accumulated depreciation—equipment	180,000
Building	250,000
Land on which building is located	110,000
Notes payable (12%, due Apr. 30, 2001)	100,000
Equipment	360,000
Accumulated depletion of oil deposit	150,000
Notes payable (10%, due Aug. 31, 1997)	30,000
Accumulated depreciation—building	75,000
Serial bonds payable (11%, due July 31, 2002, to July 31, 2007, inclusive)	300,000
Unamortized discount on term bonds payable	8,000
Accumulated depreciation—furniture and fixtures	20,000
Bond issue costs	5,000
Furniture and fixtures	50,000

INSTRUCTIONS

[a] Prepare the property, plant, and equipment and long-term liabilities sections of Oakley Oil Company's balance sheet on December 31, 1996.

[b] Indicate how Oakley Oil Company should classify any accounts that you did not use in [a].

4–32 Stockholders' Equity   The following information pertains to Friend Company on December 31 of the current year:

[1] The company has preferred and common stock outstanding. The preferred stock is $5 par value, 10%, cumulative and nonparticipating. A total of 20,000 shares was authorized, of which 10,000 shares are issued and outstanding on December 31. Friend sold its preferred stock for $6 per share.

[2] The common stock has a $1 par value. A total of 50,000 shares was authorized, of which 40,000 shares are issued and outstanding on December 31. Friend sold its common stock for $10 per share.

[3] The company has retained earnings of $2,600,000, of which $480,000 has been appropriated for plant expansion.

INSTRUCTIONS

Prepare the stockholders' equity section of Friend Company's balance sheet on December 31.

4–33 Balance Sheet The following list of accounts and balances pertains to Galyon Company on December 31, 1996, the end of the company's annual accounting period:

Accounts payable	$ 28,000
Accounts receivable	37,000
Accumulated depreciation—furniture and fixtures	10,000
Advances from customers (pertaining to goods that Galyon Company will supply in 1997)	6,000
Allowance for doubtful accounts	1,800
Bond sinking fund	110,000
Bonds payable (14%, due Jan. 1, 2009)	150,000
Cash	26,000
Common stock ($1 par, 50,000 shares authorized, 30,000 shares issued and outstanding)	30,000
Franchise	86,000
Furniture and fixtures	70,000
Merchandise inventory	48,400
Paid-in capital in excess of par	60,000
Premium on bonds payable	4,000
Prepaid rent (pertains to the first quarter of 1997)	8,400
Retained earnings	?

INSTRUCTIONS

Prepare a balance sheet in good form for Galyon Company on December 31, 1996.

4–34 Missing Amounts in Financial Statements The following *independent* cases pertain to a 1996 calendar-year accounting period:

	Case A	Case B	Case C	Case D
Revenues	$100,000	$200,000	?	?
Expenses	?	?	$ 50,000	$ 70,000
Net income	40,000	?	60,000	?
Retained earnings, Jan. 1	?	300,000	180,000	120,000
Dividends declared	50,000	70,000	?	30,000
Retained earnings, Dec. 31	120,000	310,000	?	?
Current assets, Dec. 31	?	60,000	100,000	?
Noncurrent assets, Dec. 31	420,000	?	580,000	300,000
Total assets, Dec. 31	500,000	?	?	410,000
Current liabilities, Dec. 31	?	30,000	?	20,000
Noncurrent liabilities, Dec. 31	270,000	?	170,000	?
Total liabilities, Dec. 31	?	140,000	?	?
Paid-in capital, Dec. 31	?	520,000	210,000	100,000
Total stockholders' equity, Dec. 31	200,000	?	410,000	210,000

INSTRUCTIONS

Determine the missing amounts.

4–35 Income Statement and Balance Sheet Classification Listed below are several categories that may be used in a multiple-step income statement and a balance sheet:

[a] Net sales
[b] Cost of goods sold
[c] Operating expenses
[d] Other revenues
[e] Other expenses
[f] Extraordinary items
[g] Current assets
[h] Investments and funds

[i] Property, plant, and equipment
[j] Intangible assets
[k] Other assets
[l] Current liabilities
[m] Long-term liabilities
[n] Capital stock
[o] Paid-in capital in excess of par
[p] Retained earnings

INSTRUCTIONS

Use the letters above to show where each of the following items should usually be classified.

[1] Accounts receivable.
[2] Preferred stock.
[3] Timber stand.
[4] Buildings.
[5] Interest expense.
[6] Accounts payable.
[7] Copyrights.
[8] Bonds payable (due in 20 years).
[9] Advertising.
[10] Investment in subsidiary company.
[11] Patents.

[12] Bond sinking fund.
[13] Sales discounts.
[14] Paid-in capital in excess of par—common stock.
[15] Loss of property in Iowa due to a hurricane.
[16] Write-off of inventories due to obsolescence.
[17] Transportation out.
[18] Depreciation expense.
[19] Accumulated depreciation.
[20] Goodwill.

4–36 Income Statement and Balance Sheet Classification Refer to the list of categories ([a] through [p]) in 4–35.

INSTRUCTIONS

Use the appropriate letters to show where each of the following items should usually be classified.

[1] Accumulated depletion.
[2] Allowance for doubtful accounts.
[3] Common stock dividend distributable.
[4] Merchandise inventory (ending).
[5] Note receivable (due in three months).
[6] Reserve for plant expansion.
[7] Wages payable.
[8] Premium on bonds that are payable in 10 years.
[9] Transportation in.
[10] Bond issue costs.

[11] Dividend revenue.
[12] Common stock subscriptions receivable.
[13] Organization costs.
[14] Interest payable.
[15] Sales returns and allowances.
[16] Purchase returns.
[17] Note payable (due in five years).
[18] Oil deposit.
[19] Common stock.
[20] Cash.

4–37 Income Statement and Balance Sheet Classification Refer to the list of categories ([a] through [p]) in 4–35.

INSTRUCTIONS

Use the appropriate letters to show where each of the following items should usually be classified.

[1] Raw materials.
[2] Merchandise inventory (beginning).
[3] Gain from foreign exchange transactions.
[4] Building.
[5] Treasury stock.
[6] Investment in 100 shares of Exxon's common stock that will likely be sold in three months.
[7] Prepaid insurance.
[8] Bad debts expense.
[9] Common stock subscribed.
[10] Equipment used in the business.
[11] Purchase allowances.
[12] Building site.
[13] Flood loss in an area that floods every two to three years.
[14] Pension obligations.
[15] Pension fund.
[16] Reserve for bond sinking fund.
[17] Cash surrender value of life insurance.
[18] Salaries.
[19] Premium on preferred stock.
[20] Discount on bonds payable (bonds are payable in 13 years).

4–38 Income Statement and Balance Sheet Classification   Refer to the list of categories ([a] through [p]) in 4–35.

INSTRUCTIONS

Use the appropriate letters to indicate where each of the following items should usually be classified. If an item should not be reported on either an income statement or a balance sheet, indicate where it should be reported.

[1] Work in process.
[2] Dividends declared.
[3] Purchases.
[4] Correction of an error made last year when computing depreciation expense.
[5] Deficit.
[6] Building that is being constructed for the company's own use.
[7] Small tools used in the business.
[8] Unearned rent revenue (will be earned in the first quarter of the next accounting period).
[9] Returnable containers used in the business.
[10] Machinery rearrangement costs.
[11] Bonds payable (due in six months; payment will be made from current assets).
[12] Equipment held for sale (was previously used in the business).
[13] Dividends payable.
[14] Appropriation for contingencies.
[15] Land held for future plant site.
[16] Franchise.
[17] Loss on sale of land.
[18] Taxes payable.
[19] Trademarks.
[20] Unusual and nonrecurring loss of inventories due to expropriation by a foreign government.

4–39 Statement of Cash Flows   The following information pertains to Cardosa Company during 1996:

Dividends paid	$ 10,000
Cash received from customers	135,000
Proceeds from issuing common stock	25,000
Interest received	10,000
Proceeds from sale of long-term investments	6,000
Cash paid to suppliers and employees	95,000
Purchases of long-term investments	18,000
Income taxes paid	15,000

Cardosa Company had cash of $49,400 on January 1, 1996.

INSTRUCTIONS

Prepare a statement of cash flows for 1996.

4–40 Subsequent Events   Hobby Company's accounting period ends on December 31, and the company issues its financial statements on the following February 1. Below are some events that occurred during *1997:*

Jan. 3 Sale of common stock.
  7 Write-off of an account receivable because customer was formally declared bankrupt on January 7. The bankruptcy litigation was in process on December 31, 1996.
  11 Loss of a material portion of inventories because of a sudden flood.
  18 Purchase of a competing business.
  21 Purchase of additional inventory.
  27 Write-off of an account receivable because the customer's business was destroyed by an earthquake on January 27.

INSTRUCTIONS

Indicate the appropriate treatment for each of the above events in Hobby Company's financial statements for *1996.* Assume that each event is material.

PROBLEMS

4–41 Income Statement Formats   The following list of items pertains to the 1996 calendar-year accounting period of Palladino, Inc.:

Advertising expense	$ 19,000
Gain on sale of investments	15,200
Interest expense	7,500
Interest revenue	8,900
Loss of inventory due to flood (considered unusual and nonrecurring)	21,000
Loss on write-off of plant assets due to obsolescence	21,800
Merchandise inventory, Dec. 31	80,000
Merchandise inventory, Jan. 1	62,000
Miscellaneous general and administrative expenses	7,800
Miscellaneous selling expenses	12,000
Office salaries expense	47,500
Office supplies expense	8,100
Purchases	455,000
Purchase discounts	8,700
Purchase returns and allowances	31,000
Sales	931,000
Sales discounts	15,200
Sales returns and allowances	22,800
Sales salaries expense	52,000
Transportation in	13,700
Utilities expense	10,400

Palladino, Inc., had 10,000 shares of common stock outstanding throughout 1996. The company's income tax rate is 40%.

INSTRUCTIONS

[a] Prepare a detailed, multiple-step income statement for 1996.
[b] Prepare a condensed, single-step income statement for 1996.
[c] Which of the two forms of income statements do you prefer? Explain your answer.

4–42 Corrected Income Statement and Retained Earnings Statement   The accountant for Terro Company has just handed you the income statement and retained earnings statement that appear below:

Terro Company
Income Statement
As of December 31, 1996

Revenues		
Net sales		$658,000
Extraordinary gain from expropriation of property by a foreign government		50,000
Correction of understatement of 1995 ending inventory due to error		30,000
Rent revenue		11,800
Dividend revenue		7,200
Total revenues		757,000
Expenses		
Cost of goods sold	$328,000	
Selling expenses	109,600	
General and administrative expenses	84,200	
Interest expense	12,200	
Total expenses		534,000
Net income		$223,000

Terro Company
Statement of Retained Earnings
As of December 31, 1996

Retained earnings, Jan. 1		$ 789,000
Add: Net income		223,000
		1,012,000
Less: Extraordinary loss of plant assets due to earthquake	$60,000	
Unusual loss on sale of long-term investments	23,000	
Dividends declared	37,000	120,000
Retained earnings, Dec. 31		$ 892,000

ADDITIONAL INFORMATION

[1] You have determined that the account balances in the above statements are correct. The statements, however, are not presented according to GAAP.
[2] The company had 10,000 shares of common stock outstanding throughout 1996.
[3] The company's income tax rate was 40% in 1995 and 1996.
[4] The company uses a calendar-year accounting period.

INSTRUCTIONS

[a] Prepare a condensed, multiple-step income statement for 1996 that complies with GAAP.
[b] Prepare a condensed, single-step income statement for 1996 that complies with GAAP.
[c] Prepare a statement of retained earnings for 1996 that complies with GAAP.
[d] From the standpoint of user decision making, why should extraordinary gains and losses be presented in a special section of the income statement?

4–43 Corrected Retained Earnings Statement The bookkeeper for Tweed Company recently prepared the following statement of retained earnings:

Tweed Company
Statement of Retained Earnings
December 31, 1996

Retained earnings, Jan. 1, 1996		$615,540
Add: Net income for 1996	$92,040	
Gain on sale of land	85,420	
Gain from settlement of litigation that began in 1995	25,000	
Gain from foreign currency transaction	6,000	208,460
		824,000
Less: Dividends declared during 1996	20,000	
Loss of inventory caused by a government prohibition judged to be unusual and nonrecurring	50,000	
Recognition of salaries expense incurred in 1995 but erroneously not recognized in the 1995 income statement	19,500	
Loss from write-off of equipment leased to others	15,500	105,000
Retained earnings, Dec. 31, 1996		$719,000

INSTRUCTIONS

[a] Prepare a corrected statement of retained earnings for 1996. Assume an income tax rate of 40% and 10,000 shares of common stock outstanding throughout 1996. (*Note:* The additions and deductions in the statement shown above are *before* income taxes, except for net income.)
[b] Indicate specifically where Tweed Company should report any items that do not belong on the statement of retained earnings.

4–44 Combined Statement of Income and Retained Earnings The following information pertains to the 1996 calendar-year accounting period of Cole Corporation:

Cost of goods sold	$232,600
Dividend revenue	7,590

Dividends declared	80,000
Gain on sale of investments (not considered unusual or nonrecurring for this company)	89,340
General and administrative expenses	69,587
Interest expense	12,650
Loss from expropriation of properties (considered unusual and nonrecurring)	48,000
Loss from settlement of litigation that began in 1995 (not considered unusual or nonrecurring for this company)	35,000
Loss of warehouse due to hurricane (considered unusual but recurring for this company)	42,150
Net sales	525,554
Selling expenses	63,473
Write-off of inventory due to obsolescence (considered unusual but recurring for this company)	17,024

ADDITIONAL INFORMATION

Cole Corporation reported retained earnings of $187,000 on its balance sheet dated December 31, 1995. During 1996 it was discovered that $60,000 of revenue earned in 1995 had not been reported on the 1995 income statement. The company had 5,000 shares of common stock outstanding throughout 1996.

INSTRUCTIONS

[a] Prepare a combined statement of income and retained earnings for 1996. Use the multiple-step format and assume an income tax rate of 40%.

[b] Do you favor a combined statement of income and retained earnings over separate statements of income and retained earnings? Explain your answer.

4–45 Statement of Stockholders' Equity   Adams Company reported the following amounts in the stockholders' equity section of its balance sheet dated December 31, 1995:

Preferred stock ($100 par value; 1,000 shares)	$100,000
Common stock ($25 par value; 10,000 shares)	250,000
Paid-in capital in excess of par	200,000
Retained earnings	341,580

On January 3, 1996, the company sold 2,000 additional shares of common stock for $60 per share. During 1996 it was discovered that $25,000 of revenue earned in 1995 had not been reported on the 1995 income statement.

Adams Company reported a net income for 1996 of $55,000. The company declared cash dividends of $2,500 on the preferred stock and $7,500 on the common stock at the end of *each* of the four quarters of 1996. Dividends are paid in cash 30 days after being declared.

INSTRUCTIONS

Prepare a statement of stockholders' equity for the year ended December 31, 1996. Assume an income tax rate of 40%.

4–46 Statement of Stockholders' Equity   Hawley Company reported the following amounts in the stomckholders' equity section of its balance sheet dated December 31, 1995:

Preferred stock ($150 par value; 1,000 shares)	$300,000
Common stock ($37.50 par value; 10,000 shares)	375,000
Paid-in capital in excess of par	600,000
Retained earnings	450,400

ADDITIONAL INFORMATION

[1] On January 2, 1995, Hawley sold 2,000 additional shares of common stock for $90 per share.

[2] Late in 1996, it was learned that because of a mathematical error, an overstatement of depreciation expense by $37,500 had occurred in 1995.

[3] Hawley reported net income of $82,500 for 1996.

[4] Hawley declared cash dividends of $15,000 on the preferred stock and $45,000 on the common stock during 1996.

INSTRUCTIONS

Prepare a statement of stockholders' equity for the year ended December 31, 1996. Assume an income tax rate of 40%.

4—47 Balance Sheet The following accounts and balances pertain to Louis Corporation on December 31, 1996:

Accounts payable	$ 38,300
Accounts receivable	43,900
Accumulated depletion	165,300
Accumulated depreciation	70,000
Paid-in capital in excess of par	369,000
Advances from customers (advances pertain to goods that Louis Corporation will supply in 1997)	4,500
Advances to suppliers (advances pertain to goods that suppliers will provide in 1997)	7,100
Allowance for doubtful accounts	2,600
Appropriation for plant expansion	58,500
Bond issue costs	21,300
Bond sinking fund	190,700
Bonds payable (10%, due July 1, 2007)	500,000
Building	210,000
Cash	21,100
Cash surrender value of life insurance	12,300
Common stock ($1 par, 50,000 shares authorized, 40,000 shares issued and outstanding)	40,000
Common stock subscribed (1,000 shares)	1,000
Franchise	51,840
Interest payable	3,000
Investment in bonds—long term	65,000
Land	99,500
Land held for future plant site	138,000
Marketable securities—short term	18,570
Merchandise inventory (at lower of FIFO cost or market)	41,430
Note payable (12%, due April 1, 2000)	25,000
Oil deposit	568,300
Organization costs	10,560
Prepaid insurance	4,300
Salaries payable	6,700
Stock subscriptions receivable (due in 3 months)	10,000
Unamortized discount on bonds payable	11,000
Unappropriated retained earnings	241,000

INSTRUCTIONS

Prepare a balance sheet in good form.

4—48 Balance Sheet The following information pertains to Mills Enterprises on December 31, 1996:

Patents	$ 80,000
Supplies	20,990
Common stock ($10 par, 20,000 shares authorized, 10,000 shares issued and outstanding)	100,000
Cash	50,000
Land	160,200
Machinery rearrangement costs	48,300
Unappropriated retained earnings	?
Serial 12% debenture bonds, $50,000 installments due annually from June 1, 1997, through June 1, 2006	500,000
Cash surrender value of life insurance	11,400
Trademarks	48,000

Appropriation for contingencies	80,000
Advances from customers (advances pertain to goods that Mills Enterprises will provide in 1997)	15,875
Allowance for doubtful accounts	3,300
Plant expansion fund	203,100
Accounts payable	31,000
Accumulated depreciation—building	45,000
Investment in land (held for long-term speculative purposes)	196,500
Machinery and equipment	290,800
Unearned rent revenue (Mills Enterprises will earn this revenue during the first quarter of 1997)	6,125
Paid-in capital in excess of par	400,000
Accumulated depreciation of machinery and equipment	30,000
Building	250,000
Accounts receivable	73,410
Long-term investment in common stock	84,000
Note receivable (due on May 15, 1997)	21,000
Marketable securities	37,000
Notes payable (due in 1997)	40,000
Merchandise inventory (at lower of FIFO cost or market)	58,600

INSTRUCTIONS

[a] Prepare a balance sheet in good form. Compute the missing amount of unappropriated retained earnings.

[b] What are serial 12% debenture bonds? Explain the rationale for the financial reporting treatment of these bonds.

4–49 Corrected Balance Sheet The bookkeeper for Widby Corporation has prepared the following balance sheet:

Widby Corporation
Balance Sheet
For 1996

Debits

Current Debits

Cash	$ 24,000	
Cash surrender value of life insurance	18,000	
Building fund	112,000	
Accounts receivable	58,760	
Merchandise inventory	49,010	
Unamortized discount on bonds payable	12,000	
Total current debits		$ 273,770

Noncurrent Debits

Marketable securities	25,300	
Advances to suppliers	7,500	
Prepaid rent	8,400	
Land held for future plant site	80,000	
Land	125,000	
Building	215,000	
Machinery and equipment	396,000	
Mineral deposit	327,000	
Goodwill	75,700	
Patents	41,300	
Machinery rearrangement costs	51,000	
Total noncurrent debits		1,352,200
Total debits		$1,625,970

Credits

Current Credits

Allowance for doubtful accounts	$ 4,340	
Accounts payable	42,630	
Interest payable	6,000	
Income tax payable	22,500	
Pension obligations	119,000	
Total current credits		$ 194,470

Noncurrent Credits

Accumulated depreciation of building	58,000	
Accumulated depreciation of machinery and equipment	66,000	
Accumulated depletion of mineral deposit	70,000	
Note payable	20,000	
Advances from customers	11,000	
Bonds payable	500,000	
Preferred stock	100,000	
Common stock	45,000	
Paid-in capital in excess of par	384,140	
Retained earnings	177,360	
Total noncurrent credits		1,431,500
Total credits		$1,625,970

ADDITIONAL INFORMATION

[1] You have determined that although the *dollar amounts* reported are correct, the balance sheet is not in accordance with GAAP.

[2] Merchandise inventory is reported at the lower of average cost or market value.

[3] The marketable securities are reported at fair value, and management plans to sell them in 1997.

[4] The advances to suppliers pertain to goods that will be provided during 1997.

[5] The prepaid rent applies to the first quarter of 1997.

[6] The pension obligations will be paid after 2004.

[7] The note payable is due on May 1, 1997.

[8] The advances from customers pertain to goods that Widby Corporation will provide in 1997.

[9] The bonds payable pay interest of 10% and are due on June 30, 2008.

[10] Relevant details about the preferred and common stock are as follows:

Preferred stock—$10 par value, 8%, cumulative and nonparticipating, 20,000 shares authorized, 10,000 shares issued and outstanding.

Common stock—$1 par value, 50,000 shares authorized, 45,000 shares issued and outstanding.

INSTRUCTIONS

Prepare a balance sheet in good form.

4–50 Corrected Balance Sheet The bookkeeper for Schuller Company prepared the following balance sheet on December 31, 1996:

Schuller Company
Balance Sheet
December 31, 1996

Assets

Current assets	$ 508,525
Investments and funds	28,520
Property, plant, and equipment	723,600
Intangible assets	80,355
Other assets	98,000
Total assets	$1,439,000

Liabilities and Stockholders' Equity

Current liabilities	$162,000	
Long-term liabilities	562,000	
Total liabilities		$ 724,000
Stockholders' equity		715,000
Total liabilities and stockholders' equity		$1,439,000

Upon inquiry, you learn the following additional facts:

[1] Current assets include cash, $33,000; merchandise inventory (at lower of FIFO cost or market), $75,125; note receivable (13%, due June 1, 1999), $100,000; investment in subsidiary (held for control), $215,000; and plant expansion fund, $85,400.

[2] Investments and funds include prepaid insurance (applicable to the first six months of 1997), $12,000; and bond issue costs, $16,520.

[3] Property, plant, and equipment includes land, $167,000; land held for future plant site, $146,600; building, $375,000 less accumulated depreciation, $45,000; and furniture and fixtures, $114,600 less accumulated depreciation, $34,600.

[4] Intangible assets include accounts receivable of $63,000 less an allowance for doubtful accounts of $4,125; and organization costs, $21,480.

[5] Other assets consist of goodwill, $98,000.

[6] Current liabilities include accounts payable, $23,595; interest payable, $8,405; and a note payable (12%, due May 1, 1999), $130,000.

[7] Long-term liabilities include serial 10% debenture bonds, $500,000 ($50,000 installments are payable annually from April 1, 1997, through April 1, 2006); advances from customers (advances pertain to goods that Schuller Company will ship in 1997) $12,000; and retained earnings appropriated for bond retirement, $50,000.

[8] Stockholders' equity consists of common stock ($1 par, 50,000 shares authorized, 40,000 shares issued and outstanding), $40,000; paid-in capital in excess of par, $430,000; and unappropriated retained earnings, $245,000.

INSTRUCTIONS

Prepare a balance sheet in good form.

4–51 Income Statement, Retained Earnings Statement, and Balance Sheet The information shown below was obtained from the accounting records of Schriver Company on December 31, 1996, the end of the company's annual accounting period. The account balances shown have been updated through December 31.

Accounts payable	$ 52,500
Accounts receivable	78,000
Accumulated depletion	65,000
Accumulated depreciation	70,000
Advances from customers (advances pertain to goods that Schriver Company will ship in 1997)	18,300
Allowance for doubtful accounts	3,000
Bond issue costs	31,000
Bond sinking fund	115,000
Bonds payable (10%, due June 1, 2009)	400,000
Building	275,000
Cash	71,110
Cash surrender value of life insurance	31,600
Common stock ($10 par, 20,000 shares authorized, 10,000 shares issued and outstanding throughout 1996)	100,000
Cost of goods sold	503,140
Dividend revenue	8,390
Dividends declared	100,000
Gain from expropriation of property by a foreign government (considered unusual and nonrecurring)	100,000
General and administrative expenses	253,430
Goodwill	53,100
Interest expense	50,000

Interest payable	12,500
Investment in common stock—long term	67,000
Land	196,000
Land held for future plant site	140,000
Loss of plant assets due to flood (considered unusual and nonrecurring)	70,000
Loss on sale of long-term investments (considered unusual but not nonrecurring)	10,000
Marketable securities—short term	21,890
Merchandise inventory (at lower of FIFO cost or market)	73,500
Mineral deposit	236,400
Net sales	1,532,850
Note payable (12%, due May 1, 2000)	100,000
Paid-in capital in excess of par	236,000
Patents	12,900
Prepaid insurance	8,500
Rent revenue	12,500
Salaries payable	19,700
Selling expenses	287,170
Unamortized discount on bonds payable	11,000

ADDITIONAL INFORMATION

Schriver Company had retained earnings of $157,000 on January 1, 1996. The company's income tax rate is 40%. Income taxes have already been paid.

INSTRUCTIONS

[a] Prepare an income statement (multiple-step format) for the year ended December 31, 1996.
[b] Prepare a statement of retained earnings for the year ended December 31, 1996.
[c] Prepare a balance sheet as of December 31, 1996.
[d] Provide evidence showing that the financial statements you prepared articulate with each other.

4–52 Income Statement, Retained Earnings Statement, and Balance Sheet Listed below are account balances of Chilo Company on December 31, 1996, the end of the company's annual accounting period. The account balances shown have been updated through December 31.

Paid-in capital in excess of par	$ 361,600
Net sales	1,554,750
Dividends declared	200,000
Cash	88,000
Land	114,000
Franchise	89,900
Note receivable (14%, due July 30, 2001)	50,000
Accounts payable	53,700
Bond issue costs	13,000
Common stock ($10 par, 25,000 shares authorized, 10,000 shares issued and outstanding throughout 1996)	100,000
Note payable (12%, due July 1, 2002)	200,000
Other revenue	42,250
Supplies	12,300
Plant expansion fund	115,000
Accumulated depreciation—furniture and fixtures	37,000
Organization costs	21,700
Serial 10% debenture bonds ($50,000 installments are due annually from June 1, 1997, through June 1, 2004)	400,000
Loss of inventory due to earthquake (considered unusual and nonrecurring)	100,000
Land held for future plant site	90,000
Merchandise inventory (at lower of average cost or market)	87,400
Furniture and fixtures	123,000
Advances from customers (advances pertain to goods that Chilo Company will ship in 1997)	25,300
Cost of goods sold	657,500

Loss from write-off of plant assets due to obsolescence (considered unusual but not nonrecurring)	22,000
Investment in subsidiary (held for control)	179,000
Building	375,000
Interest expense	60,000
General and administrative expenses	296,400
Accounts receivable	75,000
Selling expenses	214,100
Allowance for doubtful accounts	3,700
Interest payable	10,000
Accumulated depreciation of build1ctbing	75,000

ADDITIONAL INFORMATION

Chilo Company reported retained earnings of $193,000 on its balance sheet dated December 31, 1995. On July 14, 1996, it was discovered that $40,000 of revenue earned during 1995 had been incorrectly omitted from the 1995 income statement. The company's income tax rate was 40% in 1995 and 1996. Income taxes have already been paid.

INSTRUCTIONS

[a] Prepare an income statement (single-step format) for the year ended December 31, 1996.
[b] Prepare a statement of retained earnings for the year ended December 31, 1996.
[c] Prepare a balance sheet as of December 31, 1996.
[d] Provide evidence showing that the financial statements you prepared articulate with each other.

4–53 Statement of Cash Flows   The following events pertain to the 1996 calendar-year accounting period of Prater Company:

[1] Received cash from the following sources:

a. From issuing short-term debt	$ 11,000
b. From issuing long-term debt	25,000
c. From selling land	21,000
d. From selling equipment	30,000
e. From issuing preferred stock	15,000
f. From collecting short-term loans	15,000
g. From dividends received	4,000
h. From customers	260,000
i. From interest received	16,000

[2] Paid cash for the following purposes:

a. To make short-term loans	$ 10,000
b. To purchase land	25,000
c. To liquidate long-term note	32,000
d. To pay dividends	26,000
e. To purchase equipment	44,000
f. To liquidate short-term debt	14,000
g. To pay suppliers and employees	210,000
h. To pay interest	5,000
i. To pay income taxes	25,000

Prater Company had cash of $63,000 on January 1, 1996.

INSTRUCTIONS

Prepare a statement of cash flows for 1996.

CASES

4–54 Extraordinary Items   As an audit partner for Mack & Company, CPAs, you are responsible for many clients. The events listed below occurred during 1996:

[1] Luce Company lost some uninsured equipment because of an earthquake. This is the first earthquake to occur in the area where the equipment was located, and geologists believe that the area will not experience earthquakes in the future.

[2] Patten Company sustained a loss when it sold its computer division. Patten had been manufacturing computers and household appliances in separate divisions since 1984.

ᶜ [3] Sutch Company changed from the average cost method to the FIFO method of inventory cost determination.

ⁱⁿᵛ [4] It was discovered that Cloninger Company's bookkeeper forgot to deduct salvage value when computing straight-line depreciation for each of the two preceding years.

[5] Because of an expropriation, Nicley Company lost all of its inventory held in a Middle Eastern country.

[6] Dobbs Corporation wrote off some plant assets because of obsolescence.

[7] Raines Enterprises determined that certain depreciable assets would probably have useful lives 10 years longer than projected when the assets were purchased.

[8] Taft's Children's Wear destroyed a large portion of its inventory because of a government ban on the sale of clothing made of a flameproof fabric that causes skin irritations.

[9] White, Inc., discovered that the ending inventory for the previous year had been misstated because of a counting error.

[10] Keene Company lost some inventory because of a flood. Floods occur every three to five years in the area where the inventory was lost.

[11] Kilby, Inc., lost all of its perishable inventory because its employees went on strike.

[12] International Business Enterprises had a gain from foreign currency transactions.

[13] Maull Corporation realized a gain from an insurance settlement. The settlement pertained to the company's South American plant, which was expropriated in 1996.

[14] Based on recent collection experience, Wertz, Inc., changed the percentage used to estimate bad debts expense. The percentage was changed from 1% to 1.5% of net sales.

[15] Redmon Company sustained a loss from selling some of the common stock in the company's investment portfolio.

INSTRUCTIONS

Indicate which of the above events should be reported as extraordinary items. If an event should not be reported as an extraordinary item, indicate the appropriate financial statement category in which the event should be reported. Assume a multiple-step format and that all events are material.

4–55 Income and Cash Flows As an accountant for Milstead, Inc., you recently prepared the financial statements for the past year. The statements show that Milstead had a substantial net income for the year; however, net cash flow from operating activities was a large *negative* amount. After studying the statements carefully, Milstead's president questions whether the statements are correct. He says, "I thought that net income and net cash flow from operating activities were related concepts. I simply don't understand how we could have a large negative operating cash flow in the same period that we generated such high earnings."

INSTRUCTIONS

Assuming that Milstead's financial statements do not contain errors, present major reasons that could conceivably explain why the company's net income substantially exceeds its net cash flow from operating activities.

4–56 Estimates in Financial Statements Many companies promise to pay for their active employees' health care after they retire. Two alternative methods of accounting for the cost of medical benefits of retirees have been widely discussed in recent years. Method 1 would treat the costs as expenses when the benefits are ultimately paid to retirees (i.e., after the employees retire). Method 2 would attempt to better comply with the matching principle by *estimating* the future costs of retirees' health care benefits and treating the costs as expenses during the period over which the retirees worked for the company. Because the company recognizes the expense, it would also recognize a liability for future medical benefits.

In a *Business Week* article (September 16, 1989, p. 106), a financial analyst arguing in favor of method 1 was quoted as saying that "it is better to be correctly wrong, and have no number in the financial statements, than to be approximately correct and mislead investors."

INSTRUCTIONS

Do you agree or disagree with the financial analyst? Explain the rationale that supports your answer.

4–57 Estimates in Financial Statements Assume that you are a CPA employed by an independent auditing firm. You and an accountant who works for one of your clients (a retail clothing company) are discussing the need to make estimates in the financial statements for the period just ended. The accountant states, "Financial statements presented in conformity with generally accepted accounting principles are described in the authoritative literature of the accounting profession as historical in nature. To me, that means that historical financial statements report transactions and events that have already happened and do not attempt to impound forecasts of future events into the measurements made in the statements. This simplifies the accountant's role and reduces the responsibilities assumed by a preparer of financial statements. I have approached the preparation of our company's financial statements in that manner. In a nutshell, our historical financial statements are just that: a treatise of what has already happened, unaffected by estimates of things that might happen in the future."

INSTRUCTIONS

Do the accountant's assertions accurately describe financial statements as they are presently prepared under GAAP? Explain the rationale that supports your answer.

4–58 Financial Statement Deficiencies   The following is the complete set of financial statements prepared by Poulos Corporation:

Poulos Corporation
Statement of Earnings and Retained Earnings
For the Fiscal Year Ended August 31, 1996

Sales		$3,500,000
Less returns and allowances		35,000
Net sales		3,465,000
Less cost of goods sold		1,039,000
Gross margin		2,426,000
Less:		
Selling expenses	$1,000,000	
General administrative expenses	1,079,000	2,079,000
Operating earnings		347,000
Add other revenue:		
Purchase discounts	10,000	
Gain on increased value of investments		
in real estate	300,000	
Correction of error in last year's statement	90,000	400,000
Ordinary earnings		747,000
Add extraordinary item—gain on sale of		
fixed asset		53,000
Earnings before income tax		800,000
Less income tax expense		380,000
Net earnings		420,000
Add beginning retained earnings		3,258,000
		3,678,000
Less:		
Dividends (12% stock dividend declared		
but not yet issued)		120,000
Contingent liability [Note 2]		808,000
Ending unappropriated retained earnings		$2,750,000

Poulos Corporation
Statement of Financial Position
August 31, 1996

Assets

Current Assets		
Cash	$ 80,000	
Accounts receivable, net	110,000	
Inventory	130,000	
Total current assets		$ 320,000

Other Assets

Land and building, net	4,160,000	
Investments in real estate (current value)	1,508,000	
Goodwill [Note 1]	250,000	
Discount on bonds payable	42,000	
Total other assets		5,960,000
Total assets		$6,280,000

Liabilities and Stockholders' Equity

Current Liabilities

Accounts payable	$ 140,000	
Income taxes payable	320,000	
Stock dividend payable	120,000	
Total current liabilities		$ 580,000

Other Liabilities

Due to Powers, Inc. [Note 2]	808,000	
Bonds payable (including portion due within one year)	1,000,000	
Total other liabilities		1,808,000
Total liabilities		2,388,000

Stockholders' Equity

Common stock	1,000,000	
Paid-in capital in excess of par	142,000	
Unappropriated retained earnings	2,750,000	
Total stockholders' equity		3,892,000
Total liabilities and stockholders' equity		$6,280,000

NOTES TO THE FINANCIAL STATEMENTS

[1] As required by federal income tax laws, goodwill is not amortized. The goodwill was "acquired" in 1990.

[2] The amount due to Powers, Inc., depends on the outcome of a lawsuit that is currently pending. The amount of loss, if any, is not expected to exceed $808,000.

INSTRUCTIONS

Identify and explain the deficiencies in the presentation of Poulos' financial statements. There are *no* arithmetical errors in the statements. Organize your answer as follows:

[a] Deficiencies in the statement of earnings and retained earnings.

[b] Deficiencies in the statement of financial position.

[c] General comments.

If an item appears on both statements, identify the deficiencies for each statement separately.

(AICPA adapted)

4–59 Balance Sheet Classification   You are the controller for Pressley Lifestyles, Inc. As you plan to prepare the company's most recent financial statements, you identify an important issue that relates to balance sheet classification. During the last year, Pressley issued some bonds that are convertible into common stock at the option of the bondholders. The convertible bonds will mature in 20 years if not converted. The convertible bonds do not require the payment of interest unless the company operates profitably. Pressley's president does not want to classify these securities as debt but suggests that they be classified as part of stockholders' equity. He notes that they are similar to common stock because they do not require the payment of interest (similar to dividends) unless the company operates profitably. He also asserts that most convertible bond investors have indicated to him that they intend to convert the bonds into stock in the near future.

INSTRUCTIONS

Respond to the president regarding the balance sheet classification issues involved in this case. If you conclude that the president's suggested treatment is inappropriate, be sure to consider whether any compromises are appropriate.

4–60 Reporting Contractual Commitments   Janus, Inc., a construction contractor, has entered into two contracts during the past few days. Janus' controller has asked your advice as to how the company should report the contracts in the company's financial statements for the year just ended.

The first contract involves a commitment to buy federal securities (treasury bonds) from a securities dealer in the "when issued" market. The federal government has indicated that it will issue treasury bonds two weeks after the end of the company's year. Janus, Inc., has committed to buy and pay for $250,000 of those bonds at face amount when they are issued. Because the company entered into the contract, the value of the treasury bonds has increased in the market due to a general decrease in market interest rates. The controller wants to report the gain in value of the treasury bonds but does not wish to report the commitment as a liability and a related asset.

The second contract relates to the company's commitment to buy a tract of land within the next year. According to the contract terms, Janus, Inc., was required to pay a $25,000 option fee to secure the right to buy the land for $1,000,000 at any time during the next year. The controller asserts that the company intends to buy the land within the option period but wonders how the contract should be reported in the company's financial statements for the year just ended. She wants to report the option fee as an asset called *deposit on land* but does not want to report the remaining amount of the commitment as a liability and a related asset.

The controller does not wish to report the gross amounts of the two contracts as liabilities and assets because of the adverse effects of doing so on the relationships and ratios in the company's financial statements. For example, recording those commitments as liabilities would result in a higher debt-to-equity ratio, a relationship about which the company's bank has already expressed concern.

INSTRUCTIONS

Evaluate each of the two commitments and determine which, if either, should be reported as a liability and related asset in Janus' financial statements. Also, comment on the propriety of recording and reporting the gain in value on the contract to acquire the treasury bonds in the "when issued" market.

CHAPTER
5

The Accounting Cycle

OBJECTIVES

To discuss and illustrate the steps in the accounting cycle. These steps are the following:

1. Identify transactions.
2. Analyze transactions.
3. Record transactions in journals.
4. Post to ledger accounts.
5. Prepare an unadjusted trial balance.
6. Prepare adjusting entries.
7. Prepare an adjusted trial balance.
8. Prepare financial statements.
9. Prepare closing entries.
10. Prepare a post-closing trial balance (optional).
11. Prepare reversing entries (optional).

A recent article in Business Week began this way:

Imagine the horror. You're the chief executive of a major company attending an important meeting. Your second-in-command is called away for a moment and then returns ashenfaced. His news: Your company's last five quarters have been a lie. Reported profits never existed, and your books have been cooked for several quarters.

The article goes on to describe a recent scandal at Leslie Fay Co., a large company that makes women's apparel. Outside auditors estimated that instead of earning $23.9 million in 1992, the company lost $13.7 million.

To help ensure that the numbers reported in financial statements are based on real underlying events such as sales and purchases, a company needs a reliable accounting system in which certain steps are followed in every accounting period. These steps, collectively called **the accounting cycle,** are explained in this chapter.

"Who Played Dress-Up with the Books?" *Business Week,* March 15, 1993, p. 34.

The primary objective of financial reporting is to provide information useful in making investment, lending, and similar decisions. To provide this information, accountants follow a sequence of steps during an enterprise's accounting period, which is usually one year. This sequence is called the **accounting cycle** or the **accounting process.**

In this chapter, we review the steps in the accounting cycle. Most students have been introduced to them in previous courses. However, a thorough review of the accounting cycle will solidify the knowledge required to understand the remainder of this text.

As we explain later in this chapter, computers have profoundly affected accounting information systems in recent years. In this chapter, though, we emphasize the manual processing methods that some small businesses use. Emphasizing a manual system permits us to illustrate the accounting cycle in a way that is easiest to understand. Fundamentally, this chapter explains the basic information-processing functions of recording and summarizing business transactions. Accountants perform these functions regardless of whether a company uses a manual or a computer-based system.

STEP 1. IDENTIFY TRANSACTIONS

The initial step in the accounting cycle is transaction identification. Accountants must systematically identify all transactions so that they can be properly recorded. Broadly defined, a **transaction** is an event that (1) changes a firm's financial position *and* (2) can be measured with sufficient objectivity. For example, a cash purchase of supplies is a transaction that changes a firm's financial position by increasing one asset (supplies) and decreasing another (cash). In contrast, employing a new office manager is not presently considered a transaction under generally accepted accounting principles (GAAP). A major reason that hiring activities are not considered accountable events is that their impact on the firm's financial position is too uncertain to measure in a sufficiently reliable manner.

Transactions may be external or internal in nature. **External transactions** involve outside parties. Examples include sales, purchases, and loans. **Internal transactions** are confined to the accounting entity itself. Examples are depreciation, amortization, and conversion of production costs into inventory.

A firm's accounting system should identify pertinent information about every transaction. When a transaction occurs, a **source document,** often called a **business paper,** is prepared to evidence the transaction. For external transactions, for example, a sales invoice is a source document that supports a sale transaction, a check supports a payment transaction, and a promissory note supports a loan. Depreciation schedules, amortization schedules, and inventory schedules are common examples of source documents for internal transactions. Because entries in accounting records are based on information in the source documents, these documents must be carefully designed, prepared, and controlled. To verify the accuracy of financial statement information, an accountant should be able to trace financial statement numbers to the source documents. This tracing process is important to the auditing function. The term **audit trail** refers to the evidence that links the balances shown in the financial statements with the thousands of transactions that are summarized in those balances.

STEP 2. ANALYZE TRANSACTIONS

After identifying transactions, the accountant determines their impact on financial position as represented by the basic equation Assets = Liabilities + Owners' Equity. This analysis occurs within the **double entry system** of accounting. Under this system, which was first described in the 15th century by an Italian mathematician named Paciolo, the accountant makes entries in which debits equal credits for every transaction. These entries are made in records called **accounts;** every transaction affects at least two accounts.

Accounts have several forms. The simplest form, illustrated below, is called a **T account** because it resembles the letter T.

Account Title	
Debits (left side)	Credits (right side)

Companies actually use account forms that are more detailed than the T account. Nevertheless, the T account is a convenient and widely used instructional device. We therefore use it throughout the text.

The term **debit** (sometimes called **charge**) refers to the left-hand side of an account; **credit** refers to the right-hand side. When both sides of an account are totaled and the smaller sum is subtracted from the larger, the difference is called the **balance** of the account. Every account has a **normal balance,** which is simply the balance that one would *ordinarily* find in the account. The normal balance may be either debit or credit, depending on the type of account.

Proper analysis of a transaction requires an understanding of the major types of accounts and the manner in which debit and credit entries affect each, as summarized below:[1]

Type (Category) of Account	Balance Increased by	Balance Decreased by	Normal Balance
Asset	Debit	Credit	Debit
Liability	Credit	Debit	Credit
Owners' equity	Credit	Debit	Credit
Revenue	Credit	Debit	Credit
Expense	Debit	Credit	Debit

Note that debits and credits affect asset and expense accounts in one way and liability, owners' equity, and revenue accounts in the opposite way. Also note that the normal balance in an account coincides with what is done to increase the balance in the account. For example, we increase the balance in an asset account with a debit; the normal balance in an asset account is therefore a debit.

Remember that any transaction affects financial position as represented by the basic equation Assets = Liabilities + Owners' Equity. Revenue and expense accounts are also reflected in this equation because they are **temporary extensions of owners' equity,** as shown in Exhibit 5–1. Companies conveniently use these temporary accounts to determine net income. With these accounts, they measure revenue and expense activities in many individual accounts and thereby avoid excessive detail in the owners' equity account. At the end of the accounting period, the balances in the revenue and expense accounts are transferred to the owners' equity account via the closing process (explained at Step 9).[2]

STEP 3. RECORD TRANSACTIONS IN JOURNALS

After the information shown on source documents has been gathered and analyzed, it is entered in chronological order in a journal. Thus, a **journal** is a chronological record of trans-

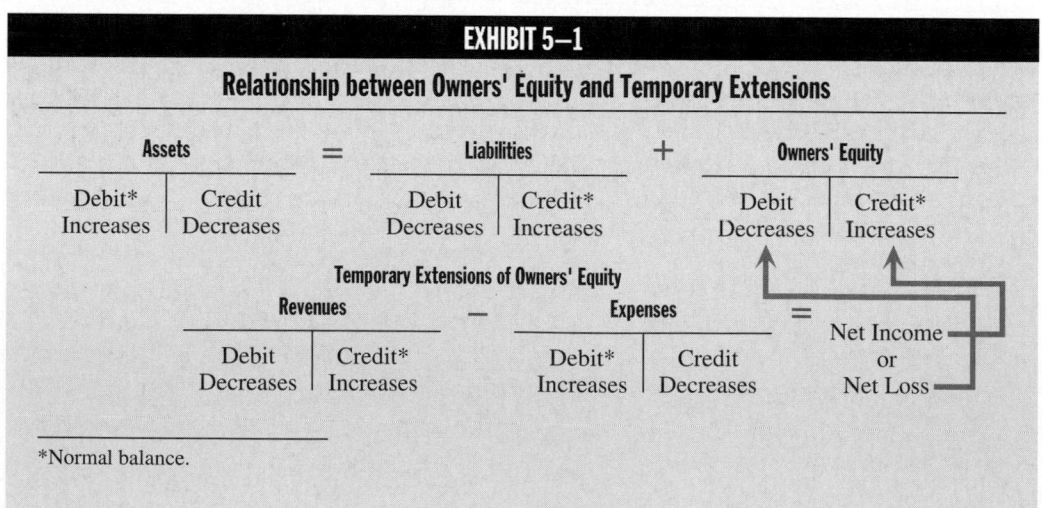

EXHIBIT 5–1

Relationship between Owners' Equity and Temporary Extensions

Assets		=	Liabilities		+	Owners' Equity	
Debit* Increases	Credit Decreases		Debit Decreases	Credit* Increases		Debit Decreases	Credit* Increases

Temporary Extensions of Owners' Equity

Revenues		−	Expenses		=	Net Income or Net Loss
Debit Decreases	Credit* Increases		Debit* Increases	Credit Decreases		

*Normal balance.

---

[1] Other types of accounts will be discussed at appropriate places in the text.

[2] Gain accounts (e.g., Gain on Sale of Land) function in the same way as revenue accounts; loss accounts (e.g., Loss of Building Caused by Fire) function in the same way as expense accounts.

actions. The process of recording transactions in a journal is called **journalizing.** Because this marks the first time that transactions are recorded in the debit-and-credit framework, a journal is often called a **book of original entry.**

General Journal

The most fundamental journal is the **general journal,** often called simply the **journal.** A general journal entry consists of the transaction date, the accounts and amounts to be debited (Dr.), the accounts and amounts to be credited (Cr.), and an explanation of the transaction. A **simple journal entry** consists of one debit and one credit. A **compound journal entry** consists of two or more debits or two or more credits. To illustrate, consider the following two transactions of Brookshire Corporation during October:

Oct. 1 Sold merchandise to Johnson Company for $1,200 on account.

4 Purchased machinery from Roberts Tool Company for $10,000. Paid $2,000 cash and signed a 90-day, 12% promissory note for the remainder of the purchase price.

These transactions would be entered in Brookshire's general journal as follows:

General Journal   Page J7

Date		Description	Post. Ref.	Dr.	Cr.
Oct.	1	Accounts Receivable	111	1,200	
		Sales	401		1,200
		Sold merchandise to Johnson Company on account.			
	4	Machinery	161	10,000	
		Cash	101		2,000
		Notes Payable	211		8,000
		Purchased machinery from Roberts Tool Company. Paid $2,000 cash and signed a 90-day, 12% promissory note.			

As shown above, the account to be debited is customarily listed before the account to be credited. The account credited is also indented to distinguish it clearly from the account debited. The Posting Reference column contains the identification numbers of the individual ledger accounts to which each part of every journal entry has been posted. These numbers are inserted in the column when posting occurs; they permit cross-referencing between the general journal and the ledger accounts. Also, account numbers in the Posting Reference column verify that journal entries have been posted.

Special Journals

Although all transactions *could* be recorded in a general journal, a business usually has several **special journals** in addition to a general journal to facilitate the efficient recording of large numbers of similar transactions. Common types of special journals and the nature of the transactions recorded in each type are listed below:

Type of Special Journal	Nature of Transactions Recorded
Sales journal	Sales of merchandise on credit
Cash receipts journal	Receipts of cash from any source
Purchases journal	Purchases of merchandise on credit[3]
Cash payments journal	Payments of cash for any purpose

---

[3]Sometimes a purchases journal is expanded to record *all credit purchases,* including merchandise, equipment, and supplies.

The number, purpose, and format of special journals vary considerably. Each business must decide on its special journals based on its needs. The topic of special journals is covered in more depth in Appendix B.

When a company uses special journals, it uses the general journal to record all transactions that do not fit the special journals. The general journal, then, is an integral part of an accounting system whether or not special journals are used. For this reason and because the general journal offers a convenient instructional format, we use it throughout the textbook to illustrate the application of various accounting concepts and principles.

STEP 4. POST TO LEDGER ACCOUNTS

General Ledger

After transactions have been journalized, the next step is to transfer the information to accounts in the general ledger. This transfer process is called **posting.** It may occur at various times during an accounting period, and it involves reorganizing information from a chronological system to a system of individual accounts. When we post, we bring all like items (e.g., all cash items) together in one place. To illustrate, the journal entries shown earlier for Brookshire Corporation are posted to the following general ledger T accounts:

	Cash	**Acct. No. 101**
	Oct. 4 J7	2,000

	Accounts Receivable	**Acct. No. 111**
Oct. 1 J7 1,200		

	Machinery	**Acct. No. 161**
Oct. 4 J7 10,000		

	Notes Payable	**Acct. No. 211**
	Oct. 4 J7	8,000

	Sales	**Acct. No. 401**
	Oct. 1 J7	1,200

As shown, the accountant must post each part of every general journal entry. The posting process consists of (1) transferring the date and amount to the appropriate side (debit or credit) of the ledger account, (2) inserting the journal page number as a posting reference in the ledger account, and (3) inserting the ledger account number in the Posting Reference column of the general journal.

The **general ledger,** often called simply the **ledger,** consists of many accounts. Each account is a record of information about a particular asset, such as Cash and Accounts Receivable; liability, such as Accounts Payable and Notes Payable; owners' equity, such as Common Stock and Retained Earnings; revenue, such as Sales and Service Fees Earned; and expense, such as Salaries and Advertising. Based on the scope of its operations and the extent of detail desired for reporting purposes, each business determines the exact nature of its accounts. The **chart of accounts** is a list of a firm's general ledger accounts. The accounts are usually numbered to permit easy identification and cross-referencing with the journals. Each asset account, for example, might be assigned a code number between 101 and 199; each liability account might be assigned a code number between 201 and 299.

In a computer-based accounting system, the general ledger information is stored on a device such as magnetic tape or disc. In a manual system, the general ledger is often a bound collection of pages. Each page represents an account. Typically, the first group of pages represents the asset accounts, followed by those of the liability, owners' equity, revenue, and expense accounts, in that order.

Certain ledger accounts are called *real accounts,* whereas others are known as *nominal accounts.* **Real** (or **permanent**) **accounts** remain open. These include asset, liability, and owners' equity accounts. Real accounts measure stocks of things, such as resources or debts, that exist at a certain point in time. **Nominal** (or **temporary**) **accounts** are closed at the end of every accounting period. These include revenue and expense accounts. Nominal accounts measure flows, such as sales or cost of goods sold, that occur over time. During an accounting period, **mixed accounts** contain both real and nominal components. At the end of the period, adjusting entries separate mixed accounts into their real and nominal components. For example, before adjusting entries, the Supplies account usually has both consumed (nominal) and unconsumed (real) portions. An adjusting entry places the consumed portion in a nominal account (Supplies Expense) and allows the unconsumed portion to remain in a real account (Supplies). After the accountant makes adjusting entries, all accounts in the ledger are either real or nominal.

The general ledger ordinarily includes certain adjunct and contra accounts. An **adjunct account** is one whose balance is added to the balance in the account to which it relates. For example, Transportation-In is an adjunct account to Purchases, and Premium on Bonds Payable is an adjunct account to Bonds Payable. A **contra** (or **offset**) **account** is one whose balance is subtracted from the balance in the account to which it relates. For instance, Sales Discounts is a contra account to Sales, and Allowance for Doubtful Accounts is a contra account to Accounts Receivable. Adjunct and contra accounts are closed at the end of an accounting period only if the accounts they relate to are also closed.

Subsidiary Ledgers

In addition to a general ledger, most businesses have one or more **subsidiary ledgers.** The purpose of a subsidiary ledger is to store the details of certain general ledger accounts. For example, a company may have thousands of credit customers. Although it is certainly necessary to know the total amount that these customers owe the company, it is also essential to know the name and address of each customer and how much each one owes. This information facilitates the billing process and is useful when the company makes credit-granting decisions. Rather than have a separate Accounts Receivable for each customer in the general ledger, firms usually create an Accounts Receivable subsidiary ledger. This ledger is often in the form of a tray of alphabetized cards, each card representing a customer's account. The Accounts Receivable account in the general ledger then becomes a **control** (or **main**) **account** that is supported by many detailed accounts in the subsidiary ledger.

When a subsidiary ledger exists, posting must appear in both the control account and the appropriate subsidiary ledger accounts. The control account is debited for the total debits and credited for the total credits made to the subsidiary ledger accounts. After all accounts have been posted, the balance in the control account should equal the total of the individual account balances in the subsidiary ledger. To ensure this equality, the accountant periodically reconciles each control account with its subsidiary ledger accounts.

Why use subsidiary ledgers? One important reason that a company uses them is to reduce the number of accounts in its general ledger. With fewer accounts, it is easier to avoid errors and to find them when they occur. Subsidiary ledgers also facilitate the division of labor in an accounting department. Individuals with limited education or experience can often be assigned responsibility for one or more subsidiary ledgers. Work on the various ledgers can thereby proceed simultaneously.

A subsidiary ledger can support any general ledger account. Subsidiary ledgers are often set up for Cash (when a company has several bank accounts), Accounts Receivable, Merchandise Inventory (when a company uses a perpetual inventory system), Plant Assets, Accounts Payable, Capital Stock, Selling Expenses, and Administrative Expenses.

STEP 5. PREPARE AN UNADJUSTED TRIAL BALANCE

A **trial balance** is a list of general ledger accounts and their debit or credit balances. It summarizes, usually on one sheet of paper, information that appears in a company's general ledger. The accountant prepares a trial balance at the end of every accounting period, before making the adjusting entries. Because the account balances do not yet reflect adjustments, the trial balance prepared at this time is often called an **unadjusted trial balance.**

A trial balance serves two main purposes:

1. It provides evidence that total debits in a company's general ledger equal total credits.

2. It provides information that helps the accountant to formulate adjusting entries.

The trial balance is a control device that helps to eliminate accounting errors. When total debits in a company's general ledger do not equal total credits, the trial balance is said to be **out of balance.** This condition alerts the accountant that one or more errors have been made. The accountant must find and correct these errors before preparing financial statements. On the other hand, a trial balance that is **in balance** does not necessarily signify the absence of errors. For example, the trial balance does not indicate the failure to record a transaction or the recording of a transaction in the wrong accounts.

The unadjusted trial balance for Eagle Company at December 31, 1996, is presented below. Information pertaining to this company, which uses a calendar-year accounting period, will be used to help explain the subsequent steps in the accounting cycle.

Eagle Company
Unadjusted Trial Balance
December 31, 1996

Account	Dr.	Cr.
Cash	$ 21,079	
Accounts receivable	60,000	
Allowance for doubtful accounts		$ 500
Note receivable	10,000	
Merchandise inventory	57,606	
Prepaid insurance	1,200	
Land	40,000	
Building	100,000	
Accumulated depreciation—building		10,000
Office equipment	120,000	
Accumulated depreciation—office equipment		24,000
Accounts payable		38,405
Unearned rent revenue		4,800
Long-term note payable		72,000
Common stock, $5 par		50,000
Paid-in capital in excess of par value		65,000
Retained earnings		34,215
Sales		523,000
Purchases	187,000	
Purchase returns		2,000
Purchase allowances		2,500
Purchase discounts		3,600

Transportation-in	7,250	
Sales salaries expense	78,000	
Advertising expense	24,000	
Transportation-out	6,000	
Miscellaneous selling expenses	5,141	
Officers' salaries expense	76,000	
Professional services	23,000	
Utilities expense	8,244	
Miscellaneous administrative expenses	5,500	
Totals	$830,020	$830,020

STEP 6. PREPARE ADJUSTING ENTRIES

Under the **cash basis of accounting,** revenue is recorded only when received in cash, and expenses are recorded only when paid in cash. In contrast, the **accrual basis of accounting** requires recognition of revenue when it is earned according to the revenue realization principle and recognition of expenses when they are incurred according to the matching principle. Under accrual basis accounting, the cash inflows typically associated with a given period's revenues may occur in past, present, or future periods. Similarly, the cash outflows typically associated with a given period's expenses may occur in past, present, or future periods. Thus, the primary difference between cash basis and accrual basis accounting is the timing of the recognition of revenues and expenses.

Revenue Realization
Matching

Current generally accepted accounting principles require accrual basis accounting, because this system generates measures of performance and financial position that are superior to those of cash basis accounting. To help implement the accrual basis of accounting, the accountant makes certain **adjusting entries** (often called **adjustments**) at the end of every accounting period. Adjusting entries are initially recorded in the general journal, and then posted to the appropriate general ledger accounts. If an entry requires an account that is not in the general ledger, the accountant simply creates (opens) a new account.

Purpose of Adjusting Entries

Adjusting entries permit an accurate measurement of earnings and financial position on the accrual basis. Adjusting entries are based on **revenue realization** and **matching** (see Chapter 2). Every adjusting entry allocates revenues or expenses between current and future periods. Moreover, every adjusting entry affects both a balance sheet account (asset or liability) and an income statement account (revenue or expense).[4]

Revenue Realization
Matching

Accumulating Adjusting Data

An external event such as a purchase or sale signals the accountant to record the transaction. At the end of the accounting period, however, no external events signal the accountant to record adjusting entries. How then does the accountant determine the nature and amounts of adjusting entries to record? Basically, the accountant carefully considers each account in the trial balance and examines certain source documents. Accounts that have mixed balances (i.e., mixed accounts) must be separated into real and nominal components. In addition, certain information not reflected on the trial balance must be entered in the accounting records. For example, the presence of Prepaid Insurance on the trial balance causes the accountant to inquire whether any insurance has expired and therefore should be charged to expense. This

---

[4]Certain **correcting entries** and **reclassification entries** are sometimes made during the adjustment process. For example, a correcting entry might be made to charge to Advertising Expense an amount that was mistakenly charged to Research and Development Expense during the year. A reclassification entry might be made to reclassify to current liability status the portion of long-term debt that will mature within the next year. As these examples suggest, a correcting or reclassification entry often affects only nominal accounts or only real accounts.

inquiry normally involves a review of the company's insurance policies. A Notes Receivable account usually leads the accountant to review the notes to determine whether any interest has been earned. Interest earned should be entered in a revenue account. Because many adjusting entries repeat from one accounting period to the next, accountants can often gain insight into the nature and amounts of this period's adjusting entries by examining the ones that were made at the end of the preceding period.

Classification of Adjusting Entries

We shall classify adjusting entries using the following three categories:

1. Accruals
2. Deferrals
3. Special items

Accruals.   Accruals are adjusting entries that normally have *one* of the following characteristics:

1. A revenue is recognized before the related cash receipt, *or*
2. An expense is recognized before the related cash payment.

Accruals are appropriate for revenues and related assets and for expenses and related liabilities that increase or accumulate gradually during the accounting period. Rather than recording these items weekly, daily, or even more frequently, the accountant records them by making adjusting entries at the end of the accounting period.

As an example of **accrued revenues** (accrued assets), on July 1, 1996, Eagle Company acquired a $10,000, one-year, 12% note receivable, with interest payable at maturity. This note represents money loaned by the company and is reflected on its trial balance. The revenue realization principle holds, in part, that revenue generated by allowing others to use enterprise assets, such as money, should be recorded as time passes. Accordingly, the company should make the following adjusting entry on December 31, 1996, the end of the company's annual accounting period:

Revenue Realization

Dec. 31	Interest Receivable	600	
	Interest Revenue		600

            To accrue interest for 6 months on note receivable.
            Accrued interest is computed as follows:
            $\$10,000 \times .12 \times {}^{6}\!/_{12} = \$600$

Revenue Realization

The adjusting entry assigns the $600 of interest revenue to 1996, the period in which the revenue was earned according to the revenue realization principle. The cash receipt associated with the interest will occur in the next accounting period, specifically on June 30, 1997. Note that the adjusting entry affects both a balance sheet account (Interest Receivable) and an income statement account (Interest Revenue). This journal entry, like all others, must be posted to the general ledger accounts affected.

As an example of **accrued expenses** (accrued liabilities), on October 1, 1996, Eagle Company issued a $72,000, 10-year, 10% note payable with interest payable annually on September 30. September 30, 1997, is therefore the first date that interest will be paid. Nevertheless, the money borrowed was used during the last three months of 1996. Accordingly, the cost of that money (interest) must be reported as an expense in 1996 to comply with the matching principle. The accountant should make the following adjusting entry:

Matching

Dec. 31	Interest Expense	1,800	
	Interest Payable		1,800

            To accrue interest for 3 months on note payable.
            Accrued interest is computed as follows:
            $\$72,000 \times .10 \times {}^{3}\!/_{12} = \$1,800$

The adjusting entry assigns the $1,800 of interest expense to the current accounting period (1996), the period in which the expense was incurred. The cash payment associated with the accrued interest will occur on September 30 of the next accounting period. Notice that the adjusting entry affects both a balance sheet account (Interest Payable) and an income statement account (Interest Expense).

Eagle Company must make one other major accrual, that of income tax expense. This is usually the final adjusting entry, because the amount depends on the size of a company's pretax income. We shall therefore make this entry later in the chapter, after we have calculated Eagle's 1996 income before taxes.

Deferrals. Deferrals are adjusting entries required to separate mixed accounts into their real and nominal components. A deferral-type adjusting entry typically has *one* of the following characteristics:

1. A revenue is recognized after the related cash receipt, *or*
2. An expense is recognized after the related cash payment (or incurrence of a liability).

In Exhibit 5–2 we compare accruals with deferrals.

Adjusting entries to reflect **deferred (unearned) revenues** are necessary for mixed accounts in which a portion of the balance represents revenue that has been earned currently and a portion represents revenue that will be earned in one or more future accounting periods. For example, Eagle Company's trial balance shows Unearned Rent Revenue of $4,800. The lease shows that the $4,800 represents one year's rent received in advance on an office in the company's building. When the amount was received on September 1, 1996, Cash was debited and Unearned Rent Revenue (a liability account) was credited.

The revenue realization principle holds, in part, that revenue generated by allowing others to use an enterprise asset, such as an office, is earned as time passes. Accordingly, on December 31, 1996, the following adjusting entry is required to reflect the fact that one-third of the $4,800 has been earned:

Revenue Realization

Dec. 31	Unearned Rent Revenue	1,600	
	Rent Revenue		1,600
	To record revenue earned on office rented, computed as follows: $4,800 × 4/12 = $1,600		

EXHIBIT 5–2
Comparison of Accruals and Deferrals

Accrued Revenue	Revenue recognition ————————————————→ *Time*	Cash receipt
Deferred (Unearned) Revenue	Cash receipt ————————————————→ *Time*	Revenue recognition
Accrued Expense	Expense recognition ————————————————→ *Time*	Cash payment
Deferred (Prepaid) Expense	Cash payment (or incurrence of liability) ————————→ *Time*	Expense recognition

As usual, the adjusting entry affects a balance sheet account (Unearned Rent Revenue) and an income statement account (Rent Revenue). After the entry has been posted, the Unearned Rent Revenue account has a $3,200 credit balance ($4,800 − $1,600 = $3,200). This balance is a liability, because it represents the company's obligation to provide the rented asset (i.e., the office) during the first eight months of the next accounting period.

Some companies follow the practice of **crediting a revenue account** when revenues are collected in advance of being earned. *If* Eagle had observed this practice, it would have debited Cash and credited Rent Revenue for $4,800 on September 1, 1996. Then on December 31, 1996, the **adjusting entry** would require a **debit to Rent Revenue** to reduce it and a **credit to the liability account Unearned Rent Revenue for $3,200.** The amounts reported on the 1996 financial statements would be the same as before, because the economic circumstances have not changed. Rent Revenue for 1996 would therefore still be $1,600 and Unearned Rent Revenue at December 31, 1996, would still be $3,200.

Adjusting entries to reflect **deferred (prepaid) expenses** are necessary for mixed accounts in which a portion of the balance represents an expense that has been incurred currently and a portion represents an expense that will be incurred in one or more future accounting periods. For example, Eagle Company's trial balance shows Prepaid Insurance of $1,200. The insurance policy shows that this amount represents the cost of fire protection for one year, paid in advance on April 1, 1996. When the original amount was paid, the company debited Prepaid Insurance and credited Cash.

Matching   The matching principle recognizes costs as expenses when the goods or services represented by the costs contribute to revenue. During 1996, three-fourths of the insurance protection presumably contributed to revenue. The expired portion of the insurance cost must therefore be entered in an expense account. The following adjusting entry is required:

Dec. 31	Insurance Expense	900	
	Prepaid Insurance		900
	To record expired portion of insurance, computed		
	as follows:		
	$1,200 \times 9/12 = \$900$		

Notice once again that the adjusting entry affects a balance sheet account (Prepaid Insurance) and an income statement account (Insurance Expense). After posting, the Prepaid Insurance account has a $300 debit balance. This balance represents an asset, specifically, the right to receive fire insurance protection during the first three months of the next accounting period.

Some companies follow the practice of **debiting an expense account** for short-term prepayments. *If* Eagle had observed this practice, it would have debited Insurance Expense and credited Cash for $1,200 on April 1, 1996. On December 31, 1996, the **adjusting entry** would require a **debit to Prepaid Insurance** and a **credit to Insurance Expense for $300.** The amounts reported on the 1996 financial statements would be the same as before; Insurance Expense for 1996 would still be $900, and Prepaid Insurance at December 31, 1996, would still be $300.

Matching   The matching principle further requires Eagle Company to record depreciation on its building and office equipment. These assets contributed to revenues throughout 1996; accordingly, a portion of their cost must be allocated to 1996 expense. Eagle uses the straight-line method to depreciate the building and office equipment over 50 and 10 years, respectively. Furthermore, the company expects each asset to have no salvage value.[5] The adjusting entry appears below:

---

[5]Under the straight-line method, we compute depreciation using the following formula:

$$\text{Annual Depreciation} = \frac{\text{Cost} - \text{Salvage Value}}{\text{Years of Service Life}}$$

Dec. 31	Depreciation Expense—Building	2,000	
	Depreciation Expense—Office Equipment	12,000	
	Accumulated Depreciation—Building		2,000
	Accumulated Depreciation—Office Equipment		12,000
	To record depreciation, computed as follows:		

$$\text{Building}\,\frac{\$100{,}000 - 0}{50\ \text{years}} = \$2{,}000$$

$$\text{Office Equipment}\,\frac{\$120{,}000 - 0}{10\ \text{years}} = \$12{,}000$$

Note that a compound entry was made to record depreciation. Two simple entries would also have been appropriate. Once again, the adjusting entry affects a balance sheet account (Accumulated Depreciation) and an income statement account (Depreciation Expense). The credits are made to accumulated depreciation accounts rather than directly to the asset accounts. Accumulated Depreciation is a contra account that permits the balance sheet to show both the cost and the accumulated depreciation of the major types of plant assets. Both pieces of information are generally considered relevant and are required disclosures.[6] The cost of an asset minus its accumulated depreciation is often called the asset's **book value** (or **net book value**).

When a company incurs costs that will likely benefit several accounting periods, such as the cost of buildings and equipment, the normal procedure is to debit an asset account instead of an expense account. Therefore, adjusting entries to record long-term cost allocations, such as depreciation, are usually similar to the one illustrated above.

Special Items.   These are adjusting entries that do not fit neatly into the accrual and deferral categories and are therefore classified separately. Common examples include the adjusting entries for bad debts expense and for cost of goods sold in a company that uses the periodic inventory system.

Companies that sell on credit do not usually expect to collect all of their accounts receivable. Therefore, some portion of credit sales made during a period and some portion of accounts receivable at the end of the period will likely never be collected in cash. To reflect these expectations, companies having credit sales make an adjusting entry to record **estimated bad debts.**

Procedures for estimating bad debts expense are covered in Chapter 7. For now, assume that all of Eagle Company's sales are on credit and that the company expects that 0.5% of its sales will never be collected. The company makes the following adjusting entry:

Dec. 31	Bad Debts Expense	2,615	
	Allowance for Doubtful Accounts		2,615
	To record estimated bad debts, computed as follows: $523,000 × .005 = $2,615		

The adjusting entry assigns Bad Debts Expense of $2,615 to the current accounting period, where it is matched on the income statement with the revenue from credit sales. Credit sales give rise to the uncollectibles. Bad debts expense is regarded as a cost of making credit sales, and recording it helps implement the matching principle. The credit in the above entry is made to the Allowance for Doubtful Accounts. We do not credit Accounts Receivable because we do not yet know which specific accounts will become uncollectible. The Allowance for Doubtful Accounts is a contra account to Accounts Receivable; we therefore subtract it from Accounts Receivable on the balance sheet. Accounts Receivable minus the Allowance for Doubtful Accounts is often called the **net realizable value** of accounts receivable. The

Matching

[6]*APB Opinion No. 12,* "Omnibus Opinion—1967," 1967, par. 5.

net realizable value of Eagle's accounts receivable at December 31, 1996, is $56,885 [$60,000 − ($500 + $2,615)]. The $500 amount is the balance in the Allowance for Doubtful Accounts before adjustments are made.

An outflow of resources is associated with most expenses. This outflow may occur in past, present, or future periods. In regard to bad debts, however, no such outflow occurs. Instead, there is simply a reduction in the inflow of cash expected. Thus, Bad Debts Expense is somewhat peculiar, and some accountants think it should be treated as a revenue contra account (perhaps called Sales Uncollectible) rather than an expense. We have treated the adjusting entry for bad debts as a special item because of its peculiar nature.

Another special item is the **adjustment for Cost of Goods Sold.** A company using the periodic inventory system debits Purchases when it makes a merchandise purchase. Furthermore, the recording of a sale does not involve entries in either the Cost of Goods Sold or Merchandise Inventory account. As a result, the Merchandise Inventory balance shown on the ending trial balance is the balance that was on hand at the *beginning* of the accounting period.[7] The objectives of the Cost of Goods Sold adjustment are therefore threefold:

1. To enter the ending inventory balance in the Merchandise Inventory account and remove the beginning inventory balance. The ending balance can then be presented on the ending balance sheet.

2. To close all of the accounts included in the calculation of net purchases. These accounts include Purchases, Purchase Returns, Purchase Allowances, Purchase Discounts, and Transportation-In.

3. To enter the Cost of Goods Sold Expense in the accounting records. One computes cost of goods sold using the following formula:

$$\text{Cost of Goods Sold} = \text{Beginning Inventory} + \text{Purchases} - \text{Purchase Returns}$$
$$- \text{Purchase Allowances} - \text{Purchase Discounts}$$
$$+ \text{Transportation-In} - \text{Ending Inventory}$$

To illustrate, Eagle Company's physical inventory count at the end of 1996 shows merchandise costing $43,756. The adjusting entry for Cost of Goods Sold appears below.

The adjusting entry accomplishes the three objectives described above. Actually, the entry is nothing more than the implementation of the basic cost of goods sold formula in general journal form. After the entry is posted, the Cost of Goods Sold account will have a $200,000 debit balance. Because Cost of Goods Sold is a nominal account, it must be closed during the closing process.

Dec. 31	Merchandise Inventory (Dec. 31)	43,756	
	Purchase Returns	2,000	
	Purchase Allowances	2,500	
	Purchase Discounts	3,600	
	Cost of Goods Sold	200,000	
	Merchandise Inventory (Jan. 1)		57,606
	Purchases		187,000
	Transportation-In		7,250
	To record cost of goods sold and ending inventory.		

The adjusting entry to Cost of Goods Sold is part adjusting and part closing. Some accountants prefer to treat it as a closing entry. Because it is peculiar, we have classified it as a special item.

---

[7]Throughout this chapter, we assume that a periodic inventory system is used. In Chapter 8, we review in detail the differences between periodic and perpetual systems.

STEP 7. PREPARE AN ADJUSTED TRIAL BALANCE

After journalizing and posting the adjusting entries, the accountant prepares a second trial balance. This is called an **adjusted trial balance** because the account balances listed reflect the company's adjusting entries. An adjusted trial balance serves three major purposes:

1. It provides evidence that, after the adjusting entries have been made, total debits in a company's general ledger equal total credits. It thus helps to control errors made during the adjustment process.
2. It enables the accountant to calculate income before taxes so that the adjusting entry to Income Tax Expense can be made.
3. It provides a convenient listing of account balances for use in the financial statements.

The adjusted trial balance of Eagle Company appears on page 174.

Note that the columns are subtotaled and an informal calculation of income before taxes is made. This calculation may be made on a calculator and need not be shown in detail on the adjusted trial balance. Income before taxes is the difference between the income statement accounts with credit balances and the income statement accounts with debit balances. For Eagle Company, this difference is $80,000.

Income tax expense is typically a major expense. Unlike most other expenses, it can be computed only after calculating income before taxes. Eagle Company's income tax rate is 48%.[8] The company therefore records the accrual of its income tax expense as follows:

Dec. 31	Income Tax Expense	38,400	
	Income Tax Payable		38,400
	To accrue income tax expense at a rate of 48%.		

As usual, this adjusting entry is journalized and posted to the affected general ledger accounts listed near the bottom of the adjusted trial balance. The columns are then totaled.

STEP 8. PREPARE FINANCIAL STATEMENTS

Using the information on the adjusted trial balance, the accountant prepares the formal **financial statements.**[9] These important statements are the output of the accounting information system and serve as input for many investment, credit, and similar decisions. Preparing the statements is therefore a crucial step in the accounting cycle.

The accountant ordinarily prepares financial statements in the following order: (1) income statement, (2) statement of retained earnings, (3) balance sheet, and (4) statement of cash flows. These are the basic financial statements explained in Chapter 4. Preparing the statement of cash flows requires more information than appears on the adjusted trial balance. In Chapter 22, we discuss and illustrate how to prepare the statement of cash flows. The income statement, statement of retained earnings, and balance sheet for Eagle Company appear in Exhibit 5–3. We present these statements for illustrative purposes; most accountants would probably combine several of the items shown, based on materiality considerations.

Materiality

---

[8]In this chapter, we review the accounting cycle without being diverted by the mechanics of calculating income taxes. We therefore assume that a tax rate of 48% applies to all income and that no differences exist between the company's pretax accounting income and its taxable income. In Chapter 19, we discuss and illustrate how to account for income taxes under more complex circumstances.

[9]Financial statements may also be prepared using a worksheet, as discussed in Appendix A. A **worksheet** is used to accumulate and organize the information required to prepare financial statements.

Eagle Company
Adjusted Trial Balance
December 31, 1996

Account	Dr.	Cr.
Cash	$ 21,079	
Accounts receivable	60,000	
Allowance for doubtful accounts		$ 3,115
Note receivable	10,000	
Interest receivable	600	
Merchandise inventory	43,756	
Prepaid insurance	300	
Land	40,000	
Building	100,000	
Accumulated depreciation—building		12,000
Office equipment	120,000	
Accumulated depreciation—office equipment		36,000
Accounts payable		38,405
Interest payable		1,800
Unearned rent revenue		3,200
Long-term note payable		72,000
Common stock, $5 par		50,000
Paid-in capital in excess of par value		65,000
Retained earnings		34,215
Sales		523,000
Interest revenue		600
Rent revenue		1,600
Cost of goods sold	200,000	
Sales salaries expense	78,000	
Advertising expense	24,000	
Transportation-out	6,000	
Miscellaneous selling expenses	5,141	
Officers' salaries expense	76,000	
Professional services	23,000	
Utilities expense	8,244	
Interest expense	1,800	
Insurance expense	900	
Depreciation expense—building	2,000	
Depreciation expense—office equipment	12,000	
Bad debts expense	2,615	
Miscellaneous administrative expenses	5,500	
Subtotal	840,935	840,935
Income tax expense	38,400	
Income tax payable		38,400
Total	$879,335	$879,335

Income before taxes = $523,000 + 600 + 1,600 − 200,000 − 78,000 − 24,000 − 6,000 − 5,141 − 76,000 − 23,000 − 8,244 − 1,800 − 900 − 2,000 − 12,000 − 2,615 − 5,500 = $80,000

Income tax expense = $80,000 × .48 = $38,400

STEP 9. PREPARE CLOSING ENTRIES

After preparing the financial statements, the accountant prepares **closing entries.** These entries are made at the end of the accounting period. They are first recorded in the general journal and then are posted to the appropriate ledger accounts.

The accountant closes *only* the nominal accounts. Furthermore, *all* nominal accounts are closed. To **close an account** means to reduce its balance to zero. Closing nominal accounts is logical, because they measure activities or flows that have occurred *during a given period of time.* At the end of the period, nominal accounts have served their purpose. Their balances must therefore be reduced to zero so that the accounts can be used to measure activities in the *next* accounting period. The measurement of any activity, whether it is sales or the 100-meter dash, logically begins at zero.

Because nominal accounts are temporary extensions of owners' equity (see Exhibit 5–1), their balances may be transferred directly to an owners' equity account (Retained Earnings in the case of a corporation) during closing. However, most accountants transfer revenue and expense balances to a clearing account called **Income Summary** (or **Revenue and Expense Summary**). This account merely summarizes the net income or loss for the period, and its balance is closed (i.e., reduced to zero and transferred) to owners' equity.[10] Closing entries are formulated based on the nominal account balances shown on the adjusted trial balance. The closing entries for Eagle Company are presented below.

Dec. 31	Sales	523,000	
	Interest Revenue	600	
	Rent Revenue	1,600	
	Income Summary		525,200
	To close revenue accounts.		
Dec. 31	Income Summary	483,600	
	Cost of Goods Sold		200,000
	Sales Salaries Expense		78,000
	Advertising Expense		24,000
	Transportation-Out		6,000
	Miscellaneous Selling Expenses		5,141
	Officers' Salaries Expense		76,000
	Professional Services		23,000
	Utilities Expense		8,244
	Interest Expense		1,800
	Insurance Expense		900
	Depreciation Expense—		
	Building		2,000
	Depreciation Expense—Office		
	Equipment		12,000
	Bad Debts Expense		2,615
	Miscellaneous Administrative		
	Expenses		5,500
	Income Tax Expense		38,400
	To close expense accounts.		
Dec. 31	Income Summary	41,600	
	Retained Earnings		41,600
	To close the Income Summary account.		

Although compound entries were used to illustrate the closing process, it would also have been appropriate to use a series of simple entries. Note that after closing entries are

---

[10]Some corporations (especially those that declare dividends quarterly) record the declaration of a dividend by debiting a **Dividends Declared** account, while others charge Retained Earnings directly. Dividends Declared is a nominal account and is presented on the statement of retained earnings. It normally has a debit balance and is closed directly to Retained Earnings at the end of the accounting period:

Dec. 31	Retained Earnings	XXX	
	Dividends Declared		XXX
	To close the Dividends Declared account.		

In sole proprietorships and partnerships, **Drawing** accounts are used instead of Dividends Declared. Drawing accounts are closed directly to Owners' Capital at the end of the accounting period.

EXHIBIT 5–3

Preparation of Financial Statements

Eagle Company
Income Statement
For the Year Ended December 31, 1996

Sales revenue			
Sales			$523,000
Cost of goods sold			
Merchandise inventory, Jan. 1, 1996		$ 57,606	
Purchases	$187,000		
Less: Purchase returns	2,000		
Purchase allowances	2,500		
Purchase discounts	3,600		
Add: Transportation-in	7,250		
Net purchases		186,150	
Cost of goods available for sale		243,756	
Merchandise inventory, Dec. 31, 1996		43,756	
Cost of goods sold			200,000
Gross margin on sales			323,000
Operating expenses			
Selling expenses			
Sales salaries	78,000		
Advertising	24,000		
Transportation-out	6,000		
Miscellaneous	5,141	113,141	
Administrative expenses			
Officers' salaries	76,000		
Professional services	23,000		
Utilities	8,244		
Insurance	900		
Depreciation of building	2,000		
Depreciation of office equipment	12,000		
Bad Debts	2,615		
Miscellaneous	5,500	130,259	
Total operating expenses			243,400
Income from operations			79,600
Other revenues			
Interest		600	
Rent		1,600	2,200
			81,800
Other expense			
Interest			1,800
Income before taxes			80,000
Income tax expense ($80,000 × .48)			38,400
Net income			$ 41,600
Earnings per share ($41,600 ÷ 10,000 shares outstanding)			$4.16

Eagle Company
Statement of Retained Earnings*
For the Year Ended December 31, 1996

Retained earnings, Jan. 1, 1996	$ 34,215
Add: Net income	41,600[†]
Retained earnings, Dec. 31, 1996	$ 75,815

Eagle Company
Balance Sheet
December 31, 1996

Assets

Current Assets

Cash		$ 21,079
Accounts receivable	$ 60,000	
Less: Allowance for doubtful accounts	3,115	56,885
Note receivable		10,000
Interest receivable		600
Merchandise inventory		43,756
Prepaid insurance		300
Total current assets		$132,620

Plant Assets

Land		40,000
Building	100,000	
Less: Accumulated depreciation	12,000	88,000
Office equipment	120,000	
Less: Accumulated depreciation	36,000	84,000
Total plant assets		212,000
Total assets		$344,620

Liabilities and Stockholders' Equity

Current Liabilities

Accounts payable		$ 38,405
Interest payable		1,800
Income tax payable		38,400
Unearned rent revenue		3,200
Total current liabilities		$ 81,805

Long-Term Liabilities

Notes payable		72,000
Total liabilities		153,805

Stockholders' Equity

Paid-in capital		
Common stock, $5 par, 10,000 shares issued and outstanding	$ 50,000	
Paid-in capital in excess of par value	65,000	
Total paid-in capital		115,000
Retained earnings		75,815[‡]
Total stockholders' equity		190,815
Total liabilities and stockholders' equity		$344,620

---

*Eagle Company declared no dividends during 1996. If dividends had been declared, they would have been subtracted on the retained earnings statement, as discussed and illustrated in Chapter 4.

[†]This number was obtained from the income statement.

[‡]This number was obtained from the statement of retained earnings.

posted, zero balances will exist in each revenue account, each expense account, and the Income Summary clearing account. Furthermore, the ending balance in the Retained Earnings account is $75,815 (34,215 + $41,600). Through no coincidence, this is the same figure reported for Retained Earnings on Eagle's balance sheet dated December 31, 1996.

STEP 10. PREPARE A POST-CLOSING TRIAL BALANCE (OPTIONAL)

After journalizing and posting the closing entries, the accountant usually prepares a **post-closing trial balance.** This is simply a list of general ledger accounts and their balances after the closing entries have been made. The post-closing trial balance therefore consists entirely of real accounts. Its purpose is to provide evidence that equal debits and credits exist in the general ledger after closing. Thus, it helps to ensure that the closing process has been performed correctly. The post-closing trial balance is not a required step in the accounting cycle, because its purpose is solely error detection.

STEP 11. PREPARE REVERSING ENTRIES (OPTIONAL)

The final step in the accounting cycle is to journalize and post **reversing entries.** These entries bear the first date of the new accounting period. They are called *reversing entries* because they are the reverse or opposite of certain adjusting entries made at the end of the preceding period. Reversing entries do not mean that the adjusting entries reversed were unnecessary or inaccurate.

The sole purpose of reversing entries is to *simplify* the subsequent recording of certain kinds of recurring transactions. Because their only purpose is simplification, reversing entries are optional. To illustrate, recall that on December 31, 1996, Eagle Company had outstanding a $72,000, 10-year, 10% note payable with interest due annually on September 30. In Exhibit 5–4, we summarize selected accounting entries pertaining to the note under alternative assumptions about reversing entries.

EXHIBIT 5–4
Effect of Reversing Entries

Event	Assumption			
	Accrued Interest Expense Is Reversed		Accrued Interest Expense Is Not Reversed	
Dec. 31, 1996 Adjusting entry to accrue interest expense	Interest Expense 1,800		Interest Expense 1,800	
	Interest Payable	1,800	Interest Payable	1,800
Dec. 31, 1996 Closing entry applicable to accrued interest expense	Income Summary 1,800		Income Summary 1,800	
	Interest Expense	1,800	Interest Expense	1,800
Jan. 1, 1997 Reversing entry	Interest Payable 1,800		No entry	
	Interest Expense	1,800		
Sept. 30, 1997 Payment of Interest	Interest Expense 7,200		Interest Expense 5,400	
	Cash	7,200	Interest Payable 1,800	
			Cash	7,200

Under either assumption, the interest expense recorded for the first nine months of 1997 is $5,400. That is, under the "reversing entry assumption," the interest expense is $5,400 ($7,200 − $1,800). Under the "no reversing entry assumption," the $5,400 is entered directly on September 30, 1997, but the accountant must remember to debit Interest Payable for $1,800 on that date. Observe that making either assumption results in the same amounts on the 1997 financial statements. Making the reversing entry on January 1, however, eliminates the need to divide the September 30 interest payment between the amount currently expensed and the amount previously accrued. This may seem like a trivial simplification for Eagle Company with its single note payable. However, some companies have many notes payable. Moreover, the recording of interest payments is often assigned to a clerical employee who may have had little more than high school bookkeeping courses. Under these circumstances, a qualified accountant may well decide to make reversing entries to simplify the recording of interest payments by the clerical employee. At the end of the period, the accountant can then analyze each note payable and formulate the appropriate adjusting entry for accrued interest.

The following types (i.e., categories) of adjusting entries *may* be reversed: (1) adjusting entries to record accruals (either revenues or expenses) and (2) adjusting entries to record deferrals when the original amount to which the adjusting entry pertains was recorded in a nominal account. For example, an adjusting entry debiting Prepaid Insurance and crediting Insurance Expense may be reversed because it is a deferral in which the original amount was recorded in a nominal account (i.e., Insurance Expense). In contrast, an adjusting entry debiting Insurance Expense and crediting Prepaid Insurance should not be reversed because, although the adjusting entry is a deferral, the original amount was recorded in a real account (i.e., Prepaid Insurance). Reversing entries should not record the cost of an asset that has expired, nor should they reinstate liabilities that no longer exist.

A company may choose to reverse any number of adjusting entries as long as they fall into one of the two categories discussed above. Because reversing entries are optional, companies should not make them unless the benefits exceed the costs.

USE OF COMPUTER TECHNOLOGY

Because it is easier to illustrate and understand, a **manual accounting system** has been emphasized in this chapter. Although some small businesses use a manual system, most companies use a **computer-based accounting system.** Both types of information systems rely on the accounting principles discussed in Chapter 2. Moreover, both types use the information-processing functions discussed in the present chapter. That is, both types identify, summarize, and classify business transactions and lead to the same financial statements.

Most companies use computer-based accounting systems because computers can usually process large amounts of data more effectively than people can. For identifying and processing many thousands of routine transactions such as purchases or sales, computers are incredibly fast, accurate, and cost effective. In accounting, computers have simplified many of the more mundane aspects of such activities as billing and payroll. They have also permitted accountants to develop useful reports in such areas as accounts receivable and inventories. The overall impact of computers on accounting has therefore been positive. Computers are no substitute for the seasoned judgments of well-educated accountants. Indeed, computers make the accountant's work more interesting and challenging.

Computer-based accounting systems may rely on **mainframe** (large) **computers, mini-computers** (medium), or **microcomputers** (small). Technological advances during the 1980s led to a significantly increased use of microcomputers in business. Microcomputers cost only a few thousand dollars and are relatively easy for people to understand and use. They allow users to perform a wide variety of functions, such as transaction processing, spreadsheet analysis, and word processing. Companies have developed various **software packages,** such as general ledger software, to satisfy each microcomputer application.

WESTERN ACCOUNTING ARRIVES IN EASTERN EUROPE

In the early 1990s Eastern Europe drew the attention of the Western world. The iron curtain came down and Western companies rushed in to set up shop in newly opened markets. The six largest international accounting firms and a handful of smaller ones moved in, sometimes on the heels of clients, sometimes forging the way and encouraging clients to follow.

Though the now independent republics that once formed the Soviet Union and its former satellites were by no means prepared for a capitalist invasion, Western investors couldn't resist the tempting market of over 300 million new consumers, a continent of raw materials and European knowhow offered at Latin American wages.

"This is probably as big as Commodore Perry opening Japan," said Paul Hoffman, a partner and Eastern European liaison in the New York office of Arthur Andersen & Co. "A whole new section of the world is entering the global economy, and the movement is coming on fast."

Arthur Andersen itself came on pretty fast in Moscow, opening an office there in the days of detente, and then closing it in the darker days of the cold war. The firm is back again, holding a 70% interest in a joint venture with Promsroy Bank, the former Soviet Union's largest industrial bank. In late June 1990, the firm announced it would be the first Western accounting firm permitted to perform audits acceptable to the Soviet government. The following day, Ernst & Young announced it, too, would perform official audits. Previously, all certified auditing of transnational joint ventures was carried out by Inaudit, a Soviet agency established for that express purpose.

But business is booming too much for Inaudit. With 1,800 joint ventures taking shape, the former Soviet agency simply cannot keep up with the workload. In fact, the agency's situation worsened when Ernst & Young hired Inaudit's second-ranking official and Arthur Andersen took on three others from the agency's staff.

A CPA in the Moscow May Day Parade

All of the six largest accounting firms have established offices in Moscow, and Ernst & Young already has a second office operating in Kiev. All the firms, however, are experiencing a predictable problem: the conversion of financial information into forms useful to Western companies and investors. The former Soviet Union's centrally controlled economy does not deal with such concepts as profitability and stockholder equity. Financial information was aimed at measuring performance against production goals, not measuring profit and loss.

C. Richard Eigenbrode, senior tax manager at Price Waterhouse, said that when he spoke to a group of upper-level managers at a seminar in Moscow, one of their questions was "What is an operating loss?"

"Even at that upper level," says Eigenbrode, "they're struggling with basic concepts."

To alleviate the accounting education problem and set things in motion for a compatible system of international accounting, the United Nations Center for Transnational Corporations (UNCTC) organized several brainstorming sessions and helped found an ongoing educational program. CPAs "donated" by the largest CPA firms are teaching in Russian universities and institutions, using a special curriculum developed by Dr. Adolf J. H. Enthoven, director of the Center for International Accounting Development at the University of Texas—Dallas.

Raymon de Reyna, a Deloitte & Touche partner who taught an intensive two-week course at Moscow State University, was invited to march in the famous May Day parade in Red Square, perhaps the first Western CPA to receive such an invitation.

SOURCE: Glenn Alan Cheney, "Western Accounting Arrives in Eastern Europe," *Journal of Accountancy* (September 1990), pp. 40–43.

Software packages contain **programs,** or sets of instructions that tell computers exactly what to do.

Clearly, the computer revolution is changing our society and is having a profound influence on accounting. Computers offer many exciting opportunities to improve accounting information in the future. For example, some have suggested a **database approach to corporate financial reporting** in which companies make electronic financial databases available to users instead of conventional financial statements. With their microcomputers and appropriate software packages, users could then access the financial databases to structure their own sets of information that would be uniquely suited to their specific information needs.[11]

Accountants should think of computers as useful tools for increasing the benefits of accounting information and lowering the cost of producing it. Again, remember that the es-

---

[11]William H. Beaver and Alfred Rappaport, "Financial Reporting Needs More Than the Computer," *Business Week* (August 13, 1984), p. 16.

sence of the accounting cycle outlined in this chapter occurs in all accounting systems, whether manual or computer based.

Of all the steps required in the accounting cycle, typical intermediate accounting students have the most trouble with the preparation of adjusting entries. The following broad principles from the theoretical model in Chapter 2 are important to remember when preparing adjusting entries:

1. **Revenue realization.** Under the accrual basis of accounting, certain adjusting entries are necessary to ensure that revenues will be recognized in the period in which they are earned, regardless of when the cash inflows associated with them occur.

2. **Matching.** Under the accrual basis of accounting, certain adjusting entries are necessary to ensure that expenses will be recognized in the period in which they are incurred, regardless of when the cash outflows associated with the expenses occur.

Together, the revenue realization and matching principles are the essence of the accrual basis of accounting. The need to implement these principles explains why adjusting entries are necessary at the end of every accounting period.

Some adjusting entries are fairly simple, but most require the accountant to exercise professional judgment. The following examples illustrate this point.

1. The bad debt expense adjustment requires the accountant to estimate the amount of a company's credit sales that will never be collected. Chapter 7 explains the procedures for estimating bad debts.
2. A company must make an adjusting entry when the market value of its inventory has declined below historical cost. Determining market value requires considerable judgment, as Chapter 8 explains.
3. The depreciation adjustment requires an estimate of historical cost (not always easy to determine), salvage value, and useful life. It also requires selecting a depreciation method. Chapter 12 explains depreciation accounting.
4. Because income tax laws and GAAP sometimes differ in their recognition and measurement of the elements of financial statements, making the accrual for income taxes can be highly complex and judgmental. Chapter 19 explains this subject.
5. Determining the adjusting entry for pension expense requires many estimates such as expected employee turnover and interest cost on the pension obligation to employees. Although they typically get considerable help from actuaries, accountants must still make many judgments, as Chapter 24 explains.

That accounting is imprecise and requires judgment is apparent throughout the process of making adjusting entries. In fact, just making sure that all necessary adjustments are made requires judgment.

1. A transaction is an event that changes a company's financial position and can be measured with sufficient objectivity. (Step 1)
2. Source documents serve as evidence that transactions have occurred. (Step 1)
3. The term *debit* refers to the left-hand side of an account; *credit* refers to the right-hand side. (Step 2)
4. A journal is a chronological record of transactions. A company should always have a general journal and may have one or more special journals. (Step 3)
5. Posting involves transferring information from journals to accounts in a ledger. A company should always maintain a general ledger and may have one or more subsidiary ledgers. (Step 4)
6. The unadjusted trial balance provides evidence that total debits in a company's general ledger equal total credits. It also provides information that helps the accountant to formulate adjusting entries. (Step 5)
7. Adjusting entries permit accurate measurement of earnings and financial position on the accrual basis. (Step 6)

8. Adjusting entries are based on the revenue realization and matching principles. (Step 6)

9. An adjusted trial balance provides a convenient list of account balances that may be used to prepare the financial statements. (Step 7)

10. The accountant usually prepares financial statements in the following order (Step 8): **a.** income statement; **b.** statement of retained earnings; **c.** balance sheet; **d.** statement of cash flows.

11. Closing entries transfer nominal account balances to owners' equity. After closing, all nominal accounts should have zero balances. (Step 9)

12. A post-closing trial balance consists entirely of real accounts. (Step 10)

13. Accountants use reversing entries to simplify the subsequent recording of certain kinds of recurring transactions, such as interest payments. (Step 11)

APPENDIX A: THE WORKSHEET

USING A WORKSHEET TO PREPARE ANNUAL STATEMENTS

The accountant often uses a *worksheet,* which is a multicolumn sheet of paper, to accumulate and organize the information required to prepare financial statements. Worksheets facilitate the preparation of financial statements by providing (1) a place where adjusting entries can be made informally before they are journalized and posted, (2) an orderly means whereby each account can be classified according to the financial statement in which it will appear, and (3) a balancing mechanism that helps to uncover accounting errors. Worksheets are never published, because they are not formal financial statements.

In practice, many different worksheet formats exist. The format used in any given case depends on individual or company preferences.

A 12-column worksheet for Eagle Company is shown in Exhibit 5–5 (pages 184–185). This worksheet includes the same basic data used earlier in the chapter. Eagle Company's worksheet consists of six pairs of amount columns. Sometimes accountants reduce the worksheet's size by eliminating the Adjusted Trial Balance columns or by combining the Retained Earnings and Balance Sheet columns. The financial statement balances, of course, are not affected by worksheet size. Eagle Company's worksheet has no columns for the statement of cash flows. Preparing this statement may require a separate worksheet, which we explain later in Chapter 22. The following steps are required to prepare the worksheet:

1. Enter the unadjusted trial balance by using the first pair of amount columns and determine that the columns balance.

2. Enter all adjusting entries, except income taxes, in the Adjustments columns. Then subtotal these columns to determine that they balance. The adjusting entries are identified by small letters (a–g) and are presented in the order in which they are discussed in the chapter. Note that when an adjustment requires an account that is not listed in the unadjusted trial balance, a new account is listed below the Unadjusted Trial Balance totals. When a worksheet is used, the adjusting entries are usually made informally in the Adjustments columns *before* they are journalized and posted. Errors can then be found and corrected before entering the formal accounting records.

3. Determine the adjusted account balances by combining the Unadjusted Trial Balance amounts with the Adjustments amounts. Extend the adjusted balances in the Adjusted Trial Balance columns. Subtotal these columns to determine that they balance.

4. Extend each debit account balance in the Adjusted Trial Balance to the Debit column of the financial statement in which the balance will appear. Similarly, extend each credit account balance to the Credit column of the financial statement in which the balance will appear.

5. Subtotal the Income Statement columns. The difference between the columns is the *pretax* income or loss for the period. For Eagle Company, the difference is $80,000 ($525,200 − $445,200), and it represents pretax income.

6. Compute the income tax expense by applying the appropriate income tax rate to the pretax income. The income tax expense for Eagle Company is $80,000 × .48 = $38,400.

7. Enter the income tax accrual in the Adjustments columns. Then extend the Income Tax Expense balance to the Debit column of the Adjusted Trial Balance and of the Income Statement. Extend the Income Tax Payable balance to the Credit column of the Adjusted Trial Balance and of the Balance Sheet. Total the Adjustments columns and the Adjusted Trial Balance columns.

8. Enter net income in the Income Statement Debit column to balance the two Income Statement columns. The balancing figure is also entered in the Retained Earnings Credit column.

9. Subtotal the Retained Earnings columns and enter the balance, which is ending retained earnings, in the Retained Earnings Debit column and the Balance Sheet Credit column.

10. Total the Balance Sheet columns and determine that they balance.

Eagle Company's financial statements may now be prepared directly from the worksheet. These statements would match those illustrated in the chapter. After the statements are prepared, the adjusting entries are journalized and posted on the basis of information shown in the Adjustments columns of the worksheet. To complete the accounting cycle, the accountant would close the nominal accounts as illustrated in the chapter. Finally, the accountant *may* prepare a post-closing trial balance and reversing entries.

USING A WORKSHEET TO PREPARE INTERIM STATEMENTS

Most companies formally prepare adjusting and closing entries only at the end of each fiscal year. Nevertheless, companies typically desire interim (e.g., monthly or quarterly) financial statements in addition to annual statements. At the end of each interim period, the accountant enters the necessary adjustments on a worksheet similar to the one of Eagle Company and does not formally record them in journals or ledgers. Adjustments shown on the year-end worksheet then pertain to the entire year; these amounts are journalized and posted to the accounts in the general ledger.

Because the balance sheet represents financial position at a point in time, the accountant obtains information about assets and equities directly from the Balance Sheet columns of an interim worksheet. Conversely, revenue and expense amounts on an interim worksheet are cumulative since the beginning of the fiscal year. Therefore, to determine revenues and expenses associated with a particular interim period, the accountant must subtract revenues and expenses attributable to previous interim periods from the corresponding amounts shown on the worksheet. To illustrate, assume that a company closes its books each December 31. To prepare an income statement for March, the accountant must subtract the revenues and expenses for January and February from the corresponding amounts shown on the March 31 worksheet. To prepare an income statement for the second quarter, the accountant must subtract the revenues and expenses for the first quarter from the corresponding amounts shown on the June 30 worksheet. Like the income statement, the retained earnings statement pertains to a certain period of time. It therefore is typically prepared like the income statement.

APPENDIX B: SPECIAL JOURNALS

The general journal format we use throughout this book deemphasizes certain procedural details and enables us to better illustrate how to apply basic accounting concepts and principles. In practice, most businesses have several special journals in addition to a general journal. Special journals typically process most of a company's transactions. This appendix will review some of the more common types of special journals.

A *special journal* is used to initially record a single type of transaction that often recurs. A company may create a special journal to handle virtually any kind of routine transaction. However, a company still needs a general journal to record transactions that do not fit the intended purpose of one of its special journals. Typically, adjusting entries, correcting entries, closing entries, reversing entries (if used), and entries for transactions that occur infrequently, such as the sale of common stock in exchange for land, are recorded in the general journal.

What are the advantages of special journals? First, special journals save time in journalizing and posting transactions. When journalizing, there is no need to rewrite account titles; when posting, transaction *totals* rather than individual amounts may be transferred to general ledger accounts. By simplifying the journalizing and posting requirements for routine transactions, special journals tend to reduce the number of errors made. Moreover, errors are easier to pinpoint once they have occurred.

Another use for special journals is to permit a division of labor within the accounting department. Instead of several people attempting to use the general journal simultaneously, certain individuals can assume responsibility for one or more special journals. This often enables the company to better utilize persons with limited education or experience in bookkeeping or accounting. Such separation of duties also strengthens the company's internal control system.

Each business must determine which types and formats of special journals it needs based on the nature of its transactions.

The types and formats presented below are for illustrative purposes only.

SALES JOURNAL

The sales journal is a chronological listing of all *credit* sales of merchandise. For a company that makes 5,000 credit sales a month, a sales journal relieves the company of (1) recording 5,000 general journal entries debiting Accounts Receivable and crediting Sales and (2) posting these entries individually to the general ledger. A sales invoice or sales ticket typically initiates an entry in a sales journal.

An abbreviated sales journal of Star-Bright, Inc., is presented in Exhibit 5–6 (page 186). Special journals are normally arranged in columns. Star-Bright's sales journal contains five columns. We assume in the illustration that the company's credit terms are 2/10, n/30.[12] If credit terms varied by customer, a journal column could easily be added to record the terms of each sale.

The process of posting from a sales journal is depicted by the arrows. Individual amounts in the sales journal are posted daily as debits to the appropriate accounts in the accounts receivable subsidiary ledger. Daily posting provides up-to-date credit records and facilitates the billing process. The check marks in the Posting Reference column indicate that individual accounts have been posted. At the end of each month, the Amount column *total* is posted in the general ledger as a debit to the Accounts Receivable control account and a credit to Sales. The notation (111/401) at the bottom of the Amount column

---

[12]In other words, a customer who pays within 10 days after the invoice date may deduct 2% from the invoice price; a customer who does not pay within the 10-day discount period must pay the gross invoice amount within 30 days after the invoice date.

EXHIBIT 5–5

Eagle Company
Worksheet
For the Year Ended December 31, 1996

Accounts	Unadjusted Trial Balance Dr.	Unadjusted Trial Balance Cr.	Adjustments Dr.	Adjustments Cr.	Adjusted Trial Balance Dr.	Adjusted Trial Balance Cr.	Income Statement Dr.	Income Statement Cr.	Retained Earnings Dr.	Retained Earnings Cr.	Balance Sheet Dr.	Balance Sheet Cr.
Cash	21,079				21,079						21,079	
Accounts receivable	60,000				60,000						60,000	
Allowance for doubtful accounts		500		(f) 2,615		3,115						3,115
Note receivable	10,000				10,000						10,000	
Merchandise inventory, Jan. 1, 1996	57,606			(g) 57,606								
Prepaid insurance	1,200			(d) 900	300						300	
Land	40,000				40,000						40,000	
Building	100,000				100,000						100,000	
Accumulated depreciation —building		10,000		(e) 2,000		12,000						12,000
Office equipment	120,000				120,000						120,000	
Accumulated depreciation —office equipment		24,000		(e) 12,000		36,000						36,000
Accounts payable		38,405				38,405						38,405
Unearned rent revenue		4,800	(c) 1,600			3,200						3,200
Long-term note payable		72,000				72,000						72,000
Common stock		50,000				50,000						50,000
Paid-in capital in excess of par value		65,000				65,000						65,000
Retained earnings, Jan. 1, 1996		34,215				34,215				34,215		
Sales		523,000				523,000		523,000				
Purchases	187,000			(g) 187,000								
Purchase returns		2,000	(g) 2,000									
Purchase allowances		2,500	(g) 2,500									
Purchase discounts		3,600	(g) 3,600									

Account	Trial Balance Dr	Trial Balance Cr	Adjustments Dr	Adjustments Cr	Adjusted Trial Balance Dr	Adjusted Trial Balance Cr	Income Statement Dr	Income Statement Cr	Retained Earnings Dr	Retained Earnings Cr	Balance Sheet Dr	Balance Sheet Cr
Transportation-in	7,250			(g) 7,250								
Sales salaries expense	78,000				78,000		78,000					
Advertising expense	24,000				24,000		24,000					
Transportation-out	6,000				6,000		6,000					
Miscellaneous selling expenses	5,141				5,141		5,141					
Officers' salaries expense	76,000				76,000		76,000					
Professional services	23,000				23,000		23,000					
Utilities expense	8,244				8,244		8,244					
Miscellaneous administrative expenses	5,500				5,500		5,500					
	830,020	830,020										
Interest receivable			(a) 600		600						600	
Interest revenue				(a) 600		600		600				
Interest expense			(b) 1,800		1,800		1,800					
Interest payable				(b) 1,800		1,800						1,800
Rent revenue			(c) 1,600		1,600			1,600				
Insurance expense			(d) 900		900		900					
Depreciation expense—building			(e) 2,000		2,000		2,000					
Depreciation expense—office equipment			(e) 12,000		12,000		12,000					
Bad debts expense			(f) 2,615		2,615		2,615					
Merchandise inventory, Dec. 31, 1996			(g) 43,756		43,756						43,756	
Cost of goods sold			(g) 200,000		200,000		200,000					
			273,371	273,371	840,935	840,935	445,200	525,200				
Income tax expense			(h) 38,400		38,400		38,400					
Income tax payable				(h) 38,400		38,400						38,400
			311,771	311,771	879,335	879,335						
Net income							41,600			41,600		
							525,200	525,200				
Retained earnings, Dec. 31, 1996									75,815			75,815
									75,815	75,815	395,735	395,735

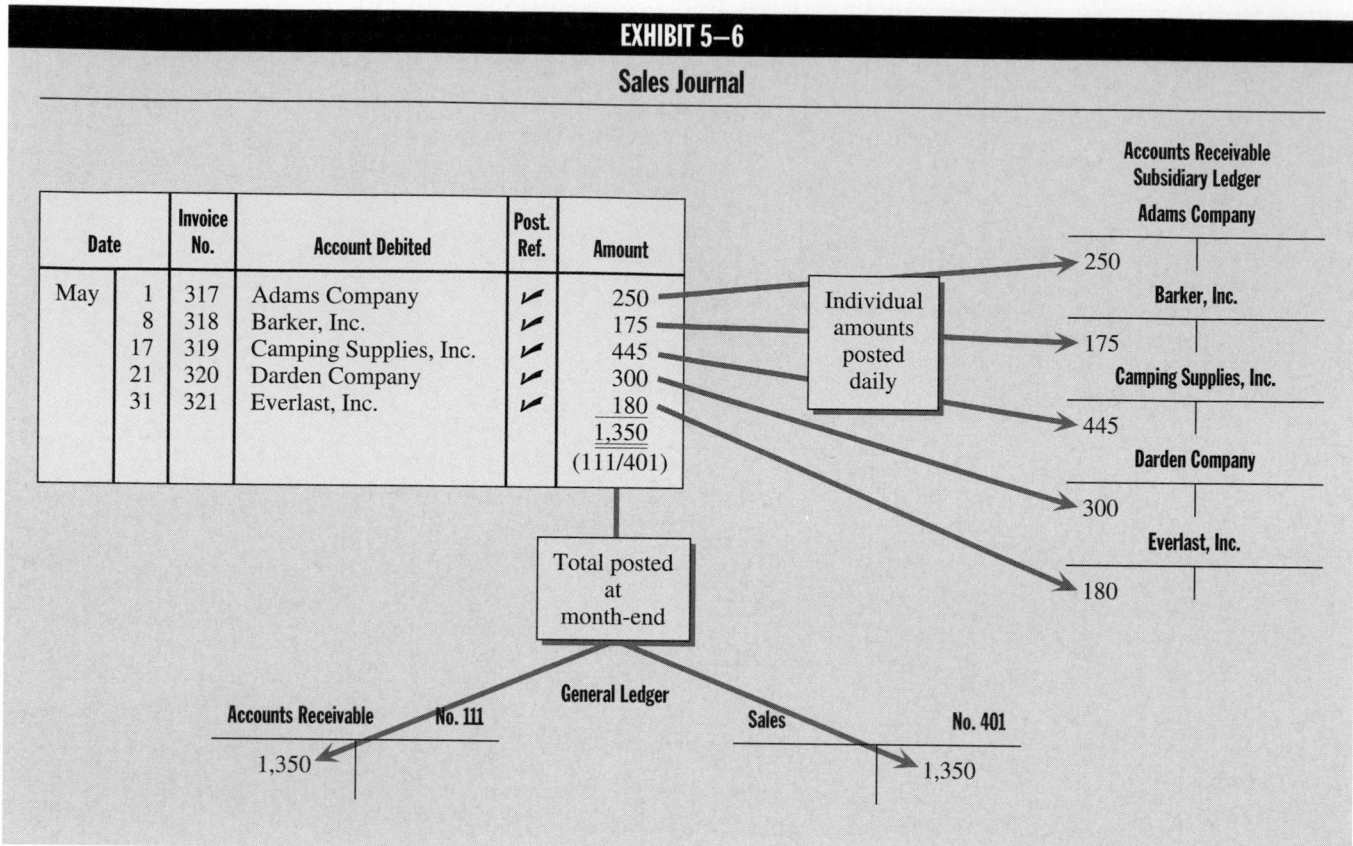

EXHIBIT 5–6

Sales Journal

Date		Invoice No.	Account Debited	Post. Ref.	Amount
May	1	317	Adams Company	✓	250
	8	318	Barker, Inc.	✓	175
	17	319	Camping Supplies, Inc.	✓	445
	21	320	Darden Company	✓	300
	31	321	Everlast, Inc.	✓	180
					1,350
					(111/401)

Individual amounts posted daily

Accounts Receivable Subsidiary Ledger

Adams Company — 250

Barker, Inc. — 175

Camping Supplies, Inc. — 445

Darden Company — 300

Everlast, Inc. — 180

Total posted at month-end

General Ledger

Accounts Receivable   No. 111   1,350

Sales   No. 401   1,350

indicates that general ledger accounts bearing these numbers have been posted. Note that if each sale were recorded in the general journal instead of the sales journal, each debit and credit would have to be separately posted to the general ledger. This would be time consuming and expensive. As the sales journal illustrates, posting any journal involves making equal debits and credits in the general ledger. Moreover, the sum of the debits (or credits) posted to subsidiary ledger accounts should equal the amount posted as a debit (or credit) to the related control account.

CASH RECEIPTS JOURNAL

The cash receipts journal records all cash receipts, including those resulting from cash sales. Star-Bright's cash receipts journal in Exhibit 5–7 consists of nine columns. Five of these columns are used to record amounts. The following posting features of the cash receipts journal are noteworthy:

1. Column *totals* for cash, sales discounts, and sales are posted at the end of each month. Individual amounts are not posted. The account numbers posted are inserted parenthetically at the bottom of these columns to indicate that posting has occurred.
2. The term *sundry accounts* means various individual accounts. Therefore, sundry accounts are posted *individually*.

Their total is not posted. The account number 211 in the Posting Reference column indicates that the Notes Payable account has been posted. The (X) notation at the bottom of the Sundry Accounts column signifies that the column total is not posted.

3. Amounts in the Accounts Receivable column are posted *individually and in total*. Individual amounts, referenced by the check marks, are posted daily as credits to the customer accounts in the accounts receivable subsidiary ledger. The column total is posted at the end of the month as a credit to the Accounts Receivable control account in the general ledger. The notation (111) at the bottom of the column indicates that the column total has been posted.

PURCHASES JOURNAL

Some companies use a purchases journal to record *all credit purchases;* others use it to record only *credit purchases of merchandise.* A purchase invoice normally initiates each entry in a purchases journal. Star-Bright's purchases journal in Exhibit 5–8 consists of six columns; its purpose is confined to recording credit acquisitions of merchandise. To record all credit acquisitions in its purchases journal, the company would have to add columns to record items such as supplies and equipment.

EXHIBIT 5-7

Cash Receipts Journal

Cash Receipts Journal

Date		Account Credited	Explanation	Post Ref.	Cash Debit	Sales Discounts Debit	Accounts Receivable Credit	Sales Credit	Sundry Accounts Credit
May	3	Sales	Cash sales		500			500	
	11	Adams Company	Payments in full	✔	245	5	250		
	14	Notes Payable	90-day, 10% loan from City National Bank	211	2,000				2,000
	27	Barker, Inc.	Payment in full	✔	175		175		
	31	Darden Company	Payment in full	✔	294	6	300		
					3,214	11	725	500	2,000
					(101)	(402)	(111)	(401)	(X)

Total debits = $3,225   Total credits = $3,225

EXHIBIT 5-8

Purchases Journal

Purchases Journal

Date		Account Credited	Invoice Date	Terms	Post Ref.	Amount
May	1	Modern Supply Company	Apr. 29	2/10, n/30	✔	200
	16	Dresser, Inc.	May 15	2/10, n/60	✔	550
	18	Office Products Distributors	May 16	n/30	✔	450
	24	Ebenezer, Inc.	May 23	1/10, n/30	✔	196
	31	Wilson Manufacturing Company	May 29	2/10, n/30	✔	254
						1,650
						(501/201)

Individual amounts in the purchases journal are posted daily as credits to the appropriate accounts in the accounts payable subsidiary ledger. The check marks in the Posting Reference column indicate that individual accounts have been posted. The column *total* is posted in the general ledger at the end of each month as a debit to the Purchases account and a credit to the Accounts Payable control account. The notation (501/201) at the bottom of the Amount column signifies a monthly posting.

CASH PAYMENTS JOURNAL

The cash payments journal records all cash payments, including those resulting from cash purchases. Star-Bright's cash payments journal in Exhibit 5–9 consists of 10 columns; 5 of these are amount columns. Significant posting features in the cash payments journal are described below:

1. Column *totals* for cash, purchase discounts, and purchases are posted at the end of each month. Individual amounts are not posted. The account numbers posted are inserted parenthetically at the bottom of these columns to indicate that posting has occurred.

2. Amounts in the Sundry Accounts column are posted *individually*. The total of these amounts is not posted. The account numbers 131 and 517 in the Posting Reference column indicate postings made to the Prepaid Insurance and Advertising Expense accounts, respectively. The (X) notation at the bottom of the Sundry Accounts column signifies that the column total is not posted.

EXHIBIT 5–9

Cash Payments Journal

Cash Payments Journal

Date		Check No.	Account Debited	Explanation	Post. Ref.	Cash Credit	Purchase Discounts Credit	Accounts Payable Debit	Purchases Debit	Sundry Accounts Debit
May	2	477	Purchases	Cash purchases		300			300	
	8	478	Modern Supply Company	Payment in full	✔	196	4	200		
	12	479	Prepaid Insurance	Fire insurance policy	131	450				450
	25	480	Dresser, Inc.	Payment in full	✔	539	11	550		
	31	481	Advertising	WACK Radio Station	517	250				250
						1,735	15	750	300	700
						(101)	(502)	(201)	(501)	(X)

Total credits = $1,750   Total debits = $1,750

3. Amounts in the Accounts Payable column are posted *individually and in total*. Individual amounts, referenced by the check marks, are posted daily as debits to the supplier accounts in the accounts payable subsidiary ledger. The column total is posted at the end of the month as a debit to the Accounts Payable control account in the general ledger. The (201) notation at the bottom of the column indicates that the column total has been posted.

OTHER SPECIAL JOURNALS

To avoid repetition, we have illustrated only the four most common special journals. Remember, however, that companies may use other types.

For example, many companies use a voucher system, in which a voucher is prepared for each transaction that requires a cash payment. A **voucher** is a business paper containing detailed information about a liability and its payment. Each voucher is recorded in a journal called a **voucher register.** This journal is similar to an expanded purchases journal and thus replaces the purchases journal. Checks are drawn only in payment of approved vouchers. A **check register,** which is merely a modified cash payments journal, replaces the cash payments journal in a voucher system.

A **payroll register** is a widely used journal for recording payroll information. A **sales returns and allowances journal** and a **purchases returns and allowances journal** are often used by companies that have many such transactions.

QUESTIONS

5–1   What is the purpose of the accounting cycle? List in sequence the steps involved.

5–2   What is the nature of source documents? List five examples.

5–3   Is the normal balance in each of the following accounts a debit or a credit?

[a] Prepaid Insurance

[b] Wages Expense

[c] Sales

[d] Accounts Payable

[e] Gain on Sale of Land

[f] Accumulated Depreciation

[g] Discount on Bonds Payable

[h] Common Stock

[i] Dividends

[j] Loss on Sale of Investments

[k] Sales Returns

5–4   Does a debit increase or decrease the balance in each of the following types of accounts?

[a] Revenue   [c] Expense   [e] Owners' Equity

[b] Liability   [d] Asset

5–5   What is a journal? Why might a company want to use several special journals?

5–6   What is an example of a general journal entry to record each of the following?

[a] An increase in an asset and an increase in a liability.
[b] A decrease in a liability and a decrease in an asset.
[c] An increase in an expense and a decrease in an asset.
[d] An increase in an asset and an increase in a revenue.
[e] An increase in an asset and an increase in owners' equity.

5–7 What is a general ledger? Why is posting to general ledger accounts necessary?

5–8 How do real, nominal, and mixed accounts differ?

5–9 What are a subsidiary ledger and a control account? Why might a company want to use several subsidiary ledgers?

5–10 What are the major purposes of an unadjusted trial balance? Does an unadjusted trial balance prove that no errors have been made during an accounting period?

5–11 How do the cash basis and the accrual basis of accounting differ?

5–12 What are adjusting entries? Why are they needed?

5–13 A company recently made an adjusting entry to record depreciation and one to record accrued interest on notes receivable. How does each entry relate to an accounting principle?

5–14 How does an accountant accumulate the information needed to prepare adjusting entries?

5–15 How do accruals and deferrals differ?

5–16 What are two examples of adjusting entries that are based on the revenue realization principle? What are two examples that are based on the matching principle?

5–17 What is an example that illustrates two ways in which an adjusting entry applicable to Prepaid Rent might be recorded?

5–18 What is an example that illustrates two ways in which an adjusting entry applicable to Unearned Subscriptions Revenue might be recorded?

5–19 What are the purposes of the cost of goods sold adjustment, assuming the use of a periodic inventory system?

5–20 What are the major purposes of an adjusted trial balance?

5–21 Why is the income tax adjustment usually the final adjusting entry prepared?

5–22 Why are the following statements usually prepared in the sequence indicated?

[a] Income statement [b] Statement of retained earnings [c] Balance sheet

5–23 How do financial statements relate to the need that users have to predict future cash flows?

5–24 What are closing entries? Why are they needed?

5–25 What types of accounts appear on a postclosing trial balance?

5–26 What are reversing entries? Why are these entries often desirable?

5–27 What is a worksheet? How does it facilitate the preparation of financial statements?

EXERCISES

5–28 Debit/Credit Rules A list of accounts appears below:

[1] Accounts Receivable.
[2] Investment in Bonds.
[3] Accounts Payable.
[4] Salaries Expense.
[5] Sales.
[6] Dividends.
[7] Accumulated Depreciation.
[8] Unearned Subscriptions Revenue.
[9] Dividends Payable.
[10] Premium on Bonds Payable.
[11] Paid-In Capital in Excess of Par Value.
[12] Allowance for Doubtful Accounts.
[13] Treasury Stock.
[14] Goodwill.
[15] Retained Earnings.
[16] Retained Earnings Appropriated for Plant Expansion.
[17] Interest Earned.
[18] Advertising.
[19] Sales Returns.
[20] Common Stock.

INSTRUCTIONS
State whether the balance in each account is increased by a debit or a credit.

5–29 Journal Entries During July, Rockman Company engaged in the transactions listed below. The company uses a periodic inventory system.

July	1	Purchased on account merchandise costing $30,000.
	1	Paid $800 of freight charges in connection with merchandise referred to above.
	6	Purchased land for $10,000.
	10	Sold merchandise for cash of $9,000.
	14	Borrowed $8,000 by signing a 90-day, 10% note.
	16	Sold 1,000 shares of $10 par value common stock for $15,000.
	19	Sold merchandise on account for $6,000.
	23	Sold land that was purchased on July 6. The cash selling price was $11,000.
	27	Received a $1,000, 90-day, 12% note from a customer on account.
	31	Paid July salaries of $5,000.

INSTRUCTIONS

Record the above transactions in general journal form.

5–30 Posting   Kerlinger, Inc., recorded the following journal entries during its first month of operations:

Aug.	1	Cash	10,000	
		Common Stock		10,000
	3	Prepaid Rent	1,200	
		Cash		1,200
	4	Equipment	5,000	
		Cash		5,000
	11	Purchases	4,000	
		Accounts Payable		4,000
	13	Accounts Receivable	7,000	
		Sales		7,000
	24	Cash	2,000	
		Accounts Receivable		2,000
	27	Accounts Payable	3,000	
		Cash		3,000
	31	Salaries Expense	1,400	
		Advertising Expense	200	
		Utilities Expense	100	
		Cash		1,700

INSTRUCTIONS

[a] Set up a general ledger and post each journal entry to appropriate T accounts.
[b] Prepare an unadjusted trial balance on August 31.

5–31 Correcting Entries   A trial balance for Jill Roth, M.D., at the end of her first month in practice is presented below:

Jill Roth, M.D.
Trial Balance
October 31

Account	Dr.	Cr.
Cash	$ 9,560	
Supplies	11,730	
Prepaid rent	6,800	
Equipment	58,000	
Accounts payable		$ 9,640
Jill Roth, capital		75,000
Revenues from patients		5,450
Salaries expense	1,300	
Utilities expense	400	
Miscellaneous office expenses	300	
Jill Roth, drawing	2,000	
	$90,090	$90,090

ADDITIONAL INFORMATION

Upon examining Roth's books, you discover the following:

[1] Cash of $300 received from a patient had been recorded as $500. (Roth renders services on a cash basis only.)

[2] A $964 purchase of supplies on account had been recorded as $469.

[3] A $2,000 purchase of equipment had been charged to prepaid rent.

[4] A $677 payment on account had been recorded as $776.

INSTRUCTIONS

[a] Journalize the necessary correcting entries on October 31. (Do not record adjusting entries.)

[b] Prepare a corrected trial balance.

5–32 Adjusting and Reversing Entries The following information pertains to Judd Company for the current year:

[1] On November 1, the company received a $10,000, 90-day, 10% note from a customer.

[2] Accrued wages as of December 31 amount to $3,250.

[3] On September 1, the company received $2,400 for rent paid in advance for eight months on a warehouse that Judd Company leases to Moore Company. Judd Company credited a nominal account.

[4] On October 1, the company paid $1,800 for a two-year fire insurance policy and debited a nominal account.

[5] The company computes $2,000 of depreciation for the year.

[6] The company estimates $2,300 of bad debts for the year.

INSTRUCTIONS

[a] Prepare the necessary adjusting journal entries on December 31, the end of the company's annual accounting period.

[b] Assuming that Judd Company wants to make reversals, prepare the reversing entries that are appropriate on January 1 of the next accounting period.

5–33 Adjusting Entries Ann Hong owns the Hong Hair Styling Center. A trial balance for the business at the end of this first year of operations appears below:

Hong Hair Styling Center
Trial Balance
December 31

Account	Dr.	Cr.
Cash	$13,000	
Supplies	14,000	
Prepaid rent	12,000	
Equipment	25,000	
Accounts payable		$ 3,000
Note payable		20,000
Hong, capital		7,000
Styling revenues		56,500
Advertising expense	7,000	
Salaries expense	13,000	
Utilities expense	2,500	
	$86,500	$86,500

ADDITIONAL INFORMATION

[1] A physical count reveals that supplies costing $2,000 are on hand at year-end.

[2] Rent on the shop was paid in advance for two years on January 1.

[3] The equipment was acquired on January 1. It has an estimated useful life of 10 years and no expected salvage value. Hong elects to use the straight-line depreciation method.

[4] The note payable relates to a one-year, 12% loan obtained from First National Bank on April 1.

[5] Salaries earned by employees but unpaid to them at year-end amount to $1,500.

INSTRUCTIONS

Using the trial balance and the additional information presented, prepare the necessary adjusting entries in general journal form at December 31.

5–34 Cost of Goods Sold and Gross Margin Selected account balances for Lovell Company on December 31 are shown below. Each account has a normal balance.

Account	Balance
Transportation-out	$ 12,000
Merchandise inventory, Dec. 31	36,000
Purchase discounts	3,000
Sales returns	11,000
Transportation-in	8,000
Sales discounts	7,000
Merchandise inventory, Jan. 1	30,000
Purchase returns	6,000
Sales allowances	9,000
Purchase allowances	4,000
Purchases	200,000
Sales	370,000

INSTRUCTIONS

[a] Prepare a schedule showing the computation of cost of goods sold.

[b] Calculate the amount of gross margin.

5–35 Financial Statements   The adjusted trial balance of Wilcox Company on December 31 appears below:

Account	Dr.	Cr.
Cash	$ 27,000	
Accounts receivable	50,000	
Allowance for doubtful accounts		$ 3,000
Note receivable (short term)	10,000	
Merchandise inventory	20,000	
Prepaid rent (for one year)	6,000	
Equipment	100,000	
Accumulated depreciation		15,000
Accounts payable		23,000
Salaries payable		2,000
Income tax payable		22,000
Common stock ($10 par value; 6,000 shares)		60,000
Paid-in capital in excess of par value		40,000
Retained earnings		50,000
Sales		215,000
Interest revenue		6,000
Cost of goods sold	100,000	
Salaries expense	20,000	
Rent expense	6,000	
Advertising expense	17,000	
Depreciation expense	10,000	
Bad debts expense	3,000	
Miscellaneous expense	5,000	
Income tax expense	22,000	
Dividends	40,000	
	$436,000	$436,000

INSTRUCTIONS

Prepare an income statement, a statement of retained earnings, and a balance sheet.

5–36 Closing Entries   Refer to the information presented for Wilcox Company in 5–35.

INSTRUCTIONS

[a] Journalize the closing entries on December 31.

[b] Prepare a post-closing trial balance.

5–37 Closing Entries   Listed below are the adjusted account balances of Melton Company on December 31. Each account has a normal balance.

Account	Balance
Accounts payable	$ 33,000
Accounts receivable	30,000
Accumulated depreciation—equipment	20,000
Advertising expense	8,000
Allowance for doubtful accounts	1,000
Bad debts expense	1,000
Cash	40,000
Common stock	40,000
Cost of goods sold	101,000
Depreciation expense—equipment	10,000
Equipment	100,000
Income tax expense	16,000
Interest expense	6,000
Interest payable	3,000
Merchandise inventory	50,000
Note payable	30,000
Prepaid rent	4,000
Rent expense	12,000
Retained earnings	53,000
Salaries expense	20,000
Sales	236,000
Sales returns	11,000
Transportation-out	5,000
Utilities expense	2,000

INSTRUCTIONS

Prepare closing entries in general journal form at December 31.

5–38 Reversing Entries Haskew Publishing Company made the following adjusting entries on December 31, 1996:

[1] Rent Receivable	3,000	
Rent Revenue		3,000
[2] Insurance Expense	700	
Prepaid Insurance		700
[3] Property Tax Expense	1,800	
Property Tax Payable		1,800
[4] Subscriptions Revenue	2,800	
Unearned Subscriptions Revenue		2,800
[5] Supplies Expense	850	
Supplies		850
[6] Amortization Expense	1,700	
Copyrights		1,700
[7] Bad Debts Expense	650	
Allowance for Doubtful Accounts		650
[8] Advertising Revenue	2,100	
Unearned Advertising Revenue		2,100

INSTRUCTIONS

Assuming that the company wants to make reversals, prepare all reversing journal entries that are appropriate on January 1, 1997.

5–39 Reversing Entries On November 1, 1996, Craft Company issued at par value $200,000 of 20-year, 12% bonds with interest payable semiannually on April 30 and October 31. The company uses a calendar-year accounting period.

INSTRUCTIONS

Record all appropriate journal entries using a table similar to the one shown below.

	Assumption	
Event	**Craft Company makes reversing entries for accrued interest.**	**Craft Company does not make reversing entries for accrued interest.**
12/31/96 adjusting entry to record accrued interest		
12/31/96 entry to close accrued interest		
1/1/97 reversing entry applicable to accrued interest		
4/30/97 entry to record payment of interest		
10/31/97 entry to record payment of interest		

5–40 Accrual Accounting A recent comparative balance sheet of Roncom, Inc., showed the following information:

	Balance	
Explanation	**12/31/95**	**12/31/96**
Interest receivable	$100	$500
Consulting fees receivable	700	300
Prepaid insurance	400	700
Supplies	400	200
Salaries payable	500	800
Utilities payable	300	200
Unearned subscriptions revenue	600	800
Unearned advertising revenue	600	200

Selected information about the company's 1996 revenues and expenses (accrual basis) appears below:

Revenues		**Expenses**	
Interest	$1,400	Insurance	$2,200
Consulting fees	5,000	Supplies	1,200
Subscriptions	7,500	Salaries	4,300
Advertising	3,000	Utilities	3,000

INSTRUCTIONS

[a] Compute the amount of 1996 cash receipts from each of the following sources: (1) interest, (2) consulting fees, (3) subscriptions, and (4) advertising.

[b] Compute the amount of 1996 cash payments for each of the following purposes: (1) insurance, (2) supplies, (3) salaries, and (4) utilities.

5–41 Accrual Accounting A recent comparative balance sheet of Cars Company revealed the following information:

	Balance	
Explanation	**12/31/95**	**12/31/96**
Interest receivable	$100	$300
Consulting fees receivable	700	200
Prepaid insurance	500	800
Supplies	400	100
Salaries payable	500	900
Utilities payable	300	100
Unearned subscriptions revenue	600	900
Unearned advertising revenue	600	400

Selected information about the company's 1996 cash receipts and disbursements appears below:

Explanation	Cash Receipts	Cash Disbursements
Interest	$3,500	
Consulting fees	3,000	
Insurance		$2,900
Supplies		1,200
Salaries		4,400
Utilities		1,000
Subscriptions	7,000	
Advertising	4,200	

INSTRUCTIONS

Compute each of the following income statement amounts for 1996 under the accrual basis of accounting: (1) interest revenue, (2) consulting fees earned, (3) insurance expense, (4) supplies expense, (5) salaries expense, (6) utilities expense, (7) subscriptions revenue, and (8) advertising revenue.

5–42 (Appendix B) **Special Journals** Ross Company uses the following journals: sales, sales returns and allowances, purchases, purchases returns and allowances, cash receipts, cash payments, and general. The following events occurred during December:

[1] Purchased merchandise on account.
[2] Paid accounts payable.
[3] Collected cash from customers on account.
[4] Made credit sales.
[5] Issued common stock for legal services received.
[6] Paid December rent.
[7] Returned defective merchandise to suppliers and received credit.
[8] Borrowed money from bank.
[9] Purchased merchandise for cash.
[10] Received defective merchandise from customers and granted credit.
[11] Discovered that a cash purchase of equipment in October had inadvertently been charged to the Land account at that time.
[12] Received payments made by customers on account.
[13] Computed annual depreciation.
[14] Made cash sales.

INSTRUCTIONS

Indicate the journal in which the company should record each of the above events.

5–43 (Appendix B) **Special Journals** Presented below are several transactions of Hopson company that occurred during December 1996. The company uses a periodic inventory system and a calendar-year accounting period.

Dec. 1 Purchased merchandise on account from Prince Company. The cost was $370.
4 Sold merchandise to Larry Gordon for $205 cash.
5 Paid Rip Company $440 on account.
8 Borrowed $10,000 from City & County Bank and signed a one-year, 12% note.
12 Sold merchandise on account for $1,400 to Hoffmann, Inc.
13 Signed a two-year, 13% note for $20,000 in exchange for land purchased from Windsor Corporation.
17 Received $275 on account from Winslow Company.
20 The company discovered that a $5,000 purchase of equipment on November 14, 1996, had inadvertently been entered in the Land account.
22 Purchased merchandise from Moore Company for $170 cash.
30 Paid a utility bill of $235 for services received in December.
31 Estimated depreciation for the year at $4,000.
31 Determined that $400 of prepaid insurance had expired during 1996.

INSTRUCTIONS

[a] Record these transactions in general journal form.
[b] Assume that Hopson Company uses the following journals: sales, cash receipts, purchases, cash payments, and general. Indicate where the company should record each transaction.

5–44 (Appendix B) Sales Journal   Loveday Company began operations on May 1 and transacted the following credit sales during May:

Date	Customer	Invoice No.	Amount
May 1	Macy Company	101	$550
8	Gresham, Inc.	102	280
16	Epling Enterprises	103	675
21	Davis Company	104	460
31	Cathey, Inc.	105	600

INSTRUCTIONS

[a] Set up a sales journal and record each of the above transactions.
[b] Post the journal entries to appropriate general and subsidiary ledger accounts.

5–45 (Appendix A) Worksheet   Presented below is the unadjusted trial balance of Sunlight Consultants, Inc., on December 31, the end of the company's annual accounting period:

Account	Dr.	Cr.
Cash	$ 26,000	
Note receivable	5,000	
Prepaid rent	12,000	
Equipment	100,000	
Accumulated depreciation		$ 20,000
Accounts payable		17,000
Common stock		30,000
Retained earnings		15,000
Consulting revenues		175,000
Salaries expense	90,000	
Travel expense	10,000	
Utilities expense	6,000	
Dividends	8,000	
	$257,000	$257,000

ADDITIONAL INFORMATION

This information is available on December 31:

[1] Accrued interest on note receivable is $250.
[2] Seventy-five percent of the prepaid rent shown above has expired.
[3] Depreciation expense for the year is $12,000.
[4] The December utility bill of $550 has not been paid or recorded.
[5] The income tax rate is 40%.

INSTRUCTIONS

Prepare a 12-column worksheet (as shown in Appendix A).

PROBLEMS

5–46 Journal Entries and Posting   Molson Company began operations on June 1. The company uses a periodic inventory system and records purchases of merchandise at gross amounts. The following transactions occurred during June:

June   1 Issued 1,000 shares of $10 par value common stock for $60,000.
        2 Borrowed $10,000 by signing a one-year, 10% note.
        3 Purchased the following for cash:

	Cost
Land	$10,000
Building	30,000
Equipment	5,000
Total	$45,000

        4 Purchased a three-year fire insurance policy for $4,800. (Debit an asset account.)
        5 Purchased office supplies for $4,000. (Debit an asset account.)

6 Received merchandise and an invoice dated June 5 from Black, Inc., for $6,000. Credit terms are 2/10, n/30.

6 Paid freight of $300 on merchandise received from Black, Inc.

8 Sold merchandise on credit to Haslem Company for $20,000. Terms are n/30.

10 Purchased merchandise from Nee, Inc., for cash of $6,000.

12 Returned $600 of defective merchandise to Nee, Inc., and received a cash refund.

14 Sold merchandise for cash of $5,000.

15 Paid Black, Inc., the amount of the June 5 invoice, less the discount.

17 Received merchandise returned by Haslem Company. Granted credit of $1,000.

20 Received one-year's rent of $4,800 in advance on a small office. (Credit a liability account.)

23 Received merchandise and an invoice dated June 21 from Small, Inc., for $7,500. Credit terms are 1/10, n/60.

25 Sold merchandise on credit to James Company for $3,000. Terms are n/30.

29 Received payment in full from Haslem Company. (See June 8 and June 17 transactions.)

30 Paid the following June expenses:

Salaries	$1,900
Advertising	600
Utilities	500
Total	$3,000

INSTRUCTIONS

[a] Record each of the June transactions in a general journal.

[b] Post each journal entry to appropriate general ledger accounts.

[c] Prepare an unadjusted trial balance on June 30.

5—47 Journal Entries and Posting Presented below is an unadjusted trial balance for Leonard Company on November 30:

Leonard Company
Unadjusted Trial Balance
November 30

Account	Dr.	Cr.
Cash	$ 14,000	
Accounts receivable	21,000	
Allowance for doubtful accounts		$ 1,000
Notes receivable	7,000	
Merchandise inventory, Jan. 1	15,000	
Prepaid insurance	3,000	
Prepaid rent	8,000	
Investment in Ace Company stock	20,000	
Equipment	60,000	
Accumulated depreciation		10,000
Accounts payable		11,000
Note payable		5,000
Common stock		40,000
Retained earnings		61,000
Sales		110,000
Sales returns	4,000	
Purchases	55,000	
Purchase returns		2,000
Purchase discounts		1,000
Transportation-in	5,000	
Salaries expense	20,000	
Advertising expense	6,000	
Utilities expense	3,000	
Interest expense	–0–	
	$241,000	$241,000

ADDITIONAL INFORMATION

The following transactions occurred during December:

Dec. 1 Sold the investment in Ace Company Stock for $14,000.
      3 Received a $4,000, 90-day, 13% note from a customer on account.
      4 Purchased merchandise for cash of $3,600.
      6 Paid the $5,000 note listed above. The note, which matured on Dec. 6, was for 120 days at 12% interest.
      7 Paid $8,000 of accounts payable. Took cash discounts of 2%.
      8 Returned $400 of defective merchandise purchased on Dec. 4 and received a cash refund.
      9 Collected $10,000 from customers on account.
     11 Wrote off uncollectible accounts receivable of $800.
     13 Purchased merchandise on account for $3,000. Terms are n/30.
     13 Paid freight of $200 on merchandise purchased.
     16 Received merchandise returned by a customer. Granted credit of $800.
     18 Sold merchandise on account for $9,000.
     22 Made cash sales of $5,000.
     23 Purchased a one-year insurance policy for $1,900.
     28 Purchased $10,000 of equipment to use in the business. Paid $2,000 cash and signed an $8,000, one-year, 12% note.
     31 Paid the following expenses:

Salaries	$1,800
Advertising	600
Utilities	300
Total	$2,700

INSTRUCTIONS

[a] Record each of the December transactions in a general journal. (Do not record adjusting entries.)
[b] Set up general ledger accounts and enter the opening balances for December. Post each journal entry to appropriate accounts.
[c] Prepare an unadjusted trial balance on December 31.

5–48 Accounting Cycle Greene Consulting Company began operations on December 1. The following transactions occurred during the first month:

Dec. 1 Sold 500 shares of $100 par value common stock for $50,000 cash.
      1 Purchased equipment for $30,000 cash. (The equipment has an estimated useful life of 10 years and no expected salvage value. The company plans to use straight-line depreciation.)
      1 Purchased a one-year insurance policy for $4,800. (The company records all pre-paid amounts in *real,* that is, balance sheet accounts.)
      1 Paid $9,600 office rent in advance for one year.
      2 Purchased on account supplies costing $8,000.
     10 Received $2,000 from a client for services rendered.
     16 Borrowed $5,000 from City Bank and signed a 90-day, 12% note.
     30 Paid half of the amount owed for the purchase of supplies on December 2.
     31 Billed clients $4,000 for services rendered during December.
     31 Paid $500 for advertisements run in the local newspaper during December.
     31 Paid the utility bill for $180 for December.
     31 Paid December salaries of $2,500.

INSTRUCTIONS

[a] Record the December transactions in general journal form.
[b] Post the journal entries to general ledger T accounts.
[c] Prepare an unadjusted trial balance at December 31.
[d] Journalize and post all necessary adjusting entries. (A count reveals that supplies costing $7,000 are on hand December 31. The income tax rate is 40%.)
[e] Prepare an adjusted trial balance.
[f] Prepare an income statement, a statement of retained earnings, and a balance sheet for December.

[g] Journalize and post closing entries.
[h] Prepare a post-closing trial balance.

5–49 Accounting Cycle   Presented below is the post-closing trial balance of Hyde Corporation on December 31, 1995:

Hyde Corporation
Post-Closing Trial Balance
December 31, 1995

Account	Dr.	Cr.
Cash	$ 12,000	
Accounts receivable	18,000	
Allowance for doubtful accounts		$ 900
Merchandise inventory	23,000	
Prepaid rent	24,000	
Equipment	50,000	
Accumulated depreciation		10,000
Accounts payable		21,000
Income tax payable		11,000
Common stock		40,000
Retained earnings		44,100
	$127,000	$127,000

Following is a summary of transactions that occurred during 1996:

[1] Purchased merchandise on account for $85,000. (The company uses a periodic inventory system.)
[2] Paid transportation charges of $4,600 on merchandise purchased.
[3] Sold merchandise as follows:

On account	$145,000
For cash	51,600
Total	$196,600

[4] Collected $136,000 of accounts receivable.
[5] Wrote off uncollectible accounts of $850.
[6] Paid the income tax liability that was reported on December 31, 1995.
[7] Paid $78,000 on accounts payable.
[8] Paid the following expenses:

Salaries	$21,000
Advertising	12,000
Utilities	8,000
Telephone and telegraph	4,400
Total	$45,400

[9] Declared dividends of $10,000. The company will pay the dividends early in 1997.

ADDITIONAL INFORMATION

This information is available on December 31, 1996:

[1] The company estimates that 1% of credit sales made during 1996 will never be collected.
[2] A physical count reveals that merchandise costing $19,000 is on hand at year-end.
[3] One-half of the prepaid rent as of December 31, 1995, expired during 1996.
[4] The equipment has an estimated useful life of 10 years and no expected salvage value. The company uses straight-line depreciation.
[5] The income tax rate for 1996 is 40%.

INSTRUCTIONS

[a] Set up general ledger T accounts for the post-closing trial balance accounts and for the following accounts: Dividends Payable, Sales, Cost of Goods Sold, Purchases, Transportation-In, Salaries Expense, Advertising Expense, Utilities Expense, Telephone and Telegraph, Bad Debts Expense,

Rent Expense, Depreciation Expense, Income Tax Expense, Dividends, and Income Summary. Enter the opening balances for 1996 in the ledger T accounts.

[b] Journalize the 1996 transactions in the order in which they are presented above. Use the number at the left of each transaction to indicate the date.

[c] Post the journal entries to the general ledger T accounts.

[d] Prepare an unadjusted trial balance.

[e] Journalize and post adjusting entries.

[f] Prepare an adjusted trial balance.

[g] Prepare an income statement, a statement of retained earnings, and a balance sheet.

[h] Journalize and post closing entries.

[i] Prepare a post-closing trial balance.

5–50 Adjusting Entries The following transactions occurred during the 1996 calendar-year accounting period of Maroni Company.

Apr.	1	Paid $4,000 to a local television station for commercial time that will be broadcast evenly over 12 months, beginning in April.
June	1	Received $6,000 from a tenant paying rent in advance for one year.
Sept.	1	Paid $1,200 for a one-year fire insurance policy.
Nov.	1	Received $24,000 from customers for subscriptions paid in advance for one year.

INSTRUCTIONS

[a] Assuming that the company has entered the above receipts and payments in *real* (balance sheet) accounts, journalize the adjustments required on December 31, 1996.

[b] Assuming that the company has entered the above receipts and payments in *nominal* (income statement) accounts, journalize the adjustments required on December 31, 1996.

[c] Under the assumption in [a], compute the adjusted account balances for the 1996 financial statements for all accounts in your adjusting entries.

[d] Under the assumption in [b], compute the adjusted account balances for the 1996 financial statements for all accounts in your adjusting entries.

5–51 Adjusting and Reversing Entries Eller Publishing Company recorded the following transactions during its 1996 calendar-year accounting period:

Mar.	1	Received $36,000 from customers for subscriptions paid in advance for one year.
Apr.	1	Paid $4,800 for a one-year fire insurance policy.
Aug.	1	Received $18,000 from a tenant paying rent in advance for six months.
Oct.	1	Paid $12,000 to a local radio station for advertising time. The station agreed to broadcast two ads each month for 12 months, beginning in October.

INSTRUCTIONS

[a] Journalize these transactions, assuming that the company enters in *real* (balance sheet) accounts the amounts that are received or paid in advance.

[b] Based on [a], journalize the necessary adjustments on December 31, 1996.

[c] Assuming that the company uses reversing entries, journalize the reversals that are appropriate for the adjusting entries in [b].

[d] Journalize the above transactions assuming that the company enters in *nominal* (income statement) accounts the amounts that are received or paid in advance.

[e] Based on [d], journalize the necessary adjustments on December 31, 1996.

[f] Assuming that the company uses reversing entries, journalize the reversals that are appropriate for the adjusting entries in [e].

5–52 Adjusting and Reversing Entries The following information pertains to Durty's Laundry Service on June 30, 1996, the end of the company's fiscal year:

[1] On March 1, 1996, the company purchased a three-year fire insurance policy for $1,800. A *real* (balance sheet) account was debited.

[2] The company's estimate of bad debts for the fiscal year is $1,750.

[3] On October 1, 1995, the company received $12,000 for rent received in advance for one year for storage space that it leases to Hill Company. A nominal account was credited.

[4] The company's estimate of depreciation for the year is $10,000.

[5] On April 1, 1996, the company paid $1,800 to the local newspaper for advertising space and debited a nominal account. The newspaper agreed to publish four ads each month for one year, beginning in April.

[6] On May 31, 1996, the company borrowed $5,000 from Citizens' Bank and signed a 120-day, 12% note.

[7] Employees have earned wages of $980 that the company has not paid or recorded as of June 30, 1996.

[8] On December 1, 1995, the company purchased at par value ten $1,000, 12%, 20-year bonds of Wynn, Inc. The bonds pay interest semiannually on May 31 and November 30.

[9] On March 1, 1996, the company received $12,000 for laundry service that it will provide for one year, beginning on that date. A *real* (balance sheet) account was credited.

[10] Property taxes owed and unrecorded as of June 30 total $1,175.

INSTRUCTIONS

[a] Prepare adjusting entries in general journal form at June 30, 1996.

[b] Assuming that the company wants to make reversing entries, identify the adjusting entries that it may appropriately reverse.

5–53 Adjusting and Reversing Entries   Presented below is the trial balance of Janeway Company at December 31, 1996; the end of the company's annual accounting period:

Account	Dr.	Cr.
Cash	$ 24,500	
Accounts receivable	25,000	
Allowance for doubtful accounts	150	
Merchandise inventory, Jan. 1	53,000	
Investment in DEBTCO, Inc., bonds	30,000	
Land	47,000	
Building	200,000	
Accumulated depreciation—building		$ 22,500
Equipment	80,000	
Accumulated depreciation—equipment		24,000
Accounts payable		19,000
Note payable		50,000
Common stock		100,000
Retained earnings, Jan. 1		174,528
Sales		452,000
Interest revenue		2,700
Rent revenue		9,000
Purchases	280,380	
Purchase returns and allowances		11,180
Transportation-in	10,000	
Salaries expense	86,200	
Rent expense	21,000	
Utilities expense	7,678	
	$864,908	$864,908

ADDITIONAL INFORMATION

[1] Eighty percent of 1996 sales were made on credit. The company estimates that 2% of credit sales will never be collected.

[2] A physical count reveals that merchandise costing $60,000 is on hand at year-end.

[3] On March 17, 1995, the company purchased thirty $1,000, 12%, 20-year bonds of DEBTCO, Inc. The bonds pay interest semiannually on March 31 and September 30.

[4] The company computes annual depreciation as follows:

Building	2.5% of cost
Equipment	5% of cost

[5] The note payable relates to a 90-day, 12% loan obtained from Walker National Bank on October 20, 1996.

[6] The company has rented a portion of its building to Robin's Retail Store since July 1, 1994. The rent is $6,000 per year, payable by Robin's in advance each July 1.

[7] As of December 31, employees had earned salaries of $5,200 that the company had not paid or recorded.

[8] The company has rented a warehouse from the Safe Storage Company since October 1, 1995. The rent is $12,000 per year, payable by Janeway Company in advance each October 1.

[9] The utility bill for December 1996 is $447. As of December 31, this amount had not been paid or recorded.

[10] The company's income taxes for the year are $26,300 to be paid in 1997.

INSTRUCTIONS

[a] Prepare the adjusting entries in general journal form on December 31, 1996.

[b] Identify the broad accounting principle that underlies each adjusting entry. (*Hint:* Review the principles discussed in Chapter 2.)

[c] Refer to the part of your answer in [b] that pertains to the cost of goods sold adjustment. Explain why the broad accounting principle you identified applies to the cost of goods sold adjustment.

[d] Assuming that Janeway Company wants to make reversing entries, identify the adjusting entries that the company may appropriately reverse.

5–54 Adjusting and Reversing Entries   Presented below is the trial balance of Debose Corporation at December 31, 1996, the end of the company's annual accounting period:

Debose Corporation
Trial Balance
December 31, 1996

Account	Dr.	Cr.
Cash	$ 12,925	
Accounts receivable	24,000	
Allowance for doubtful accounts		$ 300
Note receivable	4,000	
Merchandise inventory, Jan. 1	10,000	
Supplies	1,300	
Prepaid insurance	3,000	
Land	70,000	
Building	60,000	
Accumulated depreciation—building		6,000
Equipment	20,000	
Accumulated depreciation—equipment		4,000
Goodwill	9,375	
Accounts payable		8,600
Unearned rent revenue		7,200
Bonds payable (20-year, 10%)		100,000
Common stock		50,000
Paid-in capital in excess of par value		10,000
Retained earnings, Jan. 1		15,000
Sales		200,000
Purchases	95,000	
Purchase returns		3,000
Transportation-in	8,000	
Salaries expense	30,000	
Travel expense	7,000	
Advertising expense	16,000	
Transportation-out	10,000	
Telephone expense	5,000	
Utilities expense	11,000	
Interest expense	7,500	
	$404,100	$404,100

ADDITIONAL INFORMATION

[1] The company makes all its sales on credit. It estimates that 1.5% of sales made during 1996 will never be collected.

[2] The note receivable is a 90-day, 12% note taken from a customer on December 1, 1996.

[3] A physical inventory indicates that merchandise costing $30,000 is on hand December 31, 1996.

[4] A count reveals that supplies costing $300 are on hand December 31, 1996.

[5] The Prepaid Insurance account pertains to a three-year fire policy purchased on July 1, 1995, for $3,600.

[6] The following information concerns the building and equipment:

	Estimated Useful Life in Years	Estimated Salvage Value	Depreciation Method
Building	40	None	Straight line
Equipment	20	None	Straight line

[7] The company recorded $10,000 of goodwill when it acquired a competing firm on October 1, 1994. Debose Corporation uses the straight-line method of amortizing goodwill.

[8] On July 1, 1996, the company leased a portion of its building to Candor Company and received a check for $7,200 for one year's rent paid in advance.

[9] The company issued the bonds payable at par value on October 1, 1993. The bonds pay interest semiannually on March 31 and September 30.

[10] Salaries earned but unpaid to employees as of year-end totaled $3,200.

[11] On December 1, 1996, the company paid $1,800 for advertising time on a local television show that will be broadcast on January 12, 1997.

[12] A utility bill of $1,150 for December 1996 has been received but not yet recorded or paid.

[13] Property taxes that accrued during 1996 amounted to $3,600.

[14] The company determines that income tax expense for 1996 is $9,700. This amount will be paid in 1997.

INSTRUCTIONS

[a] Prepare adjusting entries in general journal form at December 31, 1996.

[b] Identify the broad accounting principle that underlies each adjusting entry. (*Hint:* Review the principles discussed in Chapter 2.)

[c] Refer to the part of your answer in [b] that pertains to the adjusting entry for the building and equipment (i.e., depreciation). Explain why the broad accounting principle you identified applies to this adjusting entry.

[d] Identify adjusting entries that Debose Corporation may appropriately reverse, assuming that the company wants to make reversing entries.

5–55 Reconstructing Adjusting Entries   Presented below are trial balances of Christian Company at December 31, 1996:

	Trial Balance			
	Unadjusted		Adjusted	
Account	Dr.	Cr.	Dr.	Cr.
Cash	$ 14,000		$ 14,000	
Accounts receivable	22,000		22,000	
Allowance for doubtful accounts	56			$ 2,000
Note receivable	10,000		10,000	
Interest receivable			1,000	
Supplies	6,000		3,209	
Merchandise inventory, Jan. 1	20,000			
Merchandise inventory, Dec. 31			25,000	
Prepaid rent	18,000		6,000	
Equipment	120,000		120,000	
Accumulated depreciation— equipment		$ 30,000		40,000
Accounts payable		12,000		12,000
Salaries payable				2,000
Income tax payable				16,000
Common stock		40,000		40,000
Retained earnings		67,265		67,265
Sales		205,631		205,631
Interest revenue				1,000

Account	Dr.	Cr.	Dr.	Cr.
Cost of goods sold			102,840	
Purchases	107,840			
Salaries expense	29,000		31,000	
Miscellaneous expenses	8,000		8,000	
Supplies expense			2,791	
Rent expense			12,000	
Depreciation expense			10,000	
Bad debts expense			2,056	
Income tax expense			16,000	
	$354,896	$354,896	$385,896	$385,896

INSTRUCTIONS

Based on the above information, *reconstruct* the adjusting journal entries that Christian Company made on December 31, 1996.

5–56 Effects of Adjusting Entries   At the end of 1996, Lee Company failed to record the adjusting entries indicated below:

[1] Estimate of bad debts.
[2] Depreciation of plant assets.
[3] Earned portion on one year's rent that Lee had received in advance on July 1, 1996, and recorded in a liability account.
[4] Accrued wages owed to employees.
[5] Unexpired portion of a one-year fire insurance policy that Lee paid for on September 1, 1996, and charged to a nominal account.
[6] Accrued interest on an investment in bonds.

INSTRUCTIONS

Prepare a table similar to the one shown below and indicate the effect of each error on the 1996 financial statement elements shown. Use the following code in marking your answers: O = overstated, U = understated, and NE = no effect. Assume that each error is independent of the others.

Error	Total Revenues	Total Expenses	Net Income	Total Assets	Total Liabilities	Total Stockholders' Equity
Example: Failed to record accrued interest on note payable.	NE	U	O	NE	U	O
[1]						
[2]						
[3]						
[4]						
[5]						
[6]						

5–57 (Appendix B)   General and Special Journals   Roseland Company began operations on May 1. The company uses a periodic inventory system. All credit sales are subject to terms of 2/10, n/30. The following transactions occurred during May:

May 1 Issued 10,000 shares of $5 par value common stock for $60,000.
2 Issued 1,000 shares of $5 par value common stock for land valued at $5,000.
3 Purchased a building for $30,000. Check no. 101 was issued.
5 Received merchandise and an invoice dated May 2 from Brown Company for $2,000. Terms are 1/15, n/30.
7 Sold merchandise on credit to Albert Company for $3,000. Invoice no. 1001 was issued.
9 Purchased merchandise from Dantley Company for cash of $1,500. Check no. 102 was issued.
11 Sold merchandise on credit to Hadler Company for $2,500. Invoice no. 1002 was issued.

12 Received merchandise and an invoice dated May 10 from Gatlin Company for $4,000. Terms are 2/10, n/60.

13 Sold merchandise to Roundtree Company for cash of $6,300.

15 Issued check no. 103 for $1,980 to Brown Company in payment of May 2 invoice, less the discount.

16 Received a check for $2,940 from Albert Company in payment of May 7 invoice, less the discount.

18 Received a check for $2,450 from Hadler Company in payment of May 11 invoice, less the discount.

19 Issued check no. 104 for $3,920 to Gatlin Company in payment of May 10 invoice, less the discount.

24 Received merchandise and an invoice dated May 23 from Early Company for $1,000. Terms are 2/10, n/30.

25 Sold merchandise on credit to Canton Company for $8,000. Invoice no. 1003 was issued.

28 Received merchandise and an invoice dated May 26 from Ison Company for $1,800. Terms are 3/15, n/30.

31 Sold merchandise on credit to Jasper Company for $2,800. Invoice no. 1004 was issued.

INSTRUCTIONS

[a] Record the transactions for May using the following journals (as shown in Appendix B): sales, purchases, cash receipts, cash payments, and general.

[b] Post the appropriate amounts in a general ledger and in accounts receivable and accounts payable subsidiary ledgers. Systematically number all accounts and use posting references.

[c] Prepare a trial balance on May 31.

[d] Reconcile the subsidiary ledgers with the appropriate control accounts.

5–58 (Appendix A) **Worksheet, Financial Statements, Adjusting and Closing Entries** Tomaski Company has adopted a calendar-year accounting period. The company's unadjusted trial balance on December 31, appears below:

Account	Dr.	Cr.
Cash	$ 36,775	
Accounts receivable	30,000	
Allowance for doubtful accounts	225	
Merchandise inventory, Jan. 1	42,000	
Investment in bonds (long term)	20,000	
Land	52,000	
Building	100,000	
Accumulated depreciation—building		$ 25,000
Equipment	50,000	
Accumulated depreciation—equipment		25,000
Accounts payable		32,000
Common stock ($10 par value, 10,000 shares)		100,000
Retained earnings, Jan. 1		109,500
Sales		475,000
Interest revenue		1,500
Rent revenue		12,000
Purchases	305,000	
Purchase returns		12,000
Salaries expense	88,000	
Advertising expense	22,000	
Utilities expense	6,000	
Supplies expense	30,000	
Dividends	10,000	
	$792,000	$792,000

ADDITIONAL INFORMATION

This information is available on December 31:

[1] The company estimates that bad debts expense for the year is $3,500.

[2] The December 31 merchandise inventory is $50,000.

[3] Unrecorded interest of $500 has accrued on the investment in bonds.
[4] The company estimates depreciation for the year as follows:

Building	$2,500
Equipment	$5,000

[5] One-fourth of the rent revenue shown above has *not* been earned as of December 31.
[6] Employees have earned salaries of $4,000 that the company has not paid or recorded.
[7] The cost of supplies on hand December 31 is $12,000.
[8] The income tax rate is 40%.

INSTRUCTIONS

[a] Enter the unadjusted trial balance on a 12-column worksheet (as in Appendix A).
[b] Enter the adjusting entries on the worksheet.
[c] Complete the worksheet.
[d] Prepare an income statement, a statement of retained earnings, and a balance sheet.
[e] Record the adjusting and closing entries in the general journal.

5–59 (Appendix A) Worksheet, Financial Statements, Adjusting and Closing Entries   Presented below is the unadjusted trial balance of Ritter, Inc., on December 31, the end of the company's annual accounting period:

Account	Dr.	Cr.
Cash	$ 4,500	
Accounts receivable	18,000	
Allowance for doubtful accounts		$ 300
Notes receivable (due in six months)	10,000	
Merchandise inventory, Jan. 1	23,000	
Prepaid insurance	4,800	
Land	40,000	
Building	50,000	
Accumulated depreciation—building		20,000
Equipment	20,000	
Accumulated depreciation—equipment		12,000
Accounts payable		21,000
Dividends payable		8,000
Unearned rent revenue		6,000
Common stock ($5 par value, 10,000 shares)		50,000
Retained earnings, Jan. 1		22,000
Sales		225,000
Purchases	123,000	
Transportation-in	7,000	
Salaries expense	34,000	
Advertising expense	8,000	
Utilities expense	4,000	
Dividends	18,000	
	$364,300	$364,300

ADDITIONAL INFORMATION

This information is available on December 31:

[1] Accrued interest on notes receivable totals $500.
[2] Employees have earned salaries of $1,500 that the company has not paid or recorded.
[3] One-half of the unearned rent revenue shown above was earned during the year.
[4] Three-fourths of the prepaid insurance shown above expired during the year.
[5] Depreciation for the year is as follows:

Building	$2,000
Equipment	$4,000

[6] Bad debts expense for the year is $900.
[7] The inventory on hand December 31 has a cost of $27,000.
[8] The income tax rate is 40%.

INSTRUCTIONS

[a] Enter the unadjusted trial balance on a 12-column worksheet (as in Appendix A).
[b] Enter the adjusting entries on the worksheet.
[c] Complete the worksheet.
[d] Prepare an income statement, a statement of retained earnings, and a balance sheet.
[e] Record the adjusting and closing entries in the general journal.

CASES

5–60 Accrual Accounting   Assume that you are working in the office of a small business client of your local CPA firm. The client has always maintained accounting records but has never prepared a set of financial statements completely in accordance with GAAP. Now, however, the client needs a bank loan, and the banker has required a set of financial statements prepared according to GAAP. Your client has asked you to help him to understand the meaning of accrual accounting.

INSTRUCTIONS

[a] How does accrual accounting affect the determination of income? Include in your discussion what constitutes an accrual and a deferral, and give appropriate examples of each.
[b] Compare accrual accounting and cash accounting.   (AICPA adapted)

5–61 Periodic Financial Reporting   Firms prepare annual financial statements for internal management and for distribution to outside parties. In addition, many firms prepare summary reports or statements quarterly, monthly, and weekly for both internal use and external distribution. The frequency of reporting may affect the preparation cost and the objectivity of the reports or statements.

INSTRUCTIONS

[a] Explain why the accounting period appropriate for internal and external reporting for most firms is one year.
[b] Explain in general terms why summary reports or statements are prepared for reporting periods of less than one year. Give an example why (1) internal management and (2) an outside party may want reports or statements that cover a shorter period.
[c] Adjustments to the accounting records are made when summary reports or statements are prepared annually, quarterly, or monthly.
   [1] Explain why these adjustments are needed.
   [2] Cite examples of adjustments that would have to be made to the accounting records.
[d] How is the objectivity of financial information in summary reports or statements affected when more frequent reports are prepared?   (CMA adapted)

Compound Interest Concepts

OBJECTIVES

1. To distinguish clearly between simple and compound interest.
2. To discuss and illustrate the fundamentals of compound interest.
3. To discuss and illustrate how to solve each of the following types of compound interest problems in accounting contexts:
   a. Amount and present value of a single sum.
   b. Amount and present value of an ordinary annuity.
   c. Amount and present value of an annuity due.
   d. Amount and present value of a deferred annuity.

THE MANHATTAN SAVINGS BANK

Current High Yield Certificates

Accounts		Annual Rate	Effective Annual Yield
7 Month	$2,500 minimum. Daily compounding. Interest paid quarterly and at maturity. Interest may be deferred until maturity.	3.80%	3.87%
*12 Month	$2,500 minimum. Daily compounding. Interest paid quarterly and at maturity. Interest may be deferred until maturity.	4.25%	4.34%
*24 Month	$2,500 minimum. Daily compounding. Interest paid quarterly and at maturity.	4.75%	4.86%
*3 Year	$2,500 minimum. Daily compounding.	5.60%	5.76%
*4 Year	$2,500 minimum. Daily compounding.	6.00%	6.18%
*5 Year	$2,500 minimum. Daily compounding.	6.50%	6.72%

Insured Money Director Account Under $100,000	
Annual Rate	Annual Yield
3.50%	3.56%

Insured Money Director Account $100,000 and Above	
Annual Rate	Annual Yield
3.50%	3.56%

Member F.D.I.C.

Some people have called it magic; others have called it the eighth wonder of the world. Regardless of what it's called, compound interest has an impressive power to make a sum of money grow. For example, Francis Baily, a 19th century British astronomer, determined that a British penny invested at 5% compound interest at the birth of Christ would have yielded enough gold by the year 1810 to fill 357 million earths. As another example, when Benjamin Franklin died in 1790, he left about $4,600 to the cities of Boston and Philadelphia under the condition that the money not be used for 100 years. By 1890, the $4,600 had grown to $332,000.

Compound interest will likely affect your life. Whether you are saving for retirement or paying off the mortgage on a new home, the effects of compound interest will likely be significant. Compound interest has quite an impact on accounting. It greatly affects such topics as accounting for leases and pensions. Moreover, the FASB is currently working on a financial instruments project, the outcome of which is likely to result in more use of compound interest concepts in accounting measurements.

Robert L. Rose, "Compounding: It's Boring but a Wonder," *The Wall Street Journal*, June 17, 1985, p. 23.

A dollar received today is worth more than a dollar received one year from today. This is true even if we ignore inflation, because the dollar received today can be invested to earn a return. Thus, we could place $1.00 in a 6% savings account today and have $1.06 at the end of one year. Having $1.06 one year hence is obviously better than receiving only $1.00 at that time.

Money has been regarded as a valuable resource ever since scientists first discovered that it doesn't grow on trees. It comes as no surprise, then, that money cannot be used free of charge. Money has a time value, commonly called **interest,** that people must consider when making rational investment and credit decisions.

Interest is the cost of using money over time. From the standpoint of a borrower, interest is the excess money paid over the amount that was borrowed. From a lender's point of view, interest is the excess money that is received over the amount that was loaned. Because the value of money changes over time, cash inflows and outflows that occur at different points in time are not directly comparable. Therefore, they should not be lumped together but should be compared as of a common point in time. We may choose to compare cash flows as of some future time. Usually, however, we compare cash flows as of the present time, because the present is the time within which we live and think.

To illustrate, assume that you have just decided to sell your wristwatch. Allen offers you $100, payable immediately; Baker offers $103, to be paid in one year. Assuming that you can earn a 6% return on your money, which offer should you accept? Clearly, if we compare the alternatives as of one year hence, we find that Allen's offer is worth $106 ($100 × 1.06), whereas Baker's offer is worth only $103. Making the comparison as of the present time, we find that Allen's offer is worth $100 while Baker's offer is worth less ($103 ÷ 1.06 = $97.17). In either case, Allen's offer should be accepted. Note that, because money has a time value, we could not meaningfully compare the two offers until we determined the value of each offer as of a common point in time.

In this chapter, we explain and illustrate the fundamentals of compound interest. The time value of money has so many applications in business that it often is covered in several college courses, such as accounting, finance, economics, and mathematics. Readers must acquire a working knowledge of compound interest concepts to understand many topics covered in subsequent chapters. Examples are accounting for certain notes receivable and notes payable under *Accounting Principles Board Opinion No. 21,* accounting for bonds as investments and liabilities, accounting for leases under *Financial Accounting Standards Board Statement No. 13,* accounting for pension plans under *FASB Statement No. 87,* accounting for sinking funds, and accounting for installment contracts. That money has a time value is clearly recognized in *APB Opinion No. 21,* a pronouncement that frequently requires accountants to estimate and record interest even though a long-term note may contain no stated interest rate.

In this chapter, we are not concerned with changes in general purchasing power of money over time (inflation or deflation). We will compare various sums of money without regard to the ability of those sums to buy goods and services. Assuming a 6% interest rate, for example, the question of whether $1.00 today can buy more or fewer goods and services than can $1.06 one year hence is beyond the scope of this chapter.

SIMPLE VERSUS COMPOUND INTEREST

Interest is earned over a period of time. Therefore, a stated interest rate relates to a particular time period. Because interest is normally stated as an **annual percentage rate,** such as 8%, 10%, or 12%, we assume throughout the text that a stated interest rate is a rate **per year,** unless indicated otherwise.

The two types of interest are simple and compound. **Simple interest** is earned only on the principal sum of money invested. The formula for simple interest follows:

$$i = prt$$

where i = simple interest
p = principal sum of money
r = interest rate per unit of time
t = time expressed in units that correspond to the rate

If $1,500 is borrowed at 8% for one year, the simple interest is $1,500 × .08 × 1 = $120. If the same amount is borrowed for only six months, simple interest is $1,500 × .08 ×

$^6/_{12}$ = $60. Note that r and t must correspond with one another. If r is an annual rate, t must be expressed in years; if r is a monthly rate, t must be expressed in months; and so forth.

Simple interest is used in many short-term (less than one year) business transactions. Recall that we assumed simple interest in Chapter 5 when we illustrated adjusting entries for the accrual of interest on notes receivable and notes payable.

Compound interest is earned on the principal sum of money invested *and* on the interest accumulated. In other words, the principal earns interest and the accumulated interest earns interest. To illustrate, assume that $1,500 is invested for three years at 8%. A comparison of simple versus compound interest on this investment follows:

Simple Interest

$$i = prt = \$1,500 \times .08 \times 3 = \$360$$

Accumulated amount at the end of the three years is

$$\$1,500 + \$360 = \$1,860$$

Compound Interest					
(A)	(B)	(C)	(D)	(E)	(F)
					Accumulated
				Compound	Amount
Year	Principal	Rate	Time	Interest	(B + E)
1	$1,500.00 $\times$	.08 $\times$	1 =	$120.00	$1,620.00
2	1,620.00 $\times$	.08 $\times$	1 =	129.60	1,749.60
3	1,749.60 $\times$	.08 $\times$	1 =	139.97	1,889.57
			Total	$389.57	

Notice that with compound interest, the accumulated amount at the end of each year becomes the new principal sum on which interest is earned during the next year. Notice further that $29.57 ($389.57 − $360.00 or $1,889.57 − $1,860.00) of additional interest resulted from compound interest. This is the interest on prior interest accumulations, which can be verified as shown below.

Year	Prior Interest Accumulation	Rate	Time	Interest on Prior Interest Accumulation
1	−0−* $\times$	.08 $\times$	1 =	−0−
2	$120.00† $\times$	.08 $\times$	1 =	$ 9.60
3	249.60‡ $\times$	.08 $\times$	1 =	19.97
			Total	$29.57

---

*No interest was accumulated prior to Year 1.
†This is the $120.00 interest for Year 1.
‡This is the $120.00 interest for Year 1 plus the $129.60 interest for Year 2.

Compound interest is used in most long-term (beyond one year) business transactions. Although interest is typically stated as an annual percentage rate, when compound interest is assumed, interest may be compounded (calculated and added to principal) for periods of less than one year. For example, interest may be compounded semiannually, quarterly, monthly, daily, or even continuously.[1] To avoid repetition, we make the customary assumption throughout the textbook that a stated annual interest rate is compounded annually, unless indicated otherwise.

BASIC CONCEPTS

The fundamental concepts underlying all compound interest problems are as follows:

1. **Present value (*PV*).** *Present value* usually refers to a value at the present time (today). More generally, it refers to a value at the beginning of any time span that is of concern.
2. **Future value (*FV*).** This usually refers to a value at some time in the future. More generally, future value can refer to a value at the end of any time period that is of concern.
3. **Interest rate (*i*).** This refers to a rate that corresponds to the length of each compounding period. This rate is computed by dividing the annual interest rate by the number of times a year interest is compounded.[2] For example, if interest is stated at 8%, compounded annually (once per year), the interest rate is 8% per annual period (8% ÷ 1). If interest is stated at 8%, compounded semiannually (twice per year), the interest rate is 4% per semiannual period (8% ÷ 2). And if interest is stated at 8%, compounded quarterly, (four times per year), the interest rate is 2% per quarterly period (8% ÷ 4).
4. **Time periods (*n*).** This refers to the number of compounding periods. It may be computed by multiplying the number of years involved by the number of compounding periods in each year. For example, interest for three years, compounded semiannually, involves 6 (3 × 2) compounding periods. Likewise, interest for three years, compounded quarterly, involves 12 (3 × 4) compounding periods.

Using these four fundamental concepts, we can solve compound interest problems.

Quite often, sketching the known components in the form of a **time diagram** aids in understanding and resolving the compound interest problem. The four concepts discussed above are depicted in the following time diagram:

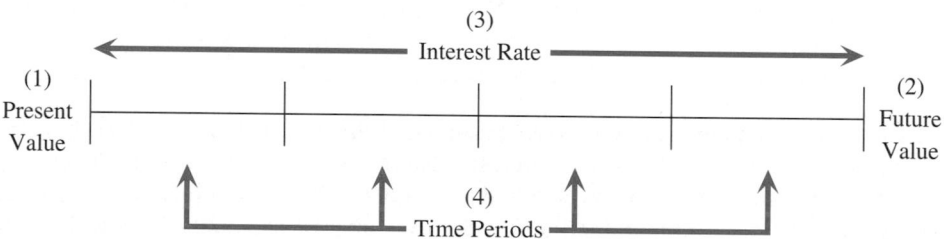

SINGLE SUM PROBLEMS

Single sum problems (sometimes called *lump-sum problems*) involve a single sum of money and generally fall into one of the following two categories:

---

[1]Continuous compounding is accomplished using logarithms.

[2]The interest rate (*i*) is called a **stated, or nominal, rate.** Furthermore, the term **frequency of compounding** (usually denoted by the letter *m*) refers to the number of times a year interest is compounded.

It is worthwhile to note that when *m* is greater than 1, the effective or true rate of interest (*r*) on an investment is greater than the stated annual rate. The **effective rate** is the rate that, when compounded annually, generates the same annual interest as the stated annual rate does when compounded *m* times per year. The effective rate may be calculated using the following formula:

$$r = (1 + i)^m - 1$$

For example, if the stated annual rate is 8% compounded quarterly, the effective annual rate is

$$
\begin{aligned}
r &= (1 + i)^m - 1 \\
&= (1 + .02)^4 - 1 \\
&= (1.02)^4 - 1 \\
&= 1.08243 - 1 \\
&= .08243 \\
&= 8.243\%
\end{aligned}
$$

1. Problems that focus on the future value of a single sum of money that is left on deposit for a certain number of periods at a certain interest rate per period.
2. Problems that focus on the present value of a single sum of money that is discounted for a certain number of periods at a certain interest rate per period.

AMOUNT (FUTURE VALUE) OF A SINGLE SUM

In everyday conversation, *amount* refers to any amount, past, present, or future. In discussions of compound interest, *amount* refers only to a future value. The amount of a single sum is therefore the future value to which the sum will accumulate if left on deposit for a certain number of periods at a certain interest rate per period. For example, in the earlier discussion of simple and compound interest, $1,889.57 (a future value) is the amount to which $1,500 (a single sum of money) will accumulate if left on deposit for three years at 8% compounded annually. The solution is illustrated in the time diagram in Exhibit 6–1. Note that the arrow points to the right, the direction of the future value.

The period-by-period approach used earlier to calculate future value ($1,889.57) is somewhat cumbersome, and it would be even more so in a problem involving more than three periods. To simplify the calculations, the following formula is often applied:

$$FV = PV(1 + i)^n$$

where FV = future value of a single sum
  PV = present value (principal sum) of a single sum
  i = interest rate per compounding period
  n = number of compounding periods

Applying this formula, we find that $1,889.57 is indeed the future value:

$$
\begin{aligned}
FV &= PV(1 + i)^n \\
&= \$1,500 \, (1 + .08)^3 \\
&= \$1,500 \, (1.08)^3 \\
&= \$1,500 \, (1.25971) \\
&= \$1,889.57
\end{aligned}
$$

The formula $FV - PV(1 + i)^n$ is the basic compound interest formula. Note that it consists of four variables: FV, PV, i, and n. If we know the values of any three, we can solve for the fourth using algebra.

Focus for a moment on the $(1 + i)^n$ part of the formula. Because of the frequent need to apply compound interest concepts in the business world, tables have been published that provide solutions for $(1 + i)^n$ for many combinations of i and n. We shall refer to each of these solutions as a **future value factor (fvf)**. Table 6–1 at the end of this chapter contains future

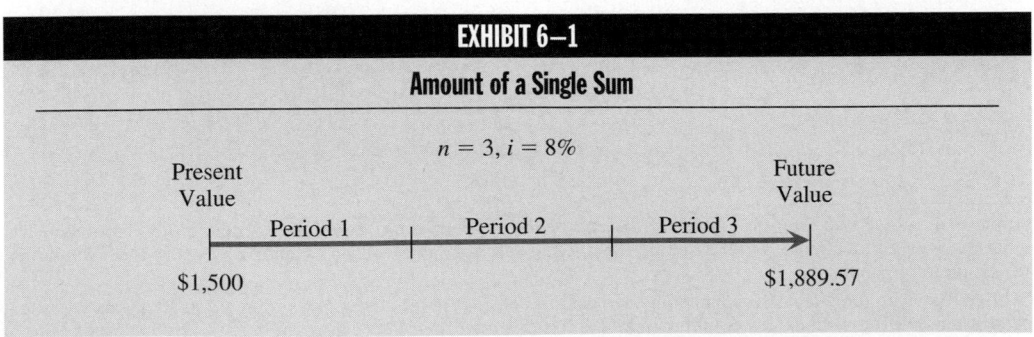

EXHIBIT 6–1
Amount of a Single Sum

$n = 3, i = 8\%$

Present Value ... Future Value

Period 1   Period 2   Period 3

$1,500 .... $1,889.57

value factors for most of the commonly encountered *i* and *n* values.[3] It can be used to save time in solving problems that involve the amount of a single sum.

Table 6–1 is entitled "Amount of 1" because it gives the amounts (future values) to which 1 (such as one dollar, one peso, or one mark) will accumulate if left on deposit for *n* periods at *i* compound interest. If we know the amount to which 1 will accumulate, we can find the amount to which any single sum will accumulate by simply multiplying the single sum by the amount to which 1 will accumulate. Note that the table consists of rows of compounding periods (*n*) and columns of interest rates (*i*). A future value factor is located at the intersection of each row and column.[4] For example, the future value factor of *n* = 5 and *i* = 10% is 1.61051. To illustrate finding a table factor, Exhibit 6–2 presents a portion of Table 6–1 with the factor circled for *n* = 5 and *i* = 10% (1.61051).

To really understand the solutions to compound interest problems, you should remember how Table 6–1 was constructed—that is, by solving $(1 + i)^n$ for different combinations of *i* and *n* values. It is no surprise that future value factors increase with each increase in *i* or *n*.

Because we know that $FV = PV(1 + i)^n$ and $(1 + i)^n = fvf$, we can now state

$$FV = PV \cdot fvf_{\overline{n}|i} \qquad (6\text{–}1)$$

where   *FV* = future value of a single sum
   PV = present value (principal sum) of a
       single sum
   $fvf_{\overline{n}|i}$ = future value factor (from Table 6–1)
       for the relevant *n* and *i*

The expression $fvf_{\overline{n}|i}$ is read as *"fvf sub n at i"* or *"fvf angle n at i."* When solving a compound interest equation, inserting the values for *n* and *i* ensures that you will locate and use the correct table factor.

Recall that we have determined, using both a period-by-period approach and a formula approach, that $1,889.57 is the future value of $1,500 deposited for three years at 8% compounded annually. Now we can use Equation 6–1 and Table 6–1 to implement a third approach to solving the problem. This approach is the easiest of all, because some of the calculations have already been performed, and the results appear in Table 6–1. First, note in Table 6–1 that the *fvf* for *n* = 3 and *i* = 8% is 1.25971. Now we can say

---

EXHIBIT 6–2

Finding the Future Value Factor of *n* = 5, *i* = 10% Using Table 6–1 (Amount of 1)

Number of Periods (*n*)	Interest Rate (*i*)		
	8%	10%	12%
1	1.08000	1.10000	1.12000
2	1.16640	1.21000	1.25440
3	1.25971	1.33100	1.40493
4	1.36049	1.46410	1.57352
5	1.46933	(1.61051)	1.76234
6	1.58687	1.77156	1.97382

---

[3]Table 6–1, as well as the other tables at the end of the chapter, are partial. In practice, more comprehensive tables are widely available. Of course, any compound interest table can be extended by using the formula on which the table is based.

[4]Notice that each table factor is rounded to five decimal places. In practice, tables rounded to 10 places are often used when dealing with extremely large numbers to minimize the effects of rounding.

$$FV = PV \cdot fvf_{\overline{n}|i}$$
$$= \$1,500 \cdot fvf_{\overline{3}|8\%}$$
$$= \$1,500 \, (1.25971)$$
$$= \$1,889.57$$

Because of the computational ease and time savings offered by compound interest tables, we emphasize a table-based solution to the problems in this chapter.

Accounting Examples

Problem 1. At the beginning of Year 1, Florida Electric Company deposited $50,000 in a special building fund that earns 8% interest compounded quarterly. How much cash will be in the fund at the end of Year 10?

Solution 1. In this problem, we know the present value ($50,000), the interest rate per period (8% ÷ 4 = 2%), and the number of periods (4 × 10 = 40). We are asked to solve for the future value, which we do with Equation 6–1 and Table 6–1:

$$FV = PV \cdot fvf_{\overline{n}|i}$$
$$= \$50,000 \cdot fvf_{\overline{40}|2\%}$$
$$= \$50,000 \, (2.20804)$$
$$= \$110,402$$

Problem 2. To keep things simple, let's modify Problem 1. Assume that Florida Electric Company wants to accumulate $110,402 for the purchase of a new building. If at the beginning of Year 1 the company deposited $50,000 in a special building fund that earns 8% interest compounded quarterly, how many years will it take for the fund to accumulate to $110,402?

Solution 2. We know the present value ($50,000), the future value ($110,402), and the interest rate per period (8% ÷ 4 = 2%). We are asked to solve for the number of years, which we can easily do using Equation 6–1 and Table 6–1. Because $FV = PV \cdot fvf_{\overline{n}|i}$, we can divide both sides of the equation by *PV*:

$$fvf_{\overline{n}|i} = \frac{FV}{PV}$$

$$fvf_{\overline{n}|2\%} = \frac{\$110,402}{\$50,000}$$

$$= 2.20804$$

Now that we know the future value factor and the interest rate per period, we simply run our finger down the 2% column of Table 6–1 until we find 2.20804. Because 2.20804 is found at *n* = 40, we conclude that it will take *10 years* (40 quarterly interest periods ÷ 4) to accumulate $110,402. If we had not found the number 2.20804 in the 2% column of Table 6–1, we could have approximated our answer using linear interpolation, a procedure explained later in the chapter.

Problem 3. Suppose that the problem were phrased this way. Florida Electric Company wants to accumulate $110,402 for the purchase of a new building. If at the beginning of Year 1 the company deposited $50,000 in a special building fund in which interest is compounded quarterly, what annual rate of interest is required for the $50,000 deposit to accumulate to $110,402 at the end of Year 10?

Solution 3. We follow the same approach taken in Problem 2, except that we look for the future value factor of 2.20804 in Table 6–1 along the row in which *n* = 40 (10 years × 4 compounding periods per year). Because 2.20804 is in the 2% column, we conclude that the required annual rate of interest is 8% (2% × 4).

PRESENT VALUE OF A SINGLE SUM

Determining the present value of a single sum is the inverse of determining the amount of a single sum. Instead of moving forward in time using accumulation to determine a future value, we move backward in time using **discounting** to determine a present value. For example, suppose that we want to know the present value of $1,889.57 to be received or paid in three years discounted at 8% compounded annually. We could prepare a decumulation table similar to the compound interest accumulation table presented earlier. Instead of going forward in time, we would go backward, and instead of multiplying each year's principal by 1.08, we would multiply by 1/1.08 (which is the same as dividing by 1.08), as shown below.

										Compound Discount		
(A)		**(B)**		**(C)**		**(D)**				**(E)**		**(F)**
				Discount						Decumulated		Compound Discount
Year		Principal		Rate		Time				Amount		(B−E)
3		$1,889.57	×	$\frac{1}{1.08}$	×	1	=			$1,749.60		$139.97
2		1,749.60	×	$\frac{1}{1.08}$	×	1	=			1,620.00		129.60
1		1,620.00	×	$\frac{1}{1.08}$	×	1	=			1,500.00		120.00
										Total		$389.57

The time diagram shown in Exhibit 6–3 illustrates the solution to the problem. The arrow in the diagram points to the left, which is the direction of the present value.

That $1,500 is the present value (the decumulated amount at the beginning of Year 1) is no surprise, because this problem was used earlier to explain the amount of a single sum. Preparing decumulation tables is tedious and time consuming. Fortunately, there are easier ways to solve the problem.

Remember the basic compound interest formula:

$$FV = PV(1 + i)^n$$

If we divide both sides of this equation by $(1 + i)^n$, we get

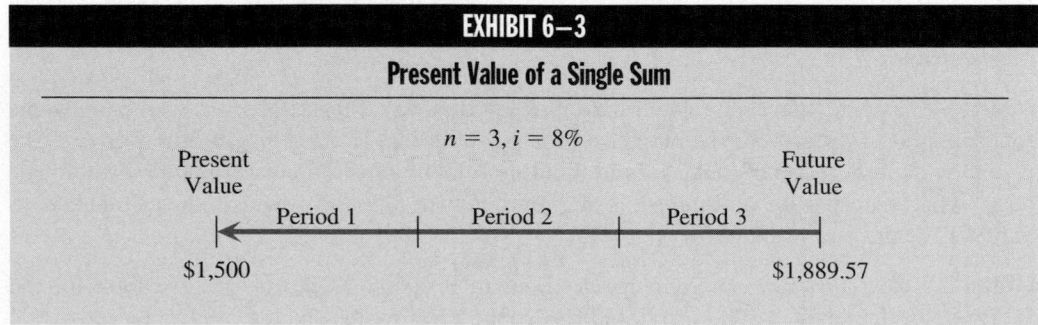

EXHIBIT 6–3

Present Value of a Single Sum

$n = 3, i = 8\%$

Present Value — Period 1 — Period 2 — Period 3 — Future Value

$1,500 $1,889.57

$$PV = \frac{FV}{(1 + i)^n}$$

We can now apply this formula to the problem and determine that $1,500 is indeed the present value:

$$
\begin{aligned}
PV &= \frac{FV}{(1 + i)^n} \\[2mm]
&= \frac{\$1,889.57}{(1.08)^3} \\[2mm]
&= \frac{\$1,889.57}{1.25971} \\[2mm]
&= \$1,500
\end{aligned}
$$

We can easily rewrite the above formula as follows:

$$PV = FV \cdot \frac{1}{(1 + i)^n}$$

The $1/(1 + i)^n$ part of the equation is simply the reciprocal (the inverse) of the formula used to calculate the amount of 1. Tables are widely available that provide solutions for $1/(1 + i)^n$ for combinations of i and n. We shall refer to each of these solutions as a **present value factor** (**pvf**). A present value factor is simply the reciprocal of the future value factor for a given i and n. Table 6–2 at the end of the chapter contains present value factors for many i and n combinations. Given the formula used to construct the table, you should not be surprised that present value factors decrease with an increase in n or i. Note that the table is entitled "Present Value of 1." If we know the present value of 1 for a certain i and n, we can easily compute the present value of any single sum by multiplying the single sum by the present value of 1.

Because we know that $PV = FV \cdot 1/(1 + i)^n$ and $1/(1 + i)^n = pvf$, we can now state the following:

$$PV = FV \cdot pvf_{\overline{n}|i} \qquad\qquad (6\text{–}2)$$

where PV = present value (principal sum)
                    of a single sum
          FV = future value of a single sum
    $pvf_{\overline{n}|i}$ = present value factor (from Table 6–2)
                    for the relevant n and i

Equation 6–2 saves time in solving problems for the present value of a single sum. To illustrate its application to the example problem, we first find in Table 6–2 that the *pvf* for $n = 3$ and $i = 8\%$ is .79383. Now we can state the following:

$$
\begin{aligned}
PV &= FV \cdot pvf_{\overline{n}|i} \\
&= \$1,889.57 \cdot pvf_{\overline{3}|8\%} \\
&= \$1,889.57\,(.79383) \\
&= \$1,500
\end{aligned}
$$

Accounting Examples

Problem 4. What is the value at the beginning of Year 1 of a noninterest-bearing note that has a maturity value of $10,000 at the end of Year 4? Assume that the market rate of interest for similar notes is 8% compounded annually.

Solution 4.   We know the future value (the $10,000 maturity value), the interest rate per period (8%), and the number of periods (4). We can solve for the present value by using Equation 6–2 and Table 6–2:

$$PV = FV \cdot pvf_{\overline{n}|i}$$
$$= \$10,000 \cdot pvf_{\overline{4}|8\%}$$
$$= \$10,000 \,(.73503)$$
$$= \$7,350.30$$

In other words, $7,350.30 is the sum that a person would pay today to receive $10,000 at the end of four years, assuming 8% interest compounded annually. That the note could be sold only at a discount ($10,000 − $7,350.30 = $2,649.70) appears reasonable because the note has no stated interest and similar notes yield 8%.

As in the examples concerning the amount of a single sum, we could alter the information in Problem 4 to illustrate solutions for other variables. However, the point should now be clear. That is, we are dealing with one basic equation of four variables. When three of the variables are known, solving for the one unknown is not difficult.

Problem 5.   One of your clients, I. M. Rich, wants to put aside some money to buy his son an $8,000 automobile when his son graduates from college in four years. Assuming that Mr. Rich will earn 6%, compounded annually, on his savings during the first two years and 8%, compounded semiannually, during the last two years, how much should he deposit at the beginning of the four-year period?

Solution 5.   Once again we are seeking the present value of a single sum ($8,000). However, in this case, the interest rate and the frequency of compounding change after the second year. We therefore need to break down the problem into two components. First, compute the present value, *as of the beginning of the third year,* of $8,000 to be received at the end of four semiannual periods discounted at 4% per period. (Remember that the 8% interest is compounded semiannually during the last two years.) Second, compute the present value, *as of the beginning of the first year,* of the value calculated in the first step when discounted for two years at 6%. Thus, we have

$$\textbf{Step 1.}\quad PV = FV \cdot pvf_{\overline{n}|i}$$
$$= \$8,000 \cdot pvf_{\overline{4}|4\%}$$
$$= \$8,000 \,(.85480)$$
$$= \$6,838.40$$

The value $6,838.40 is the present value as of the beginning of the *third year.* To determine the present value as of the beginning of the *first year,* we must perform Step 2.

$$\textbf{Step 2.}\quad PV = FV \cdot pvf_{\overline{n}|i}$$
$$= \$6,838.40 \cdot pvf_{\overline{2}|6\%}$$
$$= \$6,838.40 \,(.89000)$$
$$= \$6,086.18$$

Mr. Rich should therefore deposit $6,086.18 so that he will have the $8,000 required to purchase the automobile at the end of the four-year period.

Remember from this example that *when a compound interest problem appears complex, try to solve it by dividing it into its components.*

ANNUITY PROBLEMS

An **annuity** is a series of equal receipts or payments, called **rents,** that occur at uniform intervals at a constant interest rate.[5] This book assumes a standard annuity in which interest is

---

[5] Note that the term **rents** refers to a series of equal receipts or payments of any kind. In compound interest discussions, use of this term is not confined to its everyday connotation of payments on a leased asset.

compounded once at the end of each interval. Annuities commonly occur at annual, semiannual, quarterly, or monthly intervals. Lease payments, sinking fund payments, mortgage payments, and retirement payments are only a few examples of annuities that accountants encounter every day.

Annuities may be classified as ordinary annuities or annuities due.[6] The difference lies solely in the timing of the rents. With an **ordinary annuity,** the rents occur at the *end* of each period. With an **annuity due,** the rents occur at the *beginning* of each period. In both kinds of annuities, *one* rent occurs during each period, either at the beginning (annuity due) or at the end (ordinary annuity). For this reason, the symbol n in annuity problems refers to either the number of compounding periods or the number of rents.

As in the single sum problems discussed earlier, annuities involve present and future value concepts. Whereas earlier discussions dealt with the present and future values of a single sum, the following sections concern the present and future values of multiple sums, each of which is equal in size.

AMOUNT (FUTURE VALUE) OF AN ORDINARY ANNUITY

As shown earlier, a single sum of $1,500 left on deposit for three years at 8% will accumulate to $1,889.57. What is the amount (future value) at the end of three years of *three periodic rents of $1,500 each* that occur at the end of each year at 8% compounded annually? The question involves the amount of an ordinary annuity.

As the time diagram in Exhibit 6–4 suggests, computing the amount of an ordinary annuity involves nothing more than computing the total amount of a series of single sums.[7] Algebraically, we have

3rd Rent		2nd Rent		1st Rent		Amount of the Ordinary Annuity
$1,500	+	$1,500 (1.08)	+	$1,500 $(1.08)^2$	=	$4,869.60

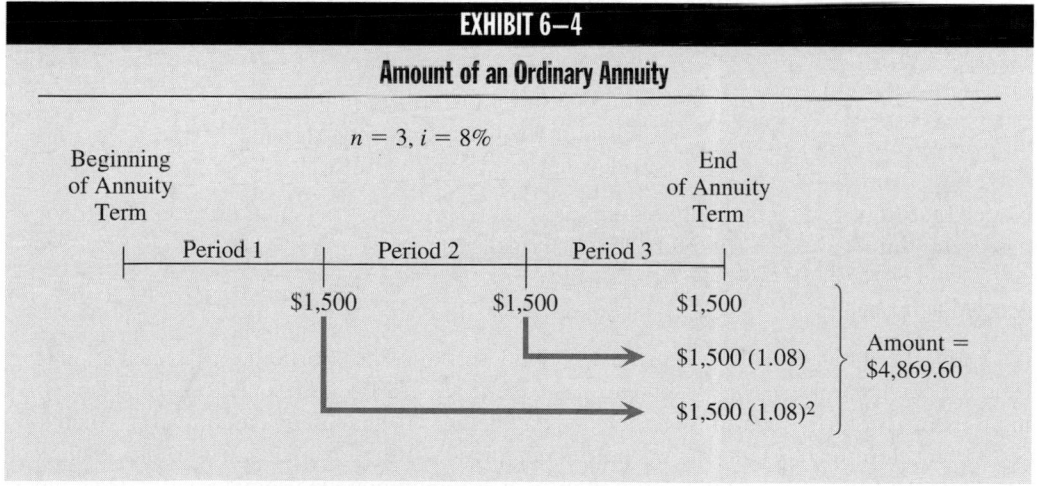

EXHIBIT 6–4

Amount of an Ordinary Annuity

---

[6]Ordinary annuities are sometimes called *annuities in arrears;* annuities due are sometimes called *annuities in advance.*

[7]You may find it helpful to verify this statement by applying Equation 6–1 and Table 6–1 to each of the $1,500 rents. This would give the following results:

1st rent	$1,500 (1.16640) =	$1,749.60
2nd rent	1,500 (1.08000) =	1,620.00
3rd rent	1,500 (1.00000) =	1,500.00
	Total	$4,869.60

Note that although the annuity encompasses three periods, only two rents earn interest. The first rent earns interest during Periods 2 and 3; the second rent earns interest during Period 3 only. The third rent earns no interest, because it occurs at the end of the three-year span. In an amount of an ordinary annuity of *n* rents, only *n* − 1 rents will earn interest, because the last rent occurs at the end of the annuity term and no interest period exists for that rent. *An amount of an ordinary annuity focuses on a future value and the last rent occurs at the end of the annuity term.*

Of course, the $1,500 rent in the preceding equation could be factored out:

$$\$1,500 \ (1 + 1.08 + 1.08^2) = \$4,869.60$$

$$\$1,500 \ (1 + 1.08 + 1.1664) = \$4,869.60$$

$$\$1,500 \ (3.24640) = \$4,869.60$$

Turn to Table 6–3 at the end of the chapter and locate the factor for *n* = 3, *i* = 8%. You will see that it is 3.24640, the number by which we multiplied $1,500 in the last equation. Note that Table 6–3, "Amount of an Ordinary Annuity of 1," contains factors for many combinations of *n* and *i*. Each factor is an **amount of an ordinary annuity factor (*aoaf*).** Each factor could have been determined by the approach used above for *n* = 3 and *i* = 8%, but the following formula was applied to save time in generating each factor:

$$aoaf_{\overline{n}|i} = \frac{(1 + i)^n - 1}{i}$$

Each table factor, then, is based on an equation that incorporates values for both *n* and *i*.

Using Table 6–3, we can find the amount to which an ordinary annuity of any size rent will accumulate. We simply multiply the size of each rent by the amount to which an ordinary annuity of 1 will accumulate. Expressed algebraically, we have

$$AOA = R \cdot aoaf_{\overline{n}|i} \qquad\qquad (6\text{–}3)$$

where   *AOA* = amount (future value) of an ordinary
                annuity of *n* rents at *i* interest rate
          R = size of each periodic rent
  aoaf$_{\overline{n}|i}$ = amount of an ordinary annuity of
                1 factor (from Table 6–3) for the
                relevant *n* and *i*

Notice that Equation 6–3 contains four variables (*AOA*, *R*, *n*, and *i*) and if we know the values of any three, we can solve for the fourth using algebra.

Accounting Examples

Problem 6. On January 1 of the current year, Control Systems Corporation creates a sinking fund to accumulate cash that will be needed to retire a $1,000,000 issue of bonds payable that matures in 10 years. Accordingly, the company decides to make 20 semiannual payments of $30,000 each into a sinking fund. The first payment will be made on June 30 of the current year, and the fund is expected to earn interest at 10% compounded semiannually. How much cash will be in the fund at the end of 10 years?

Solution 6. The problem clearly involves an annuity, because periodic payments (rents) of $30,000 each will be placed in a sinking fund. Furthermore, it is an ordinary annuity, because the initial rent occurs at the end of the first semiannual period. Because the payments are made semiannually, we know that *n* = 10 × 2 = 20 and *i* = 10% ÷ 2 = 5%. We must determine the amount of an ordinary annuity of 20 rents of $30,000 each at 5% interest. Using Equation 6–3 and Table 6–3, we have

$$AOA = R \cdot aoaf_{\overline{n}|i}$$
$$= \$30,000 \cdot aoaf_{\overline{20}|5\%}$$
$$= \$30,000 (33.06595)$$
$$= \$991,978.50$$

Unfortunately, the amount in the sinking fund at the end of 10 years will be $8,021.50 ($1,000,000 − $991,978.50) less than the company needs to retire the bonds.

Problem 7. Referring to Problem 6, how much would Control Systems Corporation have to deposit at the end of each semiannual period to accumulate $1,000,000 in the sinking fund at the end of 10 years?

Solution 7. In Problem 6, semiannual deposits of $30,000 left the company $8,021.50 short of its goal of $1,000,000. Thus, logic dictates that the company will have to deposit somewhat more than $30,000 each period. To find the exact size of each deposit, we refer to Equation 6–3, which states that $AOA = R \cdot aoaf_{\overline{n}|i}$. Dividing both sides of the equation by $aoaf_{\overline{n}|i}$ and substituting the values of the known variables, we have the following:

$$R = \frac{AOA}{aoaf_{\overline{n}|i}}$$
$$= \frac{\$1,000,000}{aoaf_{\overline{20}|5\%}}$$
$$= \frac{\$1,000,000}{33.06595}$$
$$= \$30,242.59$$

Control Systems Corporation must therefore deposit $30,242.59 at the end of each semiannual period to accumulate $1,000,000 at the end of 10 years.

Problem 8. One of your clients, Tracy Mack, tells you that she wants to accumulate a $10,000 cash gift for her new baby daughter by depositing $300 at yearly intervals beginning one year from now. The periodic deposits will be placed in a 6% savings account. When Tracy accumulates the $10,000, how old will her daughter be?

Solution 8. We know that this problem involves an ordinary annuity, because the periodic deposits of $300 begin one year from now. Furthermore, we know the desired future amount ($10,000), the size of the periodic rents ($300), and the interest rate per period (6%). The unknown that we seek is the number of periods, which we can determine by rewriting Equation 6–3 and using Table 6–3. Equation 6–3 states that $AOA = R \cdot aoaf_{\overline{n}|i}$. Dividing both sides of the equation by R and substituting the known values, we have

$$aoaf_{\overline{n}|i} = \frac{AOA}{R}$$
$$aoaf_{\overline{n}|6\%} = \frac{\$10,000}{\$300}$$
$$= 33.33333$$

We now search the 6% column of Table 6–3 for the factor 33.33333. We won't find it, but we can determine that it would lie between 30.90565 (the factor for $n = 18$) and 33.75999 (the factor for $n = 19$). Because it is closer to the factor for $n = 19$, we conclude that it will take almost 19 years for Tracy Mack to accumulate $10,000. In other words, her daughter will be almost 19 years old when she receives the $10,000 gift from her mother.

A closer approximation may be achieved by using linear interpolation. In general, when a factor is computed but does not appear in the pertinent compound interest table, interpolation may be used to find a reasonable approximation of the unknown number of periods (n) or interest rate (i).[8] The smaller the range of interpolation, the smaller the error will be. Interpolation is based on the principle of proportion, as the following format suggests:

	When n is	The corresponding $aoaf$ is		
	18	30.90565		
x			2.42768	
	?	33.33333		2.85434
	19	33.75999		

We can set up the following proportion:

$$\frac{x}{1} = \frac{2.42768}{2.85434}$$

Solving for x, we find that it equals .85. Because x is the distance between 18 and n, we conclude that $n = 18 + .85 = 18.85$. Tracy's daughter, then, will be approximately 18.85 years old when she receives her gift. Any time you want to interpolate, set up a proportion similar to the one shown above.

Problem 9.   Referring to the information in Problem 8, what interest rate would Tracy Mack have to earn on her investment so that she could give her daughter the $10,000 present on her eighteenth birthday?

Solution 9.   Logic dictates that because it would take approximately 18.85 years to accumulate $10,000 at 6% interest, Tracy will have to earn more than 6% to accumulate the same amount in less time. Once again, dividing both sides of Equation 6–3 by R, we have

$$aoaf_{\overline{n}|i} = \frac{AOA}{R}$$

Therefore, $aoaf_{\overline{18}|i} = \$10{,}000/\$300 = 33.33333$. Looking across the 18th row of Table 6–3, we determine that 33.33333 would lie between 30.90565 (the factor for $i = 6\%$) and 37.45024 (the factor for $i = 8\%$). Approximating the answer through interpolation, we have

	When i is	The corresponding $aoaf$ is		
	6%	30.90565		
2% x	?	33.33333	2.42768	6.54459
	8%	37.45024		

---

[8] An exact answer may be determined using logarithms or an electronic calculator.

Setting up a proportion, we have

$$\frac{x}{2\%} = \frac{2.42768}{6.54459}$$

Solving for x, we find that it equals .74%. Since x is the distance between 6% and i, we conclude that $i = 6\% + .74\% = 6.74\%$. Tracy Mack would thus have to earn roughly 6.74% interest if she wanted to give her daughter $10,000 on her eighteenth birthday.

AMOUNT (FUTURE VALUE) OF AN ANNUITY DUE

Earlier we stated that an annuity due is one in which the rents occur at the *beginning* of each period. Further, we saw that $4,869.60 is the amount of an *ordinary* annuity of three annual rents of $1,500 each at 8%. What is the amount at the end of three years of three annual rents of $1,500 each that occur at the *beginning* of each year at 8% compounded annually?

As the time diagram in Exhibit 6–5 suggests, an annuity due begins with a rent and ends one period *after* the last rent. Thus, if we took the amount of an ordinary annuity of three $1,500 rents at 8% and left all the money on deposit at 8% for one additional period, we would have the amount of an annuity due of three $1,500 rents at 8%. For any given values of n and i, the amount of an annuity due is greater than the amount of an ordinary annuity by the interest on the latter amount for one period. Stated differently, the amount of an annuity due for given values of n and i is equal to the amount of an ordinary annuity of $(n + 1)$ rents at i interest rate, *minus* one rent (the final rent).

An **amount of an annuity due** *focuses on a future value and last rent occurs one period before the end of the annuity term.* In an amount of an annuity due of n rents, all of the n rents earn interest. Note carefully in Exhibit 6–5 that the third rent earns interest for one period, the second rent earns interest for two periods, and the first rent earns interest for three periods. Algebraically,

$$\$1,500 \ (1.08) + \$1,500 \ (1.08)^2 + \$1,500 \ (1.08)^3 = \$5,259.17$$

Factoring out the $1,500 rent, we have

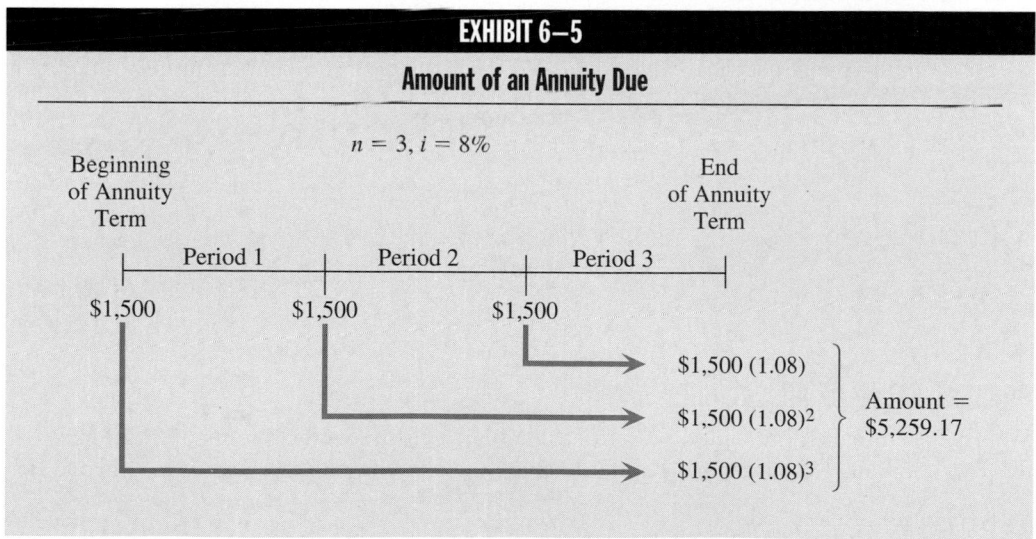

EXHIBIT 6–5
Amount of an Annuity Due

$n = 3, i = 8\%$

Beginning of Annuity Term

End of Annuity Term

Period 1 Period 2 Period 3

$1,500 $1,500 $1,500

$1,500 (1.08)
$1,500 (1.08)²
$1,500 (1.08)³

Amount = $5,259.17

$$\$1,500 \ (1.08 + 1.08^2 + 1.08^3) = \$5,259.17$$

$$\$1,500 \ (1.08 + 1.1664 + 1.25971) = \$5,259.17$$

$$\$1,500 \ (3.50611) = \$5,259.17$$

In the last equation, 3.50611 is simply a factor for computing the amount of an annuity due (*aadf*) where $n = 3$ and $i = 8\%$. We could construct a table of these factors and call it "Amount of an Annuity Due of 1." However, the relationship between the amount of an ordinary annuity and the amount of an annuity due is so straightforward that a separate table is unnecessary. We can use the "Amount of an Ordinary Annuity of 1" table (Table 6–3) to determine an *aadf* simply by finding the factor for $(n + 1)$ periods and i, and subtracting 1 from the factor we find. Stated algebraically,[9]

$$aadf_{\overline{n}|i} = aoaf_{\overline{n+1}|i} - 1$$

To illustrate, let's use Table 6–3 to calculate $aadf_{\overline{3}|8\%}$. We simply look up the table factor for $n + 1 = 4$ periods and $i = 8\%$, and we find 4.50611. Subtracting 1 from this, we get 3.50611. Now that we know how to derive an *aadf* using Table 6–3, we can state

$$AAD = R \cdot aadf_{\overline{n}|i} \qquad \qquad (6\text{–}3A)$$

where AAD = amount of an annuity due of n
rents at i interest rate

R = size of each periodic rent

$aadf_{\overline{n}|i}$ = amount of an annuity due of 1 factor
(from Table 6–3, *as adjusted*) for the
relevant n and i

Because the values of n and i determine the value of $aadf_{\overline{n}|i}$, Equation 6–3A consists of four variables: AAD, R, n, and i. Remember that if we know the values of any three, we can solve for the fourth using algebra.

Accounting Example

Problem 10.   Warren Wilson has created a fund for his retirement in 35 years. He deposits $3,000 today in a special 8% account, and he plans to make periodic deposits of $3,000 each at annual intervals over the next 34 years. How much cash will be in Wilson's retirement fund when he retires?

Solution 10.   Because the initial rent occurs at the beginning of the first year, we are dealing with an annuity due. Specifically, we are asked to calculate the amount (a future value) of an annuity due of 35 rents of $3,000 at 8%. Using Equation 6–3A and Table 6–3, as adjusted, we have

$$\begin{aligned}
AAD &= R \cdot aadf_{\overline{n}|i} \\
&= \$3,000 \cdot aadf_{\overline{35}|8\%} \\
&= \$3,000 \ (aoaf_{\overline{35+1}|8\%} - 1) \\
&= \$3,000 \ (187.10215 - 1) \\
&= \$3,000 \ (186.10215) \\
&= \$558,306.45
\end{aligned}$$

PRESENT VALUE OF AN ORDINARY ANNUITY

We have seen that the amount of an ordinary annuity of three annual rents of $1,500 each at 8% is $4,869.60. Accountants often must solve problems that are the inverse of this one, for

---

[9] A second way to derive $aadf_{\overline{n}|i}$ is as follows: $aadf_{\overline{n}|i} = aoaf_{\overline{n}|i}(1 + i)$. Although this approach is correct, it is more difficult to use when i is the unknown variable.

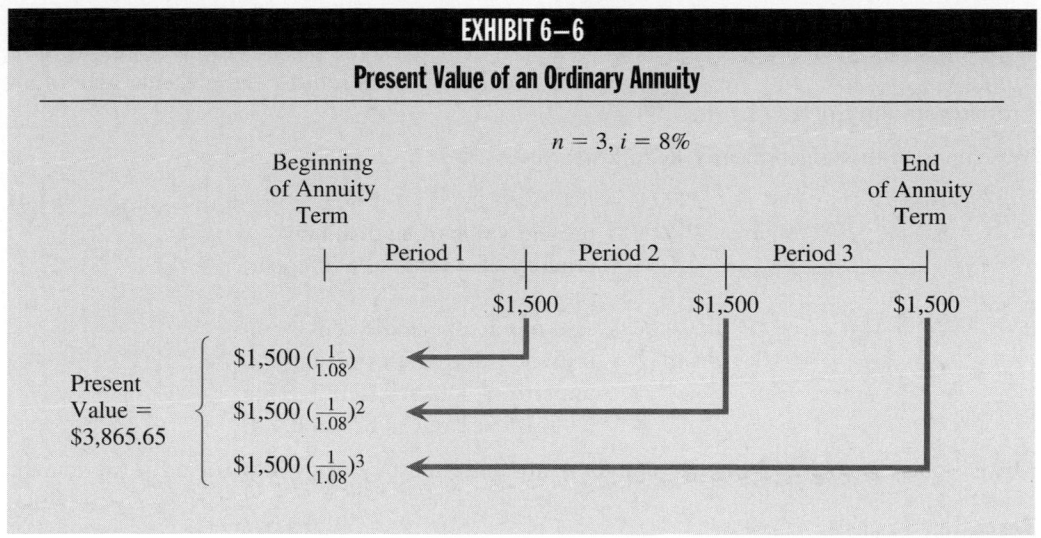

EXHIBIT 6–6

Present Value of an Ordinary Annuity

example: What is the present value of an ordinary annuity of three annual rents of $1,500 each discounted at 8%? The time diagram in Exhibit 6–6 illustrates the solution.

A **present value of an ordinary annuity** *focuses on a present value and the first rent occurs one period after the beginning of the annuity term.* Note carefully that the initial rent occurs at the end of the first time period, consistent with our definition of an ordinary annuity. When the present value of an ordinary annuity of *n* rents is computed, each rent is discounted.

In Exhibit 6–6, we compute the present value of an ordinary annuity by computing the present value of each rent and summing the results. Algebraically, we have

1st Rent	2nd Rent	3rd Rent	Present Value of the Ordinary Annuity

$$\$1,500 \left(\frac{1}{1.08}\right) + \$1,500 \left(\frac{1}{1.08}\right)^2 + \$1,500 \left(\frac{1}{1.08}\right)^3 = \$3,865.65$$

Factoring out the $1,500 rent, we have

$$\$1,500 \left[\left(\frac{1}{1.08}\right) + \left(\frac{1}{1.08}\right)^2 + \left(\frac{1}{1.08}\right)^3\right] = \$3,865.65$$

$$\$1,500 (.92593 + .85734 + .79383) = \$3,865.65$$

$$\$1,500 (2.57710) = \$3,865.65$$

Locate the table factor for $n = 3$, $i = 8\%$ in Table 6–4. Through no coincidence, it is 2.57710, the number we multiplied by $1,500 in the last equation. Table 6–4 is titled "Present Value of an Ordinary Annuity of 1." It contains many factors, each of which we shall call a **present value of an ordinary annuity factor (*pvoaf*).** Although each *pvoaf* could have been calculated by the approach illustrated above for $n = 3$ and $i = 8\%$, the following formula was used to save time:

$$pvoaf_{\overline{n}|i} = \frac{1 - \dfrac{1}{(1 + i)^n}}{i}$$

As the title indicates, Table 6–4 includes present value factors assuming an ordinary annuity of 1. For given n and i values, we can easily calculate the present value of an ordinary annuity of any size rent. We simply multiply the size of each rent by the present value of an ordinary annuity of 1.

We can state this algebraically as follows:

$$PVOA = R \cdot pvoaf_{\overline{n}|i} \qquad\qquad (6\text{--}4)$$

where $PVOA$ = present value of an ordinary
annuity of n rents at i interest
rate

R = size of each periodic rent

$pvoaf_{\overline{n}|i}$ = present value of an ordinary
annuity of 1 factor (from Table
6–4) for the relevant n and i

Of the four variables ($PVOA$, R, n, and i), any three must be known to solve for the fourth.

Accounting Example

Problem 11.   On January 1 of the current year, Allied Steel Company issues $5,000,000 of 8%, 20-year term bonds that pay interest semiannually each June 30 and December 31. How much cash will the bonds sell for if, on January 1, the market rate of interest for bonds similar to those of Allied Steel Company is 10%?

Solution 11.   Note that Allied's bonds have a **coupon interest rate** (often called **nominal rate** or **stated rate**) of 8%. This is simply the annual rate of interest stated in the bond contract. This rate is used to compute the amount of cash that will be paid as interest to bondholders each year. Note also that when the bonds are sold, the **market rate of interest** (often called the **yield rate** or the **effective rate**) for similar bonds is 10%. What would entice bond investors to purchase Allied's 8% bonds when these investors could purchase similar bonds and earn 10%?

Of course, the bonds must sell for a price that is less than their par or face value. In other words, the bonds will sell **at a discount,** the amount necessary to bring the yield rate on Allied's bonds up to the 10% market rate. Logic also dictates that when the coupon rate exceeds the market rate, the bonds will sell **at a premium.** When the two rates are equal, the bonds will sell **at par.**

Now that we have used intuition, let's formulate a more precise solution to the problem. First, recognize that because the bonds pay interest semiannually, they include $20 \times 2 = 40$ periods ($n = 40$), and the stated interest rate per period is $8\% \div 2 = 4\%$. Second, recognize that in addition to paying the $5,000,000 maturity value (a single sum) to bondholders in 20 years, Allied must also pay $200,000 ($4\% \times \$5,000,000$) interest at the end of each semiannual period for 20 years. The interest payments constitute an ordinary annuity. Finally, recognize that to compute the present value of the bonds (the price bondholders would be willing to pay on January 1), we must discount the maturity value and the interest annuity using the market rate of interest per period, so $i = 10\% \div 2 = 5\%$. Now we can determine the present value of Allied's bonds using the following two steps:

Step 1.   Compute the present value of the single
sum maturity value of $5,000,000 for $n = 40$
and $i = 5\%$. (Use Equation 6–2 and Table 6–2.)

$$PV = FV \cdot pvf_{\overline{n}|i}$$
$$= 5,000,000 \cdot pvf_{\overline{40}|5\%}$$
$$= \$5,000,000 \,(.14205)$$
$$= \$710,250$$

Step 2. Compute the present value of the ordinary interest annuity of $200,000 for $n = 40$ and $i = 5\%$. (Use Equation 6-4 and Table 6-4.)

$$PVOA = R \cdot pvoaf_{\overline{n}|i}$$
$$= \$200,000 \cdot pvoaf_{\overline{40}|5\%}$$
$$= \$200,000(17.15909)$$
$$= \$3,431,818$$

Summing the results of Steps 1 and 2, we get $710,250 + $3,431,818 = $4,142,068, which is the present value of the bonds. Thus, if bondholders pay $4,142,068 for Allied's bonds, they will earn 10%, compounded semiannually, on their investment. Note that our intuition was correct; the bonds sell at a discount of $857,932 ($5,000,000 − $4,142,068). This discount is simply extra interest that Allied must pay. To help implement the matching principle, this discount must be amortized over the life of the bond issue. We discuss discount (and premium) amortization more fully in Chapter 15. **Matching**

The bond pricing problem illustrates that *with a seemingly complex problem, it is often helpful to divide it into its components.* As the problem suggests, we sometimes need more than one equation and table. Nevertheless, the same basic compound interest concepts apply.

PRESENT VALUE OF AN ANNUITY DUE

Recall that an annuity due is one in which the rents occur at the beginning of each time period. In the previous section, we saw that $3,865.65 is the present value of an ordinary annuity of three rents of $1,500 each discounted at 8%. Now we will simply change the timing of the $1,500 rents and ask this question: What is the present value of three annual rents of $1,500 each that occur at the *beginning* of each year (an annuity due) discounted at 8%? Once again, a time diagram (Exhibit 6-7) helps us to visualize the solution. Note that the initial rent is not discounted, because it occurs at the beginning of the three-year span. In general, when the present value of an annuity due of n rents is computed, only $(n - 1)$ rents will be discounted. *A* **present value of an annuity due** *focuses on a present value and the first rent occurs at the beginning of the annuity term.*

As shown in Exhibit 6-7, an annuity due begins with a rent and ends one period *after* the last rent. Therefore, if we computed the present value of an annuity due of three $1,500 rents at 8% and then *discounted* all the money at 8% for one more period, we would have the

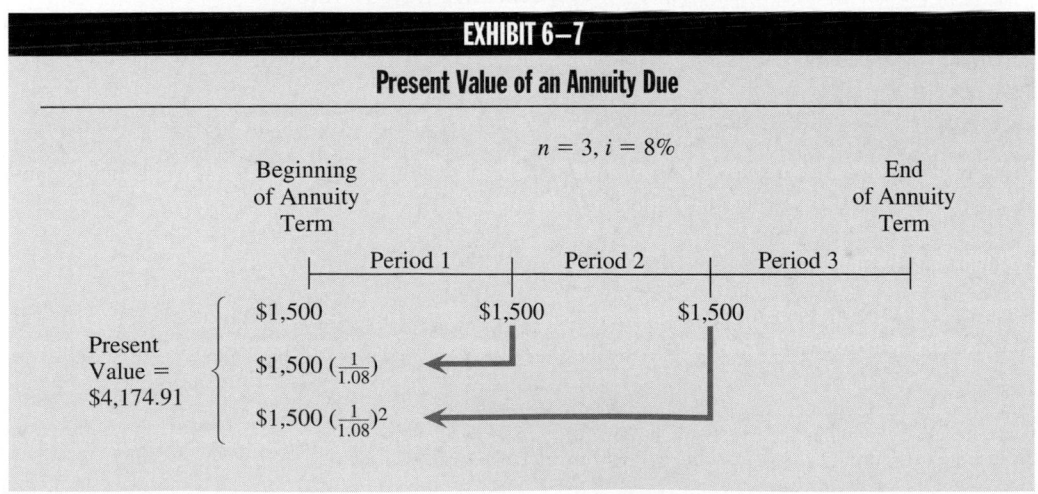

EXHIBIT 6-7

Present Value of an Annuity Due

$n = 3, i = 8\%$

present value of an ordinary annuity of three $1,500 rents at 8%. Similarly, if we computed the present value of an ordinary annuity of three $1,500 rents at 8% and then *compounded* all the money at 8% for one period into the future, we would have the present value of an annuity due of three rents of $1,500 at 8%. For any given values of *n* and *i*, the present value of an annuity due will be greater than the present value of an ordinary annuity by the interest on the latter amount for one period. Stated somewhat differently, the present value of an annuity due for any given values of *n* and *i* will be equal to the present value of an ordinary annuity of $(n - 1)$ rents at *i* interest rate, *plus* one rent (the initial rent).

As Exhibit 6–7 suggests, we could compute the present value of an annuity due by computing the present value of each rent and summing the results. Expressed algebraically,

$$\$1,500 + \$1,500\left(\frac{1}{1.08}\right) + \$1,500\left(\frac{1}{1.08}\right)^2 = \$4,174.91$$

Factoring out the $1,500 rent, we have

$$\$1,500\left[1 + \frac{1}{1.08} + \left(\frac{1}{1.08}\right)^2\right] = \$4,174.91$$

$$\$1,500\,(1 + .92593 + .85734) = \$4,174.91$$

$$\$1,500\,(2.78327) = \$4,174.91$$

The 2.78327 component in the last equation is simply a factor for computing the present value of an annuity due (*pvadf*) where $n = 3$ and $i = 8\%$. A complete table of these factors would be called a "Present Value of an Annuity Due of 1" table. We have not constructed such a table because we already have Table 6–4 and we know that a relatively simple relationship exists between the present value of an ordinary annuity and the present value of an annuity due. Thus, we can use Table 6–4 to determine a *pvadf* simply by finding the factor for $(n - 1)$ periods and *i*, and adding 1 to the factor. Stated algebraically,[10]

$$pvadf_{\overline{n}|i} = pvoaf_{\overline{n-1}|i} + 1.$$

To illustrate, let's use Table 6–4 to calculate $pvadf_{\overline{3}|8\%}$. Looking at the table, we find that the factor for $n - 1 = 2$ periods and $i = 8\%$ is 1.78326. Adding 1 to this number, we get 2.78326.

Now that we know how to use Table 6–4 to calculate a *pvadf*, we can state

$$PVAD = R \cdot pvadf_{\overline{n}|i} \qquad\qquad (6\text{–}4A)$$

where $PVAD$ = present value of an annuity due
  of *n* rents at *i* interest rate
  R = size of each periodic rent
  $pvadf_{\overline{n}|i}$ = present value of an annuity due
  of 1 factor (from Table 6–4, *as
  adjusted*) for the relevant *n* and *i*

The four variables that make up Equation 6–4A are *PVAD*, *R*, *n*, and *i*. As usual, if we know the values of any three, we can solve for the fourth.

Accounting Examples

Problem 12. On July 1 of the current year, Rockwell Drilling Company signed a 12-year, noncancelable lease with Equipment Leasing Corporation. The lease gave Rockwell the right to

---

[10]A second way to compute $pvadf_{\overline{n}|i}$ is as follows: $pvadf_{\overline{n}|i} = pvoaf_{\overline{n}|i}(1 + i)$. Although this approach is correct, it is more difficult to use when *i* is the unknown variable.

use certain drilling equipment that had a 12-year estimated useful life and no salvage value. In exchange, Rockwell agreed to make 12 annual lease payments of $15,000 each, beginning on July 1. Assuming a relevant interest rate of 10%, what is the present value of the lease on July 1?

Solution 12. Because the initial lease payment occurs at the beginning of the first interval, the lease payments represent an annuity due. To determine the present value of the lease, we compute the present value of an annuity due of 12 rents ($n = 12$) of $15,000 each at $i = 10\%$. Using Equation 6–4A and Table 6–4, we have

$$\begin{aligned}
PVAD &= R \cdot pvadf_{\overline{n}|i} \\
&= \$15,000 \cdot pvadf_{\overline{12}|10\%} \\
&= \$15,000 \, (pvoaf_{\overline{12-1}|10\%} + 1) \\
&= \$15,000 \, (6.49506 + 1) \\
&= \$15,000 \, (7.49506) \\
&= \$112,425.90
\end{aligned}$$

Observe that the *timing* of the lease payments impacts the present value of the lease. *In general, the timing of cash inflows and outflows has an important impact on the valuation of assets and liabilities and on the measurement of revenues and expenses in accounting.*

Problem 13. Jane Thomas retired today after 40 years with the Stork Candy Company. She has accumulated $187,298.32 in her retirement account, and she wants to withdraw $20,000 annually, beginning today, for as long as her retirement money lasts. Assuming that all money in Jane's account earns 10% interest, how many $20,000 annual withdrawals can she make?

Solution 13. We know that $187,298.32 is the present value of an annuity due of n rents of $20,000 each at $i = 10\%$. Dividing both sides of Equation 6–4A by R, we have

$$\frac{PVAD}{R} = pvadf_{\overline{n}|i}$$

$$\text{or} \quad pvadf_{\overline{n}|i} = \frac{PVAD}{R}$$

Substituting the known values for *PVAD*, *R*, and *i*, we have

$$pvadf_{\overline{n}|10\%} = \frac{\$187,298.32}{\$20,000}$$

$$pvadf_{\overline{n}|10\%} = 9.36492$$

Of course, we should not look for 9.36492 in Table 6–4, because we have seen that this table assumes an ordinary annuity. However, remember that $pvadf_{\overline{n}|i} = pvoaf_{\overline{n-1}|i} + 1$. Subtracting 1 from both sides of this equation, we have

$$pvadf_{\overline{n}|i} - 1 = pvoaf_{\overline{n-1}|i}$$

Substituting the known values, we have

$$9.36492 - 1 = pvoaf_{\overline{n-1}|10\%}$$

$$\text{or} \quad pvoaf_{\overline{n-1}|10\%} = 8.36492$$

Now we can search the 10% column in Table 6–4 until we find 8.36492. We find it in the row in which $n = 19$; since 19 is the *pvoaf* for ($n - 1$) rents, we conclude that Jane Thomas can make *20 withdrawals* ($19 + 1 = 20$) from her retirement account. If we had not found 8.36492, we could have interpolated to approximate n.

DEFERRED ANNUITIES

In a deferred annuity, the initial rent occurs two or more periods in the future. That is, the initial rent does not occur at either the beginning or the end of the first time period but at some later date. For computational convenience, it is customary to treat all deferred annuities as deferred ordinary annuities instead of deferred annuities due. We shall therefore omit the adjective "ordinary" when referring to deferred annuities.

The **deferral period** is the length of time between the present and the *beginning* of the first period in which a rent occurs. Remember, therefore, that the deferral period ends one period *before* the initial rent occurs. Thus, if an annuity begins to produce rents at the end of six periods, we say that it is deferred five periods. Similarly, an annuity that is deferred for 9 periods will produce its first rent at the end of 10 periods. The time diagram in Exhibit 6–8 illustrates an annuity of three annual rents of $1,500 at 8%, deferred four years.

The deferral period does not affect the calculation of an amount (future value). Because there is nothing on deposit to accumulate interest during the deferral period, the amount of a deferred annuity is the same as the amount of an annuity that is not deferred, assuming that the two annuities have the same values for n, i, and R. In the example above, the amount would be $4,869.60, the same figure computed in the discussion of the amount of an ordinary annuity.

On the other hand, assuming that the two annuities have the same values for n, i, and R, the present value of a deferred annuity is less than the present value of an annuity that is not deferred. The reason is that when we compute a present value, we must discount through the deferral period.

The easiest way to compute the present value of a deferred annuity is to find the *pvoaf* for the *total* number of periods involved, that is, the number of periods that the annuity is deferred (k) plus the number of periods in which rents occur (n). Then subtract the *pvoaf* associated with the ordinary annuity that is nonexistent during the deferral period. The resulting factor is then multiplied by the size of the periodic rent. Algebraically, we have:

$$PVDA = R \cdot (pvoaf_{\overline{k+n}|\,i} - pvoaf_{\overline{k}|\,i}) \qquad (6\text{--}5)$$

$$\begin{aligned}
\text{where} \quad PVDA =~ & \text{present value of an ordinary annuity} \\
& \text{of } n \text{ rents at } i \text{ interest rate, } \textit{deferred} \\
& k \text{ periods} \\
R =~ & \text{size of each periodic rent} \\
pvoaf_{\overline{k+n}|\,i} =~ & \text{present value of an ordinary} \\
& \text{annuity factor for the } \textit{total} \text{ number} \\
& \text{of periods involved}
\end{aligned}$$

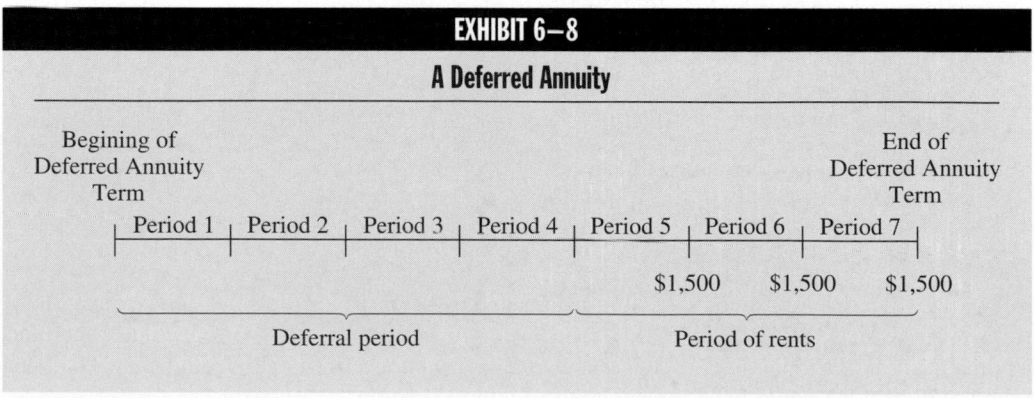

EXHIBIT 6–8

A Deferred Annuity

Begining of Deferred Annuity Term

End of Deferred Annuity Term

Period 1 | Period 2 | Period 3 | Period 4 | Period 5 | Period 6 | Period 7

$1,500 $1,500 $1,500

Deferral period

Period of rents

$$pvoaf_{\overline{k}|\,i} = \text{present value of an ordinary}$$
$$\text{annuity factor for the number of}$$
$$\text{periods in which no rents occur}$$

If we want to know the present value of an annuity of three annual rents of $1,500 at 8% deferred four years, we would proceed as follows:

$$
\begin{aligned}
PVDA &= R \cdot (pvoaf_{\overline{7}|\,8\%} - pvoaf_{\overline{4}|\,8\%}) \\
&= \$1,500\ (5.20637 - 3.31213) \\
&= \$1,500\ (1.89424) \\
&= \$2,841.36
\end{aligned}
$$

Another way to compute the present value of a deferred annuity is first to compute the present value of the annuity at the beginning of the first period in which a rent occurs (using Equation 6–4 and Table 6–4) and then to discount this single sum to the present (using Equation 6–2 and Table 6–2). Following this approach, we find that the present value of the annuity at the beginning of Period 5 is $3,865.65 ($1,500 × 2.57710). Discounting this single sum to the present, we find that it equals $2,841.37 ($3,865.65 × .73503). The $.01 discrepancy ($2,841.37 − $2,841.36) between answers is the result of rounding.

Accounting Example

Problem 14. Sam Sharpe purchases a $50,000 annuity contract that promises a return of 8% compounded annually. Sam shall receive 15 equal annual payments, the first of which is due 10 years from now. How much will each annual payment be?

Solution 14. Because the annuity begins to produce rents at the end of 10 years, we say that it is deferred nine years. Therefore, we know that $50,000 is the present value of an ordinary annuity of 15 annual rents at 8%, deferred nine years. To solve for the size of the periodic rent, we divide both sides of Equation 6–5 by $(pvoaf_{\overline{k+n}|\,i} - pvoaf_{\overline{k}|\,i})$:

$$
\begin{aligned}
R &= \frac{PVDA}{(pvoaf_{\overline{k+n}|\,i} - pvoaf_{\overline{k}|\,i})} \\[2mm]
&= \frac{\$50,000}{(pvoaf_{\overline{24}|\,8\%} - pvoaf_{\overline{9}|\,8\%})} \\[2mm]
&= \frac{\$50,000}{10.52876 - 6.24689} \\[2mm]
&= \frac{\$50,000}{4.28187} \\[2mm]
&= \$11,677.14
\end{aligned}
$$

When solving a compound interest problem, you should first determine what type of problem you are being asked to solve. Distinguishing between single sum problems and annuity problems is fairly easy, because periodic rents of equal size clearly indicate an annuity problem.

On the other hand, distinguishing between the following types of annuity problems is often difficult:

1. Amount of an ordinary annuity.
2. Amount of an annuity due.
3. Present value of an ordinary annuity.
4. Present value of an annuity due.

CONCLUDING REMARKS

To help you see the differences between these four types of annuity problems, Exhibit 6–9 compares them in one illustration. *When solving an annuity problem that seems difficult, draw a time diagram and remember the following points:*

1. An annuity problem involves a value that represents a single sum of money. This value may occur either before or after the rents. If the value (which may be the unknown variable) occurs *after* the rents, the value is an *amount* (future value). Consequently, we have an amount of an annuity problem. To determine whether the annuity is ordinary or due, note the timing of the *final rent.* If the final rent occurs *at the same time* as the value, we have an amount of an *ordinary* annuity problem. If the final rent occurs *one period before* the value, we have an amount of an annuity *due* problem.

2. If the value (which may be the unknown variable) in the problem occurs *before* the rents, the value is a *present value.* Consequently, we have a present value of an annuity problem. To determine whether the annuity is ordinary or due, observe the timing of the *first rent.* If the first rent occurs *one period after* the value, we have a present value of an *ordinary* annuity problem. If the first rent occurs *at the same time* as the present value, we have a present value of an annuity *due* problem.

A deferred annuity is not difficult to recognize, because the first rent occurs two or more periods after the beginning of the annuity term (see Exhibit 6–8).

Once you have identified the problem, you may solve it using the appropriate equation(s) and table(s). The major equations presented in the chapter are summarized in Exhibit 6–10. After you gain experience working with the equations, you may find that you can simplify the writing of them by omitting the letters that precede the letter f (for factor). For example, Equation 6–3 may be concisely written as $AOA = R \cdot f_{\overline{n}|i}$. If you simplify the writing of an equation, take care to use the correct type of factor when solving the equation.

Finally, try to form the habit of examining your answers to compound interest problems from a common sense perspective. We know, for example, that the present value of $1,000 discounted for two years at 8% could not possibly be $8,573.40. The actual present value is only $857.34. Obviously, misplacing a decimal can greatly affect the solution to a compound interest problem.

EXHIBIT 6–9

Comparison between Four Types of Annuities ($n = 3$)

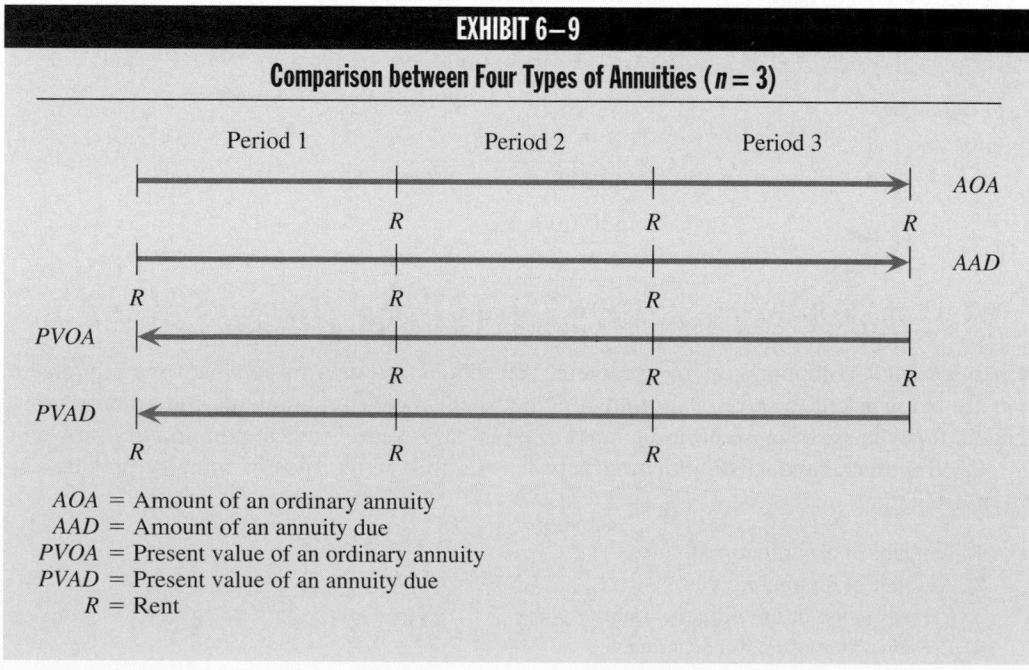

AOA = Amount of an ordinary annuity
AAD = Amount of an annuity due
PVOA = Present value of an ordinary annuity
PVAD = Present value of an annuity due
   R = Rent

TIME IS MONEY

It is said that accounting, like law, is a profession that has a rule for every situation. If that's true, then why don't accountants have a consistent standard for when, and under what circumstances, to use one of the most fundamental measurements of finance itself—the time value of money?

As anyone who has bought a bank CD knows, the yield on an investment is basically a function of how much money is invested at what rate of return for how long. In theory, both assets and liabilities of corporations can be measured in the same way. For liabilities: How much money would be needed today to pay for an obligation that does not come due for 5 or 10 years—future health obligations of not-yet-retired workers, say, or the projected pension liabilities of a firm 10 or 20 years in the future? For assets: What is the "present value" of a financial asset—a mortgage, say, or a corporate bond—that is due to mature in the year 2013? In both cases, the solution comes from taking the future value or cost of the asset or liability in question, then using an assumed rate of interest over the period of time involved to "discount" it back to its present value.

Unfortunately, the accountants who actually prepare financial reports have few—and often highly inconsistent rules for when and how to make those calculations in preparing balance sheets. "Financial statements are becoming irrelevant to business decision making," complains G. Michael Crooch, partner at Arthur Andersen. "We are not measuring items according to their economic value because we're ignoring the time value of money."

Now at last the Financial Accounting Standards Board seems willing to face the problem, by adding a discounting project to its agenda. New rules are years away, but they eventually could have a dramatic effect on corporate financials. Depending upon what FASB finally decides, present value accounting could be used for virtually any transaction that involves a long delay before final settlement. Potential targets for discounting include impaired assets, product and manufacturers' warranties, and loss reserves for property-casualty insurers.

Present value accounting could in some ways be quite a boon to corporations, by reducing the liability side of their balance sheets. How? By recognizing that $1 million payable in 1994 is not as effectively large a liability as $1 million payable in 1989. That's common sense. If you were to take $600,000 and invest it at a relatively modest 10%, it would equal $1 million by the time the liability would need to be paid. Thus the effective liability is not $1 million but $600,000.

For example, under current FASB income tax accounting rules, deferred taxes must be booked in full, rather than discounted forward to the time when they are due. Thus, General Electric had a $3.1 billion deferred tax reserve in 1987. "That $3.1 billion is more than we'll really have to pay, considering the interest effect," notes Bernard Doyle, GE's manager of corporate accounting services. We're not talking peanuts. The discounted value of that liability is hundreds of million of dollars less than book value.

In a few cases, present value accounting is already required by FASB. Under a new FASB statement regarding pension accounting, General Electric in 1987 reported only a $15.5 billion liability based on an 8.5% rate of return; without discounting for present value, the liability would have been much greater.

Present value accounting obviously helps a company put its best foot forward, and of course could be abused. How? By making unrealistically high assumptions about interest rates. "Experience has shown that, in many cases, insurers have not been adequately funded in the past," notes Denis Callaghan, analyst at Alex. Brown. "If they were allowed to use discounting, the problem could get worse." Maybe, but any company that overdiscounts the future liability risks having to take major writeoffs as the liabilities come due. All in all, present value accounting has lots to recommend it.

Arthur Wyatt, Arthur Andersen & Co. accounting partner, sums up: "Any company routinely considers present values when doing deals. Why shouldn't investors have that information in the financial statements?"

SOURCE: Penelope Wang, "Time Is Money," *Forbes*, January 9, 1989, p. 300. Reprinted by permission of *Forbes* magazine, January 9, 1989. © Forbes, Inc., 1989.

EXHIBIT 6–10

Summary of Compound Interest Equations

Equation Number	Equation	Appropriate Table
6–1	$FV = PV \cdot fvf_{\overline{n}\rvert i}$	6–1
6–2	$PV = FV \cdot pvf_{\overline{n}\rvert i}$	6–2
6–3	$AOA = R \cdot aoaf_{\overline{n}\rvert i}$	6–3
6–3A	$AAD = R \cdot aadf_{\overline{n}\rvert i}$	6–3 (adjusted)
6–4	$PVOA = R \cdot pvoaf_{\overline{n}\rvert i}$	6–4
6–4A	$PVAD = R \cdot pvadf_{\overline{n}\rvert i}$	6–4 (adjusted)
6–5	$PVDA = R \cdot (pvoaf_{\overline{k+n}\rvert i} - pvoaf_{\overline{k}\rvert i})$	6–4

EXHIBIT 6–11

Characteristics of Annuity Problems

Type of Annuity Problem	Focus	Rents
Amount of an ordinary annuity	A future value	End of each period. *Final rent occurs at same time as future value.*
Amount of an annuity due	A future value	Beginning of each period. *Final rent occurs one period before future value.*
Present value of an ordinary annuity	A present value	End of each period. *Initial rent occurs one period after the present value.*
Present value of an annuity due	A present value	Beginning of each period. *Initial rent occurs at same time as present value.*

In the remaining chapters of this textbook, you will be asked to apply many of the tools discussed in this chapter and the previous chapters on the accounting cycle. The next chapter, which covers cash and receivables, is the first of a series of seven chapters that explain asset accounting. As we move into our study of various types of assets, you will see the application of these tools.

KEY POINTS

1. Simple interest is earned only on the principal sum of money invested; compound interest is earned not only on the principal but also on the interest accumulated. (Objective 1)

2. Four fundamental concepts underlie all compound interest problems:
   a. present value (PV)   **c.** interest rate (i)
   b. future value (FV)   **d.** time periods (n)   (Objective 2)

3. In a compound interest problem, the values of i and n should reflect the number of times a year that interest is compounded. (Objective 2)

4. An amount of a single sum problem focuses on the future value to which a single sum of money will accumulate if left on deposit for a certain number of periods at a certain interest rate per period. (Objective 3)

5. A present value of a single sum problem focuses on the present value of a single sum of money that is discounted for a certain number of periods at a certain interest rate per period. (Objective 3)

6. An annuity is a series of equal receipts or payments, called *rents,* that occur at uniform time intervals at a constant interest rate. In an ordinary annuity, the rents occur at the end of each time period; in an annuity due, the rents occur at the beginning of each time period. Present value and future value concepts apply to annuities, just as these concepts apply to single sum problems. (Objective 3)

7. Important characteristics of the major types of annuity problems are summarized in Exhibit 6–11. (Objective 3)

8. A deferred annuity is one in which the initial rent occurs two or more periods in the future. A deferral period does not affect the calculation of an amount, but it does affect the calculation of a present value. (Objective 3)

9. When solving a compound interest problem, you should read the problem carefully to determine the type of problem you are dealing with, solve the problem using the appropriate equations and tables, and make sure your answer seems reasonable. (Objective 3)

10. A complex problem can usually be solved by dividing it into its components. (Objective 3)

6-1 What is meant by the time value of money?

6-2 How do simple and compound interest differ?

6-3 What is the difference between the amount of a single sum and the present value of a single sum?

6-4 What is an annuity?

6-5 How do an ordinary annuity and an annuity due differ?

6-6 How do the amount of an ordinary annuity and the amount of an annuity due differ?

6-7 What is the difference between the present value of an ordinary annuity and the present value of an annuity due?

6-8 What does the term *assets* mean? Explain the strengths and limitations of using present value concepts to measure assets.

6-9 What is a deferred annuity?

6-10 How were the factors in each of the following tables calculated?

[a] Table 6-1   [b] Table 6-2?
[c] Table 6-3   [d] Table 6-4?

6-11 How could an Amount of 1 table be converted to a Present Value of 1 table?

6-12 How could an Amount of an Ordinary Annuity of 1 table be converted to an Amount of an Annuity Due of 1 table?

6-13 How could a Present Value of an Ordinary Annuity of 1 table be converted to a Present Value of an Annuity Due of 1 table?

6-14 What are the number of compounding periods (n) and the interest rate per period (i) for each of the following?

[a] Three years, 12% compounded annually.
[b] Three years, 12% compounded semiannually.
[c] Three years, 12% compounded quarterly.
[d] Three years, 12% compounded monthly.

6-15 Assuming that $n = 15$ and $i = 10\%$, what is

[a] The amount of 1?
[b] The present value of 1?
[c] The amount of an ordinary annuity of 1?
[d] The amount of an annuity due of 1?
[e] The present value of an ordinary annuity of 1?
[f] The present value of an annuity due of 1?

6-16 To what amount will $3,500 accumulate if it is deposited for five years at 10%, assuming

[a] Simple interest?
[b] Interest compounded annually?
[c] Interest compounded semiannually?
[d] Interest compounded quarterly?

6-17 Assuming an interest rate of 8%, compounded quarterly, how many years will it take for a deposit of $1,800 to accumulate to $2,674.71?

6-18 What annual interest rate, when compounded annually, would cause an initial deposit of $6,600 to accumulate to $25,063.50 in 14 years?

6-19 Ann Long plans to send each of her two daughters to private universities. For the first daughter, Ann will need $25,000 in three years; Ann plans to accumulate this amount by depositing a certain sum today in a three-year certificate of deposit that pays 6% interest compounded annually. For the second daughter, Ann will need $50,000 in seven years; she plans to accumulate this amount by depositing a certain sum today in a seven-year certificate of deposit that pays 8% interest compounded annually. What is the total amount of cash that Ann needs to deposit today?

---

*Brief descriptions of the exercises and problems in this chapter are not given so that students may practice learning how to recognize the different types of compound interest problems. As indicated in the chapter, learning to recognize the different types of problems is very important.

6–20 Bob Roberts has deposited $3,000 on the same day of each month for the last two years in an account that pays 12% interest, compounded monthly. He made the last deposit today. How much money does Bob now have in his account?

6–21 Jim Dodd has $25,000 today as a result of having deposited equal amounts of cash in a savings account every six months for 12 years. The account pays interest of 6% compounded semiannually. Assuming that the last deposit was made today, how much was each deposit?

6–22 As of today, Sam Jones has accumulated $114,550.00 in a retirement account that pays 10% interest compounded annually. He accumulated this sum by depositing $2,000 at annual intervals during each year that he worked in the clothing business. The last deposit was made today. How many deposits did Sam make?

6–23 Joan Jetta has $9,433.42 today as a result of having deposited $750 at annual intervals the last 10 years. The last deposit was made today. Assuming annual compounding, what interest rate did Joan earn on her periodic deposits?

6–24 Brian Willoughby plans to deposit $1,250 in his savings account today and at each of the next 35 monthly intervals, for a total period of three years. Assuming that Brian's money earns interest of 12%, compounded monthly, how much money will he have in his account at the end of three years?

6–25 Cathy Archerly wants to accumulate $30,000 at the end of 18 years and will make 18 equal annual deposits into a fund that pays 8% interest, compounded annually. She will make the final deposit one year before the $30,000 sum is accumulated. How much will each deposit be?

6–26 When Ben Wiseman's son was born, Ben deposited $250 in a special savings account that pays interest at 8% compounded annually. Later, he deposited $250 on each of his son's birthdays. How old is Ben's son if today is his birthday and, just *before* Ben makes his current deposit, the amount accumulated in the account is $7,331.07?

6–27 Bill Stockman deposited $1,000 annually in an investment account for five years, ending one year ago. Assuming that interest is compounded annually and that Bill has accumulated $6,715.61 in his account as of today, what stated interest rate did he earn?

6–28 Maria Corsiano wants to earn an interest rate of 10%, compounded quarterly. How much money should she pay today to an insurance company for the right to receive $20,000 at quarterly intervals, starting three months from now, for the next eight years?

6–29 Today Homer Rice deposited $10,000 in a savings account that pays 6% interest compounded semiannually. Homer wants to liquidate the balance in his account by making equal semiannual withdrawals, starting six months from now, for four years. How large will each withdrawal be?

6–30 Regina Holt has $60,207.90 in a savings account that pays 6% interest compounded annually. How many annual withdrawals of $5,000 each can she make from the account, assuming that she makes the first withdrawal one year from now?

6–31 Elisa Frye buys an automobile having a cash price of $6,473.70 with $1,500 down and payments of $2,000 annually for three years. Assuming annual compounding, what is the stated interest rate in this transaction?

6–32 Assuming that he wants to earn interest of 12%, compounded monthly, how much money should Mario Rucci pay today to an insurance company for the right to receive $3,000 each month for 36 months, with the initial $3,000 to be received today?

6–33 Kristy Hall wants to use all the money in her $20,000 savings account to pay for her college education, which begins today. The account pays 10% interest compounded annually. What constant amount of cash can she withdraw at the beginning of each of her four years in college?

6–34 Issac Levin currently owes a debt of $3,167.46. The debt accrues interest at 10% compounded annually on the unpaid balance. How many annual payments of $500 each will Issac have to make to liquidate the debt and interest, assuming that the first payment is made today?

6–35 Connie Dawson purchased a new video recorder that had a cash price of $526.59. She made an $80 down payment and paid the balance in $80 installments at the end of each year for seven years. What is the stated annual interest rate?

6-36 Assume that it is now the beginning of Year 1. Answer each of the following questions, assuming an interest rate of 6% compounded annually.

[a] What is the amount at the end of Year 10 of 10 annual deposits of $5,000 each, the first of which is made at the end of Year 1?

[b] What is the amount at the end of Year 20 of 10 annual deposits of $5,000 each, the first of which is made at the end of Year 11?

[c] As of the beginning of Year 11, what is the present value of 10 annual receipts of $5,000 each, the first of which is received at the end of Year 11?

[d] As of the beginning of Year 1, what is the present value of 10 annual receipts of $5,000 each, the first of which is received at the end of Year 11?

[e] Why are the correct answers to [a] and [b] the same?

[f] Why are the correct answers to [c] and [d] different?

PROBLEMS*

6-37 Old Savings and Loan Association, whose slogan is "Our Interest Is More Interesting," currently pays interest at a rate of 8%, compounded quarterly. Second Savings and Loan Association, whose slogan is "Our Interest Interests More," pays 8% compounded annually. If you want to deposit $10,000 for five years, what would be the total additional interest that you could earn by depositing the money in Old Savings and Loan rather than Second Savings and Loan?

6-38 McSween Company deposited $10,000 with each of four investment companies at the following terms:

Investment Company	Annual Rate	Compounded	Investment Term in Years
W	12%	Annually	8
X	10	Quarterly	6
Y	10	Semiannually	4
Z	8	Quarterly	2

What will be the balance in each investment account at its maturity?

6-39 Joanne Hill was informed by the attorney managing her deceased uncle's estate that the following deposits would be made in her new savings account at the end of each of the following years:

Year	Deposit
1995	$5,000
1996	3,000
1997	4,000
1998	5,000

The account pays 8% interest compounded annually.

INSTRUCTIONS

[a] Assuming that Joanne makes no additional deposits or withdrawals, what will be the balance in her savings account at the end of 1998, immediately after the last deposit?

[b] What would be the balance in the savings account at the end of 1998 if, instead of the deposits shown above, a deposit of $4,300 was made at the end of each year?

[c] Explain the similarities and differences in the techniques you used to solve [a] and [b].

6-40 For many years, John Phillips has admired a refurbished Model T automobile owned by his neighbor. Thus, John quickly accepted his neighbor's recent offer to sell John the car. Which of the following two payment options offered by the neighbor should John take?

[1] $9,300 cash payable immediately.

[2] $11,000 cash payable in one sum after two years.

John knows that he can earn 8%, compounded annually, on his money.

---

*Brief descriptions of the exercises and problems in this chapter are not given so that students may practice learning how to recognize the different types of compound interest problems. As indicated in the chapter, learning to recognize the different types of problems is very important.

6–41 Your neighbor has a $5,000 noninterest-bearing note receivable that matures at the end of three years. You recently inherited $25,000, and you know that you could earn 10%, compounded annually, on investments that are similar in risk to your neighbor's note. Your goal is to maximize your income.

INSTRUCTIONS

[a] What is the maximum amount of cash that you would be willing to pay today for your neighbor's note?

[b] What is the maximum amount of cash that you would be willing to pay today if the $5,000 note paid you interest of 3% at the end of each year? (*Hint:* You will receive $5,000 × 3% = $150 at the end of Years 1, 2, and 3 and the $5,000 maturity value at the end of Year 3.)

[c] Explain why the amounts in [a] and [b] are *maximum* amounts.

6–42 On February 1, 1996, Tharpe Tool Company leased equipment from Micah Manufacturing Corporation. The lease term is three years, which equals the estimated economic life of the equipment. The lease requires Tharpe to make 36 monthly rental payments of $5,000 each, with the first payment due on February 1, 1996.

INSTRUCTIONS

[a] Assuming a relevant interest rate of 12% compounded monthly, what is the present value of the lease to Tharpe Tool Company on February 1, 1996?

[b] Answer [a], assuming that the first of the 36 monthly rental payments is made on March 1, 1996.

6–43 Harry Pangle, a local dentist, opens a tax-deferred retirement account that pays 8% interest compounded annually. He plans to deposit $2,000 at annual intervals for 25 years, with the initial deposit made today.

INSTRUCTIONS

[a] How much cash will Harry have in his account when he retires at the end of 25 years?

[b] How much of the sum that you calculated in [a] is interest?

[c] What equal-size deposits would Harry have to make at the beginning of each year to accumulate $200,000 at the end of 25 years?

6–44 Doris Kearns retired from Kelley Company today with $165,766.20 in a retirement account that pays 8% interest compounded annually.

INSTRUCTIONS

[a] How many $15,000 annual withdrawals can Doris make from her account if she makes the first withdrawal one year from now?

[b] What equal amount should she withdraw at the end of each year if she wants to make the final withdrawal 25 years from today?

[c] What equal amount should she withdraw annually if she wants to make a total of 15 withdrawals, with the initial withdrawal made today?

[d] What equal amount should she withdraw annually if she wants to make a total of 15 withdrawals, with the initial withdrawal made five years from now?

6–45 Pat Fisher plans to retire 20 years from today. She wants to build a tax-deferred retirement account by making 20 annual deposits, with the first deposit made today. Pat wants to make 20 annual withdrawals of $25,000 each from her retirement account, with the initial withdrawal made 20 years from now. The retirement account will earn 12% interest, compounded annually.

INSTRUCTIONS

[a] What equal amounts should Pat deposit in her account?

[b] What is the total amount of interest that Pat will earn on the money in her account?

6–46 Keap Trucking Company purchased a new truck from Goin Motor Company in exchange for a three-year, noninterest-bearing promissory note with a maturity value of $80,000. The market rate of interest for similar notes is 10% compounded annually.

INSTRUCTIONS

[a] What is the historical cost of the truck to Keap Trucking Company?

[b] Answer [a], assuming that the $80,000 note paid interest of 2% at the end of each year for three years. (*Hint:* The note pays interest of $80,000 × 2% = $1,600 to the holder at the end of each of the three years, and it pays the maturity value of $80,000 at the end of the third year.)

6–47 Billy Coker buys a new home today costing $67,736.39. He makes a $10,000 down payment and gets a 10-year mortgage loan for the balance. The mortgage bears interest at 10%, compounded quarterly, and calls for equal quarterly payments, starting three months from now.

INSTRUCTIONS

[a] How much will each quarterly payment be?
[b] What is the total sum of cash that Billy will spend on the down payment and the loan?
[c] What is the total amount of interest that Billy will pay on the loan?
[d] What is the total amount of interest that Billy could save if he could get the required loan at 8% compounded quarterly?

6–48 Jolla Company will need $5,000,000 at the end of 20 years to retire a maturing issue of term bonds. To accumulate the desired sum, the company deposits $125,000 at the end of each year in a sinking fund that pays 6% interest compounded annually.

INSTRUCTIONS

[a] Will the fund at the end of 20 years be sufficient to retire the bonds?
[b] If your answer to [a] is no, what equal amount of cash would the company have to deposit at the end of each of the 20 years to accumulate the desired sum?

6–49 Nypaver Company wants to purchase a new warehouse in three years. The company expects the warehouse to cost $360,000 at that time. To accumulate this amount, the company plans to make 12 quarterly deposits of $24,000 each in a special account that pays 10% interest compounded quarterly. The first deposit is made today.

INSTRUCTIONS

[a] Will the amount in the fund at the end of three years be sufficient to purchase the warehouse?
[b] If your answer to [a] is no, what equal amounts of cash would the company have to deposit at the beginning of each quarter to accumulate $360,000 at the end of three years?

6–50 Determine the stated annual interest rate in each of the following independent cases (assume annual compounding in each case):

[a] A deposit of $650 accumulates to $925.15 in nine years.
[b] A person lends $75,131 today in exchange for $100,000 to be received at the end of three years.
[c] Periodic deposits of $1,200 made at the end of each year accumulate to $25,218.08 at the end of 14 years.
[d] Periodic deposits of $2,800 made at the beginning of each year accumulate to $57,075.97 at the end of 11 years.
[e] An annuity contract purchased for $53,373.90 promises to pay $5,000 at the end of each year for the next 25 years.
[f] A person borrows $50,000 in exchange for a written promise to pay $4,821.78 at the beginning of each year for 30 years, with the first payment due now.

6–51 On April 1, 1996, Knuckles Corporation issues 10%, 20-year bonds payable with a total par value of $60,000. Interest is payable semiannually on September 30 and March 31.

INSTRUCTIONS

[a] How much will the bonds sell for if, on April 1, 1996, the market rate of interest for similar bonds is
[1] 8%? [2] 10%? [3] 12%?
[b] Make the journal entry for Knuckles Corporation to record the bond issuance under each of the three assumptions in [a].
[c] Explain the meaning and accounting treatment of Discount on Bonds Payable.

6–52 Carsdale Company has projected substantial growth in sales over the next five years. To ensure that sufficient funds are available for capital expansion, Carsdale plans to deposit $75,000 in a building fund at the end of each year for the next five years.

INSTRUCTIONS

[a] What will be the balance in the fund at the end of the fifth year if interest is earned at 8% compounded annually?
[b] How many years would it take for the fund to accumulate $348,075 if interest is earned at 10% compounded annually?
[c] What interest rate, compounded annually, would be necessary to accumulate $414,422 by the end of the fifth year?

6-53 How many *years* are involved in each of the following independent situations?

[a]   A deposit of $1,800 accumulates to $4,572.63 at 6% compounded annually.

[b]   A person lends $22,819.50 today in exchange for $50,000 to be received in the future, which includes interest at 8% compounded semiannually.

[c]   Deposits of $300 at the end of each quarter accumulate to $11,115.36 at the end of the final quarter. The interest rate is 8% compounded quarterly.

[d]   Deposits of $600 at the beginning of each year accumulate to $14,787.25 at the end of the final year. The interest rate is 4% compounded annually.

[e]   A person deposits $1,635.14 today in a savings account that pays interest at 8% compounded quarterly. The account is liquidated by withdrawals of $100 at the end of each quarter, with the initial withdrawals made at the end of the first quarter.

[f]   A person deposits $1,777.37 today in a savings account that pays interest at 6% compounded annually. The account is liquidated by annual withdrawals of $200, with the initial withdrawal made today.

6-54 On January 1, 1994, Melody Chiles buys new furniture costing $5,000. To pay for it, she signs a promissory note calling for equal monthly payments for three years. The first payment is due in one month. The note bears interest at 12% compounded monthly.

INSTRUCTIONS

[a]   How much will each monthly payment be?

[b]   How much interest will Melody pay on the furniture loan in each of the following years:
[1] 1994?   [2] 1995?   [3] 1996?

6-55 Brett Carver wants to establish a special retirement fund from which he can make five annual withdrawals of $20,000 each, with the first withdrawal to be made on January 1, 2003. Brett wants to make four equal annual contributions to the retirement fund, beginning January 1, 1996 and ending January 1, 1999. Brett wants the fund to be exhausted after the final withdrawal on January 1, 2007. The fund will earn 10% interest, compounded annually.

INSTRUCTIONS

[a]   What equal annual amount should Brett contribute to the fund?

[b]   What is the total amount of interest that Brett will earn on the money in his fund?

6-56 Morley Taste wants to establish a college fund for his son, Leslie. Morley estimates that Leslie will require $15,000 per year for four years, beginning September 1, 2002, and ending September 1, 2005. Morley wants to make three equal annual contributions to the college fund, beginning September 1, 1996, and ending September 1, 1998. Morley wants the fund to be exhausted after the final withdrawal on September 1, 2005. The fund will earn 12% interest, compounded annually.

INSTRUCTIONS

[a]   What equal annual amount should Morley contribute to the fund?

[b]   What is the total amount of interest that Morley will earn on the money in his fund?

6-57 John Bryant wants to buy a log cabin kit from Wild Homes, Inc., for $20,000 cash. The best alternative use of John's money is an investment account that pays 8% interest compounded annually. John expects that it would take him two years working part-time to complete the exterior of the cabin and an additional year to finish the interior. If John decides to buy the kit, he will leave his present part-time job of making Christmas ornaments from pine cones. As a result, he will lose $2,000 cash income at the end of each of the three years that he worked on the cabin.

The cabin would be constructed on a lake in a retirement community. John expects that the annual rent for the first five years after completion would be $2,400 and for the second five years would be $3,600. Rental payments would be due at the beginning of each year. John expects that he would sell the cabin for $26,000 after renting it for 10 years.

INSTRUCTIONS

Using appropriate compound interest concepts, determine whether the log cabin is a sound economic investment for John Bryant. Ignore income taxes.

6-58 Patrick Murphy is thinking about buying a new home that costs $125,000. He wants to make a down payment of $25,000 and finance the balance of the purchase price by using an 8%, fixed-rate mortgage loan. He is trying to decide whether the term of the loan should be 15 or 30 years. In either case, the mortgage company would require Patrick to make annual mortgage payments (for principal and interest) at the end of each year for the term of the loan.

Patrick knows that between the years 1926 and 1992, Standard & Poor's 500 index of common stocks increased at an annual rate that slightly exceeded 10%. Patrick believes that investing in a diversified portfolio of common stocks, such as the S&P 500, is a prudent long-term strategy when considering both expected return and risk. He also believes that a 10% annual earnings rate for such an investment is reasonable to assume for the future.

INSTRUCTIONS

[a] Using compound interest concepts, perform an analysis to help Patrick Murphy decide whether to obtain a 15-year loan or a 30-year mortgage loan. What is your recommendation?

[b] What additional factors should Patrick consider before making the decision in [a]?

CASES

6–59 Historical Cost In Chapter 2 we stated that the historical cost of an asset equals the cash equivalent price of acquiring the asset and putting it to its intended use. Suppose that on July 1, 1996, Cowboy Corporation buys 100 shares of common stock of Oiler Company as an investment in exchange for a three-year note. The note has a face amount of $14,049.29 and no stated interest rate. Oiler Company is a small, closely held enterprise, and the market value of its common stock is not readily determinable. On July 1, 1996, the market rate of interest for notes similar to the one issued by Cowboy is 12%.

INSTRUCTIONS

[a] How should Cowboy determine the historical cost of its investment in Oiler Company?

[b] Justify your answer to [a] from the standpoint of accounting theory.

6–60 Revenue Realization On December 31, 1996, Northern Galleries, Inc., sold a unique painting to Green Company in exchange for a five-year note receivable. The note had a face amount of $161,051 and no stated interest rate. The market rate of interest for similar notes on December 31, 1996, was 12%. The painting could not be appraised in a reliable manner.

INSTRUCTIONS

Explain how Northern Galleries should determine the amount of revenue to recognize on the sale for the period ending December 31, 1996.

6–61 State Lottery A U.S. state recently ran a full-page advertisement in the state's major newspapers announcing that it was sponsoring a lottery in which "the winner would receive $1,000,000." The fine print near the bottom of the ad indicated that "the $1,000,000 would be paid in $50,000 annual installments over 20 years."

INSTRUCTIONS

Do you believe that the state's ad is fair and reasonable, or is it misleading? Ignoring income taxes, defend your position with appropriate arguments.

TABLE 6−1

Amount of 1

$$fvf_{\overline{n}|i} = (1 + i)^n$$

Periods (*n*)	1%	2%	2.5%	3%	4%	5%
1	1.01000	1.02000	1.02500	1.03000	1.04000	1.05000
2	1.02010	1.04040	1.05062	1.06090	1.08160	1.10250
3	1.03030	1.06121	1.07689	1.09273	1.12486	1.15762
4	1.04060	1.08243	1.10381	1.12551	1.16986	1.21551
5	1.05101	1.10408	1.13141	1.15927	1.21665	1.27628
6	1.06152	1.12616	1.15969	1.19405	1.26532	1.34010
7	1.07214	1.14869	1.18869	1.22987	1.31593	1.40710
8	1.08286	1.17166	1.21840	1.26677	1.36857	1.47746
9	1.09369	1.19509	1.24886	1.30477	1.42331	1.55133
10	1.10462	1.21899	1.28008	1.34392	1.48024	1.62889
11	1.11567	1.24337	1.31209	1.38423	1.53945	1.71034
12	1.12683	1.26824	1.34489	1.42576	1.60103	1.79586
13	1.13809	1.29361	1.37851	1.46853	1.66507	1.88565
14	1.14947	1.31948	1.41297	1.51259	1.73168	1.97993
15	1.16097	1.34587	1.44830	1.55797	1.80094	2.07893
16	1.17258	1.37279	1.48451	1.60471	1.87298	2.18287
17	1.18430	1.40024	1.52162	1.65285	1.94790	2.29202
18	1.19615	1.42825	1.55966	1.70243	2.02582	2.40662
19	1.20811	1.45681	1.59865	1.75351	2.10685	2.52695
20	1.22019	1.48595	1.63862	1.80611	2.19112	2.65330
21	1.23239	1.51567	1.67958	1.86029	2.27877	2.78596
22	1.24472	1.54598	1.72157	1.91610	2.36992	2.92526
23	1.25716	1.57690	1.76461	1.97359	2.46472	3.07152
24	1.26973	1.60844	1.80873	2.03279	2.56330	3.22510
25	1.28243	1.64061	1.85394	2.09378	2.66584	3.38635
26	1.29526	1.67342	1.90029	2.15659	2.77247	3.55567
27	1.30821	1.70689	1.94780	2.22129	2.88337	3.73346
28	1.32129	1.74102	1.99650	2.28793	2.99870	3.92013
29	1.33450	1.77584	2.04641	2.35657	3.11865	4.11614
30	1.34785	1.81136	2.09757	2.42726	3.24340	4.32194
31	1.36133	1.84759	2.15001	2.50008	3.37313	4.53804
32	1.37494	1.88454	2.20376	2.57508	3.50806	4.76494
33	1.38869	1.92223	2.25885	2.65234	3.64838	5.00319
34	1.40258	1.96068	2.31532	2.73191	3.79432	5.25335
35	1.41660	1.99989	2.37321	2.81386	3.94609	5.51602
36	1.43077	2.03989	2.43254	2.89828	4.10393	5.79182
37	1.44508	2.08069	2.49335	2.98523	4.26809	6.08141
38	1.45953	2.12230	2.55568	3.07478	4.43881	6.38548
39	1.47412	2.16474	2.61957	3.16703	4.61637	6.70475
40	1.48886	2.20804	2.68506	3.26204	4.80102	7.03999

Table 6–1   **243**

TABLE 6–1

Amount of 1

6%	8%	10%	12%	16%	20%	24%	Periods (*n*)
1.06000	1.08000	1.10000	1.12000	1.16000	1.20000	1.24000	1
1.12360	1.16640	1.21000	1.25440	1.34560	1.44000	1.53760	2
1.19102	1.25971	1.33100	1.40493	1.56090	1.72800	1.90662	3
1.26248	1.36049	1.46410	1.57352	1.81064	2.07360	2.36421	4
1.33823	1.46933	1.61051	1.76234	2.10034	2.48832	2.93163	5
1.41852	1.58687	1.77156	1.97382	2.43640	2.98598	3.63522	6
1.50363	1.71382	1.94872	2.21068	2.82622	3.58318	4.50767	7
1.59385	1.85093	2.14359	2.47596	3.27841	4.29982	5.58951	8
1.68948	1.99900	2.35795	2.77308	3.80296	5.15978	6.93099	9
1.79085	2.15892	2.59374	3.10585	4.41144	6.19174	8.59443	10
1.89830	2.33164	2.85312	3.47855	5.11726	7.43008	10.65709	11
2.01220	2.51817	3.13843	3.89598	5.93603	8.91610	13.21479	12
2.13293	2.71962	3.45227	4.36349	6.88579	10.69932	16.38634	13
2.26090	2.93719	3.79750	4.88711	7.98752	12.83918	20.31906	14
2.39656	3.17217	4.17725	5.47357	9.26552	15.40702	25.19563	15
2.54035	3.42594	4.59497	6.13039	10.74800	18.48843	31.24259	16
2.69277	3.70002	5.05447	6.86604	12.46768	22.18611	38.74081	17
2.85434	3.99602	5.55992	7.68997	14.46251	26.62333	48.03860	18
3.02560	4.31570	6.11591	8.61276	16.77652	31.94800	59.56786	19
3.20714	4.66096	6.72750	9.64629	19.46076	38.33760	73.86415	20
3.39956	5.03383	7.40025	10.80385	22.57448	46.00512	91.59155	21
3.60354	5.43654	8.14027	12.10031	26.18640	55.20614	113.57352	22
3.81975	5.87146	8.95430	13.55235	30.37622	66.24737	140.83116	23
4.04893	6.34118	9.84973	15.17863	35.23642	79.49685	174.63064	24
4.29187	6.84848	10.83471	17.00006	40.87424	95.39622	216.54199	25
4.54938	7.39635	11.91818	19.04007	47.41412	114.47546	268.51207	26
4.82235	7.98806	13.10999	21.32488	55.00038	137.37055	332.95497	27
5.11169	8.62711	14.42099	23.88387	63.80044	164.84466	412.86416	28
5.41839	9.31727	15.86309	26.74993	74.00851	197.81359	511.95156	29
5.74349	10.06266	17.44940	29.95992	85.84988	237.37631	634.81993	30
6.08810	10.86767	19.19434	33.55511	99.58586	284.85158	787.17672	31
6.45339	11.73708	21.11378	37.58173	115.51959	341.82189	976.09913	32
6.84059	12.67605	23.22515	42.09153	134.00273	410.18627	1210.36292	33
7.25103	13.69013	25.54767	47.14252	155.44317	492.22352	1500.85002	34
7.68609	14.78534	28.10244	52.79962	180.31407	590.66823	1861.05403	35
8.14725	15.96817	30.91268	59.13557	209.16432	708.80187	2307.70699	36
8.63609	17.24563	34.00395	66.23184	242.63062	850.56225	2861.55667	37
9.15425	18.62528	37.40434	74.17966	281.45151	1020.67470	3548.33027	38
9.70351	20.11530	41.14478	83.08122	326.48376	1224.80964	4399.92954	39
10.28572	21.72452	45.25926	93.05097	378.72116	1469.77157	5455.91262	40

TABLE 6–2

Present Value of 1

$$pvf_{\overline{n}|i} = \frac{1}{(1 + i)^n}$$

Periods (n)	1%	2%	2.5%	3%	4%	5%
1	.99010	.98039	.97561	.97087	.96154	.95238
2	.98030	.96117	.95181	.94260	.92456	.90703
3	.97059	.94232	.92860	.91514	.88900	.86384
4	.96098	.92385	.90595	.88849	.85480	.82270
5	.95147	.90573	.88385	.86261	.82193	.78353
6	.94205	.88797	.86230	.83748	.79031	.74622
7	.93272	.87056	.84127	.81309	.75992	.71068
8	.92348	.85349	.82075	.78941	.73069	.67684
9	.91434	.83676	.80073	.76642	.70259	.64461
10	.90529	.82035	.78120	.74409	.67556	.61391
11	.89632	.80426	.76214	.72242	.64958	.58468
12	.88745	.78849	.74356	.70138	.62460	.55684
13	.87866	.77303	.72542	.68095	.60057	.53032
14	.86996	.75788	.70773	.66112	.57748	.50507
15	.86135	.74301	.69047	.64186	.55526	.48102
16	.85282	.72845	.67362	.62317	.53391	.45811
17	.84438	.71416	.65720	.60502	.51337	.43630
18	.83602	.70016	.64117	.58739	.49363	.41552
19	.82774	.68643	.62553	.57029	.47464	.39573
20	.81954	.67297	.61027	.55368	.45639	.37689
21	.81143	.65978	.59539	.53755	.43883	.35894
22	.80340	.64684	.58086	.52189	.42196	.34185
23	.79544	.63416	.56670	.50669	.40573	.32557
24	.78757	.62172	.55288	.49193	.39012	.31007
25	.77977	.60953	.53939	.47761	.37512	.29530
26	.77205	.59758	.52623	.46369	.36069	.28124
27	.76440	.58586	.51340	.45019	.34682	.26785
28	.75684	.57437	.50088	.43708	.33348	.25509
29	.74934	.56311	.48866	.42435	.32065	.24295
30	.74192	.55207	.47674	.41199	.30832	.23138
31	.73458	.54125	.46511	.39999	.29646	.22036
32	.72730	.53063	.45377	.38834	.28506	.20987
33	.72010	.52023	.44270	.37703	.27409	.19987
34	.71297	.51003	.43191	.36604	.26355	.19035
35	.70591	.50003	.42137	.35538	.25342	.18129
36	.69892	.49022	.41109	.34503	.24367	.17266
37	.69200	.48061	.40107	.33498	.23430	.16444
38	.68515	.47119	.39128	.32523	.22529	.15661
39	.67837	.46195	.38174	.31575	.21662	.14915
40	.67165	.45289	.37243	.30656	.20829	.14205

Table 6–2 **245**

TABLE 6–2

Present Value of 1

6%	8%	10%	12%	16%	20%	24%	Periods (n)
.94340	.92593	.90909	.89286	.86207	.83333	.80645	1
.89000	.85734	.82645	.79719	.74316	.69444	.65036	2
.83962	.79383	.75131	.71178	.64066	.57870	.52449	3
.79209	.73503	.68301	.63552	.55229	.48225	.42297	4
.74726	.68058	.62092	.56743	.47611	.40188	.34111	5
.70496	.63017	.56447	.50663	.41044	.33490	.27509	6
.66506	.58349	.51316	.45235	.35383	.27908	.22184	7
.62741	.54027	.46651	.40388	.30503	.23257	.17891	8
.59190	.50025	.42410	.36061	.26295	.19381	.14428	9
.55839	.46319	.38554	.32197	.22668	.16151	.11635	10
.52679	.42888	.35049	.28748	.19542	.13459	.09383	11
.49697	.39711	.31863	.25668	.16846	.11216	.07567	12
.46884	.36770	.28966	.22917	.14523	.09346	.06103	13
.44230	.34046	.26333	.20462	.12520	.07789	.04921	14
.41727	.31524	.23939	.18270	.10793	.06491	.03969	15
.39365	.29189	.21763	.16312	.09304	.05409	.03201	16
.37136	.27027	.19784	.14564	.08021	.04507	.02581	17
.35034	.25025	.17986	.13004	.06914	.03756	.02082	18
.33051	.23171	.16351	.11611	.05961	.03130	.01679	19
.31180	.21455	.14864	.10367	.05139	.02608	.01354	20
.29416	.19866	.13513	.09256	.04430	.02174	.01092	21
.27751	.18394	.12285	.08264	.03819	.01811	.00880	22
.26180	.17032	.11168	.07379	.03292	.01509	.00710	23
.24698	.15770	.10153	.06588	.02838	.01258	.00573	24
.23300	.14602	.09230	.05882	.02447	.01048	.00462	25
.21981	.13520	.08391	.05252	.02109	.00874	.00372	26
.20737	.12519	.07628	.04689	.01818	.00728	.00300	27
.19563	.11591	.06934	.04187	.01567	.00607	.00242	28
.18456	.10733	.06304	.03738	.01351	.00506	.00195	29
.17411	.09938	.05731	.03338	.01165	.00421	.00158	30
.16425	.09202	.05210	.02980	.01004	.00351	.00127	31
.15496	.08520	.04736	.02661	.00866	.00293	.00102	32
.14619	.07889	.04306	.02376	.00746	.00244	.00083	33
.13791	.07305	.03914	.02121	.00643	.00203	.00067	34
.13011	.06763	.03558	.01894	.00555	.00169	.00054	35
.12274	.06262	.03235	.01691	.00478	.00141	.00043	36
.11579	.05799	.02941	.01510	.00412	.00118	.00035	37
.10924	.05369	.02673	.01348	.00355	.00098	.00028	38
.10306	.04971	.02430	.01204	.00306	.00082	.00023	39
.09722	.04603	.02209	.01075	.00264	.00068	.00018	40

TABLE 6–3

Amount of an Ordinary Annuity of 1

$$aoaf_{\overline{n}|i} = \frac{(1 + i)^n - 1}{i}$$

Periods (n)	1%	2%	2.5%	3%	4%	5%
1	1.00000	1.00000	1.00000	1.00000	1.00000	1.00000
2	2.01000	2.02000	2.02500	2.03000	2.04000	2.05000
3	3.03010	3.06040	3.07562	3.09090	3.12160	3.15250
4	4.06040	4.12161	4.15252	4.18363	4.24646	4.31012
5	5.10101	5.20404	5.25633	5.30914	5.41632	5.52563
6	6.15202	6.30812	6.38774	6.46841	6.63298	6.80191
7	7.21354	7.43428	7.54743	7.66246	7.89829	8.14201
8	8.28567	8.58297	8.73612	8.89234	9.21423	9.54911
9	9.36853	9.75463	9.95452	10.15911	10.58280	11.02656
10	10.46221	10.94972	11.20338	11.46388	12.00611	12.57789
11	11.56683	12.16872	12.48347	12.80780	13.48635	14.20679
12	12.68250	13.41209	13.79555	14.19203	15.02581	15.91713
13	13.80933	14.68033	15.14044	15.61779	16.62684	17.71298
14	14.94742	15.97394	16.51895	17.08632	18.29191	19.59863
15	16.09690	17.29342	17.93193	18.59891	20.02359	21.57856
16	17.25786	18.63929	19.38022	20.15688	21.82453	23.65749
17	18.43044	20.01207	20.86473	21.76159	23.69751	25.84037
18	19.61475	21.41231	22.38635	23.41444	25.64541	28.13238
19	20.81090	22.84056	23.94601	25.11687	27.67123	30.53900
20	22.01900	24.29737	25.54466	26.87037	29.77808	33.06595
21	23.23919	25.78332	27.18327	28.67649	31.96920	35.71925
22	24.47159	27.29898	28.86286	30.53678	34.24797	38.50521
23	25.71630	28.84496	30.58443	32.45288	36.61789	41.43048
24	26.97346	30.42186	32.34904	34.42647	39.08260	44.50200
25	28.24320	32.03030	34.15776	36.45926	41.64591	47.72710
26	29.52563	33.67091	36.01171	38.55304	44.31174	51.11345
27	30.82089	35.34432	37.91200	40.70963	47.08421	54.66913
28	32.12910	37.05121	39.85980	42.93092	49.96758	58.40258
29	33.45039	38.79223	41.85630	45.21885	52.96629	62.32271
30	34.78489	40.56808	43.90270	47.57542	56.08494	66.43885
31	36.13274	42.37944	46.00027	50.00268	59.32834	70.76079
32	37.49407	44.22703	48.15028	52.50276	62.70147	75.29883
33	38.86901	46.11157	50.35403	55.07784	66.20953	80.06377
34	40.25770	48.03380	52.61289	57.73018	69.85791	85.06696
35	41.66028	49.99448	54.92821	60.46208	73.65222	90.32031
36	43.07688	51.99437	57.30141	63.27594	77.59831	95.83632
37	44.50765	54.03425	59.73395	66.17422	81.70225	101.62814
38	45.95272	56.11494	62.22730	69.15945	85.97034	107.70955
39	47.41225	58.23724	64.78298	72.23423	90.40915	114.09502
40	48.88637	60.40198	67.40255	75.40126	95.02552	120.79977

Table 6–3   **247**

TABLE 6–3

Amount of Ordinary Annuity of 1

6%	8%	10%	12%	16%	20%	24%	Periods (*n*)
1.00000	1.00000	1.00000	1.00000	1.00000	1.00000	1.00000	1
2.06000	2.08000	2.10000	2.12000	2.16000	2.20000	2.24000	2
3.18360	3.24640	3.31000	3.37440	3.50560	3.64000	3.77760	3
4.37462	4.50611	4.64100	4.77933	5.06650	5.36800	5.68422	4
5.63709	5.86660	6.10510	6.35285	6.87714	7.44160	8.04844	5
6.97532	7.33593	7.71561	8.11519	8.97748	9.92992	10.98006	6
8.39384	8.92280	9.48717	10.08901	11.41387	12.91590	14.61528	7
9.89747	10.63663	11.43589	12.29969	14.24009	16.49908	19.12294	8
11.49132	12.48756	13.57948	14.77566	17.51851	20.79890	24.71245	9
13.18079	14.48656	15.93742	17.54874	21.32147	25.95868	31.64344	10
14.97164	16.64549	18.53117	20.65458	25.73290	32.15042	40.23787	11
16.86994	18.97713	21.38428	24.13313	30.85017	39.58050	50.89495	12
18.88214	21.49530	24.52271	28.02911	36.78620	48.49660	64.10974	13
21.01507	24.21492	27.97498	32.39260	43.67199	59.19592	80.49608	14
23.27597	27.15211	31.77248	37.27971	51.65951	72.03511	100.81514	15
25.67253	30.32428	35.94973	42.75328	60.92503	87.44213	126.01077	16
28.21288	33.75023	40.54470	48.88367	71.67303	105.93056	157.25336	17
30.90565	37.45024	45.59917	55.74971	84.14072	128.11667	195.99416	18
33.75999	41.44626	51.15909	63.43968	98.60323	154.74000	244.03276	19
36.78559	45.76196	57.27500	72.05244	115.37975	186.68800	303.60062	20
39.99273	50.42292	64.00250	81.69874	134.84051	225.02560	377.46477	21
43.39229	55.45676	71.40275	92.50258	157.41499	271.03072	469.05632	22
46.99583	60.89330	79.54302	104.60289	183.60138	326.23686	582.62984	23
50.81558	66.76476	88.49733	118.15524	213.97761	392.48424	723.46100	24
54.86451	73.10594	98.34706	133.33387	249.21402	471.98108	898.09164	25
59.15638	79.95442	109.18177	150.33393	290.08827	567.37730	1114.63363	26
63.70577	87.35077	121.09994	159.37401	337.50239	681.85276	1383.14570	27
68.52811	95.33883	134.20994	190.69889	392.50277	819.22331	1716.10067	28
73.63980	103.96594	148.63093	214.58275	456.30322	984.06797	2128.96483	29
79.05819	113.28321	164.49402	241.33268	530.31173	1181.88157	2640.91639	30
84.80168	123.34587	181.94342	271.29261	616.16161	1419.25788	3275.73632	31
90.88978	134.21354	201.13777	304.84772	715.74746	1704.10946	4062.91304	32
97.34316	145.95062	222.25154	342.42945	831.26706	2045.93135	5039.01217	33
104.18375	158.62667	245.47670	384.52098	965.26979	2456.11762	6249.37509	34
111.43478	172.31680	271.02437	431.66350	1120.71295	2948.34115	7750.22511	35
119.12087	187.10215	299.12681	484.46312	1301.02703	3539.00937	9611.27913	36
127.26812	203.07032	330.03949	543.59869	1510.19135	4247.81125	11918.98612	37
135.90421	220.31595	364.04343	609.83053	1752.82197	5098.37350	14780.54279	38
145.05846	238.94122	401.44778	684.01020	2034.27348	6119.04820	18328.87306	39
154.76197	259.05652	442.59256	767.09142	2360.75724	7343.85784	22728.80260	40

TABLE 6–4

Present Value of an Ordinary Annuity of 1

$$pvoaf_{\overline{n}|i} = \frac{1 - \dfrac{1}{(1 + i)^n}}{i}$$

Periods (n)	1%	2%	2.5%	3%	4%	5%
1	0.99010	0.98039	0.97561	0.97087	0.96154	0.95238
2	1.97040	1.94156	1.92742	1.91347	1.88609	1.85941
3	2.94099	2.88388	2.85602	2.82861	2.77509	2.72325
4	3.90197	3.80773	3.76197	3.71710	3.62990	3.54595
5	4.85343	4.71346	4.64583	4.57971	4.45182	4.32948
6	5.79548	5.60143	5.50813	5.41719	5.24214	5.07569
7	6.72819	6.47199	6.34939	6.23028	6.00205	5.78637
8	7.65168	7.32548	7.17014	7.01969	6.73274	6.46321
9	8.56602	8.16224	7.97087	7.78611	7.43533	7.10782
10	9.47130	8.98259	8.75206	8.53020	8.11090	7.72173
11	10.36763	9.78685	9.51421	9.25262	8.76048	8.30641
12	11.25508	10.57534	10.25776	9.95400	9.38507	8.86325
13	12.13374	11.34837	10.98318	10.63496	9.98565	9.39357
14	13.00370	12.10625	11.69091	11.29607	10.56312	9.89864
15	13.86505	12.84926	12.38138	11.93794	11.11839	10.37966
16	14.71787	13.57771	13.05500	12.56110	11.65230	10.83777
17	15.56225	14.29187	13.71220	13.16612	12.16567	11.27407
18	16.39827	14.99203	14.35336	13.75351	12.65930	11.68959
19	17.22601	15.67846	14.97889	14.32380	13.13394	12.08532
20	18.04555	16.35143	15.58916	14.87747	13.59033	12.46221
21	18.85698	17.01121	16.18455	15.41502	14.02916	12.82115
22	19.66038	17.65805	16.76541	15.93692	14.45112	13.16300
23	20.45582	18.29220	17.33211	16.44361	14.85684	13.48857
24	21.24339	18.91393	17.88499	16.93554	15.24696	13.79864
25	22.02316	19.52346	18.42438	17.41315	15.62208	14.09394
26	22.79520	20.12104	18.95061	17.87684	15.98277	14.37519
27	23.55961	20.70690	19.46401	18.32703	16.32959	14.64303
28	24.31644	21.28127	19.96489	18.76411	16.66306	14.89813
29	25.06579	21.84438	20.45355	19.18845	16.98371	15.14107
30	25.80771	22.39646	20.93029	19.60044	17.29203	15.37245
31	26.54229	22.93770	21.39541	20.00043	17.58849	15.59281
32	27.26959	23.46833	21.84918	20.38877	17.87355	15.80268
33	27.98969	23.98856	22.29188	20.76579	18.14765	16.00255
34	28.70267	24.49859	22.72379	21.13184	18.41120	16.19290
35	29.40858	24.99862	23.14516	21.48722	18.66461	16.37419
36	30.10751	25.48884	23.55625	21.83225	18.90828	16.54685
37	30.79951	25.96945	23.95732	22.16724	19.14258	16.71129
38	31.48466	26.44064	24.34860	22.49246	19.36786	16.86789
39	32.16303	26.90259	24.73034	22.80822	19.58448	17.01704
40	32.83469	27.35548	25.10278	23.11477	19.79277	17.15909

Table 6–4   **249**

TABLE 6–4

Present Value of an Ordinary Annuity of 1

6%	8%	10%	12%	16%	20%	24%	Periods (*n*)
0.94340	0.92593	0.90909	0.89286	0.86207	0.83333	0.80645	1
1.83339	1.78326	1.73554	1.69005	1.60523	1.52778	1.45682	2
2.67301	2.57710	2.48685	2.40183	2.24589	2.10648	1.98130	3
3.46511	3.31213	3.16987	3.03735	2.79818	2.58873	2.40428	4
4.21236	3.99271	3.79079	3.60478	3.27429	2.99061	2.74538	5
4.91732	4.62288	4.35526	4.11141	3.68474	3.32551	3.02047	6
5.58238	5.20637	4.86842	4.56376	4.03857	3.60459	3.24232	7
6.20979	5.74664	5.33493	4.96764	4.34359	3.83716	3.42122	8
6.80169	6.24689	5.75902	5.32825	4.60654	4.03097	3.56550	9
7.36009	6.71008	6.14457	5.65022	4.83323	4.19247	3.68186	10
7.88687	7.13896	6.49506	5.93770	5.02864	4.32706	3.77569	11
8.38384	7.53608	6.81369	6.19437	5.19711	4.43922	3.85136	12
8.85268	7.90378	7.10336	6.42355	5.34233	4.53268	3.91239	13
9.29498	8.24424	7.36669	6.62817	5.46753	4.61057	3.96160	14
9.71225	8.55948	7.60608	6.81086	5.57546	4.67547	4.00129	15
10.10590	8.85137	7.82371	6.97399	5.66850	4.72956	4.03330	16
10.47726	9.12164	8.02155	7.11963	5.74870	4.77463	4.05911	17
10.82760	9.37189	8.20141	7.24967	5.81785	4.81219	4.07993	18
11.15812	9.60360	8.36492	7.36578	5.87746	4.84350	4.09672	19
11.46992	9.81815	8.51356	7.46944	5.92884	4.86958	4.11026	20
11.76408	10.01680	8.64869	7.56200	5.97314	4.89132	4.12117	21
12.04158	10.20074	8.77154	7.64465	6.01133	4.90943	4.12998	22
12.30338	10.37106	8.88322	7.71843	6.04425	4.92453	4.13708	23
12.55036	10.52876	8.98474	7.78432	6.07263	4.93710	4.14281	24
12.78336	10.67478	9.07704	7.84314	6.09709	4.94759	4.14742	25
13.00317	10.80998	9.16095	7.89566	6.11818	4.95632	4.15115	26
13.21053	10.93516	9.23722	7.94255	6.13636	4.96360	4.15415	27
13.40616	11.05108	9.30657	7.98442	6.15204	4.96967	4.15657	28
13.59072	11.15841	9.36961	8.02181	6.16555	4.97472	4.15853	29
13.76483	11.25778	9.42691	8.05518	6.17720	4.97894	4.16010	30
13.92909	11.34980	9.47901	8.08499	6.18724	4.98245	4.16137	31
14.08404	11.43500	9.52638	8.11159	6.19590	4.98537	4.16240	32
14.23023	11.51389	9.56943	8.13535	6.20336	4.98781	4.16322	33
14.36814	11.58693	9.60857	8.15656	6.20979	4.98984	4.16389	34
14.49825	11.65457	9.64416	8.17550	6.21534	4.99154	4.16443	35
14.62099	11.71719	9.67651	8.19241	6.22012	4.99295	4.16486	36
14.73678	11.77518	9.70592	8.20751	6.22424	4.99412	4.16521	37
14.84602	11.82887	9.73265	8.22099	6.22779	4.99510	4.16549	38
14.94907	11.87858	9.75696	8.23303	6.23086	4.99592	4.16572	39
15.04630	11.92461	9.77905	8.24378	6.23350	4.99660	4.16590	40

Cash and Receivables

OBJECTIVES

1. To discuss and illustrate the financial accounting and reporting requirements for cash and receivables classified as current assets.
2. To explain the accounting for a petty cash fund.
3. To discuss and illustrate the preparation of a bank reconciliation and a proof of cash.
4. To explain the accounting for credit sales.
5. To discuss and illustrate the accounting for uncollectible accounts receivable.
6. To explain certain financing methods under which companies use their accounts receivable to generate cash.
7. To discuss and illustrate the accounting for notes receivable.

In 1990 Unisys Corporation, an $8 billion company that makes computers, named James Unruh its chief executive officer. Unisys had been suffering substantial financial losses, and its debt had increased to 66% of total capitalization. The company was having trouble paying its bills. Unruh, an accountant, became very close to the company's major customers. He also formed 13 teams whose goal was to generate substantial amounts of cash that the company needed to stay in business. The "accounts receivable team" generated $250 million of cash in 1991, the "inventory team" generated another $250 million, and by year-end, the company had paid its bank indebtedness and had over $800 million of cash on its balance sheet. The accounts receivable collection period decreased from about 73 days of sales in 1990 to about 51 days in 1991. Inventories decreased by about 57%. The company was well on its way to achieving profitable operations and generating favorable cash flows.

The Unisys case illustrates the critical importance of cash to any business. Without adequate cash, a company cannot survive. In this chapter, we discuss the accounting and reporting for cash and receivables.

Wechsler Linden, "The Bean Counter as Hero," *Forbes* (October 11, 1993), pp. 46–48.

In Part I of this book, we discussed the theoretical basis for financial reporting, and in Part II we presented the tools of accounting. In Part III, our focus shifts to asset accounting. Each of the seven chapters in Part III discusses important measurement and disclosure principles that relate to certain assets, and each is related to the theoretical framework presented in Chapter 2. Recall that in Chapter 2 we defined *assets* as probable future economic benefits obtained or controlled by a particular entity as a result of past transactions or events. The Kellogg Company balance sheet printed on the endpapers shows several of the assets discussed in Part III.

This chapter focuses on cash and receivables classified as current assets. Cash and receivables classified as noncurrent assets are discussed in Chapter 10. Recall that in Chapter 3 we discussed the nature of asset valuation. Generally, the valuation of cash and short-term receivables is less complex and controversial than the valuation of most other assets.

The assets described in this chapter are highly liquid (i.e., cash or close to cash realization) and are therefore important in assessing a company's overall liquidity. An empirical study provided evidence that users of financial statements are becoming more concerned about liquidity evaluations: "While security analysts used to be concerned primarily with earnings per share, they are now devoting increased attention to the balance sheet and cash flow. Liquidity analysis plays a significant part in security analysts' evaluation of companies."[1]

CASH

COMPOSITION OF CASH

Cash is the standard medium of exchange in business transactions. It includes currency, coins, checks, bank drafts, money orders, and demand deposits (checking accounts). Savings accounts are also usually considered cash, because banks generally do not enforce their legal right to demand a notice before the depositor makes a withdrawal. As a result, savings account balances are usually available for immediate expenditure.

Most companies maintain several general ledger accounts for cash to provide management with adequate details concerning cash balances. For example, a company might establish the following:

1. A **petty cash** account for currency and coins (called a *petty cash fund*) used to make small disbursements.
2. A **cash on hand** account for undeposited cash receipts.
3. A separate **cash in bank** account for each checking account maintained.

External users of financial statements generally are interested in the total amount of cash that a company has and in the relationship between this amount and other financial statement amounts. That is the reason that companies typically combine the amounts shown in the various cash accounts and report only a single total as "cash" on the balance sheet.

Asset/Liability Measurement

The valuation of cash is not highly controversial. Cash is simply reported at its *face amount*. The classification of cash as current or noncurrent depends on management's intended use of the cash. To be classified as a current asset, cash must be available for use in current operations. Because it is highly liquid, cash is usually listed first among the current assets. A material amount of cash that has been restricted or designated for some current purpose, such as the payment of current bond interest, should be reported separately among the current assets. On the other hand, cash that is not available for current purposes, such as cash accumulated in a sinking fund to retire the principal amount of long-term bonds, should be reported in the investments and funds category, not in current assets.

Materiality

Several noteworthy considerations in accounting for cash are described below.

1. **Certificates of deposit (CDs)** are normally included in short-term investments instead of cash, because banks usually impose substantial interest penalties that discourage CD holders from making withdrawals before the CDs mature.
2. **Postdated checks, NSF checks** (not sufficient funds checks, those that cannot be covered by funds in the debtor's bank account), and **IOUs** should be reported as receivables rather than cash.

---

[1]Morton Backer and Martin L. Gosman, *Financial Reporting and Business Liquidity* (New York: National Association of Accountants, 1978), p. 251.

3. **Expense advances,** such as advances for employee travel, and **postage stamps** should be reported as prepaid expenses, not cash.

4. A **bank overdraft,** which occurs when a depositor has written checks for a sum larger than that in the depositor's bank account, should be reported as a current liability, except when the depositor has sufficient funds in another account with the *same bank* to cover the account that is overdrawn. Under these circumstances, which may arise when a company maintains a regular operating account and a payroll account with the same bank, the bank will transfer funds to the overdrawn account if the depositor fails to do so. As a result, the depositor may appropriately offset the overdraft against the cash balance and report the net amount of cash among the current assets.

5. **Undelivered checks,** as of the balance sheet date, should be considered part of a debtor's cash. Technically, checks drawn by a company should not be deducted from the company's cash balance until they have been mailed or otherwise delivered. As a result, liabilities that the checks are intended to liquidate still exist and should be reported as current payables.

6. **Compensating balances** are minimum amounts that a company agrees to maintain in a bank checking account as partial consideration for a loan or line of credit. Compensating balances limit the amount of cash that a company can spend in everyday operations. Moreover, compensating balances increase a company's effective interest cost if they are higher than the checking account balances that the company would normally maintain. For these reasons, a company should disclose information about compensating balances in the notes to its financial statements. An example of such a note is as follows: "During 1996, informal arrangements were maintained with a number of banks which generally required the Company to maintain compensating cash balances of 8% of the loan commitments plus 8% of the average daily outstanding debt balances. At December 31, 1996, the cash balance includes $9.5 million of such compensating balances."

MANAGEMENT OF CASH

Companies need cash to buy goods and services, to pay off debts, and to make distributions to owners. Because of its critical importance to any business, cash must be managed effectively. As the chief executive of Firestone Tire & Rubber Company has stated: "Cash becomes the final determinant in the way you run a company."[2] Effective cash management involves striking a delicate balance between **risk** and **profitability.** On the one hand, managers try to avoid having too little cash on hand in order to minimize the company's risk of insolvency. On the other hand, they try to avoid excessive cash balances because uninvested cash does not contribute to the company's profits. In 1992, for example, American Airlines reported cash that amounted to only 0.2% of total assets. Wal-Mart's cash at the end of 1992 represented only 0.06% of total assets.

Effective cash management requires careful **planning** and **control.** The major aspect of **cash planning** is the **cash budget,** which is an internal statement of projected cash inflows, outflows, and balances. Among other things, the cash budget enables managers to prepare in advance for such activities as the raising of additional cash through borrowing and the investing of idle cash in productive assets. Cash planning is usually covered in managerial accounting and financial management courses.

Cash control is an important part of a firm's **internal control system.** Internal control has been defined as follows: "The plan of organization and all of the coordinate methods and measures adopted within a business to safeguard its assets, check the accuracy and reliability of its accounting data, promote operational efficiency, and encourage adherence to prescribed managerial policies."[3] Internal control includes **accounting controls,** which relate to the safeguarding of assets and the reliability of financial records, and **administrative controls,** which relate to operational efficiency and adherence to managerial policies. Accountants should have a general awareness of administrative controls, including statistical analyses,

---

[2]Thomas O'Hanlon, "Less Means More at Firestone," *Fortune* (October 20, 1980), p. 116.
[3]*AICPA Professional Standards*—Volume 1 (Chicago: Commerce Clearing House), AU Sec. 320.09.

time and motion studies, performance reports, employee training programs, and quality controls.[4] In addition, accountants should have a thorough understanding of accounting controls. Several important **principles of internal accounting control** are listed below:

1. Company personnel should be competent and honest, and they should be given specific responsibilities.
2. The responsibility for a series of related events, such as receiving merchandise and paying for it, should be divided between two or more persons.
3. The accounting function should be separated from the custodianship of company assets.
4. Adequate accounting records should be kept at all times.
5. Certain clerical personnel should be rotated among various jobs.
6. Assets should be protected by insurance and by physical safeguards.
7. An internal audit staff should be maintained if management believes the benefits of such a staff exceed the costs.

Maintaining an adequate system of internal accounting control for all assets is important, particularly for cash. Cash appeals to virtually everyone and is relatively easy to steal if not properly safeguarded. If one person, for example, receives and records a company's cash, that person can easily pocket some of the receipts and fail to record them. The specific features of internal accounting controls over cash vary from company to company. Generally, however, these controls are designed to ensure that

1. Responsibilities are divided between those employees who account for cash and those who have custody of it.
2. All cash receipts are recorded when received and deposited immediately and intact in the bank.
3. All disbursements are made for authorized purposes.
4. All disbursements, except for small ones made from petty cash, are made by check.

Specific accounting controls for cash are usually covered in more depth in auditing courses. Two important control measures designed to help safeguard a company's cash—maintaining a petty cash fund and periodically reconciling the bank statement—are discussed below.

PETTY CASH

A business should generally make all payments by check. But most businesses find it inconvenient or impossible to write checks for such small items as taxi fares, newspaper delivery charges, postage, express charges, and minor supplies. A company usually pays for these kinds of items from a **petty cash fund,** often called an **imprest cash fund.** An imprest fund is established for a fixed amount and allows a company to effectively control small amounts of cash fairly simply.

The following discussion explains how a petty cash fund works.

1. A responsible employee is appointed **petty cashier.** A check payable to petty cash is cashed, and the petty cashier places the money in the petty cash fund (which is often kept in a locked box). The check that establishes the fund is usually for an amount ($300, for example) that the company estimates will last from two to four weeks. The following journal entry is required:

Petty Cash	300	
Cash		300

2. As time passes, the petty cashier disburses money from the fund. To evidence each disbursement, the petty cashier places in the fund a prenumbered receipt, signed by the person who received cash. The amount of petty cash on hand and the amounts shown on the signed re-

---

[4]*AICPA Professional Standards*—Volume 1, AU Sec. 320.10.

ceipts should always equal the original amount of the fund ($300 in our example). The company does *not* make journal entries when petty cash is disbursed.

3. When the amount of cash in the fund is low, the petty cashier submits the signed receipts and requests reimbursement from the general cashier for an amount that will increase the cash in the fund to the original amount. At this time, the receipts are canceled so that no one can use them again. In addition, the company records increases in those expenses (or other accounts) that are documented by the receipts.

Now assume that after three weeks only $25 remains in the petty cash fund. The signed receipts show the following petty cash disbursements:

Postage	$ 45
Office supplies	102
Transportation-in	125
Total	$272

Because the fund contains only $25, the general cashier must write a check for $275 ($300 − $25) to restore the fund to its original amount ($300). After the check is written, the company makes the following journal entry:

Postage Expense	45	
Office Supplies Expense	102	
Transportation-in	125	
Cash Short and Over	3	
Cash		275

The check is then cashed and the money is placed in the petty cash fund.

Cash Short and Over is a nominal account that is debited for cash shortages and credited for overages. Such shortages and overages usually result from errors in making change or failure to obtain receipts for very small amounts. A debit balance in the Cash Short and Over account at the end of a period should be reported as a miscellaneous expense and a credit balance as a miscellaneous revenue. However, a material cash shortage resulting from a cause such as theft should be charged to a receivable account if the company expects to recover the amount of the shortage. If recovery is not expected, the company should charge a loss account.

Materiality

Observe that the company debited the Petty Cash account when the fund was established and made no other entries in this account. At the end of an accounting period, therefore, the petty cash fund should ordinarily be replenished. This ensures that all expenses paid with petty cash are recorded and that the petty cash on hand corresponds with the amount shown in the Petty Cash account. If for some reason the fund is not replenished at the end of an accounting period, the company should still debit the appropriate expense accounts, but it should credit the Petty Cash account directly. Over time the pattern of petty cash disbursements may suggest that the original amount of the petty cash fund is either too low or too high. If this occurs, the amount of petty cash and the balance shown in the Petty Cash account should be increased or decreased as appropriate. For example, if the company in the above example increases the fixed amount of the petty cash fund from $300 to $400, the following journal entry is made:

Petty Cash	100	
Cash		100

CASH IN BANK

The cash that a business has on hand may include petty cash funds, change funds (funds used to make change with customers), and undeposited receipts. As stated earlier, a business normally keeps most of its cash in one or more checking accounts. The checking account gives a company a *double record* of its cash transactions, the company's own record plus that provided by the bank. The bank's record is summarized on a monthly **bank statement.**

An accountant verifies the cash on hand simply by counting it. In contrast, because the cash in a checking account cannot be conveniently counted, the accountant verifies it by preparing a bank reconciliation.

Bank Reconciliation

When a company receives a bank statement, its accountant should immediately prepare a **bank reconciliation.** This schedule explains any differences between a company's book balance of cash and the bank statement balance. A bank reconciliation helps to identify errors that the depositor or the bank made in recording cash transactions. It also helps in making journal entries to update the depositor's accounting records.

On a depositor's books (accounting records), the cash balance in a bank account is an asset. On the bank's books, the cash in the depositor's account is a liability. Because the depositor and the bank do not simultaneously record all transactions, and because either party can make mistakes, the asset balance on the depositor's books usually does not equal the liability balance on the bank statement. Many factors may explain why the two balances differ:

1. **Deposits in transit.** These are additions to cash in the bank that the depositor has recorded but that do not appear on the bank statement. For example, on the last day of the month, the depositor may place the day's cash receipts in the bank's night depository for the bank to record on the next business day. These receipts should appear on the next month's bank statement.

2. **Outstanding checks.** Checks that the depositor has issued and recorded but have not yet cleared the bank will not yet be deducted on the bank statement.

3. **Bank collections.** Promissory notes are often made payable at the payee's bank. The bank may therefore collect a note for the depositor and credit the proceeds to the depositor's account. Such collections made near the end of a month may appear on the bank statement but not on the depositor's books because the depositor is not yet aware of the collection.

4. **Bank charges.** The bank often makes various charges that are not yet recorded on the depositor's books, such as charges for bank services, checkbooks, NSF checks, and repayment of depositor loans.

5. **Bank errors.** Occasionally, a bank error might affect the depositor's account. For example, the bank might erroneously charge one company's check to another company's account. The depositor should instruct the bank to correct such errors.

6. **Depositor errors.** Sometimes an error is made in the depositor's accounting records (commonly called a **book error**). For example, the depositor may have written a check for one amount but recorded it at a different amount. The depositor should promptly correct the accounting records.

An accountant may prepare a bank reconciliation by reconciling from the bank statement balance to the book balance, or vice versa. Accountants prefer, however, to reconcile from both of these balances to the **correct cash balance.** Such a reconciliation is relatively easy to understand; it shows in one place the information needed for making journal entries, and it indicates the correct cash balance that a company can spend from its checking account (the balance after all errors are corrected and all outstanding items clear the bank). A convenient form for this type of bank reconciliation is shown in Exhibit 7–1.

Observe that the bank reconciliation is divided into two sections: "balance per bank statement" and "balance per books." The logic of the additions and deductions in each section is not difficult to understand. Both sections end with the same "correct cash balance." This is the amount of cash that the depositor can spend from the checking account and the amount that should appear on the depositor's balance sheet.

Usually, the depositor must make journal entries after the reconciliation is completed to update the depositor's accounting records. These entries are based on the items added or de-

---

EXHIBIT 7–1

Bank Reconciliation Form

Balance per bank statement		$XXX
Add: Deposits in transit	$XX	
Bank errors that understate the balance per bank statement (e.g., the bank charges someone else's check to the depositor's account)	XX	XX
		XXX
Deduct: Outstanding checks	XX	
Bank errors that overstate the balance per bank statement (e.g., the bank charges one of the depositor's checks to someone else's account)	XX	XX
Correct cash balance		$XXX
Balance per books		$XXX
Add: Deposits credited by the bank but not yet recorded by the depositor (e.g., collection of a promissory note)	$XX	
Book errors that understate the balance per books (e.g., the depositor writes a check for $10 but deducts $100 on the books)	XX	XX
		XXX
Deduct: Bank charges not yet recorded by the depositor (e.g., bank service charges and NSF checks)	XX	
Book errors that overstate the balance per books (e.g., the depositor writes a check for $100 but deducts $10 on the books)	XX	XX
Correct cash balance		$XXX

---

ducted in the "balance per books" section. Additions and deductions in the other section either have already been recorded by the depositor or represent errors that the bank must correct.

To illustrate, assume that Todd Company keeps all of its cash in a checking account. An examination of the company's accounting records and its bank statement for the month ended May 31, 1996, revealed the following information:

1. The cash balance shown as of May 31 on the bank statement was $17,631.
2. The cash balance shown as of May 31 on the company's books was $15,214.
3. A deposit of $1,500 mailed to the bank on May 31 did not appear on the bank statement.
4. On May 30, the bank collected a note receivable for Todd Company and credited the proceeds of $2,100 to the company's account. The proceeds included $100 of interest, all of which the company earned during 1996. Todd Company has not yet recorded the collection.
5. Outstanding checks as of May 31 were as follows:

No. 902	$ 132
No. 922	870
No. 923	1,645

6. The company discovered that check no. 916, written in May for $527 in payment of an account payable, had been incorrectly recorded as $257.
7. The bank returned a check for $548 that the company deposited on May 29. The check was drawn by a customer who did not have sufficient funds in his bank account to cover the check.
8. The bank statement showed a $12 service charge for May.

EXHIBIT 7-2		

Todd Company
Bank Reconciliation
May 31, 1996

Balance per bank statement		$17,631
Add: Deposit in transit		1,500
		19,131
Deduct: Outstanding checks		
No. 902	$ 132	
No. 922	870	
No. 923	1,645	2,647
Correct cash balance		$16,484
Balance per books		$15,214
Add: Note and interest collected by bank		2,100
		17,314
Deduct: Bank service charge	$ 12	
NSF check received from customer	548	
Error made in recording check no. 916 ($527 − $257)	270	830
Correct cash balance		$16,484

The bank reconciliation for Todd Company is shown in Exhibit 7–2. As stated earlier, the journal entries to update the depositor's accounting records should be based on the items added or deducted in the "balance per books" section.

Cash	2,100	
Notes Receivable		2,000
Interest Revenue		100
(To record collection of note and interest by bank.)		
Miscellaneous Expense	12	
Cash		12
(To record bank service charge.)		
Accounts Receivable	548	
Cash		548
(To record NSF check.)		
Accounts Payable	270	
Cash		270
(To correct error made in recording check no. 916.)		

These entries may be combined into a single compound entry. When the entries are posted, Todd Company's Cash account will show a balance of $16,484, the correct amount as shown on the bank reconciliation.

An accountant should reconcile the monthly bank statement for each checking account that a company maintains. If a company has more than one checking account, the amount of cash to report on a balance sheet will be the sum of the correct cash balances shown on the bank reconciliations and any cash that the depositor has on hand.

Proof of Cash

Auditors frequently prepare an expanded version of the bank reconciliation known as a **four-column bank reconciliation,** or simply a **proof of cash.** A proof of cash includes four reconciliations:

1. A reconciliation of the bank statement and book balances of cash at the end of the *previous month*.
2. A reconciliation of the cash receipts (deposits) shown on the bank statement with those shown on the books for the *current month*.
3. A reconciliation of the cash payments shown on the bank statement with those shown on the books for the *current month*.
4. A reconciliation of the bank statement and book balances of cash at the end of the *current month*.

The proof of cash is a stronger control measure than the single-column bank reconciliation. Auditors frequently prepare a proof of cash when a company is found to have weak internal control over cash. Because it provides a reconciliation of cash transactions as well as cash balances, the proof of cash makes it easier to pinpoint errors made by the company or the bank. This feature is particularly important when a company has made cash transfers from one bank account to another during the month. If a transfer is shown as a payment from one account but is not shown as a receipt by the other, an accountant or auditor would want to know why. We illustrate how to prepare a proof of cash in the appendix to this chapter.

RECEIVABLES

Receivables are claims held against others for money, goods, or services. They generally result in an inflow of cash. An enterprise should classify a receivable as a *current asset* only if collection of the receivable is expected within the next year or operating cycle, whichever is longer. Other receivables should be reported in the investments and funds category or in other assets, as we discuss in Chapter 10.

Because of the operating cycle concept, current assets include "installment or deferred accounts and notes receivable if they conform generally to normal trade practices and terms within the business."[5] These receivables are often collectible over periods that are longer than one year after the balance sheet date. Accounting for installment receivables is discussed in Chapter 21.

Proper accounting for a receivable requires an assessment of the *amount, timing,* and *uncertainty* associated with its collection. In theory, an accountant should initially value (measure) a receivable at an amount equal to the present value of the cash that the enterprise expects to collect. Such a valuation reflects the time value of money; an enterprise earns *interest* by waiting to collect money. The amount of interest is the difference between a receivable's maturity value and its present value. In practice, accountants often ignore interest for short-term receivables, because they regard the amount as immaterial.

Asset/Liability Measurement

Materiality

Valuation of a receivable at its present value is consistent with the FASB's second objective of financial reporting (see Chapter 2), which states that financial reporting should provide information useful in assessing cash flow prospects. If investors and creditors can more accurately predict the cash that a company will collect from its receivables and from other sources, this should enable them to more accurately assess their own chances of receiving cash from the company.

Receivables may be classified as **trade receivables** or **nontrade receivables,** which are generally reported separately on the balance sheet. **Trade receivables** result from sales of goods or services to customers. They usually compose most of the total dollar value of a company's receivables. All other receivables are **nontrade.** Examples of nontrade receivables are

1. Receivables from officers or employees.
2. Advances to subsidiaries.
3. Various types of deposits made with other parties.

---

[5]*Accounting Research Bulletin No. 43,* "Restatement and Revision of Accounting Research Bulletins," 1953, Ch. 3, Sec. A, par. 4.

4. Claims against insurance companies.
5. Receivables from stock subscriptions.
6. Dividends receivable (from other companies).
7. Interest receivable.

A receivable may be represented by an open account (a nonwritten promise to pay) or by a note (a written promise to pay). Thus, **accounts receivable** and **notes receivable** are reported separately on the balance sheet. They are discussed below.

ACCOUNTS RECEIVABLE

In a broad sense, the term *accounts receivable* includes all receivables not evidenced by written promises to pay. But accountants usually restrict the term to open accounts that have resulted from selling goods or services on credit. Because accounts receivable are very important assets to many companies, they must be managed effectively. Such management involves a trade-off between the revenues generated by credit sales and the costs associated with carrying the resulting accounts receivable.

Asset/Liability Measurement
Generally accepted accounting principles (GAAP) require companies to report accounts receivable at **net realizable value.** This is the amount that the company expects to collect, and it equals the face amount of the receivables less an estimated uncollectible amount. Be-
Materiality
cause of materiality, accountants generally ignore the interest inherent in the face amount of accounts receivable.

Recording Credit Sales

Revenue Realization
Recording accounts receivable is closely related to the revenue realization principle (discussed in Chapter 2). That is, a seller should record a receivable that arises from a sale of goods on the date that the sale occurs. This is also when the seller recognizes revenue. Under most circumstances, the sales revenue and the related receivable should be recorded at the precise moment that title passes from the seller to the buyer. For practical reasons, however, accounts receivable and related sales revenue are usually recorded when the seller ships the goods.

Trade Discounts.   A trade discount is an amount that a seller deducts from a list price to determine the invoice price of goods sold. List prices are quoted in the seller's catalogs or price lists; trade discounts usually appear in a separate schedule. A trade discount, then, is merely a convenient device that manufacturers and wholesalers often use to price their goods. The use of trade discounts enables a company to revise its prices periodically without having to reprint its catalogs and to set different prices for different types of customers and for different quantities sold.

Neither sellers nor purchasers should record trade discounts in their accounts. To illustrate, assume that All Star Wholesalers sells 100 footballs to Retail Sports, Inc., for the list price of $30 each, less a trade discount of 40%. The invoice price is therefore $18 ($30 − $12) per football, and the total invoice price is $1,800 ($18 × 100). Here is how All Star Wholesalers records the transaction:

Accounts Receivable	1,800	
Sales		1,800

Many sellers express trade discounts in a series such as 40/20/10. The use of multiple trade discounts allows the seller to conveniently vary the selling price based on such factors as the type of customer or the quantity purchased. If the terms are 40/20/10, a customer may receive a trade discount of (1) 40%; (2) 40% and 20%; *or* (3) 40%, 20%, and 10%, depending on the circumstances. Suppose, for example, that MCA, Inc., sells Model 21 television sets for the list price of $100 each, less the following discounts:

40%	If 50 or fewer sets are purchased.
40% and 20%	If more than 50 but fewer than 100 sets are purchased.
40%, 20%, and 10%	If 100 or more sets are purchased.

Assuming that customers Aim, Bar, and Cam purchase 30, 60, and 200 television sets, respectively, Exhibit 7–3 shows how MCA, Inc., would determine the invoice price for each customer.

Cash Discounts.   Companies frequently offer cash discounts to their credit customers. A **cash discount** is a reduction from an invoice price that is offered to buyers to encourage prompt payment. Companies use trade discounts to *establish* an invoice price and cash discounts to *reduce* the invoice price. From the seller's point of view, a cash discount is called a **sales discount;** from the purchaser's point of view, a cash discount is called a **purchase discount.** A cash discount is usually expressed in terms such as 2/10, n/30; or 2/10, EOM (end of month). Terms of 2/10, n/30 mean that the buyer may deduct 2% from the invoice price if payment is made within 10 days after the invoice date. A buyer who does not pay within the 10-day discount period must pay the gross invoice amount within 30 days after the invoice date.

Purchasers generally take cash discounts offered to them because it is usually advantageous to do so. Suppose, for example, that Sim Company sells goods to Burt Company for an invoice price of $1,000, terms 2/10, n/30. Burt Company can liquidate its debt by paying $980 within 10 days after the invoice date. In effect, $980 is the **cash price** of the goods. Instead of paying the $980 by the 10th day, Burt Company may choose to pay a $20 premium to keep the $980 for an additional 20 days (30 days − 10 days). This choice will result in an interest rate of 2.04% ($20 ÷ 980) for 20 days. This is equivalent to an effective *annual* rate of 36.7% (2.04% × 360/20). Clearly, most companies try to avoid such a high interest cost.

In theory, an account receivable and the related sales revenue should be measured net of any cash discounts allowable. This is consistent with the **net method** of recording credit sales. In Exhibit 7–4, we compare the net method with the **gross method** of recording credit sales. The net method correctly states the receivable at its realizable value on the date of sale and correctly states the amount of revenue earned on that date. Under the net method, we record the receivable and the related revenue at an amount that equals the **cash equivalent price** on the date of sale. Remember that sellers offer cash discounts to encourage buyers to pay promptly. A buyer who fails to take a cash discount has in effect decided to engage in a deferred payment transaction. The buyer therefore incurs an interest cost, and the seller

---

EXHIBIT 7–3

Trade Discount

Customer	Quantity Purchased	Applicable Trade Discount	Invoice Price per Unit	Total Invoice Price
Aim	30	40%	$100 − ($100 × 40%) = $60	$60 × 30 units = $1,800
Bar	60	40% and 20%	$100 − ($100 × 40%) = $60 $60 − ($60 × 20%) = $48	$48 × 60 units = $2,880
Cam	200	40%, 20%, and 10%	$100 − ($100 × 40%) = $60 $60 − ($60 × 20%) = $48 $48 − ($48 × 10%) = $43.20	$43.20 × 200 units = $8,640

	EXHIBIT 7–4	
	Net and Gross Methods of Recording Credit Sales	

Transaction	Net Method		Gross Method	
July 1				

Jam Company sells merchandise for $100, terms 2/10, n/30.	Accounts Receivable 98
	    Sales
		98	Accounts Receivable 100
			    Sales
				100

Alternative Assumption No. 1				
July 10				

Jam Company receives payment that buyer made within the discount period.	Cash 98
	    Accounts Receivable
		98	Cash 98
			Sales Discounts 2
			    Accounts Receivable
				100

Alternative Assumption No. 2				
July 30				

Jam Company receives payment that buyer made after the discount period.	Cash 100
	    Accounts Receivable
	    Sales Discounts Not
	      Taken
		98
		
		2
			Cash 100
			    Accounts Receivable
				100

earns interest revenue. The interest that the seller earns is reflected in the Sales Discounts Not Taken account. The seller should report the balance in this account on the income statement as financial revenue.

Most companies record credit sales at gross amounts by using the gross method. When the seller later receives the buyer's payment, the seller records any cash discounts taken in a Sales Discounts account. The seller later deducts the balance in this account from sales to arrive at net sales. Although the gross method tends to result in an overstatement of accounts receivable and sales revenue, it is practical and convenient, and it enables a company to make a year-end adjusting entry to estimate sales discounts and thereby eliminate material errors from financial statements.

Accounting for Uncollectible Accounts

Companies sell on credit rather than only for cash to increase total sales and thereby increase profits. But a company that sells on credit assumes the risk that some customers will not pay their accounts. When an account becomes uncollectible, the company has sustained a **bad debt loss.** These losses are simply one of the costs of doing business on credit. Accounting for bad debt losses would be fairly easy if they occurred in the same period as the sale. In reality, bad debt losses often occur in subsequent periods.

One method of accounting for uncollectible accounts, called the **direct write-off method,** involves debiting Bad Debts Expense and crediting Accounts Receivable in the period in which the company finally determines that the accounts are uncollectible.[6] This method is based on actual rather than estimated bad debt losses. However, the direct write-off method usually violates the matching principle. The reason is that the bad debts expense is often recognized in a later accounting period than the one in which the related sales revenue was recognized. The result is a mismatching of sales revenue and bad debts expense. In

Matching

---

[6]An entry debiting Accounts Receivable and crediting Bad Debts Expense would be made if an account that had been written off was later recovered in the *same* accounting period. If a recovery occurred in a *subsequent* accounting period, Accounts Receivable would be debited, and Bad Debts Recovered (a revenue account) would be credited. An entry debiting Cash and crediting Accounts Receivable would be made to record the collection.

addition, the direct write-off method leads to the reporting of accounts receivable at an amount higher than their net realizable value (i.e., at an amount greater than the company expects to collect), which violates the asset/liability measurement principle.

Use of the direct write-off method may be appropriate if a company's bad debt losses are immaterial or if a company is unable to reasonably estimate its losses from uncollectible receivables.[7] Generally, however, the inability to estimate bad debt losses suggests that collectibility is so uncertain that the company should defer the recognition of revenue beyond the time of sale. As we explain in Chapter 21, if a company makes a credit sale to a customer who is a relatively poor credit risk, recognition of revenue should occur after the time of sale, and either the installment sales method or the cost recovery method of accounting may be used. Most companies, however, make credit sales only to customers that have a reasonable credit standing, and accordingly, the general rule in accounting is to recognize revenue at the time of sale. Because bad debt losses usually are material, and because most companies can reasonably estimate their bad debt losses based on their own collection experience or that of similar companies, use of the direct write-off method is discouraged.

Companies that can estimate their uncollectibles use the **allowance method** to account for them.[8] Under this method, a company estimates the total amount of its uncollectible accounts at the end of every accounting period. As we discuss later in the chapter, this estimate may be based on credit sales or on accounts receivable. The company records the estimate in a year-end *adjusting entry* similar to the one shown below (the $5,200 amount is assumed):

Bad Debts Expense	5,200	
Allowance for Doubtful Accounts		5,200

The balance in Bad Debts Expense usually appears as an operating expense on the income statement where the expense is matched with sales revenue.[9] The Allowance for Doubtful Accounts (also called the *Allowance for Uncollectible Accounts* and the *Allowance for Bad Debts*) is a contra account to Accounts Receivable. The allowance is therefore deducted from Accounts Receivable on the balance sheet to estimate the net realizable value of the receivables. The use of an allowance account relieves a company of the necessity of crediting individual customer accounts each time it estimates bad debts. Obviously, when a company estimates bad debts and makes an adjusting entry, it does not yet know which accounts will become uncollectible.

The allowance method tends to overcome the matching and asset valuation problems inherent in the direct write-off method. That is the reason that accountants prefer the allowance method, even though it is based on estimated figures.

Accountants usually consult with a company's credit department personnel to estimate the amount of bad debts. As indicated earlier, the company's collection experience and that of similar companies are usually the most important factors in determining the estimate. These factors should be evaluated in the context of current and projected circumstances that may affect the company's future collection experience. Assessing the collectibility of accounts receivable is a challenging task, particularly in the difficult economic climate that

Asset/Liability Measurement

Materiality

---

[7]*FASB Statement of Financial Accounting Standards No. 5,* "Accounting for Contingencies," 1975, par. 23.

[8]For income tax purposes, most companies must use the direct write-off method for tax years beginning after 1986.

[9]Because uncollectibles are *expected* when a company makes credit sales, a strong argument can be made that uncollectibles should not be included in revenue. Therefore, the estimated amount of a company's bad debts should be treated as a revenue offset (similar to Sales Returns) rather than an expense. Following this approach, a company should debit Sales—Uncollectibles instead of Bad Debts Expense when it estimates bad debts. The balance in Sales—Uncollectibles later appears as a deduction from sales on the income statement.

In practice, companies usually debit Bad Debts expense. The rationale is that even if a receivable proves uncollectible, it existed on the date of sale and revenue was generated for the full amount of the sale.

many companies have faced in recent years. When estimating bad debts under the allowance method, accountants may use either an income statement approach or a balance sheet approach.

Income Statement Approach.   Under this approach to the allowance method, an accountant first determines the average percentage relationship between a company's *credit sales* and its actual bad debt losses. This percentage is then multiplied by credit sales for the current year to estimate bad debts expense.

The income statement approach is so called because it emphasizes the Bad Debts Expense account rather than the Allowance for Doubtful Accounts. With the income statement approach, credit sales (an income statement number) is multiplied by a percentage to estimate the amount of bad debts expense (another income statement number) as accurately as possible. This approach emphasizes the matching principle because the bad debts estimate is based directly on the related sales revenue. Exhibit 7–5 presents facts to illustrate two approaches to the allowance method for Downes Company, an enterprise that uses a calendar-year accounting period.

Matching

To illustrate the income statement approach, let us further assume that in previous years, actual bad debt losses each year have averaged 1% of credit sales and that the company expects this percentage to continue in the future. Here is the adjusting entry that the company makes on December 31, 1996:

Bad Debts Expense	2,100	
Allowance for Doubtful Accounts		2,100
($210,000 × .01 = $2,100)		

Observe that we made the entry *without considering* the previous balance ($400 credit) in the Allowance for Doubtful Accounts. The reason is that under the income statement approach, we focus on Bad Debts Expense, not on the allowance account. After the above entry is posted, Bad Debts Expense will have a balance of $2,100, and the balance in the allowance account will be $2,500 ($400 + $2,100).

In another variation of the income statement approach, bad debts expense is based on a percentage of total sales (cash and credit) rather than only credit sales. The use of a percentage based on credit sales is logical, because bad debts arise only from credit sales. Nevertheless, the use of total sales is acceptable because it would produce reasonable results if a company's mix of cash and credit sales is fairly stable over time.

Balance Sheet Approach.   The primary objective of this approach to the allowance method is to report accounts receivable on the balance sheet at net realizable value (and so the name *balance sheet* approach). To accomplish this objective, the balance sheet approach focuses on establishing a **desired balance** in the Allowance for Doubtful Accounts. The desired balance equals the estimated amount of uncollectible accounts receivable. This is the amount that, when subtracted from Accounts Receivable, will reduce the receivables to their net realizable value. Reporting accounts receivable at their net realizable value is consistent with the asset/liability measurement principle.

Asset/Liability Measurement

EXHIBIT 7–5
Downes Company **Facts to Illustrate Allowance Method**

Credit sales made during 1996	$210,000
Accounts receivable, 12/31/96	50,000
Allowance for doubtful accounts, 12/31/96, before adjustment	400 (credit balance)

1. Percentage of Accounts Receivable. A simple way to implement the balance sheet approach is to multiply the year-end Accounts Receivable balance by a percentage that the company estimates from experience will be uncollectible. The product is the desired balance in the allowance account. The adjusting entry to estimate bad debts is then recorded for the amount that is necessary to produce the desired balance.

To illustrate, return to Exhibit 7–5. Assume that instead of using the income statement approach, Downes Company elects to use the balance sheet approach and that it estimates that approximately 4% of the accounts receivable balance on December 31, 1996, will be uncollectible. The company makes the following adjusting entry on December 31, 1996:

Bad Debts Expense	1,600	
Allowance for Doubtful Accounts		1,600

Notice carefully that this entry reflects the amount necessary to produce the desired balance in the allowance account. The computation is shown below:

Desired balance in allowance account ($50,000 × .04)	$2,000
Less: Credit balance in allowance account before adjustment	400
Amount of adjusting entry	$1,600

After this entry is posted, Bad Debts Expense will have a balance of $1,600; the balance in the allowance account will be $2,000 ($400 + 1,600).

The allowance account sometimes has a *debit* balance before adjustment. As we illustrate later in the chapter, a company writes off uncollectible accounts by debiting the allowance account and crediting Accounts Receivable. A debit balance in the allowance account therefore occurs when a company has written off a greater amount of accounts receivable than it had previously estimated as uncollectible. A debit balance in the allowance account before adjustment would simply be *added* to the desired balance to determine the amount of the adjusting entry. For example, if Downes Company had a $400 *debit* balance (instead of a $400 *credit* balance) in its allowance account before adjustment, the company would make the adjusting entry on December 31, 1996, for $2,400 ($2,000 + $400).

2. Aging of Accounts Receivable. A more accurate way to implement the balance sheet approach is to determine the desired balance in the allowance account by aging the accounts receivable. Here the accountant groups a company's individual accounts receivable into categories based on how long they have been outstanding. This schedule is called an **aging of accounts receivable.** Next, the total in each category is multiplied by an estimated uncollectible percentage. The accountant then adds the products to derive a total amount that is estimated to be uncollectible. Because this is the desired total in the allowance account, the adjusting entry to estimate bad debts should be recorded for the amount necessary to produce the desired balance.

The estimated uncollectible percentages are based on a company's collection experience and on the advice of its credit department personnel. Higher percentages are usually associated with the higher-age categories because, generally, the longer that an account has been outstanding, the less likely it is to be collected.

To illustrate, refer again to Exhibit 7–5. Assume that Downes Company now elects to estimate its bad debts using the aging form of the balance sheet approach and that it prepares the information shown in Exhibits 7–6 and 7–7. The company makes the following adjusting entry on December 31, 1996:

Bad Debts Expense	1,969	
Allowance for Doubtful Accounts		1,969

EXHIBIT 7–6

Downes Company
Aging of Accounts Receivable
December 31, 1996

Customer	Accounts Receivable Balance 12/31/96	Time Outstanding				
		Under 30 Days	30–60 Days	61–120 Days	121–180 Days	Over 180 Days
Adams Company	$ 1,200	$ 900	$ 300			
Blunt & Company	600			$ 600		
Carver Enterprises	750	600	150			
Dandridge, Inc.	350					$ 350
Zimmerman Company	500				$500	
Total	$50,000	$39,300	$5,600	$3,400	$600	$1,100

Note once again that the above entry is for the amount necessary to produce the desired balance in the allowance account. The computation is shown below:

Desired balance in allowance account (total estimated amount uncollectible shown in Exhibit 7–7)	$2,369
Less: Credit balance in allowance account before adjustment	400
Amount of adjusting entry	$1,969

After the above entry is posed, Bad Debts Expense will have a balance of $1,969, and the allowance balance will be $2,369 ($400 + $1,969). If the allowance account had a $400 *debit* balance (instead of a $400 *credit* balance) before adjustment, the adjusting entry would have been for $2,769 ($400 + $2,369).

Summary and Evaluation of Approaches.   There are two basic approaches to the allowance method of accounting for uncollectible accounts. Each has two forms or variations:

1. Income statement approach
   a. Percentage of credit sales
   b. Percentage of total sales
2. Balance sheet approach
   a. Percentage of accounts receivable
   b. Aging of accounts receivable

Matching

Asset/Liability Measurement

A company may use any form of the allowance method to estimate its bad debts because all are acceptable under GAAP. The income statement approach emphasizes the matching principle; the balance sheet approach emphasizes the reporting of accounts receivable at their net realizable value. Notice that both approaches demonstrate that financial statements **articulate** with one another. Under the income statement approach, what we do to benefit the income statement directly affects the balance sheet; under the balance sheet approach, what we do to benefit the balance sheet directly affects the income statement.

Remember that all variations of the allowance method are based on **estimates** and require **judgment** to apply. A company's actual bad debt losses equal its estimates only by

EXHIBIT 7–7

Downes Company
Estimated Amount Uncollectible Based on Aging Analysis
December 31, 1996

Time Outstanding	Amount	Estimated Percentage Uncollectible	Estimated Amount Uncollectible
Under 30 days	$39,300	1%	$ 393
30–60 days	5,600	6%	336
61–120 days	3,400	25%	850
121–180 days	600	40%	240
Over 180 days	1,100	50%	550
Total	$50,000		$2,369

chance. Under the income statement approach, the percentage of credit sales usually produces the most accurate results, because bad debt losses relate only to credit sales. Under the balance sheet approach, an aging of accounts receivable generally produces the most accurate results. In practice, many companies estimate their uncollectible accounts using one approach and then apply another approach to determine whether a reasonable result is being obtained. For example, a company might use the percentage of credit sales approach and determine that a bad debts adjusting entry for $12,000 is necessary. To check the reasonableness of the $12,000 amount, the company might age the accounts receivable and determine that an adjusting entry for only $10,000 is necessary. As a result of applying these two approaches concurrently, the company might finally decide to make the adjusting entry for $11,000.

Over time, a company may determine that its estimates of bad debts were too high or too low, and the company's allowance balance before year-end adjustment thus contains an excessive credit or debit balance. When this occurs, the company should change the percentage that it uses to estimate bad debts. Such a change is an example of a **change in an accounting estimate,** and as we discussed briefly in Chapter 4 and will discuss in more depth in Chapter 20, the change should be accounted for in current and future periods. In other words, the company should begin using a revised percentage to estimate its bad debts but should not make a prior period adjustment.

Writing Off Uncollectible Accounts. When all reasonable attempts to collect an account have failed, a company's credit manager should authorize the accounting department to write off the account as uncollectible. Assume that the following balances were taken from the accounting records of Ace Enterprises:

Accounts receivable	$100,000	(Debit)
Allowance for doubtful accounts	1,700	(Credit)

If the company's credit manager decides that an account of $500 from W. Grant is uncollectible, the accountant makes the following entry:

Allowance for Doubtful Accounts	500	
Accounts Receivable		500

The accountant posts this entry to the appropriate general and subsidiary ledger accounts. After posting, the Accounts Receivable balance will be $99,500 ($100,000 − $500), and the balance in the allowance account will be $1,200 ($1,700 − $500). Notice that although the write-off reduces Accounts Receivable and the allowance account, it has no effect on the net realizable value of the receivables. Before the write-off, the net realizable value was \$98,300 (\$100,000 − \$1,700); after the write-off, it is still \$98,300 (\$99,500 − \$1,200).

Collection of Accounts Written Off.   Occasionally, a company collects all or part of an account that it wrote off as uncollectible. When this occurs, the company should first reverse, to the extent of the recovery, the entry that it made to write off the account. Then the company should record the collection in the usual manner. To illustrate, refer to the information presented in the previous section for Ace Enterprises and assume that Ace later collects the account of \$500 from W. Grant. Ace records the following entries:

Accounts Receivable	500	
Allowance for Doubtful Accounts		500
(To reinstate W. Grant's account.)		
Cash	500	
Accounts Receivable		500
(To record the collection.)		

Notice that there are two entries debiting Cash and crediting the Allowance account rather than a single entry. Making two entries is preferable because it permits Ace to accumulate in its accounts receivable subsidiary ledger a complete record of its credit experience with W. Grant.

Other Applications of the Allowance Method

Our discussion of the allowance method has thus far been confined to its use in accounting for uncollectible accounts. We have seen that through the use of estimates, the allowance **Matching** method enables a company to better match expenses and revenues and to report receivables at **Asset/Liability Measurement** their net realizable value. The same logic applies to the use of the allowance method in accounting for other items that affect the cash realization of accounts receivable. For example, a company may use the allowance method to account for

1. Sales discounts that customers will probably take (assuming that the company records accounts receivable at gross amounts).
2. Anticipated sales returns and allowances.
3. Anticipated collection costs (e.g., attorney's fees) that the company will incur when trying to collect accounts receivable.
4. Anticipated freight costs that customers will be allowed to deduct from their remittances because of the company's shipping terms.

To illustrate, assume that Allen Beam & Company determines from experience that the actual cost of collecting its accounts receivable averages 1% of the year-end accounts receivable balance. If the current year-end accounts receivable balance is \$100,000, the company makes the following adjusting entry:

Collection Expense	1,000	
Allowance for Collection Expense		1,000
(\$100,000 × .01 = \$1,000)		

Collection Expense is reported as an operating expense on the income statement, and the Allowance for Collection Expense is deducted from Accounts Receivable on the balance sheet. In a subsequent period, the company charges actual collection costs to the allowance account and credits Cash or other appropriate accounts.

Adjusting entries similar to the one shown above are appropriate to record estimated sales discounts, sales returns and allowances, and freight costs. In each case, a contra revenue account (e.g., Sales Discounts) or an expense account (e.g., Transportation-Out) is debited and the appropriate allowance account is credited. The effect of these entries is to reduce current net income and lower the net realizable value of accounts receivable reported on the balance sheet. For example, American Brands, Inc., makers of such diverse products as Master locks, Titleist golf balls, and Jim Beam bourbon, uses the allowance method to account for sales discounts, uncollectible accounts, and sales returns. In its 1992 annual report, the company provided the following information about its accounts receivable:

(In millions)	1992	1991
Accounts receivable, customers	$1,315.3	$1,396.8
Less allowances for discounts,		
doubtful accounts and returns	60.0	56.1
	$1,255.3	$1,340.7

Despite the theoretical merits of applying the allowance method to items other than uncollectible accounts, most companies do not do so. Instead of estimating these items in advance, companies usually account for them when they actually occur. This approach, which is required for income tax purposes, is justified under GAAP because of immateriality and because the amounts involved often do not fluctuate significantly from year to year.

Materiality

Use of an Allowance Account when a Right of Return Exists

Many companies allow customers to return defective merchandise. Some companies, such as those in the newspaper, perishable food, and book publishing industries, permit customers to return merchandise under certain circumstances, even when the merchandise is not defective. These circumstances may include the customer's dissatisfaction or inability to resell the product.

When customers have the right to return products, the seller recognizes revenue at the time of sale only if *all* of the following conditions are met:

1. The seller's price to the buyer is substantially fixed or determinable at the date of sale.

2. The buyer has paid the seller, or the buyer is obligated to pay the seller and the obligation is not contingent on resale of the product.

3. The buyer's obligation to the seller would not be changed in the event of theft or physical destruction or damage of the product.

4. The buyer acquiring the product for resale has economic substance apart from that provided by the seller. (That is, a separate, arm's-length relationship exists between the buyer and seller.)

5. The seller does not have significant obligations for future performance to directly bring about resale of the product by the buyer.

6. The amount of future returns can be reasonably estimated.[10]

Further discussion of these conditions appears in Chapter 21. The sixth condition stated above is particularly important for our purposes. In effect, the condition requires that if sales returns are material, companies that sell products with a right of return must use the allowance method of accounting for sales returns to properly recognize revenue at the time of sale.

Materiality

To illustrate, assume that Averill Company gives customers the right to return products. Recent experience indicates that customers will return approximately 20% of the merchandise Averill Company has sold and that the company can later resell the merchandise for approximately 60% of the original sales price. During the current year, Averill Company made sales of $100,000. Here is the adjusting entry the company makes at year-end, assuming a perpetual inventory system:

Sales Returns	20,000	
Inventory-Estimated Returns	12,000	
Allowance for Sales Returns		20,000
Cost of Goods Sold		12,000

---

[10]*FASB Statement of Financial Accounting Standards No. 48,* "Revenue Recognition When Right of Return Exists," 1981, par. 6

CARD GLUT

For an entire generation of Americans, Brooklyn's Topps Co., Inc., had the sports card market to itself. But competitors weighed in during the 1980s when collectors were paying thousands of dollars for old baseball cards, thereby helping create new interest in baseball and other sports cards. Today as many as 100 companies vie for pieces of the $1.4 billion (annual retail sales) sports and entertainment card market.

With a 32% market share Topps remains the biggest player. Its line this year included the traditional 55-cents-a-pack cards covering baseball and three other sports, as well as premium-priced packs that feature fancier photos and more sophisticated statistics and retail at $1.75 per pack. Topps' sales in fiscal 1992, ended in February, were up 4.5%, to $300 million, from 1991; net income was flat at $54.5 million, $1.15 a share. So far this year, sales and income have inched up 11% and 5%, respectively, over year-ago levels, about in line with what competitors are doing.

But trouble may be brewing for Topps. The card publishing business is inherently risky because any sales to wholesalers and retailers—which account for about 70% of cards shipped by Topps—can be returned to the manufacturer. (Only hobby dealers have no right to make returns.)

Ominously, for four consecutive quarters, Topps' accounts receivable have risen steadily. In the past two quarters, receivables have risen at over 50%, while sales have gone down. Says Howard Schilit, American University accounting professor who has looked at Topps' books: "When I see receivables going up so much faster than sales, I'm very suspicious."

Is Topps having trouble collecting from its wholesalers? Are some wholesalers waiting to see how the cards sell before they pay? And will they end up burying Topps in unwanted inventory? John Perillo, Topps' chief financial officer, says no. He says that Topps still gets paid every 21 days. He adds that receivables appear to be rising only because Topps has been shipping nearly 50% of its cards in the final few weeks of each quarter, leaving huge receivables on the books at quarter's end. The increased receivables are really just an accident of bookkeeping timing, says Perillo, who adds that Topps changed its shipping schedules in the past year.

Some of Topps' competitors find this explanation hard to swallow. And Lou J. Biggs, senior buyer for Weeke Wholesale Co. in Fairview Heights, Ill., says that in 1990 his Topps cards sold out in six months. This year, he says, it has taken him eight months to get rid of only 74% and he's returning the balance—around 30% more of the 55-cent cards than last year, and 5% to 10% more of Topps' premium-priced cards.

Topps books its sales, less a reserve for returns, as soon as it ships its products. Topps is not required to disclose its reserves in its quarterly reports, and any charges accumulated over the year are deducted from the reserve at year-end. If the actual returns are higher than the amount reserved, the difference is charged against earnings.

Perillo insists Topps' overall returns won't increase as a percentage of sales this year. But shareholders won't really know the score until after Topps' current fiscal year ends, on Feb. 27.

Right now this much is clear: The low end of the sports card market is in the doldrums, the victim of oversupply. Last year two major Topps competitors, Marvel Entertainment Group's Fleer unit and Leaf Inc.'s Donruss division, abandoned the low end of the market because dealers were returning the cheaper cards in large quantities. But Topps is betting that cheaper cards will still be an important factor in the market, and so has continued production of cheap cards as well as premium-priced ones. Topps Chairman Arthur T. Shorin says that cutting production is missing the point. "Our aim is to increase demand."

Many securities analysts who follow Topps say they expect no sizable writeoff this year. They predict fiscal 1993 earnings of $1.35 a share, versus $1.15 in 1992. But if Topps' reserves against returns prove inadequate, the company's stock, recently trading at 15 a share, will likely take a pounding. There's simply no way to tell whether Topps has enough of a cushion for a rainy day.

Since January, Topps insiders have unloaded over 700,000 shares—1.5% of the company's outstanding stock—at prices ranging from 15⅜ to 19½. They may know something.

SOURCE: Roula Khalaf, "Card Glut," *Forbes* (December 21, 1992), p. 89. Reprinted by permission of *Forbes Magazine*, December 21, 1992, © Forbes Inc., 1992.

The Inventory-Estimated Returns account is a current asset and shows the net realizable value of inventory that is expected to be returned ($100,000 × 20% × 60% = $12,000). The Allowance for Sales Returns is deducted from Accounts Receivable on the balance sheet. The effect of this entry is to reduce gross margin and current assets by $8,000.

Suppose now that during the first month of the next accounting period, a customer returns merchandise that had an original sales price of $1,000. Assuming that the customer has not paid for the goods, Averill Company makes the following entry:

Inventory-Returned Goods		600	
Allowance for Sales Returns		1,000	
Inventory-Estimated Returns			600
Accounts Receivable			1,000

Use of Accounts Receivable to Generate Cash

Instead of waiting until customers pay their accounts, companies often obtain the cash immediately by engaging in accounts receivable financing. Such financing is growing in popularity. Many companies use accounts receivable financing even though it usually entails interest rates well above prime. Accounts receivable financing helps companies to overcome short-term cash flow problems, to negotiate terms, and to have the funds more quickly than under other financing arrangements. It also allows seasonal businesses to cover their off-season expenses. Accounts receivable financing is usually accomplished by **pledging, assigning,** or **factoring** the accounts.

The key conceptual issue under each of the three alternatives is whether a **borrowing transaction** or a **sale transaction** has occurred. In a borrowing transaction, the receivables are simply used as collateral to obtain a loan. The borrowing company continues to report the receivables as assets and also reports the interest expense and the liability for the loan. In a sale transaction, the selling company receives cash, removes the receivables from the accounting records, and typically recognizes a loss on the receivables sold. The selling company does not recognize a liability because the receivables have actually been sold.

Pledging Accounts Receivable.   Companies sometimes obtain loans by pledging their accounts receivable as collateral. In a pledging arrangement, the borrower agrees to collect its accounts receivable and to use the proceeds to repay the lender. The borrower records the loan and related interest in the usual manner, and the loan balance is reduced as the borrower remits its collections. If the borrower defaults, the lender can recover the amount owed by selling the accounts pledged.

If a company has pledged some or all of its accounts receivable, it should disclose the amount pledged, either parenthetically or in a note to its financial statements.

Assigning Accounts Receivable.   An assignment of accounts receivable is a more formal type of pledging arrangement. In an assignment, a borrower (called the **assignor**) transfers its rights in some or all of its accounts receivable to a lender (called the **assignee**) in exchange for a loan. The money received from collecting the accounts is later used to pay off the loan.

An assignment is evidenced by a **financing agreement** and a **promissory note,** both of which the assignor signs. The financing agreement may indicate that the assignment is on either a **nonnotification** or a **notification** basis. When accounts are assigned on a nonnotification basis, as is usually the case, customers are not informed that their accounts have been assigned. As a result, they continue to make payments to the assignor, who in turn forwards them to the assignee. When accounts are assigned on a notification basis, customers are notified to make their payments directly to the assignee.

The assignor retains ownership of the accounts assigned. As a result, the assignor assumes the risk that accounts receivable will not be realized for their full face amount because of such factors as sales discounts, sales returns and allowances, and bad debt losses.

Before entering into an assignment, the assignee (usually a bank or a finance company) analyzes the borrower's accounts receivable. The assignee generally refuses to lend money secured by accounts believed to be too risky. Furthermore, the assignee usually lends only a certain percentage (often between 60% and 90%) of the face amount of the accounts that it is willing to lend against. This helps to insulate the assignee from collection losses that the assignor might sustain. As additional protection, the assignee frequently requires the assignor to substitute new accounts for ones that become past due or uncollectible. Naturally, the assignee charges *interest* for the loans that it makes. In addition, the assignee usually requires a *service charge* for processing the assignment.

To illustrate, assume that on December 31, 1995, Smith Company assigns $100,000 of accounts receivable to Citibank under a nonnotification arrangement. Citibank advances $80,000 less a service charge of $1,600, and Smith Company signs a promissory note that provides for interest of 1% per month on the unpaid loan balance. Smith Company makes the following entries on December 31:

Assigned Accounts Receivable	100,000	
Accounts Receivable		100,000
Cash	78,400	
Service Charge Expense	1,600	
Notes Payable		80,000

The first entry transfers the assigned accounts to a separate account. The second entry records the receipt of cash on the loan.

To continue the illustration, a series of 1996 transactions and the corresponding journal entries appear below:

1. From January 1 to January 31, Smith Company collected assigned accounts of $60,000, less sales discounts of $700 and sales returns and allowances of $1,300.

Cash	58,000	
Sales Discounts	700	
Sales Returns and Allowances	1,300	
Assigned Accounts Receivable		60,000

2. On January 31, Smith remitted the January collections to Citibank.

Notes Payable	57,200	
Interest Expense ($80,000 × .01)	800	
Cash		58,000

3. From February 1 to February 28, Smith collected $29,000 of assigned accounts and wrote off as uncollectible $3,000 of assigned accounts.

Cash	29,000	
Allowance for Doubtful Accounts	3,000	
Assigned Accounts Receivable		32,000

4. On February 28, Smith paid off the remaining loan balance and transferred the remaining balance in Assigned Accounts Receivable to Accounts Receivable.

Notes Payable ($80,000 − $57,200)	22,800	
Interest Expense ($22,800 × .01)	228	
Cash		23,028
Accounts Receivable	8,000	
Assigned Accounts Receivable		8,000
($100,000 − $60,000 − $32,000)		

Disclosure Smith Company should separately disclose the specifically assigned accounts receivable
Materiality if they are material. Moreover, it should disclose its equity in the assigned accounts, either parenthetically or in a note. A note in the 1995 financial statements, for example, might say that "on December 31, 1995, Smith Company had $20,000 ($100,000 − $80,000) equity in its assigned accounts receivable."

The preceding example provides a general view of accounting for assigned accounts receivable. In practice, the accounting requirements depend in part on the financing agreement. A general description of this agreement should be disclosed in the footnotes to the assignor's financial statements.

Factoring Accounts Receivable. In a factoring arrangement, a company (the **seller**) sells its accounts receivable to a financial institution, called a **factor.** In most cases, the factor is a bank or a finance company. Factoring differs from an assignment in that the seller actually transfers ownership of its accounts receivable to the factor. Although accounts may be factored **with recourse** (the factor may hold the seller liable if debtors do not pay), accounts are usually factored **without recourse** (the factor bears the risk that debtors will not pay). Moreover, accounts are usually factored on a notification basis.

The details of a factoring arrangement vary and should be spelled out in a factoring contract. A typical factoring arrangement is continuous. The factor maintains a credit department that performs all functions related to the seller's accounts receivable. In addition to deciding to whom the seller may extend credit, the factor assumes responsibility for billing and collecting and for bad debt losses. The seller ships merchandise to approved customers and immediately sells the receivables to the factor. Thus, the advantages of factoring to a seller are immediate cash and relief from the burden of carrying accounts receivable. Factoring arrangements are common in the textile, apparel, carpet, and furniture industries. Moreover, the use of credit cards such as American Express, VISA, and MasterCard is in essence a factoring arrangement.

Factoring is a fast-growing and often very profitable business. In Florida, for example, Capital Factors, Inc., anticipated earning between $1.3 and $1.4 billion in a recent year. In recent years more factoring companies have formed to buy the accounts receivable of smaller companies. Factoring companies bought at least $62 billion of receivables in 1993, which is up from $46 billion in 1987. And much of that amount was purchased from smaller companies that do not have the asset base to attract bank financing. Small business clients include companies involved in temporary help services, trucking, and computer products. Although the biggest factoring companies, such as Barclay's Commercial Corporation, CIT Group, and Heller Financial, Inc., dominate the market, most of the approximately 240 factoring firms are small and have been in business for less than 10 years.[11]

When accounts are factored, the factor charges a **factoring fee** for its services of credit approval, billing, collecting, and assuming bad debt losses. This fee is usually 1% to 3% of the net amount of the receivables factored. The factor then credits the seller's account for the net amount of the receivables factored less the factoring fee. The factor may also withhold some predetermined amount (usually about 10% of the net amount of receivables factored) to protect itself against sales returns and allowances.

To illustrate, assume that on September 1, 1996, Riley Company factors $20,000 of accounts receivable *without recourse* with First Finance Corporation on a notification basis. First Finance charges a factoring fee of 3% of the amount of receivables factored. In addition, First Finance withholds 10% of the amount of receivables factored to cover sales returns and allowances. Riley makes the following journal entry on September 1:

Cash	17,400	
Receivable from Factor (20,000 × 10%)	2,000	
Loss on Factoring Accounts		
Receivable ($20,000 × 3%) *Service charge.*	600	
Accounts Receivable		20,000

Riley Company classifies the Receivable from Factor as a current asset. This account is later credited when sales returns and allowances occur and when the factor remits the ending

[11]Udayan Gupta, "Factoring and Venture Firms' Roles in Financing Growth," *The Wall Street Journal* (April 18, 1994), p. B2.

balance in Riley's account. If, for example, *no* sales returns and allowances occurred, Riley makes the following entry when First Finance remits the ending balance in Riley's account:

Cash	2,000	
Receivable from Factor		2,000

Notice in this example that Riley Company factored accounts receivable *without recourse* and accounted for the factoring as a sale. Accordingly, the accounts receivable are removed from the accounting records, and no liability is recorded.

When receivables are factored *with recourse,* the transfer is recognized as a sale only if all of the following conditions are met:

1. The transferor (i.e., the company selling the accounts) surrenders control of the future economic benefits embodied in the receivables.
2. The transferor's obligation under the recourse provisions can be reasonably estimated.
3. The transferee (i.e., the company buying the accounts) cannot require the transferor to repurchase the receivables except as specified in the recourse provisions.[12]

Substance over Form
The three conditions help determine whether the transfer of receivables is in substance a sale transaction or a borrowing transaction. If the three conditions are met, then the factoring with recourse is accounted for as a sale, in the same manner as illustrated for Riley Company. On the other hand, if *any* of the three conditions is not met, the amount of the proceeds from the transfer of the receivables should be reported as a liability because the transaction is now regarded as a borrowing, not a sale. Assume that Riley Company factored its receivables *with recourse* and did not satisfy all of the three conditions. Under these circumstances, Riley Company accounts for the transfer of receivables as a borrowing and makes the following journal entry on September 1:

Cash	17,400	
Receivable from Factor (20,000 × 10%)	2,000	
Interest Expense ($20,000 × 3%)	600	
Payable to Factor		20,000

Notice that the accounts receivable of $20,000 that were factored are not removed from Riley's accounting records. These accounts are still considered Riley's assets, and now Riley has a collateralized loan for which it must account. If the transaction had incorrectly been accounted for as a sale, Riley Company would have been permitted to engage in **off-balance-sheet financing.** That is, the company would have been permitted to borrow money without having to report the liability.

The appropriate accounting practices for a factoring arrangement depend on the specific agreement. A company that enters into a factoring agreement should briefly describe the agreement in the notes to its financial statements.

NOTES RECEIVABLE

A **promissory note,** often called simply a **note,** is a written promise to pay a certain sum of money at a designated time. The **maker** signs the note and usually makes it payable to the order of a specified **payee,** who in turn may endorse the note and thereby sell (discount) it to a subsequent holder. From a payee's viewpoint, a note represents a **receivable** and therefore an asset. Notes receivable are more desirable than accounts receivable for the following reasons:

1. Notes are often easier to collect because they represent written claims. Thus, their use may reduce a company's bad debt losses.

---

[12]*FASB Statement of Financial Accounting Standards No. 77,* "Reporting by Transferors for Transfers of Receivables with Recourse," 1983, part 5.

2. Notes can usually be converted into cash by discounting them with a bank or other lender, and this process (which we explain in a subsequent section) is usually quicker and cheaper than assigning or factoring accounts receivable.

3. Notes receivable usually bear a specified rate of interest, but accounts receivable do not.

Companies often acquire notes receivable in exchange for merchandise when customers need credit for a period longer than usual for open accounts. Occasionally, companies acquire notes in exchange for account receivable claims against customers who simply need additional time to pay their accounts. Notes receivable may also result from the sale of other assets and from lending money.

Valuation of Notes Receivable

As indicated earlier in the chapter, notes receivable are valued initially at an amount equal to the present value of the cash that the company expects to collect. This approach is theoretically sound because it recognizes the time value of money.

Asset/Liability Measurement

If a company can reasonably estimate the amount of its uncollectible notes receivable, it establishes an allowance for such notes in a manner similar to that used for accounts receivable. Companies that acquire many notes as a result of selling merchandise can usually estimate their uncollectibles with reasonable accuracy.

Because money has a time value, all commercial notes contain interest. Nevertheless, notes are commonly classified as either **interest bearing** or **noninterest bearing.** Interest-bearing notes specifically state a certain interest rate; noninterest-bearing notes do not. In a noninterest-bearing note, the interest is included in the face amount of the note and is not explicitly stated.

Interest-Bearing Notes Receivable.   Because interest-bearing notes receivable specifically state a certain interest rate, the present value of the note at the time of issuance equals its face amount, assuming that the interest rate is reasonable. Consequently, such notes are initially recorded at their face amount (which equals their present value). Interest revenue is then recognized on the accrual basis as time passes.

To illustrate, assume that on October 1, 1995, Sun Company, which uses a calendar-year accounting period, sells merchandise having a sales price of $1,000 to Bin Company in exchange for a one-year *interest-bearing* note. The note has a face amount of $1,000 and a stated interest rate of 12% (equal to the going market rate for similar notes) payable at maturity. Sun Company accounts for the note as shown in Exhibit 7–8.

Noninterest-Bearing Notes Receivable.   The present value of a noninterest-bearing note receivable is less than its face amount. The reason is that the face amount includes interest even though no interest is specifically stated. Although it is theoretically correct to account for this interest, many companies fail to do so.

To illustrate, let us assume that on October 1, 1995, Sun Company (referred to in the previous section) sells merchandise having a sales price of $1,000 to Bur Company in exchange for a one-year, *noninterest-bearing* note. The note has a face amount of $1,120, and the going market rate for similar notes is 12%. The note therefore has a present value of $1,000, an amount that equals the sales price of the merchandise as well as the face amount of the note ($1,120) divided by 1.12. Sun Company accounts for the note using one of the alternative methods shown in Exhibit 7–9.

Under Method 1, the note is initially recorded at its present value of $1,000. This is done by debiting Notes Receivable for the face amount ($1,120) and crediting Discount on Notes Receivable for the total amount of interest that the note contains ($120). Notice that the interest equals 12% of the sales price of $1,000 for one year. The balance in the discount account is deducted from Notes Receivable on the balance sheet. Consequently, if Sun Company

EXHIBIT 7–8

Accounting for Interest-Bearing Notes Receivable

Transaction	Entry		
Oct. 1, 1995			
Sun Company sells merchandise having a sales price of $1,000 to Bin Company in exchange for a one-year *interest-bearing* note. The note has a face amount of $1,000 and a stated interest rate of 12% (equal to the going market rate for similar notes) payable at maturity.	Notes Receivable Sales	1,000	1,000
Dec. 31, 1995			
Sun Company computes accrued interest for three months ($1,000 × .12 × $\frac{3}{12}$ = $30).	Interest Receivable Interest Revenue	30	30
Sept. 30, 1996			

Sun Company collects principal and interest at maturity.*	Cash
	   Note Receivable
	   Interest Receivable
	   Interest Revenue
		1,120	1,000
			30
			90

*The illustration assumes that Sun Company does not make reversing entries.

prepared a balance sheet on October 1, the company reports a net amount of $1,000, which equals the present value of the note on that date.

Observe that the present value of the Bur Company note ($1,000) is the same as the present value of the Bin Company note recorded in the previous section. The reason is that these are similar one-year notes with maturity values of $1,120. Under Method 1, as shown in Exhibit 7–9, $30 of interest revenue is recorded in 1995 and $90 in 1996. These are the same amounts recorded for the Bin Company note in Exhibit 7–8. Method 1 is theoretically correct because it reflects the economic reality that money has a time value. Method 1 puts substance (i.e., the economic fact that the note contains interest) over form (i.e., the fact that the note has no stated interest rate). Notes receivable, sales, and interest revenue are all correctly reported under Method 1.

Substance over Form

In practice, many companies use Method 2 to record short-term, noninterest-bearing trade notes receivable. Using this method, these companies initially record such notes at their face amounts, not at their present values. The use of Method 2 leads to several misstatements in the financial statements. In the example shown, sales, net income, assets, and stockholders' equity would each be overstated in 1995, and interest revenue would be understated. In 1996, interest revenue and net income would be understated.

Accounting Principles Board Opinion No. 21, which we explain in Chapter 10, requires companies under certain circumstances to impute (estimate and record) interest in transactions involving receivables and payables for which there is either no stated interest or an unreasonable amount of stated interest. Applying the principles set forth in this pronouncement produces the results shown under Method 1. However, *APB Opinion No. 21* states that it is not intended to apply to "receivables and payables arising from transactions with customers or suppliers in the normal course of business which are due in customary trade terms not exceeding approximately one year."[13] Consequently, many companies use Method 2 to account

---

[13]*APB Opinion No. 21,* "Interest on Receivables and Payables," 1971, par. 3.

EXHIBIT 7–9

Accounting for Noninterest-Bearing Notes Receivable

Transaction	Method 1: Record at Present Value (theoretically correct)			Method 2: Record at Face Amount (theoretically incorrect)		
Oct. 1, 1995						

Sun Company sells merchandise having a sales price of $1,000 to Bur Company in exchange for a one-year, *noninterest-bearing* note. The note has a face amount of $1,120 and the going market rate for similar notes is 12%.	Notes Receivable
	    Sales
	    Discount on Notes
	        Receivable*
		1,120	1,000
			
			120
				Notes Receivable
				    Sales
					1,120	1,120

Dec. 31, 1995						

Sun Company computes accrued interest for three months ($1,000 × .12 × ³⁄₁₂ = $30).	Discount on Notes
	    Receivable
	        Interest Revenue
		30	30	No entry		

Sept. 30, 1996						

Sun Company collects principal and interest at maturity.†	Cash
	Discount on Notes
	    Receivable
	        Notes Receivable
	        Interest Revenue
		1,120
		
		90
			
			1,120
			90
				Cash
				    Notes Receivable
					1,120	1,120

*Some firms prefer *not* to use a discount account. These firms debit Notes Receivable for $1,000 on October 1 and for $30 on December 31. They then credit Notes Receivable for $1,030 on September 30, 1996. This approach is an acceptable variation of Method 1 because it produces essentially the same results.

†The illustration assumes that Sun Company does not make reversing entries.

for these types of notes receivable. Because the receivables are short term, an argument can be made that the amount of interest often is not material. In addition, net income may not be significantly distorted if the receivables occur fairly evenly over time. **Materiality**

Discounting Notes Receivable

Most notes are **negotiable,** which means that a payee may transfer its rights to collect a note to a subsequent holder. On the maturity date, the holder collects the amount of the note's maturity value from the maker.

When a note is negotiable, therefore, the payee may obtain cash before the maturity date by **discounting** (selling) the note at a bank or other entity. To discount the note, the payee endorses it. In rare cases, the endorsement is made **without recourse,** which means that the endorser avoids future liability on the note. Usually, however, banks require that endorsements be made **with recourse,** which means that the endorser agrees to pay the holder if the maker does not. Consequently, endorsers typically remain **contingently liable** on notes receivable that they have discounted.

Contingent liabilities, discussed more fully in Chapter 14, are obligations that must be paid if certain conditions occur. For example, if the maker of a note fails to pay the holder on the maturity date, an endorser (with recourse) must pay. Users of financial statements want to know about a company's contingent obligations. Consequently, the Financial Accounting

Standards Board (FASB), in its *Statement of Financial Accounting Standards No. 5,* requires companies to disclose contingent liabilities that relate to notes receivable discounted, even if there is only a remote chance that the company will actually have to pay.[14]

When discounting a note at a bank, a company receives cash **proceeds.** These proceeds, which the bank calculates, are equal to the **maturity value** of the note less the bank's **discount.** To calculate the discount, the bank multiplies the **maturity value** of the note by the bank's **discount rate** (the interest rate that the bank charges for discounting the note) and by the **remaining time to maturity.** These calculations are illustrated in the following example.

Suppose that on March 1, 1996, Blue, Inc., receives a $10,000, 90-day, 10% note from a customer on account. Thirty days later, on March 31, 1996, Blue discounts the note *with recourse* at Park National Bank. The bank's discount rate is 12%, and Blue receives proceeds of $10,045, computed as follows:[15]

Face amount of note	$10,000
Interest to maturity ($10,000 × .10 × 90/360)	250
Maturity value of note*	10,250
Bank discount ($10,250 × .12 × 60/360)	205
Proceeds	$10,045

*Remember that the maturity value equals the face amount of a noninterest-bearing note.

Substance over Form

How should Blue, Inc., account for the note receivable discounted? Similar to the use of accounts receivable to generate cash, the key conceptual issue in accounting for notes receivable discounted is whether a borrowing transaction or a sale transaction has in substance occurred. In practice, most notes receivable are accounted for as sales transactions because most notes are discounted with recourse, and the three conditions for recognizing a transfer of receivables with recourse as a sale usually are satisfied (see page 274). Also, those notes receivable issued without recourse are recognized as sales transactions.

Assuming that the three conditions have been met and the transfer of receivables with recourse can be recognized as a sale, Blue should account for the note receivable discounted

---

[14]*FASB Statement of Financial Accounting Standards No. 5,* par. 12.

[15]Observe in this example that the Blue note was short term (less than one year) in nature and that Park National Bank used simple interest when discounting it. As Chapter 6 indicated, simple interest is used in many short-term business transactions. When long-term notes receivable (one year and longer) are discounted, banks typically use compound interest when calculating the discount.

When a company discounts a long-term note receivable and the bank uses compound interest to calculate the discount, the proceeds equal the sum of the present value of the face amount of the note and the present value of the interest to be received at maturity. The bank uses its discount rate when computing the present values. These calculations are illustrated in the following example.

Suppose that on July 1, 1996, Blue, Inc., receives a $10,000, **18-month,** 10% note from a customer on account. Both principal and interest are due on the maturity date, which is December 31, 1997. On December 31, 1996, six months after receiving the note, Blue discounts the note with recourse at Park National Bank. The bank's discount rate is 12%, and Blue receives proceeds of $10,267.89, computed as follows:

Present value of $10,000 for 1 year at 12% ($10,000 × .89286)	$ 8,928.60
Present value of $1,500 interest ($10,000 × 10% × $1\frac{1}{2}$ years = $1,500) for 1 year at 12% ($1,500 × .89286)	1,339.29
Proceeds	$10,267.89

In this chapter, you may assume that unless stated otherwise, the bank uses simple interest when discounting short-term notes.

EXHIBIT 7–10

Accounting for Notes Receivable Discounted

Transaction	Footnote Approach			Contra Account Approach		
Mar. 1, 1996						

Blue, Inc., receives a $10,000, 90-day, 10% note from a customer on account.	Notes Receivable
	    Accounts Receivable
		10,000	10,000	Notes Receivable
				    Accounts Receivable
					10,000	10,000

Mar. 31, 1996						

Blue, Inc., discounts the note (with recourse) at Park National Bank at a discount rate of 12%.	Cash
	    Notes Receivable
	    Interest Revenue
		10,045	10,000
			45
				Cash
				    Notes Receivable
				      Discounted
				    Interest Revenue
					10,045	10,000
						45

Alternative Assumption No. 1						
May 30, 1996						

The customer pays Park National Bank.	No entry			Notes Receivable
				    Discounted
				    Notes Receivable
					10,000	10,000

Alternative Assumption No. 2						
May 30, 1996						

The customer dishonors the note and the bank charges Blue, Inc., with the maturity value plus a protest fee of $25.	Dishonored Notes
	  Receivable
	    Cash
		10,275	10,275	Dishonored Notes
				  Receivable
				    Cash
				
				Notes Receivable
				  Discounted
				    Notes Receivable
					10,275
					
					10,000
						10,275
						
						10,000

(with recourse) using one of the two approaches shown in Exhibit 7–10.[16] Because most makers pay their notes at maturity, the **footnote approach** is easier to apply. Under this approach, Notes Receivable is credited when a note is discounted, and the contingent liability is disclosed in a footnote such as: "The company is contingently liable for $10,250 on a note receivable discounted at the bank. It does not expect the maker of the note to default." The company, of course, stops making this disclosure when it is no longer contingently liable for the note. Instead of using a footnote, the company may disclose essentially the same information parenthetically on the balance sheet.

---

[16]Observe that Interest Revenue is credited for $45 on March 31. Actually, Blue, Inc., has earned $83.33 ($10,000 $\times$ .10 $\times$ 30/360 = $83.33) as a result of holding the note for 30 days. This suggests that on March 31, Blue should record $83.33 as interest revenue and debit a loss account for $38.33 ($83.33 − $45 = $38.33), as shown below:

Cash	10,045.00	
Loss from Discounting Notes Receivable	38.33	
Notes Receivable (or Notes Receivable Discounted)		10,000.00
Interest Revenue		83.33

Although this approach is logical, companies rarely use it because of materiality considerations.

Some accountants prefer the **contra account approach,** under which Notes Receivable Discounted is credited when a company discounts a note. Notes Receivable Discounted is a contra account to Notes Receivable and is deducted from Notes Receivable in the current assets section of the balance sheet to disclose the contingent liability. The contra account approach requires slightly more bookkeeping than the footnote approach. Moreover, it fails to disclose the full amount of the contingent liability. Notice in the example that the contingent liability is actually $10,250 (Principal + Interest). The Notes Receivable Discounted account, however, shows only the face amount of $10,000.

When a note has been discounted, the bank will try to collect the maturity value from the maker on the maturity date. If the maker defaults, the bank must promptly notify the endorser. Therefore, the endorser who has not heard from the bank within a few days after the maturity date may generally assume that the maker has paid the note and thereby ended the endorser's contingent liability. If, on the other hand, the maker does not pay the bank, we say that the note has been **dishonored.** In this case, the bank promptly notifies the endorser and holds the endorser liable for the full maturity value plus any **protest fee** (any reasonable cost that the bank incurs in protesting the note). The endorser pays the bank and then has a claim against the maker for the full amount paid. Because the endorser pays the note, it no longer has a contingent liability to the bank.

To illustrate the accounting entries involved, assume that on the maturity date, May 30, 1996, the customer pays Park National Bank the amount owed, thereby ending Blue's contingent liability. As shown in Exhibit 7–10, Blue does not make an entry under the footnote approach but does under the contra account approach. In practice, the entry required under the contra account approach is likely to be made a few days after the maturity date, because a company that is contingently liable on a note does not usually know on the maturity date that the maker has paid.

Assume now that instead of paying the note on May 30, 1996, the customer dishonored it and the bank charged Blue, Inc., with the maturity value plus a protest fee of $25. Under these circumstances, Blue makes the appropriate entry or entries shown in Exhibit 7–10.

Dishonored Notes Receivable is a special note receivable account and is reported separately from Notes Receivable on the balance sheet. This account is used for all dishonored notes receivable, whether or not they have been discounted. Blue, Inc., will earn interest on the amount in this account at the rate allowed by law. The Dishonored Notes Receivable account is credited if Blue collects from the maker. If the company cannot collect the dishonored note, it writes off the amount uncollectible to an Allowance for Uncollectible Notes account, assuming that it uses such an account for its notes receivable.

Remember that the above example assumes that Blue, Inc., discounted the note receivable on a *with recourse* basis and that the three conditions for recognizing a transfer of receivables with recourse as a sale had been satisfied. If the note had been discounted *without recourse,* Blue would still account for the discounting as a sale, but *no contingent liability would exist.* On the other hand, if the note had been discounted on a *with recourse* basis and any of the three conditions had *not* been met, Blue would account for the discounting transaction as a borrowing instead of a sale. Accordingly, Blue makes the following journal entry on March 31, when the note is discounted:

Cash	10,045	
Liability for Notes Receivable Discounted		10,000
Interest Revenue		45

Liability for Notes Receivable Discounted is a current liability account. In this case an actual liability, not a contingent liability, exists. The Notes Receivable account remains on Blue's books on March 31. If the customer pays Park National Bank on May 30, Blue makes the following entry:

| Liability for Notes Receivable Discounted | 10,000 | |
| Notes Receivable | | 10,000 |

On the other hand, if the customer dishonors the note on May 30, Blue makes the following entries:

Dishonored Notes Receivable	10,275	
Cash		10,275
Liability for Notes Receivable Discounted	10,000	
Notes Receivable		10,000

BALANCE SHEET PRESENTATION OF RECEIVABLES

As stated earlier, an enterprise should classify a receivable as a current asset only if it expects collection within the next year or operating cycle, whichever is longer. Within the current assets category, trade receivables should be reported separately from nontrade receivables. Moreover, a company should report separately those receivables that reflect **related-party transactions,** such as loans the company makes to officers or to affiliated companies. Accounts and notes receivable should be segregated when the amount of each is material. Exhibit 7–11 shows a receivables disclosure that Oneida Ltd. made in its 1993 annual report. Oneida is a well-known manufacturer of dinnerware, china, and crystal.

Materiality

Cash and receivables are two examples of **financial instruments.** Since 1990, GAAP has required companies to disclose information about financial instruments that have off-balance-sheet risk and about financial instruments with concentrations of credit risk. These disclosures are explained in Chapter 25.

Disclosure

The following elements of the theoretical model discussed in Chapter 2 are particularly important to the topics that we presented in Chapter 7.

1. **Asset/liability measurement principle.** Cash is measured at its face amount, accounts receivable are measured at net realizable value, and notes receivable are measured at present value on the date received. Also, the balance sheet approach to the allowance method of accounting for uncollectible accounts emphasizes this principle.

2. **Revenue realization principle.** A company ordinarily records revenue and the related receivable that arises from a sale of goods on the date that the sale occurs. Only in exceptional cases does GAAP permit the recognition of revenue either before or after the time of sale.

PROFESSIONAL JUDGMENT

Asset/Liability Measurement

Revenue Realization

EXHIBIT 7–11

Oneida Ltd.
Receivables Disclosure

Receivables

Receivables by major classification are as follows:

| | (Thousands) | |
	1993	1992
Accounts receivable	$56,587	$62,613
Other accounts and notes receivable	2,013	2,483
Less allowance for doubtful accounts and promotional allowances	(1,728)	(3,332)
Receivables	$56,872	$61,764

SOURCE: Oneida Ltd., 1993 Annual Report.

Matching

Substance over Form

3. **Matching.** The income statement approach to the allowance method of accounting for uncollectible accounts helps a company to more accurately match the expense of uncollectible accounts with the sales revenue that is associated with those accounts.

4. **Substance over form.** When receivables are transferred *with recourse* from one company to another, such as by factoring accounts receivable or discounting a note receivable, the transferor should account for the transfer as a sale of the receivables only if three conditions are met. These conditions help to establish whether the transfer of receivables is in substance a sale of the receivables or whether it is really a borrowing transaction. When accounting for noninterest-bearing notes receivable, recording the note initially at its present value is theoretically better than recording it at its face amount because substance is considered more important than form in financial accounting.

When applying these principles, accountants **must use professional judgment.** For example, an accountant uses judgment when implementing the allowance method of accounting for uncollectible accounts. Many factors could affect the amount of the adjusting entry for bad debts, including the condition and trend of the national, regional, and local economies; the extent to which accounts are concentrated in a small number of industries; and the business prospects for those enterprises that have received credit. Although the numbers reported in financial statements for bad debts expense and the allowance for doubtful accounts may look highly precise, they are really just estimates. As we explain in several places throughout the book, financial statements involve many estimates.

CONCLUDING REMARKS

Cash is the standard medium of exchange in business transactions, and receivables are claims held against others that generally result in a future inflow of cash. To be classified as a current asset, cash must be available for use in current operations. Similarly, receivables are properly classified as current assets only when they are collectible within the next year or operating cycle, whichever is longer.

Cash and receivables are two examples of monetary assets because they are fixed or determinable in terms of the number of dollars on hand or to be received, regardless of how prices change. For this reason, the valuation of cash and receivables is less controversial than the valuation of nonmonetary assets. In the next two chapters, we focus on accounting for inventory. Inventory is a current asset that is nonmonetary in nature and is considerably more challenging to value than either cash or receivables.

KEY POINTS

1. Cash includes currency, coins, checks, bank drafts, money orders, checking accounts, and savings accounts. (Objective 1)

2. On a balance sheet, cash is valued at face amount and classified as a current asset only if the cash is available for use in current operations. (Objective 1)

3. A petty cash fund is typically used to disburse relatively small amounts of currency and coins for such items as taxi fares, postage, and minor supplies. (Objective 2)

4. A bank reconciliation is a schedule that explains any differences between a company's book balance of cash in a particular bank account and the bank statement balance. (Objective 3)

5. A proof of cash is an expanded, four-column reconciliation that is a stronger control measure than the single-column bank reconciliation. (Objective 3)

6. The preparation of either a bank reconciliation or a proof of cash usually indicates that a company has to make certain adjusting entries to update its accounting records. (Objective 3)

7. Receivables are claims held against others for money, goods, or services. (Objective 1)

8. A receivable should be valued initially at an amount equal to the present value of the cash that the company expects to collect. A receivable should be classified as a current asset only if collection is expected within the next year or operating cycle, whichever is longer. (Objective 1)

9. From the standpoint of accounting theory, the net method of recording credit sales is better than the gross method. But most companies use the gross method because of convenience and materiality. (Objective 4)

10. The allowance method, rather than the direct write-off method, should be used when accounting for uncollectible accounts. (Objective 5)

11. The allowance method requires that bad debts be estimated by an income statement approach or a balance sheet approach. (Objective 5)

12. The income statement approach emphasizes the matching principle and requires that the adjusting entry for bad debts be made without considering the previous balance in the Allowance for Doubtful Accounts. (Objective 5)

13. The balance sheet approach emphasizes the reporting of accounts receivable at net realizable value and requires that the previous balance in the Allowance for Doubtful Accounts be considered in recording the adjusting entry for bad debts. (Objective 5)

14. In addition to its use in accounting for uncollectible accounts, the allowance method can be used in accounting for other items that affect the cash realization of accounts receivable (e.g., sales discounts). (Objective 5)

15. Many companies use accounts receivable to generate cash immediately by pledging, assigning, or factoring the accounts. Each method of accounts receivable financing has important financial statement implications. (Objective 6)

16. Although some notes have no stated interest rates, all commercial notes contain interest, because money has a time value. (Objective 7)

17. To be theoretically correct, we should always account for the interest component of a note receivable, whether or not the interest is explicitly stated. In practice, many companies do not separately account for the interest component of short-term, noninterest-bearing trade notes receivable because of materiality. (Objective 7)

18. A company may use either a footnote approach or a contra account approach to accounting for certain notes receivable that are discounted. (Objective 7)

APPENDIX A: PREPARING A PROOF OF CASH

As stated earlier in this chapter, auditors often prepare a *four-column bank reconciliation*, also called a *proof of cash*.

To illustrate how to prepare a proof of cash, we use the information presented earlier in the chapter when illustrating the preparation of a bank reconciliation for Todd Company for the month ended May 31, 1996. In addition, assume that the following facts pertain to Todd Company during June 1996:

1. The cash receipts (deposits) shown on the June bank statement were $78,839. These receipts included the deposit of $1,500 that was in transit on May 31.

2. The cash receipts shown on the company's books during June were $79,864.

3. The cash payments shown on the June bank statement were $76,188. These payments included the checks of $2,647 that were outstanding on May 31.

4. The cash payments shown on the company's books during June were $77,261.

5. The cash balance shown as of June 30 on the bank statement was $20,282.

6. The cash balance shown as of June 30 on the company's books was $17,817.

7. A deposit of $3,600 mailed to the bank on June 30 did not appear on the June bank statement.

8. On June 30, the bank collected a note receivable for Todd Company and credited the proceeds of $3,175 to the company's account. The proceeds included $175 of interest, all of which the company earned during 1996. Todd Company has not yet recorded the collection.

9. Outstanding checks as of June 30 totaled $2,910.

10. The bank statement showed a $20 service charge for June.

The proof of cash for Todd Company appears in Exhibit 7–12. The form is divided into two sections, like the form in Exhibit 7–1. In the "per bank statement" section, we reconcile from four amounts shown on the bank statement to the correct (true) amounts. In the "per books" section, we reconcile from four amounts shown on the company's books to the same correct amounts that are determined in the "per bank statement" section.

The first column of the proof of cash is simply the single-column bank reconciliation prepared at the end of May (see Exhibit 7–2); the fourth column is a single-column reconciliation for June. The second column reconciles the June receipts, and the third column reconciles the June payments.

To prepare a proof of cash, we may begin by completing the top line in each section. We do this simply by copying the necessary information from the bank statement and the company's books. Next, we copy in the first column the information shown in the fourth column of the proof of cash prepared for the *previous* month. We then prepare in the fourth column a single-column reconciliation for the *current* month. Finally, each reconciling item in one of the two outside columns is ordinarily added or deducted in one of the two inside columns.

A logical analysis of each reconciling item should enable you to determine whether to add or deduct the item. For example:

1. The May 31 deposit in transit of $1,500 is deducted from the June receipts shown on the bank statement. Because this amount is a *May* receipt that is shown as a receipt on the *June* bank statement, we deduct it to derive the *correct amount* of June receipts.

2. The outstanding checks of $2,910 on June 30 are added to the June payments shown on the bank statement. Because these

EXHIBIT 7–12

Todd Company
Proof of Cash
For June 1996

	May 31 Balance	June Receipts	June Payments	June 30 Balance
Per bank statement	$17,631	$78,839	$76,188	$20,282
Deposits in transit				
May 31	1,500	(1,500)		
June 30		3,600		3,600
Outstanding checks				
May 31	(2,647)		(2,647)	
June 30			2,910	(2,910)
Correct amounts	$16,484	$80,939	$76,451	$20,972
Per books	$15,214	$79,864	$77,261	$17,817
Note and interest collected by bank				
May	2,100	(2,100)		
June		3,175		3,175
Bank service charge				
May	(12)		(12)	
June			20	(20)
NSF check	(548)		(548)	
Error made in recording check no. 916	(270)		(270)	
Correct amounts	$16,484	$80,939	$76,451	$20,972

checks are June payments that simply have not cleared the bank as of June 30, we add them to derive the *correct amount* of June payments.

3. The note and interest collected by the bank in June ($3,175) are added to the June receipts shown on the company's books. Because this amount is a June receipt not yet shown on the company's books, we add it to derive the *correct amount* of June receipts.

4. The bank service charge of $12 for May is deducted from the June payments shown on the company's books. Because this amount is a *May* payment (i.e., the bank charged the company's checking account in May) that the company recorded as a payment in *June,* we deduct it to derive the *correct amount* of June payments.

Remember that a company usually prepares journal entries based on the information shown on its bank reconciliations. Our illustration assumes that Todd Company prepares such entries near the beginning of the month that follows each recon-

ciliation. In practice, many companies do this because they do not receive their bank statements in the mail on the last day of each month. When a company wants to prepare accurate financial statements (e.g., at year-end), it should record its journal entries as transactions of the month to which the bank reconciliation pertains.

As with the single-column bank reconciliation, preparation of a proof of cash usually indicates that a company has to make journal entries to update its accounting records. The entries necessary for Todd Company are suggested by the information shown in the "per books" section of the proof of cash:

Cash	3,175	
Notes Receivable		3,000
Interest Revenue		175
(To record collection of note and interest by bank.)		
Miscellaneous Expense	20	
Cash		20
(To record bank service charge.)		

QUESTIONS

7–1   What are the normal components of cash?

7–2   What are the guidelines for the valuation and classification of cash on the balance sheet?

7–3   How should a company report each of the following items?

[a] Bank overdrafts.

[b] Certificates of deposit.

[c] NSF checks received from customers.

[d] Expense advances made to employees.

[e] Postdated checks received from customers.

[f] Postage stamps.

[g] IOUs received from employees.

7–4 What do accountants mean by the term *internal control?*

7–5 Why should a company divide the responsibility for a series of related transactions between two or more persons?

7–6 What is the purpose of a petty cash fund?

7–7 What is the nature of a Cash Short and Over account?

7–8 What is a bank reconciliation? What purposes does it serve?

7–9 What is a proof of cash? What purposes does it serve?

7–10 What does the term *receivables* mean? How should receivables be classified on the balance sheet?

7–11 How should short-term receivables be valued on the balance sheet?

7–12 How does the balance sheet valuation of short-term receivables relate to the need of investors and creditors to predict the amount, timing, and uncertainty of cash flows to themselves?

7–13 What is the difference between a trade discount and a cash discount?

7–14 What is the distinction between the net method and the gross method of recording credit sales? Which method do companies generally use? Why?

7–15 How are the direct write-off method and the allowance method of accounting for uncollectible accounts similar? How do they differ?

7–16 Assume that a company uses the allowance method of accounting for uncollectible accounts. What is the major argument in favor of using the income statement approach? What is the major argument in favor of using the balance sheet approach?

7–17 Why does the Allowance for Doubtful Accounts sometimes have a debit balance?

7–18 What is the theoretical argument for using the allowance method to account for expected sales returns and allowances? (Assume that the expected amount is material.)

7–19 Why is it theoretically correct to account for interest when accounting for a noninterest-bearing note receivable?

7–20 What is the fundamental difference between the footnote approach and the contra account approach to accounting for notes receivable discounted?

7–21 Cash Components The controller of Wiser Women's Wear is trying to determine the total amount to report as *cash* on a balance sheet dated December 31. The following items are under consideration:

EXERCISES

[1] Currency and coins in a change fund (used for making change with customers) on December 31.

[2] NSF checks received during December from customers on account and returned by the bank with the December bank statement.

[3] Certificates of deposit held on December 31.

[4] Checks that the company has drawn payable to suppliers. Checks have been recorded but not mailed as of December 31.

[5] Postage stamps on hand December 31.

[6] Correct cash balance on December 31 in special checking account used for writing payroll checks.

[7] Petty cash on hand December 31.

[8] A check received from a customer and dated January 5 of the following year.

[9] IOUs from company personnel.

[10] Correct cash balance on December 31 in Chemical Bank general checking account.

INSTRUCTIONS

[a] Identify the items that the controller should report as cash on the December 31 balance sheet.

[b] Indicate the proper balance sheet reporting for items that the company should not include as cash.

7-22 Cash Components   The following information pertains to Bemis Company on December 31:

Correct cash balance in general checking account with First Bank	$ 2,142
Overdraft in special checking account with Second Bank (Bemis does not have another account with Second Bank.)	150
Cash accumulated in a special fund that will be used for plant expansion in five years	15,187
Cash surrender value of life insurance	3,265
Cash travel advances in the hands of company salespersons	1,296
Currency and coins in a petty cash fund (The company has not replenished the fund to the imprest amount of $200.)	58

INSTRUCTIONS

[a] Calculate the total amount that Bemis Company should report as *cash* in the current assets section of the balance sheet dated December 31.

[b] Indicate the proper balance sheet reporting of items that you omitted in [a].

7-23 Petty Cash   On April 1, East Insurance Agency established an imprest petty cash fund for $300 by writing a check on City National Bank. On April 23, the fund contained the following:

Currency and coins	$ 26
Receipts for office supplies expense	84
Receipts for postage expense	167
Receipts for advertising expense	18

On April 26, the agency wrote a check to increase the fund to the imprest amount.

INSTRUCTIONS

Prepare the necessary journal entries to record the petty cash transactions during April.

7-24 Cash Balance before Adjustments   The following information pertains to Traneus Company as of November 30:

Bank statement balance	$2,148
Bank service charge for November (not previously recorded on Traneus' books)	17
Checks outstanding	215
Interest on bank balance credited by bank during November (not previously recorded on Traneus' books)	37
Deposit in transit	490

INSTRUCTIONS

Based on this information, compute the general ledger cash balance on November 30 *before* adjustments.

7-25 Bank Reconciliation   The following information pertains to Travel, Inc., as of September 30:

Cash balance per general ledger	$2,385
Cash balance per bank statement	2,505
Checks outstanding	350
Bank service charge shown on September bank statement	10
Error made by Travel, Inc., in recording a check that cleared the bank in September (check was drawn in September for $145 but recorded at $185)	40
Deposit in transit	260

INSTRUCTIONS

Prepare a September bank reconciliation for Travel, Inc.

7–26 Cash to Report The bookkeeper for American Company recently prepared the following bank reconciliation:

American Company
Bank Reconciliation
September 30

Balance per bank statement			$12,642
Add: Deposit in transit		$870	
Checkbook printing charge		21	
Error made in recording check no. 1782			
(issued in September to acquire equipment)		160	
NSF check from a customer returned with the			
bank statement		500	1,551
			14,193
Deduct: Outstanding checks			
No. 1763	$235		
No. 1795	168		
No. 1796	45	448	
Note collected by bank (includes $50 interest)		950	1,398
Balance per books			$12,795

INSTRUCTIONS

[a] What amount should American report as *cash* on the balance sheet dated September 30? Assume that the company has $450 cash on hand on September 30.

[b] Prepare the necessary compound journal entry.

7–27 Bank Reconciliation Maxie Corporation keeps all its cash in a checking account. An examination of the company's accounting records and bank statement for the month ended June 30 revealed the following information:

[1] The cash balances as of June 30 are

Bank statement balance	$7,469
Book balance	7,524

[2] A deposit of $950 that was placed in the bank's night depository on June 30 does not appear on the bank statement.

[3] The bank statement shows that on June 30, the bank collected a note for Maxie and credited the proceeds of $935 to the company's account. The proceeds included $35 interest, all of which Maxie earned during the current accounting period. Maxie has not yet recorded the collection.

[4] Checks outstanding on June 30 are

No. 151	$150
No. 157	48
No. 166	72

[5] Maxie discovered that check no. 159, written in June for $183 in payment of an account payable, had been recorded in the company's records as $138.

[6] Included with the June bank statement was an NSF check for $250 that Maxie had received from Green Company on account on June 26. Maxie has not yet recorded the returned check.

[7] The bank statement shows a $15 service charge for June.

INSTRUCTIONS

[a] Prepare a June 30 bank reconciliation for Maxie.

[b] Prepare the necessary journal entries.

[c] Post the journal entries to Maxie's cash account and determine the adjusted cash balance.

7–28 (Appendix A) Proof of Cash The following information pertains to the cash of Patio Company:

[1]	July 31	August 31
Balance shown on bank statement	$2,738	$2,696
Balance shown in general ledger before		
reconciling the bank account	2,578	2,500

	July 31	August 31
Outstanding checks	863	1,015
Deposit in transit	685	1,245

[2]

	For August
Deposits shown on bank statement	$5,588
Charges shown on bank statement	5,630
Cash receipts shown on company's books	5,398
Cash payments shown on company's books	5,476

[3] The bank service charge was $18 in July (recorded by the company during August) and $24 in August (not yet recorded by the company).

[4] Included with the August bank statement was a check for $500 that had been received on August 25 from a customer on account. The returned check, marked NSF by the bank, has not yet been recorded on the company's books.

[5] During August the bank collected $750 of bond interest for Patio Company and credited the proceeds to the company's account. The company earned the interest during the current accounting period but has not yet recorded it.

[6] During August the company issued a check for $696 for equipment. The check, which cleared the bank during August, was incorrectly recorded by the company for $896.

INSTRUCTIONS

Prepare a proof of cash for August.

7–29 Recording Credit Sales   Perico, Inc., engaged in the following transactions during August:

Aug.	1	Sold merchandise to A Company for $5,000; terms 2/10, n/30.
	2	Sold merchandise to B Company for $10,000; terms 2/10, n/30.
	11	Received payment from B Company for the August 2 sale.
	30	Received payment from A Company for the August 1 sale.

INSTRUCTIONS

Prepare general journal entries for these transactions on Perico's books, using

[a] The *net method* of recording credit sales.
[b] The *gross method* of recording credit sales.

7–30 Bad Debts   The following data pertain to two companies that have calendar-year accounting periods:

	1996 Credit Sales	Accounts Receivable Dec. 31, 1996	Allowance for Doubtful Accounts Dec. 31, 1996 before Adjustment
Camp Company	$200,000	$40,000	$150 credit balance
Hope Company	500,000	55,000	250 debit balance

INSTRUCTIONS

Journalize the necessary adjusting entry on December 31, 1996, based on the following independent assumptions:

[a] For Camp Company, assuming the company estimates that 1% of credit sales are uncollectible.
[b] For Camp Company, assuming the company estimates that 6% of the accounts receivable balance on December 31, 1996, will be uncollectible.
[c] For Hope Company, assuming the company estimates that 0.5% of credit sales are uncollectible.
[d] For Hope Company, assuming the company estimates that 5% of the accounts receivable balance on December 31, 1996, will be uncollectible.

7–31 Bad Debts   The following information pertains to Logan, Inc.

[1] Sales made during 1996:

Cash	$ 80,000
Credit	340,000
Total	$420,000

[2] Accounts Receivable classified by age on December 31, 1996:

Age of Accounts	Accounts Receivable Balance
Under 30 days	$40,000
30–60 days	20,000
61–120 days	10,000
Over 120 days	5,000
Total	$75,000

[3] The Allowance for Doubtful Accounts had a $400 credit balance before adjustment on December 31, 1996.

INSTRUCTIONS

Prepare the adjusting entry on December 31, 1996, to record estimated bad debts under each of the following:

[a] The income statement approach, assuming that the uncollectible rate is 1% of *credit* sales.
[b] The income statement approach, assuming that the uncollectible rate is 0.80% of *total* sales.
[c] The balance sheet approach, assuming that the uncollectible rate is 5% of gross accounts receivable.
[d] The balance sheet approach, assuming that the following uncollectible percentages are appropriate: under 30 days, 1%; 30–60 days, 3%; 61–120 days, 10%; over 120 days, 30%.

7–32 Aging Schedule An aging of Lombardo Company's accounts receivable on December 31, 1996, reveals the following information:

Time Outstanding	Amount of Accounts Receivable
Under 30 days	$ 80,000
30–60 days	16,000
61–120 days	12,000
121–180 days	8,000
Over 180 days	4,000
Total	$120,000

Based on past experience, the company believes that the following uncollectible percentages are appropriate: under 30 days, 1.5%; 30–60 days, 3%; 61–120 days, 15%; 121–180 days, 30%; over 180 days, 60%.

INSTRUCTIONS

Using the aging of accounts receivable variation of the balance sheet approach, prepare the adjusting entry on December 31, 1996, to record estimated bad debts, assuming that the balance in the Allowance for Doubtful Accounts *before adjustment* is

[a] $410 credit
[b] $410 debit

7–33 Accounts Receivable—Selected Events Lomascolo, Inc., reported the following information on its balance sheet dated December 31, 1995:

Accounts receivable	$53,800
Less: Allowance for doubtful accounts	2,400
	$51,400

The following events occurred during 1996:

[1] Made credit sales of $210,000 and cash sales of $56,000.
[2] Collected $201,800 from customers on account.
[3] Wrote off $3,300 of accounts considered to be uncollectible.
[4] Collected $400 from customers whose accounts had been written off as uncollectible.
[5] Estimated that 5% of the accounts receivable balance at year-end would prove to be uncollectible.

INSTRUCTIONS

Prepare journal entries to record the above events.

7–34 Allowance Method for Sales Returns   Haag Company uses the allowance method to account for its sales returns. Based on past experience, Haag estimates that customers will return approximately 10% of the goods that the company sold. The company also estimates that it can resell goods returned by customers for approximately 80% of the original selling price. Haag's sales during the current accounting period were $400,000. The company uses a perpetual inventory system.

INSTRUCTIONS

[a] Prepare an adjusting journal entry to record estimated sales returns for the current accounting period.
[b] Prepare a journal entry to record the return in the next accounting period of goods that Haag sold for $4,000. Assume that the customer had not paid for the goods.

7–35 Assigning Accounts Receivable   On July 1, Morton Company assigned $50,000 of accounts receivable to its bank on a nonnotification basis. On that date, the bank advanced $40,000, less a service charge of 1% of the total accounts assigned, and Morton signed a $40,000 note bearing interest of 1% per month on the unpaid loan balance at the beginning of the month.

During July Morton collected $33,000 on assigned accounts. The company remitted this amount to the bank on July 31.

During August the company collected the remaining balance of assigned accounts. On August 31 the company paid off the remaining loan balance.

INSTRUCTIONS

Record the above events in general journal form.

7–36 Factoring Accounts Receivable   On February 1, Pryor Company factored $160,000 of accounts receivable without recourse with Fast Finance Company on a notification basis. Fast Finance charged a factoring fee of 3% of the amount of receivables factored. To cover sales returns and allowances, Fast Finance withheld 5% of the amount of receivables factored.

INSTRUCTIONS

Prepare the necessary journal entry for Pryor on February 1.

7–37 Pledging, Assigning, and Factoring   On September 30, Steele Company engaged in the following transactions:

[1] Obtained a $10,000, 30-day, 12% loan from First National Bank. The company pledged $10,000 of accounts receivable as security for the loan.
[2] Assigned $25,000 of accounts receivable on a nonnotification basis to Commerce Bank. The bank advanced $21,000, less a service charge of $420, and Steele signed a $21,000 note calling for interest of 1% per month on the unpaid loan balance.
[3] Factored $60,000 of accounts receivable without recourse on a notification basis with Quick Finance Company. Quick Finance charged a factoring fee of 2% of the amount of receivables factored and withheld 10% of the amount factored.

INSTRUCTIONS

Journalize each of the September 30 transactions.

7–38 Interest-Bearing Notes Receivable   On November 1, 1995, Burgin Manufacturing Company sold land in exchange for a $60,000, 12%, 90-day promissory note. The 12% interest rate was the going market rate for similar notes. Burgin had paid $32,000 to acquire the land in 1987. When the note matured, Burgin collected principal and interest.

INSTRUCTIONS

Prepare all journal entries (including an adjusting entry) required to record these events on Burgin's books in 1995 and 1996. Assume that Burgin uses a calendar-year accounting period and does not make reversing entries.

7–39 Recording Notes Receivable   On October 1, 1995, Tupper, Inc., sold merchandise having a sales price of $5,000 and received a one-year promissory note with a face amount of $5,500. The note had no stated interest rate, although the market rate for similar notes was 10%. When the note matured, Tupper collected the face amount. The company uses a calendar-year accounting period and does not make reversing entries.

[2] Accounts Receivable classified by age on December 31, 1996:

Age of Accounts	Accounts Receivable Balance
Under 30 days	$40,000
30–60 days	20,000
61–120 days	10,000
Over 120 days	5,000
Total	$75,000

[3] The Allowance for Doubtful Accounts had a $400 credit balance before adjustment on December 31, 1996.

INSTRUCTIONS

Prepare the adjusting entry on December 31, 1996, to record estimated bad debts under each of the following:

[a] The income statement approach, assuming that the uncollectible rate is 1% of *credit* sales.
[b] The income statement approach, assuming that the uncollectible rate is 0.80% of *total* sales.
[c] The balance sheet approach, assuming that the uncollectible rate is 5% of gross accounts receivable.
[d] The balance sheet approach, assuming that the following uncollectible percentages are appropriate: under 30 days, 1%; 30–60 days, 3%; 61–120 days, 10%; over 120 days, 30%.

7–32 Aging Schedule An aging of Lombardo Company's accounts receivable on December 31, 1996, reveals the following information:

Time Outstanding	Amount of Accounts Receivable
Under 30 days	$ 80,000
30–60 days	16,000
61–120 days	12,000
121–180 days	8,000
Over 180 days	4,000
Total	$120,000

Based on past experience, the company believes that the following uncollectible percentages are appropriate: under 30 days, 1.5%; 30–60 days, 3%; 61–120 days, 15%; 121–180 days, 30%; over 180 days, 60%.

INSTRUCTIONS

Using the aging of accounts receivable variation of the balance sheet approach, prepare the adjusting entry on December 31, 1996, to record estimated bad debts, assuming that the balance in the Allowance for Doubtful Accounts *before adjustment* is

[a] $410 credit
[b] $410 debit

7–33 Accounts Receivable—Selected Events Lomascolo, Inc., reported the following information on its balance sheet dated December 31, 1995:

Accounts receivable	$53,800
Less: Allowance for doubtful accounts	2,400
	$51,400

The following events occurred during 1996:

[1] Made credit sales of $210,000 and cash sales of $56,000.
[2] Collected $201,800 from customers on account.
[3] Wrote off $3,300 of accounts considered to be uncollectible.
[4] Collected $400 from customers whose accounts had been written off as uncollectible.
[5] Estimated that 5% of the accounts receivable balance at year-end would prove to be uncollectible.

INSTRUCTIONS

[a] Prepare all journal entries (including an adjusting entry) required to record these events on Tupper's books, assuming that the company records the note at present value.

[b] Prepare all journal entries required to record these events on Tupper's books, assuming that the company records the note at face amount.

[c] From a theoretical standpoint, is it better for Tupper to record the note at present value or at face amount? Explain your answer.

7–40 Discounting Notes Receivable   Inka Company has the following three notes receivable:

Note	Date of Note	Face Amount	Interest Rate	Time of Note
X	April 1, 1996	$10,000	8%	90 days
Y	May 1, 1996	40,000	9%	90 days
Z	May 16, 1996	60,000	10%	60 days

INSTRUCTIONS

For each note, calculate the proceeds that Inka would receive by discounting the note on May 31, 1996, at a rate of 12%.

PROBLEMS

7–41 Petty Cash   The following events pertain to Kim's Supply House:

June   1   Established an imprest petty cash fund for $300 by writing a check on Asbury County Bank.

12   Wrote a check to replenish the fund. The fund contained

Currency and coins	$ 16
Receipts for transportation-in	203
Receipts for postage expense	66

20   Wrote a check to replenish the fund and to increase the imprest amount to $400. The fund contained

Currency and coins	$ 36
Receipts for transportation-in	177
Receipts for postage expense	70
Receipts for charitable contributions	25

INSTRUCTIONS

Prepare the necessary journal entries to record the petty cash transactions during June.

7–42 Bank Reconciliation   Poppen Company keeps all its cash in a checking account. Presented below are the company's bank reconciliation prepared at the end of May, the general ledger account for cash, and a summary of the company's bank statement for June:

Poppen Company
Bank Reconciliation
May 31

Balance per bank statement	$6,250
Add: Deposits in transit	225
	6,475
Deduct: Outstanding checks	418
	$6,057
Balance per books	$6,072
Deduct: Bank service charge	15
Correct cash balance	$6,057

Cash

Balance, June 1	6,057	June disbursements	25,679
June receipts	26,182		

**Summary of Poppen Company's
Bank Statement for June**

Balance, June 1	$ 6,250
Deposits shown for June	25,692
Note and interest collected during June	1,575
Checks that cleared during June	(25,707)
June service charge	(17)
Balance, June 30	7,793

ADDITIONAL INFORMATION

[1] During June Poppen incorrectly recorded two checks. Check no. 507 was drawn for $233 but recorded as $323; check no. 521 was drawn for $180 but recorded as $18. Both checks were issued in payment of accounts payable and cleared the bank in June.

[2] During June the bank erroneously charged a $210 check of Potter Company to Poppen Company's account.

[3] Of the $1,575 note and interest collected by the bank during June, $75 represents interest, all of which Poppen earned during the current year. The company has not yet recorded the collection.

INSTRUCTIONS

[a] Prepare a June 30 bank reconciliation.
[b] Prepare journal entries to bring Poppen Company's accounting records up to date.
[c] What amount should Poppen report as *cash* on the balance sheet dated June 30?

7–43 Bank Reconciliation   Jett Company uses a calendar-year accounting period. The following information is available about the company's cash.

**First National Bank
General Account: Jett Company**

Date	Debits			Credits	Balance
4–30					4,942
5–01				610	5,552
5–02	177				5,375
5–04	248		755	1,552	5,924
5–05	437				5,487
5–09	489			3,621	8,619
5–12	705			1,986	9,900
5–20	930				8,970
5–22	423				8,547
5–26				2,549	11,096
5–29	255	NSF			10,841
5–30	20	DM	5,798		5,023
5–31	14	SC		1,290 CM	6,299
	Total debits	**$10,251**		**Total credits $11,608**	

LEGEND: DM: Debit memo   NSF: Not sufficient funds check
         CM: Credit memo   SC: Service charge

Jett Company
Bank Reconciliation
April 30

Balance per bank statement	$4,942
Add: Deposit in transit	610
	5,552

Deduct: Outstanding checks

No. 606	$177	
No. 607	248	425
Correct cash balance		$5,127

Balance per books	$5,139
Deduct: Bank service charge	12
Correct cash balance	$5,127

Jett Company's Cash Account
Taken from General Ledger

Cash

Balance, April 30	5,139	Cash Payments Journal, May 31	10,816
Cash Receipts Journal, May 31	10,583		

Information Taken from Jett Company

Cash Receipts Journal			Cash Payments Journal		
Date	**Cash Debit**		**Date**	**Check No.**	**Cash Credit**
5–03	1,552		5–01	608	755
5–08	3,621		5–03	609	473
5–12	1,986		5–06	610	489
5–25	2,549		5–11	611	705
5–31	875		5–16	612	930
	10,583		5–21	613	243
			5–27	614	511
			5–29	615	5,798
			5–30	616	346
			5–31	617	566
					10,816

ADDITIONAL INFORMATION

[1] During May the bank erroneously deducted from Jett Company's account a collection charge of $20 that was applicable to Lett Company.

[2] The credit memo shown on the bank statement relates to a note that the bank collected on Jett's behalf. The note had a face value of $1,200, and Jett earned interest of $90 during the current accounting period. The company has not yet recorded the collection.

[3] Jett failed to record the bank service charge for April (see April reconciliation).

[4] The NSF check shown on the bank statement had been received during May from a customer on account. Jett has not yet recorded the return of the check.

[5] Jett made two errors in recording cash payments during May:

Check No.	Actual Amount of Check	Amount Recorded
609	$437	$473
613	423	243

Check no. 609 was for delivery expense; check no. 613 was issued to purchase equipment.

INSTRUCTIONS

[a] Prepare a bank reconciliation dated May 31.
[b] Prepare the necessary journal entries.

7–44 (Appendix A) Proof of Cash   Refer to the information given for Jett Company in 7–43.

INSTRUCTIONS

[a] Prepare a proof of cash for May.
[b] Prepare the necessary journal entries.

7–45 Bank Reconciliation   The accounting period of Pointer Company ends on December 31. The following information is available about the company's cash.

Pointer Company
Bank Reconciliation
October 31

Balance per bank statement		$18,005
Add: Deposit in transit		1,790
		19,795
Deduct: Outstanding checks		
No. 773	$4,563	
No. 774	2,118	6,681
Correct cash balance		$13,114
Balance per books		$11,534
Add: Note collected by bank		
Principal	1,500	
Interest earned during current accounting period	100	1,600
		13,134
Deduct: Bank service charge		20
Correct cash balance		$13,114

County National Bank
General Account: Pointer Company

Date	Debits		Credits	Balance
10–31				18,005
11–01			1,790	19,795
11–02	4,563			15,232
11–04	2,118	4,567	5,967	14,514
11–05	963			13,551
11–06			3,410	16,961
11–07	2,515			14,446
11–11			1,037	15,483
11–13	2,264			13,219
11–18	3,325			9,894
11–24	964		4,255	13,185
11–28	619		750 CM	13,316
11–29	3,000	35 DM	500 CM	10,781
11–30	665 NSF	22 SC		10,094
Total debits	**$25,620**		**Total credits**	**$17,709**

LEGEND: DM: Debit memo   NSF: Not sufficient funds check
        CM: Credit memo   SC: Service charge

Pointer Company's Cash Account
Taken from General Ledger

Cash

Balance, Oct. 31	11,534	Cash payments journal, Nov. 30	21,575
Cash receipts journal, Nov. 30	18,269		

Information Taken from Pointer Company

Cash Receipts Journal			Cash Payments Journal		
Date	**Cash Debit**		**Date**	**Check No.**	**Cash Credit**
11–03	5,967		11–01	775	4,567
11–06	3,410		11–04	776	963
11–11	1,037		11–05	777	2,515
11–23	4,255		11–10	778	3,264
11–30	3,600		11–17	779	3,325
	18,269		11–22	780	694
			11–27	781	619
			11–28	782	760
			11–29	783	3,000
			11–30	784	1,868
					21,575

ADDITIONAL INFORMATION

[1] After preparing the October 31 reconciliation, Pointer failed to record the necessary journal entries.

[2] The NSF check had been received during November from a customer on account. Pointer has not yet recorded the return of the check.

[3] The credit memos shown on the bank statement pertain to $750 of bond interest that Pointer earned during the current accounting period and that the bank collected on the company's behalf (collection not yet recorded on Pointer's books) and a $500 collection made for Poynter Company that the bank erroneously credited to Pointer's account.

[4] The $35 debit memo shown on the bank statement pertains to the rental of a safe deposit box during November.

[5] Pointer made two errors in recording cash payments during November.

Check No.	Actual Amount of Check	Amount Recorded
778	$2,264	$3,264
780	964	694

Check no. 778 was issued to purchase equipment; check no. 780 was for advertising expense.

INSTRUCTIONS

[a] Prepare a bank reconciliation dated November 30.

[b] Prepare the necessary journal entries.

7–46 (Appendix A) Proof of Cash Refer to the information given for Pointer Company in 7–45.

INSTRUCTIONS

[a] Prepare a proof of cash for November.

[b] Prepare the necessary journal entries.

7–47 Recording Credit Sales McKay, Inc., began operations in 1996. During the year, the company sold merchandise with a gross invoice price of $150,000. All sales were subject to credit terms of 3/10, n/60. Of the total sales of $150,000, the company received payments for 50% within the discount period and 30% after the discount period had expired. The company had not collected the other 20% as of year-end.

INSTRUCTIONS

[a] Prepare general journal entries to record the above transactions using (1) the *net method* of recording credit sales and (2) the *gross method* of recording credit sales.

[b] What financial statement balances would McKay report on December 31, 1996, for sales, sales discounts not taken, sales discounts, and accounts receivable under (1) the net method and (2) the gross method?

[c] Which of the above methods of recording credit sales is theoretically superior? Why?

7–48 Accounts Receivable—Selected Events   Gerke Department Store reported the following information on its balance sheet dated December 31, 1995:

Accounts receivable	$138,000
Less: Allowance for doubtful accounts	7,000
	$131,000

The company engaged in the following transactions during 1996:

[1] Made cash sales of $320,000 and credit sales of $670,000.
[2] Collected $650,800 from customers on account.
[3] Wrote off $7,200 of accounts considered to be uncollectible.
[4] Collected $600 from customers whose accounts had been written off as uncollectible.

INSTRUCTIONS

[a] Prepare journal entries to record these transactions.
[b] Journalize the adjusting entry to record estimated bad debts at the end of 1996 under each of the following *independent* assumptions:
  [1] The company estimates that 2.0% of *credit* sales are uncollectible.
  [2] The company estimates that 1.5% of *total* sales are uncollectible.
  [3] The company estimates that 9% of the accounts receivable balance at the end of 1996 will be uncollectible.
  [4] The company estimates that 75% of the year-end balance of accounts receivable has an uncollectible percentage of 5%; the remaining 25% has an uncollectible percentage of 20%.
[c] Assume that the company estimates its bad debts on the basis of assumption [b-1].
  [1] Show how accounts receivable would be presented on the balance sheet prepared at the end of 1996.
  [2] What is the dollar effect of the year-end bad debt adjustment on the pretax income for 1996?
  [3] What is the dollar effect of the year-end bad debt adjustment on the working capital (current assets minus current liabilities) reported at the end of 1996?

7–49 Aging Schedule   Gildrie Corporation operates in an industry that has a high rate of bad debts. On December 31, 1996, before any year-end adjustments, Gildrie's Accounts Receivable balance was $600,000 and its Allowance for Doubtful Accounts balance was $25,000. The year-end balance reported in the statement of financial position for the Allowance for Doubtful Accounts is based on the aging schedule shown as follows:

Time Outstanding	Amount of Accounts Receivable	Probability of Collection
Under 15 days	$300,000	.96
16–30 days	200,000	.90
31–45 days	50,000	.80
46–60 days	30,000	.70
61–75 days	10,000	.65
Over 75 days	10,000	.00

INSTRUCTIONS

[a] What is the appropriate balance for the Allowance for Doubtful Accounts on December 31, 1996?
[b] Show how Accounts Receivable would be presented on the balance sheet on December 31, 1996.
[c] What is the dollar effect of the year-end bad debt adjustment on the pretax income for 1996?

(CMA adapted)

7–50 Aging Schedule   From inception of operations to December 31, 1995, Murr Corporation provided for uncollectible accounts receivable under the allowance method: provisions were made monthly at 2% of credit sales; bad debts written off were charged to the allowance account; recoveries of bad debts previously written off were credited to the allowance account; and no year-end adjustments to the allowance account were made. Murr's usual credit terms are net 30 days.

The balance in the Allowance for Doubtful Accounts was $130,000 at January 1, 1996. During 1996 credit sales totaled $9,000,000, interim provisions for doubtful accounts were made at 2% of credit sales, $90,000 of bad debts were written off, and recoveries of accounts previously written off amounted to $15,000. Murr installed a computer facility in November 1996 and prepared an aging of accounts receivable for the first time as of December 31, 1996. A summary of the aging is as follows:

Classification by Month of Sale	Balance in Each Category	Estimated % Uncollectible
Nov.–Dec. 1996	$1,140,000	2%
Jul.–Oct.	600,000	10
Jan.–June	400,000	25
Prior to 1/1/96	130,000	75
	$2,270,000	

Based on the review of collectibility of the account balances in the "prior to 1/1/96" aging category, additional receivables totaling $60,000 were written off as of December 31, 1996. Effective with the year ended December 31, 1996, Murr adopted a new accounting method for estimating the Allowance for Doubtful Accounts at the amount indicated by the year-end aging analysis of accounts receivable.

INSTRUCTIONS

[a] Prepare a schedule analyzing the changes in the Allowance for Doubtful Accounts for the year ended December 31, 1996. Show supporting computations in good form.

[b] Prepare the journal entry for the year-end adjustment to the Allowance for Doubtful Accounts balance as of December 31, 1996. (AICPA adapted)

7–51 Aging Schedule Lytle Company sells office equipment and supplies to many organizations in the city and surrounding area on contract terms of 2/10, n/30. In the past, over 75% of the credit customers have taken advantage of the discount by paying within 10 days of the invoice date.

The number of customers taking the full 30 days to pay has increased within the last year. Current indications are that less than 60% of the customers are now taking the discount. Bad debts as a percentage of gross credit sales have risen from the 1.5% provided in past years to about 4% in the current year.

The controller has responded to a request for more information on the deterioration in collections of accounts receivable with the report reproduced below.

Lytle Company
Finance Committee Report
Accounts Receivable Collections
May 31, 1996

The fact that some credit accounts will prove uncollectible is normal. Annual bad debt write-offs have been 1.5% of gross credit sales over the past five years. During the last fiscal year, this percentage increased to slightly less than 4%. The current Accounts Receivable balance is $1.2 million. The condition of this balance in terms of age and probability of collection is as follows:

Proportion of Total	Age Categories	Probability of Collection
68%	not yet due	99%
15%	less than 30 days past due	96½%
8%	30 to 60 days past due	95%
5%	61 to 120 days past due	91%
2½%	121 to 180 days past due	60%
1½%	over 180 days past due	10%

The Allowance for Doubtful Accounts had a credit balance of $30,250 on June 1, 1995. Lytle has provided for a monthly bad debts expense accrual during the current fiscal year based on the assumption that 4% of gross credit sales will be uncollectible. Total gross credit sales for the 1995–1996 fiscal year amounted to $3 million. Write-offs of bad accounts during the year totaled $108,750.

INSTRUCTIONS

[a] Prepare an accounts receivable aging schedule for Lytle Company using the age categories identified in the controller's report to the finance committee showing

[1] The amount of accounts receivable outstanding for each age category and in total.

[2] The estimated amount that is uncollectible for each category and in total.

[b] Compute the amount of the year-end adjustment necessary to bring Allowance for Doubtful Accounts to the balance indicated by the age analysis. Then prepare the necessary journal entry to adjust the accounting records.

[c] First assume a recessionary environment with tight credit and high interest rates. Then
  [1] Identify steps Lytle Company might consider to improve the accounts receivable situation.
  [2] Evaluate each step identified in terms of the risks and costs involved.   (CMA adapted)

7–52 Changing an Accounting Estimate of Bad Debts   Esman Company has been in business for five years, but its financial statements have never been audited. Engaged to perform an audit for 1996, you find that the company's balance sheet has no allowance for doubtful accounts. Bad debts have simply been expensed as written-off and recoveries credited to income as collected. The company's policy is to write off at December 31 of each year those accounts on which no collections have been received for three months. The installment contracts are for two years.

Upon your recommendation, the company agrees to revise its accounts for 1996 to reflect the allowance method of accounting for bad debts. The estimate of bad debts is to be based on a percentage of sales that is derived from the experience of prior years.

Statistics for the past five years are as follows:

Year	Charge Sales		Accounts Written Off and Year of Sale		Recoveries and Year of Sale
1992	$100,000	(1992) $ 550			
1993	250,000	(1992) 1,500	(1993) $1,000		(1992) $100
1994	300,000	(1992) 500	(1993) 4,000	(1994) $1,300	(1993) 400
1995	325,000	(1993) 1,200	(1994) 4,500	(1995) 1,500	(1994) 500
1996	275,000	(1994) 2,700	(1995) 5,000	(1996) 1,400	(1995) 600

Accounts receivable at December 31, 1996, were as follows:

1995 sales	$ 15,000
1996 sales	135,000
	$150,000

INSTRUCTIONS

Prepare the adjusting journal entry or entries with appropriate explanations to set up the Allowance for Doubtful Accounts. Support each item with organized computations. Ignore income tax implications.   (AICPA adapted)

7–53 Assigning and Factoring Accounts Receivable   The following information pertains to Cosby Carpet Company:

June 1 Assigned $37,500 of accounts receivable to City Bank on a nonnotification basis. The bank advanced $32,000, less a service charge of $800. Cosby signed a $32,000 promissory note bearing interest of 1% per month on the unpaid loan balance.
     28 Collected assigned accounts of $25,000, less sales returns and allowances of $750.
     29 Sold goods on account for $40,000.
     30 Remitted the June 28 collection to City Bank.
     30 Factored $25,000 of accounts receivable without recourse with Faith Bank on a notification basis. Faith Bank charged a factoring fee of 3% of the amount of receivables factored and withheld 10% of the amount factored to cover sales returns and allowances.

INSTRUCTIONS

[a] Journalize these events on Cosby's books.
[b] Assume that Cosby wants to prepare a balance sheet dated June 30. Discuss the financial reporting requirements for those receivables that pertain to the assignment and factoring arrangements.

7-54 Notes Receivable Discounted   The following events pertain to Farmer Company:

May 1 Farmer receives a $20,000, 90-day, 10% note in satisfaction of West Company's account receivable of $20,000.

  31 Farmer discounts the note with recourse at First Bank. The discount rate is 12%. (Relevant circumstances indicate that the discounting should be accounted for as a sale of the note.)

July 30 West Company pays First Bank the total amount owed on the note.

INSTRUCTIONS

[a] Prepare journal entries to record these events on Farmer's books using each of the following approaches to accounting for notes receivable discounted:
  [1] Footnote approach.   [2] Contra account approach.
[b] Assume that instead of paying the note on July 30, West Company dishonors it. First Bank charges Farmer with the maturity value and a $40 protest fee. Journalize the entry or entries required for Farmer on July 30 under the
  [1] Footnote approach.   [2] Contra account approach.
[c] What is the fundamental difference between these two approaches to accounting for notes receivable discounted?

7-55 Notes Receivable   The following events pertain to Arbo Company:

Dec. 31, 1995 Arbo Company sells merchandise to Ball Company. The merchandise has a selling price of $10,000, and Arbo receives a one-year promissory note that has a face amount of $11,000 and no stated interest rate. The market rate for similar notes is 10%.

Dec. 16, 1995 Arbo sells land to Bliss Company in exchange for a $90,000, 10%, 90-day promissory note. The 10% interest rate equals the going market rate for similar notes. The cost of the land to Arbo is $60,000.

Jan. 30, 1996 Arbo discounts the Bliss note with recourse at County Bank. The discount rate is 12%. (Relevant circumstances indicate that Arbo Company should account for the discounting as a sale of the note.)

Mar. 16, 1996 Bliss pays County Bank the full amount owed.

Nov. 30, 1996 Ball pays Arbo the full amount owed.

  Arbo Company uses a calendar-year accounting period and does not make reversing entries. The company records notes receivable at present value on the date received, and it uses the footnote approach to accounting for notes receivable discounted.

INSTRUCTIONS

[a] Prepare journal entries (including adjusting entries) to record these events on Arbo's books.
[b] Should Arbo recognize interest earned on the Ball note? Explain the rationale for your answer.
[c] Assume that the Ball and Bliss notes are dishonored when they mature. County Bank charges Arbo with the maturity value of the Bliss note and a $60 protest fee. Journalize the entry or entries required for Arbo on March 16, 1996, and November 30, 1996.

7-56 Notes Receivable   You are examining Topline Corporation's financial statements for the year ended December 31, 1996. Your analysis of the 1996 entries in the Trade Notes Receivable account was as follows:

Topline Corporation
Analysis of Trade Notes Receivable
For the Year Ended December 31, 1996

Date			Folio	Trade Notes Receivable Debit	Credit
Jan.	1	Balance forward		$118,000	
Feb.	28	Received $25,000 6% note due 10/29/96 from Daley, whose trade account was past due.	MEMO		
	28	Discounted Daley note at 6%.	CR		$ 24,960

Date			Folio	Trade Notes Receivable	
				Debit	Credit
Mar.	29	Received noninterest-bearing demand note from Edge, the corporation's treasurer, for a loan.	CD	6,200	
Aug.	30	Received principal and interest due from Allen and, in accordance with agreement, two principal payments in advance.	CR		34,200
Sept.	4	Paid protest fee on note dishonored by Charnes.	CD	5	
Nov.	1	Received check dated 2/1/97 in settlement of Bailey note. The check was included in cash on hand 12/31/96.	CR		8,120
Nov.	4	Paid protest fee and maturity value of Daley note to bank. Note discounted 2/28/96 was dishonored.	CD	26,031	
Dec.	27	Accepted furniture and fixtures with a fair market value of $24,000 in full settlement from Daley.	GJ		24,000
	31	Received check dated 1/3/97 from Edge in payment of 3/29/96 note. (The check was included in petty cash until 1/2/97, when it was returned to Edge in exchange for a new demand note of the same amount.)	CR		6,200
	31	Received principal and interest on Charnes note.	CR		42,437
	31	Accrued interest on Allen note.	GJ	1,200	
		Totals		$151,436	$139,917

The following information is available:

[1] Balances at January 1, 1996, were a debit of $1,400 in the Accrued Interest Receivable account and a credit of $400 in the Unearned Interest Income account. The $118,000 debit balance in the Trade Notes Receivable account consisted of the following three notes:

Allen note dated 8/31/92, payable in annual installments of $10,000 principal plus accrued interest at 6% each Aug. 31	$70,000
Bailey note discounted to Topline at 6% on 11/1/95, due 11/1/96	8,000
Charnes note for $40,000 plus 6% interest dated 12/31/95, due on 9/1/96	40,000

[2] No entries were made during 1996 to the Accrued Interest Receivable account or the Unearned Interest Income account, and only one entry for a credit of $1,200 on December 31 appeared in the Interest Income account.

[3] All notes were from trade customers unless otherwise indicated.

[4] Debits and credits offsetting Trade Notes Receivable debit and credit entries were correctly recorded unless the facts indicate otherwise.

[5] Topline Corporation uses the contra account approach when accounting for notes receivable discounted. Notes receivable are discounted with recourse and are properly accounted for as sales. The company also follows the practice of debiting Trade Accounts Receivable instead of Dishonored Notes Receivable when a customer's note is dishonored.

INSTRUCTIONS

Prepare a worksheet to adjust each entry to correct or properly reclassify it, if necessary. Enter your adjustments in the proper columns to correspond with the date of each entry. Do not combine related entries for different dates. Your completed worksheet will provide the basis for one compound journal entry to correct all entries to Trade Notes Receivable and related accounts for 1996. Formal journal entries are not required. In addition to the information shown in the above analysis, the following headings are suggested:

Adjustment or Reclassification Required

Trade Notes Receivable	Trade Accounts Receivable	Interest Income	Other Accounts	
				Amount
Debit (Credit)	Debit (Credit)	Debit (Credit)	Account Title	Debit Credit
				(AICPA adapted)

CASES

7–57 Outstanding Checks   You are the controller for Parker, Inc., a company that uses a calendar-year accounting period. Walter Brush, a new person on the accounting staff, has just prepared a bank reconciliation dated December 31, 1996, and has determined that outstanding checks are $14,895. Walter believes that this amount should be classified as liabilities on Parker's year-end balance sheet because the checks have not cleared the bank as of December 31.

INSTRUCTIONS

Explain how Parker, Inc., should account for the outstanding checks on its year-end balance sheet.

7–58 Notes Receivable and Bad Debts   Case Company has significant amounts of trade accounts receivable. The company uses the allowance method to estimate bad debts instead of the specific write-off method. During the year, some specific accounts were written off as uncollectible, and some that had been previously written off as uncollectible were collected.

Case also has some interest-bearing notes receivable for which the face amount plus interest at the prevailing rate of interest is due at maturity. The notes were received on July 1, 1995, and are due on June 30, 1997.

INSTRUCTIONS

[a] What are the deficiencies of the specific write-off method?
[b] What are the two basic allowance methods used to estimate bad debts, and what is the theoretical justification for each?
[c] How should Case account for the collection of the specific accounts previously written off as uncollectible?
[d] How should Case report the effects of the interest-bearing notes receivable on its December 31, 1996, balance sheet and its income statement for the year ended December 31, 1996? Why?

(AICPA adapted)

7–59 Notes Receivable and Bad Debts   Part 1.   On July 1, 1995, Sperl Company, a calendar-year company, sold special-order merchandise on credit and received in return an interest-bearing note receivable from the customer. Sperl Company will receive interest at the prevailing rate for a note of this type. Both the principal and interest are due in one lump sum on June 30, 1996.

INSTRUCTIONS

[a] When should Sperl Company report interest income from the note receivable? Discuss the rationale for your answer.
[b] Assume that the note receivable was discounted *without recourse* at a bank on December 31, 1995. How would Sperl Company determine the amount of the discount and what is the appropriate accounting for the discounting transaction?

Part 2.   On December 31, 1995, Sperl Company had significant amounts of accounts receivable as a result of credit sales to its customers. Sperl Company uses the allowance method based on credit sales to estimate bad debts. Based on past experience, 1% of credit sales normally will not be collected. This pattern is expected to continue.

INSTRUCTIONS

[a] Discuss the rationale for using the allowance method based on credit sales to estimate bad debts. Contrast this method with the allowance method based on the balance in the trade receivables accounts.

[b] How should Sperl Company report the allowance for bad debts account on its balance sheet at December 31, 1995? Also describe the alternatives, if any, for presentation of bad debts expense in Sperl Company's 1995 income statement. (AICPA adapted)

7–60 Notes Receivable, Assigning, and Factoring On July 1, 1995, Ridens Company sold special-order merchandise on credit and received in return an interest-bearing note receivable from the customer. Ridens will receive interest at the prevailing rate for a note of this type. Both the principal and interest are due in one lump sum on June 30, 1996.

On September 1, 1995, Ridens sold special-order merchandise on credit and received in return a noninterest-bearing note receivable from the customer. The prevailing rate of interest for a note of this type is determinable. The note receivable is due in one lump sum on August 31, 1997.

Ridens also has significant amounts of trade accounts receivable as a result of credit sales to its customers. On October 1, 1995, some trade accounts receivable were assigned to Davidson Finance Company on a with-recourse, nonnotification basis for an advance of 75% of their amount at an interest charge of 20% on the balance outstanding.

On November 1, 1995, other trade accounts receivable were factored on a without-recourse basis. The factor withheld 5% of the trade accounts receivable factored as protection against sales returns and allowances and charged a finance charge of 3%.

INSTRUCTIONS

[a] How should Ridens determine the interest revenue for 1995 on the
1. Interest-bearing note receivable? Why?
2. Noninterest-bearing note receivable? Why?

[b] How should Ridens report the interest-bearing note receivable and the noninterest-bearing note receivable on its balance sheet at December 31, 1995?

[c] How should Ridens account for subsequent collections on the trade accounts receivable assigned on October 1, 1995, and the payments to Davidson Finance? Why?

[d] How should Ridens account for the trade accounts receivable factored on November 1, 1995? Why? (AICPA adapted)

7–61 Credit Card Plan One of your corporate clients operates a full-line department store that dominates its market area, is easily accessible to public and private transportation, has adequate parking facilities, and is near a large, permanent military base. The president of the company seeks your advice on a proposal she received.

A local bank in which your client has an account recently affiliated with a popular national credit card plan and has invited your client to participate. Under the plan, affiliated banks mail credit card applications to persons in the community who have good credit ratings, regardless of whether they are bank customers. A recipient who wishes to receive a credit card completes, signs, and returns the application and installment credit agreement. Cardholders may charge merchandise or services at any participating establishment throughout the nation.

The bank guarantees payment to all participating merchants on invoices that have been properly completed, signed, and validated with the impression of credit cards that have not expired or been reported stolen or otherwise canceled. Local merchants, including your client, may turn in all card-validated sales tickets or invoices to their affiliated local bank at any time and receive immediate credits to their checking accounts of 96.5% of the face value of the invoices. If card users pay the bank in full within 30 days for amounts billed, the bank levies no added charges against them. If they elect to make their payments under a deferred payment plan, the bank adds a service charge with an effective annual interest rate of 18% on unpaid balances. Only the local affiliated banks and the franchiser of the credit plan share in these revenues.

The 18% service charge approximates what your client has been billing customers who pay their accounts over an extended period on a schedule similar to that of the credit card plan. Participation in the plan does not prevent your client from continuing its credit business.

INSTRUCTIONS

[a] What are (1) the positive and (2) the negative financial factors and accounting factors that your client should consider in deciding whether to participate in the credit card plan? Explain.

[b] If your client participates in the plan, which income statement and balance sheet accounts may change materially as the plan becomes fully operative? (Such factors as market position, sales mix, prices, and markup are expected to remain about the same as in the past.) Explain. (AICPA adapted)

7-62 Troubled Notes Receivable Ted Rooney is the chief financial officer for a small Midwestern company that manufactures farm implements and offers long-term credit to buyers. In fulfilling the financing function, the company makes a number of noninterest-bearing loans. Under the terms of these loans, the borrower signs a note for an amount larger than the funds actually lent and the interest revenue to the company is implicit in the difference between the amount lent and the amount to be repaid (i.e., the discount on the note receivable). Ted is aware of the provisions of *APB Opinion No. 21,* "Interest on Receivables and Payables," that require the company to amortize the discount on the long-term receivables, and the company has consistently recognized interest revenue in this manner.

Recently, Ted read an article in the local newspaper that described the financial implications of a recent drought in the area in which many of the company's best customers operate. Although there is no evidence that any of the company's customers are experiencing financial difficulties, the article states that many bankruptcies of farming operations are expected. Ted believes that some of the company's notes receivable may eventually become uncollectible or only partially collectible. He wonders whether his company should continue to recognize interest revenue on those loans that have some uncertainty as to their ultimate collectibility.

INSTRUCTIONS

Help Ted decide what to do. If you believe that additional evidence is necessary before making any decisions, describe the evidence that Ted should obtain in attempting to resolve the problem.

7-63 Receivable Classification You are the independent CPA for Pack, Inc., an electronic products' wholesaler. Pack has recently made an important sale to a retail company that is opening several new outlets. Due to the size of the sale, Pack has allowed the retailer to acquire the goods by signing a three-year, interest-bearing note rather than requiring the normal credit terms of 30 days. Pack uses a one-year period for classifying current assets and liabilities on its balance sheet, and this practice is still appropriate in light of the recent sale to the retailer.

When you explain to Pack's management that the receivable should be classified as noncurrent because of its maturity date, management objects, stating that the company intends to discount the receivable without recourse at a local bank fairly soon after the balance sheet date. Management asserts that although the bank it normally uses does not engage in such transactions, other banks would be quite willing to do so because they commonly do for other businesses. Pack's management further objects to classifying the receivable as a noncurrent asset because such classification would cause the company to violate one of its lending covenants that requires a minimum amount of working capital.

The retailer is a fairly small company that has been Pack's customer for many years. You recall recently reading a rather negative newspaper article about financial difficulties encountered by the retailer due to keen competition from other large chains of electronics retailers.

Your audit of Pack is now almost completed, and Pack will not accomplish the transfer of the receivable prior to the issuance of the financial statements.

INSTRUCTIONS

Would you accept classifying the receivable as a current asset? Explain your answer. If you believe that additional evidence is needed do resolve the case, be sure to identify the nature of that information as part of your solution.

7-64 Financial Reporting Case Following are the current asset sections of the 1993 balance sheets and selected disclosures of two major U.S. corporations:

The Fairchild Corporation and Consolidated Subsidiaries
Consolidated Balance Sheets

June 30	1993	1992
(in thousands)		
Assets		
Current Assets:		
Cash and cash equivalents (of which $4,200 and $30,300 is restricted)	**$ 70,099**	$ 45,946
Short-term investments	**5,425**	41,468
Accounts receivable-trade, less allowances of $1,900 and $2,275	**64,423**	71,675

June 30	1993	1992
Inventories:		
Finished goods	**51,776**	61,446
Work-in-process	**30,766**	33,358
Raw materials	**8,987**	13,573
	91,529	108,377
Prepaid expenses and other current assets	**14,308**	43,916
Total Current Assets	**245,784**	311,382

Restricted Cash

On June 30, 1993, the Company had restricted cash of $4,200,000 maintained as collateral for certain debt facilities. Cash investments are in high grade, short-term commercial paper.

Statement of Cash Flows

For purposes of the statement of cash flows, the Company considers all temporary investments with original maturity dates of three months or less as cash equivalents. Total cash disbursements (receipts) made by the Company for income taxes and interest were as follows:

For the years ended June 30, *(in thousands)*	1993	1992	1991
Interest	**$ 63,567**	$81,796	$76,463
Income Taxes	**(23,171)**	(7,017)	19,935

Northern Telecom Limited and Subsidiary Companies
Consolidated Balance Sheet
December 31

(millions of U.S. dollars)	1993	1992
Assets		
Current assets		
Cash and short-term investments at cost (approximates market value)	**$ 138**	$ 90
Accounts receivable		
Related parties	**272**	317
Trade (less provision for uncollectibles $58 for 1993, $35 for 1992)	**2,553**	2,257
Finance subsidiaries' customers (less provision for uncollectibles $12 for 1993, $15 for 1992) (note 7)	**325**	377
Inventories (note 8)	**1,145**	930
Prepaid expenses	**83**	79
Deferred income taxes	**296**	105
	4,812	4,155

(f) Cash equivalents
All highly liquid investments with original maturities of three months or less are classified as cash and short-term investments.

INSTRUCTIONS

[a] For Fairchild Corporation:
[1] What is included in the financial statement element, "Cash and cash equivalents"?
[2] What is meant by the parenthetical phrase explaining that cash is restricted? For what purpose is the cash restricted? Why is this important enough to warrant disclosure?
[3] What are the total amounts of accounts receivable, before allowances for uncollectibles, for 1993 and 1992? What do the net-of-allowance numbers presented in the balance sheet represent?
[b] For Northern Telecom:
[1] What short-term investments are combined with cash? Why do you think the company combines these items rather than presenting them separately in the balance sheet?
[2] Why do you think accounts receivable are separated into three categories: related parties, trade, and finance subsidiaries' customers?

CHAPTER

8

Inventories:
Basic Valuation Methods

OBJECTIVES

1. To discuss and illustrate the financial accounting and reporting requirements for inventories.
2. To explain the methods used to determine inventory quantities on hand.
3. To explain the nature of costs that should be included in inventory.
4. To discuss and illustrate various inventory cost flow methods.
5. To discuss and illustrate the valuation of inventory at the lower of cost or market value.
6. To indicate exceptional cases under generally accepted accounting principles of inventory valuation above cost.
7. To indicate effects of inventory errors on financial statements.
8. To explain conceptual considerations in accounting for inventories.

The strongest argument favoring historical cost measurements is that most people consider them highly reliable. Historical cost measurements are based on actual past transactions that accountants can verify using such evidence as invoices and canceled checks. As you will learn in this chapter, though, determining the historical cost of inventory is much more challenging than it may seem at first glance. One challenge is selecting an appropriate cost flow method. GAAP permits some flexibility in this area, and several methods are currently used in the business community.

Microsoft Corporation, for example, uses the first-in, first-out (FIFO) method. Walt Disney Company uses the average cost method. Nike, Inc., uses the last-in, first-out (LIFO) method. McDonnell Douglas Corporation uses the specific identification method to account for its inventory of MD-80 aircraft. Many companies, such as Quaker Oats, use more than one inventory costing method.

INVENTORIES

Inventories are goods that are held for sale in the ordinary course of business and goods that are in production or that will soon be used in production. A **service business,** such as a legal firm, normally has no inventories. In contrast, inventories are one of the most important assets of **merchandising businesses** and **manufacturing businesses,** which typically derive most of their revenues from sales of inventories. In January 1993, for example, Kroger Company had over $1.5 billion of inventory, an amount that represented about 72% of current assets and 36% of total assets. Moreover, cost of goods sold is usually the largest expense of merchandising and manufacturing businesses. It is not surprising, then, that the managers of merchandising and manufacturing companies often devote substantial resources to inventory planning and control. Furthermore, users of financial statements regard inventory information as extremely important when they make investment, lending, and similar decisions.

In this chapter and the next, we discuss the accounting valuation of inventories. Inventories are physical resources, and our primary concern is how accountants obtain a financial representation of such resources for external reporting purposes. Most of our discussion focuses on **inventory valuation methods,** often called **inventory pricing methods,** that companies use to prepare their external financial statements in accordance with GAAP. This chapter presents an overview of basic valuation methods; Chapter 9 introduces several additional methods.

ACQUISITION OF INVENTORIES

A merchandising company buys finished inventory and later resells it. In contrast, a manufacturing company produces its inventory and, in doing so, incurs the following **manufacturing (or production) costs:**

1. **Direct materials.** Raw materials costs that can be traced directly and practically to units of the firm's product. In the case of a manufacturer of wooden desks, for example, the cost of the wood is a direct materials cost.
2. **Direct labor.** Labor costs that can be traced directly and practically to units of the firm's product. For the desk manufacturer, the labor costs of the employees who assemble the desks are direct labor costs.
3. **Manufacturing overhead.** All manufacturing costs, other than direct materials and direct labor, necessary to construct the company's product. For the desk manufacturer, examples are the costs of factory maintenance, the depreciation of factory equipment, and the glue used on certain parts of each desk.

CLASSIFICATION OF INVENTORIES

A merchandising company has one class of inventory, commonly called *merchandise* (or *merchandise inventory*). A manufacturing company, however, may have the following four categories of inventory:

1. **Raw materials.** Goods that can be traced directly to units of the firm's product. An example is the desk manufacturer's inventory of wood.
2. **Factory supplies.** Goods that can be traced only indirectly to units of the firm's product. An example is the desk manufacturer's supply of glue. Generally, it is not practical to trace glue to specific desks. The cost of factory supplies used is an element of overhead that is commonly called **indirect materials.**
3. **Work (goods) in process.** Goods that are partially completed. Goods in process have been assigned appropriate manufacturing costs and will remain in production until completed.
4. **Finished goods.** Products that are completed and ready for sale. Finished goods have been assigned their full share of manufacturing costs.

FLOW OF INVENTORY COSTS

Exhibit 8–1 compares the typical flow of inventory costs in a merchandising company with that in a manufacturing concern. Note that inventory costs are initially accounted for as assets. In other words, a company's inventory is first measured at its historical cost. To implement the matching principle, the costs are expensed in the period when the inventory is sold. In this way, the revenue generated by the sale of inventory can be related to the costs incurred to purchase or produce it.

Asset/Liability Measurement

Matching

A merchandising company and a manufacturing company calculate cost of goods sold in somewhat different ways. In the comparison shown in Exhibit 8–2, we assume a periodic inventory system.

Note in Exhibit 8–2 that a merchandising company adds the cost of its net purchases to the cost of its beginning inventory to derive the cost of goods available for sale. Because a manufacturing company *produces* (rather than *purchases*) its finished goods inventory, it adds the cost of goods manufactured. We discussed the calculation of net purchases in Chapter 5. The computation of the cost of goods manufactured by Parker Company is shown in

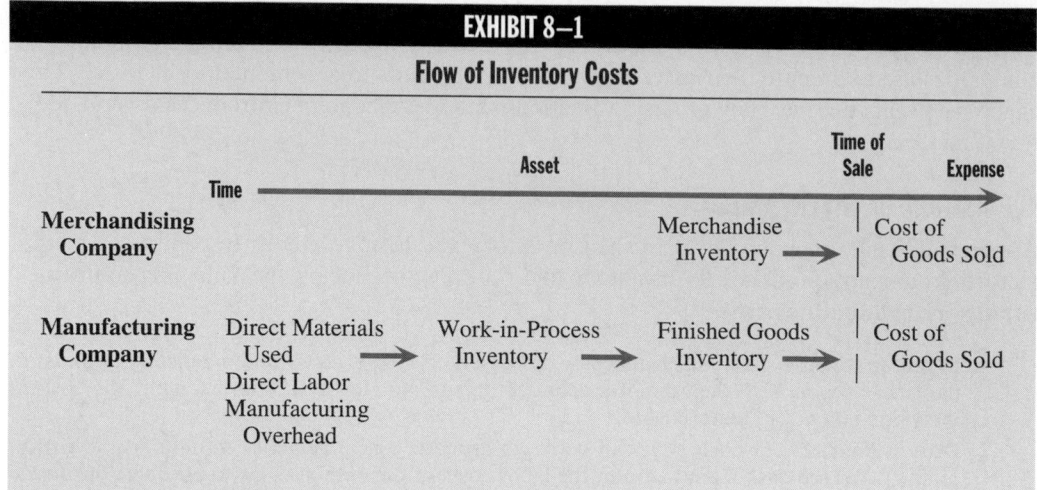

EXHIBIT 8–1

Flow of Inventory Costs

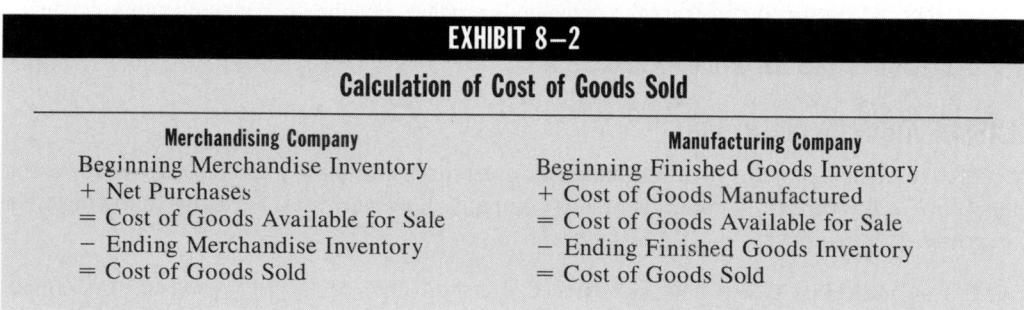

EXHIBIT 8–2

Calculation of Cost of Goods Sold

Merchandising Company	Manufacturing Company
Beginning Merchandise Inventory	Beginning Finished Goods Inventory
+ Net Purchases	+ Cost of Goods Manufactured
= Cost of Goods Available for Sale	= Cost of Goods Available for Sale
− Ending Merchandise Inventory	− Ending Finished Goods Inventory
= Cost of Goods Sold	= Cost of Goods Sold

Exhibit 8–3 (dollar amounts assumed). The schedule of cost of goods manufactured is generally used for internal purposes and is seldom published.

Observe in Exhibit 8–3 that to calculate cost of goods manufactured, we add the total manufacturing costs incurred during the period to the beginning work-in-process inventory. The total ($257,000) tells us the amount of manufacturing costs that we must account for during the period. From this total we subtract the cost of the ending work-in-process inventory (the partially completed goods on hand at the end of the period) to derive the cost of goods manufactured during the period. As noted in Exhibit 8–2, the cost of goods manufactured is included in the calculation of a manufacturing company's cost of goods sold.

As our discussion suggests, a manufacturing company accounts for inventories somewhat differently than does a merchandising company. For example, many manufacturing companies use **direct costing** (also called **variable costing**) for internal reporting purposes, because this method enables managers to better plan and control their company's operations. Under direct costing, the accountant classifies all manufacturing costs as either variable or fixed. Variable manufacturing costs vary in total in direct proportion to changes in production volume. They include direct materials, direct labor, and variable overhead. Fixed manufacturing costs, in contrast, remain constant in total as production volume changes over a relevant range of production. Fixed manufacturing costs are confined to such overhead costs as property taxes and depreciation. Under the direct costing method, the accountant records as inventory costs only the variable manufacturing costs. Fixed overhead costs are expensed in the period in which they are incurred, because it is assumed that a company incurs these costs primarily to allow production to occur.

EXHIBIT 8–3

Parker Company
Schedule of Cost of Goods Manufactured
For the Year Ended December 31

Direct materials used		
Raw materials inventory, Jan. 1	$ 23,000	
Add: Net purchases of raw materials	157,000	
Cost of raw materials available for use	180,000	
Less: Raw materials inventory, Dec. 31	25,000	$155,000
Direct labor		47,000
Manufacturing overhead		
Indirect labor	12,000	
Indirect materials	3,000	
Factory utilities	5,000	
Depreciation of factory building	3,500	
Depreciation of factory equipment	6,000	
Taxes on factory properties	7,000	
Miscellaneous factory expenses	1,500	38,000
Total manufacturing costs incurred during the year		240,000
Add: Work-in-process inventory, Jan. 1		17,000
Total manufacturing costs to account for		257,000
Less: Work-in-process inventory, Dec. 31		15,000
Cost of goods manufactured		$242,000

Direct costing contrasts with **absorption costing,** in which fixed overhead costs are treated as a part of the cost of inventory. Proponents of absorption costing point out that because both variable and fixed overhead costs are normally necessary to produce specific goods, both costs should be inventoried. Generally accepted accounting principles require the use of absorption costing for external reporting purposes, because most accountants view fixed overhead as an important component of the historical cost of inventory that is manufactured. Direct costing is not acceptable under GAAP.

Many manufacturing companies use standard costs to account for their inventories. Primarily a management tool, **standard costing** requires a company to accumulate inventory costs using amounts that *should be* incurred to manufacture the inventory rather than actual costs. Standard costing allows a company to detect variances between what it should cost to produce a product and what it actually costs. Standard costs are acceptable for external reporting under GAAP, however, if they reasonably approximate actual costs determined using a recognized cost flow method. Peculiarities in accounting for inventories of manufacturing companies, such as direct costing and standard costing, are covered more extensively in cost accounting courses.

The objective of inventory management is to maintain an adequate supply of goods while minimizing the investment in inventory and other carrying costs. If a company has too much inventory, it incurs unnecessary costs. If it has too little, however, the company may suffer costly production delays and lost sales. In recent years, the computer has become a vital part of most modern inventory systems. Some companies have used computers to implement **just-in-time (JIT) inventory systems.** When a company has a JIT system, its production, inventory, and marketing systems are linked so that the company acquires inventory only when immediately needed for production or sale. To help ensure that inventory is acquired only as needed, companies with JIT systems usually contract to purchase goods from a

NATURE OF THE INVENTORY VALUATION PROBLEM

relatively small number of vendors. Wal-Mart Stores, for example, acquires many of its household products from Procter & Gamble.

Inventory accounting problems would be relatively simple if a company instantaneously sold all the inventory that it purchased or produced. In most cases, however, even in companies that have JIT systems, there is a lag between the time goods are purchased or produced and the time they are sold. As a result, most companies have an inventory of unsold goods on hand at the end of the accounting period, and accountants must then resolve the question of how to allocate the cost of goods available for sale between (1) the goods on hand (ending inventory) and (2) the goods sold.

The accountant may determine cost of goods sold *residually,* that is, by subtracting the cost of the ending inventory from the cost of goods available for sale. To do this, the accountant must value the ending inventory directly, which means resolving the following important questions:

1. What is the physical quantity of goods on hand?
2. What is the accounting valuation of those goods?

DETERMINATION OF INVENTORY QUANTITIES

The method for determining the physical quantity of goods on hand differs depending on whether a company uses a periodic or a perpetual inventory system. Regardless of the system used, the accountant must understand the general principles to determine which goods properly belong in inventory and which goods do not.

PERIODIC VERSUS PERPETUAL INVENTORY SYSTEM

Under a **periodic inventory system,** inventory quantities are *not* maintained on a day-to-day basis in the accounting records. Instead, at the end of each accounting period, the quantity of unsold goods is determined by a physical count. The accountant then determines the inventory's cost by using one of the generally accepted inventory cost flow methods discussed later in the chapter. The inventory cost thus derived is subtracted from the cost of goods available for sale to determine the cost of goods sold. In a periodic system, therefore, cost of goods sold is a residual figure that includes the cost of goods actually sold as well as the cost of those lost by theft, spoilage, and similar causes. Although a periodic system is not ideal for inventory planning and control, it is relatively inexpensive and is often appropriate for products that turn over rapidly and have low unit costs, such as groceries and hardware.

In contrast, a **perpetual inventory system** requires the accountant to maintain continuous records of the quantity of inventory on hand. Under a perpetual system, an account may be established for each product; these accounts are kept in an **inventory subsidiary ledger.** The account for each product shows increases and decreases, as well as the balance on hand. In a complete perpetual system, the subsidiary ledger accounts are maintained in cost dollars as well as in units. Consequently, the balance in the merchandise inventory control account in the general ledger should agree with the total of the individual account balances in the subsidiary ledger.

In a perpetual system, it is still desirable to physically count the inventory at least once each year, but the count need not occur at year-end. This count tests the accuracy of the perpetual records. An actual count frequently reveals differences between the records and the physical units on hand. These differences may exist for several reasons, including theft, evaporation, and inaccurate recording. When a careful count indicates differences, the accounting records should be appropriately adjusted. If, for example, the accounting records show inventory on hand costing $10,000 but the physical count indicates only $9,885, the following entry is necessary:

Inventory Shortage   115
    Merchandise Inventory   115
    (To record inventory shortage. $10,000 − $9,885 = $115.)

A TONIC FOR THE BUSINESS CYCLE

Just-in-time has come of age. Keeping inventories lean to hold down costs was easy when business was slow and manufacturers had plenty of spare capacity to meet unexpected demand. Now, with a stronger economy, companies face the possibility of losing sales because their shelves are empty.

Nonetheless, manufacturers are resisting the temptation to refill warehouses. Instead, they are sticking with JIT, which uses automated purchasing, production, and sales systems to allow companies to receive parts just prior to assembly. The result: smaller inventories of both parts and final products. Indeed, unlike most previous recoveries, inventories have risen slower than sales.

Staying lean can save business billions of dollars freeing money for investment or dividends. And it may help explain why the recession of 1990–91 was fairly mild and why the economy was so slow getting back up to speed. In the long run, the trend to lean inventories should act as a kind of wonder drug for the business cycle, boosting the lows and tempering the highs.

Still Wary

Not too many years ago, business cycles were in good part driven by the ups and downs of inventories. As sales boomed, producers built up stocks in anticipation of ever-greater demand. But if the economy slowed, companies suddenly found themselves with warehouses full of television sets and acres of unsold cars. Workers were laid off as production fell. Only after shelves finally emptied would workers be rehired. Then, as the economy strengthened, businesses would build up inventories, and the whole circle would start again.

This time, things seem quite different. When the recession started in mid-1990, companies already had their inventories under control. So the ratio of inventories to sales rose by a meager 5%, compared with 15% during the 1981–82 recession.

Despite a big pickup in demand in recent months, businesses are being cautious. Current inventory levels are a mere 2% to 3% above optimum levels, figures economist Michael K. Evans. And he doesn't expect them to grow much more. "It looks like the inventory buildup is pretty much complete," says Evans.

That's because new inventory systems have become ingrained. General Electric Co.'s appliance division is still catching up with consumers, who have been buying refrigerators and the like at a breakneck pace. But Richard L. Burke, vice-president for purchasing, technology, and manufacturing, has no regrets about focusing on short production cycles and fast turnarounds. "It's absolutely worth the price," he says. "We're going to leanness everywhere."

No Retreat

JIT means that companies also have to get a better handle on production and quality, since they can't pull stock off the shelf to replace rejects or cover for manufacturing problems. Last fall, General Motors Corp. fell short of production goals by 90,000 cars and trucks, largely because of snafus at its Tonawanda (N.Y.) engine plant. But there won't be any inventory backsliding at GM. Says Alan S. Dawes, executive in charge of operations at GM's auto components group: "There's absolutely no way we're going away from just-in-time."

That attitude may do more than help turn around GM. It may also improve the nation's long-term economic health. Leaner inventories, says Northwestern University economist Robert J. Gordon "may have made a permanent contribution to reducing the impact of the business cycle."

SOURCE: Howard Gleckman, Zachary Schiller, and James B. Treece, "A Tonic for the Business Cycle," *Business Week,* April 4, 1994, p. 57.

Materiality

The inventory shortage is a loss account that, if material in amount, should be reported separately in the income statement. Many companies simply report inventory shortages as part of cost of goods sold. This practice is justified on the ground that some shortages may be considered a normal cost in the selling process.

Although the perpetual system is more costly than the periodic system to implement, it facilitates better inventory planning and control. In the past, perpetual records were used primarily for low-volume, high-cost items such as jewelry, fur coats, and automobiles. In recent years, however, the widespread use of electronic computers has enabled companies to maintain perpetual records for a greater variety of inventory items. With computers, companies can conveniently store and retrieve large amounts of data in a cost-effective manner. Many companies account for part of their inventories on a periodic basis and the remainder on a perpetual basis.

In a periodic inventory system, merchandise purchases are debited to the Purchases account. Throughout the accounting period, therefore, the Merchandise Inventory account contains only the balance that was on hand at the beginning of the period. At the end of the period, the accountant makes an adjusting entry to record the ending inventory as well as the cost of goods sold for the entire period, as discussed in Chapter 5. In contrast, under a perpetual system, the Merchandise Inventory and Cost of Goods Sold accounts are continually maintained. Merchandise purchases are therefore charged directly to the Inventory account. Moreover, an entry to record a sale is accompanied by an entry that reduces the Inventory account and recognizes an increase in Cost of Goods Sold. At the end of the accounting period, an adjusting entry is not required, because the Inventory account reflects the balance on hand and the Cost of Goods Sold account reflects the expense incurred during the entire period. The proper accounting for selected merchandise transactions under periodic and perpetual inventory systems is shown in Exhibit 8–4.

GOODS TO INCLUDE IN INVENTORY

The general rule for determining what items to include in inventory is that goods belong to the entity that has legal title, regardless of where they are located. Consequently, when title to goods passes from seller to buyer, the seller should record a sale and exclude the goods from inventory. The buyer in turn should record a purchase and include the goods in inventory.

The Uniform Commercial Code provides that title to goods may pass at any tme expressly agreed to by buyer and seller. When the time of title passage is not expressly agreed on, the buyer takes title when goods exist and are identified to the contract, and the seller has completed performance in regard to delivering the goods. If goods are shipped **FOB (free on board) shipping point,** title passes to the buyer when the seller delivers the goods to the carrier. Title to goods shipped **FOB destination** passes when the goods arrive at their ultimate destination. If the buyer agrees to pick up the goods at the seller's place of business, title passes when the seller has completed the goods and identified them to the contract.

Application of the legal title rule may pose problems when a company owns goods that are located elsewhere or when it holds goods that belong to someone else. We discuss these problems in the following sections.

Goods in Transit

Materiality

During an accounting period, the accountant normally records purchases when goods are received and sales when goods are shipped, regardless of the precise moment at which title passes. This procedure is expedient, and because title usually passes in the same period, no material misstatements occur in the financial statements.

EXHIBIT 8–4					
Accounting under Periodic and Perpetual Inventory Systems					
Transaction	Periodic Inventory System			Perpetual Inventory System	
Purchase merchandise costing $4,000 on account	Purchases	4,000		Merchandise Inventory	4,000	
	Accounts Payable		4,000	Accounts Payable		4,000
Pay freight of $45 on purchase	Transportation-In	45		Merchandise Inventory	45	
	Cash		45	Cash		45
Return defective merchandise costing $250	Accounts Payable	250		Accounts Payable	250	
	Purchase Returns		250	Merchandise Inventory		250
Sell goods costing $3,000 on account for $6,000	Accounts Receivable	6,000		Accounts Receivable	6,000	
	Sales		6,000	Sales		6,000
				Cost of Goods Sold	3,000	
				Merchandise Inventory		3,000

On the other hand, the accountant should carefully analyze the invoice terms of goods that are in transit at the end of an accounting period to determine who has legal title. The analysis should encompass goods purchased as well as goods sold. Goods shipped FOB shipping point belong to the buyer; those shipped FOB destination belong to the seller. When analyzing goods in transit, the accountant should examine invoices for several days before and after the end of the accounting period to ensure a proper cutoff at year-end.

CONSIGNED GOODS

A **consignment** is a method of marketing goods in which the owner (the **consignor**) transfers physical possession of certain goods to an agent (the **consignee**) who sells them on the owner's behalf. Goods on consignment should be included in the consignor's inventory and excluded from the consignee's inventory. Similarly, goods in the hands of others for sale, storage, processing, or other reasons should be included in the inventory of the party holding title. Accounting for consignments is covered in advanced accounting courses.

In accordance with the asset/liability measurement principle, the quantity of inventory on hand should be valued initially at its historical cost. Two questions must be answered when determining an inventory cost valuation:

1. What costs should be included in inventory?
2. What method should be used to associate inventory costs with the physical units on hand?

COSTS TO INCLUDE IN INVENTORY

An accountant must differentiate between product costs and period costs. **Product costs** "attach to" the inventory. These costs are initially capitalized and are regarded as assets (i.e., inventory). When the inventory is later sold, the product costs expire and are therefore charged to expense (cost of goods sold). In contrast, **period costs** are expensed in the period in which they are incurred. In other words, period costs are not inventoried, because their relationship to the product (inventory) is generally considered too difficult to trace. Selling expenses, general and administrative expenses, and income tax expense are examples of period costs.

Product costs are incurred, either directly or indirectly, to purchase or produce inventory as well as to bring the inventory to a condition and location for sale. These costs include direct materials, direct labor, and overhead. They also include the invoice cost of purchased merchandise as well as the costs of inbound transportation, insurance, inspection, handling, warehousing, and purchasing.

The specific content of product costs varies somewhat between companies. Many companies use only the invoice cost plus the cost of inbound transportation to value inventories of purchased goods. Other costs that should in theory be inventoried (such as insurance, handling, and purchasing costs) are treated as period costs. This treatment is justified on the ground that it is often impossible to meaningfully allocate certain indirect costs to inventory. The treatment is considered acceptable if a company applies it *consistently* over time to either a certain portion or to all of its inventories. Inventory costs capitalized for financial reporting purposes may differ from those capitalized for income tax purposes.

Generally accepted accounting principles do not permit a company to capitalize the interest cost associated with inventories that are routinely manufactured or otherwise produced in large quantities on a repetitive basis. However, interest cost should be capitalized if it is a material part of the cost of acquiring inventory items that are constructed as discrete projects, such as ships.[1] For these items, interest cost represents an important component of

> **INVENTORY VALUATION AT COST**
>
> Asset/Liability Measurement
>
> Consistency
>
> Materiality

---

[1] *FASB Statement of Financial Accounting Standards No. 34,* "Capitalization of Interest Cost," 1979.

historical cost. Companies should also capitalize interest as part of the historical cost of acquiring certain plant assets. We explain interest capitalization more fully in Chapter 11.

Invoice Cost

The invoice cost itself is the largest component of product cost for purchased inventory. To determine the invoice cost, **trade discounts** are subtracted from the list price and are not entered in the accounting records.[2] Theory and practice usually differ about whether the invoice cost component of product cost should also exclude **cash discounts.**[3]

In theory, the cost of purchases (and of inventory) should be measured net of cash discounts allowable. This is known as the **net method** of recording purchases; it is compared with the **gross method** in Exhibit 8–5. The cost measured under the net method represents the cash-equivalent price on the date of purchase and therefore the correct historical cost. Cash discounts encourage early payment. Any discount not taken represents the cost of engaging in a deferred payment transaction. Accordingly, this cost should be shown as a financing expense on the income statement.

In practice, most companies record purchases (and inventory) at gross invoice amounts. Cash discounts taken are recorded in the Purchase Discounts account at the time of payment, and this balance is deducted from purchases when measuring cost of goods sold.[4] This procedure is theoretically deficient in two major respects. First, it technically violates the matching principle, because discounts are recorded only when cash is paid rather than when the purchases that give rise to the discounts are made. Second, the procedure does not allocate discounts taken between goods sold and those on hand. This tends to understate cost of goods sold and overstate net income and ending inventory. Despite its theoretical shortcomings, the gross method is supported on the practical grounds that (1) it is more convenient than the net method from a bookkeeping standpoint and (2) if applied consistently over time, it usually produces no material errors in the financial statements.

Matching

Consistency

Materiality

Transportation Costs

If practical, the costs of inbound transportation should be allocated to specific units of inventory purchased. This procedure, which is facilitated by the use of a perpetual inventory system, permits transportation charges to be appropriately reflected in cost of goods sold as well as in ending inventory. Transportation costs are inventoried because they are an important part of the cost of acquiring goods. In the purchase of coal, for example, rail transportation costs constitute a substantial portion of inventoriable costs.

In a periodic inventory system, inbound transportation charges are usually accumulated in a nominal account entitled Transportation-In or Freight-In. Theoretically, the balance in this account at the end of an accounting period should be allocated in a reasonable manner between cost of goods sold and ending inventory. Instead of implementing this approach, firms often use the more expedient alternative of including all transportation-in costs in the

---

[2]A **trade discount** is a reduction from a catalog list price granted by manufacturers and wholesalers of certain products. The use of trade discounts enables a company (1) to revise its prices periodically without having to reprint its catalogs and (2) to set different prices for different types of customers.

[3]A **cash discount** is a reduction from the amount of an invoice that is offered for early payment of cash. The purpose of a cash discount is to encourage early payment. A cash discount is usually expressed in terms such as "2/10, n/30." These terms mean that the purchaser may deduct 2% from the amount of the invoice if payment is made within 10 days of the invoice date. A purchaser who fails to pay within 10 days must pay the entire invoice amount within 30 days of the invoice date. As we explained in Chapter 7, the effective annual interest cost associated with not paying within 10 days is 36.7%. It is usually advantageous for a company to take all available cash discounts, even if the company must borrow money to do so.

[4]Some companies treat purchase discounts as financial revenue similar to interest. This treatment lacks theoretical support. A purchaser of goods who pays for them within the discount period has not thereby made a loan to the seller. Because no loan has been made, no financial revenue has been realized.

EXHIBIT 8–5

Net and Gross Methods of Recording Purchases

Transaction	Net Method		Gross Method	
July 1				

ABC Company purchases merchandise for $100, terms 2/10, n/30.	Purchases* 98
	    Accounts Payable 98
			Purchases* 100
			    Accounts Payable 100	

Alternative Assumption No. 1				
July 10				

ABC Company pays within the discount period.	Accounts Payable 98
	    Cash 98
			Accounts Payable 100
			    Purchase Discounts 2
			    Cash 98	

Alternative Assumption No. 2				
July 30				

ABC Company pays after the discount period.	Accounts Payable 98
	Discounts Lost (or
	   Interest Expense) 2
	    Cash 100
			Accounts Payable 100
			    Cash 100	

*Assuming a periodic inventory system.

---

calculation of net purchases. Although the expedient approach tends to overstate cost of goods sold and understate net income and ending inventory, it is often supported on the grounds of conservatism, materiality, and consistency of application. | Conservatism
Materiality
Consistency

INVENTORY COST FLOW METHODS

Inventory costs flow into a business and are treated as assets when goods are purchased or manufactured; they flow out and are charged to expense when goods are sold. The difference between the cost inflows and the cost outflows represents the cost of the inventory on hand.

If inventory unit cost prices remained constant over time, the process of inventory cost determination would be relatively simple. That is, it would simply involve multiplying the quantity of each inventory item on hand by its constant unit cost and summing the results. In reality, of course, unit costs usually fluctuate. With inflation, they tend to rise over time. The reality of fluctuating unit costs underscores the critical importance of the various inventory cost flow methods. When reflecting on these methods, keep the following points in mind:

1. Each method leads to a determination of inventory and cost of goods sold based on historical costs. | Asset/Liability Measurement

2. A company can use one method to account for a certain portion of its inventories (such as raw materials) and other methods to account for different portions (such as finished goods).

3. The method(s) adopted should be used consistently over time and should be disclosed in the financial statements. | Consistency
Disclosure

Specific Identification Method

The **specific identification method** requires a company to maintain detailed records that permit the accountant to identify individually the actual unit costs of (1) inventory items on hand and (2) inventory items sold. The method may be used with either a periodic or a perpetual inventory system. Each item of inventory is identified (using a code on a sales tag, for example) with its actual unit cost. When an item is sold, the difference between its selling price and its actual cost represents the gross margin.

The major argument for the specific identification method is that the flow of inventory costs corresponds with the actual physical flow of goods. With specific identification, we account for the actual costs of units sold and on hand.

The major arguments against specific identification method follow:

1. It may permit management to manipulate income. Suppose, for example, that a company offers two identical gold watches for $500 each. Due to recent fluctuations in gold prices, one watch costs $250 and the other $350. Management can earn a gross profit of either $250 or $150 from the sale of one watch simply by choosing which watch to sell.

2. The method is very costly to implement, even with high-speed electronic computers. The detailed record-keeping requirements usually limit the applicability of the specific identification method to inventories that consist of relatively expensive, slow-moving items, such as automobiles, farm equipment, art objects, fur coats, jewelry, and long-term construction projects.

Cost Flow Methods Based on Assumptions

Because it is rarely feasible to specifically identify inventory unit costs, most companies make an **assumption** about the way inventory costs flow through the business. The major cost flow assumptions available under GAAP and the method of implementing each are as follows:

Cost Flow Assumption	Cost Flow Method
1. Cost flow is in the same order in which costs were incurred.	1. First-in, first out (FIFO)
2. Cost flow is an average of the costs incurred.	2. Average cost
3. Cost flow is in the reverse order in which costs were incurred.	3. Last-in, first-out (LIFO)

A 1993 survey of the annual reports of 600 companies found a total of 1,011 disclosures of inventory cost flow methods. Some companies obviously use more than one method. The use of FIFO, LIFO, and average cost was reported by 415, 358, and 193 companies, respectively.[5]

In reflecting on the FIFO, average cost, and LIFO methods, bear in mind that each method reflects an **assumed cost flow pattern.** Any method may be used *regardless of the way goods physically flow through the business.* For example, goods may (and usually do) physically flow in the FIFO manner, yet LIFO may be used as the cost flow method.

Jackson Company is a merchandising concern that, for accounting purposes, identifies its inventory items using a combination of numbers and letters. The following inventory data for the company's Product 19-C for the current year will be used to illustrate the application of the FIFO, average cost, and LIFO methods.

Date	Product 19-C	Number of Units	Unit Cost	Total Cost
Jan. 1	Inventory on hand	300	$5	$ 1,500
Mar. 21	Purchase	900	6	5,400
Aug. 19	Purchase	600	7	4,200
Nov. 3	Purchase	200	8	1,600
	Available for sale	2,000		$12,700

We will assume that 800 units of Product 19-C were sold on May 27 and another 800 units were sold on October 9. A physical count on December 31 indicates that 400 units of Product 19-C are on hand.

---

[5]*Accounting Trends & Techniques,* 47th ed. (New York: AICPA, 1993), p. 145.

First-In, First-Out (FIFO) Method.   The FIFO method is based on the assumption that inventory costs should be matched with sales revenue in the same order in which the costs were incurred. The most recent costs incurred are therefore used in determining the cost of inventory on hand. Assuming a periodic system, the cost of the 400 units of Product 19-C is determined as follows:

Most recent costs (Nov. 3 purchase)	200 units @ $8	$1,600
Next most recent costs (Aug. 19 purchase)	200 units @ $7	$1,400
Inventory, Dec. 31	400	$3,000

Recall that cost of goods sold is a residual figure determined by subtracting the cost of the ending inventory from the cost of goods available for sale. For Product 19-C, cost of goods sold under FIFO is $9,700 ($12,700 − $3,000). Note that under the FIFO method, cost of goods sold consists of the earliest costs incurred [(300 units @ $5) + (900 units @ $6) + (400 units @ $7) = $9,700].

The FIFO method produces the same cost figures regardless of whether a company uses a periodic or a perpetual system. For example, if Jackson Company maintained perpetual records for Product 19-C, it would use a form similar to the one shown in Exhibit 8–6. Observe in the exhibit that the cost of the ending inventory and the cost of goods sold are still $3,000 and $9,700, respectively.

The following summarizes the major arguments for FIFO.

1. On the balance sheet, FIFO produces an ending inventory cost based on the most recent acquisition prices. This cost frequently approximates current replacement cost, which tends to add *relevance* to the inventory measurement reported on the balance sheet.
2. FIFO's assumed cost flow pattern corresponds closely to the physical flow of goods in most businesses. Therefore, when goods physically move in a first-in, first-out manner, FIFO approximates specific identification. Unlike specific identification, however, FIFO gives management little opportunity to manipulate income.

EXHIBIT 8–6
Perpetual Inventory—FIFO Method

Date	Purchased Number of Units	Unit Cost	Total Cost	Sold Number of Units	Unit Cost	Total Cost	Balance Number of Units	Unit Cost	Total Cost
Jan. 1							300	$5	$1,500
Mar. 21	900	$6	$5,400				300	5	1,500
							900	6	5,400
May 27				300	$5	$1,500			
				500	6	3,000	400	6	2,400
Aug. 19	600	7	4,200				400	6	2,400
							600	7	4,200
Oct. 9				400	6	2,400			
				400	7	2,800	200	7	1,400
Nov. 3	200	8	1,600				200	7	1,400 } Ending
							200	8	1,600 } inventory = $3,000

Cost of goods sold $9,700

Matching

The major argument against FIFO is its failure to match current costs with current revenues on the income statement. FIFO produces a cost of goods sold figure that is based on the *earliest* costs incurred. These costs often depart considerably from current replacement costs. Observe that because the balance sheet and income statement **articulate** with each other, the "balance sheet advantage" of FIFO may be offset by the "income statement disadvantage."

Average Cost Method.   The average cost method is based on the assumption that a weighted average of all inventory costs should be used to measure inventory cost flow. This average is computed by dividing the total cost of goods available for sale by the total number of units available for sale. Assuming a periodic system, the cost of the 400 units of Product 19-C is determined as follows:

Weighted average unit cost	$12,700 ÷ 2,000 = $6.35
Inventory, Dec. 31	400 units @ $6.35 = $2,540

Cost of goods sold is therefore $10,160 ($12,700 − $2,540). We can verify this by multiplying the 1,600 units sold by $6.35 (1600 × $6.35 = $10,160). Note that a *weighted average,* rather than a *simple average,* unit cost figure is used. A weighted average reflects the number of units acquired at each price; a simple average [($5 + $6 + $7 + $8) ÷ 4 = $6.50] does not.

When used with a perpetual inventory system, the average cost method is called the **moving average method.** Under this method, a new weighted average unit cost must be *computed after every purchase;* the average is therefore said to "move." The moving average method for Product 19-C is illustrated in Exhibit 8–7.

Observe carefully that a new weighted average unit cost is computed after each purchase. This is done by dividing the total cost of goods available for sale (immediately after the purchase) by the total number of units available for sale (immediately after the purchase). For example, the weighted average unit cost after the first purchase (March 21) is computed as follows:

Jan. 1	Inventory	300 units @ $5	$1,500
Mar. 21	Purchase	900 units @ $6	$5,400
	Available for sale immediately after		
	Mar. 21 purchase	1,200 units	$6,900

Weighted average unit cost $6,900 ÷ 1,200 = $5.75

The same procedure is used to determine the weighted average unit cost after the August 19 and November 3 purchases.

Under the average cost method, the cost of the ending inventory usually differs, depending on whether a company uses a periodic or a perpetual inventory system. It follows that when ending inventories differ, cost of goods sold figures also differ. These differences are shown below for Product 19-C.

Average Cost Method	Ending Inventory	+	Cost of Goods Sold	=	Cost of Goods Available for Sale
Periodic system	$2,540		$10,160		$12,700
Perpetual system	2,900		9,800		12,700

The following are the major arguments for the average cost method:

1. It generally produces ending inventory and cost of goods sold measurements that fall between those produced under FIFO and LIFO. Thus, average cost is essentially a compromise solution to the complex question of how one should assume that inventory costs flow through a business.

EXHIBIT 8-7

Perpetual Inventory—Moving Average Method

	Purchased			Sold			Balance		
Date	Number of Units	Unit Cost	Total Cost	Number of Units	Unit Cost	Total Cost	Number of Units	Unit Cost	Total Cost
Jan. 1							300	$5.00	$1,500
Mar. 21	900	$6	$5,400				1,200	5.75*	6,900
May 27				800	$5.75	$4,600	400	5.75	2,300
Aug. 19	600	7	4,200				1,000	6.50*	6,500
Oct. 9				800	6.50	5,200	200	6.50	1,300
Nov. 3	200	8	1,600				400	7.25*	2,900 } Ending inventory = $2,900

Cost of goods sold $9,800

*Weighted average unit cost is computed after each purchase.

2. It is relatively easy to apply, especially with computers.

3. It affords management little opportunity to manipulate income.

The major arguments against average cost are as follows:

1. It is not as accurate as FIFO in approximating the current cost of the ending inventory on the balance sheet.

2. It is not as accurate as LIFO in approximating the current cost of goods sold on the income statement.

3. It corresponds with the physical flow of goods only when goods available for sale are sold in essentially a random pattern. This may occur with inventories of liquid products such as chemicals and petroleum, but does not occur with most products.

Last-In, First-Out (LIFO) Method. The LIFO method assumes that inventory costs should be matched with sales revenue in the reverse order in which the costs were incurred (the opposite of FIFO).[6] Inventory is therefore valued at the earliest costs incurred. Referring to Jackson Company and assuming a *periodic* system, we determine the LIFO cost of the ending inventory of 400 units of Product 19-C as follows:

Earliest costs (Jan. 1 inventory)	300 units @ $5	$1,500
Next earliest costs (Mar. 21 purchase)	100 units @ $6	$ 600
Inventory, Dec. 31	400	$2,100

Observe that the ending inventory of 400 units is divided into *two layers* (300 units @ $5 and 100 units @ $6). Cost of goods sold is $10,600 ($12,700 − $2,100) and consists of the most recent costs incurred [(200 units @ $8) + (600 units @ $7) + (800 units @ $6) = $10,600].

---

[6]LIFO is an outgrowth of the **base stock method,** which some companies in the United States used early in the 20th century. Because the base stock method is not acceptable for income tax purposes and is not considered an important method for financial reporting purposes, it is not illustrated in this textbook

			EXHIBIT 8–8					

Perpetual Inventory—LIFO Method

	Purchased			Sold			Balance		
Date	Number of Units	Unit Cost	Total Cost	Number of Units	Unit Cost	Total Cost	Number of Units	Unit Cost	Total Cost
Jan. 1							300	$5	$1,500
Mar. 21	900	$6	$5,400				300	5	1,500
							900	6	5,400
May 27				800	$6	$4,800	300	5	1,500
							100	6	600
Aug. 19	600	7	4,200				300	5	1,500
							100	6	600
							600	7	4,200
Oct. 9				600	7	4,200			
				100	6	600			
				100	5	500	200	5	1,000
Nov. 3	200	8	1,600				200	5	1,000 ⎱ Ending
							200	8	1,600 ⎰ inventory = $2,600

Cost of goods sold $10,100

The application of LIFO for Product 19-C using a *perpetual* system is shown in Exhibit 8–8. Under the perpetual system, units sold are costed at the time of sale. Because LIFO is therefore applied currently throughout the period rather than only at the period's end, LIFO results usually differ between a periodic and a perpetual system. These differences are shown below for Product 19-C.

LIFO Method	Ending Inventory	+	Cost of Goods Sold	=	Cost of Goods Available for Sale
Periodic system	$2,100		$10,600		$12,700
Perpetual system	2,600		10,100		12,700

Observe that for Product 19-C, cost of goods sold is higher under the periodic than under the perpetual system. This occurred because of the timing of the purchases and sales and because the unit cost prices of Product 19-C rose steadily during the current year. In our example, the cost of goods sold differences relate to the sale on October 9. Under the perpetual system, the October 9 sale was costed using the most recent cost prices at that time [(600 units @ $7) + (100 units @ $6) + (100 units @ $5) = $5,300]. Under the periodic system, the October 9 sale was costed using the most recent cost prices as of the end of the year [(200 units @ $8) + (600 units @ $7) = $5,800]. Many companies that experience rising inventory costs use LIFO for tax purposes, because it tends to produce a higher cost of goods sold and therefore less income taxes. The tax law states that companies using LIFO for tax purposes must also use it for financial reporting purposes. Consequently, a company that uses LIFO with a perpetual system often restates its cost of goods sold and inventory at year-end to conform with the results that would have occurred under a periodic system. This restatement is done for income tax and external financial reporting purposes.

Most companies that use LIFO for income tax and financial reporting purposes maintain their inventory records throughout the year using a different cost flow method, such as FIFO or average cost, to facilitate management's internal reporting preferences. At year-end, the accountant uses a LIFO allowance account to adjust the results to a LIFO basis. This account frequently is called a *LIFO reserve,* although many accountants do not like the term *reserve.* As evidence of the significant effect that LIFO can produce over time, the LIFO reserve account of some companies is actually larger than the reported LIFO inventory account.[7]

To illustrate how a LIFO reserve account works, assume that in the current year a company adopts the LIFO method for financial reporting purposes. In the past, the company used the FIFO method, and it plans to continue to maintain its inventory records on a FIFO basis for internal reporting purposes. If the ending inventory for the year is $56,000 on a FIFO basis and $50,000 on a LIFO basis, the following year-end entry is appropriate:

Cost of Goods Sold	6,000	
Allowance to Reduce Inventory		
Cost to LIFO Basis		6,000

The balance in the Allowance account is deducted from the inventory of $56,000 on the balance sheet.

Applying LIFO to each of a company's products, as we have done for Jackson Company's Product 19-C, is called the **specific goods method** of applying LIFO. This method requires that LIFO be applied to *each product* in a company's inventory. In the next chapter, we present other methods of applying LIFO.

Major Arguments for LIFO. LIFO is perhaps the most controversial inventory cost flow method. Nevertheless, certain theoretical and economic arguments support its use.

1. From a theoretical standpoint, the use of LIFO is often said to produce a better matching of cost of goods sold expense (measured using recent cost prices) with sales revenue (measured using recent selling prices). As a result, it is often claimed that LIFO produces a better measure of net income than either FIFO or average cost.

   Matching

2. When inventory costs are rising, net income normally includes a component called **inventory profits.** These profits equal the difference between the current replacement cost of sales and the cost of sales determined using a generally accepted cost flow method. Inventory profits are illusory, however, because they generally must be used to replace depleted inventories at higher costs. **The LIFO method greatly reduces inventory profits,** thereby causing net income to more accurately reflect an amount that can be distributed to stockholders and still enable the company to replace its inventories.

3. During periods of rising prices, LIFO tends to produce net income and inventory measurements that reflect conservatism.[8] Many financial analysts consider the use of LIFO as a favorable factor when they evaluate the **quality of a company's earnings.**

   Conservatism

4. LIFO is often supported on the economic ground that, during periods of rising prices, its use tends to lower taxable income and thereby postpone income tax payments until the time, if ever, that inventory unit costs or physical quantities decline. Federal income tax law permits a company to compute taxable income using LIFO only if the company also uses LIFO for financial reporting. This is known as the **LIFO conformity requirement,** and, as the name implies, this requirement pertains only to LIFO. Although Congress believed that the conformity requirement was fair and reasonable when LIFO was initially allowed for tax purposes in 1938, many people today argue that the requirement adversely affects GAAP and should be eliminated. With the major exception of LIFO, a company does not have to use the same methods for financial reporting purposes as it uses for income tax purposes or vice versa.

The LIFO conformity requirement has deterred some companies from adopting LIFO. Nevertheless, occasionally high inflation rates in the United States have made it one of the

---

[7]See James M. Reeve and Keith G. Stanga, "Balance Sheet Impact of Using LIFO: An Empirical Study," *Accounting Horizons* (September 1987), pp. 9–15.

[8]Not all companies have experienced a rising trend of inventory costs over time. Some companies in the electronics industry, for example, have experienced declining costs. For these companies, using FIFO is considered more conservative than using LIFO.

most popular accounting methods in past years. Hoover Ball & Bearing, for example, changed from FIFO to LIFO in 1974 (a year of high inflation during which many companies switched to LIFO), thereby saving the company $3.3 million in income taxes.[9] One author has estimated that the use of LIFO permitted General Electric Company to save approximately $1 billion of income taxes during a 25-year period ending in 1979.[10] Such tax savings enhance a company's availability of cash. This increased cash flow is in effect an interest-free loan of indefinite and perhaps permanent duration. It reduces borrowing requirements and thereby tends to lower interest costs, which in turn contributes even further toward improving a company's cash flow.

Major Arguments against LIFO.   Despite the theoretical and economic advantages of LIFO, the method has been attacked for several reasons. The major arguments against LIFO are summarized below.

1. LIFO inventories are often valued using outdated cost prices. Some say that LIFO-valued inventories are "unrealistic" because they fail to reflect current costs. When inventory valuations are unrealistic, related measurements such as working capital, the current ratio, and inventory turnover are also distorted.

2. The LIFO cost flow assumption is usually opposite to the physical flow of goods. Only a few types of inventories, such as coal or gravel, physically flow in a LIFO manner.

Matching

3. When a liquidation of LIFO inventory layers occurs, outdated costs tend to be matched with sales revenue, thereby reducing the matching benefits that LIFO generally produces. Matching outdated costs with current revenues is said to produce an "unrealistic" measure of net income. Frequently, the liquidation of LIFO layers is involuntary, as when a strike disrupts production or a supplier fails to deliver goods on a timely basis at the end of an accounting

Materiality

period. A LIFO liquidation can sometimes have a material impact on a company's financial statements. For example, in 1980 Bethlehem Steel Corporation had a LIFO liquidation that increased its income by 77%. In the same year, a LIFO liquidation by the Firestone Tire & Rubber Company increased its income by 65%.[11]

A study has demonstrated that LIFO layer liquidations tend to be industry specific. Companies in cyclical industries, especially primary metals and rubber/plastic products, have been most likely to experience them. When a corporate manager evaluates the desirability of a LIFO layer liquidation, the company's cost of capital and income tax expense tend to be the most important considerations.[12]

4. The use of the LIFO permits income manipulation, such as by making end-of-period purchases designed to preserve existing inventory layers. At times these purchases may not even be in the best economic interests of the company.

5. LIFO generally results in a greater administrative burden than either FIFO or average cost. As stated earlier, most companies that use LIFO for external reporting maintain their records on some other basis (such as FIFO) for internal reporting. Moreover, because LIFO involves many complex tax regulations, its use for tax purposes may cause the Internal Revenue Service (IRS) to take a closer look at a firm's inventory accounting system to determine whether all the tax requirements have been met. A LIFO election can be invalidated because of a technicality.

6. The variations in methods of applying LIFO as well as the fact that most LIFO users have adopted it at different times tend to distort intercompany comparisons, even those made between two LIFO companies in the same industry.

7. During periods of rising inventory costs, the use of LIFO for tax purposes, coupled with the conformity requirement, creates a paradox. That is, it postpones taxes and thereby makes the firm better off economically, yet it lowers reported net income and thereby makes the firm *appear worse* than it would under FIFO or average cost. One study has found that many com-

[9]"FIFO to LIFO: More and More Companies Are Making the Switch," *Barrons* (October 21, 1974), p. 5.

[10]S. Thomas Moser, "LIFO: Inflation Lifeline," *Management Focus* (March–April 1981), p. 24.

[11]Allen I. Schiff, "The Other Side of LIFO," *Journal of Accountancy* (May 1983), pp. 120–121.

[12]Philip G. Cottell, Jr., "LIFO Layer Liquidations: Some Empirical Evidence," *Journal of Accounting, Auditing and Finance* (Winter 1986), pp. 30–45.

panies "have voluntarily paid tens of millions of dollars in additional income taxes by continuing to use FIFO rather than switching to LIFO.[13] Many managers are reluctant to adopt LIFO out of fear that the reduced reported earnings will cause investors to penalize the market price of their company's stock. Although the empirical studies in this area have not produced consistent results, research suggests that this fear of managers may be unjustified, because changes to LIFO do not appear to result in unfavorable market reactions.[14] A retired chairman of General Electric Company has speculated that some managers may not want to use LIFO because "most top executive contracts are tied to reported earnings."[15]

To further illustrate that LIFO is a controversial method, many countries do not allow its use. Examples include the United Kingdom, Australia, New Zealand, Singapore, and Sweden. Some U.S. companies, such as Goodyear, Alcoa, and General Motors, use LIFO only for their domestic (U.S.) inventories and other methods for the inventories of foreign subsidiaries.

Comparison of Results between FIFO, Average Cost, and LIFO. Exhibit 8–9 summarizes the financial statement impact of the FIFO, average cost, and LIFO methods of Product 19-C of Jackson Company for the current year. We do not show the results under the specific identification method, because they depend on which units were sold and which are on hand.

As Exhibit 8–9 suggests, certain key financial statement variables for Jackson Company differ depending on which cost flow method the company adopts. These variables include inventory, total current assets, working capital, cost of goods sold, gross margin, and net income. The fact that the various cost flow methods produce different financial statement effects underscores the importance of each company disclosing the method(s) that it uses.

Disclosure

Because the unit cost of Product 19-C rose steadily during the current year, FIFO produces the lowest cost of goods sold figure; LIFO used with a periodic system produces the

---

EXHIBIT 8–9

Comparison of Results under FIFO, Average Cost, and LIFO

	FIFO		Average Cost		LIFO	
	Periodic System	Perpetual System	Periodic System	Perpetual System	Periodic System	Perpetual System
Cost of goods available for sale	$12,700	$12,700	$12,700	$12,700	$12,700	$12,700
Cost of ending inventory (Dec. 31)	3,000	3,000	2,540	2,900	2,100	2,600
Cost of goods sold	$ 9,700	$ 9,700	$10,160	$ 9,800	$10,600	$10,100

---

[13]Gary C. Biddle, "Accounting Methods and Management Decisions: The Case of Inventory Costing and Inventory Policy," *Journal of Accounting Research* (Supplement 1980), p. 273.

[14]See, for example, Shyam Sunder, "Stock Price and Risk Related to Accounting Changes in Inventory Valuation," *Accounting Review* (April 1975), pp. 305–315. It is also worth noting that the LIFO conformity requirement does *not* prohibit the disclosure of supplemental non-LIFO income information. This supplemental information, such as the amount of net income that would have been reported if the FIFO method had been used, cannot be presented on the face of the financial statements.

One difficulty in conducting empirical research on the effect of LIFO adoption is properly controlling for the many factors that cause firms that adopt LIFO to differ from those that do not.

[15]Reginald H. Jones, quoted in *Journal of Accountancy* (July 1981), p. 28.

highest. The nature of the differences produced under the various cost flow methods depends primarily on the direction and magnitude of unit cost movements as well as on the length of time that a company has used LIFO.

Selection of a Cost Flow Method

We have just seen that the various inventory cost flow methods can lead to substantially different financial statement results. We also know that accountants seek to produce information that enables users to make meaningful intercompany comparisons. To help ensure the propriety of these comparisons, differences between the financial statements of different companies should result from basic differences between the companies themselves or from the nature of their transactions and not merely from differences in accounting principles.[16] Given these facts, why does GAAP permit companies to choose among several inventory cost flow methods?

The basic reason is that circumstances may differ substantially among companies. Accountants generally believe that a company should have some leeway in selecting a cost flow method that is most appropriate in light of the company's circumstances. The accounting profession has therefore tended to favor *some flexibility,* rather than *strict uniformity,* when formulating accounting principles. Nevertheless, two of the great challenges of the Financial Accounting Standards Board (FASB) and its predecessor committees have been (1) to identify the circumstances that warrant the use of a particular accounting principle and (2) to eliminate alternative principles that are not justified by differences in circumstances.

Given the alternatives currently available under GAAP, what basic criterion should a corporate manager use in selecting an inventory cost flow method? *Accounting Research Bulletin No. 43* states that "the major objective in selecting a method should be to choose the one that, under the circumstances, most clearly reflects periodic income."[17] The phrases *under the circumstances* and *most clearly reflects periodic income* have not been well defined. As a result, they often convey significantly different meanings to different people. The FASB's conceptual framework suggests that when selecting an inventory cost flow method, a company should choose the method that is most helpful to users for the purpose of predicting future cash flows. This focus is consistent with the second objective of financial reporting, which is to provide information that helps users to accurately assess their chances of receiving cash from the reporting enterprise. Unfortunately, no one has yet determined which inventory cost determination method best predicts future cash flows in all instances. The absence of more concrete criteria for selecting a cost flow assumption has *increased the importance of judgment.* In reality, many companies appear to select a method based largely on factors such as tax minimization, steady growth in reported earnings, and so forth. Thus, it seems fair to say that financial statements today often reflect certain differences that are unrelated to basic differences among companies or their transactions.

Many research studies have attempted to explain why companies select particular accounting methods. For example, one recent study compared FIFO and LIFO users to determine the variables that explain the selection of inventory method. The study found that expected tax savings is the primary reason that companies use LIFO and that a variety of reasons helps explain why more FIFO companies have not adopted LIFO. Examples of these

---

[16]*APB Statement No. 4,* "Basic Concepts and Accounting Principles Underlying Financial Statements of Business Enterprises," 1970, par. 101.

[17]*Accounting Research Bulletin No. 43,* "Restatement and Revision of Accounting Research Bulletins," Ch. 4, Stmt. 4.

reasons include LIFO layer liquidations, LIFO bookkeeping costs, declining inventory costs, effects on debt covenants, and concern about LIFO's complexity.[18]

The author of *Accounting Research Study No. 13* concluded:

> *Specific identification of costs and, if that is not practicable, the FIFO cost flow assumption represent approaches to inventory cost determination which are sound in principle.... Enterprises using any cost flow assumption other than specific identification or FIFO should be required to disclose (1) the effect on net income for the period and on the balance sheet inventory amounts of the method used as compared with FIFO and (2) related tax effects.*[19]

The FASB has not adopted these conclusions.

When a company adopts a cost flow method for a portion or for all of its inventories, it should use the method consistently over time. As stated earlier, the accountant should disclose the method(s) in the financial statements. When a company changes to another cost flow method, the accountant should disclose the nature of the change, the justification for it, and its dollar effects on income. We explain accounting changes in Chapter 20.

Consistency
Disclosure

The accountant initially values inventory items by multiplying quantities on hand by unit costs derived under a cost flow method (specific identification, FIFO, etc.). The resulting valuation is at historical cost. In inventory accounting, GAAP requires a departure from historical cost measurement when the utility of inventory has declined below cost. This departure is known as the **lower of cost or market rule,** or simply the **LCM rule.**[20]

Accounting Research Bulletin No. 43 defines the LCM rule:

> *A departure from the cost basis of pricing the inventory is required when the utility of the goods is no longer as great as its cost. Where there is evidence that the utility of goods, in their disposal in the ordinary course of business, will be less than cost, whether due to physical deterioration, obsolescence, changes in price levels, or other causes, the difference should be recognized as a loss of the current period. This is generally accomplished by stating such goods at a lower level commonly designated as* market.[21]

A company purchases or manufactures inventory for ultimate sale. The term **utility of goods** thus refers to the ability of the goods to generate revenue via sale. Utility is a very subjective concept, and **market** is used simply as a practical means of measuring it. Therefore, if the market measure of goods on hand at the end of the current period has declined below cost, the accountant should report the difference as a loss of the period in which the decline occurred.

INVENTORY VALUATION AT THE LOWER OF COST OR MARKET (LCM)

Asset/Liability Measurement

MEANING OF MARKET

What does **market** mean? *Accounting Research Bulletin No. 43* states:

> *As used in the phrase* lower of cost or market *the term market means current replacement cost (by purchase or by reproduction, as the case may be) except that:*

---

[18]Barry E. Cushing and Marc J. LeClere, "Evidence on the Determinants of Inventory Accounting Policy Choice," *Accounting Review* (April 1992), p. 355–366.

[19]Horace G. Barden, *Accounting Research Study No. 13,* "The Accounting Basis of Inventories" (New York: AICPA, 1973), pp. 12–13.

[20]A company cannot use LCM with LIFO for federal income tax purposes. Generally accepted accounting principles, however, require a company to use LCM with LIFO for financial reporting purposes. Other differences exist between the way in which a company applies LCM for income tax versus financial reporting purposes. Readers interested in the details of how to apply LCM for income tax purposes should consult appropriate tax references.

[21]*Accounting Research Bulletin No. 43,* Ch. 4, Stmt. 5.

(1) Market should not exceed the net realizable value (i.e., estimated selling price in the ordinary course of business less reasonably predictable costs of completion and disposal); and

(2) Market should not be less than net realizable value reduced by an allowance for an approximately normal profit margin.[22]

Generally, therefore, *market* means **current replacement cost** on the balance sheet date. In the case of purchased inventories, this cost includes not only the purchase price that would have to be paid for the quantities usually purchased but also incidental acquisition costs such as freight and handling. For manufactured inventories, replacement cost is based on current materials prices, prevailing labor rates, and current overhead costs. Note that replacement cost is an **input** (or **entry**) **value**, because it represents an amount that would have to be paid to acquire inventory.

The purpose of using replacement cost to represent market (and therefore utility) is that declines in replacement cost are often associated with declines in selling prices. Selling prices, however, may be influenced by other factors. *Bulletin No. 43* therefore states that in applying the LCM rule, "judgment must always be exercised and no loss should be recognized unless the evidence indicates clearly that a loss has been sustained."[23] To help practicing accountants determine whether or not a loss has been sustained, the bulletin specifies an upper and a lower limit within which market must fall. Each limit is an **output** (or **exit**) **value,** because each is based directly on expected selling prices that the firm will receive for the goods being valued.

The upper limit on market, commonly called the **ceiling,** is **net realizable value.** The lower limit, commonly called the **floor,** is **net realizable value reduced by an allowance for an approximately normal profit margin.** These concepts are illustrated below for one unit of Inventory Item Q.

Estimated selling price in the ordinary course of business	$10
− Reasonably predictable costs of completion and disposal	1
= Net realizable value (ceiling)	9
− Allowance for an approximately normal profit margin (30% of selling price)	3
= Net realizable value less an allowance for an approximately normal profit margin (floor)	$ 6

When applying the LCM rule, *replacement cost is used as market only when it falls between the ceiling and the floor.* On the other hand, *if replacement cost is greater than the ceiling, the ceiling is used as market.* The use of a ceiling is defended on the ground that if inventory were reported at more than its net realizable value, the amount reported would exceed the inventory's utility. This would result in a loss when the inventory is sold. If *replacement cost is less than the floor, the floor is used as market.* Limiting market to the floor is defended on the basis that writing down inventory items below the floor understates the inventory's utility and thereby permits the recognition of an abnormally high profit when the inventory is sold.

From a practical standpoint, the LCM rule requires (1) selecting as market the middle amount from among the ceiling, replacement cost, and floor and (2) selecting the lower of cost or market to use for inventory valuation purposes. Exhibit 8–10 displays four inventory items. The assumed dollar amounts are on a *per-unit basis.*

Observe in Exhibit 8–10 that for each item, market is the middle value selected from among the ceiling, replacement cost, and floor. *After* we have determined market, we com-

---

[22]*Accounting Research Bulletin No. 43,* Ch. 4, Stmt. 6.
[23]*Accounting Research Bulletin No. 43,* Ch. 4, par. 9.

EXHIBIT 8–10					
The LCM Rule					

Market Determinants

Inventory Item	Ceiling[1]	Replacement Cost[2]	Floor[3]	Market[4]	Cost[5]	LCM[6]
A	$7	$6	$5	$6	$3	$3
B	7	8	5	7	9	7
C	7	6	5	6	8	6
D	7	4	5	5	8	5

[1]Net realizable value (the estimated selling price, assumed to be $10, less reasonably predictable costs of completion and disposal, assumed to be $3).

[2]The current replacement cost as of the balance sheet date.

[3]Net realizable value less a normal profit margin. (Normal profit is assumed to be 20% of the $10 selling price.)

[4]The middle amount selected from among the ceiling, replacement cost, and floor.

[5]Determined using a cost flow method (specific identification, FIFO, etc.).

[6]Lower of cost or market (the lower amount selected from the cost and market). This amount is used for inventory valuation purposes on the balance sheet.

pare it with cost. The lower of cost or market is then entered in the LCM column. Unit amounts in the LCM column are the correct ones to use for inventory valuation purposes. Note that these amounts represent the cost for Item A, the ceiling for Item B, the replacement cost for Item C, and the floor for Item D.

The LCM rule applies to goods that a company will sell in the ordinary course of business. At times a company may own damaged, deteriorated, or obsolete goods that it cannot sell in the usual manner. Such goods should be carried in a separate account and, for accounting purposes, should be valued below cost, at their estimated selling prices less disposal costs. The accounting principles that should be used for inventory received in a trade-in are discussed in Chapter 11; accounting for repossessed inventory is presented in Chapter 21.

METHODS OF APPLYING THE LCM RULE

In the preceding example, we assumed that the LCM rule was applied to each item in inventory. Actually, a company may choose to apply the rule to (1) each inventory item, (2) major categories of items, or (3) the inventory as a whole. According to *Bulletin No. 43,* the application method selected should most clearly reflect periodic income. Moreover, the method should be applied consistently over time. Most companies use the individual item method.[24]   Consistency
Regardless of the method used, the quantity of each item should initially be multiplied by (1) unit costs to derive aggregate cost and (2) unit market values to derive aggregate market.[25] This is shown in Exhibit 8–11, in which we assume the same inventory items (A, B, C, and D) as in Exhibit 8–10. For simplicity, we assume that 1,000 units of each item are on hand.

Observe in Exhibit 8–11 that the final inventory valuation is $21,000, $23,000, or $24,000, depending on how the LCM rule is applied. In certain cases, the results under the different methods may be equal. If the results are not equal, applying LCM to individual

[24]Lower of cost or market must be applied to each inventory item for federal income tax purposes.

[25]Multiplying by unit costs overcomes the problem of having to compare more than one unit cost with a single unit market value. Under the FIFO method, for example, more than one unit cost may exist for certain inventory items.

EXHIBIT 8–11

Methods of Applying the LCM Rule

	Number of Units	Unit Cost	Unit Market	Aggregate Cost	Aggregate Market	LCM Applied to (1) Individual Items	(2) Major Categories	(3) Inventory as a Whole
Category I								
Item A	1,000	$3	$6	$ 3,000	$ 6,000	$ 3,000		
Item B	1,000	9	7	9,000	7,000	7,000		
Subtotal				12,000	13,000		$12,000	
Category II								
Item C	1,000	8	6	8,000	6,000	6,000		
Item D	1,000	8	5	8,000	5,000	5,000		
Subtotal				16,000	11,000		11,000	
Total				$28,000	$24,000			$24,000
Inventory valuation						$21,000	$23,000	$24,000

items produces the lowest inventory valuation; applying it to the inventory as a whole produces the highest.

Once an inventory item has been written down to a value below cost, that value is regarded as its "new cost" for purposes of subsequent accounting. If the market value of an item that has been written down subsequently increases, the increase is *not* reflected in the accounts until a sale occurs.

RECORDING LCM IN THE ACCOUNTS

When application of the LCM rule indicates that inventory should be reported at market, how should this be recorded? Ideally, a loss account should be debited and a valuation allowance account (an inventory *contra* account) should be credited. To illustrate, let's assume the following facts for Bradley Company:

Inventory, Jan. 1, at cost	$ 50,000
Purchases during the year	200,000
Inventory, Dec. 31	
At cost	40,000
At market	33,000

If the company uses the periodic inventory system, the cost of goods sold adjusting entry is as shown:

Dec. 31	Inventory, Dec. 31	40,000	
	Loss on Reduction of Inventory Cost to Market	7,000	
	Cost of Goods Sold	210,000	
	Inventory, Jan. 1		50,000
	Allowance to Reduce Inventory Cost to Market		7,000
	Purchases		200,000

On the other hand, the following adjusting entry is made if the company uses a perpetual system:

Dec. 31	Loss on Reduction of Inventory Cost to Market	7,000	
	Allowance to Reduce Inventory		
	Cost to Market		7,000

Under either system, cost of goods sold is reported at $210,000 and the loss of $7,000 is shown in the body of the income statement (*not* as an extraordinary item). A clear distinction is therefore made between an *expense* associated with *goods sold* and a *loss* associated with holding *goods on hand*. Separating the expense from the loss is conceptually correct since the two amounts are caused by different factors. Moreover, a separate reporting of the two amounts may help financial statement users to make more accurate predictions of future cash flows.

The Allowance account is deducted from inventory on the balance sheet:

Inventory, at cost	$40,000	
Less: Allowance to reduce inventory		
cost to market	7,000	$33,000

Use of the Allowance account facilitates the disclosure of the ending inventory at both cost ($40,000) and market ($33,000).   **Disclosure**

At the end of the *next* accounting period, the Allowance account should be closed to the Beginning Inventory if a periodic system is used or to Cost of Goods Sold if a perpetual system is used. This avoids overstatement of the beginning inventory and cost of goods sold. If the market value of the ending inventory is below cost, the difference should again be entered in the Loss and the Allowance accounts.

In practice, a number of acceptable variations of these procedures are encountered. Conceptually, these variations are less desirable than the procedure described above. They may be supported, however, on the grounds of materiality and practicality. For example, the LCM rule is sometimes applied in the accounts by   **Materiality**

1. Debiting Cost of Goods Sold (instead of the Loss account) and crediting the Allowance account.
2. Debiting the Loss account and crediting the Inventory account (instead of the Allowance account).
3. Debiting Cost of Goods Sold (instead of the Loss account) and crediting the Inventory account (instead of the Allowance account).

When an Allowance account is used, some accountants leave it open and merely adjust it upward or downward at year-end so that it agrees with the difference between cost and market. An increase in the Allowance account requires the recognition of a loss. A decrease requires the recognition of a recovery of loss, sometimes called a *gain*. The balance in the Allowance account is never reduced below zero. In other words, a debit balance should never exist in the Allowance account, because it would cause the carrying value of the inventory to exceed cost.

PROS AND CONS OF LCM

The LCM rule is an example of the conservatism modifying convention. It permits accountants to recognize a loss on inventory, even though evidence of the loss does not result from a sale. The rule has a long history in accounting. Its early use was supported as a means of achieving balance sheet conservatism at a time when creditors were the primary users of external financial statements and the balance sheet was regarded as the most important financial statement. Modern financial reporting emphasizes the income statement, and the LCM rule is now supported on the basis that it produces a conservative income measure in the current period.   **Conservatism**

Many users of financial statements support the LCM rule because they think it reduces their risk of making poor decisions. In a study involving in-depth interviews of important financial statement users, Backer found that "all but one of the 74 bankers interviewed favored the lower of cost or market rule....The security analysts also overwhelmingly supported the rule. Only four of these 72 analysts interviewed opposed the rule."[26]

Despite the alleged benefits of the LCM rule, it has long been one of the most controversial elements of GAAP. Critics have leveled many arguments against it. The following are some of the major objections:

1. The rule requires a write-down to market when cost exceeds market, but it does not permit a write-up to market when market exceeds cost. Some accountants consider this inconsistent and illogical.

2. The rule permits the use of four different inventory measures. Some inventory items may therefore be valued at cost; others are valued using ceiling, replacement cost, and floor amounts. The existence of these different valuation bases may inhibit the ability of statement users to make valid intercompany and interperiod comparisons.

3. Different methods may be used to apply the LCM rule (i.e., to individual items, major categories, or the inventory as a whole) and to record it in the accounts. As a result, intercompany comparisons may be distorted.

4. Determining a "normal profit" to establish a floor is difficult and subjective. These profits vary between inventory items and over time as selling prices and cost prices change.

5. Valuing an inventory item at the floor to prevent an abnormally high profit on its sale may be closer to income manipulation than to income measurement. While management's function is to earn a profit, the accountant's function is to measure and report it.

6. The LCM rule may produce conservative results in the first year of its use. However, when the lower inventory costs are charged to cost of goods sold in a subsequent period, net income tends to be higher and therefore unconservative.

7. The rule is often complicated to apply. Furthermore, there is room to suspect that many preparers and users of financial statements may not adequately understand it.[27]

INVENTORY VALUATION ABOVE COST

Thus far we have discussed the valuation of inventory at cost and at the lower of cost or market. In Chapter 3, we discussed several alternatives to conventional historical cost measurement. These include current cost (replacement cost), current exit value in orderly liquidation, expected exit value in due course of business (net realizable value), and present value of expected cash flows. Many critics of historical cost accounting believe that accounting information would be more useful if inventories were consistently measured using any of the alternatives to conventional historical cost. Some accountants, for example, believe that inventories should be measured and reported at current cost, regardless of whether the current cost measurement is above or below historical cost. Although many theoretical arguments lend support to the valuation of inventory at amounts higher than historical cost, such valuation is permissible under GAAP only in certain exceptional cases.

For example, construction companies often engage in projects that take several years to complete, such as office buildings, ships, and dams. Instead of waiting until the end of a project to recognize income, these companies may, under GAAP, choose to recognize income *during production* using the percentage of completion method. Under this method, the inventory account Construction in Progress consists of *historical costs incurred plus income recognized to date*. The reporting of inventory in this manner is considered appropriate for these companies, given the unusual nature of the construction business. We further explain and illustrate the percentage of completion method in Chapter 21.

---

[26]Morton Backer, *Financial Reporting for Security Investment and Credit Decisions* (New York: National Association of Accountants, 1970), p. 102.
[27]Barden, p. 104.

The reporting of inventory at **net realizable value,** even though such value may be above cost, is permitted under GAAP in certain exceptional cases. Precious metals that have a fixed monetary value and no substantial marketing costs may be reported at net realizable value. Similarly, certain agricultural and mineral products, units of which are interchangeable, can be sold immediately at quoted market prices, and are difficult to cost appropriately, may be reported at net realizable value.[28] In addition, it is customary for companies within certain industries to report inventories at net realizable value, because it is virtually impossible for them to determine costs with sufficient objectivity. A meat packing company, for example, buys its raw material "on the hoof" and divides it into many cuts, such as ribs and chuck. Since any allocation of the cost of the animal to the resulting cuts would be purely arbitrary, these companies value their inventories of cuts at net realizable value.[29]

Industry Practices

A company that values its inventory above cost is considered to have earned income before the time of sale. Clearly, this is an exceptional treatment, given the revenue realization principle. Financial statements of companies that value inventories above cost should disclose the valuation basis used.

Revenue Realization

Inventory errors often occur when counting, pricing, or extending inventory amounts. Inventory errors may also arise because certain goods have been either incorrectly included or incorrectly excluded when the inventory was taken. We may better appreciate the importance of accurately accounting for inventories by focusing on the impact of certain inventory errors on financial statements. Several common types of errors made in accounting for merchandise and the effects of each are summarized below.

EFFECTS OF INVENTORY ERRORS ON FINANCIAL STATEMENTS

1. The company's accountant *incorrectly includes* in the ending inventory the cost of certain goods that do not belong to the company.
   a. If the credit purchase of the goods has *not* been recorded, the effects are an overstatement of ending inventory, an understatement of cost of goods sold, and an overstatement of net income and ending retained earnings.
   b. If the credit purchase of the goods has been recorded, *two* errors have occurred (i.e., incorrectly including the goods in inventory *and* incorrectly recording the purchase). The effects are an overstatement of ending inventory and of accounts payable. Cost of goods sold, net income, and ending retained earnings, however, are correctly stated, because both purchases and ending inventory are overstated by the same amounts and therefore offset one another in the calculation of cost of goods sold and net income.
2. The company's accountant *incorrectly excludes* from ending inventory the cost of certain goods that belong to the company.
   a. If the credit purchase of the goods has been recorded, the effects are an understatement of ending inventory, an overstatement of cost of goods sold, and an understatement of net income and ending retained earnings.
   b. If the credit purchase of the goods has *not* been recorded, *two* errors have occurred (i.e., incorrectly excluding the goods from inventory *and* incorrectly failing to record the purchase). The effect is an understatement of ending inventory and of accounts payable. Cost of goods sold, net income, and ending retained earnings, however, are correctly stated, because both purchases and ending inventory are understated by the same amounts and therefore offset one another in the calculation of cost of goods sold and net income.

When considering the effects that inventory errors have on net income, remembering the following relationships often is helpful.

$$BI + NP - EI = CGS \qquad\qquad (8\text{--}1)$$

$$S - CGS - OE = PI \qquad\qquad (8\text{--}2)$$

$$PI - T = NI \qquad\qquad (8\text{--}3)$$

---

[28]*Accounting Research Bulletin No. 43*, Ch. 4, par. 16.
[29]*Accounting Research Bulletin No. 43*, Ch. 1A, par. 1.

where BI = Beginning inventory

NP = Net purchases

EI = Ending inventory

CGS = Cost of goods sold

S = Sales

OE = Other expenses

PI = Pretax income

T = Income tax

NI = Net income

Equation (8–1) indicates that an overstatement (understatement) of either the *beginning inventory or purchases* tends to increase (decrease) cost of goods sold. Equations (8–2) and (8–3) show that an overstatement (understatement) of cost of goods sold results in an understatement (overstatement) of pretax income and net income.

In contrast, equation (8–1) indicates that an overstatement (understatement) of *ending inventory* tends to decrease (increase) cost of goods sold. Equations (8–2) and (8–3) show that an understatement (overstatement) of cost of goods sold results in an overstatement (understatement) of pretax income and net income.

The types of inventory errors discussed previously relate to purchase transactions. Similar errors may arise in relation to sales transactions. For example, the cost of certain goods that have actually been sold may erroneously be included in the ending inventory.

The various types of inventory errors just discussed affected the current accounting period. Recognize, however, that an error in the ending inventory of the current period has the opposite effect in the next period, because the ending inventory of one period is the beginning inventory of the next. If the error is not corrected in the second period, it will offset the error made in the first period.

Correcting an inventory error requires a logical analysis of the error's effects on the financial statements. The appropriate correction depends in part on when the error is detected. An error in the ending inventory of one period that is discovered near the end of the next, for example, requires a prior period adjustment. Chapter 20 discusses the topic of error correction in greater depth.

CONCLUDING REMARKS/ PROFESSIONAL JUDGMENT

Asset/Liability Measurement

Revenue Realization

Matching

Consistency

Disclosure

Throughout this text, we stress the importance of understanding the relationship between the individual topics covered and the theoretical model presented in Chapter 2. The following elements of the model are especially pertinent in inventory accounting.

1. **Asset/liability measurement principle.** The primary basis of accounting for inventories is historical cost. Remember that determining historical cost is not as easy as it may appear. Resolving important issues such as what costs should be inventoried and what cost flow method should be used is a real challenge to the practicing accountant.

2. **Revenue realization principle.** When an increase in the value of inventory is verified by a sale, revenue is usually recorded. Only in exceptional cases may accountants properly value inventory above cost and therefore recognize revenue before the time of sale.

3. **Matching principle.** The cost of the inventory sold must be charged to expense in the period in which the sale occurs. By so doing, the sales revenue is matched with the cost of the goods sold to produce the revenue.

4. **Consistency principle.** A company should account for its inventories using the same methods over time. This principle is particularly important in inventory accounting, because several alternative accounting methods exist.

5. **Disclosure principle.** Exhibit 8–12 shows recent inventory disclosures of the Goodyear Tire & Rubber Company. The following disclosure guidelines should be observed when reporting inventories on the balance sheet and in the related notes:

EXHIBIT 8–12

Example Inventory Disclosure

The Goodyear Tire & Rubber Company
Consolidated Balance Sheet
December 31, 1992

	December 31	
(Dollars in millions)	1992	1991
Assets		
Current assets:		
Cash and cash equivalents	$ 207.5	$ 163.4
Short-term securities	96.5	71.7
Accounts and notes receivable (Note 3)	1,353.3	1,315.0
Inventories (Note 5)	1,288.2	1,312.7
Prepaid expenses	364.0	255.9
Total Current Assets	$3,309.5	$3,118.7

Notes to Financial Statements

Note 1: Accounting Policies

A summary of the significant accounting policies used in the preparation of the accompanying
financial statements follows:

Inventory Pricing

Inventories are stated at the lower of cost or market. Cost is determined using the last-in,
first-out (LIFO) method for a significant portion of domestic inventories and the first-in,
first-out (FIFO) method or average cost method for other inventories. Refer to Note 5.

Note 5: Inventories

(In millions)	1992	1991
Raw materials and supplies	$ 237.9	$ 232.0
Work in process	60.2	58.1
Finished product	990.1	1,022.6
	$1,288.2	$1,312.7

The cost of inventories using the last-in, first-out (LIFO) method (approximately 36.2% of
consolidated inventories in 1992 and 35.0% in 1991) was less than the approximate current
cost of inventories by $320.6 million at December 31, 1992, and $301.9 million at December 31, 1991.

SOURCE: The Goodyear Tire & Rubber Company, 1992 Annual Report.

---

a. Report inventories in the current assets section.
b. Disclose separately (if material) each major class of inventory, such as raw materials, work in
process, finished goods, factory supplies, and goods on consignment. Remember to include
in inventory only those goods for which the company (i.e., the accounting entity) has legal
title on the balance sheet date. Kellogg Company, whose financial statements are reproduced
in the endpapers of this book, reported two categories of inventories for 1993 and 1992:
(1) raw materials and supplies and (2) finished goods and materials in process (see inside
front cover of this text). The company combined certain items based on materiality considerations.
c. List inventories in order of their liquidity.
d. Disclose parenthetically in a footnote or in a summary of significant accounting policies the
inventory cost flow method used (FIFO, average cost, etc.) as well as the basis used in pricing
the inventory (cost or LCM). Also disclose any methods used that are peculiar to the firm's
industry.
e. If the company has made a change in its inventory accounting principles, disclose the nature
of and justification for the change. The effect of the change on income should also be disclosed. We explain accounting changes in Chapter 20.

f. Subtract the amount in an inventory allowance account (such as the Allowance to Reduce Inventory Cost to Market) from the amount in the Inventory account to derive the net amount. Report all three amounts on the balance sheet or in the related notes.

g. Do not offset the cost of inventories pledged as collateral against the loan liability. These inventories are properly reported as assets. However, the nature of the pledge agreement should be disclosed.

h. Do not include in inventories advance payments made to suppliers for goods that the company has ordered but title to which has not been received as of the balance sheet date. These advances should be reported after inventories in the account Advances to Suppliers.

Industry Practices

6. Industry practices. This modifying convention sometimes requires the reporting of inventories at amounts above cost. Companies in the meat packing industry, for example, typically value their inventories of cuts at net realizable value.

Conservatism

7. Conservatism. This modifying convention is reflected in the LCM rule. Under this rule, a departure from historical cost measurement is required when the utility of inventory has declined below cost.

Throughout this book, we highlight the importance of applying judgment when resolving accounting questions. This chapter has covered several areas in which accountants must use judgment. For example, determining which costs to include in the historical cost of inventory requires judgment; some companies capitalize costs such as inventory insurance, handling, and purchasing, and other companies expense those costs when incurred. As another example, selecting an inventory cost method (FIFO, LIFO, etc.) requires judgment. Choosing the method that most clearly reflects periodic income, as *ARB No. 43* requires, is highly subjective. As a final example, applying the lower of cost or market rule can be highly judgmental. Accountants must answer such subjective questions as these: Exactly which goods have declined in utility to amounts less than historical cost? What are the ceiling, floor, and replacement cost amounts for those goods? Clearly, the measurement issues involved in accounting for inventories are very challenging.

KEY POINTS

1. Inventories are goods that are held for sale in the ordinary course of business and goods that are in production or that will soon be used in production. (Objective 1)

2. To value an inventory for financial reporting purposes, an accountant must determine (1) the physical quantity of goods on hand and (2) the accounting valuation that should be associated with those goods. (Objective 1)

3. Inventory quantities are maintained on a day-to-day basis in a perpetual inventory system but not in a periodic system. (Objective 2)

4. Inventory items should be included in the inventory of the entity that has legal title. Goods in transit at the end of an accounting period that were shipped FOB shipping point belong to the buyer; those shipped FOB destination belong to the seller. Consigned goods belong to the consignor. (Objective 2)

5. To determine the cost of an inventory, an accountant must determine (1) what costs to include in inventory and (2) what method to use in associating inventory costs with the physical units on hand. (Objective 1)

6. Product costs are inventoried; period costs are charged to expense in the period in which they are incurred. (Objective 3)

7. Trade discounts are deducted when determining product costs. In theory, cash discounts should also be deducted, but in practice, most companies account for inventory at gross invoice amounts (i.e., without deducting cash discounts). (Objective 3)

8. Inventory cost flow methods include specific identification, FIFO, average cost, and LIFO. Each method leads to a valuation of inventory and cost of goods sold based on historical cost. (Objective 4)

9. The specific identification method requires that the actual unit costs of goods on hand and goods sold be identified individually. In contrast, the FIFO, average cost, and LIFO methods reflect assumed cost flow patterns. (Objective 4)

10. A company electing to use LIFO for income tax purposes must also use it for financial reporting purposes. The LIFO method is an important exception to the general principle that a company

does not have to use the same methods for financial reporting purposes that it uses for income tax purposes. (Objective 4)

11. A company should select the inventory cost flow method that most clearly reflects its periodic income; once selected, the method should be used consistently over time and disclosed in the financial statements. (Objective 4)

12. Inventory should ordinarily be reported on a balance sheet at the lower of cost or market value. In essence, the term *market* refers to the middle value selected from among the ceiling, replacement cost, and floor amounts. (Objective 5)

13. The lower of cost or market rule may be applied to each inventory item, to major categories of items, or to the inventory as a whole. (Objective 5)

14. The lower of cost or market rule is an exception to historical cost measurement of inventories that is justified on the basis of conservatism. (Objective 5)

15. The valuation of inventory at an amount higher than historical cost is permissible under GAAP only in certain exceptional cases. (Objective 6)

16. Inventory errors can cause several important misstatements to occur in the financial statements. (Objective 7)

17. The following elements of accounting theory are especially important in the area of inventory accounting: asset/liability measurement, revenue realization, matching, consistency, disclosure, industry practices, and conservatism. (Objective 8)

QUESTIONS

8–1 What are the major differences between trading and manufacturing companies regarding the classification of inventories and the calculation of cost of goods sold? Why do these differences exist?

8–2 The primary basis of accounting for inventories under GAAP is historical cost. What are three inventory valuation methods that are alternatives to historical cost? Briefly explain why these methods are not generally accepted today.

8–3 What is a periodic inventory system? What is a perpetual system? What factors should a manager consider when deciding which system the company should use?

8–4 What general rule determines which goods properly belong in a company's inventory? How does the accountant apply this general rule to goods in transit on the balance sheet date and to consigned goods?

8–5 What is the difference between product costs and period costs?

8–6 Why is the net method of recording purchases theoretically superior to the gross method?

8–7 What are the major arguments for and against the specific identification method of inventory cost determination?

8–8 What are the major arguments for and against the FIFO method of inventory cost determination?

8–9 What are the major arguments for and against the average cost method of inventory cost determination?

8–10 What are the major arguments for and against the LIFO method of inventory cost determination?

8–11 What basic problem does the existence within GAAP of several inventory cost flow methods create for external users of financial statements? How does the accounting profession justify these alternative methods?

8–12 What basic criterion should a company manager use in selecting an inventory cost flow method? Why is this criterion difficult to apply?

8–13 How does the LCM rule relate to the need of investors and creditors to predict the amount, timing, and uncertainty of cash flows to themselves?

8–14 What are the major arguments for and against the LCM rule in accounting for inventories?

8–15 What does the term *market* mean in the context of the LCM rule?

8–16 What is the rationale for ceiling and floor limits on market under the LCM rule?

8–17 Under what circumstances, if any, is it appropriate under GAAP to value inventories at amounts higher than historical cost?

8–18 How does inventory accounting relate to the asset/liability measurement principle, revenue realization principle, and matching principle?

8–19 Why is the consistency principle especially important in inventory accounting?

8–20 How does inventory accounting relate to the conservatism modifying convention?

EXERCISES

8–21 Cost of Goods Sold   Listed below are selected accounts and their balances that appeared on the *unadjusted* trial balance of Lampen, Inc., at April 30, 1996, the end of the company's annual fiscal period. Each account has a normal balance.

Sales returns	$ 12,000
Merchandise inventory	35,000
Transportation-out	14,000
Purchase returns	5,000
Sales	300,000
Advertising	15,000
Transportation-in	8,000
Purchases	135,000
Sales discounts	4,000
Sales commissions	12,000
Officers' salaries	40,000

A physical count on April 30 indicates that merchandise costing $22,000 is on hand.

INSTRUCTIONS

[a] Prepare the adjusting journal entry to record cost of goods sold on Lampen's books at April 30, 1996.

[b] What account(s) in [a] will Lampen have to close when it prepares closing entries on April 30, 1996?

[c] Indicate where the accounts you did *not* include in [a] should appear in Lampen's financial statements.

[d] Prepare a schedule of cost of goods sold for Lampen, Inc., for the year ending April 30, 1996.

[e] Calculate the amount of gross margin.

8–22 Cost of Goods Manufactured   Information pertaining to Lott Manufacturing Corporation for the year ended December 31, 1996, appears as follows:

Indirect labor	$ 45,000
Salespersons' salaries	42,000
Raw materials inventory, Dec. 31	53,000
Depreciation of factory properties	30,000
Work in process, Jan. 1	40,000
Direct labor	110,000
Factory utilities	20,000
Finished goods, Dec. 31	96,000
Work in process, Dec. 31	33,000
Advertising expense	25,000
Raw materials inventory, Jan. 1	46,000
Indirect materials	7,000
Purchases of raw materials	400,000
Property taxes on factory	18,000
Finished goods, Jan. 1	68,000
Returned purchases of raw materials	10,000
Net sales	835,000
Miscellaneous factory expenses	4,000

INSTRUCTIONS

[a] Prepare in good form a schedule of cost of goods manufactured for the year ended December 31, 1996.

[b] Calculate the cost of goods sold.

[c] Calculate the amount of gross margin.

8–23 Direct versus Absorption Costing   The following information pertains to Darwin Manufacturing Company during its first year of business.

Sales	10,000 units
Production	13,000 units

Cost per unit produced	
Direct materials	$2.00
Direct labor	3.00
Variable overhead	2.50
Fixed overhead	1.50

INSTRUCTIONS

Calculate the cost of the company's year-end inventory, assuming (1) absorption costing and (2) direct costing.

8–24 Periodic and Perpetual Systems   Inbody, Inc., is a wholesaler of infant car seats. At the beginning of 1996, the company's inventory consisted of 900 car seats priced at $10 each. During 1996 the following events occurred:

[1] Purchased 8,000 car seats on account at $10 each, terms n/30.
[2] Returned 500 defective car seats to supplier and received credit.
[3] Paid for 6,000 of the car seats purchased in [1].
[4] Sold 7,900 car seats on account for $16 each, terms n/30.
[5] Received 200 car seats returned by a customer and gave credit. The goods were in excellent condition and were therefore returned to regular inventory.
[6] Received cash for 6,800 of the car seats sold in item [4].
[7] Physical count at year-end revealed 600 units on hand.

INSTRUCTIONS

[a] Prepare journal entries (including adjusting entries) to record these events on Inbody's books, assuming that the company uses (1) a periodic system and (2) a perpetual system.
[b] What is the company's cost of goods sold for 1996 under (1) the periodic system and (2) the perpetual system? Explain any difference you find between the two numbers.

8–25 Goods in Transit   Milsap Company had the following purchase and sale transactions near the end of 1996:

No.	Transaction	Terms	Date Merchandise Shipped by Seller	Date Merchandise Received by Buyer
1	Purchase	FOB shipping point	12/31/96	1/5/97
2	Purchase	FOB destination	12/31/96	1/5/97
3	Sale	FOB shipping point	12/31/96	1/5/97
4	Sale	FOB destination	12/31/96	1/5/97

INSTRUCTIONS

For each transaction, indicate whether Milsap Company should include the merchandise in its inventory at December 31, 1996. Assume that all dollar amounts are material. Explain your answer in each case.

8–26 Goods to Include in Inventory   As the independent CPA for Tarver Corporation, state whether the goods in each of the following 1996 events should be included in Tarver's inventory for the fiscal year ending June 30, 1996. Explain your answer in each case.

[1] Finished goods pledged as collateral for a 90-day loan from Countywide Bank were on hand June 30.
[2] An order, accompanied by cash payment for the total sales price, was received on June 29 for goods that Tarver shipped on July 2.
[3] Tarver made advance payments of $2,000 to suppliers for goods ordered but not shipped as of June 30.
[4] On June 30 Tarver shipped goods FOB destination to Glenn Corporation, which received them on July 5.
[5] On June 29 Sherly Company shipped goods FOB shipping point to Tarver, which received them on July 2.
[6] Certain raw materials owned by Tarver were at Snow Company for processing on June 30.
[7] Tarver had certain goods on hand for which it was acting as a selling agent for Soulby Company.

[8] On June 26 Wooley, Inc., shipped goods FOB destination to Tarver, which received the invoice on June 30 and the goods on July 2.

[9] On June 29 Swanner Company shipped goods FOB shipping point to Tarver, which received the invoice and the goods on July 2.

[10] On June 30 Tarver sent goods to a consignee and prepaid the freight charges. The consignee received the goods on July 5.

8-27 Goods to Include in Inventory   During an annual audit at December 31, 1996, you find the following transactions:

[1] Merchandise costing $5,160 was received on January 3, 1997, and the related purchase invoice recorded January 5. The invoice showed that the shipment was made on December 29, 1996, FOB destination.

[2] Merchandise costing $963 was received on December 28, 1996, and the invoice was not recorded. You located it in the hands of the purchasing agent; it was marked "on consignment."

[3] A packing case containing a product costing $765 was not included in the physical inventory because it was marked "hold for shipping instructions." Your investigation revealed that the customer's order was dated December 18, 1996, but the case was shipped and the customer billed on January 10, 1997. The product was a stock item of your client.

[4] Merchandise received on January 6, 1997, costing $720 was entered in the purchase register on January 7, 1997. The invoice showed that shipment was made FOB supplier's warehouse on December 31, 1996. Because it was not on hand December 31, it was not included in inventory.

[5] A special machine, made to order, was finished and in the shipping room on December 31, 1996. The customer was billed on that date, and the machine was excluded from inventory although it was not shipped until January 4, 1997.

INSTRUCTIONS

Assume that the amount is material in each case. State whether the merchandise should be included in the client's inventory, and explain your decision.   (AICPA adapted)

8-28 Net versus Gross Method   Cap Company, which uses a periodic inventory system, had the following merchandise transactions during December 1996:

Dec.   1   Purchased merchandise from Sing Company for $10,000, terms 2/10, n/30.
         2   Purchased merchandise from Song Company for $20,000, terms 3/10, n/30.
       11   Paid Song Company for Dec. 2 purchase.
       30   Paid Sing Company for Dec. 1 purchase.

INSTRUCTIONS

[a] Prepare the general journal entries to record these transactions on the books of Cap Company using (1) the *net method* of recording purchases and (2) the *gross method* of recording purchases.

[b] Discuss the accounting logic of the net method and the gross method of recording purchases.

8-29 FIFO and LIFO   Dooley, Inc., is a wholesaler of footballs. The following information pertains to the company's inventory during July 1996:

Balance, July 1	2,000 units @ $11
Purchase, July 12	2,000 units @ $12
Purchase, July 26	2,000 units @ $15
Balance, July 31	2,500 units

INSTRUCTIONS

Assuming that Dooley uses a periodic inventory system, calculate each of the following amounts for July 1996:

[a] Ending inventory under FIFO.   [c] Ending inventory under LIFO.
[b] Cost of goods sold under LIFO.   [d] Cost of goods sold under FIFO.

8-30 FIFO, LIFO, and Average Cost   Busy Bee Company sells honey. The following information is available from its inventory records for 1996:

	Jars	Cost per Jar
Inventory, Jan. 1	200	$1.00

Purchases		
Jan. 16	300	1.50
Feb. 22	600	2.00
Mar. 3	500	2.50
Mar. 19	400	3.00

During the first quarter of 1996, the company sold 1,400 jars at $7 each. The company uses a periodic system. A physical inventory on March 31 reveals 600 jars on hand.

INSTRUCTIONS

Prepare a schedule in the form shown below and compute the missing values. Show all supporting computations.

	Inventory Mar. 31, 1996	1st Quarter, 1996		
		Sales	Cost of Goods Sold	Gross Margin
LIFO	$	$	$	$
FIFO				
Average cost				

8–31 FIFO, Average Cost, and LIFO Dorani, Inc., uses raw material Z in its production process. The following changes occurred in Dorani's inventory of raw material Z during January:

Jan.	1	Balance on hand	100 units @ $27
	6	Purchased	300 units @ $25
	14	Purchased	600 units @ $28
	25	Purchased	400 units @ $21
Jan.	9	Issued to production	200 units @ ?
	28	Issued to production	800 units @ ?

INSTRUCTIONS

[a] Assuming that Dorani maintains complete *perpetual* records for raw material Z, compute the cost of the inventory at January 31 and the cost of materials issued to production during January using the (1) FIFO, (2) average cost, and (3) LIFO methods. (Round unit cost calculation to three places.)

[b] Assuming that Dorani uses a *periodic* system to account for raw material Z, compute the cost of the inventory at January 31 and the cost of materials issued to production during January using the (1) FIFO, (2) average cost, and (3) LIFO methods. (Round unit cost calculations to three places.)

8–32 Effects of LIFO and FIFO Nephi Company began operations on January 1, 1993, and adopted the LIFO method of inventory pricing. The following additional facts pertain to the company:

Year	Reported Net Income	Ending Inventory under LIFO	Ending Inventory That the Company Would Have Reported under FIFO
1993	$ 48,000	$ 8,000	$15,000
1994	66,000	12,000	22,000
1995	90,000	18,000	12,000
1996	120,000	26,000	17,000

The company's income tax expense has consistently been 40% of income before taxes.

INSTRUCTIONS

Calculate the amount of net income the company would have reported for 1993, 1994, 1995, and 1996 under the FIFO method.

8–33 Lower of Cost or Market   For each of the following *independent* cases, determine the correct unit value for inventory valuation under the LCM rule:

Case	Historical Cost	Cost to Replace	Ceiling	Floor
1	$50	$48	$60	$53
2	78	76	86	72
3	38	37	48	40
4	80	82	79	71
5	23	21	27	22
6	18	17	20	16
7	60	61	59	50
8	89	84	97	88

8–34 Lower of Cost or Market   Langman, Inc., compiled the following inventory information on June 30, 1996, the end of its fiscal year:

	Quantity	Unit Cost	Unit Market
Category 1			
Product A	400	$20	$18
Product B	500	28	32
Category 2			
Product C	700	17	19
Product D	600	18	14
Category 3			
Product E	400	35	39
Product F	300	31	28

INSTRUCTIONS

Compute Langman's inventory valuation at November 30, assuming that the company applies the LCM rule to (1) each product, (2) major categories of products, and (3) the inventory as a whole.

8–35 Lower of Cost or Market   The following information pertains to Majority, Inc., at December 31, 1996:

Inventory, Jan. 1	$ 68,000
Purchases during 1996	428,000
Inventory, Dec. 31	
Cost	60,000
Market	50,000

Before 1996, application of the LCM rule never produced a need to write down the company's inventory to an amount below cost.

INSTRUCTIONS

Prepare the necessary *adjusting* journal entries to record cost of goods sold and to reflect the application of the LCM rule under each of the following assumptions:

[a] The company uses a *periodic* inventory system and applies the LCM rule using a loss account and a valuation allowance account.

[b] The company uses a *periodic* inventory system and applies the LCM rule using neither a loss account nor a valuation allowance account.

[c] The company uses a *perpetual* inventory system and applies the LCM rule using a loss account and a valuation allowance account.

[d] The company uses a *perpetual* inventory system and applies the LCM rule using neither a loss account nor a valuation allowance account.

8–36 Inventory Errors   Bekins, Inc., began operations on January 1, 1995. The following data pertain to the company's first two years in business:

	Reported Amount	Correct Amount
Inventory		
Dec. 31, 1995	$ 20,000	$30,000
Dec. 31, 1996	35,000	35,000
Net income		
For 1995	60,000	?
For 1996	66,000	?
Retained earnings		
Dec. 31, 1995	60,000	?
Dec. 31, 1996	126,000	?

During 1995 and 1996, the company's income tax expense rate was 40%, and the company declared no dividends.

INSTRUCTIONS

Compute the correct amount for each of the following variables:

[a] Net income for 1995.
[b] Net income for 1996.
[c] Retained earnings, December 31, 1995.
[d] Retained earnings, December 31, 1996.

8–37 Inventory Errors Beretta Company uses a periodic inventory system and sells its merchandise for 100% above cost. The following events occurred near the end of the first year of operations (Year 1):

[1] The company failed to record the credit purchase of goods to which it received legal title during Year 1. Although the goods had not been sold by year-end, the company did not include them in its ending inventory.

[2] The company failed to record the credit sales of goods to which it surrendered legal title during Year 1. The company included the goods in its ending inventory.

[3] The company included certain goods to which it had not yet received legal title in its ending inventory. The company did not record a purchase of these goods.

[4] The company recorded a credit purchase of goods to which it received legal title during Year 1. Although the goods had not been sold by year-end, the company did not include them in its ending inventory.

[5] The company recorded a credit purchase of goods to which it did not receive legal title during Year 1. These goods were included in the company's ending inventory.

[6] The company recorded a credit sale of goods to which it had not surrendered legal title as of the end of Year 1. These goods were excluded from the company's ending inventory.

INSTRUCTIONS

Set up a matrix like the one shown below. At the intersection of each row and column, indicate the effect of the event on the financial statement variable at the end of Year 1, using the following code: O = Overstated, U = Understated, NE = No Effect. Treat each event independently. (*Note:* You should have 36 answers in the completed matrix.)

Event No.	Total Revenues	Total Expenses	Net Income	Total Assets	Total Liabilities	Total Stockholders' Equity
1						
2						
3						
4						
5						
6						

8–38 Accrual Basis and Cash Flows   The following data were taken from the financial statements of Beaver Brook, Inc., a calendar-year merchandising corporation:

[1] Balance sheet data:

	Dec. 31, 1995	Dec. 31, 1996
Trade accounts receivable, net	$ 84,000	$ 78,000
Inventory	150,000	140,000
Accounts payable, merchandise (credit)	(95,000)	(98,000)

[2] Total sales were $1,200,000 for 1996 and $1,100,000 for 1995. Cash sales were 20% of total sales each year.

[3] Cost of goods sold was $840,000 for 1996.

[4] Variable general and administrative (G&A) expenses for 1996 were $120,000. They have varied in proportion to sales; 50% have been paid in the year incurred and 50% the following year. Unpaid G&A expenses are *not* included in accounts payable above.

[5] Fixed G&A expenses, including $35,000 depreciation and $5,000 bad debt expense, totaled $100,000 each year. Eighty percent of fixed G&A expenses involving cash were paid in the year incurred and 20% the following year. Each year there was a $5,000 bad debt estimate and a $5,000 write-off. Unpaid G&A expenses are *not* included in accounts payable above.

INSTRUCTIONS

[a] Compute the amount of cash collected during 1996 resulting from total sales in 1995 and 1996.

[b] Compute the amount of cash disbursed during 1996 for purchases of merchandise.

[c] Compute the amount of cash disbursed during 1996 for variable and fixed general and administrative expenses.

(AICPA adapted)

8–39 Current Value Accounting   The controller of Bernstein Company is discussing a comment you made in the course of presenting your audit report.

"... And frankly," Mr. Tauzin continues, "I agree that we, too, are responsible for finding ways to produce more relevant financial statements that are as reliable as the ones we now produce. For example, suppose the company acquired a finished item for inventory for $40 when the general price-level index was 110. And, later, the item was sold for $75 when the general price-level index was 121 and the current replacement cost was $54. We could calculate a 'holding gain.'"

INSTRUCTIONS

[a] Explain to what extent and how current replacement costs already are used in generally accepted accounting principles to value inventories.

[b] Compute the amount of the holding gain in Mr. Tauzin's example.

[c] Why is the use of current replacement cost for *both* inventories and cost of goods sold preferred by some accounting authorities to the generally accepted use of FIFO or LIFO?

[d] Why do some authorities believe that the present market resale (exit or output) price is a conceptual improvement on current replacement (entry or input) cost for inventory measurement?

(AICPA adapted)

PROBLEMS

8–40 Goods to Include in Inventory   Harper, Inc., uses a periodic inventory system and a fiscal year ending September 30. On September 30, 1995, the company correctly reported inventory on hand costing $15,000. During the fiscal year ending September 30, 1996, the company recorded purchases of $56,000. A physical count on September 30, 1996, revealed that goods costing $26,000 were on hand. The following material events occurred between September 23 and October 7, 1996:

[1] Goods costing $3,000 that Harper was holding as a consignee were included in the physical count.

[2] An invoice for goods costing $4,600 was received and entered as a credit purchase on September 29. The goods arrived on October 2. The supplier shipped the goods FOB destination on September 27.

[3] An invoice for goods costing $4,100 was received and entered as a credit purchase on October 3. The goods arrived on that date and were in satisfactory condition. The invoice indicates that the supplier shipped the goods FOB shipping point on September 29.

[4] Goods that Harper specially purchased from an overseas supplier for ultimate sale to Digital Enterprises, Inc., were included in the physical count. A contract between Harper and Digital pertaining to the goods states that "title passes when buyer approves the goods." A representative from Digital Enterprises inspected and approved the goods in Harper's warehouse on September 28. Harper shipped the goods and recorded a sale on October 4. The goods cost $2,500 and were sold on credit for $3,600.

[5] Goods costing $800 and housed in a special storeroom were inadvertently overlooked when the physical count was taken.

[6] An invoice for goods costing $3,100 was received and entered as a credit purchase on September 28. The supplier shipped the goods FOB shipping point on September 26. The receiving report indicates that Harper received them on October 1.

INSTRUCTIONS

[a] Make all necessary correcting entries in general journal form for the fiscal year ending September 30, 1996. Assume that the adjusting entry for cost of goods sold has not been made and that the books for the year have not been closed.

[b] Compute the correct inventory amount for Harper's balance sheet dated September 30, 1996.

[c] Make the adjusting journal entry to record the cost of goods sold for the fiscal year ending September 30, 1996.

8–41 Goods to Include in Inventory Cheers Company of Boston uses a periodic inventory system and a fiscal year ending June 30. The company makes all its merchandise purchases and sales on credit. The following information is available from the company's inventory records:

Beginning inventory, July 1, 1995	$20,000
Purchases, July 1, 1995–June 30, 1996	90,000
Purchase returns, July 1, 1995–June 30, 1996	2,000
Ending inventory, June 30, 1996 (per physical count)	16,000

The following events occurred near the end of the fiscal year that ended on June 30, 1996:

[1] Goods costing $4,000 received on June 27 were recorded as a purchase twice.

[2] Goods shipped by rail from Boston to a Seattle customer were recorded as a sale on June 30. The goods cost $3,600; the selling price was $7,000. They were shipped on June 30, FOB Seattle. Cheers Company did not include these goods in its physical inventory.

[3] Goods costing $3,500 received on June 29 were recorded as a purchase on July 2.

[4] Goods costing $4,500 were recorded as a purchase on July 5. A Phoenix, Arizona, supplier shipped them to Boston by rail, FOB Phoenix, on June 30.

[5] Goods costing $2,400 held by Bailey Company on consignment were not counted. Cheers Company recorded a sale of $6,000 when it shipped them to Bailey on June 23.

[6] Goods costing $3,800 were received on June 18 and returned for credit on June 20 because they were not satisfactory. Cheers Company did not record these events.

INSTRUCTIONS

[a] Make all necessary correcting entries in general journal form for the fiscal year ending June 30, 1996. Assume that the adjusting entry for the cost of goods sold has not been made and that the books for the year have not been closed.

[b] Compute the correct inventory amount for Cheers Company's balance sheet dated June 30, 1996.

[c] Make the adjusting journal entry to record the cost of goods sold for the fiscal year ending June 30, 1996.

8–42 Net versus Gross Method Wong, Inc., began operations in 1996. The company maintains complete perpetual records for its merchandise inventory. During 1996 Wong purchased merchandise having a gross invoice cost of $100,000. All purchases were made under the terms 2/10, n/30. Wong paid freight charges of $5,000 for the merchandise.

During the year, Wong paid for 80% of the merchandise within the discount period; it paid for the other 20% after the discount period had expired. Wong sold 70% of the merchandise it acquired for cash of $120,000; the other 30% remains in inventory at year-end.

INSTRUCTIONS

[a] Prepare the general journal entries to record these transactions on Wong's books using (1) the *net method* of recording purchases and (2) the *gross method* of recording purchases.

[b] What financial statement balances would Wong report at December 31, 1996, for sales, cost of goods sold, gross margin, discounts lost (or interest expense), and ending inventory under (1) the *net method* and (2) the *gross method?*

[c] Which method of recording purchases (net method or gross method) is generally regarded as theoretically superior? Why?

8–43 FIFO, Average Cost, and LIFO The following information pertains to Model A–4 digital watches of Time Corporation for the month of July 1996:

Date	Calculators	Units	Unit Cost	Unit Selling Price
July 1	Beginning inventory	1,000	$52	
7	Purchase	3,000	50	
12	Sale	2,000		$90
17	Purchase	6,000	45	
22	Purchase	2,000	43	
28	Sale	7,000		90
31	Ending inventory	3,000		

INSTRUCTIONS

[a] Assuming that the company uses a *periodic* inventory system, calculate the cost of the ending inventory and the cost of goods sold using (1) the FIFO method, (2) the average cost method, and (3) the LIFO method. (Round unit cost calculations to three places.)

[b] Assuming that the company uses a *perpetual* inventory system, calculate the cost of the ending inventory *and* the cost of goods sold using (1) the FIFO method, (2) the average cost method, and (3) the LIFO method. (Round unit cost calculations to three places.)

[c] Calculate the amount of gross margin in [a-1, 2, 3] and [b-1, 2, 3].

[d] Assume that the inflation rate (i.e., the increase in the overall level of prices in the economy) was 1% during July 1996. Use your answer to [c] to logically evaluate the claim that the use of LIFO produces lower earnings during inflationary periods.

8–44 FIFO, Average Cost, and LIFO The following inventory information pertains to the Suny small-screen TVs of Circuit Town, Inc., for the year ended December 31, 1996:

Date	TVs	Units	Unit Cost	Total Cost
Jan. 1	Inventory on hand	200	$150	$ 30,000
Mar. 14	Purchase	300	175	52,500
Oct. 3	Purchase	400	200	80,000
	Available for sale	900		$162,500

The company sold 400 TVs on May 30 and 300 on December 20. A physical count on December 31 indicates that 200 TVs are on hand.

INSTRUCTIONS

[a] Assuming that the company uses a *periodic* inventory system, calculate the cost of the ending inventory *and* the cost of goods sold using (1) the FIFO method, (2) the average cost method, and (3) the LIFO method. (Round unit cost calculations to three places.)

[b] Assuming that the company uses a *perpetual* inventory system, calculate the cost of the ending inventory *and* the cost of goods sold using (1) the FIFO method, (2) the average cost method, and (3) the LIFO method. (Round unit cost calculations to three places.)

8–45 Effects of LIFO and FIFO Kenelley, Inc., began operations on January 1, 1993, and adopted the LIFO method of inventory pricing. Condensed income statements for Kenelley, Inc., for 1993–1996 appear below.

	1993	1994	1995	1996
Net sales	$250,000	$300,000	$400,000	$480,000
Cost of goods sold	125,000	150,000	200,000	240,000
Gross margin	125,000	150,000	200,000	240,000
S&A expenses	75,000	75,000	75,000	75,000
Pretax income	50,000	75,000	125,000	165,000

	1993	1994	1995	1996
Income taxes (40%)	20,000	30,000	50,000	66,000
Net income	$ 30,000	$ 45,000	$ 75,000	$ 99,000

Kenelley's comparative balance sheets showed the following LIFO inventory amounts at December 31: 1993—$25,000; 1994—$27,000; 1995—$30,000; and 1996—$38,000.

Notes to Kenelley's financial statements indicated that if the company had used the FIFO inventory method, December 31 inventories would have been as follows: 1993—$35,000; 1994—$42,000; 1995—$50,000; and 1996—$65,000.

INSTRUCTIONS

[a] Using the condensed format shown above, prepare income statements for Kenelley, Inc., for 1993–1996, assuming that the company had used FIFO since its inception.

[b] Explain the underlying factors that cause Kenelley's net income under FIFO to differ from its net income under LIFO.

8–46 Effect of Change from FIFO to LIFO Woodside Terrace Company manufactures two products: Q-1 and Q-2. On December 31, 1995, Woodside used the FIFO inventory method. On January 1, 1996, it changed to the LIFO method. The cumulative effect of this change is not determinable and, as a result, the ending inventory of 1995 under FIFO is also the beginning inventory for 1996 under LIFO. Any layers added during 1996 should be costed by reference to the first acquisitions of 1996, and any layers liquidated during 1996 should be considered a permanent liquidation.

The following information was available from Woodside's inventory records for the last two years:

	Q-1		Q-2	
	Units	Unit Cost	Units	Unit Cost
1995 Purchases				
Jan. 7	5,000	$4.00	22,000	$2.00
Apr. 16	12,000	4.50		
Nov. 8	17,000	5.00	18,500	2.75
Dec. 13	10,000	6.00		
1996 Purchases				
Feb. 11	3,000	7.00	23,000	3.00
May 20	8,000	7.50		
Oct. 15	20,000	8.00		
Dec. 23			15,500	3.50
Units on Hand				
Dec. 31, 1995	15,000		14,500	
Dec. 31, 1996	16,000		12,000	

INSTRUCTIONS

Compute the effect of the change from the FIFO to the LIFO inventory method on income before income taxes for the year ended December 31, 1996. (AICPA adapted)

8–47 Effects of FIFO, LIFO, and Average Cost The controller of Rosetta Corporation, a retail company, made three different schedules of gross margin for the first quarter ended September 30, 1996. These schedules appear below.

	Sales ($10 per unit)	Cost of Goods Sold	Gross Margin
Schedule 1	$280,000	$118,550	$161,450
Schedule 2	280,000	116,900	163,100
Schedule 3	280,000	115,750	164,250

The computation of cost of goods sold in each schedule is based on the following data.

	Units	Cost per Unit	Total Cost
Beginning inventory, July 1	10,000	$4.00	$40,000
Purchase, July 25	8,000	4.20	33,600

	Units	Cost per Unit	Total Cost
Purchase, Aug. 15	5,000	4.13	20,650
Purchase, Sept. 5	7,000	4.30	30,100
Purchase, Sept. 25	12,000	4.25	51,000

The president of the corporation cannot understand how three different gross margins can be computed from the same set of data. As controller, you have explained that the three schedules are based on three different assumptions concerning the flow of inventory costs: FIFO, LIFO, and weighted average. Schedules 1, 2, and 3 were not necessarily prepared in this sequence of cost flow assumptions.

INSTRUCTIONS

Prepare three separate schedules computing cost of goods sold and supporting schedules. Show the composition of the ending inventory under each of the three cost flow assumptions.

(AICPA adapted)

8–48 Lower of Cost or Market　USCO Company manufactures four products and prices its inventory using the lower of average cost or market value. The company maintains a normal profit margin rate of 20% of selling price. USCO's accountant gathered the following information, all on a per unit basis, at December 31, 1996:

Product	Historical Cost	Current Replacement Cost	Estimated Selling Price	Estimated Cost to Dispose
W	$23	$22	$30	$ 3
X	28	24	40	5
Y	47	48	70	10
Z	81	82	90	10

INSTRUCTIONS

[a] Prepare a schedule to determine the correct unit values for the inventory valuation of each product under the LCM rule.

[b] Explain the rationale for the use of selling prices when applying the LCM rule.

8–49 Lower of Cost or Market　Selected items of merchandise information for eight independent cases (1 through 8) appear below. In each case, the normal profit margin rate is 30% of selling price.

INSTRUCTIONS

Set up a table similar to the one shown below and compute the missing values.

Case	Estimated Selling Price	Estimated Cost to Dispose	Ceiling	Allowance for Normal Profit Margin	Floor	Replacement Cost	Market	Historical Cost	LCM
1	$60		$50			$52		$51	
2		$5		$15		28		31	
3			18	6			$16		$15
4	30	4						19	18
5	10		9			7		8	
6		6		12		35			32
7			69	24		72		70	
8	70	9				37		41	

8–50 Lower of Cost or Market　The following inventory information pertains to Tombras, Inc., at December 31, 1996:

		Per Unit			
	Quantity	Original Cost	Cost to Replace	Net Realizable Value	Floor
Small Appliances					
Product A	500	$25	$22	$27	$23
Product B	300	31	33	36	29
Garden Products					
Product C	600	14	18	20	13
Product D	800	21	21	20	15

INSTRUCTIONS

[a] Determine the inventory valuation at December 31, 1996, assuming that the company applies the LCM rule to (1) each product, (2) major categories of products, and (3) the inventory as a whole.

[b] The accountant for Tombras is trying to determine which one of the three amounts in [a] she should use in the company's published financial statements. What major factors should she consider?

8–51 Inventory Errors Condensed income statements for Twin City Company for 1991–1996 appear below.

	Year Ending December 31					
	1991	1992	1993	1994	1995	1996
Net sales	$125,000	$132,000	$141,000	$156,000	$163,000	$176,000
Cost of goods sold	75,000	80,000	85,000	94,000	98,000	106,000
Gross margin	50,000	52,000	56,000	62,000	65,000	70,000
S&A expenses	30,000	31,000	34,000	39,000	41,000	45,000
Pretax income	20,000	21,000	22,000	23,000	24,000	25,000
Income taxes (40%)	8,000	8,400	8,800	9,200	9,600	10,000
Net income	$ 12,000	$ 12,600	$ 13,200	$ 13,800	$ 14,400	$ 15,000

The previous statements were prepared without knowledge of the inventory errors shown below.

Date	Inventory
Dec. 31, 1990	Correctly stated
Dec. 31, 1991	Understated $10,000
Dec. 31, 1992	Overstated $8,000
Dec. 31, 1993	Understated $6,000
Dec. 31, 1994	Correctly stated
Dec. 31, 1995	Overstated $12,000
Dec. 31, 1996	Overstated $6,000

INSTRUCTIONS

[a] Using the condensed format shown above, prepare corrected income statements for Twin City Company for 1991–1996.

[b] Describe the overall impact that the correction of the inventory errors in [a] has on the company's earnings trend.

8–52 Inventory Errors You have been asked to review the records and prepare corrected financial statements for U-102 Corporation. The accounting records agree with the following balance sheet:

U-102 Corporation
Balance Sheet
December 31, 1996

Assets		Liabilities and Capital	
Cash	$ 5,000	Accounts payable	$ 2,000
Accounts receivable	10,000	Notes payable	4,000
Notes receivable	3,000	Capital stock	10,000
Inventory	25,000	Retained earnings	27,000
	$43,000		$43,000

A review of U-102's books indicates that the following errors and omissions had *not* been corrected during the applicable years:

Dec. 31	Inventory Overvalued	Inventory Undervalued	Prepaid Expense	Unearned Revenue	Accrued Expense	Accrued Revenue
1993	—	$6,000	$900	—	$200	—
1994	$7,000	—	700	$400	75	$125
1995	8,000	—	500	—	100	—
1996	—	9,000	600	300	50	150

According to the books, net income is $4,000 in 1994, $6,500 in 1995, and $7,500 in 1996. No dividends were declared during these years and no adjustments were made to retained earnings.

INSTRUCTIONS

Prepare a worksheet to develop the correct net income for 1994, 1995, and 1996 and the adjusted balance sheet accounts as of December 31, 1996. (Ignore possible income tax effects.)

(AICPA adapted)

8–53 Sales and Purchases Cutoff   You have been engaged to audit Midwest Company for the year ended December 31, 1996. Midwest, a wholesale chemical business, makes all sales at 25% over cost.

Shown below are portions of Midwest's sales and purchases accounts for the calendar year 1996:

Sales

Date	Reference	Amount	Date	Reference	Amount
12/31	Closing entry	700,590	Balance forward		658,320
			12/27	SI#965	5,195
			12/28	SI#966	20,000
			12/28	SI#967	1,302
			12/31	SI#969	5,841
			12/31	SI#970	7,922
			12/31	SI#971	2,010
		700,590			700,590

Purchases

Date	Reference	Amount	Date	Reference	Amount
Balance forward		360,300	12/31	Closing entry	385,346
12/28	RR#1059	3,100			
12/30	RR#1061	8,965			
12/31	RR#1062	4,861			
12/31	RR#1063	8,120			
		385,346			385,346

RR = Receiving report.
SI = Sales invoice.

You observed the taking of physical inventory of goods in the warehouse on December 31, 1996, and were satisfied that it was properly taken. When you conducted a sales and purchases cutoff test (to determine that these transactions are recorded in the proper period), you found that at December 31, 1996, the last receiving report that had been used was no. 1063 and that no shipments had been made on any sales invoices with numbers larger than no. 968. You also obtained the following additional information:

[1] Included in the physical inventory were chemicals that had been purchased and received on receiving report no. 1060 but for which an invoice was not received until 1997. The cost was $4,366.

[2] In the warehouse at December 31, 1996, were goods that had been sold and paid for by the customer but that were not shipped until 1997. They were all sold on sales invoice no. 965 and were not inventoried. (The sales agreement between Midwest Company and this customer provided

that title to the goods passes as soon as the customer pays for them and the seller processes the customer's order.)

[3] On the evening of December 31, 1996, there were two cars on Midwest Company siding:

    [a] Car #AR38162 was unloaded on January 2, 1997, and received on receiving report no. 1063. The freight was paid by the vendor.

    [b] Car #BAE74123 was loaded and sealed on December 31, 1996, and was switched off the company's siding on January 2, 1997. The sales price was $12,700 and the freight was paid by the customer. This order was sold on sales invoice no. 968.

[4] Two cars of chemicals enroute to Z Pulp and Paper Company were temporarily stranded on December 31, 1996, on a railroad siding. They were sold on sales invoice no. 966 and the terms were FOB destination.

[5] A truckload of material enroute to Midwest Company on December 31, 1996, was received on receiving report no. 1064. The material was shipped FOB destination and freight of $75 was paid by Midwest Company. However, the freight was deducted from the purchase price of $975.

[6] Chemicals exposed to rain in transit and deemed unsalable were included in the physical inventory. Their invoice cost was $1,250 and freight charges of $350 had been paid on them.

INSTRUCTIONS

[a] Compute the adjustments that should be made to Midwest Company's physical inventory at December 31, 1996.

[b] Prepare the adjusting entries required as of December 31, 1996.   (AICPA adapted)

8–54 Inventory Reconciliation   Canary Company cans two food commodities that it stores at various warehouses. The company uses a perpetual inventory system under which the finished goods inventory is charged with production and credited for sales at standard cost. The detail of the finished goods inventory is maintained on punched cards by the tabulating department in units and dollars for the various warehouses.

The accounting department receives copies of daily production reports and sales invoices. Units are then extended at standard cost and a summary of the day's activity is posted to the Finished Goods Inventory general ledger control account. Next the sales invoices and production reports are sent to the tabulating department for processing. Every month the control account and detailed tab records are reconciled and adjustments recorded. The last reconciliation and adjustments were made at November 30, 1996.

Your CPA firm observed the taking of the physical inventory at all locations on December 31, 1996. The inventory count began at 4:00 p.m. and was completed at 8:00 p.m. The company's figure for the physical inventory is $342,400. The general ledger control account balance at December 31 was $384,900, and the final "tab run" of the inventory punched cards showed a total of $403,300.

Unit cost data for the company's two products are as follows:

Product	Standard Cost
A	$2
B	3

A review of December transactions disclosed the following:

[1] Sales invoice no. 1301, Dec. 2, was priced at standard cost for $11,700 but was listed on the accounting department's daily summary at $11,200.

[2] A production report for $23,900, Dec. 15, was processed twice in error by the tabulating department.

[3] Sales invoice no. 1423, Dec. 9, for 1,200 units of product A was priced at a standard cost of $1.50 per unit by the accounting department. The tabulating department corrected the error but did not notify the accounting department of it.

[4] A shipment of 3,400 units of Product A was invoiced by the billing department as 3,000 units on sales invoice no. 1504, Dec. 27. The error was discovered by your review of transactions.

[5] On December 27 the Memphis warehouse notified the tabulating department to remove 2,200 unsalable units of Product A from the finished goods inventory, which it did without receiving a special invoice from the accounting department. The accounting department received a copy of the Memphis warehouse notification on December 29 and prepared a special invoice, which was processed in the normal manner. The units were not included in the physical inventory.

[6] A report for the production on January 3 of 2,500 units of Product B was processed for the Omaha plant as of December 31.

[7] A shipment of 300 units of Product B was made from the Portland warehouse to Ben's Markets, Inc., at 8:30 p.m. on December 31 as an emergency service. The sales invoice was processed as of December 31. Canary Company prefers to treat the transaction as a sale in 1996.

[8] The working papers of the auditor observing the physical count at the Chicago warehouse revealed that 700 units of Product B were omitted from Canary's physical count. Canary concurred that the units were omitted in error.

[9] A sales invoice for 600 units of Product A shipped from the Newark warehouse was mislaid and was not processed until January 5. The units were shipped on December 30.

[10] The physical inventory of the St. Louis warehouse excluded 350 units of Product A marked "reserved." Investigation revealed that this merchandise was being stored as a convenience for Harry's Markets, Inc., a customer. This merchandise, which has not been recorded as a sale, is billed as it is shipped.

[11] A shipment of 10,000 units of Product B was made on December 27 from the Newark warehouse to the Chicago warehouse. The shipment arrived on January 6 but had been excluded from the physical inventories.

INSTRUCTIONS

Prepare a worksheet to reconcile the balances for the physical inventory, Finished Goods Inventory general ledger control account, and the tabulating department's detail of finished goods inventory ("tab run"). Use the format shown below.

	Physical Inventory	General Ledger Control Account	Tabulating Department's Detail of Inventory
Balance per client	$342,400	$384,900	$403,300

(AICPA adapted)

8-55 Corrected Inventory You are auditing Falcon Enterprises for the year ended December 31, 1996. To reduce the workload at year-end, the company took its annual physical inventory under your observation on November 30, 1996. The company's Inventory account, which includes raw material and work in process, is on a perpetual basis and the FIFO method of pricing is used. There is no finished goods inventory. The company's physical inventory revealed that the book inventory of $58,410 was understated by $3,000. To avoid distorting the interim financial statements, the company decided not to adjust the book inventory, except for obsolete inventory items, until year-end.

Your audit revealed the following information about the November 30 inventory:

[1] Pricing tests showed that the physical inventory was overpriced by $2,200.

[2] Footing and extension errors resulted in a $150 understatement of the physical inventory.

[3] Direct labor included in the physical inventory amounted to $10,000. Overhead was included at the rate of 200% of direct labor. You determined that the amount of direct labor was correct and the overhead rate was proper.

[4] The physical inventory included obsolete materials recorded at $250. During December these obsolete materials were removed from the inventory account and charged to Cost of Sales.

Your audit also disclosed the following information about the December 31 inventory:

[1] Total debits to certain accounts during December are listed below:

Purchases	$24,700
Direct labor	12,100
Manufacturing overhead	25,200
Cost of sales	68,600

[2] The cost of sales of $68,600 included direct labor of $13,800.

[3] Normal scrap loss on established product lines is negligible. However, a special order started and completed during December had excessive scrap loss of $800, which was charged to Manufacturing Overhead.

INSTRUCTIONS

[a] Compute the correct amount of the physical inventory at November 30, 1996.

[b] Without prejudice to your solution to [a], assume that the correct amount of the physical inventory at November 30, 1996, was $55,250. Compute the amount of the inventory at December 31, 1996.

(AICPA adapted)

8–56 LIFO   Bill Fallon, president of All-Out, Inc., read an article claiming that many of the country's largest 500 companies were either adopting or considering adopting the last-in, first-out (LIFO) method for valuing inventories. The article stated that the firms were switching to LIFO to (1) neutralize the effect of inflation in their financial statements, (2) eliminate inventory profits, and (3) reduce income taxes. Fallon wonders if the switch would benefit his company.

All-Out currently uses the first-in, first-out (FIFO) method of inventory valuation in its periodic inventory system. The company has a high inventory turnover rate, and inventories represent a significant proportion of the assets.

In discussing this trend toward LIFO inventory with business friends, Fallon has been told that the LIFO system is more costly to operate and will provide little benefit to companies with high turnover. Fallon intends to use the inventory method that is best for the company in the long run and not to select a method just because it is the current fad.

INSTRUCTIONS

[a] Explain to Mr. Fallon what "inventory profits" are and how the LIFO method of inventory valuation could reduce them.

[b] Explain to Mr. Fallon the conditions that must exist for All-Out to receive tax benefits from the LIFO method.   (CMA adapted)

8–57 FIFO and LIFO   FIND Company is considering changing its inventory valuation method from FIFO to LIFO because of the potential tax savings. However, the management wishes to consider all of the effects on the company, including its reported performance, before making the final decision.

The Inventory account, currently valued on the FIFO basis, consists of 1,000,000 units at $7 per unit on January 1, 1996. There are 1,000,000 shares of common stock outstanding as of January 1, 1996, and the cash balance is $400,000.

The company has made the following forecasts for the period 1996–1998:

	1996	1997	1998
Unit sales (in millions of units)	1.1	1.0	1.3
Sales price per unit	$10	$10	$12
Unit purchases (in millions of units)	1.0	1.1	1.2
Purchase price per unit	$7	$8	$9
Annual depreciation (in thousands of dollars)	$300	$300	$300
Cash dividends per share	$.15	$.15	$.15
Cash payments for additions to and replacement of plant and equipment (in thousands of dollars)	$350	$350	$350
Income tax rate	40%	40%	40%
Operating expense (exclusive of depreciation) as a percent of sales	15%	15%	15%
Common shares outstanding (in millions)	1	1	1

INSTRUCTIONS

[a] Prepare a schedule that illustrates and compares the following data for FIND Company under the FIFO and the LIFO inventory method for 1996–1998. Assume that the company would begin LIFO at the beginning of 1996.

  [1] Year-end inventory balances.   [3] Earnings per share.
  [2] Annual net income.   [4] Cash balance.

Assume that all sales are collected in the year of sale and all purchases, operating expenses, and taxes are paid during the year incurred.

[b] Using the data above, your answer to [a], and any additional issues you believe need to be considered, prepare a report that recommends whether or not FIND Company should change to the LIFO inventory method. Support your conclusions with appropriate arguments. (CMA adapted)

8–58 Insurance Costs, LCM, and LIFO   Pasco Company purchased a significant amount of raw materials inventory for a new product that it is manufacturing. Pasco purchased insurance on these raw materials while they were in transit from the supplier.

Pasco uses the lower of cost or market rule for these raw materials. The replacement cost of the raw materials is above the net realizable value and both are below the original cost.

Pasco uses the average cost inventory method for these raw materials. In the last two years, each purchase has been at a lower price than the previous purchase, and the ending inventory quantity for each period has been higher than the beginning inventory quantity for that period.

INSTRUCTIONS

[a] What is the theoretically appropriate method that Pasco should use to account for the insurance costs on the raw materials while they were in transit from the supplier? Why?

[b] [1] At which amount should Pasco's raw materials inventory be reported on the balance sheet? Why?

[2] In general, why is the lower of cost or market rule used to report inventory?

[c] What would have been the effect on ending inventory and cost of goods sold had Pasco used the LIFO inventory method instead of the average cost inventory method for the raw materials? Why?

(AICPA adapted)

JUDGMENT CASES

8–59 Recognizing a Sale   You are the controller (head of the accounting department) for Classic Corporation, a large, publicly held manufacturer of electronic products and component parts. The company recognizes sales revenue according to the accrual basis of accounting.

Today's date is *January 20, 1996,* and you have just completed your initial draft of the financial statements for Classic's accounting period that ended on December 31, 1995. The income statement shows that the company's earnings per share (EPS) for 1995 are considerably lower than had been previously expected. In fact, the 1995 EPS are lower than EPS for 1994, and this breaks a 10-year trend of rising EPS.

Classic's chief executive officer, Don Wilkey, enters your office and lets you know that he is extremely displeased with these earnings results. He is especially concerned about the potential negative effect of the EPS decline on the company's stock price and subsequent shareholder reaction.

Mr. Wilkey then brings up the subject of a large order of compact disc players that Classic recently manufactured under a special order placed by Sound Design Corporation, a national retail electronics chain. The contract with Sound Design provided that the CD players would be manufactured according to Sound Design's precise specifications and that title to the goods would pass "on the date Sound Design approves the goods." Classic Corporation produced the goods during 1995, and a Sound Design representative inspected and approved them on January 3, 1996. Classic then shipped the goods on January 3.

Mr. Wilkey observes that the preliminary 1995 income statement does not reflect the large sale made to Sound Design. He points out that if the income statement could be revised to include the sale, EPS for 1995 would be comfortably higher than for 1994. Classic could then continue its string of unbroken EPS increases, and its stockholders would be happy. Mr. Wilkey tells you that he has a way to convince the independent auditors to go along with his plan, but he does not explain exactly what he has in mind.

You inform Mr. Wilkey that generally accepted accounting principles permit a sale to be recognized only when title to goods in inventory passes from a seller to a buyer, in this case, on January 3, 1996. Mr. Wilkey then states that "the goods in question were completed in 1995, and it only seems fair and reasonable to recognize the sales revenue in 1995. The fact that Sound Design did not inspect the goods until January 3, 1996, is trivial."

Mr. Wilkey then suggests that you revise the 1995 income statement to reflect a sale of the special order merchandise to Sound Design. As he leaves your office, he reminds you of the need for everyone at Classic to be a team player.

INSTRUCTIONS

Would you revise the 1995 income statement in accordance with Mr. Wilkey's instructions? Explain in detail the rationale that supports your decision. As a *part* of your explanation, include a discussion of the major parties who would be affected by your decision.

8–60 Lower of Cost or Market Decision   Joy Toys, Inc., typically manufactures most of its product in anticipation of the Christmas season. Sometimes the company quickly designs and manufactures a toy to take advantage of fads (such as Star Wars) that sweep the nation.

During the accounting period that just ended, the company designed and produced a large number of a toy called "Sneak Bombers," which the company anticipated rushing to market. The toy emulates a widely publicized new bomber that the federal government has recently considered funding for the armed forces. Shortly before Joy Toys was set to begin taking customer orders for the toy bombers, the U.S. Congress failed to pass enabling legislation to fund the real bomber's production. As a result, the news about the bomber has been adverse and interest in it has diminished. Market studies show that if Congress does not fund the bomber's production, little interest in it will exist and the toy bombers probably will not be marketable at a price and volume necessary for Joy Toys to recover its cost of production.

The U.S. president stated at a recent news conference that he intends to fight for the bomber and suggested that he might call Congress back into a special session to reconsider funding for production of the new aircraft. Furthermore, a hostile foreign nation recently declared war on a U.S. ally, and the president and Congress have expressed outrage. In fact, a number of congresspeople who had originally voted against the bomber have said that they are reconsidering their earlier vote in light of the latest world crisis.

Joy Toys must file its financial statements for the most recent accounting period with the SEC later this week, and its president does not want to recognize any losses in the value of the inventory of toy bombers. He believes that if Congress provides even limited funding for the bomber's production, the toy will "sell like hotcakes." He believes that the chances of Congress funding the project are "better than 75%" and observes that "it's an ill wind that blows no good" in regard to the recent outbreak of war between the two foreign countries.

INSTRUCTIONS

Do you believe that Joy Toys should recognize a loss on its inventory of Sneak Bombers in the financial statements for the accounting period just ended? Support your answer with careful analysis and reasoning.

8–61 Inventory Reporting Florida Partners, Ltd., is a limited partnership formed to fund the cultivation and sale of a variety of tropical plants. The investors provide funding to the limited partnership, which in turn advances monies to a contract grower, Green Top Growers (GTG), Inc., which is then responsible for acquiring the plants and plant materials, planting and cultivating the plants until their maturity, and then selling them on behalf of the limited partnership. GTG, a closely held company whose financial statements are not audited, is involved in a number of such arrangements and also grows plants on its own behalf. GTG has existed for 10 years, although it has expanded substantially only in the last two. The types of plants in question take between 18 months and 3 years to grow.

You are the accountant for Florida Partners and are currently preparing its financial statements for the year just ended. Because the limited partnership has only recently been formed, the project is not very far along at this time. The monies advanced to GTG so far are intended to provide only for the acquisition of the plants and plant materials and their initial planting. GTG is authorized to acquire the plant materials in the form of seeds, seedlings, or cuttings limited only in such a fashion as to meet the projected growing schedules in the partnership agreement.

As of the partnership's balance sheet date, GTG had acquired the necessary seeds and seedlings and planted them in accordance with the agreement. The cuttings will be made from stock plants owned by GTG and then planted by GTG on behalf of Florida Partners. On a recent visit to GTG's facilities, you noticed that none of the cuttings have been made, although GTG has a large number of stock plants from which, according to its president, the cuttings will soon be taken.

The general partner of the limited partnership believes that the balance sheet description of the amounts advanced to GTG should be characterized as "plant inventory." She readily agrees to disclose the fact that the inventory is held and is being cultivated by a contract grower and that the inventory will continue to be cared for by GTG on behalf of the limited partnership. You nevertheless wonder whether calling all of the amounts advanced to GTG "plant inventory" is appropriate in light of the fact that the cuttings have not yet been completed. The president responds to your concerns in the following fashion: "The cuttings exist. They simply have not yet been separated from the stock plants. Moreover, we have paid GTG and it is obligated to perform according to the contract. The plant material exists, is growing at this time, and was growing at the balance sheet date. I believe that those cuttings exist, belong to the limited partnership, and should be so reported. To do otherwise might unduly alarm the investors by causing them to believe that the project is behind schedule or otherwise troubled when, in fact, it is not. We only recently funded the partnership and things are going perfectly. Why plant any seeds of doubt if, in fact, none exist?"

INSTRUCTIONS

What should the amounts advanced to GTG by the partnership be called on the partnership's balance sheet? Do you believe that it would be acceptable to refer to the items as "plant inventory"? Defend your answers with appropriate arguments. Regardless of your answers to these questions, what information do you believe should be disclosed about the state of the inventory and costs paid to the contract grower?

8–62 Accounting for Costs   At the beginning of last year your company, Many Things, Inc., embarked on a real estate development project involving single-family dwellings. By the end of the year the company wished that it had not done so because of a substantial economic downturn caused primarily by a large plant closure near the project. The company has incurred significant acquisition and construction costs, and you are attempting to determine whether those costs now exceed the net realizable value (NRV) of the project.

You have read the authoritative accounting literature on the subject, consisting primarily of *FASB Statement No. 67,* "Accounting for Costs and Initial Rental Operations of Real Estate Projects." In particular, you are puzzled as to whether the calculation of NRV must include interest and property taxes that are incurred after the completion of the project but before the expected sale of the inventory of dwellings.

This issue is especially important because if post-completion interest and taxes are included in the NRV calculation then a loss on the project will be required so as not to value the project at more than its NRV. If those costs do not have to be included in the calculation, however, then a loss on the property will not have to be recognized during the current year.

INSTRUCTIONS

Do you believe that it is necessary to impound post-completion interest and property taxes in the calculation? Explain and support your answer in a written memorandum.

FINANCIAL REPORTING CASE

8–63 Financial Reporting Case   Armstrong World Industries is a manufacturer and marketer of interior furnishings. Its products include floor coverings, building materials, and furniture.

Armstrong's 1993 and 1992 balance sheets include a single line for inventories at $286.2 million and $319.4 million, respectively. The inventories note that accompanies that 1993 financial statements is as follows:

> **Inventories** were $33.2 million lower at the end of 1993, a 10 percent decline from the 1992 year-end position. The decrease was primarily a result of the successful ongoing process changes that reduced cycle time and improved inventory turnover from 8.0 to 8.8 turns on sales.
>
> Approximately half of the inventory reduction occurred in Europe with about $4.0 million of the reduction related to the translation of foreign currency inventories to U.S. dollars at lower exchange rates.
>
> Approximately 51% in 1993 and 48% in 1992 of the company's total inventory is valued on a LIFO (last-in, first-out) basis. Such inventory values were lower than would have been reported on a total FIFO (first-in, first-out) basis, by $109.7 million at the end of 1993 and $108.3 million at year-end 1992.

Inventories *(millions)*	1993	1992
Finished goods	**$176.8**	$203.4
Goods in process	**34.5**	34.3
Raw materials and supplies	**74.9**	81.7
Total	**$286.2**	$319.4

Inventories are valued at the lower of cost or market. Approximately two-thirds of 1993's domestic inventories are valued using the LIFO method. Other inventories are generally determined on a FIFO method.

INSTRUCTIONS

[a] What method(s) of accounting for inventories are used?
[b] What explanation does the company make for the decline in inventory from 1992 to 1993?
[c] What would be the impact on the financial statements if those inventories accounted for by the LIFO method had been accounted for by the FIFO method?
[d] Why do you think the company presents detailed information about finished goods, goods in process, and raw materials and supplies in the note rather than in the balance sheet?

Inventories: Additional Valuation Methods

OBJECTIVES

1. To discuss and illustrate the dollar-value LIFO method.
2. To discuss and illustrate the conventional retail method.
3. To discuss and illustrate the retail LIFO method.
4. To discuss and illustrate the gross margin method.

Several years ago, Stauffer Chemical Company had a dispute with the SEC concerning the manner in which the company pooled its LIFO inventories. Most manufacturing companies have fewer than five LIFO pools and many have only one, but Stauffer had set up 288. It had so many that the SEC effectively referred to them as "puddles." Stauffer argued that setting up 288 LIFO pools was needed to fairly state the company's financial position and results of operations. The SEC charged, however, that the company merely used all these "puddles" to manipulate income (e.g., by manipulating the timing of LIFO layer liquidations) and that Stauffer's 1982 net income was overstated by $31.1 million, or 25%.

As this example shows, accounting for inventories is not a precise science. Instead, considerable judgment is required. At times, two reasonable people can apply their best judgment in different ways, and the impact on financial statements can be substantial.

Geoffrey Smith, ed. Richard Greene, "Puddle Muddle," *Forbes*, October 8, 1984, p. 92.

The previous chapter provided an overview of basic inventory valuation methods. The objective of this chapter is to explain and illustrate several additional methods of inventory valuation. These methods are dollar-value LIFO, the conventional retail method, retail LIFO, and the gross margin method. Some of these methods may initially appear to be more complex than they really are. However, one reason that companies use them is to simplify the enormous clerical tasks that accounting for inventory can produce.

LIFO APPLICATION METHODS

In Chapter 8 we discussed the **specific goods method** of applying LIFO. According to this method, LIFO is applied to each product in a company's inventory. Although the specific goods method is conceptually simple, its practical application is usually confined to inventories of only a small variety of products. When a company has many kinds of products, the specific goods method can create a large clerical burden. A company that handles hundreds of different goods, for example, usually wants a more efficient method of applying the basic LIFO concept. In this chapter, we present the two most commonly used methods of applying LIFO: (1) the dollar-value LIFO method and (2) the retail LIFO method.[1] Each method is acceptable for income tax purposes and for financial reporting purposes in accordance with GAAP. We present the dollar-value LIFO method first; retail LIFO is presented in a later section on the retail method. Throughout our discussion, we focus primarily on the general concepts that underlie these methods. In practice, many detailed rules and regulations of the income tax law pertain to the use of LIFO. An accountant who wants to apply the LIFO method must thoroughly understand these rules and regulations and their implications.

As we saw in Chapter 8, the LIFO conformity requirement states that if a company uses LIFO for income tax purposes, it must also use LIFO for financial reporting purposes. However, income tax regulations allow companies to use *different methods of applying LIFO* for the two purposes as long as the methods used in the financial statements are acceptable for tax purposes. In practice, the vast majority of LIFO companies use the same methods of applying LIFO for financial reports and income taxes. When deciding how to apply LIFO for financial reporting purposes, a company should be guided by the primary objective of *providing useful information* to investors, creditors, and other users. A company should use different LIFO application methods for financial reporting purposes than used for tax purposes if the expected benefits to users of financial statements exceed the costs to the company of having to administer different LIFO application methods. An excellent discussion of many technical issues that pertain to the implementation of LIFO in practice is contained in an *Issues Paper* published by the AICPA in 1984.[2]

DOLLAR-VALUE LIFO METHOD

Under the specific goods method, LIFO is applied on the basis of changes in the *quantity of physical units of each product* in the inventory. In contrast, the dollar-value LIFO method is applied to goods in **designated pools.** Moreover, it is applied on the basis of *inventory changes measured in cost dollars, not in physical units.*

In 1938 LIFO was initially accepted as a tax method designed to allow companies to charge to expense the higher costs associated with the most recent inventory acquisitions. Dollar-value LIFO was developed during the 1940s as a way to allow companies whose products have style or design changes, such as clothing and automobiles, to obtain the tax benefits of LIFO. If these companies were required to apply LIFO on the basis of specific physical units in inventory, old inventory costs would be expensed when the number of physical units of a product declined because of style or design changes. In essence, the dollar-value LIFO method helps companies save taxes by giving them a greater opportunity to preserve old inventory costs while charging the more recent (and presumably higher) costs to expense. This opportunity to preserve old inventory costs exists because dollar-value LIFO is applied on the basis of dollars invested in broadly defined pools of goods. It is not applied to specific physical units of inventory.

A complicating factor when applying dollar-value LIFO is that the cost dollar is seldom a stable device with which to measure inventory changes. Because the ability of a dollar to acquire inventory usually changes over time, we cannot accurately measure inventory

---

[1]Yet another method of applying LIFO is the **specific goods pooling method.** Under this method, a company divides its inventory into *pools,* each of which must consist of *substantially identical goods.* Each pool, rather than each product, then becomes the basis for applying LIFO. The company applies LIFO on the basis of changes in the *quantity of physical units* in the designated inventory pools. The specific goods pooling method is not widely used in practice and, for the sake of brevity, is not illustrated in this book.

[2]Task Force on LIFO Inventory Problems, *Issues Paper,* "Identification and Discussion of Certain Financial Accounting and Reporting Issues Concerning LIFO Inventories" (New York: AICPA, Nov. 30, 1984), File 3175.

changes simply by comparing cost dollars incurred in different time periods. For this reason, the dollar-value method requires us to measure all inventory changes in **cost dollars of the same year,** commonly called the **base year.** The term *base-year cost* refers to the total cost, determined as of the *beginning* of the period in which a company adopts the dollar-value LIFO method, of all inventory items in a designated pool. Inland Steel Company, for example, adopted the dollar-value LIFO method in 1950; the company therefore determines its base-year inventory costs as of January 1, 1950. Partly because it has used LIFO for more than 40 years, the LIFO cost of Inland Steel's December 31, 1992, inventories amounted to less than half of the current replacement cost.

The accountant uses a year-end **conversion factor** to convert **cost dollars of the current year** to **cost dollars of the base year.** This factor measures changes in the level of inventory cost prices that have occurred since the base period. It is computed as follows:

$$\text{Conversion Factor} = \frac{\text{Current Year-End Specific Price Index}}{\text{Base-Year Specific Price Index}}$$

Note that the conversion factor is derived by using a **specific price index.** A specific rather than a general price index is used because the direction and magnitude of changes in a company's inventory cost prices may differ from those of the overall level of prices in the economy. Methods of determining a specific price index under dollar value LIFO are discussed later in the chapter.

Over time, the dollar-value LIFO method may produce several inventory layers, each of which is expressed in *cost dollars rather than physical units.* Therefore, because of changes in the mix of physical units in the inventory, the dollar-value LIFO cost of the ending inventory may exceed that of the beginning inventory even though the total number of physical units in the inventory has declined during the period. The accounting records must permit us to associate each layer with the conversion factor in existence when the layer was constructed.

To implement the dollar-value LIFO method, the accountant must measure in *base-year costs* both the beginning and the ending inventories of the current period. If the ending inventory exceeds the beginning inventory when each is measured in base-year costs, an inventory increment (measured in base-year costs) has occurred. Because the increment occurred in the current year, we price it at current-year costs by multiplying the increment by the current-year conversion factor to obtain a new LIFO inventory layer.[3] We then add this layer to those in existence at the beginning of the current period to get the ending dollar-value LIFO inventory amount.

Conversely, if the ending inventory is less than the beginning inventory when each is measured in base-year costs, a reduction in inventory has occurred in the current period. This reduction requires that we charge previously established LIFO layers to cost of goods sold in a last-in, first-out sequence at amounts that reflect the cost prices in existence when the layers were constructed.

Three major factors explain why many companies use the dollar-value LIFO method. First, the method greatly eases the clerical burden of applying LIFO to specific goods. Second, because the method maintains inventory layers in cost dollars instead of physical units, it gives a company some room to change the composition of inventory without expensing old (and presumably lower) inventory costs. Finally, dollar-value LIFO permits considerable flexibility when grouping inventory items into pools. Under dollar-value LIFO, pooled goods must only be **similar** in a fairly broad sense. Thus, dollar-value LIFO enables a company to

---

[3]Remember that we derive the current year conversion factor by dividing the current *year-end* specific price index by the base-year specific price index. In practice, although a year-end index is most commonly used, the use of a *beginning-of-the-year* index or an *average-for-the-year* index is also considered acceptable.

pool a reasonably large number of products. The more items that a company pools, the more room there is for increases in the quantity of certain goods to offset decreases in the quantity of others. As a result, dollar-value LIFO helps to preserve old inventory costs, thereby helping a company to realize more of the tax benefits that it usually seeks from using LIFO. Although the widespread use of computers tends to make the specific goods method of applying LIFO more feasible than it once was, companies still prefer dollar-value LIFO because of the pooling flexibility that it offers. Some companies that use dollar-value LIFO are still reporting inventory costs incurred *during the 1940s.*

To illustrate the pooling concept that may be applied under dollar-value LIFO, assume that Brian Enterprises sells 10 different models of *each* of the following product lines: sofas, chairs, lamps, tents, exercise bicycles, and canoes. Under the specific goods method of applying LIFO, pools would not exist and the company would therefore apply LIFO to each of its 60 different products (10 $\times$ 6 = 60). Under dollar-value LIFO, the company would likely apply LIFO to only two pools: home furniture (sofas, chairs, and lamps) and sporting goods (tents, exercise bicycles, and canoes).

A company may include the entire inventory in a single pool under dollar-value LIFO. In practice, most companies that use LIFO have only a few pools, presumably in an attempt to reduce the chances of LIFO layer liquidations. One empirical study found that the median number of pools used by retailers is six and for nonretailers is three. The most frequently occurring (mode) number of pools is two for retailers and one for nonretailers.[4] A company that has more than one pool must apply the dollar-value method to each pool. The ending dollar-value inventory amounts determined in the various pools are summed to get the overall ending inventory at LIFO cost.

Application Procedures

The following five steps summarize the procedures used to apply the dollar-value LIFO method to a designated pool of goods:

Step 1. Price the ending inventory at the current-year cost. A good measure of this cost is obtained by multiplying the physical quantities on hand by the actual unit costs of the goods most recently purchased or produced.

Step 2. Obtain an appropriate year-end conversion factor (as explained later in the chapter) that measures the change in inventory *cost prices* that has occurred since the base period.

Step 3. Restate the ending inventory from current-year cost (as determined in Step 1) to base-year cost by dividing the results in Step 1 by the year-end conversion factor obtained in Step 2.

Step 4. From the ending inventory priced at base-year cost (as determined in Step 3), subtract *the inventory on hand at the beginning of the current period, also priced at base-year cost.*

Step 5. Compute the cost of the ending dollar-value LIFO inventory as follows:

1. If the difference in Step 4 is zero, inventory is unchanged. Thus, the ending dollar-value LIFO inventory valuation is the same as the beginning valuation.

2. If the difference in Step 4 is positive, inventory has increased. Price the increase by multiplying the difference obtained in Step 4 by the year-end conversion factor obtained in Step 2. Then add the result to the beginning dollar-value LIFO inventory valuation to get the correct ending valuation at LIFO cost.

3. If the difference in Step 4 is negative, inventory has decreased. Subtract the decrease from the most recently acquired layer(s) at base-year cost in a last-in, first-out sequence. The correct dollar-value LIFO ending inventory valuation will be the remaining layers multiplied by their respective conversion factors.

[4]James M. Reeve and Keith G. Stanga, "The LIFO Pooling Decision: Some Empirical Results from Accounting Practice," *Accounting Horizons* (June 1987), pp. 25–33.

Application of these five steps produces the correct dollar-value LIFO ending inventory amount. One may then determine cost of goods sold residually by subtracting the ending inventory amount from the cost of goods available for sale.

An Illustration

Assume that a company adopts dollar-value LIFO on January 1, 1993. Its inventory priced at current costs on that date was $10,000, and the specific price index derived internally was 100. This inventory is subsequently regarded as the base LIFO layer from which changes may occur. The current-year cost of the ending inventory, as well as the year-end conversion factor for December 31, 1993, and for each of the succeeding three years, is given below.

December 31	Ending Inventory at Current-Year Cost*	Year-End Conversion Factor†
1993	$12,480	1.20
1994	16,950	1.50
1995	14,420	1.40
1996	14,040	1.30

*Obtained by multiplying the physical quantities on hand by the actual unit costs of the goods most recently acquired.

†Obtained by dividing the current year-end specific price index by the base-year specific price index (100). Methods used to determine a specific price index under dollar value LIFO are explained later in the chapter.

The information in Exhibit 9–1 illustrates how to compute the ending dollar-value LIFO inventory amounts. We have keyed the illustration to the five steps presented earlier. Observe carefully the following major points:

1. On December 31, 1993, the application of Step 4 shows an inventory increase of $400 expressed in *base-year costs*. In Step 5, we price this increase using the conversion factor from Step 2 (1.20). The inventory therefore consists of *two layers,* the base plus the 1993 layer, for a total LIFO cost of $10,480.

2. On December 31, 1994, applying Step 4 indicates an inventory increase of $900 expressed in *base-year costs*. Once again, we price the increase using the conversion factor from Step 2 (1.50). The inventory now consists of *three layers,* the base plus the 1993 and 1994 layers, for a total LIFO cost of $11,830.

3. On December 31, 1995, the application of Step 4 shows an inventory *decrease* of $1,000 expressed in *base-year costs*. When a decrease occurs, we must remove it from the existing LIFO inventory layers in a last-in, first-out sequence. In other words, we assume that the last layer(s) in is the first to go out. Any layer removed is charged to cost of goods sold at an amount equal to the base-year cost of the layer multiplied by the conversion factor in existence when the layer was created. Expressed in base-year costs, the $1,000 decrease eliminates all of the 1994 layer ($900) and $100 of the 1993 layer. Had the inventory decrease been larger, it could have eliminated the entire 1993 layer and some or all of the base. An inventory layer, once eliminated, cannot subsequently be reconstructed. The inventory at the end of 1995 consists of *two layers,* the base plus three-fourths of the 1993 layer, for a total LIFO cost of $10,360. Note that we do not construct a 1995 layer, because the inventory that year does not increase.

4. On December 31, 1996, applying Step 4 indicates an inventory increase of $500 expressed in *base-year costs*. As usual, we price the increase using the year-end conversion factor (1.30) derived in Step 2. The inventory now consists of *three layers:* the base, the remaining 1993 layer, and the new 1996 layer. Adding these layers produces a total LIFO cost of $11,010. Note that the entire 1994 layer and one-fourth of the 1993 layer are *not* reflected in the 1996 ending inventory; they were eliminated in 1995 and are therefore never added back.

EXHIBIT 9-1

Dollar-Value LIFO

December 31	Ending Inventory at Current-Year Cost (Step 1)	Year-End Conversion Factor (Step 2)	Ending Inventory at Base-Year Cost (Step 3)	Ending Minus Beginning Inventory, Both at Base-Year Cost (Step 4)	Cost of Ending Dollar-Value LIFO Inventory (Step 5)	
1993	$12,480	÷ 1.20	= $10,400	$10,400 − $10,000 = $ 400	$10,000 × 1.00 = $10,000	(base layer)
					400 × 1.20 = 480	(1993 layer)
					$10,480*	
1994	16,950	÷ 1.50	= 11,300	11,300 − 10,400 = 900	$10,000 × 1.00 = $10,000	(base layer)
					400 × 1.20 = 480	(1993 layer)
					900 × 1.50 = 1,350	(1994 layer)
					$11,830*	
1995	14,420	÷ 1.40	= 10,300	10,300 − 11,300 = (1,000)	$10,000 × 1.00 = $10,000	(base layer)
					300 × 1.20 = 360	(remaining 1993 layer)
					$10,360*	
1996	14,040	÷ 1.30	= 10,800	10,800 − 10,300 = 500	$10,000 × 1.00 = $10,000	(base layer)
					300 × 1.20 = 360	(remaining 1993 layer)
					500 × 1.30 = 650	(1996 layer)
					$11,010*	

*This is the correct amount to report on the ending balance sheet and to subtract from the cost of goods available for sale to measure the cost of goods sold for the year.

361

Let us now *assume* that the company's general ledger shows that it made purchases of $75,000 during 1996. The following is the adjusting journal entry that the company makes on December 31, 1996:

Inventory, December 31	11,010	
Cost of Goods Sold	74,350	
Inventory, January 1		10,360
Purchases		75,000

The company should, of course, make similar entries at the end of 1993, 1994, and 1995.

At first glance, the dollar-value LIFO method usually appears formidable. In practice, however, many companies find that it is a convenient way to apply LIFO to a large, complex inventory. The financial statement numbers it produces are ordinarily different from those produced by the specific goods method of applying LIFO. Nevertheless, dollar-value LIFO has many practical advantages, and the numbers that it produces are acceptable for financial reporting and income tax purposes. Although a specific price index is used to implement the method, dollar-value LIFO is a *method of determining an inventory's historical cost, not its current value.*

Assets/Liability Measurement

In a survey of 206 companies using LIFO, about 70% were found to use the dollar-value method exclusively. Twelve percent use the retail LIFO method (discussed later in the chapter) exclusively. Only 4% use the specific goods method or the specific goods pooling method (see footnote 1) exclusively; the rest use a combination of methods.[5]

METHODS OF DETERMINING A PRICE INDEX UNDER DOLLAR-VALUE LIFO

In practice, a variety of methods is considered acceptable to determine the price index under dollar-value LIFO. One widely used method is the **double extension method.** Under this method, which requires a company to construct its own **internal index** at the end of each year, we multiply the actual quantity of each inventory item on hand at year-end by its current year unit cost. Next, we multiply the actual quantity of each item by its base-year unit

---

EXHIBIT 9–2

Double Extension Method

		Unit Cost		Total Cost	
Item	**Actual Quantity at Year-End**	**Current Year**	**Base Year**	**Current Year**	**Base Year**
A	1,000	$16	$15	$16,000	$15,000
B	2,500	11	10	27,500	25,000
C	500	25	20	12,500	10,000
				$56,000	$50,000

Year-end specific price index = $56,000 ÷ $50,000 = 112%.

$$\text{Year-end conversion factor*} = \frac{112}{100} = 1.12.$$

---

*Observe that the base is 100 ($50,000 ÷ $50,000 = 100%, or 1.00) when a company develops its own internal index. When the base is 100, the year-end conversion factor is the same as the year-end specific price index (112% = 1.12). If the base is not 100, as is often the case when a company relies on an *external* price index, the year-end conversion factor differs from the year-end specific price index.

---

[5]Keith G. Stanga, "Methods of Applying LIFO in Practice," Working paper, The University of Tennessee, 1985.

PUDDLE MUDDLE

"Bone Char . . . that was one of the inventory accounts the Securities & Exchange Commission was concerned about," says Stauffer Chemical's counsel John Ronan. "I mean . . . bone char is not one of our more important products."

Maybe not. But the injunctive action against Connecticut-based Stauffer Chemical for fraudulently overstating its 1982 earnings, settled out of court in August, is one of the SEC's most important actions. The complaint prompted a spate of class action suits against Stauffer, but it also troubles chief finance officers from coast to coast.

Basically the SEC charged the big chemical company with three things: 1) improperly structuring some LIFO "puddles" in its inventory accounting, 2) improperly recognizing inventory profit resulting from intracompany product transfers, and 3) prematurely recognizing sales. As a result, said the commission, Stauffer's 1982 earnings were exaggerated by 25%, or $31.1 million.

This is no arcane bookkeeping hassle. There are "puddles" all over the place in corporate America. If you think of an inventory grouping containing many different products as a "pool," then it follows that a smaller grouping—often containing only one type of product—is a "puddle." Under LIFO accounting, companies assume that the products they are selling today are the newest ones in inventory. That keeps earnings down in periods of high inflation and cuts taxes as a result.

Of course, different products in an inventory pool may fare differently in the marketplace. A sharply lower supply of hot-selling gadgets might force revenues to be compared with lower prior-period costs for the whole pool, not only for gadgets but also for slow-selling widgets, where supply has not changed at all. So puddles, with narrower product ranges, generally produce a more accurate matching of revenues and costs.

The SEC has no objection to puddling. It just didn't like the way Stauffer used the technique. "They required us to take 8 of our 288 inventory puddles—one of them including Bone Char—and recombine them into other puddles," says Ronan.

Why the nitpicking? One side effect of LIFO is to create sudden surges of earnings when year-end inventory is sharply lower than at the beginning of the year. That's because digging into inventories under LIFO means offsetting today's revenues with unnaturally old, hence low, corporate costs.

The commission alleged that Stauffer was setting up puddles partly in order to hit those lower historic cost figures. It also claimed that Stauffer actually gave "presentations" to its operating people to show them how to set up puddles to maximize LIFO liquidation benefits.

Regulators charged, for example, that inventory had been shipped overseas solely because accounting there was not on a LIFO basis. This created LIFO liquidations, exaggerated by improper puddling, that were not eliminated in consolidation, they said. Earnings without sales, to get right to the point.

It's not hard to guess what triggered the SEC investigation. Look at the first three footnotes of Stauffer's 1982 annual report: The change to puddling increased earnings by $16.5 million. New pesticide sales programs "shifted" $72 million of 1983 sales back to 1982. This boosted earnings by another $18.6 million, much of it because of LIFO liquidations. Significant numbers for a company reporting $124 million in earnings for the year.

To sharp eyes, all this activity seemed suspicious. There was a steep downturn in agricultural chemical demand in 1982. Since Stauffer closed no factories, inventories should have been rising, not falling sharply enough to hit LIFO cushions. And what sort of legitimate marketing scheme would transfer sales from one year to another?

The commission says it found an "Early Order Program" that conveniently boosted profits. To encourage distributors to stock up, Stauffer guaranteed future refunds on unsold products carried at the end of the 1982–83 growing season. It sweetened the package with partial reimbursement of warehouse fees and automatic "redating" of bills until early the following year. In the 1982–83 season almost 40% of Stauffer's agricultural chemical sales were booked this way, according to the SEC.

The SEC attacked all this as "contrary to generally accepted accounting principles." So far, it hasn't lifted a finger against Stauffer's auditors, Deloitte Haskins & Sells, who specifically approved the 1982 change to puddling. Why not? That's what Representative Doug Barnard (D–Ga.), who heads the House Commerce, Consumer & Monetary Affairs Subcommittee, wants to know.

Sometimes, of course, the commission sues auditors separately at a later date. But that's still a good question, Congressman.

SOURCE: Geoffrey Smith, ed. Richard Greene, "Puddle Muddle," *Forbes* (October 8, 1984), p. 92. Reprinted by permission of *Forbes* Magazine. © Forbes, Inc., 1984.

---

cost. We now have two columns of extensions, which explains the name "double extension method." We then total the extensions and divide the total current year cost by the total base-year cost to derive the current year-end specific price index. We illustrate these procedures in Exhibit 9–2 for a simplified inventory of only three items. When applying the double extension method in practice, some companies double extend their entire ending inventory; others double extend only a representative sample of inventory items.

A significant problem may occur under the double extension method when a **new item** (i.e., an item that was not in the base inventory) is added to inventory during a particular year. Under these circumstances, the base-year cost of the new item must be estimated by using published vendor price lists, vendor quotes, or general industry indexes so that the current year's price index can be correctly determined. If a company cannot reasonably estimate the base-year cost of new items, perhaps because the base year has receded far into the past, the price index determined under the double extension method may be significantly distorted.

A second widely used approach for determining a price index under dollar-value LIFO is the **link chain method.** Under this method, a company computes an internal price index each year by multiplying the year-end inventory quantities (either the entire inventory or a representative sample) by (1) end-of-the-year unit costs and (2) beginning-of-the-year unit costs. The resulting extensions are totaled, and the totals are divided to determine the current year price change index. The current year price change index is then multiplied by the cumulative prior year index to determine the current link chain index. We illustrate these procedures in Exhibit 9–3.

Notice in Exhibit 9–3 that in the first year of using the link chain method (1995), there is no cumulative prior year index; consequently, the price change index for the first year is

---

EXHIBIT 9–3

Link Chain Method

1995 — Assumed to Be the Base Year

Item	Actual Quantity at Year-End	Unit Cost — End of Year	Unit Cost — Beginning of Year*	Total Cost — End of Year	Total Cost — Beginning of Year
X	2,000	$10	$ 9	$ 20,000	$18,000
Y	3,000	22	20	66,000	60,000
Z	1,000	18	15	18,000	15,000
				$104,000	$93,000

*The beginning-of-year unit costs for 1995 are considered to be the base-year unit costs.

1995 link chain index = $104,000 ÷ $93,000 = 111.8% (The price change index is the same as the link chain index in 1995 because 1995 is assumed to be the base year.)
1995 year-end conversion factor = 111.8 ÷ 100 = 1.118

1996

Item	Actual Quantity at Year-End	Unit Cost — End of Year	Unit Cost — Beginning of Year	Total Cost — End of Year	Total Cost — Beginning of Year
X	4,000	$12	$10	$ 48,000	$ 40,000
Y	5,000	25	22	125,000	110,000
Z	3,000	20	18	60,000	54,000
				$233,000	$204,000

1996 price change index = $233,000 ÷ $204,000 = 114.2%
1996 link chain index = 114.2% × 111.8% = 127.7%
1996 year-end conversion factor = 127.7 ÷ 100 = 1.277

the link chain index. Note also that in the second year (and subsequent years) of applying the link chain method, base-year unit costs (i.e., the beginning-of-year costs for 1995) are no longer used. An advantage of the link chain method over the double extension method is that the link chain method does not require a determination of base-year costs for new items.

The price change index computed for the second year (1996) is simply "linked to" the cumulative prior year index. Each year's link chain index becomes the cumulative prior year index in the next year. In our example, 111.8% is the link chain index for 1995, so it becomes the cumulative prior year index in 1996. Moreover, 127.7%, the link chain index for 1996, will become the cumulative prior year index in 1997.

Double extension and link chain are methods of deriving an internal price index. If a company can show that an **external index** (a published index) is a suitable measure of the change in cost prices of the specific goods that it actually purchases or produces, it can use the external index when applying dollar-value LIFO. In the survey of 206 companies that use LIFO mentioned earlier, about 54% of the companies that use the dollar-value approach reported using the link chain method; 35% use the double extension method; and 7% use the double extension and link chain methods concurrently. Only a small percentage of the companies surveyed use external indexes such as the Producer Price Indexes.

RETAIL INVENTORY METHOD

The **retail inventory method** is a reversed markup procedure of inventory pricing used by many retail businesses, such as department stores. The main advantage of the method is that it produces accounting information and facilitates inventory control at less cost than other methods that could be used in retail concerns. Ending inventory and cost of goods sold figures derived under the retail method are acceptable for financial reporting and income tax purposes.

When applying the retail method, the accountant records the beginning inventory, purchases, and sales in the accounts in the usual manner under a periodic inventory system. Moreover, supplementary records of certain additional information are kept. This information includes the beginning inventory and net purchases, each stated at **retail** (i.e., **selling**) **prices.** The accumulation of supplementary records at retail prices is facilitated by the fact that retail companies usually price their merchandise for sale soon after acquisition. The accountant divides the *cost of goods available for sale* during a period by the *retail value of the same goods* to produce a cost-to-retail percentage that is commonly called the **cost percentage.** This percentage reflects the relationship between cost and retail that prevails in the *current* period. Sales for the period are then deducted from the retail value of goods available for sale to derive an ending inventory valued at *retail prices.* The accountant multiplies the ending inventory at retail by the cost percentage to derive an *estimate* of the *historical cost* of the ending inventory to use for balance sheet reporting purposes. Cost of goods sold may then be computed in the usual manner for a periodic system. Alternatively, cost of goods sold may be computed by multiplying the sales for the period by the cost percentage. The following simplified example illustrates the essence of the retail method.

Asset/Liability Measurement

	At Cost	At Retail
Beginning inventory	$ 9,800	$ 14,000
Net purchases	65,200	86,000
Goods available for sale	$75,000	$100,000
Cost percentage ($75,000 ÷ $100,000 = 75%)		
Deduct:		
Sales		80,000
Ending inventory		
At retail		$ 20,000
At cost ($20,000 × 75%)	$15,000	
Cost of goods sold		
($9,800 + $65,200 − $15,000 = $60,000, *or*		
$80,000 × 75% = $60,000)	$60,000	

Observe that the retail method enables us to calculate the cost of the ending inventory without knowing how many physical units are actually on hand. Nevertheless, a company using the retail method *must count its physical inventory at least once each year* for good internal control. Goods counted are extended at retail prices and are compared with the inventory at retail value derived under the retail method. Differences may occur for several reasons, including theft, breakage, inaccurate records, and an inaccurate physical count. If the physical count has been performed correctly, the accounting records should be adjusted to agree with it.

The following are the main uses of the retail method:

1. The retail method enables a company to estimate its inventory at any time without a physical count, because both cost and retail figures are always available. These estimates are used for annual as well as interim reporting purposes.
2. Even when the inventory is counted, the retail method enables a company to take its physical inventory at marked selling prices, thereby expediting the work of personnel since they do not have to refer to purchase invoices.
3. The retail method provides results that are useful when determining insurance coverage and settlements.

The major limitation of the retail method is that the cost percentage is merely an average of all goods reflected in its calculation. The average yields accurate results if the same relationship between cost and selling price exists for all goods or if the mix of goods in ending inventory is the same as that in the goods available for sale. Because some departure from these conditions usually occurs, the retail method produces accounting values of ending inventory and cost of goods sold that are only *approximations.* When the relationship between cost and selling price varies substantially between departments, the accountant should apply the retail method separately to each department, thus improving the accuracy of the method. Ending inventory costs computed in each department are summed to derive the cost for the entire inventory.

A company using the retail method does not have to apply the method to its entire inventory. For example, a large department store may use the retail method when accounting for certain types of merchandise, such as men's clothing, and the specific identification method when accounting for others, such as expensive jewelry.

When applying the retail method, the accountant adds transportation-in and subtracts purchase discounts when computing net purchases in the cost column. These two items are not added or subtracted in the retail column because the original retail price of the inventory is ordinarily set in a manner that reflects them. Purchase returns and purchase allowances are subtracted in the cost and retail columns because these items reduce the amount of goods purchased.

The sales amount that should be subtracted in the retail column should be the net of any sales returns and allowances. Sales discounts, however, are not subtracted from sales because they are financial in nature and are not part of the initial markup that is applied to goods purchased. Employee discounts and normal shrinkage (due to damage, theft, etc.) should be subtracted (just as sales are) in the retail column because these items represent normal reductions of the original retail value of goods available for sale during the period.

RETAIL METHOD TERMINOLOGY

The example presented above was simplified to introduce the rationale, uses, and limitations of the retail method. To properly handle the complexities encountered in practice, the accountant must understand the meaning of the following important terms used by retailers:

1. **Original retail price.** The price at which merchandise is first marked for sale to customers. This price includes an initial markup equal to the difference between the original retail price and the cost.

2. **Additional markup.** Amount added to the original retail price.
3. **Markup cancellation.** Cancellation, either in part or in total, of an additional markup. A markup cancellation does not reduce the selling price below the original retail price.
4. **Net markup.** Amount of additional markups less markup cancellations.
5. **Markdown.** Amount subtracted from the original retail price.
6. **Markdown cancellation.** Cancellation, either in part or in total, of a markdown. A markdown cancellation does not increase the selling price above the original retail price.
7. **Net markdown.** Amount of markdowns less markdown cancellations.

Assume that a retail concern purchases a new line of summer dresses for $60 each and immediately prices each dress for sale at $100. The *original retail price* is therefore $100. This price, which actually includes an *initial markup* of $40, is now an important point of reference when labeling future changes in selling price. If, in response to great demand for the dresses, the company raises the selling price to $110, we have an *additional markup* of $10. If the price is later lowered from $110 to $106, we have a *markup cancellation* of $4. The *net markup* is now $6. Suppose that near the end of the summer, the company lowers its selling price from $106 to $90. This action represents a *markup cancellation* of $6 and a *markdown* of $10. If the company later raises the price from $90 to $92, we have a *markdown cancellation* of $2. The *net markdown* is now $8.

CONVENTIONAL RETAIL METHOD (LOWER OF AVERAGE COST OR MARKET)

The existence of additional markups, markup cancellations, markdowns, and markdown cancellations introduces new complexities to the retail method. First, a company's accounting system must permit an accurate accumulation of each of these items in supplementary records. Second, because these items represent adjustments to the original retail price, they must be included in a logical manner in the basic retail inventory procedures that we illustrated earlier.

The **conventional retail method,** the one most commonly used by retailers, requires (1) including net markups when calculating the cost percentage and (2) subtracting net markdowns along with sales when measuring the ending inventory at retail. In other words, the accountant computes the cost percentage *after* considering net markups but *before* considering net markdowns. These procedures are illustrated in the example on page 368.

The conventional retail method produces an ending inventory that approximates the **lower of average cost or market,** which we will refer to simply as *lower of cost or market.* Observe in our example that the lower of cost or market valuation is $14,400. *If* we had ignored net markups as well as net markdowns when computing our cost percentage, the cost percentage would have been 74.8% ($57,600 ÷ $77,000). Note that the $77,000 amount equals the retail value of the beginning inventory ($13,000) plus the retail value of the net purchases ($64,000). Ending inventory at cost would then have been $14,960 ($20,000 × 74.8%). *If,* on the other hand, we had included net markups *and* net markdowns when calculating our cost percentage, the cost percentage would have been 75.8% ($57,600 ÷ $76,000). Note that the $76,000 amount equals the retail value of the beginning inventory ($13,000) plus the retail value of the net purchases ($64,000) plus the net markups ($3,000) minus the net markdowns ($4,000). Ending inventory at cost would then have been $15,160 ($20,000 × 75.8%). As these numbers illustrate, the conventional retail method produces the lowest ending inventory valuation when compared with alternative methods of handling net markups and net markdowns.

Are the results under the conventional retail method simply the most conservative, or do they really approximate those achieved by applying the lower of cost or market rule? Suppose that a company began operations near the end of a year and bought only a single item of merchandise that it was unable to sell. The item cost $100 and was originally priced to sell for

	At Cost		At Retail
Beginning inventory	$10,000		$13,000
Net purchases	47,600		64,000
Additional markups		$ 7,000	
Less: Markup cancellations		4,000	
Net markups			3,000
Goods available for sale	$57,600		80,000
Cost percentage ($57,600 ÷ $80,000 = 72%)			
Deduct:			
Sales			(56,000)
Markdowns		12,000	
Less: Markdown cancellations		8,000	
Net markdowns			(4,000)
Ending inventory			
At retail			$20,000
At lower of cost or market ($20,000 × 72%)	$14,400		

$200. The retail price was subsequently raised to $250 (an additional markup of $50). Later the price was lowered to $125 (a markup cancellation of $50 and a markdown of $75). The following illustration shows how to value the ending inventory item using the conventional retail method:

	At Cost		At Retail
Beginning inventory	–0–		–0–
Net purchases	$100.00		$200
Additional markup		$50	
Less: Markup cancellation		50	
Net markup			–0–
Goods available for sale	100.00		200
Cost percentage ($100 ÷ $200 = 50%)			
Deduct:			
Sales			(–0–)
Markdown		75	
Less: Markdown cancellation		–0–	
Net markdown			(75)
Ending inventory			
At retail			$125
At lower of cost or market ($125 × 50%)	$ 62.50		

The lower of cost or market valuation produced by the conventional retail method approximates the inventory's *net realizable value less an allowance for a normal profit margin (i.e., the floor)*. In our example, the inventory item that cost $100 was originally priced at $200 to allow a 50% profit margin based on selling price. The sales price of the item was finally reduced to $125. This price indicates that the item's **utility** (its ability to produce future revenue) has declined. Observing the lower of cost or market rule requires that we recognize the decline in the current period, the one in which it occurred. This reflects the

Conservatism   conservatism modifying convention. Accordingly, the conventional retail method produces an ending inventory valuation of $62.50, an amount clearly below the historical cost of $100. Note that the lower of cost or market valuation of $62.50 represents the estimated selling price ($125) less an allowance for a normal profit margin of 50% of selling price ($125 × 50% = $62.50).

We emphasize that the conventional retail method only *approximates* an ending inventory valuation at lower of cost or market. The method does *not* measure "market" by comparing ceiling, replacement cost, and floor values. Moreover, accountants apply the method to many inventory items, not simply to a single unit. An averaging effect therefore occurs. The conventional retail method is also limited because it assumes that markdowns apply only to goods sold during a period. This assumption is justified on the ground that goods marked down are more likely than not to have been sold during the period. In reality, however, some of the goods marked down may still be in ending inventory.

RETAIL LIFO METHOD ~~Do not need~~

Many companies adapt the retail method to reflect the LIFO cost flow assumption. This adaptation is called the **retail LIFO method.** Use of this method enables retailers to secure the matching benefits and tax advantages that LIFO usually produces while, at the same time, reducing substantially the clerical burden of applying LIFO. **Matching**

Compared with the conventional retail method, the retail LIFO method requires two important changes when calculating the periodic **cost percentage.**

1. The beginning inventory is *excluded* from the calculation. Under retail LIFO, the sole purpose of the cost percentage is to price any new LIFO layer that might be added in the current period. Thus, the beginning inventory is excluded to ensure that the resulting cost percentage reflects cost and retail prices of the current period only.
2. Net markups as well as net markdowns are *included* in the calculation. In other words, the accountant computes the cost percentage *after* considering both net markups and net markdowns. The rationale for including both in the cost percentage is that LIFO is a method of arriving at *cost,* not lower of cost or market.

To illustrate these changes, assume that the following information pertains to Lite Company for the current year:

	At Cost	At Retail
Inventory, Jan. 1 (base LIFO layer)	$ 19,500	$ 30,000
Net purchases	140,000	208,000
Net markups		7,000
Net markdowns		15,000
Sales		190,000

If we now make the simplifying assumption that the level of specific retail prices remained *constant* during the year, here is how Lite Company would determine the cost percentage and the LIFO cost of the ending inventory.

	At Cost	At Retail
Net purchases	$140,000	$208,000
Net markups		7,000
Net markdowns		(15,000)
Subtotal	$140,000	200,000
Cost percentage ($140,000 ÷ $200,000 = 70%)		
Beginning inventory at retail		30,000
Goods available for sale at retail		230,000
Deduct: Sales		(190,000)
Ending inventory at retail		$ 40,000

	At Cost	At Retail
Ending inventory at retail		$ 40,000
Less: Beginning inventory at retail		30,000
Inventory increase at retail		$ 10,000
Ending inventory at LIFO cost		
Beginning inventory	$ 19,500	
Add: Inventory increase		
($10,000 × 70%)	7,000	
Ending inventory	$ 26,500	

Note that the beginning inventory was excluded and that the net markups and net markdowns were included in the calculation of the cost percentage (70%). The cost percentage was then used to convert the inventory *increase* that occurred during the year from a retail measure ($10,000) to a cost measure ($7,000). The cost of the inventory increase was then added to the cost of the beginning inventory to derive the cost of the ending LIFO inventory ($26,500).

The preceding example is very simplified; in reality, the retail dollar (like the cost dollar) is rarely a stable device for measuring inventory changes. Indeed, the level of specific retail prices usually fluctuates over time. Therefore, the retail LIFO method requires us to measure all inventory changes in **retail dollars of the base year.** The term *base year* refers to the *beginning* of the year in which a company adopts the retail LIFO method. In the remaining discussion of the retail LIFO method, we make the realistic assumption that the level of specific retail prices changes over time.

The retail LIFO method is very similar to the dollar-value LIFO method discussed earlier. In fact, the retail LIFO method is sometimes called the **dollar-value retail LIFO method.** Like dollar-value LIFO, retail LIFO is applied to **designated pools** of similar goods. In addition, retail LIFO is applied on the basis of **inventory changes measured in dollars as opposed to physical units.** In contrast with dollar-value LIFO, retail LIFO measures inventory changes in *retail dollars* rather than in cost dollars.

As with the dollar-value LIFO method, retail LIFO requires that we use a conversion factor. Again, we compute this factor by dividing a specific price index for the current year by a specific price index for the base year. However, because the retail method requires a conversion of *retail dollars,* the price index used must measure the change in the level of *retail prices* that has occurred since the base year.

For income tax and financial reporting purposes, most retailers use the Department Store Inventory Price Indexes published monthly by the Bureau of Labor Statistics (BLS). BLS index numbers measure changes in the level of retail prices of goods in 20 department groups, such as infant's wear, men's clothing, housewares, and major appliances. The accountant simply selects the index numbers that are appropriate given the nature of the inventory pool to which retail LIFO is applied. If the BLS indexes are not appropriate for a given retail concern, the company may construct its own *internal* price index using the link chain or double extension methods.

Over time, the retail LIFO method may produce several inventory layers. Each layer is expressed in *retail dollars rather than in physical units.* The accounting records must permit us to associate each layer with (1) the year-end conversion factor in existence when the layer was created and (2) the cost percentage for the year the layer was created.

To implement the retail LIFO method, the accountant must measure in *base-year retail prices* both the beginning and the ending inventories of the current period. If the ending inventory exceeds the beginning inventory when each is measured in base-year retail prices, an inventory increment (measured in base-year retail prices) has occurred. Because the increment occurred in the current year, we should price it at current year costs. To convert the increment from *base-year retail* prices to *current-year cost* prices, we must multiply it by (1) the current year-end conversion factor (this converts the increment from *base-year* retail prices to *current-year* retail prices) and (2) the current-year cost percentage (this converts the increment from current-year *retail* prices to current-year *cost* prices). The inventory increment so priced forms a layer that is added to those in existence at the beginning of the current period to determine the ending retail LIFO inventory cost.

On the other hand, if the ending inventory is less than the beginning inventory when each is measured at base-year retail prices, a reduction in inventory has occurred. This reduction requires us to charge previously established LIFO layers to cost of goods sold in a last-in, first-out sequence at amounts that reflect the cost prices in existence when the layers were constructed.

Application Procedures

The five steps summarized below are used to apply the retail LIFO method to a designated pool of goods. Note that these steps closely parallel those used to apply the dollar-value LIFO method.

Step 1. Determine the current-year cost percentage and the ending inventory at retail. Again, be sure to (1) exclude the beginning inventory and (2) include net markups and net markdowns when calculating the cost percentage.[6]

Step 2. Obtain an appropriate year-end conversion factor that measures the overall change in inventory *retail prices* that has occurred since the base period. We compute the conversion factor as follows:

$$\text{Conversion Factor} = \frac{\text{Current Year-End Specific Price Index}}{\text{Base-Year Specific Price Index}}$$

Step 3. Restate the ending inventory from current-year retail prices (as determined in Step 1) to base-year retail prices by dividing the results in Step 1 by the year-end conversion factor obtained in Step 2.

Step 4. From the ending inventory priced at base-year retail prices (as determined in Step 3), subtract *the inventory on hand at the beginning of the current period, also priced at base-year retail prices.*

Step 5. Compute the cost of the ending retail LIFO inventory as follows:

1. If the difference in Step 4 equals zero, inventory is unchanged. Consequently, the ending retail LIFO inventory valuation is the same as the beginning valuation.

2. If the difference in Step 4 is positive, inventory has increased. Price the increase at current-year *cost* by multiplying the difference in Step 4 by (1) the year-end conversion factor obtained in Step 2 *and* (2) the current-year cost percentage obtained in Step 1. Then add the result to the beginning retail LIFO inventory valuation to get the correct ending valuation at LIFO cost.

3. If the difference in Step 4 is negative, inventory has decreased. Subtract the decrease from the most recently acquired layer(s) at base-year retail prices in a last-in, first-out manner. The correct retail LIFO ending inventory valuation will then be the remaining layers multiplied by (1) their respective conversion factors *and* (2) their respective cost percentages.

An Illustration

Let's assume that a retail concern adopts the retail LIFO method on January 1, 1993. On that date, the company's inventory at retail prices is $20,000 and its cost percentage is 70%. Furthermore, an appropriate specific retail price index obtained externally is 125. The cost of

---

[6]Actually, calculating the cost percentage is required only when a LIFO layer is added in the current period. Nevertheless, we have included it as a part of Step 1 because it is relatively easy to derive in the process of calculating the ending inventory at retail.

the inventory on January 1, 1993, is therefore $14,000 ($20,000 × 1.00 × 70%).[7] This inventory layer is regarded in future years as the base. Additional information for 1993, 1994, 1995, and 1996 appears in Exhibit 9–4.

The dollar amounts shown in Exhibit 9–4 for net purchases, net markups, net markdowns, beginning inventory at retail, and sales are obtained from the company's general ledger and supplementary records. Using this information, we *calculated* each year's cost percentage and ending inventory at retail, thereby complying with Step 1 of the basic retail LIFO procedures. Step 2 requires us to obtain an appropriate year-end conversion factor. We computed these factors using the specific price index numbers shown near the bottom of Exhibit 9–4. The index numbers themselves are obtained from an appropriate external source.

Using the information shown in our example, we illustrate in Exhibit 9–5 how to compute each year's ending retail LIFO inventory valuation.

The following points are particularly noteworthy:

1. On December 31, 1993, applying Step 4 reveals an inventory increase of $800 in *base-year retail prices*. In Step 5, we price this increase at *current-year cost* by multiplying it by the year-end conversion factor (1.20) obtained in Step 2 *and* by the current-year cost percentage obtained in Step 1 (72%). The inventory therefore consists of *two layers,* the base plus the 1993 layer, for a total retail LIFO cost of $14,691.

2. On December 31, 1994, applying Step 4 indicates an inventory increase of $2,000 in *base-year retail prices*. Once again, we price the increase at *current-year cost* by multiplying it by the year-end conversion factor from Step 2 (1.40) *and* by the current-year cost percentage from Step 1 (75%). The inventory now consists of *three layers,* the base plus the 1993 and 1994 layers, for a total retail LIFO cost of $16,791.

3. On December 31, 1995, applying Step 4 shows an inventory *decrease* of $2,400 in *base-year retail prices*. When a decrease occurs, we must remove it from the existing LIFO inventory layers in a last-in, first-out sequence. In other words, we assume that the last layer(s) in is the first to go out. Any layer removed is charged to cost of goods sold at an amount equal to the base-year retail value of the layer multiplied by the conversion factor and by the cost percentage in existence when the layer was created. Expressed in base-year retail prices, the $2,400 decrease eliminates all of the 1994 layer ($2,000) and one-half ($400) of the 1993 layer. Had the inventory decrease been larger, it could have eliminated the entire 1993 layer and some or all of the base. Once eliminated, an inventory layer cannot later be reconstructed. The 1995 ending inventory consists of *two layers,* the base plus one-half of the 1993 layer, for a total retail LIFO cost of $14,346. We do not construct a 1995 layer, because the inventory that year does not increase.

4. On December 31, 1996, applying Step 4 shows an inventory increase of $1,000 expressed in *base-year retail prices*. We therefore price the increase by multiplying it by the year-end conversion factor (from Step 2) *and* by the current-year cost percentage (from Step 1). The inventory now consists of *three layers:* the base, the remaining 1993 layer, and the new 1996 layer. Summing these layers produces a total retail LIFO cost of $15,352. Observe that the entire 1994 layer and one-half of the 1993 layer are *not* reflected in the 1996 ending inventory; they were eliminated forever in 1995.

We know (from Exhibit 9–4) that the company's general ledger shows that purchases of $133,200 (at cost) were made during 1996. Here is the adjusting journal entry that the company makes on December 31, 1996:

Inventory, December 31	15,352	
Cost of Goods Sold	132,194	
Inventory, January 1		14,346
Purchases		133,200

The company should, of course, make similar entries at the end of 1993, 1994, and 1995.

---

[7]125/125 = 1.00.

During past years of relatively high inflation, many companies adopted LIFO. In 1974, for example, the inflation rate exceeded 10%, and many companies adopted LIFO in that year. Many retailers find that the retail LIFO method is a practical means to realize LIFO's costing benefits. Although the method appears complex, its use can produce substantial clerical savings. The apparent complexity of the method is greatly reduced when we focus on its similarity to the dollar-value LIFO method. This similarity can be seen more clearly in the parallel form of Exhibits 9–1 and 9–5.

The **gross margin method** (often called the **gross profit method**) is widely used to obtain the **estimated cost** of an ending inventory. The method requires adding the beginning inventory at cost to the net purchases at cost to produce the cost of goods available for sale during the period. Net sales for the period are then multiplied by a gross margin on sales percentage; the result is subtracted from net sales to produce an estimated cost of goods sold figure. This figure is then subtracted from the cost of goods available for sale to produce an estimate of the cost of the ending inventory, as shown:

GROSS MARGIN METHOD

Beginning inventory (measured at cost)		$ 30,000
Net purchases (measured at cost)		150,000
Cost of goods available for sale		180,000
Deduct:		
Net sales (measured at selling prices)	$200,000	
Less: Estimated gross margin		
($200,000 × 20%)	40,000	
Estimated cost of goods sold		160,000
Estimated cost of ending inventory		$ 20,000

Dollar amounts for the beginning inventory, net purchases, and net sales are taken directly from the company's accounting records. The estimated gross margin on sales percentage (20% in this example) is a **historical rate** (not a current rate such as the one we use under the retail method) that reflects recent past experience. Typically, it is an average of the percentages applicable to the past few years.

Notice the similarity between the procedures used in applying the gross margin method and those used in calculating cost of goods sold in a periodic inventory system. In both calculations, we begin by deriving the cost of goods available for sale. Under the gross margin method, we then subtract the estimated cost of goods sold to obtain the estimated cost of the ending inventory. Under the periodic system, we subtract the cost of the ending inventory from the cost of goods available for sale to derive the cost of goods sold.

GROSS MARGIN ON SALES PERCENTAGE

Under the gross margin method, we use a **gross margin on sales percentage** when reducing net sales to an estimated cost basis. Gross margin percentages are usually derived and expressed in relation to selling prices. To illustrate, if a soccer ball costs $8 and sells for $10, the gross margin is $2. The gross margin percentage based on selling price is therefore 20% ($2 ÷ $10 = .20 = 20%). The remaining 80% ($8 ÷ $10 = .80 = 80%) is called the **cost of goods sold percentage.** The gross margin on sales percentage and the cost of goods sold percentage always sum to 100%.

At times, a gross margin percentage may be based on cost prices instead of selling prices. Using the same basic data for the soccer ball, the gross margin percentage based on cost is 25% ($2 ÷ $8 = .25 = 25%). When we are given a gross margin on cost percentage, we first convert it to a gross margin on sales percentage to correctly apply the gross margin

EXHIBIT 9–4

Information to Illustrate Retail LIFO Method

	1993 At Cost	1993 At Retail	1994 At Cost	1994 At Retail	1995 At Cost	1995 At Retail	1996 At Cost	1996 At Retail
Net purchases	$108,000	$155,000	$120,000	$164,000	$113,150	$159,000	$133,200	$187,000
Net markups		6,000		10,000		4,000		12,000
Net markdowns		(11,000)		(14,000)		(8,000)		(19,000)
Subtotal	$108,000	150,000	$120,000	160,000	$113,150	155,000	$133,200	180,000
Cost percentage								
1993 ($108,000 ÷ $150,000 = 72%)								
1994 (120,000 ÷ 160,000 = 75%)								
1995 (113,150 ÷ 155,000 = 73%)								
1996 (133,200 ÷ 180,000 = 74%)								
Beginning inventory at retail		20,000		24,960		31,920		31,008
Goods available for sale at retail		170,000		184,960		186,920		211,008
Deduct: Sales		145,040		153,040		155,912		181,904
Ending inventory at retail		$ 24,960		$ 31,920		$ 31,008		$ 29,104
Year-end specific retail price index obtained externally		150		175		190		170
Conversion factor		150/125 = 1.20		175/125 = 1.40		190/125 = 1.52		170/125 = 1.36

EXHIBIT 9–5

Retail LIFO

December 31	Current-Year Cost Percentage (Step 1)	Ending Inventory at Current-Year Retail Prices (Step 1)		Year-End Conversion Factor (Step 2)		Ending Inventory at Base-Year Retail Prices (Step 3)	Ending Minus Beginning Inventory, Both at Base-Year Retail Prices (Step 4)	Cost of Ending Retail LIFO Inventory (Step 5)			
1993	72%	$24,960	÷	1.20	=	$20,800	$20,800 − $20,000 = $ 800	$20,000 × 1.00 × 70% = $14,000	(base layer)		
								800 × 1.20 × 72% = 691	(1993 layer)		
								$14,691*			
1994	75%	31,920	÷	1.40	=	22,800	22,800 − 20,800 = 2,000	$20,000 × 1.00 × 70% = $14,000	(base layer)		
								800 × 1.20 × 72% = 691	(1993 layer)		
								2,000 × 1.40 × 75% = 2,100	(1994 layer)		
								$16,791*			
1995	73%	31,008	÷	1.52	=	20,400	20,400 − 22,800 = (2,400)	$20,000 × 1.00 × 70% = $14,000	(base layer)		
								400 × 1.20 × 72% = 346	(remaining 1993 layer)		
								$14,346*			
1996	74%	29,104	÷	1.36	=	21,400	21,400 − 20,400 = 1,000	$20,000 × 1.00 × 70% = $14,000	(base layer)		
								400 × 1.20 × 72% = 346	(remaining 1993 layer)		
								1,000 × 1.36 × 74% = 1,006	(1996 layer)		
								$15,352*			

*This is the correct amount to report on the ending balance sheet and to subtract from the cost of goods available for sale to measure the cost of goods sold for the year.

method. The following widely used formulas enable us to convert a gross margin on cost percentage to a gross margin on sales percentage, and vice versa:

$$\text{Gross Margin on Sales Percentage} = \frac{\text{Gross Margin on Cost Percentage}}{100\% + \text{Gross Margin on Cost Percentage}}$$

$$\text{Gross Margin on Cost Percentage} = \frac{\text{Gross Margin on Sales Percentage}}{100\% - \text{Gross Margin on Sales Percentage}}$$

Obviously, only the first formula is required to find an unknown gross margin on sales percentage. Accountants nevertheless should be familiar with both types of conversions.

The following examples illustrate how to apply the formulas:

Gross Margin on Sales Percentage		Gross Margin on Cost Percentage
20% (given)	→	$\frac{20\%}{100\% - 20\%} = 25\%$
25% (given)	→	$\frac{25\%}{100\% - 25\%} = 33\frac{1}{3}\%$
$\frac{50\%}{100\% + 50\%} = 33\frac{1}{3}\%$	←	50% (given)
$\frac{100\%}{100\% + 100\%} = 50\%$	←	100% (given)

Because cost prices are less than selling prices, each gross margin on cost percentage is higher than the related percentage based on sales. The gross margin on sales percentage is often called the **markup on sales;** similarly, the gross margin on cost percentage frequently is called the **markup on cost.**

When converting a known markup on cost to an unknown markup on sales, many students find it helpful to first write out the following simple formula:

$$\text{Cost } (C) + \text{Markup } (M) = \text{Selling Price } (SP)$$

For example, when converting a 25% markup on cost to an unknown markup on sales, you may proceed as follows:

$$C \qquad\qquad + M \quad = SP$$
$$100\% \text{ (the base)} + 25\% = 125\%$$

Writing out the formula allows you to see that **markup on sales** (M/SP) is 25%/125% = 20%.

Similarly, you may convert a 20% markup on sales to an unknown markup on cost in the following manner:

$$C \quad + M \quad = SP$$
$$80\% + 20\% = 100\% \text{ (the base)}$$

Writing out the formula allows you to see that **markup on cost** (M/C) is 20%/80% = 25%.

When making either type of conversion, you must first identify the **base,** either cost or selling price, and set it equal to 100%.

USES OF THE GROSS MARGIN METHOD

Remember that we use an average *historical* (as opposed to a current) gross margin on sales percentage to implement the gross margin method. A major assumption of this method is that this percentage reasonably approximates the rate of gross margin in the current period.

Because this rate usually differs to some extent from the average historical rate, the gross margin method yields only an **estimate** of the cost of the ending inventory. This estimate generally approximates the results under whatever inventory cost flow method the company uses (FIFO, average cost, and so forth). An exception may occur when a company using LIFO liquidates layers consisting of outdated costs. In this case, the ending inventory estimate under the gross margin method may depart considerably from the actual LIFO cost; we must therefore use caution when interpreting the results produced by the gross margin method.

The estimates produced by the gross margin method are generally considered too imprecise for use in annual financial statements prepared according to GAAP. Nevertheless, many companies use the method when preparing their internal as well as external interim reports (i.e., monthly or quarterly reports). Companies that use the gross margin method in their external interim reports and companies that use other methods than those used for annual reporting purposes "should disclose the method used at the interim date and any significant adjustments that result from reconciliations with the annual physical inventory."[8]

Accountants often use the gross margin method to estimate the cost of an inventory lost by fire or other casualty. The information needed to apply the method may be taken directly from the accounting records. If the records have been lost, the accountant can sometimes construct estimates of the needed information using prior years financial statements, microfilm copies of bank records showing details of receipts and disbursements, and contact with suppliers and customers. When inventory has been lost, a company may apply the gross margin method to help determine an insurance settlement. We must remember, however, that the method produces an estimate of the *historical cost* of the inventory lost. Insurance coverage and settlements are often based on *replacement costs*. Thus, the results of the gross margin method may need adjusting to an estimated current replacement cost basis.

Auditors often use the gross margin method as a rough test of the validity of an inventory's cost determined under either a periodic or a perpetual system. If a material difference exists between the ending inventory cost determined using the gross margin method and that determined under the company's accounting system, the auditor should inquire concerning the reasons for the difference. This inquiry may simply reveal that the gross margin on sales percentage used in the gross margin method does not properly reflect current conditions. On the other hand, the inquiry may reveal errors made when determining cost within the company's accounting system.

Materiality

GROSS MARGIN METHOD APPLIED TO CLASSES OF GOODS

Gross margin percentages sometimes vary considerably between different classes of goods within a single company. When such variation occurs, the use of a single, companywide gross margin percentage assumes that goods in the various classes are sold in the same mix each period. This assumption is, of course, seldom valid. As a result, we should apply the gross margin method separately to each class of goods, thereby enhancing the method's accuracy. We can then sum the ending inventory costs determined for each class to produce an overall cost for the company's inventory.

Accountants must use judgment when applying the broad and detailed principles explained throughout this book. When applying dollar-value LIFO, for example, an accountant must categorize a company's inventories into one or more pools. *Accounting Research Bulletin No. 43* offers only general guidance in this area; it says that "in accounting for the goods in inventory at any point of time, the major objective is the matching of appropriate costs

PROFESSIONAL JUDGMENT

---

[8] *APB Opinion No. 28*, "Interim Financial Reporting," 1973, par. 14a.

against revenues in order that there may be a proper determination of the realized income."[9] Because matching is highly subjective, accountants must use judgment when forming LIFO pools. One study of companies that use LIFO found that the number of inventory pools for jewelry ranged from 1 to 215.[10]

Another instance in which the accountant must apply judgment is determining a price index under dollar-value LIFO. Here a company must choose between double extension, link chain, or an external index. If it chooses the double extension or link chain method, the accountant must decide whether to apply the method to the entire LIFO inventory or only to a sample of goods. If it is applied to only a sample, the accountant must determine how large the sample should be. If double extension is used, some reasonable approach for dealing with new items (i.e., those items not in the base inventory) must be determined. If an external index is used, determining which one requires that judgment be exercised.

These examples highlight the theme that accounting requires many estimates and judgments. In formulating these judgments, an accountant should remember that the overriding objective of financial reporting is to provide useful information for decision making and that useful information ultimately helps users to assess more accurately their chances of receiving cash from the reporting enterprise.

CONCLUDING REMARKS

The inventory methods presented in this chapter may at first appear complex and imprecise. Remember, though, that accountants seek to provide **useful information** for which the **benefits exceed the costs.** Many large companies have tens of thousands, sometimes hundreds of thousands, of products. To account for such large and diverse inventories in a cost-effective manner, the methods described in this chapter are often helpful.

Perhaps the most serious adverse consequence of modern inventory accounting is the distorted balance sheet valuations that often result under LIFO. As indicated earlier, some LIFO users are still reporting inventory costs incurred during the 1940s. In the authors' opinion, the FASB's future development of GAAP should include an attempt to improve the balance sheet valuation of inventory that occurs under LIFO.[11]

The next chapter covers the financial accounting and reporting for investments and funds.

KEY POINTS

1. The dollar-value LIFO method and the retail LIFO method help to simplify the clerical tasks associated with applying LIFO in practice. (Objectives 1 and 3).

2. Dollar-value LIFO is a way to apply LIFO on the basis of changes in base-year cost dollars associated with a pool of similar goods. Under this method, LIFO layers are expressed in cost dollars rather than in physical units. (Objective 1)

3. Dollar-value LIFO gives companies considerable flexibility when grouping their inventory items into pools. The result is that dollar-value LIFO helps to preserve old inventory costs while charging the most recent costs to expense (i.e., cost of goods sold). (Objective 1)

4. Applying dollar-value LIFO requires the use of a specific price index that measures changes in the level of a company's inventory cost prices over time. (Objective 1)

5. The retail inventory method is a reversed markup procedure of inventory pricing used by many retail businesses such as department stores. (Objectives 2 and 3)

6. The conventional retail method requires that we include net markups when calculating the cost percentage and subtract net markdowns along with sales when measuring the ending inventory at

---

[9]*Accounting Research Bulletin No. 43,* "Restatement and Revision of Accounting Research Bulletins," 1953, ch. 4, par. 4.

[10]James M. Reeve and Keith G. Stanga, "The LIFO Pooling Decision: Some Empirical Results from Accounting Practice," *Accounting Horizons* (June 1987), pp. 25–33.

[11]One possible solution for the balance sheet problem posed by LIFO is the LIFO/FIFO method, under which a company uses LIFO to measure cost of goods sold on the income statement and FIFO to report inventories on the balance sheet. The LIFO/FIFO method has been considered by the accounting profession but never accepted as GAAP. See Michael P. Bohan and Steven Rubin, "LIFO/FIFO: How Would It Work?" *Journal of Accountancy* (September 1986), pp. 106–110.

retail. The method produces an ending inventory valuation that approximates the lower of cost or market. (Objective 2)

7. The retail LIFO method is an adaptation of the retail method used by many retailers to reflect the LIFO cost flow assumption. Under this method, we apply LIFO on the basis of changes in base-year retail dollars associated with a pool of similar goods. LIFO layers are expressed in retail dollars rather than in physical units; retail LIFO is therefore very similar to dollar-value LIFO. (Objective 3)

8. When calculating the periodic cost percentage under the retail LIFO method, the beginning inventory is excluded, while net markups and net markdowns are included. (Objective 3)

9. Applying retail LIFO requires the use of a specific price index that measures changes in the level of a company's retail prices over time. (Objective 3)

10. The gross margin method is used to estimate the cost of an inventory. The method relies on the use of a historical gross margin on sales percentage. Although the estimate produced by this method is generally considered too imprecise for use in annual financial statements, the method is frequently used for interim reporting purposes, for estimating the cost of an inventory lost by fire or other casualty, and for testing the reasonableness of an inventory cost derived in some other manner. (Objective 4)

11. When we are given a gross margin on cost percentage, we should first convert it to a gross margin on sales percentage to correctly apply the gross margin method. (Objective 4)

QUESTIONS

9–1 What are the basic differences between the specific goods method of applying LIFO and the dollar-value LIFO method?

9–2 How is an incremental LIFO inventory layer determined under the specific goods method? How is it determined under dollar-value LIFO?

9–3 Why is it considered appropriate to use a specific price index rather than a general price-level index when implementing the dollar-value LIFO or the retail LIFO method?

9–4 Explain the double extension method and the link chain method of constructing an internal price index.

9–5 Briefly describe the operation of the dollar-value LIFO method.

9 6 Assume that the total number of physical units in a dollar-value LIFO pool has declined from the beginning to the end of a period. Is it possible under this condition for the dollar-value LIFO cost of the ending inventory to exceed that of the beginning inventory? Why?

9–7 Assuming that a company has decided to use LIFO, what are the major advantages of the dollar-value method?

9–8 Briefly describe the general operation of the retail inventory method.

9–9 What are the major uses of the retail method?

9–10 What major assumption about the composition of the ending inventory is inherent in the retail method?

9–11 What is the meaning of each of the following terms?

[a] Original retail price   [e] Markdown
[b] Additional markup   [f] Markdown cancellation
[c] Markdown cancellation   [g] Net markdown
[d] Net markup

9–12 Why does the conventional retail method produce an ending inventory valuation that approximates the lower of cost or market?

9–13 What are the major differences between the conventional retail method and the retail LIFO method with regard to the manner in which the periodic cost percentage is calculated? Why do these differences exist?

9–14 Briefly describe the operation of the retail LIFO method.

9–15 How, if at all, does the LIFO inventory valuation on the balance sheet relate to the need that investors and creditors have to predict the amount, timing, and uncertainty of cash flows to themselves?

9–16 Briefly describe the operation of the gross margin method.

9–17 How does a markup on cost differ from a markup on sales price?

9–18 Should we use a gross margin on cost percentage or a gross margin on sales percentage when applying the gross margin method? Why?

9–19 What are the major uses of the gross margin method?

EXERCISES

9–20 Double Extension Method   Kappa Corporation applies the dollar-value LIFO method to each of the five pools into which it has divided its inventory. The following information pertains to Pool No. 1:

| | Year-End Quantity | | Current-Year Unit Cost | | |
Product	1995	1996	1995	1996	Base-Year Unit Cost
X	1,000	900	$22	$23	$20
Y	1,700	1,800	13	14	10
Z	2,100	1,800	32	34	30

INSTRUCTIONS

Compute the year-end specific price index for Pool No. 1 for 1995 and 1996 using the double extension method. (The base-year specific price index is 100.)

9–21 Link Chain Method   Pavco Corporation applies the dollar-value LIFO method to each of the four pools into which it has divided its inventory. Pavco adopted dollar-value LIFO on January 1, 1995, and the company uses the link chain method in each LIFO pool. The following information pertains to Pool No. 1:

| | Actual Quantity at Year-End | | Unit Cost | | |
Item	1995	1996	1/1/95	12/31/95	12/31/96
A	3,000	4,000	$10	$12	$14
B	5,000	5,000	16	18	20
C	4,000	3,000	12	15	17

INSTRUCTIONS

Compute the year-end conversion factor for Pool No. 1 for 1995 and 1996 using the link chain method.

9–22 Dollar-Value LIFO   On January 1, 1994, Lincoln, Inc., adopted the dollar-value LIFO method. The company's inventory priced at current costs on that date was $50,000. Additional inventory data are as follows:

Date	Inventory at Year-End Prices	Price Index*
Dec. 31, 1994	$58,300	106
Dec. 31, 1995	59,890	113
Dec. 31, 1996	69,020	119

*Price index at Jan. 1, 1994 = 100.

INSTRUCTIONS

Compute the cost of the company's inventory at December 31, 1994, 1995, and 1996, using the dollar-value LIFO method.

9–23 Dollar-Value LIFO   Horace Company adopted the dollar-value LIFO method on January 1, 1996. The company's inventory priced at current cost on that date was $100,000. During 1996 the company purchased merchandise costing $900,000. The inventory on December 31, 1996, measured by reference to the actual unit costs of the goods most recently purchased, was $154,000. The specific price index for the company's inventory was 100 on January 1, 1996, and 110 on December 31, 1996.

INSTRUCTIONS

[a] Compute the cost of inventory at December 31, 1996, using the dollar-value LIFO method.

[b] Compute the cost of goods sold for 1996 under the dollar-value LIFO method.

9–24 Conventional Retail Method   The following information was taken from the accounting records of Eagle Department Store for the current year:

	Cost	Retail
Beginning inventory	$15,000	$20,000
Net purchases	60,000	75,000
Net markups		5,000
Net markdowns		6,000
Sales		84,000

INSTRUCTIONS

Calculate the ending inventory using the conventional retail method.

9–25 Conventional Retail Method   The following information was taken from the financial records of Hughes' Hardware Store:

Inventory, Jan. 1, 1996	
At cost	$ 6,000
At retail	10,000
Purchases during 1996	
At cost	37,540
At retail	67,000
Purchase returns during 1996	
At cost	1,140
At retail	2,000
Additional markups during 1996, at retail	6,000
Markdowns during 1996, at retail	8,000
Markup cancellations during 1996, at retail	1,000
Markdown cancellations during 1996, at retail	3,000
Transportation-in during 1996, at cost	1,600
Sales during 1996, at retail	60,000

INSTRUCTIONS

Calculate the inventory valuation at December 31, 1996, using the conventional retail method.

9–26 Conventional Retail Method   Deane Department Store uses the retail inventory method. Information relating to the computation of the inventory at December 31, 1996, appears as follows:

	Cost	Retail
Inventory, Jan. 1, 1996	$ 41,000	$ 96,000
Purchases	387,400	592,000
Freight-in	12,000	
Net markups		46,000
Net markdowns		30,000
Sales		580,000

Estimated normal shrinkage due to breakage and theft is 3% of sales.

INSTRUCTIONS

Calculate the estimated inventory on December 31, 1996, at the lower of cost or market using the retail inventory method.

9–27 Conventional Retail Method   The following data pertain to Davini Company for 1996:

	Cost	Retail
Inventory, Jan. 1	$15,000	$25,000
Net purchases	30,000	65,000
Net markups		10,000
Net markdowns		15,000
Sales		53,640

INSTRUCTIONS

Calculate the estimated ending inventory on the basis of lower of cost or market using the retail method.

9–28 Retail LIFO   Using the data presented in Exercise 9–27, calculate the cost of the ending inventory using the retail LIFO method. Assume that the inventory on January 1, 1996, is the base LIFO layer and that the retail price index increased by 12% during 1996.

9–29 Retail LIFO   The following data pertain to Curl Benny Supply Company for the current year:

	Cost	Retail
Inventory, Jan. 1 (base LIFO layer)	$18,250	$ 25,000
Sales		86,500
Net markups		7,000
Net markdowns		10,000
Net purchases	75,000	103,000

INSTRUCTIONS

Calculate the cost of the ending inventory at December 31 using the retail LIFO method. Assume no change in the level of retail prices during the year.

9–30 Retail LIFO   Using the data presented in 9–29 and assuming that the retail price index increased by 10% during the year, calculate the cost of the ending inventory at December 31 using the retail LIFO method.

9–31 Retail LIFO   Alfie Company uses the retail LIFO inventory method. The following information pertains to the company's 1996 accounting period:

	Cost	Retail
Inventory, Jan. 1, 1996	$ 30,000	$ 43,000
Purchases	140,000	180,000
Freight-in	10,000	
Net markups		35,000
Net markdowns		15,000
Sales		190,000

INSTRUCTIONS

Assuming that the inventory on January 1, 1996, is the base inventory and that there was no change in the price index during the year, compute the inventory at December 31, 1996, using the retail LIFO method.

9–32 Gross Margin Percentages   Prepare a table similar to the one shown below and fill in the missing amount for each case.

Case	Gross Margin on Sales Percentage	Gross Margin on Cost Percentage
1	20%	
2		200%
3	33⅓%	
4		20%
5	75%	
6		66⅔%

9–33 Gross Margin Method   On May 9, 1996, a fire destroyed the entire uninsured merchandise inventory of Z-93 Company. You obtained the following data:

Inventory, Jan. 1, 1996	$20,000
Purchases, Jan. 1 through May 9	70,000
Sales, Jan. 1 through May 9	80,000
Gross margin on sales percentage	25%

INSTRUCTIONS

Calculate the estimated fire loss to report in Z-93 Company's income statement for 1996.

9–34 Gross Margin Method Yoakley Company uses the gross margin method to estimate its inventories for interim reporting purposes. The following data pertain to the company:

Inventory, Jan. 1, 1996	$ 50,000
Purchases, Jan. 1 through Mar. 31, 1996	120,000
Sales, Jan. 1 through Mar. 31, 1996	180,000
Markup on cost	25%

INSTRUCTIONS

Calculate the estimated cost of the inventory at the end of the first quarter of 1996.

9–35 Gross Margin Method You are the independent auditor for Zack's Department Store. Tomorrow is the last day of the current fiscal year. The store will be closed and you will observe the taking of the physical inventory to accurately determine its cost.

Zack's accounting records as of the end of today provide the following data that pertain to the current fiscal year: sales, $446,000; sales returns, $20,000; beginning inventory, $70,000; purchases, $194,000; purchase returns, $4,000; transportation-in, $10,000.

The average rate of gross margin on sales during the last three years is 40%.

INSTRUCTIONS

Calculate an estimate of the cost of the ending inventory.

9–36 Gross Margin Method The following data were obtained from the accounting records of Black, Inc.:

Inventory, July 1	$12,000
Purchases	
July	60,000
August	70,000
September	59,600
Sales	
July	70,000
August	82,000
September	90,000

The company's markup on cost has averaged 25% during the past few years.

INSTRUCTIONS

Estimate the ending inventory costs for July, August, and September for monthly reporting purposes.

PROBLEMS

9–37 Specific Goods LIFO The following information pertains to Mertie Company, which uses a periodic inventory system.

	Product S		Product T	
	Number of Units	Unit Cost	Number of Units	Unit Cost
Inventory, Jan. 1, 1995	200	$2	300	$3
Purchases				
1995	300	3	600	4
	500	4	600	5
1996	900	5	600	7
	700	6	300	8
Sales				
1995	600		1,300	
1996	1,900		800	

INSTRUCTIONS

[a] Calculate each of the following amounts for Mertie Company using the specific goods method of applying LIFO:

[1] Cost of inventory at December 31, 1995.

[2] Cost of goods sold for 1995.

[3] Cost of inventory at December 31, 1996.

[4] Cost of goods sold for 1996.

[b] How is the existence of an incremental LIFO layer determined under the specific goods method?

[c] What are the fundamental differences between the specific goods method and the dollar-value method of applying LIFO?

9–38 Dollar-Value LIFO Merita Company adopted the dollar-value LIFO inventory method on January 1, 1993. The company's inventory on that date was $10,000, which is considered the base LIFO layer. Additional data about the company appear below.

Year	Purchases	December 31 Inventory at Current Year Prices	Price Index*
1993	$62,000	$13,200	110
1994	68,000	18,150	121
1995	71,000	14,630	133
1996	82,000	21,750	145

*Price index at Jan. 1, 1993 = 100.

INSTRUCTIONS

[a] Compute the cost of the inventory at December 31, 1993, 1994, 1995, and 1996, using the dollar-value LIFO method.

[b] Compute the cost of goods sold for 1993, 1994, 1995, and 1996, under the dollar-value LIFO method.

9–39 Dollar-Value LIFO McClellan, Inc., sells Products H, I, and J. On January 1, 1994, the company adopted the dollar-value LIFO method. The company's inventory priced at current costs on that date was $200,000. Other data about the company's inventory appear below.

Dec. 31	Quantity			Current Year Unit Cost		
	H	I	J	H	I	J
1994	1,000	500	100	$110	$220	$330
1995	1,020	510	102	121	242	225
1996	350	250	50	140	260	380

INSTRUCTIONS

Compute the ending inventories for 1994, 1995, and 1996 using the dollar-value LIFO method. The base-year unit costs are $100, $200, and $300 for Products H, I, and J, respectively. McClellan derives a price index using the double extension approach.

9–40 Dollar-Value LIFO Roll, Inc., uses the FIFO inventory method for internal reporting purposes. On January 1, 1993, the company adopted the dollar-value LIFO method for income tax and external reporting purposes. The company's inventory priced at current costs on that date was $20,000. When applying the dollar-value LIFO method, the company relies on an appropriate external price index. Additional data appear below.

Date	Inventory Priced at Current Year Cost	External Price Index
Dec. 31, 1993	$22,800	132.0
Dec. 31, 1994	34,320	145.2
Dec. 31, 1995	34,650	181.5
Dec. 31, 1996	51,480	217.8

INSTRUCTIONS

[a] Assuming that the external price index was 110 on January 1, 1993, compute the cost of the inventory at December 31, 1993, 1994, 1995, and 1996, using dollar-value LIFO.

[b] Explain why a price index is needed to implement the dollar-value LIFO method.

9–41 Conventional Retail Method   The following information pertains to Babcock Company for the fiscal year ended June 30, 1996:

	Cost	Retail
Inventory, July 1, 1995	$12,600	$20,000
Purchases	46,160	80,500
Purchase returns	1,860	3,000
Purchase allowances	900	1,500
Transportation-in	4,000	
Additional markups		8,000
Markdowns		13,000
Markup cancellations		4,000
Markdown cancellations		8,000
Gross sales		69,000
Sales returns		2,000
Employee discounts granted		1,000
Normal breakage		2,000

INSTRUCTIONS

Calculate the June 30, 1996, inventory at lower of cost or market using the conventional retail method.

9–42 Conventional Retail Method   Baird Store applies the conventional retail method to each of its three departments to estimate its monthly inventories for internal reporting purposes. The following information for January 1996 is available from the company's accounting records:

	Department					
	Men's Clothing		Women's Clothing		Infants' Wear	
	Cost	Retail	Cost	Retail	Cost	Retail
Beginning inventory	$1,003	$1,700	$2,040	$ 4,000	$1,176	$2,800
Net purchases	3,797	6,000	5,960	11,500	3,624	8,800
Net markups		300		500		400
Net markdowns		700		900		500
Sales		5,000		11,000		8,000

INSTRUCTIONS

Calculate the estimated January 31 inventory for Baird Store by applying the conventional retail method to each department separately and summing the results.

9–43 Conventional Retail Method   Ballou's Department Store uses the retail inventory method to estimate ending inventory for its monthly financial statements. The following data pertain to a single department for October 1996.

Inventory, Oct. 1		
At cost	$ 20,000	
At retail	30,000	
Purchases (exclusive of freight and returns)		
At cost	100,151	
At retail	146,495	
Freight-in	5,100	
Purchase returns		
At cost	2,100	
At retail	2,800	
Additional markups	2,500	
Markup cancellations	265	

Markdowns (net)	800
Normal spoilage and breakage	2,600
Sales	134,730

INSTRUCTIONS

[a] Using the conventional retail method, prepare a schedule computing the estimated lower of cost or market inventory on October 31, 1996.

[b] A department store using the conventional retail inventory method estimates the cost of its ending inventory at $29,000. An accurate physical count reveals only $22,000 of inventory at lower of cost or market. List the factors that may have caused the difference between the computed inventory and the physical count.

(AICPA adapted)

9–44   Retail LIFO   The information below pertains to Yin, Inc., which adopted the retail LIFO method on Jan. 1, 1993:

Date	Inventory at Retail Prices	Cost Percentage	Retail Price Index
Jan. 1, 1993	$100,000	50%	100
Dec. 31, 1993	123,200	51	110
Dec. 31, 1994	152,520	55	124
Dec. 31, 1995	133,280	54	136
Dec. 31, 1996	168,200	56	145

INSTRUCTIONS

[a] Calculate the cost of the inventory at December 31, 1993, 1994, 1995, and 1996, using the retail LIFO method.

[b] Explain why a retail price index is needed to implement the retail LIFO method, assuming that the level of retail prices changes over time.

9–45   Retail LIFO   Zimprich Company adopted the retail LIFO method on January 1, 1994. On that date, the company's inventory at retail prices was $50,000, its cost percentage was 45%, and a suitable retail price index was 100. Additional information for 1994, 1995, and 1996, appears below.

	1994	1995	1996
Beginning inventory at retail	$ 50,000	$ 61,040	$ 63,440
Net purchases			
At cost	86,000	101,200	112,800
At retail	205,000	233,000	247,000
Net markups at retail	10,000	7,000	9,000
Net markdowns at retail	15,000	20,000	16,000
Sales at retail	188,960	217,600	222,440
Year-end retail price index	109	122	135

INSTRUCTIONS

[a] Calculate the cost of ending inventory for each year using the retail LIFO method.

[b] Calculate the cost of goods sold for each year under the retail LIFO method.

9–46   Retail LIFO   Under your guidance, Ray's Sporting Goods Store installed the retail method of accounting for its merchandise inventory as of January 1, 1996. When you prepared the store's financial statements on June 30, 1996, the following data were available:

	Cost	Selling Price
Inventory, Jan. 1	$26,900	$ 40,000
Markdowns		10,500
Additional markups		19,500
Markdown cancellations		6,500
Markup cancellations		4,500
Purchases	86,200	111,800
Sales		123,000
Purchase returns and allowances	1,500	1,800
Sales returns and allowances		4,000

INSTRUCTIONS

[a] Prepare a schedule to compute the store's June 30, 1996, inventory under the retail LIFO method. Assume that the level of retail prices has remained constant.

[b] Without prejudice to your solution to [a], assume that you computed the June 30, 1996, inventory to be $45,150 at retail and the cost percentage to be 80%. The level of retail prices has increased from 100 at January 1 to 105 at June 30. Prepare a schedule to compute the June 30, 1996, inventory under the retail LIFO method.   (AICPA adapted)

9–47 Conventional Retail and Retail LIFO   Reeves Corporation, which uses the conventional retail inventory method, wishes to change to the retail LIFO method beginning with the accounting year ending December 31, 1996. Amounts indicated by the firm's accounting records are as follows:

	Cost	Retail
Inventory, Jan. 1, 1996	$ 5,210	$ 15,000
Net purchases in 1996	47,250	100,000
Net markups in 1996		7,000
Net markdowns in 1996		2,000
Sales in 1996		100,000

Assume that all net markups and net markdowns apply to 1996 purchases and that it is appropriate to treat the entire inventory as a single department. Also assume that the level of specific retail prices remained constant in 1996.

INSTRUCTIONS

Compute the inventory valuation at December 31, 1996, using:

[a] The conventional retail method.

[b] The retail LIFO method, effecting the change in method as of January 1, 1996.

                                                                    (AICPA adapted)

9–48 Conventional Retail and Retail LIFO   Underwood Department Store converted from the conventional retail method to the retail LIFO method on January 1, 1995. In your examination of the financial statements for the year ended December 31, 1996, management asks that you give a summary of certain computations of inventory costs for the past three years.

The following information is available.

[1] The inventory at January 1, 1994, had a retail value of $45,000 and a cost of $27,500, based on the conventional retail method.

[2] Transactions during 1994 were as follows:

	Cost	Retail
Gross purchases	$282,000	$490,000
Purchase returns	6,500	10,000
Purchase discounts	5,000	
Gross sales		492,000
Sales returns		5,000
Employee discounts		3,000
Freight-in	26,500	
Net markups		25,000
Net markdowns		10,000

[3] The retail value of the December 31, 1995, inventory was $56,100; the cost percentage for 1995 under the retail LIFO method was 62%; and the retail price index was 102% of the January 1, 1995, price level.

[4] The retail value of the December 31, 1996, inventory was $51,450; the cost percentage for 1996 under the retail LIFO method was 61%; and the retail price index was 105% of the January 1, 1995, price level.

INSTRUCTIONS

[a] Prepare a schedule showing the computation of the cost of inventory on hand at December 31, 1994, based on the conventional retail method.

[b] Prepare a schedule showing the computation of the cost of inventory on hand at December 31, 1994, based on the retail LIFO method. Underwood Department Store does not consider beginning inventories in computing its retail LIFO cost percentage. Assume that the retail value of the December 31, 1994, inventory was $50,000.

[c] Without prejudice to your solution to [b], assume that you computed the December 31, 1994, inventory (retail value $50,000) under the retail LIFO method at a cost of $28,000. Prepare a schedule showing the computations of the cost of the store's 1995 and 1996 year-end inventories under the retail LIFO method.   (AICPA adapted)

9–49 Gross Margin Method   A major portion of Valley Company's inventory was stolen on the night of August 16, 1996. A physical count the next day revealed that goods costing $12,000 were still on hand. Your examination of the company's accounting records reveals the following:

Inventory, Jan. 1, 1996	$ 25,000
Transactions, Jan. 1 through Aug. 16, 1996	
Purchases	97,000
Purchase returns	2,500
Transportation-in	5,400
Sales	141,500
Sales returns	5,000

The company began operations early in 1995, and its income statement for that year appears below.

Valley Company
Income Statement
For the Year Ended December 31, 1995

Net Sales		$195,000
Cost of goods sold		117,000
Gross margin on sales		78,000
Operating expenses		
Selling expenses	$11,000	
Administrative expenses	17,000	
Total		28,000
Income before income taxes		50,000
Income tax expense		20,000
Net income		$ 30,000

INSTRUCTIONS

Calculate an estimate of the cost of the inventory that was stolen.

9–50 Gross Margin Method   On the night of September 30, 1996, a fire destroyed most of the merchandise inventory of Sampson, Inc. All goods were completely destroyed except for (1) partially damaged goods that normally sell for $10,000 and that had an estimated net realizable value of $1,000 after the fire and (2) undamaged goods that normally sell for $6,000.

The following data are available from the company's accounting records, which were locked in a fireproof safe:

Inventory, Jan. 1, 1996	$ 46,000
Net purchases, Jan. 1 through Sept. 30, 1996	$423,750
Net sales, Jan. 1 through Sept. 30, 1996	525,000

Condensed income statement information for the past three years appears below.

	1995	1994	1993
Net sales	$500,000	$300,000	$100,000
Cost of goods sold	384,000	220,000	71,000
Gross margin	116,000	80,000	29,000
Operating expenses	25,000	20,000	9,000
Income before income taxes	91,000	60,000	20,000
Income tax expense	36,400	24,000	8,000
Net income	$ 54,600	$ 36,000	$ 12,000

The company estimates that the rate of gross margin on sales in 1996 is equal to the weighted average rate for the past three years.

INSTRUCTIONS

[a] Estimate the amount of the fire loss, assuming that Sampson, Inc., does not carry insurance on its inventory.

[b] Assume now that Sampson does have insurance on the inventory and that you are the adjustor for the insurance company. How might you argue that Sampson's loss is really smaller than the amount you computed in [a]?

9–51 Gross Margin Method On April 15, 1996, fire damaged the office and warehouse of Hap Wholesale Corporation. The only accounting record saved was the general ledger, from which the following trial balance was prepared.

Hap Wholesale Corporation
Trial Balance
March 31, 1996

Cash	$ 7,000	
Accounts receivable	27,000	
Inventory, Dec. 31, 1995	50,000	
Land	24,000	
Building and equipment	120,000	
Accumulated depreciation		$ 27,200
Other assets	3,600	
Accounts payable		23,700
Accrued liabilities		7,200
Capital stock		100,000
Retained earnings		47,700
Sales		90,400
Purchases	42,000	
Other expenses	22,600	
	$296,200	$296,200

The following additional information has been gathered:

[1] The fiscal year of the corporation ends on December 31.

[2] An examination of the April bank statement and canceled checks revealed that checks written April 1–15 totaled $11,600: $5,700 for accounts payable as of March 31; $2,000 for April merchandise shipments; and $3,900 for other expenses. Deposits during the same period amounted to $10,650, which consisted of receipts on account from customers, with the exception of a $450 refund from a vendor for merchandise returned in April.

[3] Correspondence with suppliers revealed unrecorded obligations at April 15 of $8,500 for April merchandise shipments, including $1,300 for shipments in transit on that date.

[4] Customers acknowledged indebtedness of $26,400 at April 15, 1996. It was also estimated that customers owe another $5,000 that will never be acknowledged or recovered. Of the acknowledged indebtedness, $600 will probably be uncollectible.

[5] The companies insuring the inventory agreed that the corporation's fire loss claim should be based on the assumption that the overall gross margin on sales percentage for the past two years was in effect during the current year. The corporation's audited financial statements disclosed the following:

	Year Ended December 31	
	1995	**1994**
Net sales	$400,000	$300,000
Net purchases	226,000	174,000
Beginning inventory	45,000	35,000
Ending inventory	50,000	45,000

[6] Inventory with a cost of $6,500 was salvaged and sold for $850. The balance of the inventory was a total loss.

INSTRUCTIONS

Prepare a schedule computing the amount of the inventory fire loss. The supporting schedule of the computation of the gross margin on sales percentage should be in good form.   (AICPA adapted)

9-52 Gross Margin Method   Apex Corporation is an importer and wholesaler. Its merchandise is purchased from a number of suppliers and is warehoused by Apex until it is sold to customers.

In conducting the audit for the year ended June 30, 1996, the company's CPA determined that the internal control system was good. Accordingly, the physical inventory was observed at an interim date, May 31, 1996, instead of at year-end.

The following information was obtained from the general ledger:

Inventory, July 1, 1995	$ 87,500
Physical inventory, May 31, 1996	95,000
Sales for 11 months ended May 31, 1996	840,000
Sales for year ended June 30, 1996	950,000
Purchases for 11 months ended May 31, 1996	950,000
(before audit adjustments)	675,000
Purchases for year ended June 30, 1996 (before audit adjustments)	790,000

The CPA's audit disclosed the following information:

Shipments received in May and included in the physical inventory but recorded as June purchases	$7,500
Shipments received in unsalable condition and excluded from physical inventory (Credit memos had not been received nor had chargebacks to vendors been recorded.)	
Total at May 31, 1996	1,000
Total at June 30, 1996 (including the May unrecorded chargebacks)	1,500
Deposit made with vendor and charged to purchases in April 1996 (Product was shipped in July 1996.)	2,000
Deposit made with vendor and charged to purchases in May 1996 (Product was shipped, FOB destination, on May 29, 1996, and was included in May 31, 1996, physical inventory as goods in transit.)	5,500

INSTRUCTIONS

In audit engagements in which interim physical inventories are observed, a frequently used auditing procedure is to test the reasonableness of the year-end inventory by the gross margin method. Prepare in good form the following schedules:

[a] Computation of the gross margin on sales percentage for the 11 months ended May 31, 1996.

[b] Computation by the gross margin method of cost of goods sold during June 1996.

[c] Computation by the gross margin method of the June 30, 1996, inventory.   (AICPA adapted)

CASES

9-53 Impact of Changing from FIFO to LIFO   Will Peak, president of Perrin Enterprises, is thinking about changing his company's method of inventory pricing from FIFO to dollar-value LIFO. Perrin Enterprises is a large, publicly held manufacturer of a wide variety of products whose costs are expected to increase steadily in the near future. Peak has learned that in such an environment, the use of LIFO can result in a material, and sometimes permanent, deferral of income taxes. Peak is concerned, though, that using LIFO could lower his company's net income, stock market price, working capital, and current ratio (current assets divided by current liabilities). He fears that although using LIFO may save income taxes, investors and creditors may not look favorably on the company in the future.

INSTRUCTIONS

Advise Peak as to whether or not Perrin Enterprises should adopt LIFO. Provide rationale for your advice, and be sure to address Peak's concerns about LIFO.

9–54 Retail Method Peccolo Paint Company, your client, manufactures paint. The company's president, Mr. Peccolo, has decided to open a retail store to sell Peccolo paint as well as wallpaper and other supplies that would be purchased from other suppliers. He has asked you for information about the retail method of pricing inventories at the retail store.

INSTRUCTIONS

Prepare a report to the president explaining the retail method of pricing inventories. Your report should include the following points:

[a] Description and accounting features of the method.
[b] Conditions that may distort the results under the method.
[c] Advantages of using the method when compared to cost methods of inventory pricing.
[d] Accounting theory underlying the treatment of net markdowns and net markups under the method. (AICPA adapted)

9–55 Inventories and Cash Basis Accounting The owner of Reno's Retail Hardware computes income on a cash basis. At the end of each year, he takes a physical inventory and computes the cost of all merchandise on hand. To this he adds the ending balance of accounts receivable, because he considers this a part of inventory on the cash basis. Using this logic, he deducts from this total the ending balance of accounts payable for merchandise and arrives at what he calls inventory (net).

The following information has been taken from Reno's cash basis income statements:

	1996	1995	1994
Cash received	$173,000	$164,000	$150,000
Cost of goods sold			
Inventory (net), Jan. 1	8,000	11,000	3,000
Total purchases	109,000	102,000	95,000
Goods available for sale	117,000	113,000	98,000
Inventory (net), Dec. 31	1,000	8,000	11,000
Cost of goods sold	116,000	105,000	87,000
Gross margin	$ 57,000	$ 59,000	$ 63,000

The following additional information is available:

	1996	1995	1994
Cash sales	$151,000	$147,000	$141,000
Credit sales	24,000	18,000	14,000
Accounts receivable, Dec. 31	8,000	6,000	5,000
Accounts payable for merchandise, Dec. 31	33,000	20,000	13,000

INSTRUCTIONS

[a] Without reference to the above, discuss the various cash basis concepts of revenue and income and indicate the conceptual merits of each.
[b] Is the gross margin for Reno's Retail Hardware being computed on a cash basis? Evaluate and explain the approach used with illustrative computations of the cash basis gross margin for 1995.
[c] Explain why the gross margin for Reno's retail Hardware shows a decrease while sales and cash receipts are increasing. (AICPA adapted)

JUDGMENT CASES

9–56 LIFO Liquidation You are the chief accountant for the O'Neil Company, a large, publicly held furniture wholesaler that uses the dollar-value LIFO inventory method. O'Neil ordinarily buys furniture from a variety of manufacturers and later resells it to numerous retailers throughout the nation. Today's date is *January 10, 1996,* and you are working hard to prepare the financial statements for the accounting period that ended on December 31, 1995. Your LIFO working papers show that O'Neil had a LIFO layer liquidation during 1995 because the year-end inventory is less than the beginning inventory when both inventories are priced at base-year cost. As a result, 1995 net income will be materially *higher* than it would have been without the liquidation.

The chief executive officer of O'Neil Company, Rhonda Hoyt, enters your office and tells you emphatically that a LIFO layer liquidation is unacceptable. Ms. Hoyt is concerned about the incremental income taxes that will have to be paid and about the potentially distortive effects on accounting net income often associated with a LIFO layer liquidation.

Ms. Hoyt then reminds you that on December 15, 1995, O'Neil placed a large furniture order with Stratford Company, a major supplier, with delivery scheduled for January 15, 1996. Because delivery is now only five days away, Ms. Hoyt tells you to call Stratford immediately and ask that Stratford date its sales invoice December 31, 1995. In this way O'Neil can assert that it owned the inventory on December 31, 1995, and thereby avoid the 1995 LIFO layer liquidation. Ms. Hoyt reminds you about how important it is for everyone at O'Neil Company to be a team player.

INSTRUCTIONS

Would you follow Ms. Hoyt's instructions by calling Stratford and asking it to predate its sales invoice? Explain in detail the rationale that supports your decision. As a *part* of your explanation, include a discussion of the major parties who would be affected by your decision.

9–57 LIFO Liquidation   You are the chief financial officer for the Howard Company, a manufacturer of small electronic devices that uses dollar-value LIFO to value inventories. In response to heightened competition and new data processing capabilities, the company recently implemented a *just-in-time* approach to managing inventories. This approach, under which the company tries to manufacture products "just in time" to make sales, has been quite successful. The company has reduced the inventory level it normally carries, resulting in a substantial savings in carrying costs. The end of the year is now approaching and the company's president is meeting with you to plan the preparation of the company's financial statements. You have just pointed out that the new inventory management method will result in reporting a rather large profit during the year due to the liquidation of several LIFO layers that have accumulated over the years.

The president responds that he has been thinking about this issue and does not want to pay the income taxes that will result from the LIFO layer liquidations, nor does he wish to report the higher net income during the current year. He states:

> We have had a really good year without considering the LIFO liquidation, and we don't need to report higher profits at this time. What really concerns me is that we are projecting a slowdown in our business next year due to the recession that many are predicting and I want to "save" those low-cost layers of LIFO inventory until we need them. Therefore, I am going to instruct the director of purchasing to acquire additional amounts of inventory necessary to prevent the liquidation of any LIFO layers for bookkeeping purposes this year. If our profits next year are not as high as I want them to be, then we'll just let the liquidation of LIFO layers take care of that problem at that time. By the way, my plan doesn't cause you any problems does it? You aren't going to suggest that we need to provide any financial statement disclosure of our actions and plans to manage our reported income, are you?

INSTRUCTIONS

Should Howard Company make any disclosures about the president's plans and actions? If so, be specific and describe the nature of the disclosures that you recommend. If not, explain why you believe that disclosures are unnecessary.

9–58 Retail Method   Carly's Kids Clothes uses the conventional retail method of valuing its inventories. In past years, the company has had a stable cost-to-retail relationship for its inventory due to buying from one manufacturer and marking up the goods by a fixed percentage. Because of excellent sales and a lack of competition, Carly's has not previously needed to mark down any of its goods.

In the current year, however, two national department store chains opened stores in the small town in which Carly's has its store. Those department stores provide intense competition, and Carly's has found itself buying products from a variety of manufacturers with lower costs, reducing markup on many of its goods, and marking down various items of inventory. Despite these adjustments, Carly's is unable to sell all of certain products.

As an independent CPA, you are beginning the audit of Carly's for the current year and have also been asked to consult on the store's problems related to the new competition. Of particular concern is determining the value of ending inventory. In past years, you have been able to determine the inventory value at retail by simply counting the items on shelves and extending the quantities of the various items by the retail prices noted on each item. The retail value of the inventory was then reduced to a lower of cost or market valuation by multiplying the retail value by the appropriate cost percentage. You had little concern with obsolete or unsalable goods, because little inventory remained at year-end and what remained was always sold rather quickly after year-end.

At the end of the current year, there is a relatively large amount of inventory on hand because Carly's had bought larger quantities to obtain lower prices and disappointing sales levels had resulted from the increased competition. You are also aware that the stable cost percentage of past years is uncertain today and that the value of some of the inventory may be impaired below its net realizable value less the normal gross margin amount. Carly Genova, the owner of the store, has stated, "Let's just get these financial statements out as quickly as possible and turn our attention to solving my business problems. By the way, I don't expect to spend any more money than last year on producing the financial statements. Times are getting real tough here."

INSTRUCTIONS

Describe the methods that you believe should be applied to value Carly's inventory at the end of the current year. Be specific in your answer and identify procedures that you believe should be applied in light of the company's changed conditions. Also comment on the owner's statement about the cost of preparing the financial statements. What should you do in regard to preparing the financial statements and concerns about your fee?

FINANCIAL REPORTING CASE

9–59 Financial Reporting Case   Below are financial statement notes concerning inventories for Deere & Company and Philip Morris Companies, Inc., from their respective 1993 financial statements:

Deere & Company

Inventories. Substantially all inventories owned by Deere & Company and its United States equipment subsidiaries are valued at cost on the "last-in, first-out" (LIFO) method. Remaining inventories are generally valued at the lower of cost, on the "first-in, first-out" (FIFO) basis, or market. The value of gross inventories on the LIFO basis represented 83 percent and 81 percent of worldwide gross inventories at FIFO value on October 31, 1993 and 1992, respectively.

Under the LIFO inventory method, cost of goods sold ordinarily reflects current production costs thus providing a matching of current costs and current revenues in the income statement. However, when LIFO-valued inventories decline, as they did in 1993 and 1992, lower costs that prevailed in prior years are matched against current year revenues, resulting in higher reported net income. Benefits from the reduction of LIFO inventories totaled $51 million ($33 million or $.43 per share after income taxes) in 1993, $65 million ($43 million or $.56 per share after income taxes) in 1992 and $128 million ($84 million or $1.11 per share after income taxes) in 1991.

Raw material, work-in-process and finished goods inventories at October 31, 1993 totaled $464 million on a LIFO-value basis compared with $525 million one year ago. If all inventories had been valued on a FIFO basis, estimated inventories by major classification at October 31 in millions of dollars would have been as follows:

	1993	1992
Raw materials and supplies	$ 192	$ 213
Work-in-process	295	377
Finished machines and parts	919	979
Total FIFO value	1,406	1,569
Adjustment to LIFO basis	942	1,044
Inventories	$ 464	$ 525

Philip Morris Companies, Inc.

Note 1. Summary of Significant Accounting Policies

Inventories. Inventories are stated at the lower of cost or market. The last-in, first-out ("LIFO") method is used to cost substantially all domestic inventories. The cost of other inventories is determined by the average cost or first-in, first-out methods. It is a generally recognized industry practice to classify the total amount of leaf tobacco inventory as a current asset although part of such inventory, because of the duration of the aging process, ordinarily would not be utilized within one year.

Note 4. Inventories

The cost of approximately 54% of inventories in 1993 and 56% of inventories in 1992 was determined using the LIFO method. The stated LIFO values of inventories were approximately $1.0 billion lower than the current cost of inventories at December 31, 1993 and 1992.

INSTRUCTIONS

[a] For Deere & Company:
   [1] What explanation does the company make for its decline in inventories from 1992 to 1993 and the impact that decline had on the 1993 income?
   [2] From the information presented in the above note, does it appear that using LIFO has a significant impact on the company's financial statements? What additional information would you like to have to better answer this question?
[b] For Philip Morris Companies, Inc.:
   [1] How does the company explain its policy concerning the classification of inventories as a current asset in relation to the common policy of conversion to cash within one year?
   [2] From the information presented in the above note, does it appear that using LIFO has a significant impact on the company's financial statements? Based only on the information you have for the two companies in this case, does it appear that using LIFO has had a greater impact on Deere & Company or Philip Morris?

Investments and Funds

OBJECTIVES

1. To discuss reasons that businesses invest in the securities of other companies.
2. To define the classifications for various types of investments for financial accounting and reporting purposes.
3. To develop the concepts and theories underlying financial accounting and reporting for investments.
4. To describe acceptable accounting practices for acquiring, holding, and disposing of investments.
5. To illustrate the financial statement disclosures for investing activities.

"SEC Is Seeking Updated Rules for Accounting"
"Accounting Body Backs Modified Rules on the Valuation of Securities by Banks"
"Some Banks Alter Investment Strategies Due to New Accounting Rule Proposal"
"FASB Votes to Make Banks and Insurers Value Certain Bonds at Current Price"

These are headlines from 1992 and 1993 issues of *The Wall Street Journal*. They refer to a new accounting standard from the FASB that requires companies to carry many of their investments at market value rather than historical cost or the even more conservative lower of cost or market, this procedure is often referred to as *mark to market;* The new standard became effective in 1994.

Will this new reporting requirement have an important impact on financial statements? The answer is a definite yes for banks, which are expected to experience the most dramatic impact. One study that attempts to determine the impact of the new standard on reported earnings of banks reveals the following:

MARKING TO MARKET: THE IMPACT

Bank	Pretax 1989 Earnings/Losses	Results with Securities at Market Value	Change in Percent
	Millions of Dollars		
CitiCorp	$1,533	$2,059	34%
J. P. Morgan	−1,100	− 921	16
Manufacturers Hanover	−362	−353	2
Chemical	−454	−516	−14
Chase Manhattan	−469	−645	−38

DATA: Center for the Study of Financial Services, Catherine Young, "The Bean Counters Have the Banks Cowering," *Business Week* (November 16, 1990), p. 56.

This new accounting standard and other aspects of accounting for investments are the subjects of this chapter. As the headlines referred to here indicate, accounting for investments is a hotly contested issue that has received much attention in recent years.

E nterprises invest in income-producing securities issued by other companies for a variety of reasons, including (1) earning a return on otherwise temporarily idle cash; (2) accumulating resources to accomplish certain objectives, such as retiring long-term bonds; and (3) acquiring ownership in another enterprise to gain influence, control, or some other business advantage. Pertinent accounting issues concern the classification (current or noncurrent), measurement (valuation basis), and disclosure of relevant information, including the accounting methods followed.

Investments in securities can generally be classified as either debt or equity. Debt investments represent a lending/borrowing relationship in which the creditor/lender lends money to the debtor/borrower in the form of a debt instrument, such as notes and bonds. The instrument ordinarily establishes the amount of the loan, the rate of interest and frequency that the borrower is required to pay it to the lender, and the maturity date. Equity investments represent ownership in the company (i.e., the investee) whose outstanding preferred or common stock is held by another company (i.e., the investor). The instrument may provide a dividend rate (e.g., dividend percentage on the par or stated value of preferred stock) and information about any priority the instrument has in the event the issuing company liquidates.

Marketable securities are those for which an active market exists for buying and selling investment securities. This ordinarily means that the securities sell on a national securities exchange, such as the New York Stock Exchange, or in an over-the-counter market. Securities that sell in foreign markets are considered marketable when those markets are of a breadth and scope comparable to those referred to above.[1]

Through 1994 companies generally accounted for marketable equity securities at the lower of cost or market value in accordance with *SFAS No. 12*.[2] Marketable debt securities were not subject to the reporting requirements of *SFAS No. 12*, but many companies accounted for them in accordance with that standard. Accounting for marketable debt and equity securities at the lower of cost or market is a conservative approach in which losses indicated by market declines were recognized immediately in income. Market increases, however, were not recognized in income unless they represented recoveries of previously recognized losses. The highest amount that could be placed on a portfolio of marketable debt and equity securities was cost.

Conservatism

In 1993 the FASB issued *SFAS No. 115* on accounting for investments in debt and equity securities. This pronouncement is particularly important because it represents a major breakthrough in the manner in which market value is used in the valuation of investments. *SFAS No. 115* extends the use of market value to a variety of debt and equity investments for measurement and recognition in the financial statements.[3] For many investments, valuation at market is no longer limited to those situations in which market has declined below cost but is also applicable when market value exceeds cost.

We noted previously that predicting future cash flows is an important use of financial statements. Measuring investments at market value is generally believed to be preferable to cost or the lower of cost or market measures for purposes of providing information concerning the future cash consequences of holding investments.

SFAS No. 115 is an important pronouncement in terms of accounting for debt and equity investments and because it delivers a signal concerning the significance of market valuations in financial reporting in general. We discuss this development and its larger implications for financial reporting later in this chapter.

---

[1] *FASB Statement of Financial Accounting Standards No. 115,* "Accounting for Certain Investments in Debt and Equity Securities," 1993, par. 3.

[2] *FASB Statement of Financial Accounting Standards No. 12,* "Accounting for Certain Marketable Securities," 1975.

[3] *FASB Statement of Financial Accounting Standards No. 115,* par. 13.

Organizationally, this chapter first defines important terminology and explores in greater depth the movement toward the use of market value in accounting for debt and equity investments. We then look at the reporting requirements of *SFAS No. 115,* including accounting for three different classifications of debt and equity investments: trading, available-for-sale, and held-to-maturity. Next we consider accounting for investments in the common stock of another company by the equity method and consolidation, approaches used when the investor holds a relatively large part of the outstanding stock of the investee. We then consider the sale and reclassification of investments. We complete our coverage of accounting for investments by considering several situations that may be encountered when debt and equity investments are held, including the receipt of stock purchase warrants, stock rights, stock dividends, and stock splits, as well as accounting for the cash surrender value of life insurance and funds accumulated for specific purposes, such as the retirement of debt.

INVESTMENT TERMINOLOGY

Before we begin our discussion of accounting for investments, we need to establish clear definitions of several terms that were used in introducing the subject of investments, as well as additional terminology that will be used throughout this chapter. A **debt security** is any security that represents a creditor relationship with an enterprise. It includes U.S. Treasury securities, U.S. government agency securities, municipal securities, corporate bonds, convertible debt, commercial paper, and a variety of other financial instruments. When a company holds as an investment a debt security issued by a government agency or another company, financial reporting issues for debt investments become an important consideration.[4]

An **equity security** represents an ownership interest in an enterprise. Examples are common and preferred stock. The term *equity security* also encompasses the right to acquire (e.g., warrants, rights, and call options) and the right to dispose of (e.g., put options) an ownership interest in an enterprise at fixed or determinable prices. When a company holds as an investment equity securities issued by another company, financial reporting issues for equity investments are an important consideration.

Fair value is a frequently encountered term in accounting for debt and equity investments. This is the amount at which a financial instrument could be exchanged in a current transaction (i.e., a current exit value) between willing parties other than in a forced or liquidation sale. If a quoted market price is available for an investment, fair value is the product of the number of trading units (e.g., shares of stock) multiplied by its market price.[5]

As we shall see when we explore the specific financial reporting requirement of *SFAS No. 115,* accounting standards have been developed around three classifications of debt and equity investments: trading securities, held-to-maturity securities, and available-for-sale securities. A clear understanding of these terms is important because different accounting methods are used for each classification of investment. **Trading securities** are bought and held principally to sell in the near term. They generally reflect active and frequent buying and selling and are used to generate profits on short-term differences in price.[6] Trading securities include both debt and equity investments. In a classified balance sheet, an investment in trading securities is a current asset.

At the other extreme are **held-to-maturity securities.**[7] These are investments that the investor has the intent and ability to hold until they mature and are, of necessity, limited to debt investments because equity investments have no fixed maturity date. The fact that a debt

---

[4]Not all debt instruments are debt securities. Securities are either in bearer or registered form, are commonly traded in a securities market, and are part of a class or series or are divisible into a class or series. (*SFAS No. 115,* par. 137) An outstanding loan is an example of a debt instrument that is not a debt security.
[5]*FASB Statement of Financial Accounting Standards No. 115,* par. 137.
[6]*FASB Statement of Financial Accounting Standards No. 115,* par. 12.
[7]*FASB Statement of Financial Accounting Standards No. 115,* par. 7.

investment has a distant maturity date does not alone make it a held-to-maturity investment. If the holder of the investment intends to hold such a security for only a short or indefinite period of time, the investment is not considered to be in the held-to-maturity category. Ordinarily, held-to-maturity investments are noncurrent assets in a classified balance sheet, but they could be current assets if the maturity date is in the near future.

The final classification of debt and equity investments is **available-for-sale securities.**[8] This category includes both debt and equity investments that are not classified as either trading or held-to-maturity. This residual definition approach makes available-for-sale securities difficult to describe, other than to say that management's intent is not to immediately sell the investment (i.e., trading) or to retain the investment until it matures (i.e., held-to-maturity). This leaves in the available-for-sale category those debt and equity investments for which management intends to retain the investment until disposal is consistent with other objectives for investing in a particular security, operating conditions dictate a need to sell, or other factors. For example, a company might hold available-for-sale securities as a secondary source of cash, as needed, in the event of lagging revenues due to a recessionary economy. Another company might hold as available-for-sale an investment in the stock of a start-up company with the intent to dispose of that investment when the other company becomes solidly established. Available-for-sale investments may be classified as current or noncurrent in a classified balance sheet, depending primarily on the intent of management.

THE MOVE TOWARD MARKET VALUE

Conservatism

For decades many accounting theorists have advocated accounting for investments at fair (e.g., market) value. Until recently, however, the primary method of accounting for marketable securities has been the conservative lower of cost or market. Those advocating a market value approach believe that it provides decision makers with current and useful information that reports the economic consequences of holding investments during an accounting period. Accounting for investments at market value requires the revaluation of investments at the end of each accounting period, based on market value at that time. It has not been widely used in the past, except in certain specialized industry situations.

Revenue Realization

Market valuation raises interesting questions of revenue realization. Some market value advocates argue that the periodic adjustment in value should be recognized in the determination of income. Others prefer that unrealized gains and losses (e.g., market changes for investments that have not been sold) be accumulated in stockholders' equity directly, without affecting the determination of income. Opponents of the market value method believe that historical cost, or the lower of cost or market, should be the valuation method of choice for marketable investments, thereby deferring the recognition of unrealized gains and losses (other than losses that are recognized under the lower of cost or market method) until the investments are sold.

Accounting theorists have advocated the use of current value for asset accounting and balance sheet presentation for many years. These include Moonitz and Sprouse,[9] Edwards and Bell,[10] Chambers,[11] Sterling,[12] and Beaver.[13] These authors have often used marketable

---

[8]*FASB Statement of Financial Accounting Standards No. 115,* par. 12.

[9]Robert T. Sprouse and Maurice Moonitz, *Accounting Research Study No. 3,* "A Tentative Set of Broad Accounting Principles for Business Enterprise" (New York: AICPA, 1962).

[10]E. O. Edwards and P. W. Bell, *The Theory of Measurement of Business Income* (Berkeley: University of California Press, 1964).

[11]R. J. Chambers, *Accounting Evaluation and Economic Behavior* (Englewood Cliffs, N.J.: Prentice-Hall, 1966).

[12]Robert R. Sterling, *The Theory of the Measurement of Enterprise Income* (Lawrence: The University Press of Kansas, 1970).

[13]William H. Beaver, "Reporting Rules for Marketable Equity Securities," *Journal of Accountancy* (October 1971), pp. 57–61.

FASB 115: IT'S BACK TO THE FUTURE FOR MARKET VALUE ACCOUNTING

Like time travel, comprehensive market value accounting still lies in the future. In an era of deregulated interest rates and massive losses from thrift and bank failures, a debate has raged over the accounting for financial instruments. Market value accounting has been called a panacea by some and a placebo by others. The Financial Accounting Standards Board, under intense pressure from the Securities and Exchange Commission and others to resolve the issue, accelerated part of its financial instruments project to focus on accounting for debt securities. In May, the FASB issued Statement No. 115, *Accounting for Certain Investments in Debt and Equity Securities.* . . .

To many, the new FASB standard may seem like déjà vu. It resembles both current accounting guidelines and various aspects of a proposal advanced by the American Institute of CPAs accounting standards executive committee several years ago. Before reviewing Statement no. 115, it's important to understand the circumstances that preceded it.

New Business Environment

The business strategies of financial institutions and other investors have become more dynamic since interest rates were deregulated over a decade ago. At one end of the spectrum are investors that manage a part of their investment portfolios as a trading account. At the other end are those that purchase debt instruments, rarely (if ever) sell them before maturity and seek only to earn an interest spread relative to their cost of funds. In the middle, however, are many other investors that buy and sell parts of their investment portfolios to manage interest rate risk, to comply with regulations, to take advantage of market opportunities and to meet other business objectives.

Because the accounting model for debt instruments was designed in simpler times, its continued relevance has been questioned, particularly in the case of portfolios carried at cost. Accounting standards that allow financial statements to overstate significantly a business enterprise's underlying economic value—as was the case with many failed banks and savings and loans—are fair game for criticism. Many believe market value accounting is the best way to move the accounting model into the future.

What to Do?

While many have called for more relevant financial reporting for financial instruments, it's clear there are no easy ways to achieve that objective. The FASB deliberated during a time of highly charged debate. The accounting profession, financial institutions, regulators, the SEC, the General Accounting Office, members of Congress and others were vocal in advancing their views on the subject.

After considering a number of different approaches, the FASB issued Statement no. 115, which turned out to be more evolutionary than revolutionary. It isn't likely to please either those who wanted to maintain the status quo or those who wanted to move to the future with comprehensive market value accounting. The new standard clearly is a compromise.

Statement No. 115

Statement no. 115 applies to all investments in debt securities and to equity securities with readily determinable fair values. It supersedes FASB Statement no. 12, *Accounting for Marketable Securities.* While it applies to financial assets in security form, it does not apply to loans or liabilities. Under Statement no. 115, securities are classified into three categories:

- **Held to maturity.** Debt securities meeting the requirements for this category are reported at amortized cost. Debt securities not included in this classification and equity securities with readily determinable market values are assigned to one of the following categories.

Asset/Liability Measurement

securities to illustrate their particular approach for the valuation of assets at current or market value. Based on extensive research in this area, Sterling concluded: "In research different people from different schools of thought using different postulates and different research methods have drawn the same conclusion: Marketable securities ought to be valued at market. That conclusion has not been challenged in the research literature."[14] In practice, however, the predominant method of measuring and reporting marketable securities has been historical cost or some variation of cost, such as the lower of cost or market or the equity method.

More recently, Foran and Foran attempted to evaluate marketable equity security accounting in light of the FASB's conceptual framework. They correctly state that one purpose of the framework is to be a standard of comparison by which current practice can be evaluated. These authors carefully analyzed market value and lower of cost or market procedures with the individual parts of the conceptual framework, concluding that it is unnecessary to delay recognition until a cash-to-cash cycle is complete. They recommended that the FASB implement its conceptual framework by revising accounting for marketable securities to be

---

[14]Robert R. Sterling, "Accounting Research, Education and Practice," *Journal of Accountancy* (September 1973), pp. 43–50.

- **Trading.** Debt and equity securities in this category are reported at fair value; changes in unrealized gains and losses are included in the income statement. These securities are bought and sold to make short-term profits as opposed to being held to realize longer-term gains from capital appreciation.
- **Available for sale.** Debt and equity securities not assigned to one of the above categories are included here. These investments also are reported at fair value, but unrealized gains and losses (net of tax effects) are reported in a separate component of shareholders' equity.

Genuine Concern

Statement no. 115 is a response to genuine concern about the relevance of current financial reporting for marketable securities. Although the new standard may lack conceptual pu-rity, it does restrict entities' ability to overstate assets and manage reported earnings.

Significant problems remain to be ironed out before some or all liabilities can be reported at fair value. Without fair value reporting for liabilities and off-balance-sheet obligations, broader application of an assets-only approach could compromise the value of financial reporting. Only time will tell whether Statement no. 115 will be an effective solution to the market value accounting dilemma. Since it's also probably not the final solution, stay tuned for "Back to the Future II."

SOURCE: James T. Parks, "FASB 115: It's Back to the Future for Market Value Accounting," *The Journal of Accountancy* (September 1993), pp. 49–56.

Executive Summary

- THE FINANCIAL ACCOUNTING Standards Board issued Statements no. 115, *Accounting for Certain Investments in Debt and Equity Securities,* to address concerns about how entities account for financial instruments.
- BECAUSE THE CURRENT accounting model was designed in simpler times, many have questioned the relevance of current financial reporting for marketable securities. Market value accounting is believed by some to be the best way to move this model into the future.
- STATEMENT NO. 115 APPLIES to all investments in debt securities and to equity securities with readily determinable fair values. It supersedes FASB Statement no. 12, Accounting for Marketable Securities. Statement no. 115 classifies securities into three categories: held to maturity, trading and available for sale.
- THE EFFECTIVE DATE for Statement no. 115 is for financial statements issued for fiscal years beginning after December 15, 1993. Earlier application is permitted but may not be applied retroactively.
- SIGNIFICANT PROBLEMS remain to be resolved before liabilities and off-balance-sheet financial instruments can be reported at fair value. Few expect Statement no. 115 to be the final word on market value accounting.

---

consistent with the current objectives, qualitative characteristics, elements, and recognition and measurement standards of financial reporting.[15]

The FASB has taken steps in *SFAS No. 115* to respond to these and other suggestions for greater use of current value information in financial statements. In the authors' opinion, investments that have no maturity date or that management does not intend to hold to maturity, and for which a ready market value exists, are a logical place to start the expanded use of current value because of the ready availability of a measurement mechanism (i.e., the market value). We view this as a very positive development in the FASB's ongoing attempts to improve financial reporting and expect it to serve as a forerunner for expanded use of current value information in financial reporting of other assets.

When investments in debt and equity securities are made, an asset account is established or increased and the Cash account is decreased. Periodically, cash representing interest revenue on debt investments and dividend revenue on equity investments is received. These

INVESTMENT PURCHASES AND PERIODIC REVENUE

---

[15]Nancy J. Foran and Michael F. Foran, "SFAS No. 12 and the Conceptual Framework," *Accounting Horizons* (December 1987), pp. 43–50.

transactions are the same for all debt and equity investments that are classified as trading, held-to-maturity, or available-for-sale. For that reason, we first cover accounting for the purchases of debt and equity investments and the recognition of periodic interest and dividend revenue. In the next section, we expand our coverage to include periodic changes in market value of investments and the implications of classifying specific investments as trading, held-to-maturity, and available-for-sale.

INVESTMENTS IN DEBT SECURITIES

In general, investments in bonds and notes are recorded at the fair market value of the consideration given for the security. When debt securities are acquired solely for cash, their value is presumed to be the amount of cash paid. If a security is exchanged for *noncash consideration,* the fair market value of the noncash consideration is presumed to represent the present value of the security. If the fair market value of the noncash consideration is not determinable, however, we must then select an appropriate interest rate and compute the present value of the security by using techniques described in Chapter 6. The interest rate to be used in valuing the transaction can be affected by several considerations, such as the issuer's credit standing and any restrictive covenants in the security, tax consequences, and collateral. Prevailing rates of interest for similar securities of issuers with similar credit ratings also help in selecting an appropriate interest rate. The objective in selecting an interest rate is to approximate the rate that would have been incurred in an arm's-length transaction involving lending cash. *Accounting Principles Board Opinion No. 21* deals with this particular phenomenon and many other areas of financial accounting.[16]

When the price paid for a debt investment is less than its face value, the security is said to have been purchased at a *discount.* If the price paid is more than face value, the bond was purchased at a premium. For example, if a bond with a face value of $1,000 is purchased for $940, a $60 discount ($1,000 − $940) exists. The purchaser has acquired the right to receive $1,000 at maturity, as well as periodic interest, and the amount of the discount is considered additional interest revenue. This circumstance implies that the interest rate stated on the instrument was not as high as other available investment opportunities, requiring the seller to reduce the price below face value.

On the other hand, if the price exceeds the face value, the investment has been purchased at a *premium.* For example, if a $1,000 face value bond is purchased for $1,075, the price includes the face value of $1,000 and a premium of $75 ($1,075 − $1,000). The purchaser would be willing to pay a premium price only if the bond's stated interest rate is higher than the rate on other available investments because the purchaser will receive only the $1,000 face value at maturity. The additional $75 paid for the investment is not returned at maturity, so it represents a reduction in interest revenue that the purchaser of the instrument receives.

Any **discount** or **premium** recognized in conjunction with a debt investment is treated as a direct increase (premium) or reduction (discount) in the carrying amount of that investment. The premium or discount is then amortized as an adjustment to interest revenue over the life of the security by using the effective rate of interest. [17] The effective rate of interest is represented by the discount rate that equates the purchase price with the two future cash flows (interest payments and face or maturity amount) obtainable from the investment. We apply the effective rate of interest to the carrying value of each period to determine annual interest. In this manner, a constant rate of interest is recognized over the life of the investment. The difference between the total interest revenue, determined by applying the effective rate of interest to the carrying amount, and the cash received during the period represents the

---

[16]*APB Opinion No. 21,* "Interest on Receivables and Payables," 1971.

[17]*APB Opinion No. 21,* par. 15.

amount of premium or discount to be amortized. This is consistent with amortization practices discussed in Chapter 6.

The straight-line method of amortizing premium or discount is not acceptable unless the results of applying that method are not materially different from the **effective interest method** (also called the **compound interest method** or the **interest method**) described above.

Materiality

The following example illustrates the provisions of *APB Opinion No. 21* as applied to investments in debt securities. Later chapters illustrate applications of this important pronouncement in other circumstances.

Assume that Foster Company acquires ten $1,000 bonds of Leverage Company on January 1, 1994, as a long-term investment at 89.2 (i.e., at 89.2% of the face amount). The bonds mature in five years and bear a stated rate of interest of 9% payable annually on December 31. The following entry records the acquisition of the bonds:

Jan. 1, 1994	Investments	8,920	
	Cash		8,920

The computations are as follows:

$$\$1,000 \times 10 \qquad\qquad = \$10,000 \;\text{Face amount}$$
$$\$1,000 \times 10 \times 89.2\% = \underline{\;\;(8,920)\;} \;\text{Cash paid}$$
$$\underline{\underline{\$\;\;1,080}} \;\;\text{Discount}$$

The determination of the interest rate implicit in this transaction requires trial and error, because it represents a present-value problem involving both an annuity and a single amount. To illustrate, note that when Foster bought the Leverage bonds, rights to two cash flows were acquired:

1. Interest payments of $900 (9% × $1,000 × 10) per year for five years.
2. The maturity value of $10,000 at the end of five years.

Since Foster paid only $8,920 for both of these rights, some interest rate (r) will equate both future cash flows (interest and principal) with the investment price or present value (PV) of $8,920. The equation may be expressed as follows:

PV of the interest payment annuity for five years at r rate
   + PV of the maturity value in five years at r rate = PV of total investment

In this case, the equation becomes

$900 yearly for five years at r + $10,000 in five years at r = $8,920

Both the present values of an annuity (series of interest payments) and an amount (single principal payment) are involved, so we must estimate the effective rate by using the present-value tables in Chapter 6. Because the bonds were acquired below par value, the effective rate is logically higher than the stated rate of 9%.

Trying 12%, we compute as follows:

$$(\$900 \times 3.60478^*) + (\$10,000 \times .56743^\dagger) \approx \$8,920$$
$$\$3,244 + \$5,674 \approx \$8,920$$
$$\$8,918 \approx \$8,920$$

---

*3.60478 is the present value of five payments of $1 at 12%. See Table 6–4.
†.56743 is the present value of a single $1 due five years from now at 12%. See Table 6–2.

The effective interest rate of 12% approximately equates the two future cash flows with the amount paid for the investment and is therefore the effective rate of interest. If a higher or lower rate had been selected originally, then the computation would have failed to equate the two numbers, thereby requiring the testing of different rates until the equation was satisfied.

At the end of the year, the 9% interest payment is received and a portion of the discount on the bonds is amortized:

Dec. 31, 1994 Cash ($10,000 × 9%)	900	
Investments	170	
Interest Revenue ($8,920 × 12%)		1,070

During the first year of the investment, Foster earns 12% on its carrying amount. Because the carrying amount of the investment during the year is $8,920, then $1,070 ($8,920.00 × 12%) total interest revenue is earned. Only $900 ($10,000 × 9%) is received in cash, however, and the difference of $170 ($1,070 − $900) represents the amount of discount to be amortized as part of interest revenue. Exhibit 10–1 presents an amortization table developed for Foster Company as an aid to accounting for this investment.

At the end of the second year, the effective interest rate (12%) is applied to the investment's carrying amount at the beginning of the *second* period. Because $170 of the discount was amortized at the end of the first year, the carrying amount of the investment increased by that amount as demonstrated in the following computation:

Investment in bonds	$10,000
Discount at Jan. 1, 1995 ($1,080 − $170)	910
Carrying amount at Jan. 1, 1995	$ 9,090

The carrying amount of the investment is $9,090 at the beginning of the second year. By multiplying the carrying value of the note by the effective interest rate (12%), we compute

EXHIBIT 10–1

Amortization Table for Investment in Bonds at Discount

Date	Explanation	(1) (12% × carrying value [Col. 6]) Total Interest Revenue	(2) (9% × $10,000) Cash Received	(3) (Col. 1 − Col. 2) Discount to Be Amortized	(4) Face Amount of Bonds	(5) (Reduced by Col. 3) Remaining Discount	(6) (Col. 4 − Col. 5) Carrying Amount
Jan. 1, 1994	Acquisition of bonds	—	—	—	$10,000	$1,080	$ 8,920
Dec. 31, 1994	Recognition of interest	$1,070	$900	$170	10,000	910	9,090
Dec. 31, 1995	Recognition of interest	1,091	900	191	10,000	719	9,281
Dec. 31, 1996	Recognition of interest	1,114	900	214	10,000	505	9,495
Dec. 31, 1997	Recognition of interest	1,139	900	239	10,000	266	9,734
Dec. 31, 1998	Recognition of interest	1,166*	900	266	10,000	—	10,000

*Minor rounding adjustment in 1998 figures to eliminate remaining discount.

the total interest revenue for the second year to be $1,091. Again, since $900 of this amount is received in cash, the difference of $191 ($1,091 − $900) represents the amount of discount to be amortized as additional interest revenue. This process continues each year until all of the discount has been amortized and the bonds mature with the discount fully amortized; no gain or loss is recognized at the maturity of the bonds as reflected in Exhibit 10–1. The carrying value of the investment at the maturity date is $10,000.

If the straight-line method of amortization had been used in this example, the amount of amortization would be $216 ($1,080/5) per year. As in the effective interest method, the carrying amount of the bond investment would increase from $8,920 to $10,000, except that the increase would accumulate in equal increments of $216. Compared to the effective interest method, the straight-line method is conceptually inferior. The interest revenue is overstated in the earlier years and understated in the latter years for a bond purchased at a discount. The opposite pattern would hold for bonds purchased at a premium. As a result, the straight-line amortization method is not generally acceptable unless the periodic difference between it and the effective interest method is immaterial.   **Materiality**

How would these procedures differ if the bonds had been acquired at a **price higher than par value?** In this case, the effective interest rate would be less than the stated rate. The effective rate is applied to the carrying amount of the investment to determine interest revenue for the period, which would be less than the cash received. The difference between the interest revenue and the cash received is amortized as a *reduction* in the carrying amount of the investment. As in the case of an investment acquired at a discount, the straight-line method of amortization is appropriate only if it renders amounts that do not vary materially   **Materiality** from those obtained from the effective interest method.

To illustrate, assume that Foster Company acquired the $10,000 par value bonds at $10,400, which results in an approximate effective interest rate of 8%. The journal entries to record the acquisition of the bonds on January 1, 1994, and to recognize interest revenue at December 31, 1994, are as follows:

Jan. 1, 1994	Investments	10,400	
	Cash		10,400
Dec. 31, 1994	Cash ($10,000 × 9%)	900	
	Interest Revenue ($10,400 × 8%)		832
	Investments		68

The December 31, 1994, entry reduces the Investments account to $10,332 ($10,400 − $68), and interest revenue for 1995 is computed as $827 ($10,332 × 8%). Amortization of the premium in this manner over the five-year period results in a carrying amount at maturity of $10,000, the bond's face amount. An amortization table similar to the one in Exhibit 10–1 can be prepared to assist in determining the periodic amortization amounts. If straight-line amortization were applied, annual amortization of the premium would be $80 ($400/5 years).

In both the discount and premium examples illustrated, we debited Investments for the purchase price of the bonds. We could have debited the face value of the bonds to Investments and recorded any discount or premium in a separate valuation account. Had we followed that approach, the discount would have carried a credit balance and *reduced* the carrying amount of the investment when combined with the face value. The premium would have carried a debit balance and *increased* the carrying amount of the investments when combined with the Investments account. Amortization of discount and premium would have been made to the separate discount or premium accounts rather than to the Investments account, as we did in this illustration. Unless stated otherwise, in this textbook and in the problem and other material at the end of this chapter, we use the approach illustrated here of combining the face value and any discount or premium into a single Investments account.

If Foster Company's year-end for financial reporting purposes were December 31 and the interest payment had not been received by that date, Interest Receivable would be debited in the entries to recognize interest revenue that is earned but not yet received. When the cash is received at a later date, Interest Receivable would be eliminated (i.e., credited) and Cash debited.

INVESTMENTS IN EQUITY SECURITIES

Accounting for investments in equity securities is more straightforward than for investments in debt securities because of the absence of a maturity date. For equity investments, the purchase price is recorded in an investment account. Any difference between that price and the par or stated value of the equity securities is reflected in the investment account and not separately recorded. Dividends are recorded as they are received.

To illustrate, we assume that Foster Company purchased 1,000 shares of the common stock of Welsch, Inc., on January 1, 1994, at $12.50 per share. The par value of the Welsch common is $10, but that has no impact on Foster's recording of the investment. The purchase is recorded as follows:

Jan. 1, 1994	Investments (1,000 × $12.50)	12,500	
	Cash		12,500

Assuming that Welsch pays a dividend of $.75 per share on September 30, 1994, Foster records that dividend as follows:

Sept. 30, 1994	Cash (1,000 × $.75)	750	
	Dividend Revenue		750

Dividends received do not change the amount recorded in the Investments account. The holder of the stock investment does not anticipate dividends and does not record them until they are received except when the company issuing the stock declares a dividend to be paid at a later date. In this case, the investor should record a receivable for the amount of the dividend receivable and the related dividend revenue. The receivable is eliminated (i.e., credited), and the Cash account is debited when the cash is received.

ACCOUNTING FOR TRADING, HELD-TO-MATURITY, AND AVAILABLE-FOR-SALE PORTFOLIOS

SFAS No. 115 uses the term *unrealized holding gains and losses* for changes in the market value of investments that are still held at the end of an accounting period. Debt and equity investments classified as trading are accounted for at fair value and any unrealized holding gains and losses are included in determining earnings. Debt and equity investments classified as available-for-sale are also accounted for at fair value, but unrealized holding gains and losses are excluded from earnings and accumulated in stockholders' equity until realized. Debt securities classified as held-to-maturity are accounted for at amortized cost.

In establishing these accounting practices, the FASB was undoubtedly influenced by many factors, including practices used in the past, political influences, and pressure from reporting companies. The procedures described in the previous paragraph also have conceptual merit, which we will discuss as we consider each type of investment in greater depth. Trading securities are held for short periods of time, so market value is a logical measure of their probable future cash flow effects. Because the sale of trading securities is likely to occur soon, including market adjustments in determining net income has conceptual merit. Available-for-sale investments will be sold at some future date that is not expected to be in the very short term. Valuing them at market value is conceptually logical in terms of their likely future cash flow prospects, and accumulating gains and losses in stockholders' equity and deferring them until the point of sale has some logic. The current market value of debt securities that are classified as held-to-maturity is of no particular relevance in judging the future cash flow effects of those investments. This is the reason that the FASB requires these investments to be carried at amortized cost, which will eventually equal maturity value.

These requirements represent significant change from previous reporting practices. Previously, marketable equity securities were separated into current and noncurrent portfolios and accounted for at the lower of cost or market. The three-category classification is different, but the most significant change is the requirement to account for trading and available-for-sale securities at market value, regardless of whether that value increases or decreases.

To illustrate these procedures, we build on the example of Foster Company presented in the previous section. Recall that in our first example on January 1, 1994, Foster acquired $10,000 face value of Leverage Company bonds for $8,920 and 1,000 shares of Welsch, Inc., common stock for $12,500. Welsch paid a $.75 per share cash dividend on September 30, and Leverage made a 9% interest payment, or $900, at December 31. We need only to add information about the market value of these investments to illustrate accounting under *SFAS No. 115.*

Exhibit 10–2 includes the cost and market value of the Leverage bonds and the Welsch common stock at the end of 1994 and 1995, the two years of our example.

TRADING SECURITIES

We first assume that the two investments are classified as trading securities. As we discussed earlier, this means that they were bought and held principally to be sold in a relatively short time. Foster's primary objective is to generate profits on short-term differences in purchase and sale prices.

Interest revenue on the bond investment and dividend revenue on the common stock investment are recorded as in our previous example. An additional year-end entry is required, however, to record the increase in market value to $23,200, as indicated in Exhibit 10–2.

Entries to record these events, assuming a trading securities classification for the two investments, follow:

Jan. 1, 1994	Investments (Trading)	8,920	
	Cash		8,920
	(To record purchase of Leverage bonds.)		
	Investments (Trading)	12,500	
	Cash		12,500
	(To record purchase of Welsch common stock.)		
Sept. 30	Cash	750	
	Dividend Revenue		750
	(To record dividend revenue on the Welsch common stock.)		
Dec. 31	Cash	900	
	Investments (Trading)	170	
	Interest Revenue		1,070
	(To record interest revenue on the Leverage bonds.)		

EXHIBIT 10–2				
Investment Information				
	1994		**1995**	
	Cost	Market Value	Cost	Market Value
Leverage bonds	$ 8,920	$ 9,700	$ 8,920	$10,800
Welsch common	12,500	13,500	12,500	13,200
	$21,420	$23,200	$21,420	$24,000

Dec. 31	Investments (Trading)	1,610	
	Unrealized Gain on Investments		1,610
	(To record the increase in market value		
	of investments.)		

Except for the last entry, these entries are the same as those we discussed earlier. We have simply combined the two investments into a single trading portfolio. The $1,610 gain in the last entry is determined as follows:

Market value at Dec. 31, 1994 (Exhibit 10–2)		$23,200
Carrying amount at Dec. 31, 1994		
Leverage bonds ($8,920 + $170)	$ 9,090	
Welsch common	12,500	21,590
Unrealized gain		$ 1,610

The gain consists of $610 on the Leverage bonds ($9,700 − $9,090 = $610) and $1,000 on the Welsch common ($13,500 − $12,500 = $1,000). When this gain is recorded, the carrying amount of the portfolio increases to $23,200 ($21,590 + $1,610), the same as the market value. The carrying amount of the portfolio consists of the following individual securities: Leverage bonds ($9,700) and Welsch common ($13,500). The $9,700 balance for the Leverage bonds represents the purchase price, amortization of discount, and increase in market value ($8,920 + $170 + $610); the $13,500 balance for the Welsch common represents the purchase price and the increase in market value ($12,500 + $1,000 = $13,500).

We need only to assume that the Welsch common pays another dividend, this time $.80 per share, on September 30 to extend the example through 1995. Using the information in Exhibit 10–2, entries for 1995 are as follows:

Sept. 30, 1995	Cash (1,000 × $.80)	800	
	Dividend Revenue		800
	(To record dividend revenue on Welsch		
	common stock.)		
Dec. 31	Cash	900	
	Investments	191	
	Interest Revenue		1,091
	(To record interest revenue on Leverage bonds.)		
	Investments	609	
	Unrealized Gain on Investments		609
	(To record the increase in market value		
	of investments.)		

The calculation of the unrealized gain that is recorded in the last entry is as follows:

Market value at Dec. 31, 1995 (Exhibit 10–2)		$24,000
Carrying amount at Dec. 31, 1995:		
Leverage bonds ($9,700 + $191)	$ 9,891	
Welsch common	13,500	23,391
Unrealized gain		$ 609

The gain consists of a $909 gain ($10,800 − $9,891 = $909) on the Leverage bonds, less a $300 loss on the Welsch common ($13,500 − $13,200 = $300). When this gain is recorded, the carrying amount of the portfolio increases to $24,000 ($23,391 + $609), the same as the market value. The carrying amount of the portfolio consists of the following individual securities: Leverage bonds ($10,800) and Welsch common ($13,200). Notice that in 1995, the market value of the Welsch common dropped, but that was more than offset by the increase in value of the Leverage bonds.

The 1994 and 1995 financial statements would include the following information about this activity:

Foster Company
Partial Balance Sheet

	FMV 1994	1995
Current Assets		
Investments	$23,200	$24,000

Foster Company
Partial Income Statement

	1994	1995
Interest revenue	$ 1,070	$ 1,091
Dividend revenue	750	800
Unrealized gain on investments	1,610	609

Foster Company
Partial Statement of Cash Flows

	1994	1995
Operating activities		
Interest received	$ 900	$ 900
Dividends received	750	800
Purchase of investments	$21,420	—

Earlier we defined trading securities as investments that generally reflect active and frequent buying and selling and noted that management's objective in holding them is to generate profits on differences in price. In this illustration, we have assumed that Foster Company held the Welsch common stock and the Leverage bonds throughout 1994 and 1995. This assumption may seem inconsistent with the definition of trading securities, but we have done this so that we could illustrate the procedures required by *SFAS No. 115* for a constant portfolio of trading securities. In fact, companies may classify securities as trading for an extended period of time if management intends to sell them when cash is needed or market conditions warrant. Actual sale of the securities is not required for them to be classified in the trading category. Cash flows from trading securities are presented in the operating activities section of the statement of cash flows.

AVAILABLE-FOR-SALE SECURITIES

Next we assume that the same securities—the Leverage bonds and the Welsch common stock—make up a portfolio of investments classified as available-for-sale. In 1994 the entries to record the purchase of the two investments, the receipt of the cash dividend on the Welsch common, and the receipt of interest revenue and amortization of discount on the Leverage bonds are the same as in the previous example in which the investments were classified as trading securities. Only the final entry is different.

Available-for-sale securities are valued at fair value, much like trading securities, but the change in value from one period to the next is *not* included in determining net income. Rather, unrealized gains and losses are accumulated as a separate component of stockholders' equity. If the net accumulated amount is a gain, the element of stockholders' equity has a credit balance and adds to the amount of total stockholders' equity. If the net accumulated amount is a loss, the element has a debit balance and reduces total stockholders' equity.

Let's continue the example of Foster Company and record the unrealized holding gain at the end of 1994. The amount is the same as in the earlier example, and it is recorded as follows:

Dec. 31, 1994	Investments (Available-for-Sale)	1,610	
	Accumulated Unrealized Gains/Losses on Investments		1,610
	(To record the increase in market value of investments.)		

Similarly, the following entry is recorded on December 31, 1995:

Dec. 31, 1995   Investments (Available-for-Sale)   609
                    Accumulated Unrealized Gains/Losses
                        on Investments   609
                    (To record the increase in market value
                        of investments.)

Notice that both of these entries involve two balance sheet accounts. The first account, Investments (Available-for-Sale), adds to the recorded amount of investments, bringing the carrying amount of investments up to market value. The second account, Accumulated Unrealized Gains/Losses on Investments, is a stockholders' equity account. In this case, it is positive (adds to total stockholders' equity) because market value has increased.

Combining these entries with those presented earlier for Foster Company's investments results in the following financial statement elements:

Foster Company
Partial Balance Sheet

	1994	1995
Assets		
Investments	$23,200	$24,000
Stockholders' equity		
Accumulated unrealized gains/losses on investments	$ 1,610	$ 2,219*

*$1,610 + $609 = $2,219

Foster Company
Partial Income Statement

	1994	1995
Interest revenue	$ 1,070	$ 1,091
Dividend revenue	750	800

Foster Company
Partial Statement of Cash Flows

	1994	1995
Operating activities		
Interest received	$ 900	$ 900
Dividends received	750	800
Investing activities		
Purchase of investments	$21,420	—

Notice that the investments in the balance sheet are simply designated as "assets" with no indication as to current or noncurrent. Either classification is possible, depending on the maturity date for the debt investment and the intent of management concerning both the debt and equity investment.

The difference in treating the unrealized holding gain in income (trading securities) and accumulating them in stockholders' equity (avaliable-for-sale securities) is evidenced in two places in the financial statements. First, the unrealized gain that was included in the income statement for trading securities is not included in determining income for the available-for-sale securities. Second, an additional element of stockholders' equity exists for the available-for-sale securities that was not present for trading securities. The statement of cash flows is the same whether the investments are treated as trading or available-for-sale except that purchases and sales of investments are classified as investing activities.

Recording the investments at market value but not including the unrealized holding gains and losses in the determination of net income is a conceptually interesting procedure because it permits recognition of fair value but does not require a change in the concept of revenue realization for purposes of determining net income. The gains and losses are simply accumulated in stockholders' equity until the securities are sold or otherwise disposed of. At that time, the unrealized gains and losses become realized and are recognized in determining net income.

Revenue Realization

HELD-TO-MATURITY SECURITIES

We stated earlier that held-to-maturity securities are limited to debt investments and are carried in the accounts at amortized cost. Because management expects to hold the investments to maturity and, thereby, receive the face or maturity value, current market value is not considered as relevant a measurement attribute as amortized cost.

If we assume that the Foster Company investment in Leverage bonds is classified as held-to-maturity, the entries for those securities that we made earlier when we assumed they were trading securities and available-for-sale securities are still appropriate, except for the entries to record the change in market value at the end of the year. Historical cost, adjusted for amortization of discount or premium, determines the carrying amount of debt investments classified as held-to-maturity. No entry is made to recognize the change in market value because that information is not considered to be the relevant basis for carrying an investment that management intends to hold to maturity and receive the maturity value in cash.

The following items would appear in Foster Company's financial statements for the Leverage bonds if they are considered in the held-to-maturity class. Remember that the equity investment in Welsch common cannot be considered a held-to-maturity investment because that category is reserved for bond investments that management intends to hold until the maturity date. Equity instruments do not have maturity dates.

Foster Company
Partial Balance Sheet

	1994	**1995**
Assets		
Investments	$9,090*	$9,281†

*$8,920 + $170 = $9,090
†$9,090 + $191 = $9,281

Foster Company
Partial Income Statement

	1994	**1995**
Interest revenue	$1,070	$1,091

Foster Company
Partial Statement of Cash Flows

	1994	**1995**
Operating activities		
Interest received	$ 900	$ 900
Investing activities		
Purchase of investments	$8,920	—

In this section, we have seen three different approaches used in accounting for debt and equity investments, depending on whether the portfolio is considered trading, available-for-sale, or held-to-maturity. The first two employ fair value accounting for both debt and equity investments but treat the unrealized gain or loss differently. Debt securities in the held-to-maturity category are carried at amortized cost and unrealized gains and losses are

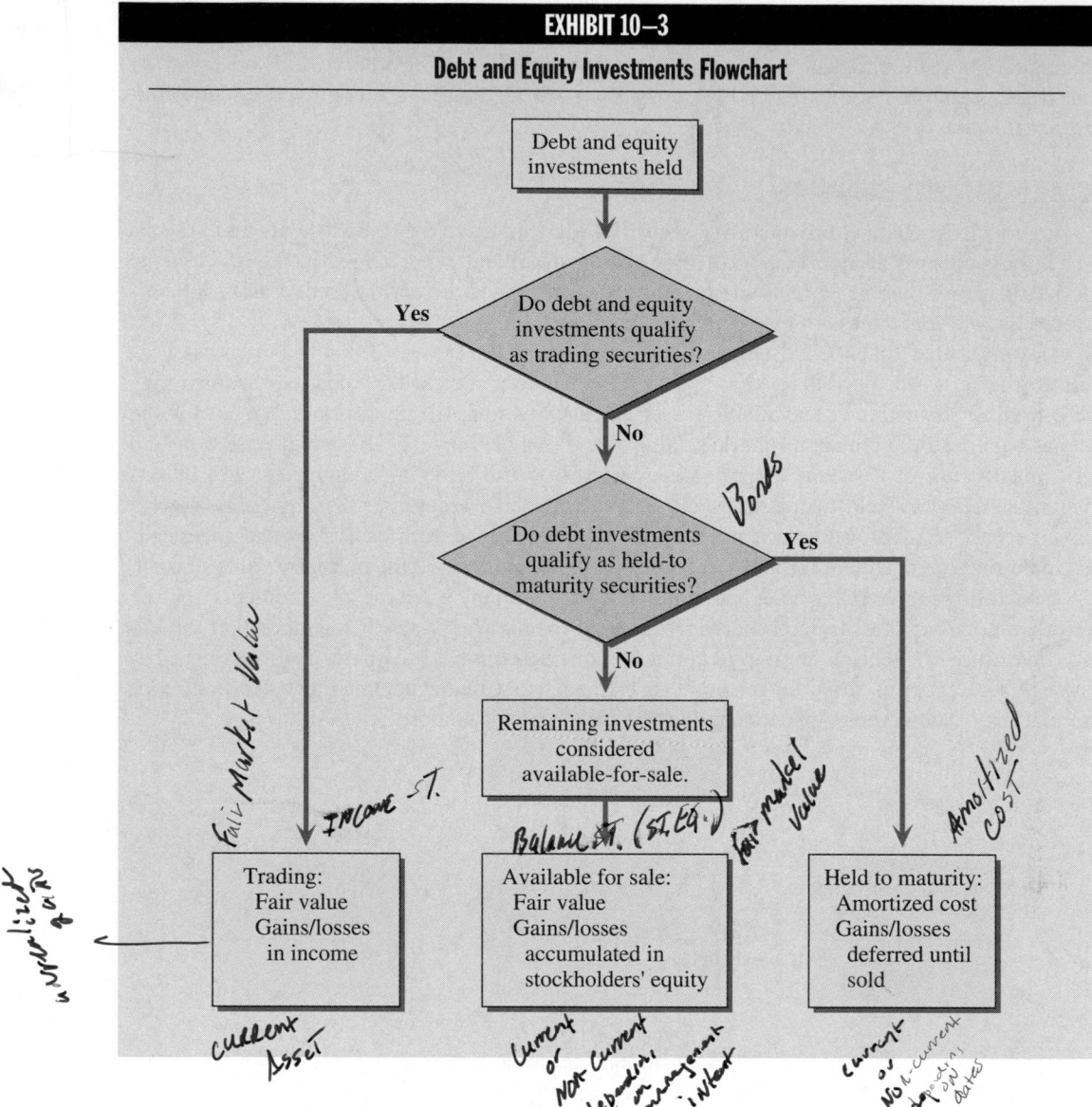

EXHIBIT 10–3

Debt and Equity Investments Flowchart

Debt and equity investments held

Do debt and equity investments qualify as trading securities?

Yes

No

Do debt investments qualify as held-to maturity securities?

Yes

No

Bonds (handwritten)

Remaining investments considered available-for-sale.

Fair Market Value (handwritten)   *Income -ST.* (handwritten)

Balance ST. (ST. EQ.) (handwritten)   *Fair market value* (handwritten)   *Amortized cost* (handwritten)

unrealized gains (handwritten)

Trading:
Fair value
Gains/losses
in income

Available for sale:
Fair value
Gains/losses
accumulated in
stockholders' equity

Held to maturity:
Amortized cost
Gains/losses
deferred until
sold

current Asset (handwritten)   *Current or Not current depending on management intent* (handwritten)   *current or Non-current depending on dates* (handwritten)

deferred until the securities are sold. Accounting for the three portfolios is summarized in Exhibit 10–3.

Exhibit 10–4 includes the note disclosure for the fair value of investments from Dow Chemical Company's 1993 annual report. Notice in particular the section on marketable equity and debt securities, which is separated into the three portfolios we have discussed in this section: trading, available-for-sale, and held-to-maturity. Also note that for each classification, cost, unrealized gains, unrealized losses, and fair value are disclosed.

THE EQUITY METHOD

Equity investments are classified as trading or available-for-sale securities, as described earlier in this chapter, when the investor owns relatively small amounts of the total outstanding equity of the investee company. Although equity investments classified as trading and available-for-sale may be large in terms of absolute dollars invested, or even in terms of the total assets of the investor company, they represent a relatively small portion of the investee's outstanding stock. The investor's role is passive because the investor does not own enough of the

---

EXHIBIT 10—4

Disclosure of Investments

S *Fair Value of Investments* (in millions)

Total investments include cash equivalents ($362), marketable securities and interest-bearing deposits ($430), and other investments ($1,726).

Marketable equities and debt securities classified as Trading and Available-for-Sale are reported at fair value. Debt securities classified as Held-to-Maturity are reported at amortized cost. Items classified as Other are not material and are reported at cost. The cost of investments sold is determined by specific identification.

Maturities for most debt securities range from 1 to 10 years for the Available-for-Sale classification and 1 to 5 years for the Held-to-Maturity classification.

The cost of investments at year-end 1992 was $1,426 with a fair value of $1,569.

Fair Value of Investments at December 31, 1993

	Cost	Unrealized Gains	Unrealized Losses	Fair Value
Interest-bearing deposits	$ 105	—	—	$ 105
Marketable equity and debt securities:				
Trading	433	$ 7	—	440
Available-for-Sale				
Debt securities	732	38	$ 3	767
Equity securities	489	205	22	672
Held-to-Maturity	177	3	3	177
Other	357	—	4	353
Total investments	$2,293	$253	$32	$2,514

SOURCE: Dow Chemical Company, 1993 Annual Report.

---

investee to be actively involved in the latter's operations or to influence its operating, financing, and investing policies.

Different accounting practices are required if the level of investment in voting equity securities, usually common stock, reaches a point that the investor can exercise significant influence over the investee. The range of business activities and purposes for which significant influence investments are made is broad. Regardless of the reasons for an investor to hold a relatively large portion of the outstanding stock of another company, the ability to significantly influence an investee provides evidence that the investee's earnings, losses, and other business activities have direct implications for the investor.

The equity method of accounting for these investments reflects the significant relationship between an investor and investee by requiring the investor to recognize a portion of the income or loss of the investee each accounting period. The amount of investee income or loss that the investor recognizes is based on the level of equity investment held and results in an increase (decrease) in the Investment account for the pro rata share of the investee's income (loss).

The **equity method** for significant influence investments is regarded as a sound accounting principle, because the carrying amount of the investment is directly affected by the results of the investee's operations. Application of the equity method represents a type of "automatic valuation" accounting. An investment in a significant portion of the voting stock of another company represents, in substance, an investment in the net assets of that company. Under the equity method, changes in the investee's net assets that result from earnings or losses and from dividend payments result in changes in the investor's Investment account.

The equity method of accounting is an extension of accrual accounting. The investor company recognizes its share of the investee earnings or losses on the income statement in

Revenue Realization   the period earned. The income is later realized either via dividend distributions by the investee or disposition of the investment by the investor. The undistributed earnings (earnings retained after dividends are distributed) of the investee represent an increase in the net assets of the investee. A profitable investee company should experience a rise in the market value of its outstanding equity as the net assets increase from undistributed earnings. Therefore, the cash flow that an investor could realize from the disposition of the investment is simply the realization of previously recognized income.

The "automatic valuation" represented by the equity method is a surrogate for measuring the investment at current value. If the equity method of accounting were *not* required for investors having significant influence, income would be recognized when dividends were received or when the investment was sold. In the latter case, if the investment was sold for a price higher than original cost, the gain would be both recognized and realized in the period of disposition. This approach would have the undesirable effect of delaying the recognition of income until the investment was sold and then recognizing in a single period the lump-sum gain (or loss). In contrast, the equity method provides for a more timely recognition of earned income from equity investments.

A recent research study supports the equity method as generally the best indicator of cash returns on nonmajority-owned intercorporate investments. Based on a study of 148 companies that had significant portions of their outstanding stock owned by other corporate entities, the authors concluded that the equity method is generally more successful than the cost method or the market value method in estimating earnings that will be realized in the future.[18]

The ability to exercise significant influence may be evident in several ways. For example, representation on the investee's board of directors, material intercompany transactions, technological dependency of the investee, and other relationships may indicate an ability to exercise significant influence. Because of the difficulties in determining whether an investor exercises significant influence over the investee, *APB Opinion No. 18* established a threshold level of investment to guide practice.[19] It states that a direct or indirect investment of 20% or more in the *voting* stock of an investee indicates, *in the absence of contrary evidence,* that an investor has the ability to exercise significant influence over an investee.[20] The *Opinion* thus establishes a presumption of significant influence arising at investment levels of 20% or more. The presumption may be rebutted, however, if evidence is available to support alternative practices. Recently, several companies have applied the equity method of accounting to holdings of investee voting stock as small as 5% to 10%, contending that even such small investments create significant influence if the rest of the investee's stock is widely distributed.

An important observation is that *APB Opinion No. 18* does not absolutely require application of the equity method if 20% or more of the voting stock of an investee is held. *FASB Interpretation No. 35* provides guidance as to what types of evidence may overcome the presumption of significant influence arising at investment levels of 20% or more of the voting stock. Specifically, it provides five examples of evidence that tend to rebut the presumption of significant influence, even if 20% or more of the voting stock is held:

Opposition by the investee, such as litigation or complaints to governmental regulatory authorities, challenges the investor's ability to exercise significant influence.

The investor and investee sign an agreement under which the investor surrenders significant rights as a shareholder.

---

[18]Sharon M. McKinnon and Katherine Taylor Harvorsen, "Accounting for Non-Majority-Owned Intercorporate Investments: A Cashflow Assessment of Alternative Methods," *Journal of Business, Finance & Accounting* (January 1993), pp. 20–21.

[19]*APB Opinion No. 18,* "The Equity Method of Accounting for Investments in Common Stock," 1971.

[20]*APB Opinion No. 18,* par. 17.

Majority ownership of the investee is concentrated among a small group of shareholders who operate the investee without regard to the views of the investor.

The investor needs or wants more financial information to apply the equity method than is available to the investee's other shareholders (for example, the investor wants quarterly financial information from an investee that publicly reports only annually), tries to obtain that information, and fails.

The investor tries and fails to obtain representation on the investee's board of directors.[21]

Finally, although the test for significant influence is based on voting stock, the equity method is applied only to investments in common stock. Thus, the investment level used to assess the existence of significant influence may differ from the investment level used in accounting for the investment. For example, an investor might own 10,000 of 100,000 shares (10%) of the common stock and all of the 25,000 shares (100%) of voting preferred stock of another company. The percentage of voting stock owned is 28% (35,000/125,000 = 28%), indicating that the equity method is appropriate. The percentage used to apply the equity method to the investment in common stock is only 10%, however, because that is the percentage of common stock held. The equity method does not apply to investments in preferred stock.

A BASIC EXAMPLE OF THE EQUITY METHOD

An investor applying the equity method to a common stock investment bases the recognition of income and the accompanying increase in the Investment account on the percentage of common stock represented by the investment. The receipt of dividends is treated as a reduction of the carrying amount of the investor's Investment account. The receipt of dividends represents a partial conversion of the investment to cash from equity in the investee's assets.

The following example illustrates accounting practices appropriate for the equity method. Assume that Foster Company acquires a 25% interest (10,000 of 40,000 shares) in the voting stock of Thomas Company in January 1, 1996. Also assume that Thomas Company has only one class of common stock, all of which is voting, and that both companies report on a calendar-year basis. If Foster paid $500,000 for the investment and Thomas reports a net income of $100,000 for 1996 and pays a $20,000 dividend on December 31, 1996, Foster will record the following entries:

Jan. 1, 1996	Investment in Equity Securities	500,000	
	Cash		500,000
	(To record acquisition of 25% voting interest in Thomas Company.)		
Dec. 31, 1996	Investment in Equity Securities	25,000	
	Investment Income		25,000
	(To record equity in investee net income. $100,000 × 25% = $25,000.)		
Dec. 31, 1996	Cash	5,000	
	Investment in Equity Securities		5,000
	(To record receipt of dividend. $20,000 × 25% = $5,000.)		

Excerpts from the 1996 balance sheet and income statement of Foster Company would appear as follows:

Foster Company
Partial Balance Sheet
December 31, 1996

Noncurrent assets
   Investment in equity securities $520,000
     ($500,000 + $25,000 − $5,000 = $520,000)

---

[21]*FASB Interpretation No. 35,* "Criteria for Applying the Equity Method of Accounting for Investments in Common Stock: An Interpretation of APB Opinion No. 18," 1981, par. 4.

Foster Company
Partial Income Statement
For the Year Ended December 31, 1996

Other revenue
    Investment income $25,000

The favorable impact of the investee's earnings are, thus, immediately reflected in the investor's financial statements. The dividends received by the investor are treated as a partial recovery or liquidation of the investment. Financial reporting for investments accounted for under the equity method contain many additional significant issues, and the following paragraphs discuss several of these.

THE EXISTENCE OF POSITIVE AND NEGATIVE DIFFERENTIAL

One issue arises in applying the equity method if the investor pays more or less for an investment than the book value of the underlying assets. For example, if the earning potential of the investee is abnormally high, the current value of the investee's net assets as represented by the market value of the investee's stock is frequently higher than the carrying amount on the investee's books.

    If an excess amount is paid to acquire an equity interest in specifically identifiable undervalued assets, the difference is amortized over the individual lives of those assets. For example, assume that the book value of the net assets (assets minus liabilities) of Thomas Company in the previous example is $1,960,000 when Foster Company acquires a 25% ownership interest for a cost of $500,000. A 25% ownership in Thomas' net assets, however, equals only $490,000 ($1,960,000 × 25%); therefore, Foster paid $10,000 more for the investment than is represented by the book value that was acquired. If Foster's management concludes that this differential represents an excess of the current value over the book value of Thomas' plant assets, which have a 10-year life, the following entry to amortize this differential is necessary at the end of each year.

Investment Income   1,000
    Investment in Equity Securities   1,000
        ($10,000 ÷ 10 years = $1,000)

Combining this entry with those above results in $24,000 being included in the net income of the investor ($25,000 − $1,000) and an investment in the balance sheet of $519,000 [$500,000 + ($25,000 − $1,000) − $5,000]. After $1,000 has been amortized each year for 10 years, the $10,000 excess of cost over book value will have been fully amortized and that adjustment will no longer be necessary.

    In practice, accountants frequently find it difficult to determine which specific assets are overvalued or undervalued and how much of the difference between the price paid and the book value acquired relates to general excess earning capacity. If the differential cannot be associated with specific assets, the excess is considered *goodwill*. *APB Opinion No. 17* specifies that amounts recorded for goodwill must be amortized over a period not to exceed 40 years.[22] Accountants frequently attribute all of the difference between the cost of an equity-method investment and the book value of the underlying net assets to goodwill because information about the value of specific assets is difficult to obtain. Furthermore, differences **Materiality** caused by this simplifying assumption are often not material. Therefore, in most situations any excess of cost over the book value of the underlying assets is amortized as goodwill over a period no longer than 40 years. For example, in Foster Company's acquisition of

---

[22]*APB Opinion No. 17*, "Intangible Assets," 1970, par. 29. The subject of goodwill and amortization of goodwill are covered in greater depth in Chapter 13.

Thomas Company—resulting in a $10,000 difference between cost and book value—if the $10,000 is interpreted as goodwill with a 20-year life, $500 would be amortized against the Equity in Investee Income account each year ($10,000/20 years = $500). Any *negative differential* (excess of book value acquired over investment cost) is usually amortized in a similar fashion; however, the amortization results in *increases,* rather than decreases, in Equity in Investee Income and Investment in Equity Securities.

INVESTEE OPERATING LOSSES

Another significant accounting issue arises if an investee company incurs operating losses to such an extent that application of the equity method reduces the investor's asset account to zero. To illustrate, assume that Thomas Company incurs $50,000 net loss; then Foster Company prepares the following entry:

Investment Loss	12,500	
Investment in Equity Securities		12,500
($50,000 × 25% = $12,500)		

This entry is appropriate unless it brings the Investment account to a credit (negative) balance. Investors ordinarily discontinue applying the equity method if the Investment account reaches zero, unless the investor (1) has guaranteed the indebtedness of the investee or (2) is otherwise committed to provide financial support. For example, if the stock of the investee were acquired from the investee at less than par, the investor may be obligated (in the event of investee dissolution) to contribute amounts that would make the investment equal to the par value of the stock. In such cases, the Investment account may properly contain a credit balance and be reported as a liability to the extent of any contingent obligation.

    The investor may suspend the use of the equity method if the recognition of investee net losses reduces the investment balance to zero and the conditions (described earlier) that would require the continued recognition of investee losses do not apply. The investor should resume applying the equity method if the investee becomes profitable again only after its share of the net income equals the net losses that were not recognized during the period of suspension.

EQUITY-METHOD DISCLOSURES

APB Opinion No. 18 requires the following disclosures for investments in common stock when such investments are significant to the financial position and results of operations of the investor:[23]

1. Name of each investee.
2. Percentage of ownership of common stock.
3. Accounting policies with respect to the investment. (In cases in which 20% or more of the voting stock is held and the equity method **is not used** or when less than 20% of the voting stock is held and the equity method **is used,** the following should be disclosed: name of the investee and the reason(s) for departure from the 20% guideline.)
4. Difference between investor's carrying value and the underlying equity in net assets, and the accounting treatment for this difference.
5. Aggregate value, based on quoted market price, of the investment in common stock of each identified investee that is not a subsidiary.
6. Summarized financial information of investees (either individually or combined).
7. Material effects of the possible exercise of options or warrants, possible conversions, and so on.

Disclosure

---

[23]*APB Opinion No. 18,* par. 20.

Exhibit 10–5 includes the equity-method disclosures from the 1993 annual report of Whirlpool Corporation. Whirlpool is a manufacturer and marketer of major home appliances. The company manufactures in 11 countries and markets in more than 120 countries under several well-known brand names, including *Whirlpool, KitchenAid, Roper, Kenmore* (through Sears, Roebuck and Co.), and others. Whirlpool's assets in the balance sheet include "Investment in Affiliated Companies" totaling $320 million in 1993 and $282 million in 1992. These amounts represent the balances resulting from applying the equity method, as described in a financial statement note identifying accounting policies employed in the preparation of the statements. The disclosure in Exhibit 10–5 includes selected balance sheet and income statement information of the affiliated companies, which is intended to comply with the disclosure requirements identified above.

EQUITY INVESTMENTS REPRESENTING CONTROL OF INVESTEE

If a company acquires an investment in the voting stock of an investee that exceeds 50%, the investor is presumed to be capable of **controlling** the investee's operating and financial policies. The investor is then called the **parent** and the investee is called the **subsidiary.** In these circumstances, accountants prepare **consolidated financial statements** for the two entities. This practice is based on the position that the two separate legal entities represent only one *economic* entity as a result of the majority investment. Therefore, financial reporting reflects the economic reality—not the mere legal form of organization—by consolidating the financial statements of the companies. Accounting and reporting practices underlying consolidated financial statements, while similar to the equity method, are discussed at length in advanced accounting texts and are discussed here only briefly.[24]

Substance over Form

Consolidating the financial statements of two or more corporations involves aggregating the adjusted trial balances of each company after eliminating the residual effects of all intercompany transactions. Such transactions may involve buying and selling, lending and borrowing, and investing activities. Furthermore, *consolidated net income* generally remains the same whether the investor applies the equity method to the investee or fully consolidates the investee into a complete set of consolidated financial statements. The difference between the equity method and the **consolidation method** is one of the degree of detail disclosed, not one of earnings measurement. Under the equity method, only one asset account and one revenue account are presented in the investor's financial statements that represent the investment in the investee. Hence, the equity method is frequently called a **single-line consolidation.** The consolidation approach combines the specific individual asset, liability, revenue, and expense accounts of the subsidiary with those of the parent for financial reporting purposes. Any **minority interest**—outstanding stock held by individuals or entities other than the parent company—is usually included as part of the stockholders' equity of the consolidated entity.

The 1993 annual report of Harcourt General, the publisher of this textbook, provides an excellent example. Harcourt General is an international publisher and specialty retailer whose core businesses are publishing and retailing. Publishing operations include educational, scientific, technical, medical, professional, and trade publications. Specialty retailing operations include Nieman Marcus stores, NM direct mail order, Bergdorf Goodman, and Contempo Casuals. The company also encompasses insurance operations and a professional services segment. All of the financial statements include the word *consolidated,* such as the consolidated balance sheets and consolidated statements of cash flows. The summary of significant accounting policies includes the following statement: "The consolidated financial statements include the accounts of Harcourt General, Inc., and its majority-owned subsidiaries."

---

[24]For an excellent discussion of financial accounting and reporting for various business combinations, see Arnold J. Pahler and Joseph E. Mori, *Advanced Accounting: Concepts and Practice,* 5th ed. (Fort Worth: The Dryden Press, Harcourt Brace & Company College Publishers, 1994).

EXHIBIT 10-5

Whirlpool Corporation
Equity Method Disclosure

---

(5) Affiliated Companies

The Company has direct voting interests, ranging from 30% to 49%, in three Brazilian companies (Brastemp S.A., Embraco S.A. and Consul S.A.) engaged in the manufacture and sale of major home appliances and related component parts and in Vitromatic, S.A. de C.V., a Mexican manufacturer of home appliances. Other significant investments include an interest in Brasmotor S.A., a Brazilian holding company that has interests in Brastemp S.A., Embraco S.A. and Consul S.A.

Equity in the net earnings (losses) of affiliated companies, net of related taxes, is as follows:

(millions of dollars)	1993	1992	1991
Brazilian affiliates	$ 21	$ (10)	$ 2
Mexican affiliate	(6)	(5)	(1)
Other	1	2	—
Total equity earnings (losses)	$ 16	$ (13)	$ 1

Combined condensed financial information for all affiliated operating companies follows:

(millions of dollars)	1993	1992	1991
Current assets	$ 700	$ 669	
Other assets	815	775	
	$1,515	$1,444	
Current liabilities	$ 442	$ 461	
Other liabilities	235	226	
Stockholders' equity	838	757	
	$1,515	$1,444	

(millions of dollars)	1993	1992	1991
Net sales	$2,062	$1,829	$1,806
Cost of products sold	$1,446	$1,583	$1,534
Net earnings	$ 90	$ 3	$ 44
Whirlpool share of net currency translation gains (losses) included in operating results	$ (12)	$ (5)	$ 6
Dividends and fees paid to Whirlpool by affiliates	$ 4	$ 3	$ 3

SOURCE: Whirlpool Corporation, 1993 Annual Report.

From time to time, an entity sells its investments or transfers them from one classification to another (e.g., from available for sale to trading). These events may have significant financial statements implications.

Sales of investments are generally handled by (1) bringing the carrying amount of the investment up to date, if appropriate (i.e., for bond investments only), (2) comparing the amount received with the revised carrying amount, and (3) recording a gain for the excess of the amount received over the carrying amount or a loss for the excess of the carrying amount over the amount received. This gain or loss is not an extraordinary item, although it may be disclosed separately in the income statement if it is particularly material or if for some other reason separate disclosure is considered particularly important.

SALES AND TRANSFERS OF INVESTMENTS

Materiality

SALE OF DEBT INVESTMENTS

If the bonds are sold before their maturity date, a gain or loss may arise. Because the premium or discount recognized at the acquisition of the bond has been subject to amortization since acquisition, the amount of gain or loss depends in part on the remaining unamortized premium or discount. Returning to the previous example in which Foster Company purchased Leverage bonds for $8,920, including a $1,080 discount, assume that Foster sells the bonds on June 30, 1996, for $10,200 plus accrued interest. The following entries are necessary to update the accounts:

June 30, 1996	Interest Receivable	450	
	Investments	107	
	Interest Revenue		557

(To accrue interest for January 1–June 30, 1996.
$10,000 × 9% × 6/12 = $450.)

Calculations for the discount amortization are as follows:

$9,281 × 12% × 6/12	= $557
Less: Amount to be received in cash	(450)
Discount to be amortized	$107

This amount may also be determined as ½ of the 1996 amortization in Exhibit 10–1 (½ × $214). A second entry is required to record the sale:

June 30, 1996	Cash	10,650	
	Gain on Sale of Bonds		812
	Investment in Bonds ($9,281 + $107)		9,388
	Interest Receivable		450

(To record receipt of cash, $10,200 + $450 = $10,650; elimination of investment in bonds; and recognition of gain.)

The gain of $812 can be verified as follows:

Cash received, excluding interest		$10,200
Carrying amount of investment at June 30, 1996:		
Face value	$10,000	
Unamortized discount ($719 − $107)	(612)	(9,388)
Gain on sale of investment		$ 812

In this illustration, we have assumed that the entire investment in the bonds held by Foster Company was sold. If only part of the bonds were sold, the entries to record interest receivable, amortization of discount, and the sale would have been made for only that part of the investment that was sold. For example, if 4 of the 10 bonds had been sold, only $180 of interest revenue would be recognized ($450 × 40%); only $43 of bond discount amortization would be recognized ($107 × 40%); and a gain of only $325 would be recognized ($812 × 40%).

In this illustration, the bond investment was sold at a gain because the cash received was *more than* the carrying amount (face value, less the unamortized discount). Had the cash received been *less than* the carrying amount, a loss would have been recognized on the sale equal to the difference between the cash received and the carrying amount.

SALE OF EQUITY INVESTMENTS

Recording the sale of equity investments is more straightforward because equity investments do not involve amortization of discount or premium. The carrying amount of the equity investment is compared with the amount received from the sale of the investment. Any difference is a gain or loss.

To illustrate the sale of equity investments, we assume that Foster Company sold the Welsch common stock on June 30, 1996, when the market value was $13,600. Remember that the carrying amount of the investment at the end of 1995 was $13,200. No further adjustment would have been made between the end of 1995 and the time of sale. Assuming that this investment was classified as a trading security, the following entry is required:

June 30, 1996	Cash	13,600	
	Investments (Trading)		13,200
	Gain on Sale of Investments		400

Had the Welsch common been classified as an available-for-sale security rather than a trading security, the entry is somewhat more complicated. Recall that the unrealized gains and losses from holding the investment have not been recorded in earnings but have been accumulated in stockholders' equity. At the time of sale, these must be recognized in determining earnings by eliminating the unrealized gain (1994) and unrealized loss (1995) from the stockholders' equity account, as well as recognizing the gain occurring in 1996. This is accomplished with the following entry:

June 30, 1996	Cash	13,600	
	Accumulated Unrealized Gains/Losses		
	on Investments ($13,200 − $12,500)	700	
	Investments		13,200
	Gain on Sale of Investments		
	($13,600 − $12,500)		1,100

The $700 debit to Accumulated Unrealized Gain/Loss on Investments in stockholders' equity clears that account of the balance at December 31, 1995, resulting from the Welsch common stock investment. The Gain on Sale of Investments recognizes the entire gain in earnings from holding the common stock from the date of purchase to the time of sale.

The sale of an equity investment accounted for by the equity method is similar. Remember, however, that the carrying amount of the investment changes frequently as a result of the investee's income or loss, receipt of dividends, and the amortization of any positive or negative differential arising at the time of purchase. To illustrate the sale of an equity-method investment, we return to our original equity-method example in which Foster Company held 25% of the common (voting) stock of Thomas Company. If the entire investment is sold on January 1, 1997, for $527,500, the following entry is made to record the sale and gain:

Jan. 1, 1997	Cash	527,500	
	Investment in Equity Securities		520,000
	Gain on Sale of Investments		7,500

Had Foster sold only a part of the investment, a pro rata share of the investment balance would have been written off. For example, if Foster had sold only 3,000 of its 10,000 shares (30%) for $160,000, the entry to record the sale is as follows:

Jan. 1, 1997	Cash	160,000	
	Investment in Equity Securities		
	(30% × $520,000)		156,000
	Gain on Sale of Investments		4,000

TRANSFERS OF INVESTMENTS

Classification of investments as trading, available-for-sale, and held-to-maturity is based primarily on management's intent. From time to time, a transfer of securities from one classification to another is required. Such transfers are generally accounted for in a manner that results in investment-related account balances that reflect what they would have been had the new classification been in effect since the investment was acquired. For example, for transfers from the trading category, any unrealized holding gain or loss will already have been recognized in income and is not reversed when the securities are sold. For transfers into the trading category, any unrealized holding gain or loss is recognized at the time of transfer. For a debt security transferred into the available-for-sale category from the held-to-maturity category, any unrealized holding gain or loss at the date of the transfer is recognized in the separate component of stockholders' equity. When a debt security is transferred into the held-to-maturity category from the available-for-sale category, any unrealized holding gain or loss included in stockholders' equity at the time of transfer is amortized over the remaining life of the security as an adjustment of interest in a manner consistent with the amortization of any premium or discount.

Similar to the transfer of investments is the situation in which an investor's ownership percentage increases to the point that the equity method should be used, or it decreases to the point that the equity method should be abandoned. In the former case, the investor must go back to the point of original purchase and reconstruct what the investment balance would have been had the equity method been used, applying the actual percentage(s) of common stock owned. The Investment account is adjusted to the calculated amount and the amount of the adjustment is also reflected in retained earnings. Should an investment balance decline to the point that the equity method should be suspended, the carrying amount of the investment at that time becomes a substitute for cost in applying the method that is appropriate for the reclassified investment (e.g., either trading or available-for-sale).

ADDITIONAL INVESTMENT CONSIDERATIONS

Companies may hold several investment instruments other than debt and equity securities. Specifically, an investing company may hold stock purchase warrants and stock rights. Also, an investor may receive shares of stock through the issuance of stock dividends and stock splits by the investee, adding to the number of shares held by the investor. In this section, we introduce these situations briefly, considering them from the perspective of the investor. In Chapters 15, 16, and 17, we cover these topics in greater depth when we consider them from the perspective of the issuing company. In this section, we also introduce accounting for loans receivable, the cash surrender value of life insurance, and the accumulation of cash in a fund for a specified future purpose, such as retirement of long-term debt.

STOCK PURCHASE WARRANTS

Stock purchase warrants convey to the holder the ability to buy a given number of shares of stock at a stated price for a specified period of time. These warrants are often issued when a company sells bonds or stock to make the primary securities more attractive.

When an investor acquires a stock purchase warrant along with another security such as a bond or share of preferred stock, we allocate the price paid between the two securities. This is accomplished by using the relative market values of the two securities as indicated in the following formula:

$$\begin{array}{c} \text{Allocated cost} \\ \text{of stock} \\ \text{warrants} \end{array} = \frac{\text{Fair market value of warrants}}{\left(\begin{array}{c}\text{Fair market}\\\text{value of}\\\text{warrants}\end{array}\right) + \left(\begin{array}{c}\text{Fair market}\\\text{value of}\\\text{other security}\end{array}\right)} \times \begin{array}{c}\text{Total cost}\\\text{of}\\\text{investment}\end{array}$$

For example, assume that Foster Company purchases ten $1,000 bonds for $1,050 each and with every bond receives 10 detachable stock purchase warrants, each of which may be used to acquire one additional share of common stock. Immediately after the securities are acquired, separate markets for the warrants and the bonds arise because the warrants are detachable and the two securities can be sold separately. The fair market value of each bond is $1,025; the fair market value of each warrant is $5. The following calculation is necessary to allocate a portion of the total cost to the 100 warrants (10 bonds $\times$ 10 warrants = 100):

$$\text{Cost of warrants} = \frac{\$5 \times 100 \text{ warrants}}{\left[\begin{array}{c} (\$5 \times 100 \text{ warrants}) \\ + \\ (\$1,025 \times 10 \text{ bonds}) \end{array}\right]} \times (\$1,050 \times 10 \text{ bonds})$$

$$= \$488.37$$

The following entry records the acquisition of the two securities:

Investment in Bonds	10,012	
Stock Purchase Warrants	488	
Cash		10,500
(To record acquisition of bonds with stock purchase warrants.)		

Each warrant has an allocated cost of $4.88 ($488 ÷ 100). Because the life of most warrants is limited, they must be exercised or sold, or they become worthless.

To illustrate the accounting for stock warrants subsequent to purchase, assume that the bond investor exercises half (50) of the warrants. Further assume that the investor can exercise each warrant by paying $50 for one share of common stock. The journal entry appears as follows:

Investments	2,744	
Stock Purchase Warrants (50 $\times$ $4.88)		244
Cash (50 $\times$ $50)		2,500
(To exercise 50 stock purchase warrants.)		

The market price of the stock when the warrants are exercised does not determine the cost of the stock acquired. Rather, the cost is determined by the $4.88 allocated cost of the warrant, plus the $50 cash paid when the warrant was exercised. If the remaining 50 warrants are sold for $6 each, a gain is recognized as follows:

Cash (50 $\times$ $6)	300	
Stock Purchase Warrants (50 $\times$ $4.88)		244
Gain on Sale of Warrants		56
(To record the sale of the remaining warrants.)		

Warrants that expire unexercised or unsold are eliminated from the accounting records by recognizing a loss equal to their allocated cost. To illustrate, assume that the investor allowed the 50 warrants that were not exercised to expire rather than selling them. A loss is recognized as follows:

Loss on Expiration of Stock Purchase Warrants	244	
Stock Purchase Warrants		244
(To record expiration of warrants.)		

STOCK RIGHTS

A corporation distributes stock rights to employees or shareholders on a pro rata basis to permit them to maintain their proportionate interest in the corporation pursuant to a new stock issue. Although one right is usually issued for each share held, the number of rights required to purchase an additional share depends on the terms of the offering. Rather than exercise the right to purchase additional shares, the stockholder may choose instead to sell the rights on the open market.

When stock rights are received, the accountant for the investor allocates the cost of the original stock investment between (1) the original investment and (2) the rights just received. This allocation is based on the relative fair market values of the rights and the stock at the time the rights are received. When separate stock rights are issued, a market price for them will exist as well as for the related stock because the two securities can be traded separately. The following formula is used to determine the amount to be assigned to the rights:

$$\text{Allocated cost of rights} = \frac{\text{Fair market value of rights}}{\left(\begin{array}{c}\text{Fair market}\\ \text{value of}\\ \text{rights}\end{array}\right) + \left(\begin{array}{c}\text{Fair market}\\ \text{value of}\\ \text{stock}\end{array}\right)} \times \text{Total cost of investment}$$

For example, assume that Foster Company acquires 100 shares of Cypress Company's common stock for $75 per share and later receives a stock right for each share of stock held. If the market value of the rights is $5 per right and the value of the stock is $88¾ per share at the time the rights are received, the following calculation is necessary:

$$\text{Allocated cost of rights} = \frac{(100 \times \$5)}{(100 \times \$5) + (100 \times \$88.75)} \times (100 \times \$75) = \$400$$

A journal entry is then made to reflect the allocation of cost to the new investment:

Investment in Stock Rights	400	
Investment in Common Stock		400
(To record receipt of stock rights.)		

If the rights are exercised and new shares are acquired, the cost of the new shares is calculated as the $4 allocated cost of the rights plus the additional amount paid for the shares. If the rights are sold, a gain or loss is recognized if the proceeds from the sale differ from the allocated cost of $4 per right ($400/100 = $4). If the rights expire and become worthless, the Investment in Stock Rights account is eliminated and a loss recognized equal to the allocated cost. The loss represents the dilution of the ownership interest experienced by the investor because of nonexercise of the rights. The journal entries to account for the disposition of stock rights whether they are exercised, sold, or allowed to expire are similar to those for stock purchase warrants presented in the previous section.

STOCK DIVIDENDS AND STOCK SPLITS

Occasionally, an investor company receives shares of stock of the investee company when the investee issues a *stock dividend* or *stock split*. In such cases, the recipient (investor) of the additional stock makes no accounting entry. Rather, a memorandum is written to indicate that the original investment cost is now allocated over the larger number of shares, thereby *lowering the cost per share.*

To illustrate, assume that Foster Company holds 200 shares of Hill Company's common stock that were purchased for $11,000 ($55 a share) when Hill declares a 10% stock dividend. Foster will receive an additional 20 shares (200 × 10%) of Hill stock. After the dividend is received, Foster holds 220 shares of stock at a cost of $11,000, or $50 per share ($11,000/220 = $50). If Foster then sells 50 shares for $60 per share, the following entry is appropriate:

Cash (50 × $60)	3,000	
Investment in Common Stock (50 × $50)		2,500
Gain on Sale of Stock		500
(To record sale of 50 shares of Hill Company's common stock.)		

Foster carries the remaining 170 shares (220 − 50) of Hill on its books at $8,500 ($11,000 − $2,500), or $50 per share ($8,500/170 = $50).

If Hill Company had issued a stock split rather than a stock dividend, the same procedure would be followed. However, the increase in shares would have been much higher than 10%; for example, it could have been 100% or 200%.

LOANS RECEIVABLE

Earlier in this chapter, loans receivable were cited as an example of a debt instrument that is not a debt security. For many enterprises, particularly financial institutions, loans are very important assets. Guidance for accounting for loans is found in *SFAS No. 114,* which defines a loan as a contractual right to receive money on demand or on fixed or determinable dates. Examples include accounts receivable with terms exceeding one year and notes receivable.[25] *SFAS No. 114* specifically deals with accounting for impaired loans and indicates that a loan is impaired when it is probable that a creditor will be unable to collect all amounts due according to the contractual terms of the loan agreement. Impaired loans are measured at the present value of expected future cash flows discounted at the loan's effective interest rate, the loan's observable market price, or the fair value of collateral if the collection of the loan is expected to depend on the collateral. Measuring impairments of loans requires judgment and estimates, and creditors have latitude in developing measurement methods that are practical in their circumstances.

CASH SURRENDER VALUE OF LIFE INSURANCE

A company may insure the lives of key executives and name itself as beneficiary. The purpose of this arrangement is to compensate the company for the loss of services arising from the untimely death of important members of management.

Two forms of insurance are commonly used: term and whole life insurance. With **term life insurance,** the company is simply buying protection for the loss of the insured individual. The insurance does not represent an investment, and the premiums are ordinarily expensed as paid. **Whole life,** on the other hand, has the unique feature of accumulating cash surrender value in addition to providing insurance protection. The cash surrender value represents an investment to the company in that it can borrow the accumulated cash value from the insurance company or terminate the policy and receive the cash surrender value outright.

When a company pays an annual premium on whole life insurance, part of the premium is recognized as Insurance Expense. The remaining portion represents an increase in cash surrender value and should, therefore, be recognized as an increase in an investment asset. The amount of the annual premium reflecting an increase in the cash surrender value is specified by the insurance contract. The insurance contract frequently includes a schedule of cash surrender values listed by the number of years the policy has been in effect. The cash surrender value should be classified on the investing company's balance sheet as a noncurrent asset, because corporations do not usually intend to terminate insurance policies within the operating cycle.

To illustrate accounting for cash surrender values, assume that Foster Company takes out a whole life policy, naming itself as beneficiary. The insurance contract calls for $200,000 coverage on the life of Foster's chief executive officer (CEO) in return for premiums of $3,500 per year. The cash surrender value schedule indicates the cash value increases for the first three years as follows:

End of Coverage Year	Cash Surrender Value
1	–0–
2	$ 500
3	1,100

---

[25]*Statement of Financial Accounting Standards No. 114,* "Accounting by Creditors for Impairment of a Loan," 1993, par. 4.

Because the first year's premium does not result in an increased cash surrender value, the entire $3,500 premium is debited to Insurance Expense when paid. The following journal entries record the second and third years' premiums:

Insurance Expense	3,000	
Cash Surrender Value of Life Insurance	500	
Cash		3,500
Insurance Expense	2,900	
Cash Surrender Value of Life Insurance ($1,100 − $500)	600	
Cash		3,500

Notice that the *increase* in the cash surrender value is debited to the investment account Cash Surrender Value of Life Insurance, and the remainder of the $3,500 premium is debited to Insurance Expense.

If Foster's CEO died at the end of the fifth year of coverage when the cash surrender value was $3,700, the following journal entry is necessary to record the receipt of the death benefit:

Cash	200,000	
Cash Surrender Value of Life Insurance		3,700
Gain from Life Insurance Settlement		196,300

A corporation may also establish life insurance coverage for the benefit of employees and their named beneficiaries. Because this type of insurance is for the benefit of the employee, not the company, all of the premium is considered a form of compensation expense. Any accumulation of cash surrender value belongs to the employee and should not be identified as a company asset.

FUNDS

Business enterprises establish special funds for a variety of purposes, including bond or other debt redemption, future plant expansion, and pension commitments. When such funds are established, several significant accounting and reporting issues arise.

Fund assets may be held and managed by corporate personnel, or fund resources may be transferred to a **fiscal agent** or **trustee,** such as a bank, for administration. Although many long-term special funds are created in compliance with such things as contractual provisions, bond indentures, or covenants in debt instruments or pension plans, others are the result of internal management decisions.

To illustrate, assume that Foster Company management decides to create a bond-retirement fund in the amount of $10,000; the following entry is necessary:

Bond-Retirement Fund Cash	10,000	
Cash		10,000
(To establish bond-retirement fund.)		

If Foster's management decides to acquire treasury bills so that the fund will earn interest, the investment is recorded at cost:

Bond-Retirement Fund Investment	10,000	
Bond-Retirement Fund Cash		10,000
(To record acquisition of treasury bills by bond-retirement fund.)		

Subsequent accounting for investments made by such a fund follows the principles previously described and depends on the nature, extent, and investment objectives of the fund. Dividends and interest earned on fund investments are debited to the Bond-Retirement Fund Investment account.

When transferred to a fiscal agent, the fund assets and related liabilities may be excluded from the financial statements. Liabilities are excluded only to the extent that the company's obligations have been discharged. Pension fund assets and liabilities are frequently accounted for in this manner. Bond sinking funds and related bonds payable are normally reported in corporate financial statements, however, even if sinking-fund assets have been transferred to a fiscal agent. Although a fund may consist of a variety of assets, such as cash and investments in several types of securities, all of these assets normally are aggregated into a single account for balance sheet presentation.

A fund is usually created by an original contribution and augmented by additional contributions and the earnings of the fund itself. A company desiring to accumulate a certain amount in the fund by some specific date needs estimates of the earning power of the assets in the fund to ascertain the specific amount of the contributions. The company may then use present-value techniques to determine the future contribution necessary to accumulate the desired amount. The accountant should monitor the performance of the fund in terms of earnings and contributions to ascertain whether the fund is accumulating resources at the level anticipated in the original present-value calculation. If fund assets earn at a level higher than anticipated, the remaining contributions may be reduced. Conversely, if the fund performs more poorly than planned, the company must increase its contributions to meet its goals for the fund. The techniques incident to evaluating the earnings performance of a fund involve the compound interest concepts discussed in Chapter 6.

PROFESSIONAL JUDGMENT

Accounting for investments is another area in which management judgment is very important. The classification of securities as trading, available-for-sale, or held-to-maturity is based primarily on management's intent. This is inherently judgmental and requires careful analysis to determine the proper classification. That classification is particularly important because of the difference in accounting methods required for different classifications of investments.

Determining whether the equity method is appropriate may require judgment. Although the authoritative accounting literature establishes 20% of the voting stock as a benchmark for determining the use of the equity method, this is not intended to be an absolute rule. In fact, a company that holds less than 20% of the voting stock may exert significant influence and, therefore, should use the equity method. Likewise, a company that holds more than 20% may lack the ability to exert significant influence because of the heavy concentration of the remaining shares or for other reasons. Both of these situations require careful judgment to determine the appropriateness of the equity method.

Once management reaches the decision to apply the equity method, the underlying cause of any positive or negative differential and the period over which that difference should be amortized require careful analysis and judgment.

CONCLUDING REMARKS

In this chapter, we have considered accounting practices and theory for a variety of investments that a company may hold. We have considered the important impact that *SFAS No. 115* is expected to have on financial statements and discussed the movement toward increased use of fair value accounting that is represented by that statement.

We complete our study of debt and equity investments with a brief summary of the basic accounting procedures followed for each major investment category:

Investment Category	Accounting Treatment
Trading securities (debt and equity)	Market value, with unrealized holding gains and losses recognized in income
Available-for-sale (debt and equity)	Market value, with unrealized holding gains and losses accumulated in stockholders' equity until the point of sale
Held-to-maturity (debt only)	Amortized cost

Investment Category	Accounting Treatment
Significant influence (equity only)	Equity method, in which the pro rata share of the investee's income, losses, and dividends are recognized
Controlling interest (equity only)	Consolidated financial statements

KEY POINTS

1. Companies invest in securities of other companies for a variety of business purposes, including earning a return on available cash, accumulating resources for specific purposes, and influencing or controlling another enterprise. (Objective 1)

2. Investments in debt and equity securities are generally classified as (a) trading, (b) available-for-sale, or (c) held-to-maturity, based primarily on management's intent concerning the investment. (Objective 2)

3. Recent FASB pronouncements extend the use of current market value as the method of valuation and recognition for many investments. (Objective 3)

4. For a number of years many accounting theorists have advocated increased use of current value rather than historical cost, particularly for investments for which a ready market is available. (Objective 3)

5. Investments in debt and equity trading securities are accounted for at market value, and any unrealized gains and losses are included in the determination of net income. (Objective 4)

6. Investments in debt securities classified as held-to-maturity are accounted for at amortized cost. (Objective 4)

7. Investments in debt and equity securities classified as available-for-sale are accounted for at market value, but accumulated unrealized gains and losses are reported in stockholders' equity and do not affect the determination of net income until the investments are sold. (Objective 4)

8. Investments in equity securities that give the investor the ability to significantly influence the investee are accounted for by the equity method. The ability to significantly influence the investee is generally considered to exist when 20% or more of voting stock is owned, absent evidence to the contrary. (Objective 4)

9. The acquisition of stock purchase warrants and the receipt of stock rights, stock dividends, and stock splits on equity investments complicate accounting procedures for equity investments and require careful analysis for proper accounting. (Objective 4)

10. The authoritative accounting literature establishes important disclosure requirements, which are usually met in notes to the financial statements, for securities classified as trading, available-for-sale, and held-to-maturity. Special disclosures are required when the equity method is applied for significant influence investments. (Objective 5)

QUESTIONS

10–1 What are several reasons that a company might invest available cash in another company's stocks and bonds?

10–2 What is the relationship between the holder of debt securities and the company that issued them?

10–3 What is the relationship between the holder of equity securities and the company that issued them?

10–4 What characteristic must a security have to be considered "marketable"?

10–5 Prior to the issuance of *SFAS No. 115,* investments in marketable securities were most often accounted for by the lower of cost or market method. Why is this method considered conservative?

10–6 Generally, how does *SFAS No. 115* alter accounting for investments in debt and equity securities from the manner in which they were accounted for prior to that pronouncement's issuance?

10–7 How is the term *fair value* defined when accounting for investments in debt and equity securities?

10–8 What distinguishes trading securities from the other classifications of debt and equity securities?

10–9 What are the distinguishing characteristics of held-to-maturity securities in contrast to the other classifications of debt and equity securities?

10–10 What do we mean when we say that available-for-sale securities are defined residually in relation to trading and held-to-maturity securities?

10–11 What conclusions have accounting researchers generally reached concerning the use of current value information in accounting for investments?

10–12 Why would a buyer of a debt investment ever be willing to pay more than the face value of a bond?

10–13 What are the accounting procedures required to account for a bond investment that is purchased at a price less than face value?

10–14 What is the relationship of discount and premium amortization on bond investments to the amount of interest revenue recognized each accounting period?

10–15 What does the term *unrealized holding gain or loss* mean as applied to investments in debt and equity securities?

10–16 How is the amount of unrealized gain or loss determined for an investment portfolio that includes both debt and equity securities and is classified as "trading"?

10–17 What is the income statement impact, if any, of unrealized gains on a portfolio of trading securities?

10–18 What is the income statement impact, if any, of unrealized losses on a portfolio of available-for-sale securities?

10–19 What is the difference in accounting for unrealized gains and losses on trading securities as compared to available-for-sale securities?

10–20 Why are held-to-maturity securities not carried at market value like trading and available-for-sale securities?

10–21 When is the equity method generally appropriate for investments in the stock of another company?

10–22 What do we mean when we refer to the equity method as an "automatic valuation" of an equity investment?

10–23 What are several forms of evidence that a company has the ability to significantly influence another company?

10–24 How are the following events handled in accounting for an investment in common stock by the equity method: purchase of the investment, receipt of dividends, amortization of positive differential, reporting of net income by investee?

10–25 How are investments that represent a controlling interest in the investee generally accounted for in the preparation of financial statements?

10–26 What is the general procedure followed in accounting for the sale of debt and equity investments?

10–27 What accounting procedure is applied when stock purchase warrants are purchased along with a debt security?

10–28 How is the cost basis for an individual share of stock computed when the investor has received either a stock dividend or a stock split on the shares owned?

10–29 When should a company recognize a loss for impairment of a loan receivable?

10–30 What is the rationale underlying the treatment of insurance on key executives, in which the company is beneficiary, as an investment?

EXERCISES

10–31 Trading Securities (Equity)   Mims Company purchased 100 shares of common stock of Farber, Inc., on January 1, 1996. The purchase price was $50 per share, the stock's par value. At December 31, 1996, the end of Mims Company's financial reporting period, the stock had a market value of $56 per share. Farber did not pay dividends during 1996. Mims considers the Farber common as a trading security.

INSTRUCTIONS

[a] Prepare the general journal entries to record all transactions for Mims Company concerning its investment in Farber common.
[b] How will this investment affect Mims Company's 1996 financial statements?

10–32 Trading Securities (Equity)   Swanson, Inc., purchased 150 shares of AMB Company common stock at $37 per share during 1996. AMB common has a $25 par value and paid a $1 per share dividend on September 30, 1996. Swanson prepares financial statements on a calendar-year basis; the market price of the AMB common stock was $42 at December 31. Swanson classifies the AMB common as a trading security.

INSTRUCTIONS

Identify all elements of the balance sheet, income statement, and statement of cash flows that are affected by these transactions, and indicate the dollar amount and direction of the change on each element.

10–33 Available-for-Sale Security (Debt)   On September 1, 1995, Adams Company purchased $300,000 face value, 8% bonds, which would mature in eight years. The bonds were purchased at a price to yield 12% compounded semiannually. Interest is payable on August 31 and February 28. Adams classifies the bonds as available-for-sale.

INSTRUCTIONS

Round amounts to the nearest dollar:

[a] Using the appropriate present-value table, compute the purchase price of the bonds and prepare the journal entry to record their purchase with any premium or discount included in the Investment account.

[b] Prepare the December 31, 1995, adjusting entry to record accrued interest revenue.

[c] Prepare the February 28, 1996, journal entry to record the interest received.

[d] Assuming that at December 31, 1995, the market value of the bonds was $245,000, record the unrealized gain or loss.

10–34 Trading Securities (Debt and Equity)   Merker Company acquired securities for its trading portfolio as follows:

January 1, 1996	Farmer bonds, 20 bonds at $500 par value, purchase price $10,000
February 1, 1996	Miller common stock, 750 shares at $8 par value, purchase price $7,500

Interest on the bonds was received at June 30 and December 31 at the stated annual rate of 8%. Dividends on the Miller common were declared and paid on September 15 at $1 per share. The market values of the securities at December 31 were

Farmer bonds: $180 per bond
Miller common: $10.50 per share

INSTRUCTIONS

Prepare general journal entries to record

[a] The purchase of the investments.

[b] Two interest and one dividend payments.

[c] The unrealized gain or loss at the end of the year.

10–35 Available-for-Sale Security (Equity)   Hunt Company purchased 500 shares of Wafford common stock on July 3, 1996, as part of its available-for-sale portfolio. Hunt reports on a fiscal year basis, ending on January 31.

Following is information about this investment:

Purchase price: $17 per share
Dividend received: $1 per share on October 31, 1996
Market value at January 31, 1997: $22

INSTRUCTIONS

[a] Prepare general journal entries to record all activities relative to the Wafford common stock investment for Hunt Company.

[b] How would your response to (a) differ if the market value of the Wafford common at January 31, 1997, had been $15?

10–36 Available-for-Sale Security (Debt)   On January 1, 1996, Whaley, Inc., purchased $30,000 face value, five-year, 12% bonds that were priced to yield 8%, with interest payable annually on December 31. Whaley uses the effective interest method of amortization and carries any discount or premium on bond investments in the Investments account.

The market price of the bonds at December 31 was $36,000.

INSTRUCTIONS

[a] Calculate the amount of the unrealized gain or loss that is recognized at December 31, 1996.

[b] Prepare the general journal entry to record this gain or loss.

10–37 Available-for-Sale Securities (Debt and Equity) On July 1, 1996, the beginning of Filliman Company's fiscal year, it purchased and classified the following investments as available-for-sale:

Arnold common stock ($10 par), 10,000 shares at $12

Palmer bonds ($1,000 maturity value), 100 bonds at $1,000

The bonds pay 7% interest annually on June 30. A cash dividend of 8% on par value of the Arnold common stock was received on March 31, 1997. Market values for the securities at June 30, 1997, are

Arnold common stock: $15 per share

Palmer bonds: $975 per bond

INSTRUCTIONS

[a] Prepare all journal entries required to record the transactions and events described above.

[b] Explain the impact of this on the stockholders' equity section of Filliman's June 30, 1997, balance sheet.

10–38 Held-to-Maturity Security The following is a partial effective interest amortization table for a bond investment that is classified as held-to-maturity and is due in eight years:

Date	Interest Revenue	Cash Received	Amortization	Present (Carrying) Value
Jan. 1, 1995				$11,000
July 1, 1995	$440	$600	$160	?
Jan. 1, 1996				

INSTRUCTIONS

[a] Is the effective rate lower or higher than the nominal rate?

[b] Is the carrying value lower or higher than the face value?

[c] What is the nominal rate?

[d] What is the effective rate?

[e] What is the carrying value on July 1, 1995?

[f] What is the face amount of bond investment?

[g] What will be the sum of the amortization column for the eight years?

[h] At the end of eight years, what will be the final carrying value?

[i] If the investment is held to maturity as planned, what will be the gain or loss, if any, that the investor will recognize when the investment is retired?

10–39 Held-to-Maturity Security (Debt) Monterrey Company acquired one thousand $1,000 face value, 8% bonds in Pedro, Inc., at a price to yield 6%. The bonds mature eight years from the date of purchase. Interest is paid annually.

INSTRUCTIONS

[a] Determine the price Monterrey was required to pay for the bonds and prepare the general journal entry to record the purchase.

[b] What is the carrying amount of the bonds one year from the date of purchase, after recognition of interest revenue for the first year? Prepare the general journal entry to record the first year's interest.

[c] Would the fact that the bonds have a market value of $1,120,000 one year after the purchase change your accounting for these held-to-maturity bonds? Why or why not?

10–40 Equity Method On February 1, 1995, Schmidhammer purchased 2,000 shares of common stock in Wesley for $12 per share. This investment represents 25% of Wesley's outstanding common stock of 8,000 shares and, accordingly, Schmidhammer determines that it should use the equity method. The purchase price of $12 per share approximates the book value of the Wesley common, so no amortization of positive or negative differential is required.

Events following this January 1, 1995, purchase are

1995: June 30—Wesley paid a dividend of $.50 per share.
         December 31—Wesley reported net income of $42,000.
1996: June 30—Wesley paid a dividend of $.10 per share.
         Wesley reported a net loss of $14,000.

INSTRUCTIONS

[a] Prepare all general journal entries that Schmidhammer should make for this investment in 1995 and 1996.

[b] What is the carrying amount of Schmidhammer's investment in Wesley at the end of 1996?

10–41 Equity Method   On January 1, 1996, Qualls Company purchased 20% of Green Company's outstanding common stock for $1,000,000 when the underlying book value of the company was $4,500,000. Forty percent of the excess is attributable to assets with a remaining life of eight years, and the remainder to unrecorded goodwill to be amortized over 40 years. Green Company reported net income of $280,000 in 1996 and declared dividends of $.90 per share on all 200,000 outstanding shares. Qualls accounts for its investment in Green by the equity method.

INSTRUCTIONS

Prepare Qualls's journal entries, relative to the Green investment, that are required after January 1, 1996.

10–42 Equity Method with Losses   On January 1, 1992, Kids Stuff Toy Company purchased a 40% influential interest in Clothes for Tots, Inc., for $110,000. The subsequent earnings and dividend distributions of Clothes for Tots were as follows:

Year	Net Income (loss)	Dividends
1992	$ 50,000	$60,000
1993	(160,000)	40,000
1994	(150,000)	10,000
1995	20,000	–0–
1996	140,000	10,000

INSTRUCTIONS

For each of the five years, determine Kids Stuff's reported income (loss) from the investment in Clothes for Tots. Determine the balance of the investment account at the end of 1996.

10–43 Equity Method   On January 1, 1996, Holland Shipbuilders, Inc., purchased a 35% interest in Vernon Iron Works at $20 per share. As a result, Holland was able to appoint two members of the board of directors. The balance of Vernon Iron Works appeared as follows on January 1, 1996:

Vernon Iron Works
Balance Sheet
January 1, 1996

Assets

Current assets		$ 20,000
Land		40,000
Fixed assets	$160,000	
Accumulated depreciation	(50,000)	110,000
Total assets		$170,000

Liabilities and Owners' Equity

Current liabilities	$ 15,000
Long-term liabilities	75,000
Common stock (no par; 6,000 shares authorized, issued, and outstanding)	50,000
Retained earnings	30,000
Total liabilities and owners' equity	$170,000

Vernon reported a net income of $25,000 and paid dividends of $10,000 during 1996. The depreciable assets of Vernon are undervalued by $30,000. The average remaining life of the depreciable assets is six years. Holland Shipbuilders amortizes goodwill over a 20-year period.

INSTRUCTIONS

Round all amounts to the nearest dollar:

[a] Provide Holland's journal entry to record the acquisition of 35% of Vernon Iron Works.

[b] Provide the journal entry to record Holland's share in the income and dividends of Vernon Iron Works.

[c] Provide the journal entry to amortize the excess of investment cost over equity. (*Hint:* Remember that Holland is purchasing only 35% of the $30,000 amount by which the depreciable assets are undervalued.)

10–44 Sales of Investments   Elkins, Inc., sold two investments during 1996. Information about each follows:

> Trading security—Johnstone common stock, purchased in 1995 for $5,000, carrying amount at the time of sale $5,500, selling price $5,600.
>
> Available-for-sale security—Gee Whiz 100 face-value bonds, purchased in 1995 for $7,500, carrying amount at the time of sale $8,250, selling price $7,900.

INSTRUCTIONS

[a] Prepare general journal entries to record each sale, assuming that differences between carrying amounts and selling prices are the result of price changes since Elkins's last financial reporting date.

[b] Explain briefly why you have handled the two sales differently.

10–45 Sales of Investments   Murray Company has an investment in bonds, described as follows:

One hundred $1,000 face-value bonds	$100,000
Discount on original purchase	(5,000)
Purchase price	$ 95,000
Amortization of discount since purchase	1,500
Recognition of unrealized gains	1,000
Current carrying amount	$ 97,500

INSTRUCTIONS

Record the sales of these bonds in each of the following independent cases:

[a] Assume that the bonds are trading securities and that the selling price is the present carrying amount of $97,500.

[b] Assume that the bonds are available-for-sale securities with a selling price of $98,500. The difference between the present carrying amount and the selling price is due to changes in value since Murray's last financial reporting date.

10–46 Stock Rights   Stout Company owns 1,200 shares of stock purchased for $75 per share. One stock right is received for each share of stock outstanding; the market values of the stock and rights at their issuance date are $90 and $4, respectively. Two rights are required to purchase one share of stock at $80. Stout classifies the investment as available for sale.

Stout exercises 500 rights one month later, sells 400 rights at $5.30 per right toward the end of the year, and allows the remaining rights to expire.

INSTRUCTIONS

Round all amounts to the nearest dollar:

[a] Provide the appropriate journal entry for
  [1] The receipt of the rights.
  [2] The exercise of 500 rights.
  [3] The sale of 400 rights.
  [4] The expiration of the remaining rights.

[b] Is the account carrying the original investment in stock reduced when stock rights are received? Why? Could the receipt of the stock rights be recorded as a memorandum entry similar to that for stock dividends? Explain your answer.

10–47 Stock Purchase Warrants   Esau Company purchased 10 units of a bond and three stock purchase warrants in Frank, Inc., at $1,050 per unit. Immediately thereafter, the bonds were selling for $1,040 and the warrants were selling for $12 each.

INSTRUCTIONS

Determine the cost that should be associated with each individual security involved in the purchase.

10-48 Sinking Fund   Krippin Manufacturing Company established a sinking fund on January 1, 1995, for the retirement to a bond issue. The following transactions occurred:

Jan.	1,	1995	Established a sinking fund with $270,000 cash.
Jan.	18		Purchased equity securities for $250,000.
July	15		Paid fund expenses of $10,000.
Sept.	9		Sold equity securities having an original cost of $60,000 for $53,000.
Dec.	20		Received dividends of $15,000 on equity securities.
Feb.	12,	1996	Purchased certificate of deposit for $50,000.
Dec.	31		Received interest and dividends of $27,000.
Dec.	31		Sold all securities in the fund for $275,000 and retired an outstanding bond issue of $300,000. The remaining fund balance was transferred back to the corporate Cash account.

The market value of the equity securities did not change during 1995 and 1996.

INSTRUCTIONS

Provide the appropriate journal entries for these transactions.

10-49 Cash Surrender Value   On January 2, 1994, Fillbert Company insured its president with a $100,000 face-value insurance policy with Fillbert as the beneficiary. Premiums are $1,900 per year and are payable each January 2, beginning in 1994. The cash surrender value after each payment is made for the first three payments is as follows:

	Cash Surrender Value
Jan. 2, 1994	–0–
Jan. 2, 1995	$300
Jan. 2, 1996	$650

Fillbert records each payment in the Prepaid Expense account, appropriately adjusting that account each December 31, the end of its financial reporting period.

INSTRUCTIONS

Prepare all general journal entries required for this insurance policy from January 2, 1994, through December 31, 1996.

PROBLEMS

10-50 Trading Securities (Equity)   Hammer, Inc., purchases stocks of other companies and holds them for short periods of time with the intent to earn a return on otherwise idle cash. Hammer classifies these investments as trading securities.

On January 15, 1995, Hammer purchased 250 shares of LLL common stock for $50 per share. On August 1, LLL paid a $2 per share cash dividend. At December 31, 1995, LLL common stock was selling for $57.

On April 1, 1995, Hammer purchased 1,000 shares of $20 par value MMM preferred stock for $22 per share. MMM paid the annual dividend of 6% of par value on September 30. At December 31, 1995, MMM preferred was selling for $24.

During 1996 Hammer sold the LLL common on March 7 at $59. LLL paid no dividend prior to that date. On September 30, 1996, MMM preferred again paid the stated dividend rate, and MMM was selling for $23 at December 31, 1996.

Also during 1996, on October 5, Hammer purchased 2,000 shares of NNN common stock at $5 per share. NNN did not pay dividends during the year, and at December 31, 1996, NNN common was selling at $4 per share.

INSTRUCTIONS

[a] Prepare the general journal entries required to record these events in chronological order.
[b] Prepare partial balance sheets, income statements, and statements of cash flows for 1995 and 1996, showing the impact of these investment transactions.

10-51 Trading Securities (Debt and Equity) During 1996 Shallowford Company made two investments in securities to create a trading portfolio. These investments are described as follows:

Jan. 1 Purchased 500, $1,000 face value bonds of Monitor, Inc., stated interest rate 10%, priced to yield 8%, interest paid annually on December 31. The bonds mature in five years.

July 1 Purchased 10,000 shares of common stock of Volity, Inc., par value $10 per share. Purchase price was $13 per share.

Market values for these two trading securities at December 31, 1996, are as follows:

Monitor bonds, $1,080 per $1,000 bond
Volity common, $12½ per share

INSTRUCTIONS

[a] Prepare the general journal entries to record the purchases of the two investments, including supporting computations for the prices paid in each case.
[b] Prepare an analysis that includes the carrying amount and any unrealized gains or losses that should be recognized in 1996.

10-52 Available-for-Sale Securities (Debt) On June 1, 1995, Warner, Inc., purchased as a long-term investment 800 of the $1,000 face value, 8% bonds of Universal Corporation for $738,300. The bonds were purchased to yield 10% interest. Interest is payable semiannually on December 1 and June 1. The bonds mature on June 1, 2000. Warner uses the effective interest method of amortization and classifies the bonds as available-for-sale. At the end of 1995, the carrying amount of the bonds approximates their market value, so no unrealized gain or loss needs to be recognized. On November 1, 1996, Warner sold the bonds for $795,000. This amount includes the appropriate accrued interest.

INSTRUCTIONS

Round all amounts to nearest dollar.

[a] Prepare a schedule of interest revenue and bond discount amortization for the original bond investment from June 1, 1995, to June 1, 2000.
[b] Prepare a schedule showing the income or loss before income taxes from the bond investment that Warner should record for the years ended December 31, 1995 and 1996. Show supporting computations in good form.   (AICPA adapted)

10-53 Available-for-Sale Securities (Equity) Piper Company invests idle cash in marketable equity securities that are classified as available-for-sale. The following table summarizes information related to its portfolio for the years 1994–1996:

Marketable Equity Securities

	Date Purchased	Shares Purchased	Purchase Price	Market Price per Share		
				12/31/94	12/31/95	12/31/96
Sax	1/15/94	700	$45	$44	$46	$47
Xon	3/1/94	400	47	50	43	49
Citco	9/21/94	1,000	56	50	51	53
STL	2/2/95	500	31	29	25	26

In 1995 Piper sold 200 shares of Sax for $28 per share and 400 shares of Citco for $52 per share.

INSTRUCTIONS

Provide all the appropriate journal entries relating to this available-for-sale equity securities portfolio for 1994 to 1996.

10-54 Held-to-Maturity Securities On May 1, 1995, Pope Company purchased for long-term funding purposes $20,000 face amount, 12% bonds, due in three years, at 105.076% of face value. The bonds pay interest on May 1 and November 1. Pope utilizes the effective interest method of amortization on interest dates and at calendar year-end.

INSTRUCTIONS

Round all amounts to the nearest dollar:

[a] Provide the appropriate journal entries for the bond investment from the date of original purchase through December 31, 1996, assuming that Pope Company does *not* use a separate

discount or premium account on bond investments. Construct an effective interest amortization table for the entire three-year life of the bond issue to support your journal entries. (*Hint:* You must first determine the effective interest rate by trial and error.)

[b] Write a brief explanation of how your answer to [a] would differ had Pope Company carried the investment account at par value with any premium or discount in a separate account. Illustrate your explanation by preparing the journal entries again for the purchase of the investment on May 1, 1995, and the November 1, 1995, interest received.

[c] Might a rational businessperson ever purchase bonds with a $20,000 face value for an amount higher than this? Why?

10–55 Held-to-Maturity Securities (Debt)   Pillar, Inc., decided to invest in bonds to achieve long-term funding objectives. On January 2, 1994, Pillar purchased $100,000 face amount, 6% bonds due in three years. The bonds were priced to yield an effective interest rate of 10%. Interest is payable semi-annually on June 30 and December 31. Pillar utilizes the effective interest method of amortization and adjusts the carrying value of the bonds on interest payment dates. On June 30, 1995, Pillar changed its intent concerning half of the bonds and sold half of them at 99% of face value.

INSTRUCTIONS

Round all amounts to the nearest dollar.

[a] Compute the price paid for the investment and provide the appropriate journal entry for the acquisition on January 2, 1994, assuming that Pillar uses a separate discount or premium account on bond investments.

[b] Provide the appropriate journal entries related to the bond investment through December 31, 1996. Construct a table similar to the one in Exhibit 10–1 to determine the proper amortization adjusted for the June 30, 1995, sale.

10–56 Equity Method   On June 30, 1994, Miller Company purchased 30% of the outstanding common voting stock of Rex Company for $1,300,000. At that time, Rex Company's net assets amounted to $4,000,000. The level of investment is sufficient to provide Miller significant influence over the activities of Rex. The difference between the purchase price and the underlying book value of Rex's net assets is due to the following:

[1] Land is undervalued by $25,000.

[2] Depreciable assets with a 10-year remaining life are worth $30,000 more than the book value.

[3] Goodwill is determined to exist for any remaining difference between cost and book value. Goodwill is estimated to have a useful life of 25 years from the date of the stock purchase described above. The following relates to Rex Company:

Year	Net Income	Dividends Declared and Paid on December 31
1994	$100,000	$25,000
1995	120,000	40,000
1996	75,000	–0–

INSTRUCTIONS

[a] Prepare all necessary journal entries for these transactions described on Miller Company's books through 1996.

[b] Compute the investment account balance on December 31, 1994, 1995, and 1996. (*Hint:* By purchasing 30% of the outstanding common stock of Rex Company, Miller has purchased only 30% of the undervalued amount of land [$25,000] and depreciable assets [$30,000]. Also, recall that land is *not* subject to amortization.)

10–57 Equity Method   Porter Company has made substantial dollar investments in several companies over the past several years to diversify and to reduce its dependence on the high-quality steel market. Porter has manufactured high-quality steel for more than 50 years. The company policy has been to acquire a substantial portion, but not a majority, of the equity issues of specialty product companies that have been identified as good performers in growth industries. Porter exercises significant influence over the managements of these companies because it has at least a 25% representation on each of their boards of directors.

The following schedule lists the companies in which Porter has invested, the percentage of ownership in each company, and the carrying amount of the investment as of December 31, 1995.

Company	Percentage Ownership	Carrying Amount of Investment as of Dec. 31, 1995
Specialty Alloy	15%	$72,000,000
Aerospace, Inc.	40	10,000,000
Temper, Inc.	30	8,000,000
Air Flow, Inc.	30	100,000

Investment performance varied greatly among the companies during 1996. The following is a schedule of the income and dividend performance of each company and the market value of its outstanding stock. An interpretation of the information follows.

1996 Performance

Company	Income (Loss)	Dividends Paid	Market Value of Outstanding Stock as of Dec. 31, 1996
Specialty Alloy	$50,000,000	$8,000,000	$540,000,000
Aerospace, Inc.	8,000,000	2,000,000	35,000,000
Temper, Inc.	(6,000,000)	500,000	10,000,000
Air Flow, Inc.	(800,000)	none	1,400,000

Temper, Inc., lost a substantial portion of the market for one of its product lines because a competitor introduced a lower-priced model based on technology not available to Temper. This was the cause of the current year's loss. Management has restructured the company so that it is expected to be profitable in the future, although the level of dollar profits will be reduced from those experienced in the past. Consequently, the market value of Temper stock is not expected to return to the levels experienced when it was purchased. The $10 million market value reflects this restructuring.

Air Flow, Inc., expects to be profitable from now on. The current year loss contains the final expenditures incurred in the redevelopment of its product lines. It has received a substantial number of orders for future deliveries.

INSTRUCTIONS

Porter Company reports on a calendar-year basis and is preparing its 1996 financial statements in accordance with generally accepted accounting principles.

[a] Determine the amount that each of the investments that Porter holds in the four companies contributes to the total investment that should be reported on the December 31, 1996, statement of financial position.

[b] Calculate the amount of income that each investment contributes to Porter's income for 1996.

(CMA adapted)

10−58 Equity Method On January 1, 1994, Overland Railroad Company established significant influence over K&K Railroad by acquiring 60,000 shares of common stock, a 30% interest, for $570,000. K&K's book value was $1,300,000 on January 1, 1994. Since this purchase, K&K earned income and paid dividends as follows:

Year	Net Income	Dividends
1994	$180,000	$100,000
1995	310,000	140,000

The market value per share on K&K common stock on December 31, 1994 and 1995, was $8 and $9, respectively. Overland Railroad incorrectly accounted for this investment as if significant influence had *not* been established and included it as an available-for-sale investment.

INSTRUCTIONS

[a] As a result of incorrectly applying accounting principles, the financial statements of Overland Railroad Company are incorrect. At December 31, 1994 and 1995, were the following accounts overstated, understated, or correct? If incorrect, by what amount? Show supporting computations. Assume that any excess of cost over book value should be amortized over 30 years.

[1] Net Investment in K&K Railroad.
[2] Net Income.

[b] If the K&K investment were sold on January 1, 1996, would a larger gain be reported under the incorrect approach or the equity method? Which method better assigns income to periods? Discuss your reasoning.

10–59 Stock Rights   Elliott, Inc., engaged in the following transactions during 1996.

Jan.   6   Purchased 500 shares of Kann Company common stock at $87 per share. Brokerage commissions were $390. The Kann stock is to be classified as available for sale.

May   24   Received notice that Kann issued a 10% stock dividend, followed by a cash dividend of $2.70 per share.

Aug.   1   Received one stock right from Kann for every share of Kann common held. Four stock rights entitled the owner to purchase one share of Kann common at $50 per share. Each right had a market value of $11, and Kann common was trading ex-rights (without rights) at $80 per share. The stock rights expire on August 1, 1997.

Sept. 21   Sold 200 Kann stock rights for $13.50 per right.

Sept. 30   Exercised 300 stock rights for the acquisition of Kann common.

Dec. 31   Determined the market value for Kann stock rights at $16.50 per right. Kann common closed at $68 per share.

INSTRUCTIONS

Provide the appropriate journal entries and year-end adjustments for the Elliott's transactions, rounding all amounts to the nearest dollar. Because of the relatively small dollar amounts involved, you may ignore recording any difference between market value and carrying value on the Kann stock rights.

10–60 Sinking Fund   For purposes of redeeming a bond issue, Whisper Company has established a sinking fund. The following transactions relate to this fund for 1996:

Jan.   1   Received dividends of $6,500 on North Company stock held in the fund.

Jan.   14   Paid expenses of $365.

Feb.   23   Transferred annual company contribution of $77,500 to the fund.

Apr.   1   Purchased at par, $120,000 of 8% bonds plus accrued interest. Interest payable June 30 and December 31.

May   31   Sold bonds purchased on April 1 at 102% of par, plus accrued interest.

Aug.   17   Sold $450,000 of sinking-fund assets for $432,700.

Nov.   30   Received dividends of $8,200 on Wood Company stock.

Dec.   22   Sold remaining fund assets for 105% of carrying value for $680,400.

Dec.   23   Used $1,200,000 of the fund cash total of $1,247,515 to retire bond issue.

Dec.   31   Returned remaining fund cash to the general Cash account.

INSTRUCTIONS

Prepare journal entries for these transactions.

CASES

10–61 Available-for-Sale Securities (Debt)   Wilson Company purchased $1,000,000 of face amount, 5%, six-year bonds at 71.22 on January 1, 1993. Calendar-year 1996 was a poor year for Wilson because of declining revenues and tighter operating margins. The company had an operating income of only $100,000 on revenues of $2,000,000 (or 5%). The treasurer decided to remedy the situation by selling the $1,000,000 face amount, 5% bonds on December 31, 1996, at 90 and recognizing a gain for that period. The following calculation determined the gain on the sale:

Proceeds	$900,000
Carrying value	712,200
Gain	$187,800

As a result of this transaction, Wilson's net income totaled $287,800, or 14.4% of sales. The treasurer was very pleased. The company was now above the industrywide profitability average for

1996, the stockholders would be satisfied, and the treasurer's year-end bonus, which is based on net income, would be almost triple what it would have been before the transaction. As the treasurer's assistant, you are not comfortable with his remedy. You confront the treasurer and tell him, "I have good news, and I have bad news."

INSTRUCTIONS

[a] What is the "good news"?
[b] What is the "bad news"?

10–62 Equity Method   A reprint from the *Forbes* "Numbers Game" column follows. The article is critical of the use of the equity method.

Under a 1971 Accounting Principles Board [APB] ruling, if company A owns between 20% and 50% of company B, A is required to report a portion of B's earnings—equal to A's percentage of ownership. Nevertheless, B continues to show 100% of its earnings. It's called equity accounting.

There's nothing equitable about equity accounting. It is grossly misleading.

The crux of the problem lies in how you define "earnings." Most investors think of earnings as the money a company has to spend—the dollars left over after all the obligations are taken care of. But that's not how the accountants define it: "Earnings are simply not synonymous with cash or working capital," explains Michael J. Walters, a partner with [KPMG Peat Marwick, a Big Six accounting firm].... So, earnings aren't necessarily dollars you can spend. They are dollars that can contribute to assets.

Fair enough, but this use of equity accounting brings in alleged earnings, not corresponding revenues. So it can throw off all the common measures of success: profit margin, return on equity, even price/earnings multiples.

Take a modest example of the resulting confusion: Giant Bendix Corp. ($3.8 billion revenues) has a 21% interest in ASARCO, a metals producer. Bendix adds on to its income statement some $25.5 million from ASARCO, driving up its earnings to $163 million. This deflates Bendix' current P/E from 8.2 to 6.9, inflates its profit margin from 3.6% to 4.2% and blows up its return on equity from 15% to a more impressive 18%.

Mark this, however: When ASARCO was losing money, Bendix carefully kept its interest below 20%. But it became apparent that ASARCO was going to make money. So in 1978 Bendix signed an antitakeover agreement with ASARCO—an increasingly common move—then picked up more stock and started to pick up earnings.

Bendix is not doing anything shady. It is simply complying with generally accepted accounting principles (GAAP).

What is happening here is an exercise in *reductio ad absurdum*. Start with a shaky premise and extend the logic further until it becomes ridiculous. Before 1971, earnings were generally brought in only when a firm achieved a 51% interest—clear control—in a second company. At that point the two balance sheets were consolidated entirely, with minority interests in earnings subtracted out. This is still the method that is used for companies with more than 50% ownership.

Now that *seems* logical. You run a company, you get the earnings. But that isn't entirely true. Even at 51% you can't simply take those earnings. However, since the statements were totally consolidated, the earnings ratios still have meaning.

But companies liked the idea of being able to report those earnings and wanted to carry it a step further and bring in earnings from minority investments. After all, they said, you can have control over the use of much of a firm's income with less than 51% of its stock. You can elect directors, and those directors mean influence over dividend policy and most other major decisions. That influence, they argued, should give them the right to show a portion of the resulting income on their own income statements. The Accounting Principles Board was compliant, and all that remained was to pick a percentage at which significant influence would be presumed.

Somewhat arbitrarily, the APB set forth 20% as the point at which you could *presume* control. Earnings could be brought in with a smaller investment if you could *prove* control. So now Saul Steinberg is taking in 3% of Reliance Group's profits, claiming that his own Leasco is run by the same group of directors and that this demonstrates control.

Steinberg is not alone. Bangor Punta, with only 7% of the stock of Lone Star Industries, is bringing in 7% of Lone Star's earnings, worth some $3 million of BP's $29 million in earnings.

The alternative to this foolishness would be to use cost accounting for partially owned companies, which allows a firm to show only dividends received as earnings—the pre-1971 method.

During the famous monkey trials, William Jennings Bryan proclaimed: "The Bible states it, it must be so." Well, equity accounting is in the accountant's bible, but that doesn't necessarily make it so.

SOURCE: Richard Greene, "Equity Accounting Isn't Equitable," *Forbes* (March 31, 1980), pp. 104–105. Reprinted by permission of *Forbes* Magazine. © Forbes Inc., 1980.

INSTRUCTIONS

Read the article carefully. Do you agree with the conclusions of this article? Why? How would you respond to the allegations presented in it?

JUDGMENT CASES

10–63 Investment Classification Issues   Your client, Come Clean, Inc., specializes in the removal and treatment of a hazardous waste that other companies create in their productive processes. This particular toxic waste was identified only five years ago. Because little was known about some of its toxic properties, liability insurance was not available prior to the most recent year. In prior years, the company was required by a state regulatory agency to perpetually maintain a large fund in lieu of liability insurance to compensate anyone injured by the activities of the company in disposing of the waste. To date no claims have been made and none are known to exist. Further, the company was successful last year in acquiring liability insurance, and the state has agreed that the fund no longer needs to be maintained.

The assets in the fund are marketable equity securities of a wide range of large corporations. At the end of the preceding year, the aggregate market value of the fund had declined below the aggregate cost due primarily to a broad and sudden decline in the stock market shortly before year-end. At that time you believed that the decline in the market value was temporary in light of the broad market decline and the intent of management to retain the fund for the foreseeable future. The fund is classified as available-for-sale, rather than trading or held-to-maturity, so the aggregate decline was reported as a direct charge to the stockholders' equity of Come Clean, Inc., rather than as a loss in income.

Since that time, the value of the portfolio has gradually risen and you believe that it will eventually equal or exceed its cost. However, the fund is no longer required, and the company has been selling the securities to expand capacity or replace obsolete equipment. The president of Come Clean, Inc., has informed you that he intends to use the fund to replace outdated plant assets and to increase the disposal capacity of the company. He therefore contends that the decline in the aggregate market value of the portfolio below its cost should continue to be considered temporary and the difference reported as a direct reduction of stockholders' equity. You further predict that the company can hold the securities for the foreseeable future.

INSTRUCTIONS

How should the difference between the aggregate cost and market value of the portfolio be reported in the financial statements for the current year? Support your answer with consideration of the relevant factors and accounting principles.

10–64 Equity Method   Hi-Flyer Airline, Inc., acquired a 25% interest in the voting stock of a large regional travel agency, We-Book-Em, Inc. Originally, the airline planned to use the travel agency as a "feeder" for a charter business it intended to develop. The airline has since abandoned the charter business program, but it continues to hold stock in the travel agency. Hi-Flyer has appropriately applied the equity method of accounting to its interest in the travel agency, and that investment has been largely profitable.

Now, however, the travel agency has lost three accounts that collectively represent 40% of its revenues. Its cash flow and profitability forecasts reveal anticipated losses through each of the next five years. The value of We-Book-Em stock has also been adversely affected and the amount of Hi-Flyer's related investment account substantially exceeds the market value of the shares and any price that might be realized in a unitary sale of the interest. You have just received the latest audited financial statements of the travel agency, which discuss the loss of the contracts but do not contain any write-down of assets or loss in the corresponding income statement.

Hi-Flyer does not intend to sell its interest and now plans to acquire an even larger share of the travel agency to gain control and finally implement its own charter and reservation service. The president tells you, "We know how to make lemonade out of lemons and that is exactly what we are going to do with We-Book-Em. While our program won't be launched for at least three years and we don't expect it to generate material amounts of revenue for five, we are quite confident that the more distant future is very, very rosy."

You are pondering the implications of the situation when you read that the FASB has initiated a project of accounting for impairments of assets. You become concerned that some kind of a write-down in the carrying amount of the We-Book-Em investment might be necessary. You are also aware that the major lending institution assisting Hi-Flyer has expressed concern about the debt/equity ratio and net income level reported recently by the airline. Any write-down of the investment in We-Book-Em would certainly increase the concerns of Hi-Flyer's lenders and would be resisted strongly by the management of Hi-Flyer.

INSTRUCTIONS

Is a write-down of the investment in We-Book-Em necessary at this time? If you believe that a current write-down of the investment is or may be necessary, describe the amount of the write-off that will be required. Draw on your knowledge of equity method accounting as well as other accounting standards and principles.

10–65 Financial Reporting Case   Coastal Corporation is a diverse corporation in the energy industry whose activities center on five basic areas: natural gas, refining and marketing, exploration and production, coal, and power. The company is based in Houston, Texas.

Coastal Corporation's 1993 balance sheet includes the item "investments—equity method" with a dollar balance of $424.7 million. The comparative 1992 amount is $330.2 million.

Following is a portion of Note 4 accompanying Coastal's 1993 financial statements. This note includes information about investments that the company has in several other enterprises.

Note 4. Investments

The Company has interests in corporations and partnerships which are accounted for on an equity basis. These investments, included in Other Assets, are Great Lakes Gas Transmission Limited Partnership (50% interest), which operates an interstate pipeline system; Pacific Refining Company (50% interest), which operates a refinery and terminal facilities in California; Javelina Company (40% interest), which operates a gas processing plant in Corpus Christi, Texas; Eagle Point Cogeneration Partnership (50% interest), which operates a cogeneration facility in New Jersey; corporate joint ventures (50% interest), which have developed gas and oil properties in Argentina; and several pipeline and other ventures. The Company's investment in these entities, including advances, amounted to $424.7 million and $330.2 million at December 31, 1993 and 1992, respectively. The Company's equity in income of the investments was $71.9 million, $63.8 million and $26.6 million in 1993, 1992 and 1991, respectively, while dividends and partnership distributions received amounted to $17.5 million, $47.8 million and $18.9 million in 1993, 1992 and 1991, respectively. The 1992 equity in income excludes the restructuring charges as discussed in Note 10.

Summarized financial information of these entities is as follows (millions of dollars)

	December 31,	
	1993	**1992**
Current assets	$ 272.9	$ 375.0
Noncurrent assets	2,208.1	1,955.2
	$2,481.0	$2,330.2
Current liabilities	$ 353.2	$ 369.3
Noncurrent liabilities	1,129.7	1,139.1
Deferred credits	155.5	113.3
Equity	842.6	708.5
	$2,481.0	$2,330.2

FINANCIAL REPORTING CASE

	Year Ended December 31,		
	1993	**1992**	**1991**
Revenues	$1,165.2	$1,126.4	$1,038.2
Operating income	192.8	194.1	74.4
Net income	123.7	108.6	25.1

INSTRUCTIONS

[a] What are the percentages of ownership that Coastal holds in the various investees described in Note 4? Do these percentages generally appear to justify the use of the equity method? Why or why not?

[b] In 1993 Coastal's net income was $115.8 million; in 1992 it lost $126.8 million. How significant are the equity-method investments in light of this information?

[c] One of the disclosure standards accompanying the use of the equity method is summarized financial information about investee companies. What information has Coastal provided to comply with that requirement? How useful do you believe this information is to a reader of a company's financial statements?

Property, Plant, and Equipment: Acquisition and Disposal

OBJECTIVES

1. To describe the roles of tangible and intangible assets in the revenue-producing process.
2. To discuss the basic accounting principles that underlie accounting for tangible and intangible assets.
3. To apply the asset/liability measurement principle to specific plant assets in a variety of circumstances.
4. To discuss the proper accounting treatment of plant asset expenditures that are incurred after the initial acquisition of the related assets.
5. To discuss transactions that result in the disposal of plant assets, including their sale, abandonment, destruction, or exchange for other plant assets.
6. To identify and discuss those limited situations in which a departure from historical cost is warranted in accounting for plant assets.

THE IMPORTANCE OF PROPERTY, PLANT, AND EQUIPMENT

Property, plant, and equipment (PPE) is an important item on the balance sheets of many companies. For example, in 1993 American Airlines reported PPE of approximately $14 billion, which represented approximately 72% of total assets! American Airlines is not an anomaly. The following are other examples that illustrate the significance of PPE:

Company	PPE	Total Assets	PPE/Total Assets
Exxon	$62.0 billion	$84 billion	74%
DuPont	21.4 billion	37.1 billion	58
Wal-Mart	9.8 billion	20.6 billion	48

Accounting for PPE is important, as well. The use of most plant assets is systematically recorded as depreciation. Depreciation is important because it represents a major expense in the determination of net income, and it represents a major deduction in the determination of the company's income taxes. Depreciation can be determined by several different methods, the choice of which may influence other transactions.

A recent study in *Management Science* determined that the decision to buy new equipment is influenced by the company's depreciation policies. Additionally, the *Journal of Property Management* traced a 20% to 40% decline in the market value of most real estate investments to the elimination of the depreciation write-off in the 1986 Tax Reform Act. This article further states that this market decline was a major determinant of the savings and loan crisis.

lant and intangible assets are used in virtually all businesses to produce and distribute goods and services. The specific assets required vary in nature because of differences in the business activities of enterprises. These assets include both tangible properties, such as equipment and buildings, and intangible assets, such as patents and franchise rights. **Tangible assets** are often called **property, plant, and equipment** or simply **plant assets** or **fixed assets**. *Assets lacking physical substance* are typically referred to as **intangible assets.**

CLASSIFICATION OF PLANT AND INTANGIBLE ASSETS

All plant and intangible assets have two primary characteristics in common:

1. **They are acquired as operating assets.** Plant and intangible assets are acquired to use in the production or distribution of goods or services. They are *not* acquired primarily for purposes of resale, even though they may later be sold.
2. **They are relatively long lived.** Plant and intangible assets are expected to have relatively long lives in terms of their contribution to the production and distribution of goods and services. In most cases, therefore, the cost of these assets is allocated as an expense over their productive lives.

Despite these similarities, characteristics of *specific* plant and intangible assets vary considerably. For example, although most are readily transferable between enterprises, others cannot be separated from the original enterprise. Furthermore, some are natural resources; others are man-made properties. Numerous classifications of plant and intangible assets are available. In this text, we use the classification that follows:

Asset Classification	Example Assets	Allocation of Cost
Tangible Plant Assets		
Property, plant, and equipment subject to depreciation	Buildings Equipment Furniture Fixtures	Depreciation
Property not subject to depreciation	Land	—
Natural resources	Oil and gas reserves Mineral deposits	Depletion
Intangible Assets		
Separately identifiable	Patents Copyrights Trademarks Franchises Leaseholds	Amortization
Not separately identifiable	Goodwill	Amortization

Chapters 11, 12, and 13 deal with accounting for plant and intangible assets. The balance sheet inside the front cover of the book lists "Property" as an asset category in the balance sheet of Kellogg Company. These assets include significant investments in tangible assets that the company uses in its day-to-day operations. We discuss plant assets in Chapters 11 and 12.

The first part of Chapter 11 presents general principles of accounting for all plant and intangible assets. We then focus on specific issues concerning the acquisition and disposal of various types of plant assets. Chapter 12 covers the depreciation and depletion of plant assets and includes several special accounting problems. Because a detailed discussion of depreciation is included in Chapter 12, Chapter 11 uses only *straight-line* depreciation. In Chapter 13, the accounting principles discussed in Chapters 11 and 12 are applied to intangible assets, and several unique problems associated with intangible assets are identified and discussed. At the end of Chapter 13, we discuss three subjects that include aspects of both plant and intangible assets: research and development costs, accounting by development stage enterprises, and accounting by oil and gas producing companies. These subjects pose particularly challenging problems for the accounting profession and illustrate the complexity of accounting for plant and intangible assets and other closely related costs.

DEFINITIONS AND BASIC ACCOUNTING PRINCIPLES

Plant assets are acquired primarily to use in the production and distribution of goods and services, are expected to be used over a relatively long period, and have tangible physical properties. Although plant assets are apparent because of their physical qualities, their value lies in their **service potential** (i.e., the positive contribution they are capable of making to the revenue-producing process of the enterprise). Service potential can also exist in an intangible asset, where it is manifested in the form of rights and privileges that accrue to the holder of the asset.

The types of plant assets that a company employs depend on the nature of that company's operations. Although most companies use certain standard plant assets (e.g., buildings, machinery), other kinds of plant assets (e.g., pipelines, containers, transportation equipment) are unique to specific businesses. Following are examples of the categories of plant assets presented in the balance sheets of four well-known U.S. corporations.

Company	Categories of Plant Assets
The Goodyear Tire & Rubber Company	Land and improvements
	Buildings
	Machinery and equipment
	Pipeline
	Construction in progress
Phillips Petroleum Company	Exploration and production
	Gas and gas liquids
	Petroleum products
	Chemicals
	Corporate and other
The Coca-Cola Company	Land
	Buildings and improvements
	Machinery and equipment
	Containers
The Dow Chemical Company	Land
	Land and waterway improvements
	Buildings
	Transportation and construction equipment
	Machinery and equipment
	Utility and supply lines

Several principles underlie accounting for all plant and intangible assets. Application of the principles to specific assets, problems encountered in applying the principles, and specified exceptions to the general principles are discussed throughout this and subsequent chapters.

Asset/Liability Measurement

Principle 1. Plant and intangible assets are initially recorded at historical cost.

Plant and intangible assets are *initially* measured and recorded at **historical cost,** which is the cash price or the cash-equivalent value of other consideration. The cash or cash-equivalent price represents the bargained value of the asset at the time of acquisition. From the viewpoint of the acquirer, the cash or cash-equivalent price represents the future value of the service potential expected from the asset.

Historical cost, as applied to plant and intangible assets, is best described as **full cost,** because it includes all costs related to the acquisition and preparation of the asset for its intended use. In addition, subsequent costs to extend the useful life of the asset (beyond that originally expected) or to increase either the quantity or quality of service rendered by the asset are considered part of the cost of the asset.

Cost includes expenditures necessary to bring assets to the appropriate location and to prepare them for their intended use. Substantial outlays for transportation, installation, remodeling, and reconditioning may be required to advance the asset to the point of becoming a positive factor in the generation of revenue.

Significant time may lapse between the purchase of the asset and its placement into service. This is particularly true in the case of buildings undergoing extensive renovation. Costs related to the asset incurred during this period (e.g., insurance, taxes, and supervisory salaries) are capitalized as part of the cost of the asset. For some assets, such as machinery, trial runs and other tests may be necessary before the asset can be put into full service. These tests may require supplies, materials, and other assets. Such costs are also part of the cost of acquiring the asset and preparing it for its intended use.

> **Principle 2.** The cost of plant and intangible assets is allocated as depreciation, depletion, or amortization in a systematic and rational manner to achieve a matching of expenses and revenues during the useful life of the asset. — **Matching**

As plant and intangible assets are used in the production of revenue, their *future* service potential declines. Because these assets are established at historical cost, this decline in service potential is measured by treating a portion of historical cost as an expense in the periods that benefit from the use of the asset. From the accountant's perspective, **depreciation** is the process of allocating the cost of property, plant, and equipment as an expense to those periods during which the asset contributes to the revenue producing process. The terms **depletion** and **amortization** are used to describe this allocation process for **natural resources** and **intangible assets,** respectively. This procedure is important to the process of matching — **Matching** revenues and expenses in the determination of net income.

Depreciation of assets is not recognized until they are placed into service, even if they were acquired at some previous date. No depreciation is recognized during a period of remodeling or renovation between the time the asset is acquired and placed into service. In compliance with the matching principle, recognition of depreciation is deferred until the — **Matching** asset becomes a part of the revenue-producing process.

Methods to determine depreciation expense must be **systematic** and **rational.** A systematic method calculates the periodic depreciation charge in advance or on the basis of the activity level during a particular period. A rational method identifies the association between the amount of depreciation expense recognized and the decline in the service potential of the asset during the period. Chapter 12 covers in detail a number of systematic methods that are widely practiced. Specific circumstances must be considered in evaluating the rational feature of a particular method.

> **Principle 3.** The establishment of cost and the subsequent allocation of that cost is necessarily based on many estimates and assumptions about the use of the plant or intangible asset.

Estimates and assumptions are an important part of accounting for plant and intangible assets. If cash transactions are not used in acquiring the assets and if costs related to acquisition are incurred, judgments must be made in determining the historical cost. Cost allocation methods (i.e., depreciation, depletion, and amortization) require an estimate of useful life in terms of calendar time, service time, or productive output. Finally, the various cost allocation methods that are used in practice require applying an estimate of residual (or salvage) value.

An additional judgment involves estimating the pattern of the decline in the service potential of a plant or intangible asset. Because the allocation method must be rational, it should reflect—to the extent possible—the estimated decline in the service potential of the asset on a periodic basis over its estimated useful life.

Principle 4. The unallocated cost of a plant or intangible asset, called *book value,* is *not* intended to approximate the current market value of the asset.

Matching

As indicated in Principle 2, the process for allocating the cost for plant and intangible assets to those periods that benefit from the assets' use is important in matching revenues and expenses to determine net income. The historical cost of the asset, less accumulated depreciation, depletion, or amortization, is called **book value.** We can define *book value* best in terms of the process followed in its calculation: the historical cost is reduced by the accumulated depreciation, depletion, or amortization recognized to date. Alternatively, book value can be defined as the *un*allocated portion of the historical cost of the asset.

Given the way book value is determined, we cannot expect it to equal the current market value of the asset. After an asset is acquired, its market value may remain constant, decline, or increase. If the market value declines, it may or may not decline at the same rate as the book value declines. The term *book value* is a misnomer, because it seems to imply that the number measures the current worth of the asset. Although *unallocated cost* is more descriptive of the number, *book value* is widely used in practice. Although book value does not equal the current value of the asset, depreciation policy should generally be applied so that the book value does not exceed the current value of the asset.

DETERMINING COST OF SPECIFIC ITEMS OF PROPERTY, PLANT, AND EQUIPMENT

Property, plant, and equipment—or simply plant assets—are established in appropriate accounts at cost. The full cost includes expenditures necessary to acquire the assets and to prepare them for their intended use. The following paragraphs develop and apply the full-cost concept to specific types of plant assets.

LAND

The cost of land includes a variety of expenditures related to its acquisition and its preparation for use as intended by the acquiring enterprise. The following expenditures should be capitalized as the cost of land:

1. The original bargained acquisition price.
2. Commissions related to acquisition.
3. Legal fees related to acquisition.
4. Cost of surveys.
5. Cost of an option to buy the acquired land.
6. Cost of removing unwanted buildings from the land, less any proceeds from salvage.
7. Unpaid taxes (to date of acquisition) assumed by the purchaser.
8. Cost of permanent improvements (e.g., landscaping) and improvements maintained and replaced by the government (e.g., street lights and sewers).

What happens when some of these costs are incurred but the land is *not* acquired? For example, in deciding whether to acquire a parcel of land, a company may pay for surveys, purchase options, and other items related to several parcels of land but eventually may buy only one. A case can be made that costs associated with land not acquired are necessary expenditures for the land acquired, but, in the authors' opinion, such costs should be expensed as incurred. The relationship between such costs and the acquired land is indirect, and care must be taken not to capitalize costs in an amount that exceeds the fair value of the acquired land.

Expenditures for land improvements that have limited lives should be capitalized in accounts other than the Land account and depreciated over their estimated useful lives. Examples are private driveways, sidewalks, fences, parking lots, and easements or rights-of-way of limited duration.

Land and other plant assets that are held for speculative or other investment purposes are properly classified as investments rather than as property, plant, and equipment. Taxes and other expenditures required to maintain these assets should be capitalized as part of the cost of the assets if they are not producing revenue while they are considered an investment. If the assets produce revenue (e.g., through rental), these expenditures should be treated as expenses and matched against the revenue that the investments generate. **Matching**

Land is generally considered to have an unlimited life and is not expected to decline in service potential as it is used. Thus, land is usually carried at the original cost figure and is not depreciated over the periods during which it is used in the operations of the enterprise.

BUILDINGS

The cost of a building includes all necessary expenditures to acquire or construct and prepare the building for its intended use. The following major expenditures are capitalized as part of the cost of buildings.

If acquired by purchase:

1. The original bargained purchase price of the building.
2. Cost of renovation necessary to prepare the building for its intended use.
3. Cost of building permits related to renovation.
4. Unpaid taxes (to date of acquisition) assumed by the purchaser.

If acquired by construction:

1. Cost of constructing new building, including material, labor, and overhead.
2. Cost of excavating land in preparation for construction.
3. Cost of plans, blueprints, specifications, and estimates related to construction.
4. Cost of building permits.
5. Architectural and engineering fees.
6. Interest cost when an extended period of time is required for construction.[1]

The cost of a building that is acquired but *immediately* removed to prepare the land for construction of a new building is treated as part of the cost of the *land* rather than as part of the cost of the new building. As we indicated earlier, the cost of *removal* is also treated as part of the land cost. Also the cost of removing an existing building that the new purchaser actually used for a time should be treated as an adjustment to the gain or loss on the disposal of the old building rather than as part of the cost of the newly constructed building.

Care must be taken to distinguish between building costs and the cost of other assets, such as removable fixtures. The latter represent separate assets that are recorded in appropriate asset accounts and depreciated over their expected useful lives. This holds even if they were acquired with the building and used in a manner closely related to it.

MACHINERY, EQUIPMENT, FURNITURE, AND FIXTURES

Machinery, equipment, furniture, and fixtures are various types of property, plant, and equipment that enterprises use in the production and distribution of goods and services. The following list includes some of the costs that should be capitalized in the appropriate asset account:

1. The original bargained acquisition price.
2. Freight, insurance, handling, storage, and other costs related to acquiring the asset.
3. Cost of installation, including site preparation, assembling, and installing.
4. Cost of trial runs and other tests required before the asset can be put into full operation.
5. Cost of reconditioning equipment acquired in a used state.

---

[1]The subjects of overhead as part of the cost of internally constructed plant assets and capitalization of interest are covered in later sections of this chapter.

Making the proper distinction in the accounting records between the types of property, plant, and equipment is important because the estimated lives of assets and the methods of depreciation may vary among the various asset categories.

NATURAL RESOURCES

Natural resources (e.g., timber, coal, and oil) represent tangible assets that are recorded at cost when they are acquired. These costs are then allocated, usually on a production basis, as depletion to the periods benefiting from the use of the natural resources, as we explain in Chapter 12.

The cost of natural resources includes the original purchase price plus exploration and development costs related to locating and extracting the resources.[2] Other plant assets, separate from the natural resource, are frequently acquired to use in developing and producing natural resources. Buildings and equipment, for example, are typically used in the successful exploitation of natural resources. These assets are established in separate accounts and depreciated over the shorter of (1) their expected useful lives or (2) the expected useful life of the related natural resource.

OTHER PLANT ASSETS

Types of property, plant, and equipment are as numerous as types of enterprises. Each enterprise must acquire those plant assets required to succeed in its line of business. In addition to the more common plant assets—land, buildings, machinery, equipment, furniture, fixtures, and natural resources—a wide variety of assets is used by some enterprises. Several of these are discussed in the following paragraphs.

Returnable containers are used in certain types of businesses to transfer products between the enterprise and its customers. Such containers may represent a significant asset, particularly when a large number are in circulation at any particular time. In some cases, the customer makes no deposit; the container is simply returned by the customer or picked up by the enterprise after it has been used. In these cases, the enterprise typically uses an inventory method whereby the asset cost is increased as units are acquired and reduced as a periodic count or estimate reveals the number of units that are no longer in use. The reduction may be due to normal wear and tear, breakage, or other causes. The amounts of deposits that are intended to be returned later represent a liability of the enterprise. This liability is often called **deposits from customers.** Returnable containers that are not returned within a reasonable

Matching   period should be treated as sales at the deposit amount. To complete the matching process, the cost of unreturned containers is then charged to an appropriate expense.

Miscellaneous tools and other small items of equipment are another type of plant asset, despite their relatively low unit cost. The practical limitations of capitalizing and depreciating a large number of inexpensive assets result in the cost of such items being treated as expenses when incurred—or later on an inventory basis similar to that for returnable containers.

Materiality   Materiality is an important consideration in these situations, and a departure from the strict
Matching   application of the matching principle may be justified if expensing small assets or using an inventory approach does not have a significant impact on the financial statements.

In a manufacturing process, various tools and other devices are used to mold, stamp, cut, and shape other materials. Such devices, commonly called *patterns and dies,* should be capitalized in appropriate asset accounts and depreciated over their estimated useful lives. If such devices are used only in a particular job rather than in a continuous manufacturing process, they should be charged to cost for that particular job.

---

[2]Unique problems associated with accounting for exploration costs in the oil and gas industry are covered in Chapter 13.

The concept of full cost, whereby plant assets are established at the cost to acquire and prepare them for intended use, is more easily stated than applied. Accountants encounter numerous problems in attempting to apply this general principle to specific situations. Judgment is required to assess which expenditures should be classified as part of the cost of assets and which costs should be treated in other ways.

This section discusses several frequently encountered problems: cash discounts, deferred-payment plans, internally constructed assets, capitalization of interest, acquisition by issuing securities, and basket purchases. Although these problems and their resolutions can apply to a wide range of plant assets, they are illustrated here in the context of specific plant assets.

CASH DISCOUNTS

The bargained purchase price of a plant asset is the cash paid or the cash-equivalent price. If cash discounts are available for early payment, should cost include or exclude the cash discount? A related question is whether the amount of the recorded cost should depend on whether the cash discount is taken.

Theoretically, the cash-equivalent price equals the original price *minus* any cash discount available, *whether or not the discount is taken,* because the net amount is the price at which the asset could be acquired in a cash transaction. If the discount is not taken, a *discount lost* is recorded and treated as an expense in the current period.

As an illustration, assume that Elmwood Company acquired equipment with a list price of $88,000 with terms 2/10, n/30. The asset is recorded at the net amount of $86,240 [$88,000 − (.02 × $88,000)]:

Equipment	86,240	
Accounts Payable		86,240

If payment is made within the 10-day discount period, the $86,240 payment of Accounts Payable is recorded. If payment is made *after* the 10-day period, however, the following entry is appropriate:

Accounts Payable	86,240	
Discount Lost	1,760	
Cash		88,000

Recording the asset at the **net amount** is preferable, because this represents the cash equivalent price. However, some accountants record the asset at the total price paid ($88,000 in the above example) if the discount is not taken. The basis for this treatment is that the total price was the actual amount paid; in certain circumstances, it may not be appropriate or possible for management to take the discount. Materiality may be an important consideration in these decisions, because relatively small discounts may not have a significant impact on the financial statements.

Materiality

DEFERRED-PAYMENT PLANS

Plant assets may be acquired on a long-term financing plan whereby periodic payments are made or a single payment is made at some future date. An asset acquired in this manner is recorded at the current cash-equivalent price and any interest included in the financing plan recognized as expense in the appropriate period(s). The objective of this practice is to distinguish properly between the portion of payments that represents the cost of the asset acquired and that portion representing interest charges for the credit received. Failure to make this distinction results in a misstatement of the cost of the asset, depreciation expense, and interest expense.

If interest is not stated in a deferred-payment contract, if the stated interest is not reasonable in view of current market conditions, or if the face amount of the obligation differs from the current selling price for the same or equivalent asset, interest may need to be *imputed.* The amount of the obligation is assumed to include the **acquisition price** of the asset and **interest charges.** The obligation is recorded at the asset's estimted fair value and the difference between the face amount of the obligation and the estimated fair value of the asset at the date of acquisition is recognized as interest over the life of the obligation. The asset and related obligation are recorded at an amount equal to (1) the fair value of the asset being acquired, (2) the market value of the obligation, or (3) the present value of the obligation determined by present-value techniques that use an estimated interest rate. If either of the first two methods is used to record the transaction, the difference between the **face value of the note** and the **recorded amount of the asset** is used to compute a rate on which the recognition of interest will be based. If the third method is used, the borrower's (i.e., the purchaser's) incremental borrowing rate is used as a basis for computing the recorded amount of the asset, the obligation, and the subsequent recognition of interest. This process is a *specific* application of the general process of imputing interest required by *Accounting Principles Board Opinion No. 21* that we discussed in Chapter 10. Exhibit 11–1 summarizes the processes used in accounting for deferred-payment acquisitions.

Two independent examples illustrate the process of imputing interest on such acquisitions. In the first example, we assume that Bryson Production Company acquired a used machine by issuing a $150,000 noninterest-bearing note. The transaction took place on December 31, 1993, and payment is due on December 31, 1996. Neither the market value of the note nor the fair value of the property is determinable. Recently, however, Bryson paid 12% interest on similar transactions.

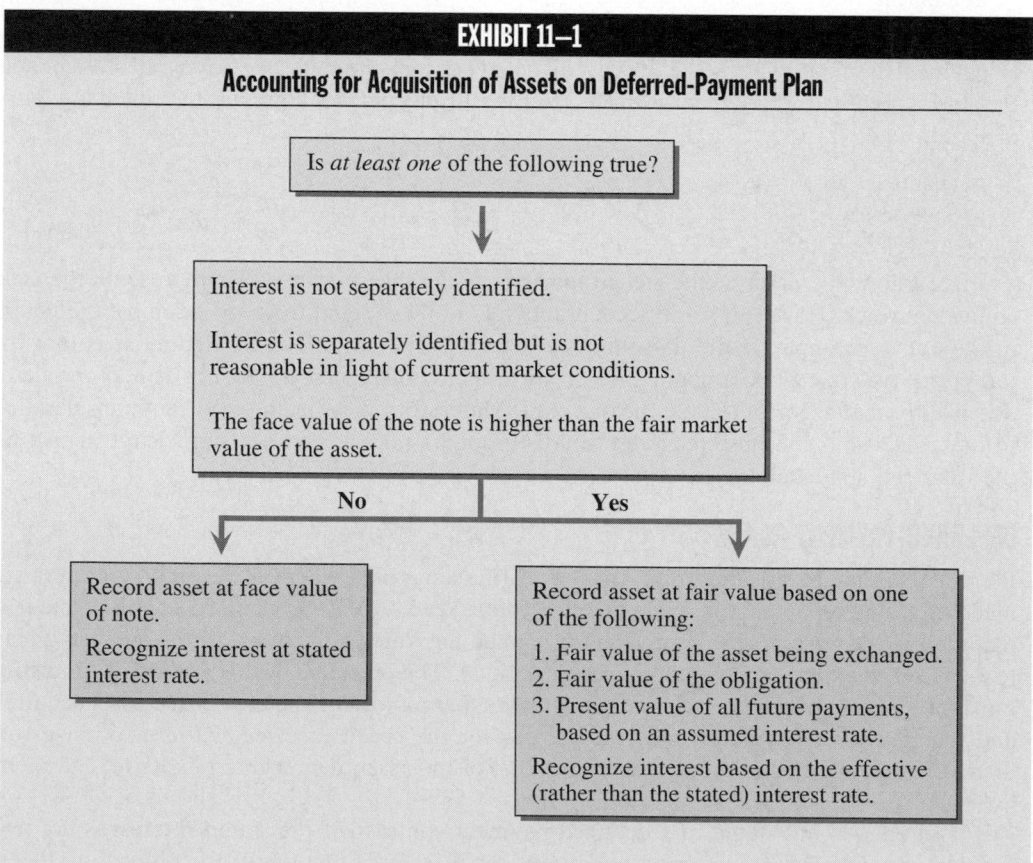

EXHIBIT 11–1

Accounting for Acquisition of Assets on Deferred-Payment Plan

Is *at least one* of the following true?

Interest is not separately identified.

Interest is separately identified but is not reasonable in light of current market conditions.

The face value of the note is higher than the fair market value of the asset.

No

Record asset at face value of note.

Recognize interest at stated interest rate.

Yes

Record asset at fair value based on one of the following:

1. Fair value of the asset being exchanged.
2. Fair value of the obligation.
3. Present value of all future payments, based on an assumed interest rate.

Recognize interest based on the effective (rather than the stated) interest rate.

Because no stated interest rate exists and market values of the note and the asset are unknown, the portion of the note representing interest must be separated by using the 12% interest rate. Using the present value of one factor from Table 6–2, we can determine the present value as follows:

$$\text{Present value of note} = \left[\frac{\text{Face}}{\text{value}} \times pvf_{\overline{n}|i} \right]$$

$$= [\$150,000] \times [pvf_{\overline{3}|12\%}]$$

$$= (\$150,000)(.71178)$$

$$= \$106,767$$

The cost of the machinery is recorded at \$106,767, and the note payable, net of a discount to reduce the face value of \$150,000 to its present value, is recorded at the same amount. This may be done by using a separate discount account as follows:

Machinery	106,767	
Discount on Notes Payable	43,233	
Notes Payable		150,000

The discount of \$43,233 is recognized as interest over the life of the note according to the following schedule:

Date	Interest Computation	Carrying Value of Obligation
		$ 106,767
Dec. 31, 1994		
Interest recognition	(12% × $106,767 = $12,812)	12,812
		119,579
Dec. 31, 1995		
Interest recognition	(12% × $119,579 = $14,349)	14,349
		133,928
Dec. 31, 1996		
Interest recognition	($150,000 − $133,928 = $16,072)	16,072
		150,000
Payment of note		(150,000)
		–0–

Interest at December 31, 1996, can also be determined by applying the 12% rate to the carrying value of the obligation, as was done in 1994 and 1995. The following computation would result: 12% × \$133,928 = \$16,071. The \$1 difference from the amount in the preceding schedule is due to a rounding difference caused by stating the amounts in whole dollars. One way to get around this rounding problem is to adjust for the difference between the face value and carrying value of the note in the last year, as we did in the schedule.

The following entry recognizes the interest at December 31 of each intervening year:

	1994	1995	1996
Interest Expense	12,812	14,349	16,072
Discount on Notes Payable	12,812	14,349	16,072

As each entry recognizing interest is made, the carrying value of the note increases—as indicated in the schedule. The final payment at December 31, 1996, is made by a debit to the Notes Payable account and a credit to the Cash account for \$150,000. The cost of the asset for purposes of depreciation and financial statement presentation is \$106,767.

Plant acquisitions resulting in *multiple* payments may also require interest imputations. To illustrate, Chesney Company acquired a used machine by issuing three $50,000 noninterest-bearing notes, payable one, two, and three years from the transaction date of December 31, 1993. Neither the market value of the notes nor the fair value of the asset is determinable. In recent similar transactions, however, Chesney paid 12% interest.

As in the previous case, no interest rate is stated and the market values of the notes and asset are not determinable. The portion of the notes representing interest must be separated by using the appropriate present-value factor for an ordinary annuity from Table 6–4, as follows:

Face value of notes (representing both principal and interest)	$150,000
Present value of notes	
[$50,000 × [$pvoaf_{\overline{3}\rvert 12\%}$]	
($50,000) × (2.40183) =	(120,092)
Amount of imputed interest	$ 29,908

The purchase of the asset and the related obligation are then recorded as follows:

Machinery	120,092	
Discount on Notes Payable	29,908	
Notes Payable		150,000

The portion of each $50,000 payment representing interest is separated and recognized periodically over the life of the notes according to the following schedule:

Date	Interest Computation	Carrying Value of Obligation
		$120,092
Dec. 31, 1994		
Interest recognition	12% × $120,092 = $14,411	14,411
Payment		(50,000)
		84,503
Dec. 31, 1995		
Interest recognition	12% × $84,503 = $10,140	10,140
Payment		(50,000)
		44,643
Dec. 31, 1996		
Interest recognition	12% × $44,643 = $5,357	5,357
Payment		(50,000)
		–0–

An entry is made to record the periodic payment and to recognize interest at December 31 of each intervening year, as follows:

	1994	1995	1996
Notes Payable	50,000	50,000	50,000
Cash	50,000	50,000	50,000
Interest Expense	14,411	10,140	5,357
Discount on Notes Payable	14,411	10,140	5,357

This series of entries completely eliminates the obligation of $120,092 recognized at the date of acquisition and the proper recognition of interest expense for the intervening accounting periods. The cost of the asset for purposes of depreciation and financial statement presentation is $120,092.

Imputing interest for a plant asset acquisition is required to distinguish between the cost **Asset/Liability Measurement** of the plant asset and interest expense. This, in turn, results in a proper measurement of the asset in the balance sheet and interest expense and depreciation expense in the income state- ment. It is also an interesting example of the principle of substance over form in that we rec- ognize interest expense on debt obligations that are noninterest bearing in form. Failure to impute interest in those situations described in Exhibit 11–1 results in improper figures for these important financial statement items. **Substance over Form**

One form of deferred payment acquisition of plant assets is a capital lease. A lease trans- action that meets certain specified criteria is treated by the leasing party (i.e., the lessee) as a purchase of the property. Both the asset acquired and the debt incurred in the form of the lease are recorded on the lessee's books. The subject of lease accounting is covered in greater depth in Chapter 23.

INTERNALLY CONSTRUCTED ASSETS

Companies may construct their own plant assets rather than acquire them from other enter- prises. Some companies do this routinely as an expected part of business operations; others do it only occasionally. Several reasons for constructing assets internally follow:

1. To acquire needed productive services at prices lower than those from external sources.
2. To use facilities and personnel that would otherwise be idle in slack periods.
3. To produce specialized assets that might not otherwise be available.
4. To ensure the privacy of information concerning future production plans.

The need to determine cost applies to plant assets that are developed internally as well as those acquired from external sources. However, measuring the cost of internally con- structed assets poses some unusual problems. Costs to produce inventory are generally iden- tified in terms of material, labor, and overhead costs. This classification also provides the basis for determining the cost of plant assets that are constructed internally.

Accountants generally agree that materials and direct labor should be included in the cost of an internally constructed asset because they represent both tangible material and pay- ment to employees directly involved in producing the asset. Overhead costs are more contro- versial, however, because they are indirect production costs that are not closely associated with any specific product or constructed plant asset.

Several positions exist concerning inclusion of manufacturing overhead in the cost of in- ternally constructed assets. One position holds that the costs of such assets should *not* include any overhead charge because of the indirect nature of overhead and the inability to associate overhead charges with the particular asset being constructed. The basis of this assumption is that overhead costs are the same whether or not assets (other than inventory) are being con- structed. However, the exclusion of overhead does not appear viable if overhead costs in- crease as a result of constructing plant assets internally. A second position, thus, requires only *incremental* overhead to be included in the cost of the internally constructed asset. While intuitively logical, isolating the increase in overhead costs that can be specifically identified with constructing a plant asset internally is often difficult.

The concept of full cost supports a third position concerning the amount of overhead, if any, to be capitalized as part of the cost of a plant asset that is constructed internally. This position holds that the asset should be charged overhead on the same basis as inventory that is also being produced. For example, if overhead is charged to the manufacture of inventory at $1.50 per hour of direct labor, the same allocation procedure is used to charge overhead to the plant asset; thus, the cost of the asset includes $1.50 of overhead per hour of direct labor. Although this method is widely used in practice, it is difficult to justify if production below capacity is a reason for constructing the asset internally. Absorbing the cost of idle capacity in the cost of the internally constructed asset relieves current income and inventory of charges that would otherwise have been made to them and results in a higher cost of the constructed asset. This process increases income of the current and near future years (by reducing costs of sales and inventory) and reduces income of distant future years (by increasing depreciation charges on the internally constructed asset).

Authoritative accounting pronouncements do not resolve the issue. Proper accounting is, thus, a matter of professional judgment in applying the concept of full cost. The authors believe that the full-cost concept should be generally followed and that the total cost of internally developed assets should include material, labor, and overhead prorated in the same manner as inventory being manufactured. A logical exception to this general policy arises if the company were operating below capacity and constructing a plant asset internally to utilize more efficiently its employees and facilities. In such a case, if it is *practical* to determine the incremental overhead, only the incremental overhead associated with the manufacture of the asset should be included in the cost of the asset.

What amount should be capitalized as the cost of an internally constructed asset when the internal costs total more than the price at which the asset could have been purchased externally? Accountants generally agree that the *maximum* amount at which the asset should be established is its *market value*. Any costs beyond that amount represent inefficiencies of internal construction and should not be included in the cost of the asset. Future periods should not be burdened by the higher depreciation charges that would result from the capitalization of those costs. Any costs beyond the external market price of the internally constructed asset should be treated as expenses in the period in which they are incurred.

CAPITALIZATION OF INTEREST

Our earlier discussion of deferred payment for plant assets emphasizes the importance of distinguishing between expenditures that represent payments for interest on money borrowed and expenditures that are made to acquire the productive services of various types of assets. Controversy has surrounded the determination of the cost of assets, however, when interest costs are incurred specifically for the acquisition and preparation of assets for their intended use.

Historically, most enterprises have treated all interest as expense when incurred. The **capitalization of interest** as part of the historical cost of assets has been a common practice among public utilities, however, because customers are charged regulated rates based on costs incurred and designed to provide stockholders of the utilities with a fair rate of return on their investments. When interest costs are incurred to construct utility facilities, interest is capitalized as part of the cost of those facilities. Therefore, utility rates on the new facilities are based on higher asset acquisition costs, and future utility users in those areas will pay rates that cover the interest costs required to finance the facilities that produce the services they consume.

The practice of capitalizing interest has not been limited to public utilities. An increasing number of other enterprises began adopting the policy of capitalizing interest in certain circumstances. Standards of accounting and reporting in this area were subsequently established by the Financial Accounting Standards Board (FASB) in its *Statement of Financial Accounting Standards No. 34.*[3] This pronouncement requires all enterprises to capitalize interest in certain circumstances on the premise that the cost of acquiring an asset includes all costs necessary to bring the asset to the condition and location required for its intended use. The capitalization of interest cost in certain circumstances is considered necessary to Matching   achieve a proper matching of revenues and expenses as the asset costs are depreciated in future periods.

Interest is capitalized as part of the cost of acquiring an asset if an **extended period** is required to prepare the asset for its intended use and **significant expenditures** related to the asset take place during that period. The objectives of capitalizing interest in such cases are (1) to obtain a cost that reflects the enterprise's total investment in the asset and (2) to recog-

---

[3]*FASB Statement of Financial Accounting Standards No. 34,* "Capitalization of Interest Cost," 1979.

nize in future periods depreciation expense that adequately measures the cost of services provided by the asset. Interest is capitalized *only* if the amounts are material and the benefits of capitalization exceed the costs of accumulating the required information. Within those constraints, capitalization of interest is appropriate in situations such as the following: **Materiality**

1. Assets are constructed by the enterprise for its own use.
2. Assets are constructed for an enterprise by another enterprise and the acquiring enterprise makes deposits or progress payments.
3. Land is under development for a particular use.
4. Assets intended for sale or lease are constructed as discrete projects.

Common characteristics of these assets are that (1) they are *not yet* being used in earning activities and (2) they are undergoing preparation for use in *future* earning activities. If the production of an asset is complete, if the asset is not being changed in some way, or if obsolescence, excess capacity, or need of repair prevents an asset from being used in earning activities, the asset does not qualify for the capitalization of interest. Also, interest is not capitalized on inventories that are routinely manufactured or otherwise produced in large quantities on a repetitive basis.

Theoretically, capitalized interest is the interest that was actually incurred during a period but that *could have been avoided* if expenditures related to the qualifying asset had not been made. Interest is based on the average accumulated expenditures for the asset during the development period, including interest capitalized in prior periods.

If specific borrowings are associated with an asset for which interest is being capitalized, the interest rates on those borrowings are used. If this direct association cannot be made, a **weighted average interest rate** on all borrowings of the company will determine the amount of interest to be capitalized. Because the interest to be capitalized is based on actual outstanding debt, the amount capitalized cannot exceed the interest incurred during the period. Interest capitalization begins when the initial expenditure related to the development of the asset is made and continues as long as the asset is undergoing active development. Interest capitalization ends when the asset is ready for its intended use, whether or not it is placed in service at that time.

To illustrate interest capitalization, assume that Harper Company is constructing a warehouse to use in its own operations. Costs of material, labor, and overhead of $160,000 have been identified and charged to the asset account. Initial expenditures in early January 1995 were $70,000. In early May of that year, $50,000 more was invested; in early October, an additional $40,000. On January 2, 1995, the company arranged for a 12%, $100,000 loan to partially finance the construction. In January the company borrowed the full amount of the loan and used it to finance the first $100,000 of expenditures in the warehouse. The remaining investment in the project came from available cash within the company. In addition to this loan, the company has the following outstanding debt throughout 1995:

$500,000, 15% notes payable due in 1997, interest payable semiannually on June 30 and December 31.

$800,000, 13% bonds payable due in 1999, interest payable quarterly on January 31, April 30, July 31, and October 31.

The amount of interest to be capitalized is as follows:

Period of Time	Investment	No. of Months	(Investment) × (No. of Months)
January–April	$ 70,000	4	$ 280,000
	50,000		
May–September	$120,000	5	600,000
	40,000		
October–December	$160,000	3	480,000
			$1,360,000

Average Expenditure for 1995
$1,360,000/12 months = $113,333

Average Interest Rate on Debt Unrelated to Construction

Amount of Debt	Interest Rate	Interest Amount
$ 500,000	15%	$ 75,000
800,000	13	104,000
$1,300,000		$179,000

Weighted average interest rate: $179,000/$1,300,000 = 13.769%

Interest Capitalization for 1995

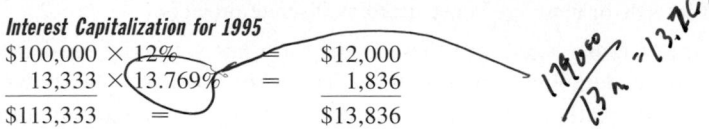

$100,000 × 12%	=	$12,000
13,333 × 13.769%	=	1,836
$113,333	=	$13,836

The average accumulated expenditure for the construction of the asset during 1995 is $113,333. This represents the amount that the company had invested in the construction project, on average, during 1995 and is the basis for determining the amount of interest to be capitalized. It is determined by computing the amount of the investment for three periods of time during the year, the end of the first two periods being determined when an additional investment was made in the asset and the end of the last period determined by the end of the financial reporting period. Interest on the average investment is determined in two steps: (1) on the first $100,000 investment in the asset at the 12% rate on the $100,000 loan taken out specifically for this project and (2) on the remaining $13,333 ($113,333 − $100,000) at the 13.769% weighted average interest rate on the remaining debt of the company.

If we assume that interest on the $100,000 debt incurred specifically for this asset is charged directly to the asset account as incurred and that other interest is allocated from interest expense previously recognized, the entry to record the capitalization of interest is as follows:

Warehouse	13,836	
Cash (or Interest Payable)		12,000
Interest Expense		1,836

Several entries totaling the amounts in the above entry may be made at different points in time. The $12,000 interest on debt incurred specifically for this asset would be charged to the asset as it was paid or accrued. The transfer of $1,836 interest previously recognized as an expense is most likely made when the asset is complete or at the end of the accounting period if the asset is still in process. This is necessary to state properly the asset cost and the interest expense for the period.

When the $13,836 interest is combined with the $160,000 of material, labor, and overhead costs that are capitalized as part of the cost of the asset, the total asset cost is $173,836 ($160,000 + $13,836). This amount is the basis for financial statement presentation and depreciation calculation.

In this case, the investment in the asset for which interest is being capitalized is higher than the debt directly related to that project. In addition, Harper has other debt outstanding that provides the basis for the capitalization of interest on the investment in excess of $100,000. If the company had no debt beyond the $100,000 directly related to the asset under construction, no additional interest could be capitalized, because the amount of capitalized interest is limited to the amount of interest actually incurred during the construction period.

Disclosure   When a company has capitalized a part of interest incurred during an accounting period in accordance with *FASB Statement No. 34,* special disclosure must be made in the financial statements. Exhibit 11–2 presents an example of this disclosure from the 1993 financial statements of The Goodyear Tire & Rubber Company. Goodyear's principal business is the

---

EXHIBIT 11–2

The Goodyear Tire & Rubber Company
Capitalization of Interest Disclosure

Note 13. Interest Expense

Interest expense includes interest and amortization of debt discount and expense less amounts capitalized as follows:

(In millions)	1993	1992	1991
Interest expense before capitalization	$167.4	$236.9	$326.1
Less capitalized interest	5.0	4.0	8.3
	$162.4	$232.9	$317.8

The Company made cash payments for interest in 1993, 1992 and 1991 of $181.1 million, $260.7 million and $349.1 million, respectively.

SOURCE: The Goodyear Tire & Rubber Company, 1993 Annual Report.

---

development, manufacture, distribution, and sale of tires throughout the world. In addition, the company produces and sells a broad spectrum of rubber, chemical, and plastic products for the transportation industry and various other industrial and consumer markets. This disclosure separates the amount of interest recognized into the amount capitalized and the amount expensed currently. The cash paid for interest is also disclosed.

ACQUISITION BY ISSUING SECURITIES

Plant assets may be acquired by issuing securities (e.g., stock certificates) rather than paying cash or transferring other assets to the seller. In such transactions, accountants record the equivalent amount of cash that would have been transferred in a comparable cash transaction. Several problems may obscure the determination of the cash-equivalent amount. Market values of either the securities or the asset(s) exchanged may not be readily available. On the other hand, although a market value of the securities may be readily determinable from a market quotation, such value may be based on a level of market activity substantially different from the number of shares involved in the acquisition. In such situations, the market price may not indicate the value of the shares if the number issued in the acquisition had been included in the transactions determining the market price.

When securities are issued in exchange for assets, the market value of the shares issued is normally used as the basis for recording both the assets acquired and the stock issued. When the market value of the property exchanged is more objectively determinable than the market value of the stock, the value of the property is used. If the market value of the stock is based on a level of market activity so far below the number of shares included in the transaction that the current market value is not appropriate, the estimated valuation of the property exchanged or an estimate of the value of the stock apart from the original market value should be made by the officers of the issuing corporation. This value is used in recording the transaction. Generally, neither the **par** (or **stated**) **value** nor the current book value of the stock is an appropriate base for recording transactions in which securities are exchanged for plant assets.

To illustrate, assume that Lyons Company purchases land from another enterprise by issuing 22,000 shares of its $25 par value stock. The market price of the stock is $32 at the time of the transaction. The 22,000 shares do not represent a substantial number of shares in relation to the volume of stock activity in the market. The purchase of the land is recorded by the following entry:

Land	704,000	
Common Stock (22,000 × $25)		550,000
Paid-In Capital in Excess of Par Value		154,000
[22,000 × ($32 − $25)]		

BASKET PURCHASES

Basket purchase is a term that refers to the acquisition of several assets for a single price. The primary accounting problem arising from the basket (lump-sum) purchase is the apportionment of the total price paid to the individual assets acquired. Sometimes several assets can be purchased in a single transaction for less than the individual assets could be acquired separately. In such cases, the allocation of the total price paid for the group of assets to the individual assets is based on the relative values of the individual assets acquired. The total cost recorded must not exceed the total price paid, even if the total appraised value exceeds that amount. The individual asset values that are assigned for allocation purposes may be based on current market prices, appraisal values, the present values of expected future benefits, or other appropriate estimations.

Asset/Liability Measurement

To illustrate, we will assume that Ledford Company acquires several assets in a single transaction from a competitor who is going out of business. The total purchase price is $855,000. The acquired assets and their individually estimated values, based on current market prices and independent appraisals, are as follows:

Inventory	$100,000
Building	500,000
Land	150,000
Fixtures	200,000

The allocation of the $855,000 cost to the individual assets is based on the relative estimated value of the individual assets, as follows:

Asset	Appraisal Value	Cost Allocation
Inventory	$100,000	(100/950) $855,000 = $ 90,000
Building	500,000	(500/950) $855,000 = 450,000
Land	150,000	(150/950) $855,000 = 135,000
Fixtures	200,000	(200/950) $855,000 = 180,000
	$950,000	$855,000

Alternatively, a percentage of cost to total appraisal value may be computed as follows: $855,000/$950,000 = 90%. This percentage is then applied to the estimated value of each asset to determine the portion of the total cost allocated to that asset. For example, Land would be allocated $135,000, as follows: $150,000 × 90% = $135,000. The entry to record the basket purchase in this example is as follows:

Inventory	90,000	
Building	450,000	
Land	135,000	
Fixtures	180,000	
Cash		855,000

Although this illustration deals with a purchase of several different classes of assets, the same procedure may be used to allocate the cost of several items of the same type to individual items. For example, several inventory items or several pieces of machinery may be purchased for a single price. The cost of each individual inventory or machinery item is determined by allocating the cost of all items on the basis of the relative value of the individual items.

When a company makes a basket purchase of assets, it may also make expenditures that relate to only one of the assets. Accountants must carefully distinguish between the common price paid for several assets and any related expenditures that apply only to a single asset. The former should be allocated among the assets acquired, as illustrated above. Any related expenditures that apply to specific assets should be associated entirely with those assets. For example, a company may acquire inventory, furniture, and land in a single purchase transaction. The price paid should be allocated among these assets based on their individual relative fair values. Legal fees paid to transfer title of the land, however, should be assigned only to the land and should not affect the recorded cost of the inventory and fixtures.

After plant assets are acquired and placed into service, additional costs may be related to the continued use of the assets. **Capital expenditures** are expected to benefit *future* periods and, thus, are recorded as assets and depreciated. **Revenue expenditures** are normal, recurring expenditures designed to sustain the usefulness of the asset through the *current* accounting period and are charged to expense as incurred.

POSTACQUISITION EXPENDITURES

In distinguishing between capital and revenue expenditures, accountants commonly identify capital expenditures as those expenditures expected to allow the related asset to render greater future benefits to the enterprise. Capital expenditures are expected to have one or both of the following positive impacts on future operations:

1. The *quantity* of services received from the asset will be increased. This may take the form of a longer useful life or more units of output.
2. The *quality* of the services from the asset will be increased.

If neither of these conditions is met, the expenditure is intended to maintain the present level and quality of services rendered by the asset. These expenditures are appropriately designated as revenue expenditures and charged to expense as incurred.

A common practice to distinguish between capital and revenue expenditures is to establish a dollar amount that represents a materiality threshold. Expenditures that are less than the designated amount are treated as expenses when incurred, even if they are beneficial to future periods. The designated level for this distinction varies with the size of the enterprise. For example, a small company might expense all amounts below $100, and a large company might follow the same practice for amounts below $10,000. Although this practice is justifiable only on grounds of materiality, it eliminates the practical problem of judging the nature of a large number of small dollar amounts.

Materiality

Companies describe their policies concerning postacquisition expenditures in their annual reports if they have a material impact on the financial statements. For example, in its 1993 financial statement notes, Federal Express Corporation explains that expenditures for major additions, improvements, flight equipment modifications, and overhaul costs are capitalized. Maintenance and repairs are charged to expense as incurred except for B747 aircraft, airframe, and engine overhaul maintenance cost, which is accrued and charged to expense on the basis of hours flown. Similarly, Parker Hannifin Corporation's 1993 annual report explains that improvements to plant and equipment that extend their useful lives are capitalized, and maintenance and repairs are expensed. When property is retired or otherwise disposed of, the cost and accumulated depreciation are removed from the accounts and any gain or loss included in income.

Expenditures related to plant assets incurred after the original acquisition may be classified in four categories: (1) additions, (2) replacements and betterments, (3) rearrangement and relocation, and (4) repair and maintenance. Additions are clearly capital expenditures and are recorded as assets and depreciated over future periods. At the other extreme are expenditures for repair and maintenance, which are revenue expenditures that are expensed as incurred. Between these two extremes are replacements/betterments and rearrangement and relocation costs. These are more difficult to categorize and may be treated as either capital or revenue expenditures, depending on the specifics of the situation. The following discussion of these four categories will help you distinguish between capital and revenue expenditures and identify the period over which the capital expenditures should be allocated.

ADDITIONS

Additions represent major expenditures that, by definition, are capital in nature because they increase the service potential of the related asset. Additions to buildings are common when the size of the asset can be increased by adding a new wing or level to the existing facility.

Two major problems exist in relation to additions. First, the period over which the expenditure is to be depreciated must be determined. If the estimated useful life of the addition is independent of the asset to which it relates, the addition is treated as a *separate* asset and depreciated over its estimated useful life, regardless of the life of the original asset. This is common practice when structures are built as components, and the addition would continue to exist even if the original structure were removed. In many cases, however, the addition is not independent of the original structure, and the period of depreciation for the addition must be determined in relation to the original structure. In such cases, the cost of the addition is depreciated over the shorter of the estimated life of the addition or the remaining life of the original asset.

The second problem related to additions is identifying the costs that are appropriately capitalized. Adding to a facility frequently requires alteration to the original structure. For example, the addition of a new wing of a building may involve removing walls or rerouting plumbing. If the original unit were constructed with a plan to expand, costs related to the original asset incurred when the addition takes place are appropriately capitalized as part of the cost of the addition. On the other hand, costs that *could have been avoided* if appropriate planning had taken place at an earlier date should be expensed rather than carried forward as part of the addition.

REPLACEMENTS AND BETTERMENTS

Replacements and betterments represent the substitution of a new part of an asset for an existing part. For example, the base of a machine may be replaced with a new one or the roof of a building may be replaced.

If the new part of the asset is similar in nature to the part being eliminated, the substitution is called a **replacement.** If the new part represents an improvement in quality over the part being eliminated, the substitution is called a **betterment.** An important consideration in determining the appropriate accounting treatment of replacements and betterments is whether the original part of the existing asset is separately identifiable. If separate identification is possible, the new expenditure should be substituted for the portion of the book value being replaced or improved.

To illustrate, we assume that Fagan Company acquires a building at a cost of $250,000. Separate identification of the cost components indicates that $30,000 of the cost relates to the roof of the building. The building is being depreciated over a 25-year life by the straight-line method, with an estimated salvage value of $20,000. The roof, however, is being depreciated over a 10-year life by the straight-line method, with no estimated salvage value. After nine years, the roof is replaced at a cost of $50,000. The replacement is expected to last for the remaining years of the original estimate of the building's life.

The replacement is substituted in the accounts as follows:

Building (new roof)	50,000	
Accumulated Depreciation	27,000	
(90% × $30,000)		
Loss on Replacement of Roof	3,000	
Building (old roof)		30,000
Cash		50,000

The roof is depreciated at $3,125 per year ($50,000/16) over the remaining 16 years of the life of the building. Depreciation of the remainder of the building is not affected by the replacement of the roof.

If separate identification is not possible or practical, the cost of replacements and betterments is treated as an increase in the book value of the asset, thereby increasing the basis for depreciation over the remaining life of the asset. If the replacement or betterment is designed primarily to enhance the *quality* of the service potential of the asset, the cost is charged to the asset account and an appropriate increase in depreciation expense is recognized in future years. Although the book value of the replaced or improved portion remains in the asset and accumulated depreciation accounts, the replacement or betterment usually takes place when the original expenditure is nearing the point of full depreciation and its book value is a relatively small amount. Any distortion in the financial statements is minimal.

If the replacement is designed primarily to *extend the length of the service life* of the asset, the book value is increased by charging Accumulated Depreciation. The accountant then depreciates the revised book value, less any salvage value, over the revised useful life.

For an illustration, we assume that Webb, Inc., replaces the electrical system in its building at a cost of $100,000. The building originally cost $800,000 and had $425,000 accumulated depreciation at the time of the replacement. The company has no record of the separate components of the building. At the time of the replacement, the asset had a remaining life of 10 years with an expected $50,000 residual value.

If the replacement is made to enhance the quality of service potential in the future, the replacement is accounted for as follows:

Building	100,000	
Cash		100,000

This entry increases the book value to $475,000, as follows:

Original cost of building	$ 800,000
Cost of replacement of electrical system	100,000
	900,000
Accumulated depreciation	(425,000)
	$ 475,000

Depreciation expense thereafter is recognized at $42,500 per year [($475,000 − $50,000) ÷ 10 years].

If replacement is made to extend the useful life, the replacement is accounted for as follows:

Accumulated Depreciation—Building	100,000	
Cash		100,000

This entry also increases the book value to $475,000, computed as follows:

Original cost of building		$800,000
Accumulated depreciation prior to replacement	$ 425,000	
Cost of replacement of electrical system	(100,000)	325,000
		$475,000

If we further assume that the replacement adds 7 years to the current estimated service period of 10 years and that the estimated residual value is unchanged, the depreciation thereafter is recognized at $25,000 per year [($475,000 − $50,000) ÷ 17].

REARRANGEMENTS AND RELOCATIONS

Rearrangements and **relocations** frequently occur to facilitate future operations. If the costs of such activities are material and can be separated from recurring operating expenses, **Materiality**

Matching they are capitalized and recognized as expenses over the periods expected to benefit in accordance with the matching principle. If the costs are *not* material, if they are *inseparable* from recurring operating expenses, or if the future benefits in terms of increased efficiency are *questionable,* they are expensed in the period in which they are incurred.

The unamortized portion of costs of previously capitalized rearrangement and relocation costs is sometimes presented as an intangible asset, but it is more appropriately described as a **deferred charge** (i.e., an unamortized balance awaiting amortization). Deferred charges are usually presented in the balance sheet as a part of an Other asset category. Chapter 13 discusses this balance sheet category in more detail.

REPAIR AND MAINTENANCE

Repair and **maintenance** expenditures are necessary to maintain the current operating capabilities of plant assets. Such expenditures range from custodial care and recurring minor repairs on buildings to periodic inspection and servicing of machinery and equipment. Repair and maintenance expenditures are treated as expenses when incurred because they are designed to ensure continued and dependable service of the asset.

Distinguishing between repair or maintenance expenditures and those expenditures that should be capitalized is sometimes difficult. Major repairs that take on the characteristics of replacements and betterments in terms of the expected future use of the asset are capitalized **Materiality** if the impact on future income is judged to be material.

The expensing of repair and maintenance when incurred is based on the assumption that such expenses are fairly evenly distributed over time and that individual expenditures are relatively small. Expenditures made in one period that provide for the use of the asset in a subsequent period are usually small and/or are offset by similar expenditures incurred during the subsequent period. If financial statements are prepared on a monthly or quarterly basis, the assumptions of immateriality and even distribution over time may be less appropriate. In these cases, repair and maintenance expense may be accrued on an estimated basis by establishing an allowance account, with actual expenditures charged to that allowance when made.

To illustrate the accrual of repair and maintenance, assume that Progolf Company incurs substantial amounts of repair and maintenance related to its equipment. Because of the size of the expenditures, their relative infrequency, and the need to prepare monthly financial statements, the company recognizes the estimated annual cost of $120,000 for the current year on a monthly basis. Actual costs incurred during January, February, and March are $500, $18,500, and $1,200, respectively. Entries to recognize the expenses and related expenditures are as follows:

January			
Various dates	Allowance for Repair and Maintenance	500	
	Cash (or other asset, liability, or expense account, as appropriate)		500
31	Repair and Maintenance Expense ($120,000/12)	10,000	
	Allowance for Repair and Maintenance		10,000
February			
Various dates	Allowance for Repair and Maintenance	18,500	
	Cash (or other appropriate account)		18,500
28	Repair and Maintenance Expense	10,000	
	Allowance for Repair and Maintenance		10,000
March			
Various dates	Allowance for Repair and Maintenance	1,200	
	Cash (or other appropriate account)		1,200
31	Repair and Maintenance Expense	10,000	
	Allowance for Repair and Maintenance		10,000

This method results in equal recognition of repair and maintenance expense of $10,000 each month, even though the pattern of the expenditures varies considerably. A question arises, however, as to the balance in the Allowance for Repair and Maintenance account at the end of a reporting period. For Progolf Company, this amount is as follows:

		Balance in Allowance Account
January	Expense recognized	$(10,000)
	Costs charged to allowance	500
	Balance in allowance at January 31	(9,500)
February	Expense recognized	(10,000)
	Costs charged to allowance	18,500
	Balance in allowance at February 28	(1,000)
March	Expense recognized	(10,000)
	Costs charged to allowance	1,200
	Balance in allowance at March 31	$ (9,800)

Diversity in practice exists in the treatment of an allowance account in balance sheets perpared at the end of each month. The nature of the item, as well as the process giving rise to it, suggests treating the allowance in the same way that accumulated depreciation is treated (i.e., as a deduction in determining the book value of the related asset). An alternative interpretation of treating the allowance as a liability is difficult to justify, because expenditure in the future depends on future events. Also, the notion that the enterprise has a liability to itself for repair and maintenance on its assets is difficult to support. A related question concerns the treatment of any balance in the allowance account at the end of the **annual** reporting period. If the estimated accrual method is used to spread the expense over the interim periods of the year, the estimated amount should be continually evaluated and adjusted in the final month or quarter so that the allowance account is eliminated at year-end. This way, the problem of balance sheet classification in annual financial statements is avoided.

Accounting for plant asset–related expenditures made subsequent to original acquisition requires careful judgment. The overriding objective is to match properly the cost of the expiration of the service potential with the revenue generated by that effort. Consistency in application is also important, because inconsistent treatment may materially affect the financial position and the results of operation. Accounting policies should reflect the most logical and realistic assumptions available.

Matching

Consistency

Materiality

Accounting for the various types of capital and revenue expenditures discussed in this section are summarized in Exhibit 11–3. In some cases, companies present their accounting policies concerning repairs, maintenance, and other postacquisition expenditures in notes to the financial statements. Exhibit 11–4 includes a section of the accounting policy statement from the 1993 annual report of H. J. Heinz Company, a worldwide provider of processed food products and nutritional services. The disclosure makes specific reference to the accounting treatment of improvements and repairs and maintenance, as well as other aspects of accounting for plant assets.

DISPOSALS OF PLANT ASSETS

Plant assets are disposed of for a variety of reasons and in a variety of ways. They may be **sold,** or they may be **abandoned** or **converted involuntarily,** as in the case of loss by fire, flood, or other natural disaster. They can also be **exchanged.** Regardless of the cause, two basic steps are followed in accounting for the disposal. First, depreciation is recognized to the date of the disposal. This is necessary to reflect properly the cost of operations for that portion of the year in which the asset is used and to correctly establish the book value of the asset at the time of disposal. Second, the cost and accumulated depreciation of the asset are

EXHIBIT 11–3

Summary of Accounting for Postacquisition Expenditures

Type of Expenditure	Circumstances	Accounting Treatment
Additions	Useful life is *independent* of original asset.	Capitalize expenditure in separate account and depreciate over the estimated useful life.
	Useful life is *limited* to remaining life of original asset.	Capitalize expenditure as part of the original asset and increase the depreciation recognized over the remaining useful life.
Replacement and Betterment	*Separate* identification of portion of asset substituted is possible.	Capitalize expenditure to asset account and depreciate over shorter of the estimated useful life of (1) the replacement/betterment or (2) the original asset. Cost and accumulated depreciation on that portion of asset being replaced are removed, and gain or loss is recognized.
	Separate identification of portion of asset substituted is *not* possible; service *potential* of asset is improved.	Charge expenditure to asset account and depreciate over the shorter of the estimated life of (1) the replacement/betterment or (2) the original asset.
	Separate identification of portion substituted is *not* possible; service *life* of asset is extended.	Charge expenditure to Accumulated Depreciation and depreciate book value over revised estimated life.
Rearrangement and Relocation	Costs are *identifiable* and *material* in amount; changes are expected to produce *discernible* future benefits.	Capitalize expenditure and amortize over the period expected to benefit.
	Costs are *not* separately identifiable, not material in amount and/or future benefits are *not* discernible.	Treat expenditure as expense when incurred.
Repair and Maintenance	Incurrence of costs is *evenly* distributed over the annual period.	Treat expenditures as expenses when incurred.
	Incurrence of costs is *not* evenly distributed over the annual period.	Accrue periodic expense on an estimated basis and charge actual expenditures to allowance. (No allowance should be carried forward from one annual period to the next.)

eliminated from the accounts, any cash received is recorded, and a gain or loss on the disposal is recognized. In exchanges, other assets are received and cash may be paid, both requiring accounting recognition.

To illustrate, assume that Gatlin Corporation acquired a building in January 1990 at a total cost of $510,000. The building has been depreciated by the straight-line method using a 20-year life with an estimated residual value of $60,000. On June 30, 1996, the building is **sold** for $425,000. The company reports on a calendar-year basis.

Depreciation must be brought up to date before recording the sale itself. To account for the half-year depreciation in 1996, the following entry is made:

June 30, 1996	Depreciation Expense	11,250	
	[½ × ($510,000 − $60,000)/20]		
	Accumulated Depreciation		11,250

This increases accumulated depreciation on the asset to $146,250, determined as follows:

Depreciation, 1990–1995
[($510,000 − $60,000)/20 years] (6 years) $135,000
Depreciation, Partial Year 1996
[($510,000 − $60,000)/20 years] (½ year)   11,250
                                                $146,250

Many companies would defer recording the depreciation of $11,250 until the end of the year, when depreciation on all plant assets is recognized. Regardless of when the entry is made, the accumulated depreciation used in recording the sale of the asset is $146,250.

The entry for the sale of the asset is then recorded as follows:

June 30, 1996	Cash	425,000	
	Accumulated Depreciation—Building	146,250	
	Building		510,000
	Gain on Sale of Building		61,250

The gain is measured by subtracting the book value from the proceeds of the sale:

$$\text{Gain} = \$425,000 - (\$510,000 - \$146,250) = \$61,250$$

Sometimes assets are **abandoned** without being sold or otherwise disposed. The process of recording a disposal by abandonment is the same as that illustrated above except that no proceeds are received. In this case, the loss equals the book value of the asset after depreciation is updated to the date of abandonment.

Sometimes an enterprise loses an asset due to factors other than its own choice, that is by **involuntary conversion.** Examples are loss by fire, flood, or other disaster. The accounting procedures parallel those for abandonment if *no* insurance proceeds are received; if insurance proceeds *are* received, the accounting procedures are much like those for the sale of plant assets.[4]

To illustrate an exchange transaction, we assume that on June 30, 1996, Gatlin Corporation exchanges the building described above for a building valued at $750,000. Gatlin paid $350,000 in the exchange. Depreciation must first be updated to the date of the transaction, as in previous examples. The exchange is then recorded as follows:

June 30, 1996	Building (new)	750,000	
	Accumulated Depreciation	146,250	
	Building (old)		510,000
	Cash		350,000
	Gain on Exchange of Buildings		36,250

This transaction is a **monetary exchange** because a significant portion of the value Gatlin is giving up is in the form of cash ($350,000/$750,000 = 46.7%).

Companies may dispose of plant assets in a *nonmonetary exchange,* which is a transaction involving little or no cash. For example, a company might exchange equipment for another company's inventory, equipment, or other assets. As a general rule, nonmonetary transactions are accounted for at fair value. This means that the asset acquired is recorded at the fair value of the asset(s) given up or the fair value of the asset(s) received, whichever is more readily determinable. Certain exceptions exist, however, to this general rule. For example, when a company trades a plant asset for another company's plant asset that serves the same purpose, the earning process is not considered complete and any gain that might be implied by the fair values in the transaction is not recorded. A loss in the same transaction

Conservatism

would be recorded, however, due to the modifying convention of conservatism. Another exception to the rule of recording nonmonetary exchanges at fair value arises when fair value cannot be determined. In this situation, the asset acquired is recorded at the book value of the asset given up. These and other complications in accounting for nonmonetary exchanges are discussed in Appendix A of this chapter.

Gains and losses on plant assets are ordinarily not considered to be extraordinary items in the income statement. Depending on the extent of detail in the income statement, such

Materiality

items may be separately disclosed, however. If a gain or loss of this type is material in amount and is judged to be **either** unusual in nature **or** infrequent in occurrence, separate disclosure should be made. *Accounting Principles Board Opinion No. 30* states that in rare instances, an event or transaction may occur that clearly meets the criteria of **unusual in nature** and **infrequent in occurrence** and that results in the disposal of a plant asset.[5] One example is the destruction of a plant asset by a natural disaster, such as an earthquake. Therefore, it is important to consider the underlying cause of a write-down or write-off of a plant asset in judging whether it is an **extraordinary** item or not.

DEPARTURES FROM COST

Asset/Liability Measurement

Cost is well established as the basis for measuring and reporting property, plant, and equipment and is supported by authoritative pronouncements. As with most accounting principles, however, exceptions exist to the general practice of recording and depreciating assets at cost. This section discusses several situations representing departures from the general concepts developed earlier in this chapter.

---

[4]Property insurance, including the computation of amounts to be received on insurance policies that include coinsurance requirements, is covered in Chapter 12. In Chapter 11, any situation involving insurance proceeds states the amount to be received from the insurance recovery.

[5]*APB Opinion No. 30,* "Reporting the Results of Operations," 1973, par. 23.

DONATED ASSETS

Enterprises may receive assets by donation, such as when land is donated to an enterprise by a city as an inducement to locate a facility there. The future advantages to the city result from increased property tax revenues, increased levels of employment, improved reputation, and other positive aspects of increased business activity.

Strict adherence to cost would result in recording the asset acquired at zero or at an amount equal to the relatively minor costs incidental to the acceptance of the land, such as the cost of transferring title. Accounting for donated assets at a zero cost, however, is not generally thought to represent the substance of the transaction in terms of the fair value of the donated asset received by the enterprise.

Accounting for **nonreciprocal transfers,** which are transfers of assets or services in one direction, either to or from the enterprise, is discussed in *APB Opinion No. 29,* which concludes that the receipt of an asset in a nonreciprocal transfer should be based on the fair value of the asset received.[6] The APB relied heavily on the modifying convention of substance over form in reaching this conclusion.

Substance over Form

To illustrate the receipt of a donated asset, we assume that Shelby Company receives land appraised at $130,000 as an inducement to locate a manufacturing facility in the city of Manchester. The receipt of the land and the related contribution by the city is recorded as follows:

Land	130,000	
Donated Capital—Plant Site		130,000

Costs incurred relative to the transfer that *would have been incurred* had the asset been purchased are also charged to the asset account. Any other costs are treated as expenses in the current period. The Donated Capital account becomes a part of the stockholder's equity of the enterprise that receives the donated asset.

PERMANENT IMPAIRMENT IN VALUE

The price that an enterprise pays for a plant asset is based on estimates of future use, of future demand for products and services, and of other considerations of future events. When circumstances dramatically change, plant assets may experience a **permanent impairment in value.**

A permanent impairment in value may occur when the demand for products or services significantly declines, when assets become obsolete or inadequate, or when other circumstances change. Depreciation (allocating cost to the periods benefiting from the use of the asset) is designed to facilitate the determination of net income via the matching principle. Although depreciation accounting is not designed primarily as a method to value an asset, generally assets are not carried in the balance sheet at amounts exceeding their value. We have already seen this practice in the rule of applying the lower of cost or market value to inventory.

Matching

In the case of plant assets, this general rule discourages carrying assets in the accounts or in the balance sheet at amounts exceeding their value. This sometimes means that the future value of the assets has been reduced from that originally expected, even though the assets will continue to be used. In other cases, the assets have become valueless for their original purpose and are worth only their salvage value.

If a permanent impairment in value has occurred, the book value of the asset is reduced by crediting the accumulated depreciation and recognizing a loss. If the asset is to continue

---

[6]*APB Opinion No. 29,* "Accounting for Nonmonetary Transactions," 1973, par. 18.

in use, future depreciation charges may require adjustment to account for revised estimates of useful life, salvage value, and other factors.

To illustrate, we assume that Fraker Company acquired machinery in 1993 for use in producing a line of toys. The asset cost $100,000 and had an expected $20,000 residual value at the end of an expected eight-year life. At the end of 1995, the machinery had a book value of $70,000, computed as follows:

Asset cost in 1993	$100,000
Accumulated depreciation at December 31, 1995 [($100,000 − $20,000)/8] (3 years)	(30,000)
Book value at December 31, 1995	$ 70,000

Because of changes in consumer demand, management determines in early 1996 that the asset is worth substantially less than originally expected. Specifically, it is determined that the book value should be reduced to $20,000; the remaining life, to two years; and the salvage value, to $2,000.

The 1996 entry to record this impairment in value is as follows:

Loss—Obsolescence of Machinery ($70,000 − $20,000)	50,000	
Accumulated Depreciation—Machinery		50,000

Materiality

Depreciation recognized in 1996 and 1997 will be $9,000 [($20,000 − $2,000)/2 years]. If material, the loss of $50,000 should be separately disclosed in the income statement on the basis that it is not a typical transaction that reflects normal business operations. However, this type of loss should *not* be treated as extraordinary.

If the book value of an asset is being reduced to the salvage value and no future use of the asset is expected, an entry similar to the one in the previous paragraph is made for the amount that leaves the estimated residual value as the book value. No further depreciation is recognized on the asset after it has been retired from active service.

In November of 1993, the FASB issued an exposure draft of a proposed statement on the subject of accounting for the impairment of long-lived assets. This exposure draft addresses accounting for long-lived assets when an entity is unable to recover the carrying amount of those assets. Currently, authoritative accounting literature includes relatively little guidance on when an impairment has occurred and the proper accounting for such impairments. The statement proposed in the exposure draft would fill that void.

The proposed statement would require long-lived assets as well as certain intangible assets that are to be held and used by an entity to be reviewed for impairment whenever certain events or changes in circumstances indicate that the carrying amount of the assets may not be recoverable. The entity would estimate the future cash flows expected to result from the use of the asset and its eventual disposal. If the sum of the expected future cash flows is less than the carrying amount of the asset, an impairment would be recognized.[7]

QUASI-REORGANIZATION

A **quasi-reorganization** is a specialized situation in which assets are reduced from their book values to lower estimates of future value. To this extent, the quasi-reorganization is similar to a permanent impairment in value.

The quasi-reorganization differs, however, in that it involves a simultaneous adjustment in the book values of several assets. It represents a general decline in the value of the enterprise rather than the decline in usefulness of one asset or a few specific assets. The quasi-

---

[7]Proposed FASB Statement of Financial Accounting Standards, "Accounting for the Impairment of Long-Lived Assets," 1993.

"YOU KNOW IT WHEN YOU SEE IT"

The following article was published in 1988 and since that time the FASB has considered the subject of asset impairment. The article is still relevant, because it clearly indicates the need for guidance in this important area.

Last winter wasn't a particularly good one for Pillsbury Company, and a footnote in the company's third-quarter report to shareholders showed why: a $113 million loss on the sale or shutdown of several restaurant operations, including its money-losing Godfather's Pizza chain. But precisely how did Pillsbury, which saw its stock jump nearly 10% in value on the day of the announced write-offs, wind up with the $113 million figure? You'll search Pillsbury's financials in vain for an answer, as indeed you would in the case of almost any other company engaged in writing off failed (or failing) assets.

The 1980s are clearly the decade of business restructurings and write-offs. But, ironically, accounting provides few rules to protect shareholders regarding when management can (or must) write off an "impaired asset," and by how much.

Since 1986 the Dow Jones industrials alone have taken at least $10 billion in writedowns, much of it related to impairment questions. A recent study by the National Association of Accountants reports that these impairment write-offs are one of the fastest-growing categories of all asset writedowns. Further, the study concludes that behind the numbers lurks a "a climate of vague accounting standards" that gives companies too much leeway in choosing when and how to write down assets. That feeling was echoed in a survey of accountants by the Financial Accounting Standards Board who ranked impairment at the top of outstanding issues warranting new standards.

Yet many corporations don't seem eager for tightened standards, arguing that management is the best guide for when an asset becomes worthless. Even so, lax accounting standards can lead to abuses. In 1986, for example, the Securities & Exchange Commission took action against Charter Co. for attempting to sell a refinery at well below book value without first writing it down on its balance sheet. Warns Edmund Coulson, chief accountant at the SEC: "There are many other such cases in the pipeline."

What are the rules governing impairment? Under current accounting principles, a long-lived asset (plant, property and so on) should be labeled "impaired" when there is no hope of recovering its book value. Of course, hope, or lack of it, is in the eye of the beholder. Comments Wayne Kolins, partner at accounting firm [BDO Seidman]: "In these situations, it's often a case of people saying, 'You know it when you see it.'"

Once an asset has been judged impaired, companies also have considerable leeway in determining what balance sheet value to assign to it. Among the acceptable methods: net realizable value (what the asset will bring if sold); a total of projected future cash flows over the life of the asset; and "discounting"—the present value of those future cash flows based on a given rate of return. Since future cash flow is worth less than cash in hand, discounting can result in lower valuations and larger write-offs.

To complicate matters, businesses have begun announcing partial writedowns based on "probable" impairment. This includes assets whose return no longer meets carrying costs but which might recover their value in the future. Thus in 1986 Squibb Corp. decided that political and economic conditions in South America and Asia had impaired its pharmaceuticals operations there. Squibb took a writedown of $68 million on those assets, declaring them "permanently" impaired. But are they really? Since Squibb concedes that there remains a "small probability" that those assets will recover, it is operating those facilities on a reduced scale.

With writedowns becoming such a common—and costly—feature of a business scene that is complex enough already, such accounting double-speak is hardly to be welcomed. But without a clarification of the rules, there seems little doubt that it will continue.

SOURCE: Penelope Wang, "You Know It When You See It," *Forbes*, July 25, 1988, p. 84. Reprinted by permission of *Forbes Magazine*. © Forbes Inc., 1988.

reorganization involves adjustments to several stockholders' equity accounts, including Retained Earnings, as part of the process by which the book values of assets are reduced. The circumstances that call for the quasi-reorganization process are considered in Chapter 17.

DISCOVERY VALUE

The value of property may increase significantly if a hidden quality is discovered subsequent to acquisition. An example is the discovery of a valuable natural resource on land subsequent to acquisition. Because the existence of the resource was unknown when the land was acquired, the original cost would not reflect the value exchanged.

The accounting treatment of assets discovered subsequent to acquisition varies considerably, ranging from nonrecognition to the complete recognition of the estimated value of the discovered assets. Accountants generally hesitate to record increases in asset values that have not been verified by transactions with other enterprises. Thus, the most common treatment of discovery value is nonrecognition. This is consistent with the APB's conclusion:

> *The Board is of the opinion that property, plant and equipment should not be written up by an entity to reflect appraisal, market or current values which are above cost to the entity....Whenever appreciation has been recorded on the books, income should be charged with depreciation computed on the written up amounts.*[8]

Some increases in value were recorded prior to this APB pronouncement. In addition, some accountants believe that the discovery of assets that were unknown at the time of acquisition differs from the appreciation in asset value that results from changing market conditions, changes in consumer tastes, or other factors occurring after acquisition. Therefore, an accountant may occasionally encounter an increase in the recorded amount of a plant asset that represents the recording of discovery value. As indicated in *APB Opinion No. 6,* depreciation (or depletion) of the asset should reflect the increased cost basis of the asset. Accountants generally agree that when such asset write-ups are appropriate, the credit side of the entry should be to the stockholders' equity rather than to a revenue or gain account.

To illustrate, we assume that Royal Mining Company acquired land for $200,000 in 1994. In 1996 Royal discovered on the land mineral deposits in the estimated amount of 7,000 tons and appraised at $40 per ton (net of anticipated extraction costs). Management estimates that the land will be worth its original cost of $200,000 after the extraction of the mineral deposits. The entries to record these events assume that 15,700 tons were extracted and sold in 1996:

1994	Land	200,000	
	Cash		200,000
1996	Land—Mineral Deposits Discovered	280,000	
	Unrealized Capital Increment—		
	Discovery of Mineral Deposits		280,000
	(7,000 tons × $40)		
	Depletion Expense	58,613	
	Land—Mineral Deposits Discovered		58,613
	[(15,700/75,000) × $280,000 = $58,613]		

The capital account, Unrealized Capital Increment—Discovery of Mineral Deposits, is presented as part of the stockholders' equity section in the balance sheet.

At the end of Chapter 12, after completing our study of plant assets and depreciation, we look more carefully at the disclosure requirements for property, plant, and equipment. Many companies include only total amounts for property, plant, and equipment in their balance sheets and then provide greater detail in notes to the financial statements. This is the approach taken by Meredith Corporation in the disclosure found in Exhibit 11–5. Meredith is a diversified media company that publishes many well-known magazines, including *Ladies Home Journal* and *Better Homes and Gardens.*

PROFESSIONAL JUDGMENT

Professional judgment is required in many instances of acquisition and disposal of plant assets. Even the characteristics of plant assets as being **primarily** for use in operations rather than for resale and having **relatively** long lives are descriptions requiring the application of professional judgment.

The principle of historical cost is often supported on the basis of its objectivity, meaning that it is a way to quantify an asset that is based on a transaction for which market price is determined in a transaction between a willing buyer and a willing seller. The establishment of cost, however, may require the application of judgment. Examples for which this is true follow:

---

[8]*APB Opinion No. 6,* "Omnibus Opinion," 1965, par. 17.

EXHIBIT 11–5

**Meredith Corporation
Plant Asset Disclosure**

5. Property, Plant, and Equipment
A comparative summary of property, plant and equipment follows:

	1993	1992	1991
			(in thousands)
Land and improvements	$ 6,239	$ 5,835	$ 5,684
Buildings and improvements	53,473	51,861	51,793
Machinery and equipment	95,604	92,166	92,858
Cable distribution system	76,116	9,167	—
Leasehold improvements	4,741	4,748	4,882
Construction in progress	2,506	746	1,333
Total (at cost)	238,679	164,523	156,550
Less accumulated depreciation	(107,792)	(95,094)	(90,553)
Net property, plant, and equipment	$ 130,887	$ 69,429	$ 65,997
Depreciation expense for the year	$ 16,014	$ 10,718	$ 11,714

For each classification of property, plant and equipment, depreciable lives are as follows:

	Depreciable Life
Buildings and improvements	5 to 45 years
Machinery and equipment	3 to 20 years
Leasehold improvements	4 to 15 years
Cable distribution system	5 to 15 years

SOURCE: Meredith Corporation, 1993 Annual Report.

1. Imputed interest—When interest must be imputed to separate a purchase price into the cost of the asset and the interest being paid, the accountant must select an imputed rate.

2. Internally constructed assets—When assets are constructed internally, accountants must make decisions concerning the material, labor, and overhead that should be associated with those assets. These decisions require judgment, particularly when the constructed asset is comingled with inventory under construction.

3. Capitalization of interest—Accountants may have to use judgment to identify outstanding debt securities that relate directly to a construction project or to determine the average investment when materials, labor, and overhead flow into the project on a continuous basis.

4. Issuance of securities—When securities are issued in exchange for a plant asset, accountants may be required to use judgment in establishing the fair value inherent in the transaction, particularly in the case of securities which do not actively trade and assets for which there is no established market value (e.g., used assets).

5. Basket purchase—When a single price is paid for a group of assets, accountants must estimate individual fair values to properly allocate the total purchase price to the individual assets.

Accounting for postacquisition expenditures may also require judgments. For example, whether a particular expenditure is capital or revenue is critically important to subsequent accounting for those expenditures. Whether an expenditure is a replacement or betterment and whether it is made to improve the quality of asset performance or to extend the useful life of the asset are judgments that affect the manner with which the expenditure is dealt. In accounting for repairs and maintenance via the allowance method, estimating the amount of the allowance to recognize is an important judgment that is based on past performance.

Many other areas of accounting for plant assets require seasoned professional judgment. Valuing donated assets, determining whether an asset has experienced an impairment in value, and estimating the amount of that impairment and assessing the value of assets discovered on previously purchased property are additional examples of judgments required.

Although historical cost may be more objective than some alternative methods of valuation (e.g., current value), these examples emphasize the significant judgment required in determining historical cost. These judgments become even more pronounced when we consider the subject of depreciation in Chapter 12.

CONCLUDING REMARKS

Asset/Liability Measurement

Several accounting principles are significant in accounting for plant assets. Chapter 11 has focused primarily on the determination of *historical cost* as the principle means of measuring plant assets. Although cost may seem to be a relatively simple and straightforward principle, complications arise in a variety of circumstances, such as the purchase of more than one asset in a single transaction, the treatment of costs related to acquisition, the internal construction of plant assets, the incurrence of interest cost in the construction of plant assets, and postacquisition expenditures that may impact the cost of plant assets. Generally accepted accounting principles in all of these situations reflect the considered judgment of accountants in determining cost.

Consistency

Materiality

In determining cost, *objectivity* is important. Accountants base their measurements on objective, verifiable evidence to the extent possible. The *consistency principle* is also important in the treatment of plant asset expenditures because similar expenditures are made from period to period. The *materiality principle* comes into play in accounting for plant assets, as it does in virtually all areas of accounting. The strict application of the principles discussed in this chapter is not required if the results are insignificant and, therefore, not cost effective.

Matching

One of the primary purposes for carefully establishing the correct cost of plant assets is to determine the appropriate amount for depreciation in accordance with the matching principle. In the next chapter, we consider depreciation of plant assets in depth, building on the general principles of cost determination discussed here.

KEY POINTS

1. Property, plant, and equipment and intangible assets are long-lived assets that are acquired for use in the production and distribution of goods and services. (Objective 1)
2. Several basic accounting principles impact the proper accounting for plant and intangible assets. Most notable are the principles of asset measurement at cost and matching. (Objective 2)
3. Several unique problems may be encountered in attempting to determine the cost of specific types of plant assets, such as land, buildings, machinery, equipment, furniture, fixtures, and natural resources. (Objective 3)
4. Particular care must be taken in establishing the cost of plant assets when the following are involved:
   a. Cash discounts.
   b. Deferred-payment plans.
   c. Internally constructed plant assets.
   d. Capitalization of interest.
   e. Acquisition by issuing securities.
   f. Basket purchases.
   g. Installation, preparation, and start-up costs. (Objective 3)
5. An important distinction in accounting for postacquisition expenditures is to separate capital expenditures from revenue expenditures. Capital expenditures are amortized over their estimated useful lives, whereas revenue expenditures are charged to expense as incurred. (Objective 4)
6. Disposals of plant assets may result from sales, abandonments, involuntary conversions, or exchanges. Disposals may result in gains or losses, which are presented as part of net income. (Objective 5)
7. Certain specialized situations dictate a departure from historical cost in accounting for plant assets. These exceptions are found in the cases of donated assets, permanent impairments in value, quasi reorganizations, and discovery value. (Objective 6)

APPENDIX A: ACQUISITIONS AND DISPOSALS BY EXCHANGE

An enterprise may be a party to an **exchange** transaction whereby it simultaneously acquires an asset and disposes of another one. For example, an enterprise may exchange land that it owns for land held by another enterprise. Also, used machinery may be exchanged for other used machinery. Transactions like this are called **nonmonetary transactions.** The Accounting Principles Board (APB) established the proper accounting for nonmonetary transactions in *Opinion No. 29,* which was cited earlier in this chapter.

CONCEPTS UNDERLYING EXCHANGE TRANSACTIONS

The general principle governing the recording of a nonmonetary exchange is to record the acquired asset at the **fair value** of the assets involved in the exchange. The fair value of the surrendered asset is used as a measure of the cost of the acquired asset, and a gain or loss may be recognized on the exchange. This principle was illustrated earlier in this chapter when we recorded the exchange of buildings. However, if the fair value of the asset received is more clearly evident than the fair value of the asset surrendered, the former amount is used. Fair value of a nonmonetary asset may be established by estimated realizable value in cash transactions of similar assets, quoted market prices, independent appraisals, and other available evidence.

Modification of this fair value concept is required in several circumstances, including instances in which fair value is not determinable or the transaction does not result in the completion of an earning process. In some circumstances, the fair value of assets surrendered or received cannot be determined within reasonably objective limits. In these cases, the acquired asset is recorded at the book value of the surrendered asset. No gain or loss on the exchange is recorded, because the new asset is simply substituted for the old asset in the accounts.

Two types of nonmonetary exchanges are not considered to result in the completion of an earning process:

1.　*An exchange of a product or property held for sale in the ordinary course of business for a product or property to be sold in the same line of business to facilitate sales to customers other than parties to the exchange.*

2.　*An exchange of a productive asset not held for sale in the ordinary course of business for a similar productive asset or an equivalent interest in the same or similar productive asset.*[9]

In the first case, inventory is exchanged for inventory. A subsequent transaction in which the inventory is sold to the ultimate customer must take place before the earning process is considered complete. In the second case, productive assets are exchanged for productive assets of the same general type performing essentially the same function. The earning process is not considered complete until these assets are used in the production of goods or services that are sold. These transactions are sometimes referred to as *swaps* of inventory or similar productive assets.

Assets acquired in swaps are generally recorded at the book value of the assets surrendered, and no gain is recognized

[9]*APB Opinion No. 29,* par. 21.

as a result of the exchange. Exchanges may include a small amount of cash, referred to as "boot," to adjust for a difference in the values of the assets exchanged. If boot is received in a transaction in which a gain is apparent (i.e., the fair value received exceeds the book value surrendered), the recipient of the boot has realized a gain to the extent that the cash received exceeds a pro rata share of the book value of the surrendered asset. This gain and the acquired asset should be recorded at a pro rata share of the book value of the surrendered asset.

In certain circumstances, the fair value inherent in a swap of inventory or plant assets may indicate that a loss would be recorded if fair value were the basis for recording the transaction. In such cases, fair value is used and the loss is recognized

Conservatism　in accordance with the modifying convention of conservatism. Methods of accounting for assets acquired through nonmonetary exchanges are summarized in Exhibit 11–6.

In summary, recording nonmonetary transactions repre-

Revenue Realization　sents an interesting application of the accounting principles of revenue realization and asset measurement and of the modifying convention

Asset/Liability Measurement　of conservatism. Transactions are generally recorded on the basis of fair value, which is consistent with revenue-realization and his-

Conservatism　torical cost if the transaction represents the completion of an earning process. If the earning process is not complete, however, the acquired asset is recorded at the book value of the surrendered asset unless a loss is apparent; in that case, the loss is recorded

Conservatism　in accordance with the modifying convention of conservatism. In a nonmonetary transaction

Revenue Realization　that does not complete the earning process and in which a gain is apparent and boot is received, the revenue-realization principle requires that a gain be recognized to the extent that boot received exceeds a proportionate share of the book value of the asset surrendered.

ILLUSTRATIONS OF EXCHANGE TRANSACTIONS

This section analyzes a number of transactions, each of which illustrates a different concept in recording exchange transactions. In each independent case, Carland Company is trading equipment. The following information is common to all cases:

Cost of equipment traded	$100,000
Accumulated depreciation to date of trade	40,000
Book value of equipment traded	$ 60,000

Example 1

Carland trades the equipment for several trucks. The value of the equipment is not determinable, but the trucks have a total estimated market value of $75,000. No cash is involved in the transaction.

This transaction is a nonmonetary exchange that represents the **completion** of an earning process, because the assets exchanged are *not similar in nature.* Because the fair value of the equipment is not determinable, the fair value of the trucks

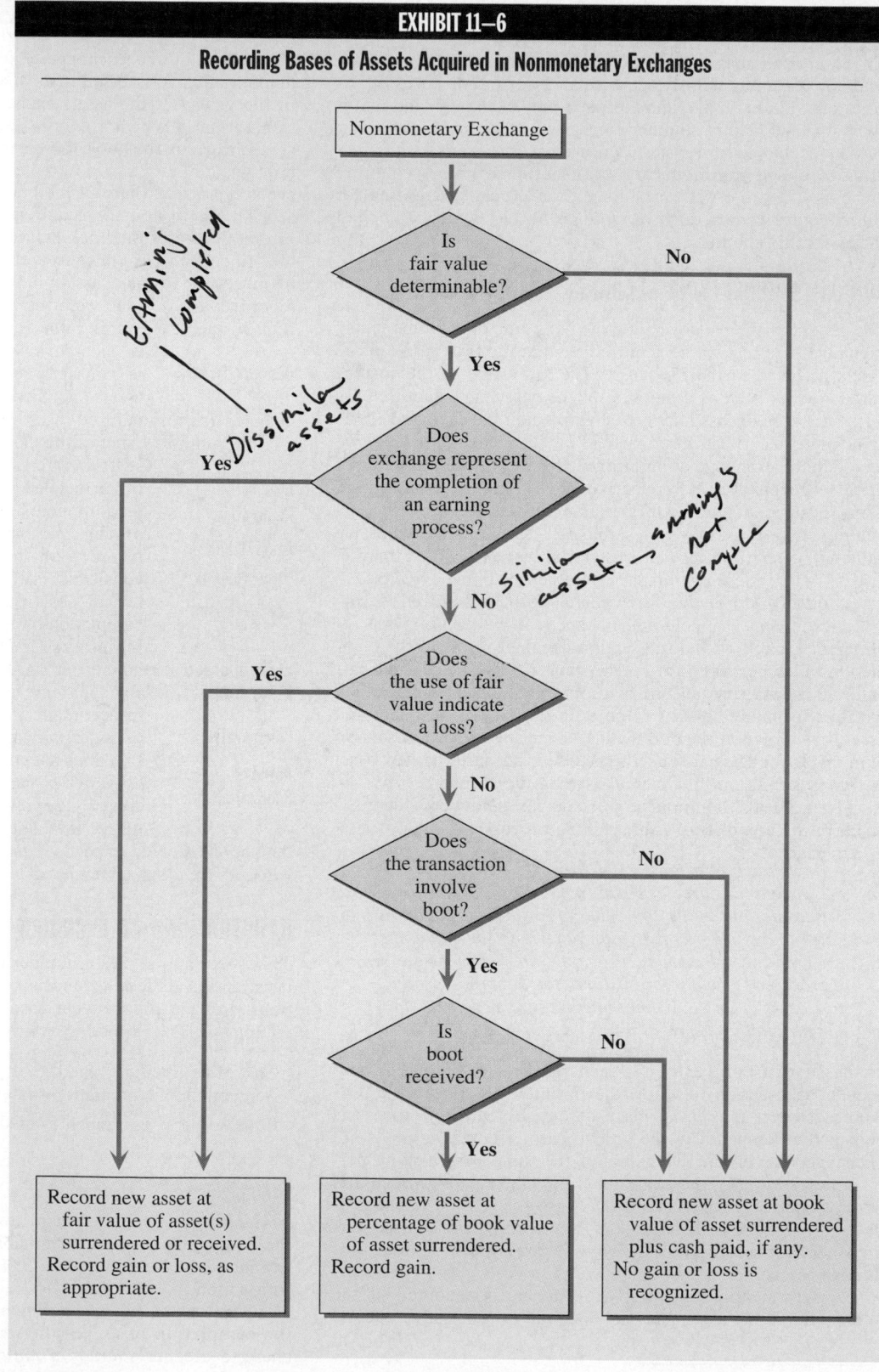

EXHIBIT 11–6

Recording Bases of Assets Acquired in Nonmonetary Exchanges

received is used as the value inherent in the transaction. The assets acquired are recorded at fair value, and any resulting gain or loss is recorded as follows:

Trucks	75,000	
Accumulated Depreciation—		
Equipment	40,000	
Equipment		100,000
Gain on Exchange of		
Assets		15,000

If boot had been either received or paid, cash would have been either debited or credited as part of the entry.

Example 2

Carland trades the equipment for office furniture. The value of neither the equipment nor the office furniture can be determined objectively.

This transaction is recorded on the basis of the book value of the assets surrendered, because the fair value being exchanged cannot be determined. No gain or loss is recognized. The following entry is appropriate:

Office Furniture	60,000	
Accumulated Depreciation—		
Equipment	40,000	
Equipment		100,000

Example 3

Carland exchanges the equipment, which has an appraised value of $50,000, and pays an additional $5,000 in exchange for similar equipment for which a value cannot be readily determined.

This transaction does not represent the completion of an earning process, because similar assets are exchanged. Although such transactions would normally be recorded on the basis of the book value of the assets surrendered, any loss indicated must be recorded. In this case, a loss is indicated, determined as follows:

Recorded amount of assets surrendered		
Equipment	$60,000	
Cash	5,000	$65,000
Fair value inherent in transaction		
Fair value of equipment surrendered	50,000	
Cash paid	5,000	(55,000)
Loss indicated		$10,000

Conservatism   Because a loss is indicated, conservatism dictates that the assets acquired be recorded at the fair value inherent in the transaction and the loss recognized, as follows:

Equipment (new)	55,000	
Loss on Exchange of Equipment	10,000	
Accumulated Depreciation—		
Equipment	40,000	
Equipment (old)		100,000
Cash		5,000

Example 4

Carland trades the equipment, valued at $67,000, for similar equipment for which no fair value is determinable. A gain is apparent in the transaction, computed as follows:

Fair value inherent in transaction	
Fair value of asset surrendered	$67,000
Recorded amount of asset surrendered	
Equipment	(60,000)
Gain indicated	$ 7,000

However, the gain is not recorded, because the *earning process has not been completed*. The transaction is recorded as follows:

Equipment (new)	60,000	
Accumulated Depreciation—		
Equipment	40,000	
Equipment (old)		100,000

Example 5

Carland exchanges the equipment (valued at $65,000) and $5,000 cash for similar equipment for which a market value is not determinable.

This transaction *does not represent the completion of the earning process*, because similar items of equipment are being exchanged. A gain is indicated because the fair value inherent in the transaction exceeds the recorded amounts of assets surrendered.

Fair value inherent in transaction		
Fair value of equipment surrendered	$65,000	
Cash	5,000	$70,000
Recorded amount of assets surrendered		
Equipment	60,000	
Cash	5,000	(65,000)
Gains indicated		$ 5,000

The **gain is not recorded,** and the equipment acquired is recorded at the book value of the equipment surrendered plus the $5,000 cash paid:

Equipment (new)	65,000	
Accumulated Depreciation—		
Equipment	40,000	
Equipment (old)		100,000
Cash		5,000

Example 6

Carland trades the equipment for similar productive equipment valued at $69,000. In addition, Carland receives $6,000 in cash.

Although this is a nonmonetary exchange that does not represent the completion of an earning process, the *receipt of boot in a gain situation* requires recognition of a gain to the extent that the cash received exceeds an appropriate portion of the book value surrendered. The gain inherent in the transaction is computed as follows:

Fair value inherent in transaction		
Cash received	$ 6,000	
Fair value of equipment received	69,000	$75,000
Recorded amount of asset surrendered		
Equipment		(60,000)
Gain indicated		$ 15,000

The portion of the transaction that represents a sale is determined by dividing the cash received by the total fair value inherent in the transaction:

$$\text{Sale }\% = \frac{\$6,000}{\$75,000} = 8\%$$

The book value of the equipment surrendered must be separated into the portion sold (8%) and the portion traded (100% − 8% = 92%):

Book value sold: $60,000 × 8% =	$ 4,800
Book value traded: $60,000 × 92% =	55,200
	$60,000

The gain recognized in the transaction is measured as follows:

Cash received	$6,000
Book value sold	(4,800)
Gain recognized	$1,200

The $1,200 can also be computed by multiplying the total gain on the transaction by the percentage of the transaction representing a sale:

$$\$15,000 \times 8\% = \$1,200.$$

The acquired equipment is recorded at the book value of that portion of the assets surrendered that is considered to have been traded ($60,000 × 92%, or $55,200):

Equipment (new)	55,200	
Accumulated Depreciation—		
Equipment	40,000	
Cash	6,000	
Equipment (old)		100,000
Gain on Exchange of		
Equipment		1,200

Asset/Liability Measurement

Conservatism

These methods reveal the influence of historical cost as a means to measure plant assets and the modifying convention of conservatism. The nonrecognition of gains in transactions that do not complete the earning process is designed to prevent artificial write-ups of assets and the recording of gains in value from holding assets that result from meaningless transactions in which similar assets are exchanged. One word of caution: The use of fair value in recording exchanges of unlike assets is *not a departure* from historical cost. Rather, it is an *application* of that method, because the cost in a noncash transaction (or part-cash transaction) is the fair value of the consideration given up to acquire that asset. If the fair value of the asset received is more clearly determinable, however, we use it as a substitute measure of cost.

Research in the area of nonmonetary exchanges has revealed some interesting interpretative findings concerning *APB Opinion No. 29*. One is that the Accounting Principles Board intended to apply the exception to the general rule to exchanges of similar nonmonetary transactions only when both parties to the transaction are either dealers or nondealers. For example, an exchange of trucks between two parties, both of which intend to use the vehicles in their operations to deliver merchandise to customers, would be considered an exchange of similar productive assets. In contrast, an exchange of trucks between a truck-dealer (for which the truck is inventory) and a retailer that will use the vehicle in its operations would be considered an exchange of nonsimilar assets.

A second observation is that as the amount of boot received in a transaction increases, the portion of the transaction representing a sale increases and, hence, the amount of the gain to be recognized increases. The general rule for exchange transactions applies to the monetary portion of the exchange, whereas the exception to the rule applies to the nonmonetary portion.[10]

---

[10]James B. Hobbs and D. R. Bainbridge, "Nonmonetary Exchange Transactions: Clarification of APB Opinion No. 29," *Accounting Review* (January 1982), pp. 171–175.

QUESTIONS

11–1   What are the two primary characteristics of all plant and intangible assets?

11–2   How do plant and intangible assets differ? Identify several types of each.

11–3   What are four principles that underlie accounting for plant and intangible assets?

11–4   What is the "full-cost" interpretation of historical cost, as applied to plant assets?

11–5   In determining the full cost of land, what expenditures in addition to the bargained acquisition price might be included?

11–6   Why is it generally desirable for land improvements to be capitalized in a separate account from the Land account?

11–7   How should land that is held for investment or speculative purposes be classified in the balance sheet?

11–8 For items of machinery, equipment, furniture, and fixtures, what expenditures may be included in the cost figure in addition to the original acquisition price?

11–9 What is the preferred treatment of cash discounts in determining the cost of plant assets?

11–10 In what circumstances may it be necessary to *impute* interest included in the payments in a deferred payment plan for plant assets? What is the purpose of imputing interest?

11–11 What distortions will exist in the financial statements of the buyer of a plant asset if interest is not imputed on an installment contract for which interest should have been imputed?

11–12 As a general rule, a careful distinction is maintained between interest and the cost of plant assets. In certain circumstances, however, it is appropriate to capitalize interest in establishing the correct cost of an asset. What are these circumstances?

11–13 When a plant asset is acquired by issuing capital stock, what is the appropriate basis for recording the asset acquired?

11–14 If several assets are acquired in a single transaction for one price, how is the recorded cost of the individual assets determined?

11–15 Enterprises may produce their own plant assets to use in future operations. Determining the cost of these assets is complicated by the fact that production activities of plant assets may be mixed with production activities of inventory items. Describe how the cost of internally developed assets should be determined, including an identification of specific costs to be included.

11–16 How do capital expenditures and revenue expenditures differ? Cite several examples of each.

11–17 How does the accounting treatment of the following three types of betterments differ?

[a] Substitution of part of an asset when separate cost identification is possible.

[b] Substitution of part of an asset when separate cost identification is not possible and the advantage of the expenditure is improved quality of future services.

[c] Substitution of part of an asset when separate cost identification is not possible and the advantage of the expenditure is an extension of the useful life of the asset.

11–18 Under what circumstances should the allowance method of recognizing repair and maintenance expense be used as an alternative to recognition as costs are incurred? What is the purpose of the allowance method?

11–19 Cardwell Company acquired a three-acre site for the construction of a new branch plant. Which of the following costs (or groups of costs) should *not* be charged to the company's Land account?

[a] Title examination fees, recording fees, and surveying fees.

[b] Costs of grading, clearing, and draining the property.

[c] Costs of removing the old, unwanted building from the land.

[d] Property taxes accruing during the period of plant construction. (AICPA adapted)

11–20 (Appendix A) Assets acquired in exchange transactions may be recorded in one of several ways, depending on the circumstances of the exchange. What are the circumstances in which each of the following bases are appropriate for recording an asset acquired in a nonmonetary exchange?

[a] Fair value inherent in the exchange.

[b] Book value of assets(s) surrendered.

[c] A percentage of the book value of asset(s) surrendered.

11–21 (Appendix A) Horwitz Company received $20,000 in cash and a used computer with a fair value of $180,000 from Harvest Corporation for Horwitz's existing computer having a fair value of $200,000 and an undepreciated cost of $160,000 recorded on its books. Which answer shows, respectively, how much gain Horwitz should recognize on this exchange and at what amount the acquired computer should be recorded?

[a] Zero and $140,000   [c] $20,000 and $160,000

[b] $4,000 and $144,000   [d] $40,000 and $180,000   (AICPA adapted)

11–22 (Appendix A) Sipp Company exchanged inventory items that cost $8,000 and normally sold for $12,000 for a new delivery truck with a list price of $13,000. At which figure should the delivery truck be recorded on Sipp's books?

[a] $8,000   [b] $8,667   [c] $12,000   [d] $13,000   (AICPA adapted)

11–23 How does the accounting for an addition to a plant asset when the addition has a useful life that is independent of the original asset compare with an addition for which the useful life is limited to the remaining life of the original asset?

11–24 Replacements and betterments may be made when identification of the portion of the original asset that is substituted is possible. In other circumstances, separate identification of the portion of the original asset that is being replaced is not possible. How do the accounting treatments for the cost of the replacement or betterment in these circumstances vary?

11–25 What is the proper accounting basis for assets that are donated to an enterprise? Explain the reasoning that underlies your answer.

11–26 How should a permanent impairment in value be accounted for and what impact does that accounting have on future depreciation charges?

EXERCISES

11–27 Building and Land Cost   Weber Company acquired land and a building for $275,000. The land was appraised at $125,000 and the building at $175,000. Weber assumed unpaid property taxes of $12,000, 40% allocated to the land and 60% to the building. Additional costs incurred were

[1] Building renovation, $57,500.
[2] Option on alternative land and building that were not acquired, $1,750.
[3] Cost of survey, $210.

INSTRUCTIONS

Determine the cost of the building and the land, identifying the individual elements of cost included in each asset.

11–28 Plant Asset Acquisition Cost   Saxon Co. recently acquired several items of property, plant, and equipment. The transactions are described as follows:

June   5   Purchased land appraised at $175,000 and machinery appraised at $50,000 for a total of $195,000.

July   16   Purchased a building for $185,000 in cash and 100,000 shares of Saxon's $7 par value common stock, which sold for $10 on the transaction date.

Aug.   21   Received a parcel of land from the city of Hillsboro as an inducement to locate a plant there. No payment was required. The land was appraised at $65,000.

Sept.   25   Acquired furniture and fixtures by issuing a $75,000, two-year, noninterest-bearing note. In similar transactions, the company has paid 12% interest.

INSTRUCTIONS

Prepare the journal entry appropriate in each case to record the acquisition of property, plant, and equipment.

11–29 Land Cost   Blauser Company acquired land on June 1, 1996, for $170,000, on which a new building will be immediately constructed. Costs related to the acquisition include the following:

[1] A commission of 4% of the price for the location of the land and the negotiation of the acquisition price.
[2] $1,700 for legal fees related to the transfer of the title of the land and other matters.
[3] $550 for a survey pursuant to the closing of the transaction.
[4] $2,500 for options acquired at an earlier date: $1,500 for the land acquired, and $1,000 for an alternative parcel of land that was seriously considered but not acquired.
[5] $16,000 for removal of an existing building. $2,750 was received from the salvage of materials.
[6] $2,400 for 1995 property taxes that were delinquent on June 1, 1996. Taxes for 1996 are expected to be $3,000 and will be paid by Blauser before December 31, 1996.

INSTRUCTIONS

Determine the total cost of the land as it should be presented in the company's balance sheet on December 31, 1996.

11–30 Fixtures Cost   Flank Company acquired several fixtures for its new building, including display cases, shelves, and hanging racks. The invoice price of the fixtures was $72,500. The company received a 2% cash discount by paying within the discount period. Freight and insurance during shipment totaled $410. Costs of assembling and installing the fixtures were $475. While installing a display case, a new employee carelessly broke a glass top. This top was replaced at a cost of $220.

INSTRUCTIONS

Determine the total cost of the fixtures, identifying the individual elements making up the total.

11–31 Equipment Transactions   On January 1, 1996, Prosser Company acquired used equipment by issuing the seller a two-year, noninterest-bearing note for $200,000. The value of the equipment is apparently less than $200,000, but a specific amount cannot be determined. In recent borrowings, Prosser has paid 10% interest.

On January 7, the company installed the equipment. Estimated costs of installation were $1,750 for labor and $670 for materials, both included in the manufacturing accounts. On January 12, the company paid $780 for freight and insurance charges during shipment.

INSTRUCTIONS

[a] Prepare general journal entries for the preceding transactions and for adjustments required on December 31, 1996. Provide supporting computations. The company plans to depreciate the asset over eight years, with the salvage value being approximately equal to the costs of removal. Straight-line depreciation should be used. Interest is recognized by the effective interest method.

[b] What amount of interest expense will be recognized at December 31, 1997, on the equipment note?

11–32 Plant Asset Transactions   Darmon, Inc., acquired the following plant assets during the current year:

Equipment.   Acquired at an invoice price of $60,000, subject to a 1% cash discount that was not taken. Freight and insurance during shipment cost $350. The equipment has a five-year life expectancy and a salvage value of 10% of the invoice price.

Land.   Acquired by issuing 10,000 shares of Darmon's $5 par value common stock when the market price of the stock was $17. The stock issued was treasury stock that had been acquired at an earlier date at $9 per share.

Machinery.   Acquired at a cost of $27,600. Installation costs were $770. Trial runs and other testing cost $510. These expenses have been included in the Manufacturing Overhead account. The machinery is expected to be useful for 10 years, at the end of which it will have a $3,200 salvage value.

INSTRUCTIONS

Prepare all general journal entries needed to record the acquisition and depreciation of the assets for the current year. Straight-line depreciation should be used with a full year recognized.

11–33 Internally Constructed Assets   Wicker Company decided to construct its own equipment rather than acquire similar assets from other companies. Management believed that building the assets would cost less than buying them. Material and labor costs were determined to be $175,000 and $220,000, respectively. Overhead is normally charged to production at the rate of 85% of the direct labor cost. The actual increment in overhead resulting from the construction was determined to be $162,000.

INSTRUCTIONS

Assuming that the company is operating at full capacity and must curtail production operations to construct the equipment, determine the appropriate amounts to be capitalized as the cost of the equipment. Justify your treatment of overhead costs.

11–34 Building Addition   Emmerson Company acquired a building in 1986 for $200,000. It depreciated the building through 1995 (10 years) by the straight-line method, assuming a 25-year life and a value at the end of that life of $50,000. In 1996 the company added a wing to the building at a cost of $250,000. The wing is expected to have a useful life of 40 years and was constructed in a way that permits its use beyond the life of the original building. No salvage value is expected on the addition.

INSTRUCTIONS

Prepare all journal entries to record the 1996 transactions, including depreciation on both the original building and the addition.

11–35 Building Addition   Wilmer, Inc., contracted for the construction of a wing on its warehouse. Work was completed during 1996, at which time Wilmer paid the entire purchase price of $100,000. The original building had a cost of $175,000, with accumulated depreciation of $85,000, at the time the new wing was completed. A facility like the new wing would ordinarily be expected to have a useful life of 25 years, but the construction design limits its useful life to the life of the original structure, which is only 10 years. No salvage value is assumed for either the original building or the addition.

INSTRUCTIONS

Prepare all journal entries to record the 1996 transactions, including depreciation on both the original structure and the new wing.

11–36 (Appendix A) Nonmonetary Exchange   Mannis Company recently swapped used machinery for similar used machinery with a competing company. Mannis's previous machinery cost $7,000 and had a book value of $5,500 at the time of the trade. The machinery's estimated value was $6,200, and Mannis paid $500 in cash as part of the transaction. Machinery received in the trade had not been appraised recently. Mannis's accountant recorded the trade as follows:

Machinery (new)	6,700	
Accumulated Depreciation	1,500	
Machinery (old)		7,000
Cash		500
Gain on Exchange of Machinery		700

INSTRUCTIONS

[a] Prepare the general journal entry you would suggest for recording the transaction.
[b] Explain the fallacy, if any, in the accountant's entry and how your entry corrects that problem.

11–37 Replacement   Warf, Inc., replaced a portion of its building for $875,000. Before the replacement, the Building and Accumulated Depreciation accounts were as follows:

Building	$3,500,000
Accumulated depreciation	(2,250,000)
	$1,250,000

INSTRUCTIONS

Prepare the general journal entry to record the $875,000 expenditure in each of the following *independent* cases:

[a] Separate identification of the portion of the building being replaced is not possible. The replacement was designed to improve the service potential of the total facility for the remainder of its original expected useful life.
[b] The portion of the building being replaced accounts for $1,000,000 and $785,000 of the Building and Accumulated Depreciation accounts, respectively.
[c] Separate identification of the portion of the building being replaced is not possible. The primary purpose of the expenditure is to lengthen the life of the building from that orginally estimated.

11–38 Miscellaneous Plant Asset Entries   Reese, Inc., engaged in the following transactions involving plant assets during the current year:

[1] A building expansion costing $350,000 is expected to provide service for 20 years, even though the original building will be useful for only 10 more years.
[2] The base of a machine was replaced for $9,000. The portion of the orginal cost allocated to the base was $5,000, and the cost of the asset was 40% depreciated at the time of the replacement. The old base was sold for $800. The new base is expected to serve the machine to the end of its useful life.
[3] Reese made a number of improvements in a building for $95,000. The cost of items replaced could not be determined. The improvements were made to ensure the original estimated useful life of the building.
[4] The relocation required to move into the new addition cost $17,500. Management believes that the relocation will benefit the company for at least five years.
[5] Servicing machinery on a regular basis resulted in expenditures of $5,200.

INSTRUCTIONS

[a] Prepare the general journal entry to record each transaction.
[b] Describe the appropriate period of depreciation or amortization of any items capitalized in each entry.

11–39 Impairment in Value   CD, Inc., invested heavily in equipment that was needed to produce a new line of stereophonic equipment. On January 1, 1996, the cost and accumulated depreciation balances on the equipment were as follows:

Equipment	$5,250,000
Accumulated depreciation	(2,700,000)
	$2,550,000

Due to changes in consumer tastes and unexpected advances in electronics, CD's management now believes that the future service potential of the equipment is greatly reduced and the useful life is much shorter than originally estimated. Specifically, management believes the future service potential of the asset is limited to $1,000,000 and the future life extends only through 1997.

INSTRUCTIONS

Determine the amounts that should be presented in the company's balance sheet and income statement relative to the equipment at December 31, 1996.

11–40 Correction of Errors Lemke, Inc., carried out a number of transactions involving the acquisition of several assets. All expenditures were recorded in the following single asset account, identified as Fixed Assets:

Fixed Assets	
Acquisition price of land and building	$120,000
Options taken out on several pieces of property	2,000
List price of machinery purchased	39,800
Freight on machinery purchased	625
Repair to machinery resulting from damage during shipment	185
Cost of removing old machinery	600
Driveways and sidewalks	12,750
Building remodeling	60,000
Utilities paid since acquisition of building	1,700
	$237,660

Based on property tax assessments, which are believed to fairly represent the relative values involved, the building is worth twice as much as the land. The machinery was subject to a 2% cash discount, which was taken and credited to Purchases Discounts. Of the two options, $750 related to the building and land purchased and $1,250 related to those not purchased. The old machinery was sold at book value.

INSTRUCTIONS

Prepare the general journal entry or entries to close out the Fixed Asset account and establish appropriate individual plant asset accounts. Provide supporting calculations for the amounts capitalized in each account. All expenditures were made in the current year and the books have not been closed.

11–41 Building Disposals Estes, Incorporated, owns a building with a book value of $85,000 on October 31, 1995, the end of the company's fiscal year.

Building	$180,000
Accumulated depreciation	(95,000)
	$ 85,000

Depreciation is computed by the straight-line method at $1,500 per month.

INSTRUCTIONS

Prepare the general jounral entry or entries to record the disposal of the building under each of the following *independent* situations:

[a] The building is sold on June 30, 1996, for $105,000.

[b] The company incurs costs of $15,800 to improve the building in preparation for its sale. The building is sold on August 31, 1996, for $97,000.

[c] The building is destroyed by fire on March 31, 1996. Proceeds from insurance total $69,800.

11–42 Capitalization of Interest Cost Houston Company entered into a contract with Dallas Company to construct a building for Houston. The contract called for work to begin on June 1, 1995, and for Houston to make an initial payment of $100,000 at that time. Houston was to pay another $50,000 at the end of each three-month period until May 31, 1996, when the final $50,000 payment was due and the building was to be completed and placed into service.

All aspects of the contract were completed on schedule. Houston made the payments from existing working capital and did not incur any additional debt for the specific purpose of financing the construction of the building. Throughout the construction period, however, Houston had $750,000 of debt outstanding at an average interest rate of 11.5%.

INSTRUCTIONS

[a] Determine the appropriate cost of the building on the books of Houston Company.

[b] Explain the rationale for the various components of cost in [a].

11–43 (Appendix A)   Machinery Disposals   Stacy Manufacturing Company plans to eliminate a machine. The machine has the following cost and accumulated depreciation at the time of the anticipated transaction:

Machinery	$75,000
Accumulated depreciation	(62,500)
	$12,500

INSTRUCTIONS

Prepare the general journal entry to record the disposal in each of these *independent* cases:

[a] The machine is appraised at $17,000 and is traded for a patent with an unknown value.

[b] The machine is appraised at $5,000 and is traded for a similar machine with an indeterminate value. In addition, cash of $27,000 is paid.

[c] The machine is sold for $13,700 cash.

[d] The machine is traded, along with $400 cash, for a similar machine with an appraisal value of $15,000.

[e] The machine is traded for a similar machine with a value of $15,000. In addition, $1,000 cash is received.

11–44   Repair and Maintenance Expense   The controller of Tucker, Inc., asked you to review the Repair and Maintenance Expense account for the year to determine whether all of the charges are appropriate. You have identified the following 10 transactions for further scrutiny. All of these transactions are considered material in amount.

Date	Amount	Description
Jan. 3	$10,000	Service contract on office equipment.
Mar. 7	10,000	Initial design fee for proposed extension of office building.
Apr. 12	7,500	New condenser for central air conditioning unit located on the roof of office building.
Apr. 20	7,000	Purchase of two executive chairs and desks.
May 12	40,850	Purchase of storm windows and screens and their installation on all office windows.
May 18	8,450	Sealing of roof leaks in production plant.
June 19	1,780	Replacement of large door to production area.
July 3	11,740	Installation of automatic door-opening system on the above door to speed opening.
Sept. 14	38,500	Overhead crane for the assembly department to speed up production.
Oct. 18	11,000	Replacement of broken gear on machine in the machining department.

INSTRUCTIONS

For each of these transactions, indicate whether the Repair and Maintenance Expense account is properly charged and, if not, indicate the appropriate account to which the transaction should be charged. Explain your reasoning in each case.   (CMA adapted)

PROBLEMS

11–45   Cost Determination   Determining historical cost may be complicated by a number of factors related to the transaction in which the asset is acquired. Chumley Company has been involved in a number of transactions in which plant assets have been acquired.

INSTRUCTIONS

In each of the following *independent* situations, determine the cost of the plant assets to Chumley Company:

[a] Land and building are acquired for $580,000. The building is demolished at a cost of $37,000 to make way for a new facility to be constructed in the future. Proceeds of $10,000 were received from salvaged materials from the old building.

[b] Land and building are acquired for $500,000 and are appraised at $200,000 and $350,000, respectively. Plans call for the renovation of the building, after which it will be used in future operations.

[c] Land is acquired at a cost of $135,000. An option had been taken out earlier for $5,000, which guaranteed the purchase price for 90 days. Another option for $5,000 was negotiated on an alternative land site that was not acquired. Legal costs related to the acquisition were $650.

[d] Land was purchased by issuing 1,200 shares of common stock. The stock has a market value of $16 per share and a par value of $10. No independent appraisal of the land has been made.

[e] Equipment was purchased by issuing a $65,000, three-year, noninterest-bearing note. The purchaser's borrowing rate is estimated to be 12%, based on other recent borrowing. Transportation and installation costs incurred by the purchase totaled $2,100.

[f] Equipment was acquired at an invoice price of $85,000. The company took a 1% cash discount by paying within the 10-day period required by the agreement. Damage to the asset during shipment required the purchaser to pay $125. The costs of installation were $2,450. Insurance on the equipment for one year ($350) was paid.

[g] On the advice of a management consulting firm, Chumley reorganized its production facilities. Costs of $15,775 were incurred for rearrangement activities. At the same time, equipment costing $47,500 was acquired, on which an available 2% cash discount was not taken due to an oversight by the bookkeeper. The equipment that was being replaced was sold at a price that resulted in a $1,000 loss.

11–46 Miscellaneous Plant Asset Transactions   Dinville Company recently acquired land and a building in a single transaction.

INSTRUCTIONS

Prepare the journal entry to record the acquired assets in each of the following *independent* situations:

[a] Paid cash of $285,000 for land appraised at $250,000 and an existing building, which will be destroyed to make room for a new one, appraised at $50,000.

[b] Paid cash of $275,000 for land appraised at $175,000 and an existing building, which will be retained and used, appraised at $125,000.

[c] Paid cash of $285,000. In addition, $15,000 was received from the salvage of an existing building that was destroyed to make room for a new one. The land was appraised at $250,000 and the old building at $35,000.

[d] Signed a $370,000 noninterest-bearing note that requires a single payment at the end of three years. No appraisal on the land is available. Dinville Company recently borrowed money at 10%.

[e] Paid cash of $500,000 for land appraised at $250,000; other assets acquired in the same transaction appraised as follows:

Equipment	$100,000
Fixtures	115,000
Patent	85,000

11–47 Miscellaneous Plant Asset Transactions   Barth Company acquired several items of property, plant, and equipment during the current year, its first year of operation:

Jan. 5 The city of Lincoln donated land to the company as an inducement to locate facilities in the city. The land was appraised at $315,000 and resulted in no cash payment by the company.

Jan. 12 Issued 50,000 shares of $20 par value common stock and paid $500,000 cash for assets appraised as follows:

Building	$1,700,000
Land	850,000
Machinery	150,000
Inventory	450,000

At the time of the transaction, the common stock was selling for $51 per share.

Feb. 5 Acquired machinery on account for $145,000, terms 2/10, n/30. Payment was made on Mar. 2.

July 17 Machinery priced at $30,000 was acquired by issuing a 90-day, 10% note. The note was paid at maturity.

Aug.   1   Machinery was purchased by issuing a noninterest-bearing note for $85,000, payable at the end of two years. In similar transactions, the company paid an interest rate of 10%.

INSTRUCTIONS

Prepare the journal entries necessary to record the acquisitions of property, plant, and equipment indicated above. Also, prepare any additional entries that would be required during the calendar year as a result of the information given. (Do not prepare adjusting entries to recognize depreciation.)

11–48 Correction of Errors   McClain Company recently acquired a building and the surrounding land. The company's accountant established a single Land and Building account and has made the following entries:

1996			Land and Building Account
Jan.	3	Acquisition price	$425,000
	3	Prepayment of insurance on building (2 years)	10,500
Feb.	1	Payment of property taxes ($2,400 delinquent for 1995; $3,600 for 1996)	6,000
Mar.	7	Renovation costs on building	42,500
Apr.	1	Cost of open house to familiarize the public with new facility opened that day	2,000
			486,000
Dec.	31	Depreciation for 1996, computed by straight-line method with 20-year life	(24,300)
			$461,700

McClain's accountant has shown the $461,700 Land and Building account in the balance sheet and the $24,300 as Depreciation Expense in the income statement. As a staff member of the independent accounting firm responsible for auditing the financial statements of the company, you must propose any adjustments you consider necessary. Your investigation reveals the following:

[1] Upon acquisition, the land was independently appraised at $115,000 and the building at $325,000.
[2] Company policy calls for depreciation by the straight-line method, computed monthly.
[3] The building is expected to have a residual value of 10% of its cost at the end of its 20-year life. The building was placed in service on April 1, 1996.
[4] Property taxes are allocated 74% to the building and 26% to the land.

INSTRUCTIONS

Prepare any adjusting entry or entries that you consider necessary. Provide computations that you would present to your supervisor to support your position. (All amounts may be rounded to the nearest dollar.)

11–49 (Appendix A)   Nonmonetary Exchanges   Jacksboro Metal Products Company has retained you to evaluate its accounting procedures in several areas. One area is nonmonetary transactions. Andy Jack, president of Jacksboro Metal, met with you concerning these transactions and indicated that in his opinion no "sale" has taken place until at least 50% of the transactions is represented in cash. Therefore, in accounting for exchanges of assets that do not meet this 50% test, he has instructed his accountant simply to transfer the book value of the surrendered asset, plus cash (if any), into the new asset account. In Andy's opinion, "This makes a lot of sense and is really easy. In addition, it does not clutter up the income statement with gains and losses that are meaningless in that they have no significant cash consequences."

In evaluating the company's financial records, you discover the following transactions:

[1] Jacksboro Metal traded metal inventory to a competitor for a small strip of land adjacent to Jacksboro's warehouse. The metal had a cost of $10,000; the strip of land had been appraised at $18,000. Jacksboro's accountant had recorded the land at $10,000 as Andy instructed.
[2] Jacksboro Metal traded several unneeded trucks to a competitor for some metal inventory that was difficult to obtain. The trucks had a book value of $45,000 (cost, $120,000; accumulated depreciation $75,000). Although no appraisal value was available for the trucks, the metal was valued at $42,000. Jacksboro paid $3,500 "boot" in addition to the trucks to complete the transaction. Andy instructed the accountant to record the metal inventory at $48,500 ($45,000 + $3,500) because the cash did not constitute 50% of the transaction.

INSTRUCTIONS

[a] React to Andy Jack's rule concerning accounting for nonmonetary exchanges. Do you agree or disagree with it? Why?

[b] Evaluate Jacksboro's accounting treatment of each of the exchanges described. What changes, if any, would you suggest to bring Jacksboro's accounting into conformity with generally accepted accounting principles?

[c] For each of the exchanges described, state briefly the theoretical justification for recording the required asset in the way you have suggested it should be recorded.

11–50 (Appendix A) Nonmonetary Exchanges Rothchild, Inc., plans to dispose of certain gymnastics equipment in one of several ways. The equipment originally cost $200,000, and depreciation recognized to date is $70,000. A recent appraisal values the equipment at approximately $150,000 on the used equipment market. Rothchild's owner wants to know the impact of various methods of disposal on the company's financial statements.

INSTRUCTIONS

Prepare the general journal entry or entries for the following *independent* alternative methods of disposal. Following each entry, comment on the impact the alternative would have on the income statement for the year in which the transaction took place.

[a] Rothchild trades the equipment for a vacant lot whose current value is not known.

[b] Rothchild trades the equipment for similar equipment valued at $160,000 and pays $10,000 in the exchange.

[c] Rothchild trades the equipment for similar equipment valued at $140,000 and receives $10,000 cash.

[d] Rothchild sells the equipment for $150,000. The proceeds are combined with an additional $50,000 cash and a $125,000, five-year, 10% note to purchase new equipment. (The 10% interest rate on the note appears fair.)

[e] Rothchild trades the equipment for similar equipment also valued at $150,000. No cash is included in the transaction.

11–51 Repair and Maintenance Astaire Company uses the allowance method of accounting for equipment repair and maintenance expenditures. A monthly amount of $1,200 is recognized as an expense and credited to the allowance on a quarterly basis. Expenditures for repairs and maintenance are charged to this allowance. Any existing balance in the allowance is adjusted to zero through the expense at the end of the company's fiscal year, March 31. Depreciation on equipment is computed at 2% of the gross asset balance at the end of each quarter. Account balances on April 1, 1995, are as follows:

Equipment	$125,000
Accumulated depreciation	(57,200)
	$ 67,800

Astaire engaged in the following transactions involving equipment from Arpil 1, 1995, through March 31, 1996:

Apr.	18	Repair costs	$ 550
May	27	Equipment acquisition	5,275
July	30	Repair costs	3,620
Oct.	19	Repair costs	5,200
Dec.	17	Equipment acquisition	10,900
Feb.	18	Repair costs	4,990

INSTRUCTIONS

[a] Determine the amounts to be included in Astaire's balance sheet based on the equipment accounts at the end of each quarter for the year April 1, 1995, through March 31, 1996. Compute all amounts to the nearest dollar.

[b] What amount of repair and maintenance expense will appear in the annual income statement on March 31, 1996?

[c] Briefly explain the rationale for the allowance method of accounting for repairs and maintenance in this situation, as opposed to simply recognizing repair and maintenance expenditures as expenses when they are incurred.

11–52 Capitalization of Interest Cost   Ritter, Inc., contracted a company to build a storage warehouse in 1995. Construction began on January 2 and Ritter paid $50,000 on that date. Ritter then made additional payments as follows, based on progress toward completion of the structure:

Apr. 1	$50,000
June 1	75,000
Sept. 1	85,000
Nov. 1	45,000

Ritter arranged for a 13½% loan of $120,000 on January 2 and borrowed the total amount at that time. The proceeds were used to partially finance the construction. Amounts invested in the project in excess of $120,000 were financed from available working capital. The company had debt obligations, other than the one related directly to the construction project, of $1,000,000 on which interest expense of $120,000 was recognized.

Completion of the project is expected sometime during 1996. Ritter's reporting period ends on December 31.

INSTRUCTIONS

[a] Prepare a schedule to determine the cost of the construction in progress at December 31, 1995.

[b] Prepare general journal entries to record these events, assuming that all interest has been charged to interest expense as incurred. Capitalized interest is to be recognized at year-end.

[c] Prepare the disclosure note to accompany the financial statements relative to this construction project.

11–53 Miscellaneous Plant Asset Transactions   Sidler Company presented the following items of property, plant, and equipment in its balance sheet on December 31, 1995:

Property, Plant, and Equipment

Equipment	$ 126,250	
Accumulated depreciation	(32,500)	$ 93,750
Buildings	751,000	
Accumulated depreciation	(251,500)	499,500
Land		162,720

During 1996 the company engaged in the following transactions involving property, plant, and equipment:

Jan. 1 Began construction of a small office building and made a $10,000 initial payment. (The project was completed on August 1.)

2 Sold bonds in the face amount of $200,000 par value. Annual interest of 12% is to be paid semiannually on June 30 and Dec. 31. Sidler plans to use the proceeds to purchase several property, plant, and equipment items in the near future and to finance construction of the small office building.

Feb. 5 Acquired a piece of equipment with a list price of $35,250. A 2% cash discount was received by paying within the 10-day discount period.

28 Made the second progress payment ($20,000) on the office building.

Apr. 30 Made the third progress payment ($20,000) on the office building.

May 1 Acquired a piece of used equipment in a trade for a similar asset that the company had owned for several years. The newly acquired asset had a market value of $18,000. The asset surrendered had a book value of $15,000 (cost, $25,000; accumulated depreciation, $10,000). Sidler paid $750 in cash.

(Hint: The proper amount for recording the newly acquired asset is the book value of the asset surrendered, plus cash paid. This transaction represents the exchange of similar productive assets in which the earning process is not complete.)

June 30 Made the fourth progress payment ($20,000) on the office building.

July 1 Acquired land by issuing a $55,000, two-year noninterest-bearing note. The note calls for two payments of $27,500, one and two years after the date of the note. A recent appraisal of the land indicates an estimated value of $46,475.

Aug. 1 Completed and placed in service the small office building. The building had been constructed by another company between Jan. 1 and Aug. 1. Sidler made the final payment of $10,000 on Aug. 1.

INSTRUCTIONS

[a] Prepare all journal entries for the preceding transactions and any additional necessary entries.

[b] Prepare any adjusting entries required on December 31, 1996. Depreciation is computed at 10% of the ending account balance for equipment and 4% of the ending account balance for buildings, approximating straight-line depreciation with 10- and 25-year lives for equipment and buildings, respectively.

[c] Prepare the presentation of property, plant, and equipment to be included in the December 31, 1996, balance sheet.

11–54 Correction of Errors Foster Company purchased land and a building, demolished the existing building, and immediately constructed a new building. All of this occurred in the first eight months of 1995. In evaluating the company's Building account at year-end, you find that the following amounts make up the $954,800 balance:

Jan.	5	Purchase price of land and building	$175,000
	15	Demolition cost of old building, net of $10,000 salvage	54,000
Sept.	1	Cost of new building	630,000
	1	Insurance on new building	12,000
	5	Display fixtures in new building	62,800
Dec.	31	Interest expense on new building	21,000
			$954,800

Upon further analysis, you discover the following explanation of these amounts:

$175,000—The land was appraised at $150,000 and the existing building, $50,000. A combined purchase price of $175,000 was negotiated because the seller was anxious to sell the property as soon as possible.

$ 54,000—The company negotiated a price of $64,000 for demolition of the old building, with the contractor retaining all salvageable materials. The latter were estimated to be worth $10,000 and will reduce the contracted price for the work.

$630,000—This represents the contract price for the new building, which was placed into service on September 1. No interest was paid directly or indirectly related to this building prior to September 1.

$ 12,000—Insurance was taken out on the building and its contents at $12,000 for a 12-month period.

$ 62,800—Display fixtures, which are separate from the building itself, were installed.

$ 21,000—A loan was taken out when the building was placed into service to cover the $630,000 contract price. Interest was calculated at $630,000 at the effective 10% interest rate for four months, or $21,000.

Foster Company depreciates all plant assets by the straight-line method. Useful lives are 20 years for buildings and 10 years for all others. Expected salvage values are 25% of cost for buildings and 10% of cost for all others. The company reports on a calendar-year basis.

INSTRUCTIONS

[a] Prepare individual correcting entries for each item in the Building account that was incorrectly charged to that account. Provide a one-sentence explanation of your reasoning in each case.

[b] Prepare depreciation adjusting entries for all plant assets, assuming that depreciation is computed to the nearest whole month.

11–55 (Appendix A) Nonmonetary Exchanges Swanson, Inc., owns Asset A, a used asset for which no current market value is readily determinable. Asset A cost $125,000 several years ago and has a book value of $65,000 at the present time. The company is considering alternative opportunities to dispose of Asset A in an exchange transaction that would result in the acquisition of another asset that would perform essentially the same function as Asset A.

INSTRUCTIONS

For each of the following *independent* cases, prepare the general journal entry necessary to record the exchange of Asset A for the appropriate alternative asset. For each alternative, briefly explain the amount at which the new asset is capitalized.

	Asset B	Asset C	Asset D	Asset E	Asset F
Original cost	$145,000	$90,000	$100,000	$ 175,000	$110,000
Accumulated depreciation	(75,000)	–0–	(25,000)	(100,000)	(10,000)
Book value	$ 70,000	$90,000	$ 75,000	$ 75,000	$100,000
Current market value	*	$90,000	$ 50,000	$ 90,000	$100,000
Cash paid by (received by) Alvarez, Inc.	–0–	$28,000	$ (3,000)	$ (10,000)	$ 45,000

*Unable to determine.

11–56 (Appendix A) Miscellaneous Plant Asset Transactions Cronan Manufacturing Company had several transactions during 1995 and 1996 concerning plant assets. Several of these transactions are described below, followed by the entry or entries made by the company's accountant.

Equipment. Several used items were acquired on February 1, 1995, by issuing a $100,000 noninterest-bearing note. The note is due one year from the date of issuance. No market value of the note or the equipment is available. Cronan's most recent borrowing rate was 8%.

Feb. 1, 1995	Equipment	100,000	
	Notes Payable		100,000
Dec. 31, 1995	Depreciation Expense	10,000	
	Accumulated Depreciation—Equipment		10,000

Buildings. A building was acquired on June 1, 1995, by issuing 100,000 shares of the company's $5 par value common stock. The common stock is not widely traded; therefore, no market price is available. The building was appraised on the transaction date at $650,000.

June 1, 1995	Building	500,000	
	Common Stock (100,000 × $5)		500,000
Dec. 31, 1995	Depreciation Expense	20,000	
	Accumulated Depreciation—Building		20,000

Inventory/Fixtures. Inventory and display fixtures were acquired for $125,000 cash on April 1, 1996, from a competitor who was liquidating her business. The estimated value of the inventory was $85,000 and the value of the fixtures was $55,000.

Apr. 1, 1996	Inventory	85,000	
	Display Fixtures	55,000	
	Cash		125,000
	Gain on Acquisition of Inventory and Fixtures		15,000

Land. Land was donated by the city of Alexandria in September 1996 as an inducement to build a facility there. Plans call for construction at an undetermined future date. The land was appraised at $65,500. No entry was made.

Machinery. Machinery was acquired in an exchange for similar equipment on October 12, 1995. The assets surrendered had orginally cost $52,000, had $16,000 accumulated depreciation, and were appraised at $45,000 on the date of the exchange. Cronan received machinery valued at $40,000 and $5,000 in cash in the transaction.

Oct. 12, 1995	Machinery	40,000	
	Cash	5,000	
	Accumulated Depreciation—Machinery	16,000	
	Machinery		52,500
	Gain on Exchange of Machinery		8,500
Dec. 31, 1995	Depreciation Expense	4,000	
	Accumulated Depreciation—Machinery		4,000

ADDITIONAL INFORMATION

Cronan uses straight-line depreciation, applied to all assets as follows:

[1] A full year's depreciation taken in the year of acquisition and no depreciation taken in the year of disposal.

[2] Estimated life: 25 years for buildings; 10 years on all other assets. (No salvage values are assumed.)

INSTRUCTIONS

For each of the preceding items of property, plant, and equipment

[a] Describe the error(s) made in recording the assets and related depreciation, if any.

[b] Prepare journal entries to correct the accounts and to properly record depreciation for 1996. The books for 1996 have not been adjusted or closed.

CASES

11–57 Internally Constructed Assets   Five years ago, Martin Manufacturing, Inc., began producing "probos," a new type of instrument it hoped to sell to doctors, dentists, and hospitals. The company was unable to produce enough probos to meet the demand, which far exceeded initial expectations.

The company was manufacturing its product with equipment built at the start of its operations. To meet demand, more efficient equipment was needed. The company decided to design and build the equipment, because the equipment currently available on the market was unsuitable.

In 1996 Martin devoted a section of the plant to development of the new equipment and hired a special staff. Within six months, the company developed a machine at a cost of $170,000 that successfully increased production and reduced labor costs. Sparked by the success, the company built three more machines at a cost of $80,000 each.

INSTRUCTIONS

[a] In addition to satisfying a need that outsiders cannot meet within the desired time, why might a firm construct plant assets for its own use?

[b] In general, what costs should be capitalized for a self-constructed plant asset?

[c] Discuss the reasonableness of including in the capitalized cost of internally constructed assets

[1] The increase in overhead caused by the construction activity.

[2] A proportionate share of overhead on the same basis as that applied to goods manufactured for sale.

[d] Discuss the proper accounting treatment of the $90,000 difference by which the cost of the first machine exceeded the cost of the subsequent machines.   (AICPA adapted)

11–58 Land and Building Cost   Robinette Company purchased land to use as its corporate headquarters. A small factory that was on the land when it was purchased was torn down before construction of the office building began. Furthermore, a substantial amount of rock blasting and removal had to be done to the site before construction of the building foundation began. Because the office building was set back on the land far from the public road, Robinette had the contractor construct a paved road that led from the public road to the office building parking lot.

Three years after the office building was occupied, Robinette added four stories to the office building. The four stories had an estimated useful life of five years more than the remaining estimated useful life of the original office building.

Ten years later, the land and building were sold at an amount more than their net book value and Robinette had a new office building constructed in another state for its new corporate headquarters.

INSTRUCTIONS

[a] Which of the above expenditures should be capitalized? How should each be depreciated or amortized? Discuss the rationale for your answers.

[b] How would the sale of the land and building be accounted for? Include in your answer how to determine the net book value at the date of sale. Discuss the rationale for your answer.   (AICPA adapted)

JUDGMENT CASES

11–59 Repair and Maintenance   Seaborne Carriers, Inc., transports petroleum by ocean-going vessels throughout the world. The company has typically accounted for its major repair and maintenance costs by charging them to expense when related liabilities were incurred. Seaborne has become aware of the generally accepted accounting practice in the airline industry by which the anticipated costs of major repairs and maintenance are charged to operations as an expense over the period that the asset is used before the actual repair or maintenance is performed. For example, jet engines must be maintained carefully and at precise points of use measured in hours. The costs of the maintenance are charged as an expense while the aircraft is used rather than only at the points that the maintenance must be performed. The propriety of this accounting is well recognized in the airline industry.

Seaborne Carriers now wishes to use the same type of accounting for the regularly scheduled maintenance and repairs performed on its vessels. The president says to you, "What is good for the goose is good for the gander and this will more closely match the costs of our operations with the revenues that are generated at the same time. Further, with all present environmental concerns, we can demonstrate our commitment to proper maintenance programs."

You have not thought about this idea before because you are not skilled in airline industry accounting. As a result of a discussion with a staff person at the AICPA, you are now aware that such accounting is considered appropriate for airlines but that other industries typically have not adopted such procedures because no liability has been incurred prior to the performance of the maintenance and no obligation exists to maintain equipment; generally, the charge for depreciation expense is thought to measure the cost of using the asset during a period of time. You are aware that airlines do depreciate their equipment in normal fashion.

INSTRUCTIONS

Would you be willing to accept the accounting proposed by Seaborne Carriers for its scheduled maintenance and repair activities? Explain the rationale for your position.

11–60 Capitalization of Interest   Adaptable, Inc., is a real estate developer that constructs and, on occasion, operates large commercial buildings (e.g., warehouses, office buildings, and apartment complexes). One of the buildings that it recently completed and operated is a medical office building near a large hospital. Interest and other construction costs were appropriately charged to the building during its construction. The original plan was to lease office space to physicians and other professionals associated with the hospital. That plan, however, has not proven successful and occupancy rates have remained relatively low.

Now, Adaptable has decided to convert the building to an apartment complex primarily to rent to hospital employees and to students enrolled in the hospital's nursing school. The company estimates that the conversion will take about a year, and it wonders whether it will be able to capitalize interest on the entire cost of the asset during its conversion period. That is, will the entire cost of the asset now recorded on the books of the company and the costs incurred on the conversion qualify as expenditures on which interest should be capitalized during the construction period? The president of Adaptable is particularly anxious to capitalize as much interest as possible. He tells you, "We are going to have a small bottom line next year anyway, and this would certainly help keep income as high as possible."

INSTRUCTIONS

Should interest be capitalized during the conversion period? If so, what amount of average accumulated expenditures should be used to calculate the amount of interest to be capitalized? That is, should the amount of average accumulated expenditures include the total cost of the asset to Adaptable or be limited to the new expenditures made to accomplish the conversion?

FINANCIAL REPORTING CASE

11–61 Financial Reporting Case   American Brands, Inc., is a global consumer products holding company. Its businesses include tobacco, distilled spirits, life insurance, hardware and home improvement products, office products, and specialty businesses.

Like many companies, American Brands presents property, plant, and equipment as a single line-item in its balance sheet and includes underlying details in notes to the financial statements. For example, for 1993 the company's balance sheet includes the following item (in millions):

Property, plant, and equipment, net $1,472.1

The comparative number for 1992 was $1,406.4.

Additional information presented elsewhere in the financial statements that helps explain the balance sheet presentation includes the following:

Excerpt from Statement of Cash Flows

For years ended December 31 *(In millions)*	1993	1992	1991
Investing Activities			
Additions to property, plant and equipment	(249.9)	(288.5)	(233.9)
Proceeds from the disposition of property, plant and equipment	19.3	18.9	32.7
Proceeds from the disposition of operations, net of cash and income taxes	9.6	13.7	—
Acquisitions, net of cash acquired	(456.7)	—	(632.6)
Purchases of investments	(2,079.7)	(1,576.8)	(890.2)
Proceeds from the maturity, call and sale of investments	1,708.2	1,142.7	472.8
Other investing activities, net	4.9	(3.5)	—
Net cash used by investing activities	(1,044.3)	(693.5)	(1,251.2)

From Significant Accounting Policies

Property, Plant and Equipment

Property, plant, and equipment are carried at cost. Depreciation is provided, principally on a straight-line basis, over the estimated useful lives of the assets. Profits or losses resulting from dispositions are included in income. Betterments and renewals which improve and extend the life of an asset are capitalized; maintenance and repair costs are expensed.

Financial Statement Note

Property, Plant and Equipment, Net

The components of property, plant and equipment, net are as follows:

(In millions)	1993 Consumer Products and Corporate	Life Insurance[a]	Total
Land and improvements	$ 92.3	$ 3.7	$ 96.0
Buildings and improvements to leaseholds	636.9	14.4	651.3
Machinery and equipment	1,847.2	33.7	1,880.9
Construction in progress	114.3	—	114.3
	2,690.7	51.8	2,742.5
Less accumulated depreciation	1,218.6	32.5	1,251.1
	$1,472.1	$19.3	$1,491.4

(In millions)	1992 Consumer Products and Corporate	Life Insurance[a]	Total
Land and improvements	$ 88.9	$ 3.7	$ 92.6
Buildings and improvements to leaseholds	593.2	11.7	604.9
Machinery and equipment	1,729.2	30.0	1,759.2
Construction in progress	102.9	—	102.9
	2,514.2	45.4	2,559.6
Less accumulated depreciation	1,107.8	29.2	1,137.0
	$1,406.4	$16.2	$1,422.6

[a]Included in Life insurance—Other assets

INSTRUCTIONS

[a] What are the major categories of property, plant, and equipment that are detailed in the company's financial statements? Why do you think "construction in progress" is listed separately?

[b] Has the relationship of the various types of plant assets changed significantly between 1992 and 1993? Provide evidence to support your answer.

[c] What do you learn from the statement of cash flows about the cash impact of transactions involving plant assets? How is the accounting policy statement helpful in understanding how the company deals with transactions involving plant assets?

Property, Plant, and Equipment: Depreciation, Depletion, and Special Problems

OBJECTIVES

1. To describe the depreciation process as an application of the matching principle in accounting for property, plant, and equipment.
2. To describe and illustrate depreciation methods that are commonly used in practice, including methods based on time and activity level.
3. To discuss accounting for natural resources and the related amortization of cost through the depletion process.
4. To illustrate typical presentations of plant assets and related disclosures of depreciation in the financial statements and related notes.
5. To introduce the accounting treatment of changes in estimates and corrections of errors affecting plant assets.

Depreciation expense is an important part of the income statement. The accumulated amount of depreciation on plant assets is an important figure in determining a company's financial position.

Following are examples of the magnitude of depreciation expense and accumulated depreciation for four well-known U.S. corporations for 1993:

	Depreciation Expense		Accumulated Depreciation	
	In Millions of Dollars	Percentage of Total Revenue	In Millions of Dollars	Percentage of Plant Asset Cost
Ameritech	$2,162	18.5%	$11,751	40.4%
Procter & Gamble	1,140	3.7	5,392	36.2
Wal-Mart	649	1.2	1,607	16.3
Federal Express	580	7.4	3,230	48.2

The amounts for depreciation expense include depletion and amortization. Of these, depreciation expense represents by far the largest amount.

Depreciation expense is an important adjustment in the operating activities section of the statement of cash flows. Depreciation expense does not require the use of cash, and in the preparation of the statement of cash flows, expenses are adjusted to eliminate depreciation expense. For example, Procter & Gamble's 1993 statement of cash flows includes earnings before prior year's effect of accounting change of $1,776 million and net cash flows from operating activities of $3,338 million. Several offsetting adjustments account for this difference of $1,562 million; by far the largest is depreciation expense (including depletion and amortization) at $2,705 million.

In this chapter we consider the subject of depreciation and depletion, including the alternative methods of calculating them and other implementation issues associated with accounting for plant assets throughout their useful lives.

REVENUE-EXPENSE ASSOCIATION

Matching

Matching **principle** is a term used to identify the process by which accountants determine net income. Matching involves the recognition of revenues associated with business activities during a certain time period and the identification of expenses related to the generation of those revenues. The difference between these revenues and expenses is the **net income** of the enterprise for that period.

Three principles govern the inclusion of an expenditure (or part of one) as an expense in the matching process for a particular time period. The principles are (1) association of cause and effect, (2) systematic and rational allocation, and (3) immediate recognition.[1]

Association of cause and effect refers to the fact that some expenditures are directly associated with specific revenues and are included in determining net income for the period in which those revenues are received. For example, certain manufacturing costs, such as direct materials and direct labor, are directly related to items of inventory produced and help to determine income when those items are sold.

Systematic and rational allocation explains the accounting recognition of those costs that do not have a direct cause and effect relationship on the generation of revenue but that are recognized as expenses in an attempt to allocate costs in a systematic and rational manner among several accounting periods. An expenditure that is made in one period but provides benefits to several accounting periods, such as the cost of a plant asset, is an example of the need for interperiod allocations in the determination of income.

Immediate recognition explains the inclusion of certain costs in determining income because expenditures of the current period (or those carried forward from previous periods) have no discernible future benefits. The recognition of certain expenses, such as research and development, and the expensing of items that do not result in increased revenues, such as the write-off of obsolete equipment, exemplify the immediate recognition of costs in determining income.

THE DEPRECIATION PROCESS

Accounting for property, plant, and equipment when they enter the productive processes of the enterprise is best described by systematic and rational allocation. We saw in Chapter 11 that plant assets are acquired for the purpose of being used in the production or distribution of other goods or services and are expected to provide service over a relatively long period. With the exception of land, plant assets are believed to possess valuable, but limited, economic usefulness to the enterprise holding the rights to the service potential of the assets.

DEPRECIATION DEFINED

Asset/Liability Measurement

Plant assets are measured and recorded at cost, and that cost is allocated to the periods benefiting from the use of the assets on the basis of several estimates concerning their use. In theory, the accountant prefers to allocate the cost of property, plant, and equipment in a manner that is proportionate to the contribution that the assets make to the generation of revenue each period. In other words, the greater the contribution to revenue for a particular accounting period, the more depreciation expense should be charged for a given asset. However, because of the uncertainties surrounding the precise pattern in which a given asset contributes to revenue, accountants estimate periodic depreciation by methods that include simplifying assumptions and that are both systematic and rational.

Cost allocation via depreciation does not measure the value of an asset; it is intended to recognize a portion of the cost of the asset as an expense each period in determining net income. **Depreciation** is defined as the process of allocating the cost of property, plant, and equipment as an expense in a systematic and rational manner to those periods expected to benefit from the use of the asset.

---

[1]*APB Statement No. 4,* "Basic Concepts and Accounting Principles Underlying Financial Statements of Business Enterprises," 1970, pars. 156–160.

The assumption that the economic usefulness or service potential of plant assets declines over time is supported by the realities of the process of producing and distributing goods and services. Declining service potential is caused by changes in both the asset and the environment in which the asset is used.

The changes in property, plant, and equipment that support the notion of declining service potential result from routine wear and tear, deterioration, and other effects of constant use in normal business operations. Over time these **physical factors** result in a decline in the future service potential of the assets and provide support for allocating the acquisition cost of plant assets as an expense. Due to the finite service potential of most plant assets, the use of the assets in one period results in a decline in the service potential available for use in future periods.

Changes in the environment in which property, plant, and equipment are used, sometimes called **functional factors,** also influence the amount of future service potential present in an asset at a given time. Business expansion and growth may render a plant asset obsolete. At that time, the asset is **inadequate for the intended purpose,** although it may still be suitable for its original purpose and may prove quite useful to another enterprise. For example, adequate buildings acquired at the inception of a business may become limited in their future service potential when unexpected growth requires larger facilities for efficient operation.

Supercession results when an enterprise acquires improved assets that are capable of providing the same service as present plant assets at an increased level of efficiency or at a significantly reduced cost. **Obsolescence** broadly refers to the decline in future service potential due to the functional factors relating to the environment in which the enterprise operates rather than to a decrease in the asset's physical utility. Functional factors include inadequacy, supercession, and other changes that affect the asset's potential to provide future service.

ESTIMATES REQUIRED IN THE DEPRECIATION PROCESS

The depreciation process requires several estimates concerning property, plant, and equipment. Measuring plant assets at cost involves estimates, assumptions, and allocations, many of which were described in Chapter 11. These include the treatment of acquisition-related costs, the capitalization of interest costs, the treatment of overhead for internally constructed assets, and others. Nevertheless, the cost of plant assets is better described as an actual or computed figure than an estimate. However, other figures necessary to apply the depreciation process (i.e., the useful life and salvage value of the asset) are clearly estimates of future events.

Asset/Liability Measurement

Allocating the cost of an asset over future periods requires an estimate of its **useful life,** which may be expressed in **time** (e.g., months or years), **productive output** (e.g., units produced), or **service quantities** (e.g., machine hours operated or miles driven). The logical basis for estimating useful life varies from asset to asset. Accountants attempt to identify the measure of useful life that is most closely associated with the decline in the service potential of the asset to the enterprise. Time is usually the measure used for buildings, furniture, and fixtures. The useful life of machinery that turns out identifiable products may be appropriately stated in terms of productive output. In still other cases, service capacity (determined by some physical quantity used or consumed) may be appropriate; for example, miles driven may provide the best estimate of the useful life of a vehicle. Regardless of the nature of the depreciable asset, however, **an estimate of the useful life must be made** to identify the period over which the asset will be depreciated. This life may be identified by a number of titles, all of which have common meanings: service life, economic life, estimated useful life, and other similar terms. When the estimates and assumptions used in computing depreciation are important in understanding the financial statements, disclosure of items such as estimated useful lives and residual values are common. For example, the 1993 annual report of Federal Express Corporation discloses the estimated useful lives of plant assets in four categories: flight equipment, package handling and ground support equipment, computer and electronic equipment, and other. It also mentions the fact that aircraft airframes and engines are assigned residual values ranging from 10% to 20% of asset cost and that all other property and equipment have no assigned residual values.

In all widely used methods, the total depreciable amount is the difference between the cost of the asset and the estimated value expected to accrue to the asset holder at the end of the useful life. This latter amount is identified by a variety of terms with common meaning, including *residual value* and *salvage value*. Any anticipated costs of preparing the asset for disposal at the end of its expected useful life are treated as reductions in the residual value for purposes of determining the total depreciable amount. Estimates of useful life and residual value are based on the expected usefulness of the asset to the present owner.

Depreciation is recorded at the end of each accounting period by an adjusting entry in which Depreciation Expense is debited and Accumulated Depreciation is credited, as discussed in Chapter 5. The depreciation expense is a component of income determination for

Matching   that period and represents an application of the matching principle. Accumulated depreciation is a contra asset to the plant asset amount(s) presented in the balance sheet. The increase in accumulated depreciation resulting from the recognition of depreciation expense further reduces the book value of the asset as presented in the balance sheet. Some companies provide a brief explanation of the relationship of cost, accumulated depreciation, and book value to help readers better understand the information presented in the balance sheet. For example, Armstrong World Industries, Inc.'s 1992 financial statements include a note indicating that property, plant, and equipment values are stated at acquisition cost, with accumulated depreciation deducted to arrive at net book value.

A common misconception is that the process of depreciation provides for the replacement of plant assets, including generating cash to acquire replacement assets at some future time. As the previous discussion indicates, and illustrations to come will demonstrate, depreciation under current GAAP is a process of cost allocation intended primarily for income-determining purposes. It is based on the asset's cost and is not intended to provide for the replacement of assets. It does not generate funds for the replacement of assets, although the need to continuously provide for the replacement of plant assets is an important managerial responsibility.

DEPRECIATION ESTIMATION METHODS: INDIVIDUAL ASSETS

Several methods have been developed to apply the general concept of depreciation to property, plant, and equipment. These methods combine the cost, the estimated useful life, and the estimated residual value of the asset with certain assumptions about the pattern of decline in the asset's service potential.

This section discusses methods for determining periodic depreciation for individual assets. These methods may be classified as those based on time and those based on activity level.

Depreciation Methods Based on Time
1. Straight line
2. Accelerated
   a. Sum-of-the-years'-digits
   b. Declining balance

Depreciation Methods Based on Activity Level
1. Productive output
2. Service quantity

Several additional depreciation methods are discussed in Appendix A of this chapter. These methods are applied to plant assets in groups rather than individually.

Depreciation expense determined by any of the methods based on time can be computed in advance and will be the same regardless of the level of activity during the period. Depreciation determined by any method based on activity level results in the determination of a constant depreciation charge **per unit of activity.** Depreciation expense for a time period is then computed at the end of that period and is based on the activity level achieved during it.

To illustrate the depreciation methods in this section, the following asset is assumed:

Asset 147

Cost	$12,000
Estimated salvage value	$ 2,000
Estimated life	
In years	5
In units of output	25,000
In service hours	60,000

It would be unusual to have a depreciable asset for which the useful life could be stated equally well in terms of years, units of output, and service hours. The example here includes all three to facilitate the illustration and comparison of the methods, and we indicate the circumstances most appropriate for applying the individual method, recognizing that all methods would usually not apply to the same asset.

STRAIGHT-LINE METHOD

The **straight-line method** of depreciation is simple and results in the same amount of depreciation expense for each full year in the life of the asset. The depreciation charge is based on the **passage of time** rather than the level of productive activity.

Periodic depreciation under the straight-line method is computed as follows (D = depreciation):

$$D = \frac{(\text{Cost}) - (\text{Salvage Value})}{\text{Number of Years in Asset's Life}}$$

Depreciation for the first year (D_1) for Asset 147 is computed as follows:

$$D_1 = \frac{\$12,000 - \$2,000}{5}$$

$$= \$2,000$$

Due to the straightforward nature of the calculation, the absence of complicating assumptions, and the ease of understanding, the straight-line method is widely practiced. The method is conceptually appropriate if the decline in service potential relates primarily to the passage of time rather than to the level of activity and if the decline is thought to be approximately the same amount each period. The straight-line method may also provide a reasonable basis for depreciation when the level of activity is important but the use of the asset is relatively constant from period to period.

Applying the straight-line method to the five-year life of Asset 147, we arrive at the schedule in Exhibit 12–1. The book value at the end of the fifth year is the $2,000 salvage

---

EXHIBIT 12–1

Depreciation Schedule for Asset 147
Straight-Line Method

End of Year	Depreciation Entry: Dr.: Depreciation Expense Cr.: Accumulated Depreciation	Balance: Accumulated Depreciation	Book Value
—	—	—	$12,000
1	$2,000	$ 2,000	10,000
2	2,000	4,000	8,000
3	2,000	6,000	6,000
4	2,000	8,000	4,000
5	2,000	10,000	2,000

value originally used to determine the total depreciation to be charged ($10,000). The book value (cost less accumulated depreciation) at the end of each year is the amount presented as an asset in the enterprise's balance sheet. The financial statement disclosure requirements for plant assets are covered in a later section of this chapter.

ACCELERATED METHODS

Accelerated depreciation methods, sometimes referred to as **reducing-charge methods,** are designed to recognize larger amounts of depreciation in the early years of an asset's life and smaller amounts in the later years. Of the several variations of accelerated depreciation, the most widely used are the declining-balance and the sum-of-the-years'-digits methods. Both are presented in this section. Even though the amount of depreciation varies from year to year with accelerated methods, depreciation is still based on the passage of time; it is computed in advance and is based on estimates of useful life and salvage value.

Accelerated depreciation methods emerged from income tax law, which allowed companies to take more depreciation in the early years in the asset's life than in later years. As we discuss later in this section, the use of accelerated depreciation for income tax purposes does not necessitate its use for financial reporting purposes. However, accelerated depreciation may be conceptually sound if the pattern of declining expense is consistent with the actual contribution the asset makes to the revenue-generating process.

Accelerated depreciation methods are conceptually attractive when one or more of the following circumstances are present:

1. *Superior performance*—The asset is expected to provide superior operating performance (i.e., operate with greater efficiency) in the early years of its life.

2. *Repair and maintenance*—Repair and maintenance are expected to follow a pattern of increased expenditures during the life of the asset. Declining depreciation expense, coupled with increasing repair and maintenance, results in a more constant total cost of operating the asset than is true with other depreciation methods.

3. *Obsolescence*—The greater the potential for obsolescence, the greater the need for increased depreciation early in the asset's life to reflect its rapidly expanding decline in service potential. This reduces the probability that a significant write-off will be required later in the asset's life.

Sum-of-the-Years'-Digits Method

The **sum-of-the-years'-digits method** is applied by computing a fraction, the denominator of which equals the *life of the asset in years plus all digits between that number and zero.* The numerator of the fraction represents the *specific number of the year* in the useful life of the asset, applied in *descending order* throughout the life of the asset; for example, if the useful life is 10 years, the number 10 would be the numerator in D_1, 9 in D_2, and so on. This fraction is then multiplied by **depreciable cost** (i.e., the cost minus salvage value). Thus, depreciation is computed:

$$D = \left(\frac{\text{Current Year Digit}}{\text{Sum-of-the-Years'-Digits}}\right) \times (\text{Cost} - \text{Salvage Value})$$

Applying these concepts to Asset 147, we find that the denominator (the sum-of-the-years'-digits, $5 + 4 + 3 + 2 + 1$) equals 15. Depreciation is determined for each year by multiplying the appropriate fraction by the depreciable amount. Remember that the numerator is selected in *reverse* (*descending*) order, resulting in the following computations:

$$D_1 = \tfrac{5}{15} \times (\$12{,}000 - \$2{,}000) = \$\ 3{,}333$$
$$D_2 = \tfrac{4}{15} \times (\$12{,}000 - \$2{,}000) = \ 2{,}667$$
$$D_3 = \tfrac{3}{15} \times (\$12{,}000 - \$2{,}000) = \ 2{,}000$$
$$D_4 = \tfrac{2}{15} \times (\$12{,}000 - \$2{,}000) = \ 1{,}333$$
$$D_5 = \tfrac{1}{15} \times (\$12{,}000 - \$2{,}000) = \ \underline{\ 667}$$
$$\underline{\$10{,}000}$$

These computations result in a schedule for Asset 147 as illustrated in Exhibit 12–2. As with straight-line depreciation, the book value of $2,000 at the end of the five years equals the salvage value anticipated at the beginning of the asset's life.

For assets with relatively long lives, determining the sum of the digits as computed above may be burdensome. In these cases, the denominator in the fraction may be determined as follows (n = years in asset's life; SYD = sum-of-the-years'-digits):

$$SYD = n\left(\frac{n + 1}{2}\right)$$

For example, for an asset with a 35-year life, the sum of the digits is computed as follows:

$$SYD = 35\left(\frac{35 + 1}{2}\right)$$
$$- 630$$

The depreciation rate is 35/630 for the first year, 34/630 for the second year, and so forth.

Declining-Balance Method

The **declining-balance method** is a second type of accelerated depreciation in which the expense in early years exceeds that of later years. In the sum-of-the-years'-digits method, a declining fraction is multiplied by a constant base. In the declining-balance method, the opposite is true: a **constant percentage** is multiplied by a **declining base.**

In the declining-balance method, a percentage is based on some multiple of the straight-line rate. The most common application of this method is **double-declining balance,** wherein the percentage is twice the straight-line rate. This fixed percentage is then applied to the declining book value of the asset, giving a depreciation figure that declines throughout the life of the asset. *The book value, however, is not reduced below the estimated salvage value.*

The double-declining balance rate is computed as twice the straight-line rate, as follows (DDB = double-declining balance):

$$DDB\% = \left(\frac{100\%}{\text{Life in Years}}\right) \times (2)$$

	EXHIBIT 12–2		

Depreciation Schedule for Asset 147
Sum-of-the-Years'-Digits Method

End of Year	Depreciation Entry: Dr.: Depreciation Expense Cr.: Accumulated Depreciation	Balance: Accumulated Depreciation	Book Value
—	—	—	$12,000
1	$3,333	$ 3,333	8,667
2	2,667	6,000	6,000
3	2,000	8,000	4,000
4	1,333	9,333	2,667
5	667	10,000	2,000

For Asset 147, this rate is 40%:

$$DDB\% = \left(\frac{100\%}{5}\right) \times (2)$$
$$= 40\%$$

Applying 40% to the declining book value of Asset 147 and ignoring salvage value until the book value is reduced to it, we compute the depreciation for each year in the asset's life as follows:

$$D_1 = 40\% \ (\$12,000) = \$4,800$$
$$D_2 = 40\% \ (\$12,000 - \$4,800) = \$2,880$$
$$D_3 = 40\% \ [\$12,000 - (\$4,800 + \$2,880)] = \$1,728$$
$$D_4 = \$10,000 - (\$4,800 + \$2,880 + \$1,728) = \$592$$

Depreciation at 40% of the book value cannot be taken in Year 4 because this would reduce book value below the $2,000 salvage value expected. Likewise, no depreciation can be taken in Year 5. Some companies avoid this problem by systematically switching to straight-line at the point where it exceeds declining balance. Exhibit 12–3 shows a schedule for Asset 147 that results from applying the double-declining balance method as computed above.

Accelerated depreciation is an area in which the determination of a company's federal income tax liability has had a significant impact on financial reporting practices. The popularity of the double-declining balance method resulted, at least in part, from the fact that for many assets, the maximum depreciation that could be deducted in computing the income tax liability was an amount equal to twice the straight-line rate in the first year, without regard to salvage value. Because this maximum has not applied to all assets, however, variations of the declining-balance method are found in practice. For example, maximum depreciation on used assets acquired before 1981 and certain other assets is 1½ times the straight-line amount. Accordingly, the declining-balance method at 150% of the straight-line rate is used in some circumstances. The mechanics of applying the declining-balance method are the same regardless of the multiple of the straight-line rate used. The use of a multiple of less than 2, however, results in a less dramatic acceleration of depreciation in the early years of the asset's life.

Companies may use different accounting methods for financial reporting and income tax purposes. Regardless of this option, many companies use their tax methods for their financial statements to avoid keeping two sets of records. The objective of selecting a deprecia-

Matching   tion method for financial reporting purposes is to properly match revenues and expenses. The inability to directly associate the decline in service potential of plant assets with revenues produced by those assets, however, precludes precise measurements of the amount of cost to treat as depreciation each period. Thus, methods designed primarily for income tax purposes frequently become a part of financial reporting on the basis that the tax methods are consistent with the general principle of matching. Also, the differences in amounts be-

Materiality   tween accounting and income tax methods may be immaterial when placed in the context of a company's financial statements. Accounting for differences in methods used for income tax and financial reporting purposes is the subject of Chapter 19.

In 1981 income tax law was changed to incorporate a new method of deciding which portion of the cost of assets could be deducted when determining a company's income tax liability. That method is called the **Accelerated Cost Recovery System (ACRS)** and permits accelerated recovery of the cost of assets over periods generally shorter than their useful lives. This system remains in effect for assets placed in service from 1981 through 1986 but was modified by the Tax Reform Act of 1986 for assets placed in service after 1986. It was

EXHIBIT 12–3

Depreciation Schedule for Asset 147
Double-Declining Balance Method

End of Year	Depreciation Entry: Dr.: Depreciation Expense Cr.: Accumulated Depreciation	Balance: Accumulated Depreciation	Book Value
—	—	—	$12,000
1	$4,800	$ 4,800	7,200
2	2,880	7,680	4,320
3	1,728	9,408	2,592
4	592	10,000	2,000
5	–0–	10,000	2,000

changed again slightly by the 1993 Tax Act. The revised method is called the **Modified Accelerated Cost Recovery System (MACRS).** In the opinion of the authors, the amounts that are written off for income tax purposes under ACRS or MACRS may not be appropriate as depreciation expense for financial reporting purposes because they are not based on the estimated useful lives of the assets. This is particularly true for real estate and other property with relatively long lives.

In situations for which companies use an acceptable depreciation method, such as straight line, for financial statement presentation and ACRS (or MACRS) for income tax purposes for the same assets, a temporary difference between financial and taxable income arises. Chapter 18 of this text discusses ACRS and MACRS in greater detail and considers more carefully the differences between the way the cost of plant assets is recognized in financial statements and the way cost is recognized in preparing tax returns. At this point, simply keep in mind that it is acceptable and, in fact, may even be mandatory for companies to use different methods in preparing financial statements from those used in the preparation of income tax returns. Depreciation is one of those areas where this frequently occurs. Companies frequently explain this difference to readers of their financial statements. An example is found in the 1993 annual report for Goodyear Tire & Rubber Company, which explains that depreciation is computed by the straight-line method in the financial statements and accelerated depreciation is used for income tax purposes. Additional information in the income tax note to the financial statements explains the dollar impact of the temporary difference for depreciation.

PRODUCTIVE-OUTPUT METHOD

The **productive-output** (or **units-of-output**) **method** uses the output of plant assets as a basis for recognizing periodic depreciation. The rationale is that some assets are capable of producing a determinable number of units of productive output and depreciation should be recognized in relation to the portion of that output that occurs in each accounting period.

A cost factor *per unit of output* is first calculated. This factor is then applied to the actual output for the period to determine the depreciation charge. Depreciation expense cannot be determined in advance, because it depends on the level of output during the period. The depreciation computation for the productive-output method is generalized as follows:

$$D = \left(\frac{\text{Cost} - \text{Salvage Value}}{\text{Life in Units of Output}} \right) \times \left(\begin{array}{c} \text{Units of Output} \\ \text{for Period} \end{array} \right)$$

The first element in the computation represents a depreciation rate per unit of output. Applying this concept to Asset 147 results in a cost per unit of $.40:

$$\begin{array}{c} \text{Estimated Cost} \\ \text{per Unit of} \\ \text{Output} \end{array} = \frac{\$12,000 - \$2,000}{25,000 \text{ units}}$$

$$= \$.40$$

We shall assume that units are produced in Years 1–5 in the following pattern: 4,000, 9,000, 8,000, 2,000, and 2,000. Depreciation may then be computed for each year by applying the $.40 cost per unit to the units of output:

$$D_1 = \$.40 \times 4,000 = \$1,600$$
$$D_2 = \$.40 \times 9,000 = \$3,600$$
$$D_3 = \$.40 \times 8,000 = \$3,200$$
$$D_4 = \$.40 \times 2,000 = \$800$$
$$D_5 = \$.40 \times 2,000 = \$800$$

Exhibit 12–4 shows the schedule that results for Asset 147 when the units-of-output method is applied to the five years in the asset's life. As in the other methods, the book value at the end of five years equals the expected salvage value of $2,000, because the total amount of the recognized depreciation expense is $10,000.

The productive-output method is suitable when the asset provides a separate, identifiable unit of product, as is the case with equipment used to manufacture items of inventory. For those assets, this method is particularly suitable if the decline in service potential is more closely tied to the production of units than to the passage of time. If an asset is used very little in a period, depreciation by the units-of-output method will be small; if the level of activity is high, depreciation will be high. If obsolescence or additional factors other than physical output are considered important in determining the pattern of decline in the asset's service potential, the productive-output method is *not* suitable.

SERVICE-QUANTITY METHOD

The productivity of some assets is best measured in terms of service quantity; for example, we state the productivity of certain machinery in terms of operating hours and the productivity of vehicles in terms of miles. The mechanics of applying the service-quantity method are similar to those of the productive-output method, but the concepts underlying the methods are somewhat different.

EXHIBIT 12–4

Depreciation Schedule for Asset 147
Productive-Output Method

End of Year	Depreciation Entry: Dr.: Depreciation Expense Cr.: Accumulated Depreciation	Balance: Accumulated Depreciation	Book Value
—	—	—	$12,000
1	$1,600	$ 1,600	10,400
2	3,600	5,200	6,800
3	3,200	8,400	3,600
4	800	9,200	2,800
5	800	10,000	2,000

Under the **service-quantity method,** the contribution to operations is stated in terms of **productive-input factors** rather than output of the production process. Accordingly, depreciation recognized in any period depends on the quantity of the productive-input factor consumed in the use of the asset during that period. The amount of the productive input is limited, and the depreciable amount (cost less salvage value) is recognized as an expense on the basis of the expiration of this limited quantity of productive inputs.

Depreciation under the service-quantity method is generalized as follows:

$$D = \left(\frac{\text{Cost} - \text{Salvage Value}}{\begin{array}{c}\text{Total Quantity of} \\ \text{Productive} \\ \text{Service}\end{array}} \right) \times \left(\begin{array}{c}\text{Productive} \\ \text{Service for} \\ \text{Period}\end{array} \right)$$

The first factor represents a depreciation rate per unit of productive service. For Asset 147, the appropriate service quantity is 60,000 service hours, resulting in a cost per hour of $.1667:

$$\frac{\text{Estimated Cost per Unit}}{\text{of Productive Service}} = \frac{\$12,000 - \$2,000}{60,000 \text{ Hours}}$$

$$= \$.1667$$

The asset is used during Years 1–5 in the following service hours: 14,000, 15,000, 20,000, 4,000, and 7,000. Depreciation is computed for each year as follows:

$$D_1 = \$.1667 \times 14,000 = \$2,334$$
$$D_2 = \$.1667 \times 15,000 = \$2,501$$
$$D_3 = \$.1667 \times 20,000 = \$3,334$$
$$D_4 = \$.1667 \times 4,000 = \$667$$
$$D_5 = \$.1667 \times 7,000 = \$1,164$$

A $3 rounding adjustment is made in the D_5 computation.

The schedule for Asset 147 that results when we apply the service-quantity method to the five years in the asset's life is illustrated in Exhibit 12–5.

Depreciation varies annually, depending on the level of use of the asset during the period. If the decline in service potential relates to the physical use of the asset, the service-quantity method is appropriate. In particular, if the use of the asset varies from period to period, this method more realistically reflects the decline in service potential through depreciation expense than does a method that recognizes depreciation based on the passage of time but disregards the level of activity. If the decline in the service potential relates more to the

	EXHIBIT 12–5		
	Depreciation Schedule for Asset 147		
	Service-Quantity Method		
End of Year	**Depreciation Entry: Dr.: Depreciation Expense Cr.: Accumulated Depreciation**	**Balance: Accumulated Depreciation**	**Book Value**
—	—	—	$12,000
1	$2,334	$ 2,334	9,666
2	2,501	4,835	7,165
3	3,334	8,169	3,831
4	667	8,836	3,164
5	1,164	10,000	2,000

passage of time or obsolescence, however, the straight-line or an accelerated method is more suitable, even when the contribution of the asset may be stated in terms of service quantities.

In our discussion of depreciation methods, we have used the same asset throughout, assuming that we could estimate useful life in terms of time, units of production, and service quantities. This was done for purposes of illustration only. As stated earlier, in practice only one of these would be used for any particular asset. In these illustrations, the fact that the exhaustion of service quantities or the completion of units of product took place precisely over a five-year period is of no particular relevance because depreciation would be based on only one of these variables (service quantities, units of production, or passage of time) for any particular asset.

What is the proper accounting treatment when an enterprise continues to use fully depreciated assets? Obviously, the estimate of useful life in terms of either time or activity level proved to be inaccurate, even if it was based on the best information available when the asset was placed in service. The cost and accumulated depreciation of fully depreciated assets should remain in the accounts as long as the assets are actively used, even though these figures effectively cancel each other out in the determination of book value. The use of fully depreciated plant assets in the revenue-producing process presents a theoretical problem, because no portion of the cost of these assets is included among expenses. This violates the matching principle. If fully depreciated assets make significant contributions to revenue, this fact should be disclosed in the financial statements. This is usually not a major problem, because fully depreciated assets still in use are usually not an important part of total assets.

Matching Disclosure

SELECTING AN APPROPRIATE DEPRECIATION METHOD

We have discussed several factors that should be considered when a company selects a depreciation method: physical use, expected obsolescence, the expected pattern of decline in usefulness, the periodic contribution of the asset to the revenue-producing process, and others. These considerations are often difficult, if not impossible, to quantify, and they sometimes offset each other, resulting in some uncertainty about the most appropriate method in a given set of circumstances.

Many times *practical,* rather than conceptual, considerations govern the selection of a depreciation method. For example, the simplicity of the straight-line method explains its frequent use in accounting practice. Companies often adopt ACRS or MACRS for income tax purposes and straight-line depreciation for financial reporting, thereby reducing taxable income and deferring income tax payments without reducing the net income reported in the early years of the assets' lives. This combination is particularly popular among rapidly expanding companies that are investing additional amounts in plant assets on a continuous basis. In other cases, however, simplicity may influence the choice, and a company will use straight-line depreciation for both income tax reporting and financial reporting to avoid the cost and inconvenience of retaining two sets of depreciation records. In many cases, depreciation methods used in the past are applied to new assets without any real consideration of the appropriateness of those methods. In some cases, depreciation methods used by other companies with which the enterprise may be compared may influence the choice of depreciation method.

The authoritative accounting literature suggests only that a depreciation method be both systematic and rational. Companies may select depreciation methods for financial reporting purposes and use those same methods for internal cost accounting purposes of valuing inventory. When technology costs (e.g., plant and equipment and information systems costs) are significant, traditional depreciation methods may mask the impact of technology on product cost, resulting in poor decisions. The problem is that technology costs are being buried in overhead, causing a distortion of overhead rates and possibly resulting in incorrect, adverse decisions, such as dropping a profitable product. As technology increases in relation to material, direct labor, and other product costs, the suitability of traditional depreciation

CUSTOMIZED ACCOUNTING

Poor Harvard. In February it announced that despite the hefty flow of income from its nearly $5 billion endowment fund it would be running $42 million in the red this year. How embarrassing. Kind of like losing to that place in New Haven.

But wait. Maybe things weren't really that bad. Or so says Harvard's own Robert Anthony, a leading expert on higher education accounting. He declares that Harvard, in fact, had a $6 million surplus. Other accountants put the figure even higher, at $11 million to $20 million.

Why all this confusion? For years, major universities, including Harvard, have prepared their books under the arcane rules of "fund accounting." These rules made it extremely difficult to figure out whether the school did or did not spend more money than it took in. For more than 10 years the Financial Accounting Standards Board, the country's chief rule setter, has been pushing for nonprofits to present their financials like for-profit businesses.

Last year Harvard did just that. For example, it consolidated its results in an operating income statement. But it did so while the FASB was still working out its new guidelines. In effect, Harvard made up its own rules—some of which are neither in accordance with existing standards nor in line with the FASB's proposals.

"I didn't want to wait for everybody else to figure out what they should or shouldn't do," affirms E. Lyndon Tefft, Harvard's director of financial systems and the architect of the new statements.

Perhaps one reason Harvard didn't want to wait was that it wanted rules that suited its own purposes. The most glaring departure from accounting norms is Harvard's aggressive $76 million provision for replacement of facilities, which Harvard says is its depreciation expense for the year. Fair enough, but Harvard doesn't figure depreciation the way the Generally Accepted Accounting Principles rules say. GAAP says depreciation should be based on what a building or piece of equipment cost originally. Now Harvard has some fine old ivy-covered buildings that cost a fraction of what it would cost to build them today, if indeed they could be built today. So, the university decided, the heck with GAAP, we'll figure depreciation our own way. Using GAAP rules, Harvard's depreciation last year would have been $29 million, not $76 million. But Harvard figured it would cost $3.5 billion to replace those buildings, so it took a much higher figure for depreciation.

Does the Harvard depreciation method give a fairer financial picture than the GAAP method? Not necessarily. Harvard accounting expert Anthony says: "I doubt they'll have to replace the facilities with money from operations. By the same token that they got the old buildings contributed [by alumni], they're going to get the new ones contributed."

Well, the bottom line of the bottom line is this: If Harvard had depreciated its buildings the way companies are required to do, it would ended with a surplus of $6 million, not a deficit of $42 million. Of Harvard's new approach, Herbert Folpe, an expert on higher education at KPMG Peat Marwick, which audits over 700 colleges and universities, says: "It's unorthodox."

Whatever else it is, the new Harvard accounting may come in handy in persuading alumni to be more generous. A lot of them think that the university is already rich. Harvard denies that was its intention, but a touch of red ink could certainly help loosen the purse strings a bit.

There's more. Harvard's endowment earned $212 million last year in interest and dividends, but the university recorded only $207 million as revenue, tucking the remaining $5 million into its endowment.

Then there is an estimated $7 million to $10 million in contributions Harvard got last year that it could have counted as income but simply decided to add to the endowment—kind of like a company crediting income directly to earned surplus instead of flowing it through the income account. Of this practice, KPMG Peat Marwick's Folpe says that these funds should be added to revenue. "Otherwise," he says, "a university has the ability to manage its own bottom line."

And that may be precisely what Harvard is doing: managing its bottom line in such a way as to appear poorer than it really is. The university is in the midst of a plan to reportedly raise $2.5 billion on top of what is already the world's largest private endowment. Harvard is a bit like the rich man who wears scuffed shoes and a frayed collar when he visits his doctor.

SOURCE: Roula Khalaf, "Customized Accounting," *Forbes* (May 25, 1992), p. 50. Reprinted by permission of *Forbes Magazine*, May 25, 1992, © Forbes, Inc., 1992.

methods, particularly straight-line and other time-based methods, becomes questionable.[2] This suggests that it is reasonable to expect more sophisticated methods of depreciation to be developed for purposes of internal cost allocation. The impact this may have on the choice of depreciation methods for external financial reporting purposes is difficult to assess, but one

---

[2]James A. Brimson, "Technology Accounting," *Management Accounting* (March 1989), pp. 47–53.

possibility is that new, more sophisticated methods developed primarily for internal use will emerge and have an impact on the methods used for external financial reporting purposes.

Consistency

Consistency is an important accounting principle when considering the depreciation of plant assets. Once a depreciation method is selected for a particular asset or class of assets, that method should be used consistently from period to period so that the net incomes of successive accounting periods are comparable.

In summary, it is difficult to generalize exactly how companies determine the depreciation methods they use. Conceptual as well as practical considerations are important, and consistency over time must also be considered.

FRACTIONAL-YEAR PROBLEMS

In the previous examples, we have assumed that the **depreciation year** and the **financial reporting period** are the same. That is, Asset 147 was acquired at the beginning of a reporting period and a full year's depreciation was taken in that year. In practice, plant assets are not always acquired at the beginning of a fiscal period. Likewise, assets are not always disposed of at the end of the period. The problem of accounting for depreciation for assets acquired and disposed of at various times during the year is frequently encountered in applying all of the methods that were discussed in the previous section. The computation of depreciation expense differs, however, only for those methods in which depreciation is based on the passage of time. Depreciation for partial years under the activity-based methods is computed in the same way as for full years of use, because the expense is based on productive output or service quantity rather than a time period.

Numerous policies are available in applying depreciation methods in reporting periods when assets have been held only part of the period. This may occur twice in the life of every asset: once in the period the asset is acquired and once in the period of its disposal. Only if acquisition and disposal transactions occur on or very close to the first and last days of the financial reporting period are the problems of depreciation for partial years avoided.

To illustrate several problems and alternative approaches to depreciation for partial years, the example of Asset 286 is used.

Asset 286

Cost	$100,000
Estimated salvage value	None
Estimated life in years	4
Date of acquisition	Aug. 10
Financial reporting period	Jan. 1–Dec. 31

A fractional-year problem exists because the four years in the asset's life do not correspond precisely to four financial reporting years:

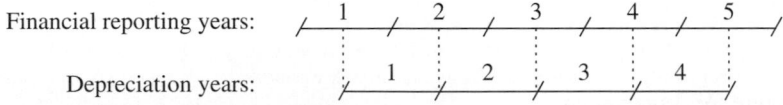

The first depreciation year begins during the first financial reporting year and ends during the second financial reporting year. This sequence continues throughout the life of Asset 286, with the financial reporting periods following a January-through-December pattern and the depreciation years following an August-to-August pattern.

A number of policies may be adopted for the fractional-year problem that exists in the first and last years in the asset's life. Several of these are applied to Asset 286 in Exhibit 12–6, which uses the straight-line method of depreciation.

Several observations are possible concerning these approaches to the fractional-year problem. Policy 1 is widely practiced and results in the most precise recognition of depreciation in terms of time. Because depreciation computations incorporate numerous assumptions

EXHIBIT 12–6

Alternative Approaches to Fractional-Year Problem for Asset 286
Straight-Line Method

Fractional-Year Policy	Depreciation Recognized in Financial-Reporting Periods				
	1	2	3	4	5
1. Recognize depreciation to nearest full month	$10,417*	$25,000[†]	$25,000	$25,000	$14,583[‡]
2. Recognize depreciation to nearest full year	–0–	25,000	25,000	25,000	25,000
3. Recognize depreciation to nearest half year	12,500[§]	25,000	25,000	25,000	12,500
4. Recognize one-half year's depreciation in period of acquisition and one-half in period of disposal	12,500	25,000	25,000	25,000	12,500
5. Recognize full year's depreciation in period of acquisition and none in period of disposal	25,000	25,000	25,000	25,000	–0–
6. Recognize no depreciation in period of acquisition and full year in period of disposal	–0–	25,000	25,000	25,000	25,000

*$5/12$ (100,000/4)
[†]$(100,000/4)$
[‡]$7/12$ (100,000/4)
[§]$(25,000 \times \frac{1}{2})$

and estimates, computations based on periods of time shorter than one month are rarely made. In the case of Asset 286, five months (August–December) of depreciation are recognized in the first financial reporting period, because the asset was acquired in the first half of August. Seven months of depreciation remain to be recognized in the fifth financial reporting period. Under Policy 2 no depreciation is taken in the first year, because the enterprise acquired the asset in the last half of the year. If the asset had been acquired in the first half, a full year's depreciation would have been taken in the first year and none in the last year. In Policy 3 depreciation is recognized to the nearest half year. Thus, if the asset is acquired in the period of January–March, a full year's depreciation is taken in the first year. If the asset is acquired in the period April–September, a half-year's depreciation is taken; and if the asset is acquired in the period October–December, no depreciation is taken. In Policies 1, 2, and 3, the date of the acquisition of the asset influences the amount of depreciation recognized in the first and last years.

Policies 4, 5, and 6 differ from Policies 1, 2, and 3 in that assets are treated the same, regardless of when they are acquired. In Policy 4, a half-year's depreciation is taken in the first year and the same in the last year. In Policy 5, a full year's depreciation is taken in the first year and none in the last year. In Policy 6, no depreciation is taken in the first year and a full year's depreciation is taken in the last year. Policies 5 and 6 resolve the fractional-year problem by forcing the depreciation year and the financial reporting year to coincide.

Applying fractional-year policies when accelerated depreciation methods are used varies only in that the amount of depreciation recognized declines each year. For example, with the sum-of-the-years'-digits method, Asset 286 would be depreciated as follows under Policies 1 and 3:

$$
\begin{array}{cc}
\textbf{Policy 1} & \textbf{Policy 3} \\
\textbf{Nearest Full Month} & \textbf{Nearest Half Year}
\end{array}
$$

Year 1: $\$100{,}000 \times \left(\dfrac{4}{10}\right) \times \left(\dfrac{5 \text{ mo.}}{12 \text{ mo.}}\right) = \underline{\underline{\$16{,}667}}$ $\qquad\qquad\qquad \$100{,}000$

$\times \left(\dfrac{4}{10}\right) \times \left(\dfrac{1}{2}\right) = \underline{\underline{\$20{,}000}}$

Year 2: $\$100{,}000 \times \left(\dfrac{4}{10}\right) \times \left(\dfrac{7 \text{ mo.}}{12 \text{ mo.}}\right) = \$23{,}333 \qquad \$100{,}000 \times \left(\dfrac{4}{10}\right) \times \left(\dfrac{1}{2}\right) = \$20{,}000$

$\$100{,}000 \times \left(\dfrac{3}{10}\right) \times \left(\dfrac{5 \text{ mo.}}{12 \text{ mo.}}\right) = \dfrac{12{,}500}{\underline{\underline{\$35{,}833}}} \qquad \$100{,}000 \times \left(\dfrac{3}{10}\right) \times \left(\dfrac{1}{2}\right) = \dfrac{15{,}000}{\underline{\underline{\$35{,}000}}}$

The same procedure is followed for the declining balance method in that the depreciation expense for each "depreciation year" is allocated between two financial reporting years. Assuming double-declining balance, we compute the following:

$$
\begin{array}{cc}
\textbf{Policy 1} & \textbf{Policy 3} \\
\textbf{Nearest Full Month} & \textbf{Nearest Half Year}
\end{array}
$$

Year 1: $\$100{,}000 \times 50\% \times \left(\dfrac{5 \text{ mo.}}{12 \text{ mo.}}\right) = \underline{\underline{\$20{,}833}} \qquad \$100{,}000 \times 50\% \times \left(\dfrac{1}{2}\right) = \underline{\underline{\$25{,}000}}$

Year 2: $\$100{,}000 \times 50\% \times \left(\dfrac{7 \text{ mo.}}{12 \text{ mo.}}\right) = \$29{,}167 \qquad \$100{,}000 \times 50\% \times \left(\dfrac{1}{2}\right) = \$25{,}000$

$(\$100{,}000 - \$50{,}000) \qquad\qquad\qquad (\$100{,}000 - \$50{,}000)$

$\times 50\% \times \left(\dfrac{5 \text{ mo.}}{12 \text{ mo.}}\right) = \dfrac{10{,}417}{\underline{\underline{\$39{,}584}}} \qquad \times 50\% \times \left(\dfrac{1}{2}\right) = \dfrac{12{,}500}{\underline{\underline{\$37{,}500}}}$

In the case of declining balance, depreciation for the second and subsequent years can be computed directly by multiplying the percentage times the book value at the beginning of the year. For example, under Policy 1, the second year's depreciation is computed as follows: $(\$100{,}000 - \$20{,}833) \times 50\% = \$39{,}584$; under Policy 3, the second year's depreciation is computed as follows: $(\$100{,}000 - \$25{,}000) \times 50\% = \$37{,}500$. The keys to applying fractional-year policies are practicality, logic, and consistency. If numerous assets are acquired and disposed of frequently and during various times of the year, all of the policies in Exhibit 12–6 are suitable for coping with the fractional-year problem.

Consistency

However, the policy selected must be applied consistently. Infrequent acquisitions and dis- **Materiality**
posals of major assets that individually have a material impact on financial position and
results of operations should be depreciated under an appropriate depreciation method to the
nearest full month.

Business operations frequently use **natural resources,** sometimes referred to as **wasting as-**
sets. Natural resources include coal, oil, ore, precious metals (e.g., silver and gold), and timber and are characterized by their removal and consumption and, thus, the loss of physical
characteristics. The replacement of natural resources comes about only by the process of nature and is not subject to human production. **Depletion** is the term used to describe the accounting procedure by which the costs of natural resources are allocated to expense as they
contribute to the revenue-producing processes.

NATURAL RESOURCES AND DEPLETION

Accounting for natural resources parallels closely accounting for property, plant, and **Asset/Liability Measurement**
equipment. The measurement of natural resource at cost is based on the sacrifice made to
acquire the asset. The allocation of cost over the quantities of the natural resource used to
produce revenue (i.e., depletion) is typically computed on a unit basis, much like the units- **Matching**
of-output method of depreciation. This allocation matches revenues with expenses in the determination of periodic income. The book value of the natural resource at any time is that
portion of the cost that has not been charged to income. Book value does not necessarily represent the current market value of the natural resource, because the book value is only a portion of the original cost of the asset. The similarity between plant assets and natural
resources is further emphasized by the fact that they are usually presented together in the
balance sheet, with separate disclosure by major categories.

The **depletion rate,** an estimate of the cost per unit of the natural resource, is based on
cost, reduced by any expected residual value after the natural resource has been fully exploited. The depletion rate is then applied to the number of units of the natural resource with-
drawn during the period.

To illustrate the depletion process, we shall assume that Universal Mining Company acquired the rights to mineral deposits for $22,500,000. Management expected 500,000 tons of
the mineral to be economically removed and sold. If, during 1996, 70,000 tons are removed
and sold, the depletion rate and depletion charge for the year are computed as follows:

$$\text{Depletion Rate per Ton} = \frac{\$22,500,000}{500,000 \text{ tons}} = \$45.00 \text{ per Ton}$$

$$\text{Cost of Mineral Removed in 1996} = (\$45.00 \times 70,000 \text{ Tons})$$

$$= \$3,150,000$$

Depletion is recognized by the following general journal entry:

Depletion Expense	3,150,000	
Accumulated Depletion		3,150,000

The natural resource and related depletion are shown in the balance sheet:

Mineral deposits	$22,500,000	
Less: Accumulated depletion	$ 3,150,000	$19,350,000

The depletion expense for the period ($3,150,000) is presented as a cost of production in the
income statement.

If some portion of the natural resource is not sold and remains in inventory, that portion
of the depletion is included in the inventory cost and not charged to income as a cost in the
period of production. For example, in the previous case, if 15,000 of the 70,000 tons extracted in 1996 remained in inventory at the end of the year, depletion expense and the cost
of the depletable resource held in inventory are as appears on the following page.

$$\begin{array}{llll}
\text{Depletion expense} & = & 55{,}000 \text{ tons} \times \$45 = & \$2{,}475{,}000 \\
\text{Inventory} & = & \underline{15{,}000} \text{ tons} \times \$45 = & \underline{675{,}000} \\
& & \underline{\underline{70{,}000}} & \underline{\underline{\$3{,}150{,}000}}
\end{array}$$

Although this process appears relatively straightforward and analogous to the depreciation process presented earlier in this chapter, several unique aspects of natural resources are frequently encountered. These aspects are discussed individually in the following paragraphs:

1. The costs of exploration, development, and restoration.
2. The discovery of natural resources subsequent to acquisition.
3. Unique tax aspects of natural resources.
4. The distribution of liquidating dividends.

EXPLORATION, DEVELOPMENT, AND RESTORATION COSTS

The cost of natural resources may include a variety of expenditures after the initial acquisition of the property or the purchase of rights to explore on another's property. **Exploration costs** are frequently incurred in attempting to locate reserves of the natural resource that can be economically extracted. Sometimes these costs result in the location of reserves that can be economically exploited, and at other times, in the failure to do so. This difference has led to two accounting methods for exploration costs. Under the **successful-efforts method,** only those exploration costs that can be associated with the discovery of producible reserves are considered to be a part of the depletion base of the natural resource; costs not associated with the discovery of producible reserves are expensed as incurred on the basis that they fail to represent future expected benefits. The alternative, the **full-cost method,** assumes that all exploration costs are necessary expenditures to discover the location of producible reserves and are a part of the cost of those producible reserves. Both methods are used in practice and a great deal of controversy has surrounded their use, particularly in the oil and gas industry. We discuss this controversy in greater depth in Chapter 13.

Development costs are expenditures that are necessary to exploit reserves of natural resources that have been located through successful exploration activities. Development costs in the form of tangible assets, such as special machinery and equipment, tunnels, shafts, and wells, are separately classified in appropriate asset accounts and depreciated over their estimated useful lives in accordance with normal depreciation policies. If these assets are limited in their usefulness to the development of a specific natural resource project, they should be depreciated over the life of that project by the same method used for the natural resource.

The property containing a natural resource may be sold after extraction activities are complete. The amount expected to be derived from such sale represents the salvage or residual value and reduces the depletion base. To prepare the property for sale, however, **restoration costs** may be necessary to return the property to its natural state. Restoration costs reduce the net amount expected to be received in the form of a salvage value and therefore increase the depletion base.

To illustrate, assume that for $4,750,000 Willow Mines acquires property believed to contain valuable minerals. The company incurs $500,000 in exploration costs and an additional $1,550,000 in tangible developmental costs before the mineral can be successfully extracted. Geological estimates indicate that 75,000 tons of the mineral is a reasonable estimate of the amount that can be economically extracted. Willow Mines expects to sell the property for $800,000 after exploitation. However, restoration costs of $150,000 will be required to prepare the property for sale. The depletion base and depletion rate per ton are computed as follows:

Initial acquisition price		$4,750,000
Exploration costs		500,000
Development costs		1,550,000
Total acquisition cost		$6,800,000
Less: Estimated residual value	$800,000	
Restoration costs	(150,000)	(650,000)
Depletion base		$6,150,000
Depletion rate per ton ($6,150,000/75,000 tons)		$82.00

DISCOVERY SUBSEQUENT TO ACQUISITION

Natural resource reserves may be discovered on previously acquired property. In this case, the cost of the property does not include a price paid for the natural resource, because that resource was not known to exist at the time of purchase. As noted in Chapter 11, diversity in recording discovery value ranges from the full recognition of the discovered amount to not recording the amount at all. In terms of including a reasonable depletion charge in the determination of income in future years, support exists for the capitalization of discovery value and its inclusion in the depletion base on which the periodic depletion charge is computed. When the existence of the natural resource is known at the time of acquisition, the cost of the asset reflects that fact and depletion is based on cost.

TAX ASPECTS OF NATURAL RESOURCES

Under certain provisions of the Internal Revenue Code, the amount of depletion that can be deducted in determining a company's income tax liability may be computed as a percentage of gross income, which is essentially the same as gross margin in financial reporting. This method is called *percentage depletion* and permits from 5% to 22% of gross income to be deducted for income tax purposes, depending on the particular natural resource involved. Percentage depletion is not available for all natural resources. For example, it cannot be used for timber or large oil and gas holdings. A company logically deducts percentage depletion instead of depletion based on cost for any year in which percentage depletion exceeds cost depletion. If gross income is large, the percentage depletion taken for income tax purposes may exceed depletion for financial reporting in an accounting period or in total over the life of the asset. Tax law allows the deduction in excess of cost as an incentive for companies to take the risk of exploring for necessary natural resources.

Despite this unique approach for determining depletion for income tax purposes, cost is the basis for measuring plant assets and applying the matching principle for financial reporting. Recent changes in the Internal Revenue Code, which have limited considerably the applicability of percentage depletion, have reduced the differences in accounting for depletion between income tax reporting and financial statement reporting.

Asset/Liability Measurement
Matching

DISTRIBUTION OF LIQUIDATING DIVIDENDS

In some cases, a company's major business activity centers around the exploitation of natural resources, and no plans exist to replace the resource upon exhaustion. A practice that may be encountered is for the company to distribute dividends to stockholders in amounts up to the total of the retained earnings plus accumulated depletion. To the extent that dividends exceed the amount of retained earnings, however, distributions represent **liquidating dividends** or a **return of stockholders' investments** to stockholders rather than a return **on** their investments.

To illustrate, we assume that Huffman Company had a retained earnings balance of $1,200,000 at December 31, 1995. Accumulated depletion on natural resources totals $1,000,000, and cash dividends of $2,000,000 are declared. The shares of common stock outstanding total 1,000,000. The entry to record the dividend is as follows, assuming that paid-in capital in excess of par of at least $800,000 exists:

Retained Earnings (or Dividends Declared)	1,200,000	
Paid-In Capital in Excess of Par	800,000	
Dividends Payable		2,000,000

Care must be taken to inform stockholders that the $2.00 dividend per share represents a $1.20 per-share return on the investment and an $.80 per-share liquidating dividend.

THE ALLOCATION PROBLEM

Matching

This chapter frequently points out that depreciation and depletion are cost allocation processes. They are an integral part of applying the matching principle to an enterprise's non-monetary inputs, such as inventories and plant assets, to accounting periods for purposes of determining net income. The costs that have not yet been assigned as expenses to an accounting period are maintained as assets in anticipation of future assignment as expenses. We are attempting to match the various **inputs** (costs) into an enterprise's revenue-producing process with the **outputs** (revenues) of that process.

As Arthur L. Thomas has indicated, however, the outputs of a process are the result of not only a number of inputs but also the *interaction* of those inputs:

> *The allocation problem has several dimensions, some of which are subtle. But one is easily described: to match costs with revenues, we must know what the contributions of the firm's individual inputs are. Unfortunately, . . . there is no way to know this.*
>
> *Seeing why this is so requires introducing a final concept, interaction. Inputs to a process interact whenever they generate an output different from the total of what they would yield separately. For instance, labor and equipment interact whenever people and machines working together produce more goods than the total of what people could make with their bare hands and machines could make untended. As this example suggests, interaction is extremely common. Almost all of a firm's inputs interact with each other—their failure to do so would ordinarily signal their uselessness.*
>
> *Surprising as it may seem, it can be proved that whenever inputs interact, calculations of how much total revenue or cash flow has been contributed by any individual input are as meaningless as, say, calculations of the proportion of a worker's services due to any one internal organ: heart, liver or lungs. Thus, despite all textbooks and American Institute of CPAs or FASB releases to the contrary—despite what you have been trained to believe—our attempts to match costs with revenues must almost always fail.[3]*

Matching

Does this interaction mean that the allocation of plant asset costs is futile and that we should not attempt to apply the matching principle? Not necessarily, but understanding the limitations of matching and cost allocation is important. Thomas further suggests that wherever possible, the Financial Accounting Standards Board (FASB) should develop accounting standards that do not rely on arbitrary allocation. Two primary allocation-free alternatives to conventional financial reporting exist: current value accounting and reporting of cash flows. When allocations cannot be eliminated in financial reporting, they should be kept simple. Complex cost allocation methods should be avoided, and care should be taken not to extend allocation methods to additional areas of financial reporting whenever possible.[4]

FINANCIAL STATEMENT PRESENTATION

Disclosure

Property, plant, and equipment have a significant impact on the financial position of business enterprises. For many enterprises, the investment in property, plant, and equipment exceeds that of any other asset category. The method of depreciation used may also significantly influence the financial position and results of operations of the reporting enterprise.

The Accounting Principles Board (APB) identified four disclosures related to property, plant, and equipment to be included in the financial statements or in related notes:[5]

---

[3]Arthur L. Thomas, "The FASB and the Allocation Fallacy," *Journal of Accountancy* (November 1975), p. 66.
[4]Thomas, p. 68.
[5]*APB Opinion No. 12*, "Omnibus Opinions," 1967, pars. 4–5.

1. Depreciation expense for the period.
2. Balances of major classes of depreciable assets, by nature or function, at the balance sheet date.
3. Accumulated depreciation, either by major classes of depreciable assets or in total, at the balance sheet date.
4. A general description in the method or methods used in computing depreciation with respect to major classes of depreciable assets.

Due to differences in assets of various enterprises and the flexibility permitted by the authoritative literature, information about plant assets is presented in numerous ways in financial statements. In Chapter 11, we reviewed the plant asset disclosure of Meredith Corporation, which presented only total amounts in the balance sheet but presented detailed amounts for types of plant assets in a note to the financial statements (Exhibit 11–5). In Exhibit 12–7, we present the plant asset disclosure from the 1993 annual report of Exxon Corporation. Exxon's principal business is energy, involving exploration for and production of

---

EXHIBIT 12–7

Exxon Corporation
Disclosure of Plant Assets

8. Investment in property, plant, and equipment

	Dec. 31, 1993		Dec. 31, 1992	
	Cost	Net	Cost	Net
		(millions of dollars)		
Petroleum and natural gas				
Exploration and production	$ 62,131	$32,263	$ 62,609	$32,880
Refining and marketing	28,103	16,185	28,166	15,898
Total petroleum and natural gas	$ 90,234	$48,448	$ 90,775	$48,778
Chemicals	9,155	5,006	9,048	5,015
Other	11,746	8,508	10,915	8,006
Total	$111,135	$61,962	$110,738	$61,799

Accumulated depreciation and depletion totaled $49,173 million at the end of 1993 and $48,939 million at the end of 1992. Interest capitalized in 1993, 1992 and 1991 was $374 million, $364 million and $331 million, respectively.

Summary of Accounting Policies Excerpt

Property, Plant and Equipment. Depreciation, depletion and amortization, based on cost less estimated salvage value of the asset, are primarily determined under either the unit of production method or the straight-line method. Unit of production rates are based on oil, gas and other mineral reserves estimated to be recoverable from existing facilities. The straight-line method of depreciation is based on estimated asset service life taking obsolescence into consideration.

Maintenance and repairs are expensed as incurred. Major renewals and improvements are capitalized, and the assets replaced are retired.

The corporation's exploration and production activities are accounted for under the "successful efforts" method. Under this method, costs of productive wells and development dry holes, both tangible and intangible, as well as productive acreage are capitalized and amortized on the unit of production method. Costs of that portion of undeveloped acreage likely to be unproductive, based largely on historical experience, are amortized over the period of exploration. Other exploratory expenditures, including geophysical costs, other dry hole costs and annual lease rentals, are expensed as incurred.

SOURCE: Exxon Corporation, 1993 Annual Report.

crude oil and natural gas, manufacturing of petroleum products, and transportation and sale of crude oil, natural gas, and petroleum products. Exxon operates in the United States and many other countries. Exhibit 12–7 includes Note 8 from the 1993 annual report and an excerpt from the summary of accounting policies concerning property, plant, and equipment, including depreciation. The consolidated balance sheet includes a single asset line, "Property, plant and equipment, at cost, less accumulated depreciation and depletion," at $61,962 million (1993) and $61,799 million (1992). These amounts tie to the totals in the "Net" columns in Exhibit 12–7. In the consolidated income statement, depreciation and depletion are presented as one of several expense items at $4,884 million, $5,044 million, and $4,824 million in 1993, 1992, and 1991, respectively.

Asset categories that are closely related are frequently combined to avoid unnecessary detail in the balance sheet. For example, land may be combined with land improvements or other assets closely related to it. Buildings may be combined with improvements, equipment, or other assets closely related to them.

Straight-line is the most widely used method of depreciation in financial reporting. *Accounting Trends & Techniques,* a summary of the financial reporting practices of 600 companies, indicates that from 1989 through 1992, approximately 94% of the companies used straight-line depreciation. During this same four-year period, approximately 19% used an accelerated depreciation method and approximately 8% used units of production. These percentages exceed 100% because some companies use different methods on various classes of assets. For example, 564 companies in 1992 reported using straight-line depreciation, 100 used an accelerated method, 47 used units of production, and 5 used other unidentified methods, a total of 716 companies. Declining-balance depreciation is the most widely used accelerated method.[6]

CHANGES IN ESTIMATES AND CORRECTIONS OF ERRORS

Matching
Asset/Liability Measurement

Companies often have to change estimates incorporated in depreciation methods. They may also have to correct errors in past cost and depreciation amounts.

CHANGES IN ESTIMATES

As we have seen in studying depreciation and depletion, matching revenues and expenses requires several estimates. Measuring the asset at cost may involve estimates, assumptions, and allocations. Furthermore, estimates of useful life—in terms of either time or service quantities—must be made, as well as estimates of the residual value of the asset.

These estimates are made when the asset is placed into service based on information available at that time. As conditions change, however, estimates of useful lives may need to be either lengthened or shortened. Likewise, estimates of salvage value may also require revision. Management has a responsibility to continuously monitor its operations and to periodically reevaluate the estimates used in recognizing depreciation and depletion.

A change in estimated life or salvage value is not a correction of an error if the estimate was originally made in good faith and was based on all information available at the time. The change simply verifies the fact that as time passes and more information becomes available, more accurate estimates are possible.

Changes in estimates of useful lives and salvage values are treated on a **prospective basis,** according to *APB Opinion No. 20.*[7] This means that the effect of the change is recognized in the period in which the change is made and in future periods. No recognition is made of the depreciation or depletion that would have been recognized in the past had different estimates been in effect.

---

[6]*Accounting Trends & Techniques* (New York: AICPA, 1993), p. 341.
[7]*APB Opinion No. 20,* "Accounting Changes," 1971, par. 31.

To illustrate the change in depreciation estimates, we assume that Mosteller Company acquired machinery in early 1993 for $275,000. The machinery was expected to have a five-year life and a salvage value of $25,000. Straight-line depreciation recognized in 1993, 1994, and 1995 was based on these estimates. In 1996, management determines that the machine can be used four more years, after which it will have an approximate $5,000 salvage value.

Depreciation for 1996 and the remaining years in the asset's life is $30,000:

Cost	$275,000
Depreciation, 1993–1995	
[($275,000 − $25,000)/5 years] × 3 years	(150,000)
Book value at beginning of 1996	125,000
Expected salvage value, end of 1999	(5,000)
Depreciation base, 1996–1999	$120,000
Depreciation expense, 1996–1999	
($120,000/4 years)	$ 30,000

The book value ($125,000) at the time of the change in estimate is used as the cost figure in the revised depreciation computation, and the depreciation method is applied as usual. At the end of 1999, the book value of the asset will be $5,000, the expected salvage value:

$$\$275{,}000 - [(\$50{,}000 \times 3 \text{ years}) + (\$30{,}000 \times 4 \text{ years})] = \$5{,}000$$

The same basic process is followed with other depreciation methods if either the useful life or the salvage value is changed.

When estimated useful lives of plant assets are important for an understanding of the financial statement, the notes to the financial statements often disclose this. In its 1992 annual report, Ford Motor Company indicates that buildings and land improvements are depreciated on a 30-year life and automotive machinery and equipment on a 14-year life. The disclosure states that a study completed in 1990 found that actual lives for certain asset categories were actually longer than those being used for depreciation purposes and, accordingly, during the third quarter of 1990, Ford changed the way it estimated useful lives. The disclosure includes the dollar effects of this change on both depreciation expense and net income (after income taxes).

CORRECTIONS OF ERRORS

Corrections of past errors in recording assets, depreciation, and depletion are treated as **prior period adjustments** in accordance with *FASB Statement of Financial Accounting Standards No. 16*.[8] Errors involving property, plant, and equipment frequently result from the expensing of asset costs that should have been capitalized and from the incorrect application of depreciation methods.

We illustrate the correction of plant-asset and depreciation errors by assuming that Watson Corporation acquired equipment in 1993 that was expected to be used for 10 years. The asset cost $150,000 and was expected to have a $10,000 salvage value at the end of its 10-year life. During the 1996 audit, management discovered that the equipment had been incorrectly expensed in 1993. Correct depreciation policy called for the use of the straight-line method of depreciation with a half-year depreciation taken in the first and last years of the asset's life.

Ignoring any income tax effects of the error, we can determine the appropriate corrections to the accounts and the proper depreciation expense for 1996:

---

[8]*FASB Statement of Financial Accounting Standards No. 16*, "Prior Period Adjustments," 1977, par. 11.

Cost of equipment	$150,000
Depreciation expense	
1993: [($150,000 − $10,000)/10]½ = $ 7,000	
1994: [($150,000 − $10,000)/10] = $14,000	
1995: [($150,000 − $10,000)/10] = $14,000	(35,000)
Book value at beginning of 1996	115,000
Depreciation expense	
1996: [($150,000 − $10,000)/10]	(14,000)
Book value at end of 1996	$101,000

The following entry corrects the asset and related depreciation of 1993–1995:

Equipment	150,000	
Accumulated Depreciation		35,000
Retained Earnings		
(or Prior Period Adjustment)		115,000

The credit to Retained Earnings represents the net effect of the $150,000 understatement of income resulting from the expensing of the asset in 1993, less the $35,000 overstatement to income in 1993, 1994, and 1995 resulting from the failure to record depreciation ($7,000 + $14,000 + $14,000).[9] The entry to record depreciation for 1996 is made as if the asset and related depreciation had been properly recorded in the past:

Depreciation Expense	14,000	
Accumulated Depreciation		14,000

The prior period adjustment is presented in the statement of retained earnings as a restatement of the beginning balance, as discussed in Chapter 4. In the Watson case the adjustment of the beginning Retained Earnings for 1996 is an addition of $115,000, the amount credited to Retained Earnings in the preceding entry.

The location of errors and the analysis required to determine the impact of errors on the financial statements may be quite complicated, particularly if comparative financial statements are presented. Companies may also change accounting methods (e.g., depreciation method), a subject not covered at this point. Accounting changes and correction of errors are covered more extensively in Chapter 20.

PROFESSIONAL JUDGMENT

In Chapter 11, we identified several areas for which professional judgment is required to determine the cost of plant assets. Professional judgment is equally important when determining depreciation expense.

Depreciation and depletion are inherently judgmental processes. Judgment may be required to determine the cost of plant assets as well as each asset's expected useful life and its residual or salvage value, if any. Useful life may be stated in terms of time (e.g., years), productive output (e.g., units of product), or service quantity (e.g., machine hours). Regardless of the basis on which useful life is estimated, professional judgment must be carefully applied in determining the period over which the depreciation or depletion process will take place.

Estimating salvage, or residual, value at the end of the asset's life is also an important judgment that is required in applying all widely used methods of depreciation and depletion. Judgment is also required when making a change in estimate of certain items, such as useful life or salvage value.

The depreciation or depletion method selected should be appropriate for the particular asset in question. In this chapter, we have identified a number of factors—both theoretical and practical—that should be considered when selecting an appropriate method. Professional judgment is particularly important when selecting an appropriate method of depreciation and

---

[9]The income tax consequences of the correction are not considered in this illustration. As we saw in Chapter 4, the correction is presented in the financial statements on a net-of-tax basis. The subject of correction of errors, including the income tax implications, is covered more extensively in Chapters 19 and 20 of this text.

depletion because of the significant impact the method has on the amount of reported net income and financial position. Generally, judgment is required in associating the contribution that the plant asset makes to the revenue-generating process by considering the decline in remaining service potential for the asset during the accounting period. Because revenue is generated by the interactive functioning of all parts of the business, the contribution any one plant asset makes is impossible to measure directly. This is when seasoned, professional judgment becomes particularly important in selecting the most appropriate method for the depreciation or depletion of each plant asset.

The *matching principle* is the primary accounting principle that explains the process of depreciation. In this chapter, we have illustrated several methods of depreciation. We have also discussed problems inherent in applying the matching principle such as partial year depreciation.

    The *consistency principle* is particularly important in depreciation inasmuch as consistent application of accounting methods over time is necessary in generating information for successive accounting periods that can be compared in evaluating the financial progress of the reporting entity. The *disclosure principle* also impacts the presentation of plant assets in the financial statements. Companies typically include important information concerning plant assets in both the financial statements and in related notes.

    We can see the problems inherent in applying the *asset/liability measurement, matching,* and *consistency principles* in situations in which errors of previous periods are discovered and in which changes in estimates required to apply these accounting principles are made. These accounting problems are only introduced in this chapter and are addressed and illustrated more completely in Chapter 19.

CONCLUDING REMARKS

Matching

Consistency

Disclosure

Asset/Liability Measurement

Matching

Consistency

KEY POINTS

1. Depreciation is the process of allocating the cost of property, plant, and equipment as an expense in a systematic and rational manner to those periods expected to benefit from the use of the asset. (Objective 1)

2. Depreciation is a necessary part of applying the matching principle to long-lived assets that are used in the production of revenue. (Objective 1)

3. Several accounting methods are used to allocate the cost of individual plant assets to the periods that benefit from their use. Those methods can be distinguished between those based on time and those based on activity level. (Objective 2)

4. Special accounting policies are adopted to handle situations in which plant assets are used for less than a complete accounting period. Consistency is an important accounting principle in handling this special accounting problem. (Objective 2)

5. Natural resources are a special type of property, plant, and equipment. The allocation of the cost of natural resources is called *depletion* and is similar to depreciation of other plant assets. (Objective 3)

6. Authoritative accounting pronouncements require several specific items of information to be disclosed in the financial statements concerning plant assets. These include the balances in major classes of depreciable assets, accumulated depreciation, depreciation expense, and a general description of the depreciation methods used. (Objective 4)

7. Changes in estimates required to recognize depreciation and depletion are handled on a prospective basis and, therefore, are recognized in the period of the change and in future periods. (Objective 5)

8. Corrections of errors in accounting for plant assets, depreciation, and depletion are treated as prior period adjustments. Previously issued financial statements are restated, and retained earnings are corrected for the past errors. (Objective 5)

APPENDIX A: GROUP DEPRECIATION METHODS

The depreciation methods discussed earlier apply the concept of depreciation to specific individual assets. In some cases, however, it is impractical or even impossible to apply one of the generally accepted depreciation methods to individual assets or to individual components of a complex asset. Several methods are available to compute depreciation for groups of assets that are treated as a single asset for purposes of determining periodic depreciation expense.

Of the many variations of group depreciation methods, the following are included in this section: inventory method, retirement and replacement methods, and group and composite systems.

INVENTORY METHOD

The **inventory method** of determining periodic depreciation of plant assets parallels closely the determination of expense and the related asset for supplies. As assets are acquired, an asset account is established or increased. At the end of the financial reporting period, an inventory count is made of the items on hand. The difference between the asset balance and the cost of the items on hand, possibly adjusted to an amount below cost to reflect wear and tear, represents the depreciation charge for the period.

The inventory method of depreciation is appropriate when a large number of items with a small unit cost are used in the productive process and applying a depreciation method to individual assets is impractical. Examples are machine tools, hand tools, and patterns used in the manufacturing process. The inventory method approximates the depreciation amount that would have resulted from depreciating the assets on an individual basis.

To illustrate, we assume that Tyson Manufacturing Company uses a large number of small hand tools in its manufacturing process. Rather than compute depreciation individually on these relatively inexpensive tools, the company uses the inventory method to depreciate them. The asset account reflects the following activity during 1996:

Small Tools Account

Balance, January 1, 1996	$12,750
Acquisitions	
March 5, 1996	1,300
August 29, 1996	5,420
October 7, 1996	3,500
	$22,970

An inventory count taken on December 31, 1996, reveals that hand tools costing $17,250 are in use. Management determines that these assets should be reduced by 20% due to wear and tear on them to date. Depreciation expense to be recognized in 1996 is determined as follows:

Balance in Small Tools account	$22,970
Value of ending inventory	
$17,250 − .20 ($17,250)	13,800
Depreciation for 1996	$ 9,170

The entry to recognize depreciation is as follows:

Depreciation Expense	9,170	
Small Tools		9,170

No accumulated depreciation account is maintained, and Depreciation Expense is debited periodically for the reduction in the asset account necessary to bring it to the appropriate balance.

Cash may be received when assets are sold. In the entry debiting Cash, the asset account is credited. This effectively reduces the difference between the ending balance in the asset account and the value of the inventory of tools on hand, thus reducing the depreciation recognized.

For example, for the Tyson case, we will assume that the beginning balance and acquisitions are the same as previously stated but that, in addition, $1,500 was received from the sale of used hand tools at December 31, 1996. The following general journal entries are required:

Cash	1,500	
Small Tools		1,500
Depreciation Expense	7,670	
Small Tools		7,670

The $1,500 from the cash sale is credited directly into the asset account (Small Tools), reducing the balance from $22,970 to $21,470. Depreciation is then computed as $7,670 ($21,470 − $13,800).

RETIREMENT AND REPLACEMENT METHODS

The retirement and replacement methods may be used in much the same situations as the inventory method. They are suitable when a large number of similar items are employed by the enterprise and the items are being replaced on a relatively constant schedule. No depreciation is recognized until items are replaced.

The retirement and replacement methods are frequently used by public utilities, which have large numbers of virtually identical items that are constantly being installed and retired: utility poles, utility lines, accessories used in utility lines, meters (gas, water, electric), and telephone receivers.

Under the **retirement method,** the cost of retired items is debited to Depreciation Expense at the time of retirement, and the asset account is reduced by the same amount. The cost of the new items that replace the existing ones is debited to the asset account. No identification of depreciation by individual unit is kept, no accumulated depreciation account is maintained, and no depreciation is taken until units are replaced.

Assume that Ozark Utility Company uses the retirement method to determine depreciation on a large number of utility poles located throughout the city of Ozark. The balance in the Utility Pole account is $250,000 at the beginning of 1996. During the year, poles originally costing $72,500 are replaced with new poles costing $97,000. In addition, new poles that are installed in a new service area cost $19,600.

The following entries are necessary to recognize these events:

Depreciation Expense	72,500	
Utility Poles		72,500
Utility Poles	97,000	
Cash		97,000
Utility Poles	19,600	
Cash		19,600

Any cash received from the salvage of the poles being replaced is treated as a reduction in the $72,500 depreciation expense.

The **replacement method** is similar to the retirement method in terms of the circumstances in which it is appropriate. Under the replacement system, however, the cost of replacing the assets—not the cost of the original assets—is treated as the periodic depreciation. In applying the replacement system to the Ozark situation, we record the following entries:

Depreciation Expense	97,000	
Cash		97,000
Utility Poles	19,600	
Cash		19,600

The original cost of the utility poles is left in the asset account and the cost of replacement ($97,000) is the depreciation amount recognized. Normally, the asset account is affected only if new poles were acquired for purposes other than replacement of existing poles (such as those for $19,600 in the Ozark case).

As is the case with the retirement method, in the replacement method, no identification or depreciation by individual unit is kept, no accumulated depreciation account is maintained, and depreciation expense is not recognized until existing units are replaced. Also, any cash received from the salvage of individual units is treated as a reduction of depreciation expense.

A criticism of both the retirement and the replacement methods is that they do not present the allocation of cost as an expense during the period of time when the assets are being used to produce revenue. The reasonableness of either method as an approximation of the allocation of cost depends on the constancy of retirement and replacement over time on a continuous basis. If continuous retirement and replacement of a large number of similar assets does not apply, these methods should not be used.

The retirement method is a type of first-in, first-out (FIFO) cost determination, since the oldest costs are charged to expense and the most recent ones are maintained in the asset account. In the case of Ozark Utility Company, the 1996 depreciation expense is $72,500 (made up of the oldest costs), and the balance sheet asset is $294,100 ($250,000 − $72,500 + $97,000 + $19,600), which includes the more recent costs of replacement. On the other hand, the replacement method is a form of last-in, first-out (LIFO) since the most recent costs are charged as an expense and the older costs are retained in the asset account. In the case of Ozark Utility Company, the 1996 depreciation expense is $97,000 (made up of the most recent

costs), and the balance sheet asset is $269,600 ($250,000 + $19,600), including the original cost of those items that have now been replaced.

GROUP AND COMPOSITE SYSTEMS

In some cases, individual assets are combined and depreciated at an average depreciation rate for the assets included. When assets are combined in this manner because of their similarity (e.g., a fleet of vehicles), the depreciation system is called a **group system.** Dissimilar assets may be combined for depreciation purposes if they are used in operations as an integrated unit (e.g., components of an integrated manufacturing assembly). In such cases, the depreciation system is called a **composite system.**

The group and composite systems differ from the methods of group asset depreciation in that an Accumulated Depreciation account is kept for the **group of assets** involved. However, the accumulated depreciation does not relate to any particular asset within the group. The mechanics of applying the group and composite systems are outlined in the following steps:

1. The cost of individual assets that compose the group are established in a single asset account.
2. An average depreciation rate is determined by stating the total of the annual depreciation of the individual assets as a percentage of a total cost of the assets included in the group.
3. Depreciation on the group of assets is charged to the Depreciation Expense account and credited to the Accumulated Depreciation account in an amount equal to the percentage computed in Step 2 multiplied by the cost of the assets.
4. The removal of an individual asset from the group is recorded as a debit to the Accumulated Depreciation account and a credit to the asset account in an amount equal to the cost of the individual asset removed. No gain or loss is recognized. Any proceeds received on the asset removal are debited to Cash and reduce the amount that would otherwise be charged to Accumulated Depreciation.

To illustrate, we shall assume that Time Manufacturing Company has a number of small production processes that operate simultaneously to produce several consumer products. The composite depreciation system is used for the assets employed in each process. Information concerning the components of the integrated production assembly for digital watches is presented in Exhibit 12–8.

EXHIBIT 12–8

Digital Watch Production Assembly

Component	Historical Cost	Estimated Salvage Value	Estimated Depreciable Amount	Useful Life in Years	Depreciation per Year
L	$ 27,000	$ 3,000	$ 24,000	8	$ 3,000
M	19,000	4,000	15,000	10	1,500
N	5,000	–0–	5,000	5	1,000
O	62,000	2,000	60,000	12	5,000
P	12,000	2,000	10,000	8	1,250
	$125,000	$11,000	$114,000		$11,750

The five components have been debited to a single asset account, Digital Watch Production Assembly. We compute the depreciation per year on each component by using the straight-line method. The average depreciation rate is 9.4%, determined by dividing the total depreciation per year of $11,750 by the cost of the assets, $125,000. The composite life is 9.7 years ($114,000/$11,750). This indicates that the group of assets will be fully depreciated in approximately 10 years if the 9.4% depreciation rate is applied to cost annually.

A single depreciation entry is made each year for the group of assets, as follows:

Depreciation Expense	11,750	
Accumulated Depreciation—		
Digital Watch Production		
Assembly		11,750

The disposal of a component of the group of assets is recorded by charging the Accumulated Depreciation account. No gain or loss is recognized, because the accumulated depreciation cannot be associated with any particular asset or component of the group. For example, if Component P is sold for $1,000 after five years of service, the following entry is made:

Cash	1,000	
Accumulated Depreciation—Digital		
Watch Production Assembly	11,000	
Digital Watch Production		
Assembly		12,000

The cost of replacing removed components is debited into the composite asset account. When the components of a composite asset change significantly, as might be the case after several components have been replaced, the depreciation rate may require revision. Periodically, a recalculation of the depreciation amount should be made based on the existing components at that time. The periodic depreciation amount is then updated to reflect the current makeup of the composite asset.

The major advantage of the group and composite method is the clerical cost savings that result from maintaining a single asset account and single accumulated depreciation account for several individual assets. In our example of the Digital Watch Production Assembly, only five components exist, so the cost savings are not very great. This example is intended to illustrate an approach, however, and if the compsite asset had many parts, the clerical savings could be significant. A major problem in the case of the composite system is the application of a single depreciation rate, based on a weighted average life, to diverse components whose lives may vary considerably. This variance is illustrated in the Time Manufacturing example, in which the estimated lives of the components range from 5 to 12 years, but the same rate of depreciation is applied to all components. This problem does not arise in the group system, because the basis for combining the assets is their similarity; therefore, the life of each asset is similar to that of the other assets in the group.

Another problem with both the group and the composite systems is that no gain or loss is recorded on the disposal of individual assets within the group. Inaccurate estimates of useful lives and individual assets that are not productive may go unnoticed more easily under the group and composite systems than they would if the assets were depreciated on an individual basis.

APPENDIX B: CASUALTY INSURANCE

To reduce the risk of financial loss due to casualties (e.g., from fires, thefts, floods, or accidents), business enterprises commonly acquire **casualty insurance.** The purpose of this insurance is to shift to an insurance company the burden of a potential loss from such unexpected occurrences. The **face value** of the insurance policy is the largest amount that the insurance company may be required to pay if a loss occurs. Payments made to the insurance company are called **premiums** and are paid in advance of the period of insurance coverage. Thus, payments initially represent prepaid expenses when they are made. Premiums are typically lower when insurance contracts provide for coverage over longer periods of time (i.e., more than one year). For this reason, the prepaid expense for insurance may include both current and noncurrent amounts.

We are accustomed to thinking in terms of cost or book value as a measurement of property, plant, and equipment. For insurance purposes, however, the relevant dollar measurement of these assets is **fair market value.** The amount recoverable from an insurance company is the lesser of the loss based on fair market value or the face value of the insurance policy, unless the policy includes a coinsurance clause, which is discussed in the next section. The recorded amount of the asset—the cost or book value—is *not* the basis for determining the insurance reimbursement and is used only to determine the book gain

or loss resulting from the asset loss and related insurance reimbursement.

Common complexities in accounting for casualty insurance are coinsurance and coverage by multiple insurance policies. These topics are discussed in the following sections, after which the accounting process for recording an insured casualty loss is illustrated.

COINSURANCE

Casualty insurance policies frequently contain **coinsurance requirements** to encourage companies to insure assets at amounts based on their fair market values. Companies realize that many casualties result in only partial destruction of plant assets. In the absence of coinsurance requirements, companies are inclined to insure assets at less than their fair market values, because they would receive full reimbursement for any losses up to the face amounts of the insurance policies.

The coinsurance requirement is stated as a percentage of fair market value of the insured asset and requires the property to be insured to at least the percentage indicated or the insured must share in any loss that occurs. For example, if an asset with a fair market value of $100,000 is insured under a policy including an 80% coinsurance requirement, the asset must be insured for at least $80,000 ($100,000 × 80%) to collect the full amount of any loss from the insurance company. The amount paid, however, will still not exceed the face value of the insurance policy.

The amount recoverable under a coinsurance situation is computed by multiplying the loss incurred (based on fair market value at the time of the casualty) by the percentage of face value of the policy to the coinsurance requirement in dollars. The amount actually reimbursed is the smallest of three amounts: the amount recoverable under the coinsurance requirements, the amount of the loss, or the face value of the policy. These relationships are presented in Exhibit 12–9.

To illustrate, we assume that Stevens Company has insurance for several of its assets under separate policies containing coinsurance requirements. These policies are described below, including losses incurred from casualties on each asset:

	Asset A	Asset B	Asset C
Fair market value of asset	$200,000	$250,000	$300,000
Face value of policy	$180,000	$150,000	$250,000
Coinsurance requirement	90%	70%	80%
Amount of loss from casualty (based on fair market value)	$150,000	$120,000	$290,000

For Asset A, the coinsurance requirement is met since the $180,000 face value of the policy is exactly equal to the coinsurance requirement ($200,000 × 90%). Thus, the computation of the amount recoverable under the coinsurance requirement is not necessary and the insurance company will pay $150,000, the smaller of the face value of the policy ($180,000) or the amount of the loss ($150,000).

For Asset B the coinsurance requirement is not met since the $150,000 face value of the policy is less than the coinsurance requirement of $175,000 ($250,000 × 70%). The maximum amount recoverable is computed as follows:

$$\frac{\$150,000}{\$250,000 \times 70\%} \times \$120,000 = \$102,857$$

Since the policy will pay the lowest of the face value of the policy ($150,000), the amount of the loss ($120,000), or the amount recoverable under the coinsurance requirement ($102,857), only $102,857 will be recovered. The insured party will share in any loss, with the insurance company paying $102,857 and the insured paying the remaining $17,143 ($120,000 − $102,857).

For Asset C, the coinsurance requirement is met, because the $250,000 face value of the policy is higher than the coinsurance requirement of $240,000 ($300,000 × 80%). Thus, the computation of the amount recoverable is not necessary and the insurance company will pay the $250,000 face value of the policy since it is less than the $290,000 loss.

COVERAGE BY MULTIPLE INSURANCE POLICIES

If more than one insurance policy covers the same property, the amount reimbursable under each policy is determined in the same way as described in the previous section. Each policy will pay the *lowest* of the following: (1) the face value of the policy, (2) an allocated portion of the loss, or (3) the maximum recoverable under a coinsurance requirement.

The allocated portion of the loss is based on the face value of the policies. For example, if a company has a $100,000 policy on a piece of property and another policy of $50,000 on the same property, the first policy is allocated two-thirds ($100,000/$150,000) of any loss and the second policy is allocated one-third ($50,000/$150,000) of the loss. The maximum recoverable under a coinsurance requirement is computed as illustrated in the previous section, with the face value of the individual policy used in the numerator of the computation.

ACCOUNTING FOR CASUALTIES

The following steps summarize the process of accounting for a casualty:

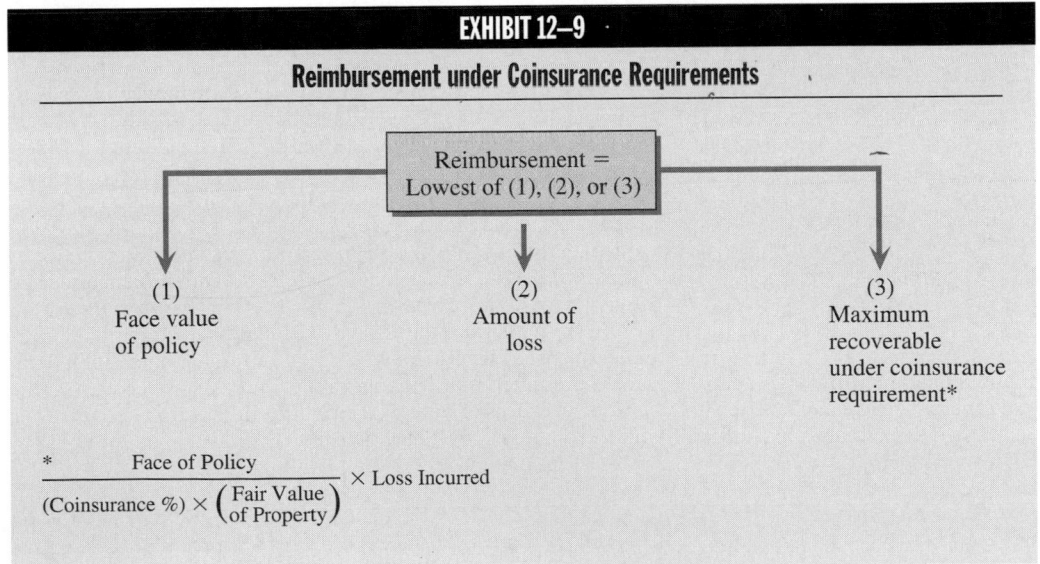

EXHIBIT 12–9
Reimbursement under Coinsurance Requirements

Reimbursement =
Lowest of (1), (2), or (3)

(1)
Face value
of policy

(2)
Amount of
loss

(3)
Maximum
recoverable
under coinsurance
requirement*

$$^* \frac{\text{Face of Policy}}{(\text{Coinsurance \%}) \times \left(\begin{array}{c}\text{Fair Value}\\ \text{of Property}\end{array}\right)} \times \text{Loss Incurred}$$

1. Depreciation expense is recognized to the date of the casualty; other adjustments, such as the expiration of prepaid insurance, are made.
2. A Casualty account is established to serve as a clearing account for amounts relative to the casualty.
3. The Casualty account is debited and credited for appropriate amounts, as follows:

   Debits: Book value of the asset(s) destroyed or damaged.
   Adjustments to Prepaid Insurance resulting from the reduction in insurance coverage for the remainder of the period for which premiums have been paid.
   Other costs incidental to the settlement.

   Credits: Amounts recoverable from insurance companies.
   Amounts recoverable from the salvage of damaged assets.

4. The Casualty account is closed to the Income Summary as a single amount representing the net loss or gain on the casualty and related insurance settlement.

Since the amounts relative to the casualty and related insurance settlement become available over an extended period of time, the Casualty account is used temporarily to house the various components as they become available. A debit balance in the account represents a loss, and a credit balance represents a gain. The latter results when insurance is based on the fair market value of assets and the final settlement from the insurance company exceeds the book value of the lost asset(s) and other costs related to the settlement.

Amounts recoverable from the insurance company are classified as current assets when collection is anticipated in the near future. The loss or gain resulting from the closing of the Casualty account is presented as an extraordinary item in the income statement only if it is both unusual in nature and infrequent in occurrence.

To illustrate the process of recording a casualty, we assume that Murray Manufacturing Company, a calendar-year corporation, has a building that was damaged by fire on May 1, 1996. Specific information on the building and the fire loss is as follows:

Cost of building		$450,000
Accumulated depreciation through December 31, 1995	125,000	$325,000
Fair value of building at May 1, 1996		$700,000
Face value of insurance policy		$500,000
Amount of fire loss (based on fair value)		$350,000
Coinsurance requirement		80%
Prepaid insurance at January 1, 1996		$1,800

Depreciation expense is computed on a monthly basis at an annual rate of $45,000. The prepaid insurance at January 1 represents the premium for the calendar year 1996 that was paid in advance in late 1995. The insurance policy continues in effect after the loss for the remainder of 1996 in an amount adjusted forward for the payment for the fire loss.

The building is determined to have been a 50% loss, based on the relationship of the fire loss to the fair value of the building ($350,000/$700,000). The following general journal entries are required to record the casualty if we assume that depreciation expense is computed to the nearest full month.

To Adjust Accounts to the Date of the Fire Loss

Depreciation Expense	15,000	
Accumulated Depreciation		15,000
[4 months × ($45,000/12) = $15,000]		
Insurance Expense	600	
Prepaid Insurance		600
(⁴⁄₁₂ × $1,800 = $600)		

To Close Accounts to Casualty Account

Casualty ($225,000 − $70,000)	155,000	
Accumulated Depreciation [½ ($125,000 + $15,000)]	70,000	
Building (½ × $450,000)		225,000
Receivable from Insurance Company	312,500	
Casualty		312,500

$$\left[\frac{\$500,000}{\$700,000 \times 80\%} \times \$350,000 = \$312,500 \right]$$

Casualty	750	
Prepaid Insurance		750
[($312,500/$500,000) × $1,200 = $750]		

To Close Casualty to Income Summary

Casualty	156,750	
Income Summary		156,750
($155,000 + $750 − $312,500)		

The entry for $750 to reduce Prepaid Insurance and adjust the Casualty account is necessary because the insurance in effect after the payment of $312,500 is reduced to $187,500 ($500,000 − $312,500). The Casualty account is charged with a pro rata share of the premium related to the remainder of the year. The balance in the Prepaid Insurance account after this adjustment is $450 ($1,200 − $750), representing the premium related to insurance coverage of $187,500 for the remainder of 1996.

In this situation, the Casualty account had a credit balance, indicating that the company had a gain rather than a loss. This gain is presented in the income statement as "proceeds from insurance in excess of book value of building destroyed by fire" or another appropriate title.

QUESTIONS   **12–1**   What is the primary theoretical justification for recognizing the cost of property, plant, and equipment as expense over their estimated useful lives?

12–2 What are the specific elements in the definition of the term *depreciation*?

12–3 Under the matching principle, what distortion in income would occur if plant assets were written off as expenses when they were acquired rather than during their estimated useful lives via depreciation?

12–4 How is depreciation an example of the principle of systematic and rational allocation in the recognition of expenses?

12–5 How do physical and functional factors differ as they relate to the decline in usefulness of property, plant, and equipment.

12–6 What specific estimates are required to apply the widely used methods of depreciation?

12–7 What is the primary justification for the straight-line depreciation method?

12–8 What are primary justifications for accelerated depreciation methods?

12–9 For an asset with a relatively long life, computing the denominator base for the sum-of-the-years'-digits depreciation method can be burdensome if done by adding the digits from zero to the number of years in the asset's life. Apply the shortcut method of determining the denominator for an asset with an estimated useful life of 18 years and indicate the fraction that would be depreciated in each of the first two years.

12–10 The double-declining balance depreciation rate can be computed by dividing the dollar amount of straight-line depreciation by the cost less the estimated salvage value of the asset and then doubling the resulting rate. How can the same rate be computed without using the dollar amount of depreciation?

12–11 What is the primary impetus behind the use of accelerated depreciation methods?

12–12 What justification exists for the use of depreciation methods based on productive output or service quantities?

12–13 Under all depreciation methods, the book value of a plant asset declines through its life. What does this declining book value represent?

12–14 What are several factors that a company might consider in choosing an appropriate depreciation method for a newly acquired asset?

12–15 When a plant asset is acquired or disposed of at a time other than the beginning or ending of a year, how should depreciation be handled for the first and last financial reporting periods during which the asset is used?

12–16 (Appendix A) What is the justification for group depreciation methods in which numerous assets are depreciated as a single asset?

12–17 (Appendix A) What amount is debited to depreciation expense in each of the following group depreciation methods?

[a] Inventory   [c] Replacement
[b] Retirement   [d] Group and composite

12–18 What is depletion and how is it different from or similar to depreciation?

12–19 What are examples of a change in accounting estimate for plant assets? Describe how such changes are treated in the financial statements of the period of change.

12–20 If an accountant determines in 1996 that a depreciable asset with a 10-year life was incorrectly treated as an expense in 1993, what accounting treatment is appropriate in 1996 and future years?

12–21 (Appendix B) What is coinsurance and how does it affect the amount that a company will receive from the insurer in the event of a loss?

12–22 Property, plant, and equipment are conventionally presented in the balance sheet at which of the following amounts?

[a] Replacement cost less accumulated depreciation.
[b] Cost less salvage value.
[c] Original cost adjusted for general price-level changes.
[d] Acquisition cost less depreciation recognized to date.   (AICPA adapted)

12–23 In general accounting usage, which statement(s) applies (apply) to depreciation?

[a] It is a process of asset valuation for balance sheet purposes.
[b] It applies only to long-lived intangible assets.
[c] It is used to indicate a decline in market value of a long-lived asset.
[d] It is an accounting process that allocates long-lived asset cost to accounting periods.
     (AICPA adapted)

12–24 Which of the following four statements is the assumption on which straight-line depreciation is based?

[a] The operating efficiency of the asset decreases in later years.
[b] Service value declines as a function of time rather than use.
[c] Service value declines as a function of obsolescence rather than time.
[d] Physical wear and tear are more important than economic obsolescence.   (AICPA adapted)

12–25 A graph is set up with "depreciation expense" on the vertical axis and the years listed along the horizontal axis. Assuming linear relationships, how would the graphs for straight-line and sum-of-the-years'-digits depreciation, respectively, be drawn?

[a] Vertically and sloping down to the right.
[b] Vertically and sloping up to the right.
[c] Horizontally and sloping down to the right.
[d] Horizontally and sloping up to the right.   (AICPA adapted)

EXERCISES

12–26 Depreciation Computations Walker Company acquired a new machine costing $147,500. The machine is expected to have a $20,000 residual value at the end of its six-year life, and it is expected to provide 17,000 hours of useful service.

INSTRUCTIONS

Determine the first full year's depreciation, to the nearest dollar, under each of the following methods. The machine was used 2,750 hours during the year.

[a] Straight line
[b] Sum-of-the-years'-digits
[c] Double-declining balance
[d] Service hours

12–27 Depreciation Computations The Wilmington *Daily News* acquired a delivery truck to distribute newspapers throughout the city. The truck cost $12,500 and is expected to last approximately four years, during which it will be driven approximately 80,000 miles. Its estimated salvage value is $1,500. The truck was driven 14,500 and 17,600 miles in its first two years.

INSTRUCTIONS

Determine annual depreciation for the first two years of the truck's life using each of the following methods:

[a] Straight line
[b] Service miles
[c] Sum-of-the-years'-digits
[d] Double-declining balance

12–28 Cost Determination and Depreciation Winfred Products Company purchased machinery that had a selling price of $175,000 by paying $85,000 cash and issuing $108,000 of face-value, noninterest-bearing notes. The company paid an additional $5,000 for delivery and installation. Winfred took a service contract with $2,500 annual payments; the first year's payment was made at the time the machinery was acquired. The machinery is expected to have a useful life of 10 years and an estimated salvage value of $20,000 at the end of that time.

INSTRUCTIONS

[a] Determine the cost of the machine for purposes of computing depreciation.
[b] Prepare general journal entries to record these events.
[c] Determine the first-year depreciation expense using each of the following methods:
   [1] Straight line
   [2] Sum-of-the-years'-digits
   [3] Declining balance at 150% the straight-line rate.

12–29 Partial Year Depreciation Roth Company acquired equipment for $500,000 on April 8, 1995. The asset is expected to have a four-year life and a salvage value of $60,000, and straight-line depreciation is to be used. The company reports on a calendar-year basis.

INSTRUCTIONS

[a] Compute depreciation to be recognized in 1995, 1996, 1997, 1998, and 1999 under each of the following *independent* fractional-year policies:
[1] Depreciation recognized to nearest full month.
[2] Depreciation recognized to nearest full year.
[3] Half-year depreciation taken in the year of acquisition and in the year of disposal.
[4] Full-year depreciation taken in the year of acquisition and none in the year of disposal.
[b] If the asset had been acquired on November 20, 1995, instead of April 8, under which policies would depreciation in 1995 and 1999 differ from that computed in [a]? Why?

12–30 Partial Year Depreciation On January 1, 1995, Fenner, Inc., purchased a new machine for $600,000. It has an estimated useful life of seven years with an expected salvage value of $25,000 at the end of that time. Fenner management specifies depreciation of machinery by the sum-of-the-years'-digits method.

INSTRUCTIONS

[a] What amount should be shown on Fenner's balance sheet on December 31, 1996, net of accumulated depreciation, for this asset?
[b] Assume that the asset was acquired on August 5, 1995, rather than January 1. Compute the projected book value of the machine on December 31, 1995, 1996, and 1997, under each of the following *independent* fractional-year policies:
[1] A half-year's depreciation is taken in the year of acquisition and disposal.
[2] Depreciation is computed to the nearest full month.

12–31 Cost Determination and Depreciation The Building account of Cochran Company includes the following items on December 31, 1996:

Building

Contract price	225,000	Gain on sale of	
Options	7,000	old building	17,500
Repair and maintenance	12,000		

The building was acquired in early 1996 and all entries have been made since the acquisition. The options include $5,000 on the building that was acquired and $2,000 on a building that was not acquired. Repair and maintenance costs relate to routine activities occurring after the building was occupied.

INSTRUCTIONS

[a] Prepare the entry (or entries) needed to correct the Building account on December 31, 1996, before the books are closed.
[b] Determine depreciation expense for 1996 using each of the following methods, assuming a 20-year life and $80,000 salvage value. A half-year depreciation is taken in the year of acquisition and the year of disposal.
[1] Straight line
[2] Sum-of-the-years'-digits
[3] Double-declining balance

12–32 Cost Determination and Depreciation Salem, Inc., a calendar-year company, purchased a machine for $65,000 on January 1, 1994. On that day, Salem incurred the following additional costs:

Loss on sale of old machinery	$1,000
Freight-in on new machinery	500
Installation	2,000
Testing before regular operation	300

The estimated salvage value of the new machine is $5,000. Salem estimates that the machine will have a useful life of 20 years, with depreciation being computed on the straight-line method. In January 1996, accessories costing $5,400 were added to the machine to reduce its operating costs. The accessories neither prolonged the machine's life nor provided salvage value.

INSTRUCTIONS

[a] Compute depreciation expense for 1994.

[b] Compute depreciation expense for 1996. (AICPA adapted)

12–33 Cost Determination and Depreciation On January 1, 1995, Phillips, Inc., purchased a machine for $50,000. Phillips paid shipping expenses of $500 and installation costs of $1,200. The machine was estimated to have a 10-year life and a salvage value of $3,000. In January 1996, additions costing $3,600 were made to comply with pollution control ordinances. These additions neither prolonged the life of the machine nor provided salvage value.

INSTRUCTIONS

Prepare a schedule showing the components of book value for the machine at the end of years 1995 through 1998 under the straight-line method of depreciation. (AICPA adapted)

12–34 Asset Exchanges and Depreciation Carter Company acquired a used machine in an exchange for a similar machine from Darter Company. Just before the exchange, the book values of the respective assets were as follows:

	Cost	Accumulated Depreciation	Book Value
Carter Company	$55,000	$25,000	$30,000
Darter Company	47,500	22,500	25,000

INSTRUCTIONS

Prepare the journal entries to record the exchange and the first year's depreciation expense on the books of both companies in the following *independent* situations:

[a] No market value of either asset is available. Carter Company uses straight-line depreciation with a six-year life for the asset acquired. Darter Company uses double-declining balance depreciation with a 10-year life for the asset acquired. No salvage value is expected from either asset. (*Hint:* Because no market value information is available, the acquired assets must be recorded at the book value of the assets surrendered.)

[b] The asset relinquished by Carter Company is valued at $22,000. (Both parties are aware of this value.) No value can be determined for the asset relinquished by Darter Company. Carter Company uses straight-line depreciation with an eight-year life and a $4,000 salvage value on the asset acquired. Darter Company uses sum-of-the-years'-digits depreciation with a six-year life and no salvage value on the assets acquired. (*Hint:* Because losses are apparent, the acquired assets must be recorded at $22,000 and those losses recognized.)

12–35 (Appendix A) Inventory Depreciation Method Stark Co. uses the inventory method to account for numerous small tools used by employees. Under this method, depreciation is based on an inventory of tools on hand at the end of the year. Expenditures are charged to the Tools account throughout the year. The balance in the Tools account at the beginning of 1996 was $35,000. The following activity concerning small tools occurred during the year:

Acquisitions (at cost)	
Mar. 12	$18,750
Aug. 28	6,300
Sale of used tools (at salvage value)	
Dec. 19	4,600

An inventory at the end of the year revealed that tools costing $38,800 were on hand and in use.

INSTRUCTIONS

[a] Prepare all general journal entries for activities related to small tools during 1996.

[b] Prepare the balance sheet and income statement for small tools for 1996.

12–36 (Appendix A) Retirement and Replacement Methods Mack Utility Company has a balance in its Water Meter account of $1,790,000 on January 1, 1996. This balance represents a large number of items, each with a small dollar value. The company is continually replacing the meters as its service employees identify units that are not functioning properly. During 1996 the company installed new meters in three different geographical areas, as follows:

Date of Job Completion	Cost of New Meters Installed	Cost of Old Meters Replaced	Proceeds from Sale of Old Meters
Feb. 17	$265,000	$192,000	$17,000
May 28	350,000	—	—
Oct. 30	160,000	93,000	5,000

The May 28 installation of new meters was in a new service area.

INSTRUCTIONS

[a] Prepare all journal entries for these transactions using the following depreciation methods:
  [1] Retirement method
  [2] Replacement method
[b] Prepare the balance sheet and income statement amounts using both of these methods for the year ended December 31, 1996.

12–37 (Appendix A) Composite Depreciation System A schedule of machinery owned by Remdal Manufacturing Company for its Assembly P is presented below:

	Total Cost	Estimated Salvage Value	Estimated Life in Years
Component P1	$440,000	$40,000	10
Component P2	280,000	20,000	5
Component P3	175,000	—	4

Remdal computes depreciation by the straight-line method.

INSTRUCTIONS

[a] Compute the composite life of the machines (in years) and the average depreciation rate for the machines (as a percentage).
[b] Prepare the general journal entry to record depreciation on the machines as a group for one year.

12–38 Correction of Errors On January 2, 1995, Denver Company exchanged a used truck with a competitor, receiving a similar truck in the transaction. The original cost of Denver's truck was $7,000. It had accumulated depreciation of $3,800 and a market value of approximately $4,200 at the time of the exchange. Denver paid an additional $4,400 cash for the "new" truck, which was valued at approximately $8,600.

The accountant for Denver Company recorded the truck at $7,600, the total of the cash paid and the book value of the old truck. He recorded depreciation on the basis of miles driven, assuming a total useful life of 50,000 miles, with 12,200 miles driven in 1995. However, he failed to consider the $2,700 expected salvage value after the 50,000-mile life.

INSTRUCTIONS

[a] At what amount should Denver have recorded the acquired truck? Why?
[b] Assume that the accountant's errors are found in 1996 before depreciation expense has been recorded for that year. Prepare the journal entries necessary to correct the accounts and to properly recognize depreciation expense for 1996, assuming that 17,200 miles were driven that year.

12–39 Cost Determination and Depreciation Melcher Company acquired a used delivery truck for $14,350. The following expenditures were made upon acquisition:

New tires	$425
Body repair and paint	750
Installation of special shelves	375
One-year insurance premium	450

Management expects the truck to be of service for four years and to be driven a total of 60,000 miles. A $3,000 salvage value is expected.

INSTRUCTIONS

[a] Determine the cost of the truck for financial accounting purposes.
[b] Determine the depreciation expense for the first and second years using each of the following methods:
  [1] Straight line
  [2] Service quantity—miles (The truck was driven 9,760 and 14,950 miles in the first and second years, respectively.)

12–40 Change in Asset Life Gatan, Inc., purchased machinery in January of 1994 and applied straight-line depreciation during 1994 and 1995. The machinery cost $128,400, had an estimated six-year life, and was expected to be worth $8,400 at the end of six years. In 1996 management reevaluated its plant assets and determined that this machinery would be useful for eight more years, including 1996. At the end of that period, a salvage value of only $2,000 is expected.

INSTRUCTIONS

[a] What amount of depreciation was recorded in 1994 and in 1995?
[b] When the change in estimated useful life is made in 1996, what entry, if any, should be made to account for the difference between annual depreciation taken in previous years and the amount that will be taken in future years?
[c] Prepare the general journal entry to record depreciation expense for 1996.

12–41 Change in Asset Life Wellman Corporation purchased a machine on January 1, 1991, for $160,000. Upon acquisition, it had an estimated useful life of 10 years with no salvage value, and it is being depreciated on a straight-line basis. On January 1, 1996, as a result of experience with the machine, management decided that the machine had an estimated useful life of 15 years from the date of purchase.

INSTRUCTIONS

[a] Prepare the general journal entry to record depreciation for 1996.
[b] Independent of your answer to [a], assume that on January 1, 1996. Wellman determines that it can extend the asset's life 10 years beyond that date only by investing an additional $15,000 in the asset. The company anticipates a residual value of $5,000 at the end of the revised life. Prepare the journal entries required in 1996, including the recognition of depreciation for the year.
(AICPA adapted)

12–42 Correction of Errors In 1994 North Company bought a piece of machinery, the cost of which was erroneously charged to Depreciation Expense in 1994. The company depreciates this class of assets by the double-declining balance method with one-half year's depreciation taken in the year of acquisition and in the year of disposal. This particular machine cost $62,000 and is expected to have an $8,000 residual value at the end of eight years, at which time the company plans to dispose of it.

The error indicated above was discovered in 1996 as a result of the periodic evaluation of the estimated useful lives of all plant assets.

INSTRUCTIONS

Prepare the general journal entries to correct the accounts and to properly record depreciation expense for 1996.

12–43 Depletion Worsham Company acquired a tract of land containing an extractable natural resource. The purchase contract requires Worsham to restore the land to a condition suitable for recreation after it has extracted the natural resource. Geological surveys estimate recoverable reserves of 500,000 tons and a land value of $1,000,000 after restoration. Relevant cost information follows:

Land purchase price	$10,000,000
Estimated restoration costs	1,200,000

INSTRUCTIONS

[a] What is the depletion charge per ton of the recoverable reserves?
[b] If the company extracts 100,000 tons in the first year and sells 75,000 tons, determine the following amounts:
  [1] Depletion expense.
  [2] Inventory cost of the recovered natural resource. (AICPA adapted)

12–44 (Appendix B) Property Insurance Information about four independent cases concerning casualty insurance on equipment is presented below:

	Case A	Case B	Case C	Case D
Fair market value of equipment at date of fire	$75,000	$100,000	$120,000	$150,000
Amount of fire loss	65,000	80,000	70,000	120,000
Face value of insurance policy	50,000	90,000	75,000	110,000
Coinsurance requirement	None	80%	90%	70%

INSTRUCTIONS

[a] For each case, determine the amount that would be recoverable from the insurance company.

[b] Prepare the general journal entry to record the fire loss and insurance recovery for Case B. Assume that the equipment destroyed had originally cost $145,000 and had accumulated depreciation of $82,700. No adjustment to Prepaid Insurance is required.

PROBLEMS

12–45 Depreciation Computations Fox Machine Company acquired heavy machinery at a cost of $160,000. In addition to the purchase price, it paid $5,000 for delivery of the machinery and $2,000 to train company personnel to operate the equipment. The machinery was expected to provide 10,000 machine hours of service for five years, after which it can be sold for approximately $17,000. Actual machine operating hours during the first five years were as follows: 2,700, 2,200, 2,400, 1,600, and 1,500.

INSTRUCTIONS

[a] Compute depreciation for each of the five years using the following depreciation methods:

[1] Straight line   [3] Sum-of-the-years'-digits
[2] Service quantity—machine hours   [4] Double-declining balance

[b] Comment briefly on the impact on book value that you see when comparing the four methods.

12–46 Plant Asset Cost and Depreciation Information pertaining to Rand Corporation's property, plant and equipment for 1996 is presented below.

Account Balances at January 1, 1996

	Debit	Credit
Land	$ 150,000	
Building	1,200,000	
Accumulated depreciation		$263,100
Machinery and equipment	900,000	
Accumulated depreciation		250,000
Automotive equipment	115,000	
Accumulated depreciation		84,600

Depreciation Method and Useful Life

Building—150% declining balance; 25 years.
Machinery and equipment—Straight line; 10 years.
Automotive equipment—Sum-of-the-years'-digits; 4 years

The salvage value of the depreciable assets is immaterial. Depreciation is computed to the nearest month.

TRANSACTIONS DURING 1996 AND OTHER INFORMATION

On January 2, 1996, Rand purchased a new car for $10,000 cash and trade-in of a two-year-old car with a cost of $9,000 and a book value of $2,700. The new car has a cash price of $12,000; the market value of the trade-in is not known.

On April 1, 1996, a machine purchased for $23,000 on April 1, 1991, was destroyed by fire. Rand recovered $15,500 from its insurance company.

On July 1, 1996, machinery and equipment were purchased at a total invoice cost of $280,000; additional costs of $5,000 for freight and $25,000 for installation were incurred.

Rand determined that the automotive equipment composing the $115,000 balance at January 1, 1996, would have been depreciated at a total amount of $18,000 for the year ended December 31, 1996.

INSTRUCTIONS

[a] For each asset classification, prepare schedules showing depreciation expense and accumulated depreciation that would appear on Rand's income statement for the year ended December 31, 1996, and balance sheet at December 31, 1996, respectively.

[b] Prepare a schedule showing gain or loss from disposal of assets that would appear in Rand's income statement for the year ended December 31, 1996.

[c] Prepare the property, plant, and equipment section of Rand's December 31, 1996, balance sheet.

(AICPA adapted)

12–47 Miscellaneous Transactions   Rosman Company entered into a series of transactions involving plant assets during 1995, its first year of operations. These transactions are summarized as follows:

Jan. 10   Acquired machinery for $10,250 on account, terms 2/10, n/30.
 12   Paid freight-in of $250 on machinery acquired on Jan. 10. The machine was immediately put into service.
 18   Paid the account related to the machinery acquired on Jan. 10.
Mar. 19   Acquired inventory, fixtures, a building, and land for a single price of $520,000. The assets were appraised as follows:

Inventory	$150,000
Fixtures	70,000
Building	250,000
Land	100,000

May   1   Completed costs for $50,000 of renovation on the building acquired on Mar. 19 and placed into service the fixtures, building, and land.
Nov. 1   Acquired a truck and immediately placed it into service. The truck had a list price of $9,000 and was purchased by issuing an $8,200, 12%, two-year note. The 12% interest rate was typical for this type of transaction and is payable annually. The truck was driven 1,600 miles in 1995.
Dec. 5   Acquired a second machine, similar to that acquired on Jan. 10. (Both machines will be used.) The machine was acquired on account for $10,700, terms 2/10, n/30. Payment was not made until 1996. Rosman did not incur a freight charge on this machine.
 31   Implemented the following policies of the executive group of Rosman Company to determine the periodic depreciation on plant assets:

Asset	Life	Salvage	Method	Fractional-Year Policy
Machinery	8 yrs.	None	Double-declining balance	Nearest full month
Fixtures	12 yrs.	$10,000	Sum-of-the-years'-digits	Half-year in years of acquisition and disposal
Building	25 yrs.	$60,000	Straight line	Half-year in years of acquisition and disposal
Truck	50,000 miles	$800	Service quantity—miles	None

INSTRUCTIONS

[a] Prepare general journal entries to record these transactions.
[b] Prepare all adjusting entries.
[c] Prepare the property, plant, and equipment section of the balance sheet for Rosman Company on December 31, 1995.
[d] Briefly describe the meaning of the book values you included in [c]. Explain their relationship to the current market value of the assets.

12–48 Cost and Depreciation Calculations   On January 1, 1995, Mock Corporation purchased a tract of land (site number 101) with a building for $650,000. Additionally, Mock paid a real estate brokers' commission of $36,000, legal fees of $6,000, and title guarantee insurance of $18,000. The closing statement indicated that the land value was $500,000 and the building value was $100,000. Shortly after acquisition, the building was razed at a cost of $75,000.

Mock entered into a $3,000,000 fixed-price contract with Smart Builders, Inc., on March 1, 1995, for the construction of an office building on land site number 101. The building was completed and occupied on September 30, 1996. Additional construction costs were incurred as follows:

Plans, specifications, and blueprints	$ 28,000
Architects' fees for design and supervision	112,000

The building is estimated to have a 40-year life from date of completion and will be depreciated using the declining balance method at 150% of the straight line rate.

To finance the construction cost, Mock borrowed $3,000,000 on March 1, 1995. The loan is payable in 10 annual installments of $300,000 plus interest at the rate of 9%. Mock's average amounts of accumulated building construction expenditures were as follows:

For the period March 1 to December 31, 1995	$ 900,000
For the period January 1 to September 30, 1996	2,300,000

INSTRUCTIONS

[a] Prepare a schedule to determine the individual costs making up the balance in the Land account for land site number 101 as of September 30, 1996.

[b] Prepare a schedule that discloses the individual costs that should be capitalized in the office building account as of September 30, 1996. Show supporting computations.

[c] Comment briefly on the rationale for capitalizing interest as part of the building that you prepared in [b].

[d] Prepare a schedule showing the depreciation expense computation of the office building for the year ended December 31, 1996.   (AICPA adapted)

12−49 Miscellaneous Transactions Cox Manufacturing Company produces tools that it sells to a variety of manufacturing companies for use in their production operations. Many items of machinery are used to manufacture these tools. Presented below are the Machinery account and the related Accumulated Depreciation account of Cox on January 1, 1996, the beginning of the company's fiscal year:

Machinery	$725,400
Accumulated depreciation	(276,100)
	$449,300

The company uses the straight-line method of depreciation. The machinery is expected to have a 10-year life and no salvage value. Each piece of machinery is accounted for individually with a half-year's depreciation taken in the years of acquisition and disposal. Depreciation is recorded on December 31 of each year.

The following transactions involving machinery took place during 1996:

Feb. 1 Sold a machine acquired in 1994 for $10,500, for $4,860.

15 Acquired new machinery costing $15,750 to replace the machine sold Feb. 1.

Mar. 25 Incurred repair and maintenance costs of $8,500.

Nov. 7 Traded a machine costing $25,500, acquired in 1993, for a similar machine. The acquired machine had a fair market value of $20,000. Cox paid $1,000 as a part of the exchange.

11 Incurred repair and maintenance costs of $6,750.

Dec. 5 Sold for $2,500 a machine acquired in 1993 for $7,250.

10 Acquired new machinery costing $12,500.

31 Recorded depreciation for all machinery for 1996.

INSTRUCTIONS

[a] Prepare general journal entries for all machine-related transactions for 1996, including the recognition of depreciation for the year. Provide supporting computations for your entries. (*Hint:* In the November 7 transaction, the machine acquired should be recorded at the book value surrendered, plus cash paid, because a gain is indicated.)

[b] Determine the balances in the Machinery and Accumulated Depreciation accounts for the December 31, 1996, balance sheet.

12−50 Miscellaneous Transactions and Corrections Wyer Company takes a full year's depreciation in the year of acquisition and no depreciation in the year of disposal for all long-lived assets.

At the beginning of 1996, Wyer had five assets, described below:

	Asset V	Asset W	Asset X	Asset Y	Asset Z
Cost	$92,000	$127,500	$27,800	$70,000	$150,000
Year of acquisition	1993	1996	1991	1992	1996
Depreciation method	Straight line	Double-declining balance	Units of production	Straight line	Sum-of-the-years'-digits
Estimated life	10 yrs.	5 yrs.	100,000 units	7 yrs.	5 yrs.
Estimated salvage value	None	$5,000	$3,800	None	$15,000

Additional information about four of the assets has been collected to facilitate making the appropriate journal entries at the end of 1996.

Asset V—Management has determined that the asset will be useful for a total of 17 years rather than the 10 years originally estimated. No salvage value is expected at the end of the asset's life.

Asset X—During 1996, the company spent $10,000 to improve the asset, adding 40,000 units of output to its total expected capacity. Before 1996, 65,000 units had been produced; during 1996 the asset produced 20,000 units. The estimated salvage value remained unchanged as a result of the improvement in 1996, which was recorded as a debit to Accumulated Depreciation.

Asset Y—During 1996 Asset Y was sold for $25,000. The bookkeeper recorded the sale as follows:

Depreciation Expense	10,000	
Cash	25,000	
Asset Y		35,000

Asset Z—Asset Z was acquired in late 1996 to replace Asset Y, which was sold.

INSTRUCTIONS

Prepare general journal entries for each asset on December 31, 1996, the end of Wyer's reporting period, to correct any errors made during the year and to properly record depreciation for the year. Show supporting computations.

12–51 Correction of Errors You have been assigned to help audit Mallard for 1995. Part of your responsibility is to evaluate the accounting procedures used to record plant assets and depreciation during 1993 and 1994, the first two years of the company's existence. No audit was made during those years.

The company applies the straight-line method of depreciation to buildings and the double-declining balance method to equipment. It takes a full year's depreciation in the year of acquisition but none in the year of disposal. Balances in these accounts at the end of 1995 (before 1995 depreciation has been recognized) are as follows:

	Building (10-year life)	Equipment (5-year life)
Cost	$400,000	$160,000
Accumulated depreciation	(75,000)	(102,400)
	$325,000	$ 57,600

Your analysis of the company's records reveals the following:

Building. The building was acquired before the beginning of operations on January 1, 1993, for $400,000. Of this amount, $50,000 should have been allocated to the land on which the building is situated. Transaction costs were an additional $25,000. Another $152,000 in renovation costs was incurred before the building was placed in service. The transaction and renovation costs were charged to expense in 1993. The building was originally expected to have a residual value of $25,000, which appears to have been a reasonable estimate at that time. Recent changes in economic conditions during 1995 indicate that the building will likely be disposable at $100,000 at the end of its 10-year life.

Equipment. No salvage value was expected from the equipment at the end of its five-year life. It now (1995) appears that the equipment will be worth $40,000 at the end of that period. It is also determined that machinery acquired during 1995 for $40,000 was incorrectly recorded as repair and maintenance expense. This mistake has not been corrected.

INSTRUCTIONS

For the Building and Equipment accounts separately, prepare all general journal entries necessary to correct the accounts and to properly record depreciation for 1995. Present supporting computations with your entries.

12–52 Correction of Errors To establish a branch of its main store, Dobson Co. acquired the assets of a competitor. Dobson paid $500,000 in cash and issued 10,000 shares of common stock that had a $25 par value and a $30 market value at the date of issuance. The market value is based on active trading of the stock in quantities far in excess of the 10,000 shares exchanged in the acquisition. To negotiate the purchase price, Dobson used an appraisal of the assets, which reveals the following values on the transaction date:

Inventory	$200,000
Accounts receivable	100,000
Display fixtures	100,000
Building	300,000
Land	100,000
	$800,000

An inexperienced bookkeeper for Dobson recorded the acquisition as follows:

Inventory	200,000	
Accounts Receivable	100,000	
Fixed Assets	450,000	
Cash		500,000
Common Stock (10,000 shares @ $25)		250,000

A further analysis of the Fixed Asset account reveals that the same bookkeeper entered the following items in the account during 1995:

Debit Entries

May 1	Acquisition price	$450,000	
May 1	Insurance on building and fixtures		
	(May 1, 1995, to April 30, 1996)	10,000	$460,000

Credit Entries

May 1	Proceeds from the sale of unneeded		
	display fixtures	17,500	
Dec. 31	Depreciation for 1995	22,125	(39,625)
	Balance, December 31, 1995		$420,375

A computation accompanying the depreciation figure for 1995 is as follows: ($460,000 − $17,500)/20 years = $22,125. You have determined that the unneeded display fixtures that were sold represent 10% of the fixtures acquired from the competitor on May 1.

You have also learned that Dobson depreciates fixtures over a 10-year life by the sum-of-the-years'-digits method and assumes a salvage value of 10% of the cost of items on hand when the depreciation calculation is made. The building is subject to straight-line depreciation over a 20-year life and has an estimated $50,000 residual value. All depreciation is computed to the nearest full month. This information was apparently ignored by the bookkeeper.

INSTRUCTIONS

[a] Prepare general journal entries to correct the accounts on December 31, 1995, assuming that the books have not been closed. For each entry, explain to the bookkeeper why the entry is necessary and what error(s) were made in the original recording of the item.

[b] Prepare the balance sheet for property, plant, and equipment on December 31, 1995.

[c] Determine the appropriate depreciation expense amounts for the display fixtures and building for 1996.

12–53 Depletion and Depreciation Rim Mine Corporation acquired property in 1996 that is believed to include valuable mineral deposits. The cost of the property was $900,000. Geological estimates indicate that approximately 10,000,000 tons of the mineral may be economically extracted. It is further estimated that the property can be sold for $250,000 to be used for commercial development following mineral extraction. For $80,000, Rim expects to restore the land to a condition appropriate for resale.

After initial acquisition, the following costs were incurred:

Exploration costs—$350,000 (related to expected producible mineral reserves).

Development costs—$325,000 (related to development of tunnels and shafts in the ground); $560,000 (related to specialized production equipment).

INSTRUCTIONS

[a] Prepare general journal entries necessary to record these transactions, beginning with the initial acquisition and including depletion and depreciation for 1996 using the following additional information:

[1] It extracted and sold 3,720,000 tons of the mineral during 1996.

[2] The specialized production equipment will be useful in ongoing production operations; it has an eight-year life expectancy and a $35,000 salvage value. Double-declining balance depreciation is to be used, with a full year's depreciation taken in 1996.

[b] How would your entries in [a] differ if the specialized production equipment is acquired solely for use in the extraction of the mineral for this project? (The $35,000 salvage value is still a reasonable estimate.)

12–54 Income Statement Wilman Mining Company went into business in January 1995 to mine and sell a mineral. Assets were acquired as follows:

Asset	Cost	Estimated Useful Life	Residual Value
Land and mineral deposit	$1,000,000*	10,000,000 tons	$200,000[†]
Mine building	75,000	life of mine	5,000
Equipment	650,000	8 years	65,000

*Additional costs

Exploration costs (related to minerals discovered)	$ 88,000
Development costs	110,000

[†]Restoration costs (estimated cost of preparing
land for sale at $200,000) 75,000

Depreciation policies of the company are as follows:
   Mineral deposits—tons extracted basis
   Mine building—same basis as mineral deposits
   Equipment—double-declining balance

Operating data for 1995 and 1996 are as follows:

	1995	1996
Tons of mineral extracted	1,500,000	2,500,000
Tons of mineral sold at $4 per ton	1,200,000	2,000,000
Costs of mineral extraction, exclusive of depreciation and depletion (labor, maintenance, etc.)	$1,175,000	$2,260,000
Selling and administrative costs	$985,000	$1,660,000

Inventory of extracted minerals is carried on the first-in, first-out basis. The cost basis for inventory produced during a given period is computed at the average production cost for that period.

Wilman had 500,000 shares of common stock outstanding in 1995 and 520,000 in 1996.

INSTRUCTIONS

Prepare comparative income statements for 1995 and 1996, providing computations to support your entries, and ignoring income taxes. The company's year-end is December 31.

12–55 (Appendix A) Composite Depreciation System Wong Manufacturing Company uses the composite depreciation system for its Production Assembly L35. The individual components in the assembly and their estimated residual values and estimated lives are presented below:

Component	Cost	Estimated Salvage Value	Estimated Useful Life in Years
L35-1	$125,000	$25,000	5
L35-2	36,000	1,000	7
L35-3	117,000	17,000	10
L35-4	42,000	–0–	6
L35-5	19,500	1,500	6
L35-6	211,250	11,250	8
L35-7	82,600	1,600	9

INSTRUCTIONS

[a] Determine the composite life of Assembly L35 and the annual depreciation rate.

[b] Prepare the adjusting entry to record depreciation for the first year of the assembly's life. Depreciation is recorded to the nearest hundred dollars.

[c] During the second year of the asset's life, Component L35-2 is determined to be incompatible with the other components and is sold for $20,000. Record the disposal of Component L35-2.

[d] Component L35-2 is replaced with a new component costing $50,000 and having an estimated nine-year life and a $500 salvage value. Record this replacement and depreciation for the second year.

[e] Disregard the information in [d]. Management determines that Component L35-2 must be replaced with a highly specialized piece of equipment, now in the experimental stage. This component costs $100,000, is expected to be useful for only two years, and will have no salvage value. Record the replacement and depreciation for the second year.

12–56 (Appendix A) **Group Depreciation Methods** Maples Company is considering the use of a group depreciation method for Asset X. The company uses many units of Asset X at all times and is constantly replacing them, the price is relatively low. Information about Asset X for 1996 has been estimated as follows:

	Units
Beginning balance	100,000
Additions	78,000
Retirements	(62,000)
Ending balance	116,000

Asset X is replaced on a FIFO basis. The beginning balance in Asset X is $250,000, indicating a $2.50 unit cost. Additions were made at a $2.60 unit cost during 1996. Retirements were salvaged for $5,000.

INSTRUCTIONS

[a] Prepare the general journal entries to record additions, retirements, and depreciation for the year using each of the following group depreciation methods:
[1] Inventory
[2] Replacement
[3] Retirement

[b] Determine the depreciation expense and the asset balance to be presented in the 1996 financial statements under each depreciation method in [a].

[c] Write a paragraph explaining why a company might choose to use a group depreciation system rather than treating each asset as an individual unit.

12–57 (Appendix B) **Property Insurance** This problem contains two *independent* parts.

Part 1. Jack Company has several assets under separate insurance policies that contain co-insurance requirements. Descriptions of these policies and insurable losses sustained on each asset are as follows:

	Asset W	Asset X	Asset Y
Fair market value of asset	$45,000	$25,000	$40,000
Face value of policy	$40,000	$22,500	$25,000
Coinsurance requirement	80%	90%	85%
Amount of casualty loss	$25,000	$24,000	$30,000

INSTRUCTIONS

Determine the amount to be reimbursed by the insurance company for Assets W, X, and Y.

Part 2. Frost Company has two insurance policies on its building. Policy 1 has a face value of $500,000; Policy 2 has a face value of $300,000. The estimated value of the building is $1,000,000. The company recently sustained a $750,000 loss when a fire destroyed a major portion of the building.

INSTRUCTIONS
Determine the amount to be received from each policy in the following independent cases:

[a] The policies contain no coinsurance requirements.
[b] Both policies have 90% coinsurance requirements.
[c] Policy 1 has a 90% coinsurance requirement and Policy 2 has a 70% coinsurance requirement.

12–58 Asset Section of Balance Sheet Mallory, Inc., manufactures a variety of medical instruments and supplies. The company uses the calendar year for reporting purposes. Information regarding Mallory's assets as of December 31, 1996, before any year-end adjustments, follows.

Short- and Long-Term Investments. Mallory invests excess funds in short-term marketable securities. The company also has long-term investments in the common stock of other companies. Mallory's holdings of common stock represent less than 5% ownership in those companies. Short-term investments are considered "trading" securities and long-term investments are considered "available-for sale" securities for purposes of applying *FASB Statement 115,* "Accounting for Certain Investments in Debt and Equity Securities." Details are shown below.

Information on Mallory's Holdings of Common Stocks

Investments	Acquisition Date	Purchase Price	Market Values Dec. 31, 1995	Dec. 31, 1996
Short-term				
PWR, Inc.	Mar. 1, 1996	$ 130,000	—	$ 123,000
Tyra Company	Aug. 15, 1996	80,000	—	75,500
Marank Company	Nov. 20, 1996	50,000	—	51,500
Total short-term investments		260,000	—	250,000
Long-term				
Grabill Corporation	July 1, 1995	117,000	$112,000	113,000
Mikott, Inc.	Mar. 1, 1994	242,000	260,000	252,000
Stanor Company	Dec. 15, 1993	165,000	168,000	170,000
Clarmit, Inc.	Aug. 22, 1992	286,000	272,000	260,000
Total long-term investments		810,000	812,000	795,000
Total investments		$1,070,000	$812,000	$1,045,000

None of the declines in market prices are considered permanent. Dividends that have been declared but have not been received as of December 31, 1996, total $10,300.

Accounts Receivable. The outstanding accounts receivable as of December 31, 1996, total $304,000. The allowance for uncollectible accounts had a credit balance of $16,800 on December 31, 1995. A total of $6,400 in uncollectible accounts was written off during 1996. An aging of the accounts receivable on December 31, 1996, shows that a total of $12,400 of the accounts receivable will be uncollectible.

Notes Receivable. Mallory holds two notes from trade customers that are due in 1997. In addition, Mallory holds a note that resulted from the sale of some of its manufacturing equipment. This note is not due until 1999. Interest is due on the anniversary date of the note and has not been accrued as of December 31, 1996. Details follow, with the two trade notes listed first.

Date of Note	Maturity Date	Face Amount	Annual Interest Rate
Apr. 1, 1996	Mar. 31, 1997	$150,000	8%
July 1, 1996	June 30, 1997	275,000	8%
Jan. 1, 1995	Dec. 31, 1999	450,000	9%
		$875,000	

Inventories. Inventories are valued at the lower of cost or market value. Cost is determined by the FIFO method. Mallory's physical count of inventory reflects that merchandise with a cost of $2,500,000 and market value of $3,200,000 was on hand on December 31, 1996. In addition to this inventory, Mallory had merchandise costing $240,000 still out on consignment. The handling and shipping charges to ship the merchandise to the consignee totaled $8,000, and the market value was $300,000.

Property, Plant, and Equipment. Mallory states all property at cost. The property and related account balances before the current year's depreciation expense are shown below. The depreciation expense for 1996 is $125,000 for the building and $150,000 for the equipment and furniture.

	Cost	Accumulated Depreciation (before adjustment)
Land	$1,450,000	—
Buildings	3,600,000	$1,425,000
Equipment and furniture	1,750,000	785,000
	$6,800,000	$2,210,000

Included in the amount for land is $250,000 for a parcel acquired on December 28, 1996, as a potential building site. As part of the contract to acquire the land, Mallory also had to pay $20,000 in delinquent property taxes; this amount was recorded as an expense.

ADDITIONAL INFORMATION

Cash. The total in the various bank accounts and imprest petty cash funds amounts to $165,000.

Insurance. Mallory has purchased insurance to protect its assets and operations. The following policies will be in effect during 1997:

Policy No.	Date of Policy	Premium Amount	Coverage in Years
JNA-XY5782	July 1, 1994	$18,000	3
DOME-NX85472	Apr. 1, 1995	30,000	3
FMC-BD287X	Oct. 1, 1996	8,000	1

Patent. Mallory acquired patent rights on January 2, 1996, for $75,000. At that time, management estimated that the patent would provide economic benefits to the company for the next five years.

INSTRUCTIONS

[a] Prepare a classified asset section of the statement of financial position for Mallory, Inc., on December 31, 1996, as it should appear in the annual report to shareholders.

[b] Describe the information pertaining to Mallory's assets, which must be disclosed in the notes to the 1996 financial statements in the annual report to its shareholders. (CMA adapted)

CASES

12–59 Expensing versus Amortizing Asset Costs Constructo Corporation sells and erects "shell houses." These are frame structures that are completely finished on the outside but are unfinished on the inside except for flooring, partition studding, and ceiling joists. Shell houses are sold chiefly to customers who are handy with tools and who have time to do the interior wiring, plumbing, wall finishing, and other work necessary to complete the houses.

Constructo buys shell houses from a manufacturer in unassembled packages consisting of all lumber, roofing, doors, windows, and similar materials. Upon commencing operations in a new area, Constructo buys or leases land for its local warehouse, field office, and display houses. Sample display houses are erected for $6,000 to $10,000. The unassembled packages constitute the majority of the expense; erection is a short, low-cost operation. Sample models are torn down or altered every three to seven years. Sample display houses have little salvage value because dismantling and moving costs amount to nearly as much as the cost of an unassembled package.

INSTRUCTIONS

[a] Constructo must make a choice between (1) expensing the costs of sample display houses in the period in which the expenditure is made and (2) spreading the costs over more than one period. Discuss the advantages of each method.

[b] Would it be preferable to amortize the cost of display houses on the basis of (1) the passage of time or (2) the number of shell houses sold? Explain. (AICPA adapted)

12–60 Depreciation Policy   Rhonda Manufacturing Company was organized January 1, 1995. During 1995 it used the straight-line method of depreciating its plant assets in its reports to management.

On November 8, you meet with Rhonda's officers to discuss the depreciation method to be used for income tax and stockholder reporting. The company's president has suggested a new method, which he believes is more suitable than the straight-line method for the period of rapid expansion of production and capacity that he foresees. Below, the proposed method is applied to a fixed asset with an original cost of $32,000, an estimated useful life of five years, and an estimated salvage value of $2,000.

Year	Years of Life Used	Fraction Rate	Depreciation Expense	Accumulated Depreciation at Year-End	Book Value at Year-End
1	1	1/15	$ 2,000	$ 2,000	$30,000
2	2	2/15	4,000	6,000	26,000
3	3	3/15	6,000	12,000	20,000
4	4	4/15	8,000	20,000	12,000
5	5	5/15	10,000	30,000	2,000

The president favors the new method because he has heard the following:

[1] It will increase the funds recovered during the years near the end of the assets' useful lives, when maintenance and replacement disbursements will be high.

[2] It will result in increased write-offs in later years and thereby reduce taxes.

INSTRUCTIONS

[a] What is the purpose of accounting for depreciation?

[b] Is the president's proposal within the scope of generally accepted accounting principles? Discuss the circumstances under which the method would be reasonable and those under which it would not be reasonable.

[c] The president asks your advice:

    [1] Do depreciation charges recover or create funds? Explain.

    [2] Assume that the IRS will accept the proposed depreciation method in this particular case. If the method were used for stockholder and tax reporting purposes, how would it affect the availability of funds generated by operations?   (AICPA adapted)

12–61 Significance of Book Value   When John Severance, president of Severance, Inc., opened his office on Monday, March 8, he discovered that a robbery had occurred over the weekend. Someone had entered the office through a back window and had stolen a computer from one of the office desks. After notifying authorities, John identified the serial number on those computers that were not taken and compared them with the plant asset records that were kept in the company vault. After doing this, he said to the employees: "Thank goodness the thief took one of our computers that was almost fully depreciated. That certainly eases our situation since the computers are not insured."

INSTRUCTIONS

[a] What is your reaction to John's evaluation of this situation?

[b] Is Severance, Inc., "better off" because a thief stole a computer on which more depreciation has already been taken in comparison with other computers? Why?

JUDGMENT CASES

12–62 Gain Recognition and Depletion   White Paper Company owns large holdings of forest lands in the Pacific Northwest that are used to supply the company's mills with various types of pulp. The company recently received an offer on some of its least productive land and has decided to sell.

Specifically, the company has received an offer to sell a portion of one large forest that it has owned for many decades. The president wants to determine how the sale will be reported in the company's financial statements and the amount of gain to be recognized. The current carrying amount of the forest on the company's books of $8,000,000 represents the cost of the forest, less charges for depletion, plus improvements (such as roads and reforestation), and cultivation costs. The portion to be sold represents about 1/8 of the total forest land and the proposed sales price is $5,000,000. The land subject to the sale is mountainous, near a river, and is in a particularly remote area that does not currently have roads developed on it. Recent geological tests, however, reveal that substantial and valuable mineral deposits exist on the land and the buyer plans to exploit them.

Your assistant has prepared the following proposed accounting for the sale. He has assigned a pro rata share of the carrying amount of the tract ($8,000,000 × 1/8), or $1,000,000, to the sale and proposes reporting a gain of $4,000,000 on the transaction. You believe that the problem is rather simple and are satisfied with this suggestion. You have arranged a meeting with the president to discuss the proposed accounting.

You are surprised when you arrive at the meeting and the president points out a number of considerations that he believes are important to the determination of the proper accounting treatment for the transaction. He states that the land has been virtually worthless to the company up to this point. He believes that the other factors and considerations as to the newly found minerals should be recognized in accounting for the sale and argues that only a nominal amount, if any, of the carrying amount of the forest should be attributed to the portion sold, resulting in a gain of virtually all of the $5,000,000 sales price. He reasons:

> *The land we are selling has never been of value to us in our productive processes. Indeed, we never would have bought it if we could have avoided doing so when we acquired the large tract from the U.S. Department of Interior many years ago. The fact that mineral deposits have now been found on it is simply fortuitous for us. The productivity of this forest to our company will remain unchanged by the sale and, therefore, the entire sales price of $5,000,000 is simply a windfall gain that we are receiving. Finally, if we allocate the cost as you suggest, this will leave a relatively small amount of original cost for us to allocate to the revenues generated by the timber production that we will sell in the future from other parts of the land. We will report much higher profitability on the sale of timber than we actually achieve and you don't want that, do you?*

INSTRUCTIONS

React to the president's proposal. Do you think that the proposed accounting for the sale is acceptable?

12–63 Depreciating and Valuing Inactive Assets   High Flyer Aviation has a group of airplanes of various designs and ages. Some older planes are not fuel efficient and have lately been used only when all other aircraft are already in use and for charter flights when other more efficient planes are not readily available in the location desired.

Very recently an oil crisis has occurred due as a result of the invasion of one small mideastern country by another. One result of this crisis has been a dramatic increase in the cost of petroleum products, including aircraft fuel. In fact, the cost of fuel has become so high that the older, less-efficient aircraft are not being used at all because they simply cannot be operated at a positive contribution margin due to the high fuel prices and the effects of intense charter competition. At the time that the company's financial statements are being prepared, the crisis shows no signs of relenting. In fact, the situation appears to be worsening, and most oil analysts predict that the price of petroleum products will remain very high for the foreseeable future.

As a result of these factors, High Flyer Aviation has mothballed all of its older, inefficient aircraft and is attempting to sell them. No buyers have been found, however, and prospects look dim for finding a buyer in the near future. You are concerned with whether the carrying amounts in the financial statements of these older aircraft should continue to be depreciated or whether they have been impaired and should be written down to lower figures than their current carrying values. The aircraft have been depreciated by a combination of methods. The engines, controls, and avionics are depreciated over flying hours while the airframes are depreciated over a period of 10 years by the straight-line method. The president of the company has indicated to you that if she cannot sell the planes at a gain, she will hold them until fuel prices come back down and things stabilize.

> *At that time we will begin again to use these plans profitably. Until then, I don't believe that any aspect of the aircraft should be depreciated or written down to some arbitrary amount that has nothing to do with their value in use. I certainly don't think that the components of the aircraft that are ordinarily depreciated over flying hours should be depreciated when no flying is conducted—that just doesn't make sense.*

Despite the president's assurances, you are still concerned about both appropriate depreciation policy and the realizability of the carrying amount of the aircraft. You are aware, for example, that replacing the old engines with new, fuel-efficient ones is one way to make the aircraft more serviceable. You also know that this is a very expensive alternative.

INSTRUCTIONS

Should any (or all) of the components of the inactive aircraft continue to be depreciated while they are not being used? Should the value of the aircraft be written down to an amount lower than their undepreciated cost? If so, describe the conceptual amount at which they should be carried on the financial statements of High Flyer Aviation. If you believe continued depreciation and/or a write-down is appropriate, how will you convince the president to accept this accounting treatment?

12–64 Depreciating a Leased Asset Stokes Petroleum Company has constructed equipment for a large offshore drilling platform that it planned to use in its exploration and production efforts. The company has now decided, however, to lease that equipment to another company because of unanticipated cash flow needs. This lease has a term of five years, and the company expects to be able to lease the equipment to other companies for its entire economic life of approximately 15 years. If fact, management believes that it will be possible to negotiate leases with higher payments through other companies after the initial 5-year lease is complete. The total amount of the lease payments that the company expects to receive over the economic life of the equipment exceeds the current carrying amount of the equipment on the financial statements of Stokes by only a small amount. If those anticipated cash receipts were discounted at any reasonable rate of interest, however, the present value of the future cash receipts would be substantially less than the carrying value of the equipment.

Stokes is in the process of preparing its annual financial statements and you wonder how the equipment that was constructed to be used, but that is now being leased, should be depreciated and whether it should be considered impaired in value at this time. That is, the net present value of the expected future cash flows from the leases, some of which are yet to be negotiated, are less than the carrying value of the asset.

INSTRUCTIONS

Should the equipment be depreciated in a normal fashion? Should any recognition be given in the selection of a depreciation method to the belief that the leases following the first lease will result in substantially greater lease payments? Should a loss be recognized now in these circumstances? If so, how will this loss affect the amount of depreciation to be recognized on the equipment in the future? If you believe that a loss should be recognized, describe how you would measure the amount of the loss.

12–65 Estimating Useful Life Fast Fuel, Inc., has just completed a marine fueling depot. As part of the necessary construction, concrete bulkheads and pilings have been put in place to provide the support for the floating fuel dock. Management of the company does not believe that it is necessary to depreciate the cost of the bulkheads or pilings. They contend that the useful life of those fixtures are unlimited, much more in the nature of land and, therefore, should not be depreciated.

When consulted, the engineers responsible for the design and construction of the facility assert that they believe that the bulkheads will last for at least 100 years and that the life of the pilings is indefinite. They point out that waterfront bulkheads have been used in seaports for hundreds of years and some of them still are in place and functioning. In addition, they note that the construction techniques used in the design and construction of the bulkheads and pilings have improved and should be even more durable than earlier ones.

INSTRUCTIONS

Do you believe that the costs associated with the bulkheads and pilings should be subjected to depreciation? Explain the basis and reasoning supporting your position. If you believe that these assets should be depreciated, describe the period over which you believe that these costs should be allocated.

FINANCIAL REPORTING CASE

12–66 Financial Reporting Case Boise Cascade Corporation is an integrated paper and forest products company headquartered in Boise, Idaho. The company operates in the United States and Canada, manufacturing and distributing paper products, office products, and building products. The company owns significant timberland to support these operations.

Below are Boise Cascade's 1993 balance sheet, with 1992 and 1991 for comparison, and excerpts from the statement of cash flows and accounting policy statement.

Boise Cascade Corporation and Subsidiaries
Balance Sheets

Assets	December 31		
	1993	**1992**	**1991**
	(expressed in thousands)		
Current			
Cash and cash items (Note 1)	$ **14,860**	$ 12,588	$ 15,156
Short-term investments at cost, which approximates market (Note 1)	**7,569**	7,744	6,855
	22,429	20,332	22,011
Receivables, less allowances of $1,264,000, $1,757,000, and $4,891,000	**366,187**	366,891	367,218
Inventories (Note 1)	**446,609**	415,930	479,432
Deferred income tax benefits	**38,831**	49,518	47,894
Other	**13,397**	12,993	16,680
	887,453	865,664	933,235
Property (Note 1)			
Property and equipment			
Land and land improvements	**56,871**	56,601	64,334
Buildings and improvements	**571,712**	556,266	593,649
Machinery and equipment	**4,642,434**	4,498,287	4,417,202
	5,271,017	5,111,154	5,075,185
Accumulated depreciation	**(2,261,360)**	(2,044,189)	(1,912,660)
	3,009,657	3,066,965	3,162,525
Timber, timberlands, and timber deposits	**366,054**	385,955	389,454
	3,375,711	3,452,920	3,551,979
Other assets (Note 1)	**249,809**	241,122	243,952
Total assets	$ **4,512,973**	$ 4,559,706	$ 4,729,166

Boise Cascade Corporation and Subsidiaries
Statements of Cash Flows (Excerpt)

	Year Ended December 31		
	1993	**1992**	**1991**
	(expressed in thousands)		
Cash provided by (used for) investment			
Expenditures for property and equipment	**(216,818)**	(275,414)	(293,609)
Expenditures for timber and timberlands	**(4,663)**	(7,537)	(5,065)
Sales of operating assets (Note 1)	**23,992**	202,156	143,374
Other	**8,867**	(31,387)	(24,831)
Cash used for investment	**(188,622)**	(112,182)	(180,131)

Summary of Significant Accounting Policies (Excerpt)

Property. Property and equipment are recorded at cost. Cost includes expenditures for major improvements and replacements and the net amount of interest cost associated with significant capital additions. Capitalized interest was $1,118,000 in 1993, $3,492,000 in 1992, and $6,498,000 in 1991. Substantially all of the Company's paper and wood products manufacturing facilities determine depreciation by the units-of-production method, and other operations use the straight-line method. Gains and losses from sales and retirements are included in income as they occur except at certain pulp and paper mills that use composite depreciation methods. At those facilities, gains and losses are included in accumulated depreciation. Estimated service lives of principal items of property and equipment range from 3 to 40 years.

Cost of the company timber harvested and amortization of logging roads are determined on the basis of the annual amount of timber cut in relation to the total amount of recoverable timber. Timber and timberlands are stated at cost, less the accumulated total of timber previously harvested.

A portion of the Company's wood requirements are acquired from public and private sources. Except for deposits required pursuant to wood supply contracts, no amounts are recorded until such time as the Company becomes liable for the timber. At December 31, 1993, based on average prices at the time, the unrecorded amount of those contracts was estimated to be approximately $210,000,000.

INSTRUCTIONS

[a] What percentage of total assets in 1993 are in the property category? Has this relationship changed significantly over the three-year period 1991–1993?

[b] How significant are expenditures of cash for property and equipment, compared to other cash expenditures, for the three-year period?

[c] What items are included in the cost of property and equipment, other than the initial purchase price of those assets?

[d] What depreciation method(s) does the company use for the various categories of property and equipment?

[e] What is the company's policy relative to recording purchases under wood supply contracts? What is the amount of the unrecorded obligation under these contracts at the end of 1993?

CHAPTER
13

Intangible Assets

OBJECTIVES

1. To distinguish between intangible assets and property, plant, and equipment and to explain how intangible assets contribute to the revenue-producing process.

2. To distinguish between separately identifiable intangible assets and goodwill, an intangible asset relating to the enterprise as a whole.

3. To apply basic accounting principles, such as matching and asset/liability measurement, in accounting for intangible assets.

4. To illustrate the preparation of the financial statement items and accompanying disclosures for intangible assets.

5. To explain the intangible asset *goodwill*, including how it arises, how to estimate its value, and how to determine its cost.

6. To discuss accounting issues that may involve intangible assets, including research and development, development-stage enterprises, and oil and gas accounting.

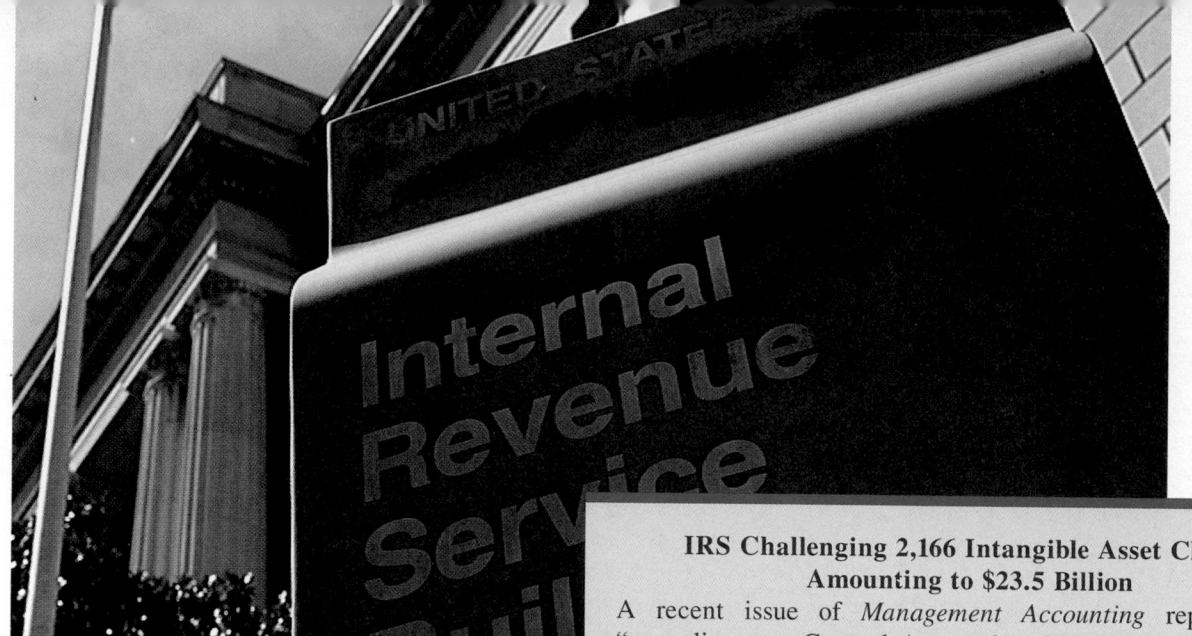

DEFINING INTANGIBLE ASSETS

Intangible assets are factors in the production and distribution of goods and services that generate revenue. Most intangible assets have relatively long lives and are subject to amortization over several periods subsequent to their acquisition. They are similar to property, plant, and equipment, but the distinguishing feature of intangible assets is their **lack of physical characteristics.** The value of an intangible asset accrues primarily from the rights or privileges that the intangible provides the owner. The uncertainty of the amount and timing of future benefits is generally thought to be greater with intangible assets than with other long-lived assets.

The absence of physical existence alone does not qualify an asset to be presented as an "intangible." Assets that lack physical existence are found in several balance sheet categories other than intangibles. For example, receivables, short-term investments, and prepaid expenses are presented as current assets; noncurrent receivables and some investments in stocks and bonds are classified as investments and funds; and long-term prepayments are presented as other assets or deferred charges. Thus, in addition to the lack of physical existence, assets classified as intangible must be used in the production or distribution of other goods or services and must have relatively long lives, making them subject to amortization.

Intangible assets are frequently segregated into those that are separately identifiable and those that lack separate identification. Examples of **separately identifiable intangible assets** are patents, copyrights, franchises, licensing agreements, trade names, and trademarks. Intangible assets lacking separate identification are inherent in a continuing business and relate to an enterprise as a whole. The name given such assets varies from entity to entity, but a common name for this type of intangible asset is **goodwill,** the term used in this chapter.

Despite the fact that intangible assets lacking separate identification vary considerably in nature from separately identifiable intangibles, the accounting profession has developed standards that guide the accounting for *all* intangibles. The most significant of these standards are included in *Accounting Principles Board Opinion No. 17,* which provides the basis for some of the material in this chapter.[1]

Generally accepted standards of accounting for intangible assets incorporate historical cost in applying the asset/liability measurement and matching principles. In much the same way as with property, plant, and equipment, intangible assets are recorded initially at historical cost, determined as the fair value at acquisition. Cost is subsequently amortized over those periods in which the intangible assets are used as factors in the production or distribution of goods and services. Accounting for intangible assets is described below in terms of acquisition, amortization, disposal, and financial statement presentation.

ACQUISITION OF INTANGIBLE ASSETS

An intangible asset is recorded at cost, which is the sacrifice in assets or the incurrence of liabilities necessary to acquire the asset. Intangible assets may be acquired from other enterprises, in which case cost is normally the fair value of consideration given in the exchange transaction. In unusual circumstances, the value of the intangible asset received may be more readily determinable than the value of the consideration given, and in these cases the former is used to record the cost of the acquired intangible asset.

Intangible assets may also be acquired as part of a group of assets or as part of the acquisition of an entire enterprise. Separately identifiable assets and liabilities, including intangible assets, acquired in such transactions are assigned part of the total cost of the group of assets or enterprise acquired. This assignment is normally based on the fair value of individual assets. The cost of an intangible asset not separately identifiable that is acquired in this manner is measured by the difference between the total cost of the group of assets and the cost assigned to the other assets, including the separately identifiable intangible assets. This process is developed in greater depth in a subsequent section of this chapter.

Some intangible assets are developed internally. Costs of developing, maintaining, and restoring intangible assets that can be separately identified and have determinate lives are capitalized in appropriate intangible asset accounts. Similar costs that do not relate to separately identifiable, intangible assets, that have indeterminate lives, or that are inherent in a continuing business should not be capitalized as intangible assets.

We must take care in distinguishing between costs of intangible assets and other expenditures that are appropriately charged to expense when incurred under generally accepted

ACCOUNTING STANDARDS FOR INTANGIBLE ASSETS

Asset/Liability Measurement

Matching

---

[1]*APB Opinion No. 17,* "Accounting for Intangible Assets," 1970.

accounting principles (GAAP). Examples of the latter are advertising, research, and development costs. Frequently, these expenses are closely related to the development of intangible assets and are sometimes confused with them.

The initial accounting for potential intangible asset acquisition costs is summarized in Exhibit 13–1. Separately identifiable intangible assets with determinable lives are capitalized in specific intangible asset accounts, whether they were acquired from another entity or developed internally. Patents, for example, may be acquired from other enterprises or developed internally. Intangible assets, such as goodwill, that cannot be separately identified but result from transactions with other entities should be established in appropriate intangible asset accounts. Costs relating to internally developed intangibles that cannot be separately identified are treated as expenses when incurred, even though they may have many of the characteristics of goodwill. For example, a company may develop an outstanding reputation, much like one that it could acquire through a business merger. Costs incurred to develop this reputation internally are normally expensed as incurred. Expenditures that are charged to expense when incurred under generally accepted accounting principles, such as research and development or advertising, are not established as intangible assets, even though they may relate closely to the development, maintenance, or enhancement of certain intangible assets.

AMORTIZATION OF INTANGIBLE ASSETS

Before the Accounting Principles Board (APB) issued *Opinion No. 17,* companies separated intangible assets into those *with* determinable lives and those *without* determinable lives. Those with determinable lives were amortized; those without determinable lives were not amortized. Under *APB Opinion No. 17,* however, all intangible assets must be amortized over the periods benefiting from their use.[2] In establishing this requirement, the APB made the following observation:

> The value of intangible assets at any one date eventually disappears and . . . the recorded costs of intangible assets should be amortized by systematic charges to income over the periods estimated to be benefited.[3]

A number of pertinent factors must be considered in establishing the periods expected to benefit from intangible assets. These include the following:[4]

1. Legal, regulatory, or contractual provisions may limit the maximum useful life.
2. Provisions for renewal or extension may alter a specified limit on useful life.
3. Obsolescence, demand, competition, and other economic factors may affect useful life.
4. Useful life may parallel the service life expectancies of individuals or groups of employees.
5. Present competitive advantage may be restricted by expected actions of competitors or others.
6. An apparent unlimited life may in fact be indefinite and benefits cannot be reasonably projected.
7. An intangible may be a composite of any individual factors with varying effective lives.

As a practical matter, the APB established a maximum period of 40 years for the amortization of intangible assets. Thus, an intangible asset should be amortized over the shorter of its economic life (which may be influenced by legal or contractual limitations) or 40 years.

---

[2]In requiring the amortization of intangible assets, the APB indicated that companies were not required to amortize intangibles acquired before November 1, 1970, the effective date of *APB Opinion No. 17.* Because some companies began amortizing intangibles that previously had not been amortized whereas others continued to carry these intangibles at their historical cost, some intangible assets are still found on some companies' balance sheets at unamortized historical cost.

[3]*APB Opinion No. 17,* par. 27.

[4]*APB Opinion No. 17,* par. 27.

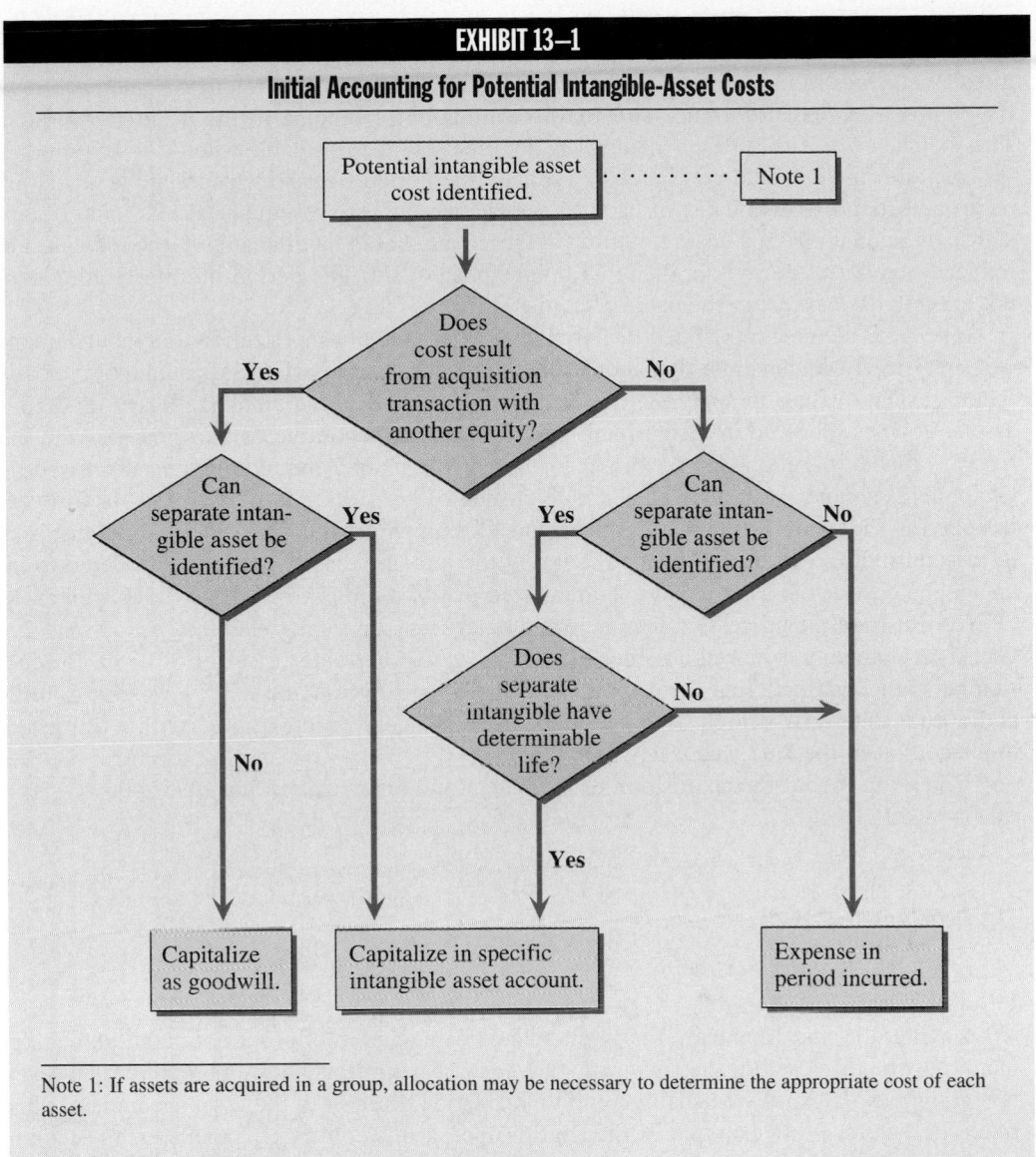

EXHIBIT 13–1

Initial Accounting for Potential Intangible-Asset Costs

Note 1: If assets are acquired in a group, allocation may be necessary to determine the appropriate cost of each asset.

The APB offered little justification for the 40-year maximum amortization period; however, several explanations appear reasonable.

Intangible assets with indeterminate lives, such as goodwill, are frequently amortized over the maximum period. These assets may relate to individual employees or groups of employees and other conditions that are of limited duration. These same conditions are not likely to continue beyond a period of 40 years. Amortization over a 40-year period, even though this is an arbitrary assignment of cost, prevents any one accounting period from being burdened with such a significant amortization charge that income is materially affected. Also, few intangible assets are useful to an enterprise for more than 40 years. In fact, the makeup of a corporation in terms of asset structure, personnel, production processes, marketing strategy, and many other aspects will generally be significantly different when viewed in 40-year intervals.

Materiality

In summary, although the 40-year maximum amortization period is somewhat arbitrary, justification exists for amortization over a relatively long period. Also, if the value of intangible assets does in fact diminish over time, the matching principle requires some portion of the cost of such assets to enter into the determination of income in the periods benefited. This is true even if the life of the asset is not precisely determinable when it is acquired.

Matching

An enterprise should continuously evaluate the period over which intangible assets are being amortized. If estimates of useful lives change due to subsequent events and circumstances, the unamortized cost remaining at that point should be allocated to the increased or reduced number of periods in the remaining expected life. The period of amortization cannot exceed 40 years from the date of acquisition.

The APB also recommended the straight-line method of amortization unless a company can specifically demonstrate that another method is more appropriate. Accountants typically ignore residual values in applying the straight-line method in the amortization of intangible assets. Policies followed in recognizing amortization for partial years vary, but the alternatives available parallel closely those for property, plant, and equipment discussed in Chapter 12. Amortization may be computed to the nearest full month, half year, or full year in applying the straight-line method in periods during which the intangible asset is disposed of or acquired. Expenditures during the life of the intangible asset that are considered to increase the cost of the asset should be amortized over the remaining life of the related asset.

To illustrate the process of acquiring and amortizing an intangible asset, we assume that Clarkson Company acquired a patent in 1995 from another enterprise for $10,000. Production personnel estimate that the patent will be used for 10 years and will be worthless at the end of that time. The straight-line method is used to amortize intangibles, with a full year's amortization in the first year.

Entries to record the acquisition of the patent and amortization for 1995 follow:

Patent	10,000	
Cash		10,000
Amortization Expense	1,000	
Patent		1,000
($10,000/10 years = $1,000)		

Chapters 11 and 12 explain that accumulated depreciation of property, plant, and equipment must be disclosed in the financial statements. No similar requirement exists, however, for intangible assets, so we usually credit amortization directly to the asset account, as illustrated in the preceding example. Although this approach is commonly practiced, an accumulated amortization account for intangible assets is certainly acceptable and is sometimes encountered in business. In fact, if a clear record of the relationship of the historical cost of an intangible asset and its related accumulated amortization is particularly important, such an account is preferable. Unless indicated otherwise, this textbook follows the procedure of crediting amortization directly to the intangible asset account.

Continuing the example of Clarkson Company, assume that in 1997 the company incurs $2,000 in legal costs in successfully defending the patent when a competitor charges that Clarkson Company's patent violates one the competitor holds. Entries to record the $2,000 additional cost of the patent and amortization expense for 1997 are as follows:

Patent	2,000	
Cash		2,000
Amortization Expense	1,250	
Patent		1,250
[($8,000 + $2,000)/8 years = $1,250]		

The $8,000 book value of the patent ($10,000 cost, less $2,000 amortization for 1995 and 1996) and the $2,000 additional cost are totaled and amortized over the remaining life of eight years. Amortization for 1997 is $1,250.

DISPOSAL OF INTANGIBLE ASSETS

Companies may sell separately identified intangible assets in the same way as other assets. When such a transaction occurs, the **unamortized cost** of the asset is removed from the books; the proceeds from the sale or exchange recorded; and a gain or loss, if any, recognized. The company's amortization policy may require the recording of amortization before the sales transaction is recorded.

The cost of intangible assets should not be written off as a loss in the period of acquisition, as was sometimes done before the issuance of *APB Opinion No. 17*. Estimates of value and future benefits of intangible assets may indicate that the unamortized cost should be reduced significantly by a charge against income at some point in the expected useful life. Unwarranted losses based on temporary conditions or other circumstances that do not support a diminished value of intangible assets are not recorded.

FINANCIAL STATEMENT PRESENTATION OF INTANGIBLE ASSETS

Financial statement disclosures include the method and the period of amortization of intangible assets. Although balance sheet presentations of intangible assets vary, typical presentations include a general category designated "intangible assets" or "other assets" in which the various specific intangible assets held by the enterprise are listed.

Exhibit 13–2 presents PepsiCo, Inc.'s disclosure of intangible assets in a note to the financial statements in the company's 1993 annual report. PepsiCo's primary product lines are beverages, snack foods, and restaurants. A single line appears in the company's 1992–1993 comparative balance sheets, labeled "Intangible assets, net." The note presented in Exhibit 13–2 details the specific intangible assets held by the company and the dollar amounts of each one. The text presents the accounting policy concerning amortization of the intangible assets and how recoverability is evaluated. Acceptable alternative presentations are to include the detailed information of individual intangible assets in the body of the balance sheet and to present the accounting policy employed in a separate policy statement rather than in an intangibles note.

Companies may acquire separately identifiable intangible assets from other enterprises or governmental entities, or they may develop them internally. Separately identifiable intangibles that are developed internally and have determinable lives or that are acquired from others should be established in intangible asset accounts that describe the nature of the right or privilege involved.

Several different types of separately identifiable intangible assets are encountered in practice. In the following discussion, we explore some of the most common types of intangibles: patents, copyrights, trade names, trademarks, franchises, licensing agreements, and leaseholds. We also discuss organization costs and deferred charges, assets that are frequently presented with or close to intangible assets in the balance sheet.

PATENTS

A **patent** is a document issued by the U.S. Patent Office that grants the holder the right to exclude others from making, using, or selling the item that is the subject of the patent.

SEPARATELY IDENTIFIABLE INTANGIBLE ASSETS

EXHIBIT 13–2

PepsiCo, Inc.
Intangible Asset Disclosure

Note 7—Intangible Assets

Identifiable intangible assets arose from the allocation of purchase prices of businesses acquired, and consist principally of reacquired franchise rights and trademarks. Reacquired franchise rights relate to acquisitions of franchised bottling and restaurant operations, and the trademarks principally relate to acquisitions of international snack food operations and KFC. Values assigned to such identifiable intangibles were based on independent appraisals or internal estimates. Goodwill represents any residual purchase price after allocation to all identifiable net assets.

	1993	1992
Reacquired franchise rights	$3,959.7	$3,476.9
Trademarks	898.5	734.2
Other identifiable intangibles	154.7	159.6
Goodwill	2,916.6	2,588.3
	$7,929.5	$6,959.0

Intangible assets are amortized on a straight-line basis over appropriate periods generally ranging from 20 to 40 years. Accumulated amortization was $1.3 billion and $1.0 billion at year-end 1993 and 1992, respectively.

The recoverability of carrying values of intangible assets is evaluated on a recurring basis. The primary indicators of recoverability are current or forecasted profitability of the related acquired business, measured as profit before interest, but after amortization of the intangible assets. Consideration is also given to the estimated disposal values of certain identifiable intangible assets compared to their carrying values. For the three-year period ended December 25, 1993, there were no adjustments to the carrying values of intangible assets resulting from these evaluations.

SOURCE: PepsiCo, Inc., 1993 Annual Report.

Patents are frequently received on new and innovative products for which a market may exist. The legal life of a patent is 17 years. A patent is not renewable, but during the legal life of the original patent, the holder can sometimes effectively extend its life by obtaining a new patent that includes slight variations to the original product.

Many of the consumer products we use every day are manufactured under patents granted to the producing companies. For example, cameras, household appliances, and hair dryers are frequently produced under patents.

Obtaining a patent does not guarantee that the holder has something of value. The value of a patent stems from its potential for creating competitive advantage, which may include the ability to produce and sell a different or superior product, obtain a higher selling price for the product, produce it at a lower cost, and exclude competition from producing a specific product or utilizing a specific process.

A patent acquired from another enterprise is recorded at the fair value of consideration given unless the fair value of the assets received is more readily determinable. The cost of internally developed patents includes legal and registration fees, including the cost of models and drawings that accompany registration applications. Research and development costs incurred in the generation of patents, however, are charged to expense as incurred. (We will cover this topic later in the chapter.)

Costs of successful legal defenses of patents are capitalized as part of the patent cost, because such action supports the inherent value of the patent. Costs of unsuccessful legal defenses of patents, however, are expensed as incurred. In addition, the unsuccessful defense of a patent raises a question concerning the existence of an asset and usually implies that the remaining unamortized patent cost should be written off as a loss. If a new patent is obtained as a result of refinement, improvement, or other modification of an existing patent, the unamortized cost of the existing patent is considered part of the cost of the new patent if the benefits provided by the two patents are essentially the same.

The cost of a patent is amortized over the shorter of the economic or legal life. Numerous factors tend to reduce the useful life of a patent, including

1. Technical progress resulting in new and more efficient inventions.
2. Substitute products for current products.
3. Changes in customer demands.
4. Developments by competitors that are sufficiently different to qualify for different patents.

Thus, the economic life of a patent is frequently less than the maximum legal life.

COPYRIGHTS

A **copyright** provides the holder with exclusive rights to the publication, production, and sale of the rights for a literary, dramatic, musical, or artistic work. **Exclusive right** means that the holder can use the work and can **preclude others from using it.** Individuals holding copyrights typically use them to reproduce the work, to sell or otherwise distribute it, and to perform or record it.

Prior to 1978, the Copyright Office (a department of The Library of Congress) granted copyrights for 28 years with a right to renew for another 28 years. Since 1978 the Copyright Office has issued copyrights for the length of the author's life plus 50 years.

The cost of acquired copyrights includes the acquisition price and any related expenditures. The cost of internally developed copyrights includes legal and other registration costs. Generally, the cost is amortized over the economic life of the copyright, which is the period over which the copyright is expected to produce revenue. If the economic life exceeds 40 years, a 40-year period is used for amortization. Due to the limited period of time over which most copyrights are expected to generate revenue, however, the economic life is usually much shorter than the legal life. As a practical matter, the cost of copyrights is often amortized over a relatively short period.

TRADE NAMES AND TRADEMARKS

A **trade name** or **trademark** is a symbol, design, word, or phrase that an enterprise uses to distinguish itself or its product from other enterprises. Trademarks frequently consist of designs or other unique symbols used to encourage public identification of products or enterprises. Legal protection for trade names and trademarks is granted by registration with the U.S. Patent Office.

We are all familiar with many trade names, such as Coca-Cola, Polaroid, Ford, and Zenith. These, along with many other recognizable trade names, create immediate product identification.

Registration of trade names and trademarks provides continuous protection, subject to periodic renewal. Capitalizable costs of trade names and trademarks include legal fees, registration costs, design costs, acquisition costs, successful legal defense, and other expenditures directly related to the acquisition of the right to use the trade name or trademark. Although advertising expenditures may enhance the value or extend the life of a trade name or trademark, this association is generally believed to be too indirect to warrant the capitalization of advertising as part of the trade name or trademark.

The cost of a trade name or trademark is amortized over the shorter of 40 years or the economic life of the asset. Due to the uncertainties inherent in estimating useful life when factors such as consumer demand are important, the cost of trade names and trademarks is typically amortized over a relatively short period of time.

FRANCHISES

A **franchise** is a contractual agreement that allows the holder to perform certain functions, to sell certain products or services, to use certain trade names or trademarks, or to do other specific things identified in the franchise agreement. Many of the businesses we encounter daily operate under franchises. Examples are Burger King, McDonald's, and Kentucky Fried Chicken restaurants.

Some enterprises enter into franchise agreements with other enterprises to sell products, use trade names, or engage in other activities in exchange for specific payments and the fulfillment of other obligations. In other cases, enterprises enter into franchise agreements with governmental units to use public property or to furnish certain types of services, such as water, gas, electric power, public transportation, and waste disposal.

The initial cost of a franchise is recorded as an intangible asset to be amortized over future periods. The franchise cost is then amortized over the shorter of 40 years or the economic life of the franchise. In computing the economic life of the franchise, the holder must consider the time (if any) specified in the franchise contract. If the entity granting the franchise has the right to terminate it, the holder should amortize the cost of the franchise over a relatively short period of time. Periodic payments made under a franchise agreement should generally be charged to expense as incurred.

LICENSING AGREEMENTS

Some enterprises obtain licensing agreements to engage in certain lines of business or to use properties or rights owned by other entities. For example, radio and television stations obtain licenses from the Federal Communications Commission. The cost of such licenses represents an intangible asset, the accounting for which parallels closely the accounting for franchises. The cost is amortized over the shorter of the economic life or 40 years.

An interesting example of licensing agreements is found in the trucking industry. Due to deregulation as a result of the Motor Carrier Act of 1980, the Financial Accounting Standards Board (FASB) issued *Statement of Financial Accounting Standards No. 44,* which requires companies to write off as an expense any unamortized costs of interstate operating rights subject to the provisions of that act. The cost of other licensing agreements, such as *intrastate* operating rights in a state that has not deregulated the industry, may still be carried as intangible assets.[5]

LEASEHOLDS

Leasehold costs are frequently found in balance sheets as either property, plant, and equipment or intangible assets. A **lease** is a contract in which the owner of the property **(lessor)** grants another party **(lessee)** the right to use the property for a specified period of time for fixed or determinable payments. The lease typically states other rights and obligations of both the lessor and lessee.

In accounting for leases, some are treated as purchases of the property by the lessee. We follow this accounting treatment if the lease contract is similar to an acquisition of the property by the lessee and includes certain specified characteristics. This practice is called the

---

[5]*FASB Statement of Financial Accounting Standards No. 44,* "Accounting for Intangible Assets of Motor Carriers," 1980, pars. 3–7.

capitalization of the lease and is a clear example of substance over form, the modifying convention discussed in Chapter 2. In these cases, the capitalized cost of the lease, which is usually the present value of the required lease payments, is presented as an asset in the lessee's balance sheet. This is a complex subject, which we treat extensively in Chapter 23 of this textbook. Leases that are not capitalized are called **operating leases.**

Substance over Form

With both capital and operating leases, lessees may have costs that are presented as intangible assets. Lease contracts frequently call for lessees to prepay lease payments. Such payments must be associated with the appropriate periods and represent intangible assets prior to amortization. Some portion of these prepayments may be appropriately classified as current assets.

Lessees frequently make expenditures that improve the quality of service rendered by leased property. Examples of such leasehold improvements include improvements to building space and improvements to land, such as the addition of driveways, shrubbery, and parking lots. Although these expenditures are made in anticipation of benefits to be derived by the lessee, the improvements typically become the property of the lessor at the end of the lease term. Leasehold improvements are capitalized by the lessee in a separate leasehold Improvement account and amortized over the shorter of the lease term, the life of the property resulting from the improvement, or 40 years.

ORGANIZATION COSTS

Organizing a business enterprise, particularly a corporation, involves numerous costs. Such **organization costs** include the following:

1. Legal fees of drafting the corporate charter and bylaws.
2. Legal fees of corporate registration.
3. Compensation to promoters of the enterprise and other promotional costs.
4. Initial stock issuance costs.
5. Miscellaneous costs of organization.

Theoretically, one can argue that all periods in which the enterprise operates benefit from the incurrence of these costs. As a practical matter, however, the life of the enterprise is not known or determinable at its inception, when these costs are incurred. Support exists for the position that the early years in the enterprise's life benefit most from organization costs and that such costs lose significance once the enterprise becomes an established operating unit.

Organization costs are frequently treated as an intangible asset and amortized over a short period in the early years of the enterprise's life. The fact that certain organization costs may be amortized for income tax purposes over a period of five years may have encouraged some enterprises to use the same period of amortization for financial reporting purposes.

Distinguishing between organization costs and costs that relate to normal operations is a difficult determination requiring the accountant to use judgment. Costs of normal operations should not be capitalized as organization costs or any other type of intangible asset.

DEFERRED CHARGES

Deferred charges, sometimes called **deferred costs** or **deferred debits,** may be found in balance sheets with or near the intangible assets. As we saw in Chapter 4, deferred charge is a broad term used to identify a number of different items with debit balances that do not fit well in any of the other asset categories of the balance sheet. Organization costs are referred to as *deferred charges* in some cases. Other costs, such as long-term prepayments, plant rearrangement costs, and deferred income taxes with debit balances, are also sometimes referred to as *deferred charges.*

EXHIBIT 13–3

Tennessee Valley Authority
Disclosure of Deferred Charge and Other Assets

Partial balance sheet presentation:
Assets (in millions)

	Power Program		All Programs	
Deferred Charges and Other Assets	**1993**	**1992**	**1993**	**1992**
Loans and other long-term receivables and other	$ 346	$ 1,452	$ 405	$ 1,501
Unamortized debt issue and reacquisition costs	1,255	1,062	1,255	1,062
Total	1,601	2,514	1,660	2,563
Total assets	$30,923	$29,319	$32,101	$30,487

SOURCE: Tennessee Valley Authority, 1993 Annual Report.

The presence of deferred charges indicates the problem of attempting to define all costs that have not been amortized in one of the common asset categories. The deferred-charge category is necessary because some debit-balance accounts do not fit elsewhere.

Exhibit 13–3 contains the "deferred charges and other assets" section from the 1992–1993 comparative balance sheets of the Tennessee Valley Authority. TVA is a unique federal corporation that supplies electricity and develops resources in a service area that covers a significant portion of the southeast region of the United States. TVA is one of America's largest producers of electric power, distributing power to more than 7 million people in an 80,000-square-mile region. The item "unamortized debt issue and reacquisition costs" is an excellent example of a deferred charge that is frequently found in corporate balance sheets.

INTANGIBLE ASSETS NOT SEPARATELY IDENTIFIABLE: GOODWILL

Certain transactions give rise to intangible assets that are not separately identifiable as are patents, copyrights, and other intangibles discussed previously. Intangible assets that cannot be separately identified relate to the enterprise as a whole. They frequently exist because of the enterprise's unique combination of separate assets and personnel, and their synergism explains why the value of an enterprise as a whole—measured in terms of its anticipated earning capacity—may be greater than the sum of the values of the individual parts of the enterprise. While such intangible assets are identified with a variety of titles, a commonly used term, *goodwill,* is used throughout this text.

GOODWILL CONCEPT

Goodwill refers to the capability of an enterprise to produce above normal earnings. This unique earning capability results from the existence of intangible qualities, such as an outstanding reputation, superior managerial capability, and ability to operate at an above-normal level of efficiency. Any characteristic or combination of characteristics that gives an enterprise a competitive advantage over other enterprises, thereby allowing a higher level of earnings than would normally be expected, supports the existence of goodwill.

Goodwill has been described as a master valuation account, meaning that it provides a reconciliation of the difference between the value of an enterprise as a whole and the aggregate value of its individual parts. When viewed in this context, goodwill explains the difference between enterprises that have above-normal earnings and those with normal earnings.

Because goodwill is identified with an enterprise as a whole, the asset Goodwill is inseparable from that enterprise. Goodwill is not exchangeable in the same manner as separately identifiable assets. It may be exchanged, however, when an entire enterprise is acquired. As depicted in Exhibit 13–1, internally developed qualities, such as an outstanding reputation for quality, that are similar to acquired goodwill are not recognized as assets.

When an enterprise contemplates the acquisition of another business, it must determine the value of that business. A starting point is to estimate the current value of all specific assets to be received and liabilities to be assumed. This amount is identified as the fair value of **net assets** received. The seller will attempt to include any existing goodwill in determining the exchange price, whether or not the goodwill has previously been recorded as an asset. Once an exchange price is agreed on and a sale takes place, the purchaser has acquired goodwill to the extent that the overall purchase price exceeds the current value of the other net assets received. The purchaser then records goodwill. *The recorded cost of the goodwill may vary from the valuation of the goodwill estimated to be inherent in the business being acquired, because the goodwill recorded is the amount necessary to reconcile the total purchase price to the current value of the other net assets received.*

Conceptually, goodwill should be measured by identifying those factors that offer a competitive advantage to an enterprise, such as superior managerial efficiency, an excellent reputation among customers, and the ability to operate at a high level of efficiency. By placing a monetary valuation on these features and aggregating these amounts, the value of goodwill could be established.

Realistically, valuing the individual intangible qualities supporting the existence of goodwill involves measurement problems too complex for present accounting practice. Accountants have therefore turned to an indirect method of valuing goodwill, whereby they estimate the total anticipated excess earning capability rather than the individual elements that support the existence of goodwill. This process involves estimating future periodic earnings from an investment in another enterprise, comparing this estimation with what would normally be expected, and aggregating the excess of anticipated earnings over normal earnings. *Excess earning capacity is estimated for purposes of determining a price to pay for the enterprise rather than for purposes of financial statement presentation.*

For example, assume that Red Company is considering the acquisition of Blue Company. Red Company will take over all of Blue Company's assets and will assume all its liabilities. Red Company estimates the current value of Blue Company's net assets (assets less liabilities) at $750,000. In addition, Red Company believes it will be able to achieve a level of earnings substantially in excess of normal on its investment due to Blue Company's outstanding reputation. Specifically, the excess earnings are estimated to total $100,000. Red Company is therefore willing to pay up to $850,000 for Blue Company's net assets. If an amount higher than $750,000 is paid, the excess is identified as the cost of goodwill resulting from the transaction. In this case, goodwill should not exceed $100,000, because that is the value estimated for goodwill. The cost of goodwill is less than $100,000, however, if the final bargained exchange price is less than $850,000. For example, if the agreed-upon purchase price is $780,000, the purchased amount of goodwill is $30,000 ($780,000 − $750,000). On the other hand, if the agreed-upon price is $840,000, the purchased amount of goodwill is $90,000 ($840,000 − $750,000).

ACCOUNTING FOR GOODWILL

Once acquired, goodwill is accounted for in much the same way as are other intangible assets because the general requirements of *APB Opinion No. 17* apply to goodwill. Exhibit 13–1 indicates that goodwill acquired from another enterprise is recorded at cost in an appropriate intangible asset account. The life of goodwill is not constrained by legal or contractual limitations and therefore may be judged by management to be indeterminate. In such cases, we amortize the goodwill over a 40-year period. In other cases, management may decide that the period over which excess earnings can be anticipated is limited to a period shorter than 40 years, and we amortize goodwill over the expected period of advantageous operations.

In taking the position that goodwill should be treated as an asset and amortized over its estimated useful life, the APB considered several alternative treatments. These included (1) retaining the cost of goodwill as an asset indefinitely unless a reduction in value becomes evident and (2) writing off the cost of goodwill immediately when it is acquired. Supporting the nonamortization approach is the notion that until the future value becomes less than cost, no loss should be recognized. The basis for writing off goodwill at the time of purchase is that the nature of goodwill differs from other assets and warrants special accounting treatment; because goodwill relates to the business as a whole and its value fluctuates widely, estimates of either its value or term of existence are too unreliable for purposes of income determination.[6] These positions were rejected by the APB in favor of the amortization approach we describe in this textbook.

Financial statement disclosures should explain the existence of goodwill and the accounting policy relative to amortization. For example, in Ford Motor Company's 1992 annual report, an accounting policy note explains that goodwill represents the excess of the purchase price over the fair value of net assets of acquired companies and is amortized on a straight-line method over 40 years. The note goes on to explain that goodwill resulted principally from that company's acquisition of Jaguar Limited and The Associates.

Interestingly, U.S. accounting standards for goodwill differ from those in the United Kingdom, where companies are permitted to write off goodwill to stockholders' equity immediately after acquiring other companies. By writing off goodwill to stockholders' equity, the income statements of U.K. companies do not reflect the annual amortization of goodwill expense as do those of U.S. companies. Writing off goodwill to stockholders' equity immediately after acquisition tends to make U.K. companies appear more leveraged than their U.S. counterparts. To counteract this effect, some U.K. companies capitalize goodwill but do not amortize it. Many observers believe that U.K. accounting standards give U.K. companies an unfair advantage over U.S. companies when the former acquire other U.S. companies. For example, they believe that U.K. accounting standards for goodwill have aided large U.K. advertising companies, such as Saatchi & Saatchi and WPP Group, when they acquired U.S. advertising agencies, because most of the purchase price was for goodwill. If this argument is correct, U.K. companies could bid more than their U.S. counterparts because accounting for goodwill in the United Kingdom does not penalize earnings. The counterargument is that because goodwill amortization is a noncash expense, investors are not misled by the differing U.S. and U.K. standards; thus, the differing standards do not give U.K. firms an unfair advantage.[7]

GOODWILL EXAMPLE: DIVERSIFIED ENTERPRISES/SINGLE PRODUCT, INC.

In the following paragraphs, we use an example involving Diversified Enterprises and Single Product, Inc., to illustrate various computational considerations in estimating the value of goodwill. Diversified is considering the acquisition of Single Product, a relatively small company that has an excellent reputation. Single Product deals with a product line into which Diversified wants to move. Diversified would acquire all the assets and assume all the liabilities of Single Product. Single Product's balance sheet is presented in Exhibit 13–4. Single Product has no cash to be transferred to Diversified.

Diversified Enterprises must answer two questions in determining a reasonable price to pay for the net assets of Single Product. First, to what extent do the balance sheet figures represent the current value of the individual assets and liabilities? Second, is goodwill evident in the past performance of Single Product? The price that Diversified is willing to pay

---

[6]*APB Opinion No. 17,* pars. 17, 19–20.

[7]Jeffrey D. Laderman and Leah J. Nathans, "Goodwill Is Making a Lot of People Angry," *Business Week* (July 31, 1989), pp. 73, 76.

EXHIBIT 13–4

Single Product, Inc.
Balance Sheet
June 30, 1995

Assets			Liabilities	
Accounts receivable		$ 28,000	Accounts payable	$ 99,000
Inventories		145,000	Bonds payable	112,000
Property, plant,				$211,000
and equipment	$275,000			
Accumulated			**Stockholders' Equity**	
depreciation	(125,000)	150,000	Capital stock	$150,000
Patents		85,000	Retained earnings	47,000
				$197,000
			Total liabilities	
			and stockholders'	
Total assets		$408,000	equity	$408,000

EXHIBIT 13–5

Current Value of the Net Assets of Single Product, Inc.

Assets		
Accounts receivable	$ 25,000	
Inventories	131,000	
Property, plant, and equipment	182,000	
Patents	100,000	$438,000
Liabilities		
Accounts payable	99,000	
Bonds payable	112,000	(211,000)
Estimated current value of net assets		$227,000

should be based on the current value of Single Product's net identifiable assets (assets less liabilities) plus the value of any excess earning capability included in the acquisition. The total of the two elements establishes an amount within which to negotiate an acquisition price.

Based on appraisals, current market prices, and the application of specific price indexes to historical cost figures, Diversified has established the values presented in Exhibit 13–5 for Single Product's assets. We shall assume that the amounts of liabilities on Single's books fairly reflect the obligations that Diversified is assuming.

Why do the recorded amounts of assets in Single's balance sheet differ from the current value estimates in Exhibit 13–5? The recorded amounts of assets are based on GAAP, which usually do not reflect the current value of the assets. The basis for measuring and recording most assets is cost. Adjustments to costs are made to reflect market declines in applying the lower of cost or market method to inventories and other assets whose realizabilities have been impaired. The balance sheet amounts for many items, however, may differ significantly from their current market values. Also, the method used to account for inventories may cause a difference between recorded amounts and current market values. If the last-in, first-out (LIFO) method is used, for example, the balance sheet amount may be well below the current value, whereas the first-in, first-out (FIFO) method normally causes the recorded amount

Asset/Liability Measurement

and the current value to be closer. If the inventory to be acquired will be used in a different way by the acquiring enterprise, it may have a higher or lesser value than the amount recorded on the books of the acquired company. Differences in the valuation of receivables most likely reflect differences in the assessment of uncollectible accounts, because the net receivables amount reflects the net realizable value of the asset.

Asset/Liability Measurement

Differences between the recorded amounts and the current values of plant assets and of separately identifiable intangible assets are due primarily to the initial measuring and recording of these assets at cost and the subsequent depreciation and amortization of the cost figures. The market prices of the assets may remain constant, decline at a different rate from the book value, or actually increase. Book values presented in the balance sheet are not intended to reflect current value.

If Diversified pays a price it believes is fair in light of the earning potential of the enterprise acquired, goodwill will emerge only if that price exceeds $227,000. For example, if the two enterprises agree on a $250,000 cash purchase price, goodwill is $23,000, computed as follows:

Purchase price	$250,000
Less: Estimated current value	
of net assets received	(227,000)
Cost of goodwill	$ 23,000

In this case, the journal entry to record the acquisition of the net assets and the assumption of Single's liabilities, by Diversified is as follows:

Accounts Receivable	25,000	
Inventories	131,000	
Property, Plant, and Equipment	182,000	
Patents	100,000	
Goodwill	23,000	
Accounts Payable		99,000
Bonds Payable		112,000
Cash		250,000

If Diversified pays a higher price, the implied amount attributed to goodwill will be higher. For example, if $275,000 is paid, the cost of goodwill will be $48,000, determined by the excess of the $275,000 purchase price over the $227,000 estimated value of the net assets received.

The Diversified illustration was hypothetical. Exhibit 13–6, however, discloses an actual purchase transaction involving goodwill. In 1991, Northern Telecom completed the acquisition of 73% of STC PLC, an English company that was subsequently renamed STC Limited. Exhibit 13–6 includes Note 11 from the 1993 financial statements that explains this purchase in 1991, one of the comparative years presented. The aggregate purchase cost was $2,609 million resulting in the recognition of $1,847 of goodwill. As the note goes on to explain, goodwill is amortized over 40 years. Note 3, which is referred to in Note 11, explains that goodwill associated with the STC PLC acquisition was written down in 1993 by $500 million as part of a restructuring. This writedown of goodwill is explained in terms of continuing weaknesses in the European economic environment and the expectation of lower growth in European sales and earnings.

A study published in 1992 investigated whether goodwill disclosures by publicly traded companies in the United States are sufficient to enable investors to determine the financial statement impact of accounting for goodwill in accordance with *APB Opinion No. 17.* Based on a study of 621 New York and American Stock Exchange companies, several interesting conclusions can be reached. One is that companies vary substantially in their goodwill asset and expense disclosures, with 21% of companies failing to disclose net goodwill, 58% not

---

EXHIBIT 13–6

Northern Telecom
Purchase of Business with Goodwill

---

11. *Acquisition of STC PLC*

On March 5, 1991, Northern Telecom completed the acquisition of the remaining outstanding ordinary shares (approximately 73 percent) of STC PLC (STC), a company incorporated under the laws of England, since renamed STC Limited, at a price of 317 pence per share. The aggregated purchase cost was $2,609 and was financed by new multi-year bank facilities. The acquisition has been accounted for as a purchase and the consolidated statement of operations includes 27 percent of STC's net earnings prior to February 28, 1991, and consolidation of STC's results thereafter. During 1991, Northern Telecom sold the Distributors Division, the Land Cable Products Division, the Electronics Distribution Division, and two smaller divisions of STC. No gain or loss was recorded on the disposals, as these amounts were included in the determination of goodwill.

The following is a summary of the purchase transaction effective March 1, 1991, relating to the acquisition of 73 percent of STC based on exchange rates effective on that date:

Aggregate purchase cost	$ 2,609
Total assets (at fair value)	(2,348)
Total liabilities (at fair value)	1,586
Goodwill	$ 1,847

Goodwill, including the net amount from the original acquisition of 27 percent of STC, is amortized on a straight-line basis over 40 years. In 1993, the goodwill was written down by $500 as described in note 3.

SOURCE: Northern Telecom, 1993 Annual Report.

disclosing accumulated goodwill amortization, and 76% not disclosing goodwill amortization expense. Nearly one-third of the companies did not disclose the period over which goodwill is amortized. These and other results of this research suggest that investors cannot easily identify the financial statement effects of current goodwill accounting rules. The authors issued a call for more complete and improved disclosures that would allow investors to more easily and accurately determine the impact of goodwill on the financial statements.[8]

ESTIMATING THE VALUE OF GOODWILL

For goodwill to exist, evidence of a capability to earn amounts in excess of that which would normally be expected must exist. An evaluation of the existence of goodwill therefore requires a comparison of expected earnings with normal earnings. If the anticipated earnings exceed the norm, evidence of goodwill is present. This process is particularly important in determining the price an entity should pay for another entity.

How is the **normal rate of earnings** for an enterprise determined? The normal rate used for goodwill estimation is typically an approximation of the rate required to attract capital into the company that is acquiring another company. The risk associated with the enterprise is a major variable in determining the cost of capital: The higher the risk associated with the company, the higher the cost of capital. Risk, in turn, is assessed by considering the company's line of business, existing debt-equity relationships, past profitability, and other variables. In determining the normal rate, a common approach is to consult financial

---

[8]Linda Duvall, Ross Jennings, John Robinson, and Robert B. Thompson II, "Can Investors Unravel the Effects of Goodwill Accounting?" *Accounting Horizons* (June 1992), pp. 10–12.

services and other sources for an average cost of capital for other companies in the same industry. Of course, care must be taken that industry figures represent companies that are truly comparable.

Projecting expected future earnings for purposes of comparison with normal earnings involves a careful analysis of past earnings and projected changes in future conditions. Although information about the past may be useful in estimating future earnings, unadjusted past earnings are normally not an appropriate measure of expected future earnings. Trends in the past, however, may be projected into the future and may serve as a reasonable basis for estimating future profitability. Extraordinary items and other infrequently recurring items included in past earnings are usually excluded when using past earnings to project future earnings.

Several methods of estimating the value of goodwill in an acquisition are discussed in this section. The following four steps are common to all methods:

Step 1. Estimate the periodic earnings that are expected to be achieved on the investment in the current value of the net assets to be received.

Step 2. Estimate the periodic earnings that are considered normal on the investment in the current value of the net assets to be received.

Step 3. Comparing amounts in Steps 1 and 2, compute the amount of **anticipated periodic excess earnings over normal earnings**

Step 4. Convert the amount computed in Step 3 from a periodic figure to an aggregate figure that represents an estimate of the **total anticipated excess earnings** (i.e., goodwill).

Several methods are available for making the conversion required in Step 4 of the **periodic** anticipated excess earnings to an **aggregate** figure that represents the total value of future anticipated excess earnings.

Estimating Expected Periodic Earnings

A starting point for **estimating expected future earnings** is past performance. However, our intent is to estimate *future* earnings, and in the future the factors influencing earnings may be different from past factors. When we base assessments of future earnings on past earnings, we should use several periods in an attempt to eliminate the impact of nonrecurring events and to identify significant trends in earnings or components of earnings.

Continuing the Diversified Enterprises example, we assume the earnings information for Single Product for the past four years as given in Exhibit 13–7. The average net income for the four years is $50,000, or a 22% return on the current value of the net assets of Single Product. These amounts are computed as follows:

$$\frac{\text{Average}}{\text{Net Income}} = \frac{\$51,000 + \$50,000 + \$43,000 + \$56,000}{4 \text{ Years}} = \$50,000$$

$$\frac{\text{\% Return on Current}}{\text{Value of Net Assets}} = \frac{\$50,000}{\$227,000} = 22\%$$

Several factors should be considered in deciding on the appropriateness of using $50,000 as an expected level of earnings in the future. The inclusion of the extraordinary items is questionable, because they are not expected to recur. Also, the accounting policies followed by Diversified to determine net income may differ from those used by Single Products. Such a difference could influence the assessment of future earnings. Other factors could also impact expected future earnings. For example, in the future, depreciation and amortization on property, plant, and equipment and patents will be based on the **new cost basis** (i.e., the estimated fair value), and their estimated lives may be extended or reduced.

To continue our example, we assume that the average earnings of Single Product during 1992–1995, after the elimination of extraordinary items and the inclusion of an additional charge of $3,850 per year for expected increases in depreciation and amortization, represent a reasonable estimate of future earnings. This amount is computed as follows:

EXHIBIT 13–7				
Single Product, Inc.				
Income Data for Years Ending June 30, 1992–1995				
	1992	**1993**	**1994**	**1995**
Revenues	$255,000	$262,000	$212,000	$238,000
Expenses	(204,000)	(224,000)	(160,000)	(182,000)
Income before extraordinary items		38,000	52,000	
Extraordinary gain (loss)		12,000	(9,000)	
Net income	$ 51,000	$ 50,000	$ 43,000	$ 56,000

Average annual income before extraordinary items

1992	$ 51,000	
1993	38,000	
1994	52,000	
1995	56,000	
	$197,000 ÷ 4 years = $49,250	
Less: Additional depreciation and amortization	(3,850)	
Estimated future annual income	$45,400	

This estimate reflects a rate of return of 20% ($45,400/$227,000 = 20%) on the estimated current value of the net assets being acquired. These amounts are used in the continuation of the Diversified Enterprise illustration.

Estimating Normal Periodic Earnings

The selection of a **normal rate of earnings** should reflect an estimate of the rate necessary to attract capital into the business under existing circumstances. As with determining all interest rates, the risk taken in the investment is an important consideration. A related consideration is the industry in which the enterprise operates.

Published rates that represent averages of a number of similar enterprises can usually be obtained from various financial services (e.g., Dun & Bradstreet or Standard & Poor's). However, rates obtained in this manner are based on historical figures and may differ from rates based on current values. Also, the unique features of the enterprise under consideration may make the identification of comparable enterprises difficult. Any valid rate must be based on companies that are similar to the one for which goodwill is being computed.

In continuing the example of Diversified Enterprises, we assume 12% as a rate that represents a normal cost of attracting capital into enterprises similar to Single Product. Thus, normal annual earnings on the $227,000 investment are $27,240 ($227,000 × 12%).

Computing the Anticipated Annual Excess Earnings

The amounts computed in Steps 1 and 2 are combined to determine the **anticipated annual earnings in excess of normal.** In the case of Single Product, this computation is made as follows:

Estimated future annual earnings ($227,000 × 20%)	$45,400
Estimated normal annual earnings ($227,000 × 12%)	(27,240)
Estimated excess of expected annual earnings over normal	$18,160

Estimating Total Excess Earnings

Several methods are available to convert the annual amount of anticipated excess earnings to an **estimate of total goodwill.** Three methods are illustrated in the following paragraphs.

Method 1. Years Multiple of Excess Earnings.   This method is based on the assumption that the excess earnings will continue for a determinable number of periods. Goodwill is computed by multiplying the excess annual earnings by the number of years the management believes it can sustain the advantages acquired.

For Diversified Enterprises, we assume (for this calculation) that management believes it can sustain the anticipated level of excess earnings for six years, in which case goodwill is valued as follows:

$$\text{Goodwill} = 6 \text{ years} \times \$18,160 = \$108,960$$

A deficiency in this method is the failure to recognize the difference between the value of the excess earnings of the first year after the acquisition and that of subsequent years (i.e., the time value of money). Also, the difficulty in accurately estimating the number of years over which the excess earnings can be sustained is an important implementation problem.

Method 2. Present Value of Excess Earnings.   Recognition of the time value of the excess earnings is an advantage of basing the value of goodwill on the **present value** of excess earnings rather than on the total amount as in Method 1. The period over which the excess earnings can be sustained must be estimated. The amount of annual excess earnings is then discounted to its present value by an appropriate interest rate.

Assuming that Diversified estimates that the excess earnings will continue for six years, we discount at the normal rate (i.e., the estimated cost of capital, which—in this case—is 12%), and goodwill is computed as follows:

$$\text{Goodwill} = 4.11141 \times \$18,160 = \$74,663$$

Table 6–4 shows that the present value of an annuity factor for six periods at 12% is 4.11141. That figure is used because the estimated excess earnings of $18,160 per year will accrue to Diversified Enterprises over a six-year period.

The greater risk inherent in the continuation of the excess earnings in the future may encourage the use of a higher interest rate in estimating the total value of goodwill. For example, if the 20% rate is used in estimating the goodwill in the Diversified acquisition of Single Product, goodwill is estimated as follows:

$$\text{Goodwill} = 3.32551 \times \$18,160 = \$60,391$$

We again use an annuity factor (3.32551 from Table 6–4) to estimate the value of goodwill. In this case, however, the factor for six periods is at *20%.*

Conceptually, the present-value method has merit because explicit recognition is given to the limited life of the excess earnings and the time value of money is considered. Practical problems of implementation are the estimations of the number of years and the interest rate. As seen in the Method 2 examples, judgments about these factors can significantly affect the resulting goodwill estimate.

Method 3. Capitalization of Excess Earnings.   The assumption that the excess earnings will continue *indefinitely* leads to estimating goodwill by capitalizing the excess earnings at an appropriate rate. If the normal rate is used in the Diversified example, then

$$\text{Goodwill} = \frac{\$18,160}{12\%} = \$151,333$$

Goodwill computed in this manner represents the amount that would have to be invested to yield a return equal to the **excess earnings in perpetuity.** In other words, an investment of $151,333 that yields a 12% return will yield $18,160 annually ($151,333 $\times$ 12% per year in perpetuity). The primary flaws in this computation are (1) that the computed goodwill figure is based on the assumption that estimated excess earnings will continue indefinitely and (2) that this perpetual advantage relates entirely to conditions that exist when goodwill is acquired.

The uncertainty concerning the continuity of excess future earnings may encourage the use of a higher interest rate, indicating the higher level of risk. In the Diversified Enterprises case, a 20% rate for capitalizing excess earnings results in the following computation:

$$\text{Goodwill} = \frac{\$18,160}{20\%} = \$90,800$$

We have used two different interest rates in the previous illustrations to point out the difficulty of selecting the appropriate rate for applying this method. One study on valuing a closely held business suggests that the rate used should represent the expected yield on an investment in the company and can be selected by either the summation or the direct market comparison methods. Under the summation method, the accountant determines the required rate of return and then adjusts that rate for any portion of the expected return that may not be reflected in the earnings stream being capitalized. To illustrate this method, the authors of the study suggest the following approach:

Long-term U.S. government bond rate	10%
Plus: Average premium return on small stocks over U.S. government bonds	8
Expected total rate of return on small publicly held stocks	18
Plus: Premium for greater risk and liquidity	10
Total required expected rate of return for subject company	28
Less: Consensus long-term inflation expectation	6
Capitalization rate to apply to current earnings	22%

The direct market comparison method requires the accountant to develop a rate, or range of rates, based on information from comparable companies. One of the implementation problems associated with this method is the difficulty of getting information about similar companies, particularly if the company for which goodwill is being estimated is not publicly held.[9]

In summary, the assumptions underlying the various methods of estimating goodwill and the judgments required in the implementation of the methods demonstrate the difficulty of measuring the asset Goodwill. *An important point to remember is that the amount recorded as goodwill is the actual cost that is implied in the purchase transaction.* The estimation procedures we have just illustrated are used to quantify the value of goodwill to assist management in determining an appropriate amount for negotiating a purchase price of another enterprise. Estimates of the value of goodwill may also be useful to auditors in assessing the appropriateness of the recorded amount of goodwill in the balance sheet.

Asset/Liability Measurement

"NEGATIVE GOODWILL"

In the previous examples, we assumed that the price paid for an enterprise *exceeds* the sum of the current value of the individual identifiable assets, less liabilities. If the sum of the values of the individual assets, less liabilities is *more* than the price paid, does "negative goodwill" exist? Presumably, the answer is no, because this would result in assets being recorded

---

[9]Warren Kissin and Ronald Zulli, "Valuation of a Closely Held Business," *The Journal of Accountancy* (June 1988), p. 42. (The illustration presented here differs from that found in this reference only in the numbers used.)

GOODWILL GAMES

Many a company would like to do what Supermarkets General Holdings Corporation just did. In one swoop the parent of Pathmark supermarkets and Rickel home-improvement stores wrote off $600 million in goodwill.

The company, which had 1992 revenues of $4.3 billion, made its move just before filing for a public offering in March. Supermarkets General probably figured that the writeoff, by boosting reported earnings, would make the issue easier to sell.

Goodwill, of course, comes with an acquisition. It is the difference between what you pay and the current value of the net assets you acquire. Thus what you pay for a brand name or reputation counts as goodwill—a so-called intangible. Under current accounting rules, U.S. companies must amortize goodwill for reporting purposes over as many as 40 years. It's a drag on earnings year after year, and until this year there was no tax benefit, since the amortization of goodwill has not been tax-deductible, as depreciation of other assets is.

Companies have argued again and again that this accounting treatment puts them at a disadvantage: Their British and German counterparts, for example, can write off goodwill against equity immediately and thus not crimp their future earnings.

How did Supermarkets General get away with its writeoff? By finding a loophole. Seems the language governing all this is murky. The accounting rule actually says that goodwill should be reevaluated more or less continually and reduced if need be. Certainly, a company that decided to sell or wind down a business it had previously acquired could get rid of the associated goodwill. The rule also gives a break to companies that suffer losses over several years and expect only lackluster results in the future. They, too, can write off part or all of the goodwill on their books.

Supermarkets General, formed in a 1987 leveraged buyout by Merrill Lynch Capital Partners, has been losing money for six years. Supermarkets General told the Securities & Exchange Commission and the company's accountants at Deloitte & Touche that its total operating income for the next 35 years, the duration of the remaining goodwill,

would not reach $600 million, the amount of goodwill remaining.

A dire forecast, you might say, for a company about to tap the public markets. But you can be sure Supermarkets General peddled a different story to investors. The dismal performance was based on results at the end of 1992. But in March Supermarkets General announced a restructuring that would slash debt, spin off the Rickel stores and offer to the public about one-third of the new company.

The restructuring gave a whole new look to the company's past and future. The company told investors to look at income after the effects of the restructuring. Instead of the flat sales and net losses it reported last year, Supermarkets General said that now Pathmark's net income was $42 million.

"Supermarkets General essentially told the SEC to ignore the restructuring in calculating the goodwill impairment, but told investors to feel good about it," says Lehman Brothers accounting expert Robert Willens. The accountants and SEC went along.

Before the writeoff, the goodwill amortization costs were $17 million per year. The writeoff eliminated the charge, enhancing aftertax income by that amount. Figure at 11 times earnings the change adds about $200 million to Pathmark's valuation. Pretty neat. Take a $600 million bookkeeping hit and increase the company's market value by $200 million.

Any company that posted losses in recent years but is now restructuring may be able to follow in Supermarkets General's lead. The recession and disappointing results from many LBOs give managements a plausible argument for writing down goodwill.

Now, if only the SEC and the Financial Accounting Standards Board would get the message and eliminate this accounting monstrosity once and for all for everybody.

SOURCE: Amy Feldman, "Goodwill Games," *Forbes*, September 13, 1993, p. 214. Reprinted by permission of *Forbes Magazine*, September 13, 1993. © Forbes, Inc., 1993.

Asset/Liability Measurement   at amounts in excess of the price paid for them, a violation of applying the asset/liability measurement principle using historical cost.

If the price paid for an enterprise is *less* than the sum of the values of the individual identifiable assets, less liabilities, the difference is allocated as a reduction of the recorded cost of those separately identifiable noncurrent assets other than investments. If, in an unusual case, this allocation reduces noncurrent assets (other than investments) to zero, the difference is recorded as a deferred credit and amortized as an *addition* to future income over a period not to exceed 40 years. Such a deferred credit would be identified as an "excess of book value over cost of purchased subsidiary" or another appropriate title. (The terms **negative goodwill** or **badwill** are not usually found in published financial statements.) This item is placed in the balance sheet among noncurrent liabilities or in a separate deferred credit section between liabilities and stockholders' equity.

At the beginning of Chapter 11, we indicated that several topics would be deferred to the end of Chapter 13 because they related to both plant and intangible assets and their coverage is enhanced by an understanding of accounting standards for both types of assets. As we complete Chapter 13, we look at the following subjects, all of which have commanded significant attention by the accounting profession in recent years: research and development costs, development-stage enterprises, and accounting by oil and gas producing companies.

Accounting for research and development costs is closely related to accounting for plant and intangible assets because both types of assets are used in research and development activities, and some intangible assets are developed internally through research and development. The term *development-stage enterprises* refers to companies that are just getting started and whose activities frequently involve research and development, particularly in high-tech enterprises. Also, questions of accounting for certain start-up costs are often related to, and sometimes confused with, accounting for plant and intangible assets. Accounting for costs in the oil and gas industry relates to both plant and intangible asset accounting and represents a continuing controversy for the accounting profession.

These three areas represent interesting extensions of the material we have covered concerning plant and intangible assets. An understanding of each is an important part of gaining a full appreciation of the complexities of financial reporting in today's environment.

RESEARCH AND DEVELOPMENT COSTS

Research and development (R & D) is an important aspect of business operations for many enterprises. Prior to 1975, R & D costs were frequently capitalized as intangible assets and amortized over several periods. *FASB Statement of Financial Accounting Standards No. 2* was issued in 1974 to establish standards for the accounting and reporting of R & D costs and related tangible and intangible assets.[10] Under this pronouncement, many costs that were previously identified as R & D are part of the cost of other tangible and intangible assets. Those costs that are identified as R & D are treated as expenses in the period incurred.

The FASB defines **research** and **development** as follows:

> *Research is planned search or critical investigation aimed at discovery of new knowledge with the hope that such knowledge will be useful in developing a new product or service . . . or a new process or technique . . . or in bringing a significant improvement to an existing product or process.*
>
> *Development is the translation of research findings or other knowledge into a plan or design for a new product or process whether intended for sale or use.*[11]

The distinction between R & D costs and expenditures that are capitalized in various tangible and intangible asset categories requires that the accountant use careful judgment. Identifying R & D costs is facilitated by understanding the activities that lead to R & D costs. Such activities typically occur *prior to the beginning of commercial production and distribution of a product or process.* Various activities can result in R & D costs.[12]

1. Laboratory research aimed at the discovery of new knowledge.
2. Searching for applications of new research findings or other knowledge.
3. Conceptual formulation and design of possible product or process alternatives.
4. Design, construction, and testing of preproduction prototypes and models.
5. Design, construction, and operation of a pilot plant that is not of a scale economically feasible for commercial production.

---

[10]*FASB Statement of Financial Accounting Standards No. 2,* "Accounting for Research and Development Costs," 1974.

[11]*FASB Statement of Financial Accounting Standards No. 2,* par. 8.

[12]*FASB Statement of Financial Accounting Standards No. 2,* par. 9.

Activities that relate to commercial production do not result in the incurrence of R & D costs, even though many are similar in nature to activities giving rise to R & D costs. The following are examples of activities that do *not* result in R & D costs:[13]

1. Engineering follow-through in an early stage of commercial production.
2. Quality control during commercial production, including routine testing of products.
3. Routine, ongoing efforts to refine, enrich, or otherwise improve the quality of an existing product.
4. Adaptation of an existing capacity to a particular requirement or customer's need as part of a continuing commercial activity.
5. Seasonal or other periodic design changes to existing products.

Several elements of costs identified with R & D activities can be identified: (1) materials, equipment, and facilities; (2) personnel; (3) intangibles purchased from others; (4) contract services; and (5) indirect costs. R & D expense of an enterprise includes some or all of these costs in a given reporting period. If a cost is considered to be R & D, it is charged to expense when incurred.

Materials, Equipment, and Facilities

Materials, equipment, and **facilities** acquired for use in R & D activities that have alternative future uses—either in other R & D activities or in non–R & D activities— are capitalized in appropriate asset categories when acquired. The costs of materials subsequently used in R & D activities and depreciation on equipment and facilities used in R & D activities are classified as R & D expense when recognized. Costs of materials, equipment, and facilities acquired for particular R & D projects that have no alternative use are expensed as R & D when incurred.

Personnel

Salaries, wages, and other **personnel costs** of employees involved in R & D activities are charged to R & D expense as incurred.

Intangibles Purchased from Others

The costs of **purchased intangible assets** used in R & D activities that have alternative future uses in other R & D activities or non–R & D activities are capitalized in appropriate asset categories. As these intangible assets are amortized, R & D expense is charged. The costs of intangible assets that are purchased for use in present R & D projects only and that have no alternative future use are charged to R & D expense as incurred.

Contract Services

Enterprises may engage others to perform R & D activities for them. The costs of such **contract services** are treated as R & D expenses when incurred.

Indirect Costs

A reasonable allocation of **indirect costs** that relate to R & D activities is included in the R & D expense in determining net income. Indirect costs include general and administrative expenses not directly related to R & D activity. To be included in R & D expense, however, general and administrative expenses must have some relationship to R & D activity.

---

[13]*FASB Statement of Financial Accounting Standards No. 2,* par. 10.

EXHIBIT 13–8

Cost Analysis for Energy-Efficient Company

Expenditure	Capitalize as	Expense as
a. Acquisition of equipment and building to be used in ongoing research activity.	Building, equipment	
b. Salaries of research staff responsible for the design of new heating unit.		R & D
c. Material, labor, and overhead of model of new heating unit.		R & D
d. Costs of testing of model of new heating unit.		R & D
e. Legal fees related to patent on new heating unit.	Patent	
f. Costs of research on marketability of new heating unit.		Operating expense
g. Cost of acquiring patent believed to compete with one on new heating unit.	Patent	
h. Costs of engineering activity necessary to advance heating unit to point of commercial production.		R & D
i. Costs of quality control in early stages of commercial production.		Manufacturing cost
j. Depreciation of equipment and building acquired in a.		R & D
k. Amortization of patent acquired in e.		Manufacturing cost
l. Salaries of salespersons selling new heating unit.		Operating expense
m. Warranty costs on heating units sold.		Operating expense

To illustrate the identification of R & D costs, we assume that Energy-Efficient Company is involved in the production of high-efficiency home heating and air conditioning equipment. Energy-Efficient incurs a number of expenditures related to its activities that are listed on the left in Exhibit 13–8. The proper accounting for these activities is described in the analysis on the right.

Numerous examples can be cited to illustrate the distinction between R & D costs and other expenditures. Most of the items in the Energy-Efficient example are obvious from the previous discussion. The capitalization of legal costs (item **e**) and the cost of acquiring a competing patent (item **g**) are appropriately capitalized in the Patent account. Because this patent is related to a product that is being produced for sale, the amortization of the cost (item **k**) is treated as a manufacturing cost. If the patent had been used in R & D activities, the amortization would have been classified as R & D expense. The cost of market research (item **f**) on the new product is not included as R & D, because the research relates to the **marketability** of the product, not to its technical development. In summary, those costs incurred prior to the beginning of commercial production are either capitalized in appropriate asset accounts or charged to R & D expense. Amortization of the cost of assets used in R & D activities is included in R & D expense when recognized.

We indicated earlier that prior to the issuance of *Statement No. 2,* companies frequently capitalized R & D costs and amortized them over future periods. Why did the FASB take the position that R & D costs are to be expensed as incurred unless they are for specific assets that have identifiable alternative future uses? The board carefully considered several capitalization alternatives for R & D expenditures: (1) capitalization of all costs when incurred,

Asset/Liability Measurement

(2) capitalization of costs when specified conditions are present, and (3) accumulation of all R & D costs in a special category until the existence of future benefits could be determined. Applying the asset/liability measurement principle is particularly difficult because the future benefits of individual R & D projects involve a high degree of uncertainty and estimates of the rates of success of R & D projects vary considerably. Also, a direct relationship between R & D costs and specific future revenue generally cannot be determined. Even if a relationship between present R & D costs and future revenue can be demonstrated, the problem of measuring the asset still exists. Generally, an expenditure is not treated as an asset unless the future economic benefits can be identified and objectively measured at the time it is made.[14]

Conservatism

For these and other reasons, the FASB determined that R & D costs should be expensed as incurred. This position is consistent with the modifying convention of conservatism, which indicates that the least favorable alternative presentation should be followed when significant doubt exists about the appropriate accounting principle to be applied.

One area of particular difficulty in accounting for R & D in recent years has been the treatment of the costs of developing computer software. If software is developed in conjunction with activities typically associated with R & D, the cost should be expensed as incurred. For example, if software is developed to create a new or significantly improved product or process without any contractual arrangement for sale or cost reimbursement, the development costs are considered R & D costs. Likewise, costs of developing software that is intended for use in the company's ongoing R & D activities are expensed as R & D as incurred.[15]

In 1985 the FASB specified the accounting for the costs of computer software to be sold, leased, or otherwise marketed as a separate product or as part of a product or process. *FASB Statement of Financial Accounting Standards No. 86* specifies that costs incurred internally in creating a computer software product should be charged to expense when incurred as R & D until its technological feasibility has been established. Technological feasibility is established upon completion of a detailed program design or working model. Thereafter, all software production costs are capitalized and subsequently reported at the lower or unamortized cost or net realizable value. Capitalized software development costs are amortized based on current and expected future revenue for each product, subject to a minimum amortization equal to straight-line amortization over the remaining estimated economic life of the product.[16]

If the treatment of computer software development costs has an important impact on the financial statements, that fact should be disclosed. Digital Equipment Corporation, for example, disclosed in its 1992 annual report its policy to capitalize software development costs beginning at the time their technological feasibility is established. These costs are then amortized over three years from the date the products are available for general release.

Research and development is an accounting area that has attracted a great deal of study in recent years. These studies have reported some interesting results on the impact of *FASB Statement No. 2* on financial reporting, as well as on management behavior. For example, Shehata found a significant structural change in R & D spending behavior after the issuance of *Statement No. 2*.[17] Similarly, Wasley and Linsmeier's research points to a decrease in

---

[14]*FASB Statement of Financial Accounting Standards No. 2,* pars. 37–44.

[15]*FASB Interpretation No. 6,* "Application of FASB Statement No. 2 to Computer Software: An Interpretation of FASB Statement No. 2," 1975, pars. 7–8.

[16]*FASB Statement of Financial Accounting Standards No. 86,* "Accounting for the Costs of Computer Software to Be Sold, Leased, or Otherwise Marketed," 1985, pars. 3, 5, 8.

[17]Mohamed Shehata, "Self-Selection Bias and the Economic Consequences of Accounting Regulation: An Application of Two-Stage Switching Regression to SFAS No. 2," *Accounting Review* (October 1991), p. 768.

R & D financing when the exposure draft of *Statement No. 2* was issued.[18] Cooper and Selto found that the accounting treatment of R & D had an effect on suboptimizing behavior, or the selection of inferior property, plant, and equipment projects over superior R & D projects.[19] Kirsch and Sakthivel's work suggests that the capitalization of internally developed software costs can provide better information for internal control purposes than expensing as required by *Statement No. 2*.[20]

These projects indicate the importance of R & D as both a business activity and a financial reporting issue. They also substantiate the conclusion that the financial statement consequences of alternative accounting practices are very important and their economic consequences may have an important impact on management behavior.

DEVELOPMENT-STAGE ENTERPRISES

A **development-stage enterprise** is an organization that either (1) is devoting substantially all of its effort to establishing a new business and that has not begun planned principal operations or (2) has begun planned principal operations but has not yet generated significant revenue from those operations. Prior to 1976, a variety of accounting and financial reporting practices existed for development-stage enterprises, including the deferral of many costs without regard to their recoverability and the offsetting of revenue against deferred costs. The FASB issued *Statement of Financial Accounting Standards No. 7* in 1975 to standardize accounting and reporting practices by newly developed companies.

Development-stage enterprises typically devote a substantial amount of effort to activities such as the following:[21]

1. Financial planning.
2. Raising capital.
3. Exploring for natural resources.
4. Developing natural resources.
5. Research and development.
6. Establishing sources of supply.
7. Acquiring property, plant, equipment, and other operating assets.
8. Recruiting and training personnel.
9. Starting up production.

Development-stage enterprises engaged in these activities incur significant costs but generate little or no revenue. Thus, development-stage enterprises typically incur operating losses during the development stage.

Matching

FASB Statement No. 7 requires development-stage enterprises to account and report on much the same basis as established operating enterprises in financial statements that purport to present financial position and results of operations. The same generally accepted accounting principles that apply to established enterprises govern the recognition of revenue and expense and the capitalization of costs for development-stage enterprises.

The financial statements issued by a development-stage enterprise should present **financial position, results of operations,** and **cash flows,** as do those issued by established

[18]Charles E. Wasley and Thomas J. Linsmeier, "A Further Examination of the Economic Consequences of SFAS No. 2," *Journal of Accounting Research* (Spring 1992), pp. 156–164.

[19]Jean C. Cooper and Frank H. Selto, "An Experimental Examination of the Effects of SFAS No. 2 on R & D Investment Decisions," *Accounting, Organizations and Society* (May 1991), p. 227.

[20]Robert J. Kirsch and Sachi Sakthivel, "Capitalize or Expense?" *Management Accounting* (January 1993), pp. 38–43.

[21]*FASB Statement of Financial Accounting Standards No. 7,* "Accounting and Reporting by Development Stage Enterprises," 1975, par. 9.

EXHIBIT 13–9

Financial Reporting Requirements of Development-Stage Enterprises

Financial Statements	Special Disclosure Requirements*
Balance sheet	Cumulative net losses reported with a descriptive title, such as "deficit accumulated during the development stage" in stockholders' equity.
Income statement	Cumulative amounts of revenues and expenses from the enterprise's inception.
Statement of cash flows	Cumulative amounts of sources and uses of cash since the enterprise's inception.
Statement of stockholders' equity	For each issuance of stock, the date, number of shares of stock, warrants, rights, or other equity securities issued.
	For each issuance, the dollar amounts assigned to the consideration received (per share and in total).
	For each issuance involving noncash consideration, the nature of the transaction and the basis for assigning a dollar amount.

*These special disclosures are required *in addition* to those normally required under generally accepted accounting principles.

---

enterprises. *Additional disclosures* that are necessary because of the unique nature of the development-stage enterprise are summarized in Exhibit 13–9.

The financial statements must clearly indicate that the enterprise is in a development stage and must also include a description of the specific development activities in which the enterprise is involved. In the first year that the enterprise is no longer considered to be in the development stage, disclosure should indicate that in previous years it had been a development-stage enterprise.

The reporting requirements of *FASB Statement No. 7* simply apply generally accepted accounting principles of established operating enterprises to development-stage enterprises. Practices such as capitalizing operating losses and nonrecoverable costs as intangible assets are not acceptable. The treatment of a cost is governed by the nature of the cost rather than the degree of maturity of the company incurring the cost. Under certain circumstances, however, a development-stage company may prepare financial statements on a basis other than generally accepted accounting principles.

In Chapter 1, we discussed the economic impact of accounting principles and raised the question of whether the FASB should be concerned with the economic impact of the standards it sets. This issue is important with respect to financial reporting by development-stage companies. Some accountants have pointed out that applying generally accepted accounting principles to developing enterprises may result in reporting net losses, which may not be fully understood by investors and creditors who could supply capital for these companies. If these reported losses influenced investors and creditors to withhold or delay investments in developing companies, new companies would have an even more difficult time getting started.

In an attempt to consider this issue, the FASB questioned officers of 15 venture-capital enterprises. The conclusion of this limited research was that the accounting treatment of pre-operating losses has little effect, if any, on the amount of capital that would be provided or the terms under which it would be provided to newly developed companies. According to these officers, the venture-capital investor typically relies on an assessment of cash flows based on an investigation of the technological, marketing, management, and financial aspects of the enterprise.[22] Other research in this general area tends to support these conclusions.

ACCOUNTING BY OIL AND GAS PRODUCING COMPANIES

Oil and gas producing companies incur substantial costs in locating and developing oil and gas reserves. Given the current state of technology, exploration requires many drilling efforts, only some of which locate producible oil and gas reserves. Other such efforts result in "dry holes" that provide no producible oil and gas.

The oil and gas industry uses two methods to account for costs incurred in exploration activities. The **successful-efforts method** is based on the theory that only the costs of locating wells from which gas and oil can economically be extracted are capitalized and amortized over future periods. In this method, costs associated with activities that do not result in the location of producible oil and gas reserves are treated as expenses when they are incurred.

In the alternative method, the **full-cost method,** the costs of *all* efforts are treated as the costs of locating producing wells. Because many unsuccessful efforts are usually necessary to locate reserves that can be successfully exploited, exploration costs that would be treated as expenses when incurred in the successful-efforts method are treated as assets and amortized over future periods in the full-cost method.

Both the successful-efforts and the full-cost methods have been widely used in accounting for the numerous costs incurred in oil and gas explorations. In practice, the successful-efforts method has been widely adopted by larger companies; smaller companies have favored the full-cost method.

In response to strong encouragement by the Securities and Exchange Commission (SEC), in December 1977 the FASB issues *Statement No. 19.*[23] In this statement, which resulted from a lengthy process of considering many diverse views, the FASB attempted to eliminate the full-cost method and establish successful-efforts as the only acceptable accounting method for oil and gas exploration costs. Costs in oil and gas producing activities fit into several classifications: acquisitions, explorations, development, production, support equipment, and facilities. Under the successful-efforts method, the costs of acquiring oil and gas rights are capitalized when incurred. These costs are amortized as a part of the cost of oil and gas produced. Exploration costs, except for the costs of drilling exploratory wells, are expensed as incurred. The costs of drilling exploratory wells are **temporarily deferred** until a determination is made of whether or not the well is producible. If producible reserves exist, the costs of the exploratory wells are capitalized and amortized as part of the cost of oil and gas produced. If producible reserves do not exist, the costs of the exploratory wells are expensed when this determination is made.

Costs of developing proved reserves are capitalized and depreciated as part of the cost of oil and gas produced. Production costs are treated as part of the cost of oil and gas produced and are expensed as incurred. Costs of support equipment and facilities are capitalized and depreciated as costs of oil and gas produced to the extent that they are used in oil and gas producing activities.

The application of the basic concept underlying the successful-efforts method is apparent in the accounting for exploration costs as previously described. All exploration costs, *except* those for drilling exploratory wells that result in producible oil and gas reserves, are expensed as incurred. Thus, costs that are capitalized and amortized over a long period

---

[22]*FASB Statement of Financial Accounting Standards No. 7,* par. 49.

[23]*FASB Statement of Financial Accounting Standards No. 19,* "Financial Accounting and Reporting by Oil and Gas Producing Companies," 1977.'

relate only to recoverable oil and gas reserves, the basic principle underlying the successful-efforts method.

An important issue that emerged in the FASB's consideration of alternative accounting methods used in the oil and gas industry was the potential negative economic impact of requiring companies to expense the costs of unsuccessful explorations. Proponents of the full-cost method argued that the required expensing of the costs of unsuccessful efforts would discourage exploration in the oil and gas industry at a time when exploration was greatly needed. A related argument was that the reduced profitability of companies under the successful-efforts method would discourage investment in oil and gas producing companies. These arguments were stated as being particularly significant for newer, developing companies that had aggressive exploration policies and, therefore, had a greater need for outside capital than established operating enterprises.

Does the accounting method used by a company for exploration activities in the oil and gas industry identify those companies that are aggressive in exploration? One researcher concluded that full-cost companies are *not* more aggressive in exploration than successful-effort companies, although full-cost companies did make a greater use of outside capital.[24] One interpretation of this research is that the method used to account for oil and gas production costs is not necessarily a factor that encourages or discourages exploration in the oil and gas industry.

A more recent study examined the circumstances surrounding voluntary changes from the successful-efforts to the full-cost methods of accounting by oil and gas producing companies. One explanation offered for such changes is that highly leveraged companies (i.e., those with high levels of debt financing) or those with high drilling risk prefer full-cost accounting in an attempt to reduce the probability of violating accounting-based debt covenant restrictions. The research conclusions suggest that full-cost adoption is associated not only with high leverage but also with current increases in debt financing and, to a lesser extent, with exploration activities. The researchers conclude that we can expect full-cost method adoptions to occur concurrently with abnormal increases in debt financing and exploration activities.[25]

Despite the fact that the FASB was cooperating with the SEC in attempting to eliminate the diversity in accounting for oil and gas producing activities, the SEC responded negatively to the FASB's position. Reacting to numerous pressures, including the strength of the small oil and gas producing companies and the fear of discouraging oil and gas exploration activities if the successful-efforts method was required, the SEC took the position that both full-cost and successful-efforts methods were unsatisfactory methods of accounting by oil and gas producing companies.

The SEC indicated its preference for the development of a method of current-value accounting that would eventually replace both existing methods. It further indicated that it would develop such a method and tentatively referred to it as **reserve-recognition accounting.** In the meantime, enterprises reporting to the SEC could continue to use either the full-cost or the successful-efforts method.

In light of these developments, the FASB issued *Statement of Financial Accounting Standards No. 25,* "Suspension of Certain Accounting Requirements for Oil and Gas Producing Companies."[26] This statement suspended the effective date of *Statement No. 19,* thereby

---

[24]Edward B. Deakin III, "An Analysis of Differences between Non-Major Oil Firms Using Successful-Efforts and Full-Cost Methods," *Accounting Review* (October 1979), pp. 722–734.

[25]W. Bruce Johnson and Ramachandran Ramanan, "Discretionary Accounting Changes from 'Successful-Efforts' to 'Full-Cost' Methods: 1970–1976," *Accounting Review* (January 1988), p. 108.

[26]*FASB Statement of Financial Accounting Standards No. 25,* "Suspension of Certain Accounting Requirements for Oil and Gas Producing Companies," 1979.

allowing companies to continue using either the full-cost or the successful-efforts method. Companies that were not required to report to the SEC, as well as those that were required to do so, continued to have the option of reporting under either method. At a later date, the SEC abandoned its plan to develop the reserve-recognition accounting method. Its decision was based primarily on the practical problems encountered in attempting to apply a current value approach to oil and gas reserves. Thus, oil and gas producing companies continue to choose either the full-cost method or the successful-efforts method.

In 1987 the SEC again considered the fact that two methods were being used in accounting by oil and gas producing companies and resolved **not to issue** a release concerning the abolishment of the full-cost method. The SEC concluded that the potential harm to struggling oil and gas producing companies of going forward with a proposal to discontinue the full-cost method would outweigh the benefits to investors.[27]

This series of events verifies the fact that the SEC has ultimate responsibility for the establishment of standards for reporting by publicly held corporations in the United States. Although the SEC has generally supported the positions of the FASB, if the two do not agree, the legal position of the SEC is superior. This series of events concerning oil and gas accounting also indicates that the reporting requirements applicable to those companies that must report to the SEC have significant influence on those enterprises that do not report to it.

PROFESSIONAL JUDGMENT

Accounting for intangible assets and for activities such as R & D and the location and development of oil and gas reserves requires significant judgment on the part of the professional accountant. Review Exhibit 13–1, which presents a number of questions that must be answered just to determine whether an intangible asset exists according to generally accepted accounting principles. Once the fact that an intangible asset exists is established, an amortization policy must be determined, which involves the most difficult judgmental decision of determining the asset's estimated useful life. This is not a simple decision, and legal or contractual limitations, competition, and other factors may affect it.

Although accounting for separate intangible assets, such as patents, copyrights, and trademarks, involves professional judgment, nowhere is the professional accountant's judgment challenged more than in the area of goodwill. We have discussed a variety of methods for estimating its value, all of which require the accountant to make or obtain important estimates of the normal and expected returns from an enterprise that is acquired, the period over which those returns can be expected, and the discount rates that are appropriate in converting those returns to an estimated value of goodwill.

Turning to the specialized areas we discussed at the end of this chapter, we learned that separating costs into those that should be expensed as R & D and those that should be capitalized in some asset account or expensed as other than R & D involves sound judgment and objectivity. We also observed that research in this area suggests that accounting for R & D has an important impact on financial reporting and management behavior. Even determining when a company has entered commercial production with a product or when technological feasibility is established for a software product may be highly judgmental. The same can be said for the area of oil and gas accounting, in which decisions to expense or capitalize various costs have very significant financial statement implications.

Asset/Liability Measurement

Accounting for intangible assets is governed primarily by the accounting principles of *asset/liability measurement, matching, and consistency,* much like accounting for plant assets. In measuring intangible assets, the accountant must exercise significant judgment, particularly in accounting for the intangible asset, goodwill.

---

[27]"SEC Votes against Change in Oil and Gas Accounting," *Journal of Accountancy* (January 1987), p. 50.

Conservatism

As with plant assets, reliable evidence is important in accounting for intangible assets. Recorded assets should be based on verifiable evidence. Also, careful distinctions must be made between the cost of intangible assets and other expenditures, such as research and development, that are expensed as incurred. The *modifying convention of conservatism* is also apparent in accounting for research and development and other costs often associated with intangible assets.

Matching

Consistency

The *matching principle* is apparent in the required amortization of intangible assets over the shortest of the asset's useful life, its legal or contractual period, or 40 years. The *consistency principle* requires that the treatment of intangible assets be the same from period to period so that the resulting financial information will be comparable.

CONCLUDING REMARKS

In studying a company's balance sheet, remember that the principles underlying accounting for different types of assets vary. These differing principles are used in recognition of the fact that the values of various assets are realized in several ways. For example, receivables are shown in the balance sheet at their net realizable value (gross amount less an estimate of the portion that will not be collected). Inventories are shown at the lower of cost or market. We have seen, however, that cost can be determined by several different flow assumptions and that variations also exist in the methods of determining the lower of cost or market once the cost has been determined.

Concerning investments, we learned that a number of different methods are applied. These methods vary, depending on whether the investment is in debt or equity securities and its classification as trading, available-for-sale, or held-to-maturity.

Now that we have studied the major asset categories, it is useful to review the significance of the dollar amounts to the various types of assets included in a company's balance sheet. A review of the primary valuation techniques included within generally accepted accounting principles is presented in Exhibit 13–10.

EXHIBIT 13–10
Review of Asset Valuation Techniques

Type of Asset	Basis of Valuation Generally Found in Balance Sheet
Current Assets	
Cash	Face amount
Trading securities	Fair value
Receivables	Net realizable value
Inventories	Lower of cost or market
Prepaid expenses	Unexpired cost
Noncurrent Investments	
Available-for-sale securities (debt and equity)	Fair value
Held-to-maturity securities (debt)	Amortized cost
Equity investments providing significant influence	Equity method
Plant and Intangible Assets	
Property, plant, and equipment	Portion of cost not yet recognized as depreciation
Natural resources	Portion of cost not yet recognized as depletion
Intangibles	Portion of cost not yet recognized as amortization
Other Assets	Miscellaneous, depending on nature of specific asset

1. Intangible assets differ from property, plant, and equipment primarily because the intangibles lack physical substance. Both types of assets have relatively long lives and are used in the production and distribution of goods and services. (Objective 1)

2. Some intangible assets (e.g., patents, copyrights, and franchises) are separately identifiable. Some intangibles, usually identified as goodwill, are associated with an enterprise as a whole and cannot be transferred apart from that enterprise. (Objective 2)

3. Intangible assets that can be separately identified and have determinable lives are recorded as assets. Other costs related to internally developed intangibles, including ones with characteristics similar to those of goodwill, are treated as expenses when they are incurred. (Objective 2)

4. Intangible assets are initially recorded at cost and then amortized over their estimated useful lives. The period of amortization cannot exceed 40 years, and the straight-line method is commonly used. (Objective 3)

5. Financial statement disclosure of intangible assets includes the method and period of amortization. Intangibles are typically presented in a separate asset section designated as "Intangible Assets" or "Other Assets." (Objective 4)

6. Goodwill is an intangible asset representing anticipated excess earning capacity. It arises when the price paid for another business exceeds the current value of the identifiable net assets acquired. Goodwill is recorded at cost and amortized over its estimated useful life in the same manner as other intangible assets. (Objective 5)

7. The value of goodwill can be estimated by several methods that are based on a comparison between anticipated earnings and normal earnings. (Objective 5)

8. Research and development costs are treated as expenses when they are incurred. Some costs related to R & D activities, however, are capitalized in appropriate asset categories and amortized as R & D expense over their estimated useful lives. (Objective 6)

9. Development-stage enterprises must apply generally accepted accounting principles in preparing financial statements purporting to present financial position and results of operations in the same way that established enterprises do. In addition, development-stage enterprises must disclose certain cumulative figures that relate to the enterprise since its inception. (Objective 6)

10. Oil and gas producing companies may account for exploration costs under either the successful-efforts or the full-cost method within current GAAP. This is an area of significant controversy in which the FASB attempted to reduce variation in accounting practice by requiring companies to use only the successful-efforts method. Under pressure from the SEC, however, the FASB suspended this requirement. (Objective 6)

QUESTIONS

In questions 13–1 through 13–4, circle the letter of the correct answer.

13–1 Which of the following procedures best describes the proper accounting of the cost of intangible assets subsequent to acquisition?

[a] Amortize over the longer of 40 years or the estimated useful life.
[b] Amortize over 40 years.
[c] Amortize over the shorter of the estimated useful life or 40 years.
[d] Amortize over 10 years.

13–2 Which of the following assets should *not* be presented in the intangible asset category of the balance sheet?

[a] Goodwill   [c] Patents
[b] Copyrights   [d] Accounts receivable

13–3 Which of the following characteristics is *not* necessary for an asset to qualify as intangible?

[a] Has a determinable life.
[b] Conveys a right or privilege.
[c] Has a relatively long life.
[d] Is used in the production of other goods or services.

13–4 Which of the following statements best describes proper accounting by development-stage companies?

[a] The same as established operating enterprises except for the capitalization of R & D.
[b] The same as established operating enterprises except for the capitalization of operating losses in early years of operations.

[c] The same as established operating enterprises except for the requirement of additional disclosures in the financial statements and related notes.

[d] The same as established operating enterprises except that the statement of cash flows is not required.

13–5 What are the key elements in the definition of *intangible asset?*

13–6 What basic feature distinguishes intangible assets from tangible plant assets?

13–7 How do intangible assets that can be separately identified differ from those that cannot be separately identified? Indicate the type(s) of transactions in which each typically arises.

13–8 What are several types of expenditures that are closely related to intangible assets but that should *not* be capitalized and amortized over periods after their incurrence?

13–9 With regard to *APB Opinion No. 17,* what was the basic rationale for requiring the amortization of intangible assets, even in cases in which the life of the intangible appears to be unlimited at the point of acquisition?

13–10 What are several factors that should be considered in estimating the useful life of a separately identifiable intangible asset?

13–11 What is the current legal life of the following intangible assets: patents, copyrights, and trademarks?

13–12 What are several examples of intangible assets whose lives may be limited through contractual arrangements between two enterprises or between an enterprise and a governmental unit?

13–13 What types of individual costs are properly included in organization costs?

13–14 How should organization costs be treated subsequent to the beginning of operations?

13–15 What does the term *goodwill* mean? Identify any specific criteria that must be met for goodwill to be established as an asset in the balance sheet.

13–16 What are specific procedures that are followed in accounting for goodwill, including the determination of cost and the recognition of periodic amortization?

13–17 What are the steps that should be followed in estimating the value of goodwill existing in a potential acquisition?

13–18 Of the various methods of estimating the value of goodwill presented in this chapter, which appears to have the greatest conceptual merit? Why?

13–19 What are the key elements in the FASB's definition of *research and development?*

13–20 What are three activities that qualify as research and development (R & D) and three that do not qualify?

13–21 What is the proper accounting for costs that are classified as R & D?

13–22 R & D costs are classified in five categories: (1) materials, equipment, and facilities; (2) personnel; (3) intangibles purchased from others; (4) contract services; and (5) indirect costs. What items are included in each category? Give one or more example(s) of each.

13–23 What does the term *development-stage enterprise* mean? Suggest several activities in which such an enterprise would typically be engaged.

13–24 To what extent do the accounting and reporting standards that are applicable to established operating enterprises apply to development-stage enterprises?

13–25 What was the nature of the economic impact concern that was raised with the FASB in conjunction with developing standards for development-stage enterprises? What did the FASB discover in its evaluation of this concern?

13–26 How do the full-cost and the successful-efforts methods of accounting by oil and gas producing companies differ?

13–27 What were the roles of the FASB and the Securities and Exchange Commission in developing current financial accounting and reporting standards for oil and gas producing companies?

EXERCISES

13–28 Franchise On January 2, 1995, East Company entered into a franchise agreement to operate a fast-food restaurant called Hot Dog Haven. The initial franchise fee was $14,000 and is expected to produce revenue as long as the company retains the right to use the designation.

The franchise contract is for a five-year period, at the end of which a new agreement will be negotiated, if desired, by the original parties. The franchise also calls for payment of 5% of gross revenues by East Company each year. Revenues for 1995 and 1996 were $97,800 and $128,600, respectively. Straight-line amortization is used on all intangible assets. East Company reports on a calendar-year basis.

INSTRUCTIONS

[a] Prepare all journal entries for East Company relative to the franchise agreement for 1995 and 1996.

[b] Determine the amounts to be included in the 1996 financial statements relative to the franchise.

13–29 Research and Development Distinguishing between R & D costs and other related costs is sometimes difficult.

INSTRUCTIONS

Identify the accounts that should be debited in each of the following transactions or adjustments:

[a] Cost of models of products under development.
[b] Cost of patent usable only in a current R & D project.
[c] Legal fees paid to successfully defend a patent used in ongoing R & D activities.
[d] Amortization of a patent on a product currently being manufactured and sold.
[e] Costs of quality control over the production process.
[f] Amortization of a patent used in ongoing R & D activities.
[g] Warranty costs on products sold.
[h] Costs of R & D contract services expected to be of continuing benefit.
[i] Materials expected to be used only in current R & D projects.

13–30 Patents Wells Manufacturing Company acquired three patents in January 1995. The patents have different lives, as indicated in the following schedule:

	Cost	Estimated Useful Life in Years	Remaining Legal Life in Years
Patent X	$12,500	10	17
Patent Y	27,250	5	7
Patent Z	65,620	Indefinite	17

Patent Z is believed to be uniquely useful as long as the company retains the right to use it. In June 1996, the company unsuccessfully attempted to defend its right to Patent Y. Legal fees of $12,700 were incurred in this action.

The company's policy is to amortize intangible assets by the straight-line method to the nearest half year. The company reports on a calendar-year basis.

INSTRUCTIONS

Determine the amount of amortization that should be recognized for 1995, 1996, and 1997.

13–31 Patent Lance Company acquired a patent on June 25, 1993, for $13,000. Management expects the patent to be useful to the company for its remaining legal life of 13 years.

On January 12, 1995, the company spent $5,000 to successfully defend the patent against a competing company.

During 1996 management determines that the estimated remaining life of the patent should be reduced to only four remaining years, including the current year. This decision was made after careful consideration of actions of various competing companies.

INSTRUCTIONS

Prepare all journal entries relating to the patent for 1993 through 1996, assuming that the company's year-end is December 31. Company policy is to amortize intangible assets by the straight-line method, computed to the nearest full month.

13–32 Organization Costs Williard Manufacturing Company was organized during 1995. In assisting in the preparation of the financial statements for the year ending December 31, you discover that the following items were debited to the Organization Cost account during early January 1995:

Legal fees of corporate registration	$27,500
Compensation of promoters of corporation	13,800
Salaries of employees before the beginning of operations	4,860
Discount on 10-year bonds issued before the beginning of operations	2,770
	$48,930

Plans call for the amortization of organization costs over a five-year period by the straight-line method. The company's accountant does not plan to begin this amortization until 1996, however, due to the large operating loss that the company sustained in 1995.

No amortization of the discount on the bonds has been made. The straight-line method is considered appropriate.

INSTRUCTIONS

Prepare all correcting and adjusting entries that you would propose on December 31, 1995. Closing entries for the year have *not* been made.

13–33 Leasehold Prosser Enterprises leased several items of equipment under a lease that does not qualify for capitalization. The lease was entered into on May 1, 1995. Prosser paid the $150,000 rental for the first year in advance; a similar payment is made each year on May 1. The lease term is 10 years; the equipment is expected to have a useful life of 25 years.

On May 1, 1995, the company spent $36,000 to make certain improvements to the equipment. These improvements are expected to guarantee the maximum usefulness of the equipment for the duration of the lease term.

Leasehold improvements are amortized by the straight-line method, computed to the nearest half year.

INSTRUCTIONS

Determine the balance sheet and income statement amounts related to the equipment lease for the years ending December 31, 1993–1996.

13–34 Goodwill Ramsey Company is considering acquisition of the net assets of Fuller Company to expand its operations. The book value and current value of Fuller Company's net assets are $165,000 and $200,000, respectively. The normal rate of return is believed to be 9%, but Ramsey believes it can earn 16% annually on its investment in Fuller due to Fuller's excellent reputation.

INSTRUCTIONS

Compute the goodwill that results from applying the following methods to the situation described above:

[a] Years multiple of excess earnings (assuming a 10-year period of excess earnings).
[b] Present value of excess earnings at the expected rate (assuming an 8-year period of excess earnings).
[c] Capitalization of excess earnings at the normal rate.
[d] Capitalization of excess earnings at 16%.

13–35 Goodwill Filson Company is considering acquisition of Roth Company's net assets as part of a diversification program. Filson management believes that Roth's excellent reputation provides an opportunity to achieve a level of earnings in excess of the normal rate of 10%. In fact, it expects to earn a rate of return of 16% on its investment.

The following information on Roth Company is available:

	Estimated Current Value
Current assets	$175,000
Noncurrent assets	280,000
Total reported assets	455,000
Liabilities	(272,000)
Net assets	$183,000

In determining the amount it should bid for Roth Company, Filson management is attempting to estimate a value for goodwill.

INSTRUCTIONS

Compute the goodwill resulting from each of the following methods:

[a] Years multiple of excess earnings (assuming a five-year period).
[b] Present value of excess earnings at the expected rate (assuming a five-year period).
[c] Capitalization of excess earnings at the normal rate.
[d] Capitalization of excess earnings at the expected rate.

13–36 Goodwill Dover Diversified acquired Simplified Products Company on January 1, 1996. Conditions of the acquisition include the following:

[1] Dover issued $1,200,000 of 20-year bonds to finance the transaction. This amount was transferred to Simplified Products to complete the acquisition. Interest is payable annually on December 31 at 13%.

[2] Dover is to take over all Simplified Products's assets (except cash) and all liabilities. Simplified is then to liquidate its assets by distributing cash to stockholders in retirement of their shares of stock.

[3] Dover has established the following current valuations on assets and liabilities to be assumed:

	Book Value on Simplified's Books	Estimated Current Value
Receivables	$ 100,000	$ 90,000
Inventory	550,000	720,000
Property, plant, and equipment	900,000	1,300,000
Current liabilities	(300,000)	(250,000)
Noncurrent liabilities	(1,000,000)	(1,000,000)
Net assets	$ 250,000	$ 860,000

[4] Dover has determined through various estimation techniques that goodwill inherent in the transaction has a value of at least $400,000. Goodwill is to be amortized over a 10-year period by the straight-line method.

INSTRUCTIONS

Prepare all journal entries on Dover Diversified's books for the year ended December 31, 1996. Include amortization of goodwill for the full year.

13–37 Research and Development An account for a research project identified as AM423 is included on the trial balance of your client, Buckley Company. The account balance consists of the following charges:

Salaries of research staff	$27,700
Patent acquired solely for use in project AM423	15,200
Patent acquired for use in several research projects, including AM423	16,200
Cost of models	8,950
	$68,050

Intangible assets are amortized by the straight-line method over the shorter of the legal life or estimated useful life. The company's patents have generally been found to be useful for approximately 10 years. You determined that both of the patents were acquired in early 1996 and that the cost of models and salaries were incurred throughout 1996.

INSTRUCTIONS

Determine the items that should be presented in the Buckley's balance sheet and income statement on December 31, 1996.

13–38 Copyright Storeytime Company incorrectly charged the $42,000 cost of a copyright acquired in early 1995 to the Retained Earnings account. The error was discovered as part of the 1996 audit. The company holds several copyrights and follows the policy of amortizing their cost over the period expected to benefit by the straight-line method, computed to the nearest whole year. The $42,000 copyright was expected to be useful in producing revenue for 12 years from the time of acquisition, even though the legal life was 27 years from that date.

INSTRUCTIONS

[a] Prepare the entry necessary in 1996 to correct the error of 1995.
[b] Prepare the entry to record amortization of the copyright for 1996.

13–39 Amortization of Intangibles Borton Company acquired three intangible assets during 1996 in transactions with other enterprises: patent, $15,270; leasehold improvement, $27,750; and goodwill,

$248,000. The patent has a remaining legal life of six years. The leasehold improvement has an expected life of 25 years. The goodwill is expected to provide benefits in the form of high earnings indefinitely. The leasehold improvement is on property that Borton has leased for 15 years; renewal depends on the intent of both parties at the end of the lease period. No further information on the lives of the various intangible assets is available or determinable.

INSTRUCTIONS

[a] State your recommendation for the useful life to be used for amortization of the three intangible assets. Justify your recommendations.

[b] Assuming that straight-line amortization is used with a full year taken in the year of acquisition, prepare the entry or entries necessary to record the amortization of the intangible assets at the end of 1996, based on your recommendation in [a].

13–40 Research and Development   For several years, Martin Manufacturing Company has accounted for R & D costs in accordance with *Statement of Financial Accounting Standards No. 2*. In 1996 research efforts materialize and three patents are acquired. Patent 93–1 will be used in the ongoing R & D activities of the enterprise. Patent 93–2 will be used in one specific research project that is currently underway. Patent 93–3 will be used in the company's manufacturing process.

Company officials suggest that the cost of the patents be established as follows:

Patent	Legal Costs of Obtaining Patents	Costs Previously Charged to R & D	Total Cost
93–1	$ 6,500	$17,625	$24,125
93–2	2,000	–0–	2,000
93–3	4,250	19,000	23,250
	$12,750	$36,625	$49,375

Because legal costs were charged to the Legal Fees account when they were incurred, the company's accountant recommends the following entry:

Patents	49,375	
Legal Fees		12,750
Retained Earnings		36,625

INSTRUCTIONS

[a] Evaluate the suggested entry to record the patents. Justify your position.

[b] Suggest alternative entries to capitalize the patents.

[c] How should the amortization of the patent costs be treated in subsequent years?

13–41 Trademark   Fisher, Inc., developed a trademark to distinguish its products from those of its competitors. Through advertising and other means, the company is seeking to establish significant product identification to increase future sales.

The similarity between the trademark costs and other intangible and operating costs has caused some confusion over proper accounting. The following items are being treated as part of the cost of the trademark:

Marketing research to study consumer tastes	$18,650
Design costs of trademark	17,800
Legal fees of registering trademark	850
Advertising to establish recognition of trademark	12,650
Registration fee with U.S. Patent Office	1,200

Through renewals, the trademark is expected to have an unlimited life.

INSTRUCTIONS

[a] Evaluate each of the costs as appropriate for capitalization in the Trademark account.

[b] Recommend the period of amortization for the cost of the trademark. Justify your recommendation.

13–42 Oil and Gas Costs   Texas Oil Company is involved in oil and gas production activities. The following costs were incurred during 1996:

Acquiring mineral rights	$13,500,000
Exploration	
Drilling exploratory wells resulting in recoverable reserves	8,400,000
Drilling exploratory wells not resulting in recoverable reserves	5,550,000
Other costs	7,890,000
Developing recoverable oil reserves	9,375,000
Producing oil and gas (after extraction)	10,550,000
Acquiring equipment for use in oil and gas producing activities	17,650,000

INSTRUCTIONS

For each of these cost categories, indicate the proper accounting treatment within the successful-efforts method by choosing among the following:

[a] Expense as incurred.
[b] Capitalize and amortize as a cost of oil and gas produced.
[c] Treat as a cost of oil and gas produced as incurred.

PROBLEMS

13–43 Intangible Asset Cost Sawyer, Inc., has accumulated a number of costs in a single Intangibles account. As a new employee in the company's accounting department, you have been asked to analyze the account and recommend any corrections you think should be made. The Intangibles account for 1996 is presented to you as follows:

Intangibles

Date	Transaction Description	Dr.	Cr.	Balance
Jan. 2	Legal fees related to organization of business	10,500		10,500
Jan. 2	Prepayment of lease on building for one year	18,000		28,500
Feb. 1	Prepayment of insurance for two years	1,800		30,300
Feb. 28	Advertising expenses (radio, television, and newspaper)	8,000		38,300
Apr. 7	Premium on bonds issued		10,500	27,800
Apr. 25	Interest paid on short-term notes	2,500		30,300
May 5	Legal fees in filing for trade name (Superco)	10,800		41,100
June 30	Cash discount on merchandise purchased		250	40,850

The company plans to present financial statements as of June 30, 1996, to a local bank to support its request for additional financing. Company policy is to amortize intangible asset costs over a 10-year period, computed to the nearest full month. The president suggests an amortization on June 30, 1996, of $1,866, computed as follows:

$$(\$40,850/10 \text{ years}) \times \tfrac{1}{2} \text{ year} = \$2,043$$

INSTRUCTIONS

[a] Prepare an analysis of the entries in the Intangibles account and indicate corrections you would propose in the account, including reclassifications of items.
[b] Based on your response to [a] above, prepare the entries to properly record amortization of intangible assets on June 30, 1996. Assume that all amounts are material and that straight-line amortization is to be used.

13–44 Miscellaneous Intangible Assets Sanders Company acquired three intangible assets before 1996. The company is preparing financial statements on June 30, 1996. Before that date no formal statements had been prepared, and the cost of intangible assets had been charged (debited) to Retained Earnings when acquired.

The following intangible assets were accounted for in this manner:

Asset	Acquisition Date	Estimated Useful Life in Years	Cost
Copyright No. 1	Jan. 2, 1992	25	$30,000
Copyright No. 2	July 15, 1993	15	33,000
Goodwill	Feb. 28, 1994	Indeterminate	50,000

Management has now decided to correct the past accounting treatment and to account for the intangibles as if they had been properly capitalized at the time of acquisition and subsequently amortized. The straight-line method of amortization is to be used, computed to the nearest half-year. The company has selected July 1 to June 30 for its financial reporting period.

INSTRUCTIONS

[a] Prepare the entries necessary to reclassify the intangible assets and to record amortization for 1996. Provide adequate support for your entries.

[b] Briefly explain in a written paragraph the process you followed in preparing the entry or entries in [a].

13–45 Research and Development Nashville Sound, Inc., has initiated an extensive research program to develop a more efficient method to record compact discs. Management expects to be able to lease its production facilities, when completely refined, to the many record-producing companies in the area.

You have been asked to assist in preparing financial statements for the year ended December 31, 1996. Costs related to the project have been accumulated in a master account identified simply as Recording since the beginning of the project in early 1996, as follows:

Debits

$225,000	Equipment purchased for use in many research projects over a five-year period.
85,000	Salaries of staff working on research project.
17,500	Computer program services purchased through a contract with another enterprise.
24,800	Legal fees related to the patent acquired on the new production process, which is expected to be useful in producing revenue for 10 years.

Credits

$ 88,000	Down payments received from other companies that have contracted to use the new production process in the future.

Management has determined that the company incurred general and administrative expenses of $190,500 during 1996. Based on the time spent on the various enterprise functions, you estimate that 25% of this amount relates to the research project identified as "Recording."

Discussions with corporate officials reveal that all long-lived assets are depreciated with a full year's amortization taken in the year of acquisition and none in the year of disposal. You determine that the process began to generate revenue in 1996 and, therefore, the amortization of the patent should begin this year.

INSTRUCTIONS

[a] Prepare all journal entries you would suggest to correct the Recording account and other accounts related to the company's research and development effort.

[b] Prepare all adjusting entries that should be made on December 31, 1996, to reflect amortization and depreciation for the year.

[c] Identify all items that will appear in the financial statements on December 31, 1996, related to plant and intangible assets and research and development.

[d] Describe in a short paragraph your treatment of items that are included in the research and development expense in [c].

13–46 Patents Phoenix Supply Company acquired two patents, several items of equipment, and a parcel of land for a total of $137,500. Appraisal values of the assets on the date of acquisition are as follows:

Patent A	$30,000
Patent B	40,000
Equipment	19,700
Land	62,000

By acquiring the assets in a group, the company was able to get a favorable price. The acquisition took place on April 27, 1994. Patent A has a 5-year remaining life and Patent B a 12-year remaining life. Amortization on intangible assets is determined on a straight-line basis, computed in whole dollars to the nearest full month.

During 1995 the company became involved in two lawsuits resulting in the successful defense of Patent B but the unsuccessful defense of Patent A. The company incurred total legal fees of $17,600. Management estimates that approximately equal effort went into defending each patent. The established date of these settlements was March 7, 1995.

No further transactions affecting the patents occurred through October 31, 1996.

INSTRUCTIONS

[a] Prepare journal entries for the years 1994, 1995, and 1996, related to the intangible asset accounts. The company's reporting year ends on October 31.
[b] Briefly explain any difference in your treatment of the legal costs of the defenses of Patents A and B.

13–47 Goodwill Washington Company is negotiating to acquire Jefferson Company. Washington manufactures and sells wood-burning stoves, and Jefferson Company produces parts that are required to manufacture the stoves. Jefferson Company enjoys an exceptional reputation, and Washington management believes it can continue Jefferson's current level of income and satisfy its own need for parts.

Under the contemplated arrangement, Washington Company will negotiate for the acquisition of the net assets of Jefferson Company. The following information has been developed to determine the appropriate price:

[1] Recorded amounts and estimated current values of Jefferson Company's assets and liabilities are as follows:

	Recorded Amounts	Estimated Current Values
Assets to be received	$1,585,000	$1,925,000
Liabilities to be assumed	570,000	510,000
	$1,015,000	$1,415,000

[2] Jefferson Company's earnings for the past five years averaged $200,000. This is believed to be a reasonable estimate of future income.
[3] The level of income normally experienced by companies similar to Jefferson Company is 9%.

INSTRUCTIONS

[a] Compute the estimated value of goodwill under each of the following methods and assumptions:
 [1] Years multiple of excess earnings, assuming a five-year period of excess earnings.
 [2] Present value of excess earnings, assuming a seven-year period of excess earnings and a 10% interest rate.
 [3] Capitalization of excess earnings at the normal rate.
 [4] Capitalization of excess earnings at 1 ½ times the normal rate.
[b] If management accepts the present value of excess earnings method as the appropriate value of goodwill for negotiation purposes, what is the maximum price Washington Company should pay for the net assets of Jefferson Company?

13–48 Goodwill Phelps Company is considering the acquisition of Martin Company. A considerable amount of information about Martin Company has been accumulated, including the following.

Net income. Net income figures are

1991	$78,500	1994	$51,500
1992	59,000	1995	72,000
1993	67,200		

Net income for 1991 included a $12,500 extraordinary gain; 1993 net income included a $14,000 extraordinary gain.

Selected Balance Sheet Data. As of the transaction date, recorded amounts and estimated current values of assets are

	Recorded Amount	Estimated Current Value
Receivables	$125,000	$120,000
Inventories	216,000	415,000
Property, plant, and equipment	300,000	425,000
Patents	10,000	75,000

Liabilities to be assumed are $665,000.

Phelps Company management believes that the investment in Martin Company will provide a return in excess of the 10% normal for the industry. Analysis of the components of earnings indicates that average net income for the past five years is a reasonable basis for estimating future income. It is believed, however, that the effect of extraordinary items should be eliminated and that depreciation and amortization can be expected to increase by $12,500 annually.

INSTRUCTIONS

[a] Estimate the amount of goodwill in the Martin Company acquisition by each of the following methods:

[1] Years multiple of estimated excess earnings, assuming a five-year period of excess earnings.

[2] Present value of estimated excess earnings, discounted at the normal rate over a five-year period.

[3] Capitalization of the estimated excess earnings at a 15% rate.

[b] For each category of assets, indicate the probable reason for the difference between the recorded amount and the estimated current value.

[c] After extended negotiations, the two companies finally agreed on a price of $405,000. Prepare the journal entry to record the acquisition by Phelps Company. You may include all liabilities in a single Liability account. The agreement calls for a cash payment of $175,000 and the issuance of 10,000 shares of $10 par value stock of Phelps Company. The current market price of the stock is $23.

13–49 Goodwill   Maxwell Company has negotiated to acquire the net assets of Robbins Company. The companies have agreed that the purchase price will be established at the fair market value of the assets, less liabilities, plus the value of the goodwill of Robbins Company. The value of the goodwill has been agreed upon as the average of the last three years' excess of income from normal operations over 10% of stockholders' equity, at the beginning of the year, discounted to the present at 10% for a five-year period. The last three years are 1993, 1994, and 1995.

The following figures have been taken from the Robbins Company's last four years of financial statements (December 31 year-end):

	1992	1993	1994	1995
Net income	$ 225,000	$ 250,000	$ 350,000	$ 550,000
Stockholders' equity				
Common stock	1,000,000	1,000,000	1,200,000	1,200,000
Paid-in capital in excess of par value	500,000	500,000	600,000	600,000
Retained earnings	125,000	250,000	400,000	500,000
	$1,625,000	$1,750,000	$2,200,000	$2,300,000

You have been engaged as an independent CPA to calculate the purchase price to which both parties have agreed. As part of your investigation, you discover the following:

[1] The two companies have agreed on the following estimates of the current value of the assets to be transferred (other than goodwill):

Receivables	$150,000	Buildings	$1,400,000
Inventory	400,000	Land	1,600,000
Equipment	500,000	Franchise	150,000

[2] Liabilities to be assumed by Maxwell Company total $1,200,000.

[3] Additional shares of stock were sold in May 1994.

[4] The following questionable items have been recorded by year:

1993. Net income included an extraordinary gain of $25,500. This represents the excess of the proceeds over cost of land purchased by the city under condemnation proceedings.

1994. A franchise agreement was entered into in January and $100,000 paid in advance. The period of the franchise is five years. No amortization has been taken. The $100,000 was debited to an intangible asset account.

1995. A sum of $15,000 was received from a customer whose account had been erroneously written off as uncollectible in 1994 by a direct charge to Bad Debts Expense. The arrangement with the customer had explicitly called for repayment in 1995. The $15,000 was credited to Miscellaneous Income when received.

An insurance recovery of $125,000 was received on inventory that was totally destroyed by a flood. The $125,000 was presented as an extraordinary gain due to the unusual circumstances surrounding the flood. The cost of the inventory, $75,000, was debited to Retained Earnings. The flood was extremely unusual; a similar event has never occurred in the location of the company this century and is not expected to recur.

An additional tax assessment of $97,000 was paid. Of this amount, $25,000 related to 1992, $35,000 to 1993, and $37,000 to 1994. Retained Earnings was debited for the total of $97,000, because this adjustment resulted from an accounting error.

INSTRUCTIONS

[a] Prepare a schedule that includes the following:
   [1] The corrected net income for 1992, 1993, 1994, and 1995.
   [2] The amount to be used for computing goodwill for 1993, 1994, and 1995. A conference with officials of the two companies reveals that the phrase *income from normal operations* appears to have meant income before extraordinary items.

[b] Prepare a schedule restating retained earnings for 1992, 1993, 1994, and 1995 at year-end.

[c] Based on information from your schedules in [a] and [b], compute goodwill as agreed upon by the two companies.

[d] Prepare the journal entry to record Robbins Company's net assets acquired by Maxwell Company, assuming that payment is made by issuing 100,000 shares of Maxwell Company common stock and the remainder in cash. The common stock had a $20 par value and a $27 market price when the transaction was finalized on January 5, 1996.

[e] Prepare the adjusting entry one year after the acquisition to record amortization on the intangible assets acquired. The franchise is expected to have a six-year life, and the goodwill is to be amortized over a period consistent with the method by which it was computed.

13–50 Miscellaneous Intangible Assets   Information concerning Wallock Corporation's intangible assets is as follows:

[1] On January 1, 1995, Wallock signed an agreement to operate as a franchisee of Rapid Copy Service, Inc., for an initial franchise fee of $85,000. Of this amount, $25,000 was paid when the agreement was signed and the balance is payable in four annual payments of $15,000 each beginning January 1, 1996. The agreement provides that the down payment is not refundable and no future services are required of the franchisor. At January 1, 1995, the present value of the four annual payments discounted at 14% (the implicit rate for a loan of this type) is $43,700. The agreement also provides that 5% of the revenue from the franchise must be paid to the franchisor annually. Wallock's revenue from the franchise for 1995 was $950,000. Wallock estimates the useful life of the franchise to be 10 years.

[2] Wallock incurred $78,000 of experimental and development costs in its laboratory to develop a patent that was granted on January 2, 1995. Legal fees and other costs associated with registration of the patent totaled $16,400. Management estimates that the useful life of the patent will be eight years.

[3] Wallock purchased a trademark from Sampson Company for $40,000 on July 1, 1992. Expenditures of $10,000 to successfully defend the trademark were paid on July 1, 1995. Management estimates that the useful life of the trademark will be 20 years from the date of acquisition.

INSTRUCTIONS

[a] Prepare a schedule showing the "intangibles" section of Wallock's balance sheet at December 31, 1995. Show supporting computations in good form.

[b] Prepare a schedule showing all expenses resulting from the transactions that would appear on Wallock's income statement for the year ended December 31, 1995. Show supporting computations in good form.

(AICPA adapted)

13–51 Miscellaneous Intangible Assets Farmer, Inc., was organized and began operations in 1996. Selected transactions for the first year of operation are listed below:

Jan. 5   Paid $7,500 to the attorneys who prepared the corporate bylaws, obtained the corporate charter, and generally advised the company on several legal matters.

Jan. 10 Issued 1,000 shares of the company's common stock to promoters of the corporation. In another recent transaction, stock sold at $12 per share. The par value of the stock is $10.

Feb. 5   Paid $10,000 to develop and acquire the exclusive right to use the company's trademark.

Mar. 21   Paid $8,500 to an advertising firm to promote the company and its products, emphasizing the trademark recently developed. A second installment is to be paid in six months.

Apr. 1   Obtained a license from the city for $12,000 to operate a shop in the local airport. The license covers a five-year period, at the end of which the company must pay $12,000 to renew it for five years. In addition, the company must pay 5% of gross revenues to the city to cover utilities, maintenance, and other operating expenses. As an estimate of this amount for April 1 to December 31, $15,000 was paid on April 15. In subsequent years, this payment will be made at the end of the calendar year.

July 25 Hired a marketing research firm to help survey potential customers and assess ways to capitalize more on consumer demand. An initial payment of $3,850 was made to the firm.

Sept. 30 Made to the advertising firm a second payment of $8,500 for promotional services rendered. The advertising is expected to enhance the value of the trademark and to generally benefit the company for several years.

Oct. 5   Acquired another company, Smitty Enterprises. In the transaction, $265,000 cash was paid to acquire assets valued as follows: inventory, $97,500; property, plant, and equipment, $180,000; franchise rights, $42,500. Noncurrent liabilities assumed totaled $96,000. Management has estimated goodwill of $80,000, based on the present value of excess future earnings over a 10-year period. The franchise has a 5-year remaining life.

Nov. 7   Paid $2,500 in legal fees to successfully defend the trademark against a competitor who had begun using a logo that differed only in color to market similar products.

INSTRUCTIONS

[a] Prepare general journal entries to record these transactions.

[b] Prepare any adjusting entries necessary for intangible assets on December 31, 1996, in anticipation of the preparation of financial statements. Consider the following information:

  [1] Revenues for 1996 were $376,000.

  [2] Intangible assets are to be amortized by the straight-line method, computed to the nearest full month. Intangibles are to be amortized over the contractual period, if any. Other intangibles, including goodwill, are to be amortized over a 10-year period.

  [3] Amortization is rounded to the nearest dollar.

[c] Indicate items and amounts relative to intangible assets that will be presented in the company's balance sheet and income statement on December 31, 1996.

13–52 Research and Development Loszynski Corporation was founded in 1983 and experienced only moderate growth during its first 10 years. However, Loszynski was able to attract several scientists and researchers with technical experience and ability and became a pioneer in the field of robotics.

Loszynski experienced a 30% annual growth in revenue for the years 1993–1995 due to the increased demand for its products and consulting services. Assured of sufficient financing, the company planned several expenditures in 1995 that would enable it to meet increased demand and continue its excellent growth rate through the rest of the decade.

Ron Griffin of Loszynski's General Accounting Department is experiencing difficulty understanding several transactions made during the first quarter of 1996, some of which include expenditures that were planned in 1995. Griffin has asked the controller for assistance in determining how to record the following six transactions and how they will affect the Loszynski's financial statements in both current and future periods. All amounts are considered material.

[1] Loszynski paid $260,000 for land on which to build a new research facility. The cost to raze and remove an old building on the site of the newly proposed research facility was $50,000. Lumber, copper tubing, and a few remaining usable fixtures from the old building were salvaged and sold for $10,000. Loszynski paid $4,000 to the architect who designed the new building, $30,000 for excavation of the basement, and $420,000 to a contractor for construction of the building. Due to the foundation, construction, and materials used, the new building is expected to last for at least 60 years. Loszynski's research director believes, however, that the building will not be appropriate for the needs of the company after 20 years.

[2] Loszynski gave a one-year noninterest-bearing note for $165,000 to Roberts Industries in exchange for a conveyor and a temperature-monitoring system (TMS) to be installed in the new research facility. The imputed interest rate on the note is 10% per year. At the date of the exchange, the remaining life of both items on Roberts' books was 7 years. The conveyor had an estimated value of $60,000 at the date of the exchange, is expected to last 30 years, and will be needed as long as the company uses the new research facility. The TMS had an estimated value of $100,000 at the date of the exchange and is expected to last five years.

[3] Loszynski incurred the following costs in securing a trademark:

Design costs	$2,000
Registration fees	300
Attorney's fees	950

Loszynski's attorney informed the company that the trademark registration system provides for an initial registration term of 20 years and an indefinite number of renewals for periods of 20 years each. Loszynski's marketing manager believes the trademark will be of value to the company for 50 years.

[4] Loszynski incurred $9,000 of legal fees in defending the rights to a patent. The patent was purchased in the first quarter of 1994 at a cost of $15,000 and is being amortized over a period of 12 years.

[5] Loszynski made improvements to a building it has occupied since the first quarter of 1992 under the terms of a 20-year lease. Carpeting installed at a cost of $4,500 is expected to last 10 years and shelving installed at a cost of $3,650 is expected to last 30 years.

[6] Loszynski spent $48,000 searching for practical applications of new research findings that are believed to be of use to the company for the next 20 years.

INSTRUCTIONS

As controller for Loszynski Corporation, review the six transactions brought to your attention by Ron Griffin. For each of the six transactions

[a] Identify whether the item is to be expensed in 1996 or capitalized.

[b] Identify the amount to be capitalized or expensed (other than depreciation or amortization).

[c] Identify the number of years to be used to write off the items that are capitalized.

[d] Justify your answers by reference to underlying accounting theory or to authoritative accounting pronouncements. You need not cite accounting pronouncements by name, number, or promulgating body.

Income tax implications and calculation of annual depreciation or amortization charges for capitalized items are to be ignored. Use the following format to present your answer.

Item Number	Amount to Be Expensed (if any)	Capitalized Items (if any)		Justification of Treatment and/or Life
		Amount	Life	

(CMA adapted)

13–53 Patents Wimple, Inc., develops, manufactures, and sells burglar alarm systems, ranging from relatively simple units for private residences to sophisticated units for large office buildings. The company's operations depend largely on an ongoing research and development program, resulting in the internal development of patents. Also, the company occasionally acquires patents from other companies.

As the accountant for Wimple, Inc., you are responsible for the proper accounting of many transactions relative to research and operating activities. The following activities have taken place over several years:

1992

Continuous	Research to develop improved alarm systems	$179,000
May 31	Acquisition of Patent A, with a 12-year remaining legal life, from a competitor	72,000

1993

Feb. 28	Costs of models of new alarm system	32,250
Oct. 31	Legal fees for acquisition of Patent B on new alarm system	38,000

1994

Continuous	Development to advance new alarm system to commercial production	38,000
June 30	Initiation of advertising campaign to promote new alarm system, enhancing the value of Patents A and B	42,000
Oct. 25	Legal expenses for the successful defense of Patent B	18,000

1995

Mar. 19	Legal expenses for the unsuccessful defense of Patent A	8,500
May 24	Acquisition of Patent C, with a six-year remaining legal life, from a competitor in anticipation that it will replace Patent A	43,500

1996

Continuous	Research on improved alarm system to replace Patent B	82,650

In 1996 management determined that the remaining life of Patent B was only four years, including the current year. Research was begun in that year to prepare for the replacement of Patent B with a new patent, presumably Patent D, at some future date.

INSTRUCTIONS

Prepare the Patent account for 1992 through December 1996, the end of Wimple's current reporting year, following these guidelines:

[a] Amortization is by the straight-line method, with no assumed residual value.

[b] Amortization is based on the shorter of the legal life or 10 years, unless indicated otherwise, computed to the nearest half year from acquisition or to disposal.

[c] The book value presented in the balance sheet on December 31 of each year should be indicated.

13–54 Miscellaneous Intangible Assets   Memphis Diversified Enterprises has been in business for several years. A trial balance prepared by the company's staff accountant for December 31, 1996, is presented on the following page.

Before 1996, Memphis Diversified Enterprises prepared financial statements for internal use only. The company has not been audited because the ownership is held completely by one family. As of 1996, however, in anticipation of seeking bank loans and a possible public offering of common stock, the company needs audited financial statements prepared in conformity with generally accepted accounting principles.

As a member of the team of independent auditors responsible for Memphis Diversified Enterprises, you have been assigned the intangible assets. You have observed that four intangible asset accounts—patents, franchise agreement, organization costs, and goodwill—appear on the unadjusted trial balance. Additional investigation reveals the following:

Patents. All patents were purchased from another company when Memphis Diversified Enterprises began operations on January 2, 1989. These patents are being amortized over an expected useful life of 14 years. Improvements made to equipment covered by the patents costing $75,000 were debited to the account in January 1993. Amortization in 1993–1995 included amortization on the $75,000 for the remaining life of the relevant patent. It is determined that the $75,000 should have been expensed in 1993. It is further determined on December 31, 1996, that one of the patents has a remaining life of only 2 years. This patent was originally assigned a cost of $210,000.

Franchise Agreement. A franchise agreement was signed on January 1, 1996. A $50,000 fee was paid, covering a five-year period, at the end of which the company may renew the agreement by paying $50,000. A decision on renewal has not been made as of December 31, 1996. The agreement calls for an annual payment of 5% of revenue. An entry debiting the account for $45,000 was made at the time of the cash payment for 1996.

Memphis Diversified Enterprises
Unadjusted Trial Balance
December 31, 1996
(In thousands of dollars)

	Dr.	Cr.
Cash	$ 20	
Accounts receivable	50	
Inventory	120	
Equipment	800	
Accumulated depreciation—equipment		$ 250
Buildings	1,200	
Accumulated depreciation—buildings		400
Patents	550	
Franchise agreement	95	
Organization costs	102	
Goodwill	345	
Accounts payable		12
Accrued wages payable		5
Accrued taxes payable		60
Bonds payable		500
Premium on bonds payable		35
Preferred stock ($100 par value)		100
Common stock ($25 par value)		1,100
Paid-in capital in excess of par value		220
Retained earnings (as of January 1)		400
Sales revenue		900
Cost of goods sold	400	
Selling and administrative expenses	300	
	$3,982	$3,982

Organization Costs. Organization costs include the unamortized portion of amounts paid to promoters for services rendered at the inception of the corporation. These fees have been amortized, since inception, over an estimated 40-year life. The decision is made, as of December 31, 1996, to reduce the total period of amortization of organization costs to 12 years.

Goodwill. The Goodwill account includes three items:

$ 45,000 —Legal expenses relative to incorporation. These were assigned to the account in January 1989.

200,000 —Excess of cost over assigned net asset values of an enterprise acquired in early 1994, expected to be of value for an indefinite period.

100,000 —Amount paid to an advertising consulting firm in early 1995 for a major advertising effort expected to be beneficial for an indefinite period.

No amortization has been taken on any amount in the Goodwill account.

INSTRUCTIONS

[a] Prepare an analysis of each intangible asset, indicating (1) the changes needed to restate each intangible account on a corrected basis for determining the amount of amortization for 1996 and (2) the proper amount of amortization for 1996.

[b] Prepare two compound journal entries (1) to correct the intangible asset account balances before the recording of 1996 amortization and (2) to record 1996 amortization for all intangible assets.

13–55 Intangible Costs Honeyall, Inc., is a large publicly held corporation. The company made the following six selected expenditures during the current fiscal year ended April 30, 1995. The proper accounting treatment of these transactions must be determined so that Honeyall's annual financial statements may be prepared in accordance with generally accepted accounting principles.

CASES

[1] Honeyall spent $2 million on a program designed to improve relations with its dealers. This project was favorably received by the dealers, and Honeyall's management believes that the company should receive significant future benefits from this program. The program was conducted during the fourth quarter of the current fiscal year.

[2] A pilot plant was constructed during 1994–1995 at a cost of $4 million to test a new production process. The plant will be operated for approximately five years. At that time, the company will determine the economic value of the process. The pilot plant is too small for commercial production, so it will be dismantled when the test is over.

[3] A new product will be introduced next year. The company has spent $3 million during the current year to design tools, jigs, molds, and dies for this product.

[4] Honeyall purchased Merit Company for $5 million in cash in early August 1994. The fair market value of Merit's identifiable assets was $4 million.

[5] A large advertising campaign was conducted during April 1995 to introduce a new product to be released during the first quarter of the 1995–1996 fiscal year. The advertising campaign cost $2.5 million.

[6] During the first six months of the 1994–1995 fiscal year, $500,000 was expended for legal work in connection with a successful patent application. The patent became effective November 1, 1994. The legal life of the patent is 17 years; its economic life is expected to be approximately 10 years.

INSTRUCTIONS

For each of the six transactions described above, determine the amount that should be included on Honeyall's April 30, 1995, balance sheet and in Honeyall's income statement for the year ended April 30, 1995.

(CMA adapted)

13–56 Research and Development   Burke Company is in the process of developing a revolutionary new product. A division of the company was formed to develop, manufacture, and market this product. As of year-end (December 31, 1996), the new product has not been manufactured for resale; however, a prototype unit is in operation.

Throughout 1996 the new division incurred certain costs, including design and engineering studies, prototype manufacturing costs, administrative expenses (including salaries of administrative personnel), and market research costs. In addition, approximately $800,000 in equipment (estimated useful life, 10 years) was purchased for use in developing and manufacturing the new product. Approximately $300,000 of this equipment was built specifically for the design development of the new product. The remaining $500,000 of equipment was used to manufacture the preproduction prototype and will be used to manufacture the new product once it is in commercial production.

INSTRUCTIONS

[a] Define *research* and *development* as defined in *Statement of Financial Accounting Standards No. 2.*

[b] Briefly indicate the practical and conceptual reasons for the conclusion reached by the FASB on accounting and reporting practices for research and development costs.

[c] In accordance with *Statement of Financial Accounting Standards No. 2,* indicate how the various costs described above should be recorded on the financial statements for the year ended December 31, 1996?

(AICPA adapted)

13–57 Development-Stage Enterprise   The president of New Company, Thomas P. New, has engaged you to assist in preparing financial statements to be used in conjunction with a proposed bank loan. Officials of the bank have requested financial statements "based on good accounting."

Mr. New has prepared the following balance sheet, which he considers adequate for purposes of the proposed bank loan. He also offers the information that accompanies the balance sheet as an explanation of some of the activities of the enterprise to date.

New Company
Balance Sheet
October 31, 1996

Assets

Cash	$ 17,650
Machinery (at cost)	59,350
Land (at cost)	15,000
Intangibles	41,400
	$133,400

Liabilities

Accrued expenses	$ 11,975
Notes payable (90-day)	21,425
	33,400

Stockholders' Equity

Common stock	100,000
	$133,400

Notes:

[1] Intangible assets consist of the following:

Research and development	$15,400
Marketing research	3,400
Personnel recruitment and training	12,600
Legal fees relative to organization of corporation	4,750
Operating expenses incurred through October 31, 1996	5,250
	$41,400

[2] Common stock has been issued as follows:

[a] Thomas P. New, president, acquired 8,000 shares at the $10 par value.

[b] George M. New, brother of Thomas, received 2,000 shares in exchange for land that he had purchased five years earlier for $15,000.

[c] One thousand shares were issued to John X. New, a cousin of both Thomas and George, for managerial services rendered in operating the enterprise to date. John will become the general manager at some future date when he quits his current position with another company.

New Company was organized during 1996. The company has been raising capital, acquiring assets, developing personnel, and developing products that it plans to market in the future. Only insignificant amounts of revenue have been generated to date.

Thomas New asks you to verify the authenticity of his balance sheet and transfer it to the bank as soon as possible so that he may proceed with his application for the much needed bank loan.

INSTRUCTIONS

[a] Identify deficiencies in Mr. New's balance sheet, considering both his draft of the statement and the additional information that he was provided. Indicate the proper treatment of each item you have listed as a deficiency.

[b] In addition to the changes you propose in [a], what items must be included to provide the bank with financial statements that are prepared in conformity with generally accepted accounting principles?

JUDGMENT CASES

13–58 Organization Costs Big Time Co., Inc., was formed during the previous year and you, the newly appointed controller of the company, have encountered a thorny issue involving a large series of payments to the founder and chief executive officer (CEO) for his work in establishing the company and attracting investors. The CEO has directed you to treat all the amounts paid to him as "organization costs" and to amortize them over a five-year period. He stated, "Without my strenuous efforts, this company wouldn't even exist. I worked night and day to find investors and put these deals together. I developed corporate bylaws, obtained the corporate charter, and simply got the wheels rolling. When we start generating revenue next year, I want to match it with these costs in an appropriate manner. If any costs were necessary to form and organize this business, they are the amounts paid to me."

You are more than a little concerned because the amounts paid to the CEO constitute 10% of the total stockholders' equity of $6,000,000 contributed by the other investors. Indeed, this is the manner by which the amounts paid to the CEO were determined. He has consistently had checks written to him in the amount of 10% of all payments received for the issuance of capital stock. The corporate charter and bylaws do not specifically prohibit such withdrawals and, in fact, provide that the CEO and other officers shall be compensated adequately for the services rendered to the company.

INSTRUCTIONS

How should you account for these amounts? If you believe that they should not be considered organization costs and reported as assets, what treatment do you recommend? Be sure to address the theoretical as well as the practical issues inherent in the case.

13-59 Capitalization versus Expense   Fast Change, Inc., has just undergone substantial personnel changes in its executive leadership. The board of directors has replaced the chief executive officer (CEO), the vice presidents for production, marketing, and finance, and a number of other high-level positions. The executive search (headhunter) costs involved in the transition, as well as severance pay (parachutes) to those whose contracts were prematurely terminated, are each individually material to the company. The changes were made because the company's poor performance in recent years has come close to violating several of its lending covenants relating to debt-equity ratios and the rate of return on assets employed (net income divided by total assets).

The new CEO would like the company to stop perceiving itself as a "loser" and wants to avoid issuing financial statements that reveal the violations of lending covenants and the attendant negotiations with the banks that will follow. He observes that if the personnel costs involved in changing the management team were capitalized rather than charged to expense, the company's financial statements would not depict a violation of the lending covenants. He has called you, the new chief accounting officer, to his office and instructs you to research the possibility of appropriately capitalizing these costs. He tells you, "All of these costs were incurred by the company to remedy a bad management situation. The result of incurring these costs is the excellent management team that is now in place and those costs will continue to benefit the company throughout our tenure. I personally believe that these costs should be reported as an intangible asset and amortized over the next five years [the length of his contract]. As you know, however, I'm not an accountant, and I don't want to do anything wrong by issuing financial statements that contain departures from GAAP. However, I also want to put our best foot forward as we move to improve the operating performance of this business. We're all new here, and I know you want to get off on the right foot. Because of the importance of this matter to me, I know I can count on you, as a valuable member of our team, to leave no stone unturned in justifying our position in treating these costs as intangible assets."

INSTRUCTIONS

Perform the research requested by the CEO. Be sure to consider the appropriate technical and conceptual issues that underly the preparation of financial statements in accordance with GAAP. Also, consider any ethical issues that come to mind as you consider the wishes of your new boss.

13-60 Accounting for Training Costs   Universal Airlines, Inc., has just finished the internal development of a software project that is to be used in the company's flight simulators. The software was created for new destinations that have recently emerged in Eastern Europe and in the former Soviet Union. The company hired software engineers to develop the initial programs. Now the company plans to have its complement of pilots undergo extensive training on the simulator. The company believes that it stands to profit handsomely by developing its routes in the emerging areas of Europe and Asia, and that by training all of its pilots to fly to and from each major city in that area, it will be able to capitalize on those opportunities.

Universal is now considering the accounting implication of these expenditures. Specifically, it wants to know which, if any, of those costs could be capitalized as assets and which should be expensed at the time they are incurred. The company understands that specific accounting standards exist to guide accounting for the software and hardware costs. The expenditures in question, however, include the salaries of the personnel responsible for operating the simulators and the salaries of the pilots during the period of time they will be undergoing the training. The company indicates that the pilots will be required to undergo retraining on all routes that they fly and those routine training costs that are incurred to maintain their skills will continue to be charged to expense as incurred. For these one-time costs, new skills will be obtained; however, the company believes that capitalizing them makes good sense.

INSTRUCTIONS

Can the company capitalize the costs as assets in accordance with generally accepted accounting principles? Be sure to describe your rationale for whatever accounting you believe to be appropriate.

13-61 Contributions to a Partnership   Randy Rich and Tammy Talented decide to begin a partnership. The business is to be a catering service that will managed by Tammy. Over the years she has built up a substantial following among the citizens of Small Town and is frequently called on to cater parties, picnics, and various other business and social functions. Tammy needs to expand her operations out of her home and Randy is to contribute $200,000 to acquire facilities, stoves, ovens, a delivery vehicle, and serving equipment. Although Tammy will not contribute any tangible assets, she is to receive a one-half interest in the net assets of the partnership. She and Randy want to recognize the value of the customer and client lists, recipes, and cooking skills that have made her catering service so successful over the years. She and Randy propose crediting her capital account for an amount equivalent to Randy's in recognition of the intangible things of value that she brings to the partnership. Randy asserts, "I certainly would not have been willing to have put up $200,000 of my jingable cash and granted Tammy an equal equity interest in the partnership if I did not believe that she is contributing every bit as much as I am. Without her, there is no business—just a bunch of equipment that I have no idea how to use productively. Surely accounting principles are reasonable enough to recognize the value of her contributions."

INSTRUCTIONS

Do you believe that the consideration that Tammy is contributing to the partnership can be recognized in accordance with generally accepted accounting principles? Be sure to support your answer with analysis and and research into this topic.

13–62 Financial Reporting Case   Following are excerpts of information about intangible assets from the 1993 annual reports of two U.S. corporations. ConAgra is a diversified, international food company. Information presented includes a statement of accounting policy and a balance sheet excerpt. American Brands is a global consumer products holding company. Information presented includes an accounting policy statement explaining intangibles resulting from business acquisitions. American Brand's 1993 balance sheet includes a single line as "Intangibles resulting from business acquisitions, net" at $1,472.1 million with a comparative amount for 1992 of $1,406.4 million.

FINANCIAL REPORTING CASE

ConAgra

Amortization of Intangibles   Brands and goodwill arising from the excess of cost of investment over equity in net assets at date of acquisition and trademarks are being amortized using the straight-line method, principally over a period of 40 years.

Consolidated Balance Sheets
May 30, 1993 and May 31, 1992
Dollars in millions except per share amount

	1993	1992
Brands, trademarks and goodwill, at cost less accumulated amortization of $283.2 and $202.2	2,670.3	2,723.6

American Brands

Intangibles Resulting from Business Acquisitions   Intangibles resulting from business acquisitions, comprising cost in excess of net assets of businesses acquired, and brands and trademarks, are being amortized on a straight-line basis over 40 years, except for intangibles acquired prior to 1971, which are not being amortized because they are considered to have a continuing value over an indefinite period. Amortization amounted to $95.7 million, $84.9 million and $75.9 million in 1993, 1992, and 1991, respectively. The cumulative amortization amounted to $476.1 million and $380.8 million at December 31, 1993 and 1992, respectively.

INSTRUCTIONS

[a]   For ConAgra, based on what you have learned in this chapter, evaluate the adequacy of disclosure about intangible assets. How might this disclosure be revised to improve your ability, as a user of financial statements, to understand this important aspect of the company's activities?

[b]   For American Brands, on what basis are intangible assets acquired prior to 1971 not being amortized? What is your opinion of this procedure? Evaluate American Brand's disclosure for adequacy and opportunity for improvement, as you did in part [a] for ConAgra.

Current and Contingent Liabilities

OBJECTIVES

1. To explain the conceptual characteristics of liabilities of business enterprises.
2. To define current liabilities and distinguish them from noncurrent liabilities.
3. To differentiate among determinable, estimated, and contingent liabilities.
4. To explain the many complex and often imprecise and subjective determinations necessary in accounting for loss contingencies.
5. To apply acceptable accounting measurement and disclosure practices to a variety of current liabilities.
6. To describe the various types of obligations arising from employee compensation.
7. To classify liabilities as current or long term, including short-term obligations expected to be refinanced.
8. To apply acceptable accounting measurement and disclosure practices to a variety of contingent and estimated liabilities.
9. To understand recent initiatives designed to convey to information users more about the imprecise and subjective nature of certain accounting measurements.

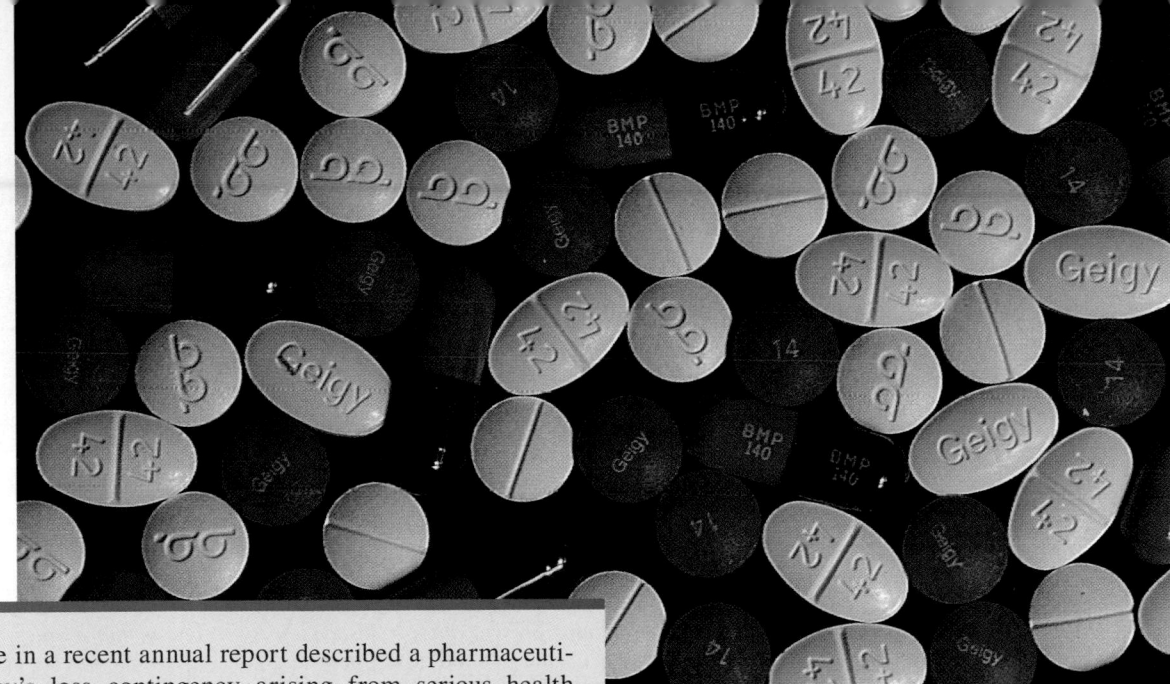

A disclosure in a recent annual report described a pharmaceutical company's loss contingency arising from serious health problems that may have resulted when customers used one of the company's products. The disclosure described "pending lawsuits...against the company...in which it is claimed by individuals infected with the human immunodeficiency virus (HIV) that their infection with HIV and, in some cases, resulting illnesses, including acquired immune deficiency syndrome–related conditions or death therefrom, may have been caused by administration of antihemophilic factor (AHF) concentrates processed" by the company. The disclosure goes on to describe a number of other lawsuits against the company, certain environmental loss contingencies, and the amount accrued in accordance with FASB accounting standards. The disclosure concludes, "Management believes that any additional liability which may ultimately be incurred with respect to these matters will not have a material adverse impact on the Company's financial position or results of operations."

Disclosures of this type illustrate the complexity of loss contingencies to which businesses are exposed and the importance of such information to investors and creditors that use the financial statements of those companies. Accounting cannot eliminate uncertainties that are an inherent part of the financial reporting process, but disclosures of the type illustrated here can allow financial statement users to intelligently include those matters in their analysis. In August 1994, *The Wall Street Journal* reported that Rhone-Poulnic Rorer, Inc., along with another company, Baxter, Inc., had reached a tentative settlement of as much as $160 million with individuals who had contracted AIDS from using blood-clotting medications of the two companies.

Rhone-Poulnic Rorer, 1992 Annual Report, note 16, p. 55 and Thomas M. Burton and G. Pascal Zachary, "Pact Reached in Hemophiliac AIDS," *The Wall Street Journal,* August 3, 1994, p. B7.

CHARACTERISTICS OF LIABILITIES

Companies often acquire goods and services and pay for them at a later date. Examples include the purchase of supplies, items of inventory, and other services and assets on account. Events and actions of organizations and individuals external to a company can also create various liabilities that eventually must be paid. Examples include obligations to taxing authorities, lawsuits that are initiated against the firm, and claims resulting from warranties and guarantees. Not all of a firm's potential obligations are necessarily reportable liabilities, however, because certain criteria must be met before an accounting liability is recognized.

As we discussed in Chapter 3, the Financial Accounting Standards Board (FASB) has defined **liabilities** as

> *probable future sacrifices of economic benefits arising from present obligations of a particular entity to transfer assets or provide services to other entities in the future as a result of past transactions or events.*[1]

To provide more guidance, the FASB established three characteristics of a liability:

1. *A liability embodies a present duty or responsibility to one or more other entities that entails settlement (of the obligation) by probable future transfer or use of assets at a specified or determinable date, on occurrence of a specified event, or on demand.*
2. *The duty or responsibility obligates a particular entity, leaving it little or no discretion to avoid the future sacrifice.*
3. *The transaction or other event obligating the entity has already happened.*[2]

Future Cash Flows

The focus of liability recognition therefore is to provide information about likely future cash outflows that the reporting entity is currently obliged to pay. Financial information users such as present and prospective creditors and investors are greatly interested in an organization's expected future cash flows. Information about present obligations that will require future cash payments is an important aspect of understanding *total* future expected cash flows. Furthermore, the amounts reported as liabilities generally require payments that the reporting entity can neither influence in amount or timing nor avoid. Such obligations differ from other expected future cash payments because they already exist and cannot be avoided easily by management decisions or actions.

Not all liabilities represent obligations that must be paid in cash. Some, such as customer order deposits and warranties, will be satisfied by providing goods or services for those to whom the obligations are owed. Nevertheless, the amounts reported on the balance sheet for all liabilities should approximate the cash that will be required to discharge whatever obligation exists.

This chapter discusses a company's obligations that represent accounting liabilities classified as **current.** We first examine current liabilities that are known to exist and whose amounts are readily determinable. Next we discuss accounting and reporting for liabilities that are contingent. **Contingent liabilities** are uncertain obligations; that is, their existence and, in many cases, their related amounts are not known precisely. Contingent liabilities include—among other things—lawsuits, claims and assessments in progress against the firm, warranties, and guarantees.

CURRENT LIABILITIES

Accounting Research Bulletin No. 43 provides the basic definition of **current liabilities:**

> *The term is used principally to designate obligations whose liquidation is reasonably expected to require the use of existing resources properly classified as current assets, or the creation of other current liabilities.*[3]

---

[1]*FASB Statement of Financial Accounting Concepts No. 6,* "Elements of Financial Statements," 1985, par. 35.
[2]*FASB Statement of Financial Accounting Concepts No. 6,* par. 36.
[3]*Accounting Research Bulletin No. 43,* "Restatement and Revision of Accounting Research Bulletins," 1953, Sec. A, Ch. 3, par. 7.

The FASB has added guidance as to how that basic definition should be applied in practice. Specifically, *SFAS No. 78* indicates that current liabilities should include obligations that are due on demand or that will become due on demand within one year (or one operating cycle, if longer) from the balance sheet date. Additionally, in some cases, debt with a long-term maturity date should also be reported as a current liability.

Debt agreements frequently contain a variety of clauses and requirements to which a debtor must adhere. Examples include covenants made at the outset of a loan by the debtor to maintain a certain level of cash, working capital, or stockholders' equity. A violation of such covenants usually provides certain additional rights to the creditor, among which is frequently an option to call the debt and demand repayment immediately. Not all loan covenants contain clear and objective criteria for determining compliance. For example, a covenant may provide that the debtor must maintain "adequate liquidity to service the debt for six months in the absence of operating profits." Determining compliance with such a provision requires much analysis, careful estimates, and seasoned judgments on the part of the company and its accountants. If it is determined that a covenant has been violated, the creditor may demand repayment in the near future. The debtor should reclassify the debt as a current liability unless the creditor has waived the violation or has lost the right to demand repayment. A creditor may lose the right to call the debt if, for example, the violation is cured *before* the right is exercised.

Additionally, long-term debt should not be reclassified as current if it is *probable* that the violation will be cured within a grace period provided by the agreement. Such determinations require particular care because they involve direct estimates of future activities and conditions. Again, considerable judgment is required on the part of accountants making such estimates. Generally, positive events or conditions that are expected to resolve a particular violation should be specifically identifiable and should demonstrate a high probability of occurence. Examples include a commitment from a willing and capable third-party buyer to purchase large amounts of goods immediately in the following period or a strong recovery of an investment portfolio subsequent to the balance sheet date that may have cured the condition of default by the time financial statements are issued. The notes to the financial statements should disclose cases in which it is believed that violations of covenants will be cured within a grace period.   **Disclosure**

The underlying theme of *SFAS No. 78* is consistent with the general provisions of *Accounting Research Bulletin No. 43.* The FASB pronouncement is simply more direct and describes specific circumstances in which debt with a noncurrent maturity is considered likely to require the use of existing working capital. In such circumstances, accountants should classify the debt as a current liability regardless of its original maturity date.[4] Therefore, current liabilities are defined in terms of claims on the company's working capital and in terms of their due dates. That is, if the satisfaction of a liability is expected to require the use of existing working capital, the obligation is considered current regardless of its maturity date.

VALUATION OF CURRENT LIABILITIES

In theory, liabilities should originally be stated at the present value of the future cash payments necessary to extinguish or satisfy the obligation. In practice, however, current liabilities are frequently recorded and presented in the financial statements at their full maturity amounts. Although this practice may result in a slight theoretical overstatement of certain current liabilities, clerical simplicity, immateriality, and conservatism support such a minor   **Materiality** overstatement of current liabilities. Generally, the time until maturity is short for current

---

[4]*FASB Statement of Financial Accounting Standards No. 78,* "Classification of Obligations That Are Callable by the Creditor," 1983.

Conservatism

liabilities and the related amount of any overstatement inherent in the face amount of the liability is trivial. Furthermore, recording current liabilities at their full amounts results in a larger charge to the goods or services acquired and thereby typically results in a more conservative measure of income. The Accounting Principles Board (APB), in its *Opinion No. 21*, requires the presentation of most liabilities at their net present value and then adds:

> *This Opinion is not intended to apply to ... receivables and payables arising from transactions with customers or suppliers in the normal course of business which are due in customary trade terms not exceeding approximately one year.*[5]

Businesses, therefore, are not required to apply present-value techniques to the valuation of most current liabilities. Current liabilities, however, may be (and, in many cases, are) presented at their net present value.

Before reading the following discussion of financial accounting and reporting for current liabilities, refer to the balance sheet of Kellogg Company on the inside front cover of your textbook. Notice that several types of current liabilities are presented, including current maturities of long-term debt, notes and accounts payable, and several accrued liabilities. These liabilities are important elements in the balance sheet, because they make up approximately 48% of total liabilities and 29% of total liabilities and equities.

SPECIFIC TYPES OF CURRENT LIABILITIES

ACCOUNTS PAYABLE

As previously indicated, there are many types of current liabilities; however, the most common is probably represented by trade accounts payable. **Accounts payable** are those liabilities that arise in acquiring goods and services in the normal course of business. Many of the accounting and reporting issues related to accounts payable have counterparts in **accounts receivable,** as discussed in Chapter 7, and we review many of them in this section.

Trade accounts payable are recognized when the acquisition of goods or services results in a liability. If Artesia Company acquires $1,000 worth of supplies on account, the following journal entry is made at the point of acquisition:

Supplies on Hand	1,000	
Accounts Payable		1,000
(To record the acquisition of supplies.)		

If the invoice amount is $1,000 and a purchase discount is allowed for early payment, other problems arise. If Artesia acquired the same supplies on terms of 2/10, n/30, the journal entry is as follows:[6]

Supplies on Hand	980	
Accounts Payable		980
(To record acquisition of supplies for invoice amount of $1,000,		
terms 2/10, n/30.)		

If the invoice is paid prior to the expiration of the 10-day discount period, Accounts Payable is charged and Cash credited for $980. If the invoice is not paid within the discount period, however, the payment of the invoice is recorded as follows:

Accounts Payable	980	
Purchase Discounts Lost	20	
Cash		1,000
(To record payment of invoice and lost discount.)		

---

[5]*APB Opinion No. 21*, "Interest on Receivables and Payables," 1971, par. 3.

[6]This entry seems theoretically preferable because $980 represents the cash-equivalent price and present value of the liability at the point of acquisition. Furthermore, the presentation of the liability at the net amount reflects management's intent to take the discount.

The Purchase Discounts Lost account is treated as an element of financing or interest expense on the income statement. Further, unpaid invoices existing at year-end should be evaluated to determine whether any discounts have been lost at that time. If, for example, it is determined at year-end that purchase discounts in the amount of $15 have already been lost on unpaid invoices, the following adjusting entry is necessary:

Purchase Discounts Lost	15	
Accounts Payable		15

As discussed in Chapter 8, "Inventories: Basic Valuation Methods," in practice we may encounter a variety of methods of accounting for purchase discounts. Generally, such amounts are immaterial and therefore the issue is relatively unimportant. The differences in these methods may accumulate to a material amount, however, and the following considerations should take precedence:

Materiality

1. The good or service acquired should be recorded at its cash-equivalent price at the point of acquisition.
2. Any difference between the cash-equivalent price at acquisition (in 1) and the payment required to settle the account should generally be treated as a financial expense.

Current Notes Payable

Current notes payable generally arise from three types of transactions:

1. **Trade notes payable** that result from the acquisition of goods or services (usually equipment or other large items).
2. **Loan notes payable** that result from cash-borrowing activities.
3. **Current maturities** of long-term notes and bonds payable that represent amounts payable from current assets. Typically, such current maturities have been previously classified as noncurrent liabilities.

Trade notes payable generally do not present significant accounting and reporting problems. The maturity date, the amount necessary to satisfy the note, and the interest rate are usually available; the major calculation required is determining the amount of interest to be accrued at the end of an accounting period.

For example, if we assume that Heyman Company reports on a calendar year and that on November 1, 1995, it acquires machinery with a value of $12,000 by issuing a $12,000 note bearing 10% interest, due in six months, the following entries are necessary:

Nov. 1, 1995	Machinery	12,000	
	Trade Notes Payable		12,000
	(To record the acquisition of machinery by issuing a six-month 10%, $12,000 note.)		
Dec. 31, 1995	Interest Expense	200	
	Interest Payable		200
	(To record accrued interest at year-end. $12,000 \times 10\% \times \frac{1}{6} = $200.)		
May 1, 1996	Trade Notes Payable	12,000	
	Interest Payable	200	
	Interest Expense	400	
	Cash		12,600
	(To record payment of note and related interest at maturity.)		

The May 1 entry assumes that no reversing entry was made at the beginning of 1996.

Interest-Bearing Notes. Notes payable that arise from cash-borrowing activities are generally of two types: **interest-bearing notes** and so-called noninterest-bearing notes. Accounting and reporting for interest-bearing notes requires the accountant to accrue interest and report a liability in the amount of the accrued interest payable plus the face value of the note. The accounting practices for such interest-bearing notes are similar to those previously described for the acquisition of equipment and, therefore, contain no additional accounting complications.

Noninterest-Bearing Notes.   Certain notes do not pay any stated rate of interest in addition to the face amount of the note. This type of liability is frequently referred to as **noninterest bearing.** The lender deducts interest on such notes, however, in advance and issues the notes at discount; that is, the borrower (the maker of the note) receives an amount that is less than the face value of the note.

To illustrate, assume that on November 1, 1995, Century Company issues a one-year note payable with a face amount of $10,000 to a bank and in return receives $8,800 in cash. This note was discounted by the bank at 12% ($10,000 × .12 = $1,200; $10,000 − $1,200 = $8,800). The effective rate of interest in the note exceeds 12%, however, as indicated below:

$$\frac{\text{Interest}}{\text{Amount Received}} = \frac{\$1,200}{\$8,800} = 13.64\% \text{ (for a one-year note)}$$

Therefore, $1,200 of interest was paid for a loan of $8,800 for a one-year period. The journal entry to record the loan, the discount representing future interest, and the amount to be repaid on November 1, 1996, is as follows:

Nov. 1, 1995	Cash	8,800	
	Discount on Notes Payable	1,200	
	Notes Payable		10,000
	(To record issuance of note and receipt of cash.)		

The Notes Payable account could have been credited with the $8,800 instead of the $10,000. In that case, no figure would be entered in the Discount on Notes Payable account. If a Discount on Notes Payable account is used, it appears on the balance sheet as a **contra account** (reduction) to the Notes Payable account. In any case, the note is reported in the balance sheet at its present value ($8,800) at the date of issuance, rather than its maturity value ($10,000).

The adjusting entry at December 31, 1995, follows:

Dec. 31, 1995	Interest Expense	200	
	Discount on Notes Payable		200
	(To record accrued interest of note payable. $1,200 × ²⁄₁₂ = $200.)		

As a result of this adjusting entry, the note is reported in the balance sheet as a $9,000 ($10,000 − $1,000) current liability at December 31, 1995. We have amortized $200 of the original discount of $1,200 and, therefore, the remaining discount is $1,000.

When the note matures and is paid during 1996, the following entry is made:

Nov. 1, 1996	Notes Payable	10,000	
	Interest Expense	1,000	
	Discount on Notes Payable		1,000
	Cash		10,000
	(To record payment of note payable and recognize interest expense.)		

This entry assumes that no reversing entry was made January 1, 1996.

Some companies amortize discount or premium during the year to facilitate preparing interim financial statements. Adjustments at the end of the year are thereby confined to the amount necessary to complete the annual amortization.

Current Maturities. **Current maturities** of long-term notes payable must frequently be reported as current liabilities to the extent they must be paid during the next year or operating cycle, whichever is longer. A sinking fund may exist to service such liabilities, and, if so, the current maturities of long-term debt should be excluded from current liabilities. Such obligations are classified as noncurrent liabilities in a manner consistent with the sinking fund. Chapter 10 discusses sinking funds in dealing with a variety of investments and funds; consequently, this chapter does not discuss these issues further. Occasionally, a company plans to refinance current debt on a noncurrent basis; such anticipated action produces some additional accounting and reporting problems, which we discuss in the following section.

Short-Term Obligations Expected to Be Refinanced

In certain circumstances, a company may wish to *refinance a short-term obligation* on a noncurrent basis. Examples include the current maturity of a previously noncurrent debt or a line of credit with a bank that a company wishes to extend. Furthermore, a short-term obligation may be refinanced on a long-term basis after the date of the balance sheet but before financial statements are issued. Because those debts may not require the use of working capital, questions arise about the proper classification at the balance sheet date.

To guide such liability classification issues, the FASB issued *Statement of Financial Accounting Standards No. 6,*[7] which calls for the following evidence when a company excludes a short-term obligation from current liabilities:

1. An indication of the *intent* to refinance the note on a noncurrent basis.
2. A demonstration of the *ability* to accomplish the long-term refinancing.

Management usually evidences its **intent** to refinance a short-term obligation with express representation or action. The **ability** to refinance a short-term obligation on a long-term basis, however, is frequently more difficult to establish. *SFAS No. 6* provides two ways for a company to demonstrate its ability to refinance a short-term obligation:

1. Subsequent to the balance sheet date but prior to the issuance of the balance sheet, the firm must issue long-term debt or equity securities to refinance the obligation; *or*
2. Prior to the issuance of the balance sheet, the firm must secure a noncancelable, long-term (the longer of one year or one operating cycle from the balance sheet date) financing agreement that clearly allows the firm to refinance the short-term liability on a long-term basis.

Obviously, if a company actually accomplishes such a refinancing transaction, it meets both the ability and the intent criteria. However, if the debt is still outstanding when the financial statements are issued, the accountant should obtain a formal declaration of intent from management and carefully read the details of the refinancing agreement. The accountant must also exercise great care in analyzing the terms of refinancing agreements to ensure proper interpretation and application.

If refinancing is accomplished, accountants use information that became available after the balance sheet date to alter accounting measurements and classification on the financial statements of the period already ended. This use of hindsight is appropriate because the newly acquired information relates to a condition that existed at the balance sheet date rather than to a new condition.

If both the intent and ability criteria are met, the accountant *must* exclude the short-term obligation from current liabilities. In this fashion, the *timing* of future cash flows is better reflected in the balance sheet classifications of liabilities. The amount of short-term debt to be excluded from current liabilities should not exceed

---

[7]*FASB Statement of Financial Accounting Standards No. 6,* "Classification of Short-Term Obligations Expected to Be Refinanced," 1975.

1. The amount available for refinancing under the agreement; *or*
2. A reasonable estimate of the minimum amount expected to be available, if the amount available for refinancing will fluctuate.

The accountant must adjust the amount to be excluded from current liabilities to reflect any financing agreement limitations or restrictions that indicate that a portion of the amount in the agreement may not be available. For example, a limitation dealing with working capital may provide that "the amounts to be refinanced will not exceed 50% of the company's working capital at the time of refinancing."

Short-term liabilities arising from transactions in the ordinary course of business and due in customary terms are not subject to these reclassification tests. Such short-term liabilities should be routinely classified as current. Examples of those liabilities include accounts payable incurred in the acquisition of inventory and supplies, collections received in advance of rendering services or providing goods, and other debts resulting from normal operating transactions.

Another question arises when a short-term obligation is repaid after the balance sheet date and the cash used to pay the debt is subsequently replenished through long-term borrowing. In its *Interpretation No. 8,*[8] the FASB observed that repayment of a short-term obligation before funds are obtained through long-term borrowing requires the use of current assets. Therefore, a short-term obligation repaid after the balance sheet date should be classified as current. This is true even if long-term debt or equity securities are subsequently issued and the proceeds are used to replenish current assets, because working capital was employed temporarily to retire the short-term debt, making the debt a current liability.

Disclosure   **Disclosure of Short-Term Obligations Classified as Long-Term Liabilities.**   *SFAS No. 6* requires total current liabilities to be presented in a classified balance sheet, regardless of whether a short-term obligation has been excluded. If a short-term obligation is classified as a noncurrent liability, the amount of and reasons for the classification should also be disclosed in the notes to the financial statements. Other required disclosures include a general description of any financing agreements, the terms of any new obligations incurred or expected to be incurred, and the terms of any equity securities issued or expected to be issued. Those disclosure requirements are illustrated in Exhibit 14–1 for the hypothetical Calico, Inc., and Darnell, Inc.

Dividends Payable

The topic of dividends is treated more fully in Chapter 17, "Stockholders' Equity: Operations, Earnings, Dividends, and Other Issues." Because many types of dividends result in current liabilities, however, the matter is discussed briefly at this time. When a company's board of directors declares a cash or property dividend, the amount to be paid to stockholders becomes a liability of the company. Once declared, dividends are usually paid within a few months. Therefore, dividends payable are usually classified as current liabilities. For example, if on December 26, 1995, Arnold Company declares a $1.50 per share dividend to be paid on January 31, 1996, to shareholders of record as of January 5, 1996, and if 10,000 shares of common stock are outstanding, the accountant makes the following entries:

Dec. 26, 1995	Dividends (or Retained Earnings)	15,000	
	Dividends Payable		15,000
	(To record declaration of cash dividend.)		
Jan. 31, 1996	Dividends Payable	15,000	
	Cash		15,000
	(To record payment of dividend.)		

---

[8]*FASB Interpretation No. 8,* "Classification of a Short-Term Obligation Repaid Prior to Being Replaced by a Long-Term Security: An Interpretation of FASB Statement No. 6," 1976.

EXHIBIT 14–1

Illustrations of Debt Refinancing

Illustration No. 1: Actual Refinancing
Excerpt from Balance Sheet of Calico, Inc.

	Dec. 31, 1995
Current Liabilities	
Accounts payable	$ 2,000,000
Accrued expenses	3,000,000
Income taxes payable	1,000,000
Current maturities of long-term debt	1,000,000
Total current liabilities	$ 7,000,000
Long-Term Debt	
Notes payable refinanced in January 1996 [Note 8]	$ 4,000,000
Other long-term debt	10,000,000
	$14,000,000

NOTE 8: On January 20, 1996, the Company issued 100,000 shares of common stock and received proceeds totaling $4,500,000 of which $4,000,000 was used to liquidate notes payable that matured on January 31, 1996. Accordingly, such notes payable have been excluded from current liabilities at December 31, 1995.

Illustration No. 2: Financing Agreement
Excerpt from Balance Sheet of Darnell, Inc.

	Dec. 31, 1995
Current Liabilities	
Accounts payable	$1,000,000
Accrued expenses	1,500,000
Income taxes payable	500,000
Total current liabilities	$3,000,000
Long-Term Debt	
8% Notes payable [Note 9]	$2,000,000

NOTE 9: The Company has entered into a financing agreement with a bank to borrow up to $3,000,000 at any time through 1997. Amounts borrowed under the agreement mature three years from the date of the loan and bear interest at 1% above the bank's prime interest rate. The agreement requires the Company to maintain working capital of at least $8,000,000 and prohibits the payment of dividends and reacquisition of the Company's common stock without prior approval of the bank. Because the Company intends to borrow $2,000,000 under the agreement to pay its 8% notes payable that mature on April 1, 1996, the notes have been classified as long-term debt.

The accountant does not record a liability for dividends until the company's board of directors declares them, because no liability exists for undeclared dividends, regardless of how profitable the company has been.

Advances from Customers

Companies may require customers to make deposits that are either refundable or applicable to future purchases. Such payments are usually designed to provide security for the company receiving the deposit. For example, a business may require a customer to make a substantial payment before the business will accept and manufacture an order designed specifically for that customer.

Revenue Realization   In transactions such as these, we do not recognize revenue at the time we receive cash, because it has not been earned. The recipient company must perform some service or provide some good to earn the revenue. Therefore, the amount of the deposit should be treated as a liability until the obligation to produce the good or service has been discharged. Such liabilities do not require cash repayment but will be satisfied by providing goods or services. To illustrate, assume that Thin Spread Company, a mill manufacturer of cloth, receives a $500,000 order to manufacture a type of cloth with an unusual design. Prior to beginning the mill run, Thin Spread requests and receives a deposit of $50,000 (10% of total order price) from the customer. The entry to record the receipt of the deposit appears as follows:

Cash	50,000	
Advances from Customers		50,000
(To record receipt of deposit.)		

Advances from customers is a liability to deliver goods or services in the future. When the mill run is complete and shipped, the following entry is necessary:

Accounts Receivable	450,000	
Advances from Customers	50,000	
Sales Revenue		500,000
(To record sale of cloth and recognition of revenue.)		

A company may receive advance payments in a variety of other circumstances as well. Examples include magazine subscriptions, construction deposits, gift certificates, airline and other travel tickets, and promotions such as ticket book sales by restaurants or theaters. Such deposits will not be refunded in the normal course of business but will be applied to the total sales price of the goods or services. Those advances should be accounted for as liabilities until the good or service is provided and the revenue earned. This is another situation in which estimates of expected future events and conditions are required before a company can prepare *historic* financial statements. In some situations, such as the advance sale of subway tokens or restaurant and theater gift certificates, the expected future utilization rates must be estimated to properly account for the revenue to be realized from the transaction. Expiration dates, if they exist, may be helpful in assessing the completion of the earnings process.

Returnable containers and refundable deposits should also be recorded as liabilities. Many states have recently enacted returnable container laws to encourage environmental cleanliness. For example, manufacturers may be required to offer a price for returned cans or bottles that exceeds their worth. In such cases, the company that is obligated to return the reward should accrue a liability for the estimated amount of the returns at the time that product sales are made. Management and the accountant must estimate future events and conditions to prepare historic financial statements. Experience in prior periods may help to assess the likely amount of returns in the future, but because many of these programs are relatively new and changes in existing ones occur rather frequently, the accountant may be faced with unusual uncertainties relating to potentially large amounts. In such cases, disclosure of the uncertain conditions is of particular importance to help financial statement users make informed decisions.

Matching   Companies also receive refundable deposits in a number of situations. For example, warehouse and space rental agreements often require the renter to make security, repair, and cleaning deposits. At the time such amounts are paid, the party receiving the deposit records a liability. The liability is reduced when the deposit is refunded. If deposits are forfeited, however, the liability should be removed and the amount recognized as revenue. If the deposit was securing an asset of the company, such as a rental security deposit on equipment that is not returned, the asset should be written off, matched with the revenue from the forfeited deposit, and a gain or loss recognized.

Tax Liabilities Other Than Income Taxes

Sales Taxes.   In many governmental jurisdictions, sales tax laws require merchants to collect and remit sales taxes to a government authority. The tax is usually added to the invoice or sales receipt, and merchants collect the sales tax along with the sales price of the good. To illustrate, if Huntington Company sells $1,000 of merchandise that is subject to a 5% sales tax, the following entry is necessary:

Cash	1,050	
Sales Revenue		1,000
Sales Tax Payable ($1,000 × 5%)		50
(To record the sale of merchandise.)		

When the sales taxes that have been collected are remitted to the taxing authority, the following entry is made:

Sales Tax Payable	50	
Cash		50
(To record remittance of sales taxes collected.)		

Note that sales taxes are expenses of the customer rather than of the business collecting them. When a company collects sales taxes, it incurs a liability to the extent of the sales taxes collected. Similarly, when it pays the sales taxes, the liability is merely removed. Neither revenue nor expense should be reported in the financial statements of the tax-collecting enterprise.

In practice, however, some businesses merely record sales taxes collected as additions to revenue and the remittance of the collected taxes as reductions in revenue. In such cases, if financial statements are prepared after sales are made but before the sales taxes are remitted, an adjusting entry is necessary to report the liability to the taxing authority and the related reduction of revenue. This simple clerical procedure facilitates recording cash sales. In the previous example, the entries appear as follows:

Cash	1,050	
Revenue		1,050
(To record sale and related sales tax.)		

Because liability accounts are not credited, the amount of the sales tax liability is unclear. Therefore, the following calculation is required:

$$X = \text{Taxable sales (cash price of goods alone)}$$

$$X + .05X = \$1,050$$

$$1.05X - \$1,050$$

$$X = \frac{\$1,050}{1.05}$$

$$X = \$1,000 \text{ (cash price of goods alone)}$$

The sales tax payable may then be determined by multiplying the tax rate (5%) times the net sales amount ($1,000). An overpayment of the sales tax occurs if one merely multiplies the tax rate times the unadjusted balance in the sales account ($1,050 × .05 = $52.50). The adjusting entry to reduce revenue and record the liability for sales taxes collected is a charge to revenue and a credit to sales tax payable.

Another problem in accounting for sales taxes arises if the taxing jurisdiction allows collecting merchants a fee to cover the cost of collecting and remitting the tax. Continuing with the previous example, if the taxing authority allows merchants a 2% fee for collecting sales taxes, we find that the $1 fee (.02 × $50) should be recorded as additional revenue at the time the taxes are remitted by charging Sales Tax Payable for the full $50, crediting Cash for $49, and crediting a revenue account for $1.

This illustration may appear to indicate that sales tax is recorded on each individual sale. In practice, many sales might be combined and sales tax recorded for the group of sales. For example, sales tax might be recorded at one time for all sales occurring during a day or week. Some customers—for example, churches or governments—may be exempt from sales taxes. In these cases, the company does not collect taxes on sales made to such customers and must take care to ensure that sales taxes are not inadvertently collected or paid to taxing authorities. Separate records of sales made to tax-exempt organizations should be kept to avoid this type of error.

Property Taxes.   Property taxes are usually based on the *assessed value* of various real and personal properties and represent a substantial source of revenue for state and local governments. Such taxes generally become a liability of the paying company at the time they become obligations to the government. This date is usually called the *lien date*. Two accounting questions arise in regard to property taxes:

1. When should the liability be recognized?
2. When should the expense be recognized?

In essence, the liability comes into existence at the lien date, whereas the expense is generally considered to be incurred throughout the period covered by the lien. Property taxes represent expenses associated with the right to use the property subject to the taxes during the tax year of the government. Two commonly encountered accounting methods are illustrated in the example that follows.

Assume that Braunegg Corporation, which uses a calendar year for financial reporting, owns some real estate that is subject to city property taxes of $24,000 per year. The taxes are levied on October 1, 1995, for the forthcoming tax year of the city government and are payable on February 1, 1996. The two methods of accounting for property taxes are illustrated in Exhibit 14–2.

Matching   Under each method, the income statement reports the same expense. That is, property taxes are charged to expense during the periods benefited. Because the FASB has stated that the primary purpose of financial reporting is to provide information about an enterprise's earnings, either method seems consistent with the overall goals of financial accounting.[9] The differences between the two methods are confined solely to the balance sheet. The differences, advantages, and disadvantages of each method are summarized below:

	Immediate Liability-Recognition Method	Accruing Liability-Recognition Method
Difference	Liability and deferred charge are recognized in total at lien date.	Liability is accrued at same amount and time as expense is recognized.
Advantage	Liability is recognized in full as legal obligation of company at time it is incurred.	Assets are not overstated as a result of recognizing a deferred charge for unpaid property taxes.
Disadvantage	An "asset" is recognized for unpaid property taxes.	Legal liability of company not recognized at time it is incurred.

The American Institute of Certified Public Accountants (AICPA) has taken the position that the accruing liability-recognition method is preferable,[10] and the authors concur with this position. A liability exists at the time the taxes are levied; however, if the property is

---

[9]*FASB Statement of Financial Accounting Concepts No. 1,* "Objectives of Financial Reporting by Business Enterprises," 1978, par. 43.

[10]*Accounting Research Bulletin No. 43,* "Restatement and Revision of Accounting Research Bulletins," 1953, Sec. A, Ch. 10, par. 14.

EXHIBIT 14–2

Property Tax Accounting Methods Compared

Explanation	Immediate Liability-Recognition Method		Accruing Liability-Recognition Method	
Oct. 1, 1995 City levies property tax for coming fiscal year, 10/1/95 to 9/30/96.	Deferred Property Taxes 24,000 Property Taxes Payable	24,000	No entry	
Dec. 31, 1995 Company records adjusted by accruing property-tax expenses for financial reporting purposes.	Property Tax Expense 6,000 Deferred Property Taxes	6,000	Property Tax Expense 6,000 Property Tax Payable	6,000
Feb. 1, 1996 Payment of property tax recorded.	Property Taxes Payable 24,000 Cash	24,000	Property Tax Payable 6,000 Deferred Property Taxes 18,000 Cash	24,000
Dec. 31, 1996 Remaining 1995–1996 levied taxes are charged to expense.	Property Tax Expense 18,000 Deferred Property Taxes	18,000	Property Tax Expense 18,000 Deferred Property Taxes	18,000

sold, the buyer is generally required to pay the seller for property taxes related to the remaining portion of the year. From an economic perspective, the liability is thus prospective and not final at the lien date. Furthermore, the accruing liability-recognition method avoids the problem of overstated assets, because it does not recognize an asset for unpaid property taxes.

Liabilities Related to Payroll Taxes. Another type of tax liability frequently encountered in practice relates to a company's payroll. Employers are required by law to withhold certain amounts from the salaries and wages of employees and to remit these amounts to the appropriate taxing authorities. Furthermore, the law places additional payroll taxes directly on employers. Accountants must be well acquainted with the various types of **payroll taxes** and **payroll withholdings.** Amounts typically withheld from employees' pay include federal, state, and city income taxes, and the employees' share of Social Security taxes. Amounts withheld to be paid directly to various government agencies are recorded as part of the employer's salary expense and as liabilities to the appropriate government agency rather than as payable to the particular employee. These amounts are subsequently paid to the appropriate government agency on behalf of the employer. Payroll-related taxes charged to the employer generally include federal and state unemployment taxes and the employer's share of Social Security taxes. Taxes levied directly on the employer that are not withheld from the pay of employees are reported as additional payroll tax expenses and as related liabilities to the appropriate government agencies. As such, the latter taxes represent payroll expenses to the employer in addition to the basic salary of the employee. A variety of payroll-related taxes and the associated financial accounting and reporting issues are discussed in more detail in Appendix A of this chapter.

Bonus and Profit-Sharing Plans

Companies often compensate key employees for superior profits made by the enterprise or for those profits attributed to the segment of the enterprise managed by the particular employee. Although there are many variations of such plans, the central theme is to motivate employees by directly relating their well-being to the company's success. These types of compensation plans result in liabilities and expenses that must be measured and reported in the financial statements. To illustrate three commonly employed formulas for computing bonuses, we assume that Claudia Company reports a net income of $100,000 before deducting income taxes and bonuses. Any bonus accrued at the end of the year is deductible for income tax purposes in the year accrued, and the company's income tax rate is 40%.

Example 1.   The bonus to be paid is expressed as 5% of net income over $60,000. The computation is made before bonus and income tax expenses are deducted. Therefore, the following computations and entries are necessary to determine and record the bonus and income taxes:
   Bonus:

$$\text{Bonus} = .05(\$100,000 - \$60,000)$$
$$\text{Bonus} = .05(\$40,000)$$
$$\text{Bonus} = \$2,000$$

   Income taxes:

$$\text{Taxes} = .40(\$100,000 - \text{Bonus})$$
$$\text{Taxes} = .40(\$100,000 - \$2,000)$$
$$\text{Taxes} = .40(\$98,000)$$
$$\text{Taxes} = \$39,200$$

Example 2.   Assume now that the bonus is to be 5% of net income in excess of $60,000 *after* deducting the bonus but *before* considering income taxes.
   Bonus:

$$\text{Bonus} = .05(\$100,000 - \$60,000 - \text{Bonus})$$
$$\text{Bonus} = .05(\$40,000 - \text{Bonus})$$
$$\text{Bonus} = \$2,000 - .05\,\text{Bonus}$$
$$1.05\,\text{Bonus} = \$2,000$$
$$\text{Bonus} = \$2,000/1.05$$
$$\text{Bonus} = \$1,905$$

   Income taxes:

$$\text{Taxes} = .40(\$100,000 - \text{Bonus})$$
$$\text{Taxes} = .40(\$100,000 - \$1,905)$$
$$\text{Taxes} = .40(\$98,095)$$
$$\text{Taxes} = \$39,238$$

Example 3.   Assume now that the bonus is to be 5% of net income after deducting *both* bonus and taxes. In this case, the bonus depends on taxes, and the amount of taxes depends on the bonus. Two equations, each containing two unknowns (bonus and income taxes), are required to determine the individual amounts of bonus and income taxes:

$$\text{Bonus} = .05(\$100,000 - \text{Bonus} - \text{Income Taxes}) \qquad (14\text{--}1)$$
$$\text{Taxes} = .40(\$100,000 - \text{Bonus}) \qquad (14\text{--}2)$$

Substitute Equation (14–2) in Equation (14–1):

$$\text{Bonus} = .05[\$100,000 - \text{Bonus} - .40(\$100,000 - \text{Bonus})]$$
$$\text{Bonus} = .05(\$100,000 - \text{Bonus} - \$40,000 + .40\,\text{Bonus})$$
$$\text{Bonus} = \$5,000 - .05\,\text{Bonus} - \$2,000 + .02\,\text{Bonus}$$
$$1.03\,\text{Bonus} = \$3,000$$
$$\text{Bonus} = \frac{\$3,000}{1.03}$$
$$\text{Bonus} = \$2,913$$
$$\text{Taxes} = .40(\$100,000 - \text{Bonus})$$
$$\text{Taxes} = .40(\$100,000 - \$2,913)$$
$$\text{Taxes} = .40(\$97,087)$$
$$\text{Taxes} = \$38,835$$

Proof:

$$\text{Bonus} = .05(\$100,000 - \text{Bonus} - \text{Taxes})$$
$$\$2,913 = .05(\$100,000 - \$2,913 - \$38,835)$$
$$\$2,913 = .05(\$100,000 - \$41,748)$$
$$\$2,913 = .05(\$58,252)$$
$$\$2,913 = \$2,913$$

Compensation expense and a related liability should be recorded in the amount of the bonus calculated. For the many other types and variations of bonus plans and profit-sharing arrangements, accountants are guided by the provisions of those agreements concerning the timing and amount of liabilities and related expenses. Careful study of such agreements is necessary to ensure comprehension and proper accounting.

The term **contingent liability** is used to describe a circumstance in which the existence of a liability is uncertain. In many cases, the precise amount of a contingent liability, if any, also may not be known. A contingent liability is thus distinguishable from an estimated liability. An **estimated liability** is known to exist, but its exact amount is unknown. If an enterprise is relatively certain that a contingent liability exists and if the amount can be reasonably estimated, the contingent liability should be recorded in the financial statements. As such, contingent liabilities represent another area in which estimates of future events are necessary to prepare historic financial statements. In fact, the estimates involved in accounting for loss contingencies in accordance with *SFAS No. 5* are among the most complex and pervasive in financial accounting. The range of events to which these contingencies relate is extremely broad and may involve matters about which the accountant is largely uninformed. Examples include contingent losses related to environmental pollution, wrongful discharge of employees, the effects of drought on the growth rate and size of plants, and other events far from the accounting and financial reporting issues typically confronted. In a number of these circumstances, the accountant consults experts on the particular issue being considered.

The FASB considered the accounting and reporting issues for many types of contingencies and issued *SFAS No. 5,* which defines a contingency as

> *An existing condition, situation, or set of circumstances involving uncertainty as to possible gain or loss to an enterprise that will ultimately be resolved when one or more future events occur or fail to occur.*[11]

CONTINGENT LIABILITIES

---

[11]*FASB Statement of Financial Accounting Standards No. 5,* "Accounting for Contingencies," 1975, par. 1.

An unsettled lawsuit provides an example of both a **gain contingency** and a **loss contingency.** For the plaintiff (the party that brings suit against another), the possibility of gain exists if it wins the suit. To the defendant (the party charged by the plaintiff of some wrongdoing), the suit represents a loss contingency because payment must be made if the plaintiff prevails. Uncertainty exists for both parties until the suit is resolved either in the courts or through a negotiated settlement.

Although *SFAS No. 5* recognizes that contingencies may involve either gain or loss, it is concerned exclusively with loss contingencies and simply carries forward the conclusions of *Accounting Research Bulletin No. 50,* stating that "gain contingencies should not be accrued since to do so might recognize revenue prior to its realization."[12] In this chapter, we consider loss contingencies. We treat revenue recognition, including contingent gains, more fully in Chapter 21 (which deals with many unusual problems of determining the timing and amount of revenue to be reported in financial statements). Nevertheless, the role of conservatism is evident in the different accounting treatments accorded gain and loss contingencies. In the following discussion, consider how the modifying convention of conservatism is applied in the specific accounting standards used by our profession in reporting loss contingencies. Also consider the complex judgments and estimates of future events that underly historic financial statements.

[margin notes: Revenue Realization; Conservatism]

CRITERIA FOR ACCRUING LOSS CONTINGENCIES

Loss contingencies involving either the impairment of an asset or the incurrence of a liability require accrual on the basis of less evidence than is required for recognizing gain contingencies. This practice is consistent with the modifying convention of conservatism found throughout the financial accounting process. The FASB set forth three conditions that, if met, require the accrual of a loss contingency:[13]

[margin note: Conservatism]

1. The likelihood of the future event or events confirming the loss must be *probable.*
2. The amount of the loss must be *reasonably estimable.*
3. The event giving rise to the loss must have *taken place* by the balance sheet date.

Thus, a loss must be *probable* of being ultimately sustained, *estimable,* and *timely* to require accrual in the financial statements. A loss contingency that meets each of those criteria also satisfies the conceptual requirements contained in *SFAC No. 6,* "Elements of Financial Statements." According to that concepts statement, liabilities are probable future sacrifices of economic resources arising from present obligations of an enterprise due to past events or transactions. Therefore, when the criteria for accruing a loss contingency according to *SFAS No. 5* are met, the concepts in *SFAC No. 6* defining a liability are also satisfied.

Probability of Contingent Losses

To help accountants evaluate the likelihood of a future event occurring and thereby confirming a loss, the FASB defined three conditions of **probability.** These categories represent a continuum ranging from an extreme of almost complete certainty that a loss has been incurred to an extreme of almost complete certainty that no loss has been incurred. Exhibit 14–3 illustrates such a continuum.

The three categories of probability established by *SFAS No. 5* are[14]

1. **Probable.** The future event or events are *likely* to occur.
2. **Reasonably possible.** The chance of the future event(s) occurring is *more than remote* but *less than likely.*
3. **Remote.** The chance of the future event or events occurring is *slight.*

---

[12]*FASB Statement of Financial Accounting Standards No. 5,* par. 17.
[13]*FASB Statement of Financial Accounting Standards No. 5,* par. 8.
[14]*FASB Statement of Financial Accounting Standards No. 5,* par. 3.

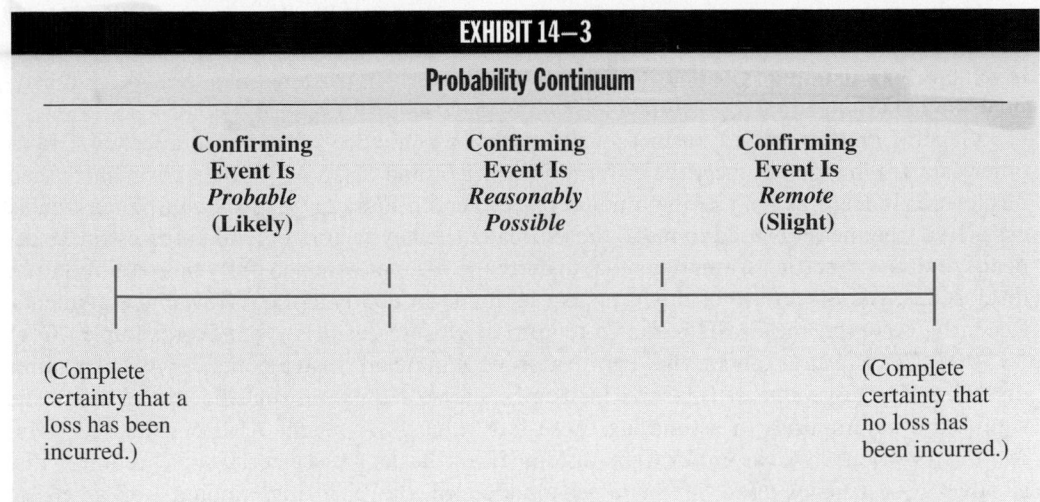

EXHIBIT 14–3

Probability Continuum

| Confirming Event Is *Probable* (Likely) | Confirming Event Is *Reasonably Possible* | Confirming Event Is *Remote* (Slight) |

(Complete certainty that a loss has been incurred.)

(Complete certainty that no loss has been incurred.)

The FASB did not assign probability percentages to those categories but relies on accounts to use professional judgment in assessing the category of probability in which a particular loss contingency should be placed. Assessing the probability of the outcome of many future events is one of the most demanding aspects of professional accounting.

Estimability of Contingent Losses

SFAS No. 5 also requires accountants to estimate the amount of contingent losses. According to an FASB interpretation,[15] if the estimated amount of a loss contingency is a range of amounts, the condition of reasonable estimability is met. Therefore, if a loss is probable, if the event giving rise to the loss has occurred by the balance sheet date, and if a range of loss can be estimated, a loss should be accrued. If one particular amount in the range represents a superior estimate of the loss ultimately to be incurred, then *that* amount should be accrued. If no specific amount in the range appears to be a better estimate, however, the *minimum* amount of the range should be selected. This practice represents the least conservative method of applying a fundamentally conservative policy. The amount of the range and the nature of the contingency should both be disclosed in such circumstances.

Conservatism

If the estimability, probability, and timeliness conditions are met, the estimated amount of the loss is charged against income in the current period and the carrying amount of the related asset is reduced or a related liability is recognized. Generally, disclosures of the nature of the contingency and the amount of the loss accrued are necessary.

Disclosure

DISCLOSURE OF LOSS CONTINGENCIES NOT ACCRUED

A loss contingency that is reasonably possible, but not probable, must be disclosed even if the loss is not reasonably estimable or if the event giving rise to the loss occurred after the balance sheet date. The disclosure should include the nature of the contingency and an estimate of the loss or a statement that such an estimate is not possible.

Disclosure

Remote Loss Contingencies

The FASB generally does not require the disclosure of remote loss contingencies. Disclosure is not prohibited, however, and if an unusually large potential loss is remotely possible,

---

[15]*FASB Interpretation No. 14,* "Reasonable Estimation of the Amount of a Loss: An Interpretation of FASB Statement No. 5," 1976, par. 3.

disclosure of the nature and amount of loss may be desirable. Furthermore, certain types of loss contingencies, including the following, must be disclosed even if the probability of loss is remote: (1) guarantees of the indebtedness of others, (2) guarantees to repurchase receivables, and (3) obligations of commercial banks under certain letters of credit.

General or unspecified business risks, such as a practice of self-insurance for fire or other catastrophe, do not meet the criteria for accrual, and *SFAS No. 5* does not *require* their disclosure. Indeed, as long as the amount of a recorded loss contingency can be reasonably estimated, the methods used to make the estimate, the key factors on which the estimate depends, and the specific assumptions that underly the estimate are generally not required to be disclosed. Little disclosure of this type can be found in contemporary financial statements.

Disclosure   Recently, however, the FASB began to require disclosures of this type. For example, *SFAS No. 107,* "Disclosures about the Fair Value of Financial Instruments," which requires disclosing the fair value of financial instruments, also requires disclosing the methods and significant assumptions in estimating those fair values.[16] A recent AICPA proposed statement of position, "Disclosure of Certain Significant Risks and Uncertainties" requires disclosing "...estimates used in the determination of the carrying amounts of assets or liabilities or disclosure of gain or loss contingencies..." when "it is at least reasonably possible that the estimate...will change in the near term."[17] Although it is not clear that the provisions of this proposal will be cleared by the FASB, its mere existence reveals the accounting profession's concern about providing financial statement users with this type of information.

Finally the FASB, in *SFAS No. 105,* "Disclosure of Information about Financial Instruments with Off-Balance Sheet Risk and Financial Instruments with Concentrations of Credit Risk," calls for disclosing concentrations of credit risk. These standards, which are discussed more fully in Chapter 25, require disclosure of a wide range of uncertainties and explain how accountants have dealt with those matters in preparing financial statements. It is significant that information about the risks and uncertainties confronted by reporting entities is beginning to be required as part of the financial statement disclosures.

Exhibit 14–4 displays the normal accounting practices for a variety of loss contingencies. Much of the table is easily understood and applied, but the problems of accounting for litigation, claims, and assessments in items 7 and 8 are more complex.

Litigation, Claims, and Assessments

Litigation has become an all too common problem for many companies, and when a company is sued, certain accounting and reporting implications are evident. If a lawsuit or other claim is filed against a company and the final outcome is not known when financial statements are issued, then a contingent liability exists and the probability of an unfavorable outcome as well as the amount of the loss, including attorneys' fees, must be estimated. Lawyers usually assist in making these estimates. However, the general criteria for accounting and reporting loss contingencies should be applied and, therefore, accountants must also be acquainted with the facts of the litigation.

One special type of loss contingency, referred to as an **unasserted claim,** requires additional analysis. An unasserted claim is a situation involving a **potential claim** or assessment in which the **potential claimant** is not aware of a right to proceed with the claim. Examples include violations of tax or customs regulations, pollution of the environment, and a variety of torts (social wrongs) involving possible lawsuits.

---

[16]*FASB Statement of Financial Accounting Standards No. 107,* "Disclosures about the Fair Values of Financial Instruments," 1991.

[17]AICPA *Statement of Position,* "Disclosure of Certain Significant Risks and Uncertainties," 1994. (Proposed for clearance by the FASB.)

EXHIBIT 14-4

Loss Contingencies

Loss Related To	Usually Should Be Accrued	Should Not Be Accrued	Accrual Depends on Circumstances*
1. Collectibility of receivables.	X		
2. Obligations related to product warranties and product defects.	X		
3. Risk of loss or damage of enterprise property by fire, explosion, or other hazards.		X	
4. General or unspecified business risks.		X	
5. Risk of loss from catastrophes assumed by property and casualty insurance companies, including reinsurance companies.		X	
6. Threat of expropriation of assets.			X
7. Pending or threatened litigation.			X
8. Actual or possible claims and assessments.†			X
9. Guarantees of indebtedness of others.			X
10. Obligations of commercial banks under "standby letters of credit."			X
11. Agreements to repurchase receivables (or the related properties) that have been sold.			X

*Should be accrued when both criteria are met (probable and reasonably estimable).
†Estimated amounts of losses incurred prior to the balance sheet date but settled subsequent thereto should be accrued as of the balance sheet date.
SOURCE: Ernst & Young, *Financial Reporting Developments*, "Accounting for Contingencies" (August 1975), p. 4.

Unasserted claims do not require disclosure in the financial statements unless (1) assertion is probable, even if no disclosures are made in those financial statements and (2) a related loss is at least reasonably possible should the claim be asserted. The rationale underlying these additional criteria for disclosure of unasserted claims is the idea that a company need not "tell on itself." That is, no disclosure regarding an unasserted claim is required unless the claim will *probably* be asserted even if the disclosures were not made in the financial **Disclosure** statements. Unasserted claims that are probable of assertion and meet the other criteria for accruing loss contingencies should be recorded as liabilities and related losses.

To illustrate the importance of items that are the subject of loss contingency disclosures, an actual circumstance taken from practice is helpful. Exhibit 14-5 is a portion of a note that appeared in the 1992 annual report of Union Carbide Corporation. In addition to the absolute amount of the matter discussed, notice the relatively long time period involved in litigating and settling the matter. Notice also that even after the protracted processes described, much uncertainty remains and will continue into the indefinite future.

Such disclosures involving extremely sensitive matters clearly require professionals with skills other than accounting to evaluate and describe. Accountants must learn about these

---

EXHIBIT 14–5

Contingency Disclosure

In February 1989, UCC&P Inc. and Union Carbide India Limited (UCIL) paid $470 million to the union of India in final settlement of all claims with respect to the Dec. 3, 1984, methyl isocyanate gas release at the UCIL plant in Bhopal, India. UCC&P Inc. is a 50.9 percent shareholder of UCIL. The Supreme Court of India discharged the previous undertaking of UCC&P Inc. in the District Court at Bhopal to maintain unencumbered assets having a fair market value of $3 billion. In December 1989, the Supreme Court of India upheld the Bhopal Act, under the Indian Constitution. The Bhopal Act was the main basis on which the Union of India represented the victims. In October 1991, the Supreme Court of India: upheld the civil settlement of $470 million in its entirety; set aside that portion of the settlement that quashed the criminal prosecutions which were pending at the time of the settlement and that precluded any future criminal proceedings; required the Union of India to purchase, out of the settlement fund, a group medical insurance policy to cover 100,000 asymptomatic persons who may later develop symptoms; required the Union of India to make up any shortfall in the settlement fund; and requested UCC&P Inc. and UCIL to fund the capital and operating costs of a hospital in Bhopal for eight years, which the Court estimated would require "around Rs. 50 crores" (approximately $17 million), with the land to be provided free by the State of Madhya Pradesh. UCC&P Inc. and UCIL announced that together they would provide the Government of India with up to Rs. 50 crores for a hospital to be built in Bhopal by the Government.

The Corporation and UCC&P Inc. created the Bhopal Hospital Trust with the Rt. Honorable Sir Ian Percival, formerly Solicitor General for England and Wales, as Trustee, and UCC&P Inc. pledged its shares of UCIL to the Trust. The Trust may call upon the shares to make payment to the Government of up to Rs. 51 crores (approximately $18 million), less the amount to be paid by UCIL, for a hospital in Bhopal. The Reserve Bank of India approved the pledge of the shares to the Trust. In June 1992, the Government of India requested Rs. 98 to Rs. 106 crores (approximately $34 to $37 million) for the hospital.

In April and May 1992, the Magistrate in Bhopal ordered that: the shares of UCIL held by UCC&P Inc. are attached; the unremitted dividends from UCIL to UCC&P Inc. for the years from 1984 through 1991 after deducting taxes payable are attached (approximately Rs. 6 crores, or $2 million); and the Reserve Bank of India not grant permission for sale or transfer of the shares or payment of the dividends to UCC&P Inc. without approval of the Court. In July 1992, the Government Prosecutor requested the Magistrate to appoint a receiver to take charge of the property of UCC&P Inc. attached by the Magistrate. UCIL appealed to the High Court to set aside the attachment of the shares and unremitted dividends, and that appeal is pending. The High Court ordered on an interim basis that no receiver be appointed for the shares and dividends. In October 1992, a victim applied to the Magistrate in Bhopal to set aside the attachment so that the funding of a hospital in Bhopal for the victims by the Bhopal Hospital Trust may proceed.

In the opinion of counsel for the Corporation, under generally recognized legal principles, the criminal proceedings in India should not have adverse financial consequences for the Corporation outside of India. The assets that might be lost from the attachment in the criminal proceedings are primarily the shares of UCIL, carried at $26 million in the consolidated financial statements of the Corporation.

All the suits with respect to the gas release that were brought in the U.S. prior to the settlement have been dismissed, except two suits in a state court, one of which was reactivated after dismissal. At an appropriate time, the settlement will be placed before that court. In October 1990, two suits were filed in Texas State Courts with respect to the gas release seeking compensatory and punitive damages. The two suits were transferred to Federal Court and dismissed, and the dismissal has been upheld by the U.S. Court of Appeals for the Second Circuit.

SOURCE: Union Carbide Corporation Annual Report, 1992.

---

matters from other professionals to assess the adequacy of accounting measurement and disclosure in the company's financial statements. The extreme breadth of these issues is one of the reasons that many people find accounting to be a demanding and fulfilling profession.

Evidence about Litigation, Claims, and Assessments

Accountants must collect sufficient competent evidence to support accounting entries. In litigation, claims, and assessments, accountants frequently rely on attorneys to study and evaluate the merits and prospects of individual lawsuits. In fact, lengthy written representations from lawyers are usually requested by accountants attempting to apply *SFAS No. 5* to loss contingencies arising from litigation, claims, and assessments. Lawyers can analyze each lawsuit and comment on the probability of an unfavorable outcome, amount of possible loss, the defendant's proposed course of action, and any other relevant issues. Accountants typically do not have the requisite legal expertise to make such determinations alone and therefore frequently rely on the knowledge and experience of members of the legal profession.

Accountants' skill and expertise are limited to the education, training, and experience they have obtained. Therefore, in many cases, including accounting for a variety of loss contingencies, accountants rely on the judgment and expertise of specialists to provide the basis for financial reporting practices. The use of specialists is thus rather common as accountants attempt to gather evidence to support the many complex and subjective assertions made in the financial statements. Examples of other accounting issues that may be resolved by relying on specialists include valuating gems, assessing recoverable oil and gas reserves, and estimating the obsolescence of technologically complex equipment and items of inventory. The key point to remember is that each financial statement account makes several assertions related to such items as existence, ownership, and valuation. The accountant must be sure that each assertion made by the financial statements is supported by adequate evidence, and sometimes expert opinions of specialists must be obtained.

WARRANTIES AND GUARANTEES

Many companies offer their customers warranties and guarantees of product performance or capability that extend well beyond the time of the sale. Reasonable estimates of the selling company's contingent liability for such commitments are usually possible. The estimated warranty expense and the related liability under the warranty should be recognized at the time of the original sale of the product. If the amount of the liability under the warranty cannot be reasonably estimated, then no expense or liability should be recognized. Revenue from the sale of the item, however, should usually be deferred in such cases until the actual amount of the warranty expense becomes known. In this manner, revenue and expense matching is accomplished even if warranty expense is not currently estimable.

Matching

To illustrate, assume that Andrews, Inc., a manufacturer of high-quality kitchen appliances, warrants its products to be "oven safe." Engineering estimates and historical analysis, however, indicate that 1% of all products sold will fail within the warranty period and about one-half of those products will be returned. If sales for Andrews are $5,000,000 for 1995 and the company's gross margin on sales is 40%, the following entry records the estimated warranty expense for 1995:

| Dec. 31, 1995 | Warranty Expense | 15,000 | |
| | Estimated Liability for Warranties | | 15,000 |

The calculations to arrive at that figure are as follows:

$$\text{Amount Originally Received for Returned Products} = \$5,000,000 \times .01 \times .5 = \$25,000$$

$$\text{Sales} - \text{Gross Margin} = \text{Cost of Goods Sold}$$

$$\$25,000 - .4(\$25,000) = \text{Cost of Goods Expected to Be Returned}$$

Therefore, $15,000 ($25,000 − $10,000) is the amount estimated to be necessary to honor warranties.

If goods costing $2,000 are drawn from inventory on January 15, 1996, to honor warranties, the following entry is appropriate:

Jan. 15, 1996	Estimated Liability for Warranties	2,000	
	Inventory		2,000

Even if some of the warranties to sales made in 1995 were honored during 1995, a similar entry is appropriate. Honoring a warranty discharges a liability of the company. The entry to adjust the Warranty Expense account at the end of the year is based on prior experience and estimated remaining warranties to be honored.

In some cases, extended warranties are available at added cost when products are purchased. Examples include automobile and appliance warranties that extend beyond the basic warranty that comes with the product. When extended warranties are sold in connection with products that already have limited warranties, revenues from the sale of the extended warranties generally should be deferred, reported as a liability, and recognized as revenue during the additional expected warranty period.

PREMIUMS

Premiums often are used to enhance product sales. Usually a company acquires an inventory of premium items and offers to "give" them away to customers upon proof that the customers have acquired a certain quantity of the primary product. Accounting for premiums of this nature is illustrated in the following example.

Assume that Suds City Soap Company initiated a premium program whereby the company sells customers a kitchen utensil at a reduced price on presentation of 10 box tops from its soap product. During the first year of the program, Suds acquired 10,000 kitchen utensils at $1 each and sold 750,000 boxes of the soap product at $2.50 per box. The company estimated that 10% of all sales would result in the return of box tops for the utensil. By the end of the year, Suds City had received 50,000 box tops and had sent the kitchen utensils to the customers. Assume that customers must send $.60 with each 10 box tops as a reduced purchased price and that shipping and handling costs are $.20 per utensil. The following entries reflect proper accounting for these events.

Inventory of Premiums (10,000 × $1.00)	10,000	
Cash		10,000
(To record acquisition of kitchen utensils.)		
Cash (750,000 × $2.50)	1,875,000	
Sales		1,875,000
(To record sale of soap.)		
Cash (5,000 × $.60)	3,000	
Premium Expense [5,000 × ($1.00 − $.60)]	2,000	
Inventory of Premiums (5,000 × $1.00)		5,000
(To record premiums sent to customers based on box tops		
received. 50,000 ÷ 10 = 5,000)		
Premium Expense (5,000 × $.20)	1,000	
Cash		1,000
(To record postage expense on premiums mailed.)		
Premium Expense	1,500	
Estimated Liability under Premium Plan		1,500
(To accrue the estimated premium liability at year end.)		

Calculations for the last entry are as follows:

Total sales (in boxes)	$750,000
Percent expected to claim premiums	× .10
Total box tops to be received	75,000

DECIDING WHAT TO DISCLOSE

Bert Avenue in Newburgh Heights, Ohio, is a long way from Wall Street. When residents of this blue-collar town think of markets, it is Polish delis, not sexy new stock issues, that typically come to mind. Some Wall Street analysts may soon be keeping a closer eye on Bert Avenue, however. It is in this unlikely place that two important and potentially explosive issues are suddenly edging closer together: environmental cleanup and how the costs of such cleanup should be disclosed to potential investors.

According to knowledgeable sources, the Securities and Exchange Commission is examining records pertaining to a trash dump in Newburgh Heights controlled by the Sunbeam-Oster Co., a Rhode Island–based manufacturer of household appliances. The SEC will neither confirm nor deny the inquiry, which is known to focus on the costs Sunbeam-Oster has estimated to clean up the Bert Avenue dump. The dump is contaminated with low-level radioactive wastes. Sunbeam-Oster, which says it is unaware of any SEC inquiry, estimates cleanup costs at $7.5 million. The company's estimated net worth is $610 million. "We have reserved funds for the cleanup," says David Fannin, special counsel for Sunbeam-Oster. "[We] don't believe it will have any significant impact on the company."

Litmus Tests. The SEC inquiry could nevertheless prove interesting. This is believed to be the first such inquiry involving the issue of nondisclosure of environmental liabilities. Sunbeam-Oster was not required to notify potential investors of the cleanup costs in the prospectus for its initial public stock offering last year, Fannin says. SEC rules do ask, however, that companies consider the *range* of possible liabilities in preparing their filings for the agency. The SEC employs several litmus tests. One says that disclosure of a potential liability is required if it is estimated to exceed 10 percent of a company's net worth. In the case of the Bert Avenue dump, disclosure would be required only if cleanup costs were likely to exceed $61 million.

Some lawyers and securities experts question this approach. A more useful standard, suggests Boston University law Prof. Tamar Frankel, is "whether the information [concerning a company's potential liability] might have a material effect on a reasonable investor. If the liability here was just $7 million, the answer is probably no. If you're talking $50 million, the answer is probably yes. The wise thing to do is to disclose the information and let the investors make their own decisions."

This is where things can get dicey. Take the Bert Avenue dump. A deep ravine with piles of contaminated soil now concealed under bright blue tarpaulins, the dump became Sunbeam-Oster's problem when the company inherited the facility in a bankruptcy-court reorganization of another company. The cleanup question arose immediately. Sunbeam-Oster's $7.5 million estimate is based on a plan to bury most of the contaminated soil at the Bert Avenue site; only the most dangerous materials would be removed to a federally licensed facility. The plan must be approved by the federal Nuclear Regulatory Commission and by Ohio's Environmental Protection Agency. The federal regulators have few objections to the Sunbeam-Oster plan, but Ohio's EPA would have to waive state laws and several state regulations that prevent disposal of hazardous wastes in or near residential neighborhoods. Additionally, some 200 people who live around the Bert Avenue dump have sued Sunbeam-Oster. The residents are challenging the plan for on-site burial. They are also seeking $110 million in damages.

These factors could raise the odds that Sunbeam-Oster may have to consider off-site burial, a much more expensive prospect. Some estimates are as high as $50 million; others are in the range of $20 million to $25 million.

Should Sunbeam-Oster be required to disclose these potential liabilities to investors thinking of plunking down money for a few of its shares? The answers may be found not in the reams of paperwork now under study by the SEC but under many tons of dirt beneath the bright blue tarps on Bert Avenue.

SOURCE: Reprinted from Dan McGraw, "Deciding What to Disclose," *U.S. News & World Report* (November 1, 1993). Copyright Nov. 1, 1993, U.S. News & World Report.

Balance carried forward	$ 75,000
Less: Box tops received	(50,000)
Estimated remaining box tops to be received	25,000
	÷ 10
Estimated premiums to be sent	2,500
Cost per premium ($.40 + $.20)	× .60
Remaining liability and expense related to annual sales	$ 1,500

As the 25,000 box tops are subsequently received and utensils shipped, the following entry is necessary:

Cash (2,500 × $.60)	1,500	
Estimated Liability under Premium Plan (2,500 × $.40)	1,000	
Inventory (2,500 × $1.00)		2,500
(To record premiums sent to customers based on box tops received.)		

Estimated Liability under Premium Plan	500
Cash (2,500 × $.20)	500

(To record postage expense on premiums mailed.)

If the original estimate of the liability under the premium plan differs from actual experience, the difference is charged or credited to income during the period in which this fact becomes evident.

COMPENSATED ABSENCES

The compensation of employees often exceeds the amount they are immediately paid for services rendered. For example, companies frequently provide retirement benefits, paid vacations, and sick leave for their employees. Sabbatical leaves are granted to employees such as physicians and college professors. Employees usually earn the right to such *compensated absences* in periods prior to the absence. If conditions described in the following paragraph are met, compensation expense for each accounting period should include the cost to the employer of future absences earned by employees during that period. Because accounting for pension plans and other post-retirement benefits is more complex and controversial, Chapter 24 is devoted to that topic. Other types of deferred payments for employee services, however, are clearly in the nature of contingent liabilities, and we discuss some of them in the following paragraphs.

FASB Statement of Financial Accounting Standards No. 43[18] addresses financial reporting for various programs of employee benefits. According to that pronouncement, compensated absences represent a type of contingency, and the recognition criteria contained in *SFAS No. 5* are expanded to encompass the special aspects of those costs. In accordance with *SFAS No. 43*, employers must accrue a liability for employees' compensation for future absences when four separate conditions exist:

1. The employer's obligation is attributable to services *already rendered* by the balance sheet date.
2. The obligation relates to *vested rights* that are not contingent on continued employment or to rights that *accumulate* from period to period even if not taken.
3. Payment of the compensation is *probable*.
4. The amount is *reasonably estimable*.

Disclosure   Disclosure of such contingencies is required when the first three conditions exist but the amount is not reasonably estimable. *SFAS No. 5* requires disclosure of loss contingencies when there is at least a reasonable possibility of loss, regardless of whether the amount of the loss is reasonably estimable. Therefore, we should consider the desirability of disclosing unaccrued compensated absence obligations for which payment is deemed reasonably possible, whether or not the amount is estimable. That logic parallels the disclosure requirements of *SFAS No. 5.*

The FASB does not require the accrual of sick leave prior to an illness unless the leave is *vested* in the employee. The payment of unvested but accumulated sick leave is contingent on a future illness; because the illness is not a condition existing at the balance sheet date, accrual is not required. However, the wording of this provision regarding sick leave is "permissive," and the accrual of accumulating but nonvesting sick leave for which payment is probable is acceptable. The authors of this text recommend disclosure of the particular ac-

Materiality   counting policy followed for material amounts of accumulating, but nonvesting, sick leave.

Occasionally, a company desires to reorganize its affairs and in doing so encourages various groups of employees to leave the firm voluntarily. The reasons for providing induce-

---

[18]*FASB Statement of Financial Accounting Standards No. 43*, "Accounting for Compensated Absences," 1980.

ments to terminate employment may relate to declining or changing markets, financial failures, or other operating difficulties. Regardless of the reasons, however, accounting issues are evident whenever management offers special termination benefits to encourage employees to leave the company. *SFAS No. 88,* "Employers' Accounting for Settlements and Curtailments of Defined Benefit Pension Plans and for Termination Benefits," provides guidance in such circumstances.

Generally, if an employer offers, for a short-period of time, special termination benefits to employees, an expense and a related liability should be recognized when two conditions are met. Those conditions are

1. The probability that the employees will accept the offer.
2. The ability to reasonably estimate the amount.

If both conditions are met, accountants should record an expense and a related liability in the amount of the present value of the estimated costs. Sometimes the special termination plan may affect additional benefit programs to which the employees would otherwise be entitled, such as pension benefits and other compensated absence rights. In such cases, the effects of the special termination plan on those other benefit programs should be considered when determining the effects of the termination benefits. In this fashion, likely future cash outflows resulting from past events are appropriately estimated and reported in the balance sheet. This assists financial statement users to assess risks and probable future flows of cash.

This book focuses on financial accounting and reporting for businesses operated for profit. Standards of financial accounting and reporting, however, also apply to nonbusiness enterprises. New pronouncements can substantially affect both profit-seeking and not-for-profit organizations. For example, cities frequently adopt very liberal policies on compensated absences to alleviate budget constraints while still providing attractive overall compensation packages. Accruing compensated absences can have a much more significant effect on governmental organizations than on business enterprises.

PROFESSIONAL JUDGMENT

Accounting for many of the current liabilities discussed in this chapter is rather straightforward. Conceptual issues exist, however, that considerably complicate accounting for a number of liabilities. Perhaps the most difficult of these issues lies in determining proper classification when loan covenants of long-term debt have or may have been violated. In such circumstances, the issues are of exceptional importance and determining whether covenants have been violated may require complex judgments. Further, determining whether a company may be able to cure such violations within a grace period may involve estimates of future events. Remember that conservatism is a part of financial accounting as related to uncertainties. Conservatism is not, however, an objective of financial accounting and care should be taken not to understate income or financial position.

Conservatism

Accounting for contingent losses is an even more complex issue. Accountants must identify events, sometimes far afield from accounting processes, that may have impaired assets or caused liabilities to possibly have been incurred and then to estimate the outcome of other future events affecting the existence and amount of the contingent losses. It is obvious that considerable knowledge of the business, its exposures to risks of various types, keen intellect, and seasoned judgment are all necessary to work effectively in this perilous area of professional accounting. Due professional care and competence are of utmost importance in these challenging and difficult circumstances.

CONCLUDING REMARKS

Accounting for current and contingent liabilities is an important part of the preparation of financial statements in accordance with generally accepted accounting principles. The authors believe that in the future, additional disclosures of a variety of risks will almost certainly be required of particular business enterprises. We believe these disclosures will be

Disclosure   made prior to actual events of loss and will thereby expand considerably the responsibility of professional accountants. The authoritative standards will be involved in these matters for many years, and accountants should be prepared to accept these changes when they occur. Indeed, consider how you can increase your awareness of deliberations such as these as your career expands and your own responsibilities increase.

KEY POINTS

1. Financial accounting and reporting for current and contingent liabilities require a good understanding of both the concepts underlying recognition and valuation of liabilities as well as the specific practices required by authoritative bodies. (All objectives)

2. As in other areas of financial reporting, broad and relatively abstract concepts guide accounting practice in the area of liabilities. (Objective 1)

3. An obligation must exhibit three characteristics to represent a reportable liability: (1) it must entail a probable future economic sacrifice, (2) it must require a transfer of resources, and (3) it must be the result of a past transaction or event. Not all obligations and commitments of an enterprise are considered reportable liabilities. (Objective 1)

4. A current liability is a liability that will be satisfied with current assets or through the creation of a new current liability, or one due on demand or that will become due on demand during the next period. (Objective 2)

5. Several major categories of current liabilities exist, including:
   a. Trade accounts payable.
   b. Notes payable.
   c. Dividends payable.
   d. Advances from customers.
   e. Various liabilities for taxes (e.g., payroll, sales, property, income).
   f. Contingent liabilities.
   (Objectives 3 and 6)

6. To exclude a short-term obligation from current liabilities, an enterprise must *intend* to refinance the obligation on a noncurrent basis and *demonstrate the ability* to accomplish the refinancing. (Objective 7)

7. A contingent liability is uncertain as to existence and, usually, as to amount. (Objectives 3 and 8)

8. Examples of contingent liabilities include the following:
   a. Litigation.
   b. Inventory obsolescence.
   c. Collectibility of receivables.
   d. Warranties.
   e. Guarantees.
   f. Compensated absences. (Objective 8)

9. For a loss contingency to require accrual, it must be probable that a liability has been incurred or an asset impaired by the balance sheet date and the amount of the loss must be reasonably estimable. (Objectives 4 and 8)

10. Loss contingencies that are at least reasonably possible must be disclosed even if the other conditions for accrual are not met. (Objectives 4 and 8)

11. The concept of conservatism suggests that liabilities and loss contingencies be accrued and reported in the financial statements on the basis of less evidence than is required for receivables and gain contingencies. (Objectives 4 and 8)

12. Complex estimates and determinations requiring seasoned professional judgment and great care are frequently encountered in accounting for contingent liabilities. (Objectives 1, 2, 3, 4, 5, 8, and 9)

APPENDIX A: LIABILITIES RELATED TO PAYROLL TAXES

The liabilities of various taxes related to payroll are a significant matter for most companies. These taxes are sometimes levied on the employee, and the employer merely withholds amounts from the employee's pay and remits those amounts to the appropriate government authority. In other cases, payroll taxes are levied on the employing company based on its payroll. In the following paragraphs, we describe the most common and significant payroll-related taxes and the accounting practices for each.

Income tax withholding laws require an employer to withhold an amount from an employee's salary that approximates the federal (and if applicable, state and local) income tax due on those earnings. The withholding requirements pertain only to **employer/employee relationships**. Payments to independent contractors, such as CPAs or attorneys in public practice who prepare tax returns and render other services to businesses, are not subject to the withholding laws since no employer/employee relationship exists.

The government determines the amount to be withheld from employee salaries. Employers use tables or formulas supplied by the government to determine the specific amounts to withhold from individual employees. Withholding amounts vary according to several factors, such as the amount of earnings, the length of the pay period, and the employee's marital status and number of dependents. The employer must remit income tax withholdings at regular intervals, the frequency of which is determined by the total amounts withheld. Income tax withholdings are taxes levied on the employee rather than the employer.

Social Security taxes—also called **Federal Insurance Contribution Act (FICA)** taxes—provide for old-age and survivor benefits for qualified people and hospitalization insurance through the Medicare program. Social Security taxes are levied on both the employer and the employee. Social Security taxes are stated as a percentage rate applied to the earnings of each employee. Certain payroll taxes are limited to a base level of earnings (e.g., 6% of earnings up to $60,000 a year) while others are applied to an individual's earnings without limitation (e.g., 1.45% of total earnings). As a result of the rising costs of operating the Social Security system, the rates and base earnings amounts have been raised frequently; future increases are almost assured. For purposes of this text, we assume Social Security taxes of 8% for both employer and employee on the first $50,000 per year of the employee's base earnings. The increase is determined through the use of a formula that is based primarily on the consumer price index. Employers are required to make periodic remittances of Social Security taxes to the federal government.

Employers pay **the federal unemployment tax (FUTA),** instituted by the **Federal Unemployment Tax Act,** to provide unemployment benefits to individuals who have lost their jobs through no fault of their own. This tax, like Social Security taxes, is expressed as a percentage (e.g., 6.2%) of a base wage (e.g., $7,000) per year. Unlike Social Security taxes, however, FUTA is levied on employers only. A credit of up to 5.4% of the total tax is allowed, however, for contributions made to a qualified state plan. Employers who pay an amount less than 5.4% to a state plan as a reward for low unemployment compensation claims are, nevertheless, allowed the full 5.4% credit against the total federal tax. As with other employment-related taxes, employers are required to make periodic remittances of FUTA.

A **state unemployment tax (SUTA)** is usually levied only on employers; however, in a few states, the tax is levied on employees as well. The greatest distinction between state plans is that most of them allow a merit reduction in the tax rate for favorable employment histories. Under these merit plans, enterprises whose former employees have made only a few unemployment claims are rewarded with reduced tax rates for stable employment. Therefore, a company may be paying a rate of only 1% or less while continuing to receive the full 5.4% credit against FUTA.

To illustrate the accounting entries necessary to record various types of payroll taxes, assume that Warder Company payroll for the month ending January 31 is $10,000; Social Security taxes, 8% of the first $50,000 earned by each employee; and unemployment taxes, 6.2% of the first $7,000 of each employee's wages with 5.4% of the total being due to the state and the balance due to the federal government. Federal withholding tax tables reveal that $1,750 is to be withheld for employee income taxes. We prepare the following entry to record the January payroll:

Jan. 31	Salary Expense	10,000	
	Payroll Tax Expense	1,420	
	Income Tax Withholding		
	Payable		1,750
	FICA (Social Security)		
	Taxes Payable		1,600
	FUTA Payable		80
	SUTA Payable		540
	Cash		7,450

(To record payment of January payroll.)

The calculations are as follows:

Taxes Paid by Employer

FICA $10,000 × .08	= $	800
FUTA $10,000 × .008 =		80
SUTA $10,000 × .054 =		540
(.008 + .054 = .062)		
		$ 1,420

Withheld from Employee

FICA $10,000 × .08	$	800
Federal income tax		
(from tables)		1,750
		$ 2,550

Cash Required

Total payroll	$10,000
Less withholding	2,550
	$ 7,450

Note that FICA taxes are levied on both employer and employee in the same amount ($800) for a total of $1,600. Therefore, $800 of this amount is withheld from employees, and the additional $800 represents a payroll tax expense of the employer. FUTA and SUTA are both taxes on the employer in this example and as such represent increases in payroll tax expense. Federal income taxes withheld, however, are not additional payroll tax expenses of employers. They are simply amounts that are withheld from employees' salaries.

Although for simplicity we assumed that only taxes were withheld, *other payroll withholdings* would be recorded as liabilities in a similar fashion. Companies frequently agree to withhold health insurance premiums, union dues, savings plan deductions, and other amounts from employees' salaries as a convenience to the employee. Such amounts should be accounted for in a fashion similar to any payroll withholding and reported as a liability until remitted to the appropriate agency. Of course, those items are reflected as part of salary expense and do not represent incremental expenses to the employer. In other cases, employers provide "fringe" benefits, such as life and hospitalization insurance; such costs are expenses in addition to the employees' basic salary.

QUESTIONS

14–1   What does the term *liability* mean? What are its three essential characteristics?

14–2   What characteristics distinguish a current liability from a noncurrent one?

14–3   What are some of the problems that arise in attempting to value current liabilities? Describe what, in your opinion, is the theoretically preferable valuation amount of liabilities. Do not consider implementation problems in your answer.

14–4   How would each of the following be reported on the balance sheet?

[a] Bank overdraft.
[b] Cash dividend declared.
[c] Dividends in arrears on preferred stock.
[d] Estimates of income taxes payable.
[e] Personal injury claim pending.
[f] Customer accounts with credit balances.
[g] Deposits received by a public utility for meter installations.
[h] Current portion of a serial bond issue.
[i] Interest on a note payable that is deducted from the face amount of the note in determining the net proceeds.
[j] Strike settlement calling for retroactive wage payments.
[k] The obligation at the balance sheet date for vacation time to be taken (and paid) during the coming year.

14–5   In what situations should a short-term note payable be reported on the balance sheet at an amount less than face (maturity) value?

14–6   When, if ever, is it proper to report a short-term obligation as a noncurrent liability?

14–7   If a company pays off a short-term obligation immediately after the balance sheet date and then replenishes the funds used through long-term borrowing, should that short-term debt be classified as a noncurrent liability on the balance sheet? Why?

14–8   Advances from customers are considered to be liabilities, even though they typically will not require a cash payment to customers in the future. How is this consistent with the definition of the term *liability?*

14–9   What are the two methods of accounting for tax collection? Describe them.

14–10   Real estate taxes become a lien on the property owned by Campbell Company on the assessment date in May. The company does not begin to accrue taxes on its books until August, which begins the city's fiscal year. What do you think of this practice?

14–11   (Appendix A) What types of liabilities commonly arise in connection with a payroll? Discuss each type briefly, indicating whether the item typically represents an expense of the employer, the employee, or both.

14–12   The sales manager for Ally Company is entitled to a bonus of "10% of company profits." What problems could arise in interpreting this agreement?

14–13   What does the term *contingent liability* mean?

14–14   The existence and evaluation of contingent claims can affect a company's working capital position. What does this statement mean?

14–15   What are five examples of contingent liabilities? For each type, discuss the desirability and usual practice of disclosure or accrual accorded it in the current period.

14–16   What are the reporting approaches employed to present contingent liabilities? Briefly discuss each approach.

14–17   What are unasserted claims and how should they be presented in the financial statements?

14–18   Warranties and premiums may require the recognition of an estimated liability for services or products to be provided in the future. What basic accounting principle explains these accounting procedures? Discuss briefly.

14–19   Under what conditions should compensated absences be recognized as an expense in the period in which the employer earns the right to the future absence?

14–20   If sick leave does not vest in employees, a company is not required to record a liability at the time the employee earns the right to be paid during an absence in the future. Why are compensated absences for sick pay benefits treated differently from compensated absences for vacations?

14–21   The FASB set forth three conditions that, if met, require the accrual of a loss contingency. What are these conditions? Briefly describe each.

14–22 Cash Discounts Magnolia Company purchased equipment on September 5, 1995, with a list price of $150,000 on terms of 2/10, n/30. The company paid the account in full on September 13, 1995.

INSTRUCTIONS

[a] Prepare the general journal entry to record the purchase and the final payment, assuming that accounts payable are recorded at their gross amount.

[b] Prepare the general journal entry to record the purchases and the final payment, assuming accounts payable are recorded at an amount net of cash discounts.

14–23 Notes Payable Harold Company borrowed $25,000 from the bank in the form of a noninterest-bearing note on August 15, 1995. The note was discounted at 15% and matures in one year. On November 30, 1995, Harold borrowed $15,000 with interest payable of 12½% per annum, due in six months.

INSTRUCTIONS

Prepare the journal entries to record these transactions and any December 31, 1995, year-end adjustments.

14–24 Notes Payable—Alternatives Warner Manufacturing Company is considering a one-year loan from Northwest State Bank. Two alternatives are available: (1) a $17,500, 15% note, issued at face value and (2) a $17,500, noninterest-bearing note, discounted at 15%. Warner plans to borrow the money on November 1. The end of the company's financial reporting year is December 31.

INSTRUCTIONS

For each alternative, complete the following requirements:

[a] Prepare the general journal entries for the note issued on November 1 and any required adjustment at December 31.

[b] Prepare the financial statement presentation at December 31.

14–25 Debt Classification On May 31, 1995, Bristol Company had the following liabilities:

Account	Amount	Description
Accounts Payable	$10,500	Payable in 10–60 days.
Accrued Expenses	7,250	Payable in 10–30 days.
Notes Payable	17,800	$7,800 note payable on July 7, 1995; $10,000 note payable on Aug. 17, 1995.
Bonds Payable	65,000	Payable on May 31, 2002.

On July 7, before the 1995 financial statements were issued, the $7,800 note payable was replaced by an 18-month note for the same amount. The company is considering similar action on the $10,000 note due on August 17, 1995. The 1995 financial statements were issued on July 19, 1995.

INSTRUCTIONS

Prepare the liability presentation for Bristol Company's May 31, 1995, balance sheet, including any required notes.

14–26 Dividends Payable Cypress Company has the following capital stock outstanding at October 31, 1995, the end of the company's fiscal year:

[1] Eight percent preferred stock, $100 par value, 100,000 shares issued and outstanding.

[2] Common stock, $50 par value, 520,000 shares issued and outstanding.

On October 31, 1995, the board of directors declared the specified preferred dividend and a $2.75 dividend per share on the common stock. These dividends were paid on November 30, 1995.

INSTRUCTIONS

[a] Prepare the general journal entries to record the declaration and payment of these dividends. Use separate liability accounts for the two classes of stock.

[b] Describe the presentation of the dividend liabilities in the October 31, 1995, balance sheet.

14–27 Customer Advances Devon Printers produces printed materials to its customers' specifications for orders of $50,000 or more. A 12% advance is required when the order is placed. The balance is due 30 days after delivery of the printed materials.

On May 13, 1995, Devon received an order totaling $178,500, including the 12% advance. The company delivered the finished products on June 3, 1995, and received final payment, including 4% sales tax, on June 30, 1995.

INSTRUCTIONS

[a] Prepare the general journal entries to record these events.

[b] Describe briefly the impact of these events on Devon's current liabilities.

14–28 Sales Tax   Total amounts received or receivable from sales by Lotus Manufacturing Company in January 1995 were $120,460, including sales tax. Seventy-five percent of the sales are normally on account.

INSTRUCTIONS

Prepare the journal entry to record these data (in whole dollars) for 1995 if the sales tax rate is 4%.

14–29 Sales Tax   Paramount Company records sales at amounts that include any state and local sales taxes. During April 1995, Paramount recorded sales of $107,100.

[1] Fifty percent of sales were subject to both 7% state sales tax and a 4% city sales tax.

[2] Forty percent of sales were subject to a 4% city sales tax only.

[3] Ten percent of sales were labor and not subject to any tax.

INSTRUCTIONS

Prepare the entry to record the sales for April 1995.

14–30 Property Tax   Monrouia Company paid $25,000 for 1994–1995 real estate property taxes. The city's fiscal year is July 1–June 30 and the company accrues property taxes quarterly over the city's fiscal period. Monrouia makes property improvements during 1995 and the real estate tax bill increases to $30,000. The company protests the increase but pays half of the $30,000 when it receives the tax bill on October 15, 1995. The company is confident it will prevail in its appeal. On March 15, 1996, Monrouia is notified that the assessment has been reduced to $28,500. The balance due is paid on April 1, 1996. Annual financial statements are prepared on June 30, 1996.

INSTRUCTIONS

Prepare any journal entries necessary to record the real estate taxes for July 1, 1995, to June 30, 1996. The company prepares quarterly financial statements and makes property tax accruals only when interim or annual financial statements are prepared.

14–31 (Appendix A) Payroll Tax   Kathryn McKenna, CPA, has five employees, each paid $300 weekly. The employer is responsible for remitting 16% of the salaries quarterly for Social Security taxes—8% each for the employee's and employer's contribution. One percent of the base salary, $8,000, is remitted quarterly for federal unemployment insurance, and 2.7% of the base salary is remitted quarterly for state unemployment insurance. Weekly federal income tax withholding per person is $70, and weekly state income tax withholding per person is $10.

INSTRUCTIONS

Prepare the entries to record the payment of a weekly salary and the quarterly remittance to the appropriate agencies. Base quarterly computations on 13 weeks, and assume that your computations are for the first quarter of a year.

14–32 Bonus Computation   Remington Company provides an incentive compensation plan under which the company president receives a bonus equal to 10% of the company's income in excess of $100,000 before income taxes are deducted but after the bonus is deducted.

INSTRUCTIONS

If income before tax and bonus is $320,000 and the effective tax rate is 40%, what amount should the bonus be?

14–33 Bonus Computation   Savannah Company's compensation agreement provides that each branch manager will receive an annual bonus of 10% of the branch's net income after taxes and bonus. The income tax rate is 40%. Branch manager A received $5,660.

INSTRUCTIONS

Determine the amount of Branch A's income before bonus and income tax.

14–34 Bonus Computation Fairview Company agrees to pay its sales manager a bonus of 6% of the company's earnings. Company income for the year before the bonus and taxes is $110,000. Income taxes are 40% of income after bonus.

INSTRUCTIONS

Compute the bonus in the following independent situations:

[a] Bonus is computed on income before bonus and income tax deductions.

[b] Bonus is computed on income after deduction for bonus but before deduction for income taxes.

[c] Bonus is computed on income before deduction for bonus but after deduction for income taxes.

[d] Bonus is computed on net income after deductions for both bonus and income taxes.

14–35 Warranty Merced Corporation grants a one-year warranty with each machine it sells. Expenses during the warranty period average $2,500. Merced sells a machine for $110,000 cash on July 1, 1995. The Product Warranty Expense account is debited at the time of sale.

INSTRUCTIONS

Prepare the entries to record the sale and subsequent payment of $1,870 on October 17, 1995, for service covered by the warranty.

14–36 Warranty In 1995 Atlantic Corporation began selling a new line of products with a two-year warranty against defects. Based on past experience, the estimated warranty costs related to dollar sales are first year of warranty, 2%; second year of warranty, 5%. Sales and actual warranty expenditures for 1995 and 1996 are presented below.

	1995	1996
Sales	$500,000	$700,000
Actual warranty expenditures	10,000	30,000

INSTRUCTIONS

Determine the estimated warranty liability at the end of 1995 and 1996.

14–37 Premium Liability Better Foods Company includes two coupons in each box of corn flakes. It offers a free kitchen utensil with 15 coupons. In 1995 Better Foods purchased 6,500 kitchen utensils at $1.10 each and sold 115,000 boxes of corn flakes. In 1995, customers redeemed 47,325 coupons. Management estimates that 65% of the coupons will be redeemed.

INSTRUCTIONS

Prepare the general journal entries to record the premium plan for 1995.

14–38 Contingent Liability Grace Company was named the defendant in a legal action. The plaintiff is asking for $500,000 in damages. The initial judgment called for $220,000 in favor of the plaintiff. Grace attorneys have appealed the case as of December 31, 1995, and expect a reversal due to errors in law and fact in the original judgment.

INSTRUCTIONS

Describe how, if at all, the financial claim resulting from this suit should be recorded on the books and disclosed in the financial statements at the end of 1995.

14–39 Contingent Liability TD Company sells football helmets. In 1995 TD discovered a defect in the helmets, which has led to lawsuits that are reasonably estimated to result in losses of $750,000. Based on its own experience and that of similar enterprises, TD believes that additional lawsuits reasonably estimated to result in losses of $1,500,000 will probably occur, even though the parties that will bring suit are not identifiable at this time.

INSTRUCTIONS

Determine the amount of expense, if any, that should be charged to income in 1995 as a result of this situation.

14–40 General Current Liabilities The following items represent common liabilities recorded on the books of an ordinary business corporation.

[1] Dividends
[2] Purchase commitments
[3] Purchase of goods on credit

[4] Officers' salaries
[5] Special bonus to employees

INSTRUCTIONS

[a] When should each item be recorded as a liability?

[b] Prepare *pro forma* entries (accounts only) to record these items as liabilities.

14–41 Current Portion of Long-Term Debt   Watson Corporation purchased a new home office building on August 1, 1995. To pay for the building, the company secured a $430,000, 12% mortgage to be repaid over 25 years with monthly payments of $4,528.90, payable on the first of each month. Each payment includes interest for the previous month.

INSTRUCTIONS

Determine how this mortgage should be shown in Watson's December 31, 1995, balance sheet, assuming the first payment is made on September 1, 1995.

PROBLEMS

 14–42 Balance Sheet Presentation   The following information about Marvin Company is available at December 31, 1995:

[1] Employee income taxes withheld, $900.

[2] Cash balance at First State Bank, $2,500.

[3] Cash overdraft at Harbor Bank, $1,350.

[4] Accounts receivable with credit balance, $2,850.

[5] Estimated expenses of meeting warranties on merchandise previously sold, $3,200.

[6] Estimated damages as a result of unsatisfactory performance on a contract, $1,250.

[7] Accounts payable, $29,750.

[8] Dividends in arrears on preferred stock, $25,000.

[9] Deferred serial bonds of $500,000, issued at par and bearing interest at 10%, payable in semi-annual installments of $50,000, due April 1 and October 1 of each year; the last bond to be paid on October 1, 2002. Interest is also paid semiannually.

[10] Par value of capital stock to be distributed as a result of a stock dividend, $40,000.

INSTRUCTIONS

[a] Prepare the current liability section of the balance sheet for Marvin Company on December 31, 1995.

[b] Briefly explain those items that you have *not* included among the current liabilities, citing reasons for their exclusion.

14–43 General Current Liabilities   The following information is available for Jamison Company for 1995:

Sales on Account. The total for the year is $201,400 (including sales tax of 6%). Accounts receivable totaling $35,800 remain uncollected at the end of the year. Seventy percent of the sales tax had been remitted by the end of 1995.

Cash Dividend. The sum of $15,000 is declared on December 1, 1995, to be paid in January 1996. Jamison's accounting period ends on December 31.

Machinery Purchased. A noninterest-bearing, $34,200 note was issued on December 31, 1995, payable in one year to acquire machinery. (An appropriate interest rate for the note is 14%.)

Note Payable. A $7,500, one-year note was discounted at the bank at 10% on November 2, 1995, to provide cash for current operations.

INSTRUCTIONS

[a] Prepare all general journal entries required to record the preceding information.

[b] Prepare the current liability section of the 1995 balance sheet for the Jamison Company, assuming that additional current liabilities are as follows:

Accounts payable	$15,200
Wages payable	10,600
Payroll taxes payable	2,150

 14–44 General Current Liabilities   Hanford Company, a calendar-year company, was involved in several transactions during 1995 that potentially involved current liabilities. These are described below.

[1] The company made two purchases of merchandise in the last half of December. The first, for $15,500, was made on December 15, subject to terms 2/10, n/30. It has not been paid at year-end. The second, for $18,800, was made on December 28, subject to terms 1/10, n/20. It has not been

paid by year-end, but management intends to pay the invoice within the discount period. The company maintains a periodic inventory system and records purchases at the net amount.

[2] On October 16, the company borrowed $10,000 from Golden State Bank by issuing a $10,000, 14% note, due one year from the date of issuance.

[3] Accrued wages for the last three days of December totaled $12,500 before the following withholdings:

Income tax	$1,560
FICA tax	875

The company must match the amount withheld from employees for FICA tax and remit both portions to the IRS.

[4] Dividends declared on December 31, 1995, payable on January 31, 1996, were $1 per share. The company has 54,250 shares of stock outstanding.

[5] On November 8, 1995, a customer signed an agreement for Hanford to produce certain specialty items to the customer's specifications. The items are currently under construction and are expected to be delivered in January 1996. The total amount of the order is $17,500. The customer paid Hanford a 15% advance on November 8, when the agreement was reached.

INSTRUCTIONS

[a] Prepare the general journal entries to record the transactions described in items 1 through 5 through the end of 1995. Include any adjustments that would be necessary at December 31, 1995.

[b] Indicate the impact of each item on the current liability section of the December 31, 1995, balance sheet of Hanford Company.

14–45 Miscellaneous Liabilities Sullivan, Inc., a publisher, is preparing its December 31, 1995, financial statements and must determine the proper accounting treatment for each of the following situations:

[1] Sullivan sells subscriptions to several magazines for a one-year, two-year, or three-year period. Cash receipts from subscribers are credited to Magazine Subscriptions Collected in Advance. This account had a balance of $2,400,000 at December 31, 1995. Outstanding subscriptions at December 31, 1995, expire as follows:

During 1996	$600,000
During 1997	900,000
During 1998	400,000

[2] On January 2, 1995, Sullivan, a large publicly held company, discontinued collision, fire, and theft coverage on its delivery vehicles and became self-insured for these risks. Actual losses of $45,000 during 1995 were charged to Delivery Expense. The 1994 premium for the discontinued coverage amounted to $100,000. The controller wants to set up a reserve for self-insurance by a debit to Delivery Expense of $55,000 and a credit to Reserve for Self-Insurance of $55,000.

[3] An author filed a suit for breach of contract seeking damages of $1,500,000 against Sullivan on July 1, 1995. The company's legal counsel believes that an unfavorable outcome is probable. A reasonable estimate of the court's award to the plaintiff is between $250,000 and $500,000. No amount within this range is a better estimate of potential damages than any other amount.

[4] During December 1995, a competitor filed suit against Sullivan for industrial espionage, claiming $2,000,000 in damages. Management and company counsel believe it is reasonably possible that damages will be awarded to the plaintiff, although the amount cannot be reasonably estimated.

INSTRUCTIONS

Prepare the journal entries for 1–4 at December 31, 1995. If you believe that no entry is required, explain your reasoning. Show supporting computations in good form.

14–46 General Current Liabilities Included in Murphy Corporation's liability account balances at December 31, 1994, is the following:

Note payable, bank	$2,800,000

Transactions during 1995 and other information relating to Murphy's liabilities are as follows:

[1] The principal amount of the note payable above is $2,800,000 and bears interest at 15%. The note is dated April 1, 1994, and is payable in four equal annual installments of $700,000 beginning April 1, 1995. The first principal and interest payment was made on April 1, 1995.

[2] On July 1, 1995, Murphy issued for $1,774,000 a $2,000,000 face amount note to a wealthy stockholder. The note was dated July 1, 1995, and matures on July 1, 1996. No explicit interest is stated in the note and the entire face amount of the note is payable at the maturity date. Murphy uses the straight-line method of amortizing discount on this note because of its short life.

INSTRUCTIONS

[a] Prepare the current liabilities section of Murphy's balance sheet at December 31, 1995.
[b] Determine the interest expense to be reported during 1995.   (AICPA adapted)

14–47 Warranty Liability   Santa Ana Company, a manufacturer of heavy machinery, grants a four-year warranty on its products. The Estimated Liability for Product Warranty account shows the following transactions for the year:

Opening balance	$ 45,000
Provision (made at interim dates)	20,000
	65,000
Cost of servicing claims	(12,000)
Ending balance (before adjustment)	$ 53,000

A review of unsettled claims and the company's experience indicates that claims have averaged 2% of net sales per year.

The following additional information is available from the company's records at the end of the current year:

Gross sales	$2,040,000
Sales returns and allowances	40,000
Cost of goods sold	1,350,000

INSTRUCTIONS

[a] Prepare any necessary adjusting journal entries, giving effect to the proper accounting treatment of product warranties. Support any entries with clearly detailed computations. The books have not been closed.
[b] Identify the amount of the expense included in the determination of net income and the amount of the liability presented in the balance sheet for warranties.

14–48 Warranty Liability   Avalon Tube Company manufactures television tubes and sells them with a six-month guarantee under which defective tubes are replaced free of charge. On June 30, 1995, the Liability for Product Warranty account had a balance of $450,000. By December 31, 1995, this amount had been reduced to $50,000 by charges for tubes returned.

Avalon has operated for many years and has consistently experienced an 8% return rate. Due to the introduction of new models, the rate increased to 10% on October 1, 1995. It is assumed that no tubes sold during a given month are returned in that month. Each tube is stamped with a date at the time of sale so that the warranty indicates the likely pattern of returns during the six-month period, starting with the month following the sale.

Month Following Sale	Percent of Total Returns Expected During That Month
First	20
Second	30
Third	20
Fourth	10
Fifth	10
Sixth	10
Total	100

For example, for January sales, 20% of the returns are expected in February, 30% in March, and so on.

Gross sales of tubes for the second half of 1995 were

Month	Amount	Month	Amount
July	$3,600,000	October	$2,850,000
August	3,300,000	November	2,000,000
September	4,100,000	December	1,800,000

The company's warranty also covers the payment of freight cost on defective tubes returned and on new tubes sent as replacements. This freight cost is 10% of the sales price of the tubes returned. The manufacturing cost of the tube is roughly 75% of the sales price, and the salvage value of the returned tubes averages 25% of their sales price.

INSTRUCTIONS

[a] Compute the Product Warranty Liability account balance as of December 31, 1995.
[b] Prepare any adjusting entries necessary.

14–49 Coupon Liability This problem consists of two *independent* parts.
   Part 1. Nutriment Food Company distributed coupons to consumers that can be presented to grocers for discounts on some of its products. The grocers are reimbursed when they send Nutriment the coupons. In Nutriment's experience, 40% of such coupons are redeemed, and generally, one month elapses between the date a grocer receives a coupon from a consumer and the date Nutriment receives it. During 1995 Nutriment issued two separate series of coupons, as follows:

Date Issued	Total Value	Amount Disbursed on Redemption as of December 31, 1995
Jan. 1, 1995	$78,000	$22,700
July 1, 1995	93,000	29,900

INSTRUCTIONS

Determine the amount that should appear in the December 31, 1995, balance sheet as a liability for unredeemed coupons. Show all computations.
   Part 2. Heartland Cereals distributes coupons to consumers that can be presented to grocers for discounts on certain cereals, on or before a stated expiration date. The grocers are reimbursed when they send the coupons to Heartland. In the company's experience, 30% of such coupons are redeemed, and on the average, one month elapses between the date a grocer receives a coupon from the buyer and the date Heartland receives it. On May 1, 1995, Heartland issued coupons with a total value of $15,000 and an expiration date of December 31, 1995. As of December 31, 1995, Heartland had disbursed $3,000 to grocers for these coupons.

INSTRUCTIONS

[a] Prepare the general journal entries to record these transactions.
[b] Briefly explain the error(s) that would exist in the financial statements if Heartland recognized the coupon expense only at the time it disbursed cash to grocers.

14–50 Coupon Liability Mrs. Stone Company manufactures a packaged pancake mix. The company offers a free spatula to customers who send in three proofs of purchase. The following data have been accumulated:

	1995	1996
Pancake mix sales ($1.25 per box)	$600,000	$500,000
Number of spatulas purchased ($.85 per spatula)	17,000	15,000
Number of spatulas distributed as premiums	16,500	12,750
Spatulas estimated to be distributed in subsequent periods	4,000	2,500
Mailing costs are $.30 per spatula		

INSTRUCTIONS

[a] Prepare the general journal entries necessary to record sales, premium purchases, redemptions, and year-end adjustments.
[b] Give the account balances that would appear in the income statements and balance sheets for 1995 and 1996.

14–51 Token Liability Rapid Transit Authority sells tokens good for one bus ride at $.50 each. Sales for 1995 are as follows:

Month	Tokens Sold	Month	Tokens Sold
January	19,500	July	18,000
February	20,000	August	20,500
March	21,000	September	30,000
April	23,000	October	28,000
May	22,000	November	25,000
June	26,000	December	23,500

Past experience has shown that 70% of the tokens are used on the month of sale, 15% in the following month, and 10% in the next. Five percent of tokens are unused and void after six months.

INSTRUCTIONS

[a] Prepare the entries for 1995, assuming a liability account is credited when the tokens are sold.
[b] Prepare the entries for 1995, assuming a revenue account is credited when the tokens are sold.

14–52 (Appendix A) General Current Liabilities Young Folks, Inc., produced quality children's apparel for over 25 years. The company's fiscal year is from April 1 to March 31. The following information relates to the obligations of Young Folks as of March 31, 1995:

Bonds Payable.   The company issued $4,000,000 of 7% bonds on July 1, 1989, at 98, which yielded proceeds of $3,920,000. The bonds will mature on July 1, 1999. Interest is paid semiannually on July 1 and January 1. Young Folks uses the straight-line method to amortize the bond discount.

Notes Payable.   Young Folks has signed several long-term notes with financial institutions and insurance companies. The maturities of these notes are given below. The total unpaid interest for all of these notes amounts to $90,000 on March 31, 1995.

Due Date	Amount Due
Apr. 1, 1995	$ 100,000
July 1, 1995	200,000
Oct. 1, 1995	100,000
Jan. 1, 1996	200,000
Apr. 1, 1996–Mar. 31, 1997	600,000
Apr. 1, 1997–Mar. 31, 1998	400,000
Apr. 1, 1998–Mar. 31, 1999	400,000
Apr. 1, 1999–Mar. 31, 2000	500,000
Apr. 1, 2000–Mar. 31, 2001	500,000
	$3,000,000

Estimated Warranties.   Young Folks has a one-year product warranty on selected items. The estimated warranty liability on sales made during the 1994 fiscal year and still outstanding as of March 31, 1994, amounted to $55,000. The warranty costs on sales made from April 1, 1994, through March 31, 1995, are estimated at $145,000. The actual warranty costs incurred during the current 1995 fiscal year are as follows:

Warranty claims honored on 1994 sales	$ 55,000
Warranty claims honored on 1995 sales	75,000
	$130,000

ADDITIONAL INFORMATION

[1] **Trade payables.**   Accounts payable for supplies, goods, and services purchased on open account amount to $325,000 as of March 31, 1995.
[2] **Payroll related items.**   The following outstanding obligations relate to Young Folks' payroll as of March 31, 1995.

Accrued salaries and wages	$145,000
FICA taxes	15,000
State and federal income taxes withheld from employees	30,000
Other payroll deductions	3,000

[3] **Taxes.** The following taxes are incurred but not due until the next fiscal year:

State and federal income taxes	$250,000
Property taxes	100,000
Sales and use taxes	185,000

[4] **Miscellaneous accruals.** Other accruals not separately classified amount to $50,000 as of March 31, 1995.

[5] **Dividends.** On March 15, 1995, the company's board of directors declared a cash dividend of $.40 per common share and a 10% common stock dividend. Both dividends were to be distributed on April 12, 1995, to the common stockholders of record at the close of business on March 31, 1995. Data regarding Young Folks' common stock are as follows:

Par value	$5 per share
Number of shares issued and outstanding	2,500,000 shares
Market value of common stock	
Mar. 15, 1995	$22.00 per share
Mar. 31, 1995	$21.50 per share
Apr. 12, 1995	$22.50 per share

INSTRUCTIONS

[a] Prepare the current liability section of the balance sheet for Young Folks, Inc., as of March 31, 1995, as it should appear in the annual report to stockholders.

[b] If you excluded any items from the presentation of current liabilities, explain why you did so.

(CMA adapted)

14–53 Current Liabilities—Classification Cromwell, Inc., is planning to refinance certain short-term obligations on a long-term basis. The company has a December 31 year-end; 1995 financial statements will be published on March 15, 1996. At December 31, 1995, before the reclassification of short-term debt, the liabilities and stockholders' equity sections of the company's balance sheet appear as follows.

Liabilities and Stockholders' Equity		
	1995	**1994**
Current liabilities		
Accounts payable	$ 7,000,000	$ 5,000,000
Notes payable to banks	12,000,000	4,000,000
Accrued liabilities	4,000,000	4,500,000
Total current liabilities	23,000,000	13,500,000
Long-term debt	4,000,000	3,000,000
Total liabilities	27,000,000	16,500,000
Stockholders' equity		
Common stock ($1 par value; authorized 4,000,000 shares; issued 2,000,000 shares in 1995 and 1994)	2,000,000	2,000,000
Paid-in capital in excess of par value	1,000,000	1,000,000
Retained earnings	6,000,000	5,000,000
Total stockholders' equity	9,000,000	8,000,000
Total liabilities and stockholders' equity	$36,000,000	$24,500,000

The company intends to refinance $9,000,000 of the $12,000,000 notes payable on a long-term basis. Although the entire $12,000,000 is due on June 30, 1996, the bank has informally agreed to extend the maturity date for up to $6,000,000 of this amount to June 30, 1997, if necessary. On January 31, 1996, the company issues 1,000,000 additional shares of the $1 par value common stock for $4,000,000 ($4 per share). After issue costs and underwriting fees, the company's net proceeds from the stock issuance were $3,500,000. On February 15, 1996, the company entered a financing agreement with a financially capable commercial bank, permitting the company to borrow up to $3,000,000 at the bank's prime interest rate. Borrowings, available at the company's option after April 1, 1996, will mature five years after the loan date. The lender can cancel the agreement only if the company's retained earnings drop below $750,000. The company must also maintain compensating balances equal to 10% of the amount borrowed.

Cromwell, Inc., uses the entire proceeds of the sale of the common stock to retire part of the current notes payable and now intends to draw down the entire available commitment of five-year debt on April 1, 1996. The company plans to refinance the rest of the notes before June 30, 1996, and is currently negotiating with various lenders.

INSTRUCTIONS

[a] Prepare the liabilities and stockholders' equity sections of Cromwell's comparative balance sheet as of December 31, 1995 and 1994, after any necessary reclassifications based on the preceding information. The statements are issued on March 15, 1996.
[b] Describe any financial statement disclosures that should be made based on this information.

CASES

14–54 Classification of Liabilities The following items are listed under "liabilities" on the balance sheet of Costa Mesa Industrial Company on December 31, 1995:

Accounts payable	$ 300,000
Notes payable	400,000
Bonds payable	1,040,000

Accounts payable represent obligations to suppliers that were due in January 1996. Notes payable mature during 1996. However, the company expects to refinance the notes. Bonds payable mature on July 1, 1996.

These liabilities must be reported on the balance sheet in accordance with GAAP governing the classification of liabilities as current and noncurrent.

INSTRUCTIONS

[a] What is the general rule for determining whether a liability is classified as current or noncurrent?
[b] Under what conditions may any of Costa Mesa Industrial Company's liabilities be classified as noncurrent? Explain your answer. (CMA adapted)

14–55 Contingent Liabilities—Litigation In May 1995 Albright Company became involved in litigation. As a result, Albright will probably have to pay $1,400,000. In July 1995, a competitor commenced a suit against Albright, alleging violation of antitrust laws and seeking damages of $2,200,000. Albright denies the allegations, and the likelihood that Albright will pay or sustain any damages is remote. In September 1995, Marion County brought action against Albright for $1,800,000 for polluting Lake Cachuma. It is reasonably possible that Marion County will be successful in its vigorous suit; however, the amount of damages Albright will have to pay is not reasonably estimable.

INSTRUCTIONS

[a] What amount, if any, should be accrued by a charge to income in 1995?
[b] Prepare any disclosures that Albright Company should make with respect to the pollution suit.

14–56 Contingent Liabilities—Litigation The sole operations of Firmin, Inc., consist of the manufacture and sale of water skis. Several uncertainties surround certain aspects of Firmin's operations for the year ended December 31, 1995. As head of Firmin's accounting department, you must determine the effect of each of these uncertainties on the company's annual financial statements. Of primary concern are the following situations.

[1] During tight turns, the skeg (keel) of the company's top-line slalom ski has a tendency to pop off and skim across the water. In the past year 10 people are known to have been hospitalized with head injuries as a result of this defect. Legal counsel believes that although no claims have been made yet, a class action suit will probably be filed soon, and although successful prosecution is unlikely, the company will probably sustain losses of $250,000.

[2] In October 1995, a worker was injured in the manufacturing plant in an accident partially the result of his own negligence. The worker has sued Firmin for $1,000,000. Counsel believes it is reasonably possible that the outcome of the action will be unfavorable and that the settlement will cost the company from $125,000 to $500,000.

INSTRUCTIONS

Discuss the appropriate accounting treatment, including any required disclosures in each circumstance. Provide the basis and logic of your conclusions.

14–57 Reclassification of Debt Gregory Corporation has notes payable of $1,500,000 among its liabilities at December 31, 1995. These notes are due as follows:

Due Date	Amount
May 1, 1996	$250,000
Oct. 1, 1996	650,000
Nov. 1, 1996	600,000

The company is considering the appropriate balance sheet classification of the liabilities at December 31, 1995, and has asked your advice.

INSTRUCTIONS

[a] Discuss briefly the conditions that must be met for short-term obligations to be excluded from the current liabilities in the balance sheet.

[b] Under each of the following independent situations, indicate your recommendation for the proper balance sheet classification of the notes payable.

[1] At March 15, 1996, before the 1995 financial statements are issued, the company is actively seeking opportunities to refinance the total $1,500,000 on a long-term basis.

[2] On March 1, 1996, before the 1995 financial statements are issued, a bank formally commits to refinance the $250,000 short-term note due on May 1, 1996. The bank has indicated its plans to consider Gregory's request to refinance the remainder of its short-term debt on a long-term basis as those obligations come due. The final decision will depend on Gregory's financial situation at the due dates of the short-term obligations.

[3] On February 1, 1996, before the 1995 financial statements are issued, the company issues 500,000 shares of capital stock at $1.25 per share. The funds are to be used to refinance the short-term debt as it comes due during 1996. The company plans another issue of stock before November 1, 1996.

[4] On February 1, 1996, before the 1995 financial statements are issued, the company enters into a long-term agreement with a local bank to refinance its short-term debt on a long-term basis. The agreement provides for refinancing up to $2,000,000 and requires the company to maintain a $50,000 cash balance with the bank.

[c] Define *current liability*. Why is it logical, in light of this definition, to exclude certain short-term obligations from current liabilities, even though they may come due very soon after the date of the financial statements?

14–58 Contingent Liabilities—Warranties Sir Maxwell Company sells two types of merchandise: collars and doghouse kits. Each carries a one-year warranty. The following is known about each warranty:

[1] Collars—Product warranty costs, based on past experience, will normally be 1% of sales.

[2] Doghouse kits—Product warranty costs cannot be reasonably estimated because this is a new product line. However, the chief engineer believes that product warranty costs are likely to be incurred.

INSTRUCTIONS

How should Sir Maxwell report the estimated product warranty costs for each of the two types of merchandise above? Explain your answer. Do not discuss disclosures that should be made in Sir Maxwell's financial statements or notes. Be sure to discuss any issues related to revenue recognition in light of the information provided about the warranty programs.   (AICPA adapted)

14–59 Contingent Liabilities—Various Playhouse Company manufactures toys. During the year, the following situations arose:

[1] A safety hazard related to one of its toy products was discovered. It is considered probable that liabilities have been incurred. Based on past experience, a reasonable estimate of the amount of loss can be made.

[2] One of its small warehouses is located on the bank of a river and could no longer be insured against flood losses. No flood losses have occurred after the date that the insurance became unavailable; however, such losses are highly probable.

[3] This year, Playhouse began promoting a new toy by including a coupon redeemable for a movie ticket in each toy's carton. The movie ticket, which cost Playhouse $2, is purchased in advance and then mailed to the customer when Playhouse receives the coupon. Playhouse estimated, based on past experience, that 60% of the coupons would be redeemed. Forty percent of the coupons were actually redeemed this year, and the remaining 20% of the coupons are expected to be redeemed next year.

INSTRUCTIONS

[a] How should Playhouse report the safety hazard? Why?

[b] How should Playhouse report the noninsurable flood risk? Why?

[c] How should Playhouse account for the toy promotion campaign in this year? (AICPA adapted)

14–60 Contingent Liabilities—Litigation Edgemont Company is being sued for $2,000,000 for an injury caused to a visitor as a result of alleged negligence while the individual was touring the Edgemont plant in March 1996. The suit was filed in July 1996. Edgemont's lawyer states that it is probable that Edgemont will lose the suit and be found liable for a judgment costing anywhere from $200,000 to $900,000. However, the lawyer states that the most probable judgment is $400,000.

INSTRUCTIONS

[a] How should Edgemont report the suit in its 1996 financial statements? Discuss the rationale for your answer. Include in your answer any disclosures that should be made in Edgemont's financial statements or notes.

[b] Assume that Edgemont is a large public company and has decided to allow its insurance coverage to expire for personal injuries to employees, customers, and others such as the visitor in the case. What disclosures, if any, would you recommend in the financial statements of Edgemont to inform readers of this decision? (AICPA adapted)

JUDGMENT CASES

14–61 Estimating a Contingent Liability Preferred Health Maintenance Organization (PHMO) provides a full range of prepaid health care services to its subscribers. PHMO has approximately 1,000,000 subscribers who are generally enrolled through group plans. In exchange for enrollment fees, usually paid by employers, members and their dependents are entitled to almost unlimited medical care at no additional charge, except for a nominal fee charged for medications.

Although PHMO offers a wide range of health services through its extensive network of clinics and hospitals, members must sometimes be referred to other health care providers. In addition, it may be necessary for some outside providers to render extended care for critically ill patients for whom PHMO is not equipped to treat. These outside referrals are often necessary when a member has a specialized medical need that his or her local PHMO clinic is not equipped to provide. A referral may also be necessary in an emergency situation when a member cannot reach a PHMO clinic on a timely basis. In such cases, the outside provider must verify the referral by calling a 24-hour telephone line to receive a billing code. Granting such a billing code authorizes the outside provider to treat the PHMO member and bill PHMO for its services.

PHMO keeps a record of billing codes granted, including the date of initial care provided by the outsider, the membership account number, the type of provider, and the identity of the provider. Billing codes on statements received from outside providers are matched against this record to verify that authorization for service was granted. However, no system exists for identifying billing codes for which services may have been provided and unbilled at any point in time. The amounts corresponding to the unbilled services may be quite significant in relation to the financial statements of PHMO.

Outside providers have varied systems for billing PHMO. Large providers may have reciprocal arrangements with PHMO, or they may provide services on a fixed fee basis. Small providers may bill secondary health insurance or Medicare initially and then bill PHMO for any remaining amounts unpaid by the other insurers. Some providers may bill PHMO at the same time they bill other insurers and later refund any duplicate or overpayments to PHMO. Some providers may require the patient to pay before treatment and reimburse the patient upon receipt of PHMO's payment.

As the controller of PHMO, you must determine the appropriate accounting treatment for these incurred but not reported (IBNR) claims against PHMO at the time the year-end financial statements are issued, generally within 45 days after close of the calendar year.

INSTRUCTIONS

Discuss the problems associated with accounting for the IBNR liability at year-end. Develop a method for estimating the liability for IBNR claims, if any, that should be accrued as of year-end. Discuss any contingent liability associated with injuries sustained prior to year-end for services that may be performed after year-end by outside providers.

14–62 Disclosing Unasserted Claims Cosco Company, a limited partnership formed last year, has just realized that the process of its formation violated certain laws and regulations of the Securities and Exchange Commission (SEC). Specifically, interests in the partnership were offered to too many individuals, thereby requiring the sale of partnership interest to come under the SEC's registration requirements. Cosco's top management was unaware of the legal limitation on the number of investors at the time the partnership was formed and has just been informed of the violation by its legal counsel. Cosco had requested legal counsel to research the propriety of some planned distributions to the limited partners and, in so doing, the attorneys then realized the problems in the formation of the partnership. The primary result of this finding is that it provides the investors in the limited partnership a right of recission; that is, the right to get their investments back from the partnership. In addition, according to the law, the partnership is required to file an offering document under the securities laws and to register Cosco appropriately.

Cosco's president and you, the controller, are attempting to determine the effects of this matter, if any, on its annual financial statements. The president, a former practicing CPA, suggests, "This seems like an unasserted claim to me. That is, the investors have not indicated an awareness of their rights to proceed in making a claim for recision of their investment. According to my recollection of *FASB Statement No. 5,* we are not required to disclose such events unless it is already probable that the investors will find out about their rights to proceed notwithstanding any disclosures in our financial statements. Therefore, I say 'Mum's the word!' We'll straighten all this out next year in any event. I was already thinking about forming a new corporation, registering it with the SEC, and having all the limited partners contribute their interests in exchange for stock. That way, we can accomplish the same thing as we would with a recision offer without all the alarming aspects of making a recision offer for no real reason but some little legal technicalities. So, I expect you to go ahead with the annual financial statements on a 'business as usual basis' without sounding any unnecessary alarms."

INSTRUCTIONS

What should you do? Be sure to consider the guidance about the disclosure of unasserted claims contained in *FASB Statement No. 5,* "Accounting for Contingencies."

14–63 Estimating Returns Gridley Manufacturing, Inc., a manufacturer of office equipment, has adopted a program to boost sales by sponsoring a number of limited partnerships that will acquire its equipment and lease that equipment to companies on a temporary basis. Gridley acts as the general partner for the limited partnerships and has the responsibility for marketing the equipment leases to customers. According to the terms of the partnership agreement, Gridley has agreed to repurchase the equipment from the limited partners at the end of three years at its then fair value at the option of the individual partners unless Gridley communicates to the partners in writing within six months of the original investment that it will not continue to act as the general partner. The president of Gridley has indicated that he expects the company to act as the general partner throughout the three-year period covered by the agreement.

Although the equipment will be in used condition at the end of three years, Gridley has stated in the offering documents that because the equipment is expected to be "out on rental" at the end of three years, thus providing an income stream, its fair value may well exceed its original cost. A sample calculation was provided that indicated a present value of future rentals at the end of three years that would exceed the original cost of the equipment. The offering document further stated that "fair value is to be determined by independent appraisal." During the past year, several of these partnerships have been funded and the equipment "sold" to the partnerships. Most of the individual partners are physicians and other skilled health care professionals.

You are the accountant for Gridley and are attempting to account for the sales of equipment to the partnerships. In particular, you are wondering how you should account for the repurchase provision (put option) available to the individual limited partners.

INSTRUCTIONS

Assess the provisions of the investment contracts and the offering documents and develop a method of accounting for the right of the individual partners to return the equipment to Gridley. Be sure to describe all of the factors that you considered in developing your suggested solution.

14–64 Accounting for Contingent Liabilities Colorful Paint Company, Inc., just learned that the method it used to dispose of solvents for a number of prior years is now considered to pose a significant health risk to the ground water supplying a nearby municipality. The U.S. Environmental Protection Agency has instructed the company to refine all of the soil at the dump site and to pay a material fine. The costs of the cleanup cannot be precisely determined in advance, but the company believes that it will be from $500,000 to perhaps $1,000,000. At the end of the reporting period, the company agreed to the cleanup and to pay the $50,000 fine; however, it had begun none of the activities necessary to clean up the contamination.

INSTRUCTIONS

How should these environmental contamination treatment costs be reported? Be sure to include in your answer whether a liability should be recognized at the end of the current year and whether any of the costs can be capitalized.

FINANCIAL REPORTING CASE

14–65 Financial Reporting Case Bristol-Myers Squibb Company is a major U.S. Corporation in the health-care industry. While the company is involved in many dimensions of this important industry, it is probably best known for its role in four core businesses: pharmaceuticals, consumer products, medical devices, and nutritionals. Included among the company's consumer products are Excedrin, Comtrex, and Bufferin.

Following is the liabilities section of the balance sheet and the disclosure of contingencies from Bristol-Myers Squibb Company's 1993 financial statements.

Liabilities
Current Liabilities:

Short-term borrowings	**$ 177**	$ 375	$ 553
Accounts payable	**649**	562	537
Accrued expenses	**1,550**	1,422	1,167
U.S. and foreign income taxes payable	**689**	941	495
Total Current Liabilities	**3,065**	3,300	2,752
Product Liability	**1,370**	63	65
Other Liabilities	**1,138**	1,245	669
Long-Term Debt	**588**	176	135
Total Liabilities	**6,161**	4,784	3,621

Note 18 Contingencies

Various lawsuits, claims, and proceedings of a nature considered normal to its businesses are pending against the company and certain of its subsidiaries. The most significant of these are described below.

As of December 31, 1993, approximately 10,000 plaintiffs have filed suit against the company, its subsidiary, Medical Engineering Corporation, and certain other subsidiaries, in federal and state courts and in certain Canadian provincial courts, alleging damages for personal injuries of various types resulting from polyurethane covered breast implants and smooth walled breast implants. Certain of these cases are class actions which seek to allege claims on behalf of all breast implant recipients. All federal court actions have been consolidated for pretrial proceedings in Federal District Court in Birmingham, Alabama. . . .

The company is a defendant in a number of actions brought against it and other pharmaceutical companies in federal and state courts by the children or grandchildren of women who ingested diethylstilbestrol (DES), a product which had been, but is no longer, manufactured or sold by an affiliate of the company.

The company is a defendant in several state antitrust actions (one of which has been removed to federal court) filed on behalf of purported classes of individual purchasers of infant formula products, and by one State Attorney General, alleging a conspiracy regarding pricing of infant formula products and other violations of state antitrust or deceptive trade practice laws and seeking treble damages, statutory and civil penalties, and injunctive relief. Six other state Attorneys General and the Canadian Bureau of Competitive Policy have commenced or stated an intention to commence investigations of pricing practices and marketing activities in the infant formula industry. The company is also a defendant in two federal court actions, one filed by the State of Louisiana on behalf of indirect purchasers of infant formula alleging a conspiracy regarding pricing of infant formula products and seeking treble damages, civil penalties and injunctive relief and the other filed by Nestlé Food Company alleging anticompetitive practices in violation of federal and state antitrust or other laws and seeking treble damages, civil penalties, and injunctive relief.

As of December 31, 1993, the company was a defendant with other major pharmaceutical manufacturers and drug wholesalers in 25 actions brought in various federal courts by retail pharmacies, individually or as representatives of purported class actions, which allege anticompetitive or unfair practices in the pricing and distribution of pharmaceuticals in violation of federal and state laws and which seek treble damages and injunctive relief. As of December 31, 1993, the company was also a co-defendant in four state court actions in California brought by retail pharmacies, individually or as representatives of purported class actions, which allege discrimination in the pricing of pharmaceuticals in violation of California laws and which seek treble damages and injunctive relief.

The company is a defendant in a purported class action filed in June 1992 in the U.S. District Court for the Southern District of New York alleging violations of federal securities laws and regulations in connection with, among other things, earnings projections.

The company, together with others, is a party to, or otherwise involved in, a number of proceedings brought by the Environmental Protection Agency under the Comprehensive Environmental Response, Compensation and Liability Act (CERCLA or Superfund) directed at the cleanup of Superfund sites.

While it is not possible to predict with certainty the outcome of these cases, it is the opinion of management that all lawsuits, claims and proceedings which are pending against the company are without merit or will not have a material adverse effect on the company's consolidated financial position.

INSTRUCTIONS

[a] Identify the major contingencies that are disclosed in Note 18 of Bristol-Myers Squibb Company's 1993 financial statements.

[b] From the balance sheet excerpt and Note 18, can you determine whether these contingencies have been recorded, or are they simply disclosed in note form? Explain.

[c] If you were analyzing the Bristol-Myers Squibb company's financial statement, how would you use the information found in Note 18?

Long-Term Debt

OBJECTIVES

1. To emphasize the distinction between long-term and current liabilities.
2. To describe the nature of bonds, notes payable, and various types of debt instruments.
3. To apply acceptable financial accounting and reporting practices to the issuance and reacquisition or retirement of debt.
4. To discuss why premium and discount frequently arise on long-term debt.
5. To account for premium and discount on long-term debt, including amortization and balance sheet presentation.
6. To apply acceptable financial accounting and reporting practices to convertible debt and debt with detachable stock-purchase rights.
7. To recognize that many securities contain complex provisions that complicate financial accounting and reporting classification and measurement.

Long-term debt can have a tremendous effect on a company's operations and financial reports. The role of debt in financing a company is controversial and continues to evolve. Historically, the terms of most bonds have not extended beyond 20 to 30 years. During 1993, however, Coca-Cola and Walt Disney companies departed from this well-established pattern. Both of these corporations issued bonds with terms of 100 years. And, six other companies sold over $1.9 billion of 50-year debt instruments. In addition, the companies were able to obtain this extremely long-term financing at surprisingly low rates.

According to one business publication, "Most newspaper accounts said the investors [in these very long-term securities] were crazy because nobody knows what the companies will look like in 100 years and because they got relatively slim yield premiums above U.S. Treasuries to take the risk. These perpetual securities are none other than fixed-rate preferred stock, a long-time investment staple." Acquiring preferred stock, like all other investments, is a good deal only if the price is right. Although many question the wisdom of investing in these very long-term bonds, the companies were delighted and, according to *Barron's,* the Disney company was able to raise twice as much money as expected.

Andrew Bary, *Barron's* (August 2, 1993), p. 42.

Most companies rely, at least to some extent, on long-term debt as a method to finance operations. Of course, equity investments contributed by owners are also important sources of long-term financing. The decision to support long-term operational needs, such as the acquisition of property, plant, and equipment, by issuing debt rather than raising funds through equity financing is a complex one and receives substantial attention in finance courses. Generally, companies attempt to secure resources at the lowest possible cost. Thus, many combinations of debt and equity financing are commonly encountered in practice.

In this chapter, we focus primarily on financial accounting and reporting for several types of long-term debt rather than on the decision to incur debt. The following section considers, among other things, the characteristics that distinguish current liabilities from long-term debt and those that separate debt from equity securities.

As we begin our study of long-term debt, turn to the balance sheet of Kellogg Company on the inside front cover of your text. Notice the large amounts of noncurrent liabilities, particularly long-term debt, included in the liability section. Many of the details of the individual debt issues making up those total amounts are presented in note 6 to the financial statements included in the appendix at the end of this book. Also, briefly review the statement of earnings also inside the front cover of your text and notice interest expense included in the determination of net income. Those items are the end result of the accounting process for long-term debt that is described in this chapter.

THE NATURE AND CHARACTERISTICS OF DEBT

DEBT/EQUITY DISTINCTIONS

The distinction between debt and equity instruments is sometimes hazy; however, certain distinguishing characteristics are usually evident. Generally, **debt instruments** contain a maturity date that establishes the time at which the face value of the debt must be repaid to the lender. Furthermore, debt instruments usually bear interest that must be paid periodically, regardless of the profitability of the borrowing company. Classifying financial instruments with such features as debt informs financial statement users of future cash outflows that will be necessary without regard to the results of operations or management discretion.

Equity securities, conversely, usually do not have maturity dates and therefore do not require redemption by the issuing company. Dividends are not paid on equity securities except at the discretion of the issuing company's board of directors.

During the last 20 years many new and complex financial instruments that contain attributes of both debt and equity securities have been introduced. Corporations have turned to creative financing to secure long-term resources at the lowest possible cost. Complex securities have characteristics of both debt and equity and include convertible bonds that are exchangeable for stock at the option of the bondholder, income bonds requiring the payment of interest only if income is earned, redeemable stock that may require reacquisition at the discretion of the investor, and participating mortgages, whose maturity amounts change in relation to some other factor such as the fair value of underlying collateral.

Substance over Form

As is the case in other areas of accounting, the determination of whether a given financing instrument represents debt or equity is based on substance rather than form. In practice, most companies account for a security as debt if it (1) requires the periodic payment of interest and (2) contains a fixed maturity date (or allows redemption at the discretion of the investor [lender]). Conversely, a security containing neither of these characteristics is generally classified as some type of corporate stockholders' equity. The determination of whether a particular security is debt or equity to the issuing enterprise can, nevertheless, be complex and require substantial judgment. In recognition of the difficulties faced by practitioners in accounting for a variety of financial instruments, the FASB initiated a project to provide much needed guidance. One part of that project deals with distinguishing between debt and equity instruments. At the time of this writing, the FASB has progressed only to the stage of issuing a discussion memorandum on that topic.[1] This project is now well underway.

Once we have classified a particular security as some type of debt, we must then further classify the item as either current or long term.

---

[1]FASB Discussion Memorandum, "Distinguishing between Liability and Equity Instruments and Accounting for Instruments with Characteristics of Both," 1990.

CURRENT AND LONG-TERM DEBT

Although Chapter 14 discussed the characteristics that distinguish between **current liabilities** and **long-term debt,** a brief review is useful. The accounting profession has defined the characteristics of current liabilities; other debt not containing those attributes is classified as long term.

Generally, if the satisfaction of a liability is expected to require presently existing working capital, or if a liability is due on demand within one year from the date of the balance sheet, a current classification is appropriate. Other liabilities not expected to require presently existing working capital for repayment are classified as long term. Remember that a primary objective of reporting and classifying liabilities is to provide information about the magnitude and timing of future cash outflows. Classifying liabilities as either current or long term contributes to meeting this objective. Not all liabilities that mature within one year, however, are expected to require the use of cash that is currently on hand or that is expected to become available through successful operations. Thus, even if a liability matures in the near future, we may consider it noncurrent if resources other than current assets are used to extinguish the debt. For example, a company may have established a sinking fund to retire a bond issue. You will recall that special funds, such as bond-redemption sinking funds, are classified as noncurrent investments. The bonds that will be redeemed with the assets in the sinking fund are classified in a manner consistent with the sinking fund. Therefore, bonds to be retired with sinking-fund assets classified as noncurrent are considered noncurrent liabilities, even if the bonds mature in the very near future. Some noncancelable financing agreements may also cause accountants to classify a liability with a current maturity date as a long-term debt.

Certain types of long-term liabilities are considered elsewhere in this book. Specifically, accounting and reporting for lease and postretirement liabilities of employees are discussed in Chapters 23 and 24, respectively. Contingent liabilities, some of which may be noncurrent, are discussed in Chapter 14. This chapter discusses a variety of long-term bonds and notes payable. Because accounting and reporting problems associated with bonds and notes are similar, the discussion centers primarily on bonds. Remember, however, that the underlying ideas apply to both notes and bonds payable.

THE NATURE OF BONDS

Bonds represent contracts of debt whereby one party, an **issuer,** borrows fund from an **investor.** Usually many individual bonds, each evidenced by a certificate, are issued, and the contractual agreement between the issuer and investors is contained in another document called a **bond indenture.** Companies generally issue bonds to borrow significant amounts while providing a large number of relatively small debt instruments. For example, a company may borrow $10,000,000 by issuing 10,000 separate $1,000 bonds covered by a single bond indenture. In this way, the issuing company obtains a large amount of needed capital while allowing many different investors to provide the funds. This system also allows investors (1) to make smaller investments in a variety of companies, thereby avoiding some risk by diversifying their investments and (2) to buy or sell additional bonds in the capital market while retaining some or all of their original holdings.

The bond indenture usually requires that an independent fiscal agent, called a **trustee,** protect the interests of both the issuer and the investors. Bond indentures also specify other terms, such as the maturity date, bond amounts (e.g., $1,000 and $10,000 denominations), any conversion or call features, sinking-fund requirements, other repayment terms, and any other special provisions or restrictions.

KITCHEN-SINK BONDS MAY OFFER EVERYTHING BUT STABILITY

There they go again.

Wall Streeters have figured out a new way to turn explosive securities into tame-looking investments. Once again, banks are the targeted buyers. But regulators fear the bonds' future may prove stormier than buyers expect.

Banks and other financial institutions have bought more than $3.5 billion [bonds] since April. The offerings are called secured investor trusts but known on the Street as "kitchen-sink bonds," because they are backed by everything but.

For securities firms and some of their clients, kitchen-sinkers are a godsend. The bonds are issued by trusts into which Wall Street dumps bits and pieces of capricious, hard-to-value mortgage-backed securities. If the market for a certain mercurial mortgage-backed bond should dry up, just pop it into a trust and get it off the investors' books.

Yet even the bonds' admirers aren't without qualms. Michael May, vice president of the Federal Home Mortgage Loan Corp., which issues mortgage-backed securities and has been considering issuing this type, concedes: "Some days I feel just fine; some days they make me nervous as hell."

Kitchen-sinkers are the offspring of mortgage-backed securities, which are backed by the interest and principal payments from pools of mortgage loans. Wall Street carves up the cash flows from those securities into quirkier bonds, known as collateralized mortgage obligations, or CMOs. There are more than $800 billion of CMOs on the market.

A More Palatable Mix

The problem is, a few CMOs are just too weird for investors to digest. These CMOs may languish in the inventories of Wall Street firms that underwrite CMOs or on the books of customers, posing risks. Kitchen-sinkers are the latest way Wall Street gussies up mercurial bonds and passes them on to other investors. The idea is to lump lots of the unpalatable CMOs into another diversified pool, then recut the underlying cash flow into pieces that appear more appetizing.

"To the extent that this creates demand for more esoteric [CMOs], the deals will improve the market overall," says Mr. May of Freddie Mac.

Because kitchen-sinkers carry triple-A ratings from credit-rating services, their risks aren't obvious. The top-notch rating, from Fitch Investors Service, Inc., and Duff & Phelps Credit Rating Co., reflects how the deals were structured, not the underlying assets' safety.

The bonds will boast the triple-A rating as long as the underlying securities throw off enough cash to pay investors as promised, a structure known as a cash-flow bond. Never mind it's a slight promise: to repay investors their principal at the trusts' expiration in some 30 years. What lures investors is the two percentage points above floating short-term rates they will get if the bonds work out.

Marketability Questioned

And what if they don't? Federal regulators and even critics on Wall Street worry that the bonds are too complex to analyze and may be unsalable as a result. The trusts contain pieces of dozens of mortgage deals—some privately placed—from as many as a dozen underwriters.

"Our concern with this product is the purchaser's ability to test the volatility of the securities," says William A. Stark, assistant director of the office of capital markets at the Federal Deposit Insurance Corp., which insures bank deposits. The Office of Thrift Supervision has determined that the bonds are high-risk holdings, which means the thrifts holding them would have to mark them to market prices.

Earlier this fall, mortgage prepayments reached record levels as interest rates fell and homeowners rushed to refinance at lower rates. That drove down the price of CMOs whose returns rely solely on interest—not principal—payments on the underlying mortgages; such bonds suffer when mortgage prepayments rise because it means the interest payments earmarked for them are cut off early.

Insurance companies feeling the heat of new regulations wanted to dump such interest-only bonds as IOs and PAC IOs, or planned amortization class, a structure intended to be more stable. When no one wanted them, the sellers couldn't get an acceptable price.

Spurred by Bank's Demand

Wall Street firms created the kitchen-sink trusts to seize on the profit opportunity created by matching up the poor-selling IOs with banks' ravenous appetite for floating-rate bonds. Bear, Stearns & Co. has issued nearly $2.5 billion since April, reaping at least $25 million in profit and savings.

Banks are especially enamored of floating-rate mortgage-backed bonds because they are exempt from stringent new rules intended to monitor the "interest-rate sensitivity" of banks' portfolios. The rules restrict bank investments in the most volatile mortgage-backed securities, but that has barely damped banks' appetites for bonds that can match their short-term liabilities. Holdings of CMOs by the 100 largest banks nearly tripled to $90 billion in the first half of 1993, according to *Inside Mortgage Securities,* a newsletter.

The Wall Street firms putting these deals together insist that the trusts provide a resale market for hard-to-analyze bonds that are prone to falling out of favor. "If there isn't a bid in the market," says one deal designer, "at least you can get the bonds off your books."

Increasingly, however, underwriters are using the trusts to absorb the risky remnants of new issues, which must be sold in order to sell the rest of the deal.

SOURCE: Laura Jereski, "Kitchen-Sink Bonds May Offer Everything but Stability," *The Wall Street Journal* (November 18, 1993), Dow Jones Company, Inc., 1993. Reprinted by permission of The Wall Street Journal, © 1993 Dow Jones & Company, Inc. All Rights Reserved Worldwide.

TYPES OF BONDS

One of the principal goals of the issuing company is to acquire long-term funds at the lowest cost. Because investment policies differ from time to time and from company to company, various provisions are found in bond issues. The following paragraphs discuss some of the most common distinguishing characteristics and types of bonds.

Bonds may be **serial bonds** or **term bonds.** All of the term bonds in a single issue mature on the same date, whereas groups of individual serial bonds mature at various scheduled times in the future. Serial bonds allow the issuing company to retire an entire bond issue in installments. Term bonds, however, may require the issuing company to establish a sinking or bond-redemption fund to provide adequate money to retire the entire bond issue at one time. We discuss term bonds throughout this chapter and serial bonds in Appendix B of this chapter.

Bonds may be **registered bonds** or **coupon bonds.** Interest and principal payments on registered bonds are paid only to the owner of the bonds as recorded in the trustee's records. Interest on coupon bonds, also called **bearer bonds,** is paid to the person submitting a detachable interest coupon. In the case of coupon bonds, the company does not maintain a record of who owns the individual bonds at any point in time.

Senior bonds are those with higher claims on a company's assets; **subordinated bonds** or **second-mortgage bonds** are those whose claim on assets is secondary. **Callable bonds** may be retired (reacquired) prior to maturity if the issuing company opts to pay a call premium to bondholders in addition to accrued interest and the face amount of the bond. **Convertible bonds,** on the other hand, may be exchanged for equity securities of the issuing company at the option of the investor.

State and local governments, as well as other nonprofit organizations, also frequently issue many types of bonds. For example, **revenue bonds** are those whose interest and principal are payable from resources generated by a particular government operation, such as an airport or a public utility. **General obligation bonds,** on the other hand, are secured by the full faith and credit of the issuing unit of government. The proceeds of general obligation bonds are used for such purposes as road or street improvement and constructing municipal buildings such as fire and police stations.

More recently, several other types of debt instruments have emerged. For example, "deep-discount" and "zero-coupon" interest rate bonds bear little or no stated rate of interest in addition to their face amount. The bonds sell initially at a very great discount to provide the investor a competitive rate of return. Investors buy the bonds by paying only a small fraction of the maturity amount and buy only the right to the maturity value of the bonds at some distant date. The difference between the amount paid for the bonds and the maturity amount received represents interest expense to the issuing company and interest revenue to the investor. Correctly structured, income taxes may be deferred until the maturity date of the bonds, when the amount invested and related interest are received by the investor in the form of the face amount. The corporation issuing the bonds does not have to make periodic interest payments, and that may also be attractive. So-called junk bonds are issued at relatively high rates of interest due to the high credit risk they represent. These bonds were used to effect high-risk corporate buyouts during the late 1980s, and defaults have resulted in much adverse publicity that continues at this writing.

Corporations issue many types of bonds and other debt instruments and, consequently, the long-term debt section of the balance sheet is frequently complex. Exhibit 15–1 presents a footnote taken from a recent annual report of Bethlehem Steel Corporation, a leading integrated steel producer in the United States. The total long-term debt amounts of $638.5 million and $618.3 million for 1993 and 1992, respectively, correspond to the long-term debt figures reported on the face of the balance sheet. The Financial Accounting Standards Board (FASB), in its *Statement of Financial Accounting Standards No. 47,* requires

EXHIBIT 15–1

Bethlehem Steel Corporation's Long-Term Debt Disclosure

Long-Term Debt	December 31	
(dollars in millions)	**1993**	**1992**
Hot-dip galvanizing lines financing	$262.0	$220.5
Revolving and other credit agreements	—	80.0
Debentures:		
6⅞% due 1999	18.8	18.8
9% due 2000	39.9	41.3
8⅜% due 2001	41.6	41.6
8.45% due 2005	90.7	90.7
Pollution control and industrial revenue bonds:		
5¼%–8%, due 1994–2002	78.1	90.7
Variable interest at 50%–70% of prime rate, due 1994–1996	27.0	35.0
Notes and loans:		
10⅜% Senior Notes, due 2003	105.0	—
9⅝%–12.75%, due 1994–1997	34.8	35.0
Unamortized debt discount	(2.0)	(2.1)
Amounts due within one year	(57.4)	(33.2)
Total long-term debt	$638.5	$618.3

Maturities and sinking fund requirements at December 31, 1993 for the next five years were $57.4 million in 1994, $61.8 million in 1995, $88.9 million in 1996, $71.9 million in 1997 and $75.6 million in 1998.

During 1993, we sold $105 million of Senior Notes to finance the construction of a coal injection facility at our Burns Harbor Division. The Notes are unsecured senior obligations and are senior in right of payment to all existing and future subordinated indebtedness of Bethlehem. As unsecured senior obligations of Bethlehem, the Notes will effectively be subordinate to secured senior indebtedness of Bethlehem. These Notes contain covenants which impose certain limitations on Bethlehem's ability to incur or repay debt, to pay dividends and make other distributions on or redeem capital stock, or to sell, merge, transfer or encumber assets. See Note M, Stockholders' Equity.

Disclosure   certain disclosures concerning long-term debt in the company's financial statements.[2] Those disclosures include the amount of long-term debt maturing in each of the next five years, as presented in the Bethlehem Steel Corporation example in Exhibit 15–1. Such disclosures are particularly helpful to financial statement users attempting to assess a company's expected future cash flows. In particular, notice the last paragraph of the disclosure in Exhibit 15–1. The fair value of the company's long-term debt exceeds the amount reported in the company's 1993 balance sheet by approximately $30 million. This may result from a number of factors such as improving the company's credit worthiness or declining rates of interest subsequent to the issuance of the company's debt.

ACCOUNTING FOR BONDS PAYABLE

Substantial time is required to plan and execute most bond issues, and many of the terms in a bond indenture are established well in advance of the sale of the bonds. Between the time that bond terms are established and the point of sale, many economic and market condi-

---

[2]*FASB Statement of Financial Accounting Standards No. 47,* "Disclosure of Long-Term Obligations," 1981.

A major portion of the costs to construct hot-dip galvanizing lines at our Sparrows Point and Burns Harbor Divisions are financed through a $270 million loan agreement. Borrowings are collateralized by the coating lines and originally incurred interest based on the London Interbank Offered Rate (LIBOR). At December 31, 1993, $112 million of this debt incurs a fixed rate of 5.99% with the balance converted to a fixed rate of 5.69% in January 1994. This loan will be repaid in equal semiannual installments over a seven-year period. Repayment on $120 million of the loan began in 1993 with repayment on the balance beginning in 1994.

Our revolving credit agreement expires on December 31, 1996, and is nonreducing with initial bank commitments of $400 million. The agreement permits additional banks to be added and the total commitment amount to be increased to $500 million. Borrowings under the revolver are subject to collateral coverage requirements and incur interest based on the prime rate, Federal Funds rate, certificate of deposit rates or LIBOR. Our accounts receivable and inventories are pledged as collateral for borrowings and letters of credit under the credit agreement and certain other obligations to participating banks. No borrowings were outstanding at December 31, 1993. We pay five eighths of 1% per annum commitment fee on the unused available credit.

Our revolving credit and hot-dip galvanizing lines financing agreements contain restrictive covenants which require Bethlehem to maintain a minimum adjusted tangible net worth. At December 31, 1993, our adjusted tangible net worth exceeded the more restrictive of these requirements by about $1 billion.

At December 31, 1993, interest rate swap agreements with notional amounts totaling $225 million effectively fix the interest rate on a like amount of our floating rate debt at 7.99% to 11.95%. These agreements expire from 1995 through 2001. Net payments or receipts under these agreements are included in interest expense.

We estimate the aggregate fair value of our debt and related obligations exceeds the total debt recorded at December 31, 1993 by approximately $30 million and approximately equals the total debt recorded at December 31, 1992. We based our estimates on quoted market prices or current rates offered for debt with similar terms and maturities.

SOURCE: Bethlehem Steel Corporation, 1993 Annual Report.

tions—as well as the financial status of the issuing company—may change substantially. Changes in conditions normally affect the desirability of the bonds as investments and cause the market value of the bonds to change.

Investors view bond purchasing as an investment that requires present-value techniques. Basically, a bond may be viewed as a set of future cash flows consisting of (1) the series of interest payments to be received representing an annuity and (2) a single repayment of principal at the maturity date. The cash received as interest is determined by multiplying the rate of interest stated on the bond times the face or maturity value of the bonds. Once the aggregate amount of both future cash flows has been determined, an investor then calculates the present value of those flows. The investor selects a discount rate that provides a satisfactory return on an investment with the risk characteristics of the company issuing the bonds. The resulting number, which represents the present value of the two types of cash flows provided by the bond, is the price that the investor is willing to pay for the bond.

If the discount rate employed by the investor differs from the rate of interest stated on the bond, then the present value of the bond determined by the investor's discount rate will differ from the face amount (i.e., par value) of the bond. Of course, in a normal bond issue, the final price to be received for the bonds is set by the market for all bonds rather than merely a single buyer's appropriate discount rate. The market price for all bonds, however, is based on a consideration of alternative investment opportunities as well as the specific characteristics of the issuing company. If the issuer of the bonds receives cash in an amount less than the face amount of the bonds, the bonds are said to be issued at a **discount.** If the issuer receives more than the face amount of the bonds, they are issued at a **premium.** The difference between the selling price and the face amount of the bonds is the premium or discount.

To illustrate a discount, assume that Baycraft Corporation decides to issue bonds with terms as described in Exhibit 15–2. If subsequent to printing the bond indenture but prior to issuance, Baycraft suffers serious financial or operating problems or if the market interest rate for similar investments rises, then the market value of Baycraft bonds will fall as they become a less desirable investment.

Exhibit 15–2 shows that interest will be paid five times in the amount of $900 each time. If we know the rate of interest demanded by investors as an adequate return on the bonds, we can then determine the issuance price. The following present-value formula illustrates how to calculate the issuance price of the bonds in order to yield a 12% rate of interest. Figures are rounded to the nearest dollar.

$$
\begin{aligned}
\text{Present value (PV) of the bonds} &= \text{(PV of interest payments)} \\
&\quad + \text{(PV of maturity amount)} \\
&= \text{(PV of 5 payments of \$900 at} \\
&\qquad \text{an annual rate of 12\%)} \\
&\quad + \text{(1 payment of \$10,000 at the end of} \\
&\qquad \text{5 years at an annual rate of 12\%)} \\
&= (3.60478 \times \$900) \\
&\quad + (.56743 \times \$10,000) \\
&= \$3,244 + \$5,674 \\
&= \$8,918
\end{aligned}
$$

The investors are willing to pay $8,918 for the Baycraft bonds to earn a return of 12% rather than the 9% rate of interest stated on the face of the bonds. The buyers of the bonds will receive repayment of $10,000 on the maturity date in addition to $900 interest per year for the years 1995–1999.

If we assume that the interest payment is to be paid semiannually rather than annually, the conversion is not difficult. In this case, the annual rate (12%) must be expressed as a semiannual rate (6%), and the 5 annual compounding periods are changed to 10 semiannual compounding periods. The interest annuity is one-half year's interest, $450, rather than $900. The present value of the bonds (rounded to the nearest dollar) can now be determined by the same technique we illustrated:

$$
\begin{aligned}
\text{PV of bonds} &= (7.36009 \times \$450) + (.55839 \times \$10,000) \\
&= \$3,312 + \$5,584 \\
&= \$8,896
\end{aligned}
$$

In this case, interest is assumed to compound more frequently, resulting in a slightly higher amount of interest than in the annual interest case and, therefore, a slightly lower present value ($8,896 compared to $8,918).

In this illustration, we calculated the price of a bond for which the stated interest rate is lower than the rate of return required by investors (market rate), resulting in sale of the bond

---

EXHIBIT 15–2

Baycraft Corporation
Bond Terms

Face amount ($1,000 each)	$10,000
Stated interest rate	9%
Annual interest payment date	January 1
Date of bonds	January 1, 1995
Date of maturity	December 31, 1999
Issue costs	$500

---

issue below its face amount (at a discount). If the stated interest rate had been higher than the rate of interest required by investors (market rate), the bond issue would sell at a premium rather than a discount. We illustrate that situation later in the chapter.

Once the selling price of a particular bond issue has been established, that price is typically stated as a percentage of the par or face value of the bonds, such as 98 or 103. For example, if a $10,000,000 face value bond issue sells for 98, the issuer of the bonds receives $9,800,000 ($10,000,000 × 98%), and the bonds are sold at a discount of $200,000. If the $10,000,000 bonds sell for 103, the issuer of the bonds receives $10,300,000 ($10,000,000 × 103%), and the bonds are sold at a premium of $300,000.

ISSUANCE OF BONDS

Issue Costs

Costs incurred in preparing and marketing a bond issue include legal and accounting fees, broker commissions, printing and engraving costs, registration fees, and promotional costs. Such issue costs are recorded as deferred charges, reported in the assets section of the balance sheet, and amortized over the life of the related debt. Issue costs are recorded as separate assets, because they are not related to the market rate of interest implicit in the bond issue. Accountants usually amortize issue costs by the straight-line method, although other methods are satisfactory and are occasionally encountered in practice. As discussed both here and in Chapter 10, a premium or a discount results from differences between the rate of interest stated on the bonds and the effective rate of interest that exists for those bonds when they are sold. We discuss the conceptual and practical accounting issues related to premium and discount more extensively later in this chapter.

A Simplified Example

The terms of bond issues generally provide (1) a long period to maturity, (2) an interest rate to be paid, and (3) other terms of the issue. The amount of consideration received when the bonds are issued provides the basis for accounting entries. To illustrate accounting for bonds payable, we continue the example of Baycraft Corporation. Assume, however, that interest is payable semiannually on January 1 and July 1.

If Baycraft sells its bonds on January 1, 1995, at their face amount, the following entries are necessary during 1995 and at the beginning of 1996.

Jan. 1, 1995	Cash	10,000	
	Bonds Payable		10,000
	(To record sale of bonds at face amount.)		
Jan. 1, 1995	Deferred Bond-Issue Costs	500	
	Cash		500
	(To record issue costs.)		

July 1, 1995	Interest Expense	450	
	Cash		450
	(To record semiannual payment of interest. $10,000 × .09 × ½ = $450.)		
Dec. 31, 1995	Interest Expense	450	
	Interest Payable		450
	(To accrue interest for second half of 1992, payable on January 1, 1996.)		
Dec. 31, 1995	Issue Cost Expense	100	
	Deferred Bond-Issue Costs		100
	(To amortize issue costs. $500 ÷ 5 = $100.)		
Jan. 1, 1996	Interest Payable	450	
	Cash		450
	(To pay interest accrued on December 31, 1995.)		

In this case, the process of recognizing interest expense and the amortization of issue costs continues each year until maturity when the retirement of the bonds is accounted for by the following entry:

Dec. 31, 1999	Bonds Payable	10,000	
	Cash		10,000
	(To account for retirement of bonds.)		

COMPLICATING FACTORS IN ACCOUNTING FOR BONDS

The previous example reflects accounting under simplified conditions. The following section illustrates several realistic circumstances that complicate financial accounting and reporting for bonds payable. Many of those problems have counterparts in Chapter 10 with respect to investments in the bonds of other corporations. A brief review is provided, however, because there are some differences between accounting for investments in bonds and accounting for the issuance of bonds. Also, certain aspects of accounting for bonds relate exclusively to the liability of issuing companies.

Issuance between Interest Payment Dates

Bonds are frequently issued at a point after the date printed on the bonds and between interest payment dates. Interest begins to accrue on the date of the bonds, however, even if the bonds have not been issued. Of course, if the bonds are never issued, no accounting entries or interest payments are made. For example, assume that the Baycraft Corporation issues the bonds described in Exhibit 15–2 on May 1, 1995, at 100 (100% of face amount) plus accrued interest. We continue our assumption that interest is paid semiannually on January 1 and July 1.

The following entry and supporting calculations are required:

May 1, 1995	Cash	10,300	
	Interest Expense		300
	Bonds Payable		10,000
	(To record issuance of bonds @ 100 plus accrued interest. $10,000 issuance price of bonds + $300: [$10,000 × .09 × ⁴⁄₁₂ = accrued interest].)		

Investors in the bonds will pay to the issuer the amount of interest accrued at the date of issuance. Interest Expense is credited for the amount of accrued interest *received* by the *issuer* at the issuance of the bonds. Although Interest Payable could just as easily have been credited, the entry as made is logical, because on July 1, 1995, when the first semiannual interest payment is made, interest for only two months (May and June) will be reflected as an expense of Baycraft Corporation. The following entry and T account analysis illustrates this procedure:

July 1, 1995   Interest Expense   450
                       Cash   450
                   (To pay semiannual interest.
                     $10,000 × .09 × ½ = $450.)

Interest Expense

1995			1995		
July 1	Payment of interest	450	May 1	Receipt of accrued interest upon issuance of bonds	300
July 1	Interest expense for six months ended July 1, 1992	150			

If the $300 for accrued interest is credited to Interest Payable at the date of issuance, Interest Payable must be debited for $300 and Interest Expense must be debited for $150 when the $450 interest is paid on July 1, 1995.

Recognition of Accrued Interest

Another complication arises if the interest payment date does not coincide with the company's year-end. Interest payable and interest expense must be accrued to apply the matching principle. The entry to record the accrued but unpaid interest expense at December 31, 1995, and related calculation follows:

Matching

Dec. 31, 1995   Interest Expense   450
                        Interest Payable   450
                    (To accrue interest expense payable on
                      January 1, 1996. $10,000 × .09 × ½ = $450.)

Because interest for the entire six months is payable on the following day (January 1), that entire amount is accrued. A lower amount is accrued if the payment date is more distant than the following day. For example, if interest is payable on February 1 and August 1, then only five months of interest is accrued at December 31.

Accounting Subsequent to Issuance

Chapter 10 notes that premium or discount on bonds is treated, respectively, as a direct addition to or deduction from the face amount of the bonds. In the Baycraft Corporation example in which bonds payable are issued at an effective interest rate of 12%, paid annually, the issue price is $8,918 with a related discount of $1,082 ($10,000 − $8,918). This illustration is based on the original assumption of annual interest payments. Thus, immediately following the bond issuance on January 1, 1995, the liability for the bonds is presented in the Baycraft balance sheet at $8,918. Because that amount represents the present value of the future cash flows—both interest and principal—on the date of issuance, the requirements of *Accounting Principles Board Opinion No. 21* are satisfied.[3] That pronouncement requires receivables and payables to be recorded at their present value when issued. The amounts so reported and maturity disclosures provide investors and creditors with useful information about future cash outflows required by the bonds and the present value of those amounts.

Disclosure

Amortization: The Effective Interest Method.   The discount that emerges as a result of a difference between the rate of interest stated on the bonds (9%) and the market rate of interest (12%) is

[3]*APB Opinion No. 21,* "Interest on Receivables and Payables," 1971.

amortized as an increase of reported interest expense over the life of the bonds. For example, during 1995 the following entries are required:

Jan. 1, 1995	Cash		8,918	
	Discount on Bonds Payable		1,082	
	Bonds Payable			10,000
	(To record issuance of bonds.)			
Dec. 31, 1995	Interest Expense		900	
	Interest Payable			900
	(To accrue annual interest payable at			
	Dec. 31, 1995.)			
Dec. 31, 1995	Interest Expense		170	
	Discount on Bonds Payable			170
	(To record amortization of discount.)			

The discount amortization is computed as follows:

Carrying amount of bonds @ Jan. 1, 1995	$8,918
Effective rate of interest expense	.12
Total annual interest expense (rounded)	1,070
Less: Interest expense recognized with Dec. 31, 1995, interest accrual	900
Amortization—1995	$ 170

The calculation demonstrates the manner in which we can determine the amount of discount or premium to be amortized. In practice, accountants, usually aided by a computer, prepare amortization tables to facilitate recording the amortization of any premium or discount related to the bonds. Such a table is presented in Exhibit 15–3 for Baycraft Corporation.

This process of amortization continues each year until the Discount on Bonds Payable account is fully amortized at the maturity date of the bonds. If the bonds are issued subsequent to the original date printed on the face of the bonds (as discussed earlier), any premium or discount is amortized over the remaining life of the bonds *beginning at the date of issuance and continuing to the maturity date.* The amortization of premium or discount in such situations does not present any significant additional problems and is treated routinely. That is, the premium or discount is amortized over the life of the debt by the **effective interest method** (also called the **compound interest method** or simply **interest method**) of amortization.

The total interest expense each year is computed by multiplying the effective rate of interest (12% in the Baycraft example) by the carrying amount of the liability at the beginning of each year. The total interest expense computed in that manner is then compared to the interest that has been paid or accrued on the bonds in accordance with the bond indenture. The difference between the amount of interest paid or payable during the year and the total interest expense to be recognized represents the discount or premium to be amortized. Remaining unamortized discount (or premium) continues to be classified as an adjustment to the maturity amount of the bonds payable to determine their carrying amount in the company's balance sheet.

The carrying amount of the bonds increases each year as the discount is amortized to interest expense until, at the maturity date of the bonds, the discount is fully amortized. At that time, the carrying amount of the bonds is their face amount. Therefore, when the bonds are retired at maturity, no gain or loss arises, because the cash required to retire the bonds is equal to the carrying amount of the bonds at that time.

Amortization: The Straight-Line Method.   Although the effective interest method of discount amortization is required by *APB Opinion No. 21* because it recognizes a constant interest rate on the bonds payable over the life of the bonds, other methods of amortization are occasionally

EXHIBIT 15–3

Baycraft Corporation
Amortization of Bond Discount
Effective Interest Method
(amounts rounded to the nearest dollar)

Date	(1) Interest Expense	(2) Cash Paid	(3) Discount Amortization	(4) Par Value Outstanding	(5) Unamortized Discount	(6) Carrying Value
Jan. 1, 1995	—	—	—	$10,000	$1,082	$ 8,918
Dec. 31, 1995	$1,070	$ 900	$ 170	10,000	912	9,088
Dec. 31, 1996	1,091	900	191	10,000	721	9,279
Dec. 31, 1997	1,113	900	213	10,000	508	9,492
Dec. 31, 1998	1,139	900	239	10,000	269	9,731
Dec. 31, 1999	1,169*	900	269	10,000	—	10,000
	$5,582	$4,500	$1,082			

(1) (Previous year Column 6) × 12%
(2) ($10,000 par value) × 9%
(3) (Column 1) − (Column 2)
(4) $10,000 par value
(5) (Previous year Column 5) − (Current year Column 3)
(6) (Column 4) − (Column 5)

*Adjusted for rounding difference.

encountered in practice. These alternative procedures are acceptable only if their results do not differ materially from the results of the effective interest method. Because the differences resulting from each method of amortization are frequently immaterial, the **straight-line method** of amortization is sometimes used in practice. The amount of discount or premium recognized at the issuance of the bonds is divided by the number of years the bonds are outstanding. The resulting amount is amortized each year in the same fashion as described here. Annual amortization by the straight-line method for the example in Exhibit 15–3 would be $216.40 ($1,082 ÷ 5).

Materiality

Bonds Issued at a Premium. Companies frequently issue bonds at amounts exceeding their face value. We refer to the excess of the price received over the face amount of the bonds as **premium.** Premium, like discount, also represents an adjustment to the stated interest rate expense on the bonds. Premium exists if the interest rate stated on the bonds is *higher* than the interest rate required by the market for similar securities. Investors are thus willing to pay more than the face amount of the bonds. Accounting for premium mirrors the procedures we employed in reporting discount.

To illustrate premium, assume that the Baycraft bonds sell on January 1, 1995, at an effective interest rate of 6% rather than 12% in the preceding example with interest being paid semiannually at January 1 and July 1 each year. The total amount received for the bonds is $11,280 (rounded to the nearest dollar), determined as follows:

$$\text{PV of bonds} = (\text{PV of interest payments}) + (\text{PV of maturity})$$
$$= (\$450 \text{ for 10 six-month periods at 6\% annual interest})$$
$$+ (\$10,000 \text{ at 6\% annual interest})$$
$$= (\$450 \times 8.53020) + (\$10,000 \times .74409)$$

$$= \$3,839 + \$7,441$$
$$= \$11,280$$

The present-value factor for the interest payments, 8.53020, is the present value of an annuity at *3% for 10 periods,* because interest is paid semiannually. The present-value factor for the maturity value of the bonds, .74409, is the present value of one at 3% for 10 periods. These values are taken from Table 6–4 and Table 6–2, respectively.

The entry to record the issuance follows:

Jan. 1, 1995	Cash	11,280	
	Bonds Payable		10,000
	Premium on Bonds Payable		1,280

The following entry records the first interest payment and amortizes six months of premium (rounded to the nearest dollar) by using the effective interest method:

July 1, 1995	Interest Expense	450	
	Cash		450
	($10,000 × .09 × ½ = $450)		
July 1, 1995	Premium on Bonds Payable	112	
	Interest Expense		112
	($11,280 × .06 × ½ = $338;		
	$450 − $338 = $112)		

The credit to interest expense resulting from amortizing the premium *reduces* reported interest expense to 6% (the effective rate) of the carrying value of the bonds ($11,280). The carrying value of the bonds during the second six-month period declines from $11,280 by the amount of the premium amortized ($112) to $11,168. Total interest expense for the second six-month period becomes $335 ($11,168 × .06 × ½). The premium amortized during the last half of 1995 is the difference between the cash paid ($450) and the total interest expense to be reported ($335), or $115.

The process of amortization continues each six-month period until the bonds mature and the premium has been fully amortized. An amortization table similar to the one presented for discount in Exhibit 15–3 may be useful in accounting for the premium over the entire life of the bonds. Such a table is presented in Exhibit 15–4. The amortization of the premium *reduces* interest expense below the $450 *cash paid* rather than increasing interest expense, as was the case in the discount example.

Materiality   As in the discount case, practitioners frequently use the straight-line method of amortizing premium rather than the more complex, but theoretically superior, effective interest method. As before, if material differences do not result from the straight-line method, there is little objection to its use. But *APB Opinion No. 21* requires the use of the effective interest method if material differences result from other methods. Semi-annual amortization by the straight-line method for the example in Exhibit 15–4 would be $128 ($1,280 ÷ 10).

Retirement of Bonds.   If bonds are retired at maturity, any premium or discount will have been amortized over their life and their carrying amount at maturity represents the amount of cash required to retire them. Therefore, no gain or loss on the retirement of bonds at maturity is recognized.

If the bonds are retired early, however, recognition of gain or loss is frequently necessary because the carrying amount of the debt, including unamortized premium or discount and issue costs, differs from the amount paid to accomplish the early retirement. A company might reacquire its own debt prior to maturity for a number of reasons. For instance, if management thinks interest rates are likely to drop in the near future, the reacquisition of bonds paying a relatively high rate of interest might be prudent. Once the interest rates drop, the

	EXHIBIT 15–4				

Baycraft Corporation
Amortization of Bond Premium
Effective Interest Method
(amounts rounded to the nearest dollar)

Date	(1) Interest Expense	(2) Cash Paid	(3) Premium Amortization	(4) Par Value Outstanding	(5) Unamortized Premium	(6) Carrying Value
Jan. 1, 1995	—	—	—	$10,000	$1,280	$11,280
July 1, 1995	$ 338	$ 450	$ (112)	10,000	1,168	11,168
Dec. 31, 1995	335	450	(115)	10,000	1,053	11,053
July 1, 1996	332	450	(118)	10,000	935	10,935
Dec. 31, 1996	328	450	(122)	10,000	813	10,813
July 1, 1997	324	450	(126)	10,000	687	10,687
Dec. 31, 1997	321	450	(129)	10,000	558	10,558
July 1, 1998	317	450	(133)	10,000	425	10,425
Dec. 31, 1998	313	450	(137)	10,000	288	10,288
July 1, 1999	309	450	(141)	10,000	147	10,147
Dec. 31, 1999	303*	450	(147)	10,000	—	10,000
	$3,220	$4,500	$(1,280)			

(1) (Previous period Column 6) $\times$ (6% $\times$ ½)
(2) ($10,000 par value) $\times$ (9% $\times$ ½)
(3) (Column 1) $-$ (Column 2)
(4) $10,000 par value
(5) (Previous period Column 5) $-$ (Current period Column 3)
(6) (Column 4) + (Column 5)

*Adjusted for rounding difference.

market would place a premium on existing instruments bearing higher interest rates, and the company would be required to pay the premium to reacquire its own bonds in an open-market purchase.

A company can retire its debt without actually repaying it in several ways. *SFAS No. 76,* "Extinguishment of Debt," provides that debt should be considered extinguished in two circumstances other than those in which the debtor repays the creditor and is relieved of all obligations under the debt. The first situation arises when the debtor is legally released from being the primary obligor under the debt, and it is probable that the debtor will not make future cash payments under the debt. For example, property that is subject to a mortgage may be sold and the related debt may be assumed by the buyer, thereby relieving the original debtor of all responsibilities under the debt instrument. This situation arises in real estate lending because mortgages are sometimes nonrecourse other than to the property securing the loan.

Another way to extinguish debt requires the debtor to establish an irrevocable trust for the retirement of the debt. The assets in the trust must be U.S. government securities or securities backed by the U.S. government. Such monetary securities are virtually risk free as to the amount and timing of repayment. The future cash flows from the securities must be adequate and timely to service the debt for which the trust was created. When such a trust exists, the related debt is considered "retired," and it is removed from the balance sheet along with the assets in the trust fund. This type of arrangement is called an **in-substance defeasance** of debt.

The accounting profession has considered the problems with reporting extinguishments of debt and issued a series of related pronouncements. The first of these pronouncements, *APB Opinion No. 26,* states

> *A difference between the reacquisition price (of the debt) and the net carrying amount of the extinguished debt should be recognized currently in income of the period of the extinguishment as losses or gains.*[4]

Some accountants believe that this rule could, in some circumstances, cause the financial statements to appear misleading. As presented in Exhibit 15–5, Aeronca, Inc. (manufacturers of aircraft and aerospace structures, jet aircraft, engine components, and environmental and aircontrol systems), departed from the requirements of *APB Opinion No. 26.* Aeronca, Inc., elected to record the difference between the carrying amount of the extinguished bonds and the value of the preferred stock issued to reacquire the bonds as paid-in capital in excess of par value rather than as a gain recognized in income. The company contended that reporting a gain in the circumstances described would have caused its financial statements to be misleading.

Following the issuance of *APB Opinion No. 26,* gains or losses from the extinguishment of debt were included in income *before* extraordinary items during the period of the extinguishment, because such items generally were not considered both unusual in nature and infrequent in occurrence. The potential materiality of those gains and losses in addition to the ability of a company to control the timing of their recognition caused concern in the business community. In essence, company managements could directly, and frequently in an arbitrary fashion, influence reported earnings through debt retirement activities. In extreme cases (such as described in Exhibit 15–5), the results reported for a debt extinguishment seemed to defy economic realities.

Materiality

Responding to those criticisms, the FASB issued *Statement of Financial Accounting Standards No. 4,* which specified precisely the reporting requirements for such items:

Materiality

> *Gains and losses from extinguishment of debt that are included in the determination of net income shall be aggregated and, if material, classified as an extraordinary item.*[5]

One exception to the FASB rule relates to cash purchases of debt made within one year of a sinking-fund requirement that an enterprise must meet.[6] For example, a typical bond indenture may specify that at December 31, 1995, a sinking fund to retire an issue of bonds must represent at least 50% of the face amount of the bonds outstanding. If a company retires some of its bonds within one year prior to December 31, 1995, to comply with that indenture requirement, gains or losses may arise. Because such gains or losses result from well-planned contractual requirements, the FASB concluded that they should *not be classified as extraordinary items.*

Remember that an extraordinary item represents a special type of gain or loss to be reported separately in the income statement. Extraordinary items are presented net of any related tax effects, and reported after operating income. Financial statement users are thereby put on notice not to expect such unusual and infrequent items of gain or loss to recur in the

---

[4]*APB Opinion No. 26,* "[Early] Extinguishment of Debt," 1972, par. 26. ("Early" is in brackets because FASB amendments increased the scope of *APB Opinion No. 26* to include extinguishments other than those taking place before the scheduled maturity of the debt.)

[5]*FASB Statement of Financial Accounting Standards No. 4,* "Reporting Gains and Losses from the Extinguishment of Debt," 1975, par. 8.

[6]*FASB Statement of Financial Accounting Standards No. 64,* "Extinguishments of Debt Made to Satisfy Sinking-Fund Requirements," 1982, par. 3.

EXHIBIT 15–5

Aeronca, Inc.
Extinguishment of Debt

Notes to Financial Statements
Note 1—Summary of Accounting Policies:

Extinguishment of Debt: In October 1973, the Company issued 50,000 shares of 6% Prior Preferred Shares, par value $100, in exchange for the outstanding $5,000,000 of 6% Senior Subordinated Notes. It also issued 18,040 shares of convertible $6 Serial Preference Shares, Series A, stated value $100 a share, in exchange for $1,300,000 and $504,000 of outstanding 6% convertible subordinate debentures and 5¾% convertible subordinated debentures, respectively. The Company expensed the unamortized balance (approximately $148,000) of the deferred financing costs associated with the issuance of each of the three classes of subordinated debt to the extent that such unamortized balances were allocable to the debt so extinguished.

Opinion No. 26 of the Accounting Principles Board of the American Institute of CPA's states that the excess of the carrying amount of the extinguished debt over the present value of the new securities issued should be recognized as a gain in the statement of operations of the period in which the extinguishment occurred. While it is not practicable to determine the present value of the new equity securities issued, such value is at least $2,000,000 less than the face amount of the debt extinguished. However, the terms and provisions of these new equity securities are substantially similar to those of the debt securities extinguished, both on the basis of the Company's continuing operations and in the event of liquidation. It is the opinion of the management, therefore, that no gain as a result of this exchange has been realized or should be recognized in the financial statements.

SOURCE: Aeronca, Inc., 1973 Annual Report.

---

foreseeable future. Although many debt extinguishments may not satisfy both of the criteria for treatment as an extraordinary item (unusual in nature and infrequent in occurrence), *SFAS No. 4* requires that gains or losses from extinguishing debt be treated as extraordinary. The rationale for this treatment, in part, is to avoid some of the problems previously discussed. By excluding gains or losses on debt extinguishments from operating income, financial statement users are made aware of their special nature.

To illustrate accounting for an extinguishment of debt, we again modify the example of Baycraft Corporation. Assume that after amortizing discount for 1995, the company—in anticipation of lower interest rates—reacquires the bonds presented in Exhibit 15–3 for $9,800 on January 4, 1996. The following entry reflects the reacquisition and recognition of the related extraordinary loss:

Loss on Retirement on Bonds—Extraordinary	1,112	
Bonds Payable	10,000	
Cash		9,800
Discount on Bonds Payable		912
Deferred Bond-Issue Costs		400
(To reflect the reacquisition of debt at an early date		
preceding maturity.)		

The remaining discount of $912 at the date of extinguishment is merely the original discount ($1,082) less the amount amortized at December 31, 1995 ($170). The $400 remaining issue costs related to those bonds are also removed from the accounting records, thereby affecting the amount of gain or loss reported.

What would be the proper accounting treatment if only part of the outstanding bonds were reacquired? The percentage of the issue reacquired would be applied to the par value, the unexpired discount or premium, and the deferred bond issue costs to determine the portion of each to be removed. Cash is then credited for the price paid and an extraordinary gain or loss recognized.

To illustrate, we assume the same facts as in the previous illustration except that only 50% of the bond issue is extinguished for $4,900. The entry to record the retirement, including a loss of $556, is presented as follows:

Loss on Retirement of Bonds—Extraordinary	556	
Bonds Payable ($10,000 × 50%)	5,000	
Cash		4,900
Discount on Bonds Payable ($912 × 50%)		456
Deferred Bond-Issue Costs ($400 × 50%)		200

A company may reacquire its own bonds but not retire them. The company intends instead to sell them at a later time. Such bonds are called **treasury bonds** and a Treasury Bonds account may be charged when the bonds are acquired rather than the liability account (Bonds Payable). An extraordinary gain or loss should still be recognized on the reacquisition, however, and the Treasury Bonds account should be deducted from the liability Bonds Payable in the balance sheet. Treasury bonds should not be reported as assets. Furthermore, interest on treasury bonds should not be paid, accrued, or otherwise recognized in the financial statements.

Companies experiencing financial and operating difficulties occasionally reach agreements with creditors to restructure liabilities or retire debts for less than their maturity amounts. Restructurings of debt occurring because of financial difficulties of the debtor present a number of accounting issues. A discussion of troubled-debt restructurings from the perspective of both creditors and debtors appears in Appendix A of this chapter.

OTHER LONG-TERM DEBT ACCOUNTING PROBLEMS

Other types of bonds and long-term debt instruments exist. The following section considers unusual accounting issues posed by several of those types of liabilities.

DEBT AND EQUITY RIGHTS COMBINED

Companies have developed various hybrid debt instruments in their efforts to obtain external financing at the lowest cost. This is obvious in accounting and reporting for debt instruments containing provisions that allow bondholders the opportunity to become stockholders under specified conditions. When such obligations are issued, we must resolve several additional accounting and reporting problems.

We may generally classify debt instruments containing equity-acqusition features as either (1) bonds issued with detachable stock purchase warrants or (2) bonds that may be converted into equity securities. The following discussion describes general accounting theory and reporting practices for each type of debt security.

Accounting Theory and Equity-Acquisition Features

The accounting profession has addressed the issue of accounting for debt with **equity-acquisition features** on several occasions, the most recent of which resulted in the issuance of *APB Opinion No. 14.*[7]

Theoretically, when an investor acquires a debt security that in some way facilitates the acquisition of equity securities, some amount of the purchase price is paid for the right to acquire the equity security in a potentially advantageous manner. The remaining amount of the purchase price relates to the liability aspects of the security. Stated alternatively, if the

---

[7]*APB Opinion No. 14*, "Accounting for Convertible Debt and Debt Issued with Stock Purchase Warrants," 1969.

same bonds were issued without the equity-acquisition feature, they would normally sell for less. The equity-acquistion feature has a value and enhances the market value of the composite security. Furthermore, to the extent that purchasers pay for the equity-acquisition feature, such payment represents a permanent contribution to equity not requiring repayment. Indeed, only the principal at maturity and related interest when earned must be paid to the investor. Therefore, in theory, some portion of the total consideration received for convertible debt and debt with detachable stock rights should be considered a contribution to equity and the remainder as the incurrence of a liability. The following discussion considers both types of securities, presents the accounting profession's position on each, and illustrates appropriate accounting and reporting techniques.

Accounting for Debt with Detachable Stock-Purchase Rights

When debt is issued with **detachable stock-purchase warrants,** the repayment of the debt at maturity is generally expected, regardless of whether the stock-purchase warrants are exercised. Because the stock-purchase warrants are detachable and may be exercised separately from the debt, a market for the warrants normally is established and provides information on the relative value of the warrants. Furthermore, because a market for the separate debt instrument is also established, we can easily determine the value of the debt portion of the composite security in an objective manner. Thus, the equity and debt instruments do not represent mutually exclusive investment alternatives, and separate values for each element exist independent of the other and should be recorded in the accounting records.

If active markets for the two securities exist immediately after issuance, the allocation of the total proceeds of the sale is based on the relative fair market values of the two securities. The portion of the total consideration to be allocated to debt is represented by the ratio of the fair market value of the debt to the total fair market value of the debt and warrants. The remaining portion of the consideration received is associated with the warrants. To understand this concept, consider the following example.

Bradfield, Inc., issues 1,000 bonds with a maturity value of $1,000 each. A detachable stock warrant, attached to each bond, may be exchanged for a share of stock with a payment of $25 per share. Bradfield, Inc., sells the bonds with the warrants attached at 102. Shortly after issuance, the bonds are traded in the market at 103 and the warrants are traded at $5 each. The following calculation presents the basis for an entry to record the issuance:

$$\text{Total consideration to be treated as debt} = \left[\frac{\text{Market value of bonds without warrants}}{\text{Market value of bonds without warrants} + \text{Market value of warrants}} \right] \times \$1,020,000$$

$$= \frac{\$1,030}{\$1,030 + \$5} \times \$1,020,000$$

$$= \frac{\$1,030}{\$1,035} \times \$1,020,000$$

$$= \$1,015,072$$

The remaining proceeds of $4,928 ($1,020,000 − $1,015,072) represent the amount included in the total price that is allocated to the detachable stock-purchase warrants.

The following entry records the issuance of the bonds and warrants, based on the preceding calculation:

Cash	1,020,000	
Bonds Payable		1,000,000
Premium on Bonds Payable		15,072
Stock-Purchase Warrants		4,928
(To record issuance of bonds and detachable warrants.)		

For purposes of financial reporting, immediately after issuance, the bonds are presented in the balance sheet with the premium added, as follows:

Long-Term Liabilities		
Bonds payable	$1,000,000	
Add: Premium on bonds payable	15,072	$1,015,072

The stock warrants appear in the stockholders' equity section of the balance sheet as a separate element of paid-in capital.

From this point forward, we account for the bonds in the manner illustrated earlier in this chapter. The premium is amortized over the life of the bonds as a reduction of interest expense. Again, the effective interest method of amortization should be used unless other amortization methods approximate the results of the effective interest method.

If market values of the bonds and attached warrants are not available, other allocation techniques are used. For example, we may select an estimated interest rate that appears reasonable for the debt security alone. In doing so, we should consider the risk class of the issuing company as well as other economic conditions. Factors such as the prime rate of interest and government security rates provide useful guides for selecting an appropriate rate. Using the estimated interest rate, we can determine the present value of the liability. The difference between the present value of the debt and the total consideration received may be appropriately attributed to the detachable warrants and reported as paid-in capital. This approach should be used only when fair market values of the bonds and the stock warrants are not available. Another possibility is that a market value is available for either the bonds or the warrants but not both. In this case, we either estimate the unknown value and allocate the total proceeds as before or assign the known value to the one security and allocate the remaining proceeds to the other security.

The amount initially attributed to the warrants is recognized as part of paid-in capital and is classified as such until the warrants are exercised or expire. Accounting for stock-purchase warrants subsequent to issuance is considered in Chapter 16, which deals with a variety of issues involving stockholders' equity.

Accounting for Convertible Debt

Different problems arise if a company issues debt containing a feature allowing conversion of that debt into some type of the company's capital stock. In considering the accounting problems of such securities, the APB stated:

> *A convertible debt security is a complex hybrid instrument bearing an option, the alternative choices of which cannot exist independently of one another. The holder ordinarily does not sell one right and retain the other. Furthermore, the two choices are mutually exclusive; they cannot both be consummated. Thus the security will either be converted into common stock or will be redeemed for cash. The holder cannot exercise the option to convert unless he foregoes the right to redemption, and vice versa.[8]*

Substance over Form   Although the APB ultimately selected the logic implicit in that statement for guiding financial accounting and reporting, an alternative argument is based on the idea of substance over form. Specifically, the APB acknowledged the following:

> *The contrary view is that convertible debt possesses characteristics of both debt and equity and that separate accounting recognition should be given to the debt characteristics and to the conversion option at the time of issuance. This view is based upon the premise that there is an economic value inherent in the conversion feature or call on the stock and that the nature and value of this feature should be recognized for accounting purposes by the*

---

[8]*APB Opinion No. 14,* par. 7.

issuer.... Similar separate accounting recognition for disparate features of single instruments is reflected in, for example...the allocation of the purchase cost in a bulk acquisition between goodwill and other assets.[9]

As indicated, the first position was ultimately adopted and consequently *no portion of the proceeds from the issuance of convertible debt should be attributed to the conversion feature.* In reaching this conclusion, the APB attributed much significance to the inseparability of the debt and conversion option of such instruments. Therefore, all the proceeds from the issuance of convertible debt are attributed to the liability. Stockholders' equity of the issuing company remains unaffected by the issuance of convertible debt until conversion takes place at a later date. Disclosure of the conversion feature in the notes is necessary, however, to inform financial statement users of the possible changes in the financial structure of the company.

Disclosure

The APB did, however, provide an exception to the general rule cited above. Recognizing that in unusual cases, an extremely high value may be placed on the conversion feature of a convertible debt instrument, the APB concluded that "when convertible debt is issued at a substantial premium, there is a presumption that such premium represents paid-in capital."[10] Thus, if a convertible debt instrument is issued at an unusually low effective rate of interest, the accountant may conclude that a portion of the premium on that issuance should be classified as paid-in capital. In that way, the effective yield on the debt portion of the instrument will become more reasonable as the amount of premium on the debt is reduced. Determining what constitutes "substantial premium" and should, therefore, cause an allocation to stockholders' equity clearly requires seasoned judgment on the part of the practitioner.

To illustrate the application of the general provisions in which there is not a "substantial premium," consider the previous example of Bradfield, Inc., but assume that convertible bonds are issued instead of bonds with detachable warrants. If convertible bonds with a face amount of $1,000,000 are issued for $1,115,000 and if each bond is convertible into 10 shares of common stock, the following entry is necessary:

Cash	1,115,000	
Bonds Payable		1,000,000
Premium on Bonds Payable		115,000
(To record issuance of convertible bonds.)		

The entire amount received is related to the bonds, and no proceeds are considered to be an addition to stockholders' equity. The liabilities section of the balance sheet at the date of issuance appears as follows:

Long-Term Liabilities		
Convertible bonds payable	$1,000,000	
Premium on bonds payable	115,000	$1,115,000

If the $115,000 was judged to be a "substantial premium," a portion of the proceeds should be allocated to stockholders' equity. One way to accomplish the allocation involves determining the present value of the debt by discounting it using a rate appropriate for similar debt not containing the conversion feature. The difference between the present value of the debt portion, so determined, and the total consideration received is attributed to stockholders' equity. Chapter 16 discusses the exchange of convertible bonds for common stock and deals with a variety of other issues involving stockholders' equity.

OTHER LONG-TERM LIABILITIES

One encounters several other types of long-term liabilities in practice. For example, companies frequently issue **serial bonds,** which mature in several scheduled maturity dates rather

---

[9]*APB Opinion No. 14,* par. 9.
[10]*APB Opinion No. 14,* par. 18.

than at a single maturity date as in the case of term bonds. Although financial accounting and reporting for serial bonds does not differ conceptually from the practices illustrated for term bonds, several complicating factors arise. Appendix B of this chapter illustrates the accounting practices unique to serial bonds. Furthermore, lease and pension obligations are frequently reported as liabilities in the financial statements of business enterprises. Because accounting classification, measurement, and reporting standards for those liabilities are complex, Chapters 23 and 24, respectively, are devoted to these topics. Chapter 19, which deals with financial reporting of income taxes, discusses noncurrent deferred tax credits. Also, certain loss contingencies, discussed in Chapter 14, may represent an enterprise's long-term liabilities. Lawsuits and other claims provide examples of contingent liabilities that may require noncurrent classification.

The present chapter discusses only a limited number of noncurrent liabilities. Although notes and bonds payable frequently represent most of a company's noncurrent liabilities, the other important items mentioned in the preceding paragraph are considered elsewhere in this book.

CREATIVE FINANCING INSTRUMENTS

One of the most significant business developments of the last several decades has been the evolution of creative financing instruments. Companies have sought to lower the cost of the resources obtained from creditors and investors, to hedge risks, to increase returns on assets employed, and to achieve a variety of other objectives through alternative, complex, and creative means of financing. In many cases, accountants are closely involved in designing and developing such arrangements. Indeed, one principal reason for developing such innovative financing instruments is to structure transactions in such a manner to obtain a desired accounting result. For example, many companies wish to avoid reporting liabilities on their balance sheets and attempt to accomplish "off-balance-sheet" financing.

Some of the securities that have been developed recently include **shared appreciation** or **participating mortgages,** in which the lender benefits from increases in the value of the asset used to secure a loan; **zero coupon convertible bonds,** for which interest is paid only if the security is held to maturity; **preferred** or **common stock** with "put" options that allow the investor to sell the security back to the issuer; and debt payable in the common stock of the issuing entity. The accounting questions that arise for such instruments relate to their classification (i.e., debt or stockholders' equity); their valuation (i.e., the amount at which the item should be recorded); and the amount, timing, and classification of the return paid on the instrument (e.g., interest expense or dividends).

Consider, for example, shared appreciation or "participating" mortgage, which generally allows the lender to share in any increases in the value of the property securing the debt. To illustrate, a clause in such an instrument might provide that after five years the property is to be appraised and 50% of any increase in the fair value of the property over its worth at the time of the loan is to become due to the lender. If the amount of the liability to the borrower increases, the property's fair value rises. Such terms are found in real estate financing because real estate commonly increases in value over time. Participating loans generally bear interest at rates less than equivalent notes that do not contain the participation feature. The lower interest compensates the borrower for relinquishing some of the rights to the property's appreciation.

The accounting questions that surround such agreements are complex and numerous. For example, at what rate should interest be recognized during the period between the inception of the loan and the appraisal date? Should annual appraisals be performed and any increase in the fair value of the property be used as a basis for increasing the liability? Should the offsetting charge resulting from any increase in the liability of the participation feature be reported as an increase in the related asset, as interest expense, or in some other way?

At this writing, there are no authoritative answers to these questions, and students should realize that the creativity of lenders and borrowers is almost unlimited. New and different financing instruments will continue to be developed in response to events and circumstances not now foreseen. *SFAS No. 105,* "Disclosure of Information about Financial Instruments with Off-Balance-Sheet Risk and Financial Instruments with Concentrations of Credit Risk" and *SFAS No. 107,* "Disclosures about Fair Value of Financial Instruments" represent recent actions of the FASB to ensure that financial statement users receive information necessary to understand terms, conditions, and risks involved in a wide variety of financial instruments including long-term debt. These standards are, however, limited to disclosure. Organizations that set accounting standards tend to trail practice in such circumstances, and accountants are frequently required to develop acceptable accounting solutions for complex financial instruments without precise authoritative guidance. Substantial seasoned judgment and analysis are necessary to appropriately address and resolve such complex accounting problems. The rights and risks that are created and assigned to the parties involved in the agreement must be well understood to successfully account for the underlying transactions. Consultation with other professional accountants is common when such problems are encountered. Indeed, the intellectual challenges implicit in circumstances such as these represent extremely interesting and important aspects of professional practice.

Disclosure

Accounting for long-term debt may be rather straightforward and not unduly complex. Recording debt when incurred and recognizing periodic interest expense, including determining the effective interest rate and amortizing any discount or premium, do not pose major problems for accountants. There are, however, a number of complex conceptual issues that accountants must resolve in preparing financial statements and that accounting standards-setting organizations are only now beginning to address. Examples include distinguishing between debt and equity instruments for purposes of balance sheet classification, accounting for participating loans, and the valuation of liabilities subsequent to issuance or incurrence. Because accounting standard setters have not acted to resolve many of these issues and because we cannot expect such organizations to keep up with the pace by which new forms of financial instruments are created, professional accountants are commonly called on to make determinations that are complex and subjective. In discharging such responsibilities, seasoned professional judgment is absolutely necessary. Experience and technical knowledge must both be brought to bear on problems of appropriately accounting for and reporting complex financial instruments.

PROFESSIONAL JUDGMENT

Students can expect to see significant changes in the professional accounting standards that may require major revisions in the manner in which we currently account for liabilities. In addition, we can expect the financial markets to continue to develop new financial instruments that contain complex rights and risks. Accountants must understand and report these changes in accordance with acceptable professional concepts and standards.

The accounting principles of asset/liability measurement, matching, and disclosure primarily govern accounting for debt. Liabilities are recorded at their historic amounts and adjusted for the accrual and payment of interest and the amortization of premium or discount, if any. Fair values of long-term debt financial instruments are disclosed. Interest expense is measured by matching the cost incurred with time periods in which the debt is outstanding. The accounting records of the issuing company do not recognize changes in the value of debt, such as bonds, occurring in financial markets. The principle of disclosure is also important in the information about debt terms and maturities provided in the notes to the financial statements.

CONCLUDING REMARKS

Asset/Liability Measurement

Matching

Disclosure

KEY POINTS

1. Long-term debts are those reportable obligations of an enterprise that do not require the use of current assets or the creation of new current liabilities for repayment and those with due dates more than one year (or operating cycle, if longer) in the future. (Objectives 1 and 7)

2. Long-term debt is usually recorded at the present value of the future cash obligations. (Objective 3)

3. When debt is extinguished, any difference between its carrying amount and its reacquisition price is treated as an extraordinary gain or loss. (Objective 3)

4. Premium and discount arise when the market rate of interest for an obligation differs from the rate of interest stated on the face of that security. (Objective 4)

5. Premium or discount is amortized over the life of the related debt by applying a constant interest rate to the carrying amount of the liability (effective interest method). The straight-line method of amortization is acceptable only if the results do not differ materially from the effective interest method. (Objective 5)

6. When a company sells a debt instrument with detachable stock-purchase warrants, it recognizes an increase in stockholders' equity and in liabilities. The proceeds from the sale of the hybrid security must be allocated between the debt and equity components based on the relative fair values of the two. (Objectives 2 and 6)

7. When a company sells a convertible debt security, the value of the equity-acquisition feature is usually not recognized in the accounts. The liability for the debt security is normally recorded in the accounting records as if the conversion feature did not exist. (Objective 6)

8. Some financial instruments issued by a company may contain provisions that complicate classification and accounting. Such instruments must be carefully analyzed to ensure appropriate treatment in the financial statements. (Objectives 1, 2, 3, and 7)

APPENDIX A: TROUBLED-DEBT RESTRUCTURINGS

A company with financial difficulties may have trouble repaying its debt on a timely basis. Furthermore, most debt instruments contain covenants requiring a company to maintain certain financial characteristics as evidenced by the financial statements. For example, a debt covenant may require the maintenance of a given debt/equity ratio, current ratio, or working capital amount. A company experiencing operating and financial difficulty may at some time violate some or all of its debt covenants. When covenant violations occur, a common practice is for creditors and debtors to renegotiate and restructure the troubled debt.

As a result of the variety and complexity of **troubled-debt restructurings,** the FASB issued *Statement of Financial Accounting Standards No. 15,* which discusses the accounting and reporting by both debtors and creditors.[11] Because there is considerable similarity between debtor and creditor accounting for such restructurings, we consider both in this appendix. First, however, we explore the steps necessary to *identify* troubled-debt restructurings.

IDENTIFYING TROUBLED-DEBT RESTRUCTURINGS

Not all debt restructurings represent troubled-debt restructurings; we must therefore exercise care in determining whether a particular debt restructuring is, in fact, a *troubled*-debt restructuring. For example, a troubled-debt restructuring is not involved if a creditor, experiencing financial difficulty, makes concessions in debt terms to induce a debtor to pay the debt at a point *earlier* than the scheduled maturity date.

In a troubled-debt restructuring, the *debtor* must be experiencing financial difficulty and the creditor, attempting to make the best of a bad situation, grants to the debtor a concession that would not be granted in a normal business relationship. Thus, creditors sustain accounting losses on troubled-debt restructurings while debtors realize accounting gains. Examples of restructurings include a modification of debt terms, such as interest rate reductions or maturity date extensions, settlement of the debt for less than its face amount, and granting equity interests in the debtor to creditors. Once a troubled-debt restructuring has occurred, appropriate accounting measurements and disclosures must be accorded the restructuring.

ACCOUNTING BY DEBTORS

Four types of troubled-debt restructurings are recognized for accounting purposes. The first two involve full settlement of the debt as a result of a debtor (1) transferring assets to the creditor or (2) granting an equity interest to the creditor; the third type involves a modification of debt terms (e.g., extension of maturities, reduction of interest); and the fourth, some combination of the first three types. We discuss each type in the following pages.

Transfer of Assets

In a troubled-debt restructuring, creditors are sometimes willing to accept various debtor assets in immediate settlement of the debt. In a *transfer of assets,* debtors must consider how much of any resulting gain or loss is related to the disposition of the assets and how much is related to the extinguishment of debt.

For example, assume that Covina Company has been experiencing poor sales of its latest real estate project and is near default on its loan from Pomona National Bank. Recognizing that

---

[11] *FASB Statement of Financial Accounting Standards No. 15,* "Accounting by Debtors and Creditors for Troubled Debt Restructuring," 1977.

if Covina defaults on its loan other creditors may file suit, Pomona has agreed to accept Covina Company's land, which has a fair value of $40,000, in full settlement of Covina's debt. If the land has a book value of $35,000 and the liability is reflected on the books at its maturity value of $50,000, the following entries are necessary on Covina's books:

Land	5,000	
Gain on Disposal of Land—		
Ordinary		5,000
(To adjust land to its fair value at		
the time of disposal.)		
Note Payable	50,000	
Land		40,000
Gain from Restructuring of		
Debt—Extraordinary		10,000
(To recognize gain on the		
extinguishment of debt.)		

These entries demonstrate that two steps may be required when assets are transferred in settlement of a debt. We first adjust the carrying amount of the asset to be transferred from its current book value to its fair value at the time of transfer with a resulting gain or loss recognized on the disposal of the asset. Such gains or losses are *not* extraordinary because gains or losses on asset disposals occur frequently and are not unusual.

After the asset has been adjusted to its fair value, we next recognize any difference between the fair value of the asset and the carrying amount of the extinguished debt as an *extraordinary gain*. This is consistent with the nature of troubled-debt restructurings wherein creditors grant concessions to debtors to provide at least some recovery of a loan.

Remember, gains on the extinguishment of debt should be reflected as extraordinary items according to *SFAS No. 4* and *SFAS No. 15.*

Grant of Equity Interest

A second method by which troubled debt may be restructured occurs when a debtor *grants an equity interest* to the creditor in consideration for the debt extinguishment. Debtors should record the fair value of the equity securities granted and recognize an extraordinary gain for any difference between the carrying amount of the debt extinguished and the fair value of the equity grant.

To illustrate, assume that instead of transferring land to Pomona National Bank, Covina Company grants 1,000 shares of $25 preferred stock to Pomona in consideration for the extinguishment of the $50,000 note. If the preferred stock has a fair value of $45,000, the following entry is necessary to reflect the transaction:

Note Payable	50,000	
Preferred Stock (1,000		
shares @ $25)		25,000
Paid-in Capital in Excess		
of Par Value		20,000
Gain from Restructuring of		
Debt—Extraordinary		5,000
(To record extinguishment of note as		
a result of equity grant with a fair		
value of $45,000.)		

We observe several important points: Only gains (not losses) are recognized on this type of transactions, because the fair market value of the equity grant will not be higher than the carrying amount of the extinguished debt. Also, the gain is treated as extraordinary in accordance with *SFAS No. 15.*

From a practical perspective, it is frequently difficult to determine the fair value of the equity interest that is granted, because the market value of the securities of a troubled company may be highly volatile or even nonexistent. This is especially true for companies whose securities are not actively traded in a public market. Therefore, accountants must exercise considerable judgment to develop reasonable estimates of fair value when debt is extinguished through an equity grant.

Modification of Terms

The third type of restructuring transaction involves a **modification of the terms** of the debt. Although the terms of a debt may be modified in many ways, accounting for all such debt alterations involves the same underlying principles. When the terms of a debt are adjusted in a troubled-debt restructuring, the *total amount* of the future cash payments should be determined. This total should include all payments for both principal and interest required in the future without using present-value techniques. In other words, the gross future cash payments for principal and interest after the modification of terms should be calculated. This number is then compared with the current carrying amount of the debt on the books of the debtor. If the carrying value of the debt is less than the aggregate future cash payments required by the debt, we amortize the difference over the life of the debt as interest expense by using the effective interest method specified in *APB Opinion No. 21.* No gain is recognized in the period of the extinguishment if the future cash flows exceed the carrying amount of the debt.

On the other hand, if the carrying amount of the debt is higher than the aggregate total future cash payments required under the modified debt agreement, we adjust the carrying value of the debt to the aggregate total future cash flows and recognize an extraordinary gain for the difference. Furthermore, no interest expense is recognized on the debt following such a write-down. All payments in satisfaction of the debt are considered payments of principal even if some portion of the payments is designated as interest in the revised debt agreement.

To illustrate, assume that the note payable to Pomona National Bank bears interest at 12% and is carried as a liability on Covina's books at $50,000. Instead of the previous restructuring examples, however, assume now that Pomona agrees to reduce the principal amount of the note by $10,000 but continues to require interest to be paid at 12% on the remaining $40,000. If the note is due in one year, the following entry is necessary:

Note Payable	5,200	
Gain from Restructuring of		
Debt—Extraordinary		5,200

The calculations are as follows:

$40,000 × .12 = $ 4,800 Interest to be paid on new
                           principal amount
       + 40,000 Remaining principal
         $44,800 Aggregate future cash
                           payments

$50,000 Current carrying amount
of liability

− 44,800 Aggregate payments
required after
restructuring

$ 5,200 Gain on restructuring

The carrying value of the liability is now $44,800 as a result of the preceding entry. Consequently, all cash payments now made in satisfaction of the note are considered payments of principal, even though a portion ($4,800) has been designated in the restructuring agreement as interest. Covina recognizes no interest expense on the note subsequent to restructuring.

Combination of Methods

The final manner in which a troubled-debt restructuring may occur involves some combination of the first three methods: transfer of assets, grant of equity interest, or modification of terms. In such a *combination restructuring,* if an asset is transferred to the creditor in partial settlement of the debt, the asset is adjusted from its carrying value to its fair value and a gain or loss is recognized on the disposal of the asset. Next, the fair value of the asset transferred is credited and the debt is reduced by a similar amount. In a combination restructuring in which some debt remains on the books after these adjustments, no extraordinary gain on the extinguishment is recognized.

An equity interest might also have been granted to the creditor. The debtor should record the fair value of the equity interest with a corresponding charge to the carrying amount of the debt. If the extinguishment is completed as a result of the asset transfer and equity grant, an extraordinary gain should normally be recognized. The amount of the gain is the difference between the carrying value of the debt prior to extinguishment and the fair values of the asset transferred and the equity grant.

If the debtor still has a residual liability on the restructured debt following a transfer of assets or grant of equity interest, or both, the provisions governing a modification of terms should be applied. That is, the gross future payments for both interest and principal still required following the asset transfer and/or grant of equity should be compared to the adjusted carrying value of the debt. If the gross future cash payments exceed the adjusted carrying amount of the debt, the difference is recognized as interest expense over the life of the debt. However, if the gross future cash payments are less than the adjusted amount of the debt, the debt should be written down to the total of the gross future cash flows with an extraordinary gain recognized to the extent of the difference.

To illustrate accounting for combination restructuring, assume that a debtor in a troubled-debt restructuring agrees to the following terms: (1) Covina will transfer land with a carrying value of $15,000 and a fair value of $12,000 to Pomona; (2) Covina will grant to the creditor 100 shares of its $10 par value stock, which has a current fair value of $6 per share; and (3) in consideration of the asset transfer and equity grant, Pomona will reduce the principal balance of the note from $30,000 to $10,000 and will reduce the interest rate on the note from 12% to 10%, compounded annually. Assume

those transactions occur on January 1, 1995, when the note payable has a carrying value of $29,000. Under the restructuring, the note matures on December 31, 1996, at which time both accrued interest (compounded annually) and principal are due. Exhibit 15–6 illustrates the necessary calculations and entries to analyze and record this restructuring on the books of Covina Company.

ACCOUNTING BY CREDITORS

Accounting and reporting practices for troubled-debt restructurings by creditors generally parallel those of debtors; however, certain differences exist. *SFAS No. 114,* "Accounting by Creditors for Impairment of a Loan," amends the provisions of *SFAS No. 15* as applied to creditors in a troubled-debt restructuring.[12] In such restructurings, creditors grant concessions to debtors because of the debtors' impaired ability to fulfill the original terms of the obligation. Because creditors are attempting to recoup as much of a receivable as possible, losses on the settlement of such receivables are likely to be sustained.

Asset Receipts

A troubled-debt restructuring may occur in several ways. From the creditor's perspective, however, there is no conceptual difference between the receipt of a debtor's asset such as inventory and the receipt of any equity interest in the debtor. Both transfers result in the creditor's *receipt of an asset.*

When a creditor receives assets in satisfaction of a receivable in a troubled-debt restructuring, the assets received should be recorded at their fair value on the date of receipt. If an allowance for uncollectible accounts has been established specifically for the receivable in question, the allowance account as well as the receivable should be removed from the books of the company with a loss recognized for any remaining difference.

To illustrate, assume that Pomona National Bank accepts land with a fair value of $40,000 in satisfaction of a note receivable with a carrying amount of $50,000, but for which a $6,000 Allowance for Uncollectible Accounts has been established. The following entry is necessary:

Land (Real Estate Owned)	40,000	
Allowance for Loan Losses	6,000	
Loss on Settlement of Receivable	4,000	
Note Receivable		50,000
(To record receipt of land in satisfaction of note receivable.)		

We can make several observations in regard to this entry. First, a loss of $10,000 has been sustained in the settlement of this receivable; $6,000 was recognized in an earlier period as a result of the use of the allowance method of recognizing bad debts; and the additional $4,000 loss is recognized in the period of the settlement. Second, these losses are not considered to be extraordinary, because—from the creditor's perspective—they

---

[12]*FASB Statement of Financial Accounting Standards No. 114,* "Accounting by Creditors for Impairment of a Loan," 1993.

EXHIBIT 15−6

Illustration of a Combination Troubled-Debt Restructuring

Journal entries:

Jan. 1, 1995	Loss on Disposal of Land	3,000	
	Land		3,000
	(To recognize loss on disposal of land.)		
Jan. 1, 1995	Note Payable	12,600	
	Discount on Common Stock	400	
	Land		12,000
	Common Stock (100 shares @ $10)		1,000
	(To attribute fair value of land transferred and		
	equity granted to an equivalent portion of debt.)		

Calculation for consideration:

Land (written down from $15,000 value)	$12,000
Equity grant (par $1,000)	600
Total fair value of consideration	$12,600

On January 1, 1995, the following test is made to determine whether further accounting entries are necessary:

Debt carrying value:	
Original carrying amount of debt	$29,000
Less: Write-down from above	12,600
Carrying value of debt	$16,400
Future cash flows:	
Maturity cash requirement	$10,000
Interest	
Dec. 31, 1995 ($10,000 × .10)	1,000
Dec. 31, 1996 ($11,000 × .10)	1,100
Total aggregate future payments required	$12,100

Since the adjusted carrying amount of the debt ($16,400) exceeds the future cash requirements ($12,100), an entry is necessary for the difference ($4,300):

Jan. 1, 1995	Note Payable	4,300	
	Gain from Restructuring of Debt—		
	Extraordinary		4,300
	(To reduce carrying amount of note to		
	aggregate of future cash payments.)		

On December 31, 1995, no entry is required; all payments represent principal following restructuring; thus, no interest should be accrued.

Dec. 31, 1996	Note Payable	12,100	
	Cash		12,100
	(To record retirement of debt at maturity;		
	no interest expense recognized.)		

---

are losses on the collection of receivables, not on the extinguishment of debt. Furthermore, if the assets received are equity securities of the debtor (equity grant), the accounting and reporting techniques are not changed; that is, the equity securities received should be recorded as an asset at their fair market value on the date received.

EXHIBIT 15–7

Disclosure of Troubled-Debt Restructurings

Debtor Disclosures	Creditor Disclosures
1. Description of changes in terms	1. Aggregate recorded investment
2. Aggregate gain and tax effects of restructuring	2. Gross interest revenue that *would* have been recognized without the troubled-debt restructuring
3. Aggregate gain or loss on asset transfers	3. Interest revenue recognized
4. Per-share amount of gain or loss on debt extinguishment	4. Commitments to lend additional funds
5. Extent of a contingent amount payable in the total liability	

(In addition, disclosures required by other standards for liabilities and assets generally apply.)

Modification of Terms

If the terms of a receivable are changed pursuant to a troubled-debt restructuring, creditors must determine the total amount of cash expected to be received in the future. This amount is then discounted to its present value using the effective interest in the original debt instrument. The present value of the expected future cash flows is then compared with the carrying amount of the receivable, net of any related allowance account.

If the present value of cash to be received in the future is less than the carrying amount of the receivable, an ordinary loss should be recognized for the difference. Remaining collections are then treated in the same fashion as described in Chapter 10. Interest revenue is recognized at the effective rate on the balance of the receivable at the beginning of each period as long as collection of future amounts is expected.

Combination of Methods

If the restructuring is a combination of a partial settlement by receipt of assets and a modification of terms, the fair value of the asset received should be used to reduce an equivalent amount of the receivable. Conversely, if the present value of the cash to be received in the future is less than the net adjusted carrying amount of the receivable, the receivable should be written down to the present value of the aggregate future cash receipts and a loss recognized. Again, interest revenue should be recognized on future cash receipts in the manner previously described.

COMPARING AND CONTRASTING DEBTOR AND CREDITOR ACCOUNTING

Although there are many similarities between debtor and creditor accounting for troubled-debt restructurings, several differ-

ences are also apparent. The differences relate primarily to timing, interest recognition, and classification. Gains on the extinguishment of debt should be classified as extraordinary by the debtor, whereas losses on the collections of receivables should not be classified as extraordinary items by the creditor.

Creditors may recognize interest revenue because of present-value calculations, but debtors do not base their accounting on present-value measurements. Creditors may recognize the impairment of a receivable and a related loss by using the allowance method of bad debt recognition at an earlier time than debtors recognize gains from the consequences of an actual restructuring. This is consistent with the accrual of loss and gain contingencies discussed in Chapter 14; that is, gain contingencies should not be accrued prior to realization, because revenue might be recognized prematurely, but loss contingencies should be recognized when it is probable that a loss has been incurred and the amount of the loss is reasonably estimable. Furthermore, these practices are themselves in harmony with the modifying convention of con-

Conservatism servatism, which requires that accounting and reporting properly recognize inherent uncertainties in the commercial process.

Different estimates of the fair value of the consideration exchanges can cause other inconsistencies in accounting treatment between debtors and creditors. Existing differences in the recorded values of receivables and payables may also result in nonsymmetrical accounting treatments.

DISCLOSURE OF TROUBLED-DEBT RESTRUCTURINGS

Exhibit 15–7 summarizes the disclosure requirements for troubled-debt restructurings. Substantial disclosures are required to ensure adequate comprehension of the underlying transactions by financial statement users.

APPENDIX B: ACCOUNTING FOR SERIAL BONDS

Serial bonds allow an issuing company to repay the principal portion of the bonds in a series of installments. When serial bonds are issued, groups of individual bonds within that issue have maturity dates different from those of the other groups. A

EXHIBIT 15—8

Facts to Illustrate
Accounting for Serial Bonds

Issuing company	Staging
Total bond issue (par value)	$1,000,000
Date of bonds and date of issue	Jan. 1, 1995
Maturity dates as shown:	

Group	Amount	Maturity Date
A	$ 250,000	Dec. 31, 1996
B	250,000	Dec. 31, 1997
C	500,000	Dec. 31, 1998
	$1,000,000	

Interest rate stated	10%
Interest payment terms	Annually on Dec. 31
Proceeds of issue	$949,200

NOTE: Bond issues usually involve much larger amounts and longer periods of time between issuance and maturity. However, for illustrative purposes, a smaller amount and shorter period of time are assumed.

---

series of maturity dates allows the issuer to retire the bonds gradually. Serial bonds may eliminate the need for a sinking fund or reduce the financial stress of meeting the maturity requirements of an entire bond issue at a single date.

Serial bonds are also attractive to state and local governments that rely on tax revenues to service debt. For example, if voters approve a bond issue and a related tax to fund a road-building project, the government may choose to issue serial bonds. The governmental unit then constructs the road with the proceeds of the bond issue and, as it receives tax revenues, retires the debt in a series of maturities rather than in a single maturity.

Several accounting and reporting problems arise when a company issues serial bonds. Generally, these problems relate to the timing of premium or discount amortization and classification of the liability for the bonds payable.

The entry to record the issuance of the bonds in Exhibit 15—8 is relatively simple and parallels the entries discussed earlier in regard to term bonds. The proceeds of the issue are debited to Cash with a credit to Bonds Payable for the face amount of the entire issue. Any difference is treated as premium or discount on the bonds. As we illustrated earlier, premium or discount represents the difference, if any, between the interest rate stated on the bonds and the effective market rate of interest for those bonds on the date of issuance. The following entry is required to record the issuance of the bonds:

Jan. 1, 1995		
Cash	949,200	
Discount on Bonds Payable	50,800	
Bonds Payable		1,000,000
(To record issuance of serial bonds.)		

We must next determine the effective rate of interest implicit in the bond issue. Although this problem is not conceptually different from that encountered for term bonds, there are complicating factors. The several maturity dates cause uneven cash flows throughout the life of the bonds, not only for principal repayments but also for interest payments. Cash flow patterns for term-bond interest payments are constant over the life of the bonds, and there is only a single maturity date. Although the application of present-value techniques to serial bonds is more difficult, the objective remains the same. Specifically, we are seeking to determine the rate of interest (effective rate) that equates the present value of the liability (cash proceeds of the issue) with the future cash flows (various principal maturities and interest payments) required under the bond indenture. We make this calculation to meet the reporting requirements of *APB Opinion No. 21*, "Interest on Receivables and Payables," which requires the effective interest method for amortizing premium or discount over the life of the debt unless other methods do not cause material differences. Remember that even the simpler straight-line method of premium or discount amortization is not acceptable unless the results are close to those obtained by using the effective interest method. Therefore, we use the effective interest method to illustrate accounting for serial bonds.

When a combination of annuity (series of payments) and single amounts of cash flows are involved, we must select a rate of interest that equates the future cash flows with the issue price of the debt. The rate should appear reasonable and can be tested by determining whether the future cash flows, discounted at that rate, approximate the present value of the liability (proceeds of the issue).

In Exhibit 15—8, because the bonds sold at a discount, we know that the effective or market rate of interest demanded must be higher than the stated interest rate of 10%. In other words, if the stated rate of interest on the bonds provided a rate of return equal to that required by the market, the bonds would have sold at their par value. Because the bonds were sold at a discount, we can conclude that the market required a higher rate of return than was stated on the bonds. Therefore, in attempting to select the appropriate rate, we should test a higher rate than the stated rate (10%). We select 12% to test, and the calculations that follow demonstrate how the effective rate of interest implicit in a serial bond issue can be determined.

General formula:

Proceeds of Bond (Present Value [PV]) = PV of Group A
Cash Flows +
PV of Group B
Cash Flows +
PV of Group C
Cash Flows

Application:

Group A = PV of $250,000 Due in 2 Years +
PV of 2 Ordinary Annuities of $25,000

+

Group B = PV of $250,000 Due in 3 Years +
PV of 3 Ordinary Annuities of $25,000

+

Group C = PV of $500,000 Due in 4 Years +
PV of 4 Ordinary Annuities of $50,000

Using a 12% effective interest rate:

Price of Bonds   Present Value at 12%

Group A

$949,200 = (.79719 × $250,000) + (1.69005 × $25,000)

Group B

+ (.71178 × $250,000) + (2.40183 × $25,000)

Group C

+ (.63552 × $500,000) + (3.03735 × $50,000)

Accumulating:

Group A

$949,200 = $199,298 + $42,251

Group B

+ $177,945 + $60,046

Group C

+ $317,760 + $151,868

$949,200 ≈ $949,168 (Approximate equality; therefore the 12% interest rate is a reasonable approximation.)

NOTE: The annuity amounts are the interest payments required under the terms of the bond. $250,000 × .10 = $25,000; $500,000 × .10 = $50,000.

Because these two amounts are virtually equal, we select 12% as an adequate approximation of the effective rate of interest. If such an approximation does not result from applying the test rate of interest, another rate is selected for testing. This pro-

---

EXHIBIT 15−9

Serial Bonds Amortization Table

Date	(1) Interest Expense	(2) Cash Paid	(3) Discount Amortization	(4) Par Value Outstanding	(5) Unamortized Discount	(6) Carrying Value
Jan. 1, 1995	—	—	—	$1,000,000	$50,800	$949,200
Dec. 31, 1995	$113,904	$100,000	$13,904	1,000,000	36,896	963,104
Dec. 31, 1996	115,572	100,000	15,572	750,000	21,324	728,676
Dec. 31, 1997	87,441	75,000	12,441	500,000	8,883	491,117
Dec. 31, 1998	58,883*	50,000	8,883	–0–	–0–	–0–
	$375,800	$325,000	$50,800			

(1) (Previous year Column 6) × 12%
(2) (Outstanding par value) × 10%
(3) (Column 1) − (Column 2)
(4) Outstanding par value
(5) (Previous year Column 5) − (Current year Column 3)
(6) (Column 4) − (Column 5)

*Adjusted for rounding difference.

cess continues until a rate is found that satisfactorily equates the present and future values of the cash flows.

In practice, computer routines search for and find the appropriate discount rate. Computers also develop amortization tables assisting further in properly accounting for the bonds payable. Nevertheless, accountants must understand the logic and techniques underlying the determination of implicit effective rates in such circumstances.

Once the effective interest rate is established (in this case, 12%), we can compute and recognize interest expense and amortize the premium or discount on the bonds. The amortization table in Exhibit 15–9 facilitates this process and illustrates how the serial maturities affect interest expense recognition.

The entries to be made at December 31 of each year are based on the table in Exhibit 15–9. Discount is amortized over the life of the serial bonds in much the same manner as is the case for term bonds. That is, a constant rate of interest (12%) is recognized on the carrying value of the liability. The entries are as follows:

Jan. 1, 1995	Cash	949,200		
	Discount on Bonds Payable	50,800		
	Bonds Payable		1,000,000	
	(To record issuance of bonds.)			
Dec. 31, 1995	Interest Expense	113,904		
	Discount on Bonds Payable		13,904	
	Cash		100,000	
	(To pay interest and amortize discount.)			

Dec. 31, 1996	Interest Expense	115,572		
	Discount on Bonds Payable		15,572	
	Cash		100,000	
	(To pay interest and amortize discount.)			
	Bonds Payable	250,000		
	Cash		250,000	
	(To retire Group A serial bonds.)			
Dec. 31, 1997	Interest Expense	87,441		
	Discount on Bonds Payable		12,441	
	Cash		75,000	
	(To pay interest and amortize discount.)			
	Bonds Payable	250,000		
	Cash		250,000	
	(To retire Group B serial bonds.)			
Dec. 31, 1998	Interest Expense	58,883		
	Discount on Bonds Payable		8,883	
	Cash		50,000	
	(To pay interest and amortize discount.)			
	Bonds Payable	500,000		
	Cash		500,000	
	(To retire Group C serial bonds.)			

QUESTIONS

15–1 What principal characteristics distinguish long-term debt and equity financing?

15–2 Why is it usually desirable for firms to issue large numbers of relatively small long-term debt instruments?

15–3 What is the definition of each of the following type of bonds?

[a] serial bonds   [d] coupon bonds
[b] term bonds   [e] zero coupon bonds
[c] registered bonds

15–4 What are "issue costs" associated with a bond issue? How should such costs be accounted for throughout the term of the bond issue?

15–5 What factors may cause the price of a bond to differ from its face amount at the date of sale?

15–6 If a company has several bond issues outstanding, each with different interest rates, due dates, and other provisions, how might the company disclose this information in the financial statements without burdening the balance sheet with undue detail?

15–7 What are the various ways in which a debt may be extinguished? Include in your answer a discussion of qualified defeasance transactions.

15–8 How are discounts and premiums on bonds payable accounted for at the following times?

[a] At issuance.
[b] During the term of the debt.
[c] At the time of the debt retirement.

15–9 How is the amount of the discount or premium computed for a bond issue?

15–10 Describe two methods of amortizing premiums or discounts on bonds payable. Which method is required? Why?

15–11 The treasurer of Wilder Company proposes that treasury bonds be recorded as assets in the investments section of the balance sheet. Do you agree? Why or why not?

15–12 What are two different types of securities representing a combination of debt and equity instruments? How does financial accounting and reporting differ for each type?

15–13 What are the primary reasons for not recognizing a separate value for the equity element in a convertible bond at the time of issuance?

15–14 How is the equity element valued in the case of debt issued with detachable stock purchase warrants?

15–15 (Appendix A) What characteristics must a debt restructuring possess before it should be considered a troubled-debt restructuring?

15–16 (Appendix A) What are the four types of troubled-debt restructurings?

15–17 (Appendix A) What disclosures should be made in the financial statements about a troubled-debt restructuring?

15–18 (Appendix A) *Statement of Financial Accounting Standards No. 15,* "Accounting for Troubled Debt Restructurings," should bring accounting for common events by debtors and creditors closer together. Discuss the symmetry of accounting by debtors and creditors for the same transaction and discuss how differences might arise.

15–19 (Appendix B) What accounting procedures are employed for serial bonds? Briefly describe them.

EXERCISES

15–20 Bond Entries Paragon, Inc., issued $1,000,000 of 20-year, 10% term bonds on January 1, 1995, at 101. Interest is payable semiannually on June 30 and December 31.

INSTRUCTIONS

Prepare general journal entries to record

[a] The issuance of the bonds.
[b] The payment of the interest for the first two six-month periods.
[c] The amortization of premium for the year. (For simplicity, use the straight-line method of premium amortization.)

15–21 Bond Retirement Bruin, Inc., called an outstanding bond issue seven years before its maturity date. At the time the bonds were called, they had a carrying value of $55,000. Furthermore, Bruin was required to pay $72,000 to reacquire the bonds.

INSTRUCTIONS

[a] What amount of gain or loss, if any, should Bruin report during the year the call provision was exercised?
[b] How should the gain or loss in [a] be classified?

15–22 Bond Retirement Triquist Corporation reports long-term debt of $1,000,000, less unamortized discount of $50,000 at December 31, 1995. Although the bonds bear a stated interest rate of 10%, they were issued at an effective yield of 12%. Interest is payable on January 1 of each year. On June 30, 1996, Triquist retires the bonds for 103 plus accrued interest. Triquist amortizes bond discount by the effective interest method.

INSTRUCTIONS

[a] What gain or loss, if any, should Triquist report from the bond retirement on its 1996 income statement?
[b] How should this gain or loss be classified?

15–23 Bond Discount—Issue Price Cleland Company sold 1,000, $100 par value bonds that had a coupon rate of interest of 14% when the market rate of interest was 16%. The bonds mature 10 years from their date of issuance.

INSTRUCTIONS

[a] Compute the price at which the bonds sold if interest is paid annually, and identify any premium or discount to be recognized.
[b] Compute the price at which the bonds sold if interest is paid semiannually, and identify any premium or discount to be recognized.

15-24 Bond Premium—Issue Price Stoddard Company sold 11% bonds when the market rate of interest for comparable securities was 10%. The company sold 10,000, $1,000 par value bonds. The bonds pay interest semiannually and mature 20 years from the date they were issued.

INSTRUCTIONS

[a] Compute the price at which the bonds sold.
[b] Prepare the general journal entry to record the sale of the bonds.

15-25 Amortization of Discount Graziano Enterprises sold 100, $1,000 par value bonds that bear interest at 12%, at a price to yield an effective 16%. Interest is paid annually on the bonds, which mature eight years from their date of issuance.

INSTRUCTIONS

[a] Compute the issue price of the bonds.
[b] Prepare the general journal entry to record the sale of the bonds.
[c] Determine interest expense and the discount or premium amortization for the first year of the bond issue by the effective interest method.
[d] Determine interest expense and the discount or premium amortization for the first year of the bond issue by the straight-line method.

15-26 Amortization of Premium Curtis, Inc., issued 10,000, $100 par value bonds that bear interest at 12% when bonds of comparable quality were paying only 10% interest. Curtis's bonds pay interest semiannually and mature 10 years from their date of issuance.

INSTRUCTIONS

[a] Determine the price at which the bonds sold.
[b] Compute interest expense and the amortization of premium or discount for the first two 6-month periods under both the effective interest and straight-line methods.

15-27 Sale of Bonds between Interest Dates Anderson, Inc., issued $1,000,000, 12%, 20-year bonds at 102 plus accrued interest on February 1, 1995. The bonds are dated January 1, 1995, and pay interest semiannually on June 30 and December 31. The premium is to be amortized by the straight-line method over the period during which the bonds are outstanding. Bond issue costs totaled $50,000.

INSTRUCTIONS

Prepare all general journal entries for the bonds for 1995, assuming that amortizations are recorded annually on December 31, the end of the company's financial reporting period.

15-28 Retiring Part of a Bond Issue Hunter Manufacturing Company had the following bonds outstanding at December 31, 1995:

Bonds payable	$1,000,000
Less: Discount	(80,000)
	$ 920,000

The bond discount was being amortized over the 10-year life of the bonds (8 years remaining after December 31, 1995) by the straight-line method.

At June 30, 1996 (a semiannual interest payment date), the company retired $600,000 of the bonds at 101% of par value.

INSTRUCTIONS

[a] Determine the appropriate carrying amount of the bonds at June 30, 1996.
[b] Prepare the general journal entry to record the retirement of the bonds at June 30, 1996.
[c] Prepare the balance sheet presentation of the remaining bonds at December 31, 1996.

15-29 Bond Entries On July 1, 1992, Kentro Company issued 1000, $1,000 par value bonds at 99. The bonds pay interest annually on June 30, at 13% and mature eight years from their date of issuance. Discount is amortized by the straight-line method.

On June 30, 1995, the company retired the bonds at 102 after interest had been paid.

INSTRUCTIONS

Prepare the entries to record the final interest payment and the retirement of the bonds. Provide computations for each entry.

15–30 Amortization of Discount   McKenna Company issued $100,000 par value, 12% bonds on January 1, 1995. The bonds mature in 10 years and pay interest semiannually on June 30 and December 31. They were sold for $89,406, which yields an effective annual interest rate of 14%.

INSTRUCTIONS

[a] Determine the amount of interest expense to be recognized in 1995 using the effective interest method of discount amortization.

[b] What amount of the interest expense is represented by the amortization of the discount?

15–31 Bonds with Detachable Warrants   On July 1, 1995, Finch Corporation issued $2,000,000 of 7% bonds payable in 10 years. The bonds pay interest semiannually. The bonds include detachable warrants giving the bondholder the right to purchase for $30 one share of $1 par value common stock at any time during the next 10 years. The bonds and warrants were sold for $2,000,000. The value of the warrants at the time of issuance was $100,000. No valuation of the bonds, separate from the warrants, is available.

INSTRUCTIONS

[a] Prepare in general journal form the entry to record the issuance of the bonds.

[b] Explain the basis of your valuation of the warrants.   (AICPA adapted)

15–32 Bonds with Detachable Warrants   Lavery Corporation issued 100 bonds, each with a $1,000 face amount, on May 31, 1995. The bonds are due in 10 years and pay interest annually at 10%. A detachable stock-purchase warrant was attached to each bond that allows the holder of each warrant to acquire a share of the company's $25 par preferred stock for $15. Each bond with the detachable warrant sold at 102. Immediately after the issuance, the stock-purchase warrants were traded in the market at $40 while the market value of the bonds (without the warrants) was 101.

INSTRUCTIONS

Prepare the entry to record the issuance of the bonds and detachable stock-purchase warrants and the later exercise of half of the warrants.

15–33 Convertible Bonds   Albright Corporation issued 100, $1,000 par value bonds that pay 12% interest on par value at a price to yield 10%. Each bond is convertible to 10 shares of Albright Corporation common stock on any interest payment date. Interest is paid semiannually on January 1 and July 1, and the bonds mature 10 years from the date of issuance.

INSTRUCTIONS

[a] Prepare the general journal entry to record the issuance of the bonds.

[b] Explain briefly your treatment of the equity element included in the bond issue.

15–34 Bonds with Detachable Warrants   Devon Corporation sold a $1,000,000, 20-year, 8% bond issue for $1,030,000. Each $1,000 bond has a detachable warrant that permits the purchase of one share of the corporation's common stock for $30. The stock has a par value of $25 per share. Immediately after the sale of the bonds, the corporation's securities had the following market values:

8% bond without warrants	$1,020
Warrants	10
Common stock	28

INSTRUCTIONS

What entry should the corporation make to record the sale of the bonds?

15–35 Bonds with Detachable Warrants   Brookhurst Development, Inc., issued $2,000,000 of $1,000 face amount, 7% bonds on January 1, 1995, for $1,920,000. Two detachable stock-purchase warrants were attached to each $1,000 bond. Each warrant conveys the right to purchase one share of $100 par value common stock at $110 per share before July 1, 1995.

When the bonds were issued, Brookhurst's common stock was selling exactly at par and the market value of the warrants was $15 each.

INSTRUCTIONS

Prepare the entry that Brookhurst Development should make at the date the bonds were issued.

15–36 Bond Accounting   On January 1, 1995, Landing Company issued $100,000 of 10% bonds, due December 31, 2014 (20 years). Interest is to be paid annually on December 31. At the time the bonds were issued, the market rate of interest was 8%.

INSTRUCTIONS

[a] Calculate and record the proceeds of the bond issue.
[b] Prepare a schedule to calculate the interest expense and amortization of the premium or discount for the first four years (through December 31, 1998) using the effective interest method.
[c] Prepare the entry to retire the bonds on January 1, 1999, at 101.

15–37 Bond Retirement   Tarbet, Inc., reports the following liability on its December 31, 1995, balance sheet:

Bonds payable (9%, due Dec. 31, 2004)	$400,000
Premium on bonds	10,800
	$410,800

The bonds were issued on December 31, 1994, at 103, with interest payable on June 30 and December 31 of each year. On March 1, 1996, Tarbet retired $200,000 of the bonds at 98 plus accrued interest.

INSTRUCTIONS

[a] Is Tarbet amortizing the premium by the effective interest or the straight-line method?
[b] Prepare the general journal entry to record the retirement of the bonds on March 1, 1996, including the payment of interest for the period January 1 through March 1, 1996.

(AICPA adapted)

15–38 (Appendix A)   Troubled-Debt Restructuring   Marshall Company is experiencing financial difficulty and is renegotiating debt restructurings with its creditors to relieve its financial stress. Marshall has a $125,000 note payable to Western State Bank. The bank is considering two alternatives:
   Alternative 1.   Acceptance of land owned by Marshall Company, valued at $100,000 and carried on Marshall's books at its historical cost of $70,000.
   Alternative 2.   Acceptance of an equity interest in Marshall Company in the form of 11,000 shares of common stock valued at $10 per share. (The common stock has an $8 par value.)

INSTRUCTIONS

Prepare the general journal entry that Marshall Company would make under each alternative. Identify any extraordinary items that would be recognized in determining Marshall's net income.

15–39 (Appendix A)   Troubled-Debt Restructuring   Due to adverse economic circumstances and poor management, Braunegg, Inc., has negotiated a restructuring of its $85,000 note payable to Paramount Bank. Paramount Bank has agreed to reduce the face value of the note from $85,000 to $60,000, reduce the interest rate from 14% to 10%, and extend the due date one year from the date of restructuring. The restructuring will occur on August 31, 1995, the last day of Braunegg's annual reporting period. There is no unpaid interest on the restructured loan at this time.

INSTRUCTIONS

[a] Prepare the general journal entry to record the restructuring on August 31, 1995. Include computations to support your figures.
[b] Prepare the general journal entry one year later to record the final repayment of the note, assuming that no interest was paid during the year.

15–40 Bond Accounting   On January 1, 1991, Germane Company issued $1,000,000 of 7% bonds due to mature in 15 years. Interest was due and payable annually on January 1. The bonds were sold to yield 8%.

PROBLEMS

INSTRUCTIONS

[a] Calculate the proceeds at the time of issuance.
[b] Prepare the amortization schedule for the years ended December 31, 1991 through 1994, using the effective interest method.
[c] On January 2, 1995, Germane purchased $250,000 of the bonds on the open market. At that time, the bonds were selling at a price to yield 10%. Prepare a journal entry to record the transaction. Support your entry by computations.

15–41 Issue Price of Bonds   Polaris Company issued bonds dated July 1, 1995, on that date. The bonds have a face value of $10,000,000 and are due in 20 years. They were sold to yield 16%, although the stated interest rate was 16½%. Interest is payable semiannually on June 30 and December 31.

INSTRUCTIONS

[a] Determine the issue price of the bonds on July 1, 1995.

[b] Comment on the relative values of each element of the future cash flow.

[c] Determine the amount of interest expense and premium or discount amortization that Polaris will recognize at each of the first two interest payment dates, assuming that the effective interest method is used.

15–42 General Bonds   Magic Music, a chain of retail stores that sell musical instruments, issued 12% bonds with a face value of $1,000,000 on January 1, 1995. Interest is payable quarterly on March 31, June 30, September 30, and December 31, of each year. The bonds mature on December 31, 2004, and were sold to yield a rate of 16% annually. Issue costs of $25,000 were incurred at the time of issuance.

INSTRUCTIONS

[a] Prepare a schedule to determine the amount that Magic Music received from the issuance of the bonds.

[b] Prepare the general journal entries to record the issuance of the bonds, including the payment of the issue costs.

[c] Prepare the long-term liability and any other necessary portions of the balance sheet at the date of issuance to reflect the above information.

15–43 Alternative Methods of Amortization   Covington Company issued 1,000, $1,000 par value bonds at a price to yield an effective rate of 12%. The bonds are dated May 1, 1995, and pay 11% interest annually on April 30. The bonds mature on April 30, 2000.

INSTRUCTIONS

[a] Prepare an amortization table showing the amount of interest expense and amortization of the discount or premium for each year of the bond issue by the effective interest method.

[b] Prepare an amortization table showing the amount of interest expense and the amortization of the discount or premium for each year of the bond issue by the straight-line method.

[c] Explain why the amortization of the discount or premium by the straight-line method exceeds that by the effective interest method in some years but not in other years.

15–44 General Bonds   Severson Company issued 10%, $3,000,000 face value bonds on October 1, 1992. Severson received $3,250,000, plus accrued interest. Interest is payable twice a year on January 1 and July 1. On December 31, 1994, the book value of the bonds, including the unamortized premium, was $3,142,000. On March 1, 1995, Severson purchased the bonds on the open market at 97 plus accrued interest. Severson used the straight-line method of premium amortization because the results did not differ materially from the effective interest method.

INSTRUCTIONS

Prepare general journal entries to record the following:

[a] The issuance of the bonds.

[b] Any adjusting entry necessary at December 31, 1992.

[c] Any entries necessary during 1995.

15–45 Convertible Bonds/Bonds with Warrants   Fleming, Inc., issued $40,000,000 of $1,000 bonds payable maturing in 20 years and bearing interest at a stated rate of 14%. The interest is payable semiannually, and each bond includes a detachable warrant enabling the holder to purchase one share of $50 par value common stock at any time prior to the year 2000 for $30. The bonds were dated and issued on January 1, 1995, for $40,500,000. The total market value of the warrants immediately after issuance was $1,000,000, and each bond (without the warrant) sold at 99.

INSTRUCTIONS

[a] Prepare a journal entry to record the issuance of these securities at January 1, 1995.

[b] Prepare the journal entry to record the subsequent exercise of the warrants.

[c] How, if at all, would your answer differ if the bonds were convertible rather than attached to a stock warrant? Assume that each bond is convertible into 10 shares of stock with no additional

charge for conversion. Answer both [a] and [b] and assume that the bonds are converted shortly after issuance.

15–46 General Bonds Osgood Company issued bonds as follows:

Two thousand $1,000 par value bonds.

Ten percent stated annual interest, payable on February 28 (or 29) and August 31 of each year.

Selling price, 103% of par value (plus accrued interest, which is credited to interest expense).

Date of bonds, March 1, 1995.

Date of sale, May 1, 1995.

Due date of bonds, February 28, 2005.

The company amortizes (by the straight-line method) any premium or discount at year-end (December 31) for the entire year. Amortization is rounded to the nearest dollar. No reversing entries are made on January 1.

INSTRUCTIONS

[a] Prepare all general journal entries required for the years 1995 and 1996.
[b] Prepare the balance sheet and income statement presentations of the bond and interest expense accounts for 1995 and 1996.

15–47 General Bonds Porter Ridge Development, Inc., issued $800,000 par value bonds on July 1, 1993. They mature eight years from the date of issuance and pay interest semiannually on December 31 and June 30. Issue costs of the bonds were $12,000 and are amortized by the straight-line method over the life of the bond issue.

The following partial amortization table accounts for the bonds and the related interest:

Date	Cash Interest Paid	Interest Expense Recognized	Amortization	Carrying Value of Bonds
July 1, 1993	—	—	—	$846,611
Dec. 31, 1993	$36,000	$33,864	$2,136	844,475
June 30, 1994	36,000	33,779	2,221	842,254
Dec. 31, 1994	36,000	33,690	2,310	839,944

The bonds are callable at 110 on any interest payment date after December 31, 1994.

INSTRUCTIONS

[a] Determine the nominal or stated interest rate on the bond issue.
[b] Determine the effective (annual) interest rate on the bond issue.
[c] Prepare all journal entries required for 1993 and 1994 concerning the bond issue.
[d] Prepare the general journal entries to record the June 30, 1995, interest payment and the reacquisition of $400,000 of the bonds at that date.

15–48 Convertible Bonds/Bonds with Warrants Two comparable companies issued bonds on January 1, 1994, as described below:

Port Company. Issued $1,000,000, 10%, 10-year bonds, at 102. Each $1,000 bond is convertible into 100 shares of the company's $5 par value common stock on any interest payment date after January 1, 1994. Immediately after the sale, the bonds were selling at 102 and the common stock at $11.

Starboard Company. Issued $1,000,000, 10% bonds, at 103. Each $1,000 bond is accompanied by two detachable warrants to purchase one share each of the company's $50 par value common stock at $100 per share. Immediately after the sale, the bonds were selling at 102, the warrants at $20, and the common stock at $112.

INSTRUCTIONS

For each company, complete the following:

[a] Prepare the general journal entry to record the sale of the bonds.
[b] Explain your treatment of the equity portion of the hybrid security that was recorded in [a].
[c] Prepare the relevant portion(s) of the balance sheet immediately following the sale of the bonds.
[d] Prepare the entry to record the conversion on July 1, 1994, of the entire debt of Port Company and the exercise of all Starboard Company warrants. Use straight-line amortization for simplicity when applicable.

15–49 General Bonds   On March 1, 1994, Luna Company sold its 100 five-year, $1,000 face value, 8% bonds dated March 1, 1994, at an effective annual interest rate (yield) of 10%. Interest is payable annually and the first interest payment date is February 28, 1995. Luna uses the interest method of amortization. Bond issue costs were incurred in preparing and selling the bond issue. The bonds can be called by Luna at 101 at any time on or after March 1, 1995.

INSTRUCTIONS

[a] [1] Determine the selling price of the bonds.

   [2] Specify how all items related to the bonds would be presented in a balance sheet prepared immediately after the bond issue was sold.

[b] What items related to the bond issue are included in Luna's 1994 income statement, and how is each determined? What amount of interest would be reported at December 31, 1994?

[c] Is the amount of bond discount amortization using the interest method of amortization lower in the second or third year of the life of the bond issue? Why?

[d] Assuming that the bonds were called in and retired on March 1, 1995, how should Luna report the retirement of the bonds on the 1995 income statement?   (AICPA adapted)

15–50 General Bonds   On July 1, 1994, Michael's Manufacturing Company sold $2,500,000 of bonds dated July 1, 1994, paying interest at 10% and issued to yield 12%. Bond issue costs totaled $28,000.

The bonds mature on June 30, 2004. They pay interest annually at June 30. The company's policy is to amortize bond premium and discount by the effective interest method and bond issue costs by the straight-line method on a monthly basis.

INSTRUCTIONS

[a] Compute the price at which the bonds sold.

[b] Prepare an amortization table for the first four years of the bond issue.

[c] Prepare all general journal entries to record bond-related events for 1994 and 1995. (No reversing entries are made on January 1.)

[d] Prepare the financial statement presentation of all bond-related items for the company's 1994 and 1995 financial statements. (Michael's accounting period ends on December 31.)

15–51 Debt Retirement   Your client, Eastern Manufacturing, Inc., is planning to issue new bonds at a lower interest rate to extinguish bonds currently outstanding. You have been asked to assist with some calculations regarding these transactions.

After reviewing the data, you realize that the decision to redeem bonds and issue new ones can be viewed as a capital budgeting decision. When using capital budgeting techniques, Eastern has adopted the following cutoff points: maximum payback period is eight years and minimum desired rate of return is 16%.

The following data relate to the original (outstanding) bonds and the new bonds to be issued:

	Original Bond Issue	New Bond Issue
Face value	$20,000,000	$20,000,000
Coupon rate	6%	5%
Call premium	4%	4½%
Expired life	5 years	—
Remaining life to maturity	15 years	15 years
Issued at	98½	100
Total issue costs	$120,000	$135,000

The new issue is to be sold and then one month later the original issue is to be redeemed. The overlapping month's interest on the original issue is *not* to be considered a miscellaneous cost of reacquisition.

All discounts and issue cost are amortized on a straight-line basis because that method is not materially different from the effective interest method of amortization. Interest is paid annually. All cash flows are assumed to occur at year-end. The federal income tax rate is 40%.

INSTRUCTIONS

[a] Compute Eastern's accounting gain or loss on the early extinguishment of the original (outstanding) bonds.

[b] Compute the net cash investment based on the difference between the net cash outflow to redeem the original issue and the amount raised by the new issue.

[c] Compute the net cash benefit per year based on the difference between the annual net cash outlay required on the original issue and that required on the new issue.

[d] Independent of your answers to [b] and [c], assume that the net cash investment was $550,000 and that the net cash benefit per year was $120,000. Evaluate this "investment" by using the following capital-budgeting methods: (1) payback and (2) present value. (AICPA adapted)

15-52 (Appendix A) Troubled-Debt Restructuring In connection with a debt restructuring on December 31, 1995, Bremerton Corporation, experiencing cash flow problems stemming from poor operations, transferred real estate to the Superior Bank in full settlement of a debt of $1,700,000. However, the real estate was carried on the books of Bremerton at $1,200,000. The current fair market value for similar real estate is $1,350,000.

INSTRUCTIONS

[a] Is the restructuring a troubled-debt restructuring? Why?

[b] Should the debtor recognize a gain or loss on the transfer of the real estate? If your answer is yes, indicate how the amount would be presented in the income statement.

[c] Should the debtor recognize a gain or loss in the restructuring? If your answer is yes, indicate the amount and how it would be treated in the income statement.

[d] What is the proper accounting treatment of this debt restructuring by the creditor?

15-53 (Appendix A) Troubled-Debt Restructuring On December 31, 1995, a $100,000 note is restructured by modifying the terms of the debt. The modifications, which are due to debtor financial difficulties, include the following:

[1] Forgiving $10,000 of principal and $6,969 of accrued interest.

[2] Extending the maturity date by five years.

[3] Reducing the interest rate from 10% to 6%.

Interest at 6% is to be paid annually on the new principal amount under the new terms. Therefore, the aggregate future cash payments under the new term total $117,000. This total represents $90,000 of principal and $27,000 of interest (6% × $90,000 × 5).

INSTRUCTIONS

[a] Is the restructuring a troubled-debt restructuring? Why?

[b] Will interest expense be recognized by the debtor in the future? If so, what is the effective interest rate under the new terms?

[c] A partial amortization schedule is provided below. Complete the schedule for the restructured debt presented in this case.

Date	(.06 × 90,000) Stated Interest Payment	Principal Payment	Reported Effective Interest Expense	Balance
12/31/95				$106,969
12/31/96	$5,400			
12/31/97	5,400			
12/31/98	5,400			
12/31/99	5,400			
12/31/2000	5,400			

[d] How should the debtor record the payment made on December 31, 1996?

[e] How should the creditor record the payment made on December 31, 1996?

15-54 (Appendix B) Serial Bonds On December 31, 1987, South Gate Company issued $1,000,000 of 8% serial bonds when the market rate was 10%. The bonds pay interest annually and will be retired according to the following schedule:

12/31/95	$ 400,000
12/31/96	300,000
12/31/97	200,000
12/31/98	100,000
Total	$1,000,000

On December 31, 1995, South Gate Company had excess cash and decided to retire the $100,000 of the bonds due December 31, 1998, on the open market. At that time, the market interest rate was 8% per annum. In accordance with GAAP, South Gate uses the effective interest method.

INSTRUCTIONS

Answer the following questions and provide supporting computations. Formal schedules are *not* necessary unless otherwise noted.

[a] Calculate the proceeds from the issuance.
[b] Prepare an amortization schedule for 1988 and 1989.
[c] Show the balance sheet presentation for the bonds at December 31, 1988 and 1989.
[d] How much did it cost to buy back the December 31, 1998, bonds at December 31, 1995?

CASES

15–55 Amortization/Extinguishment This case consists of two *independent* parts.
   Part 1. The effective interest method is appropriate for amortizing a premium or discount arising on the issuance of bonds.

INSTRUCTIONS

[a] Describe the effective interest method of amortization and how it compares with the straight-line method of amortization.
[b] How is amortization computed using the effective interest method? How do the results differ from those computed under the straight-line method, and why?

   Part 2. Gain or loss from the early extinguishment of debt that is refunded can theoretically be accounted for in three ways:

[1] Amortized over remaining life of old debt.
[2] Amortized over the life of the new debt issue.
[3] Recognized in the period of extinguishment.

INSTRUCTIONS

[a] Provide supporting arguments for each of the three methods.
[b] Which method is generally accepted, and how should the appropriate amount of gain or loss be recorded in a company's financial statements? (AICPA adapted)

15–56 Convertible Debt Blair Company recently issued $1,000,000 face value, 5%, 30-year subordinated debentures at 97. The debentures are redeemable at 103 on demand by the issuer and at any date on 30 days' notice 10 years after the issue. The debentures are convertible into $10 par value common stock of the company at the conversion price of $12.50 per share for each $500 or multiple thereof of the principal amount of the debentures.

INSTRUCTIONS

[a] Explain how the conversion feature of convertible debt is valuable to (1) the issuer and (2) the purchaser.
[b] Blair management has suggested that in recording the issuance of the debentures, a portion of the proceeds should be assigned to the conversion feature.
   [1] What are the arguments for according separate accounting recognition to the conversion feature of the debentures?
   [2] What are the arguments in favor of accounting for the convertible debentures as a single element?
[c] Assume that no value is assigned to the conversion feature on issue of the debentures. Assume further that five years after issue, debentures with a face value of $100,000 and book value of $97,500 are tendered for conversion on an interest payment date when the market price of the debentures is 104 and the common stock is selling at $14 per share. The company records the conversion as follows:

Bonds Payable	100,000	
Bond Discount		2,500
Common Stock		80,000
Paid-in Capital in Excess of Par Value		17,500

Discuss the propriety of this accounting treatment. (AICPA adapted)

15-57 Convertible Debt/Debt with Warrants Incurring long-term debt with an arrangement whereby lenders receive an option to buy common stock during all or a portion of the time the debt is outstanding is a frequently used corporate financing practice. In some situations, the result is achieved through the issuance of convertible bonds; in others, the debt instruments and the warrants to buy stock are separate.

INSTRUCTIONS

[a] Describe the differences that exist in current accounting for original proceeds of the issuance of convertible bonds and of debt instruments with separate warrants to purchase common stock.
[b] Discuss the rationale for the differences described in [a].
[c] Summarize the arguments that support the alternative accounting treatment.

(AICPA adapted)

15-58 General Debt Accounting One way for a corporation to accomplish long-term financing is through the issuance of long-term debt instruments in the form of bonds.

INSTRUCTIONS

[a] Describe how to account for the proceeds from bonds issued with detachable stock-purchase warrants.
[b] Contrast a serial bond with a term (straight) bond.
[c] For a five-year term bond issued at a premium, why would the amortization in the first year of the life of the bond differ using the effective interest method of amortization instead of the straight-line method? Indicate whether the amount of amortization in the first year of the life of the bond is higher or lower using the effective interest method instead of the straight-line method.
[d] When a bond issue is sold between interest dates at a discount, what journal entry is made and how is the subsequent amortization of the discount affected? Include an explanation of how the amounts of each debit and credit are determined.
[e] Describe how to account for and classify the gain or loss from the reacquisition of a long-term bond before its maturity. (AICPA adapted)

15-59 Convertible Debt/Debt with Warrants The equityholders of a business entity usually include both creditors and owners. These two classes of equityholders share some characteristics, and sometimes it is difficult to distinguish between them. Examples of this problem include (1) convertible debt and (2) debt issued with stock-purchase warrants. Although both examples represent the debts of a corporation, in each case there is a question as to whether there is an ownership interest that requires accounting recognition.

INSTRUCTIONS

[a] Define convertible debt and debt issued with stock-purchase warrants.
[b] Discuss the similarities and differences of convertible debt and debt issued with stock-purchase warrants.
[c] Describe the alternative accounting treatments for the proceeds from convertible debt. Explain which treatment is preferable.
[d] Describe the alternative accounting treatments for the proceeds from debt issued with stock-purchase warrants. Explain which treatment is preferable. (AICPA adapted)

15-60 Debt Refinancing Gerardi Vineyards, Inc., suffered a crop failure during the summer of 1995. As the end of its reporting year nears, Gerardi's controller is searching for ways to increase reported earnings. Among other alternatives, the controller is considering refinancing the company's long-term borrowing. Gerardi issued $500,000 of 6% notes payable to a bank at 100 several years ago when interest rates were much lower. These notes mature at December 31, 2015. The bank has since approached Gerardi with the following proposal.

In exchange for the $500,000 note now owed, the bank will allow Gerardi to issue a new note for only $475,000 maturing in 20 years at the current rate of 20%. Under each alternative, interest is paid annually on the liability.

INSTRUCTIONS

[a] Prepare a pro forma journal entry that would be made if Gerardi accepts the proposal.
[b] Describe the theoretical support for this treatment. Also, comment on any problems you see in this treatment.
[c] Suggest a way to overcome the problem(s) discussed in [b]. Do not limit your discussion to contemporary generally accepted accounting principles.

[d] Comment on the controller's decision. Should Gerardi refinance the debt? Consider present-value concepts in your answer, but do not attempt any present-value calculations.

15-61 Debt Financing vs. Leasing   The president of Today's Toy Company has decided to expand the manufacturing capacity of her company to meet increased demand for certain low-cost toys. Emily Toon, vice president for production, has located two similar plant sites on which comparable industrial buildings already exist. She has approached the president to decide which site should be selected.

The first site could be purchased for $200,000. The toy company's banker, Ms. Sullivan, indicates that an 80% loan of $160,000 for 20 years could be arranged at an interest rate of 15% to allow Today's Toy to buy the facility. Equal annual payments of $25,562 will be made to the bank under the terms of the proposed loan. The second site is available only through a long-term lease that requires a 20-year term with payments of $25,000 to be made at the end of each year.

In evaluating the two alternatives, Ms. Toon points out that under the lease, no down payment is required, the annual payments are virtually equal, and best of all, the company will not be required to record any liability for the lease on its financial statements. In this manner, the debt/equity and return on assets ratios will be maintained. Under the purchase arrangement, however, both ratios will become weaker.

INSTRUCTIONS

[a] If you were president of Today's Toy Company, would you accept Ms. Toon's advice? If not, what additional information would you request?

[b] Discuss the propriety of not recorded the lease as a liability. Do not consider current authoritative pronouncements in your answer. Rather, discuss the conceptual meaning and characteristics of liabilities in general.

15-62 Financial Statement Presentation   On January 1, 1995, Torrance Corporation issued $1,106,775 in 20-year bonds that have a maturity value of $1,000,000 and pay interest semiannually on January 1 and July 1. Bond issue costs were not material in amount. The following three presentations of the long-term liability section of the balance sheet might be used for these bonds at the issue date:

[1]	Bonds payable (maturing Jan. 1, 2015)	$1,000,000
	Unamortized premium on bonds payable	106,775
	Total bond liability	$1,106,775
[2]	Bonds payable, principal (face value $1,000,000, maturing Jan. 1, 2015)	$ 252,572*
	Bonds payable, interest (semiannual payment $40,000)	854,203†
	Total bond liability	$1,106,775
[3]	Bonds payable, principal (maturing Jan. 1, 2015)	$1,000,000
	Bonds payable, interest ($40,000 per period for 40 periods)	1,600,000
	Total bond liability	$2,600,000

---

*The present value of $1,000,000 due at the end of 40 (six-month) periods at the yield rate of 3½% per period.
†The present value of $40,000 per period for 40 (six-month) periods at the yield rate of 3½% per period.

INSTRUCTIONS

[a] Discuss the conceptual merit(s) of each of the date-of-issue balance sheet presentations shown for these bonds.

[b] Explain why investors would pay $1,106,775 for bonds with a maturity value of only $1,000,000.

[c] Assuming that a discount rate is needed to compute the carrying value of the obligations arising from a bond issue at any date during the life of the bonds, discuss the conceptual merit(s) of using for this purpose:
[1] The coupon or nominal rate.
[2] The effective or yield rate at date of issue.

[d] If the obligations arising from these bonds are to be carried at their present value, computed by means of the current market rate of interest, how would the bond valuation after the date of issue be affected by an increase or a decrease in the market rate of interest?   (AICPA adapted)

15–63 (Appendix A) Troubled-Debt Restructuring While discussing troubled-debt restructurings, a CPA commented: "The determination of whether or not a debt restructuring is a troubled-debt restructuring is simplified because the economic results of any restructuring clearly indicate what type of transaction has occurred. Little judgment is required, other than the possible determination of fair market value of assets or equity interests transferred."

INSTRUCTIONS

Describe other areas, if any, requiring interpretation and judgment in identifying and accounting for debt restructurings.

JUDGMENT CASES

15–64 Classifying Financial Instruments You are the controller of Hedges, Inc., and are preparing its financial statements. During the year, the company borrowed $10,000,000 by issuing "income bonds." The bonds mature in 20 years but require the payment of interest only if income is earned in an amount sufficient to pay the interest in each year.

You have just received a memo from the president of Hedges stating his belief that the bonds should not be reported under the balance sheet caption of liabilities due to the unusual interest-paying feature. He does not suggest that the bonds be reported as a part of stockholders' equity, but it is clear that he does not want them included in the company's liabilities on the balance sheet. He points out that the present value of the maturity amount of the bonds is just a small portion of the present value of the maturity and interest payments. That is, the present value of the interest payments represents most of the present value of the total future cash outflows of the bonds, and that amount is contingent on the ability of Hedges to earn sufficient income in each year.

INSTRUCTIONS

Develop a method to present the bonds that you believe meets professional standards but that also satisfies the wishes of your boss. If both cannot be achieved, develop a solution that meets professional standards and comes as close as possible to meeting the president's wishes.

15–65 Related-Party Obligations During the past year, your client, George Harris, Inc., borrowed $250,000 from its president and sole owner. It is now January 25 and you are preparing the December 31 financial statements for the year just ended. There is no note to support the loan, and Mr. Harris has told you that the terms were never well developed. He stated, "The company needed the money to pay one of its notes that had come due, and I had to make sure that the company didn't default. The company will pay me back when it can afford to." Now you must consider whether the borrowing should be reported as current or a long-term liability, and you have approached Mr. Harris to resolve the issue. In response to your question, he states, "If anything, the amount is a long-term liability. It is certainly not current. Wow, reporting that amount as a current liability will result in violations of working capital maintenance convenants on one of my bank loans, and that will be bad news. In fact, why don't we just consider the amount as a permanent contribution to the capital of the company? Yeah. That's it. Then the bank will be even more impressed by my debt/equity ratio. Just report the amount as an addition to the stockholders' equity of the company. I'll be happy to write you up something to that effect, if it will make you feel better." At that point, he prepares a memo that asserts that the amounts provided by him to the company are permanent contributions to the equity of the company.

You leave this meeting with mixed emotions. The terms and conditions of the transaction are clearly within Mr. Harris's authority to define, but you remember a discussion you had with him about his personal tax situation in which he spoke of withdrawing funds from his company to facilitate a payment to the Internal Revenue Service. When you call to remind him of this conversation, he responds, "I can get that money from a lot of places, and you need not worry about where or if I can pay my taxes. Just prepare the financial statements for my company along the lines we discussed and everything will be O.K." You now wonder what to make of all this information.

INSTRUCTIONS

Determine how the $250,000 amount should be reported. If you believe that additional disclosures are necessary, be sure to describe what information should be included.

15–66 Existence of a Liability You are auditing the financial statements of Maywhort Properties, Inc., a real estate developer located and operating exclusively in the San Diego area and have just stumbled across a five-year nonrecourse note payable that was incurred during the past year. The note, which has not been recorded in the general ledger, was incurred in the acquisition of a parcel of land in Arizona. However, you are not aware of any plans to begin development activities away from the San Diego area, and when you ask management about the note, the president responds as follows:

> *We didn't want to sign that note; however, that was the only way that our local bank would give us a construction loan for the shopping center project out in the Laguna suburb. The note is without recourse except for the Arizona property, which serves as the only collateral. The interest payable on the $5,000,000 note was to come from the proceeds of our large shopping center loan. So we had to sign our shopping center loan for $21,000,000 rather than the $20,000,000 that we wanted just to allow them to withhold the extra $1,000,000 as interest on the $5,000,000 nonrecourse note.*
>
> *The lending officer assured us that when the note matures in five years, we can default on it and they will take back the property at that time in accordance with the nonrecourse provisions without any prejudice to us. In fact, the president of the bank personally assured me of the acceptability of this arrangement. Because that was the only way we could get our loan, we agreed. That's all there is to this deal. We do not intend to repay the loan at its maturity. Indeed, one of our people who is familiar with land in that area told us that the property is probably worth only about $500,000. We view this deal as a way for the bank to increase the effective rate of interest on our big construction loan. We now have to repay and pay interest on an extra $1,000,000, which, of course, is reported appropriately. We don't think that we have acquired land or incurred additional debt in the amount of $5,000,000.*

When you suggest that it might be necessary to record the loan and related property, the president of Maywhort Properties responds, "No, we're not going to do that. The substance of the transaction is not the acquisition of land and the incurrence of debt. We're never going to pay the debt. At maturity, we're simply going to let the property revert to our lender. To report a liability in this circumstance would cause the financial statements to be misleading."

You have since confirmed the essence of the transaction with officials at the bank. They also stated that they acquired the land through foreclosure proceedings that resulted from a default on a loan they had made to a party completely unrelated and unknown to Maywhort. They added that the current deal was structured to accomplish certain financial reporting objectives of theirs, and that in no way should any of this reflect adversely on Maywhort Properties.

INSTRUCTIONS

Determine how you should respond to this situation. Should you insist on recording the loan and related debt? If so, at what amount should the debt and land be recorded?

15–67 Classification of Liabilities   During the year, Serious Problems, Inc., a small manufacturer, violated a number of debt covenants. Among the consequences of those events is the acceleration of the maturities of its debts due on demand. At this date, none of the creditors has demanded payment of the amounts due, but discussions are ongoing. Some type of restructuring is expected but has not yet been negotiated and finalized. You have proposed a number of disclosures and indicated that the debt should be reclassified as current rather than long term. Your client has agreed to the note disclosures but has suggested that an unclassified balance sheet be prepared this year. That is, there would be no distinction between current assets and liabilities and those that are noncurrent. You wonder whether this complies with generally acceptable accounting principles.

INSTRUCTIONS

Do you believe that it would be acceptable to prepare for the company a balance sheet that does not distinguish between current and long-term liabilities? Be sure to support your answer with appropriate analysis and research.

FINANCIAL REPORTING CASE

15–68 Financial Reporting Case   Abbott Laboratories is a diversified health-care company devoted to the discovery, development, manufacture, and marketing of innovative products that improve diagnostic, therapeutic, and nutritional practice. The company markets products in more than 130 countries and employs 5,000 people.

Below is the liabilities section of Abbott Laboratories 1993 balance sheet and Note 2 which includes information on debt and lines of credit.

Liabilities and Shareholders' Investment (dollars in thousands)	1993	December 31 1992	1991
Current Liabilities:			
Short-term borrowings	$ 841,514	$ 909,116	$ 523,526
Trade accounts payable	638,509	597,226	522,397
Salaries, wages and commissions	215,432	196,259	212,394
Other accrued liabilities	933,049	905,877	649,744
Dividends payable	139,600	125,300	106,297
Income taxes payable	324,749	41,583	194,255
Current portion of long-term debt	2,080	7,147	20,724
Total Current Liabilities	3,094,933	2,782,508	2,229,337
Long-Term Debt	306,840	110,018	125,118
Other Liabilities and Deferrals:			
Deferred income taxes	51,383	321,301	347,245
Other	560,484	379,768	350,579
Total Other Liabilities and Deferrals	611,867	701,069	697,824

Note 2—Debt and Lines of Credit (dollars in thousands)

The following is a summary of long-term debt at December 31:

	1993	1992	1991
5.6% debentures, due 2003	$200,000	—	—
Industrial revenue bonds at various rates of interest, averaging 4.0% at December 31, 1993, and due at various dates through 2023	82,600	$ 82,600	$ 82,600
Other, principally foreign affiliate borrowings at various rates of interest, averaging 4.7% at December 31, 1993, and due at various dates through 1998	24,240	27,418	42,518
Total, net of current maturities	306,840	110,018	125,118
Current maturities of long-term debt	2,080	7,147	20,724
Total carrying amount	$308,920	$117,165	$145,842
Total fair market value	$304,038	$115,568	

Payments required on long-term debt outstanding at December 31, 1993, are $19,969 in 1995, $1,399 in 1996, $4,209 in 1997, and $2,460 in 1998.

At December 31, 1993, there were $300,000 of domestic lines of credit, none of which were used. Related compensating balances, which are subject to withdrawal by the Company at its option, and commitment fees are not material. The Company may issue up to $300,000 of senior debt securities in the future under a registration statement filed with the Securities and Exchange Commission in 1993.

At December 31, 1993 and 1992, the carrying amount of short-term borrowings approximated fair value.

INSTRUCTIONS

[a] What percentage of Abbott Laboratories' liabilities are other than current for 1993? Has this relationship changed materially from 1991 through 1993?

[b] What detailed information is provided in Note 2 for the various types of debt that Abbott Laboratories has outstanding?

[c] Why do you think Abbott Laboratories has chosen to present this detailed information in Note 2 rather than incorporating it into the body of the balance sheet?

[d] What part of Note 2 is particularly useful in determining the impact that the repayment of debt is likely to have during the years immediately following 1993?

[e] What is the relationship between the total carrying amount of debt for 1993 ($308,920,000) and the amount of debt presented as current and long-term debt in the balance sheet?

Stockholders' Equity: Corporate Formation and Contributed Capital

OBJECTIVES

1. To discuss characteristics, advantages, and disadvantages of the corporate form of business enterprise.
2. To explain various stockholders' rights and different types of equity securities.
3. To identify the characteristics of common and preferred stock.
4. To explain the judgments necessary in distinguishing between debt and equity securities and among various types of equity instruments.
5. To describe and illustrate acceptable accounting and reporting practices for the issuance of capital stock for both cash and noncash consideration.
6. To describe and illustrate acceptable accounting and reporting practices for the issuance of capital stock through subscription.
7. To describe and illustrate the methods of accounting for treasury stock.
8. To describe and illustrate acceptable accounting and reporting practices for the retirement of capital stock.
9. To describe and illustrate acceptable accounting and reporting practices for property and treasury stock donations.

To obtain sufficient capital to establish or expand their operations, companies today commonly issue various classes of stock in initial public offerings. Corporations also issue stock throughout their existence to achieve many goals and objectives as well. For example, in February 1994 RJR Nabisco Holdings Corp. revealed plans to raise $2 billion through the issue of preferred stock. The plan was widely viewed as an initial step in separating its tobacco and food divisions or to facilitate a merger with another consumer products company.

Companies also use their own stock in attempts to directly acquire other enterprises. An example of this was provided by the attempts of both Viacom and QVC, Inc., to acquire the publishing and entertainment company, Paramount. But such transactions can become difficult to consumate because the value of the proposed acquirers' stock is subject to price fluctuations, which can be substantial. In the case of Paramount, Viacom was successful by reducing the amount of its common stock and increasing other securities that were not so volatile as that of Viacom.

The Wall Street Journal (February 25, 1994), pp. C19 and A3.

T he substantial growth in the corporate form of business during the industrial revolution was, in part, a response to the demands of commerce. As capital was substituted for labor and as mass production economies replaced individual craft shops, the need for larger accumulations of capital became more intense. Few individuals possessed the resources necessary to build factories, hire employees, and sustain operations until an adequate level of profitability and accumulated earnings was generated. The need emerged for a form of business organization that would permit a large number of owners to pool their resources to provide the large amounts of capital required to support these more complex business activities. One of the important characteristics of the corporate form of business organization is the widespread distribution of ownership that is accomplished when many owners purchase shares of stock in a corporation, thereby permitting a much greater accumulation of capital than is possible with the sole proprietorship and partnership forms of business organization. As a result of these and related factors, the modern corporate form of business was developed, expanded, and refined.

As we begin our two-chapter coverage of the subject of stockholders' equity, turn to the balance sheet of Kellogg on the right front endpapers of your textbook. The last section of this financial statement is titled "Stockholders' Equity" and includes common stock, capital in excess of par value, and treasury stock, all of which are subjects covered in this chapter. Other aspects of stockholders' equity, including retained earnings, are covered in Chapter 17. Notice that total stockholders' equity was over $1.7 billion in 1993, so you can see that it is a very important part of this company's balance sheet.

THE CORPORATE ENVIRONMENT

Corporations offer important advantages over other forms of business, such as sole proprietorships and partnerships. For example, the corporate organization (1) facilitates the accumulation of large amounts of capital; (2) provides for economies of scale in production due to the potential large size of corporate organizations; and (3) facilitates a capital market in which resources are easily allocated to more efficient producers. Other advantages include **limited liability,** in that stockholders have no personal liability for the corporation's debts and risk only their capital investments; and **unlimited life of the corporation,** in that the death of a stockholder does not cause the termination of the corporation, as in the case of the death of a partner in a partnership.

The advantages of limited liability and unlimited life do not come without some cost to the stockholders. One cost is in the form of **double taxation.** A corporation, unlike a partnership or a sole proprietorship, is generally subject to taxation on net income. Furthermore, individual stockholders are subject to taxation on the distributions of that corporate net income as they receive dividends. Therefore, income is taxed at the corporate level and again at the individual level.

Corporate stockholders often are not involved in the custody and management of corporate assets. Financial accounting and reporting therefore provide valuable communication between a corporation's owners and managers. The custodians of resources report on the efficiency and effectiveness of their performance to the providers of those resources. Resource providers of corporations are (1) owners or stockholders and (2) creditors. Chapters 14 and 15 discuss accounting and reporting for the corporation's liabilities. This chapter and the following one are concerned with financial accounting and reporting for stockholders' equity.

THE CORPORATE STRUCTURE

A corporation is established under the authority of state law. In most cases, a state official, frequently the secretary of state, responds to a request for a corporate charter made by **incorporators,** who will become **stockholders** of the corporation. A corporate charter and related **articles of incorporation** describe the nature of the business, the classes and types of corporate stock to be issued, and other pertinent information. After a corporate charter is granted, the **common stockholders** elect a **board of directors,** which, in turn, appoints members of corporate management, such as the president, vice presidents, and other executives. The board of directors also approves the corporate **bylaws** under which the company operates.

TYPES OF CORPORATIONS

Corporations are usually stock ownership companies that are organized for profit. There are, however, other types of corporate organizations. For example, **public corporations** may be

---

EXHIBIT 16–1

Types of Corporations

Corporation Type	Nature of Ownership
1. Public corporations	Government owned
2. Mutual companies	Consumer controlled
3. Private corporations	Stockholder owned
(a) Publicly held corporations	Widely distributed ownership by institutions and/or individuals; shares typically traded on organized exchanges
(b) Closely held corporations	Limited distribution of ownership
(1) Professional corporations	Shares restricted to members of a legally recognized profession
(2) S corporations	Designed to avoid double taxation
(3) Other closely held corporations	Limited ownership by institutions and/or individuals; shares not traded on organized exchanges

---

established and owned by a unit of government to meet a social need. Examples include the Federal Deposit Insurance Corporation, which insures deposits in certain commercial banks, and the Off Track Betting Corporation, which provides revenue to the City of New York from pari-mutuel horse race betting.

Mutual companies are cooperative organizations designed to benefit consumer groups. Shares are distributed to the organization's customers. Many life insurance companies and savings and loan associations are mutual companies. Policyholders of mutual life insurance companies and depositors of savings and loan associations are given the rights and privileges usually afforded owners in a stock company. Corporate profits can be distributed to the customers in the form of lower prices or as dividends. Because mutual companies do not have stockholders, their balance sheets have no owner contributions or stockholders' equity section.

In contrast to public corporations and mutual companies, **private corporations** are owned by individuals or institutions and may be publicly held or closely held. **Publicly held corporations** register stock and other securities with the Securities and Exchange Commission (SEC) and are usually actively traded in an organized securities market such as the New York or American Stock Exchange. Ownership of publicly held companies is usually widespread and may include thousands of shareholders. **Closely held corporations** issue stock to a limited and well-defined group. Ownership is generally closed to prospective stockholders.

Two types of closely held corporations are the **professional corporation** and the **S corporation.** Professional corporations are established by members of a legally recognized profession, such as medicine, law, and accountancy. Ownership shares are usually available only to members of the profession. This limitation is intended to ensure the integrity of the profession by minimizing conflict of interest and professional compromise. S corporations (named for subchapter S of the Internal Revenue Code) have many advantages of the corporate form, without the negative element of double taxation. To maintain this favorable tax status, S corporations can have no more than 35 stockholders.[1]

Exhibit 16–1 summarizes the types of corporations introduced here.

Because the rights and risks of the various resource providers differ greatly, accountants must clearly understand stockholders' rights and responsibilities. The basic rights of the shareholder fall into three major categories: (1) rights to management; (2) rights to corporate

STOCKHOLDERS' RIGHTS AND TYPES OF STOCKHOLDERS' EQUITY

---

[1]This limit may be increased to 70 if spouses are included as shareholders.

property; and (3) rights to decide on changes in the original contract.[2] **Rights to management** include the right to elect directors, based on the pro rata ownership share in the firm, and the right to receive financial statements. **Rights to corporate property** include the right to declared dividends and the right to a proportionate share of corporate property at dissolution. **Rights to decide on changes in the original contract** include the right to vote on changes in the corporate bylaws and the right to maintain the pro rata ownership share based on the level of the original investment. The right to maintain the pro rata ownership share is called a **preemptive right;** it enables a stockholder to purchase additional securities from a new stock offering up to the percentage that the individual owned prior to the new issuance. Accordingly, a stockholder's percentage of ownership cannot be reduced as a result of a corporation issuing additional shares of stock to different investors, unless the stockholder declines the opportunity to acquire additional shares.

Not all stockholders receive all of these rights. For example, the preemptive right has often been eliminated in recent elections, deciding changes in the corporate bylaws. Furthermore, all stockholders of a corporation may not be entitled to the same rights. Many large corporations issue several classes of stock, with different characteristics and rights (e.g., dividend preferences, dividend amounts, and voting privileges). For example, Giant Food, Inc., which operates almost 150 supermarkets, has authorized three classes of stock. Exhibit 16–2 is the footnote description of these classes of stock in the company's 1993 annual report. Each class of stock has distinct characteristics and confers certain rights. Class AC and AL common stock, for example, provide voting privileges. In this way, control of the corporation can be maintained by a select group of stockholders, while capital can be accumulated from a widespread distribution of Class A common stock. Disclosures dealing with stock option plans are presented in Chapter 17.

Accountants classify stockholders' equity as either **contributed equity** or **earned equity.** Distinguishing between these types of equity in financial reports is important, because such information enables investors to determine how much a company relies on owner contributions versus profitable operations to sustain its financial base. Earned equity, called **retained earnings,** is discussed in the following chapter. Stockholders' contributed equity, the subject of this chapter, is usually classified for accounting and reporting purposes as **preferred stock** or **common stock.** We now discuss the major characteristics of common stock and preferred stock.

CHARACTERISTICS OF CAPITAL STOCK

The term **capital stock** identifies shareholder contributions to the enterprise. It can also be used to discuss classes of common stock or preferred stock. Two of the most significant features of capital stock are the following: (1) capital stock does *not* generally have a maturity date on which the principal portion of the security must be repaid and (2) dividends are *not* required to be paid on capital stock.

These characteristics of capital stock are also the most important factors distinguishing debt financing from stockholders' contributed equity. Most debt instruments require the payment of interest on a regular basis and specify a maturity date. In contrast, equity securities generally require neither dividends nor repayment of the principal amount of the investment. Distinguishing between debt and equity instruments is not, however, as simple as it may first appear. A number of securities that are in relatively common use contain elements of both. For example, some options sold by a company may require that entity to issue shares of its own capital stock at a certain price. Does such an obligation represent a liability or part of

---

[2]For more detailed discussion, see Richard A. Scott, "Owners' Equity, the Anachronistic Element," *Accounting Review* (October 1979), pp. 750–763.

EXHIBIT 16–2

Giant Food, Inc.
Description of Capital Stock

---

6. Common Stock and Employee Incentive Plans

Shares Authorized: Common stock, $1 par value, authorized and outstanding at year-end is as follows:

| | | Outstanding | | |
Class	Authorized	1993	1992	1991
"A" non-voting	75,000,000	**59,440,440**	59,370,475	58,728,961
"AC" voting	125,000	**125,000**	125,000	125,000
"AL" voting	125,000	**125,000**	125,000	125,000
	75,250,000	**59,690,440**	59,620,475	58,978,961

Class "A" common stock has all of the rights and privileges pertaining to other classes of common stock except the right to vote. No dividends may be declared on any class of common stock without declaring at least an equal dividend on Class "A" stock. However, dividends may be declared on Class "A" stock without declaring dividends on any other class of common stock.

At February 27, 1993, the Company had reserved 3,133,068 shares of its Class "A" common stock for issuance under its stock option and stock bonus plans. In September 1991, the Company's Board of Directors approved a plan to purchase up to 200,000 shares of its Class "A" common stock in the open market. As of February 27, 1993, the Company has not purchased any shares under this plan. The company has purchased and accumulated treasury stock in order to accommodate the needs for registered common stock which may arise in connection with the exercise of stock options and the award of shares under a stock bonus plan.

SOURCE: 1993 Giant Food, Inc.

---

stockholders' equity? The question may be particularly significant if the price at which the stock must be issued is substantially less than the market price of the shares.

We discuss some of these questions in the following pages of this chapter. However, these and many other questions are currently being considered as part of a major FASB agenda project. An FASB discussion memorandum, "Distinguishing between Liability and Equity Instruments and Accounting for Instruments with Characteristics of Both," was issued in 1990 and identifies many of the important issues that need to be resolved in this area of financial reporting. Further progress on this project is expected during the next several years, and students should be alert for developments that take place. In the interim, professional accountants must use seasoned judgment in classifying and accounting for such hybrid instruments. In complex situations, financial statement disclosures should include a description of the instrument and the related accounting policies accorded it.

Minimum Legal Capital

In the event of the dissolution of a corporation, creditors receive assets to satisfy their claims before assets are distributed to stockholders. Therefore, the more assets contributed to the enterprise by stockholders, the greater the security of creditors. To protect creditors from an excessive or unwarranted distribution of assets to stockholders, states have enacted laws requiring corporations to maintain certain minimum levels of stockholders' equity. These laws prohibit enterprises from distributing assets to shareholders to such an extent that the minimum legal capital is impaired. This therefore assures creditors of at least a minimum continuing economic commitment of stockholders in the enterprise.

To ensure an adequate measure of minimum legal capital, many state laws require corporations to issue stock with a **par value.** State laws frequently require corporations (1) to assign a formal par value to stock, (2) to ensure that the stock not be sold **at discount** (i.e., at an amount less than par), and (3) to maintain a minimum amount of legal capital. Accordingly, companies frequently assign a relatively low par value to their stock and issue enough shares to meet the legal requirements. For example, if a company is required to maintain minimum legal capital of $5,000 and issues $10 par value stock, at least 500 shares should be issued at an amount no less than par to comply with this provision of state law.

In some jurisdictions, common stock may be issued at a discount. Under those circumstances, the amount of the discount is generally considered a contingent liability of the owners to the creditors of the corporation. In the event of liquidation of corporate assets, the creditors may recover unsatisfied obligations by assessing the owners for additional contributions up to the amount of the original discount. Although most stock is nonassessable, accountants should be alert to the possibility of such a problem, especially if stock has been issued at a discount on par.

A corporation may also issue **no-par stock.** State law usually requires the company to **assign** or **state a value** for no-par stock to comply with the corporate charter and minimum legal capital requirements. The use of stated or assigned value is usually legally acceptable and poses no significant accounting problems. Some jurisdictions allow the issuance of **true no-par stock,** which has no par, stated, or assigned value. In addition, true no-par stock cannot be issued at a discount and thus involves no contingent liability of the stockholders to corporate creditors.

Par, stated, or assigned value on common stock must not be confused with either fair value or book value per share. The **fair value per share of stock** is the price at which both buyer and seller agree to transact a sale. Market values for common stock are quoted for most publicly held companies in publications such as *The Wall Street Journal.* The **book value per share of stock** is the total stockholders' equity divided by the total number of shares outstanding. The book value per share is the dollar amount per share an owner would receive if assets were liquidated and obligations were satisfied at the amounts reported on the financial statements. Both the fair value and the book value per share are generally much larger than the par, stated, or assigned value. The fair value of stock is influenced by a variety of factors including analysts' and others' expectations about a company's future profits and cash flows. The par value of a stock is not a measure of the value or worth of a company but is simply a legal device frequently used by states to protect creditors. Many persons would call the concept of par or stated value an anachronism in the context of the modern corporation.

States grant corporate charters to enterprises in their jurisdictions and enforce laws governing corporate conduct. Because these laws differ, the American Bar Association (ABA) has tried to establish a unified system of law for all states. Specifically, the ABA's Committee on Corporate Laws has suggested a Model Business Corporation Act. However, not all states have adopted the provisions of the model act. Furthermore, the act contains terminology that can be interpreted differently, and certain provisions have become obsolete. Accountants should be aware of the state corporation laws affecting their employers or clients to adequately account for the rights and protections of the various resource providers.

CLASSES OF CAPITAL STOCK

Common Stock

Common stock represents the most fundamental type of equity and generally gives the owner the right to vote, to share in residual profits, and, in the event of dissolution, to share in all assets remaining after creditors' and preferred stockholders' claims have been satisfied. If there is only one class of stock, it is common stock.

Common stockholders have a residual interest in the corporation, because they receive economic benefit *only if* the corporation successfully meets its obligations to creditors and preferred stockholders. Therefore, common stockholders tend to assume more risk than other groups associated with the enterprise. Consistent with the relatively high level of risk, however, is the potential for great financial reward. Common stockholders have no upper limit on their economic rewards from profitable operations. Creditors receive only interest and principal repayment; preferred stockholders, with certain exceptions, receive a fixed or limited return on their investment regardless of profitability. Therefore, if a company is profitable in its operation, the holdings of common stockholders will become more valuable. Conversely, if a company suffers losses, the value of the common stockholders' equity will be reduced as fewer assets are available to satisfy residual claims.

Preferred Stock

Preferred stock represents equity securities that receive a preference over the claims of common stockholders in terms of dividends from earnings and assets in the event of dissolution. Therefore, preferred stock usually represents a somewhat less risky investment than common stock. Although the board of directors of a corporation is not required to declare dividends on either stock, any dividend declared must go first to preferred stockholders to the extent of their preference claims. The amount of the dividend to be paid on preferred stock is generally stated as a percentage of the par or stated value of the stock. For example, a holder of $100 par value, 12% preferred stock has the right to receive a dividend, if declared, each year of $12 ($100 $\times$ .12). Furthermore, in the event of bankruptcy or other dissolution, preferred stockholders receive the par or stated value of their investment before any distribution is made to common stockholders. Occasionally, no-par preferred stock is issued, with the dividend stated as a fixed dollar amount rather than as a percentage of par. An amount to be distributed upon dissolution is also stated in the event of the termination of the business. Preferred stock, which usually conveys no voting rights, often carries other types of preference claims.

Cumulative Preferred Stock.   A **cumulative clause** on preferred stock means that all dividends, including dividends that were not declared and paid in prior years, must be updated and paid before any dividends can be paid to common stockholders. Although stockholders cannot directly require the payment of dividends, a cumulative clause protects preferred stockholders from situations in which no dividends are paid on preferred or common shares for several years and then an exceptionally large dividend is declared. If preferred stock is not cumulative, preferred stockholders receive only the dividends attributable to the current year. If, however, preferred is cumulative, the current year's dividend and all **dividends in arrears** must be paid to preferred stockholders before the common stockholders share in a distribution. The application of the cumulative feature is illustrated in Chapter 17, where we discuss dividends in detail.

Participating Preferred Stock.   A **participation right** allows preferred stockholders not only to receive the preference dividend but also to share with common stockholders in any further dividends that are declared. Participating preferred stock may be either fully or partially participating. If the stock is **fully participating,** the preferred stockholders share dividend distributions with common stockholders without limit. With **partially participating** preferred stock, the preferred stockholders share dividends in excess of the stated rate in only a limited way. Participation features are illustrated in Chapter 17.

Callable Preferred Stock.   Some preferred stock issues are **callable,** which means the shares may be redeemed at the option of the corporation. Although the individual shareholder cannot demand the exercise of a call provision (as at the maturity date of a bond issue), the corporations can terminate the life of a callable preferred stock issue. When such a feature is present, the stock certificate states a **call price,** which is usually a few percentage points higher than the issuance price. Such a call premium is generally necessary to make the callable stock attractive to investors.

Corporations may favor a call provision, because it allows them to use the money generated from the stock issue for only as long as needed and then to call the stock and return the money to the stockholders. Excess resources are thus divested, allowing the corporation to retain only needed productive assets. Moreover, the call provision provides an escape mechanism for the corporation in the event of a market decline. Specifically, if the market cost of capital decreases significantly from the preferred stock's dividend rate, a call provision allows the corporation to redeem the preferred stock and issue a new offering at the lower financing rate. Of course, from the investor's perspective, a call provision is a negative characteristic that may cause the involuntary divestiture of an investment that is generating above-market returns. As a result, the capital market frequently demands a dividend rate on callable preferred stock above the market rate for similar noncallable preferred stock.

Convertible Preferred Stock. With this type of stock, stockholders can exchange preferred stock for common stock at a predetermined ratio or price. Convertible preferred stock may be attractive to investors, because it provides them with preferred claims on dividends and enables them to become common shareholders and participate without limitation in the earnings of the business.

The outstanding feature of convertible preferred stock is the opportunity for the preferred stock investor to participate in potential gains in the price of common shares. For example, assume that Hydrophonics Corporation issues $100 par, 10% preferred stock at par that is convertible into four common shares. If the market value per common share is $20, the preferred shareholder would not find the conversion feature attractive. Conversion would imply a trade of $100 preferred stock for common stock worth $80 (4 × $20). However, if the price of the common stock increased to $35 per share, the conversion feature would rise in value. A preferred stockholder could trade $100 of preferred stock for common shares worth $140 (4 × $35).

The preferred stockholder could realize this benefit not only through conversion but also by selling the preferred stock to someone who would be willing to pay $140 per share. Because of the attractiveness of the convertibility feature to investors, corporate issuers can frequently offer a dividend rate on convertible preferred stock that is less than the rate on similar nonconvertible shares.

Redeemable Preferred Stock. Corporations have found redeemable preferred stock an attractive means to obtain capital contributions. Redeemable preferred stock has the unique feature of *mandatory* redemption at a specified date or, less frequently, redemption at the stockholder's discretion. Remember that callable preferred stock is redeemable at the issuer's discretion, whereas redeemable preferred stock must be retired at a specified date according to the provisions of the preferred stock contract.

A question arises as to whether this type of preferred stock possesses more of the characteristics of debt than of equity. Redeemable preferred stock is not a form of permanent capitalization and must be retired or refunded at a specified date, much the same as debt. However, redeemable preferred stock does not guarantee a return on the investment, as does debt. The omission of a preferred stock dividend payment does not initiate grounds for default, as does the omission of a debt interest payment. Furthermore, redeemable preferred stock is subordinate to debt in the event of final liquidation of assets. Therefore, redeemable preferred stock has the characteristics of *both* debt and equity. If, however, we assume a viable business, the return guarantee and subordination characteristics would not seem critical to the investor. The dominant characteristic would appear to be the mandatory redemption

Substance over Form requirement. As a result, many people believe that redeemable preferred stock is in substance

IT LOOKS LIKE A STOCK BUT DEDUCTS LIKE A BOND

Two big U.S. energy producers think they may have struck a tax-saving gusher of sorts in the Turks and Caicos Islands—yes, the Turks and Caicos Islands. But some Wall Streeters believe the Internal Revenue Service might eventually cap their tropical tax loophole.

For years, this spine-shaped island cluster 90 miles due north of Haiti was best known for its Club Med and scuba diving. Lately, however, the islands have gained prominence on Wall Street as the wellspring of two preferred stock offerings that appear to give the issuers, Texaco, Inc., and Enron Corp., the best of two worlds. Normally, companies can deduct the interest costs of bond offerings but not the dividends paid on stock. Called MIPS (monthly income preferred shares), the new $25-a-share offerings—priced on Oct. 27 by Texaco and on Nov. 4 by Enron—appear to enable the issuers to deduct the "dividends" on the preferred shares as if they were interest. Rating agencies are treating the shares much like equity. A comparable debt sale might endanger the issuers' credit standing.

Long Arm

Although similar transactions have been done for European companies and financial institutions, Texaco's $600 million MIPS and Enron's $200 million issue represent the first such offerings by U.S. corporations, according to Goldman, Sachs & Co. Vice-President Christopher Hogg. Although Goldman, which sells mostly to institutions and rich individuals, led the deals, they target mainly retail investors.

Sound too good to be true? Maybe it is. A few Wall Streeters privately wonder whether Turks and Caicos are far enough away to enable the deals to escape the long arm of the IRS. Asked for comment, the IRS maintained its usual silence on specific tax situations. An IRS spokesman says the agency has not provided "general guidance" on tax treatment of such offerings. But a Big Six accounting firm tax partner says that the IRS, under pressure to produce revenue, has lately been "very aggressive" in scrutinizing large offshore tax-driven transactions.

At the moment, a number of other companies are "waiting in the wings," as a Goldman source put it, to get their issues to market. Barring an unfavorable IRS ruling, investment bankers figure that some $10 billion worth of the new instrument could hit the market over the next 12 months.

These transactions take advantage of a recently enacted provision in the corporate statutes in Turks and Caicos. According to the Goldman source, the move was engineered by Sullivan & Cromwell, Goldman's outside law firm, which also issued a tax opinion supporting the transaction.

Under the Turks and Caicos law, Texaco and Enron established subsidiaries that sold preferred shares to investors and lent the proceeds to the parent companies. In the Texaco transaction, the terms of the loan were 50 years (renewable for an additional 50 years) at 6⅛%, the same rate of interest paid to preferred shareholders. Since Texaco "borrowed" the money from Texaco Capital LLC, its offshore subsidiary, it intends to deduct the interest expense just as it would on an ordinary bank loan. By organizing these subsidiaries as partnerships, the parents avoid U.S. withholding taxes on the interest payments. Assuming that Texaco's 26% first-half-'93 effective tax rate remains constant for the life of the loan, the company's after tax interest cost would be only about 5.1%.

"Alchemy"

Thanks to the long maturity, coupon-suspension rights, and other features, rating agencies regard the exotic new offerings as having "equity characteristics" that therefore pose no threat to the issuers' ratings. Accordingly, Standard & Poor's Corp. and Moody's Investors Service reaffirmed their existing single-A ratings on Texaco's senior and preferred debt and their triple-B ratings on Enron's senior and preferred.

Regarding the tax play, Moody's Senior Vice-President Harold Goldberg quips: "It's a form of alchemy—one of the world's oldest professions," adding: "If it's tax-effective, it's an attractive way of building capital." S&P's Managing Director Solomon B. Samson says: "Our presumption is that [the deals are] going to work," adding that the underwriters feel they "will meet the criteria of the IRS."

Texaco and Enron seem quite pleased with their apparent coup. Enron Executive Vice President Edmund P. Segner says that because the Houston-based company expects its earnings to grow faster than the 8% coupon on the issue, the deal is a winner regardless of the tax benefits. A Texaco financial officer says the company wanted to sell preferred stock, and "when this structure was introduced to us, it looked like something we should analyze." As for the IRS, he says: "Suffice it to say, we're comfortable with the structure and don't consider it aggressive at all." The revenuers may look at it differently.

SOURCE: Phillip L. Zweig, *Business Week* (November 22, 1993), p. 118. Reprinted from November 22, 1993 issue of Business Week by special permission, copyright © 1993 by McGraw-Hill, Inc.

a type of pseudodebt.[3] Indeed, the SEC requires companies subject to its jurisdiction to report redeemable preferred stock outside of the stockholders' equity section of the balance sheet. As previously discussed, this subject and many other related topics are under active consideration by the FASB at this time.

---

[3]See R. D. Nair, Larry E. Rittenberg, and Jerry J. Weygandt, "Accounting for Redeemable Preferred Stock: Unresolved Issues," *Accounting Horizons* (June 1990), pp. 33–41, for a further discussion of these issues.

If redeemable preferred stock is in substance a form of debt, why doesn't the corporate issuer just issue straight debt? This question is especially intriguing because preferred stock dividends are not deductible for tax purposes, whereas debt interest payments are deductible. The answer may lie in the corporate manager's desire to avoid the violation of restrictive bond covenants prohibiting the issuance of further debt. Corporate lending agreements of publicly held companies often express restrictive covenants in terms of generally accepted accounting principles (GAAP). As a result, a corporate borrower could circumvent a restrictive covenant on the issuance of additional debt by issuing redeemable preferred stock, which has the main characteristics of debt but is not technically debt according to GAAP. In this way, the corporate borrower could obtain "near debt" financing without violating existing contracts. Furthermore, if the corporation issues the redeemable preferred stock to other corporations, a below-market dividend rate can be offered. Corporate investors may agree to accept a below-market return, because corporations can exclude most of their dividend income from federal income taxation.[4]

ACCOUNTING FOR CAPITAL STOCK

The issuance of capital stock is a fairly infrequent but highly significant event in the operation of a corporation. As an example, in late 1982, CBS, Inc., a large broadcaster in the United States, brought a new equity offering to the market for the first time in 45 years. Likewise, RCA, the consumer electronics company, issued new equity shares in 1982 for the first time since the company's inception in 1919.

The issuance of capital stock should not be confused with transactions in the **secondary market,** such as the New York or American Stock Exchange. The secondary market is represented by transactions between owners of previously issued shares of stock. The corporation is not a party to transactions involving its own stock in the secondary market, except in the case of treasury stock transactions, which are discussed later in this chapter. New issues are sold through an intermediary, called an **underwriter.** The underwriter, or more frequently an underwriting syndicate, makes the new offering available to investors, much like a retail store for new common stock offerings. Exhibit 16–3 illustrates a new issue announcement by an underwriting syndicate. These announcements are called *tombstones* (they resemble tombstones) and are placed in financial publications such as *The Wall Street Journal.*

Issuances of capital stock require the approval of a company's board of directors and must result in a total number of outstanding shares that is within the number authorized in the corporate charter granted by the state. A great deal of planning and research generally precedes a stock issue to make it attractive to investors. Although stock is usually issued for cash, other considerations may be accepted as payment. Also, subscriptions for future stock are frequently sold before the stock is issued.

STOCK ISSUED FOR CASH

Par or Stated Value Capital Stock

When capital stock is issued for cash, an entry is made to debit Cash, credit either Common Stock or Preferred Stock for the par or stated value, and recognize any Discount on Par or Paid-in Capital in Excess of Par Value on the issuance. To illustrate, if Haller Company issues 500 shares of $10 par value common stock at $15 per share on October 31, 1995, the following journal entry is necessary:

---

[4]The **exclusion rule** was established to prevent corporate profits distributed to an investor corporation from being taxed more than twice. To illustrate, assume that Corporation B has an investment in Corporation A common stock. Without the exclusion rule, Corporation A profits that were distributed to Corporation B would be taxed three times: as net income to Corporation A, as dividend income to Corporation B, and as dividend income to individual equity investors in Corporation B. The exclusion rule eliminates most of the second stage of taxation, so that most corporate profits are taxed only twice: once at the corporate level and once at the individual investor level.

EXHIBIT 16–3

People's Choice TV New Issue Announcement

This announcement is neither an offer to sell nor a solicitation of an offer to buy any of these Securities.
The offer is made only by the Prospectus.

January 27, 1994

1,250,000 SHARES

PEOPLE'S CHOICE TV CORP.

COMMON STOCK

Price $29 Per Share

Copies of the Prospectus may be obtained in any State from only such
of the undersigned as may legally offer these Securities in
compliance with the securities laws of such State.

GERARD KLAUER MATTISON & CO., INC.
OPPENHEIMER & CO., INC.

SOURCE: *The Wall Street Journal* (January 22, 1994), p. c19.

Oct. 31, 1995 Cash	7,500	
Common Stock		5,000
Paid-in Capital in Excess of Par Value		2,500
(To record issuance of stock.)		

Note that no gain or loss is recognized on the issuance of stock. Indeed, gains and losses are not recognized on any investment transactions with owners. Such increases and decreases in equity do not result from revenue-generating activities and are therefore excluded from the income statement. Changes in net assets resulting from investment transactions with owners are treated as direct changes in the appropriate contributed stockholders' equity accounts.

Paid-in capital in excess of par represents an increase in contributed capital above the par amount; a discount on par represents owner contributions in an amount less than the total par value. Neither discount on par nor paid-in capital in excess of par affects retained earnings.

Paid-in Capital in Excess of Par Value or Discount on Capital Stock, as an element of contributed capital, remains as an account during the entire time the stock is outstanding. Thus, paid-in capital in excess of par or discount on par is reported in the balance sheet from the time the stock is issued until it is reacquired and retired. Nor do the amounts in these accounts vary with changes in the market value of the company's stock. At the time of retirement, all accounts related to the issuance of the stock are removed from the contributed stockholders' equity section of the balance sheet.

Costs incurred in issuing stock are appropriately treated as reductions of the related proceeds, and only the net amount of cash received is capitalized. Preferably, such issue costs are charged directly to the Capital Stock or Paid-in Capital in Excess of Par Value account. Law sometimes prohibits this treatment, however, and Retained Earnings may be charged. We discuss the few exceptions to these rules later in this chapter.

True No-Par Capital Stock

Occasionally, a corporation issues true no-par stock. Accounting for this type of stock issuance is simple. To illustrate, assume that Haller Company issued 500 shares of no-par common stock at $15 per share on October 31, 1995. The following journal entry is appropriate:

Oct. 31, 1995 Cash	7,500	
Common Stock		7,500
(To record issuance of no-par stock.)		

In contrast to the journal entry for the par value stock, there is no credit to a Paid-in Capital in Excess of Par Value account. Indeed, the issuance of true no-par stock never results in the recording of a separate Paid-in Capital in Excess of Par Value or a Discount on Par Value account. The total proceeds of the issuance should be credited to the appropriate capital stock account (either common or preferred).

Lump-Sum Issuances

A corporation may issue multiple classes of capital stock and/or debt for a lump-sum consideration. The accounting problem is to assign the lump-sum purchase price to the various classes of securities. The solution is to allocate to each security in the package an issue price proportional to the fair market value of the security relative to the total fair market value of the package. To illustrate, assume that Haller Company issues the following securities for a lump-sum consideration of $800,000:

Security	Number of Shares	Par Value	Market Price per Share	Total Value
Common—Class A	1,000	$ 1.00	$ 30	$ 30,000
Common—Class B	10,000	0.50	36	360,000
$10 Preferred	5,000	90.00	102	510,000
				$900,000

The $800,000 issue price is allocated to each security on the basis of relative market values, calculated as follows:

Security	Proportion	×	Lump-Sum Price	=	Security Allocation	=	Par Value	+	Paid-in Capital in Excess of Par Value
Common—Class A	$\dfrac{\$30,000}{\$900,000}$		$800,000		$ 26,667		$ 1,000		$ 25,667
Common—Class B	$\dfrac{\$360,000}{\$900,000}$		800,000		320,000		5,000		315,000
$10 Preferred	$\dfrac{\$510,000}{\$900,000}$		800,000		453,333		450,000		3,333
					$800,000	=	$456,000	+	$344,000

Haller Company makes the following journal entry for the $800,000 multiple security issuance:

Cash	800,000	
Common Stock—Class A		1,000
Common Stock—Class B		5,000
$10 Preferred Stock		450,000
Paid-in Capital in Excess of Par Value, Common Stock—		
Class A		25,667
Paid-in Capital in Excess of Par Value, Common Stock—		
Class B		315,000
Paid-in Capital in Excess of Par Value, $10 Preferred Stock		3,333

STOCK ISSUED FOR CONSIDERATION OTHER THAN CASH

In general, if a company's stock is issued for consideration other than cash, the transaction should be based on the *fair market value of the consideration received or the market value of the stock issued, whichever is more clearly discernible.* To illustrate, assume that Haller Company issues 1,000 shares of its $10 par value common stock for an automobile with a fair market value of $12,500. The following journal entry is required to properly record the transaction for consideration in the form of stock:

Equipment—Transportation	12,500	
Common Stock (1,000 shares at $10)		10,000
Paid in Capital in Excess of Par Value		2,500
(To record acquisition of automobile and issuance of stock.)		

The automobile is subsequently depreciated in normal fashion, but the contributed stockholders' equity accounts are unchanged on successive balance sheets. Retained earnings will, of course, decrease through the recognition of depreciation expense over the life of the asset.

Occasionally, companies issue stock for services received that have no future benefit and do not qualify as assets. To illustrate, assume that an attorney agrees to accept 100 shares of Haller's $10 par value common stock in satisfaction of the legal fee of $1,370. The following entry records these transactions:

Professional Fees Expense	1,370	
Common Stock		1,000
Paid-in Capital in Excess of Par Value		370
(To record legal fee expense and issuance of common stock.)		

In this case, Haller's net assets are unaffected, even though an expense is reported and net income is decreased. The balance sheet effect of this transaction is confined to the stockholders' equity section. Specifically, as retained earnings decrease through the recognition of the expense, contributed stockholders' equity accounts increase. This event results in no changes in the company's assets or liabilities.

STOCK ISSUED IN THE ABSENCE OF MARKET VALUES

A company may issue stock for noncash consideration, and neither the stock issued nor the consideration received has market value. This situation commonly occurs with development-stage companies.

Developing corporations frequently issue stock in exchange for noncash consideration. For example, a development-stage high-technology firm may need highly specialized engineering skills and product patent rights to begin operations. If these costs are prohibitive, new stock may have to be offered to the engineers and patent holders in return for their cooperation. An accounting problem arises if neither the noncash consideration received nor the stock issued have an objectively determinable value.

How then does the accountant assign a dollar amount to the stock issuance if neither the stock nor the related consideration has an objective market value? The FASB requires that a

Verifiability dollar amount be assigned to any noncash consideration received in exchange for equity securities. In the case of a noncash consideration without a verifiable market value, the FASB has given the accountant wide latitude in assigning dollar amounts to both the stock and the consideration received. For example, an estimate may be made by analyzing other stocks or considerations that are similar to those being exchanged and for which objective determination of market value is possible. In addition, the financial statements of the corporation must disclose the basis for assigning dollar amounts.[5]

STOCK SUBSCRIPTIONS

Corporations often sell rights to their shares in an initial stock issue before the stock is actually issued. Such rights are called **stock subscriptions.** They provide a useful way for development-stage corporations to market equity securities to public investors in an orderly manner. Stock subscriptions are generally sold to investors at a fraction of the total cost of the stock. The subscriber pays the remaining portion of the stock price at the time the shares are issued. Questions frequently arise as to how to record stock subscriptions if cash is received prior to the issuance of stock. Further, if the subscription down payment is forfeited because the subscription is not exercised and lapses, how should that circumstance be reported?

When a stock subscription contract is initiated, the company records the cash received and a "subscription receivable" for the unpaid balance of the stock price; credits are made to reflect an increase in stockholders' equity. Although the corporation is required to issue the stock after the subscription receivable has been fully paid, a liability does not exist as a result of the subscription contract. There are no claims on the corporation's assets but only an obligation to issue capital stock when the subscription has been fully received. As such, the credit portion of the entry represents a direct increase in the equity of the company.

Another question related to stock subscriptions is whether a subscription receivable is an asset. The unpaid portion of the stock subscription represents a mutual promise of the corporation and the subscriber. The corporation promises to deliver stock in the future, and the subscriber promises to pay the balance of the subscription price. Accountants do not generally consider all such *mutual promises* (executory contracts) as an accounting event. In contrast, accounts receivable are recorded when one party to the contract delivers goods or services but remains unpaid. The delivery of goods or services on account is a partial performance of the agreement by the seller to the buyer and is considered a recordable event. The subscription receivable does not have this characteristic, because neither party has performed the agreement with respect to the unpaid portion of the subscription.

As a result, some have favored treating the subscription receivable as a reduction in stockholders' equity rather than as an asset. The stockholders' equity section then reports an increase only for the actual cash consideration. Presently, either an asset or a contra equity presentation of the subscription receivable is acceptable. If little uncertainty exists as to the collectibility of the subscription receivable, many accountants prefer to record the item as an asset. Conversely, the subscription receivable should be treated as a reduction of stockholders' equity if collection is uncertain. The preferred presentation also depends on the state laws applicable to stock subscriptions. For example, some state laws grant the subscriber all rights of stock ownership, including dividends and voting rights, for the complete subscription; others grant such rights only for the prepaid portion of the subscription. Under the former legal arrangement, the whole subscription should be disclosed as an increase in stockholders' equity; in the latter case, a net equity presentation (subscriptions receivable as contra equity) would be more appropriate.

---

[5]*FASB Statement of Financial Accounting Standards No. 7,* "Accounting and Reporting by Development Stage Enterprises," 1975, par. 11. Under SEC rules, a dollar amount may *not* be assigned to noncash consideration lacking objectively determinable market value for issuances by development-stage corporations.

To illustrate the accounting for a subscription contract, assume that Nesor Corporation issues stock subscriptions for 1,000 shares of its $10 par value common stock at a subscribed price of $125. Further assume that investors must make a 50% down payment for all subscribed stock. The following journal entry is appropriate:

Cash	62,500	
Stock Subscriptions Receivable	62,500	
Common Stock Subscribed		10,000
Paid-in Capital in Excess of Par Value		115,000
(To record receipt of stock subscriptions.)		

The increase in the stockholders' equity account originates from stock subscriptions rather than the outright sale of stock; the common stock account is therefore identified as subscribed. When Nesor receives additional cash that pays the subscription receivable in full, the following entry is recorded:

Cash	62,500	
Stock Subscriptions Receivable		62,500
(To record receipt of cash for full payment of subscribed stock.)		
Common Stock Subscribed	10,000	
Common Stock		10,000
(To record issuance of 1,000 shares of subscribed stock.)		

If the subscription is defaulted because payment is not made in the prescribed time period, the remaining Stock Subscriptions Receivable and Common Stock Subscribed are removed from the books. Three common alternatives exist to properly dispose of down payments on the forfeited shares:[6]

1. Refund the partial payment on the forfeited shares to the subscriber.
2. Retain the partial payment on the forfeited shares until the subscription is sold to another investor. (Refund the remaining cash to the original subscriber after deducting expenses of the reissue and any reductions in selling price below the subscription price.)
3. Retain the cash advance as a default penalty.

The subscription contract and applicable state laws guide the contracting parties to the appropriate solution in the event of default.

To illustrate the first alternative, assume that 100 shares of the Nesor Corporation subscription are defaulted after the cash advance is made. The entry necessary to record the default and the refund to the subscriber is as follows:

Common Stock Subscribed ($10 × 100)	1,000	
Paid-in Capital in Excess of Par Value	11,500	
Cash ($62.50 × 100)		6,250
Stock Subscriptions Receivable		6,250
(To record defaulted stock subscription and return of cash		
to subscriber.)		

If the subscription contract contains the third alternative and Nesor retained the cash advance, the journal entry is identical to the preceding one, except that cash would not be credited and the Paid-in Capital in Excess of Par Value account is debited for only $5,250. Under the second alternative, Nesor's retention of part of the cash down payment would be credited to the paid-in capital account, and the remaining refund would be credited to Cash. As these entries indicate, if the corporation retains any cash advanced under a defaulted stock subscription, the amount should be reported as an increase in contributed capital. No gain or

---

[6]A fourth alternative requires an amendment to the original contract so that a pro rata distribution of shares equal to the partial payment is made.

loss is recognized on such transactions, because their effects are totally associated with contributed equity.

Retaining the cash advance may first appear to be an unreasonably harsh penalty to the defaulting subscriber. However, the purpose of such a provision is to give the subscriber an incentive to purchase shares. Without this incentive, the subscriber could treat the stock subscription as a risk-free stock option. To illustrate, if Nesor Corporation already had stock outstanding and trading in an organized market, the investor could subscribe stock at $125 per share and exercise the subscription if the market value of the shares exceeded $125 or default if the market value of the shares were less than $125. If the investor does not stand to lose the down payment, the subscription provides a no-loss investment opportunity. Because this is not the purpose of a stock subscription, provisions for the partial or full forfeiture of the down payment are not unreasonable when previously issued shares are already trading in the secondary market.

TREASURY STOCK

Companies frequently acquire shares of their own stock through market purchases without intending to retire the stock. A company's stock that has been issued and then acquired by the company for some future purpose is referred to as **treasury stock.** These are some of the reasons that a company acquires shares of its own stock:

1. Buying out a stockholder or retiring executive.
2. Meeting provisions of stock option plans for employees.
3. Meeting the requirements of a proposed merger in which large amounts of stock are to be exchanged.
4. Preparing to meet the requirements of a stock dividend.
5. Reducing stockholder pressure for an increased dividend rate.

When treasury stock is purchased, the acquisition must be recorded in the accounting records. On rare occasions, annual reports present small amounts of treasury stock as assets. This practice, however, is generally undesirable and discouraged. A company has equity in its assets and does not have an asset in its own equity. A company cannot own itself via stock purchases. Therefore, treasury stock should be presented as a reduction of shareholders' equity, not as an asset.

TWO METHODS TO ACCOUNT FOR TREASURY STOCK

Two acceptable methods are used to record the reduction in stockholders' equity that occurs when treasury stock is acquired: (1) the **cost method,** which is more frequently encountered in practice, and (2) the **par value method.** To illustrate, consider the stockholders' equity section of the balance sheet of Bender, Inc., as presented in Exhibit 16–4. Not all of Bender's authorized common stock has been issued. The 50,000 authorized but unissued shares are *Disclosure* not presented in the financial statements. A note in the balance sheet discloses the authorization of those shares.

Cost Method

The **cost method** of accounting for treasury stock assumes the eventual reissuance of the stock. Therefore, the cost method is preferred when management intends to hold the treasury shares temporarily for later reissuance rather than for later retirement. To illustrate, assume that Bender, Inc., acquires 2,000 shares of its common stock at $145 per share to provide for a stock option plan and intends to reissue the shares at a later time. The following entry is necessary to record the transaction using the cost method:

Treasury Stock (2,000 shares × $145)	290,000	
Cash		290,000
(To record acquisition of treasury stock.)		

EXHIBIT 16–4

Bender, Inc.
Partial Balance Sheet

Stockholders' Equity [Note 1]

Preferred stock ($100 par, 7% cumulative; 100,000 shares authorized, issued, and outstanding)	$10,000,000
Common stock ($100 par; 200,000 shares authorized, 150,000 shares issued and outstanding)	15,000,000
Paid-in capital in excess of par value (common)	750,000
Contributed equity	25,750,000
Retained earnings	42,500,000
Total stockholders' equity	$68,250,000

NOTE 1: The 7% cumulative preferred stock was issued at par value and is callable at any time at 103. Fifty thousand of the 200,000 shares were reserved by the board of directors and are intended to be issued to employees as part of a recently introduced employee stock option plan.

EXHIBIT 16–5

Bender, Inc.
Partial Balance Sheet with Treasury Stock—Cost Method

Stockholders' Equity

Preferred stock ($100 par, 7% cumulative; 100,000 shares authorized, issued, and outstanding)	$10,000,000
Common stock ($100 par; 200,000 shares authorized, 150,000 shares issued, 148,000 shares outstanding, 2,000 shares held in treasury)	15,000,000
Paid-in capital in excess of par value (common)	750,000
Contributed equity	25,750,000
Retained earnings	42,500,000
Total contributed equity and retained earnings	68,250,000
Less: Cost of treasury shares	(290,000)
Total stockholders' equity	$67,960,000

The Treasury Stock account is classified as a reduction in the stockholders' equity of the company. Exhibit 16–5 presents the stockholders' equity section of Bender's balance sheet following this transaction. The Common Stock and Paid-in Capital in Excess of Par Value accounts are not affected by the treasury stock transaction if the cost method is used.

When treasury stock is reissued, its cost is removed from the books. To illustrate, assume that Bender sells the treasury stock listed in Exhibit 16–5 for $275,000 cash. The following entry records this transaction:

Cash	275,000	
Paid-in Capital in Excess of Par Value	15,000	
Treasury Stock		290,000
(To record reissuance of treasury stock at $15,000 below cost.)		

In this case, the treasury stock was sold below its cost and Paid-in Capital in Excess of Par Value was reduced by $15,000. State law may require other treatments, such as charging Retained Earnings for the difference, but the entry presented here is acceptable in most circumstances. If the company's stockholders' equity did not include any paid-in capital in excess of par value, the $15,000 difference between the acquisition and resale price of the treasury stock would have been charged to Retained Earnings. If the stock were sold for more than its cost, an additional amount of paid-in capital in excess of par would be recognized.[7] In any event, no losses or gains are recognized on treasury stock transactions because they represent transactions in a company's own equity. Because the permanent contributed capital accounts were not adjusted when the treasury stock was purchased, no further entry is needed to reestablish the status of the stock as outstanding.

Another complication in the cost method of accounting for treasury stock arises if treasury shares are acquired at different times and at different prices. Companies typically follow either a first-in, first-out (FIFO) or a weighted average cost-flow assumption, similar to that used in accounting for inventories. As with the case of inventory accounting, consistent application of the method selected is important.

Consistency

Par Value Method

The second acceptable method of accounting for treasury stock is the **par** or **stated value method.** In substance, this method is consistent with an assumption that common stock may be retired. Under this method, treasury stock is recorded at the par (or stated) value of common stock, and the paid-in capital in excess of par value from the original common stock issuance is eliminated.

We illustrated the par value method using Bender, Inc., and the acquisition and reissuance data from the previous example. Recall that Bender acquired 2,000 shares of its $100 par value common stock at $145 per share. The following entry records the acquisition of the treasury stock for $290,000, using the par value method:

Treasury Stock	200,000	
Paid-in Capital in Excess of Par Value	10,000	
Retained Earnings	80,000	
Cash (2,000 × $145)		290,000
(To record purchase of treasury shares.)		

Using this method, the treasury shares are reported at par value (2,000 shares × $100 par). The difference between the cost of the shares ($290,000) and their par value ($200,000) is treated as a reduction in Paid-in Capital in Excess of Par on a pro rata basis and next as a reduction in Retained Earnings. In this case, Bender's 150,000 shares of common stock were originally issued at an average price per share of $105, determined as follows (see Exhibit 16–4):

Par value	$15,000,000
Paid-in capital in excess of par value	750,000
	$15,750,000

$$\frac{\$15,750,000}{150,000} = \$105 \text{ per share}$$

Therefore, the pro rata portion of paid-in capital in excess of par value on the acquired treasury shares equals 2,000 × ($105 − $100), or $10,000. If the pro rata paid-in capital in excess of par value is eliminated, any remainder is treated as a reduction of Retained Earnings. Because the 2,000 shares were purchased at $145 per share, the excess $40 per share ($145 − $105) is treated as a direct reduction of Retained Earnings.

---

[7]Contributed capital arising from treasury stock transactions may be carried in a separate account, such as Paid-in Capital from Treasury Stock Transactions.

EXHIBIT 16–6

Bender, Inc.
Partial Balance Sheet
With Treasury Stock—Par Value Method

Stockholders' Equity	
Preferred stock ($100 par, 7% cumulative; 100,000 shares authorized, issued, and outstanding)	$10,000,000
Common stock ($100 par; 200,000 shares authorized, 150,000 shares issued, 148,000 shares outstanding, 2,000 shares held in treasury)	14,800,000
Paid-in capital in excess of par value (common)	740,000
Contributed equity	25,540,000
Retained earnings	42,420,000
Total stockholders' equity	$67,960,000

Exhibit 16–6 illustrates the stockholders' equity section of Bender's balance sheet after the acquisition of shares for $290,000 under the par value method. Notice that the total stockholders' equity is the same in Exhibits 16–5 and 16–6, but that the disclosure of the treasury stock differs according to the method applied.

Disclosure

If treasury stock is reissued under the par value method, accounting is again different. Continuing the Bender example, the reissuance is treated as if the stock were being issued for the first time at par value, except that the credit for par value is to the Treasury Stock account. The entry under the par value method for reissuance of the stock for $275,000 follows:

Cash	275,000	
Paid-in Capital in Excess of Par Value		75,000
Treasury Stock		200,000
(To record reissuance of treasury stock.)		

The difference between the carrying amount of the Treasury Stock, in this case its par value, and the consideration received is treated as an increase in Paid-in Capital in Excess of Par Value.

Treasury Stock Acquired in Takeover Attempts

An exception to the methods previously described involves corporate takeover attempts. In a **corporate takeover,** one company attempts to acquire another by buying a controlling interest in its stock. Companies that are the subject of takeover attempts often take defensive action; one common defense is to purchase large amounts of treasury stock—often at prices that exceed both those offered by the party attempting to accomplish the takeover and the market price of the stock. The exception to the cost and par value methods occurs if the treasury stock is acquired at a price that exceeds the market price of the stock.

The FASB has determined that only the fair value of the treasury stock should be accounted for as the cost of acquiring the stock. Amounts paid in excess of the market price to acquire shares of treasury stock should generally be treated as a loss in the income statement rather than as a reduction in the Paid-in Capital in Excess of Par Value. Amounts paid to stockholders to preclude their purchase of additional shares should be charged to expense as incurred. Further, costs incurred in defending against takeovers should not be classified as extraordinary items.[8]

---

[8]*FASB Technical Bulletin No. 85-6,* "Accounting for a Purchase of Treasury Shares at a Price Significantly in Excess of the Current Market Price of the Shares and the Income Statement Classification of Costs Incurred in Defending against a Takeover Attempt," 1985.

SUMMARY OF TREASURY STOCK ACCOUNTING

Regardless of whether the cost method or the par value method is used for treasury stock accounting, several points are important:

1. Treasury stock should not be classified as an asset.
2. Dividends are not recorded as paid or received on treasury stock (the company cannot distribute dividends to itself).
3. Retained earnings are not increased as a result of treasury stock transactions, although decreases in retained earnings are possible when applying the par value method or if shares are sold below cost when applying the cost method and no paid-in capital in excess of par exists.
4. Gains or losses are not recognized on treasury stock transactions.
5. Regardless of which method is used, total stockholders' equity remains the same, although the individual components may differ.
6. Legal minimum capital must be preserved.

RETIREMENT OF STOCK

COMMON STOCK RETIREMENT

If a company acquires stock to be retired, accounting is similar to the par value method of accounting for treasury stock. Instead of charging the Treasury Stock account for the par value of the securities, however, the original Common Stock account is charged. Such an entry effectively removes the stock from the company's accounts, which, of course, is consistent with the nature of the transaction.

For example, if Bender, Inc., acquires and retires 2,000 shares of $100 par value stock, which was originally issued for $105 per share, at $145 per share, the following entry is necessary:

Common Stock	200,000	
Paid-in Capital in Excess of Par Value	10,000	
Retained Earnings	80,000	
Cash		290,000
(To record acquisition and retirement of 2,000 shares of common stock at $145 per share, originally issued at $105 per share.)		

The disclosures of stock authorized, issued, and outstanding are adjusted to reflect the retirement of the acquired stock. The rationale, previously discussed, for the direct charge to Retained Earnings under the par value method of accounting for treasury stock is also valid here. A permanent distribution of $80,000 of earned equity has taken place as a result of the transaction.

If a company acquires and retires stock at a price below the original selling price, additional paid-in capital results from the retirement. To illustrate, assume that Bender acquired and retired 2,000 shares of its common stock at $85 per share. In this case, the following entry is appropriate:

Common Stock	200,000	
Cash (2,000 × $85)		170,000
Paid-in Capital in Excess of Par Value		30,000
(To record acquisition and retirement of 2,000 shares of common stock at $85 per share, originally issued at $105 per share.)		

The paid-in capital from the retirement arises because the company was able to retire stock that originally sold for $105 per share for only $85 per share, resulting in a permanent increase in the company's contributed equity of $20 per share ($5 recognized when the stock was sold and $15 when it was retired), even though those shares are no longer outstanding.

PREFERRED STOCK RETIREMENT

Preferred stock can be redeemed through either a call provision or a mandatory redemption provision. Other than this, the principles underlying the redemption of preferred stock are similar to those for the retirement of common stock. When preferred stock is redeemed, the Preferred Stock account and associated Paid-in Capital in Excess of Par Value on the preferred stock are eliminated. Any difference between the sum of these accounts and the cash redemption price is either charged to Retained Earnings or credited to Paid-in Capital in Excess of Par Value.

To illustrate the accounting, refer to the $10,000,000 preferred stock issue of Bender in Exhibit 16–4. Assume that Bender elects to call the preferred stock at 103 according to the provisions of the preferred stock contract (Note 1, Exhibit 16–4). Bender records the following entry for the redemption:

Preferred Stock	10,000,000	
Retained Earnings	300,000	
Cash ($10,000,000 × 1.03)		10,300,000
(To redeem the preferred stock at 103.)		

The Preferred Stock account is eliminated. Because the preferred stock was issued at par, there is no Paid-in Capital in Excess of Par Value account to eliminate. The $300,000 charge to Retained Earnings represents the distribution of earned equity to the preferred shareholders upon redemption of their shares. If the call provisions specified a call price of 97, the journal entry is as follows:

Preferred Stock	10,000,000	
Paid-in Capital in Excess of Par Value		300,000
Cash		9,700,000
(To redeem the preferred stock at 97.)		

The credit to the Paid-in Capital in Excess of Par Value account represents a contribution to the remaining stockholders' equity as a result of retiring the preferred stock at an amount less than book value.

TREASURY STOCK RETIREMENT

A firm may eventually decide to retire treasury stock if it has no plans to reissue it. Retired treasury stock becomes authorized but unissued common stock. Accounting for treasury stock retirement involves removing the Treasury Stock and Common Stock accounts from the accounting records. Because the Treasury Stock is recorded differently under the cost and par value methods, accounting for its retirement also differs under the two approaches.

Recall the Bender situation in which 2,000 shares of $100 par value common stock are purchased for the treasury at $145 a share. Assuming that the treasury stock was recorded at cost, the Treasury Stock account balance is $290,000 and the journal entry to retire these shares is as follows:

Common Stock	200,000	
Paid-in Capital in Excess of Par Value	10,000	
Retained Earnings	80,000	
Treasury Stock		290,000
(To retire treasury stock.)		

The Common Stock, related Paid-in Capital in Excess of Par Value and Treasury Stock accounts are eliminated from the accounting records. The $80,000 charge to Retained Earnings can be evaluated in the same manner as discussed previously for the par value method. The Treasury Stock account is, of course, eliminated at cost.

Under the par value method, Paid-in Capital in Excess of Par Value and Retained Earnings have already been reduced in the appropriate amounts at the time the treasury stock was acquired. The Treasury Stock account has a $200,000 balance, representing the par value of the treasury stock. All that remains is eliminating the treasury shares and outstanding common stock at their par values. The journal entry is

Common Stock	200,000	
Treasury Stock		200,000
(To retire treasury stock.)		

As expected, both the cost and par value methods produce the same results when the treasury stock purchase and treasury stock retirement transactions are combined.

PROPERTY AND TREASURY STOCK DONATIONS

In this chapter, we have discussed obtaining corporate capital through owner contributions. In Chapter 17, we discuss earnings as a source of corporate capital. A third and less common source of corporate capital is the donation of either property or stock, frequently called *donated capital*. Donated capital should not be confused with contributed capital; the terms *donated* and *contributed* have entirely different meanings in this context. **Donated capital** represents a nonreciprocal transfer of property from an outsider to the company. **Contributed capital** is cash, property, or services received by the company in exchange for ownership shares and accompanying rights.

PROPERTY DONATIONS

Cities and counties often attract new businesses and thereby stimulate their economies by donating land or property to particular enterprises. This is not a normal exchange transaction but a unilateral transfer of assets to the corporation. Because the donation is a gift, the enterprise does not release assets in the acquisition. Consequently, the enterprise has no cost related to acquiring the asset. Recall that assets given or received in unilateral transfers are

Asset/Liability Measurement

recorded at their estimated fair values. In arm's-length exchange transactions, the cost of acquiring an asset is a measure of its fair value, and that amount is used to record the acquisition of the item. Therefore, because cost is a good measure of the fair value of an asset at the time of purchase, recording *donated* assets at their estimated fair values is consistent with recording other assets acquired in exchange transactions at their cost.

To account for a donated asset, accountants charge the specific asset account for the estimated fair value of the donated item and make an offsetting credit to an account, Donated Capital. The use of this separate account is preferable to crediting Paid-in Capital in Excess of Par Value to recognize the nature of the stockholders' equity. Donated assets are not capital contributions by stockholders but capital donations from outsiders. They should therefore be given distinctive recognition.

To illustrate, consider the donation of a warehouse and adjoining land by the city of Ramsey to Valley Electric Company. If the land is appraised at $15,000 and the warehouse at $75,000, Valley Electric records the donation as

Land	15,000	
Building	75,000	
Donated Capital		90,000
(To record asset donations.)		

Disclosure

Donated capital is presented separately in the stockholders' equity section of the balance sheet.

TREASURY STOCK DONATIONS

Stockholders, or a stockholder's estate, may sometimes donate capital stock back to the company. This transfer is treated somewhat differently from property transfers, because the company should not consider the donated shares as assets. The donated shares are treasury shares to the corporation and are therefore subject to either the cost or the par value method of accounting.

Under the cost method, donated treasury shares are usually not formally entered in the records, because the firm incurred no cost in acquiring the treasury stock. The number of shares outstanding is reduced by the donated shares via a memorandum to the accounting records. Subsequent reissue of donated treasury shares requires a credit to Donated Capital for the reissue price.

Under the par value method, donated treasury shares are recorded at par value with an offsetting credit to Donated Capital. If the donated shares are reissued at a price higher (lower) than the par value, the difference is disclosed by increasing (decreasing) the Donated Capital account.

Donated treasury stock gives a business an opportunity to issue the same shares twice— first to the initial owner and then as donated treasury stock. The second issuance benefits the firm by generating additional capital. This additional capital results only because the original owner voluntarily forfeited the rights to the shares. Therefore, under both accounting methods, the increase in stockholders' equity from issuance of donated treasury shares is labeled Donated Capital.

PROFESSIONAL JUDGMENT

Accounting for activities and reporting them in the stockholders' equity section of the balance sheet require considerable professional experience and judgment. Perhaps the foremost consideration relates to analyzing specific features of complex securities to determine whether they should be included in stockholders' equity or reported as debt of the issuing company. Substantial knowledge of the authoritative accounting literature coupled with considerable professional experience is requisite to successfully resolve such issues.

In addition to determining the appropriate classification of securities issued by a company, an accountant must exercise judgment in a number of other areas. Examples include designing disclosures that effectively communicate the specific features of various securities in a complete but succinct fashion, valuing nonmonetary amounts received in exchange for a company's securities, and appropriately accounting for and reporting treasury stock transactions and donated capital. Estimating the fair value of donated assets can be particularly challenging and may call for knowledge in addition to that typically possessed by accountants.

CONCLUDING REMARKS

In this chapter, we have reviewed the basic elements of corporate organization and contributed capital. Corporate ownership capital is provided through the issuance of capital stock to acquiring individuals and institutions (e.g., banks, pension funds, and investment mutual funds). Capital stock offers owners a variety of rights and preferences, as specified by the company's board of directors.

Disclosure

The stockholders' equity section of the balance sheet should disclose not only the main classifications of ownership but also information about the rights and preferences of each class of stock. As an example, the dividend preference rate and provisions should be disclosed for preferred stock. In this way, the various classes of shareholders understand the basic rights and preferences of each ownership class in relation to other ownership classes. Furthermore, the shares authorized, issued, and outstanding should be disclosed for each class of stock.

Exhibit 16–7 illustrates the share status relationships. Authorized shares can be either issued or unissued. The unissued shares can be further divided into subscribed and unsubscribed stock. Recall that subscribed stock is authorized but unissued. Issued stock can be classified as issued and outstanding or issued and not outstanding. Shares that are issued but not outstanding result from treasury stock purchases or donations.

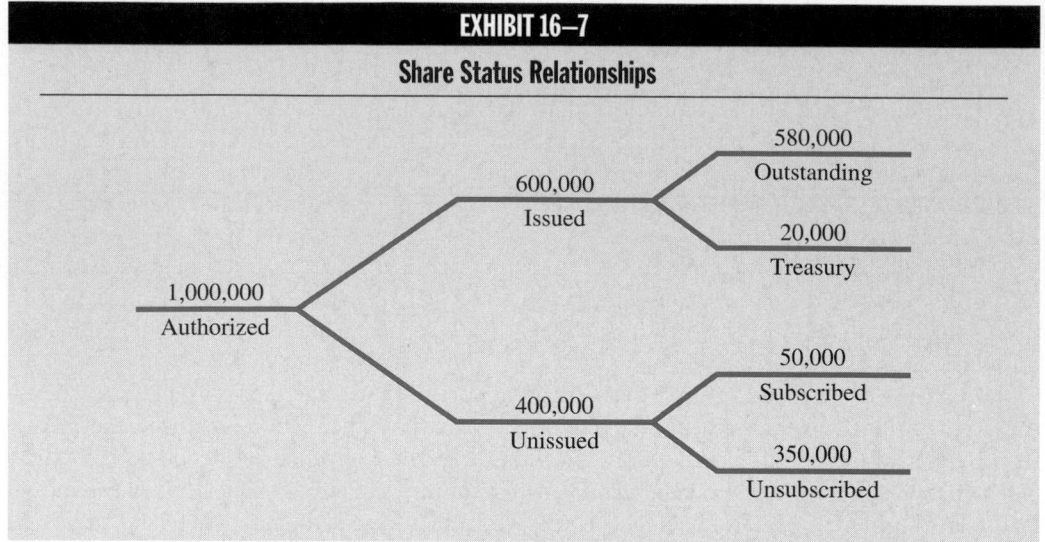

EXHIBIT 16–7

Share Status Relationships

Exhibit 16–7 includes hypothetical share amounts to aid in understanding the relationships. To illustrate how the various categories of stockholders' equity change as transactions occur, assume that the 50,000 subscribed shares are issued. In this case, the total unissued stock decreases to 350,000, the total issued stock increases to 650,000, and the total stock outstanding increases to 630,000 shares. The unsubscribed and treasury amounts are unchanged by the issuance of the 50,000 shares of subscribed stock. Other adjustments in share status may be evaluated in this way.

To illustrate the presentation of stockholders' equity in the balance sheet, review the balance sheet excerpt from the Coastal Corporation's 1993 balance sheet which is presented in Exhibit 16–8. Included are the liability and stockholders' equity sections of the 1993 and 1992 balance sheets. Coastal Corporation is an energy company that is organized in five areas: natural gas, refining and marketing, exploration and production, coal, and power. Notice that the caption, Mandatory Redemption Preferred Stock is included in a separate category located between liabilities and stockholders' equity, in a manner consistent with our discussion in this chapter. Also, notice that the amount of preferred stock redeemable within one year is included with current liabilities. Stockholders' equity follows that section, and includes one class of preferred stock, two classes of common stock, additional paid-in capital (another title for paid-in capital in excess of par value), retained earnings, followed by a deduction for treasury stock. While two classes of common stock are included in the company's capital structure, only a small part is labeled Class A Common Stock, and the majority is under the caption Common Stock. The treasury stock is accounted for at cost and consists of 4,415,394 shares of common stock for both 1993 and 1992.

KEY POINTS

1. The corporate form of business organization has certain advantages over the sole proprietorship and partnership forms, particularly in terms of allowing the accumulation of large amounts of capital from many diverse owners. (Objective 1)

2. Corporations provide limited liability to shareholders, facilitate the generation of additional equity capital, and continue in existence despite the death of one or more shareholders. (Objective 1)

3. A primary disadvantage of the corporate form of business organization is the double taxation of income, first at the corporate level and again as corporate profits are distributed to stockholders. (Objective 1)

4. Preferred stock contains a preference claim over common stock in dividend distributions and in the distribution of assets upon liquidation. Preferred stock may be fully or partially participating, cumulative, or both. (Objectives 2 and 3)

EXHIBIT 16–8

The Coastal Corporation
Stockholders' Equity Presentation

	December 31,	
(Millions of dollars)	1993	1992
Liabilities and Stockholders' Equity		
Current Liabilities		
Notes payable and preferred stock redeemable within one year	$ 271.7	$ 229.1
Accounts payable	1,649.1	1,791.3
Accrued expenses	374.0	397.2
Current maturities on long-term debt	95.1	115.4
Total Current Liabilities	2,389.9	2,533.0
Debt		
Long-term debt, excluding current maturities	3,612.8	4,106.5
Subordinated long-term debt, excluding current maturities	199.7	199.6
	3,812.5	4,306.1
Deferred Credits and Other		
Deferred income taxes	1,339.9	1,339.5
Other deferred credits	380.1	354.6
	1,720.0	1,694.1
Mandatory Redemption Preferred Stock		
Issued by subsidiaries	26.6	36.7
Common Stock and Other Stockholders' Equity		
Cumulative preferred stock (with aggregate liquidation preference of $210.1 million)	2.7	.1
Class A common stock—Issued (1993—422,857 shares; 1992—444,868 shares)	.1	.1
Common stock—Issued (1993—108,512,342 shares; 1992—107,967,176 shares)	36.2	36.0
Additional paid-in capital	1,209.3	1,006.7
Retained earnings	1,162.7	1,099.9
	2,411.0	2,142.8
Less common stock in treasury—at cost (1993 and 1992—4,415,394 shares)	132.9	132.9
	2,278.1	2,009.9
	$10,227.1	$10,579.8

SOURCE: The Coastal Corporation, 1993 Annual Report.

5. Preferred stock may be callable, convertible, or redeemable. (Objectives 2 and 3)

6. Common stock is considered the residual equity of a corporation because the claims of other investors and creditors must be satisfied before distributions may be made to common stockholders. (Objectives 2 and 3)

7. Distinguishing between debt and equity securities and among various equity securities is sometimes complex and requires substantial professional judgment. (Objective 4)

8. Common stock may be issued for cash or noncash consideration and may be subscribed prior to issuance. In the event of noncash consideration, valuation is based on the market value of the consideration or the stock, whichever is more clearly determinable. (Objectives 5, 6, and 9)

9. Treasury stock is stock that has been issued and subsequently reacquired in the secondary market by the issuing company. Treasury stock is held pending either reissuance or retirement. (Objectives 7 and 8)

10. Treasury stock acquisition and disposition can be accounted for under either the cost or the par value method. (Objective 7)

11. Capital stock that is retired should be removed from the stockholders' equity accounts of the corporation. (Objective 8)

12. Property or stock donations should be reflected as donated capital in the stockholders' equity section of the balance sheet. (Objective 9)

QUESTIONS

16–1 What are some of the operating and financing advantages of a corporation compared to a partnership or a sole proprietorship?

16–2 What is the difference between publicly held and closely held corporations?

16–3 Why do corporations frequently issue more than one class or type of stock?

16–4 What do the terms *cumulative preferred stock* and *participating preferred stock* mean?

16–5 How should cumulative dividends in arrears on preferred stock be presented (if at all) in a corporation's financial statements?

16–6 Describe redeemable preferred stock. How should redeemable preferred stock be presented in the financial statements?

16–7 What is the most important distinction between accounting for corporations and accounting for other forms of business organizations?

16–8 In what way should the term *reserve* be used, if at all, in financial accounting?

16–9 How does a company account for stock issuances in which there are no established market values for either the stock or the consideration received?

16–10 Explain the term *subscribed common stock*. How should common stock subscriptions be presented in the balance sheet?

16–11 What are some accounting alternatives related to the cash advanced on a defaulted stock subscription?

16–12 How does a company account for the difference between proceeds and cost when the company transacts in its own stock?

16–13 Describe treasury stock. How is it presented in the balance sheet?

16–14 What are the appropriate accounting practices for the acquisition of shares of a company's own stock?

16–15 What is minimum legal capital and why does state law usually require corporations to maintain a certain amount of stockholders' equity?

16–16 If a company issues shares of its own stock in consideration for property or services, at what amount should the transaction generally be recorded?

16–17 What are the acceptable accounting considerations and procedures for the receipt of (1) property donations and (2) donations of the company's stock?

16–18 Why isn't the stockholders' equity of a corporation valued at the aggregate *market* value of the outstanding stock?

EXERCISES

16–19 Stockholders' Equity Section Presentation Sanger Corporation was organized on January 1, 1993. On that date, it issued 100,000 shares of $10 par value common stock at $12 per share (200,000 shares were authorized). During the period January 1, 1993, through December 31, 1995, Sanger earned net income of $400,000 and declared and paid cash dividends of $150,000. On January 10, 1995, Sanger purchased 5,000 shares of its common stock at $10 per share. On December 29, 1995, Sanger subscribed an additional 50,000 shares for 40% down at $14 per share. On December 31, 1995, it sold 3,000 treasury shares at $15 per share. Sanger used the cost method in accounting for treasury stock.

INSTRUCTIONS

Prepare the stockholders' equity section of the Sanger Corporation balance sheet as it should appear on December 31, 1995.

(AICPA adapted)

16–20 Common Stock Transactions Ansdell Corporation was organized on January 1, 1995, with an authorization of 500,000 shares of common stock with a par value of $5 per share. The company uses the cost method of accounting for treasury stock transactions. During 1995 Ansdell had the following capital transactions:

Jan.	5	Issued 100,000 shares at $5 per share.
Apr.	6	Issued 50,000 shares at $7 per share.
June	8	Issued 15,000 shares at $10 per share.
July	28	Purchased 25,000 shares at $4 per share.
Dec.	31	Sold 25,000 shares held as treasury stock at $8 per share.

INSTRUCTIONS

Provide the appropriate journal entries for each of these transactions.   (AICPA adapted)

16–21 Lump-Sum Consideration for Capital Stock   Dowell Corporation incorporated on January 1, 1995, with an authorization of 100,000 shares of no-par common stock and 15,000 shares of $100 par preferred stock. The corporation issued 60,000 shares of common stock and 10,000 shares of preferred stock on January 7, 1995, for a lump-sum price of $2,700,000.

INSTRUCTIONS

Provide the appropriate journal entry for the capital stock issuance of January 7, 1995, under each of the following *independent* assumptions:

[a] The common stock and preferred stock traded in the secondary market at $35 and $105 per share, respectively, immediately after the issuance.

[b] The common stock traded immediately in the secondary market at $25 per share. Because the preferred stock was closely held, a market price was not established for the preferred shares.

[c] At the issuance of common stock, the board of directors established a stated value of $25 per share. Both the common and preferred stock issuances became closely held. Therefore, a market price was not established for either issue. (*Hint:* Base the allocation on par and stated values.)

16–22 Treasury Stock Transactions   Sheldon Company exchanged 100 shares of treasury stock (its $50 par common stock) for some land to be used in its business. The treasury stock had cost $60 per share, and on the exchange date, it had a fair market value of $65 per share. Sheldon received $1,200 for scrap when an existing building was immediately removed from this land.

INSTRUCTIONS

Record the acquisition of the land in the appropriate journal entry, assuming the treasury shares were originally recorded under

[a] The cost method

[b] The par value method   (AICPA adapted)

16–23 Conversion of Preferred Stock to Common Stock   In 1995 Stukey, Inc., issued 8,000 shares of $100 par value convertible preferred stock for $105 per share. One share of preferred stock can be converted into three shares of Stukey's $25 par value common stock at the option of the preferred shareholder. In August 1995, all of the preferred stock was converted into common stock. The market value of the common stock at the date of the conversion was $30 per share.

INSTRUCTIONS

[a] What is the appropriate journal entry for the issuance of the preferred stock?

[b] Record the journal entry required to convert preferred shares to common shares.

[c] Why would a company issue convertible preferred stock instead of just placing common stock directly? Why would an investor be willing to accept the conversion feature?   (AICPA adapted)

16–24 Treasury Stock Acquisition and Donation   Gerald Corporation has 25,000 shares of $5 par value stock authorized, issued, and outstanding. All of these shares were issued at a price of $11 per share. The company had retained earnings of $75,000.

INSTRUCTIONS

Identify the changes in the stockholders' equity section of the balance sheet for each of the following *independent* situations:

[a] Twenty-five hundred shares were acquired at $21 per share (assume the par value method of accounting).

[b] Twenty-five hundred shares were acquired by a stockholder donation (assume the cost method of accounting).

[c] Twenty-five hundred shares were acquired at $21 per share and then reissued at $18 per share (assume the cost method of accounting).

16–25 Stock Subscription Transactions   On January 1, 1995, Sumner Corporation subscribed 60,000 shares of its $10 par common stock. The subscription contract required a down payment equal to 40% of the total purchase price of the securities, with the remainder due in two months. The contract specified a subscription price of $22 per share. On March 2, 1995, all but 4,000 shares were issued. These shares were not issued because a subscriber defaulted. On March 2, Sumner issued these 4,000 shares to another party for $18 per share.

INSTRUCTIONS

[a] Provide the January 1, 1995, journal entry to reflect the subscribing of common stock.
[b] Provide the journal entry on March 2, 1995, to reflect the issuance of common stock.
[c] Provide the journal entry to record the default on 4,000 shares, assuming each of the following *independent* contract terms:
  [1] The partial payment is refunded.
  [2] The partial payment is refunded, less any expenses or reductions in issue price from the resale of the stock.
  [3] The partial payment is forfeited.
[d] Why would an issuing company insist on provision [c-2] or [c-3] in a subscription contract?

16–26 Treasury Stock Transactions—Cost Method   An analysis of the stockholders' equity of Juniper Corporation as of January 1, 1995, is as follows:

Common stock ($20 par value; 100,000 shares authorized, 60,000 shares issued and outstanding)	$1,200,000
Paid-in capital in excess of par value	140,000
Retained earnings	760,000
Total stockholders' equity	$2,100,000

Juniper acquired 1,000 shares of its stock for $35,000, and during 1995, it entered into the following transactions:

  Sold 600 treasury shares at $38 per share.
  Sold 200 treasury shares at $31 per share.
  Retired the remaining treasury shares.

INSTRUCTIONS

[a] Provide the appropriate journal entries to reflect the treasury transactions indicated above. Assume the use of the cost method of accounting.
[b] How should treasury stock be presented on the financial statements? Why?   (AICPA adapted)

16–27 Treasury Stock Transactions—Cost and Par Value Methods   Jamison Corporation acquired 2,000 shares of its own $5 par value stock at $21 per share on February 10, 1995. It sold 1,200 of these shares at $27 per share on May 1, 1995, and an additional 600 shares on August 17, 1995, for $14 per share. Jamison's common stock was originally issued at $16 per share.

INSTRUCTIONS

[a] Record the initial purchase of treasury shares in journal entries under
  [1] The cost method
  [2] The par value method
[b] Record the reissuances of treasury stock in the journal entries under
  [1] The cost method
  [2] The par value method

16–28 Treasury Stock Transactions   The stockholders' equity section of Walker, Inc.'s balance sheet on December 31, 1994, was as follows:

Common stock ($5 par value; 1,200,000 shares authorized, 800,000 shares issued, 700,000 shares outstanding)	$ 4,000,000
Paid-in capital in excess of par value	3,250,000
Retained earnings	5,240,000
	12,490,000

Balance carried forward	$12,490,000
Less: Treasury stock, at cost, 100,000 shares	800,000
Total stockholders' equity	$11,690,000

During 1995 Walker reissued 50,000 shares of the treasury stock at $14 per share.

INSTRUCTIONS

[a] Record the reissuance of the treasury shares in the appropriate journal entry.

[b] Revise the stockholders' equity section of Walker's balance sheet for December 31, 1995, assuming that the par value method was used for all treasury stock transactions. Net income was $300,000. (*Hint:* Restate the December 31, 1994, stockholders' equity, assuming the 100,000 shares of treasury stock had been accounted for by the par value method. Then record the reissue of the 50,000 shares. Treat the treasury stock as a reduction in common stock in stockholders' equity.) (AICPA adapted)

16–29 Various Capital Stock Retirement Transactions The stockholders' equity section of the balance sheet for Miller Products, Inc., appeared as follows on December 31, 1994:

$4 Preferred stock ($40 par value; 5,000 shares authorized, issued, and outstanding, callable at 102%)	$ 200,000
Common stock ($5 stated value; 100,000 shares authorized, 60,000 shares issued and outstanding)	300,000
Paid-in capital in excess of par value (common)	600,000
Retained earnings	1,000,000
Total stockholders' equity	$2,100,000

On February 2, 1995, Miller purchased and retired 5,000 shares of common stock at $18 per share. On March 2, it acquired 3,000 shares of common stock as treasury stock at $14 per share (use the cost method). On April 2, the shares acquired on March 2 were retired. On August 10, Miller called 3,000 shares of preferred stock.

INSTRUCTIONS

[a] Provide the journal entries for the 1995 transactions.

[b] How would total stockholders' equity be affected if the par value method was used for the March 2 treasury stock acquisition and the April 2 retirement?

16–30 Stockholders' Equity Reporting Fallon Corporation was incorporated on January 1, 1995, with an authorization of 200,000 shares of $5 par value common stock and 20,000 shares of 10%, nonparticipating, cumulative, $30 par preferred stock. On February 2, 1995, Fallon issued 100,000 shares of common stock at $24 per share and 15,000 shares of preferred stock at $29 per share. Subscriptions were taken for 40,000 common shares at a contracted price of $25 per share. The subscription contract required a 60% cash advance. The stock will be issued when the subscription price is paid in full on January 31, 1996. In 1995 Fallon received land from the City of Elmhurst for future plant expansion at no cost. The land had a cost to Elmhurst of $12,000 and a market value on the transfer date of $25,000. In 1995 Fallon purchased 15,000 shares of its own common stock for $30 per share (assume the cost method). Fallon declared cash dividends for preferred and common stock only once during 1995. The common dividend was $10,000. Net income for 1995 was $65,000.

INSTRUCTIONS

Prepare in good form the stockholders' equity section of the balance sheet on December 31, 1995.

16–31 Stock Subscriptions and Issuances The stockholders' equity section of the balance sheet for Farmer Corporation appeared as follows on December 31, 1995:

Preferred stock ($20 par value; 20,000 shares authorized, issued, and outstanding)	$ 400,000
Common stock ($2 par value; 100,000 shares authorized, 60,000 shares issued, and 50,000 shares outstanding)	120,000
Paid-in capital in excess of par value (common)	1,150,000
Paid-in capital from defaulted subscriptions	150,000
Retained earnings	70,000
Treasury stock (at par)	(20,000)
Total stockholders' equity	$1,870,000

Farmer was formed on January 1, 1995, with the issuance of 20,000 preferred shares and 10,000 common shares. It issued the common shares for $25 per share and an additional 50,000 common shares on a subscription basis. The original subscription contract was for 70,000 shares at a subscription price of $25 per share, with a required cash down payment equal to 30% of the purchase price. The subscription contract requires the cash advance on all defaulted shares to be forfeited. Farmer earned $100,000 in 1995 but declared no dividends.

INSTRUCTIONS

Provide the journal entries that must have been made in 1995, as determined from the December 31, 1995, stockholders' equity balances and related information.

16–32 Stockholders' Equity—Transaction Effects   Consider the following statement of stockholders' equity for Biotech, Inc.:

Biotech, Inc.
Stockholders' Equity
December 31, 1995

Common stock, $1 par value; authorized 3,000,000 shares; issued 1,500,000 shares; outstanding 1,400,000 shares	$ 1,400,000
Additional paid-in capital:	
In excess of par value	20,000,000
From treasury stock	200,000
Total paid-in capital	21,600,000
Unappropriated retained earnings	8,100,000
Total stockholders' equity	$29,700,000

Biotech originally issued all of the outstanding common stock and treasury stock in 1989 for $11 per share. The treasury stock is common stock reacquired on March 31, 1995. Biotech uses the par value method of accounting for treasury stock.

During 1996 the following events or transactions occurred:

Feb. 12   Issued 400,000 shares of unissued common stock for $12.50 per share.

Sept. 20   Purchased by Biotech from the retiring president 100,000 shares of Biotech's common stock for $13 per share, which was equal to market value on this date. This stock was canceled.

Dec. 31   Named as a defendant in a lawsuit by two separate parties for patent infringements. Biotech's management and outside legal counsel share the following opinions regarding these suits:

Suit	Likelihood of Losing the Suit	Estimated Loss
1	Reasonably possible	$600,000
2	Probable	400,000

INSTRUCTIONS

[a] Determine the amount by which Biotech's paid-in capital in excess of par value will increase as a result of the February 12, 1996, transaction.

[b] Determine the amount by which Biotech's paid-in capital in excess of par value will decrease as a result of the September 20, 1996, transaction.

[c] Biotech wishes to appropriate retained earnings for all loss contingencies that are not properly accruable by a charge to earnings. What amount of retained earnings should be appropriated?

(AICPA adapted)

PROBLEMS

16–33 Recording Stock Transactions   The stockholders' equity section of the January 1, 1995, balance sheet for Wilson Corporation is as follows:

12% Callable preferred stock ($100 par value; 1,000 shares issued and outstanding)	$ 100,000
Common stock ($10 par value; 40,000 shares authorized, 25,000 shares issued and outstanding)	250,000
Paid-in capital in excess of par value (preferred)	1,000
Paid-in capital in excess of par value (common)	1,200,000
Retained earnings	900,000
Total stockholders' equity	$2,451,000

The following transactions occurred in 1995:

Jan.   16   Issued 15,000 shares of common stock for $63 per share.

Feb.   18   Purchased 20,000 shares of common stock for the treasury at $54 per share (assume the cost method).

Mar.   10   The city of Watsonville donated land with an appraised value of $300,000 for use as a future plant site.

Apr.   1   Retired 10,000 shares of the treasury stock purchased in February. The market price of common shares was $57 per share at the time.

July   29   Called 250 preferred shares at a call price of $103 per share.

Aug.   17   Resold the remaining treasury shares from February at $66 per share.

Sept.   9   Acquired land and building by issuing 10,000 common shares when the common was selling for $48 per share. Appraised value of the land was $200,000 and of the building, $350,000. Consider the market value of the stock as the basis for determining the value of the acquired assets.

Oct.   9   A shareholder donated 6,000 common shares to the corporation (assume the cost method).

Dec.   7   Sold the donated shares for $80 per share.

INSTRUCTIONS

Provide the appropriate journal entries for these transactions.

16–34 Stockholder Equity Transactions   Gibralter Corporation began operations on January 1, 1995, by issuing the following shares:

5,000 shares of 12% redeemable preferred stock, $100 par value	$ 500,000
60,000 common shares, $2 par value, 100,000 shares authorized	1,080,000

In addition, the following transactions took place during the year:

Jan.   9   Subscribed an additional 20,000 common shares at $20 per share. Subscribers were required to put down 40% of the purchase price, with the remainder due in six months.

Feb.   2   Paid legal fees with respect to the stock offering by issuing 1,000 common shares when the market price was $22 per common share.

Mar.   19   Purchased 10,000 common shares for the treasury at $16 per share (assume the par value method).

July   1   Purchased and retired 5,000 common shares at $20 per share.

July   10   Received the remaining amount due on 19,000 shares of the stock subscription. The remaining 1,000 shares were defaulted. The down payment was refunded to the defaulting party. At this time the market price per share was $24.

Aug.   21   Retired 3,000 treasury shares.

Sept.   30   Reissued 7,000 treasury shares at $25 per share.

Nov.   12   The estate of a deceased stockholder donated 1,000 common shares to the company (assume the par value method).

Nov.   23   Sold the donated shares for $30 per share.

INSTRUCTIONS

Provide the appropriate journal entries for each transaction.

16–35 Stockholders' Equity Journal Entries and Financial Reporting   Minton Corporation's stockholders' equity section of the balance sheet appears as follows on January 1, 1995:

11% Callable preferred stock ($100 par value; 60,000 shares authorized, issued, and outstanding)	$ 6,000,000
Common stock ($10 par value; 400,000 shares authorized, issued, and outstanding)	4,000,000
Paid-in capital in excess of par value (common)	12,000,000
Retained earnings	15,000,000
Total stockholders' equity	$37,000,000

Common and preferred stock were issued at the corporation's inception. There were no capital stock transactions from the inception of the corporation through January 1, 1995. In 1995 the following transactions took place:

Jan.	16	Purchased 30,000 treasury shares of common stock at $52 per share (assume the cost method).
Feb.	3	Retired 10,000 treasury shares when the market price was $48 per share.
Mar.	6	Called 10,000 preferred shares at $102 per share.
May	22	Received 15,000 common shares as a donation from a stockholder when the market price was $41 per share.
Sept.	30	Purchased 10,000 common shares at $38 per share for immediate retirement.
Oct.	16	Reissued 10,000 of the treasury shares purchased in January at $47 per share.
Nov.	17	Reissued 10,000 donated common shares at $51 per share.
Dec.	1	Retired the remaining donated shares.

Net income for 1995 was $1,000,000.

INSTRUCTIONS

[a] Provide the appropriate journal entries for each transaction.
[b] Prepare the stockholders' equity section of the balance sheet for Minton as it should appear on December 31, 1995.

16–36 Comprehensive Stockholders' Equity Transactions   Grover Manufacturing Company initiated operations on January 1, 1995. On December 31, 1995, the company's stockholders' equity section of the balance sheet appeared as follows:

Common stock ($30 par value; 60,000 shares authorized, 50,000 shares issued, and 35,000 shares outstanding)	$1,500,000
Common stock subscribed (5,000 shares)	150,000
Paid-in capital in excess of par value	1,375,000
Retained earnings	800,000
Treasury stock (at cost)	(780,000)
Total stockholders' equity	$3,045,000

During 1996, 40% of the purchase price of the subscribed shares was remitted by subscribers. All but 500 of the subscribed shares were issued, because the original subscriber defaulted on the shares. These shares were issued at $50 per share to a new owner, and the remaining cash advance was returned to the original subscriber (less any price loss). The common stock subscriptions were subscribed at the same price as the original issue of 50,000 shares. Furthermore, in 1996 Grover resold 5,000 treasury shares at $56 per share. Later in the year, another 5,000 treasury shares were sold at $25 per share after a sharp drop in the company's stock price. At the end of the year, 3,000 treasury shares were retired.

INSTRUCTIONS

Provide the appropriate journal entries for Grover manufacturing Company for 1996 based on the preceding discussion.

16–37 Treasury Stock Transactions   The stockholders' equity section of Hapke Furniture Company's balance sheet appeared as follows on January 1, 1996:

Common stock ($5 par value; 80,000 shares authorized, issued, and outstanding)	$ 400,000
Paid-in capital in excess of par value	1,000,000
Retained earnings	800,000
Total shareholders' equity	$2,200,000

The following events occurred in sequence during 1996:

[1] Ten thousand common shares were purchased for the treasury at $20 per share.
[2] An additional 10,000 shares were purchased for the treasury at $30 per share.
[3] Twelve thousand treasury shares were resold at a market price of $27 per share.
[4] Five thousand Hapke common shares were donated to the company by a stockholder's estate.
[5] Eleven thousand treasury shares were reissued at a market price of $23 per share.
[6] The remaining shares were retired.

INSTRUCTIONS

[a] Provide the appropriate journal entries assuming the cost method of accounting for treasury stock and treasury stock reissuance on a first-in, first-out basis.
[b] Provide the appropriate journal entries assuming the cost method of accounting for treasury stock, and treasury stock reissuance under an average cost assumption.
[c] Provide the appropriate journal entries assuming the par value method of accounting for treasury stock.

16–38 Comparative Stockholders' Equity Analysis and Journal Entries The following are comparative stockholders' equity sections of the balance sheets for Burnside Corporation. Some items that require disclosure are not included.

	Dec. 31, 1995	Dec. 31, 1996
10% Preferred stock ($20 par value; 90,000 shares authorized)	$ 100,000	$ 120,000
Common stock ($5 par value; 150,000 shares authorized)	300.000	400,000
Common stock subscribed (10,000 shares)	–0–	50,000
Paid-in capital in excess of par value (common)	360,000	410,000
Donated capital (10,000 shares Burnside common)	–0–	50,000
Retained earnings	400,000	660,000
Treasury stock (10,000 shares of common)	–0–	(50,000)
Total stockholders' equity	$1,160,000	$1,640,000

Net income for 1996 was $300,000. The subscribed stock sold at $7.

INSTRUCTIONS

[a] Provide the journal entries to account for the 1996 changes in the stockholders' equity account balances for Burnside Corporation.
[b] How many shares of the preferred and common stock were issued and outstanding at December 31, 1995 and 1996?

16–39 Correction of Improper Stockholders' Equity Presentation Unger Corporation presented the following balance sheet for December 31, 1995:

Assets	
Current assets	$ 30,000
Treasury stock (at market; cost = $15,000)	14,000
Fixed assets	56,000
Total assets	$100,000

Liabilities and Stockholders' Equity	
Current liabilities	$ 20,000
Common stock subscribed (500 shares)	10,000
Long-term debt	8,000
Total liabilities	38,000

Total liabilities (balance carried forward)	$ 38,000
Stockholders' equity	
Common stock (4,000 shares issued)	18,000
10% Preferred stock (1,000 shares issued)	12,000
Less: Stock subscriptions receivable	(4,000)
Reserve for depreciation	16,000
Earned surplus	20,000
Total liabilities and stockholders' equity	$100,000

Your investigation of Unger Corporation's financial records indicates that all authorized shares have been either issued or subscribed. In addition, the par values for the common and preferred stock are $2 and $10, respectively. The treasury stock was originally purchased when the market price was $20 per share. During 1995, 250 treasury shares were resold for $25 per share. A Gain on Treasury Stock Transactions was credited for the difference between the original cost and the selling price. Furthermore, the excess of cost over market of the treasury shares at the end of the period was recognized as an unrealized loss on the 1995 income statement. You also discovered that the City of Stanton donated land with a market value of $9,000 to Unger during 1995.

INSTRUCTIONS

Revise the December 31, 1995, balance sheet for Unger Corporation as it should be presented according to generally accepted accounting principles.

16–40 Treasury Stock—Cost Flow Assumptions   Warner Company has 30,000 shares of $10 par value common stock authorized and 20,000 shares issued and outstanding. On August 15, 1995, Warner purchased 1,000 shares of treasury stock at $12 per share. Warner uses the cost method to account for treasury stock. On September 14, 1995, the company sold 500 shares of the treasury stock for $14 per share.

On October 20, 1995, Warner acquired another 1,000 shares of common stock for the treasury, paying $9 per share and on November 24, 1995, reissued 750 shares of treasury stock receiving $10.50 per share.

INSTRUCTIONS

[a] Prepare the journal entries to record these transactions using
    [1] The average cost method of accounting.
    [2] The FIFO method of accounting.
[b] Determine the balance to be reported in the Treasury Stock account under each method of accounting. (AICPA adapted)

16–41 Ownership Restructuring   Armstrong Company is a small, closely held corporation with three stockholders. K. Allen plans to retire, leaving N. Slezak and K. Bell to manage the business. The owners agreed to alter the capitalization of the firm to reflect this event. Allen will redeem his capital stock in return for nonvoting preferred stock. Before the agreement, the stockholders' equity section of Armstrong's balance sheet appeared as follows:

Common stock ($20 par value; 10,000 shares authorized and issued,	
9,000 shares outstanding)	$200,000
Paid-in capital in excess of par value	50,000
Retained earnings	140,000
Treasury stock (cost method)	(30,000)
Total stockholders' equity	$360,000

The three owners presently have the following ownership interests: Allen, 20%; Slezak, 40%; and Bell, 40%. The corporation will be reorganized according to the following agreement:
[1] The treasury stock will be canceled.
[2] Two new stock issues will be authorized: $10 par value common stock and 12% cumulative nonvoting preferred stock ($100 par value).
[3] The stockholders will surrender their shares for cancellation and will receive the newly authorized shares as follows:
    [a] Allen will receive only preferred stock.
    [b] Slezak will receive 40% of the common stock.
    [c] Bell will receive 60% of the common stock and the remainder of the preferred stock.
[4] The total number of shares for the preferred stock and common stock issue is 19,000.

INSTRUCTIONS

[a] Prepare the journal entry to cancel the Treasury Stock account on the company's books.

[b] Prepare a schedule computing the amount of each stockholder's equity in the company before the recapitalization.

[c] Compute the number of new common stock and new preferred stock shares to be issued, given that they total 19,000 shares.

[d] Prepare a schedule computing the number of shares of each type of newly issued stock that each stockholder will receive under the agreement described above.

16–42 Preparation of Stockholders' Equity Section Memorem, Inc., a manufacturer of restaurant and kitchen equipment, was incorporated in 1961. Its stock is publicly held. The stockholders' equity section of the balance sheet at September 30, 1995, follows.

$2 Cumulative redeemable preferred stock ($15 par value; 500,000 shares authorized, 4,000 shares issued and outstanding)	$ 60,000
Common stock ($10 par value; 1,000,000 shares authorized, 110,000 shares issued and outstanding)	1,100,000
Retained earnings	622,000
Total stockholders' equity	$1,782,000

Memorem's capital stock transactions during fiscal 1996 were as follows:

[1] On January 2, Memorem issued 8,000 preferred shares in exchange for land with an appraised value of $100,000. Six months ago 1,000 shares of Memorem preferred were exchanged "over the counter" for $14 per share.

[2] On January 17, 4,500 shares of common stock were sold to John Carter at $25 per share.

[3] On September 14, Memorem purchased dissident stockholder Carter's 4,500 shares at $27 per share. The shares are to be held as treasury shares and accounted for at cost. (Carter violently opposed Memorem's business strategy and Memorem management decided to eliminate his interest.)

[4] On September 28, Memorem contracted with Karen Singer for the sale of 10,000 previously unissued shares at $25 per share to be issued when the purchase price is fully paid. At September 30, only $195,000 had been paid. Singer agreed to pay the balance on or before November 3, 1996.

[5] On September 30, Memorem redeemed 4,000 preferred shares according to the issue agreement. The shares were redeemed at $18 per share.

[6] A cash dividend of $2 was declared on the preferred shares on March 11 and paid on March 30.

[7] A cash dividend of $1.50 per share was declared on September 15, and payable October 11.

[8] Memorem's net income for fiscal year 1996 was $250,000.

INSTRUCTIONS

Prepare the stockholders' equity section of the balance sheet for the year ended September 30, 1996. This statement should be supported by the following schedules, presented in the order given:

[a] Changes in preferred stock account.

[b] Changes in common stock account.

[c] Calculation of paid-in capital in excess of par value.

[d] Changes in retained earnings.   (AICPA adapted)

16–43 Analyzing Changes in Stockholders' Equity On January 1, 1995, the stockholders' equity section of Vernon Electronics Company's balance sheet revealed the following information:

$5 Convertible preferred stock ($40 par value; 50,000 shares authorized, 20,000 shares issued and outstanding)	$ 800,000
Common stock ($5 stated value; 200,000 shares authorized, 120,000 shares issued and outstanding)	600,000
Paid-in capital in excess of par value	3,000,000
Retained earnings	4,500,000
Total stockholders' equity	$8,900,000

In addition, the following information is known:

[1] On February 2, 1995, the company acquired 15,000 common shares for $33 per share (assume the cost method).

[2] On September 30, 1995, 5,000 preferred shares were converted to common shares. One share of preferred stock is convertible into one share of common stock. At the time of conversion, the common stock had a market value of $42 per share.

[3] On December 21, 1995, the company placed a stock subscription of 10,000 common shares at a subscription price of $33 per share. The subscription contract required a cash down payment equal to 60% of the subscription price, with the balance due on February 1, 1996.

[4] On February 1, 1996, 8,500 common shares were issued according to the subscription contract. Because of default by a subscriber, 1,500 shares were not issued. The subscription contract requires the subscriber to forfeit all cash advances.

[5] On April 15, 1996, 10,000 shares held in treasury were reissued at $50 per share.

[6] On May 16, 1996, a special dividend of preferred stock was distributed to common stockholders. One hundred shares of common stock entitled a shareholder to one share of preferred stock. The market price of preferred stock was $40 per share at the time. (*Hint:* Record this dividend at the market price of the preferred shares.)

[7] Cash dividends are declared for preferred and common shares on October 31 and April 30 of each year. Semiannual cash dividends for common shares are $0.50 per share.

[8] Net income for 1995 was $660,000, and for 1996, $890,000.

INSTRUCTIONS

Analyze the changes in Vernon Electronics stockholders' equity accounts for 1995 and 1996. Create column headings for the stockholders' equity accounts. Enter under each column heading the beginning balances and the changes in the accounts due to transactions in 1995 and 1996. Determine balances for each account for December 31, 1995, and December 31, 1996. Provide in good form a schedule supporting computations for dividend calculations.

CASES

16–44 Characteristics of Capital Stock   Capital stock is an important part of corporate equity. The term *capital stock* generally includes common and preferred stock issued by a corporation.

INSTRUCTIONS

[a] What are the basic rights of ownership of common stock? How are they exercised?

[b] What is preferred stock? Discuss the various preferences that may be afforded preferred stock.
(AICPA adapted)

16–45 Presentation of Stockholders' Equity Section   The stockholders' equity section of the balance sheet reports the ownership interest in the corporation. This interest is usually separated into contributed capital and earned capital.

INSTRUCTIONS

[a] Why is the distinction made between these two components of stockholders' equity?

[b] The contributed capital is frequently divided into legal (or stated) capital and paid-in capital in excess of par value. What is the reason for this disclosure method?

16–46 Presentation of Stock Subscriptions   Roswell Corporation presented its balance sheet to the bank prior to negotiating a loan. The balance sheet included among its current assets $300,000 in stock subscriptions receivable. The loan officer took exception to this presentation and suggested that this amount should be reported as a reduction of the stockholders' equity.

INSTRUCTIONS

[a] What arguments could the bank loan officer use for his position?

[b] What arguments could Roswell Corporation use to support its presentation method?

16–47 Characteristics of Redeemable Preferred Stock   The right side of Kemper Corporation's balance sheet at December 31, 1995, appears as follows:

Current liabilities	$ 200,000
10% Bond payable (due in 2006)	2,000,000
$5 Redeemable preferred stock ($50 par value; cumulative and nonvoting, to be redeemed in 2004 at par)	1,000,000
Common stock ($5 par value; 600,000 shares authorized, issued, and outstanding)	3,000,000
Total liabilities and stockholders' equity	$6,200,000

INSTRUCTIONS

[a] In what ways is the redeemable preferred stock similar to the 10% bond payable?

[b] In what ways is the redeemable preferred stock similar to the common stock?

[c] Is the redeemable preferred stock more like an equity or a debt?

[d] How should redeemable preferred stock be presented in the financial statements? Support your position.

16–48 Eliminating Preferred Stock   Preferred stock may be eliminated from a corporation's capital structure in several ways:

[1] The corporation may call the preferred stock.

[2] The corporation may redeem the preferred stock according to a mandatory redemption provision.

[3] The corporation may purchase the preferred stock as treasury stock and retire it at a later date.

[4] The corporation may purchase the preferred stock directly off the market for immediate retirement.

[5] The preferred stockholders may convert the preferred stock to common stock according to a conversion provision.

INSTRUCTIONS

Identify the characteristics of each of the preceding elimination methods.

16–49 Treasury Stock   Simpson Company recently entered into an agreement with Sandra Bailey, a common stockholder, in which the company reacquired her stock. The stock is to be held as treasury stock and reissued to others at a later time. Because Simpson is short of cash, however, it issued a note payable to Bailey for $100,000 payable in 18 equal monthly payments plus interest at 15%, a reasonable rate. As security for the note, Simpson agreed to allow Bailey to retain possession of the shares, receive dividends, and to vote the shares at stockholder meetings until the note has been completely paid.

Simpson's controller has called you, its external accountant, for advice on how to report this transaction. Specifically, he asks this question: "Should I record this stock as if it has been reacquired and is now treasury stock, or, if not, how should I report the note that has been issued to Ms. Bailey?"

INSTRUCTIONS

Prepare a brief report to the controller describing how you believe the transactions described should be reported in Simpson's financial statements for the year ending next week.

JUDGMENT CASES

16–50 Induced Conversion of Convertible Debt   The management of Landco, Inc., issued convertible bonds two years ago. The terms of the bonds allowed the bondholders, at their option, to convert each bond into four shares of the company's common stock. The bonds have a current market value that exceeds their carrying amount and the market value of the stock for which they could be exchanged. Therefore, few bondholders have exercised their rights to conversion. Further, Landco has an adequate number of authorized but unissued shares to effect the conversion without making any open market purchases.

Landco has decided to induce a conversion of its convertible bonds by adding a sweetener to the conversion terms and conditions. Landco hopes that this move will help the company obtain a better debt/equity ratio to meet certain lending covenants in its other debt instruments. The sweetener provides that a cash premium will be paid to each bondholder who elects to exercise the conversion option. The premium will be sufficient to provide the bondholders with stock and cash that has a fair value equivalent to the current market value of the bonds. While no time limit has been set for the sweetened conversion period, the company has reserved the right to cancel the sweetener at any time after an initial eight-month period.

Subsequently, a large number of the convertible bonds have been converted, and the company is now considering how to account for the conversion transactions.

INSTRUCTIONS

Determine how the bond conversion should be accounted for and reported in the financial statements of Landco, Inc.

16–51 Distinguishing between Debt and Equity Instruments   Canton Company, Inc., a manufacturer of electronic products, prepares a classified balance sheet and would like your assistance with an unusual problem. Canton has issued preferred stock that allows holders to redeem it at par value after an initial five-year period. The company controller tells you that he is completely aware that the Securities and Exchange Commission requires that such securities be reported outside of the stockholders' equity section of the balance sheet. The controller's boss wants to create and report a third section of the balance sheet between liabilities and stockholders' equity called "Other Sources of Financing." According to the controller, the balance sheet would contain totals for Liabilities, Other Sources of Financing, and Stockholders' Equity. In this fashion, the company believes that the balance sheet more appropriately displays the various methods the company has used and the extent to which each has financed the business.

INSTRUCTIONS

Respond to the controller. Would you be willing to accept a balance sheet that is classified in the manner described? If not, what presentation that incorporates the desires of the company would you be willing to accept?

16–52 Accounting for Call Options Payable in an Enterprise's Own Stock   Santa Barbara Company, Inc., has issued a number of call option contracts that require the company to sell shares of its common stock to the option holder for $50 per share. Each option allows the holder to acquire 100 shares of the stock through December 31, 1998, at which time the options expire. The company sold 1,000 of the option packages for $5,000 each. If the options are not exercised, the holders may redeem them for 50% of the purchase price. While the value of the stock currently is above the exercise price of the options (and the cost of the option contract), the holders have not yet chosen to exercise them and they remain outstanding.

The president of Santa Barbara wishes to classify the options as equity securities rather than debt. In developing her arguments, she states:

> Of course, none of the holders have yet exercised the option. If the stock goes up, they will exercise near the end of the expiration period due to the present value of the dollars they will have to pay when they exercise. If the stock goes way down, which, by the way, is inconceivable, then they will simply redeem the option at the 50% amount. Either way we win. If we have to issue stock, it costs us nothing. Even in the extremely unlikely case that we have to honor the redemption clause, the amount we have to pay is only one-half of what we received originally. It is clear to me that this instrument is a classic equity call option and should be so classified.

INSTRUCTIONS

Comment on the president's position. Do you believe that the options can be acceptably classified as an equity instrument? Provide supporting arguments for your position.

16–53 Equity Sweeteners   Upstart, Inc., is a company that is trying to market its first stock issuance and is experiencing difficulty in obtaining an acceptable price for those securities. It is now considering "sweetening" the terms of those securities to make them more attractive to the market. One of the ideas is to include a clause that provides that the company will distribute to those equity holders 1% of the company's gross revenues each year for the next 10 years. Because the company has several long-term contracts to perform a variety of services, the earning and collection of gross revenues in each of the next 10 years are virtually assured.

INSTRUCTIONS

The president of the company has approached you to advise her about how the issuance of such securities should be accounted for and reported in the company's financial statements. Of particular concern is whether any of the proceeds of the stock issuance should be reported as debt when issued and how the obligation to pay the 1% should be reported generally. Develop a memorandum that addresses the president's concerns. Be sure to state the basis for your positions and refer to any authoritative literature that you believe relevant to those issues.

FINANCIAL REPORTING CASE

16–54 Financial Reporting Case   National Service Industries is a diversified manufacturing and service company. Its core businesses are lighting equipment, textile rental, and specialty chemicals.

Following is the liability and stockholders' equity section of National Service Industries' 1993 balance sheet, with comparative year 1992.

(In thousands, except share data)	August 31 1993	1992
Liabilities and Stockholders' Equity		
Current Liabilities:		
Current maturities of long-term debt	$ 1,792	$ 1,434
Notes payable	4,404	—
Accounts payable	85,505	77,748
Accrued salaries, commissions, and bonuses	37,103	32,319
Self insurance reserves	71,888	61,232
Other accrued liabilities	42,981	37,035
Total Current Liabilities	243,673	209,768
Long-Term Debt, less current maturities	28,418	28,359
Deferred Income Taxes	84,289	92,654
Other Long-Term Liabilities	27,110	28,677
Stockholders' Equity:		
Series A participating preferred stock, $.05 stated value,		
500,000 shares authorized, none issued		
Preferred stock, no par value, 500,000 shares authorized, none issued		
Common stock, $1 par value, 80,000,000 shares authorized,		
57,918,978 shares issued in 1993 and 1992	57,919	57,919
Paid-in capital	7,299	6,313
Retained earnings	673,399	652,717
	738,617	716,949
Less:		
Treasury stock, at cost (8,357,539 shares in 1993 and 8,381,075 shares in 1992)	34,594	33,995
Total Stockholders' Equity	704,023	682,954
Total Liabilities and Stockholders' Equity	$1,087,513	$1,042,412

INSTRUCTIONS

[a] Why are no dollar figures presented for the two classes of preferred stock? Why do you think the company presents its preferred stock in this manner?

[b] For 1993, how many shares of common stock are authorized, issued, and outstanding? How do these amounts differ for 1992, if at all?

[c] What portion of the total liabilities and stockholders' equity consists of stockholders' equity in 1993? Has this relationship changed significantly since 1992?

Stockholders' Equity: Operations, Earnings, Dividends, and Other Issues

OBJECTIVES

1. To demonstrate acceptable accounting for several types of dividends on different classes of stock.
2. To explain appropriate accounting and reporting standards for a variety of stock option and compensation plans, stock warrants, and stock rights.
3. To explain current controversies about and a number of the important judgments necessary in accounting for stock-based compensation plans.
4. To describe the circumstances in which a quasi-reorganization is appropriate and to demonstrate the accounting procedures that are applied.
5. To describe the transactions and events directly affecting retained earnings.

Investors typically acquire the equity securities of a company with a number of goals in mind. Principal among those objectives is capital growth, through increases in the value of the securities acquired, and the receipt of periodic cash flows, from the declaration and payment of dividends by the company in which the equity investment has been made. A recent article in *Business Week* observed, however, that companies in the United States have historically paid out a larger portion of their profits as dividends than have foreign companies. Indeed, since about 1980, U.S. companies have been distributing even more of their profits than ever; in one quarter reaching almost 100% of corporate profits. The article points out that such a practice generally bodes ill for those companies' ability to boost productivity and growth.

Business Week identifies two factors that may have caused this recent increase. The first involves attempts by takeover targets to encourage stockholders to resist takeover attempts. The second relates to a change in the capital gains tax law that eliminated the gap between the tax rate at which dividends are taxed and the rates at which capital gains from—for example—selling stocks whose value has appreciated since acquisition are taxed. The outlook for dividend policy in the future, according to the article, is for reduced dividend payout ratios as companies attempt to retain capital to modernize operations and otherwise boost productivity.

Gene Koretz, "Economic Trends," *Business Week* (August 16, 1993), p. 18.

I n this chapter, we discuss the measurement of retained earnings and how it represents an equity interest in assets of the company and may be used as a source of financing as well as an equity source for dividend payments to existing stockholders. Retained earnings is generally thought of as the cumulative net income of a company that has not been distributed to equity investors as dividends. Retained earnings represents equity in assets resulting from profitable operations rather than an asset itself.

We also discuss a number of accounting issues relating to stock options, warrants, rights, appropriations of retained earnings, and quasi-reorganizations.

Occasionally, a company uses the term *earned surplus* in financial statements to describe retained earnings. However, the practice is rare and is discouraged by the accounting profession. The Committee on Terminology of the American Institute of Certified Public Accountants recommended that accountants stop using the term *surplus,* which connotes excess or unneeded equity.[1] However, *surplus* is often used in legal instruments and in statutes regulating commerce, and accountants may thus occasionally encounter the term. As used in financial statements, *surplus* connotes "the amount that remains when use or need is satisfied" (Webster)—a definition that is incompatible with the meaning of retained earnings. Accordingly, we emphasize the preferred term *retained earnings*.

RETAINED EARNINGS

Two financial statements are necessary to broadly report a company's results of operations: an income statement and a statement of changes in retained earnings. These two statements are often combined. In many cases, the statement of retained earnings is presented in a statement summarizing changes in all stockholders' equity accounts, including retained earnings. Both the income and retained earnings statements present activity for a *period of time,* in contrast to the balance sheet, which provides information about economic resources and obligations at a *point in time.* During the closing process, an accountant transfers the amount of a company's net income or loss to retained earnings.

The accounting profession has adopted standards that specify the types of transactions and events that affect income and should therefore appear initially on the income statement rather than the statement of retained earnings. Briefly, revenues, expenses, gains, and losses determine income and should always appear on the income statement. It would therefore be improper to directly charge or credit retained earnings for a revenue, expense, gain, or loss.

The statement of retained earnings is affected by a limited and defined set of items. This practice provides financial statement users with assurance that net income is determined in a comparable fashion by all reporting entities engaging in similar transactions or encountering similar events. Specifically, the items presented in Exhibit 17–1 are the most common items that are charged or credited directly to the Retained Earnings account. As explained in Chapter 16, certain treasury stock transactions cause adjustments to retained earnings. In addition, the adoption of certain accounting principles sometimes results in a retroactive adjustment through retained earnings. The FASB often requires a retroactive adjustment through retained earnings for the transition to a new accounting standard, as when *FASB Statement of Financial Accounting Standards No. 2,* "Accounting for Research and Development Costs" (1974) became effective. Retroactive adjustment through retained earnings is also appropriate when certain existing standards are adopted, such as the initial application of the equity method by an investor establishing significant influence over an investee (see Chapter 10). Furthermore, when a company is reorganized due to financial difficulty, retained earnings may also be affected. We discuss reorganizations and the other items in Exhibit 17–1 more fully later in this chapter.

THE INCOME STATEMENT AND RETAINED EARNINGS

Earlier in this textbook, we developed various concepts of income. We also discuss income determination and presentation in greater detail in Chapter 21. At the present time, the ac-

---

[1]*Accounting Terminology Bulletin No. 2,* "Review and Résumé," 1953, par. 65.

EXHIBIT 17–1

Primary Items Directly Affecting Retained Earnings*

Nature of Event	Debits to Retained Earnings	Credits to Retained Earnings
Income Summary account closed to Retained Earnings	Net loss	Net income
Distributions to stockholders (cash, property, or stock)	Dividends declared	—
Initial adoption of certain accounting principles	Retroactive negative adjustment (loss, expense)	Retroactive positive adjustment (gain, revenue)
Corrections of accounting errors made in prior years	Prior period adjustment (loss, expense)	Prior period adjustment (gain, revenue)
Reservation of earned equity for a specific purpose (e.g., plant expansion, debt service)	Appropriation	Cancellation of existing appropriation
Treasury stock transactions	Negative adjustments from treasury stock transactions	—
Quasi-reorganization	Write-down of assets to fair value	Establishment of a zero balance by charging contributed capital

*This list is not intended to be exhaustive. For example, other items that can affect retained earnings are changes in certain accounting principles and changes in the accounting entity (see Chapter 20).

counting profession supports a modified all-inclusive determination of net income in which items of revenue, expense, gain, and loss are included in the determination of net income. Thus, in measuring an enterprise's net income, only selected, well-defined items are excluded and treated as direct charges or credits to the Retained Earnings account.

Procedurally, all income statement accounts are closed to an Income Summary account, which, in turn, is closed to the Retained Earnings account. Therefore, the net income earned or loss sustained during the period is reported as a single number on the statement of retained earnings. Individual revenues, expenses, gains, and losses composing net income are displayed on the income statement. Accountants should not bypass the income statement by recording revenues, expenses, gains, and losses directly in the Retained Earnings account.

PRIOR PERIOD ADJUSTMENTS

Prior period adjustments are recorded as direct charges or credits to the Retained Earnings account and do not affect net income. **Prior period adjustments,** although quite rare, usually result from accounting errors made in previous years that have been detected and corrected in the current year. Management has a strong incentive to provide fairly stated financial information initially and, thereby, to minimize public disclosure of prior period mistakes in later reports. A prior period adjustment informs financial information users that decisions made in prior years may have been based on flawed information provided by management.

Accounting Principles Board Opinion No. 20 defines errors in financial statements as "mathematical mistakes, mistakes in the application of accounting principles, oversights or misuses of facts that existed at the time the [previous] financial statements were prepared.[2] The Accounting Principles Board (APB) also defined changes from unacceptable accounting principles to generally accepted accounting principles (GAAP) as corrections of errors. Normal recurring changes in accounting estimates, however, do not constitute corrections of errors. For example, the useful lives and salvage values of depreciable assets must be estimated in advance to calculate depreciation expense. Revisions in such estimates as a result of new or better information are not considered corrections of errors whose effects are recorded directly in retained earnings. Rather, changes in estimates affect net income of the current and, possibly, future periods. Other examples of circumstances that require accounting estimates include the recognition of bad debts and the evaluation of loss contingencies.

In sum, if available information is misused or intentional misestimates are made, an error occurs. If new information that provides for a better estimate becomes available, a change in accounting estimate results. Accountants must evaluate whether original estimates are wrong as a result of intentional action or honest misestimates. Financial accounting and reporting for each type of event differs greatly. We discuss accounting changes more fully in Chapter 20.

The presentation of prior period adjustments in the retained earnings statement is made net of any related income tax effects. For example, assume that a $3,000 advertising commission that had been incurred and should have been charged to expense in a prior period is paid and charged to expense during the current period. To facilitate proper presentation of **Matching** financial position and matching in the income statement, the correction of this error is properly treated as a prior period adjustment. The advertising expense may also be deductible for federal income taxes. Thus, a tax benefit may be associated with the prior period adjustment, and the effect of the correction of the error on retained earnings should be shown net of the related income tax effect. We discuss the techniques for calculating the tax effects of prior period adjustments in Chapters 19 and 20.

DIVIDEND DISTRIBUTIONS OF CORPORATE ASSETS

Dividends involve the unilateral transfer of items of value from a corporation to its stockholders. Corporate assets are usually the items transferred, although, in some cases, additional stock of the corporation is transferred as a stock dividend. In any event, dividends represent a reduction of retained earnings, unless the dividend is a liquidating dividend. Liquidating dividends are presumed to be paid from resources that were originally contributed by stockholders rather than earned by the enterprise. As such, contributed capital accounts are charged when liquidating dividends are declared and paid. The various classes, types, and amounts of dividends and the related accounting and reporting practices are considered next; liquidating dividends are discussed later.

The board of directors of a corporation must **declare** a dividend before a liability to pay dividends is incurred by the corporation. The day the board of directors decides that a dividend should be distributed is called the **date of declaration.** Usually, the declaration provides for a **date of record** and a **date of payment.** Exhibit 17–2 summarizes the accounting and reporting implications of each of these important dates.

The board of directors declares a dividend via a news release to the financial press and shareholders. A typical dividend announcement is provided in Exhibit 17–3 for the Walt Disney Company, an entertainment and leisure-oriented company.

Although the phrase "dividends are paid out of retained earnings" is frequently used, we should clearly recognize that dividends are paid with cash or other assets. Retained earnings merely represents the funding source or equity for the reduction of assets used to pay the dividend. For example, a company may have retained earnings far in excess of cash available

---

[2]*APB Opinion No. 20,* "Accounting Changes," 1971, par. 13.

EXHIBIT 17–2

Summary of Dividend Paying Events

Event	Explanation	Accounting Entry		
Date of declaration	Board of directors declares dividend and corporation incurs liability to pay dividend.	Retained Earnings Dividends Payable	XX	XX
Date of record	Declaration specifies that ownership of stock on record date determines the specific dividend recipient.	No journal entry required; however, a memo entry is made to specific stockholder accounts in subsidiary records.		
Date of payment	Cash (or other assets) is disbursed to appropriate stockholders of record.	Dividends Payable Cash	XX	XX

EXHIBIT 17–3

The Walt Disney Company
Dividend Announcement

 The **WALT DISNEY** Company.

Contact: Tom Deegan
(818) 560–1572

FOR IMMEDIATE RELEASE

January 24, 1994

DISNEY INCREASES DIVIDEND

Directors of the Walt Disney Company today voted to increase the company's quarterly cash dividend from 6.25 cents to 7.5 cents per share.

This marks the seventh consecutive year Disney has increased its dividend. The dividend, payable May 20, 1994, to shareholders of record April 15, 1994, represents an annual increase of 20 percent. The last dividend increase—from 5.25 cents to 6.25 cents per share—occurred in January 1993.

SOURCE: The Walt Disney Company, 1994.

for supporting operations and dividend payments. Cash generated by operations may be invested in plant assets or used to retire debt and thus not be available for distribution as dividends. To the extent that dividends declared and paid do not exceed the amount of a company's retained earnings, the dividends may generally be thought of as a distribution of profits and a return on an original investment. If the amount of dividends paid exceeds a company's retained earnings, the excess distributed is considered a return of part of the original investment and generally is called *liquidating dividends.*

Cash Dividends

When a corporation's board of directors declares a **cash dividend,** the total amount to be disbursed as well as the per share amount of the dividend is usually stated explicitly, and accounting is consistent with that described in Exhibit 17–2. When a company has more than one class of stock, allocating dividends among the classes of stock can become complex. We discuss several of these complexities in the following pages.

Dividends on Cumulative Preferred Stock.   A cumulation clause requires a company to pay all dividends to preferred stockholders, including unpaid dividends from prior years called **dividend in arrears,** before any dividends are paid to common stockholders. Dividends in arrears are not a liability until a dividend is declared by a corporation's board of directors. Accountants must be aware of such clauses to properly calculate the dividends due each stockholder class.

Exhibit 17–4, the stockholders' equity section of Sundeen Corporation's balance sheet at December 31, 1995, illustrates the difficulties that can arise and the related computations necessary to appropriately distribute dividends. Assume that on December 31, 1995, Sundeen's board of directors declares a dividend of $600,000 to be paid on January 31, 1996, to stockholders of record at January 15, 1996. Further assume that no dividends have been paid for the previous three years. The following computation demonstrates how the $600,000 dividend will be distributed if Sundeen's preferred stock outstanding was unchanged for the periods in question.

Par value of preferred stock outstanding	$1,000,000
Dividend percentage	× .07
Annual dividend to preferred stockholders	70,000
X number of years in arrears (3) + Current year's dividend	× 4
Total dividend to preferred stockholders	$ 280,000

Because the preferred stock is cumulative, the three years' dividends in arrears and the current year's dividend are paid before the common stockholders receive any dividend. Therefore, of the total dividend declared ($600,000), the preferred stockholders receive $280,000; the common stockholders receive only $320,000. The total dividends declared result in the following dividends per share:

Preferred stock	
In arrears ($210,000/100,000 shares)	$21.00
Current ($70,000/10,000 shares)	7.00
Total dividends per share (preferred)	$28.00
Common stock	
Current ($320,000/60,000 shares)	$ 5.33

The following entries record the declaration and payment of the dividend:

Dec. 31, 1995 Retained Earnings	600,000	
Dividends Payable (Preferred)		280,000
Dividends Payable (Common)		320,000
(To record declaration of dividend. Preferred 3 years in arrears.)		

EXHIBIT 17—4

Sundeen Corporation
Partial Balance Sheet

December 31, 1995

Stockholders' Equity

Preferred stock ($100 par, 7% cumulative, nonvoting; 10,000 shares authorized, issued, and outstanding)	$1,000,000
Common stock ($25 par; 100,000 shares authorized, 60,000 shares issued and outstanding)	1,500,000
Paid-in capital in excess of par value	750,000
Total paid-in capital	3,250,000
Retained earnings	2,500,000
Total stockholders' equity	$5,750,000

Jan. 31, 1996 Dividends Payable (Preferred)	280,000	
Dividends Payable (Common)	320,000	
Cash		600,000
(To record payment of dividends.)		

No formal accounting entry is necessary on the date of record, when the stockholders who will receive the dividends are determined.

Dividends on Noncumulative Preferred Stock.   Now assume the same facts except that the preferred stock is *not* cumulative. The following calculation reflects the distribution of the dividend under this condition:

Par value of preferred stock outstanding	$1,000,000
Dividend percentage	× .07
Total dividend to preferred stockholders	$ 70,000

Because the preferred stock is noncumulative, only the current year dividend is paid to the preferred stockholders. This is the case even though the preferred stockholders have received no dividends for the last three years. The common stockholders will, of course, receive the remaining $530,000. Dividends per share are

Preferred stock ($70,000/10,000 shares)	$7.00
Common stock ($530,000/60,000 shares)	8.83

The cumulative feature of preferred stock affects the value of common stock and preferred stock. When preferred stock is cumulative, dividends for common shareholders may be reduced if dividends on preferred stock fall in arrears. As a result, common stock investors will likely discount the market value of the common shares. In contrast, preferred stockholders perceive the cumulative feature as an attractive characteristic that provides some protection against omitted dividends. As a result, the market price of preferred stock will likely be higher than it would be without the cumulation clause.

Dividends on Participating Preferred Stock.   Preferred stock may be fully participating, partially participating, or nonparticipating. Participation features may also be combined with cumulation clauses. (For simplicity, we illustrate each separately.) Participating preferred stockholders share additional dividends with common stockholders after each has received an initial dividend. The initial dividend distribution is based on the preference percentage of the preferred stock. The extent of the sharing depends on whether the preferred stock is fully or partially participating.

To illustrate, consider again the stockholders' equity of Sundeen Corporation presented in Exhibit 17–4. For simplicity, however, assume that there are no dividends in arrears and that the preferred stock is fully participating. The following calculation demonstrates the manner in which the $600,000 dividend is distributed:

Step 1. Preference Distribution to Preferred Stockholders

Total preferred par value	$1,000,000
Preference rate	× .07
Initial distribution amount	$ 70,000

Step 2. Equivalency Distribution to Common Stockholders

Total common par value	$1,500,000
Equivalency rate (based on preferred rate)	× .07
Initial distribution amount	$ 105,000

Step 3. Participation Distribution

Total dividend declared		$ 600,000
Preference to preferred stockholders	$ 70,000	
Equivalency to common stockholders	105,000	
Total distributed prior to participation		175,000
Remaining participation dividend		$ 425,000

Step 4. Distribution of Remaining Dividend Based on Ratio of Total Par Values

Remaining participation dividend (Step 3)		$425,000
Ratio of total par values		
Preferred par	$1,000,000	40%
Common par	1,500,000	60%
Total combined par values	$2,500,000	100.0%
Portion of remainder to preferred stockholders (.40 × $425,000)		$170,000
Portion of remainder to common stockholders (.60 × $425,000)		255,000
Total remainder distributed		$425,000

Step 5. Summary of Total Dividend Allocation

Preferred stock		
Preference amount (Step 1)	$ 70,000	
Participation amount (Step 4)	170,000	
Total preferred dividend		$240,000
Common stock		
Preference equivalency amount (Step 2)	105,000	
Participation amount (Step 4)	255,000	
Total common dividend		360,000
Total dividend		$600,000

When preferred stock is **fully participating,** both common and preferred shareholders usually receive an equal percentage dividend on the par value of their holdings. An exception occurs if the dividend declared is too small to pay common stockholders the preference rate. In the preceding example, in which the preference rate is 7%, the percentage to be paid is calculated in the following manner:

Preferred stock ($240,000/$1,000,000) 24%
Common stock ($360,000/$1,500,000) 24%
Total (Dividend/Total par value of both classes) ($600,000/$2,500,000) 24%

The percentage paid to each class is 24%. Because the percentage in our example (24%) exceeds the preferred rate (7%), we conclude that each class of stockholder shares the dividend equally on a pro rata basis.

Several other points are significant in these calculations. First, a participation clause in preferred stock does not apply until the preferred stockholders receive the preference amount and the common stockholders receive dividends equivalent (on a weighted average) to those received by the preferred stockholders. Therefore, if a dividend fails to meet both requirements, the preferred stockholders receive only the preference amount. The participation clause applies only to dividends in excess of the original preference dividend paid on preferred stock and an equivalent dividend on common stock. Of course, if a dividend is too small to meet even the preference amount of the preferred stock, the preferred shareholders receive the entire dividend.

Once a participation clause is in effect, the number of shares outstanding must be multiplied by the related par values of each class of stock as a basis for allocating the remaining dividend. The total dividend to be received by each class of stockholder may comprise a base dividend computed on the preference clause in the preferred stock and the participating amount. Finally, if the preferred stock is both cumulative and participating, *any dividends in arrears are paid first and are not considered part of the current distribution to preferred shareholders.*

The example presented previously is based on a fully participating clause in the preferred stock issue. In such situations, preferred stockholders continue to share dividends with common stockholders regardless of the total dividends declared.

Some participating preferred stock issues are partially rather than fully participating. **Partial participation** means that preferred stockholders share, to a limited extent, in any dividends declared above the preference rate. The participation rate establishes an upper limit, not a preference.

To illustrate, assume that the participation clause of Sundeen Corporation's preferred stock specifies only partial participation. Also assume that preferred stockholders receive a 7% preference dividend and participate with common stockholders up to a maximum of 10%, including the preference amount. In this case, the first three steps are those of the previous analysis; the next two steps involve modifications.

Step 1. Preference Distribution to Preferred Stockholders

Same as fully participating ($70,000 to preferred stockholders).

Step 2. Equivalency Distribution to Common Stockholders

Same as fully participating ($105,000 to common stockholders).
(Had the undistributed dividend at this point been $105,000 or less, it would all go to the common stockholders and no future calculation would be necessary.)

Step 3. Participation Distribution

Same as fully participating ($425,000 remaining dividend).

Step 4. Distribution of Remaining Dividend

Total combined par value of stockholders' equity (preferred and common)	$2,500,000
Partial participation percentage	× .03
Participating dividend	$ 75,000

Preferred share (.03 × $1,000,000)	$ 30,000
Common share (.03 × $1,500,000)	45,000
	$ 75,000

(Had the undistributed dividend at this point been less than $75,000, it would be allocated between common and preferred in proportion to their total par value, 40% and 60%, respectively.)

Step 5. Summary of Total Dividend Allocation

Preferred stock		
Preferred amount (Step 1)	$ 70,000	
Participation amount (Step 4)	30,000	
Total preferred dividend		$100,000
Common stock		
Initial common equivalency amount (Step 2)	105,000	
Participation amount (Step 4)	45,000	
Remaining dividend ($600,000 − $250,000)	350,000	
Total common dividend		500,000
Total dividend		$600,000

(The total dividend is reduced by the preference and participation amounts previously determined: $100,000 + $105,000 + $45,000 = $250,000.)

Several observations are possible. The participation amount of 3% is applied to both common and preferred stock to determine if any nonparticipating additional dividend is available exclusively to common stockholders. In this case, $350,000 of the total dividend is available to common stockholders only. The largest dividend preferred stockholders can ever receive is 10% of the total par value of the outstanding preferred stock, or $100,000 (.10 × $1,000,000), in addition to any dividends in arrears.

If preferred stock is cumulative or participating (or both), accountants must be particularly careful in computing dividends. Note that the overall financial statements are not affected by cumulation or participation clauses. Rather, the total dividend declared is charged to retained earnings regardless of which stockholder class receives a particular amount. The question of which stockholder groups receive what amount of dividends is very important, however, and complicated calculations may be required to determine the correct distribution.

The decision to declare and pay dividends is also complex and generally involves careful planning of both the total amount of the dividends as well as the amount to be paid on each share and class of stock. For simplicity, we have assumed the total amount of a dividend and illustrated the calculations necessary to allocate the total dividend to various classes of stockholder. In practice, however, most companies attempt to select the per share amount of dividends to be paid to each class of stockholder and then calculate the total dividend necessary. Many companies strive to maintain consistent dividend policies from year to year, because management generally believes that a consistent dividend policy communicates stability and strength to the investment community. If the total dividend is too great, the per share amounts are revised to reduce the total dividend to a more reasonable amount that is consistent with management goals and corporate capabilities.

Legal Limitations on Dividends

Corporations are granted corporate charters by the states in which they are organized and thereby operate under the laws of those states. An important protection for creditors commonly found in state laws is the limits on the amount of dividends a company can declare and distribute. For example, California law, in part, provides two tests limiting the amount of a dividend. The first test limits dividends to the amount of retained earnings prior to the declaration. A company that desires to declare a dividend larger than its existing Retained Earnings balance is permitted to do so if total assets (excluding goodwill and deferred charges) is at least 25% more than total liabilities (excluding deferred taxes and other deferred credits) and current assets at least equal current liabilities. These tests are based on amounts in the company's financial statements measured in accordance with generally accepted accounting principles. Situations in which the amount of a dividend to be declared approaches the legal limits may cause accountants to consult with attorneys to ascertain whether the proposed amount to be declared and paid complies with state law.

Property Dividends

While most corporations routinely declare and pay cash dividends, other assets, such as marketable securities, may be distributed to stockholders as **property dividends.** If a corporation distributes noncash assets as dividends, accounting is based on the fair value of the property transferred. Such noncash dividends are **nonreciprocal transfers of nonmonetary assets** and may require the recognition of a gain or loss on the disposal of the asset.

To illustrate, assume that Drand, Inc., elects to declare a dividend whereby inventory with a recorded book value of $10,000 and a fair market value of $16,000 is to be distributed to stockholders. The entry to record the dividend declaration and distribution appears below:

Retained Earnings	16,000	
Inventory		10,000
Gain on Disposal of Inventory		6,000
(To record declaration and distribution of property dividend.)		

A gain is recognized only on the inventory to be distributed. Remaining amounts of inventory continue to be carried at the lower of cost or market. An exception to the general practice of recognizing gains or losses occurs if the fair value of the asset to be distributed is not determinable. In such cases, the dividend declaration and payment should be based on the recorded book values. These practices reflect the provisions of *APB Opinion No. 29,*[3] which is discussed in Chapter 11. In essence, fair values are used to record most nonmonetary transactions, including nonreciprocal transfers such as the declaration and payment of property dividends. The extent of a property dividend is best represented by the fair value of the property distributed rather than its historical cost.

An additional accounting and reporting problem arises if a property dividend is declared in one period and is to be paid in the following period. If a property dividend is declared near the end of an accounting period and is to be distributed in the next year, when should any gain or loss on the disposal of the asset be recognized? Further, should changes in the value of the asset between the date of declaration and the date of distribution be recognized and, if so, in what manner?

Although these issues are not explicitly addressed in the authoritative literature, the authors support the recognition of gain or loss when a property dividend is declared. No further adjustments should be made to the asset for later changes in its fair value prior to distribution. In the authors' judgment, the amount of the dividend to be paid is usually established at the declaration date. The board of directors' action to declare a dividend creates a liability, and the amount of the liability to be recognized should be measured by the fair value of the consideration to be given. Of course, adequate disclosure of the timing and valuation basis employed is necessary in such circumstances.

Disclosure

As an example, assume that Drand, Inc., declares a property dividend on December 31, 1995, to be paid on January 15, 1996. On December 31, the equipment to be distributed has

---

[3] *APB Opinion No. 29,* "Accounting for Nonmonetary Transactions," 1973, par. 26.

a book value of $25,000 and a fair market value of $35,000. The following entries are necessary on December 31, 1995, to record the dividend declaration and the revision in the carrying value of the asset:

Dec. 31, 1995	Retained Earnings	35,000	
	Dividend Payable		35,000
Dec. 31, 1995	Equipment	10,000	
	Gain on Disposition Commitment of Equipment		10,000
	(To record declaration of dividend and to record gain on disposal of property.)		

Note that the liability and related asset to be used in satisfying the liability are now carried on Drand's books at the same amount ($25,000 + $10,000 = $35,000). Net income rises as a result of the recognized gain, which causes a related increase in retained earnings. However, the direct charge to Retained Earnings in the first entry shown above reduces Retained Earnings by an amount equal to the sum of the gain and the carrying amount of the equipment. Thus, the direct effect of the $10,000 *gain* on retained earnings is offset by $10,000 of the $35,000 debit to Retained Earnings in the first entry.

The entry to record the payment of the dividend on January 15, 1996, is

Jan. 15, 1996	Dividends Payable	35,000	
	Equipment		35,000
	(To record distribution on property subject to the dividend.)		

If changes in the equipment's fair value occur following the declaration of the dividend and related revaluation of the property, the authors suggest nonrecognition of the change for the following reasons. First, any change in the value of the asset results in a related change in the liability, because the former is to be used to satisfy the latter. Therefore, any gains or losses on revaluing the asset would be directly offset by losses and gains on revaluing the related liability. Second, once the commitment to the asset's disposition has been made and the asset is revalued, no further gain or loss is sustained by the enterprise. This, of course, assumes that no specific event, such as fire or theft, changes the underlying circumstances and requires the dividend to be paid with other assets.

Scrip Dividends

On rare occasions, a company may be short of cash yet still wish to declare a dividend. In such cases, a company may issue **scrip dividends** in the form of written promises to pay cash in the future. Such promises are considered similar to notes payable and are accounted for as a liability. Scrip dividends may bear interest and may be traded, sold, or otherwise disposed of by the shareholder or other owner of the scrip.

Scrip dividends are usually declared only by companies that are quite profitable but for some reason are temporarily short of cash. For example, a construction company may have generated substantial net income during a period but may have only limited cash available if the other party to a contract retains a large amount of cash pending completion of the project. In such a situation, the company may elect to declare a scrip dividend.

Scrip dividends are rare in practice. Most companies that are short of cash are unwilling to incur additional claims on cash through their own unilateral action. Further, most companies that have the profitability to declare dividends either have cash available or can arrange short-term financing for such purposes.

Liquidating Dividends

Liquidating dividends represent distributions of corporate assets that are a return of contributed equity rather than a distribution of earned equity resulting from profitable operations. Such dividends are commonly encountered in the extractive industries and in situations involving corporate dissolution. If a corporation elects to dissolve, creditor claims take precedence over the claims of stockholder groups. Even prior to the repayment of all corporate debt, however, it may be possible to pay a liquidating dividend to the extent that creditors are adequately protected through compliance with state laws limiting the amounts of dividends and establishing legal minimum stated capital levels.

Accountants recognize liquidating dividends only after retained earnings have been exhausted by prior operating losses or previous dividend distributions. Once Retained Earnings is completely exhausted, further distributions of assets to stockholders are charged to Paid-in Capital in Excess of Par rather than Capital Stock accounts. Finally, in a complete dissolution, remaining assets distributed to residual equity holders result in the total elimination of both assets and corporate equity, thereby closing corporate records.

STOCK DIVIDENDS AND SPLITS

Stock dividends and stock splits are two types of stock distributions frequently encountered in practice. **Stock dividends** are dividend declarations to be satisfied in the form of additional shares of the declaring company's stock. Because each shareholder receives additional shares based on the extent of present holdings, no problems are encountered in regard to stockholders' preemptive rights.

A **stock split** occurs when a corporation exchanges a different number of shares of stock for the shares currently held by stockholders. Thus, a shareholder owns more shares after the split than before. Conversely, in a **reverse stock split,** a shareholder owns fewer shares after the split.

A primary reason for a company to declare a stock split is to influence the market for its shares of stock. When a company operates successfully, the market value of its stock may rise to a level that limits active trading. Some investors may be reluctant or unable to acquire shares with a high individual value and trading in the stock may therefore be limited. In such circumstances, the company may decide to "split" the number of shares to reduce the market price of each share and thereby encourage active trading.

Stock dividends are frequently distributed by companies that, while successful, have operating or financing needs for all available cash. For example, a highly successful company may want to build new factories and expand operations as quickly as possible. Management may therefore wish to retain all available cash. The corporation, however, may also want to distribute dividends to shareholders in recognition of the successful operating results. Stock dividends can be a solution to this dilemma.

Stock Dividends

Stock dividends have been discussed by the accounting profession for a long time, yet the subject remains somewhat controversial. The central question about stock dividends is whether a significant accountable event has transpired. The company neither disposes of assets nor acquires cash or other assets through the issuance of additional shares. The declaration of a stock dividend does not give rise to a claim on the assets of a corporation, because *additional* shares of the corporation's own stock are to be issued. The recognition of a liability is thus inappropriate. Rather, the declaration of a stock dividend generally requires a charge to Retained Earnings with a corresponding credit to Stock Dividends Distributable, also a stockholders' equity account. When the dividend is distributed, the Stock Dividend Distributable account is eliminated and the newly outstanding common stock is recorded. This event reduces retained earnings available for future dividends.

Small Stock Dividends.   If a stock dividend represents an increase of less than 20% to 25% of the previously outstanding shares of similar stock, it is called a **small stock dividend.** Such

Materiality
dividends are so small that the market value of each outstanding share is not expected to change materially. This perception is best expressed by *Accounting Research Bulletin 43,* which states the following:

> *As has been previously stated, a stock dividend does not, in fact, give rise to any change whatsoever in either the corporation's assets or its respective shareholders' proportionate interests therein. However, it cannot fail to be recognized that, merely as a consequence of the expressed purpose of the transaction and its characterization as a dividend in related notices to shareholders and the public at large, many recipients of stock dividends look upon them as distributions of corporate earnings and usually in an amount equivalent to the fair value of the additional shares received....The committee therefore believes that where these circumstances exist [small stock dividends] the corporation should in the public inter-est account for the transaction by transferring from earned surplus [retained earnings] to the category of permanent capitalization...an amount equal to the fair value of the additional shares issued. Unless this is done, the amount of earnings which the shareholder may believe to have been distributed to him will be left...in earned surplus [retained earnings] subject to possible further similar stock issuances or cash distributions.*[4] *[Emphasis added.]*

Accounting principles require accountants to record the declaration of small stock dividends by transferring from retained earnings to contributed capital an amount equal to the market value of the shares issued. The rationale for this approach is that stockholders believe they are receiving something of value, even when in reality each stockholder's proportionate interest in the company remains unchanged. Accounting policymakers were concerned that unless stock dividends were accounted for in this manner, investors would be misled into be-lieving the potential for total dividends was greater than was really the case due to the un-changed balance of retained earnings that would remain. Research into stock prices indicates that the market prices of securities will fall in proportion to stock dividend distributions and that the resulting market prices will properly reflect the underlying value of the total owner-ship. As a result, the rationale for recording small stock dividends at market value rests on tenuous, possibly incorrect, assumptions. Regardless, the procedure of transferring an amount equal to the market value of the shares issued from retained earnings to contributed capital remains a part of current accounting practice.

Large Stock Dividends. When a stock dividend increases the number of outstanding shares by more than 20% to 25%, the value of each share in the market is expected to decline. Such declarations are known as **large stock dividends.** The difference between accounting for a small stock dividend and a large stock dividend involves the amount of equity reclassified as the par or stated value of the newly issued shares. While the market value of the stock is used in small stock dividends to reduce retained earnings and increase contributed capital, the amount to be reclassified in large stock dividends from retained earnings is limited to the par or stated value of the stock.

The theory underlying large stock dividends recognizes that if the number of shares of stock outstanding substantially increases and no changes occur in total assets or liabilities, the value of each share of stock declines. As indicated previously, the same case can be made for accounting for small stock dividends, although current accounting practice does not re-flect this similarity.

Stock Splits

A **stock split,** sometimes called a **stock split-up,** is a distribution of a company's own capi-tal stock to existing stockholders with the intent of reducing the market price of the stock. For example, in a 2-to-1 stock split, stockholders receive two shares for each share they owned before the split.

---

[4]*Accounting Research Bulletin No. 43,* Ch. 7, Sec. B, par. 10.

As previously stated, the primary purpose of a stock split is to reduce the market price of the stock to a level that will encourage investment in the company. If a company has been operating successfully, the market price of its stock may have risen so high that active trading, particularly by individual investors, is discouraged. For example, the most expensive New York Stock Exchange issue in 1983 was Metromedia, which sold at more than $400 per share. An investor would need $40,000 to purchase a round lot of 100 shares. Subsequently, the price of Metromedia's stock rose to over $550 per share. Shortly thereafter, several officers of the company gained control through the acquisition of stock in a leveraged buyout. When the number of shares of a company's stock is increased through a stock split, the price of each share in the market declines. The assets and liabilities of the company remain constant while the number of ownership shares increases. Consequently, each share after the stock split represents a smaller interest in the same total ownership than existed before the stock split. By exchanging a larger number of shares for a smaller number of shares, management may restore the market price of its company's stock to a more desirable level. Most companies try to maintain their stock price in a certain range to encourage trading and wide ownership.

Some believe that the prices of securities will not adjust to the full extent of a stock split but will adjust to a price that reflects a premium after the stock split. To illustrate, they would expect a stock selling at $200 that is split 4 to 1 to sell at more than $50 ($200/4) after the split. The suggestion is that the stock split action increases the value of each shareholder's holdings, even though the theoretical value should remain unchanged. An argument in favor of this position suggests that the stock split (or large stock dividend) significantly increases the potential breadth of ownership. Advocates of this position argue that a decrease in the price of the stock increases the number of individuals able to purchase the stock and thus increases the actual demand (price) for the stock.

Some have also argued that if enough people believe a stock split will increase the total value of stockholder holdings, it will become a self-fulfilling prophecy. Empirical evidence on the adjustment of stock prices to stock splits indicates that stock prices adjust fully for the dilutive effect of stock splits. As A. Wilfred May cogently states, "A pie does not grow through its slicing."[5] Some evidence supports the proposition that there is no intrinsic value in stock splits, but that stock prices may reflect a postsplit premium because the stock split signals information to market participants about management's positive expectations for future performance.[6] Other studies, however, suggest that stock splits may be followed by a postsplit discount. Stock splits often follow a period of excess returns, and the market perceives that these excess returns cannot be sustained indefinitely.[7]

When a stock split occurs, the par or stated value of the stock is adjusted in proportion to the size of the stock split. For example, a $100 par value stock that is split 2:1 will have a $50 par value after the split; a $50 par value stock that is split 5:1 will have a $10 par value after the split.

The accounting procedure for recording a stock split is simply to prepare a memorandum entry that indicates the change in the number of shares and the par value of those shares. No formal general journal entry is required since there is no change in the balance of the capital stock accounts, only a change in the number of shares and the par value of those shares. Recall again the outstanding common stock of Sundeen Corporation presented in Exhibit 17–4

[5]A. Wilfred May, "Current Popular Delusions about the Stock Split and Stock Dividend," *The Commercial and Financial Chronicle* (November 15, 1956), p. 5.

[6]Eugene Fama, Lawrence Fisher, Micheal Jensen, and Richard Roll, "The Adjustment of Stock Prices to New Information," *International Economic Review* (February 1969), pp. 1–21. Also Guy Charest, "Split Information, Stock Returns, and Market Efficiency—I," *Journal of Financial Economics* (June/September 1978), pp. 265–296.

[7]John Bajkowski, "Corporate Actions and Stock Market Reactions," *AAII Journal* (August 1992), p. 35.

(60,000 shares of $25 par value stock). If the company declared a 2:1 stock split, the company would have 200,000 shares of common stock authorized, 120,000 of which were outstanding at a $12.50 par value. The total amount in the Common Stock account, $1,500,000, is unchanged. No amount of retained earnings is transferred to contributed capital as was done in the case of a stock dividend discussed earlier.

In a **reverse stock split** or **stock split-down,** shareholders own fewer shares after the split. An example of a stock split-down is a 1-for-2 split in which a stockholder who holds 50 shares of stock before the split owns only 25 shares after the exchange. The objective of a reverse stock split is the opposite of a stock split. That is, a reverse stock split is designed to increase the price of the stock in the market.

The distinction between a large stock dividend and a stock split is a fine one at best. Basically, a *large stock dividend* is the issuance of stock with the same par (or stated) value as the shares outstanding; hence, the increase in legal capital (credit to common stock). A *stock split* is simply the exchange of existing shares for new shares with a different par (or stated) value per share; the total par (or stated) value of the outstanding shares is maintained. The end result of the two approaches is similar: more shares are outstanding, and total stockholders' equity remains unchanged. With large stock dividends, however, the components of stockholders' equity are altered, since an amount equal to the par (or stated) value of the shares issued has been reclassified from retained earnings to contributed capital.

TREASURY STOCK AND DIVIDENDS

Cash dividends are not declared on treasury stock. To do so would imply that the corporation is an owner of itself and is able to earn income from a common stock investment in itself. If such dividends were declared, the company would essentially be reducing retained earnings and simultaneously recording dividend revenue (increasing retained earnings through income) with no corresponding change in resources. Although the economic substance of the corporation remains unchanged, the transfer of retained earnings to dividend revenue may be misleading to financial statement users. As a result, most states do not allow cash dividends to be declared on treasury shares.

Substance over Form

Stock dividends and stock splits on treasury shares are appropriate because they involve only a reclassification within the stockholders' equity accounts and do not affect income. As a result, stock dividends and stock splits may be declared on treasury shares in some states, although a few states prohibit stock dividends on treasury shares. A stock split on treasury shares has the same effect as on outstanding shares. The par value of the treasury shares is adjusted so that the total par value of all treasury shares remains unchanged after the split. Naturally, the total cost of the treasury shares is also unaffected.

APPROPRIATION OF RETAINED EARNINGS

Occasionally, the management of a company decides to commit corporate resources to some project or purpose and wishes to communicate that fact through the financial statements. For example, management may wish to retain resources to expand plant assets or repay debt rather than pay dividends to stockholders. In such situations, retained earnings may be appropriated to notify financial statement users about the intended use of the company's resources. To illustrate, if Montclair Company management decides to build a new factory at an estimated cost of $2,500,000, the following appropriation of retained earnings is acceptable:

Retained Earnings	2,500,000	
Retained Earnings Appropriated for Plant Expansion		2,500,000
(To appropriate retained earnings according		
to company plans.)		

FORD DECLARES STOCK SPLIT, LIFTS DIVIDEND 12.5%

Dearborn, Mich.—Ford Motor Co., signaling its optimism for a sustained recovery, raised its dividend 12.5% and declared a 2-for-1 stock split. Ford also said it will sell its unprofitable First Nationwide thrift unit to First Madison Bank of Dallas, Texas, for $1.1 billion.

Ford said it would take a charge of $440 million against first-quarter earnings in connection with the sale of First Nationwide. But analysts expect Ford to be solidly profitable in the quarter nonetheless. Excluding the charge, analysts anticipate Ford will earn significantly more than year-ago net income of $572 million, or $1.02 a share.

In addition, Ford, which already owned 54% of Hertz Corp., purchased the remaining 46% stake of the car-rental agency from AB Volvo and a Hertz management group. As anticipated, Ford also moved to expand truck capacity in the United States by continuing production of its Aerostar minivan.

The stock split and the dividend increase to 45 cents a presplit share from 40 cents a share caught some analysts by surprise, and sent Ford stock surging $1.375 to close at $58.50 in composite New York Stock Exchange trading. Ford last raised its dividend in 1989. The announcements followed Ford's regularly scheduled directors meeting yesterday.

Analysts said they had anticipated that Ford might boost its dividend, but later in the year. The higher dividend is payable June 1 to stock of record May 2. Ford said it will ask stockholders to approve the issuance of additional shares to allow for the 2-for-1 split at the May 12 annual meeting in Cleveland. If approved, the split will be distributed on July 5 to stock of record on June 6.

Wall Street applauded Ford's moves.

"It's a sign of confidence in the underlying environment for the corporation and it's also a sign that management believes that the worst is over in Europe," said Jack Kirnan, Salomon Brothers auto analyst.

Ford's action could also put pressure on General Motors Corp. and Chrysler Corp. to share more wealth with stockholders as the U.S. auto market recovery starts pumping up their profits.

In December, Chrysler raised its quarterly dividend 33% to 20 cents a share. GM's dividend also stands at 20 cents a share.

Steven Girsky, PaineWebber Inc.'s auto analyst, predicted that both Chrysler and GM will now declare a stock split similar to the one declared by Ford.

"The industry is turning from the cash-using to the cash-generating stage," Mr. Girsky said. However, he added that GM's severely underfunded pension plan may make it difficult for the No. 1 automaker to increase its cash dividend soon.

Bonuses Disclosed

Separately, Ford yesterday filed its preliminary proxy statement, which disclosed that its bonus-level executives will divide a pool of $79.4 million, the first bonus payments since

1990. Ford earned $2.5 billion in 1993, compared with a loss of $502 million in 1992.

Ford Chairman Alexander Trotman received total compensation for 1993 of $2.08 million, including salary of $852,709, a $1 million bonus and restricted stock valued at $229,462. Mr. Trotman also exercised stock options granted in prior years, earning $1.85 million.

Mr. Trotman, who assumed the duties of chairman, chief executive officer and president last November, will receive a salary for 1994 of $1.5 million, according to the statement.

Harold A. Poling, who retired effective Jan. 1, was paid $1.6 million in annual compensation and received a $1.1 million bonus and restricted stock totaling $923,755. Mr. Poling also exercised prior-year stock options totaling $8.13 million.

The compensation committee said in the proxy that it considered, among other things, "the key leadership roles of Mr. Poling and Mr. Trotman in the dramatically improved profitability achieved by the company" in determining their bonuses.

Vice Chairman Allan D. Gilmour earned $760,088 in annual compensation and received a $700,000 bonus and restricted stock valued at $313,069. He exercised options totaling $1.9 million.

Louis R. Ross, Ford's vice chairman and chief technical officer, was paid $740,366 in annual compensation and received a $450,000 bonus and restricted stock totaling $208,953. He exercised stock options totaling $1.1 million.

Company Is Confident

"The whole collection of announcements should be viewed as good news," said David McCammon, Ford's vice president-finance and treasurer. Mr. McCammon said the dividend increase "shows we're confident and we're looking forward to the future." He said a turnaround in vehicle sales is gradually taking place in Europe but "the real story is in the U.S. car and truck business."

Mr. McCammon said Ford is paying $145 million to purchase a 26% holding in Hertz from Volvo. He declined to say how much Ford paid for the additional 20% stake it is buying from Hertz management. "Hertz is an exceptionally well-managed company," Mr. McCammon said. "They earned over $100 million before tax last year. It's a great business to display our products."

A Ford spokesman said the company will spend an additional $275 million to ready the St. Louis assembly plant and retool other facilities to continue building the Aerostar minivan.

The account Retained Earnings Appropriated for Plant Expansion is reported as part of stockholders' equity rather than as a liability or a contra asset account. The appropriation provides financial statement users with information on corporate plans and may also help explain a reduction in dividends as resources are held to finance construction.

Appropriating retained earnings does *not* necessarily imply that resources have been set aside for the purpose indicated. The appropriation is simply a reclassification of retained earnings, which signals owners about possible reductions in dividends.

State law occasionally requires an appropriation of retained earnings in the case of treasury stock. Law sometimes requires companies to record an appropriation of retained earnings equal to the cost of any treasury stock. Such regulations are designed to protect the creditors of a company from a substantial reduction of stockholders' equity through treasury stock acquisitions.

Management may also record an appropriation of retained earnings as a reporting response to loss contingencies, as discussed in Chapter 14. An appropriation of retained earnings, however, is not considered an alternative to recording loss contingencies in accordance with *Statement of Financial Accounting Standards No. 5.*[8] Rather, accountants consider an appropriation of retained earnings as a supplement to other practices required by generally **Disclosure** accepted accounting principles, such as note disclosure.

Finally, when the reason for the appropriation no longer exists, the appropriated retained earnings should be returned directly to unappropriated retained earnings. Losses or gains should be presented in the income statement and never charged or credited to appropriated retained earnings. Similarly, the Appropriated Retained Earnings account should never be included in the determination of net income.

STATEMENT OF CHANGES IN STOCKHOLDERS' EQUITY

The issues discussed above complicate the presentation of the statement of retained earnings **Disclosure** as well as the disclosure of changes in other stockholders' equity accounts. Although a separate statement of retained earnings is frequently presented, it is also common to combine the changes in retained earnings with a statement presenting changes in other stockholders' equity accounts. The resulting statement of stockholders' equity reflects the activity that has taken place in all equity accounts during the accounting period.

A statement of changes in stockholders' equity may be presented as a financial statement, along with the balance sheet, income statement, and statement of cash flows, or it may be presented as a note to the financial statements. An illustrative statement is presented in Exhibit 17–5 for the Toro Company, whose business is lawn and turf care, maintenance, and beautification. Toro has chosen to present the statement as Footnote 5 of its 1993 financial statements. Although no single statement will illustrate all possible changes in stockholders' equity accounts, the Toro example illustrates many of the transactions we have discussed in Chapters 17 and 18, including the payment of dividends, the issuance of shares of stock under stock option plans, the purchase of treasury stock, and the reporting of net income (1990 and 1993) and net loss (1992).

CAPITAL STOCK AND EMPLOYEE COMPENSATION

Corporate management and the board of directors exercise great control over stockholders' equity. The stock of a company may be used to provide part of the remuneration of employees as well as to provide funds for capital expenditures and to finance ongoing business operations. Stock option plans and stock appreciation rights are frequently used as important incentives for employees. The primary purposes of these plans are to motivate employees,

---

[8]*FASB Statement of Financial Accounting Standards No. 5,* "Accounting for Contingencies," 1975, par. 15.

EXHIBIT 17—5

The Toro Company
Changes in Stockholders' Equity

5. Stockholders' Equity

Changes in common stock, additional paid-in capital, retained earnings, receivable from ESOP and foreign currency translation adjustment during fiscal years ended July 31, 1993, 1992 and 1991 were as follows:

(Dollars in thousands)	Common Stock	Additional Paid-in Capital	Retained Earnings	Receivable from ESOP	Foreign Currency Translation Adjustment
Balance at July 31, 1990	$11,814	$39,477	$111,741	$(10,445)	—
Common dividends paid ($0.48 per share)	—	—	(5,700)	—	—
Issuance of 133,349 shares under stock option plans	134	1,883	—	—	—
Purchase of 34,900 common shares	(35)	(621)	—	—	—
Payment received from ESOP	—	—	—	2,611	—
Net earnings	—	—	9,700	—	—
Balance at July 31, 1991	11,913	40,739	115,741	(7,834)	—
Common dividends paid ($0.48 per share)	—	—	(5,753)	—	—
Issuance of 178,848 shares under stock option plans	179	2,176	—	—	—
Purchase of 50,269 common shares	(50)	(744)	—	—	—
Net loss	—	—	(23,753)	—	—
Balance at July 31, 1992	12,042	42,171	86,235	(7,834)	—
Common dividends paid ($0.48 per share)	—	—	(5,824)	—	—
Issuance of 272,149 shares under stock option plans	272	3,499	—	—	—
Purchase of 43,242 common shares	(44)	(772)	—	—	—
Payment received from ESOP	—	—	—	2,611	—
Cumulative translation adjustment	—	—	—	—	(795)
Net earnings	—	—	13,040	—	—
Balance at July 31, 1993	**$12,270**	**$44,898**	**$93,451**	**$(5,223)**	**$(795)**

SOURCE: The Toro Company, 1993 Annual Report.

reward high performance, and reduce employee attrition. If employees own stock in their company, the success of the company becomes even more important to them. If the company operates profitably and the value of the stock increases, employees who own stock become better off.

STOCK OPTION PLANS

An **employee stock option** is a temporary right granted by the company that permits an employee to purchase a limited amount of corporate stock at a specified price, called the **exercise price.** An employee can exercise the option by purchasing the stock at the exercise price and then resell those shares at the market price to realize a gain or hold the shares for other investment purposes. Employee stock options are not transferable, so only the employee can realize the potential benefits. In addition, companies frequently prohibit the exercise of an option until the end of a prespecified **service (holding) period.** This restriction ensures a degree of employee loyalty and tenure. The stock option agreement typically establishes an exercise period and an expiration date. Exhibit 17–6 depicts a typical stock option plan.

Stock option plans may be compensatory or noncompensatory, depending on whether employee compensation is intended in the specific plan.

Noncompensatory Stock Option Plans

Stock option plans for employees are **noncompensatory** and result in no recognition of salary expense if each of four characteristics is present. To be noncompensatory, a plan must[9]

1. Involve substantially all full-time employees (executives may be excluded).
2. Be offered to eligible employees equally or on the basis of a uniform percentage of salary.
3. Limit the time permitted for exercise of an option right to a reasonable period.
4. Provide for a discount from the market price no greater than would be reasonable in an offer of stock to stockholders or others.

Accounting for noncompensatory stock option plans is relatively simple and straightforward. If an employee exercises an option to acquire shares of stock, the corporation simply records the cash received and the related issuance of the stock. Only the cash received is treated as consideration for the stock issued in a noncompensatory plan. The difference between the market price and the exercise price on the exercise date is a benefit to the employee that is disregarded in the corporate accounting records. The rationale for this treatment is that management does not intend to compensate employees for past or future services but to raise additional capital and to improve loyalty in the work force by providing employees a convenient mechanism by which they can become stockholders.

Compensatory Stock Option Plans

Compensatory stock option plans do not meet all four characteristics of noncompensatory plans. **Compensatory plans** convey a right to selected employees in return for either past or future services to the company. Many large corporations compensate their corporate officers with both salaries and stock options. In compensatory stock option plans, the consideration a corporation receives for stock issued from exercised options consists of the option price and the value of services rendered by employees above their salary levels. A major accounting difficulty is measuring the incremental value of compensation arising from the stock option plan. These services must be valued to report total compensation expense equal to the value of services rendered by employees.

Accountants measure the compensatory portion of employee stock options as the excess of the market price of the stock over the exercise price. This spread is computed on the date that *both* (1) the number of shares an individual employee is entitled to receive and (2) the option or purchase price of the shares first become known.[10] This date, called the **measurement date,** is used to determine the amount of compensation to be recognized in conjunction with the plan.

---

[9]*APB Opinion No. 25,* "Accounting for Stock Issued to Employees," 1972, par. 7.
[10]*APB Opinion No. 25,* par. 10.

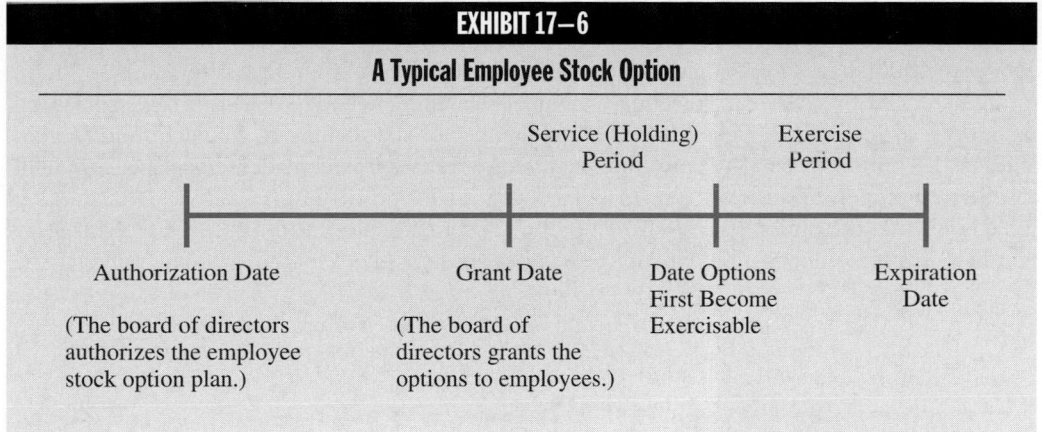

EXHIBIT 17–6

A Typical Employee Stock Option

	Service (Holding) Period	Exercise Period	
Authorization Date	Grant Date	Date Options First Become Exercisable	Expiration Date
(The board of directors authorizes the employee stock option plan.)	(The board of directors grants the options to employees.)		

As a result of the two criteria for determining the measurement date, the measurement date often coincides with the grant date. Therefore, the compensatory portion of the option is usually determined as the excess of the market value of the stock over the exercise price of the option on the grant date.

Compensation is recorded only as the services giving rise to the stock options are rendered. Thus, if an employee must perform services for several periods after the option is granted and before the stock is issued, the employer recognizes salary expense in each period in which services are performed. This principle is applied even if the total amount of compensation was known at the grant date. The procedure is simply an application of the matching principle, whereby the compensation expense is allocated to the periods in which services are performed.

Matching

One of the problems with the present method of accounting for compensatory stock options is the measurement of the compensation expense. Compensatory stock options are often granted with the exercise price equal to the market price of the stock at the measurement date. As such, generally accepted accounting principles require no compensation expense to be recorded. This treatment biases financial reporting toward understating compensation expense, because the options have obvious value. An employee who was granted a stock option with the exercise price equal to the market price would not be willing to give the options away. The options are valuable because the employee cannot lose money if the stock price decreases but can realize a substantial gain if the stock price increases.[11]

Another complication arises if the measurement date occurs after the grant date. In such cases, compensation expense should be recorded in each period from the grant date to the measurement date based on the quoted market price of the stock at the end of each period. The difference between the option price and the market value of the stock at the end of each period represents the total compensation to be recognized. Amounts previously recognized as compensation under the option plan in prior periods are subtracted from the total compensation to determine the compensation for the current period.

---

[11]Several methods have been suggested for the valuation of stock options. See, for example, Fischer Black and Myron Scholes, "The Pricing of Options and Corporate Liabilities," *Journal of Political Economy* (May/June 1973), pp. 158–162. The Black and Scholes valuation model was tested for accuracy against a set of publicly traded warrants similar to executive stock options. The valuation model was found to perform admirably. See Eric Noreen and Mark Wolfson, "Equilibrium Warrant Pricing Models and Accounting for Executive Stock Options," *Journal of Accounting Research* (Autumn 1981), pp. 384–398. These models are at the heart of a recent FASB proposal, discussed in later pages of this text, to change accounting for stock option plans.

To illustrate the accounting for compensatory stock options, assume that on January 1, 1992, Value Corporation provides a stock option plan to the president of the corporation whereby 1,000 shares of $50 par value common stock may be purchased for $40 per share immediately after five years of employment on December 31, 1996. The market price on January 1, 1992, is $75. Because both (1) the number of shares that may be acquired (1,000) and (2) the option price ($40) are known, January 1, 1992, is considered the measurement date. The compensation per share to be recognized is the difference between the market price ($75) and the option price ($40) on the measurement date. In this case, Value Corporation recognizes compensation expense of $35 per share as the services are rendered over the five-year period.

At the end of the first year, on December 31, 1992, the following entry is made:

Dec. 31, 1992   Salary Expense   7,000
                      Stock Options Exercisable   7,000
                (To record portion of compensatory stock option
                plan earned at 12/31/92. 1,000 shares × $35 =
                $35,000 × ⅕ = $7,000.)

This entry is repeated each year until the options become exercisable.[12] Market price changes in the stock *after* the measurement date are not recognized as additional compensation from the perspective of the employing corporation. The account Stock Options Exercisable is a contributed stockholders' equity account that remains open until the final exercise date on December 31, 1996. When the options are exercised and the employee remits the $40 per share option price, the following entry is necessary:

Dec. 31, 1996   Cash   40,000
                Stock Options Exercisable   35,000
                      Common Stock   50,000
                      Paid-in Capital in Excess of Par Value   25,000
                (To record issuance of stock under compensatory
                option plan: 1,000 × $40 = $40,000; 7,000 ×
                $5 = $35,000; 1,000 × $50 = $50,000;
                $75,000 − $50,000 = $25,000)

If the options are not exercised, the Stock Options Exercisable account is reclassified as part of Paid-in Capital in Excess of Par Value. The entry to record the expiration of the options is

Jan. 1, 1997   Stock Options Exercisable   35,000
                      Paid-in Capital in Excess of Par Value   35,000
                (To record expiration of options.)

Substance over Form   This treatment is acceptable even though the stock option is not exercised. The corporation, as of the grant date, transferred an item of value to the employee. The employee can then choose to exercise the option to realize its value or hold the option in an attempt to real-

---

[12]An alternative approach is to record the total future compensation expense on the measurement date as follows:

Jan. 1, 1992   Deferred Compensation Expense   35,000
                      Stock Options Exercisable   35,000

The Deferred Compensation Expense account is disclosed in stockholders' equity in the balance sheet as a contra account to the Stock Options Exercisable account. The Deferred Compensation Expense account is amortized over the five-year period of intended compensation as follows:

Dec. 31, 1992   Salary Expense   7,000
                      Deferred Compensation Expense   7,000

A similar entry is made at the end of each year until the Deferred Compensation Expense account is fully amortized on December 31, 1996.

ize further price appreciation on the security. If the employee allowed the option to lapse because the price of the stock decreased during the holding period, the speculative behavior should not affect the valuation of the option by the corporation. The paid-in capital in excess of par from nonexercise of the option is theoretically justified as the value of services contributed by the employee. In addition, this treatment is similar to that for detachable warrants issued with certain debt instruments which lapse. We discussed this topic in Chapter 15.

Stock Option Accounting Controversy

The issue of accounting for stock option plans is currently quite controversial. At this writing, the FASB has issued a proposed statement of financial accounting standards that, if adopted authoritatively, would increase significantly the compensation expense recognized in the financial statements by many corporations that offer such plans. For example, under current plans, according to *APB Opinion No. 25,* as previously discussed, compensation expense is measured on the first date (measurement date) on which both the number of shares and the exercise price available to an employee are known. Therefore, fixed stock options with an exercise price equal to the stock's market value on the date of grant result in no compensation expense to the company, unlike variable plans. As a consequence, most option plans today are fixed rather than variable, and no compensation expense is recognized in the company's financial statements.

Under the FASB proposal, compensation expense would begin to be recognized at the grant date, which is defined as the point in time that the employer and employee agree to the terms of a plan. The measurement date currently in use generally coincides with the grant date for fixed stock plans but precedes the date for variable plans. The amount of compensation to be recognized would be based on the estimated value of the option at the grant date and would be amortized over the vesting period. Compensation expense would not be recorded for options that are not expected to vest, and so estimates of forfeitures due to employee attrition and failure to achieve performance goals in the plans would be necessary. Further, the need to estimate the fair value of the options themselves poses a number of complexities. Many have asserted that the process of estimating the value of stock options is impractical and unreliable and that existing valuation models do not consider the specific features of many plans. As a result of these concerns, the FASB proposal for changing the manner in which we account for and report stock option plans is not certain of enactment, and the provisions of *APB Opinion No. 25* continue to guide practice in this area.

STOCK APPRECIATION RIGHTS

Compensatory stock options have two major disadvantages for the employee. First, the employee must make a cash outlay equal to the exercise price times the number of shares acquired. The size of the cash outlay could be burdensome to the employee acquiring a large number of optioned shares. Second, optioned shares are taxable for the difference between the market price and the exercise price (on the date of exercise). An employee is thus immediately liable for taxes on optioned shares, even though the employee may want to hold the shares beyond the date of exercise. Therefore, an employee experiences an immediate cash outflow for the exercise price coupled with a tax on the increment of market price over exercise price.

To diminish the negative characteristics of compensatory stock options, companies may grant **stock appreciation rights (SARs).** An SAR entitles an employee to either cash or corporate stock in an amount equal to the excess of the market value of the company's stock over a predetermined price for a stated number of shares. This right awards the employee participation in price appreciation for a stated number of shares of the company's stock without actually requiring the employee to remit cash, as in the case of stock options.

The FASB has provided guidance in accounting for stock appreciation rights.[13] SARs fall in the category of variable award plans, in which, according to the FASB, the number of shares of stock or the amount of cash that may be awarded to an employee is unspecified on the grant date. As a result, the criteria for determining the measurement date, as discussed earlier, remain unsatisfied on the grant date. The number of shares or amount of cash an employee is entitled to receive becomes known only on the date the employee exercises the SAR. The number of shares of stock or cash awarded is a function of the appreciation of share price over the predetermined price at the date of exercise. Therefore, the measurement date, used for determining the total compensation, is the exercise date rather than the earlier grant date.

Because the total compensation to be recognized in conjunction with the SAR is unknown until the exercise date, a question remains about how to accrue compensation expense. Total compensation to be allocated is estimated by the excess of the market value over the predetermined price. This amount is then allocated over the service period (or vesting period). During the period until exercise, subsequent increases or decreases in the market price of the shares require adjustments to the compensation accrued.

To illustrate, consider Pueblo Corporation, which granted an SAR to the chief executive officer (CEO) on January 1, 1993. After the three-year holding period, the SAR entitled the CEO to the appreciation in share price over the market value of the stock, as determined at the grant date. The SAR had the following terms:

> Service (holding) period: Jan. 1, 1993–Dec. 31, 1995
> Number of shares: 1,000
> Exercise date: Jan. 1, 1996
> Form of compensation: Cash or common stock at CEO's discretion

The quoted market prices of Pueblo's shares were as follows:

Jan. 1, 1993	$20
Dec. 31, 1993	28
Dec. 31, 1994	26
Dec. 31, 1995	32

The SAR was exercised on January 1, 1996. Exhibit 17–7 summarizes the accounting for Pueblo Corporation.

The Compensation Expense account is adjusted annually to reflect the accrued compensation to date. As of December 31, 1993, the total compensation to be allocated is the difference between the excess of the market price ($28) over the predetermined price ($20) times the number of shares specified by the SAR. However, only one-third (33½%) of this amount was earned by the CEO as of December 31, 1993. The employee must provide services over a three-year period before the right can be exercised. Therefore, the total compensation should be allocated over this period. The total compensation to be allocated is readjusted annually to reflect the new market price of the company's stock. The journal entry is recorded on December 31, 1993, as follows:

Dec. 31, 1993	Compensation Expense	2,667	
	Compensation Payable		2,667
	(To record accrual of compensation from SAR plan.)		

Similar entries are made in 1994 and 1995 for $1,333 and $8,000, respectively. The credit to Compensation Payable assumes that the appreciation will be paid in cash by the employer. If

---

[13]*FASB Interpretation No. 28,* "Accounting for Stock Appreciation Rights and Other Variable Stock Option or Award Plans," 1978.

			EXHIBIT 17–7			

Pueblo Corporation
Accrued Compensation Expense under an SAR Plan

Date	Market Price	Predetermined Price	Compensation to Be Allocated	Service Period Allocation	Compensation Accrued to Date	Annual Compensation Expense
1/1/93	$20	$20	–0–	0%	–0–	–0–
12/31/93	28	20	$ 8,000	33⅓%	$ 2,667	$2,667
					1,333	
12/31/94	26	20	6,000	66⅔%	4,000	1,333
					8,000	
12/31/95	32	20	12,000	100%	$12,000	$8,000

the plan called for the appreciation to be paid only in the company's common stock, a credit to a stockholders' equity account, such as Stock Appreciation Rights Exercisable, would be appropriate. In this case, the employee has the option of receiving either cash or shares of stock, so the liability account is appropriate.

In 1994 the market price of the shares exceeded the option price by $6 per share. This represents a total compensation of $6,000 ($6 × 1,000 shares) to be allocated. Through December 31, 1994, two-thirds (66⅔%) of the service period elapsed; therefore, 66⅔% of the compensation was earned by the CEO. The compensation accrued to date was $4,000 ($6,000 × 66⅔%), of which $2,667 has already been recognized for 1993. The remaining $1,333 is the compensation expense to be recognized in 1994. The $1,333 reflects a "catch-up" adjustment for changes in market value in 1994, as required by *FASB Interpretation No. 28.*

Notice that the market price fell between the end of 1993 and 1994. Because the market price fell below the previous period's market price, the total compensation to be allocated decreased. In the example, the total compensation to be allocated fell to $6,000 [($26 − $20) × 1,000 shares] from the previous amount of $8,000. As of the end of 1995, the employee has completely satisfied the service obligation so that the rights are now 100% earned. Therefore, $8,000 of compensation expense is recognized in 1995, determined in the same manner as 1994.[14]

On January 1, 1996, the CEO exercised the SAR. If the CEO chose to receive cash, the following journal entry is appropriate.

Jan. 1, 1996	Compensation Payable	12,000	
	Cash		12,000
	(To record exercise of SAR for cash.)		

---

[14]A decline in the market price of the stock could result in a negative Compensation Expense, although this did not occur in the case of Pueblo Corporation. To illustrate, assume that the market price of Pueblo's stock at the end of 1994 was $22 instead of $26. Total compensation to be allocated would be $2,000 ($2 × 1,000 shares). Since $2,667 compensation expense was recognized during 1993, negative compensation of $1,334 [($2,000 × 66⅔%) − 2,667 = − $1,334] should be recognized in 1994, as follows:

Dec. 31, 1994	Compensation Payable	1,334	
	Compensation Expense		1,334

If this occurs, the amount eliminated should never exceed the total amount accrued to date, even if the market price of the stock is less than the predetermined price.

If the CEO chose to receive stock, the following journal entry is appropriate, assuming the stock has a par value of $20:

Jan. 1, 1996	Compensation Payable	12,000	
	Common Stock (375 shares @ $20)		7,500
	Paid-in Capital in Excess of Par Value		4,500
	(To record exercise of SAR for common stock.)		

Notice in the last entry that the CEO does not receive 1,000 shares of common stock. The 1,000 shares included in the SAR agreement are simply a mechanism for determining the amount that the CEO will receive in either cash or common stock. In this case, if the CEO chooses to receive stock, he or she will receive 375 shares, determined by dividing the stock appreciation on 1,000 shares by the market price of the stock on the exercise date: ($12,000/ $32 = 375 shares).

STOCK OPTION PLAN DISCLOSURE

Disclosure The specific characteristics of a stock option plan are typically disclosed in a note to the financial statements. The reference should include information about the number of options outstanding, granted, and exercised during the period, as well as the option price. The stock option plan disclosure of The Great Atlantic and Pacific Tea Company, Inc (A&P), a major grocery company, presented in Exhibit 17–8, illustrates the type of information normally provided.

STOCK RIGHTS, STOCK WARRANTS, AND CONVERTIBLE SECURITIES

STOCK RIGHTS

Companies frequently issue **stock rights** conveying the right to acquire stock in the future. The terms of the rights specify the price per share of the stock (usually an amount below the market price), the number of shares subject to the rights, the expiration date of the rights, and other relevant information. Stock rights are usually valuable because they allow a person to acquire stock below the market price.

Rights are issued for various reasons. For example, if a stock dividend is declared, some stockholders may have the right to receive fractional shares, and rights may be issued to meet the obligation. Rights may also be used to protect the preemptive rights of present stockholders if a new stock issue is forthcoming. The rights allow present stockholders to maintain their existing percentage of ownership.

STOCK WARRANTS

Stock warrants are issued by a company in exchange for cash and provide the holder with the right to acquire shares of stock at a specified price. As we discussed in Chapter 15, stock warrants are often sold as part of a package of securities, and the issuing company allocates the amount received to the individual securities on the basis of their relative values. For example, if bonds and warrants are sold together for $1,500,000 and allocation based on their relative market values indicates that $100,000 should be allocated to the warrants, the following entry is required:

Cash	1,500,000	
Bonds Payable		1,400,000
Common Stock Warrants Exercisable		100,000

The Common Stock Warrants Exercisable account is presented in the stockholders' equity section of the balance sheet.

Assuming the warrants permit the acquisition of 100,000 shares of $10 par value common stock for $25 per share, the journal entry to record their exercise is

---

EXHIBIT 17–8

The Great Atlantic & Pacific Tea Company, Inc.
Employee Stock Option Disclosure

Stock Options

The Company had a 1984 Stock Option Plan for its officers and key employees, which expired on February 1, 1994. The 1984 Stock Option Plan, which provided for the granting of 1,500,000 shares, was amended as of July 10, 1990, to increase by 1,500,000 the number of options available for grant as either options or Stock Appreciation Rights ("SAR's"). Each option was available for grant at the fair value of the Company's common stock on the date the option was granted. SAR's allow the optionee, in lieu of purchasing stock, to receive cash in an amount equal to the excess of the fair market value of common stock on the date of exercise over the option price. A total of 1,270,000 SAR's was granted in fiscal 1993.

A summary of option transactions is as follows:

	Shares	Price Range Per Share
Outstanding February 29, 1992	1,190,875	$5.50–$65.13
Granted	15,000	23.00– 24.38
Cancelled or expired	(2,500)	39.75
Options exercised	(5,000)	5.50
SAR's exercised	(4,250)	21.50
Outstanding February 27, 1993	1,194,125	$21.50–$65.13
Granted	1,270,000	23.38– 26.00
Cancelled or expired	(35,000)	23.38– 52.38
Outstanding February 26, 1994	2,429,125	$21.50–$65.13
Exercisable at:		
February 27, 1993	967,375	$21.50–$65.13
February 26, 1994	1,252,125	$21.50–$65.13

On March 18, 1994, the Board of Directors approved (subject to shareholder approval) the 1994 Stock Option Plan for its officers and key employees. The 1994 Stock Option Plan provides for the granting of 1,500,000 shares as either options/SAR's. Options/SAR's issued under this plan will be granted at the fair market value of the Company's common stock at the date of grant.

Also on March 18, 1994, the Board of Directors approved (subject to shareholder approval) the 1994 Stock Option Plan for Non-Employee Directors. This plan provides for the grant of up to 100,000 stock options. Options issued under this plan will be granted at the fair market value of the Company's common stock at the date of grant. Pursuant to this plan, options for 18,000 shares were granted to nine (9) directors as of March 18, 1994.

SOURCE: The Great Atlantic & Pacific Tea Company, Inc., 1993 Annual Report.

Cash (100,000 × $25)	2,500,000	
Common Stock Warrants Exercisable	100,000	
Common Stock (100,000 × $10)		1,000,000
Paid-in Capital in Excess of Par Value		1,600,000

(To record exercise of warrants, 100,000 shares at $25 per share plus the amount paid for the warrants.)

If the owners of the warrants allow them to lapse without exercising them, however, then the necessary entry becomes

Common Stock Warrants Exercisable	100,000	
Paid-in Capital in Excess of Par Value		100,000

(To record the expiration of stock warrants.)

The amount paid for the warrants becomes part of paid-in capital in excess of par value if the warrants are not exercised.

Warrants may also be used as a "sweetener" to improve the market for other securities, such as debt, issued by the company. If debt is issued with detachable stock warrants or options, some of the consideration received for the composite security (debt and equity) is allocated to stockholders' equity. The method usually employed to accomplish the allocation is based on the relative fair market values of bonds and warrants traded individually. We discussed accounting for detachable warrants in Chapter 15.

Recall that the Stock Warrants Exercisable account appears in the contributed capital section of stockholders' equity until the warrants either are exercised or expire. In the event of exercise, additional consideration is received and the Stock Warrants Exercisable account is removed from the records. The stock issued is recorded at the sum of the carrying amount of the warrants, if any, and the exercise price received.

To illustrate, assume that Harmon Corporation originally issued 1,000 bonds, including one detachable warrant per bond. Also assume that after the proceeds of the issue had been allocated, the Stock Warrants Exercisable account had a credit balance of $15,000 (or $15 per warrant). Each warrant, upon exercise, grants the holder one share of $10 par value common stock at a cash price of $35 per share. Further assume that half of the warrants were exercised when the market price of the common stock was $60 per share. The following journal entry reflects the exercise:

Cash ($35 × 500)	17,500	
Stock Warrants Exercisable ($15 × 500)	7,500	
Common Stock ($10 × 500)		5,000
Paid-in Capital in Excess of Par Value		20,000
(To record exercise of 500 stock warrants.)		

The $60 market value of the stock when the warrant is issued is not used to record the issuance of the stock. Rather, the stock is recorded at an amount equal to the total of the cash received ($35 per share), plus the amount allocated to the warrant when it was originally issued ($15), for a total per share of $50.

If a warrant expires or lapses, the Stock Warrants Exercisable account is reclassified as Paid-in Capital in Excess of Par Value, unless a portion of the warrant is refunded; in which case the warrant account is removed to the extent of the refund and reclassified as a liability. Any residual balance in the warrant account is then reclassified as Paid-in Capital in Excess of Par Value. To illustrate, if the remaining warrants of Harmon Corporation were allowed to expire, the following journal entry is made:

Stock Warrants Exercisable ($15 × 500)	7,500	
Paid-in Capital in Excess of Par Value		7,500
(To record expiration of 500 stock warrants.)		

CONVERTIBLE SECURITIES

If the owner of a convertible security, such as a bond or preferred stock, exercises the conversion feature, certain accounting issues emerge. The carrying amount of the convertible security (par value, plus any premium or less any discount) may differ from the market value of the stock issued at the time the conversion takes place.

To illustrate, assume that Top Togs, Inc., issues convertible bonds that have a maturity value of $1,000,000 and are carried in the corporate books net of a $25,000 discount. Further assume that each $1,000 bond is convertible into 10 shares of $75 par value common stock. The current market value of the common stock is $104 per share. If all 1,000 bonds are converted on January 1, 1996, the following entry is necessary:

Jan. 1, 1996	Bonds Payable	1,000,000	
	Discount on Bonds Payable		25,000
	Common Stock (1,000 × 10 × $75)		750,000
	Paid-in Capital in Excess of Par Value		225,000
	(To record the conversion of bonds and issuance of stock.)		

Recording the conversion in this manner results in reporting the stock at the book value of the converted debt ($975,000) rather than the $1,040,000 market value of the stock ($104 per share × 10,000 shares).

The rationale for this position is provided by the treatment accorded the convertible debt when originally issued. Remember that some of the proceeds of convertible debt may be considered a permanent contribution to stockholders' equity. Due to the inseparability of the debt and equity components of a convertible security, however, the proceeds from the issuance of convertible debt are classified as debt. Therefore, when a conversion takes place, an apparent gain or loss on the extinguishment of debt may result from the accounting treatment at the issuance of the convertible security. The difference between the carrying amount of converted debt and the fair value of the stock issued upon conversion is properly treated as an adjustment to stockholders' equity rather than as a gain or loss on the debt retirement. Underlying theory suggests that if the debt is converted to stock, the security represents a permanent increase in stockholders' equity at issuance, and no gain or loss is recognized when the form of the instrument is converted.

Substance over Form

The key concept to remember in accounting for convertible securities is that the carrying amount of the security being converted is merely reclassified as the carrying amount of the new security being issued. This is the case regardless of whether the convertible security is debt or preferred stock. The conversion of one form of financing to another in accordance with the terms of the instrument does not give rise to accounting gains or losses.

EARNINGS PER SHARE

A required disclosure for publicly held corporations is the earnings per share. Basically, the **earnings per share (EPS)** of a corporation results from the division of the accounting net income available to common shareholders for a particular period by the number of *common* shares outstanding during the period. The EPS figure is a measure of the amount of net income attributable to each share of common stock. This measure can be useful to the common stockholder because the market price per share of stock is to some degree dependent upon the EPS of that stock. In addition, with EPS figures, the common stock investor can more readily evaluate the dividend policy of the company, because dividends are frequently expressed in per share terms.

Complications arise if the corporation changes the number of shares outstanding during the year or has preferred stock outstanding. If the corporation changes the number of shares outstanding during the period, either through new stock issues or purchases of treasury shares, the denominator of the EPS calculation should be adjusted to reflect a weighted average of the number of common shares outstanding during the period. If preferred stock is outstanding during the period, the numerator of the EPS calculation should be adjusted by subtracting all preferred dividends declared during the period or which accumulate under a cumulation feature. In this way, the numerator measures the net income available to common shareholders after dividend preferences for preferred stock are satisfied.

To illustrate, assume that Franklin Company reported a net income of $1,000,000 for 1995. In addition, Franklin declared preferred dividends on its preferred stock of $200,000 for 1995. Franklin had 400,000 common shares outstanding at the beginning of the year and issued an additional 400,000 shares halfway through the year, on June 30, 1995. There were no other stock transactions during the year.

OTHER STOCKHOLDERS' EQUITY CONSIDERATIONS

Disclosure

The weighted average number of common shares outstanding during 1995 is calculated as follows:

(1) Outstanding Shares	(2) Period Outstanding	(3) Share-months (Col. 1 × Col. 2)	(4) Weighted Average (Col. 3) ÷ (Col. 2)
400,000	6 mos.	2,400,000	
800,000	6 mos.	4,800,000	
	12 mos.	7,200,000	600,000

The EPS calculation for Franklin is

$$\frac{\$1,000,000 - \$200,000}{600,000 \text{ shares}} = \$1.33 \text{ per share}$$

The common stockholders have $1.33 in earnings for each share of stock.

The EPS calculation is complicated considerably by the introduction of stock dividends and stock splits. Furthermore, securities such as stock warrants, employee stock options, and securities convertible to common stock represent potential common shares (dilution) that must be considered when attempting to determine EPS. These considerations are rather involved and are therefore discussed separately and in greater detail in Chapter 18.

APPRAISAL CAPITAL

As discussed in Chapter 2, contemporary accounting theory recognizes the desirability of valuing assets held for exchange, such as inventories or marketable securities, at the lower of cost or market. Plant assets are valued at historical cost less accumulated depreciation and are not revalued upward in the normal course of financial accounting and reporting. The modifying convention of conservatism influences financial accounting extensively. At present there is little support for valuing many assets at amounts *exceeding* their original cost, because to do so might recognize gains or revenues before they are realized. During the past decade, however, increased professional interest in adjusting the carrying amounts of assets upward has been evident. One example is the market valuation of certain debt and equity investments, as described in Chapter 10. The theoretical arguments favoring this change usually are based on recognizing the effects of inflation, changing replacement costs, or changing values.

Conservatism

Notwithstanding the controversy of valuing assets above their cost, accountants generally agree that if such asset write-ups occur, a direct increase in a separate section of stockholders' equity is also appropriate. Accountants consider the direct adjustment of stockholders' equity preferable to recognizing gains in the income statement with resultant increases in retained earnings. An account title to recognize such an asset write-up might be Appreciation Capital or Appraisal Capital. This type of stockholders' equity is not frequently encountered in practice and generally would represent a departure from GAAP.

QUASI-REORGANIZATION

Occasionally, a corporation finds that it cannot operate profitably given its operating situation and asset and liability structure. In such circumstances, a possible solution is a quasi-reorganization. The term *quasi* means "the same as," and accounting for a quasi-reorganization is similar to that required in a complete reorganization of a business enterprise. A quasi-reorganization, however, costs far less than a complete legal reorganization. In a **quasi-reorganization,** the assets of a company are generally revalued at their current fair values, and the net revaluation loss is reflected in retained earnings. For example, a company may have forecasted an expanding demand for its products and invested in major plant expansion. If the forecast is not realized, excess plant assets may result. Idle or partially productive plant assets may cause the company to be unable to operate profitably. Debt repayment may become impossible under original lending terms. In such cases, the plant assets may be written down to an amount approximating their fair value, and debt may be restructured to allow additional time for repayment. In extreme cases creditors may also agree to accept reduced amounts in satisfaction of corporate debts to maximize the partial recovery of loaned funds. Quasi-reorganization, which is permitted under many state laws, requires the approval of the corporate board of directors and stockholders, and care must be exercised to ensure the maintenance of minimum legal corporate capital.

Four general conditions usually indicate the desirability of a quasi-reorganization:

1. Various assets of the company are overvalued.
2. Retained Earnings contains a deficit.
3. The future of the company from an operating perspective appears favorable if adjustments to the assets and liabilities are made.
4. A change in control of the entity takes place.

In most quasi-reorganizations, common stockholders sacrifice in terms of reduced reported equity. Preferred stockholders may sacrifice through a lack of dividends, and creditors may decide to forgo some of their legal rights to require timely payment. Those shareholders may also relinquish control of the organization to additional shareholders who are granted ownership rights in consideration for forgiving debts owed by the entity. The resource providers of the company are thus attempting to make the best of a bad situation and take action to facilitate the survival of the company.

As the carrying value of assets is reduced to a level facilitating future profitable operations, Retained Earnings is charged directly for the amount of the write-down. The Retained Earnings account usually will then have a debit balance (i.e., a deficit) due to operating losses and the asset write-down. Therefore, other entries are frequently necessary to adjust Retained Earnings to a zero balance. To remove a deficit from Retained Earnings, we credit Retained Earnings and charge Paid-in Capital in Excess of Par Value. If insufficient paid-in capital in excess of par is available to absorb the entire deficit in Retained Earnings, the par or stated value of the common stock is usually reduced. A reduction of the par value of the stock gives rise to additional paid-in capital in excess of par, which in turn is credited to the remaining debit balance in Retained Earnings.

Profitable operations following a quasi-reorganization may facilitate new stock issues and other financing sources for the troubled enterprise. Dividends may be paid from resources generated by profitable operations following a quasi-reorganization.

After a quasi-reorganization, the Retained Earnings account is dated in a manner such as "Retained Earnings from January 1, 1995." In this way, financial statement users can assess the degree of operating success attained by a company after a quasi-reorganization.

To illustrate accounting for a quasi-reorganization, the following example is provided. Exhibit 17–9 presents an abbreviated balance sheet of Static Company prior to a quasi-reorganization. Note that Static's Retained Earnings account contains a deficit even before the quasi-reorganization. This condition is typical in that operating losses usually precede the need to reorganize. Because Static has been unable to operate profitably and has experienced difficulty servicing its debt, and because profitable operations appear possible in the future if a reorganization is effected, the board of directors authorizes a quasi-reorganization.

A review of Static's property reveals that various assets should be adjusted to net realizable values as follows:

EXHIBIT 17–9

Static Company
Abbreviated Balance Sheet
Prior to Quasi-reorganization

December 31, 1995
Assets

Current Assets

Cash	$ 1,500	
Accounts receivable (net of allowance for doubtful accounts of 7,000)	10,000	
Inventory at FIFO cost	30,000	
Total current assets		$ 41,500

Property, Plant, and Equipment

Machinery (net of accumulated depreciation of $25,000)	50,000	
Building (net of accumulated depreciation of $75,000)	250,000	
Land	100,000	
Total property, plant, and equipment		400,000
Total assets		$441,500

Liabilities and Stockholders' Equity

Liabilities

Current liabilities	$ 75,000
Long-term bonds payable	250,000
Total liabilities	$325,000

Stockholders' Equity

Common stock ($10 par; 10,000 shares authorized, issued, and outstanding)	100,000
Paid-in capital in excess of par value	75,000
Total contributed equity	175,000
Retained earnings (deficit)	(58,500)
Total stockholders' equity	116,500
Total liabilities and stockholders' equity	$441,500

Assets	Current Carrying Amount	Net Realizable Value
Inventory	$ 30,000	$ 25,000
Machinery	50,000	40,000
Building	250,000	250,000
Land	100,000	90,000
	$430,000	$405,000

In this case a total assets write-down of $25,000 takes place, which increases the deficit in Retained Earnings as indicated in the following entry:

Dec. 31, 1995	Retained Earnings	25,000	
	Inventory		5,000
	Machinery		10,000
	Land		10,000
	(To reduce the carrying amounts of various assets to net realizable value in accordance with quasi-reorganization.)		

Following this entry, the deficit in retained earnings is $83,500 ($58,500 + $25,000). Because the Paid-in Capital in Excess of Par Value of $75,000 is not sufficient to absorb the $83,500 deficit in retained earnings, the par value of the common stock must be reduced. We shall assume a reduction in par value to $7.50 per share, which is reflected by the following entry:

Dec. 31, 1995	Common Stock	25,000	
	Paid-in Capital in Excess of Par Value		25,000
	(To reflect change in par value to accomplish quasi-reorganization. $2.50 × 10,000 shares.)		

Permission of the stockholders, regulatory agencies, and usually the creditors is necessary before the par value of stock is changed. The final step in completing the quasi-reorganization is elimination of the deficit in Retained Earnings of $83,500:

Dec. 31, 1995	Paid-in Capital in Excess of Par Value	83,500	
	Retained Earnings		83,500
	(To eliminate deficit balance in Retained Earnings pursuant to quasi-reorganization.)		

Following the quasi-reorganization and a year in which operations generate net income of $20,000, the stockholders' equity section of Static's balance sheet appears as presented in Exhibit 17–10. Note that retained earnings is dated and that the company reflects a reduced equity structure.

In practice, a quasi-reorganization is infrequently encountered, because it is generally an extreme measure in a company's fight for survival. The "fresh-start" provided by a quasi-reorganization does not change the underlying economic difficulties; cash flow and profitability problems usually remain. Therefore, a quasi-reorganization is generally not effective unless new management or improved products or conditions tend to support favorable future operating prospects. A quasi-reorganization does give a company the opportunity to organize in a way that allows operations to be conducted in a more realistic and orderly fashion. In this way, management may be able to generate adequate revenues to sustain the enterprise.

Several events and transactions that relate to stockholders' equity accounts demand seasoned professional judgment to successfully address and resolve. Even the area of dividends, which seems relatively straightforward, may require the exercise of judgment. For example, when property dividends are issued, valuation of the property is an important consideration and is rarely as objectively determinable as cash dividends. Knowledge of the law as well as accounting principles may also be necessary in determining that the legal limits of dividends have not been exceeded and that certain required disclosures have been made. These decisions include information about unpaid accumulated dividends on preferred stock and distributions that represent liquidations rather than returns on investments.

PROFESSIONAL JUDGMENT

EXHIBIT 17–10

Static Company
Partial Balance Sheet
One Year after Quasi-reorganization

December 31, 1996

Stockholders' Equity

Common stock ($7.50 par; 10,000 shares authorized, issued, and outstanding)	$ 75,000
Paid-in capital in excess of par value	16,500
Total contributed capital	91,500
Retained earnings (since Jan. 1, 1996)	20,000
Total stockholders' equity	$111,500

We discussed stock dividends and stock splits and observed that a fine line of distinction exists between the two. While the authoritative accounting literature suggests that distributions of 20 to 25% or more are likely to impact market price (i.e., have the basic characteristic of stock splits) and smaller distributions are not likely, or not as likely, to affect market price (i.e., have the basic characteristic of stock dividends), this is a matter of judgment. The 20 to 25% guideline must not be applied routinely, but must be approached with professional judgment and an eye toward the resulting market price reaction as a determinant of the appropriate accounting treatment.

Determining whether stock issued to employees includes an element of compensation is another area where professional judgment comes into play in appropriately accounting for stockholders' equity. While criteria are included in the authoritative literature, decisions such as whether the discount available to employees is no more than would be available to stockholders or others is a matter of professional judgment.

The whole area of disclosure of information about stockholders' equity involves backing away from details and evaluating the adequacy of information that is presented in the primary financial statements, the statement describing changes in stockholders' equity accounts, and the notes to the financial statements. Because stockholders are considered one of the most important user groups of the financial statements, adequate disclosure of information concerning transactions and events affecting stockholders' equity is particularly important for the fair presentation.

A final area where professional judgment in accounting for stockholders' equity is important is identifying and reporting corrections of errors. We discuss that subject in Chapter 20.

CONCLUDING REMARKS

Transactions affecting stockholders' equity accounts involve a wide range of activities throughout the life of an enterprise. The first economic events affecting a company upon its formation and the final acts of dissolution involve equity accounts. Furthermore, most events directly affecting stockholders' equity are usually material and require careful study to assure acceptable practices.

The equity sections of the balance sheets of most large corporations usually contain many different classes and types of stock which have been issued over a long period of time. Therefore, careful review of each issue is necessary to ensure proper accounting for dividends, new stock issues, and other activities affecting individual stockholders. In summary, the stockholders' equity section of a company's balance sheet must be considered and treated as carefully as any other element of a corporation's financial position.

KEY POINTS

1. Dividends are a company's liability only when declared by the board of directors. (Objective 1)
2. Property dividends, like other dividends, should be accounted for at fair market value, with gains and losses recognized upon disposal of the property. (Objective 1)
3. If outstanding preferred stock is cumulative or fully or partially participating, careful analysis is required to properly allocate dividends between common and preferred stockholders. (Objective 1)
4. Small stock dividends are accounted for on the basis of fair market value; large stock dividends are recorded on the basis of par or stated value. (Objective 1)
5. Stock splits require no formal accounting treatment, just a memorandum noting the new par or stated value per share and the number of shares authorized, issued, and outstanding. (Objective 1)
6. Employee stock options can be considered compensatory or noncompensatory. Compensatory stock options require the recognition of compensation expense. The total compensation is measured as the excess of the market value over the option price on the measurement date, which is usually the grant date. (Objectives 2 and 3)
7. Stock appreciation rights (SARs) entitle certain employees to stock appreciation over some specified price multiplied by a specified number of shares. SARs are compensatory and therefore require compensation recognition in the accounting records. Because the measurement date is the exercise date, accounting recognition is based on estimates until final exercise. (Objectives 2 and 3)

8. Quasi-reorganizations are appropriate only when a company is faced with severe financial or operating problems that appear to be manageable if adjustments to assets, liabilities, and stockholders' equity accounts are made. (Objective 4)

9. The major items affecting a company's retained earnings are earnings and dividends. Less frequent items are corrections of errors, certain treasury stock transactions, appropriations, initial adoption of certain accounting principles, and quasi-reorganizations. (Objective 5)

QUESTIONS

17-1 What is meant by the term *retained earnings*? Comment on the propriety of using the term *earned surplus*.

17-2 What are some of the items that affect retained earnings?

17-3 Three dates are important in evaluating dividend status: date of declaration, date of record, and date of payment. What are the accounting implications of each date?

17-4 Preferred stock may have a *cumulation clause* and/or a *participation clause*. What does each term imply to the preferred stockholder?

17-5 Can an investor unambiguously state that, for a particular investment, receiving a dividend is preferable to receiving no dividend? Why or why not?

17-6 What is a property dividend, and what are the significant accounting issues related to this kind of dividend?

17-7 What is a scrip dividend, and what are the significant accounting issues related to this kind of dividend?

17-8 What are liquidating dividends, and what are the significant accounting issues related to this kind of dividend?

17-9 What is a stock dividend? What is the economic result of a stock dividend?

17-10 Accounting authoritative pronouncements distinguish between small and large stock dividends. How is this distinction defined, what are the accounting implications, and how is this distinction justified?

17-11 What is the distinction between a large stock dividend and a stock split? What are the accounting implications of this distinction?

17-12 What is the purpose of a large stock dividend or stock split? What is the purpose of a reverse stock split?

17-13 Why aren't cash and property dividends paid on treasury stock?

17-14 Why might a company appropriate retained earnings? What does a retained earnings appropriation communicate to financial statement users?

17-15 What is an employee stock option? What is the distinction between a compensatory and noncompensatory employee stock option?

17-16 What significant accounting issues are related to compensatory employee stock options?

17-17 What is a stock appreciation right? Why is the measurement date for stock appreciation rights usually different from that for employee stock options? What are the major accounting considerations for stock appreciation rights?

17-18 What is *appraisal capital* and how is it recognized in the accounting records?

17-19 What is a *quasi-reorganization?* What is its economic impact? How is a quasi-reorganization effected in the accounting records?

17-20 Why might corporate executives wish to receive stock options or stock appreciation rights rather than cash for part of their compensation?

EXERCISES

17-21 Dividends on Common and Preferred Stock Fuller Corporation was organized on January 1, 1994. On that date, 10,000 shares of $4 preferred stock ($40 par) were issued. The preferred stock is cumulative and participating up to a maximum amount of 15%, including the preference amount. In addition, 150,000 shares of Fuller common ($10 par) were issued. No dividends were declared or paid in 1994. On July 1, 1995, Fuller declared a 5% common stock dividend to common stockholders of record on July 20, 1995, distributable on August 1, 1995. The market price of Fuller common was $28 a share on July 1, 1995, and $30 a share on August 1, 1995. On December 1, 1995, Fuller declared a $300,000 cash dividend to stockholders of record on December 10, 1995, payable on December 31, 1995.

INSTRUCTIONS

[a] Provide all journal entries relating to dividends by Fuller Corporation for 1995. Separately identify the dividends to the common and preferred shares.

[b] Discuss how the cumulation feature on the preferred affects the market value of the common.

17–22 Dividend Calculation and Journal Entries Baker Corporation has experienced a highly profitable year, and the board of directors has decided to bring all dividends in arrears up to date. The preferred stock of the company is fully participating as well as cumulative. The board wishes to accomplish three objectives with the dividend:

[1] Pay all dividends in arrears.

[2] Pay the current year preference amount.

[3] Pay the maximum possible amount of dividend to the common stockholders without invoking the participation clause of the preferred stock.

The stockholders' equity section of Baker Corporation's balance sheet is summarized as follows:

Preferred stock ($100 par, 15% cumulative, fully participating; 4 years' dividends in arrears; 10,000 shares authorized, 8,000 shares issued of which 3,000 shares are held in treasury)	$ 500,000
Common stock ($10 par; 500,000 shares authorized, 300,000 shares issued of which 50,000 shares are held in treasury)	2,500,000
Paid-in capital in excess of par value	350,000
Retained earnings	1,150,000
Total stockholders' equity	$4,500,000

The company uses the par value method of accounting for treasury stock.

INSTRUCTIONS

[a] Prepare the calculations necessary to determine the maximum dividend consistent with the three objectives of the board of directors.

[b] If such a dividend were declared, prepare the entry or entries necessary to record it.

17–23 Property Dividend Reece, Inc., owned 100,000 shares of marketable common stock of Clarke Corporation on December 31, 1995. At that time, the Reece account Investment in Marketable Equity Securities had a carrying value of $7 per share, which was the cost of the securities. The market value of the investment on that date was $8 per share. On that same date, Reece's board of directors declared a property dividend in which the shares of Clarke Corporation were to be distributed to Reece stockholders on January 17, 1996. At the time the shares were distributed, the market value of the Clarke Corporation stock had dropped to $5 per share.

INSTRUCTIONS

[a] Prepare the entries necessary to record the declaration and distribution of this property dividend.

[b] What is the proper accounting treatment, if any, of the $3 drop in market value from the declaration to the distribution date?

17–24 Dividend Calculation—Total Amount The board of directors of Diliberto, Inc., wishes to declare a dividend whereby common stockholders are to receive a total per share dividend of $4. Diliberto's stockholders' equity section appears as follows:

Preferred stock ($100 par, 7%, participating to 10%, noncumulative; 100,000 shares authorized, 25,000 shares issued and outstanding)	$ 2,500,000
Common stock ($25 par; 250,000 shares authorized, issued, and outstanding)	6,250,000
Paid-in capital in excess of par value	1,250,000
Retained earnings	5,000,000
Total stockholders' equity	$15,000,000

INSTRUCTIONS

Determine the total amount of the dividend that must be declared to meet the per share goals of the board of directors.

17-25 Large Stock Dividends and Retained Earnings Appropriation   Morgan Company has had an agreement with its bondholders that required the company to make payments to a sinking fund and to maintain a related appropriation of retained earnings to retire the bonds. The company has been required to make sinking fund contributions of $500,000 for each of the last five years. At the beginning of 1993, the bonds are repaid, the retained earnings appropriation is canceled, and a 40% common stock dividend is declared and distributed. Immediately before the declaration of the dividend, the company had 1,250,000 shares of $10 par value common stock outstanding with a per share market value of $12.50. Immediately before repaying the bonds at their carrying amount, the company's Unappropriated Retained Earnings balance was $4,000,000.

INSTRUCTIONS

Prepare the journal entries to record the removal of the appropriated retained earnings and the declaration and distribution of the stock dividend. Then compute the remaining amount of unappropriated retained earnings.

17-26 Small Stock Dividend   On February 1, 1995, the board of directors of Huling, Inc., declared a 5% common stock dividend distributable to common stockholders of record on February 15, 1995. Distribution of the dividend took place on February 28, 1995.

Market prices of the stock were as follows:

Feb. 1, 1995	$75 per share
Feb. 15, 1995	80 per share
Feb. 28, 1995	76 per share

There were 100,000 shares of $50 par value stock authorized and 75,000 of the shares were issued and outstanding prior to the stock dividend.

INSTRUCTIONS

[a] Prepare the journal entries to record the stock dividend.
[b] If prior to the stock dividend the retained earnings was $1,000,000, paid-in capital in excess of par value was $250,000, and there were no other issues of stock outstanding, prepare the stockholders' equity section of the balance sheet as of
   [1] February 1, 1995   [2] February 28, 1995

17-27 Preferred Stock Dividend   McNeill Corporation has 20,000 shares of $10 par value common stock and 1,000 shares of $100 par value, 7% preferred stock outstanding. A total dividend of $25,000 is declared by the corporation. No dividends were paid in the prior year.

INSTRUCTIONS

[a] If the preferred stock is neither participating nor cumulative, determine the amount of dividends payable to each class of stock.
[b] Assume that the preferred stock is fully participating but noncumulative. What dividends are payable to each class of stock?
[c] Assume that the preferred stock is cumulative but not participating. What dividends are payable to each class of stock?
[d] Assume that the preferred stock is both cumulative and fully participating. Compute the dividends for each class of stock.

17-28 Statement of Retained Earnings   As the accountant responsible for preparing the financial statements for Golding, Inc., you have assembled the following general ledger information related to retained earnings for the year ended December 31, 1995.

Retained Earnings

Date	Item	Dr.	Cr.
1/1/95	Beginning balance		$1,500,000
4/15/95	1st quarterly dividend for 1995 in cash	$12,000	
7/12/95	2nd quarterly dividend for 1995 in cash	10,000	
8/12/95	Small stock dividend	25,000	
10/12/95	3rd quarterly dividend for 1995 in cash	15,000	
11/15/95	Completed litigation—appropriation closed		100,000
11/29/95	Correction of error in inventory pricing of prior year		72,000
12/31/95	Net income for the year		155,000
12/31/95	Total	$62,000	$1,827,000

While reading the minutes of the December 26, 1995, meeting of the board of directors, you learn that a dividend of $13,000 was declared, which is to be paid on January 5, 1996.

INSTRUCTIONS

Prepare a retained earnings statement in good form for Golding, Inc., for 1995.

17–29 Maximum Dividend Declaration Hunt, Inc., began operations in January 1991 and had the following reported net income or loss for each of its five years of operations:

1991	$ 150,000 loss
1992	130,000 loss
1993	120,000 loss
1994	250,000 income
1995	$1,000,000 income

At December 31, 1995, the Hunt capital accounts were as follows:

Preferred stock ($100 par value; 8% fully participating, cumulative; 10,000 shares authorized, issued, and outstanding)	$1,000,000
Preferred stock ($100 par value; 4% nonparticipating, noncumulative; 1,000 shares authorized, issued, and outstanding)	100,000
Common stock ($10 par value; 100,000 shares authorized, 50,000 shares issued and outstanding)	500,000

Hunt has never paid a cash or stock dividend. The capital accounts have not changed since Hunt began operations. The appropriate state law permits dividends only from retained earnings.

INSTRUCTIONS

Prepare a worksheet showing the *maximum* amount available for cash dividends on December 31, 1995, and the way it would be distributable to holders of the common shares and each type of the preferred shares. Show supporting computations in good form. (AICPA adapted)

17–30 Scrip, Property, and Stock Dividends The balance sheet of Maseo Company appeared as follows on December 31, 1995.

Assets	
Cash	$ 10,000
Investments (trading) (market value = $60,000)	50,000
Inventory	70,000
Plant assets	200,000
Less: Accumulated depreciation	(50,000)
Total assets	$280,000

Liabilities and Stockholders' Equity	
Current liabilities	$ 10,000
Long-term debt	100,000
Common stock ($2 par; 20,000 shares authorized, 10,000 shares issued and outstanding)	20,000
Paid-in capital in excess of par value	100,000
Retained earnings	50,000
Total liabilities and stockholders' equity	$280,000

The market value of the outstanding common shares on December 31, 1995, was $25 per share. The increase in market value of the investments (trading) has taken place since the last time those investments were adjusted for market value changes at December 31, 1994.

INSTRUCTIONS

[a] Provide the appropriate journal entries for each of the following *independent* situations:

[1] On January 1, 1996, Maseo declared a property dividend of all holdings of marketable equity securities.

[2] On January 1, 1996, Maseo declared a scrip dividend of $35,000.

[3] On January 1, 1996, Maseo declared a cash dividend of $80,000.

[4] On January 1, 1996, Maseo declared a 10% stock dividend.

[5] On January 1, 1996, Maseo declared a 40% stock dividend.

[b] How do the applications of accounting principles differ for [4] and [5]? What is the rationale for the difference in procedure?

17–31 Employee Stock Options As president of Endo Company, Brenda Vance received options to buy 1,000 shares of her employer's $10 par stock on June 30, 1995. The options call for a price of $18 per share and are exercisable for five years following the grant date. Vance exercised her option on August 1, 1995, and sold the shares on November 1, 1995. The market prices of the stock on selected dates were as follows:

June 30, 1995	$18 per share
Aug. 1, 1995	25 per share
Nov. 1, 1995	28 per share

INSTRUCTIONS

[a] Provide the appropriate journal entries for Endo Company with respect to the stock options.

[b] Provide the appropriate journal entries for Endo Company with respect to the stock options, assuming the option prices to Vance were

[1] $15 per share

[2] $21 per share

[c] Provide the appropriate journal entry for the exercise of the option on August 1, 1995, under the original assumptions.

[d] What is the distinction between a compensatory and a noncompensatory stock option? How does the accounting for these types of stock options differ?

17–32 Appropriation of Retained Earnings The board of directors of Carroll, Inc., has decided to embark on substantial plant expansion. To demonstrate the need to retain assets in the company, the board agrees on December 31, 1994, to authorize an appropriation of retained earnings in the amount of $2,500,000, the anticipated cost of the plant expansion. The plant was partially constructed on December 31, 1995, and the board decided to reduce the appropriation by $800,000, the cost incurred to date. Finally, in September 1996 the plant was completed and the remaining portion of the appropriation was removed.

INSTRUCTIONS

[a] Prepare the entries to record, reduce, and finally remove the appropriation.

[b] Describe where the Appropriated Retained Earnings account should appear on Carroll's 1994 and 1995 financial statements.

[c] What does the Appropriated Retained Earnings account communicate to the financial statement user?

17–33 Warrant Exercise Johnson Company issues a series of bonds along with detachable stock warrants. Each warrant conveys the right to buy one share of $10 par value common stock for $50 per share. Ten thousand bonds were issued (each with one detachable warrant attached), and $80,000 was correctly recorded as Stock Warrants Exercisable. Eighty percent of the warrants are exercised at a time when the market value of the stock is $65 per share.

INSTRUCTIONS

Record the appropriate journal entry for the exercise of the warrants.

17–34 Stock Appreciation Rights On December 31, 1992, Cerda Textile Company offered its top management share appreciation rights with the following terms:

Option price (predetermined)	$50 per share
Number of shares	7,000
Holding period	3 years
Expiration date	Dec. 31, 1995

The share appreciation is to be paid upon exercise in Cerda common stock ($20 stated value). The market value of Cerda common was as follows:

Dec. 31, 1992	$50 per share
Dec. 31, 1993	48 per share
Dec. 31, 1994	57 per share
Dec. 31, 1995	56 per share

The stock appreciation rights were exercised on December 31, 1995.

INSTRUCTIONS

Provide the correct journal entries to accrue compensation expense for 1993, 1994, and 1995. Record the proper journal entry for the exercise of the stock appreciation rights.

17–35 Dividends and Earnings per Share   Fubar Company presented the following comparative stockholders' equity sections of the balance sheet:

Fubar Company
Partial Balance Sheet
For the Years Ended December 31

	1994	1995
Stockholders' Equity		
9% Preferred stock ($90 par value; 1,000 shares authorized, issued, and outstanding)	$ 90,000	$ 90,000
Common stock ($5 par; 100,000 shares authorized, 50,000 shares issued and outstanding on December 31, 1994, and 70,000 shares issued and outstanding on December 31, 1995)	250,000	350,000
Paid-in capital in excess of par value	250,000	450,000
Retained earnings	200,000	350,000
Total stockholders' equity	$790,000	$1,240,000

Quarterly common stock dividends of $.25 were declared on March 31, June 30, September 30, and December 31, 1995. Semiannual preferred stock dividends were declared on June 30 and December 31, 1995. On May 1, 1995, and September 1, 1995, 10,000 common shares were issued. Retained earnings were affected by only dividends and earnings for 1995.

INSTRUCTIONS

Compute the earnings per share for Fubar Company for 1995.

PROBLEMS

17–36 Journal Entries—Retained Earnings   The following transactions and events of Graffin, Inc., occurred during 1995.

[1] A former employee sued Graffin for injuries sustained in the company's parking lot. Although legal counsel considered it highly unlikely that the former employee would win the case, management decided to appropriate retained earnings of $200,000 (10% of the amount sought by the former employee) on January 31, 1995.

[2] Graffin declared a 40% stock dividend on February 10, 1995, when the market price of the stock was $25. On March 1, 1995, 4,000 shares of $10 par value common stock were issued in distributing the stock dividend. The market value of the stock on March 1, 1995, was $18.

[3] On April 15, 1995, the company created a plant expansion fund by acquiring certificates of deposit in the amount of $300,000. Retained earnings in the same amount were appropriated.

[4] On June 30, 1995, a second stock dividend of 1,000 shares of $10 par value common stock was declared. The dividend was distributed on July 15, 1995. The market values of a share of common on June 30 and July 15, 1995, were $16.00 and $16.50, respectively.

[5] The former employee dropped the lawsuit described in item [1] on September 1, 1995, with no cost to the company except attorney's fees, which have been paid and properly recorded.

[6] Graffin declared a cash dividend of $.25 per common share on September 30, 1995, and paid on October 15, 1995.

[7] On December 20, 1995, the company made an expenditure of $45,000 from the plant expansion fund using a certificate of deposit that matured earlier that month. The certificate cost $40,000 and matured with interest at $48,000 on December 15, 1995.

INSTRUCTIONS

Prepare necessary entries for the above information. You may assume that adequate paid-in capital in excess of par value and retained earnings exist to account for these transactions.

17–37 Quasi-reorganization Laker, Inc., has suffered substantial operating losses for several years. The company's ability to service its debts and pay operating expenses has been impaired. Consequently, Laker's owners, managers, and creditors have decided to execute a quasi-reorganization. An abbreviated balance sheet of Laker prior to the quasi-reorganization is presented below.

Laker, Inc.
Balance Sheet
December 31, 1995

Assets

Current Assets

Cash	$ 10,000
Accounts receivable (less allowance of $5,000)	15,000
Inventory	25,000
Total current assets	50,000

Noncurrent Assets

Plant and equipment (net of accumulated depreciation of $155,000)	340,000
Goodwill	60,000
Total noncurrent assets	400,000
Total assets	$ 450,000

Liabilities and Stockholders' Equity

Current Liabilities

Accounts payable	$ 55,000
Notes payable	25,000
Total current liabilities	80,000

Long-Term Liabilities

Mortgage payable	210,000

Stockholders' Equity

Common stock ($10 par value; 25,000 shares authorized, issued, and outstanding)	250,000
Paid-in capital in excess of par value	50,000
Retained earnings	(140,000)
Total stockholders' equity	160,000
Total stockholders' equity and liabilities	$ 450,000

The following information may bear on accounting for the quasi-reorganization. The owner of Laker, Inc., decides to reduce plant assets to a more reasonable level to increase utilization of remaining assets. He has decided to sell certain equipment that originally cost $100,000 and that has been depreciated to $40,000 by the end of 1995. The expected selling price for the equipment is $15,000, although no sale has been made yet.

An independent appraisal of the company's inventory reveals goods with a carrying value of $8,000 to be obsolete and worthless. The holder of a $25,000 note agrees to accept the proceeds from the sale of the idle equipment mentioned above in full satisfaction of the note.

The mortgage holder agrees to accept 2,000 shares of new $100 par value voting preferred stock in satisfaction of the liability. In addition, the par value of the common stock is reduced to $1 per share, and voting rights for 10 years to effect the quasi-reorganization are suspended.

INSTRUCTIONS

[a] Prepare the necessary entries to record the above events.
[b] Prepare a balance sheet for Laker as of January 1, 1996, following the quasi-reorganization.

17–38 Comprehensive Dividend Calculation Hernandez, Inc., has three classes of stock outstanding at December 31, 1995:

Preferred stock (Class A) ($100 par value, 12%, cumulative and fully participating; 2 years' dividends in arrears; 10,000 shares authorized, issued, and outstanding)	$1,000,000
Preferred stock (Class B) ($100 par value, 10%, noncumulative, participating to 12%; 10,000 shares authorized, 5,000 shares issued and outstanding)	500,000
Common stock ($50 par value; 100,000 shares authorized, 50,000 shares issued, and 40,000 shares outstanding)	2,500,000
Paid-in capital in excess of par value	750,000
Treasury stock (10,000 shares of $50 par value common)	(600,000)
Retained earnings	3,250,000
Total stockholders' equity	$7,400,000

The board of directors of Hernandez, Inc., is deliberating about the amount of dividend to pay. Because no dividends have been paid for three years, determining how a dividend should be divided is somewhat complex.

INSTRUCTIONS

The chairman of the board of directors of Hernandez, Inc., has asked you to compute the amount of dividend payable to each class of stock under each of the following assumptions:

[a] The total dividend is $600,000.
[b] The total dividend is $650,000.
[c] The total dividend is $750,000.

17–39 Quasi-reorganization   Adverse financial and operating circumstances warrant that Smith Company undergo a quasi-reorganization at December 31, 1995. The following information may be relevant in accounting for the quasi-reorganization.

[1] Inventory with a cost of $215,000 is currently recorded in the accounts at its market value of $200,000.
[2] Plant assets with a fair market value of $700,000 are currently recorded at $875,000 net of accumulated depreciation.
[3] A creditor agrees to extend the maturity date of a loan for five years, although interest as originally stated must continue to be paid.
[4] Individual stockholders contribute $600,000 to create additional paid-in capital to facilitate the reorganization. No new shares of stock are issued, although control of a majority of the company's outstanding stock passes to the company's creditors.
[5] The par value of the common stock is reduced from $25 to $15.
[6] Immediately before these events, the stockholders' equity section appears as follows:

Common stock ($25 par value; 100,000 shares authorized and outstanding)	$2,500,000
Paid-in capital in excess of par value	1,750,000
Retained earnings (deficit)	(750,000)
Total stockholders' equity	$3,500,000

INSTRUCTIONS

Prepare the stockholders' equity section of Smith Company's balance sheet after the quasi-reorganization.

17–40 Employee Stock Options   On January 2, 1994, the stockholders of Austin Company authorized a stock option plan that provided key employees with options to purchase an aggregate of 20,000 shares of the company's $10 par value common stock at $14 per share. The market value of the stock was $16 on this date.

The next day, January 3, 1994, Austin granted the president options to purchase 3,000 shares: 1,000 shares for services to be rendered in 1994, 1,000 shares for services to be rendered in 1995, and 1,000 shares for services to be rendered in 1996. The options are exercisable during the six months following the year in which the services were rendered. The market value of the stock was $17 on January 3, 1994.

The president exercised his option for 1,000 shares on April 1, 1995, when the market price was $20 per share. Subsequently, he sold the stock on September 1, 1995, at $18 per share.

The president did not exercise his options in 1995. When the options lapsed on June 30, 1995, the market value of the stock was $12 per share.

INSTRUCTIONS

[a] Prepare journal entries required in 1994 and 1995 under the plan and to record lapsing of the option in 1995 (if necessary).

[b] Explain fully the reasons or principles underlying the entries.   (AICPA adapted)

17–41 Comprehensive Changes in Stockholders' Equity   Barnet, Inc., began operations in 1992 in a state which defines minimum legal capital as $1,000 or the par value of outstanding common stock less 10% to provide for treasury stock transactions, whichever is larger. Stock dividends, once declared, become part of minimum legal capital. The company employes a calendar year for purposes of financial reporting.

Immediately after Barnet was organized, the stockholders' equity section of its balance sheet appeared as follows:

Common stock ($25 par value; 100,000 shares authorized, 25,000 shares issued and outstanding)	$625,000
Paid-in capital in excess of par value	20,000
Retained earnings	–0–
Total stockholders' equity	$645,000

Net income (loss) for the period 1992 to 1996 appears below:

1992	$ 30,000
1993	40,000
1994	8,000
1995	(10,000)
1996	30,000

Activities related to the various types of dividends are described below:

1992   Declared a cash dividend of $.75 per share on December 31, 1992, and paid it on January 15, 1993.

1993   Declared a 5% stock dividend on December 31, 1993, when the stock was selling for $26 per share. The dividend was distributed on January 20, 1994.

1994   Declared a dividend on December 31, 1994, in the amount of $.60 per share to be paid with trading investments held by Barnet as a temporary investment. The cost of each share of the investments held by Barnet was $45 and the market value at December 31, 1994, was $50. The dividend was paid on January 10, 1995, when the investments were selling for $56 per share. (*Hint:* The gain on the dividend shares should be recorded and included in 1994 income.)

1995   Declared a cash dividend on December 20, 1995, of $.50 per share despite the loss reported for the current year. The dividend was paid on January 5, 1996.

1996   Declared a 2-for-1 stock split and changed the par value of the stock to $12.50 on June 30, 1996. On December 26, 1996, the company declared a 2% stock dividend, at which time the company's stock was selling for $17.50 per share.

INSTRUCTIONS

[a] Prepare the entries necessary to record these events through December 31, 1996.

[b] Prepare an analysis of the changes in stockholders' equity accounts as a result of these events.

17–42 Comprehensive Stockholders' Equity Emphasizing Retained Earnings Presentation   Branagh Company was formed on July 1, 1993. It was authorized to issue 200,000 shares of $5 par value common stock value common stock and 50,000 shares of 6%, $10 par value, cumulative and nonparticipating preferred stock. Branagh has a July 1–June 30 fiscal year.

The following information relates to Branagh's stockholders' equity accounts.

Common Stock.   Prior to the 1995–1996 fiscal year, Branagh had 105,000 shares of outstanding common stock issued as follows:

[1] On July 1, 1993, 95,000 shares were issued for cash at $20 per share.

[2] On July 24, 1993, 5,000 shares were exchanged for a plot of land that cost the seller $70,000 in 1996 and had an estimated market value of $130,000 on July 24, 1993.

[3] On March 1, 1995, 5,000 shares were issued. The shares had been subscribed for $32 per share on October 31, 1994.

During the 1995–1996 fiscal year, the following transactions involving common stock took place:

Oct.   1, 1995   Received subscriptions for 10,000 shares at $40 per share. Cash of $80,000 was received in full payment for 2,000 shares and stock certificates were issued. The remaining subscriptions for 8,000 shares were to be paid in full by September 30, 1996, at which time the certificates were to be issued.

Nov. 30, 1995   Purchased 2,000 shares of its own stock on the open market at $38 per share. Branagh uses the cost method for treasury stock.

Dec. 15, 1995   Declared a 2% stock dividend for stockholders of record on January 15, 1996, to be issued on January 31, 1996. Branagh was having a liquidity problem and could not afford a cash dividend at the time. Branagh's common stock was selling at $43 per share on December 15, 1995. (The stock dividend was not distributed on treasury or subscribed shares.)

June 20, 1996   Sold 500 shares of its common stock that it had purchased on November 30, 1995, for $21,000.

Preferred Stock. Branagh issued 30,000 shares of preferred stock at $15 per share on July 1, 1994.

Cash Dividends. Branagh has followed a schedule of declaring cash dividends in December and June and paying stockholders of record the following month. The cash dividends that have been declared since inception of the company through June 30, 1996, are shown below.

Declaration Date	Common Stock	Preferred Stock
Dec. 15, 1994	$.10 per share	$.30 per share
June 15, 1995	$.10 per share	$.30 per share
Dec. 15, 1995	—	$.30 per share

No cash dividends were declared during June 1996 due to the company's liquidity problems.

Retained Earnings. As of June 30, 1995, Branagh's Retained Earnings account had a balance of $370,000. For the fiscal year ending June 30, 1996, Branagh reported net income of $20,000.

In March 1995, Branagh received a term loan from Guardian National Bank. The bank requires Branagh to establish a sinking fund and restrict retained earnings for an amount equal to the sinking fund deposit. The annual sinking fund payment of $40,000 is due on April 30 each year; the first payment was made on schedule on April 30, 1996.

INSTRUCTIONS

Prepare the stockholders' equity section of the statement of financial position (balance sheet), including appropriate notes, for Branagh Company as of June 30, 1996, as it should appear in the annual report to shareholders.   (CMA adapted)

17–43 Comprehensive Dividends   For the first time, Bull Products, Inc., is including a five-year summary of earnings and dividends per share in its 1996 annual report to stockholders. At January 1, 1992, the corporation had issued 7,000 shares of 4% cumulative, nonparticipating, $100 par value preferred stock and 40,000 shares of $10 par value common stock, of which 108 shares of preferred and 4,000 shares of common stock were held in treasury.

Dividends were declared and paid semiannually on the last day of June and December. Cash dividends paid per share of common stock and net income (loss) for each year were as follows:

	1992	1993	1994	1995	1996
Net income (loss)	$126,568	$(11,812)	$47,148	$115,824	$193,210
Dividend on common					
June 30	.40	.11	.10	.40	.60
Dec. 31	.48	.11	.30	.40	.40

In addition, a 10% stock dividend was declared and distributed on all common stock (including treasury shares) on April 1, 1994, and common stock was split 5 for 1 on October 1, 1996. The corporation has met a sinking fund requirement to purchase and retire 140 shares of its preferred stock on October 1 of each year, beginning in 1996 using any available treasury stock. On July 1, 1993, the corporation purchased 400 shares of its common stock and placed them in the treasury and on April 1, 1995, issued 5,000 shares of common stock to officers, using treasury stock to the extent available.

INSTRUCTIONS

[a] Prepare a schedule showing the computation of preferred stock dividends paid semiannually and annually for the five years. Use the following column headings:

		Number of Shares		Dividends Paid	
Year	Half (1st or 2nd)	Purchased and Retired	Outstanding	Semiannually	Annually

[b] Prepare a schedule that shows for each of the five years the cash dividends paid to common stock-holders and the average number of shares of common stock outstanding after adjustment for the stock dividend and split. Use the following format:

	Shares of Common Stock		Dividends Paid		Common Stock Adjusted for	
Dividend Date	In Treasury	Outstanding	Per Share	Total	10% Stock Dividend	5-for-1 Stock Split
6/30/92						
12/31/92						
Total for year						
Average for year						

(Continue this format for the next four years.) (AICPA adapted)

17–44 Comprehensive Stockholders' Equity Emphasizing Retained Earnings During May 1994, Ferretti, Inc., was organized with 3,000,000 authorized shares of $10 par value common stock, and 300,000 shares of its common stock were issued for $3,300,000. Net income through December 31, 1994, was $125,000.

On July 3, 1995, Ferretti issued 500,000 shares of its common stock for $6,250,000. A 5% stock dividend was declared on October 2, 1995, and issued on November 6, 1995, to stockholders of record on October 23, 1995. The market value of the common stock was $11 per share on the declaration date. Ferretti's net income for the year ended December 31, 1995, was $350,000.

During 1996 Ferretti had the following transactions:

[1] In February Ferretti reacquired 30,000 shares of its common stock for $9 per share. Ferretti uses the cost method to account for treasury stock.

[2] In June Ferretti sold 15,000 shares of its treasury stock for $12 per share.

[3] In September each stockholder was issued (for each share held) one stock right to purchase two additional shares of common stock for $13 per share. The rights expire on December 31, 1996.

[4] In October 250,000 stock rights were exercised when the market value of the common stock was $14 per share.

[5] In November 400,000 stock rights were exercised when the market value of the common stock was $15 per share.

[6] On December 15, Ferretti declared its first cash dividend to stockholders of $.30 per share, payable on January 10, 1997, to stockholders of record on December 31, 1996.

[7] On December 21, in accordance with the applicable state law, Ferretti retired 10,000 shares of its treasury stock and had them revert to an unissued basis. The market value of the common stock was $16 per share on this date.

[8] Net income for 1996 was $800,000.

INSTRUCTIONS

Prepare a schedule of all transactions affecting the capital stock (shares and dollar amounts), paid-in capital in excess of par value, retained earnings, and the treasury stock (shares and dollar amounts) and the amounts that would be included in Ferretti's balance sheet at December 31, 1994, 1995, and 1996, as a result of these transactions. Show supporting computations in good form.

(AICPA adapted)

17–45 Comprehensive Stockholders' Equity Worksheet   Barr Corporation is a publicly owned company whose shares are traded on a national stock exchange. At December 31, 1995, Barr had 25,000,000 shares of $10 par value common stock authorized, of which 15,000,000 shares were issued and 14,000,000 shares were outstanding.

The stockholders' equity accounts at December 31, 1995, had the following balances:

Common stock	$150,000,000
Paid-in capital in excess of par value	80,000,000
Retained earnings	50,000,000
Treasury stock	18,000,000

During 1996, Barr had the following transactions:

[1] On February 1, a secondary distribution of 2,000,000 shares of $10 par value common stock was completed. The stock was sold to the public at $18 per share, net of offering costs.

[2] On February 15, Barr issued at $110 per share, 100,000 shares of $100 par value, 8% cumulative preferred stock with 100,000 detachable warrants. Each warrant contained one right that with $20 could be exchanged for one share of $10 par value common stock. On February 15, the market price for one stock right was $1.

[3] On March 1, Barr reacquired 20,000 shares of its common stock for $18.50 per share. Barr uses the cost method to account for treasury stock.

[4] On March 15, when the common stock was trading for $21 per share, a major stockholder donated 10,000 shares.

[5] On March 31, Barr declared a semiannual cash dividend on common stock of $.10 per share, payable on April 10, 1996.

[6] On April 15, when the market price of the stock rights was $2 each and the market price of the common stock was $22 per share, 30,000 stock rights were exercised. Barr issued new shares to complete the transaction.

[7] On April 30, employees exercised 100,000 options that were granted in 1993 under a noncompensatory stock option plan. When the options were granted, each option had a preemptive right and entitled the employee to purchase one share of common stock for $20 per share. On April 30, the market price of the common stock was $23 per share. Barr issued new shares to settle the transaction.

[8] On May 31, when the market price of the common stock was $20 per share, Barr declared a 5% stock dividend distributable on July 1, 1996, to stockholders of record on June 1, 1996. The appropriate state law prohibits stock dividends on treasury shares.

[9] On June 30, Barr sold the 20,000 treasury shares reacquired on March 1 and an additional 280,000 treasury shares costing $5,600,000 that were on hand at the beginning of the year. The selling price was $25 per share.

[10] On September 30, Barr declared a semiannual cash dividend on common stock of $.10 per share and the yearly dividend on preferred stock, both payable on October 30, 1996, to stockholders of record on October 10, 1996.

[11] On December 31, the remaining outstanding rights expired.

[12] Net income for 1996 was $25,000,000.

INSTRUCTIONS

Prepare a worksheet that summarizes, for each transaction, the changes in Barr's stockholders' equity accounts for 1996. The columns on this worksheet should have the following headings:

Date of transaction (or beginning date)
Common stock—number of shares
Common stock—amount
Preferred stock—number of shares
Preferred stock—amount
Common stock warrants—number of rights
Common stock warrants—amount
Paid-in capital in excess of par value
Retained earnings
Treasury stock—number of shares
Treasury stock—amount

(AICPA adapted)

17–46 Comprehensive Stockholders' Equity   At December 31, 1994, Cadan, Inc., had 6,000,000 authorized shares of $20 par value common stock, of which 1,000,000 shares were issued and outstanding. The stockholders' equity accounts at December 31, 1994, had the following balances:

Common stock	$20,000,000
Paid-in capital in excess of par value	6,000,000
Retained earnings	5,000,000

Transactions during 1995 and other information relating to the stockholders' equity accounts were as follows:

[1] On January 5, 1995, Cadan issued at $54 per share, 100,000 shares of $50 par value, 9% cumulative convertible preferred stock. Each share of preferred stock is convertible, at the option of the holder, into two shares of common stock. Cadan had 600,000 authorized shares of preferred stock. The preferred stock has a liquidation value equal to its par value.

[2] On February 1, 1995, Cadan reacquired 10,000 shares of its common stock for $32 per share. Cadan uses the cost method to account for treasury stock.

[3] On April 30, 1995, Cadan sold 250,000 shares (previously unissued) of $20 par value common stock to the public at $34 per share.

[4] On June 18, 1995, Cadan declared a cash dividend of $2 per share of common stock, payable on July 12, 1995, to stockholders of record on July 1, 1995.

[5] On November 10, 1995, Cadan sold 5,000 shares of treasury stock for $42 per share.

[6] On December 14, 1995, Cadan declared the yearly cash dividend on preferred stock, payable on January 14, 1996, to stockholders of record on December 31, 1995.

[7] On January 20, 1996, before the books were closed for 1995, Cadan became aware that the ending inventories at December 31, 1994, were understated by $300,000 (after tax effect on 1994 net income was $180,000). The appropriate correcting entry was recorded the same day.

[8] After correcting the beginning inventory, net income for 1995 was $3,500,000.

INSTRUCTIONS

[a] Prepare a statement of retained earnings for the year ended December 31, 1995. Assume that only single-period financial statements for 1995 are presented.

[b] Prepare the stockholders' equity section of Cadan's balance sheet at December 31, 1995.

(AICPA adapted)

17–47 Relationship between Dividends and Retained Earnings   Crabb Corporation has been in business for four years. The corporation has never paid a dividend but has accumulated $600,000 of earnings over the past four years. The balance sheet on December 31, 1995, appears as follows:

CASES

Assets		
Current assets	$	50,000
Land		300,000
Plant assets		500,000
Less: Accumulated depreciation		(100,000)
Patents		400,000
Total assets		$1,150,000

Liabilities and Stockholders' Equity		
Current liabilities	$	50,000
Long-term debt		100,000
Common stock (no par; 10,000 shares authorized, issued, and outstanding)		400,000
Retained earnings		600,000
Total liabilities and stockholders' equity		$1,150,000

Net income for 1995 was $150,000. The statement of retained earnings indicates that $200,000 of retained earnings is appropriated for future plant expansion. Howie Jones, a stockholder with a

20% holding, is concerned about the lack of dividends over the last four years. Specifically, he notices that retained earnings are $600,000 and he is therefore thinking about pressuring the company to pay some of this amount in dividends. Jones believes 40%, or $240,000 of retained earnings, could be paid in dividends, leaving $200,000 for plant expansion and $160,000 as a cushion against economic downturns.

INSTRUCTIONS

Mr. Jones has come to you for advice on how best to proceed against the company.

[a] What is your advice to him?

[b] How would you alleviate his concern about the lack of dividends? In other words, show Mr. Jones that the lack of dividends may not be as bad as he thinks.

17–48 Alternative Dividend Plans   The board of directors of Southern Fixtures Company is considering several strategies for the upcoming annual dividend. Alex Hemming, the treasurer of the company, has been asked to explain to the board of directors the advantages and disadvantages of each strategy. These are the four strategies:

[1] Declare the normal cash dividend of $1.00 per share.

[2] Declare a 2% stock dividend on the outstanding common stock.

[3] Declare a 40% stock dividend on the outstanding common stock.

[4] Split the stock, 2 for 1, and declare a $.50 per share dividend on the new outstanding shares.

Southern has 100,000 shares of $2.50 par value common stock outstanding. The market price of the common stock is $50 per share.

INSTRUCTIONS

[a] Provide the information needed by the board of directors. Be sure to identify the amount to be charged to Retained Earnings for each method.

[b] The chair of the board discovers that the amount charged to Retained Earnings is the same under each alternative and therefore concludes that the methods are identical in terms of economic effect on the firm. Respond to this observation.

17–49 Stock-Based Compensation Plans   SLC Company is considering an employee incentive plan for certain key employees. The compensation committee of the board of directors is considering either a stock option plan or a stock appreciation right plan. The compensation committee wants a brief report on the advantages and disadvantages of each type of plan for both employer and employee. In addition, the compensation committee wishes to know the financial statement reporting principles for each method.

INSTRUCTIONS

Provide the information requested by the compensation committee of the board of directors.

17–50 Stock Options Measurement Date   On December 14, 1993, the board of directors of Short Company authorized a grant of nontransferable (restricted) options to company executives for the purchase of 10,000 shares of $50 par value common stock at $52½ any time during 1996 if the executives were still employed by the company. The closing price of Short common stock was $55 on December 14, 1993, $52 on January 2, 1996, and $49⅛ on December 31, 1996. None of the options was exercised.

INSTRUCTIONS

[a] Prepare a schedule computing the compensation expense attributable to the stock options that Short should recognize. Prepare any entries for 1993 through 1996.

[b] Assume that the market price of Short common stock rose to $57 (instead of declining to $52) on January 2, 1996, and that all options were exercised on that date. What cost would the company incur for executive compensation? Why? Prepare any additional entries necessary in these circumstances.

[c] Discuss the arguments for measuring compensation from executive stock options in terms of the spread between:

[1] Market price and option price when the grant is made.

[2] Market price and option price when the options are first exercisable.

[3] Market price and option price when the options are exercised.

[4] Cash value of the executives' services estimated at the grant date and the amount of their salaries.   (AICPA adapted)

17–51 Convertible Bonds   On February 1, 1992, Silver Company sold its five-year, $1,000 par value, 8% bonds, which were convertible at the option of the investor into Silver Company common stock at a ratio of 10 shares of common stock for each bond. The convertible bonds were sold by Silver Company at a discount. Interest is payable annually each February 1. On February 1, 1995, Jahr Company, an investor in Silver Company convertible bonds, tendered 1,000 bonds for conversion into 10,000 shares of Silver common stock, which had a market value of $110 per share at the date of the conversion.

INSTRUCTIONS

How should Silver Company account for the conversion of the convertible bonds into common stock under both the book value and market value methods? Discuss the rationale for each method and indicate which method Silver should use.   (AICPA adapted)

JUDGMENT CASES

17–52 Distinguishing Errors from Changes in Estimates   Your new client, Harris & Sons, Inc., fired its former chief executive officer and immediately appointed a new president. Shortly after the end of the year and following the issuance of financial statements, the company also discharged its independent auditors.

You were pleased when the new president requested your accounting firm to perform the current year's audit. In discussing the engagement with the former auditors and the new president, you have learned that a number of assets were written off shortly after the new president was appointed and the estimated lives of most of the company's assets were shortened. In fact, the company now reports few assets on its balance sheet and the charges for depreciation are extremely small. You have also determined that the former auditors had initially disagreed with those actions although they agreed with the new management in the end. That disagreement, however, was the source of the action taken to discharge the prior audit firm.

During this year's work, you have learned that one of the company's factories that was written down to its salvage value is continuing to operate at full capacity. When you ask the president about the seeming inconsistency between the write-off of the plant last year and its continued operation, the president simply smiles and states:

When we wrote off that plant, I thought we would almost immediately abandon it. The more I thought about it, however, the more I realized that my earlier estimates needed to be revised and that we could still operate the plant and make a profit. Therefore, I changed my mind shortly after the financial statements for last year were issued and decided to continue operating it. I realize that given the write-off, there won't be any depreciation expense to recognize on that facility. However, I need to report a lot of profit anyway to demonstrate the turnaround I was hired to engineer. But given the accounting for changes in estimates, I don't see any other way to report the results of our operations this year. Anyway, its an ill wind that blows no good, right?

INSTRUCTIONS

Is the president correct in his analysis of this situation? Prepare a response to the president's position. If you believe that you need additional information, describe what else you would like to determine to provide acceptable accounting in this set of circumstances.

17–53 Accounting for Redeemable Preferred Stock   You are the controller for Sanford, Inc., a private company not subject to the registration requirements of the Securities and Exchange Commission, which issued redeemable preferred stock during the current year. The stockholders have the option of redeeming the stock five years after its issuance at a stated redemption value. If redeemed, any dividends in arrears must be paid in addition to the redemption value.

The company has decided to report the stock outside the stockholders' equity section of the balance sheet as it would be required to do if the company were a public registrant. Other accounting issues have arisen, however, and you are attempting to determine acceptable financial reporting practices. The principal issue relates to the difference between the issuance price and the redemption value of the stock. The stock was issued at a substantial discount from the redemption value, and you are wondering whether this difference should be amortized as would be the case if the stock was clearly a debt instrument. Further, if the difference is to be amortized, you wonder how the annual amount should be recognized. If the instrument was a note or bond payable, any such amortization would be an adjustment to interest expense recognized on the debt. In this case, however, the stock may not even be redeemed by the stockholders.

INSTRUCTIONS

How should the difference between the issuance price and the redemption value of the stock be accounted for and reported in the company's financial statements?

17–54 Property Dividends   Your client, Expansion Minded, Inc., is in the process of planning for the end of its accounting year-end. The president, Bob Cool, is the company's sole shareholder and has realized that the company needs to report a higher level of income than it has earned if it is to comply with certain of its lending covenants. He has developed an idea that would solve this problem and is presenting it to you for your consideration:

> *My idea is to declare and later distribute to me a large property dividend. The dividend would be the land we acquired several years ago as a plant expansion site. The property has increased in value substantially since we acquired it due to growth in the nearby city. I understand that accounting for property dividends requires that, when declared, the property subject to the dividend should be revalued to its fair value with a gain or loss recognized and a liability recognized for that amount. Because we would recognize a large gain on such a revaluation, that would solve our lending covenant problem. I know that the same amount will reduce Retained Earnings, but we get a boost to earnings that is badly needed. Further, I have a number of tax losses available so receiving taxable income in this amount won't really be adverse to me personally. Finally, in a few years when the company needs the land back for plant expansion, I will contribute it to the company and account for it as paid-in capital in excess of par value. As far as I can see, this solves a lot of problems. The company is not harmed, we comply with our lending covenants, and life can go on smoothly. What do you think?*

INSTRUCTIONS

Do you believe that the accounting described by Bob Cool would comply with generally accepted accounting principles? Be specific and inclusive in developing your answer.

FINANCIAL REPORTING CASE

17–55 Financial Reporting Case   Strawbridge & Clothier operates department stores and other retail businesses in Pennsylvania, New Jersey, and Delaware. Following are excerpts from the company's statement that explains changes in stockholders' equity accounts and notes to the financial statements for the year ending January 29, 1994.

Excerpt from Consolidated Statement of Common Shareholders' Equity (in thousands)

	Series A Common Stock	Series B Common Stock	Capital in Addition to Par Value of Shares	Retained Earnings	Treasury Stock (Deduction)	Total
Balance, January 30, 1993	$6,761	$3,196	$157,591	$ 75,291	–0–	$242,839
Net earnings				17,727		17,727
Cash dividends—common (per share: $1.08 Series A; $.99 Series B)				(10,963)		(10,963)
Cash dividends—preferred				(17)		(17)
Stock dividend (3%)	203	96	6,947	(7,246)		–0–
Exercise of stock options, employee stock purchases, and contribution to Retirement Savings Plan	127	3	2,486		$ 18	2,634
Conversions	60	(60)				–0–
Treasury stock purchases					(18)	(18)
Balance, January 29, 1994	$7,151	$3,235	$167,024	$ 74,792	$–0–	$252,202

Excerpt from Consolidated Balance Sheet (in thousands)

Liabilities, Preferred Stock, and Common Shareholders' Equity	January 29 1994	January 30 1993
Preferred Stock	**$ 296**	$ 474
Series Preferred Stock—no par value: authorized— 2,000,000 shares; none issued	**–0–**	–0–
Common Shareholders' Equity		
Series A Common Stock—par value $1 a share: authorized— 20,000,000 shares; issued and outstanding 1993—7,151,254 shares, 1992—6,761,104 shares	**7,151**	6,761
Series B Common Stock—par value $1 a share, convertible: authorized—20,000,000 shares; issued and outstanding 1993— 3,235,149 shares, 1992—3,196,369 shares	**3,235**	3,196
Capital in addition to par value of shares	**167,024**	157,591
Retained earnings	**74,792**	75,291
Total Common Shareholders' Equity	**252,202**	242,839
	$663,052	$653,939

Excerpts from Notes to Consolidated Financial Statements

5. Preferred Stock

The Preferred Stock ($100 par value) provides for $5 cumulative dividends and redemption at $105 per share (1993—$311,000; 1992—$498,000). Sinking fund provisions require that on April 1 of each year, the Company shall redeem shares of at least $179,900 in par value. Par value of shares redeemed and retired was as follows: 1993—$180,300; 1992— $180,200; 1991—$186,200. Outstanding shares at fiscal year ends were: 1993—2,961; 1992—4,742; 1991—6,549.

6. Common Stock

Series A and Series B shares are entitled to one and ten votes per share, respectively. Series B shares are convertible on a share-for-share basis into Series A shares. Series A shares are freely transferable while Series B shares are only transferable to certain permitted transferees. Series A Common Stock is entitled to cash dividends at least 10% higher than any cash dividend declared on Series B Common Stock.

INSTRUCTIONS

[a] Identify the major transactions and events that changed stockholders' equity accounts during the year.

[b] To the extent possible from the information given, reconstruct the journal entries that were made, by the major category you have identified in [a], to record the transactions and events that changed stockholders' equity.

[c] Concerning preferred stock:

[1] Why do you think the company excludes preferred stock from the financial statement that explains changes in all other stockholders' equity accounts?

[2] What explains the change in preferred stock from $474,000 at the end of the 1993 fiscal year to $296,000 at the end of the 1994 fiscal year?

[3] Why does the balance sheet include the preferred stock identified as "Series Preferred Stock" in light of the fact that there are no dollar amounts involved?

Earnings per Share

OBJECTIVES

1. To explain the significance of earnings per share (EPS) figures, particularly for publicly held companies.
2. To explain the various situations that present the potential for dilution (reduction) in earnings per share.
3. To distinguish between companies with simple capital structures and those with complex capital structures and to identify the EPS requirements of each.
4. To demonstrate the computation of EPS for companies with simple capital structures and primary and fully diluted EPS for companies with complex capital structures.
5. To prepare the appropriate financial statement presentation of EPS, based on the specific circumstances of the reporting company.
6. To discuss how certain modifying conventions explain the need to incorporate potential dilution in EPS calculations.

A recent study found that the principal reason for turnover among chief executive officers (CEOs) is that their corporations experience lower than expected earnings per share figures. In this study of 408 CEOs, the earnings per share figures were primary predictors of CEO turnover.

A recent issue of *Fortune* states that in picking growth stocks, earnings per share should be expected to grow at least 20% per year over the next five years. *Financial World's* list of America's top 200 growth companies has an average annual five-year earnings per share growth rate of 31.1%.

Earnings per share figures are important measures of company performance and are widely used in making important financial decisions. *The Wall Street Journal* and other publications frequently cite them. How are these figures computed? How and where are they presented in the financial statements? These are some of the questions that this chapter answers.

S. M. Puffer and J. B. Weintrop, "Corporate Performance and CEO Turnover: The Role of Performance Expectations," *Administrative Science Quarterly* (March 1991), pp. 1–19; M. Ozarian, A. Ourusoff, M. Panchapaleesan, "America's Top 200 Growth Companies," *Finance World* (August 4, 1992), pp. 32–44; and T. P. Pare, "How to Know When to Buy Stocks," *Fortune* vol. 126, issue 9, Fall 1992, pp. 79–83.

BASIC EARNINGS PER SHARE CONCEPTS

Financial analysts, individual investors, and other financial statement users often use indexes, ratios, and percentages to relate various financial statement items to one another. Many of the commonly used measures will be discussed in Chapter 25. Although these measures are not usually included in the financial statements, the numbers needed for their computation are.

Earnings per share (EPS) figures represent an exception, because they are computed by the accountant and become an integral part of the income statement when required. This is a result of the many complexities that may exist in the computations, the specific implications of which are generally not available to an external user of the financial statements.

In its simplest form, EPS is computed by dividing the net income by the number of shares of common stock outstanding:

$$\text{EPS} = \frac{\text{Net Income}}{\text{Number of Shares of Common Stock Outstanding}}$$

The concept of EPS relates only to an enterprise's common stock and is best thought of as "earnings per *common* share." The concept of EPS does not apply to preferred stock, because preferred stock typically receives a fixed return and is not the ownership interest to which residual earnings accrue.

HISTORICAL DEVELOPMENT OF EPS

The development of EPS over the last several decades demonstrates an interesting reversal of position by the authoritative accounting organizations in reaction to the ways financial statements are used and the needs of their users. Before 1966 presentation of EPS figures was a matter of management discretion, and many years ago accountants were actually *discouraged* from being associated with EPS figures.

In 1966 the Accounting Principles Board (APB), in *APB Opinion No. 9,* "Reporting the Results of Operations," strongly *encouraged* companies to disclose EPS. In 1969 *APB Opinion No. 15 required* the disclosure of EPS and set up the relatively complicated structure of computation and presentation that now exists.[1] This pronouncement provides the basis for most of the material in this chapter.

In 1978, the Financial Accounting Standards Board (FASB) concluded in *Statement of Financial Accounting Standard No. 21*[2] that EPS figures should *not* be required in the financial statements of **nonpublic enterprises.**[3] At the present time, therefore, EPS figures are *required* only in the financial statements of public enterprises.

In no longer requiring nonpublic companies to present EPS in their income statements, the FASB carefully considered both the cost burden of preparing and presenting EPS figures and the usefulness of the information to financial statement users. A growing concern is the excessive burden placed on small or nonpublic companies when they are subject to the same financial reporting requirements as large, publicly held companies. The FASB lightened this burden somewhat by excluding the EPS requirement for nonpublic companies. As we shall see in the following section, the significance of EPS is frequently interpreted in relation to stock market prices. The lack of active trading of the stock of nonpublic companies supports the position that EPS figures are generally not of great usefulness to users of their financial statements. Even though nonpublic companies are not required to present EPS figures, if management decides to present them, the reporting standards for public companies presented in this chapter must be followed.

SIGNIFICANCE OF EPS FIGURES

Many people regard EPS as the most important single number in the financial statements. EPS figures are frequently cited in corporate annual reports, press releases, investment service publications, financial periodicals, and elsewhere as measures of an enterprise's success in achieving its profit objective. Many financial statement users believe EPS figures are useful indicators of an enterprise's management effectiveness, earnings potential, and future dividends.

Several studies support the usefulness of EPS figures in financial analysis. For example, one researcher gathered data from chartered financial analysts (CFAs) concerning the importance of items in the financial statements. He concluded:

---

[1] *APB Opinion No. 15,* "Earnings per Share," 1968.

[2] *FASB Statement of Financial Accounting Standards No. 21,* "Suspension of the Reporting of Earnings per Share and Segment Information by Nonpublic Enterprises," 1978.

[3] A **nonpublic enterprise** is one whose debt or equity securities do not trade in a public market on a foreign or domestic stock exchange or in the over-the-counter market or that is not required to file financial statements with the Securities and Exchange Commission.

Security analysts are more interested in information items that concern the income statement and affect the amount of income earned by a corporation than in balance sheet information items. Earnings per share continues to lead the list as the most important item.[4] [*Emphasis added.*]

Net income is an **aggregate earnings calculation,** reflecting the return on all of the enterprise's resources derived from many sources, such as creditors, preferred and common stockholders, and past operations. However, the extent to which creditors and investors other than common stockholders share in earnings is normally fixed in amount due to their contractual arrangements with the enterprise. For example, preferred stocks and bonds have stated dividend and interest rates that establish the return that investors expect to receive. Common stock, on the other hand, represents the **residual equity** and its return is the first to be reduced if earnings decrease and is in a position to benefit if earnings increase. Thus, EPS may have relevance to current and prospective common stockholders as income increases and decreases, because the return to creditors and preferred stockholders has already been recognized.

Because EPS is actually a measure of **earnings per common share,** we must deduct the required return to all senior securities, such as bonds and preferred stock, to derive the earnings attributable to common stock. Interest to debt holders has already been deducted (as an expense) in determining net income. One of the first adjustments we must make in computing EPS is to subtract the dividend on preferred stock from net income to determine the amount of income that should be associated with common stock. We can now modify our general notion of EPS as follows:

$$\text{EPS} = \frac{\text{Net Income} - \text{Preferred Dividend}}{\text{Number of Shares of Common Stock Outstanding}}$$

Comparing the relative desirability of common stock of different companies is particularly difficult if the analysis is based on net income and dollars invested in the company's common stock, as is the case in computing such ratios as return on stockholders' equity. Because of differences in asset structure, dollars invested by various classes of creditors and investors, rates of change in these variables over time, and other considerations, comparing companies on an aggregate basis is difficult for certain types of investment decisions. Because market prices of common stock are quoted per share, users of financial statements want a per share measure of income to facilitate comparisons among companies. This desire has resulted in the emphasis on EPS in addition to net income.

EPS figures are frequently used in conjunction with other per-share measures of an enterprise. The price/earnings ratio, for example, is computed by dividing the per-share market price of the stock by EPS. To illustrate, assume that a company has common stock with a market price of $25 and has EPS of $4.50. The related price/earnings ratio is 5.6 ($25.00/$4.50), indicating that the stock is selling at 5.6 times EPS. The price/earnings ratio must be interpreted carefully. If it is judged to be low relative to other stocks, at least two alternative explanations exist. The stock may be considered an excellent investment opportunity because of the low price at which it can be acquired in relation to earnings. Alternatively, a declining trend in the price/earnings ratio may reflect investors' negative attitude toward the enterprise's growth potential.

Another frequently cited measure is dividend payout, in which the dividend paid on a per-share basis is divided by the EPS for the same time period. For example, if a company with EPS of $4.50 pays $2.00 in dividends, the dividend payout is 44% ($2.00/$4.50), indicating that cash in an amount equal to 44% of net income was paid out as dividends to common stockholders. As a general rule, if the investor's primary objective is the periodic cash

---

[4]Gyan Chandra, "Information Needs of Security Analysts," *Journal of Accountancy* (December 1975), p. 70.

return that can be expected on the dollars invested, a company with a high dividend payout is considered a superior stock investment to a company that retains a higher portion of earnings and, therefore, has a lower dividend payout. Of course, many factors affect the relationship between a company's net income and its cash dividends paid to stockholders for the same period of time. Normally, dividends paid are less than net income as companies retain assets generated by income activities for other uses. In fact, too high a dividend payout ratio may raise significant questions about the future of the enterprise.

These illustrations demonstrate the need for per-share measures that enhance the value of comparisons among enterprises. Although the examples are not comprehensive, they show how EPS figures may be used in comparing enterprises. Caution should be taken, however, when attempting to simplify the results of complex events and transactions into a single figure that is then used as a comparative tool. Many transactions and events influence the determination of net income and other items that appear in financial statements. Many judgments and estimates must be made when reporting these transactions and events. Finally, differences in business enterprises and the economic circumstances surrounding them must also be considered.

In summary, although financial figures and ratios may provide important input into an investment or other decision about an enterprise, they should be interpreted in light of the circumstances of the enterprise and the decision maker. This is true for EPS as well as many other measures that are commonly used to evaluate and compare business enterprises.

POTENTIAL DILUTION IN EPS

The general concept of allocating income to shares of common stock is relatively simple. In certain situations, however, the existence of convertible securities, rights to acquire stock, and obligations to distribute shares of stock under various arrangements may complicate the calculation of EPS. These situations create the *potential for a decline* in EPS if certain actions are taken. This **potential dilution** is of particular concern because it may result from actions over which the enterprise has no control. For example, if outstanding stock options allow the option holders to acquire shares of common stock at a fixed or determinable price, the potential for reduced EPS exists because the number of shares of common stock outstanding will increase if the options are exercised. Similarly, outstanding convertible bonds may permit holders to convert their bond investments into common stock, thereby increasing the number of shares of common stock outstanding. In the case of both stock options and convertible bonds, the company whose outstanding stock is potentially affected does not make the decision whether options are exercised or bonds are converted. Rather, the company relinquished that authority in an earlier transaction to the holder of the options or bonds. Arrangements such as stock options and convertible bonds are identified as **potentially dilutive securities,** or simply **potential diluters,** for purposes of computing EPS.

The capital structures of some corporations include potential diluters; others do not. For purposes of computing EPS, a **simple capital structure** is one that includes no potential diluters; a **complex capital structure** includes one or more potential diluters. The capital structures of many large corporations include several types of potential diluters. It is possible, however, for a large corporation to have no potential diluters. The distinction between a simple and a complex capital structure is based not on the size of the enterprise but on whether the capital structure includes arrangements that potentially dilute EPS.

The computation of EPS for companies with simple capital structures requires understanding the treatment of the claim on income of those securities that are senior to common stock, such as preferred stock, and understanding the number of shares of common stock necessary to compute EPS. These concepts are equally important for computing EPS figures for companies with complex capital structures. EPS of companies with complex capital structures is further complicated by potential diluters. These considerations are the subjects of the following sections. In all illustrations in the textbook and in the cases, exercises, and problems at the end of the chapter, the enterprises for which information is presented are assumed to be public companies that are required to present EPS figures in their financial statements.

The computation of EPS for a company with a simple capital structure is not affected by potential diluters. Two factors, however, may complicate this computation. First, the number of shares of common stock outstanding during the reporting period may change as a result of the sale of stock, treasury stock transactions, stock splits, stock dividends, and other stock transactions. The EPS computation is based on the *weighted average number of common shares outstanding during the period.* Second, the existence of preferred stock with a prior claim on income must be considered in determining the income allocable to common stock.

WEIGHTED AVERAGE NUMBER OF COMMON SHARES

The **weighted average number of common shares,** as used in computing EPS, is a representative number of shares of common stock outstanding during the accounting period, giving consideration to the length of time specific numbers of shares were actually outstanding. The most frequently encountered activities that change the number of outstanding shares are the sale of additional shares of common stock and treasury stock transactions. The sale of new shares of stock increases the number of outstanding shares; the acquisition of treasury stock decreases the number of outstanding shares; and the resale of treasury stock increases the number of outstanding shares.

To illustrate the determination of a weighted average, assume that Diamond Company reports a net income of $178,000 and that it has the following common stock activity during 1995:

	Stock Activity	Number of Shares Outstanding
Jan. 1	Common stock outstanding	100,000
Mar. 1	Sale of common stock	20,000
		120,000
July 1	Purchase of treasury stock	(5,000)
		115,000
Nov. 1	Sale of treasury stock	3,000
Dec. 31	Common stock outstanding	118,000

The weighted average number of common shares outstanding is computed by preparing a schedule in which the number of months is multiplied by the number of shares outstanding.[5] The Months × Shares figures are totaled and divided by 12 to determine the weighted average, as shown on the following page.

---

[5]An alternative method weights the various numbers of shares outstanding by multiplying each number by the length of time outstanding, with 12 months as the denominator of the fraction. For Diamond Company in 1995, this computation is as follows:

Number of Shares	Fraction of Year Outstanding	Weighted Average
100,000	$12/12$	100,000
20,000	$10/12$	16,667
(5,000)	$6/12$	(2,500)
3,000	$2/12$	500
		114,667

Period	Months	×	Shares Outstanding	=	Months × Shares
Jan. 1–Feb. 28	2		100,000		200,000
Mar. 1–June 30	4		120,000		480,000
July 1–Oct. 31	4		115,000		460,000
Nov. 1–Dec. 31	2		118,000		236,000
	12				1,376,000

$$1,376,000/12 = 114,667$$

EPS for 1995 is then computed as follows:

$$\text{EPS} = \frac{\$178,000}{114,667} = \$1.55$$

When the enterprise issues a stock dividend or a stock split during the accounting period, the number of shares outstanding prior to the issuance of the additional shares must be *restated to retroactively apply* the stock dividend or stock split. Remember that stock splits and stock dividends do *not* increase the total stockholders' investment in the corporation. They simply represent a *reallocation of the common stock investment over a larger number of shares of common stock*. Treating the stock dividend or stock split retroactively restates the common stock activity during the year in terms of the stock at the end of the year, *after* the stock dividend or stock split.

Continuing the example of Diamond Company, assume that in 1996 it reports a net income of $220,000 and had the following common stock activity:

	Stock Activity	Number of Shares Outstanding
Jan. 1	Common stock outstanding	118,000
Mar. 1	Sale of common stock	10,000
		128,000
July 1	Purchase of treasury stock	(5,000)
		123,000
Oct. 1	Distribution of 2:1 stock split	123,000
		246,000
Nov. 1	Purchase of treasury stock	(6,000)
Dec. 31	Common stock outstanding	240,000

The weighted average number of common shares outstanding is computed much like that in the previous example, except that the number of shares outstanding prior to the 2:1 stock split must be converted to the basis of the shares at the end of the year. This is done by multiplying the number of shares by 2, as illustrated below:

					Months × Shares		
Period	Months	×	Shares Outstanding	=	Original	× Stock Split Conversion	= Restated
Jan. 1–Feb. 28	2		118,000		236,000	2	472,000
Mar. 1–June 30	4		128,000		512,000	2	1,024,000
July 1–Sept. 30	3		123,000		369,000	2	738,000
Oct. 1–Oct. 31	1		246,000				246,000
Nov. 1–Dec. 31	2		240,000				480,000
	12						2,960,000

$$2,960,000/12 = 246,667$$

EPS for 1996 is then computed as follows:

$$\text{EPS} = \frac{\$220,000}{246,667} = \$.89$$

In this illustration, the stock split conversion factor, 2, is used because the increase in shares in a 2:1 split results in twice as many shares outstanding after the split as before. This factor is based on the specific distribution made. For example, if a 3:1 split is distributed, the factor is 3; if a 10% stock dividend is distributed, a stock dividend conversion factor of 1.10 is used. This adjustment is made only to those shares outstanding prior to the stock split or stock dividend because the share activity after that event is stated on an after-split or after-dividend basis.

Con Agra is a diversified, international food company that operates major businesses in branded grocery products. During the year ended May 31, 1992, the company engaged in the following activities that changed its number of outstanding shares of common stock:

- Sold shares in connection with employee stock option and incentive plans.
- Issued shares in connection with the acquisition of a subsidiary company.
- Converted a small number of shares of preferred stock into common stock.
- Purchased shares of treasury stock.
- Issued shares in a 3:2 stock split.

Although some of these activities are beyond the scope of our current discussion of computing the weighted average number of shares outstanding, they illustrate the many types of activities that companies engage in that change the number of outstanding shares and, thereby, complicate the determination of the weighted average. In calculating the weighted average, the 3:2 stock split was applied retroactively, as illustrated earlier.

PREFERRED STOCK

Certain securities have claims that must be satisfied before dividends may be paid on common stock. These securities are called **senior securities,** indicating their preferential rights over common stock.

Debt instruments are examples of senior securities, and the return to debt holders is deducted in determining net income. Preferred stock is also a senior security, but because net income accrues to *all* owners (stockholders) of the enterprise, dividends on preferred stock are *not* deducted in determining net income. Because EPS is a concept relating only to common stock, however, the numerator in the computation must be reduced by the return on all senior securities. Accordingly, net income as reported in the income statement is reduced by the dividends on preferred stock to obtain a "residual" income figure that represents the amount allocable only to common stockholders.

To illustrate, Walls Company reports net income of $2,700,000 for 1995 and has 2,300,000 weighted average number of shares of common stock outstanding for the year. In addition, the company has preferred stock outstanding throughout 1995 as follows: 1,000,000 shares, $12 par, 7% dividend rate. The preferred dividend of $840,000 (1,000,000 × $12 × 7%) is deducted from the reported net income in determining EPS, as follows:

$$\text{EPS} = \frac{\$2,700,000 - \$840,000}{2,300,000} = \$.81$$

If the company reports a net loss rather than a net income, the preferred dividend is subtracted from the net loss in computing a loss per share on common stock. To illustrate, Walls Company reports a net loss of $1,700,000 in 1996 and still has 2,300,000 outstanding shares of common stock and an $840,000 preferred dividend requirement. The 1996 *loss per share* is computed as follows:

$$\frac{\text{Loss per}}{\text{Share}} = \frac{\$(1,700,000) - \$840,000}{2,300,000} = \frac{\$(2,540,000)}{2,300,000} = \$(1.10)$$

Observe the following guidelines when adjusting the reported net income for preferred dividends. If the preferred stock is *cumulative,* the dividends are deducted from net income or net loss **whether or not they were declared.** If preferred dividends are *not cumulative,* only dividends **actually declared** are deducted from net income or net loss in computing EPS. Any dividends in arrears on cumulative preferred stock are not subtracted in determining the income that accrues to the common stockholders.

FINANCIAL STATEMENT PRESENTATION

Investors attach a great deal of importance to EPS figures and frequently evaluate them in conjunction with other information contained in the financial statements. Accordingly, EPS figures are prominently presented on the face of the income statement, and the presentation should be consistent with the income statement presentation in which the EPS figures are included.

To illustrate the income statement presentation of EPS, consider Longwood Company, which had 110,000 shares of common stock outstanding throughout 1996 and 95,000 shares throughout 1995. Dividends on the company's cumulative preferred stock amounted to $50,000 each year. The company's income statement shows net income of $230,500 in 1996 and $208,000 in 1995, with a $44,500 gain (net of $23,000 income tax) on the refunding of long-term debt in 1996. The income and EPS figures are presented in Exhibit 18–1.

EPS figures must be presented for each of the following if they appear in the income statement: income from continuing operations, income before extraordinary items, and net income. Additionally, various authoritative accounting pronouncements require disclosure of EPS either in the body of the income statement or in related notes for specific types of items. For example, EPS must be presented for the cumulative effect of a change in accounting principle and for an extraordinary gain or loss that results from extinguishment of debt.

Exhibit 18–2 is an example of the EPS presentation for a simple capital structure from the 1993 income statement of Phillips Petroleum Company, a company dedicated primarily to petroleum exploration, production, refining, and marketing. This exhibit includes only the lower portion of the income statement and the brief explanation of income per share of com-

EXHIBIT 18–1		
Longwood Company Partial Income Statement		
	1996	**1995**
Income before extraordinary items	$186,000	$208,000
Extraordinary item—Gain on refunding of long-term debt, net of $23,000 income tax	44,500	—
Net income	$230,500	$208,000
Earnings per common share:		
Income before extraordinary items	$1.24*	$1.66†
Extraordinary item	.40‡	—
Net income	$1.64§	$1.66

*($186,000 − $50,000)/110,000 shares = $1.24.
†($208,000 − $50,000)/95,000 shares = $1.66.
‡($44,500/110,000 shares = $.40.
§($230,500 − $50,000)/110,000 shares = $1.64.

EXHIBIT 18–2

Phillips Petroleum Company
EPS Disclosure—Simple Capital Structure

Income Statement Excerpt

	Millions of Dollars		
Years Ended December 31	1993	1992	1991
Income before Extraordinary Items and Cumulative			
Effect of Changes in Accounting Principles	245	270	98
Extraordinary items	(2)	(46)	213
Cumulative effect of changes in accounting principles	—	(44)	(53)
Net Income	$ **243**	180	258
Per Share of Common Stock			
Income before extraordinary items and cumulative			
effect of changes in accounting principles	$ **.94**	1.04	.38
Extraordinary items	**(.01)**	(.18)	.82
Cumulative effect of changes in accounting principles	—	(.17)	(.21)
Net Income	$ **.93**	.69	.99
Average Common Shares Outstanding (in thousands)	**261,015**	259,979	259,458

Accounting Policy Excerpt
Income per share of common stock—Income per share of common stock is calculated based upon the daily weighted average number of common shares outstanding during the year, including shares held by the company's Long-Term Stock Savings Plan (LTSSP).

SOURCE: Phillips Petroleum Company, 1993 Annual Report.

---

mon stock, which is included in the summary of significant accounting policies that follows the financial statements in the 1993 annual report. Notice that the EPS information follows the structure of the income statement with EPS figures presented for income before extraordinary items and cumulative effect of accounting change, extraordinary items, cumulative effect, and net income.

In complex capital structures, EPS may be reduced because of one or more potential diluters. Although numerous arrangements could result in the dilution of EPS, the following three classifications are commonly encountered:

1. **Stock options, warrants, and rights.** Arrangements whereby the holder has the right to purchase common stock in accordance with the terms of the agreement or instrument upon payment of a specified amount.
2. **Convertible securities.** Senior securities, such as convertible bonds and convertible preferred stock, that allow the holder to receive shares of common stock in exchange for the senior securities.
3. **Other contingent issuances.** Potential future issuances of common stock that may depend on the satisfaction of certain future conditions. Shares of common stock that a company may be required to issue in the future as a result of a past transaction or contractual agreement are examples of other contingent issuances.

In all of these cases, the potential exists for additional shares of common stock to be issued and EPS to be reduced as the net income is distributed over a larger number of common shares.

EPS COMPUTATIONS FOR COMPLEX CAPITAL STRUCTURES

DUAL EPS PRESENTATION

For public companies with complex capital structures, dual EPS may be necessary, incorporating the potentially dilutive impact of securities and arrangements such as stock options, warrants and rights, convertible securities, and other contingent issuances. The first EPS figure, commonly referred to as **primary EPS,** is based on the outstanding common stock and securities that are determined to be equivalent to common stock, known as **common stock equivalents.** The second presentation, called **fully diluted EPS,** reflects the dilution of EPS that would have taken place if the common stock represented by *all* potential diluters had been issued. Common stock equivalents and other potential diluters are ordinarily included in the calculation of EPS only if they reduce EPS (i.e., their effect is **dilutive**). If the effect of the assumed issuance of a potential diluter is **antidilutive** (i.e., results in an **increase** in EPS or a reduction in loss per share) in a particular accounting period, the shares are *not included in the EPS computations of that period*. Also, as we shall see later in this chapter,

Materiality   immaterial amounts of dilution are not presented.

Potential diluters, therefore, are of two types: common stock equivalents and others. The relationship of this distinction to the dual presentation of EPS is depicted in Exhibit 18–3. The distinction between potential diluters that are common stock equivalents and those that are not is extremely important, because it determines which securities are treated as common stock when computing primary EPS.

At this point, we can more precisely define several terms introduced previously.

1. **Potential diluters.** Arrangements under which an enterprise *may* be required to issue shares of common stock in the future.

Substance over Form   2. **Common stock equivalents.** Potential diluters which, because of the terms of their issuance, are treated substantially *the same as* common stock. Although a common stock equivalent is not common stock in form, it derives a large portion of its value from its common stock characteristics.

3. **Primary EPS.** The amount of income attributable to each share of common stock outstanding and common stock equivalent.

4. **Fully diluted EPS.** The amount of income per common share, reflecting the maximum dilution that would result from conversions, exercises, and other contingent issuances of common stock that would have individually decreased earnings per share.

Substance over Form   In Chapter 2, we discussed the modifying convention of substance over form. We stated that when an apparent difference exists between the economic substance of an item and its legal form, accountants emphasize the economic substance. The application of this concept is evident in computing EPS when potential dilution is included. In form, potential diluters are not outstanding common stock. They are convertible bonds, stock options, and other arrangements that *may* result in additional shares of outstanding common stock in the future. In substance, however, management in such cases usually expects to eventually increase the

---

EXHIBIT 18–3

Relationship of Potential Diluters to EPS Figures

Potential Diluters		Resulting EPS Figures
Common stock equivalents that individually reduce EPS	→ Combined with outstanding common stock →	Primary EPS
All potential diluters (including common stock equivalents) that individually reduce EPS	→ Combined with outstanding common stock →	Fully diluted EPS

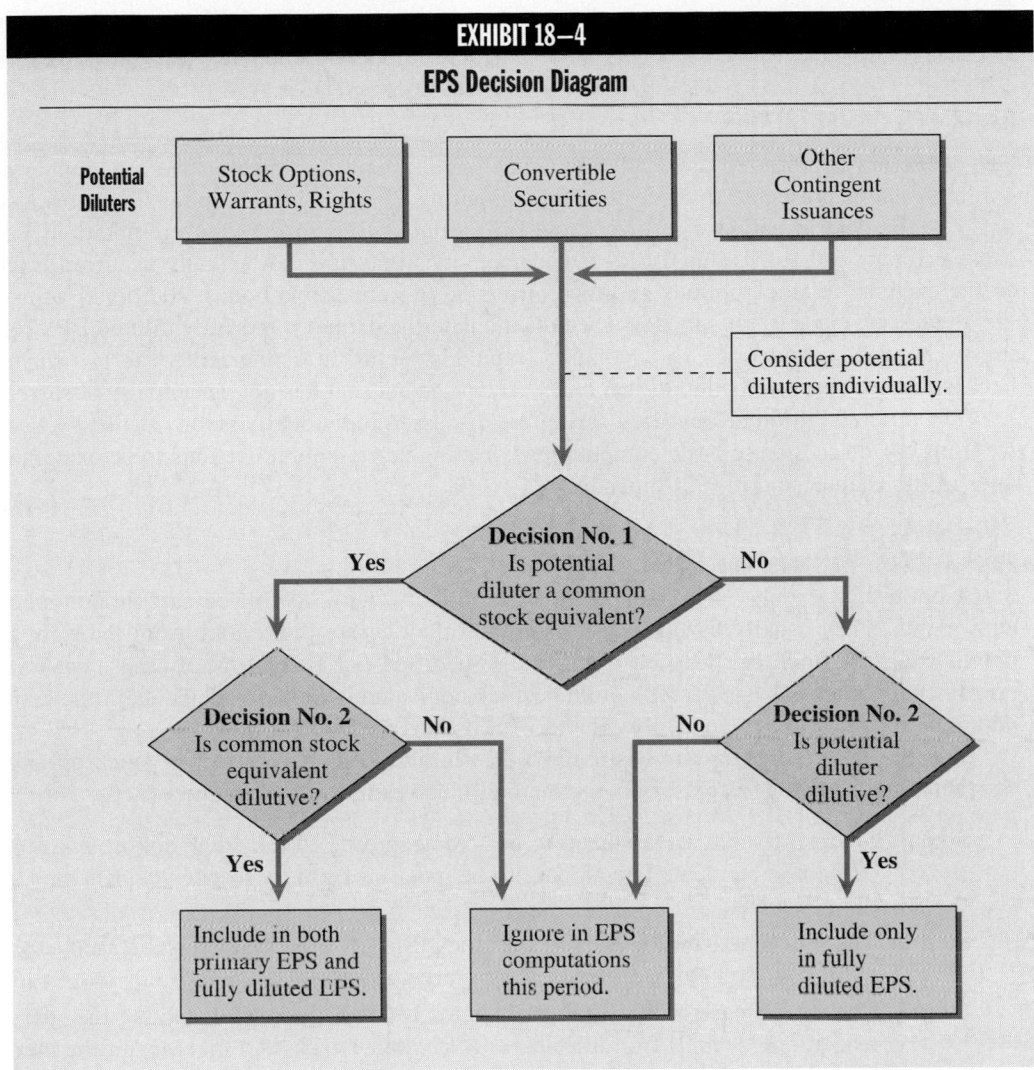

EXHIBIT 18–4

EPS Decision Diagram

Potential Diluters

Stock Options, Warrants, Rights

Convertible Securities

Other Contingent Issuances

Consider potential diluters individually.

Decision No. 1
Is potential diluter a common stock equivalent?

Yes

No

Decision No. 2
Is common stock equivalent dilutive?

No

No

Decision No. 2
Is potential diluter dilutive?

Yes

Yes

Include in both primary EPS and fully diluted EPS.

Ignore in EPS computations this period.

Include only in fully diluted EPS.

number of shares of common stock outstanding. Assuming that certain conditions are met, we anticipate an increase in outstanding shares by conservatively stating EPS at the lower figure that would have resulted if the outstanding shares had already been increased.   **Conservatism**

The treatment of the potential diluters and the resulting dual EPS presentation are summarized in Exhibit 18–4.[6]

Two major decisions must be made about each potential diluter. First, we must decide whether the potential diluter is a common stock equivalent. This decision determines whether the potential diluter will be considered in computing both primary and fully diluted EPS or only in fully diluted EPS. Second, we must decide whether the potential diluter is dilutive in the current accounting period. This decision must be made each time a company computes EPS in the context of the income or loss and the outstanding shares for that accounting period. *A potential diluter may be dilutive in one period but not in another.*

---

[6]The model in Exhibit 18–4 presents an overview of the decision-making process required to develop the primary and fully diluted EPS figures. In certain circumstances, exceptions to this general process exist. Several of these exceptions are covered later in this chapter.

The outcome of this second decision determines whether the potential diluter will be used in the EPS computations for the specific accounting period under consideration.

BASIC EPS COMPUTATIONS

The deduction of preferred dividends and the computation of the weighted average number of common shares presented in the section on computing EPS for simple capital structures also apply to the determination of primary and fully diluted EPS in the dual presentation. Because primary and fully diluted EPS include activities that have not actually occurred, such as the exercise of stock options and the conversion of convertible bonds, additional adjustments must be made to the numbers used to calculate the primary and fully diluted EPS figures. The EPS calculations in a complex capital structure are referred to as *pro forma* because they incorporate dilution that *might* take place but that has not yet actually occurred.

The potential diluters identified earlier are discussed individually below. In this section, we limit our discussion to basic computations, leaving certain complications to be explained later in the chapter and in the Appendix.

Stock Options, Warrants, and Rights

Stock options, warrants, and rights are, by definition, *always* identified as common stock equivalents. They usually have no cash yield, and they derive their value from the right to obtain common stock at specified prices for a specified period of time. Because such arrangements are always considered common stock equivalents, they are elements in the computation of both primary and fully diluted EPS if they are dilutive.

The **treasury stock method** is used to determine the dilutive effect of stock options, warrants, and rights. The treasury stock method involves the following three steps:

Step 1. Shares of stock are assumed to be sold according to the stock option, warrant, or right agreement. The amount to be received from these sales is identified as the **proceeds.**

Step 2. The proceeds from the sale of the stock (Step 1) are assumed to be used to acquire common stock at the existing market price.

Step 3. The net increase in the number of shares is determined by deducting the shares reacquired (Step 2) from the shares sold (Step 1): The *net increase* in the number of shares is added to the outstanding common shares.

This series of computations deals with **hypothetical** (assumed) transactions. The sale-of-stock assumption in Step 1 is followed by an assumption about the way the company uses the proceeds from the sale. In Step 2, we assume that shares of stock were reacquired from the market. The assumed *net* increase, computed in Step 3, is then used in the EPS computations. The treasury stock method gets its name from the basic assumption that underlies the method, namely, that the company will obtain the needed shares of common stock by acquiring *treasury stock.*

The number of shares outstanding will increase only if the market price used in Step 2 exceeds the price in Step 1 at which the holders of options, warrants, or rights can acquire stock (i.e., the exercise price). In this case, the number of shares sold will be more than the number repurchased, resulting in an increase in the number of shares outstanding. If the market price were *less than* the exercise price, the assumed exercise would be illogical, because the holder of the option, warrant, or right could purchase the stock at a lower price from the market without using the option, warrant, or right. Moreover, it would also be **antidilutive,** because the number of shares sold would be less than the number reacquired. In this case, the outstanding shares would be reduced, resulting in an increased EPS.

To illustrate the treasury stock method, assume that Palmer Company has 600,000 shares of common stock outstanding through 1996 and reported a net income of $282,500 for the year. In 1995 the company issued 100,000 options to acquire common stock in the company at the par value of $50. No options have been exercised by the end of 1996. The market price of the stock throughout 1996 was $60. No other potential diluters exist.

Remember that the stock options are common stock equivalents by definition. Also note that the options are dilutive because the market price of $60 exceeds the exercise price of $50. We know that when we apply the treasury stock method, more shares will be sold (at $50) than can be repurchased (at $60). In addition, because options are the only potential diluter and they are common stock equivalents, primary and fully diluted EPS will be the same.

The application of the treasury stock method in this situation indicates a net increase of 16,667 in the number of common shares:[7]

Step 1. One hundred thousand shares assumed sold at $50 equals $5,000,000 of proceeds.

Step 2. Five million dollars used to buy stock at $60 results in the reacquisition of 83,333 shares ($5,000,000/$60).

Step 3. Number of shares sold (100,000) exceeds the number of shares repurchased (83,333) by 16,667.

Primary and fully diluted EPS are computed as follows:

$$\text{Primary and Fully Diluted EPS} = \frac{\$282,500}{600,000 + 16,667} = \$.46$$

If options, warrants, and rights are outstanding for only part of the financial reporting period, the incremental number of shares identified by the treasury stock method is weighted for the length of time they were outstanding. For example, in the above illustration, if the options had been issued on May 1, 1996, and Palmer Company reported on a calendar-year basis, the equivalent number of shares would be 11,111, because the common stock equivalents were outstanding for only $\frac{8}{12}$ of the year:

$$\text{Common Equivalent Shares} = 16,667 \times \frac{8}{12} = 11,111$$

What market price is used in applying the treasury stock method when the price changes during the financial reporting period? In the previous illustration, we assumed a single market price of $60. Now we assume that $60 is the average market price for the year 1996 but

---

[7]A short-cut method for computing the number of shares that results from the application of the treasury stock method uses the following formula:

$$I = \left[\frac{M - E}{M}\right]N$$

where I = Incremental Number of Shares
M = Market Price per Share
E = Exercise Price per Share
N = Number of Shares Obtainable

Applying this formula to the information presented for Palmer Company, we compute the incremental number of shares obtained from the treasury stock method as follows:

$$I = \left[\frac{\$60 - \$50}{\$60}\right]100,000$$

$$I = 16,667$$

that the ending market price is a different figure. In computing **primary** EPS, we use the average market price in applying the treasury stock method to determine the dilutive effect of stock options, warrants, and rights. If the market price at the end of the accounting period is *higher than the average,* however, we use the higher (ending) figure for computing **fully diluted** EPS.

To understand the impact of this difference, recall the assumptions that underlie the treasury stock method. First, we assume that shares were sold to holders of stock options, warrants, and rights at the prices established by those agreements. Next, we assume that the company used the proceeds from this sale to acquire treasury stock. Keep in mind that the higher the market price, the fewer shares we are able to obtain with the fixed amount of money acquired from the assumed sale of shares. Finally, we determine the net increase in the number of shares of common stock outstanding that results from the sale of shares and the subsequent reacquisition of treasury shares. The **higher** the market price used to determine the number of shares that can be reacquired, the **fewer** shares will be bought. Likewise, the **fewer** shares bought, the **higher** the net increase in the number of outstanding shares and the **greater** the dilution in EPS when those shares are incorporated into the EPS calculations.

For example, in the illustration of Palmer Company, we assume that the average market price was $60 but the market price at the end of the accounting period was $95. Also, we will return to the assumption that the options were issued in 1995 and were therefore outstanding throughout 1996. Primary EPS is $.46 as computed earlier. Fully diluted EPS is $.44, however, because the use of the $95 ending market price results in a greater assumed dilution:

Step 1. One hundred thousand shares assumed sold at $50 equals $5,000,000 proceeds.

Step 2. Five million dollars used to buy stock at $95 results in the reacquisition of 52,632 shares ($5,000,000/$95).

Step 3. Number of shares sold (100,000) exceeds the number of shares repurchased (52,632) by 47,368.

$$\text{Fully Diluted EPS} = \frac{\$282,500}{600,000 + 47,368} = \$.44$$

If the ending market price of the stock is **equal to or less than** the average for the period, the average price is used to compute both primary and fully diluted EPS. In this procedure, the emphasis is on conservatism in computing EPS figures, because EPS will always be the lowest possible figure, given the assumptions of the treasury stock method.

Conservatism

In the illustrations of the treasury stock method above, we used the average market price in computing EPS, except when the higher ending market price was used in computing fully diluted EPS. The average market price might exceed the exercise price of stock options, warrants, or rights, but the market price *at the end of the period* might be below the exercise price. In this situation, the assumption that the options, warrants, and rights are exercised is not logical, because the holders could acquire shares at a lower price without the option, warrant, and right. To cover this situation, the APB determined that the assumption that stock options, warrants, and rights have been exercised should not be reflected in EPS calculations until the market price of the stock has been above the exercise price for substantially all of the last three months of the period for which EPS is being computed.[8]

The application of the treasury stock method, as we have used it here, is limited to situations in which no more than 20% of the outstanding common stock can be reacquired with

---

[8]*APB Opinion No. 15,* par. 36. If stock options, warrants, and rights are issued during the last three months of the accounting period, this stipulation is usually interpreted to mean the last three months of the period or the length of time outstanding, if shorter.

the assumed proceeds of the exercise of stock options, warrants, and rights. When the proceeds are so great that more than 20% of the outstanding stock can be acquired, a modification must be made in the application of the method. This procedure is covered in the appendix to this chapter.

Convertible Securities

Convertible securities are considered common stock equivalents if the return to the holder at the time of issuance is significantly less than the return on a comparable security without the conversion privilege. As we discussed in Chapter 15, convertible securities are complex hybrid securities that incorporate elements of more than one type of debt or ownership interest. The logic behind the treatment of convertible securities as common stock equivalents when there is a significant reduction in return is that investors' willingness to accept the reduced return to obtain the conversion privilege signifies that the conversion privilege has substantial value and, therefore, the value of the convertible security depends to a large extent on the value of common stock.

How could we determine that an investor was sacrificing a significant amount of return to acquire a security with a conversion feature? Ideally, we would compare the return on the convertible security with the return on an identical security in all respects *except* that it was not convertible. This is impractical, however, because the convertible security is not available without the conversion feature.

In its *Opinion No. 15,* the APB sought to achieve a degree of uniformity in making this important decision by stating that a convertible security was a common stock equivalent if its **cash yield**[9] at the date of issuance was *less than two-thirds of the bank prime interest rate at that date.* If this test was met, the convertible security would be treated as if conversion had already taken place for purposes of computing both primary and fully diluted EPS. If this test was not met, the convertible security would be treated as if conversion had taken place only in computing fully diluted EPS. An important feature of this test is that the classification of a convertible security is made only once—when the security is issued. This classification remains with the convertible security as long as it is outstanding and is not changed as market conditions that might affect the desirability of the conversion feature fluctuate.

Accountants criticized several aspects of this classification method, especially the use of the bank prime interest rate (a measure of the short-term borrowing cost of financially strong companies) for classifying long-term securities for purposes of computing EPS. In 1982 the FASB issued its *Statement of Financial Accounting Standards No. 55,*[10] which changed the standard for this evaluation from the bank prime interest rate to the average Aa corporate bond yield. The FASB noted that since *APB Opinion No. 15* was issued in 1968, the bank prime interest rate had become more volatile and a high degree of correlation between the bank prime interest rate, and the rates of return on long-term debt and preferred stock no longer existed. In a subsequent change, the FASB replaced the "cash yield" test with an "effective yield" test.[11] This change was made in response to problems encountered in applying the cash yield test to zero coupon convertible bonds, instruments that do not pay any interest

---

[9]The **cash yield** on a convertible bond is the effective interest rate, determined by adjusting the nominal interest rate for any premium or discount resulting from sale of the bond. This is computed by dividing the annual interest by the market price of the bond at the date of issuance. The cash yield on a preferred stock is the effective return, determined by dividing the stated dividend amount by the selling price of the stock.

[10]*FASB Statement of Financial Accounting Standards No. 55,* "Determining Whether a Convertible Security Is a Common Stock Equivalent," 1982.

[11]*FASB Statement of Financial Accounting Standards No. 85,* "Yield Test for Determining Whether a Convertible Security Is a Common Stock Equivalent," 1985.

EXHIBIT 18–5		
Aa Corporate Bond Yield Rule		
Aa corporate bond yield	12%	Convertible securities with an effective yield in this range *are not common stock equivalents.*
⅔ × 12%	8%	
Less than 8%		Convertible securities with an effective yield in this range *are common stock equivalents.*

until maturity. Under the previous cash yield test, these instruments would always be common stock equivalents due to the lack of any periodic cash yield.

Summarizing the previous discussion, under current accounting standards, a convertible security is a common stock equivalent if its *effective yield* is less than two-thirds of the *Aa corporate bond yield* at the date of issuance. This relationship is depicted in Exhibit 18–5, using a 12% Aa corporate bond yield as an example.

In selecting the average Aa corporate bond yield over the bank prime interest rate for purposes of applying this test, the FASB was influenced by the relationship of the bank prime interest rate to short-term securities and the Aa corporate bond yield to long-term securities. For example, the board cites the fact that in recent years, the United States and some other countries have experienced an inverted yield curve in which short-term interest rates have exceeded long-term rates.[12] In applying the two-thirds test, the FASB intends Aa to refer to bonds of equal quality to those rated Aa by either Moody's or Standard & Poor's. Aa bonds are defined by those organizations as bonds of high quality, issued by companies with a strong capacity to pay interest and repay principal. The average Aa bond yield should be based on bond yields for a brief period of time, such as one week preceding the date of issuance of the security being tested.

The changes in the two-thirds rule as a result of *FASB Statements Nos. 55* and *85* do not change any other aspect of the procedure. The classification is still made at the date of issuance and is not changed thereafter. In applying the two-thirds test in this textbook, including the cases, exercises, and problems at the end of the chapter, we use figures for the Aa corporate bond yield that do not necessarily reflect actual yield rates for the year specified. Also, we typically assume that the security's nominal interest rate is its effective yield.

Convertible Bonds.   To incorporate convertible securities into the EPS computations, the **"if converted" method** is applied. Under this method, convertible securities are assumed to have been converted at the beginning of the accounting period or at their date of issuance, if later. The interest (after income taxes) that would not have been paid if the security had been converted must be considered in addition to the increased number of shares of common stock that would have been outstanding. This procedure recognizes that the holders of senior securities cannot share in distributions of earnings that apply to common stock without first relinquishing their rights to the senior securities.

Because the "if converted" method results in an adjustment to both the numerator and the denominator of the EPS computation, it may not be immediately obvious whether the assumed conversion is dilutive. In such cases, EPS must be computed with and without the assumed conversion to determine whether the conversion will reduce EPS. This procedure is illustrated in the following example.

---

[12]*FASB Statement of Financial Accounting Standards No. 55,* par. 5.

Martin Company calculates EPS for 1996, without considering any potential dilution, as $2.50. This was correctly determined by dividing the $10,000,000 net income by the weighted average number of common shares outstanding, 4,000,000. However, the company has $5,000,000 par value of convertible bonds that were sold in 1995 at par and yield an 8% interest rate. The bonds are convertible into 50 shares of common stock per $1,000 bond. The Aa corporate bond yield when the bonds were issued was 11%; the company's income tax rate is 35%.

The first step is to determine whether the potential diluter is a common stock equivalent. Because the yield (8%) is greater than two-thirds of the Aa corporate bond yield at the date of issuance (11% $\times$ $\frac{2}{3}$ = 7.3%), we conclude that the security is *not a common stock equivalent.* Therefore, the assumed dilution will be incorporated only into the fully diluted EPS computation.

Next, the numbers to incorporate the effect of the conversion into the EPS figures are accumulated as follows:

Numerator Adjustment

Reduction in interest expense ($5,000,000 $\times$ 8%)	$ 400,000
Increase in income tax expense ($400,000 $\times$ 35%)	(140,000)
Increase in net income	$ 260,000

Denominator Adjustment

Number of shares of common stock (5,000 bonds $\times$ 50 shares of common stock per bond)	250,000

The bonds are convertible into 250,000 shares of common stock. If converted, Martin would incur $400,000 less interest expense, but because the interest is income tax deductible, it would incur $140,000 in additional income tax. The *net* savings is $260,000. This can be computed directly by multiplying the interest savings by 1 minus the income tax rate:

$$\text{Increase in Income} = (\text{Interest Savings}) \times (1 - \text{Income Tax Rate})$$
$$- (\$5,000,000 \times 8\%) \times (1 - .35)$$
$$= (\$400,000) \times (.65)$$
$$= \$260,000$$

Because the convertible bond is not a common stock equivalent, the EPS as originally computed by the company represents primary EPS:

$$\text{Primary EPS} = \frac{\$10,000,000}{4,000,000} = \$2.50$$

Fully diluted EPS is computed by incorporating the assumed conversion of the convertible bond into the above computation:

$$\text{Fully Diluted EPS} = \frac{\$10,000,000 + \$260,000}{4,000,000 + 250,000} = \$2.41$$

The assumed conversion of the bond is dilutive in this case, because it reduces EPS from $2.50 to $2.41.

A useful shortcut for testing dilution is to compute a **dilution index** by dividing the adjustment to the numerator by the adjustment to the denominator. In this case, the dilution index is $1.04 ($260,000/250,000). If this index is *less than EPS without considering dilution,* as it is in this case, the potential diluter is dilutive because its inclusion will reduce

EPS. The dilution index is compared with EPS assuming no dilution each time EPS is computed, because the numbers representing both the net income and the weighted average number of common shares outstanding may change from period to period. The dilution index may be used in all cases in which potential diluters result in adjustments to both the numerator and the denominator in EPS calculations.

If convertible securities are outstanding during only part of the period for which EPS figures are being calculated, the adjustments to both the numerator and denominator are weighted for the length of time the securities were actually outstanding. For example, if the convertible bonds in the previous example had been issued on March 1, 1996, and we assume that Martin reports on a calendar-year basis, the bonds were outstanding only $^{10}/_{12}$ of the year. Both the numerator and denominator are weighted accordingly and fully diluted EPS is calculated as follows:

$$\text{Fully Diluted EPS} = \frac{\$10,000,000 + \$216,667^*}{4,000,000 + 208,333^\dagger} = \$2.43$$

$^*\$260,000 \times {}^{10}/_{12} = \$216,667$
$^\dagger\$250,000 \times {}^{10}/_{12} = 208,333$ shares

In the example in this section, we have assumed that only one convertible security was present and we used a simplified dilution index to test for dilution. In situations in which multiple convertible securities are present, an additional complexity is introduced that requires a modification of the dilution index approach discussed earlier. This complexity is briefly discussed and illustrated in the Appendix of this chapter.

In disclosing information about earnings per share figures, some companies discuss considerable detail about such things as the "if converted" method. For example, AMR Corporation (American Airlines) indicates in its 1992 annual report that its convertible debt is not a common stock equivalent and, therefore, is included only in fully diluted earnings per share and then only if the effects of such inclusion are dilutive. The note goes on to explain that earnings applicable to common shares are increased to reflect the elimination of interest (less tax effect) on the convertible debt.

Convertible Preferred Stock.   Preferred stock plays a dual role in EPS computations when it is a potential diluter. On the one hand, preferred stock is a senior security for purposes of computing EPS. On the other hand, preferred stock that is convertible into common stock is a potential diluter that must be treated like a convertible security in computing primary EPS and fully diluted EPS.

In computing EPS without dilution, net income is reduced by the dividend on preferred stock, as illustrated earlier. If the preferred stock is convertible, however, the dividend is added back to net income, and the equivalent number of common shares is added to the weighted average number of common shares outstanding. This procedure is similar to the way we treated convertible bonds, with one exception. Interest on the bonds is income tax deductible, and the exclusion of interest expense results in increased income taxes. This is the reason we adjusted net income for the reduced interest expense, net of the income tax effects. Dividends that a company pays on its preferred stock are *not tax deductible*. Therefore, when the numerator in the EPS computation is adjusted for preferred dividends, the adjustment is for the full amount of those dividends and is not reduced by an income tax adjustment.

To illustrate the "if converted" method for convertible preferred stock, we use the case of Amsler Company, which reports a $5,000,000 net income for 1996 and has 500,000 shares of common stock outstanding the entire year. In addition, 100,000 shares of $100 par value, 9%, cumulative preferred stock are outstanding. Each share of preferred stock may be converted into two shares of common stock. The preferred stock was sold in 1989 at par value when the Aa corporate bond yield was 10%.

In this situation, the preferred stock is *not* a common stock equivalent, because its yield of 9% (the same as the nominal dividend rate because the stock sold at par) is higher than two-thirds of the Aa corporate bond yield at issuance (10% × ⅔ = 6.7%). EPS without assuming dilution, also primary EPS in this case, is computed by subtracting the preferred dividend in the numerator and dividing by the 500,000 shares of common stock outstanding:

$$\begin{matrix} \text{Primary EPS} \\ \text{(Also EPS without} \\ \text{Dilution)} \end{matrix} = \frac{\$5,000,000 - (9\% \times \$100 \times 100,000)}{500,000} = \$8.20$$

Fully diluted EPS is computed by adding back the preferred dividend in the numerator and adding the increased number of common shares to the figures in the primary EPS computation. Because the preferred dividend is the $900,000 subtracted above (9% × $100 × 100,000), we are simply returning to the $5,000,000 net income figure. The increased number of common shares that would result from the conversion of the preferred is 200,000 (100,000 shares of preferred × 2). Fully diluted EPS is computed as follows:

$$\text{Fully Diluted EPS} = \frac{\$5,000,000}{500,000 + 200,000} = \$7.14$$

As with convertible bonds, a dilution index can be computed to help determine whether the conversion is dilutive. Here the index is $4.50 ($900,000/200,000). Because this is less than EPS without considering dilution ($8.20), the conversion is dilutive.

Other Contingent Issuances

Other contingent issuances represent potential future distributions of common stock that may depend on the satisfaction of certain future conditions. If the shares to be issued depend merely on the passage of time or are issuable upon the attainment of certain conditions and those conditions are already met, the shares are included in computing both primary and fully diluted EPS. Shares awaiting issuance in a stock dividend are an example of a contingent issuance that is included in both primary and fully diluted EPS because the distribution depends only on the passage of time.

Other contingent issuances may occur only when certain future conditions are met, such as attaining a specified level of income. Such issuances are sometimes encountered in business combinations. If attaining a stated level of income is a condition for issuance of common stock and that condition is not currently met, the contingent shares are not common stock equivalents and, therefore, are included only in fully diluted EPS. For this computation, earnings are adjusted to include the higher level of income specified in the agreement. As in the case of all potential diluters, shares in a contingent issuance should not be included in primary or fully diluted EPS unless their effect is dilutive. Also, if the contingent issuance arose during the accounting period for which EPS is being computed, the figures are weighted for the appropriate length of time.

To illustrate, Sarasota, Inc., had 1,000,000 shares of common stock outstanding throughout 1996, a year in which the company reported a net income of $3,250,000. Dividends of $92,500 on noncumulative preferred stock were declared and paid during the year. Under the terms of a business combination of a previous year, the company is required to issue 500,000 additional shares of common stock if the net income reaches $4,000,000 and is maintained at that level between the year of the business combination and the end of 1999. This condition had not been met through 1996.

Primary EPS is computed without considering the contingent issuance resulting from the business combination, because the condition for issuance has not been met. Primary EPS is thus computed by reducing net income by the preferred dividend and dividing by the number of shares of common stock.

$$\text{Primary EPS} = \frac{\$3,250,000 - \$92,500}{1,000,000} = \$3.16$$

The computation of fully diluted EPS considers the impact of the contingent issuance, including the increase in income that must be achieved, if the contingent issuance is dilutive. In this case, dilution results, because the increases in the numerator and in the denominator result in an index below $3.16:

	Increase in Income
Required income for distribution	$4,000,000
1996 income	3,250,000
Incremental income required	$ 750,000
Increased number of shares	500,000
Dilution index ($750,000/500,000)	$1.50

Fully diluted EPS is computed as follows:

$$\text{Fully diluted EPS} = \frac{\$3,250,000 - \$92,500 + \$750,000}{1,000,000 + 500,000} = \$2.61$$

We have now seen how the questions of whether a security is a common stock equivalent and whether it is dilutive are answered for three types of potential diluters. A summary of these important decisions is found in Exhibit 18–6.

THREE PERCENT MINIMUM DILUTION PRESENTED

Companies with complex capital structures usually make the dual presentation of primary and fully diluted EPS in their income statements. As a practical matter, the dual presentation is required only if the aggregate dilution of all potential diluters is at least 3%. To assess

---

EXHIBIT 18–6
Summary of EPS Decisions

Potential Diluters	*Decision No. 1:* Is Potential Diluter a Common Stock Equivalent (CSE)?	*Decision No. 2:* Does Potential Diluter Reduce EPS?
Stock options, warrants, rights	Always CSE.	Application of the treasury stock method results in dilution if the market price of the stock exceeds the exercise price.
Convertible securities	CSE if the effective yield is less than two-thirds of the Aa corporate bond yield at the date of issuance. (If yield is equal to or exceeds this level, not CSE.)	Must be tested by computing EPS with and without assumed conversion.
Other contingent issuances	CSE if issuance depends only on passage of time or if conditions necessary for issuance are currently being met. (Not CSE if conditions necessary for issuance are not being met.)	Must be tested by computing EPS with and without assumed issuance of stock.

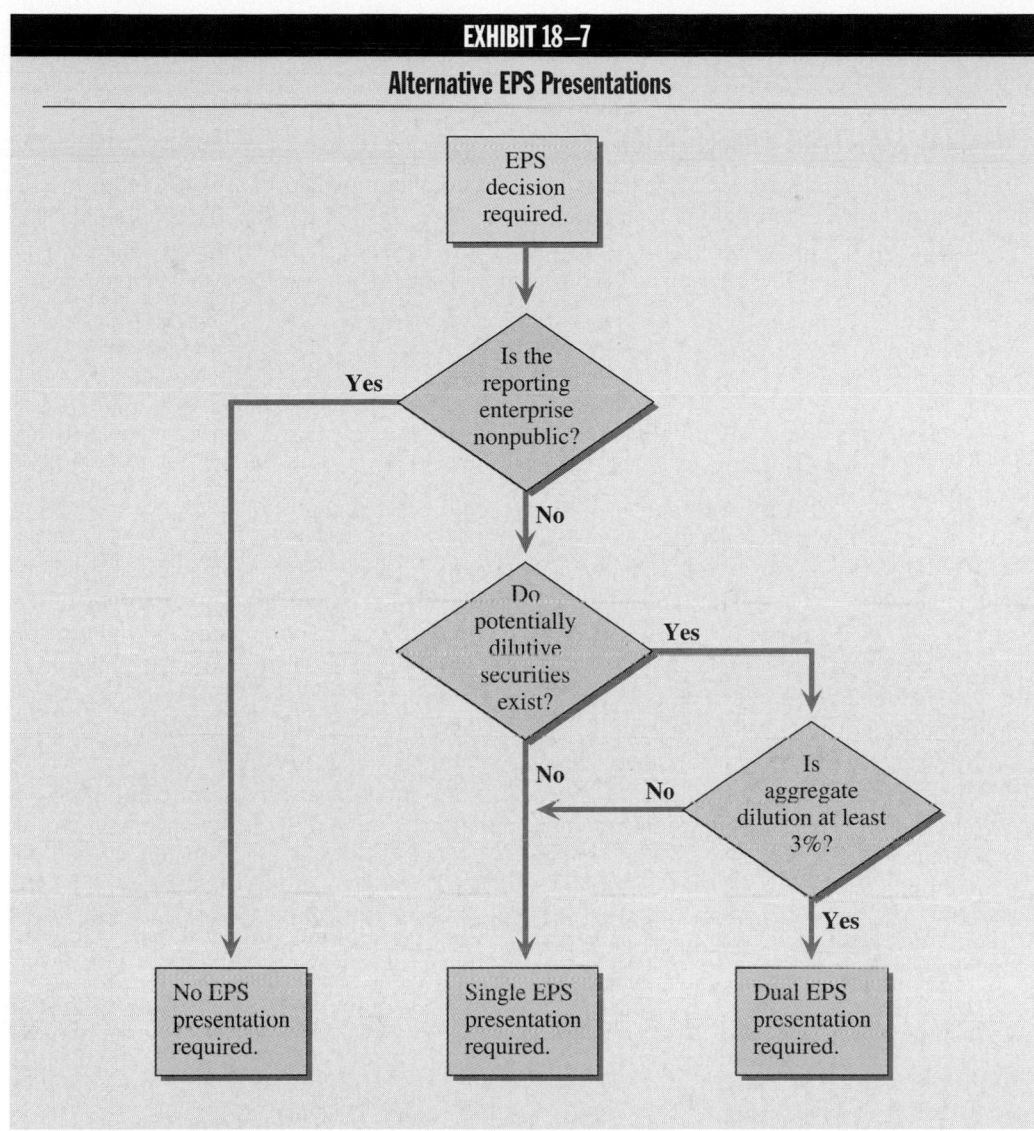

EXHIBIT 18–7

Alternative EPS Presentations

whether aggregate dilution is 3% or greater, *EPS assuming no dilution* is compared with *EPS assuming full dilution*. If the latter is 97% or less of the former, the test is met and primary and fully diluted EPS are required. The impact of the 3% test on the type of EPS presentation required is illustrated in Exhibit 18–7.

To illustrate this test, EPS assuming no dilution for Pepper Company is $1.85 for 1996. To report dual EPS, fully diluted EPS must be $1.79 (97% × $1.85) or less. For example, if the company's fully diluted EPS is $1.54, the dual presentation is required. On the other hand, if fully diluted EPS is computed to be $1.82, the 3% dilution test is not met and the dual presentation need not be made. In the latter case, EPS might be presented as follows:

Earnings per common share (no material potential dilution) $1.85

The 3% minimum dilution test is a practical application of the modifying convention of materiality. We do not further complicate the financial statements with the dual EPS figures   **Materiality** unless the dollar impact is significant. The 3% materiality standard used here is solely for purposes of presenting EPS. A similar standard for materiality in other situations is not implied by the use of 3% in the case of EPS.

FINANCIAL STATEMENT PRESENTATION

Primary and *fully diluted EPS* are terms used for computational purposes to determine the numbers to be presented in the income statement. The APB did not specify titles to identify EPS figures in the income statement. As you review financial statements, you will find that some companies use these terms and other companies use terms such as the following:

Situation	Primary EPS Concept	Fully Diluted EPS Concept
No common stock equivalents	Earnings per common share— assuming no dilution	Earnings per common share— assuming full dilution
With common stock equivalents	Earnings per common and common equivalent share	Earnings per common share— assuming full dilution

Note that these designations vary, depending on whether the capital structure of the company includes common stock equivalents.

Disclosure   In addition to disclosure in the income statement, disclosure in the notes to the financial statements is made to explain the rights and privileges of the holders of potentially dilutive securities, the bases on which primary and fully diluted EPS are computed, and other information necessary for an understanding of the EPS figures. Such information includes dividend and liquidation preferences, participating rights, call prices and dates, conversion or exercise prices or rates and dates, sinking fund requirements, and unusual voting rights.

In discussing the financial statement presentation of EPS for companies with simple capital structures, we stated that EPS figures are presented on income from continuing operations, income before extraordinary items, and net income, if these items appear in the income statement. For complex capital structures, potential diluters are included in the EPS computations on all of these income figures if they are dilutive in any one of the income figures. This is true even if they are *antidilutive* in one or both of the other income figures.

To illustrate this possibility, we assume that Barron Company reports the following items in its 1996 income statement:

Income before extraordinary item	$ 28,500,000
Extraordinary loss	(37,900,000)
Net loss	$ (9,400,000)

The company has 10,000,000 shares of common stock outstanding and no preferred stock. Applying the treasury stock method to outstanding stock options results in 1,000,000 common stock equivalent shares. This situation is dilutive for purposes of computing EPS on income before extraordinary items but antidilutive for purposes of computing EPS on net loss, as we see below:

	EPS without Dilution	EPS with Dilution
Income before extraordinary items		
$28,500,000/10,000,000 shares	$2.85	
$28,500,000/11,000,000 shares		$2.59
Net loss		
$(9,400,000)/10,000,000 shares	$(.94)	
$(9,400,000)/11,000,000 shares		$(.85)

The assumed exercise of the options is **antidilutive** in the net loss situation because it spreads the loss over a larger number of shares, thereby resulting in a *smaller loss per share*.

EXHIBIT 18–8

Unisys Corporation
EPS Disclosure—Complex Capital Structure

Income Statement Excerpt

Year ended December 31 (Millions, except per share data)	1993	1992	1991
Income (loss) before extraordinary items ** and changes in accounting principles**	**361.6**	296.2	(1,393.3)
Extraordinary items	**(26.4)**	65.0	
Effect of changes in accounting principles	**230.2**		
Net income (loss)	**565.4**	361.2	(1,393.3)
Dividends on preferred shares	**121.6**	122.1	121.2
Earnings (loss) on common shares	**$443.8**	$239.1	$(1,514.5)
Earnings (loss) per common share Primary			
Before extraordinary items and changes in accounting principles	**$ 1.46**	$ 1.06	$ (9.37)
Extraordinary items	**(.16)**	.40	
Effect of changes in accounting principles	**1.39**		
Total	**$ 2.69**	$ 1.46	$ (9.37)
Fully diluted Before extraordinary items and changes in accounting principles	**$ 1.48**	$ 1.04	$ (9.37)
Extraordinary items	**(.11)**	.36	
Effect of changes in accounting principles	**.94**		
Total	**$ 2.31**	$ 1.40	$ (9.37)

Accounting Policy Excerpt

Earnings per common share   In 1993 and 1992, the computation of primary earnings per share was based on the weighted average number of outstanding common shares and additional shares assuming the exercise of stock options. The computation of fully diluted earnings per share for both years further assumes the conversion of the 8¼% convertible subordinated notes due August 1, 2000. The computation of fully diluted earnings per share for 1993 further assumes conversion of Series A Cumulative Convertible Preferred Stock. In 1991, both primary and fully diluted earnings per common share were based on the weighted average number of outstanding common shares. The inclusion of additional shares assuming the conversion of Series A Cumulative Convertible Preferred Stock would have been antidilutive in 1992 and 1991. The shares used in the computations for the three years ended December 31, 1993 were as follows (in thousands):

	1993	1992	1991
Primary	**165,070**	163,725	161,552
Fully diluted	**246,550**	181,813	161,552

SOURCE: Unisys Corporation, 1993 Annual Report.

In this case, the exercise of the stock options would still be incorporated in all computations, even though it results in an **antidilutive effect** for one of the income (loss) figures.

Exhibit 18–8 presents the partial income statement of Unisys Corporation for 1993, along with a financial statement note explaining the EPS figures. Unisys has a complex capital structure and, therefore, presents primary and fully diluted EPS figures. Unisys is a large provider of information services, technology, and software. Notice that the EPS presentation parallels the income statement, with primary and fully diluted figures presented for income (loss) before extraordinary items and changes in accounting principles, extraordinary items, effect of changes in accounting principles, and net income. The note explains that primary EPS is calculated assuming the exercise of stock options, and fully diluted EPS further assumes the conversion of convertible notes for all years. Also, fully diluted EPS assumes conversion of convertible preferred stock for 1993, but not for 1992 and 1991 because the effect was antidilutive.

EXAMPLE EPS COMPUTATIONS

This section presents a step-by-step approach to computing EPS for a company with a complex capital structure. We illustrate this approach by preparing the EPS presentation for Holston Company for 1996. Excerpts from Holston's balance sheet and other relevant information are presented as follows:

Partial Balance Sheet at December 31, 1996

Stockholders' Equity

Convertible preferred stock ($50 par, 7% cumulative; 100,000 shares authorized, 65,000 shares issued and outstanding, each share convertible into three shares of common stock)	$ 3,250,000
Common stock ($10 par; 4,000,000 shares authorized, 1,700,000 shares issued)	17,000,000
Paid-in capital in excess of par value on common stock	4,685,000
Retained earnings	12,755,000
	$37,690,000
Less: Treasury stock (75,000 shares of common at $17 cost)	(1,275,000)
	$36,415,000

	Common Stock Activity in 1996	Number of Common Shares
Jan. 1	Number of shares outstanding	1,100,000
Apr. 1	Distribution of 10% stock dividend	110,000
May 1	Sale of previously unissued stock	490,000
Oct. 1	Acquisition of treasury stock	(300,000)
Dec. 1	Sale of treasury stock	225,000
Dec. 31	Number of shares outstanding	1,625,000

Other Information

1. Holston Company had 100,000 stock options outstanding throughout 1996; each option allowed the acquisition of one share of common stock at $15. The market price of the common averaged $24 during 1996. The market price at the end of 1996 was $30.

2. Holston had 75,000 stock purchase warrants outstanding throughout 1996; each warrant allowed the acquisition of one share of common stock at $32.

3. As the result of a business combination in 1994, Holston is required to issue 300,000 shares of common stock if income reaches the $5,000,000 level in any year through 1998. This level of income has not been reached before 1996.

4. The convertible preferred stock was originally sold at par value in 1994 and may be converted into three shares of common stock per share of preferred stock at the discretion of the preferred stockholders at any time. Through 1996, no conversions have taken place.

5. Holston has outstanding $10,000,000 of convertible bonds that were issued at par in 1992 and yield 7%. Each $1,000 bond may be converted into 40 shares of common stock. The Aa corporate bond yields since the year of issuance have been as follows:

1992	12%	1994	10%	1996	11%
1993	11%	1995	10½%		

6. Holston reported net income of $4,750,000 for 1996.

7. The income tax rate for Holston is 40%.

Step 1. Determine Weighted Average Number of Common Shares Outstanding

The weighted average number of common shares outstanding is determined by considering the amount of time various numbers of shares of common stock were outstanding during the year. The 10% stock dividend of March 31 is applied retroactively.

Period	Number of Months	×	Number of Shares Outstanding	=	Original	×	Stock Dividend Conversion	=	Restated
								Months × Shares	
Jan. 1–Mar. 31	3		1,100,000		3,300,000		1.10		3,630,000
Apr. 1–Apr. 30	1		1,210,000						1,210,000
May 1–Sept. 30	5		1,700,000						8,500,000
Oct. 1–Nov. 30	2		1,400,000						2,800,000
Dec. 1–Dec. 31	1		1,625,000						1,625,000
	12								17,765,000

$$\text{Weighted Average} = 17{,}765{,}000/12 = 1{,}480{,}417$$

Step 2. Compute Base EPS (EPS assuming no dilution)

Base EPS is computed by reducing the net income of $4,750,000 by the preferred dividend and dividing by the weighted average common shares. The preferred dividend is $227,500 (65,000 shares × $50 par × 7%).

$$\text{Base EPS} = \frac{\$4{,}750{,}000 - \$227{,}500}{1{,}480{,}417} = \$3.05$$

Notice that the conversion feature of the preferred stock does not affect this computation.

Base EPS provides the basis for comparing potential diluters to determine whether they dilute EPS if included in the computations.

Step 3. Evaluate Potential Diluters for Common Stock Equivalency Status

Each potential diluter must be evaluated to determine whether it is a common stock equivalent and therefore included in primary EPS (if dilutive). The five potential diluters of Holston Company are evaluated as follows:

Potential Diluter	Evaluation
Stock options	Common stock equivalent (by definition).
Stock purchase warrants	Common stock equivalent (by definition).
Contingent issuance resulting from business combination	Not a common stock equivalent because the conditions required for the stock to be issued have *not* been met (i.e., the $5,000,000 level of income has not been attained).
Convertible preferred stock	Not a common stock equivalent because the effective yield (7%) is more than two-thirds of the Aa corporate bond yield when the stock was issued (2/3 × 10% = 6.7%).
Convertible bonds	Common stock equivalent because the effective yield (7%) is less than two-thirds of the Aa corporate bond yield when the bonds were issued (⅔ × 12% = 8%).

Step 4. Determine Whether Potential Diluters Are Dilutive in this Accounting Period

Because potential diluters are included in EPS computations only when they are individually dilutive, each must be evaluated to determine whether it will be included in the EPS computations in the current period. This evaluation is made as follows:

Potential Diluter	Evaluation	
Stock options	Dilutive—Both the average and ending market prices ($24 and $30) exceed the exercise price ($15).	
Stock purchase warrants	Antidilutive—Both the average and ending market prices ($24 and $30) are less than the exercise price ($32).	
Contingent issuance resulting from business combination	Dilutive—The dilution index is less than base EPS:	
	Addition to numerator ($5,000,000 − $4,750,000)	$250,000
	Addition to denominator	300,000
	Dilution index ($250,000/300,000)	.83
Convertible preferred stock	Dilutive—The dilution index is less than base EPS:	
	Addition to numerator (Step 2)	$227,500
	Addition to denominator (65,000 × 3)	195,000
	Dilution index ($227,500/195,000)	1.17
Convertible bonds	Dilutive—The dilution index is less than base EPS:	
	Addition to numerator ($10,000,000 × 7%)(1 − .40)	$420,000
	Addition to denominator (10,000 bonds × 40 shares)	400,000
	Dilution index ($420,000/400,000)	1.05

Step 5. Summarize Potential Diluters

The potential diluters can now be summarized to determine how they will affect the computation of primary and fully diluted EPS for 1996. This is done for Holston Company as follows:

	Issuance Assumed in Computing	
Potential Diluter	Primary EPS	Fully Diluted EPS
Stock options (common stock equivalent, dilutive)	Yes	Yes
Stock purchase warrants (common stock equivalent, antidilutive)	No	No
Contingent issuance (not common stock equivalent, dilutive)	No	Yes
Convertible preferred stock (not common stock equivalent, dilutive)	No	Yes
Convertible bonds (common stock equivalent, dilutive)	Yes	Yes

From this summary, we see that primary EPS will include the elements of base EPS, plus the dilutive effect of the *stock options* and the *convertible bonds*. Fully diluted EPS will include the dilutive effect of these same items *plus* the contingent issuance and the convertible preferred stock. Also, the dilutive effect of the options will be greater in fully diluted EPS than in primary EPS, because the year-end market price of the stock exceeds the average price for the year.

Step 6. Compute Primary and Fully Diluted EPS and Apply 3% Test

The elements for computing primary and fully diluted EPS are calculated as follows:

Numerator

Net income	$4,750,000
Less: Preferred dividend (see Step 2)	(227,500)
Plus: Interest (after tax) on convertible debt (see Step 4)	420,000
For primary EPS	$4,942,500
Plus: Income increase for contingent issuance (see Step 4)	250,000
Preferred dividend (see Step 2)	227,500
For fully diluted EPS	$5,420,000

Denominator

Weighted average common shares outstanding (see Step 1)	1,480,417
Plus: Application of treasury stock method to stock	
options (at the average market prices)	
Proceeds from sale: 100,000 × $15 = $1,500,000	
Shares acquired: $1,500,000/$24 = 62,500	
Net increase: 100,000 − 62,500 =	37,500
Plus: Equivalent shares for convertible debt (see Step 4)	400,000
For primary EPS	1,917,917
Plus: Shares increase from contingent issuance (see Step 4)	300,000
Equivalent shares for convertible preferred stock (see Step 4)	195,000
Application of treasury stock method to stock options	
(at the ending market price)	
Proceeds from sale: 100,000 × $15 = $1,500,000	
Shares acquired: $1,500,000/$30 = 50,000	
Net increase: 100,000 − 50,000 = 50,000	
Excess of increase for fully diluted over primary:	
50,000 − 37,500 =	12,500
For fully diluted EPS	2,425,417

Primary and fully diluted EPS can now be computed using the appropriate numbers:

$$\text{Primary EPS} = \$4,942,500/1,917,917 = \$2.58$$

$$\text{Fully Diluted EPS} = \$5,420,000/2,425,417 = \$2.23$$

For the dual presentation of EPS to be required, fully diluted EPS must be 97% or less of base EPS as computed in Step 2. Because base EPS is $3.05, the dual presentation is required if fully diluted EPS is $2.96 or less ($3.05 × 97%). This condition is clearly met in this case because fully diluted EPS is $2.23.

Step 7.   Prepare the Income Statement Presentation of EPS

The dual presentation of EPS is reported after the net income figure at the bottom of the income statement. Appropriate wording depends on the circumstances of the presentation. The presentation for Holston for 1996 might appear as follows:

Net income	$4,750,000
Earnings per share	
Earnings per common and common equivalent share	$2.58
Earnings per common share, assuming full dilution	$2.23

The fact that professional accountants must use judgment when they prepare financial statements is well established. We have noted in this textbook several instances in which an accountant's judgment may affect the amount of an enterprise's net income. For example, the following choices may have an important impact on the amount and timing of net income: method of inventory valuation, method of depreciation and estimated useful life of plant and equipment, and estimated useful life of intangible assets.

PROFESSIONAL JUDGMENT

In fact, we can conclude that any judgment made in the determination of net income has a direct impact on the amount of the company's earnings per share, because net income is the basis for the numerator in the EPS calculation.

Other professional judgments involve issues that are unique to EPS calculations. For example, a company that is not publicly held may choose to present earnings per share and, if so, must conform to the principles presented in this chapter. How does that company determine the market price of its common stock for purposes of applying the treasury stock method if the stock is not sold publicly? Even if a common stock does sell regularly, determining its average market price for a year may be complicated and require the accountant's professional judgment. We have stated that a potential diluter is a common stock equivalent if the condition(s) required to issue stock have already been met. These conditions may be complex, however, and determining whether they are met may involve significant professional judgment.

Much of the material we have studied in this chapter comes from *APB Opinion No. 15,* which was issued in 1968. Since that time, companies have become very creative in designing financial instruments that did not exist in 1968. Are these instruments, which are not mentioned in the authoritative literature concerning EPS, potential diluters that must be judged by the general standards of *APB Opinion No. 15,* even though the opinion does not specifically refer to them?

In summary, we can see that calculating EPS is not the simple process that it may have seemed before we explored the entire situation surrounding the calculations. They involve complex determinations of the relationship of a company's earnings and its financing structure and frequently require a high level of professional judgment for the resulting figures to be consistent with the substance of the authoritative accounting literature.

CONCLUDING REMARKS

Earnings per share is an area of accounting in which many types of situations may be encountered. Several aspects of EPS that are beyond the scope of this textbook have been omitted in an attempt to focus our attention on basic concepts and methods of computation. Several additional complications that may be encountered in computing EPS are covered in the Appendix to this chapter.

In Chapter 2, we identified one of the objectives of financial reporting as predicting future cash flows, concluding that one of the primary goals of an enterprise is to increase its wealth over time so that it can return the maximum amount of cash to its owners. Information useful for predicting future cash flows includes information directly related to the entity's cash activities, such as the statement of cash flows. In addition, information about earnings is also regarded as important for assessing future cash flows. Information about earnings includes earnings per share amounts.

The association between earnings and the amount of common stock in a company's capital structure has been a topic of considerable research interest in the past. For example, one study attempted to determine whether common stock offering announcements convey information about the level of the company's future cash flows. Among the conclusions reached is that forecasts of current year earnings decrease when companies announce plans to issue additional shares of common stock. In contrast, forecasts of the five-year growth rate of earnings are unchanged. The researchers interpret these results as being consistent with the claim that equity offering announcements convey unfavorable information regarding the company's short-term but not its long-term earnings prospects.[13]

Substance over Form   The requirements of *APB Opinion No. 15* regarding EPS computations represent an interesting combination of the modifying conventions of substance over form and conserva-

[13]Peter Alan Brous, "Common Stock Offerings and Earnings Expectations: A Test of the Release of Unfavorable Information," *The Journal of Finance* (September 1992), pp. 1517–1535.

INVISIBLE DILUTION

Introduced with great fanfare a few weeks ago by Shearson Lehman Hutton, Inc., "unbundled stock units" are being marketed as a way to lessen the threat of takeover, cut taxes and improve earnings per share. If this gimmick is approved by the Securities & Exchange Commission, American Express Co., Pfizer, Inc., Sara Lee Corp. and Dow Chemical Co. say they will offer them to their shareholders as a swap for existing common shares of up to 20% of their capitalization.

If a shareholder takes the bait, what does he get? A package of three separate securities. One is a 30-year, deep-discount bond that will provide guaranteed interest payments equal to the current dividend on the common. The second is a preferred stock that will pay dividends equal to any dividend increases on the common. The third is a 30-year common stock warrant with a strike price equal to the maturity value of the bond—meaning that after 30 years the investor can swap the bond back to the company for a share of common stock.

So the old stockholder gets about what he started with, but in three separate pieces. Presumably, the stockholder can then decide to sell off part of the package and keep the rest. By selling the warrant, for example, he keeps the dividend but loses some future appreciation. If he sells the bond and preferred, he gives up income and some capital appreciation but gains big if the stock takes off. To institutional holders, the package is worth slightly more than the original share, because of its built-in downside protection. If 30 years from now the stock is worth less than the maturity value of the bond, the warrant expires worthless, but a holder of the units still gets the full bond maturity value. To individuals, the package has a serious downside: higher trading costs if they want to sell.

What's in it for the company? A tax saving. As *Forbes* has repeatedly pointed out, our tax laws subsidize debt and penalize common equity. By paying deductible interest rather than nondeductible dividends, the unbundled stock units will provide a nice tax saving for the company. Will Internal Revenue disallow this tax ploy? That remains to be seen. If the IRS goes along, there will be tangible gains to the companies involved—and a corresponding loss for the Treasury.

The final supposed advantage of the unbundling is, in our view, an illusion. By replacing common stock with a package of securities, the recapitalization would reduce the number of common shares outstanding and thus the divisor that determines earnings per share. If earnings remain the same, reduction of the divisor makes earnings per share seem larger.

We say "appear" for good reason. In fact, the company is incurring a potential dilution that will eventually offset much of this apparent gain.

Here's why: Years and perhaps even decades later, as rising stock prices induce holders to exercise their warrants, the warrants will be exercised and the canceled stock will reappear, reducing earnings per share.

Argues Norman Weinger, accounting analyst at Oppenheimer & Co., "There's a hidden dilution effect in these units." Abraham Briloff, accounting profession emeritus at Baruch College, agrees: "The unbundled stock unit is the equivalent of a share of common stock, period. The sum of its parts should be equal to a common share and have no earnings impact."

These accounting experts are simply saying that—not counting the hoped-for subsidy from the U.S. Treasury—two and two equals four and cannot equal five.

In the best of all worlds, issuing companies would be required to recognize the potential dilution in the common stock, which would probably cancel any gains in earnings per share. In devising the unbundled stock units, the Shearson Lehman people got around this problem. Under current accounting rules, warrants are considered "common stock equivalents" and therefore dilutive only when the exercise price of the warrant is lower than the stock price. When the situation is reversed and the warrant is "out of the money," that is, at a price above the current market—as with unbundled stock units—existing accounting rules do not require that the potential dilution be recognized. When initially issued, the 30-year USU warrants are expected to be priced far above the current stock price and thus out of the money.

But here's the rub: If they were certain to stay forever out of the money, the warrants would have no value. But presumably they will have a value. Thus the market recognizes a liability for the company even if the accounting rules don't. Calculating a warrant's value is no simple matter, but that doesn't seem to stop the options boys in Chicago with their sophisticated computers.

If unbundled stock units take hold, the accounting profession will have to address the accounting problems posed by them—in particular, how to evaluate out-of-the-money warrants. It took the accountants a long time to figure out how to deal with the more obvious kind of dilution—in-the-money warrants and convertibles. Our guess is they will be a little slow catching on to this latest trick, too.

SOURCE: Penelope Wang, "Invisible Dilution," *Forbes* (February 6, 1989). Reprinted by permission of *Forbes Magazine*, February 6, 1989. © Forbes Inc., 1989.

tism. Stressing *substance over form* in financial reporting refers to emphasizing the economic implications of events rather than their legal form. This concept is applied in an attempt to provide information in financial statements that better reflects the economic impact of activities being presented. Applying substance over form in computing EPS requires that we incorporate events and activities that have not actually occurred. This is different from traditional accounting. The adjustments to net income and to the number of shares of common stock outstanding are only for the purposes of computing diluted EPS figures. These adjustments are not entered in the accounting records except as a memorandum in conjunction with the documentation of EPS calculations.

Conservatism refers to the financial reporting practice of using the accounting alternative that results in the least favorable impact on net income when reporting in a context of significant uncertainty. Uncertainties about EPS computations center primarily on the ultimate issuance of additional shares of common stock that may reduce EPS (i.e., potential dilution). Procedures for computing EPS are designed to state EPS on a diluted basis, thereby reflecting the potential decline expected from these potential increases in the number of common shares outstanding.

Conservatism

KEY POINTS

1. Users of financial statements frequently cite EPS as one of the most important figures on which they base financial decisions. (Objective 1)

2. The term *dilution* refers to a reduction in EPS resulting from the issuance of additional shares of common stock. *Potential dilution* refers to possible future reductions in EPS. (Objective 2)

3. The potential for dilution of EPS exists when a company's capital structure includes stock options, warrants, and rights; convertible securities; and other contingent issuances of common stock. (Objective 2)

4. A company with a simple capital structure has no potential diluters. A company with a complex capital structure has one or more potential diluters. (Objective 3)

5. A publicly held company with a simple capital structure must present EPS in the income statement, based on the outstanding common stock for that period. (Objective 3)

6. A publicly held company with a complex capital structure must present EPS in the income statement based on both the outstanding common stock for that period and the potential diluters in its capital structure. (If the potential dilution is not material, however, the potential dilution is not required to be presented.) (Objective 3)

7. EPS figures are based on the weighted average number of shares of common stock outstanding. Securities whose claim on income precedes the claim of the common stockholders, such as preferred stock, must be deducted before computing EPS. (Objective 4)

8. Primary EPS is based on the outstanding common stock, plus potential diluters identified as *common stock equivalents.* Fully diluted EPS is based on the outstanding common stock plus *all potential diluters.* (Objective 4)

9. In preparing the EPS figures for complex capital structures, events that have not actually taken place are incorporated, resulting in *pro forma* figures. Methods used to incorporate these assumed events include the treasury stock method for stock options, rights, and warrants, and the "if converted" method for convertible securities. (Objective 4)

10. EPS figures are presented on the face of the income statement. The precise wording and disclosure varies, depending on the circumstances of each company. (Objective 5)

11. The modifying conventions of substance over form and conservatism explain the incorporation of potential dilution in EPS figures. We attempt to reflect the economic substance of events rather than simply their legal form. We incorporate only those events that would reduce EPS. (Objective 6)

APPENDIX A: ADDITIONAL EPS CONSIDERATIONS

In practice, many variations are encountered in computing EPS, particularly for companies with complex capital structures. This appendix discusses several additional considerations in computing EPS that were not covered in the chapter. Some relate to circumstances that were intentionally avoided in the previous discussion. Others concern points that must be understood for a more complete knowledge of EPS but that the authors consider less important than material covered earlier.

MODIFICATION OF THE TREASURY STOCK METHOD

In developing the methods for computing EPS, the Accounting Principles Board concluded that the treasury stock method should be modified when the number of shares involved with stock options and warrants exceeded 20% of the number of shares outstanding. To put that modification into practice, a company must first apply a test to determine whether or not the number of shares that might be sold by stock option and similar plans exceeds 20% of the outstanding shares at the end of the accounting period. If that test is met, a 20% limitation is in effect on the assumed stock buyback that is part of the treasury stock method.

When this situation exists, the proceeds from the assumed sale of common stock are distributed as follows:

1. As if the funds were first applied to the repurchase of common stock, up to 20% of the shares outstanding at the end of the period.
2. As if the remaining funds were used to reduce short-term or long-term borrowing and any remaining funds were invested in U.S. government securities or commercial paper.

If the net effect of these assumptions is dilutive, the results of these two steps are combined and included in EPS computations.

To illustrate, assume that Montvale Company had 200,000 shares of outstanding common stock throughout 1996; the company also had outstanding stock options allowing the purchase of 100,000 shares of common stock at $20 per share. The market price of the common stock throughout 1996 was $37. The 20% test is met because the company stock option plan permits the purchase of stock by option holders in excess of 20% of the outstanding shares (100,000 shares exceeds 20% of 200,000 shares). The 20% limitation is also in effect because the proceeds from the sale of 100,000 shares at $20 permits the buyback of more than 40,000 shares (20% × 200,000): [(100,000 × $20)/$37 = 54,054]. Assuming that Montvale has at least $520,000 of outstanding debt at a 10% interest rate, that the company's income tax rate is 35%, and that net income for 1996 was $450,000, we determine the dilutive effect of the stock options as follows:

Proceeds from assumed exercise of options (100,000 × $20)		$2,000,000
20% limitation, 20% × 200,000 = 40,000		
Reacquisition of treasury shares (40,000 × $37)		1,480,000
Proceeds available for debt reduction		$ 520,000
Interest savings, after tax ($520,000 × 10%)(1 − .35)		$33,800
Increase in outstanding shares		
Shares sold	100,000	
Shares repurchased	(40,000)	60,000

Primary EPS, incorporating the dilution caused by the assumed exercise of the options, is computed as follows:

$$\text{Primary EPS} = \frac{\$450,000 + \$33,800}{200,000 + 60,000} = \$1.86$$

APB Opinion No. 15 does not indicate the order in which the company's debt is assumed to have been retired. Also, if the

proceeds available for debt reduction ($520,000 in the above example) exceed the amount of outstanding debt, the remaining amounts are assumed to have been invested in U.S. government securities or commercial paper. This has a similar impact on income as debt reduction, because the interest, after income tax, is added to income.

In applying this modification in the treasury stock method, all options and warrants are combined, including those that are antidilutive (i.e., ones for which the exercise price exceeds the market price). The aggregate results are included in the EPS calculations, however, only if the net effect of the assumed exercise of all options and warrants is dilutive.

RETROACTIVE APPLICATION OF STOCK SPLITS AND STOCK DIVIDENDS

In computing the weighted average number of common shares outstanding, stock splits and stock dividends are applied retroactively to restate stock outstanding prior to the split or dividend on the basis of the stock at the end of the accounting period. Financial statements are typically presented on a comparative basis, with the current period set in the context of one or more additional (historical) accounting periods.

If a stock split or stock dividend takes place in the current year, the split or dividend is applied retroactively to the comparative year figures, as well as within the current period, as we studied earlier.

To illustrate this point, assume that EPS for Pioneer Company for 1995 was originally reported in that year as $3.26, determined by dividing the $326,000 net income by 100,000 shares of outstanding common stock. Assume further that in 1996 the company reported a net income of $350,000, distributed a 2:1 stock dividend during the year, and had no other common stock activity. EPS for 1996 is $1.75, determined by dividing the $350,000 net income by 200,000 shares of common stock. Remember that the stock dividend is applied retroactively and, thus, the 200,000 shares are considered outstanding for the entire period, even though 100,000 shares were issued in a stock split during the year. For comparative purposes, the 1995 EPS figure of $3.26 must be restated on a basis consistent with that of 1996, as follows:

$$\$326,000/(100,000 \text{ shares} \times 2) = \$1.63$$

EPS figures in the 1996–1995 comparative income statements are $1.75 and $1.63, respectively.

When a company declares a stock dividend or stock split and applies it retroactively by restating earnings per share figures, it should disclose this information, usually in the form of a note to the financial statements. For example, Primera Corporation, a financial services corporation, indicated in notes to its 1992 financial statements that the company's board of directors declared a 3:2 stock split in the form of a 50% stock dividend and that the current and prior years' earnings per share had been restated to reflect this event.

MULTIPLE CONVERTIBLE SECURITIES

In the text, we illustrated a simplified method for determining whether a convertible security is dilutive, a method that involves calculating a dilution index, which is compared with base EPS. If the dilution index is less than base EPS, the convertible security is dilutive. A refinement is required when the dilution index is close to the base EPS amount and multiple dilutive securities exist.

To illustrate this situation, assume that Mintz Company had a net income of $9,500 with 2,000 shares of common stock outstanding.[14] Assume further that the two classes of convertible preferred stock are outstanding as follows:

Class A—1,000 shares convertible into common on a 1:1 ratio; $2.50 dividend paid per share.

Class B—1,500 shares convertible into common on a 1:1 ratio; $1.00 dividend paid per share.

Base EPS is $2.75, computed as follows:

$$\frac{\$9,500 - (\$2,500 + \$1,500)}{2,000 \text{ shares}} = \$2.75$$

Computing a dilution index as discussed earlier, both issues of preferred stock appear to be dilutive:

Class A Dilution Index: $\dfrac{1,000 \text{ shares} \times \$2.50}{1,000 \text{ shares}} = \$2.50$

Class B Dilution Index: $\dfrac{1,500 \text{ shares} \times \$1.00}{1,500 \text{ shares}} = \$1.00$

Notice that the dilution index for the Class A preferred is $2.50, relatively close to the base EPS figure of $2.75. Rather than automatically assuming that each is dilutive, we must compute a series of EPS figures that incorporates the potential diluters, **starting with the most dilutive security.** In this example, the Class B convertible preferred stock is more dilutive than the Class A convertible preferred stock because the Class B dilution index is $1.00, lower than $2.50 for the Class A. EPS, including the dilutive effect of the Class B preferred, is determined as follows:

$$\frac{\$9,500 - \$2,500}{2,000 + 1,500 \text{ Shares}} = \$2.00$$

---

[14]This illustration is based on a similar illustration adapted from *AICPA Accounting Interpretation,* "Computing Earnings per Share," sec. 43, "Conversion Assumed for Primary Only" (New York: AICPA, 1970).

Including the Class B preferred stock reduces EPS from $2.75 to $2.00. Now we must compare the dilution index of the Class A convertible preferred stock to determine whether it will further dilute the EPS calculation. In this case, it will not because the dilution index of the Class A convertible preferred is $2.50, which exceeds $2.00. Thus, the Class A convertible preferred is not included, and diluted EPS is stated at $2.00, the maximum potential dilution. Had the dilution index of the Class A convertible preferred been less than $2.00, both classes of convertible preferred stock would have been included in the calculation.

This example illustrates a refinement in the procedure covered in the chapter text in which multiple convertible securities are entered in the EPS calculation *in order of their dilutive effect.* Each resulting EPS calculation becomes the basis for determining the dilutive status of the next convertible security. If the two (or more) convertible securities are common stock equivalents, this procedure must be applied in computing both primary and fully diluted EPS. If they are not common stock equivalents, the procedure is applied only in computing fully diluted EPS. Applying this refinement to the Holston Company comprehensive illustration in this chapter would have no effect on the resulting EPS figures because of the strong dilutive effect of each individual potential diluter.

DELAYED EFFECTIVENESS AND CHANGING RATES OR PRICES

Some convertible securities are not convertible until a future date, and in some cases conversion rates vary over time. Similarly, some options or warrants are not exercisable until a future date, and in some cases exercise prices vary over time. Conversion rates on convertible securities and exercise prices on stock options and warrants are important in applying the "if converted" and treasury stock methods to compute primary and fully diluted EPS.

In computing *primary EPS,* the conversion rate or price in effect for the period of computation is used. If the conversion or exercise privilege is delayed, the earliest rate or price in the *next five years* is used. If conversion or exercise is not available within the five-year period, the potential diluter is not used to compute primary EPS.

In computing *fully diluted EPS,* the most advantageous conversion rate or exercise price to the holder that becomes effective in the *next 10 years* is used. If conversion or exercise is not available within the 10-year period, the potential diluter is not used in computing fully diluted EPS.

QUESTIONS

18–1 What is meant by the term *dilution* as it relates to EPS?

18–2 What are three types of potential diluters? How may each reduce EPS?

18–3 What is meant by the term *senior security* when computing EPS? How does the existence of senior securities affect EPS?

18–4 What is the difference between companies with simple capital structures and those with complex capital structures? What type of EPS presentation must each make?

18–5 In computing EPS, a weighted average number of common shares outstanding is used. What is the impact, if any, of each of the following common stock transactions on the weighted average computation?

[a] Sale of additional shares.   [d] Resale of treasury stock.
[b] Acquisition of treasury stock.   [e] Distribution of a cash dividend.
[c] Distribution of a stock dividend.   [f] Distribution of a stock split.

18–6 In what circumstances is the dividend on preferred stock subtracted from net income in computing EPS? In what circumstances is this subtraction not made?

18–7 What is the difference between the two EPS figures in each pair below? Under what circumstances would the two be the same?

[a] Base EPS and primary EPS.
[b] Primary EPS and fully diluted EPS.

18–8 How do common stock equivalents differ from other potentially dilutive securities? When would each of the following be considered common stock equivalents?

[a] Convertible securities.
[b] Stock options, warrants, and rights.
[c] Other contingent issuances.

18–9 How could a common stock equivalent be included in the determination of EPS in one year but not in another year, even though it existed throughout both years?

18–10 When incorporating the dilutive impact of some potential diluters in EPS, the numerator in the computation is adjusted; in other cases, it is not. What is the reason for this difference? When is an adjustment necessary?

18–11 What is the distinction between companies that are publicly held and those that are not publicly held? What is the importance of this distinction in determining the appropriateness of presenting EPS?

18–12 The treasury stock method is used to determine the dilutive effect of the exercise of stock options, warrants, and rights. How is it possible to determine whether the application of the method will result in a reduction in EPS prior to actually making the computations to determine the amount of the dilution?

In questions 18–13 through 18–22, select the correct answers.

18–13 Which of the following best describes the presentation of EPS?

[a] Required in the financial statements of all companies.
[b] Required in the financial statements of companies whose stock is publicly held.
[c] Required in the financial statements of companies whose stock is not publicly held.
[d] Not required in the financial statements of any company.

18–14 When EPS figures are presented, where should they be located?

[a] In the income statement following net income.
[b] In the stockholders' equity section of the balance sheet.
[c] In the notes to the financial statements.
[d] In any of the three places suggested in [a], [b], and [c].

18–15 Which of the following is *not* a potential diluter of EPS?

[a] Stock options, warrants, and rights to acquire common stock.
[b] Contingent issuances of common stock.
[c] Debt that is convertible into common stock.
[d] Preferred stock that is cumulative and nonconvertible.

18–16 Which of the following best describes the number of shares used to calculate primary EPS?

[a] The number outstanding at the end of the accounting period.
[b] The weighted average number of shares outstanding plus common stock equivalents.
[c] The weighted average number of shares outstanding plus all potential diluters.
[d] The simple average of common shares outstanding.

18–17 Which of the following best describes fully diluted EPS?

[a] EPS assuming the dilutive effect of events judged by management as most likely to occur.
[b] EPS based on historical income and outstanding shares.
[c] EPS incorporating the negative effect of all possible extraordinary losses that could occur in the future.
[d] EPS based on the assumption of full dilution of all potential diluters.

18–18 (Appendix A) To what extent is treasury stock assumed to be acquired by a corporation applying the treasury stock method in EPS calculations?

[a] To the maximum extent possible.
[b] Up to 20% of earnings for the period being reported on.
[c] None until all long-term debt has been retired and then to the maximum extent possible.
[d] Up to 20% of outstanding common stock.   (AICPA adapted)

18–19 Which of the following statements best describes the impact of effective yield at issuance of convertible securities on calculating EPS?

[a] If less than two-thirds of the then current Aa corporate bond yield, these securities are used to calculate primary EPS but not fully diluted EPS.
[b] If less than two-thirds of the then current Aa corporate bond yield, these securities are used to calculate fully diluted EPS but not primary EPS.
[c] If more than two-thirds of the then current Aa corporate bond yield, these securities are used to calculate primary EPS and fully diluted EPS.
[d] If more than two-thirds of the then current Aa corporate bond yield, these securities are used to calculate fully diluted EPS but not primary EPS   (AICPA adapted)

18–20 In computing EPS, the equivalent number of shares of convertible preferred stock (cumulative) is added as an adjustment to the denominator (number of shares outstanding). If the preferred stock is preferred as to dividends, which amount should be added as an adjustment to the numerator (net earnings)?

[a] Annual preferred dividend.
[b] Annual preferred dividend $\times$ (1 − income tax rate).
[c] Annual preferred dividend $\times$ income tax rate.
[d] Annual preferred dividend $\div$ income tax rate.   (AICPA adapted)

18–21 A company issued a new class of convertible preferred stock during the year. At the date of issuance, the yield on the stock was 60% of the Aa corporate bond yield; by the end of the year, the cash yield was 90% of the Aa corporate bond yield. At the end of the year, what type of classification should this security receive for computation of EPS?

[a] Long-term debt equivalent.   [c] Convertible preferred stock.
[b] Other potentially dilutive security.   [d] Common stock equivalent security.
                                                                      (AICPA adapted)

18–22 The computation of EPS in accordance with generally accepted accounting principles may involve the consideration of securities deemed common stock equivalents. Common stock equivalents are an example of which of the following?

[a] Form over substance.   [c] Form over accounting principle.
[b] Substance over form.   [d] Substance over accounting principle.   (AICPA adapted)

18–23 How may a "dilution index" be helpful in determining whether some potential diluters will reduce EPS?

18–24 Under what conditions are potential diluters other than stock options, rights, and warrants or convertible securities considered common stock equivalents?

18–25 What is the purpose of the calculation in which a determination is made whether fully diluted EPS is 3% or more below EPS without considering dilution?

18–26 (Appendix A)   In computing primary and fully diluted EPS, why are stock splits and stock dividends treated retroactively, including the restatement of comparative years' figures, in determining the weighted average number of shares of outstanding common stock?

18–27 (Appendix A)   How are potential diluters whose effective dates are delayed (i.e., not in effect in the year for which EPS figures are being calculated) treated in determining current year EPS?

EXERCISES

18–28 Simple EPS   Sanders Company had 145,000 shares of common stock outstanding throughout 1996. The income statement for the year includes the following:

Income before extraordinary item	$195,000
Extraordinary loss	27,500
Net income	$167,500

The company had 85,000 shares of $12 par value, 7% cumulative preferred stock outstanding throughout 1996.

INSTRUCTIONS

Prepare the EPS presentation for Sanders' income statement for 1996.

18–29 Simple EPS Sims Company had 100,000 shares of common stock outstanding on January 1, 1996. During the year, the company sold and subsequently repurchased stock as follows:

July 1, 1996 — Sold 70,000 shares of common stock.

Dec. 1, 1996 — Purchased 25,000 shares of common treasury stock.

The company reported a net income for 1996 of $750,000.

INSTRUCTIONS

Compute EPS for the company for 1996.

18–30 Weighted Average Calculation Wilson, Inc., had 100,000 shares of common stock outstanding at March 1, the beginning of its current fiscal year. On June 1, it sold 10,000 additional shares. On September 1, it purchased 4,000 shares of treasury stock. No other stock activity took place during the year.

INSTRUCTIONS

Calculate the weighted average number of shares of common stock outstanding for the fiscal year beginning March 1.

18–31 Weighted Average Calculation Samson Company had 1,200,000 shares of common stock outstanding on January 1, the first day of its financial reporting year. Following is activity that took place during the year:

March 1—Sold 50,000 additional shares of common stock.
May 1—Purchased 10,000 shares of treasury stock.
October 1—Distributed a 10% stock dividend.
December 1—Resold 2,000 shares of treasury stock.

INSTRUCTIONS

Calculate the weighted average number of shares of common stock for purposes of calculating EPS.

18–32 Convertible Bonds Wilkes Company had 100,000 shares of common stock outstanding throughout 1996, a year in which the company reported a $150,000 net income. In addition to common stock, the company had the following securities in its capital structure:

Cumulative preferred stock—12,000 shares, 7%, $100 par value.
Long-term debt—$1,000,000, 6%, convertible into 90 shares of common stock per $1,000 bond. These bonds were issued when the average Aa corporate bond yield was 8%.

The company's income tax rate is 35%.

INSTRUCTIONS

Compute primary and fully diluted EPS for 1996 for Wilkes Company.

18–33 Treasury Stock Method Aaron Company had 157,000 shares of common stock outstanding at December 31, 1996. There had been 150,000 shares outstanding at January 1, 1996, and 7,000 shares were sold on August 1, 1996. Net income for the year was reported as $300,000.

Outstanding throughout the year were stock options allowing the holders to acquire 30,000 shares of common stock at $25 per share. The market price of the stock averaged $35 in 1996, was $48 at December 31, 1996, and did not fall below $25 during the year.

INSTRUCTIONS

Compute primary and fully diluted EPS for 1996 for Aaron Company.

18–34 Convertible Preferred Hammer Company has two classes of capital stock:

Cumulative preferred stock—1,000,000 shares authorized, $10 par value, 500,000 shares outstanding, 7% dividend rate, each share convertible into 5 shares of common stock.
Common stock—12,000,000 shares authorized, $6 par value, 7,000,000 shares outstanding.

In 1996, Hammer reported net income of $10,000,000. No capital stock activity took place during the year. The company's income tax rate is 35%.

The preferred stock was issued in 1994 at par value when the average Aa corporate bond yield was 10%.

INSTRUCTIONS

Compute primary and fully diluted EPS for 1996.

18–35 Weighted Average Calculation   Saffell Company had 745,000 shares of common stock outstanding at the beginning of 1996. During the year, the company had the following common stock activity:

Jan. 31   Sold 100,000 additional shares.
May 31   Acquired 10,000 shares of treasury stock.
Aug. 31   Resold 1,000 shares of treasury stock.
Oct. 31   Resold 4,000 shares of treasury stock.

INSTRUCTIONS

Compute the weighted average common shares outstanding for 1996 to be used in computing EPS.

18–36 Weighted Average Calculation   Henley Company had 1,475,000 shares outstanding at December 31, 1996, the end of its fiscal year. On March 31, 1996, the company had sold 150,000 additional shares of stock; a 2:1 stock split was declared on August 1, 1996, and distributed on September 1, 1996.

INSTRUCTIONS

Compute the weighted average common shares outstanding for 1996 to be used in computing EPS.

18–37 Denominator Calculation   At December 31, 1995, AMT, Inc., had 500,000 shares of common stock outstanding. On October 1, 1996, 150,000 additional shares of common stock were issued for cash. AMT also had $4,000,000 of 8% convertible bonds outstanding at December 31, 1996, which are convertible into 180,000 shares of common stock. The bonds were considered common stock equivalents at the time of issuance and are dilutive in the 1996 EPS computations. No bonds were issued or converted into common stock during 1996.

INSTRUCTIONS

Determine the number of shares that should be used in computing AMT's primary EPS for the year ended December 31, 1996.   (AICPA adapted)

18–38 Test for Dilution   Leach, Inc., has asked you to help compute EPS figures for its 1996 income statement. Net income for the year is $10,000,000, and the company had 2,600,000 shares of common stock outstanding the entire year. The company has no preferred stock in its capital structure.

Leach officials are attempting to determine whether the following securities will have a dilutive effect on EPS if they are assumed to have been converted or exercised:

Convertible bonds—$10,000,000 par value, 9%, each $1,000 bond convertible into 30 shares of common stock.

Stock options—1,000,000 options to acquire one share each at $16.

Leach's income tax rate is 35% and its common stock sold for $12 throughout 1996. Both the convertible bonds and the stock options were issued in 1994.

INSTRUCTIONS

Test the convertible bonds and the stock options for dilution and indicate your results.

18–39 Test for Dilution   Haskins Co. has 100,000 shares of common stock outstanding throughout 1996. The reported net income for the year is $125,000, after an income tax rate of 35%.

INSTRUCTIONS

Determine whether the potential diluters below are dilutive in 1996. Treat each item *independently*.

[a] Convertible bonds are outstanding as follows: $100,000 par value, 6%, convertible into 60 shares of common stock per $1,000 bond.
[b] Convertible bonds are outstanding as follows: $200,000 par value, 7%, convertible into 10 shares of common stock per $1,000 bond.

[c] Fifty thousand stock options are outstanding that allow the holders to purchase one share per option for $10. The stock sold for $12 throughout the year.

[d] Preferred stock (20,000 shares with a par value of $10) is outstanding. The preferred has a 7% dividend rate and is convertible into two shares of common per preferred share.

18-40 Treasury Stock Method Throughout the year, Plummer Company had stock options outstanding that allow the acquisition of 75,000 shares of common stock from the company at $10 per share. There are 1,000,000 shares of common stock outstanding in the current capital structure.

INSTRUCTIONS

Determine the number of common shares that will be used in computing both primary and fully diluted EPS resulting from the options in each of the following *independent* situations:

[a] The average market price of the common stock was $15, and the year-end price was $15.

[b] The average market price of the common stock was $16, and the year-end price was $18.

[c] The average market price of the common stock was $14, and the year-end price was $10½.

[d] The average market price of the common stock was $9, and the year-end price was $12.

18-41 (Appendix A) Treasury Stock Method Falco, Inc., had stock options outstanding throughout 1996, allowing the holders to acquire 100,000 shares of common stock from the company at the $50 par value per share. The market price of the stock was $75 throughout the year and at year-end.

The company has a 35% income tax rate and pays 8% interest on its $5,000,000 debt. Net income for 1996 was $275,000.

INSTRUCTIONS

Compute primary and fully diluted EPS for 1996 in each of the following *independent* situations:

[a] The weighted average number of outstanding shares of common stock was 600,000 during 1996, with 610,000 outstanding at December 31.

[b] The weighted average number of outstanding shares of common stock was 300,000 during 1996, with 325,000 outstanding at December 31.

18-42 "If Converted" Method Fain Company began operation in 1995 and in that year issued the following securities:

Preferred stock—175,000 shares, $100 par value, 8%, issued at $110, convertible into 4 shares of common stock per preferred share.

Bonds—$10,000,000 par value, 6½%, issued at par value and convertible into 6 shares per $100 bond.

In 1996 the preferred stock and bonds are still outstanding, none having been converted or retired. Fain's income tax rate is 35%.

INSTRUCTIONS

For both the preferred stock and the bonds, determine the adjustments that would have to be made to the 1996 EPS calculations, assuming each has a dilutive effect.

18-43 Analysis of Potential Diluters Whatley Company has two potentially dilutive securities, as follows:

Cumulative preferred stock (8%)—50,000 shares authorized and outstanding, $100 par value, issued at $140 in 1993, convertible into two shares of common per preferred share.

Convertible debt (6%)—$2,000,000 par value, issued at par in 1992, convertible into 15 shares of common stock per $1,000 bond.

Whatley's management is attempting to compute EPS for 1996 and has correctly determined that EPS, without considering potential dilution, is $3.25. The Aa corporate bond yield from 1992 to 1994 was 10½% and in 1995 and 1996 was 9%. The company's income tax rate is 35%.

INSTRUCTIONS

[a] Determine whether the potential diluters are common stock equivalents.

[b] Determine whether the potential diluters are dilutive in 1996.

18-44 3% Minimum Dilution Test Beverly, Inc., is attempting to determine whether the potential dilution in its capital structure is sufficient to warrant a dual EPS presentation in 1996. The company has not had to present primary and fully diluted EPS in the past.

Beverly reported a $500,000 net income and has 300,000 shares of common stock outstanding. The company's income tax rate is 35%. The following potentially dilutive securities exist:

Stock options—50,000 outstanding, allowing the purchase of one share each of common stock at $100. The market price of common stock throughout 1996 was $105.

Convertible debt—$500,000 par value, 6%, convertible to 30 shares of common stock per $1,000 bond.

INSTRUCTIONS

[a] Determine whether Beverly must make a dual presentation of EPS by applying the 3% guideline.
[b] Would your answer to [a] be different if the bonds were convertible into 60 shares per $1,000 bond?

18-45 Options Outstanding Part of Year The fiscal year of Whammo Company ends June 30. On September 30, 1995, the company issued 50,000 stock options to its employees, allowing them to acquire one share of common stock for each option at the $10 par value of the stock.

During fiscal year 1996, Whammo had a weighted average of 286,500 shares outstanding and reported a net income of $355,500. The stock of the company sold at $17 throughout the year.

INSTRUCTIONS

Compute primary EPS for 1996.

18-46 Convertible Bonds Outstanding Part of Year On May 31 of the last calendar year, Rolf Company issued $1,000,000 of 12% bonds at par value. Each $1,000 bond may be converted into 80 shares of common stock.

Rolf reports $135,000 of net income for the year ended December 31. The weighted average number of shares of common stock outstanding was 100,000, and the company's income tax rate is 35%.

INSTRUCTIONS

Assuming that the convertible debt is not a common stock equivalent, compute primary and fully diluted EPS for Rolf Company for the last calendar year.

18-47 (Appendix A) Stock Split The 1995 income statement of Phillip, Inc., a calendar-year company, included earnings per share of $2.29. This figure was determined as follows:

1995 net income	$1,700,000
Less: Preferred dividend	(100,000)
	$1,600,000
Divided by: Number of common shares outstanding entire year	700,000
Earnings per share	$2.29

During 1996 Phillip issued a 2:1 stock split on March 1, reported a net income of $2,450,000, and had no other capital transactions. It paid a $100,000 preferred dividend on December 31, 1996.

INSTRUCTIONS

[a] Determine EPS for 1996.
[b] Apply the stock split of 1996 retroactively to 1995 and restate the EPS for that year.

18-48 (Appendix A) Stock Dividend Parton, Inc., a company with a simple capital structure, reported EPS of $1.57 for the calendar year 1995, computed as follows:

Net income	$18,800,000
Divided by: Weighted average common shares outstanding	12,000,000
Earnings per share	$1.57

At January 1, 1996, Parton declared a 10% stock dividend on the 12,500,000 shares of common stock outstanding at that time. The dividend shares were issued on February 28, 1996.

INSTRUCTIONS

[a] Determine EPS for 1996, assuming that Parton reports net income of $26,000,000.

[b] Determine EPS for 1995 that should be presented for comparative purposes in the 1995–1996 comparative income statement.

18–49 (Appendix A) Delayed Stock Options Pickler Company has 250,000 options outstanding to acquire one share of common stock each. These options can be exercised at any time after December 31, 2003, at $50 per share.

During 1996 Pickler reports a net income of $6,500,000; has 1,000,000 shares of common stock outstanding; and has 500,000 shares of 9%, $100 par value, cumulative preferred stock outstanding. The average and year-end market price of the company's common stock was $65 during 1996.

INSTRUCTIONS

Compute primary and fully diluted EPS for Pickler for 1996.

PROBLEMS

18–50 Simple EPS Hensley Company had the following common stock activity in 1996:

	Number of Shares
Outstanding, Jan. 1	150,000
New shares issued, May 1	25,000
Treasury shares acquired, July 1	10,000
Treasury shares resold, Dec. 1	7,500
Outstanding, Dec. 31	172,500

Hensley had 100,000 shares of cumulative preferred stock outstanding during 1996. The preferred stock has a $10 par value and an 8% dividend rate.

INSTRUCTIONS

[a] Prepare the EPS presentation for 1996, assuming income before extraordinary items is $600,000 and net income is $675,000. There is one extraordinary item in 1996.

[b] Independent of [a], prepare the earnings (loss) per share presentations for 1996, assuming that the company sustained a $420,000 net loss for 1996, with no extraordinary item.

18–51 Simple EPS Sander Company had the following common stock activity in 1995:

	Number of Shares
Outstanding, Jan. 1	500,000
New shares issued, Mar. 1	50,000
Stock issued in 2:1 split, June 1	550,000
Treasury shares acquired, Nov. 1	40,000
Outstanding, Dec. 31	1,060,000

Sander had 200,000 shares of $20 par value cumulative preferred stock outstanding throughout 1995. The dividend rate of this stock is 8%. The company reports a net income of $1,750,000 for 1995 with no extraordinary items.

The accountant for Sander indicates that EPS should be reported as $1.65, determined by dividing the reported net income by 1,060,000 shares of common stock.

INSTRUCTIONS

[a] Write a paragraph indicating your reaction to the accountant's computation. What specific items, if any, has the accountant not considered?

[b] Recompute EPS for Sander for 1995. Provide supporting schedules for the amounts used in your computation.

18–52 Seven-Step EPS Calculation Powell Company had 175,000 shares of common stock outstanding at July 1, 1995, the beginning of its fiscal year. On September 30, 1995, the company sold an additional 25,000 shares. On May 31, 1995, 15,000 shares of treasury stock were acquired off the market.

The company had 25,000 shares of preferred stock outstanding throughout the year ended June 30, 1996. The preferred stock has a $10 par value and an 8% dividend rate and is cumulative and nonconvertible.

In addition to the common and preferred stock, Powell has the following securities outstanding:

[1] Ten percent short-term notes payable of $35,000 due in varying amounts in 30, 60, and 90 days.

[2] Stock options that allow employees to purchase 35,000 shares of common stock at $25 per share. The stock sold for $32.50 throughout the 1996 fiscal year. The options were originally issued in 1992.

[3] Convertible bonds, issued at the par amount of $500,000 in 1993. The bonds yield 10% interest, payable semiannually, and each $100 bond is convertible into 15 shares of common stock on any interest payment date (December 31 and June 30).

For the year ended June 30, 1996, the following items have been determined to be appropriate for inclusion in Powell's income statement:

Income before tax	$320,000
Income tax expense	112,000
Net income	$208,000

The Aa corporate bond yield was 8% in 1992 and increased 1% each year from 1993–1996.

INSTRUCTIONS

[a] Following the seven-step process outlined in the chapter, prepare the financial statement presentation of EPS for Powell Company for the year ended June 30, 1996.

[b] Explain the difference between primary and fully diluted earnings per share, using information from your calculations in [a] to illustrate your points.

18–53 EPS—Alternative Financing Plans Toyex Corporation is considering several plans for increasing its long-term capitalization to provide funds for an expansion of facilities. One consideration is the impact of each plan on EPS.

Toyex Corporation reported EPS of $2.25 for the most recent fiscal year, determined on the basis of $1,687,500 net income and 750,000 shares of common stock outstanding.

The plans under consideration for obtaining approximately $1,000,000 include the following alternatives:

[1] Sell 200,000 additional shares of common stock at approximately $5 per share.

[2] Sell $1,000,000 of 9% bonds approximately at par value.

[3] Sell 100,000 shares of 8% preferred stock approximately at $10 par value, each share convertible into 2 shares of common stock.

[4] Sell $1,000,000 of 7½% convertible bonds approximately at par value, each $1,000 bond convertible into 50 shares of common stock.

Toyex management expects to earn 15% (before income tax) on the increased funds available. The 35% income tax rate for the company is expected to continue. The Aa corporate bond yield throughout the period is expected to be 11%.

INSTRUCTIONS

[a] Determine the EPS that Toyex may be expected to present in the income statement under each of the four alternative plans.

[b] Identify factors that Toyex should consider in addition to the specific figures in [a] above.

[c] From the viewpoint of a current common stockholder, which alternative method of financing the $1,000,000 is preferable? Why?

18–54 (Appendix A) Simple EPS Weber Corporation is preparing the comparative financial statements to be included in the annual report to stockholders. Weber employs a fiscal year ending May 31.

Income from operations before income taxes for Weber was $1,600,000 and $785,000, respectively, for fiscal years ended May 31, 1996 and 1995. Weber experienced an extraordinary loss of $600,000 due to an earthquake on March 3, 1996. A 40% combined income tax rate pertains to any and all of Weber Corporation's profits, gains, and losses.

Weber's capital structure consists of preferred stock and common stock. The company has not issued any convertible securities or warrants, and there are no outstanding stock options.

Weber issued 50,000 shares of $100 par value, 6% cumulative preferred stock in 1982. All of this stock is outstanding, and no preferred dividends are in arrears.

There were 2,000,000 shares of $1 par common stock outstanding on June 1, 1994. On September 1, 1994, Weber sold an additional 500,000 shares of the common stock at $17 per share.

Weber distributed a 20% stock dividend on the common shares outstanding on December 1, 1995. These were the only common stock transactions during the past two fiscal years.

INSTRUCTIONS

[a] Determine the weighted average number of common shares to be used in computing earnings per share on the current comparative income statement for
 [1] The year ended May 31, 1995.
 [2] The year ended May 31, 1996.
[b] Starting with income from operations before income taxes, prepare a comparative income statement for the years ended May 31, 1996 and 1995. The statement will be part of Weber's annual report to stockholders and should include appropriate earnings per share presentation.
[c] The capital structure of a corporation is the result of its past financing decisions. Furthermore, the earnings per share data presented on a corporation's financial statements depends on the capital structure.
 [1] Explain why Weber is considered to have a simple capital structure.
 [2] Describe how earnings per share data would be presented for a corporation that has a complex capital structure. (CMA adapted)

18–55 Complex Capital Structure Warner company is attempting to determine its primary and fully diluted EPS for 1996. The controller believes that it may be necessary to consider the following securities, all of which were issued prior to 1996.

Security	Number or Par Value (in dollars)	Interest/Dividend Rate	Aa Corporate Bond Yield at Issuance	Convertibility (in total) or Purchase Option
Bonds A	$100,000	10%	12%	10,000 shares
Bonds B	$200,000	9%	9½%	None
Bonds C	$500,000	7%	11%	15,000 shares
Preferred stock	$500,000	7½%	10%	50,000 shares
Options	45,000	—	12½%	1 share per option at $30

The controller has correctly determined that the net income for 1996 is $650,000 and the weighted average number of outstanding shares is 475,000. The company's income tax rate is 35% and the Aa corporate bond yield in 1996 was 11½%. The common stock sold for $47 throughout 1996. The preferred stock is cumulative.

INSTRUCTIONS

[a] Prepare a schedule indicating the common stock equivalency status of each security listed and whether each security is dilutive in 1996.
[b] Compute primary and fully diluted EPS for 1996.
[c] Discuss briefly your reason for omitting any of the securities in the preceding table that you did not use in computing EPS.
[d] Explain the difference in your treatment of income taxes in dealing with the interest on the convertible bonds and the dividend on preferred stock.

18–56 Comprehensive EPS Calculations Shipley Corporation's capital structure is as follows:

	Dec. 31, 1996	Dec. 31, 1995
Outstanding shares of:		
Common stock	336,000	300,000
Nonconvertible preferred stock	10,000	10,000
8% convertible bonds	$1,000,000	$1,000,000

ADDITIONAL INFORMATION

[1] On September 1, 1996, Shipley sold 36,000 additional shares of common stock.
[2] Net income for the year ended December 31, 1996, was $750,000.
[3] During 1996 Shipley paid dividends of $3 per share on its nonconvertible preferred stock.
[4] The 8% bonds are convertible into 40 shares of common stock for each $1,000 bond and were not considered common stock equivalents at the date of issuance.
[5] Unexercised stock options to purchase 30,000 shares of common stock at $22.50 per share were outstanding throughout 1996. The average market price of Shipley's common stock was $36 per share during 1996. The market price was $33 per share at December 31, 1996.

[6] Warrants to purchase 20,000 shares of common stock at $38 per share were attached to the preferred stock at the time of issuance. The warrants, which expire on December 31, 2001, were outstanding at December 31, 1996.

[7] Shipley's effective income tax rate was 40% for 1995 and 1996.

INSTRUCTIONS

[a] Determine the number of shares that should be used to compute Shipley Corporation's primary EPS for the year ended December 31, 1996.

[b] Compute the primary EPS for the year ended December 31, 1996.

[c] Determine the number of shares that should be used to compute fully diluted EPS for the year ended December 31, 1996.

[d] Compute the fully diluted EPS for the year ended December 31, 1996.   (AICPA adapted)

18–57 Comprehensive EPS Calculations   Dobson Company's statement of income and the stockholders' equity section of the statement of financial position for the fiscal year ended September 30, 1996, are presented as follows:

Dobson Company
Statement of Income
For the Fiscal Year Ended September 30, 1996
(dollars in thousands)

Sales		$1,000,000
Cost of goods sold		750,000
Gross margin		250,000
Operating expenses (including interest expense of $6,000)		50,000
Income before income taxes		200,000
Income taxes (40%)		
Current	$60,000	
Deferred	20,000	80,000
Income before extraordinary item		120,000
Extraordinary gain, net of income taxes of $20,000		30,000
Net income		$ 150,000

Dobson Company
Stockholders' Equity Section of the
Statement of Financial Position
September 30, 1996
(dollars in thousands)

Preferred stock ($50 par value, 6%; 10,000,000 shares authorized, 5,000,000 shares issued and outstanding)	$250,000
Common stock ($1 par value; 100,000,000 shares authorized with 54,250,000 issued and 53,250,000 shares outstanding)	54,250
Paid-in capital in excess of par value	275,000
Retained earnings	200,000
Total equity	$779,250
Less: Treasury stock—at cost (1,000,000 shares)	40,000
Total stockholders' equity	$739,250

ADDITIONAL INFORMATION

[1] Dobson issued 6% convertible debentures during the 1992–1993 fiscal year at par value of $1,000 each. Each debenture is convertible into 30 shares of common stock. No conversions were made during the fiscal year ended September 30, 1996, and the value of the outstanding debentures is $100,000,000.

[2] A 5% common stock dividend was declare in January 1996 and issued during February 1996 to all stockholders of record: 2,250,000 shares were issued.

[3] Dobson's management has the following options to purchase shares of the company's common stock, adjusted for all dividends declared to date:

Option	Number of Shares	Option Price	Expiration Date
A	2,000,000	$25	Sept. 30, 1998
B	3,000,000	45	Sept. 30, 1999

[4] Market price information for Dobson Company common stock and data on the Aa corporate bond yield are as follows:

	For the Year Ended Sept. 30			
	1993	**1994**	**1995**	**1996**
Average price of common stock	$28	$35	$38	$40
Year-end market price of common stock	$25	$38	$35	$40
Average Aa corporate bond yield	8%	9%	10%	10%

[5] Changes in the number of common shares outstanding during the current fiscal year are summarized below:

Date	Shares Outstanding	Explanation
Oct. 1, 1995	45,000,000	Shares outstanding at the beginning of the year.
Feb. 1, 1996	47,250,000	Shares after a 5% stock dividend was issued.
June 1, 1996	53,250,000	Shares after 6,000,000 new shares were issued for $42.

[6] The outstanding preferred stock is noncumulative and no preferred dividend was declared or paid during 1996.

INSTRUCTIONS

[a] Calculate the weighted average number of common shares outstanding for Dobson for the fiscal year ended September 30, 1996.

[b] Prepare an analysis of the potentially dilutive securities included in Dobson's capital structure. Indicate whether they are included in only primary EPS or in both primary and fully diluted EPS, or excluded from EPS computations.

[c] Compute primary and fully diluted EPS for the year ended September 30, 1996. *Hint:* When a stock dividend is distributed, the number of shares into which the convertible debentures may be converted should be adjusted to an after-dividend basis. (CMA adapted)

18–58 Comprehensive EPS Calculations The controller of Hamby, Inc., has asked you to help to determine both primary and fully diluted EPS for presentation in the company's income statement for the year ended September 30, 1996.

Your working papers disclose the following opening balances and transactions in the company's capital stock accounts during the year:

[1] Common stock (at October 1, 1995, stated value $10, authorized 300,000 shares; effective December 1, 1995, stated value $5, authorized 600,000 shares):

Balance Oct. 1, 1995—issued and outstanding 60,000 shares.
Dec. 1, 1995—60,000 shares issued in a 2:1 stock split.
Dec. 1, 1995—280,000 shares (stated value $5) issued at $39 per share.

[2] Treasury stock—common:

Mar. 1, 1996—purchased 40,000 shares at $38 per share.
Apr. 1, 1996—sold 40,000 shares at $40 per share.

[3] Stock purchase warrants, Series A (initially each warrant was exchangeable with $60 for one common share; effective December 1, 1995, each warrant became exchangeable for two common shares at $30 per share):

Oct. 1, 1995—25,000 warrants issued at $6 each.

[4] Stock purchase warrants, Series B (each warrant is exchangeable with $45 for one common share):

Apr. 1, 1996—20,000 warrants authorized and issued at $10 each.

[5] First mortgage bonds, 5½%, due 2003 (nonconvertible; priced to yield 5% when issued):

Balance, Oct. 1, 1995—authorized, issued, and outstanding at $1,400,000 face value.

[6] Convertible debentures, 7%, due 2015 (initially each $1,000 bond was convertible at any time until maturity into 12½ common shares; effective December 1, 1995, the conversion rate became 25 shares for each bond):

Oct. 1, 1995—authorized and issued at their face value (no premium or discount) of $2,400,000.

The following table shows market prices for the company's securities and the assumed Aa corporate bond yield during 1995–1996:

	Price (or Rate)			Average for Year Ended
	Oct. 1, 1995	Apr. 1, 1996	Sept. 30, 1996	Sept. 30, 1996
Common stock	66	40*	42*	37½*
First mortgage bonds	88½	87	86	87
Convertible debentures	100	120	119	115
Series A warrants	6	22	19½	15
Series B warrants	—	10	9	9½
Aa corporate bond yield	8%	7¾%	7½%	7¾%

*Adjusted for stock split.

INSTRUCTIONS

Assuming that net income for the year was $850,000 and that the income tax rate was 35%, prepare computations of primary and fully diluted EPS. Provide schedules and analyses to support your conclusions on each of the following:

[a] Common stock equivalency status of all potential diluters.
[b] Dilutive status of all potential diluters.
[c] Consideration of the minimum materiality standard for a dual presentation of EPS.

(AICPA adapted)

CASES

18–59 Concept of Substance over Form   Financial accounting usually emphasizes the economic substance of events, even though the legal form may differ and suggest different treatment. For example, under accrual accounting, expenses are recognized when they are incurred (substance) rather than when cash is disbursed (form).

Although substance over form dominates most generally accepted accounting principles and practices, form sometimes prevails over substance.

INSTRUCTIONS

Discuss EPS for a complex capital structure, identifying specific instances in which substance or form prevails.   (AICPA adapted)

18–60 Stockholders' Equity and EPS   Orten Company had the following accounts on its December 31, 1995, trial balance:

    6% Cumulative Convertible Preferred Stock, $100 par value
    Premium on Preferred Stock
    Common Stock, $1 stated value
    Premium on Common Stock
    Retained Earnings

The following additional information is available for the year ended December 31, 1995:

[1] Two million shares of preferred stock were authorized, of which 1,000,000 were outstanding. All shares outstanding were issued on January 2, 1992, for $120 a share. The Aa corporate bond yield was 8.5% on January 2, 1992, and 10% on December 31, 1995. The preferred stock is convertible

into common stock on a one-for-one basis until December 31, 2001, after which the preferred stock ceases to be convertible and is callable at par value by the company. No preferred stock has been converted into common stock, and there were no dividends in arrears at December 31, 1995.

[2] The common stock has been issued at amounts above stated value per share since Orten's incorporation in 1977. Of the 5,000,000 shares authorized, 3,500,000 shares were outstanding at January 1, 1995. The market price of the outstanding common stock has increased slowly, but consistently, for the last five years.

[3] The company has an employee stock option plan whereby certain key employees and officers may purchase shares of common stock at 100% of the market price at the date of the option grant. All options are exercisable in installments of one-third each year, beginning one year after the date of the grant, and expire if not exercised within four years of the grant date. On January 1, 1995, options for 70,000 shares were outstanding at prices ranging from $47 to $83 a share. Options for 20,000 shares were exercised at $47 to $79 a share during 1995. No options expired during 1995 and additional options for 15,000 shares were granted at $86 a share during the year. The 65,000 options outstanding at December 31, 1995, were exercisable at $54 to $86 a share; of these, 30,000 were exercisable at that date at prices ranging from $54 to $79 a share.

[4] The company also has an employee stock purchase plan whereby the company pays one-half and the employee pays the other half of the market price of the stock at the date of the subscription. During 1995 employees subscribed to 60,000 shares at an average price of $87 a share. All 60,000 shares were paid for and issued late in September 1995.

[5] On December 31, 1995, a total of 355,000 shares of common stock was set aside for future stock options and future purchases under the employee stock purchase plan.

The only changes in the stockholders' equity for 1995 were those described above, 1995 net income, and cash dividends paid.

INSTRUCTIONS

[a] Prepare the stockholders' equity section of Orten's balance sheet at December 31, 1995. Substitute Xs, where appropriate, for unknown dollar amounts. Use good form and provide full disclosure. Write appropriate footnotes as they should appear in the published financial statements.

[b] Explain how the denominator should be determined to compute *primary* EPS for presentation in the financial statements. Be specific about the handling of each item. If additional information is needed to determine whether an item should be included and to what extent, identify the information needed and how the item would be handled if the information were known. Assume that Orten had substantial net income for the year ended December 31, 1995. (AICPA adapted)

18–61 (Appendix A) Advanced EPS Concepts EPS is one of the most frequently featured financial statistics of modern corporations. Daily quotations of stock prices have recently been expanded for many securities to include a "times earnings" figure that is based on EPS. Analysts often focus their discussions on the EPS of corporations in which they are interested.

INSTRUCTIONS

[a] Explain how dividends or dividend requirements on any class of preferred stock that may be outstanding affect the computation of EPS.

[b] One of the technical procedures used in computing EPS is the treasury stock method.
　　[1] Briefly describe the circumstances in which the treasury stock method should be applied.
　　[2] Identify the limit to the applicability of the treasury stock method. Briefly indicate the procedures that should be followed beyond the limit of the treasury stock method.

[c] Under some circumstances, convertible debentures are considered common stock equivalents.
　　[1] When should convertible debentures be treated as common stock equivalents? In such cases, what is the effect on the computation of EPS?
　　[2] When convertible debentures are not considered common stock equivalents, how are they handled in EPS computations? (AICPA adapted)

JUDGMENT CASES

18–62 Managing EPS You are the controller of Litigious, Inc., which last year won and collected a large judgment from a competitor for unfair market infringement. The company is a small publicly held corporation with approximately 10 major stockholders and a large number of additional shares outstanding that are widely held. The financial statements for the preceding year appropriately reported the large gain from the litigation as part of income from continuing operations and before extraordinary items. The effects on the company's reported earnings per share of that gain were also large and favorable. Now the president of Litigious wishes to continue to report a high earnings per share number in the current year; however, operating results have been disappointing, and you expect that the rest of the current year will not show much improvement.

The large cash fund resulting from the judgment described above is still held in short-term investments; however, a number of desirable long-term projects are available to the company that would probably result in highly profitable results in approximately three years. Notwithstanding these desirable potential uses of the resources, the president has tentatively decided to use the funds to reacquire a large block of the company's outstanding stock. He states:

> *Why don't we simply reacquire a lot of our stock off the market with the proceeds from the litigation? That way we will be able to report a high earnings per share for the current year as well. That is particularly desirable from my personal perspective because my compensation and retirement agreements are based, in large measure, on the company's reported earnings per share. Further, I am scheduled to retire at the end of next year, and my retirement formula is highly weighted to the last three years of the company's performance as indicated by its earnings per share. I know a large number of attractive long-term projects are available for the company, but I simply don't have the time to wait for them to bear fruit. I am, therefore, going to begin the stock reacquisition program immediately because, as you know, the calculation is based on outstanding shares.*

INSTRUCTIONS

What, if anything, should you do? Can you ethically participate in the plan to reacquire the shares as the president intends? What considerations should affect your course of action?

18–63 Information Content of EPS A friend of yours, Roger Jones, is a financial analyst for a national brokerage firm with offices in the same building as your public accounting firm. Occasionally, he calls to ask you "accounting type" questions that usually require only a simple, brief answer. Today, however, he has called to discuss the concept of fully diluted earnings per share. He states:

> *I am considering investing in a company whose fully diluted earnings per share is much less than the number it reports for primary earnings per shares. The difference between the two, as best as I can tell, relates to a large number of bonds that can be converted into common stock. Because the company is currently troubled, its stock is trading at a low amount, and the bondholders clearly won't be converting their bonds any time soon. Therefore, I think that the acquisition of common stock today makes a lot of sense because there is no way that the fully diluted earnings per share number is realistic. That is, the value of the shares may be depressed by the possible conversion of the bonds, but I just don't think that will happen. Therefore, the shares are very likely undervalued. What do you think of my analysis?*

You are aware that your friend does not have a strong accounting background having majored in general business in college and worked for the brokerage firm for the past two years. He sometimes feels insecure in his position because he does not understand the assumptions and practices under which financial statements are prepared in conformity with generally accepted accounting principles.

INSTRUCTIONS

Respond to your friend's views. Remember, you have your own work to do and cannot spend a lot of time at work coaching him.

FINANCIAL REPORTING CASE

18–64 Financial Reporting Case Ralston Purina Company was founded in 1894 and is the world's largest producer of dry dog food and dry and soft-moist cat foods. In addition, Ralston Purina is a large wholesale baker, manufacturer of dry cell battery products, and a producer of breakfast cereals and other food products.

Following is Ralston Purina Company's 1992 income statement, with comparative years 1991 and 1990. The earnings per share note from the summary of significant accounting policies accompanying the 1992 financial statements follows the income statement.

Ralston Purina Company and Subsidiaries
Consolidated Statement of Earnings
(Dollars in millions except per share data)

Year ended September 30	1992	1991	1990
Net Sales			
Costs and Expenses	**$7,752.4**	$7,375.8	$7,101.4
Cost of products sold	**4,223.1**	3,974.3	3,864.1
Selling, general and administrative	**1,784.9**	1,643.3	1,511.8
Advertising and promotion	**931.3**	870.5	845.1
Interest	**242.9**	208.7	207.7
Other (income)/expense, net	**28.1**	31.2	17.7
	7,210.3	6,728.0	6,446.4
Earnings before Income Taxes and			
Extraordinary Item	**542.1**	647.8	655.0
Income Taxes	**221.4**	255.9	258.7
Earnings before Extraordinary Item	**320.7**	391.9	396.3
Extraordinary Item – Loss on			
Early Retirement of Debt	**(7.5)**		
Net Earnings	**313.2**	391.9	396.3
Preferred Stock Dividend, Net of Taxes	**21.0**	20.7	20.5
Earnings Available to Common Shareholders	**$ 292.2**	$ 371.2	$ 375.8
Earnings per Share			
Primary			
Earnings before Extraordinary Item	**$ 2.82**	$ 3.34	$ 3.23
Extraordinary Item	**(.07)**		
Net earnings	**$ 2.75**	$ 3.34	$ 3.23
Fully Diluted			
Earnings before Extraordinary Item	**$ 2.65**	$ 3.12	$ 3.03
Extraordinary Item	**(.06)**		
Net earnings	**$ 2.59**	$ 3.12	$ 3.03

Earnings per Share

Primary earnings per share are based on the average number of shares outstanding during the year (106,314,000 in 1992, 111,189,000 in 1991 and 116,308,000 in 1990). Fully diluted earnings per share assumes the conversion of the Series A 6.75% Preferred Stock (Redeemable Preferred Stock) and other dilutive securities into Company common stock. For purposes of calculating fully diluted earnings per share, net earnings have been adjusted for the additional contribution to the Company's employee stock ownership plans and their related trust (ESOP) that would have been required had the Redeemable Preferred Stock been converted as of the beginning of the period.

    All related common per share information and average share data has been restated, for all periods presented, to reflect the effects of the two-for-one stock split declared in 1991.

INSTRUCTIONS

[a] Does Ralston Purina Company have a simple or complex capital structure? How can you tell?

[b] Explain how the EPS presentation at the bottom of the income statement parallels the items included earlier in that statement.

[c] What explanation does the note offer to help readers of the financial statements to understand the difference between primary and fully diluted EPS?

[d] How are the numbers presented affected by the 2:1 stock split explained in the financial statement note? Explain how this is consistent with what we have learned in Chapter 18 about the treatment of stock splits. Estimate the impact the split had on EPS for 1990 and 1991.

Income Taxes

OBJECTIVES

1. To explain differences in the determination of net income for financial reporting purposes (financial income) and income for purposes of determining a company's income tax liability to the government (taxable income).

2. To explain the conceptual justification for recognizing deferred tax assets and liabilities and demonstrate accounting for permanent and temporary differences between financial and taxable income.

3. To illustrate the impact that income tax laws have on the elements of the financial statements related to income taxes.

4. To evaluate the recognition of deferred taxes on temporary differences and introduce alternatives to current practices of accounting for income taxes.

5. To explain and illustrate accounting for operating loss carrybacks and carryforwards.

You may have heard the statement that only two things are certain: death and taxes! We often think of income taxes as being paid by individuals, but corporations also pay income taxes. Information about income taxes constitutes an important part of a company's financial statements and related explanatory notes. The impact that income taxes has on companies' financial statements varies, depending primarily on profitability.

As an example of the impact of income taxes on the financial statements of a profitable company, consider the case of The Coca-Cola Company. The 1993 income statement includes income tax expense of $997 million of which approximately $650 million were paid in cash during the year. Coca-Cola's balance sheet includes a liability for "deferred income taxes" of $113 million. *Deferred* in this context means what it generally does: delayed. The company has taken advantage of certain alternatives in tax law that permit it to delay the payment of taxes, thereby retaining the use of cash that would otherwise have been paid to the government.

Delta Air Lines, Inc., on the other hand, has sustained net losses for several years and faces a quite different situation with regard to income taxes. In 1993 Delta's income statement reports the recovery of income taxes of $233 million previously paid. The company actually received a net amount of $166 million cash back from the government during the year. Delta's balance sheet includes no deferred income taxes among its liabilities, as does Coca-Cola's but includes over $504 million in deferred taxes as a noncurrent asset. Rather than representing the delay of payment of income taxes, these deferred taxes represent delayed benefits to the company in terms of having to pay fewer dollars in taxes in the future.

Relative to other amounts in the financial statements of both Coca-Cola and Delta Air Lines, the dollar amounts mentioned are quite significant. You can see, however, that they impact the two companies very differently: Coca-Cola recognized tax expense, paid cash for taxes, and had deferred tax liabilities; Delta recognized a recovery of income taxes, received cash for taxes, and had deferred tax assets.

INTRODUCTION TO INCOME TAX REPORTING

Income taxes represent a major expense for many businesses. Although income taxes are comparable to other expenses in many respects, several unusual and complicating features of accounting for income taxes and the presentation of those taxes in the financial statements exist. These complications result from the fact that the amount of income taxes to be paid must be in accordance with legal requirements of the Internal Revenue Code. This requires complex determinations of the amounts of income taxes to be paid that then become the basis for several items that appear in the financial statements and accompanying notes of the enterprise.

As you begin this chapter, turn to the Kellogg financial statements on the inside front and back covers of this text or in the text appendix. These statements contain several references to income taxes. The income statement includes an expense labeled income taxes for $353.4 million. The subtotal before that figure denotes income before income taxes and the one following that figure denotes income after income taxes. Several items in the balance sheet relate to income taxes: deferred income taxes of $85.5 million among the current assets and $188.9 million among the noncurrent liabilities, and an accrued liability for income taxes of $65.9 million. At this point, you may wonder how the same item, deferred income taxes, can be both a current asset and a noncurrent liability. We explain that, as well as other complications related to income taxes, in this chapter. In the text appendix, you will also find Note 10 of the Kellogg financial statements, which includes a great deal of tax-related information. The relevance of this information will come into clearer focus as you work through this chapter.

Going Concern

Asset/Liability Measurement

Matching

Several underlying accounting principles are important in forming specific accounting practices relating to the financial reporting of income taxes. The going-concern assumption is important because we assume that the enterprise will remain in existence in the foreseeable future and will continue to pay income taxes as profits are earned. The proper determination of assets and liabilities is influenced greatly by income taxes. Payables and receivables for income taxes are frequently included among liabilities and assets, as are deferred income taxes, a subject we consider in this chapter. The determination of income is influenced by the matching principle, in that expenses associated with revenues being recognized are included in the income statement as a part of the determination of the net income figure. Some people view income taxes as a *distribution* of income of the enterprise, but the generally accepted interpretation is that income taxes are appropriately viewed as a *determinant* of income of the enterprise. Thus, *income taxes are an expense* and are subject to accrual accounting methods in the same manner as other expenses. Accordingly, the income tax effects of revenue and expense transactions must be recognized in the income statement in the same accounting period in which those revenues and expenses affect net income, even if the items appear in the income tax return in a different accounting period. Thus, a direct association exists between income tax expense in a given accounting period and the revenues and other expenses recognized in that same period.

The objectives of financial reporting and the accounting principles that underlie financial reporting were carefully considered in developing the rules that govern presentation of income taxes in the financial statements. The basic objective of financial reporting is to provide useful information to investors, creditors, and other financial statement users for making financial decisions. Income tax laws, on the other hand, have been developed through government action to reach quite different ends, such as the generation of income for the government, the redistribution of wealth within the economy, and the encouragement of the long-run growth of the economy. Given the different objectives of financial reporting and the income tax laws, it is not surprising that the timing of the recognition of revenue and expense items sometimes varies between income tax law and GAAP.

Corporations are subject to federal income tax rates that vary from time to time as changes are made in income tax laws. At the time this textbook was written, most corporate taxpayers were subject to four progressive income tax rates, as follows:

15% on the first $50,000 of taxable income.
25% on the next $25,000 of taxable income.
34% on additional taxable income up to $10 million.
35% on taxable income exceeding $10 million.

Surtaxes are used, however, to alter these rates. For example, a 5% surtax exists on corporate taxable income between $100,000 and $335,000, effectively increasing the rate in that range to 39%. Similarly, an additional 3% surtax applies to taxable income between $15 million and $18,333,333, creating a 38% rate in that range. Combining the basic rates and surtaxes, as taxable income rises, the marginal tax rate increases progressively from 15% to 39%, drops back to 34%, and then increases to 35% and 38%, and finally settles back at 35%. Our purpose in explaining this dimension of income tax law is to make you generally aware of progressive income tax rates and to explain, as we do in the following paragraph, our use of single rates in most of the material in this chapter.

As you are probably aware from reading newspapers and listening to radio and television news, tax laws change from time to time. The authors expect that many students studying this chapter will not yet have taken a course in corporate income taxation. Accordingly, in this chapter, we focus on basic principles of reporting income tax information in financial statements and do not attempt to explain every financial reporting and income tax problem that can occur. We simplify certain income tax procedures to facilitate our study of financial reporting. For example, we generally assume simplified single income tax rates, such as 34%, 36%, and 40%, as a basis for determining income tax amounts, rather than using the graduated income tax rate schedule mentioned above. We also limit our coverage of income taxation to the federal level and do not cover, for example, accounting for state income taxes.

Through the years, several important authoritative accounting pronouncements have been issued that deal with accounting and reporting income taxes in the financial statements. From 1967 to 1987, guidance was provided by *APB Opinion No. 11*,[1] which emphasized the matching process. That pronouncement was replaced by *FASB Statement of Financial Accounting Standards No. 96*,[2] which required an asset/liability valuation approach to determining the elements of financial statements concerning income taxes. The FASB encountered great resistance in practice in its attempts to implement *SFAS No. 96*, however, and the effective date of that pronouncement was delayed three times. *FASB Statement No. 109*[3] was issued in early 1992 to replace *SFAS No. 96*, effective in 1993. In addition to these primary authoritative pronouncements, several other pronouncements on specialized areas of accounting for income taxes have been issued since *APB Opinion No. 11* was issued in 1967.

Matching

In this chapter, we discuss several important aspects of the subject of accounting for income taxes. The material is generally consistent with current authoritative literature but has been simplified to permit us to focus on basic principles of financial reporting rather than on detailed application of income tax procedures.

The remainder of this chapter is presented in three major sections. First, we consider the subject of deferred tax assets and liabilities brought about by temporary differences in the way certain items are treated in determining pretax financial income and taxable income.

[1]*APB Opinion No. 11*, "Accounting for Income Taxes," 1967.
[2]*FASB Statement of Financial Accounting Standards No. 96*, "Accounting for Income Taxes," 1987.
[3]*FASB Statement of Financial Accounting Standards No. 109*, "Accounting for Income Taxes," 1992.

Next, we explore the area of loss carrybacks and carryforwards, a unique feature of income tax law that permits a company to move losses from one year back or forward in time to offset income of other years, thereby reducing the amount of income taxes that would otherwise have to be paid. Finally, we consider a comprehensive illustration that incorporates the recognition of deferred tax assets and liabilities and operating loss carrybacks and carryforwards and focuses on the impact that these have on the primary financial statements. Appendix A discusses another unique feature of income tax law, the investment tax credit.

TEMPORARY DIFFERENCES AND DEFERRED INCOME TAX ASSETS AND LIABILITIES

Earlier in this chapter, you were introduced to the idea that certain transactions affect financial income and taxable income in different accounting periods. An important objective of accrual accounting for income taxes is to recognize the appropriate amount of current *and deferred* income taxes payable or refundable in the balance sheet for these differences.

Differences between the amount of income for financial reporting purposes and taxable income are caused by temporary and permanent differences. Both relate to differences in the way certain items are treated in determining financial income and taxable income; both are important in understanding financial reporting of income taxes. A discussion of each of these follows, including an explanation of how they affect the determination of deferred tax assets and liabilities.

TEMPORARY DIFFERENCES

The tax consequences of most events recognized in a company's financial statements are included in determining income taxes payable in the same period. Despite this general similarity in treatment, tax laws and GAAP sometimes differ in their recognition and measurement of assets, liabilities, owners' equity, revenues, expenses, gains, and losses. An important assumption inherent in an enterprise's balance sheet prepared in accordance with GAAP is that assets will be recovered at their reported amounts and liabilities will be settled at their reported amounts. Building on that assumption, we further assume that a difference between the income tax basis of an asset or a liability and its reported amount in the balance sheet will result in taxable or deductible amounts in determining taxable income in some future year. Differences that will result in taxable or deductible amounts in the future are called **temporary differences.** A difference is a **taxable temporary difference** when the item causes financial income to exceed taxable income, with the expectation that the difference will be offset in future periods. Likewise, a difference is a **deductible temporary difference** when it causes taxable income to exceed financial income, with the expectation that the difference will be offset in future periods.

Temporary differences result from differences in the pattern or timing of recognition of certain items in reporting financial income and taxable income. For every temporary difference, eventually that item's treatment will be the same in financial and taxable income. Temporary differences are said to *originate* in one accounting period (the period in which the difference is first determined) and *reverse* in a later accounting period (the later period in which the difference is offset).

The most frequently encountered temporary difference is the one resulting from plant asset write-off for tax purposes and depreciation for financial reporting purposes. The Economic Recovery Act of 1981 made significant changes in the manner in which companies write off the cost of plant assets in determining their income tax liability. That law introduced a system called the **Accelerated Cost Recovery System (ACRS),** which permitted rapid write-off of asset costs over predetermined periods that were generally shorter than the estimated useful lives of the property.

Those procedures were modified in the Tax Reform Act of 1986 and further refined by the 1993 tax act, but the system remains essentially the same. Under the **Modified Accelerated Cost Recovery System (MACRS),** the cost of eligible property is recovered over a 3-,

5-, 7-, 10-, 15-, 20-, 27.5-, 31.5-, or 39-year period, depending on the type of property, at preestablished percentage rates for each year. For example, the 5-year category includes such assets as cars, light general-purpose trucks, and computer equipment. The 7-year category includes office furniture and fixtures. The 20-year and longer periods are generally reserved for various types of real estate.

Accelerated cost recovery is an area of difference between income tax law and generally accepted accounting principles that illustrates clearly the nature of temporary differences. The periods of write-off for tax purposes are often not consistent with the useful lives of the assets and, as a result, accelerated cost recovery is usually not acceptable for financial reporting purposes. When the company uses a different method in determining financial income, such as straight-line, temporary differences occur.

We separate temporary differences into those that, at their origin, result in financial income that exceeds taxable income and those that result in taxable income that exceeds financial income. First, types of temporary differences that result in financial income higher than taxable income at the time of the origination of the temporary differences include the following:

1. Revenues or gains that are taxable after they are recognized in financial income. An example is an installment sale that is recognized as revenue in financial income at the time of the sale and included in taxable income when cash is later collected.

2. Expenses or losses that are deductible for income tax purposes before they are recognized in financial income. An example is the write-off of plant assets on an accelerated basis for income tax purposes with straight-line depreciation being used in the financial statements.

These result in what we defined earlier as *taxable temporary differences*.

Other temporary differences have the opposite effect when they originate, in that taxable income exceeds financial income. Examples include the following:

1. Revenues and gains that are taxable before they are recognized in financial income. An example is a cash advance received for services to be provided in the future that is taxable when received but is recognized in financial income when later earned.

2. Expenses and losses that are deductible for income tax purposes after they are recognized in financial income. An example is a litigation loss that is recognized in financial income when it is probable and measurable but deducted for income tax purposes later, when the litigation is settled.

These result in what we defined earlier as *deductible temporary differences*.

In practice, a number of other temporary differences exist. These are generally beyond the scope of this text and, accordingly, in the examples that follow, as well as in the assignment material at the end of the chapter, we limit our consideration to these four temporary differences. This means you do not need an in-depth knowledge of income tax laws and advanced financial accounting topics to understand the financial reporting implications of income taxes.

PERMANENT DIFFERENCES

Permanent differences result from differences in the definitions of financial and taxable income. Certain items of revenue and expense are included in either financial or taxable income but will *never* be included in the other. Permanent differences do not originate and reverse as do temporary differences. Thus, permanent differences do not give rise to deferred tax assets or liabilities because they have no future tax consequences.

In this text, we limit permanent differences included in the illustrations and end-of-chapter materials to two specific items:

1. Interest received on state and local government securities. This type of interest received is included in determining financial income but is not included in determining taxable income.

2. Insurance premiums paid when company is the beneficiary. This type of expense is included in determining financial income but is not deductible in determining taxable income.

PRINCIPLES OF ACCOUNTING FOR DEFERRED INCOME TAXES

In this chapter, we discuss a general approach to recognizing deferred income taxes called the *asset/liability method* (sometimes simply called the *liability method*). The FASB has worked extensively to implement the asset/liability method in practice. The approach used in the following sections is generally consistent with the FASB's approach but is simplified to focus on basic principles of recognizing income tax assets, liabilities, and expense. Our primary focus is on developing analytical and conceptual thinking rather than memorizing an ever-expanding set of professional standards.

Asset/Liability Measurement   Recall from our discussion of accounting theory in Chapter 3 that the asset/liability view of earnings defines revenues, expenses, gains, and losses in terms of certain changes that occur in assets and liabilities. The asset/liability method of determining deferred income taxes and income tax expense is consistent with the asset/liability view of earnings.

In contrast, another method called the *deferred method* was widely used in the past under *APB Opinion No. 11*. That method represents an excellent example of the revenue/expense view of earnings, also discussed in Chapter 3. Under the deferred method of accounting for income taxes, primary emphasis is placed on the amount of income tax expense. That is, the accountant computed the amount of income tax expense directly by multiplying the pretax accounting income subject to tax by the income tax rate. If this amount differed from the current tax liability owed to the government (i.e., taxable income multiplied by the tax rate), the difference was recognized as deferred income taxes. Under that approach, deferred income taxes represent the residual effects of recognizing the amount of income tax expense. In computing income tax expense, only the current period's income tax rate was used; future rates were ignored even when they had already been enacted. The deferred method was prominent in the past, but it is rapidly disappearing from practice because it is inconsistent with the current emphasis being placed on measuring and reporting assets and liabilities in the balance sheet under *SFAS No. 109*. For that reason, we do not cover that method extensively in this chapter.

Following are several broad principles that are important to keep in mind as we consider in more detail proper accounting for deferred tax assets and liabilities under the generalized asset/liability approach illustrated in the next section.

1. A deferred tax asset or liability is recognized for the income tax consequences of *all temporary differences* that have been recognized in either financial income or taxable income.
2. Deferred tax assets and liabilities are determined on the basis of *enacted income tax rates*. No attempt is made to estimate future income tax rates that are not yet enacted.
3. When enacted future tax rates change, deferred taxes are remeasured at the end of the next accounting period to incorporate the new rates.

EXAMPLES OF DEFERRED TAX ASSETS AND LIABILITIES

In this section, we illustrate accounting for permanent and temporary differences, focusing our attention on the determination of deferred tax assets and liabilities. We shall see that the related income tax expense is determined by combining the amount of income tax currently payable and the *change* in the amount of deferred tax assets or liabilities. Using the asset/liability method, we directly measure the assets and liabilities related to income taxes and then determine income tax expense residually.

Example 1: First Year of Operations

Pinson Company has determined its pretax financial income for 1995, its first year of operations, to be $130,000. Included in that amount are the following permanent and temporary differences from taxable income:

Permanent difference: Interest received on investments in municipal bonds, $5,000.

Temporary differences: (1) Excess of accelerated asset write-off for income tax purposes over straight-line depreciation in determining financial income, $25,000; (2) recognition of loss from litigation against the company in financial income that will not be tax deductible until settled in the future, $10,000.

For purposes of recognizing current income taxes payable, as well as deferred tax assets and liabilities, we assume that the 1995 income tax rate is 35% and the enacted rate for all future years is 38%. The following analysis facilitates our preparation of the appropriate year-end tax accrual:

	1995	Future Years
Pretax financial income	$130,000	—
Permanent difference:		
Municipal interest	(5,000)	—
Pretax financial income subject to income tax	$125,000	—
Temporary differences:		
Depreciation	(25,000)	$ 25,000
Litigation	10,000	(10,000)
Taxable income	$110,000	$ 15,000
Income tax rate	35%	38%
Income tax payable (receivable)		
Current	$ 38,500	
Deferred		$ 5,700

The depreciation temporary difference is a future taxable amount; the litigation temporary difference is a future deductible amount. You can tell this by the manner in which they are presented in the Future Years column. Based on this analysis, we can now prepare the 1995 year-end income tax accrual for Pinson, as follows:

Dec. 31, 1995 Income Tax Expense ($38,500 + $5,700)   44,200
                 Income Tax Payable   38,500
                 Deferred Income Tax   5,700

Several observations are important concerning this accrual. Notice that we have not attempted to predict future income tax rates, but have based the future year figures on enacted rates at the time of the accrual. Notice that the permanent difference is eliminated from consideration (i.e., not included in the amount of "pretax financial income subject to income tax") and has no impact on the amount of deferred income taxes. Finally, as a result of this accrual, we have two tax liabilities: the *current* income tax payable of $38,500 and the *deferred* income tax of $5,700. The amount of income tax expense is determined by simply combining these two liabilities.

Example 2: Second Year of Operations/No Tax Rate Change

We now extend Example 1 to add the complication of dealing with accounting for deferred taxes when a beginning balance exists and temporary differences reverse, as well as originate. Recall that an assumption of Example 1 was that 1995 was Pinson Company's first year of operations and, thus, no deferred tax assets or liabilities existed at the beginning of the year. We now consider 1996, the company's second year of operations, keeping in mind that the year begins with a credit balance of $5,700 in deferred income taxes.

New information for 1996 follows:

Permanent difference: Interest on investments in securities issued by municipalities totals $6,000.

Temporary differences: (1) Accelerated write-off for income tax purposes exceeds straight-line depreciation by $30,000; in addition, $12,000 of the temporary difference from depreciation from 1995 reverses in 1996. (2) The litigation loss from 1995 is settled at the $10,000 estimated amount.

Pretax financial income for 1996 is $156,000, and for this illustration, we maintain our assumption that all years beginning with 1996 are subject to a 38% income tax rate. We are now ready to analyze 1996 in a manner similar to that of 1995:

	1996	Future Years
Pretax financial income	$156,000	—
Permanent difference:		
Municipal interest	(6,000)	—
Pretax financial income subject to income tax	$150,000	—
Temporary differences:		
Depreciation:		
1996 originating	(30,000)	$30,000
1995 reversing	12,000	13,000*
Litigation:		
1995 reversing	(10,000)	—
Taxable income	$122,000	$43,000
Income tax rate	38%	38%
Income tax payable (receivable)		
Current	$ 46,360	
Deferred		$16,340

*$25,000 originating in 1995, less $12,000 reversing in 1996.

The amount of deferred income tax indicated at the end of 1996 is $16,340, representing a liability for income taxes on temporary differences that are taxable amounts in the future. The *increase* in deferred income taxes for 1996 is $10,640, however, because the 1995 balance was $5,700: $16,340 − $5,700 = $10,640. The accrual for income taxes for 1996, to record the current payable and the *net increase in deferred income taxes,* is as follows:

Dec. 31, 1996	Income Tax Expense ($46,360 + $10,640)	57,000	
	Income Tax Payable ($122,000 × 38%)		46,360
	Deferred Income Tax ($16,340 − $5,700)		10,640

Example 3: Second Year of Operations/Tax Rate Change

In Example 3, we add one more complication to accounting for deferred tax assets and liabilities—a change in the enacted future income tax rate. All information from Example 2 is repeated in Example 3 except that we now assume that during 1996, the enacted income tax rate for all future years is changed to 40%. Applying this rate to the accumulated temporary differences, we determine that the net change in deferred income taxes for 1996 is $11,500:

Accumulated net temporary differences (see analysis from Example 2)	$43,000
Income tax rate	40%
Ending balance in deferred income taxes	$17,200
Beginning balance of deferred taxes	(5,700)
Increase for 1996	$11,500

Alternatively, the $11,500 change in deferred taxes can be computed as follows:

Origination of 1996 excess depreciation: $30,000 × 40%	$12,000
Reversal of 1995 excess depreciation: $12,000 × 38%	(4,560)
Reversal of 1995 litigation: ($10,000) × 38%	3,800
Change in tax rate on temporary difference carried forward from prior year: $13,000 × (40% − 38%)	260
	$11,500

The 1996 accrual under this new tax rate assumption is as follows:

Dec. 31, 1996　Income Tax Expense ($46,360 + $11,500)　　　57,860
　　　　　　　　Income Tax Payable ($122,000 × 38%)　　　　　　　　　46,360
　　　　　　　　Deferred Income Taxes ($17,200 − $5,700)　　　　　　　11,500

The use of currently enacted income tax rates and the procedure followed when the enacted rate changes represent an interesting example of accounting for a change in accounting estimate. Changes in estimate were introduced in Chapter 12 when we considered changes in the estimated useful lives of plant assets; the subject is considered again in Chapter 20. In the case of accounting for income taxes, the change in income tax rate is incorporated into the determination of income tax expense by simply adjusting the amount of expense that would otherwise have been recognized. The increase in deferred income taxes in Example 3 compared to Example 2, due to the increase in the income tax rate, is $860:

Deferred income taxes, Example 3 (40%)　　　$ 17,200
Deferred income taxes, Example 2 (38%)　　　 (16,340)
Increase [$43,000 × (40% − 38%)]　　　　　　$　860

Of this amount, $600 is due to 1996 originating differences ($30,000 × 2%); $260 is attributable to the increased income tax rate applicable to temporary differences originating in 1995 but not reversing in 1996 ($13,000 × 2%). The $260 amount, although not recognized as a separate component in determining 1996 net income, is an adjustment to income tax expense for the change in income tax rate and, thus, represents a change in accounting estimate. Had the enacted income tax rate been *reduced,* this would have resulted in a *decrease* in income tax expense recognized on the accumulated temporary differences, as well as a lower current payable on the taxable income of 1996.

The examples of deferred income taxes arising from temporary differences in this section have focused on deferred tax credits or liabilities. When tax law gives companies the latitude to select methods that defer taxable income, prudent management will naturally elect to do that. For that reason, the typical position for a company relative to deferred income taxes is a net liability position, indicating that it has deferred or delayed the payment of income taxes on some transactions that have already been included in pretax financial income. Inasmuch as the most common temporary difference, and frequently the largest one, arises from the use of accelerated write-off of plant assets in taxable income and the straight-line depreciation of those same assets in pretax financial income, we expect many companies to reflect a net liability deferred income tax position in their balance sheets. In the year-end analysis to establish the amount of deferred income taxes, a situation could arise in which taxable income exceeds pretax accounting income. For example, that situation would result from a taxable amount entering taxable income from the reversal of an earlier temporary difference that caused financial income to exceed taxable income. If this is the case, an existing deferred tax liability would be debited. Another possibility is that an originating temporary difference results in a future deductible amount and, thus, taxable income exceeds financial income. In this case, a deferred tax asset is debited in the income tax accrual.

In illustrating the application of the asset/liability method of accounting for deferred income taxes, we have avoided certain complications to permit us to focus on basic underlying principles. For example, one simplifying assumption we have made is that once the enacted future income tax rate is changed, the new rate applies to all future years. That assumption would not always hold true, because a series of rate changes could be enacted, resulting in different income tax rates in effect in different future years. Also, we have avoided net loss situations that involve loss carrybacks and carryforwards, subjects of a later section in this chapter. We combine the subjects of deferred tax assets and liabilities and loss carrybacks and carryforwards in the comprehensive illustration at the end of this chapter.

EXHIBIT 19–1

Deferred Income Taxes of Selected Companies

Company	Noncurrent Deferred Income Tax Credits	
	Millions of Dollars	As Percent of Liabilities Plus Stockholders' Equity
Union Pacific Corporation	$ 2,676.0	17.8
Shell Oil Company	3,754.0	14.0
Exxon Corporation	10,939.0	13.0
Tenneco	1,225.0	8.0
General Mills, Inc.	262.0	5.6
IBM	1,803.0	2.2
The Procter and Gamble Company	183.0	0.7
Kellogg Company	188.9	0.5

SOURCE: 1993 Annual Reports.

DEFERRED TAXES: INTERPRETATIONS AND ALTERNATIVES

Are deferred income taxes significant items in corporate balance sheets? Although the answer to this question varies from company to company, on average the response is yes. Exhibit 19–1 indicates the noncurrent deferred income tax credits, where most deferred taxes reside, for selected companies for 1993 in dollars and as a percentage of total equities (liabilities plus stockholders' equity).

The dollar amounts and relative sizes of the noncurrent deferred income tax accounts vary, but Exhibit 19–1 indicates that they may be significant balance sheet items. Of the companies presented, Union Pacific Corporation has the highest percentage of deferred taxes included in total equities—17.8%. The smallest percentage is 0.5% for Kellogg Company. The large noncurrent deferred income tax credit balances are due primarily to temporary differences caused by accelerated write-off of plant asset cost for income tax purposes, coupled with the use of straight-line depreciation for financial reporting purposes.

Accounting for deferred income tax assets and liabilities arising from temporary differences has been a controversial subject in the accounting profession for many years. Procedures resulting in the recognition of deferred tax assets and liabilities were initiated several decades ago when relatively simple temporary differences (related primarily to alternative depreciation methods) emerged.[4] As the concept expanded and was applied to a wide variety of differences between financial income and taxable income, a number of questions arose. Several authoritative pronouncements commenting on specific aspects of deferred income taxes have been issued since the basic concept was initially developed.

The Accounting Principles Board favored *comprehensive interperiod income tax allocation,* meaning that deferred taxes are recognized on all temporary differences, regardless of whether they are recurring or nonrecurring in nature. That decision was based on several general concepts and assumptions relative to the nature of income taxes and their relationship to the determination of net income. These concepts and assumptions are summarized as follows:[5]

---

[4]Homer A. Black, *Accounting Research Study No. 9,* "Interperiod Allocation of Corporate Income Taxes" (New York: AICPA, 1966), pp. 12, 64.

[5]*APB Opinion No. 11,* par. 14.

1. The operations of an entity subject to income taxes are expected to continue on a going con-cern basis, in the absence of evidence to the contrary. Accordingly, income taxes are ex-pected to continue to be assessed in the future.

2. Income taxes are an expense of business enterprises earning income subject to income taxes.

3. Accounting for income tax expense requires measurement and identification with the appro-priate time period. Accruals, deferrals, and estimations are involved in the same manner as these concepts are applied in the measurement and time period identification of other expenses.

4. Matching—perhaps the most basic principle of income determination—involves the associa-tion of specific costs with specific revenues or time periods. Expenses of the current period consist of those costs that are identified with revenue of the current period and those costs that are identified with the current period on some basis other than revenues.

Going Concern

Periodicity

Matching

As we stated earlier, the APB stressed an approach called the **deferred method,** which emphasized the determination of income tax expense. Under that approach, deferred income tax accounts were residual amounts that resulted from the determination of income tax ex-pense and were not directly determined by measuring the assets and liabilities that resulted from individual temporary differences. Income tax expense under the deferred method was based only on the income tax rate of the period of the origination of the underlying tempo-rary differences. This posed a particular problem in situations in which temporary differ-ences originated when one tax rate was in effect and reversed when another tax rate was in effect.

The FASB has recently changed the orientation of accounting for deferred income taxes to the *asset/liability method,* as described earlier in this chapter. Although the FASB would agree with the APB in terms of the general conclusion that income taxes are an expense and that operations are expected to continue on a going concern basis, the FASB's emphasis is on *asset and liability determination* as a means to determine income tax expense. In this approach, income tax expense is the amount obtained when the current income tax payable is combined with the change in deferred income taxes. Thus, the expense is a residual amount that results from the measurement of the income tax assets and liabilities. Heavy em-phasis is placed on the reversal of temporary differences and the currently enacted future in-come tax rates.

Going Concern

Alternative Methods to Comprehensive Allocation

Generally accepted accounting principles require that deferred income tax accounts include the tax effects of *all* temporary differences between financial and taxable income. This pro-cedure, often referred to as *comprehensive income tax allocation,* is a well-established ac-counting practice. Several alternatives have been suggested, however, that warrant at least brief mention before we leave the subject of deferred taxes arising from temporary differences.

One alternative to comprehensive allocation is **partial allocation.** Partial allocation as-sumes that for a particular period, income tax expense should be the same as income tax payable except for the impact of *nonrecurring* temporary differences. Proponents of partial allocation reason that recurring differences between financial income and taxable income, such as those resulting from depreciation, give rise to the *indefinite* postponement of income taxes, and, thus, the recognition of the tax effects of such recurring temporary differences should *not* be required. For example, a company may engage in a continuous investment policy in plant assets, coupled with the use of accelerated write-off for income tax purposes, and straight-line depreciation for financial reporting purposes. The reversal of temporary differences (when the tax write-off falls below straight-line depreciation on older assets) is offset by the origination of temporary differences (when the tax write-off exceeds straight-line depreciation on newer assets). The net effect is that income taxes on temporary differ-ences are continuously deferred and effectively never paid. Temporary differences from depreciation then take on the characteristics of permanent differences.

Proponents of partial allocation believe that only **nonrecurring** temporary differences between financial income and taxable income should give rise to deferred income taxes.

Materiality

Because the reversal of a nonrecurring difference is not expected to be offset by the origination of another difference (due to the nonrecurring nature of the revenue or expense), income tax expense may be materially misstated if the tax effects of the temporary difference are ignored. Under partial allocation, the income tax expense of the period is increased or decreased by income taxes on nonrecurring temporary differences that can reasonably be expected to affect taxable income in the foreseeable future. A five-year period has been suggested as an appropriate time frame for the application of this concept.[6]

Another alternative is **nonallocation** of income tax. Within this relatively simple method, the total of income tax paid during the period and payable at the end of the period would constitute income tax expense, regardless of differences in methods of recognizing revenues and expenses in the financial statements as compared with the tax return. Because this approach omits deferred income tax assets and liabilities from the balance sheet, some accountants question its appropriateness. On the other hand, historically, the methods of determining income for financial reporting and income tax purposes were quite similar. Some accountants believe that the two have gradually drifted so far apart that attempting to link them together via the recognition of deferred tax assets and liabilities is no longer appropriate.

Materiality

One final issue concerning interperiod income tax allocation is whether deferred income taxes should be *discounted* and reported in the balance sheet at their present value. We have not discounted deferred income taxes in the illustrations in this chapter. Present authoritative accounting pronouncements indicate that deferred income taxes should *not* be discounted to their present value in measuring the elements of financial statements.[7] The FASB is currently studying the broad issue of discounting in the financial statements, including discounting deferred income taxes. We may see change in this area when that study is completed. If discounting were required, it would likely have a material effect on the financial statements of those companies that carefully manage their income taxes so that significant amounts are indefinitely deferred to future periods.

OPERATING LOSS CARRYBACKS AND CARRYFORWARDS

Certain provisions of income tax law allow companies to offset losses of one year against income of other years to reduce the total income tax burden of the company. **Operating loss carrybacks** result when the loss of a particular year is taken back in time and used to reduce income taxes of past years. The carryback gives the enterprise the right to a refund of income taxes that have already been paid. **Operating loss carryforwards** result when the loss of a particular year is taken forward in time and used to reduce income taxes of future years. The effect of the carryforward is an *anticipated* reduction of income taxes that would otherwise have to be paid if operations of future years result in income subject to income taxes. Because carrybacks are based on past income and related income taxes that have already been paid and carryforwards are based on expected future income and related income taxes that *may* have to be paid, the value of carryforwards to an enterprise is more speculative or uncertain than carrybacks.

THE ALTERNATIVES: CARRYBACK/CARRYFORWARD OR CARRYFORWARD ONLY

A loss of a particular year can be carried *back* if the enterprise has reported income and paid income taxes within a specified period (three years under present tax law). If the enterprise has not had income and therefore has not paid income taxes within the specified carryback period, the loss of a particular year can be carried *forward* and offset against income of future periods for a specified period of time (15 years under present tax law). If the loss of the current period exceeds the income reported during the carryback period, the portion that cannot be carried back can be carried forward. Finally, the enterprise has the option to carry

---

[6]*APB Opinion No. 11*, par. 27.
[7]*APB Opinion No. 10*, "Omnibus Opinion—1966," 1966, par. 6.

the entire loss of a particular period forward instead of back. This election must be made in the loss year and cannot be changed once an option has been selected. However, a company may use one option for one loss year and the other option for another loss year. Once the option is selected, the income of the earliest year possible is reduced by the loss of the year in question. These alternatives are illustrated in Exhibit 19–2.

Under the *carryback/carryforward option,* the loss of 1995 in Exhibit 19–2 would be used to reduce income and income taxes of 1992, 1993, and 1994, in that order. Income taxes paid in those years are refundable to the enterprise to the extent that the 1995 loss offsets part or all of the incomes reported in those years. If the 1995 loss is so great that it more than offsets the incomes of 1992, 1993, and 1994, the remainder can be carried forward to offset income in 1996, 1997, and so on. The refund of past income taxes for which the company is eligible is based on actual income taxes paid in those years. Any reduction in future income taxes is uncertain, however, since it is to be based on future income.

Under the *carryforward-only option,* Exhibit 19–2 indicates that the loss of 1995 is not carried back but is carried forward and applied in consecutive order to the carryforward years beginning with 1996. You may wonder why a company would choose the speculative carryforward option if it could carry back the loss of a particular period and have the certainty of the refund of past income taxes. The answer lies in the *anticipation* that future income will be taxed at *higher* income tax rates than in the past. Because the amount of refund (if the loss is carried back) or the reduction in future income taxes (if the loss is carried forward) is based on actual taxes paid in the carryback year or to be paid in the carryforward year, the income tax rates in effect in the year(s) for which income is reduced by the loss are very important. Income taxes in the future may be higher than those in the past because (1) enacted income tax rates may increase or (2) a higher level of future income may place the company in a higher income tax bracket. If either of these is expected to take place, the company that sustains a loss might logically select the option of carrying forward the entire loss and forfeiting the certainty of the carryback option.

Another consideration in choosing between the carryback/carryforward option or the carryforward-only option is the timing of the receipt of the tax benefit. If the loss is carried back, the company expects to receive the refund in the near future. If the loss is carried forward, however, the company forfeits the right to the cash until some future time—after the company has earned future taxable income. If the company needs immediate cash, the carryback option may be attractive, even if income tax rates are expected to increase in the future. Throughout this chapter, including the assignment material at the end, we assume that companies choose the carryback/carryforward option unless specifically indicated otherwise.

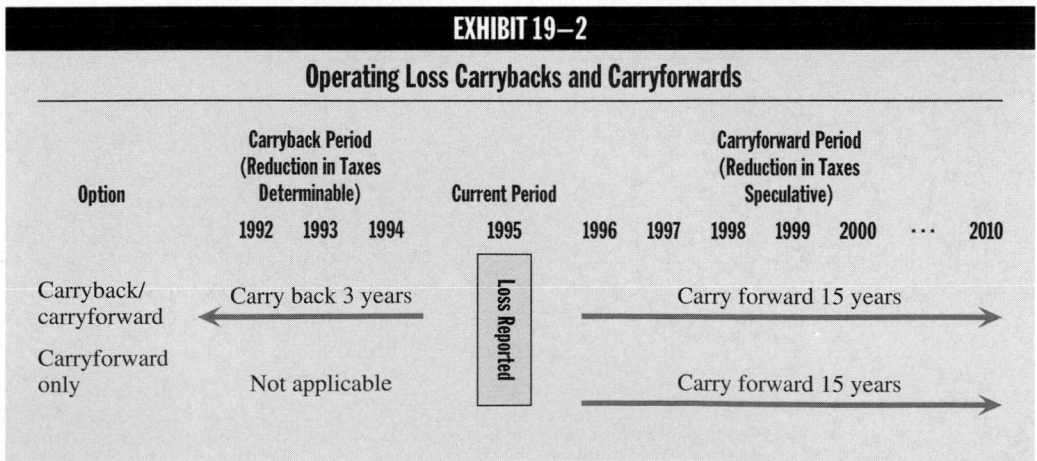

EXHIBIT 19–2

Operating Loss Carrybacks and Carryforwards

Option	Carryback Period (Reduction in Taxes Determinable)			Current Period	Carryforward Period (Reduction in Taxes Speculative)						
	1992	1993	1994	1995	1996	1997	1998	1999	2000	⋯	2010
Carryback/ carryforward	← Carry back 3 years			Loss Reported	Carry forward 15 years →						
Carryforward only	Not applicable				Carry forward 15 years →						

This discussion of loss carrybacks and carryforwards has focused on the provisions of income tax law that govern the actual payment of income taxes to the government. Our primary interest, however, is on the reporting of loss carrybacks and carryforwards in the financial statements of the enterprise. The reduction in income taxes resulting from loss carrybacks is recognized in the determination of the net loss in the loss year. That is, the loss is reduced by the income taxes of past years that will be refunded because of the carryback, and a receivable for past taxes is included in the balance sheet. This accounting treatment is

Revenue Realization   logical, because the refund of past income taxes is both realizable and measurable.

The subject of loss carryforwards, on the other hand, represents a more difficult conceptual problem and has been a subject of debate in the accounting profession in recent years. One alternative is to recognize carryforwards in the same manner as carrybacks with the realizability of the asset subject to the condition that future taxable income will be present

Conservatism   within the carryforward period. A more conservative approach is to delay the recognition of the carryforward until realization is assured, meaning that taxable income against which the carryforward can be used has already been reported.

Under *SFAS No. 109,* deferred tax assets are established for all carryforwards. Once established, however, those assets are subject to reduction via a valuation allowance for that portion that is not expected to be realized. This process is similar to the estimation of a portion of receivables that will not be collected. To account for uncollectible receivables, we record all receivables and then reduce their total by an allowance to reduce the total to net realizable value. Similarly, *SFAS No. 109* requires that we record deferred tax assets for all carryforwards and then reduce those assets to the amount expected to be realized via a valuation allowance. In this section, we focus on the recognition of receivables for loss carrybacks and deferred tax assets for loss carryforwards. We illustrate the process of the valuation allowance for deferred tax assets later in this chapter.

AN ILLUSTRATION OF CARRYBACKS AND CARRYFORWARDS

To illustrate the way operating loss carrybacks and carryforwards work, we assume that Allen Company has pretax financial income (loss) and income tax rates for 1993 through 1996 as follows:

	1993	1994	1995	1996
Pretax financial income (loss)	$75,000	$80,000	$55,000	$(165,000)
Income tax rate	40%	36%	35%	38%

Allen selects the carryback/carryforward option for purposes of applying the 1996 loss to reduce income taxes. Accordingly, the amount of refund to which the company is immediately entitled as a result of the 1996 loss is $62,300, computed as follows:

Year	Income		Income Tax Rate		Refund
1993	$ 75,000	×	40%	=	$30,000
1994	80,000	×	36%	=	28,800
1995	10,000	×	35%	=	3,500
	$165,000				$62,300

Only $10,000 of 1995 income is included in the refund to reach the level of $165,000 to offset the 1996 loss of that amount. The remaining $45,000 of 1995 income ($55,000 − $10,000) may be used as a basis for the refund of income taxes in the future if additional losses in 1997 or 1998 are carried back. The journal entry to record income tax for 1996 is as follows:

Receivable for Past Income Taxes	62,300	
Tax Benefit of Net Operating Loss		62,300

The receivable of past income taxes is presented in the balance sheet as a current asset because it represents a refund that will be received in the near future. The credit entry, Tax Benefit of Net Operating Loss, is presented in the income statement in lieu of income tax expense, resulting in the following presentation:

Loss before income tax	$(165,000)
Tax benefit of net operating loss	62,300
Net loss	$(102,700)

As long as the amount of 1996 loss is $210,000 or less, accounting for the income tax effects of the loss is essentially the same with only the numbers differing for losses other than $165,000. (The total of the pretax financial incomes of the three years prior to the loss year is $210,000: $75,000 + $80,000 + $55,000 = $210,000.) Had Allen Company's loss in 1996 exceeded $210,000, however, the portion in excess of $210,000 is available for carryforward to offset future income. Let's assume that the 1996 loss is $250,000, $210,000 of which is carried back and $40,000 of which is available for carryforward purposes. If we recognized the carryforward in 1996, as required by *SFAS No. 109,* the journal entry to recognize income taxes is as follows:

Receivable for Past Income Taxes	78,050	
Deferred Income Tax (Asset)	15,200	
Tax Benefit of Net Operating Loss		93,250

The $78,050 receivable is calculated in the same manner as in the previous example:

Year	Income		Income Tax Rate		Refund
1993	$ 75,000	×	40%	=	$30,000
1994	80,000	×	36%	=	28,800
1995	55,000	×	35%	=	19,250
	$210,000				$78,050

This represents all of the income taxes paid during the three-year carryback period, 1993–1995. The deferred tax asset of $15,200 is computed by multiplying the $40,000 carryforward amount ($250,000 − $210,000) by the current (1996) income tax rate: $40,000 × 38% = $15,200. The net loss reported in 1996 is $156,750 ($250,000 − $93,250). As you can see, we have assumed that the enacted 1996 income tax rate of 38% also applies to future years and that rate was used in computing the tax benefit of the $40,000 loss carryforward. We use a future rate, rather than the current rate, only when the future rate has already been enacted. The deferred tax asset of $15,200 that resulted from the recognition of the operating loss carryforward in the preceding entry is combined with any deferred tax asset that exists as a result of temporary differences, as we discussed in the previous section of this chapter. We illustrate the interaction of deferred tax assets and liabilities from temporary differences and the effects of operating loss carrybacks and carryforwards in a comprehensive illustration in the following section.

We have considered separately the subjects of temporary differences that give rise to deferred tax assets and liabilities and accounting for operating loss carrybacks and carryforwards. We have considered these subjects separately for purposes of instruction, but they are intertwined in practice. To understand accounting for income taxes in accordance with *SFAS No. 109,* in this section we first review some of that pronouncement's underlying principles and then combine these two topics in a comprehensive illustration.

SFAS No. 109 clearly places priority on the balance sheet when it indicates the following two objectives of accounting for income taxes:

ACCOUNTING FOR INCOME TAXES UNDER *SFAS No. 109*

1. To recognize the amount of *taxes payable or refundable* for the current year.
2. To recognize *deferred tax liabilities and assets* for the future tax consequences of events that have been recognized in the financial statements or tax returns.[8]

To implement these objectives, four basic principles are applied in accounting for income taxes under *SFAS No. 109:*

1. A tax liability or asset is recognized for the amount of taxes currently payable or receivable on the current year's tax returns.
2. A deferred tax liability or asset is recognized for the estimated future tax effects attributed to temporary differences and carryforwards.
3. The measurement of tax liabilities and assets is based on provisions of enacted tax law. The effects of future anticipated changes in tax law are not considered.
4. The measurement of deferred tax assets is reduced, if necessary, by the amount of any tax benefits that are not expected to be realized.[9]

At the end of each accounting period, the enterprise must calculate the amount of deferred tax liabilities and assets on the basis of cumulative temporary differences and carryforwards. This process involves completing the following steps:

1. Identify the types and amounts of all temporary differences and the amounts and remaining periods of all carryforwards.
2. Measure the total deferred tax liabilities based on taxable temporary differences, applying enacted tax law.
3. Measure the total deferred tax assets based on deductible temporary differences and carryforwards, applying enacted tax law.
4. Reduce the deferred tax assets by a valuation allowance if it is *more likely than not* that some portion of all of the deferred tax assets will not be realized.[10]

Applying the first three steps is similar to the examples we studied earlier in this chapter. We will discuss the valuation allowance procedure of *SFAS No. 109* later in this section.

Comprehensive Illustration

In the following example, we illustrate many of the important aspects of *SFAS No. 109* by considering three consecutive years of Zorc Company. Our assignment is to prepare the year-end income tax accrual and income tax information for the company's financial statements. Zorc Company's first year of operations is 1994. During that year, the company reported $160,000 of pretax financial income. Permanent and temporary differences are combined with pretax financial income to derive taxable income, as follows:

Pretax financial income	$160,000
Permanent differences:	
Interest on municipal securities	(5,000)
Pretax financial income subject to tax	$155,000
Temporary differences:	
Depreciation	(28,000)
Warranties	10,000
Revenue received in advance	7,000
Taxable income	$144,000

The $5,000 interest on municipal securities represents nontaxable income, and the $28,000 depreciation temporary difference represents the excess of accelerated write-off for tax pur-

---

[8]*SFAS No. 109,* par. 6.

[9]*SFAS No. 109,* par. 8.

[10]*SFAS No. 109,* par. 17. This paragraph also includes the impact of tax credit carryforwards, a subject that is beyond the scope of this presentation.

poses over straight-line depreciation for financial reporting purposes. Warranties are expensed at the time of sale on an estimated basis but are deductible for income tax purposes only when paid. In 1994, $10,000 more was accrued than paid. Revenue received in advance is taxable at the time received, but is deferred for financial reporting purposes until earned. In 1994, $7,000 was received that was not earned by year-end. Depreciation is a *taxable temporary difference* that reduces current tax payable and gives rise to a deferred tax liability. The warranties and revenue received in advance are *deductible temporary differences* that increase current tax payable and give rise to deferred tax assets (i.e., prepaid taxes).

Exhibit 19–3 presents analyses that facilitate the preparation of the year-end tax accrual, as well as information for the financial statements. We will use similar analyses for each of the three years in this example. The top analysis in Exhibit 19–3 simply "rolls forward" the amount of the temporary differences from the beginning to the end of the year. Because 1994 is the first year for Zorc Company, the beginning balances are all zero. The Change column includes the amounts used in the previous calculation to determine taxable income from pretax financial income. The numbers without brackets are deductible temporary differences; those in brackets are taxable temporary differences. The company is in a net taxable temporary difference position at the end of the year because the net amount of temporary differences is $(11,000), due to the large amount of the depreciation difference.

The lower portion of Exhibit 19–3 converts the temporary differences in the top analysis to amounts of deferred income taxes. The beginning balances are zeroes and the ending balances are computed at 34%, the assumed income tax rate for 1994 in this illustration. Each ending balance is computed by multiplying the tax rate by the ending amount of the temporary difference (e.g., for depreciation, $28,000 × 34% = $9,520). The change

---

EXHIBIT 19–3

Zorc Company
Analysis of Cumulative Temporary Differences
and Deferred Taxes
1994

Cumulative Temporary Differences (TD)

	Beginning Balance 1994	Change	Ending Balance 1994
Deductible TD			
Warranties	–0–	$ 10,000	$ 10,000
Revenue received in advance	–0–	7,000	7,000
(Taxable) TD			
Depreciation	–0–	(28,000)	(28,000)
	–0–	$(11,000)	$(11,000)

Deferred Income Taxes

	Beginning Balance @ —%	Ending Balance @34%	Change	Classification of Ending Balances Current	Classification of Ending Balances Noncurrent
Assets					
Warranties	–0–	$ 3,400	$ 3,400		$ 3,400
Revenue received in advance	–0–	2,380	2,380	$2,380	
(Liabilities)					
Depreciation	–0–	(9,520)	(9,520)		(9,520)
	–0–	$(3,740)	$(3,740)	$2,380	$(6,120)

amounts are the differences between the beginning and ending balances. The bracketed numbers are deferred tax liabilities based on taxable temporary differences. The amounts without brackets are deferred tax assets based on deductible temporary differences.

The Classification columns on the right side of the lower analysis separate the ending balances into current and noncurrent for balance sheet classification purposes. This distinction is based on the asset or liability underlying the temporary difference. In this example, we assume that the warranty period is five years, so the related temporary difference is considered noncurrent, as is depreciation, because of the noncurrent classification of the underlying plant assets. We also assume that the revenue received in advance is expected to be earned in the coming period and, thus, is a current liability.

The December 31, 1994, entry to record the income tax accrual for Zorc Company is as follows:

Dec. 31, 1994	Income Tax Expense ($48,960 + $3,740)	52,700	
	Deferred Income Tax—Current	2,380	
	Income Tax Payable ($144,000 × 34%)		48,960
	Deferred Income Tax—Noncurrent		6,120

Notice that the amounts of Deferred Income Tax—Current and Noncurrent are taken from the lower analysis in Exhibit 19–3. The Income Tax Payable is determined by multiplying the $144,000 taxable income by the 34% tax rate. An important point to understand is the way Income Tax Expense is determined—it is the net of the other three numbers and can only be computed after the remaining elements of the entry have been determined. Referring again to the analysis of deferred income taxes in the lower section of Exhibit 19–3, the change in deferred taxes is a $3,740 increase in the net liability (total of the Change column). That is the net of the increases in the noncurrent liability and the current asset for deferred taxes: $(6,120) − $2,380 = $(3,740).

An important step to complete before moving to 1995 is a proof of our numbers that is commonly referred to as a **statutory rate reconciliation.** In this procedure, the product of the pretax financial income and the statutory tax rate is reconciled to the income tax expense for the period. For Zorc Company for 1994, this calculation is as follows:

Pretax financial income @ statutory rate ($160,000 × 34%)	$54,400
Less: Permanent differences ($5,000 × 34%)	(1,700)
Income tax expense	$52,700

The tax effect of the permanent differences is the only reconciling item for 1994. Even though the interest is included in pretax accounting income, it is not subject to tax and that alone accounts for the difference between $54,400 and the income tax expense of $52,700.

We will look at how the balance sheet and income statement are affected by these calculations after we have completed all three years of analysis.

Zorc Company's second year of operations is 1995, in which pretax financial income is $150,000. Municipal interest is $12,000, and temporary differences for depreciation and warranties are $(35,000) and $12,000, respectively. Of the revenue received in advance in 1994, $5,000 is earned and an additional $9,000 is received in 1995 that is expected to be earned in 1996. A new temporary difference is the litigation loss that results from the $10,000 accrual on an estimated basis for accounting purposes. This loss will be deductible for tax purposes when the suit is settled, which is expected in 1996.

Taxable income is determined as follows for 1995:

Pretax financial income	$150,000
Permanent difference:	
Interest on municipal securities	(12,000)
Pretax financial income subject to tax	$138,000

Balance carried forward	$138,000
Temporary differences:	
Depreciation	(35,000)
Warranties	12,000
Revenue received in advance ($9,000—$5,000)	4,000
Litigation loss	10,000
Taxable income	$129,000

Exhibit 19–4 includes an analysis for 1995 similar to the 1994 analysis in Exhibit 19–3 for Zorc Company. Notice that the ending balances of both cumulative temporary differences and deferred income taxes from 1994 become the beginning balances for 1995. We also assume that during 1995, new tax legislation increases the income tax rate for 1995 and all future years to 40%. The amounts in Exhibit 19–4 are simply moved forward for one additional year. In both analyses in Exhibit 19–4, the columns identified as Change are forced or "plugged" by determining the amount of change required to move the beginning balance to the desired ending balance. The litigation loss is classified as current because of its expected settlement in 1996.

The entry to record income taxes at the end of 1995 is as follows:

Dec. 31, 1995	Income Tax Expense ($51,600 + $4,260)	55,860	
	Deferred Income Tax—Current ($8,400 − $2,380)	6,020	
	Income Tax Payable ($129,000 × 40%)		51,600
	Deferred Income Tax—Noncurrent		
	($16,400 − $6,120)		10,280

EXHIBIT 19–4

Zorc Company
Analysis of Cumulative Temporary Differences
and Deferred Taxes
1995

Cumulative Temporary Differences (TD)

	Beginning Balance 1995	Change	Ending Balance 1995
Deductible TD			
Warranties	$ 10,000	$ 12,000	$ 22,000
Revenue received in advance	7,000	4,000	11,000
Litigation	–0–	10,000	10,000
(Taxable) TD			
Depreciation	(28,000)	(35,000)	(63,000)
	$(11,000)	$ (9,000)	$(20,000)

Deferred Income Taxes

	Beginning Balance @34%	Ending Balance @40%	Change	Classification of Ending Balances	
				Current	Noncurrent
Assets					
Warranties	$ 3,400	$ 8,800	$ 5,400		$ 8,800
Revenue received in advance	2,380	4,400	2,020	$4,400	
Litigation loss	–0–	4,000	4,000	$4,000	
(Liabilities)					
Depreciation	(9,520)	(25,200)	(15,680)		(25,200)
	$(3,740)	$ (8,000)	$ (4,260)	$8,400	$(16,400)

Notice that the debits and credits to Deferred Income Tax—Current and Noncurrent, respectively, are calculated as the changes in those accounts. We did not have to deal with that consideration in 1994 because it was the company's first year. The desired ending balances of current and noncurrent deferred income taxes from Exhibit 19–4 are compared with the balances from Exhibit 19–3 and the differences debited or credited into the deferred tax accounts, as appropriate, to produce the desired ending balances. For example, Deferred Income Tax—Noncurrent must have a credit (liability) balance of $16,400 at the end of 1995. The account began with a credit balance of $6,120, requiring a credit of $10,280 in the year-end tax accrual. Similarly, the required debit (asset) balance for Deferred Income Taxes—Current is $8,400; with a debit balance of $2,380 at the end of 1994, the adjustment is $6,020 ($8,400 − $2,380). This illustrates the basic approach of the asset/liability method of accounting for income taxes—the desired balance sheet figures are first determined and the expense is recognized in the amount required to meet the balance sheet objective.

The statutory reconciliation has an additional component in 1995, due to the tax rate change from 34% to 40%. This change has the effect of increasing deferred taxes and, therefore, tax expense, as indicated in the following reconciliation:

Pretax financial income @ statutory rate ($150,000 × 40%)	$60,000
Less: Permanent differences ($12,000 × 40%)	(4,800)
Plus: Tax increase on beginning cumulative temporary differences [$11,000 × (40% − 34%)]	660
Income tax expense	$55,860

Notice that the adjustment for the tax increase is calculated only for the beginning balance of cumulative temporary differences. The temporary differences originating in 1995 have already been taxed at 40%. As we indicated earlier, we will consider the balance sheet and income statement presentation of deferred tax information when we have completed our analysis of 1996.

We consider the third year of our illustration of Zorc Company by considering 1996, a year in which the company's activities took a significant downturn. Due to negative economic trends and a loss of several important contracts, the company reported a pretax financial *loss* of $275,000. Interest earned on municipal securities was $15,000. Temporary differences consisted of the following: (1) write-off of plant assets for tax purposes exceeded depreciation expense by $40,000; (2) warranty expense by the accrual method for accounting purposes exceeded amounts paid to honor warranty commitments by $18,000; (3) revenue of $10,000 received in advance that was previously taxed was recognized in accounting income and an additional $15,000 was received that was deferred for accounting purposes but taxed currently; and (4) the litigation of 1995 was completed and the $10,000 loss was deducted for tax purposes.

An analysis of the pretax financial loss, permanent and temporary differences, and the amount of loss for tax purposes are analyzed as follows:

Pretax financial (loss)	$(275,000)
Permanent difference:	
Interest on municipal securities	(15,000)
Pretax financial (loss) subject to tax	$(290,000)
Temporary differences:	
Depreciation	(40,000)
Warranties	18,000
Revenue received in advance ($15,000 − $10,000)	5,000
Litigation loss	(10,000)
Taxable (loss)	$(317,000)

This analysis is similar to those for 1994 and 1995, except for the negative amount entered as pretax financial loss.

Notice that the loss for tax purposes is $317,000. We shall assume that Zorc Company decides to carry back the loss to the extent possible and receives a refund for income taxes paid in the carryback period. From our discussion in this chapter, we know that a loss can be carried back three years. In this case, the company has existed for only two years, however, so the loss can be carried back only to 1994 and 1995. Remember, also, that in determining the amount of the refund, the tax rate in effect in the year to which the loss is carried back is used to calculate the amount of the refund. For Zorc Company for 1996, the amount of the refund to be received is $100,560:

1994	$144,000 × 34% =	$ 48,960
1995	$129,000 × 40% =	51,600
		$100,560

The determination of deferred tax balances in Exhibit 19–5 is similar to those in the two previous exhibits with modifications necessary to include the loss carryforward of $44,000, which is determined by subtracting the amount of loss that is carried back from the total loss for tax purposes for 1996:

$$\$317,000 - (\$144,000 + \$129,000) = \$44,000$$

EXHIBIT 19–5

Zorc Company
Analysis of Cumulative Temporary Differences
and Deferred Taxes
1996

Cumulative Temporary Differences (TD) and Loss Carryforward

	Beginning Balance 1996	Change	Ending Balance 1996
Deductible TD			
Warranties	$ 22,000	$ 18,000	$ 40,000
Revenue received in advance	11,000	5,000	16,000
Litigation	10,000	(10,000)	–0–
(Taxable) TD			
Depreciation	(63,000)	(40,000)	(103,000)
Loss Carryforward			
1996 Loss*	–0–	44,000	44,000
	$(20,000)	$ 17,000	$ (3,000)

Deferred Income Taxes

	Beginning Balance @40%	Ending Balance @40%	Change	Classification of Ending Balances Current	Classification of Ending Balances Noncurrent
Assets					
Warranties	$ 8,800	$ 16,000	$ 7,200		$ 16,000
Revenue received in advance	4,400	6,400	2,000	$6,400	
Litigation	4,000	–0–	(4,000)		
Loss Carryforward	–0–	17,600	17,600		17,600
(Liabilities)					
Depreciation	(25,200)	(41,200)	(16,000)		(41,200)
	$ (8,000)	$ (1,200)	$ 6,800	$6,400	$ (7,600)

*[$317,000 − ($144,000 + $129,000)]

Notice in Exhibit 19–5 that a category for the loss carryforward has been added to the analysis at the top of the exhibit and the $44,000 1996 loss carryforward has been included. This item should be identified by year because other years may result in loss carryforwards and each year will have a different expiration year. The loss carryforward gives rise to a deferred tax asset, as indicated in the analysis at the bottom of Exhibit 19–5. We have classified this item as noncurrent on the assumption that, given the large loss encountered by Zorc Company in 1996, it will be several years before the company returns to profitable operations and is able to recognize the benefit of the loss carryforward. That item is treated in the same manner as a deductible temporary differences for purposes of determining deferred tax assets and liabilities.

The journal entry to record income taxes at the end of 1996 is as follows:

Dec. 31, 1996	Receivable for Past Income Taxes	
	[($144,000 × 34%) + ($129,000 × 40%)]	100,560
	Deferred Income Tax—Noncurrent	
	($16,400 − $7,600)	8,800
	Deferred Income Tax—Current	
	($8,400 − $6,400)	2,000
	Income Tax Benefit ($100,560 + $6,800)	107,360

Comparing the two right columns in Exhibits 19–4 and 19–5, we see that the balances of both Deferred Income Taxes—Current (debit) and Deferred Income Taxes—Noncurrent (credit) declined from 1995 to 1996. The two most significant differences are the reversal of the temporary difference from the litigation loss and the inclusion of the loss carryforward, both of which are relatively large amounts.

Notice in the journal entry above that Income Tax Expense has been replaced by the account, Income Tax Benefit, which indicates the positive impact (loss reduction) resulting from using the 1996 loss to receive the refund of 1994 and 1995 income taxes and to offset income taxes that would otherwise have to be paid after 1996.

We can now prepare the statutory rate reconciliation, as follows:

Pretax financial (loss) at statutory rate [$(275,000) × 40%]	$(110,000)
Less: Permanent differences ($15,000 × 40%)	(6,000)
Plus: Loss carryback at 34% [$144,000 × (40% − 34%)]	8,640
Income tax (benefit)	$(107,360)

The last item in the reconciliation, identified as Loss carryback at 34%, is required because the 1994 part of the carryback was determined at 34%, the 1994 income tax rate, rather than the current (1996) rate of 40%.

Now that we have completed our three-year analysis of cumulative temporary differences and the loss carryforward, the related deferred tax assets and liabilities, and the year-end journal entries to record income taxes, we can focus attention on the amounts that will be presented in the balance sheet and income statement. That information is presented in Exhibit 19–6. For each year, a portion of deferred taxes appears in the current asset section of the balance sheet. This amount represents the net amount of deferred taxes on temporary differences that are classified as current assets and liabilities in the balance sheet. In addition, in 1996, a current asset is presented for the $100,560 receivable of 1994 and 1995 taxes resulting from the 1996 carryback. For 1994 and 1995, a current liability is presented for income taxes payable—$48,960 and $51,600 in 1994 and 1995, respectively.

Among noncurrent liabilities, each year is a deferred tax amount that represents deferred taxes resulting from temporary differences classified as noncurrent and from the loss carryforward. The decline in the amount of noncurrent deferred taxes between 1995 and 1996 is due to the loss carryforward, which partially offsets the large deferred tax liability related to the depreciation temporary difference for the first time in 1996.

EXHIBIT 19-6

Zorc Company
Financial Statement Presentation of Income Taxes
1994–1996

	Balance Sheet 1994	1995	1996
Current Assets			
Receivable for past income taxes	—	—	$ 100,560
Deferred income taxes	$ 2,380	$ 8,400	6,400
Current Liabilities			
Income taxes payable	48,960	51,600	—
Noncurrent Liabilities			
Deferred income taxes	6,120	16,400	7,600
	Income Statement		
Income (loss) before income tax	$160,000	$150,000	$(275,000)
Income tax expense (benefit):			
Current	48,960	51,600	(100,560)
Deferred	3,740	4,260	(6,800)
	52,700	55,860	(107,360)
Net income (loss)	$107,300	$ 94,140	$(167,640)

The income statement presentation each year displays pretax financial income (loss), followed by income tax expense (benefit), separated into current and deferred components. In 1994 and 1995, income tax expense reduces the amount of net income reported, as we would expect given the profitability reported by the company in those years. In 1996, however, the benefit of the carryback and carryforward results in a reduction in the amount of loss that would otherwise have been reported. That reduction in loss results from the refund of past taxes and the anticipation of reduced taxes in the future when the carryforward is realized.

Valuation Allowance

Earlier we identified one additional step in determining the items and amounts that are presented in the financial statements relative to income taxes: to determine if it is *more likely than not* that some or all of the deferred tax assets will not be realized and, if so, to recognize that decline in value via a valuation allowance. This is an important step in applying *SFAS No. 109* and requires a great deal of judgment on the part of the accountant.

Under *SFAS No. 109,* deferred tax assets are recorded for all deductible temporary differences and loss carryforwards. For these assets to be realized, income, against which the deductible temporary differences and loss carryforwards can be offset, must exist. The need for and amount of a valuation allowance is, therefore, based on the evidence that there will or will not be sufficient income to permit the recognition of the deferred tax assets.

Sources of income, against which deductible temporary differences and loss carryforwards can be recognized, include the following:[11]

1. Past income against which future losses can be carried back.
2. Future reversals of existing taxable temporary differences.
3. Future taxable income from sources other than the reversals of existing temporary differences.
4. Tax-planning strategies.

---

[11]*SFAS No. 109,* par. 21.

Tax planning strategies are actions that could be taken for the specific purpose of recognizing the benefits of deferred tax assets. These actions must be prudent and feasible and, while management might not ordinarily take them, it would take them to prevent the loss of a deferred tax asset, such as the expiration of an unused loss carryforward. Examples are to accelerate the reversal of taxable temporary differences to offset a loss carryforward and to transfer dollars invested in tax-exempt investments into taxable investments for the same purpose.

Negative evidence may exist that implies a great deal of doubt concerning future income and, thus, the realizability of deferred tax assets. Examples include the following:[12]

- A series of net loss years.
- A history of loss carryforwards expiring unused.
- Losses projected in near future years.
- Unsettled circumstances, such as lawsuits, which would adversely affect future operations and profitability if unfavorably resolved.
- A change in tax law resulting in a shortened carryforward period.

On the other hand, evidence may exist that projects a much more positive picture and may lead to the decision that realization of deferred tax assets is likely and that a valuation allowance is not required:[13]

- A strong historical earnings history.
- Existing contracts or other revenue-generating transactions that will produce future taxable income in sufficient quantities to permit realization of deferred tax assets.
- Assets whose value exceeds their tax basis, which, when realized, will result in significant future income.

Management must use considered, professional judgment in determining the need for and amount of the valuation allowance. Because the decision is based primarily on the predictability of future income, the decision is of necessity highly judgmental. Both positive and negative factors, such as those described above, must be carefully analyzed in making this important judgment.

To illustrate the accounting procedures required when a valuation allowance is established for deferred tax assets, we return to the Zorc Company illustration for 1996. We assume that, after careful consideration, management determines that it is more likely than not that 25% of the deferred tax assets will not be realized. This requires a valuation allowance of $10,000, determined as follows, based on information obtained from Exhibit 19–5:

Current deferred tax assets		
Revenue received in advance		$ 6,400
Noncurrent deferred tax assets		
Warranties	$16,000	
Loss carryforward	17,600	33,600
		$40,000
Valuation allowance:		
25% × $40,000		$10,000
Allocation to current/noncurrent:		
Current: ($6,400/$40,000) × $10,000		$ 1,600
Noncurrent: ($33,600/$40,000) × $10,000		8,400
		$10,000

---

[12]*SFAS No. 109,* par. 23.
[13]*SFAS No. 109,* par. 24.

READ THOSE FOOTNOTES!

Hidden reserves, which allow managements to smooth out reported earnings, are making a quiet comeback. Their vehicle: the Financial Accounting Standards Board's new Statement 109, which tells companies how to account for tax credits. Some companies have already adopted the new rule, but most will adopt it by the first quarter of 1993.

Suppose that as the result of a big restructuring, a company generates a $1 billion loss. For tax purposes, losses can be carried forward for 15 years. Assuming the company makes money after the restructuring and pays taxes at the full corporate income tax rate of 34%, that $1 billion loss could save the company $340 million.

The accounting question is: When and how should the company account for that potential tax savings?

According to the FASB's Statement 109, managements must peer into the future. If management believes it is "more likely than not" that the company will generate enough earnings in the future to warrant the use of the credits, then the company must book the value of the tax credit as income immediately, and label the earnings infusion as a one-time accounting change.

What if management isn't so sure about future earnings? Then Statement 109 tells the company to set the tax credit aside in a reserve. This reserve can be dipped into in future years at management's discretion—and thus could be used to offset earnings disappointments.

Companies looking to set up tax credit reserves won't encounter much resistance from their auditors. That's because Statement 109 gives managements a great deal of latitude as to the outlook for future earnings. "The 'more likely than not' provision is perhaps the most judgmental clause in accounting," says Ernst & Young partner Norman Strauss.

Statement 109 certainly won't make it easy to compare companies' financial statements. Consider how computer systems maker Unisys (1992 revenues, $8.4 billion) and information services provider Ceridian (estimated 1992 revenues, $825 million) are following the new rule.

As a result of its 1991 restructuring, Unisys is sitting on tax-loss carryforwards that could save it up to $500 million (about $3 a share) in taxes. Unisys management believes the earnings outlook is reasonably bright; therefore Unisys will book most of its tax credit as income up front. The company recently said it will record a one-time gain of between $325 million and $425 million in its quarter ending Mar. 31. The remainder of the credit will most likely go into a reserve and could be taken into income slowly, over the next several years.

Now look at Ceridian, which is the successor company to the moneylosing computer systems maker Control Data. Last year Ceridian spun off its unprofitable operations, leaving it with a profitable core business in information ser-

vices — and tax credits worth over $450 million, about $10.60 a share. Ceridian will book its $450 million tax credit as a reserve, and take a fresh look at the reserve after several profitable years.

Result: Unisys' reported net income will get a big, nonrecurring infusion this year. Ceridian's aftertax earnings will get nothing this year but could instead enjoy a steady stream of infusions in the future—assuming, of course, Ceridian makes money.

Not all companies will rush to set up reserves. Those trying to build their capital accounts—banks, for example—will attempt to recognize as much of a gain as possible early; most of the gain will flow into the balance sheet as retained earnings. Others, faced with huge charges against earnings to fund reserves for retiree health benefits, will also want to book big gains immediately to mitigate the negative impact of these charges on equity. But other companies will set up reserves and use the reserves to offset unwelcome charges—or simply to make a particular quarter's earnings look better.

"With Statement 109, accounting rulemakers have created an incredible earnings management tool," charges Shearson Lehman Brothers tax and accounting expert Robert Willens. "This reserve is a mass with which you can do whatever you want."

Morale: Starting next month, read those income tax footnotes extra carefully.

Companies to Watch

Company	Net Operating Loss Carryforward* ($millions)
Armco	$1,031
Black & Decker	596
Data General	490
Michigan National Corp	215
Occidental Petroleum	990
Penn Central	940
PHM Corp	638
Southland Corp	916
Temple-Inland	598
Wang Laboratories	1,800

*For financial reporting. Numbers as of most recent fiscal year available.

NOTE: All these firms have large operating loss carryforwards that can reduce taxes in future earnings periods.

SOURCE: Roula Khalaf, "Read those Footnotes!" *Forbes* (February 15, 1993), p. 154. Reprinted by permission of *Forbes*. © Forbes, Inc., 1993.

This allocation results in a $1,600 *reduction* in the current deferred tax asset and a $8,400 *addition* to the *net* noncurrent deferred tax liability. In the following comparative analysis, the impact of the valuation allowance is determined as indicated in the right columns and is compared with the figures presented earlier without a valuation allowance in the left columns.

	Without Valuation Allowance	With Valuation Allowance
Current deferred tax asset	$ 6,400	$ 6,400
Less: Allowance	–0–	(1,600)
	$ 6,400	$ 4,800
Noncurrent deferred tax liability		
Asset component	$ 33,600	$ 33,600
Less: Allowance	–0–	(8,400)
	$ 33,600	$ 25,200
Liability component	(41,200)	(41,200)
Net noncurrent	$ (7,600)	$(16,000)
Total deferred tax	$ (1,200)	$(11,200)

Notice that the difference between the totals in the two columns is $10,000, exactly the amount of the valuation allowance.

The journal entry to record income taxes at the end of 1996 under these revised assumptions and including the valuation allowance is as follows:

Dec. 31, 1996	Receivable for Past Income Taxes	
	[($144,000 × 34%) + ($129,000 × 40%)]	100,560
	Deferred Income Tax—Noncurrent	
	($16,400 − $7,600)	8,800
	Allowance to Reduce Deferred Tax Assets to Lower Recoverable Value	10,000
	Deferred Income Tax—Current ($8,400 − $6,400)	2,000
	Income Tax Benefit ($100,560 + $6,800 − $10,000)	97,360

The statutory rate reconciliation for 1996, including the recognition of the valuation allowance, is as follows:

Pretax financial income (loss) at statutory rate [($275,000) × 40%]	$(110,000)
Less: Permanent differences ($15,000 × 40%)	(6,000)
Plus: Loss carryback at 34% [$144,000 × (40% − 34%)]	8,640
Increase in valuation allowance	10,000
Income tax (benefit)	$ (97,360)

The valuation allowance will be evaluated at the end of each year, as is done with valuation allowances on other assets. At the end of 1997, for example, a determination will be made concerning the continuing need for the $10,000 valuation allowance and, if needed, the amount required to reduce deferred tax assets from their recorded amounts to their lower realizable value. At that time, the allowance will either be increased or reduced; reduction could result in the complete elimination of the allowance if positive evidence indicates that the value of the deferred tax assets are no longer impaired and the allowance is no longer required.

FINANCIAL STATEMENT DISCLOSURE

In this chapter, we have seen that information about income taxes is imbedded in the financial statements in several places, including assets, liabilities, and expenses. A great deal of information about income taxes is also presented in notes to the financial statements. In fact, *SFAS No. 109* requires companies to report detailed underlying information about the amounts of deferred tax assets and liabilities and of temporary differences, the components of tax expense or benefit, and other information. The identification and illustration of disclosure of all aspects of accounting for income taxes are beyond the scope of this text, but it is important for you to have a general understanding of the impact that income taxes have on the financial statement, including notes to those statements.

Exhibit 19–7 includes the disclosure of income tax information in accordance with *SFAS No. 109* for Gannett Co., Inc., for 1993 and comparative years 1992 and 1991. Gannett Co., Inc., is a diversified news and information company that publishes newspapers, operates broadcasting stations and outdoor advertising businesses, and is engaged in research, marketing, commercial printing, a newswire service, data services, and news programming. The company operates in 41 states and several foreign countries. It is the nation's largest newspaper group, publishing 83 newspapers including *USA Today*. As Note 7 in Exhibit 19–7 indicates, the company adopted *SFAS No. 109* in 1992.

The financial summaries in Exhibit 19–7 describe the following, in the order presented: the sources of income before income taxes separated into domestic and foreign; the amount of provision for income taxes (i.e., expense) separated into federal, state, and foreign for 1993, 1992, and 1991; a statutory rate reconciliation showing how the U.S. statutory rate can be reconciled to the company's effective rate for each year; and the impact of various temporary differences on the amount of deferred tax assets and liabilities. The written explanation indicates that adopting *SFAS No. 109* in 1992 resulted in a $34 million noncash credit (i.e., increase) in earnings, described as the cumulative effect of adopting *SFAS No. 109*. We explain that type of accounting adjustment in greater detail in Chapter 20 of this text.

As you can see from this illustration, not only do income taxes have a significant impact on the primary financial statements, but also they result in one of the most expansive note disclosures in the financial statements. This is clearly an area in which notes play a very important role in understanding the financial activities of the reporting enterprise.

PROFESSIONAL JUDGMENT

One aspect of professional accounting that we emphasize throughout this text is the importance of professional judgment. We have already discussed the importance of carefully applied professional judgment in many areas, including inventories, plant assets, liabilities, and stockholders' equity. Accounting and reporting for income taxes are other areas for which professional judgment is very important.

Because income taxes are, by definition, based on a company's income, all of the judgments inherent in the determination of net income are also judgments that impact the proper accounting for income taxes. A unique aspect of income taxes that we have discussed in this chapter involves the differences between financial reporting and income tax reporting, that is temporary differences that give rise to deferred tax assets and liabilities. Distinguishing between those differences that are permanent and those that are temporary, as well as the current/noncurrent classification, and monitoring changes in amounts of temporary differences require careful judgment on the part of the professional accountant. The same is true for determining and monitoring the amounts of operating loss carrybacks and carryforwards.

Perhaps the most significant judgment required in applying *SFAS No. 109* is the need for a valuation allowance on deferred tax assets. The standard indicates that a valuation allowance is required when it is "more likely than not" that some or all of the deferred tax assets will not be realized. Although the FASB has provided some guidance to assist the professional accountant in making this evaluation, it is still largely a matter of professional judgment. Once a decision is reached that an allowance is required, the amount of that allowance represents another level of judgment that must be made. The allowance may be for only part of the amount of deferred tax assets, as we illustrated in the comprehensive illustration in this chapter. Information must be accumulated and retained in support of the decision reached concerning both the need for and amount of valuation allowance.

Finally, accumulating and presenting the information concerning income taxes for the financial statement note require additional judgment. Because of the comprehensive nature of the note and the complexity of the underlying transactions and events, particular care must be employed to present this information in a manner that assists readers of the financial statements in understanding the impact of income taxes rather than adding another layer of complexity that makes understanding even more difficult.

EXHIBIT 19–7

Gannett Co., Inc.
Disclosure of Income Taxes

Note 7   Income Taxes

The sources of income before income taxes consist of the following:

In thousands of dollars

	1993	1992	1991
Domestic	$650,896	$559,971	$489,928
Foreign	17,556	14,309	12,821
Total	$668,452	$574,280	$502,749

The provision for income taxes on income before the cumulative effects of accounting principle changes consists of the following:

In thousands of dollars

1993	Current	Deferred	Total
Federal	$204,733	$19,333	$224,066
State	38,750	1,232	39,982
Foreign	6,902	(250)	6,652
Total	$250,385	$20,315	$270,700

In thousands of dollars

1992	Current	Deferred	Total
Federal	$200,192	$(14,381)	$185,811
State	40,343	(2,846)	37,497
Foreign	5,292	—	5,292
Total	$245,827	$(17,227)	$228,600

In thousands of dollars

1991	Current	Deferred	Total
Federal	$179,042	$ (8,635)	$170,407
State	33,342	(2,027)	31,315
Foreign	(484)	(138)	(622)
Total	$211,900	$(10,800)	$201,100

The provision for income taxes exceeds the U.S. federal statutory tax rate as a result of the following differences:

CONCLUDING REMARKS

Income taxes have a significant impact on the financial position and results of operations of business enterprises. Accounting for income taxes represents a unique blend of accounting principles and legal compliance.

The presentation of income taxes in this chapter has intentionally simplified certain aspects of income tax law and omitted others to focus on the *financial reporting of income taxes.* Moreover, the income tax implications of certain financial reporting topics that are beyond the scope of intermediate accounting (e.g., business combinations, foreign currency translation, and tax credit carryforwards) have not been presented. Current GAAP require that we carefully measure the amount of income tax assets and liabilities that a company has

Going Concern

within the framework of the going concern assumption and accrual accounting principles. Based on the amounts of those assets and liabilities, we determine the amount of the company's income tax expense. This emphasis on the balance sheet represents a change from the income statement orientation of earlier authoritative pronouncements.

Fiscal year	1993	1992	1991
U.S. statutory tax rate	35.0 %	34.0 %	34.0 %
Increase (decrease) in taxes resulting from:			
State income taxes net of federal income tax benefit	3.9	4.3	4.2
Goodwill amortization not deductible for tax purposes	1.6	2.0	2.4
Other, net	(0.0)	(0.5)	(0.6)
Effective tax rate	40.5 %	39.8 %	40.0 %

In 1992, the Company adopted the provisions of Statement of Financial Accounting Standards No. 109, "Accounting for Income Taxes" (SFAS 109). Under the provisions of SFAS 109, the Company adjusted previously recorded deferred taxes to reflect then-enacted statutory rates. The Company has reflected the cumulative effect of adopting SFAS 109 as a change in accounting principle at the beginning of 1992. This adjustment was recorded as a non-cash credit to earnings of $34 million or $.24 per share. Prior years' financial statements were not restated; however, previously reported first quarter 1992 results have been restated to reflect this adjustment. The adoption of SFAS 109 had no effect on the provision for income taxes for 1992.

Deferred income taxes reflect temporary differences in the recognition of revenue and expense for tax reporting and financial statement purposes.

Deferred tax liabilities and assets were comprised of the following at the end of 1993 and 1992:

In thousands of dollars

	Dec. 26, 1993	Dec. 27, 1992
Liabilities		
Accelerated depreciation	$ 223,000	$ 239,000
Accelerated amortization of deductible intangibles	88,000	—
Pension	20,000	15,000
Other	39,512	23,100
Total deferred tax liabilities	370,512	277,100
Assets		
Accrued compensation costs	(18,000)	(26,000)
Postretirement medical and life	(119,000)	(122,000)
Other	(28,198)	(35,661)
Total deferred tax assets	(165,198)	(183,661)
Net deferred tax liabilities	$ 205,314	$ 93,439

SOURCE: Gannett Co., Inc., 1993 Annual Report.

The specific standards of accounting for income taxes will undoubtedly continue to evolve as income tax laws change, new situations emerge that give rise to temporary differences, and the conceptual basis for financial statements becomes more clearly determined by the FASB through interpretation of its conceptual framework. The authors believe it is reasonable to expect continuing change and refinement in this important and pervasive area of financial reporting as managers, corporate accountants, and auditors learn more about the implementation problems of accounting for income taxes under current and future authoritative accounting pronouncements.

KEY POINTS

1. The elements of financial statements related to income taxes are unlike other elements in the financial statements because their recognition and measurement are strongly affected by income tax law. (Objective 1)

2. Two areas in which income tax law has a particularly important impact on the elements of the financial statements are temporary differences between financial and taxable income and operating loss carrybacks and carryforwards. (Objective 1)

3. Temporary differences between pretax financial income and taxable income give rise to deferred tax assets and liabilities. The going concern assumption is important in justifying the inclusion of certain future income tax events in the financial statements. (Objective 2)

4. The tax effects of temporary differences are projected into the future and income taxes payable or receivable are calculated based on enacted tax rates. (Objective 2)

5. Current GAAP require the recognition of deferred tax assets and liabilities for all temporary differences. Several alternative methods exist, including partial allocation and nonallocation. (Objectives 3 and 4)

6. Operating loss carrybacks and carryforwards allow the loss of one year to be used to reduce income taxes that have already been paid (carrybacks) or that will otherwise have to be paid in the future (carryforwards). Loss carrybacks give rise to tax receivables that are generally presented as a current asset in the balance sheet. Loss carryforwards give rise to deferred tax assets that may be either current or noncurrent assets and are subject to reduction via a valuation allowance. (Objective 5)

APPENDIX A: INVESTMENT TAX CREDIT

Income tax policy is frequently used to accomplish certain economic and social objectives, as well as to serve as a source of governmental revenue and meet various other objectives. Since 1962, Congress has occasionally attempted to stimulate investment in capital assets by allowing a reduction in income taxes equal to a specified percentage of the cost of qualifying assets. Since its inception, the **investment tax credit (ITC)** has been suspended and restored several times to accomplish various objectives. The Revenue Act of 1978 established the ITC at 10% of the cost of qualifying assets. Additionally, limitations were placed on the amount of the ITC that could be used in any one year to offset income taxes that would otherwise be paid that year. These limitations changed from time to time. Any ITC resulting from the acquisition of assets in one year but that cannot be used to reduce taxes in that particular year due to these limitations, could be carried forward to future years. This works much like the operating loss carryforward provisions of the tax law, which were covered earlier in this chapter.

The Tax Reform Act of 1986 repealed the ITC from the tax law. Despite this development, we cover the ITC in this appendix for several reasons. It has been suspended and restored several times in the past and it is reasonable to assume that the same may occur in the future. As we will see in the following examples, the ITC may be accounted for by the deferred method, in which the effect of the credit is spread over the life of the asset. Even though the ITC may not be a part of the income tax law in a given year, amortization of previously recognized ITC may be an important factor for financial reporting. Finally, the ITC symbolizes the nature of political influences on the formation of financial reporting standards. The series of events leading up to the current accounting procedures for the ITC are explained in the latter part of this appendix to help you appreciate how politics may affect the determination of generally accepted accounting principles.

ALTERNATIVE ACCOUNTING METHODS

Two methods of accounting for the impact of the ITC on the income tax *expense* are used in practice: the **deferred method** and the **flow-through method.** The impact on the income tax liability is the same, regardless of the method of expense recognition used, because the ITC reduces taxes payable, within specified limitations, in the period in which the qualifying asset is acquired. In determining the appropriate amount of income tax expense for the income statement, the deferred and the flow-through methods differ. With the deferred method, the benefit of the ITC is recognized as a reduction in income tax expense throughout the life of the asset. With the flow-through method, however, the entire reduction in income tax expense is recognized in the year the asset qualifying for the ITC is acquired.

To illustrate these two methods, we will assume that Kapp Company acquired an item of equipment costing $200,000 in 1985 before the ITC was eliminated from the tax law. This asset qualified for the 10% ITC and had an expected useful life of eight years. During 1985 Kapp Company earned $182,000 before income tax, and the appropriate income tax rate was 46%. Entries to account for the ITC under the two alternative methods are illustrated in Exhibit 19–8.

The initial acquisition of the equipment (first entry) and the payment of income taxes (fourth entry) are identical under the two methods. The difference is found in the treatment of the impact of the ITC on the income tax expense in the second and third entries. The reduced income taxes are treated as a reduction in tax expense of $20,000 in 1985 under the flow-through method but deferred and allocated over the asset's life under the deferred method. Thus, only one-eighth, or $2,500, of the benefit is recognized as a reduction in income tax expense in 1985 under the deferred method.

Continuing the example of Kapp Company, we find that the income statement and balance sheet amounts for 1985 relative to the investment tax credit are as follows:

	Deferred Method	Flow-Through Method
Income Statement		
Income tax expense	$81,220	$63,720
Balance Sheet		
Deferred investment tax credit	17,500	NONE

EXHIBIT 19–8

Example of Alternative Methods: Investment Tax Credit

Journal Entries: Deferred Method			Transaction Description	Journal Entries: Flow-Through Method		
Equipment	200,000		Acquisition of equipment	Equipment	200,000	
Cash		200,000		Cash		200,000
Tax Expense	83,720		Income tax accrual for 1985	Tax Expense	63,720	
Deferred ITC		20,000		Tax Payable		63,720
Tax Payable		63,720				
Computation				*Computation*		
Tax on $182,000				Tax expense		
$182,000 \times .46 =$	$83,720			$83,720 - $20,000 = $63,720		
Deferred ITC						
$200,000 \times .10 =$	$20,000					
Tax payable						
$83,720 - $20,000 = $63,720						
Deferred ITC	2,500		Amortization of ITC	None		
Tax Expense		2,500				
Computation						
$20,000/8 years =$	$2,500					
Tax Payable	63,720		Payment of tax liability	Tax Payable	63,720	
Cash		63,720		Cash		63,720

Under the deferred method, the income tax expense of each year in the asset's life is reduced by the allocation of the deferred investment tax credit. For 1985, this results in an income tax expense of $81,220 ($83,720 − $2,500). The declining balance in the Deferred Investment Tax Credit account is presented in the balance sheet as a deferred income tax credit until it is fully amortized. Under the flow-through method, the full impact of the ITC is reflected in 1985, the year of the acquisition of the asset. Thus, no deferred investment tax credit appears in the balance sheet under this method.

THE CONTROVERSY OVER ACCOUNTING METHODS

The origin of the investment tax credit, the emergence of two methods of accounting for it, and the response of the Accounting Principles Board to this new feature of financial reporting resulted in a significant controversy. Both accounting methods that emerged for the ITC—deferred and flow-through—have merit and thus were attractive to individual accountants. Advocates of the deferred method held that the credit represents a reduction in the cost of the asset, because management was aware of the availability of the credit, considering it in deciding to acquire the asset. They believed that income is generated through the *use,* not the acquisition, of assets. Spreading the credit over the life of the asset was logical and consistent with allocating the asset's cost over its useful life in a systematic and rational manner, much like the method for depreciation. Matching is a major part of the justification for this method.

Matching

Furthermore, this treatment was consistent with the recapture feature of the income tax law that required the company to repay some or all of the ITC if the asset were not held and used for a specified period of time.

Other accountants advocated the tax reduction or flow-through method primarily on the basis that the ITC represented a selective income tax reduction that was available only to those who met certain specified conditions. They argued that the ITC was a feature of income tax law that did not alter the inherent value of the related asset but was more like a permanent difference between pretax accounting income and taxable income than a reduction in the cost and related depreciation on the asset.

Professional accounting standards for the investment tax credit were originally developed in *APB Opinion No. 2* in 1962 and subsequently modified in *APB Opinion No. 4* in 1964.[14] These opinions were issued when the APB was attempting to establish itself as the major authoritative body responsible for guiding the development of financial accounting standards in the United States. The general acceptance of its pronouncements was an important element in establishing this authority.

Initially, the APB advocated the deferred or cost reduction method. Many corporate managers and practicing CPAs, however, favored the flow-through or tax reduction method. The flow-through method has an advantage in terms of the early recognition of income in the financial statements, because the full effect of the reduction in income tax expense is recognized in the initial year.

Two significant developments during this period had a negative impact on the authoritative position of the APB and

---

[14]*APB Opinions Nos. 2 and 4,* "Accounting for the Investment Tax Credit," 1962 and 1964.

resulted in the board's subsequent acceptance of *either* method of accounting for the investment tax credit. First, the American Institute of Certified Public Accountants (AICPA) made an urgent plea to members to issue an unqualified audit opinion *only* if clients used the deferred method, because the flow-through method was not consistent with *APB Opinion No. 2*. Despite this plea, many unqualified opinions were issued for financial statements in which the flow-through method was used. Second, the Securities and Exchange Commission (SEC) took a position that allowed either method. In light of these setbacks, the APB issued *Opinion No. 4,* in which it voiced its acceptance of the flow-through method, even though it continued to maintain a *preference* for the deferred method.

In a reconsideration of the two methods in 1971, when Congress reinstated the ITC, the APB again attempted to limit accounting to the deferred method. A great deal of political pressure emerged as influential businesspeople were successful in lobbying Congress to stipulate in the income tax law that no specific method of accounting for the ITC could be required by a standard-setting body such as the APB.

This history of accounting for the investment tax credit is of considerable concern to the accounting profession. The lack of general acceptance of the deferred method under *APB Opinion No. 2* and the subsequent changes in *APB Opinion No. 4,* in which the board adjusted its position to parallel accounting practice, had a detrimental impact on the credibility of the APB. In the opinion of many, this action reduced the effectiveness of the board. The imposition of political pressure and the intervention of Congress in allowing alternative accounting procedures in this one area of accounting caused considerable

concern. Historically, accounting principles have developed within the private sector under the careful observation of the SEC. The precedent set by the situation surrounding the ITC is of concern to those who feel strongly that the future development of financial reporting standards should continue in the private sector to the maximum extent possible.

In reflecting on the events of late 1971, when the second series of episodes concerning the investment tax credit took place, an APB member suggested that the board should perhaps have been renamed the "Accounting Principles—Political Action Board." The following statements summarize his feelings:

> *Will lobbying become the* modus operandi *for generating or blocking the accounting pronouncements of the 1970's?...Congress has no monopoly on obtaining "correct" answers. The long-run implications for external financial reporting of the increasing tendencies to contact Congress on every issue are frightening.*
>
> *This may be a sad story but it illustrates why some members of the APB are supersensitive to industry reaction. We live in a democracy, and setting accounting principles is indeed subject to popularity testing. That is why we will continue to see an evolution of accounting principles. A natural resistance to change seems widespread. Radical changes may occur occasionally, but only when there is no widespread hostility among the reporting companies.*[15]

---

[15]Charles T. Horngren, "Accounting Principles: Private or Public Sector?" *Journal of Accountancy* (May 1972), pp. 40–41.

QUESTIONS

19-1   What is the significance of the conclusion that income taxes are an expense rather than a distribution of income?

19-2   What do we mean when we say that corporations are subject to progressive income tax rates?

19-3   How do the objectives of financial reporting and income tax reporting differ?

19-4   How do the following two features of income tax law significantly influence financial reporting of income tax information?

[a] Temporary differences.

[b] Operating loss carrybacks and carryforwards.

19-5   What are three examples of temporary differences between financial income and taxable income? How do they give rise to deferred income taxes?

19-6   After a projection of the tax effect of temporary differences has been completed, what is the process by which the accountant properly records the year-end income tax accrual?

19-7   What impact, if any, does an enacted change in the tax rate have on the elements of the balance sheet and income statement?

19-8   Why might a company forgo the certainty of a loss carryback to receive a refund of past income taxes in favor of carrying a current-year loss forward to reduce future taxable income?

19-9   If the item deferred income taxes appears in a company's balance sheet as a liability, what does this indicate about past relationships between pretax financial income and taxable income?

19-10 In what ways are permanent differences unlike temporary differences? Give an example of a permanent difference. Why do permanent differences not give rise to deferred income tax assets and liabilities?

19-11 What is the difference between taxable and deductible temporary differences? Give an example of each.

19-12 How does accounting for deferred income taxes under the asset/liability method differ from that under the deferred method?

19–13 Using installment sales as an example, what is meant by the "origination" and "reversal" of temporary differences?

19–14 Are deferred tax amounts significant balance sheet items for U.S. corporations? Justify your response.

19–15 What are alternatives that have been considered to the current methods of accounting for deferred taxes on temporary differences? Describe them.

19–16 In what circumstances might the Deferred Income Tax Liability account be debited rather than credited as part of the year-end accrual yet still appear in the company's balance sheet?

19–17 What is the income statement impact of recognizing a loss carryback?

19–18 In considering the impact on the balance sheet, how does a loss carryback differ from a loss carryforward?

19–19 What is the basis for classifying deferred income taxes as current and noncurrent in the balance sheet?

19–20 What is a statutory rate reconciliation? What does it accomplish?

19–21 How does a temporary difference for a loss contingency that is recognized earlier in the financial statements than in the tax return affect the financial statements?

19–22 How does a temporary difference for depreciation in which higher amounts are recognized in the tax returns early in the asset's life than are recognized in the financial statements affect the financial statements?

19–23 How might a company have more than one deferred income tax account in its balance sheet at the same time?

19–24 Under what circumstances is a valuation allowance required on deferred tax assets?

19–25 What are some of the important professional judgments that are required to apply current accounting standards in accounting for income taxes?

19–26 (Appendix A) What are the differences in concept underlying the deferred (cost reduction) method and the flow-through (tax reduction) methods of accounting for the investment tax credit?

19–27 (Appendix A) What impact do the deferred (cost reduction) and flow-through (tax reduction) methods of accounting for the investment tax credit have on the recognition of the elements of financial statements?

EXERCISES

19–28 Income Tax Accrual During 1995 Fowler, Inc., had the following differences between pretax accounting income and taxable income:

[1] Premiums on an insurance policy taken out on the company's president that are not deductible for income tax purposes, $2,000.
[2] Plant asset write-off for income tax purposes that exceeded depreciation for financial reporting, $7,800.

Pretax accounting income was $29,750, and the enacted income tax rate for 1995 and all future years was 36%. Fowler, Inc., had no previous deferred taxes.

INSTRUCTIONS
[a] Compute taxable income for 1995.
[b] Prepare the journal entry to record income taxes for 1995.

19–29 Permanent and Temporary Differences Waller Company includes the following items in pretax accounting income for 1996:
[1] Litigation loss of $25,000 (estimated), which will become tax deductible when settled in the future.
[2] Insurance premiums of $10,000, which will never be deductible for income tax purposes.
[3] Revenue from an installment sale of $45,000, which will be recognized in taxable income as received over the next three years.

Pretax financial income is $175,000.

INSTRUCTIONS
[a] Determine the amount of pretax financial income subject to income tax and the amount of taxable income for 1996.

[b] Briefly explain the difference in the way you have treated the preceding three items and justify that difference.

19–30   Calculating Financial Income from Taxable Income   The controller of Hauser, Inc., is attempting to determine the amount of pretax financial income for 1996 by making adjustments to taxable income from the company's 1996 income tax return. The tax return indicates taxable income of $190,000, on which a tax liability of $66,500 has been recognized ($190,000 × 35% = $66,500).

The controller has prepared the following list of items that may be required to determine pretax financial income from the amount of taxable income:

[1] Accelerated write-off for income tax purposes was $67,000; straight-line depreciation on the same assets is $40,000.
[2] Insurance premiums were not included as a deduction in the tax return but may be required in the income statement. The appropriate amount, if required, is $22,500.
[3] Several expenses were included in the income tax return on an estimated basis. These items will be in the income statement at these same amounts, but they are subject to change if new information in the future indicates that the original estimates were inaccurate.
[4] Interest on municipal securities was not included in the tax return. During the year, $12,350 was received on these investments.

INSTRUCTIONS

Determine the amount of pretax financial income and pretax financial income subject to tax, working from the amount of taxable income. Carefully explain each adjustment to taxable income to determine the required figures.

19–31   Income Tax Accrual with Temporary Differences   Foster, Inc., reports pretax financial income for 1996 of $88,000. Included are the following items:

[1] Depreciation on plant assets, determined by the straight-line method, of $38,000. Accelerated cost recovery, taken for income tax purposes, totaled $55,000.
[2] Interest on municipal bonds of $15,000, which is not subject to income tax.
[3] A litigation loss, recognized on an estimated basis, of $12,000. This item will not be deductible for income tax purposes until final settlement is reached in a future year.

Enacted income tax rates are 30% for 1996 and 35% for all future years.

INSTRUCTIONS

Analyze the company's income for financial and tax purposes in a manner that facilitates the preparation of the 1996 income tax accrual, and prepare that accrual in general journal form.

19–32   Income Tax Accrual with Temporary Differences   Saunders Company has correctly determined its 1996 pretax financial income to be $950,000. Included in that figure are two items that do not have tax consequences: insurance premiums paid of $25,000 and interest received on investments in municipal bonds of $10,000.

In addition, the company has two temporary differences: accelerated write-off for income tax purposes exceeds straight-line depreciation on the same plant assets by $135,000, and $50,000 cash received in advance for an order of merchandise is taxable in 1996 but will be recognized in accounting income in 1997.

The income tax rate for 1996 is 35%; the enacted rate for years after 1996 is 38%.

INSTRUCTIONS

[a] Prepare an analysis of Saunders' financial and taxable income for 1996, which provides the amount of the current income tax payable and the balance needed in deferred income taxes at the end of the year.
[b] Prepare the income tax accrual for 1996.

19–33   Reversing Temporary Difference with Income Tax Rate Change   Sprouse, Inc., had $20,000 of deferred income taxes (credit balance) at the beginning of 1996. During that year, pretax financial income and taxable income were determined by the company's accountant to be as follows:

Pretax financial income	$255,000
Temporary difference:	
Depreciation:	
1996 originating	(75,000)
Pre-1996 reversing	48,500
Taxable income	$228,500

The enacted income tax rate for 1996 was 30%. During 1996 the enacted rate for all future years increased to 36%. Depreciation temporary differences arising prior to 1996 that will reverse after 1996 totaled $60,000.

INSTRUCTIONS

[a] Prepare the income tax accrual at December 31, 1996, the end of the company's financial reporting period.

[b] Calculate the impact of the income tax rate change for years after 1996 on the amount of income tax expense recognized in 1996.

19–34 Accounting for Income Taxes by *SFAS No. 109* Francisco, Inc., has determined its 1996 pretax financial income to be $160,000. The following differences between accounting income and taxable income have also been identified: (1) insurance expense in accounting income of $12,000 that cannot be deducted for income tax purposes; (2) excess of tax write-off of plant assets over depreciation in financial income of $40,000: (3) revenue received in advance that is taxed currently but deferred for purposes of financial income of $10,000. This revenue will be earned in 1997. The income tax rate is 40% and no previous temporary differences exist.

INSTRUCTIONS

Prepare the income tax accrual entry for 1996, distinguishing between current and noncurrent deferred taxes.

19–35 Accounting for Income Taxes by *SFAS No. 109* Fosteur Company's pretax financial income for 1996 is $790,000. Temporary differences have been identified as follows:

Depreciation: Tax write-off exceeds financial depreciation by $100,000.

Litigation: Loss taken for financial reporting purposes of $45,000 will be deducted for tax purposes in the distant future.

Warranty: Amount expensed for financial reporting purposes exceeds amount currently deductible for tax purposes by $25,000.

The warranty liability is classified as a current liability in the company's balance sheet. The income tax rate is 35%, and this is Fosteur's first year of operations.

INSTRUCTIONS

[a] Prepare the income tax accrual entry for 1996, distinguishing between current and noncurrent deferred taxes.

[b] Identify the income tax elements, including dollar amounts, for the 1996 balance sheet and income statement.

19–36 Temporary Differences and Statutory Reconciliation *(SFAS No. 109)* Welsch, Inc., determines its pretax financial income to be $550,000 for 1996. The only temporary difference is for depreciation, where the amount written off for tax purposes exceeds straight-line depreciation recognized for financial reporting purposes by $70,000. At the beginning of 1996, the cumulative temporary difference for depreciation was $250,000, for which a $75,000 deferred tax liability has been recognized. The income tax rate is 40%.

INSTRUCTIONS

[a] Identify the income statement elements relative to income taxes for 1996.

[b] Prepare a statutory rate reconciliation for 1996, carefully labeling each item.

19–37 Loss Carryback Welch Company reported the following figures for the years 1993, 1994, and 1995.

	1993	1994	1995
Income (loss) before income tax	$100,000	$130,000	$(160,000)
Income tax rate	32%	34%	36%

The entire loss of 1995 is available to offset income taxes paid or becoming payable. No permanent or temporary differences exist in any of the three years.

INSTRUCTIONS

Prepare the income statement for each year, beginning with "income (loss) before income tax." Assume the carryback/carryforward option is employed.

19–38 Loss Carryback   Dunn Company reported the following for 1994 and 1995:

	1994	1995
Income (loss) before income tax	$257,000	$(163,000)
Income tax rate	38%	36%

The entire 1995 loss is available to offset income taxes paid or becoming payable. No permanent or temporary differences exist for either year.

INSTRUCTIONS

Prepare the income statement for each year, beginning with "income (loss) before income tax," applying the carryback/carryforward option.

19–39 Loss Carryback and Carryforward   Income and loss figures, accompanied by income tax rates, for Elder, Inc., for the first four years of operations are as follows:

	1993	1994	1995	1996
Income (loss) before income tax	$175,000	$182,000	$(405,000)	$121,000
Income tax rate	36%	32%	38%	35%

The entire loss in 1996 is available to reduce income taxes paid or that would otherwise be paid. No permanent or temporary differences exist in any of the years.

INSTRUCTIONS

Prepare the income statement for each year, beginning with "income (loss) before income tax," applying the carryback/carryforward option. The 1996 income tax rate is applicable to future years.

19–40 Loss Carryback and Carryforward   Wolfe, Inc., had taxable income (loss) figures as follows for 1993, 1994, and 1995, respectively: $100,000, $78,000, and ($25,000). Income tax rates are 35% for 1993 and 1994 and 32% for 1995. No permanent or temporary differences existed in any of the years.

INSTRUCTIONS

[a] Prepare the year-end income tax accrual for 1995, assuming that the company selects the option to carry back the loss.
[b] Prepare the year-end tax accrual for 1995, assuming that the company selects the option to carry the loss forward and that the future enacted income tax rate is 34%.

19–41 Loss Carryforward   Thronebary Company had a loss of $100,000 in 1994, its first year of operation. In 1995, the company had pretax financial income of $28,500, followed by $155,000 in 1996. The appropriate income tax rate is 34% for all years.

INSTRUCTIONS

Prepare the general journal entries required at the end of each year to properly account for income taxes.

19–42 (Appendix A) Investment Tax Credit   Filburg Manufacturing Company acquired several items of machinery costing a total of $175,000 during 1985. The company expects to use the machinery for 10 years. The machinery qualified for the 10% investment tax credit, reducing taxes paid in 1985 by $17,500. Pretax financial income for 1985 and 1986 was $98,500 and $125,600, respectively. The income tax rate for both years was 30%.

INSTRUCTIONS

Determine the amount of income tax expense in the income statement in 1985 and 1986 under the following methods of accounting for the investment tax credit:

[a] Flow-through (tax reduction) method.
[b] Deferred (cost reduction) method.

19–43 (Appendix A) Investment Tax Credit   Dataquick Company acquired a computer for $262,000 in early 1985. The computer was expected to be useful for 20 years. It was subject to a 10% investment tax credit, reducing taxes that would otherwise have been paid in 1985. Income before income taxes in 1985 totaled $192,500, which was subject to a 40% income tax rate. The company depreciated the computer by the straight-line method with no salvage value for both book and tax purposes.

INSTRUCTIONS

Prepare general journal entries under both the deferred and the flow-through methods for all transactions and events relating to the computer, including the impact of the acquisition on income tax expense.

19–44 Temporary Differences and Deferred Income Taxes Tucker, Inc., has correctly determined its 1995 pretax financial income as $500,000. Included in that amount is a litigation loss of $45,000 that will not be resolved in the courts until sometime in the distant future, at which time it will be deductible for income tax purposes. Also, during 1995 the company purchased equipment that is being written off on an accelerated basis for income tax purposes. The $100,000 temporary difference will reverse over the useful life of the asset. No deferred income taxes existed prior to 1995. The enacted income tax rate for all years is 40%.

INSTRUCTIONS

[a] Prepare a summary to assist Tucker in determining the amounts of its current income tax liability and any deferred income taxes.
[b] Prepare the year-end income tax accrual at December 31, 1995, including supporting computations for the amounts in your entry.
[c] What impact, if any, would an enacted change in income tax rate for 1996 and future years have on your answers to previous questions? (Provide a discussion answer and then repeat [b], assuming that the enacted income tax rate for 1996 and all future years is 38%.

19–45 Temporary and Permanent Differences Trout, Inc., reports pretax financial income of $750,000 for 1996. The following differences between financial income and taxable income have been correctly identified:

[1] A $25,000 deposit received in 1996 is taxable immediately but will be reported in financial income in the future.
[2] Insurance expense of $50,000 is expensed in financial income but not deductible for income tax purposes.
[3] Accelerated write-off of plant assets for tax purposes exceeds straight-line depreciation for financial reporting purposes by $175,000. This difference will reverse over the estimated useful lives of the assets.
[4] A litigation loss of $65,000 was recognized on an estimated basis in financial income but will become tax deductible only after final settlement in the future.

Deferred income taxes on all temporary differences are considered noncurrent.

INSTRUCTIONS

[a] Prepare an analysis that results in a computation of income taxes currently payable and deferred income taxes, assuming an enacted 34% income tax rate for all years.
[b] Prepare the income tax accrual for 1996, assuming no deferred income taxes are carried forward from 1995.
[c] Prepare the income tax accrual for 1996, assuming that a credit (liability) balance of $13,500 is carried forward from 1995.
[d] Explain the difference between permanent and temporary differences in pretax financial and taxable income, using your answer to [a] to illustrate your point(s).

19–46 Temporary and Permanent Differences Dry Gulch, Inc., has determined the following information concerning pretax financial income and taxable income for its first two years of operations:

1995

Pretax financial income is $175,000.

Interest revenue on municipal securities is $5,500.

Depreciation temporary differences of $50,000 originate during the year.

Installment sale temporary differences of $10,000 originate during the year.

The enacted income tax rate for 1995 is 30% and for all future years is 35%.

1996

Pretax financial income is $190,000.

Interest revenue on municipal securities is $7,200.

Depreciation temporary differences of $70,000 originate during the year; 25% of the 1995 originating differences reverse during the year.

Installment sales temporary differences of $12,000 originate during the year; 50% of the 1995 originating differences reverse during the year.

The enacted income tax rate for all years after 1996 is changed to 38% during the year.

INSTRUCTIONS

[a] Prepare an analysis for 1995 to determine the amount of current and deferred income taxes payable. (*Hint:* Keep in mind that at the end of 1995, you are not aware of the 1996 information given in the problem.) Combine all deferred taxes in a single account (i.e., you do not need to distinguish between current and noncurrent deferred taxes).

[b] Prepare an analysis for 1996 to determine the amount of current income taxes payable and deferred income taxes.

[c] Prepare the journal entries to record income taxes for 1995 and 1996, assuming that no balance exists in deferred income taxes prior to 1995.

19–47 Loss Carryback and Carryforward   Dexter, Inc., experienced a $550,000 pretax financial loss in 1995, a year in which the income tax rate was 34%. The following data pertain to the period 1993 to 1995:

Year	Income (Loss) before Income Taxes	Income Tax Rate
1993	$ 192,000	30%
1994	465,000	32%
1995	(550,000)	34%

Management estimates that the income tax rate beyond 1995 will be approximately 36%. The end of Dexter's financial reporting period is December 31.

INSTRUCTIONS

[a] Prepare the general journal entry to record income taxes at the end of 1995, assuming the following:
   [1] Dexter carries the 1995 loss back.
   [2] Dexter forgoes the opportunity to carry the loss back and, instead, carries the 1995 loss forward.

[b] Explain why a company might choose option [2] when option [1] results in almost immediate cash.

19–48 Loss Carryback and Carryforward   Smothers, Inc., is trying to decide whether to exercise the carryback/carryforward option or the carryforward-only option in recognizing the income tax refundable as a result of its 1995 loss (before income taxes) of $85,000. The company began operations in 1994 and reported an income before income taxes of $28,000 that year.

An important consideration is the impact of the two options on the income statement and the balance sheet for 1995 and 1996. The company is optimistic about future operations, but income is *not* believed to be assured. The company does expect, however, to report an income of approximately $75,000 in 1996 and anticipates profitable operations in future years.

The appropriate income tax rate for 1994 and 1995 was 35%. No change is expected in the income tax rate for the foreseeable future. The end of the company's financial reporting period is December 31.

INSTRUCTIONS

[a] Explain the difference between the carryback/carryforward option and the carryforward only option. Indicate why each might be a desirable alternative for Smothers, Inc.

[b] Determine the balance sheet and income statement presentation for 1994 (based on actual data) and for 1995 (based on projected data), assuming that management decides to exercise the carryback/carryforward option.

19–49 Accounting for Income Taxes by *SFAS No. 109*   Montgomery, Inc., has correctly determined its 1995 pretax financial income to be $190,000. This year is the first year of operations and four temporary differences between financial and taxable income originated during the year. They are described below:

[1] An installment sale of $15,000 was recognized in financial income, although it will not be taxable until it is collected. The company anticipates collection in 1997.

[2] Revenue received in advance amounted to $8,000 during the year. While this is taxable in 1995, it will be recognized for financial reporting purposes when it is earned, which is expected to be 1998.

[3] Depreciation for income tax purposes exceeded that for financial reporting by $40,000. This difference is expected to reverse $20,000 in 1996 and $10,000 in each of 1997 and 1998.

[4] The company became involved in litigation that resulted in a $30,000 loss recognized in financial income. That amount will not be deductible for income tax purposes, however, until the litigation is completed, which is expected to be 1997.

   The enacted income tax rates are 34% for 1995 and 36% for all years thereafter. Pretax financial income for 1995 also includes $5,000 of interest revenue on municipal securities, which is not taxable. Montgomery, Inc., accounts for income taxes in accordance with *SFAS No. 109.*

INSTRUCTIONS

[a] Prepare a schedule determining taxable income for 1995, beginning with the $190,000 of pretax financial income. Identify the adjustments you make to reach taxable income.

[b] Prepare a schedule for computing the amount of deferred taxes at the end of 1995. Distinguish between current and noncurrent deferred tax assets and liabilities.

[c] Prepare the income tax accrual at December 31, 1995, the end of Montgomery, Inc.'s reporting year.

19–50 Accounting for Income Taxes by *SFAS No. 109*   Business Analysts, Inc., has determined its pretax financial income to be $50,000 for 1995 and $85,000 for 1996, its first two years of operations. Temporary differences are as follows:

1995

[1] An installment sale for $15,000 is included in financial income but will not be included in taxable income until 1996 when it will be collected.

[2] Revenue received in advance of $7,000 will not be included in financial income until it is earned in 1998 but is taxable in 1995.

1996

[3] Assets purchased in 1996 are being written off for income tax purposes on an accelerated basis, resulting in an excess of write-off for income tax purposes over financial statement depreciation by $30,000. That amount will reverse over the period 1997 to 1999.

[4] A litigation loss, recognized in financial income in 1996, will not be deductible for income tax purposes until the litigation is complete, which is expected in 1999. The amount is $12,000.

In 1995, the income tax rate enacted for 1995 and all future years is 34%. During 1996 new rates were enacted that increased the percentages for 1996 and future years to 40%. The company ends its reporting year on December 31. There are no permanent differences between pretax financial and taxable income. Business Analysts, Inc., accounts for income taxes in accordance with *SFAS No. 109.*

INSTRUCTIONS

[a] Compute the amount of taxable income for 1995 and 1996, beginning with pretax financial income and adjusting for temporary differences. Assume that the 1995 installment sale was collected in 1996.

[b] Prepare an analysis of cumulative temporary differences and deferred taxes (similar to the one in Exhibit 19–3) to support the year-end income tax accrual for 1995, assuming that you know only the information that would be available at the end of 1995 (i.e., you are not aware of actual events pertaining to 1996 because those events have not yet occurred). Prepare the income tax accrual and statutory reconciliation at December 31, 1995, using the information in your analysis.

[c] Repeat [b] for 1996, incorporating the additional information that is now available, using Exhibit 19–4 as a model.

[d] Prepare in comparative columns the elements of the income statement and balance sheet that would appear in the 1995 and 1996 financial statements relative to income taxes.

19–51 Accounting for Income Taxes by *SFAS No. 109*   Grant Company applies *SFAS No. 109* in accounting for income taxes. At the end of 1995, the following balances of temporary differences and deferred taxes exist:

	Cumulative Temporary Differences	Deferred Tax Assets (Liabilities)	Classification
Depreciation	$(125,000)	$(47,500)	Noncurrent
Installment sales	(75,000)	(28,500)	Current
Litigation loss	60,000	22,800	Noncurrent
	$(140,000)	$(53,200)	

For 1996, pretax financial income is $400,000, including municipal interest of $25,000. Additional temporary difference activity during the year is as follows:

Depreciation:	Originating $35,000 from use of accelerated write-off for tax purposes and straight-line depreciation for financial reporting.
Installment sales:	$65,000 of the amount included in the temporary difference was collected and included in taxable income; $90,000 of new installment sales were recognized for accounting purposes and deferred for tax purposes.
Warranty expense:	Short-term warranties were offered for the first time on products sold. The amount expensed in the income statement exceeded the amount currently deductible for income tax purposes by $10,000.

INSTRUCTIONS

[a] Prepare the 1996 income tax accrual entry and statutory reconciliation, including detailed documentation of all calculations. The enacted income tax rate for 1996 and future years is 34%.

[b] During 1997, Grant Company determines its pretax financial loss to be $100,000, including municipal interest of $20,000 and temporary differences, as follows:

Depreciation:	Additional originating difference of $45,000.
Installment sales:	$75,000 of previous balance collected; 1997 sales amounts uncollected at year-end of $98,000.
Warranty:	Additional originating difference of $15,000.

The loss for income tax purposes is carried back to 1995 when the income tax rate was 38%. (Assume that 1994 was a break-even year.)

Using this additional information, repeat requirement [a] for 1997.

[c] For this requirement, repeat [b] for 1997 with the following changes in information: The pretax financial loss is $620,000 rather than $100,000. Taxable income in 1995 was $250,000, which was subject to income taxes at 38%. The deferred tax asset arising from the operating loss carryforward is classified as noncurrent.

(*Hint:* This problem does not require analyses for each year like the one included in Exhibits 19–4 and 19–5. You may find that useful, however, in completing [a] through [c].)

19–52 (Appendix A)   Investment Tax Credit   Hall, Inc., acquired heavy construction equipment in 1985 for $880,000, which qualified for a 10% investment tax credit. The equipment is expected to be useful for 10 years, and straight-line depreciation will be used. Operating information for 1985 and 1986 is as follows:

	1985	1986
Pretax financial income	$982,500	$1,050,000
Income tax rate	40%	38%

INSTRUCTIONS

[a] Prepare all journal entries for 1985 and 1986 to account for equipment, depreciation, and income taxes. The flow-through (tax reduction) method is to be used in accounting for the investment tax credit.

[b] Prepare the journal entries in [a] that would be different if the deferred (cost reduction) method were used in accounting for the investment tax credit instead of the flow-through method.

[c] Compute the amount of net income that would be recognized in 1985 and 1986 under the flow-through method and the deferred method.

19–53 (Appendix A)   Investment Tax Credit   Pepper Company, which began operations in 1983, continuously invests in equipment for use in its manufacturing process. This equipment qualifies for the investment tax credit (ITC), thereby reducing income taxes paid by 10% of the cost of qualifying assets in the year of acquisition.

Information related to the company during its first three years of operation follows:

	1983	1984	1985
Pretax financial income	$500,000	$528,000	$617,000
Income tax rate	40%	42%	42%
Equipment acquisitions eligible for ITC	$424,000	$370,000	$360,000
Estimated life of equipment acquisitions	8 years	10 years	9 years

Pretax financial income includes $18,000 in insurance premiums each year that are not deductible for income tax purposes. In addition, 1984 pretax income includes $5,000 of interest received by Pepper on investments in municipal securities.

INSTRUCTIONS

[a] Prepare a detailed calculation of income tax expense for each year, assuming that the deferred method of accounting for the ITC is used.

[b] The president of Pepper Company has asked you to determine the impact of the flow-through method on net income by preparing pro forma calculations for 1983, 1984, and 1985 under that method.

[1] Prepare pro forma calculations showing what net income would have been in 1983, 1984, and 1985 if the flow-through method had been used.

[2] Outline the items you would include in an explanation of the impact of the two alternative methods on the company's financial statements.

CASES

19–54 Relationship of Financial and Taxable Income

Jack Frost, the president of a company that is one of your clients, has confronted you with something in the company's financial statements that he does not understand. You have correctly prepared the income statement from information provided by the company's accountant. That statement shows pretax income of $100,000 and income tax expense of only $20,400. The income tax payable in the balance sheet is also $20,400, despite the fact that the enacted income tax rate is 34%. The company has been profitable in the past, and no loss carrybacks or carryforwards exist to explain this relationship.

Frost's reaction is mixed. On the one hand, he is glad that you have computed the income tax that the company must pay to be only $20,400 because of the benefit of the reduced cash outflow from what he had expected. On the other hand, he is concerned whether you have correctly determined the amount of income tax expense and payable and that users of the company's financial statements may be confused by this unusual-looking relationship in the income statement.

INSTRUCTIONS

[a] What is the most likely explanation for the relationship Frost sees in the income statement and how will you explain this "problem" to him?

[b] What financial reporting requirement is useful in explaining to readers of the financial statements why the income tax expense recognized may not equal the enacted income tax rate multiplied by the pretax financial income in the income statement?

19–55 Justification for Deferred Income Taxes

Mr. Gordo, the president of Greekline, Inc., your client, has come to you with questions concerning amounts in the financial statements regarding income taxes. He is particularly interested in how the amount of the income tax expense could possibly be more than the liability for income taxes currently payable to the government for income of 1995, the current year.

In expressing his concern, he notes that he has seen an amount for deferred income taxes in the balance sheet. He also points out that you would certainly not include in this year's financial statements amounts that do not come due until future years, and thus he sees no justification for those amounts.

You are having a conference with Mr. Gordo tomorrow and are reasonably certain that the matter will come up, because the purpose of the meeting is to finalize amounts in the financial statements prior to their distribution to the company's investors and creditors.

INSTRUCTIONS

How will you explain the financial statement elements related to income taxes to Mr. Gordo?

19–56 Using Future Tax Rates   Hart, Inc., recently hired you as auditor for the company's annual financial statements. When you were at the client's office familiarizing yourself with the accounting system and making preliminary plans for the upcoming audit, Sylvia Hart, president of Hart, Inc., stopped by for a brief conversation.

You quickly learned that although Hart is not an accountant, she is an astute reader of financial statements and takes pride in being relatively well informed about important financial reporting issues. She quickly moves the conversation toward income tax reporting and the complexities of *FASB Statement of Financial Accounting Standards No. 109*. Although she has not read the statement, she has read in *The Wall Street Journal* about its likely impact on financial statements.

Hart is concerned about the incorporation of enacted income tax rates, other than the present rate, in the numbers that affect the financial statements. Her position is that enacted tax rates may change frequently and to base important financial statement numbers on future income tax rates seems to be counter to the accounting objective of recording items on the basis of reliable information. Also, she believes that to incorporate into current financial statements the income tax rates that do not go into effect until some future date is not consistent with the historical orientation of the financial statements.

INSTRUCTIONS

How would you respond to Hart's conclusions?

JUDGMENT CASES

19–57 Materiality of Deferred Income Taxes   Laid-back, Inc., has been your employer for a number of years and your boss, the company president, is not too enthusiastic about the preparation of financial statements in conformity with GAAP. The company's bank, however, requires two-year comparative financial statements as a condition of a large loan.

In previous years, the company's president did not wish to go to the trouble to determine the proper amount of deferred income taxes, and you have acquiesced because the amounts have not seemed material. Although you did not compute the exact tax effects of temporary differences, you roughly estimated them and, although they have increased in recent years, you never believed that the total amount could be material to the financial statements taken as a whole.

During the current year, however, the company has acquired a large amount of new equipment and due to the originating temporary difference related to depreciation, you are convinced that the determination of deferred income taxes and the inclusion of them in the financial statements will be necessary this year. In fact, your preliminary calculations indicate that the amount of deferred income taxes for the current year are a material amount. To your dismay, you also observe that the amount of deferred income taxes that would have been classified as a current liability last year, had deferred taxes been recognized, would have reduced the company's working capital and current ratio to a level that would have caused the company to be in violation of one of its lending covenants with the bank. You wonder whether the deferred income tax amounts that existed at the end of the preceding year should be restated as a correction of an error. The effect of the omitted deferred income taxes on last year's financial statements taken as a whole is negligible, other than the impact on the current liabilities, working capital, and the current ratio. As you discuss this matter with your boss, he makes the following statement:

> *Look, this thing just wasn't material to last year's income or to the balance sheet taken as a whole. Furthermore, the change from last year to this year is merely a change in accounting estimate in any event. Last year we estimated deferred income taxes were immaterial and this year they are material. The entire effect of that change should be picked up in the year of the change, right? Regardless of what some theoretical analysis might suggest, we are not going to restate our financial statements over some trivial event and unduly alarm the bank. Last year's statements are just ancient history and we aren't going to rewrite them now.*

INSTRUCTIONS

Respond to the position taken by the president. Be sure to include in your answer what you believe the appropriate accounting for this matter should be. Assuming that your solution differs from that of your boss, what course of action do you believe you should take?

19–58 Valuation Allowance for Deferred Tax Assets   Your client, Spirit Franchise Company, has just completed its financial statements for 1996, the first year in which it has applied *SFAS No. 109* in accounting for income taxes. As you begin your audit of those financial statements, you immediately notice a significantly smaller balance in the noncurrent liability for deferred income taxes than in previous years.

You approach Sharon Vorner, controller for the company, in search of an explanation. Vorner responds with the following statement:

> *Applying* SFAS No. 109 *has really improved our financial position. That statement changes accounting for income taxes in two important ways that help us. First, it requires that we recompute deferred taxes at the end of each accounting period on the basis of newly enacted income tax rates. Since our deferred tax balances have been growing for many years and were initially recorded when corporate tax rates were in the 46% to 50% range, we benefited a great deal by being able to reduce our liability balance when we recomputed these items at the current 38%. Second,* SFAS No. 109 *requires the recognition of deferred tax assets for all deductible temporary differences and for operating loss carryforwards. We have had significant operating losses that were so large that we could not carry them back because of the short carryback period. We do intend, however, to use them sometime in the next 15 years as our fortunes improve and we become profitable.*

INSTRUCTIONS

You are impressed with Vorner's knowledge of *SFAS No. 109* and realize that much of what she has said is, in fact, correct. On the other hand, you are concerned about the "too favorable" impact that *SFAS No. 109* may have had on the company's financial statements and wonder if you and she are missing something in applying *SFAS No. 109*. What will you do to alleviate this uneasy feeling you have? If you believe changes are required in the financial statements to make them conform to the standards of *SFAS No. 109,* how will you convince Vorner and other representatives of the company?

19–59 Scheduling Temporary Differences   Riviera, Inc., determines its pretax financial income to be $88,500 for 1995. During the year, the company purchased assets that it plans to write off for income tax purposes on an accelerated basis while using straight-line for financial reporting purposes. The difference between the two is $25,000 in 1995, and that amount is expected to reverse over the next five years at an equal amount per year. The currently enacted income tax rate for all years is 35%.

The company's chief accountant has prepared the following analysis and accrual for income taxes for 1995:

Riviera, Inc.
Analysis of Income Tax Information for 1995–2000

	1995	1996	1997	1998	1999	2000
Pretax financial income	$ 88,500	—	—	—	—	—
Temporary difference:						
Depreciation	(25,000)	$5,000	$5,000	$5,000	$5,000	$5,000
Taxable income	$ 63,500	$5,000	$5,000	$5,000	$5,000	$5,000
Income tax rate	35%	35%	35%	35%	35%	35%
Income tax liability	$ 22,225	$1,750	$1,750	$1,750	$1,750	$1,750

1995	Income Tax Expense ($22,225 + $8,750)	30,975	
	Income Tax Payable ($63,500 × 35%)		22,225
	Deferred Income Tax ($1,750 × 5 years)		8,750

You are fascinated with the accountant's year-by-year analysis and decide to talk with her about why she went to the trouble to consider each future year separately rather than combining all future years together. When you meet to discuss this, she states: "I realize that considering each individual future year was not important in this situation. The accrual would be the same had I treated the entire $25,000 as a single temporary difference, applied the 35% income tax rate, and recorded deferred income taxes of $8,750. There are circumstances, however, in which scheduling each individual future year may be helpful, and even required, to apply *SFAS No. 109.*"

INSTRUCTIONS

To what circumstances do you think the chief accountant is referring? In other words, in applying *SFAS No. 109,* when might it be useful, even mandatory, to consider future years individually or in groups rather than in the aggregate?

FINANCIAL REPORTING CASE

19–60 Financial Reporting Case Philip Morris Companies, Inc., is a major U.S. corporation that produces many well-known products, including Marlboro cigarettes, Kraft foods, Jell-O items, Oscar Mayer meats, and Maxwell House coffee. The company's 1993 income statement includes a provision for income taxes of $2,628 million. (Comparable numbers for 1992 and 1991 are $3,669 million and $3,044 million, respectively.)

Following are the paragraph from the Summary of Significant Accounting Policies concerning income taxes and Note 10, which provides detailed income tax information.

Note 1 Summary of Significant Accounting Policies:

Income taxes Effective January 1, 1993, the Company adopted the method of accounting for income taxes prescribed by Statement of Financial Accounting Standards ("SFAS") No. 109, "Accounting for Income Taxes." The Company previously had accounted for income taxes in accordance with the method prescribed by SFAS No. 96, "Accounting for Income Taxes." See Note 10.

Note 10 Pretax Earnings and Provision for Income Taxes:

As discussed in Note 1, the Company adopted SFAS No. 109 effective January 1, 1993. SFAS No. 109 is a modification of SFAS No. 96, which had been the accounting standard previously followed by the Company. The effect of adoption of SFAS No. 109 was immaterial to the Company's 1993 financial position and results of operations.

Pretax earnings and provision for income taxes consisted of the following:

(in millions)	1993	1992	1991
Pretax earnings:			
United States	$4,078	$6,367	$5,166
Outside United States	2,118	2,241	1,805
Total pretax earnings	$6,196	$8,608	$6,971
Provision for income taxes:			
United States federal:			
Current	$1,199	$1,630	$1,764
Deferred	278	514	119
	1,477	2,144	1,883
State and local	311	464	355
Total United States	1,788	2,608	2,238
Outside United States:			
Current	830	992	711
Deferred	10	69	95
Total outside United States	840	1,061	806
Total provision for income taxes	$2,628	$3,669	$3,044

At December 31, 1993, applicable United States federal income taxes and foreign withholding taxes have not been provided on approximately $3.8 billion of accumulated earnings of foreign subsidiaries that are expected to be permanently reinvested abroad. If these amounts were not considered permanently reinvested, additional deferred income taxes of approximately $229 million would have been provided.

The effective income tax rate on pretax earnings differed from the U.S. federal statutory rate for the following reasons:

	1993	1992	1991
Provision computed at U.S. federal statutory rate	35.0%	34.0%	34.0%
Increases resulting from:			
State and local income taxes, net of federal tax benefit	3.3	3.6	3.5
Rate differences—foreign operations	0.6	1.9	2.4
Goodwill amortization	3.0	2.0	2.4
Other	0.5	1.1	1.4
Provision for income taxes	42.4%	42.6%	43.7%

The tax effects of temporary differences that gave rise to consumer products deferred income tax assets and liabilities consisted of the following:

(in millions)	December 31, 1993	1992
Deferred income tax assets:		
Accrued postretirement and postemployment benefits	$ 995	$ 670
Accrued liabilities	464	432
Restructuring reserves	472	270
Other	445	379
Gross deferred income tax assets	2,376	1,751
Valuation allowance	(62)	
Total deferred income tax assets	2,314	1,751
Deferred income tax liabilities:		
Property, plant and equipment	(1,573)	(1,634)
Prepaid pension costs	(203)	(178)
Total deferred income tax liabilities	(1,776)	(1,812)
Net deferred income tax asset (liability)	$ 538	$ (61)

Financial services and real estate temporary differences are primarily attributable to deferred income tax liabilities from investments in finance leases.

INSTRUCTIONS

[a] Despite a statutory rate of 35%, Philip Morris recognized income taxes in 1993 at a rate in excess of 42%. What explains this difference in rates? Has this relationship changed significantly in the period 1991 to 1993?

[b] For 1993, what are the two most important temporary differences that underlie the company's deferred tax assets and liabilities? Is the company in a net asset or liability position concerning deferred assets at the end of 1993? Has this relationship changed between 1992 and 1993? Explain.

[c] For 1993, a disclosure that is part of the statement of cash flows indicates that cash paid for income taxes was $2,092 million. How does this relate to the information included in Note 10 presented above?

Accounting Changes and Corrections of Errors

OBJECTIVES

1. To describe the nature of accounting changes and errors.

2. To develop the theoretical and practical aspects of financial reporting for accounting changes and correction.

3. To demonstrate financial accounting and reporting practices for each type of change and correction.

4. To discuss the calculations necessary to restate financial statements, including comparative statements of income and retained earnings.

5. To illustrate the analysis and correction of common errors that are made when recording transactions and year-end adjustments.

ACCOUNTING CHANGES CAN HAVE BIG IMPACT ON COMPANY FINANCIALS!

Accounting changes can have a tremendous impact on a company's financial statements and perhaps, more important, the company's attractiveness to potential investors.

A recent issue of *Fortune* reported that an accounting change announced by Chambers Development would cut earnings in half. After this announcement, the company's stock fell 64%. Even more dramatic examples exist, however. Perhaps the most significant accounting change relates to funding employee benefits. In 1992, General Motors adopted *SFAS No. 106,* which changed the method of accounting for health care, life insurance, and other postretirement benefits. The effect was a loss of nearly $21 billion that accounted for most of the company's $24 billion net loss for that year.

As you might expect, much research has been done in the area of accounting changes. *The Accounting Review* reports, after reviewing 500 firms, that security analysts were much less accurate with their forecasts in years of accounting changes than in years without accounting changes.

As you can see, accounting changes are very important and can affect investor decisions. This chapter focuses on the different ways to account for accounting changes and to present them in the financial statements.

Will Rogers claimed that the only thing certain about the weather was that "it's bound to change." The same might be said for financial accounting and reporting. Indeed, accounting changes may occur frequently and may be caused by a variety of factors. Examples include the effects of new authoritative pronouncements, new business transactions or forms, changes in the environment, changes in estimates, and changes in the reporting entity. Occasionally mistakes are found in financial statements and correction is required.

In this chapter we discuss the nature of accounting changes, distinguish among the various types of accounting changes, and explain the appropriate accounting practices for each type of change. We also examine various types of errors and describe how corrections to financial statements that have already been issued are made. Previous chapters occasionally mention accounting for certain types of changes and errors; for example, Chapter 12, in dealing with depreciation of plant assets, discusses changes in the useful life of a plant asset. Each of these previous illustrations was introduced in accordance with practices that are covered in greater depth in this chapter.

ACCOUNTING CHANGES AND CORRECTIONS OF ERRORS: A CONCEPTUAL ANALYSIS

In *Opinion No. 20,* the Accounting Principles Board (APB) classified the effects of all accounting-related changes in three categories:[1]

1. Changes in accounting principle.
2. Changes in accounting estimate.
3. Changes in the reporting entity.

A similar type of event requiring accounting recognition is the correction of an error. Although not considered an accounting change, the correction of an error requires analysis and accounting similar to accounting changes. We must carefully classify all accounting changes by type and carefully distinguish accounting changes from corrections of errors because different accounting and reporting practices are required for each.

CHANGES IN ACCOUNTING PRINCIPLE

A **change in accounting principle** occurs when a company selects a different generally accepted accounting principle (GAAP) from the one used in prior reporting periods. Examples include a change from the specific identification method to the first-in, first-out method of inventory pricing or a change from the sum-of-the-years'-digits to the straight-line method of depreciating plant assets. The term **accounting principle** as used here is broad and includes not only specific practices and procedures but also methods of applying them. For example, a company may continue to base its inventory valuation on the lower of cost or market value but change the *application* of the method from the inventory as a whole to individual inventory items. Although the lower of cost or market principle is still used, the method of applying the principle has changed. Such changes are considered to be changes in accounting principle.

Materiality

If we initially adopt an accounting principle for items that were previously immaterial or because of new transactions or events, a change in accounting principle does not occur. Furthermore, some changes in accounting methods that are *initially planned* as part of an overall accounting policy do not represent changes in accounting principle. For example, a change from an accelerated depreciation method to the straight-line method at some specific point in an asset's life may be planned at the time the asset is acquired. Consistent application of this policy does not represent a change in accounting principle when the straight-line method is applied.

Consistency

CHANGES IN ACCOUNTING ESTIMATE

Changes in accounting estimate arise because the preparation of financial statements requires accountants to estimate the outcome of many future events. Those estimates may require accounting adjustments as new information is gained or as different conditions arise. For example, estimates of the useful lives and salvage values of plant assets, collectibility of receivables, and the outcome of current or pending litigation represent situations in which

---

[1]*APB Opinion No. 20,* "Accounting Changes," 1971, par. 6.

management and accountants must forecast the outcome of future events to prepare financial statements at a point in time. If differences arise between estimates and the subsequent outcome of the events being estimated, we must recognize the effects of those differences in the accounting records.[3]

Although estimates of future events require substantial judgment, most estimates are quite accurate. As the accountant acquires experience and as new information becomes available, however, revisions of some estimates may be necessary.

Occasionally, the effects of a change in estimate are commingled with a change in accounting principle. For example, a company may decide to begin expensing certain costs associated with self-constructed assets when they are incurred rather than capitalizing and depreciating the costs. Such a change may be made partially to recognize more doubtful future benefits (change in estimate) of the asset being constructed and partially as a result of a different philosophy about the measurement of periodic earnings and related cost of the asset (change in principle). Accountants consider the effects of such mixed-type changes to be changes in estimate rather than changes in accounting principle.[2] They are usually caused by the acquisition of new information or changing circumstances and are closely associated with the continuing evolution of existing practices.

CHANGES IN THE REPORTING ENTITY

A **change in the reporting entity** occurs when the current year financial statements are those of a new, or at least substantially different, operating enterprise from the one reporting in previous years. Changes of this type arise if the individual companies included in consolidated or combined financial statements are changed or if consolidated statements are presented for a group of companies that previously reported individually. Our coverage of changes in entity is brief because we leave extensive treatment of this subject to advanced accounting courses.[3]

CORRECTIONS OF ERRORS

Errors in financial statements result from mistakes or omissions in the financial accounting process. Examples of errors include "mathematical mistakes, mistakes in the application of accounting principles, or oversight or misuse of facts" existing at the time the financial statements were prepared.[4] A change from an accounting principle that is *unacceptable* to a generally *acceptable* accounting principle is also considered to be the correction of an error. A *misuse* of available facts results in an **error,** whereas *newly available* information or the acquisition of *new* facts results in a **change of estimate.** This distinction is important because different accounting practices are required for changes in estimates and corrections of errors.

Three fundamental approaches are available to account for the effects of accounting changes and corrections of errors: the restatement method, the cumulative effect method, and the current and prospective method. In current practice, however, only one of the alternatives is acceptable for each type of change or correction. In this section, we discuss the three methods in terms of their general description and their strengths and weaknesses, and we identify those types of changes or corrections associated with each alternative. Later in the chapter, we illustrate the specific accounting application of each alternative.

REPORTING ALTERNATIVES FOR CHANGES AND CORRECTIONS

---

[2]*APB Opinion No. 20,* par. 11.

[3]The subject of business combinations and changes in the reporting entity are considered extensively in advanced accounting courses. For an excellent discussion of the theoretical issues, concepts, and financial accounting and reporting standards in this area, see Arnold J. Pahler and Joseph E. Mori, *Advanced Accounting: Concepts and Practice,* 5th ed. (Ft. Worth, TX: Dryden, 1994).

[4]*APB Opinion No. 20,* par. 13.

Users of financial statements are able to gain better insights and make more informed decisions if comparative statements for several accounting periods are presented. Comparative statements may reveal trends and relationships that would not be detected from single-year statements. Although generally accepted accounting principles do not specifically require comparative financial statements, *Accounting Research Bulletin No. 43* strongly recommends such comparisons:

> *The presentation of comparative financial statements in annual and other reports enhances the usefulness of such reports and brings out more clearly the nature and trends (of events affecting the enterprise). . . . Such presentation emphasizes the fact that statements for a series of periods are far more significant than those for a single period and that the accounts for one period are but an installment of what is essentially a continuous history.*[5]

Most annual reports of business enterprises contain comparative financial statements. Managements recognize that financial statement users need comparative information. The Securities and Exchange Commission (SEC) also requires comparative financial statements of registrants, as do most banks as a condition of loan agreements. Consequently, most companies routinely prepare annual reports containing financial statements for two or more periods. This is a particularly important point to keep in mind as we consider alternative methods of treating accounting changes and corrections of errors. An important difference in the restatement, cumulative effect, and current and prospective methods is the extent to which previously issued financial statements, which are now being presented as comparative information, are altered from the way they were initially presented.

RESTATEMENT METHOD

One way to account for the effects of changes is retroactive **restatement.** Previously issued financial statements that are being presented for comparative purposes are revised to show the figures that would have appeared in them if the change had been in effect at the time of their original issuance. For example, if a company changes its method of accounting for inventory from last-in, first-out (LIFO) to first-in, first-out (FIFO), the difference between the figures for beginning inventory as computed under each method is treated as an adjustment to prior years reported earnings. The effect of the change on past years does not alter current year income. The effect of the change at the beginning of the earliest year being presented is treated as an adjustment of the beginning balance of retained earnings for that year rather than being recorded as a component of income of the current year.

Advantages of Restatement

The restatement alternative has several advantages. For example, previously issued financial statements, when reissued after restatement, are "better" than they originally were. Because the prior financial statements are changed for events subsequent to their issuance, more complete or accurate information underlies the reissued statements, thereby resulting in an improved presentation.

Another advantage is that current year financial statements contain no impact of events not actually affecting those statements. Under the restatement approach, a "clean slate" is assumed each time an event occurs that would have altered the original statements if the information had been available when they were issued. The effects of events relating to a prior period are confined to the prior period only; therefore, the current income statement excludes any of the effects of the past event. Because the restatement method results in the retroactive revision of previously issued financial statements, those statements issued for

---

[5]*Accounting Research Bulletin No. 43,* "Restatement and Revision of Accounting Research Bulletins," 1953, Ch. 2, Sec. A, par. 1.

comparative purposes are presented in conformity with the accounting principle of consistency. In the earlier example of changing from the LIFO method to the FIFO method, if this change were made in 1996, the comparative statements for 1994 and 1995 would be restated and prepared on the FIFO basis, thereby making the three periods comparable.

Disadvantages of Restatement

A disadvantage of restatement is the possible loss of credibility in published financial statements. If an individual relies on information contained in financial statements while making decisions and then observes the restatement of that information in comparative financial statements in a later year, the reliability and validity of the financial accounting and reporting process may be questioned.

Another problem associated with restatement is that revenue and expense items affecting the enterprise may never be reported as a determinant of *any* year's net income. To illustrate, assume that a company fails to report a material liability and related expense resulting from losing a lawsuit and discovers the error only after financial statements for the year have been issued. Unless comparative financial statements are presented, the loss from the lawsuit is never reported as an expense and related reduction in the net income of any year. The restatement approach causes the loss to be reported as an adjustment of the beginning balance of retained earnings. Management might intentionally ignore unfavorable events in the year they arise and instead report their effects as adjustments to beginning retained earnings in later years. The presentation of restated individual prior years for comparative purposes back to the year of the error resolves this disadvantage of the restatement method.

CUMULATIVE EFFECT METHOD

An alternative to the restatement method involves recording the **cumulative effect** of the event as an adjustment to current year income. Under this approach, the cumulative effect of the change is determined as of the beginning of the year of change, and that amount is presented in the current year income statement in a special nonoperating category, much like an extraordinary item. The new method of accounting is applied at the beginning of that year in which the change takes place. For example, if a company changes from the straight-line depreciation method to an accelerated method, we determine what the accumulated depreciation would have been at the beginning of the year if the company had been using the accelerated method in the past. We then compare the balance in the Accumulated Depreciation account at the beginning of the year with the amount that would have been in Accumulated Depreciation if the new method had been used. The difference between the two balances, stated on a net-of-tax basis, represents the cumulative effect of the change and is reported as a separate component of current net income. Depreciation expense for the year in which the change occurs is based on the new method and reported in normal fashion.

Advantages of the Cumulative Effect Method

Advantages of the cumulative effect method include the fact that the effects of the event are completely accounted for in the year of the change. That is, the accountant prepares entries that adjust the affected accounts and brings them up to date as if the new method had been used in the past. Future reported earnings and financial position are determined as if the new (and presumably preferable) accounting method had been consistently employed. Future financial statement amounts are unaffected by changes taking place in prior periods. Advocates of the cumulative effect method contend that financial statement users are more likely to notice and comprehend the nature and significance of the change if its effects are included as a special item in the current year's income. Such a treatment spotlights the change and ensures that readers of the statements are adequately informed.

Disadvantages of the Cumulative Effect Method

A disadvantage of the cumulative effect method is that financial statements of years prior to the change are presented in their old form for comparative purposes. The old methods or assumptions on which prior financial statements were based have been discontinued or updated in the current year statements. Thus, the financial position and results of operations reported after the event are not presented on a basis consistent with the information presented for periods prior to the change because previous years are not restated as they are in the restatement method.

Consistency

CURRENT AND PROSPECTIVE METHOD

A third approach to account for the effects of accounting changes spreads the cumulative effect of the change over current and future reporting periods. For example, a company may decide that a plant asset will have a longer life than originally estimated. Using the **current and prospective approach,** the company bases depreciation for the *current* and *future* years on the remaining undepreciated cost of the asset and the revised estimate of the asset's life. No attempt is made to apply the new estimate to past statements nor to adjust the existing balances for the effect of the change.

Advantages of the Current and Prospective Method

Supporters of the current and prospective approach observe that many accounting changes are inevitable and as such should be reported in a normal fashion without focusing on the effect of the change as do the two previously discussed methods. When changes are due to new or recently available information, one can make a strong case that only the current and future periods are actually affected.

The current and prospective approach ensures that each event that normally affects net income is included in the income of *some* particular period or periods. Thus, this method also overcomes one of the objections to the restatement method.

Disadvantages of the Current and Prospective Method

Critics note that if new information indicates that previous estimates or accounting methods were deficient, that information should be used to adjust the statements completely, including any cumulative or retroactive effect. Effects of informational deficiencies on past financial statements can affect current and future financial statements if no adjustment is made to bring the statements up to date with regard to the new information. Another criticism of the current and prospective method is that the nature and effect of the event may be overlooked by financial statement users because no special financial statement category or presentation is employed. The items that are normally presented in the financial statements are simply presented in dollar amounts that are different from those that would have been shown had the change not been made.

COMPARING AND EVALUATING THE ALTERNATIVES

The accounting profession has carefully considered these three alternatives and concluded that *each is appropriate in certain circumstances.* The accounting situations to which each method is applied are identified at the bottom of Exhibit 20–1. The restatement method is used for corrections of errors, certain specified changes in accounting principle, and changes in entity. The cumulative effect method is the general rule for most changes in accounting principle. The current and prospective method is used for changes in estimates.

Before we look more carefully at the three methods of accounting for changes and corrections of errors, let's consider the significance of these events in the broader picture of financial reporting. We have discussed the principle of materiality and mentioned several

EXHIBIT 20-1

Analysis of Alternatives of Accounting for Changes and Errors

Issue	Restatement Method	Cumulative Effect Method	Current and Prospective Method
Description of method	The effect of the change is used to restate any prior period financial statements presented for comparative purposes. Any remaining effect is charged or credited to beginning Retained Earnings of the earliest period presented.	The cumulative effect of the change is reported as a component of current year income. A special category of gain or loss is used to bring the statements up to date.	The effect of the change is spread over income of current and future years. No special gain or loss is used in reporting the effect of the change, and no catch-up entry is made.
Current year nominal accounts affected	None. (Effects adjusted directly to Retained Earnings.)	Special nonoperating income statement account is charged or credited.	Normal income statement account is charged or credited.
Major advantages	Statements are ultimately presented "correctly." Items affecting prior years are associated individually with those years. All years presented for comparative purposes are consistent.	Financial statements are brought up to date, and future amounts are computed as if the new method had been used consistently. Users may easily focus on and understand the effects of the change.	Many changes are normal and recur frequently; such events do not justify catch-up entries or separate presentation. Many changes are due to new information, and only current and future periods should be adjusted.
Major disadvantages	May erode the credibility of the accounting process. Decisions are made by users of financial statements, and later changes in those statements may cause a lack of faith in financial reporting.	Current and prior financial statements lack comparability. Events affecting prior years are reflected in current income.	The effect of previous "deficiencies" are allowed to affect current and prospective financial position and income. The nature and effects of the changes are obscure because no special category or presentation of the event is required.
Applicable situations	Corrections of errors. Changes in principle (special cases). Changes in entity.	Changes in principle (general rule).	Changes in estimate.

times that strict adherence to GAAP is required only when the resulting financial statement numbers are significant. One research study used the audit reports of companies that changed accounting principles—an important reported event—to provide evidence on how auditors interpret the materiality principle. Because auditors are required to modify their audit reports for material changes in accounting principle, and because changes in accounting principle are reported in the financial statements and related notes, one may identify circumstances considered immaterial as those in which financial statement disclosure of a change in accounting principle is made but the audit report is not modified. Results of this study indicate that modified audit reports are issued for accounting changes whose income statement effects are lower than would be implied by other research in the area of materiality. Also, discretionary changes, such as LIFO adoption, resulted in a significantly higher percentage

Materiality

of modified opinions than did nondiscretionary changes. These results suggest that changes in accounting principle are considered particularly important financial reporting events.[6]

Another study investigated the impact of reported accounting changes on analysts' forecasts and found that the presence of accounting changes increased the amount of the forecast error. This study adds to the body of knowledge that suggests that earnings forecasts are more dispersed and less accurate in a year with an accounting change.[7]

THE RESTATEMENT METHOD: EXPANSION AND ILLUSTRATION

Consistency

The distinguishing characteristic of the restatement method is that when it is applied, financial statements of previous accounting periods that are presented for comparative purposes are restated. Elements of those statements that would have been different if the new accounting assumption had been made earlier are changed to reflect that new assumption. The primary advantage of the restatement method over the alternatives is *consistency* in that all financial statements presented are prepared by the same accounting assumption. Their elements are not affected by artificial differences that do not represent real economic phenomena.

The reader of the financial statements is made aware of the restatement by a special item presented in the statement of retained earnings, or in the retained earnings column of the statement of stockholders' equity, which restates the beginning Retained Earnings of each period presented for the impact of the changed assumption on all previous periods. The journal entry to record an event by the restatement method includes an adjustment to Retained Earnings. That account is credited (increased) if net incomes of earlier periods would have been higher under the new assumption; it is debited (decreased) if net incomes of earlier periods would have been lower.

The following items are accounted for by the restatement method:

1. Corrections of errors in financial statements of previous periods.
2. Selected special changes in accounting principle.
3. Changes in accounting entity.

The second item in this list refers to the fact that the authoritative accounting literature specifies a small number of changes in accounting principle whose impact is believed to be so significant that only the restatement method results in acceptable financial statement information. These include changes *away from* the LIFO method of accounting for inventory and changes in the revenue recognition methods used in accounting for long-term construction projects. (The latter subject is covered in greater depth in Chapter 21 of this textbook.) Other changes in accounting principle that require the restatement method are beyond the scope of this textbook and are not identified or covered here.

Another type of accounting event that may require the restatement method is the first-time adoption of a new FASB Statement of Financial Accounting Standards. In each new SFAS, the FASB identifies the transition method to be followed in changing from the current accounting practice to that specified in the new SFAS. Frequently this involves applying the restatement method, although in some instances the FASB requires other methods of implementation or gives a choice of transition method.

THE RESTATEMENT METHOD ILLUSTRATED

To illustrate accounting by the restatement method, we assume that Murphy Company has never accounted for uncollectible receivables by the estimation method, opting instead to

---

[6] Gene Chewning, Kurt Pany, and Stephen Wheeler, "Auditor Reporting Decisions Involving Accounting Principle Changes: Some Evidence on Materiality Thresholds," *Journal of Accounting Research* (Spring 1989), p. 94.

[7] John A. Elliott and Donna R. Philbrick, "Accounting Changes and Earnings Predictability" *Accounting Review* (January 1990), p. 173.

simply write off accounts directly as they are deemed uncollectible by management. This has not been a problem for the company in the past, because financial statements have been distributed on a very limited basis, primarily to management and to a bank that provides financial services for the company. In 1995, however, the company decides to apply for a loan that requires audited financial statements and must now fully comply with generally accepted accounting principles. Remember that one type of event that is considered a correction of an error is a change from an *unacceptable* accounting method to an *acceptable* one. Changing from the direct write-off method of accounting for uncollectibles to a method that estimates uncollectibles, matches that expense against revenue, and measures receivables at net realizable value is one example of such a change.

Matching
Asset/Liability Measurement

A study of Murphy's historical records indicates that uncollectible accounts constitute approximately 5% of sales. The following analysis compares the difference between the accrual of estimated uncollectibles and the direct write-off of uncollectible accounts for years prior to 1995, the year in which the change is being made.

Year(s)	Accrual Based on 5% Estimate	Direct Write-off	Difference
Before 1993	$50,000*	$43,750	$ 6,250
1993	7,500†	4,500	3,000
1994	8,750‡	6,000	2,750
	$66,250	$54,250	$12,000

*$1,000,000 sales $\times$ 5% = $50,000
† $150,000 sales $\times$ 5% = $ 7,500
‡ $175,000 sales $\times$ 5% = $ 8,750

This analysis reveals that an allowance for doubtful accounts of $12,000 is required to state receivables at net realizable value at the beginning of 1995. Had the estimated amount of uncollectibles been properly recognized in the past, additional expense of $6,250 would have been recognized before 1993, $3,000 in 1993, and $2,750 in 1994. We will assume that all amounts are material.

Because the change is being made in 1995, and 1993 and 1994 will be presented separately for comparative purposes, the impact of the change must be separately determined for those years. All years prior to the earliest year presented may be combined, as is done in the line identified above as before 1993.

In addition to the preceding information, we assume that the retained earnings statements presented in Exhibit 20–2 were included in the previously issued financial statements of Murphy Company for 1994.

Now we are ready to record the correction. First we shall ignore income tax effects and record the change as follows:

EXHIBIT 20–2		
Murphy Company Statement of Retained Earnings (as previously reported)		
	1994	**1993**
Retained earnings, beginning balance	$110,000	$100,000
Net income	40,000	25,000
Dividends declared	(25,000)	(15,000)
Retained earnings, ending balance	$125,000	$110,000

Retained Earnings	12,000	
Allowance for		
Doubtful Accounts		12,000

Observe in this entry that Retained Earnings is reduced with the debit entry, representing the additional expense that would have been recognized in previous years had the estimation method been used. The account, Allowance for Doubtful Accounts, is a contra account to Accounts Receivable and serves to reduce the amount at which that account is presented in the balance sheet from the face value of the receivables to their net realizable value.

Now let's add income tax considerations to this situation by assuming a 35% income tax rate. Also, we assume that a $25,000 deferred tax liability exists from other temporary differences and that the direct write off method of accounting for uncollectibles will continue to be used for income tax purposes. The entry to record the correction under these revised assumptions is as follows:

Retained Earnings	7,800	
Deferred Income Taxes	4,200	
Allowance for Doubtful Accounts		12,000

The deferred tax amount of $4,200 is computed as the $12,000 adjustment to the Allowance for Doubtful Accounts times the income tax rate: $12,000 × 35% = $4,200. The debit to Retained Earnings is the net-of-tax amount of that adjustment: $12,000 × (1 − .35) = $7,800. We stated earlier that a Deferred Income Tax balance of $25,000 existed, so the debit of $4,200 to that account reduces that balance to $20,800 ($25,000 − $4,200). This adjustment is required because restated financial income exceeds taxable income for past years by $12,000 due to the temporary difference between the estimation and direct write-off methods of accounting for uncollectible accounts.

We are now ready to prepare a revised statement of retained earnings for 1994 and 1993. The change in method of accounting for uncollectible accounts, which we have recorded as a correction of an error, results in a restatement of beginning retained earnings of *each year affected by the error at a different amount.* Also, net income for each year affected is restated to reflect the reduction that results from the additional expense recognized by the estimation method of accounting for uncollectible accounts. Amounts of net income and dividends for 1995 that are stated on the basis of the new (accepted) method have been added. The revised statement is presented in Exhibit 20–3.

Observe that for each year, the restatement for correction of error is limited to the impact of the change on income of previous years on a net-of-tax basis. For 1993, restatement is based on previous years incomes of $6,250; for 1994, restatement is based on previous years incomes of $9,250 ($6,250 + $3,000). For 1995, this amount is $12,000 ($6,250 + $3,000 + $2,750). Also, observe that the ending retained earnings of 1993 ($103,987) reconciles with the *restated* beginning Retained Earnings of 1994 rather than the beginning Retained Earnings as previously stated. The same is true for 1995 ($117,200). The net income figures of each year are also restated to reflect the additional expense, on a net-of-tax basis, that is required under the estimation method of accounting for uncollectible accounts. Net income for 1995 will be computed based on the allowance method of accounting for uncollectible accounts.

A PRACTICE EXAMPLE OF THE RESTATEMENT METHOD

Restatements of beginning retained earnings in published financial statements are relatively rare in practice. In the authors' opinion, this is because companies prefer not to restate financial statements and are particularly careful to avoid those situations that require restatement unless they are unavoidable, as when a new FASB statement requires that transition ap-

EXHIBIT 20–3			

Murphy Company
Statement of Retained Earnings
(restated)

	1995	1994	1993
Retained earnings, beginning as previously stated	$125,000	$110,000	$100,000
Restatement for correction of error*	(7,800)	(6,013)	(4,063)
Retained earnings, restated	$117,200	$103,987	$ 95,937
Net income†	50,000	38,213	23,050
Dividends	(30,000)	(25,000)	(15,000)
Retained earnings, ending	$137,200	$117,200	$103,987

*1993: $6,250 × (1 − .35) = $4,063
 1994: ($6,250 + $3,000) × (1 − .35) = $6,013
 1995: ($6,250 + $3,000 + $2,750) × (1 − .35) = $7,800
† 1993: $25,000 − [$3,000 × (1 − .35)] = $23,050
 1994: $40,000 − [$2,750 × (1 − .35)] = $38,213

proach. Also, many error corrections may be judged immaterial to the financial statements taken as a whole. **Materiality**

Exhibit 20–4 includes a restatement from the 1987 financial statements of Matrix Science Corporation, taken from the AICPA's *Accounting Trends & Techniques*. The accounting method in question involves recording sales prior to shipment and has been accounted for as a correction of an error. Notice that the last sentence in the explanation states that retained earnings has been restated to $27,326,800 and that figure appears as the June 30, 1984, balance in the Retained Earnings column of the consolidated statement of shareholders' equity.

Changes in accounting principle are the only events that are accounted for and reported in financial statements by the cumulative effect method. Except for those few special changes in principle that require the restatement method, all changes in accounting principle are accounted for as described in this section.

Recall that changes in accounting principle are *changes from one generally accepted accounting principle to another,* including methods of applying principles. Common examples are changes in methods of accounting for inventories (e.g., FIFO to LIFO) and change in methods of depreciation (e.g., straight-line to units of production). A change from LIFO to another accepted inventory method is one of the exceptions that requires the restatement method. A change from an accounting method that is not generally accepted to one that is in accordance with GAAP is considered a correction of error and requires the restatement method.

The following steps outline proper accounting for changes in accounting principle by the cumulative effect method:

THE CUMULATIVE EFFECT METHOD: EXPANSION AND ILLUSTRATION

1. The cumulative effect of the change on all previous years' income is computed. That amount, net of income taxes, if applicable, is presented in the income statement of the year of change as a special gain or loss, immediately following extraordinary items, if any. This special income statement item is computed as if the change occurred at the beginning of the year during which the decision to change was made.
2. Items in the income statement that are affected by the change (e.g., cost of goods sold for an inventory method change or depreciation expense for a depreciation method change) are computed by the new method in the year of the change.

EXHIBIT 20–4

Matrix Science Corporation
Example Correction of Error

Consolidated Statements of Shareholders' Equity

	Common Stock Number of Shares	Amount	Additional Paid-in Capital	Retained Earnings
Balance at June 30, 1984 (Note 2)...............................	3,946,010	$39,500	$5,015,400	$27,326,800
Cash dividends...	—	—	—	(394,600)
Net income...	—	—	—	7,802,100
Balance at June 30, 1985 (Note 2)...............................	3,946,010	39,500	5,015,400	34,734,300
Cash dividends...	—	—	—	(394,600)
Net income...	—	—	—	7,853,200
Balance at June 30, 1986 (Note 2)...............................	3,946,010	39,500	5,015,400	42,192,900
Cash dividends...	—	—	—	(631,400)
Shares issued under stock option plan...........................	550	—	14,400	—
Stock split, 2 for 1..	3,946,560	39,400	(39,400)	—
Net income...	—	—	—	1,883,700
Balance at June 30, 1987......................................	7,893,120	$78,900	$4,990,400	$43,445,200

Notes to Consolidated Financial Statements

2. Special Investigation and Accounting Practices

In August 1987, it became known that the Company had followed a practice of recording sales prior to the shipment of goods. In connection therewith, the Board of Directors engaged special legal counsel and the Company's auditors to conduct an investigation of the Company's accounting practices. Additionally, in September 1987, it was determined that substantial amounts of credit memorandums, primarily for customer returns, had not been processed in a timely manner.

The above practices involved certain senior officers and other employees of the Company. In October 1987, the former president, executive vice president and chief financial officer resigned their positions and entered into consulting agreements as of the date of their resignations with the Company. The consulting agreement with the former president ended on January 8, 1988, and the other two agreements are on a month-to-month basis.

The results of the investigation concluded that the sales recording and credit memo practices discussed above resulted in the incorrect recording of sales. While the Company does not believe the resulting adjustments were material to its financial statements, when taken as a whole in any prior year, the Company has determined that a restatement of prior years' financial statements is appropriate. Accordingly, the financial statements for 1982 through 1986 have been restated. A summary of the impact of restatement for fiscal 1986 and 1985 is shown below:

	1986 Reported	1986 Restated	1985 Reported	1985 Restated
Net Sales.....................	$75,094,500	$74,676,500	$67,134,200	$64,809,200
Net Income...................	8,271,100	7,853,200	8,056,200	7,802,100
Working Capital...............	45,198,500	43,319,000	37,370,100	35,908,600
Total Assets..................	59,294,100	56,918,400	52,828,000	50,732,900
Shareholders' Equity...........	49,127,300	47,247,800	41,250,800	39,789,200
Earnings per Share............	1.05	1.00	1.02	.99

At June 30, 1984, retained earnings, as previously reported, was $28,534,300. Retained earnings, as restated, is $27,326,800.

SOURCE: AICPA, *Accounting Trends & Techniques,* 1988, p. 312.

3. Comparative financial statements of previous periods are *not restated* to apply the new method retroactively, as would be done in the restatement method. This results in the income statement items affected by the change being presented by different methods in the current year statement, as compared with comparative year statements.

4. Required disclosures include the retroactive restatement of income and earnings per share for all years presented on a *pro forma basis* at the bottom of the income statement to supplement information presented in the body of that statement. Also, notes to the financial statements report the reason and justification for the change and the impact of the change on income and earnings per share for the year of the change.

Justifications for changes in accounting principle vary considerably. Some focus on the idea that the change brings the reporting entity in conformity with standard industry practices. Other justifications refer to preference for the newly adopted method on the basis that it produces better information with regard to an underlying accounting principle (e.g., matching principle). The FASB often indicates that a new pronouncement should be implemented in a manner consistent with the cumulative effect method of accounting as specified in *APB Opinion No. 20.* This requires the company to compute the amounts of the elements of the financial statements on the basis of the new accounting standard promulgated by the FASB and to incorporate those amounts into the financial statements by taking the cumulative effect on all past years through income of the year the new standard is adopted.

Matching

In Chapter 1, we discussed the GAAP hierarchy established in the auditing literature for purposes of defining the phrase "generally accepted accounting principles." Recall that the hierarchy has several levels, and accountants are required to apply, for a particular situation, the standard included in the highest level of the hierarchy. A change in accounting principle required to conform the financial statements of an enterprise to the GAAP hierarchy would also require use of the cumulative effect method.

GENERAL CHANGE IN ACCOUNTING PRINCIPLE ILLUSTRATED

To illustrate accounting for a general change in accounting principle, assume that during 1995, Northern Company elects to change from the straight-line method of computing the depreciation on an important machine to the service quantity/machine hours method. The company uses accelerated write-off for income tax purposes and will continue to do so in the future. The change is justified on the basis that the straight-line method depreciates the asset at too rapid a rate and that the service potential declines more closely in relation to the actual usage of the machine that varies significantly from year to year. The machine cost $140,000 in 1992 and has been depreciated through 1994 by the straight-line method, assuming an 8-year life with no salvage value. Management believes that the machine's total life in machine hours is 20,000, and plant records indicate that the machine was used 1,000, 2,600, and 1,300 hours in 1992, 1993, and 1994, respectively. Northern's income for 1995, before depreciation and income taxes, is $75,000. To simplify the calculations, we assume that applying a 35% income tax rate produces amounts that are consistent with current GAAP. We also assume that the percentages presented in the explanation of the tax write-off amounts in Exhibit 20-5 are appropriate in light of income tax law in effect when the asset was placed in service. The machine was used 1,600 hours in 1995.

Exhibit 20-5 includes information necessary to prepare the journal entries required to implement this change in accounting principle. The $7 per machine hour rate is determined as follows: $140,000/20,000 hours = $7 per hour.

For a moment, let's ignore income taxes and record the accounting change and the 1995 depreciation expense:

Accumulated Depreciation ($52,500 − $34,300)	18,200	
Cumulative Effect of Change in Accounting Principle		18,200
Depreciation Expense	11,200	
Accumulated Depreciation		11,200

Notice that the first entry includes the difference between the two methods *as of the beginning of the year of change,* regardless of when the change was made during that year. The $18,200 amount is the difference between Accumulated Depreciation under the straight-line

---

EXHIBIT 20–5

Accounting for a Change in Accounting Principle
(Based on Northern Company Illustration)

Year	Tax Write-off*	Straight-Line Depreciation**	Machine Hours Depreciation†
1992	$ 21,000	$17,500	$ 7,000
1993	30,800	17,500	18,200
1994	29,400	17,500	9,100
	$ 81,200	$52,500	$34,300
1995	29,400	17,500	11,200
	$110,600	$70,000	$45,500

*1992: $140,000 × 15% = $21,000   †1992: 1,000 hrs. × $7 = $ 7,000
 1993: $140,000 × 22% = 30,800   1993: 2,600 hrs. × $7 = 18,200
 1994: $140,000 × 21% = 29,400   1994: 1,300 hrs. × $7 = 9,100
 1995: $140,000 × 21% = 29,400   1995: 1,600 hrs. × $7 = 11,200
**1992–1995: $140,000/8 years = $17,500

---

and machine hours methods for 1992–1994: $52,500 − $34,300 = $18,200. The debit to Accumulated Depreciation reduces that account balance and the Cumulative Effect of Change in Accounting Principle represents a *gain* due to the reversal of past depreciation charges. The 1995 depreciation expense is recorded at $11,200 on the basis of the new depreciation method. Observe also that the Accumulated Depreciation balance is now exactly what it would have been had the company applied the machine hours method:

Depreciation recorded 1992–1994	$52,500
Adjustment for accounting change	(18,200)
Depreciation recorded 1995	11,200
Accumulated Depreciation balance, 1995	$45,500

How does the incorporation of income taxes alter this recording of the change in accounting principle? Remember that Northern Company uses accelerated write-off for income tax purposes and will continue to do so. Because temporary differences have existed between taxable income and pre-tax financial income for 1992–1994, deferred income taxes of $10,045 have already been recorded [($81,200 − $52,500) × .35 = $10,045]. Had the company been on the machine hours depreciation method since 1992, however, deferred income taxes would have been even higher because of the larger temporary differences resulting from the fact that the machine hours depreciation amounts are less than under the straight-line method. In fact, deferred income taxes through 1994 would have been $16,415, determined as follows: [($81,200 − $34,300)] × .35 = $16,415. These additional deferred income taxes must be recorded at the time the change in principle is recorded and the cumulative effect presented on a net-of-tax basis, as follows:

Accumulated Depreciation	18,200	
Deferred Income Taxes [($52,500 − $34,300) × .35]		6,370
Cumulative Effect of Change in Accounting Principle		11,830

Deferred income taxes are now $16,415, as follows:

Deferred income tax balance before change [($81,200 − $52,500) × .35]	$10,045
Adjustment recorded as part of accounting change	6,370
Deferred income tax balance after change [($81,200 − $34,300) × .35]	$16,415

EXHIBIT 20-6

Northern Company
Partial Income Statements

	1995	1994
Income before income tax and cumulative effect of change in accounting principle	$63,800*	$46,154
Income tax expense (35%)	22,330	16,154
Income before cumulative effect of change in accounting principle	41,470	30,000
Cumulative effect of change in accounting principle, net of $6,370 income tax	11,830	—
Net income	$53,300	$30,000
Earnings per share		
Income before cumulative effect of change in accounting principle	$.41	$.30
Cumulative effect of change in accounting principle	.12	—
Net income	$.53	$.30
Pro forma restatement of income and earnings per share, applying machine hour depreciation retroactively		
Net income	$41,470†	$35,460‡
Earnings per share	$.41	$.35

---

*Computed as follows:

1995 income before deducting depreciation	$75,000
Machine hour depreciation	(11,200)
	$63,800

†Same as income before cumulative effect of change in accounting principle.

‡Computed as follows:

1994 net income	$30,000
1994 difference between straight-line depreciation and machine-hour depreciation, net of 35% income tax [($17,500 − $9,100) × (1 − .35)]	5,460
	$35,460

The purpose of this adjustment to the deferred income tax account is to place the accounting records precisely where they would have been, had the newly adopted method been used from the beginning, and had such indirect effects as income taxes been included. The additional consideration of income taxes does not change the entry to record depreciation expense for 1995 as $11,200.

Exhibit 20-6 includes partial comparative income statements for Northern Company for 1994 and 1995, with the assumption that net income was properly reported in 1994 at $30,000. Income before income taxes and the cumulative effect was $46,154 [$30,000/(1 − .35)], and income tax expense was $16,154 ($46,154 × .35). These amounts include depreciation expense determined by the straight-line method. The pro forma amounts at the bottom of the statement show what net income would have been had the new (machine hours) method been used in both years. The earnings per share are based on 100,000 shares of common stock outstanding and no preferred stock.

The 1995 income before income tax and cumulative effect of change in accounting principle ($63,800) is determined by using the newly adopted machine hours method. The cumulative effect gain of $11,830 is presented on a net-of-tax basis, and income is presented before and after that item. For 1995 the pro forma restated income consists of income before the effect of the change in accounting principle. The 1994 pro forma restated income is computed by restating the 1994 income for the difference between the two depreciation methods on a net-of-tax basis. In the body of the financial statement, the inconsistency resulting from the use of straight-line depreciation in 1994 and machine hours depreciation in 1995 remains because the 1994 statement is not restated under the cumulative effect method. However, the effect of restatement is included in the pro forma figures.

In addition to this income statement presentation, a note to the financial statements will explain and justify the change and indicate the impact of the change on 1995 income. The impact of the change on 1995 income is twofold: (1) the impact on depreciation expense and the related difference this causes in income tax expense and (2) the inclusion of the cumulative effect "gain" in 1995 net income. Depreciation expense for 1995 is $11,200 rather than $17,500, causing income tax expense to be $2,205 higher [($17,500 − $11,200) × .35 = $2,205]. Netting these two causes net income to be $4,095 higher [($17,500 − $11,200) × (1 − .35) = $4,095]. Also, the cumulative effect increases net income by a net-of-tax amount of $11,830. Combining the two positive effects on 1995 net income means that the change in accounting principle raised 1995 net income by $15,925 ($4,095 + $11,830).

Cumulative Effect Not Determinable

In some circumstances, we may be unable to determine the cumulative effect of certain accounting changes. Perhaps the best example of such a circumstance involves a change *to* the LIFO method of inventory pricing. If we attempt to change from another method of inventory pricing to the LIFO method, we may find it difficult or even impossible to establish what the amount of inventory at the beginning of the year would have been if the LIFO method had previously been used. Remember that the LIFO method treats the cost of the last inventory acquired as the cost of the first items sold. The cost of the earliest items of inventory acquired are considered to remain in ending inventory. Therefore, LIFO inventory costs may include inventory cost layers that are very old. Determining the cost of exceptionally old LIFO cost layers is difficult or even impossible unless the accounting system was specifically designed to capture that information.

Disclosure

If the cumulative effect of a change in accounting principles is not determinable, we simply apply the new method to the existing account balances and report no cumulative effect of the change. For example, if we change from FIFO to LIFO, the ending inventory of the previous year under the FIFO pricing method is treated as if it were the beginning inventory under the LIFO pricing method. Disclosures in the notes to the financial statements must point out that no cumulative effect or pro forma amounts can be determined.

A PRACTICE EXAMPLE OF A GENERAL CHANGE IN ACCOUNTING PRINCIPLE

An example of the reporting of a change in accounting principle from the 1990 annual report of The Sun Company is presented in Exhibit 20–7. Sun Company explores for, develops, produces, and markets crude oil and natural gas outside the United States, primarily in Canada and the North Sea. Sun also mines coal in the United States, refines crude oil, and markets a full range of petroleum products; the company is also involved in real estate development. The change in accounting principle involves the method of accounting for the cost of mainte-

EXHIBIT 20–7

The Sun Company
Example Change in Accounting Principle

Partial Income Statement and Note

Consolidated Statements of Income
Sun Company, Inc., and Subsidiaries

For the Years Ended December 31 (millions of dollars except per share amounts)	**1990**	**1989**	**1998**
Income (loss) before provision (credit) for income taxes and cumulative effect of change in accounting principle	**390**	211	(43)
Provision (credit) for income taxes (Note 5)	**191**	113	(50)
Income before cumulative effect of change in accounting principle	**199**	98	7
Cumulative effect of change in accounting principle (Note 6)	**30**	—	—
Net Income	**$229**	**$ 98**	**$ 7**
Earnings per share of common stock:*			
Income before cumulative effect of change in accounting principle	**$1.86**	$.92	$.06
Cumulative effect of change in accounting principle	**.28**	—	—
Net Income	**$2.14**	$.92	$.06
Pro forma amounts assuming the accounting change had been retroactively applied (Note 6):			
Net income	**$199**	$113	$13
Net income per share of common stock*	**$1.86**	$1.06	$.12
Cash dividends paid on common stock	**$192**	$192	$286
Cash dividends per share of common stock	**$1.80**	$1.80	$2.70

*Based on the weighted average number of shares outstanding (in thousands) of 106,848 in 1990, 106,870 in 1989, and 106,139 in 1988.

6. Change in Accounting Principle

Effective January 1, 1990, Sun changed its method of accounting for the cost of maintenance and repairs incurred in connection with major maintenance shutdowns at its refineries (turnaround costs). Turnaround costs are comprised principally of amounts paid to third parties for materials, contract services and other related items. Under the new method, turnaround costs on projects exceeding $500 thousand are capitalized when incurred and then charged against income over the period benefited by the major maintenance shutdown (usually 3 to 4 years). Prior to this change in accounting, turnaround costs were charged against income as incurred. Sun believes that the new method of accounting is preferable in that it provides for a better matching of turnaround costs with future refined product revenues. Decisions regarding major maintenance shutdowns are generally based on engineering studies and economic analyses (such as discounted cash flow techniques) performed in connection with the capital budgeting process. As a result, management of Sun believes that the investment in turnaround costs enhances the reliability and performance of the refinery unit and therefore economically benefits future periods.

    The cumulative effect of this accounting change for years prior to 1990, which is shown separately in the consolidated statement of income for 1990, resulted in a benefit of $30 million (after related income taxes of $15 million), or $.28 per share of common stock. Excluding the cumulative effect, this change increased net income for 1990 by $16 million or $.15 per share of common stock. The pro forma amounts shown on the consolidated statements of income reflect net income and net income per share of common stock as if the accounting change had been retroactively applied.

SOURCE: The Sun Company, 1990 Annual Report.

nance and repairs incurred in connection with major maintenance shutdowns at its refineries. The cumulative effect gain is included in the 1990 income statement at $30 million, which is $.28 per share. The note disclosure and the pro forma disclosures that are included in the income statement clearly explain the impact of the change on net income.

EXHIBIT 20–8
The Sun Company Example Change in Accounting Principle with No Cumulative Effect

Partial Financial Statement Note

Effective January 1, 1991, Sun changed its method of accounting for the cost of crude oil and refined product inventories at Suncor from the FIFO method to the LIFO method. Sun believes that the use of the LIFO method better matches current costs with current revenues. The cumulative effect of this accounting change for years prior to 1991 is not determinable, nor are the pro forma effects of retroactive application of the LIFO method to prior years. This change decreased the 1991 net loss and net loss per share of common stock by $3 million and $.03, respectively.

SOURCE: The Sun Company, 1993 Annual Report.

In 1991 Sun Company, Inc., changed its method of accounting for the cost of crude oil and refined products inventory from the FIFO to the LIFO method. Exhibit 20–8 presents the 1993 financial statement note that explains this change. The cumulative effect of the change to LIFO on years prior to 1991 could not be determined, so no cumulative effect is included in the income statement and no pro forma earnings per share disclosures are made. The effect on 1991 income (loss) is explained in the last sentence of the disclosure.

THE CURRENT AND PROSPECTIVE METHOD: EXPANSION AND ILLUSTRATION

Changes in accounting estimate result from uncertainties in forecasting future events and their effects. Many financial statement elements require current estimates of future events. Examples include the collectibility of receivables, obsolescence of inventory, and useful lives and salvage values of plant and intangible assets. After financial statements have been issued, if new or additional evidence indicates that previous estimates should be revised, changes affecting the financial statements must be recorded. A change in accounting estimate is accounted for in the current period if the change affects only that period. If it also affects the future, it is accounted for in the period of change and applicable future periods.[8] This treatment is called the **current and prospective method.** Changes in estimate are the only accounting events that are normally accounted for by this method.

CHANGES IN ESTIMATE ILLUSTRATED

To illustrate, assume that Simmons Company has consistently estimated its bad debt expense to be 2% of credit sales. During 1995, however, the company recognizes that the estimate for the last two years has been too low and that an additional amount of $100,000 should be recognized to present the accounts receivable at their net realizable value. The entry at December 31, 1995, to record the additional provision is as follows:

Bad Debt Expense	100,000	
Allowance for Uncollectible		
Accounts		100,000

The entire amount of the changed estimate is included in income during 1995 because no future periods are affected by the change. Also, no special account is established to record the change. If the change in estimate affects future periods, however, the analysis is more complex.

Assume that Simmons Company also determines during 1995 that one of its buildings will have a longer useful life than originally expected. The building, acquired in early 1985

---

[8]*APB Opinion No. 20*, par. 31.

at a cost of $300,000, was originally estimated to have a 25-year useful life and a salvage value of $50,000. Simmons Company, which uses the straight-line depreciation method, now estimates that the building will be used for a total of 40 years and that a salvage value of $20,000 appears reasonable. The depreciation expense to be recorded in 1995 is computed as follows:

Depreciation Recognized on Building Prior to 1995

Original cost	$300,000
Less: Salvage value	50,000
Depreciable cost	250,000
÷ Original estimate of useful life in years	÷ 25
Depreciation expense per year	10,000
× Number of years depreciated (1985–1994)	× 10
Total depreciation expense through 1994	$100,000

Remaining Depreciable Cost at Beginning of 1995

Original cost	$300,000
Less: Depreciation taken 1985–1994	100,000
Remaining cost	$200,000
Less: Salvage value (revised)	20,000
Remaining depreciable cost	$180,000
÷ Number of years of useful life remaining at Jan. 1, 1995	÷ 30
Revised depreciation expense per year (1995–2024)	$ 6,000

In 1995 Simmons Company records the depreciation expense by using the revised estimated life as follows:

Depreciation Expense	6,000	
Accumulated Depreciation		6,000

Each year thereafter Simmons records depreciation in the amount and manner indicated above. Critics of the current and prospective method observe that the straight-line depreciation of a building with an original depreciable cost of $280,000 ($300,000 − $20,000) and a useful life of 40 years is $7,000 per year ($280,000 ÷ 40). This amount of depreciation expense, however, is not recognized in any of the income statements of Simmons Company. Application of generally accepted accounting principles in accounting for the effects of this change in estimate results in depreciation expense of $10,000 per year for the first 10 years and $6,000 per year for the next 30 years, a total of $280,000.

In contrast to the restatement and cumulative effect methods, no special financial statement item exists to account for the effect of a change in an accounting estimate. The accounts affected by the change, such as Bad Debt Expense and Depreciation Expense, are simply recorded at different amounts from those that would have been recorded had the change in estimate not been made.

We saw in the previous section that a change in accounting principle may result in an adjustment to deferred income tax. The same is true for changes in accounting estimates. For example, a company that uses straight-line depreciation for plant assets in its financial statements but accelerated cost recovery for income tax purposes will have temporary differences between pre-tax accounting income and taxable income in the early years of the assets' lives. These differences reverse as the asset continues to be depreciated for financial reporting purposes and after the cost has been completely written off for income tax purposes. If the company, for financial reporting purposes, extends the life of the asset from its original estimate (as illustrated in the previous example), it will probably continue to write off the asset's cost for income tax purposes in accordance with the accelerated percentages prescribed by tax law. With an extended asset life, resulting in reduced income statement depreciation charges and fixed percentages for income tax purposes, deferred income taxes will increase more rapidly than before the change in estimate was made—until the tax write-off is complete. Then deferred income taxes will decline as the asset continues to be depreciated for financial reporting purposes and after its cost has been completely written off for tax purposes.

A PRACTICE EXAMPLE OF A CHANGE IN ESTIMATE

An example of the disclosure of a change in accounting estimate is shown in Exhibit 20–9 for Delta Air Lines, Inc. Delta is a major air carrier providing scheduled air transportation for passengers, freight, and mail over a network of routes throughout the United States and abroad. The nature of the change is the lengthening of the estimated useful lives of flight equipment from 10 to 15 years. As the note indicates, the impact of the change was a $130 million decrease in depreciation expense and a $69 million increase in net income for the year ended June 30, 1987.

ERROR ANALYSIS AND CORRECTION

Materiality

Errors in financial statements include "mathematical mistakes, mistakes in the application of accounting principles, or oversight or misuse of facts that existed at the time the financial statements were prepared."[9] Changes from unacceptable accounting principles to generally accepted accounting principles are also defined as corrections of errors.

Accountants frequently discover minor errors that occur in the accounting process. If an error is immaterial and is not expected to have any impact on the decisions made by financial statement users, it does not necessarily require correction. Several small errors can, however, amount to a material misstatement of the financial statements. Accountants therefore should keep track of all the errors they detect to determine which, if any, should be corrected. Effects of errors that are individually material must be accounted for and reported. Errors in the financial statements are corrected by retroactively reporting the effect of the error as a prior period adjustment, net of any income tax effect. Thus, any previously issued financial statements that are presented with the current year statements for comparative purposes are restated to remove the effects of material errors.

Important considerations concerning the correction of errors are the **timing of the error** and the **timing of its correction.** We frequently refer in this chapter to the correction of errors **in previously issued financial statements.** Errors that are made and discovered within an accounting period can ordinarily be corrected easily by adjusting the financial statement elements affected by the errors, including revenue and expense accounts, because they have not been closed to Retained Earnings. Errors in *previously issued financial statements,* on the other hand, are generally more complex and require an adjustment to Retained Earnings, because the nominal accounts (revenues and expenses) of the period in which the error was made have been closed to Retained Earnings. Care must be taken in analyzing errors to determine the period in which the error was made so that the appropriate accounts can be properly corrected.

GENERAL TYPES OF ERRORS

Certain errors affect only one financial statement, whereas others affect two or more. Errors that affect only a single financial statement are frequently called *classification errors.* Another important distinction is whether an error is self-correcting or permanent.

Classification Errors

Classification errors may occur on any financial statement. Corrections of this type of error are usually straightforward and relatively simple. For example, a particular note payable in

---

[9]*APB Opinion No. 20,* par. 13.

EXHIBIT 20—9

Delta Air Lines, Inc.
Disclosure of Change in Accounting Estimate

Depreciation and Amortization—Prior to July 1, 1986, substantially all of the Company's flight equipment was being depreciated on a straight-line basis to residual values (10% of cost) over a 10-year period from dates placed in service. As a result of a comprehensive review of its fleet plan, effective July 1, 1986, the Company increased the estimated useful lives of substantially all of its flight equipment. Flight equipment that was not already fully depreciated is now depreciated on a straight-line basis to residual values (10% of cost) over a 15-year period from dates placed in service. The effect of this change was a $130 million decrease in depreciation expense, and a $69 million ($1.54 per share) increase in net income, for the year ended June 30, 1987. Ground property and equipment are depreciated on a straight-line basis over their estimated service lives, which range from three to 30 years.

SOURCE: Delta Air Lines, Inc., 1989 Annual Report.

---

10 years might have been classified improperly in previously issued financial statements as a current liability. To correct this error, an accountant reclassifies the note as a noncurrent liability in both the current year balance sheet and any previously issued balance sheets that are presented for comparative purposes with the current financial statements.

Because this type of error does not affect income for either the current year or prior years, no adjustments to prior years income statements or the statement of retained earnings are required.

Self-correcting Errors

The correction of certain other errors is also fairly straightforward. In fact, many errors are self-correcting over a two-year period. For example, if the ending inventory for 1995 is overstated, cost of goods sold is understated and net income is overstated for 1995. Because 1995 ending inventory becomes 1996 beginning inventory, the error affects 1996 as well. In 1996, however, the beginning inventory is overstated, causing the goods available for sale and the related cost of goods sold to be overstated. Net income for 1996 is consequently understated. The effect of this self-correcting error is to overstate net income for 1995 and understate net income for 1996 by the same amount. Even if the error is never detected, net income for 1997 and later years will be properly stated.

Most errors eventually correct themselves. Consider an extreme example: If an item of equipment acquired in 1995 is inadvertently charged to an expense account, net income for 1995 is understated. Net income in later years, however, is overstated, because no depreciation expense on the equipment is recognized. Assuming no salvage value, we find that the effect of the error made in 1995 is self-corrected over the life of the asset. Eventually the effects of the error are eliminated from the financial statements, even though the financial statements for all intervening years contain an error.

Permanent Errors

Not all errors are self-correcting. For example, if a parcel of land is acquired and inadvertently charged to expense, the effect of this error is not self-correcting. Because land is *not* a depreciable asset, the Land and Retained Earnings accounts on the balance sheet are understated indefinitely unless the error is corrected.

ANALYSIS OF SELECTED ERRORS

Many types of errors may exist in the accounting records. In this section, we discuss three common types of errors: (1) in recording deferrals and accruals, (2) in inventories, and (3) in plant assets and depreciation. Following the discussion, we illustrate the recording error corrections.

Failure to Record Deferrals and Accruals

Matching

Financial statements prepared according to GAAP apply the accrual concept as required by the matching principle. **Accrual accounting** refers to the process whereby revenues are recognized in income determination when they are earned rather than when cash is received. Likewise, expenses are recognized in the determination of income when their benefit is received, not necessarily when cash is paid out.

Four types of **deferrals** and **accruals** exist: (1) accrued revenues, (2) unearned revenues, (3) accrued expenses, and (4) prepaid expenses. The purpose of recognizing these items is to adjust the recognition of revenues and expenses from the period in which cash is received or paid to the period in which the item should be recognized in the determination of income. If the accrual or deferral is not recognized, the related revenue or expense will be recognized when the cash is received or paid but in the wrong accounting period.

The accruals (accrued revenues and accrued expenses) and deferrals (unearned revenues and prepaid expenses) are described as follows:

Accrued Revenues.   Revenues for which earning is complete but cash has not been received (e.g., interest receivable).

Unearned Revenues.   Revenues for which cash has been received but earning is incomplete (e.g., rent collected in advance).

Accrued Expenses.   Expenses for which benefit has been received but cash has not been paid (e.g., wages payable).

Prepaid Expenses.   Expenses for which cash has been paid but benefit has not been received (e.g., prepaid insurance).

Exhibit 20–10 includes a summary of the impact on the financial statements from the *failure* to recognize the four types of deferrals and accruals and of the adjustments required to correct for the omitted deferral or accrual, assuming the error is detected *before* the books for that accounting period are closed.

Inventory Errors

Inventory errors usually result from miscounting inventory, incorrectly pricing inventory, or miscalculating the dollar amount of inventory as physical amounts and dollar prices are combined to determine the total dollar amount of inventory.

Inventory errors affect *ending* inventory first and, if not corrected, *become errors in the beginning inventory of the next accounting period*. An understanding of inventory errors rests on an understanding of the process by which we determine cost of goods sold within a periodic inventory system. Recall from our earlier discussion of inventory that beginning inventory plus the net cost of purchases equals goods available for sale. At the end of the accounting period, these goods have either been sold or are still in inventory. We see these relationships in the following abbreviated calculation of gross margin, for which assumed dollar amounts are used:

Sales		$1,000
Cost of goods sold		
Beginning inventory	$ 150	
Net cost of purchases	700	
Goods available for sale	850	
Ending inventory	(320)	530
Gross margin		$ 470

EXHIBIT 20-10

Analysis of Deferrals and Accruals

Error—Failure to Record	Income Statement Errors*	Balance Sheet Errors*	Journal Entry Needed to Correct Error	
Accrued Revenue				
Example: Accrued interest receivable	− Interest Revenue − Net Income	− Interest Receivable − Retained Earnings	Interest Receivable X Interest Revenue	X
Unearned Revenue[†]				

Example: Rent received in advance	+ Rent Revenue
	+ Net Income
		− Unearned Rent Revenue
		+ Retained Earnings
			Rent Revenue X
			  Unearned Rent
			  Revenue
				X

Accrued Expenses				
Example: Accrued wages payable	− Wages Expense + Net Income	− Wages Payable + Retained Earnings	Wages Expense X Wages Payable	X
Prepaid Expenses[‡]				
Example: Prepaid insurance	+ Insurance Expense − Net Income	− Prepaid Insurance − Retained Earnings	Prepaid Insurance X Insurance Expense	X

* + = overstatement; − = understatement.

[†]This analysis assumes that the total unearned rent revenue was credited to Rent Revenue when received. Alternatively, the amount could have been credited to Unearned Rent Revenue, in which case the adjusting entry would be

Unearned Rent Revenue	X	
Rent Revenue		X

The failure to make this adjustment would cause an understatement of net income, an overstatement of Unearned Rent Revenue, and an understatement of Retained Earnings.

[†]This analysis assumes that the total expense paid was debited to Insurance Expense. Alternatively, the amount could have been debited to Prepaid Insurance, in which case the adjusting entry would be

Insurance Expense	X	
Prepaid Insurance		X

The failure to make this adjustment would cause overstatements of net income, Prepaid Insurance, and Retained Earnings.

Notice that the *ending inventory is deducted* and *beginning inventory is added* in determining cost of goods sold. Thus, an error in ending inventory has the opposite effect on cost of goods sold as the same error in beginning inventory. This example explains why an error in inventory that is not corrected will be offset in the next accounting period as the error moves from the ending inventory of the first period to the beginning inventory of the next period.

Exhibit 20-11 summarizes the impact of inventory errors, beginning with ending inventory errors and continuing to beginning inventory errors.

Errors in Recording Depreciation

Errors in recording **depreciation** are generally of three types: (1) recording it at an incorrect amount, (2) failing to record it, and (3) expensing plant assets at acquisition. We consider each of these in the following paragraphs.

Recording Depreciation at an Incorrect Amount. When depreciation is recorded at an **incorrect amount,** the financial statement elements affected are Depreciation Expense and net income

EXHIBIT 20–11

Analysis of Inventory Errors

Errors	Income Statement Errors*	Balance Sheet Errors*
Ending Inventory		
Overstatement	− Cost of Goods Sold + Net Income	+ Inventory + Retained Earnings
Understatement	+ Cost of Goods Sold − Net Income	− Inventory − Retained Earnings
Beginning Inventory		
Overstatement	+ Cost of Goods Sold − Net Income	None[†]
Understatement	− Cost of Goods Sold + Net Income	None[†]

* + = overstatement; − = understatement.
[†]This assumes that the error in beginning inventory is the reversal of an error in ending inventory of the previous period.

in the income statement and Accumulated Depreciation and Retained Earnings in the balance sheet. An understatement of Depreciation Expense results in an overstatement of net income, an understatement of Accumulated Deprecation (which causes an overstatement of the net plant asset balance), and an overstatement of Retained Earnings. An overstatement of Depreciation Expense results in an understatement of net income, an overstatement of Accumulated Depreciation (which causes an understatement of the net plant asset balance), and an understatement of Retained Earnings.

Failing to Record Depreciation. **Failure to record depreciation** has the same impact on the financial statements as an understatement of Depreciation Expense: an overstatement of net income, an understatement of Accumulated Depreciation, and an overstatement of Retained Earnings.

If depreciation is not recorded for a series of accounting periods, the effect of the errors accumulates in the balance sheet while only the amount of depreciation expense omitted each year affects the income statement. For example, if $10,000 of Depreciation Expense is ignored in 1995 and $9,000 in 1996, net income will be overstated by $10,000 and $9,000 in 1995 and 1996, respectively. The impact of the errors accumulates in the balance sheet, however, and Accumulated Depreciation will be understated and Retained Earnings will be overstated by $10,000 and $19,000 ($10,000 + $9,000) in 1995 and 1996, respectively.

Expensing Plant Assets at Acquisition. The erroneous **expensing of a plant asset at acquisition** results in an understatement of net income of that period and an offsetting overstatement of net income throughout the asset's life because Depreciation Expense is not recorded.

To illustrate, assume that a $10,000 asset with a five-year life and no salvage value was erroneously treated as an expense when it was acquired. If straight-line depreciation is appropriate and a full year's depreciation would have been taken in 1992, the year of acquisition, the impact of the series of errors on the five years is as presented in Exhibit 20–12.

RECORDING CORRECTIONS OF ERRORS

In this section, we illustrate the correction of multiple errors for Everett Company, which began operations on January 1, 1994. The company reports on a calendar-year basis. In review-

EXHIBIT 20–12					
Example Analysis of Plant-Asset Error					
	1992	1993	1994	1995	1996
Overstatement of Depreciation expense and understatement of income from original error—expensing $10,000 plant asset	$10,000	—	—	—	—
Reversal of error via understatement of Depreciation Expense ($10,000/5 years)	(2,000)	$(2,000)	$(2,000)	$(2,000)	$(2,000)
Accumulated understatement of net plant assets and Retained Earnings:					
1992	$ 8,000	8,000			
1993		$ 6,000	6,000		
1994			$ 4,000	4,000	
1995				$ 2,000	2,000
1996					–0–

ing the financial records of the company in early 1996, we discover the following errors and omissions:

1. Merchandise Inventory at December 31, 1994, was *overstated* by $10,000.
2. Merchandise Inventory at December 31, 1995, was *understated* by $8,000.
3. Wages Payable of $4,200 at December 31, 1995, were not recorded.
4. Interest Receivable of $2,750 was overlooked at December 31, 1994.
5. A machine purchased in 1994 for $45,000 was incorrectly expensed in that year rather than being capitalized and depreciated over its estimated 10-year life. Straight-line depreciation is appropriate, with a full-year's depreciation taken in the year of acquisition.

Everett Company's accountant has determined that 1994 net income was $75,000 and 1995 net income was $87,500 before correcting the errors.

First, we analyze each error to determine its impact on 1994 and 1995 net income and compute a *corrected* net income figure for each year.

	1994	1995
Net income as previously determined	$ 75,000	$87,500
1. Overstatement of 12/31/94 inventory	(10,000)	10,000
2. Understatement of 12/31/95 inventory	—	8,000
3. Wages payable at 12/31/95	—	(4,200)
4. Interest receivable at 12/31/94	2,750	(2,750)
5. Machinery errors		
Cost incorrectly expensed	45,000	—
Depreciation Expense omitted	(4,500)	(4,500)
Corrected net income	$108,250	$94,050

Notice in this analysis that the $10,000 overstatement of Merchandise Inventory in 1994 is offset by an opposite adjustment in 1995. The same is true for the 1994 interest receivable adjustment because the interest receivable that was not recorded at the end of 1994 would have been recorded as interest revenue when received in 1995.

Recording Assuming 1995 Books Are Closed

We first record these corrections, assuming that they are discovered well into 1996 and that the 1995 books are closed. We shall also ignore income tax considerations. The compound general journal entry to record the corrections follows:

Merchandise Inventory	8,000	
Machine	45,000	
Wages Payable		4,200
Accumulated Depreciation ($4,500 × 2)		9,000
Retained Earnings		39,800

The $8,000 debit to Merchandise Inventory corrects the inventory currently carried on the company's books by increasing that account by $8,000. The machine is established in the accounts with the $45,000 debit, and the Accumulated Depreciation for two years is established with the $9,000 credit. The credit to Wages Payable recognizes the liability for accrued wages. The $39,800 credit to Retained Earnings is verified as follows:

Corrected net income figures:	1994	$108,250	
	1995	94,050	$202,300
Incorrect net income figures:	1994	75,000	
	1995	87,500	(162,500)
Required Retained Earnings adjustment			$ 39,800

To incorporate income taxes into this analysis, we first assume that the previously reported net income figures ($75,000 for 1994 and $87,500 for 1995) are after-tax figures. Assuming that Everett will file amended income tax returns to correct the errors and that no temporary differences exist, corrected net income figures are as follows, applying a 30% income tax rate:

	1994	1995
Corrected net income (previous analysis)	$108,250	$94,050
Incremental income tax expense		
($108,250 − $75,000) × .30	(9,975)	
($94,050 − $87,500) × .30		(1,965)
	$ 98,275	$92,085

The compound general journal entry to record the correction of these errors, including the impact on income taxes, follows:

Merchandise Inventory	8,000	
Machine	45,000	
Wages Payable		4,200
Accumulated Depreciation		9,000
Income Taxes Payable ($9,975 + $1,965)		11,940
Retained Earnings		27,860

Again, the $27,860 credit to Retained Earnings can be verified by subtracting the incorrect net income totals of 1994 and 1995 from the revised figures [($98,275 + $92,085) − ($75,000 + $87,500) = $27,860].

Recording Assuming 1995 Books Are Open

Again, we ignore income taxes but assume that the errors are discovered early in 1996 as part of the 1995 audit and that the 1995 books are still open. Adjustments to 1995 revenue and expense accounts can be made rather than adjusting them through Retained Earnings as we did in the previous illustration. Remember, however, that revenues and expenses for 1994 have been closed and cannot be adjusted.

The compound general journal entry to record the corrections follows:

Merchandise Inventory	8,000	
Machine	45,000	
Depreciation Expense	4,500	
Wages Expense	4,200	
Interest Revenue	2,750	
Cost of Goods Sold ($10,000 + $8,000)		18,000
Accumulated Depreciation ($4,500 × 2)		9,000
Wages Payable		4,200
Retained Earnings ($108,250 − $75,000)		33,250

Notice that the adjustment to Retained Earnings is limited to the correction of income for 1994 only, $33,250.

Now let's impose income taxes on the situation; again, assuming that the income tax rate is 30%, that Everett will file amended income tax returns to correct the errors, and that no temporary differences exist. The compound general journal entry to record the corrections, including income taxes, follows:

Merchandise Inventory	8,000	
Machine	45,000	
Depreciation Expense	4,500	
Wages Expense	4,200	
Interest Revenue	2,750	
Income Tax Expense	1,965	
Cost of Goods Sold ($10,000 + $8,000)		18,000
Accumulated Depreciation		9,000
Wages Payable		4,200
Income Taxes Payable ($9,975 + $1,965)		11,940
Retained Earnings ($98,275 − $75,000)		23,275

The income tax expense recognized in 1995 is only $1,965, the adjustment related to that year. The income tax expense adjustment for 1994 is incorporated into the Retained Earnings adjustment of $23,275, which is the difference between corrected 1994 net income and the amount of income for 1994 as previously determined.

These illustrations all include adjustments to Retained Earnings to correct the errors discovered in 1996. This procedure is consistent with the discussion earlier in the chapter concerning the use of the restatement method for corrections of errors.

PROFESSIONAL JUDGMENT

As with the other subjects we have studied in *Intermediate Accounting,* identifying and properly accounting for changes and corrections of errors require significant professional judgment. The judgmental process begins when the accountant identifies those situations involving accounting changes and corrections of errors. Once identified, the accountant must analyze the change or error to properly classify the event, which also requires judgment. For example, a change in accounting estimate and the correction of an error may have similar characteristics and may require careful analysis and judgment.

Accounting estimates are an important part of the process of accounting for events and transactions that have current and future effects on the enterprise's financial statements. Ironic as it may seem, accountants must estimate future events to report historically on an enterprise's financial activities. For example, to report on the historical activities of an enterprise, the accountant must estimate the useful lives and residual values of all long-lived assets. Those estimates are inherently judgmental as are changes in them.

When a change or correction requires retroactive restatement of previous years' financial statements, the professional accountant may make judgments. Reconstructing after-the-fact the impact of applying a different accounting principle or method, for example, may be difficult if the accounting system used was not designed for that purpose. Generally, the further

EARNINGS HELPER

No one ever said accounting was an exact science. How inexact it can be has been illustrated in two recent cases: Cineplex Odeon (*Forbes*, May 29) and Blockbuster Entertainment. Both companies minimized the amortization of assets to the benefit of reported earnings.

In the case of Cineplex Odeon, the movie theater circuit amortizes its leasehold improvements—seats, carpet, equipment and the like—over an average of 27 years, despite the fact that many of these assets will almost certainly be on the scrap heap long before 27 years have elapsed.

In Blockbuster's case, the aggressive videotape rental store chain recently spread the amortization period for its tapes from a fast writeoff over 9 months to a slow one over 36 months. That bookkeeping gimmick added $3 million, or nearly 20%, to Blockbuster's reported 1988 income. Last month a Bear, Stearns report critical of Blockbuster's accounting policies sliced over $226 million off the company's market value within two days.

Questions about proper amortization and depreciation schedules even involve companies that have never been accused of dubious accounting practices, as Cineplex and Blockbuster have. Consider General Motors. Until 1987 GM wrote off tools and dies at by far the fastest rate in the car business. But in that year the company slowed amortization of its tools and dies down to a level comparable with those of Ford and Chrysler. GM was in no wise cooking the books, but the move did increase GM's reported earnings by $2.55 per share; total earnings came to $10.06 per share that year.

In 1984 IBM shifted from accelerated depreciation to the straight-line method for its rental machines, plant and other property. According to Thornton O'glove, author of the *Quality of Earnings Report*, the change increased IBM's reported earnings by $375 million, or 37 cents a share.

What's going on here? When it comes to amortization and depreciation, Generally Accepted Accounting Principles provide only the vaguest of guidelines. Management is supposed to write off assets over their estimated useful lives. But asset life expectancy is highly subjective, and is influenced by myriad factors. A state-of-the-art computer that will function mechanically for 50 years could become technologically obsolete in 5. Is its estimated useful life 5 years, 50 years or somewhere in between?

Another tough question: If something happens that will reduce (or lengthen) an asset's useful life, should management be required to change the depreciation schedule, to better reflect economic reality?

In a situation like this, where there can be honest differences of opinion, there is clearly room for the kind of abuse that prevailed in the Cineplex case. Many depreciation abuses are probably going undetected. Howard Hodges, chief accountant for the SEC's corporation finance division, cites lump sum writeoffs. "All of the restructuring charges—with big, lump sum writeoffs—are recognition that companies haven't been depreciating fast enough," says Hodges.

Why doesn't the SEC insist upon more conformity in companies' depreciation and amortization policies? Hodges replies, "We try to be observant, but when a company says it's depreciating its plant over 3 to 40 years, we don't know the intimate details. And there's no practical way we could. I'd like the accountants to take more responsibility for it."

For their part, the accountants retort that they're doing the best they can—that when reviewing depreciation, they look at engineering reports, industry practices and the company's historical use of its assets. Even so, they say, it is difficult to pass judgment on how much value can be squeezed from the assets. As Robert Fenimore, a partner at the accounting firm KPMG Peat Marwick, puts it: "You can count fixed assets and make sure they're there, but what are they worth? It's hard to say. There could be numerous studies done, all of which could give you reasonable answers with different conclusions."

As a result, the corporation's auditors will probably go along with management's judgment as long as the writeoff period doesn't diverge too much from general industry practice. Yet the permissible variations are so great as to make it difficult to compare two companies' earnings without intimate knowledge of their accounting practices.

Take the case of the airlines, which write off the same kinds of equipment over very different periods, with significant consequences for their bottom lines. Delta Air Lines depreciates its planes over 15 years and figures on a 10% residual value. Pan Am estimates a life of 25 years for the same 727s that Delta writes off in 15—and assumes a 15% residual value. Texas Air also writes off its planes over up to 25 years.

Are Pan Am and Texas Air being too aggressive? Is Delta too conservative? "There is a justification for lives well beyond 20 years, if the planes are properly maintained," says KPMG Peat Marwick's Fenimore, an airline specialist. "But in reality, it's obvious that the airlines with less financial strength are the ones with longer depreciation lives."

What can an investor do? Under Generally Accepted Accounting Principles, whenever a company stretches out the lives of its assets, management must note (but not justify) any material change in the reported earnings in the footnotes to the annual report. And an accounting shift from accelerated to straight-line depreciation must be both footnoted and justified—although the justification can be vague. When IBM changed its depreciation schedule on its rental machines five years ago, for example, it cited only "evolving changes in our operations, maintenance costs and technology."

In December 1987 the SEC asked the American Institute of Certified Public Accountants to consider having any change in the length of depreciation highlighted in the auditor's report accompanying financial statements. Presumably this would draw attention to the change and put investors on the alert.

But the accountants retort that disclosure in the footnotes is enough. Says Daniel Guy, vice president for auditing for the American Institute of Certified Public Accountants: "Footnotes are very important. Why is it necessary to highlight them? I can't imagine anyone being hoodwinked by changes in depreciation anyway." Maybe so, but some pretty smart investors were taken in by the Cineplex Odeon and Blockbuster Entertainment amortization schedules.

SOURCE: Dana Wechsler, "Earnings Helper," *Forbes* (June 12, 1989), pp. 150, 153. Reprinted by permission of *Forbes Magazine*, June 12, 1989. © Forbes Inc., 1989.

back in time the restatement is made, the more difficult the judgment that is required to apply the retroactive restatement approach for an accounting change or correction of an error.

When a change in accounting principle is made for reasons other than the requirements of a new authoritative pronouncement, judgment has been applied. Someone in a position of authority to make the decision has determined that a different accounting principle or method is preferable to one previously used. This, too, is an inherently judgmental process; such decisions are made on the basis of a careful weighing of subjective factors.

In summary, we can see that accounting for changes and errors involves applying professional judgment at several levels: properly identifying and classifying changes and errors, determining the correct amounts required to implement the change or correction in accordance with generally accepted accounting principles, and making the full disclosure required by those principles. Accounting for these events may have a significant impact on the financial position and results of operations of companies and the users of their financial statements, thereby placing a significant responsibility on accountants who prepare and audit those financial statements.

CONCLUDING REMARKS

Many new pronouncements by the FASB require the implementation of accounting changes. Most of these pronouncements also describe the manner in which such changes should be reported. The methods of transition contained in a new pronouncement may differ from the requirements of *APB Opinion No. 20*. In such circumstances, the provisions of the new pronouncement govern and should be followed. If the new pronouncement does not specify how to account for the transition to the new practices, however, the general provisions of *APB Opinion No. 20* that we have discussed in this chapter should be followed.

Financial accounting and reporting for various types of accounting changes and corrections of errors are complex. Although logic and reason underlie the standards of accounting and reporting for changes and errors, many rules must be applied to comply successfully with generally accepted accounting principles. Most knowledgeable accountants refer frequently to the technical literature for guidance when they encounter changes or errors. To help you remember and apply the standards of financial accounting and reporting in this area, Exhibit 20–13 presents a useful summary.

KEY POINTS

1. There are three types of accounting changes: (1) changes in accounting principle, (2) changes in accounting estimate, and (3) changes in the reporting entity. (Objective 1)

2. Errors result from mathematical mistakes, mistakes in the application of accounting principles, oversight or misuse of facts that existed at the time the financial statements were prepared, and using an unaccepted accounting principle. (Objective 1)

3. Three approaches are available for integrating an accounting change into the financial records: (1) the restatement method, (2) the cumulative effect method, and (3) the current and prospective method. (Objective 2)

4. The cumulative effect of *general* types of changes in accounting principle is reported in a separate special category of the income statement in the year of the change. (Objective 3)

5. The cumulative effect of *special* changes in accounting principle is retroactively reported by restating previously issued financial statements. (Objective 3)

6. The nature and justification of each change in accounting principle must be disclosed as well as the monetary effects of the change. (Objective 5)

7. Changes in accounting estimate are reported currently if only the current period is affected, or currently and prospectively if both the current and future periods are affected. (Objective 3)

8. Changes in reporting entity are reported by restating previously issued financial statements. (Objective 3)

9. The effects of errors in financial statements are reported by restating previously issued financial statements. (Objective 3)

10. The restatement method requires that previous years financial statements be restated and is appropriate for certain "special" changes in accounting principle, changes in entity, and corrections of errors. (Objective 4)

EXHIBIT 20–13

Summary of Accounting Changes and Corrections of Errors

Type	Basic Accounting Treatment	Summary Accounting and Disclosure Requirements
Changes in principle:		
General	Cumulative effect method	1. Cumulative effect in income, immediately following extraordinary items, if any. 2. Disclosure of impact on income and EPS. 3. Pro forma restatement of prior years' income and EPS.
Special*	Restatement method	1. Previous years' statements restated. 2. Disclosure of effect on income and EPS for all years presented.
Changes in estimate	Current and prospective method	1. Appropriate financial statement elements accounted for at revised amounts. 2. Disclosure of effect on income and EPS.
Changes in entity	Restatement method	1. Previous years statements restated. 2. Disclosure of effect on income and EPS for all years presented.
Corrections of errors	Restatement method	1. Previous years statements restated. 2. Disclosure of effect on income and EPS for year of error.

*The FASB has designated certain changes in accounting principle "special" changes, requiring the restatement method rather than the cumulative effect method. Examples are a change from LIFO to another inventory method and a change in the method of accounting for long-term construction contracts.

---

11. Errors must be carefully analyzed and appropriate corrections made to establish the accounts at amounts that would have existed if the errors had not been made. (Objective 5)

QUESTIONS

20–1 What is a change in accounting principle? Give one example of such a change.

20–2 What is a change in accounting estimate? Give one example of such a change.

20–3 What is a change in reporting entity? Give one example of such a change.

20–4 What are several situations that result in accounting errors?

20–5 How does the restatement method handle accounting changes and corrections?

20–6 What types of accounting events are incorporated into the financial records by the restatement method in accordance with generally accepted accounting principles?

20–7 How does the cumulative effect method handle accounting changes?

20–8 What types of accounting changes are incorporated into the financial records by the cumulative effect method?

20–9 How does the current and prospective method handle accounting changes?

20–10 What types of accounting changes are incorporated into the financial records by the current and prospective method?

20–11 Is it a correct statement that all changes of the same category (i.e., changes in principle, estimate, or entity) are implemented in the same manner?

20–12 In comparative financial statements, which of the three methods of incorporating accounting changes into the financial records is most compatible with the accounting principle of consistency? Justify your answer.

20–13 In applying the cumulative effect method of incorporating an accounting change into the accounting records, how does the accountant determine the cumulative effect and how is this item presented in the income statement?

20-14 What is the purpose of the pro forma disclosure that is presented in the cumulative effect method?

20-15 What procedure is followed when the cumulative effect of a change in accounting principle cannot be determined? What financial statement disclosure is appropriate in these circumstances?

20-16 If a company—after depreciating a plant asset for several years—determines that the asset's life should be shortened, how is depreciation expense for each year after the change determined?

20-17 What is meant by *self-correcting error?* Cite an example of a self-correcting error.

20-18 What is meant by *permanent error?* Cite an example of a permanent error.

20-19 Assume that an error in previously issued financial statements is detected in 1996, after the books have been closed for 1995. In the comparative statements for 1995 and 1996, how should this item be presented? (Assume that the error correction results in a decrease of net income in both 1995 and 1996 and in the beginning retained earnings of 1995.)

20-20 What impact does each of the following errors have on the financial statements of the period of the error?
[a] Failure to record accrued wages payable at the end of the year.
[b] Failure to adjust the Prepaid Insurance account for the portion of the prepaid insurance premiums that has expired.
[c] An overstatement of ending merchandise inventory.
[d] Failure to record depreciation expense for the year.

20-21 If a company inadvertently expensed the cost of a plant asset that should have been capitalized, what impact will this error have on the financial statements in the year of the error and the next year? (You may assume that the company's policy calls for recording a half-year depreciation in the year of acquisition.)

20-22 How does a change in accounting estimate differ from an error? How does accounting for the two differ?

20-23 A change in accounting principle is defined as a change from one generally accepted accounting principle or method to another accepted principle or method. How does a company account for a change from an accounting method or principle that is *not* accepted to one that is generally accepted? Under what circumstances might a company apply accounting principles that are not accepted?

20-24 What will the financial statement impact be if a company erroneously omits a consideration of estimated salvage value in accounting for depreciation of a machine? How should that error be corrected when it is found?

20-25 *APB Opinion 20* is an authoritative pronouncement that establishes general rules of dealing with accounting changes and corrections of errors. Many new pronouncements issued by the FASB specify new accounting principles to be applied in the future and transition rules for changing to the new principles. How should an accountant deal with a situation in which the transition rules specified in a new FASB statement seem to contradict the appropriate method of accounting in accordance with *APB Opinion 20?*

EXERCISES

20-26 Change in Depreciation Estimate Wampler Corporation purchased a machine for $300,000 on January 1, 1993. The machine had an estimated useful live of 8 years with no expected salvage value, and Wampler depreciates it by the straight-line method. As a result of experience using the machine, on January 1, 1996, management determines that the machine will have a total useful life of 10 years from the time of acquisition rather than 8 years as originally expected.

INSTRUCTIONS
Compute the amount of depreciation expense on this machine to be recognized in 1996.

20-27 Change in Depreciation Method On January 1, 1993, Reed Company purchased machinery at a cost of $175,000. The machine was depreciated by the double-declining balance method, assuming a 10-year life and no salvage value, from 1993 through 1995. During 1996, management decided to change depreciation methods to straight line.

INSTRUCTIONS
[a] Ignoring income tax considerations, compute the amount of the cumulative effect of the accounting change to be recognized during 1996.

[b] Prepare the general journal entries required to record the cumulative effect of the change and depreciation expense for 1996.

20-28 Change in Depreciation Estimate Maxy Company purchased a machine for $3,000,000 on January 1, 1993, when the machine had an estimated useful life of six years with no salvage value. The machine is being depreciated on a straight-line basis. On January 1, 1996, Maxy determined, as a result of additional information, that the machine had an estimated useful life of eight years from the date of acquisition with no salvage value. An accounting change was made in 1996 to reflect this additional information.

INSTRUCTIONS

[a] Assume that the direct effects of this change are limited to the effect on depreciation and the related income tax provision. For simplicity, we will assume that applying a 35% income tax rate produces appropriate income tax amounts under current GAAP. Show what should be reported in Maxy's income statement for the year ended December 31, 1996, as the cumulative effect on prior years of changing the estimated useful life of the machine. Explain your answer.

[b] What amount of depreciation expense on this machine should be recognized in Maxy's income statement for the year ended December 31, 1996? (AICPA adapted)

20-29 Change in Inventory Method On January 1, 1996, Belmont Company changed its inventory cost-flow method to the FIFO cost method from the LIFO cost method. Belmont can justify the change, which was made for both financial statement and income tax reporting purposes. Inventories totaled $4,000,000 on the LIFO basis at December 31, 1995. Supplementary records showed that the inventories would have totaled $4,950,000 at December 31, 1995, on the FIFO basis.

INSTRUCTIONS

[a] Ignoring income taxes, compute the 1996 adjustment for the effect of changing to FIFO.

[b] Prepare the journal entry to record this inventory change in January 1996. (AICPA adapted)

20-30 Correction of Errors Palmer Company has (incorrectly) determined its 1995 and 1996 net income to be $115,000 and $105,000, respectively. In a first-time audit of the company's financial statements, you find the following errors:

[1] Merchandise inventory was incorrectly determined as follows: $5,000 overstatement for 1995 and $15,000 overstatement for 1996.

[2] Revenue of $25,000 received in advance in 1995 was credited to a revenue account when received. Of this amount, $5,000 was earned in 1995, $12,000 was earned in 1996, and the remainder is expected to be earned in 1997.

[3] Accrued expenses of $11,500 were omitted at the end of 1996.

INSTRUCTIONS

[a] Determine the correct amount of net income for 1995 and 1996.

[b] Prepare the correcting entry in early 1997, assuming that the 1996 books have been closed.

[c] Prepare the correcting entry in early 1997, assuming that the 1996 books have not been closed.

20-31 Change in Depreciation Estimate Fowler Company acquired machinery on January 1, 1993, for $75,000. For three years the company depreciated the asset by the straight-line method over an eight-year life with a $5,000 salvage value. Then Fowler determined that the asset's useful life will be only five years rather than eight years, with no salvage value.

INSTRUCTIONS

Prepare the general journal entry to record depreciation in the fourth year of the asset's life and provide computations to support the depreciation amount.

20-32 Change in Uncollectible Estimate Hull Company estimated uncollectible accounts at 2% of credit sales for several years, including 1996—when credit sales totaled $135,000. During 1996 management decided the percentage estimate should be changed to 3%. Credit sales for 1996 totaled $195,000.

INSTRUCTIONS

[a] Hull's accountant recommends a prior period adjustment of $1,350 to apply the new 3% estimate retroactively to 1995 sales, some of which have not been collected by the end of 1996. (The $1,350 was determined by applying an additional 1% to the $135,000 credit sales for 1995.) Do you agree with the accountant's recommendation? Why?

[b] Prepare the journal entry to record uncollectible accounts for 1996.

20–33 Change in Warranty Estimate   KUB Company sells appliances with a two-year warranty. Historically, the company established a liability for product warranties of 2% of sales at the time of the sale to provide for the warranty. (This amount has been debited to an expense and credited to a liability account. Payments have been charged to the liability account.) The company's controller is concerned that 2% of sales does not provide an adequate amount for warranties because of the rapidly increasing warranty costs.

In evaluating the adequacy of this estimate, the following information has been accumulated in early 1995.

Year	Sales	Warranty Payments through Dec. 31, 1994	Revised Estimated Warranty Payments after Dec. 31, 1994
1991	$185,000	$3,800	—
1992	198,500	4,550	—
1993	251,000	5,000	$1,025
1994	262,800	3,000	3,800

INSTRUCTIONS

[a] Compute to the nearest half percentage of sales the amount of warranty expense you would provide for 1995 sales, which totaled $295,000.

[b] Prepare the journal entry to record the warranty expense and year-end liability for 1995.

[c] What adjustment, if any, would you make for years prior to 1995?

20–34 Change in Income Recognition Method   The following information represents a comparison of net income computed by the percentage-of-completion and completed contract methods for Bailey Company's long-term contracts for the years 1991–1995.

	Net Income	
	Percentage-of-Completion Method	Completed Contract Method
1991	$100,000	$ 80,000
1992	150,000	135,000
1993	195,000	206,000
1994	190,000	175,000
1995	205,000	192,000

At the end of 1995, management decided to change from the completed contract to the percentage-of-completion method on its long-term contracts because of the availability of new engineering estimates of the degree of completion.

INSTRUCTIONS

[a] Ignoring income taxes, show the retroactive adjustments that should be made to beginning retained earnings figures for 1994 and 1995.

[b] The company presented retained earnings for 1994 as follows:

Beginning balance	$400,000
Net income	175,000
	575,000
Dividends	(75,000)
Ending balance	$500,000

Assuming dividends for 1995 were $90,000, prepare comparative retained earnings statements for 1994 and 1995.

20–35 Change in Inventory Overhead Method   Mann, Inc., changed its procedure for associating manufacturing overhead with inventory items. The previous procedure for allocating overhead to inventory was based on a percentage of direct labor dollars. The company will now allocate overhead at a predetermined rate based on a fixed amount per direct labor hour.

The change is being implemented in 1996. Comparisons of amounts related to ending inventory for 1993–1996 are as follows:

	Inventory Costs Other Than Overhead	Overhead by Previous Method	Overhead by New Method
1993	$100,000	$ 50,000	$ 45,000
1994	150,000	75,000	80,000
1995	200,000	100,000	125,000
1996	250,000	125,000	132,000

INSTRUCTIONS

[a] What kind of accounting change is Mann, Inc., making?

[b] Ignoring income taxes, compute the cumulative effect of this change in 1996. Prepare the journal entry to recognize the change.

[c] What amount should be used for the ending inventory in computing the cost of goods sold for the 1996 income statement?

20–36 Correction of Error   On May 1, 1995, Iver Company prepaid an insurance policy to cover the year beginning on that date. The bookkeeper debited Insurance Expense and credited Cash for the $3,600 payment. No adjustment was made at October 31, the end of Iver's fiscal year. For the year ending October 31, the company reported net income of $17,300.

INSTRUCTIONS

Ignore income taxes.

[a] Compute the correct net income for the year ended October 31, 1995.

[b] Assuming the 1995 books have not yet been closed, prepare the entry to record the correction of the error.

[c] Assuming that the 1995 books have been closed, prepare the entry to record the correction of the error.

20–37 Correction of Error   Calvin Company included in manufactured inventory only direct materials and direct labor and treated all manufacturing overhead as an expense of the period in which it was incurred. On advice of its auditors, the company changed in 1996 to full absorption costing to conform with generally accepted accounting principles.

Beginning inventory for 1996 was $152,000, made up of $100,000 of material and $52,000 of labor. Ending inventory was $247,500, made up of $125,000 of material, $70,000 of labor, and $52,500 of overhead. Overhead applied to finished goods is 75% of the direct labor cost. The ending inventory for 1996 was properly determined, but it has not been recorded because adjusting and closing entries have not been made.

INSTRUCTIONS

[a] Ignoring income taxes, prepare the general journal entry to implement this change in accounting policy for determining the cost of manufactured inventory during 1996.

[b] Briefly explain your adjustment to the beginning inventory.

20–38 Impact of Errors   While examining the December 31, 1996, financial statements of Hickey Company, a new client, you discover the following:

[1] Inventory at January 1, 1996, was overstated by $2,000.

[2] Inventory at December 31, 1996, was understated by $5,000.

[3] A three-year insurance policy was purchased on January 2, 1995, for $1,500. The entire amount was charged as an expense in 1995.

[4] During 1996 Hickey received a $1,000 cash advance from a customer for merchandise to be manufactured and shipped during 1997. The $1,000 was credited to Sales Revenue. Hickey's gross profit on sales is 50%.

[5] Net income reported on the 1996 income statement (before reflecting any adjustments for the above items) is $34,200.

INSTRUCTIONS

Determine the proper net income for 1996 and label any adjustments to the reported net income.

(AICPA adapted)

20–39 Impact of Errors Fulton Corporation began operations on January 1, 1995. Financial statements for the years ended December 31, 1995 and 1996, contained the following errors:

	1995	**1996**
Ending inventory	$16,000 understated	$15,000 overstated
Depreciation expense	$ 6,000 understated	—
Insurance expense	$10,000 overstated	$10,000 understated
Prepaid insurance	$10,000 understated	—

In addition, on December 31, 1996, fully depreciated machinery was sold for $10,500 cash, but the sale was not recorded until 1997. There were no other errors during 1995 or 1996, and no corrections for any of the errors have been made.

INSTRUCTIONS

[a] Ignoring income taxes, determine the total effect of the errors on 1996 net income.
[b] Ignoring income taxes, determine the total effect of the errors on the amount of working capital (i.e., excess of current assets over current liabilities) at December 31, 1996.   (AICPA adapted)

20–40 Impact of Errors Sharp Company received $12,000 of inventory items on the last day of its fiscal year, May 31, 1995. The company employs a periodic inventory system.

INSTRUCTIONS

Determine the impact of the error(s) on the company's 1995 net income in each of the following independent cases:

[a] The items were included in inventory at May 31, but the purchase was not recorded until June 3.
[b] The items were excluded from the May 31 inventory, but the purchase was recorded on May 31.
[c] The items were excluded from the May 31 inventory; the purchase was not recorded until June 3.

20–41 Impact of Errors Welsley, Inc., acquired a machine in 1995 for $500,000 and erroneously charged the cost to an expense account. Correct accounting treatment would have called for the depreciation of the asset over its estimated useful life of five years with a 10% salvage value by the straight-line method. Welsley's policy is to take one-half year depreciation in the year of acquisition and one-half in the year of disposal.

INSTRUCTIONS

Ignoring income taxes, determine the impact of this error on 1995 and 1996 net income.

20–42 Correction of Errors Fallom Company's bookkeeper is not familiar with accrual accounting concepts. He determined net income for 1996 to be $124,500. In your audit of the company, you determine the following:

[1] Accrued, but unpaid, wages at the end of 1996 amounted to $4,575 and have not been recorded.
[2] Insurance premiums paid in 1996 totaled $18,000, only one-third of which relate to coverage for 1996. The other two-thirds relates to coverage in future years. (The complete amount was expensed when paid.)
[3] Accounts receivable of $50,000, which have been properly recorded, are expected to result in losses from uncollectibility of $3,000. (No specific accounts have been written off as of the end of the year.)
[4] Cash of $11,500, received in late 1996, was recorded as revenue, although the work to be performed under the related contract will take place in 1997.

INSTRUCTIONS

[a] Prepare a revised net income figure for 1996.
[b] Assuming that the 1996 books have *not* been closed, prepare separate general journal entries to correct each of the four items.
[c] How will these adjustments affect the 1996 balance sheet?

20–43 Impact of Errors The bookkeeper of Nafford Company, which has an accounting year ending December 31, made the following errors:

[1] A $1,000 collection from a customer on account was received on December 29, 1995, but not recorded until the date of its deposit in the bank, January 4, 1996.
[2] A supplier's $1,600 invoice for inventory items received in December 1995 was not recorded until January 1996. (Inventories at December 31, 1995 and 1996, were based on physical count and stated correctly.)

[3] Depreciation for 1995 was understated by $900.

[4] In September 1995, a $200 invoice for office supplies was charged to the Utilities Expense account. Office supplies are expensed as purchased.

[5] Sales on account of $3,500 for December 31, 1995, were recorded in January 1996.

INSTRUCTIONS

Determine the effect of these errors on each of the following financial statement items and provide your explanations.

[a] Net income for 1995.

[b] Working capital at December 31, 1995.

[c] Total assets at December 31, 1995.   (AICPA adapted)

20–44 Converting Cash to Accrual   Atkins Company has cash receipts and disbursement records that are summarized as follows for 1996, its first year of operations:

Cash receipts	$162,500
Cash disbursements	110,000
	$ 52,500

Management wants you to compute its income by accrual accounting principles.

You have identified the following items that may impact your computation:

[1] Depreciation of plant assets for 1996 computed by the straight-line method is $10,500.

[2] Prepaid insurance of $1,800, two-thirds of which relates to 1997, is included in the 1996 cash disbursement figure. This amount was recognized as insurance expense when it was paid.

[3] Atkins received $12,000 in advance rent for space in its building. The entire amount is included in the cash receipts figure and was recognized as rent revenue when received. However, $7,000 of it was for space that will be provided in 1997.

[4] Employees are due $2,800 at the end of 1996.

[5] Interest amounting to $3,170 from investments is receivable at the end of 1996.

[6] You estimate that your 1996 fee for accounting services that have not been billed will be $500.

INSTRUCTIONS

[a] Compute the correct income before income tax for 1996 by accrual accounting concepts.

[b] Prepare a journal entry to record the items that have not been properly recorded, assuming that the 1996 books are open.

20–45 Impact of Errors   Hoping to understand the impact of errors on the financial statement, your client has prepared a schedule with the following column headings:

Error	
1995	**1996**
Net Income	Net Income
Assets	Assets
Liabilities	Liabilities
Stockholders' Equity	Stockholders' Equity

INSTRUCTIONS

For each of the following errors, indicate whether the item at the head of each column is overstated (+), understated (−), or not affected (0) by the error:

[a] Omission of wages payable at the end of 1995.

[b] Failure to record depreciation expense for 1995.

[c] Failure to adjust insurance expense recognized in 1995 for amounts representing prepaid insurance for 1996.

[d] Overstatement of ending 1995 inventory.

[e] Understatement of ending 1996 inventory.

[f] Failure to record interest receivable at the end of 1995.

[g] Failure to adjust earned portion of amounts credited to unearned rent in 1995.

[h] Mathematical error in which $10,000 of amortization on an intangible asset was recorded at $1,000 at the end of 1995.

20–46 Change in Accounting Principle Jarvis, Inc., began operations in 1994 and used straight-line depreciation on its single piece of machinery, which cost $500,000 in early 1994. The machine was being depreciated over a 10-year period with no expected salvage value. For income tax purposes, the machinery was written off on an accelerated basis at the rates of 15%, 22%, and 21% of cost in the first three years, respectively.

Income information for 1994–1996, assuming straight-line depreciation, is as follows:

	1994	1995	1996 (preliminary)
Income before depreciation and taxes	$250,000	$365,000	$280,000
Depreciation expense—straight line	(50,000)	(50,000)	(50,000)
Income before income tax	200,000	315,000	230,000
Income tax expense at 35%	(70,000)	(110,250)	(80,500)
Net income	$130,000	$204,750	$149,500

In 1996 management decided to change to the units-of-production method, due to the high variability of use of the machine. The machine is expected to produce 500,000 units of output and have no material residual value. Units produced in 1994, 1995, and 1996 were 15,000, 65,000, and 25,000, respectively.

Because Jarvis, Inc., is a nonpublic company, no earnings per share figures are presented.

INSTRUCTIONS

[a] Prepare an analysis similar to the one in Exhibit 20–5, identifying the amount of depreciation expense under the units-of-production and straight-line methods and showing the amount of tax write-off taken in 1994–1996.

[b] Prepare the journal entries required to record the accounting change in 1996 and depreciation expense for 1996. You may assume that the 35% income tax rate produces income tax amounts that are consistent with accepted accounting standards.

[c] Prepare the income statement for 1996, with comparative year 1995, including the pro forma disclosures required by *APB Opinion No. 20*.

[d] Describe the difference in the entry in [b] to record this change if the units of production for 1994, 1995, and 1996 had been 75,000, 55,000, and 85,000, respectively.

20–47 Impact of Errors Sherrill, Inc., is a calendar-year corporation. Its financial statements for the years 1996 and 1995 contained errors as follows:

	1996	1995
Ending inventory	$1,000 understated	$4,000 overstated
Depreciation expense	$700 understated	$2,500 overstated

INSTRUCTIONS

[a] Assume that the proper correcting entries were made at December 31, 1995, for the errors affecting 1995 income. Determine the amount by which 1996 income will be overstated or understated and provide supporting computations. (Ignore income taxes.)

[b] Assume that no correcting entries were made at December 31, 1995. Ignoring income taxes, compute the amount by which Retained Earnings will be overstated or understated at December 31, 1996. (Provide supporting computations.)

[c] Assume that no correcting entries were made at December 31, 1995, nor at December 31, 1996, and that no additional errors occurred in 1997. Ignoring income taxes, compute the amount by which December 31, 1997, working capital will be overstated or understated and provide supporting computations or explanation. (*Hint:* Working capital is the excess of current assets over current liabilities.)

(AICPA adapted)

20–48 Accounting Changes and Correction of Errors This problem consists of four *independent* parts, but each company's accounting period ends on December 31. Ignore income taxes except where they are mentioned.

Part 1. At the beginning of 1993, Orange Company acquired, for $250,000, equipment that is being depreciated over an 8-year life with a salvage value of 10% of historical cost. In 1996 the decision was made to extend the useful life to 10 years with no salvage value.

INSTRUCTIONS

Prepare the journal entry, if any, to record this change and the 1996 depreciation expense.

Part 2.   Red Company has consistently expensed warranty costs as they were incurred rather than recognize them on an estimated basis in the period in which the products are sold. During 1996 management decided to change to the accrual basis in which estimates of warranty expense are made annually on the basis of sales and past warranty experience. Red Company officials estimate that the liability for warranty at the beginning of 1996 was $35,600. Warranty costs for 1996 are estimated at 2% of sales of $1,500,000. During 1996, $18,000 of warranty costs were paid, $14,500 of which relate to pre-1996 sales. Warranty Expense was debited with $18,000. The company's income tax rate has consistently been 34%, and you may assume that use of that rate produces appropriate income tax amounts. Red will continue to deduct warranty costs for income tax purposes as actual cash payments are made.

INSTRUCTIONS

Prepare the general journal entry, if any, to record this change and warranty expense for 1996.

Part 3.   Blue Company determined in 1996 that repair and maintenance expense of 1994 included the cost of a $75,000 machine that had a five-year estimated useful life with no expected salvage value. If the asset had been properly accounted for in 1994, a half-year depreciation would have been taken in that year by the straight-line method.

INSTRUCTIONS

Prepare the general journal entry, if any, to correct this oversight and to record depreciation expense in 1996.

Part 4.   White Company changed inventory methods from FIFO to LIFO in 1996. Inventory figures are as follows:

	FIFO	LIFO
Beginning 1996	$86,500	—
Ending 1996	92,800	$79,800

The beginning 1996 inventory under the LIFO method cannot be determined.

INSTRUCTIONS

Prepare the general journal entry, if any, to record the change and the 1996 ending inventory.

20–49 Change in Accounting Principle   Bill Reeves, accountant for Reynolds, Inc., has contacted you concerning a financial reporting situation in a subsidiary company. Bill describes the situation as follows:

The subsidiary company changed from the weighted average to the FIFO method during 1996. Inventory amounts under each method are as follows:

	Weighted Average	FIFO
Beginning 1996 inventory	$88,800	$82,600
Ending 1996 inventory	97,600	84,700

The subsidiary's accountant has recorded the change as follows:

Retained Earnings ($88,800 − $82,600)	6,200	
Inventory		6,200
(To restate the 1996 beginning inventory.)		

The accountant then computed the 1996 cost of goods sold as follows:

Beginning FIFO inventory	$ 82,600
Net cost of purchases	200,000
	282,600
Ending FIFO inventory	84,700
Cost of goods sold	$197,900

The subsidiary's income tax rate is 35% and you may assume that the use of that rate produces acceptable amounts. The weighted average method has been used for income tax purposes in the past, and this practice will be continued in the future.

INSTRUCTIONS

[a] Identify the type of accounting change that has taken place and briefly describe the proper accounting treatment for that change (without regard to the approach taken by the subsidiary's accountant).

[b] List the errors you can identify in the accountant's recording of the accounting change.

[c] Prepare a revised entry to record the accounting change in 1996.

[d] Has the accountant properly computed cost of goods sold? Give reasons for your answer.

[e] How should the effect of this change in inventory method be presented in the company's 1996 income statement?

20–50 Impact of Errors Warm-Glow Company manufactures kerosene heaters for home use. The company's December 31 year-end financial statements contained the following errors:

	Dec. 31, 1995	Dec. 31, 1996
Ending inventory	$2,000 understated	$1,800 overstated
Depreciation expense	$400 understated	—

An insurance premium of $1,500 was prepaid in 1995 to cover 1995, 1996, and 1997. The entire amount was charged to expense in 1995. On December 31, 1996, fully depreciated machinery was sold for $3,200 cash, but the sale was not recorded until 1997. There were no other errors during 1995 or 1996, and no corrections have been made for any of the errors. Ignore income tax considerations.

Before any of these errors were corrected, the company's 1995 and 1996 net income figures were determined to be $15,300 and $24,700, respectively.

INSTRUCTIONS

[a] Compute revised net income figures for 1995 and 1996 and label any adjustments to the previously determined figures.

[b] What is the effect of these errors on the amount of Warm-Glow's working capital at December 31, 1996? (*Working capital* is defined as the excess of current assets over current liabilities.)

[c] What is the effect of these errors on the amount of Warm-Glow's retained earnings at December 31, 1996?   (AICPA adapted)

20–51 Correction of Errors LED Corporation is negotiating a loan for expansion. Its books had never been audited and the bank requested an audit. LED then prepared the following comparative financial statements for the years ended December 31, 1996 and 1995:

LED Corporation
Balance Sheet
As of December 31

	1996	1995
Assets		
Current Assets		
Cash	$163,000	$ 82,000
Accounts receivable	392,000	296,000
Allowance for uncollectible accounts	(37,000)	(18,000)
Marketable securities, at cost	78,000	78,000
Merchandise inventory	207,000	202,000
Total current assets	803,000	640,000
Fixed Assets		
Property, plant, and equipment	167,000	169,500
Accumulated depreciation	(121,600)	(106,400)
Total fixed assets	45,400	63,100
Total assets	$848,400	$703,100

Liabilities and Stockholders' Equity	1996	1995
Liabilities		
Accounts payable	$121,400	$196,100
Stockholders' Equity		
Common stock ($10 par value; 50,000 shares authorized, 20,000 shares issued and outstanding)	260,000	260,000
Retained earnings	467,000	247,000
Total stockholders' equity	727,000	507,000
Total liabilities and stockholders' equity	$848,400	$703,100

LED Corporation
Statement of Income
For the Years Ended December 31

	1996	1995
Sales	$1,000,000	$900,000
Cost of sales	430,000	395,000
Gross profit	570,000	505,000
Operating expenses	210,000	205,000
Administrative expenses	140,000	105,000
	350,000	310,000
Net income	$ 220,000	$195,000

ADDITIONAL INFORMATION

After auditing LED's books and records, the auditor wrote the following information:

[1] An analysis of collections and losses on accounts receivable during the past two years indicates a drop in anticipated losses due to bad debts. After consultation with management, it was agreed that the loss experience rate on sales should be reduced from the recorded 2% to 1%, beginning with the year ended December 31, 1996.

[2] An analysis of marketable securities revealed that this investment portfolio consisted entirely of short-term investments in marketable equity securities that were acquired in 1995. The total market valuation for these investments as of the end of each year was as follows:

Dec. 31, 1995	$78,000
Dec. 31, 1996	$62,000

[3] The merchandise inventory at December 31, 1995, was overstated by $4,000, and the merchandise inventory at December 31, 1996, was overstated by $6,100.

[4] On January 2, 1995, equipment costing $12,000 (estimated useful life of 10 years and residual value of $1,000) was incorrectly charged to operating expenses. LED records depreciation on the straight-line method. In 1996 fully depreciated equipment (with no residual value) that originally cost $17,500 was sold as scrap for $2,500. LED credited the proceeds of $2,500 to property and equipment.

[5] An analysis of 1995 operating expenses revealed that LED charged to expense a three-year insurance premium of $2,700 on January 15, 1995.

INSTRUCTIONS

[a] Prepare the journal entries to correct the books at December 31, 1996. The books for 1996 have not been closed. (Ignore income taxes.)

[b] Assuming that any adjustments will be reported on comparative statements for the two years, prepare a schedule showing the corrected net income for the years ended December 31, 1996 and 1995. The first item on your schedule should be reported income for each year. (Ignore income taxes.)

[c] Explain the offsetting nature of the inventory errors.   (AICPA adapted)

20–52 Correction of Errors   During 1996, Harris, Inc., discovered that a plant asset acquired in 1992 had been erroneously charged to expense rather than capitalized and depreciated over its estimated useful life. The specifics of the asset are as follows:

[1] Machine cost, $75,000.

[2] Estimated residual value, $5,000.
[3] Estimated useful live, seven years.
[4] Intended method of depreciation, straight line (full year taken in year of acquisition).
Harris's retained earnings statements for 1994–1995 are summarized as follows:

	1994	1995
Retained earnings, beginning	$140,500	$165,500
Net income	40,000	38,500
	180,500	204,000
Dividends declared	(15,000)	(15,000)
Ending balance	$165,500	$189,000

INSTRUCTIONS

[a] Prepare an analysis showing the impact of this error on the retained earnings balance for each year from 1992 through 1995.
[b] Ignoring income taxes, prepare a 1996 general journal entry to correct this error.
[c] Prepare comparative retained earnings statements for 1995 and 1996. The company declared dividends of $12,000 in 1996 and has determined that its 1996 income, before correction of the error described above, is $50,000.
[d] How would you respond to [b] and [c] if Harris determined that it must file corrected income tax returns for 1992–1995 and its income tax rate was 35%? You may assume that use of that rate produces amounts consistent with GAAP.

20–53 Change in Accounting Principle   To save money and keep the nature of its plant assets from being widely known, Rolf, Inc., constructed many of its plant assets. During 1996 the company changed the way it determines the cost of these assets by including in the cost those amounts that were previously treated as expenses when incurred. Both the previous method and the newly adopted method are generally accepted. Management believes that the new method more closely approximates the company's investment in the assets and that the depreciation on the new cost method provides a superior matching of revenues and expenses. The previous method had been used since 1994, when the company began operations.
Information for 1994–1996 has been accumulated as follows:

	1996	1995	1994
Income information			
Net income (by old method)	—	$175,000	$180,000
Income before cumulative effect of accounting change (by new method)	$200,000	—	—
Depreciation expense (including depreciation on additional capitalized costs in 1993 figure)	60,000	40,000	35,000
Expenditures incorporated in accounting change			
Expensed in 1994 and 1995	—	45,000	50,000
Capitalized in 1996	40,000	—	—

The plant assets affected by the change in accounting principle are depreciated over a five-year life with no salvage value. A full year depreciation is taken in the year the assets are constructed. The impact of the change in accounting principle is limited to the capitalization of expenditures and the related impact on depreciation expense. The company had 210,000 shares of common stock outstanding throughout the 1994–1996 period.
The company's effective income tax rate for purposes of recognizing income tax expense and deferred income taxes is 35%. The previous method of determining the cost of its assets will continue to be used to determine the income tax liability.

INSTRUCTIONS

[a] Compute the cumulative effect of the change in accounting principle that should be included in 1996 net income.
[b] Prepare comparative income statements, beginning with income before the cumulative effect of the accounting change, for 1995 and 1996. Include earnings per share figures and the pro forma disclosures required by *APB Opinion No. 20*.
[c] Briefly identify the problems in comparing the information in the body of the comparative income statements. Explain how the pro forma disclosures remedy these problems.

20–54 Accounting Changes   Mentor Company decided in preparing its 1996 financial statements to make two changes from the procedures used in previous years:

Inventory—Mentor has always used the weighted average method, but management has now decided to change to the FIFO method. Comparative inventory figures for 1994, 1995, and 1996 are as follows:

	1994	1995	1996
Ending inventories			
Weighted average method	$138,000	$150,000	$180,000
FIFO method	$152,000	$162,500	$187,800

Uncollectible accounts—Mentor has recognized expense for uncollectible accounts at 2% of sales, virtually all of which are on credit. Based on past records and the anticipation of relaxed credit-granting standards, Mentor has decided that the percentage should be increased to 3%.

Mentor Company's bookkeeper was unaware of these decisions made by management and has prepared the following preliminary income statements, based on the previous methods and assumptions:

Mentor Company
Income Statements
For the Years Ended December 31, 1995 and 1996

	1996	1995
Sales	$800,000	$750,000
Cost of goods sold	(500,000)	(485,000)
Gross margin	300,000	265,000
Operating expenses	(235,000)	(212,000)
Income before income tax	65,000	53,000
Income tax expense (40%)	(26,000)	(21,200)
Net income	$ 39,000	$ 31,800
Earnings per share	$.78	$.64

The expense for uncollectible accounts is included in the operating expense figure, and earnings per share figures are based on the 50,000 shares of common stock that were outstanding throughout the two-year period. For simplicity, you may assume that the 40% income tax rate was used to determine the tax effects of the change in accounting principle, in accordance with GAAP.

Mentor plans to continue to use the weighted average method of inventory valuation for income tax purposes, as it has done in the past. The change in percentage used to estimate uncollectible receivables will be applied for both income tax and financial reporting purposes.

INSTRUCTIONS

[a] Prepare revised income statements for 1995 and 1996, incorporating the impact of the change in inventory valuation and bad debt estimation. Include the pro forma disclosures required by *APB Opinion No. 20*.

[b] Explain the difference in approach you have applied for the two types of accounting changes.

[c] Describe the lack of comparability in these statements and explain how the pro forma disclosures improve comparability.

20–55 Correction of Errors   Humble Manufacturing Company has an inexperienced bookkeeper who has maintained records on the basis of cash transactions. She recognizes expenses when cash is paid and revenues when cash is received. Operating results, recorded on this basis, are summarized for 1996 as follows:

Revenues		$88,000
Expenses		
Salaries	$18,000	
Equipment	60,000	
Insurance	15,000	93,000
Net loss		$ (5,000)

You have accumulated the following information concerning these revenue and expense items:

Revenues.　Of the $88,000 cash received in 1996, $18,500 was related to sales transactions in 1995 and $10,000 was a one-year loan from a bank on December 1, 1996. The interest rate for this loan is 15%. Additional 1996 revenues for which cash has not yet been received amount to $25,000.

Salaries.　Of the $18,000 paid in 1996, $1,850 represents salaries for the last four days of 1995. The company owes salaries of $2,200 at the end of 1996 that will be paid in early 1997.

Equipment.　The $60,000 cash paid represents the price of a new machine purchased in 1996. This machine should be depreciated over a five-year period with a full-year depreciation taken in 1996 and no salvage value. Pre-1996 acquisitions amounted to $110,000. If the appropriate depreciation policies had been followed, depreciation prior to 1996 would have been $45,000 and 1996 depreciation would have been $22,000 on pre-1996 acquisitions.

Insurance.　Of the $15,000 paid in 1996, $10,000 represents prepaid insurance for 1997. Also, $4,000 of $8,000 paid for insurance in 1995 represented prepaid insurance for 1996.

INSTRUCTIONS

[a] Compute a correct income figure for 1996, applying appropriate accrual accounting procedures and ignoring income taxes.

[b] Assuming the 1996 books are not closed, prepare the general journal entries for 1996 to correct the accounts and place them on an accrual basis.

[c] Explain how accrual accounting differs from cash accounting and why accrual accounting is an important underlying principle of financial statements.

20–56 Impact of Errors　You have been engaged to examine the financial statements of Willis Corporation for the year ended December 31, 1996. In the course of your examination, you have ascertained the following information:

[1] A check for $1,500 representing the repayment of an employee advance was received on December 29, 1996, but was not recorded until January 2, 1997.

[2] Willis uses the allowance method of accounting for uncollectible trade accounts receivable. The allowance is based on 3% of past due accounts (over 120 days) and 1% of current accounts as of the close of each month. Due to a changing economic climate, the amount of past due accounts has increased significantly, and management has decided to make a one-time adjustment to eliminate the negative allowance balance and to increase the percentage based on past due accounts to 5%. The following balances are available:

	As of Nov. 30, 1996 Dr. (Cr.)	As of Dec. 31, 1996 Dr. (Cr.)
Accounts receivable	$390,000	$430,000
Past due accounts (included in accounts receivable)	12,000	30,000
Allowance for uncollectible accounts	(28,000)	9,000

[3] The merchandise inventory on December 31, 1995, did *not* include merchandise (costing $7,000) that was stored in a public warehouse. Merchandise costing $3,000 was erroneously counted twice and included twice in the merchandise inventory on December 31, 1996. Willis uses a periodic inventory system.

[4] On January 2, 1996, a new machine was installed in the main factory. Its cost was $97,000, and it is being depreciated on the straight-line method over an estimated useful life of 10 years. When the new machine was installed, Willis paid for the following items that were not included in the cost of the machine but were charged to repairs and maintenance:

Delivery expense	$ 2,500
Installation costs	8,000
Rearrangement of related equipment	4,000
	$14,500

[5] On January 1, 1995, Willis leased a building for 10 years at a monthly rental of $12,000. On that date, Willis paid the landlord the following amounts:

Rent deposit	$ 6,000
First month's rent	12,000
Last month's rent	12,000
Installation of new walls and offices	80,000
	$110,000

The entire amount was charged to rent expense in 1995.

[6] In January 1995 Willis issued $200,000 of 8%, 10-year bonds at 97. The discount was charged to interest expense in 1995. Interest on the bonds is payable on December 31 of each year. Willis has recorded interest expense of $22,000 for 1995 and $16,000 for 1996.

[7] On May 3, 1996, Willis exchanged 500 shares of treasury stock (its $50 par value common stock) for a parcel of land to be used as a site for a new factory. The treasury stock cost $70 per share when it was acquired, and on May 3, 1996, it had a fair market value of $80 per share. Willis received $2,000 when an existing building on the land was sold for scrap. The land was capitalized at $40,000, and Willis recorded a gain of $5,000 on the sale of its treasury stock.

[8] The Advertising and Promotion account included $75,000, which represented the cost of printing sales catalogs for a special promotional campaign in January 1997.

[9] Willis was named as a defendant in a lawsuit by a former customer. Legal counsel advised management that Willis has a good defense and it does *not* anticipate that there will be any impairment of assets or that any significant liabilities will be incurred as a result of this litigation. Management, however, has conservatively established a $100,000 loss contingency.

INSTRUCTIONS

Prepare a schedule showing the effect of errors on the financial statements for 1996. The items in the schedule should be presented in the same order as the facts are given, with corresponding numbers 1 through 9. Use the following columnar headings for your schedule:

		Income Statement		Balance Sheet Dec. 31, 1996		
No.	Explanation	Dr.	(Cr.)	Dr.	(Cr.)	Account

(AICPA adapted)

CASES

20–57 Accounting Changes and Error Corrections   Walker Manufacturing is preparing its year-end financial statements. The controller is confronted with several decisions about statement presentation with regard to the following items:

[1] On making the year-end physical inventory adjustment for the current year, the prior year physical inventory sheets for an entire warehouse were discovered to have been mislaid and excluded from last year's count.

[2] The method of accounting used for financial reporting purposes for certain receivables has been approved for tax purposes during the current tax year by the Internal Revenue Service. This change for tax purposes will cause both deferred and current taxes payable to change substantially.

[3] Management has decided to switch from the FIFO inventory valuation method to the LIFO inventory valuation method for all inventories.

[4] Walker's Custom Division manufactures large-scale, custom-designed machinery on a contract basis. Management decided to switch from the completed-contract method to the percentage-of-completion method of accounting for long-term contracts.

[5] The vice president of sales has indicated that one product line has lost its customer appeal and will be phased out over the next three years. Therefore, a decision has been made to lower the estimated lives on related production equipment from the remaining five years to three years.

[6] Estimating the lives of new products in the Leisure Products Division has become very difficult due to the highly competitive conditions in this market. Therefore, the practice of deferring and amortizing preproduction costs has been abandoned in favor of expensing such costs as they are incurred.

[7] The Miller Building was converted from a sales office to offices for the Accounting Department at the beginning of this year. Therefore, the expense related to this building will now appear as an administrative expense rather than a selling expense on the current year income statement.

INSTRUCTIONS

[a] *APB Opinion No. 20,* "Accounting Changes," identifies three types of accounting changes—in accounting principle, estimates, and entity. Corrections of errors—which are not in themselves

accounting changes—make up a fourth type of event accountants may encounter. For each of these four categories

[1] Describe the change or correction.

[2] Explain the general accounting treatment required according to *APB Opinion No. 20* with respect to the current year and prior years financial statements.

[b] For each of the seven situations described for Walker Manufacturing, identify and explain whether the event is a correction of an error or the result of a change in accounting principle, in estimate, or in entity. If one of these four categories does not accurately describe the situation, explain why. (CMA adapted)

20–58 Accounting Changes   Riggs Company has made two accounting changes during 1995 that affect its 1995 income statement. These changes are described below:

Change in Life of Machinery.   During 1995 the decision was made to depreciate all machinery over a 10-year life rather than over the 8-year life used in the past for both book and income tax purposes. The company's bookkeeper determined that accumulated depreciation would have been $37,800 less under the 10-year life than under the 8-year life as of the beginning of 1995. The bookkeeper, therefore, made the following entry during 1995:

Accumulated Depreciation	37,800	
Cumulative Effect of Change in Accounting Estimate		37,800

Depreciation expense of $12,200 (assuming a 10-year life from acquisition) was recorded during 1995.

Change in Inventory Method.   During 1995 a change was made from the FIFO to the weighted average method of costing merchandise inventory. The ending 1994 inventory was $61,750 under FIFO. When management decided to change to the weighted average method in mid-1995, the beginning inventory was recalculated as $67,510, and the bookkeeper made the following entry:

Inventory ($67,510 − $61,750)	5,760	
Retained Earnings		5,760

INSTRUCTIONS

[a] What type of accounting change is the change in the life of the machinery? Do you agree with the bookkeeper's entry? Why? How would you have recorded this accounting change?

[b] What type of accounting change is the change in inventory methods? Do you agree with the bookkeeper's entry? Why? How would you have recorded this accounting change?

20–59 Accounting Changes   A change in the method of accounting may be classified as a change in accounting principle, a change in accounting estimate, or a change in reporting entity. Listed below are three *independent* situations relating to accounting changes:

Situation 1.   Shuler Company determined that the depreciable lives of its plant assets were too long to fairly match the cost of the assets with the revenue they generated. The company decided at the beginning of the current year to reduce the depreciable lives of all of its existing plant assets by five years.

Situation 2.   On December 31, 1995, Gary Company owned 70% of Allen Company. At that time, Gary used the cost method to report its investment because of political uncertainties in the country in which Allen is located. On January 2, 1996, Gary Company management was satisfied that the political uncertainties had been resolved and that the assets of the company were no longer in danger of nationalization. Accordingly, Gary plans to prepare consolidated financial statements for Gary and Allen Companies for the year ended December 31, 1996.

Situation 3.   Felker Company decides in January 1996 to adopt the straight-line method of depreciation for plant assets. The straight-line method will be used for new acquisitions as well as for previously acquired assets for which depreciation has been recorded on an accelerated basis.

INSTRUCTIONS

For each of these situations, provide the following information. Complete [a] through [d] for each situation before going to the next situation.

[a] Type of accounting change.

[b] Manner of reporting the change under current generally accepted accounting principles, including a discussion, when applicable, of how amounts are computed.

[c] Effect of the change on the statement of financial position (balance sheet) and income statement.

[d] Any necessary note disclosure.   (AICPA adapted)

20–60 Accounting Change Concepts   Connie Prince, president of Prince, Inc., contacted you recently concerning several things that occurred in her company during the current year. Specifically, the company made several accounting changes and corrected several errors that were identified during the year. Now the company is attempting to prepare its financial statements and is in need of assistance.

Connie has always prepared financial statements for her company based on procedures that she thought were appropriate. Because the statements were primarily for her own use, along with management personnel, she saw no particular reason to prepare statements in accordance with generally accepted accounting principles. To quote Connie, "I have always prepared statements in accordance with good common sense and have simply tried to handle transactions in the most logical way possible." In a recent phone conversation, Connie revealed to you that in anticipation of a bank loan, she needs to be sure that she understands certain accounting procedures and that this year's statements follow acceptable accounting procedures.

Specifically, she made the following statements to you:

[1] Changes in accounting estimates and corrections of errors are essentially the same things and, therefore, should be accounted for in the same manner.

[2] Once financial statements have been prepared and distributed outside the company, they should never be altered when they are presented in a later financial report for comparative purposes.

[3] All changes of a particular type—for example, changes in accounting principle—should be accounted for in the same way so that persons studying the financial statements will not be confused by different accounting methods for similar changes.

INSTRUCTIONS

In anticipation of your upcoming meeting with Connie Prince in which you will be required to explain generally accepted accounting principles for several accounting changes and corrections that the company has made during the year, write a brief paragraph in reaction to each of Connie's statements.

JUDGMENT CASES

20–61 Inventory Accounting and Revenue Recognition   You have just been appointed the new controller for Just-Rite Machine, Inc. Your predecessor worked for the company for only two months before being discharged; however, he had replaced another individual who had retired after serving as the company's chief financial officer for 20 years. During the two months that your predecessor served as controller, the company issued year-end financial statements that were distributed to its primary lender, The Last National Bank. To familiarize yourself with the company, you decided to carefully review the just issued financial statements prepared by the previous controller. Now, you are beginning to wish that you had not done so. You have found a number of deficiencies and changes from accounting principles that the company had previously used.

Specifically, Just-Rite changed the method used to value ending inventory. It had used FIFO for the last 10 years, but the new controller prepared the financial statements on a weighted average basis applied to purchases during the year and the beginning inventory. He left a memo stating that change was made to increase reported earnings for the year. Worse, the previous controller recognized revenue on a special order of machine parts that had not yet been produced by year-end. You have found his memo that explained:

> The manufacture of the machine is routine, and management has tried to get this order for
> a number of months. Therefore, obtaining the order represents the critical event in earning
> this revenue, and I consider it appropriate to record the revenue immediately. Of course, the
> estimated cost of goods sold will also be recorded to achieve a proper matching.

Neither of these matters is disclosed in the financial statements beyond the summary of significant policies that indicates that the company uses the average cost method of determining ending inventory.

You note that the effect of each of these two items is to increase income by a material amount for the year just ended. You are also aware that Just-Rite greatly values its relationship with the bank and doesn't wish to do anything that could cause the bank to question its operations or financial statements.

INSTRUCTIONS

[a] Without regard to part [b], describe how the matters mentioned above should be resolved. Be specific in your response. If, for example, you believe that the bank should be notified about either of these matters, prepare the necessary communication. Be sure to address all relevant accounting considerations.

[b] Now assume that you have brought the matter to the attention of the president of Just-Rite along with your suggested solution to the problems. With regard to your answer to part [a], assume that you believe that the bank should be informed of the two matters. The president of the company, however, states:

> *Your concern about these matters shows me that you are a very thorough person, and I like that in a controller. In fact, that's why the last guy is no longer here. I just had a bad feeling about him from the start. However, there is no way that we are now going to tell the bank that the financial statements it just received are wrong. I can't imagine a worse course of action. To do so would destroy the credibility of this company. The bank would never be able to accept information from us without questioning whether it was right or wrong. No, we'll just let sleeping dogs lie on this one. You just go back to your office and worry about things that have happened since you got here.*

What do you do now?

20–62 Organization Costs At the end of the current year, the limited partnership for which you are the controller is "converted" to a corporation when the limited partners transfer their interests in the partnership for shares of stock in the corporation. In such a transaction, the corporation generally records its assets and liabilities at amounts that are the same as the amounts on the partnership's books. You have prepared the entries necessary to effect the change in the form of the business and have presented them to the president of the corporation (previously the general partner), who responds to your proposal by stating:

> *This all looks pretty good except for the organization costs that were on the books of the partnership. I don't want them carried forward on the books of the corporation because they don't have any further benefit. They probably should not have been capitalized even on the books of the partnership because they represented commissions to our salespeople for finding investors. Let's get rid of them now while we are forming a new entity and not carry forward the same mistake.*

You are aware that the last financial statements for the limited partnership have not been issued yet but are due in the near future. As they are now prepared, they will report the commissions as organization costs. You have been the controller of the partnership for only the last two years and are surprised to hear about the origin of those costs. You wonder whether the last financial statements of the partnership should continue to show the organization costs as assets given what you now know about their composition.

INSTRUCTIONS

Decide what you should do, if anything, to account for the organization costs on the final financial statements of the limited partnership. Should this information have any effect on the financial statements of the new corporation?

FINANCIAL REPORTING CASE

20–63 Financial Reporting Case   Union Pacific Corporation, a major company in the U.S. transportation industry, had the unusual situation in 1993 of reporting three changes in accounting principle in the same income statement. An excerpt from that income statement and a note to the 1993 financial statements follows.

Millions of Dollars, Except per Share Amounts	1993	1992	1991
Income before income taxes and the cumulative effect of accounting changes	**1,155**	1,101	112
Income taxes (Notes 2 and 7)	**(450)**	(373)	(48)
Income before cumulative effect of changes in accounting principles	**705**	728	64
Cumulative effect to January 1, 1993, of changes in accounting principles (Note 2)	**(175)**	—	—
Net Income	**$ 530**	$ 728	$ 64

Per Share

Income before cumulative effect of changes in accounting principles	**$ 3.43**	$ 3.57	$ 0.31
Cumulative Effect to January 1, 1993, of changes in accounting principles	**(0.85)**	—	—
Net Income	**2.58**	3.57	0.31
Dividends	**1.54**	1.42	1.305

Note 2.   Accounting Changes

The Corporation adopted the following accounting changes with a cumulative adjustment—which resulted in a $175 million or $0.85 per share after-tax charge to earnings—in January 1993:

In Millions, Except per Share Amounts	OPEB	Income Taxes	Revenue Recognition	Total
Railroad	$ (171)	$ 121	$ (22)	$ (72)
Natural resources	(44)	(15)	—	(59)
Trucking	(47)	(25)	(7)	(79)
Waste management	—	—	—	—
Corporate services and other operations	(9)	44	—	35
Consolidated	$ (271)	$ 125	$ (29)	$ (175)
Per share	$(1.32)	$0.61	$(0.14)	$(0.85)

Other Postretirement Benefits (OPEB): The Financial Accounting Standards Board (FASB) issued Statement No. 106, "Employers' Accounting for Postretirement Benefits Other Than Pensions," which requires that the cost of non-pension benefits for retirees be accrued during their period of employment. The adoption of this Statement will not affect future cash funding requirements for these benefits (see Note 10).

Income Taxes: The FASB issued Statement No. 109, "Accounting for Income Taxes," which requires the balance sheet approach of accounting for income taxes, whereby assets and liabilities are recorded at the tax rates currently enacted. The Corporation's results were not significantly affected by the adoption of this Statement; however, future results may be affected by changes in the corporate income tax rate. 1993's income tax expense (before accounting changes) rose $73 million as a result of the Omnibus Budget Reconciliation Act of 1993 (the 1993 Tax Act) (see Note 7).

Revenue Recognition: The Corporation changed its method of transportation revenue and expense recognition from accruing both revenues and expenses at the inception of service to the industry practice of allocating revenues between reporting periods based on relative transit time, while recognizing expenses as incurred. The Corporation's results were not significantly affected by this accounting change.

INSTRUCTIONS

[a] Describe the three changes that make up the $175 million cumulative effect loss recognized in 1993 income. Are these changes that the company was required to make, or were they made at the discretion of management?

[b] In your opinion, are the effects of these three changes material in the aggregate and individually in determining 1993 income? Justify your position.

[c] One of the subjects that we study later in this book is line-of-business, or segment, reporting. This refers to the disclosure of financial activities of the business along product lines or industries. Notice in Note 2 that Union Pacific identifies five segments and discloses the impact of the three changes on each segment. What can you learn from this disclosure that you would not know if only the consolidated totals were presented?

Revenue Measurement and Income Presentation

OBJECTIVES

1. To discuss the theory and concepts underlying contemporary revenue-recognition practices.
2. To apply the theory of revenue realization to several special situations, including long-term contracts, installment sales, and buyers' right of return.
3. To discuss the purposes of income presentation and to consider alternatives to the present approach to income presentation.
4. To review several dimensions of income presentation that have been covered in intermediate accounting.
5. To expand our understanding of income presentation by considering the subjects of intraperiod income tax allocation and discontinued operations.

Revenue recognition is an important determinant of net income. For example, consider companies with large long-term contracts, such as Boeing and McDonnell Douglas. These companies have flexibility in the way they report revenues from long-term contracts. A survey of 1992 financial reporting practices reported in the AICPA's *Accounting Trends & Techniques* found that 129 companies used a form of the percentage-of-completion method, which provides for revenue recognition on an estimated basis at interim points during a long-term contract. Only five companies reported using the alternative method, completed contracts, which defers the recognition of revenue until the contract is complete. This difference, which can have a very significant impact on net income, and other revenue-recognition issues such as installment sales and the right of return, are important topics covered in this chapter.

Methods of revenue recognition are important for proper reporting of net income, and generally accepted accounting principles include many requirements that deal with the form and content of the income statement. In 1992 Ford Motor Company reported a net loss of over $7.3 billion. However, $6.8 billion of that net loss came from extraordinary items, discontinued operations, and the effect of accounting changes. These items caused the net loss to be 12 times as great as the loss from normal, recurring operations. These items were reported separately, after income from continuing operations, so that readers of the income statement are better able to understand the diverse transactions that affected the company's net income. In this chapter, we look carefully at the important subject of income presentation, building on our knowledge from previous chapters and adding some new subjects not previously studied.

COMPLEXITIES IN INCOME DETERMINATION

Revenue Realization

Matching

Determining and reporting income are among the most important topics in contemporary financial reporting. The timing of the recognition of revenue and related expenses is crucial in determining net income. Applying the revenue realization principle, accountants must make many decisions about the timing and extent to which revenue is recognized. In applying the matching principle, we must also identify the expenses to be included in the determination of income. Once these issues of recognition and measurement have been resolved, we must establish the appropriate form, organization, and content of the income statement.

Practices governing the recognition of revenue can be complicated. Consider, for example, accounting and reporting problems of aerospace companies (such as Boeing, Lockheed, and McDonnell Douglas), which agree—under a variety of long-term contracts—to provide research and development services and to produce aircraft, missiles, space vehicles, and the support systems. Determining when and in what amount to recognize revenue and identifying the related expenses to be matched against the revenue in determining net income are especially difficult problems.

After accountants decide how to recognize revenue and identify expense, they must prepare income statements to reflect the earning performance of their enterprises. In earlier chapters, you learned a great deal about income presentation and how some transactions complicate the presentation of income. Accountants must often exercise seasoned judgment to choose the most appropriate format and the extent of detail in presenting income.

This chapter begins by developing concepts of accounting theory underlying the recognition of revenue and by illustrating the application of these concepts in several practical situations. Then we look more closely at theoretical questions underlying the determination and presentation of income and introduce some considerations that complicate the presentation of income, including intraperiod income tax allocation and discontinued operations. Finally, a comprehensive model income statement summarizes our knowledge of income presentation.

REVENUE RECOGNITION: A CONCEPTUAL ANALYSIS

Revenue Realization

Before beginning our discussion, you need to have a good understanding of the term **revenue.** The word is derived from the French word *revenir,* which means "to return" or "to come again." Thus, *revenue* has its roots in a return-on-investment concept; that is, the business invests resources in a particular project or endeavor in the hope of earning a return on that effort.

Many attempts have been made to define the conceptual meaning of revenue. The Financial Accounting Standards Board gives a particularly useful definition in its *Statement of Financial Accounting Concepts No. 6:* "Revenues are inflows or other enhancements of assets of an entity, or settlements of its liabilities (or a combination of both) from delivering or producing goods, rendering services, or other activities that constitute the entity's ongoing major or central operations."[1] Careful study of this definition reveals several important characteristics that an event must possess to qualify for accounting recognition as an element of revenue.

Revenue Realization

Accountants generally believe that revenue results from productive activity and therefore is earned or realized in a continuous fashion. For revenue to quality for accounting recognition, however, at least three essential criteria must be met. The revenue must be (1) earned, (2) measurable, and (3) collectible. Revenue should be recognized for accounting purposes at the earliest point at which all three of these critical tests are met. Often the earliest point is the time of sale. Thus, in many situations, the recognition of revenue at the point of sale most closely follows the principles underlying the accrual basis of accounting.

---

[1]*FASB Statement of Financial Accounting Concepts No. 6,* "Elements of Financial Statements," 1985, par. 78.

Chapter 2 states that revenue is typically recognized at the point of sale, because the sale signifies the completion of the earning process and the sale transaction establishes the amount of revenue to be recognized. Only collectibility remains in question, and most sales are not made unless collectibility is reasonably certain. At a minimum, companies can make reasonably accurate estimates of the extent to which credit sales will not be collected, and they establish credit and collection policies to minimize the collectibility problem. Thus, revenue recognition at the point of sale is an established practice that works well in most situations.

To illustrate, consider a company that manufactures and sells television sets to retail customers. From an economic perspective, the manufacturer combines raw materials and component parts with labor and overhead to construct a functioning television set, thereby enhancing value. Stated simply, the productive process creates wealth and enhances value. The end product—a functioning television set—is worth more than the sum of the value of its parts. This process alone, however, does not provide sufficient evidence of the realization **Revenue Realization** of revenue to support accounting recognition. Until an external sale takes place, there is inadequate evidence as to how much (measurable) revenue was earned in the manufacturing process and whether the enhancement in value will ever be realized (collected).

This description of revenue realization is similar to that presented in *SFAC No. 5*. Specifically, the FASB indicates that for recognition, revenue must be realized (or realizable) and earned. Revenue is realized when products, merchandise, or other assets are exchanged for cash or claims to cash; they are realizable when related assets received are readily convertible into cash or claims to cash. Revenue is earned when the entity has substantially accomplished what it must do to be entitled to the benefits represented by the revenues.[2]

Consider the evidence supporting revenue recognition provided by a sale to an external party:

1. The seller retains few or no continuing obligations (earned).
2. The relative value of the product sold is established by a market transaction between independent parties (measurability).
3. The buying party, who is deemed capable of paying the agreed-upon price, either pays or promises to pay the contract price (collectibility).

For sales situations in which all of these criteria are not met, the recognition of revenue should be deferred.

Sometimes sales are made to relatively poor credit risks with a condition that the seller may regain control of the property if the buyer defaults. Such practices are common, for example, in the real estate industry. Repossession of the property pursuant to a loan default is not difficult, because real estate cannot be transported or hidden. Thus, certain types of real estate are frequently sold to relatively poor credit risks. Such sales are similar to short-term leases in terms of their economic substance. In these cases, the real estate sale completes the **Substance over Form** earning process and provides a measure of the profit to be recognized, but the collectibility of that revenue is not deemed adequately predictable. Recognition of revenue is therefore deferred until collectibility is more assured. This is an example of the application of the general principles of revenue recognition in a specific situation.

As another example, magazine, book, and encyclopedia companies frequently sell annual or even longer-term subscriptions, collecting the full fee in advance. The amount of revenue to be recognized ultimately is both collected and measurable; however, it remains unearned until the materials have been provided to the customers. Therefore, recognition is deferred until the revenue has been earned. In this situation, the earning process follows the point of sale.

---

[2]*FASB Statement of Financial Accounting Concepts No. 5,* "Recognition and Measurement in Financial Statements of Business Enterprises," 1984, par. 83.

Accountants must carefully analyze specific transactions to avoid recognizing revenue prematurely. They should accumulate and analyze objective evidence in light of the three criteria to ensure compliance with GAAP. Many businesses conduct operations in a fashion compatible with recording revenue at the point of sale; many others require unique or unusual revenue-recognition practices such as those discussed in the following section.

SPECIAL REVENUE-RECOGNITION PROBLEMS

Industries and businesses with special revenue-recognition requirements frequently depend on complex, lengthy, or unusual earnings processes or contractual relationships between buyers and sellers. In this section, we present several circumstances in which revenue is *not* recognized at the point of sale. Specifically, we consider the revenue recognition problems inherent in long-term construction contracts, installment sales, and sales transactions involving the right of return. The appendix to this chapter discusses revenue recognition in specialized situations involving real estate sales, retail land sales, and franchises, all of which have unique complexities.

LONG-TERM CONSTRUCTION CONTRACTS

In many industries, such as shipbuilding, aircraft design and production, and building construction, an enterprise's earning activities are related to relatively few large projects extending over several accounting periods. Accounting and reporting problems of such activities relate primarily to the timing and extent of revenue to be recognized in each accounting period and the treatment of costs incurred in the productive process. Because of the variety of circumstances and contractual relationships in construction projects, alternative financial accounting methods have been developed. We now turn to those methods and the circumstances in which each is appropriate.

Accounting and Reporting Issues

The methods used to account for long-term contracting activity should not be viewed as equally acceptable in the same circumstances. Rather, each method is appropriate only when certain conditions are present.

When a large construction project is contemplated, the buyer and the builder usually prepare a contract prior to beginning the construction. When such contracts are signed, one of the criteria necessary to recognize revenue is usually met. The construction company usually does not sign the contract if it has significant doubt about the buyer's ability to pay. For example, when an airplane manufacturer signs a contract with the U.S. Department of Defense to develop and produce a new type of aircraft, the collectibility of the contract amount is virtually ensured. Although not all long-term contracts involve government buyers, construction companies usually accept only customers with an ensured ability to pay the contract amount. At that point, the earning process is not complete, however, and the amount of earnings to be ultimately realized in excess of costs incurred may still not be determinable. Therefore, the recognition of revenue must wait until both the earnings and measurability criteria are met.

Revenue Realization As previously stated, the principle that revenue is realized through the productive process is widely accepted in practice. Therefore, as development and production of the contract item proceed, revenue is said to be "earned." The final criterion of measurability, however, may still remain uncertain, and revenue should not be recognized in the accounting records until all three criteria are met.

Measuring the amount of revenue earned is particularly difficult in the area of long-term construction contracts. Even if the revenue is collectible and earned through production, the amount that has been earned and the related costs associated with the earning process may still not be determinable. The amount of revenue and expenses recognized each accounting period during the production process relate to the **degree of completion** of the project and to the remaining costs and effort to be incurred in finishing the project.

Routine projects lend themselves to reliable predications of costs and productive efforts. Other developmental projects may involve many uncertainties. Furthermore, some contracts specify how final sales prices are determined. For example, a contract may guarantee to reimburse the contractor for all costs incurred plus some amount of profit. The profit portion may be stated as a certain number of dollars, a percentage above costs incurred, or an amount based on some other variable, such as days or hours of direct labor expended on the project. On the other hand, a contract may specify a total fixed amount to be received regardless of costs incurred. All these factors are considered in determining the appropriate accounting treatment for any specific situation.

Two basic methods are used to account for long-term construction contracts: the percentage-of-completion method and the completed-contract method. The **percentage-of-completion method** provides for the recognition of profit on an estimated basis as production takes place. The **completed-contract method** defers recognition of profit until all production is complete and the customer's acceptance of the project is finalized.

Under the percentage-of-completion method, revenue and expenses are recognized to the extent that production has progressed. Therefore, estimates of costs and effort to complete the project are necessary to determine the amount of profit that should be recognized at interim points during construction. Specifically, *Accounting Research Bulletin No. 45* states:

> *When estimates of costs to complete and extent of progress toward completion of long-term contracts are reasonably dependable, the percentage-of-completion method is preferable. When lack of dependable estimates or inherent hazards cause forecasts to be doubtful, the completed-contract method is preferable. Disclosure of the method followed should be made.*[3]

Disclosure

According to this statement, the selection of the method requires analysis of the *quality* of available evidence, primarily regarding the measurability of revenue earned. When effort has been expended on a long-term construction contract, we generally agree that both the earning process and the collectibility criteria have been satisfactorily met. Therefore, the measurability of the revenue earned is the last critical prerequisite for the recognition of revenue. If the construction company can satisfactorily estimate the amount of revenue earned, it should employ the percentage-of-completion method.

A more recent pronouncement confirms this position. Specifically, *FASB Statement of Financial Accounting Standards No. 56* states, "The percentage-of-completion and completed-contract methods are not intended to be free choice alternatives for the same circumstances."[4] A Statement of Position (SOP) by the American Institute of Certified Public Accountants provides important guidance about the circumstances in which each method should be selected and the manner to apply each method. A company should use the percentage-of-completion method of accounting if estimates are reasonably dependable and three other conditions exist:[5]

1. The contract specifies the enforceable rights of each party, the amount of consideration to be exchanged, and the manner and terms of settlement.
2. The buyer can be expected to honor the obligations of the contract.
3. The contractor can be expected to perform according to the terms of the contract.

---

[3]*Accounting Research Bulletin No. 45*, "Long-Term Construction-Type Contracts," 1955, par. 15.

[4]*FASB Statement of Financial Accounting Standards No. 56*, "Designation of AICPA Guide and Statement of Position (SOP) 81–1 on Contractor Accounting and SOP 81–2 Concerning Hospital-Related Organizations as Preferable for Purposes of Applying APB Opinion No. 20," 1982, par. 6.

[5]*AICPA Statement of Position 81–1*, "Accounting for Performance of Construction-Type and Certain Production-Type Contracts," 1981, par. 23.

Contractors are usually able to make the necessary reliable estimates and consequently should report most contracting activities by the percentage-of-completion method. This presumption is based on the notion that contractors will refuse contracts if reasonable estimates are impossible. However, if the construction company cannot meet the criteria for the percentage-of-completion method, the completed-contract method is appropriate.

Percentage-of-Completion Method.   In practice, contractors use two basic methods to measure the progress of the construction:

1. **Input measures** (e.g., ratio of costs incurred to total estimated costs).
2. **Output measures** (e.g., units of delivery).

A common input measure bases the progress on the ratio of the costs *already* incurred to the total *estimated* costs. In using costs incurred as a measure of degree of completion, the accountant must be cautious, because the costs may not be spread evenly over the contract period. For example, if a disproportionate amount of the costs is required in the early part of the contract period, costs incurred may not be a suitable measure of the degree of completion.

Output measures base the progress on the results achieved. One common output measure, the units-of-delivery approach, recognizes revenue when specific, discrete components of the project are completed and accepted by the buyer. The units-of-delivery approach to applying the percentage-of-completion method is most useful in contracts that require several large, but discrete, components of production. For example, the construction of a condominium complex or a group of similar ships or aircraft may be accounted for on a units-of-delivery basis. Revenue is recognized as components of the entire project are completed and delivered to or accepted by the customer. For example, if a construction company signs a contract to provide 10 condominium units and has completed 4 of them at the end of the first year, then 40% of the total revenue provided under the contract is recognized. The treatment of costs incurred under the contract, however, is not so obvious. In many contracts, certain costs incurred relate to all the units to be constructed. In the preceding example, the contractor should prorate such costs among the 10 units rather than charge them immediately to expense. Costs of planning and design are especially significant in state-of-the-art production, such as the design and construction of defense or scientific projects that have never before been attempted. In the early stages, such projects frequently incur many **learning curve costs** (i.e., expenditures necessary to learn how to do a particular construction project). Once learned, the productive process may be replicated more easily and efficiently. Careful analysis and allocation of such costs to appropriate accounting periods are necessary to ensure a proper matching of revenues and expenses.

Matching

Completed-Contract Method.   When reasonable estimates of the degree of completion are not possible, the completed-contract method of accounting for long-term contracts is applied. Under completed-contract accounting, no profit is recognized until the contract is complete and the buyer has accepted all of the contracted products or services. At that time, all profit earned on the contract is recorded. Prior to the recognition of profit, contract costs are accumulated in the balance sheet as Construction in Progress, an inventory account.

When costs are incurred under a contract and charged to an inventory account, such as Construction in Progress, we must ascertain that the amount reported as an asset does not exceed the net realizable value of the contract. Recall from Chapter 8 that the **net realizable value** of an inventory item is defined as the sales (contract) value of the item less any costs still to be incurred to complete and sell the product. Thus, even under completed-contract accounting, estimates of the remaining costs are necessary to ensure that the Construction in Progress account is not overvalued. If we determine that the costs included as an asset under a particular contract exceed the net realizable value of the contract, we must write down the asset to its net realizable value and recognize a loss at that time.

A Long-Term Contract Example. To illustrate the appropriate accounting procedures for the percentage-of-completion and completed-contract methods, we consider the following example. Dryden Construction Company agrees to build a large apartment building for Cozy Homes, Inc., for a total contract price of $5,000,000. Cozy Homes will make annual payments to Dryden, but the amounts of these payments cannot exceed the direct costs incurred by Dryden. The contract is signed on October 1, 1994; Dryden's year-end is December 31. The contract provides Cozy with a final inspection right to ensure compliance with the contract terms prior to accepting the completed project. Exhibit 21–1 provides further information about the contract.

Dryden bases its percentage-of-completion method on costs incurred rather than units delivered, because the contract calls for one large project rather than discrete parts. Dryden assumes that costs incurred accurately measure the progress. Exhibit 21–2 presents the current year gross profit calculations for the percentage-of-completion method. To illustrate the difference in the methods, Exhibit 21–3 shows the accounting entries for each contract year for both the percentage-of-completion and completed-contract methods. The resulting financial statement presentations for both methods are summarized in Exhibit 21–4.

These exhibits reveal that the only difference between the two methods is the timing of the recognition of gross profit on the contract. Both methods ultimately result in the recognition of the same total amount of gross profit ($600,000). The only balance sheet differences between the two methods relate to the carrying value of the Construction in Progress (inventory) and Retained Earnings accounts. Under the percentage-of-completion method, the amount of gross profit recognized is reflected as an increase in Construction in Progress and in Retained Earnings after being reported as an increase in net income in the income statement.

Under the percentage-of-completion method, we calculate the amount of revenue to be recognized by determining the gross profit to be recognized during the current year and adding that figure to the actual costs incurred during the year. As Exhibit 21–2 shows, a

EXHIBIT 21–1

Long-Term Contracts—Illustrative Information

Total contract price	$5,000,000			
Total anticipated costs (at 10/1/94)	4,000,000			
Item	**1994**	**1995**	**1996**	**Total**
Costs incurred each year	$ 500,000	$2,500,000	$1,400,000	$4,400,000
Estimated costs to complete (at year-end)	3,500,000	1,250,000	–0–	–0–
Progress billings each year	400,000	2,000,000	2,600,000	5,000,000
Progress payments received each year	275,000	2,100,000	2,625,000*	5,000,000

*Since the contract was completed and accepted during 1996, the buyer paid the remaining balance of the total contract amount, computed as follows:

Contract amount		$5,000,000
Prior progress payments		
1994	$ 275,000	
1995	2,100,000	2,375,000
Remaining amount		$2,625,000

EXHIBIT 21–2

Revenue Recognized by Percentage-of-Completion Method

	1994	1995	1996
Total contract price	$5,000,000	$5,000,000	$5,000,000
Costs incurred to date	500,000	3,000,000	4,400,000
Anticipated costs to complete	3,500,000	1,250,000	–0–
Total estimated costs	4,000,000	4,250,000	4,400,000
Expected gross profit	$1,000,000	$ 750,000	$ 600,000
Percentage of completion			
$500,000/$4,000,000	12.5%		
$3,000,000/$4,250,000		70.6%	
$4,400,000/$4,400,000			100%
Gross profit earned to date			
$1,000,000 × 12.5%	$ 125,000		
$750,000 × 70.6%		$ 529,500	
$600,000 × 100%			$ 600,000
Less: Gross profit previously recognized	—	(125,000)	(529,500)
Current year gross profit	$ 125,000	$ 404,500	$ 70,500

revised estimate of the cumulative percentage of completion is computed each year. This percentage is applied to the expected gross profit, which varies as revised estimates of expected costs to be incurred are made. The difference between the cumulative gross profit and the gross profit recognized in the previous year(s) is the current year gross profit. The final entry in Exhibit 21–3 for each year under the percentage-of-completion method records revenues, costs, and the increase in Construction in Progress for the gross profit recognized.

Under the completed-contract method, we defer the recognition of revenue until the project is completed. In the case of Dryden Construction Company, the $5,000,000 of revenue and the $4,400,000 of costs are recognized in 1996 when the contract is complete and the uncertainties that preclude the use of the percentage-of-completion method are resolved. Actual companies may employ different account titles and certain other minor variations, but the procedures illustrated here are representative of the two methods.

Exhibit 21–4 shows the difference between the inventory account, Construction in Progress, and the Contract Billings as a *current* asset. The "current" classification of this item is based on the operating cycle definition. An asset is current if it is expected to be sold, consumed, or converted to cash within the next year (or operating cycle if the cycle exceeds one year). The period of the accounting cycle for long-term contracts—which frequently exceeds one year—is typically used to identify current assets.

If the contract provided for billings in excess of costs incurred, the Construction in Progress account could be less than the Contract Billings account. In this case, the difference would be presented as a *current liability* labeled Excess of Contract Billings over Construction in Progress or a similar title.

Although the comparison of the percentage-of-completion and completed-contracts methods in the Dryden example demonstrate the similarities and differences, *the methods are not equally acceptable in the same circumstances.* We must consider the circumstances and available evidence and select the *appropriate* method. We use the completed-contract method only when reliable estimates of effort and resources to complete the project are not available. The percentage-of-completion method is required when reasonably dependable

EXHIBIT 21–3

Comparison of Completed-Contract and Percentage-of-Completion Journal Entries

| | | | Journal Entries | | | |
| | | | Completed-Contract Method | | Percentage-of-Completion Method | |
Date	Event	Accounts	Dr.	Cr.	Dr.	Cr.
1994	Contract signed	(No entry necessary to record contract commitment.)				
	Costs incurred	Construction in Progress	500,000		500,000	
		Cash		500,000		500,000
	Progress billings	Accounts Receivable	400,000		400,000	
		Contract Billings		400,000		400,000
	Billing collections	Cash	275,000		275,000	
		Accounts Receivable		275,000		275,000
	Revenue recognition	Construction in Progress	—		125,000	
		Cost of Earned Revenue	—		500,000	
		Construction Revenue		—		625,000
1995	Costs incurred	Construction in Progress	2,500,000		2,500,000	
		Cash		2,500,000		2,500,000
	Progress billings	Accounts Receivable	2,000,000		2,000,000	
		Contract Billings		2,000,000		2,000,000
	Billing collections	Cash	2,100,000		2,100,000	
		Accounts Receivable		2,100,000		2,100,000
	Revenue recognition	Construction in Progress	—		404,500	
		Cost of Earned Revenue	—		2,500,000	
		Construction Revenue		—		2,904,500
1996	Costs incurred	Construction in Progress	1,400,000		1,400,000	
		Cash		1,400,000		1,400,000
	Progress billings	Accounts Receivable	2,600,000		2,600,000	
		Contract Billings		2,600,000		2,600,000
	Billing collections	Cash	2,625,000		2,625,000	
		Accounts Receivable		2,625,000		2,625,000
	Revenue recognition	Construction in Progress	—		70,500	
		Cost of Earned Revenue	—		1,400,000	
		Construction Revenue		—		1,470,500
	Elimination of inventory	Contract Billings	—		5,000,000	
		Construction in Progress		—		5,000,000
	Recognition of costs and revenues on entire contract	Contract Billings	5,000,000		—	
		Cost of Earned Revenue	4,400,000		—	
		Construction Revenue		5,000,000		—
		Construction in Progress		4,400,000		—

estimates of the degree of completion can be made, because it presents the economic substance of the company's transactions and events more clearly and in a more timely fashion than does the completed-contract method. The percentage-of-completion method informs financial statement users of the volume of the company's economic activity.[6] The

Substance over Form

---

[6]*AICPA Statement of Position 81–1*, par. 22.

EXHIBIT 21–4

Comparison of Completed-Contract and Percentage-of-Completion Financial Statement Presentations

	Dec. 31, 1994		Dec. 31, 1995		Dec. 31, 1996	
	Completed Contract	Percentage of Completion	Completed Contract	Percentage of Completion	Completed Contract	Percentage of Completion
Balance Sheet						
Current assets						
Accounts receivable	$125,000	$125,000	$ 25,000	$ 25,000	–0–	–0–
Inventory						
Construction in progress	500,000	625,000	3,000,000	3,529,500	–0–	–0–
Less:						
Contract billings	(400,000)	(400,000)	(2,400,000)	(2,400,000)	–0–	–0–
Construction in progress in excess of billings	100,000	225,000	600,000	1,129,500	–0–	–0–
Income Statement						
Construction revenue	—	$625,000	—	$2,904,500	$5,000,000	$1,470,500
Cost of earned revenue	—	(500,000)	—	(2,500,000)	(4,400,000)	(1,400,000)
Gross margin	—	$125,000	—	$ 404,500	$ 600,000	$ 70,500

completed-contract method is based on results as finally determined rather than on estimates, but it does not reflect current performance when contract periods extend beyond one accounting period, and it may result in irregular recognition of income.[7]

A Hybrid Method.   In certain types of contracts (e.g., cost-plus contracts in which the revenue is determined by the costs incurred plus a specified percentage), the contractor is assured of no loss. If the contractor is protected in this manner but is unable to make reasonable estimates of the percentage of completion, *SOP 81–1* recommends a **hybrid method** described as the percentage-of-completion method based on a **zero profit margin.**[8] Under this method, revenue is recognized in an amount exactly equal to costs incurred until reasonably objective estimates of the percentage of completion are available. In the earlier example, if Dryden Construction Company had used this method, revenue and costs would be recognized in 1994 and 1995 for $500,000 and $2,500,000 (the amount of costs incurred), respectively:

1994	Cost of Earned Revenue	500,000	
	Construction Revenue		500,000
1995	Cost of Earned Revenue	2,500,000	
	Construction Revenue		2,500,000

In 1996, the year in which the contract is complete, the entire gross profit is recognized, much as in the completed-contract method:

1996	Construction in Progress	600,000	
	Cost of Earned Revenue	1,400,000	
	Construction Revenue		2,000,000
	Contract Billings	5,000,000	
	Construction in Progress		5,000,000

[7]*AICPA Statement of Position 81–1*, par. 30.
[8]*AICPA Statement of Position 81–1*, par. 33.

The first three entries in Exhibit 21–3 for each year also apply to the hybrid method. The significant difference between the hybrid method and the completed-contract method is that the hybrid method requires the inclusion of both revenues and costs in the income statement for 1994 and 1995. Performance during the period is included in the income statement, although the method does not impact net income because revenue and costs recognized are equal. The zero profit margin approach indicates to financial statement users the volume of the company's business while deferring the recognition of gross profit until more reliable estimates of the degree of completion can be made.

Anticipated Losses on Contracts.   During a contract period, the fact that a loss will be incurred on the contract may become apparent. Under all the methods presented above, a projected loss on a contract must be recognized immediately in conformity with the modifying convention of conservatism.

Conservatism

To illustrate, assume that Johnson Construction Company is using the completed-contract method on a project. At the end of 1996, the balance in the Construction in Progress account is $2,500,000, representing the costs incurred to date. If the company now projects a $350,000 loss on the contract because of unexpected increases in materials, labor, and overhead, the following entry is appropriate:

| 1996 | Loss on Construction Contract | 350,000 | |
| | Construction in Progress | | 350,000 |

From this point, construction costs are charged to the Construction in Progress account, and the balance in that account at the end of the contract equals the contract revenue if the loss estimate is accurate. If the loss estimate is not accurate, an adjustment is made when the appropriate amounts are determinable.

Assume that on another contract, Johnson is using the percentage-of-completion method. The Construction in Progress account at the end of 1996 has a balance of $6,500,000:

Construction costs incurred through 1996	$5,700,000
Gross profit recognized in previous years	800,000
Construction in Progress balance	$6,500,000

At the end of 1996, the company expects a $300,000 loss on the contract. The following entry should be made:

| 1996 | Loss on Contraction Contract | 1,100,000 | |
| | Construction in Progress | | 1,100,000 |

The $1,100,000 loss represents a reversal of the $800,000 gross profit recognized in previous years, plus the $300,000 loss that is now expected on the contract. From this point, construction costs are charged to the Construction in Progress account, and the balance in that account at the end of the contract equals the contract revenue if the loss estimate is accurate. As in the completed-contract method, if the loss estimate is inaccurate, further adjustment must be made in the future as the appropriate amounts are determinable.

INSTALLMENT SALES

The collectibility of credit sales is usually predictable and reasonably ensured as a result of credit approval, collection procedures, and historical evidence. In these cases, revenue is appropriately recognized at the point of sale. However, if a company makes credit sales to customers of relatively poor credit risk, recognition of revenue at the point of sale may be inappropriate. Although such revenue may be deemed to have been earned and measurable, collectibility remains uncertain. Therefore, the creditor defers the recognition of revenue until collecting the amount due. This practice is supported by the professional literature:

There are exceptional cases where receivables are collectible over an extended period of time, and because of the terms of the transactions or other conditions, there is no reasonable basis for estimating the degree of collectibility. When such circumstances exist, and as long as they exist, either the installment method or the cost recovery method of accounting may be used. (Under the cost recovery method, equal amounts of revenue and expense are recognized as collections are made until all costs have been recovered, postponing any recognition of profit until that time.)[9]

The **installment sales method** recognizes a portion of each cash collection as revenue and the remaining amount of cash collected as a recovery of cost. The **cost recovery method** treats all cash collected as a recovery of cost of the item sold until the full cost of the item sold is collected. Subsequent collections are treated entirely as revenue. The cost recovery method is even more conservative than the installment method, and application of the cost recovery technique is most desirable when the collectibility of receivables is extremely uncertain.

Conservatism

Under the installment sales method, revenue is recognized on a pro rata basis as each installment is received. To illustrate, assume that EZ Credit Auto Sales Company sells a $6,000 automobile to a customer on November 1, 1996, with the following terms: The customer will pay $600 down and $150 per month for 36 months plus interest at 15%. Because EZ Credit paid $4,200 for the automobile, it will make a gross profit of $1,800 on the sale. For simplicity, we ignore the interest revenue, because it is not related to the recognition of profit on the sale.

Because of the significant uncertainty of collection resulting from granting credit to relatively poor credit risks, EZ Credit Company uses the installment sales method of revenue recognition. Exhibit 21–5 presents the entries necessary to record the sale, collection of cash, and recognition of revenue. The gross profit percentage, which indicates the gross profit included in each payment received, is 30%, computed by dividing the gross profit by the sales price [($6,000 − $4,200)/$6,000 = 30%].

The Deferred Gross Profit account established at the point of sale is treated either as a contra account to Notes Receivable or as a deferred revenue (liability) account. The entry on December 31, 1996, which reflects the portion of cash collected that is recognized as revenue, may be made as each cash receipt occurs. If this practice is selected, each cash receipt of $150 (ignoring interest) is recorded in the following manner:

Cash	150	
Deferred Gross Profit	45	
Notes Receivable		150
Realized Gross Profit ($150 × 30% = $45)		45

If different sales transactions result in different gross profit percentages, separate gross profit records for each sale must be kept. For example, if installment sales in 1995 result in a gross profit percentage of 32% and installment sales in 1996 result in a gross profit percentage of 34%, the receivables and deferred gross profit amounts related to 1995 sales must be kept separate from the 1996 sales so that a proper accounting may be made of the gross profit recognized as receivables are collected.

Considering the uncertainty of collection for installment sales, it is not surprising that sellers typically retain a right of repossession (the right to take the property and resell it) if the buyer defaults. When inventory is acquired this way, the installment receivable and any deferred gross profit on the original sale must be eliminated. If the resale value of the repossessed property is greater or less than the carrying amount of the receivable (face amount, less the deferred gross profit), a gain or loss is recognized.

---

[9]*APB Opinion No. 10,* "Omnibus Opinion—1966" 1966, par. 12.

EXHIBIT 21-5

Installment Sales Accounting—Illustrative Entries

Date	Accounts	Dr.	Cr.
Nov. 1, 1996	Cash	600	
	Notes Receivable	5,400	
	Inventory		4,200
	Realized Gross Profit* ($600 × 30%)		180
	Deferred Gross Profit ($5,400 × 30%)		1,620
	(To record sale of automobile under installment sales method.)		
Nov. 30, 1996	Cash	150	
	Notes Receivable		150
	(To record receipt of payment.)		
Dec. 31, 1996	Cash	150	
	Notes Receivable		150
	(To record receipt of payment.)		
Dec. 31, 1996	Deferred Gross Profit ($300 × 30%)	90	
	Realized Gross Profit*		90
	(To record revenue for the year based on cash received.)		

*For income statement presentation purposes, the components of realized gross profit may be presented rather than the net amount of $270 ($180 + $90). In this situation, sales of $900 ($600 + $150 + $150) are included in sales revenue and $630 ($900 × 70%) is included in Cost of Goods Sold.

To illustrate, assume that Careyville Appliance Company sells a refrigerator for $500 on an installment contract calling for 25 monthly payments of $20, plus interest. The refrigerator cost Careyville $420, resulting in a gross profit percentage of 16% [($500 − $420)/ $500]. After 10 payments, the customer discontinued paying and Careyville repossessed the refrigerator. The carrying amount of the receivable is as follows:

Receivable balance [$500 − 10 ($20)]	$300
Less: Deferred gross profit balance {$80 − [10 ($20) × 16%]}	48
Carrying amount of installment receivable	$252

If the estimated resale value of the refrigerator is only $200, the entry to record the repossession is as follows:

Repossessed Inventory	200	
Deferred Gross Profit	48	
Loss on Repossession	52	
Installment Receivables		300

If the estimated resale value of the refrigerator had been higher than $252, a gain on repossession would have been recorded.

Although the installment sales method is part of generally accepted accounting principles and may be appropriate in certain circumstances, it is not widely used in practice. Credit sales are standard practice in most business settings. Selling companies carefully analyze the debt-paying ability of other companies with which they enter into credit transactions. Collectibility may not be certain, but little doubt exists in most circumstances of the buyer's intent and ability to pay. If significant doubt exists about a particular customer, the seller does not enter into a credit sale.

In certain circumstances, significant doubt concerning collection exists, however, and recognition of revenue at the point of sale is questionable. A land development transaction is one type of transaction that has experienced some abuse in the past in terms of recognition of the seller's revenue with little evidence of the buyer's intent or ability to pay. In Appendix A of this chapter, we discuss several special revenue recognition situations, including several for which the installment sales method may be appropriate. These include certain real estate transactions and franchise activities.

REVENUE RECOGNITION WHEN THE RIGHT OF RETURN EXISTS

A company may sell items with the provision that the customer return them under certain circumstances. For example, a manufacturer may sell its products to a retailer with the **right to return** any that are unsatisfactory to the consumer. In such circumstances, the manufacturer should not recognize revenue until six conditions are met:

1. The seller's price to the buyer is substantially fixed or determinable at the date of sale.
2. The buyer has paid or is obligated to pay the seller and the obligation is not contingent on resale of the product.
3. The buyer's obligation to the seller would not be changed in the event of theft or physical destruction or damage of the product.
4. The buyer acquiring the product for resale has economic substance apart from that provided by the seller. [That is, a separate, arm's-length relationship between the parties is evident.]
5. The seller does not have significant obligations for future performance to directly bring about resale of the product by the buyer.
6. The amount of future returns can be reasonably estimated.[10]

Disclosure Sales revenue and related expense that are deferred because at least one of these six conditions does not exist are recognized when all the conditions are met. Disclosure of the circumstances and the enterprise's accounting policies are necessary to adequately inform the users of the financial statements.

To illustrate the recognition of revenue when the right of return exists, we assume the following information about Rockford Corporation for 1996:

Sales	$500,000	Actual returns during year (at selling price)	$6,000
Cost of goods sold	$325,000	Cash collected on receivables	$285,000
Expected returns	2% of sales		

Because Rockford is able to make a reasonable estimate of returns, we assume that all of the conditions for revenue recognition are met in the entries required to record sales and related transactions for 1996.

To record sales and cost of goods sold:

Accounts Receivable	500,000	
Cost of Goods Sold	325,000	
Sales		500,000
Inventory		325,000

To record estimated sales returns:

Sales Returns ($500,000 × .02)	10,000	
Inventory—Estimated Returns ($10,000 × 65%)	6,500	
Allowance for Sales Returns		10,000
Cost of Goods Sold		6,500

(The 65% represents the cost-to-sales percentage in the sales: $325,000/$500,000 = 65%.)

---

[10]*FASB Statement of Financial Accounting Standards No. 48,* "Revenue Recognition When Right of Return Exists," 1981, par. 6.

To record collection of receivables:

Cash	285,000	
Accounts Receivable		285,000

To record sales returns and reclassification of inventory:

Allowance for Sales Returns	6,000	
Inventory ($6,000 × 65%)	3,900	
Accounts Receivable		6,000
Inventory—Estimated Returns		3,900

As a result of the recording of these transactions, net sales and cost of goods sold are presented at $490,000 and $318,500, respectively, maintaining the 65% cost-to-sales ratio, as shown in the following computations:

Sales	$500,000	
Sales returns	(10,000)	$490,000
Cost of goods sold ($325,000 − $6,500)		318,500
Gross margin		$171,500

This treatment is consistent with the matching principle. Accounts Receivable is presented at a net amount of $205,000, after considering $6,000 of returns received, $285,000 of collections, and $4,000 of estimated future returns: **Matching**

Accounts receivable ($500,000 − $285,000 − $6,000)	$209,000	
Allowance for sales returns ($10,000 − $6,000)	(4,000)	$205,000

The cost of inventory expected to be returned is presented in a special inventory classification, Inventory—Estimated Returns, at $2,600 ($4,000 × 65%).

In this illustration, we assumed that the conditions for revenue recognition were met and the question then became one of estimating returns and appropriately adjusting cost of goods sold so that the 65% cost-to-sales relationship is maintained in the income statement. Had the conditions for revenue recognition not been met, the sales and cost of goods sold amounts recognized in the first entry would have been deferred and recorded only when the conditions for revenue recognition were met.

OTHER UNUSUAL REVENUE-RECOGNITION CIRCUMSTANCES

The timing and magnitude of revenue recognition remain areas of complexity and controversy for the accounting profession. Judgments are frequently required in determining when revenue should be recognized and in what amount. These circumstances raise the possibility of manipulation and the "management" of earnings. Because of the central importance of revenue in the financial statements and the susceptibility to *abuse,* accountants must remain alert to the possibility of misstatement.

In our study of revenue recognition, we have emphasized situations involving physical products. Service industries, such as insurance, medical services, legal services, accounting services, management consulting, moving and storage, and banking, also encounter revenue-recognition problems. The questions of income determination for service industries are similar to those for product-related industries: When is revenue earned, measurable, and collectible? How should costs related to the generation of service revenue be treated? Few authoritative accounting pronouncements presently exist to help accountants answer these important questions. Theoretically, service revenue is recognized when services are performed (earned), amounts can be objectively determined (measurable), and collection is reasonably assured (collectible). Expenses should be recognized as the revenues they helped to create are

BUYER, DO THY HOMEWORK

The initial public offering prospectus for Oregon-based Protocol Systems, a maker of medical monitoring devices, shows a 77% jump in sales in 1991, to $23 million, and an 11% rise in the company's net earnings, to $2.2 million.

Now that's impressive—until you read the prospectus closely. You'll find that 25% of the revenue surge was the result of a one-time sale of equipment to the U.S. military during the Persian Gulf war. A little math will tell you that the sale contributed close to $500,000 to income. Discounting this one-off military deal, the company would have earned around $1.7 million in 1991, *down* from $2 million the year before.

Even so, the offering went off without a hitch—with the company selling 2.7 million shares at $11 late last month. That says a lot about the strength of this stock market—as well as the need for investors to give extra scrutiny to the numbers of companies about to go public. According to IDD Information Services, some $6.8 billion already has been raised this year, with at least another 92 companies waiting to raise another $4.5 billion by year-end.

In such a market, investors have to do more homework than ever. "Remember," says Kenneth Heebner of Boston's Capital Growth Management, "underwriters are hired to sell the stock, so they'll write the best prospectus they can."

Not doing your homework can be hazardous to your financial health. Watch for aggressive accounting, says Howard Schilit, an accounting professor at Washington, D.C.'s American University and an expert on IPOs. An example: Brite Voice Systems, which makes computerized voice systems for telephone services, went public at $12.50 a share in September 1989, raising $19 million.

Brite Voice had just introduced a new system and had signed a couple of large contracts. Because one of the systems was going to take a year to be fully installed, Brite Voice started booking revenues under the "percentage of completion" method. This allows companies to record a percentage of the revenue as parts of the work are performed.

Out of the $8.7 million in revenue shown in Brite Voice's offering prospectus for the first six months of 1989, $3.4 million was for the partially completed contract. But guess what happened the next year? Brite Voice fought with its other customer, and had to take a $460,000 writeoff for revenue recognized but still uncollected. Brite Voice now trades at less than half its offering price.

Last October's preliminary prospectus for apparel maker Warnaco Group's initial public offering showed a healthy surge of earnings improvement: 1990 profits were $5 million, following two years of losses. But on Oct. 11, the very day Warnaco sold 6 million shares for $20 each, the company sent investors a new and revised prospectus. Surprise! That $5 million profit had suddenly turned into a $17 million loss.

What happened to Warnaco's profits? While reviewing the company's registration materials, the Securities & Exchange Commission found that Warnaco had not assigned any goodwill to the 1990 sale of its Activewear division to a group of investors that included Warnaco officials.

The result was a last-minute, $22 million writeoff, which reduced the company's earnings by a like amount. Warnaco is now trading well above its offering price, thanks to the strong market. But investors should be asking questions about managers who overlooked a $22 million writedown.

Normally, material changes should be disclosed to investors before an issue is priced. But if a company springs a surprise on you, reputable underwriters usually give you up to five days to cancel your order if you find something in the final prospectus you don't like.

Here's another red flag: rising inventory levels, or accumulating receivables. Consider Laser-Pacific Media, which provides TV networks with postproduction services such as sound effects. Laser-Pacific went public last summer at $6 a share, raising $6.6 million.

In the prospectus, the company disclosed that $750,000 of its $2.5 million in trade receivables for the six months ended June 30, 1991 were past due, and that nearly $500,000 of those were 90 days past due. In other words, its customers weren't paying up for the company's services. "That's the sign of a big problem," says American University's Schilit. The stock was recently at $3.

It's no fun wading through the modern offering prospectus. But unless you're willing to do some homework, you shouldn't even think about buying newly issued stock, especially in a frothy market like this one.

SOURCE: Roula Khalaf, "Buyer, Do Thy Homework," *Forbes* (April 13, 1993), pp. 47–48. Reprinted by permission of *Forbes Magazine*, April 13, 1993, © Forbes Inc., 1993.

Matching   recognized, in accordance with the matching principle. Accountants must apply judgment in this important area of business activity. As the FASB continues to refine accounting practices, particularly in specialized industries, more guidance concerning the recognition of revenue and the determination of income in service industries may be forthcoming.

As previously mentioned, many industries engage in transactions and business relationships that require unusual accounting and reporting practices. The appendix to this chapter discusses financial accounting and reporting for several additional situations involving unique revenue-recognition problems.

The first part of this chapter has dealt with the criteria and circumstances influencing the recognition of revenue. Accounting and reporting standards have also been established in regard to the presentation of various items of revenue and expense in the income statement. The following section considers theories, standards, and practices relevant to the format, organization, and content of the income statement.

A major objective of financial reporting is to provide information to investors and creditors about **financial performance** during the reporting period. Although **performance** may refer to numerous aspects of an enterprise's operations, the FASB has clearly designated **earnings** as a focal point for financial reporting:

> *The primary focus of financial reporting is information about an enterprise's performance provided by measures of* earnings *and its* components. *Investors, creditors, and others who are concerned with assessing the prospects of net cash flows are especially interested in that information. Their interest in an enterprise's future cash flows and its ability to generate favorable cash flows leads primarily to an interest in information about its* earnings *rather than information about its cash flows.*[11] *[Emphasis added.]*

We could cite many objectives of reporting earnings. In Chapter 3, we examined the usefulness of accounting income figures and discussed net income as a measure of operating efficiency and a predictor of future cash flows.

The ability of management is a major factor in the success of a business enterprise, and income is the primary measure of business performance. Therefore, one objective of earnings is to *evaluate management efficiency* by comparing the results of management effort with some standard or goal. The objectives of business activity vary from enterprise to enterprise. A profit-oriented enterprise attempts to achieve some desired level of earnings as the basis for providing a desired level of cash flow to investors and creditors. Net income is a valuable measure of progress toward that goal. Periodic measures of earnings are useful in evaluating how well management has employed the resources at its disposal to achieve the desired level of earnings. The desired level of earnings may be determined in several ways, including management-established goals, industry averages, or individual investor expectations.

Inherent to the presentation of net income is the distinction between investment and income. **Investment** refers to the accumulated resources that the enterprise has as a result of contributions by investors. **Income** is the net result of the inflow of resources resulting from the employment of that investment. Another objective of reporting earnings is *to distinguish between the accumulation of investments and the accumulation of additional resources that result from the employment of investments.* These additional resources are either retained by the enterprise or distributed as dividends to the owners of the enterprise.

ALTERNATIVE INCOME CONCEPTS

Current accounting practice uses a transaction approach to income measurement. Under this approach, positive and negative asset and liability changes are measured and recognized in conformity with accounting principles, such as revenue realization and matching. The combined results of these changes is the determination of net income, one of the most prominent figures in financial reporting. Accounting theorists have suggested several alternative definitions of income. The primary differences among these definitions are found in the treatment of wages, income taxes, interest, and preferred dividends.

**INCOME
PRESENTATION**

Revenue Realization

Matching

---

[11]*FASB Statement of Financial Accounting Concepts No. 1,* "Objectives of Financial Reporting by Business Enterprises," 1978, par. 43.

Net Income to Stockholders

The current concept of income is founded on the notion that the amount identified as net income is that amount that accrues to *all* stockholders. **Determinants** of income are those revenues, gains, expenses, and losses that are included in the computation of net income, such as sales revenue, cost of goods sold, operating expenses, interest expense, and income tax expense. **Distributions** of income are transfers of assets to owners of the enterprise, including both common and preferred stockholders. This concept of income, which is strongly emphasized in traditional accounting thought, is often identified as **net income to stockholders.** All expenses incurred in the generation of revenue are deducted in determining income, but no distributions to owners are deducted. Several alternative approaches to this concept are explained in the following paragraphs.

Value Added Income

Under the value added concept of income, various interested parties are identified as the **recipients** of the income of the enterprise. The **value added** is the sales price of the enterprise's products or services minus the cost of the goods and services paid to other enterprises that produced those goods and services. Other groups who receive the advantages of enterprise operations—employees, creditors, government, and owners—are recipients of the income of the enterprise. Cost of goods sold is a determinant of income, but expenditures such as income taxes, interest, and dividends are considered distributions of that income to the various recipients.

Enterprise Net Income

Under the concept of **enterprise net income,** income taxes and interest expense, as well as dividends, are considered distributions of income. Recipients of the enterprise's income are the government, creditors, and owners. The resulting income is much like the operating income figure commonly appearing in income statements today, because taxes and interest are frequently presented after that amount.

Net Income to Investors

Another variation of net income is **net income to investors.** Within this concept, all interest payments to creditor and dividend payments to stockholders are considered distributions of the enterprise's income and all other distributions are considered determinants of income. This interpretation of income varies from current reporting practice only in that interest paid to creditors is treated as a distribution, rather than a determinant, of income.

Net Income to Residual Stockholders

The **residual** (or **common**) **stockholders** are typically thought of as the ultimate owners of the enterprise. Although the claim represented by preferred stock is legally that of an owner, there is some support for income to be regarded as the amount that accrues to the **residual** stockholders. This concept is reflected in the computation of earnings per share in which the net income (to all stockholders), as reported in the income statement, is reduced by the preferred dividend to derive an income figure accruing to the common stockholders. The resulting amount then becomes the basis for computing earnings per share. This view of income is consistent with the theory that common stockholders are the ultimate riskbearers and the group to whom the long-run profitability of the enterprise ultimately accrues.

Exhibit 21–6 summarizes the concepts of income and shows whether wages (return to employees), income taxes (return to government), interest (return to creditors), and preferred dividends (return to preferred stockholders) are treated as determinants or distributions of income under each concept. The concept of income reflected in current income presentation, **net income to stockholders,** is included in the fourth column.

EXHIBIT 21–6

Comparative Income Presentations
(in thousands of dollars)

	(1) Value Added Income	(2) Enterprise Net Income	(3) Net Income to Investors	(4) Net Income to Stockholders	(5) Net Income to Residual Stockholders
Sales	$2,000	$2,000	$2,000	$2,000	$2,000
Determinants of income					
Cost of goods sold	1,000	1,000	1,000	1,000	1,000
Wages	—	400	400	400	400
Income taxes	—	—	150	150	150
Interest	—	—	—	200	200
Preferred dividends	—	—	—	—	50
	1,000	1,400	1,550	1,750	1,800
Income	$1,000	$ 600	$ 450	$ 250	$ 200
Distributions of income					
Wages	$400	—	—	—	—
Income taxes	150	$150	—	—	—
Interest	200	200	$200	—	—
Preferred dividends	50	50	50	$ 50	—
Common dividends	100	100	100	100	$100
Total distributions of income	$900	$500	$350	$150	$100
Groups to whom income accrues					
Employees	X				
Government	X	X			
Creditors	X	X	X		
Preferred stockholders	X	X	X	X	
Common stockholders	X	X	X	X	X

CURRENT OPERATING PERFORMANCE VERSUS ALL-INCLUSIVE INCOME

A continuing question about the presentation of income concerns which specific transactions, if any, should be *excluded* from income determination because of their unique nature. Accountants generally agree that sales, cost of goods sold, and other similar revenue and expense items should be *included* in the determination of net income. They also generally agree that the results of capital transactions, such as dividends and stock transactions, should be *excluded* in determining net income. Opinions differ, however, on the proper treatment of items that differ in nature from normal revenues and expenses, that do not recur in any established pattern, or that represent adjustments of the income of some past accounting period. Suppose, for example, that a company sustains a loss from an earthquake. Such a loss is unusual and will not recur in any predictable pattern. If an objective of reporting earnings is to provide information for predicting future events, should the company include this loss in the measurement of income? Assume that in 1996 the company finds an error in the determination of 1994 net income. Should it include the gain or loss necessary to correct this error in the determination of 1996 net income? Special or irregular events such as these are clearly part of the history of the enterprise's earnings, but their unique characteristics have led to disagreement on the most appropriate way to present them in the financial statements. The presentation of items like these has produced two opposing schools of thought: the **current operating performance** view and the **all-inclusive** view.

Proponents of the current operating performance view believe that a company's income should be based on its normal, recurring operations. Unusual items, nonrecurring items, and items relating to other accounting periods should be *excluded* from the current year measurement of income and reported as direct increases or decreases in retained earnings. These types of items should appear in the statement of retained earnings rather than the income statement. Proponents of this view believe that financial statement users rely heavily on reported measurements of *net income* but that they lack the knowledge necessary to understand the detailed components of an income statement. They also believe that financial statement users can make more accurate predictions and more meaningful evaluations of management performance if net income reflects only the normal, recurring activities of the business.

The opposite perspective is the all-inclusive view. Proponents of this position believe that net income for a period should equal the change in owners' equity during the period, except for dividends and capital stock transactions. They contend that unusual items, events not recurring frequently, and items related to other accounting periods should be reported in the current income statement. Advocates of this view assume that financial statement users will not focus excessively on the bottom-line net income figure and that they will appropriately consider the components of net income when they interpret the enterprise's performance. All-inclusive advocates claim that irregular items tend to be unnoticed if they are not reported in the income statement. Considerable judgment is required to determine which items should be included under the current operating performance approach, which—according to all-inclusive proponents—allows management to manipulate reported income by including or excluding items as desired. This problem is avoided with an all-inclusive approach.

A careful analysis of authoritative accounting pronouncements reveals an evolution[12] in thought from a strong all-inclusive position in 1941 (*Accounting Research Bulletin No. 8*[13]) to an equally strong current operating performance position in 1948 (*Accounting Research Bulletin No. 35*[14]). By 1953 the pendulum had begun to swing away from the current operating performance position. A strong step in the direction of the all-inclusive approach came in 1966 when the Accounting Principles Board, in *Opinion No. 9*, concluded that "net income should reflect all items of profit and loss recognized during the period with the sole exception of prior period adjustments."[15] The APB opinion further stated that extraordinary items should be shown separately from the results of ordinary operations in the income statement and that prior period adjustments should be reported as adjustments to the beginning balance of retained earnings. Finally, it listed criteria for identifying both extraordinary items and prior period adjustments. These criteria have subsequently been changed, however, by other authoritative pronouncements.

In 1977, the FASB moved a step closer to an all-inclusive income statement when it issued *Statement of Financial Accounting Standards No. 16*.[16] Previously, companies were allowed to treat a variety of items as prior period adjustments. Under *Statement No. 16*, the number of items properly treated as adjustments to retained earnings was reduced considerably. In view of all these events, we can conclude that current accounting practice supports a *modified* all-inclusive view within which all income items except limited prior period adjustments are included in the determination of net income.

---

[12]For a discussion of the evolutionary process of income presentation, see Jack E. Kiger and Jan R. Williams, "An Emerging Concept of Income Presentation," *Accounting Historians Journal* (Fall 1977), pp. 63–77.

[13]*ARB No. 8*, "Combined Statement of Income and Earned Surplus," 1941.

[14]*ARB No. 35*, "Presentation of Income and Earned Surplus," 1948.

[15]*APB Opinion No. 9*, "Reporting the Results of Operations," 1966, par. 17.

[16]*FASB Statement of Financial Accounting Standards No. 16*, "Prior Period Adjustments," 1977.

In 1984 the FASB issued *Statement of Financial Accounting Concepts No. 5*, "Recognition and Measurement in Financial Statements of Business Enterprises." In this statement, the concept of *comprehensive income* is introduced and a distinction is drawn between comprehensive income and earnings.

Comprehensive income is defined as follows:

> *A broad measure of the effects of transactions and other events of an entity, comprising all recognized changes in equity (net assets) of the entity during a period from transactions and other events and circumstances except those resulting from investments by owners and distributions to owners.*[17]

The term *earnings*, on the other hand, is similar to *net income* in current practice. **Earnings** is a measure of performance for a period and to the extent feasible *excludes* items that are extraneous to that period. One example of an item that is included in present net income but excluded from this definition of earnings is the cumulative effect of a change in accounting principle.[18] Although the FASB expects that *net income, profit, net loss,* and other equivalent terms will continue to be used in financial statements for *earnings,* we can reasonably expect some future changes in income statement content and display as the FASB implements in practice the concepts of comprehensive income and earnings as described in *SFAC No. 5.* One possible outcome of this distinction is a move back to a current operating performance approach as extraneous transactions are identified as part of comprehensive income but excluded from earnings.

INCOME PRESENTATION UNDER CURRENT GAAP

Contemporary income presentation practices are based on the concept of income to stockholders (see Column 4, Exhibit 21–6). Emphasis is placed on the all-inclusive definition of income with limited exceptions. Concern for the presentation of the results of current operations, however, is apparent in the many separate classifications and subtotals required in the statement if certain types of events have taken place.

In this section, we cover several topics important to your understanding of income presentation under current generally accepted accounting principles. First, the subject of intraperiod income tax allocation is covered because it is important to understand the way an income statement is constructed, and it is important to understand prior to covering the other subjects that follow. Second, we review a number of important items that you have already studied in this text. Because these items have been covered at different points in the text and are particularly important for a comprehensive understanding of income presentation, we review them here. Finally, we cover discontinued operations, an important element of the income statement when a company has disposed of a part of its operations.

Intraperiod Income Tax Allocation

Intraperiod income tax allocation refers to the allocation of the total income tax expense recognized in an accounting period among the various components of income and changes in stockholders' equity recognized during that same period. Earlier chapters explain that certain items are granted special treatment in financial reporting, including presentation on a net of tax basis. These include, but are not limited to, the following items:

1. **Extraordinary items.** Presented in a separate income statement category immediately preceding the income statement amount, "net income."
2. **Prior period adjustments.** Presented as adjustments to beginning retained earnings of the period in which the correction or other adjustment is made.

---

[17]*Statement of Financial Accounting Concepts No. 5,* "Recognition and Measurement in Financial Statements of Business Enterprises," 1984, par. 39.

[18]*SFAC No. 5,* pars. 33–34.

In discussing intraperiod income tax allocation, we refer to these as "special items." Intraperiod income tax allocation is a problem of **financial statement presentation.** It does not affect the total *amount* of income tax expense recognized during a period; rather, it involves the manner of presentation of income tax expense in the various sections of the income statement and the retained earnings statement.

Intraperiod income tax allocation requires the presentation of special items on a **net of tax basis.** The rationale underlying this requirement is that for disclosure of special items to be complete, separate presentation requires that they be on a net of tax basis to maintain the appropriate relationship between the various elements of income and stockholders' equity. The income tax effect of special items is computed by determining the amount of income tax expense that would be recognized *with and without the special item.* The difference *between* these two tax amounts is the tax effect of the special item.

Examples of Intraperiod Allocation.   Several situations involving the application of intraperiod income tax allocation procedures may be encountered. These involve situations of income or loss before income tax, combined with one or both of the special items described earlier. In the following examples, three representative situations are illustrated.

Three companies, Red, White, and Blue, are currently determining the appropriate financial statement presentation of income tax expense for 1995. During the year, the companies reported the following information:

	Income (Loss) before Income Tax and Special Item	Special Items	Basis for Computing Total Tax
Red Company	$20,000	$27,000 extraordinary gain	$47,000
White Company	35,000	$(15,000) extraordinary loss	20,000
Blue Company	(30,000)	$42,000 positive correction of error	12,000

The appropriate income tax rate on all items is assumed to be 35%.

The amount presented as a separate item and identified as income tax expense is based on income before income tax and special items. For example, in the case of Red Company, the income before income tax and special items is $20,000; the extraordinary gain is $27,000, resulting in $47,000 as the basis for computing total income tax expense. The total income tax is separated into two components for presentation in the financial statements: (1) the portion associated with income before the special item and (2) the portion associated with the special item. Income tax expense represents the aggregate income tax effect of all items included in income (loss) before income tax and the special item and is determined without regard to the special item. The special item is then presented on a net of tax basis. This process is illustrated for the three companies in Exhibit 21–7.

In all three cases, we see that the income tax effect of the special item is computed by comparing the income tax to be recognized with and without the special item and assigning the difference to the special item. If a single income tax rate applies to all items subject to income tax, this computation is simplified, because the income tax associated with each item can be computed directly, as follows for Red, White, and Blue Companies:

Red Company:	$27,000 × 35% = $9,450	Additional income taxes associated with extraordinary gain.
White Company:	$15,000 × 35% = $5,250	Reduction in income taxes associated with extraordinary loss.
Blue Company:	$42,000 × 35% = $14,700	Additional income taxes associated with prior period adjustment.

EXHIBIT 21–7

Examples of Intraperiod Income Tax Allocation

Red Company—Extraordinary Gain

Total income tax to be recognized ($47,000 × 35%)	$ 16,450
Less: Income tax expense associated with income before extraordinary gain ($20,000 × 35%)	7,000
Additional income tax associated with extraordinary gain	$ 9,450

Red Company
Partial Income Statement
For the Year Ended December 31, 1995

Income before income taxes and extraordinary item	$ 20,000
Income tax expense	7,000
Income before extraordinary gain	13,000
Extraordinary gain, net of $9,450 income tax expense	17,550
Net income	$ 30,550

White Company—Extraordinary Loss

Total income tax to be recognized ($20,000 × 35%)	$ 7,000
Less: Income tax expense associated with income before extraordinary loss ($35,000 × 35%)	12,250
Reduction in income tax associated with extraordinary loss	$ (5,250)

White Company
Partial Income Statement
For the Year Ended December 31, 1995

Income before income taxes and extraordinary item	$ 35,000
Income tax expense	12,250
Income before extraordinary loss	22,750
Extraordinary loss, net of $5,250 income tax savings	(9,750)
Net income	$ 13,000

Blue Company—Prior Period Adjustment

Total income tax to be recognized ($12,000 × 35%)	$ 4,200
Plus: Income tax savings associated with loss before considering prior period adjustment ($30,000 × 35%)	10,500
Additional income tax associated with correction of error	$ 14,700

Blue Company
Partial Income Statement
For the Year Ended December 31, 1995

Loss before income taxes	$(30,000)
Income tax savings	10,500
Net loss	$(19,500)

The correction of error is presented in the retained earnings statement as a positive adjustment to the beginning balance. The amount of this adjustment is $27,300, which represents the $42,000 positive adjustment, net of $14,700 income tax associated with that item.

Complications in Applying Intraperiod Allocation.   Several complications may be encountered in applying the principles of intraperiod income tax allocation. We next look at the determination of the tax effect of a special item with differential tax rates.

Green Company determines its income to be $20,000 before an extraordinary gain of $16,000 and before income taxes. Appropriate income tax rates are 25% on the first $25,000 of income and 38% on all income in excess of $25,000. The determination of the income tax expense, the income tax associated with the extraordinary gain, and the related income statement presentation at December 31, 1995, are presented in Exhibit 21–8. The direct computation of the income tax associated with the extraordinary gain is more complex in this case, because all income is not taxed at the same rate. We determine the income tax effect of the extraordinary item by applying the **marginal tax rate(s).** This simply means that the extraordinary gain is considered to come *after* the income before extraordinary items. For Green Company, the income tax effect of the extraordinary gain can be computed by applying the marginal income tax rates as follows:

Taxable at 38%

$36,000 − $25,000 = $11,000

$11,000 × 38% = $4,180

Taxable at 25%

$16,000 − $11,000 = $5,000

$5,000 × 25%   =   1,250

Income tax applicable to special item $5,430

The existence of more than one special item in the same accounting period presents another complication in determining the tax related to special items. For example, a company might have both an extraordinary item and a prior period adjustment. In this situation, the income tax effect of the two or more special items is determined as a single amount by computing the amount of income tax without *any* of the special items and comparing it with the

---

EXHIBIT 21–8

Example of Intraperiod Income Tax Allocation:
Differential Income Tax Rates

Green Company

Total income tax expense		
$25,000 × 25%	$6,250	
11,000 × 38%	4,180	$10,430
$36,000		
Income tax expense associated with income before extraordinary item		
($20,000 × 25%)		(5,000)
Additional income tax expense associated with extraordinary gain		$ 5,430

Green Company
Partial Income Statement
For the Year Ended December 31, 1995

Income before income taxes and extraordinary item	$20,000
Income tax expense	5,000
Income before extraordinary gain	15,000
Extraordinary gain, net of $5,430 income tax expense	10,570
Net income	$25,570

amount of income tax including *all* of the special items. The difference between these two amounts, representing the tax effect of all special items in the aggregate, is then allocated among the individual items. This allocation is based on the ratio of the amount of each special item to the total of all special items.

Review of Principles of Income Presentation

Throughout this text, various aspects of income statement presentation have been discussed and illustrated. The following paragraphs briefly review several important features of the income statement that were considered earlier.

Single- and Multiple-Step Income Statements. A **single-step income statement** is a relatively simple presentation in which all revenues and gains included in pretax income are grouped together at the top of the statement. All expenses and losses included in pretax income are then grouped together and subtracted from the total of revenues and gains. This subtotal, reduced by income tax expense, is net income. A **multiple-step income statement** presents revenues from sales first. From this amount, cost of goods sold is deducted to determine gross margin. Operating expenses, which may be classified into specific categories such as selling and administrative expenses, are deducted from the gross margin to obtain income from operations. Other income and expense items are added to or deducted from the income from operations to obtain net income. The resulting net income figure is the same for both statements, and the difference lies in the format and extent of detail. Both types of presentations are acceptable, and each is frequently encountered. You may wish to refresh your memory about these two forms of income statement presentation by reviewing Exhibits 4–1 and 4–2.

Individually Identified Gains and Losses. Gains and losses that are unusual in nature *or* infrequent in occurrence are individually identified in the income statement. Under the multiple-step format, these items are usually displayed among other gains and losses, following income from operations. Examples of this type of item are gains and losses from the sale of plant assets or investment securities. Care should be taken not to present these items in a way that implies that they are extraordinary items. They are *not* presented on a net of tax basis, and earnings per share figures are not presented on them.

Extraordinary Gains and Losses. Gains and losses that are judged to be *both* unusual in nature *and* infrequent in occurrence are defined as **extraordinary** and are presented in a separate income statement category on a net of tax basis. This presentation is required in both single- and multiple-step income statements. An income subtotal immediately preceding extraordinary items entitled Income before Extraordinary Items must be included in the income statement. This caption is followed by the extraordinary gain or loss, presented net of its tax effect, and then by the net income amount.

To illustrate the presentation of an extraordinary item, Exhibit 21–9 includes the partial income statement and a related note to the financial statements for the 1993 annual report of Unisys Corporation. Unisys is one of the largest providers of information services, technology, and software in the world. The company employs about 49,000 people and does business in approximately 100 countries. Note 2 of the financial statements, which is presented in Exhibit 21–9 following the income statement, explains that the extraordinary items (loss) relate to the settlement of lawsuits. Notice also that the income statement includes the cumulative effect of a change in accounting principles following the extraordinary item. We review that income statement item in the following section.

Cumulative Effect of a Change in Accounting Principle. When an enterprise changes from one generally accepted accounting principle (or method of applying a principle) to another, the **cumulative effect** of that change on retained earnings at the beginning of the period of change is usually

---

EXHIBIT 21–9

Example Extraordinary Item

Unysis Corporation
Partial Income Statement

Year Ended December 31 (Millions, except per share data)	1993	1992	1991
Income (loss) before income taxes	503.4	435.6	(1,288.3)
Estimated income taxes	141.8	139.4	105.0
Income (loss) before extraordinary items and changes in accounting principles	361.6	296.2	(1,393.3)
Extraordinary items	(26.4)	65.0	
Effect of changes in accounting principles	230.2		
Net income (loss)	565.4	361.2	(1,393.3)
Dividends on preferred shares	121.6	122.1	121.2
Earnings (loss) on common shares	$443.8	$239.1	$(1,514.5)
Earnings (loss) per common share			
Primary			
Before extraordinary items and changes in accounting principles	$ 1.46	$ 1.06	$ (9.37)
Extraordinary items	(.16)	.40	
Effect of changes in accounting principles	1.39		
Total	$ 2.69	$ 1.46	$ (9.37)
Fully diluted			
Before extraordinary items and changes in accounting principles	$ 1.48	$ 1.04	$ (9.37)
Extraordinary items	(.11)	.36	
Effect of changes in accounting principles	.94		
Total	$ 2.31	$ 1.40	$ (9.37)

Note 2—Accounting Changes and Extraordinary Items

Effective January 1, 1993, the Company adopted the Financial Accounting Standard Board's Statement of Financial Accounting Standards ("SFAS") 106, "Employers' Accounting for Postretirement Benefits Other Than Pensions," and SFAS 109, "Accounting for Income Taxes." The adoption of SFAS 106 decreased net income $194.8 million, net of $124.5 million of income tax benefits, or $.79 per fully diluted common share, and the adoption of SFAS 109 increased net income by $425.0 million, or $1.73 per fully diluted common share. For further discussion of SFAS 106 and 109, see notes 14 and 4, respectively.

In 1993, the Company settled lawsuits with Honeywell, Inc., in connection with its sale of the Sperry Aerospace Group in December 1986. As a result of the settlement, the Company recorded an extraordinary charge of $26.4 million, net of $16.8 million of income tax benefits, or $.11 per fully diluted common share.

In 1992, the Company recorded an extraordinary item of $65.0 million, or $.36 per fully diluted common share, related to the tax benefit of book operating loss carryforwards. See note 4.

SOURCE: Unysis Corporation, 1993 Annual Report.

---

included in income of the period of the change.[19] The cumulative effect may be a gain or loss, depending on the nature of the specific change. The cumulative effect immediately follows extraordinary items, if any, and is presented on a net of tax basis.

---

[19]As seen in Chapter 20, the effects of certain *special types of changes in an accounting principle* are presented by retroactively restating previous financial statements rather than by including the cumulative effect of the change in the income of the period of change. Also, in rare circumstances it may not be possible to compute the cumulative effect of a change in accounting principle for inclusion in the income statement.

Prior Period Adjustments. Corrections of errors in previously issued financial statements and certain other adjustments are *not* included in the determination of net income. Primarily because they do not relate to the period in which they are recorded, these items (presented on a net of tax basis) belong in the retained earnings statement as adjustments to the beginning balance of the period, even though they are part of the enterprise's total earnings history.

Several types of events and transactions that are presented as prior period adjustments were discussed in Chapter 20. These include corrections of errors and certain retroactive adjustments resulting from the application of authoritative accounting pronouncements.

Earnings per Share. **Earnings per share** figures are included in the income statement of all publicly held companies. Other companies may choose to present earnings per share data, and several authoritative pronouncements require the presentation of earnings per share figures for certain income statement items.

When presented, earnings per share figures appear on the face of the income statement and may also be explained in related notes. A common practice is to present an earnings per share schedule (which parallels the income statement presentation) at the bottom of the income statement.

Exhibit 21–10 illustrates this method of presentation with the hypothetical Foster Company's 1995–1996 comparative income statements, which include a typical earnings per share presentation at the bottom. The exhibit assumes that 100,000 shares of common stock were outstanding throughout 1995 and 1996.

As we discussed in Chapter 18, the existence of convertible securities, stock options, and other potentially dilutive securities may require a dual presentation of primary and fully diluted earnings per share.

Discontinued Operations

When an enterprise has disposed of a major portion of its operations, the results of *continuing operations* should be separated from the results of the *discontinued segment*. Any gain or loss on the disposal of the discontinued part of the business is also shown separately. Prior to the development of this income statement presentation technique, the most frequent extraordinary items in financial reports were gains and losses from the disposal of portions of

EXHIBIT 21–10		
Foster Company Partial Income Statement For the Fiscal Years Ended October 31, 1995 and 1996		
	1995	**1996**
Income before extraordinary item and cumulative effect of change in accounting principle	$870,000	$740,000
Extraordinary loss—Major casualty loss, net of $70,000 income tax benefit	—	(130,000)
Cumulative effect of change in depreciation method, net of $28,000 income taxes	52,000	—
Net income	$922,000	$610,000
Earnings per common share		
Income before extraordinary item and cumulative effect of change in accounting principle	$8.70	$7.40
Extraordinary loss	—	(1.30)
Cumulative effect of change in accounting principle	.52	—
Net income	$9.22	$6.10

business enterprises.[20] The frequency of these items, combined with their tendency to represent large dollar amounts, prompted the APB to establish the reporting standards for discontinued operations as a part of *APB Opinion No. 30.*[21]

Income or loss from the operations of a segment prior to its disposal and any gain or loss on the disposal are *not* extraordinary items under current accounting standards. These items are combined in a section of the income statement identified as **discontinued operations.** This section is *preceded* by an income subtotal, **income from continuing operations.** The income or loss from the operations of the disposed segment and the gain or loss from the actual disposal are presented separately on a net of tax basis. This section is followed by "net income" or "income before extraordinary item and/or cumulative effect of change in accounting principles," as appropriate.

Earnings per share figures for income from continuing operations and net income are presented on the face of the income statement for publicly held companies. In practice, earnings per share figures are also frequently presented for the two components of discontinued operations or for the discontinued operations section as a single figure.

What constitutes a *segment* disposal? A **segment** is a component of an enterprise whose activities represent a separate major line of business or a separate class of customer. A segment may be a subsidiary or other investee, a division, or a department; the disposal may be accomplished by sale or abandonment. A major criterion distinguishing the disposal of a segment from other transactions is that the assets and results of operations of the discontinued part of the business can be clearly distinguished physically, operationally, and for financial accounting purposes from other assets, results of operations, and activities of the enterprise. The inability to identify separately the results of operations of the discontinued unit suggests that the transaction is not a disposal of a *segment* of the business.

To illustrate the accounting and reporting for the disposal of a segment, assume that Ball Company has determined its preliminary aggregate operating figures for 1996 as follows:

Revenue from sales	$8,000,000
Cost of goods sold	3,500,000
Operating expenses	2,000,000
	5,500,000
Income before income tax	$2,500,000

At the end of the year, the company disposed of its nuts and bolts division, which was operationally separate from the rest of the business. Operating results of this division, which are included in these aggregate figures, are as follows:

Revenue from sales	$1,500,000
Cost of goods sold	1,400,000
Operating expenses	800,000
	2,200,000
Income before income tax	$ (700,000)

In addition, the actual disposal of the nuts and bolts division resulted in a $450,000 nonoperating loss before income tax, which is *not* included in the preceding figures:

Proceeds from the sale of nuts and bolts division	$ 6,500,000
Net book value of assets of nuts and bolts division	(6,950,000)
Loss on sale before income tax	$ (450,000)

The appropriate income tax rate for all items is 40%.

---

[20]Leopold A. Bernstein, "Reporting the Results of Operations—A Reassessment of APB Opinion No. 9," *Journal of Accountancy* (July 1970), pp. 57–58.

[21]*APB Opinion No. 30,* "Reporting the Results of Operations," 1973, par. 13–18.

EXHIBIT 21–11

Ball Company
Income Statement
For the Year Ended December 31, 1996

Revenue from sales		$6,500,000
Cost of goods sold	$2,100,000	
Operating expenses	1,200,000	3,300,000
Income from continuing operations before income tax		3,200,000
Income tax expense (at 40%)		1,280,000
Income from continuing operations		1,920,000
Discontinued operations		
Loss from operations of discontinued nuts and bolts		
division, less applicable income taxes of $280,000	(420,000)	
Loss on disposal of nuts and bolts division, less		
applicable income taxes of $180,000	(270,000)	(690,000)
Net income		$1,230,000
Earnings per share		
Income from continuing operations		$1.92
Discontinued operations		
Loss from operations of nuts and bolts division	$(.42)	
Loss on disposal of nuts and bolts division	(.27)	(.69)
Net income		$1.23

The presentation of discontinued operations for Ball Company is illustrated in the income statement in Exhibit 21–11. The revenue and expense amounts for continuing operations are determined by removing the figures for the discontinued division. For example, revenues of $6,500,000 are determined by eliminating the $1,500,000 revenues of the discontinued segment from the $8,000,000 of total revenues ($8,000,000 − $1,500,000 = $6,500,000). The earnings per share figures are computed on the basis of 1,000,000 shares of common stock outstanding with no preferred stock.

The disposal of a major segment of a business enterprise frequently takes place over an extended period of time. It is not unusual for such a disposal to begin in one accounting period and extend into one or more future accounting periods. In this situation, two dates are particularly important:

Measurement Date—The date on which the management having the authority to approve the action commits itself to a formal plan to dispose of a segment of the business, whether by sale or abandonment. The plan of disposal should include, as a minimum, identification of the major assets to be disposed of, the expected manner of disposal, the period expected to be required for completion of the disposal, an active program to find a buyer if disposal is to be by sale, the estimated results of operations of the segment from the measurement date to the disposal date, and the estimated proceeds or salvage to be realized by disposal.

Disposal Date—The date of closing the sale if the disposal is by sale or the date that operations cease if the disposal is by abandonment.[22]

If the **measurement date** is in one accounting period and the **disposal date** is in a subsequent accounting period, accounting for the disposal of the segment is more complex.

In presenting discontinued operations, any operating results after the measurement date are included in the gain or loss from *disposal* of the discontinued segment, rather than as the

---

[22]*APB Opinion No. 30,* par. 14.

results of operations. At the measurement date, if a loss is expected from the planned disposal, the estimated loss is recognized immediately. On the other hand, an anticipated gain from the disposal is not recognized until the gain is realized, which is usually at the disposal date. This procedure results in a *conservative* presentation of income.

Conservatism

In estimating whether a gain or loss will result from the disposal of the segment, the net amount expected to be received from the disposal includes any estimated costs and expenses directly associated with the disposal. Additionally, if the disposal will take time and if continued operations of the segment are planned during a phaseout period, any estimated income or loss from operations is included in the estimated gain or loss on the disposal. Amounts of income or loss from operations included in the gain or loss on disposal are limited to amounts that can be reasonably projected. Normally, such projections should not exceed one year.

Disclosure

In addition to the information presented in the discontinued operations section of the income statement, the notes to the financial statements must disclose the following information:[23]

1. The identity of the segment of the business that has been or will be discontinued.
2. The expected disposal date, if known.
3. The expected manner of disposal.
4. A description of the remaining assets and liabilities of the segments at the financial statement date.
5. The income or loss from operations and any proceeds from disposal of the segment during the period from the measurement date to the financial statement date.

Many of the items that must be disclosed are also necessary to establish the measurement date. Such information is frequently made available only through management action and estimates. Accountants, therefore, should attempt to gather additional objective evidence to support the assertions and disclosures contained in the financial statements.

When discontinued operations are presented in comparative financial statements, the operating results of the discontinued part of the business must be reclassified for the comparative year(s) for purposes of comparability and an amount of income from continuing operations presented for all years that are included in the statement.

Reporting discontinued operations has provided the backdrop for interesting accounting research. One study observes that the definitions in *APB Opinion No. 30* are sufficiently ambiguous to permit companies substantial latitude in reporting the effect of discontinued operations as components of income from continuing operations or separately as discontinued operations. The authors raise the question of whether by reporting relatively more gains in income from continuing operations and relatively more losses as discontinued operations, companies may convey a greater likelihood of recurring positive future prospects than would be the case if both gains and losses were reported as discontinued operations. The results of investigating 504 discontinued operations in 1985–1986 indicate that, in fact, more gains were presented as part of continuing operations (61%) than were losses (39%). Consistent with this conclusion is the fact that discontinued operations resulting in losses were more likely presented separately as discontinued operations (57%) rather than as part of continuing operations (43%). The authors conclude that the ambiguity in the authoritative literature surrounding the definition of what constitutes a disposal of a segment, as well as criteria for distinguishing a segment's activities from the rest of the company, may be leading to incon-

---

[23]*APB Opinion No. 30*, par. 18.

sistent application of *APB Opinion No. 30,* thereby blurring the distinction between recurring and nonrecurring events that affect net income.[24]

Exhibit 21–12 presents the disclosure of discontinued operations from the income statement of Sears, Roebuck and Company for 1991–1993. As explained in the note, which is also presented in Exhibit 21–12, the company sold Coldwell Banker Residential business and the Sears Mortgage Banking operations, resulting in a $64 million after-tax loss that is included in the discontinued operations section of the statement. The income statements also include an extraordinary loss (1993) and a cumulative effect of accounting change (1992).

COMPREHENSIVE MODEL INCOME STATEMENT

The income statement in Exhibit 21–13 incorporates many of the revenue, expense, gain, and loss items discussed in this chapter and in previous chapters. The influence of the all-inclusive approach can be seen in the inclusion of the discontinued operations, extraordinary gain, cumulative effect of change in depreciation method, and other revenues and expenses not directly related to operations. On the other hand, the influence of the current operating performance approach can be seen in the separation of these items from normal, recurring transactions and the resulting subtotals, such as income from operations, income from continuing operations, and income before extraordinary item and cumulative effect of change in accounting principle.

The following aspects of this statement are particularly worthy of attention and provide a review of several concepts covered earlier:

1. The provision for income tax (e.g., $761 in 1996) incorporates the income tax effects of all transactions presented above that item in the income statement. All items in the statement below this item are presented on a net of tax basis.

2. The major types of irregular items are presented in the following order: discontinued operations, extraordinary item, and cumulative effect of a change in accounting principle. Appropriate titles are assigned to the income figures that *precede* each of these items.

3. The discontinued segment is presented immediately before the extraordinary item and is divided into the results of *operations* of the discontinued segment and the loss on the *disposal* of the discontinued segment. This section is preceded by the caption "income from continuing operations." All items in this section are presented on a net of tax basis.

4. The extraordinary gain is separately disclosed after the discontinued operations section and is presented on a net of tax basis.

5. The cumulative effect of the change in depreciation method follows the extraordinary item and is presented on a net of tax basis.

6. The earnings per share and pro forma effects of the retroactive application of the newly adopted accounting principle are presented at the bottom of the income statement, following net income.

Although it is unlikely that a single income statement would contain all the irregular items in Exhibit 21–13, it is important to understand the relation of each item to the others and to the income statement as a whole. The fictitious Morrow Company statement is presented to facilitate this understanding.

As we approach the end of our discussion of revenue measurement and income presentation, we again consider areas in which professional judgment is important in applying generally accepted accounting principles. Early in this chapter, we established the importance of revenue being earned, measurable, and collectible as prerequisites for recognition. All of these may involve judgment on the part of the accountant. Whether revenue is earned is a matter of

PROFESSIONAL JUDGMENT

---

[24]Donna Rapaccioli and Allen Schiff, "Reporting Sales of Segments under APB Opinion No. 30," *Accounting Horizons* (December 1991), pp. 51–59.

EXHIBIT 21–12

Sears, Roebuck and Co.
Presentation of Discontinued Operations

Income Statement Excerpt

(in millions, except per common share data)	Year Ended December 31		
	1993	**1992**	**1991**
Income (loss) from continuing operations	**2,409.1**	(2,566.8)	915.6
Discontinued operations (note 3)			
Operating income, less income tax expense of $167.7, $299.2 and $231.0	**240.1**	507.9	363.3
Loss on disposal, including income tax expense of $22.0	**(64.0)**	—	—
Income (loss) before extraordinary loss and cumulative effect of accounting changes	**2,585.2**	(2,058.9)	1,278.9
Extraordinary loss related to early extinguishment of debt (note 10)	**(210.8)**	—	—
Cumulative effect of accounting changes (note 2)	—	(1,873.4)	—
Net income (loss)	**$2,374.4**	$(3,932.3)	$1,278.9
Earnings (loss) per common share, after allowing for dividends on preferred shares (note 14)			
Income (loss) from continuing operations	**$6.22**	$ (7.02)	$2.65
Discontinued operations	**0.46**	1.37	1.06
Income (loss) before extraordinary loss and cumulative effect of accounting changes	**6.68**	(5.65)	3.71
Extraordinary loss	**(0.55)**	—	—
Cumulative effect of accounting changes	—	(5.07)	—
Net income (loss)	**$6.13**	$(10.72)	$3.71
Average common and common equivalent shares outstanding	**382.9**	369.6	343.8

Financial Statement Note
Note 3   Discontinued operations

In March 1993, Dean Witter completed a primary initial public offering of 19.9% of its common stock. The Company did not recognize a gain on this transaction. On June 18, 1993, the Company's Board of Directors approved a tax-free spin-off of Dean Witter to the Company's common shareholders. Sears common shareholders of record on June 28, 1993 received, effective June 30, 1993, .3903 shares of Dean Witter for each Sears common share owned. This transaction resulted in a noncash dividend to Sears common shareholders totaling $2.29 billion.

In May 1993, the Company entered into separate agreements to sell the Coldwell Banker Residential business and the Sears Mortgage Banking operations. A $64.0 million after-tax loss was recorded in the second quarter of 1993 primarily due to adverse income tax effects related to the sale of Sears Savings Bank. These sales were completed in the fourth quarter of 1993.

The operating results of the discontinued operations are summarized below:

(in millions)	Year Ended December 31		
	1993	**1992**	**1991**
Dean Witter, Discover & Co.			
Revenues	$2,832.2	$5,233.1	$4,942.0
Income	247.8	434.3	336.9
Coldwell Banker Residential Services			
Revenues	$1,203.7	$1,523.4	$1,392.2
Income (loss)	(7.7)	73.6	26.4

SOURCE: Sears, Roebuck and Co., 1993 Annual Report.

EXHIBIT 21–13

Morrow Company
Income Statements
For the Years Ended December 31, 1995 and 1996
(in thousands of dollars except earnings-per-share figures)

	1996	1995
Sales	$5,525	$5,108
Cost of goods sold	2,100	1,950
Gross margin	3,425	3,158
Selling and administrative expenses	1,250	1,200
Income from operations	2,175	1,958
Other income		
Gain on sale of plant assets	—	100
Dividend income	75	80
Other expenses		
Interest on long-term debt	(255)	(307)
Unrealized loss on investments	(92)	—
Income before income tax	1,903	1,831
Provision for income tax	761	732
Income from continuing operations	1,142	1,099
Discontinued operations		
Loss from operations of business segment, net of applicable income tax savings of $44 in 1996 and $48 in 1995	(66)	(72)
Loss on disposal of business segment, net of applicable income tax savings of $80	(120)	—
Income before extraordinary item and cumulative effect of change in accounting principle	956	1,027
Extraordinary item—gain on forced sale of assets to state municipality, net of applicable income taxes of $350	—	525
Cumulative effect of change in method of depreciation, net of applicable income taxes of $68	(102)	—
Net income	$ 854	$1,552
Earnings per common share		
Income from continuing operations	$11.42	$10.99
Discontinued operations	(1.86)	(.72)
Income before extraordinary item and cumulative effect of accounting change	9.56	10.27
Extraordinary gain	—	5.25
Cumulative effect of change in accounting principle	(1.02)	—
Net income	$ 8.54	$15.52
Pro forma amounts assuming retroactive application of new depreciation method		
Income before extraordinary item	$ 956	$ 967
Earnings per common share	$ 9.56	$ 9.67
Net income	$ 956	$1,492
Earnings per common share	$ 9.56	$14.92

net of Tax

judgment concerning whether the primary economic activity that results in the creation of revenue has been completed. Whether revenue is measurable is a matter of judgment concerning whether amounts are sufficiently objective to permit formal incorporation into the company's accounts and its financial statements. Collectibility, too, requires judgment as to whether the receivable resulting from a sales transaction can reasonably be expected to be received or an estimate of the uncollectible amount can be objectively made. Other judgments may be required when a selection must be made among available alternative methods of recognition (e.g., percentage-of-completion versus completed-contracts accounting and whether circumstances warrant use of the installment sales method). Applying revenue-recognition methods may also require judgment, such as the need to estimate returns when a right of return exists. In short, revenue recognition is a highly judgmental process that requires careful analysis by the accountant.

Classifying transactions in special categories for income presentation may also require judgment. We have learned, for example, that extraordinary items are "unusual in nature" and "infrequent in occurrence." Both of these descriptions require judgment in application. Discontinued operations presentation is based, in part, on a judgment concerning future profitability of the discontinued business unit. We learned that current research suggests that ambiguity in the authoritative accounting literature concerning definitions of discontinued operations may have resulted in reporting practices that distort the intent of the authoritative literature to distinguish between recurring and nonrecurring gains and losses in the income statement. These ambiguous definitions require even more careful analysis and judgment by professional accountants than would be the case if the definitions contained greater clarity.

Not only is professional judgment very important in measuring revenue and presenting income but also the implications of the judgments are particularly important due to the significance of income in the overall picture of financial reporting. Determining and reporting income is well established as one of the most important objectives of financial reporting, placing great responsibility on the judgment of accountants in analyzing revenue-generating activities and presenting information in the income statement and related notes.

CONCLUDING REMARKS

Income presentation is one of the central themes of corporate financial reporting. In meeting the objectives of financial reporting, the income statement and information derived from that statement are particularly important. In this chapter, we have discussed revenue realization at the point of sale as the norm, and we have identified and illustrated several situations in which revenue is logically recognized at times other than the point of sale. We have also seen that careful preparation of the income statement and the proper ordering and wording of items within that statement are important in meeting the objectives of financial reporting. Although there is evidence in recent years that the FASB is placing increased emphasis on the balance sheet in developing financial reporting standards, the income statement remains a vital part of financial reporting. Careful recognition of revenue and preparation of the income statement will undoubtedly continue to be a major responsibility of accountants in the future.

KEY POINTS

1. Revenue is not recognized until it is earned, measurable, and collectible. In many situations, these conditions are met at the point of sale, although departures from revenue recognition at the point of sale are found in certain circumstances. (Objective 1)

2. The percentage-of-completion and completed-contract methods of accounting for long-term contracts are acceptable in different circumstances. Within the percentage-of-completion method, revenue is recognized throughout the construction period as objective evidence indicates the proper amount to be recognized. Within the completed-contract method, all revenue is deferred and recognized at the completion of the contract. (Objective 2)

3. The installment sales method defers the recognition of revenue until cash is collected, and this method is acceptable in financial reporting only when collectibility is highly uncertain. (Objective 3)

4. When customers have the right to return products, six conditions must be met before the revenue can be recognized. These conditions relate to the transfer of the risks and rewards of ownership from the seller to the buyer and the ability of the seller to make a reasonably objective estimate of the amount of returns. (Objective 4)

5. A major objective of financial reporting is to present information to investors and creditors concerning an enterprise's financial performance. The primary focus is information concerning earnings and its components. (Objective 5)

6. The presentation of income is carefully defined and structured in the authoritative literature. At the present time, income is presented in a manner consistent with a modified all-inclusive concept in that all items of profit and loss, except prior period adjustments, are included in the income statement. (Objective 6)

7. "Discontinued operations"—which follows the caption Income from Continuing Operations—is a separate section of the income statement and includes both the gain or loss from the disposal of a discontinued segment of the business and the operating income or loss of that segment. These items are separated from the income or loss from ongoing business activities. (Objective 6)

8. Discontinued operations, extraordinary items, and the cumulative effect of a general change in accounting principle are presented in separate income statement categories on a net of tax basis. (Objective 6)

APPENDIX A: SPECIAL REVENUE-RECOGNITION PRACTICES

This appendix considers the unique circumstances and business practices in several industries that require unusual or complex revenue-recognition practices. The general criteria for revenue recognition developed in the body of this chapter apply equally to special industries and routine situations. Therefore, when studying the appendix, consider carefully how each of the practices specified by the accounting profession is consistent with general concepts of revenue recognition. Although specific practices are discussed, the purpose of this appendix is to develop a conceptual understanding of these special industry circumstances rather than detailed knowledge of the accounting procedures that are applied.

REAL ESTATE TRANSACTIONS

A unique aspect of real estate transactions is that risk of uncollectible receivables is reduced by the nature of the asset sold. Land and other real property are relatively easily repossessed if the purchasing party fails to comply with the terms of the sales agreement. Real estate is not readily transportable, does not generally depreciate in value, and is frequently not susceptible to damage and destruction. Although these characteristics are usually associated with land, many structural improvements and buildings possess similar characteristics.

Because sellers of real estate recognize these characteristics of real estate, a greater credit risk may be assumed without creating an unacceptable risk of loss to the selling enterprise. Although the recovery of the investment in real estate may be ensured to a greater degree than in other types of sales, the recognition of additional sales revenue should be carefully considered when the buyer is a poor credit risk.

The AICPA considered these circumstances and issued an *Industry Accounting Guide*,[25] which subsequently became part of *FASB Statement of Financial Accounting Standards No. 66*. In addition to the issues already mentioned, the guide recognized that many real estate transactions are exceptionally complex and that the legal form of the transaction may often obscure the real economic substance of an event.

Substance over Form

The accounting guide and the subsequent *SFAS No. 66* establish general criteria for the timing of recognition of revenue and provide modifying conventions for use when the conceptual criteria for revenue recognition are not met at the time of the sale.

> *[Revenue should be recognized] in full when real estate is sold, provided (a) the profit is measurable, that is, the collectibility of the sales price is reasonably assured or the amount that will not be collectible can be estimated, and (b) the earning process is virtually complete, that is, the seller is not obliged to perform significant activities after the sale to earn the profit. Unless both conditions exist, recognition of all or part of the profit shall be postponed.*[26]

If the collectibility of the sales price is uncertain, as is the case in many real estate transactions, the installment sales method of revenue-recognition or the even more conservative

---

[25]*AICPA Industry Accounting Guide*, "Accounting for Profit Recognition on Sales of Real Estate," 1973.

[26]*FASB Statement of Financial Accounting Standards No. 66*, "Accounting for Sales of Real Estate," 1982, par. 3.

cost recovery method should be used. In certain circumstances involving the collectibility of the sales price, the seller should use "deposit accounting," wherein no sale is presumed to have occurred and all cash received is treated as deferred revenue (liability) in the balance sheet. Furthermore, if the earning process is incomplete, recognition of revenue moves from the time of sale to the time of the seller's performance of the earning process. Finally, no profit is recognized until a sale is actually consummated.

Certain requirements must be met to recognize revenue when the receivables are material after the sale and completion of the earning process. These criteria relate to (1) the amount of the down payment, (2) the composition of the down payment, and (3) the terms regarding the receivable portion of the consideration.

In regard to the amount of the initial payment, a range from 5% to 25% of the purchase price, depending on the nature of the property sold, has been established for purposes of profit recognition.[27]

Even if a down payment is large enough to qualify for the recognition of profit, the composition of the payment and terms of collection must also be considered. Generally, the down payment must consist of cash or notes supported by irrevocable letters of credit from established lending institutions to support the immediate recognition of revenue. Buyers must also maintain a continuing financial commitment in that the payments being made must be sufficient to pay the total indebtedness, including interest, within 20 years for land and within normal first mortgage terms of financial institutions for other real estate.

If a buyer's down payment amount or quality or continuing investment is not adequate, the installment sales method is normally used to recognize revenue on the sale. However, if there is uncertainty as to whether cost will be recovered if a buyer defaults or if cost has already been recovered through down payment but future collections are uncertain, the cost recovery method of revenue recognition is employed.

ACCOUNTING FOR RETAIL LAND SALES

Land developers frequently acquire a large parcel of land, develop a master plan for subdivision and improvement, obtain construction approval, perform necessary improvements, and sell lots. Furthermore, certain characteristics inherent in retail land sales create special problems concerning the recognition of revenue and related expenses. Examples are small down payments, unenforceable sales contracts, and cancellation periods during which buyers can obtain refunds.

Consideration of the foregoing problems encouraged the AICPA to develop another *Industry Accounting Guide;* this one pertains to the timing and magnitude of revenue recognition.[28] This guide also became part of *SFAS No. 66.* In essence, *SFAS No. 66* contains the following requirements for recording a sale:[29]

1. The buyer must make a down payment and regular subsequent payments throughout the period covered by any cancellation with refund right.

2. The aggregate payments, including interest, must at least equal 10% of the contract sales price.

3. Collection experience on similar sales must indicate that collection of the receivable is reasonably ensured.

4. Generally, the receivable from the sale must not be subject to subordination to new loans on the property.

5. The seller must not be obligated to complete improvements of lots sold not to construct facilities applicable to lots sold.

For transactions in which the first four criteria are met and substantial progress has been made toward the completion of improvements and facilities (mentioned in requirement 5), the percentage-of-completion method is applicable.

ACCOUNTING FOR FRANCHISE ACTIVITIES

The growth of franchising as a means of commerce began intense acceleration during the 1960s and continues today. Such activities pose many contentious accounting and reporting issues which are addressed in *FASB Statement of Financial Accounting Standards No. 45.*[30] **Franchises** generally involve the creation or extension of a business in which two parties join together in a continuing contract with a joint public identity. Each party normally contributes resources. The **franchisor** frequently contributes products, processes, equipment, company reputation, and trademarks. The **franchisee** generally provides operating capital and managerial and operational resources. Franchise activities are extremely broad; they cut across industry lines and may vary in terms of organization, concept, and philosophy. For example, some franchise agreements provide for a relatively passive franchisor role, while others require extensive participation or the supply of products and skill on a continuing basis. Therefore, precise accounting and reporting standards are not possible. *FASB Statement No. 45* provides certain broad guidelines, however.

The franchise agreement contains the general bases for accounting and reporting practices. Most agreements require the franchisee to make a substantial initial payment, called a *franchise fee,* to the franchisor in consideration for the reputation, skill, products, and processes contributed by the franchisor. Properly accounting for the franchise fee in terms of revenue recognition requires careful study of the franchise agreement.

FASB Statement No. 45 notes that the problem of recognizing revenue in regard to franchise fees generally results from two issues: (1) the point at which the fee is to be considered earned and (2) the assessment of collectibility of any unpaid portion of the fee. Initial fees are generally quite specific and, therefore, the amount of the initial fee is usually known. Most franchise agreements also call for continuing payments related to the level of franchisee business. For example, continuing payments to franchisors are usually based on the sales of products to franchisees or on a percentage of the franchisee's sales or profits.

---

[27]*FASB Statement of Financial Accounting Standards No. 66,* par. 54.

[28]*AICPA Industry Accounting Guide,* "Accounting for Retail Land Sales," 1973.

[29]*FASB Statement of Financial Accounting Standards No. 66,* par. 45.

[30]*FASB Statement of Financial Accounting Standards No. 45,* "Accounting for Franchise Fee Revenue," 1981.

The three revenue-recognition practices that are used with franchises are summarized as follows:

1. **Cash basis.** This method calls for recording revenue when cash is received. Proponents cite its simplicity, the complexity of franchise agreements, and collection problems as support for this practice.
2. **Spread over life of agreement.** This method treats the initial fee as a prepayment for the privilege of using franchise rights. The prepayment is recognized ratably over the life of the franchise agreement. Franchisors agree that the franchise fee is payment for a confirmation of initial and continuing services and transfers of rights.
3. **Inception of the franchise agreement.** This method treats the sale of a franchise in a manner similar to the sale of any other commercial property, tangible or intangible. The sale represents the transfer of specified rights in exchange for specified consideration and thus supports the recognition of revenue at the point of sale.

FASB Statement No. 45 finds merit in each argument under certain separate circumstances and indirectly supports each in specific individual situations. Revenue is recognized when a franchise sale occurs *and* when all material obligations of the franchisor have been *substantially performed.* Substantial performance may take place at different points in time under different franchise agreements. Even if the franchise agreement requires no further franchisor services, revenue is not recognized if business conditions or informal policy indicate that the franchisor is likely to render substantial voluntary services.

Any unpaid franchise fees must also be assessed as to collectibility prior to the recognition of revenue. If collection of the franchise fee is uncertain, the installment method or cost recovery method may be necessary to avoid premature recognition of revenue.

QUESTIONS

21–1 What three conditions must be met for revenue to be recognized?

21–2 Why is the point of sale frequently used as the point of revenue recognition?

21–3 Why do long-term contracts pose a difficult revenue-recognition problem?

21–4 Under what circumstances should the percentage-of-completion method of recognizing revenue on long-term contracts be used?

21–5 Under what circumstances should the completed-contract method of recognizing revenue on long-term contracts be used?

21–6 What is the difference in accounting treatment of contract revenues and costs under the percentage-of-completion and completed-contract methods?

21–7 Assuming that a contract was started in 1993 and is completed in 1995, explain the procedure for estimating the amount of gross profit in each year if the percentage of completion is determined based on costs incurred to date as a percentage of total expected costs.

21–8 Under what circumstances is the installment sales method appropriate for financial reporting purposes? How does this method differ from recognizing revenue at the point of sale?

21–9 What are the six criteria that must be met for revenue to be recognized if the customer has the right to return the purchased products? If one or more of these conditions are not met, what accounting procedures are appropriate?

21–10 How does the presentation of income contribute to meeting the primary objectives of financial reporting?

21–11 How does the presentation of income assist in judging management efficiency?

21–12 Explain the concept of *value added income.* How does it differ from the concept of income underlying the income statement as currently prepared?

21–13 What is the difference between *income to stockholders* and *income to residual stockholders?*

21–14 Distinguish between the all-inclusive and current operating performance definitions of income in terms of the meaning of the final income figure resulting from each.

21–15 Distinguish between the FASB's concepts of *comprehensive income* and *earnings.*

21–16 What is the basic objective of intraperiod income tax allocation? Why is this procedure needed and how does it affect the content of financial statements?

21–17 What determines a "segment" in deciding whether the disposal of a portion of a business qualifies for separate disclosure in a discontinued operations section of the income statement?

21–18 What is the meaning of the income subtotal "income from continuing operations"?

21–19 How does *measurement date* differ from *disposal date?* Explain their significance in reporting discontinued operations in the income statement.

21–20 What is a rule for identifying those revenues, expenses, gains, and losses that must be presented on a net of tax basis in the income statement?

21–21 Which of the following is an example of an extraordinary item in reporting results of operations?

[a] A loss incurred because of a strike by employees.

[b] The write-off of deferred research and development costs believed to have no future benefit.

[c] A gain resulting from the devaluation of the U.S. dollar.

[d] A gain resulting from the state exercising its right of eminent domain on a piece of land used as a parking lot. (AICPA adapted)

21–22 Which of the following is *not* a generally practiced method of presenting the income statement?

[a] Including prior period adjustments in determining net income.

[b] Using the single-step income statement.

[c] Including the cumulative effect of a change in accounting principle in determining net income.

[d] Including gains and losses from discontinued operations of a segment of a business in determining net income. (AICPA adapted)

21–23 Which of the following shows how the gain or loss from an event or transaction that meets the criteria for infrequent occurrence but not unusual nature should be disclosed?

[a] Separately in the earnings statement immediately after earnings from continuing operations.

[b] On a net of tax basis in the earnings statement immediately after earnings from continuing operations.

[c] As an extraordinary item and treated accordingly in the earnings statement.

[d] Separately in the earnings statement as a component of earnings from continuing operations. (AICPA adapted)

21–24 When a company discontinues an operation and disposes of the discontinued segment, the transaction should be included in the earnings statement as a gain or loss on disposal reported as which of the following?

[a] A prior period adjustment.

[b] An extraordinary item.

[c] An amount after continuing operations and before extraordinary items.

[d] A bulk sale of fixed assets included in earnings from continuing operations. (AICPA adapted)

EXERCISES

 21–25 Long-Term Contract   Matthews Construction Company began work on a contract in 1995 and completed the contracted work in 1996. The total contract price was $4,200,000. Information concerning the contract for 1995 and 1996 is as follows:

	1995	1996
Costs incurred during year	$ 800,000	$3,150,000
Estimated costs to complete at end of year	2,400,000	–0–
Billings during year	720,000	3,280,000
Collections during year	400,000	3,000,000

INSTRUCTIONS

[a] Determine the amount of the $4,200,000 contract price to be recognized each year under the completed-contract method.

[b] Determine the amount of the $4,200,000 contract price to be recognized each year under the percentage-of-completion method.

21–26 Long-Term Contract   Foster Construction Company contracted to construct a building for $450,000. Foster began construction in 1995 and completed the project in 1996. Cost information for the project is as follows:

	1995	1996
Costs incurred	$200,000	$140,000
Estimated costs to complete	100,000	—

Foster uses the percentage-of-completion method for recognizing income on the contract.

INSTRUCTIONS

[a] Determine the amount of income that the company should recognize in 1995 and 1996.

[b] Prove the amount of income you have computed in [a] by computing the total income on the contract and comparing it with the incomes you have computed for 1995 and 1996.

[c] Prepare the journal entry required at the end of each year to recognize that year's income.

21–27 Installment Sales Mall Company, which began business on January 1, 1995, appropriately uses the installment sales method to recognize revenue because of the uncertainty of the collection of its receivables. The following data pertain to 1995 and 1996:

	1995	1996
Installment sales	$350,000	$420,000
Cost of installment sales	280,000	315,000
General and administrative expenses	35,000	42,000
Cash collections on installment sales of:		
1995	150,000	135,000
1996	—	225,000

INSTRUCTIONS

[a] Determine the balance in the Deferred Gross Profit account at December 31, 1996.

[b] A 1995 sale resulted in a default in 1996. At the date of default, the balance of the installment receivable was $6,400, and the repossessed merchandise had a fair value of $4,800. Assuming the repossessed merchandise is recorded at fair value, determine the amount of gain or loss on the repossession. (AICPA adapted)

21–28 Installment Sales Ratner Company sells appliances through installment contracts. Because of the uncertainty of collection and the relatively high potential for repossession, the company appropriately recognizes revenue on an installment basis, deferring revenue recognition until cash is collected.

During 1995 Ratner determined that its gross profit percentage was 40%; during 1996 this percentage increased to 42%. Of $150,000 sales in 1995, Ratner collected $70,000 in 1995 and $50,000 in 1996. Of $170,000 sales in 1996, Ratner had collected $105,000 by year-end.

INSTRUCTIONS

For 1995 and 1996, compute the amounts of gross profit to be recognized and the amounts to be deferred at the end of the year.

21–29 Rent Collected in Advance On August 1, 1996, Wilcox Company received $110,000 for one year's advance rent on space that it leases to another company. Wilcox Company's fiscal year ends on October 31.

INSTRUCTIONS

[a] Determine the portion of the $110,000 that should be recognized as revenue for the fiscal year ending October 31, 1996.

[b] Prepare the adjusting journal entry Wilcox should make on October 31, 1996, if the $110,000 was credited to Unearned Rent Revenue when it was received.

[c] Prepare the adjusting journal entry the company should make on October 31, 1996, if the $110,000 was credited to Rent Revenue when it was received.

21–30 Right of Return Clark Company sold $225,000 of merchandise on credit to its customers during 1996. The cost of this merchandise was $153,000, and Clark uses a perpetual inventory system. Based on past trends, Clark expects returns of 2.5% of sales within 90 days of the sales transaction. During 1996 cash collections of receivables were $185,000, and the selling price of merchandise returned totaled $3,100.

INSTRUCTIONS

[a] Prepare journal entries for all transactions and events for Clark Company for 1996, its first year of operations.

[b] Indicate the items and dollar amounts that will appear in the 1996 income statement as a result of these events.

21–31 Intraperiod Income Tax Allocation Robin, Inc., has properly determined its taxable income for 1995 to be $650,500, including a gain of $125,000 resulting from a transaction that will be presented as "extraordinary." The appropriate income tax rate for all items is 36%.

INSTRUCTIONS

[a] Determine the income tax expense to be included in the 1995 income statement.

[b] Describe the disclosure of the extraordinary gain to be included in the 1995 income statement.

21–32 Intraperiod Income Tax Allocation   Mowery Company has determined the following items for 1995:

Pretax financial income	$158,500
Income (loss) items not included in pretax financial income:	
Correction of error in 1994 financial statements	7,500
Extraordinary loss	(16,250)
Retained earnings, Jan. 1, 1995, as previously stated	525,000
Dividends declared during 1995	40,000
Income tax rate	30%

The company's reporting period is January 1–December 31.

INSTRUCTIONS

[a] Prepare the income statement, beginning with "income before income tax," for 1995, properly recognizing intraperiod income tax allocation requirements.

[b] Prepare the retained earnings statement for 1995, properly recognizing intraperiod income tax allocation requirements.

21–33 Extraordinary Item   Tilson Production Company determines its pretax financial income for 1995 to be $1,420,000. The appropriate income tax rate for all income items is 35%, and no permanent or temporary differences are involved. The company's reporting period ends on December 31. Included in pretax financial income are the following items:

[1] A loss of $335,000 on the destruction of a plant facility from a natural disaster. This item is considered both unusual in nature and infrequent in occurrence.

[2] A gain of $25,700 on the sale of stock owned in another company. Although Tilson does not buy and sell stock investments often, this type of transaction is common for companies of this type.

INSTRUCTIONS

Prepare the income statement to the extent possible from the information given, beginning with "income before income tax."

21–34 Special Income Items   Fairfield Fashions, Inc., has correctly determined the following information related to operations for 1995:

Revenue from sales	$650,000
Expenses	415,000
Income before income tax	$235,000

In reviewing the company's records, you discover the following items:

[1] During 1995 the company discovered an error in the amount of depreciation recognized in 1993 and 1994. The correction of this error, which has not been recorded, will result in an increase in depreciation for 1993 of $42,000 and for 1994 of $37,000.

[2] During 1995 an inventory loss of $37,800 was due to a government ban on certain highly flammable fabrics. This loss was considered both unusual and infrequent and has not been recorded.

During 1995 dividends of $62,500 were paid on 62,500 shares of common stock, which were outstanding throughout 1995. Income taxes are to be recognized at 30% on all income items.

INSTRUCTIONS

Assuming that retained earnings at January 1, 1995, were previously reported as $415,500, prepare a partial income statement and a retained earnings statement for Fairfield Fashions, Inc., for calendar year 1995.

21–35 Discontinued Operations   Presley Company, a holding company, has two operating subsidiaries: one manufacturing wheelbarrows and the other manufacturing toothbrushes. The wheelbarrow subsidiary has been unprofitable, and in late December 1995, management contracted to sell that subsidiary to another company for $60,000. The sale will be effective on April 1, 1996. Presley will operate the wheelbarrow subsidiary during the first three months of 1996, even though those operations are expected to result in a $10,000 loss (before income taxes).

At December 31, 1995, the carrying amount of Presley's investment in the wheelbarrow subsidiary is $100,000. Both the $40,000 loss on the sale of the investment and the $10,000 operating loss will be deductible on Presley's 1996 income tax return, resulting in an anticipated tax savings at an assumed 34% tax rate.

INSTRUCTIONS

Determine the amount of the "loss on disposal of wheelbarrow subsidiary, net of applicable income tax benefit," which should be presented in Presley's income statement for the year ended December 31, 1995. (AICPA adapted)

21–36 Extraordinary Items The December 31, 1996, financial statements of Smyth Corporation reported a total of $325,000 under the caption "extraordinary losses." An analysis further revealed that the $325,000 in losses comprised the following items:

[1] Smyth recorded a loss of $82,000 in the abandonment of equipment formerly used in the business.

[2] In an unusual and infrequent occurrence, a warehouse sustained a loss of $70,000 as a result of hurricane damage.

[3] During 1996 several factories were shut down during a major strike by employees. Shutdown expenses totaled $140,000.

[4] Accounts receivable of $33,000 were written off as uncollectible.

INSTRUCTIONS

[a] Ignoring income taxes, compute the amount of loss that Smyth should report as extraordinary on its 1996 statement of income.

[b] Explain the proper disclosure, if any, for any of the four items that should not be reported as extraordinary items. (AICPA adapted)

21–37 Discontinued Operations The following condensed statement of income of Banner Corporation, a diversified company, is presented for the two years ended December 31, 1996 and 1995.

	1996	1995
Net sales	$5,000,000	$4,800,000
Cost of sales	3,100,000	3,000,000
Gross profit	1,900,000	1,800,000
Operating expenses	1,100,000	1,200,000
Operating income	800,000	600,000
Gain on sale of division	450,000	–0–
Income before income taxes	1,250,000	600,000
Provision for income taxes	437,500	210,000
Net income	$ 812,500	$ 390,000

On January 1, 1996, Banner entered into an agreement to sell for $1,600,000 the assets and product line of one of its separate operating divisions. The sale was consummated on December 31, 1996, and resulted in a pretax gain on disposition of $450,000. This division's contribution to reported operating income before income taxes for each year was as follows:

1996	$(320,000) loss
1995	(250,000) loss

Assume an income tax rate of 35%.

INSTRUCTIONS

[a] What amounts should Banner present in a revised comparative statement of income for "income from continuing operations" for 1995 and 1996?

[b] What amounts should Banner present in a revised comparative statement of income for "discontinued operations" for 1995 and 1996? (AICPA adapted)

21–38 Special Income Items Fowler Company reports income before income tax of $952,000 for 1996. This figure *includes* the following items, which may require adjustment and/or reclassification before the formal income statement can be prepared:

[1] A change in depreciation method from the straight-line to the accelerated method resulted in a $40,000 loss that was due to the cumulative effect on previous years. Depreciation for 1996 was computed on the accelerated method.

[2] A gain of $127,500 on the excess of insurance recovery over the book value of a plant destroyed by a hurricane. This was the first hurricane in the county in over a century.

[3] A gain of $18,700 on the sale of noncurrent marketable equity securities.

All items are subject to 38% income tax except the gains on insurance recovery and on the sale of securities, which are subject to 25% income tax. The end of the fiscal year is November 30, 1996.

INSTRUCTIONS

Prepare the income statement, beginning with "income before income tax," and provide computations. You may omit earnings per share figures.

21–39 Income Statement Presentation   Brooks Company has accumulated information to be used to prepare its income statement of the year ended December 31, 1996. All items are on a pretax basis.

Sales	$7,750,000
Cost of goods sold	4,200,000
Operating expenses	1,600,000
Interest revenue	125,000
Extraordinary loss from major casualty	55,000
Cumulative effect (gain) of change in accounting principle	138,000
Number of outstanding shares of common stock throughout 1996	120,00
Income tax rate applicable to all items	35%

INSTRUCTIONS

Prepare a multiple-step income statement for 1996 to conform with GAAP.

21–40 Correction of Income Statement   Valler, Inc., has prepared a preliminary income statement for 1996 as follows:

Valler, Inc.
Income Statement
For the Year Ended December 31, 1996

Sales		$545,000
Cost of goods sold		241,000
Gross profit		304,000
Operating expenses		110,000
Income before special items		194,000
Special items		
Gain on the sale of land	$60,000	
Interest expense	(12,500)	
Cumulative effect of change in method of overhead recognition	(35,800)	11,700
Income before income tax		205,700
Income tax expense		73,280
Net income		$132,420

You have been engaged to review this statement and revise it as appropriate. You determine that the gain on the sale of land should be presented as an extraordinary item because it resulted from the forced sale caused by newly enacted legislation. All items are subject to a 40% income tax except this gain, which is subject to a special 25% rate.

INSTRUCTIONS

Prepare a revised income statement based on generally accepted accounting principles. (You may ignore earnings per share calculations.)

21–41 Financial Statement Classification   The following classification codes are to be used in completing this exercise:

Income Statement Categories/Items
1. Revenue.
2. Cost of goods sold.
3. Operating expenses.

4. Other revenues, expenses, gains, losses.
5. Discontinued operations.
6. Extraordinary items.
7. Cumulative effect of change in accounting principle.

Items Omitted from the Income Statement
8. Included in balance sheet.
9. Included in retained earnings statement.
10. Included in notes to the financial statements.
11. Omitted from the financial statements.

INSTRUCTIONS

Indicate the preferred code number for each of the following items. If an explanation is necessary, state it briefly. If more than one classification is needed, list all appropriate code numbers.

[a] Accumulated depreciation—buildings.
[b] Interest revenue.
[c] Loss of plant from hurricane.
[d] Revenues and expenses from segment disposed of during current year.
[e] Dividends declared.
[f] Gain on the sale of plant assets.
[g] Loss on expropriation of assets by foreign government.
[h] Annual bonus paid store manager.
[i] Impact on previous years earnings of changing depreciation method.
[j] Correction of error in inventory that was carried forward from previous year.
[k] Depreciation expense on manufacturing equipment.
[l] Loss on disposal of a segment of the business.
[m] Interest paid on outstanding debt.
[n] Loss on sale of temporary marketable securities.
[o] Accounting policies.
[p] Adjustment for change from unacceptable to acceptable accounting method.
[q] Details of outstanding debt issues.
[r] Revenue received in advance (to be earned in next accounting period).

PROBLEMS

21–42 Long-Term Contracts Buildco Construction Company began operations January 1, 1996. During the year, Buildco entered into a contract with Pepperdine Company to construct a manufacturing facility. At that time, Buildco estimated that it would take five years to complete the facility at a total cost of $4,800,000. The total contract price for construction of the facility is $5,800,000.

During 1996 Buildco incurred $1,250,000 in construction costs related to the project. Because of rising material and labor costs, the estimated cost to complete the contract at the end of 1996 is $3,750,000. Pepperdine was billed for and paid 30% of the contract price in accordance with the contract agreement.

INSTRUCTIONS

Prepare schedules to compute the amount of gross profit to be recognized for the year ended December 31, 1996, and the amount to be shown as "cost of uncompleted contract in excess of related billings" or "billings on uncompleted contracts in excess of related costs" at December 31, 1996, under each of the following methods:

[a] Completed-contract method.
[b] Percentage-of-completion method.

Provide supporting computations in good form.   (AICPA adapted)

21–43 Installment Sales Long Corporation sells farm machinery on the installment plan. On July 1, 1996. Long entered into an installment sale contract with Agriculture, Inc., for an eight-year period. Equal annual payments under the installment sale are $100,000 and are due on July 1. The first payment was made on July 1, 1996.

Additional information is as follows:

[1] The amount to be realized on an outright sale of similar farm machinery is $556,000.
[2] The cost of the farm machinery sold to Agriculture is $417,000.

[3] The finance charges relating to the installment period are $163,000 based on a stated interest rate of 8%, which is appropriate.

[4] The collection of installments due under the contract is reasonably ensured.

INSTRUCTIONS

What income or loss before income taxes should Long record for the year ended December 31, 1996, as a result of the above transaction? Show supporting computations in good form.

(AICPA adapted)

21–44 Long-Term Contracts   Scott Construction Company recognizes income under the percentage-of-completion method on its long-term contracts. During 1994 the company entered into a fixed-price contract to construct a bridge for $15,000,000. Contract costs incurred and estimated costs to complete the bridge were

	Cumulative Contract Costs Incurred	Estimated Costs to Complete
At Dec. 31, 1994	$ 1,000,000	$8,000,000
At Dec. 31, 1995	5,500,000	5,500,000
At Dec. 31, 1996	10,000,000	2,000,000

INSTRUCTIONS

[a] Prepare a schedule and determine the estimated percentage of completion at the end of each year. (Round percentage to nearest two decimal points.)

[b] Prepare a schedule and determine the amount of revenue to be recognized each year. (Round dollars to the nearest thousand.)

[c] Prepare a schedule and determine the amount of income to be recognized each year.

[d] Prepare journal entries to record transactions for 1994 using the percentage-of-completion method, assuming that Scott billed its client $1,325,000 in 1994, of which $1,200,000 has been collected by the end of the year.

(AICPA adapted)

21–45 Installment Sales   Mann Company sells computers. On January 1, 1996, Mann entered into an installment sale contract with Banner Company for a seven-year period expiring December 31, 2002. Equal annual payments under the installment sale are $1,000,000 and are due on January 1. The first payment was made on January 1, 1996.

ADDITIONAL INFORMATION

[1] The cash selling price of the computer (i.e., the amount that would be realized on an outright sale) is $5,355,000.

[2] The cost of sales relating to the computer is $4,284,000.

[3] The finance charges relating to the installment period are $1,645,000—based on a stated interest rate of 10%, which is appropriate. For tax purposes, Mann appropriately uses the accrual basis for recording finance charges.

[4] Circumstances indicate that the collection of the installment sale is reasonably ensured.

[5] The installment sale qualifies for the installment method of reporting for tax purposes.

[6] Assume that the income tax rate is 30%.

INSTRUCTIONS

[a] What income (loss) before income taxes should Mann record as a result of this transaction for the year ended December 31, 1996? Show supporting computations in good form.

[b] What provision for deferred income taxes, if any, should Mann record as a result of this transaction for the year ended December 31, 1996? Show supporting computations in good form.

(AICPA adapted)

21–46 Long-Term Contracts   The directors of Platt Construction Company are meeting to determine which method of accounting for long-term construction contracts it should use in the company's financial statements, completed-contract or percentage-of-completion. You have been engaged to assist Platt's controller in preparing a presentation for the meeting.

The controller provides you with the following information:

[1] Platt commenced business on January 1, 1995.

[2] Construction activities for the year ended December 31, 1995, are summarized as follows:

Project	Total Contract Price	Billings through Dec. 31, 1995	Cash Collections through Dec. 31, 1995	Contract Costs Incurred through Dec. 31, 1995	Estimated Additional Costs to Complete Contracts
A	$ 520,000	$ 350,000	$ 310,000	$ 424,000	$106,000
B	670,000	210,000	210,000	126,000	504,000
C	475,000	475,000	395,000	315,000	—
D	200,000	70,000	50,000	112,750	92,250
E	460,000	400,000	400,000	370,000	30,000
	$2,325,000	$1,505,000	$1,365,000	$1,347,750	$732,250

[3] All contracts are with different customers.

[4] Any work remaining to be done on the contracts is expected to be completed in 1996.

INSTRUCTIONS

[a] Prepare a schedule by project to compute the amount of revenue and income (or loss) before selling, and general and administrative expenses for the year ended December 31, 1995, that would be reported under
[1] The completed-contract method.
[2] The percentage-of-completion method (based on estimated costs).

[b] Following is a balance sheet that compares balances resulting from the use of the two methods of accounting for long-term contracts. For each numbered blank space on the statement, supply the correct balance [indicating Dr. (Cr.) as appropriate]. Disregard income taxes.

Platt Construction Company
Balance Sheet
December 31, 1995

Assets	Completed-Contract Method	Percentage-of-Completion Method
Cash	$XXXX	$XXXX
Accounts receivable		
Due on contracts	(1)	(5)
Cost of uncompleted contracts in excess of billings	(2)	—
Costs and estimated earnings in excess of billings on uncompleted contracts	—	(6)
Property, plant, and equipment, net	XXXX	XXXX
Other assets	XXXX	XXXX
	$XXXX	$XXXX

Liabilities and Stockholders' Equity		
Accounts payable and accrued liabilities	$XXXX	$XXXX
Billings on uncompleted contracts in excess of costs	(3)	—
Billings in excess of costs and estimated earnings	—	(7)
Estimated losses on uncompleted contracts	(4)	—
Notes payable	XXXX	XXXX
Common stock	XXXX	XXXX
Retained earnings	XXXX	XXXX
	$XXXX	$XXXX

(AICPA adapted)

21–47 Income Statement   Newbert, Inc., has prepared an income statement for the year ended June 30, 1996. This statement is presented for your evaluation as follows:

Newbert, Inc.
Income Statement
For the Fiscal Year Ended June 30, 1996

Sales		$765,000
Cost of goods sold	$400,000	
Operating expenses	250,000	
Income tax expense	46,000	696,000
Income before extraordinary item		69,000
Extraordinary loss		24,000
Net income		$ 45,000

In reviewing the statement, you determine the following:

[1] The extraordinary loss resulted from the sale of a division of the company at $24,000 less than its book value. The division had been operating at a loss for several years, including a $15,000 operating loss contained in the sales and expense figures in the company's income statement. The income tax benefit of the operating loss has been considered in computing the $46,000 income tax expense. The accountant who prepared the statement was not aware, however, that the loss on disposal would result in a 40% income tax benefit and has included the entire $24,000 loss as an extraordinary item.

[2] The company sold 40,000 shares of common stock on October 31, 1995, resulting in a total of 120,000 shares outstanding. The company has no preferred stock. The accountant was unaware of the need to present earnings per share figures.

[3] All income items are subject to a 40% income tax rate.

INSTRUCTIONS

[a] Prepare a revised income statement beginning with "income before income tax" for the year ended June 30, 1996. Provide computations to support your figures.

[b] Comment on why the operating results of a discontinued segment is presented as part of "discontinued operations."

21–48 Income and Retained Earnings Statements   Parish Corporation is accumulating the last portions of financial data needed to prepare the financial statements for the year ended December 31, 1995. The retained earnings totaled $1,700,000 at January 1, 1995. Cash dividends of $39,000 were declared during 1995, but only $30,000 of these were paid in 1995. The 1995 estimated income before income taxes without considering the five activities described below is $920,000. The information regarding the following activities has been taken from the company's records:

[1] A lawsuit arising from a 1993 claim was settled by the company during 1995 for $70,000. The loss has not been accrued and is due for payment in March 1996.

[2] The company sold one of several buildings in its finishing division at a gain of $20,000.

[3] Parish experienced a $200,000 loss of timber in 1995 due to a flood resulting from the eruption of a volcano that had been inactive for over 50 years. The loss was not covered by insurance.

[4] The company changed its method for depreciating its buildings in 1995 from an accelerated method to straight line. Total depreciation on the buildings through the end of 1994 would have been $260,000 lower by using the straight-line method. The change was made for both book and tax purposes.

[5] Office equipment purchased in January 1994 for $36,000 was incorrectly debited to Office Supplies Expense. The straight-line method is used to depreciate office equipment for book and tax purposes. The office equipment was estimated to have a three-year life with no expected scrap value. This error has not been corrected.

Assume Parish Corporation is subject to a 40% income tax rate on all transactions.

INSTRUCTIONS

[a] [1] Calculate the 1995 income from operations before income tax for Parish Corporation identifying adjustments, if any, that need to be made to the estimated income of $920,000.

[2] Prepare a partial income statement for Parish for the year ended December 31, 1995, beginning with the amount for adjusted income from operations before income taxes as calculated above.

[b] Prepare a retained earnings statement for Parish for the year ended December 31, 1995.

(CMA adapted)

21–49 Income Statement Presented below is information concerning the results of operations of Palmer Corporation for the calendar year 1996:

Cost of goods sold	$2,985,000
Administrative expenses	1,300,000
Gain on the sale of marketable securities	15,000
Loss on sale of discontinued segment of business	95,000
Interest expense	65,000
Selling expenses	1,500,000
Sales	8,650,000
Loss on sale of plant assets	25,500
Cumulative effect (gain) resulting from change in depreciation method from double-declining balance to straight-line method	157,000
Correction of error (loss) in previous year's income, due to capitalization of research and development costs	76,000

The following additional information is available:

[1] All income items are subject to a 35% income tax rate except the loss on disposal of a segment of the company's operations, which is subject to a 20% income tax rate.

[2] The company had 1,000,000 shares of common stock outstanding from January 1 to June 30, when an additional 200,000 shares were sold. There was no other stock activity during 1996.

[3] The following amounts related to the disposed segment are included in the appropriate revenue and cost figures:

Sales	$750,000
Cost of goods sold	600,000
Selling expenses	100,000
Administrative expenses	350,000
Interest expense	10,000

INSTRUCTIONS

[a] Prepare an income statement for Palmer Corporation for the year ended December 31, 1996.

[b] Comment on why income items such as the cumulative effect of an accounting change and components of discontinued operations, are presented in the income statement on a net of tax basis.

21–50 Intraperiod Income Tax Allocation Utah Company is preparing comparative income and retained earnings statements for 1995 and 1996. The following selected information has been developed to date:

	Fiscal Year 1995	Fiscal Year 1996
Retained earnings, Nov. 1	$575,000	?
Pretax financial income	162,000	$135,000
Dividends declared	40,000	42,000
Extraordinary gain	18,700	—
Correction of prior periods—correction of error in 1994 financial statements (loss)	—	(24,000)
Effective income tax rate	38%	36%

There are no permanent or temporary differences in 1995 or 1996. Utah Company's fiscal year-end is October 31. The company had 78,000 shares of common stock outstanding throughout 1995 and 1996. The 1994 income tax rate was 38%. The items in the preceding schedule are included at their total amounts, before income tax consideration.

INSTRUCTIONS

[a] Prepare comparative statements of income and retained earnings for 1995 and 1996.

[b] Briefly explain the rationale for intraperiod income tax allocation.

21–51 Discontinued Operations Manson Company, a diversified manufacturing company, had four separate operating divisions engaged in the manufacture of products in each of the following areas: food products, health aids, textiles, and office equipment.

Financial data for the two years ended December 31, 1995 and 1996, are as follows:

	Net Sales		Cost of Sales		Operating Expenses	
	1996	**1995**	**1996**	**1995**	**1996**	**1995**
Food products	$3,500,000	$3,000,000	$2,400,000	$1,800,000	$ 550,000	$ 275,000
Health aids	2,000,000	1,270,000	1,100,000	700,000	300,000	125,000
Textiles	1,580,000	1,400,000	500,000	900,000	200,000	150,000
Office equipment	920,000	1,330,000	800,000	1,000,000	650,000	750,000
	$8,000,000	$7,000,000	$4,800,000	$4,400,000	$1,700,000	$1,300,000

On January 1, 1996, Manson adopted a plan to sell the assets and product line of the office equipment division and expected to realize a gain on this disposal. On September 1, 1996, the division's assets and product line were sold for $2,100,000 cash, resulting in a gain of $640,000 (exclusive of operations during the phase-out period).

Manson's textiles division had six manufacturing plants, which produced a variety of textile products. In April 1996, the company sold one of these plants and realized a gain of $130,000. After the sale, the operations at the plant that was sold were transferred to the remaining five textile plants, which the company continued to operate.

In August 1996, the main warehouse of the food products division, located on the banks of the Lewis River, was flooded when the river overflowed. The resulting damage of $420,000 is not included in the preceding financial data. Historical records indicate that the Lewis River normally overflows every four to five years, causing flood damage to adjacent property.

For the two years ended December 31, 1996 and 1995, the company had interest revenue of $70,000 and $40,000, respectively, which was earned on investments.

The provision for income tax expense for each of the two years should be computed at a rate of 35%.

INSTRUCTIONS

Prepare in proper form a comparative statement of income of Manson Company for the two years ended December 31, 1996 and 1995. (AICPA adapted)

21–52 Income Statement Larsen Company has always prepared its income statement on the current operating performance basis. Because the statements have been used strictly for internal purposes, adherence to GAAP has not been a major consideration.

In early 1996 the company's accountant contacts you for advice in preparing income and retained earnings statements for 1995 in accordance with generally accepted accounting principles for use with a bank loan application. The accountant presents you with the following statements, which had been prepared for internal use:

Larsen Company
Income Statement
For the Year Ended December 31, 1995

Sales revenue	$851,000
Cost of goods sold	415,000
Gross profit	436,000
Operating expenses	305,000
Income before income tax	131,000
Income tax expense	55,020
Net income	$ 75,980

Larsen Company
Retained Earnings Statement
For the Year Ended December 31, 1995

Retained earnings, January 1, 1995		$1,405,000
Additions		
Gain on the sale of investments*	$157,000	
Correction of error—income earned in 1994 but		
erroneously omitted*	120,000	
Net income for 1995	75,980	352,980
		1,757,980
Deductions		
Extraordinary loss—major casualty*	72,500	
Cumulative effect of change in accounting principle		
in 1995*	67,000	
Cash dividends, 1995	75,000	
Stock dividends, 1995	50,000	(264,500)
Retained earnings, December 31, 1995		$1,493,480

---

*Presented on net of tax basis.

You determine that all items are appropriately described and that all items subject to income tax appropriately reflect a 42% income tax rate and that the company had 112,500 shares of common stock outstanding throughout 1995.

INSTRUCTIONS

Prepare income and retained earnings statements for 1995 in accordance with generally accepted accounting principles, including all relevant disclosures that can be determined from the given data. Provide computations to support your financial statement items.

21–53 Income Statement The following trial balance of Farmer Corporation at December 31, 1995, has been adjusted except for income tax expense.

Farmer Corporation
Trial Balance
December 31, 1995

	Dr.	Cr.
Cash	$ 675,000	
Accounts receivable (net)	1,695,000	
Inventory	2,185,000	
Property, plant, and equipment (net)	8,660,000	
Accounts payable and accrued liabilities		$ 1,895,000
Income tax payable		360,000
Deferred income tax		285,000
Common stock		2,300,000
Paid-in capital in excess of par value		3,675,000
Retained earnings, January 1, 1995		3,350,000
Net sales—Regular		10,750,000
—Plastics Division		2,200,000
Cost of sales—Regular	5,920,000	
—Plastics Division	1,650,000	
Selling and administrative expenses—Regular	2,600,000	
—Plastics Division	660,000	
Interest income—Regular		65,000
Gain on litigation settlement—Regular		200,000
Depreciation adjustment from accounting change—Regular	350,000	
Gain on disposal of Plastics Division		150,000
Income tax expense	835,000	
	$25,230,000	$25,230,000

Other financial data for the year ended December 31, 1995:

Income Tax Expense

Estimated tax payments	$475,000
Accrued	360,000
Total charged to income tax expense (estimated)	$835,000
Tax rate on all types of income	40%

Gain from litigation settlement is a taxable gain and is not considered infrequent.

The $835,000 does not properly reflect current or deferred income tax expense or intraperiod income tax allocation for financial statement purposes.

Temporary Difference (not related to Plastics Division)

Depreciation per tax return	$750,000
Depreciation per financial statements (excluding cumulative effect of accounting change)	575,000

Discontinued Operations

On October 31, 1995, Farmer sold its Plastics Division for $2,950,000 when the carrying amount was $2,800,000. For financial statement reporting, this sale was considered a disposal of a segment of a business. Because there was no phase-out period, the measurement date was October 31, 1995.

Change in Depreciation Method

On January 1, 1995, Farmer changed to the 150% declining balance method from the straight-line method of depreciation for certain of its plant assets. The pretax cumulative effect of this accounting change was determined to be a charge of $350,000. There was no change in depreciation method for income tax purposes.

Capital Structure

Common stock, $10 par, traded on a national exchange:

	Shares
Outstanding at January 1, 1995	250,000
Issued on July 1, 1995, as a 15% stock dividend	37,500
	287,500

INSTRUCTIONS

Using the multiple-step format, prepare a formal income statement for Farmer Corporation for the year ended December 31, 1995. All components of income tax expense should be appropriately shown.

(*Hint:* The 15% stock dividend should be treated as outstanding for the entire year in computing earnings per share figures.)   (AICPA adapted)

CASES

21–54 Methods of Revenue Recognition   Baxter Industries has three operating divisions—Queenswood Construction Division, Paperback Publishing Division, and Protection Securities Division. Each division maintains its own accounting system and method of revenue recognition.

Queenswood Construction Division.   During the fiscal year ended November 30, 1996, Queenswood Construction Division had one construction project in process. A $24,000,000 contract for construction of a civic center was granted on June 19, 1996, and construction began on August 1, 1996. Estimated costs of completion at the contract date were $20,000,000 over a two-year time period from the date of the contract. On November 30, 1996, construction costs of $6,000,000 had been incurred, and progress billings of $6,600,000 had been made. The construction costs to complete the remainder of the project were reviewed on November 30, 1996, and were estimated to amount to only $12,000,000 due to an expected decline in raw materials costs. Revenue recognition is based on a percentage-of-completion method.

Paperback Publishing Division.   The Paperback Publishing Division sells large volumes of novels to a few book distributors, which in turn sell to several national chains of bookstores. Paperback allows distributors to return up to 30% of sales, and distributors give the same terms to book-stores. Although returns from individual titles fluctuate greatly, the returns from distributors have averaged 20% in each of the past five years. A total of $8,000,000 of paperback novel sales was made to distributors during fiscal 1996. On November 30, 1996, $3,000,000 of fiscal 1996 sales were still subject to return privileges over the next six months. The remaining $5,000,000 of fiscal 1996 sales had actual returns of 21%. Sales from fiscal 1995 totaling $2,000,000 were collected in fiscal 1996 less 18% returns. This division records revenue according to the method referred to as revenue recognition when the right of return exists.

Protection Securities Division.   Protection Securities Division works through manufacturers' agents in various cities. Orders for alarm systems and down payments are forwarded from agents, and the division ships the goods F.O.B. factory directly to customers (usually police departments and security guard companies). Customers are billed directly for the balance due plus actual shipping costs. The firm received orders for $6,000,000 of goods during the fiscal year ended November 30, 1996; it received down payments of $600,000 and billed and shipped $5,000,000 of goods. It also billed actual freight costs of $100,000. Commissions of 10% on product price are paid to manufacturing agents after goods are shipped to customers. Such goods are warranted for 90 days after shipment, and warranty returns have been about 1% of sales. Revenue is recognized at the point of sale by this division.

INSTRUCTIONS

[a] A variety of methods for revenue recognition can be used. Define and describe each of the following methods and indicate whether each is in accordance with GAAP.

[1] Point of sale.   [3] Percentage of completion.
[2] Completed contracts.   [4] Installment contract.

[b] Compute the revenue to be recognized in fiscal year 1996 for each of the three operating divisions of Baxter Industries in accordance with generally accepted accounting principles.

(CMA adapted)

21–55 Income Statement Presentation   Raleigh Company is a major manufacturer of foodstuffs that are sold in grocery and convenience stores throughout the United States. The company's name is well known and respected because its products have been marketed nationally for over 50 years.

In April 1996 the company was forced to recall one of its major products. A total of 35 persons in Phoenix were treated for severe intestinal pain, and eventually three people died from complications. All of them had consumed Raleigh's product.

The product causing the problem was traced to one specific lot. Raleigh keeps samples from all lots of foodstuffs. After thorough testing, company management and legal authorities confirmed that the product had been tampered with after it had left the company's plant and was no longer under the company's control.

All of the product was recalled from the market—the only time a Raleigh product has been recalled nationally and the only time for tampering. Persons who still had the product in their homes, even though it was not from the affected lot, were encouraged to return the product for credit or refund. The company designed and implemented a media campaign to explain what had happened and what it was doing to minimize any chance for recurrence. Raleigh decided to continue the product with the same trade name and same wholesale price. However, the packaging was redesigned completely to be tamper resistant and safety sealed. This required the purchase and installation of new equipment.

The corporate accounting staff recommended that the costs associated with the tampered product be treated as an extraordinary charge on the 1996 financial statements. Corporate accounting was asked to identify the various costs that could be associated with the tampered product and related recall. These costs ($000 omitted) are as follows.

[1] Credits and refunds to stores and consumers	$20,000
[2] Insurance to cover lost sales and idle plant costs for possible future recalls	4,000
[3] Transportation costs and off-site warehousing of returned product	4,000
[4] Future security measures for other Raleigh products	6,000
[5] Testing returned product and inventory	800
[6] Destroying returned product and inventory	2,400
[7] Public relations program to reestablish brand credibility	1,800
[8] Communication program to inform customers, answer inquiries, prepare press releases, etc.	1,600
[9] Higher cost arising from new packaging	700

[10] Investigation of possible involvement of employees, former employees, competitors, etc.	500
[11] Packaging redesign and testing	2,000
[12] Purchase and installation of new packaging equipment	5,000
[13] Legal costs for defense against liability suits	600
[14] Lost sales revenue due to recall	22,000

Raleigh's estimated earnings before income taxes and before consideration of any of these items for the year ending December 31, 1996, are $200 million.

INSTRUCTIONS

[a] Raleigh Company plans to recognize the costs associated with the product tampering and recall as an extraordinary charge.

[1] Explain why Raleigh could classify this occurrence as an extraordinary charge.

[2] Describe the placement and terminology used to present the extraordinary charge in the 1996 income statement.

[b] Refer to the 14 cost items identified by Raleigh's corporate accounting staff.

[1] Identify the cost items by number that should be included in the extraordinary charge for 1996.

[2] For any item not included in the extraordinary charge, explain why it would not be included in the extraordinary charge.   (CMA adapted)

21–56 Income Statement Classification   Cowboy Company, a publicly held regional manufacturer of western-style clothing, uses a calendar year for financial reporting. During 1994 Cowboy purchased a small chain of retail specialty clothing stores that were privately owned and that had been a good customer of Cowboy for a number of years.

Susan Helms was hired as controller of Cowboy Company in May 1995. In preparation for the 1996 budget, she completed a detailed comparison of the 1995 performance with the 1994 figures as reported. This analysis revealed the following items, which affected the reported figures for 1994:

[1] The accounts receivable at December 31, 1994, were understated by $65,000. A subsidiary ledger had a balance with a transposed number. The Accounts Receivable control account was reduced by this amount in the adjusting entries of 1994.

[2] In May 1995, $60,000 was received in settlement for a $175,000 claim against a vendor for defective merchandise. The claim was filed in March 1994, but no receivable was recorded by Cowboy because the vendor's financial condition was very weak.

[3] In 1993 Cowboy paid $57,000 for additional federal income tax that was determined to be due for 1991 by an IRS audit.

[4] Cowboy paid $75,000 in August 1995 to settle an employee discrimination suit filed in September 1994 by a labor union that charged bias in promotion practices. No liability had been recorded in 1994, but the suit had been disclosed in the notes to the 1994 financial statements.

[5] The retail chain Cowboy acquired in 1994 recorded its bad debts on the direct write-off basis even though the chain had significant credit sales and bad debt losses. The chain was included in the consolidated earnings of Cowboy for 1994. Susan Helms estimated that the chain would have had an allowance for doubtful accounts of $72,000 if an allowance system had been used.

INSTRUCTIONS

Discuss how Susan should handle each of the five situations in preparing the 1995 financial statements, paying particular attention to whether the items should be treated as prior period adjustments or as part of 1995 income.   (CMA adapted)

JUDGMENT CASES

21–57 Bad Debt Accounting and Revenue Recognition   Foreign Ideas, Inc., is a wholesaler of electronic products such as television sets, stereo equipment, and microwave ovens. The company, located in south Texas, wishes to discuss an accounting and financial reporting issue with you because your firm is the company's auditor. The company sells many of its products to retail outlets located in Mexico. The receivables that arise from these sales are denominated in U.S. dollars. That is, although the Mexican retailers sell the products to Mexican nationals for pesos, those retailers have to convert the pesos into U.S. dollars to pay Foreign Ideas the amounts owed.

Near the end of the past year, the exchange rate between the two currencies changed abruptly and significantly. From a relatively stable ratio of about 2 to 1, the exchange rate is now about 4 to 1. This change adversely affects the ability of the Mexican retailers to pay Foreign Ideas the amounts due. Before, when pesos were exchanged for dollars, an individual would receive one dollar for two pesos; now it takes four pesos to acquire one dollar. To illustrate, suppose Foreign Ideas sold a Mexican retailer a television set for $350. If the Mexican retailer sold the product to one of its customers for 1,200 pesos, those pesos could be converted to $600 dollars and the obligation to Foreign Ideas could easily be settled. Now, however, 1,200 pesos will bring only $300 dollars when converted by the Mexican retailer. The loss in the conversion rate limits the ability of the Mexican retailers to sell U.S. products, convert their proceeds, and pay for the products.

The chief financial officer of your client describes these conditions and acknowledges that estimating the amount of bad debts expected from the Mexican receivables has proved difficult. He then states the company's intentions, as follows:

> *What we propose to do is to follow* FASB Statement No. 5, *"Accounting for Contingencies," very carefully. We are also mindful of* FASB Interpretation No. 14, *"Reasonable Estimation of the Amount of a Loss," which provides that the amount of a loss that should be reported is the best estimate of the expected loss within the range when only a range of loss can be estimated. If no amount of loss within the range appears to be a better estimate than any other, however, the low end of the range should be accrued. That is what we propose to do.*
>
> *The range of loss that we face this year extends from the total amount of our Mexican receivables to the amount that proved uncollectible in past years. Because the change in the exchange rate was so recent, abrupt, and significant, we are unable to identify any amount within the range that appears to be more likely than any other amount. We just don't have enough experience with a situation like this. By the way, we have stopped anything other than C.O.D. shipments to most of our international customers. So, only the receivables that existed at the end of the year are in question. Therefore, in accordance with* FASB Interpretation No. 14, *we are going to accrue the same amount we did last year. That is the low end of the range that seems to us to meet the requirements of the authoritative accounting literature.*
>
> *We need to know if you agree with our analysis because we are going to inform our banker of our preliminary operating results later this week and don't want to struggle with this issue when the audit begins.*

INSTRUCTIONS

Do you agree with this analysis and resolution? (You may wish to consult the coverage of accounting for loss contingencies, which is discussed primarily in Chapter 14 of this textbook.)

21–58 Income Statement Presentation Paper & Things, the manufacturer of a wide variety of paper products, owns and operates forest lands in several locations in the western United States. Recently, a volcano erupted and destroyed a large forest owned by the company in Oregon. That forest is the only timber that the company owned near the volcano. The loss of the forest is very large relative to the company's financial statements, and the company is concerned about the preparation of its income statement for the year and the manner in which the loss should be reported.

The president of Paper & Things maintains that the loss has never happened before and it is clearly unusual. Furthermore, the president believes that the mere size of the item suggests that it should be presented as an extraordinary loss.

You are the engagement partner of the company's auditor and have been consulted as to whether the loss can be considered an extraordinary item. As you are reviewing the relevant authoritative accounting literature, you happen to hear a newscast that states that eruptions of the volcano are expected to continue into the foreseeable future. You have directed your assistant to consult the U.S. Geological Survey, and that research confirms that eruptions are, in fact, expected to continue indefinitely.

INSTRUCTIONS

Determine whether you believe the loss can be reported as an extraordinary item in Paper & Things' income statement and justify your position. Be sure to cite the appropriate authoritative accounting literature in your answer and provide your reasoning as to how that literature should be applied in this particular situation.

21–59 Loss of a Customer Your audit client, Quick Shot, Inc., is a small nonpublic photography shop that provides photographic services to a number of customers. Most of its customers are groups that engage Quick Shot to photograph individuals that attend church picnics, company parties, and other social events.

In addition, the company serves two companies by taking photographs of all their employees and producing security badges from those photographs. Because of relatively rapid employee turnover, each of the companies requires semi-annual updated security badges. Quick Shot, therefore, photographs each employee of each company and prepares new security badges twice each year.

The two businesses for which security badges are produced are, by far, the most profitable of their customers and Quick Shot values them greatly. One of those clients, however, has recently been acquired by another company and has notified Quick Shot that the annual contract for security badges will not be renewed for the next year.

You are in the process of auditing Quick Shot's financial statements for the year just ended and realize that the results of operations for the year just ended contain the profits from the customer that has just been lost. You approach your client, Ms. Flash, and suggest that the financial statements should probably contain some disclosure of the fact that approximately 10% of the company's revenues and 20% of its net income before income taxes for the year were obtained from a customer that no longer will use the services of the company. She responds:

> *The financial statements that you are auditing are historical in nature. The revenues and earnings that are contained in those statements occurred and are measured accurately. They faithfully report what we earned during the year just ended. I do not believe that any disclosure of the loss of this customer is necessary for any reason. Besides, we are negotiating with a new financial institution to begin making employee photographs for them and if we are successful, they will replace the revenues and profits that we will not earn from our former customer. Unless you can show me some unequivocal support in the authoritative accounting literature to confirm the validity of your suggestion, I will not agree to provide the disclosures that you suggest.*

INSTRUCTIONS

Does the authoritative accounting literature require that the circumstances described above be disclosed in accordance with generally accepted accounting principles? Regardless of whether the authoritative accounting literature specifically requires this event to be disclosed, do you believe that disclosure of the loss of this customer is necessary? Be sure to state the underlying reasons for your belief and suggest specific wording for a note to the financial statements if you believe that some disclosure is necessary.

21–60 A Sale That Wasn't   During 1996, collection of accounts receivable from a particular customer became questionable. As a result your client, Improvident, Inc., took back the inventory that had been reported as sold during 1995. The inventory had an invoice sales price of $1,800,000, which included a 30% profit margin based on the sales revenue recognized.

INSTRUCTIONS

How should the return of the inventory be accounted for by Improvident in its financial statements for the year ended December 31, 1996? Be specific and prepare the journal entry that you recommend. In addition, be sure to prepare a memorandum for your files that explains the rationale supporting your entry.

FINANCIAL REPORTING CASE

21–61 Financial Reporting Case   Bristol-Myers Squibb Company is a large U.S. corporation that operates in the health-care industry. During 1992, the company completed the sale of The Drackett Company and reported as indicated in Note 3 of the 1993 financial statements. That note, and an excerpt from the company's 1993 income statement, follow.

Note 3   Discontinued Operations

On December 31, 1992, the company completed the sale of The Drackett Company, its household products business, to S.C. Johnson & Son, Inc., for $1.15 billion in cash. The sale resulted in a gain of $952 million before taxes, $605 million after taxes, or $1.17 per share. Drackett has been reported as a discontinued operation.

Summary results of Drackett's operations in 1992 and 1991 were

Year Ended December 31, (in millions of dollars)	1992	1991
Net sales	$571	$588
Earnings before income taxes	$103	$103
Provision for income taxes	38	38
Net earnings	$ 65	$ 65

Income Statement Excerpt

(in millions of dollars except per share amounts)	Year Ended December 31,		
	1993	**1992**	**1991**
Earnings from continuing operations before income taxes	**2,571**	1,987	2,784
Provision for income taxes	**612**	449	793
Earnings from continuing operations	**1,959**	1,538	1,991
Discontinued operations, net	—	670	65
Earnings before cumulative effect of accounting change	**1,959**	2,208	2,056
Cumulative effect of accounting change (net of income tax benefit of $144)	—	(246)	—
Net earnings	**$1,959**	$1,962	$2,056
Per common share:			
Earnings from continuing operations	**$3.80**	$2.97	$3.82
Discontinued operations	—	1.29	.13
Earnings before cumulative effect of accounting change	**3.80**	4.26	3.95
Cumulative effect of accounting change	—	(.47)	—
Net earnings	**$3.80**	$3.79	$3.95

INSTRUCTIONS

[a] Briefly explain the nature of the transaction giving rise to the discontinued operations line in the income statement.

[b] Explain the numbers related to discontinued operations: $670 million in 1992 and $65 million in 1991.

[c] Without any specific knowledge about the accounting change that occurred in 1992, what can you conclude about it in terms of its impact on retained earnings at the beginning of 1992?

[d] What subtotals preceding net income are on the income statement? What does each represent and how do they assist you in better understanding the results of operations? Focus your attention in particular on 1992.

Reporting Cash Flow Information

OBJECTIVES

1. To identify the role that cash flow information plays in meeting the objectives of financial reporting.
2. To discuss the importance of cash flow information to users of financial statements.
3. To define the three categories of cash flows of business enterprises—operating, investing, and financing—and explain how they are presented in a statement of cash flows.
4. To explain the nature of investing and financing transactions that do not affect cash flows directly and to explain the manner of reporting such events.
5. To present procedures for preparing a statement of cash flows in a relatively complex situation.

Cash is a very important asset. A company's ability to generate cash is so important, in fact, that some analysts consider cash flow analysis as the investor's best guide to a stock's worth:

> When investors go bargain hunting, they look for stocks that appear cheap in comparison with standard benchmarks. The two most common are price/earnings ratios and price/book-value ratios. But both have shortcomings and, as a result, top stock pickers are increasingly turning to a less well-known vital sign: cash flow. In simplest terms, this is the amount of cash a company actually generates from its operations.*

How does an investor learn about a company's cash flow? One way is through the statement of cash flows. Other financial statements and disclosures, however, include information that is relevant to analyzing a company's cash flow situation. This information is sometimes confusing, however, and warrants careful consideration by serious accounting students. Consider, for example, the case of Procter & Gamble Company in 1993 when net income before the effect of an accounting change was $269.0 million, but cash flow provided by operating activities was $3,338 million, over 12 times as high. Even more difficult to comprehend is General Motors' 1992 results, which indicate a net loss of $2.6 billion before cumulative effect of an accounting change but cash of over $10 billion provided by operating activities!

Net income and cash from operating activities are related concepts, but they obviously measure different aspects of a company's performance. One of our objectives in this chapter is to explore these and other issues to better understand financial statements in general and, specifically, how they assist investors and other financial statement users to understand a company's cash flows.

---

*Andrea Rock, "Cash Flow Can Be the Investor's Best Guide to a Stock's Worth," *Money* (March 1989), p. 161.

OBJECTIVES OF FINANCIAL REPORTING AND CASH FLOW INFORMATION

When the FASB specified the objectives of financial reporting in *SFAC No. 1,* information useful in assessing cash flow prospects was identified as being particularly important. Subsequently, *SFAC No. 5* specified cash flow information as a requirement for a full set of financial statements, and the statement of cash flows became a reporting requirement in *SFAS No. 95.* In this chapter, we study the background of the current reporting requirements associated with the statement of cash flows and illustrate the preparation of that statement at two levels of complexity.

The FASB identified three broad types of information as necessary to meet the objectives of financial reporting:

1. *Information useful in investment and credit decisions.* Financial reporting should assist present and potential investors and creditors and other users in making rational investment, credit, and similar decisions.[1]

2. *Information useful in assessing cash flow prospects.* Financial reporting should provide information to help present and potential investors and creditors and other users in assessing the amounts, timing, and uncertainty of prospective cash receipts to them from dividends or interest and the proceeds from the sale, redemption, or maturity of securities or loans.[2]

3. *Information about enterprise resources, claims to those resources, and changes in them.* Financial reporting should provide information about an enterprise's economic resources, obligations, and owners' equity. That information helps users identify the enterprise's financial strengths and weaknesses and assess its liquidity and solvency.[3]

An enterprise's ability to generate cash to meet its financial obligations and other cash operating needs, to reinvest in operations, and to pay cash dividends may affect the market prices of the enterprise's securities. Thus, financial reporting should provide information to help investors, creditors, and other users to assess the amounts, timing, and uncertainty of prospective cash flows to the enterprise in which they have an economic interest.[4] Cash flow information about the reporting entity is believed to help investors, creditors, and other users of financial information to assess cash flow prospects from the entity to them.

In *SFAC No. 5,* the FASB indicates that the amount and variety of information that financial reporting should provide about an entity requires several financial statements. Specifically, a full set of financial statements should show the following:

1. Financial position at the end of the period.
2. Earnings (net income) for the period.
3. Comprehensive income (total nonowner changes in equity) for the period.
4. *Cash flows for the period.*
5. Investments by and distributions to owners during the period.[5]

Earlier we stated that the FASB's concepts statements, which constitute the conceptual framework for financial reporting, are partially normative in that they do not necessarily describe specific accounting practices at the time the concept statements were issued. Subsequent to *Statements of Financial Accounting Concepts Nos. 1* and *5,* cited above, the FASB issued *Statement of Financial Accounting Standards No. 95,* "Statement of Cash Flows."[6] This pronouncement established the statement of cash flows as a requirement, thereby bring-

---

[1]*FASB Statement of Financial Accounting Concepts No. 1,* "Objectives of Financial Reporting by Business Enterprises," 1978, par. 34.

[2]*SFAC No. 1,* par. 37.

[3]*SFAC No. 1,* par. 41.

[4]*SFAC No. 1,* par. 37.

[5]*Statement of Financial Accounting Concepts No. 5,* "Recognition and Measurement in Financial Statements of Business Enterprises," 1984, par. 13.

[6]*Statement of Financial Accounting Standards No. 95,* "Statement of Cash Flows," 1987.

ing accounting practice into closer conformity with the conceptual framework. Much of this chapter is based on this important and recent authoritative accounting pronouncement.

Before we consider more carefully the specific objectives and reporting requirements of the statement of cash flows, let's refresh our memory of the basic structure of the statement. Exhibit 22–1 repeats the statement of cash flows from the review of financial statements in Chapter 4. Notice that it is prepared in three major sections: cash flows from operating, investing, and financing activities. Also, at the bottom of the statement, the change in cash is used to reconcile the beginning and ending cash balances for the period. This example is simplified in several ways, including the fact that it does not present all of the required disclosures that must accompany a statement of cash flows in conformity with *SFAS No. 95*. We will consider those details in more depth later in this chapter.

The primary purpose of the statement of cash flows is stated very simply in *SFAS No. 95:* to provide relevant information about the cash receipts and payments of an enterprise during a period of time. The information included in the statement, when used in conjunction

---

EXHIBIT 22–1

Sunrise Corporation
Statement of Cash Flows
For the Year Ended December 31, 1996

Cash Flows from Operating Activities		
Cash received from customers	$538,700	
Interest received	2,100	
Dividends received	5,200	
Rent received	8,400	
Cash provided by operating activities		$554,400
Cash paid to suppliers and employees	455,900	
Interest paid	14,200	
Taxes paid	47,300	
Cash disbursed for operating activities		517,400
Net cash flow from operating activities		37,000
Cash Flows from Investing Activities		
Short-term loans made	(18,000)	
Collections on short-term loans	8,000	
Purchases of long-term investments	(14,000)	
Proceeds from sale of long-term investments	10,900	
Purchases of property, plant, and equipment	(38,800)	
Proceeds from disposals of property, plant, and equipment	76,400	
Net cash provided by investing activities		24,500
Cash Flows from Financing Activities		
Proceeds of short-term debt	23,000	
Payments to settle short-term debt	(25,000)	
Proceeds of long-term debt	50,000	
Payments to settle long-term note	(110,000)	
Proceeds from issuing common stock	55,000	
Dividends paid	(16,000)	
Net cash used by financing activities		(23,000)
Net increase in cash and cash equivalents		38,500
Cash and cash equivalents, Jan. 1, 1996		24,000
Cash and cash equivalents, Dec. 31, 1996		$ 62,500

with related disclosures and information in the other financial statements, should help investors, creditors, and others to assess

1. The enterprise's ability to generate positive future net cash flows.
2. The enterprise's ability to meet its obligations and pay dividends and assess its needs for external financing.
3. The reasons for differences between net income and associated cash receipts and payments.
4. The effects on the enterprise's financial position of its investing and financing transactions during the period.[7]

Keep in mind as we study the statement of cash flows that it is designed to report a process that is continuously taking place in a business enterprise. Cash is continuously flowing through operating, financing, and investing activities. Although we tie the reporting of this process to the cash balance at a point in time (i.e., the end of the accounting period), the major thrust of the statement is to explain a continuous flow of transactions over time within the enterprise. The statement of cash flows is closely tied to the other major financial statements, but it presents information prepared on a cash, rather than an accrual, basis. It should be viewed as presenting equally important, instead of competing, information when compared with that presented in the other major financial statements.

HISTORICAL DEVELOPMENT OF THE STATEMENT OF CASH FLOWS

For many years, the income statement, the balance sheet, and the retained earnings statement constituted a complete set of financial statements when accompanied by disclosures in the form of notes and supplementary schedules. "Funds flow" information was primarily a tool of financial statement users to assist them in understanding how an enterprise's balance sheet changed between two points in time. Recognizing that important information is not disclosed when only these three statements are presented, the American Institute of Certified Public Accountants (AICPA) published *Accounting Research Study No. 2* in 1961.[8] This research study explored many of the financial reporting issues that led to the requirement of a statement of changes in financial position and later a statement of cash flows. That study was followed in 1963 by *Accounting Principles Board Opinion No. 3,* which discussed the need for a statement to complete the disclosure of changes in financial position and encouraged publication of such a "funds" statement.[9] This voluntary disclosure gained popularity between 1963 and 1971, when the Accounting Principles Board (APB) issued *Opinion No. 19,*

Disclosure

which *required* the presentation of a financial statement to fill the disclosure gap existing when only a balance sheet, income statement, and statement of retained earnings are presented.[10] The suggested title of the statement was statement of changes in financial position.

In a 1980 *Discussion Memorandum,* the FASB emphasized the importance of information concerning cash flows, liquidity, and financial flexibility. The memorandum was prepared to serve as a basis for the discussion of these types of information in anticipation of changing reporting requirements. The importance of information on cash flows, liquidity, and financial flexibility is summarized in statements from the 1980 *Discussion Memorandum:*

Funds Flows
Information about past cash flows or other funds flows may help users of financial statements improve their understanding of the activities of an enterprise, understand the effects on funds flows of income-generating activities, and evaluate the investing and financing activities of an enterprise. In those and other ways the information may be used as a basis for making assessments of future cash flows associated with operating, investing, and financing activities.

---

[7]*SFAS No. 95,* pars. 4–5.

[8]Perry Mason, *Accounting Research Study No. 2,* "Cash Flow Analysis and the Funds Statement" (New York: AICPA, 1961).

[9]*APB Opinion No. 3,* "The Statement of Sources and Application of Funds," 1963.

[10]*APB Opinion No. 19,* "Reporting Changes in Financial Position," 1971, par. 7.

Liquidity

Liquidity is an indication of the "nearness to cash" of the assets and liabilities of an enterprise. Nearness to cash can be regarded as the time that must elapse before assets and liabilities result in cash receipts and payments through normal operations. Information about liquidity may help to identify the relationship between income-generating activities and the related receipts and payments of cash. It also may help to identify the pay-back period on investments in operating assets. A short pay-back period may indicate a high level of financial flexibility.

Financial Flexibility

Financial flexibility is the capacity to adapt to favorable and unfavorable changes in operating conditions. For example, financial flexibility may enable an enterprise to undertake a new investment or to introduce a new product line. Equity investors may be particularly interested in this aspect of financial flexibility. When change has an adverse effect, financial flexibility may be critical to the survival of an enterprise. Declining funds flows from operations and reduced liquidity may signal an impending cash flow problem. The solvency of an enterprise may depend on its financial flexibility.... Sources of financial flexibility include the ability to generate additional cash flows by financing, by liquidating assets, and by modifying operations. Information about past funds flows and the liquidity of assets and liabilities may be useful in assessing financial flexibility.[11]

The lack of comparability among the financial statements of various companies, concern about the basic purpose of the statement of changes in financial position, and increased recognition of the importance of cash flow information led the Financial Accounting Standards Board to issue *Statement of Financial Accounting Standards No. 95,* "Statement of Cash Flows," in 1987. This statement replaced *APB Opinion No. 19* and requires a statement of cash flows.

Although the statement of cash flows may be viewed as the result of the evolutionary process just described, it represents a significant change from past financial reporting practices. It shifts the focus from information prepared on an accrual basis, as found in the other major financial statements, to information prepared on a cash basis. It also takes an important step away from the disclosure objective of the previous statement of changes in financial position as a means of reconciling all balance sheet changes. Finally, it significantly narrows areas of difference in practice by establishing specific reporting requirements and carefully defining operating, investing, and financing cash flow categories.

Disclosure

In the opinion of the authors, the renewed emphasis on cash flow reporting represents one of the most exciting and constructive developments in the accounting profession in many decades. In the past, an extreme emphasis on accrual accounting has limited efforts to improve the quality of financial reporting. We view the renewed emphasis on cash flow information *in conjunction with accrual accounting information* as a positive move that will enhance the presentation of useful information to investors, creditors, and other users in making economic decisions.

Businesses continuously convert assets into goods and services or into other assets and obligations. In a simplified situation, this conversion process can be viewed as a series of short-term conversions and a series of long-term conversions. In the short-term conversion cycle, cash is converted into inventory that is subsequently converted into receivables and then back into cash. Typically, several of these cycles take place during a single reporting period. The long-term conversion cycle involves investments of cash in machinery, equipment, furniture, fixtures, buildings, land, and other operating assets. These assets contribute to the operations of the enterprise over several accounting periods, but they subsequently are converted back into cash through successful generation of goods and services that are provided for customers. These long-lived assets may eventually be sold for cash when they are no longer

THE STATEMENT OF CASH FLOWS

---

[11]*FASB Discussion Memorandum,* "Reporting Funds Flow, Liquidity, and Financial Flexibility," 1980, pp. 2, 4.

useful to the company, but the amounts may be nominal. Both cycles are continuous, and at any point in time, the enterprise will be involved in several short- and long-term cycles simultaneously. Financing these short- and long-term cycles may involve external debt and equity in addition to the use of cash provided by operations.

Exhibit 22–2 demonstrates the major categories of transactions that affect the amount of cash held by a company. Business enterprises make many decisions on the basis of availability of cash. For example, the availability of cash influences credit policies and dividend distributions. Thus, in attempting to judge prospective cash flows, investors and creditors are particularly interested in the impact of financing and investing activities on the flow of cash in and out of the business enterprise.

In *SFAS No. 95,* the FASB established the categories of operating, investing, and financing activities for presentation of cash flows. This classification was used in Exhibit 22–1 and is also the basis for describing the types of cash flows in Exhibit 22–2. In the paragraphs that follow, we explore each of these major categories in greater depth and introduce several other reporting requirements of *SFAS No. 95.*

OPERATING ACTIVITIES

All transactions affecting cash that are *not considered investing or financing activities* are included in the operating activities category of the statement of cash flows. Generally, these transactions represent the cash flow effects of transactions affecting net income. Another way to look at the types of transactions classified as operating activities is to think of them as revenues collected in cash and expenses paid in cash. Although the terms *revenues* and *expenses* should be used only when describing accrual accounting, the cash flow equivalents of those items typically represent operating activities in the statement of cash flows.

Cash inflows from operating activities are as follows:

1. Cash receipts from sales of goods or services, including collections of receivables from customers.
2. Cash receipts from returns on loans and debt and equity instruments of other entities (e.g., interest and dividend revenue).

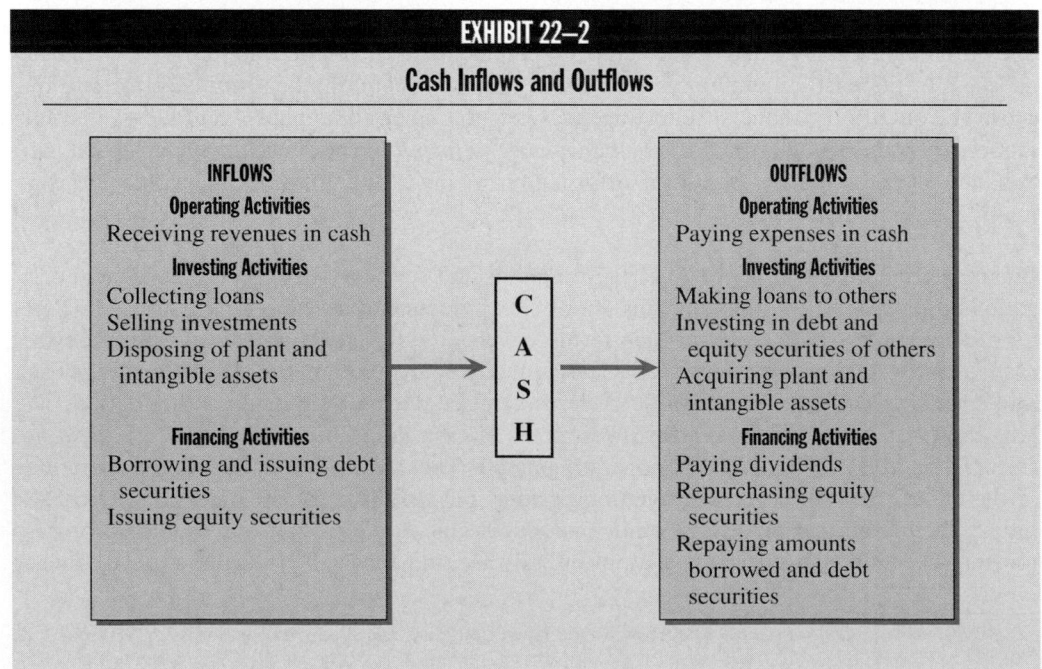

EXHIBIT 22–2

Cash Inflows and Outflows

INFLOWS

Operating Activities
Receiving revenues in cash

Investing Activities
Collecting loans
Selling investments
Disposing of plant and
  intangible assets

Financing Activities
Borrowing and issuing debt
  securities
Issuing equity securities

CASH

OUTFLOWS

Operating Activities
Paying expenses in cash

Investing Activities
Making loans to others
Investing in debt and
  equity securities of others
Acquiring plant and
  intangible assets

Financing Activities
Paying dividends
Repurchasing equity
  securities
Repaying amounts
  borrowed and debt
  securities

3. All other cash receipts that do not result from transactions classified as investing or financing activities.

Cash outflows from operating activities are as follows:

1. Cash payments to acquire materials for manufacture or resale, including payments on payables to suppliers.
2. Cash payments to other suppliers and employees for goods or services.
3. Cash payments to governments for taxes, duties, fines, and other fees or penalties.
4. Cash payments to lenders and other creditors for interest.
5. All other cash payments that do not result from transactions classified as investing or financing activities.[12]

FASB Statement No. 95 permits two ways to present cash flows from operating activities, the direct and the indirect (or reconciliation) methods. Both are discussed in the following sections of this chapter. Regardless of the method of presenting cash flows from operating activities, a *schedule reconciling net income to net cash provided by or used in operating activities* is required. Also, *interest paid* (net of amounts capitalized) and *income taxes paid* during the period *must be disclosed* in the financial statement or related notes.

Disclosure

Care must be taken in distinguishing operating activities from investing and financing activities. For example, the cash effect of the transaction that gives rise to depreciation expense is the acquisition of the asset. Because the acquisition of the asset being depreciated benefits many accounting periods, however, the purchase of that asset is considered an investing activity rather than an operating activity. On the other hand, cost of goods sold, which represents goods acquired and disposed of, is an operating expense, and the cash purchase of inventory is considered an operating cash flow. Thus, even though both plant assets and items of inventory may be acquired and paid for during one period and charged to expense in a future period or periods, the acquisition of plant assets is considered an investing activity; the acquisition of inventory is considered an operating activity. The key to understanding this distinction is that inventory is acquired to be sold while plant assets are acquired as an investment to be used internally by the company for a relatively long period of time.

Refer once more to Exhibit 22–1 and study the operating activities category of Sunrise Corporation's statement of cash flows. Notice that the company reports a positive net cash flow of $37,000 from operating activities. That amount compares to the net income of $74,400 reported by Sunrise for the same period. (Sunrise Corporation's income statement is presented in Chapter 4 in Exhibits 4–1 and 4–2.) Remember that although both numbers are important, they address different economic phenomena and the differences between the two can be substantial. The principal reasons for the difference can be determined by a careful analysis of the income statement and the statement of cash flows.

INVESTING ACTIVITIES

The investing activities of a company are presented in a separate category of the statement of cash flows following operating activities. These activities focus on asset transactions and involve cash inflows and outflows resulting from those transactions. Cash inflows from investing activities are as follows:

1. Receipts from collections or sales of loans made by the enterprise and of other entities' debt instruments that were purchased by the enterprise.
2. Receipts from sales of equity instruments of other enterprises and from returns of investments in those instruments.
3. Receipts from sales of property, plant, and equipment and other productive assets.

---

[12]*FASB Statement of Financial Accounting Standards No. 95*, pars. 22–23.

Cash outflows from investing activities are described in the following categories:

1. Disbursements for loans made by the enterprise and payments to acquire debt instruments of other entities.
2. Payments to acquire equity instruments of other enterprises.
3. Payments to acquire property, plant, and equipment and other productive assets.[13]

When a company pays cash for a plant asset, that transaction is reported as a use of cash in the investing activities category of the statement of cash flows. Similarly, when that asset is later sold in a used condition, the amount of cash received is reported as a source of cash from investing activities. Remember, any gain or loss on the disposal of the asset is reported in the income statement. The actual proceeds from the disposal are reported in the investing activities category of the statement of cash flows, and any gain or loss on the sale is removed from net income in the operating section of the statement (discussed below). If a company makes a loan to another company, including the purchase of that other company's debt securities, the money lent is reported as a use of cash in the investing activities category of the statement of cash flows. When the loan is collected, cash received (other than interest) is reported as a source of cash in the investing activities category of the statement.

Dividends received in cash from investments in equity securities of another company—and cash collected as interest revenue on loans made to another company—are **not** considered investing activities. Rather, amounts received as dividend revenue or collected as interest revenue are reported in the operating activities category of the statement of cash flows because they are included in net income.

At this time, you may wish to refer back to Exhibit 22–1 and review the presentation of the investing activities category for Sunrise Corporation. Notice that Sunrise made short-term loans and collected amounts on those types of loans, purchased long-term investments and sold some of them, and purchased and disposed of certain items of plant assets. The net cash provided by all of these activities was $24,500. Notice that in the investing activities category, both increases and decreases in cash from the various types of transactions are reported.

FINANCING ACTIVITIES

Cash flow effects of financing activities are presented in a separate category of the statement of cash flows, much as are investing activities. Cash inflows from financing activities are as follows:

1. Proceeds from issuing equity instruments.
2. Proceeds from issuing bonds, mortgages, notes, and other short-term or long-term borrowings.

Cash outflows from financing activities are as follows:

1. Payments of dividends or other distributions to owners, including outlays to reacquire the enterprise's equity instruments (e.g., purchases of treasury stock).
2. Repayments of amounts borrowed.
3. Other principal payments to creditors who have extended long-term credit (e.g., seller-financed debt related to the purchase of plant assets).[14]

Notice that although interest paid to creditors is not considered to be a financing activity of the company, dividends paid to equity investors are. The difference in treatment here is related to the basic concept discussed in Chapter 21—that dividends are a *distribution* of net

---

[13]*FASB Statement of Financial Accounting Standards No. 95,* pars. 16–17.
[14]*FASB Statement of Financial Accounting Standards No. 95,* pars. 19–20.

income, but the interest cost of borrowed funds is a *determinant* of income. Therefore, interest costs paid in cash are defined as part of operating activities rather than as a financing activity based primarily on the fact that interest expense is a determinant of net income.

Another review of Exhibit 22–1 shows that Sunrise Corporation reports a net negative cash flow of $23,000 as a result of financing activities taking place during the year. Observe that Sunrise obtained cash from short-term borrowing and made payments to settle short-term debts. In addition, the company repaid a large long-term loan ($110,000) but also borrowed additional amounts by issuing new long-term debt ($50,000). The company also issued common stock in the amount of $55,000. The payment of dividends of $16,000 also contributed to the net use of cash reported in the financing activities category of the statement.

CASH AND CASH EQUIVALENTS

The FASB indicates that when presenting cash flow information, the term *cash* should actually be interpreted as *cash and cash equivalents.* **Cash equivalents** are short-term, highly liquid investments having the following characteristics:

1. They are readily convertible to known amounts of cash.
2. They are so near their maturity that they present insignificant risk of changes in value because of changes in interest rates.

Examples of securities that meet these criteria are Treasury bills, commercial paper, money market funds, and similar investments whose original maturities are three months or less. Longer-term securities that are purchased within 90 days of their maturity also qualify as cash equivalents. Transactions involving the purchase and sale of these securities are generally considered part of the enterprise's cash management activities rather than part of its operating, investing, and financing activities.

Not all investments that meet these criteria are required to be treated as cash equivalents in the preparation of the statement of cash flows. The enterprise must establish a policy concerning short-term, highly liquid investments and treat them consistently as either cash **Consistency** equivalents or part of the enterprise's investing activities. Any change in that policy is a change in accounting principle that requires restatement of financial statements of previous years presented for comparative purposes.[15]

NONCASH TRANSACTIONS

Certain financing and investing activities do not involve the payment or receipt of cash. Even though these transactions do not affect cash flows directly, their disclosure is necessary to **Disclosure** provide supplemental information about all financing and investing activities. An example of such transactions is financing the acquisition of a plant asset directly from the seller rather than from an external source, such as a bank. The acquisition of the asset is an investing activity, and the loan from the seller is a financing activity, but no cash is involved. Transactions such as these are disclosed in a separate schedule accompanying the statement of cash flows. Other examples of transactions that require disclosure are the conversion of debt securities into common stock and the issuance of stock in exchange for plant assets. The FASB does not specifically require the disclosure of stock dividends and stock splits, but the authors suggest that their disclosure as noncash activities is desirable.

Preparing the statement of cash flows involves three basic steps:

1. Determine the net change in cash by comparing the beginning and ending amounts of cash.
2. Identify all transactions that resulted in increases or decreases in cash and all noncash financing and investing activities.

---

[15]*FASB Statement of Financial Accounting Standards No. 95,* pars 8–10.

PREPARING THE STATEMENT OF CASH FLOWS: A SIMPLIFIED EXAMPLE

3. Use the information from steps 1 and 2 to prepare a formal financial statement that conforms with the presentation and disclosure requirements of the FASB.

Information to complete these steps is found in the other basic financial statements and in the underlying accounting records of the reporting enterprise. Because this information is accumulated primarily for purposes of preparing balance sheets and income statements on an accrual basis, adjustments may be necessary to prepare the information needed for the statement of cash flows. In a sense, we begin with the ending balance sheet and work backward to determine the causes of the changes in cash during the period.

To illustrate the preparation of a simplified statement of cash flows, we assume that Hamilton Company has prepared comparative balance sheets and a condensed income statement for 1995 and 1996 along with selected additional information, all as presented in Exhibit 22–3. The following paragraphs apply the three steps identified earlier to produce the required statement of cash flows.

DETERMINING THE CHANGE IN CASH

We determine the change in cash by comparing the 1996 cash balance of $50,000 with the $100,000 balance for 1995. Cash decreased $50,000, so cash paid out must have exceeded cash received by $50,000. The $50,000 decline in cash provides an important check as we identify the underlying causes of the net change.

TRANSACTION ANALYSIS

Next we analyze the changes in all balance sheet accounts other than cash to determine the causes of the changes in cash. Exhibit 22–4 illustrates one way to identify the individual changes that in the aggregate caused cash to decline by $50,000. This approach involves a simple worksheet that analyzes the change in each account in terms of its impact on the three categories of activities presented in the statement of cash flows. An alternative approach,

---

EXHIBIT 22–3

Financial Information for Hamilton Company

Hamilton Company
Comparative Balance Sheets
December 31, 1995 and 1996
(in thousands of dollars)

	1995	1996
Assets		
Cash	$ 100	$ 50
Accounts receivable	400	300
Plant assets	1,000	1,700
Accumulated depreciation	(100)	(200)
	$1,400	$1,850
Equities		
Accrued expenses	$ 150	$ 200
Bonds payable	650	800
Capital stock	500	600
Retained earnings	100	250
	$1,400	$1,850

Hamilton Company
Income Statement
For the Year Ended December 31, 1996
(in thousands of dollars)

Revenue		$1,500
Expenses		
Depreciation	$ 100	
Other	1,100	1,200
Net income		$ 300

Additional Information

Capital stock was sold at par value for $100,000,

Bonds of $100,000 were retired, and $250,000 of new bonds were issued.

Machinery of $800,000 was acquired.

Land with a book value of $100,000 was sold for $100,000.

Cash dividends of $150,000 were declared and paid.

which some people prefer, is the T-account approach and is presented for the Hamilton Company in Appendix A.

First, we consider current assets and current liabilities other than cash. The $100,000 decrease in accounts receivable is shown as a positive adjustment to operating activities (revenues) as a source of cash. To understand this treatment, we must look beyond the balance sheet account and consider the income statement implications of that account. Accounts receivable are tied directly to sales when they increase and to cash when they decrease. If accounts receivable decreased during the period ($100,000 in this case), the cash received on accounts exceeds the amount of sales included in the income statement by that amount. We must add $100,000 to revenues in determining cash provided by selling activities to include the collection of cash on accounts that were recognized from sales in a previous accounting period. Here we see a fundamental difference between information prepared on an accrual basis and a cash flow basis.

The $50,000 increase in accrued expenses requires a similar analysis. If accrued expenses increased during the period ($50,000 in this case), the cash paid for expenses is less than the amount of expenses recognized in the income statement. Again we see a difference between accrual and cash flow information. The increase in accrued expenses

---

EXHIBIT 22–4

Hamilton Company
Cash Analysis by Worksheet
(In thousands of dollars)

| | Trial Balance | | | Cash | Sources and (Uses) of Cash | | |
	1995	1996	Increase (Decrease)	Increase (Decrease)	Operating	Investing	Financing
Assets							
Cash	$ 100	$ 50	$ (50)	$(50)	—	—	—
Accounts receivable	400	300	(100)		$100		
Plant assets	1,000	1,700	700ᵃ			$ 100	
						(800)	
Accumulated depreciation	(100)	(200)	100		100		
	$1,400	$1,850					
Equities							
Accrued expenses	$ 150	$ 200	50		50		
Bonds payable	650	800	150ᵇ				(100)
							250
Capital stock	500	600	100				100
Retained earnings	100	250	150		300		(150)
	$1,400	$1,850					
Decrease in cash				$(50) =	$550	(700)	100

ᵃOffsetting investing transactions: acquisition of machinery ($800 decrease in cash), less sale of land ($100 increase in cash).

ᵇOffsetting financing transactions: sale of bonds ($250 increase in cash), less retirement of bonds ($100 decrease in cash).

requires a subtraction from expenses (addition to net income) to determine cash used in operating activities.

We now turn our attention to the analysis of nonworking capital accounts that changed during the period. The changes in Plant Assets, Bonds Payable, and Capital Stock accounts indicate that investing and financing transactions have taken place during the year.

Capital stock was sold for $100,000 (an increase in cash), which we know from the additional information and can check by computing the change in the Capital Stock account balance from $500,000 to $600,000. In a like manner, we also know and can check that the company issued bonds payable in the amount of $250,000 (a cash increase) and retired bonds payable in the amount of $100,000 (a cash decrease). Cash was paid out for dividends of $150,000. These transactions are financing activities that, in the aggregate, provided cash of $350,000 ($100,000 + $250,000) and used cash of $250,000 ($100,000 + $150,000).

We also know from the additional information that the company paid $800,000 to acquire machinery (a cash decrease) and sold land for $100,000 (a cash increase) during the year. These transactions are investing activities, identified as such in Exhibit 22–4.

The change in the Accumulated Depreciation account and the related amount of depreciation expense during the year do not affect cash and, therefore, do not affect the cash flows from operating activities. Recall, however, that depreciation expense has been deducted in determining net income. We complete the worksheet in Exhibit 22–4 by adjusting the change in accumulated depreciation against depreciation expense, effectively removing that expense as a reduction from revenues in computing cash from operations. Also, net income (the excess of revenues over expenses) is carried over into the Operating column to complete our analysis of the change in retained earnings. In determining cash from operating activities, net income will be adjusted for the other operating source and use amounts—decrease in receivables, increase in accrued expenses and depreciation expense—all of which represent differences between accrual accounting amounts and the cash flow consequences of the same items.

PREPARING THE STATEMENT OF CASH FLOWS

The statement of cash flows for Hamilton Company is presented in Exhibit 22–5. Notice that the statement is presented in the three required sections. Operating activities provided $550,000 in cash, which differs from the reported net income of $300,000 as explained in the reconciliation at the bottom of the statement; investing activities used $700,000; financing activities provided $100,000. Disclosure is not presented for noncash transactions, interest paid, or income taxes paid because we have no information concerning these activities.

The conversion of information maintained on an accrual basis to a cash basis is sometimes difficult to understand. The following analysis will help illustrate these important relationships for Hamilton Company's 1996 financial statements.

	Accrual Amounts	Accrual-to-Cash Adjustments	Cash Flows
Revenues	$1,500	+ $100*	$1,600
Expenses			
Depreciaton	100	− 100†	–0–
Other	1,100	− 50‡	1,050
	1,200	− $150	1,050
Net income	$ 300		
Cash flows from operating activities			$ 550

*Increased positive cash flows from collection of receivables.
†Reduced negative cash flows from depreciation expense.
‡Reduced negative cash flows from increase in accrued expenses.

EXHIBIT 22–5

Hamilton Company
Statement of Cash Flows
For the Year Ended December 31, 1996
(amounts in thousands)

Cash Flows from Operating Activities		
Cash received from customers	$1,600	
Cash disbursed for operating activities	1,050	
Net cash provided by operating activities		$550
Cash Flows from Investing Activities		
Purchases of plant assets	(800)	
Proceeds from sale of land	100	
Net cash used by investing activities		(700)
Cash Flows from Financing Activities		
Proceeds of bond issuance	250	
Payments to retire bonds	(100)	
Proceeds from issuing capital stock	100	
Dividends paid	(150)	
Net cash provided by financing activities		100
Net decrease in cash		$ (50)
Cash, January 1, 1996		100
Cash, December 31, 1996		$ 50
Reconciliation of net income to net cash provided by operating activities:		
Net income		$300
Adjustments to reconcile net income to net cash provided by operating activities:		
Depreciation expense		100
Decrease in accounts receivable		100
Increase in accrued expenses		50
Net cash provided by operating activities		$550

This section provides a comprehensive illustration of the preparation of the statement of cash flows in a relatively complex situation. Several items not covered in the previous example of Hamilton Company are included. Financial statement information for Miller, Inc., presented in Exhibit 22–6 for 1995 and 1996, includes balance sheets for both years, an income statement for 1996, and additional information required to prepare the statement of cash flows.

In some situations, the analysis of transactions becomes quite complicated. This is particularly true in cases, such as for Miller, Inc., that include extraordinary items, deferred income taxes, bond discounts and premiums, and gains and losses on the sales of assets. A useful tool for accumulating the necessary information for the statement of cash flows is a four-column worksheet, which we use in this section. The worksheet is used here primarily as a device for learning the material. It may also be used in solving some of the more comprehensive problems at the end of the chapter, or for preparing a statement of cash flows in relatively complex situations in practice.

DETERMINING THE CHANGE IN CASH

The comparative balance sheets for 1995 and 1996 for Miller, Inc., reveal that cash decreased by $2,600 during 1996 ($70,000 − $67,400). This *net change* is caused by many operating, investing, and financing activities. The statement of cash flows that we will prepare

COMPREHENSIVE ILLUSTRATION: STATEMENT OF CASH FLOWS

EXHIBIT 22–6

Financial Information for Miller, Inc.

Miller, Inc.
Comparative Balance Sheets
December 31, 1995 and 1996

	1996	1995
Assets		
Cash	$ 67,400	$ 70,000
Accounts receivable, net	60,000	65,000
Inventory	94,600	62,000
Total current assets	222,000	197,000
Property, plant, and equipment	190,000	200,000
Accumulated depreciation	(33,000)	(30,000)
Patents	9,000	10,000
Total noncurrent assets	166,000	180,000
Total assets	$388,000	$377,000
Liabilities		
Dividends payable	$ 17,000	$ 10,000
Accounts payable	35,300	50,000
Income taxes payable	40,000	42,000
Notes payable	–0–	20,000
Total current liabilities	92,300	122,000
Deferred income taxes	11,400	10,000
Convertible bonds payable	60,000	100,000
Unamortized bond discount	(5,300)	(10,000)
Total noncurrent liabilities	66,100	100,000
Stockholders' Equity		
Preferred stock	10,000	10,000
Common stock	75,000	60,000
Paid-in capital in excess of par value	18,000	15,000
Retained earnings	126,600	70,000
Total stockholders' equity	229,600	155,000
Total liabilities and stockholders' equity	$388,000	$377,000

in this section separates those changes into the three basic categories and presents the cash inflows and outflows from each. We know in advance, however, that the increases in cash from all activities must be less than the decreases by $2,600.

TRANSACTION ANALYSIS

The worksheet for Miller's 1996 statement of cash flows is presented in Exhibit 22–7. The purposes of this worksheet are (1) to identify the specific operating, investing, and financing cash flows that took place during the year and (2) to identify any noncash financing and investing activities that require disclosure. The worksheet is simply a device to facilitate the

Miller, Inc.
Statement of Income
For the Year Ended December 31, 1996

Revenues		$1,200,000
Expenses		
Cost of goods sold	$500,000	
Selling expenses	300,000	
General and administrative expenses	250,000	
Interest expense	40,000	1,090,000
Income before income tax		110,000
Income tax expense		
Current	38,200	
Deferred	1,400	39,600
Income before extraordinary item		70,400
Extraordinary gain—retirement of long-term debt, net of $1,800 applicable income tax		3,200
Net income		$ 73,600

Additional Information

[1] Income before income tax includes the following items:

Depreciation expense ($2,000 in selling expenses and $6,000 in general and administrative expenses)	$8,000
Amortization of patents (included in general and administrative expenses)	1,000
Amortization of bond discount (included in interest expense)	800
Loss on sale of plant assets (included in selling expenses)	3,000

[2] Plant assets were purchased for $10,000 during 1996.

[3] Plant assets with a historical cost of $20,000 and a book value of $15,000 were sold at a $3,000 loss during 1996.

[4] Bonds with a $20,000 face value and a book value of $18,100 were retired with a cash outlay of $13,100 during 1996.

[5] Bonds with a $20,000 face value and a book value of $18,000 were converted into 1,500 shares fo $10 par value common stock during 1996.

[6] Notes payable represent bank loans of short-term duration.

[7] The dividend liability of $10,000 at December 31, 1995, was paid in early 1996. Dividends of $17,000, which were declared in late 1996, are to be paid in early 1997.

[8] Accounts payable all relate to merchandise purchased for resale.

accumulation of information needed to prepare the statement of cash flows. Entries made on the worksheet are *not recorded* in the company's formal accounting records. That is, they are neither journalized nor posted to ledger accounts.

The worksheet in Exhibit 22–7 is organized as follows:

1. The extreme left and right columns are trial balances of the real (balance sheet) accounts as of the beginning of the period (left) and the end of the period (right).

2. Debits and Credits columns are placed in the center columns and are used to enter transactions and changes that took place during the accounting period.

3. The nominal (income statement) accounts are listed below the real accounts in the middle two columns with the amount of net income flowing into retained earnings (see arrow).

EXHIBIT 22-7

Miller, Inc.
Worksheet for Statement of Cash Flows

Real Accounts	Balances Dec. 31, 1995	Changes Debits		Changes Credits		Balances Dec. 31, 1996
Debits						
Cash	70,000			(o)	2,600	67,400
Accounts receivable, net	65,000			(a)	5,000	60,000
Inventory	62,000	(b)	32,600			94,600
Property, plant, and equipment	200,000	(k)	10,000	(c)	20,000	190,000
Patents	10,000			(f)	1,000	9,000
Unamortized bond discount	10,000			(h)	800	
				(j)	1,900	
				(l_1)	2,000	5,300
	417,000					426,300
Credits						
Accumulated depreciation	30,000	(c)	5,000	(d)	2,000	
				(f)	6,000	33,000
Dividends payable	10,000	(m_1)	10,000	(m_3)	17,000	17,000
Accounts payable	50,000	(b)	14,700			35,300
Income taxes payable	42,000	(i)	2,000			40,000
Notes payable	20,000	(n)	20,000			-0-
Deferred income taxes	10,000			(i)	1,400	11,400
Convertible bonds payable	100,000	(j)	20,000			
		(l_1)	20,000			60,000
Preferred stock	10,000					10,000
Common stock	60,000			(l_2)	15,000	75,000
Paid-in capital in excess of par value	15,000			(l_2)	3,000	18,000
Retained earnings	70,000	(m_2)	17,000		73,600	126,600
	417,000		151,300		151,300	426,300

Nominal Accounts		Debits		Credits	
Revenues				(a)	1,200,000
Cost of goods sold		(b)	500,000		
Selling expenses		(c)	3,000		
		(d)	2,000		
		(e)	295,000		
General and administrative expenses		(f)	7,000		
		(g)	243,000		
Interest expense		(h)	40,000		
Income tax expense, before extraordinary item		(i)	39,600		
Extraordinary gain on debt extinguishment (net of tax)		(i)	1,800	(j)	5,000
			1,131,400		1,205,000
			73,600		
			1,205,000		1,205,000

4. At the bottom of the worksheet, the basic categories of the statement of cash flows are identi-fied, with space left below each:

| Operating activities | Financing activities |
| Investing activities | Noncash financing and/or investing activities |

Cash Flow Catagories		Changes		
		Debits		Credits
Operating Activities				
Cash collected from customers	(a)	1,205,000		
Cash paid for goods to be resold			(b)	547,300
Cash paid for selling expenses			(e)	295,000
Cash paid for general and administrative expenses			(g)	243,000
Cash paid for interest expense			(h)	39,200
Cash paid for income taxes			(i)	42,000
Investing Activities				
Cash received from sale of property, plant, and equipment	(c)	12,000		
Cash paid to acquire plant assets			(k)	10,000
Financing Activities				
Cash paid to retire bonds payable			(j)	13,100
Cash paid for dividends			(m_1)	10,000
Cash paid to retire notes payable			(n)	20,000
Noncash Financing and/or Investing Activities				
Retirement of bonds by conversion			(l_1)	18,000
Issuance of common stock for bonds	(l_2)	18,000		
Declaration of dividends			(m_2)	17,000
Dividends to be paid	(m_3)	17,000		
		1,252,000		1,254,600
Decrease in cash	(o)	2,600		
		1,254,600		1,254,600

5. Mechanical checks provided by the worksheet are
   a. The trial balance debit total must equal the trial balance credit total; this is true for both the beginning (left) and ending (right) trial balance amounts.

   b. In the changes (middle) columns, the debit total must equal the credit total after all transactions have been entered on the worksheet. This is true for categories (real accounts, nominal accounts, and statement of cash flows categories) and for the two columns in total.

   c. Each real account must "crossfoot" (i.e., the beginning balance, plus and minus changes, must equal the ending balance) after all transactions are identified and recorded.

The process by which transactions are analyzed and entered on the worksheet is illustrated in the following sections by letters corresponding to the entries in the changes columns of the worksheet in Exhibit 22–7.

Operating Activities

We begin our analysis with operating activities. To identify all cash flows from operating activities, we must analyze each of the revenue and expense accounts, keeping in mind that each account increased from zero at the beginning of the year to the balance that the account contained at the end of the year.

The increases in revenue and expense accounts occurring during the year are usually not explained completely by corresponding changes in cash. For example, the amount of revenue reported in the income statement of Miller, Inc., is not necessarily equal to the amount of cash collected from customers during the period. Some sales may have been made on account and remain uncollected at the end of the year. On the other hand, some sales made in the previous year may have been collected during the current year. Some expenses that did not require current cash payment may be recognized, and some current cash payments may have been made for expenses reported earlier (e.g., accrued expenses) or later (e.g., prepaid expenses). Therefore, we must adjust the amount of individual revenue or expense accounts from an accrual basis, as presented in the income statement, to the amount of cash flowing in or out during the year. To accomplish this logically and systematically, we analyze revenue and expense accounts in the order in which they appear on the worksheet to determine their cash flow consequences.

Revenues

(a)	Operating Activities—Cash Collected from Customers	1,205,000	
	Revenues		1,200,000
	Accounts Receivable		5,000

This worksheet entry adjusts the Revenue account for the collection of cash, as indicated by the decrease in accounts receivable, to determine cash collected from customers during the year. Miller, Inc., reported revenue of $1,200,000 for 1996 in the income statement. However, because accounts receivable decreased by $5,000 during the year, the actual cash collected from customers was more than the revenue recognized in the income statement. Analytically, we can assume that the company collected cash equal to all of the sales made during the current year (revenue for the year), plus the amount of the decline in accounts receivable.

Cost of Goods Sold

(b)	Cost of Goods Sold	500,000	
	Inventory	32,600	
	Accounts Payable	14,700	
	Operating Activities—Cash Paid for Goods to Be Resold		547,300

The amount of cost of goods sold for the year is $500,000. That amount, however, is not equal to the cash disbursed to acquire merchandise for sale. Two other balance sheet accounts affect the cash paid during the year for goods held for resale: Inventory and Accounts Payable.

The increase in Inventory indicates that more cash was paid to acquire inventory than the cost of inventory that was sold and included in Cost of Goods Sold. We adjust for this additional cash payment by debiting Inventory and crediting Operating Activities—Cash Paid for Goods to Be Resold for $32,600.

Similarly, the decrease in Accounts Payable indicates that more cash was paid to acquire inventory than the amount of purchases that was included in Cost of Goods Sold. We adjust for this additional cash payment by debiting Accounts Payable and crediting Operating Activities—Cash Paid for Goods to Be Resold for $14,700.

Entry (b) combines these related items and reflects the fact that $547,300 cash was paid for inventory-related activities—$500,000 costs of goods sold during the year, $32,600 to increase the inventory and $14,700 to pay off a portion of accounts payable.

Selling Expenses   The analysis of selling expenses is more complex because certain transactions either have caused that expense account to increase without consuming cash, or they represent activities other than operating activities. We consider each of these types of transactions separately as we determine the cash consumed by selling expenses.

(c) Investing Activities—Cash Received from Sale of		
Property, Plant, and Equipment	12,000	
Selling Expenses (Loss on Sale of Equipment)	3,000	
Accumulated Depreciation	5,000	
Property, Plant, and Equipment		20,000

This entry removes the loss recognized on the sale of equipment from the cash flows associated with the selling expenses. Recall that *sales of equipment are classified as investing activities* rather than operating activities, even though any resulting gain or loss is included in net income. Notice that entry (c) does not make any adjustment for the income tax effects of the loss on the sale of equipment. The income tax effects of gains and losses such as this one are included in the income tax expense figure in the income statement. The FASB reasoned that all income taxes should be presented in the operating activities section of the statement of cash flows, including the income tax effects of transactions presented in the statement of cash flows as financing or investing activities. (We discuss this unique classification requirement later in this chapter when we prepare the worksheet entry for the extraordinary gain from the extinguishment of debt.)

(d) Selling Expenses (Depreciation Expense)	2,000	
Accumulated Depreciation		2,000

The recognition of depreciation expense does not require or provide cash. Therefore, the effects of this noncash transaction must be identified to determine cash disbursed for selling activities. Entry (d) simply identifies the noncash depreciation expense included in selling expenses and adjusts accumulated depreciation for the change.

(e) Selling Expenses	295,000	
Operating Activities—Cash Paid for Selling		
Expenses		295,000

This entry establishes the amount of cash used to pay selling expenses. The amount is determined by subtracting the selling expenses that did not require cash (depreciation of $2,000) and the loss on the sale of equipment ($3,000) from the total selling expenses. The difference represents those selling expenses that required the use of cash.

General and Administrative Expenses   General and administrative expenses, like selling expenses, contain noncash components, and we must identify the amounts of those items before we can determine the cash consumed in paying the expenses. From the additional information, we find that two types of noncash expenses are included in general and administrative expenses: depreciation of plant assets and amortization of patents.

(f)   General and Administrative Expenses   7,000
               Patents   1,000
               Accumulated Depreciation   6,000

This entry is similar to the one in (d) and represents the noncash expenses included in general and administrative expenses. We may conclude that the remaining amount of general and administrative expenses required the disbursement of cash because nothing in the additional information indicates otherwise.

(g)   General and Administrative Expenses   243,000
               Operating Activities—Cash Paid for General and
                  Administrative Expenses   243,000

This entry establishes the amount of general and administrative expenses that required the payment of cash. This amount is determined by subtracting the expenses that did not require cash from the total general and administrative expenses: $250,000 − $7,000 = $243,000.

Interest Expense

(h)   Interest Expense   40,000
               Unamortized Bond Discount   800
               Operating Activities—Cash Paid for Interest
                  Expense   39,200

The next account appearing in the income statement is Interest Expense. If bonds are sold at a discount or premium, the interest expense for the period is not the same as the amount of cash paid for interest costs. If a *discount* is being amortized, interest expense exceeds cash interest paid, and the worksheet entry must recognize the amortization to determine the amount of cash actually paid. The preceding worksheet entry therefore includes a credit to Unamortized Bond Discount, the appropriate balance sheet account. As in the case of depreciation and amortization recognized in previous entries, the amortization of bond discount does not require the use of cash. Rather, the discount amortized is an adjustment to the amount of cash paid for interest.

If a premium were being amortized, the interest expense included in the determination of net income is not as large as the cash interest paid during the period. In that case, the worksheet entry reveals that the amount of cash paid for interest *exceeds* interest expense. The following pro forma worksheet entry shows how amortization of a premium would be handled:

Interest Expense   XXX
Unamortized Bond Premium   XXX
      Operating Activities—Cash Paid for Interest Expense   XXX

The credit to Operating Activities—Cash Paid for Interest Expense is the sum of the interest expense and the premium amortized for the period.

Income Tax Expense

(i)   Income Tax Expense   39,600
               Extraordinary Gain on Debt Extinguishment   1,800
               Income Taxes Payable   2,000
               Operating Activities—Cash Paid for Income Taxes   42,000
               Deferred Income Taxes   1,400

The next account appearing in the income statement section of the trial balances is Income Tax Expense. Four accounts affect the amount of cash paid for income taxes: Income Tax Expense, the Extraordinary Gain on Debt Extinguishment, Income Taxes Payable, and

Deferred Income Taxes. The changes in Deferred Income Taxes and Income Taxes Payable cause the amount of income tax expense to differ from the amount of cash paid for income taxes during the current period. We consider the changes in Deferred Income Taxes and Income Taxes Payable independently in the following paragraphs.

The decrease in the Income Taxes Payable account indicates that more cash was paid for income taxes than the income tax expense included in determining net income. Thus, cash used to pay income taxes is more than the combined $39,600 of income tax expense and $1,800 of tax on the extraordinary gain.

The change in the Deferred Income Taxes account can be analyzed in a similar fashion. Because that account increased, we conclude that tax expense is $1,400 *more than* the cash paid to taxing authorities. Temporary differences cause the Deferred Income Taxes account to increase by that amount.

For Miller in 1996, the actual cash paid for income taxes was $42,000, detailed as follows:

Income tax expense	$39,600
Income tax on extraordinary gain	1,800
Reduction in income tax payable	2,000
Increase in deferred income taxes	(1,400)
	$42,000

Extraordinary Gain on Debt Extinguishment The Extraordinary Gain on Debt Extinguishment, although included in the determination of net income, is excluded from the operating activities category of the statement of cash flows. Rather, the amount of cash paid to retire the bonds is reported in the *financing activities* category of the statement. The following worksheet entry accomplishes these purposes.

(j)	Convertible Bonds Payable	20,000	
	Unamortized Bond Discount		1,900
	Extraordinary Gain on Debt Extinguishment		5,000
	Financing Activities—Cash Paid to Retire Bonds		
	Payable		13,100

Recall from entry (i) that we have already included the income tax effects of the debt extinguishment in the amount paid for income taxes and classified that amount as an operating cash flow. The FASB requires that *all income taxes be classified as operating activities,* even though some portion of the total taxes may have resulted from investing or financing activities. In reaching this decision, the FASB concluded that allocation of income taxes paid to operating, investing, and financing activities would be so complex and arbitrary that the benefits, if any, would not justify the costs involved.[16]

To summarize the procedures followed in implementing this unusual classification decision, if a gain or loss is presented in the income statement at the gross amount, the item is removed from net income and reclassified at that amount and no adjustment is made to income tax expense. If the gain or loss is presented in the income statement at a net of tax amount, the item is removed from net income and reclassified at the gross amount, and cash paid for income taxes in the operating activities section is adjusted for the related amount of income taxes paid (gain) or saved (loss).

This completes the analysis of the income statement accounts, and we may conclude that we have identified all cash provided or consumed in operatng activities. We have also identified two other transactions included in income that represent investing and financing activities. Specifically, we have reclassified the loss on sale of equipment as an investing activity and the gain on the extinguishment of debt as a financing activity.

---

[16]*FASB Statement of Financial Accounting Standards No. 95,* par. 92.

Financing and Investing Activities

Our next step is to proceed through the balance sheet accounts of the trial balance and determine the cash flow implications of any remaining changes that our analysis has not fully explained to this point. We begin by analyzing changes in balance sheet accounts other than Cash. The first accounts following Cash on the trial balance in Exhibit 22–7 are Accounts Receivable and Inventory. Because of our earlier work in determining cash provided by operating activities, we have completely explained the changes in those two accounts. We know this because they crossfoot. For example, Accounts Receivable started the period with a $65,000 debit balance, was credited for $5,000, and ended with a $60,000 debit balance. Similarly, Inventory started with a $62,000 debit balance, was debited $32,600, and ended with a $94,600 debit balance.

Purchase of Property, Plant, and Equipment   The next account on the trial balance is Property, Plant, and Equipment. Our analysis of the income statement accounts has explained only a portion of the changes in that account. Therefore, we conclude that additional analysis is necessary to determine whether these additional changes represent investing activities affecting cash.

(k)	Property, Plant, and Equipment	10,000	
	Investing Activities—Cash Paid to Acquire Plant		
	Assets		10,000

From the additional information, we can determine that Miller, Inc., purchased plant assets of $10,000 during the year. That purchase represents a cash payment related to investing activities. Once this entry is recorded, we have completed our analysis of Property, Plant, and Equipment because that account now crossfoots on the worksheet ($200,000 + $10,000 − $20,000 = $190,000).

The next account in the trial balance is Patents. The change in that account has already been fully explained in our analysis of income statement accounts. Recall that the amortization expense related to patents was treated as a noncash transaction in determining cash used to pay general and administrative expenses.

Unamortized Bond Discount   The change in the Unamortized Bond Discount account has been only partially explained in our analysis to this point. Additional work is therefore necessary.

From the additional information, we learn that $20,000 of Miller, Inc., bonds were converted into common stock. The additional information also provides other data that allow us to prepare the worksheet entries presented below. For example, the additional information indicates that 1,500 shares of stock were issued with a par value of $10. That allows us to determine that the proper credit to Common Stock is $15,000 (1,500 shares @ $10). Because the carrying value of the bonds is $18,000 ($20,000 − $2,000), we also are able to determine that Paid-in Capital in Excess of Par Value of $3,000 was recognized ($18,000 − $15,000). The conversion of bonds payable to common stock is an example of a noncash financing transaction that is disclosed in a separate schedule accompanying the statement of cash flows.

Disclosure

To illustrate the two aspects of this type of financing activity—issuance of common stock and retirement of bonds payable—we divide entry (1) into two parts as follows:

(l₁)	Convertible Bonds Payable	20,000	
	Unamortized Bond Discount		2,000
	Noncash Financing Activities—Retirement of		
	Bonds by Conversion		18,000
(l₂)	Noncash Financing Activities—Issuance of Common		
	Stock for Bonds	18,000	
	Common Stock		15,000
	Paid-In Capital in Excess of Par Value		3,000

This permits us to see the dual aspects of this noncash financing activity, which must be disclosed with the statement of cash flows. In the formal statement that follows, you will see how this transaction is disclosed. Notice that we have now fully accounted for the change in the Unamortized Bond Discount account.

We have now completed our analysis of the balance sheet accounts with debit balances and can turn our attention to those with credit balances. The change in Accumulated Depreciation has been completely reconciled by our previous work. Note that the change in Accumulated Depreciation is caused by both depreciation expense and the depreciation adjustment related to the asset that was sold.

Dividends The next account, Dividends Payable, increased during 1996 by a net amount of $7,000. From the additional information, we determine that the change was caused by two different transactions. First, the $10,000 dividends declared during 1995 were paid during the current year. Second, dividends of $17,000 were declared during 1996 and are to be paid during 1997, the next year.

(m_1)	Dividends Payable	10,000	
	Financing Activities—Cash Paid for Dividends		10,000

This entry records the payment of the 1995 dividend, representing a negative cash flow during 1996.

The declaration of the dividend during 1996 to be paid in 1997 is somewhat more difficult to understand on the worksheet for the statement of cash flows. The declaration of a dividend represents a transfer from stockholders' equity to debt because Retained Earnings is reduced and Dividends Payable is increased. The declaration of a dividend is a significant financing activity, despite the fact that it does not require a cash flow until payment is made. We enter the dividend declaration as follows:

(m_2)	Retained Earnings	17,000	
	Noncash Financing Activities—Declaration of Dividends		17,000
(m_3)	Noncash Financing Activities—Dividends to Be Paid	17,000	
	Dividends Payable		17,000

The first of these two entries recognizes the declaration of the dividend as a reduction in stockholders' equity. The second recognizes the liability the company assumes with the declaration of the dividend. In the formal statement of cash flows that we prepare at the end of this illustration, you will see how this noncash financing activity is disclosed.

Notes Payable

(n)	Notes Payable	20,000	
	Financing Activities—Cash Paid to Retire Note		20,000

The change in notes payable is caused by the repayment of the note, which is a financing activity that consumes cash.

All of the changes in the remaining accounts presented in the trial balances have now been fully explained with the exception of cash itself. By providing the worksheet entry for the change in cash, we complete the analysis necessary to prepare the statement of cash flows.

Cash

We must make the final worksheet entry to determine the net change in cash. That amount is then included in the accounts used to prepare the statement of cash flows.

(o)	Decrease in Cash	2,600	
	Cash		2,600

This entry completes the worksheet and provides us with the information necessary to prepare the statement of cash flows. Cash is credited for $2,600, representing the net decrease in cash during the year, and Decrease in Cash is debited at the bottom of the worksheet to balance the statement.

PREPARING THE STATEMENT OF CASH FLOWS

Our next step is to prepare the statement of cash flows. Exhibit 22–8 presents Miller's 1996 statement in the three categories of activities: operating, investing, and financing. Information to prepare the statement is taken from the bottom of the worksheet in Exhibit 22–7.

EXHIBIT 22–8

Miller, Inc.
Statement of Cash Flows
For the Year Ended December 31, 1996

Cash Flows from Operating Activities		
Cash received from customers		$1,205,000
Less: Cash paid for goods to be sold	$547,300	
Cash paid for selling expenses	295,000	
Cash paid for general and administrative expenses	243,000	
Cash paid for interest	39,200	
Cash paid for taxes	42,000	
Cash disbursed for operating activities		1,166,500
Net cash provided by operating activities		38,500
Cash Flows from Investing Activities		
Sale of property, plant, and equipment	12,000	
Purchase of property, plant, and equipment	(10,000)	
Net cash provided by investing activities		2,000
Cash Flows from Financing Activities		
Payment of dividends	(10,000)	
Repayment of notes payable	(20,000)	
Repayment of convertible bonds payable	(13,100)	
Net cash used by financing activities		(43,100)
Net decrease in cash		(2,600)
Cash, January 1, 1996		70,000
Cash, December 31, 1996		$ 67,400

Reconciliation of Net Income to Net Cash Provided by Operating Activities

Net Income	$ 73,600	
Adjustments to Reconcile Net Income to Net Cash		
Provided by Operating Activities		
Depreciation expense	8,000	
Amortization expense	1,000	
Amortization of bond discount	800	
Loss on sale of equipment	3,000	
Increase in deferred income taxes	1,400	
Decrease in accounts receivable	5,000	
Increase in inventory	(32,600)	
Decrease in accounts payable	(14,700)	
Decrease in income taxes payable	(2,000)	
Extraordinary gain—retirement of long-term debt	(5,000)	
Net cash provided by operating activities	$ 38,500	

Supplemental Schedule of Noncash Investing and Financing Activities

Declaration of dividend in 1996 to be paid in 1997	$ 17,000
Conversion of bonds payable into common stock	$ 18,000

The operating activities section shows the cash provided by revenues and used by the various expense classifications, resulting in $38,500 positive cash flows (excess of cash receipts over cash payments). This method of determining cash flows from operating activities, when positive cash flows from revenues are reduced by negative cash flows from expenses, is identified as the **direct method.** We have used this method in the Miller, Inc., example because it is the method favored by the authors and encouraged by the FASB. Notice that we have complied with the requirement that the *amounts paid for taxes and interest be separately disclosed.*

The next section of the statement of cash flows presents Miller's investing activities during 1996. As you can see, the company both purchased and sold plant assets during the year, and those activities provided the company with a net amount of $2,000 cash.

The financing activities section of the statement shows that Miller paid dividends, repaid notes payable, and retired bonds payable, all resulting in negative cash flows. The combined effect of these events was a cash decrease of $43,100 during the year.

As we expected, the total decrease in cash of $2,600 (resulting from the combined operating, investing, and financing activities) corresponds to the decrease in cash we determined by comparing the beginning and ending cash balances.

Two important disclosures accompany the statement of cash flows in Exhibit 22–8. First **Disclosure** is the reconciliation of net income to cash flows from operating activities. In this disclosure, net income is adjusted for noncash items that are included in the determination of income following the guidelines in Exhibit 22–9. This calculation results in $38,500, which is exactly the amount of cash from operating activities in the statement of cash flows determined by the direct approach.

The second disclosure accompanying the statement of cash flows is the presentation of noncash financing and investing activities. In this illustration, the declaration of a cash

---

EXHIBIT 22–9

Adjustments to Net Income in Determining Net Cash Flows from Operating Activities

	Additions to Net Income	Deductions from Net Income
Noncash Expenses	Asset depreciation Asset depletion Asset amortization Bond discount amortization Deferred income tax increase	Bond premium amortization Deferred income tax decrease
Reclassifications	Loss—plant asset sale Loss—investment sale Loss—debt extinguishment	Gain—plant asset sale Gain—investment sale Gain—debt extinguishment
Accrual-to-Cash Adjustments	Decrease in operating current assets (e.g., accounts receivable, inventory, prepaid expenses) Increase in operating current liabilities (e.g., accounts payable, accrued expenses)	Increase in operating current assets (e.g., accounts receivable, inventory, prepaid expenses) Decrease in operating current liabilities (e.g., accounts payable, accrued expenses)
Other	Equity method loss recognized	Equity method income recognized

dividend to be paid in the following accounting period and the conversion of debt securities into common stock are examples.

The FASB permits an alternative to the direct method, identified as the **indirect method,** in presenting cash flows from operating activities. The indirect method of determining cash flows from operating activities is the approach followed in the supplemental disclosure in Exhibit 22–8, in which net income is adjusted for noncash items included in its determination. If the indirect method is followed in the preparation of the statement of cash flows, the supplemental disclosure simply becomes the operating activities section of the statement. The indirect method is widely used in practice, despite the FASB's preference for the direct method, because it was widely used before *SFAS No. 95* was issued. When the indirect method is used, supplemental disclosure of noncash investing and financing activities is still required. Also, the amount of interest and taxes paid is usually made in a note because that information is not apparent from the indirect (reconciliation) presentation.

AN EXAMPLE FROM PRACTICE

Throughout this textbook, we have provided examples from published financial statements of major corporations to illustrate the reporting practices of actual companies. Exhibit 22–10 presents the statement of cash flows of Inland Steel Industries for 1993 with comparative years 1992 and 1991. Inland Steel is a company whose businesses are leaders in value-added steel and materials distribution. Inland Steel Company, a subsidiary of Inland Steel Industries, Inc., is the fifth largest integrated steel producer in the United States, and Inland materials Distribution Group, Inc., is the nation's largest metal distribution network.

Notice that the statement of cash flows is presented in the three sections we have discussed in this chapter—operating, investing, and financing. The operating activities section is prepared by the indirect method. Cash flows in each major category include both positive and negative amounts. For example, in the financing activities category, positive cash flows came from the sale of common stock and the issuance of long-term debt; negative cash flows came from the retirement of long-term debt, the payment of dividends, and the acquisition of treasury stock.

The amounts of cash paid for interest and income taxes are presented at the bottom of the statement. The note at the bottom of the exhibit is taken from the statement of accounting policies and explains the definition of cash equivalents.

CASH FLOW CLASSIFICATION ISSUES

Several interesting classification issues exist in preparing a statement of cash flows.[17] In this section, we briefly explore some of these issues, including how the FASB dealt with them in *SFAS No. 95,* to indicate the complexity that underlies the statement of cash flows and the articulation of that financial statement with the other primary statements.

We have learned that dividends paid by a company to its stockholders are presented as negative cash flows in the *financing* activities section. Interest paid on debt obligations is presented, however, as a negative *operating* cash flow, despite the similarity of interest and dividends. The primary reason for this treatment is that interest expense is a component in the determination of net income while dividends paid are treated as a distribution rather than a determinant of net income.

Cash inflows from interest and dividend revenues are presented in the statement of cash flows as operating activities because these items enter into the determination of net income. Other transactions involving the debt and equity investments to which the interest and dividends relate are presented as investing activities; some would argue that cash inflows from interest and dividend revenues should be classified as investing as well. Apparently, the fact

---

[17]For a comprehensive discussion of the classification issues discussed here, as well as other ambiguities in the preparation of the statement of cash flows, see Hugh Nurnberg, "Inconsistencies and Ambiguities in Cash Flow Statements under FASB Statement No. 95," *Accounting Horizons* (June 1993), pp. 60–75.

EXHIBIT 22–10

Inland Steel Industries, Inc.
Statement of Cash Flows

Consolidated Statement of Cash Flows

(dollars in millions)	Increase (Decrease) in Cash Years Ended December 31		
	1993	**1992**	**1991**
Operating Activities			
Net loss	$ (37.6)	$ (815.6)	$(275.1)
Adjustments to reconcile net loss to net cash provided from (used for) operating activities:			
Depreciation	131.8	129.6	118.2
Facility shutdown and restructuring provisions	18.9	—	212.4
Deferred income taxes	(36.8)	(455.7)	(93.7)
Deferred employee benefit cost, including cumulative effect of change in accounting principle	38.1	1,066.7	(14.3)
Stock issued for coverage of employee benefit plan expense	19.1	13.4	14.0
Gain on sale of partial interest in joint venture	—	(22.5)	—
Change in: Receivables	(46.4)	(27.1)	53.8
Inventories	(4.2)	5.6	72.1
Accounts payable	34.0	22.8	(74.0)
Accrued salaries and wages	1.6	(1.8)	(6.7)
Other accrued liabilities	4.9	30.0	4.0
Other deferred items	(11.4)	33.2	14.3
Net adjustments	149.6	794.2	300.1
Net cash provided from (used for) operating activities	112.0	(21.4)	25.0
Investing Activities			
Capital expenditures	(105.6)	(64.4)	(140.2)
Investments in and advances to joint ventures, net	(1.9)	(6.3)	(24.9)
Proceeds from sales of assets	6.5	28.1	13.9
Net cash used for investing activities	(101.0)	(42.6)	(151.2)
Financing Activities			
Sale of common stock	178.7	97.9	—
Sale of preferred stock	—	—	72.8
Long-term debt issued	46.8	145.4	121.4
Long-term debt retired	(78.5)	(49.4)	(39.3)
Dividends paid	(35.7)	(35.8)	(37.6)
Acquisition of treasury stock	(9.5)	(3.5)	(2.3)
Net cash provided from financing activities	101.8	154.6	115.0
Net increase (decrease) in cash and cash equivalents	112.8	90.6	(11.2)
Cash and cash equivalents—beginning of year	137.7	47.1	58.3
Cash and cash equivalents—end of year	$ 250.5	$ 137.7	$ 47.1
Supplemental Disclosures			
Cash paid (received) during the year for:			
Interest (net of amount capitalized)	$ 76.0	$ 53.1	$ 40.4
Income taxes, net	1.9	(12.3)	(12.5)

Cash Equivalents

Cash equivalents reflected in the Statement of Cash Flows are highly liquid, short-term investments with maturities of three months or less that are an integral part of the Company's cash management portfolio. The carrying amount of cash equivalents approximates fair value because of the short maturity of those instruments.

SOURCE: Inland Steel Industries, Inc., 1993 Annual Report.

that these items enter into the determination of net income was a strong incentive for the FASB to require that they be included as operating cash flows.

Earlier, we briefly discussed the tax consequences of certain gains and losses that are included in the determination of net income, pointing out that the total income tax paid is considered an operating cash flow. This is true, even if some portion of the tax results from transactions that are classified as financing or investing activities. This is a questionable treatment, in the minds of the authors, because the financial effects of gains and losses are overstated and cash flows from operations are distorted when the gains and losses and their related tax effects are separated. The FASB relied heavily on the cost-benefit argument to support its decision not to allocate income taxes among the categories in the statement of cash flows; in its decision it also weighed the complexity of the calculations that would be involved if allocation were required. Tax considerations may also have been factors in the FASB's decision to include interest expense, dividend revenue, and interest revenue in operations; including them avoids the distortion that might result if these items were presented as financing and investing activities with their tax effects presented in operations.

In the authors' opinion, these classification issues point out the complexity of financial statement classification and the fact that the terminology used in the income statement does not correspond precisely with the more recent terminology that has been developed for the statement of cash flows. Undoubtedly, as we gain additional experience in the preparation of statements of cash flows, we will refine our definitions and classifications of items over time.

CONTINUING REFINEMENTS OF SFAS NO. 95

After *SFAS No. 95* had been in effect only a short time, the FASB issued two pronouncements that amended it in special circumstances. Detailed coverage of these specialized situations is beyond the scope of this text, but they provide an opportunity to understand the difficulty the FASB faces in its attempts to anticipate problems of implementing new financial reporting requirements. The fact that the Board must amend and refine its earlier pronouncements after some experience from practice is not unusual.

Briefly, the following changes have been implemented since *SFAS No. 95* was originally issued:

1. A statement of cash flows is not required to be presented by defined benefit pension plans that present information in accordance with *SFAS No. 35*. Also, if certain specified conditions are met, investment companies are not required to present a statement of cash flows.[18]

2. Cash receipts and payments resulting from purchases and sales of securities and other assets of banks, brokers, and dealers in securities shall be classified as operating cash flows if those assets were acquired specifically for resale and are carried at market value in a trading account.[19]

3. Although gross cash flow information is generally preferred over net cash flow information, banks, savings institutions, and credit unions are not required to report gross amounts of cash receipts and payments for specified deposits and loans.[20]

4. Cash flows resulting from futures contracts, forward contracts, option contracts, or swap contracts that are accounted for as hedges of identifiable transactions or events may be classified in the same category as the cash flows from the items being hedged, provided that accounting policy is disclosed.[21]

Throughout this chapter, we have emphasized the direct method of presentation for cash provided by or used in operating activities. Briefly, the direct method presents both positive and negative cash flows by category of operating activities in a manner similar to that used

---

[18]*FASB Statement of Financial Accounting Standards No. 102,* "Statement of Cash Flows—Exemption of Certain Enterprises and Classification of Cash Flows from Certain Securities Acquired for Resale," 1989, pars. 5–7.

[19]*SFAS No. 102,* par. 8.

[20]*FASB Statement of Financial Accounting Standards No. 104,* "Statement of Cash Flows—Net Reporting of Certain Cash Receipts and Cash Payments and Classification of Cash Flows from Hedging Transactions," 1989, par. 7.

[21]*SFAS No. 104,* par. 7.

for investing and financing activities. The indirect method, on the other hand, begins with net income and reconciles that figure to the amount of cash provided by or used in operating activities by adjusting noncash items and reclassifying items as investing or financing, as required by *SFAS No. 95*. We also stated that the FASB preferred the direct method but permitted the indirect method.

The debate over whether to require the direct method or permit both methods was an important part of the standard-setting process from which *SFAS No. 95* emerged. The FASB apparently believed that the direct method has considerable merit in that it shows operating cash receipts and payments by category, information that may be useful in estimating future operating cash flows.[22] Interestingly, a majority of respondents to the exposure draft for *SFAS No. 95* expressed a preference for the direct method and asked the FASB to make it mandatory.[23] Many financial statement preparers cited the difficulty and cost of accumulating the information required for the direct method as reasons for permitting either the direct or the indirect method. They said that they do not presently collect information in a manner that allows the determination of gross cash flows by operating categories and that to do so would require costly changes in their accounting systems.

In the final analysis, the FASB did permit either the direct or indirect method to be used. The authors strongly advocate the direct method, both from the perspective of investors and creditors who seek to understand a company's activities and from the perspective of students attempting to learn about the statement of cash flows and its relationship to the other financial statements. Although the FASB has not yet amended *SFAS No. 95* in this important area, we see this as fertile ground for continuing consideration and experimentation as both preparers and users of financial statements gain experience with the statement of cash flows, particularly the direct method of presenting cash flows from operating activities.

Even the definition of cash may be subject to refinement in the future. Although *cash* seems to be an easily defined term, research indicates that its lack of a consistent definition results in a lack of comparability among companies, particularly companies in different countries. Wallace and Collier did research described as a multicountry comparison of cash flow statements.[24] They specifically examined how national accounting standard-setting bodies that have issued pronouncements on reporting cash flow information defined cash. Their research highlights inadequacies in the definitions of cash and cash equivalents in these standards and in the interpretations of standards by preparers of financial statements. They conclude that defining cash has not proven to be simple and that national and global intercompany comparisons of financial figures will not necessarily be improved by cash flow information. Given these results, the authors of this textbook believe that it is reasonable to expect continued monitoring of the definition of cash with potential clarification coming at some time in the future.

PROFESSIONAL JUDGMENT

One of the merits of cash flow information is that it is relatively objective and does not involve many of the assumptions and judgments inherent in accrual accounting information. Despite the relative objectivity of cash flow information, professional judgment must be applied when preparing the statement of cash flows.

Cash equivalents are treated as cash for purposes of preparing a statement of cash flows. Cash equivalents are short-term, highly liquid investments that are readily convertible to known amounts of cash and are so near to maturity that they present insignificant risk of changes in value because of changes in interest rates. Examples of cash equivalents are Treasury bills, commercial paper, and money market funds. Each type of investment must be

---

[22]*SFAS, No. 95,* par. 107.

[23]*SFAS No. 95,* par. 111.

[24]R. S. Olusegun Wallace and Paul A. Collier, "The 'Cash' in Cash Flow Statements: A Multi-Country Comparison," *Accounting Horizons* (December 1991), pp. 44–52.

LIES OF THE BOTTOM LINE

For decades we've made the most fundamental and far-reaching economic decisions on the basis of that supposedly magic number, the bottom line.

As investors, we buy and sell stocks depending on whether a company's earnings are growing or shrinking. As managers, we decide what investments to make based largely on what earnings the projects will yield.

Our entire economy, like any free market, allocates the nation's collective wealth through a series of rational decisions about where it can best be invested to create more wealth. We base those decisions, above all, on what the bottom line provides.

We're making a big mistake. Reported earnings have become virtually worthless in terms of their ability to tell us what's really going on at a company. This is not only the result of a business environment in which managers obsessed with how investors will react to the quarterly numbers are tempted to fiddle. Blame must also go to the accountants who, in their well-meaning attempts to cure abuses, have in many cases made it even easier for companies to hide the ball.

"As long as investors—including supposedly sophisticated institutions—place fancy valuations on reported 'earnings' that march steadily upward," wrote Berkshire Hathaway Chairman Warren Buffett to his shareholders last year, "you can be sure that some managers and promoters will exploit GAAP [generally accepted accounting principles] to produce such numbers, no matter what the truth may be."

David Hawkins, professor of accounting at Harvard Business School, does not doubt that the time is ripe for a decline in the quality of reported earnings—a decline, he says, "that may or may not be detectable from the outside."

Take Prime Motor Inns, until a few months ago the world's second-largest hotel operator. Last year Prime reported a healthy net income of $77 million—18% of revenues—up nearly 15% from the year before.

In September Prime filed for Chapter 11 bankruptcy.

What happened? Could the bankruptcy filing have been foreseen? Prime's problem was that it didn't have enough cash coming in. Much of its reported 1989 bottom line came from selling hotels. But outside financing for those sales had dried up, and Prime had to finance many of those deals itself—leaving it without enough cash to pay its debt service, including debt for the properties it had "sold." According to banking consultants Financial Proformas, Inc., Prime had a $15 million cash *outflow* from operations in 1989—the year it reported a $77 million profit—compared with a positive cash flow of $58 million the year before.

Prime has had plenty of company over the years. W. T. Grant, Penn Central, Crazy Eddie, Miniscribe and more than a few savings and loan associations all reported impressive earnings and still went bankrupt.

As with hairdos and hemlines, fads in accounting come and go. In the 1920s, when stocks traded mostly on the basis of asset values (shades of the 1930s!), accountants devoted their skills to inflating asset values. In the 1960s the focus was on revenues. Many franchisors, for example, would book "sales" immediately after signing a franchise agreement, even though many franchisees failed ever to deliver any cash. In the 1980s the big problem was banks and savings and loans overstating the value of their assets. (The Securities & Exchange Commission is now pushing a major accounting change—keeping many of these assets on the books at market value rather than cost.)

Today, net income—the bottom line—is making a comeback. So are what Buffett likes to call "white lies" aimed at making reported profits look better than they really are.

One popular white lie is the so-called big bath method of suddenly cleansing balance sheets of past sins, after years of insisting that everything was just fine. Among other things, the big bath often positions a company for accelerated future growth (and executives for big bonuses based on increases in earnings or returns on equity), since the company starts from a base of smaller earnings in the year of the big writeoff. Ironically, a big writeoff tends to boost immediately a company's stock—presumably investors like such "candor." According to Kidder, Peabody & Co., $3.4 billion of writeoffs occurred in this year's first and second quarters, nearly twice last year's record level.

Marriott Corp. took a big bath last year with a $256 million charge that included writeoffs of advances to purchasers of its hotels over the years—as well as writedowns in the value of the hotels Marriott owned.

Why did it take management so long to own up to the problems? The accounting rules are vague. They say only that companies must write down the assets as soon as management realizes that the assets are "permanently impaired." Plenty of room for interpretation there.

"The problems were evident for years, because the partnerships were running cash flow deficits," avers Robert Renck Jr. of the New York research firm R. L. Renck & Co.

During the 1970s the accountants tried to eliminate managements' use of balance sheet reserves to smooth earnings. Yet companies still find ways to squirrel away funds to handle unexpected earnings turbulence—often by accelerating depreciation in profitable quarters, and tucking the money away in hidden accounting reserves for a rainy day.

"If push comes to shove, and the chairman wants a nickel more per share," warns accounting expert Lee Seidler, "any good controller knows where to find it."

Oil companies are champions of income smoothing. One of their favorite methods: Simply add to (or delay adding to) reserves for future environmental cleanups.

Look how well it works. Amoco Corp. announced in July that it had an extraordinary gain of $471 million in

carefully analyzed and professional judgment applied to determine whether cash flow activity for each security is part of the change in cash itself, or whether it is appropriately classified in the investing activities section of the statement of cash flows.

the second quarter from settling claims dating from Iran's seizure of the company's assets in the late 1970s. The company simultaneously added $477 million to its reserves for environmental damage.

Texaco had a $362 million gain last year from selling a stock interest in a subsidiary. In the same quarter, it booked a $355 million charge for future environmental programs.

"In the last two years, any time a major oil company has recognized a nonoperating gain, it has tended to find offsetting, nonrecurring charges to hide those profits," says Bernard Picchi, petroleum analyst at Salomon Brothers. "By the time the third- and fourth-quarter [1990] results are announced, you'll see a lot of others."

Accounting rules allow companies to wait to book future environmental expenses until they are certain that they are going to incur the expenses and know roughly what they will be. But that gives management a lot of leeway. Agrees a prominent oil company official who requested anonymity: "If we're going to have a horrible fourth quarter, we can come up with an argument to put them [the accountants] off. When we have a profitable quarter, that's when we tend to clean up our balance sheet."

Where did all this subjective judgment about the shape of the bottom line start? Go no further back than the 17th-century trading companies like the East India Company, chartered by Queen Elizabeth I in 1600 and one of the first "joint stock" companies. Initially, the company distributed all profits (if any) at the end of each spice-trading voyage. But in 1661 the company's governor announced that future distributions would consist of periodic dividends paid out of retained earnings.

All of a sudden, measuring profits was a job for the accountants, who had to start making judgment calls. Assets and profits had to be apportioned among many voyages in different stages of completion. Many subjective judgments were required before calculating each period's bottom line—the life expectancy of ships, how much capital to retain to keep the ships in tip-top shape, when to write off bad debts, etc.

In short, trading companies like the East India Company introduced accrual accounting, the bottom line and most of the bookkeeping problems we face today. With a system that at its core relies on arbitrary judgments on such questions as when (and whether) a ship will arrive, curbing abuses is an impossible task.

Part of the problem is this: Recently the more the accountants have tried to fix things by rewriting the rules, the more complicated and less useful financial statements have become.

Five years ago, for example, the Financial Accounting Standards Board, the profession's rulemaking body, decided to change the way companies handled their pension plans. It took 11 years and 132 pages to present rules putting the company's entire pension liability on the balance sheet.

The major aerospace companies all implemented the rules differently, causing huge variations in their bottom lines and making comparisons among them all but impossible. A recent analysis of Patricia McConnell, editor of Bear, Stearns & Co.'s *Accounting Issues* and adviser to the Financial Accounting Standards Board, found the new rules boosted Grumman's net income last year by 84%, Lockheed's by 112%, Boeings's by 1% and Northrop's by 26%. How much is the business really making? Good luck at figuring it out.

The FASB has also required companies that build new factories or other fixed assets to capitalize their interest expense rather than deduct it from income as they spend it. The theory is that this puts the full cost of the factory on the company's balance sheet. The reality is, it moves net income further away from that objectively measurable thing, the expenditure of hard cash.

So what's the answer? Even the loftiest academics are hard-pressed to prescribe a new way of measuring corporate health. And nobody is ready to start over with a completely new conceptual approach to accounting.

Perhaps the best approach is using cash flow as a check on the reliability of earnings. One of the most helpful things the FASB has done in recent years was to require that companies publish cash flow statements along with their income statements and balance sheets. You can't blame the FASB if the cash flow is ignored by many investors.

Start with the line labeled "cash flow from operations." If net income is moving up while cash from operations is sliding down, something is probably wrong.

But if you're interested in how this company is going to do over the long haul, don't stop there. Cash from operations leaves out a crucial part of the story, capital expenditures, without which any company will wither and die. Subtract from operating cash flow the company's capital expenditures. This will give you a reasonably clear picture of how much cash is available to distribute to owners over the long run.

The bottom line and cash flow numbers give a good fix on last year and today. But they won't tell you where the company is going. "The accountants don't know how to do that," says Buffett. "That is not a science, it's an art. And it's the job of the fellow who lays out the money, not his bookkeeper." The whole game, he adds, is "figuring out net cash flows after all required captial investments over the next five or ten years. If you're right about that and you don't pay too much [for a company], you can't lose." Investors probably understood that better in Queen Elizabeth I's day than they do now.

SOURCE: Dana Wechsler Linden, "Lies of the Bottom Line," *Forbes* (November 12, 1990), pp. 106, 108, 112. Reprinted by permission of *Forbes Magazine*, November 12, 1990. © Forbes Inc., 1990.

An important characteristic of the statement of cash flows is the classification of cash flows into operating, investing, and financing activities. These classifications create the primary basis for information useful in assessing future cash flow prospects. Most cash flows are clearly identifiable in one of these categories. The classification issues identified in the previous section indicate that some difficulties exist and judgment must be carefully applied. An important presentation decision that must be made is whether cash flows from operating activities will be presented by the direct or the indirect method. This decision requires carefully applied professional judgment in evaluating the availability of information required by each method and in determining which method produces information that is most useful for users of a company's financial statements.

Finally, we have illustrated a number of situations involving investing and financing activities that do not affect cash. These transactions are, nevertheless, important in assessing the financial position and results of operations of a company and require disclosure. Care must be taken that each transaction of this type has been identified and disclosed in a manner that permits an understanding of the nature of the transaction while carefully distinguishing it from transactions that affect cash flows.

CONCLUDING REMARKS

The emergence of the statement of cash flows as one of the primary financial statements is a major event for the accounting profession. Rarely do reporting requirements in an area change as dramatically as was the case when *SFAS No. 95* was issued, replacing the statement of changes in financial position with the statement of cash flows.

Throughout this chapter, we have emphasized the preparation of the statement of cash flows by making appropriate adjustment to accrual accounting information. A logical question is why we would not simply open a company's cash disbursement records and prepare the statement directly from that source. Logically, one might argue that this should be the most direct and easiest manner in which to prepare the statement.

The other financial statements are prepared on the basis of accrual concepts. Procedures to implement accrual accounting have been a part of practice for many years. The emergence of the statement of cash flows, which represents a break from a strict accrual orientation in financial reporting, is relatively new. At the present time, the authors believe that most accounting systems produce information designed first to produce the other major financial statements. Statements of cash flow are then prepared by adjusting accrual accounting information.

In the future, as we gain experience with cash flow information, we may design accounting systems specifically intended to produce information to prepare the statement of cash flows. For example, cash disbursement journals might require classification of all payments into operating, investing, and financing categories at the time of initial recording. An even more dramatic change might be for accounting systems to move toward cash-based recording with financial statements based on accrual concepts being prepared "outside the system," without formal recording, as we have done in this chapter in preparing the statement of cash flows. In short, we see the changing orientation toward cash flow information as a very important development that will have long-term and far-reaching implications for financial reporting.

KEY POINTS

1. The statement of cash flows has one primary objective: to provide information about a company's liquidity in terms of its cash receipts and cash payments. (Objective 1)
2. Cash flow information is generally thought to be important to users of financial statements—particularly investors and creditors—in assessing the company's cash flow, liquidity, and financial flexibility. (Objective 2)
3. The statement of cash flows is presented in three major categories that parallel the major types of cash flows for a company: operating activities, investing activities, and financing activities. (Objective 3)
4. Some investing and financing activities do not affect cash but are still important in explaining changes in financial position. Such transactions must be disclosed in a schedule accompanying the statement of cash flows. (Objective 4)

5. Three essential steps for preparing a statement of cash flows are (1) determining the change in cash for the period; (2) performing transaction analysis in which cash receipts and payments are identified and classified, as are noncash financing and investing activities; and (3) preparing a formal statement in accordance with standards promulgated by the FASB. For relatively complex situations, a worksheet is a valuable tool in analyzing transactions and accumulating the information necessary to prepare a statement of cash flows. (Objective 5)

APPENDIX A: T-ACCOUNT APPROACH OF CASH FLOW TRANSACTION ANALYSIS

An alternative to using a worksheet to identify the causes of changes in cash during an accounting period is the T-account approach. This relatively simple procedure calls for establishing a T account for each real and nominal account and identifying changes in those accounts in terms of their impact on operating, investing, and financing activities.

Exhibit 22–11 demonstrates the application of this approach for the information presented in the chapter for Hamilton Company. Notice that for each real and nominal account, the net change for the period is identified beside the account title (e.g., Accounts Receivable includes [−100], which means that the account went down by $100 during the year).

Entries to identify all changes in real and nominal accounts in terms of their impact on the three cash flow classifications and then to reclassify the net income and the change in cash are described as follows (SCF = statement of cash flows):

(a)	SCF/Operating	1,600	
	Revenues		1,500
	Accounts Receivable		100

To identify cash receipts from sales and collections of receivables as positive operating cash flow.

(b)	Plant Assets	800	
	SCF/Investing		800

To record purchase of plant assets as investing negative cash flow.

(c)	SCF/Investing	100	
	Plant Assets		100

To record sale of plant assets as investing positive cash flow.

(d)	Expense (Depreciation)	100	
	Accumulated Depreciation		100

To record depreciation expense. (No impact on cash flows.)

(e)	Expenses (other)	1,100	
	Accrued Expenses		50
	SCF/Operating		1,050

To record operating expenses and increase in accrued expenses as negative operating cash flow.

(f)	SCF/Financing	250	
	Bonds Payable		250

To record the issue of bonds as positive financing cash flow.

(g)	Bonds Payable	100	
	SCF/Financing		100

To record the retirement of bonds as negative financing cash flow.

(h)	SCF/Financing	100	
	Capital Stock		100

To record the sale of capital stock as positive financing cash flow.

(i)	Retained Earnings	150	
	SCF/Financing		150

To record the cash dividend as negative financing cash flow.

(j)	Income Summary	300	
	Retained Earnings		300

To transfer net income to real account, Retained Earnings.

(k)	SCF Summary	50	
	Cash		50

To transfer the net effect of operating, investing, and financing activities to the real account, Cash.

The entries account for the entire change in the balance of each real and nominal account (e.g., Bonds Payable increased by $250 from one transaction, decreased by $100 from another transaction, netting to an increase of $150 as indicated at the top of the T account). The analysis is complete when all changes in real and nominal accounts have been accounted for, the amount of net income reconciles the change in retained earnings (entry **(j)** above), and the net amount of all cash changes reconciles the change in cash (entry **(k)** above).

QUESTIONS

22–1 The FASB recently identified several reasons that information concerning cash flows is useful to financial statement users. What reasons did it give?

22–2 What are the objectives of a statement of cash flows?

22–3 What information is included in a statement of cash flows that is not available in comparative income statements, balance sheets, and retained earnings statements for the same reporting period?

EXHIBIT 22–11

Hamilton Company
Cash Analysis of T accounts
(in thousands of dollars)

Real Accounts   **Nominal Accounts**

Cash (− 50)		
	(k)	50

Accounts Receivable (− 100)		
	(a)	100

Revenues (+ 1,500)		
	(a)	1,500

Plant Assets (+ 700)			
(b)	800	(c)	100
	(100)		
	700		

Accumulated Depreciation (+ 100)		
	(d)	100

Expense (depreciation) (+ 100)		
(d)	100	

Accrued Expenses (+ 50)		
	(e)	50

Bonds Payable (+ 150)			
(g)	100	(f)	250
			(100)
			150

Expenses (other) (+ 1,100)		
(e)	1,100	

Capital Stock (+ 100)		
	(h)	100

Retained Earnings (+ 150)			
(i)	150	(j)	300
			(150)
			150

Income Summary:

Revenues		1,500
Expenses:		
Depreciation		(100)
Other		(1,100)
Net income		300
Reclassification (j)		(300)
		–0–

Cash Flow Classifications

Operating				
(a)	1,600	(e)	1,050	
	(1,050)			
	550			

Investing				
(c)	100	(b)	800	
			(100)	
			700	

Financing				
(f)	250	(g)	100
(h)	100	(i)	150
	350		250
	(250)		
	100		

SCF Summary:

Operating	550
Investing	(700)
Financing	100
Net decrease in cash	(50)
Reclassification (k)	50
	–0–

22-4 Why must adjustments be made to net income to determine "cash provided by or used in operating activities"?

22-5 What are three major categories of transactions that may result in increases in cash? State a general conclusion about the circumstances in which an increase in cash would actually result.

22-6 What are three major categories of transactions that may result in decreases in cash? State a general conclusion about the circumstances in which a decrease in cash would actually result.

22-7 Is depreciation a use of cash? Explain.

22-8 How should gross and net cash flows from investing and financing activities be presented in a statement of cash flows?

22-9 What are noncash investing and financing transactions? How are they presented in the statement of cash flows?

22-10 How may net income be a source of cash? How may a net loss be a use of cash?

22-11 Is it possible for a net loss for a period to result in a source of cash for that same period? Explain.

22-12 A plant asset was sold at a loss during the current year. The loss was included in income before extraordinary item on the enterprise's income statement. What is the proper presentation of this transaction in the statement of cash flows?

22-13 A plant asset was sold in a condemnation proceeding, resulting in a substantial gain. The gain was appropriately presented as an extraordinary item in the enterprise's income statement. What is the proper presentation of this transaction in the statement of cash flows?

22-14 What is the relationship between the change in cash during a period and the three types of cash flows—operating, investing, and financing?

22-15 What is the definition of *cash* as that term is used in a statement of cash flows?

22-16 How are the following transactions treated in a statement of cash flows?

[a] Declaration of a cash dividend to be paid in the next period.
[b] Declaration and payment of a cash dividend in the current period.

22-17 Describe the cash flow effects of income tax expense, income taxes payable, and deferred income taxes.

22-18 The controller of Fallow Company, your audit client, argues that the refunding of outstanding 10% debt by issuing 8% debt does not materially affect the company's financial position, because the difference between the net amount of debt outstanding is not great (i.e., not material in relation to the other balance sheet items). The controller argues, therefore, that the transaction does not need to be included in the statement of cash flows, particularly because cash is not affected. Do you agree or disagree with the controller? Why?

22-19 Which of the following financial statements has as its primary function the presentation of information about cash receipts and payments and financing and investing aspects of all significant transactions?

[a] Retained earnings statement   [c] Statement of cash flows
[b] Income statement   [d] Statement of financial position   (AICPA adapted)

22-20 In 1996 Ashley Company retired convertible bonds for which stock was issued pursuant to a conversion option. The exchange took place on an interest payment date and except for the interest payment, no cash changed hands. In preparing a statement of cash flows, the exchange in securities should be treated in which of the following ways?

[a] Ignored because the "book value" method was used to record the exchange.
[b] Added to net income to arrive at cash provided by operating activities.
[c] Subtracted from net income to arrive at cash provided by operating activities.
[d] Disclosed separately as a noncash financing activity.   (AICPA adapted)

22-21 Which of the following items represents a potential decrease in cash?

[a] Goodwill amortization.
[b] Sale of plant assets at a loss.
[c] Net loss from operations.
[d] Declaration of a stock dividend.   (AICPA adapted)

22-22 When preparing a statement of cash flows, an increase in ending inventory over beginning inventory results in an adjustment to reported net income in computing cash flows from operating activities by the indirect method because

[a] Cash was increased because inventory is a current asset.

[b] The net increase in inventory reduced cost of goods sold but represents an assumed use of cash.

[c] Inventory is not an expense deducted in computing net income but is not a use of cash.

[d] All changes in noncash accounts must be disclosed.   (AICPA adapted)

22–23 Wilmer, Inc.'s income statement includes income tax expense of $170,000, of which $137,000 was paid by year-end and $33,000 was deferred because of the use of accelerated cost recovery for income tax purposes and straight-line depreciation for financial reporting. How will these facts affect the presentation of cash provided by operating activities in the statement of cash flows?

EXERCISES

22–24 Cash Flow from Operating Activities   Vernon Company reported $185,000 of net income in 1996. Expenses reported in the determination of this income included the following: salaries, $200,000; cost of sales, $400,000; interest, $50,000; depreciation and amortization, $127,000; and income taxes, $400,000 (none of which was deferred). All sales are made for cash, expenses (other than depreciation and amortization) were paid in cash, and the balance of inventory was unchanged during the year.

INSTRUCTIONS

Using only the above information, compute cash provided by operating activities during 1996 by the indirect method.

22–25 Cash Flow from Operating Activities   Brown Company's income statement for the year ended December 31, 1996, is as follows:

Brown Company
Income Statement
For the Year Ended December 31, 1996

Revenue		
Sales	$110,000	
Services	75,000	$185,000
Expenses		
Cost of goods sold	$ 96,000	
Selling and administrative expenses	45,000	
Depreciation expense	25,000	
Amortization of intangibles	7,000	173,000
Income before income taxes		12,000
Income tax expense		4,360
Net income		$ 7,640
Earnings per common share		$.78

INSTRUCTIONS

Compute the amount of cash from operating activities for the year by the direct method, assuming the following:

[a] A sale of $18,000 resulted in the acceptance of a three-year, 8% note receivable. All other sales were for cash.

[b] The $4,360 provision for income taxes is distributed as follows:

Paid during 1996	$2,940
Deferred	1,420
	$4,360

The deferral relates to the temporary difference resulting from the use of accelerated cost recovery system for tax purposes and straight-line method for income statement reporting purposes.

[c] All current assets (other than cash) and current liabilities remained constant during 1996.

22–26 Cash Flow from Operating Activities   Telecom Company reports the following summarized income statement data for 1996:

Revenue	$1,950,000
Expenses	1,625,000
Net income	$ 325,000

Accounts receivable resulting from revenue-producing transactions increased by $56,000 from January 1 to December 31, 1996. Depreciation expense amounted to $172,000.

INSTRUCTIONS

Using only the explicit preceding information, compute cash provided by operating activities during 1996, applying the direct method.

22–27 Cash Flow from Operating Activities Net income of Jane Company for 1996 was reported as $162,000. The following related information is available:

	At Dec. 31, 1995	At Dec. 31, 1996
Accrued interest payable recognized	$10,000	$12,500
Depreciation expense recognized	18,200	19,300
Prepaid expenses recognized	775	1,235

INSTRUCTIONS

Using this information, determine the cash provided by operating activities during 1996 by the indirect method.

22–28 Cash Flow from Operating Activities Sanford Company's income statement for 1996 is presented below with explanatory information for selected items:

Sanford Company
Income Statement
For the Year Ended December 31, 1996

Revenue from sales [1]		$5,498,000
Cost of goods sold		3,150,000
Gross profit		2,348,000
Expenses		
Selling	$246,000	
Depreciation	235,000	
Amortization of intangibles	52,000	
Salaries and wages [2]	400,000	
Interest [3]	72,000	
Miscellaneous operating	5,000	1,010,000
Income before income taxes		1,338,000
Income tax expense [4]		445,000
Net income		$ 893,000
Earnings per common share		$.19

ADDITIONAL INFORMATION

[1] All sales were for cash except a $120,000 sale resulting in the acceptance of a three-year, 9% note receivable and a $75,000 sale resulting in the acceptance of a tract of land valued at $75,000.

[2] Accrued salaries and wages at December 31, 1995 and 1996, were $40,000 and $45,600, respectively.

[3] Interest expense includes $6,800 of amortization of bond discount. All interest, other than the discount amortization, was paid during 1996.

[4] Income tax expense includes $110,000 of taxes deferred due to the use of the accelerated cost recovery system for tax purposes and the straight-line method for reporting purposes. All other tax expense was paid during the year.

INSTRUCTIONS

Compute the cash provided by operating activities for 1996 by the direct method.

22–29 Cash Flow from Investing Activities   Sedano Company has the following account balances:

	1996	1995
Property, plant, and equipment	$313,000	$297,000
Accumulated depreciation	125,000	103,000

INSTRUCTIONS

Compute the cash flows from investing activities, assuming that Sedano sold for $53,000 assets with a cost of $52,000 and accumulated depreciation of $2,500.

22–30 Cash Flow from Financing Activities   Ueno Company had the following transactions in 1996:

[1] Sold 20,000 shares of common stock at $8 per share.
[2] Declared and paid cash dividends of $87,000.
[3] Declared and issued a stock dividend of $14,000.
[4] Paid an outstanding note payable for $21,200.
[5] Purchased $9,500 of treasury stock.

INSTRUCTIONS

Compute the cash flows from financing activities.

22–31 Statement of Cash Flows Preparation (Indirect)   Smart Company reported net income of $188,200 for 1996 with no extraordinary items. The following information is available:

[1] Current assets other than cash increased by $27,500 and current liabilities increased by $12,250 during the year—all related to operating activities and affected net income.
[2] Dividends of $37,500 were declared and paid to stockholders.
[3] Depreciation expense recognized was $25,600.
[4] Treasury stock was acquired for $10,000.
[5] Long-term debt was retired at $59,150.
[6] New items of property, plant, and equipment were acquired for $20,000.
[7] Cash increased by $71,900, from $110,000 to $181,900.

INSTRUCTIONS

Prepare a statement of cash flows for 1996. The company's fiscal year ends on December 31. Use the indirect method of presenting cash flows from operating activities.

22–32 Statement of Cash Flows Preparation (Direct)   Comparative data taken from the balance sheets of Randall Company at December 31, 1995 and 1996, are as follows:

	1995	1996
Assets		
Cash	$ 10,000	$ 15,000
Receivables, short term	35,000	26,700
Inventory	60,000	85,000
Property, plant, and equipment, net	75,000	70,000
Intangibles	12,000	10,000
	$192,000	$206,700
Equities		
Current liabilities	$ 6,500	$ 6,200
Noncurrent liabilities	60,000	40,000
Capital stock	100,000	125,000
Retained earnings	25,500	35,500
	$192,000	$206,700

During 1996 capital stock was sold, noncurrent debt was retired, and dividends of $5,000 were declared and paid. The income statement showed $7,000 of depreciation and amortization combined.

INSTRUCTIONS

[a] Determine the net change in cash during 1996.
[b] Assuming that revenues for 1996 totaled $100,000 and operating expenses totaled $85,000, prepare the 1996 statement of cash flows, applying the direct method of determining cash flows from operating activities. Accompanying disclosures are not required.

22–33 Statement of Cash Flows Preparation (Direct and Indirect) Marker Company's balance sheets at December 31, 1995 and 1996, are as follows:

	1995	1996
Assets		
Cash	$ 17,000	$ 2,300
Accounts receivable, net	45,000	42,000
Inventory	23,000	36,200
Property, plant, and equipment, net	165,000	147,000
Intangibles	—	17,500
	$250,000	$245,000
Equities		
Current liabilities	$ 40,000	$ 50,000
Noncurrent liabilities	90,000	95,000
Capital stock	100,000	120,000
Paid-in capital in excess of par value	40,000	40,000
Retained earnings	(20,000)	(60,000)
	$250,000	$245,000

The following additional information has been accumulated about 1996 activities:

[1] Patents were acquired by issuing a $5,000 long-term note payable and paying the remainder in cash; however, no amortization was taken because the acquisition took place at year-end.
[2] The only entries to property, plant, and equipment accounts were for depreciation and the acquisition of a $10,000 machine.
[3] No dividends were declared.
[4] Capital stock of $20,000 was issued at par.
[5] Revenues were $160,000; expenses totaled $200,000.

INSTRUCTIONS

[a] Prepare a statement of cash flows for 1996, applying the direct method of determining cash flows from operating activities. The net cash flows from operating activities to net income reconciliation disclosure is not required.
[b] Prepare a statement of cash flows for 1996, applying the indirect method of determining cash flows from operating activities.

22–34 Statement of Cash Flows—Noncash Transactions (Direct) Information from Rogoff Company's balance sheets at December 31, 1995 and 1996, indicate the following:

	Dollar Change Dec. 31, 1995– Dec. 31,1996
Assets	
Cash	+ 15,000
Accounts receivable	− 5,000
Inventory	+ 17,000
Property, plant, and equipment, net	+ 25,000
	+ 52,000
Equities	
Current liabilities	− 7,000
Bonds payable	+ 16,000
Capital stock	+ 20,000
Paid-in capital in excess of par value	+ 2,000
Retained earnings	+ 21,000
	+ 52,000

Depreciation of $7,000 was recognized in the income statement. Additional bonds were sold during the year. Land valued at $22,000 (included in property, plant, and equipment) was acquired by the issuance of stock. No dividends were declared. Revenues for 1996 were $125,000 and operating expenses were $104,000. The cash balance at the beginning of 1996 was $37,500.

INSTRUCTIONS

Prepare a statement of cash flows for 1996, using the direct method for operating activities, including all required disclosures.

22–35 Statement of Cash Flows Classifications   The following items may appear in the statement of cash flows:

[1] Revenues and operating expenses.
[2] Depreciation expense.
[3] Acquisition of treasury stock.
[4] Exchange of common stock for land.
[5] Declaration and payment of cash dividend.
[6] Payment of cash dividend declared in previous period.
[7] Acquisition of property, plant, and equipment.
[8] Retirement of long-term debt.
[9] Conversion of bonds into common stock.
[10] Amortization of intangible assets.
[11] Increase in inventory from previous year-end.
[12] Decrease in accounts receivable from previous year-end.
[13] Sale of property, plant, and equipment.
[14] Sale of capital stock.
[15] Declaration and distribution of stock dividend.

INSTRUCTIONS

For each item, indicate the proper classification in a statement of cash flows, using the following code. When an item is treated differently by the direct and indirect methods of determining cash flows from operating activities, indicate the answers for both.

	Code
Operating activities	A
Investing activities	B
Financing activities	C
Separate schedule	D
Not required to be included in the statement of cash flows	E

22–36 Statement of Cash Flows Preparation (Indirect)   The beginning and ending balances for Jeremy Company for 1996 are as follows:

	Jan. 1, 1996	Dec. 31, 1996
Cash	$10,000	$17,000
Other current assets	20,000	24,000
Fixed assets	20,000	20,000
Accumulated depreciation	(4,000)	(5,000)
Investments	10,000	10,000
Intangible assets	5,000	4,000
	$61,000	$70,000
Current liabilities	$10,000	$13,000
Long-term liabilities	13,000	12,000
Capital stock	25,000	25,000
Retained earnings	13,000	20,000
	$61,000	$70,000

An analysis of the company's records reveals the following additional information.

[1] Included $1,000 of depreciation and $1,000 of amortization of intangibles in the determination of net income.
[2] Declared and paid $1,500 of dividends during the year.
[3] Retired $1,000 of long-term liabilities during the year.

INSTRUCTIONS

Prepare a statement of cash flows, applying the indirect method of determining cash flows from operating activities.

22–37 Statement of Cash Flows Preparation (Indirect)   The beginning and ending balances for Santone Company for 1996 are as follows:

	Jan. 1, 1996	Dec. 31, 1996
Current assets	$25,000	$28,500
Fixed assets	20,000	25,000
Accumulated depreciation	(5,000)	(6,500)
Investments	10,000	10,000
Intangible assets	4,000	3,000
	$54,000	$60,000
Current liabilities	$13,000	$16,000
Long-term liabilities	12,000	8,000
Capital stock	25,000	30,000
Retained earnings	4,000	6,000
	$54,000	$60,000

An analysis of the company's records reveals the following additional information.

[1] Included $1,500 of depreciation and $1,000 amortization of intangibles in the determination of net income.
[2] Declared and paid $1,500 of dividends during the year.
[3] Sold $5,000 of capital stock, $4,000 of which was subsequently used to retire long-term liabilities.
[4] Acquired fixed assets for $5,000.
[5] Increased cash, included in the current asset figures, $2,500 during 1996. The ending balance was $10,000.

INSTRUCTIONS

[a] Prepare a statement of cash flows for 1996, applying the indirect method of determining cash from operating activities.
[b] What information that is not available would be required to be able to calculate cash flows from operating activities by the direct method?

22–38 Statement of Cash Flows Preparation (Direct)   During 1996 Moser Company reported revenues of $150,000 and expenses of $127,500. The following information is available:

[1] Current assets changed as follows:

Accounts receivable	+ $12,500
Inventory	− $ 7,500
Prepaid expenses	+ $ 2,000

Current liabilities changed as follows:

Accounts payable	+ $ 8,200
Accrued expenses	− $ 5,300

[2] Nonoperating activities are reported as follows:
   [a] Bonds payable with a book value of $10,000 were retired for cash.
   [b] Land was acquired by issuing common stock. The value attributed to the transaction was $25,000.
   [c] Machinery was sold at book value of $7,500.

INSTRUCTIONS

Prepare a statement of cash flows for the year, applying the direct method for operating activities. The reconciliation of net income to net cash flows from operating activities may be omitted. The beginning cash balance was $42,600.

22–39 Cash Flow from Operating Activities   Durand Company reported the following information in its income statement for 1996.

Revenues		$305,000
Cost of goods sold	$185,000	
Operating expenses	50,000	(235,000)
Income from operations		70,000
Loss from sale of equipment		(7,000)
Net income		$ 63,000

During the year, accounts receivable declined by $12,000, inventory increased by $17,500, accounts payable increased by $8,000, and accrued expenses declined by $6,250. The loss on the sale of equipment resulted from the sale of equipment with a $27,000 book value for $20,000 cash.

INSTRUCTIONS

Compute cash from operating activities by the direct method, including calculations to support the numbers that would appear in the statement of cash flows for cash provided by revenues and used for expenses.

22–40 Statement of Cash Flows Preparation   Telecom, Inc., has determined its cash flows from operating activities as $53,500. During 1996 the company had the following investing and financing activities:

[a] Cash dividends of $35,000 were declared and paid. An additional $14,000 of cash dividends were declared but remained unpaid at the end of the year.

[b] Machinery with a book value of $17,500 was sold for that amount. Additional machinery of $26,000 was acquired to replace that sold.

[c] Notes payable of $42,000 were taken out at the local bank early in the year. By the end of the year, $12,000 of this amount had been repaid.

[d] Bonds payable with a book value of $25,000 were converted into common stock.

INSTRUCTIONS

Prepare a statement of cash flows for the year, including only a single amount for cash flows from operating activities. (You do not have the information to determine the components of this number.) Assume the beginning cash balance was $65,000.

PROBLEMS

22–41 Statement of Cash Flows Preparation (Direct)   Information taken from the detailed trial balance sheet of Mason Company is as follows:

	Dr. (Cr.) Balances At December 31	
	1995	1996
Cash	$ 20,000	$ 30,000
Accounts receivable	45,000	78,000
Investments	15,000	–0–
Property, plant, and equipment	92,600	118,100
Accumulated depreciation	(27,100)	(33,600)
Intangible assets	17,000	16,000
Accrued expenses	(7,500)	(7,000)
Bonds payable	(25,500)	(25,500)
Common stock, $10 par	(75,000)	(100,000)
Paid-in capital in excess of par value	(40,000)	(55,000)
Retained earnings	(14,500)	(21,000)
	–0–	–0–

Other information relating to various financing and investing activities of the company is as follows:

[1] Investments were sold at their carrying value.

[2] Items of equipment costing $27,500 and having $18,000 accumulated depreciation were sold at book value. New equipment was acquired to replace the outdated models that were sold.

[3] During the year, 2,500 shares of common stock were sold for cash.

[4] Dividends of $8,500 were declared and paid during the year. No other entries were made to the Retained Earnings account except the recognition of net income, which included revenues of $107,000 and operating expenses of $92,000.

INSTRUCTIONS

[a] Prepare a statement of cash flows for 1996. Use the direct method to determine cash flows from operating activities and include all required disclosures for which you have information.

[b] Why is the reconciliation of net income to net cash provided by or used in operating activities a required disclosure when the direct method is used?

22–42 Statement of Cash Flows Preparation (Direct)   Watanabe Company is preparing a statement of cash flows for 1996. Information has been accumulated concerning changes in account balances during 1996 as follows:

	Change in Dr. (Cr.) 1996
Cash	$ (5,500)
Accounts receivable, net	12,000
Inventory	60,500
Property, plant, and equipment	17,650
Accumulated depreciation	(7,300)
Intangible assets	11,000
Accrued expenses	(1,600)
Accounts payable	(10,750)
Notes payable, 90-day	(31,150)
Bonds payable	(10,000)
Common stock	(10,000)
Paid-in capital in excess of par value	(3,000)
Retained earnings	(21,850)
	–0–

The following explanations of account changes are available:

Property, Plant, and Equipment.   Fully depreciated equipment with a cost of $7,500 was discarded. Equipment with a cost of $6,250 and accumulated depreciation of $4,000 was sold for $2,250. Depreciation expense was $18,800. Additional items of new equipment were acquired during the year.

Intangible Assets.   A patent was acquired during the year in exchange for 1,000 shares of the company's $10 par value common stock. The market value of the shares on the date of the exchange was $13. Amortization of existing intangible assets was recognized during the year.

Bonds Payable.   Retired $100,000 of 10% bonds payable at book value and issued $110,000 of 8% bonds.

Retained Earnings.   The only entries during the year were to recognize net income and dividends declared of $25,000. Revenues for 1996 totaled $285,000 and expenses totaled $238,150.

INSTRUCTIONS

[a] Prepare a statement of cash flows for 1996, including all required disclosures for which you have information. Use the direct approach for determining cash from operating activities and assume that the beginning cash balance was $14,285.

[b] Although Watanabe Company earned revenues of $285,000, the net cash flow was negative ($5,500). Discuss why this occurred.

22–43 Analysis of Cash Flow Transactions   Fallone Company recorded the items listed below during 1996. The controller believes that some or all of the items may have an impact on the company's statement of cash flows.

[1] Net income is $145,000. This amount includes a $15,000 extraordinary loss resulting from the condemnation of land by the city. The company received $165,000 for land carried on the books at $180,000. (Assume no income tax effect of the extraordinary loss.)

[2] Intangible assets increased by $28,000 during the year, representing the acquisition of a patent for $34,000 and amortization of intangibles of $6,000.

[3] Cash dividends of $12,500 were declared and paid.

[4] Treasury stock with a par value of $17,000 was acquired for $31,000 and recorded by the cost method. None of the treasury shares have been resold as of the end of the year.

[5] An analysis of the Accumulated Depreciation account reveals the following:

Balance, end of year	$210,000
Balance, beginning of year	175,000
Increase	$ 35,000
Accumulated depreciation on fully depreciated assets retired during year	$ 11,250

[6] Convertible bonds issued at $100,000 par value in 1994 were converted into common stock during the year. The par value of the stock issued was $50,000; paid-in capital in excess of par value was increased by $50,000.

[7] The balance of various noncurrent asset accounts changed during the year as follows (assume no gains or losses, other than the extraordinary loss in [1] above):

Land	decrease	$ 50,000
Equipment	increase	60,000
Building	increase	100,000

[8] An analysis of working capital accounts reveals that working capital increased by $9,750 during the year. (Working capital is the excess of current assets over current liabilities.)

INSTRUCTIONS

In preparing your responses to the following questions, assume that the amounts of all current assets and current liabilities, other than cash, were unchanged during the year.

[a] Describe how each of the eight items should be presented in Fallone's statement of cash flows for 1996.

[b] Compute the following items:
[1] Net cash provided (used) by operating activities.
[2] Net cash provided (used) by investing activities.
[3] Net cash provided (used) by financing activities.

22–44 Statement of Cash Flows Preparation (Indirect)   Trial balances at December 31, 1995 and 1996, for Cain Company are presented below, along with additional information necessary for the preparation of a statement of cash flows.

	1995	1996
Debits		
Cash	$ 19,235	$ 27,471
Accounts receivable, net	42,515	41,760
Inventory	55,600	59,255
Prepaid expenses	1,200	1,100
Property, plant, and equipment	125,450	200,450
Intangible assets	57,200	55,000
Treasury stock	–0–	12,000
	$301,200	$397,036
Credits		
Accrued expenses	$ 5,400	$ 6,200
Accounts payable	29,800	27,119
Note payable, 60 day	43,350	23,350
Accumulated depreciation	47,100	44,600
Note payable, 5 year	–0–	10,000
Common stock	125,000	160,000
Paid-in capital in excess of par value	10,000	25,000
Retained earnings	40,550	100,767
	$301,200	$397,036

During 1996 a fire resulting from an electrical storm completely destroyed a building with a cost of $75,000 and $30,000 of accumulated depreciation. Insurance proceeds of $60,000 were received. The event was considered both unusual in nature and infrequent in occurrence. The building was replaced by a new facility at a cost of $100,000. In addition, 3,500 shares of $10 par value stock were exchanged for equipment during the year. The stock was not actively traded; the equipment had a listed selling price of $50,000.

Dividends of $10,000 were declared and paid during 1996. All notes payable represent bank loans.

INSTRUCTIONS

Prepare a statement of cash flows for 1996, including all required disclosures for which you have information, applying the following assumptions:

[a] The 60-day note payable represents a bank loan that the company does not consider part of cash provided by or used in operations.

[b] The indirect method is used to compute cash from operating activities.

22–45 Revised Statement of Cash Flows Preparation (Indirect)   The accountant for Cliff Enterprises has drafted the following financial statement for 1996. The accountant was unaware of the FASB's statement concerning the statement of cash flows.

Cliff Enterprises
Working Capital Statement
December 31, 1996

Sources of Working Capital		
Net income	$762,750	
Depreciation	19,775	
Issuance of preferred stock	50,000	
Book value of fixed asset sold	$ 35,000	$867,525
Uses of Working Capital		
Acquisition of fixed assets	375,000	
Acquisition of patents	50,000	
Purchase of treasury stock	75,250	
Retirement of bonds	150,000	
Dividends on preferred stock	5,000	
Dividends on common stock	72,000	727,250
Increase in working capital		$140,275

The company's accountant accepted a position as a ski instructor at a Canadian ski resort and left town on short notice. The president of Cliff Enterprises has engaged you to evaluate the preceding statement and to revise it, if necessary, in accordance with current FASB standards. You have found the items included in the statement to be accurate. Additional information apparently not incorporated into this statement, however, includes the following:

[1] In addition to the bonds retired for $150,000, bonds of $350,000 were converted into common stock during the year.

[2] An analysis of changes in current assets and current liabilities reveals the following:

	Dollar Change in Account Balance during 1996
Cash	− 53,650
Marketable securities	+ 15,750
Accounts receivable, net	+ 85,623
Inventory	+ 97,245
Accounts payable	− 4,762
Income taxes payable	+ 9,455

[3] The fixed asset sold during the year resulted in a $15,000 gain that was included in net income. No extraordinary items were recognized during 1996.

[4] The Patent account increased $50,000 during the year. This change included the acquisition of one patent for $37,500, the successful defense of an existing patent for $19,250, and amortization for the year.

INSTRUCTIONS

[a] Identify all errors and omissions in the financial statement prepared by the previous accountant for Cliff Enterprises.

[b] Prepare a revised statement of cash flows for 1996, applying the indirect method for determining cash from operating activities. You may assume a beginning cash balance of $105,000. Include all required disclosures for which you have information.

22–46 Statement of Cash Flows Preparation with Worksheet (Direct)   Breaux Company has not yet prepared a formal statement of cash flows for 1996. Comparative statements of financial position as of December 31, 1995 and 1996, and a statement of income and retained earnings for the year ended December 31, 1996, are presented below:

Breaux Company
Statement of Financial Position
December 31, 1995 and 1996
(in thousands)

	1995	1996
Assets		
Current Assets		
Cash	$ 100	$ 60
U.S. Treasury notes	50	–0–
Accounts receivable	500	610
Inventory	600	720
Total current assets	1,250	1,390
Long-Term Assets		
Land	70	80
Buildings and equipment	600	710
Accumulated depreciation	(120)	(180)
Patents (less amortization)	130	105
Total long-term assets	680	715
Total assets	$1,930	$2,105
Liabilities and Ownership		
Current Liabilities		
Accounts payable	$ 300	$ 360
Income taxes payable	20	25
Notes payable	400	400
Total current liabilities	720	785
Term Notes Payable, Due 1998	200	200
Total liabilities	920	985
Owners' Equity		
Common stock outstanding	700	830
Retained earnings	310	290
Total owner's equity	1,010	1,120
Total liabilities and equity	$1,930	$2,105

Breaux Company
Statement of Income and Retained Earnings
For the Year Ended December 31, 1996
(in thousands)

Sales		$2,408
Less expenses and interest		
Cost of goods sold	$1,100	
Salaries and benefits	850	
Heat, light, and power	75	
Depreciation	60	
Property taxes	18	
Patent amortization	25	
Miscellaneous expense	10	
Interest	55	2,193

(continued)

(continued)

Income before income taxes	215
Income taxes	105
Net income	110
Retained earnings, Jan. 1, 1996	310
	420
Stock dividend	(130)
Retained earnings, Dec. 31, 1996	$ 290

INSTRUCTIONS

[a] Prepare a worksheet using the format of Exhibit 22–7 to facilitate the preparation of a statement of cash flows for 1996.

[b] Prepare a statement of cash flows for 1996, using the direct method for determining cash from operating activities. Treat the U.S. Treasury notes as a cash equivalent. You may omit the schedule reconciling net income to cash flows from operating activities, but include all other required disclosures for which you have information. (CMA adapted)

[c] Discuss the difference in cash flow statement treatment of the declaration and payment of a cash dividend versus the issuance of a stock dividend.

22–47 Worksheet Entries The following information is to be used in developing worksheet entries for the preparation of a statement of cash flows. Each item should be treated *independently* in complying with the problem instructions as stated. In all cases the year is 1996.

Company 1. Net income for the year includes the effect of the following transactions involving the sale of fixed assets:

Sales Price	Cost	Accumulated Depreciation	Gain (Loss)
$15,000	$75,000	$70,000	$10,000
42,500	92,000	43,000	(6,500)

Company 2. Income taxes are presented in the income statement as follows:

Income before income taxes		$XXX,XXX
Provision for income taxes		
Payable currently	$203,920	
Deferred	81,440	285,360
Net income		$XXX,XXX

Company 3. Equipment and the related depreciation accounts for 1996 are as follows:

	Debit	Credit	Balance Dr. (Cr.)
Equipment			
Balance, Jan. 1			$472,000
Cost of equipment sold for $72,800		$126,000	346,000
Cost of equipment purchased	$266,000		612,000
Cost of fully depreciated equipment discarded		27,850	584,150
Accumulated Depreciation			
Balance, Jan. 1			(255,000)
Depreciation on equipment sold	102,000		(153,000)
Depreciation on fully depreciated equipment discarded	27,850		(125,150)
Depreciation expense for 1996		86,000	(211,150)

Company 4. Interest expense was recorded during 1996 with the following entry:

Interest Expense	107,000	
Cash		102,000
Unamortized Bond Discount		5,000

Company 5.   Interest expense was recorded during 1996 with the following entry:

Interest Expense	398,000	
Unamortized Bond Premium	12,000	
Interest Payable		410,000

Company 6.   Income statement data for the company for 1996 are as follows:

Income before extraordinary items	$150,000
Extraordinary loss—retirement of bonds, net of $8,750 income tax	16,250
Net income	$133,750

The extraordinary loss resulted from the retirement of bonds payable with a face value of $300,000 and a related unamortized discount of $2,000 at a cost of $323,000. The tax rate for the transaction is 35%.

Company 7.   Land was acquired by issuing preferred stock with $105,000 par value. The preferred stock is not actively traded. The land had a current appraisal value of $117,500.

INSTRUCTIONS

Analyze the information given for each company and prepare the entry in general journal form to account for the item on a worksheet similar to that in Exhibit 22–7. Treat each item independently and provide a brief explanation for each entry.

22–48 Statement of Cash Flows Preparation (Indirect)   Wright Company has requested your assistance in the preparation of a statement of cash flows for the year ended June 30, 1996. Comparative trial balances as of June 30, 1995 and 1996, are presented below:

	Dr. (Cr.)	
	June 30, 1995	June 30, 1996
Cash	$ 2,825	$ 3,612
Accounts receivable, net	25,600	17,401
Inventory	42,700	33,250
Equipment	126,000	120,750
Accumulated depreciation, equipment	(42,700)	(52,700)
Building	122,000	207,000
Accumulated depreciation, building	(25,000)	(43,500)
Land	90,000	67,500
Patent	–0–	34,500
Accrued expenses	(2,453)	(1,100)
Accounts payable	(12,462)	(11,400)
Notes payable	(50,000)	(40,000)
Deferred income taxes	(5,430)	(6,550)
Bonds payable	(75,000)	(75,000)
Premium on bonds payable	(2,000)	(1,750)
Common stock ($10 par)	(125,000)	(150,000)
Paid-in capital in excess of par value	(25,000)	(35,000)
Retained earnings	(44,080)	(67,013)
	–0–	–0–

The following information also pertains to the fiscal year ending June 30, 1996:

Income/Dividends.   Net income for the year ended June 30, 1996, was $42,933. No extraordinary items were reported in the income statement. Dividends of $20,000 were declared and paid to common stockholders.

Property, Plant, and Equipment.   Equipment costing $25,000 with accumulated depreciation of $20,000 was sold at book value. Depreciation of $30,000 was recognized during the year. Additional equipment of $19,750 was acquired.

An addition to the building was made during the year at a cost of $85,000. Depreciation of $18,500 was recognized during the year.

Land with cost of $57,500 was sold for $97,800. Additional land was acquired by issuing 2,500 shares of common stock that had a total value of $35,000. A recent appraisal value of the land was not available.

Patent.   A patent was acquired for $34,500 during the year.

Notes payable.   A series of short-term loans was taken out under a revolving line of credit with a local bank. These loans are for nonoperating purposes.

INSTRUCTIONS

[a] Prepare a statement of cash flows for 1996, applying the indirect method of determining cash from operating activities. Include all required disclosures for which you have information.

[b] In determining net cash provided by operating activities, explain your treatment of the $1,120 increase in deferred income taxes and the $250 decrease in premium on bonds payable.

22–49 Statement of Cash Flows Preparation (Indirect)   Dove Company's statement of cash flows has not yet been prepared for the year ended December 31, 1996. The schedule below compares the net change in the balance sheet accounts between December 31, 1996 and 1995.

	Net Change Increase (Decrease)
Debit Balance Accounts	
Cash	$ (400,000)
Acounts receivable, net	500,000
Inventories	580,000
Property, plant, and equipment	1,800,000
Total	$2,480,000
Credit Balance Accounts	
Accumulated depreciation	$ 950,000
Accounts payable	1,250,000
Notes payable, current	(150,000)
Serial bonds payable	(2,000,000)
Common stock, $10 par value	9,000,000
Capital contributed in excess of par value	1,300,000
Retained earnings	(7,870,000)
Total	$2,480,000

ADDITIONAL INFORMATION

[1] Dove incurred a net after-tax loss from regular operations of $500,000 for the year ended December 31, 1996. It also had an extraordinary gain from the sale of condemned land in the amount of $1,400,000 net of income tax of $600,000. The condemned land had a book value of $2,500,000.

[2] Accounts receivable of $650,000 were written off during 1996 by charging Allowance for Doubtful Accounts. The provision for bad debts during 1996 was $1,250,000.

[3] Machinery acquired in 1991 at a cost of $2,000,000 was sold for $550,000. The machinery had a net book value of $350,000 at the date of sale.

[4] A new parcel of land was purchased during April 1996. The market value of the land was $6,300,000. Cash of $1,500,000 and 400,000 shares of Dove's common stock were given in exchange for the land.

[5] The serial bonds mature at a rate of $2,000,000 each year. The bonds were sold at par value.

[6] A 5% stock dividend was declared January 15, 1996, on 10,000,000 shares of Dove's common stock. The stock dividend was issued on February 10, 1996, to all stock holders of record as of January 31, 1996. The market value of the stock at these three dates was as follows:

Jan. 15, 1996	$11.00 per share
Jan. 31, 1996	$10.45 per share
Feb. 10, 1996	$10.60 per share

[7] A cash dividend of $.30 per share of common stock was declared on June 30, 1996, to all stockholders of record as of July 15, 1996. The dividend was paid on July 31, 1996.

[8] The notes payable resulted from extended terms granted by one of Dove Company's major suppliers of inventory.

[9] Dove's cash balance at the beginning of 1996 was $978,000.

INSTRUCTIONS

[a] Prepare a statement of cash flows for the year ended December 31, 1996. Dove Company uses the indirect method in determining cash from operating activities. Include all required disclosures permitted by the information you have.   (CMA adapted)

[b] Describe the changes to Dove Company's cash flow statement if Dove had acquired the new parcel of land described in [4] by paying $1,500,000 in cash and borrowing $4,800,000 from a local bank.

22–50 Statement of Cash Flows Preparation with Worksheet (Direct)   Young Company has prepared its financial statements for the year ended December 31, 1995, and for the three months ended March 31, 1996. The company's balance sheet at December 31, 1995, and March 31, 1996, and its income statement data for the three months ended March 31 are presented below. You are satisfied that the amounts presented are correct.

Balance Sheet

	December 31, 1995	March 31, 1996
Cash	$ 25,300	$ 87,400
Marketable investments	16,500	7,300
Accounts receivable, net	24,320	49,320
Inventory	31,090	48,590
Total current assets	97,210	192,610
Land	40,000	18,700
Building	250,000	250,000
Equipment	—	81,500
Accumulated depreciation	(15,000)	(16,250)
Investment in 30% owned company	61,220	67,100
Other assets	15,100	15,100
Total	$448,530	$608,760
Accounts payable	$ 21,220	$ 17,330
Dividend payable	—	8,000
Income taxes payable	—	34,616
Total current liabilities	21,220	59,946
Other liabilities	186,000	186,000
Bonds payable	50,000	115,000
Discount on bonds payable	(2,300)	(2,150)
Deferred income taxes	510	846
Preferred stock	30,000	—
Common stock	80,000	110,000
Dividends declared	—	(8,000)
Retained earnings	83,100	147,118
Total	$448,530	$608,760

Income Statement

	For the Three Months Ended March 31, 1996
Sales	$242,807
Gain on sale of marketable investments	2,400
Equity in earnings of 30% owned company	5,880
Gain on condemnation of land	10,700
	261,787
Cost of sales	138,407
General and administrative expenses	22,010
Depreciation	1,250
Interest expense	1,150
Income taxes	34,952
	197,769
Net income	$ 64,018

Your discussion with the company's controller and a review of the financial records revealed the following information:

[1] On January 8, 1996, the company sold marketable securities for cash of $11,600. These securities had been held for more than six months.

[2] The company's preferred stock is convertible into common stock at a rate of one share of preferred for two shares of common. The preferred stock and common stock have par values of $2 and $1, respectively.

[3] On January 17, 1996, three acres of land were condemned. An award of $32,000 in cash was received on March 22, 1996. Purchase of additional land as a replacement is not anticipated.

[4] On March 25, 1996, the company purchased equipment for cash.

[5] On March 29, 1996, bonds payable were issued by the company at par for cash.

[6] The investment in the 30% owned company included $3,220 attributable to goodwill at December 31, 1995. Goodwill is being amortized at an annual rate of $480.

INSTRUCTIONS

[a] Prepare a worksheet similar to Exhibit 22–7 to be used in preparing a statement of cash flows for the three months ended March 31, 1996.

[b] Prepare a statement of cash flows, based on your worksheet from part [a]. Use the direct method of determining cash from operating activities and include all required disclosures.

(AICPA adapted)

22–51 Statement of Cash Flows Preparation with Worksheet (Direct)   Presented below are the comparative statements of position of McFarland Corporation as of December 31, 1996 and 1995, together with the income statement for the year ended December 31, 1996.

McFarland Corporation
Statement of Financial Position

	December 31, 1996	1995	Increase (Decrease)
Assets			
Current assets			
Cash	$ 100,000	$ 90,000	$ 10,000
Accounts receivable (net of allowance for uncollectible accounts of $10,000 and $8,000, respectively)	210,000	140,000	70,000
Inventories	260,000	220,000	40,000
Total current assets	570,000	450,000	120,000
Land	325,000	200,000	125,000
Plant and equipment	580,000	633,000	(53,000)
Less: Accumulated depreciation	(90,000)	(100,000)	10,000
Patents	30,000	33,000	(3,000)
Total assets	$1,415,000	$1,216,000	$199,000
Liabilities and Shareholders' Equity			
Liabilities			
Current liabilities			
Accounts payable	$ 260,000	$ 200,000	$ 60,000
Accrued salaries and wages	200,000	210,000	(10,000)
Total current liabilities	460,000	410,000	50,000
Deferred income taxes	140,000	100,000	40,000
Long-term bonds (due Dec. 15, 1998)	130,000	180,000	(50,000)
Total liabilities	730,000	690,000	40,000
Shareholders' equity			
Common stock, par value $5; authorized 100,000 shares; issued and outstanding 50,000 and 42,000 shares, respectively	250,000	210,000	40,000

(continued)

	December 31,		Increase
Shareholders' equity *(continued)*	**1996**	**1995**	**(Decrease)**
Paid-in capital in excess of par value	233,000	170,000	63,000
Retained earnings	202,000	146,000	56,000
Total shareholders' equity	685,000	526,000	159,000
Total liabilities and shareholders' equity	$1,415,000	$1,216,000	$199,000

McFarland Corporation
Income Statement
For the Year Ended December 31, 1996

Sales	$1,000,000
Expenses	
Cost of sales	560,000
Salary and wages	190,000
Depreciation	20,000
Amortization	3,000
Loss on sale of equipment	4,000
Interest	16,000
Miscellaneous	8,000
Total expenses	801,000
Income before income taxes and extraordinary item	199,000
Income taxes	
Current	50,000
Deferred	40,000
Provision for income taxes	90,000
Income before extraordinary item	109,000
Extraordinary item—gain on repurchase of long-term bonds (net of $10,000 income tax)	12,000
Net income	$ 121,000
Earnings per share	
Income before extraordinary item	$2.21
Extraordinary item	.24
Net income	$2.45

ADDITIONAL INFORMATION

[1] On February 2, 1996, McFarland issued a 10% stock dividend to shareholders of record on January 15, 1996. The market price per share of the common stock on February 2, 1996, was $15.
[2] On March 1, 1996, McFarland issued 3,800 shares of common stock for land. The common stock and land had current market values of approximately $40,000 on March 1, 1996.
[3] On April 15, 1996, McFarland repurchased long-term bonds with a face value of $50,000. The gain of $22,000 was reported as an extraordinary item on the income statement.
[4] On June 30, 1996, McFarland sold equipment costing $53,000, with a book value of $23,000, for $19,000 cash.
[5] On September 30, 1996, McFarland declared and paid a $.04 per share cash dividend to shareholders of record August 1, 1996.
[6] On October 10, 1996, McFarland purchased land for $85,000 cash.
[7] Deferred income taxes represent temporary differences relating to the use of accelerated cost recovery system for income tax reporting and straight-line depreciation for financial reporting.

INSTRUCTIONS

[a] Analyze McFarland's transactions and prepare a worksheet similar to Exhibit 22–7 for use in preparing a statement of cash flows for 1996.
[b] Prepare a statement of cash flows for McFarland Corporation for 1996, applying the direct method for determining cash flows from operations. You may omit the schedule reconciling net income to net cash provided by operating activities, but include all other disclosures.

(AICPA adapted)

22–52 Statement of Cash Flows Preparation (Indirect) The management of Romper Co., concerned over a decrease in working capital, has provided you with the following comparative analysis of changes in account balances at December 31, 1995 and 1996:

	December 31,		Increase
	1996	1995	(Decrease)
	Debit Balances		
Cash	$ 157,000	$ 186,000	$ (29,000)
Accounts receivable	253,000	273,000	(20,000)
Inventories	483,000	538,000	(55,000)
Securities held for plant expansion purposes	150,000	—	150,000
Machinery and equipment	927,000	647,000	280,000
Leasehold improvements	87,000	87,000	—
Patents	27,800	30,000	(2,200)
Totals	$2,084,800	$1,761,000	$323,800

	December 31,		Increase
	1996	1995	(Decrease)
	Credit Balances		
Allowance for uncollectible accounts receivable	$ 14,000	$ 17,000	$ (3,000)
Accumulated depreciation of machinery and equipment	416,000	372,000	44,000
Allowance for amortization of leasehold improvements	58,000	49,000	9,000
Accounts payable	232,800	105,000	127,800
Cash dividends payable	40,000	—	40,000
Current portion of 6% serial bonds payable	50,000	50,000	—
6% serial bonds payable	250,000	300,000	(50,000)
Preferred stock	90,000	100,000	(10,000)
Common stock	500,000	500,000	—
Retained earnings	434,000	268,000	166,000
Totals	$2,084,800	$1,761,000	$323,800

ADDITIONAL INFORMATION

During 1996 the following transactions occurred:

[1] New machinery was purchased for $386,000, and obsolete machinery, with a book value of $61,000, was sold for $48,000. No other entries were recorded in Machinery and Equipment or related accounts other than provisions for depreciation.

[2] The company paid $2,000 legal costs in the successful defense of a new patent. Amortization of patents amounting to $4,200 was recorded.

[3] Preferred stock, par value $100, was purchased at 110 and subsequently canceled. The premium was charged to retained earnings.

[4] On December 10, 1996, the board of directors declared a cash dividend of $.20 per share payable to holders of common stock on January 10, 1997.

[5] A comparative analysis of retained earnings as of December 31, 1996 and 1995, is presented below:

	December 31,	
	1996	1995
Balance, Jan. 1	$268,000	$131,000
Net income	207,000	172,000
	475,000	303,000
Dividends declared	(40,000)	(35,000)
Premium on preferred stock repurchased	(1,000)	—
	$434,000	$268,000

INSTRUCTIONS

[a] Prepare a statement of cash flows for Romper Co. for the year ended December 31, 1996. Use the indirect method of presenting cash from operating activities and include all required disclosures for which you have information.

[b] Explain your treatment of the $13,000 loss on the sale of obsolete equipment ($61,000 − $48,000) in computing net cash flows from both operating and investing activities.   (AICPA adapted)

CASES

22–53 Sources and Uses of Cash   Jackson Electronics Corp. (JEC) is a young and growing producer of electronic measuring instruments and technical equipment. You have been asked to help prepare a statement of cash flows for the fiscal year ended October 31, 1995. You have obtained the following information concerning certain events and transactions:

[1] The amount of reported earnings for the fiscal year was $800,000, which included a deduction for an extraordinary loss of $93,000 (See item [5]).

[2] Depreciation expense of $265,000 was included in the earnings statement.

[3] Uncollectible accounts receivable of $40,000 were written off against the allowance for uncollectible accounts. Also, $47,000 of bad debts expense was included in determining earnings for the fiscal year, and the same amount was added to the allowance for uncollectible accounts.

[4] A gain of $4,700 was realized on the cash sale of a machine; it originally cost $75,000, of which $25,000 was undepreciated on the date of sale.

[5] On April 1, 1995, a freak lightning storm caused an uninsured building loss of $93,000 ($180,000 loss, less reduction in income taxes of $87,000). This extraordinary loss was included in determining earnings, as indicated in item [1].

[6] On July 3, 1995, building and land were purchased for $600,000. JEC paid $100,000 cash and issued $200,000 market value of its unissued common stock and a $300,000 purchase money mortgage.

[7] On August 3, 1995, $700,000 face value of JEC's 6% convertible debentures were converted into $140,000 par value of its common stock. The bonds were orginally issued at face value.

[8] The board of directors declared a $265,000 cash dividend on October 20, 1995, payable on November 15, 1995, to stockholders of record on November 5, 1995.

INSTRUCTIONS

Explain whether each of these eight items is a source or use of cash. Describe how the item should be disclosed in JEC's statement of cash flows for the fiscal year ended October 31, 1995. If the item is neither a source nor a use of cash, explain why, and indicate the disclosure, if any, that should be made.   (AICPA adapted)

22–54 Interpretation of Statement of Cash Flows   Black and Blue companies operate in the same industry and are similar in size, in terms of investment in assets and sales volume. The ratio of current assets to current liabilities at the 1996 balance sheet date is the same for both companies, approximately 2.4 to 1. This is very close to the average for all companies in the industry.

Selected data from the statements of cash flows of the two companies are presented as follows (amounts in thousands):

	Black Company			
	1993	**1994**	**1995**	**1996**
Net Cash Provided				
Operating activities	$ 100	$ 125	$ 115	$ 128
Investing activities				
Sale of assets	15	12	50	25
Financing activities				
Long-term borrowing	10	—	—	15
Issuance of capital stock	—	25	—	—
	125	162	165	168
Net Cash Used (Various)	(115)	(150)	(170)	(164)
Net increase (decrease) in cash	10	12	(5)	4

Blue Company

	1993	1994	1995	1996
Net Cash Provided				
Operating activities	$ 50	$ 30	$ (60)	$ 10
Investing activities				
Sale of assets	10	25	50	50
Financing activities				
Long-term borrowing	75	15	70	—
Issuance of capital stock	—	75	100	75
	135	145	160	135
Net Cash Used (Various)	(125)	(133)	(165)	(131)
Net increase (decrease) in cash	10	12	(5)	4

INSTRUCTIONS

[a] Identify similarities in the two companies.

[b] Identify differences between the two companies.

[c] Which company appears to be in a stronger position from the viewpoint of potential investors in the company's stock and major creditors? Why?

22–55 Deficiencies in Statement of Cash Flows The following financial statement was prepared by Sanchez Company's accountant:

Sanchez Company
Statement of Source and Application of Cash
For the Year Ended September 30, 1995

Source of Funds	
Net income	$ 52,000
Depreciation and depletion	59,000
Increase in long-term debt	178,000
Common stock issued under employee option plans	5,000
Changes in current receivables and inventories, less current liabilities	
(excluding current maturities of long-term debt)	3,000
	$297,000
Application of Funds	
Cash dividends	$ 33,000
Expenditures for property, plant, and equipment	202,000
Investments and other uses	9,000
Change in cash	53,000
	$297,000

The following additional information is available for the year ended September 30, 1995.

[1] Sanchez Company's balance sheet distinguishes between current and noncurrent assets and liabilities.

[2]

Depreciation expense	$56,000
Depletion expense	3,000
	$59,000

[3]

Increase in long-term debt	$620,000
Retirement of debt	442,000
Net increase	$178,000

[4] Sanchez Company received $5,000 in cash from its employees on its employee stock option plans, and wage and salary expense attributable to the plan (which has not been recorded) was an additional $22,000.

[5]

Expenditures for property, plant, and equipment	$240,000
Proceeds from retirements of property, plant, and equipment	38,000
Net expenditures	$202,000

[6] A stock dividend of 10,000 shares of Sanchez Company's common stock was distributed to common stockholders on April 1, 1995, when the per share market price was $6 and par value was $1.

[7] On July 1, 1995, when its market price was $5 per share, 16,000 shares of Sanchez Company common stock were issued in exchange for 4,000 shares of preferred stock.

INSTRUCTIONS

[a] Explain the objectives of a statement of the type shown above.

[b] Identify the weaknesses in the form and format of Sanchez Company's statement, without reference to the additional information.

[c] For each item of additional information, indicate the preferable treatment in the statement of cash flows and explain why it is preferable.

(AICPA adapted)

JUDGMENT CASES

22–56 Cash Equivalents   The president of Prudent, Inc., has directed that a plant replacement and improvement fund be created to finance needed improvements in the manufacturing processes for the company's principal product in the coming years. The current processes are rather obsolete and have caused some of the company's oldest customers to place orders with competitors.

Specifically, the president wants to set aside $250,000 a year for the next five years, at which time the company will obtain a loan for approximately $5,000,000 to rebuild and improve the efficiency of several machines and to acquire several new ones. The board of directors (which the president dominates) agreed to the idea during its December board meeting and on December 31, 1995, the company established a fund in the amount of $250,000. The fund is currently composed of short-term Treasury bills that mature in 60 days. Upon maturity of these amounts, the president plans to invest the proceeds in a forthcoming municipal bond issue as a gesture of support to the small town in which the company is located.

The company's accountant, Roger Readytick, is compiling the company's general-purpose financial statements and is in the midst of preparing the statement of cash flows. He is unsure about how the recently created plant replacement fund should be reported on that statement. He discussed the issue with the company president, who responded:

> *Roger, I just don't see the problem. The fund is clearly a cash equivalent at this time. The investments are even specifically mentioned in the FASB statement as a cash equivalent. As for the purpose of the fund, we created it and we can discontinue it at any time we wish. We can use these assets for any purpose we want. It isn't as if we were dealing with a sinking fund that some lender required as a condition of a loan. I want the fund treated as part of our cash and cash equivalents at the end of the year. Besides, we need to show a high liquidity anyway, because one of our banks is making noises about not renewing our annual line of credit.*

INSTRUCTIONS

Help Roger resolve this reporting issue. How should the fund be reported in the statement of cash flows? Also, be sure to consider how the fund should be presented in the balance sheet of the company.

22–57 Reporting Financing and Operating Activities   On January 1, 1995, Deep Vee, Inc., borrowed $5,000,000 by issuing a "noninterest-bearing" note with a face (maturity) amount of $7,500,000. The entire face amount of the note is due on January 1, 2000. Assume, for purposes of simplicity, that the discount is being amortized on a straight-line basis over the five-year term of the note. (*APB Opinion No. 21* requires use of the effective rate method rather than the straight-line method if the differences are material.)

INSTRUCTIONS

[a] How should Deep Vee report the $5,000,000 received in 1995 and the $7,500,000 cash payment in 2000 on its statements of cash flows?

[b] Assume that Deep Vee pays the note off early for $5,400,000 on January 1, 1996. How should the company report the cash payment on its statement of cash flows for the year ending December 31, 1996?

22–58 Investing and Operating Activities Classic Video Rentals, a nonpublic company, acquires videotapes of older classic movies at a variety of locations throughout the Southwest. The tapes are rented for short periods of time, but the company has found that many customers choose occasionally to buy them. Although the company does not advertise the tapes for sale and had not originally intended to sell tapes, it does not object to selling them when approached and has developed pricing policies for that purpose. The company depreciates the tapes in its rental collection and considers the rentals to be operating rather than capital leases.

INSTRUCTIONS

How should the purchases of the tapes be presented on the company's statement of cash flows? Also, how should the proceeds from the sales of the tapes be presented on the statement of cash flows? Explain your conclusions.

22–59 Borrowing and Repaying Debt The company for which you work as controller, Wonderous Wheat, Inc., is an agricultural producer. Its normal business practice is to borrow cash from a bank at the beginning of the season, to use those monies to prepare the land for planting, nourishing, weeding, irrigating, harvesting, and, finally, marketing the crops. The company receives the cash from the bank at the time of borrowing and expends the money as needed. The terms of the loan provide that the bank has a lien on the growing plants and on the harvested crop at the time it is sold. The buyer of the harvested crop is aware of the lien and withholds from the company the amounts due the bank to repay the loan. In this fashion, the bank is assured of receiving repayment on a timely basis and the company receives only the net proceeds from the sale.

The company's auditor, Polly Prudent, has indicated that the manner in which the company does business may affect its statement of cash flows. Specifically, she has stated that she believes that the original borrowing should be shown as a positive source of cash from financing activities. The amount of cash that is to be shown from operating activities, however, does not contain the cash that is withheld by the crop buyer and remitted directly to repay the lending bank. Further, the repayment itself will also be considered a noncash event and the repayment of the loan will not be shown on the statement of cash flows. The president of Wonderous is very disturbed to hear these views and tells Polly the following:

> I cannot believe that you are right in your interpretation of the provisions of SFAS No. 95. If we prepare our statement of cash flows as you describe, then we show a large borrowing each year, a net use of cash from operating activities, and never report the repayment of the debt. I believe that a statement prepared in that manner would be very misleading. We would look like we are zooming toward bankruptcy. Every year we borrow large amounts that we never pay back and we lose cash each year in operating the company. In reality, nothing could be further from the truth. We are profitable and always repay our debt on a timely basis. You must be mistaken. I'm going to have my people research this issue and see if you can be right.

After the meeting, the president assigns you the task of determining if Polly is right.

INSTRUCTIONS

Is Polly right? Prepare a memorandum to the president that sets forth your views on these issues. Be sure to address each of the concerns that have been raised and provide support for your views by references to the appropriate accounting standards.

22–60 Financial Reporting Case Abbott Laboratories is a diversified health-care company devoted to the discovery, development, manufacture, and marketing of innovative products that improve diagnostic, therapeutic, and nutritional practices. The company markets products in more than 130 countries and employs 50,000 people.

FINANCIAL REPORTING CASE

Abbott Laboratories' statement of cash flows for 1993, with comparative information for 1992 and 1991, are presented below. Note 1 of the financial statements—Summary of Significant Accounting Policies—includes the following:

Cash and Cash Equivalents—Cash equivalents consist of time deposits and certificates of deposit with original maturities of three months or less. The carrying amount of cash and cash equivalents approximated fair value as of December 31, 1993 and 1992.

Consolidated Statement of Cash Flows
Abbott Laboratories and Subsidiaries
(dollars in thousands)

	Year Ended December 31		
	1993	**1992**	**1991**
Cash Flow from (Used in) Operating Activities:			
Net earnings	**$1,399,126**	$1,239,057	$1,088,745
Adjustments to reconcile net earnings to net cash from operating activities—Depreciation and amortization	**484,081**	427,782	379,017
Exchange (gains) losses, net	**41,795**	24,925	7,830
Investing and financing (gains) losses, net	**(6,038)**	36,511	35,370
Trade receivables	**(192,451)**	(181,085)	(139,768)
Inventories	**(91,490)**	(109,087)	(44,818)
Prepaid expenses and other assets	**(93,759)**	(114,009)	(221,698)
Trade accounts payable and other liabilities	**375,645**	121,741	344,516
Provision for product withdrawal	**(70,000)**	215,000	—
Gain on sale of investment	**—**	(271,986)	—
Extraordinary gain	**—**	—	(202,250)
Accounting change	**—**	—	206,265
Net cash from operating activities	**1,846,909**	1,388,849	1,453,209
Cash Flow from (Used in) Investing Activities:			
Acquisitions of property, equipment, and businesses	**(952,732)**	(1,007,247)	(770,611)
Purchases of investment securities	**(335,915)**	(178,727)	(284,092)
Proceeds from sales of investment securities	**447,983**	496,120	398,682
Other	**46,826**	22,277	13,915
Net cash used in investing activities	**(793,838)**	(667,577)	(642,106)
Cash Flow from (Used in) Financing Activities:			
Proceeds from borrowings with original maturities of more than three months	**289,429**	196,487	344,162
Repayments of borrowings with original maturities of more than three months	**(197,090)**	(213,833)	(241,735)
Proceeds from (repayments of) other borrowings	**30,124**	381,848	(211,991)
Purchases of common shares	**(465,822)**	(607,598)	(317,811)
Proceeds from stock options exercised	**27,536**	74,027	57,898
Dividends paid	**(548,044)**	(488,413)	(410,345)
Net cash used in financing activities	**(863,867)**	(657,482)	(779,822)
Effect of exchange rate changes on cash and cash equivalents	**(5,104)**	(7,609)	(4,920)
Net increase in cash and cash equivalents	**184,100**	56,181	26,361
Cash and cash equivalents, beginning of year	**116,576**	60,395	34,034
Cash and cash equivalents, end of year	**$ 300,676**	$ 116,576	$ 60,395
Supplemental Cash Flow Information:			
Income taxes paid	**$ 332,834**	$ 702,897	$ 651,442
Interest paid	**52,477**	58,709	59,915

The accompanying notes to consolidated financial statements are an integral part of this statement.

INSTRUCTIONS

[a] What is the amount of cash and cash equivalents in the company's consolidated balance sheets for 1993, 1992, and 1991?

[b] How does the company define cash equivalents? Why would these investments be considered the same as cash for financial reporting purposes?

[c] In preparing the statement of cash flows, has Abbott Laboratories employed the direct or indirect method of presenting the cash flow effects of operating activities? Explain.

[d] Why is depreciation and amortization of $484,081 thousands added to net income in determining net cash from operating activities in 1993?

[e] Develop an explanation to a naive reader of Abbott Laboratories' 1993 statement of cash flows to show how a company with approximately $1.4 billion of net earnings and $1.8 billion of net cash from operating activities experienced an increase in cash of only slightly over $184 million.

[f] What were the major uses of cash, other than operations, for Abbott Laboratories for 1993?

[g] *SFAS No. 95* requires companies to disclose the amount of interest and income taxes paid during the year? How has Abbott Laboratories chosen to make that disclosure and what are the amounts paid for income taxes and interest, respectively, in 1993?

CHAPTER

23

Leases

OBJECTIVES

1. To discuss why many businesses use leasing to acquire service rights to assets.
2. To describe the controversial financial accounting and reporting issues that underlie leasing.
3. To discuss the conditions that cause the economic substance of a lease to change from the rental of property to a presumed sale and purchase.
4. To classify leases for accounting purposes from the perspectives of both lessees and lessors.
5. To demonstrate the application of appropriate accounting recognition, measurement, and disclosure principles to various types of leases.

Many companies choose to lease equipment, buildings, and other long-lived assets rather than purchase them. In fact, in certain industries, leases account for a significant portion of the assets that companies use. An example is the airline industry in which fleets, such as American, Delta, and United, include many leased airplanes. According to a recent article in *Barron's,* worldwide commercial airline fleet leases amounted to $80 billion in 1992, making up about half of the total world market.

Aviation Week & Space Technology states that leases have become popular in the airline industry because, among other things, they:

- Do not require a large capital investment.
- Represent a form of off-balance-sheet financing.
- Do not require the airline to incur the risks involved in owning the asset.

Leasing is also a popular form of financing in other industries. A recent issue of *Forbes* reported that leases accounted for 25% of all new cars that were "driven away by customers" in 1992.

Leases are important to both businesses and consumers. Businesses may lease assets to others (as the lessor) or receive leased assets for their own use (as the lessee). In this chapter, we discuss leasing as a financing method and consider the impact leasing plays in financial reporting for both lessor and lessee companies.

"Airlines Prosper under Tight Management: Leasing Transforms Commercial Transport," *Aviation Week & Space Technology,* vol. 130, issue 22 (May 28, 1989), pp. 90–93; Brigid McMenamin, "The True Cost of Leasing," *Forbes,* vol. 151, issue 3 (February 1, 1993), pp. 98–99; and Jonathan R. Laing, "Losing Altitude: The Sky's No Longer the Limit for Aircraft Leasing Companies," *Barron's,* vol. 72, Issue 43 (October 26, 1992), pp. 8–9, 22–25.

A **lease** is an agreement in which the owner of property, identified as the **lessor,** allows another party, identified as the **lessee,** to use the property in exchange for periodic payments. The lease agreement usually specifies responsibilities of each party to the lease, such as maintenance costs, taxes, and insurance, as well as the period of time during which the agreement is in effect.

LEASING AS A BUSINESS TRANSACTION

Leasing has become a very important mechanism by which companies acquire the resources needed to effectively operate their businesses. Many companies gain access to machinery, equipment, and other needed plant assets by leasing rather than purchasing assets outright. The dollar magnitude of assets that are the subject of leases, as well as the significance of leasing as a method of financing business transactions, justifies our study of this important topic in reasonable depth.

A variety of changes in our economy explains the increased popularity of leasing during the last few decades. One of the most beneficial aspects of leasing is the flexibility it provides the contracting parties to divide the risks and rights of ownership. In most purchase transactions, the principal rights and risks of ownership are transferred from the seller to the buyer—although the seller may retain certain risks, such as product guarantees or warranties. Leasing provides the parties to the agreement much greater flexibility than is possible in an outright sale and purchase.

For example, the rapid rate of technological advance in the computer industry has caused many potential buyers to lease rather than purchase equipment to avoid the risk of obsolescence. If the equipment becomes obsolete and more modern capabilities become available, the lessee can allow the lease to expire and acquire or lease new equipment. The lessee is not limited by a long-term purchase obligation and old, out-of-date equipment. In such cases, the lessor retains the risk of obsolescence. The lessor, who may also be the manufacturer of the product, may be better able to assess the possibility of obsolescence and, therefore, be willing to accept greater risk to more effectively market the product. Also, after an initial lease period, the lessor may be able to lease the property to a second lessee who does not require the latest technology. Some of the rights of ownership, such as the salvage value of the equipment at the end of the lease, may be retained by the lessor as compensation for accepting the increased risks of leasing. Rental rates are usually set at levels that recognize the relative distribution of the risks and rights of ownership to the two parties to the lease.

The income tax implications of leasing may also prove attractive; for example, lease payments may be deductible before the same amounts of depreciation could be deducted if the asset had been purchased. Lessors may be able to depreciate assets that are leased to others and report only the lease payments received as revenue. If those assets had been sold, gross profit on the sale would have been recognized and taxed immediately. Although the subject of structuring transactions for favorable tax results is beyond the scope of this text, we should recognize the significant role income taxes play in influencing the manner in which business affairs are conducted. This includes leasing as a means of financing the use or purchase of long-lived assets.

Another reason that companies may choose to lease assets, rather than buy them, relates to avoiding the need to disburse large amounts of cash to acquire needed assets. Cash preserved in that manner may then be used for other profitable projects. Companies may also enter into leases to avoid reporting large liabilities incurred in the purchase of an asset. Companies often attempt to lease assets to avoid reporting the liability and the related asset that would have resulted from a purchase. This practice is referred to as **off-balance-sheet financing** and is advantageous from a financial reporting perspective because of its effect on the company's reported financial position and results of operations. For example, the debt/equity ratio and the rate of return on assets employed improve if the company leases assets in a manner that permits it to avoid reporting the assets and related liabilities in its balance sheet. Furthermore, if some of the liabilities would have been current, leasing may improve reported working capital and the current ratio. The accounting profession has recognized the possibility of abusive accounting practices in this area and has acted to eliminate some of the ability to achieve off-balance-sheet financing, as we shall see later in this chapter.

The decision to lease, rather than purchase, is a complex business decision that requires careful analysis on the part of the lessee. The following represent the types of questions that must be answered before an informed decision can be made:

1. Are the rates firm or subject to interest rate change?
2. Is the lease noncancelable?
3. Does the acquiring company pay maintenance and taxes?
4. Are the monthly payments made at the beginning or end of the month?
5. Is casualty insurance included?
6. Are equipment upgrades guaranteed, and what is the cost?
7. What flexibility does the acquiring company have at the end of the lease?[1]

To properly account for and report leasing activities in financial statements, accountants must understand both the economics of these transactions and the motivations of the individuals who design and enter into them. The accounting profession has studied carefully the issue of leasing and has attempted to design standards that distinguish among various types of leases.

THE PRIMARY ACCOUNTING ISSUES

The primary goal in accounting for all types of leases is to recognize the economic substance of a particular lease rather than its legal form. When a lease contains provisions that change the substance of a transaction from merely the periodic payment of money for the use of property (rent) to an installment acquisition of substantial economic rights or benefits (purchase), the lease should be treated by the lessee as the purchase of an asset and the incurrence of a liability. According to the Financial Accounting Standards Board (FASB),

Substance over Form

> *A lease that transfers substantially all of the benefits and risks incident to the ownership of property should be accounted for as the acquisition of an asset and the incurrence of an obligation by the lessee.*[2]

In such cases, the lessor should record a sale of the property and recognize a receivable for the future rent, in recognition of the economic substance of the transaction. Likewise, the lessee should record the purchase of an asset and the incurrence of a liability for the obligation assumed. The concept of substance over form in regard to leases has been long established, well understood, and generally accepted. However, the specific circumstances in which leases should be treated as sales by lessors and purchases by lessees have been the subject of debate for many years.

A long history of problems is associated with accounting for leases. The Accounting Principles Board (APB) issued four separate major opinions dealing with different aspects of the subject. More recently, the FASB issued *Statement of Financial Accounting Standards No. 13,* which superseded all four of the *APB Opinions* and established comprehensive financial accounting and reporting requirements for both lessees and lessors. However, further demonstrating the complexity of this area of accounting, the FASB has amended and interpreted *SFAS No. 13* many times.

Financial reporting for complex lease agreements is a technical challenge, and current authoritative pronouncements contain many subtle provisions and implications. Before accountants can resolve the many practical and conceptual leasing problems, they must understand basic leasing terms and concepts employed in the FASB pronouncements. Therefore, before proceeding to a discussion of lease classification, accounting, and financial statement presentation, we shall establish a common ground and understanding in regard to some important leasing terms and concepts.

IMPORTANT LEASING TERMS

We begin our discussion by considering the basic types of leases and how each is distinguished from the others. Various other concepts and terms, less central to the overall theories

---

[1]Ralph L. Benke, Jr., and Charles P. Baril, "The Lease vs. Purchase Decision," *Management Accounting* (March 1990), p. 46.

[2]*FASB Statement of Financial Accounting Standards No. 13,* "Accounting for Leases," 1976, par. 91.

underlying lease accounting, are introduced throughout the chapter when necessary and relevant to the particular issues being discussed.

LESSEES

In financial accounting, lessees initially classify leases as either operating or capital.

An **operating lease** is a rental agreement requiring periodic payments for the use of an asset. An operating lease, in substance, does *not* represent the purchase of an asset; consequently, the lease itself is not recorded and no new assets or liabilities are included in the accounting records of the lessee. Instead, rent expense is recognized as the leased asset is used by the lessee.

Substance over Form   A **capital lease** is a rental agreement that *represents, in substance, the purchase of an asset and the incurrence of a liability.* In concept, when the rights and risks of ownership of a particular asset are transferred from a lessor to a lessee in a lease transaction, the lease is considered a capital lease and is a recordable transaction. To illustrate, assume that Maddox Company enters into a capital lease properly valued at $10,000. At the beginning of the lease term, Maddox makes the following entry to record the acquisition of the asset and incurrence of the liability.

Equipment	10,000	
Lease Liability		10,000

This asset and liability are subject to accounting requirements that are identical to other long-lived assets and liabilities we have studied. Whether a lease is treated as an operating or a capital lease may have important implications on the financial statements of the lessee. Therefore, the classification of the lease requires careful analysis and consideration of many factors. Several specific criteria on *SFAS No. 13* are used to distinguish between operating and capital leases and are discussed in a later section of this chapter.

LESSORS

Lessors are required to classify a lease agreement into one of four possible types: operating, sales-type, direct-financing, and leveraged leases.

An **operating lease** is the direct counterpart of a lessee's operating lease. From the perspective of the lessor, an operating lease merely represents an agreement in which rent is received for the use of property owned by the lessor. *The property is not presumed to have been sold* by the lessor to the lessee. The lessor recognizes rent revenue during the time the lessee uses the leased asset. Furthermore, the lessor depreciates the leased asset in a normal fashion because the asset has not been sold to the lessee.

The three remaining lease types represent leasing circumstances that, in substance, indicate that the lessor has "sold" the property (or the property rights) and obtained a receivable from the lessee. Once a lessor concludes that a particular lease is one of the three types of **capital leases,** rather than an operating lease, further classification as a sales-type, direct-financing, or leveraged lease is necessary.

A **sales-type lease** is a form of capital lease that gives manufacturer's or dealer's gross profit (or loss) to the lessor. That is, the fair value of the leased property at the inception of the lease is greater (or less) than its cost or carrying value on the books of the lessor. When the lease takes effect, the property is considered to be sold. The difference between the cost of the property on the books of the lessor and the fair value of the property is recorded as gross profit (loss) on the sale at that time. Normally, a sales-type lease occurs when manufacturers or dealers use leasing as a means to market their products. In sales-type leases, the lessor earns profit both from the sale of the property and as interest revenue from financing the sale. To illustrate, assume that Luper Company, a lessor, enters into a sales-type lease properly valued at $16,000. The cost of the leased asset to Luper was $12,500. The entry to record the lease (i.e., sale), to remove the leased equipment from its books, and to recognize the manufacturer or dealer profit on the sale follows:

Lease Receivable	16,000	
Cost of Goods Sold	12,500	
Equipment		12,500
Sales		16,000

The difference between the cost of goods sold ($12,500) and the sales revenue ($16,000) is the gross profit ($3,500) resulting from the sales-type lease. The entry to record a sales-type lease is similar to recording the sale of merchandise in a perpetual inventory system, as explained in Chapter 8 of this textbook.

A **direct-financing lease** is a form of capital lease that does *not* give rise to manufacturer's or dealer's gross profit (or loss) on the assumed sale of the property to the lessee. In a direct-financing lease, the cost or carrying amount of the property on the lessor's books and the fair value of the leased property at the inception of the lease are not materially different. The revenue to the lessor in a direct-financing lease consists solely of *interest* revenue from the *financing function* the lessor provides. To illustrate, assume that a lessor, Reese Company, enters into a direct-financing lease properly valued at $15,500. The entry to record the lease receivable and remove the leased equipment follows:

Materiality

Lease Receivable	15,500	
Equipment		15,500

A **leveraged lease** is a three-party lease agreement involving a lessee, a long-term creditor (such as a bank), and a lessor, in which the long-term creditor provides financing to the lessor. For example, if a shipyard agrees to build a supertanker and lease it to an oil company, construction financing may be needed. In such circumstances, a bank may lend money to the shipbuilder (lessor) but require repayment from the oil company (lessee). The lessor constructs the tanker with a relatively small amount of its own cash and the money provided by the bank. Once the asset is constructed, the oil company operates the ship under a long-term lease, repays the bank, and makes an additional payment to the shipbuilder. Leveraged leases are complex financing arrangements, details of which are generally beyond the scope of this text. However, a brief explanation is offered in the final section of this chapter.

Exhibit 23–1 summarizes the lease categories that are acceptable for financial accounting and reporting. The terms we have just discussed relate to the basic issues of lease classification; several other terms are also important for a general understanding of accounting for leases.

The **fair value** of the leased property is the price for which it could be sold in an arm's-length transaction. If the lessor is a manufacturer or dealer, fair value is ordinarily the asset's

---

EXHIBIT 23–1

Lease Classification Summary

General Lease Type	Lessor	Lessee
Noncapitalized (no sale and purchase of asset presumed)	Operating lease	Operating lease
Capitalized (sale and purchase of asset presumed)	Sales-type lease Direct-financing lease Leveraged lease	Capital lease

normal selling price less any applicable volume or trade discounts. If the lessor is not a manufacturer or dealer, fair value is ordinarily its cost or carrying amount. Fair value is determined in light of prevailing market conditions at the inception of the lease.

The **estimated residual value** is the expected fair value of the property at the end of the lease term. The estimated residual value, like estimated salvage value for purposes of depreciating plant assets, encompasses consideration of both diminished productivity and obsolescence.

Accountants use several methods to estimate the residual value of a leased asset. For example, appraisals, dealer quotations, engineering estimates, and previous experience with similar assets may prove helpful in formulating residual value estimates. In making such estimates, one should not attempt to anticipate increases in value or changes in price level. Amortization of leased assets, like depreciation of plant assets, is a cost allocation process that is required to apply the matching principle rather than an asset valuation process.

Matching

Residual value may be **guaranteed** to the lessor, in which case the lessee or a third party ensures that the lessor will realize a specified amount at the end of the lease term. If the leased asset's value is not as great as the guaranteed residual value at the end of the lease, the guarantor must make up the difference in cash. An **unguaranteed residual value** represents a residual value that has not been guaranteed by the lessee or other third party.

LEASE CLASSIFICATION

A lease meeting *any one* of the following four criteria is treated as a *capital lease* by lessees and *tentatively* classified as a type of capital lease by the lessors:

1. *The lease transfers ownership of the property to the lessee by the end of the lease term.* When a lease contains a transfer of title clause, the lease is presumed to be a sale by the lessor and a purchase by the lessee. Such leases are clearly installment sales/purchases of assets.

2. *The lease contains a bargain purchase option.* A bargain purchase option is a lease provision that allows the lessee to purchase the property at a price substantially lower than the expected fair value of the property at the time the option becomes exercisable. Because determining whether a particular purchase option represents a *bargain* purchase option is important to both lease classification and financial accounting, the economic substance of all purchase clauses must be carefully assessed.

Substance over Form

3. *The lease term is equal to 75% or more of the estimated economic life of the property at the beginning of the lease term.* When a lessee acquires the use of a leased asset for *most of its useful life,* accountants conclude that, in substance, a sale has taken place.

4. *The present value of the minimum lease payments at the inception of the lease is 90% or more of the fair value of the leased asset.* When the value of the lease is enough that it represents *most of the fair value of the property,* the lease is considered, in substance, a sale/purchase transaction. In applying this criterion, minimum lease payments are reduced by any executory costs to be paid by the lessee to the lessor, and fair value is reduced for any investment tax credit retained and expected to be realized by the lessor. *Executory costs* are expenses necessary to operate and maintain the leased property, such as taxes, insurance, and maintenance. A lease agreement may require the lessee to pay such costs directly to taxing authorities or insurance companies. In other cases, the lease may provide that the lessor is to retain formal responsibility for paying executory costs while the property is being used by the lessee. In that way, the lessor is assured that taxes are being paid and that the asset is adequately insured. In such circumstances, lease payments made by the lessee are presumed to include both a lease payment for the use of the property and a reimbursement to the lessor of executory expenses.

In the following sections, we refer to these four criteria by the following abbreviated titles: (1) the **transfer-of-title** criterion, (2) the **bargain-purchase-option** criterion, (3) the **length-of-lease-term** criterion, and (4) the **amount-of-lease-payment** criterion.

To illustrate these capitalization criteria, we consider the case of Waller Corporation, a lessor, that enters into a lease with Sacramento Company, a lessee. The 10-year lease has minimum lease payments with a present value of $150,000. The lease involves the use of machinery that has a 12-year estimated useful life and is valued at $160,000. The lease contains no transfer of ownership clause and no purchase or renewal options. We draw the following conclusions when we consider each capitalization criterion:

Lease Criteria	Conclusions
1. Transfer of title	This criterion is *not* met because no clause transferring title to the lessee is included in the lease.
2. Bargain purchase option	This criterion is *not* met because no purchase option is included in the lease.
3. Length of lease term	This criterion is *met,* because the lease term of 10 years exceeds 75% of the asset's expected life (75% × 12 years = 9 years).
4. Amount of lease payment	This criterion is *met,* because the amount of the lease, $150,000, exceeds 90% of the value of the leased asset (90% × $160,000 = $144,000).

This is a *capital lease* because at least one capitalization criterion is met.

Now that we have an understanding of some lease terminology and the lease capitalization criteria of *SFAS No. 13,* let us consider the rationale that underlies these concepts. The primary financial reporting problem that the lease capitalization criteria are attempting to resolve is that of off-balance-sheet financing by lessees. If the lessee enters into a lease that is *in substance the equivalent of a purchase* and that obligates the lessee in a manner equivalent to that of debt financing, the obligation must be included among the liabilities in the lessee's balance sheet. Of course, if the liability is included, then the asset acquired must also be included. Incurring obligations equivalent to debt but not presenting those obligations as liabilities in the balance sheet is what we mean when we refer to "off-balance-sheet financing." Prior to *SFAS No. 13,* this was a prevalent practice and, in fact, was a very attractive feature of leasing. The four capitalization criteria previously presented attempt to identify those conditions in leases that strongly suggest that the lease is so similar to the purchase of the asset and the incurrence of related debt that the entire transaction should be treated as a purchase by the lessee rather than as a lease. On the other hand, if none of the capitalization criteria are met, the lease is *not* considered equivalent to a purchase and the related asset and liability are not included in the lessee's balance sheet.

Substance over Form

We emphasize the lessee and the issue of off-balance-sheet financing, but we should not overlook the importance of the lease criteria to the lessor. From the lessor's viewpoint, the criteria are important in resolving revenue realization issues concerning the timing of lease revenue recognition in the income statement. For the lessor, the lease capitalization criteria govern the pattern of the amounts recognized and whether revenue from leases is recognized at the beginning of the lease or over the life of the lease. For example, in an operating lease, rent revenue is recognized by the lessor in a straight-line pattern, usually based on the receipt of payments from the lessee. In a direct-financing lease, the lessor recognizes no profit from the sale of the property; however, the lessor recognizes interest (based on the investment in the lease and the rate of interest implicit in the lease) over the lease term. In a sales-type lease, the lessor recognizes a gross profit or loss in the period of the inception of the lease and then recognizes interest revenue (based on the investment in the lease and the rate of interest implicit in the lease) over the lease term. Therefore, *whether* a lease is capitalized, and if it is, *how* it is capitalized, are important factors in the recognition of revenue by the lessor. Later sections of this chapter illustrate the specific accounting procedures for these various kinds of leases

Revenue Realization

In addition to being concerned about the off-balance-sheet financing dimensions of lessee accounting and the revenue recognition dimensions of lessor accounting, we are also interested in compatible accounting treatment of the same lease by both parties. *Symmetry* is a word that is sometimes used to describe the desirable outcome in which a lease that is treated

LOSING ALTITUDE: THE SKY'S NO LONGER THE LIMIT FOR AIRCRAFT LEASING COMPANIES

During the endless summer of the Easy Money 'Eighties, all manner of financial flora and fauna flourished. Few of these efflorescences were as remarkable as the aircraft leasing market. For in the matter of a decade, it was transmuted from a cottage industry dominated by a few large banks and insurance companies into a vast international money game. Today an estimated $80 billion of the $200 billion worldwide commercial fleet is leased. This compares with just a pittance of the total aircraft 15 years ago.

In the interim, plane leasing came to be regarded as a no-lose proposition. Passenger traffic rose smartly during the decade and so did lease opportunities. And even if lease margins sometimes proved modest, one always had the fat residual value of the aircraft at the end of the lease to fall back on. In a seller's market, aircraft prices bore little relation to their depreciated book value. Market values always seemed to be higher.

There were warnings that bad times lay ahead (*Barron's*, Dec. 10, 1990). Overcapacity was building and the industry was contracting, threatening a collapse in airplane asset values. But those warnings were easy to shrug off by those big-time players that during the 'Eighties either entered the leasing market or dramatically increased their exposure.

The Japanese financial institutions, trading companies and other major corporations were, of course, a given. Add to that, however, the cream of Corporate America—companies like AT&T, Ford, Philip Morris, the Baby Bells, General Electric, Disney, Whirlpool, General Motors' EDS unit, and utilities like Potomac Electric and Florida Progress. Even Fannie Mae and Sallie Mae caught the bug. Many of the large U.S. and London banks that once dominated the action were content to withdraw from the fray and garner fees by syndicating lease deals for clients. The banks had found their own brand of poison in commercial real estate and loans for leveraged transactions.

Likewise, a number of newer concerns, short on capital but long on dreams, were able to muscle their way into airplane leasing. Such outfits as Polaris Aircraft Leasing (now a unit of General Electric) availed themselves of the public partnership to finance their fleets.

Even more remarkable has been the growth of the 'Seventies start-up companies GPA Group PLC of Shannon, Ireland, and International Lease Finance Corp., headquartered in Beverly Hills, Calif. They began small, but through their nimbleness and the complaisance of their lenders, the two companies now boast world-class airfleets. Last year, the pair took delivery on more than 10% of the total commercial aircraft from the likes of Boeing Co., Europe's Airbus Industrie consortium and McDonnell Douglas Corp. In recognition of its new stature, ILFC was acquired in 1990 by the insurance giant American International Group, Inc., for $1.3 billion in cash and stock.

The 'Eighties boom in aircraft leasing was ignited by several phenomena. U.S. airline deregulation and worldwide prosperity spurred strong growth in passenger traffic. As a consequence, demand for new and used airplanes surged.

After a time, the process became self-reinforcing. Avid bidding for aircraft attracted torrents of new lease money, which, in turn, prompted more speculation in airplane ownership. Cause and effect ultimately blurred. This much is for sure: The aircraft cycle would never have reached such zany levels of excess without the availability of a seemingly inexhaustible supply of lease funds.

The major independent lessors like GPA and ILFC played a crucial role in the system. For they were willing to supply airplanes to lesser credits like the new airlines and charter companies that were springing up all over the globe. Their lease rates tended to be high. But the trade-offs were irresistible. No down payments were required beyond certain maintenance reserves and two months' rent in security deposits. And the independents offered short-term "operating" leases of five years or so rather than the more traditional 20–25-year finance leases, which allowed for the recovery of the bulk of the equipment's cost. Who could tell, after all, how long many of the new carriers would last? In a bull market, new rental customers are easy to find.

Likewise, the major U.S. airlines and flag carriers around the globe increasingly resorted to leasing as the decade wore on. Most of the lease deals were kept off the carrier's balance sheets even though the long-term leases they preferred were for all intents and purposes debt obligations. And the airlines needed the capital relief afforded by leasing as they gunned up their fleet expansion programs. The red-hot market in new and used aircraft allowed the airlines to realize gains and raise cash by selling airplanes to investor groups at inflated prices, then leasing back the equipment.

But mostly, it was the rock-bottom rental rates that attracted major airlines. The blue-chip corporations and financial institutions streaming into the 'Eighties leasing market boasted lower costs of capital than the airlines. They also had the earnings capacity to take better advantage of handsome depreciation and other tax benefits that attach to ownership of capital equipment like airliners. These benefits were then largely passed back to the airlines in lower rental rates.

The profusion of lease products rolled out during the decade was mind-boggling. There were Tax Benefit Transfer, Safe Harbor, Shogan, RIC, NIC, PIC and Foreign Sales Corporation leases. Many were leveraged with ownership and debt tranches. Like layers in a vast sedimentary deposit, each type of lease bore a trace of some quirk in the ever-mutating U.S. Tax Code. The life and then demise of the Investment Tax Credit in the early 'Eighties, for example. The schemes reached their zenith of rococo sophistication with the widely used double dip lease in the late 'Eighties. This permitted both a Japanese and U.S. lessor to simultaneously depreciate in full the very same airplanes. The Japanese tax authorities closed this loophole several years ago.

These days, however, damage control has replaced financial engineering as the primary preoccupation of the airplane-leasing crowd. For with the onset of the 'Nineties, airline industry fundamentals took a vicious turn for the worse.

Worldwide passenger traffic suddenly stumbled after decades of uninterrupted growth. Last year's 2.3% drop in global passenger traffic was the first actual decline in the entire post-World War II era. And this year's rebound has been achieved at the cost of ruinous fare wars in the U.S. and on certain international routes.

Indeed, over the past three years, U.S. carriers have racked up losses of around $7 billion. Over the same period, airlines like Continental, TWA, and America West fell into Chapter 11 bankruptcy, a process that Pan Am, Eastern, Braniff II, and Midway weren't able to survive. A number of small carriers and charter companies around the world also augered into the ground. Almost all were heavy users of leased equipment.

Nonetheless, new equipment, ordered in the salad days of the late 'Eighties, has continued to roll out of the plants of Boeing and the other airframe manufacturers at record rates. This year's deliveries will exceed 800 planes for the second year in a row, or nearly twice the level required to accommodate normal fleet expansion, replacement, and retirement. The three previous delivery years also exceeded putative world demand by a wide measure.

Lest anyone doubt the current disequilibrium between supply and demand, there's the mute testimony of some 950 airplanes, or approximately 10% of the world commercial fleet (excluding Russia), that have been taken out of service and grounded. Many have been parked in remote desert locations out West to guard against metal corrosion and cabin mildew. And not all the planes are scrap or Stage 2 aircraft, like Boeing 727s, that will no longer meet federal noise-reduction and engine-emission standards by the year 2000. Plenty of newer planes, including some "white tails" new from the factory, are currently available for sale or rent. They'll go in either direction like the hoboes of the 'Thirties. Just make a bid.

Near unanimity of opinion exists in the aviation community as to the causes of this sad state of affairs. They are repeated mantra-like in speech after speech, annual report after annual report—the Persian Gulf war, fear of terrorism and the worldwide economic slump. Comfort is undoubtedly drawn from the external or "exogenous" nature of these factors. The industry bears little blame. It was just an unfortunate run of bad cards.

Morten Beyer, president of Morten Beyer & Associates and a veteran aviation industry consultant, takes a more jaundiced view, however. He notes several insidious secular trends that tend to get short shrift in the trade.

The growth in worldwide passenger traffic has steadily declined in each decade since the dawn of the Jet Age in 1960. One can see it clearly displayed in Boeing's own charts, which have become the bible of the industry. It only stands to reason, of course. The biggest market, the U.S., with its greater-than-40% market share, has achieved a measure of saturation. The same phenomenon appears to be occurring in such affluent, fast-growing traffic areas as the Pacific Rim and Europe, he adds. "Through a natural evolu-

tion, we're fast reaching an era of diminishing returns," he averred in an interview in his suburban Washington, D.C., office. "Much of the replacement of steamships, railroad and auto travel has already taken place. Even with all their fancy hub and spokes systems, computerized reservation services, yield management techniques and frequent-flier programs, U.S. carriers haven't been able to arrest the steady decline in real terms of their yields, or revenues per passenger miles."

According to Beyer, the aviation industry is currently paying the price for a certain tulip mania that developed in the 'Eighties. Aircraft orders exploded to giddy heights as carriers and investors alike bought into the Boeing scenario of uninterrupted compounded passenger growth of better than 5% a year through 2010.

The Boeing chart still looks compelling. The disastrous traffic slowdown of the past two years shows up as a barely perceptible air pocket in the line's steep ascent through the first decade of the next millennium. The compounding gets pretty dramatic when one assumes away cycles in world economic growth, disposable income and, therefore, traffic. Like Boeing's projection of $857 billion in future commercial airplane deliveries, excluding Russia, over the next 18 years.

In the late 'Eighties, competition was fierce among the airlines and lessors like GPA and ILFC for control of prime delivery slots at Boeing and the other airframe companies. GPA used to claim that their prime position in the Boeing order queue was the lessor's greatest asset. GPA accounted

Top Lessees of Jet Aircraft

	Number of Leased Aircraft	Total Value ($millions)
American	328	$8,390.8
Delta	258	6,356.2
United	211	5,887.7
USAir	223	3,495.4
Continental	227	3,241.2
Northwest	149	3,017.6
KLM	51	2,589.2
Singapore Airlines	26	1,782.4
America West	74	1,624.7
British Airways	60	1,617.2
Air France	38	1,513.7
Federal Express	54	1,442.0
Varig	29	1,264.9
Lufthansa	21	1,239.4
Trans World	117	1,012.3
SAS	41	883.5
Aeromexico	41	869.7
Southwest	58	828.5
Garuda	19	763.2
Canadian International	38	751.8

(continued)

(Continued from p. 1047)

for 10% of Boeing's backlog as late as this past summer. A secondary market even developed for a time in which airlines and lessors traded delivery slots at premium prices.

But no more. In the past years, U.S. air carriers and others have delayed some $20 billion in new aircraft orders. GPA bit the bullet in recent weeks and pushed back more than $5 billion of its $12 billion in future orders through 2000. The queue has gotten so soft that the airplane producers are said to be offering ILFC preferential delivery on billions of dollars worth of planes over the next few years.

Invariably, the order cutbacks are depicted as deferrals rather than cutbacks. That way both parties to the transaction save face. It's strictly a matter of semantics, though. For in the long run, we're all dead, economist John Maynard Keynes once observed.

The leasing community is already feeling the pain from the commercial aviation slump. Lease defaults spiraled as a result of the demise of Eastern, Braniff, Pan Am and Midway. Many lessors were unable to find new homes for all the aircraft that rubber-banded back to them. Meanwhile, bankrupt carriers like TWA, Continental and America West have extorted drastic cuts of 50% or more in their rental rates from some of their lessors. Continental, for example, is well into its third round of rent concessions. In a glutted market, lessors have little choice but to acquiesce. The alternative is a parked airplane that earns no revenue.

But perhaps most worrisome has been the accompanying slump in aircraft values, particularly the older models.

George Batchelor, the wily owner of International Air Leases in Miami who has been leasing planes into South America for more than four decades, cites several examples. Boeing wide-body 747-200s, which commanded a $40 million price tag a year ago, are now going for $15 million. DC 10-30s have halved in price over the same period. And many older Stage 2 airplanes have sunk to their scrap value. "It's the worst cycle I've ever experienced since the 'Forties, and things only seem to be getting worse," he grouses. "When a conservative guy like me is overextended, then you know that the leasing industry is really overextended."

The pain is even extending to the portfolios of high-class corporate investors, who own the newest airplanes and lease to the best credits. Their leases may be intact. But they can no longer count on the glossy residual value of their equipment once it goes off lease. In many transactions, they paid "grossed-up" fair market prices for the aircraft in sale-lease-back arrangements with the airlines. Prices have since fallen faster than depreciated values. Many corporate investors borrowed 80% of the purchase price in leveraged leases to magnify the tax benefits.

as a capital lease by the lessor is also treated as a capital lease by the lessee. The same is true for operating leases. Symmetrical treatment of leases is a desired goal of financial reporting, and the authoritative accounting literature has been written to encourage symmetry.

CLASSIFICATION-RELATED TERMS

Additional definitions that are important in understanding the lease capitalization criteria presented earlier are as follows:

1. The **lease term** is the fixed noncancelable term of the lease plus all of the following periods:[3]
    a. Those covered by bargain renewal options. A **bargain renewal option** allows the lessee to renew the lease for an amount substantially lower than the fair rental of the property at the date the option becomes exercisable. Determining whether a particular renewal option is a *bargain* renewal option requires substantial judgment and is important because lease classification and related accounting treatments are influenced directly.

---

[3]*A noncancelable lease* is a lease that is cancelable only under one or more of the following conditions:

1. Upon the occurrence of some remote contingency.
2. With the permission of the lessor.
3. If the lessee enters into a new lease with the same lessor.
4. Upon payment by the lessee of a large penalty so that continuation of the lease appears reasonably assured.

Even if a lessor has the ability to permit the lease to be canceled, the lease is still considered noncancelable by both the lessee and lessor. This treatment is consistent with accounting practices in other areas, such as convertible debt, and is proper because the lessor can compel the lessee to pay the lease payments and meet the other terms of the lease.

b. Periods for which failure to renew the lease imposes a penalty on the lessee in an amount such that renewal appears, at the inception of the lease, to be reasonably assured.

c. Periods covered by ordinary renewal options during which a guarantee by the lessee of the lessor's debt related to the leased property is expected to be in effect.

d. Periods covered by ordinary renewal options preceding the date a bargain purchase option is exercisable.

e. Periods representing renewals or extensions of the lease at the lessor's option. Accountants always consider the lease term to end at the date a bargain purchase option becomes exercisable.

2. The **estimated economic life** of leased property is the remaining period the property is expected to be economically usable in its intended function without limitation by the lease term.

3. **Minimum lease payments** are the payments that the lessee is obligated to make in connection with the leased property. If the lease contains a bargain purchase option, only the **minimum rental payments** over the lease term preceding that option and the payment called for by the option are minimum lease payments. If the lease does *not* contain a bargain purchase option, *minimum lease payments include* all of the following:

a. The *minimum rental payments* over the lease term.

b. Any *guarantee of the residual value* of the leased property at the expiration of the lease term.

c. Any *payment that the lessee must make* or can be required to make upon failure to renew or extend the lease at the expiration of the lease term.

An appendix to *SFAS No. 13* provides that "the period covered by a bargain renewal option is included in the lease term . . . and the option rentals [required under a bargain renewal option] are included in the minimum lease payments."[4]

From the standpoint of lessors, minimum lease payments are the same as those described from the standpoint of the lessee, plus any guarantee of residual value or rental payments beyond the lease term by a third party unrelated to either the lessee or the lessor.

OTHER LEASE CLASSIFICATION ISSUES

The transfer-of-title and bargain-purchase-option criteria are applied to all leases; however, the length-of-lease-term and amount-of-lease-payment criteria are *not* applied if the lease term begins within the last 25% of the total estimated life of the the property. This exception is included in the authoritative literature in recognition of the fact that the criteria using percentages are subject to distortion and may result in leases that begin late in the asset's life being treated as capital leases, whereas identical leases earlier in the asset's life were treated as operating leases.

We stated earlier that a lease meeting one (or more) of the four basic capitalization criteria was *tentatively* classified by the lessor as a capital lease. Lessors must apply two additional criteria to permanently classify a lease as a capital lease. These criteria concern the evidence necessary to record a receivable and the ability to predict any future expenses associated with the leased property. When a lease is classified as a capital lease, lessees record additional assets and liabilities and begin to reflect expenses such as depreciation and interest. When lessors record capital leases, they reclassify assets from plant or inventory to receivables and may recognize gross profit. Interest revenue also begins to be earned and recognized in the income statement.

Consistent with the modifying convention of conservatism, generally accepted accounting principles require more evidence to record receivables than to record payables, and the same relationship exists between revenues and expenses. Therefore, lessors are required to assess the **collectibility of rent** *and* future **predictability of costs** prior to recording a capital lease. Unless future rental collections are reasonably assured *and* future costs to be

Conservatism

---

[4]*FASB Statement of Financial Accounting Standards No. 13,* par. 88.

incurred under the lease are reasonably predictable, even a lease meeting one of the initial four criteria is accounted for as an operating lease by the lessor. The collectibility of rent and predictability of costs criteria must be met prior to recording a receivable and recognizing gross profit or interest revenue, considerations that have relevance only to the lessor.

If a lease meets *one* or more of the four initial classification criteria and *both* the rental collectibility and cost predictability criteria, it is classified as a capital lease by the lessor. Remaining lessor classification criteria in *SFAS No. 13* relate to what type of capital lease a given lease is, not whether it is an operating or capital lease.

To summarize, both the lessor and lessee must consider the four primary capitalization criteria in classifying a lease as either capital or operating. If one or more of those criteria are met, the lessor must further consider the two revenue-recognition criteria before making a final classification decision. Exhibit 23–2 serves as a learning aid to summarize the classification process (excluding leveraged leases) for both the lessor and lessee.

ACCOUNTING AND REPORTING STANDARDS FOR LESSEES

We now turn to financial accounting and reporting practices for various types of leases. First we consider how lessees account for and report operating and capital leases.

OPERATING LEASES

From the perspective of lessees, operating leases are relatively simple to account for and pose few financial reporting problems. Rent expense is usually recognized as lease payments are made. The lease itself is not considered a recordable transaction, and no new assets or liabilities are reflected in the financial statements of the lessee at the inception of the lease.

When an operating lease requires unequal cash payments, rent expense should be recognized on a straight-line basis and determined by the total cash payments to be made over the lease term. According to *FASB Technical Bulletin 85–3,* "Accounting for Operating Leases with Scheduled Rent Increases," lessees should recognize rent expense on a straight-line basis unless some other allocation method is more representative of the time pattern over which the property is employed. For example, if an operating lease has a term of 10 years and requires an initial payment of $15,000 followed by eight annual payments of $10,000 and a final payment of $5,000, the total rent expense to be recognized and cash to be paid over the 10-year period is $100,000, or an average of $10,000 per year. If the lease is executed with the $15,000 payment on January 1, 1995, and the first $10,000 payment is due on January 1, 1996, the following entries to record the first and second cash payments and recognize rent expense are appropriate:

Jan. 1, 1995	Rent Expense	10,000	
	Prepaid Rent	5,000	
	Cash		15,000
Jan. 1, 1996	Rent Expense	10,000	
	Cash		10,000

The prepaid rent arising in the 1995 entry is classified as a noncurrent asset and remains on the balance sheet until the final payment is due on January 1, 2004. An entry like that for January 1, 1996, is made each year through the year 2003. The final entry on January 1, 2004, is as follows:

Jan. 1, 2004	Rent Expense	10,000	
	Cash		5,000
	Prepaid Rent		5,000

This approach recognizes an equal $10,000 amount of rent expense each year.

If the opposite situation exists and cash payments are deferred at the beginning of the lease, a liability is recorded for the unpaid portion of the expense recognized on the straight-**Materiality** line basis. Thus, when there is a material difference between the straight-line recognition of

EXHIBIT 23–2

Criteria for Lease Classification

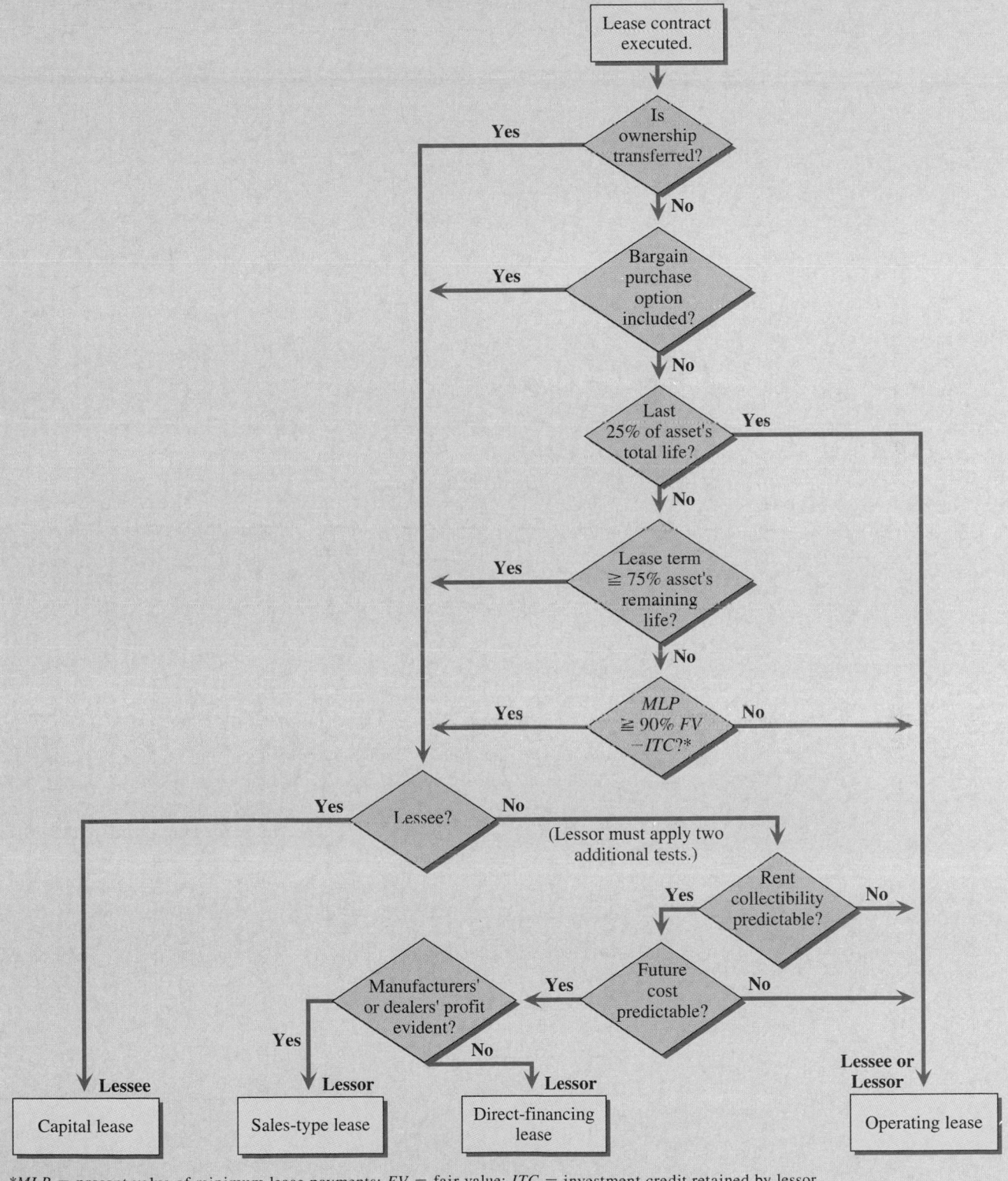

MLP = present value of minimum lease payments; *FV* = fair value; *ITC* = investment credit retained by lessor.
Adapted from Raymond J. Clay and William W. Holder, "A Practitioner's Guide to Accounting for Leases," *Journal of Accountancy* (August 1977), p. 63. Copyright © 1977 by the American Institute of Certified Public Accountants, Inc.

rent expense and the individual cash payments required by an operating lease, we recognize the balance sheet implications of the difference as either prepaid expense or accrued payable. Present-value techniques are not appropriate for operating leases. Executory costs, such as insurance and property taxes incurred directly by lessees, are accrued and allocated to the periods benefited in accordance with generally accepted accounting principles in the same manner as other similar expenses.

CAPITAL LEASES

Substance over Form

Financial accounting and reporting for capital leases by lessees are more involved. When a lessee signs a capital lease, the transaction is, in substance, a purchase of the asset. The lessee records the asset and a liability at the beginning of the lease term, at the present value of the minimum lease payments. However, the amount assigned as the cost of the asset cannot exceed the fair value of the asset at that time. Therefore, it is possible for the carrying amounts of the asset and liability to be the fair value of the asset rather than the present value of the lease payments.

Accounting for Lease Assets

Substance over Form

Lessees must address several other issues of significance in accounting for capital leases. For example, the amortization of the asset and interest relating to the lease obligation poses substantial accounting problems. The general principles that govern the systematic depreciation of other assets also apply to assets recorded under capital leases. If either the transfer of title or bargain purchase option classification tests is met, the lessee has, in substance, acquired all of the property rights inherent in the asset, which is properly classified as a plant asset. The lessee is acquiring not only the right to use the asset for the lease term but also is expected to become legal owner and, thus, control the use of the asset after the lease term. If the transfer-of-title or bargain-purchase-option tests are not met, and the lease meets either the length-of-lease-term or amount-of-lease-payment test, the lease is still classified as a capital lease. The lessee's capitalized right to the use of the property during the lease term, however, is properly considered an intangible asset and identified as "leasehold rights" or other similar designation. Inherent in these criteria is the assumption that the lessor will retain rights to the asset at the end of the lease term.

Matching

In applying the matching principle, a company depreciates and amortizes leased assets in the same manner that it does other assets it owns. However, certain modifications may be necessary in the case of a capitalized leased asset. If either the transfer-of-title or bargain-purchase-option criterion is met, the leased asset is depreciated over the estimated useful life of the asset without regard to the lease term. Also, the asset should not be depreciated below its estimated salvage value. In these circumstances, the entire asset, including the residual value, has been acquired by the lessee. The lease term is relevant only to accounting for the liability aspects of the lease. On the other hand, if the lease is capitalized because it meets either the length-of-lease-term or amount-of-lease-payment criterion, the asset is amortized over the shorter of the lease term or the life of the asset. It may seem illogical to enter into a lease for a longer period than the life of the asset, but such transactions do occur in some operations. For example, in fast-food and similar industries, lessees sometimes intend to refurbish leased facilities several times during a single, relatively long, lease term.

Accounting for Lease Liabilities

Accounting for the liability in a capital lease presents several accounting issues. Foremost among these is the determination of interest on the lease obligation. We usually record a liability for capital leases at the **present value of the minimum lease payments.** The difference between the sum of the minimum lease payments and their present value is the interest to be recognized over the lease term. The effective interest method is used so that a constant rate of interest is recognized each period throughout the lease term. This treatment is consistent with that required by *APB Opinion No. 21* and is discussed in Chapters 10 and 15.[5]

The interest rate that the lessee applies to determine the present value of the future minimum lease payments is the lower of the lessee's incremental borrowing rate or the rate implicit in the lease, assuming the lessee has knowledge of the rate used by the lessor in establishing the lease payments. The **lessee's incremental borrowing rate** is the rate that the lessee would have incurred if the funds to purchase the asset had been borrowed from a bank or other financial institution. The **interest rate implicit in the lease** is the rate that causes the gross future minimum lease payments to equal the fair value of the leased asset. Any residual value that the lessee guarantees to the lessor is included in the minimum lease payments. Executory costs that are included in the lease payments are subtracted in determining the minimum lease payments. If the lessee does not know the rate implicit in the lease, the lessee's incremental borrowing rate is used.

In this section, we illustrate lessee accounting for a capital lease by considering a contract entered into by King Company for a machine. The first $10,000 lease payment was made on December 31, 1994, and a similar payment will be made at the end of each of the following five years to compensate the lessor for use of the machine during the year following payment. The lease does not contain a purchase option or a transfer of title to the lessee at the end of the lease. The fair market value of the machine at December 31, 1994, was $55,000, its estimated useful life is nine years, and its residual value at the end of the lease is expected to be $7,800. In fact, the lessee has guaranteed that value to the lessor at the end of the six-year lease term. Both King Company's incremental borrowing rate and the lessor's rate implicit in the lease are 10%.

We must first evaluate the lease in terms of the four capitalization criteria. The transfer-of-title and bargain-purchase-option criteria are not applicable in this lease. In testing for the length-of-lease-term criterion, we find that the lease represents 66⅔% of the asset's estimated useful life (6/9 = 66⅔%) and, therefore, the 75% standard is not met. Finally, to determine whether the amount-of-lease-payment criterion is met, we must compute the present value of the lease payments and determine whether that amount equals or exceeds 90% of the $55,000 fair value of the asset. Thus, the "benchmark" figure for that determination will be $49,500 ($55,000 × 90%).

The present value of the lease is computed as follows:

Present value of six $10,000 payments:	
$10,000 × (1.00000 + 3.79079)	= $47,908
Present value of $7,800 residual value:	
$7,800 × .56447	= 4,403
Present value of lease	$52,311

Comparing the $52,311 present value of the lease with the benchmark figure of $49,500, we determine that the 90% criterion is met and *the lease is a capital lease*. In calculating the present value of the lease, the first $10,000 payment is assigned a present value of 1.00000 because it represents a down payment and includes no interest. The second through sixth payments are represented by the annuity of 3.79079 ($pvoaf_{\overline{5}|10\%}$). In other words, the six $10,000 payments represent an annuity due, as explained in Chapter 6. The residual value guarantee is a single payment at the end of the sixth year, so the appropriate factor (.56447) is the present value of 1, six years later ($pvf_{\overline{6}|10\%}$). These present value factors are taken from Tables 6–4 (present value of an annuity) and 6–2 (present value of 1).

---

[5]*APB Opinion No. 21,* "Interest on Receivables and Payables," 1971.

ILLUSTRATION OF ACCOUNTING FOR A CAPITAL LEASE

			EXHIBIT 23–3		

King Company
Lease Amortization Table

Date	Payment	Interest	Decline in Net Liability	Net Liability
Dec. 31, 1994	—	—	—	$52,311
	$10,000	—	$10,000	42,311
Dec. 31, 1995	10,000	$ 4,231	5,769	36,542
Dec. 31, 1996	10,000	3,654	6,346	30,196
Dec. 31, 1997	10,000	3,020	6,980	23,216
Dec. 31, 1998	10,000	2,322	7,678	15,538
Dec. 31, 1999	10,000	1,554	8,446	7,092
Dec. 31, 2000	7,800	708*	7,092	–0–
	$67,800	$15,489		

*Rounding difference included in this number to clear accounts.

Exhibit 23–3 is a table that separates each payment into the portion that is interest and the portion that is a reduction in the outstanding debt represented by the lease. Notice that the first $10,000 payment has no interest because it is made at the beginning of the lease and no interest has yet accrued. In all subsequent payments, the amount of interest is 10% of the net liability for the period since the last payment was made. For example, the payment at December 31, 1995, includes $4,231 of interest, which is 10% times the $42,311 net liability for that period. The net liability of the lease at the beginning is its present value of $52,311; the total amount of the payments is $67,800 (six $10,000 payments, plus the $7,800 residual value); the total amount of interest recognized is the difference between these two figures: $67,800 − $52,311 = $15,489.

The following entries are required for the year 1994:

Dec. 31, 1994	Leasehold Rights	52,311	
	Lease Liability		52,311
	(To record capital lease.)		
	Lease Liability	10,000	
	Cash		10,000
	(To record first lease payment.)		

At the end of the first year of the lease, entries are required to amortize the asset purchased by lease, recognize interest expense, and record the second lease payment.

Dec. 31, 1995	Amortization Expense	7,419	
	Leasehold Rights		7,419
	(To record amortization on asset acquired by capital lease.)		
	Interest Expense	4,231	
	Lease Liability		4,231
	(To recognize interest expense for 1995 on capital lease.)		
	Lease Liability	10,000	
	Cash		10,000
	(To record second lease payment.)		

The amount of amortization is the $52,311 cost of the asset (i.e., the present value of the lease), less the $7,800 residual value, divided by the number of years in the lease term:

($52,311 − $7,800)/6 years = $7,419. The $4,231 amount of interest expense recognized is taken from the December 31, 1995, line from Exhibit 23–3. Identical entries are made each year except that the dollar amount of interest expense declines, as indicated in the Interest column of Exhibit 23–3.

At the end of the lease term, after recording amortization and interest expense but before settlement of the residual value, the asset Leasehold Rights will have a $7,800 balance, the same as the Lease Liability. Assuming that the asset is valued at $7,800 or more and is returned to the lessor, the lessee will make the following entry:

Dec. 31, 2000 Lease Liability	7,800	
Leasehold Rights		7,800
(To record settlement of residual value of capital lease.)		

Alternatively, if the asset is appraised at only $5,000, the lessee must pay $2,800 ($7,800 − $5,000) and the appropriate entry is

Dec. 31, 2000 Lease Liability	7,800	
Loss on Transfer of Residual Value	2,800	
Cash		2,800
Leasehold Rights		7,800
(To record settlement of residual value on capital lease.)		

The lessee does not record a gain on the settlement of the residual value unless the lease contains a provision to return to the lessee a refund of lease payments equal to any excess of the appraised residual value over the guaranteed amount. For example, if the King Company lease contained this provision and the appraisal resulted in a value of $9,000 for the machine at the end of the lease term, the following entry is appropriate:

Dec. 31, 2000 Lease Liability	7,800	
Cash ($9,000 − $7,800)	1,200	
Leasehold Rights		7,800
Gain on Transfer of Residual Value		1,200
(To record settlement of residual value on capital lease.)		

The lease may permit the lessee to pay the residual value in cash and retain the asset. In this case, the guaranteed residual value is essentially a purchase option. If this alternative is chosen, the lessee must eliminate the Lease Liability and Leasehold Rights balances, record the cash payment, and establish the acquired asset in an appropriate account, as follows:

Dec. 31, 2000 Lease Liability	7,800	
Machinery	7,800	
Leasehold Rights		7,800
Cash		7,800
(To record purchase of leased asset.)		

Balance sheet presentation for the lessee involves determining the amount and classification of the asset acquired by the lease and the liability represented by it. The asset is classified as an intangible asset because the basis for capitalization is the amount-of-lease-payment criterion (i.e., the present value of the lease equals or exceeds 90% of the fair value of the asset). The liability is subject to current and noncurrent classification, like any other liability that will be retired in installments.

The intangible asset, Leasehold Rights, is presented in the balance sheet at its net amount each year. At December 31, 1994, this amount is $52,311 because no amortization will have been recognized yet. At December 31, 1995 and 1996, the net asset balances are determined as follows:

$$1995: \$52,311 - \$7,419 = \$44,892$$
$$1996: \$52,311 - (\$7,419 \times 2) = \$37,473$$

Similar calculations are required each year, with an additional year's amortization recognized each time.

Separating the liability into current and noncurrent portions is more complicated. The preferred method for determining the current portion of the liability is to compute the present value of the next payment, as follows:

$$\$10,000 \times .90909(pvf_{\overline{1}|10\%}) = \$9,091$$

This is the amount that will be presented as current each year, with the remainder of the liability classified as noncurrent. For example, at December 31, 1994, the current liability is $9,091 and the noncurrent portion is $33,220 ($42,311 − $9,091). A year later at December 31, 1995, the current liability is $9,091 and the noncurrent portion is $27,451 ($36,542 − $9,091). The total liability figures, which are reduced by $9,091 each year to determine the noncurrent portion, are taken from the Net Liability column of Exhibit 23–3.

A second method to separate the liability into current and noncurrent portions is to associate with the current portion all interest to be included in the next payment. Once the current portion has been determined in this way, the remainder is presented as noncurrent. For example, at December 31, 1994, we would determine the current and noncurrent portions as follows:

$$\text{Current: } \$10,000 - \$4,231 = \$\ 5,769$$
$$\underline{\text{Noncurrent: } \$42,311 - \$5,769 = \$36,542}$$
$$\$42,311$$

The $4,231 subtracted from $10,000 to determine the current portion is the interest amount from the December 31, 1995, line in Exhibit 23–3. The $42,311 amount is the total liability from the December 31, 1994, line. Notice that the total liability of $42,311, presented as $5,769 current and $36,542 noncurrent, reconciles with the Net Liability column at the date of presentation, December 31, 1994.

In evaluating the two methods to separate the liability into current and noncurrent portions, the authors prefer the first method because it consistently places the same value on the current liability, the present value of $10,000 payable one year later. Applying the second method in successive years, the current liability increases in amount as the interest portion of future $10,000 payments declines because the carrying amount of the obligation declines. In solving exercises and problems at the end of this chapter, the authors have chosen the first approach unless specifically indicated otherwise.

King Company's income statement presentation of this capital lease involves recognition of amortization expense on the leasehold rights and interest expense, as reflected in the year-end journal entries recorded earlier. Notice that the $10,000 payments are not recorded as an expense as they would be in an operating lease. Rather, they represent reductions in the liability balance. The payments are presented as a negative cash flow from financing activities in the statement of cash flows.

Accounting for capital leases has been illustrated here using a simplified approach in which the liability is presented at a net amount. Alternatively, the lease liability may be recorded at its total dollar or gross amount and the interest portion recorded in a separate discount account. Interest expense is then recognized by amortizing that discount. For the King Company illustration, we would record the lease at December 31, 1994, and the recognition of interest at the end of the first year of the lease as follows:

Dec. 31, 1994 Leasehold Rights	52,311	
Discount on Lease Liability	15,489	
Lease Liability		67,800
(To record capital lease.)		
Dec. 31, 1995 Interest Expense	4,231	
Discount on Lease Liability		4,231
(To recognize interest for 1995 on capital lease.)		

All other 1994 and 1995 entries are the same as presented earlier. The Discount on Lease Liability account is a contra account to the Lease Liability, so the net liability balances are the same whether the accounts are combined, as in the earlier presentation, or separated as done here.

The capital lease example just presented was based on a lease that met the amount-of-lease-payment criterion. As such, the amortization period for the leasehold rights was logically the lease term because the use of the asset reverts to the lessor at the end of the lease. If the lease had been capitalized because of either the transfer-of-title or bargain-purchase-option criteria, the lessee would classify the leased asset as a plant asset (e.g., machinery) and depreciate it over its estimated useful life by the same depreciation method used for similar assets. Notice that if either the transfer-of-title or bargain-purchase-option criteria is met, the lessee is acquiring not only the right to use the asset for the lease term but also is expected to have legal ownership in the future and, thereby, control the use of the asset after the end of the lease term until the end of its useful life.

The earlier example did not make specific reference to executory costs, such as insurance, property taxes, and maintenance. The implicit assumption we made was that the lessee was responsible for these costs and paid them directly, recognizing appropriate expenses at that time. Alternatively, the lease may require the lessee to make payment directly to the lessor for these costs with the lessor having responsibility for payment to the appropriate outside parties.

If the amount of the lease payments is adjusted for a reimbursement to the lessor for executory costs, that amount is excluded in calculating the present value of the lease. As each lease payment is made, executory expenses are recognized by the lessee. Assume, for example, that the $10,000 payments in the King Company example had been $11,500, with $1,500 designated for the coverage of executory costs. The present value of the lease would be calculated and the asset and liability recorded exactly as we did before. Each payment, however, would be separated into that portion representing a reduction in the liability and that portion representing executory costs, as follows:

Lease Liability	10,000	
Executory Expenses on Capital Lease	1,500	
Cash		11,500
(To record first lease payment.)		

In the King Company example, we dealt with a single lease. In practice, lessees often acquire the services of many assets by leasing, and the amounts described here in the balance sheet, the income statement, and the statement of cash flows represent aggregate amounts for many leases. In these more complex situations, computer programs are particularly helpful in determining lease amortization figures, such as those in Exhibit 23–3, as well as current and noncurrent portions of payables, asset amortization amounts, and other important information. In addition to the lease-related items included in the financial statements, the authoritative accounting literature requires a significant amount of additional disclosure, which is typically included in notes to the financial statements.

MISCELLANEOUS LESSEE CONSIDERATIONS

Exhibit 23–4 presents the lease disclosure from the 1993 annual report of AMR Corporation, the parent company of American Airlines, a major U.S. air carrier. Relative to the amount of operating leases ($21,213 million), the amount of capital leases ($2,233 million) is small. As we learned in this chapter, the $21,213 million of operating leases is not included among the liabilities in the balance sheet and is apparent to users of the financial statements only through the note presented in Exhibit 23–4. These leases represent an excellent example of off-balance-sheet financing.

EXHIBIT 23–4

AMR Corporation
Lessee Disclosure (American Airlines)

4. Leases

AMR's subsidiaries lease various types of equipment and property, including aircraft, passenger terminals, equipment, and various other facilities. The future minimum lease payments required under capital leases, together with the present value of net minimum lease payments, and future minimum lease payments required under operating leases that have initial or remaining non-cancelable lease terms in excess of one year as of December 31, 1993, were (in millions):

Year ending December 31,	Capital Leases	Operating Leases
1994	$ 268	$ 982
1995	281	957
1996	268	939
1997	250	954
1998	245	961
1999 and subsequent	2,404	16,420
	3,716*	$21,213*
Less amount representing interest	1,483	
Present value of net minimum lease payments	$2,233**	

---

*Future minimum payments required under capital leases and operating leases include $384 million and $6.0 billion, respectively, guaranteed by AMR relating to special facility revenue bonds issued by municipalities.

**The present value of future minimum lease payments includes $132 million guaranteed by American.

At December 31, 1993, the Company had 235 jet aircraft and 144 turboprop aircraft under operating leases and 80 jet aircraft and 63 turboprop aircraft under capital leases.

The aircraft leases can generally be renewed at rates based on fair market value at the end of the lease term for one to five years. Most aircraft leases have purchase options at or near the end of the lease term at fair market value, but generally not to exceed a stated percentage of the defined lessor's cost of the aircraft. Of the aircraft American has under operating leases, 15 Boeing 767-300ERs are cancelable upon 30 days' notice during the initial 10-year lease term. At the end of that term in 1998, the leases can be renewed for periods ranging from 10 to 12 years. In 1993, American agreed to forfeit its right to cancel leases for 25 Airbus A300-600R aircraft upon 30 days' notice and extended the terms of the leases for periods ranging from 18 to 19 years.

Rent expense, excluding landing fees, was $1.3 billion for 1993 and 1992, and $1.0 billion for 1991.

SOURCE: AMR Corporation, 1993 Annual Report.

Ideally, accounting for operating and capital leases by lessors should mirror accounting by lessees. Lease revenue for the lessor in operating leases replaces the lessee's lease expense. In capital leases, sales and/or interest revenue recognition by the lessor replaces the purchase of assets and interest expense recognition by the lessee. Earlier in this chapter, we referred to this as symmetry between lessor and lessee accounting.

In the following sections, we discuss lessor accounting, considering first operating leases and then two types of capital leases: direct financing and sales type. We build on the examples presented earlier when we considered lessee accounting, looking now at the lessor side of the transaction.

OPERATING LEASES

In an operating lease, lessors usually recognize rent revenue on a straight-line basis over the lease term, even if the cash received under the terms of the lease varies from a straight-line pattern. In such cases, a deferred revenue account is established on the balance sheet if the cash received exceeds straight-line recognition of revenue. If the cash received is less than the rent revenue recognized on a straight-line basis, a receivable is established.

The asset leased to the lessee is usually classified as part of the plant assets section of the balance sheet of the lessor and depreciated in normal fashion. Because an operating lease does not presume that a sale has taken place, the asset is depreciated over its useful life rather than over the lease term. Revenue from an operating lease is rent revenue, and expenses incurred under such leases include depreciation expense on the leased asset. Any **initial direct costs** incurred by a lessor are capitalized and amortized over the term of the operating lease as an expense to be matched against the rental revenue. **Initial direct costs** are those costs incurred by lessors that are essential in and directly related to originating a lease and that were incurred only because the particular leasing transaction occurred. Activities giving rise to initial direct costs include evaluating the prospective lessee's financial condition, evaluating and securing guarantees and other collateral, negotiating lease terms, preparing and processing lease documents, and closing the transactions. Initial direct costs do not include amounts expended for advertising, soliciting potential lessees, servicing existing leases, rent, depreciation, and supervisory and administrative functions.[6]

Matching

To illustrate lessor accounting for an operating lease, consider again the earlier example in which the lessee paid $15,000 in the first year of a 10-year operating lease, $10,000 per year for the second through the ninth years, and $5,000 in the tenth year. We also assume that on January 1, 1995, the first year of the lease, the lessor incurs $6,000 of initial direct costs that are to be amortized by the straight-line method over the 10-year lease term. Selected journal entries to record these transactions are as follows:

Jan. 1, 1995	Cash	15,000	
	Rent Revenue		10,000
	Deferred Rent Revenue		5,000
	Prepaid Initial Direct Costs	6,000	
	Cash		6,000
Dec. 31, 1995	Lease Expense	600	
	Prepaid Initial Direct Costs		600
Jan. 1, 1996	Cash	10,000	
	Rent Revenue		10,000

In the first entry, the $15,000 is separated into the $10,000 that is revenue for 1995 and the $5,000 that is deferred and will be recognized in the tenth year of the lease. The Deferred

---

[6]*FASB Statement of Financial Accounting Standards No. 91,* "Accounting for Nonrefundable Fees and Costs Associated with Originating or Acquiring Loans and Initial Direct Costs of Leases," 1986, par. 24.

Rent Revenue account is a noncurrent liability until the ninth year when it is a current liability. The initial direct costs are capitalized as prepaid expenses and $600 ($6,000/10 years) is recognized each year. The prepaid amount of initial direct costs is an asset that declines each year as amortization is recognized. Assuming that the amounts are material, $600 is appropriately classified as a current asset and the remainder as a noncurrent asset in each year's balance sheet. For the second through the ninth years, an entry like the one at January 1, 1996, is made to record receipt of each $10,000 rent amount, and $600 of prepaid initial direct costs are amortized as was done December 31, 1995.

Materiality

Notice that the lease transaction itself is not recorded. Rather, only the cash payments (initial direct costs) and the cash receipts (rent revenue) are recorded, with adjustment to result in recognition over the lease term by the straight-line method.

CAPITAL LEASES

Capital leases from the viewpoint of the lessor are those leases that are treated as if the asset that is the subject of the lease had been sold to the lessee. The asset on the books of the lessor that results from recording a capital lease is a lease receivable, which mirrors the lease liability recorded by the lessee for a capital lease.

Before we delve into the details of recording capital leases and presenting them in the financial statements of lessors, let's review briefly the criteria that must first be met for a lease to be subject to this treatment. A capital lease for a lessor must meet one or more of the four basic capitalization criteria: transfer of title to the lessee, bargain purchase option, lease term that equals or exceeds 75% of the asset's expected useful life, or the present value of the lease equals or exceeds 90% of the fair value of the asset. If one or more of these criteria are met, the lessor must consider two additional revenue recognition criteria: the costs related to the lease are known or reasonably estimable and collection of the lease payments is reasonably assured. Once these conditions are met, the lessor must further classify the lease as a sales-type or a direct-financing lease.

Lessors may earn two types of revenue from capital leases: gross profit and interest revenue. In a sales-type lease, the lessor earns both types of revenue; in a direct-financing lease, the lessor earns only interest revenue. To determine what type of capital lease the lessor is engaged in requires consideration of the role the lessor plays in the leasing transaction and the relationship of the present value of the lease to the carrying amount of the leased assets on the lessor's books. That carrying amount is usually the cost of the asset to the lessor.

If the lessor is the manufacturer of the asset, the lease is most likely a sales-type capital lease. The lessor/manufacturer may offer its customers the opportunity to purchase the asset outright or, alternatively, to lease the asset. For the lease alternative, the lessor establishes a payment schedule so that the present value of the lease approximates the amount at which the customer (lessee) could have purchased the asset. Had the property been sold outright rather than leased, a gross profit would have been earned equal to the difference between the sales price and the manufactured cost of the asset to the lessor. In a sales-type lease, approximately the same thing takes place with the present value of the lease payments substituting for the sales price of the asset. The lessor earns a gross profit equal to the difference between the present value of the lease payments and the manufactured cost of the asset.

In addition to the gross profit on the sales-type lease, the lessor is also providing a financing function for the lessee because the lessor extends credit in the form of the deferred lease payment schedule. The difference between the total lease payments that are required and the present value of those payments represents interest revenue to the lessor, mirroring the interest expense recognized by the lessee.

In a direct-financing lease, the lessor has usually purchased the asset rather than having manufactured it. The lessor's function is to provide financing to the lessee. The lease payment schedule is established so that the present value of the lease payments approximates the carrying amount or cost of the asset and, therefore, there is no gross profit on the transaction. Rather, the lessor simply recognizes interest revenue over the lease term equal to the difference between the total lease payments and the present value of the lease.

Recall the specifics of the King Company lease in which that company agreed to make six annual $10,000 payments, beginning on December 31, 1994, for the use of a machine that is expected to have a nine-year useful life. The lessee guaranteed a residual value of $7,800 at the end of the sixth year. Finally, both the interest rate implicit in the lease and the lessee's incremental borrowing rate were 10%. We shall now assume that the lessor is Queen Company and that the lease amortization schedule presented in Exhibit 23–5 correctly separates each lease payment into interest revenue and the portion representing a reduction in the receivable. Information in Exhibit 23–5 is identical to that in Exhibit 23–3, except for the columnar headings, which reflect lessor terminology (i.e., receivable) rather than lessee terminology (i.e., payable). The lessor receives $67,800 in total payments, of which $15,489 is interest revenue, resulting in a net receivable (i.e., the present value of the lease) at December 31, 1995, the inception of the lease, of $52,311. We shall use this information to illustrate both the sales-type and the direct-financing lease.

Sales-Type Lease

For this illustration, we assume that Queen Company manufactures the machinery that is the subject of the lease. Queen Company incurred a cost of $30,000 to manufacture the asset and offers it to customers at $55,000. Customers have the alternative to lease the machine from Queen Company; when this alternative is chosen, a lease payment schedule is negotiated that results in a present-value amount approximately equal to the normal selling price, subject to good customer discounts of up to 5%. Recall from our earlier example that the present value of this lease, including the six $10,000 payments and the guaranteed residual value of $7,800 at the end of the sixth year, was $52,311. Because this amount exceeds 90% of the fair value of the asset, we treated this lease as a capital lease for King Company, the lessee. We further assume here that the lessor is confident of collection of the lease payments and has determined all costs relative to the lease. Therefore, this is also a capital lease for the lessor, and we can further classify it as a sales-type lease because the present value of the lease ($52,311) differs considerably from the cost to manufacture the asset ($30,000).

EXHIBIT 23–5				
Queen Company Lease Amortization Table				
Date	**Payment**	**Interest**	**Decline in Net Receivable**	**Net Receivable**
Dec. 31, 1994	—	—	—	$52,311
	$10,000	—	$10,000	42,311
Dec. 31, 1995	10,000	$ 4,231	5,769	36,542
Dec. 31, 1996	10,000	3,654	6,346	30,196
Dec. 31, 1997	10,000	3,020	6,980	23,216
Dec. 31, 1998	10,000	2,322	7,678	15,538
Dec. 31, 1999	10,000	1,554	8,446	7,092
Dec. 31, 2000	7,800	708*	7,092	–0–
	$67,800	$15,489		

*Rounding difference included in this number to clear accounts.

The lessor records this sales-type lease as follows:

Dec. 31, 1994	Lease Receivable	52,311	
	Cost of Goods Sold	30,000	
	Sales		52,311
	Machinery Inventory		30,000
	(To record sales-type lease.)		
	Cash	10,000	
	Lease Receivable		10,000
	(To record receipt of first lease payment.)		
Dec. 31, 1995	Lease Receivable	4,231	
	Interest Revenue		4,231
	(To record interest revenue on sales-type lease for 1995.)		
	Cash	10,000	
	Lease Receivable		10,000
	(To record receipt of second lease payment.)		

When the sales and the cost of goods sold amounts from the December 31, 1994, entry are carried into the lessor's income statement, a gross profit of $22,311 is recognized as follows:

Sales	$52,311
Cost of goods sold	(30,000)
Gross profit on sale	$22,311

Interest revenue for 1995 is $4,231; entries similar to those of December 31, 1995, will be made at the end of each year, with the amount of interest revenue declining as indicated in the Interest column of Exhibit 23–5. The lessor is recognizing two forms of revenue in this sales-type lease: gross profit on the sale in 1994 only and interest revenue over the lease term as the financing function is fulfilled. Notice that the asset is removed from the records of the lessor and no depreciation is recorded.

In Queen Company's balance sheet, the net receivable is subject to current and noncurrent classifications, much like the net payable for the lessee. In fact, those considerations are identical and are not repeated here. (You may want to refer to the earlier discussion of separating the lease payable into current and noncurrent portions.) Following the method preferred by the authors for making this distinction, $9,091 is presented as a current receivable in each balance sheet, and the remainder of the net receivable is presented as a noncurrent receivable.

At the end of the six-year lease, the lessor will receive asset(s) valued at $7,800 in some combination of the machine and cash. If the machine's value is $7,800 or more, the following entry is appropriate:

Dec. 31, 2000	Machinery Inventory	7,800	
	Lease Receivable		7,800
	(To record return of machine at end of lease term.)		

Recall that when we considered this lease from the lessee's perspective, in one case we assumed that the machine was valued at $5,000 and the lessee was required to pay $2,800 in cash ($7,800 − $5,000) in addition to returning the machine. In that situation, the lessor records receipt of the machine and cash, as follows:

Dec. 31, 2000	Machinery Inventory	5,000	
	Cash	2,800	
	Lease Receivable		7,800
	(To record return of machine and cash at end of lease term.)		

Direct-Financing Lease

Accounting for a direct-financing lease can be easily illustrated by changing a few assumptions. We assume that Queen Company purchases assets for lease as contracts are negotiated with lessees, rather than manufacturing those assets as indicated earlier. Queen Company establishes the lease payment schedules so that present value of the lease equals the cost of the asset. We assume that the cost of the machine to the lessor is $52,311.

The lease amortization schedule in Exhibit 23–5 can again be used in accounting for this lease. The major difference is in the first entry to record the lease transaction, in which the Machinery Inventory is simply reclassified as a receivable and no sales or cost of goods sold is recorded.

Dec. 31, 1994	Lease Receivable	52,311	
	Machinery Inventory		52,311
	(To record direct-financing lease.)		
	Cash	10,000	
	Lease Receivable		10,000
	(To record receipt of first lease payment.)		
Dec. 31, 1995	Lease Receivable	4,231	
	Interest Revenue		4,231
	(To record interest revenue on direct-financing lease for 1995.)		
	Cash	10,000	
	Lease Receivable		10,000
	(To record receipt of second lease payment.)		

Thereafter, all entries are identical to those appropriate for recording the sales-type lease as presented earlier. The only form of revenue recognized by the lessor is interest revenue, following the schedule in the Interest column in Exhibit 23–5. As with the sales-type lease, the lessor records no depreciation because the asset is assumed to have been transferred to the lessee.

ADDITIONAL LESSOR CONSIDERATIONS

In the Queen Company illustration of both the sales-type and the direct-financing leases, we recorded the receivable at the net amount, which represents the present value of the lease. An alternative procedure is to record the receivable at the gross amount, equal to the total future payments, and record the amount, which represents interest in a separate contra account identified as Unearned Income. Assuming a sales-type lease, the entry to record the lease by this approach is as follows:

Dec. 31, 1994	Lease Receivable	67,800	
	Cost of Goods Sold	30,000	
	Sales		52,311
	Unearned Income		15,489
	Machinery Inventory		30,000

If the lease is a direct-financing lease, the entry to record the lease by this approach is as follows:

Dec. 31, 1994	Lease Receivable	67,800	
	Machinery Inventory		52,311
	Unearned Income		15,489

In either case, the net amount of the receivable is $52,311 ($67,800 − $15,489) and as interest revenue is recognized each period, the Unearned Income account is debited rather than the Lease Receivable account. In all other respects, the entries for the net receivable approach presented earlier apply.

For operating leases, we discussed accounting for initial direct costs. Those same costs arise for capital leases and require special treatment. Initial direct costs related to sales-type leases are charged to expense at the beginning of the lease term and, thereby, reduce the amount of gross profit recognized on the lease. In the case of direct-financing leases, initial direct costs are debited to the amount of unearned income (gross method of recording) or the net receivable (net method of recording). In either case, the impact is to reduce the amount of interest included in the net receivable and, accordingly, the amount of interest revenue that will be recognized over the lease term. The lessor must then impute a new (lower) interest rate that will be used to amortize the interest over the lease term at a constant rate. This indirectly results in the amortization of initial direct costs in a pattern that parallels the recognition of interest revenue.

Matching
Initial direct costs are treated differently in each type of lease by the lessor. The objective of matching revenues and expenses explains each treatment in light of different leasing circumstances. For operating leases, these costs are deferred and amortized over the lease term, thereby matching the costs with the lease revenue as it is recognized. For sales-type leases, initial direct costs are taken directly into income and reduce the amount of gross profit recognized on the lease. For direct-financing leases, initial direct costs reduce the amount of future interest revenue that will be recognized.

Like lessees, lessors are required to disclose significant information about leases in their financial statements and related notes. Exhibit 23–6 presents the note disclosure of Ford Motor Company for 1993 for leasing transactions for which it is the lessor. Ford Motor Company, known primarily as a manufacturer of cars and trucks, also does business in electronics, glass, plastics, castings, climate-control systems, service and replacement parts, vehicle leasing and rental, space technology, satellite communications, defense systems, and land development.

Information about capital leases is included in a broader note identified as Receivables and Lease Investments—Financial Services. The second set of columnar information is about the company's direct-financing leases, which ties to information presented in the asset sections of the balance sheet. The third set of columnar information is about operating leases in which the company serves as lessor. These leases are *not* included in Ford's balance sheet.

ADVANCED LEASING TOPICS

Leasing is a very important and complex business activity. For the lessee, leasing is a primary source of financing assets needed to support ongoing business operations. For the lessor, leasing is a primary source of revenue generation and may be an essential mechanism through which the sale of assets to customers is accomplished.

Substance over Form
To this point in our study of leases, we have attempted to focus attention on important underlying principles. Perhaps the most compelling principle in explaining accounting for leases is the notion of substance over form. Accountants attempt to understand the true substance or intent of the business transaction being carried out via lease and account for it accordingly, rather than allowing the legal form of the transaction to dictate the accounting treatment.

Situations involving leases may become very complex. Many authoritative accounting pronouncements that attempt to explain these complexities and to address the accounting issues inherent in them have been issued and are currently in effect. Although our intent here is not to provide comprehensive coverage of all dimensions of accounting for leases, in this section we briefly introduce some of the more common complexities that may be encountered in applying accounting standards for leases.

UNGUARANTEED RESIDUAL VALUE

Our earlier example of lessee/lessor accounting included a residual value guarantee. Recall the lease in which the lessee, King Company, guaranteed a value of $7,800 to the lessor,

EXHIBIT 23–6

Ford Motor Company
Lessor Disclosure

Note 3. Net Receivables and Lease Investments — Financial Services

Included in net receivables and lease investments at December 31 were net finance receivables, investments in direct financing leases and investments in operating leases. The investments in direct financing and operating leases relate to the leasing of motor vehicles and various types of transportation and other equipment and facilities.

Net finance receivables at December 31 were as follows (in millions):

	1993	1992
Automotive	$ 58,738	$54,807
Real estate, mainly residential	24,152	24,421
Other	24,968	19,945
Total finance receivables	107,858	99,173
Loan origination costs	124	158
Unearned income	(9,037)	(8,325)
Allowance for credit losses	(2,017)	(1,948)
Unearned insurance premiums and unpaid insurance claims related to finance receivables	(139)	(199)
Net finance receivables	$ 96,789	$88,859
Fair value	$ 98,505	$90,992

Included in finance receivables was a total of $1.5 billion for 1993 and $1.9 billion for 1992 owed by three customers with the largest receivable balances. Other finance receivables consisted primarily of commercial and consumer loans, collateralized loans, credit card receivables, general corporate obligations, and accrued interest. Also included in other finance receivables at December 31, 1993, and 1992, were $2,430 million and $1,767 million, respectively, of accounts receivable purchased by certain Financial Services operations from Automotive operations.

Contractual maturities of automotive and other finance receivables are as follows (in millions): 1994—$41,376; 1995—$16,316; 1996—$11,321; thereafter—$14,693. Experience indicates that a substantial portion of the portfolio generally is repaid before contractual maturity dates.

The fair value of most receivables was estimated by discounting future cash flows using an estimated discount rate which reflected the credit, interest rate, and prepayment risks associated with similar types of instruments. For receivables with short maturities, the book value approximated fair value.

Sales of finance receivables increased net income by $60 million in 1993, $7 million in 1992, and $84 million in 1991. Allowances for anticipated credit losses are made where limited guarantee provisions of the sales contracts exist.

Investments in direct financing leases at December 31 were as follows (in millions):

	1993	1992
Minimum lease rentals	$ 7,382	$ 7,673
Estimated residual values	2,764	2,395
Lease origination costs	69	47
Unearned income	(2,010)	(2,169)
Allowance for credit losses	(133)	(154)
Net investments in direct financing leases	$ 8,072	$ 7,792

Minimum direct financing lease rentals (including executory costs of $68 million) are as follows (in millions): 1994—$2,485; 1995—$1,731; 1996—$1,031; 1997—$576; thereafter—$1,627.

(*Continued on p. 1066*)

(Continued from p. 1065)
Investments in operating leases at December 31 were as follows (in millions):

	1993	1992
Vehicles and other equipment, at cost	**$18,589**	$12,231
Lease origination costs	**23**	8
Accumulated depreciation	**(3,736)**	(2,591)
Allowance for credit losses	**(202)**	(155)
Net investments in operating leases	**$14,674**	$ 9,493

Future minimum rentals on operating leases are as follows (in millions): 1994—$3,719; 1995—$1,837; 1996—$387; 1997—$77; thereafter—$118.

Depreciation expense on operating leases reflects primarily the straight-line method over the term of the leases and was as follows (in millions): 1993—$2,984; 1992—$2,000; 1991—$1,400.

Allowances for Credit Losses. Allowances for credit losses are established as required based on historical experience. Other factors that affect collectibility also are evaluated, and additional amounts may be provided. Finance receivables and lease investments are charged to the allowances for credit losses when an account is deemed to be uncollectible, taking into consideration the financial condition of the borrower, the value of the collateral, recourse to guarantors and other factors. Recoveries on finance receivables and lease investments previously charged off as uncollectible are credited to the allowances for credit losses.

Changes in the allowances for credit losses were as follows (in millions):

	1993	1992	1991
Beginning balance	**$2,257**	$2,078	$1,847
Additions	**1,019**	1,218	1,485
Net losses	**(903)**	(993)	(1,304)
Other changes	**(21)**	(46)	50
Ending balance	**$2,352**	$2,257	$2,078

SOURCE: Ford Motor Company, 1993 Annual Report.

Queen Company, at the end of the six-year lease term. The content of leases is typically governed by the lessor, so the inclusion of a guarantee of the residual value is common. It protects the lessor from unexpected obsolescence, excess usage, unexpected market changes, and other factors that might affect the value of the used asset that will be returned to the lessor at the end of the lease term.

If the residual value is guaranteed, it is included in the determination of the present value of the lease and in the lease amortization schedule as a final payment, as we saw in the earlier examples. If the residual value is not guaranteed, however, procedures must be altered to reflect this difference for both the lessee and lessor.

The most obvious difference in accounting for a capital lease with an *unguaranteed* residual value is the fact that no final amount to cover the residual value is included in the computation of the lease liability for the lessee. The lessor, however, computes the present value of the lease to include the residual value because the asset will be returned to the lessor at the end of the lease term. Assuming a sales-type lease, if the residual value is not guaranteed, the present value of the residual is not included in the sales figure recorded by the lessor. To offset the reduction in the sales amount caused by the omission of the present value of the residual, the lessor must also reduce cost of goods sold by the present value of the residual.

The following example illustrates accounting for an unguaranteed residual value and contrasts it with that for a guaranteed residual value. Topper Company (lessor) leases equipment under a standard leasing arrangement that begins on December 31, 1995, and calls for $5,000 payments at the beginning of each year for five years. The interest rate implicit in the lease is 12% and the asset is expected to be worth $3,000 at the end of the five-year term. In Case A, we assume that the residual value is guaranteed; in Case B, we assume that the residual value is not guaranteed.

The present value of the lease under both circumstances is computed as follows:

> Present value of five $5,000 payments:
> $5,000 × (1.00000 + 3.03735*) = $20,187
> Present value of $3,000 residual:
> $3,000 × .56743[†]   =   1,702
> Present value of lease $21,889

---

*$pvoaf_{\overline{4}|12\%}$

[†]$pvf_{\overline{5}|12\%}$

The lease is amortized according to the amounts indicated in Exhibit 23–7. Whether the residual value is guaranteed or not, the lessor includes the residual value in the recorded asset because that value accrues to the lessor in either case.

We assume that Topper manufactured the equipment at a cost of $15,000. When the residual value is guaranteed, the lessor's asset is appropriately labeled *receivable;* when the residual value is not guaranteed, the authors prefer the label *investment* because it includes two diverse elements: a receivable plus the lessor's interest in the used asset to be returned at the end of the lease term. That terminology is used in the following selected entries regarding this lease:

		Case A— Guaranteed Residual	
Dec. 31, 1995	Lease Receivable	21,889	
	Cost of Goods Sold	15,000	
	Sales		21,889
	Equipment Inventory		15,000
	(To record sales-type lease with guaranteed residual value.)		
	Cash	5,000	
	Lease Receivable		5,000
	(To record first lease payment.)		
Dec. 31, 2000	Lease Receivable	321	
	Interest Revenue		321
	(To recognize interest revenue for last year of lease.)		
	Cash/Equipment Inventory	3,000	
	Lease Receivable		3,000
	(To record final settlement of lease residual value.)		

On December 31 of 1996–1999, an interest revenue accrual (DR: Lease Receivable; CR: Interest Revenue) is made according to the amounts reflected in Exhibit 23–7. Also, a cash receipt (DR: Cash; CR: Lease Receivable) of $5,000 is recorded each December 31.

EXHIBIT 23-7

Topper Company
Lease Amortization Schedule (Lessor)

Date	Payment	Interest	Decline in Net Receivable	Net Receivable
Dec. 31, 1995	—	—	—	$21,889
	$ 5,000	—	$5,000	16,889
Dec. 31, 1996	5,000	$2,027	2,973	13,916
Dec. 31, 1997	5,000	1,670	3,330	10,586
Dec. 31, 1998	5,000	1,270	3,730	6,856
Dec. 31, 1999	5,000	823	4,177	2,679
Dec. 31, 2000	3,000	321	2,679	-0-
	$28,000	$6,111		

The final entry shows a debit to Cash/Equipment Inventory to indicate that some combination of cash and used equipment will be returned to the lessor at a total of $3,000. The precise amount of each depends on the appraised value of the used asset, as discussed in our earlier example.

The following entries are appropriate for the same lease if the *residual value is not guaranteed.* Entries to accrue interest revenue and the receipt of cash are made each December 31. The amounts of sales and cost of goods sold in Case B are based on the same amounts included in Case A, except that each is reduced by the present value of the residual, as follows:

Sales: $21,889 − $1,702 = $20,187
Cost of Goods Sold: $15,000 − $1,702 = $13,298

		Case B—Unguaranteed Residual	
Dec. 31, 1995	Investment in Lease	21,889	
	Cost of Goods Sold	13,298	
	Sales		20,187
	Equipment Inventory		15,000
	(To record sales-type lease with unguaranteed residual value.)		
	Cash	5,000	
	Investment in Lease		5,000
	(To record first lease payment.)		
Dec. 31, 2000	Investment in Lease	321	
	Investment Revenue		321
	(To recognize interest revenue for last year of lease.)		
	Equipment Inventory	3,000	
	Investment in Lease		3,000
	(To record final settlement of lease residual value.)		

Comparing the accounting treatment of the sales-type lease with and without the residual value guarantee, we find that the amount of gross profit and interest revenue recognized are the same, as indicated on the following page:

	Case A Guaranteed	Case B Unguaranteed
Gross Profit		
Sales	$21,889	$20,187
Cost of goods sold	(15,000)	(13,298)
Gross profit	$ 6,889	$ 6,889
Interest Revenue		
Receivable (gross)	$28,000	—
Investment (gross)	—	$28,000
Present value of lease	(21,889)	(21,889)
Interest revenue	$ 6,111	$ 6,111

DIFFERENT INTEREST RATES

In the primary illustrations in this chapter, we made the simplifying assumption that the lessor's rate implicit in the lease and the lessee's incremental borrowing interest rate were the same. This would certainly not be the case in every instance. We further stated that the general policy to be followed is that the lessor accounts for the lease using the interest rate implicit in the lease. The lessee, however, is required to use the lower of the lessor's implicit rate or the lessee's incremental borrowing rate if the lessor's rate is known to the lessee. If the rate implicit in the lease is not known to the lessee, the lessee's incremental borrowing rate is used by the lessee.

An important observation is that the use of different rates results in different present-value amounts and potentially important differences in the way leases are treated by the two parties to the lease. In our earlier examples, we used the same amortization figures to separate payments into interest and receivable/payable reduction because the two parties were using the same interest rate. If different interest rates are used, however, the lessor and lessee will have different amounts recorded for the lease receivable and payable and the amounts of interest revenue and expense recognized will differ.

Recall that the fourth capitalization criterion indicates that a lease is classified as a capital lease if the present value of the lease equals or exceeds 90% of the fair value of the asset. The use of different interest rates could result in a difference in lease capitalization if, for example, one party's present-value calculation is at or above the 90% of fair value standard; the other party's present-value calculation is below that amount; and none of the other capitalization criteria are met.

To illustrate these differences in treatment with varying interest rates, assume that Franklin Company, a lessor, leases equipment to Jefferson Company, a lessee, for $7,000 annually, with payments due on the first day of each of the next seven years. Franklin establishes the lease payment schedule based on an assumed rate of return (interest rate) of 16%; Jefferson Company's incremental borrowing rate is 10%. In this case, whether Jefferson Company is aware of the rate implicit in the lease, a 10% rate is used for the lessee, and the two present-value calculations are as follows:

	10%	16%
$7,000 × (1.00000 + 4.35526*)	$37,487	—
$7,000 × (1.00000 + 3.68474†)	—	$32,793

----

*$pvoaf_{\overline{6}|10\%}$

†$pvoaf_{\overline{6}|16\%}$

Assuming that 90% of the fair value of the asset is $32,793 or less, both parties will treat this lease as a capital lease. The amounts of the receivable/payable and interest revenue/expense will be different, however, because of the differences in present-value calculation and interest rates used to amortize the lease. If 90% of the fair value of the asset is an amount between the two figures, the lease would be accounted for as an operating lease by the lessor (using the 16% rate) and as a capital lease by the lessee (using the 10% rate). For example, if the fair value of the asset is $40,000, the cutoff for capital lease evaluation is $36,000 ($40,000 × 90%), and the outcome described above will exist. This is one situation in which the accounting treatment of the lease lacks symmetry in that the lessee treats the lease as a purchase, but the lessor does *not* treat the same lease as a sale.

LEVERAGED LEASES—LESSOR ACCOUNTING

Leveraged leases, which apply only to lessors, have been used more and more in recent years. This growth is a response to the increasing burden of income taxes and to a desire by lessors to avoid reporting the large liabilities that result from the acquisition of property that, in turn, is leased to others under long-term leases. From the standpoint of the lessee, leveraged leases are accounted for in the same manner as nonleveraged leases. To the lessor, leveraged leases are **direct-financing leases** that meet the following four additional criteria:

1. The lease involves three parties: a lessee, a long-term creditor, and a lessor.
2. The financing provided by the long-term creditor must be nonrecourse as to the general credit of the lessor. (The leased property may, however, be subject to a mortgage.)
3. The lessor's net investment in the lease must decline in the early years of the lease and rise during the later years before final elimination.
4. The lessor's investment tax credit must be deferred and allocated to income over the life of the lease. (The investment tax credit was eliminated from law in the Tax Reform Act of 1986; therefore, this criterion is generally inoperative for leases subsequent to 1985.)

If any of these criteria are not met, the lease is considered a direct-financing lease rather than a leveraged lease. Before proceeding to a technical discussion of the financial accounting and reporting aspects of leveraged leases, we need a firm conceptual understanding of the economic sense and meaning of this form of leasing. We should understand why a leveraged lease is desirable from the lessor's perspective, because an appreciation of the benefits will aid the comprehension of the related accounting and reporting practices. The following list enumerates some of the benefits that accrue to the lessor in a leveraged lease:

1. Most funds necessary to purchase the leased asset are supplied by a long-term creditor.
2. The loan from the long-term creditor provides for no recourse against the lessor (other than a possible mortgage on the leased property).
3. The lessor receives the benefit of the investment tax credit related to the leased asset.
4. During the early years of the lease arrangement, the tax deductions for depreciation on the leased asset and interest on the nonrecourse long-term debt exceed the annual lease rental revenue. This provides the lessor with excess deductions to be applied against other taxable income.
5. At the conclusion of a leveraged lease agreement, the equipment is returned to the lessor. This benefit may also exist in a direct-financing lease but *must* be present in a leveraged lease.

For these reasons, many lessors desire a leveraged lease rather than a direct-financing lease and structure the transaction to achieve a leveraged lease classification. We now turn our attention to recording a leveraged lease. To illustrate, we assume that the present value of the minimum lease payments and the unguaranteed residual value accruing to Frost, Inc., a lessor, at the end of the lease is $50,000 ($60,000 gross payments + $7,800 residual value − $17,800 unearned income) and that the equipment cost Frost, Inc., $50,000. Further, assume that the lease now qualifies as a leveraged lease because Frost acquired the equipment recently with a nonrecourse loan of $46,000. The entry to record that acquisition of the equipment at the inception of the lease appears as follows:

Investment in Lease*	21,800	
Unearned Revenue		17,800
Cash		4,000
(To record the inception of leveraged lease.)		

---

*The Investment in Lease account is determined as follows:

Gross lease payments	$60,000
Unguaranteed residual value accruing to the lessor	7,800
Total investment	67,800
Less:	
Nonrecourse note	46,000
Investment in lease	$21,800

The Investment in Lease account is charged for the gross amount of lease rentals *net* of the total amount of the nonrecourse debt. The estimated residual value is the fair value of the leased property at the end of the lease term. This amount accrues to the benefit of the lessor in a leveraged lease.

The Unearned Revenue account consists of the estimated pretax deferred revenue after deductions for the initial direct costs remaining to be allocated to income over the lease term. The credit to cash in the transaction represents the investment made by the lessor in the leased property and is the difference between the cost of the leased property and the nonrecourse debt secured from the long-term creditor ($50,000 − $46,000 = $4,000).

The long-term debt is offset against the lease receivable. From the lessor's perspective, this treatment is desirable, because it improves the debt/equity ratio and rate of return on assets employed. Such an offsetting of receivable and payable is appropriate only because the creditor financing is nonrecourse to the lessor.

Subsequent to this entry, for income tax purposes, the leased asset is depreciated and interest expense on the nonrecourse liability to the creditor is recognized. Rent revenue is recognized as cash is received. From an income tax perspective, therefore, the lease is treated much like an operating lease. As a result, temporary differences emerge, because in the early years of the leveraged lease, the tax expense computed on the accounting income exceeds the taxes payable, which are based on the tax return. The resulting deferred credits serve to reduce the investment balance. This aspect of leveraged leasing causes a fluctuating investment balance. The *tax effects* of accelerated depreciation, along with interest expense on the third-party creditor loan, contribute to a declining investment account as a result of tax losses and emerging deferred tax credits in the early years of the lease. Later—when depreciation charges and interest expense become less than the gross lease payments being received—taxable income is recognized, thereby causing the deferred tax credits to reverse, and the Investment account rises.

Perhaps the most difficult aspect of leveraged leases to apply involves calculating the appropriate rate of interest for use in allocating total cash flow between the recovery of the investment and interest revenue. The amortizing rate represents that rate of interest that, when applied to the Investment account balance in the years that the net investment is positive, will fully amortize the unearned revenue as interest revenue over the life of the lease. This process usually involves considerable trial and error, because (1) the annuity amounts (cash flow after taxes) are uneven; (2) during some years, the investment account may be zero or negative (so the annuity series is broken); and (3) the residual value represents a single amount at the conclusion of the lease. In complex situations, computers are frequently used to ascertain the appropriate amortizing rate for leveraged leases.

SALE-LEASEBACK

A **sale-leaseback transaction** involves property that is simultaneously sold and leased back by the seller. Many times such arrangements are desirable because they provide a large amount of liquid resources to the seller while the seller-lessee still retains the *use* of the asset sold. Standards of accounting for sales with leasebacks are established in *FASB Statement of Financial Accounting Standards No. 28.*[7]

Generally, a seller-lessee classifies leases arising in sale-leaseback transactions in accordance with the four classification criteria previously discussed. For a capital lease, any profit on the sale is deferred and amortized in proportion to the amortization of the leased asset; for an operating lease, profit on the sale is recognized in proportion to the related gross rent expense recognized over the lease term. If the fair market value of the asset sold is less than its cost or carrying amount, however, a loss on the sale should be recognized in the period of the sale and leaseback. Other types of losses on the transaction should generally be deferred and amortized over the lease term. If only a minor portion of the property is leased back, then profit or loss on the sale is generally recognized in a normal fashion at the time of the transaction.

SUBLEASES

The central concept establishing subleases as a special type of lease is that a lessee, now acting as a sublessor, cannot transfer to a sublessee more rights than were obtained in the original lease. For example, if a lessee treats an original lease as an operating lease, any sublease of that property granted by the original lessee (now a sublessor) can be considered only as an operating lease.

If the original lease contains either a transfer of ownership or a bargain purchase option, the original lessee (now a sublessor) is presumed to have acquired all of the rights associated with the property. The original lessee is therefore capable of completely disposing of those rights. In determining the proper classification of a sublease, the lessor should apply all four of the normal classification criteria and the two additional criteria of rent collectibility and cost predictability.

If the original lease does not transfer title to the lessee, a sublease of the property from that lessee cannot contain a transfer of title to a sublessee. If either the length of lease term or the amount of lease payment criterion is met in the original lease but neither a transfer of title nor a bargain purchase option is provided, then the sublease should be subjected only to new length of lease term and amount of lease payment criteria. Of course, the new rent collectibility and cost predictability tests must also be met.

RELATED-PARTY LEASES

Substance over Form   *SFAS No. 13* states that economic substance, rather than mere form, governs accounting for all leases, including those between related parties. **Related parties** include a parent company and its subsidiaries, joint ventures, partnerships and partners, and investors and investees, provided that the parent company, owner, or investor has the ability to exercise **significant influence** over the operating and financial policies of the other party. The test for significant influence is also consistent with the concept of significant influence discussed in Chapter 10 and contained in *APB Opinion No. 18.*[8] Other situations and circumstances may also create related-party conditions. Examples include the extension of credit, guarantees of indebtedness, and other relationships and economic dependencies. Accountants should gain an understanding of the business purpose and the economics of related-party leases to report properly the substance of those transactions. This is especially true when the form of the agreement is unusual or does not represent normal business practice.

---

[7] *FASB Statement of Financial Accounting Standards No. 28,* "Accounting for Sales with Leasebacks," 1979.
[8] *APB Opinion No. 18,* "The Equity Method of Accounting for Investments in Common Stock," 1971.

REAL ESTATE LEASES

The unusual characteristics of the asset land cause most of the differences underlying financial accounting and reporting for real estate leases. Basically, the problem stems from the fact that land is considered to have an unlimited life for purposes of financial accounting. It is not logical, therefore, to consider a lease of land to be a sale unless either the transfer-of-title or bargain-purchase-option criterion has been met. In other words, it is impossible for a lease of land to meet the lease term criterion of 75% of useful life, because land is presumed to have an unlimited life. Furthermore, the fact that the present value of the minimum lease payments exceeds 90% of the fair value of the leased land does not indicate that the lease is in substance a sale of the land. Indeed, the land does not expire; it reverts to the lessor at the end of the lease; and it may be worth a great deal more at the conclusion of a lease than at the beginning. Given a conceptual understanding of the unusual aspects of real estate leases, we now consider the technical requirements of *SFAS No. 13* that are related to a variety of real estate leases.

Leases of Land Only

To account for real estate leases, accountants must carefully consider the types of real estate being leased. For lessees and lessors to consider a lease of land a capital lease, the lease agreement must contain a transfer of title or a bargain purchase option. Furthermore, lessors must also meet the rent collectibility and cost predictability tests. Because real estate lease terms frequently extend for periods of time in excess of 20 years, the assessment of the collectibility of rent is unusually complex. Accordingly, a lease of real estate should not be classified as a sales-type lease with manufacturer's or dealer's profit recognized unless specific criteria are met.[9] The criteria, related to predicting the collectibility of rent, require a certain amount of down payment, which must consist of cash or marketable securities readily convertible to cash. The amount of the required down payment ranges from 5% to 25% of the total purchase price for different types of real estate. Because few leases contain initial balloon payments, in which large amounts of the total lease payable must be paid at the beginning of the lease term, many real estate leases that otherwise qualify as sales-type leases are properly accounted for as operating leases because of a failure to meet the down payment quantity and quality criteria.

Leases of Land and Buildings

When a lease involves both land and a building, accountants must assess the magnitude of the portion of the assets represented by the land. If the fair value of the land portion of the leased assets equals or exceeds 25% of the total fair value of the leased assets, the land is considered separately in accordance with the provisions for leases of land only. To determine the portion of the minimum lease payments associated with the land, the incremental borrowing rate is multiplied by the estimated fair value of the land. This is done because the land is assumed to have an unlimited life and is, therefore, capable of earning that rate of return perpetually. The amount of the rental payment attributable to the land is considered to represent an operating lease unless the lease contains a transfer of title or a bargain purchase option. The remaining amount of the lease payment is related to the building and that portion of the lease is classified using the same criteria as are applied to any other leased asset.

If the fair value of the land portion of the leased assets is less than 25% of the total fair value of both the land and building, however, the land portion can be ignored for purposes of

---

[9]*FASB Statement of Financial Accounting Standards No. 26,* "Profit Recognition in Sales Type Leases of Real Estate," 1979, states that the criteria for recognizing profit contained in the AICPA *Industry Accounting Guide,* "Accounting for Profit Recognition on Sales of Real Estate," should be applied to leases of real estate.

lease classification. Therefore, if land represents less than 25% of the fair value of the combined real estate assets leased and if the lease contains neither a transfer of title nor a bargain purchase option, the lease may still be classified as a capital lease if one of the two remaining classification criteria is met. In that case, the land is considered sold, and the lessee would amortize the leased assets *(including land)* over the life of the lease or the life of the building, whichever is shorter. However, the asset would not be the land but a right to *use* the land. The 25% land portion limitation ensures that the amount of the intangible asset represented by land is relatively small. In such situations, lessors remove the leased asset (including land) from the plant assets section of the balance sheet and record an investment in the lease. The residual value of the assets should be added to the investment by the lessor because the residual value of the leased asset is presumed to revert to the lessor when a transfer of title and a bargain purchase option are absent from the lease.

Leases of Portions of a Building

Another complex issue arises if the leased asset is a *part* of a building. Such situations are common in leases involving shopping centers or high-rise office buildings and occur frequently in practice.

When only a part of a building is leased, the cost and fair value amounts required to apply the fourth classification test (amount of lease payment) are often difficult to estimate. For example, what is the cost of the fortieth floor of a high-rise office building? Without such estimates, application of the amount-of-lease-payment test, which relies on estimates of fair value, is impossible. Furthermore, without cost estimates, a lessor may have trouble determining whether a given capital lease is a sales-type or direct-financing lease. Because gross profit (or loss) and interest revenue are recognized on sales-type leases whereas only interest revenue is recognized on direct-financing leases, the cost of the property subject to the lease has a direct bearing on the classification of a lease and the nature and timing of the revenue to be recognized.

FASB Interpretation No. 24 provides guidance on how to estimate the cost and fair value when only a portion of a building is leased.[10] It states that estimates of cost and fair market value are usually possible and suggests that appraisals and replacement cost estimates may be appropriate in determining the fair value and cost of portions of a building. Therefore, although precise figures may be impossible to obtain, accountants must attempt to develop reasonable estimates of value and cost.

PROFESSIONAL JUDGMENT

Professional judgment is very important in lease accounting. As we have discussed in this chapter, the critical decision for both lessees and lessors is whether a lease is a capital or operating lease. This classification then determines the appropriate accounting application. This decision may have a significant impact on the content of the reporting entity's financial statements.

Deciding whether a lease is a capital or operating lease is an inherent judgmental process. For capital leases, the essence of ownership must be determined. If basic characteristics of ownership pass from the lessor to the lessee, the lease is a capital lease and the accounting treatment follows that of a sale (by the lessor) and purchase (by the lessee). Otherwise, the lease is an operating lease and is not accounted for as a sale and purchase.

To help in making this decision, the FASB has established certain tests: transfer of title, bargain purchase option, lease term extending 75% or more of the estimated useful life of the asset, and the present value of the lease representing 90% or more of the fair value of the leased asset. Notice the words in these criteria that require judgment: *bargain, estimated*

---

[10]*FASB Interpretation No. 24,* "Leases Involving a Part of a Building," 1978.

useful life, and *fair value of the leased asset.* The criteria established by the FASB provide guidance on sorting leases into capital and operating, but they still require judgment. For example, whether the lessee's option to purchase the asset at a distant future date is a "bargain" requires an assessment of the value of the asset at that future date. Informed judgments by different accountants could vary with regard to whether a particular option included in a lease is a *bargain* purchase option. Similarly, judgment might vary among accountants concerning the estimated useful life, the fair value of the asset, and other factors required to apply the FASB criteria.

Once a lease is judged to meet at least one of these criteria, the lessor must make additional judgments concerning the collectibility of lease payments and future costs to be incurred relative to the lease. In certain leases, the lessee may be required to estimate the interest rate implicit in the lease. For many capital leases, the lessee must make essentially the same estimates to properly account for the lease that are required for all long-lived assets, such as useful life and salvage value. These estimates do not form a comprehensive list but illustrate estimates that may be required by both the lessee and lessor in applying current financial reporting standards for leases.

Is the issue of capitalization versus noncapitalization of leases as important as the authoritative accounting literature implies? One way to answer this question is to determine the impact on financial statements of capitalizing leases that are presently accounted for as operating leases.

We ordinarily think of operating leases as relatively short-term rental arrangements. Imhoff, Lipe, and Wright observed that many companies report very large noncancelable operating lease commitments extending many years into the future. These authors developed a method of constructive capitalization, which attempts to estimate the impact of capitalization of leases that were accounted for as operating leases and, therefore, not included in the financial statements. Their results suggest a significant impact on important financial statement numbers and ratios that are often calculated using those numbers. They conclude that constructive capitalization of material long-term operating leases may be necessary for an effective evaluation of financial results within and across firms and industries.[11]

CONCLUDING REMARKS

In this chapter, we focused attention on lease capitalization because this is where the primary controversy concerning lease accounting exists. In *SFAS No. 13* and the many authoritative pronouncements that have resulted since its issuance, the FASB took the position that leases with certain characteristics require capitalization. These characteristics are described in the four basic capitalization criteria that we discussed in this chapter. Some have suggested that to specify criteria to this extent simply invites companies to negotiate leases that fail all four criteria, thereby preserving a major advantage of leasing, off-balance-sheet financing. In fact, the large dollar amounts of operating leases that can be discovered only by a careful reading of the notes to the financial statements provides some support for this assertion.

Assuming that lease capitalization is believed to be appropriate, what alternatives to current practice exist to correct the situation described in the previous paragraph? Some have argued in favor of capitalizing all leases that have certain characteristics (e.g., are noncancelable and have terms of at least one year), thereby removing most, if not all, of the judgment factor in classifying a lease as capital or operating.[12] Another alternative is to permit the legal form of the transaction to govern and to treat all leases as we currently treat operating

---

[11]Eugene A. Imhoff, Jr., Robert C. Lipe, and David W. Wright, "Operating Leases: Impact of Constructive Capitalization," *Accounting Horizons* (March 1991), pp. 51–63.

[12]For an excellent discussion of this recommendation, see Arthur R. Wyatt, "Leases Should Be Capitalized," *CPA Journal* (September 1974), pp. 35–38.

leases, with expanded note disclosure as a means to communicate the nature of obligations to users of financial statements.

The complexity of lease accounting has also been the source of much criticism, prompting one practitioner to make the following observations about applying current lease pronouncements:

> *Clearly, from a practitioner's viewpoint,* Statement 13 *has created practice problems and difficulties by forcing one to rummage through rules, amendments and interpretations when analyzing a lease. Conclusions on lease accounting seem to reach the lowest common denominator in practice, so that practitioners have concluded that the objectives of* Statement 13 *and substance over form give way to a literal interpretation of the rules of* Statement 13. *No white knights are appearing to invoke the Board's objectives, since the Board itself, through its amendments and interpretations, has opted, for the most part, to apply the arbitrary rules and percentages literally.*[13]

Earlier we identified *symmetry* as a desirable objective of lease accounting, referring to the compatible treatment by the two parties to the lease. One situation was cited that might result in the lack of symmetry—the use of different interest rates in computing the present value of the lease by the lessor and the lessee. Recall, also, that the lessor has two revenue realization criteria to apply that are not applied by the lessee—the ability to determine or estimate costs associated with the lease and the predictability of lease payments. A lease could clearly meet one of the four basic criteria but fail one or more of these additional lessor criteria and be treated as a capital lease by the lessee and as an operating lease by the lessor. Finally, the four capitalization criteria certainly leave room for judgment when they base lease capitalization on such determinations as "bargain" purchase option, "estimated" useful life of the leased asset, and "fair value" of the leased asset. Differences in applying the judgment required to make these assessments could result in differences in classification between the two parties to the lease.

Although FASB has developed a sizable body of literature concerning lease accounting, it has not answered all questions, nor do all accountants agree with the answers that are currently offered. This important subject will undoubtedly continue to be a source of interest and controversy to practitioners and standard setters in the future.

KEY POINTS

1. The first step in accounting for leases requires lessees and lessors to classify leases according to the substance of the transaction. (Objectives 1, 2, and 3)

2. Lessees classify leases as either operating leases or capital leases. Operating leases result in the recognition of rent expense. Capital leases require the recognition of the asset acquired, liability incurred, amortization or depreciation expense on the asset, and interest expense on the liability. (Objectives 3 and 4)

3. Lessors classify leases as either operating leases or one of three types of capital leases (direct-financing, sales-type, and leveraged leases). (Objectives 3 and 4)

4. A capital lease must meet at least one of four separate criteria: (1) it includes a transfer of title; (2) it includes a bargain purchase option; (3) the lease term is equal to or greater than 75% of the asset's remaining life; or (4) the present value of the minimum lease payments exceeds 90% of the asset's fair value. (Objectives 3 and 4)

5. In addition to meeting one of the four initial classification tests, lessors must apply two additional criteria to classify a lease as a capital lease: (1) rent collectibility must be reasonably certain and (2) future costs must be reasonably predictable. (Objectives 3 and 4)

6. Lessees recognize rent expense on operating leases on a straight-line basis over the lease term. (Objective 5)

7. Lessees recognize depreciation or amortization expense, interest expense, and executory costs on capital leases over the lease term. The capitalized lease liability is separated into current and noncurrent components in the balance sheet. (Objective 5)

---

[13]Richard Dieter, "Is Lessee Accounting Working?" *CPA Journal* (August 1979), p. 19.

8. Lessors recognize rental revenue on a straight-line basis and continue to depreciate assets subject to operating leases. (Objective 5)

9. Lessors recognize only interest revenue on direct-financing and leveraged leases, whereas gross profit and interest revenue are recognized on sales-type leases. Investments in capital leases (or lease receivables) are subject to current and noncurrent balance sheet classifications. (Objective 5)

10. Many other unusual circumstances in regard to leasing activities require careful consideration and analysis to properly report such transactions. (Objective 5)

QUESTIONS

23–1 The issue of "substance over form" is central in financial accounting and reporting for leases. What do we mean by substance and form as they relate to lease accounting?

23–2 What are the usual two parties to a lease? Describe their roles.

23–3 What is a capital lease? Under what circumstances do lessees classify leases as capital leases? If a lease fails to meet the requirements for a capital lease, what type of lease is it?

23–4 Under what circumstances does a lessor classify a lease as a sales-type lease?

23–5 How should a lessee account for and report a capital lease?

23–6 How should lessors account for and report sales-type leases?

23–7 Define both a lessee's incremental borrowing rate and the interest rate implicit in a lease. How would a difference between the two rates be treated by the lessor and the lessee?

23–8 What happens in a sale-leaseback transaction? Discuss the event from the perspective of both parties to the lease.

23–9 Mark Company is a major automobile dealer and is required to lease large parking lots to house its inventory. The owner, Mark William, has approached you about the accounting problems he faces in regard to these leases. You ascertain that several of the leases contain bargain purchase options, but several others do not. What are the classification and accounting problems presented by these real estate leases?

23–10 Application of *FASB Statement of Financial Accounting Standards No. 13,* "Accounting for Leases," generally results in symmetrical treatment of the same lease by both lessee and lessor (i.e., both treat the lease as an operating lease or as some form of capital lease). Give two examples of circumstances and situations in which a departure from symmetrical treatment may arise.

23–11 An estimate of residual value is sometimes necessary when applying *SFAS No. 13.* Under what circumstances is it necessary for a lessor and lessee to estimate residual value?

23–12 What are initial direct costs? When is it important to determine initial direct costs under a lease? Explain your answer.

23–13 Are the following statements true (T) or false (F) in regard to leases?

[a] The unguaranteed residual value accrues to the lessor only if the lease contains a bargain purchase option.

[b] For a capital lease, initial direct costs incurred by lessees are deferred and allocated over the lease term in proportion to depreciation recognized on the leased asset.

[c] Leveraged leases require third-party creditor involvement unless the lessee guarantees the residual value of the asset.

[d] For a sales-type lease, the lessor uses the incremental borrowing rate of the lessee, if known, to compute the present value of the lease.

[e] From the lessor's perspective, minimum lease payments include the residual value guarantee of the lessee.

[f] From the lessee's perspective, a lease of land will not result in a capital lease even when the lease contains a bargain purchase option.

23–14 Are the following statements are true (T) or false (F) in regard to leases?

[a] Under a leasing arrangement, it is possible for lessees to amortize as an expense the full cost of a leased asset, including land and residual values.

[b] If the original lessee enters into a sublease or if the original lease agreement is sold or transferred by the original lessee to a third party, the original lessor must reevaluate the accounting treatment of the lease and make adjustments as required by the sublease arrangement.

[c] If a lease involving real estate also includes equipment, the portion of the minimum lease payments applicable to the equipment element of the lease shall be estimated by whatever means are appropriate in the circumstances.

[d] From the standpoint of the lessee, leveraged leases shall be classified and accounted for in the same manner as nonleveraged leases.

[e] During the term of a capital lease, each minimum lease payment is allocated between a reduction of the obligation and interest expense to produce a constant periodic rate of interest on the remaining balance of the obligation.

[f] The lessee usually records a capital lease as an asset and an obligation at an amount equal to the current cost of the leased property.

[g] Any profit or loss experienced by the seller-lessee in a sale-leaseback transaction must be included in income at the date of the lease agreement.

[h] In a sales-type lease, the lessor realizes a profit (or loss) at the beginning of the lease.

[i] In an operating lease, the lessee assigns rent expense to the periods benefiting from the use of the asset and does not record the commitment to make future payments.

23–15   Skyscraper Corporation owns a large building complex and leases portions of the complex for offices, retail stores, and a bank. Skyscraper substantially alters the physical layout of a part of the complex to induce Carolyn's Clothing, a high-fashion retailer, to sign a five-year lease. How should the costs of altering the building be treated if the following conditions are true?

[a] Tenants subsequent to Carolyn's Clothing will probably find the alterations desirable.

[b] Tenants subsequent to Carolyn's Clothing will not be able to use the facility until the modifications are removed.

23–16   Leasing activity has been increasing in our economy for some time. What are three reasons that help explain the popularity of leasing as a means to acquire the service rights of an asset?

23–17   *SFAS No. 13* explicitly defines a leveraged lease and prescribes the accounting practice for this type of lease. What criteria must be met for a lease to be classified as a leveraged lease?

23–18   What are the primary economic differences that distinguish between sales-type leases and direct-financing leases?

23–19   What circumstances in an original lease would preclude a sublease from being accounted for as a capital lease by the sublessor?

23–20   What two methods may be used to separate the amount of a lease liability into current and noncurrent elements? Which method is theoretically preferable? Why?

23–21   What are executory costs and what impact, if any, do they have on the calculation of the present value of the minimum lease payments?

23–22   How are initial direct costs accounted for under an operating lease?

23–23   How are initial direct costs accounted for under a sales-type lease? A direct-financing lease?

EXERCISES

23–24   Lessee and Lessor—Operating Lease   Miller Company agreed to lease a building from Light Company on January 1, 1995, for three years. There is no renewal option, and no purchase option is exercisable. The building, with a book value of $325,000, has a remaining useful life of 10 years and no salvage value. Miller's incremental borrowing rate is 10%, and the company has no knowledge of Light's implicit rate. Payments of $93,000 per year are due on December 31 of each year. Miller and Light both use straight-line depreciation.

INSTRUCTIONS

Record this transaction for 1995 on Miller's books and Light's books.

23–25   Lease Payment Computation   Kiko Corporation leased machinery, which had a sales price of $250,000. Kiko's interest rate was 10% and the lease was for eight years with payments due at the end of each year for the life of the lease. Title is transferred to Kiko at the end of the lease.

INSTRUCTIONS

Compute the annual payment required by the lease.

23–26   Lessee and Lessor—Operating Lease   On July 1, 1995, King Company leased a new building valued at $4,500,000 to Prince Company for five years. Five equal payments of $220,000 are due on December 31 of each year starting in 1995. Depreciation is calculated on a straight-line basis by both parties, and the building has an expected useful life of 25 years. Both companies recognize a full year's depreciation in the year a new asset is acquired.

INSTRUCTIONS

Prepare journal entries to record all aspects of this transaction for 1995 on Prince Company's books and King Company's books.

23–27 Lessor—Operating Lease On April 1, 1995, Jackson Corporation leased assets with a book value of $1,200,000 to Long Corporation for three years for an annual lease payment of $180,000 due each March 31. The equipment has a useful life of 16 remaining years. At the end of the lease term, the equipment returns to Jackson. Long Corporation has an incremental borrowing rate of 10% and has no knowledge of Jackson Corporation's implicit rate. Depreciation is recorded on a straight-line basis by both companies, and both companies report on a calendar-year basis.

INSTRUCTIONS

Record this transaction for Jackson for 1995 and 1996.

23–28 Lease Classification Wisteria Florist leases a watering system from Aquaflow Company. The system cost Aquaflow $64,000. There is no transfer of title at the end of the lease; there is also no bargain purchase option. The lease term is for 3 years, at 10% interest; the expected life of the system is 5 years. Wisteria pays Aquaflow $21,202 at the beginning of each year of the lease.

INSTRUCTIONS

Determine whether this lease is an operating lease or a capital lease.

23–29 Direct-Financing Lease On January 1, 1995, Frost Company, the lessee, signs a six-year lease with Pawn Company for equipment with annual payments of $43,263 due on December 31 of each year. The fair value of the equipment as well as the carrying amount on Pawn's books is $200,000. Frost's incremental borrowing rate is 9%. The lease is a direct-financing lease; Pawn's implicit interest rate is 8%.

INSTRUCTIONS

Record all lease-related transactions on Pawn's books for 1995 and 1996. (Round all amounts to the nearest dollar.)

23–30 Lessee-Lease Amortization Diamond Corporation leased equipment from Argo Company on January 1, 1995, for four years on a noncancelable lease. The equipment cost $1,000,000, which is its fair value at the inception of the lease. Diamond pays all maintenance costs, and at the end of the lease, the equipment reverts to Argo. The incremental borrowing rate for the lessee is 12%, and the useful life of the equipment is five years. Annual lease payments are $329,234.54, payable December 31 each year.

INSTRUCTIONS

Prepare a schedule in whole dollars showing the amortization of the lease by Diamond over the four-year lease term.

23–31 Lessor—Capital Lease Brad Corporation leased equipment costing $230,000 to White Company for an implied profit of $45,000. Brad's implied interest rate is 10% and the lease is for 10 years, which equals the economic life of the equipment. The lease is noncancelable, costs are predictable, and payment is reasonably assured at the end of each lease year.

INSTRUCTIONS

[a] Determine the annual payment that Brad will collect from White Company.
[b] What is the total amount of the lease payments and the amount of interest included in those payments?
[c] Prepare the journal entry to record the lease on Brad's books.

23–32 Direct-Financing Lease On January 1, 1995, Jackson Company leased a machine to Shaker Company. The lease was for 10 years, which approximated the useful life of the machine. Jackson purchased the machine for $80,000 and expects to earn a 10% return on its investment, based on an annual rental of $11,836 payable in advance each January 1.

INSTRUCTIONS

Assuming that this is a direct-financing lease, prepare Jackson's entry on December 31, 1995, to recognize interest revenue.

23-33   Lessee and Lessor—Operating Lease   Hinkle Corporation leases from Gray Company a building with a book value of $350,000. The building has a five-year useful life remaining. The lease calls for annual payments of $87,500, to be paid at the beginning of the year. The lease has a three-year term and is considered an operating lease. Gray Company spends $17,500 a year on maintenance and uses straight-line depreciation.

INSTRUCTIONS

Record journal entries for Gray Company and Hinkle Corporation on January 1 and December 31 of the first year of the lease.

23-34   Implicit Interest Rate   Wilkins Company buys equipment for $100,000 cash and leases it to James Corporation for three years. Lease payments of $25,000 are to be made at the beginning of each year. At the end of the third year, the equipment is to be returned to Wilkins when its value is estimated to be $46,000.

INSTRUCTIONS

Approximate the interest rate implicit in the Wilkins Company lease. (Round computations to the nearest dollar.)

23-35   Lessee and Lessor—Operating Lease   On March 20, 1995, Barnes, Inc., purchased a machine for $1,200,000 for the purpose of leasing it to others. The machine is expected to have a 10-year life and no residual value; it will be depreciated on the straight-line basis, computed to the nearest month. The machine was leased to Rally Company on April 1, 1995, for four years, at a monthly rental of $18,000. There is no provision for the renewal of the lease or purchase of the machine by the lessee upon expiration of the lease. Barnes paid $60,000 on commissions associated with negotiating the lease in March 1995.

INSTRUCTIONS

[a] What expense will Rally record for the year ended December 31, 1995? Show supporting computations.

[b] What income or loss before income taxes will Barnes record for the year ended December 31, 1995? Show supporting computations.   (AICPA adapted)

23-36   Lessee—Capital Lease   On January 1, 1995, Alan Corporation signed a 10-year noncancelable lease for certain machinery. The terms of the lease call for annual payments of $35,000 for 10 years, with title to pass to Alan at the end of this period. The machinery has an estimated remaining useful life of 15 years and no salvage value. Alan uses straight-line depreciation for all of its fixed assets, and it accounted for this capital lease in a similar manner. The lease payments have a present value of $234,853 and an effective interest rate of 8%. Payments are made each December 31.

INSTRUCTIONS

With respect to this lease, what entries will Alan make for 1995? (Round all amounts to the nearest dollar and record the lease liability in a single account, net of any discount.)   (AICPA adapted)

23-37   Lessee—Capital Lease Accounting and Classification   The trial balance of Sanford, Inc., for the year ended December 31, 1995, includes the following liability:

Lease liability $456,376

The minimum lease term is for a period of 10 years and began on December 31, 1993. Equal annual payments of $100,000 are due on December 31 of each year, and the interest rate implicit in this lease is 12%. The present value of the seven lease payments remaining on December 31, 1995, is the $456,376 reported above.

INSTRUCTIONS

[a] Determine the amount of interest expense that would appear in the Sanford, Inc., income statement for the year ended December 31, 1996.

[b] Prepare the current and long-term liability sections of the balance sheet of Sanford, Inc., related to this lease at December 31, 1996. The current portion of the lease liability should be computed as the present value of the December 31, 1997, payment.

23-38   Sales-Type Lease   Wofford Company leased equipment from Burnette Company on July 1, 1995, for an eight-year period expiring June 30, 2003. Equal annual payments of $525,000 are due on

July 1. The first payment was made on July 1, 1995. The rate of interest contemplated by both parties is 10%. The cash selling price of the equipment is $3,080,920, and the cost of the equipment on Burnette's accounting records was $2,500,000. Burnette properly accounted for the lease as a sale.

INSTRUCTIONS

Determine the amount of profit on the sale and the interest revenue that Burnette Company will recognize for the year ended December 31, 1995.   (AICPA adapted)

23–39 Sales-Type Lease Mize Company leased equipment to Murray, Inc., on January 1, 1995. The lease is for an eight-year period expiring December 31, 2002. The first of eight equal annual payments of $625,000 was made on January 1, 1995. Mize had purchased the equipment on December 29, 1994, for $3,200,000. Mize appropriately accounts for the lease as a sales-type lease. The present value at January 1, 1995, of all rent payments over the lease term, discounted at a 10% interest rate, is $3,667,762.

INSTRUCTIONS

Determine the amount of interest revenue that Mize will record for 1996, the second year of the lease period.   (AICPA adapted)

23–40 Lessee—Capital Lease On January 2, 1995, Walker, Inc., signed a 10-year noncancelable lease for a heavy-duty drill press. Annual payments of $15,000 are made at the end of each year, with title passing to Walker at the expiration of the lease. Walker treated this transaction as a capital lease. The drill press has an estimated useful life of 15 years and no salvage value. Walker uses straight-line depreciation for all of its fixed assets. Aggregate lease payments were determined to have a present value of $96,265, based on implicit interest of 9%.

INSTRUCTIONS

For 1995 and 1996, determine the amount Walker will recognize as interest expense and depreciation expense. (Round all computations to the nearest dollar.)   (AICPA adapted)

23–41 Implicit versus Incremental Interest Rate Marc Company leases a press costing $106,700 to Tobler Company for eight years for an annual lease payment of $20,000, to be paid at the end of each year. Tobler's incremental borrowing rate is 9.5%.

INSTRUCTIONS

[a] What specific rate should Marc Co. use in recording this lease? Why?
[b] What rate should Tobler Co. use in recording this lease? Why?

PROBLEMS

23–42 Leasehold Improvements On January 1, 1996, Uptown Clothes leased a warehouse in which large amounts of clothing inventory are to be stored. Because the warehouse is located in a high crime area, Uptown Clothes installed bars on windows and an expensive silent alarm system. The improvements acquired on March 1, 1996, which will not be removed when the lease expires, cost $115,000 and have a useful life of 10 years. The lease on the warehouse is for one year, although it contains a renewal option for additional one-year periods, up to a maximum of four renewals. The lease payments under each renewal are to be renegotiated but cannot rise more than 20% each year. Consequently, the option is clearly not a *bargain* renewal option. Uptown Clothes intends to lease the property throughout the renewal periods. The salvage value of the improvements is $90,000 at the end of one year, $20,000 at the end of five years, and $1,000 at the end of 10 years.

INSTRUCTIONS

In your answers to the following, round amounts to the nearest dollar.

[a] Prepare the entry to record the acquisition of the security devices on March 1, 1996.
[b] Prepare the entry at December 31, 1996, if any is necessary, for the security devices. Explain your answer.

23–43 Lessee—Capital Lease Stamper Woodworks signed a six-year lease in which it agreed to pay $12,000 per year for the use of a piece of equipment. At the end of the lease term, the equipment becomes the property of Stamper Woodworks. The equipment is expected to be useful to the company for eight years.

Lease payments are due each May 1, beginning in 1995. The company's fiscal year is from May 1 to April 30. Management estimates that $700 of each lease payment is designated for executory costs that the lessor pays. The lease was executed on May 1, 1995.

Stamper Woodworks recently acquired financing at 12% for other equipment it was acquiring.

INSTRUCTIONS

In your answers to the following, round amounts to the nearest dollar.

[a] At what amount should Stamper Woodworks capitalize this lease in its balance sheet?

[b] Prepare an amortization table for the recognition of interest expense for the six-year lease term?

[c] Prepare the balance sheet presentation of this lease for Stamper Woodworks as of April 30, 1997.

23–44 Lessee and Lessor—Capital Lease   Ace Trucking Company manufactures diesel trucks for interstate transportation and leases a number of them to All-the-Way Trucking. The trucks have an estimated life of 16 years and the leases are for 14 years. The normal selling price of each truck is $215,000, and the estimated residual value at the end of the lease is $20,000. All-the-Way pays all maintenance costs, insurance, and taxes in connection with these trucks. Ace Trucking paid $170,000 to manufacture each truck. It requires an implicit rate of 10%, based on the normal selling price and ignoring any salvage value to the lessor. Payments are assumed to be collectible and are paid at the end of each year. The lease is initiated on January 1, 1995.

INSTRUCTIONS

In your answers to the following, round amounts to the nearest dollar.

[a] What type of lease is this from the viewpoint of Ace Trucking Company and All-the-Way Trucking? Explain your answer.

[b] Calculate the amount of the annual lease payment.

[c] Prepare the entry to record the lease on Ace's books.

[d] Prepare All-the Way's initial entry for this lease.

23–45 Lessee and Lessor—Income Effect of Capital Leases   Tulip Company leased equipment from Rose Company on October 1, 1995. The lease is appropriately accounted for as a purchase by Tulip and as a sale by Rose. The lease is for eight years and expires on September 30, 2003. Equal annual payments under the lease are $620,000 due on October 1. The first payment was made on October 1, 1995. The cost of the equipment on Rose's accounting records was $3,000,000. It has an estimated useful life of eight years with no residual value. A full year's depreciation is taken in the year that Tulip Company acquired the assets. The appropriate rate of interest for both Tulip and Rose is 10%.

INSTRUCTIONS

[a] What expenses should Tulip appropriately record for the year ended December 31, 1995? Show supporting computations in good form and round amounts to the nearest dollar.

[b] What income or loss before income taxes should Rose appropriately record for the year ended December 31, 1995? Show supporting computations in good form and round amounts to the nearest dollar.   (AICPA adapted)

 23–46 Lessor and Lessee—Capital Lease   Shea Company leases equipment to Faldo Company for four years. The equipment, valued at $1,000 (which is also the cost of the equipment to Shea Company), is to be transferred to Faldo on January 1, 1995, and lease payments are to be made on December 31, 1995, 1996, 1997, and 1998 in the amount of $330 per year. Salvage value at the end of the four years is negligible, and Faldo may buy the property at the end of the lease for $1.

INSTRUCTIONS

In your answers to the following, round all amounts to the nearest dollar.

[a] Determine the appropriate interest rate implicit in this lease.

[b] Prepare necessary entries for Shea's books on January 1, 1995, December 31, 1995, and December 31, 1996. Assume that Shea records the gross receivables and unearned income in separate accounts.

[c] Prepare the relevant portion of Shea's balance sheet and income statement at December 31, 1996 and 1997.

[d] Prepare the necessary entries for Faldo's books on January 1, 1995, December 31, 1995, and December 31, 1996. Assume that the lease is treated as an intangible asset. Faldo Company records the lease liability and the related discount in separate accounts.

[c] Prepare the relevant portion of Faldo's balance sheet and income statement on December 31, 1996 and 1997.

23-47 Lessor—Capital Lease On January 1, 1995, Shea Company leased equipment costing $700 to Faldo Company. The sales price of the equipment is $1,000. Annual lease payments of $330 are made on December 31 for the next four years. There is no salvage value and the equipment may be purchased after the four years for $1.

INSTRUCTIONS

[a] Prepare the necessary entries for Shea's books at January 1, 1995, December 31, 1995, and December 31, 1996.

[b] Prepare the relevant portion of Shea's balance sheet and income statement at December 31, 1995 and 1996. Assume that Shea records the gross receivables and unearned income in separate accounts.

[c] Discuss any differences in accounting and reporting that the change in circumstances from Problem 23-46 will cause for Shea Company and Faldo Company.

23-48 Lessee—Capital Lease In 1995 Handel Food Company signed a long-term lease for new warehousing equipment, including conveyors and lifts. The equipment was installed according to Handel's specifications and was placed in operation on October 1, 1995.

Handel could have purchased the equipment for $1.5 million but instead decided on a noncancelable lease with the option to purchase the equipment at the end of the lease. The equipment has an estimated useful life of 20 years.

The terms of the lease are as follows:

[1] Lease period 10 years, October 1, 1995, through September 30, 2005.

[2] Rental payments of $300,000 payable to the lessor on October 1 of each of the first five years of the lease.

[3] Rental payments of $120,000 payable to the lessor on October 1 of each of the last five years of the lease.

[4] Lessee is responsible for all payments of property taxes, insurance, and maintenance. (Handel estimates that the total amount will be $30,000 annually.)

[5] Upon termination of the lease, the lessee has the option to purchase the equipment for $41,250.

Handel's independent auditor has established that the leased equipment and related obligation should be accounted for as an installment purchase. Handel uses double-declining-balance depreciation for plant assets. The lease yields a 12% rate of return to the lessor. Handel's incremental borrowing rate exceeds 12%.

Use the following present-value factors in making the necessary computations:

Discount Factors for 12% (rounded)

Period	Present Value of $1.00	Present Value of $1.00 per Period Received at End of Period
1	.89	.89
2	.80	1.69
3	.71	2.40
4	.64	3.04
5	.57	3.60
6	.51	4.11
7	.45	4.56
8	.40	4.97
9	.36	5.33
10	.32	5.65

INSTRUCTIONS

[a] Prepare Handel's balance sheet presentation of this lease on September 30, 1996. Provide supporting computations in good form.

[b] Prepare Handel's income statement presentation of this lease for the year ended September 30, 1996. Provide supporting computations in good form.   (CMA adapted)

23-49 Lessee and Lessor—Classification and Accounting Oil-Patch, Inc., leases a truck to Rogers Company for petroleum exploration. Such trucks normally last 10 years, but because of the intense use and primitive conditions in oil exploration, the expected useful life is no more than six years. The terms of the lease and other information are as follows:

Beginning of the lease term	May 1, 1995
Lease term	5 years
Lease payments	$4,300/year, beginning May 1, 1995
Cost of truck to Oil-Patch	$14,000
Fair value of truck on May 1, 1995	$18,000
Interest rate implicit in the lease	12%
Residual value of asset at Apr. 30, 2000 (estimated)	$1,000

There is no bargain purchase option or transfer of title in the lease. No significant uncertainties exist about the collectibility of lease payments or any future costs to be incurred by Oil-Patch.

Rogers Company has an incremental borrowing rate of 18%. Rogers can compute the interest rate implicit in the lease and normally depreciates and amortizes assets on a straight-line basis to the nearest month.

INSTRUCTIONS

[a] From the viewpoint of Oil-Patch, Inc.:
   [1] What type of lease is this? Why?
   [2] Prepare the entries to record the lease at May 1, 1995, and December 31, 1995, and any other entries required during 1995. (Round amounts to the nearest dollar.) Oil-Patch records the lease in a single investment account, net of any unearned income.
[b] From the viewpoint of Rogers Company:
   [1] What type of lease is this? Why?
   [2] Prepare the entries to record the lease at May 1, 1995, and December 31, 1995, and any other entries necessary during 1995. Rogers records the lease liability in a single account, net of any discount. (Round amounts to the nearest dollar.)

23-50   Lessee and Lessor—Capital Lease   Denver Company leased an asset to United Company on January 1, 1995. Conditions of the lease and other information include the following:

Lease term	6 years
Annual payments made on Jan. 1 of each year, including $1,000 of executory costs	$11,000
Estimated residual value at the end of lease term	$5,000
Initial direct costs	$1,500
Estimated life of property	10 years
Selling price of comparable assets	$53,500
Interest rate implicit in lease	8%
Incremental borrowing rate of lessee	10%
Cost of the asset to lessor	$37,500
Fiscal year of lessor	Jan. 1–Dec. 31
Fiscal year of lessee	Oct. 1–Sept. 30

United is aware of the 8% interest rate implicit in the lease.

INSTRUCTIONS

In your answers to the following, round amounts to the nearest dollar.

[a] Denver's accounting:
   [1] Prepare all journal entries during 1995, assuming the lessee guarantees the residual value of the leased property.
   [2] Prepare all journal entries during 1995, assuming the residual value is not guaranteed by the lessee or otherwise.
[b] United's accounting:
   [1] Prepare all journal entries during 1995, assuming the lessee guarantees the residual value of the leased asset.
   [2] Prepare the asset and liability presentations for United's September 30, 1995, balance sheet. Assume for this problem only that the discount related to the current portion of the liability is the amount of interest to be recognized in the next payment.
[c] Discuss briefly how your answer in [b] would differ, if at all, if the lessee's incremental borrowing rate had been 7% instead of 10%.

23-51 Lessee and Lessor—Capital Lease Goggans Corporation, a lessor of office machines, purchased a new machine for $520,000 on December 31, 1995. The machine was delivered the same day to Krull Company, the lessee. The following information relating to the lease transaction is available:

[1] The asset has an estimated useful life of seven years, which coincides with the lease term.
[2] At the end of the lease term, the machine will revert to Goggans, at which time it is expected to have a residual value of $60,000 (none of which Krull guarantees).
[3] Krull is aware of the 12% implicit interest rate on Goggans's net investment.
[4] Krull's incremental borrowing rate is 14% at December 31, 1995.
[5] Lease rentals consist of seven equal annual payments, the first of which was paid on December 31, 1995.
[6] The lease is appropriately accounted for as a direct-financing lease by Goggans and as a capital lease by Krull. Both lessor and lessee are calendar-year corporations and depreciate all fixed assets on the straight-line basis.

INSTRUCTIONS

Compute the following to the nearest dollar and show supporting computations in good form.

[a] The annual rental under the lease. (*Hint:* Determine the *net amount* that must be recovered by Goggans and then divide by the appropriate present-value factor.)
[b] The amounts of the gross lease rentals receivable and the unearned interest revenue for Goggans on December 31, 1995.
[c] What expense should Krull record for the year ended December 31, 1996?   (AICPA adapted)

23-52 Lessee and Lessor—Capital Lease On January 1, 1995, Overton Company entered into a five-year lease with Weeter Company. Overton transferred a machine to Weeter on that date, and Weeter agreed to make annual payments on January 1 of $10,000. The first payment was made on January 1, 1995. Approximately $1,000 of each payment is designated for taxes, insurance, and other costs related to the machine that are to be paid by the lessor.

Overton sells as well as leases machines. The following information relates to Overton's operations:

Normal selling price of machine	$39,710
Costs to manufacture machine	$26,000
Initial direct cost—sales commission	$1,300
Interest rate implicit in lease	10%

Weeter expects the machine to be useful for six years. Weeter has an incremental borrowing rate of 12% and is aware that the rate implicit in the lease is 10%. In addition to the annual $10,000 payments, Weeter has guaranteed the residual value at the end of the five-year lease at $3,500. The lease contains no purchase or renewal options.

INSTRUCTIONS

In your answers to the following, round amounts to the nearest dollar. Assume that both companies report on a calendar-year basis.

[a] What is the present value of the lease for both the lessor and the lessee?
[b] What is the proper classification of this lease by the lessee? By the lessor?
[c] Prepare an amortization table appropriate for both the lessor and lessee for the five-year lease term.
[d] Prepare the journal entries for the lessee through January 1, 1996. Weeter records the lease liability, net of discount, in a single account.
[e] Prepare the journal entries for the lessor through January 1, 1996.

23-53 Sales-Type and Operating Lease (Lessor) Icarus Company, which started operating in 1994, leases medical equipment to hospitals. All of its leases are appropriately accounted for as operating leases, except for a major lease entered into on January 1, 1996, which is appropriately accounted for as a sale.

For the year ended December 31, 1996, the following information is available:

Operating Leases. Revenues from operating leases were $800,000. The cost of the related leased equipment is $3,700,000, which is being depreciated on a straight-line basis over a five-year period. The estimated residual value of the leased equipment after five years is $200,000. No leased equipment was acquired or constructed in 1996. Maintenance and other related costs and the costs of any other services rendered under the provisions of the leases were $70,000 in 1996.

Lease Recorded as a Sale. The January 1, 1996, lease recorded as a sale is for a six-year period expiring December 31, 2001. The cost of this leased equipment is $3,500,000. The equipment is estimated to have no residual value at the end of the lease. Maintenance and other related costs and the costs of any other services rendered under the provisions of this lease, all of which were paid by the lessee, were $120,000 in 1996. Equal annual payments of $750,000 are due on January 1. The first payment was made on January 1, 1996. The present value of an annuity of $1 in advance at 10% is as follows:

Number of Periods	Present Value
5	4.170
6	4.791
7	5.355

Selling, general, and administrative expenses, exclusive of amounts specified above earlier, were $600,000 in 1996.

Other revenue, exclusive of amounts specified above, was $50,000 in 1996.

INSTRUCTIONS

Prepare an income statement for Icarus Company for the year ended December 31, 1996, stopping at income (loss) before income taxes. Show supporting computations in good form. (Ignore income tax and deferred tax considerations. Use the rounded present-value factors presented in the problem to make necessary computations.)   (AICPA adapted)

CASES

23–54   Advantages of Leasing   The controller of Ocean Repair Service, in discussing various financing alternatives, made the following statement:

> *Leasing is consistently the most attractive method of financing. Not only does it normally provide 100% financing with no down payment or compensating balance requirements, but also it allows us to acquire only the particular asset rights we want. For example, we may not wish to buy an asset because we have no wish to own it when it becomes obsolete. The lessor is better able to dispose of such an asset at the end of a lease than we would be if we had bought it outright. Furthermore, we avoid tying up our cash unnecessarily. Therefore, the asset we lease, as well as the cash we conserve, can both be used productively. Finally, our balance sheet appears more favorable, because we do not record additional liabilities or lose liquidity when we lease assets.*

INSTRUCTIONS

Evaluate the controller's comments.

23–55   General Leases—Lessor and Lessee   Iva Corporation entered into a lease arrangement with Shapner Leasing Corporation for a certain machine. Shapner's primary business is leasing; it is not a manufacturer or dealer. Iva will lease the machine for three years, which is 50% of the machine's economic life. Shapner will take possession of the machine at the end of the initial three-year lease and lease it to a smaller company that does not need the most current version of the machine. Iva does not guarantee any residual value for the machine and will not purchase the machine at the end of the lease term.

Iva's incremental borrowing rate is 10%, and the implicit rate in the lease is 8.5%. Iva has no way to know the implicit rate used by Shapner. Using either rate, the present value of the minimum lease payments is between 90% and 100% of the fair value of the machine at the date of the lease agreement.

Iva has agreed to pay all executory costs directly. No allowance for these costs is included in the lease payments.

Shapner is reasonably certain that Iva will meet all lease payments, and because Iva has agreed to pay all executory costs, there are no important uncertainties regarding costs to be incurred by Shapner.

INSTRUCTIONS

[a] With respect to Iva, answer the following:
   [1] What type of lease has been entered into? Explain the reason for your answer.
   [2] How should Iva compute the appropriate amount to record for the lease or asset acquired?
   [3] What accounts will be created or affected by this transaction? How will the lease or asset and other costs related to the transaction be matched with earnings?
   [4] What disclosures must Iva make regarding this lease or asset?

[b] With respect to Shapner, answer the following:
[1] What type of lease has been entered into? Explain the reason for your answer.
[2] How should this lease be recorded by Shapner? How are the appropriate amounts determined?
[3] How should Shapner determine the appropriate amount of earnings to be recognized from each lease payment?
[4] What disclosures must Shapner make regarding this lease? (AICPA adapted)

23–56 Lessee Accounting Paulsen Corporation is a diversified company with nationwide interests in commercial real estate developments, banking, copper mining, and metal fabrication. The company has offices and operating locations in major cities throughout the United States. The corporate headquarters for Paulsen is located in a metropolitan area of a midwestern state, and executives connected with various phases of company operations travel extensively. Corporate management is presently evaluating the feasibility of acquiring a business aircraft that company executives can use to expedite business travel to areas not adequately served by commercial airlines. Proposals for either leasing or purchasing a suitable aircraft have been analyzed, and the leasing proposal is considered to be more desirable.

The proposed lease agreement involves a twin-engine turboprop Viking that has a fair market value of $900,000. This plane would be leased for a period of 10 years beginning January 1, 1995. The lease agreement is cancelable only upon accidental destruction of the plane. An annual lease payment of $127,600 is due on January 1 of each year; the first payment is to be made on January 1, 1995. Maintenance operations are strictly scheduled by the lessor, and Paulsen Corporation will pay for these services as they are performed. Estimated annual maintenance costs are $6,200. The lessor will pay all insurance premiums and local property taxes, which amount to $3,600 annually and are included in the annual lease payment of $127,600. Upon expiration of the 10-year lease, Paulsen Corporation can purchase the Viking for $40,000. The estimated useful life of the plane is 15 years, and its salvage value in the used plane market is estimated to be $100,000 after 10 years. The salvage value probably will never be less than $75,000 if the engines are overhauled and maintained as the manufacturer prescribes. If the purchase option is not exercised, possession of the plane will revert to the lessor, and there is no provision for renewing the lease agreement beyond its termination on December 31, 2004.

Paulsen Corporation can borrow $900,000 under a 10-year term loan agreement at an annual interest rate of 12%. The lessor's implicit interest rate is not expressly stated in the lease agreement, but this rate appears to be approximately 8% based on 10 net rental payments of $124,000 per year and the initial market value of $900,000 for the plane. On January 1, 1995, the present value of all net rental payments and the purchase option of $40,000 is $800,000 if the 12% interest rate is used. The present value of all net rental payments and the $40,000 purchase option on January 1, 1995, is $920,000 if one uses the 8% interest rate implicit in the lease agreement. The financial vice president of Paulsen Corporation has established that this lease agreement is a capital lease as defined in *Statement of Financial Accounting Standards No. 13*, "Accounting for Leases."

INSTRUCTIONS

[a] What is the appropriate amount that Paulsen should recognize for the leased aircraft on its statement of financial position after the lease is signed?
[b] Without prejudice to your answer in [a], assume that the annual lease payment is $127,600 (as stated in the preceding information), that the appropriate capitalized amount for the leased aircraft is $1,000,000 on January 1, 1995, and that the interest rate is 9%. How will the lease be reported in the December 31, 1995, statement of financial position and related income statement? (Ignore income tax implications.)
[c] Explain the four factors that differentiate a capital lease from an operating lease. (CMA adapted)

23–57 Theoretical Constructs of Leasing On January 1, 1995, Thacker Company entered into a noncancelable lease for a machine to be used in its manufacturing operations. The lease transfers ownership of the machine to Thacker at the end of the lease term. The term of the lease is eight years. The minimum lease payment made by Thacker on January 1, 1995, was one of eight equal annual payments. At the inception of the lease, the criteria established for classification as a capital lease by the lessee were met.

INSTRUCTIONS

[a] What is the theoretical basis for the accounting standard that requires certain long-term leases to be capitalized by the lessee? Do not discuss the specific criteria for classifying a specific lease as a capital lease.

[b] How should Thacker account for this lease at its inception and how should management determine the amount to be recorded?

[c] What expenses related to this lease will Thacker incur during the first year of the lease, and how will they be determined?

[d] How should Thacker report the lease transaction on its December 31, 1995, balance sheet?

(AICPA adapted)

JUDGMENT CASES

23-58   Consideration of Lease Provisions   Your client is a chain of fast-food restaurants known as Slick Chick, which specializes in sauteed chicken dishes. During a recent expansion of operations, the company executed a number of real estate leases to serve as sites for new restaurants. The lessor has constructed the buildings as part of the lease agreement.

These leases all contain the same basic terms. None of the leases contain a transfer of title or a bargain purchase option. The fair value of the land portion of the lease is considered more than 25% of the total fair value of the leased property. Each of the leases contains a 20-year term with a right to renew the lease for an additional 20 years. You have satisfied yourself that the renewal options are not bargain renewal options as defined by *SFAS No. 13* and that the life of the buildings is approximately 40 years. The present value of the lease payments attributable to the building portion of the leases during the minimum lease terms represent only about 80% of the fair value of those portions of the assets being leased.

During lunch you have informed the president of the company that your preliminary determination is that none of the leases require treatment as capital leases. He responds:

> *Well, that is good news. If there is one thing we can't have, it's cluttering up our balance sheet with a lot of liabilities and assets that are just leased items. We are really excited about these new locations. We expect to open them within a month and predict great results from this expansion. We are planning to operate them for 15 years and then to renovate the buildings entirely in anticipation of renewing the leases at the end of the first lease term. That way, when we exercise the renewal option, the facilities will be ready to go, and we won't miss a beat. We have tied up 40 years of access to these locations and will be able to use them productively during that entire period.*

INSTRUCTIONS

The president's statement has made you lose interest in your dessert! Why? Do the president's comments have any implications for the classification of the leases? If so, why?

23-59   Revising Transactions   Your client, Hot Boats, Inc., a manufacturer of traditional family watercraft, has decided to begin producing small personal watercraft, called jet skis, in addition to its existing product line. The company has decided to use a contract source for the fiberglass hulls of the new watercraft because it does not have the ability or desire to produce them. The contractor that Hot Boats approached to produce the hulls has indicated that additional advanced computers will be necessary to ensure appropriate design. The computers are rather expensive and will be useful only to produce the hulls for Hot Boats.

As a result of these considerations, Hot Boats originally considered an agreement with the contractor to lease the computers on a long-term basis and place them in the contractor's facilities. The controller of Hot Boats approached you, the auditor for the company, to determine the accounting treatment for the proposed lease agreement. You determined that because the lease required the lessee to guarantee the residual value of the computers, the lease would have to be treated as a capital lease. The controller was clearly disappointed and subsequently approached you concerning another lease that differed from the first one in that it had a longer lease term.

Careful analysis of the revised lease proposal revealed that the new length term clearly exceeded 75% of the life of the computer and, therefore, would also be considered a capital lease. The controller was quite concerned and indicated that Hot Boats wished to avoid recording a large liability and related asset for the acquisition of the computers. She then appeared with a third agreement in hand and wants your opinion.

The new agreement has the contractor leasing the equipment from the computer manufacturer with Hot Boats entering into an unconditional and noncancelable purchase obligation with the contractor for a specified number of watercraft hulls to be produced over the next 10 years. The controller is quite excited and states:

> *Because this is not a lease, we are confident that we won't have to record the commitment as a liability and the related asset. This is nothing more than an executory contract much like a construction contract and, as you know, generally accepted accounting principles do not require recording such executory contracts in the accounting records.*

In analyzing the three alternatives, you become aware that the purchase commitment will result in Hot Boats paying the largest amount of the three agreements to acquire the hulls. When told this, the controller responds:

> *Yes, we determined that in our analysis, as well. The way we look at it is that the excess is just the cost of achieving the accounting result we prefer. Sometimes you just have to pay a price for the financial position you want, and this is one of those times.*

INSTRUCTIONS

Should the unconditional and noncancelable purchase obligation be recorded and included in the balance sheet of Hot Boats? How would you respond to the comments of the controller? Would your answer to the above questions differ if Hot Boats had originally proposed the purchase obligation and you were not aware of the previous lease proposals and the company's desire to avoid reporting the liability that would have resulted from the lease agreements?

23–60 Financial Reporting Case   Johnson Controls is a global market leader in automotive sealing systems, facilities services and control systems, plastic packaging, and automotive batteries. The company was founded in 1885 and operates in more than 500 locations nationwide.

Johnson Controls' statement of financial position for the year ended September 30, 1993, includes current portion of long-term debt of $21.6 million as a current liability and $500.4 million of long-term debt as a noncurrent liability. Following are Notes 3 and 5 from Johnson Controls' 1993 financial statements in which leases and long-term debt, respectively, are discussed.

Note 3—Leases

Certain administrative and production facilities and equipment are leased under long-term agreements. Most leases contain renewal options for varying periods, and certain leases include options to purchase the leased property during or at the end of the lease term. Leases generally require the Company to pay for insurance, taxes, and maintenance of the property. Leased capital assets included in net property, plant and equipment, primarily buildings and improvements, were $41 million and $51 million at September 30, 1993 and 1992, respectively.

Other facilities and equipment are leased under arrangements which are accounted for as operating leases. Total rental expense was $72 million in 1993, $65 million in 1992 and $62 million in 1991.

Future minimum capital and operating lease payments and the related present value of capital lease payments at September 30, 1993, are as follows:

(in millions)	Capital Leases	Operating Leases
1994	$ 7.6	$ 39.0
1995	6.7	31.2
1996	6.0	22.9
1997	6.2	14.0
1998	4.1	8.4
After 1998	23.7	37.1
Total minimum lease payments	54.3	$152.6
Interest	14.7	
Present value of net minimum lease payments	$39.6	

Note 5—Long-Term Debt

(in millions)	September 30, 1993	September 30, 1992
Unsecured notes		
6.15% due in 1996	$ 30.0	$ —
8⅞% due in 1998	149.8	149.7
Industrial revenue bonds due through 2009, net of unamortized discount of $3.7 million in 1993 and $4.1 million in 1992	52.8	61.5
Medium-term notes due in 1995 and 1996 at an average interest rate of 8.65%	54.8	54.8
Guaranteed ESOP debt due in increasing annual installments through 2004 at an average interest rate of 6.5% (tied in part to LIBOR)	153.4	159.4
Capital lease obligations	39.6	49.2
Other	41.6	54.7
	522.0	529.3
Less current portion	21.6	26.0
Long-term debt	$500.4	$503.3

Industrial revenue bond financed facilities have been accounted for as plant and equipment. The related bonds issued by the government units are recorded as long-term debt. Fixed rate industrial revenue bonds totalling $29 million at September 30, 1993, and $37 million at September 30, 1992, had weighted average interest rates of 6.9% and 7.2%, respectively. Variable rate bonds of $28 million at September 30, 1993, and $29 million at September 30, 1992, had weighted average interest rates of 3.2% and 3.6%, respectively.

In 1989 the Company established an employee stock ownership plan (ESOP). The ESOP was financed with $175 million in debt issued by the ESOP. The ESOP debt is guaranteed by the Company as to payment of principal and interest and, therefore, the unpaid balance is recorded as long-term debt. The dividends on the Series D Preferred Stock held by the ESOP plus Company contributions to the ESOP are used by the ESOP to service the debt. Interest incurred on the ESOP debt during 1993, 1992, and 1991 of $10 million, $11 million and $13 million, respectively, is therefore not reflected as interest expense in the Company's Consolidated Statement of Income.

The installments of long-term debt maturing in each of the next five years (including the guaranteed ESOP debt) are 1994—$22 million, 1995—$67 million, 1996—$69 million, 1997—$20 million and 1998—$171 million.

The indentures for the unsecured notes and the guaranteed ESOP debt include various financial covenants, none of which are expected to restrict future operations.

The fair value of the Company's long-term debt at September 30, 1993, is estimated to be $542 million based on current market interest rates and discounted future cash flows.

INSTRUCTIONS

[a] What are the options and responsibilities of Johnson Controls under the various leases for which it is the lessee?

[b] What are the capitalized amounts of leased assets for 1992 and 1993, and where are these found in the statements of financial position?

[c] What was the total rent expense paid under operating leases for 1991, 1992, and 1993?

[d] Current and noncurrent liabilities for capital leases are not separately disclosed in Johnson Controls' 1993 statement of financial position. By analyzing Notes 3 and 5, identify the total amount of lease liabilities included in the balance sheet and how much of that total is included as current and noncurrent.

[e] What is the total amount of lease payments and other debt that matures in each year from 1994 through 1998?

Pensions and Other Employment Benefits

OBJECTIVES

1. To describe the nature of modern pensions and other retirement benefits.
2. To explain the complexities in determining the cost of retirement benefits to employers.
3. To identify and compute the primary components of net periodic pension cost and net postretirement benefit cost.
4. To specify and illustrate situations that require the balance sheet recognition of assets and liabilities related to retirement plans.
5. To explain the information about retirement plans that must be maintained by employers that does not appear in the employer's financial statements.
6. To introduce several other aspects of accounting and financial statement disclosure for pension and other employee benefit plans.

Chrysler Corporation's 1993 income statement includes a cumulative effect loss of almost $5 billion to account for a change in its accounting for health care and other postretirement benefits. This transformed a $2,415 million income before the cumulative effect of the change in accounting principles to a $2,551 net loss for the year.

Although this event is a one-time charge required to adopt *SFAS No. 106*, "Employers' Accounting for Postretirement Benefits Other Than Pensions," on an ongoing basis, companies incur substantial expenses in the form of employee benefits. For example, the same financial statements for Chrysler Corporation include an expense for pension plans of $756 million and for other postretirement plans of $768 million for 1993 alone, a total of over $1.5 billion.

These figures demonstrate the significance of pension and other employee benefits as an expense of operations for U.S. corporations. We explore these and related issues in Chapter 24.

THE EVOLUTION AND SIGNIFICANCE OF RETIREMENT PLANS

Retirement commitments made by employers to employees are a common characteristic of modern employment agreements. A pension commitment represents an agreement in which an employer promises payments to employees after they retire. Pension plans range from relatively simple employer commitments to make specific periodic payments to a retirement fund, to promises to provide a certain level of income to employees after retirement based on a variety of factors. For example, the pension benefits a person receives may be a function of the years of service rendered to the employer, earnings levels prior to retirement, changes in the general price level, and the life span of the retired employee. In addition to pension plans, many employers provide other types of retirement benefits for former employees, including health care, life insurance, and similar benefits. Retirement benefits are best thought of as *deferred compensation arrangements* in which employees receive a portion of their previously earned compensation during their retirement years. Retirement benefits are **not** gratuities from the employer to the employee but are part of the cost of compensation for employment services rendered.

Retirement plans have become increasingly significant in our economy during the last 50 years. Before then, the responsibility for one's welfare after retirement was generally considered a function of individual savings and family duty. Events such as the industrial revolution and the Great Depression, as well as changing social perceptions of governmental and business responsibilities, have increased social awareness of the need to provide relatively comfortable and secure retirement for long-term employees. Today it is common for an individual's largest asset to be the value of a retirement plan. Employers contribute resources to the plan on behalf of employees. These resources are then available for investment, and investment earnings increase the amounts available for retirement benefits.

The assets controlled and invested by pension plans are substantial, and they represent a significant part of the available investment capital in the United States. For this reason, the activities of corporate sponsors of pension plans are of interest to businesses and employees, as well as to governments and other institutional and individual investors.

Exhibit 24–1 presents information drawn from notes to the financial statements of four large corporations that helps illustrate the magnitude of pension plans. The fair value of plan assets measures the worth of the stocks, bonds, and other investments. Stated as a percentage of total assets, these investments range from 6.1% to 47.8% for these four companies. The projected benefit obligation is one way to measure the pension obligation of the company to present and retired employees for pension benefits they have already earned. Stated as a percentage of stockholders' equity, the projected benefit obligations for these four companies range from 13.8% to 230.1%. As we shall see as we explore accounting for pension plans, you must carefully read notes to the financial statements to determine these amounts because present accounting requirements result in netting many amounts in the financial statements, including the fair value of plan assets and the projected benefit obligation. The figures in Exhibit 24–1, however, demonstrate clearly that pension plans involve material amounts in relation to other key financial statement figures.

Accounting standards for pensions have been in existence for many years, but the FASB has recently revised them and provided authoritative guidance on accounting and reporting for other types of retirement benefits. Our primary emphasis in this chapter is on pension accounting as the primary example of retirement benefit plans. We briefly examine accounting for other retirement benefits at the end of this chapter.

The relationships and responsibilities of the various parties in a typical employer-sponsored pension plan are illustrated in Exhibit 24–2. The employer frequently has primary responsibility to the employee for the capacity of the pension plan to meet contracted payments. The employer ensures the plan's solvency by making periodic contributions to it. The pension

THE NATURE OF PENSION PLANS

EXHIBIT 24–1

Selected Pension Information
(dollar figures in millions)

	Fair Value of Plan Assets	% of Total Assets	Projected Benefit Obligation	% of Stockholders' Equity
Coca-Cola (U.S. plans)	$ 731	6.1	$ 633	13.8
Federal Express	1,591	26.6	1,677	100.4
Chevron	3,831	11.0	3,456	24.7
United Technologies	7,469	47.8	8,279	230.1

SOURCE: 1993 Annual Reports.

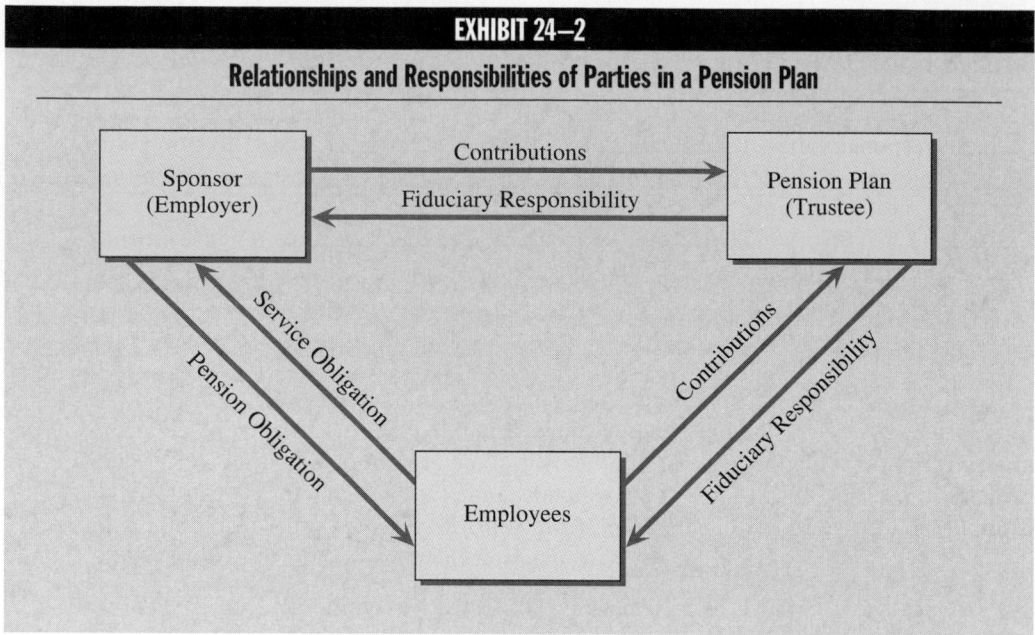

plan is usually administered by a trustee, such as an insurance company or bank, which is independent of the sponsor and responsible for stewardship of the plan's assets. In addition, the trustee determines the contributions that are needed to maintain the plan.

Pension plans may be broadly classified as either *defined contribution plans* or *defined benefit plans*. Financial accounting and reporting is usually much more simple and straightforward for defined contribution plans. Defined benefit plans, on the other hand, are more complicated and involve additional considerations in administering and accounting for the plan.

DEFINED CONTRIBUTION PLANS

Defined contribution plans contain provisions that allow employers to determine the resources that must be contributed to a pension plan each year. Defined contribution plans usually require employers to contribute a percentage of company income or employee salaries to a pension fund. Once the defined contribution is paid, the sponsor has no additional liability to provide pension benefits. Pension expense for the period is the amount of the required contribution. Pension benefits are distributed in the future from the assets accumulated in the trust fund. If the defined contribution for the period has not been paid at the balance sheet date, a liability is accrued in that amount. The liability is normally classified as current, because the defined contribution must be paid promptly.

In defined contribution plans, the *employees accept the risk* of the plan's investment performance. In a sense, the accumulated contributions plus earnings belong to the employees. Therefore, if the plan provides exceptional investment performance, employees share in the gains in the form of increased pension benefits. Likewise, if the plan does poorly, employees share in the losses by receiving smaller pension benefits. The benefits that are ultimately paid to retirees in a defined contribution plan are based on the amounts available, given the defined level of employer contribution and the earnings performance of the plan's portfolio of investments.

DEFINED BENEFIT PLANS

Many pension plans are referred to as **defined benefit plans** because they specify the benefits to be received by retirees in terms of factors such as employee age, years of service, and salary levels. The benefits are usually expressed in terms of a formula that incorporates the above factors and other factors specified in the employment agreement. For example, the formula may calculate the annual pension cost as a percentage rate times the number of years of service times the final salary (or average of several years' salary) before retirement. As an example, a pension that credited an employee with 2% of final salary for each year worked would grant a pension of 60% of final salary for an employee with 30 years of service.

Defined benefit pension plans describe the benefits employees are to receive. The pension expense of the sponsor is based on estimates of the cost of providing those benefits. Employer and employee contributions to the plans, plus earnings on investments made with plan assets, are designed to provide the benefits promised. Because the liability and related pension expense for defined benefit plans usually depend on final compensation levels and years of service, the accounting issues become more complex than under a defined contribution plan. Many variables must be estimated to determine the periodic pension contribution required and the pension expense to recognize in the determination of net income. These estimates are based on **actuarial assumptions,** which are important considerations in applying the **actuarial cost method** to determine amounts employers must fund and recognize as pension expense in the determination of net income.

In contrast to defined contribution plans, in defined benefit plans, the *employer accepts the investment risk* of the plan. The employee does not own an accumulated fund but instead is promised a contractual pension based on a formula. If the investment performance of the plan is good enough to exceed the actuarially determined pension obligation according to the formula, the employer may reduce further contributions. Likewise, if the plan's investment performance is poor, the employer must make additional contributions to ensure that formula benefits are funded. In effect, *investment gains and losses accrue to the employer,* not the employees.

OTHER ASPECTS OF PENSION PLANS

Qualified Plans

If pension plans meet certain criteria contained in the federal income tax laws, substantial tax benefits are available. A **qualified plan** (i.e., one meeting the tax law criteria) has features that allow employees to avoid paying taxes on benefits until they are actually received by employees. Employers are allowed a tax deduction at the time contributions are made to the fund. Earnings on fund assets are also not taxed until distributed to beneficiaries many years in the future. Clearly, our national tax policy encourages well-run pension plans, as you can see in these favorable tax alternatives.

Funded and Unfunded Plans

Funded Plans. Most large pension plans in the United States are either fully or partially funded. A **funded plan** means that the resources from which future pension benefits are to be paid have been transferred to a trustee or fiscal agent. If the complete amount that has been recognized as an expense has been transferred to a trustee or fiscal agent, the plan is called **fully funded.** If only part of the expense recognized has been transferred, the plan is considered **partially funded.**

Most private pension plans are subject to the provisions of the **Employee Retirement Income Security Act of 1974 (ERISA).** This law requires companies to establish certain minimum funding, participation, and vesting policies. Employers make annual contributions to pension plans that are sufficient to fully fund them in accordance with an acceptable actuarial cost method. If funding in a reasonable fashion does not occur, sponsoring companies are subject to substantial fines and penalties. The sponsoring company usually pays cash to the funding agent, who then invests the moneys and pays beneficiaries as retirement or separations occur.

One way of funding a plan is to purchase annuity contracts from an insurance company. The insurance company then pays the defined benefits as they come due. The sponsoring company pays a premium to the insurance company and, in many cases, effectively transfers the risk of honoring the pension commitments to the insurance company. Such plans are called **insured plans.**

Unfunded Plans.   Pension plans that do not require sponsoring companies to transfer funds to a trustee are considered to be **unfunded.** Unfunded plans are frequently referred to as **pay-as-you-go plans,** because funding takes place when pension benefits are paid to retirees rather than when pension expense was recognized during the period of active employment. Although such plans are rare today, they are still occasionally found in certain industries, such as certain nonbusiness organizations. If the assets set aside to pay the pension plan are retained and controlled by the plan sponsor (employing company), the plan is generally considered *nonfunded.*

Financial Reporting by Employers and by Pension Plans

Issues of financial reporting exist for employers (sponsors) who maintain pension plans and for pension plans themselves. In this chapter, we confine our discussion to financial accounting and reporting for pensions by employers that sponsor pension plans. Thus, we emphasize the recognition of pension assets and liabilities, pension expense, and funding procedures for employer-companies. Pension plans, on the other hand, prepare financial statements that are available for employee-participants in the plans and other interested parties. Accounting standards governing the financial reporting of pension plans as separate reporting entities are beyond the scope of this textbook.

PRINCIPLES UNDERLYING PENSION PLANS

A pension plan is merely an arrangement whereby an employer provides a mechanism for employees to receive a portion of their compensation after retirement. In most pension plans, the amounts an employee will receive are not precisely known before retirement. Financial accounting and reporting issues parallel those for similar economic circumstances, such as compensated absences for vacation and illness, which we discussed in Chapter 14.

An employee renders services for many years prior to retirement, but some of the remuneration for those services is paid only *after retirement.* The cost of those services to the employer, however, must be recognized as an obligation to pay retirement benefits as the employee renders services that qualify for those benefits. In this way, the financial reporting

Matching

principle of matching is achieved. Stated differently, the cost to a company of an employee's labor includes not only the direct salaries and benefits currently paid but also an amount representing the right to a pension earned by the employee during the year. As an employee works, pension benefits increase each year. The expense and related liability of the company to the employee for these pension benefits require accounting recognition in the employer's records *at the time the benefits are earned* to properly state the elements of the financial statements, particularly expenses and liabilities.

The nature of the pension liability, however, remains controversial. Does the employer's liability extend merely to making adequate contributions to the plan, or does the liability extend to the employees directly? In the former case, a pension liability would arise only for the excess of the actuarially determined obligation over the actual assets available in the plan. In the latter case, the pension liability would remain with the employer until actual cash payments were made *to the employee after retirement.* Historically, generally accepted accounting principles (GAAP) have embraced the notion of the liability arising only from contribution shortfalls to the plan. Because many corporations fund their pension plans to avoid contribution shortfalls, many corporate balance sheets do not include pension assets and liabilities. Critics of this approach assert that the employer has an obligation to the employees, not to the plan itself, and that to exclude that obligation from the balance sheet is a form of "off-balance-sheet financing," much like operating leases. In their view, the present value of outstanding pension commitments, as well as the pension assets, should be included in the employer's balance sheet. The pension obligation would then be satisfied only as pension payments from the accumulated pension assets are made to the employees.

A CONCEPTUAL ILLUSTRATION

As a simple illustration of the concepts underlying a pension plan, consider the highly simplified pension plan of Burr Corporation, which adopted a pension plan for its single employee, A. Burr, 10 years before A. Burr retires at age 65. When Burr retires, the plan will provide for 10 equal annual payments of $10,000. The first pension payment begins one year after Burr retires. If we assume that the pension plan accumulated interest at 10% compounded annually, the present value (*PV*) of the pension agreement *as of the retirement date* is computed as follows:

$$PV = \$10,000 \times [pvoaf_{\overline{10}|\,10\%}]$$
$$= \$10,000\,(6.14457)$$
$$= \$61,446$$

Because A. Burr will receive $10,000 each year, we are dealing with an annuity computation. Because we want to know the value of that annuity at A. Burr's retirement date (after which the payments to him will begin), we compute the present value of the annuity. The appropriate present value factor, 6.14457, is taken from the 10% column, 10-period row of Table 6–4. To simplify this example, we assume that the payments are to be made annually, at the end of each year.

The amount of $61,446 must be accumulated in the pension plan by the retirement date for the plan to be fully funded at the employee's retirement. Burr Corporation has 10 years in which to accumulate this amount. If the corporation wants to accumulate $61,446 by making contributions annually for 10 years, with the first contribution beginning one year from today, the following equation will solve for the amount of the equal contributions (*R* = required annual contribution):

$$AOA = (R)\,[aoaf_{\overline{n}|\,i}]$$
$$R = \frac{\$61,446}{aoaf_{\overline{10}|\,10\%}}$$
$$R = \frac{\$61,446}{15.93742}$$
$$R = \$3,855.45$$

The amount of an ordinary annuity factor for 10 periods at 10% (15.93742) is taken from Table 6–3.

Burr Corporation can accumulate $61,446 in 10 years by making equal annual contributions of $3,855.45 into a fund that earns interest at 10% compounded annually. Exhibit 24–3 illustrates the accumulation and payment phases of the pension plan. The plan can pay out much more than the amount of the contributions because of the interest earned.

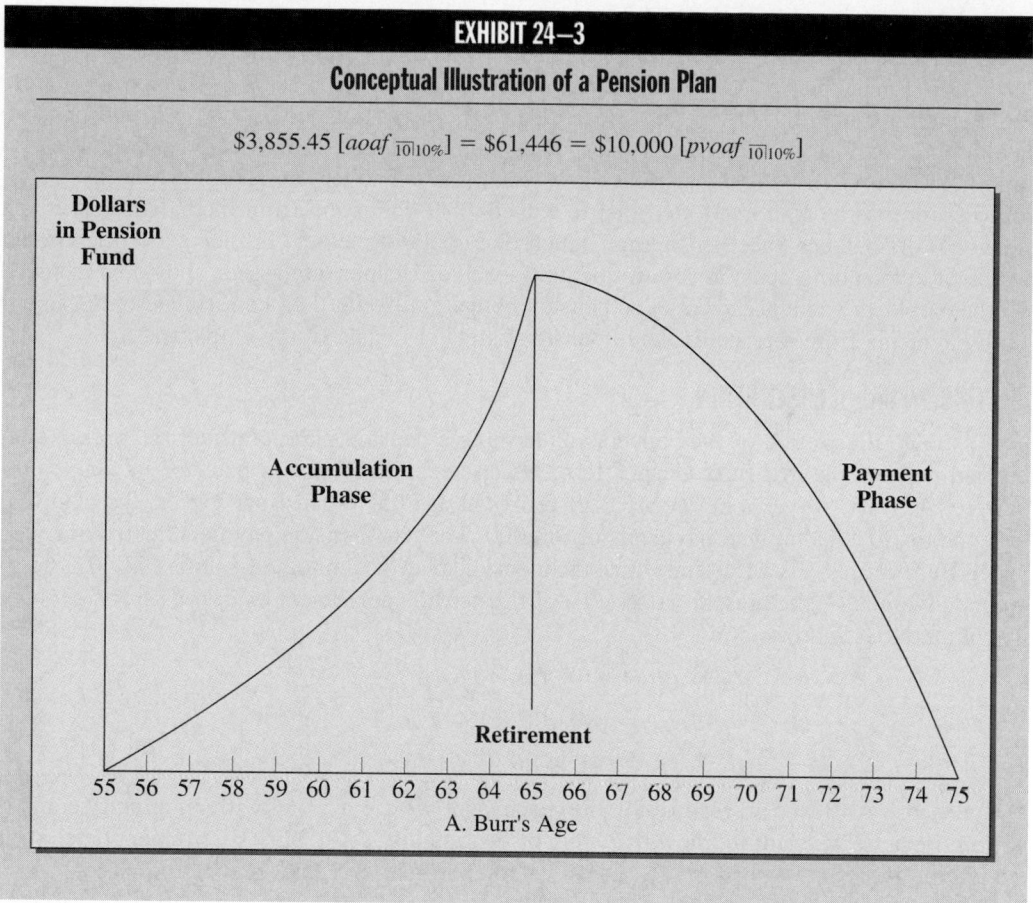

EXHIBIT 24–3

Conceptual Illustration of a Pension Plan

$$\$3,855.45\ [aoaf\ _{\overline{10}|10\%}] = \$61,446 = \$10,000\ [pvoaf\ _{\overline{10}|10\%}]$$

Notice in this example the uncertainties that are assumed away but that would have to be estimated in a real-life situation. We assumed that retirement would begin in 10 years, whereas retirements actually vary among employees and are usually not known until much closer to the retirement date. We assumed an exact payment ($10,000 per year) for an exact period of time (10 years). In reality, pension payments may be based on employees' incomes between the time benefits are earned and the time of retirement. Also, payments ordinarily continue until the employee's death rather than being limited to a specific number of years. Another uncertainty we assumed away was the interest rate on assets invested in the pension fund (10%). This rate varies, depending on investment policy, economic conditions, and other factors. In practice, actuarial assumptions must deal with these uncertainties that are inherent in pension plans.

MEASUREMENT OF PENSION EXPENSE

Recall from the discussion in Chapter 2 on financial accounting theory and in Chapter 21 on revenue measurement and income presentation that an objective of financial reporting by enterprises is to provide information about earnings and its components. Earnings are composed of revenues, expenses, gains, and losses. The cost incurred by a business each year for its pension commitments represents a type of operating expense. Recall further that **expenses** are defined in *Statement of Financial Accounting Concepts No. 6* as "outflows or other using up of assets or *incurrences of liabilities . . . during a period . . .* [and] represent actual or *expected* cash outflows that have occurred or *will eventuate* as a result of the enterprise's . . . operations."[1] (Emphasis added.)

Pension expense meets this definition and is considered a component of income during each accounting period, even though the person earning the pension may not receive benefits for many years. Most accountants agree on these conceptual issues; however, determining the *amount of pension expense* to be recognized during a period in applying the matching principle has created substantial controversy.

Matching

That an employee earns the right to a pension in the current period but may not receive the payment for many years causes uncertainties. A formal pension agreement may exist setting forth criteria for receiving a pension (e.g., years of service) and the basis on which pension benefits are computed (e.g., salary at date of retirement). Pension plans vary extensively, however, and reflect a "complex array of social concepts and pressures, legal considerations, actuarial techniques, income tax laws and regulations, business philosophies, and accounting concepts and practices."[2] Therefore, many uncertainties exist about the actual cost a business incurs each year due to its pension plan. Consequently, many estimates are required in applying a pension benefit formula to develop the amounts used for recording pension expense and to determine the amounts of related pensions assets and liabilities. Various items must be estimated to properly account for pension commitments, such as

1. Employee turnover rates.
2. Employee mortality ages.
3. Employee compensation levels.
4. Employee retirement ages.
5. Pension fund earnings.

Actuarial science is an applied branch of mathematics. Actuaries are skilled in studying and making estimates about pension commitments. Accountants commonly rely on actuaries to provide information for estimating pension expense and determining other information needed to appropriately present pensions in the financial statements of employers. Accountants are not expected to be experts in actuarial science. We are, however, required to understand basic principles upon which actuaries perform their work and to be in a position to understand and evaluate the reasonableness of assumptions made by actuaries.

A BRIEF HISTORY OF PENSION ACCOUNTING

Pension accounting has long been a controversial topic in the accounting profession and among users of accounting information. One of the earliest pronouncements on the subject, *Accounting Research Bulletin No. 47,* stated that pension costs based on current and future services "should be systematically accrued during the expected period of active service of the covered employees, generally upon the basis of actuarial calculations."[3] *ARB No. 47* provided little additional guidance to accountants and, consequently, accounting practices differed greatly.

In an attempt to clarify accounting principles and narrow the practices applicable to pension plans, the Accounting Principles Board (APB) issued *Opinion No. 8,* which superseded *ARB No. 47* and provided more precise guidance for practitioners. *APB Opinion No. 8* provided for a range of acceptable amounts that could be charged as pension expense. All APB members agreed that "the entire cost of benefit payments ultimately to be made should be

---

[1]*FASB Statement of Financial Accounting Concepts No. 6,* "Elements of Financial Statements," 1985, pars. 80–81.

[2]*APB Opinion No. 8,* "Accounting for the Cost of Pension Plans," 1966, par. 1.

[3]*Accounting Research Bulletin No. 47,* "Accounting for Costs of Pension Plans," 1956, par. 5.

charged against income subsequent to the adoption or amendment of a plan and that no portion of such costs should be charged directly against retained earnings."[4] Individual board members differed substantially, however, on how best to measure the annual cost of a pension plan. There was little controversy over the conceptual aspects of accounting for pensions, but disagreement arose in putting the concepts into practice. To account for this divergence, the APB allowed wide latitude in how the cost of a particular pension plan could be

Matching   measured and matched with revenue.

In the 1970s, concern arose in the accounting and investment communities over suspected deficiencies in financial accounting and reporting under *APB Opinion No. 8.* Specifically, the wide latitude allowed in the determination of pension expense and the potential for companies to have an unrecorded pension obligation were of primary concern. In 1980 the FASB issued *SFAS No. 36,* "Disclosure of Pension Information," to temporarily alleviate the pressure for improved financial reporting by requiring additional information in notes to

Disclosure   the financial statements.[5] At that time, no changes were made in the accounting procedures used in measuring and recording the elements of the financial statements. The FASB determined, however, that a major effort should be made to reevaluate pension accounting under *APB Opinion No. 8.*

After a great deal of effort and debate, the FASB issued *SFAS No. 87,* "Employers' Accounting for Pensions," in 1985.[6] This pronouncement substantially changed the financial accounting and reporting procedures for defined benefit pension plans by employers in ways that were intended to address the problems noted in the previous paragraph. The remainder of this chapter is based primarily on *SFAS No. 87* and, as such, deals with accounting procedures and reporting requirements that are relatively new to accounting practice.

AN OVERVIEW OF PENSION ACCOUNTING

Financial accounting and reporting of pension obligations involves a complicated process of determining the cost of offering pension benefits to employees and associating that cost with specific accounting periods. In addition, the presentation of financial position is very important, and a minimum pension liability and related intangible pension asset may be required. At this point, we discuss these requirements briefly and then develop them more completely in the remainder of this chapter.

The pension expense of an accounting period, referred to as **net periodic pension cost** in *SFAS No. 87,* is made up of several components that reflect different aspects of the employers' pension plan. The primary components of net periodic pension cost are identified as follows:

1. Service cost.
2. Interest cost.
3. Return on plan assets.
4. Recognition of gain or loss.
5. Amortization of unrecognized prior service cost.

In a defined benefit pension plan, the employer's estimate of its pension obligation results from many actuarial assumptions. Net periodic pension cost is based on the present value of the pension obligation as of a particular date, including all benefits attributed by the pension benefit formula to employee services rendered prior to that date. According to *SFAS No. 87,* this obligation, referred to as the **projected benefit obligation,** is measured using assumptions concerning future compensation levels if the pension benefits are to be based on those future levels.

---

[4]*APB Opinion No. 8,* par. 17.

[5]*FASB Statement of Financial Accounting Standards No. 36,* "Disclosure of Pension Information," 1980.

[6]*FASB Statement of Financial Accounting Standards No. 87,* "Employers' Accounting for Pensions," 1985.

Another important factor in calculating net periodic pension cost is the **fair value of plan assets.** Plan assets are investments—usually stocks and bonds—that have been purchased with the funds contributed into the pension plan. The fair value of the assets is the amount that the pension plan could reasonably expect to receive in the sale of its investment and, therefore, represents a measure of funds available to satisfy pension benefit requirements. Increases in the value of the plan assets represent reductions in the amounts that otherwise have to be contributed so that sufficient funds are available to satisfy pension demands. The projected benefit obligation, the fair value of plan assets, and other factors discussed later in this chapter interact to determine the net periodic pension cost to be recognized in the determination of net income for each accounting period.

When must a company recognize pension assets and liabilities in its financial statements? First, when the pension funding differs from the amount of pension expense recognized, an accrued pension cost (a liability representing underfunding) or a prepaid pension cost (an asset representing overfunding) is recognized. Second, if the amount of the pension obligation exceeds the fair value of the plan's assets, a minimum pension liability and a related intangible asset must be recognized. The **accumulated benefit obligation** is used to calculate pension liability, however, rather than the projected benefit obligation that is used to compute net periodic pension cost. The accumulated benefit obligation calculation differs from the projected benefit obligation in that the former does *not* take future salary levels into consideration.

In the following sections, we discuss the nature and illustrate the determination of the components of net periodic pension cost and illustrate the pension liabilities and assets resulting from the application of *SFAS No. 87* and the related financial statement disclosures. Our intent is to gain a conceptual understanding of pension accounting rather than a comprehensive understanding of all the technical aspects of *SFAS No. 87.* As you study the following material, the authors suggest that you pay particular attention to the definitions of important terms that are introduced throughout the discussion and the basic accounting principles that are being applied.

Disclosure

In this section, we use a simplified example to introduce the determination of important financial statement elements concerning pensions. We will limit our discussion to three of the components of net periodic pension cost—service, interest, and return on assets—deferring consideration of the other components and the recognition of the additional pension liability until a more advanced illustration is presented in a later section.

In approaching the study of pension accounting, a helpful frame of reference is to view the employer's interest in a pension plan as a subentity within a primary entity. The subentity is the pension plan; the primary entity is the employer company. Information is maintained about the subentity that does not appear in the financial statements of the primary entity. We refer to the specialized records of the subentity or interest in the pension plan as *memorandum* records because they are maintained outside the general ledger accounts of the primary company. As we will see, the memorandum records articulate directly with the financial statement elements of the primary entity and are very important even though they are labeled *memorandum.* The idea of the interest in a pension plan as a subentity of the primary entity is analogous to an equity-method investment that we covered in Chapter 10.

Note the relationships in the following illustration:

ACCOUNTING FOR PENSIONS: BASIC PRINCIPLES

Memorandum Records		**Financial Statement Element**
Fair Value of Plan Assets [*FVPA*]	− Projected Benefit Obligation [*PBO*]	= Prepaid/Accrued Pension Cost [*P/APC*]

In this simplified example, the relationship indicates that the fair value of the plan assets, less the company's projected benefit obligation, equals the prepaid/accrued pension cost that appears in the employer's financial statements. The first two items—fair value of plan assets and pension obligation—are memorandum records that do not appear in the balance sheet of the employer. The *FVPA* is analogous to an off-balance-sheet asset with a debit balance; the *PBO* is analogous to an off-balance sheet liability with a credit balance. They are offset and only the difference in the form of the prepaid/accrued pension cost is shown in the employer's balance sheet.

To develop these concepts further, we assume that Bean Company has a pension plan in which the fair value of plan assets is $15,000, the projected benefit obligation is $18,500, and thus the accrued pension cost (a liability) is $3,500. This is logical because even though the value of the assets and the pension obligation are both omitted from the employer's balance sheet, the employer has an unsatisfied obligation to the extent that the assets are insufficient to meet the obligation. The assumption is made that by transferring $15,000 of assets to a plan that will be used to satisfy pension benefits in the future, the employer has effectively provided for (already paid) $15,000 of the pension obligation and only $3,500 remains to be included among the employer's liabilities as a shortfall in funding of the pension plan.

We now assume that during the following year, service cost of $3,750 is incurred, interest cost at 10% is recognized, a return on plan assets of 10% is earned, and the employer contributes (funds) $3,000 to the pension plan. An analysis to accumulate information for the memorandum records and the financial statement elements appears in Exhibit 24–4.

Observe the relationship of the three components of net periodic pension cost in this illustration. Service and interest cost are combined and *reduced* by the return on the assets to determine net periodic pension cost. The following general journal entry records the pension plan transactions for the year, including the $3,000 funding:

Pension Expense ($3,750 + $1,850 − $1,500)	4,100	
Cash		3,000
Prepaid/Accrued Pension Cost ($4,600 − $3,500)		1,100

A liability increase of $1,100 is required because the pension expense of $4,100 was not completely funded. Combining the $3,500 liability balance at the beginning of the period with the $1,100 increase during the period, the prepaid/accrued pension cost appears in the balance sheet as a liability of $4,600 at the end of the period.

Let's look more closely at the three components of net periodic pension cost illustrated in this example. **Service cost** is the actuarial present value of benefits attributed by the pension benefit formula to employee services rendered during the period.[7] Determining the service cost for a period requires actuarial assumptions that reflect the time value of money (such as the discount or interest rate) and assumptions reflecting the probability of payment (such as mortality rates, turnover, attrition, and retirement age). This involves a complicated set of actuarial calculations for which accountants typically rely on actuaries. In the analysis in Exhibit 24–4, entry (a) recognizes service cost for the period as a component of pension expense (debit) and as an increase in the company's pension obligation (credit).

The **interest cost** component of net periodic pension cost is determined as the increase in the projected benefit obligation due to the passage of time. At any given time, the **projected benefit obligation** is the present value of all future retirement payments attributed by the pension benefit formula to employee services rendered prior to that date.[8] If the pension benefit formula specifies retirement benefits in terms of future salary levels, expected salaries are incorporated into the present value calculations. Notice that no assumption is

---

[7]*SFAS No. 87,* par. 21.
[8]*SFAS No. 87,* par. 264.

EXHIBIT 24-4

Analysis of Pension Accounting Information
Simplified Case

Memorandum Records	Beginning Balance*	Adjustments		Ending Balance*
		Debit	Credit	
Fair value of plan assets *(FVPA)*	$ 15,000	(c)$ 1,500		
		(d) 3,000		$ 19,500
Projected benefit obligation *(PBO)*	(18,500)		(a)$ 3,750	
			(b) 1,850	(24,100)
Financial Statement Elements				
Prepaid/Accrued Pension Cost	$ (3,500)	4,500	5,600	$ (4,600)

Pension Expense:			
Service	(a)	3,750	
Interest†	(b)	1,850	
Return on Assets‡			(c) 1,500
Cash			(d) 3,000
		$10,100	$10,100

Pension Expense:	
Service	$ 3,750
Interest	1,850
Return on assets	(1,500)
	$ 4,100

†Interest cost: $18,500 *(PBO)* × 10%
‡Return on plan assets: $15,000 *(FVPA)* × 10%
*Debit (Credit)

made about future employee services that have not yet been rendered. Rather, the assumption concerns only future compensation levels upon which benefits already earned will be based. Determination of the interest cost component requires accrual of interest at the rates equal to the assumed discount rates used in determining the service component of net periodic pension cost. Referring again to the analysis in Exhibit 24-4, entry (b) recognizes the interest cost component of pension expense (debit) and the related increase in the pension obligation (credit).

Plan assets are stocks, bonds, and other investments that have been transferred to the pension fund or have been acquired with cash that has been transferred to the fund. To qualify as a plan asset, the investment must have been segregated in a pension fund and not be available for use by management except for the payment of pension benefits. The **return on plan assets** is a reduction in the amount of net periodic pension cost; it is subtracted from the service and interest components because the return reduces the employer's net cash outflow required to satisfy the pension obligation. In Exhibit 24-4, the return is recognized in entry (c) as a reduction in pension expense (credit), indicating the offset against the service and interest components; also the fair value of plan assets is increased (debit) to indicate the enhanced value of the assets based on earnings during the year.

Entry (d) in Exhibit 24–4 records the cash payment into the pension plan, which increases the fair value of the assets (debit) and reduces cash (credit).

In this simple illustration, we have assumed that the obligation exceeded the value of the assets and that the pension expense of the period was not fully funded. We could have made alternate assumptions. For example, we could have assumed that the value of the assets in the plan exceeded the obligation and that the company included a prepaid pension cost (asset) in its balance sheet rather than an accrued pension cost (liability). We could have assumed overfunding of the pension expense rather than underfunding. These changes would not alter the basic principles illustrated in the example. Records of the value of the plan assets and the pension obligation are maintained on a memorandum basis and only the prepaid/accrued pension cost item appears in the employer's balance sheet. The net periodic pension cost, or pension expense, appears in the employer's income statement.

We have omitted two important components of net periodic pension cost in this illustration—recognition of gain or loss and amortization of unrecognized prior service cost—and we have not yet encountered the recording of the additional pension liability introduced earlier. We explain these complexities in the more advanced discussion and examples that appear in the following section.

ADDITIONAL PENSION ACCOUNTING CONSIDERATIONS

In the illustration in the previous section, we discussed the interaction of the service, interest, and return on assets components of net periodic pension cost. In this section, we identify two more components and illustrate their application: recognition of gain or loss, and amortization of unrecognized prior service cost. At that point, we will have completed our discussion of the five components of net periodic pension cost and we will summarize the calculation of this important financial statement element, after which we discuss and illustrate the recording of an additional pension liability.

RECOGNITION OF GAIN OR LOSS

Gains and losses represent changes in the amount of the projected benefit obligation and/or the value of plan assets that result from experience that differs from projections. They include amounts that have been realized (for example, by sale of a security) as well as amounts that have not been realized (for example, market-value changes in a security that has not yet been sold).

Recognition of gain or loss is required as a component of net periodic pension cost for a year if, *at the beginning of the year,* the absolute value of the net unrecognized gain or loss exceeds 10% of the greater of the projected benefit obligation or the value of the plan assets.

Materiality This 10% amount is referred to as the **corridor** in *SFAS No. 87* and represents a materiality threshold for determining when gains and losses are sufficiently large to require recognition. If accumulated gains or losses are less than the amount of the corridor, they are not recognized in net periodic pension cost for that particular accounting period. The rationale for this procedure is that gains and losses associated with pension plans offset over time and ordinarily should not be included in net periodic pension cost due to the amount of volatility they would introduce. Only when the unrecognized amount of gain or loss reaches a high level (i.e., exceeds the corridor) does this element of net periodic pension cost come into play.

If recognition of gain or loss is required, the amount is the excess of the accumulated unrecognized gain or loss over the corridor amount divided by the average remaining service period of active employees expected to receive benefits from the plan.[9] If a *gain* is being rec-

---

[9]*SFAS No. 87,* par. 32.

EXHIBIT 24-5

Lancaster, Inc.
Gain/Loss Recognition

	1994			1995			1996		
	Expected	Actual	Accumulated Gain/Loss	Expected	Actual	Accumulated Gain/Loss	Expected	Actual	Accumulated Gain/Loss
Projected benefit obligation	$165,000	$175,000	$10,000 L						
Fair value of plan assets	$165,000	$185,000	20,000 G						
			$10,000 G						
Recognition*			–0–			$10,000 G			
Projected benefit obligation				$190,000	$195,000	5,000 L			
Fair value of plan assets				$195,000	$225,000	30,000 G			
						$35,000 G			
Recognition*						(1,250)			$ 33,750 G
Projected benefit obligation							$215,000	$200,000	15,000 G
Fair value of plan assets							$240,000	$150,000	90,000 L
									$ 41,250 L
Recognition*									(2,125)
Unrecognized Loss to 1997									$ 39,125 L

---

*Recognition calculations:

Year	Corridor	Accumulated Gain/Loss	Excess of Gain/Loss over Corridor	Recognition†
1994	10% × $185,000 = $18,500	$10,000 G	–0–	–0–
1995	10% × $225,000 = $22,500	$35,000 G	$12,500	$1,250
1996	10% × $200,000 = $20,000	$41,250 L	$21,250	2,125

†(Excess of Gain/Loss over corridor)/10

---

ognized, net periodic pension cost is *reduced* by the amount; if a *loss* is being recognized, net periodic pension cost is *increased* by the amount.

A common instance of gain or loss occurs when a change in the value of plan assets differs from the expected return on those assets.[10] The expected return on plan assets gives rise to the return-on-plan-assets component of net periodic pension cost. But when changes in the value of the plan assets are other than the expected return, then the recognition-of-gain-or-loss component of net periodic pension cost is called for if the corridor test is met. In the same manner, assumptions upon which the projected benefit obligation is based may prove inaccurate and may require adjustment. As a result of these adjustments to the value of plan assets and to the projected benefit obligation, an accumulated net gain or loss will be continuously carried forward from one accounting period to the next, with recognition of part of that amount as a component of net periodic pension cost only if the corridor (materiality) test is met.   **Materiality**

To illustrate the recognition of gain or loss in determining net periodic pension cost, we assume the projected benefit obligation and fair value of plan assets amounts in Exhibit 24-5

---

[10]Specifically, *SFAS No. 87* indicates that the expected return on plan assets shall be computed on the basis of the expected long-term rate of return on plan assets and the *market-related value of plan assets.* The market-related value of plan assets may be either the fair value or a calculated value that recognizes changes in fair value in a systematic and rational manner over not more than five years (*SFAS No. 87,* par. 30). In this text, we assume for illustration purposes that the expected long-term rate of return is based on the fair value of the plan assets.

for Lancaster, Inc., *at the beginning of* 1994, 1995, and 1996. For simplicity, we also assume that prior to 1994 no accumulated gain or loss existed.

For 1994, the actual amount of the projected benefit obligation (*PBO*) exceeds the expected amount by $10,000 ($175,000 − $165,000). Because the actual obligation is greater than expected, this represents a loss in the accumulated gain/loss column. Conversely, the fair value of plan assets ($185,000) exceeds their expected value ($165,000) by $20,000, a gain. Netting the gain and loss results in an accumulated $10,000 gain. Referring to the recognition calculation at the bottom of Exhibit 24–5, no recognition is required in 1994 because the $10,000 accumulated gain is not as large as the corridor. In this year, the corridor is determined as 10% of the fair value of plan assets because their amount exceeds the projected benefit obligation. In other words, applying the corridor test, the accumulated gain is

Materiality not a sufficiently material amount to require recognition.

Moving to 1995, the $10,000 gain is carried forward from 1994 and combined with a $5,000 loss on the projected benefit obligation and a $30,000 gain on the fair value of plan assets for a net gain of $35,000. In 1995, the corridor is determined as 10% of the fair value of plan assets, because that amount ($225,000) exceeds the projected benefit obligation

Materiality ($195,000). In this case, the accumulated gain is material and the difference between that accumulated gain and the corridor is recognized over the estimated remaining service life of active employees. We use an assumed 10 years in this illustration. The $1,250 amount requiring recognition reduces net periodic pension cost because it represents a gain.

Continuing to 1996, a similar process is followed. The unrecognized gain of $33,750 is carried forward and combined with the $15,000 gain on the projected benefit obligation and the $90,000 loss on the fair value of plan assets to render an accumulated unrecognized loss of $41,250. Notice that in 1996, the corridor is defined as 10% of the projected benefit obligation (rather than the fair value of plan assets as in 1994 and 1995) because of its higher dollar amount. Because a loss is being recognized, the $2,125 calculated amount results in an increase in net periodic pension cost.

To summarize the impact of these calculations, gains and losses are an expected part of pension accounting because of the inherent uncertainty of the variables that make up the fair value of plan assets and the projected benefit obligation. In addition, over time, gains and losses tend to offset and, effectively, cancel out. Only when the accumulated unrecognized amount reaches a size that is considered material is a part of the gain or loss included as a

Materiality component in net periodic pension cost. The corridor test is used to make this materiality assessment. If gain recognition is appropriate, net periodic pension cost is reduced; if loss recognition is appropriate, net periodic pension cost is increased. Whether gain or loss is recognized, the accumulated unrecognized amount is carried forward to the next accounting period.

AMORTIZATION OF UNRECOGNIZED PRIOR SERVICE COST

New or amended pension plans often include provisions that grant increased benefits to employees based on services rendered before the change. The cost of such amendments to employers is referred to as **prior service cost**.[11] Despite their association with past services, retroactive adjustments in the employer's pension obligation are granted with the expectation that the employer will realize benefits in the future. For example, in union contract negotiations, management may agree to a specified increase in employee compensation and allow the union to decide how it should be applied. Granting increased benefits with a plan amendment on the basis of past services is logical because the employer expects increased employee loyalty and quality of performance in the future.

---

[11]*SFAS No. 87,* par. 264.

The amount of prior service cost associated with a new plan or a plan amendment is the increase in the projected benefit obligation resulting from the change. Rather than include the entire amount of prior service cost in the net periodic pension cost in the period of the change, the FASB specifies that it is to be *amortized over certain periods after the change.* Specifically, prior service cost is amortized by assigning an equal amount to each future period of service of each employee active at the date of the change who is expected to receive plan benefits.

While this amortization approach may involve a complicated set of calculations, the following example serves to illustrate an amortization scheme consistent with the above requirement. We shall assume that Lumpkin, Inc., amends its pension plan such that a prior service cost of $165,000 is incurred (i.e., the amendment increases the projected benefit obligation by $165,000). This amendment was made on January 1, 1994. The company has 10 employees and one will retire at the end of each year beginning in 1994. The calculations described in Exhibit 24–6 satisfy the amortization requirements of *SFAS No 87.*

Applying a procedure similar to the sum-of-the years'-digits method of depreciation, the $165,000 of prior service cost is amortized by a fraction, the numerator of which is the columnar total indicating the number of employees active in that particular year and the denominator of which is the total of the column of Future Service Years Remaining. For this example, prior service cost amortization for 1994 (Year 1) would be

$$10/55 \times \$165,000 = \$30,000$$

For 1995 (Year 2), amortization would be

$$9/55 \times \$165,000 = \$27,000$$

This procedure is continued until the $165,000 is completely amortized at the end of the 10th year in which 1/55 of the $165,000, or $3,000, is amortized.

To simplify the computation, the FASB allows the consistent use of alternative amortization plans—*if they more rapidly reduce* the unrecognized cost of retroactive amendments. In the previous example, Lumpkin, Inc., might choose to amortize the $165,000 prior

Consistency

EXHIBIT 24–6

Amortization of Prior Service Cost

Employee	Future Service Years Remaining	Years									
		1	2	3	4	5	6	7	8	9	10
A	1	1									
B	2	1	1								
C	3	1	1	1							
D	4	1	1	1	1						
E	5	1	1	1	1	1					
F	6	1	1	1	1	1	1				
G	7	1	1	1	1	1	1	1			
H	8	1	1	1	1	1	1	1	1		
I	9	1	1	1	1	1	1	1	1	1	
J	10	1	1	1	1	1	1	1	1	1	1
	55	10	9	8	7	6	5	4	3	2	1

Amortization fractions:
Year 1   10/55
Year 2   9/55
. . .
Year 10   1/55

service cost over a five-year period at the rate of $33,000 per year ($165,000/5 years = $33,000) rather than use the procedure outlined in Exhibit 24–6. For simplicity, in this text and in the assignment material at the end of the chapter, we assume a simplified average service life unless otherwise indicated.

SUMMARY OF COMPONENTS OF NET PERIODIC PENSION COST

Now that we have completed our discussion of recognition of gains and losses and amortization of prior service cost, we are able to summarize the five components of net periodic pension cost as follows:

Component	Probable Impact on Net Periodic Pension Cost
Service	Increase
Interest	Increase
Return on assets	Decrease
Recognition of gain or loss	Decrease (if gain)
	Increase (if loss)
Amortization of prior service cost	Increase

After we consider the recording of an additional pension liability in the following section, we end the chapter with a comprehensive multiple-year example that demonstrates the interaction of these five components in arriving at the annual pension expense (i.e., net periodic pension cost) and in updating the memorandum pension records that must be maintained by companies sponsoring pension plans for their employees.

RECOGNITION OF PENSION ASSETS AND LIABILITIES

Management may decide to fund the pension plan at the same rate as net periodic pension cost is recognized. Alternatively, the plan may be funded more rapidly or less rapidly than the recognition of the net periodic pension cost. If the expense recognized exceeds the amount funded, a liability arises; if the expense recognized is less than the amount funded, an asset arises.

To illustrate, assume that Wallen Company determines its net periodic pension cost for 1995 to be $200,000; the company's policy is to fund the amount of expense that is recognized. The general journal entry to record the expense and funding is as follows:

Pension Expense	200,000	
Cash		200,000

Rather than fully funding the amount of expense recognized, let's assume that Wallen funds only $175,000 of the expense. The entry to record the recognition of pension expense, the funding, and the resulting liability is as follows:

Pension Expense	200,000	
Cash		175,000
Prepaid/Accrued Pension Cost		25,000

On the other hand, if the company had funded $225,000, the entry would be as follows:

Pension Expense	200,000	
Prepaid/Accrued Pension Cost	25,000	
Cash		225,000

In addition to the prepaid/accrued pension cost that may be recognized because the expense is over- or underfunded, an *additional liability* may also be required. If, at the end of the accounting period, the *accumulated benefit obligation* exceeds the fair value of the plan assets, the employer must include a liability equal to the unfunded accumulated benefit obligation in the balance sheet. The amount of the liability recorded because of this situation is adjusted by the amount of the prepaid/accrued pension cost that has already been recorded as a result of the over- or underfunding of the net periodic pension cost. If this additional liability is required, an equal amount is usually recorded as an intangible asset. The amount of the intangible asset, however, is limited to the amount of unrecognized prior service cost. If the amount of liability that must be recorded exceeds the amount of the intangible asset, the excess is charged to a special stockholders' equity account with a negative balance.[12]

The **accumulated benefit obligation** referred to in the previous paragraph is the actuarial present value of benefits attributed by the pension benefit formula to employee services rendered before a specified date and based on employee services and compensation prior to that date. It differs from the projected benefit obligation, referred to earlier while discussing net periodic pension cost, in that the accumulated benefit obligation includes *no assumption about future compensation levels.*[13]

In the following illustration, we demonstrate the recognition of pension assets and liabilities as described above.[14] Turpen Manufacturing Company maintains a defined benefit pension plan for its employees. The company has accumulated the following information concerning that plan as of December 31, 1994, 1995, and 1996, the end of the company's financial reporting period.

	At December 31		
	1994	1995	1996
		(amounts in thousands)	
Plan assets at fair value	$1,200	$1,304	$1,450
Accumulated benefit obligation	1,320	1,395	1,480
Net periodic pension cost	141	144	151
Contribution made by company	125	186	120
Unrecognized prior service cost	92	86	80

First, we record the net periodic pension cost (pension expense) and the company's contribution to the plan for 1994:

Dec. 31, 1994	Pension Expense	141	
	Cash		125
	Prepaid/Accrued Pension Cost		16

Neither the assets invested in the pension fund ($1,200) nor the accumulated benefit obligation to employees ($1,320) will appear on the employer's balance sheet. The funding of net periodic pension cost is recorded *as if the employer's responsibility to employees has been satisfied,* except to the extent that funding of the expense has not taken place ($16). This is referred to as the *offsetting* feature of accounting for pensions and is criticized by some as understating both the employer's assets (amounts in the pension fund) and liabilities (obligation for future pension benefits).

Next, we determine whether the situation requires the recording of an additional liability. We do this by comparing the accumulated benefit obligation with the fair value of the plan assets:

Accumulated benefit obligation	$1,320
Plan assets at fair value	1,200
Required liability	$ 120

Remember that we already have a liability balance (Prepaid/Accrued Pension Cost) of $16. To include the required liability of $120, we must record $104 as an *additional liability*

---

[12]*SFAS No. 87,* par. 36–37.

[13]*SFAS No. 87,* par. 264.

[14]This example is a modified version of Illustration 4 of Appendix B of *SFAS No. 87.*

($120 − $16 = $104). As stated earlier, when we record this liability, we establish an intangible asset; that intangible asset, however, is limited to the amount of the unrecognized prior service cost ($92). Any excess amount of the liability is recorded in a negative stockholders' account, as follows:

Dec. 31, 1994	Intangible Pension Asset	92	
	Excess of Additional Pension Liability		
	over Unrecognized Prior Service Cost	12	
	($104 − $92)		
	Additional Pension Liability		104

This entry is required because the accumulated benefit obligation exceeds the fair value of the plan assets by more than $16. If the fair value of the plan assets had been greater than the accumulated benefit obligations, or if the accumulated benefit obligation had exceeded the fair value of plan assets by $16 or less, no additional liability would be required.

The direct charge (debit) to stockholders' equity represents a reduction in the equity of owners that is not recognized as part of net income. Recall that in Chapter 10 we discussed a similar adjustment when the aggregate market value of investments classified as available-for-sale fell below their aggregate cost. We reduced stockholders' equity directly and simultaneously reduced the Investments account to market value. The adjustment described here for pensions is similar to that adjustment in terms of its impact on stockholders' equity. The recognition of the additional liability is strictly a balance sheet procedure. If the amount of the additional liability is equal to or less than the amount of unrecognized prior service cost, no adjustment to stockholders' equity is required.

As a result of these entries, we will include pension expense of $141 in the income statement. In the balance sheet, we will have the following items:

Assets	
Intangible pension asset	$92
Liabilities	
Net pension liability	120
Stockholders' equity	
Excess of additional pension liability over unrecognized	
prior service cost	(12)

The net pension liability is the total of the accrued pension cost and the additional pension liability ($16 + $104 = $120). This liability will ordinarily be noncurrent; if the company intends to fund a portion of it during the next year, that portion is current.

Now, let's continue our example by recording the pension information for 1995. Again, we must record pension expense and funding:

Dec. 31, 1995	Pension Expense	144	
	Prepaid/Accrued Pension Cost	42	
	Cash		186

Observe that the Prepaid/Accrued Pension Cost now has a debit balance of $26, resulting from the combination of the $42 debit of 1995 and the $16 credit of 1994 ($42 − $16 = $26). This represents a change from a net liability position in 1994 to a net asset position in 1995.

Again we determine whether an additional liability is required and, if so, the amount of that liability. We do that by comparing the accumulated benefit obligation with the fair value of plan assets.

Accumulated benefit obligation	$1,395
Plan assets at fair value	1,304
Required liability	$ 91

Remember that we have a $26 *debit balance* in Prepaid/Accrued Pension Cost, representing a *net asset* position. To include a net liability of $91, we must combine the additional liability and the Prepaid/Accrued Pension Cost, and then apply the resulting subtotal to the net liability; the result is that we must increase the additional pension liability by $13 in 1995.

Net liability required		$91
Existing balances		
Additional pension liability	$104	
Prepaid/accrued pension cost	(26)	78
1995 *increase* in additional liability		$13

Because the intangible asset, which has a balance of $92, cannot exceed the amount of unrecognized prior pension cost, it must be reduced by $6 ($92 − $86 = $6). The entry to record these items is as follows:

Dec. 31, 1995 Excess of Additional Pension Liability Over		
Unrecognized Prior Service Cost	19	
Intangible Pension Asset		6
Additional Pension Liability		13

In the 1995 income statement, we will include pension expense of $144. The balance sheet will include the following pension items:

Assets	
Intangible pension asset	$86*
Liabilities	
Net pension liability	91[†]
Stockholders' equity	
Excess of additional pension liability over unrecognized prior service cost	(31)[‡]

---

*$92 − $6 = $86
[†][($104 + $13) − $26] = $91
[‡]$(12) + $(19) = $(31)

We will now complete our example of recording pension assets and liabilities by recording the appropriate journal entries for 1996. Again, we record the recognition of pension expense and the related funding, as follows:

Dec. 31, 1996 Pension Expense	151	
Cash		120
Prepaid/Accrued Pension Cost		31

Prepaid/Accrued Pension Cost now has a $5 credit (liability) balance: $31 − $26 = $5. As before, we determine the need for an additional liability by comparing the accumulated benefit obligation with the fair value of plan assets:

Accumulated benefit obligation	$1,480
Plan assets at fair value	1,450
Required liability	$ 30

In 1996 the liability must be *reduced* by $92, determined as follows:

Net liability required		$ 30
Existing balances		
Additional pension liability	$117	
Prepaid/accrued pension cost	5	(122)
1996 *decrease* in additional liability		$ 92

We reduce the liability by $92, eliminate the negative stockholders' equity account, and reduce the intangible pension asset simultaneously as follows:

Dec. 31, 1996	Additional Pension Liability	92	
	Excess of Additional Pension Liability Over		
	Unrecognized Prior Service Cost		31
	Intangible Pension Asset		61

With this adjustment, the intangible pension asset balance is $25 ($86 − $61 = $25), less than the amount of unrecognized prior service cost of $80.

In the 1996 income statement, we include $151 of pension expense and the balance sheet will include the following:

Assets	
Intangible pension asset	$25*
Liabilities	
Net pension liability	30†

---

*$86 − $61 = $25
†[($117 − $92) + $5] = $30

To summarize, the Prepaid/Accrued Pension Cost account is a cumulative difference between the expense recognized and the amount funded. The account has a debit balance, representing an asset, when pension expense has been *overfunded;* it has a credit balance, representing a liability, when pension expense has been *underfunded.* An additional liability is recognized when, at the end of the accounting period, the accumulated benefit obligation exceeds the fair value of the plan assets by more than the total of existing recorded pension liabilities. In recognizing an additional pension liability, we establish or increase an intangible pension asset that is limited in amount to the unrecognized prior service cost. Any reconciling difference is adjusted to the negative stockholders' equity valuation account.

What is the logic behind the recording of an intangible pension asset when an additional pension liability is required? Recall that companies grant retroactive credit when a pension plan is amended because of the expectation of future services from employees. By granting the plan amendment retroactively, the company is purchasing something of future value in terms of employee motivation, morale, and other factors (i.e., "employee goodwill"). The intangible asset is a measure of that value, but it is limited to the amount of prior service cost, which is an actuarial computation of the cost of that asset.

The intangible pension asset is not amortized directly as we would amortize other intangible assets. The amount of the intangible pension asset may vary considerably from year to year as we compare the accumulated benefit obligation and the fair value of plan assets at the end of each year and adjust for the amount of prepaid/accrued pension cost. As in the previous example, the amount may go up or down. Remember, however, that the intangible pension asset balance cannot exceed the unamortized balance of prior service cost. The intangible pension asset will eventually be eliminated as the prior service cost is amortized as part of net periodic pension cost over the remaining service period of employees expected to benefit from the plan amendment. In any one period, however, the change in the intangible pension asset and the amortization of prior service cost component of net periodic pension cost will not necessarily be the same.

EXPANDED PENSION RELATIONSHIPS

Now that we have covered the five primary components of net periodic pension cost and we have discussed prior service costs and the recognition of gains and losses, we can expand the relationships introduced earlier. Remember that pension expense is the result of the netting of several diverse components. Also, the difference between the fair value of the plan assets and the projected benefit obligation equals the balance sheet item, prepaid/accrued pension cost. These conclusions were reached, however, before we added prior service costs and the recognition of gains and losses to our body of knowledge. Remember also that when there are prior service costs, an *unamortized balance exists,* and when there are gains and losses, an *accumulated unrecognized balance exists.* These become part of the memorandum records that are maintained by the employer but do not appear in the employer's financial statements.

We expand our definition of net periodic pension cost or pension expense as follows:

$$\text{Net Periodic Pension Cost} \atop \text{(Pension Expense)} = \left[{\text{Service Cost} + \text{Interest Cost} - \text{Return on Plan Assets} \pm \atop \text{Loss or Gain Recognition} + \text{Prior Service Cost Amortization}} \right]$$

The relationship of the memorandum records that must be kept for the pension plan and the accounts on the employer's financial statements can be expanded:

Memorandum Records				Financial Statement Element

$$\text{Fair Value of} \atop \text{Plan Assets} - \left[{\text{Projected Benefit} \atop \text{Obligation}} - {\text{Unamortized Prior} \atop \text{Service Cost}} \right] \pm {\text{Unrecognized} \atop \text{Loss or Gain}} = {\text{Prepaid/Accrued} \atop \text{Pension Cost}}$$

This relationship indicates that in the memorandum records, the fair value of plan assets, less the projected benefit obligation reduced by the unamortized prior service cost, adjusted up or down for the unrecognized loss or gain, equal the balance sheet element, prepaid/accrued pension cost. The amount representing unamortized prior service cost is included in the projected benefit obligation, but it has not yet been recognized in net periodic pension cost. The projected benefit obligation must be reduced by the unamortized balance to reconcile the memorandum records with the prepaid/accrued pension cost account. The same is true for the unrecognized loss or gain, which represents an adjustment to either the fair value of plan assets, the projected benefit obligation, or both.

Analytically, the fair value of plan assets can be viewed as an unrecorded (off-balance-sheet) asset with a debit balance and the projected benefit obligation as an unrecorded (off-balance-sheet) liability with a credit balance. Similarly, unamortized prior service cost can be viewed as a contra liability to the projected benefit obligation that is awaiting amortization and, thus, has a debit balance. Unrecognized loss or gain represents either a debit balance (unrecognized loss) or credit balance (unrecognized gain) that awaits recognition in a manner similar to unamortized prior service cost. Making these analogies of the memorandum records with similar financial statement elements, including the assumption of normal debit and credit balances, helps explain the mechanics underlying the relationship of the memorandum records and the financial statement element, prepaid/accrued pension cost.

In this section, we work through a comprehensive two-year illustration for Roberts Company that summarizes many of the principles in this chapter. The illustration demonstrates the relationship of the five primary components of net periodic pension cost and the articulation of the memorandum records with the financial statement elements related to the employer's pension plan.

We will again use a worksheet approach that is an expanded version of the one found in Exhibit 24–4. The authors suggest that you study the worksheets in Exhibits 24–7 and 24–8 in conjunction with the related text discussion, which provides the numbers in the worksheet as well as the underlying explanation. Each worksheet begins with a beginning balance. Notice that the column starts with the fair value of plan assets, subtracts the projected benefit obligation, adds unamortized prior service cost and adds or subtracts unrecognized losses or gains, respectively.

A COMPREHENSIVE PENSION ACCOUNTING ILLUSTRATION

		EXHIBIT 24–7		

Analysis of Roberts Company Pension Accounting Information
Advanced Case—Year 1

Memorandum Records	Beginning Balance*	Adjustments Debit	Adjustments Credit	Ending Balance*
Fair value of plan assets	$ 50,000	(c)$ 2,000 (f) 20,000	(h)$17,500	$ 54,500
Projected benefit obligation	(75,000)	(h) 17,500	(a) 12,000 (b) 7,500 (g) 15,000	(92,000)
Unamortized prior service cost	15,000		(d) 1,000	14,000
Unrecognized loss (gain)	(9,000)	(c) 3,000 (e) 100 (g) 15,000		9,100
Financial Statement Elements				
Prepaid/Accrued Pension Cost	$(19,000)	57,600	53,000	$(14,400)

Pension Expense:	Debit	Credit
Service	(a) 12,000	
Interest	(b) 7,500	
Return on assets		(c) 5,000
Prior service cost	(d) 1,000	
Gain		(e) 100
Cash		(f) 20,000
	$78,100	$78,100

Key (see text pp. 1114–1116):
  (a) Service cost recognition
  (b) Interest cost recognition
  (c) Return on asset recognition
  (d) Amortization of prior
       service cost
  (e) Recognition of gain
  (f) Funding of pension plan
  (g) Adjustment of projected
       benefit obligation
  (h) Payment of benefits

Pension Expense:	
Service	$ 12,000
Interest	7,500
Return on assets	(5,000)
Prior service cost	1,000
Gain	(100)
	$ 15,400

*Debit (Credit)

We will now work through the adjustments in the worksheet, following the key letters indicated in Exhibit 24–7.

YEAR 1 ANALYSIS

(a) Recognition of Service Cost

Service cost of $12,000 (assumed) is recorded by debiting pension expense and crediting the projected benefit obligation to recognize the increased obligation of the employer for employee services rendered in the current period.

(b) Recognition of Interest Cost

Interest cost is recognized at 10% (assumed) on the projected benefit obligation at the beginning of the year: $75,000 × 10% = $7,500. Pension expense is debited and the projected benefit obligation is credited.

(c) Recognition of Return on Assets

Recall that the return on asset component of net periodic pension cost is the expected return. We assume in this example that the expected return on the assets is 10%, and the actual return was only $2,000 for the year:

Expected return ($50,000 × 10%)	$5,000
Actual return	(2,000)
Unexpected loss	$3,000

We record the return by debiting the assets for the $2,000 increase in value, debiting the unrecognized loss (gain) item for the $3,000 loss and crediting pension expense for the $5,000 expected return.

(d) Amortization of Prior Service Cost

Prior service cost is being amortized over the remaining service period of active employees who will benefit from the plan amendment, 15 years in this case (assumed). Amortization is $1,000, determined as follows: $15,000/15 = $1,000. Pension expense is debited and unamortized prior service cost is credited.

(e) Recognition of Gain

Recall that gain or loss is recognized only if the unrecognized amount *at the beginning of the year* exceeds the corridor, which is 10% of the greater of the fair value of the plan assets or the projected benefit obligation. In this case, the corridor is defined by the projected benefit obligation, and we will recognize over 15 years (assumed):

Unrecognized gain	$9,000
Corridor ($75,000 × 10%)	(7,500)
Gain subject to recognition	$1,500
Recognized in current year ($1,500/15)	$ 100

The partial gain is recognized by debiting the unrecognized gain and crediting pension expense.

(f) Funding of Pension Plan

We make the assumption that the company funds $20,000 by transferring cash to the pension fund trustee. The entry is a debit to the fair value of plan assets and a credit to cash.

(g) Adjustment to Projected Benefit Obligation

Adjustment to the projected benefit obligation is required when assumptions made do not parallel actual experience. In this case, we assume that the company's obligation increased $15,000 (i.e., a loss) because of revisions in the actuarial assumptions used to compute the projected benefit obligation. The adjustment is recorded by debiting the unrecognized loss (gain) and crediting the projected benefit obligation.

(h) Payment of Benefits

When retirees receive benefits, the memorandum accounts are adjusted but the financial statements of the employer are unaffected. When $17,500 (assumed) of benefits is paid, for example, the projected benefit obligation is debited (reduced) and the fair value of plan assets is credited (reduced).

YEAR 1 SUMMARY

We are now ready to summarize our worksheet information in the form of a journal entry to record pension expense for the year. Combining the components of net periodic pension cost, we see that the expense is $15,400, cash paid is $20,000, and the entry to record the pension plan for the year is as follows:

Pension Expense	15,400	
Prepaid/Accrued Pension Cost	4,600	
Cash		20,000

Observe that $4,600 is exactly the amount required to reconcile the beginning and ending balance of the Prepaid/Accrued Pension Cost in Exhibit 24–7: $19,000 − $14,400 = $4,600.

When we began this illustration, we did not consider the issue of the additional pension liability. Assuming that the accumulated benefit obligation at the beginning of the year was $65,000 (logically less than the projected benefit obligation), we determine the liability status at that time as follows:

Fair value of plan assets	$ 50,000
Accumulated benefit obligation	(65,000)
Required minimum pension liability	($15,000)
Prepaid/accrued pension cost	($19,000)

On the basis of these numbers, no additional liability was required at the end of the previous year because a sufficient liability was already in the balance sheet.

We will now assume that at the end of the year, the accumulated benefit obligation is $80,000. An analysis similar to the one just given is as follows:

Accumulated benefit obligation	$80,000
Fair value of plan assets	(54,500)
Minimum required liability	$25,500
Present liability position:	
Prepaid/accrued pension liability	(14,400)
Required additional liability	$11,100

The amount of the intangible asset that can be established is limited to the amount of unamortized prior service cost of $14,000. Because we must record an additional liability of only $11,100, we can record the additional liability as follows:

Intangible Pension Asset	11,100	
Additional Pension Liability		11,100

When this liability is combined with the $14,400 Prepaid/Accrued Pension Cost already in the balance sheet, the total liability is the difference between the accumulated benefit obligation and the fair value of plan assets: $14,400 + $11,100 = $25,500.

YEAR 2 ANALYSIS

For the second year of the Roberts Company example, we turn our attention to the pension information analysis in Exhibit 24–8. Observe that the beginning balances are the ending balances in Exhibit 24–7. Several of the adjustments are identical to those for year 1, except for different assumed amounts: (a) service cost of $25,000; (b) interest on the projected benefit obligation at 10%, or $9,200; (d) amortization of prior service cost at $1,000; (f) funding of the pension plan at $25,000; and (h) payment of pension benefits at $21,750.

We will now focus our attention to the worksheet adjustments that differ from those in the first year of the Roberts Company example.

EXHIBIT 24–8

Analysis of Roberts Company Pension Accounting Information
Advanced Case—Year 2

Memorandum Records	Beginning Balance*	Adjustments Debit	Adjustments Credit	Ending Balance*
Fair value of plan assets	$ 54,500	(c)$ 7,000	(h)$21,750	$ 64,750
		(f) 25,000		
Projected benefit obligation	(92,000)	(g) 2,000	(a) 25,000	
		(h) 21,750	(b) 9,200	(102,450)
Unamortized prior service cost	14,000		(d) 1,000	13,000
Unrecognized loss (gain)	9,100		(c) 1,550	5,550
			(e) –0–	
			(g) 2,000	
Financial Statement Elements				
Prepaid/Accrued Pension Cost	$(14,400)	55,750	60,500	$ (19,150)

Pension Expense:		
Service	(a) 25,000	
Interest	(b) 9,200	
Return on assets		(c) 5,450
Prior service cost	(d) 1,000	
Loss	(e) –0–	

Cash		(f) 25,000
	$90,950	$90,950

Key (see text p. 1117–1118):
- (a) Service cost recognition
- (b) Interest cost recognition
- (c) Return on asset recognition
- (d) Amortization of prior service cost
- (e) Recognition of loss
- (f) Funding of pension plan
- (g) Adjustment of projected benefit obligation
- (h) Payment of benefits

Pension Expense:	
Service	$ 25,000
Interest	9,200
Return on assets	(5,450)
Prior service cost	1,000
Loss	–0–
	$ 29,750

*Debit (Credit)

(c) Return on Plan Assets

In this year, we assume that the return on plan assets was $7,000 while the expected return was 10% of $54,500, or $5,450. This means that the company had an unanticipated gain rather than a loss as in the first year. The worksheet adjustment debits the fair value of plan assets for the increase of $7,000. The unrecognized loss (gain) item is credited for the unexpected part of that return ($1,550) and the expected return of $5,450 is credited to pension expense, reducing the amount that would otherwise be recognized.

(e) Recognition of Loss

In the second year, Roberts Company begins in a loss position rather than a gain position as in the first year. The amount is not sufficient, however, to require recognition because the accumulated unrecognized loss of $9,100 is less than 10% of the projected benefit obligation ($92,000 × 10% = $9,200). Notice that the corridor is again established by the projected benefit obligation rather than the fair value of plan assets because of its larger size. The entry −0− in the worksheet simply indicates the nature of the adjustment that would be made had one been required.

(g) Adjustment of Projected Benefit Obligation

Again we assume that the projected benefit obligation requires adjustment for experience differences from the assumptions made. This adjustment, however, is a gain of $2,000 (assumed) in that the projected benefit obligation is reduced. For example, salary increases may not have been as large as expected or turnover may have accelerated, resulting in more individuals leaving the company's work force before qualifying for pension benefits. The adjustment is recorded as a debit to the projected benefit obligation and a credit to the unrecognized loss (gain).

YEAR 2 SUMMARY

To complete this example, we must again recognize pension expense and determine the need to adjust the additional pension liability. The pension expense is recorded as follows:

Pension Expense	29,750	
Prepaid/Accrued Pension Cost		4,750
Cash		25,000

Assuming that the accumulated benefit obligation is now $91,000, the required liability position of the company is as follows:

Accumulated benefit obligation		$91,000
Fair value of plan assets		(64,750)
Minimum required liability		$26,250
Present liability position:		
Additional pension liability from Year 1	$11,100	
Prepaid/accrued pension liability	19,150	(30,250)
Required reduction in additional pension liability		$ 4,000

We record this reduction as follows:

Additional Pension Liability	4,000	
Intangible Pension Asset		4,000

Notice that the balance in the intangible asset is now $7,100 ($11,100 − 4,000), which is within the constraint of the unamortized prior service cost balance of $13,000.

Summarizing for the two-year period for Roberts Company, the following financial statement elements will appear in the income statement and balance sheet:

	First Year	Second Year
Income statement:		
Pension expense	$15,400	$29,750
Balance sheet:		
Asset: Intangible pension asset	$11,100	$ 7,100
Liabilities: Net pension liability	$25,500*	$26,250[†]

---

*$14,400 + $11,100 = $25,500
[†]$19,150 + $7,100 = $26,250

We have thus far centered our efforts on the basics of pension accounting, focusing primarily on the computation of net periodic pension cost and the assets and liabilities related to pensions that may appear in the employer's financial statements. We complete our study by considering several miscellaneous aspects of accounting for pensions that have not been covered earlier.

FINANCIAL STATEMENT DISCLOSURE

An employer's financial statements shall include the following information concerning defined benefit pension plans:[15]

1. A description of the plan, including:
    a. Employee groups covered.
    b. Type of benefit formula.
    c. Funding policy.
    d. Types of assets held.
    e. Significant nonbenefit liabilities.
    f. Effect of significant matters affecting comparability of information for all periods presented.
2. The amount of net periodic pension cost for the period, showing separately the service cost component, the interest cost component, the return on plan assets for the period, and the net total of all other components.
3. A schedule reconciling the funded status of the plan with amounts reported in the employer's statement of financial position, showing separately:
    a. The fair value of plan assets.
    b. The projected benefit obligation, the accumulated benefit obligation, and the vested benefit obligation.[16]
    c. The amount of unrecognized prior service cost.
    d. The amount of unrecognized net gain or loss.
    e. The amount of any remaining unrecognized net obligation or net asset existing at the date of initial application of *SFAS No. 87*. (This item is discussed briefly in a later section of this chapter.)
    f. The amount of any additional liability recognized.
    g. The amount of net pension asset (prepaid pension cost) or liability (unfunded accrued pension cost) recognized in the statement of financial position.

As we shall soon see, accounting for retirement benefits other than pensions follows procedures very similar to those we have just studied for pensions. Because of the close relationship of pensions and other retirement benefits, companies often combine disclosure of information about the two in a single note to their financial statements Exhibit 24–9, which follows our coverage of other types of employee benefits, includes the combined disclosure of several types of employee benefits in a single note to the financial statements of Oneida Ltd. for 1993. You may want to take a brief look at the first section of that exhibit now; we will defer more thorough discussion of it until we have completed our study of all types of employee benefits.

PROCEDURES TO REDUCE VOLATILITY IN NET PERIODIC PENSION COST

A concern of the FASB and others in accounting for the cost of pension plans by employers is the volatility in earnings that might take place in certain circumstances. For example, the determination of net periodic pension cost requires many actuarial assumptions about future events that are subject to change over time—employee turnover, life expectancies, interest rates, future salary levels, and so on. Pension expense would be particularly susceptible

---

[15]*SFAS No. 87*, par. 54.

[16]Vested benefits are benefits for which the employee's right to receive present or future pension benefits is not contingent on remaining in the service of the employer. (*SFAS No. 87*, par. 264)

to volatility when a change in actuarial assumption results in a gain in one period and a loss in another period, if both were required to be recognized in full in the determination of pension expense.

The FASB is sensitive to this problem and permits certain procedures that are designed to *reduce volatility*. Some of these are beyond the scope of this text, but we have studied two specific procedures intended to reduce volatility—the recognition of gain or loss and the amortization of prior service cost.

Materiality
The FASB requires that gains or losses are to be incorporated into net periodic pension expense *only when they exceed a defined materiality threshold* (i.e., the corridor). Even if the accountant determines that this materiality threshold has been met, the entire gain or loss is not recognized. Rather, a fraction of the *excess* of the gain or loss over the corridor is recognized, based on the remaining service period of the employees to receive benefits under the plan. This *limited recognition* requirement has the effect of spreading fluctuations over time, permitting gains and losses to offset each other, rather than being fully recognized as they occur.

The second example of a procedure to reduce volatility is the amortization of prior service costs. These costs are amortized over the remaining service period of employees expected to receive benefits from the plan amendment, thereby preventing the total cost of the plan amendment from impacting income in any one accounting period.

FINANCIAL STATEMENT ARTICULATION

We learned in Chapter 4 that the basic financial statements articulate. They are fundamentally related and are based on the same underlying accounting information. Changes in one financial statement may affect changes in other financial statements.

In the case of pension accounting under *SFAS No. 87,* we see an interesting—and perhaps even confusing—example of articulation. Rarely do we find the determination of an expense that requires the combining of five distinct components as we do in the case of pension expense. Once that expense is determined, however, the articulation of balance sheet and income statement works much as we would expect. If the expense is paid (i.e., funded), cash is reduced; if the expense is not funded, a liability is established. The recognition of the additional liability, however, where the accumulated benefit obligation exceeds the fair value of plan assets, is unique in terms of asset/liability recognition. We would not typically recognize an intangible asset while simultaneously recognizing a liability. In this instance, the intangible asset is not amortized through the income statement as would ordinarily be the case but is *adjusted again* at the end of the next accounting period based on a subsequent comparison of the accumulated benefit obligation and the fair value of plan assets. As we saw in an earlier example, prior service cost is amortized, but that amortization is not based on a reportable asset.

Remember that net periodic pension cost is determined in part by the *projected* benefit obligation—which considers expected future salary levels. The recording of the additional liability, however, is based on the *accumulated* benefit obligation, which does not consider expected future salary levels. Again, we have a unique aspect of this accounting model, in that ordinarily both the income statement and balance sheet implications of a particular event or transaction are computed on the basis of the same underlying methods and assumptions. The recording of the additional liability and the related intangible asset is strictly a

Disclosure
balance sheet disclosure, inasmuch as the pension expense (net periodic pension cost) is computed separately, by applying different underlying assumptions. In addition, the requirement to include among liabilities any excess of the accumulated benefit obligation over the fair value of plan assets may result in an adjustment to stockholders' equity that is not taken through the income statement as an expense or loss. This apparent anomaly results from the limit on the intangible asset to an amount no greater than the unrecognized prior service cost.

TRANSITION TO *SFAS NO. 87*

In this chapter, we have focused attention almost entirely on *SFAS No. 87* and have said little about the previous accounting requirements under *APB Opinion No. 8.* The procedures described in this chapter represent dramatic change from the past and have been a subject of considerable debate for many years.

Under *APB Opinion No. 8,* the projected benefit obligation and the fair value of plan assets did not enter into the determination of balance sheet assets and liabilities as they do under *SFAS No. 87.* As a result, an additional component of net periodic pension cost will be included for several years as part of the transition process. Under *APB Opinion No. 8,* a Prepaid Pension Cost or an Accrued Pension Cost account existed if the amount funded was either more or less than the amount of pension expense recognized. During the transition period, that amount is combined with the difference between the projected benefit obligation and the fair value of plan assets at the time *SFAS No. 87* was adopted and the total (or net) amount amortized over the average remaining service period of employees expected to receive benefits under the plan. If that period is less than 15 years, however, the company may amortize the balance over a 15-year period.[17] This transition adjustment was included among the many disclosure requirements described earlier in the chapter. Again, you can see in this procedure the interest of the FASB in reducing volatility in the amount of pension expense recognized in any one accounting period.

SETTLEMENT AND CURTAILMENT OF PENSION PLANS

At the same time that the FASB issued *SFAS No. 87,* it also issued *SFAS No. 88,* which deals with the settlement and curtailment of pension plans.[18] A *settlement* of a pension plan is defined as an irrevocable action that relieves the employer (or the plan) of primary responsibility for an obligation and eliminates significant risks related to the obligation and the assets used to effect the settlement. A *curtailment* of a pension plan is defined as a significant reduction in, or elimination of, defined benefit accruals for present employees' future services.[19]

Although an underlying philosophy of *SFAS No. 87* is to delay the recognition in determining net periodic pension cost of certain gains and losses, the effects of changes in assumptions, and the cost of retroactive plan amendments, *SFAS No. 88* requires immediate recognition of certain gains and losses related to the settlement and curtailment of pension plans. The maximum gain or loss subject to recognition in earnings when a pension obligation is settled is the unrecognized net gain or loss, plus any remaining unrecognized net asset existing at the date of initial application of *SFAS No. 87.* The maximum amount is recognized in earnings if the entire projected benefit obligation is settled. If only part of the projected benefit obligation is settled, a pro rata portion of the maximum amount is recognized equal to the percentage reduction in the projected benefit obligation.[20]

SFAS No. 88 also deals with **special termination benefits** offered as an inducement for employees to terminate their employment (e.g., take early retirement). An employer that offers such benefits recognizes a liability and a loss when it is *probable* that employees will be entitled to benefits and the amount can be *reasonably estimated.* The amount of liability and related loss that are recognized is the amount of any lump-sum payments and the present value of any expected future payments.[21]

---

[17]*SFAS No. 87,* par. 77.

[18]*FASB Statement of Financial Accounting Standards No. 88,* "Employers' Accounting for Settlements and Curtailments of Defined Benefit Pension Plans and for Termination Benefits," 1985.

[19]*SFAS No. 88,* pars. 3, 6.

[20]*SFAS No. 88,* par. 9.

[21]*SFAS No. 88,* par. 15.

RETIREMENT BENEFITS OTHER THAN PENSIONS

In this chapter, we have focused our attention primarily on accounting and reporting for pension plans. Pension plans are perhaps the most significant retirement plans offered by employers, but they are by no means the only such plans. In addition to pension benefits, employers often offer other benefits to employees upon their retirement, such as health care, life insurance, tuition assistance, day care, legal services, and housing subsidies. The FASB has issued its *Statement of Financial Accounting Standards No. 106* to provide accounting standards for retirement benefits other than pensions.[22]

SFAS No. 106 parallels closely accounting for pensions under *SFAS No. 87* in most important respects. For that reason, and in an effort to limit the technical complexity of our coverage of accounting for retirement benefits, we provide only an overview of accounting for other retirement benefits.[23]

A defined benefit postretirement plan is one that defines the postretirement benefits in terms of monetary amounts (e.g., a fixed dollar amount of life insurance) or benefits covered (e.g., a maximum dollar per day of hospitalization). Such agreements represent an exchange between the employer and the employee. The employee provides services currently and the employer promises to provide certain retirement benefits in addition to current wages. Retirement benefits are appropriately viewed as a form of deferred compensation, the cost of which the employer logically recognizes during the period of active employment of the individual who will receive benefits or whose beneficiaries or dependents will receive benefits.

The *expected postretirement benefit obligation* for an employer is the actuarial present value as of a particular date of the postretirement benefits expected to be paid to the employee, the employee's beneficiaries, and any covered dependents. This measurement is based on the expected amount and timing of future benefits, considering the expected future cost of providing the benefits and the extent to which those costs are shared by the employer, the employee, and others. The *accumulated postretirement benefit obligation* is the present value of all future benefits attributed to an employee's service rendered to the date of the evaluation. Prior to the time that an employee attains full eligibility for the benefits in the plan, the accumulated obligation is a portion of the expected obligation. Once full eligibility is reached by the employee, the two are the same.

Net postretirement benefit cost, the name assigned the periodic expense associated with providing retirement benefits other than pensions, is made up of five diverse and offsetting components that parallel those we have already studied in accounting for pensions. These are summarized as follows:

Cost Component	Impact on Net Postretirement Benefit Cost
Service Cost The portion of the expected postretirement benefit obligation attributed to employee services during that period.	Increase
Interest Cost The increase in the accumulated postretirement benefit obligation to recognize the effects of the passage of time.	Increase
Return on Plan Assets The change in the value of the plan assets, adjusted for contributions and benefit payments.	Decrease

---

[22]*FASB Statement of Financial Accounting Standards No. 106,* "Employers' Accounting for Postretirement Benefits Other Than Pensions," 1990.

[23]For excellent discussion of the similarities and differences between these pronouncements, including a parallel illustration of their application, see Jack L. Smith, "Pensions and Other Postretirement Benefits: Accounting Similarities and Differences," *CPA Journal* (April 1993), pp. 52–57.

Cost Component	Impact on Net Postretirement Benefit Cost
Prior Service Cost	
The effects of plan amendments which increase or reduce benefits to employees.	
If benefits are increased	Increase
If benefits are reduced	Decrease
Gains and Losses	
Changes in the amount of the accumulated postretirement benefit obligation or plan assets resulting from experience different from that assumed or from changes in assumptions.	
If loss is recognized	Increase
If gain is recognized	Decrease

A sixth element of net periodic postretirement benefit cost may be required as part of the transition to the reporting requirements of *SFAS No. 106*. In the past, most companies accounted for postretirement benefits other than pensions on a cash basis. That is, they expensed benefits as they were paid rather than as they were earned by employees, provided no funding in advance of the time benefits were paid, and recognized no obligation of the provision of benefits. One alternative for implementing *SFAS No. 106* is to recognize the previously unrecognized obligation for retirement benefits gradually over time as an increase in the amount of net periodic postretirement cost. When this is done, the addition to the amount of expense recognized is the sixth component.

As is the case in accounting for pensions, detailed disclosures are required for other retirement benefits. These focus on the components of the periodic expense recognized in the determination of income and the funded status of the plan. We illustrate the disclosure of information concerning postretirement benefits other than pensions in Exhibit 24–9.

Our primary focus in this chapter has been on benefits that accrue to former employees after they retire from active employment. We have focused primarily on pensions but have also introduced accounting for health and life insurance and other postretirement benefits.

An additional type of benefit is paid to former employees who have not yet retired. To distinguish these benefits from postretirement benefits, they are labeled *postemployment benefits* and include all types of benefits provided to former or inactive employees, such as salary continuation, supplemental unemployment benefits, severance benefits, disability benefits, job training, and continuation of health and life insurance benefits.

In *SFAS No. 112*, the FASB established standards of accounting for postemployment benefits by referring to other existing standards for situations similar to postemployment benefits. The employer must accrue a liability for postemployment benefits if the four criteria stated in *SFAS No. 43*, "Accounting for Compensated Absences," are met. We covered the subject of compensated absences in Chapter 14 as part of our coverage of current and contingent liabilities. The criteria for recognition of a liability and related expense found in *SFAS No. 43* are summarized as follows:[24]

1. The employers's obligation relates to employee services that have already been rendered.
2. The obligation relates to rights that vest or accumulate.
3. Payment is judged to be probable.
4. The amount can be reasonably estimated.

OTHER POSTEMPLOYMENT BENEFITS

---

[24]*FASB Statement of Financial Accounting Standards No. 112*, "Employers' Accounting for Postemployment Benefits," 1992, par. 6.

EXHIBIT 24–9

Oneida, Ltd.
Employee Benefits Disclosure

9. RETIREMENT BENEFIT AND EMPLOYEE SECURITY PLANS

Pension Plans

The Company maintains defined contribution and defined benefit plans covering substantially all domestic employees and employees of the Company's Canadian operation. Employees of the Silversmiths Division are covered under an Employee Stock Ownership Plan (ESOP), which functions in tandem with a defined benefit plan. Under this plan, the Company makes an annual allocation of previously contributed shares of its stock as part of its annual contribution. The Company also maintains salary deferral (401-K) plans covering substantially all employees.

Employees of the Company's industrial wire subsidiary are covered under a defined contribution plan, for which contributions are determined based upon a percentage of that subsidiary's operating income. The Company's chinaware subsidiary employees and employees of the Company's Canadian operation are covered by defined benefit plans.

The net periodic pension cost for the Company's various defined benefit plans for 1993, 1992, and 1991 were as follows:

	(Thousands)		
	1993	1992	1991
Service cost—benefits earned during the year	$ 965	$ 604	$ 559
Interest cost on projected benefit obligation	1,405	1,070	912
Actual return on plan assets	(1,303)	(1,128)	(816)
Net amortization and deferral	28	(27)	(331)
Net periodic pension cost	$ 1,095	$ 519	$ 324

Plan assets consist primarily of stocks, bonds, and cash equivalents. The following table presents a reconciliation of the funded status of the plans and assumptions used at January 1993 and 1992.

	(Thousands)			
	U.S. Plans		Foreign Plan	
	1993	1992	1993	1992
Plan assets at fair value	$ 8,830	$ 4,256	$5,933	$6,559
Actuarial present value of benefit obligations:				
Vested benefits	12,252	5,427	4,060	3,919
Nonvested benefits	196	59	42	18
Accumulated benefit obligation	12,448	5,486	4,102	3,937
Projected future salary increases	4,056	3,432	560	577
Projected benefit obligation	16,504	8,918	4,662	4,514
Plan assets more (less) than projected benefit obligation	(7,674)	(4,662)	1,271	2,045
Unrecognized net gains (losses)	7,256	3,651	481	(171)
Unrecognized prior service cost	(3,681)	(3,963)	20	(25)
Unrecognized net asset	(1,854)	(1,735)	(708)	(879)
Accrued pension asset (liability)	$ (5,953)	$(6,709)	$1,064	$ 970
Discount rate	8.00%	8.75%	8.50%	10.00%
Expected long-term rate of return on assets	8.50%	8.50%	9.50%	9.50%
Rate of increase in compensation levels	5.25%	5.25%	5.00%	6.50%

The net pension cost associated with the Company's defined contribution plans, including the cost of shares allocated to the ESOP, was $3,136,000, $3,151,000, and $2,983,000 for 1993, 1992 and 1991, respectively.

Postretirement Health Care and Life Insurance Benefits

The Company reimburses a portion of the health care and life insurance benefits for retired employees. During the year ended January 1993, the Company adopted FAS No. 106, "Employers' Accounting for Postretirement Benefits Other Than Pensions." The Company elected to immediately recognize the cumulative effect of this change in accounting of $35,400,000 ($55,800,000 before income tax benefit) which represents the accumulated postretirement benefit obligation at January 26, 1992. In addition to the cumulative effect, postretirement benefit costs increased by $2,600,000 ($4,150,000 before income tax benefit) or $.26 per share, as a result of adopting the new standard.

Net periodic postretirement benefit cost for 1993 included the following components:

		(Thousands)		
	Medical	Prescription Drugs	Life	Total
Service cost of benefits earned	$ 960	$ 780	$ 14	$1,754
Interest cost on accumulated postretirement benefit obligation	2,192	2,146	134	4,472
Net periodic postretirement benefit cost	$3,152	$2,926	$148	$6,226

The following table sets forth the status of the Company's postretirement plans, which are unfunded, at January 30, 1993:

	Medical	Prescription Drugs	Life	Total
Accumulated postretirement benefit obligation:				
Retirees	$14,223	$15,620	$1,469	$31,312
Fully eligible active plan participants	3,650	3,696	139	7,485
Other active plan participants	11,543	9,414	169	21,126
Accrued postretirement benefit costs	$29,416	$28,730	$1,777	$59,923

The discount rate used in determining the accumulated postretirement benefit obligation was 8.25% at January 30, 1993. The assumed health care cost trend rate used was 12% for 1993; the rate was assumed to decrease gradually to 6% by the year 2051 and remain at that level thereafter. An increase in the assumed health care cost trend rates by 1% per year would increase the accumulated postretirement benefit obligation at January 30, 1993, by $5,938,000 and the net periodic postretirement benefit cost for 1993 by $672,000.

Prior to 1993, the cost of providing health care and life insurance benefits to retired employees was recognized as expense as claims were paid. These costs totaled $2,290,000 and $2,050,000 for 1992 and 1991, respectively.

Postemployment Benefits
During the year ended January 1993, the Company adopted *FAS No. 112, "Employers' Accounting for Postemployment Benefits."* This statement requires employers to recognize the obligation to provide postemployment benefits to former or inactive employees prior to retirement. These benefits include severance, disability related benefits and continuation of benefits such as health care and life insurance coverage. The cumulative effect of adopting this standard at January 26, 1992, resulted in a charge to income of $1,564,000 ($2,537,000 before income tax benifit).

Employee Security Plan
The Company maintains an employee security plan which provides severance benefits for all eligible employees of the Company and its subsidiaries who lose their jobs in the event of a change in control as defined by the plan. Employees are eligible if they have one year or more of service and are not covered by a collective bargaining agreement. The plan provides two and one half months of pay for each year of service, up to twenty-four months maximum, and a continuation of health care and life insurance benefits on the same basis.

SOURCE: Oneida, Ltd., 1993 Annual Report.

For an obligation for postemployment benefits to be recognized under these criteria, all four must be met. For postemployment benefits that do not meet all of these criteria, accounting is in accordance with *SFAS No. 5,* "Accounting for Contingencies," which we also covered in Chapter 14. Recall that *SFAS No. 5* requires recognition of a liability and related expense if both of the following conditions are met:[25]

1. Information available prior to issuance of the financial statements indicates that it is probable that an asset has been impaired or a liability has been incurred at the date of the financial statements.
2. The amount of the loss can be reasonably estimated.

We illustrate the disclosure of postemployment benefits along with pensions and other postretirement benefits in Exhibit 24–9.

FINANCIAL STATEMENT DISCLOSURE

Earlier we referred to the fact that companies often combine disclosures of pensions, other postretirement, and other postemployment benefits in notes to their financial statements because of the similarity of these items. Exhibit 24–9 includes an example of this type of note from the 1993 financial statement for Oneida, Ltd., a company that manufactures and markets tableware and industrial wire products.

The first section of the note explains the company's pension plans. Notice the separate disclosure of the service, interest, and asset return components of net periodic pensions cost. The other components are combined under the description "net amortization and deferral." Details about the plan assets and obligation follow, separated into U.S. plans and foreign plans. This information reconciles with the accrued pension asset (liability) that is included in the company's balance sheet.

The second section of the note explains the company's postretirement health care and life insurance benefits. The disclosure is similar to that for pensions, with the components of net periodic postretirement benefit cost presented first, followed by the accrued postretirement benefit cost. Following that disclosure is a discussion of the assumed health care cost trend rate that was used in determining the information that is presented, including the impact of a 1% increase in that rate. This is a disclosure required by *SFAS No. 106* and is intended to alert financial statement readers to the impact this important estimate has on the amounts in the financial statements and notes.

The third section explains the impact of *SFAS No. 112,* which was adopted by Oneida, Ltd. during 1993, to account for postemployment benefits. This is followed by a brief section on an employee security plan, which provides severance benefits for selected employees.

PROFESSIONAL JUDGMENT

You have been reminded consistently throughout this textbook of the importance of applying seasoned, professional judgment in preparing financial statements and related disclosures. Pensions and other postretirement and postemployment benefits are no exception to this general rule. In fact, these important employee benefit plans often represent some of the most significant obligations and expenses recognized by companies, and the uncertainties surrounding their measurement require an even higher level of professional judgment than many of the other areas of financial reporting we have studied.

One aspect of accounting for employment benefits that creates uncertainty, which in turn requires judgment for accountants, is the long time period between the recognition of an obligation and expense and the subsequent settlement of that obligation. Consider the case of a pension plan in which the company is estimating its pension obligation for employees. Estimates for a 25-year-old person must be made for benefits to be paid as many as 40 years later and may be based on events that have yet to occur (e.g., future compensation levels). Measur-

---

[25]*SFAS No. 112,* par. 6.

ing the financial statement impact of events now, even though the completion of the transaction may occur in the future, is essentially what accrual accounting is all about, but nowhere else is the procedure challenged in terms of difficulty of application than in the case of employment benefits. We deal with this, in part, by relying heavily on other professionals, namely actuaries. Actuaries make many important judgments about the future in determining amounts that have an important impact on financial statements and their notes. Does this mean that, as accountants, we accept the work of actuaries without question? The answer to this is clearly no. Accountants are not expected to be experts in actuarial science, but they are expected to generally understand the models used by actuaries and, most important, the underlying assumptions that actuaries are making in developing the amounts used to record and disclose information about employee benefit plans. Perhaps here, more than anywhere else in financial reporting, healthy skepticism is appropriate for accountants. Participating-ing in making important actuarial judgments and assumptions, and questioning their appropriateness in a particular financial reporting situation, is an important accounting function.

Three distinct features of accounting under *SFAS No. 87* and *No. 106* warrant noting as we complete our study of accounting for retirement benefits—the delayed recognition feature, the net cost feature, and the offsetting feature.

CONCLUDING REMARKS

The *delayed recognition* feature means that changes in the obligation and the value of plan assets are not recognized in the employer's financial statements as they occur but are recognized systematically and gradually over subsequent periods. All changes are eventually recognized except to the extent that they are offset by subsequent other changes, but at any point changes that have been identified and quantified await subsequent accounting recognition as net cost components and as liabilities and assets.

The *net cost* feature means that the recognition consequences of events and transactions affecting a retirement plan are reported as a single net amount in the employer's income statement. This approach results in the aggregation of at least three items that might be reported separately for any other part of an employer's operations: the compensation (service) cost, the interest cost related to deferred payment of benefits, and the results of investing what are often significant amounts of assets (return on plan assets).

Finally, the *offsetting* feature means that values of assets contributed to a plan, and obligations for pensions and other benefits, are shown *net* in the employer's statement of financial position (balance sheet), even though the liability has not been settled and the assets may be controlled, and substantial risks and rewards associated with both are clearly borne by the employer.[26]

KEY POINTS

1. Retirement plans are complex arrangements whereby employers provide pension payments and other benefits to retired employees for services rendered during their periods of active employment. (Objective 1)

2. For employers with defined benefit pension plans, determining the cost of such plans involves a series of complex actuarial calculations that rely to a significant degree on actuarial assumptions, such as mortality rates, employee turnover, interest rates, future compensation levels, and so on. (Objective 2)

3. Net periodic pension cost is determined by combining five distinct components—service cost, interest cost, return on plan assets, recognition of gain or loss, and amortization of prior service cost. Determining pension expense is necessary because of the matching principle. (Objective 3)

4. Prepaid/accrued pension cost is recognized for the difference between pension expense and the amount of assets funded into the pension plan to satisfy the pension obligation. (Objective 4)

5. An additional liability may be required if the amount of accumulated benefit obligation at the end of the accounting period exceeds the fair value of the plan assets. To offset that liability, an intangible asset is recorded, but that asset is limited to the amount of unrecognized prior service cost.

[26]*SFAS No. 87,* Summary.

HONEST BALANCE SHEETS, BROKEN PROMISES

Accounting rules, an abstract realm known to few, have introduced a harsh new reality into Clifford Davis' retirement. Navistar International Corp., where Davis worked as a maintenance man for 32 years, has long picked up the medical bills for its 40,000 pensioners. But starting Jan. 1, an accounting-rule change requires many large companies to include on their balance sheets immense sums for these ever-more-costly health benefits.

So the Chicago-based truckmaker wants to cut back its two-decade-old plan, forcing Davis and fellow retirees on fixed incomes to fork over a hefty chunk of money for their coverage. Money-losing Navistar says it will go bust if former workers don't pick up part of their health costs. Yet Davis, who lives in a trailer in McCordsville, Ind., and is not yet 65, contends that he would have to shell out 25% of his monthly $1,400 pension check. Says Davis: "I can't afford to pay."

Lots of other corporations are axing or curtailing retiree health benefits hoping to minimize the financial broadside of the so-called 106 rule, as well as curb runaway health costs in general. The rule was adopted in 1990 by the Financial Accounting Standards Board, the overseer of U.S. accounting criteria. As FASB sees it, failing to recognize the steadily growing health-care liability misleads investors about a company's financial condition.

Some large companies with strong balance sheets that can afford the hit are simply taking a one-time earnings and net worth write-off. But others, often less robust outfits like Navistar, are finding ways to circumvent the full force of 106 at their retirees' expense.

McDonnell Douglas Corp. is replacing its health plan for white-collar retirees by giving each a one-time payment of $18,000, using surplus pension-fund money. This will halve the St. Louis plane-maker's liability under the FASB rule, to $700 million. But after 1996, most bets are that payments to new retirees will be eliminated. According to a survey by the consulting firm A. Foster Higgins & Co., almost two-thirds of U.S. companies will have scaled back or eliminated the benefits by next year. "Employers are backpedaling like crazy from their commitments to workers," complains Clare Hushbeck, a senior analyst at the American Association of Retired Persons.

Certainly, retirees are the easiest target: They can't strike or quit for another job. Management "is picking on a group that can fight back the least," says Jerry Feldscher, a pensioner at Unisys Corp., which intends to phase out its plan entirely by 1995.

Retirees slammed with health-care cuts do have an option. Many are fighting back in court, although too few cases have been decided to discern a trend. Thus far, the key legal issue is how explicit the company has been in promising medical benefits (box). As a result, most employers steer away from cutting programs for union retirees because those plans are usually written into labor contracts. General Motors Corp., for instance, imposed 80% reimbursement limits on white-collar pensioners' bills but left Untied Auto Workers retirees alone.

Miscalculation

Navistar is bolder. Aiming to save 71% on retiree health-care costs, it tried to ram through the benefits reduction for both union and nonunion pensioners. But the UAW launched a legal counterstrike that threatened to tie the company up in court for years. As a compromise, the union and the truck manufacturer have agreed to reopen their contract now, a year before the pact expires, to negotiate health issues.

Retiree health plans first came into vogue in the late 1960s and early 1970s, after medicare was enacted. The idea was that the plans would take care of areas not covered by

---

To the extent that the required liability exceeds the amount of unrecognized prior service cost, stockholders' equity is reduced. (Objective 4)

6. Employers must maintain records of the value of plan assets, projected benefit obligation, unrecognized gain or loss, and unamortized prior service cost to properly account for pension plans, even though these items do not appear in the employer's financial statements. (Objective 5)

7. Several financial statement disclosures are required for defined benefit pension plans. These disclosures focus on the components of net periodic pension cost and the funded status of the plan. (Objective 6)

8. Accounting for retirement benefits other than pensions parallels closely accounting for pension benefits. (Objective 6)

9. Accounting for postemployment benefits for individuals who have not retired is similar to accounting for compensated absences and contingencies. (Objective 6)

QUESTIONS

24–1   What is the nature of the relationship among the employer, employee, and pension plan?

24–2   What is a defined **contribution** pension plan? What are the major characteristics of such a plan?

the federal medical program for the elderly: prescription drugs, home nursing care, and hospital stays beyond 90 days. "They thought the cost to supplement medicare would be small," says Richard Ostuw, a vice-president at consultant Towers Perrin Foster & Crosby. Wrong. For the past few years, the cost of corporate retiree health plans has been surging at a 15% annual clip.

Employers have two unappetizing choices under the new rule. They can either amortize the cost of the benefits over 20 years or take the entire charge to earnings in the first year. IBM took its $2.6 billion earnings hit in the first quarter of 1991. Analyst Philip C. Rueppel of Sanford C. Bernstein & Co. says Big Blue wanted to show that the rule "wouldn't be a big deal for them." Despite rocky times, IBM has not announced any benefit reductions....

"Soft Number"

Saving the day, of course, would be some form of national health insurance to bridge the gaps left by medicare.... Whether the legislative process will get to the plight of corporate retirees is an open question. Still, McDonnell Douglas hopes that by 1996, when its $18,000 subsidies to retirees will likely end, some government measure will be in place. "We don't know what will happen by then, but we can hope," says spokeswoman Barbara Anderson.

...On the plus side, no money for health-care liabilities need be immediately diverted from operations or capital spending. "This is the ultimate soft number," says Solomon Samson, S&P's managing director for corporate finance.

Eventually, though, affected companies must come up with cold cash. That's why, bean-counting contrivance or no, the rule has led companies to limit the liability by slicing retiree health plans. And that's how the abstract art of accounting has a real and painful impact.

Handling the Health-Care Hits

Company	Charge to Earnings (in millions of dollars)
General Motors	$16,000–24,000

Likely 20-year phase-in. Will announce plans in February. Has imposed health-care reimbursement limits for white-collar retirees

Hewlett-Packard	544

Taking charge-off now. Looking at making retirees pick up more of medical tab in 1994

McDonnell Douglas	700

Currently taking hit. Ending company subsidy of health care. Until 1996, nonunion retirees will get $18,000 each to fund care. Program may not continue after that

Navistar	2,500

Phasing in charge-off over 20 years. Tried to make retirees pick up part of medical expenses, but union thwarted move in court. Now negotiating with union

Unisys	170

Hit, being taken now, will be offset by tax savings. Phasing out subsidy of health plan by 1995, when nonunion retirees will have to foot their entire insurance bill

SOURCE: Larry Light, Kelley Holland, and Kevin Kelley, "Honest Balance Sheets, Broken Promises," *Business Week* (November 23, 1992), pp. 106–107. Reprinted from Nov. 22, 1992, p. 118 issue of *Business Week* by special permission, copyright © 1993 by McGraw-Hill, Inc.

24–3 What is a defined **benefit** pension plan? How do the major characteristics of a defined benefit plan differ from those of a defined contribution plan?

24–4 What are some of the uncertainties in estimating the employer's future pension commitment for a defined benefit pension plan? Describe them.

24–5 Why is accrual accounting appropriate for pension plans?

24–6 What is the "service cost" of a pension plan?

24–7 For financial reporting purposes under *SFAS No. 87,* when is it appropriate to recognize a pension liability?

24–8 What are the five primary components of net periodic pension cost? Briefly describe each.

24–9 Under what circumstances must a component of net periodic pension cost be included for the recognition of gain or loss?

24–10 How are prior service costs accounted for?

24–11 Why does the FASB provide for the amortization of prior service cost over future periods rather than by immediate recognition?

24–12 What components make up the balance sheet account Prepaid/Accrued Pension Cost?

24–13 How does the accountant determine whether an additional pension liability is required (i.e., a liability in addition to the difference between the expense recognized and the cash paid into the pension fund)?

24–14 What is the rationale for recognizing an intangible pension asset when an additional pension liability is established?

24–15 How do interest rate assumptions affect the pension expense recognized for the period?

24–16 What is the relationship between the two following components of net periodic pension cost: *return on plan assets* and *gain or loss.*

24–17 Two of the components of net periodic pension cost are often negative costs (i.e., reductions in pension expense). Which components are these, and why do they reduce pension expense?

24–18 What procedures included in *SFAS No. 87* are specifically designed to reduce volatility in the recognition of pension expense from year to year?

24–19 Briefly explain the net cost feature of *SFAS No. 87.*

24–20 Briefly explain the offsetting feature of *SFAS No. 87.*

24–21 Describe the concepts of *settlement* and *curtailment* in regard to a pension plan.

24–22 What is the nature of retirement benefits other than pensions? Briefly outline the accounting procedures for these benefits as indicated in *SFAS No. 106.*

EXERCISES

24–23 Expense and Funding Entries   Rosser, Inc., has correctly determined its net periodic pension cost as $215,000 for the current year.

INSTRUCTIONS

Prepare the general journal entries to record pension expense and funding under each of the following situations:

[a] Rosser, Inc., funds the same amount as the expense.

[b] Rosser, Inc., funds $235,000.

[c] Rosser, Inc., funds $198,000.

24–24 Defined Contribution Benefit Plan   Rapper, Inc., has a defined contribution pension plan that covers its three employees. The terms of the plan require Rapper to contribute 5% of each employee's annual salary to the pension fund each year. In 1995 the employee salaries were as follows:

Employee	Salary
A	$72,000
B	50,000
C	44,000

INSTRUCTIONS

[a] Prepare the general journal entries to record Rapper's pension expense for 1995.

[b] Discuss the reasons that an employer's financial risk is reduced by having a defined contribution pension plan versus a defined benefit pension plan.

24–25 Expense and Funding Entries   R&B Company determines its net periodic pension cost to be $85,000 in 1995 and $102,000 in 1996.

INSTRUCTIONS

[a] If the company funds $72,000 in 1995 and $95,000 in 1996, prepare the appropriate general journal entries and determine the amount of any prepaid or accrued expense to be reported in the balance sheet for each year.

[b] If the company funds $98,000 in 1995 and $110,000 in 1996, prepare the appropriate general journal entries and determine the amount of any prepaid or accrued expense to be reported in the balance sheet for each year.

24–26 Financial Statement Elements   Barlow, Inc., has the following balances in pension-related accounts as of January 1, 1995.

Fair value of plan assets	$100,000
Projected benefit obligation	(80,000)
Prepaid/accrued pension cost	$ 20,000

During the year, the company's accountant determines that service cost is $31,000. Interest cost is to be recognized as 10% on the projected benefit obligation and the estimated and actual return on plan assets is also 10%.

INSTRUCTIONS

[a] Determine pension expense for the year, identifying the individual components.
[b] Determine the amount of prepaid/accrued pension cost that will appear in the balance sheet at the end of 1995 under each of the following independent situations:
   [1] The company funds $30,000 into the pension plan at the end of the year.
   [2] The company funds $15,000 into the pension plan at the end of the year.

24–27 Financial Statement Elements   Stoudt, Inc., has the following balances in pension-related items on June 1, the first day of its 1995 fiscal year:

Fair value of plan assets	$575,000
Projected benefit obligation	(628,000)
Prepaid/accrued pension cost	$ (53,000)

The company's actuary has determined service cost for the year beginning June 1, 1995, as $59,500. He also informs Stoudt's accountant that the interest cost and return on asset components of net periodic pension cost should be calculated at 10%.

INSTRUCTIONS

[a] Determine the amount of pension expense that will be recognized during the year beginning June 1, 1995, identifying the amounts of the individual components.
[b] Determine the amount of prepaid/accrued pension cost that will appear in the balance sheet at May 31, 1996, under each of the following independent assumptions:
   [1] Stoudt funds $50,000 into the pension fund at the end of the year.
   [2] Stoudt funds $90,000 into the pension fund at the end of the year.

24–28 Financial Statement Elements   On January 1, 1996, Reeder Co. has the following pension-related balances:

Fair value of plan assets	$1,345,000
Projected benefit obligation	(1,515,000)
Prepaid/accrued pension cost	$ (170,000)

Service cost for the year is estimated to be $290,000. Interest cost on the projected benefit obligation is to be recognized at 10%, and the return on plan assets is to be calculated at 8%.

INSTRUCTIONS

[a] Determine pension expense for 1996, and identify the individual components.
[b] Calculate the amount of prepaid/accrued pension cost that will appear in the balance sheet at the end of 1996 under each of the following *independent* situations:
   [1] The company funds $302,000 into the pension plan at the end of the year.
   [2] The company funds $347,000 into the pension plan at the end of the year.

24–29 Service and Interest Cost   On January 1, 1995, Delta Company agrees to pay a lump-sum pension to George Parker, the company's only employee, equal to 5% of his final year's pay times the number of years worked after January 1, 1995. You estimate the George's salary for 2003, his last year with the company, will be $85,000.

INSTRUCTIONS

Determine the service and interest portions of net periodic pension cost for 1995 and 1996, assuming an appropriate interest rate of 12%.

24–30 Expected Return on Plan Assets   Harmony, Inc., has a defined benefit pension plan with plan assets having a fair value of $100,000 at January 1, 1995. The company expects a 12% return on plan assets and the expected value of those assets at January 1, 1995, is also $100,000. The fair value of the plan assets increased to $135,000 at January 1, 1996.

INSTRUCTIONS

[a] Determine the expected return on plan assets component of net periodic pension cost for 1995 and 1996.

[b] Will the computation of net periodic pension cost include a component for recognition of gain or loss in either 1995 or 1996? Explain your answer for both years.

24–31 Recognition of Gain and Loss Ray, Inc., has a defined benefit pension plan with an expected value of plan assets and a projected benefit obligation of $1,800,000 at the beginning of 1995. The company has determined that its average remaining service period of active employees at that date is 10 years.

INSTRUCTIONS

Determine the amount of gain or loss to be recognized, if any, in each of the following *independent* situations:

[a] The fair value of plan assets at January 1, 1995, is $1,500,000.
[b] The fair value of plan assets at January 1, 1995, is $2,400,000.

24–32 Prior Service Cost Amortization McIvey, Inc., amends its pension plan, resulting in a prior service cost of $110,000. The company has three employees who are expected to retire as follows:

Employee	Expected Retirement
Jones	Two years from plan amendment
Rogers	Four years from plan amendment
Wallace	Five years from plan amendment

INSTRUCTIONS

Prepare an amortization schedule for the prior service cost, assuming amortization over the future service period of the three employees.

24–33 Balance Sheet Presentation of Pension Liability Berton Company has a defined benefit pension plan that has been in existence for several years. As of the end of 1995, a total of $125,000 of net periodic pension cost has been recognized in previous years, of which $121,000 has been funded.

At the end of 1995, the accumulated benefit obligation totals $165,000, and the fair value of plan assets is $180,000.

INSTRUCTIONS

Determine the item(s) and amount(s) that will appear in the company's balance sheet at the end of 1995, relative to the pension plan. Briefly explain your answer.

24–34 Expected Return and Gain/Loss At January 1, 1995, Whitt, Inc., has a defined benefit pension plan with plan assets as follows:

Fair value	$275,000
Expected value	200,000

Other relevant information is as follows:

[1] The projected benefit obligation is less than the fair value of the plan assets.
[2] Administrators of the plan expect an 8% return on plan assets.
[3] Service cost and interest components of net periodic pension expense for 1995 have been computed as $87,300 and $35,000, respectively.
[4] The average service period of employees benefiting from the plan is 15 years.
[5] No prior service costs exist.

INSTRUCTIONS

Determine net periodic pension cost for 1995, identifying each component separately.

24–35 Prior Service Cost Amortization MBZ Corporation amends its defined benefit pension plan, resulting in a significant amount of prior service cost due to the retroactive application of certain plan amendments that increased employee benefits.

The employees affected by the plan amendments are described as follows:

Group	Number of Employees	Remaining Years of Service
A	2	4
B	5	7
C	6	9

INSTRUCTIONS

[a] Prepare a schedule that identifies the amortization fraction to be used, assuming that the company decides to amortize the prior service cost over the remaining service period of those employees expected to benefit from the plan amendment. Specifically indicate the amortization fraction for the first, fifth, and ninth years.

[b] If management indicates a preference for the straight-line amortization method, what would you propose as the maximum appropriate number of years? Justify your answer.

24–36 Recognition of Loss   Four independent companies have determined their projected benefit obligation and fair value of plan assets for 1995 as follows:

Company	Projected Benefit Obligation	Fair Value of Plan Assets	Remaining Service Period of Affected Employees
A	$1,000,000	$ 800,000	10
B	1,300,000	1,070,000	6
C	1,550,000	1,600,000	5
D	1,600,000	1,900,000	7

The amount of unrecognized loss for companies A, B, C, and D, respectively, is $70,000, $180,000, $185,000, and $150,000.

INSTRUCTIONS

Prepare a table determining the amount of recognition of loss that is required, if any, for each company. Include in your table the following columnar headings: Projected Benefit Obligation, Fair Value of Plan Assets, Corridor, Unrecognized Loss, and Amount Recognized.

24–37 Recognition of Gain   The following four independent companies have gains in the pension plans for 1995. Relevant pension plan information for each company is as follows:

Company	Projected Benefit Obligation	Fair Value of Plan Assets	Remaining Service Period of Affected Employees	Gain
Shaker	$ 825,000	$750,000	4	$ 90,000
Goad	1,120,000	980,000	10	100,000
Mineau	560,000	620,000	7	60,000
Dullem	235,000	230,000	8	30,000

INSTRUCTIONS

Compute the amount of recognition of gain that is required, if any, for each company.

24–38 Additional Liability Entries   Mills, Inc., has had a defined benefit pension plan for several years. In the past, the company has funded the amount of net periodic pension cost recognized. Also, the accumulated benefit obligation had always been less than the fair value of the plan assets.

In 1995, however, these variables changed. Net periodic pension cost was computed at $240,000, but the company funded only $200,000 due to a cash shortage. Also, at the end of the year, the accumulated benefit obligation was $1,488,000, but the fair value of plan assets was only $1,400,000. The unrecognized prior service cost at the end of 1995 totaled $50,000.

INSTRUCTIONS

Prepare the general journal entries necessary to record pension expense and funding and the pension liabilities at the end of 1995.

24–39 Additional Liability Entries   Winston, Inc., has always funded the amount of its net periodic pension cost each year in the past, and the amount of its accumulated benefit obligation has consistently been less than the fair value of the pension plan's assets. In 1995, however, the company placed $340,000 in its pension plan, even though the expense for the year was only $325,000.

In preparing the adjusting entries at the end of the year, the following additional information has been accumulated:

Fair value of plan assets at December 31	$1,415,000
Amount of unrecognized prior service cost at December 31	65,000
Accumulated benefit obligation at December 31	1,575,000

INSTRUCTIONS

Prepare the general journal entries required to record pension expense and funding and the pension liabilities at the end of 1995.

24–40 Pension Expense Determination with Entry   Missoula, Inc., is preparing its entries to record pension expense and funding for 1995 and has determined the following information:

[1] Service cost for the year is $119,000.

[2] Both interest cost and the return on plan assets are $12,500 for the year.

[3] An unrecognized loss of $48,000 exists at the beginning of 1995. The corridor has been computed as $25,000 and the recognition is to be over an eight-year period.

[4] Unrecognized prior service cost totals $30,000, and the amortization fraction for 1995 is 5/18.

[5] The company plans to fund $100,000 for the year.

INSTRUCTIONS

[a] Determine the amount of net periodic pension cost for 1995, indicating the amount of each component and including required calculations.

[b] Prepare the general journal entry to record the expense and funding for 1995.

24–41 Pension Expense Determination with Entry   Frank Company has determined the following concerning its defined benefit pension plan as of June 30, 1995, the end of its fiscal year:

Service cost component of pension expense for 1995	$525,000
Interest cost component of pension expense for 1995	60,000
Expected return on plan assets for 1995	95,000
Recognition of gain or loss for 1995 (see instructions)	10,000
Amortization of unrecognized prior service cost for 1995	15,000

INSTRUCTIONS

Identify the components of pension expense and prepare the general journal entry to record the pension expense and funding for 1995 in each of the following *independent* situations:

[a] The recognition of gain or loss represents a *gain* and the company pays $475,000 into the pension plan.

[b] The recognition of gain or loss represents a *loss* and the company pays $550,000 into the pension plan.

PROBLEMS

24–42 Financial Statement Elements   Ashland, Inc., has the following pension-related account balances on January 1, 1995:

Fair value of plan assets	$157,500
Projected benefit obligation	(174,200)
Prepaid/accrued pension cost	($16,700)

During 1995 the service cost as measured by the pension plan's actuary was $28,500 and the appropriate interest rate assumption for determining interest cost is 12%. In addition, the return on plan assets (both expected and actual) was 10%. Ashland funded $25,000 into the pension plan during the year.

INSTRUCTIONS

[a] Prepare the general journal entry to record pension expense and funding for 1995. Provide supporting computations for the amounts in your entry.

[b] Determine the financial statement elements related to pensions for the 1995 statements.

[c] Why did the accrued pension expense increase during the year? (Explain briefly.)

[d] Reconcile the balance in the Prepaid/Accrued Pension Cost account with the memorandum record amounts of fair value of plan assets and projected benefit obligation.

24–43 Financial Statement Elements   Ojo, Inc., has pension-related accounts in its memorandum records as follows:

Fair value of plan assets	$580,000
Projected benefit obligation	(475,000)
Prepaid/accrued pension cost	$105,000

During 1995 service cost was $78,750, interest cost is to be recognized at 10%, and the return on assets is also 10%. The company has no prior service cost or accumulated unrecognized gain or loss.

INSTRUCTIONS

[a] Determine the amount of pension expense, carefully identifying each component and providing computations where appropriate.

[b] Prepare the general journal entry to record pension expense and funding, assuming $75,000 was deposited in the pension fund at the end of the year. Provide a reconciliation of the memorandum records for the projected benefit obligation and the fair value of plan assets and the amount of the prepaid/accrued pension cost at the end of 1995.

[c] Repeat instruction [b], assuming that the company funded only $60,000 at the end of 1995.

[d] Briefly explain the difference in the impact on the financial statements in [b] and [c].

24–44 Components of Net Periodic Pension Cost   The management of Drakos, Inc., makes a pension commitment to an employee to pay 10% of her terminal salary per year for each year of service. The commitment is made at the beginning of 1995; the employee is expected to retire at the end of 2001. A single payment is to be made at retirement.

Actuarial estimates indicate that 12% is the appropriate rate to use in determining the interest component of net periodic pension cost. The expected salary for the employee for 2001 is $78,000. A 15% rate of return is expected on plan assets.

Each year the net periodic pension cost is fully funded. The fair value of the plan assets is as follows:

Year-end	Fair Value of Plan Assets
1995	$ 3,952
1996	9,500
1997	15,000

The fair value of plan assets includes the amount funded on the last day of each year, as well as the accumulation of amounts, plus earnings, from previous years.

INSTRUCTIONS

Determine the amount of net periodic pension cost for Drakos, Inc., for 1995, 1996, and 1997. Carefully detail your computations, including appropriate explanations for components that are not included in any year.

24–45 Prior Service Cost Amortization   On May 1, 1995, Agee Company established a pension plan for its seven employees. An actuary engaged by the company has calculated the past service cost to be a total of $108,000. The employees are expected to work the following numbers of years to retirement:

Employee	Years to Retirement
A, B	2
C, D, E	3
F	6
G	8

INSTRUCTIONS

[a] Prepare the schedule needed to compute the amortization fraction for each year over which the prior service cost will be amortized. Assume amortization is to be over the expected remaining period of active employment of the seven employees.

[b] Determine the dollar amount of amortization of prior service cost for each fiscal year, assuming the company's financial reporting period is May 1–April 30.

[c] What is the longest period over which prior service costs could be amortized if Agee chose to use the straight-line method?

[d] Briefly explain how the amortization of prior service costs results in less volatility in net periodic pension cost when compared with alternative accounting treatments.

24–46 Expected Return/Gain and Loss Recognition   Shibaki, Inc., has a defined benefit pension plan for its employees. At the beginning of 1995, both the actual and expected amounts of the projected benefit obligation were $100,000. Both amounts grew at a rate of 12% per year through 1996 and 1997.

At the beginning of 1995, the fair value of the plan assets was $120,000, while the expected value was only $100,000. The company expects a return of 15% on the beginning fair value of plan assets for each year. The actual values of the plan assets at the end of 1995 and 1996 were $200,000 and $260,000, respectively.

During 1995–1997 actuaries expect employees who worked during each year to remain active for approximately six more years.

INSTRUCTIONS

[a] Prepare a schedule comparing the expected and actual amounts of the projected benefit obligation and the value of plan assets. Include in your schedule an amount representing the under- or overperformance of the plan assets at the beginning of each year, 1995–1997.

[b] Determine the amount of the gain or loss that should be recognized, if any, for each year as part of net periodic pension cost. If none should be recognized, explain why. Specifically identify the corridor for each year.

[c] Prepare a schedule indicating the amounts of the following components of net periodic pension cost for each year: return on plan assets, interest, and gain or loss recognition. (For purposes of this problem, you may ignore the service and prior service cost amortization components.)

[d] Briefly explain how the procedure you have applied for recognizing gain or loss reduces the volatility in the amount of pension expense recognized each year.

24–47 Pension Component Analysis   Onker, Inc., has a balance in its Prepaid/Accrued Pension Cost account of ($116,000) at the beginning of 1995, a liability position. The fair value of plan assets totals $785,000 and the projected benefit obligation totals $901,000.

During 1995 the company's actuary determines service cost of $120,000. The interest cost component of net periodic pension cost is determined at 12% on the projected benefit obligation and the return on assets is also determined at 12%. (Expected and actual return are the same, no prior service cost exists, and no unrecognized gain or loss exists.)

At the end of 1995, management decides to fund $128,000 into the pension plan even though this is not the same amount as the expense to be recognized for the year.

INSTRUCTIONS

[a] Prepare a worksheet analysis of the pension accounts similar to that in Exhibit 24–4. Provide an explanation for the entries in your worksheet and for the calculations that are required to determine the components of net periodic pension cost.

[b] Prepare the general journal entry to record pension expense for 1995.

[c] Reconcile the difference between the pension expense recognized and the pension funding with the change in the prepaid/accrued pension cost during the period.

24–48 Additional Pension Liability   Boatman, Inc., has a defined benefit pension plan that covers all of its salaried employees. At the beginning of 1996, the Prepaid/Accrued Pension Cost account had a $10,000 credit balance. Management has accurately determined the following information for 1996 and 1997:

	1996	1997
Net periodic pension cost for year	$124,500	$132,000
Funding into pension plan at end of year	115,000	120,000
Accumulated benefit obligation at end of year	560,000	625,000
Fair value of plan assets at end of year	528,000	530,000
Unrecognized prior service cost at end of year	40,000	35,000

INSTRUCTIONS

[a] Record the recognition of pension expense and the funding into the pension plan for each year, as well as the recognition of the additional pension liability, if required. Provide details of your computations.

[b] In comparative columns for 1996 and 1997, indicate the amounts that will appear in the income statements and balance sheets at the end of each year that relate directly to the pension plan.

24–49 Correction of Pension Error/Additional Liability   You have been selected as auditor for Bigtree, Inc., as of 1996. The company has a defined benefit pension plan for its employees that has been in operation for several years. Prior to 1995, the company's accountant had properly accounted for the recognition of net periodic pension cost. In 1995, however, due to a change in personnel, an inexperienced bookkeeper had simply recorded the pension expense as the amount of cash funded into the plan—$8,000. The proper amount of expense for the year was $10,000. You also determine that the amount of accumulated benefit obligation was less than the fair value of plan assets. (The inexperienced bookkeeper had not recorded an additional liability.) A credit balance of $1,000 is carried forward from previous years in the account Prepaid/Accrued Pension Cost.

You have accumulated the following information for 1996.

Net periodic pension cost	$12,000
Funding into pension plan	9,000
Accumulated benefit obligation	91,000
Fair value of plan assets	82,500
Unrecognized prior service cost	26,000

INSTRUCTIONS

[a] Prepare the general journal entries required to correct for the 1995 error in recording the pension and to record the 1996 pension expense and funding and the additional liability.

[b] Assume the following information for 1997:

Net periodic pension cost	$ 13,000
Funding into pension plan	10,500
Accumulated benefit obligation	100,000
Fair value of plan assets	101,000
Unrecognized prior service cost	24,000

Prepare the general journal entries required to record the pension for 1997.

[c] Describe how your answer to part [b] would have been different if the fair value of plan assets had been only $91,000, rather than $101,000.

24–50 Additional Pension Liability Vester Manufacturing Company has a defined benefit pension plan that has been in operation for several years. At the end of 1995, the company's balance sheet includes the following items related to this pension plan:

Prepaid/Accrued pension cost (debit balance)	$31,400
Additional pension liability (credit balance)	72,000
Intangible pension asset (debit balance)	72,000

Management has correctly determined the following information for 1996 and 1997:

	1996	1997
Net periodic pension cost for year	$150,000	$162,500
Funding into pension plan for year	150,000	150,000
Accumulated benefit obligation at end of year	751,000	865,000
Fair value of plan assets at end of year	655,000	835,000
Unrecognized prior service cost at end of year	67,000	60,000

INSTRUCTIONS

[a] For 1996, prepare the general journal entries required to record the annual expense and funding and the adjustment to the additional liability. Indicate the financial statement amounts that relate to the pension plan, including detailed calculations.

[b] Repeat requirement [a] for 1997.

24–51 Components of Net Periodic Pension Cost Hviding, Inc., initiated a pension plan for its president, Karl Hviding, on January 1, 1995. Hviding is expected to work through the end of 2005. Terms of the pension plan and other information concerning the plan are as follows:

[1] The plan was originally designed to pay Hviding 4% per year of service, times his terminal salary in a single lump-sum on his retirement date. At the beginning of 1997, the company decided to increase the percentage to 6%, with all other aspects of the pension remaining the same. This amendment is to be applied retroactively.

[2] Management expects Hviding's salary in the year 2005 to be $150,000.

[3] An interest rate of 10% is determined to be appropriate for purposes of calculating the interest component of net periodic pension cost.

[4] A 12% return is expected on assets invested in the pension plan. The amount invested in the plan each year and the fair value of the plan assets at the end of each year are as follows:

Year-end	Amount Invested	Accumulated Fair Value
1995	$2,000	$2,000
1996	2,000	5,500
1997	3,000	8,800

INSTRUCTIONS

[a] For each year, 1995–1997, determine the five components of net periodic pension cost: service, interest, prior service amortization, return on plan assets, and gain or loss recognition. If no amount exists for one or more component(s) in any year, indicate that fact.

[b] Prepare the general journal entries to record the pension expense and funding for each year.

24–52 Pension Component Analysis   Jollay, Inc., began 1995 with the following balances in pension-related accounts: fair value of plan assets, $95,000 debit; projected benefit obligation, $110,000 credit; unamortized prior service cost, $25,000 debit; unrecognized gain, $17,000 credit; prepaid/accrued pension cost, $7,000 credit.

During 1995 the following events and transactions take place:

[a] Service cost is $18,500, as determined by the company's actuary.

[b] Interest cost on the projected benefit obligation is to be determined at 12%.

[c] Return on assets is 12% (both expected and actual).

[d] Prior service cost is to be amortized over a 10-year period.

[e] Gain and loss recognition, if required, is to be over a 10-year period.

[f] The company funds $27,000 into the pension plan at year-end.

[g] The projected benefit obligation is reevaluated at the end of the year, resulting in a $2,800 loss (i.e., the projected benefit obligation requires a $2,800 increase due to unexpected changes in various actuarial assumptions).

[h] Pension benefits are paid in the amount of $19,900.

INSTRUCTIONS

[a] Prepare a pension information analysis, similar to that in Exhibits 24–7 and 24–8, for Jollay, Inc., for 1995. Key your entries to the items of information presented in the preceding problem.

[b] Prepare the general journal entry to record the pension plan for the year, indicating the detailed computation of the components of net periodic pension cost (i.e., pension expense).

[c] Assume that no additional pension liability was required at the beginning of 1995 and that the accumulated benefit obligation at the end of 1995 is $119,000. Prepare the general journal entry, if any, required to record the additional pension liability.

[d] Determine the financial statement elements that will appear in the company's 1995 balance sheet and income statement.

24–53 Pension Component Analysis   Serano, Inc., has the following pension-related items in its memorandum records at the beginning of 1995.

	Balances	
	Debit	**Credit**
Fair value of plan assets	$425,000	
Projected benefit obligation		$375,000
Unamortized prior service cost	17,000	
Unrecognized loss	50,000	

During the year, the company determined that its service cost was $50,000 and that interest cost should be recognized at 10% on the projected benefit obligation. The expected return on plan assets was 10% but the actual return during the year was 12%. Prior service cost and any gain or loss is to be recognized over eight years.

Additional information is as follows:

Pension funding at the end of 1995	$60,000
Reevaluation of projected benefit obligation for experience differences (gain)	10,000
Benefits paid during 1995	20,000

INSTRUCTIONS

[a] Prepare an analysis of pension information for Serano, Inc., for 1995 similar to that in Exhibits 24–7 and 24–8. Prepare details of the computed amounts included in the worksheet and identify your entries with an appropriate letter with description.

[b] Prepare the journal entry to recognize pension expense and funding for 1995.

[c] Identify the elements of the financial statements related to the pension plan for 1995.

[d] Describe the circumstances in which Serano would be required to record an additional pension liability. Is this likely to be required for Serano for 1995?

CASES

24–54 Miscellaneous Pension Concepts Jack Murphy, a young CPA who recently joined the accounting firm of Johnson, Smith and Jones, PC, has been asked to speak to the local chapter of a professional banking organization. Jack was an outstanding student at the local university, graduated two years ago with high honors, and received a commendation for high achievement on the CPA examination.

In asking Jack to speak to the group, the president asked him to address the pension accounting requirements of *FASB Statement of Financial Accounting Standards No. 87.* The president indicated that many companies encountered by the bankers have defined benefit pension plans that may significantly affect their financial statements.

Specifically, Jack determines that the following should be covered:

[1] Why accrual accounting is appropriate, rather than simply charging to expense the amount funded into the plan for the accounting period or the benefits paid employees during the period.

[2] A brief discussion of the components of net periodic pension cost.

[3] The major financial statement items that could appear in the financial statements that the bankers will encounter.

INSTRUCTIONS

[a] Help Jack prepare his response by summarizing what you believe should be covered for the identified areas of pension accounting.

[b] Identify other areas of concern that you think the bankers should understand.

24–55 Financial Statement Presentation You are the auditor for High Fashion Company. The company's president, Gail West, has approached you with some questions concerning pension accounting. West is not an accountant, but she is an astute reader of financial statements and has obviously been doing her "homework" before your conversation. Her comments to you are as follows:

I observe what seems to me to be some inconsistency in reporting pensions by different companies. For example, some show Prepaid/Accrued Pension Expense as an asset and others show it as a liability. Surely it can't be both! Also, I notice that some companies have the following accounts in their balance sheets and others do not—Intangible Pension Asset, Additional Pension Liability, and Excess of Additional Pension Liability over Unrecognized Prior Service Cost. The accounting profession must be in some degree of turmoil over pension accounting since companies are apparently using different systems of accounting for their pension plans.

You have a meeting scheduled with West tomorrow and you are certain that some of these issues will come up. Since you are uncertain which topics she will bring up, you feel it necessary to be prepared on all fronts.

INSTRUCTIONS

How will you respond to the specific criticisms West has leveled at the accounting profession?

24–56 Unique Features of Pension Accounting As an experienced professional, Margaret Fowler, CPA, is frequently called on by members of her firm to present authoritative accounting pronouncements to staff personnel as part of the firm's continuing professional education program.

Soon after the FASB issued its new pension pronouncements, the firm scheduled a seminar. Fowler prepared her presentation, wrote an outline of *FASB Statements of Financial Accounting Standards Nos. 87* and *88* and scheduled a half-day seminar on the subject. After an overview lecture by Fowler, a young staff accountant asked the following questions:

Hasn't the FASB incorporated some rather revolutionary approaches in these pronouncements? For example, it seems to me that the periodic pension expense is a conglomerate of several distinctly different items, some of which actually offset the others. Also, there seems to be a conscious attempt on the part of the FASB to avoid the recognition of certain items that took place during the accounting period by requiring that they be deferred and recognized over a long period of time. Is this correct? Finally, the FASB seems to encourage offsetting of assets and liabilities. Isn't it true that assets and liabilities are usually presented separately rather than being offset against each other?

INSTRUCTIONS

If you were in Fowler's position as instructor for this seminar, how would you respond to these assertions?

JUDGMENT CASES

24–57 Unusual Operating Conditions and Pension Reporting   Hi-Tech, Inc., has a highly skilled work force of scientists and engineers who are young, highly motivated, and well compensated. Little turnover or attrition in this group is expected. These factors result in an actuarial determination that recognizes a relatively small pension expense in the early years of the plan but will rise dramatically in later years as this work force nears retirement. This expense pattern results generally from the FASB–mandated actuarial benefit method that is used to attribute pension costs to accounting periods.

The president and the board of directors of Hi-Tech have decided to fund amounts for the pension in excess of the amounts attributed by the benefit formula. This is being done for what you consider sound business purposes. That is, the company wishes to use a cost-based actuarial method for funding rather than the benefit-based method that, according to the FASB, must be used for financial reporting purposes. This allows the company to fund relatively similar amounts over the life of the work force rather than small amounts in the early years and rapidly increasing amounts in later years.

The president, however, does not wish to report the large prepaid cost that will result from the company's funding policy. He would prefer to recognize the larger of the attribution amounts or the amount funded each year as net periodic pension cost. The president has recently stated,

Aren't you guys supposed to be conservative? What could warm the accountant's heart more than stating expenses at a higher amount than you absolutely have to? Further, I think it might be misleading to report such a large prepaid pension cost because it will be many years before we really know what the actual obligation will be. Won't it be acceptable to recognize a larger expense in this case?

INSTRUCTIONS

Respond to the president's questions. Is his suggestion permissible? What ideas can you identify that might help the president in his desire to recognize a larger pension expense, if any?

24–58 Relying on Actuaries   As controller of Ocean Topics, Inc., you are interested in and responsible for seeing that the company's financial statements are presented fairly in conformity with GAAP. In the current period, the company's operations have not lived up to expectations and promises made by the president. The company was still profitable, but the president had asserted in a speech made to the shareholders at the beginning of the year that higher operating profits would be achieved than now appear possible.

Against this background, the president has recently fired the firm of actuaries that performed the actuarial valuation of the company's defined benefit pension plan each year. She also sent you a new actuarial valuation of the plan conducted by other actuaries with whom you are not familiar. The new study reports a substantially lower net periodic pension cost than the study of the previous actuaries. The president has directed you to record the pension cost for the year on the basis of the new actuarial report without considering the old report. Out of concern for the change, you phone the old actuarial firm and talk with the actuary with whom you had previously worked. He states:

We were fired because the president did not like our numbers. She suggested that we were being overly conservative in a number of our assumptions about several actuarial factors. When we indicated that the amounts we had used were and continued to be our best estimates of the factors in question, she stated that unless we were willing to reconsider our position, she would have to obtain the opinion of other, more reasonable, actuarial experts. My boss told her that our position was final, and we immediately received a letter informing us that our services were no longer needed.

When you question the previous actuary about the new firm of actuaries, he responds,

> *Those guys have been around for a couple of years, but I don't know much about them. They don't seem interested in participating in the profession much. I certainly don't suggest that they are incompetent or dishonest. We have lost a couple of other clients to them. They seem to be willing to be quite aggressive in their assumptions. I certainly could not support some of the things they have come up with, but I am not aware of their response to your specific situation.*

INSTRUCTIONS

What course of action should you take at this time? Can you accept the work of the new actuaries without reservation or question? What responsibility does the accountant have when relying on specialists who have knowledge of matters that affect accounting measurements?

24–59 Financial Reporting Case   Bristol-Myers Squibb Company has defined benefit pension plans for its employees. These plans are described in Note 13 to the 1993 financial statements:

FINANCIAL REPORTING CASE

Note 13—Retirement Benefit Plans

The company and certain of its subsidiaries have defined benefit pension plans for regular full-time employees. The principal pension plan is the Bristol-Myers Squibb Retirement Income Plan. The company's funding policy is to contribute amounts to provide for current service and to fund past service liability.

Cost for the company's defined benefit plans included the following components:

Year Ended December 31 (in millions of dollars)	1993	1992	1991
Service cost—benefits earned during the year	$104	$ 94	$ 79
Interest cost on projected benefit obligation	152	144	131
Actual earnings on plan assets	(232)	(119)	(328)
Net amortization and deferral	54	(73)	172
Net pension expense	$ 78	$ 46	$ 54

The weighted average actuarial assumptions for the company's pension plans were as follows:

December 31	1993	1992	1991
Discount rate	7.0%	8.2%	8.6%
Compensation increase	4.5%	5.0%	5.0%
Long-term rate of return	11.0%	12.0%	12.0%

The funded status of the plans was as follows:

December 31 (in millions of dollars)	1993	1992	1991
Actuarial present value of accumulated benefit obligation:			
Vested	$(1,758)	$(1,354)	$(1,226)
Nonvested	(201)	(155)	(147)
	$(1,959)	$(1,509)	$(1,373)
Total projected benefit obligation	$(2,339)	$(1,892)	$(1,730)
Plan assets at fair value	1,702	1,681	1,694
Plan assets less than projected benefit obligation	(637)	(211)	(36)
Unamortized net assets at adoption	(103)	(129)	(145)

(continued on following page)

(*continued from previous page*)

December 31

(in millions of dollars)	1993	1992	1991
Unrecognized prior service cost	**96**	105	112
Unrecognized net losses	**510**	313	137
Adjustment required to recognize minimum pension liability	**(171)**	—	—
(Accrued) Prepaid pension expense	**$ (305)**	$ 78	$ 68

In 1993, the increase in the actuarial present value of accumulated benefit obligation and in plan assets less than projected benefit obligation was primarily due to a lower discount rate and the effect of the voluntary retirement program offered to the company's U.S. employees.

In 1993, $112 million of the adjustment required to recognize minimum pension liability was recorded in Other Assets and $59 million was recorded as a reduction in Stockholders' Equity.

Plan benefits are primarily based on years of credited service and on participant's compensation. Plan assets principally consist of equity securities and fixed income securities.

INSTRUCTIONS

[a] What are the three primary components of net pension expense for 1991–1993? Describe what is included in each component.

[b] What major actuarial assumptions underlie the amounts in the financial statements? What have been the trends in these assumptions from 1991 through 1993 and what impact have these changes generally had on the amount of net pension expense?

[c] Based on information in Note 13, would you expect to find a pension asset or liability in the company's statement of financial position for 1991, 1992, and 1993? Explain.

[d] For 1993, what is the amount of Bristol-Myers Squibb Company's accumulated benefit obligation? What is the amount of its projected benefit obligation? Why are these two amounts different?

[e] Briefly describe how this disclosure illustrates the delayed recognition, net cost, and offsetting features of accounting for pension benefits under *SFAS No. 87.*

CHAPTER
25

Additional Disclosure Issues and Financial Analysis

OBJECTIVES

1. To explain interim reporting of financial information.
2. To explain the reporting of financial information for segments of a business enterprise.
3. To explore the nature of related-party transactions and the disclosures required by GAAP.
4. To explore the nature of financial instruments and the disclosures required by GAAP.
5. To explain the analysis of financial statements.

Related-party transactions are common within the sports industry. For example, the television properties that broadcast the games of the Atlanta Braves and the Chicago Cubs are owned by the same persons who own the respective baseball teams. The teams benefit from the television exposure; the television properties benefit from the appeal and stability of the sports programming.

Some companies use their sports ownership connections to sell stadium concessions and to market their products. Anheuser-Busch, for example, owns the St. Louis Cardinals baseball team and uses the connection to promote its beer. The Coors Brewing Company sought to promote its beer when it recently acquired an interest in the Colorado Rockies baseball franchise.

Although related-party relationships such as those described frequently make good business sense, one must not presume that transactions between related parties are conducted at arm's length. Thus, an accountant needs to understand clearly where one business ends and another business begins. Moreover, disclosures must communicate this understanding adequately to the users of a company's financial statements. Related-party disclosures and several other disclosure topics are covered in this chapter.

Jerry Gorman and Richard Stein, "Keeping the Financial Scorecard—Accounting for a Sports Franchise," *The CPA Journal* (June 1992), pp. 18–27.

Disclosure

Recall from Chapter 1 that the *objectives* of financial reporting are (1) to provide useful information in investment, credit, and similar decisions, (2) to provide information helpful in assessing cash flow prospects, and (3) to provide information about enterprise resources, claims to those resources, and changes in them. In Chapter 2, we discussed the **disclosure principle,** which calls for revealing information that will be useful in the decision-making processes for reasonably informed users. We also explained that complying with the disclosure principle requires a knowledge of GAAP, a knowledge of the circumstances involved, and professional judgment. As a part of most chapters that followed Chapter 2, we covered specific disclosure requirements related to such topics as inventories, depreciation, leases, pensions, and so forth.[1]

This chapter has two primary objectives: (1) to discuss and illustrate several important disclosure issues that we have not yet presented and (2) to explain the analysis of financial statements. These objectives are related in that information disclosed by accountants is an important part of the information that investors, creditors, and others use to assess the financial health and prospects of particular enterprises. In this chapter, we cover the disclosure of interim information, financial reporting for segments of a business enterprise, related-party transactions, disclosures about financial instruments, and analysis of financial statements.

INTERIM REPORTING

Annual financial statements are often not *timely* enough for investors and creditors, who make decisions throughout a year. **Interim reporting** means the presentation of financial information for periods of less than one year. **Interim reports** may be presented for semiannual, quarterly, or monthly periods. Quarterly periods are the most common. Although quarterly reports are usually much more condensed than annual reports, empirical research indicates that quarterly information is useful in decision making.[2] Interim reports provide information that helps users to assess more accurately the amount, timing, and uncertainty of prospective cash flows.

As explained in Chapter 1, the SEC requires certain companies to file a Form 10–Q report, which includes quarterly financial information that has been reviewed but not audited by an independent CPA. These companies also typically distribute interim reports to their shareholders. The SEC also requires these companies to disclose certain quarterly information in the notes to their *annual* financial statements.

In 1973 the APB issued *Opinion No. 28*, which deals with interim financial reports.[3] This pronouncement provides accounting principles for companies to use when preparing interim reports. It also provides a list of the minimum information that publicly held companies must disclose in their interim reports.[4]

ALTERNATIVE INTERIM PERIOD VIEWS

Determining the results of business operations for intervals of less than a year is difficult. Wide fluctuations in revenue that are due to seasonal business patterns, for example, or substantial fixed costs incurred in a single interim period for the benefit of several periods complicate the determination of earnings on a short-term basis. Although the same problems may exist in annual reporting, the longer period allows the business cycle to more nearly complete its course, thereby offsetting some of the fluctuations.

The unique features of interim reporting have resulted in two basic positions concerning the nature of interim financial statements. These positions are the **discrete** or **independent view** and the **integral** or **dependent view.** Advocates of the discrete view of interim reporting

---

[1]The nature of required disclosures is so extensive that most accountants use a **disclosure checklist** to ensure that all important disclosures have been made in a set of financial statements. Such a checklist summarizes the disclosures required by GAAP.

[2]For example, see George J. Foster, "Quarterly Accounting Data: Time Series Properties and Predictive-Ability Results," *Accounting Review* (January 1977), pp. 1–21, and Jane Baldwin and G. William Glezen, "Bankruptcy Prediction Using Quarterly Financial Statement Data," *Journal of Accounting, Auditing and Finance* (Summer 1992), pp. 269–289.

[3]*APB Opinion No. 28*, "Interim Financial Reporting," 1973.

[4]A publicly held company is one whose securities trade in a public market, either a stock exchange or the over-the-counter market. The minimum disclosures are discussed later in this chapter.

regard each interim period as a basic accounting period, regardless of the length of time involved. The results of operations for each interim period would be determined in essentially the same way as for an annual period. In the determination of income, those accruals, deferrals, and estimations that would normally be applied for annual periods are also applied for interim periods.

Advocates of the integral view see each interim period as an important part of the annual period and emphasize this feature in reporting results of operations. Accruals, deferrals, and estimates required at the end of each interim period are applied in the context of expected annual results of operations. Allocations among interim periods are sometimes made to reflect the relationship of the interim period to the annual period, whereas the same allocation between annual periods would not be appropriate.

To illustrate the difference between the discrete and integral views, assume that a company launches a major advertising campaign in January. Although the costs are incurred entirely in the first quarter, the company expects results throughout the year. Applying the discrete view of interim reporting, the entire cost of the advertising campaign should be expensed in the first quarter because advertising is ordinarily not carried forward as a prepaid expense at the end of an accounting period. Within the integral view of interim reporting, however, an expense such as advertising might be allocated among four quarters to more clearly reflect the relationship of each quarter's results of operations to the annual period.

The APB took the position that the usefulness of interim financial information depends on the **relationship that it has to annual results of operations.** Therefore, the board concluded that each interim period should be viewed as an **integral part** of the corresponding annual period. In general, financial information presented in interim reports should be based on the accounting principles used by the enterprise in its annual reporting unless an accounting change has occurred. However, because of the unique nature of the interim period as a part of a longer period, certain modifications in accounting principles may be necessary for the interim information to better relate to annual results of operations.

BASIC ACCOUNTING PRINCIPLES FOR INTERIM REPORTING

Revenues from products sold or services rendered are generally recognized for interim periods on the same basis as for the annual period. Methods of revenue recognition that are used in annual reporting, such as the percentage-of-completion method on long-term contracts, should be followed in interim reports as well.

The recognition of expenses in interim periods is more complex. Expenses for interim reporting purposes are classified in two categories: (1) those associated directly with revenue and (2) all other expenses.

Matching

Expenses associated directly with revenue are matched against revenue in those interim periods in which the related revenue is recognized. Examples of expenses associated directly with revenue are costs of materials; wages, salaries, and related fringe benefits; manufacturing overhead; and warranties.

The application of traditional inventory methods in determining the inventory and cost of goods sold at the end of interim periods raises some interesting questions. The practical problems are significant. Also, the application of annual inventory procedures for interim periods may produce interim figures that would not, when added together, equal the annual figures. As a result, practices vary in determining the cost of inventory at the end of interim periods. While essentially the same procedures used for annual reporting should also be used at interim dates, several exceptions are appropriate at interim dates:[5]

---

[5]*APB Opinion No. 28*, par. 14.

1. Some companies use estimated gross margin rates to determine the cost of goods sold during interim periods or use other methods different from those used at annual inventory dates. (We discussed this method of inventory estimation in Chapter 9.) These companies should disclose the method used at the interim date and any significant adjustments that result from reconciliations with the annual physical inventory.

2. Companies that use LIFO may encounter a liquidation of base period inventories at an interim date that is expected to be replaced by the end of the annual period. In such cases, the inventory at the interim reporting date should not give effect to the LIFO liquidation, and cost of sales for the interim reporting period should include the *expected cost of replacing* the liquidated LIFO base.

3. Inventory losses from market declines should not be deferred beyond the interim period in which the decline occurs. Recoveries of such losses on the same inventory in later interim periods of the same fiscal year through market price recoveries should be recognized as gains in the later interim period. Such gains should not exceed losses recognized in previous interim periods. Some market declines at interim dates, however, can reasonably be expected to be restored in the fiscal year. Such *temporary* market declines need not be recognized at the interim date because no loss is expected for the fiscal year.

4. Companies that use standard cost accounting systems for determining inventory and product costs should generally follow the same procedures in reporting purchase price, wage rate, and usage or efficiency variances from standard cost at the end of an interim period as followed at the end of a fiscal year. Purchase price variances or volume or capacity cost variances that are planned and expected to be absorbed by the end of the annual period should ordinarily be deferred at interim reporting dates. The effect of unplanned or unanticipated purchase price or volume variances, however, should be reported at the end of an interim period following the same procedures used at the end of a fiscal year.

The influence of the integral view of financial reporting is evident in these procedures. For example, in the case of the last-in, first-out (LIFO) liquidation (item 2 of the preceding list), the procedure to be followed in the interim period is based on the desire to apply LIFO on an annual basis. Therefore, any LIFO liquidation that takes place in an interim period but that is expected to be replaced by the end of the annual period is not treated as a LIFO liquidation in the interim period. Similarly, if market declines in inventory at interim dates are temporary and are expected to be recovered by the end of the annual period (item 3 of the preceding list), no loss is recognized in the interim period. In these cases, the interim report should present figures that are most indicative of expected annual results rather than those obtained by strictly applying GAAP in each interim period as they would be applied in an annual period.

All other expenses (i.e., those not directly associated with revenue) should be recognized in interim periods as incurred or allocated among interim periods on the basis of an estimate of time expired, benefit received, or activity associated with the period. The objective of recognizing expenses is to achieve a fair measure of *results of operations for the annual period* and to present fairly the *financial position at the end of the annual period*. To meet this objective, procedures may be followed at the end of an interim period that would normally not be followed at the end of an annual period. Assume, for example, that a cost (such as repair and maintenance) usually expensed for annual reporting purposes is incurred in one interim period but clearly benefits two or more interim periods. Accruals or deferrals should then be used to charge an appropriate portion of the annual cost to each interim period. However, if no discernible benefits exist, arbitrary amounts should not be allocated among interim periods.

The amounts of certain expenses that can be reasonably estimated at interim dates are subject to year-end adjustments. Examples are inventory shrinkage, uncollectible receivables, and discretionary year-end bonuses. As the year progresses, more reliable estimates of annual amounts are usually possible. Estimates should be made at interim dates, with consideration given to all available information that is expected to influence the amount of expense to be recognized for annual reporting purposes. When possible, estimated expenses should be assigned to interim periods so that the interim periods bear a reasonable portion of the anticipated annual amount.

At this point, you may want to refer to Appendix A of Chapter 5, where we discussed using a worksheet to prepare interim financial statements.

SPECIAL PRINCIPLES OF INTERIM REPORTING

The general principles just described apply to the recognition of a wide range of revenues and expenses in interim reports, but a number of unique problems are encountered when accounting principles that were originally designed for annual reporting are applied to interim reports. Several of these problems are discussed below.

Seasonal Revenues and Expenses

Revenues and expenses of certain businesses are subject to material **seasonal variations.** In these circumstances, to avoid the possible misinterpretation that interim results indicate estimated annual results, companies should disclose the seasonal nature of their business activities.

Disclosure

To further emphasize the relationship of interim information to information relating to the annual period, *APB Opinion No. 28* requires that companies present information either for year to date or for the last 12 months to date along with quarterly information. We discuss these and other specific disclosure requirements later in this chapter.

Income Taxes

Interim period income tax expense should reflect the same general principles of income tax accounting that apply for annual reporting. At the end of each interim period, an estimate is made of the effective income tax rate expected for the annual period. This rate is then applied to income earned to date for that year. Any income tax recognized in previous interim periods is subtracted from the amount resulting from the preceding computation, and the difference is recognized as income tax expense in the current interim period. The estimate of the annual effective income tax rate should reflect anticipated investment tax credits, capital gains rates, and other information available from tax planning techniques. In arriving at this rate, no effect should be included for the income tax related to extraordinary or other items that will be reported on a net-of-tax basis when they are recognized.

For example, assume that during the first quarter of 1996, Atkins Company estimated its effective annual income tax rate to be 34%. Income before income tax for the first quarter was $485,000. During the second quarter of 1996, the estimate of the effective annual income tax rate was reduced to 32% because of revised plans to take advantage of certain income tax credits. Pretax financial income for the second quarter of 1996 was $650,000. The income tax expense for the first two quarters is determined in the following schedule:

First Quarter		
Pretax financial income for first quarter of 1996		$ 485,000
Estimated annual income tax rate		34%
Income tax expense for first quarter		$ 164,900
Second Quarter		
Pretax financial income for first quarter of 1996	$485,000	
Pretax financial income for second quarter of 1996	650,000	$1,135,000
Estimated annual income tax rate		32%
Income tax for first and second quarters of 1996		$ 363,200
Income tax expense recognized in first quarter		(164,900)
Income tax expense for second quarter		$ 198,300

The same process is followed for subsequent quarters as additional information on pretax financial income and the annual effective income tax rate becomes available.

Operating losses recognized in interim periods are subject to carryback and carryforward treatment similar to that discussed in Chapter 19 for annual periods. Operating losses of an interim period may be carried back to an earlier annual period or an earlier interim period of the year of the interim period loss. If carryback is not possible, interim period operating losses may be carried forward and recognized when the interim period loss is recognized if the tax benefits are expected to be (1) realized during the year or (2) recognizable as a deferred tax asset at the end of the year in accordance with the provisions of *SFAS No. 109.*

Disclosure of Irregular Income Items

Extraordinary items should be separately disclosed in the interim period in which they occur. The materiality of extraordinary items should be judged in relation to estimated income for the entire year. Gains and losses on disposal of a segment of a business and unusual or infrequently occurring transactions that are material with respect to the operating results of the interim period should be separately disclosed. Extraordinary items, gains and losses from segment disposals, and unusual or infrequently occurring items should *not be allocated* over several interim periods of the year in which they occur. Irregular income items that would be presented on a net of tax basis in an enterprise's annual financial statements, such as extraordinary items, are presented in the same manner in its interim financial statements.

Materiality

Disclosure

Accounting Changes

The Accounting Principles Board recommended that accounting changes be made in the first interim period of a fiscal year. This recommendation is supported by the APB's belief that changes in accounting principles and methods made in later interim periods of a fiscal year tend to obscure operating results and complicate disclosure in interim periods. Accounting changes in interim periods should generally be accounted for in the same way as they would be in annual reporting. Chapter 20 discussed the proper procedures for accounting changes.

An exception is a change in accounting principle for which there is a cumulative effect that must be recognized in income in the period of change. If the change is made in the first interim period, accounting for the change is the same as in annual reporting, because the cumulative effect to the beginning of the first interim period is the same as the cumulative effect to the beginning of the annual period in which the change is made. However, a problem arises if a change in accounting principle is made in a subsequent interim period, because the cumulative effect to the beginning of the interim period of change is not the same as the cumulative effect to the beginning of the annual period. This difference is due to the additional time encompassed by the interim periods prior to the interim period of change. *FASB Statement of Financial Accounting Standards No. 3* gave special consideration to this problem and concluded that a cumulative effect type accounting change made in other than the first interim period should be accounted for *as if the change had been made in the first interim period.*[6] Income of previous interim periods of the fiscal year in which such a change is made should be restated, with consideration given to the impact of the change in the first interim period. This procedure is consistent with the *integral view* of interim reporting, because it makes the amount of the cumulative effect included in interim income the same as the amount to be included in the determination of annual income.

Adjustments of Previous Interim Periods

An item of profit or loss that occurs in an interim period may relate to previous annual periods or previous interim periods of the same year, or both. Examples are settlements of

---

[6]*FASB Statement of Financial Accounting Standards No. 3,* "Reporting Accounting Changes in Interim Financial Statements," 1974, par. 10.

litigation and adjustments of income taxes. If this type of event is recorded in an interim period other than the first interim period, the following guidelines should be followed:[7]

1. The portion of the item that is directly related to business activities of the current interim period should be included in the determination of net income for that period.
2. The portion of the item that relates to previous interim periods of the same annual period should be included in restated income of those periods.
3. The portion of the item that relates to previous annual periods should be included in the determination of net income of the first interim period of the year of the change.

DISCLOSURE REQUIREMENTS FOR INTERIM REPORTS

Disclosure   Most companies disclose interim financial information in considerably less detail than that provided in annual financial statements. When a company reports summarized financial information at interim dates, *at least* the following should be presented:[8]

1. Selected income statement items, as applicable:
   a. Sales or gross revenues.
   b. Provision for income taxes.
   c. Unusual or infrequently occurring items.
   d. Disposal of a segment of a business.
   e. Extraordinary items, including related income tax effects.
   f. Cumulative effect of an accounting change.
   g. Net income.
   h. Earnings per share.
2. Seasonal revenues, costs, or expenses.
3. Contingent items.
4. Changes in accounting principles or estimates, including significant changes in estimates or provision for income taxes.
5. Significant changes in financial position.

This list shows the *minimum* information that *APB Opinion No. 28* requires of publicly traded companies that report quarterly information on a regular basis. The APB encouraged such companies to publish condensed balance sheet and cash flow information at interim dates because such information is often helpful to users of interim financial information in understanding and interpreting the income data that are reported.

When summarized financial information is regularly reported on a quarterly basis, information for the current quarter and the current year to date or last 12 months to date should be presented. In addition, similar information for the preceding year should be presented on a comparative basis. These disclosures are designed to facilitate **comparison** of the current quarter with a longer period of time (year to date or last 12 months) and with the comparable quarter of the previous year.

Many companies that report on a quarterly basis do not provide a separate fourth quarter statement, because the end of the fourth quarter coincides with the end of the annual reporting period. Where a separate fourth quarter report is not issued, significant events occur-
Disclosure   ring in the fourth quarter should be separately disclosed in the notes to the annual financial statements.

The interim report for Wal-Mart Stores for the three months that ended on April 30, 1993, is presented in Exhibit 25–1. Observe that Wal-Mart reported a condensed income statement, balance sheet, and statement of cash flows. The condensed statements are unaudited, and comparative amounts are reported for the three months that ended on April 30, 1992.

---

[7]*FASB Statement of Financial Accounting Standards No. 16,* "Prior Period Adjustments," 1977, par. 14.
[8]*APB Opinion No. 28,* par. 30.

FIRMS GET STINGY WITH QUARTERLY REPORTS

Your stock's quarterly report is *not* in the mail.

That's because a growing number of U.S. companies are making it harder for investors to get quarterly financial reports. Wall Street is steaming over this practice, and the Securities and Exchange Commission has launched an inquiry.

Dozens of major companies—including American Express Co., American Telephone & Telegraph Co., General Electric Co., International Business Machines Corp. and Walt Disney Co.—no longer routinely send out reports to investors who keep their shares at brokerage firms. This is known as holding stock in "street name", rather than registering the shares with the issuing company itself.

Those losing out are the estimated 75% of U.S. investors who keep their shares in street name and get financial reports and dividends forwarded to them by their brokers. Though publicly traded corporations are required only to send out annual reports and proxies, they have traditionally sent out quarterly reports to all shareholders as well. But no more.

The companies say they are saving hundreds of thousands of dollars—$800,000 a year at AT&T, for example, and $150,000 at Disney. "I'm amazed; I've gotten no complaints," says Luther Marr, head of shareholder affairs at Disney, which cut off reports to street-name holders last year.

But now, both a New York Stock Exchange committee and the SEC are looking at the issue. The SEC, if it chooses, could require companies to treat all shareholders equally in disseminating reports. An SEC spokesman in Washington won't comment on the inquiry, except to acknowledge: "We have asked some questions about the corporate practice in this area."

The Securities Industry Association, Wall Street's major trade group, calls the report cut-off "a potentially serious breach" of corporate responsibility and has urged the SEC to require corporations to send quarterly reports to all holders.

"It's just not fair," says Peter Quick, an executive at discount broker Quick & Reilly Group Inc. who is spearheading the securities association's efforts. "We see it as a small-investor problem," he says. Street-name investors "are no longer being given the same information as institutions and registered shareholders."

To critics, the cut offs are the latest example of how small investors are often discriminated against. Big institutional investors already have better access to high-technology trading and breaking financial news than do most individual investors.

Despite their dull reputation, quarterly financial reports often include more than just earnings results. Some, including American Express's, run detailed comments from the chairman; IBM's third-quarter 1991 report included 14 news items from the computer giant. Disney's provides updates on its coming movies.

Still, corporations say investors aren't clamoring to get quarterly reports. "It isn't that we don't care about holders; it's that holders don't care about the reports," says Disney's Mr. Marr. Nearly half of Disney's investors are street-name holders, Mr. Marr says, and "all they care about is [the stock] making money."

Relevant or Not?

At American Express, a spokeswoman says quarterly reports are "perceived by recipients as not important and somewhat stale" because a company's earnings have already been announced. Many companies want Congress to get rid of quarterly reporting requirements entirely.

Other companies that have cut back quarterly reports for street-name investors include Allied-Signal Inc., Bethlehem Steel Corp., Du Pont Co., Eastman Kodak Co., McDonald's Corp., Minnesota Mining & Manufacturing Co., Texaco Inc. and Westinghouse Electric Corp.

Are quarterly reports really that irrelevant? Not all investors think so.

"If you're going to have an investment in something, why, you're entitled to receive the quarterly reports," says Robert T. Willis, a 64-year-old investor in Bainbridge, Ga., who keeps his stocks in street name. Mr. Willis says he doesn't like a lot of government regulation, but this is one area that needs it—"and that's not taking some wild-eyed liberal standpoint."

Some companies have set up alternate ways for street-name holders to get quarterly reports, such as by submitting a written request. Corporations also will provide a batch of quarterly reports to brokerage firms that request them so that the brokers can forward them to investors. But these companies won't reimburse the brokers for mailing costs.

That is a key issue, because brokerage firms argue that holding shares in street name already saves corporations the cost of engraving stock certificates and mailing dividends checks.

"Look at all the companies that couldn't talk enough to shareholders when facing takeover threats" in the 1980s, says Mr. Quick of Quick & Reilly. "Now that they don't face the threat, they've decided not to talk to their holders."

SOURCE: William Power, "Firms Get Stingy with Quarterly Reports," *The Wall Street Journal*, February 13, 1992, pp. C1, C9. Reprinted by permission of The Wall Street Journal, © 1992 Dow Jones & Company, Inc. All Rights Reserved Worldwide.

In financial analysis, an important consideration is the industry in which the enterprise operates. The markets in which an enterprise buys and sells vary by industry. The risks and potential rewards of business operation vary considerably by industry. If an enterprise operates

SEGMENT REPORTING

EXHIBIT 25–1

Wal-Mart Stores, Inc.
Interim Reporting Example

Wal-Mart Stores, Inc., and Subsidiaries Condensed Consolidated Statements of Income
(Unaudited—Amounts in thousands except per share data)

	Three Months Ended April 30,	
	1993	1992
Net sales	**$13,920,407**	$11,649,430
Rental and other income	**144,791**	104,911
Total Revenues	**14,065,198**	11,754,341
Cost of sales	**11,016,745**	9,256,326
Operating, selling, and general and administrative expenses	**2,246,260**	1,807,942
Interest costs:		
Debt	**54,416**	33,266
Capital leases	**46,342**	42,593
Total costs and expenses	**13,363,763**	11,140,127
Income before income taxes	**701,435**	614,214
Provision for taxes on income	**250,785**	227,259
Net income	**$ 450,650**	$ 386,955
Net income per share	**$ .20**	$ .17
Dividends per share	**.0325**	.0263
Beginning of the year shareholders' equity	**$ 8,759,180**	$ 6,989,710
Return for the period on beginning of the year shareholders' equity	**5.14%**	5.54%

Wal-Mart Stores, Inc., and Subsidiaries Condensed Consolidated Balance Sheets
(Unaudited—Amounts in thousands)
Assets

	April 30,	
	1993	1992
Current assets		
Cash	**$ 7,685**	$ 24,752
Receivables	**924,386**	1,179,520
Inventories	**10,630,737**	7,883,379
Other	**87,515**	76,815
Total current assets	**11,650,323**	9,164,466
Net property, plant and equipment	**9,052,414**	5,446,599
Net property under capital leases	**1,517,306**	1,401,312
Other assets	**618,463**	426,488
Total assets	**$22,838,506**	$16,438,865

in a single industry, consideration of industry factors is relatively straightforward; if an enterprise operates in more than one industry, the consideration of industry factors in financial analysis is more complex.

During the 1960s, a significant trend toward diversification developed, and many **diversified companies** (i.e., companies operating in several different industries) emerged. Many

Liabilities and Shareholders' Equity	April 30,	
	1993	1992
Current liabilities		
Commercial paper	$ 1,929,247	$ 873,878
Accounts payable	4,814,833	3,588,443
Other	1,161,974	1,147,963
Total current liabilities	7,906,054	5,610,284
Long-term debt	3,817,207	1,720,209
Long-term obligations under capital leases	1,762,110	1,610,416
Deferred income taxes	217,730	181,763
Shareholders' equity	9,135,405	7,316,193
Total liabilities and shareholders' equity	$22,838,506	$16,438,865

Wal-Mart Stores, Inc., and Subsidiaries Condensed Consolidated Statements of Cash Flow

(Unaudited—Amounts in thousands)	Three Months Ended April 30,	
	1993	1992
Cash flows from operating activities:		
Net income	$ 450,650	$ 386,955
Adjustments to reconcile net income to net cash provided by operating activities:		
Depreciation and amortization	187,122	140,755
Increase in inventory	(1,362,428)	(499,080)
Increase in accounts payable	941,502	134,914
Increase (decrease) in other	(202,467)	26,916
Net cash provided by operating activities	14,379	190,460
Cash flows from investing activities:		
Capital expenditures	(975,173)	(545,873)
Other investing activities	(47,199)	2,383
Net cash used in investing activities	(1,022,372)	(543,490)
Cash flow from financing activities:		
Increase in commercial paper	340,422	419,914
Proceeds from issuance of long-term debt	750,200	29
Dividends paid	(74,749)	(60,332)
Other financing activities	(12,558)	(12,478)
Net cash provided by financing activities	1,003,315	347,133
Net decrease in cash and cash equivalents	(4,678)	(5,897)
Cash and cash equivalents at beginning of year	12,363	30,649
Cash and cash equivalents at end of first quarter	$ 7,685	24,752

SOURCE: Wal-Mart Stores, Inc., *Quarterly Report,* for the three months ended April 30, 1993.

companies that previously operated in a single industry moved into additional industries as a result of natural growth or by acquiring other companies. These companies diversified their operations for several reasons, including the desire of corporate management to spread the risks of investment over a number of industries and product lines to reduce dependence on any one set of suppliers and customers.

For more than a decade, the APB, and then the FASB, considered whether special information relative to operations in different industries should be required. This type of disclosure was called **segment reporting.** The authoritative boards identified many advantages and disadvantages of segment reporting and carefully considered the problems of separating aggregate financial information into components.

In 1976 the FASB issued *Statement of Financial Accounting Standards No. 14.* Although the major consideration centered around information along industry or product lines, the separation of information on other bases was also considered. *SFAS No. 14* resulted in disclosure requirements in three different areas:[9]

1. The enterprise's *operations in different industries.*
2. The enterprise's *foreign operations and export sales.*
3. The enterprise's *dependence on major customers.*

In subsequent pronouncements, the applicability of these requirements has been limited in several ways. A major limitation was the suspension of segment reporting requirements for nonpublic enterprises, as indicated in *SFAS No. 21.*[10] As a result of this pronouncement, the disclosure requirements discussed here were limited to publicly held companies. Another limitation states that segment disclosures are not required in interim financial presentations.[11]

Empirical research has shown that segment information is useful in decision making. One study, for example, found that segment disclosures help financial analysts to make more accurate forecasts of a company's earnings per share.[12] Another has found that segment cash flow statements, which are not presently required by GAAP, are relevant in lending decisions under certain circumstances.[13] Segment reporting provides information that helps users to assess more accurately the amount, timing, and uncertainty of prospective cash flows. It allows users to determine which business segments are doing well and which are doing poorly.

Disclosure   In deciding to require segment reporting for selected companies, the FASB determined that disaggregated information along industry or product lines, by geographic area, and by major customers is useful for purposes of assessing the risk and return inherent in investment and credit decisions. Therefore, these three areas of disclosure specified in *SFAS No. 14* are discussed in the following sections of this chapter. Although the FASB identified specific disclosure requirements, considerable flexibility exists in the manner of accumulating the necessary information that underlies these disclosures. This fact, coupled with the fact that each enterprise has unique operating characteristics, led the FASB to conclude that segment information may be of limited usefulness in attempting to compare the information of one enterprise with similar information of other enterprises.

INFORMATION ABOUT DIFFERENT INDUSTRIES

Information about industry segments is required if the enterprise has significant operations in more than one industry. An **industry segment** is a component of an enterprise that tries to earn a profit by providing a product or service or a group of related products or services primarily to customers outside the enterprise. Industry segments are determined by identify-

---

[9]*FASB Statement of Financial Accounting Standards No. 14,* "Financial Reporting for Segments of a Business Enterprise," 1976, par. 3.

[10]*FASB Statement of Financial Accounting Standards No. 21,* "Suspension of the Reporting of Earnings per Share and Segment Information by Nonpublic Companies," 1978, par. 12.

[11]*FASB Statement of Financial Accounting Standards No. 18,* "Financial Reporting for Segments of a Business Enterprise—Interim Financial Statements," 1977, par. 7.

[12]Bruce A. Baldwin, "Segment Earnings Disclosure and the Ability of Security Analysts to Forecast Earnings per Share," *Accounting Review* (July 1984), pp. 376–389.

[13]Donna L. Street and Keith G. Stanga, "The Relevance of a Segment Cash Flow Statement in Lending Decisions: An Empirical Study," *Accounting and Business Research* (Autumn 1989), pp. 353–361.

ing the products and services of an enterprise and grouping those products and services by industry lines. Those industry segments that meet the materiality guidelines described below are then identified as **reportable segments.**

Several standardized systems exist for classifying business activities. These include the **Standard Industrial Classification (SIC)** and the **Enterprise Standard Industrial Classification (ESIC),** both of which are used by the U.S. government. The SIC is a system of classifying business enterprises by the type of economic activity in which they engage. The ESIC system is based on the form of business organization. The FASB has indicated that these systems may help an enterprise to identify its industry segments and reportable segments. Because no single system of classification is universally applicable for determining the industry segments of all enterprises, identification of an enterprise's industry segments *depends largely on judgment.* In determining whether products and services are related or unrelated for purposes of identifying reportable segments, factors such as the following should be considered: the nature of the products and services, the nature of the production process, and markets and marketing methods for the distribution of the products and services.

Management's primary responsibility in identifying industry segments is to separate the enterprise's operations into those components that will be most meaningful to the users of the financial statements. As examples of the kinds of industry segments, Anheuser-Busch Companies have beer and beer-related products, food products, and entertainment; Georgia-Pacific Corporation has building products, pulp and paper, and other operations; and the Procter & Gamble Company has laundry and cleaning, personal care, food and beverage, and pulp and chemicals.

In identifying reportable segments and preparing the information to be presented, the terms *revenue, operating profit or loss,* and *identifiable assets* are important:

1. *Revenue.* The revenue of an industry segment includes both sales to unaffiliated customers and intersegment sales or transfers of products or services similar to those sold to unaffiliated customers.

2. *Operating profit or loss.* The operating profit or loss of an industry segment is its revenue less all operating expenses. Operating expenses include expenses that relate to revenues as defined above. Operating expenses that are not directly traceable to an industry segment are allocated on a reasonable basis among the segments benefiting from the expense. Revenues and expenses of a general corporate nature but not associated with the operations of specific industry segments are not included in the determination of operating profit or loss of industry segments.

3. *Identifiable assets.* The identifiable assets of an industry segment are the assets used by the segment, including those assets used exclusively by the segment and an allocated portion of assets used jointly by two or more industry segments. Assets used for general corporate purposes but not used in the operation of any industry segment are not allocated to industry segments.

The criteria for translating *industry segments* into *reportable segments* are based on the revenues, operating profits or losses, and identifiable assets of the industry segments. An industry segment constitutes a reportable segment (i.e., a segment for which information must be disclosed separately) if *any one* of the following criteria is met:

1. Revenue of the segment is 10% or more of the combined revenue of all industry segments.
2. The absolute amount of the operating profit or loss of the segment is 10% or more of the greater (in absolute amount) of the following:
   a. The combined operating profit of all industry segments with an operating profit.
   b. The combined operating loss of all industry segments with an operating loss.
3. The identifiable assets of the segment are 10% or more of the combined identifiable assets of all industry segments.

Let's consider an example in which we apply these criteria to identify reportable segments. Assume that Diversity, Inc., has identified five industry segments in which it operates.

Revenue, operating profit (loss), and identifiable assets in millions of dollars for each industry are as follows:

Industry	Revenue	Operating Profit (Loss)	Identifiable Assets
Food products	$150	$ 17	$250
Publishing	125	5	108
Metal products	62	(10)	38
Lumber	30	2	18
Electrical machinery	18	(1)	40
	$385	$ 13	$454

Any one of the three criteria of 10% of revenue, operating profit or loss, and identifiable assets is sufficient for an industry segment to qualify as a reportable segment. In this example, all three criteria apply to the process of identifying reportable segments.

Based on revenue alone, food products, publishing, and metal products are reportable segments, because revenue associated with each of these exceeds $38.5 million ($385 million × 10%). Based on identifiable assets, food products and publishing are reportable segments, because identifiable assets associated with each of these exceed $45.4 million ($454 million × 10%).

Applying the criterion of 10% of operating profit or loss is somewhat more complicated, because some segments have an operating profit and others have an operating loss. The operating profits must be combined and the operating losses must be combined to determine which is larger (based on the absolute amounts of the two). For Diversity, Inc., total operating profits are $24 million and total operating losses are $11 million, determined as follows (in millions of dollars):

Industry Segment	Absolute Amount of Operating	
	Profit	Loss
Food products	$17	
Publishing	5	
Metal products		$10
Lumber	2	
Electrical machinery		1
	$24	$11

Because the total profit figure exceeds the total loss figure, $24 million is the basis for identifying the reportable segment. Any industry with an *operating profit or loss* of $2.4 million or higher ($24 million × 10%) qualifies as a reportable segment. Therefore food products, publishing, and metal products are reportable segments.

Summarizing for Diversity, Inc., we have identified the industry segments of food products, publishing, and metal products as reportable segments. The other two industries (lumber and electrical machinery) may be combined, because they do not meet any one of the **Materiality** materiality criteria for identification as reportable segments.

An accountant **must use judgment** to identify reportable segments. Comparability between periods is important. Accordingly, an industry segment that does not meet any of the above criteria in a particular year but that has been significant in the past and is expected to be significant in the future might be considered a reportable segment. Also, an industry that is significant by these criteria in one year but has not been significant in the past and is not expected to be significant in the future may be excluded as a reportable segment. We can see the elusive nature of the materiality decision and the significance of applying judgment in **Materiality** making important materiality decisions.

SFAS No. 14 requires that *reportable segments account for 75% or more of the combined revenue from sales to unaffiliated customers of all industry segments.* If this criterion is not met, industry segments should be redefined to include additional industries as reportable segments so that the amount of revenue from sales to unaffiliated customers accounted for by reportable segments equals at least 75% of the combined total. This requirement exists to ensure that the reportable segments account for the major portion of business activity of the enterprise as a whole.

For example, assume that Newton Company has identified three reportable segments by applying the criteria of 10% of revenue, operating profit or loss, and identifiable assets. These segments are tobacco, chemicals, and rubber. ("Miscellaneous other" includes amounts from several smaller segments.) Revenue information (in millions of dollars) for these segments is as follows:

Segment	Sales to Unaffiliated Companies	Intersegment Sales	Total Revenue
Tobacco	$ 812	$ 38	$ 850
Chemicals	311	114	425
Rubber	128	125	253
Miscellaneous other	140	8	148
	$1,391	$285	$1,676

To determine whether the reportable segments represent a sufficient portion of enterprise operations, 75% of the sales to unaffiliated companies must be accounted for by the reportable segments. This criterion is met in the case of Newton Company, because sales to unaffiliated companies of the reportable segments total $1,251 ($812 + $311 + $128), and this exceeds 75% of the total of all sales to unaffiliated companies ($1,251/$1,391 = 89.9%). If this condition had not been met, some industry segments included in "miscellaneous other" would need to be combined with each other or with the previously identified reportable segments until the reportable segments accounted for 75% or more of sales to unaffiliated companies.

Once the reportable segments are identified, *the following information must be presented for each reportable segment and for other segments in the aggregate:*

1. Revenue.
2. Operating profit or loss.
3. Identifiable assets.
4. Depreciation, depletion, and amortization expense.
5. Expenditures for property, plant, and equipment.
6. Equity in the net income and net assets of vertically integrated investees that are either unconsolidated subsidiaries or accounted for by the equity method.
7. Effects of changes in accounting principle.

Disclosure

Companies may disclose this information in the body of the primary financial statements, in accompanying notes, or in separate supplemental schedules. If the latter approaches are used, the information should be related to consolidated information in the primary financial statements.

As a practical matter, the number of industry segments presented should not be so large that it causes information overload. The FASB indicates a preference for *no more than 10 segments.* If the number of industry segments exceeds 10, closely related segments may be combined to reduce the number of reportable segments.

A company that operates in several industries may be dominated by operations in a single industry. A single industry segment is considered dominant if it accounts for more than 90% of revenue, operating profit or loss, *and* identifiable assets and if no other industry segment meets any of the 10% tests discussed earlier. When an enterprise operates predominantly in a single industry, this industry should be identified in the financial statements. Although the reporting requirements of *SFAS No. 14* are limited to publicly held companies, a desirable financial reporting practice is for *all* companies to clearly identify the industry in which they operate. Many small companies do this as part of their Summary of Significant Accounting Policies.

INFORMATION ON FOREIGN OPERATIONS AND EXPORT SALES

In the current global economic environment, many companies derive significant revenue from operations in foreign countries and from exporting goods and services from the United States to foreign countries. **Foreign operations** refers to the presence of production and distribution facilities in countries other than the United States. **Export sales** refers to the operation of facilities in the United States from which goods and services are distributed to foreign countries.

Due to differences in the economic and political environments in foreign countries, significant uncertainty may be associated with foreign operations and export sales. For example, companies with operations in certain Middle Eastern and South American countries have found their operations in jeopardy because of political unrest. *SFAS No. 14* establishes certain disclosure requirements that apply even if the industry segment disclosures and major customer disclosures do not. A publicly held company is required to present information concerning foreign operations if *either* of the following conditions is met:[14]

Disclosure

1. Revenue generated by foreign operations from sales to unaffiliated customers is 10% or more of consolidated revenue as reported in the enterprise's income statement.
2. Identifiable assets of the enterprise's foreign operations are 10% or more of consolidated total assets as reported in the enterprise's balance sheet.

If a significant portion of foreign operations is conducted in two or more geographic areas, the information should be presented for each area separately. A geographic area is considered significant if its revenue from sales to unaffiliated customers or its identifiable assets are 10% or more of related consolidated amounts. The determination of what constitutes a **geographic area** is a management decision and should reflect such factors as proximity, economic relationship, similarity of business environment, and the nature and interrelationship of business activities in various foreign locations.

Information concerning foreign operations that should be presented (by geographic area, if appropriate) includes (1) revenues, (2) operating profit or loss or some other measure of profitability, and (3) identifiable assets.

If products and services exported from a company's domestic operations to foreign countries make up 10% or more of the total revenue from sales to unaffiliated customers, that amount of revenue must be separately disclosed. If significant exports are made into different geographic areas, separate disclosure by geographic area should be made as considered appropriate in the circumstances.

For example, assume that Proffitt Company is a publicly held U.S. company with both foreign operations and export sales. The total revenue of $230,000,000 for 1996, all of which is to unaffiliated customers, is distributed over various components of the company's operations as follows:

	Revenue (in millions of dollars)
Domestic operations	
Sales in United States	$105
Export sales	45
	$150

---

[14]*FASB Statement of Financial Accounting Standards No. 14*, par. 32.

	Revenue (in millions of dollars)
Foreign operations	
France	25
Germany	30
Miscellaneous other countries	25
	80
Total revenue	$230

Assume further that the $45 million of export sales is made in a single geographic area and that the $25 million of revenues from "miscellaneous other countries" represents sales in five countries, none of which exceed $7 million. In addition, none of the foreign operations from which these sales are derived represent an investment in 10% or more of identifiable assets.

Proffitt Company should make the following separate disclosures:

Segment	Information Disclosed	Justification
Export portion of domestic operations	Revenue	Exports make up more than 10% of total revenue ($45/$230 = 19.6%)
Foreign operations in France and Germany	Revenue Operating profit Identifiable assets	Revenues in France and Germany exceed 10% of total revenues (France: $25/$230 = 10.9%; Germany: $30/$230 = 13.0%)

Because all export sales are made to a single geographic area, no further separation of this revenue amount is necessary. Because foreign operations in countries other than France and Germany do not meet the significance tests of 10% of revenues ($7/$230 = 3%) or identifiable assets, no further separation of the amounts attributable to operations in these countries is necessary.

As with industry segment disclosure, information concerning foreign operations and export sales may be presented in the body of the primary financial statements or in the notes or supplementary schedules that accompany the financial statements.

Disclosure

MAJOR CUSTOMER INFORMATION

If an enterprise derives 10% or more of its revenue from sales to a single customer, that fact and the amount of revenue from each customer meeting this criterion must be disclosed. The purpose of this disclosure is to make the users of the financial statements aware of the extent of reliance of the enterprise on a small number of customers. The identity of the customer is not required.

Disclosure

To illustrate, suppose a company produces seat belts, which it sells to a major automobile manufacturer and to independent automobile parts suppliers throughout the United States. If 10% or more of sales are made to a single customer, such as the manufacturer, this fact may be important to users of the company's financial statements, because future sales are linked to the success of the automobile manufacturer.

The disclosure of reliance on **major customers** is required even if the other segment reporting requirements do not apply. If industry segment information is presented and major customer disclosure is also required, the industry segment making the sales should be disclosed.

For purposes of applying the major customer disclosure, a group of entities under common control is considered a single customer. In dealings with domestic governments, the federal government, an individual state government, or an individual local government is considered a single customer. The governments of individual foreign countries are considered single customers. The major customer disclosure usually appears in the footnotes to the financial statements. The disclosure of major customers is a desirable practice for all companies,

---

EXHIBIT 25–2

Simpson Industries, Inc.
Example Major Customer Disclosure

Note I—Major Customers

The Company's operations, as briefly described on page 3 of this Annual Report, are conducted within one business segment. Sales to customers outside the United States are not material.

Net sales to major customers:

(In thousands)

	1992	1991	1990
General Motors Corporation	$89,800	$75,300	$63,100
Ford Motor Company	39,200	30,700	31,500
Chrysler Corporation	32,400	32,200	37,800
Consolidated Diesel Company	21,900	25,300	27,800

Aggregate receivables for these customers at December 31, 1992 and 1991 approximate the same percent of total receivables as aggregate sales to these customers bear to total sales.

SOURCE: Simpson Industries, Inc., 1992 Annual Report.

---

even though the specific requirements of *SFAS No. 14* are limited to publicly held companies. Exhibit 25–2 shows a major customer disclosure of Simpson Industries, a company that produces machined parts, assemblies, and modules for manufacturers of automobiles, trucks, diesel engines, and heavy equipment.

EXAMPLE OF SEGMENT DISCLOSURE

The segment reporting disclosures of Bristol-Myers Squibb Company for 1992 with comparative years 1991 and 1990 are shown in Exhibit 25–3. The information presented for each of the company's four industry segments includes net sales, profit, year-end assets, capital expenditures, and depreciation. Bristol-Myers Squibb also reports its net sales, profit, and year-end assets in different geographic areas, as shown in Exhibit 25–3.

REPORTING DISAGGREGATED INFORMATION: CHANGE IS LIKELY

The FASB is currently working on a major project to reexamine the existing standards for reporting disaggregated information. It recently published a Research Report that examines many issues that have been raised in this area. Although users of financial statements believe that the segment information currently reported under *SFAS No. 14* is *useful,* they believe that *improvements are needed.* Examples of recommendations for improvement are as follows:[15]

1. Disclose information for each industry and geographic segment *quarterly,* instead of just annually.
2. Disclose revenues and profits by product and service line, even for those companies that operate in a single industry.
3. Provide additional guidance to help companies identify their industry and geographic segments. This guidance would be designed to allow companies to disaggregate into a larger number of segments. It would also allow more uniformity in segmentation by comparable companies.
4. Disclose additional segment information, such as cash flow, identifiable liabilities, identifiable net assets, and so forth.

---

[15]Paul Pacter, "Reporting Disaggregated Information," Research Report (FASB, 1993).

EXHIBIT 25–3

Bristol-Myers Squibb Company
Segment Reporting Example

Note 16—Segment Information

The company's products are reported in four industry segments as follows:

Pharmaceutical Products—prescription medicines, mainly cardiovascular drugs and anti-infectives, which comprise about forty percent and twenty-five percent, respectively, of the segment's sales, anti-cancer and central nervous system drugs, diagnostic agents and other pharmaceutical products.

Medical Devices—orthopaedic implants, which comprise about forty percent of the segment's sales, ostomy and wound care products, surgical instruments and other medical devices.

Nonprescription Health Products—infant formulas and other nutritional products, which comprise about sixty-five percent of the segment's sales, analgesics, cough/cold remedies and skin care products.

Toiletries and Beauty Aids—haircoloring and hair care preparations, which comprise about sixty-five percent of the segment's sales, deodorants, anti-perspirants and beauty appliances.

Unallocated expenses principally consist of general administrative expenses and net interest income, and in 1992 include a portion of the charge for restructuring. Other assets are principally cash and cash equivalents, time deposits and marketable securities. Inter-area sales by geographic area for each of the three years ended December 31, 1992, 1991, and 1990, respectively, were: United States—$915 million, $807 million and $741 million; Europe, Middle East, and Africa—$382 million, $448 million and $360 million; Other Western Hemisphere—$36 million, $28 million and $34 million; and Pacific—$26 million, $30 million and $3 million. These sales are usually billed at or above manufacturing costs.

Net assets relating to operations outside the United States amounted to approximately $1,369 million, $1,323 million and $1,186 million at December 31, 1992, 1991, and 1990, respectively.

Industry Segments (in millions of dollars)	Net Sales 1992	Net Sales 1991	Net Sales 1990	Profit[a] 1992	Profit[a] 1991	Profit[a] 1990	Year-End Assets 1992	Year-End Assets 1991	Year-End Assets 1990
Pharmaceutical Products	$ 6,313	$ 5,908	$5,261	$1,584	$1,844	$1,548	$ 4,622	$4,215	$3,972
Medical Devices	1,665	1,559	1,436	305	354	346	1,063	1,033	906
Nonprescription Health Products	1,959	1,901	1,773	268	435	390	839	827	727
Toiletries and Beauty Aids	1,219	1,203	1,271	10	203	235	547	745	686
Net sales, operating profit and assets	$11,156	$10,571	$9,741	$2,167	$2,836	$2,519	$ 7,071	$6,820	$6,291

Geographic Areas (in millions of dollars)	Net Sales 1992	Net Sales 1991	Net Sales 1990	Profit[b] 1992	Profit[b] 1991	Profit[b] 1990	Year-End Assets 1992	Year-End Assets 1991	Year-End Assets 1990
United States	$ 7,362	$ 7,172	$6,540	$1,467	$2,016	$1,677	$ 4,587	$4,430	$4,251
Europe, Middle East, and Africa	3,163	2,905	2,668	534	641	629	1,813	1,858	1,590
Other Western Hemisphere	939	862	859	138	171	189	426	424	382
Pacific	1,051	945	812	86	97	72	717	689	550
Inter-area eliminations	(1,359)	(1,313)	(1,138)	(58)	(89)	(48)	(472)	(581)	(482)
Net sales, operating profit and assets	$11,156	$10,571	$9,741	$2,167	$2,836	$2,519	$ 7,071	$6,820	$6,291
Unallocated expenses and other assets				(180)	(52)	(86)	3,733	2,596	2,924
Earnings from continuing operations before income taxes and total assets				$1,987	$2,784	$2,433	$10,804	$9,416	$9,215

Industry Segments (in millions of dollars)	Capital Expenditures 1992	Capital Expenditures 1991	Capital Expenditures 1990	Depreciation 1992	Depreciation 1991	Depreciation 1990
Pharmaceutical Products	$ 426	$ 402	$ 360	$ 186	$ 145	$ 144
Medical Devices	84	81	51	34	30	26
Nonprescription Health Products	70	54	43	28	30	29
Toiletries and Beauty Aids	34	37	38	28	26	31
Identifiable industry totals	614	574	492	276	231	230
Other	40	59	34	19	15	14
Consolidated totals	$ 654	$ 633	$ 526	$ 295	$ 246	$ 244

[a]The 1992 operating profit of the company's industry segments included the charge for restructuring as follows: Pharmaceutical Products—$371 million; Medical Devices—$155 million; Nonprescription Health Products—$150 million; and Toiletries and Beauty Aids—$150 million.

[b]The 1992 earnings from continuing operations before income taxes included the charge for restructuring as follows: United States—$595 million; Europe, Mid-East and Africa—$134 million; Other Western Hemisphere—$51 million; Pacific—$46 million; and unallocated expenses—$64 million.

SOURCE: Bristol-Myers Squibb Company, 1992 Annual Report.

5. Disaggregate all foreign operations by industry segment.
6. Provide more descriptive and explanatory information about the industry segments and geographic areas in which the company operates, in addition to the financial data.

The FASB's Research Report reviews nearly 80 research studies that have been conducted on segment reporting and identifies the following major issues related to disaggregated disclosures:

1. What bases (e.g., industries, legal entities, borrowing units) should companies use to disaggregate financial information?
2. How should financial information be disaggregated?
3. What disclosures should the FASB require in this area?
4. How should disclosures about disaggregated information be presented?
5. When should disclosures about disaggregated information be presented (i.e., annually, quarterly)?
6. What types of entities should present disclosures about disaggregated information?
7. Are any other problems (e.g., disclosures harmful to the company's competitive position) associated with reporting disaggregated information?

The FASB issued an Invitation to Comment on this subject and plans to issue an Exposure Draft near the end of 1994. Considerable due process is anticipated before the FASB changes the accounting standards that now exist in this area.

RELATED-PARTY TRANSACTIONS

Materiality

Many companies engage in transactions with related parties; such transactions, if material, must be disclosed. **Related parties** include "affiliates of the enterprise; entities for which investments are accounted for by the equity method by the enterprise; trusts for the benefit of employees, such as pension and profit-sharing trusts that are managed by or under the trusteeship of management; principal owners of the enterprise; its management; members of the immediate families of principal owners of the enterprise and its management; and other parties...which control or can significantly influence the management or operating policies of the other."[16]

Of course, all entities have related parties; however, not all entities engage in related-party transactions. The management of a company should establish procedures to identify related parties and enumerate any material related-party transactions.

Although types of related-party transactions are almost limitless, several examples occur frequently in practice: Related parties commonly lend money to and borrow money from each other; they may sell products to and buy products from each other; and one related party may provide services to another without charge. When such related-party transactions are material, several accounting issues arise.

Substance over Form

As a general rule, *accountants attempt to recognize the substance of a related-party transaction rather than its mere form.* Many transactions between related parties differ in substance and purpose from normal transactions merely because the participants in the transaction are related. Accountants must understand the business purposes of such transactions to account for and disclose the events properly.

For example, one party may lend money to a related second party without specifying the timing and amount of repayment. In such a case, the proper classification (current or noncurrent) and valuation (imputation of interest) are uncertain. To understand the underlying purpose of the event, an accountant may need to have extensive discussions with the related parties.

Substance over Form

Another common related-party transaction arises when an asset is sold at an amount that differs substantially from its market value. When such transactions occur, accountants em-

---

[16]*FASB Statement of Financial Accounting Standards No. 57,* "Related Party Disclosures," 1982, par. 24.

phasize the *substance* of the event, which is sometimes highly unusual. For example, a major shareholder may sell an asset to a closely held corporation at a price substantially lower than the market value of the property. The shareholder may be providing assistance to a financially troubled business; if so, that fact may need to be disclosed.

After identifying a related-party transaction and understanding it, the accountant should disclose the following aspects of the event.[17]

Disclosure

1. The nature of the relationship between the transacting parties.
2. The nature and description of the transaction.
3. The amount of the transaction and any changes in terms and effects from the preceding period.
4. Any amounts due from or to the related parties.

In addition, the disclosure of common control may be necessary even if no related-party transactions occur, because common control of several entities can itself cause the operating results and financial position of each controlled entity to differ.[18] For example, assume that Rhonda Rich owns two clothing stores that operate as separate corporate entities. Rhonda also has a contract to provide all uniforms to a city's street maintenance, police, and fire departments. In some years, she decides, one of the clothing stores will fulfill the contract, whereas in other years the other store fulfills the contract. The contract is large enough to materially affect the financial statements of either company. Thus, even though neither company transacts business with the other, the existence of common control clearly affects each of them. Disclosure of the common control and other details of these circumstances is necessary.

Economic dependency may create higher risk if one enterprise relies on another for a material amount of financing or operational support. For example, if much of the output of a small factory is purchased by a large retail department store chain, the chain can probably exert significant influence over the management and operating policies of the small factory. Even if significant influence is not exerted, disclosure of economic dependency may be desirable to adequately inform financial statement users of the risk of relying on a limited number of customers or suppliers.

Disclosure

Information about material related-party transactions is sometimes quite sensitive; however, such information is also vital to an intelligent use of the financial statements. An accountant's responsibility to external users of financial statements cannot be subordinated to management's desire for privacy. Indeed, in extreme cases, the lack of adequate disclosure of related-party transactions and their effects has harmed independent CPAs in later litigation.[19]

Materiality

In recent years, Wall Street innovators have developed many new types of financial instruments in response to market volatility, deregulation, tax law changes, and other stimuli. These innovative financial instruments, which bear such clever names as carrot-and-stick bonds, ZEBRAs, butterfly spreads, and OPPOSSMS, have raised many interesting accounting and reporting questions.[20] Among these questions are concerns about off-balance-sheet financing (i.e., borrowing money without fully reporting the liability), unjustified deferral of

DISCLOSURES ABOUT FINANCIAL INSTRUMENTS

---

[17]*FASB Statement of Financial Accounting Standards No. 57,* par. 2.

[18]*FASB Statement of Financial Accounting Standards No. 57,* par. 4.

[19]For example, in the case of Continental Vending Company, Inc., independent CPAs were held guilty of criminal fraud. Material loans made by a company to another commonly controlled company were not repaid. The court held that disclosure of more facts and circumstances regarding the loan and its questionable collectibility was necessary, and the findings of the court contributed to the issuance of *Statement on Auditing Standards No. 6,* "Related Party Transactions."

[20]The number of innovative financial instruments seems to increase every day, and this book will not catalog the many types. Readers who want more details about some of the new instruments should see "Glossary of Selected Financial Instruments," *Journal of Accountancy* (November 1989), pp. 59–60. This issue of the *Journal of Accountancy* contains several other good articles on financial instruments.

losses, premature recognition of gains, and inadequate disclosure about a company's risks. Moreover, many questions have been raised about the adequacy of current accounting standards for *traditional* financial instruments such as bonds and common stock. Accordingly, the FASB is currently working on a major project dealing with financial instruments.

A **financial instrument** is cash, evidence of an ownership interest in an entity, or a contract that has *both* of the following characteristics:

1. The contract imposes on one entity a contractual obligation (a) to deliver cash or another financial instrument to a second entity *or* (b) to exchange other financial instruments on potentially unfavorable terms with the second entity.

2. The contract conveys to the second entity a contractual right (a) to receive cash or another financial instrument from the first entity *or* (b) to exchange other financial instruments on potentially favorable terms with the first entity.[21]

The definition emphasizes the future receipt, payment, or exchange of cash or other financial instrument that ultimately results in cash.

The broad term *financial instrument* includes traditional financial instruments such as cash, receivables, payables, debt and equity securities, and investments in debt or equity securities, as well as the more innovative financial instruments such as financial guarantees and interest rate swaps. Examples of items that are *not* financial instruments are inventory, prepaid expenses, advances to or from suppliers, warranty obligations, plant assets, intangible assets, and deferred revenue. Some financial instruments, such as forward, futures, swap, and option contracts are commonly called **derivatives** because their value is derived from the value of some underlying security such as a stock or a bond. Many companies use derivatives to manage their business risks, and the markets for derivative financial instruments have grown considerably in recent years.

The FASB has divided its financial instruments project into three major phases: disclosure, recognition and measurement, and distinguishing between liabilities and owners' equity. *SFAS No. 105* is the FASB's initial pronouncement in this area of accounting. It requires

Disclosure *disclosure of information about financial instruments that have off-balance-sheet risk and about financial instruments with concentrations of credit risk. SFAS No. 105* does not contain new standards for the recognition, measurement, or classification of financial instruments. These new standards are expected to come from future FASB work on financial instruments.

The disclosures required by *SFAS No. 105* are designed to help users assess a company's *risks.* One risk is the **risk of accounting loss,** which has three components: **credit risk,** or the risk that the other party will not perform according to the contract, **market risk,** or the risk that future changes in market prices could make a financial asset less valuable or a financial liability more burdensome, and the **risk of theft or physical loss.** *SFAS No. 105* addresses credit and market risk only.

Risk of accounting loss differs from the risk of economic loss. Suppose, for example, that a company has an investment in common stock. The historical cost (book value) is $14,000, and the current market value is $20,000. If the stock becomes worthless, the accounting loss is $14,000 while the economic loss is $20,000. *SFAS No. 105* deals only with the accounting loss.

Another type of risk that sometimes pertains to a financial instrument is **off-balance-sheet (OBS) risk.** OBS risk exposes a company to a risk of accounting loss that exceeds the amount recognized for the instrument in the balance sheet. For example, if the ultimate obligation under a financial guarantee exceeds the amount that the company has recognized as a liability, the company has OBS risk.

---

[21]*Statement of Financial Accounting Standards No. 105,* "Disclosure of Information about Financial Instruments with Off-Balance-Sheet Risk and Financial Instruments with Concentrations of Credit Risk," 1990, par. 6.

SFAS No. 105 requires disclosures in three major areas.[22] First, the pronouncement requires that for those financial instruments with OBS risk, a company should disclose (1) the face or contract amount (or notional principal amount if there is no face or contract amount), and (2) the nature and terms. In disclosing the nature and terms of financial instruments with OBS risk, a company should disclose, at a minimum, the credit and market risk, the cash requirements, and accounting policies used for those instruments.

Disclosure

Second, *SFAS No. 105* requires that for those financial instruments with OBS credit risk, a company should disclose the *maximum* accounting loss that the company could incur and information about the collateral that supports the financial instruments.

Finally, *SFAS No. 105* requires all companies to disclose concentrations of credit risk for all financial instruments. Specifically, a company should disclose information about the (shared) activity, region, or economic characteristic that identifies the concentration of credit risk, the maximum accounting loss that the company could incur, and information about the collateral that supports the financial instruments. Concentrations of credit risk can exist in even the smallest of companies. For example, a small retailer that has granted credit exclusively to customers who are local residents has concentration of credit risk.

In December 1991, the FASB issued *SFAS No. 107,* which requires all entities to disclose, either in the body of the financial statements or the notes, the *fair value of those financial instruments for which it is practicable to estimate fair value.*[23] This disclosure requirement applies to both assets and liabilities and encompasses those that are recognized as well as those that are not recognized in the company's balance sheet. Generally, quoted market prices are the best evidence of the fair value of financial instruments. However, in those cases in which quoted market prices are not available, a company may use other ways (e.g., present value techniques) to estimate fair value.

In October 1994, while this textbook was in press, the FASB issued *SFAS No. 119,* which requires expanded disclosures about all derivative financial instruments, even those that do not have off-balance-sheet risk of accounting loss.[24] *SFAS No. 119* requires companies to distinguish between those derivative financial instruments held or issued for trading purposes and those held or issued for purposes other than trading. Certain disclosures are required for each of these two categories. *SFAS No. 119* also encourages, but does not require, quantitative information about the market risks of derivative financial instruments. In issuing *SFAS No. 119,* the FASB's intent was to improve disclosures about derivative financial instruments while the board continues to wrestle with the considerable complexity of issues about how financial instruments should be recognized and measured in financial statements.

Basic financial statements provide information that is *useful* in decision making by financial analysts, stockholders, bondholders, bank lending officers, and others. Although they are responsible for *preparing* financial statements, corporate managers also *use* them to make planning and control decisions. Moreover, accountants and auditors not only prepare and attest to financial statements but also *interpret* those statements. Thus, accountants and auditors must understand financial statement analysis. For convenience, all parties who analyze financial statements will be called *analysts* in the remainder of this chapter.

ANALYSIS OF FINANCIAL STATEMENTS

---

[22]Certain financial instruments that are subject to the disclosure requirements of other FASB pronouncements are excluded from the disclosure requirements of *SFAS No. 105.* These include certain insurance contracts, unconditional purchase obligations, pensions and other forms of deferred compensation, and extinguished debt and related assets held in trust. For certain other financial instruments, companies are not required to disclose information about OBS risk but must disclose information about concentrations of credit risk. These instruments include lease contracts and certain payables that result in amounts recorded in foreign currencies. The items excluded are described more fully in *SFAS No. 105,* pars. 14–15.

[23]*SFAS No. 107,* "Disclosures about Fair Value of Financial Instruments," 1991.

[24]*SFAS No. 119,* "Disclosure about Derivative Financial Instruments and Fair Value of Financial Instruments," 1994.

Financial statement analysis provides insights about a company's financial position and performance. These insights can help an analyst to make predictions, assess risk, and evaluate profitability, solvency, and management's performance.

An analyst studies current and past information in an attempt to gain insight into the future. Nowhere does the old adage that "those who are ignorant of the past are condemned to repeat it" seem more appropriate than in the analysis of financial statements. A basic premise is that "relationships among data may reasonably be expected to exist and continue in the absence of known conditions to the contrary."[25] This section of the chapter provides an overview of the most widely used techniques of financial statement analysis.

FUNDAMENTAL ANALYSIS OF FINANCIAL STATEMENTS

An analyst who simply focused on single amounts reported in financial statements would likely have difficulty forming rational judgments about a company. Imagine, for example, the difficulty of trying to evaluate a company's profitability by focusing only on the company's current net income. An analyst can evaluate profitability much more meaningfully by *relating* net income to such other measures as stockholders' equity, total assets, and shares of common stock. Financial statement analysis, which requires considerable judgment, seeks to clarify relationships between items of financial information.

Financial statement analysis often identifies major *changes,* or *turning points,* in amounts, trends, and relationships. The analyst then investigates the reasons for these changes because they may provide important clues about the company's future prospects. Unusual relationships indicate "red flags" that the analyst should investigate further to understand the *underlying causes.*

Financial statement analysis can take many forms. In this textbook, we discuss and illustrate **ratio analysis,** the most widely used form. Ratios are computed by dividing an item in the financial statements by another related item. Most ratios are expressed as percentages or as times per period. In this chapter, we discuss only some of the more commonly used ratios. Any number of ratios could conceivably be computed from financial statements.

Considered alone, a single ratio may not mean much. *Interpreting a ratio* therefore requires *comparing the ratio with certain benchmarks,* such as (1) the corresponding ratio for the same company in previous periods, (2) the corresponding ratio that was planned for the same company in the current period, (3) the corresponding ratio for a similar company in the current period, and (4) the average corresponding ratio of all companies in the same industry in the current period. A popular source for obtaining industry averages is *Robert Morris Associates Annual Statement Studies.* Even after comparing a given ratio with these four benchmarks, the analysis usually does not provide conclusive evidence of good or bad performance. It simply suggests an area that may need further investigation.

Analysts use financial ratios to gain insight about a company's *return* and the *risk* associated with that return. An analyst ordinarily accepts a higher risk only in exchange for a higher expected return.

One way to classify financial ratios is based on whether a ratio focuses primarily on *short-term solvency, long-term solvency,* or *profitability.* Solvency relates to risk; profitability relates to return. As explained in Chapter 1, profitability and solvency are two company attributes that analysts ordinarily evaluate. That is, an analyst usually wants to know about a company's ability to generate earnings (profitability) and its ability to pay debts when due (solvency). A company can remain viable over the long run only if it is sufficiently profitable and able to remain solvent. Of course, profitability and solvency are interrelated and therefore the three categories of ratios *are not completely independent.*

---

[25]*Statement on Auditing Standards No. 56,* "Analytical Procedures" (New York: AICPA, 1988), par. 2.

Exhibit 25–4 shows the basic financial statements of Ventura, Inc. The information needed to compute each ratio is found in this exhibit. In the following discussion, we focus on ratios for 1996, the latest year in Ventura's financial statements.

Short-Term Solvency Ratios

The ratios in this category help the analyst to assess a company's short-term debt paying ability and, therefore, the company's chances of remaining solvent in the short run.

Current Ratio.   As discussed in Chapter 4, a company's **working capital** is the *difference* between its current assets and current liabilities. Although working capital represents a dollar amount, an analyst may compute a **current ratio** to provide a **relative measure of short-term solvency,** as shown below for Ventura:

$$\text{Current Ratio} = \frac{\text{Current Assets}}{\text{Current Liabilities}} = \frac{\$185,680}{\$85,200} = 2.18$$

The current ratio, sometimes called the **working capital ratio,** provides a relative measure of the extent to which a company's current assets cover its current liabilities. Although widely used in financial analysis, especially by short-term creditors, the current ratio is a static measure that considers only whether existing current assets are sufficient to pay existing current liabilities. It implies that current assets will be liquidated and the proceeds used to pay current liabilities, which is highly unlikely in a going concern. To maintain its short-term solvency, a company must generate *future* cash inflows that are sufficient to cover its *future* cash outflows.

Quick (Acid-Test) Ratio.   The quick ratio, also called the **acid-test ratio,** is a more conservative measure of short-term solvency than the current ratio. Of a company's current assets, only cash, temporary investments, and current receivables are considered "quick" assets. The quick ratio recognizes that inventory may contain some slow-moving goods that will require considerable time to convert to cash. Moreover, although prepaid expenses benefit current operations, they will not be converted directly into cash. Thus, the quick ratio *excludes* inventory and prepaid expenses. Ventura's quick ratio is shown below:

$$\text{Quick Ratio} = \frac{\text{Cash} + \frac{\text{Temporary}}{\text{Investments}} + \frac{\text{Short-Term}}{\text{Receivables}}}{\text{Current Liabilities}} = \frac{\$52,000 + \$10,000 + \$48,000}{\$85,200}$$
$$= 1.29$$

The quick ratio indicates a company's ability to cover its current liabilities with cash and assets that can be converted quickly to cash. A limitation of this ratio is that some short-term receivables may require a lengthy collection period and may have to be factored at less than their carrying amount to obtain cash. Another limitation is that fluctuating market conditions may adversely affect the market prices of temporary investments.

Ratio of Net Cash Flow from Operating Activities to Current Liabilities.   The current and quick ratios are based on amounts that existed on the balance sheet date. Both ratios are distorted if the amounts on that date do not reflect normal conditions. A ratio that avoids this limitation is the **ratio of net cash flow from operating activities to current liabilities,** which is computed on the following page.[26]

---

[26]In those ratios that rely on an annual average, we compute the average by using the beginning and ending balances. In practice, an average using monthly balances may be computed when the beginning and ending balances are not considered representative of the entire year.

EXHIBIT 25–4

Ventura, Inc.
Basic Financial Statements

Ventura, Inc.
Comparative Balance Sheets
December 31, 1996 and 1995

	1996	1995
Assets		
Cash	$ 52,000	$ 56,000
Marketable securities	10,000	10,000
Accounts receivable, net	48,000	52,000
Inventory	75,680	49,600
Total current assets	185,680	167,600
Property, plant, and equipment	152,000	160,000
Accumulated depreciation	(26,400)	(24,000)
Patents	7,200	8,000
Total noncurrent assets	132,800	144,000
Total assets	$318,480	$311,600
Liabilities		
Dividends payable	$ 13,600	$ 8,000
Accounts payable	28,240	40,000
Income taxes payable	43,360	33,600
Notes payable	–0–	16,000
Total current liabilities	85,200	97,600
Deferred income taxes	6,880	8,000
Convertible bonds payable	–0–	32,000
Bonds payable	48,000	48,000
Unamortized bond discount	(4,240)	(8,000)
Total noncurrent liabilities	50,640	80,000
Total Liabilities	135,840	177,600
Stockholders' Equity		
Common stock ($10 par, Notes 1 and 2)	60,000	48,000
Additional paid-in capital	14,400	12,000
Retained earnings	108,240	74,000
Total stockholders' equity	182,640	134,000
Total liabilities and stockholders' equity	$318,480	$311,600

Ventura, Inc.
Income Statement
For the Year Ended December 31, 1996

Sales		$960,000
Expenses		
Cost of goods sold	$400,000	
Selling expenses	240,000	
General and administrative expenses	200,000	
Interest expense	32,000	872,000
Income before income tax		88,000
Income tax expense		42,240
Income before extraordinary item		45,760
Extraordinary gain—retirement of long-term debt, net of $1,920 applicable income tax		2,080
Net income		$ 47,840
Earnings per share:		
Income before extraordinary item		$7.62
Extraordinary gain, net of tax		.35
Net income		$7.97

Ventura, Inc.
Statement of Retained Earnings
For the Year Ended December 31, 1996

Retained earnings, Jan. 1, 1996		$ 74,000
Add: Net income		47,840
		121,840
Less: Dividends declared ($2.27 per share)		13,600
Retained earnings, Dec. 31, 1996		$108,240

Ventura, Inc.
Statement of Cash Flows
For the Year Ended December 31, 1996

Cash Flows from Operating Activities

Cash received from customers		$964,000
Less: Cash paid for goods to be sold	$437,840	
Cash paid for selling expenses	236,000	
Cash paid for general and administrative expenses	194,400	
Cash paid for interest	31,360	
Cash paid for taxes	35,520	
Cash disbursed for operating activities		935,120
Net cash flow from operating activities		28,880

Cash Flows from Investing Activities

Sale of property, plant, and equipment	9,600	
Purchase of property, plant, and equipment	(8,000)	
Net cash provided by investing activities		1,600

Cash Flows from Financing Activities

Payment of dividends	(8,000)	
Repayment of notes payable	(16,000)	
Repayment of convertible bonds payable	(10,480)	
Net cash used by financing activities		(34,480)
Net decrease in cash		(4,000)
Cash, January 1, 1996		56,000
Cash, December 31, 1996		$ 52,000

Reconciliation of Net Income to Net Cash Provided by Operating Activities

Net income	$ 47,840
Adjustments to reconcile net income to net cash provided by operating activities	
Depreciation expense	6,400
Amortization	1,440
Loss on sale of equipment	2,400
Decrease in deferred income taxes	(1,120)
Decrease in accounts receivable	4,000
Increase in inventory	(26,080)
Decrease in accounts payable	(11,760)
Increase in income taxes payable	9,760
Extraordinary gain	(4,000)
Net cash provided by operating activities	$ 28,880

Supplemental Schedule of Noncash Investing and Financing Activities

Declaration of dividend in 1996 to be paid in 1997	$ 13,600
Conversion of bonds payable into common stock on January 2, 1996	$ 14,400

NOTES
1. The market price per share of common stock on December 31, 1996, was $87.67.
2. On January 2, 1996, 1,200 shares of common stock were issued when certain convertible bondholders exercised their conversion privilege.

$$\text{Ratio of Net Cash Flow} \atop {\text{from Operating Activities} \atop \text{to Current Liabilities}} = \frac{\text{Net Cash Flow from Operating Activities}}{\text{Average Current Liabilities}} = \frac{\$28,880}{(\$85,200 + \$97,600)/2}$$

$$= .32$$

Observe that the numerator pertains to the entire year and comes from the statement of cash flows. To be consistent with the numerator, the denominator also pertains to the entire year by reflecting an annual average that is based on the ending and beginning amounts of current liabilities.

This ratio shows the extent to which a company has been able to cover its current liabilities by generating cash through its operating activities. A limitation is that net cash provided by operations in the past may not be a good predictor of the future amount of this variable.

Long-Term Solvency Ratios

By indicating a company's long-term debt-paying ability, the ratios in this category help the analyst to assess the risk that the company will become insolvent in the long run.

Debt to Total Assets.   Analysts use certain ratios to assess a company's relative reliance on debt and equity financing. The debt-to-total-assets ratio relates a company's total liabilities to its total assets, as shown for Ventura:

$$\text{Debt to Total Assets} = \frac{\text{Total Liabilities}}{\text{Total Assets}} = \frac{\$135,840}{\$318,480} = .43, \text{ or } 43\%$$

The ratio shows that 43% of Ventura's assets has come from creditors, implying that the owners provided 57%. The debt-to-total-assets ratio indicates creditor protection in the event of a corporate liquidation. A high ratio suggests that although the company tries to secure benefits from financial leverage, it also faces increased risk of becoming insolvent. Companies with low debt-to-total-assets ratios are generally better able to pay their liabilities at maturity, but they may miss good opportunities to use financial leverage favorably. The optimal mix of debt and equity financing depends on many factors, such as the stability of a company's income and the company's consistency in generating net cash inflows from operating activities.

A similar ratio frequently encountered in practice is the **debt-to-equity ratio,** which equals total liabilities divided by total stockholders' equity. Ventura's debt-to-equity ratio is 74% ($135,840/$182,640 = .74, or 74%).

Times Interest Earned.   Interest charges are fixed and must be paid when due. A company's ability to pay interest from the assets generated by its earnings process is therefore very important. The times interest earned ratio reveals the number of times that a company's annual earnings before interest and taxes cover its annual interest expense. The higher the ratio, the lower the risk that the company cannot make its interest payments. We illustrate this ratio below:

$$\text{Times Interest Earned} = \frac{\text{Income before Interest and Taxes}}{\text{Interest Expense}}$$

$$= \frac{\$47,840 + \$32,000 + \$42,240 + \$1,920}{\$32,000} = 3.88 \text{ times}$$

Observe that the numerator is income before interest and taxes because this is the amount of earnings that can cover interest charges. A company does not owe income taxes unless interest charges are met.

Cash Flow Interest Coverage. This ratio, which is based on information reported in the statement of cash flows, indicates the number of times per year that a company can cover interest payments from the net cash flow from operating activities. In essence, it is the cash flow counterpart of the times interest earned ratio. The cash flow interest coverage is potentially more useful than the times interest earned ratio because it recognizes that a company pays interest with *cash,* not earnings. The ratio for Ventura follows:

$$\begin{array}{l} \text{Cash Flow} \\ \text{Interest} \\ \text{Coverage} \end{array} = \frac{\text{Net Cash Flow from Operating Activities} + \text{Interest Paid} + \text{Taxes Paid}}{\text{Interest Paid}}$$

$$= \frac{\$28,880 + \$31,360 + \$35,520}{\$31,360} = 3.05 \text{ Times}$$

In this case, the ratio shows that, when the relevant variables are expressed on a cash flow basis, Ventura could cover its interest payments somewhat fewer times than indicated by the accrual-based, times interest earned ratio.

Ratio of Cash Provided by Operating Activities to Sales. This ratio indicates the percentage of sales that is available for spending. In other words, it reveals the cash flow effects of a company's sales. The ratio, shown below, reflects the company's success in making sales, collecting cash from operating sources, and using cash for operating purposes.

$$\begin{array}{l} \text{Ratio of Net} \\ \text{Cash Flow} \\ \text{from} \\ \text{Operating} \\ \text{Activities} \\ \text{to Sales} \end{array} = \frac{\text{Net Cash Flow from Operating Activities}}{\text{Net Sales}} = \frac{\$28,880}{\$960,000} = .03, \text{ or } 3\%$$

Ratio of Net Cash Flow from Operating Activities to Net Income. This ratio shows how much operating cash flow is represented by each dollar of net income. Generally, the cash flows from operating activities represent the cash effects of transactions that are reflected in net income. Thus, the numerator of this ratio is a cash-basis number and the denominator is a closely related measurement on the accrual basis, as follows:

$$\begin{array}{l} \text{Ratio of Net} \\ \text{Cash Flow from} \\ \text{Operating} \\ \text{Activities to} \\ \text{Net Income} \end{array} = \frac{\text{Net Cash Flow from Operating Activities}}{\text{Net Income}} = \frac{\$28,880}{\$47,840} = .60, \text{ or } 60\%$$

The fact that this ratio is less than 1 indicates that Ventura had more success earning income than in generating cash from its operating activities. In general, the higher this ratio, the higher the perceived quality of a company's earnings in a given year.

Profitability Ratios

The ratios in this category provide information about the success of the company's earnings activities. For a company to be profitable, management must use the company's assets (i.e., receivables, inventories, and other assets) productively to generate revenue. Moreover, management must control expenses to ensure a reasonable net income.

Receivables Turnover Ratio. The **receivables turnover ratio** is computed by dividing net credit sales by the average accounts receivable. Frequently, only the net sales figure (instead of net *credit* sales) is available in published financial statements. Nevertheless, if an analyst consistently uses net sales and no material changes occur in the mix of cash and credit sales, the ratio using net sales is still useful. The receivables turnover ratio indicates the number of times a year the company collects its accounts receivable.

A low receivables turnover ratio may indicate such factors as large amounts of uncollectible accounts, a weak collections policy, or credit terms that are too lenient. On the other hand, a high ratio could be the result of overly restrictive credit terms that are reducing profitability by causing the company to lose sales. The receivables turnover ratio for Ventura is as follows:

$$\text{Receivables Turnover} = \frac{\text{Net Credit Sales}}{\text{Average Accounts Receivable (net)}}$$

$$= \frac{\$960,000}{(\$48,000 + \$52,000)/2} = 19.2 \text{ times per year}$$

Observe that Ventura collects its accounts receivable about 19.2 times per year. A similar measure is the **number of days' sales in receivables,** which equals 365 divided by the receivables turnover ratio. For Ventura, this ratio equals 365/19.2 = 19.01 days. In other words, Ventura takes, on average, about 19 days to collect its accounts receivable.[27]

Inventory Turnover. A company's **inventory turnover** is computed by dividing cost of goods sold by the average inventory. This ratio indicates the average number of times the company sells its inventory in a year.

A low inventory turnover may suggest such factors as poor inventory management, ineffective marketing programs, or a weakening economy. Although a high turnover may suggest the opposite factors, it could also mean that the company does not carry enough inventory and is missing opportunities to sell goods. Moreover, inventory cost-flow methods directly affect this ratio. Suppose that an analyst wants to compare a LIFO company with a FIFO company. The analyst would likely use the LIFO company's *footnote disclosures* of FIFO inventory to estimate the inventory turnover of the LIFO company on a FIFO basis. This makes the two ratios more comparable. Remember that ratios provide important clues to ask further questions but alone do not provide conclusive answers.

Ventura's inventory turnover ratio is computed as follows:

$$\text{Inventory Turnover} = \frac{\text{Cost of Goods Sold}}{\text{Average Inventory}} = \frac{\$400,000}{(\$75,680 + \$49,600)/2}$$

$$= 6.39 \text{ Times per Year}$$

Note that the numerator is the cost of goods sold, not sales, because inventory is ordinarily measured at cost, not selling price.

A measure similar to inventory turnover is the **number of days' sales in inventory,** which equals 365 divided by the inventory turnover ratio. For Ventura, this ratio equals 365/6.39 = 57.12 days.

Asset Turnover. Receivables and inventories are two of a typical company's most important assets. Managers use receivables, inventories, and other assets to generate revenues. Asset turnover, computed by dividing net sales by average total assets, shows how efficiently a company has used its assets to generate revenues. Ventura's asset turnover ratio is computed as follows:

---

[27]In computing the number of days' sales in accounts receivable (and other ratios that are expressed as a number of days), we use calendar days in this book. Some analysts prefer a numerator of 360; others prefer 300, which is the approximate number of *business days* in a year. *Consistency in calculating comparative figures* is particularly important in these types of measurements.

$$\text{Asset Turnover} = \frac{\text{Net Sales}}{\text{Average Total Assets}} = \frac{\$960,000}{(\$318,480 + \$311,600)/2}$$

$$= 3.05 \text{ Times per Year}$$

A low asset turnover suggests an inefficient use of assets; therefore, a reduction in assets may be warranted. On the other hand, an important limitation of this ratio is that net sales are measured at recent prices, although certain assets may be measured at costs incurred many years ago. Thus, a high asset turnover may occur simply because a company acquired certain assets long ago when prices were considerably below current replacement costs.

Profit Margin on Sales. An analyst computes the profit margin on sales by dividing net income by net sales, as shown:

$$\text{Profit Margin on Sales} = \frac{\text{Net Income}}{\text{Net Sales}} = \frac{\$ 47,840}{\$960,000} = .05, \text{ or } 5\%$$

This ratio shows the percentage of each sales dollar earned as net income. It therefore provides an approximate measure of management's efficiency. When a company's profit margin on sales is too low, the company should try to increase sales, reduce expenses, or both. A detailed analysis of each expense can help identify those expenses to target for reduction.

Observe that in computing Ventura's profit margin on sales, our numerator is "all-inclusive" in the sense that it includes an extraordinary gain from retirement of long-term debt. This is really a *special type of extraordinary item.* As discussed in Chapter 15, *SFAS No. 4* requires that a gain or loss from debt extinguishment be classified as an extraordinary item, even though the gain or loss may *not* be unusual and nonrecurring. Some analysts prefer an income numerator that ignores all kinds of extraordinary gains and losses; others go even further and ignore *any* income statement item believed to be nonrecurring. *When you are comparing ratios, remember to make sure that they have been computed in a comparable manner.*

The profit margin on sales ratio is similar to the ratio of net cash flow from operating activities to net income, except that the numerator is computed on an accrual rather than a cash flow basis. Note that for Ventura, the profit margin on sales is 5%; the ratio of net cash flow from operating activities to sales is only 3%. During 1996 the company had more success earning net income than it did in generating cash from operating activities.

Rate of Return on Assets. This ratio, computed by dividing net income by average total assets, relates the amount of return achieved to the assets used in the earnings process.[28] Ventura's rate of return on assets is computed as follows:

$$\frac{\text{Rate of Return}}{\text{on Assets}} = \frac{\text{Net Income}}{\text{Average Total Assets}} = \frac{\$47,840}{(\$318,480 + \$311,600)/2} = .15, \text{ or } 15\%$$

If a company's rate of return on assets is considered too low, the company should try to find ways to (1) increase net income without increasing the asset base and/or (2) reduce the asset base without reducing net income. An analyst may gain additional insight into this ratio by separating it into components, as shown below:

$$
\begin{array}{ccc}
\text{Rate of Return} & \text{Profit Margin} & \text{Asset} \\
\text{on Assets} & = \quad \text{on Sales} & \times \text{ Turnover} \\
& = \qquad .05 & \times \quad 3.05 \\
& = .15, \text{ or } 15\% &
\end{array}
$$

---

[28] Some analysts prefer a numerator equal to net income plus interest expense (net of tax savings because of the interest expense). Their rationale is that because the denominator is assets that creditors and owners have provided, the numerator should show the return on both debt and equity capital.

In other words, a company's rate of return on assets depends on the amount of net income it earns on each sales dollar and on its efficiency in using its assets to generate sales. Some companies (e.g., discount stores, variety stores, large grocers) have low profit margins and high asset turnovers; others (e.g., expensive jewelry stores, fine furniture stores, furriers) have high profit margins and low asset turnovers.

For some companies, the rate of return on assets may be somewhat high merely because the company acquired certain assets long ago when prices were considerably below current replacement costs. Moreover, net income may be "too high" in the sense that depreciation is based on historical costs, rather than higher replacement costs.

Return on Common Stockholders' Equity.   The rate of return on common stockholders' equity reveals the profitability of the common shareholders' investment in the company. It is computed by dividing the net income minus preferred dividends, by the average common stockholders' equity, as shown:

$$\text{Return on Common Stockholders' Equity} = \frac{\text{Net Income} - \text{Preferred Dividends}}{\text{Average Common Stockholders' Equity}}$$

$$= \frac{\$47,840 - \$0}{(\$182,640 + \$134,000)/2} = .30, \text{ or } 30\%$$

A company finances its assets using debt and shareholder investments (Assets = Liabilities + Stockholders' Equity). Debt and preferred stock ordinarily require fixed interest or dividend payments. **Financial leverage** or **trading on the equity** mean using debt and preferred stock financing to increase the return to common stockholders. **Favorable financial leverage** occurs when a company earns more on the assets acquired with the funds than the fixed cost of obtaining the funds. **Unfavorable financial leverage** occurs when the company earns less than the fixed cost of the funds. In the case of Ventura, the return on common stockholders' equity is 30%; the return on assets is 15%. The company is therefore using debt capital wisely to generate additional returns for common stockholders.

Earnings per Share (EPS).   One measure of profitability, EPS, is already shown on the face of Ventura's income statement (see Exhibit 25–4). When a company has no potentially dilutive securities outstanding, EPS is computed by dividing net income minus preferred dividends, by the weighted average number of common shares outstanding. When potentially dilutive securities exist, EPS calculations may become considerably more complex, as discussed in Chapter 18. Note in Exhibit 25–4 that because Ventura had an extraordinary gain, the company's income statement shows *three* EPS amounts. For brevity, only the final EPS amount is shown here:[29]

$$\text{Earnings per Share} = \frac{\text{Net Income} - \text{Preferred Dividends}}{\text{Weighted Average Common Shares Outstanding}}$$

$$= \frac{\$47,840 - \$0}{6,000} = \$7.97$$

A limitation of EPS as a measure of profitability is that it ignores the amount invested in the firm. Two companies may have identical net incomes and earnings per share and therefore appear equally profitable. Yet if one company has twice the asset base as the other, the smaller company is really the more profitable in the sense that it earned the same amount on a smaller investment.

Another EPS limitation involves the denominator. Two companies may be alike in all major respects. Yet if one company has fewer shares outstanding than the other, perhaps be-

---

[29]Ventura had 6,000 common shares outstanding during 1996.

cause the shares were arbitrarily assigned a higher par value, the first company will have a higher EPS. Moreover, EPS can be increased merely by purchasing treasury stock and thereby reducing the denominator.

Users of financial statements perceive EPS as extremely important. Large increases (decreases) in the price of a company's stock frequently occur when the company reports EPS that are significantly above (below) financial analysts' previous estimates. Despite its importance, the analyst should understand the limitations of EPS and avoid focusing on only this single measure of a company's performance.

Price/Earnings Ratio.   Analysts frequently compare a company's market price per common share with the company's earnings per share by computing a price/earnings (P/E) ratio, as shown below:

$$\text{Price/Earnings Ratio} = \frac{\text{Market Price per Share}}{\text{Earnings per Share}} = \frac{\$87.67}{\$7.97} = 11$$

Analysts use the P/E ratio as an indication of the company's future earning power. Companies believed to have high growth potential usually have high P/E ratios; those believed to have low growth potential generally have low P/E ratios. Of course, market prices change, sometimes very quickly. If a company has a low P/E ratio and the analyst believes that the company's growth prospects are much better than the P/E ratio suggests, the analyst may wish to buy the company's stock. P/E ratios are published in *The Wall Street Journal* on each business day. On December 17, 1993, for example, the P/E ratios for some well-known companies were Goodyear, 13; Exxon, 15; Home Depot, 40; Phillips Van Heusen, 25; Shoneys, 20; and Union Carbide, 26.

Book Value per Share.   The common stockholders' equity of a profitable enterprise ordinarily increases over time. An analyst may compute the book (accounting) value of each common share by dividing the stockholders' equity attributable to common stockholders by the number of shares of common stock outstanding, as shown below:

$$\text{Book Value per Share} = \frac{\text{Common Stockholders' Equity}}{\text{Number of Common Shares Outstanding}}$$

$$= \frac{\$182,640}{6,000} = \$30.44$$

Book value per share shows the value of each common share *assuming* that assets are liquidated and liabilities settled at their recorded amounts (book values). Because accounting valuations rely largely on historical costs, the book value of a company's stock seldom equals its current market value. Book values reflect historical valuations; market values reflect future prospects. When the market price of a company's common stock is less than book value, this suggests that investors are relatively pessimistic about the company's prospects. Of course, investor pessimism is not always justified, and stocks selling below book values are sometimes good buys.

Dividend Payout Ratio.   The dividend payout ratio shows the percentage relationship between cash dividends declared on common stock and net income attributable to common stockholders, as shown for Ventura:

$$\text{Dividend Payout Ratio} = \frac{\text{Cash Dividends Declared on Common Stock}}{\text{Net Income} - \text{Preferred Dividends}}$$

$$= \frac{\$13,600}{\$47,840 - \$0} = .28, \text{ or } 28\%$$

EXHIBIT 25–5

Summary of Financial Ratios

Ratio	Formula	Computation
Short-Term Solvency Ratios		
1. Current ratio	$\dfrac{\text{Current Assets}}{\text{Current Liabilities}}$	$\dfrac{\$185,680}{\$85,200} = 2.18$
2. Quick ratio	$\dfrac{\text{Cash} + \dfrac{\text{Temporary}}{\text{Investments}} + \dfrac{\text{Short-Term}}{\text{Receivables}}}{\text{Current Liabilities}}$	$\dfrac{\$52,000 + \$10,000 + \$48,000}{\$85,200} = 1.29$
3. Ratio of net cash flow from operating activities to current liabilities	$\dfrac{\begin{array}{c}\text{Net Cash Flow from}\\ \text{Operating Activities}\end{array}}{\text{Average Current Liabilities}}$	$\dfrac{\$28,880}{(\$85,200 + \$97,600)/2} = .32$
Long-Term Solvency Ratios		
4. Debt to total assets	$\dfrac{\text{Total Liabilities}}{\text{Total Assets}}$	$\dfrac{\$135,840}{\$318,480} = .43,\ \text{or}\ 43\%$
5. Times interest earned	$\dfrac{\begin{array}{c}\text{Income before}\\ \text{Interest and Taxes}\end{array}}{\text{Interest Expense}}$	$\dfrac{\$47,840 + \$32,000 + \$42,240 + \$1,920}{\$32,000} = 3.88\ \text{Times}$
6. Cash flow interest coverage	$\dfrac{\begin{array}{c}\text{Net Cash Flow from Operating}\\ \text{Activities} + \text{Interest Paid}\\ + \text{Taxes Paid}\end{array}}{\text{Interest Paid}}$	$\dfrac{\$28,880 + \$31,360 + \$35,520}{\$31,360} = 3.05\ \text{Times}$
7. Ratio of net cash flow from operating activities to sales	$\dfrac{\begin{array}{c}\text{Net Cash Flow from}\\ \text{Operating Activities}\end{array}}{\text{Net Sales}}$	$\dfrac{\$28,880}{\$960,000} = .03,\ \text{or}\ 3\%$
8. Ratio of net cash flow from operating activities to net income	$\dfrac{\begin{array}{c}\text{Net Cash Flow from}\\ \text{Operating Activities}\end{array}}{\text{Net Income}}$	$\dfrac{\$28,880}{\$47,840} = .60,\ \text{or}\ 60\%$

Common stock investors who seek high current income may prefer companies that pay dividends equal to a relatively high percentage of net income. Investors who seek long-term growth tend to favor companies that retain a relatively high percentage of net income to finance continued growth and expansion.

A closely related ratio is **dividend yield,** computed by dividing the dividend per common share by the market price per common share. For Ventura, the dividend yield is 2.6% ($2.27/$87.67 = .026, or 2.6%). A company that reinvests most of the assets generated by its earnings process will have a relatively low dividend yield.

Exhibit 25–5 summarizes the financial ratios presented in this chapter.

Profitability Ratios

9. Receivables turnover

$$\frac{\text{Net Credit Sales}}{\text{Average Accounts Receivable (net)}} \qquad \frac{\$960,000}{(\$48,000 + \$52,000)/2} = 19.2 \text{ Times per Year}$$

10. Inventory turnover

$$\frac{\text{Cost of Goods Sold}}{\text{Average Inventory}} \qquad \frac{\$400,000}{(\$75,680 + \$49,600)/2} = 6.39 \text{ Times per Year}$$

11. Asset turnover

$$\frac{\text{Net Sales}}{\text{Average Total Assets}} \qquad \frac{\$960,000}{(\$318,480 + \$311,600)/2} = 3.05 \text{ Times per Year}$$

12. Profit margin on sales

$$\frac{\text{Net Income}}{\text{Net Sales}} \qquad \frac{\$47,840}{\$960,000} = .05, \text{ or } 5\%$$

13. Rate of return on assets

$$\frac{\text{Net Income}}{\text{Average Total Assets}} \qquad \frac{\$47,840}{(\$318,480 + \$311,600)/2} = .15, \text{ or } 15\%$$

14. Return on common stockholders' equity

$$\frac{\text{Net Income} - \text{Preferred Dividends}}{\text{Average Common Stockholders' Equity}} \qquad \frac{\$47,840 - \$0}{(\$182,640 + \$134,000)/2} = .30, \text{ or } 30\%$$

15. Earnings per share

$$\frac{\text{Net Income} - \text{Preferred Dividends}}{\text{Weighted Average Common Shares Outstanding}} \qquad \frac{\$47,840 - \$0}{6,000} - \$7.97$$

16. Price/Earnings ratio

$$\frac{\text{Market Price per Share}}{\text{Earnings per Share}} \qquad \frac{\$87.67}{\$7.97} = 11$$

17. Book value per share

$$\frac{\text{Common Stockholders' Equity}}{\text{Number of Common Shares Outstanding}} \qquad \frac{\$182,640}{6,000} = \$30.44$$

18. Dividend payout ratio

$$\frac{\text{Cash Dividends Declared on Common Stock}}{\text{Net Income} - \text{Preferred Dividends}} \qquad \frac{\$13,600}{\$47,840 - \$0} = .28, \text{ or } 28\%$$

LIMITATIONS OF FINANCIAL STATEMENT ANALYSIS

The analysis of financial statements has several important limitations, the most important of which are the following:

1. The analysis ignores the effects of changing prices. When a company has operated for many years, these effects can be very important, as will be explained in Chapter 26.
2. Corporate managers can sometimes manipulate financial ratios. A manager can increase the current ratio, for example, merely by accelerating the payment of some current liabilities at year-end. Although such an action would not affect working capital, the current ratio increases.

3. The use of different accounting principles may reduce the comparability of financial ratios between two companies. For example, if one company uses FIFO for its inventories but another has used LIFO for many years, many ratios will not likely be comparable.

4. Comparing financial ratios of a single company over time can be misleading because of underlying changes in the company (e.g., new products).

5. Comparing financial ratios of a company with a similar company can be misleading because, although the companies may appear similar, certain underlying differences may exist between them (e.g., somewhat different product lines).

6. Comparing financial ratios of one company with industry averages can be misleading because many companies operate in more than one industry.

These limitations underscore the fact that analysis of financial statements is more an art than a science. Interpreting the results of financial statement analysis requires a sound understanding of the **company,** the **industry** in which it operates, and the general **economic environment.** The analyst frequently acquires this understanding by studying information obtained from sources other than financial statements.

OTHER SOURCES OF FINANCIAL INFORMATION

An analyst may obtain information from many sources. **Published corporate information** includes such materials as annual and interim reports sent to stockholders, various reports filed with the SEC, corporate prospectuses, company newsletters and bulletins, and financial advertising. The AICPA is responsible for the National Automated Accounting Research System (NAARS). A NAARS subscriber may use an on-line computer to obtain examples of many types of financial disclosures that have appeared in corporate annual reports. Information may also be obtained by **personal contact with corporate officials,** such as conversations, speeches, corporate tours, correspondence with companies, and attending stockholders' meetings. Various **noncompany sources of information** may also be helpful, including financial services (e.g., Moody's or Standard & Poor's), business and industry journals, investment advisory services, newspapers, analysts' reports, and economic statistics. Basic financial statements, although important, are only one source of information for analysts.

FINANCIAL STATEMENT ANALYSIS IN AN EFFICIENT CAPITAL MARKET

As explained in Chapter 1, extensive empirical research in accounting and finance suggests that the stock market (especially the New York Stock Exchange) is highly efficient. In such an environment, stock prices behave as if they fully reflect *publicly available information,* including information in basic financial statements. If this information is quickly reflected in a company's stock price, as efficient-market theory suggests, is financial statement analysis still useful? The answer is yes, for the following major reasons:

1. Not everyone believes that the stock market is highly efficient. First, many believe that the evidence that points to a high degree of market efficiency is inconclusive. Second, even if the market is highly efficient, its efficiency implies that sophisticated analysts consistently try to gain a market advantage, partly by applying techniques of financial statement analysis soon after the statements are published. Paradoxically, for the stock market to *be* highly efficient, investors *must behave* as though it is not.

2. The stocks of many companies are not traded in large, well-defined markets. Efficient-market research does not apply to these companies.

3. Efficient-market research pertains only to the stock market. It does not apply to the numerous nonstock market users of financial statements (e.g., bank lending officers or labor unions).

PROFESSIONAL JUDGMENT

Throughout this book, we have made the point that accounting requires making many estimates and judgments. In this chapter, many topics have illustrated this point. For example, some companies use the gross margin method to determine ending inventories and cost of goods sold at interim reporting dates. The gross margin method requires too much estimation to be acceptable for annual reporting purposes. As another example, determining the expected cost of replacing a liquidated LIFO base layer at an interim reporting date requires making an estimate and a judgment. Also, determining whether a market decline in the value of an interim period inventory is only temporary (and therefore need not be recognized) requires judgment.

In the area of segment reporting, considerable judgment is required to determine which segments to report separately. A major argument of those who seek to improve segment reporting is that the FASB should provide additional guidance to help companies identify their industry and geographic segments. Presently, companies with similar industry and geographic operations do not always define their segments similarly. The allocation of common expenses between reportable segments also requires estimation and judgment.

The entire area of analysis of financial statements requires judgment. All financial ratios must be interpreted carefully. An analyst must use caution and judgment, for example, when comparing the current ratio of a FIFO company with the current ratio of a company that has used LIFO for many years. In this case, the two ratios will simply not be comparable. As another example, judgment is required when comparing the financial ratios of one company with industry averages because many companies operate in more than one industry.

CONCLUDING REMARKS

Consistent with present GAAP, the financial information presented in this chapter and previous chapters has emphasized the historical cost measurement attribute denominated in nominal dollars. We have not extensively discussed the effects on financial statements of changing specific and general prices, although these concepts were introduced in Chapter 3. In Chapter 26, we discuss accounting for changing prices, one of the most important and pervasive topics in financial accounting. Although the general kinds of information in the next chapter are only encouraged and not required by the FASB at this time, this study will help you to better understand the nature and limitations of conventional financial statements as well as important changes in GAAP that could occur in the future.

KEY POINTS

1. Interim reporting means presenting financial information for periods of less than one year. (Objective 1)
2. Current accounting standards reflect the integral view of interim reporting, in which the interim period is viewed as an important part of the annual period. Accounting and reporting requirements are designed to help the user of the interim information to assess progress of the enterprise toward its annual results. (Objective 1)
3. Although certain minimum disclosures are required in interim reports, these reports tend to be much less detailed than annual reports. (Objective 1)
4. Publicly held companies must provide disaggregated information about several important aspects of their operations: operations in different industries, operations in different geographic areas, and reliance on major customers. (Objective 2)
5. Industry segment information must be reported if a material part of a company's operations extends over more than one industry segment or product line. (Objective 2)
6. Geographic area information must be presented if a material part of a company's operations is carried out in more than one geographic area. (Objective 2)
7. Major customer disclosure is required if a company generates a substantial portion of its sales revenue from a single customer. (Objective 2)
8. Material related-party transactions, such as transactions between a company and its management, require special disclosures in the financial statements. (Objective 3)
9. Current accounting standards require disclosure of information about financial instruments that have off-balance-sheet risk and about financial instruments with concentrations of credit risk. (Objective 4)
10. Financial statement analysis is designed to reveal important relationships between items of financial information and thereby provide insights about a company's short-term solvency, long-term solvency, and profitability. (Objective 5)

11. Financial statement analysis requires considerable judgment and has several limitations. (Objective 5)

12. Published financial statements are only one source of financial information about a company. (Objective 5)

13. Financial statement analysis is useful even in an efficient-market environment. (Objective 5)

QUESTIONS

25–1   What is meant by the term *interim reporting*?

25–2   How does interim financial reporting relate to the need that users have to predict the amount and timing of net cash inflows they will receive as a result of their investment or credit decisions?

25–3   What is the difference between the discrete (independent) and integral (dependent) views of interim financial reporting periods?

25–4   Which of the two concepts of interim reporting—the discrete or the integral—appears to be supported by the authoritative accounting pronouncements? Support your position by references to specific interim reporting practices.

25–5   Describe the process by which income tax expense should be determined in interim periods.

25–6   Should separately classified income statement items, such as extraordinary items, be prorated over several interim periods or recognized in a single interim period? Explain.

25–7   *APB Opinion No. 28* identifies several items of information that must be presented when publicly traded companies provide interim information to security holders on a regular basis. In addition to current period information, for what additional time periods must information be presented? What is the purpose of this additional information?

25–8   In considering interim financial reporting, the APB concluded that such reporting should be viewed in which of the following ways?

[a] As a special type of reporting that need *not* follow GAAP.
[b] As useful only *if* activity is evenly spread throughout the year so that estimates are unnecessary.
[c] As reporting for a basic accounting period.
[d] As reporting for an integral part of an annual period.   (AICPA adapted)

25–9   Which of the following is an inherent difficulty in the determination of the results of operations on an interim basis?

[a] Cost of sales reflects only the amount of product expense allocable to revenue recognized as of the interim date.
[b] Depreciation on an interim basis is a partial estimate of the actual annual amount.
[c] Costs expensed in one interim period may benefit other periods.
[d] Revenues from long-term construction contracts accounted for by the percentage-of-completion method are based on annual completion, and interim estimates may be incorrect.
                                          (AICPA adapted)

25–10   Which of the following reporting practices is permissible for interim financial reporting?

[a] Use of the gross-profit method for interim inventory pricing.
[b] Use of the direct-costing method for determining manufacturing inventories.
[c] Deferral of unplanned variances under a standard-cost system until year-end.
[d] Deferral of inventory market declines until the end of the year.   (AICPA adapted)

25–11   Discuss the basic rationale underlying the need of financial statement users for information by industry for an enterprise that operates in several industries at the same time.

25–12   How does segment reporting relate to the need of investors and creditors to predict the amount and timing of net cash inflows they will receive in the future as a result of their decisions?

25–13   The FASB outlines disclosure requirements in three different areas: industry operations, foreign operations and export sales, and major customers. Are these requirements independent of each other?

25–14   Which of the following is the primary purpose of segment reporting information?

[a] Interperiod comparisons of the particular enterprise.
[b] Comparisons between different enterprises.

25–15   What is the distinction between the terms *industry segment* and *reportable segment*? How is each determined?

25–16   What guidelines exist to ensure that industry segment information conforms with each of the following?

[a] It incorporates the majority of total enterprise operations.

[b] It does not become overly detailed by the presentation of an excessive number of industries.

25–17 What is the basic rationale underlying the requirement for disclosure of foreign operations and export sales?

25–18 Define major customer. What is the purpose of major customer disclosure?

25–19 What is a related-party transaction? What disclosures does GAAP require about related-party transactions?

25–20 What is a financial instrument?

25–21 What special disclosures about financial instruments does *SFAS No. 105* require?

25–22 What special disclosures about financial instruments does *SFAS No. 107* require?

25–23 What is the main purpose of financial statement analysis?

25–24 How should an analyst determine whether a financial ratio computed for a given company is "good" or "bad"?

25–25 What are the meaning and formula for each of the following ratios: current, quick, and net cash flow from operating activities to current liabilities?

25–26 What are the meaning and formula for each of the following ratios: debt to total assets, times interest earned, cash flow interest coverage, net cash flow from operating activities to sales, and net cash flow from operating activities to net income?

25–27 What are the meaning and formula for each of the following ratios: receivables turnover, inventory turnover, asset turnover, profit margin on sales, rate of return on assets, return on common stockholders' equity, earnings per share, price/earnings ratio, book value per share, and dividend payout ratio?

25–28 What are the most important limitations of financial statement analysis?

25–29 What major sources of information are potentially available to a person who wants to perform a financial analysis?

25–30 Assuming that the stock market is highly efficient, is it still worthwhile to learn about financial statement analysis? Explain your answer.

EXERCISES

25–31 Interim Reporting In January 1996 Tyler, Inc., estimated that its year-end bonus to executives would be $480,000 for 1996. The amount paid for the year-end bonus for 1995 was $448,000. The estimate for 1996 is subject to year-end adjustment.

INSTRUCTIONS

Determine the amount of bonus expense that should be reflected in Tyler's quarterly income statement for the three months ended March 31, 1996, and justify your answer.   (AICPA adapted)

25–32 Interim Reporting In August 1995 Mose Company spent $150,000 on an advertising campaign for subscriptions to its magazine on preparing for the skiing season. There are only two issues: one in October and one in November. The magazine is sold only on a subscription basis, and the subscriptions started in October 1995. Mose's fiscal year ends on March 31, 1996.

INSTRUCTIONS

Determine the amount of expense that should be included in Mose's quarterly income statement for the three months ended December 31, 1995, as a result of this expenditure. Justify your answer.

(AICPA adapted)

25–33 Interim Reporting In May 1996 an inventory loss of $300,000 occurred from a market decline. Cox Company recorded this loss in May 1996 after its March 31, 1996, quarterly report was issued. None of this loss was recovered by the end of the year.

INSTRUCTIONS

Explain the general treatment of market declines in inventory in interim reports. How should the $300,000 loss be recognized in Cox's 1996 quarterly financial statements?   (AICPA adapted)

25–34 Interim Reporting In May 1996 Coyle Company spent $100,000 on an advertising campaign for subscriptions to the school magazine it sells. The subscriptions do not start until September 1996, and the magazine is sold only on a yearly subscription basis.

INSTRUCTIONS

How would you recognize the $100,000 advertising expense in the interim periods of 1996? Determine the amount of the advertising expense that should be included in Coyle's quarterly income statement for the three months ended June 30, 1996, and justify your answer.   (AICPA adapted)

25–35 Interim Reporting Coppi Company reported income before income tax of $100,000 and $124,000 for the first two quarters of 1996. The company's estimate of the annual effective income tax rate was 36% at the end of the first quarter and 34% at the end of the second quarter.

INSTRUCTIONS

Determine the income tax expense for the first two quarters of 1996.

25–36 Interim Reporting Coykendall Company's revenue, standard cost of goods sold, and variance information for the four quarters of 1996 are as follows:

| | Quarter Ending | | | |
	Mar. 31, 1996	June 30, 1996	Sept. 30, 1996	Dec. 31, 1996
Revenue	$445,000	$480,000	$510,000	$505,000
Standard cost of goods sold	200,000	220,000	240,000	250,000
Variance from standard*				
Planned	10,000	(15,000)	20,000	—
Unplanned	12,000	(7,000)	5,000	8,000

*Amounts in parentheses represent favorable variances or cost reductions. Other amounts represent unfavorable variances or additions to cost.

INSTRUCTIONS

Determine the amount of gross margin to be recognized in each quarter's income statement.

25–37 Major Customer Disclosure Black Company made sales in 1996 to customers as follows:

Blue Company	$ 8,300,000
White Company	4,200,000
Brown Company	2,500,000
Red Company	1,850,000
Domestic governments	9,500,000
Foreign governments	7,260,000
Other	19,890,000
	$53,500,000

The following additional information is available:

[1] "Other" sales include sales to many customers, none of which exceed $1,000,000.

[2] Red and White Companies are both subsidiaries of Purple Company. Sales to Purple Company amounted to $850,000 and are included in the "other" amount.

[3] Sales to domestic governments include $7,150,000 to federal governmental agencies, $1,100,000 to state governmental agencies, and $1,250,000 to local governmental agencies.

[4] Sales to foreign governments consisted of $4,200,000 to the government of Country Yellow and $3,060,000 to the government of Country Maroon.

INSTRUCTIONS

Identify the customers for which major customer disclosure must be made, justifying each.

25–38 Industry Disclosure Dominick Company operates in three industries. Information on industry operations for 1996 is as follows:

	Identifiable Assets	Revenue	Operating Profit
Industry X	$620,000	$695,000	$49,500
Industry Y	50,000	55,000	2,750
Industry Z	12,000	15,000	975
	$682,000	$765,000	$53,225

INSTRUCTIONS

Identify the reporting requirements for the company in terms of industry segments in accordance with *SFAS No. 14.*

25–39 Industry Disclosure DocuRim Company operates in four industries. Operating statistics (in millions of dollars) for the four industries are as follows for 1996:

Industry	Revenue	Operating Profit	Identifiable Assets
Plastics	$112	$27	$120
Metals	75	24	75
Tobacco	18	4	20
Glass	7	1	10

There were no sales between segments in 1996.

INSTRUCTIONS

Determine the reportable industry segments for DocuRim for 1996, applying all relevant criteria from *SFAS No. 14.* Present figures to support your conclusions.

25–40 Foreign Operations Disclosure Venetian, Inc., is a publicly held company with domestic (U.S.) operations as well as several operating units in foreign countries. Information (in millions of dollars) concerning these operations is summarized below:

	Revenue	Operating Profit	Identifiable Assets
Domestic operations	$545	$ 60	$508
Foreign operations			
Country W	160	20	250
Country X	80	8	106
Country Y	45	24	50
Country Z	30	(5)	71
Consolidated totals	$860	$107	$985

INSTRUCTIONS

[a] Identify the separate disclosures related to foreign operations that must be presented in accordance with *SFAS No. 14,* justifying each item requiring disclosure.

[b] Prepare the disclosure of information concerning foreign operations for Venetian, Inc., based on the limited information given, in a format of your choice.

25–41 Export Sales Disclosure In its U.S. production facility, Peninsula Technology Company produces a single product, which it sells in several domestic and foreign markets. In 1996 sales totaled $12,000,000, of which $4,500,000 were export sales in the following geographic areas:

European Common Market countries	$2,000,000
South American countries	1,700,000
Miscellaneous other countries	800,000
	$4,500,000

INSTRUCTIONS

Determine the specific information concerning domestic and export sales that must be presented with the 1996 financial statements to comply with the reporting requirements of *SFAS No. 14.*

25–42 Industry Disclosure Pekadee Company is subject to industry segment reporting requirements. Operating figures for 1996 are as follows:

Industry	Revenue	Operating Profit	Identifiable Assets
Metal containers	$ 850,000	$177,000	$ 628,000
Recording	700,000	5,000	919,000
Stereophonic equipment	200,000	22,000	275,000
Lawn equipment	172,000	32,000	250,000
Household appliances	658,000	90,000	400,000
Electronic calculators	230,000	11,000	198,000
	$2,810,000	$337,000	$2,670,000

Interindustry sales are as follows: metal containers to household appliances, $80,000; recording to stereophonic equipment, $35,000.

INSTRUCTIONS

Determine the industries that require separate disclosure in the 1996 financial statements. Present computations to support your conclusions.

25–43 Industry Disclosure   Operating profit and loss figures for the seven industries in which the Doan Company operates are as follows:

	1996 Operating Profit (Loss)
Industry A	$1,100,000
Industry B	100,000
Industry C	650,000
Industry D	(208,000)
Industry E	(28,000)
Industry F	5,000
Industry G	(2,000)
	$1,617,000

INSTRUCTIONS

Identify those industries that meet the criterion of 10% or more of operating profit or loss for Doan Company for 1996.

25–44 Short-Term Solvency Ratios   The following information was extracted from the financial statements of Yoshida Corporation.

	1996	1995
Cash	$ 55,142	$ 61,543
Current assets	163,240	178,456
Current liabilities	64,173	71,227
Net cash flow from operating activities	36,250	48,342
Short-term receivables	15,125	18,158
Temporary investments	38,546	42,590

INSTRUCTIONS

Compute each of the following ratios for 1996:

[a] Current.
[b] Quick.
[c] Net cash flow from operating activities to current liabilities.

25–45 Long-Term Solvency Ratios   The following information was taken from the 1996 financial statements of Zumstein Enterprises.

Cash paid for income taxes	$ 45,960
Cash paid for interest	35,050
Income tax expense	43,150
Interest expense	31,940
Net cash flow from operating activities	76,242
Net income	63,490
Net sales	989,000
Total assets	351,142
Total liabilities	145,310

INSTRUCTIONS

Compute each of the following ratios for 1996:

[a] Debt to total assets.
[b] Times interest earned.
[c] Cash flow interest coverage.

[d] Net cash flow from operating activities to sales.

[e] Net cash flow from operating activities to net income.

25–46 Profitability Ratios The following information was obtained from the financial statements of Cortez, Inc.

	1996	1995
Accounts receivable (net)	$ 37,000	$ 43,000
Cash dividends on common stock	3,000	3,000
Common stockholders' equity	115,000	107,000
Cost of goods sold	516,200	464,550
Merchandise inventory	58,000	62,000
Net income	55,960	52,125
Net sales (all on credit)	890,000	815,000
Preferred dividends	5,000	5,000
Total assets	215,000	207,000

Cortez had 10,000 shares of common stock outstanding throughout 1995 and 1996. The market price of the company's common stock was $73.60 at the end of 1996.

INSTRUCTIONS

Compute each of the following ratios for 1996:

[a] Receivables turnover.

[b] Inventory turnover.

[c] Asset turnover.

[d] Profit margin on sales.

[e] Rate of return on assets.

[f] Return on common stockholders' equity.

[g] Earnings per share.

[h] Price/earnings ratio.

[i] Book value per share.

[j] Dividend payout ratio.

25–47 Miscellaneous Ratios Financial information for Slepecki Company for 1996 and 1995 is shown below:

	December 31	
	1996	1995
Cash	$ 10,000	$ 80,000
Accounts receivable (net)	50,000	150,000
Merchandise inventory	90,000	150,000
Short-term marketable securities	30,000	10,000
Land and buildings (net)	340,000	360,000
Mortgage payable (no current portion)	270,000	280,000
Accounts payable (trade)	70,000	110,000
Short-term notes payable	20,000	40,000

	Year Ended December 31	
	1996	1995
Cash sales	$1,800,000	$1,600,000
Credit sales	500,000	800,000
Cost of goods sold	1,000,000	1,400,000

INSTRUCTIONS

Compute the following ratios for 1996 from the information given:

[a] Acid test. [c] Inventory turnover.

[b] Receivables turnover. [d] Current. (AICPA adapted)

25–48 Impact of Inventory Methods on Ratios The controller of O'Mary, Inc., is analyzing her company's inventory accounting policy and asks you to perform certain calculations. She is particularly concerned with the effects a proposed change to LIFO may have on certain key ratios. The following information is available to you.

	December 31	
	1996	**1995**
Inventory using present FIFO method	$ 500,000	$ 450,000
Inventory using proposed LIFO method	400,000	375,000
Current assets (using FIFO)	1,000,000	800,000
Current liabilities	500,000	425,000
Cost of goods sold (using FIFO)	2,100,000	1,900,000

INSTRUCTIONS

[a] Compute the following items for the year ended December 31, 1996, by using the current inventory method and the proposed method:

[1] Current ratio.   [2] Working capital.   [3] Inventory turnover.

[b] Comment on the analysis you have performed.

25–49 Miscellaneous Ratios   The following is information from the financial records of the Fury Company:

Net accounts receivable at Dec. 31, 1995	$1,500,000
Net accounts receivable at Dec. 31, 1996	1,800,000
Inventories at Dec. 31, 1995	2,200,000
Inventories at Dec. 31, 1996	2,500,000
Accounts receivable turnover	10
Inventory turnover	4

INSTRUCTIONS

[a] How much were sales during 1996? (Assume that all sales were on credit.)
[b] How much was cost of goods sold for 1996?
[c] Assuming a 365-day year, compute the number of days' sales in average receivables for 1996.
[d] Assuming a 365-day year, compute the number of days' sales in average inventory for 1996.

25–50 Miscellaneous Computations Based on Ratios   The December 31, 1996, balance sheet of Ferro Company is presented below. These are the only accounts in the company's balance sheet. Amounts indicated by a question mark (?) can be calculated from the additional information given.

Assets	
Cash	$ 25,000
Accounts receivable (net)	?
Inventory	?
Property, plant, and equipment (net)	294,000
	$432,000

Liabilities and Stockholder's Equity	
Accounts payable (trade)	$?
Income taxes payable (current)	25,000
Long-term debt	?
Common stock	300,000
Retained earnings	?
	$?

ADDITIONAL INFORMATION THAT PERTAINS TO 1996

Current ratio	1.5 to 1
Total liabilities divided by total stockholders' equity	.8
Inventory turnover based on sales and ending inventory	15 times
Inventory turnover based on cost of goods sold and ending inventory	10.5 times
Gross margin	$315,000

INSTRUCTIONS

Compute the following items for Ferro Company:

[a] Balance in trade accounts payable.
[b] Balance in retained earnings.
[c] Balance in inventory. (AICPA adapted)

25–51 Test of Reasonableness and Disclosure Claus Company had interest-bearing debt of $1,000,000 on its balance sheet at December 31, 1996, which represented an increase of $500,000 over interest-bearing debt at December 31, 1995. The company had interest expense of $50,000 for the year ended December 31, 1996. The market rate of interest for 1996 was 12%.

INSTRUCTIONS

[a] Comment on the reasonableness of Claus' interest expense to debt ratio. Give possible explanations for any unreasonable relationships that exist.
[b] Assume the same information except that the market rate of interest was 10% and the $500,000 additional debt represented an interest-free loan from Santa Company, a major customer of Claus. The two-year Santa loan was granted on January 1, 1996, in exchange for Claus' agreement to sell its special production equipment to Santa at a 5% discount during 1996 and 1997. Santa is expected to purchase from Claus equipment with a fair value of $2,000,000 over the two-year period.
    Prepare the entry that Claus should have made at the end of 1996.
[c] Prepare any footnote disclosure that should be included in Claus' financial statements as a result of the situation in [b].

25–52 Miscellaneous Computations Based on Ratios Collignon, Inc., generated sales revenue of $5,000,000 during 1996. Collignon's statistical summary indicates the following ratios for the year ended December 31, 1996.

Rate of return on year-end stockholders' equity	15%
Rate of return on year-end assets	10%
Net income/sales	8%
Debt/equity	50%

INSTRUCTIONS

Based on this information, compute the following:

[a] Total assets.   [d] Total debt.
[b] Stockholders' equity.   [e] Total expenses.
[c] Net income.

PROBLEMS

25–53 Interim Period Income Colgate Company reports quarterly to its stockholders. Condensed financial information is presented, emphasizing quarterly results of operations. The company reports on a calendar-year basis with quarterly reports provided on March 31, June 30, September 30, and December 31.

Selected information for the four quarters of 1996 is shown below. All "other costs and expenses" are to be recognized in the period incurred except the following:

[1] Machinery repairs of $90,000 incurred in the first quarter are expected to benefit each quarter equally.
[2] Advertising costs are allocated among the remaining quarters of the annual period, including the quarter in which the costs are incurred, on the basis of the historical pattern of sales: 20%, 30%, 15%, and 35% in the first through fourth quarters, respectively. Advertising expense amounted to $120,000 of the other costs and expenses incurred in the second quarter.

	Quarter			
	1	2	3	4
Revenue	$560,000	$675,000	$352,000	$875,000
Costs associated directly with revenue	280,000	337,000	176,000	438,000
Other costs and expenses (indicated in the period incurred)	110,000	165,000	45,000	162,000

INSTRUCTIONS

Determine income before income taxes for each quarter of 1996.

25–54 Interim Period Income Tax   Amos Company makes a quarterly estimate of the annual income tax rate and recognizes income tax expense on a cumulative year-to-date basis in the interim reports at the end of each quarter. For 1996, the expected income tax rate gradually declined as the company took advantage of certain tax credits and other methods of reducing income taxes that had not previously been anticipated.

Figures for the four quarters of 1996 are as follows:

End of Quarter	Anticipated Annual Income Tax Rate at this Date	Income for Quarter Ending on this Date
March 31, 1996	46%	$150,000
June 30, 1996	44	182,000
September 30, 1996	42	127,000
December 31, 1996	40	185,000

INSTRUCTIONS

Determine the amount of income tax expense that should be recognized in determining net income for each quarter of 1996.

25–55 Interim Period Income   Ferretti Corporation is preparing information for its 1996 second quarter interim report provided to stockholders. The company is on a calendar-year basis. Information that has been accumulated to date includes the following:

[1] Revenue for the second quarter totaled $2,894,000, including a reduction for a loss on the sale of securities of $28,000, which is considered infrequent but not unusual.
[2] Expenses directly related to revenues are $1,600,000. During the first quarter of 1996, a loss of $125,000 on inventory declines below cost was recognized. During the second quarter, inventory market values increased to a level in excess of cost. This increase in market is not reflected in the revenue or expense figures described above.
[3] Other costs and expenses incurred during the second quarter totaled $285,000. None of these are allocable to other quarters. In the first quarter, however, other costs and expenses of $40,000 were allocated to the second quarter.
[4] Income tax expense of $86,250 was recognized in the first quarter report. This was determined in the following way:

Income before income tax to Mar. 31, 1996	$187,500
Estimated annual income tax rate	46%
	$ 86,250

At June 30, 1996, the estimate of the annual effective income tax rate was revised to 42%.

INSTRUCTIONS

Determine net income for the quarter ended June 30, 1996.

25–56 Interim Period Income Statement   Kessler Company is publicly held and provides stockholders with quarterly financial information prepared in accordance with GAAP.

Selected data for the four quarters of 1996 are presented in the following schedule:

	Quarter Ended			
	Mar. 31	**June 30**	**Sept. 30**	**Dec. 31**
Revenue	$1,150,000	$1,068,000	$875,000	$1,245,000
Expenses				
Directly associated with revenue	$655,000	$548,000	$389,000	$625,000
Other	50,000	180,000	125,000	258,000
Expenses other than tax	$705,000	$728,000	$514,000	$883,000

You determine the following information concerning these data and other items of importance to Kessler's interim reporting.

[1] Included in third quarter revenue is an extraordinary gain of $212,000 (before income tax), which resulted from the involuntary conversion of a plant asset. The gain is subject to a 25% income tax rate.

[2] Included among other expenses of the second quarter are annual machinery repair costs of $120,000, which are expected to benefit all periods equally.

[3] Estimates of the annual effective income tax rate made at the end of each quarter are as follows: March 31, 46%; June 30, 40%; September 30, 44%; December 31, 42%.

[4] One hundred thousand shares of common stock were outstanding throughout 1996. The company has no preferred stock.

[5] Sales and costs directly associated with sales in 1996 followed a relatively normal seasonal pattern based on the past performance of Kessler Company.

INSTRUCTIONS

[a] Prepare condensed income statements for each quarter of 1996, including schedules to support your figures.

[b] Based on the limited information given in this problem, prepare a schedule for the quarter ending September 30, 1996, which includes the minimum disclosures required to be presented to stockholders.

25–57 Industry Segment Disclosure   Owenby, Inc., is a publicly held corporation subject to the reporting requirements of *SFAS No. 14*. The company's controller has asked your assistance in determining whether industry segment information is necessary in the 1996 financial statements. The controller presents you with the following information:

Industry	Identifiable Assets	Revenues	Expenses Directly Allocable to Industry
Wholesale	$ 9,500,000	$8,300,000	$6,850,000
Retail	400,000	265,000	180,000
Manufacturing	300,000	420,000	263,800
Construction	300,000	197,000	125,200
	$10,500,000	$9,182,000	$7,419,000

General expenses are as follows:

Operating expenses associated with all industry segments	$ 762,000
General corporate expenses associated with corporate office	1,225,000
	$1,987,000

Further investigation reveals that all figures are accurate and that the operating expenses associated with all industry segments are allocable as follows: 70% to wholesale and 10% to each of the other industries.

INSTRUCTIONS

[a] Prepare a recommendation concerning the need to present industry segment information. Provide computations to support your opinion.

[b] Identify the financial statement disclosures, if any, that are needed in relation to the company's operations in different industries.

25–58 Industry Segment Disclosure   Direct Supply is attempting to determine the operating profit (loss) of each of its industry segments. The following information (in millions of dollars) relative to industry segments for 1996 has been accumulated:

Industry Segment	Revenue	Expenses Directly Associated with Industry
Transportation equipment	$108	$ 67
Rubber products	80	60
Apparel	22	17
Lumber and wood products	7	5
Paper products	13	12
	$230	$161

The following additional revenue and expense information has been accumulated:

Revenue earned at the corporate level	$10,500,000
General corporate expenses	7,850,000
Operating expenses allocable to industry segments	22,000,000

The operating expenses allocable to industry segments relate to the rubber products, lumber and wood products, and paper products industries. Allocation is to be based on the relative amounts of revenue generated by each industry.

INSTRUCTIONS

[a] Determine the operating profit or loss of each segment for purposes of segment reporting requirements.

[b] Apply the 10% of revenue and operating profit tests to determine the reportable segments for Direct Supply for 1996. (For purposes of this problem, ignore the 10% of identifiable assets test.)

[c] Assuming that no intersegment sales were made, does your identification of reportable segments in [b] comply with the requirements of *SFAS No. 14?* You may assume that there are no comparability problems with previous years.

25–59 Foreign Operations and Export Sales   A. L. Clark Corporation has significant domestic and foreign operations. Revenues from the domestic operations result from sales within the United States and export sales.

You have been asked to help identify disclosure requirements in conformity with GAAP. As a part of your work, you determine the following:

[1] A. L. Clark Corporation is a publicly held company whose stock is traded in the over-the-counter market.

[2] Revenue from sales for the year 1996 totaled $138,000,000 ($85,000,000 from domestic operations and $53,000,000 from foreign operations).

[3] Seventy percent of the domestic revenues were derived from sales within the United States. The remaining 30% resulted from export sales distributed as follows:

England	$16,000,000
Sweden	1,800,000
Canada	4,600,000
Mexico	3,100,000
	$25,500,000

[4] Activities from foreign operations are summarized in the following schedule:

	Revenue	Operating Profit	Identifiable Assets
South American operations	$44,000,000	$7,000,000	$52,000,000
African operations	5,000,000	100,000	4,000,000
Australian operations	4,000,000	(500,000)	4,500,000
	$53,000,000	$6,600,000	$60,500,000

[5] Summary figures from A. L. Clark's 1996 consolidated income statement and other company records are as follows:

Revenues (including $2,000,000 general corporate revenues)		$140,000,000
Expenses		
Operating expenses—Domestic operations	$65,000,000	
Operating expenses—Foreign operations	46,400,000	
General corporate expenses	13,600,000	125,000,000
Income before income tax		$ 15,000,000

Assets are as follows:

Identified with domestic operations	$ 78,000,000
Identified with foreign operations	60,500,000
Identified with corporate headquarters	10,500,000
	$149,000,000

INSTRUCTIONS

[a] Identify the information, if any, that must be presented concerning export sales.

[b] Identify the information, if any, that must be presented concerning foreign operations.

[c] Prepare a supplementary schedule incorporating the information you have identified in [a] and [b]. Design the schedule so that the disclosure of export sales and foreign operations relate to aggregate amounts taken from the company's financial statements.

25–60 Industry Segment Disclosure   In the early 1970s, Kenjo Company (a publicly held corporation), entered a diversification program, which resulted in its involvement in six different industries. In attempting to apply appropriate accounting and disclosure requirements in the 1996 financial statements, accountants have accumulated the data (in millions of dollars) on Kenjo's industry operations as shown:

Industry	Total Revenue	Expenses Directly Incurred by Industry	Assets Used Directly by Industry
Agriculture	$110	$ 60	$120
Mining	80	55	140
Construction	70	60	80
Transportation	20	21	17
Wholesale trade	5	2	4
Retail trade	3	2	2
	$288	$200	$363

Additional operating expenses allocable to industry operations total $45,000,000. You determine that these expenses should be allocated as follows: 40% to agriculture, 20% each to mining and construction, 10% to transportation, and 5% each to wholesale trade and retail trade.

General corporate expenses total $12,500,000. Interest income at the corporate level was $1,780,000. Equity in earnings of an investment in an affiliated company was $2,450,000.

An analysis of Kenjo's assets reveals that $38,500,000 of assets is used at the corporate level. This includes the $18,000,000 equity accounting basis in the affiliated company. Also, assets of $27,000,000 are used jointly by three industries and are allocable to them as follows: agriculture, 60%; mining, 30%; and wholesale trade, 10%.

Interindustry sales during 1996 are as follows: mining industry to construction industry, $7,000,000; transportation industry to agriculture industry, $15,500,000.

INSTRUCTIONS

[a] Identify the reportable segments for 1996 for Kenjo Company, applying all relevant tests of significance included in *SFAS No. 14*.

[b] Prepare a supplementary schedule, based on the information presented in the problem and your response in [a], to be used to present industry segment information in the 1996 financial statements.

[c] What additional information, not available in this problem, would be required to complete the industry segment disclosure requirements of *SFAS No. 14*?

25–61 Related Party Transaction Disclosures   The Pugh, Inc., annual report dated December 31, 1996, contained the following consolidated statements of changes in stockholders' equity along with a footnote on related-party transactions:

Pugh, Inc.
Consolidated Statements of Changes in Stockholders' Equity

	Preferred Stock		Common Stock		Paid-in Capital	Retained Earnings	Total
	Shares	Value	Shares	Value			
Balances at Jan. 1, 1996	29,058	$290,580	63,660	$318,300	$92,410	$ 740,457	$1,441,747
Issuance of common stock for services	—	—	—	—	—	—	—
Redemption of preferred stock in exchange for property	(29,058)	(290,580)	—	—	—	(67,400)	(357,980)
Issuance of common stock	—	—	—	—	—	—	
Net earnings	—	—	—	—	—	1,179,742	1,179,742
Balances at Dec. 31, 1996	—	—	63,660	$318,300	$92,410	$1,852,799	$2,263,509

Related-Party Transactions

In August 1995, the company issued 1,518 shares of common stock to an officer in exchange for a proven oil and gas property valued at $100,000, the property's approximate cost. The company incurred costs of approximately $61,000 to further develop the oil and gas property. In April 1996 the company entered into an agreement with the officer whereby the company exchanged the proven oil and gas property. (which then had an estimated fair market value of $300,000) for a drilling rig and related equipment. The transaction resulted in a gain for the company of approximately $139,000 and is included in gain on sale of property and equipment in the consolidated statements of earnings.

In February 1995, the company issued 29,058 shares of preferred stock to an officer and forgave him for an indebtedness of an $88,000 note receivable in exchange for a drilling rig and related equipment having a fair market value of $375,580. In January 1996, the company redeemed all of the outstanding preferred stock for $11 per share and paid accrued dividends aggregating $38,342 in exchange for certain proven oil and gas properties carried on the books at $105,140, their approximate current value. This transaction resulted in a gain of approximately $253,000 and is included as a gain on the sale of property and equipment in the consolidated statements of earnings.

INSTRUCTIONS

[a] Prepare the entries to record the transactions that are described in the footnote.

[b] Discuss the propriety of the treatment accorded these events. Be sure to include a discussion of the basic theoretical issues involved.

25–62 Ratio Computations   Comparative balance sheets, income and retained earnings statements, and additional information pertaining to the Ramada Company appear below.

Ramada Company
Balance Sheet
December 31, 1996 and 1995

Assets

Current Assets	1996	1995
Cash	$ 3,500,000	$ 3,600,000
Marketable securities, at cost which approximates market	13,000,000	11,000,000
Accounts receivable, net of allowance for doubtful accounts	105,000,000	95,000,000
Inventories, lower of cost or market	126,000,000	154,000,000
Prepaid expenses	2,500,000	2,400,000
Total current assets	250,000,000	266,000,000
Noncurrent Assets		
Property, plant, and equipment, net of accumulated depreciation	311,000,000	308,000,000
Investments, at equity	2,000,000	3,000,000
Long-term receivables	14,000,000	16,000,000
Goodwill and patents, net of accumulated amortization	6,000,000	6,500,000
Other assets	7,000,000	8,500,000
Total assets	$590,000,000	$608,000,000

Liabilities and Stockholders' Equity

Current Liabilities	1996	1995
Notes payable	$ 5,000,000	$ 15,000,000
Accounts payable	38,000,000	48,000,000
Accrued expenses	24,500,000	27,000,000
Income taxes payable	1,000,000	1,000,000
Payments due within one year on long-term debt	6,500,000	7,000,000
Total current liabilities	75,000,000	98,000,000
Noncurrent Liabilities		
Long-term debt	169,000,000	180,000,000
Deferred income taxes	74,000,000	67,000,000
Other liabilities	9,000,000	8,000,000
Total liabilities	327,000,000	353,000,000
Stockholders' Equity		
Common stock, par value $1 per share; authorized 20,000,000 shares; issued and outstanding 10,000,000 shares	10,000,000	10,000,000
5% cumulative preferred stock, par value $100 per share; $100 liquidating value; authorized 50,000 shares; issued and outstanding 40,000 shares	4,000,000	4,000,000
Additional paid-in capital	107,000,000	107,000,000
Retained earnings	142,000,000	134,000,000
Total stockholders' equity	263,000,000	255,000,000
Total liabilities and stockholders' equity	$590,000,000	$608,000,000

Ramada Company
Statement of Income and Retained Earnings
For the Years Ended December 31, 1996 and 1995

	1996	1995
Net sales	$600,000,000	$500,000,000
Cost and expenses		
Cost of goods sold	490,000,000	400,000,000
Selling, general, and administrative expenses	66,000,000	60,000,000
Other, net	7,000,000	6,000,000
Total costs and expenses	563,000,000	466,000,000
Income before income taxes	37,000,000	34,000,000
Income taxes	16,800,000	15,800,000
Net income	20,200,000	18,200,000
Retained earnings at beginning of period	134,000,000	126,000,000
Dividends on common stock	12,000,000	10,000,000
Dividends on preferred stock	200,000	200,000
Retained earnings at the end of period	$142,000,000	$134,000,000

ADDITIONAL INFORMATION

1. Market price per share of Ramada's common stock on 12-31-96 — $10.00
2. Interest expense for 1996 (included among the costs and expenses on the income statement) — $19,500,000
3. Net cash flow from operating activities during 1996 — $48,000,000
4. Cash paid for interest during 1996 — $19,500,000
5. Cash paid for income taxes during 1996 — $16,800,000

INSTRUCTIONS

Compute the following ratios for 1996 and show supporting computations in good form:

[a] Current.
[b] Quick.
[c] Net cash flow from operating activities to current liabilities.
[d] Debt to total assets.
[e] Debt to equity.
[f] Times interest earned.
[g] Cash flow interest coverage.

[h] Net cash flow from operating activities to sales.
[i] Net cash flow from operating activities to net income.
[j] Receivables turnover.
[k] Number of days' sales in receivables (assume 365 days in a year).
[l] Inventory turnover
[m] Number of days' sales in inventory (assume 365 days in a year)

[n] Asset turnover
[o] Profit margin on sales
[p] Rate of return on assets
[q] Return on common stockholders' equity
[r] Earnings per share
[s] Price/earnings ratio
[t] Book value per share
[u] Dividend payout ratio
[v] Dividend yield.

25–63 Ratio Computations and Revised Financial Statements   Graham Company manufactures and sells children's plastic toys. The company has experienced continued growth over the past three years and has forecast sales of $3,000,000 for 1997. Graham applied to Hampton State Bank for a short-term loan of $50,000 to cover expanding working capital needs. This is the first loan application Hampton State Bank has ever received from Graham, and the bank is anxious to develop a lasting relationship.

The following financial and other information has been supplied by Graham at the bank's request or developed by bank personnel.

Graham Company—Balance Sheet
December 31, 1995 and 1996
(in thousands)
(unaudited)

Assets	1995	1996
Current assets		
Cash	$ 85	$ 60
Marketable securities (cost)	20	20
Accounts receivable (net)	520	600
Inventories	365	475
Prepaid items	40	45
Total current assets	1,030	1,200
Investments (cost)	80	80
Property, plant, and equipment (net)	590	520
Total assets	$1,700	$1,800
Equities		
Current liabilities		
Notes payable (trade)	$ 90	$ 80
Notes payable (officers)	100	100
Accounts payable	190	280
Accrued expenses and taxes	50	40
Total current liabilities	$ 430	$ 500
Long-term debt, 7%	420	400
Total liabilities	$ 850	$ 900
Stockholders' equity	850	900
Total equities	$1,700	$1,800

Graham Company—Income Statement
For the Year Ended December 31, 1995 and 1996
(in thousands)
(unaudited)

	1995	1996
Net sales	$2,500	$2,800
Cost of goods sold	1,750	2,100
Gross margin	750	700
Operating expenses		
Advertising	145	155
Bad debts estimate	25	28

	1995	1996
Depreciation	70	70
Insurance	35	36
Lease payment	—	8
Salaries	185	190
Supplies	13	8
Taxes (nonincome)	25	25
Interest	42	40
Total operating expenses	540	560
Earnings before income taxes	210	140
Income taxes	105	70
Net income	$ 105	$ 70

ADDITIONAL INFORMATION

[1] **Accounts receivable.** Sales are highly seasonal, with most sales occurring in the summer and fall for the upcoming Christmas season. Graham allows many customers to wait until January or February to settle their accounts (a common practice in the industry).

The allowance for uncollectible accounts had a balance of $30,000 on December 31, 1995, and $40,000 on December 31, 1996.

The aged accounts receivable balance on December 31, 1996, is shown as follows:

Days Past Due	Amount	Industry Collection Experience
Not due	$340,000	99% collected
1–60	120,000	97% collected
61–120	40,000	90% collected
121–180	70,000	80% collected
Over 181	70,000	50% collected
	$640,000	

[2] **Inventory.**

	1995	1996
Raw materials (LIFO)	$100,000	$100,000
Work-in-process (FIFO)	50,000	300,000
Finished goods (FIFO)	215,000	75,000

The raw materials consist primarily of plastic. Plastic prices rose approximately 10% in 1995 and by the same amount in 1996. Graham began its LIFO program on January 1, 1995.

[3] **Employment contract.** The company president has a five-year contract at $45,000 per year with three years remaining.

[4] **Insurance.** The company has purchased ordinary life insurance on its key officers. The policies have accrued a total of $5,000 cash surrender value.

[5] **Marketable securities.** The marketable securities were worth $21,000 at December 31, 1996.

[6] **Investments.** The investments of $80,000 consist of 800 shares of Fisher Company, which is owned in part by several of Graham's directors. Fisher discontinued one of its major products as a result of a legal suit concerning product safety standards. The stock declined to $60 per share following this action.

[7] **Property, plant, and equipment.** The company uses the same depreciation methods for book and tax purposes. The straight-line method is used on the plant, and the double declining-balance method is used on all equipment.

A purchase agreement for a parcel of land was signed in September 1996. Payment was to be made on January 10, 1997. The check for $10,000 was written on December 27, 1996, and delivered to the seller. The transaction was not recorded in December.

In January 1996, a noncancellable lease for equipment was signed by Graham. The lease calls for Graham to make annual payments of $8,000 for five years. The equipment can be purchased at the end of the lease for $10,000. The purchase price of the equipment was $40,000. At the date the lease was signed, the value of the lease payments and option price was $40,000 (using a 10% rate), and the present value of the remaining lease payments and option price at December 31, 1996, is $35,000.

[8] **Notes payable (officers).** The officers loaned the company $100,000 early in 1994. The notes have been renewed each year, and it is expected that they will be renewed annually for the next three years. The notes are subordinated to other notes outstanding.

[9] **Dividends.** The company paid dividends of $20,000 to its stockholders during 1996.

INSTRUCTIONS

[a] Calculate the following ratios for 1996 by using the preceding financial information:

[1] Return on total assets.

[2] Acid-test ratio.

[3] Average collection period for receivables.

[4] Inventory turnover.

[5] Times interest earned.

[b] Revise the balance sheet on a *pro forma* basis as of December 31, 1996, to make it more useful for the bank's needs.

[c] Prepare a summary of estimated cash flows for 1996.   (CMA adapted)

25–64 Financial Statements Derived from Ratios Ratio analysis is often applied to test the reasonableness of the relationships among current financial data against those of prior financial data. Given prior financial relationships and a few key amounts, an accountant can prepare estimates of current financial data to test the reasonableness of current financial information.

Star Company has in recent years maintained the following relationships among the data in its financial statements:

Gross profit rate on net sales	40%
Net profit rate on net sales	10%
Rate of selling expenses to net sales	20%
Accounts receivable turnover	8 per year
Inventory turnover	6 per year
Acid-test ratio	2 to 1
Current ratio	3 to 1
Quick-asset composition:	
8% cash	
32% marketable securities	
60% accounts receivable	
Asset turnover	2 per year
Ratio of total assets to intangible assets	20 to 1
Ratio of accumulated depreciation to cost of fixed assets	1 to 3
Ratio of accounts receivable to accounts payable	1.5 to 1
Ratio of working capital to stockholders' equity	1 to 1.6
Ratio of total debt to stockholders' equity	1 to 2

The corporation had a net income of $120,000 for 1996, which resulted in earnings of $5.20 per share of common stock.

ADDITIONAL INFORMATION

[1] Capital stock authorized, issued (all in 1988), and outstanding: common, $10 per share par value, issued at 10% premium; preferred, 6% nonparticipating, $100 per share par value, issued at 10% premium.

[2] Market value per share of common stock at December 31, 1996: $78.

[3] Preferred dividends paid in 1996: $3,000.

[4] Times interest earned in 1996: 33.

[5] The amounts of the following were the same at December 31, 1996, as at January 1, 1996: inventory, accounts receivable, 5% bonds payable—due in 2001—and total stockholders' equity.

[6] All purchases and sales were "on account."

INSTRUCTIONS

[a] Prepare in good form the condensed balance sheet and income statement for the year ended December 31, 1996, presenting the amounts you would expect to find in Star's financial statements based on the ratios and other information provided.

Major captions appearing on Star's balance sheet are Current Assets, Fixed Assets, Intangible Assets, Current Liabilities, Long-Term Liabilities, and Stockholders' Equity. In addition to the accounts divulged in the problem, you should include accounts for Prepaid Expenses, Accrued

Expenses, and Administrative Expenses. Supporting calculations should be in good form. You may ignore income taxes.

[b] Compute the following ratios for 1996 and show your computations:

[1] Rate of return on stockholders' equity.
[2] Price/earnings ratio for common stock.
[3] Dividends paid per share of common stock.
[4] Dividends paid per share of preferred stock.
[5] Yield on common stock.   (AICPA adapted)

CASES

25–65 Interim Reporting   Ivey Manufacturing Company, a California corporation listed on the Pacific Coast Stock Exchange, budgeted activities for 1996 as follows:

	Amount	Units
Net sales	$6,000,000	1,000,000
Cost of goods sold	3,600,000	1,000,000
Gross margin	2,400,000	
Selling, general, and administrative expenses	1,400,000	
Operating earnings	1,000,000	
Nonoperating revenues and expenses	–0–	
Earnings before income taxes	1,000,000	
Estimated income taxes (current and deferred)	550,000	
Net earnings	$ 450,000	
Earnings per share of common stock	$4.50	

Ivey has operated profitably for many years and has experienced a seasonal pattern of sales volume and production similar to the following amounts forecasted for 1996. Sales volume is expected to follow a quarterly pattern of 10%, 20%, 35%, and 35%, respectively, because of the seasonality of the industry. Because of production and storage limitations, production is expected to follow a pattern of 20%, 25%, 30%, and 25%, per quarter, respectively.

At the end of the first quarter of 1996, the controller of Ivey prepared and issued the following interim report for public release:

	Amount	Units
Net sales	$ 600,000	100,000
Cost of goods sold	360,000	100,000
Gross margin	240,000	
Selling, general and administrative expenses	275,000	
Operating loss	(35,000)	
Loss from warehouse fire	(175,000)	
Loss before income taxes	(210,000)	
Estimated income taxes	–0–	
Net loss	$(210,000)	
Loss per share of common stock	$(2.10)	

The following additional information is available for the first quarter just completed but was not included in the public information released:

[1] The company uses a standard cost system in which standards are set at currently attainable levels on an annual basis. At the end of the first quarter, there was underapplied fixed factory overhead (volume variance) of $50,000 that was treated as an asset at the end of the quarter. Production during the quarter was 200,000 units, of which 100,000 were sold.

[2] The selling, general, and administrative expenses were budgeted on a basis of $900,000 fixed expenses for the year plus $.50 variable expenses per unit of sales.

[3] The warehouse fire loss met the conditions of an extraordinary loss. The warehouse had an undepreciated cost of $320,000; $145,000 was recovered from insurance on the warehouse. No other

gains or losses are anticipated this year from similar events or transactions, nor has Ivey had any similar losses in preceding years; thus, the full loss will be deductible as an ordinary loss for income tax purposes.

[4] The effective income tax rate, for federal and state taxes combined, is expected to average 55% of earnings before income taxes during 1996. There are no permanent differences between pretax financial earnings and taxable income.

[5] Earnings per share were computed on the basis of 100,000 shares of capital stock outstanding. Ivey has only one class of stock issued, no long-term debt outstanding, and no stock option plan.

INSTRUCTIONS

[a] Without reference to the specific situation described above, what are the standards of disclosure for interim financial data (published interim financial reports) for publicly traded companies? Explain.

[b] Identify the weakness in form and content of Ivey's interim report without reference to the additional information.

[c] For each of the five items of additional information, indicate the preferable treatment for each item for interim reporting purposes and explain why that treatment is preferable.

(AICPA adapted)

25–66 Segment Reporting   Dozier, Inc., manufactures a wide variety of pharmaceuticals, medical instruments, and other related medical supplies. Eighteen months ago the company developed and began to market a new product line of antihistamine drugs under various trade names. Sales and profitability of this product line during the current fiscal year greatly exceeded management's expectations. The new product line will account for 10% of the company's total sales and 12% of the company's operating income for the fiscal year ending June 30, 1996. Management believes sales and profits will be significant for several years.

Dozier fears that disclosure in its annual financial statements about the volume and profitability of its new product line will adversely affect its market position in relation to its competitors. Management is not sure how *FASB Statement of Financial Accounting Standards No. 14,* "Financial Reporting for Segments of a Business Enterprise," applies in this case.

INSTRUCTIONS

[a] Why should segment information be disclosed in financial statements?

[b] Explain the factors that should be considered when attempting to decide how products should be grouped to determine a single business segment.

[c] What options, if any, does Dozier, Inc., have regarding the disclosure of its new antihistamine product line? Explain your answer.

(CMA adapted)

25–67 Meaning and Limitations of Ratios   As the CPA responsible for the audit engagement of a small client, the client requests that you provide him at the earliest possible date with some key ratios based on the final audited figures appearing on the comparative financial statements. The information is to be used to convince creditors that the client's business is solvent and to justify a request for continued financial support. The client wishes to save time by concentrating on only these key data.

The requested data and the computations taken from the financial statements follow:

	Last Year	This Year
Current ratio	2.0:1	2.5:1
Quick (acid-test) ratio	1.2:1	.7:1
Ratio of property, plant, and equipment to owners' equity	2.3:1	2.6:1
Ratio of sales to owners' equity	2.8:1	2.5:1
Net income	Down 10%	Up 30%
Earnings per common share	$2.40	$3.12
Book value per common share	Up 8%	Up 5%

INSTRUCTIONS

[a] The client asks that you prepare a list of brief comments stating how each of these items supports the solvency and going-concern potential of his business. He wishes to use these comments to support his presentation of data to his creditors. Prepare the comments by listing the implications and the limitations of each item separately. Then explain the collective inference that one may draw from them about the client's solvency and going-concern potential.

[b] Prepare a brief list of additional ratio analysis–type data that you think this client's creditors will request to supplement the data provided in [a]. Explain why the additional data will be helpful to these creditors in evaluating this client's solvency.

[c] What warnings should you offer these creditors about the limitations of ratio analysis for the purpose stated here?   (AICPA adapted)

25–68 Use of Ratios in Financial Decision   Paper Chase Corporation was formed in 1991 through a public subscription of common stock. Ann Downing, who owns 15% of the common stock, was one of the organizers of Paper Chase and is its current president. The company has been successful, but currently it is experiencing a shortage of funds. On June 10, 1996, Downing asked First National Bank for a 24-month extension of two $30,000 notes, which were due on June 30, 1996, and September 30, 1996. Another note of $7,000 is due on December 31, 1996, but she expects no difficulty in meeting that due date. Downing explained that Paper Chase's cash flow problems are due primarily to the company's desire to finance a $300,000 plant expansion over the next two fiscal years through internally generated funds.

The commercial loan officer of First National requested financial reports for the last two years. These reports were provided, as follows:

Paper Chase Corporation
Statement of Financial Position
For the Fiscal Years Ended March 31, 1995 and 1996

Assets	1995	1996
Cash	$ 12,500	$ 16,400
Notes receivable	104,000	112,000
Accounts receivable (net)	68,500	81,600
Inventories (at cost)	50,000	80,000
Plant and equipment (net of depreciation)	646,000	680,000
Total assets	$881,000	$970,000
Liabilities and Owners' Equity		
Accounts payable	$ 72,000	$ 69,000
Notes payable	54,500	67,000
Accrued liabilities	6,000	9,000
Common stock (60,000 shares, $10 par)	600,000	600,000
Retained earnings*	148,500	225,000
Total liabilities and owners' equity	$881,000	$970,000

*Cash dividends were paid at the rate of $1.00 per share in fiscal year 1995 and $1.25 per share in fiscal year 1996.

Paper Chase Corporation
Income Statement
For the Fiscal Years Ended March 31, 1995 and 1996

	1995	1996
Sales	$2,700,000	$3,000,000
Cost of goods sold[†]	1,720,000	1,902,500
Gross margin	980,000	1,097,500
Operating expenses	780,000	845,000
Income before taxes	200,000	252,500
Income taxes (40%)	80,000	101,000
Net income	$ 120,000	$ 151,500

[†]Depreciation charges of $100,000 and $102,500 on the plant and equipment for fiscal years ended March 31, 1995 and 1996, respectively, are included in cost of goods sold.

INSTRUCTIONS

[a] Calculate the following items for Paper Chase Corporation:

[1] Current ratio for fiscal years 1995 and 1996.

[2] Acid-test (quick) ratio for fiscal years 1995 and 1996.

[3] Inventory turnover for fiscal year 1996.

[4] Return on year-end assets for fiscal years 1995 and 1996.

[5] Percentage change in sales, cost of goods sold, gross margin, and net income from fiscal year 1995 to 1996.

[b] Identify and explain what other financial reports and/or financial analyses might be helpful to the commercial loan officer of First National Bank in evaluating Downing's request for a time extension on Paper Chase's notes.

[c] Assume that the percentage changes (when comparing fiscal year 1996 with fiscal year 1995) for sales, cost of goods sold, gross margin, and net income will be repeated in each of the next two years. Is Paper Chase's desire to finance the plant expansion from internally generated funds realistic? Explain your answer.

[d] Should First National Bank grant the extension on Paper Chase's notes, in light of Downing's statement about financing the plant expansion through internally generated funds? Explain your answer.

(CMA adapted)

25–69 Financial Decision Based on Ratios East Company is considering extending credit to West Company. It is estimated that sales to West would amount to $2,000,000 annually. East wholesales throughout the Midwest, and West (a retail chain) also has a number of stores there. East has had a gross margin of approximately 60% in recent years and expects to have a similar gross margin on the West order, which would be approximately 15% of East Company's present sales.

Information derived from West's financial statements for 1994–1996 is as follows:

	1994	1995	1996
Rate of return on total assets	1.96%	1.12%	(.87)%
Return to sales	1.69%	.99%	(.69)%
Acid-test ratio	1.73/1	1.36/1	1.19/1
Current ratio	2.39/1	1.92/1	1.67/1
Inventory turnover (times)	4.41	4.32	4.52
Equity relationships			
Current liabilities	36.0%	43.0%	48.0%
Long-term liabilities	16.0	10.5	5.0
Shareholders' equity	48.0	46.5	47.0
	100.0%	100.0%	100.0%
Asset relationships			
Current assets	77.0%	72.5%	69.5%
Property, plant, and equipment	23.0%	27.5%	30.5%
	100.0%	100.0%	100.0%

INSTRUCTIONS

[a] For each of the first five items of information given, indicate whether the statistic is favorable, unfavorable, or neutral in the decision to grant credit to West.

[b] Based on the information provided, would you grant credit to West? Support your answer with facts given for the case.

[c] What additional information, if any, would you want before making a final decision?

(CMA adapted)

JUDGMENT CASES

25–70 Interim Reporting Clean-Up, Inc., a hazardous waste disposal company, holds a large portfolio of marketable equity securities that management has classified as available for sale, not as trading securities. The company acquired the securities several years ago to provide a surety bond because insurance for the company's activities was not available at the time. The state had required the portfolio as a condition of granting the company's corporate charter. In the first quarter of the current year, insurance coverage became available, and the company obtained the coverage required by the state. This means that the portfolio is no longer required and can be used for other corporate purposes.

The portfolio now has a market value significantly below its cost due to a widespread decline in the market values of securities in a variety of industries subsequent to year-end. Most analysts believe the broad market decline will last for about 12 to 18 months.

Management has tentatively decided to accelerate a much needed plant modernization with the resources now available. Competitors have recently begun to take business away from Clean-Up, and it is clear that state-of-the-art technology is necessary if the company is to remain successful.

Most of the securities will likely be sold beginning in the third quarter of the current year and continuing ratably for approximately six more months. As the accountant for Clean-Up, you recommend that the securities that will be sold within the next 12 months should be reclassified as trading securities instead of securities available for sale. You also suggest that the losses on these securities should be reported as losses in the current (first) quarter's income statement. The president of the company simply smiles and states:

> *You just don't know how to manage generally accepted accounting principles. First, our plans are tentative, and we might not begin the plant modernization. Second, we will never sell securities below their original cost to us. We are not in the business of taking such losses. We will just hold those securities until their values rise. You know that the recent decline is just a temporary overall market correction. We will take great care to select for sale this year only those securities whose market values are equal to or in excess of their current carrying amount in the accounting records.*
>
> *Third, if the value of securities doesn't rise, then we will borrow the money to finance the plant expansion and use the securities as collateral. Fourth, this is just an interim determination and we can treat the decline in value similar to a temporary LIFO layer liquidation that will be restored before year-end.*
>
> *Now, what's the problem? Nothing that I can see, and I don't think you can find any reasons not to go for it either, can you? If this was an annual reporting situation, I would probably agree with you, but in interim statements, you can defer these drastic accounting decisions until the end of the year. And that is what I plan to do. As luck would have it, we issue only an income statement at interim reporting dates. Thus, we don't even have to report the decline in our portfolio, which is confined to the balance sheet.*

INSTRUCTIONS

Prepare an appropriate response to the accounting that Clean-Up's president has proposed.

25–71 Related-Party Transaction Leon Distefano serves as the general partner for a number of real estate limited partnerships. You are the accountant for one of those partnerships, Builders LTD., which is a real estate development company. At the previous annual partners' meeting, Mr. Distefano asserted that the partnership's principal project, a small office building named Commerce Center, would soon be completed and sold, with profit distributions to the limited partners to follow quickly.

Builders LTD., completed the construction of the complex early in the past year as anticipated and has attempted to sell it for the last eight months. Until the last week of December, those efforts were unsuccessful, due primarily to factors beyond the control of the general partner. Rapid, significant, and unforeseen rises in interest rates and the closure of a major local corporation that produced a large office vacancy rate have adversely affected commercial real estate generally.

You are aware that Distefano has felt considerable pressure to sell the building at the price anticipated and to provide the promised distributions to the limited partners. Only a single offer on the building for $265,000 (an amount that was $10,000 less than the building's cost) had been received recently, and it was declined. During the last week of December, Distefano sold the building to another limited partnership for which he acts as the general partner. That partnership, which was organized to acquire and operate troubled commercial real estate projects, paid $575,000 in cash for the building, an amount that was $25,000 less than the anticipated sales price.

You have pointed out to Distefano that the transaction will have to be disclosed as a related-party transaction in accordance with *FASB Statement No. 57,* "Related Party Disclosures" and Distefano agrees. Accordingly, you have drafted the following proposed note to the financial statements:

> *During the year, the company sold its principal asset, Commerce Center, to a limited partnership operated by the same general partner as Builders LTD. The sales price of $575,000 resulted in a reported profit to Builders of $300,000. The transaction was consummated for cash, and no amounts receivable or payable remain at year-end. The only offer received on the property from an unrelated third party was for $265,000, which probably represents the*

fair value of the property. The sale took place between two entities that are under the common control of a single general partner, and, accordingly, the transaction cannot be considered to have occurred at arm's length.

When you present Distefano with the proposed language of the disclosure, he takes exception to your presentation and asserts:

This goes far beyond anything that FASB Statement No. 57 requires. The description of that other lowball offer just confuses the issue. I know what this property is worth, and I know how to operate it at a profit to all involved. I paid a fair price for it, and I am confident that I will be able to operate it profitably for the new owners. Anyway, why do the partners of Builders care about any of this? They got their money and are quite happy even though the amount was less than anticipated. In fact, almost all of them have just agreed to contribute to a second Builders partnership that will construct a sister complex to Commerce Center. If you insist on this adverse disclosure, they may have second thoughts and try to back out of the deal. There is simply no way that I will accept the disclosure that you have suggested.

INSTRUCTIONS

What should you do? If you believe that it would be appropriate to revise your disclosure, prepare a new note in its entirety. If you believe that the information contained in the note presented in the case is all necessary, respond to Mr. Distefano's beliefs and assertions.

FINANCIAL REPORTING CASE

25–72 Financial Reporting Case   Disclosing disaggregated information may be important for understanding a company's financial position and results of operations. While disaggregated information may take on several forms, two types of information are often presented in financial statements: information about different industry segments and interim periods.

Following is information about industry segments and interim periods for two large publicly held corporations.

Industry Segment Information — Oneida Ltd.

12.   Operations by Industry Segment   The Company's operations and assets are in two principal industries: tableware products and industrial wire products. The Company's tableware operations, which are located in the United States, Canada, Mexico, Italy, and the United Kingdom, involve the manufacture and distribution of stainless, plated and sterling flatware and silverplated and stainless holloware. These products are sold directly or through distributors to a broad base of retail outlets including department stores, mass merchandisers and chain stores. Additionally, these products are sold to special sales markets, which include customers who use them as premiums, incentives and business gifts. The Company also sells flatware, holloware and commercial chinaware to foodservice operations in North America and Europe, including hotels, restaurants, airlines, schools and health care facilities.

The Company's industrial wire division produces copper conducting wire, as well as tin or alloy plated wire for a wide range of customers in electronics, transportation, industrial/energy, construction and consumer products markets.

Information as to the Company's operations by industry segment for 1993, 1992 and 1991 is summarized below:

	(Thousands)		
	1993	**1992**	**1991**
Net Sales and Other Operating Revenues			
Tableware products	$329,201	$317,694	$302,442
Industrial wire products	150,763	129,379	126,453
Total	$479,964	$447,073	$428,895

Operating Profit	1993	1992	1991
Tableware products	$ 17,920	$ 26,412	$ 25,365
Industrial wire products	3,226	4,235	3,125
Operating profit	21,146	30,647	28,490
Corporate expense	(4,903)	(5,685)	(4,815)
Interest expense	(10,304)	(10,452)	(11,173)
Income before income taxes and cumulative effect of accounting changes	$ 5,939	$ 14,510	$ 12,502

Cumulative Effect of Accounting Changes (Net of Income Tax Benefit $21,373)

Tableware products	$ (31,842)		
Industrial wire products	(5,122)		
Total	$ (36,964)		

Identifiable Assets

Tableware products	$245,103	$252,033	$226,793
Industrial wire products	70,373	75,793	63,551
Total	315,476	327,826	290,344
Corporate Assets—Cash	2,203	787	1,879
Total	$317,679	$328,613	$292,223

Depreciation Expense

Tableware products	$ 9,136	$ 9,037	$ 7,806
Industrial wire products	4,292	4,131	3,851
Total	$ 13,428	$ 13,168	$ 11,657

Property, Plant and Equipment Additions

Tableware products	$ 9,986	$ 15,591	$ 14,862
Industrial wire products	4,177	3,164	4,602
Total	$ 14,163	$ 18,755	$ 19,464

Foreign operations of the Company are not material and are therefore not separately set forth.

Quarterly Information—Wal-Mart
Note 8 Quarterly Financial Data (Unaudited)

Quarters Ended

1993	April 30	July 31	October 31	January 31
Net sales	$11,649,430,000	$13,028,445,000	$13,683,824,000	$17,122,072,000
Cost of sales	9,256,326,000	10,416,519,000	10,884,911,000	13,616,929,000
Net income	386,955,000	420,448,000	437,804,000	749,587,000
Net income per share	$.17	$.18	$.19	$.33

1992				
Net sales	$9,280,570,000	$10,339,972,000	$10,627,500,000	$13,638,860,000
Cost of sales	7,330,165,000	8,208,077,000	8,402,750,000	10,845,127,000
Net income	306,953,000	345,893,000	353,200,000	602,430,000
Net income per share	$.13	$.15	$.16	$.26

INSTRUCTIONS

For each of the two disclosures presented above, write a concise report (approximately 150–200 words) in which you indicate how the information disclosed is helpful in better understanding the company's aggregated information in its 1993 financial statements.

Financial Reporting and Changing Prices

OBJECTIVES

1. To discuss the nature and measurement of price changes.
2. To explain the difference between a general price-level change and a specific price change.
3. To discuss and illustrate constant dollar accounting.
4. To explain the major forms of current value accounting.
5. To discuss and illustrate current cost accounting.
6. To discuss and illustrate current cost/constant dollar accounting.
7. To present an overview of the current recommendations of the Financial Accounting Standards Board in the area of accounting for changing prices.

A recent *Wall Street Journal* article explains that the inflation rate in Serbia is currently about 10% *per day*. That equals an annual rate in the quadrillions! A Snickers bar costs six million dinars, and "Serbs complain that the dinar is as worthless as toilet paper. But for the moment, at least, there is plenty of toilet paper to go around."

Another *Wall Street Journal* article explains that in 1984, the annual inflation rate in Bolivia was about 116,000%! Bank tellers simply stopped counting cash deposits; instead they just took their client's word about how much money was in the sack. The 1,000-peso bill cost more to print than it could buy in the marketplace.

While the U.S. inflation rate has been dramatically lower than that in Serbia or Bolivia, it nonetheless has been a major concern of accountants, economists, politicians, and others. And as this chapter explains, the subject of accounting for changing prices has been one of the most pervasive and controversial topics in the United States during the 20th century. Moreover, it is a subject that students interested in international accounting need to understand.

Roger Thurow, "Special, Today Only: Six Million Dinars for a Snickers Bar," *The Wall Street Journal,* August 4, 1993, pp. A1, A7; and Sonia L. Nozario, "When Inflation Rate Is 116,000%, Prices Change by the Hour," *The Wall Street Journal,* February 7, 1985, pp. 1, 22.

C onventional financial statements often are criticized because they do not reflect current values and are not reported in dollars of the same purchasing power. These criticisms are particularly strong because of the magnitude of price changes that have occurred in the United States and elsewhere. In this chapter, we discuss the nature of price changes and illustrate how financial statements can be adjusted for them. We also discuss the current recommendations of the Financial Accounting Standards Board in the area of accounting for changing prices.

This book does not cover all the FASB's requirements, nor is it limited to those requirements. Today the FASB merely *encourages,* but does not require, companies to disclose supplementary information on the effects of changing prices. In this chapter, we explain and illustrate comprehensive financial statements adjusted for changing prices. An understanding of these comprehensive statements will help you to better understand the nature and limitations of conventional financial statements as well as the FASB's current disclosure recommendations concerning the effects of changing prices. It will also help you to more easily understand the kinds of information that may be required in the future, especially if the inflation rate should increase from its present, relatively low level. As you study this chapter, keep in mind how pervasive the subject matter is. That is, it applies to the entire set of financial statements, not merely to a few selected accounts. Accounting for changing prices has probably been the most widely discussed topic in financial accounting during the 20th century.

Multinational companies must be concerned with accounting for the effects of changing prices, even though their primary operations are in the United States or another country that has experienced relatively low inflation in recent years. Current cost accounting, for example, is permitted in the Netherlands. Moreover, accounting adjustments for general price-level changes are required in many countries, such as Brazil and Argentina, that have experienced high inflation. Accountants in these countries believe that constant dollar financial statements are more useful than nominal dollar statements.

NATURE AND MEASUREMENT OF PRICE CHANGES

A **price change** is an increase or decrease in the price of a good or service in a given market, such as a wholesale market or a retail market. Two major types of price changes are general price-level changes and specific price changes. Some of the concepts relating to these price changes were initially explained in Chapter 3.

GENERAL PRICE-LEVEL CHANGES

A **general price-level change** is an increase or decrease in the overall level of prices of goods and services throughout the economy. An increase in the general price-level means that money's **purchasing power** (its ability to buy goods and services) has decreased; this is known as **inflation.** A decrease in the general price-level, known as **deflation,** means that money's purchasing power has increased. During most of the 20th century, inflation has occurred much more frequently than deflation in the United States and most other countries. For this reason, most of the illustrations and problem assignments in this chapter assume the existence of inflation. Recognize, however, that the same general principles apply when deflation occurs.

General price-level changes are measured by using a **general price-level index** constructed by the federal government. Such an index is designed to show how much the overall level of prices in the economy has changed over time. Theoretically, a general price-level index should be constructed by monitoring changes in the prices of *all* goods and services in the economy. For practical reasons, however, the federal government derives a general price-level index by considering price changes in only a sample of goods and services. The government derives several different indexes, and each one is calculated in relation to a predetermined "market basket" of goods and services.

In constructing an index, a base period is selected and assigned an index number of 100. All other periods in the index are then assigned index numbers that relate to the base. Suppose, for example, that 1980 is selected as the base period of a particular index and that prices in the "market basket" composing the index rise by an average of 25% during 1981. Under these circumstances, 1980 and 1981 would be assigned index numbers of 100 and 125, respectively. Dividing 125 by 100 indicates that prices have risen by 25% during 1981 ($125 \div 100 = 1.25$). The reciprocal of this ratio ($100 \div 125 = .80$) indicates that a dollar in

1981 could buy only 80% of what a dollar in 1980 could buy. General price-level indexes in use today provide only rough approximations of general price-level changes, because they are not based on all prices in the economy. Furthermore, these indexes do not accurately reflect changes in the quality of products over time.

The most comprehensive general price-level index in the United States is the **Gross National Product Implicit Price Deflator (GNP Deflator)**, which is published quarterly by the U.S. Department of Commerce. Perhaps the most widely publicized index of general prices is the **Consumer Price Index for all Urban Consumers (CPI-U)**, published monthly by the U.S. Department of Labor. Generally, the inflation rates measured by the GNP Deflator and the CPI-U are similar over the long run. For this reason and because the CPI-U is calculated more frequently and is more widely publicized than the GNP Deflator, the FASB required companies to use the CPI-U when disclosing information under *SFAS No. 33*. Exhibit 26–1 shows the average annual level of the CPI-U and the annual inflation rate for each year from 1972 until 1992. The Department of Labor currently uses 1982–84 as the base for deriving the CPI-U. To simplify the calculations involved, we will merely assume certain values of the CPI-U in the illustrations and assignment material in this chapter.

SPECIFIC PRICE CHANGES

A second type of price change is known as a **specific price change.** A specific price change is an increase or decrease in the price of a specific good or service, such as food or entertainment. Specific price changes occur primarily because of changes in the demand for or supply of particular goods or services. An increase in the demand for Buick Skylarks, for example,

EXHIBIT 26–1		
Average Consumer Price Index for All Urban Consumers		
	Annual Average	Percent Change from Previous Year
1972	41.8	3.2
1973	44.4	6.2
1974	49.3	11.0
1975	53.8	9.1
1976	56.9	5.8
1977	60.6	6.5
1978	65.2	7.6
1979	72.6	11.3
1980	82.4	13.5
1981	90.9	10.3
1982	96.5	6.2
1983	99.6	3.2
1984	103.9	4.3
1985	107.6	3.6
1986	109.6	1.9
1987	113.6	3.6
1988	118.3	4.1
1989	124.0	4.8
1990	130.7	5.4
1991	136.2	4.2
1992	140.3	3.0

SOURCE: U.S. Department of Labor.

tends to increase the automobile's price. On the other hand, an increase in their supply tends to decrease their price. Forces of supply and demand interact to determine the specific price of each good and service in the economy.

Distinguishing clearly between a general price-level change and a specific price change is important. The price of a specific good or service may change at a different rate and even in the opposite direction from the overall level of prices in the economy. In a particular year, for example, the general price level might increase by 10% while the price of medical care rises by 16%, the price of new cars rises by 7%, the price of fuel oil remains stable, and the price of home video games falls by 20%. To assume that the price of a particular product will increase by 10% during a given year merely because the inflation rate is 10% in that year is incorrect.

Specific price changes may be measured by using the following methods of determining an asset's current cost:

1. **Direct pricing.**   This method requires the use of current market prices to calculate an asset's current cost. Current market prices may be obtained by referring to current invoice prices, vendors' price lists, current standard manufacturing costs, and appraisals. Suppose, for example, that a company acquired an inventory item for $100 at the beginning of the current year and that a seller's price list shows that the same item would cost $130 if purchased at year-end. Under these circumstances, the specific price increase for the inventory item is $30 ($130 − $100).

2. **Indexing.**   This method requires an appropriate specific price index to restate an asset's historical cost to a current cost basis. A company may obtain the index internally or externally. Specific price indexes for many different kinds of assets are available from a variety of government and industry sources. Unlike a general price-level index, which measures changes in the overall level of prices in the economy, a specific price index applies only to a particular good or service. Suppose that a company purchased a building at the beginning of a year for $100,000 and that an appropriate specific price index indicates that the cost of similar buildings increased by 20% during the year. Under these circumstances, a specific price increase of $20,000 [($100,000 × 1.20) − $100,000] has occurred.

ATTRIBUTE MEASURED AND MEASURING UNIT

FOUR BASES OF ACCOUNTING

Asset/Liability Measurement

Monetary Unit

To prepare financial statements according to GAAP, accountants must ordinarily measure nonmonetary assets, such as inventories, plant assets, and intangible assets, at **historical cost** until the assets are sold. Moreover, the monetary unit principle requires accountants to use the **nominal dollar** (a dollar that has not been adjusted for inflation) measuring unit. The combined effect of emphasizing historical costs and measuring those costs in nominal dollars is that neither specific price changes nor general price-level changes are recognized separately in conventional financial statements. Critics of the conventional accounting model contend that financial statements would be more *useful* for decision-making purposes if the statements were adapted to reflect specific price changes, general price-level changes, or both types of price changes.

The approaches to accounting under conditions of changing prices are shown in Exhibit 26–2.[1] The exhibit shows that either the historical cost attribute or the current value attribute of the elements of financial statements may be measured and reported. The exhibit also indicates that either nominal dollars or **constant dollars** (dollars that have been adjusted for inflation) may be used as the measuring unit.

Cell 1 of the matrix shown in Exhibit 26–2 represents the intersection of historical cost and nominal dollars (HC/ND). HC/ND financial statements are the type that accountants presently produce under GAAP. These financial statements are not adjusted for either specific

---

[1]Paul Rosenfield, "The Confusion between General Price-Level Restatement and Current Value Accounting," *Journal of Accountancy* (October 1972), pp. 63–68.

EXHIBIT 26–2

Four Bases of Accounting

Measuring Unit Used in Financial Statements	Attribute Measured in Financial Statements	
	Historical Cost (HC)	Current Value (CV)
Nominal Dollars (ND)	1	2
Constant Dollars (CD)	3	4

price changes or general price-level changes. HC/ND financial statements were discussed in previous chapters of this textbook and are therefore not covered extensively in this chapter.

Cell 2 of the matrix depicts current value/nominal dollar (CV/ND) accounting. CV/ND financial statements are adjusted to reflect specific price changes, because current values are used instead of historical costs. Because nominal dollars are the measuring unit, however, CV/ND financial statements are not adjusted for general price-level changes.

Cell 3 presents the intersection of historical costs and constant dollars (HC/CD). HC/CD financial statements are adjusted for general price-level changes, because constant dollars are used. But these statements are not adjusted for specific price changes, because the attribute measured is historical cost, not current value.

Cell 4 of the matrix shows the current value/constant dollar (CV/CD) basis of accounting. CV/CD financial statements include adjustments for both specific price changes (because current values are used) *and* general price-level changes (because constant dollars are used).

A SIMPLIFIED EXAMPLE

To illustrate the income statement results that would occur under each of the four bases of accounting shown in Exhibit 26–2, assume the following facts about Carter Company:[2]

1. The company was organized on January 1, 1995. On that date, the company sold common stock for $10,000 and immediately invested the proceeds in land costing $10,000.
2. On December 31, 1995, the land held by Carter Company was estimated to have a market value of $12,000.
3. On December 31, 1996, Carter Company sold the land for $15,000 and used the proceeds to retire all the common stock. The company terminated its operations at that time.
4. The inflation rate was zero in 1995 and 10% in 1996.

Based on these facts, the income statement results that Carter Company would report in 1995 and 1996 under each of the four bases of accounting are shown in Exhibit 26–3. Under HC/ND accounting (the conventional accounting model), Carter Company reports no gain or loss in 1995, because the company did not sell the land in that year. In 1996 the company reports a $5,000 gain ($15,000 − $10,000), because it sold the land.

Under CV/ND accounting, Carter Company reports a $2,000 gain in 1995. This amount equals the $12,000 market price at the end of 1995 minus the historical cost of $10,000. In 1996 the company reports a $3,000 gain, because it sold the land for $15,000, which is

---

[2]The idea for this example is based on Rosenfield, pp. 67–68.

EXHIBIT 26–3

Carter Company
Income Statement Results
under Four Bases of Accounting

	(1) Results under HC/ND Accounting		(2) Results under CV/ND Accounting
1995	–0–	1995	$2,000 gain
1996	$5,000 gain	1996	$3,000 gain
Total	$5,000 gain	Total	$5,000 gain

	(3) Results under HC/CD Accounting, Measured in 1996 Constant Dollars		(4) Results under CV/CD Accounting, Measured in 1996 Constant Dollars
1995	–0–	1995	$2,200 gain
1996	$4,000 gain	1996	$1,800 gain
Total	$4,000 gain	Total	$4,000 gain

$3,000 more than the land's market price at the beginning of 1996. Observe that when we sum Carter Company's income statement results for *both* 1995 and 1996 under either HC/ND accounting or CV/ND accounting, we derive a *total gain* of $5,000.

The key to understanding the results under HC/CD accounting and CV/CD accounting is to recognize that these results are not measured in nominal dollars but in 1996 *constant dollars*. The income statement results are reported in the 1996 annual report, *after* the purchasing power of the 1996 dollar is known. The 1995 results are reported in 1996 constant dollars for comparative purposes.

Under HC/CD accounting, Carter Company reports no gain or loss in 1995, because no sale occurred in that year. In 1996, when the land is sold, the company reports a $4,000 gain. This amount equals the $15,000 selling price minus the $10,000 historical cost adjusted for the 10% inflation that has occurred since the land was acquired [$15,000 − ($10,000 × 1.10) = $4,000].

Under CV/CD accounting, Carter Company reports a $2,200 gain for 1995. This amount equals the $12,000 market price at the end of 1995 minus the historical cost of $10,000, adjusted for the 10% inflation that occurred during *1996* [($12,000 − $10,000) × 1.10 = $2,200]. Remember that we are measuring the 1995 results in *1996 constant dollars;* of course, we can do this only at the end of 1996, *after* we know the 1996 inflation rate. In 1996 Carter Company reports a gain of $1,800 under the CV/CD approach. This amount equals the selling price of $15,000 minus the market price at the beginning of 1996 adjusted for the 1996 inflation of 10% [$15,000 − ($12,000 × 1.10) = $1,800]. Observe carefully that when we sum Carter Company's income statement results for *both* 1995 and 1996 under either HC/CD accounting or CV/CD accounting, we calculate a $4,000 *total gain.*

The Carter Company example is highly simplified, but it allows us to see more clearly the following major differences between the four bases of accounting:

1. Changing from historical cost accounting to current value accounting *changes the timing but not the total amount of income recognized over the life of a firm.* When the measuring unit is nominal dollars, Carter Company's *total gain* is $5,000, but it is allocated differently between 1995 and 1996, depending on whether historical cost (HC/ND) or current value (CV/ND) measurement is used. Measured in constant dollars, Carter Company's total gain is $4,000, but once again, the manner in which the total gain is allocated between years depends on whether historical cost (HC/CD) or current value (CV/CD) measurement is used. The reason that current value accounting produces a timing change is because under historical cost accounting, we generally recognize income only when a sale occurs, whereas under current value accounting, we recognize income when specific prices change. The timing of income recognition can make a big difference to investors and creditors when they evaluate the amount, timing, and uncertainty of the cash flows they expect to receive from their investments.

2. Changing from nominal dollar measurement to constant dollar measurement *changes the total amount of income recognized over the life of a firm.* Carter Company's total gain is $5,000 when expressed in nominal dollars (HC/ND and CV/ND) and $4,000 when measured in 1996 constant dollars (HC/CD and CV/CD). The reason for the difference is that the measuring unit itself has changed.

Later in this chapter, we illustrate complete financial statements prepared under the HC/CD, CV/ND, and CV/CD bases of accounting. In practice, these statements may be prepared by using the conventional HC/ND financial statements and certain additional information. Journal entries to record adjustments for general price-level changes or specific price changes are unnecessary.

Spurred on by the SEC, the FASB in 1979 issued *SFAS No. 33,* "Financial Reporting and Changing Prices." *SFAS No. 33* applied only to certain large companies, specifically "to public enterprises that have either (1) inventories and property, plant, and equipment (before deducting accumulated depreciation) amounting to more than $125 million or (2) total assets amounting to more than $1 billion (after deducting accumulated depreciation)."[3] *SFAS No. 33* applied to about 1,300 publicly held U.S. corporations. It did *not* change the primary financial statements, which are based on historical cost/nominal dollar accounting. Instead, the pronouncement required the disclosure of selected items of **supplementary information** in published annual reports. When it was originally issued, *SFAS No. 33* required that most of the supplementary items be prepared in accordance with the historical cost/constant dollar basis and the current value/constant dollar basis of accounting. As we explain later in the chapter, there are really three forms of current value accounting, and the FASB decided on the *current cost* form.

When it issued *SFAS No. 33,* the FASB stated that the supplementary information required was experimental and that the pronouncement would be reviewed extensively within five years. The idea was to require certain companies to report the supplementary information adjusted for changing prices and then assess the usefulness of the information from the perspectives of preparers and users of financial statements. Only large companies were affected because many people regularly use these companies' financial statements and because these companies are more capable than smaller companies of bearing the costs of producing the information. The FASB provided assistance for several research studies about *SFAS No. 33* information and in mid-1983 formed a task force to help it decide whether to continue the *SFAS No. 33* experiment beyond the initial five-year period. As a result of numerous studies of the usefulness of *SFAS No. 33* information, the FASB concluded that historical cost/constant dollar information is generally less useful than information about current costs. Accordingly, the board in 1984 issued *SFAS No. 82,* an amendment to *SFAS No. 33,* which eliminated the requirements to report certain information on a historical cost/constant dollar

MAJOR FASB ACTIVITIES IN ACCOUNTING FOR CHANGING PRICES

---

[3]*FASB Statement of Financial Accounting Standards No. 33,* "Financial Reporting and Changing Prices," 1979, Summary.

basis.[4] The FASB continued to study the usefulness of accounting information adjusted for changing prices and near the end of 1986 concluded in *SFAS No. 89* that companies should be *encouraged,* but *not required,* to disclose supplementary information about the effects of changing prices.[5] *SFAS No. 89* was a controversial pronouncement that received the assenting votes of only four of the seven members of the FASB. The three FASB members who were outvoted believed that supplementary accounting information adjusted for changing prices should continue to be required. Interestingly, a few years after *SFAS No. 89* was issued, the FASB changed the number of assenting votes required to issue a standard from four (a simple majority) to five (a supermajority).

In a later section of this chapter, we explain the disclosures that the FASB encourages. In the meantime, we discuss comprehensive financial statements adjusted for changing prices and present examples of them. The primary goal of this chapter is to explain the most important models that the accounting profession has seriously considered for dealing with the issue of accounting for changing prices. The FASB has encouraged but has never required comprehensive statements such as those we are about to discuss. Nevertheless, to adequately understand the topic of accounting for changing prices and the specific disclosures that the FASB currently encourages, you should understand the complete process of adjusting financial statements for changing prices. With this understanding, you will be able to quickly grasp not only the present disclosure recommendations of the FASB but also the requirements of professional pronouncements that may be issued in the future.

CONSTANT DOLLAR ACCOUNTING

NATURE AND OBJECTIVE

Historical cost/constant dollar accounting, represented by Cell 3 of the matrix in Exhibit 26–2, is commonly called **constant dollar accounting.** It is sometimes referred to as **general price-level accounting** or **general purchasing-power accounting.** Under constant dollar accounting, the attribute measured in financial statements is historical cost, and the measuring unit is the constant dollar.

The objective of constant dollar accounting is to report the elements of financial statements in dollars that have the same purchasing power. To accomplish this objective, the amounts reported in the conventional historical cost/nominal dollar financial statements are restated in constant dollars by using a general price-level index, such as the CPI-U. The financial statement amounts are converted to constant dollars by using the following general formula:

$$\begin{aligned} \text{Constant Dollar Amount} \atop \text{(HC/CD Amount)} &= \text{Nominal Dollar Amount} \atop \text{(HC/ND Amount)} \\ &\times \frac{\text{General Price-Level Index Adjusting To}}{\text{General Price-Level Index Adjusting From}} \end{aligned}$$

The quotient obtained by dividing the general price-level index we are adjusting *to* by the one we are adjusting *from* is called a **conversion factor** because it is used to convert nominal dollar amounts to constant dollar amounts. The general price-level index to adjust *from* is the one that existed at the time of origination of the financial statement amount being converted. The general price-level index to adjust *to* could be an index as of any date, although the dates most commonly suggested are the base period of the CPI-U (currently 1982–1984), the average CPI-U for the current accounting period, and the ending CPI-U for the current period. In an effort to focus on the underlying concepts and avoid needless confusion, we will convert to the year-end CPI-U in the examples and problem assignments in this chapter.

---

[4]*FASB Statement of Financial Accounting Standards No. 82,* "Financial Reporting and Changing Prices: Elimination of Certain Disclosures," 1984.

[5]*FASB Statement of Financial Accounting Standards No. 89,* "Financial Reporting and Changing Prices," 1986.

To illustrate the basic idea behind constant dollar conversion, suppose that Rupp Company acquired a parcel of land on January 1, 1996, for $10,000. On that date, the CPI-U was 100. Here is how Rupp Company would express the acquisition price of the land in year-end constant dollars, assuming that the CPI-U is 115 on December 31, 1996:

$$\$10,000 \times \frac{115}{100} = \$11,500$$

Rupp Company would report the land at $10,000 on a conventional (HC/ND) balance sheet dated December 31, 1996, and at $11,500 on a constant dollar balance sheet with the same date. Be careful to interpret the $11,500 correctly. This amount represents the land's *historical cost* expressed in 1996 year-end constant dollars. In effect, we are saying that because the inflation rate during 1996 was 15% (115 ÷ 100 = 1.15), $11,500 would be needed at the end of 1996 to buy the same quantity of goods and services that $10,000 could buy at the beginning of the year.

How much would Rupp Company have to pay at the end of 1996 if the company had to replace the land? How much could Rupp Company sell the land for on December 31, 1996? What is the present value on December 31, 1996, of the net cash receipts that the land will generate for Rupp Company in the future? These are interesting questions that cannot be answered by constant dollar information, because the answers depend on what has happened to the specific price of Rupp Company's land during the year. Remember that constant dollar accounting adjusts for general price-level changes but not for specific price changes. Constant dollar accounting is not a departure from historical cost accounting but merely a system for reporting historical cost financial statements in units that have the same purchasing power.

MONETARY AND NONMONETARY ITEMS

When preparing constant dollar financial statements, monetary and nonmonetary items must be distinguished. A **monetary item** is cash, assets that represent a fixed number of dollars to be received, or obligations that represent a fixed number of dollars to be paid. Examples of monetary assets include cash, accounts receivable, and notes receivable; examples of monetary liabilities include accounts payable, notes payable, and bonds payable.

Simply stated, a **nonmonetary item** is any financial statement item that is not monetary in nature. Examples of nonmonetary assets include inventories, plant assets, and intangible assets; examples of nonmonetary equities include obligations under product warranties and common stock. Although they are liabilities, obligations under product warranties are nonmonetary because they do not require settlement in a fixed number of dollars but rather in goods and services (or a price that reflects the value of the goods or services).

The distinction between monetary and nonmonetary assets and liabilities is *not* the same as the distinction between current assets and current liabilities. Inventories, for example, are nonmonetary assets even though classified as current, while a 10-year note payable is monetary even though classified as a long-term liability.

Monetary items are automatically stated in current purchasing power and therefore do not require restatement when preparing constant dollar financial statements. Cash, for example, is always stated in current dollars. Consequently, if an enterprise has cash of $5,000 on December 31, 1996, the amount represents $5,000 of general purchasing power at that time, and the correct amount of cash to report on a constant dollar balance sheet dated December 31, 1996, is $5,000. The same rationale applies to other monetary items.

In contrast with monetary items, nonmonetary items are not automatically stated in current purchasing power and therefore must be restated when preparing constant dollar financial statements. Each nonmonetary item is restated to reflect the total change in the general

SPECIAL, TODAY ONLY: SIX MILLION DINARS FOR A SNICKERS BAR

THE BIZARRE ECONOMY OF SERBIA CREATES AN INFLATION RATE WELL INTO THE QUADRILLIONS

Belgrade, Yugoslavia—At the Luna boutique, a Snickers bar costs six million dinars. Or at least it does until manager Tihomir Nikolic reads the overnight fax from his boss.

"Raise prices 99%," the document tersely orders. It would be an even 100% except that the computer at the boutique, which would be considered a dime store in other parts of the world, can't handle three-digit changes.

So for the second time in three days Mr. Nikolic sets about raising prices. He jams a mop across the door frame to keep customers from getting away with a bargain. The computer spits out the new prices on perforated paper. The manager and two assistants rip the paper into tags and tape them to the shelves. They used to put the prices directly on the goods, but there were so many stickers it was getting difficult to read the labels.

Counting Zeros

After four hours, the mop is removed from the door. The customers wander in, rub their eyes and squint at the tags, counting the zeros. Mr. Nikolic himself squints as the computer prints another price, this one for a video recorder.

"Is that billions?" he asks himself. It is: 20,391,560,223 dinars, to be precise. He points to his T-shirt, which is emblazoned with the words "Far Out," the name of a fruit juice he once sold. He suggests it is an ideal motto for Serbia's bizarre economic situation. "It fits the craziness," he says.

How else would you describe it? Since the international community imposed economic sanctions, the inflation rate has been at least 10% *daily*. This translates to an annual rate in the quadrillions—so high as to be meaningless. In Serbia, one U.S. dollar will get you 10 million dinars at the Hyatt hotel, 12 million from the shady money-changers on Republic Square and 17 million from a bank run by Belgrade's underworld. Serbs complain that the dinar is as worthless as toilet paper. But for the moment, at least, there is plenty of toilet paper to go around.

Hot off the Presses

The government mint, hidden in a park behind the Belgrade race track, is said to be churning out dinars 24 hours a day furiously trying to keep up with the inflation that is fueled, in turn, by its own nonstop printing. The government, which believes in throwing around money to dampen dissent, needs dinars to pay workers for not working at closed factories and offices. It needs them to buy the harvest from the farmers. It needs them to finance its smuggling forays and other ways to evade the sanctions, bringing in everything from oil to Mr. Nikolic's Snickers bars. It also needs them to supply brother Serbs fighting in Bosnia-Herzegovina and Croatia.

The money-changers, whose fingertips detect the slightest change in paper quality, insist that the mint is even contracting out to private printers to meet demand.

"We're experts. They can't fool us," says one of the changers as he hands over 800 million worth of five-million dinar bills. "These," he notes confidently, "are fresh from the mint." He says he got them from a private bank, which got them from the central bank, which got them from the mint—an unholy circuit linking the black market with the Finance Ministry. "It's collective lunacy," the money-changer says, laughing wickedly.

Lest he lose his place on this dinar merry-go-round, the changer refuses to be identified. The finance minister refuses to be interviewed. So does the governor of the central bank and the director of the mint. Bankers bar reporters from their offices. One will grant an interview, but only for several hundred dollars.

Stanko Ivkovic, the deputy director of Serbia's financial supervision office, agrees to talk, mainly so he can lambaste the U.S. and Europe for putting the Serbs through such misery by taking away their international credit. "We've been forced by the world to work more with cash than we're used to," he says.

price-level that has occurred since the time of origin of the item being restated. The restatement of nonmonetary items does not produce any gains or losses. Instead, the restatement merely alters the measuring unit from nominal dollars to constant dollars.

PURCHASING POWER GAINS AND LOSSES

Purchasing power gains and losses occur as a result of holding monetary items during periods of inflation or deflation. These gains and losses occur because monetary items are receivable or payable in a *fixed number of dollars* whose *purchasing power* changes when inflation or deflation occurs. Purchasing power gains and losses are measured and reported in the income statement when the measuring unit is constant dollars, but not when it is nominal dollars.

To illustrate, suppose that Brown Company keeps its cash of $10,000 in a checking account throughout a year in which the CPI-U increases from 105 to 210. The actual number of dollars of cash remains constant at 10,000 while the prices of goods and services steadily rise. Clearly, the company has lost purchasing power by holding the cash during the period. With an inflation rate of 100%, Brown Company would need $20,000 at the end of the year to be able to buy the same quantity of goods and services that it could buy with $10,000 at the beginning of the year. Because the company has only $10,000 at year-end, the purchasing power *loss* expressed in terms of the year-end price level is $10,000 [($10,000 × 210/105) − $10,000].

To generalize, maintaining a positive monetary position (in which monetary assets exceed monetary liabilities) results in a purchasing power loss during periods of inflation and a purchasing power gain during periods of deflation. On the other hand, maintaining a negative monetary position (in which monetary liabilities exceed monetary assets) results in a purchasing power gain when inflation occurs and a purchasing power loss when deflation occurs. These outcomes are shown in Exhibit 26–4.

PREPARATION OF CONSTANT DOLLAR FINANCIAL STATEMENTS

Now that the general principles underlying constant dollar accounting have been explained, the process of preparing a set of comprehensive constant dollar financial statements will be illustrated. The information shown in Exhibits 26–5, 26–6, and 26–7 pertains to Craig Company and is used for the illustration.

A Constant Dollar Combined Statement of Income and Retained Earnings

Based on the facts presented for Craig Company, a combined statement of income and retained earnings restated in 1996 year-end constant dollars is reported as shown in Exhibit 26–8. The following sections explain the calculation of each constant dollar amount shown in the exhibit.

Sales.   As indicated in Exhibit 26–5, Craig Company's sales were made evenly throughout 1996. The nominal dollar sales of $400,000 are therefore stated in terms of the average price index for 1996. To restate the nominal dollar amount of sales in year-end constant dollars, we must multiply by the conversion factor 1.10. This conversion factor restates sales from the average index (143) to the December 31 index (157.3).

Of course, sales are generally made on each business day. To be precise, each day's sales should be restated separately in year-end constant dollars. But general price-level indexes are not published daily, and even if they were, the benefits of using daily indexes would probably

---

EXHIBIT 26–4

Purchasing Power Gains and Losses under Different Circumstances

	Economic Condition	
Monetary Position	Inflation	Deflation
Positive (monetary assets > monetary liabilities)	Loss	Gain
Negative (monetary liabilities > monetary assets)	Gain	Loss

EXHIBIT 26–5

Basic Information about Craig Company
---

1. Craig Company was organized and began operations on January 1, 1996.
2. The company's comparative balance sheets on January 1 and December 31, 1996, are shown in Exhibit 26–6.
3. The company's combined statement of income and retained earnings for 1996 is shown in Exhibit 26–7.
4. Selected values of the CPI-U during 1996 are as shown:

January 1	130.0
Average for 1996	143.0
December 31	157.3

5. Conversion factors required to restate financial statement amounts to year-end constant dollars are computed:

Conversion Factors to Restate From

January 1 index	$157.3/130.0 = 1.21$
Average index for 1996	$157.3/143.0 = 1.10$
December 31 index	$157.3/157.3 = 1.00$

6. Sales and purchases were made evenly throughout 1996.
7. Operating expenses and income tax expense were incurred evenly throughout 1996.
8. The company declared and paid dividends on December 31, 1996.
9. The company acquired the beginning inventory, land, and equipment on January 1, 1996.
10. The company uses the first-in, first-out (FIFO) method of determining inventory cost. The ending inventory was acquired when the CPI-U was 143.
11. The company uses the straight-line method to depreciate the equipment. A 10-year useful life and no salvage value are assumed.

---

not outweigh the costs. Therefore, companies usually assume that sales are made evenly throughout the year when preparing their constant dollar financial statements. This assumption, which is also typically made in regard to costs incurred throughout the year (such as purchases, salaries, and taxes), simplifies the constant dollar restatement process by permitting a conversion from the average price index for the year.

Cost of Goods Sold. The beginning inventory was acquired on January 1, 1996, when the CPI-U was 130. Therefore, to restate the nominal dollar amount of the beginning inventory in year-end constant dollars, we multiply by the conversion factor 1.21. This conversion factor equals the December 31 index of 157.3 divided by the January 1 index of 130.

When preparing constant dollar financial statements, purchases are generally assumed to have occurred evenly throughout the year. Because Craig Company's purchases were made evenly, the company would restate them by multiplying by the conversion factor of 1.10 (the December 31 index of 157.3 divided by the average index of 143).

Craig Company uses the first-in, first-out (FIFO) inventory costing method, and the company's ending inventory was acquired when the CPI-U was 143. Therefore, to restate the ending inventory in year-end constant dollars, we multiply by the conversion factor 1.10 (the December 31 index of 157.3 divided by the average index of 143).

The calculation of cost of goods sold and ending inventory on a constant dollar basis is affected by the inventory costing method that a company uses. If, for example, Craig Company had used last-in, first-out (LIFO) instead of FIFO, the company would restate its ending inventory of $90,000 by using the conversion factor 1.21 (the December 31 index of 157.3

EXHIBIT 26—6

Craig Company
Comparative Balance Sheets
Historical Cost/Nominal Dollar Basis
January 1 and December 31, 1996

Assets

	Jan. 1	Dec. 31
Cash	$ 10,000	$ 40,000
Accounts receivable	–0–	67,000
Inventory	100,000	90,000
Land	70,000	70,000
Equipment	120,000	120,000
Less: Accumulated depreciation	–0–	(12,000)
Total assets	$300,000	$375,000

Liabilities and Stockholder's Equity

	Jan. 1	Dec. 31
Accounts payable	–0–	$ 35,000
Long-term note payable	$ 90,000	90,000
Total liabilities	90,000	125,000
Common stock	210,000	210,000
Retained earnings	–0–	40,000
Total stockholders' equity	210,000	250,000
Total liabilities and stockholders' equity	$300,000	$375,000

EXHIBIT 26—7

Craig Company
Combined Statement of Income and Retained Earnings
Historical Cost/Nominal Dollar Basis
For 1996

Sales		$400,000
Cost of goods sold		
Beginning inventory	$100,000	
Purchases	210,000	
Goods available	310,000	
Ending inventory	90,000	220,000
Gross margin on sales		180,000
Operating expenses	68,000	
Depreciation expense	12,000	80,000
Income before taxes		100,000
Income tax expense		40,000
Net income		60,000
Retained earnings, Jan. 1		–0–
Less: Dividends		20,000
Retained earnings, Dec. 31		$ 40,000

EXHIBIT 26–8

Craig Company
Combined Statement of Income and Retained Earnings
Historical Cost/Constant Dollar Basis
For 1996

Sales ($400,000 × 1.10)		$440,000
Cost of goods sold		
Beginning inventory ($100,000 × 1.21)	$121,000	
Purchases ($210,000 × 1.10)	231,000	
Goods available	352,000	
Ending inventory ($90,000 × 1.10)	99,000	253,000
Gross margin on sales		187,000
Operating expenses ($68,000 × 1.10)	74,800	
Depreciation expense ($12,000 × 1.21)	14,520	89,320
Income before taxes		97,680
Income tax expense ($40,000 × 1.10)		44,000
Income before purchasing power gain		53,680
Purchasing power gain (see Exhibit 26–9)		8,600
Net income		62,280
Retained earnings, Jan. 1		–0–
Less: Dividends ($20,000 × 1.00)		20,000
Retained earnings, Dec. 31		$ 42,280

divided by the January 1 index of 130), instead of 1.10. Under the LIFO assumption, the ending inventory of $90,000 would be assumed to be part of the $100,000 of inventory that was on hand on January 1.

Operating Expenses. Operating expenses were incurred evenly throughout 1996 and are therefore restated by multiplying by the 1.10 conversion factor used to restate from the average index for the year.

Depreciation Expense. The historical cost/nominal dollar depreciation expense of $12,000 represents an allocation of a cost ($120,000) incurred on January 1, 1996. To restate the nominal dollar amount in year-end constant dollars, we multiply by the 1.21 conversion factor used to restate from the January 1 index.

Observe that to restate depreciation expense, we use a conversion factor that adjusts from the acquisition date of the asset being depreciated. Most businesses have many depreciable assets acquired at various dates. Under these circumstances, we must multiply the historical cost/nominal dollar depreciation expense for each asset by a conversion factor that adjusts from the price index in existence when the asset was purchased. This process results in several layers of constant dollar depreciation amounts that must be summed to derive the total constant dollar amount of depreciation expense.

Income Tax Expense. Income tax expense was incurred evenly throughout the year and is restated by multiplying by the 1.10 conversion factor used to restate from the average index. Observe that income tax expense in constant dollar financial statements is derived in relation to the amount shown in the conventional historical cost/nominal dollar income statement. It is not based directly on the amount of the pretax constant dollar income, because general price-level adjustments are not allowed for income tax purposes.

Purchasing Power Gain. Earlier in the chapter, we explained the nature of purchasing power gains and losses and gave a simple example of a purchasing power loss sustained by a com-

EXHIBIT 26–9

Craig Company
Schedule Showing Computation of Purchasing Power Gain
For 1996

	Nominal Dollar Basis	Conversion Factor	Constant Dollar Basis
Net monetary items, Jan. 1	$ (80,000)*	1.21	$ (96,800)
Add: Sources of net monetary items			
Sales	400,000	1.10	440,000
Deduct: Uses of net monetary items			
Purchases	(210,000)	1.10	(231,000)
Operating expenses	(68,000)	1.10	(74,800)
Income tax expense	(40,000)	1.10	(44,000)
Dividends	(20,000)	1.00	(20,000)
Net monetary items, Dec. 31, actually on hand	$ (18,000)†		
Net monetary items, Dec. 31, that should be on hand if no purchasing power gain or loss exists			$ (26,600)
Purchasing power gain ($26,600 − $18,000)			$ 8,600

---

*Net monetary items, Jan. 1 (amounts obtained from Exhibit 26–6):

Cash	$ 10,000
Long-term note payable	(90,000)
Net monetary items, Jan. 1	$(80,000)

†Net monetary items, Dec. 31 (amounts obtained from Exhibit 26–6):

Cash	$ 40,000
Accounts receivable	67,000
Accounts payable	(35,000)
Long-term note payable	(90,000)
Net monetary items, Dec. 31	$(18,000)

pany that held cash during a period of inflation. In reality, all monetary assets, monetary liabilities, and the changes in them that occur during an accounting period must be considered when calculating purchasing power gains and losses. To facilitate the calculation, an accountant prepares a separate schedule or working paper that is not usually published.

A schedule showing the computation of Craig Company's purchasing power gain is shown in Exhibit 26–9. The preparation of a schedule showing the calculation of purchasing power gains and losses requires three major steps that are explained as follows:

1. On a conventional nominal dollar basis, start with the net monetary items (monetary assets minus monetary liabilities) on hand at the beginning of the period; then add the sources and deduct the uses of net monetary items during the period to derive the net monetary items on hand at the end of the period.

   As shown in Exhibit 26–9, Craig Company's monetary liabilities exceed its monetary assets by $80,000 on January 1. The company's only source of net monetary items during the period was sales. When sales occur, either cash or accounts receivable increases; thus, an increase in net monetary items occurs. Other frequently encountered sources of net monetary items are the sale of nonmonetary assets, such as land or equipment, and the issuance of capital stock.

Craig Company's uses of net monetary items during the period consisted of purchases, operating expenses, income tax expense, and dividends. Notice that each of these uses represents either a decrease in monetary assets or an increase in monetary liabilities (and therefore a decrease in *net* monetary items). A purchase, for example, either decreases cash (a monetary asset) or increases accounts payable (a monetary liability); in either case, a decrease in net monetary items occurs. In addition to the uses listed by Craig Company, other frequently encountered uses of net monetary items are the acquisition of nonmonetary assets and the purchase of treasury stock. Depreciation expense does not represent a use of net monetary items, because the credit side of the depreciation entry (i.e., accumulated depreciation) does not affect either monetary assets or monetary liabilities.

After adding the sources and deducting the uses of Craig Company's net monetary items, the company's monetary liabilities exceed its monetary assets by $18,000 on December 31. The accuracy of this amount should be verified by determining the net monetary items that appear on the historical cost/nominal dollar balance sheet dated December 31; this verification is shown in the second footnote to Exhibit 26–9. If the two amounts are not equal, an error must have been made in preparing the schedule.

2. Restated in terms of year-end constant dollars, start with the net monetary items on hand at the beginning of the period; then add the sources and deduct the uses of net monetary items during the period to derive the net monetary items that should be on hand at the end of the period if no purchasing power gain or loss has occurred. To comply with this step, we multiply each of the nominal dollar amounts listed in Step 1 by a conversion factor that adjusts from the time that the measurement of the amount was made.

For Craig Company, net monetary assets on January 1 are multiplied by 1.21 (the December 31 index of 157.3 divided by the January 1 index of 130). Sales, purchases, operating expenses, and income tax expense are each multiplied by 1.10 because this is the conversion factor that adjusts from the average price index for the year. Finally, the dividends are multiplied by 1.00 (157.3 ÷ 157.3) because they were declared and paid on December 31 and therefore are already stated in terms of year-end constant dollars. After converting to year-end constant dollars and then adding the sources and deducting the uses of Craig Company's net monetary items, we find that Craig Company's monetary liabilities *would exceed* its monetary assets by $26,600 on December 31 *if no purchasing power gain or loss occurred during the year.*

3. The final step is to compare (1) the net monetary items actually on hand at the end of the period with (2) the net monetary items that should be on hand if no purchasing power gain or loss exists. If (1) exceeds (2), a purchasing power gain has occurred; if (2) exceeds (1), a purchasing loss has occurred.

In the case of Craig Company, (1) exceeds (2), because a negative $18,000 is larger than a negative $26,600. A purchasing power gain of $8,600 therefore exists, as shown in Exhibit 26–9. An important factor contributing to this gain was Craig Company's indebtedness (the long-term note payable of $90,000) throughout a period of inflation. The company can now pay the debt with dollars that have less purchasing power than the dollars received when the debt was incurred.

Including the $8,600 purchasing power gain in the constant dollar income statement results in a constant dollar net income of $62,280 for Craig Company. In this example, the purchasing power gain is the major reason that the constant dollar net income ($62,280) exceeds the conventional nominal dollar net income ($60,000).

Dividends.   In this example, the nominal dollar dividends of $20,000 are also stated in year-end constant dollars, because the dividends were declared on December 31. Consequently, we simply multiply the nominal dollar amount by the conversion factor 1.00 (157.3 ÷ 157.3) to obtain the year-end constant dollar amount shown in Exhibit 26–8. Dividends are always restated in constant dollars by using a conversion factor that adjusts from the date on which they were declared. Thus, if Craig Company had declared dividends on a date other than December 31, we would have used a conversion factor that adjusts from the date of declaration.

Craig Company's constant dollar retained earnings balance on December 31, 1996, may now be computed by adding the constant dollar net income to the constant dollar retained earnings balance on January 1 and deducting the constant dollar dividends. As shown in Exhibit 26–8, the December 31 balance is $42,280. This is the correct amount of retained earnings to report in a constant dollar balance sheet dated December 31, 1996.

Craig Company had no retained earnings on January 1, 1996, because it began operations on that date. If it had been operating for several years and had retained earnings on January 1, the constant dollar retained earnings balance on January 1 to include in Exhibit 26–8 would be the December 31, 1995, constant dollar retained earnings balance multiplied by 1.21 (157.3 ÷ 130).

A Constant Dollar Balance Sheet

A constant dollar balance sheet for Craig Company on December 31, 1996, is shown in Exhibit 26–10. The following sections explain the calculation of each balance sheet amount.

Monetary Items.   The monetary items (cash, accounts receivable, accounts payable, and long-term note payable) are already stated in year-end constant dollars and therefore do not require restatement for the constant dollar balance sheet. The amounts reported for these items on a constant dollar balance sheet (Exhibit 26–10) are the same as on a nominal dollar balance sheet (Exhibit 26–6).

Inventory.   Craig Company uses the FIFO costing method, and the ending inventory was acquired when the CPI-U was 143. The nominal dollar amount of $90,000 is therefore restated in year-end constant dollars by multiplying by 1.10 (157.3 ÷ 143). As we pointed out earlier when discussing the calculation of cost of goods sold, we would restate Craig Company's inventory using the conversion factor of 1.21 instead of 1.10 if the company had used LIFO instead of FIFO.

EXHIBIT 26–10

Craig Company
Balance Sheet
Historical Cost/Constant Dollar Basis
December 31, 1996

Assets

Cash		$ 40,000
Accounts receivable		67,000
Inventory ($90,000 × 1.10)		99,000
Land ($70,000 × 1.21)		84,700
Equipment ($120,000 × 1.21)	$145,200	
Less: Accumulated depreciation ($12,000 × 1.21)	(14,520)	130,680
Total assets		$421,380

Liabilities and Stockholders' Equity

Accounts payable	$ 35,000
Long-term note payable	90,000
Total liabilities	125,000
Common stock ($210,000 × 1.21)	254,100
Retained earnings (see Exhibit 26–8)	42,280
Total Stockholders' equity	296,380
Total liabilities and stockholders' equity	$421,380

Land.   Craig Company acquired the land on January 1, 1996. The constant dollar amount to report for the land therefore equals the nominal dollar amount of $70,000 multiplied by the conversion factor 1.21 (157.3 ÷ 130) that adjusts from the price index on January 1.

Equipment and Accumulated Depreciation.   The equipment costing $120,000 was acquired on January 1, 1996, and the $12,000 of accumulated depreciation has resulted from charging one-tenth of the equipment's cost to expense during 1996. Accordingly, both amounts are restated to constant dollars by multiplying by the 1.21 (157.3 ÷ 130) conversion factor that adjusts from the price index on January 1.

Common Stock.   The common stock of $210,000 was issued on January 1 and is therefore multiplied by 1.21 (157.3 ÷ 130) to convert the nominal dollar measurement to year-end constant dollars. Again we use a conversion factor that adjusts from the price index on January 1, which is when Craig Company issued the common stock.

Retained Earnings.   The ending balance of retained earnings is obtained directly from the constant dollar statement of income and retained earnings shown in Exhibit 26–8. Recall that in Chapter 5 we used the same general approach to derive the ending retained earnings balance in a conventional nominal dollar balance sheet (i.e., we added net income to the beginning retained earnings balance and deducted dividends). The ending balance of retained earnings shown on the combined statement of income and retained earnings should cause total assets to equal total liabilities and stockholders' equity; if this equality does not exist, an error must have been made.

Subsequent Years

When preparing constant dollar financial statements in subsequent years, Craig Company should follow the same general approach illustrated thus far. If the company prepares *comparative financial statements* at the end of 1997, the individual amounts shown in the constant dollar financial statements prepared at the end of 1996 would simply be **rolled forward** (adjusted) for comparative purposes to the price index that exists at the end of 1997. This would be done to permit a meaningful comparison of the 1996 and 1997 financial statements expressed in terms of the same 1997 constant dollar measuring unit. To roll forward the 1996 constant dollar financial statements to 1997 year-end constant dollars, each amount shown in Exhibits 26–8 and 26–10 (including the monetary items) is simply multiplied by a conversion factor, the numerator of which is the price index at the end of 1997 and denominator of which is the price index at the end of 1996 (157.3).

ARGUMENTS FOR AND AGAINST CONSTANT DOLLAR ACCOUNTING

Accountants have actively debated the pros and cons of constant dollar accounting during most of the 20th century. The following arguments are used to support constant dollar accounting:

1. Constant dollar accounting provides measurements that can be added and subtracted logically, because a uniform measuring unit is used. In contrast, nominal dollar measurements reflect dollars of mixed purchasing power; adding and subtracting nominal dollars in financial statements is similar to adding and subtracting apples and oranges.
2. Constant dollar accounting enables users of financial statements to make more meaningful comparisons between different companies. Under constant dollar accounting, each company reports a set of financial statements expressed in the same measuring unit.
3. Constant dollar accounting permits users to make more meaningful comparisons of a given company's performance over time, because each year's financial statements are expressed in the same measuring unit.
4. Constant dollar accounting does not depart from historical cost accounting. Historical cost information has been used for many years, is widely understood in the financial community, and is generally perceived as highly reliable.

On the other hand, opponents of constant dollar accounting use the following arguments against it:

1. Constant dollar accounting does not reflect adjustments for specific price changes. The general price-level index used in constant dollar accounting may bear little relation to the changes in the specific prices of the goods and services that a particular company actually purchases or manufactures.

2. Constant dollar accounting may confuse users of financial statements. These users may erroneously believe that constant dollar financial statements present current values instead of historical costs.

3. Purchasing power gains and losses, which are included in constant dollar net income, are never received or paid in cash. Unlike purchasing power gains and losses, other income statement elements are associated with past, present, or expected future cash receipts or disbursements.

4. Inflation in the United States has not been severe enough to warrant constant dollar accounting. Nominal dollar financial statements are not materially distorted unless the inflation rate is sufficiently high over a sustained period.

Materiality

CONSTANT DOLLAR ACCOUNTING IN THE INTERNATIONAL SCENE

Although constant dollar accounting is not currently required in the United States, many countries that have experienced relatively high inflation rates do require it. For example, companies in Argentina, Brazil, and other South American countries are required to report constant dollar financial statements. Although the procedures for implementing inflation adjustments are not identical in all countries, the basic idea is to adjust the conventional historical cost statements to reflect the impact of general price-level changes.

The International Accounting Standards Committee (IASC), which is similar to the FASB in the United States, encourages companies to report information that has been adjusted for changing prices. Moreover, the IASC requires companies in countries that have hyperinflationary economies to express financial statements in constant dollars.

U.S. accountants working with the financial statements of companies in the Western hemisphere will likely need to become more familiar with inflation-adjusted financial statements, particularly as the effects of the North American Free Trade Agreement become widespread.

NATURE AND OBJECTIVE

Suppose that a company buys some land for $50,000 at the beginning of a year and sells it 10 years later for $150,000. Assume further that the land's market value increased by $10,000 during each of the 10 years it was held. Under these circumstances, the land is reported on a conventional historical cost balance sheet at $50,000 during the entire time it was held, and a $100,000 gain ($150,000 − $50,000) is reported on the income statement prepared at the end of the 10th year. The reason for reporting these amounts is that historical cost accounting is based on completed transactions. Increases that occur in the market values of a company's assets are ignored until the assets are sold.

Proponents of current value accounting believe that ignoring changes in market values when they occur is misleading. In the example cited in the preceding paragraph, current value proponents argue that the company is actually *better off* by $10,000 each year the land is held. Consequently, the usefulness of year-end balance sheets is enhanced by increasing the carrying value of the land by $10,000 each year it is held. Moreover, periodic income statements are more useful if they reflect $10,000 of income each year. Why postpone the recognition of all the income until the 10th year merely because the land was sold at that time? Although current value accounting may be somewhat less reliable than historical cost accounting, advocates argue that it is much more relevant, and more useful, to users of financial statements.

CURRENT VALUE ACCOUNTING

Current value/nominal dollar accounting is represented by Cell 2 of the matrix presented earlier in Exhibit 26–2. Under this system of accounting, the attribute measured in financial statements is current value; the measuring unit is the nominal dollar. Because the nominal dollar is the conventional measuring unit used in financial statements, current value/nominal dollar accounting is often simply called **current value accounting.**

The objective of current value accounting is to report financial statements that reflect the effects of specific price changes. In a set of current value financial statements, assets and liabilities are reported at their current values (instead of their historical costs) on the balance sheet date, and holding gains and losses (discussed below) are reported as the specific prices of a company's assets and liabilities change.[6] As explained earlier, specific price changes are commonly measured by direct pricing or indexing methods.

Fundamentally, the **current value** of an item refers to its value at the present time. But the term *value* can have many different meanings, and the term *current value accounting* therefore can mean different things to different people. In the accounting literature, *current value accounting* refers to three major forms or types of accounting: (1) present value accounting, (2) exit value accounting, and (3) current cost accounting. Just as historical cost accounting is based primarily (but not exclusively) on the historical cost attribute, each form of current value accounting is based primarily (but not exclusively) on an attribute other than historical cost.

PRESENT VALUE ACCOUNTING

In **present value accounting,** an asset is measured at the present discounted amount of the net cash inflows that the asset is expected to generate in the future. Income consists of three components: (1) an amount determined when an asset is acquired by subtracting the asset's cost from its present value; (2) interest revenue that is earned on the asset over time; and (3) holding gains and losses that are based on changes that occur in the asset's present value while it is held.

Determining an asset's present value requires that we discount all the net cash inflows that the asset is expected to generate in the future. The discounting process requires estimates of the amount of the net cash inflows, the timing of those flows, and the discount rate to use in computing the present value.

A strong theoretical case can be made that present value accounting information would be extremely relevant to users of financial statements. The existence of expected future economic benefits is the essence of an asset, and the asset's present value is a measure of how much those benefits currently are worth. A major weakness of present value accounting is that the information generally lacks reliability. Because of uncertainty about the future and because it is usually impossible to determine exactly how much cash inflows are associated with each one of a company's many interacting assets, accountants cannot reliably measure present values for most types of nonmonetary assets, such as equipment, buildings, and patents.

EXIT VALUE ACCOUNTING

Under **exit value accounting,** an asset is measured at the amount of cash it could be sold for in an orderly liquidation. Income consists of two components: (1) an amount determined when an asset is acquired by subtracting the asset's cost from its exit value, and (2) holding gains and losses that are based on changes that occur in the asset's exit value while it is held.

The exit value of an asset indicates the opportunity cost that a company incurs by holding rather than selling the asset. Proponents argue that exit values are relevant because they

---

[6]In this chapter, we cover current value accounting primarily from the standpoint of assets. Current value accounting for liabilities has not been widely discussed in the accounting literature and has never been required by the FASB.

indicate the ability of a company to adapt to its changing environment by selling assets and investing the money elsewhere. Exit values are also considered more objective and reliable than present values.

Opponents of exit value accounting believe that exit values lack relevance for assets, such as equipment, that a company intends to use rather than sell. Opponents also point out that many assets, such as goodwill, work-in-process inventory, and specialized plant assets, do not usually have readily determinable exit values.

CURRENT COST ACCOUNTING

In **current cost accounting,** an asset is measured at the amount of cash (or cash equivalent) that a company would currently have to pay to acquire the same asset in its existing condition. Income consists of two components: (1) holding gains and losses based on changes that occur in the asset's current cost while it is held and (2) an amount determined when an asset is sold by subtracting the asset's current cost on the date of sale from its selling price.

Proponents argue that current cost information is relevant because it helps users to make more accurate predictions of future cash flows and more meaningful evaluations of a company's financial position and performance. Opponents tend to question the reliability of current cost measurements in relation to those based on historical costs.

Although all forms of current value accounting are highly controversial and still in the early stages of their development, current cost accounting appears to be the most widely supported form of current value accounting today. The FASB opted for current cost measurements in *SFAS No. 33.* Many people prefer current cost accounting because they see current costs as more reliable than other types of current value measurements. Moreover, although current costs are used instead of historical costs, current cost accounting still represents an approach based on costs rather than selling prices. Conventional historical cost accounting is also, of course, a cost-based approach. Finally, present value accounting and exit value accounting systems allow income to be recognized when goods are purchased or manufactured. Thus, under these systems, all of the income associated with an asset such as inventory may be recognized before the time of sale. In contrast, when current cost accounting is used, holding gains and losses are recognized before the time of sale, but additional income is also recognized when a sale occurs based on the difference between the selling price and the current cost of the asset sold. The current cost approach therefore requires a less radical departure from the age-old general rule in accounting that income should be recognized only at the time of sale.

We will emphasize current cost accounting in the rest of this chapter because of the support it has received and because it may be even more widely accepted in the future.

HOLDING GAINS AND LOSSES UNDER CURRENT COST ACCOUNTING

Holding gains and losses in current cost accounting result from changes in the current cost of an asset while it is held over time. Suppose, for example, that a company invests in land costing $10,000 on January 1, 1994. Assume further that the company holds the land on December 31, 1994, when the land's current cost is $14,000, and on December 31, 1995, when its current cost is $19,000. On December 31, 1996, the land is determined to have a current cost of $25,000, and the company sells it for that amount. Under current cost accounting, the company reports a holding gain of $4,000 in 1994 ($14,000 − $10,000), $5,000 in 1995 ($19,000 − $14,000), and $6,000 in 1996 ($25,000 − $19,000). The rationale for reporting these amounts as gains is that the company's management has been smart enough or lucky enough to achieve a cost saving by purchasing the land before its price increased. Holding gains sometimes are called **cost savings.** The *total* holding gain reported during the three-year period is $15,000 ($4,000 + $5,000 + $6,000). In conventional historical cost accounting, all of the $15,000 gain is reported in 1996, the year in which the land was sold. The amount of the gain, of course, is determined in 1996 by subtracting the land's cost of $10,000 from its selling price of $25,000.

Holding gains and losses may be either unrealized or realized. **Unrealized holding gains and losses** pertain to assets still on hand at the end of a period. The adjective *unrealized* is appropriate because the assets have not yet been sold or used in operations. The *total* unrealized holding gain or loss equals the difference between the current cost and the historical cost of the asset on hand. However, the amount of unrealized holding gain or loss to recognize in a current cost income statement in any year is the *increase or decrease* in the *total* unrealized holding gain or loss during the year. This increase or decrease is computed by subtracting the total unrealized holding gain or loss at the beginning of the period from the total unrealized holding gain or loss at the end of the period.

To illustrate, suppose that a company buys an inventory item costing $100 on January 1, 1994, and that the company continues to hold the item on December 31, 1994, when the current cost is $120, and on December 31, 1995, when the current cost is $150. Under these circumstances, the *total* unrealized holding gain is $0 on January 1, 1994 ($100 − $100), $20 on December 31, 1994 ($120 − $100), and $50 on December 31, 1995 ($150 − $100). The correct amount of unrealized holding gain to report in a current cost income statement is $20 for 1994 ($20 − $0) and $30 for 1995 ($50 − $20). Notice carefully that $50 is *not* the correct amount of unrealized holding gain to report in 1995, because $20 of that amount pertains to an increase in current cost during 1994.

Realized holding gains and losses pertain to assets sold or consumed in operations during a period. The adjective *realized* applies because the assets to which the gains or losses pertain have been sold or consumed. The amount of realized holding gain or loss to report in a current cost income statement is the difference between the current cost and the historical cost of the asset sold or consumed. If the inventory item described in the previous paragraph is sold in 1996 for $200 at a time when the current cost is $170, the realized holding gain to report in 1996 is $70 (the current cost on the date of sale of $170 minus the historical cost of $100).

CURRENT COST VERSUS HISTORICAL COST INCOME STATEMENTS

To illustrate the major elements of a current cost income statement and to compare the statement with a historical cost income statement, assume that Miles Company acquires an inventory item on January 1, 1995, for $300. The item has a current cost of $500 on December 31, 1995; Miles Company sells the item for $1,000 on December 31, 1996, at which time its current cost is $900. A comparison of the income statement results under historical cost accounting and current cost accounting is shown in Exhibit 26–11. For simplicity, we will assume that cost of goods sold is the only expense.

Under historical cost accounting, Miles Company reports no income in 1995 because it did not sell the inventory in that year. In 1996, it sells the inventory and reports net income of $700, which equals the inventory's selling price of $1,000 minus the historical cost of $300.

Observe the major components of the current cost income statement in Exhibit 26–11. Under current cost accounting, cost of goods sold is measured at the current cost on the date of sale and is deducted from sales revenue to derive **current operating income.** Realized holding gains and losses are then added and subtracted to derive **conventional income** (often called **realized income**). Note that Miles Company had a realized holding gain of $600 in 1996. This amount was calculated by subtracting the historical cost of the inventory item ($300) from its current cost ($900) on the date of sale. Unrealized holding gains and losses are then added and subtracted to derive **current cost net income.** Miles Company reported an unrealized holding gain of $200 in 1995; this amount equals the total unrealized holding gain of $200 at the end of 1995 minus the total unrealized holding gain of $0 at the beginning of 1995. In 1996 the company reported an unrealized holding loss of $200. This amount

---

EXHIBIT 26–11

Miles Company
Historical Cost and Current Cost Income Statements

Historical Cost Basis

	For 1995	For 1996
Sales	–0–	$1,000
Cost of goods sold	–0–	300
Net income	–0–	$ 700

Current Cost Basis

	For 1995	For 1996
Sales	–0–	$1,000
Cost of goods sold	–0–	900
Current operating income	–0–	100
Realized holding gain	–0–	600
Conventional income	–0–	700
Unrealized holding gain (loss)	$200	(200)
Net income	$200	$ 500

---

was calculated by subtracting the total unrealized holding gain of $200 at the end of 1995 from the total unrealized holding gain of $0 at the end of 1996. (The total unrealized holding gain was $0 at the end of 1996 because the inventory was sold in 1996 and is therefore not on hand at year-end.)

Several observations about current cost income statements can now be made:

1. Current operating income is measured by matching current costs (not historical costs) with current revenues. Proponents of current cost accounting believe that requests from labor organizations for higher wages, from governments for additional taxes, and from stockholders for higher dividends should be based on current operating income, not on historical cost net income. In our example, $600 of Miles Company's historical cost net income resulted from specific price changes; only $100 was due to operations. If Miles Company distributed the $700 of historical cost income to employees, governments, and stockholders, the company could not replace the inventory item that was sold. The company's physical capacity would therefore contract. In a broader sense, any company that pays out cash equal to its historical cost net income during periods in which the current costs of inventories and plant assets increase will not be able to maintain its physical capacity without obtaining outside financing.

   Proponents of current cost accounting also believe that current operating income is a better measure for predictive purposes than is historical cost net income. They believe that current operating income more accurately reflects an amount that the company can expect to earn from future operations.

2. Conventional income in a current cost income statement always equals historical cost net income. Observe in Exhibit 26–11 that these amounts equal $0 in 1995 and $700 in 1996. The equality exists because historical cost net income actually consists of income from operations and realized holding gains. But these two components are not separately identified in a historical cost income statement, which means that users of the statement cannot determine how much of the historical cost net income was due to operations and how much was due to specific price changes.

3. Realized and unrealized holding gains and losses are reported separately on a current cost income statement. Current cost advocates believe this is desirable because holding gains and losses are generally less predictable than current operating income and are not caused by the same factors.

4. Unrealized holding gains and losses are included in the calculation of current cost net income but not historical cost net income. Proponents believe that current cost net income provides a better measure than historical cost net income of how much better or worse off a company is each period.

5. The total amount of net income reported over the life of a company is the same under current cost accounting as under historical cost accounting, but the timing differs. Note in Exhibit 26–11 that if we add Miles Company's net incomes for 1995 and 1996, we obtain the same total under either historical cost accounting or current cost accounting ($0 + $700 = $700; $200 + $500 = $700).

PREPARATION OF CURRENT COST FINANCIAL STATEMENTS

We will now illustrate the process of preparing a set of comprehensive current cost financial statements. The illustration is based on the information presented earlier in the chapter for Craig Company (see Exhibits 26–5, 26–6, and 26–7) and on the *current cost* amounts in Exhibit 26–12.

We will assume that the current cost amounts of financial statement items not shown in Exhibit 26–12 are the same as their historical cost amounts. The methods used to obtain current cost measurements such as the ones shown in Exhibit 26–12 were explained earlier in the chapter. When solving the assignment materials at the end of this chapter, you will be given current cost amounts.

A Current Cost Combined Statement of Income and Retained Earnings

A combined statement of income and retained earnings presented on a current cost basis for Craig Company is shown in Exhibit 26–13. In the following sections, we explain the current cost amounts shown in the exhibit.

Sales. Sales are made at current selling prices throughout the period. Craig Company's historical cost/nominal dollar sales of $400,000 are therefore not restated when preparing a current cost income statement.

Cost of Goods Sold. In current cost accounting, cost of goods sold equals the current costs of the units sold at the time of sale. In practice, cost of goods sold is usually based on the average current costs of the units sold during the period. An average is considered appropriate because sales generally are made fairly evenly throughout a period. Craig Company's current cost of goods sold is $260,000.

Operating Expenses. The historical cost/nominal dollar operating expenses of $68,000 are measured at current costs when incurred. Accordingly, these expenses are already stated on a current cost basis.

Matching | **Depreciation Expense.** Recall that depreciation expense is recorded because of the matching principle. Because sales are made at current selling prices throughout the period, we measure

EXHIBIT 26–12
Craig Company
Current Cost Information

	Current Cost
Cost of goods sold for 1996	$260,000
Inventory, Dec. 31, 1996	102,000
Land, Dec. 31, 1996	160,000
Equipment (gross), Dec. 31, 1996	140,000

EXHIBIT 26-13

Craig Company
Combined Statement of Income and Retained Earnings
Current Cost/Nominal Dollar Basis
For 1996

Sales		$400,000
Cost of goods sold		260,000
Gross margin on sales		140,000
Operating expenses	$68,000	
Depreciation expense	13,000	81,000
Income before taxes		59,000
Income tax expense		40,000
Current operating income		19,000
Realized holding gain*		41,000
Conventional income		60,000
Unrealized holding gain†		120,000
Net income		180,000
Retained earnings, Jan. 1		–0–
Less: Dividends		20,000
Retained earnings, Dec. 31		$160,000

---

*Realized holding gain for 1996:

Inventory sold ($260,000 – $220,000)	$ 40,000
Equipment used ($13,000 – $12,000)	1,000
Total	$ 41,000

†Unrealized holding gain for 1996:

Inventory on hand ($102,000 – $90,000)	$ 12,000
Land on hand ($160,000 – $70,000)	90,000
Equipment on hand—net ($126,000 – $108,000)	18,000
Total on Dec. 31	120,000
Less: Unrealized holding gain, Jan. 1	–0–
Amount to recognize in 1996	$120,000

depreciation expense based on the average current cost of the service potential of the assets used during the period. For Craig Company, the 1996 current cost depreciation expense is calculated as follows:

$$\frac{\$120,000 + \$140,000}{2} = \$130,000 \text{ Average Current Cost of Equipment during 1996}$$

$$\$130,000 \div 10 \text{ Years} = \$13,000 \text{ Current Cost Depreciation Expense for 1996}$$

Income Tax Expense. Income tax expense on a current cost basis is computed in relation to pre-tax historical cost/nominal dollar income. Accordingly, Craig Company's income tax expense is shown at $40,000 in Exhibit 26–13.

Realized Holding Gain. As explained earlier, realized holding gains and losses pertain to assets sold or consumed during a period and equal the difference between the current cost and the historical cost of the assets sold or consumed. As shown in the first footnote of Exhibit 26–13, Craig Company has a realized holding gain of $40,000 on the inventory sold (the current cost of goods sold of $260,000 minus the historical cost of goods sold of $220,000) and a realized holding gain of $1,000 on the equipment used in operations (the current cost depreciation expense of $13,000 minus the historical cost depreciation expense of $12,000). The total realized holding gain is $41,000.

Unrealized Holding Gain.   Earlier we explained that unrealized holding gains and losses pertain to assets still on hand at the end of a period and that the correct amount to report in a given year equals the increase or decrease in the total unrealized holding gain or loss during the year. As shown in the second footnote of Exhibit 26–13, Craig Company's unrealized holding gain for 1996 is attributable to the inventory, land, and equipment on hand at year-end. The unexpired historical cost of each asset on December 31, 1996, is subtracted from the unexpired current cost on that date to derive the total unrealized holding gain for each asset. These totals are then summed to derive the total unrealized holding gain of $120,000 on December 31, 1996. Because no unrealized holding gains or losses existed on January 1, 1996 (when the company began operations), $120,000 is the correct amount of unrealized holding gain to report for 1996.

The calculation of the unrealized holding gain of $18,000 on the equipment deserves additional explanation. Note that we derived the $18,000 amount by subtracting the historical cost book value of $108,000 from the current cost book value of $126,000 on December 31, 1996. But remember that the current cost of the equipment before accumulated depreciation is $140,000 and the current cost depreciation expense is $13,000. Why then is the current cost book value *$126,000* instead of *$127,000* ($140,000 − $13,000 = $127,000)? The answer is that the depreciation expense of $13,000 is based on an *average* of beginning and ending current cost amounts, while the accumulated depreciation to report at year-end is based on only the *ending* current cost amount and equals $14,000 ($140,000 × 10% = $14,000). The year-end accumulated depreciation ($14,000) must be based on the year-end current cost ($140,000) so that the ending balance sheet will correctly show the current cost of the asset's remaining service potential of $126,000 ($140,000 − $14,000 = $126,000; $140,000 × 90% = $126,000).

Dividends.   The historical cost/nominal dollar dividends of $20,000 were declared at year-end and are already stated in terms of year-end current costs.

A Current Cost Balance Sheet

A current cost balance sheet for Craig Company on December 31, 1996, is shown in Exhibit 26–14. The amounts are explained in the following sections.

Cash and Accounts Receivable.   These items are normally reported on a current value basis in conventional financial statements and are therefore not restated when preparing a current cost balance sheet.

Inventory and Land.   These items are reported at their respective current cost amounts determined at year-end.

Equipment and Accumulated Depreciation.   The equipment is shown at the current cost amount of $140,000 determined at year-end. Accumulated depreciation of $14,000 ($140,000 ÷ 10 years = $14,000) is subtracted so that the equipment's remaining service potential is reported at a current cost book value of $126,000 on December 31, 1993.

Accounts Payable and Long-Term Note Payable.   Accounts payable are conventionally reported on a current value basis and therefore do not require restatement in a current cost balance sheet. We shall assume that the market rate of interest on the long-term note payable has not changed during the year; therefore, the current cost amount to report for the note is the same

---

EXHIBIT 26—14

Craig Company
Balance Sheet
Historical Cost/Nominal Dollar Basis
December 31, 1996

Assets

Cash		$ 40,000
Accounts receivable		67,000
Inventory		102,000
Land		160,000
Equipment	$140,000	
Less: Accumulated depreciation	(14,000)	126,000
Total assets		$495,000

Liabilities and Stockholders' Equity

Accounts payable	$ 35,000
Long-term note payable	90,000
Total liabilities	125,000
Common stock	210,000
Retained earnings (see Exhibit 26–13)	160,000
Total Stockholders' equity	370,000
Total liabilities and stockholders' equity	$495,000

---

as the amount shown in a historical cost/nominal dollar balance sheet. Current cost accounting for liabilities has not been widely discussed in the accounting literature and has never been required by the FASB. We do not discuss this topic in detail in this chapter.

Common Stock.   This item is reported on a current cost balance sheet at the amount originally paid in by the stockholders. This is the same amount reported on a historical cost/nominal dollar balance sheet.

Retained Earnings.   The amount of this item is obtained directly from the current cost combined statement of income and retained earnings shown in Exhibit 26–13. For Craig Company, the amount is determined as follows:

Current cost retained earnings, Jan. 1	–0–
Add: Current cost net income	$180,000
Subtotal	180,000
Less: Current cost dividends	20,000
Current cost retained earnings, Dec. 31	$160,000

The ending balance of retained earnings shown on the combined statement of income and retained earnings should be the amount that causes total assets to equal total liabilities and stockholders' equity on the current cost balance sheet. If these totals are not equal after including retained earnings, an error has been made.

ARGUMENTS FOR AND AGAINST CURRENT COST ACCOUNTING

Current cost accounting has been widely discussed in the financial community in recent years. Here are the major arguments in favor of current cost accounting:

   1. Current cost accounting leads to income statements that are useful for predictive purposes. Current operating income is more predictable than holding gains and losses; these two kinds of income are reported separately on a current cost income statement. Ultimately, current cost financial statements help users to predict more accurately the amount, timing, and uncertainty of prospective cash flows.

2. Current cost accounting leads to income statements that are useful for evaluating management's performance. The separation of current operating income from holding gains and losses allows users of financial statements to evaluate management's **operating activities** (activities directly related to producing and selling products) separate from **holding activities** (holding assets while specific prices change).

3. Current cost accounting can help a company to maintain its physical capacity. During periods of rising costs, current operating income indicates the maximum amount that a company can distribute and still maintain its capacity to produce and sell products without obtaining new debt or equity capital.

4. Current cost balance sheets are relevant because they reflect current valuations of a company's resources and equities.

Here are the major arguments against current cost accounting:

1. Current cost measurements are too subjective and unreliable. This argument is particularly strong in the case of specialized assets that do not have a ready market.

2. Current cost financial statements are denominated in dollars of mixed purchasing power. Holding gains and losses are therefore not adjusted for inflation, and purchasing power gains and losses are not even reported. Suppose that a company buys land for $10,000 on January 1, 1996, and holds it on December 31, 1996, when the current cost is $11,000. The company is better off by $1,000 on December 31 only if no inflation occurred during the year. If, in fact, the inflation rate for the year was 20%, the company is actually $1,000 *worse off* at year-end [$11,000 − ($10,000 × 1.20) = ($1,000)].

CURRENT COST ACCOUNTING IN THE INTERNATIONAL SCENE

Although current cost accounting is not required in the United States, it is advocated in certain other countries. For example, Dutch companies may report current cost financial statements although they are not required to do so. Philips Group is a large Dutch appliance company that has reported current cost information for many years. In general, economic theory and research have had a greater impact on accounting in the Netherlands as compared to most other countries. Certain other countries, such as Australia, Belgium, Canada, and New Zealand also permit or encourage supplementary current cost financial information. Recently, the FASB extended current value accounting principles to encompass the accounting and reporting for certain categories of debt and equity securities, as we explained in Chapter 10.

CURRENT COST/ CONSTANT DOLLAR ACCOUNTING

NATURE AND OBJECTIVE

We have discussed constant dollar accounting, in which the attribute measured is historical cost and the measuring unit is the constant dollar. We have also discussed current cost accounting, in which the attribute measured is current cost and the measuring unit is the nominal dollar. In this section, we shall see that it is possible to combine current cost and constant dollar accounting in a single set of financial statements. Current cost accounting and constant dollar accounting are not mutually exclusive but are highly compatible with one another.

Current cost/constant dollar accounting is represented by Cell 4 of the matrix presented earlier in Exhibit 26–2. The objective of this system of accounting is to measure the current cost attribute of the elements of financial statements using dollars that have the same purchasing power. Current cost/constant dollar financial statements reflect adjustments for general price-level changes and for specific price changes. These statements therefore contain complete adjustments for the effects of changing prices and are regarded as theoretically sound.

PURCHASING POWER GAINS AND LOSSES AND HOLDING GAINS AND LOSSES ADJUSTED FOR INFLATION

Purchasing power gains and losses are measured and reported under constant dollar accounting, and holding gains and losses are measured and reported under current cost accounting. Both types of gains and losses are measured and reported under current cost/constant dollar accounting. Purchasing power gains and losses are measured in the same manner as in constant dollar accounting. Holding gains and losses in current cost/constant dollar accounting are reported net of inflation. To illustrate, suppose that a company buys an inventory item for $100 on January 1, 1996. Assume further that the 1996 inflation rate is 8% and that the company holds the inventory item on December 31, 1996, when the item's current cost is $120. In current cost accounting, a holding gain of $20 ($120 − $100) is reported for 1996. But in current cost/constant dollar accounting, the holding gain is adjusted for inflation and reported at $12 [$120 − ($100 × 1.08)]. Under current cost/constant dollar accounting, we say that only $12 of the $20 nominal dollar holding gain is a *real holding gain*. The other $8 is merely a *fictional holding gain* due to inflation.

PREPARATION OF CURRENT COST/CONSTANT DOLLAR FINANCIAL STATEMENTS

Using the same information given earlier for Craig Company (see Exhibits 26–5, 26–6, 26–7, and 26–12), we now illustrate how to prepare a set of current cost/constant dollar financial statements.

A Current Cost/Constant Dollar Combined Statement of Income and Retained Earnings

A combined statement of income and retained earnings reported on a current cost/constant dollar basis for Craig Company is shown in Exhibit 26–15. The amounts shown in the exhibit are explained as follows:

Sales. Craig Company's sales of $400,000 were made at current selling prices throughout the year and are adjusted to year-end constant dollars by multiplying by 1.10. Recall that 1.10 (157.3 ÷ 143) is the conversion factor used to restate amounts *from* the average price-level index of 143 *to* the December 31 index of 157.3.

Cost of Goods Sold. Cost of goods sold expense was incurred throughout the year. Therefore, the current cost amount of $260,000 is adjusted to year-end constant dollars by multiplying by 1.10.

Operating Expenses. The operating expenses were incurred throughout the year; the current cost amount is restated in year-end constant dollars by multiplying by 1.10.

Depreciation Expense. The current cost depreciation expense is based on the average current cost of the equipment during the year. Accordingly, this amount is multiplied by 1.10 to adjust to year-end constant dollars.

Income Tax Expense. Income tax expense is incurred throughout the year. Therefore, the current cost amount of $40,000 is restated in year-end constant dollars by multiplying by 1.10.

Purchasing Power Gain. As indicated earlier, purchasing power gains and losses under current cost/constant dollar accounting are calculated in the same manner as under constant dollar accounting. The $8,600 amount shown in Exhibit 26–15 is calculated exactly as shown in Exhibit 26–9.

Realized Holding Gain, Adjusted for Inflation. Recall that realized holding gains and losses pertain to assets sold or consumed during a period. In a current cost/constant dollar system, these gains and losses are reported net of inflation.

EXHIBIT 26–15

Craig Company
Combined Statement of Income and Retained Earnings
Current Cost/Constant Dollar Basis
For 1996

Sales ($400,000 × 1.10)		$440,000
Cost of goods sold ($260,000 × 1.10)		286,000
Gross margin on sales		154,000
Operating expenses ($68,000 × 1.10)	$74,800	
Depreciation expense ($13,000 × 1.10)	14,300	89,100
Income before taxes		64,900
Income tax expense ($40,000 × 1.10)		44,000
Current operating income		20,900
Purchasing power gain (see Exhibit 26–9)		8,600
Current operating income after purchasing power gain		29,500
Realized holding gain, adjusted for inflation*		32,780
Conventional income, adjusted for inflation		62,280
Unrealized holding gain, adjusted for inflation†		73,620
Net income		135,900
Retained earnings, Jan. 1		–0–
Less: Dividends ($20,000 × 1.00)		20,000
Retained earnings, Dec. 31		$115,900

*Realized holding gain, adjusted for inflation, for 1996:

	CC/CD	HC/CD	Difference
Inventory sold	$286,000	$253,000	$33,000
Equipment used	14,300	14,520	(220)
Total			$32,780

†Unrealized holding gain, adjusted for inflation, for 1996:

	CC/CD	HC/CD	Difference
Inventory on hand	$102,000	$ 99,000	$ 3,000
Land on hand	160,000	84,700	75,300
Equipment on hand—net	126,000	130,680	(4,680)
Total on Dec. 31			73,620
Less: Unrealized holding gain, adjusted for inflation, Jan. 1			–0–
Amount to recognize in 1996			$73,620

As shown in the first footnote of Exhibit 26–15, Craig Company has a realized holding gain, adjusted for inflation, of $33,000 on the inventory sold. The $33,000 amount equals the current cost/constant dollar cost of goods sold of $286,000 (as shown in Exhibit 26–15) minus the historical cost/constant dollar cost of goods sold of $253,000 (as shown in Exhibit 26–8). Observe that both cost of goods sold amounts are expressed in *constant dollars;* therefore, the difference between them equals a realized holding gain *adjusted for inflation.* Craig Company also has a realized holding loss, adjusted for inflation, of $220 on the equipment used in operations. The $220 amount equals the current cost/constant dollar depreciation expense of $14,300 (as shown in Exhibit 26–15) minus the historical cost/

constant dollar depreciation expense of $14,520 (as shown in Exhibit 26–8). The difference between the two depreciation amounts represents a realized holding loss *adjusted for inflation,* because both amounts are expressed in *constant dollars.* The total realized holding gain, adjusted for inflation, is $32,780.

Notice that after including the $32,780 amount in the combined statement of income and retained earnings, we derive a conventional income adjusted for inflation of $62,280. Through no coincidence, this amount equals the net income shown in Craig Company's constant dollar combined statement of income and retained earnings (as shown in Exhibit 26–8).

Unrealized Holding Gain, Adjusted for Inflation.   Unrealized holding gains and losses are also reported net of inflation in current cost/constant dollar financial statements. Remember that unrealized holding gains and losses pertain to assets still on hand at the end of a period.

As shown in the second footnote of Exhibit 26–15, Craig Company has a total unrealized holding gain, adjusted for inflation, of $73,620 at the end of 1996. This amount is associated with the inventory, land, and equipment on hand at year-end. Notice that for each asset, we subtracted the historical cost/constant dollar amount (as shown in Exhibit 26–10) from the current cost/constant dollar amount (as shown in Exhibit 26–16). Because the two amounts for each asset are expressed in *constant dollars,* the differences between them represent holding gains (or losses) *adjusted for inflation.* The total holding gain, adjusted for inflation, of $73,620 is also the correct amount to report for 1996, because Craig Company began operations on January 1, 1996, and no unrealized holding gains or losses adjusted for inflation existed at that time.

Dividends.   Craig Company's dividends were declared at year end and are already stated in terms of year-end constant dollars. We therefore simply multiply by a conversion factor of 1.00 (157.3 ÷ 157.3), as shown in Exhibit 26–15.

EXHIBIT 26–16

Craig Company
Balance Sheet
Current Cost/Constant Dollar Basis
December 31, 1996

Assets

Cash		$ 40,000
Accounts receivable		67,000
Inventory		102,000
Land		160,000
Equipment	$140,000	
Less: Accumulated depreciation	(14,000)	126,000
Total assets		$495,000

Liabilities and Stockholders' Equity

Accounts payable	$ 35,000
Long-term note payable	90,000
Total liabilities	125,000
Common stock ($210,000 × 1.21)	254,100
Retained earnings (see Exhibit 26–15)	115,900
Total Stockholders' equity	370,000
Total liabilities and stockholders' equity	$495,000

A Current Cost/Constant Dollar Balance Sheet

A current cost/constant dollar balance sheet for Craig Company is shown in Exhibit 26–16. Notice the similarity between this balance sheet and the current cost balance sheet in Exhibit 26–14. Each asset and liability are reported at the same amount on a current cost/constant dollar balance sheet as on a current cost balance sheet. The reason for this is that the current cost measurements of the assets and liabilities are obtained *at year-end* and are therefore automatically expressed in year-end constant dollars.

The differences between a current cost balance sheet and a current cost/constant dollar balance sheet are in the stockholders' equity section. As shown in Exhibit 26–16, Craig Company's common stock balance of $210,000 is adjusted to year-end constant dollars by multiplying by 1.21. Recall that this conversion factor is the one used to restate amounts *from* the January 1 price-level index of 130 *to* the December 31 price-level index of 157.3 (157.3/130 = 1.21). The 1.21 conversion factor is appropriate to use because the common stock balance originated on January 1.

The ending balance of retained earnings for a current cost/constant dollar balance sheet is obtained, as usual, directly from the combined statement of income and retained earnings. The amount for Craig Company is calculated as follows:

Current cost/constant dollar retained earnings, Jan. 1	–0–
Add: Current cost/constant dollar net income	$135,900
Subtotal	135,900
Less: Current cost/constant dollar dividends	20,000
Current cost/constant dollar retained earnings, Dec. 31	$115,900

ARGUMENTS FOR AND AGAINST CURRENT COST/CONSTANT DOLLAR ACCOUNTING

The major argument in favor of current cost/constant dollar accounting is that it combines the most desirable features of the current cost and constant dollar approaches. The use of current costs enhances the relevance of financial statements; the use of constant dollars provides a stable measuring unit that helps users make better comparisons over time and between companies.

Opponents of current cost/constant dollar accounting argue that the measurements are unreliable, relatively costly to derive, and likely to confuse most users.

THE FASB'S DISCLOSURE RECOMMENDATIONS

Earlier in the chapter, we explained that *SFAS No. 33* applied only to certain large companies, did not change the primary financial statements, and required the disclosure of selected items of supplementary information in published annual reports. We also indicated that the FASB has encouraged but never required the reporting of comprehensive statements such as those we have discussed and illustrated in this chapter. Although comprehensive statements have never been required, the FASB *may decide* to require them in the future. Even if comprehensive statements are never required, an understanding of them helps a person to appreciate the issues involved in accounting for changing prices. Moreover, a knowledge of comprehensive statements can help a person to more easily grasp the current disclosure recommendations of the FASB.

RESULTS OF THE *SFAS NO. 33* EXPERIMENT

The original disclosure requirements of *SFAS No. 33* called for the supplementary disclosure of both historical cost/constant dollar and current cost/constant dollar information. The FASB's rationale for requiring both approaches was to allow preparers and users of financial statements to experiment with both kinds of information. After a reasonable period (not to exceed five years), the FASB felt that it would be better able to evaluate the benefits and costs of these major approaches to accounting for changing prices.

After *SFAS No. 33* information became available, many research studies were conducted to determine whether the information is useful. The results generally suggested that (1) basic historical cost information as required by GAAP is more useful than either current cost/constant dollar or historical cost/constant dollar information and (2) current cost/constant dollar information is more useful than historical cost/constant dollar information.[7] Accordingly, in 1984 the FASB eliminated the original *SFAS No. 33* requirement to report historical cost/constant dollar information. Late in 1986, the FASB decided that companies should be *encouraged,* but *not required,* to disclose supplementary information on the effects of changing prices.

Here are some reasons that may explain why accounting information adjusted for changing prices was not considered more useful than it was during the early years of the *SFAS No. 33* experiment:

1. Users may simply have needed more time to become familiar with the relatively new types of measurements.
2. The FASB's initial approach of requiring both historical cost/constant dollar and current cost/constant dollar information may have been too complex and may have caused users of financial statements to become confused.
3. The U.S. inflation rate declined after *SFAS No. 33* was issued. User interest in accounting information adjusted for changing prices may increase if inflation increases significantly.
4. Many users make their own evaluations of the impact of changing prices on a business and are not convinced that *SFAS No. 33* measurements are better than their own.
5. A longer time series of *SFAS No. 33* measurements may be needed if the information is to become more useful. Information is more useful for assessing trends when several periods are presented.
6. The initial *SFAS No. 33* disclosures may have contained measurement errors that can be reduced if preparers are encouraged to continue reporting the information.

Regarding item 6, one study investigated the sign, magnitude, and sources of the potential measurement error in the current cost estimates that companies derive with different levels of specificity of the producer price indexes (PPIs). Many companies have used PPIs to estimate the current cost of various plant assets. The study's results show that the measurement error tends to produce an overstatement of new current cost and that the sources of the measurement error are product mix errors, pricing errors, and inadequate adjustments for quality change in the PPIs.[8]

After experimenting with accounting information adjusted for changing prices for several years, the FASB decided that the benefits of the information were not greater than the

---

[7]Accounting research studies are generally divided on the question of whether accounting information adjusted for changing prices is useful. Some studies suggest that the information is not useful; others suggest that it is. Examples of studies that question the usefulness of *SFAS No. 33* information are those by William H. Beaver and Wayne R. Landsman, *Incremental Information Content of Statement 33 Disclosures* (Stamford, Conn.: FASB, 1983); Mostafa M. Maksy, "The Use of Inflation-Adjusted Accounting Data by U.S. Banks," *Accounting and Business Research* (Winter 1984), pp. 37–43; Thomas E. McCaslin and Keith G. Stanga, "Accounting Information Adjusted for Changing Prices: How Do Users React?" *Journal of Commercial Bank Lending* (July 1983), pp. 50–60; and R. David Mautz, Jr., "Inflation-Adjusted Disclosures and the Determination of Ability to Pay in Collective Bargaining," *Accounting, Organizations and Society* 15, no. 4 (1990), pp. 273–295. For examples of studies that suggest that accounting information adjusted for changing prices may be useful, see Bruce Bublitz, Thomas J. Frecka, and James C. McKeown, "Market Association Tests and *FASB Statement No. 33* Disclosures: A Reexamination," *Journal of Accounting Research* (Supplement 1985), pp. 1–23; Jon W. Bartley and Calvin M. Boardman, "The Relevance of Inflation Adjusted Accounting Data to the Prediction of Corporate Takeovers," *Journal of Business Finance and Accounting* (Spring 1990), pp. 53–72; and Ibrahim M. Aly, H. A. Barlow, and Richard W. Jones, "The Usefulness of *SFAS No. 82* (Current Cost) Information in Discriminating Business Failure: An Empirical Study," *Journal of Accounting, Auditing* and Finance (Spring 1992), pp. 217–229.

[8]Keith A Shriver, "An Empirical Examination of the Potential Measurement Error in Current Cost Data," *Accounting Review* (January 1987), pp. 79–96. See also Keith A. Shriver, "Further Evidence on the Marginal Gains in Accuracy of Alternative Levels of Specificity of the Producer Price Indexes," *Journal of Accounting Research* (Spring 1986), pp. 151–165.

costs of providing it. Accordingly, the FASB's present position is merely to *encourage* companies to present the information. In the following paragraphs, we explain the general disclosure guidelines that the FASB advises. Because the information is merely encouraged and is still considered experimental in nature, the FASB's guidelines are reasonably flexible. Companies are not discouraged from experimenting with other forms of disclosure.

DISCLOSURE RECOMMENDATIONS

The FASB encourages companies to report the following *major* items of supplementary information:[9]

1. The purchasing power gain or loss on net monetary items for the current fiscal year.
2. Income from continuing operations for the current fiscal year on a current cost/constant dollar basis.
3. The current cost/constant dollar amounts of inventory and property, plant, and equipment at the end of the current fiscal year.
4. Increases or decreases for the current fiscal year in the current cost amounts of inventory and property, plant, and equipment, net of inflation. (These are essentially the total holding gains or losses adjusted for inflation, as measured in a current cost/constant dollar system. Realized and unrealized amounts are simply combined and reported as a single amount.)
5. A summary for each of the five most recent years of
   a. Net sales and other operating revenues.
   b. Income from continuing operations on a current cost/constant dollar basis.
   c. Income per common share from continuing operations on a current cost/constant dollar basis.
   d. Net assets at fiscal year-end on a current cost/constant dollar basis.
   e. Increases or decreases in the current cost amounts of inventory and property, plant, and equipment, net of inflation (the total of the realized and unrealized holding gains or losses adjusted for inflation, as measured under current cost/constant dollar accounting).
   f. Purchasing power gain or loss on net monetary items.
   g. Cash dividends declared per common share.
   h. Market price per common share at fiscal year-end.

In essence, these items had been required by the FASB immediately before it decided late in 1986 to make the information optional.

The SEC also encourages its registrants to voluntarily present quantified disclosures about the impact of inflation. Moreover, the SEC requires registrants to discuss the impact of inflation, when the impact is material, in the section of the annual report that presents management's discussion and analysis of financial condition and the results of operations. This discussion, however, need not include quantified information about the impact of inflation.

Materiality

PROFESSIONAL JUDGMENT

Accounting requires many estimates and judgments, as the topic of accounting for changing prices illustrates. In fact, many people believe that the estimates and judgments in this area are so extensive that the resulting information is too unreliable for use in financial reporting. For example, what is the current cost of a specialized machine that a company acquired five years ago? How should the company assign this current cost to depreciation expense during the period that it uses the machine? The estimates and judgments required to answer these and other questions help to explain why current cost accounting has not become more popular, even when many people consider it more relevant than historical cost accounting. Continued worldwide experimentation with accounting information adjusted for changing prices may result in systems and processes that will improve the reliability of the information. However, the nature and significance of the estimates and judgments in this area of accounting will likely always be challenging for accountants.

---

[9]*FASB Statement of Financial Accounting Standards No. 89*, pars. 7–13.

Accounting for changing prices has been one of the most widely debated financial accounting topics during the 20th century. The topic deals with fundamental issues of accounting measurement and has far-reaching implications concerning the types of information that companies may be required to report in the future. Should the FASB require companies to report comprehensive financial statements adjusted for changing prices? If so, should these statements replace or merely supplement the conventional financial statements? Also, should the financial statements reflect adjustments for general price-level changes, specific price changes, or both? Ultimately, the answers to these and similar questions depend on the relevance and reliability of the information and on whether the benefits of information exceed the costs of providing it. Although current value accounting would likely cause companies to report more volatile earnings, the SEC chairman believes that "if you are in a volatile business, then your balance sheet and income statement should reflect that volatility."[10] Your textbook authors agree with the SEC chairman on this point.

After conducting an experiment from 1979 through 1985 in which certain large companies were required to make supplementary disclosures of accounting information adjusted for changing prices, the FASB has decided that companies should be encouraged, but not required, to disclose this kind of information. Since *SFAS No. 89* was issued, the vast majority of companies have elected *not* to report the information about changing prices that the FASB encourages. Recently, however, "there has been a growing interest by companies that invest in and operate real estate properties in presenting supplementary current value information."[11]

In the future, as the FASB continues to learn more about the uses, limitations, and costs of accounting information adjusted for changing prices, the FASB could decide to make the information mandatory once again, perhaps even in the primary financial statements. Considerable research on the usefulness of accounting information adjusted for changing prices is still in progress, despite the fact that the information is no longer mandatory. If the inflation rate should increase from its present, relatively low level, this would probably increase the chances of the FASB deciding to make the information mandatory. Readers of this textbook should be prepared to actively participate in the debate about accounting for changing prices and to understand the additional changes that could occur in this area.

CONCLUDING REMARKS

KEY POINTS

1. A price change is an increase or decrease in the price of a good or service that occurs in a given market. (Objective 1)
2. A general price-level change is an increase or decrease in the overall level of prices of goods and services throughout the economy. It is measured by using a general price-level index, such as the CPI-U, constructed by the federal government. (Objective 2)
3. A specific price change is an increase or decrease in the price of a good or service. It may be measured by applying direct pricing or indexing methods. (Objective 2)
4. Constant dollar accounting calls for historical cost measurements in dollars having the same purchasing power. Adjustments are made for general price-level changes, but not for specific price changes. (Objective 3)
5. Purchasing power gains and losses are measured and reported when constant dollars are used as the measuring unit in financial statements. They occur as a result of holding monetary items during periods of inflation or deflation. (Objective 3)
6. Current value accounting calls for current value measurements in dollars that are not adjusted for inflation or deflation. Adjustments are made for specific price changes, but not for general price-level changes. (Objective 4)
7. The three major forms of current value accounting are
   [a] Present value accounting, in which an asset is measured at the present discounted amount of the net cash inflows that the asset is expected to generate in the future.

---

[10]Dana Wechler Linden, "If Life Is Volatile, Account for It," *Forbes* (November 12, 1990), p. 114.
[11]Gerald Searfoss and Judith Fellner Weiss, "Current Value Reporting for Real Estate," *Journal of Accountancy,* (October 1990), p. 69.

1240 Part VI ◆ Chapter 26   Financial Reporting and Changing Prices

[b] Exit value accounting, in which an asset is measured at the amount of cash it could be sold for in an orderly liquidation.

[c] Current cost accounting, in which an asset is measured at the amount of cash that a company would currently have to pay to acquire the same asset in its existing condition. (Objective 4)

8. The disclosure requirements of *SFAS No. 33* reflected the current cost version of current value accounting. (Objectives 5 and 7)

9. Holding gains and losses are measured and reported when current costs are used in financial statements. They occur as a result of changes in the current cost of an asset held over time. (Objective 5)

10. Unrealized holding gains and losses pertain to assets still on hand at the end of a period; realized holding gains and losses pertain to assets sold or consumed in operations during a period. (Objective 5)

11. Current cost/constant dollar accounting calls for current cost measurements in dollars having the same purchasing power. Adjustments are made for general price-level changes and specific price changes. (Objective 6)

12. Current cost/constant dollar accounting requires the reporting of purchasing power gains or losses *and* holding gains or losses adjusted for inflation. (Objective 6)

13. *SFAS No. 33* applied only to large public companies, did not change the primary financial statements, and requires certain supplemental disclosures. (Objective 7)

14. The supplemental disclosures required by *SFAS No. 33* originally reflected both the historical cost/constant dollar and current cost/constant dollar approaches. Later only the current cost/constant dollar approach was emphasized. (Objective 7)

15. Today the FASB *encourages,* but does *not require,* companies to disclose supplementary information on the effects of changing prices. (Objective 7)

QUESTIONS

26–1 How does a general price-level change differ from a specific price change?

26–2 What is the basic nature of a general price-level index?

26–3 What methods may be used to determine an asset's current cost? Explain them.

26–4 What is constant dollar accounting?

26–5 What is the difference between a monetary item and a nonmonetary item? Include four examples of each type of item in your explanation.

26–6 What are purchasing power gains and losses?

26–7 What are the major arguments for and against constant dollar accounting?

26–8 What is current value accounting?

26–9 What is current cost accounting?

26–10 How does current cost accounting relate to the need that investors and creditors have to predict the amount, timing, and uncertainty of net cash inflows that they will receive from their investments?

26–11 What are holding gains and losses in current cost accounting?

26–12 How do realized holding gains and losses in current cost accounting differ from unrealized holding gains and losses?

26–13 Why does conventional income for any given year under current cost accounting always equal net income for that year under historical cost accounting?

26–14 What are the major arguments for and against current cost accounting? Explain them.

26–15 What is current cost/constant dollar accounting?

26–16 What are holding gains and losses, adjusted for inflation, in current cost/constant dollar accounting?

26–17 What are the major arguments for and against current cost/constant dollar accounting? Explain them.

26–18 What was the nature and purpose of *SFAS No. 33?*

26–19 What are the major disclosure recommendations for the FASB in the area of accounting for changing prices? Summarize them.

26–20 Conversion Factors Listed below are selected items that pertain to Rope Company on December 31, 1996.

[1] Land acquired on July 31, 1979.
[2] Purchases made evenly throughout 1996.
[3] Common stock issued on April 30, 1976.
[4] Accounts receivable resulting from credit sales made on November 30, 1996.
[5] Bonus expense incurred on March 31, 1996.
[6] Twenty-year bonds payable issued on August 31, 1992.
[7] Interest expense applicable to the 20-year bonds payable issued on August 31, 1992.
[8] Cash in bank.
[9] Depreciation expense applicable to equipment purchased on January 31, 1989.
[10] Investment in common stock acquired on May 31, 1994.
[11] Sales made evenly throughout 1996.
[12] Income tax expense for 1996.
[13] Cash dividends declared on June 30, 1996.
[14] Inventory acquired evenly throughout 1996.
[15] Note receivable acquired on October 31, 1995.

Selected values of the CPI-U follow:

Apr. 30, 1976	64	Mar. 31, 1996	192
July 31, 1979	80	June 30, 1996	194
Jan. 31, 1989	112	Nov. 30, 1996	199
Aug. 31, 1992	147	Dec. 31, 1996	200
May 31, 1994	167	Average for 1996	195
Oct. 31, 1995	187		

INSTRUCTIONS

Indicate the numerator and the denominator of the conversion factor that should be used to restate each of the preceding items to 1996 year-end constant dollars.

26–21 Constant Dollar Cost of Land Roane Company acquired land on April 30, 1987, for $200,000. The CPI-U was 110 on April 30, 1987, and 176 on December 31, 1996.

INSTRUCTIONS

[a] At what amount is the land reported in a December 31, 1996, balance sheet prepared in constant end-of-year dollars?
[b] Explain the meaning of your answer to [a].
[c] Based only on the information presented above, can you calculate how much Roane Company could sell the land for on December 31, 1996? Explain your answer.

26–22 FIFO—Constant Dollar Basis Ripley Company began operations on January 1, 1996. Information about the company's inventory during 1996 follows:

	Number of Units	Unit Cost
Inventory, Jan. 1, 1996	300	$10
Purchases made evenly during 1996	900	12
Sales made evenly during 1996	800	
Inventory, Dec. 31, 1996	400	

The CPI-U during 1996 was as follows:

Jan. 1, 1996	90
Average for 1996	120
Dec. 31, 1996	135

INSTRUCTIONS

Compute the ending inventory and cost of goods sold for Ripley Company in 1996 year-end constant dollars, assuming that the company uses the FIFO method of inventory pricing.

26–23 LIFO—Constant Dollar Basis   Refer to the information presented for Ripley Company in Exercise 26–22.

INSTRUCTIONS

Compute the ending inventory and cost of goods sold for Ripley Company in 1996 year-end constant dollars, assuming that the company uses the LIFO method of inventory pricing.

26–24 Equipment—Constant Dollar Basis   Hamrick Company wants to prepare constant dollar financial statements on December 31, 1996. An analysis of the company's Equipment and related Accumulated Depreciation accounts on December 31, 1996, after adjusting entries have been made, reveals the following information:

Item	Equipment Cost	When Acquired	Accumulated Depreciation
A	$200,000	Dec. 1989	$160,000
B	50,000	Dec. 1991	30,000
C	175,000	Dec. 1992	87,500
	$425,000		$277,500

Selected values of the CPI-U at the end of the years appear as follows:

Year	CPI-U
1989	100
1990	106
1991	120
1992	132
1993	141
1994	149
1995	156
1996	165

INSTRUCTIONS

Compute the 1996 year-end constant dollar amount to report for (1) equipment and (2) accumulated depreciation.

26–25 Purchasing Power Gain or Loss   The following information pertains to Holt Company for 1996:
[1] The company had net monetary items of $40,000 on January 1.
[2] Sales of $300,000 and purchases of $120,000 were made evenly throughout the year.
[3] Operating expenses of $90,000 and income tax expense of $60,000 were incurred evenly throughout the year.
[4] Cash dividends of $20,000 were declared on December 31. Selected values of the CPI-U during 1996 appear as follows:

Jan. 1	110.0
Average for year	121.0
Dec. 31	133.1

INSTRUCTIONS

Prepare a schedule showing the computation of Holt Company's purchasing power gain or loss for 1996 expressed in constant end-of-year dollars.

26–26 Purchasing Power Gain or Loss   Chun Company's financial position, shown below, did not change during January 1996. The CPI-U was 90 on January 1, 1996, and 108 on January 31, 1996.

Chun Company—Balance Sheet
January 1 and January 31, 1996

Assets

Cash	$ 5,000
Accounts receivable	10,000
Short-term investment in common stock	8,000
Inventory	50,000
Land	27,000
Total assets	$100,000

Equities

Accounts payable	$ 40,000
Common stock	50,000
Retained earnings	10,000
Total equities	$100,000

INSTRUCTIONS

[a] Compute the purchasing power gain or loss in constant January 31 dollars.

[b] Explain why Chun Company had a purchasing power gain (or loss) during January.

26–27 Constant Dollar Combined Statement of Income and Retained Earnings At the end of its first year in business, Dineen Company prepared the combined statement of income and retained earnings shown below:

Dineen Company
Combined Statement of Income and Retained Earnings
Historical Cost/Nominal Dollar Basis for 1996

Sales		$180,000
Cost of goods sold		
Beginning inventory	$10,000	
Purchases	88,000	
Goods available	98,000	
Ending inventory	8,000	90,000
Gross margin on sales		90,000
Operating expenses	15,000	
Depreciation expense	25,000	40,000
Income before taxes		50,000
Income tax expense		20,000
Net income		30,000
Retained earnings, Jan. 1		–0–
Less: Dividends		3,000
Retained earnings, Dec. 31		$ 27,000

ADDITIONAL INFORMATION

[1] Sales, purchases, operating expenses, and income tax expense occurred evenly throughout 1996.

[2] Dineen Company uses the LIFO method of inventory pricing. The company acquired the beginning inventory on January 1, 1996.

[3] Depreciation expense relates to machinery acquired on March 1, 1996.

[4] Dividends were declared on November 1, 1996.

[5] Dineen Company had a purchasing power gain of $1,800 during 1996.

[6] The CPI-U on various dates during 1996 appears below.

January 1	100
March 1	150
November 1	250
December 1	300
Average for year	200

INSTRUCTIONS

Prepare a combined statement of income and retained earnings in constant end-of-year dollars for 1996.

26–28 Constant Dollar Balance Sheet   Camisa Company prepared the following balance sheet in accordance with GAAP.

Camisa Company
Balance Sheet
December 31, 1996

Assets

Cash	$ 24,000
Receivables	28,000
Inventory	34,000
Plant assets (net)	67,000
Total assets	$153,000

Equities

Payables	$ 68,000
Common stock	50,000
Retained earnings	35,000
Total equities	$153,000

ADDITIONAL INFORMATION

[1] The cash, receivables, and payables originated when the CPI-U was 105.
[2] The inventory and plant assets were acquired when the CPI-U was 99.
[3] The common stock was issued when the CPI-U was 90.
[4] The average CPI-U for 1996 was 100, and the ending CPI-U was 108.9.

INSTRUCTIONS

Prepare a balance sheet on December 31, 1996, in constant end-of-year dollars.

26–29 Roll Forward Procedure — Constant Dollar Basis   Stepp Company has prepared constant dollar financial statements for five years and is currently preparing the statements for 1996. The company's balance sheet prepared at the end of 1994, and expressed in 1995 year-end constant dollars, appears below:

Stepp Company
Constant Dollar Balance Sheet
December 31, 1995

Assets

Cash	$ 6,000
Accounts receivable	33,000
Temporary investments	15,000
Inventory	60,000
Equipment (net)	55,000
Total assets	$169,000

Equities

Accounts payable	$ 19,000
Bonds payable	55,000
Common stock	80,000
Retained earnings	15,000
Total equities	$169,000

The CPI-U increased from 100 on December 31, 1995, to 200 on December 31, 1996.

INSTRUCTIONS

[a] Prepare a balance sheet, dated December 31, 1995, expressed in terms of 1996 year-end constant dollars.

[b] Assuming that Stepp Company prepares a constant dollar balance sheet as of December 31, 1996, why would the balance sheet you prepared in [a] be useful to the company at the end of 1996?

26–30 Holding Gains and Losses Bolieau Company purchased land costing $10,000 on January 1, 1994. The current cost of the land was $15,000 on December 31, 1994, and $25,000 on December 31, 1995. The company sold the land on December 31, 1996, for $37,000, an amount equal to the land's current cost on that date.

INSTRUCTIONS

Compute the unrealized and realized holding gains or losses to report for 1994, 1995, and 1996.

26–31 Historical Cost and Current Cost Income Statements Garland Company purchased inventory costing $5,000 on January 1, 1994. The company sold the inventory for $15,000 on December 31, 1996. By examining the prices quoted in supplier's catalogs, Garland determined that the current cost of the inventory was $6,000 on December 31, 1994, $8,000 on December 31, 1995, and $11,000 on December 31, 1996.

INSTRUCTIONS

Prepare income statements for 1994, 1995, and 1996 under the accounting bases listed below. You may assume that cost of goods sold is Garland Company's only expense.

[a] Historical cost/nominal dollar basis.
[b] Current cost/nominal dollar basis.

26–32 Holding Gains and Losses—Unadjusted and Adjusted Hobby Company acquired land costing $100,000 on January 1, 1996. The company continued to hold the land on December 31, 1996, and on that date an independent appraisal indicated that the land's current cost was $130,000. The CPI-U was 110 on January 1, 1996, and 121 on December 31, 1996.

INSTRUCTIONS

[a] Compute the amount of holding gain or loss for 1996 under current cost accounting.
[b] Compute the amount of holding gain or loss, adjusted for inflation, for 1996 under current cost/constant dollar accounting.
[c] Explain your answers to [a] and [b].

26–33 Gain or Loss—Historical Cost and Current Cost The Davis and Mavis partnership was formed on January 1, 1995. On that date, Davis and Mavis each contributed $20,000 to their partnership, and the partnership immediately invested the $40,000 in a parcel of land. The partnership continued to hold the land on December 31, 1995, at which time the land was appraised at $45,000. On December 31, 1996, the partnership sold the land for $55,000, distributed the proceeds to the partners, and ended operations.

INSTRUCTIONS

Compute the gain or loss attributable to the land for 1995 and for 1996 under (1) historical cost accounting and (2) current cost accounting.

26–34 Gain or Loss—Constant Dollar and Current Cost/Constant Dollar Refer to the information presented in Exercise 26–33 for the Davis and Mavis Partnership. Assume that the CPI-U was as follows:

January 1, 1995	100
December 31, 1995	100
December 31, 1996	132

INSTRUCTIONS

Expressed in terms of December 31, 1996, constant dollars, compute the gain or loss attributable to the land for 1995 and for 1996 under (1) constant dollar and (2) current cost/constant dollar accounting.

26–35 Current Cost Income Statement On January 1, 1996, Hawley Company acquired inventory for $20,000. The inventory consisted of 10,000 identical units. The current cost of the inventory was $30,000 on July 1, 1996; on that date Hawley sold three-fourths of the inventory for $28,000. On December 31, 1996, the current cost of the inventory on hand was $7,500.

INSTRUCTIONS

Prepare a current cost income statement for 1996. Assume that cost of goods sold is Hawley Company's only expense.

26–36 Current Cost/Constant Dollar Income Statement   Refer to the information presented for Hawley Company in Exercise 26–35. The CPI-U on various dates is as follows:

January 1, 1996	110.0
July 1, 1996	121.0
December 31, 1996	133.1

INSTRUCTIONS

Prepare a current cost/constant dollar income statement for 1996. Assume that cost of goods sold is Hawley Company's only expense and that no purchasing power gain or loss exists.

26–37 Depreciation Expense under Four Bases   McKee Company acquired a machine on January 1, 1996, for $50,000. Depreciation will be computed using the straight-line method, assuming a five-year useful life and no salvage value. A specific price index applicable to the machine was 150 on January 1, 1996, and 225 on December 31, 1996. The CPI-U was 100 on January 1, 1996, and 121 on December 31, 1996. The average CPI-U for 1996 was 110.

INSTRUCTIONS

Compute the amount of depreciation expense for 1996 under each basis of accounting that follows:

[a] Historical cost/nominal dollar basis.
[b] Historical cost/constant dollar basis.
[c] Current cost/nominal dollar basis.
[d] Current cost/constant dollar basis.

PROBLEMS

26–38 Purchasing Power Gain or Loss   The following information pertains to Lopez Company:

Sales (all on account) made evenly throughout 1996	$220,000
Equipment purchased for cash on May 1, 1996	50,000
Purchases (all on account) made evenly throughout 1996	80,000
Cash received evenly throughout 1996 from customers on account	190,000
Cash dividends declared on Sept. 1, 1996, and paid on Oct. 1, 1996	20,000
Land acquired for cash on June 1, 1996	30,000
Depreciation expense for 1996	10,000
Common stock issued for cash on Mar. 1, 1996	60,000
Operating expenses paid evenly throughout 1996	40,000
Income tax expense paid evenly throughout 1996	25,000
Purchase of treasury stock for cash on Nov. 1, 1996	17,000
Sale of investment in common stock on Aug. 1, 1996, for cash (cost = $5,000; selling price = $8,000)	8,000
Cash paid evenly throughout 1996 on accounts payable	60,000
Monetary assets	
Jan. 1, 1996	35,000
Dec. 31, 1996	71,000
Monetary liabilities	
Jan. 1, 1996	10,000
Dec. 31, 1996	30,000

The following values of the CPI-U for 1996 are available:

1/1	100		8/1	114
2/1	102		9/1	116
3/1	104		10/1	118
4/1	106		11/1	120
5/1	108		12/1	122
6/1	110		12/31	124
7/1	112	Average for year	112

INSTRUCTIONS

Prepare a schedule showing the computation of Lopez Company's purchasing power gain or loss for 1996 in end-of-year dollars.

26–39 Current Cost Financial Statements Beno Company was formed on January 1, 1996. Financial statements pertaining to the company's first year of operations are as follows:

Beno Company
Comparative Balance Sheets
Historical Cost/Nominal Dollar Basis
January 1 and December 31, 1996

	Jan. 1	Dec. 31
Assets		
Cash	$ 22,000	$112,000
Accounts receivable	–0–	147,400
Inventory	220,000	198,000
Land	154,000	154,000
Equipment	264,000	264,000
Less:		
Accumulated depreciation	–0–	(26,400)
Total assets	$660,000	$849,000
Liabilities and Stockholders' Equity		
Accounts payable	–0–	$ 77,000
Note payable	$198,000	198,000
Total liabilities	198,000	275,000
Common stock	462,000	462,000
Retained earnings	–0–	112,000
Total stockholders' equity	462,000	574,000
Total liabilities and stockholders' equity	$660,000	$849,000

Beno Company
Combined Statement of Income and
Retained Earnings
Historical Cost/Nominal Dollar Basis
For 1996

Sales		$920,000
Cost of goods sold		
Beginning inventory	$220,000	
Purchases	462,000	
Goods available	682,000	
Ending inventory	198,000	484,000
Gross margin on sales		436,000
Operating expenses	149,600	
Depreciation expense	26,400	176,000
Income before taxes		260,000
Income tax expense		104,000
Net income		156,000
Retained earnings, Jan. 1		–0–
Less: Dividends		44,000
Retained earnings, Dec. 31		$112,000

The following current cost information pertains to Beno Company:

[1] The current cost of the equipment (before deducting accumulated depreciation) on December 31, 1996, was $308,000.

[2] The current cost of the land on December 31, 1996, was $352,000.

[3] The current cost of the inventory on December 31, 1996, was $224,400.

[4] Cost of goods sold on a current cost basis at the time of sale for 1996 was $572,000.

Additional information pertaining to Beno company is as follows:

[1] Sales, purchases, operating expenses, and income tax expense occurred evenly throughout 1996.

[2] The beginning inventory, land, and equipment were purchased on January 1, 1996.

[3] The LIFO method of inventory pricing is used.

[4] The equipment is being depreciated over a 10-year life using the straight-line method. No salvage value is assumed.

[5] Dividends were declared when the CPI-U was 132. Selected values of the CPI-U during 1996 follow:

January 1	110.0
Average for 1996	132.0
December 31	158.4

INSTRUCTIONS

[a] Prepare a combined statement of income and retained earnings for 1996 under the current cost/nominal dollar basis of accounting.

[b] Prepare a balance sheet as of December 31, 1996, under the current cost/nominal dollar basis of accounting.

26–40 Constant Dollar Financial Statements   Refer to the information presented in Problem 26–39 for Beno Company.

INSTRUCTIONS

[a] Prepare a schedule showing the computation of Beno Company's purchasing power gain or loss for 1996. The gain or loss should be expressed in constant end-of-year dollars.

[b] Prepare a constant dollar combined statement of income and retained earnings for 1996 in end-of-year dollars.

[c] Prepare a constant dollar balance sheet as of December 31, 1996, in end-of-year dollars.

26–41 Current Cost/Constant Dollar Financial Statements   Refer to the information presented in Problem 26–39 for Beno Company.

INSTRUCTIONS

[a] Prepare a current cost/constant dollar combined statement of income and retained earnings for 1996 in end-of-year dollars.

[b] Prepare a current cost/constant dollar balance sheet as of December 31, 1996, in end-of-year dollars.

26–42 Historical Cost and Current Cost Financial Statements   Shafer Company began operations on January 1, 1996. A balance sheet prepared on the opening day of business appears as follows:

Shafer Company
Balance Sheet
Historical Cost/Nominal Dollar Basis
January 1, 1996

Assets		Equities	
Cash	$ 10,000	Common stock	$170,000
Inventory	30,000		
Land	50,000		
Equipment	80,000		
Total assets	$170,000		

Additional information pertaining to Shafer Company is as follows:

[1] Sales (all on account) of $300,000 were made evenly throughout 1996. Seventy-five percent of the credit sales were collected during 1996; the remaining 25% is expected to be collected in 1997.

[2] Purchases (all on account) of $150,000 were made evenly throughout 1996. Eighty percent of the credit purchases were paid during 1996; the remaining 20% will be paid in 1997.

[3] Operating expenses of $40,000 and income tax expense at a rate of 40% of pretax income were incurred and paid in cash evenly throughout 1996.

[4] Cash dividends of $14,000 were declared and paid on December 31, 1996.

[5] The company uses the FIFO method of inventory pricing. The 1996 ending inventory of $20,000 was acquired when the CPI-U was 210.

[6] The company uses the straight-line method of depreciation for the equipment. An eight-year useful life and no salvage value are assumed.

The following *current cost* information pertains to Shafer.

Cost of goods sold for 1996	$190,000
Inventory, Dec. 31, 1996	24,000
Land, Dec. 31, 1996	65,000
Equipment (before deducting accumulated depreciation), Dec. 31, 1996	96,000

Selected values of the CPI-U during 1996 appear below:

Jan. 1	200.0	Average for year	210.0	Dec. 31	220.5

INSTRUCTIONS

[a] Prepare a combined statement of income and retained earnings for 1996 under the historical cost/nominal dollar basis of accounting.

[b] Prepare a balance sheet on December 31, 1996, under the historical cost/nominal dollar basis of accounting.

[c] Prepare a combined statement of income and retained earnings for 1996 under the current cost/nominal dollar basis of accounting.

[d] Prepare a balance sheet on December 31, 1996, under the current cost/nominal dollar basis of accounting.

[e] Briefly describe the major conceptual differences between the historical cost/nominal dollar financial statements and the current cost/nominal dollar statements. (You need not refer to dollar amounts.)

26–43 Constant Dollar Financial Statements Refer to the information presented for Shafer Company in Problem 26–42.

INSTRUCTIONS

[a] Prepare a schedule showing the computation of Shafer's purchasing power gain or loss for 1996 in end-of-year dollars.

[b] Prepare a historical cost/constant dollar combined statement of income and retained earnings for 1996 in end-of-year dollars.

[c] Prepare a historical cost/constant dollar balance sheet on December 31, 1996, in end-of-year dollars.

[d] Briefly describe the major conceptual differences between the historical cost/nominal dollar financial statements for Shafer Company and the historical cost/constant dollar statements. (You need not refer to dollar amounts.)

26–44 Current Cost/Constant Dollar Financial Statements Refer to the information presented for Shafer Company in Problem 26–42.

INSTRUCTIONS

[a] Prepare a current cost/constant dollar combined statement of income and retained earnings for 1996 in end-of-year dollars.

[b] Prepare a current cost/constant dollar balance sheet on December 31, 1996, in end-of-year dollars.

[c] Briefly describe the major conceptual differences between the historical cost/nominal dollar financial statements and the current cost/constant dollar statements. (You need not refer to dollar amounts.)

26–45 Financial Statement Amounts under Four Bases Several transactions concerning one asset of a calendar-year company are summarized as follows:

1994   Purchased land for $80,000 cash on Dec. 31. Current cost at year-end was $80,000.
1995   Held the land all year. Current cost at year-end was $104,000.
1996   Dec. 31—sold the land for $154,000.

Selected values of the CPI-U appear below:

Dec. 31, 1994   100   Dec. 31, 1995   110   Dec. 31, 1996   125

INSTRUCTIONS

[a] Determine the balance sheet valuation that should be assigned to the land *at the end of 1994, 1995, and 1996* under (1) the historical cost basis, (2) the constant dollar basis, (3) the current cost basis, and (4) the current cost/constant dollar basis of accounting.

[b] Determine the amount of net income that should be reported *at the end of 1994, 1995, and 1996* under (1) the historical cost basis, (2) the constant dollar basis, (3) the current cost basis, and (4) the current cost/constant dollar basis of accounting.

[c] Why is the timing of income recognition for the land under current cost accounting different from the timing under constant dollar accounting?   (AICPA adapted)

26–46 Constant Dollar Financial Statements   Rhoda Company (a retailer) was organized on December 15, 1995. The company's initial statement of financial position is presented as follows:

Rhoda Company
Statement of Financial Position
December 31, 1995

Assets

Cash	$250,000
Inventory (at historical cost, which equals market value; FIFO; periodic)	400,000
Furniture and fixtures	200,000
Land (held for future store site)	100,000
Total assets	$950,000

Liabilities and Stockholders' Equity

Accounts payable	$300,000
Capital stock ($5 par, 200,000 shares authorized; 130,000 issued and outstanding)	650,000
Total liabilities and stockholders' equity	$950,000

The statement of income and the statement of financial position prepared at the close of business on December 31, 1996, are as follows:

Rhoda Company
Statement of Income
For the Year Ended December 31, 1996

Sales		$1,100,000
Cost of goods sold		
Inventory 1/1/96	$ 400,000	
Purchases	1,000,000	
Goods available	1,400,000	
Inventory 12/31/96	600,000	800,000
Gross profit		300,000
Operating expenses		
Rent	36,000	
Depreciation	20,000	
Other (all required cash expenditures)	44,000	100,000
Income before taxes		200,000
Income tax expense		80,000
Net income		$ 120,000
Earnings per share		$1.00

Rhoda Company
Statement of Financial Position
December 31, 1996

Assets

Cash	$ 290,000
Accounts receivable	400,000
Inventory (at historical cost; FIFO; periodic)	600,000
Furniture and fixtures (net)	180,000
Land (held for future store site)	100,000
Total assets	$1,570,000

Liabilities and Stockholders' Equity

Accounts payable	$ 800,000
Capital stock ($5 par, 200,000 shares authorized; 130,000 issued and outstanding)	650,000
Retained earnings	120,000
Total liabilities and stockholders' equity	$1,570,000

Rhoda Company rents its showroom facilitates on an operating lease basis at a cost of $3,000 per month. The rent would be $5,000 per month if it were based on the current cost of the facility. All sales and cash outlays for costs and expenses occur uniformly throughout the year.

The following information is indicative of the changing prices since Rhoda Company began its operations.

[1] The CPI-U for the following times is

Dec. 31, 1995	200
Oct. 1, 1996	216
Dec. 31, 1996	220
Average for 1996	212

[2] The ending inventory was acquired on October 1, 1996.
[3] Inventory at current cost on December 31, 1996, is $700,000.
[4] Cost of goods sold at current cost as of date of sale is $875,000.
[5] Current cost of the land on December 31, 1996, is $150,000.
[6] The sales and purchases occurred uniformly throughout 1996.

INSTRUCTIONS

[a] Calculate Rhoda Company's purchasing power gain or loss for 1996 in terms of December 31, 1996, dollars. Round all computations to the nearest $100.
[b] Prepare a constant dollar income statement for 1996 for Rhoda Company in terms of December 31, 1996, dollars. Round all computations to the nearest $100.
[c] Identify and explain the advantages and disadvantages of constant dollar financial statements.

(CMA adapted)

26–47 Constant Dollar Adjustments Starr, Inc., a retailer, was organized during 1993. Starr's management has decided to supplement its December 31, 1996, nominal dollar financial statements with constant dollar financial statements. The following general ledger trial balance (nominal dollar) and additional information have been furnished:

Starr, Inc.
Trial Balance
December 31, 1996

	Dr.	Cr.
Cash and receivables (net)	$ 540,000	
Marketable securities (common stock)	400,000	
Inventory	485,000	
Equipment	650,000	
Equipment—Accumulated depreciation		$ 164,000
Accounts payable		345,000
6% First mortgage bonds, due 2011		500,000
Common stock, $10 par		1,000,000
Retained earnings, Dec. 31, 1995	46,000	
Sales		1,900,000
Cost of sales	1,508,000	
Depreciation	65,000	
Other operating expenses and interest	215,000	
	$3,909,000	$3,909,000

[1] Monetary assets (cash and receivables) exceeded monetary liabilities (accounts payable and bonds payable) by $400,000 at December 31, 1995.

[2] Purchases ($1,840,000 in 1996) and sales are made uniformly throughout the year.

[3] Depreciation is computed on a straight-line basis, with a full year's depreciation being taken in the year of acquisition and none in the year of retirement. The depreciation rate is 10% and no salvage value is anticipated. Acquisitions and retirements have been made fairly evenly over each year, and the retirements in 1996 consisted of assets purchased during 1994 that were scrapped. An analysis of the equipment account reveals the following:

Year	Beginning Balance	Additions	Retirements	Ending Balance
1994	—	$550,000	—	$550,000
1995	$550,000	10,000	—	560,000
1996	560,000	150,000	$60,000	650,000

[4] The bonds were issued in 1994 and the marketable securities were purchased fairly evenly over 1996. Other operating expenses and interest are assumed to be incurred evenly throughout the year.

[5] Assume that values of the CPI-U were as follows:

Annual Averages	Index	Conversion Factors (1996 4th Qtr. = 1.000)
1993	113.9	1.128
1994	116.8	1.100
1995	121.8	1.055
1996	126.7	1.014
End-of-Quarter		
1995 4th	123.5	1.040
1996 1st	124.9	1.029
2nd	126.1	1.019
3rd	127.3	1.009
4th	128.5	1.000

INSTRUCTIONS

[a] Prepare a schedule to convert the Equipment account balance at December 31, 1996, from nominal dollars to 1996 year-end constant dollars.

[b] Prepare a schedule to analyze in nominal dollars the Equipment—Accumulated Depreciation account for 1996.

[c] Prepare a schedule to analyze in 1996 year-end constant dollars the Equipment—Accumulated Depreciation account for 1996.

[d] Prepare a schedule to compute Starr's purchasing power gain or loss on its net holdings of monetary assets for 1996 (ignore income tax implications). The schedule should consider appropriate items on or related to the balance sheet and the income statement. (AICPA adapted)

26-48 Constant Dollar Adjustments To obtain a more realistic appraisal of her investment, Doris Klein, your client, has asked you to adjust certain financial data of Strader Company for price-level changes. On January 1, 1994, she invested $50,000 in Strader Company in return for 10,000 shares of common stock. Immediately after her investment, the trial balance appeared as follows:

	Dr.	Cr.
Cash and receivables	$ 65,200	
Merchandise inventory	4,000	
Building	50,000	
Accumulated depreciation—building		$ 8,000
Equipment	36,000	
Accumulated depreciation—equipment		7,200
Land	10,000	
Current liabilities		50,000
Capital stock, $5 par		100,000
	$165,200	$165,200

Balances in certain selected accounts as of December 31 of each of the next three years were as follows:

	1994	1995	1996
Sales	$39,650	$39,000	$54,450
Inventory	4,500	5,600	5,347
Purchases	14,475	16,350	18,150
Operating expenses (excluding depreciation)	10,050	9,050	9,075

[1] Assume the 1994 price level as the base year and that all changes in the price level take place at the beginning of each year. Further assume that the 1995 price level is 10% above the 1994 price level and that the 1996 price level is 10% above the 1995 level.
[2] The building was constructed in 1990 at a cost of $50,000, with an estimated life of 25 years. The price level at that time was 80% of the 1994 price level.
[3] The equipment was purchased in 1992 at a cost of $36,000, with an estimated life of 10 years. The price level at that time was 90% of the 1994 price level.
[4] The LIFO method of inventory valuation is used. The original inventory was acquired in the same year the building was constructed and was maintained at a constant $4,000 until 1994. In 1994 a gradual buildup of the inventory was begun in anticipation of an increase in the volume of business.
[5] Klein considers the return on her investment as the dividend she actually receives. In 1994 and again in 1996, Strader paid cash dividends in the amount of $10,000.
[6] On July 1, 1995, there was a reverse stock split-up of the company's stock in the ratio of 1:10.

INSTRUCTIONS

[a] Compute the 1996 earnings per share of common stock in terms of 1994 dollars.
[b] Compute the percentage return on investment for 1994 and 1996 in terms of 1994 dollars.
(AICPA adapted)

26-49 Constant Dollar Adjustments Hulsey Company purchased a tract of land as an investment in 1993 for $100,000. Late that year the company decided to construct a shopping center on the site. Construction began in 1994 and was completed in 1996; one-third of the construction was completed each year. Hulsey originally estimated that the costs of the project would be $1,200,000 for materials, $750,000 for labor, $150,000 for variable overhead, and $600,000 for depreciation.

Actual costs (excluding depreciation) incurred for construction were as follows:

	1994	1995	1996
Materials	$418,950	$434,560	$462,000
Labor	236,250	274,400	282,000
Variable overhead	47,250	54,208	61,200

Shortly after construction began, Hulsey sold the shopping center for $3,000,000, with payment to be made in full on completion in December 1996. One hundred and fifty thousand dollars of the sales price was allocated for the land.

The transaction was completed as scheduled and now a controversy has developed between the two major stockholders of the company. One thinks that the company should have invested in land, because a high rate of return was earned on the land. The other believes that the original decision was sound and that unanticipated changes in the price level affected the original cost estimates.

You were engaged to furnish guidance to these stockholders in resolving their controversy. As an aid, you obtained the following information:

[1] Using 1993 as the base-year, price-level indexes for relevant years are as follows:

1990	90
1991	93
1992	96
1993	100
1994	105
1995	112
1996	120

[2] The company allocated $200,000 per year for depreciation of fixed assets allocated to this construction project. Of that amount, $25,000 was for a building purchased in 1990 and $175,000 was for equipment purchased in 1992.

INSTRUCTIONS

[a] Prepare a schedule to restate in base-year (1993) costs the actual costs, including depreciation, incurred each year. Disregard income taxes and assume that each price-level index was valid for the entire year.

[b] Prepare a schedule comparing the originally estimated costs of the project with the total actual costs for each element of cost (materials, labor, variable overhead, and depreciation) adjusted to the 1993 price level.

[c] Prepare a schedule to restate the amount received on the sale in terms of base-year (1993) purchasing power. The gain or loss should be determined separately for the land and the building in terms of base-year purchasing power and should exclude depreciation.   (AICPA adapted)

CASES

26–50 Constant Dollar Financial Statements   *Two independent parts follow.*

Part 1.   Constant dollar financial statements are prepared in an effort to eliminate the effects of inflation or deflation. An integral part of determining restated amounts and applicable gain or loss from restatement is the segregation of all assets and liabilities into monetary and nonmonetary classifications. One reason for this classification is that purchasing power gains and losses for monetary items are currently matched against earnings.

INSTRUCTIONS

What factors determine whether an asset or a liability is classified as monetary or nonmonetary? Include in your response the justification for recognizing gains and losses from monetary items, *not* for nonmonetary items.

Part 2.   Proponents of price-level restatement maintain that a basic weakness of financial statements not adjusted for price-level changes is that they are made up of "mixed dollars."

INSTRUCTIONS

[a] Define *mixed dollars* and explain why is this a weakness of unadjusted financial statements.

[b] Explain how financial statements restated for price-level changes eliminate this weakness. Use property, plant, and equipment as your example in this discussion.   (AICPA adapted)

26–51 Constant Dollar Financial Statements   Published financial statements of U.S. companies are currently prepared on a stable dollar assumption, even though the general purchasing power of the dollar has declined considerably because of inflation in recent years. To account for this changing value of the dollar, many accountants suggest that financial statements should be adjusted for general price-level changes. Three *independent* statements about general price-level adjusted financial statements follow. Each statement contains some fallacious reasoning.

Statement 1.   The accounting profession has not seriously considered price-level-adjusted financial statements before because the rate of inflation usually has been so low from year to year that the adjustments would have been immaterial in amount. Price-level-adjusted financial statements represent a departure from historical cost accounting. Financial statements should be prepared from facts, not estimates.

Statement 2.   If financial statements were adjusted for general price-level changes, depreciation charges in the earnings statement would permit the recovery of dollars of current purchasing power and thereby equal the cost of new assets to replace the old ones. General price-level-adjusted data would yield statement of financial position amounts closely approximating current values. Furthermore, management can make better decisions if general price-level-adjusted financial statements are published.

Statement 3.   When adjusting financial data for general price-level changes, a distinction must be made between monetary and nonmonetary assets and liabilities, which, under historical cost accounting, have been identified as "current" and "noncurrent." When using historical cost accounting, no purchasing power gain or loss is recognized in the accounting process, but when financial statements are adjusted for general price-level changes, a purchasing power gain or loss will be recognized on monetary and nonmonetary items.

INSTRUCTIONS

Evaluate each of the independent statements. Identify the areas of fallacious reasoning in each, and explain why the reasoning is incorrect. Complete your discussion of each statement before proceeding to the next statement.   (AICPA adapted)

26–52 Constant Dollar and Current Value Statements   Kimball Corporation, a manufacturer with large investments in plant and equipment, began operations in 1953. The company's history has been one of expansion in sales, production, and physical facilities. Recently, some concern has been expressed that the conventional financial statements do not provide sufficient information for decisions by investors. After consideration of proposals for various types of supplementary financial statements to be included in the 1996 annual report, management has decided to present a balance sheet as of December 31, 1996, and a statement of income and retained earnings for 1996, both restated for changes in the general price level.

INSTRUCTIONS

[a] On what basis can it be contended that Kimball's conventional statements should be restated for changes in the general price level?
[b] Distinguish between financial statements restated for general price-level changes and current value financial statements.
[c] Distinguish between monetary and nonmonetary assets and liabilities as the terms are used in general price-level accounting. Give examples of each.
[d] Outline the procedures that Kimball should follow in preparing the proposed restatements.
[e] Indicate the major similarities and differences between the proposed supplementary statements and the corresponding conventional statements.
[f] Assuming that in the future Kimball will want to present comparative supplementary statements, can the 1996 supplementary statements be presented in 1997 without adjustment? Explain.
                                                                    (AICPA adapted)

26–53 Four Bases of Accounting   This case consists of two *independent* parts.

Part 1.   Advocates of current value accounting propose several methods for determining the valuation of assets to approximate current values. Two of the methods proposed are replacement cost and present value of future cash flows.

INSTRUCTIONS

Describe each method cited above and discuss the pros and cons of the various procedures used to arrive at the valuation of each method.

Part 2.   The financial statements of a business entity could be prepared on the basis of historical cost or current value. In addition, the basis could be stated in terms of unadjusted dollars or dollars restated for changes in purchasing power. The variations of these two distinct areas are shown in the following matrix:

	Unadjusted Dollars	Dollars Restated for Changes in Purchasing Power
Historical cost	1	2
Current value	3	4

Cell 1 of the matrix represents the traditional method of accounting for transactions; the absolute (unadjusted) amount of dollars given up or received is recorded for the asset or liability obtained **(relationship between resources).** Amounts recorded in the method represented by Cell 1 reflect the original cost of the asset or liability and do not give effect to any change in value of the unit of measure **(standard of comparison).** This method assumes the validity of the accounting concepts of going concern and stable monetary unit. Any gain or loss (including holding and purchasing power gains or losses) resulting from the sale or satisfaction of amounts recorded under this method is deferred in its entirety until sale or satisfaction.

INSTRUCTIONS

For each of the remaining cells (2, 3, and 4), respond to the following questions. *Limit your discussion to nonmonetary assets only.* Complete your discussion of *each cell* before proceeding to the next one.

[a] How will this method of recording assets affect the relationship between resources and the standard of comparison?

[b] What is the theoretical justification for using this method?

[c] How will this method of asset valuation affect the recognition of gain or loss during the life of the asset and ultimately from the sale or abandonment of the asset? Your response should include a discussion of the timing and magnitude of the gain or loss and conceptual reasons for any difference from the gain or loss computed using the traditional method.   (AICPA adapted)

JUDGMENT CASE

26–54 Fair Value in Financial Statements   As the controller of a highly successful real estate holding company, you are now preparing the financial information needed by the company's bank to facilitate a large loan that would allow the company to acquire additional property and refinance certain current holdings. The bank loan officer has requested that the financial statements of the company measure the real estate holdings at fair value (that is, the amount the assets could be sold for in an orderly liquidation). In this case, fair value clearly exceeds historical cost less accumulated depreciation. Your boss, the president of the company, also wants the real estate valued at its fair value to "better communicate the realities and strength of our financial position" and to "avoid presenting old and stale numbers that have no validity or usefulness today to anyone who might use our financial reports."

You wonder whether it would be acceptable to measure the real estate of the company at fair value. It seems that everyone that wishes to use the financial statements wants the real estate measured at its fair value rather than its historical cost.

INSTRUCTIONS

Would it be acceptable to measure the real estate at its fair value in the company's financial statements prepared in conformity with GAAP? If your answer is yes, explain why. If it is no, explain the financial reporting alternatives that are available to the company.

FINANCIAL REPORTING CASE

26–55 Financial Reporting Case   Publicly held companies frequently include a section in their annual reports in which management offers a discussion and analysis of the financial statements and notes to those statements. One of the subjects that is often discussed is the impact of changing prices on the company's activities.

Following are excerpts from management's discussion of this type from the 1993 annual reports of three major U.S. corporations:

AMR Corporation (American Airlines)

Inflation   Adjustment of historical cost data to reflect the impact of general inflation and specific price changes would lower AMR's operating results, principally because of the increased depreciation and amortization resulting from the replacement, at current cost, of equipment and property with assets that have the same service potential. However, because AMR's monetary liabilities exceed monetary assets, the reduced operating results would be partially offset by the gain from the decline in purchasing power of the net amounts owed.

The Coca-Cola Company

Impact of Inflation and Changing Prices   Inflation is a factor in many markets around the world and consequently impacts the way the Company operates. In general, management believes the Company is able to increase prices to counteract the effects of increasing costs and generate sufficient cash flows to maintain its productive capability.

Sunoco

Inflation Accounting   In recent years, the rate of inflation has declined to a more modest rate; however, continued inflation over a period of years distorts conventional measures of financial performance and condition. Financial statements report historical costs and do not reflect subsequent price changes in the general purchasing power of the dollar or the price changes of specific assets.

Sun's results of operations adjusted for inflation would be significantly less than historical cost results of operations due to the higher inflation-adjusted depreciation, depletion and amortization resulting from the inflation-adjusted amount of properties, plants and equipment exceeding the historical amount.

Inflation also affects monetary assets, such as cash and receivables, since these assets will purchase fewer goods and services in time. Conversely, debtors benefit during periods of higher-than-expected inflation because less purchasing power will be required to satisfy their obligations. Since Sun's monetary liabilities are greater than its monetary assets, there are unrealized purchasing power gains.

INSTRUCTIONS

For each company:

[a] Identify the primary conclusion(s) reached by management concerning the impact of inflation on the company's financial position and results of operations.

[b] Write a brief paragraph that indicates how this information is useful to you in interpreting the company's financial statements.

Appendix A

Kellogg Company
1993 Annual Report

Financial Highlights

(dollar amounts in millions, except per share data)	1993	Change	1992	Change	1991	Change
Net sales	$6,295.4	+ 2%	$6,190.6	+ 7%	$5,786.6	+12%
Earnings before cumulative effect of accounting change*	680.7	—	682.8	+13%	606.0	+21%
Net earnings	680.7	+58%	431.2	−29%	606.0	+21%
Earnings per share before cumulative effect of accounting change*	2.94	+ 3%	2.86	+14%	2.51	+21%
Net earnings per share	2.94	+62%	1.81	−28%	2.51	+21%
Dividends per share	1.32	+10%	1.20	+12%	1.075	+12%
Cash provided by operations	800.2	+ 8%	741.9	−21%	934.4	+14%
Capital expenditures	449.7	− 5%	473.6	+42%	333.5	+ 4%
Return on average equity before cumulative effect of accounting change*	37%		31%		30%	
Debt to total capital	35%		21%		18%	
Average shares (millions) outstanding	231.5		238.9		241.2	

*See Note 9 within Notes to Consolidated Financial Statements.

10-Year Growth in Earnings per Share

(before accounting change)

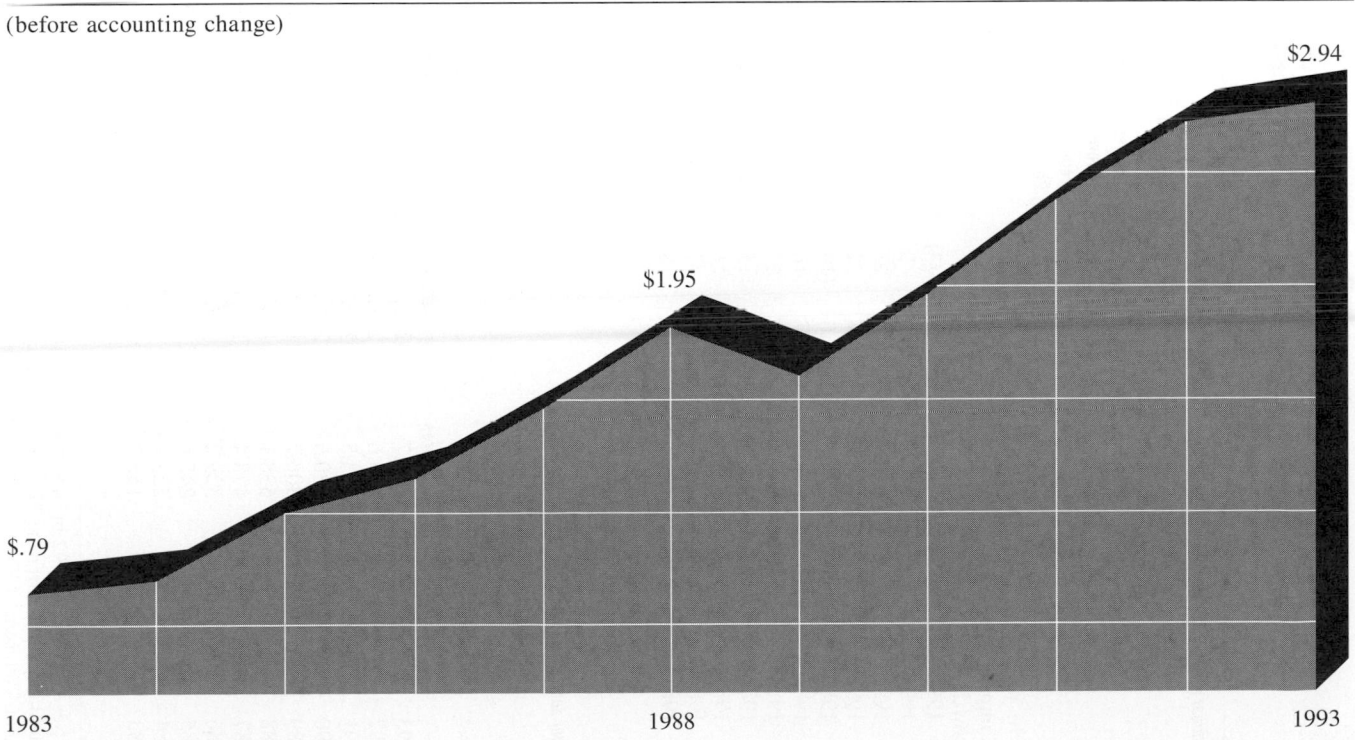

$.79 $1.95 $2.94

1983   1988   1993

Selected Financial Data

(dollar amounts in millions, except per share data)

Summary of Operations

	Net Sales	% Growth	Pretax Earnings	% Growth	Earnings Before Accounting Change	% Growth	(a) Net Earnings	% Growth	Per Common Share Data — Earnings Before Accounting Change	(a) Net Earnings	Cash Dividends	Book Value	Average Shares Outstanding (millions)	Shareholders' Equity
10-Year Compound Growth Rate	10%		9%		11%		11%		14%	14%	13%			
1993	$6,295.4	2	$1,034.1	(3)	$680.7	—	$680.7	58	$2.94	$2.94	$1.32	$7.52	231.5	$1,713.4
1992	6,190.6	7	1,070.4	9	682.8	13	431.2	(29)	2.86	1.81	1.20	8.20	238.9	1,945.2
1991	5,786.6	12	984.2	21	606.0	21	606.0	21	2.51	2.51	1.075	8.98	241.2	2,159.8
1990	5,181.4	11	814.7	22	502.8	19	502.8	7	2.08	2.08	.96	7.88	241.6	1,901.8
1989	4,651.7	7	667.0	(14)	422.1	(12)	470.2	(2)	1.73	1.93	.86	6.70	244.2	1,634.4
1988	4,348.8	15	774.7	16	480.4	21	480.4	21	1.95	1.95	.76	6.03	246.4	1,483.2
1987	3,793.0	14	665.7	13	395.9	24	395.9	24	1.60	1.60	.64	4.91	247.4	1,211.4
1986	3,340.7	14	586.6	11	318.9	13	318.9	13	1.29	1.29	.51	3.63	247.0	898.4
1985	2,930.1	13	527.4	11	281.1	12	281.1	12	1.14	1.14	.45	2.77	246.6	683.0
1984	2,602.4	9	476.1	7	250.5	3	250.5	3	.84	.84	.42	1.98	298.8	487.2
1983	2,381.1	1	444.0	8	242.7	7	242.7	7	.79	.79	.40	3.20	305.8	977.9

Other Information and Financial Ratios

	Property, Net	Capital Expenditures	Depreciation	Total Assets	Number of Employees	Current Ratio	Pretax Interest Coverage (times)	Return on Average Equity	Debt to Total Capital	Cash Provided by Operations	Long-term Debt
1993	$2,768.4	$449.7	$265.2	$4,237.1	16,151	1.0	27	37%	35%	$800.2	$521.6
1992	2,662.7	473.6	231.5	4,015.0	16,551	1.2	33	21%	21%	741.9	314.9
1991	2,646.5	333.5	222.8	3,925.8	17,017	.9	17	30%	18%	934.4	15.2
1990	2,595.4	320.5	200.2	3,749.4	17,239	.9	11	28%	26%	819.2	295.6
1989	2,406.3	508.7	167.6	3,390.4	17,268	.9	10	30%	34%	533.5	371.4
1988	2,131.9	538.1	139.7	3,297.9	17,461	.9	13	36%	32%	492.3	272.1
1987	1,738.8	478.4	113.1	2,680.9	17,762	.9	14	38%	27%	523.5	290.4
1986	1,281.1	329.2	92.7	2,084.2	17,383	1.1	13	40%	31%	542.7	264.1
1985	1,035.9	245.6	75.4	1,726.1	17,082	1.4	11	48%	38%	449.7	392.6
1984	856.0	228.9	63.9	1,667.1	17,239	1.1	26	27%	59%	331.5	364.1
1983	743.2	156.7	62.8	1,467.2	18,293	1.8	64	26%	4%	347.1	18.6

(a) Net earnings for 1992 include a $251.6 million charge ($1.05 per share) resulting from the adoption of Statement of Financial Accounting Standards 106, "Employers' Accounting for Postretirement Benefits Other Than Pensions," as of January 1, 1992. Net earnings for 1989 include a $48.1 million gain ($.20 per share) resulting from the adoption of Statement of Financial Accounting Standards 96, "Accounting for Income Taxes," as of January 1, 1989.

Management's Discussion and Analysis

STRATEGIC AND FINANCIAL OBJECTIVES

Management's primary objective is to increase shareholder value over time. To achieve this objective, the Company has implemented a long-term business strategy which focuses on continuing aggressive investment in new cereal markets, increasing returns on existing investments, maximizing cash flows, and minimizing the cost of capital through appropriate financial policies. The success of this strategy is reflected in the Company's superior earnings, return on equity, total return to shareholders, and its overall strong financial condition.

GLOBAL MARKETPLACE

Because of its strong global market share leadership, the Company is uniquely positioned to benefit from the continued increase in cereal consumption around the world. As of December 31, 1993, our market share was 43% globally, 38% in North America, 47% in Asia-Pacific, 50% in Europe, and 78% in Latin America. This favorable positioning in existing markets is accompanied by leadership in entering new markets with substantial long-term potential. Kellogg opened a new cereal plant in Latvia in 1993 and has plants scheduled to begin production in India in 1994 and in China in 1995. We plan to make our products available to a billion new consumers by early in the next century, more than doubling our present reach.

Lifestyle and demographic changes in major markets around the world favor a continued increase in consumption of ready-to-eat cereal, our core product line. Two particularly important trends are ever-increasing recognition by consumers around the world of the nutritional value of cereal and the accelerating move of the "baby boom" generation from young adulthood, where cereal consumption is relatively low, to middle age, where cereal consumption grows steadily. The Company believes it has developed the worldwide infrastructure and financial resources needed to continue its leadership of category growth.

RESULTS OF OPERATIONS

1993 Compared to 1992

Revenues Kellogg revenues are obtained primarily from the sale of ready-to-eat cereals in more than 150 countries. Kellogg has been marketing cereals since 1906 and is the global market share leader by nearly a three-to-one advantage. Increased revenues are obtained by reaching consumers in both new and developed markets with products that are both nutritious and superior in quality. The introduction of new products is vital to the Company's long-term financial strength. For 1993, the Company introduced 24 new products worldwide.

Despite intense competition, continued recessions in several major markets, and unfavorable currency movements, worldwide revenues increased by 2% for 1993, marking the 49th consecutive annual increase. The increase was achieved through higher selling prices and a 2% increase in cereal volume, being negatively impacted by foreign currency movements. Forty percent of all revenues are derived from outside the United States and are subject to foreign currency fluctuations. Excluding the negative effects of currency movements, 1993 sales would have increased 6%. During 1993, sales within the United States rose by 6% from increased selling prices and volume for both cereal and convenience foods.

1993 European sales, which were significantly affected by unfavorable foreign currency fluctuations, were down 8%. If the effects of foreign currency are excluded, European sales would have risen 4%. Sales for other areas grew by 2% from increased volume and higher selling prices, being partially offset by the negative impact of currency fluctuations. Excluding the effects of negative currency movements, other area sales would have increased 6%.

Other revenue for 1993 includes a total pretax gain of $65.9 million ($.20 per share) from the sale of the Company's British carton-container division ($.10 per share) and its Argentine snack food business ($.10 per share). In recent years the Company has divested units that do not fit with its long-term strategic plan. Other deductions for 1993 includes pre-tax charges of $64.3 million ($.18 per share) from the write-down of certain assets in Europe and North America.

Expenses and Profit Margins Cost of goods sold as a percent of sales was 47% for the year, the lowest in the last decade. Higher selling prices, increased volume, and worldwide productivity gains in factory operations are among the factors that contributed to this lower ratio.

Intense global competition requires heavy investment in value-added marketing. Selling and administrative expense represented 36% of each sales dollar in 1993. The Company is committed to building strong, long-term brand franchises through effective advertising.

Gross interest expense, prior to amounts capitalized, increased to $40.4 million for 1993, compared to $33.6 million for 1992. Higher debt levels caused the increase. The Company expects average borrowing levels and related interest expense to be slightly higher during 1994.

The Company's effective tax rate was 34.2% for the year, compared to 36.2% for 1992. The tax rate declined for a number of reasons. Decreased statutory rates in countries such as Germany, Australia, Canada, and South Africa more than offset the United States tax rate increase of 1993. The Company's 1994 effective tax rate is expected to be approximately 38%.

For 1993, earnings per share were $2.94 and earnings were $680.7 million, compared to 1992's earnings per share of $1.81 and earnings of $431.2 million. Excluding all one-time events for both years, earnings per share were $2.92, up 6% over $2.75 in 1992; and net earnings were $675.5 million, up 3%. Without the negative impact of foreign currency fluctuations, earnings per share would have been up 10% and net earnings up 6%.

Geographically, earnings before the cumulative effect of an accounting change were lower by 1% for the United States and by 1% for Europe, and up 7% for other areas. Excluding all one-time events for both years, the United States would have been up 7%, Europe down 9%, and other areas up 2%. Without the negative impact of foreign currency movements, Europe would have been up 4% rather than down 9%.

Statement of Financial Accounting Standards 112, "Employers' Accounting for Postemployment Benefits," was issued in November 1992. This statement had no material effect on the Company's financial condition or results of operations.

1992 Compared to 1991

Worldwide revenues for 1992 increased 7% to $6.2 billion on the strength of a 5% gain in cereal volume and higher selling prices. During January 1992, the Company sold Fearn International Inc., a U.S. food-service subsidiary. Excluding 1991 sales by Fearn, 1992 sales would have increased by 9% instead of 7%. Foreign currency fluctuations had a minimal impact on 1992 worldwide revenues.

Sales within the United States increased by 5%; however, excluding Fearn sales from 1991, the increase was 8%. This increase resulted from increased volume coupled with higher selling prices. European sales were up a solid 14% for the year due to a volume gain of 6% coupled with higher selling prices and the positive impact of foreign currency fluctuations. Sales for other areas grew by 6% from improved volume and selling prices, partially offset by negative foreign currency movements.

Other revenue includes a total pre-tax gain of $58.5 million ($.16 per share) from the sale of Fearn International Inc. Other deductions includes a pre-tax charge of $22.4 million ($.05 per share) from the disposition of convenience foods operations in Canada and other North America assets.

Cost of goods sold as a percent of sales was 48%, compared to 49% in 1991. Factors such as improved volume, positive inventory management, and improved factory productivity contributed to the decline. Selling and administrative expense represented 35% of each sales dollar in 1992, compared to 33% in 1991.

Gross interest expense, prior to amounts capitalized, decreased to $33.6 million, compared to $60.7 million in 1991. Lower interest rates and debt levels led to the decline. The Company's effective tax rate was 36.2%, compared to 38.4% for 1991. The decline in the rate resulted from lower effective tax rates in certain international locations.

For 1992, earnings per share were $1.81 and earnings were $431.2 million, compared to earnings per share of $2.51 and earnings of $606 million in 1991. Excluding all one-time events and the accounting change, earnings per share were $2.75, up 10%, and earnings were $657.1 million, up 8%.

Effective January 1, 1992, the Company adopted Statement of Financial Accounting Standards (FAS) 106, "Employers' Accounting for Postretirement Benefits Other Than Pensions." This standard requires that the estimated cost of postretirement benefits, principally health care, be accrued over the period earned rather than expensed as incurred. The transition effect of adopting FAS 106 on the immediate recognition basis, as of January 1, 1992, resulted in an after-tax charge of $251.6 million or $1.05 per share.

Geographically, earnings before the cumulative effect of the accounting change were up 18% for the United States, up 9% for Europe, and down 6% for other areas. Excluding the sale of Fearn and the one-time asset writeoffs, United States earnings would have been up 9% and other areas up 5%.

LIQUIDITY AND CAPITAL RESOURCES

The financial condition of the Company remained strong during 1993. Company operations have historically provided a strong, positive cash flow which, along with the program of issuing commercial paper and maintaining worldwide credit facilities, provides adequate liquidity to meet the Company's operational needs. Cash and cash equivalents totaled $98 million at December 31, 1993, compared to $126 million at December 31, 1992.

Cash provided by operating activities amounted to $800 million in 1993, compared to $742 million in 1992 and $934 million in 1991. The Company's current ratio (current assets over current liabilities) was 1.0:1.0 for 1993 and 1.2:1.0 for 1992.

The Company maintains credit facilities with banking institutions in the United States and other countries where it conducts business. At year-end, the Company had $613 million of short-term lines of credit, of which $569 million were available.

Funds expended for capital improvements in 1993 totaled $450 million, compared to $474 million in 1992 and $333 million in 1991. In 1994, capital expenditures are expected to be approximately $400 million as the Company continues to invest globally in expansion and modernization of its facilities. The capital program remains focused on producing the highest quality product at the lowest possible cost.

The Company's debt to total capital ratio was 35% at December 31, 1993, compared to 21% in 1992. The Company's increased share repurchase program led to higher debt levels resulting in the higher ratio. The Company continues to enjoy the highest available debt ratings on both its commercial paper and long-term debt.

At December 31, 1993, the Company had on file a "shelf registration" of $200 million with the Securities and Exchange Commission to provide for the issuance of debt in the United States. The net proceeds from any offering under the "shelf" would be added to the Company's working capital and be available for general corporate purposes.

In October of 1993, the Company issued $265 million Canadian Eurodollar 5-year Notes with a 6.25% interest rate. During 1992, $300 million 5-year notes were issued with a 5.9% interest rate. The first two years of both notes were swapped into variable rate debt. In March 1992, the Company's $200 million 9.5% Eurodollar Notes matured.

Notes payable are comprised principally of floating interest rate obligations that had an average interest rate of 4% in 1993, compared to 6% during 1992.

Dividends paid per share of common stock rose 10% in 1993, marking the 37th consecutive year of increase. The trend of increased dividends is expected to continue in 1994.

During 1993, the Company purchased 9,487,508 shares of its common stock at an average cost of $58 per share. In 1992, a total of 3,497,000 shares were purchased at an average cost of $63 per share. Treasury stock purchases were made under plans authorized by the Company's Board of Directors. At December 31, 1993, an additional $353 million of stock could be purchased through December 1994 under current Board authorization.

LOOKING FORWARD

Management is not aware of any adverse trends that would materially affect the Company's strong financial position. Should suitable investment opportunities or working capital needs arise that would require additional financing, management believes that the Company's triple A credit rating, strong balance sheet, and history of exceptional earnings provides a solid base for obtaining additional financial resources at competitive rates and terms.

Kellogg is a global market leader backed with a solid financial infrastructure that provides a competitive advantage. The Company is committed to long-term earnings per share growth with above average return on equity.

Kellogg Company and Subsidiaries
Consolidated Earnings and Retained Earnings
Year ended December 31

(in millions, except per share amounts)	1993	1992	1991
Net sales	**$6,295.4**	$6,190.6	$5,786.6
Other revenue (deductions), net	**(1.5)**	36.8	14.6
	6,293.9	6,227.4	5,801.2
Cost of goods sold	**2,989.0**	2,987.7	2,828.7
Selling and administrative expense	**2,237.5**	2,140.1	1,930.0
Interest expense	**33.3**	29.2	58.3
	5,259.8	5,157.0	4,817.0
Earnings before income taxes and cumulative effect of accounting change	**1,034.1**	1,070.4	984.2
Income taxes	**353.4**	387.6	378.2
Earnings before cumulative effect of accounting change	**680.7**	682.8	606.0
Cumulative effect of change in method of accounting for postretirement benefits other than pensions—$1.05 a share (net of income tax benefit of $144.6)		(251.6)	
Net earnings—$2.94, $1.81, $2.51 a share	**680.7**	431.2	606.0
Retained earnings, beginning of year	**3,033.9**	2,889.1	2,542.4
Dividends paid—$1.32, $1.20, $1.075 a share	**(305.2)**	(286.4)	(259.3)
Retained earnings, end of year	**$3,409.4**	$3,033.9	$2,889.1

See notes to consolidated financial statements.

Kellogg Company and Subsidiaries
Consolidated Balance Sheet
At December 31

(in millions)	1993	1992
Current assets		
Cash and temporary investments	$ 98.1	$ 126.3
Accounts receivable, less allowances of $6.0 and $6.2	536.8	519.1
Inventories:		
Raw materials and supplies	148.5	167.7
Finished goods and materials in process	254.6	248.7
Deferred income taxes	85.5	66.2
Prepaid expenses	121.6	108.6
Total current assets	1,245.1	1,236.6
Property		
Land	40.6	40.5
Buildings	1,065.7	1,021.2
Machinery and equipment	2,857.6	2,629.4
Construction in progress	308.6	302.6
Accumulated depreciation	(1,504.1)	(1,331.0)
Property, net	2,768.4	2,662.7
Intangible assets	59.1	53.3
Other assets	164.5	62.4
Total assets	$ 4,237.1	$ 4,015.0
Current liabilities		
Current maturities of long-term debt	$ 1.5	$ 1.9
Notes payable	386.7	210.0
Accounts payable	308.8	313.8
Accrued liabilities:		
Income taxes	65.9	104.1
Salaries and wages	76.5	78.0
Advertising and promotion	233.8	228.0
Other	141.4	135.2
Total current liabilities	1,214.6	1,071.0
Long-term debt	521.6	314.9
Nonpension postretirement benefits	450.9	407.6
Deferred income taxes	188.9	184.6
Other liabilities	147.7	91.7
Shareholders' equity		
Common stock, $.25 par value		
Authorized: 330,000,000 shares		
Issued: 310,292,753 shares in 1993 and 310,193,228 in 1992	77.6	77.5
Capital in excess of par value	72.0	69.2
Retained earnings	3,409.4	3,033.9
Treasury stock, at cost: 82,372,409 and 72,874,738 shares	(1,653.1)	(1,105.0)
Minimum pension liability adjustment	(25.3)	
Currency translation adjustment	(167.2)	(130.4)
Total shareholders' equity	1,713.4	1,945.2
Total liabilities and shareholders' equity	$ 4,237.1	$ 4,015.0

See notes to consolidated financial statements.

Kellogg Company and Subsidiaries
Consolidated Statement of Cash Flows
Year ended December 31

(in millions)	1993	1992	1991
Operating activities			
Net earnings	$ 680.7	$ 431.2	$ 606.0
Items in net earnings not requiring (providing) cash:			
Cumulative effect of accounting change		251.6	
Depreciation	265.2	231.5	222.8
Pre-tax gain on sale of subsidiaries	(65.9)	(58.5)	
Deferred income taxes	8.7	9.7	(5.4)
Other	(19.1)	25.1	16.8
Change in operating assets and liabilities:			
Accounts receivable	(17.7)	(99.1)	10.2
Inventories	13.3	(15.3)	(41.4)
Prepaid expenses	(32.3)	(.9)	(22.9)
Accounts payable	(5.0)	24.0	42.7
Accrued liabilities	(27.7)	(57.4)	105.6
Net cash provided from operating activities	800.2	741.9	934.4
Investing activities			
Additions to properties	(449.7)	(473.6)	(333.5)
Proceeds from sale of subsidiaries	95.6	115.0	
Property disposals	19.0	18.8	25.2
Other	(25.1)	(10.6)	(11.6)
Net cash used in investing activities	(360.2)	(350.4)	(319.9)
Financing activities			
Borrowings of notes payable	468.2	192.3	182.1
Reduction of notes payable	(291.5)	(170.7)	(274.0)
Issuance of long-term debt	208.3	311.7	4.3
Reduction of long-term debt	(1.7)	(270.2)	(126.0)
Issuance of common stock	2.9	13.4	17.7
Purchase of treasury stock	(548.1)	(224.1)	(83.6)
Cash dividends	(305.2)	(286.4)	(259.3)
Other	2.9	11.4	1.1
Net cash used in financing activities	(464.2)	(422.6)	(537.7)
Effect of exchange rate changes on cash	(4.0)	(20.6)	.7
Increase (decrease) in cash and temporary investments	(28.2)	(51.7)	77.5
Cash and temporary investments at beginning of year	126.3	178.0	100.5
Cash and temporary investments at end of year	$ 98.1	$ 126.3	$ 178.0

See notes to consolidated financial statements.

KELLOGG COMPANY AND SUBSIDIARIES
NOTES TO CONSOLIDATED FINANCIAL STATEMENTS

Note 1 Accounting Policies

Consolidation
The consolidated financial statements include the accounts of Kellogg Company and its wholly owned subsidiaries. Intercompany balances and transactions are eliminated.

Certain amounts in the prior year financial statements have been reclassified to conform to the current year presentation.

Cash and temporary investments
Highly liquid temporary investments with original maturities of less than three months are considered to be cash equivalents. The carrying amount approximates fair value.

Inventories
Inventories are valued at the lower of cost (principally average) or market.

Property
Fixed assets are recorded at cost and depreciated over estimated useful lives using straight-line methods for financial reporting and accelerated methods for tax reporting. Interest cost capitalized as part of the construction cost of capital assets amounted to $7.1 million in 1993, $4.4 million in 1992, and $2.4 million in 1991.

Intangible assets
Intangible assets consist principally of the underfunded amount of certain pension plans.

Notes payable and long-term debt
The carrying amounts of the Company's notes payable, long-term debt, and other financial instruments approximate fair value. The fair values are based primarily on quoted market prices.

Net earnings per share
Net earnings per share is determined by dividing net earnings by the weighted average number of common shares outstanding. All per share amounts have been restated to reflect the two-for-one stock split, effective December 4, 1991.

Note 2 Leases

Operating leases generally are for equipment and warehouse space. Rent expense on all operating leases, which generally are renewable at the Company's option, amounted to $46.8 million in 1993, $42.4 million in 1992, and $39.3 million in 1991. There are no significant future minimum rental commitments under non-cancelable leases.

Note 3 Research and Development

Research and development costs charged to earnings approximated $39.8 million in 1993, $36.6 million in 1992, and $34.7 million in 1991.

Note 4 Divestitures and Other Nonrecurring Items

All gains from divestitures and nonrecurring charges are recorded in other revenue (deductions). None of the divestitures are significant to the Company's consolidated revenues and earnings.

During 1993, the Company recognized a pre-tax gain of $32.2 million ($.10 per share) from the sale of Cereal Packaging Ltd., a wholly owned subsidiary of Kellogg Company of Great Britain, Limited, and a pre-tax gain of $33.7 million ($.10 per share) from the sale of the Argentine snack food business. During 1992, the Company sold Fearn International Inc., a foodservice subsidiary, resulting in a pre-tax gain of $58.5 million ($.16 per share).

During 1993, the Company recognized pre-tax charges of $64.3 million ($.18 per share) from the write-down of certain assets in Europe and North America. For 1992, other deductions includes a pre-tax charge of $22.4 million ($.05 per share) from the disposition of convenience foods operations in Canada and other North America assets.

Note 5 Shareholders' Equity

On December 3, 1991, shareholders approved an increase in the authorized shares of common stock from 165 million to 330 million and approved a two-for-one stock split to shareholders of record on December 4, 1991. The stated par value per share of common stock was not changed from $.25. All share and per share amounts have been restated to retroactively reflect the stock split.

In 1993, the Company purchased 9,487,508 shares of its common stock at an average cost of $58; in 1992, purchased 3,497,000 shares at an average cost of $63; and in 1991, purchased 1,515,600 shares at an average cost of $52. All purchases are included in treasury stock. A summary of shareholders' equity is shown on page 1267.

Most effects of exchange rate changes are reflected as a currency translation adjustment in shareholders' equity. Exchange adjustments attributable to operations in highly inflationary economies are reflected in earnings along with those adjustments related to foreign currency transactions that affect cash flows.

Note 6 Debt

Notes payable consist of borrowings in the United States of $352.9 million at 3.2% at December 31, 1993, and $148.3 million at 3.4% at December 31, 1992, and bank loans of foreign subsidiaries at competitive market rates. The majority of the borrowings within the United States are commercial paper which has the highest debt rating available. The Company has credit agreements providing for borrowing an aggregate of approximately $613 million on an unsecured basis, $569 million of which was unused at December 31, 1993.

As of January 1, 1992, the Company had on file a "shelf registration" of $300 million of debt securities with the Securities and Exchange Commission. Under this registration statement, the Company issued $300 million of 5.9% notes in July 1992. In August 1993, the Company filed a $200 million "shelf registration" with the Securities and Exchange Commission which remains unused at December 31, 1993.

A summary of long-term debt follows.

Summary of Shareholders' Equity

(millions)	Common stock	Capital in excess of par value	Retained earnings	Treasury stock	(a) Minimum pension liability adjustment	Currency translation adjustment
Balance, January 1, 1991	$38.6	$ 81.2	$2,542.4	($ 797.3)		$ 36.9
Stock options exercised	.1	17.7				
Two-for-one stock split	38.7	(38.7)				
Net earnings			606.0			
Dividends			(259.3)			
Exchange adjustments						(22.9)
Treasury stock purchased				(83.6)		
Balance, December 31, 1991	77.4	60.2	2,889.1	(880.9)		14.0
Stock options exercised	.1	9.0				
Net earnings			431.2			
Dividends			(286.4)			
Exchange adjustments						(144.4)
Treasury stock purchased				(224.1)		
Balance, December 31, 1992	77.5	69.2	3,033.9	(1,105.0)		(130.4)
Stock options exercised	.1	2.8				
Net earnings			680.7			
Dividends			(305.2)			
Exchange adjustments						(36.8)
Minimum pension liability adjustment					($25.3)	
Treasury stock purchased				(548.1)		
Balance, December 31, 1993	**$77.6**	**$ 72.0**	**$3,409.4**	**($1,653.1)**	**($25.3)**	**($167.2)**

(a) Refer to Note 8 for explanation of the minimum pension liability adjustment.

(millions)	1993	1992
5.9% Five-Year Notes due 1997(a)	**$299.4**	$299.1
6.25% Five-Year Canadian Eurodollar Notes due 1998(a)	**200.0**	
Other	**23.7**	17.7
	523.1	316.8
Less current maturities	**(1.5)**	(1.9)
Balance, December 31	**$521.6**	$314.9

(a) The 6.25% Canadian Eurodollar Notes were issued in October 1993. The first two years of both five-year notes were swapped into variable rate debt, indexed to the London Interbank Offered Rate.

Principal payments are due as follows (in millions): 1995–$2; 1996–$2; 1997–$302; 1998–$207.

Interest paid, net of amounts capitalized, approximated interest expense in each of the three years ended December 31, 1993.

Note 7 Stock Options

In 1991, shareholders approved the adoption of the Key Employee Long-Term Incentive Plan. The plan provides for benefits to be awarded in the form of stock options, performance shares, performance units, incentive stock options, restricted stock awards, and other stock-based awards. Under this plan, options are granted at the fair market value of the Company's common stock at the time of grant. Such options are exercisable when granted and expire ten years from date of grant. The plan also contains a reload option feature. When Company stock is surrendered to pay for the exercise price of a stock option, the holder of the option is granted a new option for the number of shares surrendered. For all options reloaded, the expiration date is not changed, but the option price becomes the fair market value of the Company's stock on the date the new reload option is granted.

Options for 10,756,690 and 10,620,578 shares were available for grant at January 1, 1993, and December 31, 1993, respectively. A summary of transactions under the plan follows.

	Shares	Average price
Under option, January 1, 1992	1,526,972	$40.72
Granted	1,569,150	61.83
Exercised	1,181,640	48.12
Cancelled	5,100	25.99
Under option, December 31, 1992	1,909,382	$52.92
Granted	848,885	62.40
Exercised	293,494	45.46
Cancelled	30,186	59.10
Under option, December 31, 1993	**2,434,587**	**$56.95**

Note 8 Pension Benefits

The Company has a number of U.S. and worldwide pension plans to provide retirement benefits for its employees. Benefits for salaried employees are generally based on salary and years of service, while union employee benefits are generally a negotiated amount for each year of service. Plan funding strategies are influenced by tax regulations. Plan assets consist primarily of equity securities with smaller holdings of bonds, real estate, and other investments.

Pension expense includes the following components.

(millions)	1993	1992	1991
Service cost	$ 24.9	$ 23.7	$ 23.6
Interest cost	57.8	57.2	52.9
Actual (return) loss of plan assets	(76.3)	(22.8)	(88.0)
Net amortization and deferral	26.7	(27.3)	42.3
Pension expense–Company plans	33.1	30.8	30.8
Pension expense–multiemployer plans	3.1	1.5	1.6
Total pension expense	$ 36.2	$ 32.3	$ 32.4

The reconciliation of the funded status of the plans at year-end follows.

(millions)	Underfunded 1993	Underfunded 1992	Overfunded 1993	Overfunded 1992
Accumulated benefit obligation:				
Nonvested	$ 35.3	$ 23.8	$ 26.9	$ 18.1
Vested	288.8	229.3	322.3	266.8
Total	324.1	253.1	349.2	284.9
Projected salary increases	13.8	12.3	86.3	85.0
Projected benefit obligation	337.9	265.4	435.5	369.9
Plan assets at fair value	279.5	214.3	404.4	362.0
Assets (less) greater than projected benefit obligation	(58.4)	(51.1)	(31.1)	(7.9)
Unrecognized net (gain) loss	41.3	6.5	25.7	8.8
Unrecognized transition amount	19.3	22.0	(14.6)	(18.1)
Unrecognized prior service cost	46.3	30.7	21.3	21.7
Minimum liability adjustment	(96.0)	(50.8)		
Prepaid (accrued) pension	($ 47.5)	($ 42.7)	$ 1.3	$ 4.5

The 1993 projected benefit obligation was impacted by plan improvements that covered most U.S. employees.

All gains and losses are recognized over the average remaining service period of active employees.

The unfunded liability in excess of the unamortized prior service cost and the net transition obligation was recorded as a reduction in Shareholders' Equity of $25.3 million, net of tax, as of December 31, 1993. Intangible assets included $56.9 million as of December 31, 1993, and $50.8 million as of December 31, 1992, relating to the underfunded pension plans.

The weighted averages for all worldwide plans of the actuarially assumed discount rate, long-term rate of compensation increase, and long-term rate of return on plan assets were 7.9, 5.4, and 9.5 percent in 1993; 9.2, 6.7, and 9.6 percent in 1992; and 9.3, 6.8, and 9.7 percent in 1991, respectively.

The Company and certain of its subsidiaries sponsor 401K plans for some active employees. These costs are not significant.

Note 9 Nonpension Postretirement Benefits

Effective January 1, 1992, the Company adopted Statement of Financial Accounting Standards (FAS) 106, "Employers' Accounting for Postretirement Benefits Other Than Pensions." This standard requires that the estimated cost of postretirement

benefits, principally health care, be accrued over the period earned rather than expensed as incurred.

The transition effect of adopting FAS 106 on the immediate recognition basis, as of January 1, 1992, resulted in a charge of $251.6 million ($1.05 per share) to 1992 earnings, net of approximately $144.6 million of income tax benefit. The Company adopted FAS 106 on a worldwide basis; however, costs associated with subsidiaries outside of the United States are insignificant.

The Company's U.S. subsidiaries provide health care and certain other benefits to substantially all retired employees, their covered dependents, and beneficiaries. Generally, employees are eligible for these benefits when one of the following service/age requirements are met: 30 years and any age; 20 years and age 55; 5 years and age 62. Net periodic postretirement benefit cost includes the following components:

(millions)	1993	1992
Service cost	$12.1	$10.9
Interest cost	38.6	34.9
Net amortization and deferral	1.0	
Net periodic postretirement benefit cost	$51.7	$45.8

Actuarial assumptions used to determine the accumulated postretirement benefit obligation include a discount rate of 7.75% for 1993 and 9.0% for 1992. The assumed health care cost trend was 9.5% for 1993, decreasing gradually to 5.25% by the year 2003 and remaining at that level thereafter. These trend rates reflect the Company's prior experience and management's expectation that future rates will decline. Increasing the assumed health care cost trend rates by 1 percentage point in each year would increase the accumulated postretirement benefit obligation as of December 31, 1993, by $70.4 million and net periodic postretirement benefit cost for 1993 by $8.5 million. All gains and losses are recognized over the average remaining service period of active plan participants. The Company's postretirement health care plans currently are not funded.

The following table sets forth the plans' combined status with the amount included in the consolidated balance sheet at year-end.

(millions)	1993	1992
Accumulated benefit obligation:		
Retirees	$251.7	$211.2
Active plan participants	265.0	227.9
	516.7	439.1
Unrecognized experience loss	(47.2)	(14.3)
Unrecognized prior service cost	(.5)	
Accrued postretirement benefit cost	$469.0	$424.8

Note 10 Income Taxes

Effective January 1, 1992, the Company adopted FAS 109, "Accounting for Income Taxes." This standard requires the use of the asset and liability approach for financial accounting and reporting of income taxes. The Company previously accounted for income taxes in conformity with FAS 96. The effect of the accounting change was not material except for allowing recognition of the tax benefit associated with the cumulative effect of adopting FAS 106 (refer to Note 9). The following table summarizes the provision for U.S. federal, state, and foreign taxes on income.

(millions)	1993	1992	1991
Earnings before income taxes and cumulative effect of accounting change:			
United States	$ 703.3	$ 727.3	$626.0
Foreign	330.8	343.1	358.2
	$1,034.1	$1,070.4	$984.2
Income taxes:			
Currently payable:			
Federal	$ 233.0	$ 226.8	$191.0
State	38.0	27.8	26.8
Foreign	104.7	132.9	136.1
	375.7	387.5	353.9
Deferred:			
Federal	(19.4)	(4.2)	7.9
State	(2.2)	(1.0)	2.0
Foreign	(.7)	5.3	14.4
	(22.3)	.1	24.3
Total income taxes	$ 353.4	$ 387.6	$378.2

The difference between the U.S. federal statutory tax rate and the Company's effective rate is as follows.

(millions)	1993	1992	1991
U.S. statutory rate	35.0%	34.0%	34.0%
Foreign rates varying from 35%	(1.5)	1.2	1.9
State income taxes, net of federal benefit	2.2	1.7	1.9
Other	(1.5)	(.7)	.6
Effective income tax rate	34.2%	36.2%	38.4%

The deferred tax assets and deferred tax liabilities recorded on the balance sheet as of year-end are as follows.

(millions)	Deferred tax assets 1993	1992	Deferred tax liabilities 1993	1992
Current:				
Promotion and advertising	$ 53.4	$ 34.1		
Wages and payroll taxes	10.7	10.8		
Pension			$ 9.0	$ 10.7
Health and postretirement benefits	13.0			
State and property taxes	9.6	7.8	6.8	6.6
Other	17.8	26.8	4.8	4.4
	104.5	79.5	20.6	21.7
Noncurrent:				
Depreciation and asset disposals	12.1		304.5	302.9
Postretirement benefits	157.4	155.1	13.8	
Capitalized interest			27.1	26.9
State taxes	8.0	5.3		15.7
Other	6.2	7.6	13.1	7.1
	183.7	168.0	358.5	352.6
Total deferred taxes	$288.2	$247.5	$379.1	$374.3

At December 31, 1993, $1,145 million of foreign subsidiary earnings was considered permanently invested in those businesses. Accordingly, U.S. income taxes have not been provided for such earnings. If all these earnings were remitted, foreign withholding taxes would amount to $54 million.

Cash paid for income taxes was as follows (in millions): 1993—$425; 1992—$361; 1991—$334.

Note 11 Financial Instruments and Credit Risk Concentration

The Company enters into foreign exchange contracts to hedge against the adverse impacts of fluctuations of foreign currency-denominated receivables, payables, and other commitments. Foreign exchange contracts generally have maturities of six months or less and are entered into with major international financial institutions. The Company's risk in these transactions is the cost of replacing, at current market rates, these contracts in the event of default by the institutions. Management believes that the risk of such losses is remote. At December 31, 1993 and 1992, the notional amounts of open forward exchange contracts and other financial market instruments were $301 million and $168 million, respectively.

Financial instruments which potentially subject the Company to concentrations of credit risk are primarily cash and temporary investments and accounts receivable. The Company places its investments in highly rated financial institutions and investment grade short-term debt instruments, and limits the amount of credit exposure to any one entity. Concentrations of credit risk with respect to accounts receivable are limited due to the large number of customers, generally short payment terms, and their dispersion across geographic areas.

Note 12 Quarterly Financial Data (Unaudited)

(millions, except per share data)	Net sales 1993	1992	Gross profit 1993	1992
First	$1,518.4	$1,515.1	$ 793.4	$ 791.0
Second	1,541.6	1,584.0	785.7	838.9
Third	1,669.2	1,670.7	897.3	874.3
Fourth	1,566.2	1,420.8	830.0	698.7
	$6,295.4	$6,190.6	$3,306.4	$3,202.9

	Earnings before cumulative effect of accounting change 1993	1992	Earnings per share before cumulative effect of accounting change 1993	1992
First	$179.2	$191.6	$ .76	$ .80
Second	142.7	163.6	.62	.68
Third	209.3	199.7	.90	.84
Fourth	149.5	127.9	.66	.54
	$680.7	$682.8	$2.94	$2.86

	Net earnings 1993	1992	Earnings per share 1993	1992
First	$179.2	($60.0)	$ .76	($ .25)
Second	142.7	163.6	.62	.68
Third	209.3	199.7	.90	.84
Fourth	149.5	127.9	.66	.54
	$680.7	$431.2	$2.94	$1.81

As discussed in Note 9, the Company adopted FAS 106 in the first quarter of 1992.

Dividend payments for the year totaled $1.32 per share, up 10 percent from 1992, marking the 37th consecutive year of increase. The trend of increased dividends is expected to continue in 1994. The principal market for trading Kellogg shares is the New York Stock Exchange. The shares are also traded on the Boston, Cincinnati, Midwest, Pacific, and Philadelphia Stock Exchanges. The closing price (on the NYSE) on December 31, 1993, was $56¾. As of December 31, 1993, there were approximately 29,381 shareholders of record. Dividends paid and the quarterly price ranges on the New York Stock Exchange during the last two years are as follows.

1993 — Quarter	Dividend	High	Low
Fourth	$ .34	$61.88	$48.75
Third	.34	54.88	47.25
Second	.32	61.00	51.00
First	.32	67.88	59.38
	$1.32		
1992			
Fourth	$ .32	$75.38	$65.88
Third	.32	73.38	62.75
Second	.28	66.88	54.63
First	.28	67.00	54.38
	$1.20		

Note 13 Operating Segments

The Company operates in a single industry—manufacturing and marketing convenience food products throughout the world. Information presented below describes operations by geographic area. Included are the schedules of net sales and earnings before the cumulative effect of the accounting change for the years 1993, 1992, and 1991, and the related year-end identifiable assets, including corporate assets that are comprised principally of cash and temporary investments.

Net Sales (millions)	1993	% change	1992	% change	1991	% change
United States	**$3,783.9**	**+ 6**	$3,564.9	+ 5	$3,411.0	+ 12
% of total	**60%**		57%		59%	
Europe	**1,505.9**	**− 8**	1,643.6	+ 14	1,447.0	+ 9
% of total	**24%**		27%		25%	
Other areas	**1,005.6**	**+ 2**	982.1	+ 6	928.6	+ 14
% of total	**16%**		16%		16%	
Consolidated	**$6,295.4**	**+ 2**	$6,190.6	+ 7	$5,786.6	+ 12

Earnings before cumulative effect of accounting change (millions)	1993	% change	1992	% change	1991	% change
United States	**$452.2**	**− 1**	$458.4	+ 18	$388.3	+ 19
% of total	**66%**		67%		64%	
Europe	**139.8**	**− 1**	141.7	+ 9	130.1	+ 20
% of total	**21%**		21%		22%	
Other areas	**88.7**	**+ 7**	82.7	− 6	87.6	+ 26
% of total	**13%**		12%		14%	
Consolidated	**$680.7**	**—**	$682.8	+ 13	$606.0	+ 21

Identifiable assets (millions)	1993	% change	1992	% change	1991	% change
United States	$2,340.4	+ 13	$2,064.4	+ 11	$1,859.6	+ 1
% of total	55%		51%		47%	
Europe	1,022.6	− 5	1,076.6	+ 3	1,110.8	+ 1
% of total	24%		27%		28%	
Other areas	766.4	+ 4	738.4	− 4	767.4	+ 8
% of total	18%		18%		20%	
Corporate assets	107.7	− 21	135.6	− 28	188.0	+ 72
% of total	3%		4%		5%	
Consolidated	$4,237.1	+ 6	$4,015.0	+ 2	$3,925.8	+ 5

Report of Independent Accountants

Price Waterhouse

To the Shareholders and Board of Directors of Kellogg Company

In our opinion, the accompanying consolidated balance sheet and the related consolidated statements of earnings and retained earnings and of cash flows present fairly, in all material respects, the financial position of Kellogg Company and its subsidiaries at December 31, 1993 and 1992, and the results of their operations and their cash flows for each of the three years in the period ended December 31, 1993, in conformity with generally accepted accounting principles. These financial statements are the responsibility of the Company's management; our responsibility is to express an opinion on these financial statements based on our audits. We conducted our audits of these statements in accordance with generally accepted auditing standards which require that we plan and perform the audit to obtain reasonable assurance about whether the financial statements are free of material misstatement. An audit includes examining, on a test basis, evidence supporting the amounts and disclosures in the financial statements, assessing the accounting principles used and significant estimates made by management, and evaluating the overall financial statement presentation. We believe that our audits provide a reasonable basis for the opinion expressed above.

As discussed in Notes 9 and 10 to the financial statements, the Company changed its methods of accounting for postretirement benefits other than pensions and for income taxes during 1992.

Price Waterhouse

Battle Creek, Michigan
February 4, 1994

Appendix B

A Listing of Official Accounting Pronouncements of the AICPA and FASB

The major accounting pronouncements of the AICPA and FASB are listed below in the order in which they were issued. Many of these pronouncements have been amended partially or completely superseded. The purpose of providing this listing is to demonstrate the flow and frequency of authoritative accounting literature as well as the specific subjects considered by authoritative bodies during different periods of time. Services provided by the AICPA and FASB should be consulted concerning the current applicability of specific authoritative pronouncements.

Number	Title	Date Issued
Accounting Research Bulletins (ARBs), Accounting Procedures Committee, AICPA		
43	Restatement and Revision of Accounting Research Bulletin Nos. 1–42	June 1953
	Chapter	
	1 Prior Opinions	
	2 Form of Statements	
	3 Working Capital	
	4 Inventory Pricing	
	5 Intangible Assets	
	6 Contingency Reserves	
	7 Capital Accounts	
	8 Income and Earned Surplus	
	9 Depreciation	
	10 Taxes	
	11 Government Contracts	
	12 Foreign Operations and Foreign Exchange	
	13 Compensation	
	14 Disclosure of Long-Term Leases in Financial Statements of Leases	
	15 Unamortized Discount, Issue Cost, and Redemption Premium on Bonds Refunded	
44	Declining-Balance Depreciation (Revised July 1958)	October 1954
45	Long-Term Construction-Type Contracts	October 1955
46	Discontinuance of Dating Earned Surplus	February 1956
47	Accounting for Costs of Pension Plans	September 1956
48	Business Combinations	January 1957
49	Earnings per Share	April 1958
50	Contingencies	October 1958
51	Consolidated Financial Statements	August 1959
Accounting Terminology Bulletins, Committee on Terminology, AICPA		
No. 1	Review and Résumé (of eight original terminology bulletins)	August 1953
No. 2	Proceeds, Revenue, Income, Profit, and Earnings	March 1955
No. 3	Book Value	August 1956
No. 4	Cost, Expense, and Loss	July 1957
Accounting Principles Board (APB) Statements, AICPA		
No. 1	Statement by the Accounting Principles Board	April 1962
No. 2	Disclosure of Supplemental Financial Information by Diversified Companies	September 1967
No. 3	Financial Statements Restated for General Price-Level Changes	June 1969
No. 4	Basic Concepts and Accounting Principles Underlying Financial Statements of Business Enterprises	October 1970
Accounting Principles Board (APB) Opinions, AICPA		
No. 1	New Depreciation Guidelines and Rules	November 1962
No. 2	Accounting for the "Investment Credit"	December 1962
No. 3	The Statement of Source and Application of Funds	October 1963
No. 4	Accounting for the "Investment Credit" (Amending No. 2)	March 1964

Number	Title	Date Issued
No. 5	Reporting of Leases in Financial Statements of Lessee	September 1964
No. 6	Status of Accounting Research Bulletins	October 1965
No. 7	Accounting for Leases in Financial Statements of Lessors	May 1966
No. 8	Accounting for the Cost of Pension Plans	November 1966
No. 9	Reporting the Results of Operations	December 1966
No. 10	Omnibus Opinion—1966	December 1966
No. 11	Accounting for Income Taxes	December 1967
No. 12	Omnibus Opinion—1967	December 1967
No. 13	Amending Paragraph 6 of the *APB Opinion No. 9,* Application to Commercial Banks	March 1969
No. 14	Accounting for Convertible Debt and Debt Issued with Stock Purchase Warrants	March 1969
No. 15	Earnings per Share	May 1969
No. 16	Business Combinations	August 1970
No. 17	Intangible Assets	August 1970
No. 18	The Equity Method of Accounting for Investments in Common Stock	March 1971
No. 19	Reporting Changes in Financial Position	March 1971
No. 20	Accounting Changes	July 1971
No. 21	Interest on Receivables and Payables	August 1971
No. 22	Disclosure of Accounting Policies	April 1972
No. 23	Accounting for Income Taxes—Special Areas	April 1972
No. 24	Accounting for Income Taxes—Investments in Common Stock Accounted for by the Equity Method	April 1972
No. 25	Accounting for Stock Issued to Employees	October 1972
No. 26	Early Extinguishment of Debt	October 1972
No. 27	Accounting for Lease Transactions by Manufacturer or Dealer Lessors	November 1972
No. 28	Interim Financial Reporting	May 1973
No. 29	Accounting for Nonmonetary Transactions	May 1973
No. 30	Reporting the Results of Operations—Reporting the Effects of Disposal of a Segment of a Business, and Extraordinary, Unusual and Infrequently Occurring Events and Transactions	June 1973
No. 31	Disclosure of Lease Commitments by Lessees	June 1973

Financial Accounting Standards Board (FASB) Statements of Financial Accounting Standards

No. 1	Disclosure of Foreign Currency Translation Information	December 1973
No. 2	Accounting for Research and Development Costs	October 1974
No. 3	Reporting Accounting Changes in Interim Financial Statements	December 1974
No. 4	Reporting Gains and Losses from Extinguishment of Debt	March 1975
No. 5	Accounting for Contingencies	March 1975
No. 6	Classification of Short-Term Obligations Expected to Be Refinanced	May 1975
No. 7	Accounting and Reporting by Development Stage Enterprises	June 1975
No. 8	Accounting for the Translation of Foreign Currency Transactions and Foreign Financial Statements	October 1975
No. 9	Accounting for Income Taxes—Oil and Gas Producing Companies	October 1975
No. 10	Extension of "Grandfather" Provisions for Business Combinations	October 1975
No. 11	Accounting for Contingencies—Transition Method	December 1975
No. 12	Accounting for Certain Marketable Securities	December 1975
No. 13	Accounting for Leases	November 1976
No. 14	Financial Reporting for Segments of a Business Enterprise	December 1976
No. 15	Accounting by Debtors and Creditors for Troubled Debt Restructurings	June 1977
No. 16	Prior Period Adjustments	June 1977
No. 17	Accounting for Leases—Initial Direct Costs	November 1977
No. 18	Financial Reporting for Segments of a Business Enterprise—Interim Financial Statements	November 1977
No. 19	Financial Accounting and Reporting by Oil and Gas Producing Companies	December 1977
No. 20	Accounting for Forward Exchange Contracts	December 1977
No. 21	Suspension of the Reporting of Earnings per Share and Segment Information by Nonpublic Enterprises	April 1978
No. 22	Changes in the Provisions of Lease Agreements Resulting from Refundings of Tax-Exempt Debt	June 1978
No. 23	Inception of the Lease	August 1978
No. 24	Reporting Segment Information in Financial Statements That Are Presented in Another Enterprise's Financial Report	December 1978
No. 25	Suspension of Certain Accounting Requirements for Oil and Gas Producing Companies	February 1979

Number	Title	Date Issued
No. 26	Profit Recognition on Sales-Type Leases of Real Estate	April 1979
No. 27	Classification of Renewals or Extensions of Existing Sales-Type or Direct Financing Leases	May 1979
No. 28	Accounting for Sales with Leasebacks	May 1979
No. 29	Determining Contingent Rentals	June 1979
No. 30	Disclosure of Information about Major Customers	August 1979
No. 31	Accounting for Tax Benefits Related to U.K. Tax Legislation Concerning Stock Relief	September 1979
No. 32	Specialized Accounting and Reporting Principles and Practices in AICPA Statements of Position and Guides on Accounting and Auditing Matters	September 1979
No. 33	Financial Reporting and Changing Prices	September 1979
No. 34	Capitalization of Interest Cost	October 1979
No. 35	Accounting and Reporting by Defined Benefit Pension Plans	March 1980
No. 36	Disclosure of Pension Information	May 1980
No. 37	Balance Sheet Classification of Deferred Income Taxes	July 1980
No. 38	Accounting for Preacquisition Contingencies of Purchased Enterprises	September 1980
No. 39	Financial Reporting and Changing Prices: Specialized Assets—Mining and Oil and Gas	October 1980
No. 40	Financial Reporting and Changing Prices: Specialized Assets—Timberlands and Growing Timber	November 1980
No. 41	Financial Reporting and Changing Prices: Specialized Assets—Income-Producing Real Estate	November 1980
No. 42	Determining Materiality for Capitalization of Interest Cost	November 1980
No. 43	Accounting for Compensated Absences	November 1980
No. 44	Accounting for Intangible Assets of Motor Carriers	December 1980
No. 45	Accounting for Franchise Fee Revenue	March 1981
No. 46	Financial Reporting and Changing Prices: Motion Picture Films	March 1981
No. 47	Disclosure of Long-Term Obligations	March 1981
No. 48	Revenue Recognition When Right of Return Exists	June 1981
No. 49	Accounting for Product Financing Arrangements	June 1981
No. 50	Financial Reporting in the Record and Music Industry	November 1981
No. 51	Financial Reporting by Cable Television Companies	November 1981
No. 52	Foreign Currency Translation	December 1981
No. 53	Financial Reporting by Producers and Distributors of Motion Picture Films	December 1981
No. 54	Financial Reporting and Changing Prices: Investment Companies	January 1982
No. 55	Determining Whether a Convertible Security Is a Common Stock Equivalent	February 1982
No. 56	Designation of AICPA Guide and SOP 81-1 on Contractor Accounting and SOP 81-2 on Hospital-Related Organizations as Preferable for Applying APB Opinion 20	February 1982
No. 57	Related Party Disclosures	March 1982
No. 58	Capitalization of Interest Cost in Financial Statements that Include Investments Accounted for by the Equity Method	April 1982
No. 59	Deferral of the Effective Date of Certain Accounting Requirements for Revision Plans of State and Local Governmental Units	April 1982
No. 60	Accounting and Reporting by Insurance Enterprises	June 1982
No. 61	Accounting for Title Plant	June 1982
No. 62	Capitalization of Interest Cost in Situations Involving Certain Tax-Exempt Borrowings and Certain Gifts and Grants	June 1982
No. 63	Financial Reporting by Broadcasters	June 1982
No. 64	Extinguishment of Debt Made to Satisfy Sinking-Fund Requirements	September 1982
No. 65	Accounting for Certain Mortgage Bank Activities	September 1982
No. 66	Accounting for Sales of Real Estate	October 1982
No. 67	Accounting for Costs and Initial Rental Operations of Real Estate Projects	October 1982
No. 68	Research and Development Arrangements	October 1982
No. 69	Disclosures about Oil and Gas Producing Activities	November 1982
No. 70	Financial Reporting and Changing Prices: Foreign Currency Translation	December 1982
No. 71	Accounting for the Effects of Certain Types of Regulation	December 1982
No. 72	Accounting for Certain Acquisitions of Banking or Thrift Institutions	February 1983
No. 73	Reporting a Change in Accounting for Railroad Track Structures	August 1983
No. 74	Accounting for Special Termination Benefits Paid to Employees	August 1983
No. 75	Deferral of the Effective Date of Certain Accounting Requirements for Pension Plans of State and Local Governmental Units	November 1983
No. 76	Extinguishment of Debt	November 1983
No. 77	Reporting by Transferors for Transfers of Receivables with Recourse	December 1983
No. 78	Classifications of Obligations that Are Callable by the Creditor	December 1983
No. 79	Elimination of Certain Disclosures for Business Combinations by Nonpublic Enterprises	February 1984
No. 80	Accounting for Futures Contracts	August 1984

Number	Title	Date Issued
No. 81	Disclosure of Postretirement Health Care and Life Insurance Benefits	November 1984
No. 82	Financial Reporting and Changing Prices: Elimination of Certain Disclosures	November 1984
No. 83	Designation of AICPA Guides and Statement of Position on Accounting by Brokers and Dealers in Securities, by Employee Benefit Plans, and by Banks as Preferable for Purposes of Applying APB Opinion 20	March 1985
No. 84	Induced Conversions of Convertible Debt	March 1985
No. 85	Yield Test for Determining Whether a Convertible Security Is a Common Stock Equivalent	March 1985
No. 86	Accounting for the Costs of Computer Software to be Sold, Leased, or Otherwise Marketed	August 1985
No. 87	Employers' Accounting for Pensions	December 1985
No. 88	Employers' Accounting for Settlements and Curtailments of Defined Benefit Pension Plans and for Termination Benefits	December 1985
No. 89	Financial Reporting and Changing Prices	December 1986
No. 90	Regulated Enterprises—Accounting for Abandonments and Disallowances of Plant Costs	December 1986
No. 91	Accounting for Nonrefundable Fees and Costs Associated with Originating or Acquiring Loans and Initial Direct Costs of Leases	December 1986
No. 92	Regulated Enterprises—Accounting for Phase-in Plans	August 1987
No. 93	Recognition of Depreciation by Not-for-Profit Organizations	August 1987
No. 94	Consolidation of All Majority-Owned Subsidiaries	October 1987
No. 95	Statement of Cash Flows	November 1987
No. 96	Accounting for Income Taxes	December 1987
No. 97	Accounting and Reporting by Insurance Enterprises for Certain Long-Duration Contracts and for Realized Gains and Losses from the Sale of Investments	December 1987
No. 98	Accounting for Leases: Sale-Leaseback Transactions Involving Real Estate; Sales-Type Leases of Real Estate; Definition of the Lease Term; Initial Direct Costs of Direct Financing Leases	June 1988
No. 99	Deferral of the Effective Date of Recognition of Depreciation by Not-for-Profit Organizations	September 1988
No. 100	Accounting for Income Taxes—Deferral of the Effective Date of FASB Statement No. 96	December 1988
No. 101	Regulated Enterprises—Accounting for the Discontinuation of Application of FASB Statement No. 71	December 1988
No. 102	Statement of Cash Flows—Exemption of Certain Enterprises and Classification of Cash Flows from Certain Securities Acquired for Resale	February 1989
No. 103	Accounting for Income Taxes—Deferral of the Effective Date of FASB Statement No. 96	December 1989
No. 104	Statement of Cash Flows—Net Reporting of Certain Cash Receipts and Cash Payments and Classification of Cash Flows from Hedging Transactions	December 1989
No. 105	Disclosure of Information about Financial Instruments with Off-Balance-Sheet Risk and Financial Instruments with Concentrations of Credit Risk	March 1990
No. 106	Employers' Accounting for Postretirement Benefits Other Than Pensions	December 1990
No. 107	Disclosure about Fair Value of Financial Instruments	December 1991
No. 108	Accounting for Income Taxes—Deferral of the Effective Date of *FASB Statement No. 96*	December 1991
No. 109	Accounting for Income Taxes	February 1992
No. 110	Reporting by Defined Benefit Pension Plans of Investment Contracts	August 1992
No. 111	Rescission of *FASB Statement No. 32* and Technical Corrections	November 1992
No. 112	Employers' Accounting for Postemployment Benefits	November 1992
No. 113	Accounting and Reporting for Reinsurance of Short-Term and Long-Term Contracts	December 1992
No. 114	Accounting by Creditors for Impairment of a Loan	May 1993
No. 115	Accounting for Certain Investments in Debt and Equity Securities	May 1993
No. 116	Accounting for Contributions Received and Contributions Made	June 1993
No. 117	Financial Statements of Not-for-Profit Organizations	June 1993
No. 118	Accounting by Creditors for Impairment of a Loan—Income Recognition and Disclosure	October 1994
No. 119	Disclosure about Derivative Financial Instruments and Fair Value of Financial Instruments	October 1994

Financial Accounting Standards Board (FASB) Statements of Financial Accounting Concepts

No. 1	Objectives of Financial Reporting by Business Enterprises	November 1978
No. 2	Qualitative Characteristics of Accounting Information	May 1980
No. 3	Elements of Financial Statements of Business Enterprises	December 1980
No. 4	Objectives of Financial Reporting by Nonbusiness Organizations	December 1980
No. 5	Recognition and Measurement in Financial Statements of Business Enterprises	December 1984
No. 6	Elements of Financial Statements (a replacement of *FASB Concepts Statement No. 3,* incorporating an amendment of *FASB Concepts Statement No. 2*)	December 1985

Number	Title	Date Issued

Financial Accounting Standards Board (FASB) Interpretations

Number	Title	Date Issued
1	Accounting Changes Related to the Cost of Inventory (an interpretation of *APB Opinion No. 20*)	June 1974
2	Imputing Interest on Debt Arrangements Made under the Federal Bankruptcy Act (an interpretation of *APB Opinion No. 21*)	June 1974
3	Accounting for the Cost of Pension Plans Subject to the Employee Retirement Income Security Act of 1974 (an interpretation of *APB Opinion No. 8*)	December 1974
4	Applicability of *FASB Statement No. 2* to Business Combinations Accounted for by the Purchase Method (an interpretation of *FASB Statement No. 2*)	February 1975
5	Applicability of *FASB Statement No. 2* to Development Stage Enterprises (an interpretation of *FASB Statement No. 2*)	February 1975
6	Applicability of *FASB Statement No. 2* to Computer Software (an interpretation of *FASB Statement No. 2*)	February 1975
7	Applying *FASB Statement No. 7* in Financial Statements of Established Operating Enterprises (an interpretation of *FASB Statement No. 7*)	October 1975
8	Classification of a Short-Term Obligation Repaid Prior to Being Replaced by a Long-Term Security (an interpretation of *FASB Statement No. 6*)	January 1976
9	Applying *APB Opinion Nos. 16* and *17* When a Savings and Loan Association or a Similar Institution Is Acquired in a Business Combination Accounted for by the Purchase Method (an interpretation of *APB Opinions Nos. 16 and 17*)	February 1976
10	Application of *FASB Statement No. 12* to Personal Financial Statements (an interpretation of *FASB Statement No. 12*)	September 1976
11	Changes in Market Value after the Balance Sheet Date (an interpretation of *FASB Statement No. 12*)	September 1976
12	Accounting for Previously Established Allowance Accounts (an interpretation of *FASB Statement No. 12*)	September 1976
13	Consolidation of a Parent and Its Subsidiaries Having Different Balance Sheets Dates (an interpretation of *FASB Statement No. 12*)	September 1976
14	Reasonable Estimation of the Amount of a Loss (an interpretation of *FASB Statement No. 5*)	September 1976
15	Translation of Unamortized Policy Acquisition Costs by a Stock Life Insurance Company (an interpretation of *FASB Statement No. 8*)	September 1976
16	Clarification of Definitions and Accounting for Marketable Equity Securities That Become Nonmarketable (an interpretation of *FASB Statement No. 12*)	February 1977
17	Applying the Lower of Cost or Market Rule in Translated Financial Statements (an interpretation of *FASB Statement No. 8*)	February 1977
18	Accounting for Income Taxes in Interim Periods (an interpretation of *APB Opinion No. 28*)	March 1977
19	Lessee Guarantee of the Residual Value of Leased Property (an interpretation of *FASB Statement No. 13*)	October 1977
20	Reporting Accounting Changes under AICPA Statements of Position (an interpretation of *APB Opinion No. 20*)	November 1977
21	Accounting for Leases in a Business Combination (an interpretation of *FASB Statement No. 13*)	April 1978
22	Applicability of Indefinite Reversal Criteria to Timing Differences (an interpretation of *APB Opinion Nos. 11 and 23*)	April 1978
23	Leases & Certain Property Owned by a Governmental Unit or Authority (an interpretation of *FASB Statement No. 13*)	August 1978
24	Lease Involving Only Part of a Building (an interpretation of *FASB Statement No. 13*)	September 1978
25	Accounting for an Unused Investment Tax Credit (an interpretation of *APB Opinion Nos. 2, 4, 11, and 16*)	September 1978
26	Accounting for Purchase of a Leased Asset by the Lessee during the Term of the Lease (an interpretation of *FASB Statement No. 13*)	September 1978
27	Accounting for a Loss on a Sublease (an interpretation of *FASB Statement No. 13*)	November 1978
28	Accounting for Stock Appreciation Rights and Other Variable Stock Option or Award Plans (an interpretation of *APB Opinion Nos. 15 and 25*)	December 1978
29	Reporting Tax Benefits Realized on Disposition of Investments in Certain Subsidiaries and Other Investees (an interpretation of *APB Opinion Nos. 23 and 24*)	February 1979
30	Accounting for Involuntary Conversions of Nonmonetary Assets to Monetary Assets (an interpretation of *APB Opinion No. 29*)	September 1979
31	Treatment of Stock Compensation Plans in EPS Computations (an interpretation of *APB Opinion No. 15* and a modification of *FASB Interpretation No. 28*)	February 1980
32	Application of Percentage Limitations in Recognizing Investment Tax Credit (an interpretation of *APB Opinion Nos. 2, 4, and 11*)	March 1980
33	Applying *FASB Statement No. 34* to Oil and Gas Producing Operations Accounted for by the Full Cost Method (an interpretation of *FASB Statement No. 34*)	August 1980

Number	Title	Date Issued
34	Disclosure of Indirect Guarantees of Indebtedness of Others (an interpretation of *FASB Statement No. 5*)	March 1981
35	Criteria for Applying the Equity Method of Accounting for Investments in Common Stock (an interpretation of *APB Opinion No. 18*)	May 1981
36	Accounting for Exploratory Wells in Progress at the End of a Period (an interpretation of *FASB Statement No. 19*)	October 1981
37	Accounting for Translation Adjustments upon Sale of Part of an Investment in a Foreign Entity (an interpretation of *FASB Statement No. 52*)	July 1983
38	Determining the Measurement Date for Stock Option, Purchase, and Award Plans Involving Junior Stock (an interpretation of *APB Opinion No. 25*)	August 1984
39	Offsetting of Amounts Related to Certain Contracts (an interpretation of *APB Opinion No. 10* and *FASB Statement No. 105*)	March 1992
40	Applicability of Generally Accepted Accounting Principles to Mutual Life Insurance and Other Enterprises (an interpretation of *FASB Statement Nos. 12, 60, 97,* and *113*)	April 1993

National Accounting Boards and Organizations

American Accounting Association (AAA)
5717 Bessie Drive
Sarasota, FL 34233
(813) 921-7747

American Institute of Certified Public Accountants (AICPA)
1211 Avenue of The Americas
New York, NY 10036
(212) 596-6200

Association of Government Accountants (AGA)
2200 Mount Vernon Avenue
Alexandria, VA 22301
(703) 684-6931

Financial Accounting Standards Board (FASB)
401 Merritt 7
P.O. Box 5116
Norwalk, CT 06856
(203) 847-0700

Financial Executives Institute (FEI)
10 Madison Avenue
P.O. Box 1938
Morristown, NJ 07962-1938
(201) 898-4609

Governmental Accounting Standards Board (GASB)
401 Merritt 7
P.O. Box 5116
Norwalk, CT 06856-5116
(203) 847-0700

Institute of Certified Management Accountants
10 Paragon Drive
Montvale, NJ 07645-1760
(201) 573-9000

Institute of Internal Auditors (IIA)
249 Maitland Avenue
Altamonte Springs, FL 32701-4201
(407) 830-7600

Institute of Management Accountants (IMA)
10 Paragon Drive
Montvale, NJ 07645-1760
(201) 573-9000

Securities and Exchange Commission (SEC)
450 Fifth Street NW
Washington, DC 20549
(202) 942-8088

Photo Credits

Financial Statement Excerpts Index

Company & Professional Organization Index

Subject Index

Kellogg Company and Subsidiaries

Consolidated Earnings and Retained Earnings

Year ended December 31, (in millions, except per share amounts)	1993	1992	1991
Net sales	**$6,295.4**	$6,190.6	$5,786.6
Other revenue (deductions), net	**(1.5)**	36.8	14.6
	6,293.9	6,227.4	5,801.2
Cost of goods sold	**2,989.0**	2,987.7	2,828.7
Selling and administrative expense	**2,237.5**	2,140.1	1,930.0
Interest expense	**33.3**	29.2	58.3
	5,259.8	5,157.0	4,817.0
Earnings before income taxes and cumulative effect of accounting change	**1,034.1**	1,070.4	984.2
Income taxes	**353.4**	387.6	378.2
Earnings before cumulative effect of accounting change	**680.7**	682.8	606.0
Cumulative effect of change in method of accounting for postretirement benefits other than pensions—$1.05 a share (net of income tax benefit of $144.6)		(251.6)	
Net earnings—$2.94, $1.81, $2.51 a share	**680.7**	431.2	606.0
Retained earnings, beginning of year	**3,033.9**	2,889.1	2,542.4
Dividends paid—$1.32, $1.20, $1.075 a share	**(305.2)**	(286.4)	(259.3)
Retained earnings, end of year	**$3,409.4**	$3,033.9	$2,889.1

See notes to consolidated financial statements.